ON THE ROAD AGAIN

with

MAN'S BEST FRIEND

United States

ON THE ROAD AGAIN

with

MAN'S BEST FRIEND

United States

Dawn and Robert Habgood

Dawbert Press, Inc.
Duxbury, Massachusetts

To Our Children

Second Edition

ISBN: 0-933603-11-8

Editor: Jeanne Dooley

Cover Photography: Anne Henning
Line Art: Glynn Brannan
            Priscilla McMillan

Manufactured in Canada

10 9 8 7 6 5 4 3 2

Table of Contents

Introduction

Like millions of others, we cherish our pets and their unique place in our family. Seventeen years ago, our two Golden Retrievers were the only "children" in our lives, and we wanted to include them in our travel adventures whenever possible. We were living in California at the time, where there are many wonderful places to stay. Yet only a few of them welcomed our furry, four-legged friends. We began to gather information on pet-friendly accommodations, and then tried to select the most interesting to visit. While many of the brochures made wonderful promises, we often found upon arrival that the accommodation did not live up to our expectations. While our dogs did not care, we did. Our experiences identified a clear problem, but they also gave us an idea for the solution.

In 1984, we released *On the Road Again with Man's Best Friend*. This guide was the first book in the country dedicated exclusively to dog-friendly lodgings. We created far more than a book of lists — *On the Road Again with Man's Best Friend* included detailed reviews of the best places to stay with your dog, based on our personal visits. As it turned out, this book was just the first in the bestselling and long-running series that spans fifteen years, tens of thousands of travel miles, and thousands of visits to the country's most interesting, pet-friendly accommodations.

We waited many years to release our first national book, *On the Road Again With Man's Best Friend*, but feel it was well worth the wait. In this second edition, we continue to balance quality and quantity. With over 18,000 accommodations — from mom-and-pop motels to luxurious resorts — you'll find an array of intriguing places to stay with your favorite canine or feline.

When you want to plan a special trip, look for our logo. This designation indicates our choices for each state's best pet accommodations. We were selective, highlighting only those that we personally visited or that received multiple reader recommendations. Our information is that of an insider, with inclusion based on merit. Please note that none of the places we've highlighted has paid a fee for inclusion in this book, or in any of our other travel guides.

We think you'll be pleased with the results. Whether you're traveling cross-country, along the coasts, or to all 50 states — this resource will guide you down the road with your own best friend.

More Than Simple Facts — Details

We chose a wide variety of pet-friendly lodgings by sifting through tens of thousands of accommodations. The entries range from economical motels and motor lodges to charming bed & breakfasts, historic inns, and exquisite five-star resorts. We provide pertinent information, including address, telephone numbers, number of rooms, rates, and web sites. We delve into each accommodation's pet policy, giving you information on fees, size requirements, and special programs.

Our "Creature Comforts" section describes amenities such as cable or satellite television, air-conditioning, kitchens, fireplaces, and restaurants, as well as swimming pools, whirlpools, health clubs, tennis courts, and lawn games. In addition to these standard features, we'll tell you if the property is historic; is located by a lake, river, or ocean; or if it provides any special pet or people amenities.

So Many Choices...

While there are a vast number of available accommodations, choosing the right one is important. The United States edition of *On The Road Again with Man's Best Friend* includes everything from charming "mom & pop" B&Bs to exquisite five-star hotels. The following classifications will guide you to the perfect accommodation.

Bed and Breakfasts

These accommodations are often private homes, so guests should approach this experience as if they were staying with a friend. Usually B&Bs are short on in-room amenities such as televisions, telephones, or Jacuzzi tubs. Yet you often get plenty of personal attention, as well as comfortable guest rooms and a common area that might include a television, a stereo, and a fireplace. While guests are offered breakfast, most B&Bs do not serve lunch or dinner. Best of all, there are always friendly hosts who will make you feel like family.

Inns

Some travelers confuse inns with B&Bs. While most inns have the same type of intimate feeling as a B&B, they usually contain more rooms. In addition, inns typically have a restaurant or serve at least one meal in addition to breakfast. Inns are more highly regulated and must meet the various state and national health and access building codes. They also provide a wider array of activities and creature comforts beyond those found at a traditional B&B.

Cottages/Cabins

The cottage and cabin complexes we feature vary greatly in size, amenities, and activities. When we recommend a cottage, even the most rustic, it is always clean and well-maintained. We often find the cottage complexes to be an advantage, as they offer a picturesque setting with plenty of open space for both guests and their pets to explore. These complexes usually have a main lodge with a common area and/or a restaurant. In some cases, all guests eat at the main lodge, while other complexes have kitchenettes.

Motels/Motor Lodges

These facilities vary in cost and features, although guests can expect fairly basic and boxy rooms, a handful of amenities, and perhaps a pool or restaurant (either on the premises or nearby). Usually these properties do not offer much in the way of additional features or noteworthy attributes beyond good value and convenience.

Hotels and Resorts

Hotels usually have 50 or more rooms and are located in large towns and cities. They typically deliver a full range of amenities, which could include an indoor or outdoor swimming pool, concierge services, multiple restaurants, a high staff-to-guest ratio, and a health club. On the other hand, resorts provide a similar level of amenities but usually are located on the outskirts of popular tourist destinations or in a country setting. Resorts also offer a wider variety of guest rooms, as well as an extensive list of activities and on-site programs.

Not All Rooms are Created Equal

Traveling with your pet might mean compromises, but not on the quality and cleanliness of your room. You are a paying guest, who often pays extra for your pet. You can, and should, ask many questions about the kind of room you are reserving. Some establishments have "pet rooms," which can mean the rooms have private entrances; are on the first floor; are smoking rooms; or are set off by themselves. We prefer to pick our room. However, if you are placed in a "pet room," you might want to ask some of the following questions. We've found most reservation agents to be remarkably straightforward with their responses.

- *Is this room as nice as, or better than, the average hotel room?*
  You don't want to stay somewhere that relegates you to the least desirable room.

- *Is this room a smoking room or pet room?*
  Those people who are non-smokers and/or allergic to animals (other than their own) will find these rooms problematic.

- *Is the carpet soiled or are the furnishings worn?*
  We've visited many pet rooms that are not up to par due to soiling, odors, or well-worn furnishings.

- *Does the room have a separate outside entrance?*
  We usually don't like navigating a labyrinth of hallways to reach the great outdoors.

- *How big is the room?*
  Large pets can present a problem in small spaces.

- *Are there safe and convenient places to walk your dog near the property?*
  We've discovered lovely hotels in unsafe neighborhoods, which can make it unwise to walk your dog at night. If your dog likes to take her daily constitutional near green spaces, the cement sidewalks that surround some city hotels might not work.

Since guest rooms vary considerably, be very specific about your personal requirements. Before calling, carefully read through the listing's summary of amenities. Before you make a reservation, inquire about the specifics.

Location, location, location is an important issue.
Is the hotel located on a busy street? If so, can you reserve a quiet room? Are there recently updated rooms in the hotel? If so, can you reserve them if accompanied by your pet? Can you reserve a room with all sorts of extra amenities, or do you prefer the stripped-down version?
Be polite, but be firm.

Money Matters

Rates

While rates often fluctuate with tourism's seasonal highs and lows, you should be able to find a room within the listing's given range. Rates are based on double occupancy and do not include taxes or meals, unless noted. Travelers also should inquire about special programs or seasonal discounts. Many of these accommodations offer terrific discount packages, off-season rates, weekly rates, or interesting theme weekends. We recommend traveling during the "shoulder" season — the time after high season when the crowds are gone; the rates are lower; and the room selection is extensive.

Pet Fees

We note if an accommodation requires a pet fee or deposit. These fees range from $2 to $500. Be clear with the reservation agent about this added pet charge. If it is a deposit, it is refundable. If it is a fee, it is non-refundable. We talked with many lodgings that charged non-refundable deposits. Don't let this term fool you — the charge is a fee that will not be returned at the end of your stay. You can clarify the fee or deposit policy by asking the following questions.

- Is there a pet fee?

- If so, is it a daily fee or a one-time fee?

- If it is a deposit, is it refundable or non-refundable?

Some of the more exclusive hotels and long-term residence inns charge both a daily fee and a hefty, non-refundable deposit ($150-500). While this charge might work for a week-long stay, it does not make sense for a night or two.

Pet Etiquette

We note various pet policies in the pet section of each listing. Small pets are universally welcome, while many establishments exclude larger pets. Although they fall in the small pet category, cats are not always welcome.

You often will be interviewed about your pet. Be patient and take the extra time to talk with the manager about your pet. This discussion also permits you to review the accommodation's pet policies and programs with a live person. Some establishments offer pet treats and other special amenities for their four-legged guests, such as homemade biscuits, meals, beds, or bowls.

Always assume that the following rules exist, unless the manager or written policies indicate otherwise:

- Never leave your pet alone in the room. If management makes an exception to this policy, you can do a few simple things to keep your furry friend comfortable. Provide your pet with an assortment of toys and turn on the television or radio to give her some sense of companionship.

- Bring bedding or a portable carrier for your pet.

- Do not allow your pet on the furniture or beds.

- Feed and provide water for your pet in the bathroom or on a tiled or hardwood floor. Not all pets are neat and tidy at meal time.

- Walk your dogs off the property and always clean up after them.

• Health regulations prohibit pets from areas where food is prepared or served. Don't bring your pet to breakfast and don't assume that she is welcome in the accommodation's public areas.

• Keep your pet leashed on the accommodation's property. While your pet may be under perfect voice control, other guests may become apprehensive when they see an unleashed pet.

Creature Comforts

Each listing includes a number of creature comforts, otherwise known as amenities. We've used the following code:

CCTV/SATV (cable/satellite television) — Most of the accommodations offer cable television. While some offer satellite television, there are still a few old-fashioned, rabbit-ear varieties around the country.

VCR (videocassette recorder) — Many of the luxury hotels and long-term residence inns offer VCRs. These units may be in the room, or rentable. Inquire when making your reservation.

A/C (air-conditioning) — As with televisions, most of the lodgings have air-conditioning. For those accommodations without this staple, we recommend packing a small fan to ensure that you and your pet are comfortable if the temperatures rise.

Refrig (refrigerator) — Many guest rooms provide refrigerators that double as honor bars in most hotels. If not standard, refrigerators usually can be rented for a small fee (generally $5 per day). Some small motels and most B&Bs offer a common guest refrigerator for perishables.

Micro (microwave) — Microwaves also are becoming a standard feature in many hotels and inns. Again, some establishments allow you to rent them for a small fee ($5-10 per day). Some accommodations put microwaves in their common areas or lobbies for guests' use.

Kit (kitchenette/kitchen) — Some accommodations offer simple kitchenettes with a refrigerator, microwave, and sink, while others contain state-of-the-art kitchens with marble countertops and every gadget imaginable. When you see the "kit" designation in a listing, you will get a kitchenette at the very least. More often, you will be pleasantly surprised by a full kitchen.

Jacuzzi or Whirlpool — While these terms often are used interchangeably, we separate them into two categories. A Jacuzzi® designation in a listing means that the room has a private, in-room tub. Whirlpools (also known as spas and hot tubs) generally are open to the public and often are located next to a pool or on a deck.

Fireplace — We have included fireplaces in a listing if they are in a common area or in a guest room. Generally, the word "fireplace" means there is just one fireplace at the establishment — possibly in the lobby or in one of the rooms or suites. If the word "fireplaces" is used, guests will find fireplaces throughout the facility, both in the guest rooms and in the common areas.

Restaurant (restaurant and cafes) — We note a "restaurant" when the facility is located within the accommodation's complex.

Cont. or Full Breakfast — Continental breakfasts are light meals consisting of fresh fruit, baked goods, juices, and coffee or tea. Full breakfasts (also known as gourmet, farm, plantation, etc.) not only include a Continental portion of the meal, but also a hot meal ranging from egg dishes to pancakes, waffles, crepes, and blintzes.

Health Club — A "health club" can range from a simple exercise room with a few weights to a full-blown facility with a spa, masseuse, and trainers, as well as a host of high-tech, weight-training equipment. If exercise facilities are important to you, we recommend asking for specifics when making your reservation. Sometimes a hotel will not have its own health club, but has health club privileges in the area. In these cases, you will see the term "hlth club access" in the listing.

Pools and Saunas — While these terms are self-explanatory, they do vary greatly in terms of setting and privacy.

Access to Tennis, Golf, or Riding — While some lodgings offer these diversions directly, others have access or privileges to local facilities that offer them. We always mention on-site activities, and try to note any off-site ones as well.

Meal Plans

The following are a few of the traditional meal plans offered by most accommodations:

- Bed and Breakfast (B&B) rates include a Continental or full breakfast.
- European Plan (EP) does not include any meals.
- Modified American Plan (MAP) includes both breakfast and dinner.
- American Plan (AP) is all-inclusive, providing breakfast, lunch, and dinner.

Guests should inquire as to whether these plans are available. Careful selection of a particular plan can save guests a good deal of money in the long run.

Virtual Lodgings? — Sneak Previews

We include web addresses for many entries. While you don't have to take advantage of this information, we think web sites provide wonderful sneak previews of the accommodations. When combined with our recommendations, you have an unbeatable resource.

Web sites are often far more detailed than the best brochure, offering firsthand glimpses into rooms, common areas, and grounds. As an added feature, you also can learn about the establishment's current specials, activities, and new programs. Web sites are a great way for travelers to obtain relevant and timely information about their destination.

Before you jump onto the web, we'd like to clarify some of the web-site features. Some of the strengths of the Internet are its capabilities to change information rapidly and to provide visuals immediately. Yet these capacities also present problems in tracking web addresses and changed domain names. Although many of the accommodations do not have their own web sites as we go to press, sites are opening daily. Moreover, accommodations with web sites may change their addresses.

In short, when you type in certain web addresses, you might have trouble gaining access to the site. If so, try a global search for the accommodation. It still exists, and often can be cross-referenced through several other sites. By using your Internet search engines, you usually can find an amazing amount of information about your destination by just typing in the name of the accommodation.

On the Road Again with Man's Best Friend Guides You Through Cyberspace

You can get updated information for *On the Road Again with Man's Best Friend, U.S.* at http://www.petsonthego.com. This site not only provides expertise in all areas of pet travel, but also updates web addresses and links to many accommodations found in our national book. Just log on to pets on the go to find out what's hot and what's not for vacationing pets. Since we're not just cyber-travelers, we still spend months on the road searching for new and unusual accommodations for our readers. We'll give you a sneak preview of the best — just log on.

As you travel down your own road, we invite your help. If you find a new place that accepts pets, or one that no longer welcomes our furry friends, please let us know via e-mail at dawbert@mindspring.com. You also may write to our editor, Allison Elliott, at Dawbert Press Inc., Box 67, Duxbury, Massachusetts 02331.

Vacation Hesitation
For Some Pets, There's No Place Like Home

Before you contemplate heading out on the road with your favorite furry friend, ask yourself a few questions.

- *Does my pet like to travel?* Dogs who lock all four legs when invited to jump in the car, or cats who hide under the bed when their carrier appears, are not going to be any happier on the road. Some pets are homebodies who prefer the comfort of their bed to life on the road.

- *Is the destination a "pet-appropriate" one?* In other words, is this trip pet-oriented or people-oriented? If you are planning a ski trip where you will be gone for eight hours a day — leave your pet at home. If you are touring museums or other non-pet-oriented destinations, please leave your furry friend at home with a loving pet-sitter or at the kennel. While cats are self-sufficient creatures who can handle long periods of solitude, dogs are pack animals who usually do not like being left alone for long periods of time.

- *Is this trip a leisurely one?* When traveling with a pet, especially a dog, you have to stop every two hours for walking and stretching. If you have limited time and are rushing from place to place, leave your pet at home.

- *Is your pet friendly and calm?* For obvious reasons, hoteliers will not allow a high-strung or barking dog as a guest. You know your dog — if she fits into this category, or is edgy around new people, leave her at home.

- *Are you traveling to an extremely hot or cold climate?* Many accommodations do not allow you to leave your pet alone in the room. When you leave, the pet comes with you. This reality can pose a problem in extremely hot or cold climates, since it is unsafe to leave your pet in the car for even a few minutes.

Modes of Transportation
Planes, Trains, and Automobiles

Car Travel

If you've never traveled with your pet before, there are a few simple things you can do to get her ready for a vacation. To ease the uninitiated pet into a comfortable travel mode, start with day trips. Then proceed to an overnight or weekend jaunt, followed by a week away. We recommend travel crates for most pets, and/or a gate to confine pets to the rear of the car. All pets need to be confined away from the driver, for safety purposes.

Before setting out on your trip, take your pet for a leisurely walk. Let her work off a little energy, and you may tire her out so she can sleep. Do not feed her or give her substantial amounts of water just before leaving. Once in the car, make sure your pet's area is either well-ventilated or amply air-conditioned. Plan frequent pit stops (every two hours or so) to exercise your pet on a leash.

Even if the day is not hot, a car can heat to very high temperatures in very little time. Take the following precautions to prevent heat stroke, brain damage, or even death:

- Never leave your pet in a hot car!

- Try to park the car in the shade and leave the windows open to provide ample ventilation. Many specialty shops/catalogues sell small, portable, battery-operated fans that affix to a partially opened window to help the car stay cooler.

- Do not leave your dog for long intervals. Check on her frequently to ensure her safety and to see that the sun hasn't shifted to shine directly on your car.

- Before you leave the car, fill her bowl with cold water to ease any effects of the heat. Heat Stroke: If your pet exhibits the effects of prolonged heat exposure (heavy breathing, unstable walking, or dazed affect), consult a veterinarian immediately (see Pet Emergencies).

- Freezing winter temperatures are also cause for concern. Make sure your pet has enough blankets or bedding to keep her warm in the car.

Plane Travel

There are certain legal guidelines and restrictions for pet air travel. The United States Department of Agriculture (USDA) and the International Air Transport Association (IATA) govern air travel for pets. The airlines themselves have varying regulations; always contact your airline well in advance to review their particular procedures and requirements.

We prefer airlines that have written rules for pet travel. Written rules are evidence that the airline has given long, careful thought to transporting animals. Small pets often can be crated and taken right on board the plane with you, while larger animals must stay in the cargo area. Regardless of your airline carrier, these are important guidelines to consider:

- The pet should be at least eight weeks old and fully weaned.
- The pet cannot be ill, violent, or in physical distress.
- Some pets may be more comfortable if they are mildly sedated during flights. Consult your veterinarian. Also make sure that your pet's nails are trimmed to avoid snagging on the travel crate's door or some other object.
- The pet should have all the necessary health certificates and documentation.
- The travel crate must meet the airline's standards and be large enough for the pet to lie down comfortably, turn around, and stand freely. Mark the crate with "Live Animal — This Side Up," as well as with your name, address, and telephone number (should she get lost or misplaced in transit), as well as the name, address, and telephone number of your destination. Your pet may enjoy an old towel, blanket, or newspaper in the crate to make her more comfortable.
- Try to book a non-stop flight, and take temperatures into consideration. In the summer, fly at night when it's often cooler; in the winter, fly during the day, when it's warmer.
- Certain short-nosed dogs such as pugs cannot breathe well in airplane cargo areas. Avoid flying with these particular breeds.
- Do not feed your pet before traveling, due to the potential for an upset stomach during the flight. Give your pet frozen water or, if possible, some ice cubes that will melt slowly and, hopefully, not dump out during boarding.
- Plan your trip well in advance and make sure you follow all the airline regulations.

Trains, Buses, and Boats

Almost without exception, dogs are not allowed on trains or buses. Dogs may be allowed on local subways, such as in New York and Boston. Generally, dogs are allowed on ferry boats, as long as they are leashed and kept out of the food areas. You may be arriving at your destination by car or plane, but once you arrive, there is generally plenty of local transportation options that allow pets. Always call in advance to check specific policies.

On the Road — Again
What Your Pet Needs to Enjoy the Trip

Just as you have to pack appropriately for your vacation, your pet will need certain items to ensure her comfort and enjoyment. Consider:

- A leash and collar with ID tags. (Create a local tag giving your local address and a telephone number.) It also may be helpful to bring along a photograph of your pet in the event that you become separated.
- A few favorite toys, chew bones, balls, and treats.
- A large container of fresh drinking water from home.
- A supply of her regular dog food (and a can opener, if needed).
- Food and water bowls.
- A pet bed, whether it is a towel, mat, pillow, or travel crate.
- Grooming brushes/aids.
- Any medication your veterinarian has prescribed or suggested.
- The pet's vaccination records, especially a rabies certificate or tag. Many overnight establishments, state forests, and parks now require current vaccination records for visiting pets. Your pet may need special inoculations when visiting regions with high incidence rates of diseases such as Lyme disease and rabies.
- Pooper-scooper or plastic bags.
- A flashlight for evening walks.
- Paper towels for clean-up and old towels for drying wet dogs.

A great resource when traveling with your pet is titled *Pet First Aid*. Authored by Bobbie Mammato, the book is published by the American Red Cross and the Humane Society of the United States. The ISBN (reference number) for the book is 1-57857-000X. For more information on this valuable tome, link to the Humane Society's web site at http://www.hsus.org/books.html.

Pet Emergencies

While *Pet First Aid* is a great book, there are times when you might need a veterinarian. We recommend calling the American Animal Hospital Association at (800) 883-6301 to find a local veterinarian. You also may contact them through their web site at www.healthypet.com. The association screens each of the veterinary hospitals it endorses to ensure high quality care.

If you like to plan ahead, find a veterinarian or two before you set off on your travels. Prepare yourself with their names, addresses, and telephone numbers in case an emergency presents itself.

Lost Pets

If your pet is lost or missing, stay calm and consider the following options:

- Contact your hotel and let the staff know that your pet is missing. Anyone who finds your pet may look at the vacation tag; notice the name, address, and telephone number of your hotel; and contact it directly.

- If you have just lost your pet in a busy area, take a few minutes to visit some of the surrounding shops, restaurants, and buildings. Leave them your name and hotel telephone number so that you can easily be reached.

- Telephone the local animal control officer, veterinary hospital, police, and humane society. One of these departments is the likely contact for stray or lost pets.

- Place a number of lost pet flyers in the area where your pet first disappeared. The most effective locations are major street intersections, churches, grocery stores, post offices, and other, heavily trafficked areas. Include a description of your pet and a photograph, as well as your local hotel phone number, your home phone number, and your work contact number. It can take time to locate your pet, and you might be called after you have finished your vacation and returned home.

- If some time has passed without any success in locating your pet, contact the local newspaper and radio stations and place an ad or notice about your pet.

- You also may want to contact the following three resources:
    Pet Finders: (800) 666-5678 - (http://www.petclub.org)
    Pet Loss Support Hot Line: (530) 752-4200
    Lost Dog: Post a description of your lost dog - (http://www.lostdog.com)

Helpful Telephone Numbers

American Animal Hospital Association..(303) 986-2800
American Humane Association..(800) 227-4645
American Kennel Club..(919) 233-9767
A.S.P.C.A...(212) 876-7700
Humane Society for the United States...(202) 452-1100
National Animal Poison Control Center...(800) 548-2423

Pet Import and Export
General Requirements

Dogs and cats that arrive in Hawaii or Guam, both of which are free of rabies, are subject to the state's or territory's quarantine requirements, in addition to whatever other Public Health Service requirements, above, apply.

Dogs, cats, and turtles are free of duty. Other pets imported into the United States, if subject to a customs duty, may be included in your customs exemption if they accompany you and are imported for your personal use and not for sale.

All animal importation are subject to health, agriculture, wildlife, and customs requirements which are monitored by three agencies — U.S. Customs, the Center for Disease Control (CDC), and the United States Department of Agriculture Animal and Plant Health Inspection Service (APHIS).

Exporting pets is an entirely different matter and the rules vary according to the country of eventual importation. We advise checking with the embassy or consulate of the country that you will be visiting and inquiring about their domestic pet importation requirements.

While APHIS and the CDC have a number of criteria that must be met for pets to enter the United States, you will most likely be talking to U.S. Customs' officials when crossing any U.S. border. The following information should be of help. It was taken directly from materials published by the Customs Department and outlines pet importation requirements. Please read it carefully and contact the U.S. Customs Department if you should have any questions.

U.S. Customs Department
Importation Requirements

"Travelers frequently inquire about taking their pets with them to the United States. All such importation are subject to health, quarantine, agriculture, wildlife, and customs requirements and prohibitions. Pets taken out of the United States and returned are subject to the same requirements as those entering for the first time.

Sadly, pets excluded from entry into the United States must either be exported or destroyed. While awaiting disposition, pets will be detained at the owner's expense at the port of arrival.

The U.S. Public Health Service requires that pet dogs and cats brought into this country be examined at the first port of entry for evidence of diseases that can be transmitted to humans. Dogs coming from areas not free of rabies must be accompanied by a valid rabies vaccination certificate.

We also suggest that you also check with state, county, and municipal authorities for local restrictions on importing pet."

Dog and Cat Importation

Domestic dogs must be free of evidence of diseases communicable to humans when examined at the port of entry. If the animal is not in apparent good health, further examination by a licensed veterinarian may be required at the owner's expense.

Dogs and cats must be vaccinated against rabies at least 30 days before entering the United States. This requirement does not apply, however, to puppies or kittens less than three months of age or to dogs and cats originating or located for at least six months in areas designated by the U.S. Public Health Service as being rabies-free.

The following procedures pertain to dogs arriving from areas that are not free of rabies:

- A valid rabies vaccination certificate should accompany the animal. This certificate should be in English or be accompanied by a translation. It should identify the animal, the dates of vaccination and expiration, and be signed by a licensed veterinarian. If no expiration date is specified, the certificate is acceptable if the date of vaccination is no more than 12 months before the date of arrival.

- If a vaccination has not been performed, or if the certificate is not valid, the animal may be admitted if it is confined immediately upon arrival at a place of the owner's choosing. The dog must be vaccinated within four days after arrival at the final destination, but no more than 10 days after arrival at the port of entry. The animal must remain in confinement for at least 30 days after being vaccinated.

- If the vaccination was performed less than 30 days before arrival, the animal may be admitted but must be confined at a place of the owner's choosing until at least 30 days have passed since the vaccination.

- Young puppies must be confined at a place of the owner's choosing until they are three months old, then they must be vaccinated. They must remain in confinement for 30 days.

Dogs and cats that arrive in Hawaii or Guam, both of which are free of rabies, are subject to the state's or territory's quarantine requirements, in addition to whatever other Public Health Service requirements, above, apply.

Dogs, cats, and turtles are free of duty. Other pets imported into the United States, if subject to a customs duty, may be included in your customs exemption if they accompany you and are imported for your personal use and not for sale.

Disclaimer

Always call ahead to confirm an accommodation's pet policy. Please keep in mind that the hosts, managers, and innkeepers are under no obligation to accept your pet. The management of each establishment in our guides has welcomed pets in the past and has indicated that they will accept them in the future if they are well behaved.

We cannot guarantee against last-minute changes of heart. Sometimes circumstances may prevent the welcoming of our furry friends. For example, the hotel may already have a few pets visiting, or may be hosting a special function that would make it impractical for staff to have your pet in residence.

Unfortunately, we also have encountered a number of establishments that have changed their pet policies due to a few bad experiences. To reduce the numbers of accommodations who are forced to change their policies, try to follow this section's guidelines on traveling with your pet. We also recommend that you notify the management that you are traveling with a pet and discuss their policies concerning pets before you arrive.

ON THE ROAD AGAIN

with

MAN'S BEST FRIEND

United States

Alabama

ABBEVILLE
Best Western Inn
(800) 528-1234, (334) 585-5060
http://www.bestwestern.com
Rtes. 431 & 27
40 rooms - $44-98
Pets: Welcome
Creature Comforts: CCTV,
refrig, micro, cont. brkfst,
whirlpool, pool

ALABASTER
Shelby Motor Lodge
(205) 663-1070
Route 31
21 rooms - $35-45
Pets: Small pets welcome
Creature Comforts: CCTV, a/c

ALEXANDER CITY
Bob White Motel
(256) 234-4215
1020 Airport Rd.
22 rooms - $35-49
Pets: Welcome
Creature Comforts: CCTV, a/c

Jameson Inn
(800) 541-3268, (256) 234-7099
4335 Rte. 2080
62 rooms - $54-75
Pets: Welcome
Creature Comforts: CCTV, a/c,
refrig, pool,

ANDALUSIA
Comfort Inn
(800) 228-5150, (334) 222-8891
http://www.comfortinn.com
1311 E. Bypass Rd.
50 rooms - $49-89
Pets: Welcome
Creature Comforts: CCTV, a/c,
refrig, micro, Jacuzzis, pool

Days Inn
(800) DAYS INN, (334) 427-0050
http://www.daysinn.com
1604 E. Bypass Rd.
100 rooms - $50-99
Pets: Welcome w/$6 fee
Creature Comforts: CCTV, a/c,
refrig, micro, Jacuzzi, cont. brkfst,
pool

Charter House Inn
(334) 222-7511
Route 84
62 rooms - $35-68
Pets: Welcome w/$25 dep.
Creature Comforts: CCTV, a/c,
refrig, cont. brkfst, pool

ANNISTON
Motel 6
(800) 466-8356, (256) 831-5463
http://www.motel6.com
202 Grace St.
116 rooms - $39-53
Pets: Under 30 lbs. welcome
Creature Comforts: CCTV, a/c,
pool

Econo Lodge
(800) 55-Econo, (256) 831-9480
http://www.econolodge.com
25 Elm St.
111 rooms - $47-69
Pets: Small pets welcome
Creature Comforts: CCTV, a/c,
cont. brkfst, pool

Holiday Inn
(800) HOLIDAY, (256) 831-3410
http://www.holiday-inn.com
Rtes. 78 & 21
195 rooms - $65-1099
Pets: Welcome
Creature Comforts: CCTV, a/c,
refrig, micro, Jacuzzis, restaurant,
pool, whirlpool

Howard Johnson Inn
(800) I-Go-Hojo, (256) 835-3988
http://www.hojo.com
Rtes. 78 & 21
45 rooms - $45-89
Pets: Welcome
Creature Comforts: CCTV, a/c,
restaurant, pool, whirlpool

Ramada Inn
(800) 2-Ramada, (256) 237-9777
http://www.ramada.com
300 Quintard Ave.
97 rooms - $45-139
Pets: Welcome
Creature Comforts: CCTV, a/c,
kit, restaurant, cont. brkfst, pool,
whirlpool

ARDMORE
Budget Inn
(256) 423-6699
Route 65
30 rooms - $35-59
Pets: Welcome
Creature Comforts: CCTV, a/c,
refrig, micro, cont. brkfst

ATHENS
Best Western Inn
(800) 528-1234, (256) 233-4030
http://www.bestwestern.com
1329 Rte. 72
88 rooms - $45-90
Pets: Small pets welcome
Creature Comforts: CCTV, a/c,
refrig, micro, cont. brkfst, pool

Bomar Inn
(800) 824-6384, (256) 232-6944
1101 Route 31
80 rooms - $40-58
Pets: Welcome w/$10 fee
Creature Comforts: CCTV, a/c,
refrig, restaurant, pool

Comfort Inn
(800) 228-5150, (256) 232-2704
http://www.comfortinn.com
1218 Kelli Dr.
63 rooms - $55-99
Pets: Welcome
Creature Comforts: CCTV, a/c,
cont. brkfst, pool

Days Inn
(800) DAYS INN, (256) 233-7500
http://www.daysinn.com
1322 Rte. 72
95 rooms - $39-129
Pets: Welcome w/$10 fee
Creature Comforts: CCTV, a/c,
kit, Jacuzzis, cont. brkfst, pool

Holiday Inn
(800) HOLIDAY, (256) 232-1520
http://www.holiday-inn.com
1500 Route 72
50 rooms - $50-87
Pets: Small pets w/$5 fee
Creature Comforts: CCTV,
refrig, micro, whirlpools, pool

The Mark Hotel
(256) 232-6200
210 Route 31
24 rooms - $35-68
Pets: Welcome
Creature Comforts: CCTV, a/c,
refrig

Town & Country Motel
(256) 232-2700
2414 Route 31
29 rooms - $34-59
Pets: Welcome w/$5 fee
Creature Comforts: CCTV, a/c,
refrig, micro, pool

ATTALLA
Colombia Inn
(256) 570-0117
915 E. Fifth Ave.
50 rooms - $39-59
Pets: Welcome
Creature Comforts: CCTV, a/c

Holiday Inn Express
(800) HOLIDAY, (256) 538-7861
http://www.holiday-inn.com
801 Cleveland Ave.
144 rooms - $49-107
Pets: Under 25 Lbs. welcome
Creature Comforts: CCTV,
refrig, micro, pool

AUBURN
Auburn University Hotel
(800) 228-2876, (334) 821-8200
http://www.auhcc.com
241 S. College St.
250 rooms - $69-275
Pets: Welcome
Creature Comforts: Lovely six
story Georgian-style hotel, sun-
drenched lobby, southern
ambiance, CCTV, a/c, refrig,
micro, handsome guest rooms,
restaurant, pool, hlth clb

Comfort Inn
(800) 228-5150, (334) 821-6699
http://www.comfortinn.com
2283 S. College St.
49 rooms - $56-89
Pets: Welcome
Creature Comforts: CCTV, a/c,
refrig, micro, cont. brkfst, pool

Heart of Auburn Inn
(800) 843-5634 , (334) 887-3462
333 So. College St.
108 rooms - $38-68
Pets: Welcome w/$5 fee
Creature Comforts: CCTV, a/c,
refrig, pool

Quality Inn
(800) 228-5151, (334) 821-7001
http://www.qualityinn.com
1577 So. College St.
122 rooms - $44-170
Pets: Welcome
Creature Comforts: CCTV, a/c,
refrig, micro, restaurant, pool, hlth
clb

BAY MINETTE
Days Inn
(800) DAYS INN, (334) 580-8111
http://www.daysinn.com
1819 Route 31
49 rooms - $75-99
Pets: Welcome
Creature Comforts: CCTV, a/c,
refrig, micro, Jacuzzis, cont.
brkfst, pool

Quality Inn
(800) 228-5151, (334) 937-9521
http://www.qualityinn.com
1402 Route 31
50 rooms - $45-80
Pets: Small pets w/$5 fee
Creature Comforts: CCTV, a/c,
refrig, cont brkfst, and a pool

BESSEMER
Days Inn
(800) DAYS INN, (205) 424-6078
http://www.daysinn.com
1121 - 9th Ave. SW
78 rooms - $57-109
Pets: Welcome w/$6 fee
Creature Comforts: CCTV, a/c,
restaurant, cont. brkfst, hlth club,
pool

Motel 6
(800) 466-8356, (205) 426-9646
http://www.motel6.com
1000 Shiloh Lane
120 rooms - $34-44
Pets: Under 30 lbs. welcome
Creature Comforts: CCTV, a/c,
pool

Ramada Inn
(800) 2-Ramada, (205) 272-6232
http://www.ramada.com
1021 - 9th Ave SW
78 rooms - $52-160
Pets: Welcome
Creature Comforts: CCTV, a/c,
refrig, restaurant, cont. brkfst,
pool, billiards

BIRMINGHAM
Baymont Inns
(800) 4-Budget, (205) 995-9990
http://www.baymontinns.com
513 Cahaba Park Circle
103 rooms - $46-75
Pets: Small pets welcome
Creature Comforts: CCTV, a/c,
refrig, micro

Best Suites of America
(800) 237-8466, (205) 940-9990
http://www.bestinns.com
140 State Farm Parkway
106 rooms - $64-120
Pets: Small pets welcome
Creature Comforts: CCTV, a/c,
refrig, micro, cont. brkfst, pool,
whirlpool, hlth clb

Best Western Inn
(800) 528-1234, (205) 328-6320
http://www.bestwestern.com
2230 Civic Center Blvd.
240 rooms - $68-114
Pets: Small pets welcome
Creature Comforts: CCTV, a/c,
refrig, micro, restaurant, pool

Clarion Hotel
(800) 252-7466, (205) 591-7900
http://www.clarioninn.com
5216 Airport Hwy.
193 rooms - $80-119
Pets: Welcome
Creature Comforts: CCTV, a/c,
restaurant, pool, hlth clb,
whirlpool

Comfort Inn
(800) 228-5150, (205) 444-9200
http://www.comfortinn.com
110 Cahaba Valley Pkwy.
62 rooms - $55-120
Pets: Welcome
Creature Comforts: CCTV, a/c,
cont. brkfst, pool

Days Inn
(800) DAYS INN, (205) 849-0111
http://www.daysinn.com
616 Decatur Hwy.
98 rooms - $55-99
Pets: Welcome w/$5 fee
Creature Comforts: CCTV, a/c,
restaurant, cont. brkfst, pool

Embassy Suites
(800) 362-2779, (205) 879-7400
http://www.embassy-suites.com
2300 Woodcrest Place
244 rooms - $110-160
Pets: Welcome w/$50 dep.
Creature Comforts: CCTV, a/c,
refrig, micro, restaurant, htd pool,
hlth clb access, sauna, whirlpools

Hampton Inn
(800) Hampton, (205) 822-2224
http://www.hampton-inn.com
1466 Montgomery St.
124 rooms - $55-85
Pets: Small pets welcome
Creature Comforts: CCTV, a/c,
pool, hlth clb access

Holiday Inn
(800) HOLIDAY, (205) 822-4350
http://www.holiday-inn.com
1548 Montgomery Hwy.
165 rooms - $70-108
Pets: Welcome w/$25 fee
Creature Comforts: CCTV, a/c,
cont. brkfst, restaurant, pool, lake-
dock, walking trail

Howard Johnson Inn
(800) I-Go-Hojo, (205) 942-0919
http://www.hojo.com
275 Oxmoor Rd.
200 rooms - $59-79
Pets: Welcome w/$15 dep.
Creature Comforts: CCTV, pool

La Quinta Inn
(800) 531-5900, (205) 324-4510
http://www.laquinta.com
905 - 11th Ct. West
105 rooms - $50-99
Pets: Small pets welcome
Creature Comforts: CCTV, a/c,
refrig, micro, cont. brkfst, pool

Microtel
(800) 275-8047, (205) 945-5550
http://www.microtelinns.com
251 Summit Pkwy.
102 rooms - $30-50
Pets: Welcome w/signed waiver
Creature Comforts: CCTV, a/c,
micro

Motel Birmingham
(800) 338-9275, (205) 956-4440
7905 Crestwood Blvd.
244 rooms - $50-115
Pets: Welcome w/$15 fee
Creature Comforts: CCTV, a/c,
refrig, micro, kit, pool

Mountain Brook Inn
(800) 523-7771, (205) 870-3100
www.mountainbrookinn.com
2800 Rte. 280
130 rooms - $99-329
Pets: W/$20 fee on pool level
Creature Comforts: Centrally
located inn with bi-level suites,
CCTV, a/c, refrig, restaurant, pool,
hlth clb access

Pickwick Hotel
(800) 255-7304, (205) 933-9555
http://www.pickwickhotel.com
1023 - 20th St.
64 rooms - $79-150
Pets: Welcome w/$25 fee
Creature Comforts: Located near
hospitals, Art Deco decor, inviting
ambiance, CCTV, a/c, kit, cont.
brkfst, writing desks, hlth clb
access

Ramada Inn
(800) 2-Ramada, (205) 591-7900
http://www.ramada.com
5216 Airport Hwy.
190 rooms - $48-79
Pets: Small pets welcome
Creature Comforts: CCTV,
refrig, micro, restaurant, pool, hlth
clb

Red Roof Inn
(800)843-7663, (205) 942-9414
http://www.redroof.com
151 Vulcan Rd.
94 rooms - $48-79
Pets: Small pets welcome
Creature Comforts: CCTV, a/c

Residence Inn
(800) 331-3131, (205) 991-8686
http://www.residenceinn.com
3 Green Hill Rd.
128 rooms - $79-175
Pets: Small pets welcome
Creature Comforts: CCTV, a/c,
refrig, micro, fireplace, kit, pool,
hlth clb access, volleyball,
whirlpools

Super 8 Motel
(800) 800-8000, (205) 956-3650
http://www.super8.com
1813 Crestwood Blvd.
120 rooms - $45-89
Pets: Welcome
Creature Comforts: CCTV, a/c,
cont. brkfst, pool

The Tutwiler
(877) 999-3223, (205) 322-2100
http://www.wyndham.com
2021 Park Place North
147 rooms - $119-255
Pets: Small pets welcome
Creature Comforts: Elegantly
restored historic hotel w/antiques,
detailed woodworking, marble
accents, CCTV, a/c, refrig,
excellent restaurant, pub, cont.
brkfst, hlth clb access

BOAZ
Best Western Inn
(800) 528-1234, (256) 593-8410
http://www.bestwestern.com
751 Rte. 431 South
50 rooms - $40-69
Pets: Welcome
Creature Comforts: CCTV,
VCR, a/c, cont. brkfst, pool

Boaz Inn Motel
(800) 443-9096, (256) 593-2874
Rte. 431 North
30 rooms - $30-50
Pets: Welcome w/$5 fee
Creature Comforts: CCTV, a/c,
refrig, micro

Key West Inn
(800) 833-0555, (256) 593-0800
http://www.keywestinns.com
10535 Rte. 168
42 rooms - $45-62
Pets: Welcome w/$5 fee
Creature Comforts: CCTV, a/c,
refrig, micro

CALERA
Days Inn
(800) DAYS INN, (205) 668-0560
http://www.daysinn.com
11691 Rte. 25
42 rooms - $45-75
Pets: Welcome
Creature Comforts: CCTV, a/c,
restaurant, pool

CAMDEN
Days Inn
(800) DAYS INN, (334) 682-4555
http://www.daysinn.com
39 Camden Bypass
46 rooms - $49-90
Pets: Welcome
Creature Comforts: CCTV, a/c,
refrig, micro, cont. brkfst, pool

CEDAR BLUFF
Cedar Bluff Motel
(205) 779-6868
Route 9
15 rooms - $39-55
Pets: Welcome
Creature Comforts: CCTV, a/c,
kit

Riverside Motel
(800) 292-9324, (205) 779-6117
Rte. 1, Box 83
14 rooms - $40-65
Pets: Welcome
Creature Comforts: CCTV,
VCR, a/c, kit, cont. brkfst, pool

CHILDERSBURG
Days Inn
(800) DAYS INN, (256) 378-6007
http://www.daysinn.com
33669 Rte 280
40 rooms - $40-60
Pets: Under 50 lbs. w/$10 fee
Creature Comforts: CCTV, cont.
brkfst, and a pool

CLANTON
Best Western Inn
(800) 528-1234, (205) 280-1006
http://www.bestwestern.com
801 Bradberry Lane
53 rooms - $49-75
Pets: Welcome w/$5 fee
Creature Comforts: CCTV, a/c,
refrig, micro, cont. brkfst, pool

Holiday Inn
(800) HOLIDAY, (205) 755-0510
http://www.holiday-inn.com
Rtes. 31 & 22
99 rooms - $49-88
Pets: Welcome
Creature Comforts: CCTV, a/c,
cont. brkfst, restaurant

Key West Inn
(800) 833-0555, (205) 755-8500
http://www.keywestinns.com
2045 - 7th Street
44 rooms - $44-56
Pets: Small pets in smoking rms.
Creature Comforts: CCTV, a/c,
refrig, micro

Rodeway Inn
(800) 228-2000, (205) 755-4049
http://www.rodeway.com
2301 7th Street
46 rooms - $35-57
Pets: Welcome
Creature Comforts: CCTV, a/c,
pool

Shoney's Inn
(800) 222-2222, (205) 280-0306
http://www.shoneysinn.com
946 Lake Mitchell Rd.
74 rooms - $42-59
Pets: Welcome w/$10 dep.
Creature Comforts: CCTV, a/c,
restaurant, pool

COLLINSVILLE
HoJo Inn
(800) I-Go-Hojo, (256) 524-2114
http://www.hojo.com
Route 68
32 rooms - $35-60
Pets: Small pets welcome
Creature Comforts: CCTV, a/c,
refrig, micro, pool

CULLMAN
Best Western Fairwinds Inn
(800) 528-1234, (256) 737-5009
http://www.bestwestern.com
1917 Commerce Ave. NW
50 rooms - $55-135
Pets: Small pets w/$30 dep.
Creature Comforts: CCTV, a/c,
refrig, micro, cont. brkfst, pool

Days Inn
(800) DAYS INN, (256) 739-3800
http://www.daysinn.com
1841 - 4th St. SW
120 rooms - $44-65
Pets: Welcome w/$3 fee
Creature Comforts: CCTV, a/c,
restaurant, cont. brkfst, pool

Economy Inn
(256) 734-0122
1834 Second Ave. NW
46 rooms - $39-55
Pets: Welcome w/$5 fee
Creature Comforts: CCTV, a/c

Holiday Inn Express
(800) HOLIDAY, (256) 734-2691
http://www.holiday-inn.com
60 rooms - $48-88
Pets: Welcome
Creature Comforts: CCTV, a/c,
cont. brkfst

Howard Johnson Lodge
(800) I-Go-Hojo, (256) 737-7275
http://www.hojo.com
98 rooms - $40-90
Pets: Welcome w/$5 fee
Creature Comforts: CCTV, a/c,
refrig, micro, restaurant, pool

Ramada Inn
(800) 2-Ramada, (256) 737-7275
http://www.ramadainn.com
Rtes. 65 & 69
126 rooms - $50-98
Pets: Welcome
Creature Comforts: CCTV, a/c,
refrig, kit, micro, Jacuzzi,
restaurant, pool

Alabama

Super 8 Motel
(800) 800-8000, (256) 734-8854
http://www.super8.com
Rtes. 157 & 65
44 rooms - $45-75
Pets: Welcome w/notice
Creature Comforts: CCTV, a/c,
Jacuzzis, cont. brkfst, pool

DALEVILLE
Econo Lodge
(800) 55-ECONO, (334) 598-6304
http://www.econolodge.com
444 No. Daleville Ave.
92 rooms - $40-56
Pets: Small pets welcome
Creature Comforts: CCTV, a/c,
refrig, micro, pool

Green House Inn
(334) 598-1475
501 So. Daleville Ave.
75 rooms - $35-64
Pets: Welcome w/$4 fee
Creature Comforts: CCTV, a/c,
kit

DAPHNE
Eastern Shore Motel
(334) 626-6601
29070 Rte. 98
63 rooms - $45-59
Pets: Welcome w/$6 fee
Creature Comforts: CCTV, a/c,
refrig, micro

DECATUR
Days Inn
(800) DAYS INN, (256) 355-3520
http://www.daysinn.com
810 - 6th Ave. NE
114 rooms - $44-78
Pets: Welcome w/$10 fee
Creature Comforts: CCTV, a/c,
restaurant, Olympic pool

Holiday Inn
(800) HOLIDAY, (256) 355-3150
http://www.holiday-inn.com
1101 - 6th Ave. NE
220 rooms - $75-119
Pets: Small pets on 1st flr
Creature Comforts: CCTV, a/c,
refrig, micro, restaurant, pool, hlth
clb access, whirlpools

Ramada Limited
(800) 2-Ramada, (256) 353-0333
http://www.ramada.com
1317 East Rte. 67
84 rooms - $54-69
Pets: Small pets welcome
Creature Comforts: CCTV, a/c,
refrig, micro, pool, hlth clb

DEMOPOLIS
Heritage Motel
(334) 289-1175
1324 Rte. 80
45 rooms - $30-45
Pets: Welcome
Creature Comforts: CCTV, a/c

Riverview Inn
(334) 289-0690
1301 N. Walnut St.
25 rooms - $45-59
Pets: Welcome w/$3 fee
Creature Comforts: CCTV, a/c,
refrig, micro

Windwood Inn
(800) 233-0841, (334) 289-1760
web site pending
628 Rte. 80
90 rooms - $34-45
Pets: Welcome
Creature Comforts: CCTV, a/c,
refrig, pool

DOTHAN
Comfort Inn
(800) 228-5150, (334) 793-9090
http://www.comfortinn.com
3593 Ross Clark Circle
122 rooms - $65-95
Pets: Welcome
Creature Comforts: CCTV,
VCR, a/c, refrig, micro, Jacuzzis,
cont. brkfst, hlth clb, pool

Days Inn
(800)DAYS-INN, (334) 793-2550
http://www.daysinn.com
2841 Ross Clark Drive
120 rooms - $44-64
Pets: Welcome w/$5 fee
Creature Comforts: CCTV, a/c,
refrig, micro, hlth club, pool

Dothan Natnl Golf Club Hotel
(800) 451-1986, (334) 677-3321
http://www.dngch.com
7410 Route 231
96 rooms - $35-75
Pets: Welcome w/$10 fee
Creature Comforts: CCTV, a/c,
kit, restaurant, cont. brkfst,
olympic-size pool, mineral hot
springs, golf, spa, and whirlpool

Eastgate Inn
(334) 794-6643
1885 Ross Clark Circle
58 rooms - $35-50
Pets: Welcome w/$10 fee
Creature Comforts: CCTV, a/c,
kit, pool

Hampton Inn
(800) Hampton, (334) 671-3700
http://www.hampton-inn.com
3071 Ross Clark Circle
112 rooms - $69-80
Pets: Welcome
Creature Comforts: CCTV, a/c,
cont. brkfst, pool

Holiday Inn
(800) HOLIDAY, (334) 794-8711
http://www.holiday-inn.com
2195 Ross Clark Circle SE
144 rooms - $48-78
Pets: Welcome
Creature Comforts: CCTV, a/c,
refrig, micro, restaurant, pool

Motel 6
(800) 466-8356, (334) 793-6013
http://www.motel6.com
2907 Ross Clark Circle
102 rooms - $34-48
Pets: Small pets welcome
Creature Comforts: CCTV, a/c,
pool

Ramada Inn
(800) 2-Ramada, (334) 692-0031
http://www.ramada.com
3011 Ross Clark Circle
158 rooms - $50-86
Pets: Welcome
Creature Comforts: CCTV,
VCR, a/c, refrig, micro, restaurant,
pool

Town Terrace Motel
(334) 792-1135
251 N. Oates St.
40 rooms - $35-57
Pets: Welcome w/$15 fee
Creature Comforts: CCTV, a/c, refrig

ELBA
Riviera Motel
(334) 897-2204
154 Yelverton St.
20 rooms - $39-50
Pets: Welcome
Creature Comforts: CCTV, a/c, refrig, micro

ENTERPRISE
Comfort Inn
(800) 228-5150, (334) 395-2304
http://www.comfortinn.com
615 Boll Weevil Circle
78 rooms - $58-108
Pets: Welcome w/$7 fee
Creature Comforts: CCTV, a/c, kit, cont. brkfst, pool

Ramada Inn
(800) 2-Ramada, (334) 347-6262
http://www.ramada.com
630 Glover Ave.
102 rooms - $56-84
Pets: Welcome
Creature Comforts: CCTV, a/c, refrig, micro, restaurant, pool, hlth clb access, whirlpools

EUFAULA
Best Western Inn
(800) 528-1234, (334) 687-3900
http://www.bestwestern.com
1337 Rte. 31 So.
42 rooms - $40-70
Pets: Small pets welcome
Creature Comforts: CCTV, VCR, a/c, refrig, micro, Jacuzzis, cont. brkfst, pool

Days Inn
(800) DAYS-INN, (334) 687-1000
http://www.daysinn.com
1521 S. Eufaul Ave.
44 rooms - $45-99
Pets: Welcome
Creature Comforts: CCTV, a/c, refrig, micro, Jacuzzis, restaurant, pool, whirlpools

Holiday Inn
(800) HOLIDAY, (334) 687-2021
http://www.holiday-inn.com
631 E. Barbour Rd.
98 rooms - $42-64
Pets: Small pets welcome
Creature Comforts: CCTV, a/c, refrig, restaurant, pool

EUTAW
Kirkwood B&B
(205) 372-9009
111 Kirkwood Dr.
2 rooms - $75-95
Pets: Welcome
Creature Comforts: CCTV, a/c, refrig, full brkfst

EVERGREEN
Comfort Inn
(800) 228-5150, (334) 578-4701
http://www.comfortinn.com
Rtes. 65 & 83
58 rooms - $49-65
Pets: Small pets w/$5 fee
Creature Comforts: CCTV, a/c, cont brkfst, pool

Days Inn
(800) DAYS-INN, (334) 578-2100
http://www.daysinn.com
901 Liberty Hill Rd.
40 rooms - $40-85
Pets: Welcome w/$5 fee
Creature Comforts: CCTV, a/c, refrig, micro, free cont. brkfst

FAIRHOPE
Bay Breeze Guest House
(334) 928-8976
www.bbonline.com/al/baybreeze
PO Box 526
4 rooms - $95-120
Pets: Welcome
Creature Comforts: Charming accommodations, country decor, pine paneling, wicker and rattan furnishings, antiques, family heirlooms, brass beds-colorful quilts, hooked rugs, white pine paneling, stained glass, CCTV, VCR, a/c, kit, fireplace, Jacuzzi, full brkfst, herb garden,460 ft. pier

Marcella's Inn
(334) 990-8520
114 Fairhope Ave.
3 rooms - $85-160
Pets: Welcome
Creature Comforts: 1914 home overlooking bay, interior designer accents and warm hospitality CCTV, a/c, antiques, gourmet brkfst, tea room

Oak Haven Lodge
(334) 928-5431
355 So. Mobile St.
18 rooms - $45-65
Pets: Welcome w/$5 fee
Creature Comforts: CCTV, a/c, kit

FAYETTE
Journey's Inn
(205) 932-6727
2502 N. Temple Ave.
40 rooms - $45-60
Pets: Welcome
Creature Comforts: CCTV, a/c, refrig

FLORENCE
Best Western Inn
(800) 528-1234, (256) 766-2331
http://www.bestwestern.com
504 S. Court St.
118 rooms - $50-65
Pets: Small pets w/$5 fee
Creature Comforts: CCTV, a/c, refrig, restaurant, pool

Comfort Inn
(800) 228-5150, (256) 760-8888
http://www.comfortinn.com
400 S. Court St.
88 rooms - $46-58
Pets: Welcome
Creature Comforts: CCTV, a/c, refrig, hlth clb

Days Inn
(800) DAYS INN, (256) 383-3000
http://www.daysinn.com
2700 Woodward Ave.
79 rooms - $40-75
Pets: Welcome
Creature Comforts: CCTV, a/c, cont. brkfst, pool

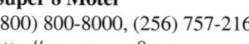

Super 8 Motel
(800) 800-8000, (256) 757-2167
http://www.super8.com
Rtes. 72 & 43
34 rooms - $46-66
Pets: Welcome w/$5 fee
Creature Comforts: CCTV, a/c,
kit, Jacuzzis, pool

FOLEY
Key West Inn
(800) 833-0555, (334) 943-1241
http://www.keywestinns.com
2520 S. McKenzie St.
44 rooms - $38-88
Pets: Welcome
Creature Comforts: CCTV, a/c,
refrig, micro, pool, whirlpools

FORT PAYNE
Adams Outdoors
(256) 845-2988
6102 Mitchell Rd. NE
10 rooms - $40-99
Pets: Leashed pets welcome
Creature Comforts: A/c, kit

Best Western Inn
(800) 528-1234, (256) 982-1113
http://www.bestwestern.com
100 Bishop Circle
60 rooms - $55-84
Pets: Under 40 lbs. welcome
Creature Comforts: CCTV, a/c,
refrig, Jacuzzis, cont. brkfst, pool

Mountain View Motel
(256) 845-2303
2302 Gault Ave. So.
7 rooms - $30-49
Pets: Welcome
Creature Comforts: CCTV, a/c

Quality Inn
(800) 228-5151, (256) 845-4013
http://www.qualityinn.com
1412 Glenn Blvd.
79 rooms - $44-69
Pets: Welcome
Creature Comforts: CCTV,
VCR, a/c, refrig, pool

GADSDEN
Days Inn
(800) DAYS-INN, (256) 442-7913
http://www.daysinn.com
1612 W. Grand Ave.
60 rooms - $50-79
Pets: Welcome
Creature Comforts: CCTV, a/c,
refrig, cont. brkfst, pool

Red Roof Inn
(800) THE ROOF, (256) 543-1105
http://www.redroof.com
1600 Rainbow Dr.
100 rooms - $49-89
Pets: Small pets w/$10 fee
Creature Comforts: CCTV, a/c,
refrig, pool

GREENVILLE
Best Western Inn
(800) 528-1234, (334) 382-9200
http://www.bestwestern.com
106 Cahaba Rd.
46 rooms - $49-69
Pets: Welcome w/$5 fee
Creature Comforts: CCTV, a/c,
refrig, micro, cont. brkfst, pool

Econo Lodge
(800) 55-ECONO, (334) 382-3118
http://www.econolodge.com
946 Fort Dale Rd.
40 rooms - $50-69
Pets: Welcome w/$2 fee
Creature Comforts: CCTV, a/c

Holiday Inn
(800) HOLIDAY, (334) 382-2651
http://www.holiday-inn.com
941 Fort Dale Rd.
96 rooms - $54-93
Pets: Under 10 lbs. welcome
Creature Comforts: CCTV, a/c,
restaurant, pool

Thrifty Inn
(334) 382-6671
105 Bypass Rd.
45 rooms - $44-66
Pets: Welcome
Creature Comforts: CCTV a/c

GULF SHORES
Bon Secor Lodge
(334) 968-7814
16730 Oyster Bay Place
7 cottages - $55-75
Pets: Welcome w/$6 fee
Creature Comforts: CCTV, kit,
river/dock

Comfort Inn
(800) 228-5150, (334) 968-8604
http://www.comfortinn.com
3049 W. 1st St.
49 rooms - $45-255
Pets: Welcome
Creature Comforts: CCTV, a/c,
refrig, cont. brkfst, pool

Gulf Pines Motel
(334) 968-7911
245 E. 22nd Ave.
17 rooms - $50-85
Pets: Welcome
Creature Comforts: CCTV, a/c,
kit

Lighthouse Motel
(334) 948-6188
http://www.gulfcoastrooms.com
455 E. Beach Blvd, Box 233
200 rooms - $55-155
Pets: Welcome w/$60 fee
Creature Comforts: CCTV, a/c,
kit, 3 pools, whirlpool, on beach

Roger's Castle
(334) 948-6954
809 W. Beach Rd.
6 apts. - $99-189
Pets: Welcome
Creature Comforts: CCTV, a/c,
kit, pool

Harris Properties
(800) 634-1429, (334) 968-8423
1709 Gulf Shore Rd.
http://www.harrisproperties.com
100 houses - $400-2,000/wk
Pets: In several houses
Creature Comforts: CCTV,
VCR, a/c, kit, fireplaces, Jacuzzis,
pools

GUNTERSVILLE
Days Inn
(800) DAYS-INN, (256) 582-3200
http://www.daysinn.com
14040 Rte. 431
52 rooms - $42-75
Pets: Small pets w/$10 dep.
Creature Comforts: CCTV, a/c,
refrig, micro, pool

Mac's Landing
(256) 582-1000
7001 Val Monte Dr.
54 rooms - $48-74
Pets: Welcome
Creature Comforts: CCTV, a/c,
kit, cont. brkfst, pool

Overlook Mountain Lodge
(256) 582-3256
13045 Rte. 431
51 rooms - $42-59
Pets: Welcome
Creature Comforts: CCTV, a/c,
refrig, micro, pool

HAMILTON
Best Western Inn
(800) 528-1234, (205) 921-7831
http://www.bestwestern.com
2031 Military St So.
80 rooms - $65-89
Pets: Welcome
Creature Comforts: CCTV, a/c,
refrig, micro, restaurant, pool

Days Inn
(800) DAYS INN, (205) 921-1790
http://www.daysinn.com
1849 Military St.
38 rooms - $65-99
Pets: Welcome w/$5 fee
Creature Comforts: CCTV, a/c,
Jacuzzis, cont. brkfst, pool

Holiday Motel
(205) 921-2171
315 Bexar Ave.
25 rooms - $30-58
Pets: Welcome
Creature Comforts: CCTV, a/c

HANCEVILE
Motel I-65
(205) 287-1114
14466 Route 91
10 rooms - $30-39
Pets: Welcome
Creature Comforts: TV, a/c

HALEYVILLE
Haleyville Motel
(205) 486-2263
Rte. 6, Box 449
15 rooms - $35-48
Pets: Welcome w/$5 fee
Creature Comforts: CCTV, a/c,
refrig

HEFLIN
Howard Johnson Express Inn
(800) I-Go-Hojo, (256)463-2900
http://www.hojo.com
Route 20
32 rooms - $39-68
Pets: Welcome w/$5 fee
Creature Comforts: CCTV, a/c,
Jacuzzis, cont. brkfst

HOMEWOOD
La Quinta Inn
(800) 531-5900, (205) 290-0150
http://www.laquinta.com
60 State Farm Pkwy.
132 rooms - $70-135
Pets: Under 25 lbs. welcome
Creature Comforts: CCTV, a/c,
refrig, micro, cont. brkfst,
whirlpool, hlth club, pool

HOOVER
La Quinta Inn
(800) 531-5900, (205) 403-0096
http://www.laquinta.com
120 Riverchase Pkwy.
133 rooms - $70-120
Pets: Under 25 lbs. welcome
Creature Comforts: CCTV, a/c,
refrig, micro, cont. brkfst,
whirlpool, hlth club, pool

HUNTSVILLE
Baymont Inns
(800) 4-Budget, (256) 830-8999
http://www.baymontinns.com
4890 University Dr.
100 rooms - $45-67
Pets: Welcome
Creature Comforts: CCTV, a/c,
refrig, micro, pool

Days Inn
(800) DAYS INN, (256) 772-9550
http://www.daysinn.com
102 Arlington Dr.
143 rooms - $53-79
Pets: Welcome w/$10 fee
Creature Comforts: CCTV, a/c,
refrig, micro, cont. brkfst, hlth
club, pool

Executive Lodge Suite Hotel
(800) 248-4722, (256) 830-8600
http://www.executivelodge.com
1535 Sparkman Dr.
212 rooms - $75-175
Pets: W/$2 fee and a CC dep.
Creature Comforts: A variety of
intriguing suite configurations,
CCTV, a/c, kit, Jacuzzis,
restaurant, cont. brkfst, 2 pools,
hlth clb access

Hilton Inn
(800) HILTONS, (256) 533-1400
http://www.hilton.com
401 Williams Ave.
277 rooms - $95-145
Pets: Welcome w/$25 dep.
Creature Comforts: CCTV, a/c,
refrig, restaurant, hlth clb,
whirlpool, pool

Holiday Inn Express
(800) HOLIDAY, (256) 721-1000
http://www.holiday-inn.com
3808 University Dr.
62 rooms - $54-74
Pets: Welcome w/$50 dep.
Creature Comforts: CCTV, a/c,
pool

Holiday Inn
(800) HOLIDAY, (256) 837-7171
http://www.holiday-inn.com
3810 University Dr.
112 rooms - $59-85
Pets: Welcome w/$50 dep.
Creature Comforts: CCTV, a/c,
refrig, restaurant, hlth clb access,
pool

Howard Johnson
(800) I-Go-Hojo, (256) 837-3250
http://www.hojo.com
4404 University Dr.
140 rooms - $49-155
Pets: Welcome
Creature Comforts: CCTV, a/c,
refrig, micro, Jacuzzis, restaurant,
pool, hlth clb

La Quinta Inn
(800) Nu-Rooms, (256) 830-2070
http://www.laquinta.com
4870 University Dr.
130 rooms - $55-79
Pets: Small pets welcome
Creature Comforts: CCTV, a/c,
refrig, micro, cont. brkfst, pool

La Quinta Inn
(800) Nu-Rooms, (256) 533-0756
http://www.laquinta.com
3141 University Dr.
130 rooms - $55-89
Pets: Small pets welcome
Creature Comforts: CCTV, a/c,
refrig, micro, cont. brkfst, pool

Marriott Hotel
(800) 228-9290, (256) 830-2222
http://www.marriott.com
Tranquility Base
290 rooms - $96-166
Pets: Small pets welcome
Creature Comforts: CCTV, a/c, restaurant, pool, hlth clb, sauna, whirlpool

Motel 6
(800) 466-8356, (256) 539-8448
http://www.motel6.com
3200 University Dr.
99 rooms - $40-59
Pets: Under 30 lbs. welcome
Creature Comforts: CCTV, a/c, pool

Ramada Inn
(800) 2-Ramada, (256) 881-6120
http://www.ramada.com
3502 So. Memorial Pkwy.
138 rooms - $46-106
Pets: Small pets w/$25 fee
Creature Comforts: CCTV, a/c, refrig, restaurant, pool

Residence Inn
(800) 331-3131, (256) 837-8907
http://www.residenceinn.com
4020 Independence Dr.
112 rooms - $80-140
Pets: Welcome w/$50 fee
Creature Comforts: CCTV, a/c, kit, restaurant, hlth clb, pool, whirlpools

Villager Lodge
(800) 328-7829, (256) 553-0610
http://www.villager.com
3100 University Dr.
100 rooms - $30-58
Pets: Welcome
Creature Comforts: CCTV, a/c, refrig, micro, pool

JASPER
Travel-Rite Inn
(205) 221-1161
200 Mallway Dr.
64 rooms - $42-55
Pets: Welcome
Creature Comforts: CCTV, a/c, micro

LEEDS
Days Inn
(800) DAYS-INN, (205) 699-9833
http://www.daysinn.com
1835 Ashville Rd.
54 rooms - $50-138
Pets: Welcome w/$5 nightly fee
Creature Comforts: CCTV, a/c, refrig, Jacuzzi, cont. brkfst, pool

Super 8 Motel
(800) 800-8000, (205) 640-7091
http://www.super8.com
2451 Moody Pkwy.
50 rooms - $45-76
Pets: Small pets w/$5 fee
Creature Comforts: CCTV, a/c

LOXLEY
Wind Chase Inn
(334) 964-4444
13156 No. Hickory Rd.
55 rooms - $52-65
Pets: Welcome w/$6 fee
Creature Comforts: CCTV, a/c, refrig

MADISON
Days Inn
(800) DAYS-INN, (256) 772-9550
http://www.daysinn.com
102 Arlington Dr.
143 rooms - $58-75
Pets: Welcome w/$10 fee
Creature Comforts: CCTV, a/c, refrig, micro, cont. brkfst, pool

Federal Square Motel
(800) 458-1639, (256) 772-8470
http://www.federalsquare.com
8781 Rte. 20
77 rooms - $50-85
Pets: Welcome w/$4 fee
Creature Comforts: CCTV, a/c, refrig, micro, bars, kit, pool

Motel 6
(800) 466-8356, (256) 772-7479
http://www.motel6.com
8995 Rte. 20
91 rooms - $40-49
Pets: Small pets welcome
Creature Comforts: CCTV, a/c, pool

MOBILE
Best Inns of America
(800) 237-8466, (334) 343-4911
http://www.bestinns.com
156 Beltline Hwy.
73 rooms - $45-75
Pets: Small pets welcome
Creature Comforts: CCTV, a/c, refrig, cont. brkfst, pool, whirlpool

Best Suites of America
(800) 237-8466, (334) 343-4949
http://www.bestinns.com
150 Beltline Hwy.
94 rooms - $60-140
Pets: Small pets welcome
Creature Comforts: CCTV, VCR, a/c, kit, Jacuzzis, cont. brkfst, pool, hlth clb

Best Western Inn
(800) 528-1234, (334) 432-2703
http://www.bestwestern.com
2701 Battleship Rd.
100 rooms - $60-88
Pets: Small pets welcome
Creature Comforts: CCTV, a/c, refrig, restaurant, pool, along river

The Clarion Hotel
(800) 252-7466, (334) 476-6400
http://www.clarioninn.com
3101 Airport Blvd.
250 rooms - $76-150
Pets: Small pets w/$25 fee
Creature Comforts: CCTV, VCR, a/c, refrig, micro, restaurant, pool, hlth clb access, whirlpools

Days Inn
(800) DAYS INN, (334) 334-3410
http://www.daysinn.com
3650 Airport Blvd.
162 rooms - $45-89
Pets: Welcome w/$5 fee
Creature Comforts: CCTV, a/c, kit, restaurant, cont. brkfst, pool

Days Inn
(800) DAYS-INN, (334) 661-8181
http://www.daysinn.com
5480 Inn Dr.
100 rooms - $59-75
Pets: Welcome w/$8 fee
Creature Comforts: CCTV, a/c, refrig, cont. brkfst, pool

Drury Inn
(800)325-8300, (334) 344-7700
http://www.drury-inn.com
824 So. Beltline Hwy.
110 rooms - $58-85
Pets: Small pets welcome
Creature Comforts: CCTV, a/c,
refrig, micro, pool

Econo Lodge
(800) 55-ECONO, (334) 479-5333
http://www.econolodge.com
1 So. Beltline Hwy.
80 rooms - $35-55
Pets: Small pets welcome
Creature Comforts: CCTV, a/c

Holiday Inn
(800) HOLIDAY, (334) 666-5600
http://www.holiday-inn.com
6257 Rte. 90 West
162 rooms - $60-95
Pets: Welcome
Creature Comforts: CCTV, a/c,
refrig, restaurant, two pools,
whirlpool

Holiday Inn
(800) HOLIDAY, (334) 342-3220
http://www.holiday-inn.com
850 So. Beltline Hwy
200 rooms - $60-88
Pets: Welcome
Creature Comforts: CCTV, a/c,
refrig, micro, restaurant, two
pools, hlth clb, whirlpool

Holiday Inn Express
(800) HOLIDAY, (334) 694-0100
http://www.holiday-inn.com
301 Government St.
210 rooms - $60-155
Pets: Small pets w/$25 deposit
Creature Comforts: CCTV, a/c,
restaurant, pool, hlth clb access

Howard Johnson Lodge
(800) I-Go-Hojo, (334) 471-2402
http://www.hojo.com
3132 Government Blvd.
160 rooms - $35-85
Pets: Small pets welcome
Creature Comforts: CCTV, a/c,
restaurant, tennis, pool, hlth clb
access, whirlpool

La Quinta Inn
(800) 531-5900, (334) 343-4051
http://www.laquinta.com
816 So. Beltline Hwy
124 rooms - $50-87
Pets: Small pets welcome
Creature Comforts: CCTV, a/c,
pool

Motel 6, Airport
(800) 466-8356, (334) 343-8448
http://www.motel6.com
400 So. Beltline Hwy.
93 rooms - $47-59
Pets: Under 30 lbs. welcome
Creature Comforts: CCTV, a/c,
pool

Motel 6, West
(800) 466-8356, (334) 660-1483
http://www.motel6.com
5488 Inn Rd.
98 rooms - $39-48
Pets: Under 30 Lbs welcome
Creature Comforts: CCTV, a/c,
pool

Motel 6, East
(800) 466-8356, (334) 473-1603
http://www.motel6.com
1520 Matzenger Dr.
141 rooms - $39-48
Pets: Under 30 lbs welcome
Creature Comforts: CCTV, a/c,
pool

Olsson's Motel
(800) 332-1004, (334) 661-5331
4137 Government Blvd.
25 rooms - $28-38
Pets: Small pets welcome
Creature Comforts: CCTV, a/c,
refrig, micro

Radisson Admiral Semmes
(800) 333-3333, (334) 432-8000
http://www.radisson.com
251 Government St.
170 rooms - $89-175
Pets: Small pets welcome
Creature Comforts: Historic
hotel, CCTV, VCR, a/c, refrig,
restaurant, pool, whirlpool, hlth
clb access

Ramada Inn on the Bay
(800) 2-Ramada, (334) 626-7200
http://www.ramada.com
1525 Battleship Pkwy.
169 rooms - $48-88
Pets: Small pets welcome
Creature Comforts: CCTV,
VCR, a/c, refrig, micro, restaurant,
pool

Red Roof Inn, North
(800) 843-7663, (334) 476-2004
http://www.redroof.com
33 So. Beltline Hwy.
110 rooms - $46-69
Pets: Small pets welcome
Creature Comforts: CCTV, a/c

Red Roof Inn, South
(800) 843-7663, (334) 666-1044
http://www.redroof.com
5450 Coca Cola Rd.
110 rooms - $44-66
Pets: Small pets welcome
Creature Comforts: CCTV, a/c

Shoney's Inn
(800) 222-2222, (334) 660-1520
http://www.shoneysinn.com
5472 Tillman's Corner Pkwy
120 rooms - $59-85
Pets: Welcome w/$5 dep.
Creature Comforts: CCTV, a/c,
refrig, micro, restaurant, cont.
brkfst, pool

Towle House Inn
(800) 938-6953, (334) 432-6440
http://www.towle-house.com
1104 Montauk Avenue
6 rooms - $75-120
Pets: Welcome in the guest house
Creature Comforts: Charming
home dating back to 1874, oldest
B&B in the city, in historic
district, CCTV, a/c, fans, four
poster beds, fireplace, hors
d'oeurves, Oriental carpets, kit,
antiques, gourmet brkfst, porches,
gardens-fountain

MONTEVALLO
Ramsey Conference Center
(205) 665-6280
6280 Vine St.
38 rooms - $30-59
Pets: Welcome
Creature Comforts: CCTV, a/c,
restaurant

MONTGOMERY

Baymont Inns
(800) 4-Budget, (334) 277-6000
http://www.baymontinns.com
5225 Carmichael Rd.
102 rooms - $46-66
Pets: Small pets welcome
Creature Comforts: CCTV, a/c,
refrig, micro, pool

Best Suites of America
(800) 237-8466, (334) 270-3223
http://www.bestinns.com
5155 Carmichael Rd.
110 rooms - $70-135
Pets: Small pets welcome
Creature Comforts: CCTV,
VCR, a/c, refrig, micro, Jacuzzis,
cont. brkfst, pool, hlth clb

Best Western Statehouse Inn
(800) 528-1234, (334) 265-0741
924 Madison Ave.
http://www.bestwestern.com
162 rooms - $65-95
Pets: Small pets w/carrier
Creature Comforts: CCTV, a/c,
restaurant, cont. brkfst, pool

Best Western Lodge
(800) 528-1234, (334) 288-5740
http://www.bestwestern.com
977 West South Blvd.
100 rooms - $50-85
Pets: Small pets-$10 fee, $10 dep.
Creature Comforts: CCTV, a/c,
refrig, micro, cont. brkfst, pool

Best Western Inn
(800) 528-1234, (334) 277-4442
http://www.bestwestern.com
5837 Monticello Ave.
49 rooms - $55-85
Pets: Small pets welcome
Creature Comforts: CCTV, a/c,
refrig, micro, cont. brkfst, pool

Carriage House Inn
(334) 215-0380
11091 Atlanta Hwy.
4 rooms - $75-99
Pets: Welcome w/$20 fee
Creature Comforts: CCTV, a/c,
kit, cont. brkfst, pool, 88 acres

Comfort Inn
(800) 228-5150, (334) 281-5090
http://www.comfortinn.com
1035 W. South Blvd.
55 rooms - $80-139
Pets: Welcome
Creature Comforts: CCTV, a/c,
refrig, cont. brkfst, pool

Days Inn
(800) DAYS-INN, (334) 269-9611
http://www.daysinn.com
2625 Zelda Rd.
120 rooms - $55-99
Pets: Welcome w/$5 fee
Creature Comforts: CCTV, a/c,
refrig, restaurant, cont. brkfst, hlth
club, pool

Days Inn
(800) DAYS-INN, (334) 284-9944
http://www.daysinn.com
4180 Troy Hwy.
50 rooms - $55-109
Pets: Welcome w/$5 fee
Creature Comforts: CCTV, a/c,
refrig, Jacuzzis, cont. brkfst, pool

Econo Lodge
(800) 55-ECONO, (334) 284-3400
http://www.econolodge.com
4135 Troy Hwy.
46 rooms - $35-63
Pets: In certain rooms w/$8 fee
Creature Comforts: CCTV, a/c,
Jacuzzis

Holiday Inn
(800) HOLIDAY, (334) 272-0370
http://www.holiday-inn.com
1185 Eastern Bypass
214 rooms - $70-98
Pets: Small pets welcome
Creature Comforts: CCTV, a/c,
refrig, restaurant, pool, sauna,
whirlpool, putting green

La Quinta Inn
(800) 531-5900, (334) 271-1620
http://www.laquinta.com
1280 East Blvd.
125 rooms - $55-88
Pets: Small pets welcome
Creature Comforts: CCTV, a/c,
cont. brkfst, pool

Motel 6
(800) 466-8356, (334) 277-6748
http://www.motel6.com
1051 Eastern Bypass
94 rooms - $38-48
Pets: Small pets welcome
Creature Comforts: CCTV, a/c,
pool

Ramada Inn
(800) 2-Ramada, (334) 277-2200
http://www.ramada.com
1355 Eastern Bypass
155 rooms - $55-78
Pets: Welcome w/$30 fee
Creature Comforts: CCTV, a/c,
refrig, restaurant, cont. brkfst,
pool, and hlth clb access

Ramada Inn
(800) 2-Ramada, (334) 265-0741
http://www.ramada.com
924 Madison Ave.
162 rooms - $55-80
Pets: Welcome
Creature Comforts: CCTV, a/c,
refrig, restaurant, cont. brkfst,
pool, hlth clb access

Residence Inn
(800) 331-3131, (334) 270-3300
http://www.residenceinn.com
1200 Hilmar Ct.
96 rooms - $99-165
Pets: Small pets w/credit card dep
Creature Comforts: CCTV,
VCR, a/c, kit, pool, hlth clb,
sauna, whirlpool

Scottish Inns
(800) 251-1962, (334) 288-1501
7237 Troy Tpke.
66 rooms - $38-47
Pets: Welcome
Creature Comforts: CCTV, a/c

Super 8 Motel
(800) 800-8000, (334) 281-8000
http://www.super8.com
1150 W. South Blvd.
165 rooms - $44-69
Pets: Small pets welcome
Creature Comforts: CCTV, a/c,
kit, cont. brkfst, pool

Villager Lodge
(800) 328-7829, (334) 834-4055
http://www.villager.com
2750 Chestnut St.
100 rooms - $36-48
Pets: Welcome w/$50 deposit
Creature Comforts: CCTV, a/c, refrig, kit, micro

MUSCLE SHOALS
Days Inn
(800) DAYS-INN, (205) 383-3000
http://www.daysinn.com
2700 Woodward Ave.
80 rooms - $44-56
Pets: Welcome
Creature Comforts: CCTV, a/c, refrig, micro, pool, hlth clb

NORTHPORT
Best Western Inn
(800) 528-1234, (205) 339-5200
http://www.bestwestern.com
2015 Rte. 82
37 rooms - $49-75
Pets: Under 25 lbs. in smkng rms
Creature Comforts: CCTV, a/c, kit, cont. brkfst, pool, sauna, whirlpool, hlth clb access

OPELIKA
Best Western Mariner Inn
(800) 528-1234, (334) 749-1461
http://www.bestwestern.com
1002 Columbus Pkwy.
100 rooms - $36-55
Pets: Small pets w/$5 fee
Creature Comforts: CCTV, a/c, pool, whirlpool

Days Inn
(800) DAYS-INN, (334) 749-5080
http://www.daysinn.com
1014 Amanda Ave.
43 rooms - $55-225
Pets: Welcome w/$5 fee
Creature Comforts: CCTV, a/c, refrig, micro, Jacuzzis, cont. brkfst, pool

Motel 6
(800) 466-8356, (334) 745-0988
http://www.motel6.com
1015 Columbus Pkwy.
78 rooms - $32-40
Pets: 30 lbs. or less welcome
Creature Comforts: CCTV, a/c, pool

OXFORD
Econo Lodge
(800) 55-ECONO, (256) 831-9480
http://www.econolodge.com
25 Elm St.
114 rooms - $48-108
Pets: Welcome
Creature Comforts: CCTV, a/c, refrig, kit, micro, cont. brkfst, pool

Holiday Inn
(800) 465-4329, (256) 831-3410
http://www.holiday-inn.com
Rte. 78 & 431
194 rooms - $45-85
Pets: Small pets welcome
Creature Comforts: CCTV, VCR, a/c, kit, restaurant, cont. brkfst, pool, whirlpool

Howard Johnson
(800) I-Go-Hojo, (256) 835-3988
http://www.hojo.com
Route 20
44 rooms - $44-65
Pets: Welcome
Creature Comforts: CCTV, a/c, refrig, micro, restaurant, pool

OZARK
Best Western Ozark Inn
(800) 528-1234, (334) 774-5166
http://www.bestwestern.com
Rte. 231 & Deese Rd.
62 rooms - $45-70
Pets: Small pets welcome
Creature Comforts: CCTV, a/c, cont. brkfst, pool

Candlelight Motel
(334) 774-4947
2015 Rte. 231
25 rooms - $29-43
Pets: Welcome w/$10 dep.
Creature Comforts: CCTV, a/c, refrig

Holiday Inn
(800) HOLIDAY, (334) 774-7300
http://www.holiday-inn.com
151 Rte. 231
100 rooms - $54-88
Pets: Under 10 lbs. welcome
Creature Comforts: CCTV, a/c, kit, restaurant, pool

PELHAM
Best Western Oak Mtn.
(800) 528-1234, (205) 982-1113
http://www.bestwestern.com
100 Bishop Circle
60 rooms - $55-89
Pets: Under 50 lbs. welcome
Creature Comforts: CCTV, a/c, refrig, Jacuzzis, cont. brkfst, pool

Comfort Inn
(800) 228-5150, (205) 444-9200
http://www.comfortinn.com
110 Cahaba Valley Pkwy.
63 rooms - $60-88
Pets: Welcome
Creature Comforts: CCTV, a/c, refrig, micro, hlth club, pool

PELL CITY
Best Western Riverside Inn
(800) 528-1234, (205) 338-3381
http://www.bestwestern.com
11900 Rte. 78
70 rooms - $50-87
Pets: Small pets welcome
Creature Comforts: CCTV, a/c, refrig, restaurant, pool, lake/dock

PHENIX CITY
Best Western American Lodge
(800) 528-1234, (334) 298-8000
http://www.bestwestern.com
1600 Rte. 280 (bypass)
44 rooms - $40-74
Pets: Welcome w/$20 dep.
Creature Comforts: CCTV, a/c, refrig, micro, pool, whirlpools

PRATTVILLE
Days Inn
(800) DAYS-INN, (334) 365-3311
http://www.daysinn.com
Rtes. 65 & 31
100 rooms - $45-119
Pets: Welcome w/$6 fee
Creature Comforts: CCTV, a/c, refrig, restaurant, cont. brkfst, pool

Holiday Inn
(800) HOLIDAY, (334) 285-3420
http://www.holiday-inn.com
2598 Cobbs Ford Rd.
128 rooms - $55-89
Pets: Welcome
Creature Comforts: CCTV, a/c, refrig, restaurant, two pools

SCOTTSBORO

Days Inn
(800) DAYS-INN, (256) 574-1212
http://www.daysinn.com
23945 John T. Reid Pkwy.
83 rooms - $45-79
Pets: Welcome
Creature Comforts: CCTV, a/c, refrig, micro, pool, hlth clb

Hampton Inn
(800) Hampton, (256) 259-4300
http://www.hampton-inn.com
46 Micah Way
52 rooms - $45-66
Pets: Small pets w/$25 dep.
Creature Comforts: CCTV, VCR, a/c, refrig, micro, pool

SELMA

Best Western Inn
(800) 528-1234, (334) 872-1900
http://www.bestwestern.com
1915 W. Highland Ave.
52 rooms - $48-72
Pets: Small pets welcome
Creature Comforts: CCTV, VCR, a/c, kit, cont. brkfst, pool

Grace Hall B&B
(800)45-SELMA, (334) 875-5744
http://www.olcg.com/selma/
gracehal.html
506 Lauderdale St.
6 rooms - $75-125
Pets: In first flr rms. w/$10 fee
Creature Comforts: Exquisitely restored Nat'l Historic Regis. 1857 antebellum mansion, elegant decor, antiques, Persian rugs, crystal chandeliers, original paintings, lovely furnishings, four poster beds, CCTV, VCR, a/c, refrig, fireplaces, full brkfst, walled-in garden, mansion tours

Graystone Motel
(334) 874-6681
1200 West Highland St.
19 rooms - $35-49
Pets: Welcome
Creature Comforts: CCTV, a/c

Holiday Inn
(800) HOLIDAY, (334) 872-0461
http://www.holiday-inn.com
1806 Rte. 80
166 rooms - $50-68
Pets: Welcome
Creature Comforts: CCTV, a/c, restaurant, two pools

Passport Inn
(800) 251-1962, (334) 872-3451
http://www.reservahost.com
601 Highland Ave.
88 rooms - $35-65
Pets: Welcome w/$5 fee
Creature Comforts: CCTV, a/c, cont. brkfst, pool

SHEFFIELD

Holiday Inn
(800) HOLIDAY, (256) 381-4710
http://www.holiday-inn.com
4900 Hatch Blvd.
200 rooms - $70-85
Pets: Welcome
Creature Comforts: CCTV, a/c, refrig, micro, restaurant, cont. brkfst, pool, whirlpool, hlth clb

Ramada Inn
(800) 2-Ramada, (256) 381-3743
http://www.ramada.com
4205 Hatch Blvd.
145 rooms - $55-79
Pets: Small pets welcome
Creature Comforts: CCTV, a/c, refrig, micro, restaurant, cont. brkfst, pool, whirlpool, hlth clb access

SHORTER

Days Inn
(800) DAYS-INN, (334) 727-6034
http://www.daysinn.com
327 Shorter Depot Rd.
65 rooms - $45-90
Pets: Welcome
Creature Comforts: CCTV, a/c, cont. brkfst, pool

STEVENSON

Budget Inn
(256) 437-2215
42973 Rte. 72
30 rooms - $42-54
Pets: Small pets welcome
Creature Comforts: CCTV, a/c, refrig, micro, cont. brkfst

THOMASVILLE

Best Western Inn
(800) 528-1234, (334) 636-0614
http://www.bestwestern.com
1200 Mosely Ave.
34 rooms - $44-65
Pets: Welcome w/$10 deposit
Creature Comforts: CCTV, a/c, rerig, cont. brkfst, pool

TROY

Days Inn
(800) DAYS-INN, (334) 566-1630
http://www.daysinn.com
1260 Rte. 231
62 rooms - $43-109
Pets: Welcome w/$5 fee
Creature Comforts: CCTV, a/c, refrig, micro, Jacuzzis, cont. brkfst, pool

Econo Lodge
(800) 55-ECONO, (334) 566-4960
http://www.econolodge.com
1013 Rte. 231
69 rooms - $45-60
Pets: Welcome
Creature Comforts: CCTV, a/c, refrig, pool

Holiday Inn Express
(800) HOLIDAY, (334) 670-0012
http://www.holiday-inn.com
Rtes. 29 & 231
60 rooms - $55-85
Pets: Small pets welcome
Creature Comforts: CCTV, a/c, pool

Holiday Inn
(800) HOLIDAY, (334) 566-1150
http://www.holiday-inn.com
Rtes. 29 & 231
99 rooms - $59-89
Pets: Small pets welcome
Creature Comforts: CCTV, a/c, refrig, restaurant, pools

Scottish Inns
(800) 251-1962, (334) 566-4090
186 Rte. 231
88 rooms - $45-55
Pets: Welcome w/$5 fee
Creature Comforts: CCTV, a/c, cont. brkfst

TUSCALOOSA

Best Western Catalina Inn
(800) 528-1234, (205) 339-5200
http://www.bestwestern.com
2015 McFarland Blvd.
37 rooms - $45-79
Pets: Small pets welcome
Creature Comforts: CCTV, a/c, kit, pool

La Quinta Inn
(800) Nu-Rooms, (205) 349-3270
http://www.laquinta.com
4122 McFarland Blvd.
125 rooms - $50-75
Pets: Small pets welcome
Creature Comforts: CCTV, a/c,
refrig, cont. brkfst, pool

Key West Inn
(800) 833-0555, (205) 556-3232
http://www.keywestinns.com
4700 Doris Pate Dr.
60 rooms - $50-79
Pets: Welcome in smoking rooms
Creature Comforts: CCTV,
VCR, a/c, refrig, cont. brkfst

Masters Inn
(800) 633-3434, (205) 556-2010
3600 McFarland Blvd.
152 rooms - $40-75
Pets: Welcome w/$6 fee
Creature Comforts: CCTV, a/c,
refrig, micro, pool

Motel 6
(800) 466-8365, (205) 759-4942
http://www.motel6.com
4700 McFarland Blvd.
78 rooms - $34-49
Pets: Welcome
Creature Comforts: CCTV, a/c,
pool

Ramada Inn
(800) 2-Ramada, (205) 759-4431
http://www.ramadainn.com
631 Skyland Blvd.
108 rooms - $38-135
Pets: Welcome
Creature Comforts: CCTV, a/c,
refrig, restaurant, pool, hlth clb
access

TUSCUMBIA
Key West Inn
(800) 833-0555, (256) 383-0700
http://www.keywestinns.com
1800 Rte. 72
44 rooms - $42-54
Pets: Under 50 lbs. w/$5 fee
Creature Comforts: CCTV,
VCR, a/c, refrig, micro, cont.
brkfst, pool

YORK
Days Inn
(800) DAYS-INN, (205) 392-5485
http://www.daysinn.com
17700 Rte. 17
50 rooms - $53-105
Pets: Welcome w/$25 deposit
Creature Comforts: CCTV, a/c,
refrig, micro, Jacuzzis, cont. brkfst

Alaska

ANCHOR POINT

Anchor River Inn
(800) 435-8531
Box 154
20 rooms - $55-85
Pets: Welcome
Creature Comforts: CCTV, refrig, restaurant

ANCHORAGE

A Cousin of Mine
(907) 248-3462
4406 Forest Rd.
3 rooms - $85-99
Pets: Welcome w/$10 fee
Creature Comforts: CCTV, a/c, kit, cont. brkfst

Adam's Place B&B
(907) 346-3604
5701 E. 97th Ave.
2 rooms - $75-85
Pets: Welcome
Creature Comforts: CCTV, a/c, kit, cont. brkfst

Alaskan Frontier Gardens
(907) 345-6556
http://www.alaska1.com/akfrontier
1101 E. Tudor Rd, #160
3 rooms - $100-175
Pets: Welcome
Creature Comforts: Terrific cedar house, beautiful gardens, and grounds, intriguing collectibles, CCTV, VCR, a/c, refrig, fireplace, Jacuzzis, full brkfst, access to boating

Alaskan Wilderness Plantation
(800) 478-9657, (907) 243-3519
http://www.jakesalaska.com
2910 W. 31st Ave.
8 rooms - $80-300
Pets: Welcome
Creature Comforts: A lovely 10,000 sq. ft. mansion on over 3 wooded acres, CCTV, VCR, a/c, fireplace, kit, Jacuzzis, full brkfst, pool

Anchorage Eagle Nest Hotel
(800) 848-7852, (907) 243-3433
4110 Spenard Rd.
28 rooms - $50-210
Pets: Welcome w/$50 dep.
Creature Comforts: CCTV, a/c, refrig, micro, kit

Aurora Winds B&B
(800) 642-9640
http://www.aurorawinds.com
7501 Upper O'Malley
5 rooms - $60-185
Pets: Welcome
Creature Comforts: A 5,200 sq. ft. home with beautifully appointed guest rooms, CCTV, VCR, a/c, Jacuzzis, fireplaces, kit, full brkfst, pool, whirlpool, sauna, hlth clb, theater, billiard table

Best Western Barratt Inn
(800) 528-1234, (907) 243-3131
http://www.bestwestern.com
4616 Spenard Rd.
217 rooms - $79-89
Pets: Small pets-$5 fee, $50 dep.
Creature Comforts: CCTV, a/c, kit, restaurant, hlth club

Comfort Inn
(800) 228-5150, (907) 277-6887
http://www.comfortinn.com
111 W. Ship Creek Ave.
100 rooms - $75-275
Pets: Welcome
Creature Comforts: CCTV, VCR, a/c, kit, cont. brkfst, pool

Days Inn
(800) DAYS-INN, (907) 276-7226
http://www.daysinn.com
321 E. 5th Ave.
130 rooms - $50-175
Pets: Welcome w/$25 dep.
Creature Comforts: CCTV, a/c, refrig, micro, restaurant

Eighth Avenue Hotel
(800) 478-4837, (907) 274-6213
Box 200089
28 rooms - $80-150
Pets: Welcome
Creature Comforts: CCTV, a/c, kit

Hillside On Gambell
(800) 478-6008, (907) 258-6006
www.servcom.com/hillside
2150 Gambell St.
26 rooms - $50-105
Pets: Welcome $5 fee, $20 dep.
Creature Comforts: CCTV, VCR, a/c, refrig, micro, kit, cont. brkfst

Ivy Inn B&B
(907) 345-4024
13570 Westwind Dr.
2 suites - $85-109
Pets: Welcome w/permission
Creature Comforts: CCTV, a/c VCR, kit, antiques, cont. brkfst

Merrill Field Inn
(800) 898-4547, (907) 276-4547
420 Sitka St.
40 rooms - $50-110
Pets: Welcome w/$7 fee
Creature Comforts: CCTV, kit, restaurants, cont. brkfst

Parkwood Inn
(907) 563-3590
4455 Juneau St.
29 rooms - $109-145
Pets: $5 fee & $50 dep.
Creature Comforts: CCTV, VCR, kit

Poppy Seed B&B
(907) 344-2286
616 E. 72nd Ave.
3 rooms - $55-90
Pets: Welcome
Creature Comforts: CCTV, a/c, kit, cont. brkfst, and scenic trails

Puffin Inn
(800) 478-3346, (907) 243-4044
4400 Spenard Rd.
42 rooms - $65-120
Pets: Welcome
Creature Comforts: CCTV, a/c,
cont. brkfst

Regal Alaskan Hotel
(800) 544-0553, (907) 243-2300
http://www.regal-hotels.com
4800 Spenard Rd.
248 rooms - $135-325
Pets: Welcome w/$50 dep.
Creature Comforts: Wonderful
setting on the water surrounded
by mountains, CCTV, a/c, refrig,
Jacuzzis, steam showers,
restaurant, sauna, whirlpools,
hlth club, on a lake

Sixth and B B&B
(907) 279-5293
145 W. Sixth Ave.
3 rooms - $40-105
Pets: Welcome
Creature Comforts: CCTV, a/c,
cont. brkfst.

Sourdough Visitors Lodge
(800) 777-3716, (907) 279-4148
801 E. Erikson St.
32 suites - $75-175
Pets: Welcome w/$50 dep.
Creature Comforts: CCTV, a/c,
kit

Super 8 Motel
(800) 800-8000, (907) 276-8884
http://www.super8.com
3501 Minnesota Dr.
84 rooms - $75-99
Pets: Welcome
Creature Comforts: CCTV, a/c,
cont. brkfst, and access to tennis

Swan House B&B
(800) 921-1900, (907) 346-3033
http://www.alaska.net/~swan1
6480 Crooked Tree Dr.
3 rooms - $135-150
Pets: Small pets on occasion
Creature Comforts: An
exquisite home w/swan motifs
and over 125 windows, CCTV,
VCR, refrig, fireplace, spa

Tess's Place
(907) 248-4704
3013 Kingfisher Dr.
3 rooms - $55-70
Pets: Welcome if crated
Creature Comforts: CCTV, a/c,
refrig, fireplace, cont. brkfst,
whirlpool

12th & L B&B
(907) 276-1225
http://www.goalaska.com
1134 L St.
4 rooms - $80-109
Pets: Welcome
Creature Comforts: CCTV, a/c,
kit

Westmark Inn
(800) 544-0970, (907) 272-7561
http://www.westmarkhotels.com
115 E. 3rd Ave.
90 rooms - $129-199
Pets: Welcome w/$10 fee
Creature Comforts: CCTV,
refrig, restaurant

BETTLES
Bettles Lodge Cabins
(800) 770-5111, (907) 692-5111
Box 27
18 rooms - $95-155
Pets: Welcome
Creature Comforts: CCTV, kit,
restaurant

BIG LAKE
Big Lake Motel
(907) 892-7976
S. Big Lake Rd, Box 520728
20 rooms - $65-85
Pets: Welcome w/$20 dep.
Creature Comforts: CCTV, a/c,
restaurant, refrig

CANTWELL
Reindeer Mountain Lodge
(907) 768-2420
MP 210 Parks Hwy.
7 rooms - $69-85
Pets: Welcome
Creature Comforts: CCTV, a/c,
refrig, micro

CIRCLE SPRINGS
Circle Hot Springs Resort
(907) 520-5113
Box 254
12 cabins - $110-190
Pets: Welcome
Creature Comforts: CCTV,
fireplace, kit, restaurant

COOPER LANDING
Sunrise Inn
(907) 595-1222
MP 45-A (Sterling Hwy.)
12 rooms - $45-120
Pets: Welcome w/$10 fee
Creature Comforts: CCTV and
restaurant

DELTA JUNCTION
Alaska 7 Motel
(907) 895-4848
www.alaskan.com/ak7motel
3548 Richardson Hwy
16 rooms - $60-75
Pets: Welcome
Creature Comforts: CCTV, a/c,
and refrig

DENALI NATIONAL PARK
Earthsong Lodge
(907) 683-2863
http://www.earthsong.com
Box 89
10 cabins - $95-125
Pets: Welcome
Creature Comforts: CCTV,
VCR, cont. brkfst, library, shop,
fireplace

Sourdough Cabins
(907) 683-2773
Box 118
51 cabins - $80-150
Pets: Welcome
Creature Comforts: none

EAGLE RIVER
Eagle River Motel
(907) 694-5000
111 Old Eagle River Rd.
12 rooms - $60-89
Pets: Welcome
Creature Comforts: CCTV, kit

FAIRBANKS

AAA Care B&B
(800) 478-2705, (907) 489-2447
557 Fairbanks St.
11 rooms - $70-150
Pets: Welcome w/$5 fee
Creature Comforts: CCTV,
VCR, kit, deck, full brkfst

Alaska Motel
(907) 456-6393
web site pending
1546 Cushman St.
36 rooms - $65-85
Pets: Welcome w/$5 fee
Creature Comforts: CCTV, a/c,
and refrig

A Pioneer B&B
(907) 452-5393
1119 Second Ave.
3 rooms - $70-90
Pets: Welcome w/CC deposit
Creature Comforts: Restored
1900's cabin, CCTV, kit, cont.
brkfst

Chena Hot Springs Resort
(800) 478-4681, (907) 452-7867
http://www.chenhotsprings.com
Box 73440
54 units - $65-155
Pets: Welcome w/$100 dep.
Creature Comforts: CCTV,
refrig, fireplace, Jacuzzis,
restaurant, pool, shop, whirlpool,
and 440 acres

Chena River B&B
(907) 479-2532
1001 Dolly Varden Ln.
5 rooms - $50-120
Pets: Welcome
Creature Comforts: CCTV,
VCR, fireplace, on 10-acres
along a river

Comfort Inn
(800) 228-5150, (907) 479-8080
http://www.comfortinn.com
1908 Chena Landings Loop
74 rooms - $65-220
Pets: Welcome
Creature Comforts: CCTV, a/c,
Jacuzzis, fireplaces, cont. brkfst,
pool

Fox Creek B&B
(907) 457-5494
http://www.ptialaska.net/
~foxcreek
2498 Elliott Hwy.
2 rooms - $55-90
Pets: Welcome
Creature Comforts: CCTV, a/c,
wood stove, full brkfst

North Woods Lodge
(800) 478-5305
web site pending
PO Box 83615
8 units - $45-99
Pets: Welcome
Creature Comforts: CCTV,
fireplaces, kit, Jacuzzi, whirlpool

Old F. E. Gold Camp
(907) 389-2414
5550 Old Steese Hwy
31 rooms - $55-75
Pets: Welcome
Creature Comforts: CCTV,
Jacuzzi, restaurant, bar

Regency Fairbanks Hotel
(800) 348-1340, (907) 452-3200
http://regencyfarbankshotel.com
95 Tenth Ave.
129 rooms - $75-275
Pets: Welcome w/$50 dep.
Creature Comforts: CCTV, a/c,
refrig, micro, kit, Jacuzzi,
restaurant

Seven Gables Inn
(907) 479-0751
http://www.7gablesinn.com
Box 99708
12 rooms - $55-140
Pets: Welcome
Creature Comforts: Old-
fashioned B&B w/country decor,
guest rooms & apts, CCTV, a/c,
VCR, ceiling fans, fireplaces,
Jacuzzis, country quilts, four
poster beds, cont. brkfst

Super 8 Motel
(800) 800-8000, (907) 451-8888
http://www.super8.com
1909 Airport Rd.
77 rooms - $75-99
Pets: Welcome
Creature Comforts: CCTV, a/c,
cont. brkfst

GLENNALLEN

The New Caribou Hotel
(800) 478-3302, (907) 822-3302
Box 329
82 rooms - $80-199
Pets: Welcome w/$10 fee
Creature Comforts: CCTV, a/c,
kit, Jacuzzis, restaurant

GUSTAVUS

Bear Track Inn
(888) 697-2284, (907) 697-3017
http://www.alaska1.com/beartrac
255 Rink Creek Rd.
14 rooms - $425-575 (MAP)
Pets: Welcome w/$50 dep.
Creature Comforts: Great log
cabin inn w/wrap-around
windows and huge bedrooms,
down comforters, CCTV, a/c,
refrig, fireplaces, restaurant, a
cont. brkfst, fishing, kayaking,
whale watching, access to golf

Gustavus Inn at Glacier Bay
(800) 697-2254, (907) 697-2254
PO Box 60
13 rooms - $125-145
Pets: Welcome
Creature Comforts: CCTV,
VCR, restaurant, bikes, fishing,
and waterviews

A Puffin's B&B
(800) 478-2258, (907) 697-2260
http://ourworld.comuserve.com/
homepages/puffin
1/4 Mile Logging Rd.
4 rooms - $85-125
Pets: Welcome
Creature Comforts: Lovely
modern cottages set on seven
acres, TV, VCR, full brkfst,
fishing, cafe, kayaking

Tri B&B
(907) 697-2425
Box 214
3 cottages - $75-99
Pets: Welcome
Creature Comforts: micro

HAINES
Captain's Choice Motel
(800) 247-7153, (907) 766-3111
http://www.kcd.com/captain
108 - 2nd Ave.
40 rooms - $70-160
Pets: Welcome w/$10 fee
Creature Comforts: CCTV,
VCR, refrig, Jacuzzis, water
view

Eagle's Nest Motel
(800) 354-6009, (907) 766-2891
http://www.haines.com
1069 Haines Hwy.
10 rooms - $60-100
Pets: Welcome
Creature Comforts: CCTV,
refrig, micro, fireplace, kit

Ft. Seward Lodge
(800) 478-7772, (907) 766-2009
http://www.haines.com
Box 307
10 rooms - $50-90
Pets: Welcome w/$50 deposit
Creature Comforts: CCTV,
refrig, micro, kit, restaurant,
cont. brkfst, and ocean views

Ft. Wm. H. Seward B&B
(800) 615-Norm, (907) 766-2856
http://www.haines.ak.us/norm/
Box 5
6 rooms - $60-135
Pets: Welcome
Creature Comforts: On National
Register of Historic Places, CCTV,
a/c, fireplace, Jacuzzi, full.brkfst,
mtn bikes, water views

Mountain View Motel
(800) 478-2902, (907) 766-2900
Box 62
10 rooms - $50-90
Pets: Welcome
Creature Comforts: CCTV, kit

Thunderbird Motel
(800) 327-2556, (907) 766-2131
http://www.kcd.com/t-bird
242 Dalton St
20 rooms - $60-70
Pets: Welcome
Creature Comforts: CCTV, kit

HEALY
Dome Home B&B
(907) 683-1239
http://www.AlaskaOne.com/
delanidome
Box 262
7 rooms - $40-95
Pets: Welcome
Creature Comforts: CCTV,
VCR, refrig, fireplace, full brkfst

Earth Song Lodge
(907) 683-2863
http://www.akpub.com/aktt/
earth.html
PO Box 89
10 cabins - $95-125
Pets: Welcome
Creature Comforts: VCR,
fireplace, cont. brkfst

HOMER
Anna's Guest House
(907) 235-2716, 235-2265
e-mail: doughboy@xyz.net
460 Bonanza Ave.
1 cottage - $65-75
Pets: Welcome
Creature Comforts: CCTV, kit,
charming yard

Best Western Bidarka Inn
(800) 528-1234, (907) 235-8148
http://www.bestwestern.com
575 Sterling Hwy.
74 rooms - $80-148
Pets: Welcome w/$20 fee
Creature Comforts: CCTV,
refrig, restaurant, whirlpools, hlth
club

Driftwood Inn
(800) 478-8019, (907) 235-8019
135 W. Brunnell Ave.
21 rooms - $45-155
Pets: Welcome w/$5 fee
Creature Comforts: CCTV,
VCR, kit, cont. brkfst

Heritage Hotel
(907) 235-7787
147 E. Pioneer Ave.
32 rooms - $50-99
Pets: Welcome w/$10 fee
Creature Comforts: CCTV, a/c

Lakewood Inn
(907) 235-6144
984 Ocean Dr. #1
35 rooms - $60-75
Pets: Welcome w/$10 fee
Creature Comforts: CCTV, a/c,
kit, Jacuzzis, restaurant

Land's End Resort
(800) 478-0400, (907) 235-2500
http://www.akms.com/landsend
4786 Homer Spit Rd.
61 rooms - $69-150
Pets: Welcome
Creature Comforts: CCTV,
VCR, a/c, refrig, fireplace,
restaurant, beach

Ocean Shores Motel
(800) 770-7775
3500 Crittenden Dr.
32 rooms - $55-135
Pets: Welcome w/$50 dep.
Creature Comforts: CCTV, a/c,
kit

Sundmarks B&B
(907) 235-5188
East Hill Farm Rd.
8 rooms - $80-105
Pets: Welcome in outside rooms
Creature Comforts: TV, VCR,
kit, full brkfst

HOPE
Bear Creek Cabins
(907) 782-3730
http://www.alaska.net~advenak
PO Box 64
7 cabins - $80-100
Pets: Welcome
Creature Comforts: Rustic
cabins

JUNEAU

Best Western Country Lane Inn
(800) 528-1234, (907) 789-5005
http://www.bestwestern.com
9300 Glacier Hwy.
55 rooms - $85-149
Pets: Welcome-$10 fee, $50 dep.
Creature Comforts: CCTV, kit, cont. brkfst

The Driftwood Lodge
(800) 544-2239, (907) 586-2280
435 Willoughby Ave.
63 rooms - $65-105
Pets: Welcome w/$5 fee
Creature Comforts: CCTV, a/c, refrig, restaurant

The Prospector Inn
(800) 331-2711, (907) 586-3737
375 Whittier St.
60 rooms - $75-150
Pets: $10 fee & $50 dep.
Creature Comforts: CCTV, kit, restaurant

Super 8 Motel
(800) 800-8000, (907) 789-4858
http://www.super8.com
2295 Trout St.
75 rooms - $75-99
Pets: Small pets welcome
Creature Comforts: CCTV, cont. brkfst

KENAI

Capt. Bligh's Beaver Creek Ldg
(907) 283-7550, 262-7919
www.alaskaone.com/cptbligh
Box 4300
6 rooms - $1,300-1,500/wk
Pets: Welcome
Creature Comforts: Log cabins on 5 acres, TV, VCR, refrig, micro, fireplace, kit, restaurant, and fly fishing

KENAI PENINSULA

Kenai Magic Lodge
(888) 262-6644, (907) 279-4341
http://www.alaska-online.com/kml/index
2440 E. Tudor Rd., #205
10 rooms - $95-175
Pets: Welcome
Creature Comforts: CCTV, VCR, kit, Jacuzzi, restaurant, fishing

Kenai Peninsula Condos
(800) 362-1383
www.aonline.com/business/kenai
PO Box 3416 VP
8 units - $85-105
Pets: Welcome in 1st flr rms
Creature Comforts: CCTV, a/c, kit

Kenai River Lodge
(907) 262-4292
http://www.alaskais.com/kenailodge
393 Riverside Dr.
12 rooms - $99-130
Pets: Welcome
Creature Comforts: Horseback riding, trout fishing, back country flights

Kenai Wilderness Lodge
(907) 262-4390
3074 Commercial Dr.
5 cabins - $45-105
Pets: Welcome
Creature Comforts: Kit, boats

Morgan's Landing Rentals
(907) 262-8343
web site pending
Box 422
3 units - $80-135
Pets: Welcome
Creature Comforts: CCTV, kit

KETCHIKAN

Best Western Landing
(800) 528-1234, (907) 225-5166
http://www.bestwestern.com
3434 Tongass Ave.
76 rooms - $90-175
Pets: Welcome-$10 fee, $50 dep.
Creature Comforts: CCTV, refrig, micro, fireplaces, restaurant, and hlth club

The Gilmore Hotel
(800) 275-9423, (907) 225-9423
Box 6814
38 rooms - $50-120
Pets: Welcome w/$50 dep.
Creature Comforts: CCTV, refrig, micro, cont. brkfst

Ingersol Hotel
(800) 478-2124, (907) 225-2124
303 Mission St.
60 rooms - $60-100
Pets: Welcome
Creature Comforts: CCTV

Ketchikan B&B
(907) 225-8550
1508 Water St.
2 rooms - $65-165
Pets: Welcome w/approval
Creature Comforts: CCTV, refrig, full brkfst

Super 8 Motel
(800) 800-8000, (907) 225-9088
http://www.super8.com
2151 Sea Level Dr.
82 rooms - $70-90
Pets: Small pets welcome
Creature Comforts: CCTV, cont. brkfst, water views

KODIAK

Briskin River Inn
(800) 544-2202, (907) 487-2700
1395 Airport Rd.
50 rooms - $115-175
Pets: Welcome w/$25 fee
Creature Comforts: A charming inn along a river, CCTV, VCR, refrig, restaurant, whirlpool

Kalsin Inn
(907) 486-2659
Box 1696
11 rooms - $65-80
Pets: Welcome if friendly
Creature Comforts: Refrig, restaurant

Kodiak B&B
(907) 486-5367
308 Cope St.
2 rooms - $75-89
Pets: Welcome
Creature Comforts: TV and cont. brkfst

Kodiak Inn
(907) 486-5712
226 W. Rezanof Dr.
82 rooms - $125-199
Pets: Welcome w/$50 dep.
Creature Comforts: CCTV, a/c, refrig, restaurant

Northland Ranch Resort
(907) 486-5578
web site pending
Box 2376
14 rooms - $59-85
Pets: Welcome
Creature Comforts: TV, game rm, restaurant, (horse/fishing packages)

Westmark Kodiak
(800) 544-0970, (907) 486-5712
http://www.westmarkhotels.com
236 W. Rezanof Dr.
80 rooms - $120-150
Pets: Welcome
Creature Comforts: CCTV,
VCR, restaurant

SITKA
Super 8 Motel
(800) 800-8000, (907) 747-8804
http://www.super8.com
404 Sawmill Creek Rd.
35 rooms - $80-110
Pets: Small pets w/permission
Creature Comforts: CCTV,
refrig, cont. brkfst

Snowshoe Motel
(907) 883-4511
Box 559
24 rooms - $45-80
Pets: Welcome
Creature Comforts: CCTV,
refrig, cont. brkfst

Tok Lodge
(907) 883-2851
Box 135
48 rooms - $85-125
Pets: Welcome
Creature Comforts: TV, VCR,
fireplace, restaurant, store

Westmark Tok Hotel
(800) 544-0970, (907) 883-5174
http://www.westmarkhotels.com
Rtes. 1 & 2
92 rooms - $95-165
Pets: Welcome w/$25 dep.
Creature Comforts: CCTV, a/c,
refrig, restaurant

PALMER
Hatcher Pass B&B
(907) 745-4210
HC01, Box 6797
3 rooms - $55-100
Pets: Welcome w/approval
Creature Comforts: refrig, full
brkfst

SKAGWAY
Westmark Inn
(800) 544-0970, (907) 835-4391
http://www.westmarkhotels.com
Spring & 3rd streets
220 rooms - $125-150
Pets: Small pets welcome
Creature Comforts: CCTV
restaurant

VALDEZ
Lake House B&B
(907) 835-4752
PO Box 1499
10 rooms - $90-109
Pets: Welcome
Creature Comforts: CCTV, a/c,
refrig, micro, cont. brkfst,
overlooks a lake

PETERSBURG
Scandia House
(907) 772-4281
110 Nordic Dr.
33 rooms - $85-105
Pets: Welcome w/$5 fee
Creature Comforts: CCTV, a/c,
refrig, cont. brkfst

SOLDOTNA
B&B Cottages
(800) 582-7829
PO Box 1626
6 cottages - $65-90
Pets: Welcome
Creature Comforts: CCTV, kit

Tiekel River Lodge
(907) 822-3259
Richardson Hwy, Mile 56
7 rooms - $50-90
Pets: Welcome w/$10 fee
Creature Comforts: Restaurant,
store

SALCHA
Aroka Inn
(907) 224-8975
Box 2448
web site pending
9 rooms - $105-120
Pets: Welcome in pet units
Creature Comforts: CCTV, kit

TALKEETNA
Latitude 62 Lodge
(907) 733-2262
Box 478
13 units - $60-105
Pets: Welcome w/$10 dep.
Creature Comforts: CCTV, kit,
Jacuzzi, fireplace, restaurant, cont.
brkfst, bar

Totem Inn
(907) 835-4443
web site pending
Box 648
20 rooms - $60-125
Pets: Welcome w/$5 fee
Creature Comforts: CCTV, a/c,
refrig, micro, restaurant

SELDOVIA
Swan House B&B
(800) 921-1900, (907) 234-8888
http://www.alaska.net/~swan1
175 Augustine Ave. North
5 rooms - $129-169
Pets: Small pets on occasion
Creature Comforts: An
enchanting 3,000 sq. ft. home w/
multi level decks, TV, VCR,
refrig, full brkfst, whirlpool,
kayaks, plush furnishings,
telescopes-water/wildlife views

TOK
Cleft of the Rock B&B
(907) 883-4219
5 Sundog Trail
6 rooms - $60-120
Pets: $5 fee & $25 dep.
Creature Comforts: Nicely
furnished log cabins, SATV, VCR,
kit, Jacuzzis, cont. brkfst,
canoeing, hiking, lawn sports,
bikes, xc-skiing

Westmark Hotel
(800) 544-0970, (907) 835-4391
http://www.westmarkhotels.com
100 Fidalgo Dr.
100 rooms - $95-165
Pets: Welcome w/$25 dep.
Creature Comforts: CCTV, a/c,
refrig, restaurant

WASILLA
Best Western Lake Lucille Inn
(800) 528-1234, (907) 373-1776
http://www.bestwestern.com
1300 W. Lake Lucille Dr.
55 rooms - $75-125
Pets: $10 fee & $25 dep.
Creature Comforts: CCTV,
VCR, refrig, micro, restaurant,
sauna, whirlpool, beach, and dock-
boat rentals

Yukon Don's B&B
(800) 478-7472, (907) 376-7472
http://www.Yukondon.com
1830 E. Parks Hwy., #386
7 rooms - $99-135
Pets: Selectively welcomed
Creature Comforts: Home of the
International Iditarod Sled Dog
Race, the inn also offers a pleasing
array of amenities, CCTV, VCR,
a/c, kit, fireplace, Jacuzzi, cont.
brkfst, sauna, hlth club, pool table

WRANGELL
Harding's Old Sourdough Ldge.
(800) 874-3613
http://www.akgetaway.com
Box 1062
16 rooms - $75-120
Pets: Welcome
Creature Comforts: TV, kit,
Jacuzzi, restaurant, sauna

Arizona

AJO

La Siesta Motel
(520) 387-5659
2561 N. Ajo-Gila Bend Hwy.
12 rooms - $35-59
Pets: Welcome w/$5 fee
Creature Comforts: CCTV, a/c,
refrig

Marine Motel
(520) 387-7626
1966 No. 2nd Ave.
20 rooms - $40-80
Pets: Small pets welcome
Creature Comforts: CCTV, a/c,
refrig

ALPINE

Coronado Trails Cabins
(520) 339-4772
25302 Rte. 191
5 cabins - $45-59
Pets: Welcome w/$10-20 fee
Creature Comforts: CCTV, kit

Tal-Wi-Wi-Lodge
(800) 476-2695, (520) 339-4319
http://www.talwiwilodge.com
40 Country Rd. #2220
20 rooms - $55-105
Pets: Leashed dogs welcome with
a $5 nightly fee
Creature Comforts: White Mtns.
lodge 8,500 ft., bucolic setting,
main lodge w/animal trophy
saloon, cabins w/knotty pine
walls, fireplaces, Jacuzzis,
restaurant, whirlpools, riding,
hiking

ASH FORK

Stagecoach Motel
(520) 637-2514
1137 Rte. 66
32 rooms - $28-45
Pets: Welcome w/$3 fee
Creature Comforts: CCTV, a/c

BENSON

Best Western Quail Hollow Inn
(800) 528-1234, (520) 586-3646
http://www.bestwestern.com
699 N. Octotillo St.
90 rooms - $54-75
Pets: Small pets welcome
Creature Comforts: CCTV,
VCR, a/c, refrig, fireplace, pool,
whirlpools

Holiday Inn Express
(800) HOLIDAY, (520) 586-8800
http://www.holiday-inn.com
630 S. Village Loop
62 rooms - $60-110
Pets: Under 40 lbs.
Creature Comforts: CCTV, a/c,
refrig, micro, Jacuzzi, cont. brkfst,
pool, whirlpool

BISBEE

Bisbee Inn B&B
(888) 432-5131, (520) 432-5131
45 OK Street
35 rooms - $50-90
Pets: Welcome w/$40 dep.
Creature Comforts: Restored
1917 historic boarding house,
turn-of-the-century furnishings,
iron bedsteads w/colorful quilts,
CCTV, VCR, a/c, kit, full brkfst

The Calumet Guest House
(520) 432-4815
608 Powell St.
6 rooms - $60-75
Pets: Welcome in one rm.
Creature Comforts: 1906 bright
pink stucco home, orig. details
beautifully preserved, Victorian
decor and array of collectibles,
claw foot tubs, antiques, CCTV,
VCR, a/c, refrig, fireplaces, kit,
gourmet brkfst, spa

The Inn at Castle Rock
(800) 566-4449, (520) 432-4449
http://www.theinn.org
112 Tombstone Canyon Rd
16 rooms - $40-125
Pets: Medium pets w/$10 fee
Creature Comforts: Eclectic
1890's Victorian inn, former
miner's boarding hse, sculptures,
collectibles, theme bedrooms,
CCTV, VCR, a/c, woodstove,
atrium, kit, bar, patios and
balconies, gardens, rock grotto,
gallery, full brkfst

The OK Street Jailhouse
(800) 821-0678, (520) 432-7435
http://www.okproperty.com
9 OK Street
1 jailhouse - $75-120
Pets: Welcome with notice
Creature Comforts: Historic
1910 jail w/original cell doors,
authentic but inviting decor, drunk
tank is now living room, western
collectibles, beamed ceilings,
skylights, CCTV, a/c, kit, Jacuzzi,
cont. brkfst

Mile High Court
(520) 432-4636
901 Tombstone Canyon
5 suites - $55-60
Pets: Welcome
Creature Comforts: CCTV, a/c,
kit, cont. brkfst

Park Place B&B
(800) 456-0682, (520) 990-0682
200 E. Vista Rd.
4 rooms - $50-75
Pets: Small pets w/notice
Creature Comforts: CCTV, a/c,
refrig, fireplaces, kit, Jacuzzi, full
brkfst

San Jose Lodge
(520) 432-5761
1002 Naco Hwy.
43 rooms - $45-70
Pets: Welcome w/$10 fee
Creature Comforts: CCTV, a/c,
kit, restaurant, pool

Sunridge Hotel
(520) 754-4700
839 Landon Dr.
150 rooms - $30-85
Pets: Welcome w/$100 dep.
Creature Comforts: CCTV, a/c, kit, cont. brkfst, pool, hlth clb, sauna, whirlpool

White House B&B
(520) 432-7215
800 Congdon Ave.
4 suites - $65-109
Pets: Welcome
Creature Comforts: CCTV, a/c, refrig, Jacuzzis, full brkfst, whirlpool

BULLHEAD CITY
Arizona Bluffs
(800) 258-3370, (520) 763-3839
220 Karis Dr.
54 rooms - $30-65
Pets: Under 25 lbs. welcome
Creature Comforts: CCTV, a/c, kit

Best Western Bullhead City
(800) 528-1234, (520) 754-3000
http://www.bestwestern.com
2360 4th St.
90 rooms - $38-54
Pets: $5 fee $25 dep.
Creature Comforts: CCTV, a/c, refrig, micro, pool, whirlpool

Colorado River Resort
(520) 754-4101
434 Riverglen Dr.
33 apts. - $39-85
Pets: Welcome w/$10 fee
Creature Comforts: CCTV, a/c, kit, pool

Days Inn
(800) DAYS-INN, (520) 758-1711
http://www.daysinn.com
2200 Karis Dr.
70 rooms - $60-80
Pets: Small pets w/$10 fee
Creature Comforts: CCTV, a/c, refrig, fireplace, kit, micro, pool, whirlpool

Desert Rancho Motel
(520) 754-2578
1041 Rte. 95
74 rooms - $40-60
Pets: Welcome w/$5 fee
Creature Comforts: CCTV, a/c, refrig, pool

Lake Mohave Resort
(800) 752-9669, (520) 754-3245
Katherine Landing
50 rooms - $60-90
Pets: W/$5 fee & $25 dep.
Creature Comforts: CCTV, a/c, kit, restaurant, lake-beach, boat rentals

Motel 6
(800) 4-MOTEL6, (520) 763-1002
http://www.motel6.com
1616 Rte. 95
118 rooms - $29-45
Pets: Under 30 lbs. welcome
Creature Comforts: CCTV, a/c, pool

River Queen Resort
(800) 227-3849, (520) 754-3214
http://www.riversideresort.com
125 Long Ave.
98 rooms - $40-75
Pets: Small pets in certain rooms
Creature Comforts: CCTV, a/c, kit, restaurant, pool

Sunridge Hotel
(800) 977-4242, (520) 754-4700
839 Landon Dr.
155 rooms - $35-89
Pets: Small pets w/$100 dep.
Creature Comforts: CCTV, a/c, refrig, restaurant, pool, hlth clb, sauna, whirlpools

CAMERON
Cameron Trading Post
(520) 679-2231
Route 89
66 rooms - $79-185
Pets: Welcome
Creature Comforts: CCTV, VCR, a/c, kit, restaurant

CAMP VERDE
Comfort Inn
(800) 228-5150, (520) 567-9000
http://www.comfortinn.com
340 N. Industrial Ave.
85 rooms - $65-89
Pets: Welcome w/$10 fee
Creature Comforts: CCTV, a/c, pool, whirlpool, cont. brkfst

CAREFREE
The Boulders
(800) 553-1717, (480) 488-9009
http://www.grandbay.com/
properties/boulders/default.html
34631 N. Tom Darlington Dr.
195 rooms - $230-1,200
Pets: Welcome w/$100 fee
Creature Comforts: Exquisite five-star resort overlooking high desert, elegant decor, Native American accents, down comforters, latilla and viga ceilings, CCTV, VCR, a/c, refrig, kiva fireplaces, kit, Jacuzzis, 5 restaurants, 2 pools, steam rooms, 36 holes of golf, tennis, ballooning, hiking, hlth clb, full spa, riding

Carefree Inn
(480) 488-5300
37220 Mule Train Rd.
190 rooms - $75-225
Pets: Small pets welcome
Creature Comforts: CCTV, a/c, refrig, micro, restaurant, two pools, tennis, hlth clb, whirlpools

CASA GRANDE
Best Western Casa Grande
(800) 528-1234, (520) 836-1600
http://www.bestwestern.com
665 Via del Cielo
82 rooms - $59-125
Pets: Welcome w/$25 dep.
Creature Comforts: CCTV, VCR, a/c, refrig, micro, kit, pool, whirlpool

Francisco Grande Resort
(800) 237-4238, (520) 836-6444
http://www.franciscogrande.com
26000 Gila Bend Hwy.
114 rooms - $60-150
Pets: Small pets w/$25 fee
Creature Comforts: CCTV, a/c, restaurant, 2 pools, tennis, golf

Holiday Inn
(800) HOLIDAY, (520) 426-3500
http://www.holiday-inn.com
777 N. Pinal Ave.
175 rooms - $60-90
Pets: Welcome
Creature Comforts: CCTV, a/c, refrig, restaurant, pool, whirlpool

Motel 6
(800) 4-MOTEL6, (520) 836-3323
http://www.motel6.com
4965 N. Sunland Gin Rd.
97 rooms - $48-75
Pets: Under 30 lbs. welcome
Creature Comforts: CCTV, a/c, pool

Sunland Inn
(520) 836-5000
7190 S. Sunland Rd.
100 rooms - $35-50
Pets: Welcome
Creature Comforts: CCTV, a/c, bar, pool

CHAMBERS
Best Western Chieftain
(800) 528-1234, (520) 688-2754
http://www.bestwestern.com
Route 191
50 rooms - $55-85
Pets: Small pets w/$5 fee
Creature Comforts: CCTV, a/c, restaurant, pool

CHANDLER
Hawthorn Suites
(800) 225-5466, (480) 705-8881
http://www.hawthorn.com
5858 W. Chandler
100 rooms - $65-110
Pets: Small pets w/$50 fee
Creature Comforts: CCTV, VCR, a/c, fireplaces, kit, restaurant, pool, whirlpool, exercise rm.

Holiday Inn Express
(800) HOLIDAY, (480) 785-8500
http://www.holiday-inn.com
15221 S. 50th St.
125 rooms - $70-120
Pets: Under 40 lbs. w/$50 fee
Creature Comforts: CCTV, a/c, refrig, micro, pool, cont. brkfst, whirlpool, hlth clb.

Homewood Suites
(800) 225-5466, (480) 753-6200
http://www.homewoodsuites.com
7373 W. Detroit St.
125 rooms - $100-210
Pets: Welcome
Creature Comforts: CCTV, VCR, a/c, refrig, micro, pool, hlth clb access, whirlpools, exercise rm.

La Quinta Inn, Chandler
(800) 531-5900, (480) 961-7700
http://www.laquinta.com
15241 S. 50th St.
115 rooms - $85-110
Pets: Small pets welcome
Creature Comforts: CCTV, a/c, refrig, micro, pool, whirlpool, exercise rm.

Red Roof Inn
(800) 843-7663, (480) 857-4969
http://www.redroof.com
7400 W. Boston St.
130 rooms - $45-85
Pets: Small pets welcome
Creature Comforts: CCTV, a/c, pool

Sheraton San Marcos Resort
(800) 325-3535, (480) 963-6655
http://www.sheraton.com
1 San Marcos Place
299 rooms - $99-255
Pets: Welcome w/$50 dep.
Creature Comforts: CCTV, VCR, a/c, refrig, restaurant, pool, sauna, whirlpool, steamroom, racquetball, tennis, golf, hlth clb

Super 8 Motel
(800) 800-8000, (480) 961-3888
http://www.super8.com
7171 W. Chandler Blvd.
72 rooms - $45-70
Pets: Small pets welcome
Creature Comforts: CCTV, a/c, cont. brkfst, pool

Wellesley Inn and Suites
(800) 444-8888, (480) 753-6700
www.wellesleyinnandsuites.com
5035 E. Chandler Blvd.
130 rooms - $70-110
Pets: $250 deposit, $150 refundable
Creature Comforts: CCTV, a/c, kit, cont. brkfst, pool, exercise rm.

Windmill Inns
(800) 547-4747, (480) 812-9600
http://www.windmillinns.com
3535 W. Chandler Blvd.
125 rooms - $89-119
Pets: Welcome
Creature Comforts: Spanish style hotel w/attractive public areas/courtyards, lodge pole beds and furnishings, southwest decor, many amenities, CCTV, a/c, refrig, micro, cont. brkfst, pool, whirlpool, hlth clb., bicycles

CHINLE
Holiday Inn
(800) HOLIDAY, (520) 634-5575
http://www.holiday-inn.com
Rte 7, Canyon de Chelly Monument
106 rooms - $75-155
Pets: Welcome
Creature Comforts: CCTV, a/c, refrig, restaurant, pool

COTTONWOOD
Best Western Inn
(800) 528-1234, (520) 634-5575
http://www.bestwestern.com
993 So. Main St.
78 rooms - $55-85
Pets: Small pets welcome
Creature Comforts: CCTV, VCR, a/c, refrig, micro, restaurant, pool, whirlpools

Little Daisy Motel
(520) 634-7865
34 S. Main St.
web site pending
21 rooms - $49-60
Pets: $3 fee & $20 dep.
Creature Comforts: CCTV, a/c, kit

The View Motel
(520) 634-7581
818 S. Main St.
34 rooms - $38-58
Pets: Small pets w/$3 fee
Creature Comforts: a/c, pool, whirlpool

DOUGLAS
Motel 6
(800) 4-MOTEL6, (520) 364-2457
http://www.motel6.com
111 - 16th St.
137 rooms - $35-49
Pets: Under 30 lbs. welcome
Creature Comforts: CCTV, a/c, pool

Price Canyon Ranch
(520) 558-2383
http://www.pricecanyon.com
PO Box 1065
9 rooms - $100-125
Pets: Welcome
Creature Comforts: Working ranch on 18,000 mountain acres set at an elevation of 5,600 ft., worm-wood paneled walls, western collectibles, rawhide chairs, Mexican pottery, satTV, a/c, fireplace, kit, dining room, pool table, games, cookouts, pool & fish pond, round-up rides

Thrift Lodge
(800) 525-9055, (520) 364-8434
http://www.travelodge.com
1030 - 19th St.
44 rooms - $40-59
Pets: Small pets welcome
Creature Comforts: CCTV, a/c, pool

EAGAR
Best Western Sunrise Inn
(800) 528-1234, (520) 333-2540
http://www.bestwestern.com
128 N. Main St.
40 rooms - $59-125
Pets: Welcome w/$25 dep.
Creature Comforts: CCTV, a/c, refrig, micro, pool, whirlpool

EHRENBERG
Best Western Flying J
(800) 528-1234, (520) 923-9711
http://www.bestwestern.com
Route 10
86 rooms - $55-125
Pets: Welcome w/$25 dep.
Creature Comforts: CCTV, VCR, a/c, refrig, micro, restaurant, pool, whirlpool

FLAGSTAFF
Arizona Mountain Inn
(800) 239-5236, (520) 774-8959
www.arizonamountaininn.com
685 Lake Mary Rd.
20 rooms/cabins - $75-125
Pets: In cabins w/$5 daily fee
Creature Comforts: A-frame cabins set in Ponderosa pine forest at 7,000 ft. on 13 acres, vaulted walls, knotty pine walls, fireplaces, kit, decks, old-fashioned camp shower

Best Western Kings House
(800) 528-1234, (520) 774-7186
http://www.bestwestern.com
1560 E. Rte. 66
58 rooms - $50-89
Pets: Welcome
Creature Comforts: CCTV, VCR, a/c, pool

Comfort Inn
(800) 228-5150, (520) 774-7326
http://www.comfortinn.com
914 So. Milton Rd.
68 rooms - $44-95
Pets: Welcome
Creature Comforts: CCTV, a/c, pool

Days Inn
(800) DAYS-INN, (520) 774-5221
http://www.daysinn.com
1000 W. Rte. 66
158 rooms - $52-86
Pets: Small pets welcome
Creature Comforts: CCTV, a/c, restaurant, pool

Embassy Suites
(800) 362-2779, (520) 774-4333
http://www.embassy-suites.com
706 S. Milton Rd.
100 rooms - $80-235
Pets: Welcome w/$25 fee
Creature Comforts: CCTV, a/c, refrig, micro, restaurant, cont. brkfst, pool

Frontier Motel
(520) 774-8993
1700 E. Rte. 66
31 rooms - $35-75
Pets: Welcome
Creature Comforts: CCTV, a/c

Holiday Inn
(800) HOLIDAY, (520) 526-1150
http://www.holiday-inn.com
2320 E. Lucky Lane
158 rooms - $50-140
Pets: Welcome
Creature Comforts: CCTV, a/c, restaurant, pool, whirlpool

Howard Johnson Hotel
(800)I-Go-Hojo, (520) 779-6944
http://www.hojo.com
2220 E. Butler Ave.
100 rooms - $70-129
Pets: Welcome w/$50 dep.
Creature Comforts: CCTV, VCR, a/c, refrig, restaurant, pool, sauna, whirlpool

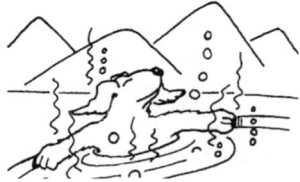

InnSuites
(800) 842-4242, (520) 774-7356
http://www.innsuites.com
1008 E. Santa Fe Blvd.
130 rooms - $55-109
Pets: Welcome w/$25 dep.
Creature Comforts: CCTV, VCR, a/c, refrig., micro, Jacuzzis, restaurant, pool

Knights Inn
(800) 654-4667, (520) 774-4581
http://www.knightsinn.com
502 West Rte. 66
68 rooms - $45-139
Pets: Welcome w/$10 fee
Creature Comforts: CCTV, a/c, pool, whirlpool

La Quinta Inn
(800) 531-5900, (520) 556-8666
http://www.laquinta.com
2015 S. Beulah Blvd.
128 rooms - $80-129
Pets: Small pets welcome
Creature Comforts: CCTV, a/c, refrig, micro, pool, whirlpools

Master Hosts Inn
(800) 535-2466, (520) 526-1339
2610 E. Rte. 66
88 rooms - $55-85
Pets: Welcome
Creature Comforts: CCTV, a/c,
refrig, restaurant, pool

Monte Vista Hotel
(520) 779-6971
100 N. San Francisco St.
48 rooms - $45-129
Pets: Welcome w/$10 dep.
Creature Comforts: CCTV, a/c,
restaurant

Motel 6
(800) 4-MOTEL6, (520) 779-3757
http://www.motel6.com
2745 S. Woodlands Rd.
88 rooms - $ 34-54
Pets: Welcome w/$ fee
Creature Comforts: CCTV, a/c,
pool

Motel 6
(800) 4-MOTEL6, (520) 779-6164
http://www.motel6.com
2500 E. Lucky Lane
90 rooms - $39-54
Pets: Welcome
Creature Comforts: CCTV, a/c,
pool

Motel 6
(800) 4-MOTEL6, (520) 774-1801
http://www.motel6.com
2010 E. Butler Ave.
150 rooms - $39-54
Pets: Under 30 lbs. welcome
Creature Comforts: CCTV, a/c,
pool

Motel 6
(800) 4-MOTEL6, (520) 779-6184
http://www.motel6.com
2500 E. Lucky Lane
121 rooms - $39-54
Pets: Under 30 lbs. welcome
Creature Comforts: CCTV, a/c,
pool

Motel 6
(800) 4-MOTEL6, (520) 774-8756
http://www.motel6.com
2400 E. Lucky Lane
103 rooms - $39-54
Pets: Under 30 lbs. welcome
Creature Comforts: CCTV, a/c,
pool

Motel 6
(800) 4-MOTEL6, (520) 779-3757
http://www.motel6.com
2745 S. Woodland Village
150 rooms - $39-54
Pets: Under 30 lbs. welcome
Creature Comforts: CCTV, a/c,
pool

Pinecrest Motel
(520) 526-1950
2818 E. Rte. 66
18 rooms - $50-65
Pets: Welcome w/$15 fee
Creature Comforts: CCTV a/c

Quality Inn
(800) 228-5151, (520) 774-871
http://www.qualityinn.com
2000 S. Milton Rd.
98 rooms - $58-138
Pets: Small pets welcome
Creature Comforts: CCTV, a/c,
pool

Ramada Limited
(800) 2-Ramada, (520) 773-1111
http://www.ramada.com
2755 Woodlands Village
92 rooms - $65-135
Pets: Welcome w/$25 dep.
Creature Comforts: CCTV,
VCR, a/c, refrig, micro, Jacuzzi,
cont. brkfst, pool, hlth clb, sauna,
whirlpool

Ramada Limited
(800) 2-Ramada, (520) 779-3614
http://www.ramada.com
2350 E. Lucky Lane
100 rooms - $52-99
Pets: Welcome
Creature Comforts: CCTV, a/c,
pool

Residence Inn
(800) 331-3131, (520) 526-5555
http://www.residenceinn.com
3440 N. Country Club Rd
102 rooms - $55-99
Pets: Small pets w/$10 fee
Creature Comforts: CCTV, a/c,
refrig, micro, fireplace, restaurant,
pool, whirlpool, hlth. club

Rodeway Inn
(800) 228-2000, (520) 526-2200
http://www.rodeway.com
2650 Rte. 66
68 rooms - $35-69
Pets: Welcome w/$5 fee
Creature Comforts: CCTV, a/c,
cont. brkfst

Super 8
(800) 800-8000, (520) 526-0818
http://www.super8.com
3725 Kasper Ave.
90 rooms - $45-75
Pets: Welcome
Creature Comforts: CCTV,
VCR, a/c, whirlpools

Travelodge
(800) 578-7878, (520) 779-5121
http://www.travelodge.com
2520 East Lucky Ln.
140 rooms - $70-99
Pets: Small pets w/$50 dep.
Creature Comforts: CCTV, a/c,
refrig, micro, cont. brkfst, pool,
sauna, whirlpool

Travelodge
(800) 578-7878, (520) 774-3381
http://www.travelodge.com
801 W. Rte. 66
49 rooms - $30-99
Pets: Welcome w/$20 dep.
Creature Comforts: CCTV, a/c,
refrig, micro, cont. brkfst, pool,
whirlpool

Western Hills Motel
(520) 774-6633
1580 E. Rte. 66
28 rooms - $45-75
Pets: Welcome w/$10 fee
Creature Comforts: CCTV, a/c,
kit, restaurant, pool

FLORENCE
Inn at Rancho Sonora
(800) 205-6817, (520) 868-8000
go-native.com/Inns/0044.html
9198 N. Rte. 79
7 rooms - $69-145
Pets: Medium-sized pets welcome
Creature Comforts: A charming
1930's adobe inn, lovely Ralph
Lauren style decor, collectibles,
antiques, hand-crafted furnishings,
bentwood chairs, four poster beds,
CCTV, VCR, a/c, fireplace, kit,
patios, cont. brkfst, pool, hiking

FOREST LAKES
Forest Lakes Lodge
(520) 535-4727
Route 260
20 rooms - $45-85
Pets: Welcome w/$10 fee
Creature Comforts: CCTV,
refrig, micro

FREDONIA
Crazy Jug Motel
(520) 643-7752
465 S. Main St.
web site pending
14 rooms - $43-59
Pets: Welcome
Creature Comforts: CCTV, a/c

GILA BEND
Best Western Space Age Lodge
(800) 528-1234, (520) 683-2273
http://www.bestwestern.com
401 E. Pina St.
42 rooms - $59-95
Pets: Welcome
Creature Comforts: CCTV, a/c,
refrig, restaurant, pool, whirlpool

Yucca Motel
(520) 683-2211
836 E. Pima St
19 rooms - $32-45
Pets: Welcome
Creature Comforts: CCTV,
refrig, micro, cont. brkfst, pool

GLENDALE
Windmill Inns
(800) 547-4747, (602) 583-0133
http://www.windmillinns.com
125345 W. Bell Rd.
128 rooms - $99-170
Pets: Small pets welcome
Creature Comforts: CCTV, a/c,
refrig, micro, restaurant, pool,
whirlpool

GLOBE
Cedar Hill B&B
(520) 425-7530
175 E. Cedar St.
2 rooms - $45-55
Pets: Welcome
Creature Comforts: CCTV, a/c,
refrig, porch w/ swing, picket
fence emclosed yard

Cloud Nine Motel
(800) 256-8399, (520) 425-5741
1649 E. Ash St
80 rooms - $45-95
Pets: Welcome
Creature Comforts: CCTV, a/c,
refrig, Jacuzzis, restaurant, pool,
whirlpool

Comfort Inn
(800) 228-5150, (520) 425-7575
http://www.comfortinn.com
1515 South St.
54 rooms - $55-85
Pets: Welcome
Creature Comforts: CCTV, a/c,
refrig, micro, pool, whirlpool

Holiday Inn Express
(800) HOLIDAY, (520) 425-7008
http://www.holiday-inn.com
2119 Rte 60
80 rooms - $49-85
Pets: Welcome
Creature Comforts: CCTV, a/c,
refrig, micro, pool, whirlpool

GOODYEAR
Best Western Phoenix
(800) 528-1234, (623) 932-3210
http://www.bestwestern.com
1100 N. Litchfield Rd.
88 rooms - $60-129
Pets: Small pets welcome
Creature Comforts: CCTV,
VCR, a/c, refrig, micro, cont.
brkfst, restaurant, pool

Holiday Inn
(800) HOLIDAY, (623) 535-1313
http://www.holiday-inn.com
1313 Litchfield Rd.
175 rooms - $60-90
Pets: Welcome w/$20 dep.
Creature Comforts: CCTV, a/c,
refrig, pool, whirlpool, exercise
rm.

Super 8 Motel
(800) 800-8000, (623) 932-9622
http://www.super8.com
1710 N. Dysart Rd.
90 rooms - $42-64
Pets: Welcome
Creature Comforts: CCTV, a/c,
cont. brkfst, Jacuzzi, pool

GRAND CANYON NAT. PARK
Telephone: *(520) 638-2526*
Pets: *Pets visting the park are not
allowed in lodge rooms, but are
required to stay in the kennels
Cert. of vaccination required.
$8 per day per pet
$4 for half days*

Bright Angel Lodge
(520) 638-6284
PO Box 699
89 rooms/cabins - $45-105
Pets: Welcome in kennel
Creature Comforts: CCTV, a/c,
refrig, micro, fireplace, pool

El Tovar
(520) 638-2631
PO Box 699, Rte 64
78 rooms - $125-285
Pets: Welcome in kennel
Creature Comforts: Historic
hotel on canyon rim, CCTV, a/c,
refrig, dining room

Kachina Lodge
(520) 638-6284
PO Box 699
49 rooms - $99-129
Pets: Welcome in kennel
Creature Comforts: Modern
lodge set along canyon rim

Maswik Lodge
(520) 638-2631
PO Box 699
278 cabins/motel units - $85-129
Pets: Welcome in kennel
Creature Comforts: Cafeteria,
bar

Rodeway Red Feather Lodge
(800) 538-2345, (520) 638-2414
http://www.rodeway.com
Rte 64, Box 1460
234 rooms - $55-135
Pets: Welcome w/$40 dep.
Creature Comforts: CCTV, a/c,
refrig, restaurant, pool, hlth clb,
whirlpool

Thunderbird Lodge
(520) 638-2631
PO Box 699
55 rooms - $115-138
Pets: Welcome
Creature Comforts: Modern
lodge along canyon rim

Yavapi Lodge
(520) 638-2631
PO Box 699
358 rooms - $94-119
Pets: Welcome
Creature Comforts: Surrounded
by a wooded setting, cafeteria

GREEN VALLEY
Best Western Green Valley
(800) 528-1234, (520) 625-2259
http://www.bestwestern.com
111 So. La Canada Dr.
110 rooms - $55-120
Pets: Welcome w/$25 dep.
Creature Comforts: CCTV, a/c,
refrig, restaurant, pool, whirlpool

Holiday Inn Express
(800) HOLIDAY, (520) 625-0900
http://www.holiday-inn.com
19200 S. I-19 Frontage Rd.
60 rooms - $70-140
Pets: Welcome
Creature Comforts: CCTV, a/c,
refrig, Jacuzzi, cont. brkfst, pool,
whirlpool

GREER
Greer Lodge
(520) 735-7216
Route 373
17 units - $80-285
Pets: Welcome in cabins
Creature Comforts: Riverside
setting, CCTV, refrig, fireplace,
kit, restaurant, fishing, xc-skiing,
skating

Molly Butler Lodge
(520) 735-7226
PO Box 70
11 rooms - $35-85
Pets: Welcome w/$10 fee
Creature Comforts: Restaurant,
bar

White Mountain Lodge
(888) 493-7568, (520) 735-7568
http://www.wmlodge.com
140 Main St.
10 rooms/cabins - $69-155
Pets: One pet per room w/$20 fee
Creature Comforts: Little
Colorado River runs through the
property of this charming 1890's
historic lodge, fieldstone
fireplaces, knotty pine accents,
southwestern artwork, CCTV,
VCR, a/c, kit, full brkfst, pool,
hlth clb access, sauna, whirlpool

HEBER
Best Western Sawmill Inn
(800) 528-1234, (520) 535-5053
http://www.bestwestern.com
1877 Rte. 260
44 rooms - $50-85
Pets: Welcome w/$25 dep.
Creature Comforts: CCTV,
VCR, a/c, refrig, micro, hlth clb,
whirlpool

HOLBROOK
Best Western Adobe Inn
(800) 528-1234, (520) 524-3948
http://www.bestwestern.com
615 West Hopi Dr.
55 rooms - $39-70
Pets: Welcome w/$25 dep.
Creature Comforts: CCTV, a/c,
pool

Best Western Arizonian
(800) 528-1234, (520) 524-2611
http://www.bestwestern.com
2508 E. Navajo Blvd.
70 rooms - $39-70
Pets: Welcome w/$25 dep.
Creature Comforts: CCTV, a/c,
refrig, micro, restaurant, pool

Budget Host Holbrook
(800) Bud-Host, (520) 524-3809
http://www.budgethost.com
235 West Hopi Dr.
25 rooms - $28-49
Pets: Welcome w/$2 fee, $5 dep.
Creature Comforts: CCTV,
VCR, a/c, kit, pool

Comfort Inn
(800) 228-5150, (520) 524-6131
http://www.comfortinn.com
2602 Navajo Blvd.
60 rooms - $44-85
Pets: Welcome w/$25 dep.
Creature Comforts: CCTV,
VCR, a/c, refrig, micro, restaurant,
pool

Econo Lodge
(800) 55-ECONO, (520) 524-1448
http://www.econolodge.com
2596 E. Navajo Blvd.
64 rooms - $36-69
Pets: Welcome w/$25 dep.
Creature Comforts: CCTV, a/c,
refrig, micro, pool

Holiday Inn Express
(800) HOLIDAY, (520) 524-1466
http://www.holiday-inn.com
1308 Navajo Blvd.
60 rooms - $49-85
Pets: Welcome
Creature Comforts: CCTV, a/c,
refrig, micro, pool, whirlpool

Motel 6
(800) 4-MOTEL6, (520) 524-6101
http://www.motel6.com
2514 Navajo Blvd.
126 rooms - $32-49
Pets: Small pets welcome
Creature Comforts: CCTV, a/c,
pool

Rainbow Inn
(800) 551-1923, (520) 524-2654
2211 East Navajo Blvd.
40 rooms - $38-69
Pets: Welcome w/$25 dep.
Creature Comforts: CCTV, a/c,
refrig

Ramada Limited
(800) 2-Ramada, (520) 524-2566
http://www.ramada.com
2608 E. Navajo Blvd.
40 rooms - $42-75
Pets: In smoking rooms w/$10 fee
Creature Comforts: CCTV,
VCR, a/c, refrig, micro, pool,
whirlpool

Travelodge
(800) 578-7878, (520) 524-6815
http://www.travelodge.com
2418 E. Navajo Blvd.
66 rooms - $35-70
Pets: Small pets welcome
Creature Comforts: CCTV, a/c,
refrig, Jacuzzi, playground

JEROME
The Surgeon's House B&B
(800) 639-1452, (520) 990-0682
http://www.azjerome.com/
surgeonshouse/index.htm
101 Hill St.
5 rooms - $90-135
Pets: In guest house w/$25 fee
Creature Comforts: Historic
1915 Mediterranean-style B&B
with incredible views, family
heirlooms, collectibles, festive
fabrics, CCTV, a/c, fireplace, kit,
gourmet brkfst, sun drenched
atrium, patio, high tea, massage,
walking tours, great cookbook

KEARNEY
General Kearney Inn
(520) 363-5505
PO Box 188
47 rooms - $39-70
Pets: Welcome
Creature Comforts: CCTV, a/c,
refrig, restaurant, pool

KINGMAN
Best Western Wayfarers
(800) 528-1234, (520) 753-6271
http://www.bestwestern.com
2815 East Andy Devine Rd.
100 rooms - $58-89
Pets: Welcome w/$20 dep.
Creature Comforts: CCTV, a/c,
refrig, micro, pool, whirlpool

Best Western Kings
(800) 528-1234, (520) 753-6101
http://www.bestwestern.com
2930 East Andy Devine Rd.
54 rooms - $50-83
Pets: Welcome
Creature Comforts: CCTV, a/c,
refrig, pool, sauna, whirlpool

Days Inn East
(800) DAYS-INN, (520) 757-7337
http://www.daysinn.com
3381 East Andy Devine Rd.
44 rooms - $43-74
Pets: Small pets w/$10 fee
Creature Comforts: CCTV, a/c,
refrig, micro, pool, whirlpools

Days Inn West
(800) DAYS-INN, (520) 753-7500
http://www.daysinn.com
3023 East Andy Devine Rd.
60 rooms - $36-69
Pets: Small pets w/$10 fee
Creature Comforts: CCTV, a/c,
refrig, micro, pool, whirlpool

High Desert Inn
(520) 753-2935
2803 East Andy Devine Rd.
15 rooms - $32-55
Pets: Welcome w/$10 dep.
Creature Comforts: CCTV, a/c

Hilltop Motel
(520) 753-2198
1901 E. Andy Devine Rd.
29 rooms - $35-40
Pets: Welcome
Creature Comforts: CCTV, a/c,
refrig, pool

Holiday Inn
(800) HOLIDAY, (520) 753-6262
http://www.holiday-inn.com
3100 E. Andy Devine Rd.
116 rooms - $57-89
Pets: Welcome
Creature Comforts: CCTV, a/c,
restaurant, pool

Motel 6
(800) 4-MOTEL6, (520) 757-7151
http://www.motel6.com
3351 W. Andy Devine Rd.
118 rooms - $34-50
Pets: Under 30 lbs. welcome
Creature Comforts: CCTV, a/c,
pool

Motel 6
(800) 4-MOTEL6, (520) 753-9222
http://www.motel6.com
424 W. Beale St.
80 rooms - $35-54
Pets: Small pets welcome
Creature Comforts: CCTV, a/c,
pool

Quality Inn
(800) 228-5151, (520) 753-4747
http://www.qualityinn.com
1400 East Andy Devine Rd.
99 rooms - $46-77
Pets: Small pets welcome
Creature Comforts: CCTV, a/c,
refrig, micro, pool, sauna,
whirlpool

Silver Queen Motel
(520) 757-4315
http://www.ctaz/~silverqueen
3285 E. Andy Devine Rd.
146 rooms - $40-55
Pets: Welcome w/$10 dep.
Creature Comforts: CCTV, a/c,
refrig, micro, pool

Super 8 Motel
(800) 800-8000, (520) 757-4808
http://www.super8.com
3401 E. Andy Devine Rd.
62 rooms - $35-69
Pets: Small pets welcome
Creature Comforts: CCTV, a/c,
refrig, micro, cont. brkfst.

LAKE HAVASU CITY
Best Western Lake Place
(800) 528-1234, (520) 855-2146
http://www.bestwestern.com
31 Wing's Loop
40 rooms - $54-109
Pets: Welcome w/$5 fee
Creature Comforts: CCTV, a/c,
pool

Bridgeview Motel
(520) 855-5559
101 London Bridge Rd.
37 rooms - $45-124
Pets: Welcome w/$50 dep.
Creature Comforts: CCTV, a/c, refrig, pool

EZ-8 Motel
(520) 855-4023
41 S. Acoma Blvd.
64 rooms - $38-79
Pets: Welcome
Creature Comforts: CCTV, a/c, refrig, micro, cont. brkfst, pool

Holiday Inn
(800) HOLIDAY, (520) 855-4071
http://www.holiday-inn.com
245 London Bridge Rd.
164 rooms - $65-140
Pets: Welcome w/$10 fee
Creature Comforts: CCTV, a/c, refrig, micro, pool, game room, whirlpools

Island Inn
(800) 243-9955, (520) 680-0606
1300 W. McCulloch Blvd.
115 rooms - $68-99
Pets: Small pets w/$10 fee
Creature Comforts: CCTV, a/c, refrig, micro, pool, whirlpool

Lakeview Motel
(520) 855-3605
440 London Bridge Rd.
15 rooms - $50-75
Pets: "Cute" pets only
Creature Comforts: CCTV, a/c, refrig, micro

Pecos II Condominiums
(520) 855-7444
451 B Lake Havasu Rd.
16 rooms - $70-105
Pets: Welcome w/$20 fee
Creature Comforts: CCTV, VCR, a/c, kit, pool, whirlpool

Pioneer Hotel
(800) 528-5169, (520) 855-1111
web site pending
197 rooms - $59-135
Pets: Welcome w/$25 fee
Creature Comforts: CCTV, VCR, a/c, refrig, micro, fireplaces, restaurant, whirlpool, spa

Sandman Inn
(800) 835-2410, (520) 855-7841
1700 N. McCulloch
90 rooms - $35-99
Pets: Welcome w/$5 fee
Creature Comforts: CCTV, a/c, kit, pool

Super 8 Motel
(800) 800-8000, (520) 855-8844
http://www.super8.com
305 London Bridge Rd.
60 rooms - $43-79
Pets: Welcome
Creature Comforts: CCTV, a/c, refrig, micro, Jacuzzi, pool

Windsor Inn
(800) 245-4135, (520) 855-4135
451 London Bridge Rd.
60 rooms - $34-75
Pets: Welcome w/$5 fee
Creature Comforts: CCTV, a/c, refrig, micro, kit, Jacuzzi, pool, whirlpool

LAKESIDE
Bartram's B&B
(800) 257-0211, (520) 367-1408
http://www.wmonline.com/wmbba/bartrams.htm
1916 W. Woodland Ave.
5 rooms - $65-89
Pets: Female dogs preferred
Creature Comforts: A 1940's ranch-style house w/summer cottage decor, four poster beds, southwestern collectibles, antiques, CCTV, VCR, a/c, fireplaces, kit, 7-course gourmet brkfst, fenced yard, and an animal menagerie

Lake of the Woods
(520) 368-5353
http://www.l-o-w.com
2244 W. White Mountain Blvd.
28 cabins - $49-275
Pets: Well-behaved pets welcome
Creature Comforts: Mountain cabins with lake views, log walls and honey-colored knotty pine, rqst lakeside cabins, CCTV, refrig, micro, fireplace, kit, pool, porches or patios, spas, sauna, recreation halls-ping pong & pool, boats, and lawn sports

Lake Oaks Resort
(520) 368-6203
Rte 2, Box 1215
15 cabins - $65-145
Pets: Welcome
Creature Comforts: CCTV, kit

Moonridge Lodge
(520) 367-1906
PO Box 1058
http://www.wmonline.com/lodging/moonrdg.htm
18 cabins - $95-185
Pets: $5 fee, $50 deposit
Creature Comforts: Fully-equipped housekeeping cottages in White Mtns., knotty pine walls, CCTV, a/c, kit, whirlpool

The Place Resort Cabins
(520) 368-6777
Rte 3, Box 2675
web site pending
19 cabins - $75-129
Pets: Small dogs w/$12 fee
Creature Comforts: CCTV, a/c, fireplaces, kit, lawn sports

LITCHFIELD PARK
The Wigwam Resort
(800) 327-0396, (623) 935-3811
http://www.wigwamresort.com
300 Indian School Rd.
331 rooms - $140-500
Pets: $25 fee, $50 dep.
Creature Comforts: Classic five-star 1918 resort w/luxurious amenities, charming casitas, inviting decor, festive lithographs, CCTV, VCR, a/c, refrig, stone fireplaces, micro, Jacuzzis, three restaurants, cont. brkfst, two pools, waterslide, hlth clb, saunas, whirlpools, putting greens, skeet, 3 golf courses, tennis program, lawn sports, riding, bikes, trap shooting, kids camp

MARBLE CANYON
Lees Ferry Lodge
(520) 355-2231
HC67 #541, Box 1
9 rooms - $55-75
Pets: Welcome
Creature Comforts: CCTV, a/c, restaurant, store

Marble Canyon Lodge
(800) 726-1789, (520) 355-2225
Route 89A
58 rooms - $45-77
Pets: Welcome
Creature Comforts: CCTV, a/c, refrig, micro, kit, restaurant

MESA
Arizona Golf Resort
(800) 528-8282, (480) 832-3202
http://www.azgolfresort.com
425 S. Power Rd.
188 rooms - $85-460
Pets: Welcome
Creature Comforts: Spanish-style resort set on 150 acres, Scandinavian decor, soft earth tones, CCTV, VCR, a/c, refrig, micro, kit, restaurant, pool, hlth clb, sauna, whirlpool, volleyball, golf, basketball, tennis

Best Western Mesa Inn
(800) 528-1234, (480) 964-8000
http://www.bestwestern.com
1625 E. Main St.
100 rooms - $40-100
Pets: Small pets w/$10 dep.
Creature Comforts: CCTV, VCR, a/c, refrig, pool, whirlpool

Best Western Superstition Sprgs
(800) 528-1234, (480) 641-1164
http://www.bestwestern.com
1342 S. Power Rd.
60 rooms - $55-215
Pets: Welcome w/$25 dep.
Creature Comforts: CCTV, a/c, refrig, micro, pool, hlth clb, whirlpool

Holiday Inn
(800) HOLIDAY, (480) 964-7000
http://www.holiday-inn.com
1600 S. Country Club Rd.
246 rooms - $59-125
Pets: Under 40 lbs. w/$100 fee
Creature Comforts: CCTV, VCR, a/c, refrig, micro, restaurant, pool, whirlpool, exercise rm.

Homestead Village
(888) STAY-HSD, (480) 752-2266
http://www.homesteadvillage.com
1920 W. Isabella
125 rooms - $40-60
Pets: Welcome w/$100 dep.
Creature Comforts: CCTV, VCR, a/c, kit

La Quinta Inn
(800) 531-5900, (480) 844-8747
http://www.laquinta.com
902 W. Grove Ave.
129 rooms - $53-200
Pets: Small pets welcome
Creature Comforts: CCTV, a/c, refrig, micro, cont. brkfst, pool, whirlpool, exercise rm.

La Quinta, Superstition Spgs.
(800) 531-5900, (480) 654-1970
http://www.laquinta.com
6530 Superstition Springs Blvd.
107 rooms - $53-200
Pets: Small pets welcome
Creature Comforts: CCTV, a/c, refrig, micro, cont. brkfst, pool, whirlpool, exercise rm.

Motel 6
(800) 4-MOTEL6, (480) 844-8899
http://www.motel6.com
336 W. Hampton Ave.
162 rooms - $44-55
Pets: Under 30 lbs. welcome
Creature Comforts: CCTV, a/c, pool

Motel 6
(800) 4-MOTEL6, (480) 834-0066
http://www.motel6.com
1511 S. Country Club Dr.
91 rooms - $40-55
Pets: Under 30 lbs. welcome
Creature Comforts: CCTV, a/c, pool

Motel 6
(800) 4-MOTEL6, (480) 969-8111
http://www.motel6.com
630 W. Main St.
104 rooms - $44-58
Pets: Under 30 lbs. welcome
Creature Comforts: CCTV, a/c, pool

Ramada Inn Suites
(800) 2-Ramada, (480) 964-2897
http://www.ramada.com
1410 S. Country Club Rd.
125 rooms - $44-99
Pets: Small pets $10 fee, $50 dep.
Creature Comforts: CCTV, a/c, refrig, kit, pool, whirlpool

Ramada Limited
(800) 2-Ramada, (480) 969-3600
http://www.ramada.com
1750 E. Main St.
64 rooms - $45-99
Pets: Small pets w/$10 fee
Creature Comforts: CCTV, a/c, pool

Residence Inn
(800) 228-9290, (480) 610-0100
http://www.residenceinn.com
941 W. Grove Ave.
117 suites - $50-150
Pets: $50 fee, $250 deposit
Creature Comforts: CCTV, VCR, a/c, kit, cont. brkfst, fireplace, pool, whirlpool, hlth clb access

MIAMI
Best Western Copper Hills
(800) 528-1234, (520) 425-7151
http://www.bestwestern.com
Route 60
70 rooms - $55-99
Pets: Under 20 lbs. w/$5 fee
Creature Comforts: CCTV, a/c, refrig, micro, restaurant, pool

MUNDS PARK
Motel in the Pines
(520) 286-9699
80 W. Pinewood Rd.
24 rooms - $35-70
Pets: Small pets w/$30 dep.
Creature Comforts: CCTV, a/c, kit, fireplaces, golf, tennis

NOGALES
Americana Motor Hotel
(520) 287-7211
639 N. Grand Ave.
90 rooms - $39-70
Pets: Small pets w/$5 fee
Creature Comforts: CCTV, a/c, refrig, restaurant, pool

Best Western Siesta
(800) 528-1234, (520) 287-4671
http://www.bestwestern.com
673 North Grand Ave
48 rooms - $35-59
Pets: Welcome
Creature Comforts: CCTV, a/c, refrig, pool, whirlpool

Best Western Time
(800) 528-1234, (520) 287-4627
http://www.bestwestern.com
921 North Grand Ave.
44 rooms - $38-67
Pets: Welcome
Creature Comforts: CCTV,
VCR, a/c, pool, whirlpool

Motel 6
(800) 4-MOTEL6, (520) 281-2951
http://www.motel6.com
141 W. Mariposa Rd.
79 rooms - $40-55
Pets: Under 30 lbs. welcome
Creature Comforts: CCTV, a/c,
pool

PAGE
Best Western Arizona Inn
(800) 528-1234, (520) 645-2466
http://www.bestwestern.com
716 Rimview Dr.
104 rooms - $40-99
Pets: Welcome w/$10 fee
Creature Comforts: CCTV, a/c,
refrig, restaurant, pool, whirlpool

Best Western Lake Powell
(800) 528-1234, (520) 645-5988
http://www.bestwestern.com
208 N. Lake Powell Blvd.
134 rooms - $35-109
Pets: Welcome w/$100 dep.
Creature Comforts: CCTV, a/c,
refrig, micro, pool, whirlpool

Econo Lodge
(800) 55-ECONO, (520) 645-2488
http://www.econolodge.com
121 S. Lake Powell Rd.
64 rooms - $40-89
Pets: Small pets w/$5 fee
Creature Comforts: CCTV, a/c,
pool

Empire Hotel
(520) 645-2406
web site pending
100 S. Lake Powell Rd.
70 rooms - $50-65
Pets: Welcome
Creature Comforts: CCTV, a/c,
restaurant, pool

Lake Powell Motel
(800) 528-6154, (520) 645-2477
Route 89
24 rooms - $80-99
Pets: Small pets w/$10 fee
Creature Comforts: CCTV, a/c,
lake views

Wahweap Lodge
(800) 528-6154, (520) 645-2433
http://www.visitlakepowell.com
100 Lake Shore Dr.
350 rooms - $75-250
Pets: Small pets welcome
Creature Comforts: A neat lodge
w/nice clean rms on Lake Powell,
CCTV, a/c, refrig, micro,
restaurant, 2 pools, hlth clb,
whirlpool, lake/boat/marina/float
trips

Weston's Empire House
(800) 551-9005, (520) 645-2406
107 S. Lake Powell Blvd.
70 rooms - $65-80
Pets: Welcome
Creature Comforts: CCTV, a/c,
access to a pool

PARKER
Havasu Springs Resort
(520) 667-3361
Rte. 2, Box 624
44 rooms - $45-80
Pets: Welcome
Creature Comforts: CCTV, a/c,
refrig, restaurant, pool, marina/
houseboats

Holiday Inn
(800) HOLIDAY, (520) 669-2133
http://www.holiday-inn.com
604 California Ave.
40 rooms - $40-68
Pets: Welcome w/$5 fee
Creature Comforts: CCTV, a/c,
refrig, micro

PATAGONIA
Stage Stop Inn
(520) 394-2211
300W. McKeown St.
44 rooms - $50-109
Pets: Welcome w/$5 fee
Creature Comforts: CCTV, a/c,
kit, restaurant, pool

PAYSON
Christopher Creek Lodge
(520) 478-4300
Star Rte., Box 119
24 rooms - $55-99
Pets: Welcome
Creature Comforts: CCTV
fishing/hunting

Grey Hackle Cabins
(520) 478-4392
Box 145
11 cabins - $45-95
Pets: Welcome w/$10 fee
Creature Comforts: CCTV, kit,
fireplace

Holiday Inn Express
(800) HOLIDAY, (520) 472-7484
http://www.holiday-inn.com
206 S. Beeline Rd.
44 rooms - $45-139
Pets: Small pets w/$25 dep.
Creature Comforts: CCTV,
VCR, a/c, refrig, micro, pool,
whirlpools

Inn of Payson
(800) 247-9477, (520) 474-3241
http://www.innofpayson.com
801 Beeline Hwy.
100 rooms - $85-165
Pets: Welcome w/$10 daily fee
Creature Comforts: CCTV,
VCR, a/c, refrig, micro, fireplace,
patios/balconies, hlth clb, refrig,
restaurant, pool, whirlpool

Kohl's Guest Ranch
(800) 331-5645,(520) 478-4211
web site pending
East Rte. 260
48 rooms - $75-225
Pets: In kennel w/$20 fee
Creature Comforts: CCTV,
VCR, a/c, refrig, micro, fireplace,
hlth clb, kit, Jacuzzi, restaurant,
pool, sauna, lawn sports, fishing,
horseback riding, hunting

Majestic Mountain Inn
(800) 408-2442, (520) 474-0185
http://www.rimcountry.com/
majestic.htm
602 East Rte.260
37 rooms - $55-148
Pets: In 1st floor smking rooms
Creature Comforts: Stone/timber
lodge, rqst. rms. w/pine cathedral
ceilings, stained glass wdws, stone
fireplace, CCTV, VCR, a/c, refrig,
micro, cont. brkfst, nice grounds

Payson Pueblo Inn
(800) 888-9828, (520) 474-5241
http://www.puebloinn.com
809 E. Rte. 260
40 rooms - $45-149
Pets: Small pets w/$5 fee
Creature Comforts: Lodge w/
vaulted lodge pole ceilings,
CCTV, VCR, a/c, refrig, micro,
fireplace, Jacuzzis

Swiss Village Lodge
(800) 247-9477, (520) 474-3241
801 N. Beeline Hwy.
99 rooms - $64-125
Pets: Welcome w/$10 fee
Creature Comforts: CCTV, a/c,
refrig, fireplace, restaurant, pool,
hot tub

Travelodge
(800) 578-7878, (520) 474-1929
http://www.travelodge.com
101 West Phoenix St.
40 rooms - $42-89
Pets: Small pets w/$10 fee
Creature Comforts: CCTV, a/c,
refrig

PEACH SPRINGS
Grand Canyon Caverns Inn
(520) 422-3223
Route 66
48 rooms - $55-60
Pets: Welcome w/$50 dep.
Creature Comforts: a/c

PEORIA
Comfort Inn
(800) 228-5150, (623) 334-3993
http://www.comfortinn.com
8473 W. Paradise Ln.
80 rooms - $65-135
Pets: Welcome
Creature Comforts: CCTV,
refrig, micro, cont. brkfst, pool,
whirlpool

La Quinta Inn
(800) 531-5900, (623) 487-1900
http://www.laquinta.com
16321 N. 83rd Ave.
108 rooms - $55-200
Pets: Welcome
Creature Comforts: CCTV, a/c,
refrig, micro, cont. brkfst, pool,
whirlpool

Residence Inn
(800) 228-9290, (623) 979-2074
http://www.residenceinn.com
8435 W. Paradise Ln.
90 rooms - $100-220
Pets: $100 deposit
Creature Comforts: CCTV, a/c,
kit, pool, whirlpool, exercise rm.

PHOENIX
Amerisuites
(800) 833-1516, (602) 997-8800
http://www.amerisuites.com
10838 N. 25th Ave.
128 rms - $70-125
Pets: Small pets welcome
Creature Comforts: CCTV,
VCR, a/c, kit, cont. brkfst, pool

Arizona Biltmore Resort
(800) 950-0086, (602) 955-6600
http://www.arizonabiltmore.com
Missouri & 24th Sts.
732 rms/villas - $115-2,200
Pets: Under 15 Lbs. w/$50 fee,
$250 deposit
Creature Comforts: Classic and
exquisite Frank Lloyd Wright
designed five-star resort, luxurious
rooms, soaring ceilings, polished
woods, Native American
collectibles, intimate European
ambiance, CCTV, VCR, a/c,
refrig, micro, fireplace, kit,
Jacuzzi, restaurants, pool, sauna,
whirlpool, marble baths, kids
camp, golf, tennis, lawn games,
hlth clb, trails

Best Western Bell
(800) 528-1234, (602) 993-8300
http://www.bestwestern.com
17211 N. Black Canyon Rd.
104 rooms - $56-125
Pets: Small pets w/$10 fee
Creature Comforts: CCTV, a/c,
refrig, pool, cont. brkfst, whirlpool

Comfort Inn Black Canyon
(800) 228-5150, (602) 242-8011
http://www.comfortinn.com
5050 N. Black Canyon Rd.
152 rooms - $45-135
Pets: Welcome
Creature Comforts: CCTV, a/c,
refrig, micro, cont. brkfst, pool,
whirlpool

Crowne Plaza Phoenix
(800) HOLIDAY, (602) 943-2341
http://www.holiday-inn.com
2532 W. Peoria Ave.
250 rooms - $70-125
Pets: Welcome w/$25 dep.
Creature Comforts: CCTV, a/c,
refrig, micro, fireplace, restaurant,
pool, sauna, whirlpool, volleyball,
tennis, hlth clb

Days Inn
(800) DAYS-INN, (602) 244-8244
http://www.daysinn.com
3333 E. Van Buren Rd.
220 rooms - $59-125
Pets: Welcome w/$10 fee
Creature Comforts: CCTV, a/c,
refrig, micro, kit, restaurant, pool,
whirlpool, hlth clb

Days Inn
(800) DAYS-INN, (602) 244-8244
http://www.daysinn.com
2420 W. Thomas Rd.
150 rooms - $55-120
Pets: Welcome
Creature Comforts: CCTV, a/c,
refrig, micro, pool, whirlpool

Econo Lodge
(800) 55-ECONO, (602) 273-7121
http://www.econolodge.com
3541 E. Van Buren St.
90 rooms - $38-58
Pets: Welcome
Creature Comforts: CCTV, a/c,
restaurant, pool

Embassy Suites Biltmore
(800) 362-2779, (602) 955-3992
http://www.embassy-suites.com
2630 E. Camelback Rd.
235 rooms - $100-250
Pets: Welcome w/$ 25 dep.
Creature Comforts: CCTV, a/c,
refrig, micro, restaurant, cont.
brkfst, pool, whirlpool

Embassy Suites, Airport
(800) 362-2779, (602) 957-1910
http://www.embassy-suites.com
2333 E. Thomas Rd.
180 rooms - $70-179
Pets: Welcome w/$10 fee
Creature Comforts: CCTV, a/c,
refrig, micro, restaurant, cont.
brkfst, pool, whirlpool, hlth clb

Hampton Inn
(800) Hampton, (602) 864-6233
http://www.hampton-inn.com
8101 Black Canyon Rd.
150 rooms - $55-115
Pets: Welcome
Creature Comforts: CCTV, a/c,
refrig, pool, whirlpool

Hilton Suites
(800) HILTONS, (602) 222-1111
http://www.hilton.com
10 E. Thomas Rd.
225 rooms - $115-255
Pets: Welcome w/$100 dep.
Creature Comforts: Atrium w/
ponds, CCTV, VCR, a/c, refrig,
micro, restaurant, pool, sauna,
whirlpool, hlth clb

Holiday Inn, Airport
(800) HOLIDAY, (602) 273-7778
http://www.holiday-inn.com
4300 E. Washington St.
300 rooms - $60-165
Pets: Small pets
Creature Comforts: CCTV,
VCR, a/c, refrig, restaurant, pool,
whirlpool, hlth clb

Holiday Inn Express, Airport
(800) HOLIDAY, (602) 453-9900
http://www.holiday-inn.com
3401 E. University Dr.
115 rooms - $70-190
Pets: Welcome w/dep.
Creature Comforts: CCTV,
VCR, a/c, refrig, Jacuzzi,
restaurant, pool, whirlpool, hlth
clb

Holiday Inn, West
(800) HOLIDAY, (602) 484-9009
http://www.holiday-inn.com
1500 N. 51st Ave.
144 rooms -$75-100z
Pets: Small pets w/dep.
Creature Comforts: CCTV, a/c,
refrig, Jacuzzi, restaurant, pool,
whirlpool, sauna, exercise rm.

Homestead Village
(888) STAY-HSD, (602) 944-7828
http://www.homesteadvillage.com
2102 W. Dunlap
140 rooms - $40-60
Pets: Welcome w/$100 dep.
Creature Comforts: CCTV,
VCR, a/c, kit

Homestead Village, North
(888) STAY-HSD, (602) 843-1151
http://www.homesteadvillage.com
18405 N. 27th Ave.
140 rooms - $40-60
Pets: Welcome w/$100 dep.
Creature Comforts: CCTV,
VCR, a/c, kit

Homewood Suites
(800) 225-5466, (602) 508-0937
http://www.homewoodsuites.com
2001 E. Highland Ave.
125 rooms - $165-225
Pets: Welcome
Creature Comforts: CCTV,
VCR, a/c, fireplaces, kit,
restaurant, pool, hlth clb access,
whirlpools

Howard Johnson
(800) 446-4656, (602) 264-9164
http://www.hojo.com
3400 Grand Ave.
134 rooms - $55-89
Pets: Welcome w/$5 fee
Creature Comforts: CCTV, a/c,
refrig, micro, pool, whirlpool

Howard Johnson
(800) 446-4656, (602) 244-8221
http://www.hojo.com
124 S. 24th St.
99 rooms - $65-95
Pets: Welcome w/$5 fee
Creature Comforts: CCTV, a/c,
refrig, micro, restaurant, pool

Inn Suites
(800) 841-4242, (602) 997-6285
http://www.innsuites.com
1615 E. Northern Ave.
170 rooms - $65-159
Pets: Welcome w/$25 deposit
Creature Comforts: CCTV, a/c,
kit, Jacuzzis, restaurant, pool,
whirlpool

La Quinta Inn, Coliseum
(800) 531-5900, (602) 258-6271
http://www.laquinta.com
2725 N. Black Canyon Hwy.
140 rooms - $55-100
Pets: Small pets welcome
Creature Comforts: CCTV, a/c,
refrig, pool

La Quinta Inn, North
(800) 531-5900, (602) 993-0800
http://www.laquinta.com
2510 W. Greenway Rd.
140 rooms - $55-105
Pets: Small pets welcome
Creature Comforts: CCTV, a/c,
refrig, restaurant, tennis, two pools

Lexington Hotel
(800) 537-8483, (602) 279-9811
100 W. Clarendon St.
180 rooms - $70-189
Pets: Welcome w/$125 dep.
Creature Comforts: CCTV,
VCR, a/c, refrig, micro, restaurant,
pool, sauna, steamrooms,
whirlpool, racquetball, basketball,
and sports clb

Los Olivos Hotel
(800) 776-5560, (602) 258-6911
202 E. McDowell Rd.
50 rooms - $40-125
Pets: Small pets w/$30 fee
Creature Comforts: CCTV,
VCR, a/c, refrig, micro, kit,
restaurant, tennis, whirlpool

Motel 6-West
(800) 4-MOTEL6, (602) 267-7511
http://www.motel6.com
1530 N. 52nd Dr.
147 rooms - $48-75
Pets: Under 30 lbs. welcome
Creature Comforts: CCTV, a/c,
pool

Motel 6
(800) 4-MOTEL6, (602) 267-7511
http://www.motel6.com
2323 E. Van Buren St.
245 rooms - $39-50
Pets: Under 30 lbs. welcome
Creature Comforts: CCTV, a/c,
pool

Motel 6
(800) 4-MOTEL6, (602) 267-8555
http://www.motel6.com
5315 E. Van Buren St.
80 rooms - $45-60
Pets: Under 30 lbs. welcome
Creature Comforts: CCTV, a/c

Motel 6, Airport
(800) 4-MOTEL6, (602) 244-1155
http://www.motel6.com
214 S. 24th St.
61 rooms - $44-57
Pets: Under 30 lbs. welcome
Creature Comforts: CCTV, a/c,
pool

Motel 6
(800) 4-MOTEL6, (602) 267-5501
http://www.motel6.com
4130 N. Black Canyon Hwy.
246 rooms - $39-57
Pets: Under 30 lbs. welcome
Creature Comforts: CCTV, a/c,
pool

Motel 6
(800) 4-MOTEL6, (602) 995-7592
http://www.motel6.com
8152 N. Black Canyon Hwy.
142 rooms - $48-69
Pets: Under 30 lbs. welcome
Creature Comforts: CCTV, a/c,
pool

Motel 6
(800) 4-MOTEL6, (602) 248-8881
http://www.motel6.com
2548 W. Indian St.
245 rooms - $39-53
Pets: Under 30 lbs. welcome
Creature Comforts: CCTV, a/c,
pool

Motel 6
(800) 4-MOTEL6, (602) 942-5030
http://www.motel6.com
2735 W. Sweetwater Ave.
130 rooms - $49-75
Pets: Under 30 lbs. welcome
Creature Comforts: CCTV, a/c,
pool

Motel 6
(800) 4-MOTEL6, (602) 993-2353
http://www.motel6.com
2330 W. Bell Rd.
139 rooms - $54-75
Pets: Under 30 lbs. welcome
Creature Comforts: CCTV, a/c,
pool

Phoenix Sunrise Motel
(800) 432-6483, (602) 275-7661
3644 E. Van Buren St.
41 rooms - $36-53
Pets: Small pets w/$20 dep.
Creature Comforts: CCTV, a/c,
refrig, pool

Pointe Hilton at Tapatio Cliffs
(800) HILTONS, (602) 866-7500
http://www.hilton.com
11111 North 7th St.
589 rooms - $189-575
Pets: Under 30 lbs. w/$100 dep.
Creature Comforts: A unique
reosrt that is terraced on the slopes
of the Phoenix North Mtn.
Preserve, CCTV, VCR, a/c, refrig,
micro, Southwestern decors,
fireplaces, balconies, restaurant,
pools & falls, sauna, whirlpool,
hlth clb, sauna, steamroom, spa,
stables, and golf

Premier Inn
(800) 786-6835, (602) 943-2371
10402 Black Canyon Hwy.
250 rooms - $50-125
Pets: Welcome in certain rooms
Creature Comforts: CCTV, a/c,
Jacuzzi, cont. brkfst, two pools

Quality Hotel
(800) 228-5151, (602) 248-0222
http://www.qualityinn.com
3600 N. Second Ave.
280 rooms - $70-140
Pets: Small pets w/$25 dep.
Creature Comforts: CCTV,
VCR, a/c, refrig, micro, restaurant,
four pools (one w/sandy bch),
whirlpools, hlth clb access

Quality Inn South Mountain
(800) 228-5151, (480) 893-3900
http://www.qualityinn.com
5121 La Puente Ave.
194 rooms - $55-109
Pets: Welcome w/$20 fee
Creature Comforts: CCTV, a/c,
refrig, micro, restaurant, pool,
whirlpool

Residence Inn
(800) 228-9290, (602) 864-1900
http://www.residenceinn.com
8242 N. Black Canyon Hwy
168 rooms - $120-250
Pets: $50 fee, $250 deposit
Creature Comforts: CCTV,
VCR, a/c, refrig, micro, kit, cont.
brkfst, pool, whirlpool, hlth clb

Sheraton Crescent Hotel
(800) 325-3535, (602) 943-8200
http://www.sheraton.com
2620 W. Dunlap Ave.
345 rooms - $99-725
Pets: Welcome
Creature Comforts: Expansive
resort property, CCTV, VCR, a/c,
refrig, restaurant, pool, sauna,
whirlpool, steamroom,
racquetball-squash, lighted tennis,
hlth clb, volleyball, access to golf

Wellesley Inn/Suites, Metro Ctr.
(800) 444-8888, (602) 870-2999
www.wellesleyinnandsuites.com
11211 N. Black Canyon Hwy.
212 rooms - $40-110
Pets: $250 deposit, $100
refundable
Creature Comforts: CCTV, a/c,
kit, cont. brkfst, pool, exercise rm.

Wellesley Inn/Suites, Airport
(800) 444-8888, (602) 225-2998
www.wellesleyinnandsuites.com
4375 E. Oak St.
139 rooms - $70-100
Pets: $150 deposit
Creature Comforts: CCTV, a/c,
kit, cont. brkfst, pool, exercise rm.

Wellesley Inn/Suites, Park Ctrl.
(800) 444-8888, (602) 279-9000
www.wellesleyinnandsuites.com
217 W. Osborn Rd.
129 rooms - $65-100
Pets: $250 deposit
Creature Comforts: CCTV, a/c,
kit, cont. brkfst, pool, exercise rm.

PINETOP
Best Western Inn
(800) 528-1234, (520) 367-6667
http://www.bestwestern.com
404 E. White Mountain Blvd.
40 rooms - $85-115
Pets: Welcome w/$5 fee
Creature Comforts: CCTV,
VCR, a/c, refrig, micro, whirlpool

Buck Springs Resort
(520) 369-3554
Buck Springs Rd.
24 rooms/cottages - $65-85
Pets: Small pets w/$10 fee
Creature Comforts: CCTV,
refrig, fireplace, kit

Double B Lodge
(520) 367-2747
Box 747
10 rooms - $45-79
Pets: Welcome
Creature Comforts: CCTV,
fireplaces, kit, pool, whirlpool

Econo Lodge
(800) 55-ECONO, (520) 367-3636
http://www.econolodge.com
458 E. White Mountain Blvd.
44 rooms - $50-120
Pets: Welcome w/$25 dep.
Creature Comforts: CCTV, a/c,
refrig, micro, cont. brkfst,
whirlpool

Lazy Oaks Resort
(520) 368-6203
1075 Larson Rd.
15 rooms - $55-110
Pets: Small pets with notice
Creature Comforts: CCTV,
refrig, micro, kit, fireplace, lake-
fishing/boat rentals

Meadow View Lodge
(520) 367-4642
Box 325
10 rooms - $55-80
Pets: Welcome
Creature Comforts: CCTV, kit

Northwoods Resort
(800) 813-2966, (520) 367-2966
http://www.northwoodsaz.com
165 E. White Mountain Blvd.
12 rooms/cottages - $75-155
Pets: Welcome w/$12 daily fee
Creature Comforts: Four-season
resort w/Bavarian-style cottages,
country ambiance, traditional
furnishings, CCTV, refrig, micro,
fireplaces, kit, lawn games,
whirlpool, hiking, access to skiing,
golf, tennis, volleyball, and riding

PRESCOTT
Antelope Hills Inn
(888) 547-7614, (520) 778-6000
6200 N. Rte 89
65 apts - $65-105
Pets: Welcome w/$25 fee
Creature Comforts: CCTV,
VCR, a/c, kit, pool, whirlpool

Best Western
(800) 528-1234, (520) 445-3096
http://www.bestwestern.com
1317 East Gurley St.
120 rooms - $55-125
Pets: Small pets in smoking rms.
Creature Comforts: CCTV, a/c,
refrig, micro, restaurant, pool,
whirlpool

Cascade Motel
(520) 445-1232
805 White Spar Rd.
12 rooms - $45-65
Pets: Welcome w/$10 fee
Creature Comforts: CCTV, a/c,
kit

Days Inn
(800) DAYS-INN, (520) 772-8600
http://www.daysinn.com
7875 E. Rte. 69
88 rooms - $59-119
Pets: Welcome w/$50 dep.
Creature Comforts: CCTV, a/c,
refrig, restaurant, cont. brkfst,
pool, spa

Forest Villas Inn
(800) 23-3449, (520) 717-1200
3645 Lee Circle
60 rooms - $75-169
Pets: Small pets w/$150 dep.
Creature Comforts: CCTV, a/c,
refrig, pool, whirlpool

Heritage House Motel
(520) 445-9091
819 E. Gurley St.
20 rooms - $42-85
Pets: Welcome w/$10 fee
Creature Comforts: CCTV, a/c,
kit

Juniper Well Ranch
(520) 442-3415
http://juniperwellranch.com
Conteras and Tonto Rds.
3 rooms - $105-145
Pets: Welcome
Creature Comforts: Log cabins
with charming decor set on 50
acres, bleached wood interiors,
soothing earth tones, mirrored
armoires, CCTV, VCR, a/c, refrig,
micro, fireplace, kit, Jacuzzi,
antiques, restaurant, cont. brkfst,
pool, sauna, whirlpool, hlth clb
access, horses and llamas

Lynx Creek Farm B&B
(888) 778-9573, (520) 778-9573
www.vacation-lodging.com/lcf
PO Box 4301
6 rooms - $85-155
Pets: Welcome w/$10 fee
Creature Comforts: 20-acre
western farm with Victorian
summer house ambiance, canopy
beds, down comforters, country
quilts, antique riding collectibles,
white wicker, picture windows,
dried flowers and wreaths, CCTV,
VCR, refrig, micro, fireplaces, kit,
gourmet brkfst, pool, whirlpool,
lawn sports, tennis access

Motel 6
(800) 4-MOTEL6, (520) 776-0160
http://www.motel6.com
1111 E. Sheldon St.
79 rooms - $45-70
Pets: Small pets welcome
Creature Comforts: CCTV, a/c,
pool

Prescott Sierra Inn
(520) 445-1250
809 White Spar Rd.
25 rooms - $45-75
Pets: Welcome w/credit card dep.
Creature Comforts: CCTV, a/c,
kit, fireplace, cont. brkfst, pool,
whirlpool

Senator Inn Motel
(520) 445-1440
1117 E. Gurley St.
47 rooms - $45-155
Pets: Welcome
Creature Comforts: CCTV, a/c,
refrig, micro, Jacuzzis, cont.
brkfst, pool

Super 8 Motel
(800) 800-8000, (520) 776-1282
http://www.super8.com
1105 E. Sheldon St.
70 rooms - $45-70
Pets: Dogs welcome w/$10 fee
Creature Comforts: CCTV, a/c,
micro, cont. brkfst, pool

PRESCOTT VALLEY
Days Inn
(800) DAYS-INN, (520) 772-8600
60 rooms - $55-125
Pets: Welcome w/$50 dep.
Creature Comforts: CCTV, a/c,
refrig, micro, pool, whirlpool

Motel 6-West
(800) 4-MOTEL6, (520) 772-2200
http://www.motel6.com
8383 E. Rte. 69
120 rooms - $46-69
Pets: Under 30 lbs. welcome
Creature Comforts: CCTV, a/c,
pool

Prescott Valley Motel
(520) 772-9412
8350 E. Rte. 69
24 rooms - $50-99
Pets: Welcome w/$5 fee
Creature Comforts: CCTV, a/c,
restaurant

RIO RICO
Rio Rico Resort
(800) 288-4746, (520) 281-1901
http://mmm.arizonaguide.com/
rio.rico/index.html
1069 Camino Caralampi
185 rooms - $80-169
Pets: Small pets w/$50 dep.
Creature Comforts: CCTV, a/c,
refrig, kit, restaurant, pool, sauna,
whirlpool, golf, tennis, horseback
riding, hlth clb

SAFFORD
Best Western Desert Inn
(800) 528-1234, (520) 426-0521
http://www.bestwestern.com
1391 Thatcher Blvd.
70 rooms - $60-75
Pets: Small pets welcome
Creature Comforts: CCTV, a/c,
refrig, pool

Comfort Inn
(800) 228-5150, (520) 428-5851
http://www.comfortinn.com
1578 W. Thatcher Blvd.
48 rooms - $45-80
Pets: Welcome w/$25 dep.
Creature Comforts: CCTV, a/c,
refrig, micro, kit, pool

Ramada Inn
(800) 2-Ramada, (520) 428-3200
http://www.ramadainn.com
420 East Rte. 70
102 rooms - $49-220
Pets: In smkng rms w/$5 fee
Creature Comforts: CCTV, a/c,
refrig, micro, 2 restaurants, cont.
brkfst, pool, whirlpool, hlth clb

SCOTTSDALE
Amerisuites
(800) 833-1516, (480) 423-9944
http://www.amerisuites.com
7300 E. Third Ave.
128 rms - $60-180
Pets: Welcome w/$20 fee
Creature Comforts: CCTV,
VCR, a/c, kit, cont. brkfst, pool

Country Inn by Carlson
(800) 456-4000, (480) 314-1200
http://www.countryinns.com
10801 N. 89th Place
165 rooms - $80-185
Pets: Small pets w/$25 fee
Creature Comforts: CCTV,
VCR, a/c, refrig, micro, fireplace,
kit, two pools, whirlpool, hlth clb

Doubletree La Posada Resort
(800) 222-TREE, (480) 952-0420
http://www.doubletreehotels.com
4949 E. Lincoln Dr.
254 rooms - $129-799
Pets: Under 20 lbs. welcome
Creature Comforts: Nestled on
32 acres against foothills of
Camelback Mtn., CCTV, a/c,
refrig, Jacuzzis, 2 restaurants,
immense lagoon pools, hlth clb,
whirlpool, sauna, lawn games,
tennis, racquetball, putting green

Four Seasons Resort
(800) 819-5053, (480) 515-5700
http://www.fourseasons.com
10600 E. Crescent Moon Dr.
210 rooms - $250-725
Pets: Under 15 lbs. welcome
Creature Comforts: Luxurious
new resort, private casitas,
bedrooms w/duvets, down
pillows, European toiletries,
CCTV, VCR, a/c, stereo, refrig,
fireplace, soaking tubs, European
toiletries, fine restaurants, spa w/
sauna, steam, whirlpool, massage,
tennis, freeform swimming pools

Gainey Suites Hotel
(800) 970-4666, (480) 922-6969
www.gaineysuiteshotel.com
7300 E. Gainey Suites Dr.
164 suites - $90-200
Pets: Welcome
Creature Comforts: Extended
stay suite hotel, CCTV, VCR, a/c,
kit, cont. brkfst, pool, whirlpool,
hlth clb

Holiday Inn
(800) 465-4329, (480) 951-4000
http://www.holiday-inn.com
7515 E. Butherus Dr.
120 suites - $90-145
Pets: Welcome
Creature Comforts: Very
attractive all-suite hotel, CCTV, a/
c, refrig, micro, Jacuzzi,
restaurant, pool, whirlpool, hlth
clb access

Homestead Village
(888) STAY-HSD, (480) 752-2266
http://www.homesteadvillage.com
3560 N. Marshall Hwy.
125 rooms - $40-100
Pets: Welcome w/$100 dep.
Creature Comforts: CCTV,
VCR, a/c, kit

Hospitality Suite Resort
(800) 445-5115, (480) 949-5115
http://www.hospitalitysuites.com
409 N. Scottsdale Rd.
210 rooms - $50-225
Pets: Under 20 lbs. w/$100 dep.
Creature Comforts: CCTV, a/c,
refrig, micro, kit, restaurant, three
pools, whirlpools, tennis,
basketball court., and a hlth clb

Inn at the Citadel
(800) 927-8367, (480) 585-6133
www.arizonaguide.com/citadelinn
8700 E. Pinnacle Peak Rd.
11 suites - $99-335
Pets: Dogs welcome
Creature Comforts: Set on
Sonoran desert, lovely chambers
appointed with antiques-luxurious
amenities, European pensione
ambiance, Empire furnishings,
some hand-painted pieces, CCTV,
VCR, a/c, refrig, kiva fireplace,
kit, balconies w/whirlpools, 3
restaurants, cont. brkfst, hlth clb
access

InnSuites
(800) 238-8851, (480) 941-1202
http://www.innsuites.com
7707 E. McDowell Rd.
100 rooms - $65-135
Pets: Small pets w/$25 fee
Creature Comforts: CCTV, a/c,
refrig, micro, Jacuzzi, full brkfst,
pool, spa, whirlpool, hlth clb
access

Marriott's Mt. Shadows Resort
(800) 228-9290, (480) 948-7111
http://www.marriott.com
5641 East Lincoln Dr.
340 rooms - $99-375
Pets: Small pets welcome
Creature Comforts: Full service
resort w/ appealing guest rooms,
CCTV, a/c, refrig, kit, two
restaurants, three pools, sauna,
whirlpool, spa, golf, tennis, lawn
games, game room, hlth clb

Marriott Camelback Inn
(800) 24CAMEL, (480) 948-1700
http://www.camelbackinn.com
5402 E. Lincoln Dr.
425 rooms - $175-2,100
Pets: Small pets preferred
Creature Comforts: Lavish
desert resort on 125 acres at base
of Mummy Mountain, Pueblo-
style casitas, beamed ceilings,
soothing colors, earth tone fabrics,
Native Am. accents, CCTV, a/c,
refrig, micro, fireplaces, kit,
balconies, Jacuzzis, restaurant,
cont. brkfst, pool, massage, sauna,
tennis, whirlpool, kids programs,
hlth clb access, 36 holes of golf,
lawn games, bikes, spa

Motel 6
(800) 4-MOTEL6, (480) 946-2280
http://www.motel6.com
6848 E. Camelback Rd.
122 rooms - $46-75
Pets: Under 30 lbs. welcome
Creature Comforts: CCTV, a/c,
pool, whirlpool

The Phoenician Resort
(800) 888-8234, (480) 941-8200
http://www.thephoenician.com
600 E. Camelback Rd.
647 rooms villas - $180-1,800
Pets: Under 30 lbs. in the casitas
Creature Comforts: Five star-
resort with exquisite amenities,
beautifully maintaned grounds,
sculptures, rooms w/McGuire
furnishings, original artwork, earth
tones, CCTV, VCR, a/c, refrig,
micro, fireplaces, bathrooms w/
Italian marble, kit, Jacuzzis, 3
restaurants, 6 pools, waterslide,
sauna, whirlpool, golf, tennis,
putting green, lawn games, hlth
clb, and croquet

Ramada Valley Ho Hotel
(800) 2-Ramada, (480) 945-6321
http://www.ramada.com
6850 Main St.
290 rooms - $55-160
Pets: Welcome w/$ 50 dep.
Creature Comforts: CCTV,
VCR, a/c, refrig, restaurant, 3
pools, whirlpools, hlth clb

Renaissance Cottonwoods
(800) 468-3571, (480) 991-1414
http://www.renaissancehotels.com
6160 N. Scottsdale Rd.
105 rooms - $109-425
Pets: Under 20 lbs. w/$50 dep.
Creature Comforts: Hotel set
against Camelback Mtn,
Southwestern decor coupled w/
many amenities, CCTV, VCR, a/c,
refrig, micro, fireplace, kit,
restaurant, two pools, whirlpools,
lawn games, tennis, putting green,
elegant shopping area-Borgata
Shops

Residence Inn
(800) 331-3131, (480) 948-8666
http://www.residenceinn.com
6040 North Scottsdale Rd
125 rooms - $85-280
Pets: Small pets w/$6 fee
Creature Comforts: CCTV,
VCR, a/c, refrig, micro, fireplace,
kit, pool, whirlpool, hlth clb
access

Royal Inn
(800) 599-5885, (480) 947-5885
2934 N. Scottsdale Rd.
40 rooms - $45-119
Pets: Welcome
Creature Comforts: CCTV, a/c,
refrig, micro, kit, pool

Scottsdale Pima Inn
(800) 344-0262, (480) 948-3800
arizonaguide.com/pimasuites
7330 N. Pima Rd.
125 rooms - $45-245
Pets: Small pets w/$100 dep.
Creature Comforts: CCTV, a/c,
refrig, micro, kit, two pools,
sauna, whirlpool, hlth clb

SEDONA
Best Western
(800) 528-1234, (520) 282-3072
http://www.bestwestern.com
1200 West Rte. 89A
110 rooms - $85-140
Pets: Welcome w/$10 fee
Creature Comforts: CCTV,
VCR, a/c, refrig, fireplace, pool,
whirlpool

Canyon Mesa Country Club
(520) 284-2176
web site pending
500 Jacks Canyon Rd.
60 units - $650-1,100/wk
Pets: Welcome
Creature Comforts: CCTV,
VCR, a/c, kit, golf, tennis, pool,
whirlpool

Desert Quail
(800) 385-0927, (520) 284-1433
http://www.desertquailinn.com
6626 Route 179
42 rooms - $59-140
Pets: Under 20 lbs. are welcome
w/$10 daily fee
Creature Comforts: Centrally
located w/traditional southwestern
charm and decor, Native Am.
fabrics, hand-crafted pine
furnishings, log beds, copper
paddle fans, sculptures, CCTV, a/
c, refrig, micro, fireplace, pool,
hlth club access, whirlpool

Forest House Resort
(520) 282-2999
Oak Creek Canyon
12 cabins - $75-125
Pets: Leashed pets welcome
Creature Comforts: Wonderful
rock and timber cottages nestled in
picturesque Oak Creek Canyon,
some riverside, walls of windows
and skylights, original artwork,
eclectic furnishings, refrig,
fireplace, cont. brkfst, hiking

Greyfire Farm B&B
(800) 579-2340, (520) 284-2340
http://www.greyfirefarm.com
1240 Jacks Canyon Rd.
2 rooms - $85-225
Pets: Welcome
Creature Comforts: Low-lying
farm house, CCTV, VCR, a/c,
antiques, fireplace, colorful quilts,
patio, full brkfst, teddy bear
collection, great views of red rock
landmarks, birds and horses

Holiday Inn Express
(800) HOLIDAY, (520) 284-0711
http://www.holiday-inn.com
6175 Rte. 179
104 rooms - $85-145
Pets: Welcome w/$25 fee
Creature Comforts: CCTV,
VCR, a/c, pool, whirlpool

Matterhorn Motor Lodge
(520) 282-7176
230 Apple Ave.
24 rooms - $50-95
Pets: Small pets welcome
Creature Comforts: CCTV, a/c,
refrig, pool, whirlpool

New Earth Lodge
(520) 282-2644
665 Sunset Dr. #26
22 rooms - $85-120
Pets: $5 fee, $25 dep.
Creature Comforts: CCTV,
VCR, a/c, fireplaces, kit

Oak Creek Terrace
(800) 224-2229, (520) 282-3562
http://www.sedona.net/resorts/oct
Rte. 89, Box 1100
20 rooms - $75-175
Pets: Small pets in ltd. rooms w/
$25 fee
Creature Comforts: Intimate
resort overlooking Oak Creek,
canyon, CCTV, traditional decor,
VCR, a/c, refrig, fireplaces, decks,
micro, kit, Jacuzzis, cont. brkfst,
fishing

Quail Ridge Resort
(520) 284-9327
http://www.quailridgeresort.com
120 Canyon Circle Dr.
13 units - $75-140
Pets: Welcome
Creature Comforts: CCTV, a/c,
kit, pool, whirlpool, tennis

Quality Inn King's Ransom
(800) 228-5151, (520) 282-7151
http://www.qualityinn.com
771 Rte. 179
80 rooms - $55-135
Pets: Small pets welcome
Creature Comforts: CCTV, a/c,
refrig, restaurant, pool, whirlpool

Sky Ranch Lodge
(888) 708-6400, (520) 282-6400
http://www.sed-biz.com/skyranch
Airport Rd., Box 2579
95 rooms - $80-175
Pets: Welcome w/$10 fee
Creature Comforts: Set on mesa
with incredible views, nicely
landscaped, bleached woods, light
pine furnishings-southwestern
decor, hand-painted pieces,
beamed ceilings, CCTV, refrig,
fireplace-woodstove, kit, pool,
spa, whirlpool, best rooms are
cottages and rooms 18-20

White House Inn
(520) 282-6680
2986 W. Rte. 89
22 rooms - $45-119
Pets: Welcome
Creature Comforts: CCTV, a/c,
refrig

SELIGMAN
Canyon Shadows Motel
(520) 422-3255
114 E. Chino Rd.
16 rooms - $35-50
Pets: Welcome in smoking rooms
Creature Comforts: CCTV, a/c,
refrig, micro

SHOW LOW
Days Inn
(800) DAYS-INN, (520) 537-4356
http://www.daysinn.com
480 W. Deuce of Clubs Ave.
124 rooms - $50-80
Pets: Small pets w/$5 fee
Creature Comforts: CCTV, a/c,
refrig, micro, restaurant, pool
access

Kiva Motel
(520) 537-4542
261 E. Deuce of Clubs Ave.
20 rooms - $50-75
Pets: Welcome
Creature Comforts: CCTV, a/c,
refrig, whirlpool

Snowy River Motel
(520) 537-2926
1640 E. Deuce of Clubs Ave.
18 rooms - $30-54
Pets: Small dogs w/$5 fee
Creature Comforts: CCTV, a/c,
refrig

Super 8
(800) 800-8000, (520) 537-7694
http://www.super8.com
1941 E. Deuce of Clubs Ave.
42 rooms - $40-50
Pets: Welcome w/$20 dep.
Creature Comforts: CCTV, a/c,
refrig, micro, whirlpools

SIERRA VISTA
Best Western Mission Inn
(800) 528-1234, (520) 458-8500
http://www.bestwestern.com
3460 E. Fry Blvd.
40 rooms - $55-68
Pets: Small pets welcome
Creature Comforts: CCTV, a/c,
pool

Motel 6
(800) 4-MOTEL6, (520) 459-5035
http://www.motel6.com
1551 E. Fry Blvd.
103 rooms - $34-49
Pets: Under 30 lbs. welcome
Creature Comforts: CCTV, a/c,
pool

Sierra Suites
(520) 459-4221
391 East Fry Blvd.
100 rooms - $50-80
Pets: Small pets w/$50 dep.
Creature Comforts: CCTV, a/c,
refrig, micro, pool, whirlpool

Sun Canyon Inn
(800) 822-6966, (520) 459-0610
260 N. Garden Ave.
82 rooms - $50-65
Pets: Welcome w/$6 fee
Creature Comforts: CCTV, a/c,
refrig, micro, restaurant, pool,
whirlpool

Thunder Mountain Inn
(800) 222-5811, (520) 458-7900
1631 South Rte. 92
100 rooms - $40-60
Pets: Welcome w/$50 dep.
Creature Comforts: CCTV, a/c,
refrig, restaurant, pool, whirlpool

Vista Inn
(520) 458-6711
201 W. Fry Blvd.
71 rooms - $39-55
Pets: Welcome
Creature Comforts: CCTV, a/c,
restaurant, cont. brkfst

Wyndemere Hotel
(800) 825-4656, (520) 459-5900
2047 South Rte. 92
150 rooms - $65-260
Pets: Welcome w/$50 dep.
Creature Comforts: CCTV,
VCR, a/c, refrig, micro, restaurant,
pool, whirlpool, hlth clb access

SPRINGERVILLE
El-Jo Motor Inn
(520) 333-4314
425 E. Main St.
30 rooms - $44-55
Pets: Welcome w/$5 fee
Creature Comforts: CCTV, a/c,
refrig, micro, whirlpool access

Reed's Motor Lodge
(520) 333-4323
514 E. Main St.
37 rooms - $39-55
Pets: Welcome
Creature Comforts: CCTV,
VCR, a/c, fireplace, whirlpool

ST. JOHNS
Days Inn
(800) DAYS-INN, (520) 337-4422
http://www.daysinn.com
185 E. Commercial St.
39 rooms - $35-49
Pets: Small pets welcome
Creature Comforts: CCTV, a/c,
restaurant, cont. brkfst

Super 8 Motel
(800) 800-8000, (520) 337-2990
http://www.super8.com
75 E. Commercial St.
66 rooms - $39-55
Pets: Welcome w/$25 dep.
Creature Comforts: CCTV, a/c,
cont. brkfst

STRAWBERRY
The Strawberry Lodge
(520) 476-3333
HCR 1, Box 331
12 rooms - $45-55
Pets: Welcome w/$10 fee
Creature Comforts: Restaurant

SUN CITY
Best Western Sun City
(800) 528-1234, (623) 933-8211
http://www.bestwestern.com
11201 Grand Ave.
77 rooms - $45-110
Pets: Small pets welcome
Creature Comforts: CCTV,
VCR, a/c, refrig, micro, pool

Motel 6
(800) 4-MOTEL6, (623) 977-1318
http://www.motel6.com
Rtes. 60 & 89
62 rooms - $55-79
Pets: Under 30 lbs. welcome
Creature Comforts: CCTV, a/c,
pool

SURPRISE
Windmill Inns
(800) 547-4747, (623) 583-0133
http://www.windmillinns.com
12545 W. Bell Rd.
125 rooms - $55-125
Pets: Welcome
Creature Comforts: CCTV, a/c,
refrig, micro, pool, whirlpool, lake

TEMPE
Amerisuites
(800) 833-1516, (480) 831-9800
http://www.amerisuites.com
1520 W. Baseline Rd.
128 rms - $80-125
Pets: Small pets w/$25 fee
Creature Comforts: CCTV,
VCR, a/c, kit, cont. brkfst, pool,
exercise rm.

Best Western, Tempe
(800) 528-1234, (480) 784-2233
http://www.bestwestern.com
670 N. Scottsdale Rd.
102 rooms - $70-135
Pets: Small pets welcome
Creature Comforts: CCTV, a/c,
refrig, micro, restaurant, pool,
whirlpool, hlth clb

Best Western
(800) 528-1234, (480) 784-2233
http://www.bestwestern.com
670 N. Scottsdale Rd.
103 rooms - $90-149
Pets: Small pets welcome.
Creature Comforts: CCTV, a/c,
cont. brkfst, pool

The Wyndham Buttes
(800) 843-1986, (480) 225-9000
http://www.wyndham.com
2000 Westcourt Way
352 rooms - $99-1,500
Pets: Under 25 lbs. w/$25 dep.
Creature Comforts: Award-winning design wrapped around mountainside on 25 acres, honey toned woods, southwestern colors, residential ambiance, best rooms overlook grotto, plantation shutters, CCTV, VCR, a/c, refrig, fireplace, kit, Jacuzzi, three restaurants, two terraced pools, waterslide, whirlpools, saunas, kids program, volleyball, lighted tennis, hlth clb

Country Suites by Carlson
(800) 456-4000, (480) 345-8585
http://www.countryinns.com
1660 W. Elliott Rd.
140 rooms - $50-159
Pets: Under 25 lbs. w/$50 fee
Creature Comforts: CCTV, a/c, refrig, micro, kit, restaurant, cont. brkfst, pool, whirlpool

Econo Lodge
(800) 55-ECONO, (480) 966-5832
http://www.econolodge.com
2101 E. Apache Blvd.
40 rooms - $35-95
Pets: Welcome
Creature Comforts: CCTV, a/c, refrig, pool

Fiesta Inn
(800) 528-6481, (480) 967-1441
2100 S. Priest Dr.
275 rooms - $75-175
Pets: Welcome
Creature Comforts: CCTV, a/c, refrig, kit, restaurant, pool, hlth clb, sauna, whirlpools, tennis, golf range

Holiday Inn
(800) HOLIDAY, (480) 968-3451
http://www.holiday-inn.com
915 E. Apache Blvd.
192 rooms - $65-129
Pets: Welcome
Creature Comforts: CCTV, a/c, refrig, kit, restaurant, pool, whirlpool, exercise rm.

Holiday Inn Express
(800) HOLIDAY, (480) 820-7500
http://www.holiday-inn.com
5300 S. Priest Dr.
160 rooms - $125-465
Pets: Welcome
Creature Comforts: CCTV, a/c, refrig, pool, whirlpool

Homestead Village
(888) STAY-HSD, (480) 414-4470
http://www.homesteadvillage.com
4909 S. Wendler Dr.
150 rooms - $40-60
Pets: Welcome w/$100 dep.
Creature Comforts: CCTV, VCR, a/c, kit

Innsuites
(800) 842-4242, (480) 897-7900
http://www.innsuites.com
1651 W. Baseline Rd.
175 rooms - $60-149
Pets: Welcome w/$50 dep.
Creature Comforts: CCTV, a/c, fireplace, kit, restaurant, pool, hlth clb access, sauna, whirlpool, tennis, putting green, tennis, and volleyball

La Quinta
(800) 531-5900, (480) 967-4465
http://www.laquinta.com
911 S. 48th St.
130 rooms - $59-105
Pets: Small pets welcome
Creature Comforts: CCTV, a/c, refrig, pool, putting green

Mission Palms Hotel
(800) 547-8705, (480) 894-1400
http://www.missionpalms.com
60 E. Fifth St.
303 rooms - $100-300
Pets: Small pets w/$25 fee, $75 deposit
Creature Comforts: Distinctive hotel, Southwestern designed rms, CCTV, a/c, refrig, Jacuzzi, restaurant, pool, whirlpools, hlth clb., tennis

Motel 6
(800) 4-MOTEL6, (480) 945-9506
http://www.motel6.com
1612 N. Scottsdale Rd.
101 rooms - $46-69
Pets: Under 30 lbs. welcome
Creature Comforts: CCTV, a/c, cont. brkfst, pool

Motel 6
(800) 4-MOTEL6, (480) 968-4401
http://www.motel6.com
1720 So. Priest Dr.
131 rooms - $44-69
Pets: Under 30 lbs. welcome
Creature Comforts: CCTV, a/c, cont. brkfst, pool

Motel 6
(800) 4-MOTEL6, (480) 967-8696
http://www.motel6.com
513 W. Broadway Rd.
61 rooms - $45-75
Pets: Under 30 lbs. welcome
Creature Comforts: CCTV, a/c, cont. brkfst, pool

Ramada Plaza Hotel
(800) 2-Ramada, (480) 967-6600
http://www.ramada.com
1600 S. 52nd St.
215 rooms - $60-175
Pets: Small pets w/$100 dep.
Creature Comforts: CCTV, a/c, refrig, pool, whirlpool

Residence Inn
(800) 331-3131, (480) 756-2122
http://www.residenceinn.com
5075 So. Priest Dr.
125 rooms - $85-225
Pets: Welcome w/$6 fee, $50 dep.
Creature Comforts: CCTV, a/c, refrig, fireplace, kit, restaurant, pool, whirlpool

Rodeway Inn
(800) 228-2000, (480) 967-3000
http://www.rodeway.com
1550 S. 52nd St.
100 rooms - $70-150
Pets: Welcome w/$5 fee
Creature Comforts: CCTV, a/c, refrig, pool, whirlpool

Super 8 Motel
(800) 800-8000, (480) 967-8891
http://www.super8
1020 E. Apache Blvd.
88 rooms - $65-90
Pets: Welcome
Creature Comforts: CCTV, a/c, cont. brkfst, pool

43

Travelodge
(800) 578-7878, (480) 968-7871
http://www.travelodge.com
1005 E. Apache Blvd.
54 rooms - $48-88
Pets: Small pets w/$4 fee
Creature Comforts: CCTV, a/c, pool

TOLLESON
Econo Lodge
(800) 55-ECONO, (623) 936-4667
http://www.econolodge.com
1520 N. 84th Dr.
120 rooms - $55-130
Pets: $10 fee, $25 dep.
Creature Comforts: CCTV, a/c, refrig, pool

TOMBSTONE
Best Western
(800) 528-1234, (520) 457-2223
http://www.bestwestern.com
Route 80
42 rooms - $55-90
Pets: W/$5 fee CC dep.
Creature Comforts: CCTV, a/c, pool

Tombstone Motel
(520) 457-3478
502 E. Fremont St.
11 rooms - $35-75
Pets: Welcome w/$25 dep.
Creature Comforts: CCTV, a/c, refrig

TUBAC
Tubac Golf Resort
(800) 848-7893, (520) 398-2211
mmm.arizonaguide.com/tubac
1 Otero Rd.
17 casitas - $69-185
Pets: Welcome w/$5 fee
Creature Comforts: Neat, old-fashioned resort w/casitas, old Arizona style bedrooms, beamed ceilings, Mexican accents,TV, a/c, kiva fireplaces, kit, restaurant, pool, whirlpool, volleyball, tennis, and golf

TUBA CITY
Quality Inn
(800) 228-5151, (520) 283-4545
http://www.qualityinn.com
Main & Moenave Sts.
84 rooms - $70-145
Pets: Small pets w/$20 dep.
Creature Comforts: CCTV, a/c, refrig, micro, restaurant

TUCSON
Baymont Inn & Suites
(800) 789-4103, (520) 889-6600
http://www.baymontinns.com
2548 E. Medina Rd.
98 rooms - $65-110
Pets: Welcome under 50 lbs.
Creature Comforts: CCTV, a/c, refrig, micro, restaurant, pool

Best Western Executive Inn
(800) 528-1234, (520) 791-7551
http://www.bestwestern.com
333 W. Drachman St.
129 rooms - $45-125
Pets: Small pets welcome
Creature Comforts: CCTV, VCR, a/c, refrig, restaurant, pool, whirlpool

The Cat & The Whistle B&B
(800) 456-0682, (520) 990-0682
www.azres.com/host/5502.htm
22nd & Kolb St.
2 rooms - $65-90
Pets: Small pets in suite
Creature Comforts: Charming home w/southwestern decor, Native American carvings, lovely artwork, CCTV, a/c, kiva fireplace, kit, patio, full brkfst

Chateau Sonata
(800) 597-8483, (520) 886-2468
www.arizonaguide.com/chateau
550 S. Camino Seco
144 suites - $65-235
Pets: Welcome w/$100 dep.
Creature Comforts: CCTV, a/c, kit, pool, whirlpool, sauna, hlth club, tennis

Clarion Hotel
(800) 252-7466, (520) 746-3932
http://www.clarioninn.com
6801 S. Tucson Blvd.
190 rooms - $55-149
Pets: Welcome w/$30 dep.
Creature Comforts: CCTV, a/c, refrig, restaurant, pool, hlth clb, whirlpool

Doubletree Hotel
(800) 222-TREE, (520) 881-4200
http://www.doubletreehotels.com
445 South Alvernon Blvd.
290 rooms - $69-475
Pets: Small pets w/$50 dep.
Creature Comforts: CCTV, a/c, refrig, restaurant, pool, hlth clb, whirlpool, tennis

Econo Lodge
(800) 55-ECONO, (520) 623-5881
http://www.econolodge.com
3020 S. 6th Ave.
86 rooms - $40-89
Pets: Welcome
Creature Comforts: CCTV, a/c, pool, whirlpool

Embassy Suites, Airport
(800) 362-2779, (520) 573-0700
http://www.embassy-suites.com
7051 S. Tucson Blvd.
200 rooms - $80-145
Pets: Welcome w/$25 dep.
Creature Comforts: CCTV, a/c, refrig, restaurant, pool, whirlpool

Embassy Suites
(800) 362-2779, (520) 745-2700
http://www.embassy-suites.com
5225 E. Broadway Rd.
144 rooms - $90-175
Pets: Welcome w/$10 fee
Creature Comforts: CCTV, a/c, refrig, micro, restaurant, pool, whirlpool

Flamingo Travelodge
(800) 578-7878, (520) 770-1910
http://www.travelodge.com
1300 N. Stone Ave.
80 rooms - $45-95
Pets: Small pets w/$50 dep.
Creature Comforts: CCTV, a/c, refrig, micro, pool, hlth clb access, whirlpool

Ghost Ranch Lodge
(800) 456-7565, (520) 791-7565
http://www.ghostranchlodge.com
801 W. Miracle Mile
83 rooms - $40-100
Pets: Small pets welcome
Creature Comforts: Set on 8-acres w/famous cactus garden, adobe and shingle casitas, CCTV, VCR, a/c, kit, restaurant, pool, whirlpool

Golf Villas at Oro Valley
(877) 845-5688, (520) 498-0098
http://www.thegolfvillas.com
10950 N. La Canada Dr.
65 villas - $100-489
Pets: Under 40 lbs. w/$400 deposit, $200 refundable
Creature Comforts: Luxury vacation villas, decorated in attractive contemporary Southwestern style, CCTV, VCR, a/c, down pillows, designer linens, Jacuzzi, robes, fireplace, gourmet kitchen, pools, spa and health club, golf

Hampton Inn
(800) Hampton, (520) 889-5789
http://www.hampton-inn.com
6971 S. Tucson Blvd.
125 rooms - $55-109
Pets: Welcome
Creature Comforts: CCTV, a/c, pool, whirlpool

Hampton Inn
(800) Hampton, (520) 206-0602
http://www.hampton-inn.com
1375 W. Grant Rd.
90 rooms - $55-109
Pets: Welcome
Creature Comforts: CCTV, a/c, pool, whirlpool

Holiday Inn
(800) HOLIDAY, (520) 624-8711
http://www.holiday-inn.com
181 W. Broadway Rd.
305 rooms - $55-175
Pets: Welcome w/$25 dep.
Creature Comforts: CCTV, a/c, refrig, restaurant, pool, hlth clb

La Quinta
(800) 531-5900, (520) 622-6491
http://www.laquinta.com
665 N. Freeway
132 rooms - $55-109
Pets: Small pets welcome
Creature Comforts: CCTV, a/c, refrig, pool

La Quinta
(800) 531-5900, (520) 747-1414
http://www.laquinta.com
6404 E. Broadway Rd.
140 rooms - $55-105
Pets: Small pets welcome
Creature Comforts: CCTV, a/c, refrig, pool, whirlpool

Motel 6
(800) 4-MOTEL6, (520) 628-1339
http://www.motel6.com
960 S. Freeway
111 rooms - $39-60
Pets: Under 30 lbs. welcome
Creature Comforts: CCTV, a/c, cont. brkfst, pool

Motel 6
(800) 4-MOTEL6, (520) 624-2516
http://www.motel6.com
1222 S. Freeway
99 rooms - $36-55
Pets: Under 30 lbs. welcome
Creature Comforts: CCTV, a/c, cont. brkfst, pool

Motel 6
(800) 4-MOTEL6, (520) 774-9300
http://www.motel6.com
4630 W. Ina Rd.
118 rooms - $44-69
Pets: Under 30 lbs. welcome
Creature Comforts: CCTV, a/c, cont. brkfst, pool

Motel 6
(800) 4-MOTEL6, (520) 628-1264
http://www.motel6.com
1031 E. Benson Hwy.
146 rooms - $34-52
Pets: Under 30 lbs. welcome
Creature Comforts: CCTV, a/c, cont. brkfst, pool

Motel 6
(800) 4-MOTEL6, (520) 622-4614
http://www.motel6.com
755 E. Benson Hwy.
120 rooms - $36-47
Pets: Under 30 lbs. welcome
Creature Comforts: CCTV, a/c, cont. brkfst, pool

Motel 6
(800) 4-MOTEL6, (520) 746-0030
http://www.motel6.com
4950 S. Outlet Ctr. Dr.
120 rooms - $ 39-68
Pets: Under 30 lbs. welcome
Creature Comforts: CCTV, a/c, cont. brkfst, pool

Quality Inn
(800) 228-5151, (520) 622-3000
http://www.qualityinn.com
475 N. Granada Ave.
285 rooms - $55-129
Pets: Welcome w/$50 dep.
Creature Comforts: CCTV, a/c, refrig, restaurant, two pools

Raddison Suite Hotel
(800) 333-3333 , (520) 721-7100
http://www.radisson.com
6555 E. Speedway Blvd.
300 rooms - $65-189
Pets: Small pets w/$25 fee
Creature Comforts: CCTV, a/c, refrig, micro, restaurant, pool, hlth clb access, whirlpool

Ramada Inn
(800) 2-Ramada, (520) 886-9595
http://www.ramada.com
6944 E. Tanque Verde Rd.
112 rooms - $55-149
Pets: Welcome w/$10 fee
Creature Comforts: CCTV, a/c, refrig, restaurant, pool, sauna, whirlpool

Ramada Inn
(800) 2-Ramada, (520) 623-6666
http://www.ramada.com
1601 N. Oracle Rd.
199 rooms - $65-93
Pets: Welcome w/$5 fee
Creature Comforts: CCTV, a/c, refrig, restaurant, pool

Ramada Inn
(800) 2-Ramada, (520) 294-5250
http://www.ramada.com
5251 S. Julian Dr.
172 rooms - $55-189
Pets: Welcome w/$10 fee
Creature Comforts: CCTV, a/c, refrig, micro, restaurant, pool, hlth clb, whirlpool

Red Roof Inn
(800) 843-7663, (520) 571-1400
http://www.redroof.com
3700 E. Irvington Rd.
120 rooms - $39-72
Pets: Small pets welcome
Creature Comforts: CCTV, a/c, restaurant, pool, whirlpool

Residence Inn
(800) 331-3131, (520) 721-0991
http://www.residenceinn.com
6477 East Speedway Blvd.
125 rooms - $65-225
Pets: Welcome w/$150 dep.
Creature Comforts: CCTV, VCR, a/c, refrig, fireplace, kit, pool, whirlpool

Rodeway Inn
(800) 228-2000, (520) 884-5800
http://www.rodeway.com
1365 W. Grant Rd.
145 rooms - $49-129
Pets: Welcome w/$10 fee
Creature Comforts: CCTV, a/c, refrig, restaurant, pool

Rodeway Inn
(800) 228-2000, (520) 884-5800
http://www.rodeway.com
810 E. Benson Rd.
100 rooms - $55-129
Pets: Welcome w/$25 dep.
Creature Comforts: CCTV, a/c, refrig, pool

Sheraton El Conquistador
(800) 325-7832, (520) 544-5000
http://www.sheraton.com
100 N. Oracle Rd.
428 rooms - $85-1,200
Pets: Welcome in the casitas
Creature Comforts: Expansive resort nestled alongside Pusch Ridge, flower gardens, rooms w/ pickled pine furnishings-contemporary decor, patios, CCTV, VCR, a/c, refrig, fireplace, kit, restaurant, two pools, hlth clb, sauna, kid's camp, massage, whirlpools, racquetball, golf, tennis

Sheraton Four Points
(800) 325-3535, (520) 622-6611
http://www.sheraton.com
350 S. Freeway
174 rooms - $50-129
Pets: Welcome w/$50 fee
Creature Comforts: CCTV, a/c, kit, restaurant, pool, whirlpool, access to golf/tennis

Super 8 Motel
(800) 800-8000, (520) 622-6446
http://www.super8.com
1248 N. Stone St.
40 rooms - $45-99
Pets: Welcome w/approval
Creature Comforts: CCTV, a/c

Travelodge Suites
(800) 578-7878, (520) 797-1710
http://www.travelodge.com
401 W. Lavery Lane
50 rooms - $55-155
Pets: Welcome w/$35 fee
Creature Comforts: CCTV, a/c, refrig, pool

Wayward Winds Lodge
(800) 791-9503, (520) 791-7526
http://mmm.arizonaguide.com/
wayward.winds
707 W. Miracle Mile
40 rooms - $49-105
Pets: Welcome
Creature Comforts: CCTV, a/c, refrig, kit, restaurant, lawn games, pool

Westward Look Resort
(800) 722-2500, (520) 297-1151
http://www.westwardlook.com
245 East Ina Road
244 rooms - $105-395
Pets: Lower casitas w/credit card deposit
Creature Comforts: Recently renovated resort on 80 acres with incredible views of Tucson, charming casitas w/viga ceilings, CCTV, a/c, refrig, fireplace, stereos, restaurant, three pools, hlth clb, whirlpool, hiking trails, golf access, lawn sports, renowned tennis program and spa

Windmill Inns
(800) 547-4747, (520) 577-0007
http://www.windmillinns.com
St. Phillips Plaza-4250 N. Campbell Ave.
120 rooms - $75-135
Pets: Welcome
Creature Comforts: CCTV, a/c, kit, pool, whirlpool, library

WICKENBURG
Best Western Rancho Grande
(800) 528-1234, (520) 684-5445
http://www.bestwestern.com
293 East Wickenburg Way
82 rooms - $60-95
Pets: Welcome
Creature Comforts: CCTV, VCR, a/c, kit, pool, whirlpool, tennis

Days Inn
(800) DAYS-INN, (520) 384-4222
http://www.daysinn.com
724 N. Bisbee Ave.
61 rooms - $39-99
Pets: Welcome
Creature Comforts: CCTV, cont. brkfst, pool

Super 8 Motel
(800) 800-8000, (520) 684-0808
http://www.super8.com
1021 N. Tegner Rd.
40 rooms - $54-75
Pets: Small pets welcome
Creature Comforts: CCTV, a/c, micro, cont. brkfst

Westerner Motel
(520) 684-2493
680 W. Wickenburg Way
12 rooms - $59-105
Pets: Welcome
Creature Comforts: CCTV, a/c,
refrig, restaurant

WILCOX
Best Western Plaza
(800) 528-1234, (520) 384-3556
http://www.bestwestern.com
1100 W. Rex Allen Dr.
90 rooms - $65-93
Pets: Small pets w/$8 fee
Creature Comforts: CCTV, a/c,
refrig, pool, whirlpool

Days Inn
(800) DAYS-INN, (520) 384-4222
http://www.daysinn.com
724 N. Bisbee Ave.
72 rooms - $42-75
Pets: Welcome w/$4 fee
Creature Comforts: CCTV, a/c,
refrig, cont. brkfst, pool

Econo Lodge
(800) 55-ECONO, (520) 384-4222
http://www.econolodge.com
724 N. Bisbee Ave.
72 rooms - $38-85
Pets: Welcome
Creature Comforts: CCTV, a/c,
refrig, micro, pool

Motel 6
(800) 4-MOTEL6, (520) 384-2201
http://www.motel6.com
921 N. Bisbee Ave.
88 rooms - $39-55
Pets: Small pets welcome
Creature Comforts: CCTV, pool

WILLIAMS
Royal American Inn
(520) 635-4591
134 E. Bill Williams Ave.
14 rooms - $30-45
Pets: Welcome w/$5 fee
Creature Comforts: CCTV, a/c,
refrig

Budget Host Inn
(800) 283-4678, (520) 635-4415
620 W. Bill Williams Ave.
26 rooms - $35-89
Pets: Welcome
Creature Comforts: CCTV,
refrig

Canyon Motel
(520) 635-9371
Old E. Rte. 66
18 rooms - $30-65
Pets: Welcome
Creature Comforts: CCTV, a/c

Grand Motel
(520) 635-4601
234 E. Bill Williams Ave.
24 rooms - $59-75
Pets: Welcome
Creature Comforts: CCTV, a/c

Highlander Motel
(800) 800-8288, (520) 635-2541
533 W. Bill Williams Ave.
12 rooms - $29-69
Pets: Small pets welcome
Creature Comforts: CCTV, a/c

Holiday Inn
(800) HOLIDAY, (520) 635-4114
http://www.holiday-inn.com
950 N. Grand Canyon Blvd.
125 rooms - $55-119
Pets: Small pets welcome
Creature Comforts: CCTV, a/c,
refrig, restaurant, pool, sauna,
whirlpool

Motel 6
(800) 4-MOTEL6, (520) 635-9000
http://www.motel6.com
831 W. Bill Williams Ave.
52 rooms - $45-99
Pets: Small pets welcome
Creature Comforts: CCTV,
VCR, a/c, kit, pool, whirlpool

Quality Inn - Mountain Ranch
(800) 228-5151, (520) 635-2693
http://www.qualityinn.com
Rte. 40 & Deer Farm Rd.
74 rooms - $58-109
Pets: Small pets welcome
Creature Comforts: CCTV,
VCR, a/c, refrig, restaurant, pool,
whirlpool, tennis

Ramada Inn
(800) 2-Ramada, (520) 635-4431
http://www.ramada.com
642 E. Bill Williams Ave.
98 rooms - $69-108
Pets: Welcome
Creature Comforts: CCTV, a/c,
restaurant, pool, whirlpool

Rodeway Inn
(800) 228-2000, (520) 635-9127
http://www.rodeway.com
750 N. Grand Canyon Blvd.
20 rooms - $24-78
Pets: $10 fee & $5 dep.
Creature Comforts: CCTV, a/c,
refrig, micro

Super 8 Motel
(800) 800-8000, (520) 635-4700
http://www.super8.com
2001 E. Bill Williams Ave.
40 rooms - $49-108
Pets: Welcome
Creature Comforts: CCTV, a/c,
refrig, pool

Travelodge
(800) 578-7878, (520) 635-2651
http://www.travelodge.com
430 E. Bill Williams Ave.
41 rooms - $39-175
Pets: Welcome
Creature Comforts: CCTV, a/c,
refrig, pool

Westerner Motel
(800) 835-8608, (520) 635-9313
530 W. Bill Williams Ave
25 rooms - $29-58
Pets: Small pets welcome
Creature Comforts: CCTV, a/c,
refrig

WINDOW ROCK
Navajo Nation Inn
(800) 662-6189, (520) 871-4108
48 W. Rte. 264
58 rooms - $62-85
Pets: Small pets welcome w/$50
fee, $100 dep.
Creature Comforts: CCTV, a/c,
refrig, restaurant, hlth clb access

Arkansas

ALMA
Days Inn
(800) DAYS-INN, (501) 632-4595
http://www.daysinn.com
250 N. Rte. 71
48 rooms - $43-59
Pets: Welcome w/$15 fee
Creature Comforts: CCTV, a/c, cont. brkfst, pool

ARKADELPHIA
Best Western Continental Inn
(800) 528-1234, (870) 246-5592
http://www.bestwestern.com
136 Valley Rd.
58 rooms - $50-69
Pets: Welcome
Creature Comforts: CCTV, a/c, refrig, pool

College Inn
(870) 246-2404
1015 Pine St.
25 rooms - $29-48
Pets: Small pets welcome
Creature Comforts: CCTV, a/c, pool

Comfort Inn
(800) 228-5150
http://www.comfortinn.com
50 Crystal Palace Dr.
55 rooms - $57-75
Pets: Welcome
Creature Comforts: CCTV, a/c, refrig, micro, Jacuzzis, cont. brkfst, whirlpool, pool

Days Inn
(800) DAYS-INN, (870) 246-3031
http://www.daysinn.com
Rte. 67 North
53 rooms - $54-75
Pets: Welcome w/$4 fee
Creature Comforts: CCTV, a/c, refrig, pool, whirlpool

Econo Lodge
(800) 55-ECONO, (870) 246-8026
http://www.econolodge.com
106 Crystal Palace Dr.
60 rooms - $49-65
Pets: Welcome
Creature Comforts: CCTV, a/c

Holiday Inn Express
(800) HOLIDAY, (870) 246-5831
http://www.holiday-inn.com
Rtes. 67 & 7
100 rooms - $65-85
Pets: Welcome w/permission
Creature Comforts: CCTV, a/c, refrig, cont. brkfst, pool

Quality Inn
(800) 228-5151, (870) 246-5855
http://www.qualityinn.com
Rtes. 30 & 7
63 rooms - $40-59
Pets: Welcome
Creature Comforts: CCTV, a/c, refrig, restaurant, pool

ASHDOWN
Budget Inn
(870) 898-3357
Route 71
12 rooms - $22-35
Pets: Welcome
Creature Comforts: CCTV, a/c

BATESVILLE
Economy Inn
(501) 793-3871
Route 233
14 rooms - $25-35
Pets: Welcome
Creature Comforts: CCTV, a/c, refrig

Ramada Inn
(800) 2-Ramada, (501) 698-1800
http://www.ramada.com
1325 N. St. Louis St.
122 rooms - $55-105
Pets: Small pets welcome
Creature Comforts: CCTV, a/c, refrig, micro, Jacuzzis, restaurant, pool, whirlpool

BENTON
Best Western Inn
(800) 528-1234, (501) 778-9695
http://www.bestwestern.com
17036 Rte. 30
65 rooms - $45-65
Pets: Small pets welcome
Creature Comforts: CCTV, a/c, pool

Days Inn
(800) DAYS-INN, (501) 776-3200
http://www.daysinn.com
1501 Rte. 30
117 rooms - $44-65
Pets: Welcome w/$5 fee
Creature Comforts: CCTV, a/c, pool

Econo Lodge
(800) 55-ECONO, (501) 776-1515
http://www.econolodge.com
1221 Hot Springs Rd.
43 rooms - $35-54
Pets: Welcome
Creature Comforts: CCTV, a/c

Ramada Inn
(800) 2-Ramada, (501) 776-1900
http://www.ramada.com
16732 Rte. 30
110 rooms - $40-75
Pets: Small pets welcome
Creature Comforts: CCTV, a/c, kit, restaurant, pool, hlth club

Trout Motel
(501) 778-3633
15438 Rte. 30
20 rooms - $25-38
Pets: Small pets w/$7 fee
Creature Comforts: CCTV, a/c, and refrig

BELLA VISTA

Inn at Bella Vista
(877) 876-5645, (501) 876-5645
http://www.innatbellavista.com
1 Chelsea Rd.
5 rooms - $95-145
Pets: Welcome in quiet periods
Creature Comforts: An unbelievable 9,000 sq. ft house nestled into 14 mountaintop acres, CCTV, VCR, a/c, fireplaces, refrig, micro, Jacuzzi, full brkfst, access to country club-golf, skeet

BENTONVILLE

Best Western Inn
(800) 528-1234, (501) 273-9727
http://www.bestwestern.com
2307 SE Walton Blvd.
55 rooms - $49-68
Pets: Welcome
Creature Comforts: CCTV, a/c, refrig, pool

Clarion Hotel
(800) 252-7466, (501) 464-4600
http://www.clarioninn.com
205 SE Walton Blvd.
106 rooms - $74-120
Pets: Welcome
Creature Comforts: CCTV, a/c, refrig, restaurant, pool, hlth clb

Comfort Inn
(800) 228-5150, (501) 271-9400
http://www.comfortinn.com
3609 Moberly Ln.
63 rooms - $60-165
Pets: Welcome
Creature Comforts: CCTV, a/c, refrig, micro, Jacuzzis, cont. brkfst, hlth clb, pool

Days Inn
(800) DAYS-INN, (501) 271-7900
http://www.daysinn.com
3408 S. Moberly Ln.
63 rooms - $59-120
Pets: Welcome w/$25 dep.
Creature Comforts: CCTV, a/c, cont. brkfst, pool, whirlpool

Ramada Inn
(800) 2-Ramada, (501) 273-2451
http://www.ramada.com
1209 N. Walton Rd.
150 rooms - $55-99
Pets: Small pets welcome
Creature Comforts: CCTV, a/c, refrig, restaurant, pool, hlth club, sauna, steamroom, whirlpool

Superior Inn
(501) 273-1818
2301 SE Walton Blvd.
54 rooms - $49-85
Pets: Welcome
Creature Comforts: CCTV, a/c, cont. brkfst, pool

BISMARK

Degray Lakeview Cottages
(501) 865-3389
Rte. 3, Box 450
4 cottages - $45-85
Pets: Welcome w/$5 fee
Creature Comforts: CCTV, a/c, fireplace, kit, access to golf

Granny's Cottages
(501) 865-4872
Route 3
8 cottages - $35-65
Pets: Welcome
Creature Comforts: CCTV, kit

BLYTHEVILLE

Best Budget Inn
(870) 763-4588
357 S. Division St.
75 rooms - $40-60
Pets: Welcome w/$5 fee
Creature Comforts: CCTV, a/c, kit, pool

Comfort Inn
(800) 228-5150, (870) 763-7081
http://www.comfortinn.com
Route 55
104 rooms - $49-75
Pets: Welcome
Creature Comforts: CCTV, a/c, refrig, restaurant, pool

Days Inn
(800) DAYS-INN, (870) 763-1241
http://www.daysinn.com
Rtes. 55 & 18
122 rooms - $47-72
Pets: Welcome w/$4 fee
Creature Comforts: CCTV, a/c, cont. brkfst, pool

Drury Inn
(800) 325-8300, (870) 763-2300
http://www.drury-inn.com
201 Rte. 55 (Access Rd.)
50 rooms - $50-70
Pets: Welcome
Creature Comforts: CCTV, a/c, hlth clb access

Holiday Inn
(800) HOLIDAY, (870) 763-5800
http://www.holiday-inn.com
Route 55
150 rooms - $50-75
Pets: Small pets w$10 fee
Creature Comforts: CCTV, a/c, refrig, restaurant, sauna, hlth club, pool, whirlpool

BOLES

Y-C Mountain Inn
(501) 577-2211
HCR 69, Box 69
12 rooms - $35-50
Pets: Welcome
Creature Comforts: CCTV, a/c, refrig, pool, stream

BRINKLEY

Best Western Inn
(800) 528-1234, (870) 734-1650
http://www.bestwestern.com
1306 Route 17
99 rooms - $57-75
Pets: Small pets in smoking rms
Creature Comforts: CCTV, a/c, refrig, cont. brkfst, Jacuzzi, hlth club, pool

Days Inn
(800) DAYS-INN, (870) 734-1055
http://www.daysinn.com
Rtes. 40 & 49
38 rooms - $49-72
Pets: Welcome w/$7 fee
Creature Comforts: CCTV, a/c, refrig, micro, cont. brkfst, pool

Econo Lodge
(800) 55-ECONO, (870) 734-2035
http://www.econolodge.com
Rtes. 40 & 49
39 rooms - $39-110
Pets: Welcome
Creature Comforts: CCTV, a/c, cont. brkfst

Heritage Inn
(870) 734-2121
1507 Rte. 17
46 rooms - $39-60
Pets: Welcome w/$5 fee
Creature Comforts: CCTV, a/c, pool

Super 8 Motel
(800) 800-8000, (501) 734-4680
http://www.super8.com
Rtes. 40 & 49
100 rooms - $45-65
Pets: Welcome w/permission
Creature Comforts: CCTV, a/c,
cont. brkfst, pool

BULL SHOALS
Dogwood Lodge
(870) 445-4311
Shorecrest Dr.
http://natconet.com/~dogwood
10 rooms - $45-65
Pets: Welcome
Creature Comforts: CCTV, a/c,
kit, pool

Mar-Mar Resort
(800) 332-2855, (870) 445-4444
http://bullshoals.com/maramar
Shorecrest Dr., Box 178
13 rooms - $38-60
Pets: Welcome
Creature Comforts: CCTV, a/c,
kit, pool

CABOT
Days Inn
(800) DAYS-INN, (501) 843-0145
http://www.daysinn.com
1114 W. Main St.
42 rooms - $49-65
Pets: Welcome w/$5 fee
Creature Comforts: CCTV, a/c,
refrig, micro, cont. brkfst,
Jacuzzis, pool

CADDO GAP
Arrowhead Cabins
(870) 356-2944
HCR 65, Box 2
7 cabins - $35-75
Pets: Welcome
Creature Comforts: Kit, a/c,
river/boating

CALICO GAP
Jenkins Motel
(870) 297-8987
605 Rte. 56
13 rooms - $35-69
Pets: Welcome
Creature Comforts: CCTV, a/c,
and kit

Wiseman Motel
(870) 297-3733
Rte. 5, Box 546
22 rooms - $50-65
Pets: Welcome w/$3 fee
Creature Comforts: CCTV, a/c,
kit, and lawn games

CARLISLE
Best Western Inn
(800) 528-1234, (870) 552-7566
http://www.bestwestern.com
Rtes. 40 & 13
60 rooms - $50-69
Pets: Small pets welcome
Creature Comforts: CCTV, a/c,
Jacuzzi, pool

CLARKRIDGE
Treasure Cove Resort
(870) 425-4325
902 County Rd.
5 cottages - $49-89
Pets: Welcome
Creature Comforts: CCTV, a/c,
kit, lawn games, and lake/dock

CLARKSVILLE
Best Western Inn
(800) 528-1234, (501) 754-7900
http://www.bestwestern.com
Rtes. 40 & 58
58 rooms - $40-69
Pets: Small pets welcome
Creature Comforts: CCTV, a/c,
pool, whirlpool

Comfort Inn
(800) 228-5150, (501) 754-3000
http://www.comfortinn.com
1167 S. Rogers Ave.
54 rooms - $47-89
Pets: Small pets welcome
Creature Comforts: CCTV, a/c,
cont. brkfst, pool

Days Inn
(800) DAYS-INN, (501) 754-8555
http://www.daysinn.com
2600 W. Main St.
50 rooms - $43-82
Pets: Welcome w/$5 fee
Creature Comforts: CCTV, a/c,
refrig, restaurant, pool

Super 8 Motel
(800) 800-8000, (501) 754-8800
http://www.super8motels.com
1238 S. Rogers Ave.
57 rooms - $39-59
Pets: Welcome w/permission
Creature Comforts: CCTV, a/c,
pool

Taylor Motel
(501) 754-2106
Route 64
18 rooms - $25-40
Pets: Welcome
Creature Comforts: CCTV, a/c,
and refrig

CLINTON
Best Western Hillside Inn
(800) 528-1234, (501) 745-4700
http://www.bestwestern.com
Route 65
36 rooms - $36-65
Pets: Small pets welcome
Creature Comforts: CCTV, a/c,
cont. brkfst, pool

Super 8 Motel
(800) 800-8000, (501) 745-6810
http://www.super8.com
Route 65
44 rooms - $45-65
Pets: Welcome w/$5 fee
Creature Comforts: CCTV, a/c,
cont. brkfst

COLTER
White Sands Motel
(870) 435-2244
PO Box 216
25 rooms - $41-80
Pets: Welcome
Creature Comforts: CCTV, a/c,
refrig, micro, restaurant, pool

COMPTON
Misty Mountain B&B
(870) 420-3731
www.mcrush.com/mistymountain
MC 33, Box 100-B
3 rooms - $55-75
Pets: In carriers
Creature Comforts: CCTV, a/c,
cont. brkfst

CONWAY

Best Western Inn
(800) 528-1234, (501) 329-9855
http://www.bestwestern.com
Rtes. 40 & 64
70 rooms - $46-77
Pets: Small pets welcome
Creature Comforts: CCTV, a/c, refrig, pool

Comfort Inn
(800) 228-5150, (501) 329-0300
http://www.comfortinn.com
150 Rte. 65
60 rooms - $50-74
Pets: Small pets w/$25 dep.
Creature Comforts: CCTV, VCR, a/c, Jacuzzis, restaurant, cont. brkfst, pool

Economy Inn
(501) 327-4800
Route 40
40 rooms - $39-69
Pets: Small pets w/$20 deposit
Creature Comforts: CCTV, a/c, Jacuzzi, cont. brkfst, pool

Holiday Inn
(800) HOLIDAY, (501) 329-2961
http://www.holiday-inn.com
Rtes. 65 & 40
108 rooms - $40-85
Pets: Under 10 lbs. welcome
Creature Comforts: CCTV, a/c, refrig, restaurant, sauna, steamroom, pool, whirlpool

Motel 6
(800) 4-MOTEL6, (501) 327-6623
http://www.motel6.com
1105 Rte. 65
88 rooms - $34-45
Pets: Under 30 lbs. welcome
Creature Comforts: CCTV, a/c, pool

Ramada Inn
(800) 2-Ramada, (501) 329-8392
http://www.ramada.com
Route 40
77 rooms - $49-79
Pets: Small pets w/$20 deposit
Creature Comforts: CCTV, a/c, refrig, restaurant, pool

COTTER

Chamberlain's Trout Dock
(870) 435-6535
89 Chamberlain Rd.
http://www.whiteriver.net/chamberlains
8 cottages - $54-105
Pets: Welcome
Creature Comforts: CCTV, a/c, kit, boat rentals, guided trout fishing trips, set on river

Rainbow Drive Resort
(870) 430-5217
http://www.whiteriver.net/rainbow
Rainbow Dr., Box 1185
8 cabins - $89-165
Pets: Welcome w/$5 fee
Creature Comforts: CCTV, a/c VCR, fireplace, kit, Jacuzzis, river

CROSSETT

The Ashley Inn
(800) 276-7738, (501) 364-4911
Route 72
75 rooms - $40-59
Pets: Welcome
Creature Comforts: CCTV, a/c, refrig, micro, pool

DARDANELLE

Western Frontier Motel
(501) 229-4118
Rtes. 22 & 27
45 rooms - $39-55
Pets: Small pets w/$10 deposit
Creature Comforts: CCTV, a/c, refrig, restaurant

DEQUEEN

Scottish Inns
(800) 251-1962, (501) 642-2721
www.reservahost.com
1314 Rte. 71
74 rooms - $26-40
Pets: Welcome
Creature Comforts: CCTV, a/c, cont. brkfst

DEVALLS BLUFF

Palaver Place B&B
(870) 998-7206
Rte. 1, Box 29-A
5 rooms - $45-65
Pets: Welcome
Creature Comforts: CCTV, a/c, refrig, country brkfst, pool

DOG PATCH

Erbie Lodge
(870) 446-5851
www.ozarkmtns.com/erbie-lodge
HCR 73, Box 145
3 rooms - $90-125
Pets: Welcome
Creature Comforts: Charming B&B on 100 acres near the Buffalo River Nat'l Forest, antiques, handmade quilts, brass beds, kit, CCTV, VCR, stereo-CDs, a/c, Jacuzzi, fenced pet area, trails, lots of friendly wildlife

DOVER

Mack's Pines
(501) 331-3261
22816 Rte. 7
8 rooms - $30-55
Pets: Welcome
Creature Comforts: CCTV, a/c

DUMAS

Days Inn
(800) DAYS-INN, (501) 382-4449
http://www.daysinn.com
501 Rte. 65
64 rooms - $52-994
Pets: Welcome
Creature Comforts: CCTV, a/c, kit, cont. brkfst, whirlpool, pool

Executive Inn
(870) 382-5115
310 Rte. 65
57 rooms - $35-50
Pets: Welcome
Creature Comforts: CCTV, a/c, refrig, micro, pool

EL DORADO

Best Western Inn
(800) 528-1234, (870) 862-1234
http://www.bestwestern.com
1920 Junction City Rd.
131 rooms - $69-89
Pets: Welcome
Creature Comforts: CCTV, a/c, refrig, sauna, hlth club, tennis, 2 pools

Comfort Inn
(800) 221-2222, (870) 863-6677
http://www.comfortinn.com
2303 Junction City Rd.
72 rooms - $55-75
Pets: Welcome
Creature Comforts: CCTV, a/c, Jacuzzis, pool, whirlpool

Whitehall Motel
(870) 863-4136
840 W. Hillsboro Rd.
48 rooms - $29-40
Pets: Welcome
Creature Comforts: CCTV, a/c, and kit

ELIZABETH
Holiday Hills Resort
(870) 488-5303
Rte 1, Box 22
16 cabins - $45-70
Pets: Welcome w/$5 fee
Creature Comforts: TV, a/c, fireplace, kit, restaurant, pool, lawn games, rec. center

Keller's Cove Resort
(870) 488-5360
Rte. 1, Box 45
6 cabins - $40-89
Pets: Welcome w/$10 fee
Creature Comforts: CCTV, a/c, kit, restaurant, pool

EUREKA SPRINGS
Alpendorf Motel
(800) 771-9876, (501) 253-9475
http://www.eureka-usa.com/alpendorf
Route 4, Box 580
30 rooms - $45-109
Pets: Welcome w/$3 fee
Creature Comforts: CCTV, VCR, a/c, fireplace, kit, Jacuzzis, restaurant, cont. brkfst, pool

Basin Park Hotel
(800) 643-4972, (501) 253-7837
http://www.basinpark.com
12 Spring St.
61 rooms - $40-185
Pets: Welcome
Creature Comforts: Centrally located historic hotel dating back to 1905, CCTV, VCR, a/c, kit, Jacuzzis, restaurant w/great views

Best Western Ozark Inn
(800) 528-1234, (501) 253-9768
http://www.bestwestern.com
Route 62
122 rooms - $40-95
Pets: Small pets welcome
Creature Comforts: CCTV, a/c, tennis, pool, whirlpools, and lawn games

Best Western Swiss Inn
(800) 528-1234, (501) 253-9501
http://www.bestwestern.com
Route 62
35 rooms - $35-95
Pets: Small pets welcome
Creature Comforts: CCTV, a/c, pool, whirlpool

Brackenridge Lodge
(501) 253-6803
Rtes. 62 & 23
12 rooms - $40-75
Pets: Small pets welcome
Creature Comforts: CCTV, VCR, a/c, fireplaces, refrig, micro, Jacuzzis, whirlpool

Carriage House
(800) 253-5259, (501) 253-5259
www.eureka.com/carriage
75 Lookout Ln.
1 cottage - $99-120
Pets: Welcome
Creature Comforts: 1800's carriage house, handmade qults, country antiuqes, CCTV, VCR, a/c, kit, fireplace, stereo, Jacuzzi, clawfoot tub, cont. brkfst, pool, and a whirlpool

Cliff Cottage
(800) 799-7409
http://www.cliffcottage.com
42 Armstrong St.
4 suites - $109-199
Pets: Flea free, $30 fee
Creature Comforts: Charming 1892 Victorian cottage, eclectic collectibles, family heirlooms, refrig-stocked w/champagne, fireplace, sleigh bed, CCTV, VCR, a/c, porches overlooking garden fountain, Jacuzzi, massages, gourmet brkfst

Colonial Mansion Inn
(800) 638-2622, (501) 253-7300
www.eureka-springs-usa.com
Route 23
32 rooms - $32-135
Pets: Welcome in ltd. rms
Creature Comforts: CCTV, a/c, refrig, Jacuzzis, cont. brkfst, pool

Cottage Inn
(501) 253-5282
www.cottageinneurekaspgs.com
Rte. 6, Box 115
3 cabins - $65-99
Pets: Welcome
Creature Comforts: CCTV, a/c, Jacuzzi, cont. brkfst

Crescent Hotel
(800) 342-9766, (501) 253-6905
http://www.crescent-hotel.com
75 Prospect Ave.
64 rooms - $75-159
Pets: Small pets welcome
Creature Comforts: Landmark hotel, Victorian turrets, beautifully restored, rqst renovated rooms, Victorian furnishings and attractive color scheme, modern baths have antique touches, CCTV, a/c, refrig, restaurant, pool, whirlpool, hlth clb, Swedish massage, yoga and tai-chi instruction

Days Inn
(800) DAYS-INN, (501) 253-7885
http://www.daysinn.com
102 Kings Hwy.
24 rooms - $45-129
Pets: Welcome w/$10 fee
Creature Comforts: CCTV, VCR, a/c, refrig, cont. brkfst, Jacuzzis, pool

Dogwood Inn
(501) 253-7200
Route 23
33 rooms - $25-69
Pets: Small pets w/$10 fee
Creature Comforts: CCTV, a/c, refrig, pool, whirlpool

1876 Inn
(800) 643-3030, (501) 253-7183
http://www.eureka-usa.com/1876inn
Rtes. 62 & 23
73 rooms - $35-72
Pets: Welcome w/$10 fee
Creature Comforts: CCTV, VCR, a/c, refrig, Jacuzzis, restaurant, pool, whirlpool

Eureka Sunset
(888) 253-9565, (501) 253-9565
http://www.eureka-usa.com/
sunset/
10 Dogwood Ridge
2 rooms - $90-135
Pets: Welcome w/deposit
Creature Comforts: CCTV,
VCR, stereos-CDs, a/c, fireplaces,
kit, Jacuzzis, full brkfst, whirlpool

Harvest House
(800) 293-5665, (501) 253-9363
www.eureka-usa.com/harvest
104 Wall St.
4 rooms - $80-125
Pets: Welcome in 2 rooms
Creature Comforts: Elegant
1890 Victorian B&B in Historic
Dist., antiques, period wall
treatments, knotty pine & floral
accents, homey décor, CCTV,
VCR, refrig, Jacuzzis, full brkfst,
screened porch and gazebo

Hidden Valley Guest Ranch
(888) HIDDEN-V, (501) 253-9777
www.hiddenvalleyguestranch.com
777 Hidden Valley Ranch Rd.
6 houses - $129-195
Pets: Welcome in farm house
Creature Comforts: A wonderful
rustic oasis on over 600 acres of
dense woods w/creeks, terrific log
cabins, fireplaces, living rooms w/
vaulted ceilings, stained glass,
CCTV, VCR, a/c, kit, Jacuzzis,
whirlpool

**Hillside Haven &
Tree House Cottages**
(501) 253-8667
http://www.virtualcities.com/
vacation/ar/e/are97v1.htm
63 Kings Hwy.
2 cottages - $99-125
Pets: Welcome
Creature Comforts: Charming
two-bedroom English-style cedar
cottages perched on a hillside,
suspended bridge, antiques, four
poster beds, stained glass, CCTV,
VCR, stereos-CDs, fireplace, kit,
claw foot tubs, Jacuzzi, cont.
brkfst, whirlpool, waterfall

Howard Johnson Express
(800) I-Go-Hojo, (501) 253-6665
http://www.hojo.com
Rte. 62, Box 309
30 rooms - $44-109
Pets: Welcome
Creature Comforts: CCTV, a/c,
refrig, cont. brkfst, whirlpool, pool

Kings Hi-Way Inn
(501) 253-7311
92 Kings Hwy.
17 rooms - $49-60
Pets: In certain rooms w/$4 fee
Creature Comforts: CCTV, a/c

Lake Leather Wood Park
(501) 253-8624
Route 62
5 cabins - $45-65
Pets: Welcome
Creature Comforts: a/c, kit, lake/
boating

Lazee Daze Resort
(501) 253-8085
Rte. 1, Box 196
5 rooms - $95-125
Pets: Welcome w/$50 deposit
Creature Comforts: CCTV,
VCR, a/c, fireplaces, kit, Jacuzzis

Log Cabin Inn
(800) 254-9411, (501) 253-9400
42 Kings Hwy.
14 rooms - $35-70
Pets: Welcome
Creature Comforts: CCTV, a/c,
kit

Oak Crest Cottages
(501) 253-9493
Rte. 6, Box 126
8 rooms - $45-70
Pets: Welcome
Creature Comforts: CCTV, a/c,
kit

Pine Lodge
(501) 253-8065
Rte. 2, Box 18
8 rooms - $75-120
Pets: In one room
Creature Comforts: CCTV,
VCR, a/c, kit, Jacuzzis

Pointe West Resort
(800) 352-6616, (501) 253-9050
http://www.eureka-net.com/
pointewest
11881 Rte. 187
20 rooms - $45-125
Pets: In ltd. rms
Creature Comforts: Set on
picturesque Beaver Lake, basic
rms, CCTV, VCR, a/c, Jacuzzis,
pool, cont. brkfst, great views

Pond Mtn Lodge & Resort
(800) 583-8043, (501) 253-5877
http://www.eureka-usa.com/
pondmtn
Rte. 1, Box 50
7 suites - $80-135
Pets: Welcome w/$7 daily fee,
$25 one-time charge
Creature Comforts: Ranch
surrounded by150 acres, pine
paneling, homey décor, CCTV,
VCR, fireplace, kit, Jacuzzi, full
brkfst on veranda, pool, billiards,
fishing ponds-dock, riding,
whirlpools

Potter's House Motel
(501) 253-7398
Passion Play Rd.
4 rooms - $25-39
Pets: Welcome
Creature Comforts: A/C

Road Runner Inn
(888) 253-8166, (501) 253-8166
RR 2, Box 158
12 rooms - $28-49
Pets: Small pets welcome
Creature Comforts: CCTV, kit,
overlooks a lake

Scandia Inn
(800) 523-8922, (501) 253-8922
http://www.eureka-usa.com/
scandia
33 Avo St.
6 rooms - $79-159
Pets: Welcome
Creature Comforts: Unassuming
1940's-style cottages w/ lovely
décor, elegant ambiance,
coordinated chintz fabrics, white
wicker, CCTV, VCR, a/c, refrig,
fireplace, Jacuzzi, full brkfst

Statue Road Inn
(800) 501-7666, (501) 253-9163
Rte. 1, Box 965
53 rooms - $35-62
Pets: Small pets welcome
Creature Comforts: CCTV, a/c,
micro, cont. brkfst

Swiss Village Inn
(800) 447-6525, (501) 253-9541
Rte. 62, Box 5
55 rooms - $55-165
Pets: Welcome w/$5 fee
Creature Comforts: CCTV,
VCR, a/c, refrig, cont. brkfst,
pool, whirlpool

Taylor Page B&B
(501) 253-7315
33 Benton St.
3 suites - $60-105
Pets: Welcome
Creature Comforts: CCTV, a/c,
kit, cont. brkfst

Tradewinds Motel
(800) 242-1615, (501) 253-9774
http://www.member.aol.com/
tradewyndz
77 Kings Hwy.
18 rooms - $35-89
Pets: Welcome w/$5 fee
Creature Comforts: CCTV,
VCR, a/c, kit, Jacuzzis, pool

Traveler's Inn
(800) 643-5566, (501) 253-8386
http://www.travelersinn.com
Rte. 1, Box 269
60 rooms - $29-49
Pets: Welcome
Creature Comforts: CCTV, a/c,
kit, cont. brkfst, pool

Whispering Oaks
(501) 253-9459
Rte. 6, Box 338
2 rooms - $30-40
Pets: Welcome
Creature Comforts: CCTV, a/c,
and refrig

White Dove Manor B&B
(800) 261-6151, (501) 253-6151
http://www.eurekasprings.com/
whitedove
8 Washington St.
7 rooms - $85-115
Pets: Under 20 lbs. welcome
Creature Comforts: A gracious
1890's Victorian home w/lovely
ambiance, four-poster beds,
antiques, CCTV, VCR, a/c,
fireplace, kit, refrig, micro,
Jacuzzi, restaurant, cont. brkfst,
pool, hlth clb access, sauna,
whirlpool, access to golf

Wildflower Cottage
(501) 253-9173
22 Hale St.
1 cottage - $95-100
Pets: Welcome
Creature Comforts: CCTV,
VCR, a/c, kit, deck, whirlpool

FAYETTEVILLE
Best Western Continental Inn
(800) 528-1234, (501) 587-1400
http://www.bestwestern.com
1122 S. Futrall Dr.
68 rooms - $68-145
Pets: Under 10 lbs. welcome
Creature Comforts: CCTV, a/c,
refrig, cont. brkfst, pool, whirlpool

Chief Motel
(501) 442-7326
1818 N. College Ave.
31 rooms - $35-45
Pets: Welcome
Creature Comforts: CCTV, a/c,
refrig, micro, pool

Days Inn
(800) DAYS-INN, (501) 443-4223
http://www.daysinn.com
2402 N. College Ave.
150 rooms - $48-129
Pets: Welcome w/$50 dep.
Creature Comforts: CCTV, a/c,
cont. brkfst, pool

Hilton Hotel
(800) HILTONS, (501) 587-8600
http://www.hilton.com
70 N. East Ave.
235 rooms - $65-139
Pets: Small pets welcome
Creature Comforts: CCTV, a/c,
refrig, micro, Jacuzzis, restaurant,
pool, hlth clb

Holiday Inn Express
(800) HOLIDAY, (501) 444-6006
http://www.holiday-inn.com
1251 N. Shiloh Dr.
112 rooms - $55-99
Pets: Small pets welcome
Creature Comforts: CCTV, a/c,
refrig, micro, cont. brkfst,
whirlpool

Inn of Fayetteville
(501) 442-3041
1000 Route 71
104 rooms - $45-75
Pets: Welcome w/$10 fee
Creature Comforts: CCTV, a/c,
refrig, micro, cont. brkfst, pool,
whirlpool

Motel 6
(800) 4-MOTEL6, (501) 443-4351
http://www.motel6.com
2980 N. College Ave.
100 rooms - $38-49
Pets: Under 30 lbs. welcome
Creature Comforts: CCTV, a/c,
pool

Ramada Inn
(800) 2-Ramada, (501) 443-3431
http://www.ramada.com
3901 N. College Ave.
120 rooms - $50-75
Pets: Welcome w/$10 dep.
Creature Comforts: CCTV, a/c,
restaurant, pool, basketball, and
tennis

Sleep Inn
(800) Sleep-Inn, (501) 587-8700
http://www.sleepinn.com
728 Millsap Rd.
62 rooms - $52-148
Pets: Small pets welcome
Creature Comforts: CCTV, a/c,
cont. brkfst

FLIPPIN
Seawright's Motel
(870) 453-2555
First & Sunset Sts.
5 rooms - $25-30
Pets: Welcome
Creature Comforts: CCTV, a/c,
refrig

Shady Oaks Cottages
(800) 467-6257, (870) 626-5474
HCR 62, Box 128
6 cottages - $360-1,200/wk
Pets: Welcome w/$5 fee
Creature Comforts: CCTV, a/c,
fireplace, kit

Sportsman's Resort
(800) 626-3474, (870) 453-2424
http://www.stlweb.com/sportmans
HCR 62, Box 96
22 rooms - $55-199
Pets: Welcome w/$10 fee
Creature Comforts: CCTV,
VCR, a/c, kit, restaurant, pool, on
a river

White Hole Resort
(870) 453-2913
HCR 62, Box 100
8 cabins - $60-225
Pets: Small pets w/$10 fee
Creature Comforts: TV, a/c, kit,
on a river

Wildcat Shoals Resort
(870) 453-2321
PO Box 1032
http://www.wildcatshoals.com
11 rooms - $79-99
Pets: Welcome
Creature Comforts: CCTV, a/c,
kit, on a river

FOREST CITY
Best Western Colony Inn
(800) 528-1234, (870) 633-0870
http://www.bestwestern.com
2333 N. Washington Ave.
104 rooms - $59-95
Pets: Welcome
Creature Comforts: CCTV,
VCR, a/c, Jacuzzis, pool,
whirlpool

Econo Lodge
(800) 55-ECONO, (870) 633-6900
http://www.econolodge.com
204 Holiday Dr.
85 rooms - $40-55
Pets: Welcome
Creature Comforts: CCTV, a/c,
and restaurant

Holiday Inn
(800) HOLIDAY, (870) 633-6300
http://www.holiday-inn.com
200 Holiday Dr.
80 rooms - $59-80
Pets: Small pets welcome
Creature Comforts: CCTV, a/c,
restaurant, pool

Luxury Inn
(870) 633-8990
315 Barrowhill Rd.
20 rooms - $35-50
Pets: Welcome w/$4 fee
Creature Comforts: CCTV, a/c

Save Inn
(870) 633-3214
105 NW St.
30 rooms - $34-50
Pets: Welcome
Creature Comforts: CCTV, a/c,
and refrig

FORT SMITH
Baymont Inns
(877)BAYMONT, (501) 484-5770
http://www.baymontinns.com
2123 Burnham Rd.
100 rooms - $35-55
Pets: Small pets welcome
Creature Comforts: CCTV, a/c,
refrig, micro, cont. brkfst, pool

Best Western Kings Row
(800) 528-1234, (501) 785-4200
http://www.bestwestern.com
5801 Rogers Ave.
111 rooms - $49-80
Pets: Under 10 lbs. welcome
Creature Comforts: CCTV,
VCR, a/c, refrig, cont. brkfst, pool

Best Western Trade Winds Inn
(800) 528-1234, (501) 785-4121
http://www.bestwestern.com
101 N. 11th St.
129 rooms - $50-69
Pets: Small pets welcome
Creature Comforts: CCTV,
VCR, a/c, refrig, micro, Jacuzzis,
restaurant, cont. brkfst, pool

Comfort Inn
(800) 228-5150, (501) 484-0227
http://www.comfortinn.com
2120 Burnham Rd.
89 rooms - $53-82
Pets: Small pets welcome
Creature Comforts: CCTV, a/c,
refrig, micro, cont. brkfst, hlth
club, pool

Days Inn
(800) DAYS-INN, (501) 783-0548
http://www.daysinn.com
1021 Garrison Ave.
53 rooms - $38-59
Pets: Welcome w/$5 fee
Creature Comforts: CCTV, a/c,
cont. brkfst, pool

Fifth Season Inn
(800) 643-4567, (501) 452-4880
2219 S. Waldron St.
136 rooms - $60-99
Pets: Welcome w/$10 fee
Creature Comforts: CCTV, a/c,
refrig, micro, Jacuzzis, restaurant,
pool, sauna, whirlpool

Guest House Inn
(501) 646-5100
3600 Grinnell Ave.
65 rooms - $50-69
Pets: Small pets w/$15 fee
Creature Comforts: CCTV, a/c,
refrig, pool

Holiday Inn Civic Center
(800) HOLIDAY, (501) 783-1000
http://www.holiday-inn.com
700 Rogers Ave.
254 rooms - $75-109
Pets: Welcome
Creature Comforts: CCTV,
VCR, a/c, refrig, Jacuzzis,
restaurant, cont. brkfst, pool, hlth
clb, sauna, and whirlpools

Motel 6
(800) 4-MOTEL6, (501) 484-0576
http://www.motel6.com
6001 Rogers Ave.
109 rooms - $36-48
Pets: Under 30 lbs. welcome
Creature Comforts: CCTV, a/c, pool

Points Inn
(800) 356-7046, (501) 452-4110
3711 Rogers Ave.
228 rooms - $75-99
Pets: Welcome w/$10 fee
Creature Comforts: CCTV, a/c, refrig, restaurant, pool, hlth clb

Quality Inn
(800) 228-5151, (501) 785-1401
http://www.qualityinn.com
2301 Towson Ave.
88 rooms - $46-99
Pets: Welcome
Creature Comforts: CCTV, a/c, refrig, restaurant, cont. brkfst, pool

GAMALIEL
Bayou Resort
(870) 467-5277
http://www.norfok.com/bayou
HCR 66, Box 390
10 rooms - $240-400/wk
Pets: Welcome w/$5 fee
Creature Comforts: CCTV, a/c, kit, pool

Castaways Resort
(870) 467-5348
http://www.castawaysresort.com
Route 101
10 cabins - $35-65
Pets: Leashed w/$5 fee
Creature Comforts: CCTV, VCR, a/c, kit, restaurant, bar, pool

Driftwood Resort
(870) 467-5330
http://www.norfolk.com/driftwood
242 Driftwood Lane
6 cabins - $55-69
Pets: Welcome w/$6 fee
Creature Comforts: CCTV, a/c, kit, on the lake

Lucky 7 Resort
(870) 467-5451
HCR 66, Box 1345
6 cabins - $45-60
Pets: Welcome w/$5 fee
Creature Comforts: CCTV, a/c, and kit

Shady Valley Resort
(870) 467-5350
http://www.geocities.com/
TheTropics/Harbor/1748/
index.html
HCR 66, Box 220
5 cabins - $40-55
Pets: Welcome
Creature Comforts: CCTV, a/c, kit

Twin Gables Resort
(870) 467-5686
HCR 66, Box 1385
6 cabins - $50-65
Pets: Welcome
Creature Comforts: CCTV, a/c, and kit

GASVILLE
Red Bud Rock Motel
(870) 435-6303
http://www.redbudrock.com
Rte. 2, Box 541
2 houses - $60-80
Pets: Welcome
Creature Comforts: TV, a/c, kit

GILLETT
Rice Paddy Motel
(870) 548-2223
PO Box 536
19 rooms - $28-39
Pets: Welcome
Creature Comforts: CCTV, a/c

GREERS FERRY
Budget Inn
(888) 297-7955, (501) 362-8111
616 W. Main St.
25 rooms - $40-55
Pets: Welcome in smoking rooms
Creature Comforts: CCTV, a/c, refrig, pool

Cole's Ozark Motel
(501) 825-6607
7650 Edgemont Rd.
15 rooms - $45-69
Pets: Welcome
Creature Comforts: CCTV, a/c, kit, pool, and lawn games

HAMPTON
Smith's Motel
(870) 798-2755
PO Box 823
8 rooms - $25-34
Pets: Welcome
Creature Comforts: CCTV, a/c

HARDY
Razorback Motel
(870) 856-2465
Rte. 1, Box 234
15 rooms - $29-45
Pets: Welcome
Creature Comforts: CCTV, a/c

Weaver Motel
(870) 856-3224
Rte. 1, Box 2
18 rooms - $45-50
Pets: Welcome w/$10 fee
Creature Comforts: CCTV, a/c

HARRISON
Comfort Inn
(800) 228-5150, (870) 741-7676
http://www.comfortinn.com
1210 Rte. 62
93 rooms - $50-74
Pets: Welcome
Creature Comforts: CCTV, a/c, refrig, cont. brkfst, pool

Family Budget Inn
(870) 743-1000
401 S. Main St.
55 rooms - $35-49
Pets: Welcome w/$4 fee
Creature Comforts: CCTV, a/c, refrig, micro, pool

Holiday Inn
(800) HOLIDAY, (870) 743-2391
http://www.holiday-inn.com
816 N. Main St.
119 rooms - $60-85
Pets: Small pets welcome
Creature Comforts: CCTV, a/c, restaurant, cont. brkfst, sauna, hlth club, pool, whirlpool

Little Switzerland
(800) 510-0691, (870) 446-2693
http://www.oztech.com/
littleswitzerland
Jasper Star Rte.
5 rooms - $49-75
Pets: Welcome w/$5 fee
Creature Comforts: CCTV, a/c, refrig, cont. brkfst

Merry Otter B&B
(870) 743-9010
103 W. South St.
8 rooms - $35-55
Pets: Welcome
Creature Comforts: CCTV, a/c,
fireplace, cont. brkfst, pool table,
sauna

Ramada Inn
(800) 2-Ramada, (870) 7417611
http://www.ramada.com
1222 N. Main St.
100 rooms - $45-79
Pets: Welcome w/$25 deposit
Creature Comforts: CCTV, a/c,
pool

Scenic 7 Motel
(870) 741-9648
Rte. 1, Box 16
20 rooms - $30-50
Pets: Welcome
Creature Comforts: CCTV, a/c,
refrig, micro, pool

Super 8 Motel
(800) 800-8000, (501) 741-1741
http://www.super8.com
1330 Rte. 62
50 rooms - $45-72
Pets: Welcome w/permission
Creature Comforts: CCTV, a/c,
Jacuzzis, cont. brkfst, pool

HEBER SPRINGS
Barnett Motel
(501) 362-8111
616 W. Main St.
25 rooms - $39-49
Pets: Welcome in smoking rooms
Creature Comforts: CCTV, a/c,
refrig, micro, pool

Lake and River Inn
(501) 362-3161
2322 Rte. 25
21 rooms - $35-49
Pets: Small pets w/$5 fee
Creature Comforts: CCTV, a/c,
refrig, micro, pool, whirlpool

Lakeshore Resort Motel
(501) 362-2315
801 Case Ford Rd.
8 rooms - $55-129
Pets: Welcome
Creature Comforts: CCTV, a/c,
kit, dock

Pines Motel
(501) 362-3176
1819 Rte. 25
12 rooms - $50-65
Pets: Welcome
Creature Comforts: CCTV, a/c,
refrig, micro

HELENA
The Edwardian Inn
(800) 598-4749, (870) 338-9155
317 Biscoe St.
12 rooms - $65-110
Pets: Welcome
Creature Comforts: 1904
Colonial Revival mansion on the
National Register, wrap-around
porch, CCTV, a/c, fireplace, refrig,
full brkfst, mature trees dot
beautifully maintained grounds

HETH
Best Western Lake Side
(800) 528-1234, (870) 657-2101
http://www.bestwestern.com
Rtes. 40 & 149
94 rooms - $44-62
Pets: Under 50 lbs. welcome
Creature Comforts: CCTV, a/c,
refrig, pool

HOPE
Best Western Inn
(800) 528-1234, (870) 777-9222
http://www.bestwestern.com
Rtes. 30 & 4
75 rooms - $46-65
Pets: Welcome
Creature Comforts: CCTV, a/c,
refrig, pool

Days Inn
(800) DAYS-INN, (870) 722-1904
http://www.daysinn.com
1500 N. Hervey Rd.
56 rooms - $43-74
Pets: Welcome
Creature Comforts: CCTV, a/c,
restaurant, cont. brkfst, pool

Holiday Inn Express
(800) HOLIDAY, (870) 722-6262
http://www.holiday-inn.com
Rtes. 4 & 30
61 rooms - $49-99
Pets: Welcome
Creature Comforts: CCTV, a/c,
refrig, micro, Jacuzzis, fireplace,
cont. brkfst, pool

Quality Inn
(800) 228-5151, (870) 777-0777
http://www.qualityinn.com
Rtes. 30 & 29
54 rooms - $39-62
Pets: Welcome
Creature Comforts: CCTV, a/c,
refrig, restaurant, cont. brkfst,
whirlpool, pool

HORSESHOE BEND
Box Hound Resort
(870) 670-4496
1313 Tri-Lake Dr.
4 cabins - $45-60
Pets: Welcome
Creature Comforts: CCTV, a/c,
kit, fireplaces, marina

HOT SPRINGS
Apple Tree Inn
(501) 624-4672
805 E. Grand Ave.
51 rooms - $33-45
Pets: Welcome w/$25 dep.
Creature Comforts: CCTV, a/c

Holiday Motel
(501) 624-1440
642 Ouachita Ave.
40 rooms - $35-45
Pets: Welcome
Creature Comforts: CCTV, a/c,
kit

Kings Inn
(888) 386-4466, (501) 623-8824
http://kingsinn-hotsprings.com/
2101 Central Ave.
44 rooms - $45-60
Pets: Welcome
Creature Comforts: CCTV, a/c,
kit, pool

Kloss Motel
(501) 623-3119
811 Park Ave.
44 rooms - $40-55
Pets: Welcome
Creature Comforts: CCTV, a/c,
and kit

Majestic Resort-Spa
(800) 643-1504, (501) 623-5511
http://www.themajestichotel.com
101 Park Ave.
249 rooms - $55-75
Pets: Welcome w/$20 fee
Creature Comforts: Legendary
hot springs resort, very attractive
traditionally furnished rms, CCTV,
a/c, refrig, restaurants, pool,
thermal mineral baths, wonderful
old fashioned soda fountain

Mt. Springs Inn
(888) 298-3200, (501) 624-7131
1127 Central Ave.
62 rooms - $49-65
Pets: Welcome w/$5 fee
Creature Comforts: CCTV, a/c,
kit, restaurant, pool

Park Hotel
(800) 895-7275, (501) 624-5323
211 Fountain St.
65 rooms - $70-175
Pets: Welcome
Creature Comforts: Historic
country inn, CCTV, a/c, restaurant,
cont. brkfst

Patton's Lake Resort
(501) 525-1678
100 San Carlos Pt.
9 cottages - $55-80
Pets: Small pets welcome
Creature Comforts: CCTV, a/c,
kit

Royale Vista Inn
(501) 624-5551
http://www.hotspringsusa.com/
rvihotel
2204 Central Ave.
207 rooms - $50-75
Pets: Welcome
Creature Comforts: CCTV, a/c,
refrig, restaurant, pool

Vagabond Motel
(501) 525-2769
http://www.vagabond-
arkansas.com
4708 Central Ave.
23 rooms - $39-50
Pets: Welcome
Creature Comforts: CCTV, a/c,
refrig, pool

HOT SPRINGS PARK
Avanelle Motor Lodge
(501) 321-1332
1204 Central Ave.
87 rooms - $52-79
Pets: Welcome
Creature Comforts: CCTV, a/c,
kit, restaurant, pool

Buena Vista Resort
(800) 255-9030, (501) 525-1321
201 Abernia Rd.
50 rooms - $55-135
Pets: Small pets w/$15 fee
Creature Comforts: CCTV, a/c,
kit, pool

Clarion Resort
(800) CLARION, (501) 525-1391
http://www.clarioninn.com
4813 Central Ave.
151 rooms - $58-169
Pets: Welcome
Creature Comforts: CCTV, a/c,
refrig, micro, restaurant, pool, hlth
clb, whirlpool, tennis, and boating

Dogwood Manor
(870) 624-0896
906 Malvern Hwy.
5 rooms - $50-90
Pets: Welcome
Creature Comforts: Lovely
Victorian listed on National
Historic Register, CCTV, VCR,
cont. brkfst

Lake Hamilton Resort
(800) 426-3184, (501) 767-5511
http://lakehamiltonresort.com
2803 Albert Pike Rd.
105 rooms - $80-175
Pets: Welcome
Creature Comforts: Set on
picturesque Lake Hamilton,
contemporary décor w/lake view
balconies, CCTV, a/c, refrig,
restaurant, live entertainment,
pool, massage, tennis, sandy
beach/boat dock

Margarete Hotel
(501) 623-1192
217 Fountain St.
12 rooms - $39-80
Pets: Small pets welcome
Creature Comforts: CCTV, a/c,
refrig

Quality Inn
(800) 228-5151, (501) 624-3321
http://www.qualityinn.com
1125 E. Grand Ave.
132 rooms - $57-75
Pets: Welcome
Creature Comforts: CCTV, a/c,
refrig, micro, restaurant, whirlpool
and a pool

Ramada Inn
(800) 2-Ramada, (501) 623-3311
http://www.ramada.com
218 Park Ave.
190 rooms - $75-120
Pets: Under 20 lbs. welcome
Creature Comforts: CCTV, a/c,
refrig, restaurant, pool

Shorecrest Resort
(800) 447-9914, (501) 525-8113
360 Lakeland Dr.
23 cottages - $49-65
Pets: Small pets w/$50 dep.
Creature Comforts: CCTV, kit

Travelier Inn
(501) 624-4681
1045 E. Grand Ave.
55 rooms - $33-59
Pets: Welcome
Creature Comforts: CCTV, a/c,
kit, restaurant, pool

HUNTSVILLE
Kings River Valley "The Barn"
(501) 559-2966
http://www.eureka-net.com/
kingsriver/barn.html
2 Park McClain Rd.
1 barn - $85-165
Pets: Welcome
Creature Comforts: Renovated
barn near creek, a sunny space w/
walls of windows, some antiques,
original art created by host, cozy
sitting area warmed by blue
enamel woodstove, handmade
quilts on beds, TV, VCR, stereo,
kit, close to King's River and
fishing, boating, swimming

JACKSONVILLE

Days Inn
(800) DAYS-INN, (501) 982-1543
http://www.daysinn.com
1414 J. Harden Dr.
40 rooms - $49-73
Pets: Welcome w/$5 fee
Creature Comforts: CCTV, a/c, refrig, micro, cont. brkfst, pool

JASPER

Lookout Mt. Cabins
(800) 596-5409, (501) 446-6224
HCR 31, Box 90
3 cabins - $55-90
Pets: Small pets welcome
Creature Comforts: 180-acre setting, a/c, fireplace, kit

JESSIEVILLE

Ouachita Motel
(501) 984-5363
6127 N. Rte. 7
5 rooms - $29-38
Pets: Welcome
Creature Comforts: CCTV

JONESBORO

Best Western Inn
(800) 528-1234, (870) 932-6000
http://www.bestwestern.com
2901 Phillips Dr.
60 rooms - $56-75
Pets: Welcome
Creature Comforts: CCTV, a/c, refrig, cont. brkfst, whirlpool, pool

Comfort Inn
(800) 228-5150, (870) 972-8686
http://www.comfortinn.com
2904 Phillips Dr.
50 rooms - $52-89
Pets: Small pets welcome
Creature Comforts: CCTV, a/c, cont. brkfst, pool

Holiday Inn
(800) HOLIDAY, (870) 935-2030
http://www.holiday-inn.com
3006 S. Caraway Rd.
180 rooms - $64-89
Pets: Welcome
Creature Comforts: CCTV, a/c, refrig, restaurant, cont. brkfst, pool

Jami Bee Motel
(870) 932-1611
3423 E. Nettleton Ave.
32 rooms - $29-39
Pets: Welcome
Creature Comforts: CCTV, a/c

Motel 6
(800) 4-MOTEL6, (870) 932-1050
http://www.motel6.com
2300 S. Caraway Rd.
80 rooms - $36-48
Pets: Under 30 lbs. welcome
Creature Comforts: CCTV, a/c, pool

Ramada Limited
(800) 2-Ramada, (870) 932-5757
http://www.ramada.com
3000 Apache Dr.
62 rooms - $59-85
Pets: Small pets w/$5 fee
Creature Comforts: CCTV, a/c, refrig, pool

Scottish Inns
(800) 251-1962, (870) 972-8300
3116 Mead Dr.
48 rooms - $35-55
Pets: Small pets welcome
Creature Comforts: CCTV, a/c, refrig

Super 8 Motel
(800) 800-8000, (870) 972-0849
http://www.super8.com
2500 S. Caraway Rd.
68 rooms - $39-59
Pets: Welcome w/permission
Creature Comforts: CCTV, a/c, cont. brkfst, restaurant

Wilson Inn
(870) 972-9000
2911 Gilmore Dr.
109 rooms - $45-69
Pets: Welcome
Creature Comforts: CCTV, VCR, a/c, refrig, micro, cont. brkfst, hlth club access

KINGSTON

Fools Cove Ranch B&B
(501) 665-2986
HCR 30, Box 198
3 rooms - $60-80
Pets: Welcome
Creature Comforts: TV, refrig, fireplace, country brkfst (other meals by rqst), whirlpool, trails

KIRBY

Daisy Motel
(870) 398-5173
HCR 71, Box 255
10 rooms - $34-48
Pets: Welcome
Creature Comforts: CCTV, kit

Lakeside Motel
(870) 398-5304
HCR 71, Box 67
9 rooms - $35-49
Pets: Welcome
Creature Comforts: CCTV, a/c, kit, grocery store

LAKE VILLAGE

La Villa Motel
(870) 265-2277
Rtes. 65 & 82
40 rooms - $40-55
Pets: Welcome
Creature Comforts: CCTV, a/c, and kit

LAKE VIEW

Cedar Oaks Resort
(870) 431-5351
Rte. 1, Box 694
10 cottages - $54-85
Pets: Welcome w/$5 fee
Creature Comforts: CCTV, a/c, fireplaces, kit

Gaston's White River Resort
(870) 431-5202
http://www.gastons.com
1777 River Rd.
74 cottages - $65-159
Pets: Welcome
Creature Comforts: Picturesque setting along White River w/300 acres and charming cottages, homey decor, w/old tools, bikes, and memorabilia, CCTV, a/c, fireplaces, kit, restaurant, pool, tennis, golf access, trout fishing river, trails

Newland Lodge
(800) 334-5604, (870) 431-8620
55 River Rd.
6 rooms - $105-150
Pets: Welcome
Creature Comforts: CCTV, a/c, kit, tennis, and riverside

Twin River Resort
(870) 431-5377
PO Box 218
10 cottages - $276-599/wk
Pets: Welcome w/$7 fee
Creature Comforts: CCTV, a/c,
fireplace, kit, Jacuzzi

LEAD HILL
Bon Terre Inn
(870) 436-7318
Route 281
10 rooms - $45-55
Pets: Welcome w/$10 fee
Creature Comforts: CCTV, a/c,
kit, and cont. brkfst

Hill Top Cottages
(870) 436-5365
Rte. 1, Box 280
7 cottages - $38-50
Pets: Welcome w/$10 fee
Creature Comforts: CCTV, a/c,
and kit

LITTLE ROCK
Baymont Inns
(877)BAYMONT, (501) 225-7007
http://www.baymontinns.com
1010 Breckenridge Rd.
101 rooms - $49-70
Pets: Small pets welcome
Creature Comforts: CCTV, a/c,
refrig, cont. brkfst

Cimarron Inn
(501) 565-1171
10200 Rte. 30
35 rooms - $35-49
Pets: Welcome w/$2 fee
Creature Comforts: CCTV, a/c,
pool

Comfort Inn
(800) 228-5150, (501) 490-2010
http://www.comfortinn.com
3200 Bankhead Dr.
122 rooms - $52-105
Pets: Small pets welcome
Creature Comforts: CCTV, a/c,
kit, cont. brkfst, pool

Days Inn
(800) DAYS-INN, (501) 851-3297
http://www.daysinn.com
7200 Bicentennial Rd.
45 rooms - $52-120
Pets: Welcome w/$8 fee
Creature Comforts: CCTV, a/c,
Jacuzzis, cont. brkfst, hlth club

Days Inn
(800) DAYS-INN, (501) 562-1122
http://www.daysinn.com
2600 W. 65th St.
83 rooms - $38-69
Pets: Welcome
Creature Comforts: CCTV, a/c,
restaurant, pool

Holiday Inn
(800) HOLIDAY, (501) 376-4000
http://www.holiday-inn.com
617 S. Broadway
272 rooms - $75-129
Pets: Small pets welcome
Creature Comforts: CCTV, a/c,
refrig, micro, Jacuzzis, restaurant,
cont. brkfst, sauna, hlth club, pool

Holiday Inn Select
(800) HOLIDAY, (501) 223-3000
http://www.holiday-inn.com
210 S. Shackleford Rd.
260 rooms - $85-120
Pets: Small pets welcome
Creature Comforts: CCTV, a/c,
refrig, restaurant, pool

La Quinta
(800) 531-5900, (501) 664-7000
http://www.laquinta.com
901 Fair Park Blvd.
125 rooms - $59-75
Pets: Small pets welcome
Creature Comforts: CCTV, a/c,
refrig, cont. brkfst, pool

La Quinta
(800) 531-5900, (501) 568-1030
http://www.laquinta.com
2401 W. 65th St.
110 rooms - $57-70
Pets: Small pets welcome
Creature Comforts: CCTV, a/c,
refrig, cont. brkfst, pool

La Quinta
(800) 531-5900, (501) 455-2300
http://www.laquinta.com
11701 Rte. 30
145 rooms - $59-75
Pets: Small pets welcome
Creature Comforts: CCTV, a/c,
refrig, cont. brkfst, pool

Legacy Hotel
(501) 374-0100
625 W. Capitol Rd.
115 rooms - $70-85
Pets: Welcome
Creature Comforts: CCTV, a/c,
refrig, restaurant

Markham Inn
(800) 654-0161, (501) 666-0161
5120 W. Markham Rd.
125 rooms - 45-75
Pets: Welcome
Creature Comforts: CCTV, a/c,
refrig, micro

Motel 6
(800) 4-MOTEL6, (501) 758-5100
http://www.motel6.com
400 W. 29th St.
118 rooms - $42-53
Pets: Under 30 lbs. welcome
Creature Comforts: CCTV, a/c,
pool

Motel 6
(800) 4-MOTEL6, (501) 568-8888
http://www.motel6.com
7501 Rte. 30
130 rooms - $37-49
Pets: Under 30 lbs. welcome
Creature Comforts: CCTV, a/c,
pool

Motel 6
(800) 4-MOTEL6, (501) 225-7366
http://www.motel6.com
10524 W. Markham St.
146 rooms - $43-55
Pets: Under 30 lbs. welcome
Creature Comforts: CCTV, a/c,
pool

Ramada Limited
(800) 2-Ramada, (501) 568-6800
http://www.ramada.com
9709 Rte. 30
59 rooms - $44-75
Pets: Small pets welcome
Creature Comforts: CCTV, a/c,
refrig, cont. brkfst

Red Roof Inn
(800) 843-7663, (501) 562-2694
http://www.redroof.com
7900 Scott Hamilton Dr.
182 rooms - $44-75
Pets: Welcome
Creature Comforts: CCTV, a/c,
cont. brkfst

Wilson Inn
(501) 376-2466
4301 E. Roosevelt Ave.
108 rooms - $40-69
Pets: Small pets welcome
Creature Comforts: CCTV, a/c,
kit, cont. brkfst, sauna

LONOKE
Perry's Motel
(501) 676-3181
200 Nathan Dr.
45 rooms - $39-48
Pets: Welcome
Creature Comforts: CCTV, a/c,
restaurant

MAGNOLIA
Best Western Coachman's Inn
(800) 528-1234, (870) 234-6122
http://www.bestwestern.com
420 E. Main St.
84 rooms - $56-70
Pets: Welcome
Creature Comforts: CCTV, a/c,
refrig, restaurant, cont. brkfst, pool

MALVERN
Town House Motel
(501) 332-5437
304 E. Page Ave.
38 rooms - $35-44
Pets: Welcome
Creature Comforts: CCTV, a/c,
refrig, cont. brkfst

MAMMOTH SPRING
Riverview Motel
(870) 625-3218
PO Box 281
50 rooms - $45-50
Pets: In first flr. smoking rms
Creature Comforts: CCTV, a/c

MARION
Best Western Regency Inn
(800) 528-1234, (870) 739-3278
http://www.bestwestern.com
Rtes. 55 & 64
59 rooms - $43-65
Pets: Welcome
Creature Comforts: CCTV, a/c,
refrig, cont. brkfst, pool

McGEHEE
Senator Motel
(870) 222-5511
222 Rte. 65
39 rooms - $35-50
Pets: Welcome
Creature Comforts: CCTV, a/c,
refrig, pool

MENA
Aerie B&B
(501) 394-6473
Route 375
2 rooms - $65-75
Pets: Small pets welcome
Creature Comforts: A 5,000 sq.
ft. mtn. home, CCTV, a/c,
fireplace, refrig, cont. brkfst

Best Western Limetree Inn
(800) 528-1234, (501) 394-6350
http://www.bestwestern.com
804 Rte. 71
78 rooms - $45-69
Pets: Small pets welcome
Creature Comforts: CCTV, a/c,
refrig, cont. brkfst, hlth club, pool

Holiday Motel
(501) 394-2611
1162 Rte. 71
13 rooms - $32-44
Pets: Welcome
Creature Comforts: CCTV, a/c,
and kit

Ozark Inn
(501) 394-1100
2102 Rte. 71
34 rooms - $34-49
Pets: Small pets welcome
Creature Comforts: CCTV, a/c

MIDWAY
Hoiday Shores Resort
(800) 365-4089, (870) 431-5370
http://www.bullshoals.com/
holidayshoreresort
Rte. 1, Box 283
13 cabins - $55-75
Pets: Welcome w/$3 fee
Creature Comforts: CCTV, a/c,
kit, lake/dock

Howard Creek Resort
(870) 431-5371
Rte. 1, Box 282
2 cabins - $50-76
Pets: Welcome w/$5 fee
Creature Comforts: CCTV, a/c,
kit, boating, lake/dock

Red Arrow Resort
(800) 548-8724, (870) 431-5375
www.bullshoals.com/redarrow
Rte. 1, Box 281
10 cabins - $299-485
Pets: Welcome w/$5 fee
Creature Comforts: CCTV, a/c,
kit, pool, lake

Sunset Point Resort
(800) 336-8113, (870) 431-5372
http://www.sunsetresort.com
Rte. 1, Box 290
8 cabins - $55-75
Pets: Welcome w/$7 fee
Creature Comforts: CCTV, a/c,
kit, pool, lake/dock

MONTICELLO
Best Western Inn
(800) 528-1234, (870) 367-6271
http://www.bestwestern.com
306 Rte. 425
70 rooms - $45-75
Pets: Small pets welcome
Creature Comforts: CCTV, a/c,
refrig, micro, cont. brkfst, pool

Hiway Host Inn
(870) 367-8555
617 W. Gaines Rd.
25 rooms - $33-40
Pets: Welcome
Creature Comforts: CCTV, a/c,
refrig

MORRILTON
Best Western Inn
(800) 528-1234, (501) 354-0181
http://www.bestwestern.com
365 Rte. 95
55 rooms - $45-75
Pets: Small pets welcome
Creature Comforts: CCTV, a/c,
refrig, micro, cont. brkfst

Days Inn
(800) DAYS-INN, (501) 354-5101
http://www.daysinn.com
1506 N. Rte 95
53 rooms - $39-60
Pets: Welcome
Creature Comforts: CCTV, a/c,
Jacuzzis, cont. brkfst, pool

MOUNT IDA
Colonial Home Motel
(501) 867-2431
HC 63, Box 306
12 rooms - $49-69
Pets: Welcome w/$10 fee
Creature Comforts: CCTV, a/c,
kit, groc. store

Denby Point Resort
(501) 867-3651
HC 1, Box 241
20 rooms - $59-105
Pets: Welcome w/$13 fee
Creature Comforts: CCTV, a/c,
kit, pool, lake/marina

Mount Ida Motel
(501) 867-3456
HC 67
17 rooms - $30-42
Pets: Small pets welcome
Creature Comforts: CCTV, a/c,
and refrig

MOUNTAIN HOME
Best Western Carriage Inn
(800) 528-1234, (870) 425-6001
http://www.bestwestern.com
963 Rte. 62
82 rooms - $53-75
Pets: Small pets welcome
Creature Comforts: CCTV, a/c,
refrig, cont. brkfst, pool

Blackburns Resort
(870) 492-5115
http://www.northfork.com/
blackburns-resort
Rte. 6, Box 280
13 cabins - $310-575/wk
Pets: Welcome w/$6 fee
Creature Comforts: CCTV, a/c,
kit, pool, lake/dock

Blue Paradise Resort
(870) 492-5113
Rte 6, Box 379
17 cottages - $35-59
Pets: Welcome w/$8 fee
Creature Comforts: CCTV, a/c,
kit, pool, lake/dock

Chit-Chat-Chaw Resort
(870) 431-5584
http://www.chitchatchaw.com
9476 Promise Land Rd.
8 cottages - $65-82
Pets: Dogs welcome w/$4 fee
Creature Comforts: CCTV, a/c,
kit, pool, lake/dock

Comfort Inn
(800) 228-5150, (870) 424-9000
http://www.comfortinn.com
1031 Highland Cir.
80 rooms - $48-65
Pets: Small pets welcome
Creature Comforts: CCTV, a/c,
cont. brkfst, pool

Durbon's Noe Creek Resort
(800) 264-5574, (870) 431-5574
Rte. 1, Box 128
5 cottages - $65-79
Pets: Welcome
Creature Comforts: CCTV, a/c,
kit, lake/dock

Edgewater Resort
(870) 431-5222
http://www.bullshoals.com/
edgewater
Rte. 1, Box 150
14 cottages - $59-105
Pets: Welcome w/$10 fee
Creature Comforts: CCTV, a/c,
kit, pool, boat, and lake/dock

Fish & Fiddle Resort
(870) 491-5161
http://www.norfork.com/fish-
fiddle
Rte. 1, Box 430
6 cabins - $320-500/wk
Pets: Welcome w/$6 fee
Creature Comforts: CCTV, a/c,
kit, and lake

Gene's Trout Resort
(800) 256-DOCK, (870) 499-5381
http://www.norfork.com/genes
Rte. 3, Box 348
12 units - $54-75
Pets: Welcome w/$10 fee
Creature Comforts: CCTV, a/c,
kit, fishing river

Holiday Inn
(800) HOLIDAY, (870) 425-5101
http://www.holiday-inn.com
1350 Rte. 62
100 rooms - $56-79
Pets: Welcome
Creature Comforts: CCTV, a/c,
refrig, restaurant, cont. brkfst, pool

Ozarks Motel
(870) 425-4881
147 S. Main St.
16 rooms - $35-45
Pets: Welcome
Creature Comforts: CCTV, a/c,
refrig, micro, access to a pool/
tennis

Peal's Resort
(870) 499-5215
Rte. 3, Box 252
32 cottages - $45-125
Pets: Leashed pets w/$3 fee
Creature Comforts: CCTV, a/c,
kit, pool

Promise Land Resort
(870) 431-5576
Rte. 1, Box 140
9 cottages - $60-89
Pets: Welcome w/$4 fee
Creature Comforts: CCTV, a/c,
kit, pool, whirlpool

Rocking Chair Ranch
(870) 492-5157
http://www.norfork.com/
rockingchair
Rte. 6, Box 445
6 cabins - $45-109
Pets: Welcome w/$5 fee
Creature Comforts: CCTV, a/c,
kit, pool, boat

Rocking Ridge Resort
(870) 491-5665
http://www.norfork.com/rocky-
ridge
Rte. 10, Box 610
9 units - $50-85
Pets: Welcome w/$5 fee
Creature Comforts: CCTV, a/c,
kit, pool, lake/dock

Royale Resort
(870) 492-5288
http://www.norfok.com/royale
Rte. 6, Box 610
8 units - $50-155
Pets: Welcome
Creature Comforts: CCTV, a/c,
kit, pool, lake/dock

Scott Valley Dude Ranch
(870) 425-5136
http://www.scottvalley.com
PO Box 1447
26 rooms - $85-185
Pets: Welcome w/$6 fee
Creature Comforts: Set on 600
bucolic acres, this resort has won
the Family Circle "Family Resort
of the Year" 3 years running,
CCTV, a/c, restaurant, riding,
canoeing/boats/fishing

Sunrise Point Resort
(870) 491-5188
http://www.norfork.com/sunrise
Rte. 10, Box 620
10 cabins - $305-425
Pets: Welcome w/$35 fee
Creature Comforts: TV, VCR,
a/c, kit, pool, lake/dock

Teal Point Resort
(870) 492-5145
715 Teal Pt. Rd.
16 rooms - $58-125
Pets: Welcome w/$7 fee
Creature Comforts: CCTV, kit,
pool

Y Cabins
(870) 499-5294
Rtes. 5 & 177
9 cabins - $50-65
Pets: Small pets welcome
Creature Comforts: CCTV, a/c,
kit

MOUNTAIN VIEW
Days Inn
(800) DAYS-INN, (870) 269-3287
http://www.daysinn.com
Rtes. 5 & 14
71 rooms - $42-95
Pets: Welcome w/$5 fee
Creature Comforts: CCTV, a/c,
Jacuzzis, cont. brkfst, pool

Dogwood Inn
(870) 269-3847
Route 14
31 rooms - $45-76
Pets: Small pets welcome
Creature Comforts: CCTV, a/c,
refrig, cont. brkfst, pool

Hidden Valley Cabins
(870) 269-2655
http://www.obsezzion.com/
hiddenvalley
PO Box 270
27 cabins - $55-139
Pets: Welcome w/$25 dep.
Creature Comforts: CCTV, a/c,
kit, pool

Jack's Fishing Resort
(870) 585-2211
Route 5
4 units - $55-69
Pets: In certain units
Creature Comforts: CCTV, a/c,
kit

Sylamore Lodges
(800) 538-2221, (870) 585-2221
http://aros.com/sylamorelodges
PO Box 1016
10 cabins - $69-175
Pets: Welcome w/$10 fee
Creature Comforts: CCTV, a/c,
kit, fireplaces, along a river

MURFREESBORO
American Heritage Inn
(870) 285-2131
705 N. Washington St.
24 rooms - $45-75
Pets: Welcome w/$5 fee
Creature Comforts: CCTV, a/c,
refrig, cont. brkfst, pool

Little Shamrock Motel
(870) 285-2342
919 N. Washington St.
22 rooms - $35-48
Pets: Welcome
Creature Comforts: CCTV, a/c,
refrig

NASHVILLE
Holiday Motor Lodge
(870) 845-2953
Route 27
42 rooms - $34-45
Pets: Small pets welcome
Creature Comforts: CCTV, a/c

NEWPORT
Days Inn
(800) DAYS-INN, (870) 523-6411
http://www.daysinn.com
101 Olivia Dr.
40 rooms - $45-72
Pets: Welcome
Creature Comforts: CCTV, a/c,
pool

Lakeside Inn
(870) 523-2787
203 Malcolm Ave.
40 rooms - $38-45
Pets: Small pets welcome
Creature Comforts: CCTV, a/c,
refrig, pool

Newport Motel
(870) 523-2768
1504 Rte. 67
14 rooms - $32-44
Pets: Welcome
Creature Comforts: CCTV, a/c,
refrig, micro

Park Inn International
(800) 437-7275, (870) 523-5851
901 Rte. 67
59 rooms - $49-75
Pets: Welcome
Creature Comforts: CCTV,
VCR, a/c, refrig, micro, restaurant,
pool

NORFOLK
Woodman's Motel
(870) 499-7454
HCR 61, Box 461
5 cabins - $40-85
Pets: Welcome
Creature Comforts: CCTV, a/c,
kit, along a river

NORTH LITTLE ROCK
Baymont Inns
(877)BAYMONT, (501) 758-8888
http://www.baymontinns.com
4311 Warden Rd.
101 rooms - $48-69
Pets: Small pets welcome
Creature Comforts: CCTV, a/c,
refrig, cont. brkfst, pool

Days Inn
(800) DAYS-INN, (501) 945-4100
http://www.daysinn.com
5800 Pritchard Dr.
41 rooms - $47-99
Pets: Welcome w/$10 fee
Creature Comforts: CCTV, a/c,
Jacuzzis, cont. brkfst

Hampton Inn
(800) Hampton, (501) 771-2090
http://www.hampton-inn.com
500 W. 29th St.
124 rooms - $59-95
Pets: Welcome
Creature Comforts: CCTV, a/c,
refrig, micro, pool

Holiday Inn
(800) HOLIDAY, (501) 758-1440
http://www.holiday-inn.com
111 W. Pershing Blvd.
205 rooms - $57-85
Pets: Welcome
Creature Comforts: CCTV, a/c,
refrig, restaurant, cont. brkfst, pool

La Quinta
(800) 531-5900, (501) 945-0808
http://www.laquinta.com
4100 E. McCain Blvd.
122 rooms - $59-75
Pets: Small pets welcome
Creature Comforts: CCTV, a/c,
refrig, cont. brkfst, pool

Masters Economy Inn
(800) 633-3434, (501) 945-4167
2508 Jacksonville Hwy.
150 rooms - $39-50
Pets: Welcome w/$5 fee
Creature Comforts: CCTV, a/c,
refrig, micro, pool

Motel 6
(800) 4-MOTEL6, (501) 758-5100
http://www.motel6.com
400 W. 29th St.
118 rooms - $42-53
Pets: Under 30 lbs. welcome
Creature Comforts: CCTV, a/c,
pool

Ramada Inn
(800) 2-Ramada, (501) 758-1851
http://www.ramada.com
120 W. Pershing Blvd.
145 rooms - $64-85
Pets: Small pets welcome
Creature Comforts: CCTV, a/c,
refrig, restaurant, pool

Super 8 Motel
(800) 800-8000, (501) 945-0141
http://www.super8.com
1 Gray Rd.
75 rooms - $44-60
Pets: Welcome
Creature Comforts: CCTV, a/c,
cont. brkfst

OAKLAND
Black Oak Resort
(870) 431-8363
http://www.blackoakresort.com
PO Box 100
9 cabins - $60-105
Pets: Welcome w/$6 fee
Creature Comforts: CCTV, a/c,
fireplaces, kit, Jacuzzis, lake, pool,
hlth clb access, sauna, whirlpool

Henry's Resort
(870) 431-5626
Rte. 1, Box 320
6 cabins - $45-65
Pets: Leashed pets w/$2 fee
Creature Comforts: CCTV, a/c,
kit, and river/fishing

Persimmon Pt. Resort
(870) 431-8877
http://www.ozarkmtns.com/
persimmon
Rte. 1, Box 169
6 rooms - $45-50
Pets: Welcome
Creature Comforts: CCTV, a/c,
kit, lake

OMAHA
Aunt Shirley's Sleeping Loft
(870) 426-5408
Rte. 1, Box 84
1 cabin - $50-60
Pets: Welcome
Creature Comforts: CCTV, a/c,
kit, full brkfst, swimming-creek

OZARK
Lamplighter B&B
(501) 667-3889
905 W. River St.
4 rooms - $40-65
Pets: Welcome in ltd. rms
Creature Comforts: CCTV, a/c,
refrig, Jacuzzi, full brkfst

Oxford Inn
(501) 667-1131
305 N. 18th St.
32 rooms - $42-65
Pets: Small pets w/$5 fee
Creature Comforts: CCTV, a/c,
pool

PARAGOULD
Linwood Motel
(870) 236-7671
1611 Linwood Dr.
25 rooms - $29-35
Pets: Welcome w/$20 dep.
Creature Comforts: CCTV, a/c

PEA RIDGE
Battlefield Inn
(501) 451-1188
14753 Rte. 62
11 rooms - $39-48
Pets: Welcome
Creature Comforts: CCTV, a/c

PIGGOTT
Open Roads Motel
(870) 598-5941
148 Independence St.
25 rooms - $40-55
Pets: Welcome
Creature Comforts: CCTV, a/c,
refrig, micro

PINE BLUFF

Admiral Benbow Motel
(870) 535-8300
Box 5009
120 rooms - $40-59
Pets: Welcome
Creature Comforts: CCTV, a/c, refrig, restaurant, and pool

Best Western Pines
(800) 528-1234, (870) 535-8640
http://www.bestwestern.com
2700 E. Harding Rd.
117 rooms - $54-79
Pets: Welcome w/$25 dep.
Creature Comforts: CCTV, a/c, refrig, Jacuzzis, cont. brkfst, steambath, pool

Classic Inn
(870) 535-1200
4125 Rhinehart Rd.
49 rooms - $35-50
Pets: Welcome
Creature Comforts: CCTV, a/c, refrig, pool

The Inn
(870) 534-7222
Rtes. 65 & 79
90 rooms - $50-65
Pets: Welcome
Creature Comforts: CCTV, a/c, refrig, micro, cont. brkfst, pool, hlth clb

POCAHONTAS

Scottish Inns
(800) 251-1962, (501) 892-4527
http://www.reservahost.com
1501 Rte. 67
75 rooms - $35-50
Pets: Welcome w/$2-6 fee
Creature Comforts: CCTV, a/c, cont. brkfst

PONCA

Lost Valley Lodging
(870) 861-5522
Route 43
3 rooms - $75-99
Pets: Welcome
Creature Comforts: Fireplace, kit, Jacuzzis, restaurant, river

ROGERS

Beaver Lake Lodge
(800) 367-4513, (501) 925-2313
14733 Dutchman Dr.
25 units - $59-75
Pets: Welcome w/$10 fee
Creature Comforts: CCTV, a/c, kit, cont. brkfst, pool

Days Inn
(800) DAYS-INN, (501) 636-3820
http://www.daysinn.com
2102 S. 8th St.
55 rooms - $45-140
Pets: Welcome w/$5 fee
Creature Comforts: CCTV, a/c, restaurant, cont. brkfst, pool

Park Inn International
(800) 437-7275, (501) 631-7000
3714 W. Walnut St.
31 rooms - $40-59
Pets: Welcome
Creature Comforts: CCTV, a/c

Ramada Inn
(800) 2-Ramada, (501) 636-5850
http://www.ramada.com
1919 Rte. 71
125 rooms - $65-89
Pets: Small pets w/$10 fee
Creature Comforts: CCTV, a/c, refrig, restaurant, pool

Second Home Beaver Lake
(501) 631-1000
100 W. Locust Ave.
8 townhouses - $95-145
Pets: Welcome w/$200 dep.
Creature Comforts: CCTV, VCR, a/c, stereo, kit, and great lake views

Super 8 Motel
(800) 800-8000, (501) 636-9600
http://www.super8.com
915 S. 8th St.
82 rooms - $44-60
Pets: Welcome
Creature Comforts: CCTV, a/c, cont. brkfst

Tanglewood Lodge
(501) 925-2100
http://www.ar-business.com/lodge
Route 6
30 rooms - $45-55
Pets: Welcome w/$10 fee
Creature Comforts: TV, a/c, kit, pool, lake

RUSSELLVILLE

Best Western Inn
(800) 528-1234, (501) 967-1000
http://www.bestwestern.com
Rtes. 7 & 40
100 rooms - $45-67
Pets: Under 12 lbs. welcome
Creature Comforts: CCTV, a/c, refrig, cont. brkfst, pool

Comfort Inn
(800) 228-5150, (501) 967-7500
http://www.comfortinn.com
3019 E. Parkway Dr.
61 rooms - $47-69
Pets: Small pets welcome
Creature Comforts: CCTV, a/c, refrig, micro, cont. brkfst, pool

Holiday Inn
(800) HOLIDAY, (501) 958-4300
http://www.holiday-inn.com
2407 N. Arkansas Ave.
152 rooms - $59-75
Pets: Welcome
Creature Comforts: CCTV, a/c, refrig, restaurant, cont. brkfst, pool

Lakeside Resort Motel
(501) 968-9715
3320 N. Arkansas Ave.
12 rooms - $28-35
Pets: Welcome
Creature Comforts: CCTV, a/c, kit

Motel 6
(800) 4-MOTEL6, (501) 968-3666
http://www.motel6.com
215 W. Birch St.
80 rooms - $35-49
Pets: Under 30 lbs. welcome
Creature Comforts: CCTV, a/c, pool

Park Motel
(501) 968-4862
2615 W. Main St.
24 rooms - $39-54
Pets: Welcome
Creature Comforts: CCTV, a/c, and kit

Southern Inn
(501) 968-1450
704 Dyke Rd.
52 rooms - $39-64
Pets: Welcome w/$5 fee
Creature Comforts: CCTV, a/c, refrig, Jacuzzis, pool

Sunrise Motel
(501) 968-7200
154 E. Aspen Rd.
96 rooms - 35-45
Pets: Welcome
Creature Comforts: CCTV, a/c

Woody's Classic Inn
(501) 968-7774
1522 E. Main St.
45 rooms - $30-42
Pets: Welcome w/$20 dep.
Creature Comforts: CCTV, a/c

SEARCY
Comfort Inn
(800) 228-5150, (501) 279-9100
http://www.comfortinn.com
107 S. Rand Dr.
59 rooms - $67-89
Pets: Small pets welcome
Creature Comforts: CCTV, a/c,
cont. brkfst, pool

Hampton Inn
(800) Hampton, (501) 268-0654
http://www.hampton-inn.com
3204 E. Race Ave.
104 rooms - $63-139
Pets: Welcome
Creature Comforts: CCTV, a/c,
refrig, micro, restaurant, cont.
brkfst, sauna, hlth club, pool

SILOAM SPRINGS
Eastgate Motor Lodge
(501) 524-5157
1951 Rte. 412
52 rooms - $29-43
Pets: Small pets w/$10 fee
Creature Comforts: CCTV, a/c,
kit, pool

Super 8 Motel
(800) 800-8000, (501) 524-8898
http://www.super8.com
1800 Rte. 412
30 rooms - $53-65
Pets: Welcome
Creature Comforts: CCTV, a/c,
cont. brkfst, pool

SPRINGDALE
Baymont Inns
(877)BAYMONT, (501) 451-2626
http://www.baymontinns.com
1300 S. 48th St.
104 rooms - $59-80
Pets: Small pets welcome
Creature Comforts: CCTV, a/c,
refrig, cont. brkfst, pool
66

Econo Lodge
(800) 55-ECONO, (501) 756-1900
http://www.econolodge.com
2001 S. Thompson Ave.
82 rooms - $45-65
Pets: Welcome
Creature Comforts: CCTV, a/c,
restaurant

Executive Inn
(800) 544-6086, (501) 756-6101
2005 Rte. 71
100 rooms - $50-75
Pets: Welcome
Creature Comforts: CCTV, a/c,
refrig, micro, restaurant, cont.
brkfst, pool

Hampton Inn
(800) Hampton, (501) 756-3500
http://www.hampton-inn.com
1700 S. 48th St.
100 rooms - $76-95
Pets: Welcome
Creature Comforts: CCTV, a/c,
kit, pool

Holiday Inn
(800) HOLIDAY, (501) 751-8300
http://www.holiday-inn.com
1500 S. 48th St.
204 rooms - $129-189
Pets: Welcome
Creature Comforts: CCTV, a/c,
refrig, restaurant, cont. brkfst, pool

ST. JOE
Maplewood Motel
(870) 439-2525
PO Box 1
12 rooms - $35-55
Pets: Welcome
Creature Comforts: CCTV, a/c,
kit

STORY
Aqua Motel
(501) 867-2123
HCR 64, Box 105
6 rooms - $35-44
Pets: Welcome w/$10 fee
Creature Comforts: TV, a/c, kit

STUTTGART
Best Western Duck Inn
(800) 528-1234, (870) 673-2575
http://www.bestwestern.com
704 W. Michigan Ave.
72 rooms - $57-99
Pets: Small pets welcome
Creature Comforts: CCTV, a/c,
refrig, cont. brkfst

TEXARKANA
Baymont Inns
(877)BAYMONT, (870) 773-1000
http://www.baymontinns.com
5102 State Line Ave.
105 rooms - $44-69
Pets: Small pets welcome
Creature Comforts: CCTV, a/c,
refrig, cont. brkfst, pool

Best Western Kings Row
(800) 528-1234, (870) 774-3851
http://www.bestwestern.com
4200 State Line Rd.
116 rooms - $49-69
Pets: Under 10 lbs. welcome
Creature Comforts: CCTV, a/c,
refrig, cont. brkfst, pool

Four Points Hotel
(800) 325-3535, (870) 792-3222
http://www.sheraton.com
5301 N. State Line Ave.
149 rooms - $65-125
Pets: Small pets welcome
Creature Comforts: CCTV, a/c,
refrig, restaurant, pool, hlth clb,
whirlpool

Howard Johnson
(800) I-Go-Hojo, (870) 774-3151
http://www.hojo.com
200 Realtor Rd.
74 rooms - $34-55
Pets: Welcome
Creature Comforts: CCTV, a/c,
refrig, cont. brkfst, pool

Motel 6
(800) 4-MOTEL6, (870) 772-0678
http://www.motel6.com
900 Realtor Ave.
121 rooms - $34-48
Pets: Under 30 lbs. welcome
Creature Comforts: CCTV, a/c,
pool

Ramada Inn
(800) 2-Ramada, (870) 794-3131
http://www.ramada.com
Route 30
126 rooms - $55-75
Pets: Small pets welcome
Creature Comforts: CCTV, a/c,
refrig, restaurant, pool

Shoney's Inn
(800) 222-2222, (870) 772-0070
http://www.shoneysinn.com
5210 State Line Ave.
74 rooms - $49-90
Pets: Small pets welcome
Creature Comforts: CCTV, a/c,
refrig, micro, Jacuzzis, pool, and
a hlth clb

Super 8 Motel
(800) 800-8000, (870) 774-8888
http://www.super8.com
325 E. 51st St.
104 rooms - $49-59
Pets: Welcome
Creature Comforts: CCTV, a/c,
fireplace, cont. brkfst, pool

VAN BUREN
Comfort Inn
(800) 228-5150, (501) 474-2223
http://www.comfortinn.com
3131 Cloverleaf St.
48 rooms - $47-72
Pets: Small pets welcome
Creature Comforts: CCTV, a/c,
refrig, micro, cont. brkfst, pool

Holiday Inn Express
(800) HOLIDAY, (501) 474-8100
http://www.holiday-inn.com
1903 N. 6th Ave.
60 rooms - $62-80
Pets: Welcome w/$10 fee
Creature Comforts: CCTV, a/c,
refrig, cont. brkfst, pool

Super 8 Motel
(800) 800-8000, (501) 471-8888
http://www.super8.com
106 N. Plaza Ct.
44 rooms - $47-64
Pets: Welcome
Creature Comforts: CCTV, a/c,
Jacuzzis, cont. brkfst, pool

WALNUT RIDGE
Alamo Court Motel
(800) 541-5590, (870) 886-2441
http://www.canweb.com/snapp
Route 67
34 rooms - $42-55
Pets: Welcome
Creature Comforts: CCTV, a/c,
refrig, micro, restaurant

Phillips Motel
(870) 886-6767
501 Rte. 67
15 rooms - $30-40
Pets: Welcome
Creature Comforts: CCTV, a/c

WEST MEMPHIS
Best Western Inn
(800) 528-1234, (870) 735-7185
http://www.bestwestern.com
3401 Service Rd.
39 rooms - $47-105
Pets: Welcome
Creature Comforts: CCTV, a/c,
cont. brkfst, pool

Econo Lodge
(800) 55-ECONO, (870) 732-2830
http://www.econolodge.com
2315 S. Service Rd.
150 rooms - $49-65
Pets: Welcome
Creature Comforts: CCTV, a/c

Motel 6
(800) 4-MOTEL6, (870) 735-0100
http://www.motel6.com
2501 Service Rd.
86 rooms - $39-50
Pets: Under 30 lbs. welcome
Creature Comforts: CCTV, a/c,
pool

Super 8 Motel
(800) 800-8000, (870) 735-8818
http://www.super8.com
901 ML King Jr. Blvd.
62 rooms - $50-65
Pets: Welcome
Creature Comforts: CCTV, a/c,
cont. brkfst

WHITE HALL
Days Inn
(800) DAYS-INN, (870) 247-1339
http://www.daysinn.com
8006 Sheridan Rd.
43 rooms - $53-77
Pets: Welcome w/$6 fee
Creature Comforts: CCTV, a/c,
refrig, micro, Jacuzzis, cont. brkfst

YELLVILLE
Wild Bill's Cabins
(800) 554-8657, (501) 449-6235
http://www.ozark-float.com
HCR 66, Box 380
5 cabins - $75-89
Pets: Welcome w/$5-25 fee
Creature Comforts: CCTV, a/c,
refrig, micro, river

California

AGOURA HILLS
Radisson Hotel
(800) 333-3333, (818) 707-1220
http://www.radisson.com
30100 Agoura Rd.
280 rooms - $70-140
Pets: Small pets w/$50 fee
Creature Comforts: CCTV, a/c,
refrig, micro, restaurant, pool,
whirlpool

AHWAHNEE
Silver Spur B&B
(209) 683-2896
44625 Silver Spur Tr.
2 rooms - $55-75
Pets: Crated pets welcome
Creature Comforts:
Southwestern decor, a/c, cont.
brkfst

ALTURAS
Best Western Trailside
(800) 528-1234, (530) 233-4111
http://www.bestwestern.com
343 North Main St.
40 rooms - $45-75
Pets: Welcome
Creature Comforts: CCTV, a/c,
kit, cont. brkfst, pool

Hacienda Motel
(530) 233-3459
201 E. 12th St.
20 rooms - $35-60
Pets: Welcome w/$4 fee
Creature Comforts: CCTV, a/c,
refrig, micro, cont. brkfst

ANAHEIM
Anaheim Hilton
(800) HILTONS, (714) 750-4321
http://www.hilton.com
777 Convention Way
1575 rooms - $125-1,650
Pets: Small pets welcome
Creature Comforts: CCTV,
a/c, refrig, four restaurants, two pools,
saunas, whirlpools, hlth club,
steam rooms

Best Western Raffles Inn
(800) 528-1234, (714) 750-6100
http://www.bestwestern.com
2040 S. Harbor Blvd.
125 rooms - $80-100
Pets: $10 fee and $100 deposit
Creature Comforts: CCTV, a/c,
refrig, micro, pool, whirlpools

Best Western Stardust
(800) 528-1234, (714) 774-7600
http://www.bestwestern.com
1057 West Ball Rd.
102 rooms - $50-95
Pets: Welcome w/$50 dep.
Creature Comforts: CCTV, a/c,
refrig, micro, pool, whirlpool

Cavalier Inn
(800) 821-2768, (714) 750-1000
11811 S. Harbor Blvd.
100 rooms - $40-75
Pets: Welcome w/$20 dep.
Creature Comforts: CCTV, a/c,
refrig, micro, Jacuzzi, pool

Days Inn
(800) DAYS-INN, (714) 527-7993
http://www.daysinn.com
916 S. Beach Blvd.
82 rooms - $45-86
Pets: Welcome w/$5 fee
Creature Comforts: CCTV, a/c,
refrig, micro, cont. brkfst, pool

Holiday Inn at the Park
(800) HOLIDAY, (714) 772-0900
http://www.holiday-inn.com
1221 S. Harbor Blvd.
255 rooms - $90-109
Pets: Welcome w/$10 fee
Creature Comforts: CCTV, a/c,
refrig, restaurant, pool, whirlpool

Marriott Hotel
(800) 228-9290, (714) 750-8000
http://www.marriott.com
700 W. Convention Way
1033 rooms - $160-190
Pets: Welcome on ground floor
Creature Comforts: CCTV, a/c,
refrig, two restaurants, two pools,
hlth clb, game room, sauna,
whirlpool

Motel 6
(800) 4-MOTEL6, (714) 520-9696
http://www.motel6.com
921 S. Beach Blvd.
227 rooms - $34-48
Pets: Under 30 lbs. welcome
Creature Comforts: CCTV, a/c,
restaurant, pool, spa

Motel 6
(800) 4-MOTEL6, (714) 220-2866
http://www.motel6.com
1440 N. State College Rd.
127 rooms - $32-40
Pets: Under 30 lbs. welcome
Creature Comforts: CCTV, a/c,
spa

Quality Inn
(800) 228-5151, (714) 750-3131
http://www.hotelchoice.com
616 Convention Way
285 rooms - $70-125
Pets: Small pets welcome
Creature Comforts: CCTV, a/c,
refrig, micro, restaurant, pool

Ramada Limited
(800) 628-3400, (714) 995-5700
http://www.ramada.com
800 S. Beach Blvd.
73 rooms - $59-109
Pets: Welcome w/$10 fee
Creature Comforts: CCTV, a/c,
refrig, micro, jacuzzis, pool, and a
whirlpool

Raffles Inn
(800) 654-0196, (714) 750-6100
2040 S. Harbor Blvd.
122 rooms - $45-150
Pets: Welcome w/$10 fee
Creature Comforts: CCTV, a/c,
refrig, Jacuzzi, pool

Residence Inn
(800) 331-3131, (714) 533-3555
http://www.residenceinn.com
1700 S. Clementine St.
200 rooms - $175-275
Pets: $6 fee, $275 deposit
Creature Comforts: CCTV,
VCR, a/c, fireplace, kit, restaurant,
cont.brkfst, pool, whirlpools

Rodeway Inn
(800) 228-2000, (714) 761-4200
http://www.rodeway.com
705 S. Beach Blvd.
71 rooms - $40-70
Pets: Welcome
Creature Comforts: CCTV, a/c,
kit, cont. brkfst, pool, whirlpools

Travelodge at the Park
(800) 578-7878, (714) 774-7817
http://www.travelodge.com
1166 W. Katella Ave.
58 rooms - $40-85
Pets: Welcome w/$25 dep.
Creature Comforts: CCTV, a/c,
pool, whirlpool

ANAHEIM HILLS
Best Western
(800) 528-1234, (714) 779-0252
http://www.bestwestern.com
5710 East La Palma Ave.
120 rooms - $70-85
Pets: Welcome w/$5 fee (pet run)
Creature Comforts: CCTV, a/c,
refrig, micro, pool, hlth clb, sauna,
whirlpool, steamroom

ANDERSON
Amerihost Inn
(916) 365-6100
2040 Deschutes Rd.
60 rooms - $50-75
Pets: Small pets welcome
Creature Comforts: CCTV, a/c,
pool, hlth clb, sauna, whirlpool

Anderson Valley Inn
(916) 365-2566
2861 McMurray Dr.
60 rooms - $44-90
Pets: Welcome w/$25 dep.
Creature Comforts: CCTV, a/c,
pool

Best Western Knight's Inn
(800) 528-1234, (916) 365-2753
http://www.bestwestern.com
2688 Gateway Dr.
40 rooms - $45-65
Pets: Small pets welcome
Creature Comforts: CCTV, a/c,
refrig, pool

ANGELS CAMP
Angels Inn Motel
(888) 753-0226, (209) 736-4242
600 N. Main St.
38 rooms - $55-90
Pets: Welcome w/$40 dep.
Creature Comforts: CCTV,
VCR, a/c, refrig, micro, pool

Gold Country Inn
(800) 225-3764, (209) 736-4611
720 S. Main St.
40 rooms - $50-65
Pets: Welcome
Creature Comforts: CCTV, a/c,
refrig, micro

ANTIOCH
Best Western
(800) 528-1234, (510) 778-2000
http://www.bestwestern.com
3210 Delta Fair Blvd.
77 rooms - $55-65
Pets: Small pets welcome w/$15
fee & $50 dep.
Creature Comforts: CCTV, a/c,
refrig, micro, pool, whirlpool

Ramada Inn
(800) 2-Ramada, (510) 754-6600
http://www.ramada.com
2436 Mahogany Way
120 rooms - $60-100
Pets: Welcome w/$10 fee
Creature Comforts: CCTV, a/c,
refrig, micro, pool, whirlpool

APTOS
Apple Lane Inn
(800) 649-8988, (408) 475-6868
http://www.applelaneinn.com
6265 Soquel Dr.
5 rooms - $95-175
Pets: In Wine Cellar rm w/$25 fee
Creature Comforts: Quaint,
historic 1870's Victorian-style
farmhouse with wrap-around
porch, antiques, stained glass
accents, wicker, four poster beds,
beamed ceilings, CCTV, VCR, a/c,
fireplace, piano, kit, full brkfst,
gazebo, barn animals

Best Western Seacliff Inn
(800) 528-1234, (408) 688-7300
http://www.bestwestern.com
7500 Old Dominion Ct.
140 rooms - $75-125
Pets: Small pets welcome
Creature Comforts: CCTV, a/c,
refrig, micro, restaurant, pool,
whirlpool

ARCADIA
Hampton Inn
(800) Hampton, (626) 574-5600
http://www.hampton-inn.com
311 E. Huntington Dr.
130 rooms - $65-99
Pets: Welcome w/$5 fee
Creature Comforts: CCTV, a/c,
refrig, micro, pool, cont. brkfst

Motel 6
(800) 4-MOTEL6, (626) 446-2660
http://www.motel6.com
225 Colorado Pl.
87 rooms - $44-56
Pets: Under 30 lbs. welcome
Creature Comforts: CCTV, a/c,
pool

Residence Inn
(800) 331-3131, (626) 446-5824
http://www.residenceinn.com
321 E. Huntington Dr.
120 rooms - $120-195
Pets: $6 fee & $75 dep.
Creature Comforts: CCTV,
VCR, a/c, fireplace, kit, hlth club
prvldges, cont.brkfst, pool, and a
whirlpool

ARCATA

Arcata Hotel
(707) 826-0217
708 - 9th St.
33 rooms - $55-130
Pets: Welcome w/$50 dep.
Creature Comforts: CCTV
restaurant

Best Western Arcata
(800) 528-1234, (707) 826-0313
http://www.bestwestern.com
4827 Valley West Blvd.
62 rooms - $55-90
Pets: Welcome w/$5 fee
Creature Comforts: CCTV, a/c,
refrig, micro, cont. brkfst, pool,
whirlpool

Comfort Inn
(800) 228-5150, (707) 826-2827
http://www.comfortinn.com
4701 Valley West Blvd.
44 rooms - $35-85
Pets: Welcome with notice
Creature Comforts: CCTV,
VCR, a/c, refrig, micro, whirlpool

Motel 6
(800) 4-MOTEL6, (707) 822-7061
http://www.motel6.com
4755 Valley W. Blvd.
81 rooms - $44-53
Pets: Under 30 lbs. welcome
Creature Comforts: CCTV, a/c,
pool

Quality Inn
(800) 228-5151, (707) 822-0409
http://www.qualityinn.com
3535 Janes Rd.
64 rooms - $75-120
Pets: Welcome w/$5 fee
Creature Comforts: CCTV, a/c,
refrig, micro, restaurant, pool, hlth
clb, whirlpools, tennis, playground

Super 8
(800) 800-8000, (707) 822-8888
http://www.super8.com
4887 Valley West Blvd.
62 rooms - $34-59
Pets: Welcome w/$50 dep.
Creature Comforts: CCTV, a/c,
pool

ARNOLD

Ebbett's Pass Lodge
(800) 225-3764, ext. 313,
(209) 795-1563
1173 Rte. 4, Box 2591
25 rooms - $44-64
Pets: Welcome w/$5 fee
Creature Comforts: CCTV, kit

Meadowmont Lodge
(800) 225-3764, ext 314,
(209) 795-1394
2011 Rte. 4
19 rooms - $48-78
Pets: Welcome w/$10 fee
Creature Comforts: CCTV, kit

Sierra Vacation Rentals
(800) 225-3764 x:341
P.O. Box 1080
15 rentals - $150-325
Pets: Welcome w/$150 deposit
Creature Comforts: CCTV,
VCR, fireplace, kit, Jacuzzi, game
room, whirlpool

ARROYO GRANDE

Best Western Casa Grande
(800) 528-1234, (805) 481-7398
http://www.bestwestern.com
850 Oak Park Rd.
112 rooms - $55-125
Pets: Welcome w/$10 fee
Creature Comforts: CCTV, a/c,
refrig, micro, restaurant, pool, hlth
clb, sauna, whirlpools

ATASCADERO

Best Western Colony Inn
(800) 528-1234, (805) 466-4449
http://www.bestwestern.com
3600 El Camino Real
77 rooms - $45-130
Pets: Small pets w/$100 dep.
Creature Comforts: CCTV, a/c,
refrig, micro, restaurant, pool, hlth
clb access, saunas, whirlpool

Motel 6
(800) 4-MOTEL6, (805) 466-6701
http://www.motel6.com
9400 El Camino Real
117 rooms - $30-40
Pets: Under 30 lbs. welcome
Creature Comforts: CCTV, a/c,
pool

Rancho Tee Motel
(805) 466-2231
6895 El Camino Real
28 rooms - $45-100
Pets: Welcome w/$5 fee, $25 dep.
Creature Comforts: CCTV, a/c,
kit, pool

Super 8 Motel
(800) 800-8000, (805) 466-0794
http://www.super8.com
6505 Morro Rd.
30 rooms - $45-120
Pets: Welcome w/$10 fee
Creature Comforts: CCTV, a/c,
refrig, and micro

AUBURN

Best Western Golden Key
(800) 528-1234, (916) 885-8611
http://www.bestwestern.com
13450 Lincoln Way
66 rooms - $55-65
Pets: Welcome w/$10 dep.
Creature Comforts: CCTV, a/c,
refrig, cont. brkfst, pool

Holiday Inn
(800) HOLIDAY, (916) 887-8787
http://www.holiday-inn.com
120 Grass Valley Hwy.
96 rooms - $70-150
Pets: Welcome w/$10 fee, $100
deposit
Creature Comforts: CCTV,
VCR, a/c, restaurant, pool,
whirlpools

AVALON

Hotel Monterey
(310) 510-0264
108 Summer Ave., Box 1372
6 rooms - $65-175
Pets: Welcome
Creature Comforts: CCTV,
VCR, a/c, refrig, whirlpools

BAKER

Bun Boy Motel
(760) 733-4363
Rtes. 15 & 127
22 rooms - $30-65
Pets: Small pets w/credit card dep
Creature Comforts: CCTV, a/c,
restaurant

 California

BALDWIN PARK
Motel 6
(800) 4-MOTEL6, (818) 960-5011
http://www.motel6.com
14510 Garvey Ave.
75 rooms - $39-48
Pets: Under 30 lbs. welcome
Creature Comforts: CCTV, a/c, pool

BAKERSFIELD
Best Western Heritage Inn
(800) 528-1234, (805) 764-6268
http://www.bestwestern.com
253 Trask St.
48 rooms - $50-65
Pets: Small pets welcome
Creature Comforts: CCTV, a/c, pool, whirlpool

Best Western Hill House
(800) 528-1234, (805) 327-4064
http://www.bestwestern.com
700 Truxtun Ave.
100 rooms - $45-65
Pets: Welcome w/$3 fee
Creature Comforts: CCTV, a/c, refrig, restaurant, pool, hlth clb

Best Western Inn
(800) 528-1234, (805) 327-9651
http://www.bestwestern.com
2620 Pierce Rd.
200 rooms - $50-90
Pets: Welcome w/$10 fee
Creature Comforts: CCTV, a/c, refrig, micro, restaurant, pool, whirlpool

Best Western Oak Inn
(800) 528-1234, (805) 324-9686
http://www.bestwestern.com
889 Oak St.
44 rooms - $45-60
Pets: Welcome w/$5 fee
Creature Comforts: CCTV, a/c, refrig, micro, pool

California Inn
(805) 834-3377
1030 Wible Rd.
60 rooms - $38-48
Pets: Small pets w/$20 deposit
Creature Comforts: CCTV, a/c, refrig, micro, pool, sauna, whirlpools

Comfort Inn
(800) 228-5150, (805) 831-1922
http://www.comfortinn.com
830 Wible Rd.
54 rooms - $35-45
Pets: Welcome w/$5 fee
Creature Comforts: CCTV, VCR, a/c, kit, pool, whirlpools

Comfort Inn
(800) 228-5150, (805) 833-8000
http://www.comfortinn.com
2514 White Lane
64 rooms - $35-55
Pets: Welcome w/$5 fee
Creature Comforts: CCTV, a/c, refrig, micro, pool, whirlpool

Inns of America
(800) 826-0778, (805) 392-1800
http://www.innsofamerica.com
6100 Knudsen Dr.
155 rooms - $24-40
Pets: Welcome
Creature Comforts: CCTV, a/c, pool

Inns of America
(800) 826-0778, (805) 831-9200
http://www.innsofamerica.com
6501 Colony St.
155 rooms - $24-40
Pets: Welcome
Creature Comforts: CCTV, a/c, pool

La Quinta
(800) Nu-Rooms, (805) 325-7400
http://www.laquinta.com
3232 Riverside Dr.
130 rooms - $55-65
Pets: Small pets welcome
Creature Comforts: CCTV, a/c, pool

Lone Oak Inn
(805) 589-6600
10614 Rosedale Hwy.
20 rooms - $40-55
Pets: Welcome w/$20 dep.
Creature Comforts: CCTV, a/c, and kit

Motel 6
(800) 4-MOTEL6, (805) 834-2828
http://www.motel6.com
2727 White Lane
rooms - $34-47
Pets: Under 30 lbs. welcome
Creature Comforts: CCTV, a/c, pool

Motel 6
(800) 4-MOTEL6, (805) 327-1686
http://www.motel6.com
1350 Easton Dr.
107 rooms - $34-45
Pets: Under 30 lbs. welcome
Creature Comforts: CCTV, a/c, pool

Motel 6
(800) 4-MOTEL6, (805) 392-9700
http://www.motel6.com
5241 Olive Tree Ct.
109 rooms - $34-44
Pets: Under 30 lbs. welcome
Creature Comforts: CCTV, a/c, pool

Motel 6
(800) 4-MOTEL6, (805) 366-7231
http://www.motel6.com
8223 E. Brundage Lane
111 rooms - $33-42
Pets: Under 30 lbs. welcome
Creature Comforts: CCTV, a/c, pool

Oxford Inn
(800) 822-3050, (805) 324-5555
4500 Buck Owens Blvd.
209 rooms - $44-69
Pets: Welcome w/$20 fee
Creature Comforts: CCTV, a/c, kit, pool, sauna, and golf

Quality Inn
(800) 228-5151, (805) 325-0772
http://www.qualityinn.com
1011 Oak St.
90 rooms - $45-70
Pets: Welcome
Creature Comforts: CCTV, a/c, refrig, cont. brkfst, pool, hlth clb, sauna, whirlpool

Quality Inn
(800) 228-5151, (805) 324-5555
http://www.qualityinn.com
4500 Pierce Rd.
90 rooms - $40-50
Pets: Small pets welcome
Creature Comforts: CCTV, a/c,
pool, sauna, whirlpool

Red Lion Inn
(800) RED-LION, (805) 323-7111
http://www.redlion.com
3100 Camino del Rio Ct.
260 rooms - $85-105
Pets: Welcome
Creature Comforts: CCTV, a/c,
refrig, two restaurants, pool,
whirlpool

Residence Inn
(800) 331-3131, (805) 321-9800
http://www.residenceinn.com
4241 Chester Ln.
115 rooms - $120-175
Pets: Welcome w/$6 fee
Creature Comforts: CCTV, a/c,
VCR, fireplace, kit, cont.brkfst,
pool, hlth clb, sauna, whirlpool,
putting green

Rio Bravo Tennis Resort
(888) 517-5500, (805) 872-5000
http://www.riobravoresort.com
11200 Lake Ming Rd.
103 rooms - $75-225
Pets: Small pets w/$50 dep.
Creature Comforts: The lodge
overlooks the Sierras as well as
Lake Ming and Kern River,
CCTV, VCR, a/c, fireplace, refrig,
Jacuzzis, restaurant, cont. brkfst,
pool, hlth clb, sauna, whirlpool,
tennis club, lawn sports, nature
trails, access to golf

BANNING
Travelodge
(800) 578-7878, (909) 849-1000
http://www.travelodge.com
1700 W. Ramsey St.
40 rooms - $38-48
Pets: Welcome w/$50 dep.
Creature Comforts: CCTV, a/c,
pool, whirlpools

Super 8
(800) 800-8000, (760) 256-8443
http://www.super8.com
1690 W. Ramsey St.
52 rooms - $40-55
Pets: Welcome w/$3 fee
Creature Comforts: CCTV,
VCR, a/c, pool

BARSTOW
Barstow Inn
(760) 256-7581
1261 E. Main St.
32 rooms - $25-50
Pets: Welcome w/$3 fee
Creature Comforts: CCTV, a/c,
pool

Econo Lodge
(800) 55-ECONO, (760) 256-2133
http://www.econolodge.com
1230 E. Main St.
50 rooms - $40-80
Pets: Welcome w/$5 fee
Creature Comforts: CCTV, a/c,
kit, pool

Motel 6
(800) 4-MOTEL6, (760) 256-1752
http://www.motel6.com
150 N. Yucca Ave.
121 rooms - $34-46
Pets: Under 30 lbs. welcome
Creature Comforts: CCTV, a/c,
pool

Quality Inn
(800) 228-5151, (760) 256-6891
http://www.qualityinn.com
1520 E. Main St.
88 rooms - $50-75
Pets: Welcome
Creature Comforts: CCTV, a/c,
restaurant, pool

Super 8
(800) 800-8000, (760) 256-8443
http://www.super8.com
170 Coolwater Lane
50 rooms - $50-65
Pets: Welcome w/$3 fee
Creature Comforts: CCTV, a/c,
pool

BASS LAKE
Forks Resort
(209) 642-3737
39150 Rte. 222
11 cabins - $75-135
Pets: Welcome w/$25 fee
Creature Comforts: CCTV,
fireplace, kit, restaurant, store, on
lake/boats

BELLFLOWER
Motel 6
(800) 4-MOTEL6, (562) 531-3933
http://www.motel6.com
17220 Downey Ave.
155 rooms - $42-54
Pets: Under 30 lbs. welcome
Creature Comforts: CCTV, a/c,
pool

BELMONT
Motel 6
(800) 4-MOTEL6, (650) 591-1471
http://www.motel6.com
1101 Shoreway Rd.
195 rooms - $59-75
Pets: Under 30 lbs. welcome
Creature Comforts: CCTV, a/c,
pool

BENICIA
Best Western Heritage Inn
(800) 528-1234, (707) 746-0401
http://www.bestwestern.com
1955 East 2nd St.
100 rooms - $60-75
Pets: Small pets w/$25 dep.
Creature Comforts: CCTV, a/c,
kit, pool, whirlpools

The Painted Lady B&B
(707) 746-1646
http://www.placestostay.com/
Benicia-PaintedLady
141 E. F St.
2 rooms - $75-99
Pets: Crated pets on occasion
Creature Comforts: Victorian
themes, CCTV, a/c, refrig, Jacuzzi,
full brkfst

BENNETT VALLEY
Cooper's Grove Ranch B&B
(707) 571-1928
5763 Somona Mtn. Rd.
2 cottages - $100-265
Pets: Welcome
Creature Comforts: CCTV,
woodstove, kit, pool, pond/
redwood grove

BERKELEY

Beau Sky Hotel
(510) 540-7688
2520 Durant Ave.
20 rooms - $60-90
Pets: Welcome
Creature Comforts: CCTV, a/c, cont. brkfst

Golden Bear Motel
(800) 252-6770, (510) 525-6770
1620 San Pablo Ave. 44
40 rooms - $45-65
Pets: Small pets w/$5 fee
Creature Comforts: CCTV

BEVERLY HILLS

Beverly Hills Plaza Hotel
(800) 800-1234, (310) 275-5575
10300 Wilshire Blvd.
115 rooms - $140-425
Pets: $100 fee and $500 deposit
Creature Comforts: CCTV, VCR, a/c, refrig, micro, restaurant, cont. brkfst, pool, hlth clb, sauna, whirlpool

The Beverly Hilton Hotel
(800) HILTON, (310) 274-7777
http://www.hilton.com
9876 Wilshire Blvd.
580 rooms - $190-1,500
Pets: Small pets welcome
Creature Comforts: CCTV, VCR, a/c, kit, Jacuzzi, two restaurants, two pools, hlth clb, whirlpools

Regent Beverly Wilshire
(800) 545-4000, (310) 275-5200
http://www.rih.com
9500 Wilshire Blvd.
300 rooms - $255-4,600
Pets: Small pets welcome
Creature Comforts: Elegant Four Seasons hotel w/exquisite décor, amenities, ambiance overlooking Rodeo Drive, very spacious accommodations w/great views, very popular w/celebrities and dignitaries, antiques, marble floors, lavish flower arrangements, CCTV, VCR, a/c, fireplace, kit, soaking tubs, Jacuzzi, restaurants, pools-some rooms overlook pool, hlth clb access, sauna, deep, steam rooms, whirlpools

Hotel Nikko
(800) Nikko-US, (310) 247-0400
http://www.nikkohotels.com
465 S. La Cienega Blvd.
303 rooms - $275-1,850
Pets: In patio rms w/$100 fee.
Creature Comforts: Serene Japanese hotel with state-of-the-art gadetry, understated room décor-rice screens, black lacquered furnishings, and naturally stained woods, CCTV, VCR, a/c, refrig, micro, Jacuzzi, restaurant w/vibrant color schemes, pool, hlth clb, sauna, whirlpool

L'Ermitage Hotel
(800) 800-2113, (310) 278-3344
http://www.lermitagehotel.com
9291 Burton Way
124 rooms - $295-4,000
Pets: Small pets welcome
Creature Comforts: Revitalized elegance after $60 million renovation, contemporary decor using English woods coupled w/ Asian accents, CCTV, VCR, stereos-CDs, a/c, fax/printers, kit, Jacuzzi, restaurant, pool, hlth clb, sauna, whirlpools, terrific 360 degree views

BERRY CREEK

Lake Oroville B&B
(800) 455-5253, (916) 589-0700
http://www.now2000.com/lakeoroville
240 Sunday Dr.
6 rooms - $95-145
Pets: Welcome w/$10 fee
Creature Comforts: Hillside home w/distant lake views, deck and terraces leading to rolling lawn, rms. decorated w/traditional furnishings, CCTV, VCR, a/c, fireplace, Jacuzzi, gourmet brkfst, billiards, amazing sunsets

BIG BEAR LAKE

Big Bear Cabins
(909) 866-2723
39774 Big Bear Blvd.
14 rooms - $50-110
Pets: Welcome w/$10 fee
Creature Comforts: CCTV, fireplace, kit, pool, and whirlpool

Black Forest Resort
(800) 255-4378, (909) 866-2166
Box 156
65 rooms - $40-125
Pets: Welcome
Creature Comforts: CCTV, fireplace, kit, whirlpools

Boulder Creek Resort
(800) 244-2327, (909) 866-2665
http://www.800bigbear.com
Box 492
35 units - $45-300
Pets: Ltd. units w/$10 fee
Creature Comforts: CCTV, VCR, a/c, fireplace, kit, Jacuzzi, pool

Cal-Pine Chalets
(909) 866-2574
41545 Big Bear Blvd.
http://www.bigbear.net/calpines
20 cabins - $60-195
Pets: Welcome
Creature Comforts: CCTV, VCR, fireplace, kit

Cozy Hollow Lodge
(800) 882-4480, (909) 866-9694
40409 Big Bear Blvd.
13 rooms - $50-175
Pets: $5 fee, $50 deposit
Creature Comforts: Great cabin complex just a short drive from town, knotty pine walls accented w/festive prints, flower boxes and planters, good-size porches, CCTV, VCR, fireplace, kit, Jacuzzi, hlth clb access, playground, whirlpool, boating, a variety of rental homes are also available

Eagle's Nest B&B
(888) 866-6465, (909) 866-6465
http://www.bigbear.com/enbb
41675 Big Bear Blvd.
8 rooms - $85-175
Pets: Welcome in one cottage suite
Creature Comforts: A charming log cabin home and cottages surrounded by tall pines, CCTV, refrig, micro, claw foot tubs, Western or Victorian decor, stained glass windows, country antiques and quilts, down comforters, beamed ceilings, river rock fireplaces, full breakfast, whirlpools, western decor

Edgewater Inn
(909) 866-4161
40570 Simonds Dr.
8 rooms - $55-90
Pets: Welcome w/$10 fee
Creature Comforts: CCTV, kit,
next to marina

Frontier Lodge
(800) 457-6401, (909) 866-5888
40472 Big Bear Blvd.
45 rooms - $65-310
Pets: Welcome w/$10 fee, 75 dep.
Creature Comforts: CCTV,
fireplace, kit, Jacuzzi, pool,
whirlpools, boat dock, and
playground

Golden Bear Cottages
(909) 866-2010
39367 Big Bear Blvd.
22 rooms - $50-130
Pets: Welcome w/$5 fee
Creature Comforts: CCTV,
VCR, fireplace, kit, Jacuzzi, pool,
whirlpool, basketball, playground

Grey Squirrel Resort
(909) 866-4335
39372 Big Bear Blvd.
18 rooms - $75-125
Pets: $5 fee, $100 dep.
Creature Comforts: CCTV,
fireplace, kit, pool, whirlpool

Grizzly Inn
(800) 423-2742, (909) 866-4666
39756 Big Bear Blvd.
8 cabins - $55-125
Pets: Welcome w/$5 fee
Creature Comforts: CCTV,
fireplace, kit, pool, whirlpool

Happy Bear Village
(800) 352-8581, (909) 866-2415
40154 Big Bear Blvd.
12 rooms - $50-175
Pets: $10 fee, $100 deposit
Creature Comforts: CCTV,
VCR, fireplace, kit, pool,
playground, whirlpool

Honey Bear Lodge
(800) 628-8714, (909) 866-7825
40994 Pennsylvania Ave.
20 rooms - $45-160
Pets: Welcome w/$5 fee, $50 dep.
Creature Comforts: CCTV,
fireplace, kit, whirlpool

Motel 6
(800) 4-MOTEL6, (909) 585-6666
http://www.motel6.com
42899 Big Bear Blvd.
120 rooms - $38-48
Pets: Under 30 lbs. welcome
Creature Comforts: CCTV, a/c,
pool

Quail Cove Lodge
(909) 866-5957
39117 N. Shore Dr.
http://www.quailcove.com
9 cabins - $70-109
Pets: Welcome w/$10 fee
Creature Comforts: CCTV,
VCR, a/c, fireplace, kit

Robinhood Inn
(800) 990-9956, (909) 866-8200
www.robinhoodinn.com
40797 Lakeview Drive
22 rooms - $50-215
Pets: $10 fee, $200 dep.
Creature Comforts: CCTV,
VCR, fireplace, kit, restaurant,
pool, massage, whirlpools

Shore Acres Lodge
(800) 524-6600, (909) BIG-BEAR
http://www.bigbearvacations.com
40432 Big Bear Blvd.
61 rooms - $65-325
Pets: Welcome w/$5 fee
Creature Comforts: Great old-
fashioned weather-shingled
cottage resort right on the lake,
CCTV, VCR, knotty pine walls,
cozy decors, fireplace, kit, pool,
whirlpool, lawn sports, boat dock

Smoketree Resort
(800) 352-8581, (909) 866-2415
40210 Big Bear Blvd.
10 rooms - $60-200
Pets: Welcome w/$10 fee
Creature Comforts: CCTV,
fireplace, kit, Jacuzzi, whirlpool

Snuggle Creek Lodge
(909) 866-2555
40440 Big Bear Blvd.
6 cottages - $89-105
Pets: Welcome w/$10 fee
Creature Comforts: CCTV,
fireplace, kit

Thundercloud Resort
(909) 866-7594
40598 Lakeview Drive
65 rooms - $65-110
Pets: Welcome w/$50 dep.
Creature Comforts: CCTV,
fireplace, kit, Jacuzzi, pool, sauna,
whirlpool

Timber Haven Lodge
(909) 866-3568 or 7207
877 Tulip Lane
8 rooms - $80-175
Pets: Welcome w/$10 fee, $50
deposit
Creature Comforts: CCTV,
fireplace, kit, whirlpools, tennis,
and lawn games

Wildwood Resort
(888) 294-5396, (909) 878-2178
www.wildwoodresort.com
40210 Big Bear Blvd.
16 rooms - $50-200
Pets: Welcome w/$10 fee
Creature Comforts: CCTV,
fireplace, kit, Jacuzzi, cont. brkfst,
pool, whirlpool, and lawn games

Wishing Well Motel
(800) 541-3505, (909) 866-3505
540 Pine Knot Blvd.
16 rooms - $50-100
Pets: Welcome w/$50 dep.
Creature Comforts: CCTV

BIG PINE
Big Pine Motel
(760) 938-2282
370 South Main St.
15 rooms - $34-50
Pets: Welcome w/$5 fee
Creature Comforts: CCTV, kit

BISHOP
Best Western Creekside
(800) 528-1234, (760) 872-3044
http://www.bestwestern.com
725 N. Main St.
90 rooms - $90-145
Pets: Welcome w/$10 fee
Creature Comforts: CCTV, kit,
pool, whirlpool

Best Western Holiday Spa
(800) 528-1234, (760) 873-3543
http://www.bestwestern.com
1025 North Main St.
90 rooms - $60-105
Pets: Small pets welcome
Creature Comforts: CCTV,
VCR, refrig, micro, pool, and a
whirlpool

Comfort Inn
(800) 228-5150, (760) 873-4284
http://www.comfortinn.com
805 N. Main St.
53 rooms - $55-80
Pets: Welcome
Creature Comforts: CCTV, a/c,
refrig, micro, pool, whirlpool

Days Inn
(800) DAYS-INN, (760) 872-1095
http://www.daysinn.com
724 W. Line St.
34 rooms - $55-86
Pets: Welcome
Creature Comforts: CCTV, a/c,
refrig, micro, Jacuzzis, cont. brkfst

Paradise Lodge
(760) 387-2370
Lower Ranch Creek Rd.
16 cabins - $55-90
Pets: Welcome w/$10 fee
Creature Comforts: Kit,
restaurant

Rodeway Inn
(800) 228-2000, (760) 873-3564
http://www.rodeway.com
150 East Elm St.
55 rooms - $45-60
Pets: Small pets welcome
Creature Comforts: CCTV, a/c,
refrig, pool

Sierra Foothills Motel
(760) 872-1386
535 South Main St.
44 rooms - $40-70
Pets: Welcome
Creature Comforts: CCTV, a/c,
pool, sauna, whirlpool

Thunderbird Motel
(760) 873-4215
190 W. Pine St.
22 rooms - $35-69
Pets: Welcome w/$4 fee
Creature Comforts: CCTV, a/c,
refrig, and micro

Vagabond Inn
(800) 522-1555, (760) 873-6351
http://www.vagabondinns.com
1030 North Main St.
80 rooms - $55-75
Pets: Welcome w/$5 fee
Creature Comforts: CCTV, a/c,
pool, sauna

BLAIRSDEN
Feather River Resort
(530) 836-2328
Rte. 89
35 cabins - $85-195
Pets: $5 fee, $100 deposit
Creature Comforts: TV,
fireplace, kit, restaurant

BLYTHE
Best Western Sahara Motel
(800) 528-1234, (760) 922-7105
http://www.bestwestern.com
825 W. Hobson Way
48 rooms - $45-120
Pets: Welcome
Creature Comforts: CCTV,
VCR, a/c, refrig, micro, cont.
brkfst, pool, whirlpool

Best Western Tropics Motel
(800) 528-1234, (760) 922-5101
http://www.bestwestern.com
9274 E. Hobson Way
55 rooms - $45-65
Pets: Welcome w/$20 dep.
Creature Comforts: CCTV, a/c,
refrig, micro, pool, whirlpool

Comfort Inn
(800) 228-5150, (760) 922-4146
http://www.comfortinn.com
903 W. Hobson Way
68 rooms - $60-120
Pets: Small pets welcome
Creature Comforts: CCTV, a/c,
refrig, micro, cont. brkfst, pool,
and a whirlpool

Econo Lodge
(800) 55-ECONO, (760) 922-3161
http://www.econolodge.com
1020 W. Hobson Way
46 rooms - $35-95
Pets: Welcome
Creature Comforts: CCTV, a/c,
pool

Hampton Inn
(800) Hampton, (760) 922-9000
http://www.hampton-inn.com
900 W. Hobson Way
60 rooms - $60-120
Pets: Welcome
Creature Comforts: CCTV,
VCR, a/c, refrig, micro, pool, hlth
clb

Holiday Inn Express
(800) HOLIDAY, (760) 921-2300
http://www.holiday-inn.com
600 W. Donlon St.
66 rooms - $50-120
Pets: Welcome w/$10 fee
Creature Comforts: CCTV,
VCR, a/c, refrig, micro, pool,
whirlpool

Motel 6
(800) 4-MOTEL6, (760) 922-6666
http://www.motel6.com
500 W. Donlon St.
126 rooms - $34-46
Pets: Under 30 lbs. welcome
Creature Comforts: CCTV, a/c,
pool

Super 8 Motel
(800) 800-8000, (760) 922-8881
http://www.super8.com
550 W. Donlon St.
66 rooms - $45-65
Pets: Welcome
Creature Comforts: CCTV, a/c,
and a pool

BODEGA BAY
Bodega Coast Inn
(800) 346-6999 (CA),
(707) 875-2217
http://www.bodegacoastinn.com
521 Highway 1
45 rooms - $80-225
Pets: Welcome w/$10 fee
Creature Comforts: CCTV,
VCR, refrig, fireplace, pool,
whirlpool, water views

BOLINAS
Elfriede's Brighton Beach Haus
(415) 868-9778
59 Brighton Ave.
3 rooms - $80-160
Pets: Welcome w/$10 fee
Creature Comforts: Turn-of-the-century beach house w/European flair, Victorian tub, brass beds, French door to deck, window boxes, CCTV, VCR, a/c, refrig, fireplace, gourmet brkfst on garden patio, trails

BORREGO SPRINGS
Borrego Springs Resort
(888) 826-7734, (760) 767-5700
1112 Tilting T Rd
102 rooms - $99-145
Pets: Welcome w/$100 deposit
Creature Comforts: CCTV, VCR, a/c, refrig, micro, pool, restaurant, cont. brkfst, tennis, golf, and a hlth clb

BRAWLEY
Town House Lodge
(760) 344-5120
135 Main St.
40 rooms - $45-55
Pets: Small pets welcome
Creature Comforts: CCTV, VCR, a/c, refrig, micro, pool

BREA
Hyland Motel
(714) 990-6867
727 S. Brea Blvd.
25 rooms - $40-50
Pets: Welcome
Creature Comforts: CCTV, a/c, refrig

Woodfin Suites Hotel
(800) 237-8811, (714) 579-3200
www.woodfinsuitehotels.com
3100 E. Imperial Hwy.
88 rooms - $85-130
Pets: Welcome w/$5 fee
Creature Comforts: CCTV, VCR, a/c, fireplace, kit, pool, hlth clb access, whirlpool

BRIDGEPORT
Best Western Ruby Inn
(800) 528-1234, (760) 932-7241
http://www.bestwestern.com
333 Main St.
30 rooms - $60-150
Pets: Small pets welcome
Creature Comforts: CCTV, a/c, whirlpool

Redwood Motel
(760) 932-3292
425 Main St.
15 rooms - $50-100
Pets: Small pets welcome
Creature Comforts: CCTV, a/c

Silver Maple Inn
(760) 932-7383
310 Main St.
22 rooms - $55-95
Pets: Welcome
Creature Comforts: CCTV, lawn games

Walker River Lodge
(800) 688-3351, (760) 932-7021
100 Main St.
35 rooms - $50-210
Pets: Welcome
Creature Comforts: CCTV, a/c, refrig, micro, pool, whirlpool

BUELTON
Econo Lodge
(800) 55-ECONO, (805) 688-0022
http://www.econolodge.com
630 Ave. of the Flags
60 rooms - $30-78
Pets: Small pets welcome
Creature Comforts: CCTV, a/c, kit

BUENA PARK
Colony Inn
(800) 982-6566, (714) 527-2201
7800 Crescent Ave.
100 rooms - $35-60
Pets: Small pets welcome
Creature Comforts: CCTV, a/c, refrig, two pools, sauna

Days Inn
(800) DAYS-INN, (714) 522-8461
http://www.daysinn.com
7640 Beach Blvd.
68 rooms - $45-95
Pets: Welcome w/$7 fee
Creature Comforts: CCTV, a/c, refrig, micro, Jacuzzis, cont. brkfst, pool, whirlpool

Motel 6
(800) 4-MOTEL6, (714) 522-1200
http://www.motel6.com
7051 Valley View Rd.
150 rooms - $34-40
Pets: Under 30 lbs. welcome
Creature Comforts: CCTV, a/c, pool

BUELLTON
Motel 6
(800) 4-MOTEL6, (805) 688-7797
http://www.motel6.com
333 McMurray Rd.
59 rooms - $44-52
Pets: Under 30 lbs. welcome
Creature Comforts: CCTV, a/c, pool

BUENA PARK
Motel 6
(800) 4-MOTEL6, (714) 522-1200
http://www.motel6.com
7051 Valley View Rd.
188 rooms - $39-52
Pets: Under 30 lbs. welcome
Creature Comforts: CCTV, a/c, pool

BURBANK
Hilton Hotel (Airport)
(800) HILTONS, (818) 843-6000
http://www.hilton.com
2500 Hollywood Way
485 rooms - $120-500
Pets: Welcome
Creature Comforts: CCTV, VCR, a/c, refrig, restaurant, two pools, hlth clb, sauna, whirlpool

Holiday Inn
(800) HOLIDAY, (818) 841-4770
http://www.holiday-inn.com
150 East Angeleno Rd.
491 rooms - $95-165
Pets: Welcome
Creature Comforts: CCTV, a/c, kit, restaurant, pool, hlth clb, saunas, whirlpool

Safari Inn
(818) 845-8586
1911 W. Olive St.
102 rooms - $60-90
Pets: Small pets welcome
Creature Comforts: CCTV, VCR, a/c, kit, restaurant, pool, whirlpool

BURLINGAME

Doubletree Hotel
(800) 222-TREE, (415) 344-5500
http://www.doubletreehotels.com
835 Airport Blvd.
290 rooms - $100-135
Pets: Welcome w/$20 fee
Creature Comforts: CCTV,
VCR, a/c, refrig, restaurant, pool,
hlth clb, and bay views

Embassy Suites
(800) EMBASSY, (415) 342-4600
http://www.embassy-suites.com
150 Anza Blvd.
344 rooms - $120-180
Pets: Welcome w/$25 fee
Creature Comforts: CCTV,
VCR, a/c, refrig, micro, restaurant,
pool, hlth clb, sauna, whirlpool

Marriott-Airport
(800) 228-9290, (415) 692-9100
http://www.marriott.com
1800 Old Bayshore Hwy.
682 rooms - $109-189
Pets: Small pets welcome
Creature Comforts: CCTV,
VCR, a/c, refrig, micro, restaurant,
pool, hlth clb, sauna, whirlpool

Red Roof Inn
(800) 843-7663, (415) 342-7772
http://www.redroof.com
777 Airport Blvd.
200 rooms - $75-120
Pets: Welcome w/$10 fee
Creature Comforts: CCTV, a/c,
pool

Vagabond Inn
(800) 522-1555, (415) 692-4040
http://www.vagabondinns.com
1640 Old Bayshore Dr.
90 rooms - $70-105
Pets: Welcome w/$ fee
Creature Comforts: CCTV, a/c,
refrig, micro

BURNEY

Charm Motel
(916) 335-2254
37363 Main St.
41 rooms - $45-70
Pets: Welcome w/$5 fee
Creature Comforts: CCTV, a/c,
kit

Green Gables Motel
(916) 335-2264
37385 Main St.
24 rooms - $45-85
Pets: Small pets w/$5 fee
Creature Comforts: CCTV, a/c,
kit

Shasta Pines Motel
(916) 335-2201
37386 Main St.
17 rooms - $35-65
Pets: Welcome w/$20 dep.
Creature Comforts: CCTV, a/c,
kit, pool

BUTTONWILLOW

Good Nite Inn
(805) 764-5121
20645 Tracy Road
82 rooms - $30-45
Pets: Welcome
Creature Comforts: CCTV,
VCR, a/c, kit, pool, hlth clb,
sauna, whirlpool

Motel 6
(800) 4-MOTEL6, (805) 764-5153
http://www.motel6.com
20638 Tracy Road
123 rooms - $35-49
Pets: Under 30 lbs. welcome
Creature Comforts: CCTV, a/c,
pool

Super 8 Motel
(800) 800-8000, (805) 764-5117
http://www.super8.com
20681 Tracy Road
85 rooms - $30-45
Pets: Welcome
Creature Comforts: CCTV, a/c,
refrig, micro, pool, whirlpool

CALIPATRIA

Calipatria Inn
(760) 348-7348
Route 111
42 rooms - $50-75
Pets: Welcome w/$10 dep.
Creature Comforts: CCTV, a/c,
refrig, micro, pool, whirlpool

CALISTOGA

Hillcrest B&B
(707) 942-6334
3225 Lake County Hwy.
4 rooms - $45-95
Pets: Welcome
Creature Comforts: Lovely
hilltop location amid 40-acres and
great views, CCTV, VCR,
fireplace, full brkfst, pool,
whirlpool

Meadow Lark Country House
(800) 942-5651, (707) 942-5651
http://www.meadowlarkinn.com
601-605 Petrified Forest Rd.
7 rooms - $100-165
Pets: Welcome
Creature Comforts: Charming
guest house tucked onto 20 acres,
lovely furnishings and décor,
Oriental carpets, English hunt
prints, rattan and wicker pieces,
four poster and sleigh beds,
CCTV, VCR, a/c, fireplace, kit,
patios w/canvas umbrellas, full
brkfst, pool, stables-European
sport horses, gardens

The Pink Mansion
(800) 238-PINK, (707) 942-0558
http://www.pinkmansion.com
1415 Foothill Blvd.
6 rooms - $85-195
Pets: In garden room w/$15 fee
Creature Comforts: An 1875
turreted Victorian mansion
perched on a hillside, Victorian
and Oriental collectibles, antiques,
high ceilings, claw foot tubs,
theme rooms, CCTV, VCR, a/c,
fireplace, kit, full brkfst, pool,
whirlpool, massage-facials, great
biking

Washington Street Lodging
(707) 942-6968
1605 Washington St.
5 cottages - $80-115
Pets: Welcome w/$15 fee
Creature Comforts: Intimate
cottages w/country décor, down
comforters, pine furnishings,
French doors open to decks
overlooking river, CCTV, a/c, kit,
cont. brkfst

CALPINE
Sierra Valley Lodge
(800) 858-0322, (916) 994-3367
Main St., Box 115
12 rooms - $40-50
Pets: Welcome
Creature Comforts: CCTV,
fireplace, restaurant, and bar

CAMARILLO
Motel 6
(800) 4-MOTEL6, (805) 388-3467
http://www.motel6.com
1641 E. Daily Dr.
82 rooms - $40-52
Pets: Under 30 lbs. welcome
Creature Comforts: CCTV, a/c,
pool

CAMBRIA
Cambria Pines Lodge
(800) 445-6868, (805) 927-4200
2905 Burton Dr.
125 rooms - $60-135
Pets: Welcome
Creature Comforts: CCTV,
refrig, micro, restaurant, cont.
brkfst, pool, whirlpool

Cambria Shores Inn
(800) 433-9179, (805) 927-8644
http://www.cambriashoresinn.com
6276 Moonstone Beach Dr.
25 rooms - $45-120
Pets: Welcome w/$5 fee
Creature Comforts: CCTV,
refrig, micro, cont. brkfst, across
from beach

Fog Catcher Inn
(800) 425-4121, (805) 927-1400
http://www.cambria-online.com
6400 Moonstone Beach Dr.
60 rooms - $50-150
Pets: Welcome in several rooms
Creature Comforts: CCTV,
refrig, micro, fireplace, pool,
whirlpool

Mariners Inn
(805) 927-4624
6180 Moonstone Beach Dr.
25 rooms - $45-145
Pets: Welcome w/$10 fee
Creature Comforts: CCTV,
refrig, fireplace, whirlpool

CAMERON PARK
Best Western Cameron Park
(800) 528-1234, (916) 677-2203
http://www.bestwestern.com
3361 Coach Lane
62 rooms - $60-80
Pets: Small pets welcome
Creature Comforts: CCTV, a/c,
kit, pool

CAMPBELL
Campbell Inn
(800) 582-4449, (408) 374-4300
675 E. Campbell Ave.
94 rooms - $99-235
Pets: Welcome w/$10 fee
Creature Comforts: CCTV,
VCR, a/c, refrig, fireplaces,
Jacuzzis, full brkfst, pool, tennis,
whirlpool

Motel 6
(800) 4-MOTEL6, (408) 371-8870
http://www.motel6.com
1240 Camden Ave.
49 rooms - $58-73
Pets: Under 30 lbs. welcome
Creature Comforts: CCTV, a/c,
pool

Residence Inn
(800) 331-3131, (408) 559-1551
http://www.residenceinn.com
2761 S. Bascom Ave.
80 rooms - $80-140
Pets: Welcome w/$5 fee &50 dep.
Creature Comforts: CCTV, a/c,
fireplace, kit, cont. brkfst, pool,
whirlpool

CANOGA PARK
Best Western
(800) 528-1234, (818) 883-1200
http://www.bestwestern.com
20122 Vanowen St.
45 rooms - $70-128
Pets: Welcome w/$25 fee
Creature Comforts: CCTV, a/c,
kit, restaurant, pool, sauna,
whirlpool

Days Inn
(800) DAYS-INN, (818) 341-7200
http://www.daysinn.com
20128 Roscoe Blvd.
58 rooms - $45-105
Pets: Welcome w/$5 fee
Creature Comforts: CCTV, a/c,
kit, pool, hlth clb, whirlpool

CAPITOLA
Capitola Inn
(408) 462-3004
822 Bay Ave.
58 rooms - $55-185
Pets: Small pets welcome w/$20
fee, $100 deposit
Creature Comforts: CCTV, a/c,
refrig, fireplaces, Jacuzzis, kit,
pool, whirlpools

El Salto by the Sea B&B
(408) 462-6365
620 El Salto Dr.
17 rooms - 125-175
Pets: Welcome
Creature Comforts: CCTV, a/c,
refrig, cont. brkfst, game rm

CARLSBAD
Four Seasons Resort
(800) 332-3442, (760) 603-6800
http://www.fshr.com
7100 Four Seasons Point
330 rooms - $275-3,500
Pets: Welcome - special pet
amenities and goodies
Creature Comforts: Newly
opened, exquisite hotel on 1,000
acres w/beautiful mtn. and water
views, lovely ambiance and
furnishings, antiques, CCTV,
VCR, a/c, fireplaces, kit, Jacuzzi,
two restaurants, pool, hlth clb,
saunas, steamrooms, whirlpools,
Arnold Palmer golf course, tennis
program, kids camp, massage-spa

Inns of America
(800) 826-0778, (760) 931-1185
http://www.innsamerica.com
751 Raintree Dr.
125 rooms - $35-75
Pets: Welcome
Creature Comforts: CCTV, a/c,
cont. brkfst, pool

Motel 6
(800) 4-MOTEL6, (760) 434-7135
http://www.motel6.com
1006 Carlsbad Village Dr.
109 rooms - $40-52
Pets: Under 30 lbs. welcome
Creature Comforts: CCTV, a/c,
pool

Motel 6
(800) 4-MOTEL6, (760) 438-1242
http://www.motel6.com
6117 Paseo del Norte
142 rooms - $40-52
Pets: Under 30 lbs. welcome
Creature Comforts: CCTV, a/c,
pool

Motel 6
(800) 4-MOTEL6, (760) 431-0745
http://www.motel6.com
750 Raintree Dr.
160 rooms - $40-53
Pets: Under 30 lbs. welcome
Creature Comforts: CCTV, a/c,
pool

Travel Inn Motel
(800) 900-0275, (760) 729-4941
3666 Pio Pico Dr.
40 rooms - $40-70
Pets: Welcome w/$35 fee
Creature Comforts: CCTV, a/c,
kit, pool

CARMEL-BY-THE-SEA
Best Western
Carmel Mission Inn
(800) 528-1234, (831) 624-1841
http://www.bestwestern.com
3665 Rio Rd.
162 rooms - $80-380
Pets: Welcome
Creature Comforts: CCTV, a/c,
refrig, restaurant, pool, whirlpool

Carmel Country Inn
(800) 215-6343, (831) 625-3263
http://monterey.gpmag.com
3rd and Dolores Sts.
12 rooms - $65-200
Pets: In ltd. rms w/$20 fee
Creature Comforts: Intimate inn
w/lovely ambiance in the heart of
town, country décor, wing chairs,
pine furnishings, dried wreaths,
flowering plants, CCTV, VCR,
refrig, fireplace, wet bars, cont.
brkfst, lovely gardens

Carmel Garden Court Inn
(831) 624-6942
Fourth and Torres, Box 6226
9 rooms - $125-265
Pets: Under 20 lbs. w/$25 fee
Creature Comforts: Award
winning garden setting, CCTV,
VCR, fireplaces, kit, full brkfst,
and patios

Carmel Tradewinds Inn
(800) 624-6665, (831) 624-2776
Mission and Third, Box 3403
28 rooms - $70-240
Pets: Welcome w/$15 fee
Creature Comforts: CCTV,
refrig, pool, whirlpool

Coachman's Inn
(800) 336-6421, (831) 624-6421
San Carlos St.
30 rooms - $85-160
Pets: Small pets w/$15 fee
Creature Comforts: CCTV,
fireplaces, kit, cont. brkfst

Cypress Inn
(800) 443-7443, (831) 624-3871
http://www.cypress-inn.com
Lincoln and 7th streets
34 rooms - $99-375
Pets: Welcome w/$17 fee – great
pet goodies and pet sitters
Creature Comforts: Classic
1920's California Mediterranean-
style inn — Doris Day is part
owner — white walls, beamed
ceilings, floor-to-ceiling
windows, very attractive décor,
CCTV, refrig, micro, fireplace,
cont. brkfst, whirlpools, inviting
living room, award-winning
garden courtyard

Forest Lodge Cottages
(831) 624-7023
http://www.carmel-
california.com/index.html
Box 1316
3 cottages - $80-250
Pets: Welcome w/$10 fee
Creature Comforts: CCTV,
VCR, a/c, fireplaces, kit,
Jacuzzis, cont. brkfst, putting
green

Highlands Inn
(800) 538-9525, (831) 624-3801
http://www.highlands-inn.com
144 rooms - $265-650
Pets: Small pets w/$75 fee
Creature Comforts: Wonderful
inn perched on hillside with
spectacular ocean views, terrific
living room w/beamed ceilings
and fieldstone fireplaces, utilizes
natural components in décor-
rock, bleached woods, and earth-
tone fabrics, CCTV, VCR, stereo,
fireplaces, kit, double Jacuzzis,
thick robes, binoculars, two
restaurants, pool, hlth clb, sauna,
whirlpools, switch-back paths

Quail Lodge
(800) 538-9516, (831) 624-1581
http://www.peninsula.com
8205 Valley Greens Dr.
104 rooms - $205-940
Pets: Welcome
Creature Comforts: Intimate,
low-lying inn on picturesque golf
course, lake and mountain views,
footbridges, rms. w/earth-tones,
vaulted ceilings, rattan
furnishings, canopy and four
poster beds, CCTV, VCR, refrig,
micro, fireplaces, two restaurants,
two pools, hlth clb, sauna,
whirlpool, putting green, golf,
tennis, extensive jogging trails

Sunset House
(831) 624-4884
http://www.sunset-carmel.com
Ocean Ave & 7th St.
4 rooms - $160-220
Pets: Welcome w/$20 fee
Creature Comforts: Intimate inn
— two blocks from the ocean in
village, vaulted beamed ceilings,
antiques, dried flowers, canopy
beds, international collection of
furnishings, country décor,
CCTV, VCR, refrig, brick
fireplaces, Jacuzzis, cont. brkfst,
cobblestone courtyard, fountain

Vagabond's House and Lincoln Green Inns
(800) 262-1262, (831) 624-7738
Fourth & Dolores Sts.
14 rooms & cottages - $85-185
Pets: Welcome w/$10 fee
Creature Comforts: Quaint English-style accommodations, intriguing patios and courtyards, vaulted beamed ceilings, inviting country décor, lovely gardens, CCTV, a/c, fireplace, kit, cont. brkfst, whirlpools

Wayside Inn
(800) 433-4732, (831) 624-5336
http://www.innsbythesea.com
Mission & 7th Sts.
22 rooms - $80-280
Pets: Small pets welcome
Creature Comforts: Intimate Williamsburg-style motor inn, informal atmosphere, family find, early American reproductions, CCTV, VCR, fireplaces, kit

CARMEL VALLEY
Blue Sky Lodge
(831) 659-2935
10 Flight Rd.
15 rooms - $58-105
Pets: Welcome
Creature Comforts: CCTV, a/c, pool, whirlpool

Carmel Valley Inn
(800) 541-3113, (831) 659-3131
Carmel Valley Rd., Box 115
http://www.carmelvalleyinn.com
48 rooms - $55-135
Pets: Welcome w/$10 fee
Creature Comforts: CCTV, a/c, refrig, restaurant, pool, whirlpool, and tennis

Carmel Valley Ranch
(800) 4-Carmel, (831) 625-9500
1 Old Ranch Rd.
http://www.grandbay.com
144 suites - $ 345-875
Pets: Welcome w/$75 fee
Creature Comforts: Lovely resort nestled on1,700 acres in the Santa Lucia Mtns, contemporary ranch-style suites w/ original artwork, assorted antiques, CCTV, VCR, fireplaces-wood stoves, kit, restaurants, cont. brkfst, pools, hlth clb, sauna, whirlpools, tennis, and golf

Valley Lodge
(800) 641-4646, (408) 659-2261
http://www.valleylodge.com
Carmel Valley & Ford Rds.
31 rooms & cottages- $ 99-299
Pets: Welcome w/$10 fee
Creature Comforts: Low-key redwood lodge and cottages nestled into a wooded hillside, vaulted rough-hewn beam ceilings, finial beds, pine and oak furnishings, assorted antiques, CCTV, VCR, fireplaces-wood stoves, kit, cont. brkfst, pool, hlth clb, sauna, whirlpool

CARPINTERIA
Best Western Carpinteria Inn
(800) 528-1234, (805) 684-0473
http://www.bestwestern.com
4558 Carpinteria Ave.
145 rooms - $90-155
Pets: Welcome
Creature Comforts: CCTV, a/c, pool, whirlpool

Motel 6
(800) 4-MOTEL6, (805) 684-6921
http://www.motel6.com
4200 Via Real
124 rooms - $39-52
Pets: Under 30 lbs. welcome
Creature Comforts: CCTV, a/c, pool

Motel 6
(800) 4-MOTEL6, (805) 684-8602
http://www.motel6.com
5550 Carpinteria Ave.
138 rooms - $39-60
Pets: Under 30 lbs. welcome
Creature Comforts: CCTV, pool

CASTAIC
Castaic Inn
(800) 628-5252, (805) 257-0229
31411 North Ridge Rt.
50 rooms - $36-86
Pets: Small pets welcome
Creature Comforts: CCTV, VCR, a/c, refrig, pool, whirlpool

CATHEDRAL CITY
Days Inn
(800) DAYS-INN, (760) 324-5939
http://www.daysinn.com
69-151 E. Palm Canyon Dr.
98 rooms - $55-175
Pets: Welcome
Creature Comforts: CCTV, a/c, kit, pool, whirlpool

Doubletree Resort
(800) 222-TREE, (760) 322-7000
http://www.doubletreehotels.com
67-967 Vista Chino St.
290 rooms - $75-145
Pets: Small pets w/$100 dep.
Creature Comforts: CCTV, VCR, a/c, refrig, restaurant, pool, hlth clb, massage, whirlpool, golf, racquetball, and tennis

CAYUCOS
Cypress Tree Motel
(805) 995-3917
125 S. Ocean Ave.
12 rooms - $32-82
Pets: Welcome w/$10 fee
Creature Comforts: CCTV, VCR, and kit

Dolphin Inn
(800) 540-4276 (CA),
(805) 995-3810
399 S. Ocean Ave.
20 rooms - $55-115
Pets: Welcome
Creature Comforts: CCTV, VCR, a/c, kit, Jacuzzi, cont. brkfst

Estero Bay Motel
(800) 736-1292, (805) 995-3614
25 S. Ocean Ave.
12 rooms - $36-120
Pets: Welcome w/$15 fee
Creature Comforts: CCTV, VCR, and kit

Shoreline Motel
(805) 995-3681
1 N. Ocean Ave.
28 rooms - $70-130
Pets: Welcome w/$10 fee
Creature Comforts: CCTV, refrig, fireplace, on the beach

CAZADERO
Cazanoma Lodge
(707) 632-5255
100 Kidd Creek Rd.
2 cabins- $125-145
Pets: Welcome
Creature Comforts: CCTV,
Jacuzzi, fireplace, kit, restaurant,
cont. brkfst, trout pond/waterfall

CEDARVILLE
Sunrise Motel
(916) 279-2161
Rte. 299
14 rooms - $35-60
Pets: Welcome
Creature Comforts: CCTV, a/c,
and refrig

CERRITOS
Sheraton Hotel
(800) 325-3535, (562) 809-1500
http://www.sheraton.com
12725 Center Court Dr
202 rooms - $85-425
Pets: Small pets w/$25 fee
Creature Comforts: CCTV, a/c,
refrig, restaurant, pool, hlth clb,
whirlpool

CHATSWORTH
Summerfield Suites
(800) 833-4353, (818) 773-0707
www.summerfieldsuites.com
21920 Lassen St.
115 rooms - $95-195
Pets: Welcome w/$10 fee, credit
card deposit
Creature Comforts: CCTV,
VCR, a/c, fireplace, kit, pool, hlth
clb, whirlpool

CHICO
Esplanade B&B
(530) 345-8040
620 The Esplanade
http://now2000.com/esplanade
5 rooms - $65-95
Pets: Welcome w/CC deposit
Creature Comforts: CCTV,
VCR, a/c, fireplace, kit, garden
patio, jacuzzi, hearty breakfast

Holiday Inn of Chico
(800) HOLIDAY, (530) 345-2491
http://www.holiday-inn.com
685 Manzanita Ct.
174 rooms - $60-175
Pets: Welcome
Creature Comforts: CCTV,
VCR, a/c, refrig, restaurant,
whirlpool, hlth club access, pool

Motel 6
(800) 4-MOTEL6, (530) 345-5500
http://www.motel6.com
665 Manzanita Ct.
78 rooms - $36-45
Pets: Under 30 lbs. welcome
Creature Comforts: CCTV, a/c,
pool

Oxford Suites
(800) 870-7848, (530) 899-9090
2035 Business Lane
183 rooms - $60-115
Pets: Welcome w/$15 fee
Creature Comforts: CCTV,
VCR, a/c, refrig, micro, fireplace,
cont. brkfst, pool, hlth clb access,
whirlpool

Town House Motel
(530) 343-1621
2231 Esplanade
30 rooms - $34-48
Pets: Small dogs w/$25 dep.
Creature Comforts: CCTV, a/c,
kit, pool

Vagabond Inn
(800) 522-1555, (530) 895-1323
http://www.vagabondinns.com
630 Main St.
42 rooms - $42-90
Pets: Welcome
Creature Comforts: CCTV, a/c,
kit, hlth club access, pool

CHINO
Motel 6
(800) 4-MOTEL6, (909) 591-3877
http://www.motel6.com
12266 Central Ave.
95 rooms - $36-49
Pets: Under 30 lbs. welcome
Creature Comforts: CCTV, a/c,
pool

CHOWCHILLA
Days Inn
(800) DAYS-INN, (209) 665-4821
http://www.daysinn.com
220 E. Robertson Blvd.
30 rooms - $45-65
Pets: Welcome
Creature Comforts: CCTV, a/c,
refrig, micro, cont. brkfst, pool

CHULA VISTA
Good Nite Inn
(619) 425-8200
394 Broadway St.
120 rooms - $32-58
Pets: Small pets welcome
Creature Comforts: CCTV, a/c,
refrig, micro, restaurant, pool

La Quinta
(800) Nu-Rooms, (619) 691-1211
http://www.laquinta.com
150 Bonita Rd.
140 rooms - $55-75
Pets: Welcome
Creature Comforts: CCTV, a/c,
pool

Motel 6
(800) 4-MOTEL6, (619) 422-4200
http://www.motel6.com
745 E St.
176 rooms - $38-45
Pets: Under 30 lbs. welcome
Creature Comforts: CCTV, a/c,
pool

Travelodge
(800) 578-7878, (619) 420-6600
http://www.travelodge.com
394 Broadway at G St.
78 rooms - $34-68
Pets: Small pets w/$50 dep.
Creature Comforts: CCTV, a/c,
refrig, micro, restaurant, pool

Vagabond Inn
(800) 522-1555, (619) 422-8305
http://www.vagabondinns.com
230 Broadway St.
91 rooms - $38-58
Pets: Welcome w/$5 fee
Creature Comforts: CCTV, a/c,
refrig, micro, restaurant, cont.
brkfst, two pools

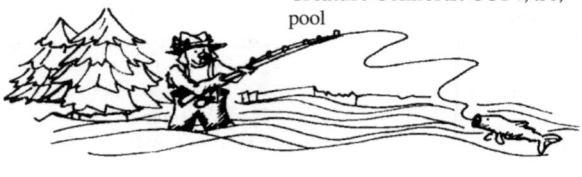

CITRUS HEIGHTS
Olive Grove Suites
(916) 725-0100
6143 Auburn Blvd.
80 rooms - $55-80
Pets: Welcome w/$50 dep.
Creature Comforts: CCTV, a/c,
kit

CLAREMONT
Howard Johnson
(800) I-Go-Hojo, (909) 626-2431
http://www.hojo.com
721 S. Indian Hill Blvd.
62 rooms - $45-70
Pets: Welcome
Creature Comforts: CCTV, a/c,
refrig, cont. brkfst, pool

Ramada Inn & Tennis Club
(800) 2-Ramada, (909) 621-4831
http://www.ramada.com
840 S. Indian Hill Rd.
122 rooms - $55-75
Pets: Welcome w/$85 dep.
Creature Comforts: CCTV, a/c,
refrig, cont. brkfst, two pools,
tennis, whirlpool, hlth club access

CLEAR LAKE
Muktip Manor
(707) 994-9571
12540 Lakeshore Dr.
1 rooms - $65-70
Pets: Welcome
Creature Comforts: CCTV, a/c,
kit, deck, cont. brkfst

Ship n Shore Resort
(707) 994-2248
http://www.lakeweb.com/
shipnshore
13885 Lakeshore Dr.
19 cabins - $40-85
Pets: Welcome w/credit card dep.
Creature Comforts: CCTV, a/c,
kit, pool, billiards, lake/beach

CLEARLAKE OAKS
Blue Fish Cove Resort
(707) 998-1769
http://www.jps.net/lost_coast/clc/
bluefish
10573 E. Rte. 20
7 cabins - $39-105
Pets: Welcome
Creature Comforts: CCTV, kit,
lawn games, lake/beach/dock

Lake Point Lodge
(707) 998-4350
13440 E. Rte. 20
40 rooms - $55-110
Pets: Small pets welcome
Creature Comforts: CCTV, a/c,
refrig, micro, pool, whirlpool

COALINGA
Big Country Inn
(209) 935-0866
Rte. 198
50 rooms - $45-64
Pets: Welcome w/$3 fee
Creature Comforts: CCTV,
VCR, a/c, pool

Inn at Harris Ranch
(800) 942-BEEF, (209) 935-0717
http://www.harrisranch.com
Rte. 1, Box 777
151 rooms - $85-245
Pets: Welcome w/$10 fee
Creature Comforts: A Spanish
hacienda-style resort set on 18,000
acres w/southwestern flair,
Palladian windows, CCTV, VCR,
a/c, finial beds, floral fabrics,
western décor, pine furnishings,
Jacuzzis, restaurants, Olympic
pool, hlth clb, whirlpools, airstrip

Motel 6
(800) 4-MOTEL6, (209) 935-2063
http://www.motel6.com
25278 W. Doris Ave.
122 rooms - $34-45
Pets: Under 30 lbs. welcome
Creature Comforts: CCTV, a/c,
pool

Motel 6
(800) 4-MOTEL6, (209) 935-2063
http://www.motel6.com
25008 W. Doris Ave.
198 rooms - $34-45
Pets: Under 30 lbs. welcome
Creature Comforts: CCTV, a/c,
pool

COLEVILLE
Andruss Motel
(530) 495-2216
106964 Rte. 395
12 rooms - $39-58
Pets: Welcome w/$5 fee
Creature Comforts: CCTV, kit,
pool, lawn games

COLTON
Days Inn
(800) DAYS-INN, (909) 788-9900
http://www.daysinn.com
2830 Iowa St.
150 rooms - $49-135
Pets: Welcome w/credit card dep.
Creature Comforts: CCTV, a/c,
refrig, micro, Jacuzzis, cont.
brkfst, whirlpool, pool

COMMERCE
Ramada Inn
(800) 2-Ramada, (562) 806-4777
http://www.ramada.com
7272 Gage Ave.
157 rooms - $60-85
Pets: Small pets welcome
Creature Comforts: CCTV, a/c,
refrig, micro, pool, hlth clb

Wyndham Garden Hotel
(800) Wyndham, (562) 887-8100
http://www.wyndham.com
5757 Telegraph Rd.
200 rooms - $70-145
Pets: Small pets w/$25 fee
Creature Comforts: CCTV,
VCR, a/c, refrig, micro, restaurant,
pool, hlth clb, sauna, whirlpool

CONCORD
Holiday Inn
(800) HOLIDAY, (510) 687-5500
http://www.holiday-inn.com
1050 Burnett Ave.
190 rooms - $75-110
Pets: Welcome
Creature Comforts: CCTV,
VCR, a/c, refrig, micro, restaurant,
pool, hlth clb, whirlpool

Sheraton Hotel
(800) 325-3535, (510) 825-7700
http://www.sheraton.com
45 John Glenn Dr.
325 rooms - $80-175
Pets: Welcome w/$10 fee
Creature Comforts: CCTV,
VCR, a/c, refrig, micro, restaurant,
pool, hlth clb, whirlpool, putting
green

CORNING
Corning Olive Inn
(800) 221-2230, (916) 824-2468
2165 Solano St.
40 rooms - $30-45
Pets: Welcome
Creature Comforts: CCTV, a/c,
pool

Days Inn
(800) DAYS-INN, (916) 824-2000
http://www.daysinn.com
3475 Rte. 99 West
62 rooms - $35-50
Pets: W/$5 fee & $25 dep.
Creature Comforts: CCTV,
VCR, a/c, refrig, micro, cont.
brkfst, pool

Shilo Inn
(800) 222-2244, (916) 824-2940
http://www.shiloinns.com
3350 Sunrise Way
80 rooms - $60-100
Pets: Welcome w/$8 fee
Creature Comforts: CCTV,
VCR, a/c, refrig, micro, pool, hlth
clb, sauna, whirlpool

CORONA
Dynasty Suites
(800) 842-7899, (909) 371-7185
http://www.dynastysuites.com
1805 W. 6th St.
55 rooms - $38-65
Pets: Small pets w/$10 fee
Creature Comforts: CCTV, a/c,
kit, Jacuzzis, pool, hlth club
access, whirlpools

Motel 6
(800) 4-MOTEL6, (909) 735-6408
http://www.motel6.com
200 N. Lincoln Ave.
126 rooms - $34-45
Pets: Under 30 lbs. welcome
Creature Comforts: CCTV, a/c,
pool

Travelodge
(800) 578-7878, (909) 735-5500
http://www.travelodge.com
1701 W. 6th St.
45 rooms - $35-50
Pets: Welcome
Creature Comforts: CCTV,
VCR, a/c, refrig, micro, pool

CORONADO
Crown City Inn
(800) 422-1173, (619) 435-3116
520 Orange Ave.
32 rooms - $60-129
Pets: Welcome w/$8 fee
Creature Comforts: CCTV,
VCR, a/c, kit, restaurant, pool

Loews Coronado Bay Resort
(800) 81-LOEWS, (619) 424-4400
http://www.loewshotels.com
4000 Coronado Bay Rd.
430 rooms - $195-1,600
Pets: Small pets welcome
Creature Comforts: Luxury
shingle-style hotel with bay views
and contemporary decor, CCTV,
VCR, a/c, bleached rattan and
wood furnishings, vibrant floral
fabrics, Palladian and French
doors lead to balconies, refrig,
micro, Jacuzzi, two restaurants,
cont. brkfst, three pools, hlth clb,
saunas, whirlpools, tennis, marina-
boat rentals, children's program

Marriott Coronado Resort
(800) 228-9290, (619) 435-3000
http://www.marriott.com
2000 - 2nd St.
300 rooms - $90-850
Pets: Small pets welcome
Creature Comforts: Luxury
resort surrounded by lagoons,
nicely landscaped grounds, and
exotic wildlife, French accents w/
a southern Californian ambiance,
CCTV, a/c, VCR, refrig, micro,
restaurant, pool, hlth clb, sauna,
whirlpool, tennis, scuba,
snorkling, and windsurfing

COSTA MESA
Ana Mesa Suites
(800) 767-2519, (714) 662-3500
3597 Harbor Blvd.
50 rooms - $60-90
Pets: Welcome w/$5 fee
Creature Comforts: CCTV, a/c,
refrig, micro, cont. brkfst, pool

Best Western Newport Mesa
(800) 528-1234, (714) 650-3020
http://www.bestwestern.com
2642 Newport Blvd.
95 rooms - $50-85
Pets: Small pets welcome
Creature Comforts: CCTV, a/c,
refrig, micro, pool, hlth clb, sauna,
whirlpools

Comfort Inn
(800) 228-5150, (714) 650-3020
http://www.comfortinn.com
2430 Newport Blvd.
57 rooms - $40-65
Pets: Small pets welcome
Creature Comforts: CCTV, a/c,
refrig, cont. brkfst, pool, whirlpool

Doubletree Hotel
(800) 222-TREE, (714) 540-7000
http://www.doubletreehotels.com
3050 Bristol St.
485 rooms - $99-695
Pets: Small pets w/$25 fee
Creature Comforts: CCTV, a/c,
refrig, micro, restaurant, pool, hlth
clb, sauna, whirlpool

La Quinta
(800) Nu-Rooms, (714) 957-5841
http://www.laquintainn.com
1515 S. Coast Dr.
160 rooms - $45-60
Pets: Welcome
Creature Comforts: CCTV, a/c,
refrig, pool

Motel 6
(800) 4-MOTEL6, (714) 957-3063
http://www.motel6.com
1441 Gisler Ave.
96 rooms - $42-54
Pets: Under 30 lbs. welcome
Creature Comforts: CCTV, a/c,
pool

Ramada Limited
(800) 2-Ramada, (714) 645-2221
http://www.ramada.com
1680 Superior Ave.
140 rooms - $50-175
Pets: Small pets welcome
Creature Comforts: CCTV, a/c,
refrig, micro, restaurant, cont.
brkfst, pool, whirlpool

Red Lion Hotel
(800) RED-LION, (714) 540-7000
http://www.redlion.com
3050 Bristol St.
485 rooms - $80-125
Pets: Small pets w/$25 fee
Creature Comforts: CCTV, a/c,
refrig, restaurant, pool, hlth clb,
sauna, whirlpool

Residence Inn
(800) 331-3131, (714) 241-8800
http://www.residenceinn.com
881 W. Baker St.
145 rooms - $100-195
Pets: Welcome w/$5 fee and a
credit card dep.
Creature Comforts: CCTV,
VCR, a/c, fireplaces, kit,
restaurant, cont. brkfst, pool, hlth
clb, sauna, whirlpool

Vagabond Inn
(800) 522-1555, (714) 557-8360
http://www.vagabondinns.com
3205 Harbor Blvd.
125 rooms - $45-70
Pets: Small pets w/$5 fee
Creature Comforts: CCTV,
VCR, a/c, refrig, micro, pool, hlth
clb, whirlpool

Westin South Coast Hotel
(800) 228-3000, (714) 540-2500
http://www.westin.com
686 Anton Blvd.
390 rooms - $169-999
Pets: Small pets welcome
Creature Comforts: CCTV, a/c,
refrig, restaurant, pool, hlth clb
access, whirlpool

Wyndham Garden Hotel
(800) Wyndham, (714) 751-5100
http://www.wyndham.com
3350 Ave. of the Arts
235 rooms - $69-925
Pets: Small pets w/$25 fee
Creature Comforts: CCTV, a/c,
refrig, restaurant, pool, hlth clb,
tennis, sauna, whirlpool, lake

CRESCENT CITY
Days Inn
(800) DAYS-INN, (707) 464-9553
http://www.daysinn.com
220 M St.
25 rooms - $45-80
Pets: In pet rooms w/$7 fee
Creature Comforts: CCTV, a/c,
refrig, cont. brkfst

Econolodge
(800) 55-ECONO, (707) 464-2181
http://www.econolodge.com
48 rooms - $50-75
Pets: WIn certain rms. w/$5 fee
Creature Comforts: CCTV, a/c,
cont. brkfst.

Pacific Motor Hotel
(800) 323-7917, (707) 464-4141
440 Rte. 101 North
64 rooms - $40-75
Pets: Small pets w/$5 fee
Creature Comforts: CCTV,
VCR, refrig, micro, pool, sauna,
whirlpool

Super 8 Motel
(800) 800-8000, (707) 464-4111
http://www.super8.com
685 Route 101
50 rooms - $45-89
Pets: Small pets welcome
Creature Comforts: CCTV

CULVER CITY
Red Lion Hotel-LA Airport
(800) RED-LION, (310) 649-1776
http://www.redlion.com
6161 Centinela Blvd.
370 rooms - $80-125
Pets: Small pets w/$50 dep.
Creature Comforts: CCTV,
VCR, a/c, refrig, restaurant, pool,
hlth clb, whirlpool

DANVILLE
Danville Inn
(800) 654-1050, (510) 838-8080
803 Camino Ramon
60 rooms - $60-85
Pets: Welcome
Creature Comforts: CCTV, a/c,
pool

DAVIS
Best Western University Lodge
(800) 528-1234, (530) 756-7890
http://www.bestwestern.com
123 B Street
54 rooms - $58-86
Pets: Welcome w/$5 fee
Creature Comforts: CCTV, a/c,
kit, pool, whirlpool

Econolodge
(800) 55-ECONO, (530) 756-1040
http://www.econolodge.com
26 rooms - $50-75
Pets: Welcome w/$5 fee
Creature Comforts: CCTV, a/c,
pool

Motel 6
(800) 4-MOTEL6, (530) 753-3777
http://www.motel6.com
4835 Chiles Rd.
103 rooms - $35-49
Pets: Under 30 lbs. welcome
Creature Comforts: CCTV, a/c,
pool

University Inn B&B
(800) 756-8648, (530) 756-8648
340 A Street
4 rooms - $55-130
Pets: Welcome
Creature Comforts: CCTV,
VCR, a/c, refrig, micro, fireplace,
and cont. brkfst

DEATH VALLEY
Stove Pipe Wells Village
(760) 786-2387
Route 190
82 rooms - $55-84
Pets: Welcome w/$25 dep.
Creature Comforts: a/c, refrig,
restaurant, pool, and an airstrip

DELANO
Comfort Inn
(800) 228-5150, (805) 725-1022
http://www.comfortinn.com
2211 Girard St.
44 rooms - $44-64
Pets: Small pets welcome
Creature Comforts: CCTV, a/c,
pool, whirlpool

Shilo Inn
(800) 222-2244, (805) 725-7551
http://www.shiloinns.com
2231 Girard St.
48 rooms - $50-75
Pets: Welcome w/$6 fee
Creature Comforts: CCTV,
VCR, a/c, pool, whirlpool

DEL MAR
Del Mar Hilton
(800) HILTONS, (619) 792-5200
http://www.hilton.com
15575 Jimmy Durante Blvd.
244 rooms - $80-145
Pets: Welcome w/$200 dep.
Creature Comforts: CCTV, a/c,
refrig, restaurant, pool, whirlpools

Del Mar Inn
(619) 755-9765
720 Camino Del Mar
77 rooms - $75-145
Pets: Small pets w/$10 fee
Creature Comforts: CCTV,
refrig, restaurant, cont. brkfst,
pool, whirlpools

DESERT HOT SPRINGS
Las Primaveras Resort Spa
(800) 400-1677, (760) 251-1677
www.lasprimaveras.qpg.com/
66-659 6th St.
7 rooms - $55-115
Pets: Welcome
Creature Comforts: CCTV, a/c,
fireplace, kit, Jacuzzis, pool,
sauna, whirlpool

Motel 6
(800) 4-MOTEL6, (760) 251-1425
http://www.motel6.com
63-950 20th Ave.
66 rooms - $36-48
Pets: Under 30 lbs. welcome
Creature Comforts: CCTV, a/c,
pool

Stardust Spa Motel
(800) 482-7835, (760) 329-5443
66634 - 5th St.
16 rooms - $38-64
Pets: Welcome
Creature Comforts: CCTV, a/c,
kit, pool, mineral whirlpool

DINUBA
Best Western Americana
(800) 528-1234, (209) 595-8401
http://www.bestwestern.com
38 rooms - $45-69
Pets: Welcome w/notice
Creature Comforts: CCTV, a/c,
pool, whirlpool

DIXON
Best Western Inn
(800) 528-1234, (916) 678-1400
http://www.bestwestern.com
1345 Commercial Way
54 rooms - $50-85
Pets: Medium pets w/$50 dep.
Creature Comforts: CCTV, a/c,
refrig, micro, pool, sauna,
whirlpool

DOWNEY
Embassy Suites
(800) EMBASSY, (562) 861-1900
http://www.embassy-suites.com
8245 Firestone Blvd.
220 rooms - $115-145
Pets: Welcome w/$16 fee
Creature Comforts: CCTV,
VCR, a/c, refrig, micro, restaurant,
pool, hlth clb, sauna, whirlpool,
steamroom

DOWNIEVILLE
Downieville River Inn & Rsrt
(800) 696-3308, (530) 289-3308
121 River St.
30 rooms - $75-165
Pets: Welcome
Creature Comforts: CCTV, a/c,
VCR, kitchens, restaurant, river,
pool, fireplace, and a variety of
outdoor recreational opportunities

DUARTE
Travelodge
(800) 578-7878, (818) 357-0907
http://www.travelodge.com
1200 E. Huntington Dr.
68 rooms - $39-76
Pets: Welcome
Creature Comforts: CCTV, a/c,
refrig, cont. brkfst, pool, whirlpool

DUNNIGAN
Best Western Inn
(800) 528-1234, (916) 724-3471
http://www.bestwestern.com
Route 5
54 rooms - $50-84
Pets: Small pet welcome
Creature Comforts: CCTV, a/c,
kit, restaurant, pool, whirlpool

IMA Value Lodge
(800) 341-8000, (916) 724-3333
http://www.imalodging.com
Route 5
40 rooms - $40-64
Pets: Small pets welcome
Creature Comforts: CCTV, a/c,
refrig, pool

DUNSMUIR
Cave Springs
(530) 235-2721
http://www.cavesprings.com
4727 Dunsmuir Ave.
30 units - $48-75
Pets: Leashed pets w/$5 fee
Creature Comforts: CCTV, a/c,
kit, pool, whirlpool

Cedar Lodge Motel
(530) 235-4331
4201 Dunsmuir Ave.
18 rooms - $32-65
Pets: Small pets welcome
Creature Comforts: CCTV,
VCR, a/c, refrig, fireplace, and
kit

Railroad Park Resort
(800) 974-RAIL, (530) 235-4440
http://www.rrpark.com
100 Railroad Park Dr.
27 rooms - $60-90
Pets: Welcome w/$7.50 fee
Creature Comforts: Neat,
restored rail cars that are
charmingly furnished, set near the
base of Castle Crags, knotty
cedar interiors, floral tab curtains,
original ladders, pipes, and
fittings, traditional furnishings
and brass beds, CCTV, a/c, kit,
dining cars-restaurant w/loads of
nostalgia, cont. brkfst, pool,
whirlpool

River Walk Inn
(800) 954-4300, (530) 235-4300
http://www.dunsmuir.com
4300 Dunsmuir Ave.
4 rooms - $49-80
Pets: Welcome w/$10 fee
Creature Comforts: 1918
renovated Cape home, antiques
and family heirlooms, sweater
chests, four poster bed, children's
room filled w/toys and secret
passage to parents' room, CCTV,
a/c, refrig, fireplaces, kit, piano,
full brkfst, lawn games

Travelodge
(800) 578-7878, (530) 235-4395
http://www.travelodge.com
5400 Dunsmuir Ave.
18 rooms - $40-90
Pets: Welcome w/$5 fee
Creature Comforts: CCTV, a/c

EL CAJON
Best Western
(800) 528-1234, (619) 440-7378
http://www.bestwestern.com
1355 East Main St.
48 rooms - $40-65
Pets: Small pets w/$6 fee
Creature Comforts: CCTV, a/c,
refrig, pool, whirlpool

Days Inn
(800) DAYS-INN, (619) 688-8808
http://www.daysinn.com
1250 El Cajon Blvd.
48 rooms - $38-54
Pets: Welcome
Creature Comforts: CCTV, a/c,
refrig, micro, cont. brkfst, pool,
hlth whirlpool

Motel 6
(800) 4-MOTEL6, (619) 588-6100
http://www.motel6.com
550 Montrose Ct.
182 rooms - $39-52
Pets: Under 30 lbs. welcome
Creature Comforts: CCTV, a/c,
pool

Travelodge
(800) 578-7878, (619) 447-3999
http://www.travelodge.com
471 N. Magnolia Ave.
48 rooms - $35-74
Pets: Under 20 lbs. w/$15 fee
Creature Comforts: CCTV, a/c,
VCR, refrig, micro, cont. brkfst,
and a pool

EL CENTRO
Barbara Worth Golf Resort
(800) 356-3806, (760) 356-2806
2050 Country Club Road
102 rooms - $52-74
Pets: Small pets w/$5 fee
Creature Comforts: CCTV, a/c,
kit, restaurant, two pools,
whirlpools, golf course

Best Western John Jay Inn
(800) 528-1234, (760) 337-8677
http://www.bestwestern.com
2352 S. Fourth St.
58 rooms - $52-68
Pets: Welcome
Creature Comforts: CCTV, a/c,
refrig, pool, sauna, whirlpool

Brunner's
(760) 352-6431
215 N. Imperial Ave.
88 rooms - $45-85
Pets: Welcome
Creature Comforts: CCTV,
VCR, a/c, refrig, restaurant, pool,
hlth clb, whirlpool

Days Inn
(800) DAYS-INN, (760) 352-5511
http://www.daysinn.com
1425 Adams Ave.
50 rooms - $45-79
Pets: Small pets w/$10 fee
Creature Comforts: CCTV, a/c,
refrig, micro, restaurant, cont.
brkfst, whirlpool, pool

Executive Inn
(800) 553-5083, (760) 352-8500
725 State St.
42 rooms - $28-65
Pets: Small pets welcome
Creature Comforts: CCTV, a/c,
kit, cont. brkfst, pool

Laguna Inn
(760) 353-7750
2030 Cottonwood Cir.
28 rooms - $44-62
Pets: Small pets welcome
Creature Comforts: CCTV, a/c,
kit, pool, whirlpool

Motel 6
(800) 4-MOTEL6, (760) 353-6766
http://www.motel6.com
395 Smoketree Dr.
110 rooms - $36-48
Pets: Under 30 lbs. welcome
Creature Comforts: CCTV, a/c,
pool

Ramada Inn
(800) 2-Ramada, (760) 352-5152
http://www.ramada.com
1455 Ocotillo Dr.
148 rooms - $45-99
Pets: Small pets welcome
Creature Comforts: CCTV, a/c,
refrig, micro, restaurant, two
pools, hlth clb, whirlpool

Travelodge
(800) 578-7878, (760) 352-7333
http://www.travelodge.com
1464 Adams Ave.
72 rooms - $35-50
Pets: Welcome
Creature Comforts: CCTV,
VCR, a/c, kit, pool

Vacation Inn
(800) 328-6289, (760) 352-9523
2015 Cottonwood Circle
190 rooms - $50-99
Pets: Welcome w/$25 dep.
Creature Comforts: CCTV, a/c,
kit, restaurant, pools, whirlpool

EL CERRITO
Freeway Motel
(510) 234-5581
11645 San Pablo Ave.
16 rooms - $45-75
Pets: Welcome
Creature Comforts: CCTV, a/c

EL MONTE
Motel 6
(800) 4-MOTEL6, (818) 448-6660
http://www.motel6.com
3429 Peck Rd.
68 rooms - $39-48
Pets: Under 30 lbs. welcome
Creature Comforts: CCTV, a/c,
pool

EL PORTAL
Yosemite View Motel
(800) 321-5261, (209) 379-2681
http://www.yosemitemotels.com
11136 Rte. 140
158 rooms - $85-175
Pets: Welcome w/$5 fee
Creature Comforts: CCTV, a/c,
fireplaces, kit, 2 restaurants, pool,
whirlpool

EL SEGUNDO
Embassy Suites
(800) EMBASSY, (310) 640-3600
http://www.embassy-suites.com
1440 E. Imperial Ave.
352 rooms - $99-189
Pets: Welcome w/$25 fee
Creature Comforts: CCTV,
VCR, a/c, refrig, micro, restaurant,
pool, hlth clb, whirlpool

Summerfield Suites
(800) 833-4353, (310) 725-0100
www.summerfieldsuites.com
810 So. Douglas Ave.
122 rooms - $159-199
Pets: $10 fee, $75 deposit
Creature Comforts: CCTV,
VCR, a/c, kit, pool, hlth clb,
whirlpool

Travelodge
(800) 578-7878, (310) 615-1073
http://www.travelodge.com
1804 E. Sycamore Rd.
95 rooms - $45-75
Pets: Small pets w/$25 dep.
Creature Comforts: CCTV, a/c,
kit, pool

ELK
Greenwood Pier Inn
(707) 877-9997 or 877-3423
www.greenwoodpierinn.com
5928 Highway 1, Box 36
15 rooms - $90-224
Pets: Welcome in certain rooms
Creature Comforts: An artist's
delight—gardens, fountains,
handmade furnishings, whimsical
signs, electic and delightful rms.
overlooking ocean, beamed
ceilings, hand-painted tiles,
stained glass windows, bathtubs
w/wonderful views, painted
furniture, CCTV, VCR, a/c, refrig,
micro, fireplace, kit, restaurant,
cont. brkfst, intriguing country
store

EMIGRANT GAP
Rancho Sierras Resort
(530) 389-8572
43440 Laing Rd.
15 rooms - $45-90
Pets: Welcome
Creature Comforts: A/C,
restaurant, bar

ESCONDIDO
Best Western
(800) 528-1234, (760) 740-1700
http://www.bestwestern.com
1700 Seven Oaks Rd.
102 rooms - $60-99
Pets: Small pets welcome
Creature Comforts: CCTV, a/c,
refrig, micro, pool, whirlpool

Castle Creek Inn
(800) 253-5341, (760) 751-8800
http://www.castlecreekresort.com
29850 Circle R Way
30 rooms - $85-165
Pets: Welcome w/$50 dep.
Creature Comforts: Originally
built as a Bavarian health resort,
antiques, furnishings from
Germany, CCTV, VCR, a/c,
fireplaces, Jacuzzi, gourmet
restaurant, cont. brkfst, pool, hlth
clb, whirlpool, tennis, golf

Welk Resort Center
(800) 932-9355, (760) 749-3000
http://www.welkresort.com
8860 Lawrence Welk Dr.
140 rooms - $120-565
Pets: In 1 bldg. w/$50 dep.
Creature Comforts: Nestled in
secluded valley on 600 acres, golf
course, rooms w/subtle earth
tones, Scandinavian-style
furnishings, CCTV, VCR, a/c,
refrig, restaurant, two pools, hlth
clb, two golf courses, lighted
tennis, whirlpools

Motel 6
(800) 4-MOTEL6, (760) 745-9252
http://www.motel6.com
900 N. Quince St.
131 rooms - $39-50
Pets: Under 30 lbs. welcome
Creature Comforts: CCTV, a/c,
pool

Motel 6
(800) 4-MOTEL6, (760) 745-9252
http://www.motel6.com
900 N. Quincy St.
99 rooms - $30-42
Pets: Under 30 lbs. welcome
Creature Comforts: CCTV, a/c,
pool

Pine Tree Lodge
(760) 745-7613
425 W. Mission St.
39 rooms - $45-55
Pets: Welcome w/$4 fee, $20 dep.
Creature Comforts: CCTV, a/c,
fireplace, kit, pool

Super 8 Motel
(800) 800-8000, (760) 747-3711
http://www.super8.com
528 W. Washington St.
45 rooms - $38-64
Pets: Small pets w/$10 fee
Creature Comforts: CCTV, a/c,
pool, whirlpool

EUREKA
A Weaver's Inn
(800) 992-8119, (707) 443-8119
http://www.humboldt1.com/
~weavrinn
1440 B St.
4 rooms - $65-129
Pets: Small pets w/$15 fee
Creature Comforts: Gracious
1883 Queen-Anne Colonial,
Victorian furnishings, detailed
woodworking, period wallpapers,
Persian rugs, pine chests, CCTV,
VCR, a/c, refrig, micro, fireplaces,
kit, full brkfst, two-person Jap.
soaking tub, Jap. contemplation
garden

Best Western Bayshore
(800) 528-1234, (707) 268-8005
http://www.bestwestern.com
3500 Broadway
82 rooms - $95-155
Pets: Small pets are welcome in
smoking rms/ $100 dep.
Creature Comforts: CCTV, a/c,
refrig, micro, restaurant, pool,

Carson House Inn
(800) 772-1622, (707) 443-1601
1209 Fourth St.
60 rooms - $75-220
Pets: Welcome
Creature Comforts: CCTV, a/c,
kit, Jacuzzis, cont. brkfst, pool,
sauna, whirlpools

The Eureka Inn
(800) 862-4906, (707) 442-6441
http://www.humboldt1.com/
~ekainn
518 Seventh St.
105 rooms - $100-260
Pets: Welcome on the first floor
Creature Comforts: Historic
English Tudor hotel, Nat'l Historic
Register w/inviting ambiance,
high redwood-beamed ceilings in
lobby, CCTV, refrig, grass or
paneled wall treatments, Queen-
Anne style furnishings, fireplaces,
Jacuzzis, restaurant, pool, and
whirlpool

Matador Motel
(800) 404-9751, (707) 443-9751
129 - 4th St.
24 rooms - $35-50
Pets: Welcome w/$4 fee
Creature Comforts: CCTV,
refrig, whirlpools

Motel 6
(800) 4-MOTEL6, (707) 445-9631
http://www.motel6.com
1934 Broadway St.
98 rooms - $33-42
Pets: Under 30 lbs. welcome
Creature Comforts: CCTV, a/c

Quality Inn
(800) 847-2211, (707) 443-1601
http://www.qualityinn.com
1209 - 4th St.
60 rooms - $99-160
Pets: Welcome
Creature Comforts: CCTV, a/c,
refrig, cont. brkfst, pool

Ramada Inn
(800) 2-Ramada, (707) 443-2206
http://www.ramada.com
270 - 5th St.
40 rooms - $70-95
Pets: Small pets w/$8 fee
Creature Comforts: CCTV, a/c,
kit, cont. brkfst, whirlpool

Red Lion Inn
(800) RED-LION, (707) 445-0844
http://www.redlion.com
1929 Fourth St.
176 rooms - $77-199
Pets: Welcome
Creature Comforts: CCTV,
VCR, a/c, restaurant, pool,
whirlpool

Sunrise Inn
(707) 443-9751
129 - 4th St.
25 rooms - $65-78
Pets: Welcome w/$4 fee
Creature Comforts: CCTV, a/c,
refrig,

Town House Motel
(800) 445-6888, (707) 444-2099
933 - 4th St.
20 rooms - $35-90
Pets: Welcome
Creature Comforts: CCTV, a/c,
refrig, micro, Jacuzzi

Travelodge
(800) 578-7878, (707) 443-6345
http://www.travelodge.com
Four - 4th St.
rooms - $35-95
Pets: Welcome
Creature Comforts: CCTV, a/c,
refrig, cont. brkfst, pool

Vagabond Inn
(800) 522-1555, (707) 443-8041
http://www.vagabondinns.com
1630 - 4th St.
88 rooms - $38-68
Pets: Welcome w/$5 fee
Creature Comforts: CCTV, a/c,
cont. brkfst, pool

FAIRFIELD
Best Western Cordelia
(800) 528-1234, (707) 864-2029
http://www.bestwestern.com
4873 Central Pl.
60 rooms - $50-70
Pets: Small pets welcome
Creature Comforts: CCTV, a/c,
refrig, micro, pool, whirlpool

Motel 6
(800) 4-MOTEL6, (707) 425-4565
http://www.motel6.com
1473 Holiday Lane
89 rooms - $37-49
Pets: Under 30 lbs. welcome
Creature Comforts: CCTV, a/c,
pool

Motel 6
(800) 4-MOTEL6, (707) 427-0800
http://www.motel6.com
2353 Magellan Rd.
66 rooms - $30-40
Pets: Under 30 lbs. welcome
Creature Comforts: CCTV, a/c,
pool

FALLBROOK
Best Western Franciscan Inn
(800) 528-1234, (760) 728-6174
http://www.bestwestern.com
1635 S. Mission Rd.
50 rooms - $50-80
Pets: Small pets w/$5 fee
Creature Comforts: CCTV, a/c,
kit, pool, whirlpool

La Estancia Inn
(760) 723-2888
3135 S. Old Hwy.
40 rooms - $50-85
Pets: Welcome w/$25 fee
Creature Comforts: CCTV, a/c,
kit, restaurant, pool, whirlpool

FALL RIVER MILLS
Lava Creek Lodge
(530) 336-6288
1 Island Rd.
7 rooms, 5 cottages - $55-145
Pets: Welcome w/$12 fee
Creature Comforts: CCTV, kit,
and a restaurant

FELTON
Inn at Felton Crest
(800) 474-4011, (831) 335-4011
http://www.feltoncrestinn.com
780 El Solyo Heights Dr.
4 rooms - $275-345
Pets: Well behaved pets welcome
Creature Comforts: A great oasis
set amidst the redwoods, elegant
retreat, lovely furnishings, feather
beds, CCTV, fireplaces, jacuzzi,
a/c, VCR refrig, micro, beamed
vaulted ceilings, cutwork linens,
French doors, cont. brkfst, and a
whirlpool

FIREBAUGH
Shilo Inn
(800) 222-2244, (209) 659-1444
http://www.shiloinns.com
46290 W. Panoche Rd.
74 rooms - $44-64
Pets: Welcome w/$3 fee
Creature Comforts: CCTV, a/c,
refrig, micro, cont. brkfst, pool

FISH CAMP
Tenaya Lodge
(800) 635-5807, (209) 683-6555
http://www.tenayalodge.com
1122 Rte. 41, Box 159
262 rooms - $135-425
Pets: Welcome w/$50 fee
Creature Comforts: Neat
mountain lodge on 35-acres, close
to Yosemite Nat'l Park entrance,
lobby contains stone fireplace,
bentwood chairs, Native American
fabrics and vaulted beamed
ceilings; rooms w/southwestern
décor, Adirondack chairs, four
poster beds, fireplaces, Jap.
sunken tubs, CCTV, refrig, micro,
restaurant, 3 pools, hlth clb,
saunas, whirlpools, steamrooms,
spa, xc-skiing, rec. programs,
trails, access to riding, fishing,
tennis, golf

FONTANA
Motel 6
(800) 4-MOTEL6, (909) 823-8686
http://www.motel6.com
10195 Sierra Ave.
101 rooms - $39-48
Pets: Under 30 lbs. welcome
Creature Comforts: CCTV, a/c, pool

FORT BRAGG
Beachcomber Motel
(800) 400-7873, (707) 964-2402
www.thebeachcombermotel.com
1111 North Main St.
28 rooms - $45-255
Pets: Welcome w/$10 fee
Creature Comforts: CCTV, kit, Jacuzzis, oceanviews

Cleone Gardens Inn
(800) 400-2189, (707) 964-2788
www.cleonegardensinn.com
24600 North Hwy. 1
12 rooms - $77-155
Pets: Welcome w/$4 fee per dog in ltd. rooms
Creature Comforts: Cottages set on 5 acres of parklike grounds, attractive rooms w/CCTV, stereo, kit, fireplaces, full brkfst, hlth club access, whirlpool

Ebb Tide Lodge
(800) 974-6730, (707) 964-5321
250 S. Main St.
31 rooms - $40-110
Pets: Welcome w/$25 fee
Creature Comforts: CCTV, a/c, cont. brkfst, whirlpool

Old Stewart House Inn
(800) 287-8392, (707) 961-0775
www.oldstewarthouseinn.com
511 Stewart St.
10 rooms - $80-140
Pets: Welcome in the cottage
Creature Comforts: A quaint 1870s Victorian, reproductions and family heirlooms, four poster beds, CCTV, a/c, fireplace, kitchen, buffet brkfst, 2-person jacuzzi

Pudding Creek Inn
(800) 227-9529, (707) 964-9529
www.PuddingCreekInn.com
700 N. Main St.
10 rooms - $80-140
Pets: Welcome in one room
Creature Comforts: Intimate, Victorian-style bungalow w/ intriguing history, homey décor, reproductions & family heirlooms, CCTV, a/c, fireplace, refrig, buffet brkfst, rec. room, lovely garden

The Rendezvous Inn
(800) 491-8142, (707) 964-8142
http://www.rendezvousinn.com
647 N. Main St.
4 rooms & 1 cottage - $89-145
Pets: Welcome in the cottage
Creature Comforts: A charming historic home, CCTV, woodstove, electric heat, homey decor, porch, full brkfst, restaurant, in town

Shoreline Vacation Rentals
(888)what-a-view, (707) 964-1444
www.shorelinevacations.com
18200 Old Coast Hwy.
5 houses - $155-350
Pets: $10 fee and a $100 dep.
Creature Comforts: An agency that represents a number of great rental prperties, contemporary decors, cathedral ceilings, CCTV, VCR, a/c, stereo, fireplace, kit, Jacuzzi, decks, ocean views

Wishing Well Cottages
(800) 362-9305, (707) 961-5450
31430 Rte. 20
2 cottages - $60-75
Pets: Welcome w/$5 fee
Creature Comforts: CCTV, a/c, fireplace, kit, trails

FORTUNA
Best Western Country Inn
(800) 528-1234, (707) 725-6822
http://www.bestwestern.com
1528 Kenmar Rd.
65 rooms - $45-125
Pets: Small pets w/$50 dep.
Creature Comforts: CCTV, a/c, refrig, micro, pool, whirlpool

Fortuna Motor Lodge
(707) 725-6993
275 - 12th St.
25 rooms - $36-64
Pets: Small pets welcome
Creature Comforts: CCTV

Holiday Inn Express
(800) HOLIDAY, (707) 725-5500
http://www.holiday-inn.com
1859 Alamar Way
45 rooms - $45-85
Pets: Welcome w/$25 dep.
Creature Comforts: CCTV, VCR, a/c, refrig, micro, pool

Super 8 Motel
(800) 800-8000, (707) 725-2888
http://www.super8.com
1805 Alamar Way
48 rooms - $44-78
Pets: Welcome w/$5 fee
Creature Comforts: CCTV, a/c, VCR, refrig, micro, whirlpool

FOUNTAIN VALLEY
Ramada Inn
(800) 2-Ramada, (714) 847-3388
http://www.ramada.com
9125 Recreation Circle
68 rooms - $60-80
Pets: Small pets w/$10 fee
Creature Comforts: CCTV, a/c, kit, pool, whirlpool

Residence Inn
(800) 331-3131, (714) 965-8000
http://www.residenceinn.com
9930 Slater Ave.
124 rooms - $72-154
Pets: Small pets w/$100 dep.
Creature Comforts: CCTV, VCR, a/c, refrig, micro, restaurant, cont. brkfst, pool, hlth clb, whirlpool

FREMONT
Best Western Thunderbird Inn
(800) 528-1234, (510) 792-4300
http://www.bestwestern.com
5400 Mowry Ave.
124 rooms - $50-85
Pets: Welcome w/$50 dep.
Creature Comforts: CCTV, a/c, refrig, pool, sauna, whirlpool

Motel 6
(800) 4-MOTEL6, (510) 793-4848
http://www.motel6.com
34047 Fremont Blvd.
66 rooms - $30-44
Pets: Under 30 lbs. welcome
Creature Comforts: CCTV, a/c, pool

Motel 6
(800) 4-MOTEL6, (510) 490-4528
http://www.motel6.com
46101 Research Ave.
159 rooms - $44-59
Pets: Under 30 lbs. welcome
Creature Comforts: CCTV, a/c, pool

Residence Inn
(800) 331-3131, (510) 794-5900
http://www.residenceinn.com
5400 Farwell Pl.
80 rooms - $75-175
Pets: $10 fee & $75 dep.
Creature Comforts: CCTV, a/c, kit, cont.brkfst, pool, hlth club access, whirlpool

FRESNO
Best Western Tradewinds
(800) 528-1234, (559) 237-1881
http://www.bestwestern.com
2141 North Parkway Dr.
112 rooms - $50-74
Pets: Welcome w/$5 fee
Creature Comforts: CCTV, a/c, refrig, micro, pool, whirlpool

Brooks Ranch Inn
(559) 275-2727
4278 W. Ashian Ave.
120 rooms - $34-54
Pets: Welcome w/$5 fee, $25 dep.
Creature Comforts: CCTV, a/c, pool

Days Inn
(800) DAYS-INN, (559) 268-6211
http://www.daysinn.com
1101 N. Parkway Dr.
98 rooms - $45-109
Pets: Welcome w/$5 fee
Creature Comforts: CCTV, a/c, refrig, micro, Jacuzzis, cont. brkfst, pool

Economy Inns of America
(800) 826-0778, (559) 486-1188
http://www.innsofamerica.com
2570 S. East St.
120 rooms - $28-47
Pets: Welcome
Creature Comforts: CCTV, a/c, pool

Hilton Hotel
(800) HILTONS, (559) 485-9000
http://www.hilton.com
1055 Van Ness Ave.
190 rooms - $80-545
Pets: Small pets welcome
Creature Comforts: CCTV, a/c, refrig, restaurant, pool, hlth clb, whirlpool

Holiday Inn
(800) HOLIDAY, (559) 268-1000
http://www.holiday-inn.com
2233 Ventura St.
323 rooms - $80-120
Pets: Welcome
Creature Comforts: CCTV, VCR, a/c, refrig, restaurant, pool, hlth clb, sauna, whirlpool

Howard Johnson
(800) I-Go-Hojo, (559) 277-3888
http://www.hojo.com
4071 N. Blackstone Ave.
96 rooms - $38-54
Pets: Welcome
Creature Comforts: CCTV, a/c, refrig, cont. brkfst, pool

La Quinta
(800) Nu-Rooms, (559) 442-1110
http://www.laquinta.com
2926 Tulare St.
130 rooms - $50-74
Pets: Small pets welcome
Creature Comforts: CCTV, a/c, refrig, micro, pool

Motel 6
(800) 4-MOTEL6, (559) 485-5011
http://www.motel6.com
445 N. Pkwy Dr.
92 rooms - $28-42
Pets: Under 30 lbs. welcome
Creature Comforts: CCTV, a/c, pool

Motel 6
(800) 4-MOTEL6, (559) 233-3913
http://www.motel6.com
933 N. Pkwy Dr.
107 rooms - $34-48
Pets: Under 30 lbs. welcome
Creature Comforts: CCTV, a/c, pool

Motel 6
(800) 4-MOTEL6, (559) 221-0800
http://www.motel6.com
4245 N. Blackstone Ave.
82 rooms - $36-48
Pets: Under 30 lbs. welcome
Creature Comforts: CCTV, a/c, pool

Motel 6
(800) 4-MOTEL6, (559) 222-2431
http://www.motel6.com
4080 N. Blackstone Ave.
140 rooms - $36-44
Pets: Under 30 lbs. welcome
Creature Comforts: CCTV, a/c, pool

Motel 6
(800) 4-MOTEL6, (559) 237-0855
http://www.motel6.com
1240 Crystal Ave.
98 rooms - $36-44
Pets: Under 30 lbs. welcome
Creature Comforts: CCTV, a/c, pool

Residence Inn
(800) 331-3131, (559) 222-8900
http://www.residenceinn.com
5322 N. Diana Ave.
120 rooms - $88-175
Pets: Welcome w/$6 fee, $75 dep.
Creature Comforts: CCTV, a/c, kit, cont. brkfst, pool, whirlpool

Rodeway Inn
(800) 228-2000, (559) 268-0363
http://www.rodeway.com
949 N. Parkway Dr.
48 rooms - $39-55
Pets: Welcome w/$5 fee
Creature Comforts: CCTV, a/c, refrig, cont. brkfst, pool

Super 8
(800) 800-8000, (559) 268-0741
http://www.super8.com
1087 North Parkway Dr.
48 rooms - $38-56
Pets: Welcome w/$5 fee
Creature Comforts: CCTV, a/c, refrig, micro, pool

Travelodge
(800) 578-7878, (559) 268-0711
http://www.travelodge.com
2345 N. Parkway Dr.
117 rooms - $36-48
Pets: Welcome
Creature Comforts: CCTV, a/c,
refrig, restaurant, pool

FULLERTON
Fullerton Inn
(714) 773-4900
2604 W. Orangethorpe Ave.
44 rooms - $35-59
Pets: Small pets welcome
Creature Comforts: CCTV, a/c,
refrig, micro, pool, whirlpool

Marriott Hotel
(800) 228-9290, (714) 738-7800
http://www.marriott.com
2701 E. Nutwood Ave.
225 rooms - $90-285
Pets: Small pets welcome
Creature Comforts: CCTV, a/c,
refrig, micro, restaurant, pool, hlth
clb, sauna, whirlpool

Motel 6
(800) 4-MOTEL6, (714) 992-0660
http://www.motel6.com
1415 S. Euclid St.
47 rooms - $36-44
Pets: Under 30 lbs. welcome
Creature Comforts: CCTV, a/c,
pool

GARBERVILLE
Best Western Humboldt House
(800) 528-1234, (707) 923-2771
http://www.bestwestern.com
701 Redwood Dr.
77 rooms - $50-95
Pets: Small pets welcome
Creature Comforts: CCTV, a/c,
kit, pool, whirlpool

Motel Garberville
(707) 923-2422
948 Redwood Dr.
30 rooms - $40-65
Pets: Welcome
Creature Comforts: CCTV, a/c,
kit

Sherwood Forest Motel
(707) 923-2721
814 Redwood Dr.
34 rooms - $56-95
Pets: Small pets welcome
Creature Comforts: CCTV, a/c,
kit, pool, whirlpool

GEORGETOWN
American River B&B
(800) 245-6566, (916) 333-4499
http://www.pcweb.net/ari
Orleans St., Box 43
rooms - $90-160
Pets: Welcome in certain rooms
Creature Comforts: Intriguing
Gold Country inn w/wrap-around
porches, down comforters, feather
beds, CCTV, a/c, refrig, fireplaces,
full brkfst, croquet field, gardens
and 80-ft redwoods surround pool
and whirlpool, wine tasting and
dinners can be arranged

GEYERSVILLE
Isis Oasis
(800) 679-PETS, (707) 857-3524
http://www.isisis.com/oasis.htm
20889 Geyersville Ave.
20 units - $60-215
Pets: Welcome
Creature Comforts: Eclectic,
assorted accommodations-from
yurts and teepees to wine cask rm
and trad. lodge rms, New Age
atmosphere, 500-year old fir tree,
Americana furnishings, stained
glass, handmade quilts, CCTV,
fireplaces, kit, restaurant, pool,
sauna, whirlpool, and small exotic
animal zoo

GILROY
Leavesley Inn
(800) 624-8225, (408) 847-5500
8430 Murray Ave.
48 rooms - $40-65
Pets: Welcome w/$10 dep.
Creature Comforts: CCTV,
VCR, a/c, refrig, micro, cont.
brkfst, pool, whirlpool

Motel 6
(800) 4-MOTEL6, (408) 842-6061
http://www.motel6.com
6110 Monterey Hwy.
94 rooms - $36-44
Pets: Under 30 lbs. welcome
Creature Comforts: CCTV, a/c,
pool

Rodeway Inn
(800) 228-2000, (408) 847-0688
http://www.rodeway.com
611 Leavesley Rd.
44 rooms - $35-85
Pets: Small pets w/$25 dep.
Creature Comforts: CCTV,
VCR, a/c, refrig, micro, pool,
whirlpool

Super 8 Motel
(800) 800-8000, (408) 848-4108
http://www.super8.com
8495 San Ysidro St.
52 rooms - $40-65
Pets: Small pets w/$30 dep.
Creature Comforts: CCTV, a/c,
refrig, pool

GLENDALE
Days Inn
(800) DAYS-INN, (818) 956-0202
http://www.daysinn.com
600 N. Pacific Ave.
120 rooms - $69-80
Pets: Welcome
Creature Comforts: CCTV, a/c,
refrig, pool, whirlpool

Red Lion
(800) RED-LION, (818) 956-5466
http://www.redlion.com
100 W. Glenoaks Rd.
346 rooms - $89-189
Pets: Welcome w/$15 fee
Creature Comforts: CCTV,
VCR, a/c, refrig, micro, Jacuzzi,
two restaurants, cont. brkfst, pool,
hlth clb, sauna, whirlpool

Vagabond Inn
(800) 522-1555, (818) 240-1770
http://www.vagabondinns.com
120 W. Colorado St.
52 rooms - $55-74
Pets: Welcome w/$5 fee
Creature Comforts: CCTV, a/c,
refrig, micro, pool

GOLETA
Motel 6
(800) 4-MOTEL6, (805) 964-3596
http://www.motel6.com
5897 Calle Real
87 rooms - $46-59
Pets: Under 30 lbs. welcome
Creature Comforts: CCTV, a/c,
pool

GRAEAGLE
Gray Eagle Lodge
(800) 635-8778, (530) 836-2511
http://www.grayeaglelodge.com
5000 Gold Lake Rd., Box 38
18 cabins - $150-235
Pets: Leashed pets w/$10 fee
Creature Comforts: A wonderful old-fashioned family owned and run resort, creek and pondside setting, simple accommodations and decor, CCTV, fireplaces, great restaurant, bar, swimming hole, mtn. bike trails, game room-billiards, fishing, access to golf, riding, rafting, waterfall

GRASS VALLEY
Alta Sierra Motel
(530) 273-9102
11858 Tammy Way
14 rooms - $40-150
Pets: Welcome w/$5 fee
Creature Comforts: CCTV, a/c, kit, pool, and golf/tennis privileges

Best Western Gold Country Inn
(800) 528-1234, (530) 273-1393
http://www.bestwestern.com
11972 Sutton Way
85 rooms - $50-98
Pets: Welcome w/$10 fee
Creature Comforts: CCTV, a/c, kit, pool, whirlpool

Coach & Four Motel
(530) 273-8009
628 S. Auburn St.
17 rooms - $50-80
Pets: Welcome
Creature Comforts: CCTV, a/c, refrig, micro, cont. brkfst

Golden Chain Motel
(530) 273-7279
Route 49
22 rooms - $40-80
Pets: Welcome w/$6 fee
Creature Comforts: CCTV, a/c, pool, and putting green

Holiday Lodge
(800) 742-7125, (530) 273-4406
1221 E. Main St.
38 rooms - $40-65
Pets: Welcome w/$10 fee
Creature Comforts: CCTV, a/c, cont. brkfst, pool

Swan-Levine House
(530) 272-1873
www.innsofthegoldcountry.com/
swan.htm
328 S. Church St.
4 rooms - $75-110
Pets: Welcome
Creature Comforts: 1867 Victorian B&B, artistic hosts created an eclectic and whimsical ambiance, handmade quilts, family heirlooms, intriguing collectibles and antiques, rooms w/white wicker, four poster beds, claw foot tubs, CCTV, VCR, fireplaces, kit, Jacuzzi, full brkfst, pool, badminton, print making studio

GROVELAND
The Groveland Hotel
(800) 273-3314, (209) 962-4000
http://www.groveland.com
18767 Main St.
17 rooms - $95-185
Pets: Welcome w/$10 fee
Creature Comforts: Restored historic mansion with antiques and decorative accents, old photographs, floral accents, handmade quilts, English and French antiques, down comforters, marble-topped dressers, teddy bears found throughout, CCTV, VCR, a/c, fireplace, Jacuzzis, restaurant, golf/tennis privileges

Hotel Charlotte
(800) 961-7799, (209) 962-6455
Main St.
11 rooms - $50-75
Pets: Welcome
Creature Comforts: Historic building with a pensione atmosphere, simple western appeal, striped and floral wallpapers, brass beds, claw foot tubs, CCTV, refrig, restaurant, cont. brkfst

Yosemite West Gate Motel
(800) 253-9673, (209) 962-5281
http://www.tales.com/ca/
yosemitewestgatemotel
7633 Route 120
45 rooms - $75-185
Pets: Welcome w/$10 fee
Creature Comforts: CCTV, a/c, refrig, micro, restaurant, pool, whirlpool, along a river

GUALALA
Gualala Country Inn
(800) 564-4466, (707) 884-4343
http://www.gualala.com
47955 Hwy. 1
20 rooms - $70-155
Pets: Welcome w/$10 fee
Creature Comforts: CCTV, fireplaces, kit, cont. brkfst, Jacuzzis, and ocean views

Surf Motel
(888) 451-SURF, (707) 884-3571
http://www.gualala.com
39170 Hwy. 1
20 rooms - $80-155
Pets: Welcome
Creature Comforts: CCTV, kit, and ocean views

GUERNEVILLE
Avalon Inn
(707) 869-9566
16484 - 4th St.
9 rooms - $50-139
Pets: Welcome
Creature Comforts: CCTV, kit, pool

Creekside Inn & Resort
(800) 776-6586, (707) 869-3623
http://www.creeksideinn.com
16180 Neeley Rd.
16 rooms - $65-180
Pets: Welcome w/credit card dep.
Creature Comforts: Charming inn and cottages, nestled under the redwoods along the Russian River, rms. w/handmade quilts, brass lamps, white wicker, American country antiques, CCTV, VCR, fireplace, kit, pool, Jacuzzi, creek views

Fern Grove Cottages
(707) 869-8105
http://www.ferngrove.com
16650 Hwy. 16
15 cabins - $69-145
Pets: "Good natured" pets welcome by arrangement
Creature Comforts: Classic 1920s cottages, knotty pine interior, TV, fireplace, Jacuzzi, cont. brkfst, pool

The Highlands
(707) 869-0333
http://www.travel.org/
HighlandsResort
14000 Woodland Dr.
15 cabins - $60-145
Pets: Welcome w$25 fee
Creature Comforts: TV, VCR,
fireplace, kit, pool, whirlpool

Santa Nella House
(707) 869-9488
12130 Rte. 116
4 rooms - $95-120
Pets: Welcome
Creature Comforts: 1870 Vict.,
CCTV, fireplace, refrig, full brkfst

HACIENDA
Motel 6
(800) 4-MOTEL6, (818) 968-9462
http://www.motel6.com
1154 S. 7th Ave.
154 rooms - $39-54
Pets: Under 30 lbs. welcome
Creature Comforts: CCTV, a/c

HALF MOON BAY
Holiday Inn Express
(800) HOLIDAY, (650) 726-3400
http://www.holiday-inn.com
230 Cabrillo Hwy.
48 rooms - $79-149
Pets: Welcome w/$10 fee
Creature Comforts: CCTV, a/c

Ramada Ltd.
(800) 2-Ramada, (650) 726-9700
http://www.ramada.com
3020 No. Cabrillo Hwy.
20 rooms - $70-125
Pets: Welcome w/$15 fee
Creature Comforts: CCTV, a/c,
refrig, micro, whirlpool

The Zaballa House
(650) 726-9123
www.whistlere.com/zaballa.rooms
324 Main St.
12 rooms - $75-285
Pets: Welcome w/$10 fee
Creature Comforts: Nicely
refurbished 1800's historic
landmark, homey appeal, four-
poster beds, vaulted ceilings and
detailed moldings, original
paintings, country décor, wicker,
ghost reputedly in residence,
CCTV, VCR, a/c, fireplaces, kit,
Jacuzzis, full brkfst, wine, gardens

HANFORD
Irwin St. Inn
(888) 583-8000, (559) 583-8000
http://www.kings.net/
irwinst2.html
522 N. Irwin St.
30 rooms - $70-110
Pets: Welcome w/$15 fee
Creature Comforts: Victorian
1880's inn w/antiques and stained
glass, Victorian ambiance, four-
poster beds, antiques, lace
curtains, potted plants, CCTV, a/c,
refrig, micro, covered verandah w/
umbrella tables, restaurant, full
brkfst, pool

Sequoia Inn
(559) 582-0338
1655 Mall Dr.
58 rooms - $75-110
Pets: Small pets w/$100 dep
Creature Comforts: CCTV, a/c,
refrig, cont. brkfst, and a pool

HARBOR CITY
Motel 6
(800) 4-MOTEL6, (310) 549-9560
http://www.motel6.com
820 W. Sepulveda Blvd.
57 rooms - $44-58
Pets: Under 30 lbs. welcome
Creature Comforts: CCTV, a/c,
pool

HAYWARD
Executive Inn
(800) 553-5083, (510) 732-6300
20777 Hesperian Blvd.
145 rooms - $78-99
Pets: Welcome
Creature Comforts: CCTV, a/c,
refrig, cont. brkfst, pool

Motel 6
(800) 4-MOTEL6, (510) 489-8333
http://www.motel6.com
30155 Industrial Pkwy SW
175 rooms - $44-58
Pets: Under 30 lbs. welcome
Creature Comforts: CCTV, a/c

Phoenix Lodge
(510) 786-2844
2286 Industrial Pkwy
70 rooms - $40-54
Pets: Welcome w/$25 dep.
Creature Comforts: CCTV, a/c,
refrig

Phoenix Lodge
(510) 786-0417
500 West A St.
70 rooms - $38-52
Pets: Welcome w/$25 dep.
Creature Comforts: CCTV, a/c,
refrig, restaurant

Vagabond Inn
(800) 522-1555, (510) 785-5480
http://www.vagabondinns.com
20455 Hesperian Blvd.
99 rooms - $50-75
Pets: Welcome w/$5 fee
Creature Comforts: CCTV, a/c,
refrig, cont. brkfst, pool, whirlpool

HEALDSBURG
Best Western Dry Creek Inn
(800) 528-1234, (707) 433-0300
http://www.bestwestern.com
198 Dry Creek Rd.
100 rooms - $60-105
Pets: Welcome w/$10 fee
Creature Comforts: CCTV, a/c,
refrig, pool, hlth clb, whirlpool

Fairview Motel
(707) 433-5548
74 Healdsburg Ave.
18 rooms - $45-90
Pets: Small pets w/CC dep.
Creature Comforts: CCTV, a/c,
refrig, pool, whirlpool, playground

Madrona Manor Country Inn
(800) 258-4003, (707) 433-4231
http://www.madronamanor.com
21 rooms & cottages - $140-265
Pets: Welcome w/$20 fee
Creature Comforts: Historic
Victorian landmark on eight
manicured acres, picturesque
gardens, Persian rugs, lovely
music room w/rosewood piano,
French objets d' art, four-poster
beds, high ceilings, Oriental
accents, CCTV, VCR, a/c, refrig,
fireplaces, Jacuzzi, lovely
restaurant, billiards, full brkfst,
pool, lawn games

HELENA
Trinity Canyon Lodge
(800) 354-9297, (530) 623-6318
http://www.virtualcities.com/ons/
ca/n/can95021.htm
Rte. 299, Box 51
10 cabins - $59-135
Pets: Welcome w/$5 fee
Creature Comforts: Set in the
heart of Shasta Trinity Nat'l
Forest, riverside, CCTV, fireplace,
kit, lodge-restaurant, river-pools,
great fishing, kayaking, rafting

HEMET
Best Western
(800) 528-1234, (909) 925-6605
http://www.bestwestern.com
2625 West Florida Ave.
69 rooms - $40-74
Pets: Welcome w/$10 fee
Creature Comforts: CCTV, a/c,
refrig, micro, pool, whirlpool

Coach Light Motel
(800) 678-0124, (909) 658-3237
1640 Florida Ave.
33 rooms - $30-45
Pets: Welcome w/$4 fee
Creature Comforts: CCTV,
VCR, a/c, refrig, micro, pool

Hemet Inn
(909) 929-6366
800 W. Florida Ave.
66 rooms - $35-45
Pets: Welcome w/$5 fee
Creature Comforts: CCTV, a/c,
kit, pool, whirlpool

Super 8 Motel
(800) 800-8000, (909) 658-2281
http://www.super8.com
3510 W. Florida Ave.
68 rooms - $40-52
Pets: Small pets welcome
Creature Comforts: CCTV,
VCR, a/c, refrig, micro, pool,
whirlpool

Travelodge
(800) 578-7878, (909) 766-1902
http://www.travelodge.com
1201 W. Florida Ave.
45 rooms - $40-54
Pets: Welcome w/$5 fee
Creature Comforts: CCTV, a/c,
refrig, micro, pool, whirlpool

HESPERIA
Days Inn
(800) DAYS-INN, (760) 948-0600
http://www.daysinn.com
14865 Bear Valley Rd.
24 rooms - $40-80
Pets: Welcome w/$10 fee
Creature Comforts: CCTV, a/c,
refrig, whirlpool

HIGHLAND
Super 8 Motel
(800) 800-8000, (909) 864-0100
http://www.super8.com
26667 E. Highland Ave.
39 rooms - $40-52
Pets: Small pets welcome
Creature Comforts: CCTV, a/c,
refrig, pool

HOLLISTER
Cinderella Motel-IMA
(800) 341-8000, (408) 637-5761
http://www.imalodging.com
110 San Felipe Rd.
20 rooms - $55-70
Pets: Welcome
Creature Comforts: CCTV, a/c,
refrig, cont. brkfst, pool

HOLLYWOOD
Best Western
(800) 528-1234, (213) 464-5181
http://www.bestwestern.com
6141 Franklin Ave.
80 rooms - $70-100
Pets: Small pets w/$25 fee
Creature Comforts: CCTV, a/c,
refrig, restaurant, pool

Motel 6
(800) 4-MOTEL6, (213) 464-6006
http://www.motel6.com
1738 N. Whitley Ave.
101 rooms - $46-59
Pets: Under 30 lbs. welcome
Creature Comforts: CCTV, a/c

HOMEWOOD
Homeside Motel
(530) 525-9990
5205 W. Lake Blvd.
9 rooms - $75-225
Pets: Welcome
Creature Comforts: CCTV,
refrig, micro, fireplace, hot tub

HOPE VALLEY
Sorensen's
(800) 423-9949, (530) 694-2203
http://www.virtualcities.com/ons/
ca/g/cag3601.htm
14255 Route 88
30 cabins - $65-350
Pets: Welcome in 4 cabins
Creature Comforts: Cabins
encircled by picturesque mtns,
lakes, and forests, rooms w/
fireplaces or woodstoves, informal
ambiance, kit, restaurant, game
room, xc-skiing, sauna, whirlpool,
walking trails, sleigh rides

HUNTINGTON LAKE
Lakeview Cottages
(562) 697-6556
58374 Huntington Lodge Rd.
11 cabins - $50-90
Pets: Welcome
Creature Comforts: CCTV, kit,
lake/boats

IDYLLWILD
Fireside Inn
(909) 659-2966
54540 N. Circle Dr.
7 units - $55-105
Pets: Small pets welcome
Creature Comforts: CCTV,
VCR, kit

Idyllwild Inn
(909) 659-2552
http://www.idyllwildinn.com
Box 115
20 cabins - $50-125
Pets: Welcome
Creature Comforts: CCTV,
fireplace, kit

Knotty Pine Cabins
(909) 659-2933
54340 Pine Crest Dr.
8 cabins - $55-130
Pets: Welcome
Creature Comforts: CCTV, a/c,
kit, and fireplaces

IMPERIAL
Best Western Imperial Inn
(800) 528-1234, (760) 355-4500
http://www.bestwestern.com
1093 Airport Blvd.
90 rooms - $45-85
Pets: Small pets welcome
Creature Comforts: CCTV, a/c,
refrig, micro, restaurant, pool, hlth
clb, sauna, whirlpool

 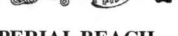 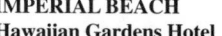
IMPERIAL BEACH
Hawaiian Gardens Hotel
(800) 334-3071, (619) 429-5303
http://www.hawaiian-gardens.com
1031 Imperial Beach Blvd.
40 rooms - $65-125
Pets: Small pets w/$50 dep.
Creature Comforts: CCTV, kit, pool, sauna

INDEPENDENCE
Courthouse Motel
(800) 801-0703
157 N. Edwards St.
10 rooms - $38-55
Pets: Welcome w/$6 fee
Creature Comforts: CCTV, a/c

Ray's Den Motel
(760) 878-2122
405 N. Edwards St.
8 rooms - $48-60
Pets: Welcome
Creature Comforts: CCTV, a/c

INDIO
Best Western Date Tree Hotel
(800) 528-1234, (760) 347-3421
http://www.bestwestern.com
81-909 Indio Blvd.
122 rooms - $75-180
Pets: Welcome w/$50 dep.
Creature Comforts: CCTV, VCR, a/c, refrig, micro, cont. brkfst, pool, hlth club, whirlpool, playground

Comfort Inn
(800) 228-5150, (760) 347-4044
http://www.comfortinn.com
43-505 Monroe St.
64 rooms - $45-110
Pets: Welcome
Creature Comforts: CCTV, a/c, refrig, pool, whirlpool

Motel 6
(800) 4-MOTEL6, (760) 342-6311
http://www.motel6.com
82195 Indio Blvd.
138 rooms - $39-50
Pets: Under 30 lbs. welcome
Creature Comforts: CCTV, a/c, pool

Palm Shadow Inn
(760) 347-3476
80-761 Hwy. 111
18 rooms - $50-135
Pets: Welcome w/$5 fee
Creature Comforts: CCTV, a/c, refrig, micro, pool, whirlpool

Penta Inn
(800) 897-9555, (760) 342-4747
84-115 Indio Blvd.
64 rooms - $30-45
Pets: Welcome w/credit card dep.
Creature Comforts: CCTV, a/c, cont. brkfst, pool

Royal Plaza Inn
(800) 228-9559, (760) 347-0911
http://www.royalplazainn.com
82-347 Hwy. 111
99 rooms - $55-99
Pets: Welcome
Creature Comforts: CCTV, a/c, refrig, restaurant, pool, whirlpool

Super 8 Motels
(800) 800-8000, (760) 342-0264
http://www.super8.com
81-753 Hwy. 111
70 rooms - $35-65
Pets: Welcome w/$20 dep.
Creature Comforts: CCTV, a/c, cont. brkfst, pool

INGLEWOOD
Econo Lodge
(800) 55-ECONO, (310) 674-8596
http://www.econolodge.com
439 Manchester Blvd.
26 rooms - $40-69
Pets: Welcome w/$8 fee
Creature Comforts: CCTV, a/c, refrig, pool

Hampton Inn
(800) Hampton, (310) 337-1000
http://www.hampton-inn.com
10300 La Cienega Blvd.
149 rooms - $65-90
Pets: Welcome
Creature Comforts: CCTV, a/c, hlth clb sauna

Motel 6
(800) 4-MOTEL6, (310) 419-1234
http://www.motel6.com
5101 W. Century Blvd.
253 rooms - $50-69
Pets: Small pets welcome
Creature Comforts: CCTV, a/c, pool

INVERNESS
Dancing Coyote Beach
(415) 669-7200
12794 Sir Francis Drake Blvd.
4 rooms - $100-140
Pets: Welcome in Acacia cottage
Creature Comforts: Unusual two-story cottages with floor-to-ceiling widows on Tomales Bay, cathedral ceilings-sky lights, wicker and rattan furnishings, seashore collectibles, fireplace, kit, cont. brkfst, hammocks, beach and dock

Manka's Inverness Lodge
(800) 58-LODGE, (415) 669-1034
http://www.mankas.com
Argyle Rd., Box 1110
10 rooms and cottages - $115-395
Pets: In certain rooms w/$50 fee
Creature Comforts: 1917 hunting and fishing lodge, bucolic hillside setting, hunting lodge ambiance, cypress beds, flannel fabrics, down comforters, Native American blankets, CCTV, VCR, fireplace, refrig, micro, restaurant w/innovative menu, full brkfst, whirlpool, decks w/Adirondack chairs

Point Reyes Cottages
(800) 808-9338, (415) 663-9338
PO Box 273
http://www.rosemarybb.com
3 cottages - $130-225
Pets: Welcome w/$25 fee
Creature Comforts: Spacious cottages with eclectic decor set on wooded hillsides, cathedral ceilings, Oriental and dhurrie rugs, country antiques, down comforters, Japanese accents, CCTV, stereo, fireplaces, kit, cont. brkfst, decks, garden spa

IRVINE
Atrium Hotel
(800) 854-3012, (949) 833-2770
http://www.atriumhotel.com
1870 MacArthur Blvd.
208 rooms - $70-120
Pets: Small pets w/$50 dep.
Creature Comforts: CCTV, VCR, a/c, refrig, micro, restaurant, pool, hlth clb and billiards

Holiday Inn
(800) HOLIDAY, (949) 863-1999
http://www.holiday-inn.com
17941 Von Karman Ave.
333 rooms - $130-295
Pets: $10 fee, $150 deposit
Creature Comforts: CCTV, a/c,
refrig, restaurant, two pools, hlth
clb, sauna, whirlpool

Homestead Village
(888) STAY-HSD, (949) 727-4228
http://www.stayhsd.com
30 Tecnology Dr.
149 rooms - $89-129
Pets: Welcome w/$75 fee
Creature Comforts: CCTV, a/c,
kit, and a cont. brkfst

La Quinta
(800) Nu-Rooms, (949) 551-0909
http://www.laquinta.com
14972 Sand Canyon Ave.
145 rooms - $55-85
Pets: Small pets welcome
Creature Comforts: CCTV, a/c,
refrig, micro, pool, hlth clb,
whirlpool

Marriott Hotel
(800) 228-9290, (714) 553-0100
http://www.marriott.com
18000 Von Karman Ave.
490 rooms - $79-789
Pets: Welcome
Creature Comforts: CCTV, a/c,
refrig, micro, restaurant, pool, hlth
clb, sauna, whirlpool, and tennis

Motel 6
(800) 4-MOTEL6, (714) 261-1515
http://www.motel6.com
1717 E. Dyer Rd.
144 rooms - $49-52
Pets: Under 30 lbs.welcome
Creature Comforts: CCTV, a/c,
pool

Residence Inn
(800) 331-3131, (714) 380-3000
http://www.residenceinn.com
10 Morgan St.
112 rooms - $79-159
Pets: Welcome w/$250 dep.
Creature Comforts: CCTV, a/c,
fireplace, kit, cont. brkfst, pool,
hlth clb, whirlpool

JACKSON
Amador Motel
(209) 223-0970
12408 Kennedy Flat Rd.
10 rooms - $40-65
Pets: Welcome
Creature Comforts: CCTV, a/c,
refrig, pool

El Campo Casa Motel
(209) 223-0100
12548 Kennedy Flat
15 rooms - $35-80
Pets: Welcome
Creature Comforts: CCTV, a/c,
pool

Jackson Holiday Lodge
(209) 223-0486
850 N. Rte. 49
35 rooms - $40-80
Pets: Welcome w/$10 dep.
Creature Comforts: CCTV, a/c,
kit, pool

JAMESTOWN
National Hotel
(800) 893-3446 (CA),
(209) 984-3446
http://www.national-hotel.com
77 Main St.
11 rooms - $65-95
Pets: /$5 fee & $50 dep.
Creature Comforts: Restored
historic property, authentic, period
wallpapers, antique wash basins,
country quilts, pull-chain
commodes, antique models,
CCTV, a/c, restaurant, massive
redwood bar, cont. brkfst, and a
resident ghost

Quality Sonora Country Inn
(800) 847-2211, (209) 984-0315
http://www.qualityinn.com
18755 Chanbroullian Ln.
61 rooms - $55-80
Pets: Welcome
Creature Comforts: CCTV, a/c,
cont. brkfst, pool

JENNER
Jenner Inn & Cottages
(800) 732-2377, (707) 865-2377
http://www.jennerinn.com
Coastal Hwy. 1
19 rooms & cottages - $85-275
Pets: In certain rooms w/$25 fee
Creature Comforts: Charming,
old-fashioned coastal inn and
cottages, Victorian/country decor,
antique beds, country quilts, white
wicker, French doors open to
decks, CCTV, VCR, fireplace, kit,
restaurant, cont. brkfst, whirlpools

Stillwater Cove Ranch
(707) 847-3227
22555 Hwy. 1
10 rooms & cottages - $55-85
Pets: Welcome w/$4 fee
Creature Comforts: A
refurbished old school set above
the craggy coastline— eclectic
and rustically inviting rms, seaside
collectibles, country décor,
fireplaces, kit, resident peacocks,
walks along boulder laden grassy
hills

JOSHUA TREE
Joshua Tree Inn
(800) 366-1444, (760) 366-1188
61259 - 29 Palms Ave.
10 rooms - $90-225
Pets: Welcome w/$10 fee
Creature Comforts: CCTV,
VCR, a/c, refrig, micro, cont.
brkfst, pool

JULIAN
Apple Tree Inn
(760) 765-0222
4360 Route 78
16 rooms - $60-85
Pets: Welcome w/credit card dep.
Creature Comforts: CCTV, a/c,
cont. brkfst, pool

Leelin Wikiup B&B
(800) 6-WIKIUP, (760) 765-1512
http://www.wikiupbnb.com
1645 Whispering Pines Dr.
3 rooms - $99-155
Pets: Under 10 lbs welcome
Creature Comforts: A wonderful
B&B w/decors ranging from
Native American to Victorian,
brass and canopy beds, bentwood
furnishings, Mexican pottery
fireplaces, CCTV, VCR, a/c,
Jacuzzis, full brkfst, whirlpool

 California

JUNE LAKE
Gull Lake Lodge
(760) 648-7516
Knoll and Bruce Sts.
14 rooms - $60-99
Pets: Welcome w/$5 fee
Creature Comforts: CCTV and kit

June Lake Motel and Cabins
(800) 648-6835 (CA),
(760) 648-6547
2716 Boulder Dr.
26 rooms - $50-96
Pets: Welcome w/$5 fee
Creature Comforts: CCTV, fireplaces, kit, whirlpool

June Lake Villager
(760) 648-7712
Route 158
22 rooms - $35-75
Pets: Small pets w/$5 fee
Creature Comforts: CCTV, fireplaces, kit, whirlpool

Reverse Creek Lodge
(800) 762-6440, (760) 648-7535
http://reversecreeklodge.com
15 rooms & cabins - $45-110
Pets: Summer only w/$25 fee
Creature Comforts: CCTV, a/c, fireplace, kit

KELSEYVILLE
Bell Haven Resort
(707) 279-4329
3415 White Oak Way
8 rooms - $85-105
Pets: Welcome w/$25 dep.
Creature Comforts: CCTV, VCR, kit, and beach/dock-boating

KENWOOD
The Little House B&GYODB
(707) 833-2536
http://www.kazwinery.com
215 Adobe Canyon Rd.
2 rooms - $125-165
Pets: Welcome w/$10 fee
Creature Comforts: An inventive and charming B&B with a home based winery, beamed ceilings, country décor, braided rugs, tab curtains, ceiling fans, fresh flowers, CCTV, VCR, a/c, kit, "Get Your Own Damn Breakfast", fenced back yard, smallest winery in Sonoma

KERNVILLE
Hi-Ho Resort Lodge
(760) 376-2671
11901 Sierra Way
8 rooms - $60-85
Pets: Welcome w/$10 fee
Creature Comforts: CCTV, woodstove, kit

Kern Lodge Motel
(760) 376-2223
67 Valley View Rd.
14 rooms - $50-105
Pets: Welcome w/$10 fee
Creature Comforts: CCTV, kit, pool

River View Lodge
(760) 376-6019
2 Sirretta St.
10 rooms - $50-99
Pets: Welcome w/$5 fee
Creature Comforts: CCTV, VCR, refrig, micro

KETTLEMAN
Best Western Olive Tree Inn
(800) 528-1234, (209) 386-4526
http://www.bestwestern.com
33415 Powers Dr.
55 rooms - $40-95
Pets: Small pets w/$45 dep.
Creature Comforts: CCTV, cont. brkfst, pool, whirlpool

KING CITY
Courtesy Inn
(800) 350-5616, (408) 385-4646
4 Broadway Circle
63 rooms - $40-145
Pets: Welcome w/$10 fee
Creature Comforts: CCTV, VCR, a/c, refrig, micro, Jacuzzis, pool, whirlpool

Motel 6
(800) 4-MOTEL6, (408) 385-5000
http://www.motel6.com
3 Broadway Circle
100 rooms - $35-44
Pets: Under 30 lbs. welcome
Creature Comforts: CCTV, a/c, pool

KINGS BEACH
Falcon Lodge
(916) 546-2583
8258 N. Lake Blvd.
30 rooms - $35-110
Pets: Welcome w/$50 dep.
Creature Comforts: CCTV, kit, pool, whirlpool

Stevenson's Holiday Inn
(800) 634-9141, (916) 546-2269
8742 N. Lake Blvd.
22 rooms - $45-100
Pets: Welcome w/$25 dep.
Creature Comforts: CCTV, refrig, micro, pool, whirlpool

KINGSBURG
Swedish Inn
(209) 897-1022
401 Conejo St.
48 rooms - $35-60
Pets: Welcome
Creature Comforts: CCTV, kit, pool, whirlpool

KLAMATH
Camp Marigold Motel
(800) 621-8513, (707) 482-3585
16101 Rte. 101
15 cabins - $42-160
Pets: Welcome
Creature Comforts: CCTV, kit

Requa Inn
(888) 788-1706, (707) 482-8205
451 Requa Rd.
10 rooms - $75-100
Pets: Welcome
Creature Comforts: Historic inn on river, CCTV, full brkfst, massage

LAGUNA BEACH
Best Western Laguna Brisas
(800) 528-1234, (949) 497-8306
http://www.bestwestern.com
1600 S. Coast Hwy.
64 rooms - $85-290
Pets: Small pets welcome
Creature Comforts: CCTV, a/c, refrig, cont. brkfst, pool, whirlpool

97

The Carriage House
(949) 494-8945
http://www.carriagehouse.com
1322 Catalina St.
6 suites - $95-165
Pets: Welcome w/$10 fee
Creature Comforts: Colonial saltbox in quiet neighborhood, inviting brick courtyard w/ fountain, finches and tropical setting, theme bedrooms, brass and four poster beds, antiques, Japanese accents, claw foot tubs, hand-painted tiles, CCTV, kit, full brkfst

Casa Laguna Inn
(800) 233-0449, (949) 494-2996
2510 S. Coast Hwy.
21 rooms - $70-255
Pets: Welcome w/$5 fee
Creature Comforts: Mission-style inn set on terraced grounds with tropical ambiance and water views, subterranean library, antique and rattan furnishings, traditional décor w/seaside twist, beamed ceilings, CCTV, fireplaces, balconies, kit, full brkfst, pool

Vacation Village
(800) 843-6895, (949) 494-8566
647 S. Coast Hwy.
125 rooms - $80-295
Pets: In the wintertime w/$10 fee
Creature Comforts: CCTV, refrig, micro, restaurant, cont. brkfst, two pools, whirlpool

LAGUNA HILLS
Laguna Hills Lodge
(800) 782-1188, (714) 830-2550
23932 Paseo de Valencia
120 rooms - $50-80
Pets: Welcome w/$5 fee
Creature Comforts: CCTV, a/c, refrig, micro, pool, sauna, whirlpool

LA HABRA
Motel 6
(800) 4-MOTEL6, (310) 694-2158
870 N. Beach Blvd.
88 rooms - $34-54
Pets: Under 30 lbs. welcome
Creature Comforts: CCTV, a/c, pool

LA JOLLA
Andrea Villa Inn
(800) 411-2141, (619) 459-3311
www.andreavilla.com
2402 Torrey Pines Rd.
50 rooms - $70-175
Pets: $10 fee, $25 deposit
Creature Comforts: CCTV, a/c, kit, cont. brkfst, pool, whirlpool

Holiday Inn Express
(800) HOLIDAY, (619) 552-1234
http://www.holiday-inn.com
6705 La Jolla Blvd.
60 rooms - $80-175
Pets: Welcome w/$10 fee
Creature Comforts: CCTV, a/c, kit, pool, whirlpools

La Jolla Marriott
(800) 228-9290, (619) 587-1414
http://www.marriott.com
4240 La Jolla Village Dr.
360 rooms - $129-695
Pets: Small pets welcome
Creature Comforts: CCTV, VCR, a/c, refrig, micro, restaurant, pool, hlth clb, sauna, whirlpool

Residence Inn
(800) 331-3131, (619) 587-1770
http://www.residenceinn.com
8901 Gilman Dr.
288 rooms - $95-325
Pets: $6 fee, $150 deposit
Creature Comforts: CCTV, VCR, a/c, fireplace, kit, restaurant, cont. brkfst, two pools, hlth clb, whirlpools, and sport courts

LAKE ARROWHEAD
Tree Top Lodge
(800) 358-8733, (909) 337-2311
27992 Rainbow Dr.
20 rooms - $60-135
Pets: Welcome
Creature Comforts: CCTV, VCR, fireplaces, refrig, pool, whirlpool, and hiking trails

Lake Arrowhead Resort
(800) 800-6792, (909) 336-1511
27984 Route 189
261 rooms - $119-425
Pets: Welcome w/$75 dep.
Creature Comforts: CCTV, a/c, fireplace, restaurant, pool, hlth clb, sauna, whirlpool, racquetball, tennis, and a lake

Prophets' Paradise B&B
(800) 987-2231, (909) 336-1969
26845 Modoc Lane
3 rooms - $90-165
Pets: Welcome
Creature Comforts: A charming Tudor-style B&B w/homey ambiance, CCTV, VCR, a/c, fireplace, Jacuzzi, full brkfst, hlth club, billiards

LAKE ELSINORE
Lakeview Inn
(909) 674-9694
31808 Casino Dr.
55 rooms - $65-80
Pets: Small pets welcome
Creature Comforts: CCTV, VCR, a/c, refrig, micro, pool, whirlpool

LAKE TAHOE (Area)
Alder Inn
(800) 544-0056, (530) 544-4485
1072 Ski Run Blvd.
(S. Lake Tahoe)
25 rooms - $40-115
Pets: Welcome w/$10 fee
Creature Comforts: CCTV, kit, pool, whirlpool

Beachside Inn
(800) 884-4920, (530) 544-2400
930 Park Ave.
18 rooms - $40-125
Pets: Welcome w/$5 fee, $50 dep.
Creature Comforts: CCTV, sauna, whirlpool

Best Western Lake Tahoe Inn
(800) 528-1234, (530) 541-2010
http://www.bestwestern.com
4110 Lake Tahoe Blvd.
(S. Lake Tahoe)
400 rooms - $49-169
Pets: Welcome
Creature Comforts: CCTV, a/c, refrig, cont. brkfst, 2 pools, whirlpool

Blue Jay Lodge
(800) 258-3529, (530) 544-5232
4133 Cedar Ave. (S. Lake Tahoe)
65 rooms - $45-180
Pets: W/$10 fee, $100 deposit
Creature Comforts: CCTV, fireplace, kit, Jacuzzi, pool, whirlpool

Blue Lake Motel
(530) 541-2399
1055 Ski Run Blvd.
(S. Lake Tahoe)
22 rooms - $45-110
Pets: Welcome w/$10 fee
Creature Comforts: CCTV, pool,
whirlpool

Calvadero Motel
(530) 541-3900
988 Stateline Ave. (S. Lake Tahoe)
20 rooms - $42-105
Pets: Welcome
Creature Comforts: CCTV, a/c,
refrig, and beach access

Days Inn
(800) DAYS-INN, (530) 541-4800
http://www.daysinn.com
968 Park Ave. (S. Lake Tahoe)
59 rooms - $55-105
Pets: Welcome w/$5 fee, $25 dep.
Creature Comforts: CCTV, cont.
brkfst, pool, sauna, whirlpool

Echo Creek Mtn. Ranch
(800) 462-5397, (530) 544-5397
www.tahoevacationguide.com
Myers Grade Rd., Box 20088
(S. Lake Tahoe)
1 house - $835-1,200
Pets: Welcome
Creature Comforts: A handsome
mtn. log cabin on 16 acres, log
beds, knotty pine walls, CCTV,
VCR, fireplaces, skylights,
gourmet kit, Jacuzzi, hot tub,
creek, game room, golf pool table,
steam train

Falcon Motor Lodge
(530) 546-2583
8258 N. Lake Blvd.
(Kings Beach)
30 rooms - $45-110
Pets: Welcome w/$50 dep.
Creature Comforts: CCTV, kit,
pool, whirlpool, beach

High Country Lodge
(530) 541-0508
1227 Emerald Bay Rd.
(S. Lake Tahoe)
15 rooms - $30-80
Pets: Welcome w/$5 fee, $50 dep.
Creature Comforts: CCTV,
refrig, micro, whirlpool

Holiday House Chalets
(800) 294-6378, (530) 546-2369
http://www.tahoeguide.com/go/
holidayhouse
7276 N. Lake Blvd. (Tahoe Vista)
7 suites - $95-165
Pets: Welcome
Creature Comforts: CCTV, kit,
fireplace, knotty pine walls,
whirlpool on water, on lake/decks/
private beach

Inn at Heavenly
(800) MY-CABIN
http://www.800mycabin.com
1261 Ski Run Blvd.
(S. Lake Tahoe)
14 rooms - $90-355
Pets: W/$20 fee & $100 dep.
Creature Comforts: Log cabins
w/knotty pine accents and country
décor, stenciling, fieldstone
fireplaces, dried flowers and
wreaths, log furnishings, country
quilts, CCTV, VCR, a/c, kit,
Jacuzzi, cont. brkfst, game room,
and water views

La Baer Inn
(800) 544-5575, (530) 544-2139
4133 Lake Tahoe Blvd.
(S.Lake Tahoe)
33 rooms - $50-120
Pets: Welcome w/$10 dep.
Creature Comforts: CCTV

Lakepark Lodge
(530) 541-5004
4081 Cedar Ave. (S. Lake Tahoe)
21 rooms - $40-70
Pets: Small pets w/$10 fee
Creature Comforts: CCTV, a/c,
refrig, whirlpool

Lampliter Motel
(530) 544-2936
4143 Cedar Ave.(S. Lake Tahoe)
28 rooms - $40-110
Pets: Welcome w/$8 fee and
credit card deposit
Creature Comforts: CCTV
whirlpool

Matterhorn Motel
(530) 541-0367
2187 Lake Tahoe Blvd.
(S. Lake Tahoe)
19 rooms - $55-90
Pets: Welcome w/$10 fee
Creature Comforts: CCTV, kit,
cont. brkfst, pool, whirlpool

The Montgomery Inn
(800) 624-8224, (530) 544-3871
http://tahoemontgomeryinn.com
966 Modesto Ave. (S. Lake Tahoe)
22 rooms - $30-54
Pets: Welcome w/$5 fee
Creature Comforts: CCTV, kit

Motel 6
(800) 4-MOTEL6, (530) 542-1400
http://www.motel6.com
2375 Lake Tahoe Blvd.
(S. Lake Tahoe)
143 rooms - $39-54
Pets: Under 30 lbs. welcome
Creature Comforts: CCTV, a/c,
pool

Norfolk Woods Inn
(530) 525-5000
http://www.tahoecountry.com/
wslodging/nw.html
6941 W. Lake Tahoe Blvd.
(Tahoma)
14 rooms & cottages - $75-175
Pets: Welcome w/$10 fee
Creature Comforts: Knotty pine
lodge with beamed ceilings and
cozy cottages, CCTV, VCR, stone
fireplaces, kit, restaurant, bar,
cont. brkfst, pool, whirlpool, rqst
Amy's Cottage— our favorite

Ravenwood Hotel
(800) 659-4185
4075 Manzanita Ave.
21 rooms - $80-75
Pets: Welcome w/$10 fee
Creature Comforts: CCTV,
VCR, fireplaces, refrig, micro,
Jacuzzis, cont. brkfst, lap pool,
and spa

Rodeway Inn
(800) 228-2000, (530) 541-7900
http://www.rodeway.com
4082 Lake Tahoe Blvd.
(S. Lake Tahoe)
99 rooms - $40-85
Pets: Welcome w/$15 fee
Creature Comforts: CCTV, pool,
whirlpool

Rustic Cottages
(530) 546-3523
7449 N. Lake Blvd. (Tahoe Vista)
http://www.rusticcottages.com
18 cottages - $55-159
Pets: Welcome w/$10 fee
Creature Comforts: CCTV,
VCR, fireplace, kit, cont. brkfst,
sledding/mtn bikes

Super 8 Motel
(800) 800-8000, (530) 544-3476
http://www.super8.com
3600 Lake Tahoe Blvd.
(S. Lake Tahoe)
110 rooms - $45-115
Pets: Welcome w/$10 fee
Creature Comforts: CCTV, kit,
restaurant, pool, whirlpool,
playground

Tahoe Colony Inn
(530) 655-6481
http://www.americana-inns.com
3794 Montreal St. (S. Lake Tahoe)
104 rooms - $45-115
Pets: Welcome
Creature Comforts: CCTV, a/c,
cont. brkfst, pool, whirlpool

Tahoe Keys Resort
(800) 438-8246, (916) 544-5397
http://www.tahoekeysresort.com
599 Tahoe Keys Blvd.
(S. Lake Tahoe)
70 condos & homes - $125-1,800
Pets: Welcome w/$25 fee, credit
card dep.
Creature Comforts: A great
assortment of year-round
waterfront vacation home rentals
and condos, 750-acre waterfront
resort, CCTV, cathedral ceilings-
skylights, rock fireplaces, kit,
pool, hlth clb, whirlpools, pool
tables, private dock-boating,
tennis

Tahoe Lake Cottages
(800) 824-6348
7018 W. Lake Blvd.
10 cottages - $150-265
Pets: In certain units
Creature Comforts: Fireplace,
kit, pool, whirlpool, lawn games

Tahoe Marina Inn
(530) 541-2180
930 Bal BiJou Rd.
(S. Lake Tahoe)
78 rooms - $70-190
Pets: Small pets welcome
Creature Comforts: CCTV,
fireplace, kit, pool, sauna

Tahoe Valley Motel
(800) 669-7544, (530) 541-0353
2241 Lake Tahoe Blvd.
(S. Lake Tahoe)
20 rooms - $95-200
Pets: Small pets w/$10 fee
Creature Comforts: CCTV,
fireplace, refrig, pool, whirlpool

Torchlite Inn
(800) 455-6060, (530) 541-2363
965 Park Ave. (S. Lake Tahoe)
32 rooms - $40-85
Pets: Welcome w/$10 dep.
Creature Comforts: CCTV
whirlpool

Tradewinds Motel
(800) 624-1829, (530) 544-6459
944 Friday St. (S. Lake Tahoe)
70 rooms - $30-90
Pets: Welcome w/$5 fee, $50 dep.
Creature Comforts: CCTV, pool,
whirlpools

LAKEHEAD
Antler's Resort
(800) 238-3924, (530) 238-2553
Box 140
3 cabins/15 houseboats - $90-175
Pets: Welcome w/$5 fee
Creature Comforts: CCTV,
fireplace, kit, store, pool, spa, and
a marina

Sugarloaf Cabins
(530) 238-2448
http://www.shastacabins.com
19667 Lake Shore Dr.
16 cabins - $60-130
Pets: Welcome
Creature Comforts: CCTV, kit,
pool

Tsasdi Resort
(800) 995-0291, (530) 238-2575
http://www.snowcrest.net/tsasdi
19990 Lakeshore Dr.
20 cabins - $50-195
Pets: Welcome, one per cabin, not
left unattended
Creature Comforts: CCTV, a/c,
kit, pool, sport courts, dock

LA MESA
Comfort Inn
(800) 228-5150, (619) 698-7747
http://www.comfortinn.com
8000 Parkway Dr.
125 rooms - $45-70
Pets: Welcome w/$50 dep.
Creature Comforts: CCTV, a/c,
refrig, pool, whirlpool

E-Z 8 Motel
(800) 326-6835, (619) 698-9444
7851 Fletcher Pkwy
105 rooms - $35-65
Pets: Welcome
Creature Comforts: CCTV, a/c,
refrig, pool, whirlpool

Motel 6
(800) 4-MOTEL6, (619) 464-7151
http://www.motel6.com
7621 Alvarado Rd.
120 rooms - $34-48
Pets: Under 30 lbs. welcome
Creature Comforts: CCTV, a/c,
pool

LA MIRADA
Residence Inn
(800) 331-3131, (714) 523-2800
http://www.residenceinn.com
14419 Firestone Blvd.
145 rooms - $125-195
Pets: Small pets welcome w/$5
fee, credit card deposit
Creature Comforts: CCTV,
VCR, a/c, fireplace, kit, cont.
brkfst, pool, hlth clb, whirlpool,
sports court

LANCASTER
Best Western Antelope Inn
(800) 528-1234, (805) 948-4651
http://www.bestwestern.com
44055 N. Sierra Hwy.
150 rooms - $60-135
Pets: Welcome w/$25 fee
Creature Comforts: CCTV, a/c,
refrig, micro, pool, hlth club,
whirlpool

Desert Inn Motor Hotel
(805) 942-8401
44219 North Sierra Hwy.
145 rooms - $60-85
Pets: Welcome w/$25 dep.
Creature Comforts: CCTV,
VCR, a/c, kit, restaurant, pool,
hlth clb, sauna, whirlpool, and
sports court

Motel 6
(800) 4-MOTEL6, (805) 948-0435
http://www.motel6.com
43540 - 17th St. W.
72 rooms - $34-48
Pets: Under 30 lbs. welcome
Creature Comforts: CCTV, a/c,
pool

LA PALMA
La Quinta Inn
(800) Nu-Rooms, (714) 670-1400
http://www.la quinta.com
3 Centerpointe Dr.
155 rooms - $50-69
Pets: Small pets welcome
Creature Comforts: CCTV, a/c,
refrig, pool, hlth clb, whirlpool

LA QUINTA
La Quinta Resort & Club
(800) 598-3828, (619) 564-4111
http://www.laquintaresort.com
640 rooms - $160-2,400
Pets: Under 50 Lbs. w/$100 fee
Creature Comforts: Lavish
Spanish-style resort w/picturesque
mountainside setting, 45
beautifully landscaped acres w/
fountains, streams, and gardens;
luxuriously appointed casitas,
four-poster beds, antiques, desert
décor, beamed ceilings, Native
American accents, CCTV, VCR,
a/c, fireplaces, kit, Jacuzzis,
restaurant, 24 pools, hlth clb,
saunas, spa, whirlpools, tennis
program, shops, 72 holes of golf

LASSEN NAT'L PARK
Drakesbad Guest Ranch
(530) 529-1512
CR Chester Warner Valley
19 units - $100-210 (AP)
Pets: Leashed dogs welcome
Creature Comforts: A rustic old-
fashioned ranch w/out electricity,
booked 2-years in advance,
woodstove, restaurant, showers in
bungalows, horses, bathhouses,
pool heated by hot springs

LATHROP
Days Inn
(800) DAYS-INN, (209) 982-1959
http://www.daysinn.com
14750 S. Harlan Rd.
55 rooms - $75-90
Pets: Welcome w/$8 fee
Creature Comforts: CCTV, a/c,
cont. brkfst, whirlpool

LAYTONVILLE
Gentle Valley Ranch
(707) 984-8456
Box 1535
14 rooms - $36-45
Pets: Welcome w/$3 fee
Creature Comforts: Sat-TV, a/c

LEBEC
Flying J Inn
(805) 248-2700
42810 Frazier Mtn Park Rd.
80 rooms - $50-75
Pets: Welcome w/$20 dep.
Creature Comforts: CCTV,
VCR, a/c, refrig, restaurant, pool,
whirlpool

LEE VINING
Murphey's Motel
(800) 334-6316, (760) 647-6316
Route 395
44 rooms - $40-99
Pets: Welcome w/$5 fee
Creature Comforts: CCTV, kit,
sauna, pool, whirlpool

LEMOORE
Best Western Vineyard Inn
(800) 528-1234, (209) 924-1261
http://www.bestwestern.com
877 East D St.
66 rooms - $50-64
Pets: Welcome w/$50 dep.
Creature Comforts: CCTV,
VCR, a/c, refrig, pool

LEWISTON
Lakeview Terrace Resort
(530) 778-3803
http://www.campgrounds.com/
lakeview
Star Rte., Box 250
12 cabins - $50-109
Pets: Welcome w/$3 fee
Creature Comforts: CCTV, kit,
pool, lawn games, lake/boats

Trinity Alps Resort
(916) 286-2205
http://www.trinityalps.com
43 cabins - $455-875/week
Pets: Welcome
Creature Comforts: Great old-
fashioned 1923 cabin resort set in
90 acres of woods, on Stuart Forks
— a 95% return rate, informal
family atmosphere, casual
mountain decor, fireplace, dining
room, soda fountain, general store,
tennis, panning for gold, bonfires,
lawn sports, game room,
community center-square dances,
swimming bridge, riding

LINDSAY
Olive Tree Inn
(800) 366-4469, (209) 562-5188
390 North Route 65
50 rooms - $40-52
Pets: Welcome w/$5 fee
Creature Comforts: CCTV, a/c,
refrig, micro, pool, whirlpool

LITTLE RIVER
Inn at School House Creek
(800) 731-5525, (707) 937-5525
www.schoolhouse creek.com
7051 N. Hwy. 1
13 cottages - $115-190
Pets: In ltd. cottages w/$15 fee
Creature Comforts: Set on 8
hillside acres, 1930's inn tucked
behind white picket fence, part of
historic ranch, main inn has
redwood paneled walls and
coffered ceilings, overstuffed
furnishings, dhurrie rugs, CCTV,
fireplaces, kit, dining rm, cont.
brkfst, lawn games, whirlpool,
gardens and giant cypress

S.S. Seafoam Lodge
(800) 606-1827, (707) 937-1827
http://www.seafoamlodge.com
6751 N. Rte. 1
24 rooms - $95-225
Pets: Welcome w/$10 fee
Creature Comforts: Rustic motor
lodge set on grassy hillside w/
distant water views, cheery
country décor, paneled walls,
CCTV, fireplaces, kit, baskets of
potpourri and salt water taffy,
whirlpool, cont. brkfst

LIVERMORE
Motel 6
(800) 4-MOTEL6, (925) 443-5300
http://www.motel6.com
4673 Lassen Rd.
102 rooms - $34-44
Pets: Under 30 lbs. welcome
Creature Comforts: CCTV, a/c,
pool

Hampton Inn,
(800) Hampton, (925) 606-6400
http://www.hampton-inn.com
8250 Constitution Dr.
80 rooms - $89-129
Pets: Small pets welcome
Creature Comforts: CCTV, a/c,
refrig, micro, pool, whirlpool

Residence Inn
(800) 331-3131, (925) 373-1800
http://www.residenceinn.com
1000 Airway Blvd.
98 rooms - $90-169
Pets: Welcome w/$7 fee, $75 dep.
Creature Comforts: CCTV, a/c,
kit, cont. brkfst, pool, hlth clb,
sauna, whirlpool

LODI
Best Western Royal Host
(800) 528-1234, (209) 369-8484
http://www.bestwestern.com
710 So. Cherokee Lane
48 rooms - $45-80
Pets: Small pets in smoking rms
Creature Comforts: CCTV, a/c,
refrig, Jacuzzis, cont. brkfst, pool

Comfort Inn
(800) 228-5150, (209) 367-4848
http://www.comfortinn.com
118 North Cherokee Lane
54 rooms - $60-110
Pets: Welcome w/$5 fee
Creature Comforts: CCTV,
VCR, a/c, refrig, micro, pool, hlth
clb, whirlpool

Wine and Roses Country Inn
(209) 334-6988
http://www.winerose.com
2505 W. Turner Rd.
10 rooms - $129-175
Pets: Welcome in 3 rooms
Creature Comforts: Classic 1902
country inn on five acres, lovely
8,000 sq. ft. main house, country
furnishings and decor, antiques,
beamed and vaulted ceilings,
handmade quilts, brass and four-
poster beds, white wicker, floral
accents, brass lamps, CCTV, a/c,
refrig, decks, fireplace, restaurant-
patio w/umbrella tables, full
brkfst, comp. wine, and lovely
rose gardens

LOMITA
El Dorado Coast Hotel
(310) 534-0700
2037 Pacific Coast Hwy.
60 rooms - $45-65
Pets: Welcome w/$50 dep.
Creature Comforts: CCTV, a/c,
refrig, pool, sauna, whirlpool

LOMPOC
Best Western Vandenberg Inn
(800) 528-1234, (805) 735-7731
http://www.bestwestern.com
940 E. Ocean Ave.
82 rooms - $45-65
Pets: Small pets w/$10 fee
Creature Comforts: CCTV, a/c,
refrig, micro, pool, hlth clb, sauna,
and a whirlpool

Inn of Lompoc
(805) 735-7744
1122 North H St.
90 rooms - $50-75
Pets: Welcome w/$15 fee
Creature Comforts: CCTV, a/c,
refrig, pool, hlth clb, whirlpool

Motel 6
(800) 4-MOTEL6, (805) 735-7631
http://www.motel6.com
1521 N. H St.
132 rooms - $28-35
Pets: Under 30 lbs. welcome
Creature Comforts: CCTV, a/c,
pool

Quality Inn
(800) 228-5151, (805) 735-8555
http://www.qualityinn.com
1621 North H St.
220 rooms - $60-99
Pets: Welcome w/$20 fee
Creature Comforts: CCTV, a/c,
refrig, micro, cont. brkfst, pool,
hlth clb access, whirlpool, and
massage

Tally Ho Motor Inn
(805) 735-6444
1020 E. Ocean Ave.
54 rooms - $30-70
Pets: Welcome w/$10 fee
Creature Comforts: CCTV,
VCR, a/c, refrig, micro, sauna,
whirlpool

LONE PINE
Alabama Hills Inn
(800) 800-5026, (760) 876-8700
http://www.touringusa.com
1920 S. Main St.
59 rooms - $50-65
Pets: Welcome w/$5 fee
Creature Comforts: CCTV, a/c,
refrig, micro, cont. brkfst, pool

Best Western Frontier Motel
(800) 528-1234, (760) 876-5571
http://www.bestwestern.com
1008 So. Main St.
73 rooms - $40-85
Pets: Welcome in 1 room
Creature Comforts: CCTV, a/c,
refrig, pool, whirlpools

Dow Villa Motel
(800) 824-9317, (760) 876-5521
www.dowvillamotel.com
310 S. Main St.
39 rooms - $55-105
Pets: Welcome w/credit card dep.
Creature Comforts: CCTV,
VCR, a/c, refrig, micro, pool,
whirlpool

National 9 Trails Motel
(760) 876-5555
633 S. Main St.
18 rooms - $30-90
Pets: Small pets w/$5 fee
Creature Comforts: CCTV, a/c,
refrig, micro, pool

LONG BEACH

Best Western
(800) 528-1234, (562) 599-5555
http://www.bestwestern.com
1725 Long Beach Blvd.
100 rooms - $58-99
Pets: Small pets welcome
Creature Comforts: CCTV,
VCR, a/c, refrig, micro, cont.
brkfst, pool

Comfort Inn
(800) 221-2222, (562) 597-3374
http://www.comfortinn.com
3201 E. Pacific Coast Hwy.
65 rooms - $50-78
Pets: Welcome
Creature Comforts: CCTV, a/c,
refrig, pool, whirlpool

Days Inn
(800) DAYS-INN, (562) 591-0088
http://www.daysinn.com
1500 E. Pacific Coast Hwy.
78 rooms - $45-90
Pets: Welcome w/$5 fee
Creature Comforts: CCTV, a/c,
refrig, micro, Jacuzzis, cont.
brkfst, whirlpool

Guesthouse Hotel
(800) 990-9991, (562) 597-1341
5325 E. Pacific Coast Hwy.
144 rooms - $90-155
Pets: Welcome w/$50 dep.
Creature Comforts: CCTV,
VCR, a/c, refrig, micro, Jacuzzis,
cont. brkfst, pool, and health club
access

Hilton Hotel
(800) HILTONS, (562) 983-3400
http://www.hilton.com
Two World Trade Center
392 rooms - $100-1,450
Pets: Under 25 lbs. welcome
Creature Comforts: CCTV, a/c,
refrig, restaurant, pool, hlth clb,
whirlpool, steam room, and ocean
views

Holiday Inn, Airport
(800) HOLIDAY, (562) 597-4401
http://www.holiday-inn.com
2640 Lakewood Blvd.
232 rooms - $60-135
Pets: Small pets welcome
Creature Comforts: CCTV, a/c,
refrig, restaurant, pool, hlth clb

Motel 6
(800) 4-MOTEL6, (562) 597-1311
http://www.motel6.com
5665 E. 7th St.
42 rooms - $48-59
Pets: Under 30 lbs. welcome
Creature Comforts: CCTV, a/c

Ramada Inn
(800) 2-Ramada, (562) 597-1341
http://www.ramada.com
5325 E. Pacific Coast Hwy.
148 rooms - $80-169
Pets: Welcome w/$25 dep.
Creature Comforts: CCTV, a/c,
kit, restaurant, pool, whirlpools

Travelodge Resort and Marina
(800) 578-7878, (562) 435-2471
http://www.travelodge.com
80 Atlantic Ave.
63 rooms - $50-110
Pets: Welcome w/$5 fee
Creature Comforts: CCTV, a/c,
refrig, restaurant, pool

Vagabond Inn
(800) 522-1555, (562) 435-7621
http://www.vagabondinns.com
185 Atlantic Ave.
50 rooms - $45-70
Pets: Welcome w/$5 fee
Creature Comforts: CCTV, a/c,
cont. brkfst, pool

LOS ANGELES

Best Western Hollywood Hills
(800) 528-1234, (213) 464-5181
http://www.bestwestern.com
6141 Franklin Ave.
82 rooms - $59-99
Pets: Small pets w/$10 fee
Creature Comforts: CCTV, a/c,
kit, restaurant, cont. brkfst, pool

Best Western Mission Hills
(800) 528-1234, (818) 891-1771
http://www.bestwestern.com
11250 Santa Monica Blvd.
115 rooms - $60-79
Pets: Welcome w/adv. notice
Creature Comforts: CCTV, a/c,
refrig, cont. brkfst, pool

Beverly Hills Plaza Hotel
(800) 800-1234, (310) 278-3325
http://www.placestostay.com
10300 Wilshire Blvd.
116 suites - $160-295
Pets: $100 fee, $500 deposit
Creature Comforts: CCTV, a/c,
refrig, restaurant, pool, hlth clb,
sauna, whirlpool

Beverly Laurel Motor Hotel
(800) 962-3824, (213) 651-2441
8018 Beverly Blvd.
52 rooms - $55-75
Pets: Welcome w/$5 fee
Creature Comforts: CCTV, a/c,
kit, restaurant, pool

Century Plaza Hotel
(800) 228-3000, (310) 277-2000
http://www.westin.com
2025 Ave. of the Stars
1075 rooms - $140-2,500
Pets: Small pets welcome
Creature Comforts: CCTV,
VCR, a/c, refrig, micro, Jacuzzis,
restaurant, two pools, hlth clb,
sauna, whirlpools

Century Wilshire Hotel
(800) 421-7223, (310) 474-4506
http://centurywilshirehotel.com
10776 Wilshire Blvd.
99 rooms - $65-95
Pets: Welcome w/$150 fee
Creature Comforts: CCTV, a/c,
kit, cont. brkfst, pool

Chateau Marmont Hotel
(800) 242-8328, (213) 656-1010
8221 Sunset Blvd.
63 rooms - $150-1,275
Pets: Welcome w/$100 fee
Creature Comforts: Neo-Gothic
chateau, built in 1929 and still a
quiet favorite among Hollywood's
famous, understated decor, CCTV,
VCR, a/c, kit, restaurant, pool,
hlth clb

Checkers Hotel
(800) Wyndham, (213) 624-0000
http://www.wyndham.com
535 S. Girard Ave.
195 rooms - $109-1,000
Pets: Welcome w/$25 fee
Creature Comforts: Boutique hotel, recent restoration, inviting décor w/French, English, and Oriental furnishings, marble foyer, Chinese lacquered boxes, Japanese screens, our favorite rooms are the "08" (corner) chambers, CCTV, VCR, a/c, refrig, micro, Jacuzzis, restaurant, pool, hlth clb, sauna, whirlpools

Continental Plaza LAX
(800) 529-4683, (310) 645-4600
9750 Airport Blvd.
575 rooms - $75-135
Pets: Welcome w/$10 & $75 dep.
Creature Comforts: CCTV, VCR, a/c, refrig, micro, restaurant, pool, hlth clb

Four Seasons Hotel
(800) 332-3442, (310) 273-2222
http://www.fshr.com
300 S. Doheny Dr.
274 rooms - $295-4,400
Pets: Under 15 lbs. welcome
Creature Comforts: Exquisite European-style hotel with pastel colors set a few minutes from Beverly Hills, residential décor, high-ceilings, French doors open to balconies, four poster beds, CCTV, VCR, a/c, fireplace, refrig, micro, Jacuzzis, restaurant, pool, hlth clb, massage, sauna, whirlpools

Hilton Hotel (Lax)
(800) HILTONS, (310) 410-4000
http://www.hilton.com
5711 W. Century Blvd.
1234 rooms - $99-499
Pets: Small pets w/$15 fee
Creature Comforts: CCTV, VCR, a/c, refrig, restaurant, pool, hlth clb, saunas, whirlpools

Holiday Inn (City Center)
(800) HOLIDAY, (213) 748-1291
http://www.holiday-inn.com
1020 S. Figueroa St.
195 rooms - $99-159
Pets: Small pets welcome
Creature Comforts: CCTV, a/c, refrig, restaurant, pool, hlth clb, sauna, whirlpool

Holiday Inn (Downtown)
(800) HOLIDAY, (213) 628-5242
http://www.holiday-inn.com
750 Garland Ave.
204 rooms - $65-139
Pets: Welcome w/$15 fee
Creature Comforts: CCTV, a/c, restaurant, pool

Holiday Inn
(800) HOLIDAY, (310) 476-6411
http://www.holiday-inn.com
170 N. Church St.
211 rooms - $65-29
Pets: Small pets welcome
Creature Comforts: CCTV, a/c, restaurant, pool, hlth clb, whirlpools

Hollywood Celebrity Hotel
(800) 222-7090, (213) 850-6464
1775 Orchid Ave.
38 rooms - $65-85
Pets: Welcome
Creature Comforts: CCTV, a/c, refrig, and micro

Hotel Intercontinental
(800) 442-5251, (213) 617-3300
http://www.interconti.com
251 S. Olive St.
432 rooms - $170-1,700
Pets: Welcome w/credit card dep.
Creature Comforts: CCTV, a/c, refrig, restaurant, pool, hlth clb, sauna, steamroom, whirlpools

Hotel Sofitel
(800) 763-4835, (310) 278-5444
http://www.sofitel.com
8555 Beverly Blvd.
310 rooms - $149-375
Pets: Welcome w/fee
Creature Comforts: CCTV, VCR, a/c, refrig, micro, restaurant, pool, hlth clb, sauna, whirlpools

Kawada Hotel
(800) 752-9232, (213) 621-4455
200 S. Hill St.
116 rooms - $75-125
Pets: Welcome
Creature Comforts: CCTV, VCR, a/c, refrig, micro, restaurant, access to a pool/hlth clb

Marriott (Lax)
(800) 228-9290, (310) 641-5700
http://www.marriott.com
5855 W. Century Blvd.
1,000 rooms - $85-495
Pets: Welcome
Creature Comforts: CCTV, a/c, refrig, micro, two restaurants, pool, hlth clb, saunas, whirlpools

Radisson Wilshire Hotel
(800) 333-3333, (213) 381-7411
http://www.radisson.com
3515 Wilshire Blvd.
380 rooms - $79-229
Pets: Small pets w/$100 dep.
Creature Comforts: CCTV, a/c, refrig, restaurant, cont. brkfst, pool, hlth clb

Sheraton Gateway
(800) 325-3535, (310) 642-1111
http://www.sheraton.com
6101 West Century Blvd.
805 rooms - $135-290
Pets: Welcome
Creature Comforts: CCTV, VCR, a/c, refrig, restaurant, pool, hlth clb, whirlpool

Summerfield Suites
(800) 833-4353, (310) 657-7400
www.summerfieldsuites.com
1000 Westmount Dr.
95 rooms - $199-325
Pets: Welcome w/$6 daily fee, $50 cleaning fee, $250 deposit
Creature Comforts: CCTV, a/c, refrig, micro, fireplaces, cont. brkfst, pool, and hlth clb access

Travelodge (Lax)
(800) 578-7878, (310) 469-4000
http://www.travelodge.com
5547 W. Century Blvd.
150 rooms - $60-95
Pets: Welcome
Creature Comforts: CCTV, VCR, a/c, micro, restaurant, pool

Vagabond Inn
(800) 522-1555, (310) 746-1531
http://www.vagabondinns.com
3101 S. Figueroa St.
72 rooms - $59-89
Pets: Welcome w/$5 fee
Creature Comforts: CCTV, a/c,
refrig, cont. brkfst, pool

Westin Bonaventure
(800) 228-3000, (310) 624-1000
http://www.westin.com
404 S. Figueroa St.
1,365 rooms - $99-199
Pets: Small pets welcome
Creature Comforts: CCTV,
VCR, a/c, refrig, micro, restaurant,
pool, hlth clb, whirlpool

Westin Century Plaza Hotel
(800) 228-3000, (310) 277-2000
http://www.westin.com
2025 Ave. of the Stars
1,075 rooms - $229-5,200
Pets: Small pets welcome
Creature Comforts: A landmark
hotel with a newer 30-story tower,
distant ocean views, CCTV, VCR,
a/c, refrig, micro, restaurant, pool,
sauna, hlth clb, whirlpool,
massage, and tennis and health
club privileges

Westwood Marquis Hotel
(800) 421-2317, (310) 208-8765
http://www.preferredhotels.com
930 Hilgard Ave.
258 rooms - $195-755
Pets: Welcome w/$100 fee
Creature Comforts: CCTV,
VCR, a/c, refrig, micro, Jacuzzis,
restaurant, two pools, hlth clb
access, massage, saunas,
whirlpools

Wyndham Hotel-LAX
(800) Wyndham, (310) 670-9000
http://www.wyndham.com
6225 West Century Blvd.
595 rooms - $90-169
Pets: Small pets welcome
Creature Comforts: CCTV,
VCR, a/c, refrig, micro, Jacuzzis,
restaurant, pool, hlth clb, saunas,
whirlpools

LOS BANOS
Best Western John Jay Inn
(800) 528-1234, (209) 827-0954
http://www.bestwestern.com
301 W. Pacheco Blvd.
58 rooms - $45-95
Pets: Welcome w/$25 dep.
Creature Comforts: CCTV, a/c,
refrig, micro, pool, hlth clb, sauna,
whirlpool

Regency Inn
(209) 826-3871
349 W. Pacheco Blvd.
40 rooms - $30-55
Pets: Small pets w/$4 fee
Creature Comforts: CCTV, a/c,
pool

LOS GATOS
Los Gatos Lodge
(800) 231-8676, (408) 354-3300
50 Saratoga Ave.
122 rooms - $99-179
Pets: Welcome w/$100 fee
Creature Comforts: CCTV, a/c,
kit, restaurant, pool, whirlpool,
and lawn games

Los Gatos Motor Inn
(408) 354-9191
55 Saratoga Ave.
60 rooms - $60-80
Pets: Small pets welcome
Creature Comforts: CCTV, a/c,
refrig, pool

LOST HILLS
Days Inn
(800) DAYS-INN, (805) 797-2371
http://www.daysinn.com
14684 Aloma St.
76 rooms - $35-74
Pets: Welcome
Creature Comforts: CCTV, a/c,
pool

Motel 6
(800) 4-MOTEL6, (805) 797-2346
http://www.motel6.com
14685 Warren St.
105 rooms - $32-46
Pets: Under 30 lbs. welcome
Creature Comforts: CCTV, a/c,
pool

LOTUS
Golden Lotus B&B
(530) 621-4562
1006 Lotus Rd.
2 cottages - $110-135
Pets: Welcome w/$20 fee
Creature Comforts: TV, VCR,
refrig, restaurant, cont. brkfst

LUCERNE
Beachcomber Resort
(707) 274-6639
6345 E. Rte. 20
9 rooms - $40-95
Pets: Small pets welcome
Creature Comforts: CCTV, a/c,
kit, lake/dock

MADERA
Best Western Madera Valley
(800) 528-1234, (209) 673-5164
http://www.bestwestern.com
317 N. G St.
94 rooms - $60-115
Pets: Welcome
Creature Comforts: CCTV, a/c,
refrig, restaurant, and hlth clb
access

Economy Inns of America
(800) 826-0778, (209) 661-1131
http://www.innsofamerica.com
1855 W. Cleveland Ave.
80 rooms - $34-55
Pets: Small pets welcome
Creature Comforts: CCTV, a/c,
cont. brkfst, pool

Days Gateway Inn
(800) DAYS-INN, (209) 674-8817
http://www.daysinn.com
25327 Ave. 16
50 rooms - $45-75
Pets: Welcome
Creature Comforts: CCTV, a/c,
refrig, cont. brkfst, pool

MAMMOTH LAKES

Austria Hof Lodge
(800) 922-2966, (760) 934-2764
http://www.VisitMammoth.com
924 Canyon Blvd.
24 rooms - $70-145
Pets: In a few rooms w/CC dep.
Creature Comforts: CCTV, kit,
fireplace, restaurant, spa, full
brkfst, walk to ski resort

Convict Lake Resort
(800) 992-2260, (760) 934-3800
Rte. 1, Box 204
23 cabins - $65-375
Pets: Welcome w/$10 fee
Creature Comforts: Altitude of
7,600 ft., TV, fireplace, kit, great
restaurant, lake-trout, boats, bikes

Crystal Crag Lodge
(888)GoMammoth,(760)934-2436
http://www.VisitMammoth.com
307 Crystal Crag Dr.
10 rooms - 60-195
Pets: Welcome
Creature Comforts: CCTV,
fireplace, kit

Condominiums
(800) 538-4751, (760) 934-6410
25 Lee Rd.
64 rooms - $80-195
Pets: Welcome in certain units
Creature Comforts: CCTV,
VCR, fireplace, kit, sauna, spa

Econo Lodge
(800) 55-ECONO, (760) 934-6855
http://www.econolodge.com
Rte. 203
33 rooms - $45-109
Pets: Welcome w/$5 fee
Creature Comforts: CCTV,
refrig, micro, restaurant, cont.
brkfst, pool, sauna, cont. brkfst,
and a spa

Edelweiss Lodge
(888)GoMammoth,(760)934-2445
http://www.VisitMammoth.com
Old Mammoth Rd.
8 rooms - $95-150
Pets: Welcome in some rooms
Creature Comforts: CCTV,
VCR, fireplace, kit, spa

Executive Inn
(888) 500-4SKI, (760) 934-8892
54 Sierra Blvd.
40 rooms - $40-95
Pets: Welcome in some rooms
Creature Comforts: CCTV, kit,
cont. brkfst, sauna, and spa

Katherine's House
(800) 934-2991, (760) 934-2991
http://www.katherineshouse.com
PO Box 2173
2 rooms & cottages - $85-245
Pets: "Welcomed and loved" w/a
$10 fee (includes bones, love and
walking)
Creature Comforts: Chalet in
quiet neighborhood, antiques, pine
furnishings, original artwork,
brass beds, CCTV, VCR, a/c,
gourmet kit, down feather beds,
fireplace, refrig, Jacuzzi, full
brkfst, great mtn. views, a friendly
dog (Cleo) in residence

Mammoth Ski & Racquet Club
(888) 762-6668, (760) 934-7368
http://www.mammothdirect.com
Canyon Blvd.
133 rooms - $99-245
Pets: Welcome in certain units
Creature Comforts: A dark
wood-paneled lodge w/a variety of
well appointed condos, CCTV,
VCR, a/c, country décor w/pine
furnishings, fireplace, kit, pool,
sauna, tennis, spa

Motel 6
(800) 4-MOTEL6, (760) 934-6660
http://www.motel6.com
3372 Main St.
152 rooms - $44-69
Pets: Under 30 lbs. welcome
Creature Comforts: CCTV, a/c,
pool

North Village Inn
(800) 257-3781, (760) 934-2535
http://www.mm.qnet.com/
~northviln
103 Lake Mary Rd.
18 rooms - $55-125
Pets: Welcome in some rooms
Creature Comforts: CCTV, a/c,
fireplace, kit, cont. brkfst

Pinecliff Resort
(760) 934-2447
http://www.visitmammoth.com
Woodman St.
16 rooms - $80-125
Pets: Welcome
Creature Comforts: CCTV,
VCR, fireplace, kit, and spa

Royal Pines Resort
(800) 457-1997, (760) 934-2306
http://www.mammothweb.com/
royalpines
3814 View Point Rd.
28 rooms - $50-99
Pets: Welcome w/$5 fee
Creature Comforts: CCTV,
VCR, kit, fireplace, spa

Shilo Inn
(800) 222-2244, (760) 934-4500
http://www.shiloinns.com
2963 Main St.
70 rooms - $80-165
Pets: Welcome w/$7 fee
Creature Comforts: CCTV,
fireplace, cont. brkfst, pool, sauna,
hlth club, spa

Sierra Nevada Rodeway Inn
(800) 824-5132, (760) 934-2515
http://www.mammothsnri.com
164 Old Mammoth Rd.
159 rooms - $69-169
Pets: Welcome in some rooms
Creature Comforts: CCTV,
VCR, fireplace, kit, cont. brkfst,
pool, sauna, spa

Thrift Lodge
(800) 525-9055, (760) 934-2416
http://www.travelodge.com
6209 Mineret Rd.
89 rooms - $65-99
Pets: Welcome w/$50 dep.
Creature Comforts: CCTV,
fireplace, kit, pool, sauna, spa

Zwart House Lodge
(760) 934-2217
76 Lupin St., Box 174
2 rooms - $50-85
Pets: Welcome w/$3 fee
Creature Comforts: CCTV, kit,
central living room

 California

MANHATTAN BEACH
Barnaby's Hotel
(800) 552-5285, (310) 545-8466
http://www.barnabys-hotel.com
3501 N. Sepulveda Blvd.
123 rooms - $125-189
Pets: Pampered pet program
Creature Comforts: Turn-of-the-century European style hotel w/ antiques, Victorian décor, carved beds w/canopies, crystal chandeliers, balconies look out on the courtyard, CCTV, VCR, a/c, refrig, fireplace, restaurant, pub, cont. brkfst, whirlpool, pool

Residence Inn
(800) 331-3131, (310) 546-7627
http://www.residenceinn.com
1700 N. Sepulveda Blvd.
175 rooms - $99-239
Pets: Welcome w/$75 fee
Creature Comforts: CCTV, VCR, a/c, fireplace, refrig, micro, cont. brkfst, pool, hlth clb access, sauna, whirlpool

MANTECA
Best Western Inn
(800) 528-1234, (209) 825-1415
http://www.bestwestern.com
1415 E. Yosemite Ave.
100 rooms - $55-90
Pets: Small pets w/$20 dep.
Creature Comforts: CCTV, VCR, a/c, refrig, micro, pool, hlth clb, sauna, whirlpools

MARINA
Motel 6
(800) 4-MOTEL6, (408) 384-1000
http://www.motel6.com
100 Reservation Rd.
126 rooms - $39-54
Pets: Under 30 lbs. welcome
Creature Comforts: CCTV, a/c

Travelodge
(800) 578-7878, (408) 883-0300
http://www.travelodge.com
3290 Dunes Dr.
84 rooms - $60-125
Pets: Small pets welcome
Creature Comforts: CCTV, a/c, cont. brkfst

MARIPOSA
Best Western Yosemite
(800) 528-1234, (209) 966-7546
http://www.bestwestern.com
4999 Rte. 140
82 rooms - $60-85
Pets: Small pets w/$10 fee
Creature Comforts: CCTV, a/c, refrig, micro, cont. brkfst, pool, and a spa

IMA Mariposa Lodge
(800) 341-8000, (209) 966-3607
http://www.imalodging.com
5052 Rte. 140
45 rooms - $45-80
Pets: Welcome w/$6 fee
Creature Comforts: CCTV, VCR, a/c, refrig, micro, pool, whirlpool

Miners Inn
(800) 321-5261, (209) 742-7777
Routes 49 & 140
65 rooms - $60-169
Pets: Welcome w/$5 fee
Creature Comforts: CCTV, a/c, refrig, pool, whirlpool

The Pelennor B&B
(209) 966-2832
3871 Rte. 49
4 rooms - $40-50
Pets: Welcome
Creature Comforts: Kit, full brkfst, pool, sauna, whirlpool

MARKLEEVILLE
Marklee Toll Station Hotel
(530) 694-2507
14856 Rte. 89
6 rooms - $45-55
Pets: Welcome w/$6 fee
Creature Comforts: CCTV, a/c, restaurant, near hot springs

MARYSVILLE
Marysville Motor Lodge
(530) 743-1531
904 E St.
40 rooms - $30-45
Pets: Welcome w/$5 fee
Creature Comforts: CCTV, a/c, refrig, pool

Vada's
(800) 593-4666, (530) 671-1151
545 Colusa Ave.
39 rooms - $35-80
Pets: W/$10 fee & $50 dep.
Creature Comforts: CCTV, a/c, kit, cont. brkfst

The Vagabond Inn
(800) 522-1555, (530) 742-8586
http://www.vagabondinss.com
721 - 10th St.
44 rooms - $39-59
Pets: Small pets w/$5 fee
Creature Comforts: CCTV, a/c, pool

McCLOUD
Stoney Brook Inn B&B
(800) 369-6118, (916) 964-2300
http://www.touristguide.com/b&b/ca/stoneybrook
309 W. Colombero Dr.
2 rooms - $65-75
Pets: Welcome w/$10 fee
Creature Comforts: A 1922 inn w/wrap-around front porch, set under Ponderosa pines along foothills of Mt. Shasta, CCTV, VCR, a/c, woodstove, kit, cont. brkfst, Finish sauna, Native American sweat lodge, whirlpool, octagonal kiva

McKINLEYVILLE
Seaview Cabins
(707) 839-1321
1186 Central Ave.
10 cabins- $39-129
Pets: Welcome
Creature Comforts: Kit, living rooms, ocean views

MENDOCINO
Blackberry Inn
(707) 937-5281
http://www.innaccess.com/bbi
44951 Larkin Rd.
18 rooms - $95-175
Pets: Under 30 Lbs. w/$10 fee
Creature Comforts: Charming interiors with an exterior that looks like a miniature old west movie set, CCTV, VCR, fireplaces, 4-poster beds, refrig, whirlpools, delux cont. brkfst, ocean views

Hill House Inn
(707) 937-0554
http://www.hillhouseinn.com
10701 Palette Dr.
44 rooms - $110-245
Pets: Welcome
Creature Comforts: CCTV,
VCR, a/c, fireplace, refrig,
restaurant, and cont. brkfst

MacElroys B&B
(707) 937-1734
998 Main St.
4 rooms - $80-115
Pets: Welcome
Creature Comforts: CCTV,
fireplace, refrig, views of gardens
and ocean

Mendocino Seaside Cottage
(800) 94-HEART, (707) 485-0239
www.romancebythesea.com
10940 Lansing St.
6 cottages - $190-340
Pets: Welcome in one rustic
cottage with a new kitchen
Creature Comforts: Very
romantic cottages, lovely country
décor, balloon draperies, white
wicker, dried wreaths, sundecks,
CCTV, VCR, raised fireplaces,
skylights, kit, cont. brkfst, Jacuzzi,
stereo-CD, flotation bed,
champagne, incredible views of
headlands, ocean, and sunsets

Mendocino Village Cottages
(707) 937-0866
45320 Little Lake St.
2 cottages - $60-125
Pets: Welcome w/$10 fee
Creature Comforts: Set in a
quiet part of town with views of
the headlands, charming rustic
ambiance, CCTV, fireplace/
woodstove, Oriental carpet,
skylights, kit, cont. brkfst, garden

Sallie & Eileen's Place
(707) 937-2028
http://www.q-net.com/
sallieandeileensplace
Box 409
2 units - $75-95
Pets: Welcome in cabins w/$5 fee
Creature Comforts: A cozy oasis
for women, secluded, A-frame and
cabin w/plenty of windows, great
yard, Jacuzzi, kit, fireplace-wood
stove, porch, rockers, hot tub

Stanford Inn by the Sea
(800) 331-8884, (707) 937-5615
http://www.stanfordinn.com
Comptche-Ukiah Rd. & Rte. 1
25 rooms - $190-355
Pets: Welcome w/$25 fee
Creature Comforts: An oasis
nestled into wooded hillside,
organic gardens, llamas, and ocean
views, cozy rooms w/lovely décor,
four poster and sleigh beds,
antiques, French doors open to
balconies, CCTV, VCR,
fireplaces, kit, Jacuzzi, cont.
brkfst, tropical greenhouse-pool,
hlth clb, sauna, whirlpool, canoes,
kayaks, and bicycles

MERCED
Best Western Sequoia Inn
(800) 528-1234, (209) 723-3711
http://www.bestwestern.com
1213 V St.
99 rooms - $50-75
Pets: Welcome w/$10 dep.
Creature Comforts: CCTV, a/c,
refrig, micro, restaurant, cont.
brkfst, pool, and hlth clb access

Days Inn
(800) DAYS-INN, (209) 722-2726
http://www.daysinn.com
1199 Motel Dr.
24 rooms - $50-95
Pets: Welcome w/credit card dep.
Creature Comforts: CCTV,
VCR, a/c, refrig, micro, pool,
whirlpool

Holiday Inn Express
(800) HOLIDAY, (209) 380333
http://www.holiday-inn.com
730 Motel Dr.
66 rooms - $75-99
Pets: Small pets welcome
Creature Comforts: CCTV, a/c,
refrig, micro, pool, sauna,
whirlpool

Motel 6
(800) 4-MOTEL6, (209) 722-2737
http://www.motel6.com
1215 R St.
76 rooms - $33-44
Pets: Under 30 lbs. welcome
Creature Comforts: CCTV, a/c

Motel 6
(800) 4-MOTEL6, (209) 384-2181
http://www.motel6.com
1410 V St.
77 rooms - $35-48
Pets: Under 30 lbs. welcome
Creature Comforts: CCTV, a/c,
pool

MIDPINES
The Homestead Guest Ranch
(209) 966-2820
PO Box 13
1 house - $95-125
Pets: Welcome
Creature Comforts: Private,
rustic ranch house on 23 acres,
knotty pine walls, fieldstone
fireplace, country antiques,
barbecue, kit

MILLBRAE
Clarion Hotel
(800) 252-7466, (415) 692-6363
http://www.clarioninn.com
401 E. Millbrae Ave.
440 rooms - $90-140
Pets: Welcome in certain rooms
Creature Comforts: CCTV, a/c,
refrig, restaurant, pool, hlth clb
whirlpool

Westin Hotel
(800) 228-3000, (415) 692-3500
http://www.westin.com
1 Old Bayshore Hwy.
395 rooms - $180-395
Pets: Small pets welcome
Creature Comforts: CCTV,
VCR, a/c, Jacuzzi, restaurant,
pool, hlth clb, sauna, whirlpool,
hiking, and bay views

MILPITAS
Best Western Brookside Inn
(800) 528-1234, (408) 263-5566
http://www.bestwestern.com
400 Valley Way
69 rooms - $60-90
Pets: Welcome in certain rooms
Creature Comforts: CCTV, a/c,
refrig, micro, restaurant, pool

Beverly Heritage Hotel
(408) 943-9080
1820 Barber Ln.
199 rooms - $85-125
Pets: Small pets w/$15 fee
Creature Comforts: CCTV, a/c, refrig, restaurant, pool, hlth clb, whirlpool

Economy Inns of America
(800) 826-0778, (408) 946-8889
http://www.innsofamerica.com
270 So. Abbott Ave.
125 rooms - $55-89
Pets: Small pets welcome
Creature Comforts: CCTV, a/c, pool

MIRANDA
Miranda Gardens Resort
(707) 943-3011
http://www.mirandagardens.com
6766 Avenue of the Giants
16 cabins- $65-185
Pets: In certain rooms w/$10 fee
Creature Comforts: Fireplaces, kit, pool, whirlpool, trails

Whispering Pines Lodge
(707) 943-3182
6582 Ave. of the Giants
2 rooms - $40-70
Pets: Welcome
Creature Comforts: CCTV, VCR, refrig, cont. brkfst

MISSION HILLS
Best Western Mission Hills
(800) 528-1234, (818) 891-1771
http://www.bestwestern.com
10621 Sepulveda Blvd.
120 rooms - $60-99
Pets: Welcome w/credit card dep.
Creature Comforts: CCTV, VCR, a/c, refrig, cont. brkfst, pool

MI-WUK VILLAGE
Country Inn
(800) 292-2093, (209) 586-4615
http://www.mlode.com/~thcc/countryinn
19958 Middle Cap Rd., Box 1235
5 rooms - $75-95
Pets: Welcome w/$10 fee
Creature Comforts: Ridgetop B&B w/country décor, country quilts, dried flowers, CCTV, VCR, a/c, refrig, full brkfst, views of river

Mi-Wuk Motor Lodge
(209) 586-3031
Route 108
24 rooms - $50-120
Pets: Welcome w/$10 fee
Creature Comforts: CCTV, VCR, a/c, fireplace, kit, pool, whirlpool

MODESTO
Best Western Mallard Inn
(800) 528-1234, (209) 577-3825
http://www.bestwestern.com
1720 Sisk Rd.
126 rooms - $85-129
Pets: Welcome w/credit card dep.
Creature Comforts: CCTV, a/c, refrig, micro, restaurant, pool, whirlpool

Best Western Town House
(800) 528-1234, (209) 524-7261
http://www.bestwestern.com
909 - 16th St.
56 rooms - $50-70
Pets: Small pets w/$20 fee
Creature Comforts: CCTV, VCR, a/c, refrig, micro, pool, sauna, whirlpool

Doubletree
(800) 222-TREE, (209) 526-6000
http://www.doubltreehotels.com
1150 - 9th St.
259 rooms - $79-525
Pets: Small pets welcome
Creature Comforts: CCTV, a/c, refrig, restaurant, pool, hlth clb, sauna, whirlpool

Howard Johnson Inn
(800) I-Go-Hojo, (209) 537-4821
http://www.hojo.com
1672 Herndon Rd.
88 rooms - $65-85
Pets: Small pets w/$15 fee
Creature Comforts: CCTV, a/c, cont. brkfst, pool

Motel 6
(800) 4-MOTEL6, (209) 522-7271
http://www.motel6.com
1920 W. Orangeburg Ave.
100 rooms - $30-39
Pets: Under 30 lbs. welcome
Creature Comforts: CCTV, a/c, pool

Red Lion Hotel
(800) RED-LION, (209) 526-6000
http://www.redlion.com
1150 - 9th St.
260 rooms - $89-425
Pets: Welcome w/$100 dep.
Creature Comforts: CCTV, a/c, refrig, micro, two restaurants, pool, hlth clb whirlpool

Vagabond Inn
(800) 522-1555, (209) 521-6340
http://www.vagabondinns.com
1525 McHenry Ave.
99 rooms - $55-75
Pets: Welcome w/$5 fee
Creature Comforts: CCTV, a/c, pool

MOJAVE
Motel 6
(800) 4-MOTEL6, (805) 824-4571
http://www.motel6.com
16958 Rte. 58
121 rooms - $34-49
Pets: Under 30 lbs. welcome
Creature Comforts: CCTV, a/c, pool

Scottish Inns
(800) 251-1962, (805) 824-9317
http://www.reservahost.com
16352 Sierra Hwy.
25 rooms - $35-55
Pets: Small pets w/$5 fee
Creature Comforts: CCTV, a/c, refrig, micro, pool, whirlpool

Vagabond Inn
(800) 522-1555, (805) 824-2463
http://www.vagabondinns.com
2145 Rte. 58
33 rooms - $30-55
Pets: Welcome w/$5 fee
Creature Comforts: CCTV, a/c, pool

MONO HOT SPRINGS
Mono Hot Springs Resort
(559) 325-1710, (559) 325-1710
http://www.monohotsprings.com
72000 Rte 168
99 rooms - $45-75
Pets: Welcome w/$4 fee
Creature Comforts: Rustic cabins set along the San Joaquin River, fireplace, Jacuzzi, hot tub, restaurant, fishing-boating, gen. store, great vistas

MONROVIA
Holiday Inn
(800) HOLIDAY, (626) 357-1900
http://www.holiday-inn.com
924 W. Huntington Dr.
175 rooms - $75-125
Pets: Welcome w/$50 dep.
Creature Comforts: CCTV, a/c,
refrig, micro, restaurant, pool,
whirlpool

MONTECITO
San Ysidro Ranch
(800) 368-6788, (805) 969-5046
http://www.sanysidroranch.com
1425 Munras Ave.
67 rms./21 cottages - $375-3,000
Pets: Welcome w/$75 fee
("privileged pets program" - all
sorts of delectible goodies,
massages, and pampering)
Creature Comforts: Lavish
cottage resort set on 500 acres in
hills south of Santa Barbara,
CCTV, VCR, a/c, fireplace,
vaulted beamed ceilings, French
doors open to private decks, four-
poster beds w/chintz comforters,
Oriental rugs, kit, Jacuzzis,
excellent restaurant, pool w/ocean
views, hlth clb, saunas,
whirlpools, spa, tennis, lawn
bowling, picturesque gardens and
citrus groves, nature trails

MONTEREY
Bay Park Hotel
(800) 338-3564, (831) 649-1020
1425 Munras Ave.
80 rooms - $95-165
Pets: Small pets w/$5 fee
Creature Comforts: CCTV,
refrig, restaurant, pool, whirlpool

Best Western Monterey Beach
(800) 528-1234, (831) 394-3321
http://www.bestwestern.com
2600 Sand Dune Dr.
196 rooms - $69-189
Pets: Small pets welcome
Creature Comforts: CCTV,
refrig, pool, hlth clb

Best Western Victorian Inn
(800) 528-1234, (831) 373-8000
http://www.bestwestern.com
487 Foam St.
70 rooms - $99-329
Pets: $25 fee and credit card dep.
(special pet program)
Creature Comforts: Victorian
inn with welcome amenities,
CCTV, VCR, fireplaces,
featherbeds, refrig, pool,
whirlpools

Carmel Hill Lodge
(888) 551-4445, (831) 373-3252
1372 Munras Ave.
38 rooms - $90-190
Pets: In smk rms w/ $10 fee
Creature Comforts: CCTV,
cont. brkfst, pool

Cypress Gardens Motel
(800) 433-4732, (831) 373-2761
http://www.innsbythesea.com
1150 Munras Ave.
45 rooms - $65-250
Pets: Welcome
Creature Comforts: CCTV,
VCR, fireplace, kit, cont. brkfst,
pool, whirlpool

El Adobe
(800) 433-4732, (831) 372-5409
http://www.innsbythesea.com
936 Munras Ave.
26 rooms - $60-125
Pets: Welcome
Creature Comforts: CCTV,
refrig, cont. brkfst, whirlpool

Holiday Inn Resort
(800) HOLIDAY, (831) 373-6141
http://www.holiday-inn.com
1000 Aguajito Rd.
202 rooms - $90-199
Pets: Welcome w/$10 fee
Creature Comforts: CCTV, a/c,
refrig, restaurant, pool, hlth clb,
sauna, whirlpool, tennis, and
putting green

Marriott Hotel
(800) 228-9290, (831) 649-4234
http://www.marriott.com
350 Calle Principal
340 rooms - $190-600
Pets: Welcome w/$10 fee
Creature Comforts: CCTV, a/c,
refrig, Jacuzzi, restaurant, pool,
hlth clb, whirlpool

Monterey Bay Lodge
(800) 588-1900, (831) 372-8057
55 Camino Aguajito
45 rooms - $85-185
Pets: $10 fee, credit card dep.
Creature Comforts: CCTV,
VCR, refrig, micro, pool

Monterey Fireside Lodge
(831) 373-4172
1131 - 10th St.
24 rooms - $75-265
Pets: Welcome w/$10 fee
Creature Comforts: CCTV,
VCR, fireplace, kit, whirlpool

Motel 6
(800) 4-MOTEL6, (831) 646-8585
http://www.motel6.com
2124 N. Freemont St.
52 rooms - $48-60
Pets: Under 30 lbs. welcome
Creature Comforts: CCTV, a/c,
pool

Munras Lodge
(831) 646-9696
1010 Munras Rd.
30 rooms - $65-220
Pets: Welcome w/$40 dep.
Creature Comforts: CCTV,
fireplace, refrig, cont. brkfst, pool,
sauna, whirlpool

Way Station Inn
(800) 858-0822, (831) 372-2945
1200 Olmstead Rd.
45 rooms - $49-169
Pets: Small pets welcome
Creature Comforts: CCTV,
fireplaces, and refrig

MONTEREY PARK
Days Inn
(800) DAYS-INN, (213) 728-8444
http://www.daysinn.com
434 Potrero Grande Dr.
88 rooms - $60-89
Pets: Small pets welcome
Creature Comforts: CCTV,
VCR, a/c, refrig, micro, pool, hlth
clb, whirlpool

MONTE RIO
Highland Dell Inn B&B
(800) 767-1759, (707) 865-1759
http://www.netdex.com/~highland
21050 River Blvd.
8 rooms - $85-250
Pets: Welcome w/$100 dep.
Creature Comforts: Historic 1906 inn and restaurant on the Russian River, country ambiance, brass beds, beamed ceilings, rattan w/floral cushions, CCTV, VCR, a/c, claw foot tubs, stereos-CDs, Jacuzzis, fireplace, refrig, full brkfst, pool, views of river and redwoods

MORENO VALLEY
Motel 6
(800) 4-MOTEL6, (909) 656-4451
http://www.motel6.com
23581 Alessandro Blvd.
60 rooms - $34-45
Pets: Under 30 lbs. welcome
Creature Comforts: CCTV, a/c, pool

MORGAN HILL
Best Western Country Inn
(800) 528-1234, (408) 779-0447
http://www.bestwestern.com
16525 Condit Rd.
85 rooms - $55-99
Pets: Small pets welcome
Creature Comforts: CCTV, a/c, refrig, pool, whirlpool

MORRO BAY
Adventure Inn on the Sea
(805) 772-5607
http://www.adventureinn.net
1148 Front St.
16 rooms - $45-159
Pets: Welcome w/$10 fee
Creature Comforts: CCTV, refrig, Jacuzzi, restaurant, cont. brkfst, pool, whirlpool

Best Value Inn
(800) 549-2022 (CA),
(805) 772-3333
220 Beach St.
33 rooms - $30-110
Pets: Small pets w/$6 fee
Creature Comforts: CCTV, refrig

Best Western El Rancho Motel
(800) 528-1234, (805) 772-2212
http://www.bestwestern.com
2460 Main St.
28 rooms - $50-140
Pets: Welcome w/$10 fee
Creature Comforts: CCTV, a/c, refrig, micro, pool, whirlpool

Best Western Tradewinds
(800) 528-1234, (805) 772-7376
http://www.bestwestern.com
225 Beach St.
25 rooms - $40-115
Pets: Small pets w/$6 fee
Creature Comforts: CCTV, a/c, refrig, whirlpool

Days Inn
(800) DAYS-INN, (805) 772-2711
http://www.daysinn.com
1095 Main St.
46 rooms - $70-125
Pets: Welcome w/$10 fee
Creature Comforts: CCTV, a/c, refrig, pool, whirlpool

Gold Coast
(805) 772-7740
670 Main St.
18 rooms - $35-100
Pets: Small pets w/$5 fee
Creature Comforts: CCTV, refrig

Golden Pelican Inn
(805) 772-7135
3270 Main St.
26 rooms - $40-75
Pets: Welcome
Creature Comforts: CCTV, cont. brkfst

Motel 6
(800) 4-MOTEL6, (805) 772-5641
http://www.motel6.com
298 Atascadero Rd.
70 rooms - $35-48
Pets: Under 30 lbs. welcome
Creature Comforts: CCTV, a/c, pool

Sundown Motel
(800) 696-6928, (805) 772-7381
640 Main St.
18 rooms - $30-95
Pets: Small pets w/$5 fee
Creature Comforts: CCTV and refrig

Sunset Travelodge
(800) 578-7878, (805) 772-1259
http://www.travelodge.com
1080 Market Ave.
31 rooms - $95-195
Pets: Small pets w/$10 fee, and a credit card dep.
Creature Comforts: CCTV, VCR, refrig, micro, cont. brkfst, pool

MOUNTAIN VIEW
Best Western Tropicana Lodge
(800) 528-1234, (415) 961-0220
http://www.bestwestern.com
1720 El Camino Real
60 rooms - $70-95
Pets: Welcome w/notice
Creature Comforts: CCTV, a/c, refrig, pool, sauna

Residence Inn
(800) 331-3131, (415) 940-1300
http://www.residenceinn.com
1854 El Camino Real
110 rooms - $89-189
Pets: Welcome w/$6 fee and credit card dep.
Creature Comforts: CCTV, a/c, fireplace, kit, cont. brkfst, pool, hlth club access, whirlpool

MOUNT SHASTA
Alpine Lodge Motel
(530) 926-3145
908 S. Mt. Shasta Blvd.
20 rooms - $35-60
Pets: Welcome w/$20 dep.
Creature Comforts: CCTV, a/c, kit, pool, whirlpool

Best Western Tree House
(800) 528-1234, (530) 926-3101
http://www.bestwestern.com
Mount Shasta Blvd.
95 rooms - $60-175
Pets: Small pets welcome
Creature Comforts: CCTV, a/c, refrig, pool, restaurant

Evergreen Lodge
(530) 926-2143
1312 S. Mt. Shasta Blvd.
20 rooms - $35-65
Pets: Welcome w/$5 fee
Creature Comforts: CCTV, a/c, kit, pool, whirlpool

Dream Inn
(877) 375-4744, (530) 926-1536
http://home.att.net/~dreaminn
326 Chestnut St.
5 rooms - $60-95
Pets: Welcome
Creature Comforts: A charming
1904 restored Victorian, patio,
rose gardens, CCTV, VCR, refrig,
micro, claw footed tub, antiques,
grand piano, Oriental rugs,
country quilts, and a cont. brkfst

Mt. Shasta Ranch
(530) 926-3870
1008 W.A. Barr Rd.
9 rooms - $55-100
Pets: Welcome w/$10 fee
Creature Comforts: CCTV,
refrig, country brkfst, whirlpool,
lawn games, game room

Mountain Air Lodge
(530) 926-3411
1121 Mount Shasta Blvd.
40 rooms - $40-130
Pets: Welcome w/$7 fee
Creature Comforts: CCTV, a/c,
kit, pool, rec. room

Pine Needles Motel
(530) 926-4811
1340 Mt. Shasta Blvd.
30 rooms - $35-66
Pets: Welcome w/$5 fee
Creature Comforts: CCTV, a/c,
kit, pool, whirlpool

Shasta Lodge Motel
(800) 742-7821, (530) 926-7821
724 N. Mt. Shasta Blvd.
30 rooms - $30-60
Pets: Welcome
Creature Comforts: CCTV, pool

Swiss Holiday Lodge
(530) 926-3446
2400 S. Mt. Shasta Blvd.
20 rooms - $35-70
Pets: Small pets welcome
Creature Comforts: CCTV, a/c,
fireplace, kit, cont. brkfst, pool

NAPA
Budget Inn
(877) 872-6272, (707) 257-6111
3380 Solano Ave.
58 rooms - $65-129
Pets: Welcome w/$10 fee
Creature Comforts: CCTV, a/c,
refrig, cont. brkfst, pool

NATIONAL CITY
E-Z 8 Motel
(800) 326-6835, (619) 474-6491
1700 E. Plaza St.
34 rooms - $35-55
Pets: Welcome
Creature Comforts: CCTV, a/c,
micro

Holiday Inn
(800) HOLIDAY, (619) 474-2800
http://www.holiday-inn.com
700 National City Blvd.
180 rooms - $50-85
Pets: Welcome w/$20 dep.
Creature Comforts: CCTV, a/c,
fireplace, restaurant, pool,
whirlpool

Radisson Suites
(800) 333-3333, (619) 474-2800
http://www.radisson.com
801 National City Blvd.
170 rooms - $65-109
Pets: Small pets w/$20 dep.
Creature Comforts: CCTV,
VCR, a/c, fireplace, kit, refrig,
micro, Jacuzzi, restaurant, cont.
brkfst, pool, hlth clb access, sauna,
whirlpool

NEEDLES
Best Western Colorado River
(800) 528-1234, (760) 326-4552
http://www.bestwestern.com
2371 West Broadway St.
64 rooms - $50-75
Pets: Small pets welcome
Creature Comforts: CCTV, a/c,
refrig, micro, pool, sauna,
whirlpool

Days Inn
(800) DAYS-INN, (760) 326-5836
http://www.daysinn.com
1215 Hospitality Lane
102 rooms - $35-90
Pets: Welcome
Creature Comforts: CCTV, a/c,
refrig, micro, cont. brkfst, pool,
whirlpool

Imperial 400 Motor Inn
(760) 326-2145
644 Broadway St.
30 rooms - $30-45
Pets: Small pets welcome
Creature Comforts: CCTV, a/c,
refrig, pool

Motel 6
(800) 4-MOTEL6, (760) 326-3399
http://www.motel6.com
1420 J St.
81 rooms - $34-42
Pets: Under 30 lbs. welcome
Creature Comforts: CCTV, a/c,
pool

River Valley Inn
(800) 346-2331 (CA),
(760) 326-3829
1707 W. Broadway St.
28 rooms - $25-40
Pets: Welcome w/$5 fee
Creature Comforts: CCTV, a/c,
refrig, micro, pool

Super 8
(800) 800-8000, (760) 326-4501
http://www.super8.com
1102 East Broadway St.
30 rooms - $35-65
Pets: Welcome w/$20 dep.
Creature Comforts: CCTV, a/c,
pool

NEVADA CITY
Nevada Street Cottages
(530) 265-8071, 265-2808
http://www.netshel.net/~nscotts
690 Nevada St.
4 cottages - $75-120
Pets: Welcome w/$10 fee
Creature Comforts: Four
charming cottages w/casual
ambiance amidst pine, maple, and
oak trees, CCTV, VCR, a/c,
Persian rugs, books-games,
fireplace, kit

NEWARK
Motel 6
(800) 4-MOTEL6, (510) 791-5900
http://www.motel6.com
5600 Cedar St.
217 rooms - $42-55
Pets: Under 30 lbs. welcome
Creature Comforts: CCTV, a/c,
pool

NEWARK
Park Inn
(510) 795-7995
5977 Mowry Ave.
36 rooms - $95-125
Pets: Welcome w/$10 fee
Creature Comforts: CCTV, a/c,
cont. brkfst, pool

NEWPORT BEACH

Balboa Inn
(949) 675-3412
105 Main St.
34 rooms - $129-185
Pets: Small pets welcome
Creature Comforts: CCTV,
VCR, a/c, fireplace, refrig,
Jacuzzi, cont. brkfst

Four Seasons Hotel
(800) 332-3442, (949) 759-0808
http://www.fshr.com
690 Newport Center Dr.
285 rooms - $145-2,500
Pets: Under 15 Lbs. welcome
Creature Comforts: Centrally
located luxury hotel overlooking
water, earth tones, Louis XV
antiques, exquisite ambiance,
CCTV, VCR, a/c, fireplace, kits,
refrig, micro, Jacuzzis, restaurant,
pool, hlth clb, saunas, whirlpools,
massage, golf access, and tennis

Hyatt Newporter
(800) 233-1234, (949) 729-1234
http://www.hyatt.com
1107 Jamboree Rd.
415 rooms - $125-975
Pets: Welcome w/$50 fee
Creature Comforts: CCTV,
VCR, a/c, refrig, fireplaces,
Jacuzzis, restaurant, 3 pools, hlth
clb, sauna, whirlpool, tennis, lawn
games, golf

Marriott Hotel & Tennis Club
(800) 228-9290, (949) 640-4000
http://www.marriott.com
900 Newport Center Dr.
585 rooms - $145-1,000
Pets: Small pets welcome
Creature Comforts: Full service
resort with great golf course and
water views, CCTV, VCR, a/c,
fireplace, kit, Jacuzzi, restaurant,
cont. brkfst, 2 pools, hlth clb,
sauna, terraced gardens, tennis,
whirlpool, golf, Kids Club, and
jogging paths

Marriott Suites
(800) 228-9290, (949) 854-4500
http://www.marriott.com
500 Bayview Circle
245 rooms - $109-550
Pets: Welcome
Creature Comforts: CCTV,
VCR, a/c, refrig, restaurant, pool,
hlth clb, sauna, whirlpools

Oakwood Corporate Housing
(800) 456-9351, (949) 574-3725
http://www.oakwood.com
880 Irvine Ave.
A variety of rms/houses—daily
and monthly rates are available
Pets: Welcome in certain units
Creature Comforts: CCTV,
VCR, a/c, fireplaces, kit, Jacuzzis,
pool, hlth clb, sauna, whirlpools

NICE

Talley's Family Resort
(707) 274-1177
3827 E. Rte. 20
10 cabins - $55-99
Pets: Welcome
Creature Comforts: CCTV,
fireplace, kit

NORTH HIGHLANDS

Motel 6
(800) 4-MOTEL6, (916) 973-8673
http://www.motel6.com
4600 Watt Ave.
63 rooms - $39-54
Pets: Under 30 lbs. welcome
Creature Comforts: CCTV, a/c

NORWALK

Motel 6
(800) 4-MOTEL6, (562) 864-2567
http://www.motel6.com
10646 E. Rosecrans Ave.
55 rooms - $40-49
Pets: Under 30 lbs. welcome
Creature Comforts: CCTV, a/c

NOVATO

Days Inn
(800) DAYS-INN, (415) 897-7111
http://www.daysinn.com
8141 Redwood Blvd.
55 rooms - $55-80
Pets: Small pets welcome
Creature Comforts: CCTV,
VCR, a/c, refrig, micro, restaurant,
pool, whirlpool

Travelodge
(800) 578-7878, (415) 892-7500
http://www.travelodge.com
7600 Redwood Blvd.
53 rooms - $45-75
Pets: Welcome w/$5 fee
Creature Comforts: CCTV, a/c,
refrig, cont. brkfst, pool, whirlpool

OAKHURST

Best Western Yosemite Hotel
(800) 528-1234, (559) 683-2378
http://www.bestwestern.com
40530 Hwy. 41
120 rooms - $45-125
Pets: Small pets welcome
Creature Comforts: CCTV,
VCR, a/c, kit, cont. brkfst, 2 pools,
hlth clb, saunas, whirlpools

Comfort Inn
(800) 228-5150, (559) 683-8282
http://www.comfortinn.com
40489 Rte. 41
112 rooms - $60-140
Pets: Small pets w/$50 dep.
Creature Comforts: CCTV,
VCR, a/c, refrig, pool, whirlpool

Ramada Inn
(800) 2-Ramada, (559) 658-5500
http://www.ramada.com
48800 Royal Oaks Dr.
70 rooms - $70-100
Pets: Welcome
Creature Comforts: CCTV,
VCR, a/c, refrig, micro, Jacuzzis,
cont. brkfst, pool, saunas,
whirlpools

OAKLAND

Clarion Suites
(800) 933-4683, (510) 832-2300
http://www.clarioninn.com
1800 Madison St.
51 rooms - $89-175
Pets: $75 fee, $150 dep.
Creature Comforts: CCTV, a/c,
kit, cont. brkfst, hlth clb access,
whirlpool, overlooks Lake Merritt

Days Inn
(800) DAYS-INN, (510) 568-1880
http://www.daysinn.com
8350 Edes Ave.
88 rooms - $59-99
Pets: Small pets welcome
Creature Comforts: CCTV, a/c,
refrig, restaurant, cont. brkfst,
pool, whirlpool

Hampton Inn (Airport)
(800) Hampton, (510) 632-8900
http://www.hampton-inn.com
8465 Enterprise Dr.
150 rooms - $69-129
Pets: Small pets welcome
Creature Comforts: CCTV, a/c,
refrig, micro, pool, whirlpool

Hilton Hotel, Airport
(800) HILTONS, (510) 635-5000
http://www.hilton.com
1 Hegenberger Rd.
360 rooms - $109-650
Pets: Welcome w/$200 dep.
Creature Comforts: CCTV,
VCR, a/c, refrig, restaurant, pool,
whirlpool

Motel 6 (Airport)
(800) 4-MOTEL6, (510) 638-1180
http://www.motel6.com
8480 Edes Ave.
285 rooms - $46-59
Pets: Under 30 lbs. welcome
Creature Comforts: CCTV, a/c,
pool

Motel 6
(800) 4-MOTEL6, (510) 436-0103
http://www.motel6.com
1801 Embarcadero St.
97 rooms - $53-65
Pets: Under 30 lbs. welcome
Creature Comforts: CCTV, a/c,
pool

OAK VIEW
Oakridge Inn
(805) 649-4018
780 N. Ventura Ave
3 rooms - $55-90
Pets: Welcome w/$10 fee
Creature Comforts: CCTV, a/c,
refrig, micro, cont. brkfst

O'BRIEN
Holiday Harbor
(800) 776-2628, (916) 238-2383
http://www.lakeshasta.com
Box 112
70 houseboats - $295-1,450
(2-night minimum)
Pets: Welcome
Creature Comforts: Well-
maintained houseboats provide an
intriguing vacation getaway on
Lake Shasta, all amenities — kit,
barbecues, general store, Toy Box-
variety of rec. watercraft, and
some great fishing

OCCIDENTAL
Occidental Lodge
(707) 874-3623
3610 Bohemian Hwy.
25 rooms - $60-78
Pets: Small pets w/$5 fee
Creature Comforts: CCTV, pool

OCEANSIDE
Days Inn
(800) DAYS-INN, (760) 722-7661
http://www.daysinn.com
1501 Carmelo Dr.
82 rooms - $50-85
Pets: Welcome w/$10 fee
Creature Comforts: CCTV, a/c,
refrig, pool, whirlpool, ocean vws

Motel 6
(800) 4-MOTEL6, (760) 941-1011
http://www.motel6.com
3708 Plaza Dr.
136 rooms - $42-55
Pets: Under 30 lbs. welcome
Creature Comforts: TV, a/c, pool

Sandman Motel
(760) 722-7661
1501 Carmelo Dr.
80 rooms - $35-55
Pets: Small pets welcome
Creature Comforts: CCTV, pool

OJAI
Best Western Casa Ojai
(800) 528-1234, (805) 646-8175
http://www.bestwestern.com
45 rooms - $55-140
Pets: Welcome
Creature Comforts: CCTV,
VCR, a/c, refrig, pool, whirlpool

Blue Iguana Inn
(800) 528-1234, (805) 646-8175
http://www.blueiguanainn.com
12 rooms - $125-190
Pets: Welcome w/$20 fee
Creature Comforts: Neat old
misssion style architecture,
Mexican furnishings, orig. works
of art, great interiors, CCTV,
VCR, a/c, kit, hot tub, pool

Los Padres Inn
(800) 228-3744, (805) 646-4365
1208 E. Ojai Ave.
30 rooms - $60-119
Pets: $10 fee, $100 dep.
Creature Comforts: CCTV, a/c,
refrig, micro, pool, whirlpool

Oakridge Inn
(805) 649-4018
780 North Ventura Ave.
33 rooms - $75-145
Pets: Small pets w/$10 fee and
credit card dep.
Creature Comforts: CCTV,
VCR, a/c, kit

Ojai Valley Inn
(800) 422-OJAI, (805) 646-5511
http://www.ojairesort.com
Country Club Rd.
215 rooms - $195-875
Pets: Welcome w/$25 fee
Creature Comforts: Exquisite
resort on 220 acres tucked into
mountain valley, southwestern
influence, Native American
artwork, CCTV, VCR, a/c, rattan
and brass accents, fireplaces, kit,
Jacuzzi, restaurants, 3 pools, hlth
clb, saunas, whirlpools, golf,
lovely new spa, lighted tennis,
riding, lawn sports, walking &
bike trails

OLEMA
Ridgetop Inn & Cottages
(415) 663-1500
9865 Sir Francis Drake Blvd.
2 cottages - $95-175
Pets: In cottage w/$25 fee
Creature Comforts: CCTV,
fireplace, kit, full brkfst, great
views

ONTARIO
Best Ontario Inn
(909) 391-6668
1045 W. Missouri Blvd.
44 rooms - $35-55
Pets: Small pets welcome
Creature Comforts: CCTV, a/c,
refrig, micro, pool, whirlpool

Country Inn
(800) 770-1887, (909) 923-1887
2359 S. Grove St.
72 rooms - $40-55
Pets: Welcome
Creature Comforts: CCTV, a/c,
pool

Country Suites by Ayres
(800) 248-4661, (909) 983-8484
231 N. Vineyard Ave.
120 rooms - $69-129
Pets: Welcome w/credit card dep.
Creature Comforts: CCTV, a/c,
refrig, micro, cont. brkfst, Jacuzzi,
pool, whirlpool

Good Nite Inn
(800) 724-8822, (909) 983-3604
1801 E. G St.
185 rooms - $35-55
Pets: Small pets welcome
Creature Comforts: CCTV, a/c,
refrig, micro, restaurant, pool, hlth
clb access, whirlpool

Holiday Inn - Airport
(800) HOLIDAY, (909) 466-9600
http://www.holiday-inn.com
3400 Shelby St.
150 rooms - $79-189
Pets: Welcome w/$75 dep.
Creature Comforts: CCTV, a/c,
kit, restaurant, pool, hlth clb
access, whirlpool

Marriott Hotel
(800) 228-9290, (909) 986-8811
http://www.marriott.com
2200 E. Holt Blvd.
300 rooms - $79-199
Pets: Under 25 Lbs. w/$250 dep.
Creature Comforts: CCTV,
VCR, a/c, refrig, micro, restaurant,
pool, hlth clb, sauna, whirlpool,
tennis, sports courts

Motel 6
(800) 4-MOTEL6, (909) 984-2424
http://www.motel6.com
1560 E. Fourth St.
69 rooms - $39-52
Pets: Under 30 lbs. welcome
Creature Comforts: CCTV, a/c,
pool

Red Lion Inn
(800) RED-LION, (909) 983-0909
http://www.redlion.com
222 N. Vineyard Ave.
340 rooms - $99-139
Pets: Welcome
Creature Comforts: CCTV, a/c,
refrig, 2 restaurants, pool, hlth clb,
sauna, spa

Red Roof Inn
(800) The-Roof, (909) 988-8466
http://www.redroof.com
1818 E. Holt Blvd.
105 rooms - $45-65
Pets: Welcome w/$25 dep.
Creature Comforts: CCTV, a/c,
refrig, micro, pool, sauna,
whirlpool

Residence Inn
(800) 331-3131, (909) 983-6788
http://www.residenceinn.com.com
2025 E. D St.
200 rooms - $129-199
Pets: Welcome $6 daily fee, $50
one-time fee
Creature Comforts: CCTV, a/c,
fireplaces, kit, cont. brkfst, pool,
hlth clb access, sauna, whirlpool

ORANGE
Hilton Suites
(800) HILTONS, (714) 938-1111
http://www.hilton.com
400 N. State College Blvd.
228 rooms - $115-175
Pets: Small pets welcome
Creature Comforts: CCTV,
VCR, a/c, refrig, micro, restaurant,
cont. brkfst, pool, hlth clb, sauna,
whirlpool

Motel 6
(800) 4-MOTEL6, (714) 634-2441
http://www.motel6.com
2920 W. Chapman Ave.
153 rooms - $39-48
Pets: Under 30 lbs. welcome
Creature Comforts: CCTV, a/c,
pool

Residence Inn
(800) 331-3131, (714) 978-7700
http://www.residenceinn.com
201 N. State College Blvd.
104 rooms - $99-229
Pets: Welcome w/credit card dep.
Creature Comforts: CCTV,
VCR, a/c, refrig, micro, restaurant,
cont. brkfst, pool, whirlpool

ORLAND
Amber Light Inn
(530) 865-7655
828 Newville Rd.
40 rooms - $29-49
Pets: Small pets welcome
Creature Comforts: CCTV, a/c,
pool, and whirlpool

Orland Inn
(530) 865-7632
1052 South St.
40 rooms - $34-48
Pets: Welcome
Creature Comforts: CCTV, a/c,
pool

OROVILLE
Best Western Grand Manor Inn
(800) 528-1234, (530) 533-9673
http://www.bestwestern.com
1470 Feather River Blvd.
55 rooms - $65-110
Pets: Welcome w/$100 dep.
Creature Comforts: CCTV, a/c,
refrig, pool, hlth clb, sauna,
whirlpool

Days Inn
(800) DAYS-INN, (530) 533-3297
http://www.daysinn.com
1745 Feather River Blvd.
69 rooms - $49-105
Pets: Welcome w/$7 fee
Creature Comforts: CCTV, a/c,
refrig, micro, Jacuzzis, cont.
brkfst, pool

Econo Lodge
(800) 55-ECONO, (530) 533-8201
http://www.EconLodge.com
1835 Feather River Blvd.
40 rooms - $33-59
Pets: Small pets welcome
Creature Comforts: CCTV, a/c,
refrig, cont. brkfst, pool

Motel 6
(800) 4-MOTEL6, (530) 532-9400
http://www.motel6.com
505 Montgomery St.
102 rooms - $34-45
Pets: Under 30 lbs. welcome
Creature Comforts: CCTV, a/c,
pool

Travelodge
(800) 578-7878, (530) 533-7070
http://www.travelodge.com
580 Oro Dam Blvd.
71 rooms - $45-75
Pets: Welcome w/$5 fee and
credit card deposit
Creature Comforts: CCTV, a/c,
refrig, micro

OXNARD
Best Western Oxnard Inn
(800) 528-1234, (805) 483-9581
http://www.bestwestern.com
1156 So. Oxnard Blvd.
80 rooms - $65-125
Pets: Small pets welcome
Creature Comforts: CCTV, a/c,
refrig, micro, pool, whirlpool

Oxnard Hilton
(800) HILTONS, (805) 485-9666
http://www.hilton.com
600 Esplanade Dr.
160 rooms - $85-145
Pets: Welcome
Creature Comforts: CCTV, a/c, refrig, micro, restaurant, pool, whirlpool, and tennis

Radisson Suite Hotel
(800) 333-3333, (805) 988-0130
http://www.radisson.com
2101 Vineyard Ave.
120 rooms - $99-179
Pets: Small pets welcome w/credit card dep.
Creature Comforts: CCTV, VCR, a/c, fireplaces, kit, Jacuzzi, restaurant, 2 pools, hlth clb, whirlpool, and tennis

Vagabond Inn
(800) 522-1555, (805) 983-9251
http://www.vagabondinns.com
1245 N. Oxnard Blvd.
70 rooms - $45-75
Pets: Welcome w/$5 fee
Creature Comforts: CCTV, a/c, refrig, restaurant, pool

PACIFICA
Best Western Lighthouse Hotel
(800) 528-1234, (415) 355-6300
http://www.bestwestern.com
105 Rockaway Beach Ave.
92 rooms - $99-199
Pets: $10 fee, $50 deposit
Creature Comforts: CCTV, a/c, refrig, pool, whirlpool, and beach

PACIFIC GROVE
Andril Fireplace Cottages
(831) 375-0994
http://www.andrilcottages.com
569 Asilomar Blvd.
16 cottages - $75-325
Pets: Welcome w/$14 daily fee
Creature Comforts: Intimate cottage complex, strong repeat clientele since 1950s, eclectic mix of furnishings from pine to contemporary pieces, tab curtains, CCTV, VCR, a/c, fireplace, kit, cont. brkfst, the beach is just down the road

Best Western Lighthouse Lodge
(800) 528-1234, (831) 655-2111
http://www.lhls.com
1150-1249 Lighthouse Dr.
99 rooms & suites - $69-850
Pets: $10 fee and $50 deposit
Creature Comforts: CCTV, VCR, fireplace, kit, Jacuzzis, cont. brkfst & wine, pool, sauna, whirlpool

Bid-a-wee Motel
(831) 372-2330
221 Asilomar Blvd.
20 rooms - $49-99
Pets: Welcome w/$10 fee
Creature Comforts: CCTV, refrig, micro

Old St. Angela Inn
(800) 748-6306, (831) 372-3246
http://www.sueandlewinns.com
321 Central Ave.
8 rooms - $100-165
Pets: Welcome in two garden level rooms w/$10 fee
Creature Comforts: Lovely 1900's shingle-style Victorian w/ waterviews, beamed ceilings, detailed wainscoting, pine and rattan furnishings, country décor, teddy bears and intriguing collectibles, CCTV, a/c, fireplace, refrig, buffet brkfst, redwood solarium, garden whirlpool, pool, beach access

Olympia Motor Lodge
(408) 373-2777
1140 Lighthouse Ave.
38 rooms - $59-135
Pets: Welcome w/$10 fee
Creature Comforts: CCTV, a/c, refrig, cont. brkfst, pool, ocean views

PALMDALE
Holiday Inn
(800) HOLIDAY, (805) 947-8055
http://www.holiday-inn.com
38630 - 5th St. West
155 rooms - $75-100
Pets: Welcome w/$15 dep.
Creature Comforts: CCTV, VCR, a/c, refrig, micro, restaurant, pool, hlth clb access, whirlpool

Motel 6
(800) 4-MOTEL6, (805) 272-0660
http://www.motel6.com
407 W. Palmdale Blvd.
103 rooms - $35-49
Pets: Under 30 lbs. welcome
Creature Comforts: CCTV, a/c, pool

PALM DESERT
Casa Larrea Resort Motel
(760) 568-0311
73-771 Larrea St.
12 rooms - $50-125
Pets: Welcome w/$100 dep.
Creature Comforts: CCTV, VCR, a/c, kit, pool, whirlpool

Casa Larrea Motel
(760) 568-0311
73-811 Larrea St.
11 rooms - $49-99
Pets: Leashed welcome
Creature Comforts: CCTV, a/c, kit, indv. decorated rooms, cont. brkfst, pool, whirlpool

Deep Canyon Inn
(800) 253-0004, (760) 346-8061
http://www.desertgold.com/inn/ inn.html
74470 Abronia Trail
34 rooms - $75-140
Pets: Welcome
Creature Comforts: CCTV, a/c, kit, cont. brkfst, pool

Desert Patch Inn
(800) 350-9758, (760) 346-9161
73758 Shadow Mountain
14 rooms - $69-119
Pets: Welcome
Creature Comforts: CCTV, VCR, a/c, kit, pool, whirlpool, putting green

Inn at Deep Canyon
(800) 253-0004, (760) 346-8061
http://www.desertresorts.com
74740 Abronia Trail
30 rooms - $70-180
Pets: Welcome
Creature Comforts: CCTV, a/c, refrig, Jacuzzi, cont. brkfst, pool

Motel 6
(800) 4-MOTEL6, (760) 345-0550
http://www.motel6.com
78100 Varner Rd.
82 rooms - $39-55
Pets: Under 30 lbs. welcome
Creature Comforts: CCTV, a/c

Palm Desert Lodge
(800) 300-3875, (760) 346-3875
74-527 Rte. 111
40 rooms - $45-85
Pets: Welcome
Creature Comforts: CCTV, a/c,
kit, Jacuzzi, pool

PALM SPRINGS
Alpine Gardens Hotel
(760) 323-2231
http://www.alpinegardens.com
1586 E. Palm Canyon Dr.
10 rooms - $75-115
Pets: Welcome
Creature Comforts: CCTV, a/c,
kit, cont. brkfst, pool, whirlpool

A Sunbeam Inn
(800) 328-3812, (760) 323-3812
291 Camino Monte Vista
14 rooms - $35-115
Pets: Small pets welcome
Creature Comforts: CCTV, a/c,
kit, pool

Bermuda Palms Resort
(800) 869-1132, (760) 323-1839
650 E. Palm Canyon Dr.
22 rooms - $39-109
Pets: Welcome w/$50 dep.
Creature Comforts: CCTV, a/c,
fireplace, kit, Jacuzzi, pool

Casa Cody Country Inn
(800) 231-CODY, (760) 320-9346
http://www.palmsprings.com/
hotels/casacody
175 S. Cahuilla Rd.
26 rooms - $65-200
Pets: Welcome w/$10 fee and a
$100 deposit
Creature Comforts: Restored
historic inn draped in
bougainvillea and surround by
gardens, Santa Fe accents and
country decor, Mexican tile floors
w/braided and throw rugs, CCTV,
a/c, fireplaces, kit, Jacuzzis, cont.
brkfst, 2 pools surrounded by
umbrella tables, French doors
open to patios, whirlpools

Chandler Inn
(760) 320-8949
http://www.thelastplanet.com/
chandler.htm
1530 N. Indian Canyon Dr.
21 rooms - $80-115
Pets: Welcome w/$20 dep.
Creature Comforts: CCTV,
VCR, a/c, refrig, pool, whirlpools

Colibri Inn
(800) 445-8916, (760) 327-4000
http://www.cyberg8t.com/~marlot/
312 Camino Monte Vista
10 rooms - $45-90
Pets: Small pets welcome
Creature Comforts: CCTV, a/c,
kit, Jacuzzi, pool, whirlpool

Days Inn
(800) DAYS-INN, (760) 324-5939
http://www.daysinn.com
69-151 E. Palm Canyon Dr.
97 rooms - $45-150
Pets: Welcome
Creature Comforts: CCTV, a/c,
kit, cont. brkfst, pool, whirlpool

Estrella Inn at Palm Springs
(800) 237-3687, (760) 320-4117
http://www.estrella.com
415 S. Belardo Rd.
68 rooms - $79-299
Pets: $20 fee and credit card dep.
Creature Comforts: 1930's
Spanish-style inn at base of the
San Jacinto Mtns., antiques,
fireplaces, CCTV, a/c, kit, 3 pools,
whirlpools, tennis, lawn games,
hlth club access, sport courts,
fountain and gardens, pet area

Hilton Resort
(800) HILTON, (760) 320-6868
http://www.hilton.com
400 E. Tahquitz Canyon Way
260 rooms - $70-695
Pets: Welcome w/$300 dep.
Creature Comforts: CCTV,
VCR, a/c, refrig, micro, Jacuzzi,
restaurant, pool, hlth clb, saunas,
whirlpools, and tennis

Howard Johnson Inn
(800) I-Go-Hojo, (760) 320-2700
http://www.hojo.com
701 E. Palm Canyon Dr.
204 rooms - $45-99
Pets: Welcome
Creature Comforts: CCTV, a/c,
restaurant, pool, whirlpool

La Serena Villas
(760) 325-3216
http://www.palmsprings.com
339 S. Belardo Rd.
45 rooms - $75-99
Pets: Welcome
Creature Comforts: CCTV,
VCR, a/c, kit, pool

McLean Company Rentals
(800) 777-4606, (760) 322-2500
http://www.ps4rent.com
477 S. Palm Canyon Dr.
200 condos - $60-350
Pets: Welcome in ltd. units
Creature Comforts: CCTV,
VCR, a/c, fireplace, kit, Jacuzzi,
pool, hlth clb

Motel 6
(800) 4-MOTEL6, (760) 327-4200
http://www.motel6.com
660 S. Palm Canyon Dr.
149 rooms - $42-55
Pets: Under 30 lbs. welcome
Creature Comforts: CCTV, a/c,
pool

Motel 6
(800) 4-MOTEL6, (760) 325-6129
http://www.motel6.com
595 E. Palm Canyon Dr.
125 rooms - $39-45
Pets: Under 30 lbs. welcome
Creature Comforts: CCTV, a/c,
pool

Motel 6
(800) 4-MOTEL6, (760) 251-1425
http://www.motel6.com
63950 - 20th Ave.
96 rooms - $42-55
Pets: Under 30 lbs. welcome
Creature Comforts: CCTV, a/c,
pool

Musicland Hotel
(800) 428-3939, (760) 325-1326
1342 S. Palm Canyon Dr.
47 rooms - $30-105
Pets: Small pets welcome
Creature Comforts: CCTV, a/c,
kit, pool, spa

Place in the Sun
(800) 779-2254, (760) 325-0254
http://www.desert-resorts.com/sun
754 San Lorenzo Rd.
15 rooms - $60-159
Pets: Small pets welcome
Creature Comforts: CCTV, a/c,
kit, pool, whirlpool, and putting
green

Quality Inn
(800) 228-5150, (760) 323-2775
http://www.qualityinn.com
1269 E. Palm Canyon Dr.
145 rooms - $45-175
Pets: Small pets welcome
Creature Comforts: CCTV, a/c,
refrig, micro, pool, whirlpool

Ramada Inn Resort
(800) 2-Ramada, (760) 323-1711
http://www.ramada.com
1800 E. Palm Canyon Dr.
255 rooms - $69-179
Pets: Welcome w/credit card dep.
Creature Comforts: CCTV,
VCR, a/c, refrig, micro, Jacuzzi, 2
restaurants, pool, hlth clb, saunas,
massage, whirlpool

Riviera Resort & Racquet Club
(800) 444-8311, (760) 327-8311
www.desertresorts.com/riviera
1600 N. Indian Canyon Dr.
480 rooms - $129-875
Pets: Welcome w/$100 dep.
Creature Comforts: An
expansive resort set on 24 acres,
contemporary décor, CCTV, a/c,
refrig, micro, Jacuzzis, restaurant,
2 pools, hlth and racquet clb,
sauna, whirlpool, tennis program,
putting green, croquet, bocci ball,
massage, lawn games, kids camp

Royal Sun
(760) 327-1564
170 S. Palm Canyon Dr.
65 rooms - $50-120
Pets: Small pets w/$10 fee
Creature Comforts: CCTV, a/c,
refrig, micro, pool, sauna,
whirlpool

Super 8 Motel
(800) 800-8000, (760) 322-3757
http://www.super8.com
1900 N. Palm Canyon Dr.
61 rooms - $49-79
Pets: Welcome w/$10 fee
Creature Comforts: CCTV, a/c,
refrig, micro, pool, whirlpool

Ville Orleans Resort Hotel
(760) 864-6200
269 Chuckwalla Rd.
15 rooms - $70-250
Pets: Small pets w/$10 fee
Creature Comforts: CCTV,
VCR, a/c, kit, pool, whirlpool

Wyndham Palm Springs
(800) Wyndham, (760) 322-6000
http://www.wyndham.com
888 Tahquitz Canyon Way
410 rooms - $75-295
Pets: Welcome w/$25 dep.
Creature Comforts: CCTV, a/c,
refrig, restaurant, pool, hlth clb,
sauna, whirlpool

PALO ALTO
Cardinal Hotel
(650) 323-5101
235 Hamilton Ave.
59 rooms - $65-185
Pets: Welcome
Creature Comforts: CCTV, a/c

Days Inn
(800) DAYS-INN, (650) 493-4222
http://www.daysinn.com
4238 El Camino Real
22 rooms - $65-130
Pets: Welcome w/$10 fee
Creature Comforts: CCTV,
VCR, a/c, kit, cont. brkfst

Holiday Inn
(800) HOLIDAY, (650) 328-2800
http://www.holiday-inn.com
625 El Camino Real
340 rooms - $140-185
Pets: Small pets welcome
Creature Comforts: CCTV, a/c,
kit, restaurant, pool, hlth clb,
whirlpool

Hyatt Rickeys
(800) 233-1234, (650) 493-8000
http://www.hyatt.com
4219 El Camino Real
345 rooms - $89-329
Pets: Welcome w/$50 dep.
Creature Comforts: CCTV, a/c,
refrig, fireplaces, pool, hlth clb,
lawn games, putting green

Motel 6
(800) 4-MOTEL6, (650) 949-0833
http://www.motel6.com
4301 El Camino Real
71 rooms - $59-75
Pets: Under 30 lbs. welcome
Creature Comforts: CCTV, a/c,
pool

Sheraton Suites
(800) 325-3535, (650) 328-2800
http://www.sheraton.com
625 El Camino Real
359 rooms - $220-390
Pets: Welcome w/$50 fee
Creature Comforts: CCTV,
VCR, a/c, micro, restaurant, pool,
and hlth clb access

PARADISE
Lime Saddle Marina
(800) 834-7571 (CA),
(530) 877-2414
3428 Pentz Rd.
25 boats - $70-485
Pets: Welcome w/$35 fee
Creature Comforts: CCTV, a/c,
kit, Jacuzzi, restaurant, cont.
brkfst, pool, hlth clb access, sauna,
whirlpool

Paradise Inn
(530) 877-2127
5423 Skyway
18 rooms - $35-50
Pets: Welcome w/$5 fee
Creature Comforts: CCTV, a/c,
kit, pool

Ponderosa Gardens Motel
(530) 872-9094
7010 Skyway
48 rooms - $50-70
Pets: Welcome w/$5 fee
Creature Comforts: CCTV, a/c,
refrig, pool, whirlpool

PASADENA

Holiday Inn
(800) HOLIDAY, (818) 449-4000
http://www.holiday-inn.com
303 E. Cordova St.
315 rooms - $99-365
Pets: Small pets w/$50 dep.
Creature Comforts: CCTV, a/c,
refrig, restaurant, pool, and tennis

Holiday Inn Express
(800) HOLIDAY, (818) 796-9291
http://www.holiday-inn.com
3321 E. Colorado Blvd.
72 rooms - $50-75
Pets: Welcome w/$10 fee
Creature Comforts: CCTV, a/c,
refrig, pool, sauna, whirlpool

Pasadena Inn
(818) 795-8401
400 S. Arroyo Pkwy.
62 rooms - $55-90
Pets: Welcome
Creature Comforts: CCTV, a/c,
cont. brkfst, pool

Vagabond Inn
(800) 522-1555, (818) 577-8873
http://www.vagabondinns.com
1203 E. Colorado Blvd.
55 rooms - $45-75
Pets: Welcome w/$5 fee
Creature Comforts: CCTV, a/c,
kit, pool

Westaway Inn
(818) 304-9678
1203 E. Colorado Blvd.
60 rooms - $45-60
Pets: Welcome w/$5 fee
Creature Comforts: CCTV, a/c,
refrig, pool, sauna, whirlpool

PASO ROBLES

Motel 6
(800) 4-MOTEL6, (805) 239-9090
http://www.motel6.com
1134 Black Oak Dr.
121 rooms - $39-48
Pets: Under 30 lbs. welcome
Creature Comforts: CCTV, a/c,
pool

Travelodge Paso Robles
(800) 578-7878, (805) 238-0078
http://www.travelodge.com
2701 Spring St.
32 rooms - $39-85
Pets: Welcome w/$5 fee
Creature Comforts: CCTV, a/c,
refrig, micro, pool

PEBBLE BEACH

The Lodge at Pebble Beach
(800) 654-9300, (831) 624-3811
http://www.pebble-beach.com
17-Mile Dr.
161 rooms - $350-2,000
Pets: Small pets welcome
Creature Comforts: World
famous historic resort and golf
course, rooms w/sophisticated
decor, luxurious furnishings, soft
earth tone fabrics and walls, rqst
rooms w/ocean or fairway views,
CCTV, VCR, a/c, fireplace, refrig,
micro, Jacuzzis, two restaurants,
pool, hlth clb, saunas, whirlpools,
tennis, 4 golf courses, general
store, beach, par-courses, trails-
hiking/riding, massage, riding

PETALUMA

Motel 6
(800) 4-MOTEL6, (707) 765-0333
http://www.motel6.com
1368 N. McDowell Blvd.
121 rooms - $39-52
Pets: Under 30 lbs. welcome
Creature Comforts: CCTV, a/c,
pool

Quality Inn
(800) 228-5151, (707) 664-1155
http://www.qualityinn.com
5100 Montero Way
110 rooms - $65-145
Pets: Welcome w/$20 dep.
Creature Comforts: CCTV,
VCR, a/c, cont. brkfst, pool,
sauna, whirlpool

PETROLIA

Mattole River Resort
(800) 845-4607, (707) 629-3445
42354 Mattole Rd.
7 cabins - $45-107
Pets: Welcome
Creature Comforts: TV, kit,
woodstove, trails, river views

PIERCY

Hartsook Inn
(707) 247-3305
900 Rte. 101
62 cottages - $50-130
Pets: Welcome w/$5 fee
Creature Comforts: TV,
fireplace, refrig, restaurant, cont.
brkfst

PICO RIVERA

Travelodge
(800) 578-7878, (562) 949-6648
http://www.travelodge.com
7222 Rosemead Blvd.
48 rooms - $45-60
Pets: Small pet welcome
Creature Comforts: CCTV, a/c,
refrig, pool, whirlpool

PINOLE

Motel 6
(800) 4-MOTEL6, (510) 222-8174
http://www.motel6.com
1501 Fitzgerald Dr.
102 rooms - $52-65
Pets: Under 30 lbs. welcome
Creature Comforts: CCTV, a/c,
pool

PISMO BEACH

Cottage Inn by the Sea
(888) 440-8400, (805) 773-4617
http://www.cottage-inn.com
2351 Price St.
80 rooms - $45-155
Pets: In non-view rms. w/$10 fee
Creature Comforts: Inn w/
country decor and great views,
CCTV, a/c, vaulted ceilings,
fireplace, refrig, micro, cont.
brkfst, oceanview pool, whirlpool

Motel 6
(800) 4-MOTEL6, (805) 773-2665
http://www.motel6.com
860 - 4th St.
136 rooms - $36-49
Pets: Under 30 lbs. welcome
Creature Comforts: CCTV, a/c,
pool

Oxford Suites Resort
(800) 982-SUITE, (805) 773-3773
www.oxfordsuitesresorts.com
651 Five Cities Dr.
135 rooms - $69-139
Pets: Welcome w/$10 fee
Creature Comforts: CCTV,
VCR, a/c, refrig, micro, full brkfst,
pool, whirlpool

Sandcastle Inn
(800) 822-6606, (805) 773-2422
http://www.sandcastleinn.com
100 Stimson Ave.
60 rooms - $69-259
Pets: Welcome w/$10 fee
Creature Comforts: CCTV,
VCR, a/c, refrig, whirlpool,
waterviews

Shell Beach Motel
(805) 773-4373
653 Shell Beach Rd.
10 rooms - $40-135
Pets: Welcome w/$10 dep.
Creature Comforts: CCTV,
refrig, pool

Spyglass Inn
(800) 824-2612 (CA),
(805) 773-4855
http://www.spyglassinn.com
2705 Spyglass Dr.
80 rooms - $65-175
Pets: Welcome w/$10 fee
Creature Comforts: Bluffside
resort overlooking Pismo Beach,
cathedral beamed ceilings,
bleached wood furnishings,
contemporary décor, CCTV, VCR,
refrig, fieldstone fireplaces,
restaurant-oceanside deck, pool,
hlth club, whirlpool, mini-golf,
ocean views

PITTSBURG
Motel 6
(800) 4-MOTEL6, (510) 427-1600
http://www.motel6.com
2101 Loveridge Rd.
176 rooms - $40-53
Pets: Under 30 lbs. welcome
Creature Comforts: CCTV, a/c,
pool

PLACENTIA
Residence Inn
(800) 331-3131, (714) 996-0555
http://www.residenceinn.com
700 W. Kimberly Ave.
110 rooms - $69-179
Pets: $5 fee and credit card dep.
Creature Comforts: CCTV,
VCR, a/c, fireplaces, kit, cont.
brkfst, pool, whirlpool

PLACERVILLE
Gold Trail Lodge
(530) 622-2906
1970 Broadway St.
33 rooms - $39-55
Pets: Welcome w/$5 fee
Creature Comforts: CCTV, pool

Mother Lode Motel
(530) 622-0895
1940 Broadway St.
22 rooms - $32-52
Pets: Welcome w/$5 fee
Creature Comforts: CCTV, a/c,
refrig, pool

PLEASANT HILL
Residence Inn
(800) 331-3131, (925) 689-1010
http://www.residenceinn.com
700 Ellinwood Way
125 rooms - $94-169
Pets: $6 fee and credit card dep.
Creature Comforts: CCTV,
VCR, a/c, kit, cont. brkfst, pool,
hlth clb, sauna, whirlpool

PLEASANTON
Candlewood Suites
(800) 946-6200, (925) 463-1212
http://www.candlewoodsuites.com
5535 Johnson Way
125 rooms - $99-139
Pets: Welcome w/$75 cleaning
charge and a $10 daily fee
Creature Comforts: CCTV,
VCR, a/c, kit, cont. brkfst, pool,
hlth clb, sauna, whirlpool

Hilton Hotel
(800) HILTON, (925) 463-8000
http://www.hilton.com
7050 Johnson Dr.
295 rooms - $99-625
Pets: Welcome w/$25 dep.
Creature Comforts: CCTV,
VCR, a/c, refrig, restaurant, 2
pools, hlth clb, whirlpool,
racquetball, and tennis

Holiday Inn Select
(800) HOLIDAY, (925) 847-6000
http://www.holiday-inn.com
11950 Dublin Canyon Rd.
245 rooms - $69-139
Pets: Welcome w/$15 fee
Creature Comforts: CCTV, a/c,
refrig, restaurant, pool, hlth clb,
whirlpool

Motel 6
(800) 4-MOTEL6, (925) 463-2626
http://www.motel6.com
5102 Hopyard St.
76 rooms - $55-65
Pets: Under 30 lbs. welcome
Creature Comforts: CCTV, a/c,
pool

PLYMOUTH
Far Horizons 49er
(800) 339-6981
18265 Rte. 49
329 rooms - $30-45
Pets: Welcome
Creature Comforts: CCTV, a/c,
restaurant, pool, whirlpool

POINT REYES STATION
Berry Patch Cottage
(888) 663-1942, (415) 663-1942
http://www.coastalgetaways.com
68 Mesa Rd.
1 cottage - $100-125
Pets: Welcome w/$5 nightly fee
Creature Comforts: Light and
airy cottage set among fruit tees,
gardens, rambling yard, CCTV,
VCR, woodstove, kit, redwood
deck, cont. brkfst

Knob Hill Cottage
(888) 663-1784, (415) 663-1784
PO Box 1108
http://www.knobhill.com
2 units - $65-115
Pets: Welcome
Creature Comforts: Fireplace,
Irish woodstove, tab curtains,
braided rugs, refrig, stereo, cont.
brkfst

**Jasmine Cottage and
Gray's Retreat**
(415) 663-1166
PO Box 56
2 cottages - $145-185
Pets: Welcome w/$15 fee
Creature Comforts: Delightfully
eclectic cottages just up the hill
from town, an 1879 schoolhouse
has kitchen w/hand-painted tiles,
stencils, hand-painted caricatures,
rattan, country antiques, four-
poster bed, dried wreaths, CCTV,
fireplace, full brkfst, patio and
garden spa, bucolic views

Pt. Reyes Station Inn
(415) 663-9372
http://www.p-r-s-i.com
11591 Rte. 1
4 rooms - $110-200
Pets: In Garden Room
Creature Comforts: A charming old-fashioned inn set behind a picket fence, traditional decor w/ floral accents, antiques, CCTV, a/c, fireplaces, sliding doors to private decks, vaulted ceilings, refrig, modern bathrooms w/ skylights and Jacuzzis, fireplaces, cont. brkfst, views of hills

Seven Gray Foxes
(415) 663-1089
145 Mesa Rd.
3 rooms - $75-139
Pets: Welcome
Creature Comforts: CCTV, a/c, fireplace, kit, cont. brkfst, garden & fields

Thirty-Nine Cypress
(415) 663-1709
http://www.point-reyes-inn.com/
39 Cypress Rd., Box 176
1 cottage - $115-160
Pets: Welcome
Creature Comforts: An expansive redwood cottage nestled amid gardens, bucolic views, Oriental rugs, country quilts, original artwork, country antiques, seashore collectibles displayed, fieldstone fireplace, kit, great brkfst, whirlpool, binoculars, bicycles, and trails

The Tree House
(800) 495-8720, (415) 663-8720
http://www.treehousebnb.com
73 Drake Summit
3 rooms - $100-135
Pets: Welcome
Creature Comforts: An inviting B&B perched on a hillside w/ terrific views, antiques, brass and finial beds, homey décor w/floral accents, decorative hats, CCTV, VCR, fireplace, kit, cont. brkfst, gardens, whirlpool, birding

POLLOCK PINES
Stagecoach Motor Inn
(916) 644-2029
5940 Pony Express Tr.
25 rooms - $50-135
Pets: Welcome w/$5 fee
Creature Comforts: a/c, kit

POMONA
Motel 6
(800) 4-MOTEL6, (909) 591-1871
http://www.motel6.com
2470 S. Garey Ave.
120 rooms - $31-40
Pets: Under 30 lbs. welcome
Creature Comforts: CCTV, a/c, pool

Sheraton Suites
(800) 325-3535, (909) 622-2220
http://www.sheraton.com
600 W. McKinley Ave.
250 rooms - $60-130
Pets: Welcome w/$10 fee
Creature Comforts: CCTV, VCR, a/c, micro, restaurant, pool, hlth clb, sauna, whirlpool

Shilo Inn
(800) 222-2244, (909) 598-0073
http://www.shiloinns.com
3200 Temple Ave.
160 rooms - $75-140
Pets: Welcome w/$7 fee
Creature Comforts: CCTV, a/c, kit, restaurant, full brkfst, pool, hlth clb, sauna, whirlpool

PORTERVILLE
Best Western Porterville Inn
(800) 528-1234, (209) 781-7411
http://www.bestwestern.com
350 W. Montgomery Ave.
116 rooms - $55-75
Pets: Small pets welcome
Creature Comforts: CCTV, a/c, refrig, micro, restaurant, pool, hlth clb, whirlpool

Motel 6
(800) 4-MOTEL6, (209) 781-7600
http://www.motel6.com
935 W. Morton Ave.
107 rooms - $34-44
Pets: Under 30 lbs. welcome
Creature Comforts: CCTV, a/c, pool

POWAY
Poway Country Inn
(800) 648-6320, (619) 748-6320
13845 Poway Rd.
45 rooms - $42-69
Pets: Small pets welcome
Creature Comforts: CCTV, a/c, kit, cont. brkfst, pool, whirlpool

QUINCY
Gold Pan Motel
(800) 804-6541, (916) 283-3686
200 Crescent St.
57 rooms - $39-69
Pets: Welcome w/$2 fee
Creature Comforts: CCTV, a/c, refrig, and micro

RAMONA
Ramona Valley Inn
(760) 789-6433
416 Main St.
40 rooms - $45-90
Pets: Welcome w/$50 dep.
Creature Comforts: CCTV, a/c, kit, pool

RANCHO BERNARDO
La Quinta Inn
(800) Nu-Rooms, (619) 484-8800
http://www.laquinta.com
10185 Paseo Montril
120 rooms - $50-75
Pets: Welcome
Creature Comforts: CCTV, a/c, refrig, pool

Radisson Suite Hotel
(800) 333-3333, (619) 451-6600
http://www.radisson.com
11520 W. Bernardo Ct.
175 rooms - $89-169
Pets: Small pets welcome
Creature Comforts: CCTV, VCR, a/c, refrig, micro, restaurant, full brkfst, pool, hlth clb access, whirlpool

Rancho Bernardo Travelodge
(800) 578-7878, (619) 487-0445
http://www.travelodge.com
16929 W. Bernardo Dr.
50 rooms - $50-75
Pets: $5 fee & $25 dep.
Creature Comforts: CCTV, a/c, refrig, micro, pool

Residence Inn
(800) 331-3131, (619) 673-1900
http://www.residenceinn.com
11002 Rancho Carmel Dr.
125 rooms - $89-159
Pets: Welcome w/$5 fee and
credit card dep.
Creature Comforts: CCTV,
VCR, a/c, refrig, cont. brkfst,
pool, hlth clb, whirlpool

RANCHO CORDOVA
Best Western Heritage Inn
(800) 528-1234, (916) 635-4040
http://www.bestwestern.com
11269 Point East Dr.
120 rooms - $60-99
Pets: Small pets w/$10 fee
Creature Comforts: CCTV, a/c,
refrig, micro, restaurant, pool,
sauna, whirlpool

Comfort Inn
(800) 228-5150, (916) 363-3344
http://www.comfortinn.com
3240 Mather Field Rd.
112 rooms - $49-69
Pets: Welcome w/credit card dep.
Creature Comforts: CCTV, a/c,
kit, pool, whirlpool

Economy Inns of America
(800) 826-0778, (916) 351-1213
http://www.innsofamerica.com
12249 Folsom Blvd.
124 rooms - $40-55
Pets: Welcome
Creature Comforts: CCTV, a/c,
pool

Motel 6
(800) 4-MOTEL6, (916) 635-8784
http://www.motel6.com
10694 Olson Dr.
68 rooms - $40-59
Pets: Under 30 lbs. welcome
Creature Comforts: CCTV, a/c

RANCHO MIRAGE
Motel 6
(800) 4-MOTEL6, (760) 324-8475
http://www.motel6.com
69-750 Rte. 111
104 rooms - 42-55
Pets: Under 30 lbs. welcome
Creature Comforts: CCTV, a/c,
pool

Westin Mission Hills Resort
(800) 228-3000, (760) 328-5955
http://www.westin.com
71-333 Dinah Shore Dr.
512 rooms - $109-1,350
Pets: Welcome w/credit card dep.
Creature Comforts: Expansive
resort set in desert amid 360 acres,
CCTV, VCR, a/c, refrig, micro,
Jacuzzis, restaurant, 3 pools,
waterslides, hlth clb, saunas,
whirlpools, steamrooms, golf,
tennis, trails, and lawn games

RANCHO SANTA FE
Inn at Rancho Santa Fe
(800) The-Inn-1, (619) 756-1131
www.theinnatranchosantafe.com
5951 Linea Del Cielo
90 rooms - $85-600
Pets: Welcome in cottage rooms
Creature Comforts: Lovely and
classic California resort in toney
hamlet, 20 manicured acres,
beamed-ceiling living room w/
antiques, ship models, chintz
furnishings, CCTV, VCR, a/c,
fireplaces, rms. w/pastel colors,
wicker and reproductions, kit,
Jacuzzis, restaurant, pool, hlth clb,
saunas, whirlpool, tennis, lawn
games, beach cottage, paths
around inn

Rancho Valencia Resort
(800) 548-3664, (619) 756-1123
http://www.ranchovalencia.com
5921 Valencia Cir.
43 rooms - $325-2,000
Pets: Welcome w/$75 daily fee
Creature Comforts: Luxurious
casitas on wooded hillsides,
exclusive enclave, 40 acres of
beautifully landscaped grounds,
festive fabrics, French doors open
to patios w/umbrella tables,
beamed ceilings, bleached woods,
plantation shutters, CCTV, VCR,
a/c, fireplaces, kit, Jacuzzis,
restaurant, pool, hlth clb, saunas,
complete spa, whirlpools, tennis
program, lawn games, golf access,
polo

RED BLUFF
Cinderella Riverview Motel
(530) 527-5490
600 Rio St.
40 rooms - $29-59
Pets: Welcome
Creature Comforts: CCTV, a/c,
refrig, pool, river views

IMA Value Lodge
(800) 341-8000, (530) 529-2028
http://www.imalodging.com
30 Gilmore Rd.
60 rooms - $39-65
Pets: Welcome
Creature Comforts: CCTV, a/c,
refrig, micro, pool

Kings Lodge
(800) 426-5655, (530) 527-6020
38 Antelope Blvd.
40 rooms - $35-45
Pets: Welcome
Creature Comforts: CCTV, a/c,
refrig, pool

Motel 6
(800) 4-MOTEL6, (530) 527-9200
http://www.motel6.com
20 Williams Ave.
61 rooms - $34-46
Pets: Under 30 lbs. welcome
Creature Comforts: CCTV, a/c

Red Bluff Inn
(530) 529-2028
30 Gilmore Rd.
60 rooms - $39-65
Pets: Welcome w/$20 dep.
Creature Comforts: CCTV, a/c,
refrig, micro, pool

Super 8
(800) 800-8000, (916) 527-8882
http://www.super8.com
203 Antelope Blvd.
72 rooms - $49-69
Pets: Welcome w/$25 dep.
Creature Comforts: CCTV, a/c,
pool

REDDING
Americana Lodge
(800) 626-1900, (530) 241-7020
1250 Pine St.
55 rooms - $29-39
Pets: Welcome w/$25 dep.
Creature Comforts: CCTV, a/c,
refrig, micro, pool

Best Western Inn
(800) 528-1234, (530) 241-6464
http://www.bestwestern.com
532 N. Market St.
61 rooms - $45-78
Pets: $7 fee and $25 dep.
Creature Comforts: CCTV, a/c,
refrig, micro, pool

Best Western Ponderosa
(800) 528-1234, (530) 241-6300
http://www.bestwestern.com
2220 Pine St.
70 rooms - $45-80
Pets: Welcome w/credit card dep.
Creature Comforts: CCTV, a/c,
refrig, micro, pool

Bridge Bay Resort
(800) 752-9669, (530) 241-6464
http://www.sevencrown.com
10300 Bridge Bay Rd.
40 rooms - $55-155
Pets: $5 fee and $25 dep.
Creature Comforts: CCTV, a/c,
kit, restaurant, pool, marina-boat
rentals

Capri Motel
(800) 626-1900, (530) 241-1156
4620 Rte. 90
59 rooms - $30-45
Pets: Welcome w/$100 dep.
Creature Comforts: CCTV, a/c,
refrig, micro, pool

Comfort Inn
(800) 228-5150, (530) 221-6530
http://www.comfortinn.com
2059 Hilltop Dr.
90 rooms - $45-80
Pets: Welcome w/$100 dep.
Creature Comforts: CCTV, a/c,
refrig, cont. brkfst, pool

Doubletree Hotel
(800) 222-TREE, (530) 221-8700
http://www.doubletreehotels.com
1830 Hilltop Dr.
194 rooms - $85-250
Pets: Welcome in 1st flr rms.
Creature Comforts: CCTV,
VCR, a/c, refrig, micro, Jacuzzis,
restaurant, cont. brkfst, pool,
whirlpool

Fawndale Lodge
(800) 338-0941, (530) 275-800
http://www.fawnresort@suno.com
15215 Fawndale Rd.
11 rooms - $44-75
Pets: Welcome
Creature Comforts: CCTV, kit,
cont. brkfst, pool

Holiday Inn Express
(800) 465-4329, (530) 241-5500
http://www.holiday-inn.com
1080 Twin View Blvd.
50 rooms - $79-99
Pets: Welcome w/$10 fee
Creature Comforts: CCTV,
VCR, a/c, refrig, pool

La Quinta Inn
(800) Nu-Rooms, (530) 221-8200
http://www.laquinta.com
2180 Hilltop Dr.
140 rooms - $53-142
Pets: Small pets welcome
Creature Comforts: CCTV, a/c,
refrig, micro, restaurant, pool,
whirlpool

Motel 6
(800) 4-MOTEL6, (530) 246-4470
http://www.motel6.com
1250 Twin View Blvd.
97 rooms - $39-53
Pets: Under 30 lbs. welcome
Creature Comforts: CCTV, a/c

Motel 6
(800) 4-MOTEL6, (530) 221-1800
http://www.motel6.com
1640 Hilltop Dr.
80 rooms - $39-53
Pets: Under 30 lbs. welcome
Creature Comforts: CCTV, a/c

Motel 6
(800) 4-MOTEL6, (530) 221-0562
http://www.motel6.com
2385 Bechelli Ln
105 rooms - $39-53
Pets: Under 30 lbs. welcome
Creature Comforts: CCTV, a/c

Oxford Suites
(800) 762-0133, (530) 221-0100
1967 Hilltop Dr.
139 rooms - $65-120
Pets: Welcome w/$15 fee
Creature Comforts: CCTV,
VCR, a/c, refrig, micro, full brkfst,
pool, hlth clb access, whirlpool

Paradise B&B
(530) 223-5305
120 Palisades Ave.
2 rooms - $65-100
Pets: Welcome
Creature Comforts: CCTV, a/c,
cont. brkfst, fireplace, whirlpool,
mtn views, long the river

Red Lion Inn
(800) RED-LION, (530) 221-8010
http://www.redlion.com
1830 Hilltop Dr.
195 rooms - $85-275
Pets: Small pets welcome
Creature Comforts: CCTV, a/c,
refrig, restaurant, pool, whirlpool,
putting green

River Inn
(800) 995-4341, (530) 241-9500
1835 Park Marina Blvd.
80 rooms - $70-105
Pets: Welcome w/$5 fee
Creature Comforts: CCTV,
VCR, a/c, refrig, micro, Jacuzzis,
pool, sauna, whirlpool

Vagabond Inn
(800) 522-1555, (530) 223-1600
http://www.vagabondinns.com
536 E. Cypress Ave.
70 rooms - $55-85
Pets: Welcome w/$5 fee
Creature Comforts: CCTV, a/c,
pool

REDLANDS
Best Western Sandman Motel
(800) 528-1234, (909) 793-2001
http://www.bestwestern.com
1120 W. Colton Ave.
65 rooms - $40-75
Pets: Welcome w/permission
Creature Comforts: CCTV, a/c,
refrig, cont. brkfst, pool, whirlpool

Good Nite Inn
(909) 793-3723
1675 Industrial Park Ave.
100 rooms - $30-45
Pets: Small pets welcome
Creature Comforts: CCTV, a/c,
pool, whirlpool

Super 8 Motel
(800) 800-8000, (909) 792-8779
http://www.super8.com
1160 Arizona St.
80 rooms - $36-55
Pets: Welcome
Creature Comforts: CCTV, a/c, pool

RED MOUNTAIN
Old Owl Inn
(888) 653-6954
701 Rte. 395
2 cabins - $50-105
Pets: Welcome
Creature Comforts: CCTV, a/c, cont. brkfst

REDONDO BEACH
Vagabond Inn
(800) 522-1555, (310) 378-8555
http://www.vagabondinns.com
6226 Pacific Coast Hwy.
40 rooms - $45-60
Pets: Welcome w/$5 fee
Creature Comforts: CCTV, a/c, refrig, cont. brkfst, pool

REDWAY
Redway Inn
(800) 732-5380 (CA),
(707) 923-2660
3223 Redwood Dr.
12 rooms - $45-65
Pets: Welcome
Creature Comforts: CCTV, a/c, refrig, micro, cont. brkfst

REDWOOD CITY
Good Nite Inn
(650) 365-5500
485 Veterans Blvd.
125 rooms - $40-75
Pets: Small pets welcome
Creature Comforts: CCTV, a/c, refrig, micro, pool

Hotel Sofitel
(800) 763-4835, (650) 598-9000
http://www.sofitel.com
223 Twin Dolphin Dr.
320 rooms - $100-450
Pets: Small pets w/$25 fee
Creature Comforts: CCTV, a/c, refrig, restaurant, pool, hlth clb, sauna, whirlpools

Super 8 Motel
(800) 800-8000, (650) 366-0880
http://www.super8.com
84 Woodside Rd.
40 rooms - $40-65
Pets: Welcome
Creature Comforts: CCTV, a/c, refrig, and micro

REEDLEY
Edgewater Inn
(559) 637-7777
1977 W. Manning Ave.
49 rooms - $45-130
Pets: Small pets w/$5 fee
Creature Comforts: CCTV, VCR, a/c, refrig, pool, whirlpool

RIALTO
Best Western Empire Inn
(800) 528-1234, (909) 877-0690
http://www.bestwestern.com
475 W. Valley Blvd.
100 rooms - $59-79
Pets: Welcome w/$5 fee
Creature Comforts: CCTV, a/c, restaurant, pool, whirlpools

RICHMOND
Civic Center Motel
(510) 235-8300
e-mail: ccmpwang@aol.com
425 - 24th St.
48 rooms - $35-55
Pets: Welcome
Creature Comforts: CCTV, a/c

RIDGECREST
Econo Lodge
(800) 55-ECONO, (760) 446-2551
http://www.econolodge.com
201 Inyokem Rd.
55 rooms - $35-60
Pets: Small pets welcome
Creature Comforts: CCTV, a/c, refrig, micro

Heritage Inn & Suites
(800) 843-0693, (760) 446-6543
1050 N. Norma Dr.
169 rooms - $80-125
Pets: Welcome
Creature Comforts: CCTV, VCR, a/c, kit, restaurant, pool, hlth clb, whirlpools

Motel 6
(800) 4-MOTEL6, (760) 375-6866
http://www.motel6.com
535 S. China Lake Blvd.
76 rooms - $35-48
Pets: Under 30 lbs. welcome
Creature Comforts: CCTV, a/c, pool

RIVERSIDE
Dynasty Suites
(800) 842-7899, (909) 369-8200
http://www.dynastysuites.com
3735 Iowa Ave.
32 rooms - $35-65
Pets: Small pets w/$10 fee
Creature Comforts: CCTV, VCR, a/c, refrig, micro, pool, whirlpool

Motel 6
(800) 4-MOTEL6, (909) 784-2131
http://www.motel6.com
1260 University Ave.
61 rooms - $35-58
Pets: Under 30 lbs. welcome
Creature Comforts: CCTV, a/c

Motel 6
(800) 4-MOTEL6, (909) 351-0764
http://www.motel6.com
3663 La Sierra Ave.
149 rooms - $33-55
Pets: Under 30 lbs. welcome
Creature Comforts: CCTV, a/c, pool

Motel 6
(800) 4-MOTEL6, (909) 681-6666
http://www.motel6.com
6830 Valley Way
60 rooms - $38-59
Pets: Under 30 lbs. welcome
Creature Comforts: CCTV, a/c, pool

Motel 6
(800) 4-MOTEL6, (760) 375-6866
http://www.motel6.com
535 S. China Lake Blvd.
76 rooms - $30-45
Pets: Under 30 lbs. welcome
Creature Comforts: CCTV, a/c

Super 8 Motel
(800) 800-8000, (909) 682-1144
http://www.super8.com
1350 University Ave.
82 rooms - $32-59
Pets: Welcome
Creature Comforts: CCTV, a/c, pool

ROCKLIN
First Choice Inn
(800) 462-2400, (916) 624-4500
http://www.firstchoiceinns.com
4420 Rocklin Rd.
125 rooms - $60-135
Pets: Under 25 lbs. w/$20 fee and a credit card deposit
Creature Comforts: CCTV, VCR, a/c, refrig, micro, pool, hlth clb, whirlpool

ROHNERT PARK
Best Western
(800) 528-1234, (707) 584-7435
http://www.bestwestern.com
6500 Redwood Dr.
145 rooms - $45-80
Pets: Welcome
Creature Comforts: CCTV, cont. brkfst, pool, whirlpool

Motel 6
(800) 4-MOTEL6, (707) 585-8888
http://www.motel6.com
6145 Commerce Blvd.
127 rooms - $39-50
Pets: Under 30 lbs. welcome
Creature Comforts: CCTV, a/c

Red Lion Hotel
(800) RED-LION, (707) 584-5466
http://www.redlion.com
1 Red Lion Dr.
244 rooms - $100-199
Pets: Welcome w/credit card dep.
Creature Comforts: CCTV, a/c, refrig, 2 restaurants, pool, whirlpool, and tennis

ROSAMOND
Devonshire Motel
(805) 256-3454
2076 Rosamond Blvd.
30 rooms - $50-75
Pets: Small pets welcome
Creature Comforts: CCTV, a/c, refrig, pool, whirlpool

ROSEMEAD
Motel 6
(800) 4-MOTEL6, (818) 572-6076
http://www.motel6.com
1001 S. San Gabriel Blvd.
130 rooms - $30-39
Pets: Under 30 lbs. welcome
Creature Comforts: CCTV, a/c, pool

Vagabond Inn
(800) 522-1555, (818) 288-6661
http://www.vagabondinns.com
3633 N. Rosemead Blvd.
100 rooms - $45-60
Pets: Welcome w/$5 fee
Creature Comforts: CCTV, a/c, restaurant, pool, whirlpool

ROSEVILLE
Best Western Roseville Inn
(800) 528-1234, (916) 782-4434
http://www.bestwestern.com
220 Harding Blvd.
125 rooms - $50-75
Pets: Welcome w/$10 fee
Creature Comforts: CCTV, a/c, refrig, cont. brkfst, pool, whirlpool

ROWLAND HEIGHTS
Giant Oaks Lodge
(800) 786-1689, (909) 867-2231
32180 Hilltop Blvd.
12 rooms - $75-135
Pets: Welcome w/$10 fee
Creature Comforts: CCTV, a/c, fireplace, refrig, micro, Jacuzzi, pool, whirlpool

Motel 6
(800) 4-MOTEL6, (909) 964-5333
http://www.motel6.com
18970 E. Labin Ct.
125 rooms - $39-49
Pets: Under 30 lbs. welcome
Creature Comforts: CCTV, a/c, pool

SACRAMENTO
Best Western Expo Inn
(800) 528-1234, (916) 922-9833
http://www.bestwestern.com
1413 Howe Ave.
127 rooms - $69-109
Pets: Small pets welcome
Creature Comforts: CCTV, a/c, kit, cont. brkfst, pool, whirlpool

Best Western Harbor Inn
(800) 528-1234, (916) 371-2100
http://www.bestwestern.com
1250 Halyard Dr.
138 rooms - $69-99
Pets: Small pets w$10 fee and credit card dep.
Creature Comforts: CCTV, a/c, refrig, cont. brkfst, pool, whirlpool

Beverly Garland Hotel
(800) 972-7900, (916) 929-7900
1780 Tribute Rd.
205 rooms - $69-129
Pets: Welcome w/$25 dep.
Creature Comforts: CCTV, a/c, refrig, restaurant, pool, whirlpool

Clarion Hotel
(800) 443-0880, (916) 444-8000
http://www.clarioninn.com
700 - 16th St.
240 rooms - $89-139
Pets: Small pets w/$50 dep.
Creature Comforts: CCTV, VCR, a/c, refrig, micro, pool, whirlpool

Days Inn
(800) DAYS-INN, (916) 488-4100
http://www.daysinn.com
3425 Orange Grove Ave.
142 rooms - $65-89
Pets: Welcome w/$25 fee
Creature Comforts: CCTV, a/c, refrig, restaurant, cont. brkfst, pool

Doubletree Hotel
(800) 222-TREE, (916) 929-8855
http://www.doubletreehotels.com
2001 Pt. West Way
450 rooms - $99-550
Pets: Welcome
Creature Comforts: CCTV, VCR, a/c, refrig, micro, Jacuzzis, restaurant, cont. brkfst, pool, whirlpool

Econo Lodge
(800) 55-ECONO, (916) 443-6631
http://www.econolodge.com
711 - 16th St.
40 rooms - $40-90
Pets: Welcome w/$6 fee
Creature Comforts: CCTV, VCR, a/c, refrig, restaurant, cont. brkfst

Guest Suites
(800) 227-4903, (916) 641-2617
http://www.guestsuites.com
2804 Grasslands Dr.
55 suites - $85-129
Pets: Welcome w/$50 fee
Creature Comforts: Spacious
accommodations w/contemporary
décor, CCTV, VCR, a/c, fireplace,
kit, Jacuzzi, restaurant, cont.
brkfst, pool, hlth club, tennis,
sauna, whirlpool, trails

Hilton Inn
(800) HILTONS, (916) 922-4700
http://www.hilton.com
2200 Harvard St.
328 rooms - $99-489
Pets: Welcome w/$25 fee
Creature Comforts: CCTV, a/c,
refrig, restaurant, pool, hlth clb,
sauna, whirlpool

Host Hotel, Airport
(800) 903-HOST, (916) 929-8636
http://www.hostairporthotel.com
6945 Airport Blvd.
85 rooms - $75-109
Pets: Welcome
Creature Comforts: CCTV, a/c,
cont. brkfst, hlth clb

Howard Johnson
(800) I-Go-Hojo, (916) 366-1266
http://www.hojo.com
3343 Bradshaw Rd.
124 rooms - $65-85
Pets: Welcome
Creature Comforts: CCTV, a/c,
fireplace, refrig, restaurant, pool,
hlth clb, sauna, whirlpool

Inns of America
(800) 826-0778, (916) 386-8408
http://www.innsofamerica.com
25 Howe Ave.
101 rooms - $35-50
Pets: Welcome
Creature Comforts: CCTV, a/c,
pool

La Quinta Inn
(800) Nu-Rooms, (916) 348-0900
http://www.laquinta.com
4604 Madison Ave.
125 rooms - $60-75
Pets: Small pets welcome
Creature Comforts: CCTV, a/c,
pool

La Quinta Inn
(800) Nu-Rooms, (916) 448-8100
http://www.laquinta.com
200 Jibboom St.
166 rooms - $60-85
Pets: Small pets welcome
Creature Comforts: CCTV, a/c,
restaurant, hlth clb, pool

Motel 6
(800) 4-MOTEL6, (916) 383-8110
http://www.motel6.com
7850 College Town Dr.
118 rooms - $39-55
Pets: Under 30 lbs. welcome
Creature Comforts: CCTV, a/c,
pool

Motel 6
(800) 4-MOTEL6, (916) 457-0777
http://www.motel6.com
1415 - 30th St.
94 rooms - $42-59
Pets: Under 30 lbs. welcome
Creature Comforts: CCTV, a/c,
pool

Motel 6
(800) 4-MOTEL6, (916) 331-8100
http://www.motel6.com
5110 Interstate Ave.
82 rooms - $43-60
Pets: Under 30 lbs. welcome
Creature Comforts: CCTV, a/c,
pool

Motel 6
(800) 4-MOTEL6, (916) 441-0733
http://www.motel6.com
227 Jibboom St.
105 rooms - $44-59
Pets: Under 30 lbs. welcome
Creature Comforts: CCTV, a/c,
pool

Motel 6
(800) 4-MOTEL6, (916) 689-9141
http://www.motel6.com
7780 Stockton Blvd.
59 rooms - $37-54
Pets: Under 30 lbs. welcome
Creature Comforts: CCTV, a/c

Motel 6
(800) 4-MOTEL6, (916) 689-6555
http://www.motel6.com
7407 Elsie Ave.
118 rooms - $39-46
Pets: Under 30 lbs. welcome
Creature Comforts: CCTV, a/c,
pool

Motel 6
(800) 4-MOTEL6, (916) 372-3624
http://www.motel6.com
1254 Halyard Dr.
116 rooms - $35-54
Pets: Under 30 lbs. welcome
Creature Comforts: CCTV, a/c,
pool

Radisson Hotel
(800) 333-3333, (916) 922-2020
http://www.radisson.com
500 Leisure Ln.
305 rooms - $79-425
Pets: Welcome w/credit card dep.
Creature Comforts: CCTV,
VCR, a/c, refrig, restaurant, pool,
hlth clb, whirlpool, par course, and
lake

Ramada Inn
(800) 2-Ramada, (916) 487-7600
http://www.ramada.com
2600 Auburn Blvd.
180 rooms - $49-89
Pets: Welcome w/credit card dep.
Creature Comforts: CCTV, a/c,
restaurant

Red Lion Hotel
(800) RED-LION, (916) 929-8855
http://www.redlion.com
2001 Point West Way
450 rooms - $79-199
Pets: Welcome w/$25 dep.
Creature Comforts: CCTV, a/c,
refrig, restaurant, pools, hlth clb,
sauna

Red Lion's Inn
(800) RED-LION, (916) 922-8041
http://www.redlion.com
1401 Arden Way
375 rooms - $69-135
Pets: Welcome w/$25 dep.
Creature Comforts: CCTV, a/c,
refrig, restaurant, 3 pools, hlth clb,
putting green

Residence Inn
(800) 331-3131, (916) 920-9111
http://www.residenceinn.com
1530 Howe Ave.
175 rooms - $99-199
Pets: Welcome w/$6 fee and
credit card dep.
Creature Comforts: CCTV,
VCR, a/c, kit, cont. brkfst, pool,
whirlpool

Sands Motel
(916) 925-8584
2160 Auburn Blvd.
20 rooms - $38-54
Pets: Welcome
Creature Comforts: CCTV, a/c, pool

Super 8 Motel
(800) 800-8000, (916) 427-7925
http://www.super8.com
7216 - 55th St.
61 rooms - $39-59
Pets: Welcome
Creature Comforts: CCTV, a/c, pool

Travelodge Capitol Center
(800) 578-7878, (916) 444-8880
http://www.travelodge.com
1111 H St.
71 rooms - $39-85
Pets: Welcome
Creature Comforts: CCTV, a/c

Vagabond Inn
(800) 522-1555, (916) 446-1481
http://www.vagabondinns.com
909 - 3rd St.
105 rooms - $65-89
Pets: Welcome w/$5 fee
Creature Comforts: CCTV, a/c, refrig, micro, pool

ST. HELENA
El Bonita
(800) 541-3284, (707) 963-3216
http://www.elbonita.com
195 Main St.
42 rooms - $99-225
Pets: Small pets w/$5 fee
Creature Comforts: CCTV, a/c, kit, Jacuzzi, pool, sauna, whirlpool, and massage

Harvest Inn
(800) 950-8466, (707) 963-WINE
http://www.harvestinn.com
1 Main St.
55 cottages - $100-525
Pets: Welcome in king fireplace rooms w/$75 fee
Creature Comforts: Great English Tudor-style cottages with w/wine-country ambiance, expansive lobby w/beamed ceilings, antique popcorn maker, wine tasting counter, CCTV, VCR, a/c, English country cottage décor, reproductions, brick fireplaces, ceiling fans, vaulted ceilings, refrig, micro, brick patios, rocking chairs, Jacuzzis, cont. brkfst, 2 pools, hlth clb, whirlpool, on 14 acres of gardens and vineyards

Wine Country
Victorian and Cottages
(707) 963-0852
http://www.anotherplanet.to
400 Meadowwood Lane
2 cottages - $150-175
Pets: Welcome w/$10 daily fee
Creature Comforts: A cozy "kit" cottage from 1940s w/Ralph Lauren decor and more contemp. 2-bedrm cottage w/a "Pottery Barn" look, both nestled in woods near Victorian main house, fireplace, country antiques and collectibles, kit, cont. brkfst, garden patio, pool, whirlpool

SALINAS
Best Western John Jay Inn
(800) 528-1234, (831) 784-0176
http://www.bestwestern.com
175 Kern St.
58 rooms - $55-120
Pets: Welcome
Creature Comforts: CCTV, a/c, refrig, cont. brkfst, pool, hlth clb, sauna, whirlpool

El Dorado Motel
(800) 523-6506, (831) 449-2442
1351 N. Main St.
42 rooms - $32-65
Pets: Welcome w/$5 fee
Creature Comforts: CCTV, refrig

Motel 6
(800) 4-MOTEL6, (831) 753-1711
http://www.motel6.com
140 Kern St.
121 rooms - $39-45
Pets: Under 30 lbs. welcome
Creature Comforts: CCTV, a/c, pool

Motel 6
(800) 4-MOTEL6, (831) 757-3077
http://www.motel6.com
1257 De La Torre Blvd.
128 rooms - $34-45
Pets: Under 30 lbs. welcome
Creature Comforts: CCTV, a/c, pool

Travelodge
(800) 578-7878, (831) 424-1741
http://www.travelodge.com
555 Airport Blvd.
96 rooms - $39-129
Pets: Welcome
Creature Comforts: CCTV, a/c, kit, pool

Vagabond Inn
(800) 522-1555, (831) 758-4693
http://www.vagabondinns.com
131 Kern St.
70 rooms - $45-90
Pets: Welcome w/$5 fee
Creature Comforts: CCTV, a/c, refrig, pool

SAN ANDREAS
Black Bart Inn
(800) 225-3764 x:331,
(209) 754-3808
35 Main St.
50 rooms - $48-58
Pets: Welcome
Creature Comforts: CCTV, a/c, refrig, Jacuzzis, restaurant, bar, pool

SAN ANSELMO
San Anselmo Inn
(800) 598-9771, (415) 455-5366
http://www.sainn.com
339 San Anselmo Ave.
15 rooms - $65-130
Pets: Welcome w/$50 dep.
Creature Comforts: CCTV, a/c, refrig, micro, country accents, Italian restaurant, full brkfst

SAN BERNARDINO

La Quinta Inn
(800) Nu-Rooms, (909) 888-7571
http://www.laquinta.com
205 E. Hospitality Ln.
154 rooms - $59-135
Pets: Welcome in smoking rms
Creature Comforts: CCTV, a/c, pool

Motel 6
(800) 4-MOTEL6, (909) 887-8191
http://www.motel6.com
1960 Ostrems Way
104 rooms - $38-49
Pets: Under 30 lbs. welcome
Creature Comforts: CCTV, a/c, pool

Motel 6
(800) 4-MOTEL6, (909) 825-6666
http://www.motel6.com
111 Redlands Ave.
120 rooms - $36-52
Pets: Under 30 lbs. welcome
Creature Comforts: CCTV, a/c, pool

Sands Motel
(909) 889-8391
606 No. H St.
55 rooms - $40-59
Pets: Small pets welcome
Creature Comforts: CCTV, VCR, a/c, restaurant, pool, whirlpool

SAN BRUNO

Summerfield Suites Hotel
(800) 833-4353
www.summerfieldsuites.com
1350 Huntington Ave.
118 rooms - $129-199
Pets: Under 40 lbs. w/$50 fee
Creature Comforts: CCTV, a/c, kit, Jacuzzi, cont. brkfst, pool

SAN CLEMENTE

Holiday Inn-San Clemente
(800) 465-4329, (714) 361-3000
http://www.holiday-inn.com
111 S. Avenida de Estrella
72 rooms - $79-150
Pets: Welcome w/$10 fee
Creature Comforts: CCTV, VCR, a/c, refrig, Jacuzzis, restaurant, pool, hlth clb access, sauna, whirlpool

SAN DIEGO

Beach Haven Inn
(800) 831-6323 , (619) 272-3812
4740 Mission Blvd.
24 rooms - $50-150
Pets: Small pets w/$50 dep.
Creature Comforts: CCTV, VCR, a/c, kit, Jacuzzi, cont. brkfst, pool, whirlpool

Best Western Hanalei Hotel
(800) 528-1234, (619) 297-1101
http://www.bestwestern.com
2270 Hotel Circle North
416 rooms - $79-129
Pets: Small pets w/$50 dep.
Creature Comforts: CCTV, VCR, a/c, refrig, micro, restaurant, cont. brkfst, pool, hlth clb, whirlpool

Crown Point View Suites
(800) 338-3331, (619) 272-0676
http://www.crownpoint-view.com
4088 Crown Point Dr.
20 rooms - $79-199
Pets: Small pets w/$50 dep.
Creature Comforts: CCTV, refrig, and micro

Days Inn
(800) DAYS-INN, (619) 578-4350
http://www.daysinn.com
9350 Kearney Mesa Rd.
60 rooms - $45-95
Pets: Welcome
Creature Comforts: CCTV, a/c, refrig, restaurant, cont. brkfst, pool

E-Z 8 Motel
(800) 326-6835, (619) 291-8252
2484 Hotel Circle Place
111 rooms - $35-55
Pets: Welcome
Creature Comforts: CCTV, a/c, refrig, Jacuzzi, pool

E-Z 8 Motel
(800) 326-6835, (619) 294-2512
4747 Pacific Hwy.
98 rooms - $35-55
Pets: Welcome
Creature Comforts: CCTV, a/c, refrig, Jacuzzi, pool

Doubletree Mission Valley Hotel
(800) 222-TREE, (619) 297-5466
http://www.doubletreehotels.com
7450 Hazard Center
300 rooms - $169-495
Pets: Small pets in smk.. rms.
Creature Comforts: CCTV, a/c, refrig, micro, hlth club, sauna, restaurant, pools, whirlpools

Doubletree Carmel Highland
(800) 222-TREE, (619) 297-5466
http://www.doubletreehotels.com
14455 Penasquitos Dr.
175 rooms - $129-295
Pets: Small pets in smk.. rms.
Creature Comforts: CCTV, a/c, refrig, micro, hlth club, sauna, restaurant, pools, whirlpools, golf, and lighted tennis

Four Points Hotel
(800) 325-3535, (619) 277-8888
http://www.sheraton.com
8110 Aero Dr.
228 rooms - $79-170
Pets: Welcome w/credit card dep.
Creature Comforts: CCTV, a/c, refrig, micro, restaurant, pool, hlth clb, sauna, whirlpool, lawn sports, and game rooms

Glory's Holiday House
(619) 225-0784
3330 Ingelow St.
3 rooms - $99-129
Pets: Welcome w/$10 fee
Creature Comforts: Warm and inviting B&B, hilltop location, great ambiance, affable hostess, CCTV, VCR, a/c, sliding glass doors reveal bay views, kit, full brkfst, pool, whirlpool

Good Nite Inn
(800) NITE-INN, (619) 286-7000
4545 Waring Rd.
90 rooms - $35-60
Pets: Welcome
Creature Comforts: CCTV, a/c, refrig, micro, pool

Good Nite Inn Seaworld
(800) NITE-INN, (619) 543-9944
3880 Greenwood St.
150 rooms - $35-60
Pets: Welcome
Creature Comforts: CCTV, a/c, refrig, micro

Grosvenor Inn

(800) 232-1212, (619) 233-8826
http://www.netsv.com/gindustries/
grosvenorinn
810 Ash St.
55 rooms - $40-69
Pets: Welcome w/$25 fee
Creature Comforts: CCTV,
VCR, a/c, kit, pool, whirlpool

Handlery Hotel

(800) 676-6567, (619) 298-0511
http://www.handlery.com
950 Hotel Circle No.
217 rooms - $89-269
Pets: Welcome w/$50 fee
Creature Comforts: CCTV, a/c,
refrig, restaurant, 3 pools, hlth clb,
sauna, whirlpool, paddle tennis,
golf, tennis, and massage

Hilton Hotel

(800) HILTONS, (619) 543-9000
http://www.hilton.com
1901 Camino del Rio So.
350 rooms - $169-2469
Pets: Under 30 Lbs. w/$50 dep.
Creature Comforts: CCTV,
VCR, a/c, refrig, micro, jacuzzis,
restaurant, pool, hlth clb, sauna,
whirlpool

Holiday Inn on the Bay

(800) HOLIDAY, (619) 232-3861
http://www.holiday-inn.com
1355 N. Harbor Dr.
600 rooms - $99-199
Pets: Welcome
Creature Comforts: CCTV,
VCR, a/c, refrig, micro, restaurant,
pool, hlth clb, whirlpool

The Horton Grand Hotel

(800) 542-1886, (619) 544-1886
http://www.hortongrand.com
311 Island Ave.
152 rooms - $139-369
Pets: Welcome w/$50 fee
Creature Comforts: A delightful
1886 hotel set in Old Town's
Gaslamp Quarter, life-size papier
mache horse, CCTV, VCR,
antiques, canopy beds, high
ceilings and Palladian windows,
a/c, fireplaces, period décor, kit,
restaurant, festive Victorian bar w/
murals, friendly ghost, hlth clb
access

Howard Johnson

(800) I-Go-Hojo, (619) 293-7792
http://www.hojo.com
1631 Hotel Circle South
80 rooms - $45-85
Pets: Welcome w/$50 dep. fee
Creature Comforts: CCTV, a/c,
cont. brkfst, pool, whirlpool

Lamplighter Inn

(800) 545-0778, (619) 582-3088
6474 El Cajon Blvd.
64 rooms - $40-89
Pets: Small pets w/$5 fee
Creature Comforts: CCTV, a/c,
kit, pool

Marriott San Diego Marina

(800) 228-9290, (619) 234-1500
http://www.marriott.com
333 West Harbor Dr.
1,350 rooms - $169-549
Pets: Welcome
Creature Comforts: CCTV,
VCR, a/c, kit, Jacuzzis, restaurant,
pools, hlth clb, saunas, whirlpools,
tennis, and marina-boat rentals

Marriott Suites

(800) 228-9290, (619) 696-9800
http://www.marriott.com
701 A St.
264 suites - $169-275
Pets: Welcome w/$50 dep.
Creature Comforts: CCTV,
VCR, a/c, refrig, Jacuzzis,
restaurant, whirlpool

Motel 6

(800) 4-MOTEL6, (619) 296-1612
http://www.motel6.com
2424 Hotel Circle North
204 rooms - $47-60
Pets: Under 30 lbs. welcome
Creature Comforts: CCTV, a/c,
pool

Motel 6

(800) 4-MOTEL6, (619) 268-9758
http://www.motel6.com
5592 Claremont Mesa Blvd.
65 rooms - $45-63
Pets: Under 30 lbs. welcome
Creature Comforts: CCTV, a/c

Old Town Inn

(800) 643-3025, (619) 260-7105
4444 Pacific Hwy.
85 rooms - $35-120
Pets: Welcome
Creature Comforts: CCTV, a/c,
kit, cont. brkfst

Pacific Shores Inn

(800) 826-0715, (619) 483-6300
4802 Mission Blvd.
54 rooms - $55-100
Pets: Welcome w/$25 fee
Creature Comforts: CCTV, a/c,
kit, pool

Park Manor Suites

(800) 874-2649, (619) 291-0999
http://www.parkmanorsuites.com
525 Spruce St.
80 suites - $75-300
Pets: Welcome
Creature Comforts: Suite hotel
w/a sense of "old world" style,
original art, eclectic yet appealing
decor, some antique furnishings,
CCTV, a/c, kit, cont. brkfst,
restaurant

Radisson Harbor View

(800) 333-3333, (619) 239-6800
http://www.radisson.com
1646 Front St.
333 rooms - $60-139
Pets: Welcome w/$25 dep.
Creature Comforts: CCTV, a/c,
refrig, micro, Jacuzzis, restaurant,
pool, hlth clb, sauna, whirlpool,
and tennis

Ramada Inn

(800) 2-Ramada, (619) 278-0800
http://www.ramada.com
5550 Kearny Mesa Rd.
150 rooms - $75-175
Pets: Welcome w/C dep.
Creature Comforts: CCTV,
VCR, a/c, kit, Jacuzzi, restaurant,
pool, hlth clb, whirlpool

Red Lion Hotel

(800) RED-LION, (619) 297-5466
http://www.redlion.com
7450 Hazard Center Dr.
300 rooms - $95-169
Pets: Small pets welcome
Creature Comforts: CCTV, a/c,
refrig, micro, Jacuzzis, restaurant,
2 pools, hlth clb, sauna,
whirlpools, and tennis

Residence Inn Kearny Mesa
(800) 331-3131, (619) 278-2100
http://www.residenceinn.com
5400 Kearny Mesa Rd.
144 rooms - $89-159
Pets: Welcome w/$5 fee and credit card dep.
Creature Comforts: CCTV, VCR, a/c, kit, cont. brkfst, Jacuzzi, pool, hlth clb access, whirlpools

San Diego Hilton & Tennis
(800) HILTONS, (619) 276-4010
http://www.hilton.com
1775 E. Mission Bay Dr.
356 rooms - $139-739
Pets: Under 20 Lbs. w/$50 dep.
Creature Comforts: CCTV, VCR, a/c, refrig, micro, Jacuzzis, restaurant, pool, hlth clb, sauna, massage, whirlpool, lighted tennis, putting green, beach-boat rentals

San Diego Marriott
(800) 228-9290, (619) 692-3800
http://www.marriott.com
8757 Rio San Diego Dr.
350 rooms - $109-199
Pets: Welcome w/$50 fee and credit card dep.
Creature Comforts: CCTV, a/c, refrig, restaurant, pool, hlth clb, sauna, whirlpool, and tennis

San Diego Paradise Point Resort
(800) 344-2626, (619) 274-4630
http://www.paradisepoint.com
1404 W. Vacation Rd.
462 rooms - $170-475
Pets: Welcome CC dep.
Creature Comforts: Expansive resort occupies 44 acres along the inland waterway, waterfalls, lagoons, tropical gardens, CCTV, a/c, kit, Jacuzzi, restaurants, five pools, hlth clb, saunas, whirlpools, tennis, beach, bikes, putting green, lawn sports, trail, sandy beach, kids camp, marina-boat rentals

Super 8 Mission Bay
(800) 800-8000, (619) 274-7888
http://www.super8.com
4540 Mission Bay Dr.
116 rooms - $45-75
Pets: Welcome
Creature Comforts: CCTV, a/c, pool

U.S. Grant Hotel
(800) 237-5029, (619) 232-3121
http://www.grandheritage.com
326 Broadway St.
278 rooms - $135-1,600
Pets: Welcome (Pampered Pet Program)
Creature Comforts: Restored 1910 historic property, downtown, visited by more than a dozen Presidents, expansive lobby—Palladian columns supporting hand-painted ceilings, crystal chandeliers, Chinese porcelains, imported marbles, CCTV, VCR, a/c, refrig, antiques-reproductions, Queen-Anne furnishings, balconies w/views, restaurant, pub, hlth clb access

Vagabond Inn
(800) 522-1555, (619) 297-1691
http://www.vagabondinns.com
625 Hotel Circle South
88 rooms - $45-85
Pets: Welcome w/$10 fee
Creature Comforts: CCTV, a/c, refrig, and 2 pools

Vagabond Inn
(800) 522-1555, (619) 232-6391
http://www.vagabondinns.com
1655 Pacific Hwy.
33 rooms - $39-70
Pets: Welcome w/$5 fee
Creature Comforts: CCTV, a/c, refrig, pool

Vagabond Inn
(800) 522-1555, (619) 224-3371
http://www.vagabondinns.com
1325 Scott St.
40 rooms - $49-75
Pets: Welcome w/$10 fee
Creature Comforts: CCTV, a/c, refrig, pool

SAN DIMAS
Motel 6
(800) 4-MOTEL6, (909) 592-5631
http://www.motel6.com
502 W. Arrow Hwy.
119 rooms - $39-48
Pets: Under 30 lbs. welcome
Creature Comforts: CCTV, a/c

Red Roof Inn
(800) THE ROOF, (909) 589-1111
http://www.redroof.com
204 N. Village Ct.
135 rooms - $40-55
Pets: Small pets welcome
Creature Comforts: CCTV, a/c, refrig, pool, whirlpool

SAN FRANCISCO
Beresford Arms
(800) 533-6533, (415) 626-0200
http://www.beresford.com
701 Post St.
96 suites - $89-199
Pets: Under 25 lbs. welcome
Creature Comforts: CCTV, VCR, kit, restaurant, cont. brkfst, whirlpools

Beresford Hotel
(800) 533-6533, (415) 673-9900
http://www.beresford.com
635 Sutter St.
114 rooms- $89-159
Pets: Under 25 lbs. welcome
Creature Comforts: Victorian hotel, CCTV, VCR, restaurant, cont. brkfst, and hlth clb access

Best Western Civic Center
(800) 528-1234, (415) 621-2826
http://www.bestwestern.com
364 - 9th St.
57 rooms - $69-129
Pets: Small pets welcome
Creature Comforts: CCTV, a/c, refrig, pool

Campton Place
(800) 235-4300, (415) 781-5555
http://www.camptonplace.com
340 Stockton St.
127 rooms - $230-1,250
Pets: Under 40 lbs. w/$25 fee
Creature Comforts: Exquisite boutique hotel set just off Union Square, rated on of the top hotels in the U.S., luxurious amenities, Oriental objects d'art, hallways encircle open-air atrium, Henredon furnishings, limited edition artwork, CCTV, VCR, a/c, kit, marble bathrooms-Jacuzzis, restaurant, hlth clb access and pool

The Clift Hotel
(800) 65-CLIFT, (415) 775-4700
http://www.clifthotel.com
495 Geary St.
329 rooms - $145-950
Pets: $40 nightly fee (pet goodies)
Creature Comforts: Historic landmark, intimate interior spaces, famous Art Deco Redwood Room, Oriental artwork, carved wood ceilings and crystal chandeliers, Georgian-style furnishings, CCTV, VCR, a/c, refrig, micro, Jacuzzis, restaurant, pool access, hlth clb

Days Inn
(800) DAYS-INN, (415) 922-2010
http://www.daysinn.com
2358 Lombard St.
22 rooms - $75-130
Pets: Welcome w/credit card dep.
Creature Comforts: CCTV, a/c, refrig, cont. brkfst

Executive Suites
(888) 8-SUITES, (415) 495-5151
www.executive-inns-suites.com
1 St. Francis St.
55 units - $210-399
Pets: Under 10 lbs. welcome
Creature Comforts: Nicely furnished studios apartments in the heart of the city, CCTV, VCR, a/c, kit, cont. brkfst, courtyard, fireplaces, hlth club, sauna, pool

Fairmont Hotel
(800) 527-4727, (415) 772-5000
http://www.fairmont.com
950 Mason Street
300 rooms - $230-1,950
Pets: Under 20 lbs. welcome
Creature Comforts: Classic 1906 gracious hotel perched atop Nob Hill, great city and bay views, luxurious amenities, objects d'art, Victorian decor, CCTV, VCR, a/c, kit, Jacuzzis, restaurants, limited edition artwork, hlth clb -spa, pool

Golden Gate Hotel
(415) 392-3702
775 Bush St.
23 rooms - $75-95
Pets: Welcome selectively
Creature Comforts: Charming and affordable hotel, bird cage elevator, white wicker, claw foot tubs, a/c, CCTV, cont brkfst

Grosvenor House
(800) 999-9189, (415) 421-1899
http://www.bestlodgings.com/sites/grosvenor/index.shtml
899 Pine St.
200 suites - $99-355
Pets: Welcome w/$175 fee
Creature Comforts: Newly renovated high-rise set on Nob Hill, residential décor, CCTV, VCR, a/c, kit, cont. brkfst

Hotel Nikko
(800) Nikko-US, (415) 394-1111
http://www.nikkohotels.com
222 Mason St.
275 rooms - $175-1,850
Pets: Welcome
Creature Comforts: Serene Japanese hotel with state-of-the-art gadetry, understated room décor-rice screens, black lacquered furnishings, and naturally stained woods, CCTV, VCR, a/c, refrig, micro, Jacuzzi, restaurant w/vibrant color schemes, pool, hlth clb, sauna, whirlpool

Hotel Tritron
(800) 433-6611, (415) 394-0555
http://www.hoteltriton.com
342 Grant Ave.
142 rooms - $145-325
Pets: Welcome w/$50 fee
Creature Comforts: Art Deco style hotel w/whimsical twist, suites named after popular artists, European décor, trendy furnishings, memorabilia, biodegradable products used, air-filtration system, CCTV, VCR, a/c, refrig, micro, restaurant, hlth clb, variety of publicity stunts

INN 1890
(888) INN-1890, (415) 386-0486
http://adamsnet.com/inn1890
1890 Page St.
8 rooms - $90-155
Pets: Quiet dogs welcome
Creature Comforts: CCTV, VCR, a/c, kitchen, brass beds, down comforters, antiques, bay windows, 12-ft high ceilings, fireplaces, robes & slippers, cont. brkfst, near Golden Gate Park

The Inn San Francisco
(800) 359-0913, (415) 641-0188
943 S. Van Ness Ave.
22 rooms - $85-255
Pets: Welcome selectively
Creature Comforts: Lovely 27-room Victorian inn set on Mansion Row, detailed mahogany woodworking, elegantly appointed pair of parlors, VCR, a/c, marble fireplaces, Oriental carpets, period wallpapers, kit, Jacuzzis, full brkfst, garden fountain, redwood hot tub

Laurel Motor Inn
(415) 567-8467
444 Presidio Ave.
49 rooms - $75-109
Pets: Welcome
Creature Comforts: CCTV, a/c, kit, cont. brkfst

La Quinta
(800) Nu-Rooms, (415) 583-2223
http://www.laquinta.com
20 Airport Blvd.
174 rooms - $55-75
Pets: Under 25 lbs. welcome
Creature Comforts: CCTV, a/c, cont. brkfst, pool, hlth clb, whirlpool

The Mansions Hotel
(800) 826-9398, (415) 929-9444
http://www.themansions.com
2220 Sacramento St.
21 rooms - $139-375
Pets: Welcome
Creature Comforts: Whimsically eclectic 1887 Queen-Anne Victorian mansion set in a quiet residential neighborhood, stained glass, Oriental objects d'art, crystal chandeliers, elegantly garbed staff and mannequins, resident ghost—Claudia, canopy beds, CCTV, VCR, a/c, fireplaces, refrig, billiard room, assortment of collectibles displayed, restaurant, full brkfst, whirlpool, cabaret theater, sculpture garden

Marriott
(800) 228-9290, (415) 896-1600
http://www.marriott.com
55 Fourth St.
1,500 rooms - $139-2,500
Pets: Welcome
Creature Comforts: CCTV, a/c,
refrig, restaurants, pools, hlth clb

Marriott - Fisherman's Wharf
(800) 228-9290, (415) 775-7555
http://www.marriott.com
1250 Columbus Ave.
285 rooms - $129-750
Pets: Welcome w/$ fee
Creature Comforts: CCTV, a/c,
refrig, restaurants, hlth clb

Monaco Hotel
(800) 214-4220, (415) 292-0100
http://www.hotelmonaco.com
201 rooms - $175-459
Pets: Welcome w/$25 fee
Creature Comforts: CCTV, a/c,
VCR, kit, restaurant, cont. brkfst,
hlth club, massage

Pacific Heights Inn
(800) 523-1801, (415) 776-3310
http://www.pacificheightsinn.com
1555 Union St.
40 rooms - $65-155
Pets: Welcome
Creature Comforts: CCTV,
VCR, a/c, residential decor, kit,
Jacuzzis, cont. brkfst

The Pan Pacific Hotel
(800) 327-8585, (415) 732-7747
http://www.panpac.com
500 Post St.
330 rooms - $199-1,750
Pets: Under 30 lbs. w/$75 fee
Creature Comforts: Striking 17-
story atrium highlights this elegant
city hotel, bronze sculpture,CCTV,
VCR, a/c, marble fireplace, refrig,
soaking tubs/Jacuzzis, restaurant,
hlth clb, whirlpool

Pensione San Francisco
(415) 864-1271
1668 Market St.
36 rooms - $45-75
Pets: Welcome w/credit card dep.
Creature Comforts: A simple no
frills pensione-style inn, low-key
ambiance, theme rooms, wicker
and rattan, throw rugs, painted
furnishings, CCTV, refrig, cont.
brkfst
132

Ramada Inn
(800) 2-Ramada, (415) 589-7200
http://www.ramada.com
245 S. Airport Blvd.
177 rooms - $95-145
Pets: Welcome w/$25 dep.
Creature Comforts: CCTV, a/c,
restaurant, cont. brkfst, pool

San Francisco Airport Hilton
(800) HILTONS, (415) 589-0770
http://www.hilton.com
Route 101
527 rooms - $109-199
Pets: Under 25 lbs. welcome
Creature Comforts: CCTV, a/c,
refrig, restaurant, 2 pools, hlth clb

Travelodge
(800) 578-7878, (415) 673-0691
http://www.travelodge.com
1450 Lombard St.
73 rooms - $55-140
Pets: Welcome
Creature Comforts: CCTV, a/c,
and restaurant

Vagabond Inn
(800) 522-1555, (415) 692-4040
http://www.vagabondinn.com
222 S. Airport Blvd.
51 rooms - $49-99
Pets: Welcome w/$5 fee
Creature Comforts: CCTV, a/c

The Westin St. Francis
(800) 228-3000, (415) 397-7000
http://www.westin.com
335 Powell St. (Union Sq.)
1,189 rooms - $189-1,900
Pets: Welcome w/port. kennel
Creature Comforts: Renowned
historic grand hotel on Union
Square, wood-paneled reception
area w/ornately carved ceilings
and lovely antiques, floor-to-
ceiling windows, brass fixtures,
chintz fabrics, formal English
furnishings, popular "09" guest
rooms, CCTV, VCR, a/c, refrig,
Jacuzzis, restaurants, hlth clb

SAN JACINTO
Crown Motel
(909) 654-7133
138 South Ramona Blvd.
22 rooms - $35-55
Pets: Small pets welcome
Creature Comforts: CCTV, a/c,
refrig, micro, pool, whirlpool

SAN JOSE
Airport Inn
(408) 453-5340
1355 North 4th St.
192 rooms - $55-75
Pets: Welcome w/$10 fee
Creature Comforts: CCTV, a/c,
refrig, micro, pool, hlth clb

Best Western San Jose Lodge
(800) 528-1234, (408) 453-7750
http://www.bestwestern.com
1440 N. First St.
75 rooms - $60-78
Pets: Welcome
Creature Comforts: CCTV, a/c,
cont. brkfst, pool

Crowne Plaza
(800) HOLIDAY, (408) 998-0400
http://www.holiday-inn.com
282 Almaden Blvd.
230 rooms - $90-195
Pets: Welcome w/credit card dep.
Creature Comforts: CCTV, a/c,
restaurant, pool

Doubletree Hotel
(800) 222-TREE, (408) 453-6200
http://www.doubletreehotels.com
1350 North 1st St.
324 rooms - $99-695
Pets: Welcome w/$50 dep.
Creature Comforts: CCTV, a/c,
refrig, micro, restaurant, pool,
whirlpool

Hanford Hotel
(408) 453-3133
1755 North 1st St.
95 rooms - $55-105
Pets: Welcome w/$ 50 dep.
Creature Comforts: CCTV, a/c,
refrig, micro, restaurant, pool

Hilton Hotel
(800) HILTONS, (408) 287-2100
http://www.hilton.com
300 Almaden Blvd.
350 rooms - $99-395
Pets: Welcome w/$25 fee
Creature Comforts: CCTV,
VCR, a/c, refrig, micro, restaurant,
pool, whirlpool

Homewood Suites
(800) 225-5466, (408) 428-9900
http://www.homewoodsuites.com
10 West Trimble Rd.
140 rooms - $89-250
Pets: $75 fee and $275 deposit
Creature Comforts: CCTV,
VCR, a/c, kit, restaurant, pool,
racq. court, whirlpool

Hyatt Hotel
(800) 233-1234, (408) 885-1234
http://www.hyatt.com
302 South Market
169 rooms - $89-795
Pets: Welcome
Creature Comforts: CCTV,
VCR, a/c, refrig, Jacuzzis,
restaurant, whirlpools

Motel 6, Airport
(800) 4-MOTEL6, (408) 436-8180
http://www.motel6.com
2081 N. 1st St.
74 rooms - $55-73
Pets: Under 30 lbs. welcome
Creature Comforts: CCTV, a/c

Motel 6
(800) 4-MOTEL6, (408) 270-3131
http://www.motel6.com
2560 Fontaine Rd.
202 rooms - $52-68
Pets: Under 30 lbs. welcome
Creature Comforts: CCTV, a/c,
pool

Red Lion Hotel
(800) RED-LION, (408) 453-4000
http://www.redlion.com
2050 Gateway Pl.
500 rooms - $99-275
Pets: Welcome w/credit card dep.
Creature Comforts: CCTV, a/c,
refrig, restaurant, pool, hlth clb,
sauna, whirlpool

Summerfield Suites
(800) 833-4353, (408) 436-1600
www.summerfieldsuites.com
1602 Crane St.
99 rooms - $79-169
Pets: $10 fee, $75 deposit
Creature Comforts: CCTV,
VCR, a/c, fireplaces, kit, cont.
brkfst, steambath, pool, hlth club,
whirlpool

SAN JUAN BAUTISTA
San Juan Inn
(408) 623-4380
410 Alameda St.
44 rooms - $44-88
Pets: Welcome w/$6 fee
Creature Comforts: CCTV,
VCR, a/c, refrig, micro, pool,
whirlpool

SAN JUAN CAPISTRANO
Best Western Capistrano Inn
(800) 528-1234, (949) 493-5661
http://www.bestwestern.com
27174 Ortega Hwy.
108 rooms - $65-89
Pets: Small pets w/$25 fee
Creature Comforts: CCTV, a/c,
kit, cont. brkfst, pool, whirlpool

SAN LUIS OBISPO
Best Western Royal Oak
(800) 528-1234, (805) 544-4410
http://www.bestwestern.com
214 Madonna Rd.
99 rooms - $50-90
Pets: Small pets welcome
Creature Comforts: CCTV, a/c,
refrig, restaurant, cont. brkfst,
pool, whirlpool

Best Western Somerset Manor
(800) 528-1234, (805) 544-0973
http://www.bestwestern.com
1895 Monterey St.
39 rooms - $55-110
Pets: Welcome
Creature Comforts: CCTV, a/c,
refrig, micro, restaurant, full
brkfst, pool, whirlpool

Campus Motel
(800) 447-8080 (CA),
(805) 544-0881
404 Santa Rosa St.
36 rooms - $39-169
Pets: Welcome w/$7 fee
Creature Comforts: CCTV,
VCR, a/c, refrig, micro, Jacuzzis,
cont. brkfst, pool, whirlpool

Days Inn
(800) DAYS-INN, (805) 549-9911
http://www.daysinn.com
2050 Garfield St.
43 rooms - $59-145
Pets: $10 fee and $50 dep.
Creature Comforts: CCTV, a/c,
refrig, micro, Jacuzzi, cont. brkfst,
pool, whirlpool

Heritage Inn B&B
(805) 544-7440
http://www.slo-online.com/
heritageinn
978 Olive St.
9 rooms - $90-155
Pets: Well behaved w/$25 dep.
Creature Comforts: B&B with
country décor antique accents,
Victorian ambiance, fireplaces,
pocket doors, pastel colors,
antique brass and white iron beds,
antique photos, refrig, claw foot
tub, cont. brkfst

Howard Johnson
(800) I-Go-Hojo, (805) 544-5300
http://www.hojo.com
1585 Calle Joaquin
65 rooms - $49-99
Pets: Small pets w/$10 fee
Creature Comforts: CCTV, a/c,
refrig, micro, restaurant, and 2
pools

Motel 6
(800) 4-MOTEL6, (805) 541-6992
http://www.motel6.com
1625 Calle Joaquin
117 rooms - $34-48
Pets: Under 30 lbs. welcome
Creature Comforts: CCTV, a/c,
pool

Motel 6
(800) 4-MOTEL6, (805) 549-9595
http://www.motel6.com
1433 Calle Joaquin
86 rooms - $39-52
Pets: Under 30 lbs. welcome
Creature Comforts: CCTV, a/c,
pool

Sands Motel
(800) 441-4657, (805) 544-0500
1930 Monterey St.
72 rooms - $45-135
Pets: Small pets welcome
Creature Comforts: CCTV,
VCR, a/c, refrig, micro, cont.
brkfst, pool, whirlpool

Travelodge
(800) 578-7878, (805) 543-5110
http://www.travelodge.com
1825 Monterey St.
38 rooms - $45-109
Pets: Small pets welcome
Creature Comforts: CCTV, a/c,
pool

Vagabond Inn
(800) 522-1555, (805) 544-4710
http://www.vagabondinns.com
210 Madonna Rd.
59 rooms - $45-75
Pets: Welcome w/$5 fee
Creature Comforts: CCTV, a/c, pool

SAN MARCOS
Quails Inn
(800) 447-6556, (760) 744-0120
http://www.quailsinn.com
1025 La Bonita Dr.
144 rooms - $85-325
Pets: Welcome w/$10 fee
Creature Comforts: Lakefront property surrounded by giant pines and rolling hills, CCTV, VCR, a/c, charming country décor, rms. along pool and lake, refrig, micro, restaurant, 2 pools, hlth clb, whirlpool, paddle tennis cts, tennis, and boating

SAN MATEO
Best Western Los Prados
(800) 528-1234, (650) 341-3300
http://www.bestwestern.com
2940 South Norfolk St.
113 rooms - $99-149
Pets: Under 25 Lbs. w/$50 dep.
Creature Comforts: CCTV, a/c, refrig, cont. brkfst, hlth clb whirlpool

Dunfey Hotel
(650) 573-7661
1770 S. Amphlett Blvd.
272 rooms - $125-375
Pets: Welcome w/$75 dep.
Creature Comforts: CCTV, a/c, refrig, restaurant, pool

Residence Inn
(800) 331-3131, (650) 574-4700
http://www.residenceinn.com
2000 Winward Way
160 rooms - $129-199
Pets: $5 fee & CC dep.
Creature Comforts: CCTV, VCR, a/c, fireplaces, kit, cont. brkfst, pool, whirlpool

Villa Hotel
(800) 341-2345, (650) 341-0966
http://www.villahotel.com
101 West Hillsdale Blvd.
287 rooms - $85-220
Pets: Welcome w/$50 or CC dep.
Creature Comforts: CCTV, a/c, refrig, micro, pool, hlth clb, whirlpool

SAN PEDRO
Vagabond Inn
(800) 522-1555, (310) 831-8911
http://www.vagabondinns.com
215 S. Gaffey St.
70 rooms - $50-75
Pets: Welcome w/$5 fee
Creature Comforts: CCTV, a/c, refrig, pool

SAN RAFAEL
Villa Inn
(888) VILLA-IN , (415) 456-4975
http://www.rodeway.com
1600 Lincoln Ave.
60 rooms - $65-135
Pets: Welcome w/$20 dep.
Creature Comforts: CCTV, a/c, kit, restaurant, cont. brkfst, pool, whirlpool

Wyndham Garden Hotel
(800) Wyndham, (415) 479-9800
http://www.wyndham.com
1010 Northgate Dr.
225 rooms - $79-255
Pets: Welcome w/$50 dep.
Creature Comforts: CCTV, a/c, refrig, micro, pool, hlth clb, whirlpool

SAN RAMON
Marriott/Bishop Ranch
(800) 228-9290, (510) 867-9200
http://www.marriott.com
2600 Bishop Dr.
368 rooms - $79-149
Pets: Welcome
Creature Comforts: CCTV, a/c, refrig, micro, restaurant, pool, hlth clb, sauna, whirlpool, jogging

Residence Inn
(800) 331-3131, (510) 277-9292
http://www.residenceinn.com
1071 Market Pl.
105 rooms - $69-179
Pets: $5 fee & $75 clean fee
Creature Comforts: CCTV, a/c, fireplaces, kit, cont. brkfst, pool, hlth clb, racquet ct., whirlpool

SAN SIMEON
Best Western Courtesy Inn
(800) 528-1234, (805) 927-4691
http://www.bestwestern.com
9450 Castillo Dr.
117 rooms - $50-135
Pets: Small pets w/$10 fee
Creature Comforts: CCTV, a/c, refrig, cont. brkfst, pool, whirlpool, game room

Best Western Oceanfront
(800) 528-1234, (805) 927-4688
http://www.bestwestern.com
9415 Hearst Dr.
90 rooms - $69-179
Pets: Small pets
Creature Comforts: CCTV, VCR, a/c, refrig, fireplaces, restaurant, cont. brkfst, hlth club, pool, whirlpool

Motel 6
(800) 4-MOTEL6, (805) 927-8691
http://www.motel6.com
9070 Castillo St.
100 rooms - $43-56
Pets: Under 30 lbs. welcome
Creature Comforts: CCTV, a/c, pool

Silver Surf Motel
(800) 621-3999, (805) 927-4661
9390 Castillo Dr.
73 rooms - $40-93
Pets: Welcome w/$5 fee
Creature Comforts: CCTV, fireplaces, refrig, pool, whirlpool

SANTA ANA
Holiday Inn Express
(800) HOLIDAY, (714) 835-3051
http://www.holiday-inn.com
1600 E. First St.
150 rooms - $70-94
Pets: Very small pets w/$100 dep.
Creature Comforts: CCTV, VCR, a/c, refrig, restaurant, pool, hlth clb, sauna, whirlpool

Motel 6
(800) 4-MOTEL6, (714) 558-0500
http://www.motel6.com
1623 E. 1st St.
79 rooms - $39-50
Pets: Under 30 lbs. welcome
Creature Comforts: CCTV, a/c, pool

Red Roof Inn
(800) Red-Roof, (714) 542-0311
http://www.redroof.com
2600 N. Main St.
126 rooms - $40-65
Pets: Welcome
Creature Comforts: CCTV, a/c,
pool, whirlpool

SANTA BARBARA
Beachcomber Inn
(800) 965-9776, (805) 965-4577
http://www.oceanpalms.com
202 W. Cabrillo Blvd.
32 rooms - $55-335
Pets: Welcome
Creature Comforts: CCTV, a/c,
cont. brkfst, pool

Beach House Inn
(805) 966-1126
320 W. Yanonali St.
12 rooms - $85-265
Pets: Welcome w/permission
Creature Comforts: CCTV, a/c,
kit, beach access

Blue Sands Motel
(805) 965-1624
421 S. Milpas St.
11 rooms - $75-169
Pets: Under 10 lbs. w/$5 fee
Creature Comforts: CCTV, a/c,
refrig, cont. brkfst, pool

Casa Del Mar Inn
(800) 433-3097, (805) 963-4418
http://www.casadelmar.com
18 Bath St.
21 rooms - $69-235
Pets: Small pet w/$10 fee
Creature Comforts: A 1929
Mediterranean-style inn set just a
block from the ocean, recently
refurbished, festive lithographs,
wicker accents, floral coverlets,
bleached woods, CCTV, a/c, terra
cotta fireplaces, kit, cont. brkfst,
courtyard whirlpool

Fess Parker's Doubletree Rsrt
(800) 222-TREE, (805) 564-4333
http://wwwdoubletreehotels.com
633 E. Cabrillo Blvd.
360 rooms - $189-850
Pets: Welcome on 1st floor
Creature Comforts: Enormous
24-acre Spanish-style resort just a
stone's throw from the beach,
reproductions and English
antiques, earth tone colors, rqst
700/800 rms facing ocean, CCTV,
VCR, a/c, refrig, Jacuzzis, 2
restaurants, pools, hlth clb, saunas,
whirlpools, tennis, basketball,
lawn games, putting green

Four Seasons Biltmore
(800) 332-3442, (805) 969-2261
http://www.fsrh.com
1260 Channel Dr.
234 rooms - $199-1,800
Pets: Under 15 Lbs. welcome
Creature Comforts: An exquisite
resort w/lavish furnishings and
elegant décor, on 20 acres of
beautifully maintained grounds,
vaulted beamed ceilings, chintz
furnishings, CCTV, VCR,
fireplaces, refrig, micro, Jacuzzis,
restaurant, 2 pools, hlth clb,
saunas, spa, whirlpools, tennis,
croquet, lawn sports, ocean-side
Coral Casino Club

Holiday Inn
(800) HOLIDAY, (805) 964-6241
http://www.holiday-inn.com
5650 Calle Real
159 rooms - $69-189
Pets: $25 fee & $100 dep.
Creature Comforts: CCTV, a/c,
refrig, restaurant, cont. brkfst, pool

Ivanhoe Inn
(805) 963-8832
http://www.travel-seek.com/
sb_cust/ivanhoe/info.htm
1406 Castillo St.
5 units - $99-195
Pets: Small pets welcome
Creature Comforts: Charming
1880's Victorian set behind a
picket fence amid flower gardens,
gazebo, spacious lawn, CCTV, a/c,
kit, four poster beds, country
décor, patio, cont. brkfst

The Mary May Inn
(805) 682-3199
http://www.marymayinn.com
111 W. Valerio St.
12 rooms - $85-195
Pets: Small dogs w/$10 fee
Creature Comforts: 1880's
Queen-Anne Victorian and
Federal houses, high ceilings,
lovely furnishings, canopy and
rice beds, Persian rugs, pine
pieces, dried flowers, white
wicker, CCTV, VCR, a/c,
Jacuzzis, fireplaces, refrig, full
brkfst, whirlpools

Motel 6
(800) 4-MOTEL6, (805) 687-5400
http://www.motel6.com
3505 State St.
59 rooms - $49-60
Pets: Under 30 lbs. welcome
Creature Comforts: CCTV, a/c

Motel 6
(800) 4-MOTEL6, (805) 864-1392
http://www.motel6.com
443 Corona Del Mar
51 rooms - $53-65
Pets: Under 30 lbs. welcome
Creature Comforts: CCTV, a/c,
pool

Ocean Palms Hotel
(800) 350-2326, (805) 966-9133
232 W. Cabrillo Blvd.
43 rooms - $85-255
Pets: Welcome w/$5 fee, $25 dep.
Creature Comforts: CCTV,
VCR, fireplaces, kit, pool,
whirlpool

Pacifica Suites
(800) 338-6722, (805) 683-6722
5490 Hollister Ave.
75 rooms - $99-210
Pets: Small pets welcome
Creature Comforts: Historic site,
CCTV, a/c, refrig, micro, cont.
brkfst, pool, whirlpool

SANTA CLARA
Econo Lodge
(800) 55-ECONO, (408) 241-3010
http://www.econolodge.com
2930 El Camino Real
70 rooms - $65-160
Pets: Welcome w/$6 fee
Creature Comforts: CCTV,
VCR, a/c, refrig, micro, full brkfst,
pool

Guest House Suites
(408) 241-3010
2930 El Camino Real
70 rooms - $89-260
Pets: Welcome
Creature Comforts: CCTV,
VCR, a/c, refrig, micro, cont.
brkfst, and hlth club access

Howard Johnson Lodge
(800) I-Go-Hojo, (408) 446-4656
http://www.hojo.com
5405 Stevens Creek Blvd.
95 rooms - $80-125
Pets: Small pets w/$10 fee
Creature Comforts: CCTV, a/c,
refrig, micro, and 2 pools

Madison Street Inn
(800) 491-5541, (408) 249-6676
http://www.santa-clara-inn.com
1390 Madison St.
6 rooms - $69-109
Pets: Small pets welcome
Creature Comforts: B&B set on
beautifully landscaped lot, CCTV,
VCR, fireplace, refrig, four-poster
and brass beds, Jacuzzi-Japanese
tub, full brkfst under arbor, pool,
floral gardens, murder mysteries,
access to tennis

Marriott Hotel
(800) 228-9290, (408) 988-1500
http://www.marriott.com
2700 Mission College Blvd.
755 rooms - $99-469
Pets: Small pets welcome
Creature Comforts: CCTV,
VCR, a/c, refrig, restaurant, pool,
whirlpool, tennis & racquet court

Motel 6
(800) 4-MOTEL6, (408) 241-0200
http://www.motel6.com
3208 El Camino Real
99 rooms - $56-69
Pets: Under 30 lbs. welcome
Creature Comforts: CCTV, a/c,
pool

Silicon Valley Suites
(408) 241-3010
2930 El Camino Real
70 rooms - $95-209
Pets: Welcome
Creature Comforts: CCTV, a/c,
refrig, micro, cont. brkfst, hlth
club access, pool

Vagabond Inn
(800) 522-1555, (408) 241-0771
http://www.vagabondinns.com
3580 El Camino Real
72 rooms - $55-75
Pets: Welcome w/$5 fee
Creature Comforts: CCTV, a/c,
refrig, micro, pool

Westin Hotel
(800) 228-3000, (408) 986-0700
http://www.westin.com
5101 Great American Pkwy.
505 rooms - $89-599
Pets: Small pets welcome
Creature Comforts: CCTV, a/c,
refrig, restaurant, pool, sauna,
whirlpool, golf, and access to a
hlth club and tennis

SANTA CRUZ
Days Inn
(800) DAYS-INN, (831) 423-8564
http://www.daysinn.com
325 Pacific St.
38 rooms - $85-170
Pets: Small pets welcome
Creature Comforts: CCTV, a/c,
refrig

Edgewater Beach Motel
(831) 423-0440
http://edgewaterbeachmotel.com
525 Second St.
17 rooms - $85-190
Pets: Welcome w/$10 fee
Creature Comforts: CCTV,
VCR, a/c, fireplace, kit, pool,
beach views

Inn at Pasatiempo
(831) 423-5000
555 Route 17
55 rooms - $80-185
Pets: Welcome w/$10 fee
Creature Comforts: CCTV,
VCR, refrig, restaurant, pool

Ocean Front Vacation Rental
(800) 801-4453, (831) 266-4453
http://www.oceanfronthouse.com
1600 W. Cliff Dr.
1 house - $1,650-1,900/wk
Pets: Selectively welcomed w/
credit card dep.
Creature Comforts: A lovely 3-
bedroom home overlooking the
ocean, lovely décor, CCTV, VCR,
stereo-CDs, a/c, kit, fireplace,
white washed walls, rattan and
pine furnishings, Persian rugs,
patio, enclosed yard, quiet beach
and tidepools, ocean-side path

Ocean Pacific Lodge
(800) 995-0289, (831) 457-1234
120 Washington St.
58 rooms - $69-145
Pets: Small pets welcome on the
first floor w/$20 fee
Creature Comforts: CCTV,
VCR, a/c, refrig, micro, cont.
brkfst, pool, hlth clb, saunas,
whirlpools

Pacific Inn
(831) 425-3722
330 Ocean St.
35 rooms - $80-155
Pets: Welcome w/$25 dep.
Creature Comforts: CCTV, a/c,
refrig, pool, whirlpool

Travelodge Riviera
(800) 578-7878, (831) 423-9515
http://www.travelodge.com
619 Riverside Ave.
61 rooms - $85-229
Pets: Welcome
Creature Comforts: CCTV, a/c,
kit, pool, whirlpool

SANTA FE SPRINGS
Dynasty Suites
(800) 842-7899, (562) 921-8571
13530 E. Firestone Blvd.
48 rooms - $39-55
Pets: Small pets w/$5 fee
Creature Comforts: CCTV,
VCR, a/c, refrig, micro, cont.
brkfst, pool, whirlpool

Motel 6
(800) 4-MOTEL6, (562) 921-0596
http://www.motel6.com
13412 Excelsior Dr.
80 rooms - $38-49
Pets: Under 30 lbs. welcome
Creature Comforts: CCTV, a/c

 California

SANTA MARIA
Best Western Inn
(800) 528-1234, (805) 922-5200
http://www.bestwestern.com
1725 N. Broadway St.
106 rooms - $55-100
Pets: Welcome
Creature Comforts: CCTV, VCR, a/c, refrig, micro, restaurant, cont. brkfst, pool, whirlpool

Comfort Inn
(800) 228-5150, (805) 922-5891
http://www.comfortinn.com
210 Nicholson Ave.
64 rooms - $45-89
Pets: Small pets w/$10 fee
Creature Comforts: CCTV, a/c, refrig, cont. brkfst, pool, whirlpool

Hunter's Inn
(800) 950-2123, (805) 922-2123
1514 S. Broadway St.
70 rooms - $40-84
Pets: Small pets w/$5 fee
Creature Comforts: CCTV, refrig, micro, pool, whirlpool

Motel 6
(800) 4-MOTEL6, (805) 928-8111
http://www.motel6.com
2040 N. Preisker Lane
126 rooms - $38-52
Pets: Under 30 lbs. welcome
Creature Comforts: CCTV, a/c, pool

Ramada Suites
(800) 2-Ramada, (805) 928-6000
http://www.ramada.com
2050 N. Preisker Ln.
210 rooms - $60-175
Pets: Welcome w/$15 fee
Creature Comforts: CCTV, a/c, kit, restaurant, pool, hlth clb, whirlpool

Rose Garden Inn
(805) 922-4505
1007 E. Main St.
80 rooms - $60-99
Pets: Welcome w/$5 fee
Creature Comforts: CCTV, a/c, refrig, micro, pool, whirlpool, and tennis

SANTA MONICA
The Georgian Hotel
(800) 538-8147, (310) 395-9945
http://www.georgianhotel.com
1415 Ocean Blvd.
85 rooms - $169-329
Pets: $100 fee and credit card dep.
Creature Comforts: Historic hotel w/Art Deco ambiance, barrel-ceiling foyer w/marble and rattan, lovely décor, wicker and bleached woods, windows w/ ocean views, CCTV, VCR, refrig, micro, restaurant, and hlth club access

Holiday Inn
(800) HOLIDAY, (310) 451-0676
http://www.holiday-inn.com
120 Colorado Blvd.
133 rooms - $89-259
Pets: Small pets w/$50 dep.
Creature Comforts: CCTV, VCR-games, a/c, refrig, restaurant, pool

Loews Beach Hotel
(800) 23-LOEWS, (310) 458-6700
http://www.loewshotels.com
1700 Ocean Ave.
349 rooms - $250-395
Pets: Under 50 Lbs. in 1st flr rms.
Creature Comforts: CCTV, VCR, a/c, refrig, micro, Jacuzzis, 2 restaurants, pool, hlth clb, saunas, steamrooms, whirlpools, playground, lobby bar, kids club

SANTA NELLA
Best Western Andersen's Inn
(800) 528-1234, (209) 826-5534
http://www.bestwestern.com
12367 S. Rte. 33
94 rooms - $59-79
Pets: Small pets w/$10 fee
Creature Comforts: CCTV, a/c, cont. brkfst, pool

Holiday Inn Express
(800) HOLIDAY, (209) 826-8282
http://www.holiday-inn.com
28976 West Plaza Dr.
100 rooms - $50-79
Pets: Welcome
Creature Comforts: CCTV, a/c, refrig, cont. brkfst, pool, hlth clb, whirlpool

Motel 6
(800) 4-MOTEL6, (209) 826-6644
http://www.motel6.com
12733 S. Rte. 33
111 rooms - $34-50
Pets: Under 30 lbs. welcome
Creature Comforts: CCTV, a/c, pool

Ramada Inn Mission de Oro
(800) 2-Ramada, (209) 826-4444
http://www.ramada.com
13070 S. Rte. 33
160 rooms - $55-89
Pets: Welcome w/$10 fee
Creature Comforts: CCTV, a/c, refrig, restaurant, pool, whirlpool

Super 8 Motel
(800) 800-8000, (209) 827-8700
http://www.super8.com
28821 W. Gonzaga Rd.
64 rooms - $39-75
Pets: Small pets welcome
Creature Comforts: CCTV, a/c, pool, whirlpool

SANTA ROSA
Best Western Garden Inn
(800) 528-1234, (707) 546-4031
http://www.bestwestern.com
1500 Santa Rosa Ave.
78 rooms - $59-159
Pets: Small pets w/$10 fee
Creature Comforts: CCTV, a/c, refrig, restaurant, pool, whirlpool

Hillside Inn
(707) 546-9353
2901 - 4th St.
35 rooms - $50-75
Pets: Welcome
Creature Comforts: CCTV, a/c, kit, restaurant, pool

Holiday Inn Express
(800) HOLIDAY, (707) 545-9000
http://www.holiday-inn.com
870 Hopper Ave.
98 rooms - $69-109
Pets: Small pets w/$50 dep.
Creature Comforts: CCTV, a/c, refrig, cont. brkfst, pool, hlth clb, whirlpool

Los Robles Lodge
(800) 255-6330, (707) 545-6330
1985 Cleveland Ave.
102 rooms - $59-129
Pets: Welcome
Creature Comforts: CCTV,
VCR, a/c, refrig, micro, restaurant,
pool, hlth clb, whirlpool

Motel 6
(800) 4-MOTEL6, (707) 525-9010
http://www.motel6.com
3145 Cleveland Ave.
119 rooms - $40-54
Pets: Under 30 lbs. welcome
Creature Comforts: CCTV, a/c,
pool

Motel 6
(800) 4-MOTEL6, (707) 546-1500
http://www.motel6.com
2760 Cleveland Ave.
100 rooms - $42-55
Pets: Under 30 lbs. welcome
Creature Comforts: CCTV, a/c,
pool

Santa Rosa Travelodge
(800) 578-7878, (707) 542-3472
http://www.travelodge.com
1815 Santa Rosa Ave.
31 rooms - $35-50
Pets: Small pets w/$25 dep.
Creature Comforts: CCTV, a/c,
refrig, pool

SANTA YNEZ
Santa Cota Motel
(805) 688-5525
3099 Mission Dr.
23 rooms - $85-109
Pets: Welcome w/$5 fee
Creature Comforts: CCTV, a/c,
refrig

SANTEE
Carlton Oaks Country Club
(800) 831-6757, (619) 448-4242
9200 Inwood Dr
60 rooms - $59-90
Pets: Welcome w/$100 dep.
Creature Comforts: CCTV,
VCR, a/c, refrig, restaurant, cont.
brkfst, pool, and golf

SAN YSIDRO
International Motor Inn
(619) 428-4486
190 E. Calle Primera
197 rooms - $45-55
Pets: Welcome
Creature Comforts: CCTV,
VCR, a/c, kit, pool, whirlpool

Motel 6
(800) 4-MOTEL6, (619) 690-6663
http://www.motel6.com
160 E. Calle Primera
103 rooms - $29-37
Pets: Under 30 lbs. welcome
Creature Comforts: CCTV, a/c,
pool

SCOTTS BEACH
Best Western Inn
(800) 528-1234, (408) 438-6666
http://www.bestwestern.com
6020 Scotts Valley Dr.
58 rooms - $65-135
Pets: Small pets in smoking rms.
Creature Comforts: CCTV, a/c,
refrig, pool, whirlpool

SEAL BEACH
Radisson Inn of Seal Beach
(800) 333-3333, (562) 493-7501
http://www.radisson.com
600 Marina Dr.
70 rooms - $99-159
Pets: Welcome w/credit card dep.
Creature Comforts: CCTV,
VCR, a/c, pool, hlth clb, whirlpool

SEASIDE
Bay Breeze Inn
(800) 899-7129, (408) 899-7111
2049 Fremont Blvd.
50 rooms - $35-110
Pets: Welcome
Creature Comforts: CCTV,
fireplace, kit, cont. brkfst

Thunderbird Motel
(800) 848-7841, (408) 394-6797
1933 Fremont Blvd.
32 rooms - $30-125
Pets: Welcome w/$10 fee
Creature Comforts: CCTV, kit,
cont. brkfst, pool

SELMA
Best Western John Jay Inn
(800) 528-1234, (559) 891-0300
http://www.bestwestern.com
2799 Floral Ave.
57 rooms - $49-120
Pets: Small pets welcome
Creature Comforts: CCTV, a/c,
refrig, cont. brkfst, pool, sauna,
hlth clb, whirlpool

Super 8 Motel
(800) 800-8000, (559) 896-2800
http://www.super8.com
3142 S. Highland Ave.
40 rooms - $40-65
Pets: Small pets welcome
Creature Comforts: CCTV, a/c,
pool

SEPULVEDA
Motel 6
(800) 4-MOTEL6, (818) 894-9341
http://www.motel6.com
15711 Roscoe Blvd.
114 rooms - $40-54
Pets: Under 30 lbs. welcome
Creature Comforts: CCTV, a/c,
pool

SHASTA LAKE
Bridge Bay Resort
(800) 752-9669, (530) 241-6464
http://www.sevencrown.com
10300 Bridge Bay Rd.
40 rooms - $55-160
Pets: Welcome w/$5 fee, $25 dep.
Creature Comforts: CCTV, a/c,
kit, restaurant, and boat-rentals

SHELTER COVE
Shelter Cove Inn
(888) 570-9676, (707) 986-7521
205 Wave Dr.
16 rooms - $75-115
Pets: Welcome
Creature Comforts: CCTV, a/c,
refrig

SIERRA CITY
Herrington's Sierra Pines
(530) 862-1151
Route 49
22 rooms - $55-109
Pets: Welcome
Creature Comforts: CCTV,
fireplaces, kit, restaurant, and river

SIMI VALLEY
Motel 6
(800) 4-MOTEL6, (805) 526-3533
http://www.motel6.com
2566 N. Erringer Rd.
60 rooms - $48-69
Pets: Under 30 lbs. welcome
Creature Comforts: CCTV, a/c,
pool

Radisson Simi Valley
(800) 333-3333, (805) 583-2000
http://www.radisson.com
999 Enchanted Way
196 rooms - $79-139
Pets: Welcome w/$35 fee
Creature Comforts: CCTV, a/c,
refrig, micro, restaurant, cont.
brkfst, 2 pools, hlth clb, whirlpool

SMITH RIVER
Casa Rubio Beach House
(800) 357-6199
http://www.moriah.com/casarubio
17285 Crissey Rd.
4 units - $79-99
Pets: Female dogs are preferred
Creature Comforts: CCTV, kit,
view of the water, beach

SOLVANG
Best Western
(800) 528-1234, (805) 688-2383
http://www.bestwestern.com
1440 Mission Dr.
39 rooms - $45-105
Pets: Small pets welcome
Creature Comforts: CCTV, a/c,
refrig, cont. brkfst, pool, whirlpool

Danish Country Inn
(800) 447-3529, (805) 688-2018
1445 Mission Dr.
82 rooms - $140-209
Pets: Under 25 lbs. w/$25 fee
Creature Comforts: CCTV,
VCR, a/c, refrig, restaurant, cont.
brkfst, pool, whirlpool

Hamlet Motel
(800) 253-5033, (805) 688-4413
1532 Mission Dr.
15 rooms - $35-130
Pets: Very small w/$10 fee
Creature Comforts: CCTV, a/c,
refrig, cont. brkfst

Meadowlark Motel
(800) 549-4658, (805) 688-4631
2644 Mission Dr.
20 rooms - $40-75
Pets: Welcome
Creature Comforts: CCTV, a/c,
kit

Viking Motel
(800) 368-5611 (CA),
(805) 688-1337
1506 Mission Dr.
12 rooms - $35-90
Pets: Small pets welcome
Creature Comforts: CCTV, a/c,
refrig, cont. brkfst

SONOMA
Best Western Sonoma Valley
(800) 528-1234, (707) 938-9200
http://www.bestwestern.com
550 W. Second St.
72 rooms - $99-259
Pets: Welcome w/$10 fee
Creature Comforts: CCTV, a/c,
refrig, micro, cont. brkfst, pool,
hlth clb, whirlpool

Martha's Cottage B&B
(707) 996-6918
19377 Orange St.
1 cottage - $110-140
Pets: Welcome
Creature Comforts: A charming
750 sq. ft. house, cathedral ceiling,
living room w/bay window,
CCTV, a/c, kit, cont. brkfst, deck

Sparrow's Nest B&B
(707) 996-3750
http://www.bbchannel.com/bbc/
p214318.asp
424 Denmark St.
1 cottage - $100-150
Pets: Welcome w/$10 fee
Creature Comforts: A charming
California bungalow w/English
country decor, very clean, garden
& courtyard, CCTV, VCR, a/c, kit,
china, full breakfast, geese, ducks,
chickens

SONORA
Aladdin Motor Inn
(209) 533-4971
14260 Mono Way
60 rooms - $55-100
Pets: Welcome w/$5 fee
Creature Comforts: CCTV,
VCR, a/c, refrig, pool, whirlpool

Best Western Sonora Oaks
(800) 5128-1234, (209) 533-4400
http://www.bestwestern.com
19551 Hess Ave.
100 rooms - $69-89
Pets: Welcome w/$10 fee and
credit card dep.
Creature Comforts: CCTV, a/c,
fireplaces, pool, whirlpool

Days Inn
(800) DAYS-INN, (209) 532-2400
http://www.daysinn.com
106 S. Washington St.
65 rooms - $55-120
Pets: Welcome w/$20 fee
Creature Comforts: CCTV, a/c,
restaurant, pool

Hammons House Inn
(888) 666-5329, (209) 532-7921
http://hammonshouseinn.com
22963 Robertson Ranch Rd.
4 rooms - $85-175
Pets: Welcome
Creature Comforts: Neat ranch
house set on 7 acres of pines,
meadows, and pond, country
quilts, etched glass doors, CCTV,
VCR, a/c, rock fireplace,
woodstove, ceiling fans, kit,
Jacuzzi, full country brkfst, sliding
glass doors lead to deck, gazebo,
pool

Miner's Motel
(800) 451-4176, (209) 532-7850
18740 Rte. 108
19 rooms - $40-85
Pets: Small pets welcome
Creature Comforts: CCTV,
VCR, a/c, refrig, pool

Mountain View B&B
(800) 446-1333, (209) 533-0628
http://www.mtvu.com
12980 Mt. View Rd.
4 rooms - $65-85
Pets: Welcome w/$10 fee
Creature Comforts: CCTV, a/c,
refrig, fireplace, full brkfst, pool

Sonora Gold Lodge
(800) 363-2154
http://www.goldlodge.com
480 Stockton St.
42 rooms - $39-119
Pets: Welcome w/$10 fee
Creature Comforts: CCTV, a/c,
refrig, micro, pool

STANTON

Motel 6
(800) 4-MOTEL6, (714) 891-0717
http://www.motel6.com
7450 Katella Ave.
206 rooms - $37-49
Pets: Under 30 lbs. welcome
Creature Comforts: CCTV, a/c,
pool

STATELINE

Harrah's Hotel & Casino
(800) HARRAHS, (702) 588-6611
http://www.harrahstahoe.com
Rte. 50 - Casino Center
532 rooms - $179-1,250
Pets: Welcome in hotel kennel
Creature Comforts: CCTV, a/c,
refrig, micro, Jacuzzi, 5
restaurants, pool, hlth clb,
massage, sauna, whirlpool, mtn
and lake views

STOCKTON

Best Western Charter Way Inn
(800) 528-1234, (209) 948-0321
http://www.bestwestern.com
550 West Charter Way
80 rooms - $48-69
Pets: Welcome
Creature Comforts: CCTV, a/c,
refrig, micro, pool, whirlpool

Days Inn
(800) DAYS-INN, (209) 948-6151
http://www.daysinn.com
33 N. Center St.
93 rooms - $50-75
Pets: Welcome
Creature Comforts: CCTV, a/c,
refrig, cont. brkfst, pool

Econo Lodge
(800) 55-ECONO, (209) 466-5741
http://www.econolodge.com
2210 S. Manthey Rd.
70 rooms - $35-85
Pets: Welcome w/$25 dep.
Creature Comforts: CCTV, a/c,
refrig, pool

Holiday Inn
(800) HOLIDAY, (209) 474-3301
http://www.holiday-inn.com
111 East March Lane
205 rooms - $50-65
Pets: Welcome w/$50 dep.
Creature Comforts: CCTV, a/c,
refrig, restaurant, cont. brkfst,
pool, hlth clb access, whirlpool

La Quinta

(800) Nu-Rooms, (209) 952-7800
http://www.laquinta.com
2710 West March Lane
155 rooms - $50-65
Pets: Small pets welcome
Creature Comforts: CCTV, a/c,
pool

Motel 6
(800) 4-MOTEL6, (209) 467-3600
http://www.motel6.com
1625 French Camp Tpke
125 rooms - $38-50
Pets: Under 30 lbs. welcome
Creature Comforts: CCTV, a/c,
pool

Motel 6
(800) 4-MOTEL6, (209) 946-0923
http://www.motel6.com
817 Navy Dr.
76 rooms - $34-50
Pets: Under 30 lbs. welcome
Creature Comforts: CCTV, a/c,
pool

Motel 6
(800) 4-MOTEL6, (209) 951-8120
http://www.motel6.com
6717 Plymouth Rd.
76 rooms - $38-52
Pets: Under 30 lbs. welcome
Creature Comforts: CCTV, a/c,
pool

Ramada Inn
(800) 2-Ramada, (209) 474-3301
http://www.ramada.com
111 E. March Lane
79 rooms - $55-90
Pets: Welcome w/$50 fee
Creature Comforts: CCTV, a/c,
refrig, micro, restaurant, pool, and
a whirlpool

Residence Inn
(800) 331-3131, (209) 472-9800
http://www.residenceinn.com
3240 W. March Lane
200 rooms - $99-189
Pets: $60 fee and $6/nightly fee
Creature Comforts: CCTV,
VCR, a/c, kit, cont. brkfst, pool,
hlth clb, whirlpool

SUN CITY

Travelodge
(800) 578-7878, (909) 672-9573
http://www.travelodge.com
27955 Encanto Dr.
58 rooms - $35-55
Pets: Welcome
Creature Comforts: CCTV, a/c,
pool, whirlpool

SUN VALLEY

Scottish Inns
(800) 251-1962, (818) 504-2671
http://www.reservahost.com
8365 Lehigh Ave.
55 rooms - $40-60
Pets: Welcome
Creature Comforts: CCTV, a/c

SUNNYVALE

Best Western Sunnyvale Inn
(800) 528-1234, (408) 734-3742
http://www.bestwestern.com
940 Weddell Dr.
88 rooms - $99-159
Pets: Small pets welcome
Creature Comforts: CCTV, a/c,
refrig, cont. brkfst, pool

Maple Tree Inn
(800) 423-0243, (408) 262-2624
711 E. El Camino Real
182 rooms - $60-160
Pets: Welcome w/$10 dep.
Creature Comforts: CCTV, a/c,
cont. brkfst, pool, hlth clb

Motel 6
(800) 4-MOTEL6, (408) 736-4595
http://www.motel6.com
775 N. Mathilda Ave.
146 rooms - $54-70
Pets: Under 30 lbs. welcome
Creature Comforts: CCTV, a/c,
pool

Motel 6
(800) 4-MOTEL6, (408) 720-1222
http://www.motel6.com
806 Ahwanee Ave.
58 rooms - $54-70
Pets: Under 30 lbs. welcome
Creature Comforts: CCTV, a/c,
pool

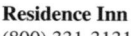

Residence Inn
(800) 331-3131, (408) 720-1000
http://www.residenceinn.com
750 Lakeway Dr.
231 rooms - $79-189
Pets: $10 fee and $75 dep.
Creature Comforts: CCTV,
VCR, a/c, kit, restaurant, cont.
brkfst, pool, hlth clb, whirlpool,
racquet ct.

Residence Inn
(800) 331-3131, (408) 720-8893
http://www.residenceinn.com
1080 Stewart Dr.
247 rooms - $79-199
Pets: $10 fee, $75 dep.
Creature Comforts: CCTV,
VCR, a/c, kit, restaurant, cont.
brkfst, pool, hlth clb, whirlpool,
basketball, racquet ct.

Summerfield Suites
(800) 833-4353, (408) 745-1515
www.summerfieldsuites.com
900 Hamlin Ct.
138 rooms - $79-225
Pets: Under 40 lbs. w/$10 daily
fee and $75 cleaning fee
Creature Comforts: CCTV,
VCR, a/c, fireplaces, kit, cont.
brkfst, pool, hlth club, whirlpool

Vagabond Inn
(800) 522-1555, (408) 734-4607
http://www.vagabondinns.com
816 Ahwanee Ave.
60 rooms - $50-75
Pets: Welcome w/$5 fee
Creature Comforts: CCTV, a/c,
refrig, micro, pool

SUSANVILLE
Best Western Trailside
(800) 528-1234, (916) 257-4123
http://www.bestwestern.com
2785 Main St.
90 rooms - $49-79
Pets: Welcome
Creature Comforts: CCTV, a/c,
refrig, Jacuzzis, restaurant, pool,
whirlpool

River Inn Motel
(916) 257-6051
1710 Main St.
50 rooms - $34-58
Pets: Welcome w/$5 fee
Creature Comforts: CCTV, a/c,
pool

Super Budget Motel
(916) 257-2782
2975 Johnsonville Rd.
70 rooms - $40-75
Pets: Welcome w/$5 fee
Creature Comforts: CCTV, a/c,
pool

SYLMAR
Motel 6
(800) 4-MOTEL6, (818) 362-9491
http://www.motel6.com
12775 Encinitas Ave.
158 rooms - $44-54
Pets: Under 30 lbs. welcome
Creature Comforts: CCTV, a/c,
pool

TEHACHAPI
Best Western Mountain Inn
(800) 528-1234, (805) 822-5591
http://www.bestwestern.com
416 W. Tehachapi Blvd.
74 rooms - $50-69
Pets: Welcome
Creature Comforts: CCTV, a/c,
refrig, micro, restaurant, pool,
whirlpool

Resort Science Springs
(800) 244-0864, (805) 822-5581
18100 Lucaya Rd.
64 rooms - $75-205
Pets: Welcome w/$20 dep.
Creature Comforts: CCTV, a/c,
kit, restaurant, cont. brkfst, pool,
hlth clb, sauna, tennis, lawn
games, golf, whirlpool

The Resort at Stallion Springs
(800) 244-0864, (805) 822-5581
http://www.stallionsprings.com
18100 Lucaya Rd.
63 rooms - $ 79-220
Pets: Welcome w/$20 dep.
Creature Comforts: Set on 2,300
acres, CCTV, a/c, kit, four poster
beds, country decor, restaurant,
cont. brkfst, pool, hlth clb, sauna,
lighted tennis, lawn games, golf,
whirlpool, lake

Travelodge (Tehachapi Summit)
(800) 578-7878, (805) 823-8000
http://www.travelodge.com
500 Steuber Rd.
81 rooms - $40-69
Pets: Welcome
Creature Comforts: CCTV, a/c,
refrig, micro, restaurant, pool

TEMECULA
Comfort Inn
(800) 228-5150, (909) 699-5888
http://www.comfortinn.com
27338 Jefferson Ave.
72 rooms - $50-75
Pets: Welcome w/$10 fee
Creature Comforts: CCTV, a/c,
refrig, pool, whirlpool

Motel 6
(800) 4-MOTEL6, (909) 676-7199
http://www.motel6.com
41900 Moreno Dr.
135 rooms - $36-49
Pets: Under 30 lbs. welcome
Creature Comforts: CCTV, a/c,
pool

Ramada Inn
(800) 2-Ramada, (909) 676-8770
http://www.ramada.com
28980 Front St.
70 rooms - $55-89
Pets: Welcome w/$35 dep.
Creature Comforts: CCTV, a/c,
refrig, micro, pool, whirlpool

Temecula Creek Inn
(909) 694-1000
44501 Rainbow Canyon Rd.
80 rooms - $99-189
Pets: Small pets welcome
Creature Comforts: CCTV, a/c,
refrig, restaurant, pool, whirlpool,
and tennis

THOUSAND OAKS
E-Z 8 Motel
(800) 326-6835, (805) 499-0755
2434 W. Hillcrest Dr.
128 rooms - $55-69
Pets: Small pets welcome
Creature Comforts: CCTV, a/c,
refrig, micro, pool, spa

Motel 6
(800) 4-MOTEL6, (805) 499-0711
http://www.motel6.com
1516 Newbury Rd.
175 rooms - $39-52
Pets: Under 30 lbs. welcome
Creature Comforts: CCTV, a/c,
pool

Thousand Oaks Inn
(800) 600-6878, (805) 497-3701
75 W. Thousand Oaks Blvd.
105 rooms - $60-85
Pets: Welcome w/$50 dep.
Creature Comforts: CCTV,
VCR, a/c, refrig, micro, restaurant,
pool, whirlpool, and hlth clb/golf/
tennis access

THREE RIVERS
Best Western Holiday Lodge
(800) 528-1234, (559) 561-4119
http://www.bestwestern.com
40105 Sierra Drive
54 rooms - $59-95
Pets: Welcome
Creature Comforts: CCTV,
VCR, a/c, refrig, pool, whirlpool

Buckeye Tree Lodge
(559) 561-5900
46000 Sierra Dr.
12 rooms - $40-115
Pets: Welcome w/$5 fee
Creature Comforts: CCTV,
refrig, micro, pool

IMA Lazy J Ranch Motel
(800) 341-8000, (559) 561-4449
http://www.imalodging.com
39625 Sierra Dr.
18 rooms - $45-175
Pets: Welcome
Creature Comforts: CCTV, a/c,
kit, pool, hiking

Sequoia Village Inn
(559) 561-3652
45971 Sierra Dr.
6 rooms - $55-100
Pets: Welcome
Creature Comforts: CCTV, a/c,
fireplace, kit, pool, whirlpool

Sierra Lodge
(800) 367-8879, (559) 561-3681
http://www.threerivers.com
43175 Sierra Dr.
22 rooms - $45-170
Pets: Small pets welcome
Creature Comforts: CCTV, a/c,
fireplaces, kit, cont. brkfst, pool

The River Inn
(559) 561-4367
45176 Sierra Dr.
12 rooms - $40-70
Pets: Welcome w/$4 fee
Creature Comforts: CCTV,
refrig

TORRANCE
Residence Inn
(800) 331-3131, (310) 543-4566
http://www.residenceinn.com
3701 Torrance Blvd.
248 rooms - $89-199
Pets: Welcome w/$5 fee and
credit card dep.
Creature Comforts: CCTV,
VCR, a/c, kit, fireplaces, cont.
brkfst, pool, hlth clb, whirlpool

Summerfield Suites
(800) 833-4353, (310) 371-8525
www.summerfieldsuites.com
19901 Prairie Ave.
145 rooms - $129-189
Pets: Welcome w/$5 fee and
credit card dep.
Creature Comforts: CCTV,
VCR, a/c, fireplaces, kit, cont.
brkfst, pool, hlth clb, whirlpool

TRACY
Motel 6
(800) 4-MOTEL6, (209) 836-4900
http://www.motel6.com
3810 Tracy Blvd.
111 rooms - $34-53
Pets: Under 30 lbs. welcome
Creature Comforts: CCTV, a/c,
pool

Phoenix Lodge
(209) 835-1335
3511 Tracy Blvd.
60 rooms - $40-56
Pets: Small pets w/$30 dep.
Creature Comforts: CCTV, a/c,
refrig, micro, pool

TRINIDAD
Bishop Pine Lodge
(707) 677-3314
1481 Patricks Point Rd.
12 rooms - $50-99
Pets: Welcome w/$7 fee
Creature Comforts: CCTV, kit,
hot tub

Shadow Lodge
(707) 677-0532
687 Patrick's Point Rd.
10 rooms - $50-110
Pets: Welcome w/$10 fee
Creature Comforts: CCTV, kit

TRINITY CENTER
Cedar Stock Resort
(800) 982-2279 (CA),
(530) 286-2225
http://www.cedarstock.com
45810 Rte. 3
Cabins/hseboats - $350-2,395/wk
Pets: Welcome
Creature Comforts: Houseboats
and rustic cabins, restaurant,
grocery store, marina-boating,
access to hiking and riding

TRONA
Desert Rose Motel
(619) 372-4572
84368 Trona Rd.
14 rooms - $38-60
Pets: Welcome
Creature Comforts: CCTV, a/c,
restaurant

TRUCKEE
Alpine Village Motel
(800) 933-1787, (916) 587-3801
12660 Deerfield Dr.
27 rooms - $50-85
Pets: Welcome
Creature Comforts: CCTV cont.
brkfst

Super 8 Motel
(800) 800-8000, (916) 587-8888
http://www.super8.com
11506 Deerfield Dr.
43 rooms - $65-115
Pets: Welcome
Creature Comforts: CCTV, a/c,
cont. brkfst, sauna, whirlpool

TULARE
Best Western Town & Country
(800) 528-1234, (559) 688-7537
http://www.bestwestern.com
1051 North Blackstone Dr.
93 rooms - $49-69
Pets: Small pets w/$10 fee
Creature Comforts: CCTV,
VCR, a/c, refrig, micro, cont.
brkfst, pool, whirlpool

Friendship Inn
(800) 424-4777, (559) 688-0501
http://www.hotelchoice.com
26442 Rte. 99
55 rooms - $38-55
Pets: Welcome w/$20 dep.
Creature Comforts: CCTV, a/c, micro, cont. brkfst, pool

Green Gable Inn
(559) 686-3432
1010 E. Prosperity Ave.
59 rooms - $45-79
Pets: Small pets welcome
Creature Comforts: CCTV, a/c, refrig, micro, pool, hlth clb, sauna, whirlpool

Inns of America
(800) 826-0778, (559) 686-1611
http://www.innsofamerica.com
1183 N. Blackstone Dr.
90 rooms - $35-59
Pets: Welcome
Creature Comforts: CCTV, a/c, pool

Motel 6
(800) 4-MOTEL6, (559) 686-1611
http://www.motel6.com
1111 N. Blackstone Dr.
111 rooms - $35-58
Pets: Under 30 lbs. welcome
Creature Comforts: CCTV, a/c, pool

TURLOCK
Best Western Orchard Inn
(800) 528-1234, (209) 667-2827
http://www.bestwestern.com
5025 N. Golden State Blvd.
72 rooms - $54-69
Pets: Small pets w/$10
Creature Comforts: CCTV, a/c, kit, pool, whirlpool

Best Western Gardens Inn
(800) 528-1234, (209) 632-0231
http://www.bestwestern.com
1119 Pedras Rd.
94 rooms - $54-100
Pets: Small pets welcome
Creature Comforts: CCTV, VCR, a/c, refrig, cont. brkfst, pool, whirlpool

Comfort Inn
(800) 221-2222, (209) 668-3400
http://www.comfortinn.com
200 West Glenwood Ave.
92 rooms - $45-70
Pets: Small pets welcome
Creature Comforts: CCTV, pool, whirlpool

Motel 6
(800) 4-MOTEL6, (209) 667-4100
http://www.motel6.com
250 S. Walnut Ave.
101 rooms - $32-49
Pets: Under 30 lbs. welcome
Creature Comforts: CCTV, a/c, pool

TWENTY NINE PINES
Circle C Motel
(760) 367-7615
6340 El Rey Ave.
12 rooms - $70-90
Pets: Small pets welcome
Creature Comforts: CCTV, VCR, a/c, kit, pool, whirlpool

Motel 6
(800) 4-MOTEL6, (760) 367-2833
http://www.motel6.com
72562 Twentynine Palms Hwy.
124 rooms - $40-56
Pets: Under 30 lbs. welcome
Creature Comforts: CCTV, a/c, pool

29 Palms Inn
(760) 367-3505
http://www.cyberspike.com/29palmsinn
73950 Inn Ave.
18 cabins - $60-280
Pets: Welcome
Creature Comforts: Old-fashioned adobe and wood frame cottages, CCTV, a/c, kit, restaurant, cont. brkfst, fireplaces, pool, pond, massage, houseboat, loads of wildlife and photographic opportunities

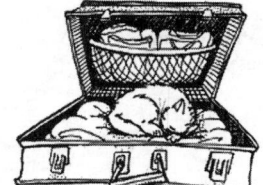

TWIN PEAKS
Arrowhead Pine Rose Cabins
(800) 429-PINE, (909) 337-2341
www.lakearrowheadcabins.com
Rte. 189 & Grand View
17 cabins - $59-215
Pets: In ltd. cabins w/$5 fee
Creature Comforts: Old-fashioned theme cabin resort set on 5 acres, CCTV, VCR, knotty pine walls and beamed ceilings, country décor, handmade quilts, four poster, sleigh and brass beds, comfortable furnishings and rockers, fireplace, kit, pool, whirlpool, lawn games

UKIAH
Days Inn
(800) DAYS-INN, (707) 462-7584
http://www.daysinn.com
950 N. State Rd.
54 rooms - $65-85
Pets: Welcome w/$5 fee
Creature Comforts: CCTV, a/c, restaurant, cont. brkfst, pool

Holiday Lodge
(800) 300-2906, (707) 462-2906
1050 S. State St.
45 rooms - $35-60
Pets: Small pets w/$5 fee
Creature Comforts: CCTV, a/c, pool

Motel 6
(800) 4-MOTEL6, (707) 468-5404
http://www.motel6.com
1208 S. State St.
62 rooms - $34-49
Pets: Under 30 lbs. welcome
Creature Comforts: CCTV, a/c, pool

Western Traveler Motel
(707) 468-9167
693 S. Orchard Ave.
55 rooms - $35-75
Pets: Welcome w/$5 fee
Creature Comforts: CCTV, VCR, a/c, refrig, pool, whirlpool

VACAVILLE
Best Western Heritage Inn
(800) 528-1234, (707) 448-8453
http://www.bestwestern.com
1420 East Monte Vista Ave.
41 rooms - $56-77
Pets: Welcome w/$25 dep.
Creature Comforts: CCTV, a/c, refrig, micro, pool

Motel 6
(800) 4-MOTEL6, (707) 447-5550
http://www.motel6.com
107 Lawrence Dr.
97 rooms - $37-49
Pets: Under 30 lbs. welcome
Creature Comforts: CCTV, a/c,
pool

VALENCIA
Hilton Garden Inn (at Six Flags)
(800) HILTONS, (805) 254-8800
http://www.hilton.com
27710 The Old Rd.
150 rooms - $99-275
Pets: Welcome
Creature Comforts: CCTV,
VCR, a/c, refrig, micro, restaurant,
cont. brkfst, pool, hlth clb,
whirlpool

VALLEJO
Best Western at Marine World
(800) 528-1234, (707) 554-9655
http://www.bestwestern.com
1595 Fairgrounds Dr.
59 rooms - $75-100
Pets: Small pets welcome
Creature Comforts: CCTV, a/c,
refrig, pool

E-Z 8 Motel
(800) 326-6835, (707) 554-1840
4 Mariposa St.
85 rooms - $29-44
Pets: Welcome
Creature Comforts: CCTV, a/c,
refrig, pool, whirlpool

Holiday Inn
(800) HOLIDAY, (707) 644-1220
http://www.holiday-inn.com
1000 Fairgrounds Dr.
165 rooms - $85-145
Pets: Welcome w/$10 fee
Creature Comforts: CCTV, a/c,
refrig, micro, restaurant, pool,
sauna, whirlpool

IMA Royal Bay Inn
(800) 643-8887, (707) 643-1061
http://www.imalodging.com
44 Admiral Callaghan Ln.
78 rooms - $39-75
Pets: Welcome w/$10 fee
Creature Comforts: CCTV, a/c,
refrig, restaurant, pool

Motel 6
(800) 4-MOTEL6, (707) 643-7611
http://www.motel6.com
1455 Marine World Pkwy
54 rooms - $37-49
Pets: Under 30 lbs. welcome
Creature Comforts: CCTV, a/c,
pool

Motel 6
(800) 4-MOTEL6, (707) 642-7781
http://www.motel6.com
458 Fairgrounds Dr.
97 rooms - $37-49
Pets: Under 30 lbs. welcome
Creature Comforts: CCTV, a/c,
pool

Motel 6
(800) 4-MOTEL6, (707) 552-2912
http://www.motel6.com
597 Sandy Beach Rd.
149 rooms - $34-50
Pets: Under 30 lbs. welcome
Creature Comforts: CCTV, a/c,
pool

Ramada Inn
(800) 2-Ramada, (707) 643-2700
http://www.ramada.com
1000 Admiral Callaghan Ln.
130 rooms - $65-130
Pets: Welcome w/$20 fee
Creature Comforts: CCTV, a/c,
kit, pool, whirlpools

Thriftlodge
(800) 525-9055, (707) 552-7220
http://www.travelodge.com
160 Lincoln Rd.
60 rooms - $35-85
Pets: Welcome
Creature Comforts: CCTV, a/c,
kit pool, whirlpool

VENTURA
Best Western Inn
(800) 528-1234, (805) 648-3101
http://www.bestwestern.com
708 E. Thompson Blvd..
75 rooms - $69-110
Pets: Welcome w/$25 dep.
Creature Comforts: CCTV, a/c,
refrig, pool

La Quinta
(800) Nu-Rooms, (805) 658-6200
http://www.laquinta.com
5818 Valentine Rd.
140 rooms - $50-65
Pets: Small pets welcome
Creature Comforts: CCTV, a/c,
refrig, pool, whirlpool

Motel 6
(800) 4-MOTEL6, (805) 643-5100
http://www.motel6.com
2145 E. Harbor Blvd.
200 rooms - $39-50
Pets: Under 30 lbs. welcome
Creature Comforts: CCTV, a/c,
pool

Motel 6
(800) 4-MOTEL6, (805) 650-0080
http://www.motel6.com
3075 Johnson Dr.
151 rooms - $40-55
Pets: Under 30 lbs. welcome
Creature Comforts: CCTV, a/c,
pool

Vagabond Inn
(800) 522-1555, (805) 648-5371
http://www.vagabondinns.com
756 E. Thompson Blvd.
80 rooms - $45-90
Pets: Welcome w/$5 fee
Creature Comforts: CCTV, a/c,
refrig, pool, whirlpool

VICTORVILLE
Holiday Inn
(800) HOLIDAY, (760) 245-6565
http://www.holiday-inn.com
15494 Palmdale Rd.
164 rooms - $70-99
Pets: Welcome
Creature Comforts: CCTV, a/c,
restaurant, pool

Motel 6
(800) 4-MOTEL6, (760) 243-0666
http://www.motel6.com
16901 Stoddard Wells Rd.
62 rooms - $35-48
Pets: Under 30 lbs. welcome
Creature Comforts: CCTV, a/c,
pool

Red Roof Inn
(800) Red-Roof, (760) 241-1577
http://www.redroof.com
13409 Mariposa Rd.
95 rooms - $35-60
Pets: Welcome
Creature Comforts: CCTV, a/c,
refrig, micro, pool, whirlpools

Travelodge
(800) 578-7878, (760) 243-7700
http://www.travelodge.com
16868 Stoddard Wells Rd.
75 rooms - $49-75
Pets: Welcome
Creature Comforts: CCTV, a/c,
refrig, pool

VISALIA
Best Western Visalia Inn
(800) 528-1234, (559) 732-4561
http://www.bestwestern.com
623 Main St.
41 rooms - $60-80
Pets: Small pets w/$5
Creature Comforts: CCTV, a/c,
refrig, pool

Holiday Inn Plaza Park
(800) HOLIDAY, (559) 651-5000
http://www.holiday-inn.com
9000 W. Airport Dr.
257 rooms - $75-129
Pets: Welcome w/credit card dep.
Creature Comforts: CCTV, a/c,
refrig, restaurant, 2 pools, hlth clb,
whirlpool, putting green

Thriftlodge
(800) 525-9055, (559) 732-5611
http://www.travelodge.com
4645 W. Mineral King Ave.
78 rooms - $49-75
Pets: Welcome
Creature Comforts: CCTV, a/c,
refrig, hlth clb, lawn games, pool

VISTA
La Quinta Inn
(800) Nu-Rooms, (760) 727-8180
http://www.laquinta.com
630 Sycamore Ave.
105 rooms - $55-75
Pets: Small pets welcome
Creature Comforts: CCTV, a/c,
refrig, pool, and hlth clb access

VOLCANO
St. George Hotel
(209) 296-4458
http://www.stgeorgehotel.com
16104 Main St.
20 rooms - $55-85
Pets: Welcome in certain rms.
Creature Comforts: CCTV,
fireplace, refrig, restaurant, full
brkfst, pool, piano, game room,
sauna, whirlpool, lawn games

WALNUT CREEK
Embassy Suites Hotel
(800) EMBASSY, (925) 934-2500
http://www.embassy-suites.com
1345 Treat Blvd.
250 rooms - $99-195
Pets: Welcome
Creature Comforts: CCTV,
VCR-video gms, a/c, refrig,
restaurant, pool, hlth clb, sauna,
whirlpools

Holiday Inn
(800) HOLIDAY, (925) 932-3332
http://www.holiday-inn.com
2730 North Main St.
148 rooms - $99-189
Pets: Welcome
Creature Comforts: CCTV, a/c,
refrig, restaurant, pool, whirlpool

Motel 6
(800) 4-MOTEL6, (510) 935-4010
http://www.motel6.com
2389 N. Main St.
71 rooms - $49-65
Pets: Under 30 lbs. welcome
Creature Comforts: CCTV, a/c,
pool

Walnut Creek Motor Lodge
(800) 824-0334, (925) 932-2811
1960 North Main St.
70 rooms - $50-80
Pets: $5 fee and 50 dep.
Creature Comforts: CCTV, a/c,
kit, pool, whirlpool

WATSONVILLE
Best Western Inn
(800) 528-1234, (831) 724-3367
http://www.bestwestern.com
740 Freedom Blvd.
43 rooms - $55-130
Pets: Small pets welcome
Creature Comforts: CCTV, a/c,
refrig, cont. brkfst, pool, whirlpool

Motel 6
(800) 4-MOTEL6, (831) 728-4144
http://www.motel6.com
125 Silver Leaf Dr.
124 rooms - $39-52
Pets: Under 30 lbs. welcome
Creature Comforts: CCTV, a/c,
pool

National 9 Motel
(831) 724-1116
1 Western Dr.
19 rooms - $35-120
Pets: Welcome w/$10 fee
Creature Comforts: CCTV pool

WEAVERVILLE
49er Motel
(530) 623-4937
718 Main St.
14 rooms - $35-60
Pets: Welcome
Creature Comforts: CCTV, a/c,
kit, pool

Motel Trinity
(530) 623-2129
1112 Main St.
25 rooms - $50-85
Pets: Small pets welcome
Creature Comforts: CCTV, a/c,
kit, pool, whirlpools

Victorian Inn
(530) 623-4432
1709 Main St.
60 rooms - $50-110
Pets: Welcome w/$10 dep.
Creature Comforts: CCTV,
VCR, a/c, refrig, pool, whirlpool

WEED
Lake Shastina Golf Resort
(800) 358-GOLF, (530) 938-3201
http://www.lakeshastinagolf.com
5925 Country Club Dr.
29 condos - $95-160
Pets: Welcome
Creature Comforts: Great golf
course and nicely decorated
condos near the base of Mt Shasta,
CCTV, a/c, refrig, Jacuzzi,
restaurant, pool, tennis, nearby
Lake Shastina

Motel 6
(800) 4-MOTEL6, (916) 938-4101
http://www.motel6.com
466 N. Weed Dr.
118 rooms - $35-44
Pets: Under 30 lbs. welcome
Creature Comforts: CCTV, a/c, pool

Sis-Q-Inn Motel
(916) 938-4194
1825 Shastina Dr.
21 rooms - $39-59
Pets: Welcome w/$5 fee
Creature Comforts: CCTV, a/c, refrig, micro, whirlpool

WEST COVINA
Hampton Inn
(800) Hampton, (818) 967-5800
http://www.hampton-inn.com
3145 E. Garvey Dr.
125 rooms - $49-75
Pets: Welcome
Creature Comforts: CCTV, a/c, refrig, micro, cont. brkfst, pool

WEST HOLLYWOOD
Le Montrose Suite Hotel
(800) 776-0666, (310) 855-1115
http://www.travel2000.com
900 Hammond St.
125 rooms - $145-595
Pets: Under 14 lbs., w/$75 cleaning fee
Creature Comforts: European-style hotel w/warm ambiance, traditional décor, CCTV, VCR, a/c, fireplaces, kit, Jacuzzis, restaurant, roof top pool and terrace dining, hlth clb, sauna, whirlpool, and tennis

Le Parc Hotel
(800) 578-4837, (310) 855-8888
http://www.travel2000.com
733 N. West Knoll Dr.
154 rooms - $135-295
Pets: Welcome w/$50 fee and credit card dep.
Creature Comforts: CCTV, VCR, a/c, fireplaces, kit, Jacuzzis, restaurant, pool, hlth clb, sauna, whirlpool, and tennis

Summerfield Suites
(800) 833-4353 (310) 657-7400
www.summerfieldsuites.com
1000 Westmount Dr.
110 rooms - $139-199
Pets: Welcome w/$50-100 fee and a $250 dep.
Creature Comforts: CCTV, VCR, a/c, kit, restaurant, pool, hlth clb, sauna, whirlpools

Wyndham Bel Age Hotel
(800) Wyndham, (310) 854-1111
http://www.wyndham.com
1020 N. San Vincente Blvd.
200 rooms - $149-499
Pets: Welcome w/$50 dep.
Creature Comforts: CCTV, a/c, refrig, Jacuzzis, restaurant, pool, hlth clb, whirlpools

WESTLEY
Days Inn
(800) DAYS-INN, (209) 894-5500
http://www.daysinn.com
7144 McCracken Rd.
34 rooms - $40-70
Pets: $5 fee and $25 dep.
Creature Comforts: CCTV, a/c, pool, whirlpool

WESTMINSTER
Motel 6
(800) 4-MOTEL6, (714) 895-0042
http://www.motel6.com
13100 Goldenwest Rd.
127 rooms - $39-50
Pets: Under 30 lbs. welcome
Creature Comforts: CCTV, a/c, pool

Motel 6
(800) 4-MOTEL6, (714) 891-5366
http://www.motel6.com
6266 Westminster Ave.
98 rooms - $39-50
Pets: Under 30 lbs. welcome
Creature Comforts: CCTV, a/c, pool

WESTPORT
Blue Victorian Inn
(800) 400-6310 (CA),
(707) 964-6310
38921 N. Rte. 1
5 rooms - $85-135
Pets: Welcome w/$10 fee
Creature Comforts: The owners are instilling charm to this already lovely B&B, CCTV, fireplace, kit, cont. brkfst, whirlpool, pet area

Howard Creek Ranch
(707) 964-6725
www.howardcreekranch.com
40501 N. Rte. 1
10 rooms - $60-175
Pets: Welcome
Creature Comforts: A wonderful old 40-acre ranch, heirlooms, country décor w/warm ambiance, fireplaces-wood stoves, American antiques, colorful quilts, four poster and canopy beds, clawfoot tub, beamed ceilings, sky lights, Oriental and braided rugs, Jacuzzis, kit, full brkfst, massage, spa, sauna, massage, 75 foot swinging bridge and ocean views

WHITTIER
Motel 6
(800) 4-MOTEL6, (562) 692-9101
http://www.motel6.com
8221 S. Pioneer Blvd.
98 rooms - $37-49
Pets: Under 30 lbs. welcome
Creature Comforts: CCTV, a/c, pool

Vagabond Inn
(800) 522-1555, (562) 698-9701
http://www.vagabondinns.com
14125 E. Whittier Blvd.
48 rooms - $40-75
Pets: Welcome w/$5 fee
Creature Comforts: CCTV, a/c, refrig, cont. brkfst, pool

WILLIAMS
Granzella's Inn
(530) 473-3310
391 - 6th St.
44 rooms - $55-75
Pets: $10 fee & $50 dep.
Creature Comforts: CCTV, a/c, restaurant, pool, whirlpool

Motel 6
(800) 4-MOTEL6, (530) 473-5337
http://www.motel6.com
455 - 4th St.
121 rooms - $34-49
Pets: Under 30 lbs. welcome
Creature Comforts: CCTV, a/c, pool

  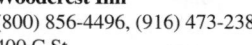

Woodcrest Inn
(800) 856-4496, (916) 473-2381
400 C St.
60 rooms - $50-65
Pets: Welcome w/$5 fee
Creature Comforts: CCTV, a/c,
refrig, micro, cont. brkfst, pool,
whirlpool

WILLITS
Baechtel Creek Inn
(800) 459-9911, (707) 459-9063
101 Gregory Ln.
46 rooms - $59-115
Pets: Small dogs w/$10 fee
Creature Comforts: CCTV,
VCR, a/c, refrig, micro, cont.
brkfst, pool, whirlpool

Holiday Lodge
(800) 835-3972, (707) 459-5361
1540 S. Main St.
16 rooms - $40-70
Pets: Small pets w/$5 fee
Creature Comforts: CCTV, a/c,
kit, cont. brkfst, pool

WILLOW CREEK
Willow Creek Motel
(530) 629-2115
375 Rte. 65
12 rooms - $38-52
Pets: Welcome
Creature Comforts: CCTV, a/c,
kit, pool, gold panning

WILLOWS
Best Western Golden Pheasant
(800) 528-1234, (530) 934-4603
http://www.bestwestern.com
249 N. Humboldt Ave.
104 rooms - $59-159
Pets: Welcome w/$10 fee
Creature Comforts: CCTV,
VCR, a/c, refrig, full brkfst, 2
pools, whirlpool

Blue Gum Inn
(530) 934-5401
Route 99
30 rooms - $29-49
Pets: Welcome w/$5 fee
Creature Comforts: CCTV, a/c,
kit, pool

Cross Roads West Inn
(800) 814-6301, (530) 934-7026
452 N. Humboldt Ave.
40 rooms - $30-49
Pets: Welcome
Creature Comforts: CCTV, a/c,
cont. brkfst, pool

Days Inn
(800) DAYS-INN, (530) 934-4444
http://www.daysinn.com
475 N. Humboldt Ave.
50 rooms - $55-75
Pets: Welcome w/$5 fee
Creature Comforts: CCTV, a/c,
refrig, micro, cont. brkfst, pool,
whirlpool

Super 8 Motel
(800) 800-8000, (530) 934-2871
http://www.super8.com
457 Humboldt Ave.
41 rooms - $45-65
Pets: Welcome w/$25 dep.
Creature Comforts: CCTV, a/c,
pool

WOODLAND
Cinderella Motel
(800) 782-9403, (916) 662-1091
99 W. Main St.
30 rooms - $40-65
Pets: Welcome w/$25 dep.
Creature Comforts: CCTV, a/c,
refrig, pool, whirlpool

Motel 6
(800) 4-MOTEL6, (916) 666-6777
http://www.motel6.com
1564 Main St.
79 rooms - $38-55
Pets: Under 30 lbs. welcome
Creature Comforts: CCTV, a/c,
pool

WOODLAND HILLS
Country Inn
(800) 447-3529, (818) 222-5300
23627 Calabassas Rd.
124 rooms - $135-325
Pets: Welcome w/$50 fee
Creature Comforts: CCTV,
VCR, a/c, refrig, micro, full brkfst,
pool, hlth clb access

Vagabond Inn
(800) 522-1555, (818) 347-8080
http://www.vagabondinns.com
20175 Ventura Blvd.
95 rooms - $60-95
Pets: Welcome w/$5 fee
Creature Comforts: CCTV, a/c,
refrig, micro, pool, whirlpool

YORKVILLE
Sheep Dung Estates
(707) 894-5322
http://www.sheepdung.com
Rte. 128, Box 49
5 cottages - $125-150
Pets: Very welcome — $15 fee
Creature Comforts: Terrific
energy-efficient cottages on 550
acres, perched on picturesque
hillsides w/great views, very
private, lovely decors and
comfortable furnishings, cathedral
ceilings, terra cotta floors and
throw rugs, intimate porches,
walls of windows, stereos, down
comforters, woodstoves, kit, cont.
brkfst, pond, great hiking, featured
in *Home Magazine*

YOSEMITE
The Redwoods
(209) 375-6666
8038 Chilnualna Falls Rd.
125 rooms - $99-495
Pets: Welcome in some rooms
Creature Comforts: CCTV,
VCR, fireplace, kit, and
swimming holes

YOUNTVILLE
Vintage Inn
(800) 351-1133, (707) 944-1112
http://www.vintageinn.com
6541 Washington St.
80 rooms - $175-349
Pets: Welcome w/$25 fee
Creature Comforts: French
Provincial inn amid vineyards,
rms. w/vaulted ceilings, plantation
shutters, French doors open to
verandas, rattan and lightly stained
oak pieces, handmade furnishings
w/hand-painted fabrics, CCTV,
VCR, a/c, fireplaces, refrig,
Jacuzzis, massages, cont. brkfst,
pool, hlth club access, whirlpool-
terry robes, tennis, bikes

The Webber Place
(800) 647-7177, (707) 944-8384
6610 Webber St.
4 rooms - $125-195
Pets: Welcome w/$20 fee
Creature Comforts: Lovingly
refurbished 1850's farmhouse
country accents, Folk Art
collectibles, Oriental and braided
rugs, fireplace, refrig, claw foot
tub, full brkfst, sunroom w/vaulted
ceilings and paneled walls, lattice
trimmed veranda, hammock

YREKA
Best Western Miner's Inn
(800) 528-1234, (916) 842-4355
http://www.bestwestern.com
122 E. Miner St.
134 rooms - $45-89
Pets: Welcome
Creature Comforts: CCTV, a/c,
kit, pool

Motel 6
(800) 4-MOTEL6, (916) 842-4111
http://www.motel6.com
1785 S. Main St.
102 rooms - $34-49
Pets: Under 30 lbs. welcome
Creature Comforts: CCTV, a/c,
pool

Super 8
(800) 800-8000, (916) 842-5781
http://www.super8.com
136 Montague Rd.
61 rooms - $44-65
Pets: Welcome
Creature Comforts: CCTV, a/c,
Jacuzzi, cont. brkfst, pool

Wayside Inn
(800) 303-4855, (916) 842-4412
1235 So. Main St.
45 rooms - $35-155
Pets: Welcome w/$4 fee
Creature Comforts: CCTV,
VCR, a/c, fireplace, kit, Jacuzzi,
restaurant, pool, whirlpool

YUBA CITY
Days Inn
(800) DAYS-INN, (530) 674-1711
http://www.daysinn.com
700 N. Palora Ave.
50 rooms - $50-105
Pets: Welcome w/$5 fee
Creature Comforts: CCTV, a/c,
refrig, micro, Jacuzzis, cont.
brkfst, pool

Motel Orleans
(800) 626-1900, (916) 674-1592
730 Palora Ave.
52 rooms - $35-55
Pets: Welcome w/$4 fee
Creature Comforts: CCTV, a/c,
refrig, micro, pool

Vada's Motel
(916) 671-1151
545 Colusa Ave.
40 rooms - $39-79
Pets: Small pets welcome w/credit
card dep.
Creature Comforts: CCTV, a/c,
and kit

YUCCA VALLEY
Oasis of Eden Inn
(800) 606-6686, (916) 473-2381
http://desertgold.com/eden/
eden.html
56377 Twentynine Palms Rd.
40 rooms - $65-195
Pets: $10 fee & $25 dep.
Creature Comforts: Theme
rooms, CCTV, VCR, a/c, kit, cont.
brkfst, Jacuzzi, pool, whirlpool

Super 8
(800) 800-8000, (760) 228-1773
http://www.super8.com
Barberry Ave.
48 rooms - $44-65
Pets: Welcome
Creature Comforts: CCTV, a/c,
cont. brkfst, pool

Colorado

ALAMOSA
Best Western Inn
(800) 528-1234, (719) 589-2567
http://www.bestwestern.com
1919 Main St.
120 rooms - $49-109
Pets: Under 25 lbs. welcome
Creature Comforts: CCTV, a/c, restaurant, whirlpool

Cottonwood Inn
(719) 589-3882
123 San Juan Ave.
9 rooms - $50-109
Pets: Welcome
Creature Comforts: CCTV, a/c, full brkfst

Holiday Inn
(800) HOLIDAY, (719) 589-5833
http://www.holiday-inn.com
333 Santa Fe Ave.
125 rooms - $75-100
Pets: Welcome w/$25 dep.
Creature Comforts: CCTV, VCR, a/c, refrig, restaurant, pool, sauna, whirlpool

ANTONITO
Conejos River Guest Ranch
(719) 376-2464
25390 Rte. 17
8 rooms - $70-90
Pets: Welcome
Creature Comforts: Set along a river, restaurant, full brkfst, bikes, hiking

ASPEN
Aspen Club Lodge
(800) 882-2582, (970) 925-6760
http://www.aspenclubfamilys.com
709 Durant St.
90 rooms - $79-550
Pets: Small pets w/$100 dep.
Creature Comforts: CCTV, VCR, a/c, refrig, Jacuzzis, restaurant, cont. brkfst, pool, whirlpool, skiing, hiking

Beaumont Inn
(800) 344-3853, (970) 925-7081
1301 E. Cooper Ave.
http://www.thebeaumont.com
30 rooms - $85-385
Pets: Welcome w/$20 fee
Creature Comforts: Informal yet elegant inn, rms. w/sophisticated Western motif, nightly turndown, CCTV, refrig, fireplace, gourmet brkfst, restaurant, pool, hot tub

Hotel Jerome
(800) 331-7213 (970) 920-1000
http://www.aspen.com/jerome
330 E. Main St.
95 rooms - $155-1,500
Pets: $70 fee and credit card dep.
Creature Comforts: Highly recommended, historic 1889 Victorian-style hotel with antiques and loads of appeal, CCTV, VCR, a/c, refrig, Jacuzzis, restaurant, pool, hlth club, whirlpool

Limelite Lodge
(800) 433-0832, (970) 925-3025
http://www.aspen.com/limelite
228 E. Cooper St.
63 rooms - $60-245
Pets: Welcome
Creature Comforts: CCTV, VCR, a/c, refrig, 2 pools, sauna, whirlpools

The Little Nell
(800) 525-6200, (970) 920-4600
http://www.thelittlenell.com
765 E. Durant Ave.
90 rooms - $245-4,900
Pets: Welcome w/personalized pet program, toy baskets, dog-sitters
Creature Comforts: Exquisite ski-on/off resort, lovely gardens, overlooking Aspen Mtn, beautifully and individually decorated rooms, Belgian wool carpets, down comforters, CCTV, VCR, a/c, fireplaces, refrig, micro, Jacuzzis, marble bathrooms, restaurant, sauna, spa, pool, whirlpool, golf/tennis access

St. Regis
(800) 325-3535, (970) 920-3300
http://www.sheraton.com
315 E. Dean St.
258 rooms - $125-875
Pets: Small pets welcome
Creature Comforts: Luxury property, CCTV, VCR, a/c, refrig, micro, Jacuzzis, restaurant, pool, hlth clb, saunas, whirlpool, golf/tennis access

AURORA
La Quinta
(800) 531-5900, (303) 337-0206
http://www.laquinta.com
1011 S. Abilene St.
122 rooms - $65-85
Pets: Welcome
Creature Comforts: CCTV, a/c, refrig, pool

Motel 6
(800) 4-MOTEL6, (303) 873-0286
http://www.motel6.com
14031 E. Iliff Ave.
121 rooms - $39-49
Pets: Under 30 lbs. welcome
Creature Comforts: CCTV, a/c, pool

BEAVER CREEK
Comfort Inn
(800) 228-5150, (970) 949-5511
http://www.comfortinn.com
161 W. Beaver Creek Blvd.
149 rooms - $99-550
Pets: Welcome w/$15 fee
Creature Comforts: CCTV, a/c, refrig, micro, pool, whirlpool

BOULDER
Best Western Inn
(800) 528-1234, (303) 449-3800
http://www.bestwestern.com
770 - 28th St.
96 rooms - $65-110
Pets: Under 20 Lbs w/ CC dep.
Creature Comforts: CCTV, a/c, refrig, cont. brkfst, pool, sauna, hot tub

Boulder Mountain Lodge
(800) 458-0882, (303) 444-0882
91 Four Mile Canyon Rd.
23 rooms - $45-90
Pets: Welcome w/$50 dep.
Creature Comforts: CCTV, kit, pool, whirlpool

The Broker Inn
(800) 338-5407, (303) 444-3330
http://www.bldr.broker_inn
555 - 30th St.
115 rooms - $95-199
Pets: Welcome
Creature Comforts: CCTV, a/c, refrig, Jacuzzis, restaurant, pool, and a whirlpool

Days Inn
(800) DAYS-INN, (303) 499-4422
http://www.daysinn.com
5397 S. Boulder Rd.
75 rooms - $65-95
Pets: Small pets welcome
Creature Comforts: CCTV, a/c, refrig, micro, pool

Foot of the Mountain
(303) 442-5688
200 Arapahoe Ave.
18 log cabins - $55-75
Pets: Welcome w/$5 fee
Creature Comforts: CCTV, refrig

Holiday Inn
(800) HOLIDAY, (303) 443-3322
http://www.holiday-inn.com
800 - 28th St.
165 rooms - $75-110
Pets: Welcome w/$20 fee
Creature Comforts: CCTV, a/c, refrig, restaurant, pool, sauna, whirlpool

Homewood Suites
(800) 225-5466, (303) 499-9922
http://www.homewoodsuites.com
4950 Baseline Rd.
110 rooms - $99-179
Pets: Welcome w/$50 fee
Creature Comforts: CCTV, a/c, VCR, fireplace, micro, whirlpool

Pearl Street Inn
(888) 810-1302, (303) 444-5584
http://www.pearlstreetinn.com
1820 Pearl St.
8 rooms - $90-150
Pets: Welcome w/$10 fee
Creature Comforts: Historic inn w/Victorian charm, wicker furnishings, period antiques, floral fabrics, CCTV, a/c, fireplaces in all rms, excellent restaurant, gourmet brkfst, whirlpool

Residence Inn
(800) 331-3131, (303) 449-5545
http://www.residenceinn.com
3030 Center Green Dr.
130 rooms - $129-199
Pets: Welcome w/$5 fee
Creature Comforts: CCTV, VCR, a/c, kit, restaurant, cont. brkfst, whirlpool

Super 8 Motel
(800) 800-8000, (303) 443-7800
http://www.super8.com
970 - 28th St.
69 rooms - $55-90
Pets: Welcome
Creature Comforts: CCTV, a/c, kit, pool

BRUSH
Best Western Inn
(800) 528-1234, (970) 842-5146
http://www.bestwestern.com
1208 N. Colorado Ave.
45 rooms - $45-70
Pets: Small pets welcome
Creature Comforts: CCTV, a/c, cont. brkfst, pool

BUENA VISTA
Topaz Lodge Motel
(719) 395-2427
115 N. Rte. 2
18 rooms - $45-109
Pets: Welcome w/$5 fee
Creature Comforts: CCTV, cont. brkfst, access to tennis

BURLINGTON
Burlington Inn
(719) 346-5555
450 S. Lincoln St.
112 rooms - $29-49
Pets: Welcome w/$5 fee
Creature Comforts: CCTV, a/c, restaurant, pool

Chapparal Budget Host
(800) Bud-Host, (719) 346-5361
http://www.budgethost.com
405 S. Lincoln St.
40 rooms - $39-55
Pets: Small pets welcome
Creature Comforts: CCTV, a/c, pool

Sloan's Motel
(800) 362-0464, (719) 346-5333
1901 Rose Ave.
28 rooms - $25-45
Pets: Small pets welcome
Creature Comforts: CCTV, a/c, refrig, micro, pool

CANON CITY
Best Western Inn
(800) 528-1234, (719) 275-3377
http://www.bestwestern.com
1925 Freemont St.
68 rooms - $45-110
Pets: Small pets welcome
Creature Comforts: CCTV, a/c, refrig, micro, pool, whirlpool

Canon Inn
(800) 525-7727, (719) 275-8676
http://www.canoninn.com
3075 E. Rte. 50
150 rooms - $55-95
Pets: Small pets w/$50 dep.
Creature Comforts: CCTV, a/c, refrig, micro, restaurant, pool, whirlpool

Holiday Motel
(719) 275-3317
1502 Main St.
15 rooms - $29-49
Pets: Small pets w/$25 dep.
Creature Comforts: CCTV, a/c, kit, pool

Travelodge
(800) 578-7878, (719) 275-0461
http://www.travelodge.com
2990 E. Main St.
40 rooms - $35-79
Pets: Welcome
Creature Comforts: CCTV, a/c, refrig, whirlpool

CASTLE ROCK

Super 8 Motel
(800) 800-8000, (303) 688-0880
http://www.super8.com
1020 Park St.
60 rooms - $38-52
Pets: Welcome w/permission
Creature Comforts: CCTV, a/c

CLIFTON

Best Western Inn
(800) 528-1234, (970) 434-3400
http://www.bestwestern.com
3228 Rte. 70
49 rooms - $52-85
Pets: Under 25 lbs. welcome
Creature Comforts: CCTV, a/c,
refrig, cont. brkfst, hlth clb,
whirlpool

COLORADO SPRINGS

Antlers Hotel
(800) 222-TREE, (719) 473-5600
http://www.doubletreehotels.com
4 S. Cascade St.
292 rooms - $69-179
Pets: Under 50 lbs. w/$50 dep.
Creature Comforts: CCTV, a/c,
refrig, Jacuzzis, restaurant,
whirlpool

Apollo Park Executive Suites
(800) 279-3620, (719) 635-1539
805 S. Circle Dr., 2-B
88 rooms - $59-95
Pets: Welcome w/$100 dep.
Creature Comforts: CCTV, a/c,
kit, pool

Best Western Palmer House
(800) 528-1234, (719) 636-5201
http://www.bestwestern.com
3010 N. Chestnut St.
150 rooms - $50-90
Pets: $10 fee, $25 dep
Creature Comforts: CCTV, a/c,
refrig, micro, restaurant, pool,
putting green

Chief Motel
(719) 473-5228
1624 S. Nevada Ave.
24 rooms - $30-68
Pets: Small pets w/$5 fee
Creature Comforts: CCTV, a/c,
kit, whirlpool

Days Inn
(800) DAYS-INN, (719) 527-0800
http://www.daysinn.com
2850 S. Circle Dr.
120 rooms - $40-89
Pets: Welcome w/$25 dep.
Creature Comforts: CCTV, a/c,
restaurant, pool

Doubletree Hotel
(800) 222-TREE, (719) 576-8900
http://www.doubletreehotels.com
1775 E. Cheyenne Mtn. Dr.
298 rooms - $99-575
Pets: Welcome w/$10 daily fee
Creature Comforts: CCTV, a/c,
refrig, restaurant, pool, hlth club,
whirlpool

Drury Inn
(800) 325-8300, (719) 598-2500
http://www.drury-inn.com
8155 N. Academy Blvd.
118 rooms - $80-115
Pets: Welcome
Creature Comforts: CCTV,
VCR, a/c, refrig, micro, whirlpool

Econo Lodge
(800) 55-ECONO, (719) 636-3385
http://www.econolodge.com
714 N Nevada Ave.
38 rooms - $35-100
Pets: Small pets w/$10 fee
Creature Comforts: CCTV, a/c,
refrig, micro, Jacuzzis, pool

Economy Inn
(800) 235-1545, (719) 634-1545
1231 S. Nevada Ave.
42 rooms - $29-88
Pets: Small pets w/$10 fee
Creature Comforts: CCTV, a/c,
kit, Jacuzzis, pool, whirlpool

Hampton Inn
(800) Hampton, (719) 593-9700
http://www.hampton-inn.com
7245 Commerce Center Dr.
128 rooms - $55-115
Pets: Small pets w/$25 dep.
Creature Comforts: CCTV, a/c,
refrig, micro, pool

Holiday Inn
(800) HOLIDAY, (719) 598-7656
http://www.holiday-inn.com
505 Pope's Bluff
200 rooms - $55-110
Pets: Welcome w/$50 dep.
Creature Comforts: CCTV,
VCR, a/c, refrig, Jacuzzis,
restaurant, pool, whirlpool, tennis

Holiday Inn Express
(800) HOLIDAY, (719) 473-5530
http://www.holiday-inn.com
725 W. Cimarron Rd.
205 rooms - $50-100
Pets: Small pets welcome
Creature Comforts: CCTV, a/c,
kit, pool, sauna

Howard Johnson Lodge
(800) I-Go-Hojo, (719) 598-7793
http://www.hojo.com
5056 N. Nevada Ave.
50 rooms - $40-80
Pets: Welcome
Creature Comforts: CCTV, a/c,
pool

La Quinta Inn
(800) 531-5900, (719) 528-5060
http://www.laquinta.com
4385 Sinton Dr.
105 rooms - $50-95
Pets: Welcome
Creature Comforts: CCTV, a/c,
refrig, cont. brkfst, pool

Marriott Hotel
(800) 228-9290, (719) 260-1800
http://www.marriott.com
5580 Tech Center Dr.
303 rooms - $99-179
Pets: Welcome
Creature Comforts: CCTV,
VCR, a/c, refrig, restaurant, pool,
saunas, whirlpools, volleyball

Motel 6
(800) 4-MOTEL6, (719) 520-5400
http://www.motel6.com
3228 N. Chestnut St.
83 rooms - $33-54
Pets: Under 30 lbs. welcome
Creature Comforts: CCTV, a/c,
pool

Radisson Inn North
(800) 333-3333, (719) 598-5770
http://www.radisson.com
8110 N. Academy Blvd.
202 rooms - $79-175
Pets: Under 20 lbs. w/$50 dep.
Creature Comforts: CCTV, a/c,
refrig, micro, Jacuzzis, restaurant,
cont. brkfst, pool, sauna, whirlpool

Radisson Inn, Airport
(800) 333-3333, (719) 597-7000
http://www.radisson.com
1645 N. Newport Dr.
144 rooms - $79-125
Pets: Under 50 lbs. w/$50 dep.
Creature Comforts: CCTV, a/c,
refrig, micro, Jacuzzis, restaurant,
cont. brkfst, pool, sauna, whirlpool

Raintree Inn
(719) 632-4600
2625 Ore Mill Rd.
115 rooms - $40-80
Pets: Welcome
Creature Comforts: CCTV, a/c,
pool, whirlpools

Ramada Inn-East
(800) 2-Ramada, (719) 596-7660
http://www.ramada.com
520 N. Murray Blvd.
102 rooms - $45-100
Pets: Welcome w/$20 dep.
Creature Comforts: CCTV, a/c,
refrig, whirlpool

Ramada Inn-North
(800) 2-Ramada, (719) 272-6232
http://www.ramada.com
4440 Rte. 25
220 rooms - $45-100
Pets: Welcome w/$25 dep.
Creature Comforts: CCTV, a/c,
refrig, pool, game room

Red Lion Hotel
(800) RED-LION, (719) 576-8900
http://www.redlion.com
1775 E. Cheyenne Mtn. Blvd.
300 rooms - $79-169
Pets: Welcome
Creature Comforts: CCTV, a/c,
refrig, restaurants, pool, saunas,
whirlpools

Red Roof Inn
(800) The-Roof, (719) 598-6700
http://www.redroof.com
8280 Rte. 83
112 rooms - $55-109
Pets: Small pets welcome
Creature Comforts: CCTV, a/c,
refrig, pool

Residence Inn
(800) 331-3131, (719) 574-0370
http://www.residenceinn.com
3880 N. Academy Rd.
95 rooms - $99-189
Pets: Welcome w/$10 fee
Creature Comforts: CCTV,
VCR, a/c, fireplace, kit, pool,
whirlpool, volleyball

Residence Inn
(800) 331-3131, (719) 576-0101
http://www.residenceinn.com
2765 Geyser Dr.
70 rooms - $88-179
Pets: $5 daily fee, $25 clean. fee
Creature Comforts: CCTV, a/c,
kit, pool, whirlpool

Rodeway Inn
(800) 228-2000, (719) 471-0990
http://www.rodeway.com
2409 E. Pikes Peak Ave.
112 rooms - $45-75
Pets: Welcome w/$50 dep.
Creature Comforts: CCTV, a/c,
kit, pool

Sheraton Hotel
(800) 325-3535, (719) 576-5900
http://www.sheraton.com
2886 S. Circle Dr.
500 rooms - $79-239
Pets: Welcome
Creature Comforts: CCTV,
VCR-games, a/c, refrig, Jacuzzis,
restaurant, pool, saunas,
steamrooms, whirlpool, tennis,
basketball, putting green, lawn
games

Stagecoach Motel
(719) 633-3894
1647 S. Nevada Ave.
18 rooms - $35-70
Pets: Small pets w/$5 fee
Creature Comforts: CCTV, a/c,
refrig

Swiss Chalet
(719) 471-2260
3410-342 W. Colorado Ave.
18 rooms - $25-77
Pets: Small pets w/$25 dep.
Creature Comforts: CCTV, a/c,
kit

CORTEZ
Anasazi Motor Inn
(800) 727-6232, (970) 565-3773
640 S. Broadway St.
88 rooms - $45-75
Pets: Welcome w/$50 dep.
Creature Comforts: CCTV, a/c,
VCR, kit, restaurant, pool, spa

Arrow Motor Inn
(800) 727-7692, (970) 565-7778
440 S. Broadway St.
42 rooms - $30-65
Pets: Small pets w/credit card dep
Creature Comforts: CCTV, a/c,
refrig, micro, pool, whirlpool

Bel Rau Lodge
(970) 565-3738
2040 E. Main St.
40 rooms - $30-66
Pets: Small pets welcome
Creature Comforts: CCTV, a/c,
kit, whirlpool

Best Western Turquoise
(800) 528-1234, (970) 565-3778
http://www.bestwestern.com
535 E. Main St.
77 rooms - $45-165
Pets: Under 25 lbs. welcome
Creature Comforts: CCTV, a/c,
refrig, micro, cont. brkfst, pool,
whirlpool

Comfort Inn
(800) 228-5150, (970) 565-3400
http://www.comfortinn.com
2321 E. Main St.
140 rooms - $49-105
Pets: Welcome w/$4 fee
Creature Comforts: CCTV, a/c,
refrig, Jacuzzis, cont. brkfst, pool,
whirlpool

Days Inn
(800) DAYS-INN, (970) 565-8577
http://www.daysinn.com
Rtes. 160 & 145
77 rooms - $39-88
Pets: Small pets welcome
Creature Comforts: CCTV, a/c,
Jacuzzis, restaurant, pool,
whirlpool

Holiday Inn Express
(800) HOLIDAY, (970) 565-6000
http://www.holiday-inn.com
2121 E. Main St.
100 rooms - $79-109
Pets: Small pets welcome
Creature Comforts: CCTV, a/c,
Jacuzzi, restaurant, pool, hlth club,
whirlpool

Ramada Limited
(800) 2-Ramada, (970) 565-3474
http://www.ramada.com
2020 E. Main St.
72 rooms - $39-88
Pets: Small pets w/$25 dep.
Creature Comforts: CCTV, a/c,
pool, whirlpool

CRAIG
A Bar Z Motel
(800) 458-7228, (970) 824-7066
2690 W. Rte. 40
44 rooms - $32-68
Pets: Welcome w/$5 fee
Creature Comforts: CCTV, a/c,
refrig, micro, Jacuzzis, cont.
brkfst, whirlpool, volleyball,
horseshoes

Best Western
(800) 528-1234, (970) 824-8101
http://www.bestwestern.com
755 E. Victory Way
33 rooms - $30-60
Pets: Welcome
Creature Comforts: CCTV, a/c,
refrig, cont. brkfst

Black Nugget Motel
(800) 727-2088, (970) 824-8161
2855 W. Victory Way
22 rooms - $35-55
Pets: Small pets welcome
Creature Comforts: CCTV, a/c,
refrig, micro, cont. brkfst, lawn
games

Holiday Inn
(800) HOLIDAY, (970) 824-4000
http://www.holiday-inn.com
300 S. Rte. 40
168 rooms - $50-129
Pets: Welcome w/$50 dep.
Creature Comforts: CCTV, a/c,
refrig, micro, restaurant, pool, rec.
dome, whirlpool

Ramada Inn
(800) 2-Ramada, (970) 824-9282
http://www.ramada.com
262 Commerce St.
44 rooms - $40-79
Pets: Welcome w/$50 dep.
Creature Comforts: CCTV, a/c,
kit, Jacuzzis, pool, whirlpool

Super 8 Motel
(800) 800-8000, (970) 824-3473
http://www.super8.com
200 Rte. 13
59 rooms - $35-75
Pets: Welcome
Creature Comforts: CCTV, a/c

DEL NORTE
Del Norte Motel & Cafe
(800) 372-2331, (719) 657-3581
1050 Grand Ave.
18 rooms - $29-49
Pets: Welcome
Creature Comforts: CCTV, a/c,
restaurant

CRIPPLE CREEK
Victor Hotel
(800) 748-0870, (719) 689-3553
www.indra.com/falline/vh/vh.htm
4th St. & Victor Ave.
30 rooms - $89-109
Pets: Welcome in ltd. rms
Creature Comforts: An 1890's
bank, refurbished and is now a
delightful inn w/Victorian accents,
CCTV, a/c, antiques, restaurant,
cont. brkfst, great mtn. views

DELTA
Best Western Sundance
(800) 528-1234, (970) 874-9781
http://www.bestwestern.com
903 Main St.
41 rooms - $42-66
Pets: Small pets welcome
Creature Comforts: CCTV, a/c,
restaurant, pool, hlth clb,
whirlpool

DENVER
Adam's Mark
(303) 623-0303
http://www.adamsmark.com
1550 Court Place
1,224 rooms - $155-1,200
Pets: Welcome w/$100 dep.
Creature Comforts: Nestled in
the heart of the city's business and
retail districts, CCTV, a/c, refrig,
micro, restaurant, pool, hlth clb,
sauna, whirlpool

Best Western Executive Inn
(800) 528-1234, (303) 373-5730
http://www.bestwestern.com
4411 Peoria St.
199 rooms - $89-169
Pets: Welcome
Creature Comforts: CCTV, a/c,
refrig, pool, hlth clb

Cameron Motel
(303) 757-2100
4500 E. Evan Ave.
35 rooms - $48-75
Pets: Small pets w/$5 fee
Creature Comforts: CCTV, a/c,
kit

Days Inn
(800) DAYS-INN, (303) 571-1715
http://www.daysinn.com
620 Federal Blvd.
185 rooms - $33-62
Pets: Small pets welcome
Creature Comforts: CCTV, a/c,
refrig, micro, restaurant

Doubletree Hotel
(800) 222-TREE, (303) 321-3333
http://www.doubletreehotels.com
3203 Quebec St.
572 rooms - $99-575
Pets: Small pets welcome
Creature Comforts: CCTV,
VCR, a/c, refrig, restaurant, pool,
sauna, hlth club, whirlpool

Drury Inn
(800) 325-8300, (303) 373-1983
http://www.drury-inn.com
4400 Peoria St.
138 rooms - $49-75
Pets: Welcome
Creature Comforts: CCTV, a/c,
refrig, micro, pool, hlth clb

Embassy Suites, Airport
(800) 345-0087, (303) 375-0400
http://www.embassy-suites.com
4444 N. Havana St.
210 rooms - $89-149
Pets: Small pets w/$25 dep.
Creature Comforts: CCTV, a/c,
kit, restaurant, full brkfst, pool,
hlth clb, sauna, steamroom,
whirlpool

Executive Tower Hotel
(800) 525-6651, (303) 571-0300
http://www.exectowerhotel.com
1405 Curtis St.
335 rooms - $85-199
Pets: Welcome
Creature Comforts: CCTV,
VCR, a/c, refrig, micro, Jacuzzi,
restaurant, cont. brkfst, pool, hlth
clb access, sauna, steamroom,
whirlpool, racquet cts

Holiday Chalet B&B
(800) 626-4497, (303) 321-9975
web site pending
1820 E. Colfax Ave.
10 rooms - $69-139
Pets: Welcome w/$5 fee, $50 dep.
Creature Comforts: Restored
Victorian brownstone mansion in
historic district, CCTV, VCR, a/c,
kit, full brkfst

Holiday Inn, Airport
(800) HOLIDAY, (303) 573-1450
http://www.holiday-inn.com
15500 - 40th Ave.
256 rooms - $99-199
Pets: Small pets w/CC dep.
Creature Comforts: CCTV, a/c,
refrig, restaurant, pool, hlth clb,
whirlpool

Holiday Inn, West
(800) HOLIDAY, (303) 279-7611
http://www.holiday-inn.com
14707 W. Colfax Ave.
225 rooms - $99-199
Pets: Small pets w/CC dep.
Creature Comforts: CCTV, a/c,
refrig, restaurant, pool, hlth clb,
whirlpool, putting green

Holiday Inn
(800) HOLIDAY, (303) 279-7611
http://www.holiday-inn.com
1450 Glenarm Pl.
394 rooms - $99-199
Pets: Small pets w/CC dep.
Creature Comforts: CCTV, a/c,
refrig, restaurant, pool

Holiday Inn, Southeast
(800) HOLIDAY, (303) 745-6958
http://www.holiday-inn.com
3200 S. Parker Rd.
475 rooms - $99-199
Pets: Small pets w/CC dep.
Creature Comforts: CCTV, a/c,
refrig, restaurant, pool, hlth clb,
whirlpool

La Quinta Inn
(800) 531-5900, (303) 371-5640
http://www.laquinta.com
3975 Peoria Way
110 rooms - $65-90
Pets: Welcome
Creature Comforts: CCTV, a/c,
refrig, micro, cont. brkfst, pool

La Quinta Inn
(800) 531-5900, (303) 458-1222
http://www.laquinta.com
3500 Fox St.
106 rooms - $65-90
Pets: Welcome
Creature Comforts: CCTV, a/c,
refrig, cont. brkfst, pool

La Quinta Inn
(800) 531-5900, (303) 758-8886
http://www.laquinta.com
1975 S. Colorado Blvd.
129 rooms - $65-90
Pets: Welcome
Creature Comforts: CCTV, a/c,
refrig, micro, cont. brkfst, pool

Loews Giorgio Hotel
(800) 81-LOEWS, (303) 782-9300
http://www.loewshotels.com
4150 E. Mississippi Ave.
190 rooms - $90-989
Pets: Welcome
Creature Comforts: Lovely city
hotel w/Italian accents, marble
trim, antiques, original artwork,
CCTV, VCR, a/c, refrig, micro,
restaurant, cont. brkfst, hlth club

Marriott Hotel
(800) 228-9290, (303) 297-1300
http://www.marriott.com
1701 California St.
610 rooms - $79-189
Pets: Small pets welcome
Creature Comforts: CCTV, a/c,
refrig, restaurants, pool, hlth clb,
sauna, steamroom, whirlpool

Marriott Hotel - Southeast
(800) 228-9290, (303) 758-7000
http://www.marriott.com
6363 E. Harrington Ave.
595 rooms - $59-129
Pets: Small pets welcome
Creature Comforts: CCTV, a/c,
refrig, restaurant, pool, whirlpool

Marriott Hotel Tech Center
(800) 228-9290, (303) 779-1100
http://www.marriott.com
4900 S. Syracuse Rd.
627 rooms - $69-159
Pets: Small pets welcome
Creature Comforts: CCTV,
VCR, a/c, refrig, Jacuzzi,
restaurant, pool, hlth clb, sauna,
steamroom, whirlpool, racquet cts.

Motel 6, Central
(800) 4-MOTEL6, (303) 455-8888
http://www.motel6.com
3050 W. 49th Ave.
191 rooms - $33-54
Pets: Under 30 lbs. welcome
Creature Comforts: CCTV, a/c,
pool

Motel 6, East
(800) 4-MOTEL6, (303) 371-1980
http://www.motel6.com
12020 E. 39th Ave.
138 rooms - $36-48
Pets: Under 30 lbs. welcome
Creature Comforts: CCTV, a/c,
pool

Quality Inn
(800) 228-5151, (303) 758-2211
http://www.qualityinn.com
6300 E. Hampden St.
185 rooms - $60-125
Pets: Welcome w/$5 fee
Creature Comforts: CCTV, a/c,
refrig, restaurant, pool, sauna,
whirlpool

Ramada Inn (Airport)
(800) 2-Ramada, (303) 388-6161
http://www.ramada.com
3737 Quebec St.
149 rooms - $75-99
Pets: Small pets w/$50 dep.
Creature Comforts: CCTV, a/c,
refrig, restaurant, pool

Ramada Inn (Downtown)
(800) 2-Ramada, (303) 433-8331
http://www.ramada.com
1975 Bryant St.
166 rooms - $75-99
Pets: Small pets w/$50 dep.
Creature Comforts: CCTV, a/c,
refrig, restaurant, pool

Ramada Inn, Airport
(800) 2-Ramada, (303) 831-7700
http://www.ramada.com
1150 E. Colfax St.
145 rooms - $75-99
Pets: Small pets w/$25 dep.
Creature Comforts: CCTV, a/c,
restaurant, pool

Residence Inn
(800) 331-3131, (303) 683-5500
http://www.residenceinn.com
93 W. Centennial Ave.
78 rooms - $99-189
Pets: Welcome w/CC dep.
Creature Comforts: CCTV, a/c,
kit, pool, whirlpool

Residence Inn, Downtown
(800) 331-3131, (303) 458-5318
http://www.residenceinn.com
2777 Zuni St.
155 rooms - $99-189
Pets: Welcome w/$10 fee
Creature Comforts: CCTV,
VCR, a/c, kit, pool, whirlpool

Super 8 Motel
(800) 800-8000, (303) 433-6677
http://www.super8.com
2601 Zuni St.
175 rooms - $35-55
Pets: Welcome
Creature Comforts: CCTV, a/c,
pool

Super 8 Motel
(800) 800-8000, (303) 296-3100
http://www.super8.com
5888 N. Broadway St.
106 rooms - $38-54
Pets: Welcome
Creature Comforts: CCTV, a/c,
pool

Westin Hotel
(800) 228-3000, (303) 572-9100
http://www.westin.com
1672 Lawrence St.
420 rooms - $99-999
Pets: Small pets welcome
Creature Comforts: Luxury city
hotel, CCTV, VCR, a/c, refrig,
Jacuzzis, restaurant, pool, saunas,
racquetball, whirlpool

DILLON
Best Western Lodge
(800) 528-1234, (970) 468-2341
http://www.bestwestern.com
652 Lake Dillon Dr.
69 rooms - $55-155
Pets: Welcome w/$15 fee
Creature Comforts: CCTV, a/c,
kit, restaurant, cont. brkfst, sauna,
pool, whirlpool

DOLORES
Dolores Mtn. Inn
(800) 842-8113, (970) 882-7203
http://www.dminn.com
701 Railroad Ave.
30 rooms - $35-59
Pets: Welcome w/$5 fee
Creature Comforts: CCTV, a/c,
kit, river

Lebanon Schoolhouse B&B
(800) 349-9829, (970) 882-4461
http://www.subee.com/sch_house/
home.html
24925 County Rd.
5 rooms - $65-125
Pets: Welcome in the suite
Creature Comforts: 1907
historic landmark, country setting,
antiques, antique pool table,
CCTV, VCR, refrig, fireplace,
Jacuzzi, gourmet brkfst, whirlpool

Outpost Motel
(800) 382-4892, (970) 882-7271
1800 Central Ave.
13 rooms - $39-89
Pets: Welcome
Creature Comforts: CCTV, a/c,
fireplace, kit, river

DURANGO
Adobe Inn
(970) 247-2743
2178 Main Ave.
www.dww.net/laplatadiscounts
25 rooms - $45-120
Pets: Welcome w/$6 fee
Creature Comforts: CCTV, a/c,
refrig, cont. brkfst, pool, whirlpool

Alpine Motel
(800) 818-4042, (970) 247-4042
3515 N. Main Ave.
25 rooms - $30-90
Pets: Welcome
Creature Comforts: CCTV, a/c,
refrig, micro

Best Western Purgatory Lodge
(800) 528-1234, (970) 247-9669
http://www.bestwestern.com
49617 Rte. 550
31 rooms - $99-189
Pets: Welcome w/$6 fee
Creature Comforts: CCTV, a/c,
refrig, micro, Jacuzzi, cont. brkfst,
pool, whirlpool

Budget Inn
(800) 257-2222, (970) 247-5222
3077 Main Ave.
35 rooms - $55-79
Pets: Welcome w/$4 fee, $10 dep.
Creature Comforts: CCTV, a/c,
refrig, pool

Doubletree Hotel
(800) 222-TREE, (970) 259-6580
http://www.doubletreehotels.com
501 Camino Del Rio Rd.
160 rooms - $129-375
Pets: Under 20 lbs. welcome in
smoking rooms w/$10 fee
Creature Comforts: CCTV, a/c,
refrig, restaurant, pool, hlth club,
sauna, whirlpool, whirlpool

Holiday Inn
(800) HOLIDAY, (970) 247-5393
http://www.holiday-inn.com
800 Camino Del Rio Rd.
140 rooms - $60-129
Pets: Welcome
Creature Comforts: CCTV, a/c,
restaurant, pool, sauna, whirlpool

Iron Horse Inn
(800) 748-2990, (970) 259-1010
http://www.ironhorsedurango.com
5800 N. Main Ave.
144 rooms - $75-129
Pets: Welcome
Creature Comforts: CCTV, a/c,
fireplaces, refrig, micro,
restaurant, pool, saunas, whirlpool

Leland House
(800) 664-1920, (970) 385-1920
www.creativelinks.com/rochester
721 E. 2nd Ave.
10 rooms - $99-169
Pets: In ltd. rms w/$15 fee
Creature Comforts: A charming
1927 brick building accented with
historic memorabilia, rooms
named after historic characters,
CCTV, a/c, kit, library, gourmet
brkfst

Red Lion Inn
(800) RED-LION, (970) 259-6580
http://www.redlion.com
501 Camino Del Rio Rd.
160 rooms - $75-179
Pets: Under 20 lbs. welcome in
smoking rooms w/$10 fee
Creature Comforts: CCTV,
VCR, a/c, refrig, micro, Jacuzzis,
restaurant, pool, hlth clb, sauna,
whirlpool

Rochester Hotel
(800) 664-1920, (970) 385-1920
http://www.rochesterhotel.com
726 E. Second St.
24 rooms - $89-199
Pets: Welcome w/$15 daily fee
Creature Comforts: 1890's
historic B&B with creative Old
West decor, CCTV, VCR, kit,
Jacuzzis, library, full brkfst

Rodeway Inn
(800) 228-3000, (970) 259-2540
http://www.rodewayinn.com
2701 Main Ave.
32 rooms - $40-100
Pets: Welcome w/$5 fee
Creature Comforts: CCTV, a/c,
refrig, micro, whirlpool

Travelodge
(800) 578-7878, (970) 247-1741
http://www.travelodge.com
2970 Main Ave.
49 rooms - $40-145
Pets: Welcome
Creature Comforts: CCTV, a/c,
kit

EAGLE
Best Western Lodge
(800) 528-1234, (970) 328-6316
http://www.bestwestern.com
200 Loren Lane
50 rooms - $49-155
Pets: Welcome w/CC dep.
Creature Comforts: CCTV, a/c,
refrig, micro, Jacuzzis, steambaths

EDWARDS
The Inn at Riverwalk
(888) 926-0606, (970) 926-0606
http://www.vail.net/riverwalk
22 Main St.
60 rooms - $69-275
Pets: In certain rooms w/$10 fee
Creature Comforts: Set on banks
of Eagle River in Victorian
village, CCTV, VCR, a/c, refrig,
micro, restaurant, pool, whirlpool

The Lazy Ranch B&B
(800) 655-9343, (970) 926-3876
http://vail.net/lodging/lazy/
index.html
57 Lake Creek Rd.
4 rooms - $70-125
Pets: Welcome
Creature Comforts: Award-
winning 100-year-old ranch on 60
acres, old-fashioned western
appeal, comforters, quilts, country
antiques, full country brkfst,
fishing, riding

ENGLEWOOD
Embassy Suites
(800) 362-2779, (303) 792-0433
http://www.embassy-suites.com
10250 E. Costilla Ave.
235 rooms - $99-169
Pets: Small pets w/$10 fee
Creature Comforts: CCTV, a/c,
refrig, micro, restaurant, pool, spa

Hampton Inn
(800) Hampton, (303) 792-9999
http://www.hampton-inn.com
9231 E. Arapahoe Rd.
152 rooms - $85-109
Pets: Welcome
Creature Comforts: CCTV,
VCR, a/c, refrig, micro, pool

La Quinta Inn
(800) 531-5900, (303) 649-9969
http://www.laquinta.com
7077 S. Clinton St.
150 rooms - $79-129
Pets: Welcome
Creature Comforts: CCTV, a/c,
refrig, micro, pool, whirlpool

Residence Inn
(800) 331-3131, (303) 740-7177
http://www.residenceinn.com
6565 S. Yosemite St.
128 rooms - $60-159
Pets: Welcome w/$10 fee
Creature Comforts: CCTV,
VCR, a/c, fireplaces, kit, cont.
brkfst, pool, hlth clb access

Super 8 Motel
(800) 800-8000, (303) 771-8000
http://www.super8.com
5150 S. Quebec St.
80 rooms - $45-79
Pets: Welcome
Creature Comforts: CCTV, a/c

Woodfield Suites
(303) 799-4555
9009 E. Arapahoe Rd.
133 rooms - $99-149
Pets: Small pets w/$10 fee
Creature Comforts: CCTV,
VCR, a/c, kit, pool, whirlpool

ESTES PARK
Castle Mtn. Lodge
(800) 852-PINE, (970) 586-3664
http://www.estes-park.com/castle
1520 Fall River Rd.
24 cottages - $45-325
Pets: Welcome w/$15 fee
Creature Comforts: Great mtn.
views, lustrous wood paneling,
homey atmosphere, CCTV, VCR,
vaulted ceilings, stone fireplaces,
kit, saunas, whirlpool, near a river

Four Winds Motor Lodge
(970) 586-3313
1120 Big Thompson Ave.
54 rooms - $40-225
Pets: Welcome w/$5 fee
Creature Comforts: CCTV,
fireplaces, kit, pool, sauna,
whirlpool

Machin's Cottages in the Pines
(970) 586-4276
www.estespark.com/machins
2450 Eagle Cliff Rd.
17 cottages - $80-175
Pets: Small pets welcome
Creature Comforts: Set on 14
acres, CCTV, kit

Olympus Lodge
(800) 248-8141, (970) 586-8141
Route 34
14 rooms - $45-135
Pets: Small pets w/$10 fee
Creature Comforts: CCTV,
VCR, a/c, refrig, micro, Jacuzzis,
whirlpool

The Stanley
(800) 976-1377, (970) 586-3673
http://www.grandheritage.com
333 Wonderview Rd.
132 rooms - $129-325
Pets: Welcome w/$25 fee
Creature Comforts: Historic
Georgian-style hotel w/great mtn.
views, CCTV, a/c, refrig, micro,
restaurant, cont. brkfst, pool, hlth
clb, concert series, tennis,
whirlpool, volleyball, golf, trails

Triple R Cottages
(970) 586-5552
1000 Riverside Dr.
7 cottages - $50-130
Pets: Welcome w/$5 fee
Creature Comforts: CCTV,
fireplace, kit

EVANS
Motel 6
(800) 4-MOTEL6, (970) 351-6481
http://www.motel6.com
3015 - 8th Ave.
114 rooms - $29-44
Pets: Under 30 lbs. welcome
Creature Comforts: CCTV, a/c,
pool

Sleep Inn
(800) 753-3746, (970) 356-2180
http://www.sleepinn.com
3025 - 8th Ave.
60 rooms - $60-75
Pets: Welcome w/$10 fee
Creature Comforts: CCTV, a/c,
refrig, micro, whirlpool

FAIRPLAY
The Western Inn
(719) 836-2026
Route 9
22 rooms - $40-65
Pets: Welcome
Creature Comforts: CCTV,
refrig

FT. COLLINS
Days Inn
(800) DAYS-INN, (970) 221-5490
http://www.daysinn.com
3625 E. Mullberry St.
75 rooms - $35-110
Pets: Welcome w/$5 fee
Creature Comforts: CCTV,
VCR, a/c

Holiday Inn
(800) HOLIDAY, (970) 484-4660
http://www.hoiday-inn.com
3836 E. Mulberry St.
198 rooms - $65-99
Pets: Welcome
Creature Comforts: CCTV, a/c,
refrig, restaurant, pool, sauna,
whirlpool

Motel 6
(800) 4-MOTEL6, (970) 482-6466
http://www.motel6.com
3900 E. Mulberry St.
126 rooms - $29-45
Pets: Under 30 lbs. welcome
Creature Comforts: CCTV, a/c,
pool

Mulberry Inn
(970) 493-9000
4333 Mulberry St.
122 rooms - $40-129
Pets: Welcome w/$5 fee
Creature Comforts: CCTV,
VCR, a/c, refrig, Jacuzzis, pool

Sleep Inn
(800) 753-3746, (970) 484-5515
http://www.sleepinn.com
3808 E. Mulberry St.
64 rooms - $50-65
Pets: Small pets w/$10 fee
Creature Comforts: CCTV, a/c

Super 8 Motel
(800) 800-8000, (970) 493-7701
http://www.super8.com
409 Centro Way
71 rooms - $45-69
Pets: Welcome
Creature Comforts: CCTV, a/c,
cont. brkfst, sauna, whirlpool

University Park Holiday Inn
(800) HOLIDAY, (970) 482-2626
http://www.holiday-inn.com
425 W. Prescott Rd.
260 rooms - $80-99
Pets: Welcome
Creature Comforts: CCTV, a/c,
Jacuzzi, restaurant, pool, sauna,
whirlpool

FORT MORGAN
Best Western Inn
(800) 528-1234, (970) 867-8256
http://www.bestwestern.com
725 Main St.
24 rooms - $50-75
Pets: Welcome w/credit card dep.
Creature Comforts: CCTV, a/c,
restaurant, pool, whirlpool

Central Motel
(970) 867-2401
201 W. Platte Ave.
20 rooms - $35-65
Pets: Welcome
Creature Comforts: CCTV,
VCR, a/c, refrig, micro

Econo Lodge
(800) 55-ECONO, (970) 867-9481
http://www.econolodge.com
1409 Barlow Rd.
42 rooms - $40-65
Pets: Welcome w/$5 fee
Creature Comforts: CCTV, a/c,
refrig, micro, restaurant, pool

FRISCO

Best Western
(800) 528-1234, (970) 668-5094
http://www.bestwestern.com
1202 Summit Blvd.
125 rooms - $50-175
Pets: Welcome w/$50 dep.
Creature Comforts: CCTV,
VCR, a/c, restaurant, pool,
whirlpool

New Summit Inn
(800) 745-1211, (970) 668-3220
web site pending
1205 N. Summit Blvd.
32 rooms - $38-55
Pets: Welcome w/$5 fee, $20 dep.
Creature Comforts: CCTV, a/c,
micro, cont. brkfst, hlth clb, sauna,
whirlpool

Snowshoe Motel
(970) 668-3444
521 Main St.
38 rooms - $30-99
Pets: Welcome w/$5 fee
Creature Comforts: CCTV,
VCR, a/c, kit, Jacuzzi, sauna,
whirlpool

FRUITA

Motel H
(970) 858-7198
333 Rte. 6
15 rooms - $30-55
Pets: Welcome w/$20 dep.
Creature Comforts: CCTV, a/c

GEORGETOWN

Georgetown Motor Inn
(303) 569-3201
1100 Rose St.
33 rooms - $50-70
Pets: Welcome w/$25 dep.
Creature Comforts: CCTV,
refrig, whirlpool

GLENWOOD SPRINGS

B&B on Mitchell Creek
(970) 945-4002
http://www.bbhost.com/
mitchellcreekb&b
1686 Mitchell Creek Rd.
1 room - $85-109
Pets: Welcome in garage
Creature Comforts: Set in a
canyon alongside a spring, large
rooms w/ vaulted natural wood
beam ceilings, refrig, full brkfst/
dinner, massage, hiking

Best Western Caravan Inn
(800) 528-1234, (970) 945-7451
http://www.bestwestern.com
1826 Grand Ave.
70 rooms - $60-89
Pets: Welcome w/$5 fee
Creature Comforts: CCTV, a/c,
kit, cont. brkfst, pool, whirlpool

Glenwood Motor Inn
(800) 543-5906, (970) 945-5438
141 W. 6th St.
45 rooms - $49-65
Pets: Small pets welcome
Creature Comforts: CCTV, a/c,
refrig, micro, pool, sauna,
whirlpool

National 9-Homestead Inn
(800) 458-6685, (970) 945-8817
52039 Rte. 9
36 rooms - $35-85
Pets: Small pets w/$25 dep.
Creature Comforts: CCTV, a/c,
refrig, micro, whirlpool

Hotel Colorado
(800) 544-3998, (970) 945-6511
http://www.hotelcolorado.com
526 Pine St.
128 rooms - $75-155
Pets: Welcome
Creature Comforts: 1893 hist.
landmark, Teddy Roosevelt's
western White House, Victorian
accents, antiques, CCTV, refrig,
Jacuzzi, restaurant, pool, hlth clb,
sauna, steamrooms, spa,
whirlpool, Bell tower suites with
staircases, views and 4 poster beds

Ramada Inn
(800) 2-Ramada, (970) 945-2500
http://www.ramada.com
124 W. 6th St.
124 rooms - $45-125
Pets: Welcome w/credit card dep.
Creature Comforts: CCTV—
video games, a/c, refrig, micro,
steambaths, restaurant, pool,
whirlpool

Silver Spruce Motel
(970) 945-5458
162 W. 6th St.
90 rooms - $35-110
Pets: Welcome w/$5 fee
Creature Comforts: CCTV, a/c,
fireplace, kit, Jacuzzi, whirlpool

GOLDEN

Days Inn
(800) DAYS-INN, (303) 277-0200
http://www.daysinn.com
15059 W. Colfax Ave.
150 rooms - $65-99
Pets: Small pets w/$5 fee
Creature Comforts: CCTV, a/c,
refrig, micro, restaurant, pool,
sauna, whirlpool

Holiday Inn
(800) HOLIDAY, (303) 279-7611
http://www.holiday-inn.com
14707 W. Colfax Ave.
225 rooms - $80-119
Pets: Welcome w/credit card dep.
Creature Comforts: CCTV, a/c,
restaurant, pool, whirlpool, putting
green

La Quinta Inn
(800) 531-5900, (303) 279-5565
http://www.laquintainn.com
3301 Youngfield Service Rd.
130 rooms - $68-89
Pets: Welcome
Creature Comforts: CCTV, a/c,
refrig, pool

Marriott Hotel
(800) 228-9290, (303) 279-9100
http://www.marriott.com
1717 Denver West Blvd.
305 rooms - $89-179
Pets: Welcome w/$10 fee
Creature Comforts: CCTV,
VCR, a/c, refrig, restaurant, pool,
saunas, whirlpools, massage

GRANBY

Inn at Silver Creek
(800) 926-4386, (970) 887-2131
http://www.innatsilvercreek.com
62927 Rte. 40
344 rooms - $95-245
Pets: Welcome w/$12 fee
Creature Comforts: CCTV, a/c,
fireplace, refrig, Jacuzzi,
restaurant, pool, hlth clb, sauna,
tennis, racquetball, whirlpool

Trail Riders
(970) 887-3738
215 E. Agate Ave.
16 rooms - $36-74
Pets: Welcome
Creature Comforts: CCTV, a/c,
refrig, micro

GRAND JUNCTION

Best Western Sandman Hotel
(800) 528-1234, (970) 243-4150
http://www.bestwestern.com
708 Horizon Dr.
79 rooms - $40-65
Pets: Small pets w/$5 fee
Creature Comforts: CCTV, a/c,
VCR, refrig, pool, sauna,whirlpool

Best Western Horizon Inn
(800) 528-1234, (970) 245-1410
http://www.bestwestern.com
754 Horizon Dr.
99 rooms - $40-65
Pets: Small pets w/$5 fee
Creature Comforts: CCTV,
VCR, a/c, refrig, pool, sauna,
whirlpool

Days Inn
(800) DAYS-INN, (970) 245-7200
http://www.daysinn.com
733 Horizon Dr.
105 rooms - $45-75
Pets: Small pets w/ CC dep.
Creature Comforts: CCTV, a/c,
restaurant, pool

Grand Vista
(800) 800-7796, (970) 241-8411
web site pending
160 rooms - $79-120
Pets: Welcome w/$10 fee
Creature Comforts: CCTV, a/c,
refrig, restaurant, cont. brkfst,
pool, hlth clb access, whirlpool

Hilton Hotel
(800) HILTONS, (970) 241-8888
http://www.hilton.com
750 Horizon Dr.
264 rooms - $99-310
Pets: Welcome w/$50 dep.
Creature Comforts: CCTV, a/c,
refrig, Jacuzzi, restaurant, pool,
whirlpool, hlth clb, tennis, lawn
sports

Holiday Inn
(800) HOLIDAY, (970) 243-6790
http://www.holiday-inn.com
755 Horizon Dr.
292 rooms - $60-119
Pets: Welcome
Creature Comforts: CCTV, a/c,
refrig, micro, restaurant, pool,
sauna, whirlpool, putting green

Howard Johnson
(800) I-Go-Hojo, (970) 243-5150
http://www.hojo.com
752 Horizon Dr.
99 rooms - $40-75
Pets: Small pets w/$10 fee
Creature Comforts: CCTV,
VCR, a/c, refrig, restaurant, pool,
tennis access

Motel 6
(800) 4-MOTEL6, (970) 243-2628
http://www.motel6.com
776 Horizon Dr.
100 rooms - $31-46
Pets: Under 30 lbs. welcome
Creature Comforts: CCTV, a/c,
pool

Peachtree Inn
(800) 525-0030, (970) 245-5770
http://www.peachtreehotel.com
1600 North Ave.
75 rooms - $29-55
Pets: Welcome
Creature Comforts: CCTV, a/c,
refrig, pool

Super 8 Motel
(800) 800-8000, (970) 248-8080
http://www.super8.com
728 Horizon Dr.
132 rooms - $35-60
Pets: Under 30 lbs. welcome
Creature Comforts: CCTV, a/c,
pool

West Gate Inn
(800) 453-9253, (970) 241-3020
http://www.gi.net/wgi
2210 Rte. 6
100 rooms - $39-77
Pets: Welcome w/$25 dep.
Creature Comforts: CCTV, a/c,
restaurant, pool

GRAND LAKE

Columbine Creek Ranch
(970) 627-2429
web site pending
14814 Rte. 34
4 cabins - $44-109
Pets: Welcome
Creature Comforts: CCTV,
VCR, a/c, fireplaces, kit, full
brkfst, whirlpool, trout ponds

GREELEY

Best Western Ramkota
(800) 528-1234, (970) 353-8444
http://www.bestwestern.com
701 - 8th St.
148 rooms - $70-165
Pets: Small pets welcome
Creature Comforts: CCTV, a/c,
refrig, micro, restaurant, pool, hlth
clb access, whirlpool

Holiday Inn
(800) HOLIDAY, (970) 330-7495
http://www.holiday-inn.com
2563 W. 29th St.
65 rooms - $60-85
Pets: Welcome w/$10 fee
Creature Comforts: CCTV, a/c,
refrig, micro, pool, whirlpool

GREENWOOD VILLAGE

Motel 6 - South
(800) 4-MOTEL6, (303) 790-8220
http://www.motel6.com
9201 E. Arapahoe Rd.
139 rooms - $44-58
Pets: Under 30 lbs. welcome
Creature Comforts: CCTV, a/c,
pool

GUNNISON

Days Inn
(800) DAYS-INN, (970) 641-0608
http://www.daysinn.com
701 Rte. 50
45 rooms - $35-75
Pets: Welcome w/$5 fee
Creature Comforts: CCTV, a/c,
pool, whirlpool

Char-B-Resort
(970) 641-0751
Route 742
16 cottages - $75-120
Pets: Welcome
Creature Comforts: CCTV,
fireplace, kit, whirlpool

Harmel's Guest Ranch
(800) 235-3402, (970) 641-1740
http://www.harmels.com
Box 955
37 units - $80-189 (MAP)
Pets: Welcome
Creature Comforts: Set in Taylor
River Valley, family-oriented dude
ranch w/wonderful views, kit,
restaurant, pool, mtn. bikes,
rafting, riding, hunting, store, river
rafting, fishing

Hylander Inn
(970) 641-0700
412 E. Tomichi Ave.
24 rooms - $40-85
Pets: Welcome w/$5 fee
Creature Comforts: CCTV, a/c

HOTCHKISS
Hotchkiss Inn
(970) 872-2200
406 Rte. 133
25 rooms - $40-65
Pets: Welcome w/$5 fee
Creature Comforts: CCTV, a/c

HOT SULPHUR SPRINGS
Canyon Motel
(970) 725-3395
221 Byers Ave.
12 rooms - $40-64
Pets: Welcome w/$5 fee
Creature Comforts: CCTV, kit

Stagecoach Country Inn
(970) 725-3910
412 Nevada St.
9 rooms - $40-75
Pets: Welcome
Creature Comforts: CCTV, restaurant

IDAHO SPRINGS
H&H Motor Lodge
(800) 445-2893, (303) 567-2838
2445 Colorado Blvd.
25 rooms - $35-79
Pets: Welcome
Creature Comforts: CCTV, a/c, kit, restaurants, sauna, whirlpool

LA JUNTA
Quality Inn
(800) 228-5150, (719) 384-2571
http://www.qualityinn.com
1325 E. 3rd St.
76 rooms - $39-80
Pets: Welcome
Creature Comforts: CCTV, a/c, refrig, micro, restaurant, pool, and a hlth clb

Stagecoach Inn
(719) 384-5476
905 W. 3rd St.
30 rooms - $39-55
Pets: Small pets w/$5 fee
Creature Comforts: CCTV, a/c, refrig, micro, pool

LAKE CITY
Crystal Lodge
(800) 984-1234, (970) 944-2201
e-mail: crylodge@rmi.net
Route 149
18 units - $59-120
Pets: Welcome w/$25 dep.
Creature Comforts: CCTV, VCR, restaurant, whirlpool

LAKEWOOD
Comfort Inn
(800) 228-5150, (303) 989-5500
http://www.comfortinn.com
3440 S. Vance St.
122 rooms - $59-119
Pets: Welcome w/CC dep.
Creature Comforts: CCTV, a/c, refrig, micro, cont. brkfst, pool, hlth clb, whirlpool

Foothills Executive Lodging
(800) 456-0425, (303) 232-2932
web site pending
7150 W. Colfax Ave.
100 units - $45-99
Pets: Welcome w/$250 dep.
Creature Comforts: CCTV, VCR, a/c, fireplaces, kit, Jacuzzis, pools, hlth clb access, whirlpool

Motel 6
(800) 4-MOTEL6, (303) 232-4924
http://www.motel6.com
3050 W. 49th Ave.
191 rooms - $33-49
Pets: Under 30 lbs. welcome
Creature Comforts: CCTV, a/c, pool

Rodeway Inn
(800) 228-2000, (303) 238-1251
http://www.rodeway.com
7150 W. Colfax St.
92 rooms - $59-99
Pets: Welcome w/$50 dep.
Creature Comforts: CCTV, a/c, restaurant, pool

Super 8 Motel
(800) 800-8000
http://www.super8.com
100 W. Jefferson Ave.
87 rooms - $38-54
Pets: Welcome
Creature Comforts: CCTV, a/c, micro, refrig, pool, whirlpool

LAMAR
Best Western Cow Palace
(800) 528-1234, (719) 336-7753
http://www.bestwestern.com
1301 N. Main St.
97 rooms - $75-110
Pets: Welcome
Creature Comforts: CCTV, VCR, a/c, refrig, Jacuzzi, pool, sauna, whirlpool

Blue Spruce Motel
(800) 835-6323, (719) 336-7454
1801 S. Main St.
25 rooms - $30-49
Pets: Welcome w/$5 fee
Creature Comforts: CCTV, a/c, cont. brkfst, pool

LAS ANIMAS
Best Western Cow Palace
(800) 528-1234, (719) 456-0011
http://www.bestwestern.com
Route 50
38 rooms - $49-65
Pets: Welcome
Creature Comforts: CCTV, VCR, a/c, refrig, Jacuzzi, pool, sauna, whirlpool

LEADVILLE
Silver King Motor Inn
(800) 871-2610, (719) 486-2610
2020 N. Poplar St.
60 rooms - $45-65
Pets: Welcome
Creature Comforts: CCTV, a/c

LIMON
Best Western Limon Inn
(800) 528-1234, (719) 775-0277
http://www.bestwestern.com
925 T Ave.
48 rooms - $35-85
Pets: Small pets welcome
Creature Comforts: CCTV, a/c, refrig, Jacuzzi, cont. brkfst, pool, whirlpool

Econo Lodge
(800) 55-ECONO, (719) 775-2867
http://www.econolodge.com
985 Rte. 24
48 rooms - $35-59
Pets: Small pets w/$10 dep.
Creature Comforts: CCTV, a/c

Preferred Motor Inn
(719) 775-2385
158 E. Main St.
58 rooms - $35-109
Pets: Welcome w/$5 fee
Creature Comforts: CCTV, a/c,
pool, whirlpool

Safari Motel
(800) 330-7021, (719) 775-2363
637 Main St.
28 rooms - $35-66
Pets: Welcome w/$5 fee
Creature Comforts: CCTV, a/c,
pool

Super 8 Motel
(800) 800-8000, (719) 775-2889
http://www.super8.com
Route 70
31 rooms - $38-52
Pets: Welcome
Creature Comforts: CCTV, a/c,
cont. brkfst

LONGMONT
First Interstate Inn
(800) 462-4667, (303) 772-6000
3940 Rte. 119
30 rooms - $39-49
Pets: Small pets w/$5 fee
Creature Comforts: CCTV, a/c

Raintree Plaza Hotel
(800) 843-8240, (303) 776-2000
1900 Ken Pratt Blvd.
215 rooms - $99-259
Pets: Welcome w/$50 dep.
Creature Comforts: CCTV,
VCR, a/c, kit, restaurant, cont.
brkfst, pool, sauna, hlth club,
whirlpool

Super 8 Motel
(800) 800-8000, (303) 772-0888
http://www.super8.com
10805 Turner Ave.
36 rooms - $45-69
Pets: Welcome
Creature Comforts: CCTV, a/c,
cont. brkfst

Super 8 Motel
(800) 800-8000, (303) 772-8106
http://www.super8.com
2446 N. Main St..
64 rooms - $42-79
Pets: Welcome
Creature Comforts: CCTV, a/c,
hlth clb, cont. brkfst

LOVELAND
Best Western Limon Inn
(800) 528-1234, (970) 667-7810
http://www.bestwestern.com
542 E. Rte. 34
88 rooms - $55-85
Pets: Small pets welcome
Creature Comforts: CCTV, a/c,
refrig, Jacuzzis, cont. brkfst,
whirlpools, tennis

Budget Host
(800) Bud-Host, (970) 667-5202
http://www.budhost.com
2716 SE Frontage Rd.
30 rooms - $29-75
Pets: Small pets welcome
Creature Comforts: CCTV, a/c,
refrig, pool, whirlpool

MANCOS
Mesa Verde Motel
(970) 533-7741
191 W. Railroad Ave.
15 rooms - $35-55
Pets: Small pets welcome
Creature Comforts: CCTV, a/c,
whirlpool

MANITOU SPRINGS
Red Wing Motel
(800) RED-9547, (719) 685-5656
56 El Paso Blvd.
28 rooms - $55-120
Pets: Small pets welcome
Creature Comforts: CCTV, a/c,
kit, pool

MARBLE
Ute Meadows Inn B&B
(888) 883-6323
http://www.utemeadows.com
2880 County Rd.
7 rooms - $95-150
Pets: Dogs welcome in ground
floor rms, reasonable but
extensive pet policy; horses
welcome too
Creature Comforts: Beautiful
contemp. home w/stunning
panoramic views, luxurious
interior w/exposed beams, down-
filled leather couches, western
style rms, SATV, radiant heat,
gourmet ranch brkfst, hiking,
fishing, skiing

MESA VERDE NAT'L PARK
Far View Lodge
(800) 449-2288, (970) 529-4421
Box 277
150 rooms - $60-110
Pets: Welcome w/$20 dep.
Creature Comforts: CCTV,
refrig, store, restaurant

MONARCH
Monarch Mtn. Lodge
(800) 332-3668, (719) 539-2581
http://www.rmi.net/monarch
1 Powder Pl.
100 rooms - $60-179
Pets: Welcome
Creature Comforts: CCTV,
VCR, a/c, kit, restaurant, pool,
hlth clb, sauna, racquetball,
whirlpool

MONTE VISTA
Comfort Inn
(800) 228-5150, (719) 852-0612
http://www.comfortinn.com
1519 Grand Ave.
44 rooms - $60-95
Pets: Welcome
Creature Comforts: CCTV, a/c,
Jacuzzis, pool, hlth clb, sauna,
whirlpool

MONTROSE
Black Canyon Motel
(800) 348-3495, (970) 249-3495
www.innfiders.com/blackcyn
1605 E. Main St.
49 rooms - $35-99
Pets: Welcome w/$4 fee
Creature Comforts: CCTV, a/c,
micro, Jacuzzi, cont. brkfst, pool,
whirlpool

San Juan Inn
(970) 249-6644
1480 Rte. 550
50 rooms - $40-70
Pets: Welcome w/$5 fee
Creature Comforts: CCTV, a/c,
micro, pool, whirlpool

Super 8 Motel
(800) 800-8000, (970) 249-9294
http://www.super8.com
1705 E. Main St.
42 rooms - $38-55
Pets: Welcome w/credit card dep.
Creature Comforts: CCTV, a/c,
whirlpool

Uncompahgre B&B
(800) 318-8127, (970) 240-4000
http://www.travelguides.com/bb/
uncompahgre
21049 Uncompahgre Rd.
8 rooms - $55-80
Pets: Welcome
Creature Comforts: A former
school, circa 1914, charmingly
updated, CCTV, VCR, a/c, refrig,
dining rm, full brkfst

NEDERLAND
Nederhaus Motel
(800) 422-4629, (303) 444-4705
686 Rte. 119
12 rooms - $35-95
Pets: Small pets welcome
Creature Comforts: CCTV, a/c,
restaurant

NORTHGLENN
Days Inn
(800) DAYS-INN, (303) 457-0688
http://www.daysinn.com
36 E. 120th Ave.
120 rooms - $45-95
Pets: Small pets w/$5 fee
Creature Comforts: CCTV, a/c,
refrig, pool

Holiday Inn
(800) HOLIDAY, (303) 452-4100
http://www.holiday-inn.com
10 E. 120th Ave.
233 rooms - $70-105
Pets: Welcome on 1st floor
Creature Comforts: CCTV,
VCR, a/c, refrig, restaurant, pool,
whirlpool

Ramada Inn
(800) 2-Ramada, (303) 451-1234
http://www.ramada.com
110 W. 104th Ave.
144 rooms - $60-100
Pets: Welcome w/$25 dep.
Creature Comforts: CCTV, a/c,
refrig, Jacuzzis, pool, saunas, spa

OURAY
Ouray Cottage Motel
(970) 325-4370
4th & Main Sts.
13 cottages - $55-109
Pets: Welcome
Creature Comforts: CCTV, a/c,
kit

Ouray Victorian Inn
(800) 84-OURAY, (970) 325-7222
http://www.ouraylodging.com
50 - 3rd Ave.
48 rooms - $50-99
Pets: Welcome w/credit card dep.
Creature Comforts: Centrally
located, set along a river, CCTV,
kit, cont. brkfst, whirlpools

PAGOSA SPRINGS
Best Western Oak Ridge
(800) 528-1234, (970) 264-4173
http://www.bestwestern.com
158 Hot Springs Blvd.
80 rooms - $55-85
Pets: Under 20 lbs. welcome
Creature Comforts: CCTV, a/c,
refrig, sauna, pool

Davidson's Country Inn
(970) 264-5863
PO Box 87
8 rooms - $65-100
Pets: Welcome
Creature Comforts: Log house
on 30-acres, country western
decor, game rm, country brkfst

Pagosa Springs Inn
(888) 221-8088, (970) 731-8400
3565 Rte. 160
98 rooms - $79-120
Pets: Welcome
Creature Comforts: CCTV, a/c,
refrig, micro, Jacuzzi, cont. brkfst,
pool, whirlpool

Super 8 Motel
(800) 800-8000, (970) 731-4005
http://www.super8.com
34 Piedra Rd.
31 rooms - $35-55
Pets: Welcome w/$5 fee
Creature Comforts: CCTV, a/c

PARACHUTE
Super 8 Motel
(800) 800-8000, (970) 285-7936
http://www.super8.com
252 Green St.
102 rooms - $38-65
Pets: Welcome w/credit card dep.
Creature Comforts: CCTV, a/c

PINE
Anchorage Farm
(303) 838-5430
http://www.anchoragefarm.com/
12889 Parker Ave.
4 rooms - $80-140
Pets: B&B for horses
Creature Comforts: Exceptional
guest ranch w/beautifully
decorated rooms, bright colors,
quilts, canopy beds, Southwestern
Room w/kiva fireplace, viga
ceilings, Elk Room w/feather
beds, green/blue floral color
scheme, priv. entrances, SATV,
a/c, gourmet brkfst, hot tub,
riding, horse camps, and hiking

PUEBLO
Best Western Town House
(800) 528-1234, (719) 543-6530
http://www.bestwestern.com
730 N. Santa Fe
88 rooms - $60-100
Pets: Small pets welcome
Creature Comforts: CCTV, a/c,
refrig, cont. brkfst, pool, hlth clb,
whirlpool

Hampton Inn
(800) Hampton, (719) 544-4700
http://www.hampton-inn.com
4703 N. Fwy.
110 rooms - $65-110
Pets: Welcome w/CC dep.
Creature Comforts: CCTV, a/c,
refrig, micro, pool

Holiday Inn
(800) HOLIDAY, (719) 543-8050
http://www.holiday-inn.com
4001 N. Elizabeth St.
195 rooms - $69-99
Pets: Welcome in smoking rooms
Creature Comforts: CCTV,
VCR, a/c, refrig, restaurant, pool,
whirlpool

Motel 6
(800) 4-MOTEL6, (719) 543-8900
http://www.motel6.com
960 Rte. 50
87 rooms - $32-49
Pets: Under 30 lbs. welcome
Creature Comforts: CCTV, a/c,
pool

Motel 6
(800) 4-MOTEL6, (719) 543-6221
http://www.motel6.com
4103 N. Elizabeth St.
122 rooms - $30-47
Pets: Under 30 lbs. welcome
Creature Comforts: CCTV, a/c, pool

Ramada Inn
(800) 2-Ramada , (719) 542-3750
http://www.ramada.com
2001 N. Hudson St.
185 rooms - $65-99
Pets: Welcome w/$75 dep.
Creature Comforts: CCTV, a/c, restaurant, pool

REDSTONE
Avalanche Ranch B&B
(970) 963-2846
12863 Rte. 133
12 cabins - $99-165
Pets: Welcome w/$10 fee
Creature Comforts: CCTV, VCR, kit, lawn games

Redstone Inn
(800) 748-2524, (970) 963-2526
http://www.historic-hotels.com/
Redstone.html
82 Redstone Blvd.
35 rooms - $50-185
Pets: Welcome w/$25 fee
Creature Comforts: Four-season resort on 22 acres, CCTV, a/c, fireplace, refrig, restaurant, pool, hlth clb, sauna, tennis, whirlpool, mtn. bikes, stables-sleigh rides, xc-skiing

RIDGEWAY
Super 8 Motel
(800) 800-8000, (970) 626-5444
http://www.super8.com
373 Palomino Tr.
52 rooms - $50-95
Pets: Welcome w/$50 dep.
Creature Comforts: CCTV, a/c, fireplace, cont. brkfst, Jacuzzi, pool, sauna, spa, whirlpool

RIFLE
Rusty Cannon Motel
(800) 341-8000, (970) 625-4004
http://www.imalodging.com
701 Taughenbaugh Blvd.
88 rooms - $35-60
Pets: Small dogs w/$10 dep.
Creature Comforts: CCTV, a/c, kit, pool, sauna

SALIDA
Aspen Leaf Lodge
(719) 539-6733
7350 Rte. 50
18 rooms - $30-75
Pets: Small pets w/$5 fee
Creature Comforts: CCTV, a/c, refrig, micro, restaurant, pool, whirlpool

Circle R Motel
(800) 755-6296, (719) 539-6296
304 E. Rainbow Blvd.
18 rooms - $30-60
Pets: Welcome w/$5 fee
Creature Comforts: CCTV, a/c, whirlpool

Rainbow Inn
(719) 539-4444
105 E. Rte. 50
20 rooms - $25-65
Pets: Welcome
Creature Comforts: CCTV, a/c, kit, whirlpool

Redwood Lodge
(719) 539-2528
7310 Rte. 50
28 rooms - $40-85
Pets: Small pets w/$5 fee
Creature Comforts: CCTV, a/c, refrig, Jacuzzis, whirlpool

The Tudor Rose B&B
(800) 379-0889 (719) 539-2002
http://www.bbonline.coma/co/
tudorose/index.html
6720 Paradise Rd.
6 rooms - $50-125
Pets: Outside pets only — in the pen w/$4 fee
Creature Comforts: A 4,600 sq. ft. 1890's Tudor-style manor house set on 36-acres w/mtn. views, Jacuzzis, full brkfst, hlth club, whirlpool

Western Holiday Motel
(719) 539-2553
545 W. Rainbow Rd.
40 rooms - $40-92
Pets: Small pets w/$5 fee
Creature Comforts: CCTV, a/c, kit, pool, whirlpool

Woodland Motel
(800) 488-0456, (719) 539-4980
http://www.woodlandmotel.com
903 W. 1st St.
18 rooms - $30-85
Pets: Welcome
Creature Comforts: CCTV, kit, whirlpool

SILVER CREEK
The Inn at Silver Creek
(800) 926-4386, (970) 887-2131
http://www.innatsilvercreek.com
Rte. 40, Box 4222
342 rooms - $40-299
Pets: Welcome
Creature Comforts: Family-oriented resort, CCTV, a/c, kit, Jacuzzis, steambaths, fireplaces, restaurant, pool, hlth clb, tennis, sauna, whirlpool, skating, access to river rafting/riding/skiing

SILVERTHORNE
Days Inn
(800) DAYS-INN, (970) 468-8661
http://www.daysinn.com
580 Silverthorne Ln.
88 rooms - $45-175
Pets: Welcome
Creature Comforts: CCTV, a/c, fireplaces, kit, Jacuzzi, pool, spa, whirlpool

SILVERTON
Alma House Inn
(970) 387-5336
220 E. 10th St.
10 rooms - $50-105
Pets: Welcome
Creature Comforts: Historic home with loads of character, CCTV, VCR, fireplace, cont. brkfst

Wyman Hotel & Inn
(800) 609-7845, (970) 387-5372
www.silverton.org/wymanhotel
1370 Greene St.
20 rooms - $45-140
Pets: Small pets w/$12 fee
Creature Comforts: Nat'l Historic Register, classic 1899 Victorian furnished w/antiques, CCTV, VCR, down comforters, canopy beds, fireplace, Jacuzzis, buffet brkfst

SNOWMASS VILLAGE
Silvertree Hotel
(800) 837-4255, (303) 923-3520
http://www.silvertreehotel.com
100 Elbert Ln.
262 rooms - $145-550
Pets: Welcome
Creature Comforts: Set on Snowmass Village Plaza, CCTV, VCR, refrig, Jacuzzis, fireplace, restaurants, pool, hlth clb, sauna, steamroom, massage, tanning, skiing, whirlpools, lawn games

Wildwood Lodge
(800) 837-4255, (970) 923-3550
http://www.silvertreehotel.com
40 Elbert Ln.
150 rooms - $75-625
Pets: Welcome w/credit card dep.
Creature Comforts: Wonderful mountain lodge just steps from Snowmass, CCTV, VCR, refrig, micro, fireplace, Jacuzzis, restaurant, cont. brkfst, pool, hlth clb, massage, whirlpool

SOUTH FORK
Wolf Creek Ski Lodge
(800) 874-0416, (719) 873-5547
31042 W. Rte. 160
50 rooms - $49-75
Pets: Welcome
Creature Comforts: CCTV, kit, restaurant, whirlpool

STEAMBOAT SPRINGS
The Alpiner Lodge
(800) 538-7519, (970) 879-1430
http://steamboat-lodging.com
424 Lincoln Ave.
33 rooms - $60-135
Pets: Welcome
Creature Comforts: CCTV, a/c

Harbor Hotel
(970) 879-1522
PO Box 774109
113 rooms - $40-190
Pets: Welcome in the annex
Creature Comforts: CCTV, a/c, kit, whirlpool

Holiday Inn
(800) HOLIDAY, (970) 879-2250
http://www.holiday-inn.com
3190 S. Lincoln Ave.
80 rooms - $60-170
Pets: Welcome w/$25 dep.
Creature Comforts: CCTV, VCR, refrig, micro, restaurant, pool, whirlpool

Rabbit Ears Motel
(800) 828-7702, (970) 879-1150
201 Lincoln Ave.
66 rooms - $55-175
Pets: Welcome
Creature Comforts: CCTV, refrig, micro, cont. brkfst, hot springs pool access

Sky Valley Lodge
(800) 538-7519, (970) 879-7749
www.steamboat-lodging.com
31490 Rte. 40
25 rooms - $75-225
Pets: Small pets w/$15 fee
Creature Comforts: English country manor set on mountainside overlooking town, brass and feather beds, CCTV, refrig, restaurant, cont. brkfst, sauna, whirlpool, hiking, xc-skiing

Super 8 Motel
(800) 800-8000, (970) 879-5230
http://www.super8.com
Route 40
60 rooms - $45-95
Pets: Welcome
Creature Comforts: CCTV, a/c, sauna, cont. brkfst

STERLING
Best Western Sundowner
(800) 528-1234, (970) 522-6265
http://www.bestwestern.com
Overland Trail St.
29 rooms - $70-99
Pets: Pets w/permission.
Creature Comforts: CCTV, VCR, a/c, cont. brkfst, hlth clb, whirlpool

Colonial Motel
(970) 522-3382
915 S. Division St.
14 rooms - $29-48
Pets: Small pets w/$7 fee
Creature Comforts: CCTV, a/c, refrig, micro

Days Inn
(800) DAYS-INN, (970) 522-6660
http://www.daysinn.com
12881 Rte. 61
93 rooms - $39-69
Pets: Welcome
Creature Comforts: CCTV, a/c, restaurant, pool, hlth clb, whirlpool

Ramada Inn
(800) 2-Ramada, (970) 522-2625
http://www.ramada.com
Route 6
100 rooms - $55-88
Pets: Welcome w/credit card dep.
Creature Comforts: CCTV, a/c, refrig, micro, restaurant, pool, sauna, whirlpool

Super 8 Motel
(800) 800-8000, (970) 522-0300
http://www.super8.com
12883 Rte. 61
72 rooms - $45-75
Pets: Welcome w/permission
Creature Comforts: CCTV, a/c, pool

STRATTON
Best Western Inn
(800) 528-1234, (970) 348-5311
http://www.bestwestern.com
700 Colorado Ave.
40 rooms - $39-89
Pets: Small pets welcome
Creature Comforts: CCTV, a/c, micro, refrig, hlth clb, whirlpool

TELLURIDE
Hotel Columbia
(800) 201-9505, (970) 728-0660
www.columbiatelluride.com/
300 San Juan Ave.
21 rooms - $195-1,800
Pets: Welcome
Creature Comforts: Luxurious hotel on San Miguel River, sophisticated Western-inspired rms w/stunning fabrics and colors, down comforters, fireplace, clawfoot tubs, steam showers, excellent service and amenities, CCTV, VCR, cont. brkfst, gourmet restaurant, exercise rm, hot tub

The Peaks Resort & Spa
(800) 789-2220, (970) 728-6800
http://www.slh.com/slh/index.html
136 Country Club Dr.
180 rooms - $170-440
Pets: Welcome w/$20 fee
Creature Comforts: Exquisite resort w/Victorian accents, beautifully appointed rms., CCTV, VCR, fireplaces, kit, Jacuzzis, restaurant, pool, hlth clb, sauna, spa, whirlpool, steamroom, tennis, squash, skiing, children's program

THORNTON
Motel 6
(800) 4-MOTEL6, (303) 429-1550
http://www.motel6.com
6 W. 83rd Pl.
121 rooms - $33-49
Pets: Under 30 lbs. welcome
Creature Comforts: CCTV, a/c, pool

TRINIDAD
Best Western Inn
(800) 528-1234, (719) 846-2215
http://www.bestwestern.com
900 W. Adams St.
54 rooms - $50-109
Pets: Small pets welcome
Creature Comforts: CCTV, a/c, restaurant, hlth clb, pool, whirlpool

Budget Host
(800) Bud-Host, (719) 846-3307
http://www.budgethost.com
10301 Santa Fe Trail
25 rooms - $30-75
Pets: Small pets w/$4 fee
Creature Comforts: CCTV, a/c, refrig, micro, whirlpool

Days Inn
(800) DAYS-INN, (719) 846-2271
http://www.daysinn.com
702 W. Main St.
60 rooms - $45-89
Pets: Small pets w/$20 dep.
Creature Comforts: CCTV, a/c, restaurant, pool, hlth clb, whirlpool

Holiday Inn
(800) HOLIDAY, (719) 846-4491
http://www.holiday-inn.com
9995 County Rd.
112 rooms - $50-99
Pets: Small pets welcome
Creature Comforts: CCTV, a/c, refrig, micro, rest, pool, whirlpool

Super 8 Motel
(800) 800-8000, (719) 846-8280
http://www.super8.com
1924 Freedom Rd.
42 rooms - $39-89
Pets: Welcome w/permission
Creature Comforts: CCTV, VCR, Jacuzzis, a/c, pool

TWIN LAKES
Mt. Elbert Lodge
(800) 381-4433, (719) 486-0594
http://mount-elbert.com/
10764 Rte. 82
6 cabins - $88-144
Pets: Welcome in cabins w/$8 fee
Creature Comforts: Character-filled log cabins nestled into mountain meadows w/scenic views, private, Trail's End most secluded, Waterwheel near babbling creek, fireplaces, kit

VAIL
Antlers at Vail
(800) 258-8619, (970) 476-2471
http://www.vail.net/antlers
680 W. Lionshead Pl.
70 rooms - $125-550
Pets: In ltd. units w/$10 fee
Creature Comforts: Spacious contemp. condos - creekside, CCTV, VCR, fireplaces, kit, heated pool, saunas, whirlpool

Lifthouse Condominiums
(800) 654-0635, (970) 476-2340
http://www.toski.com/lifthouse/index.html
555 E. Lionshead Pl.
12 condos - $175-320
Pets: Welcome
Creature Comforts: Studio apts., CCTV, VCR, fireplaces, kit, restaurant, whirlpool

WALDEN
North Park Motel
(970) 723-4271
625 Main St.
21 rooms - $35-70
Pets: Welcome
Creature Comforts: CCTV, a/c, kit

WALENSBURG
Best Western Rambler
(800) 528-1234, (719) 738-1121
http://www.bestwestern.com
457 Rte. 85
32 rooms - $50-99
Pets: Small pets in certain rooms
Creature Comforts: CCTV, a/c, pool

WESTCLIFFE
Westcliffe Inn
(800) 284-0850, (719) 783-9275
Hermit Rd.
28 rooms - $35-79
Pets: Welcome in 14 rooms
Creature Comforts: CCTV, a/c, sauna, hot tub

WESTMINSTER
La Quinta - North
(800) 531-5900, (303) 252-9800
http://www.laquinta.com
345 W. 120th Ave.
130 rooms - $65-89
Pets: Welcome
Creature Comforts: CCTV, a/c, refrig, pool

La Quinta - Mall
(800) 531-5900, (303) 425-9099
http://www.laquinta.com
8701 Turnpike Dr.
130 rooms - $65-89
Pets: Welcome
Creature Comforts: CCTV, a/c, refrig, pool

WHEAT RIDGE
Holiday Inn
(800) HOLIDAY, (303) 423-4000
http://www.holiday-inn.com
4700 Kipling St.
120 rooms - $60-90
Pets: Small pets w/$25 dep.
Creature Comforts: CCTV, a/c, restaurant

Motel 6 - South
(800) 4-MOTEL6, (303) 467-3172
http://www.motel6.com
10300 S. Rte. 70
113 rooms - $30-42
Pets: Under 30 lbs. welcome
Creature Comforts: CCTV, a/c,
pool

Quality Inn
(800) 228-5151, (303) 467-2400
http://www.qualityinn.com
12100 W. 44th Ave.
99 rooms - $45-85
Pets: Small pets welcome
Creature Comforts: CCTV, a/c,
refrig, restaurant, pool, whirlpool

WINTER PARK
High Mountain
(800) 772-9987, (970) 726-5958
web site pending
RR 50
12 rooms - $100-175
Pets: Welcome w/$5 fee
Creature Comforts: CCTV,
VCR, fireplaces, refrig, micro,
cont. brkfst, pool, hlth clb, sauna,
whirlpool, lawn games

Vintage Hotel
(800) 472-7017, (970) 726-8801
http://rkymtnhi.com/vintage
100 Winter Park Dr.
120 rooms - $85-545
Pets: Welcome
Creature Comforts: Set in the
midst of Winter Park ski resort,
spacious rooms w/wood accents,
traditional furnishings, CCTV,
fireplaces, kit, restaurant, cont.
brkfst, pool, sauna, whirlpools,
sleigh rides, xc-skiing

YELLOW JACKET
Wilson's Pinto Bean Farm
(303) 562-4476
21434 Rd. #16
3 rooms - $45-55
Pets: Welcome
Creature Comforts: Fields of
crops, farm animals, full brkfst

Connecticut

AVON
Avon Old Farms
(800) 836-4000, (860) 677-1651
www.avonoldfarmshotel.com
Rtes. 44 & 10
160 rooms - $89-275
Pets: Welcome in ltd. rms
Creature Comforts: CCTV,
VCR, a/c, refrig, restaurant, cont.
brkfst, pool, hlth clb, sauna

BARKHAMSTEAD
Rose & Thistle B&B
(860) 379-4744
24 Woodacres Rd.
2 rooms - $95-105
Pets: Small pets welcome
Creature Comforts: A charming
English-style cottage, 10 pondside
acres, CCTV, VCR, a/c, fireplace,
kit, game room, full brkfst,
swimming, skating

BERLIN
Hawthorne Inn
(860) 828-4181
2387 Wilbur Cross Hwy.
68 rooms - $70-85
Pets: Welcome
Creature Comforts: CCTV, a/c,
refrig, restaurant, cont. brkfst,
pool, hlth clb

BRANFORD
Motel 6
(800) 4-MOTEL6, (203) 483-5828
http://www.motel6.com
320 E. Main St.
99 rooms - $42-52
Pets: Under 30 lbs. welcome
Creature Comforts: CCTV, a/c

BRIDGEPORT
Holiday Inn
(800) HOLIDAY, (203) 334-1234
http://www.holiday-inn.com
1070 Main St.
185 rooms - $85-475
Pets: Small pets welcome
Creature Comforts: CCTV, a/c,
refrig, restaurant, hlth club, pool

CHESTER
Inn at Chester
(800) 949-STAY, (860) 526-9541
http://www.innatchester.com
318 W. Main St.
43 rooms - $99-275
Pets: Welcome
Creature Comforts: Expansive
1776 farmhouse, handsomely
refurbished, CCTV, VCR, a/c,
fireplaces, refrig, Jacuzzis,
restaurant, tavern, cont. brkfst,
hlth clb, sauna, tennis, and lawn
games

CORNWALL
Cornwall Inn
(800) 786-6884, (860) 672-6884
270 Kent Rd.
14 rooms - $55-165
Pets: Welcome in ltd. rms
Creature Comforts: A nicely
refurbished historic 1810 country
inn, CCTV, a/c, fireplace, refrig,
restaurant, bar, cont. brkfst, pool

CROMWELL
Comfort Inn
(800) 228-5150, (203) 635-4100
http://www.comfortinn.com
111 Berlin Rd.
75 rooms - $55-85
Pets: Welcome
Creature Comforts: CCTV, a/c,
cont. brkfst

Radisson Hotel
(800) 333-3333, (860) 635-2000
http://www.radisson.com
100 Berlin Rd.
210 rooms - $79-159
Pets: Small pets w/$10 fee
Creature Comforts: CCTV, a/c,
restaurant, pool

Super 8 Motel
(800) 800-8000, (860) 632-8888
http://www.super8.com
1 Industrial Park Rd.
116 rooms - $45-70
Pets: Welcome
Creature Comforts: CCTV, a/c

DANBURY
Hilton and Towers
(800) HILTONS, (203) 794-0600
http://www.hilton.com
18 Old Ridgebury Rd.
244 rooms - $99-185
Pets: Welcome w/$10 fee
Creature Comforts: CCTV,
VCR, a/c, restaurant, pool, hlth
clb, sauna, whirlpool, and tennis

Holiday Inn
(800) HOLIDAY, (203) 792-4000
http://www.holiday-inn.com
80 Newtown Rd.
115 rooms - $75-109
Pets: Welcome
Creature Comforts: CCTV, a/c,
refrig, restaurant, pool

Ramada Inn
(800) 2-Ramada, (203) 792-3800
http://www.ramada.com
Route 84
180 rooms - $69-149
Pets: Welcome
Creature Comforts: CCTV, a/c,
kit, restaurant, pool

EAST HARTFORD
Holiday Inn
(800) HOLIDAY, (860) 528-9611
http://www.holiday-inn.com
363 Roberts St.
130 rooms - $85-125
Pets: Welcome
Creature Comforts: CCTV, a/c,
restaurant, pool

Ramada Inn
(800) 2-Ramada, (860) 528-9703
http://www.ramada.com
100 E. River St.
199 rooms - $89-129
Pets: Small pets w/$50 dep.
Creature Comforts: CCTV, a/c,
restaurant, pool

Wellesley Inn
(800) 444-8888, (860) 289-4950
www.wellesleyinnandsuites.com
333 Roberts St.
102 rooms - $50-95
Pets: Welcome w/$5 fee
Creature Comforts: CCTV, a/c, cont. brkfst, and hlth clb access

EAST WINDSOR
Best Western Colonial Inn
(800) 528-1234, (860) 623-9411
http://www.bestwestern.com
161 Bridge St.
121 rooms - $50-125
Pets: Small pets w/$25 deposit
Creature Comforts: CCTV, a/c, Jacuzzi, restaurant, cont. brkfst, pool, hlth clb, game rm

Ramada Inn
(800) 2-Ramada, (860) 623-9494
http://www.ramada.com
161 Bridge St.
148 rooms - $55-90
Pets: Welcome
Creature Comforts: CCTV, a/c, refrig, pool, hlth clb, play grnd

ENFIELD
Motel 6
(800) 4-MOTEL6, (860) 741-3685
http://www.motel6.com
11 Hazard Ave.
121 rooms - $37-49
Pets: Under 30 lbs. welcome
Creature Comforts: CCTV, a/c

Red Roof Inn
(800) The-Roof, (860) 741-2571
http://www.redroof.com
5 Hazard Rd.
110 rooms - $35-75
Pets: Small pets welcome
Creature Comforts: CCTV, a/c

Super 8 Motel
(800) 800-8000, (860) 741-3636
http://www.super8.com
1543 King St.
64 rooms - $44-62
Pets: Under 30 lbs. welcome
Creature Comforts: CCTV, VCR, a/c, kit, cont. brkfst

ESSEX
The Griswold Inn
(860) 767-1776
http://www.griswoldinn.com
36 Main St.
30 rooms - $95-195
Pets: Welcome
Creature Comforts: 1700's inn set in historic district, sloping floors and beamed ceilings, nautical paraphernalia, maritime paintings, antiques, four poster and brass beds, CCTV, a/c, fireplaces, refrig, restaurant, great pub, cont. brkfst, charming hamlet

FARMINGTON
The Centennial Inn
(800) 852-2052, (860) 677-4647
http://www.centennialinn.com
5 Spring St.
112 rooms - $85-225
Pets: Welcome w/$10 fee
Creature Comforts: Great suite hotel, 12-acre rural setting, variety of suite configurations, traditional decor, CCTV, VCR, a/c, brick fireplaces, kit, cont. brkfst, pool, hlth clb, whirlpool, skylights, ceiling fans, trails

Farmington Inn
(800) 648-9804, (860) 677-2821
827 Farmington Ave.
74 rooms - $89-179
Pets: Welcome w/in smkg. rooms
Creature Comforts: CCTV, VCR, a/c, restaurant, tennis, hlth club access

GREENWICH
Howard Johnson Motor Lodge
(800) I-Go-Hojo, (203) 637-3691
http://www.hojo.com
1114 Boston Post Rd.
102 rooms - $80-129
Pets: Welcome w/$10 fee
Creature Comforts: CCTV, a/c, pool

GROTON
Clarion Inn
(800) 443-0611, (860) 446-0660
http://www.clarioninn.com
156 Kings Hwy.
69 rooms - $190-175
Pets: Welcome w/dep.
Creature Comforts: CCTV, a/c, kit, Jacuzzis, restaurant, pool, hlth clb access, sauna, whirlpool

GUILFORD
B&B at B
(203) 453-6490
279 Boston St.
3 rooms - $79-105
Pets: Welcome
Creature Comforts: CCTV, VCR, a/c, refrig, full brkfst, pool, fenced yard

HARTFORD
Days Inn
(800) DAYS-INN, (860) 247-3297
http://www.daysinn.com
207 Brainard Rd.
68 rooms - $39-99
Pets: Welcome
Creature Comforts: CCTV, a/c, refrig, micro, Jacuzzi, cont. brkfst

Goodwin Hotel
(860) 246-7500
1 Haynes St.
125 rooms - $80-255
Pets: Small dogs w/CC deposit
Creature Comforts: CCTV, a/c, restaurant

Holiday Inn Downtown
(800) HOLIDAY, (860) 549-2400
http://www.holiday-inn.com
50 Morgan St.
344 rooms - $90-255
Pets: Small pets welcome
Creature Comforts: CCTV, VCR, a/c, restaurant, hlth club, pool

Ramada Inn
(800) 2-Ramada, (860) 246-6591
http://www.ramada.com
440 Asylum St.
95 rooms - $50-95
Pets: Small pets welcome
Creature Comforts: CCTV, a/c, restaurant

Red Roof Inn
(800) The-Roof, (860) 724-0222
http://www.redroof.com
100 Weston St.
114 rooms - $45-85
Pets: Small pets welcome
Creature Comforts: CCTV, a/c

Super 8 Motel
(800) 800-8000, (860) 246-8888
http://www.super8.com
57 W. Service Rd.
104 rooms - $42-65
Pets: W/permission
Creature Comforts: CCTV, a/c

LAKEVILLE
Inn at Iron Master
(860) 435-9844
http://www.innatironmasters.com
229 Main St.
25 rooms - $70-139
Pets: Welcome
Creature Comforts: Charming
accommodations in country
setting, CCTV, a/c, floral accents,
fieldstone fireplace, restaurant,
cont. brkfst, pool, English country
garden and Victorian gazebo

Interlaken Inn
(800) 222-2909, (860) 435-9878
http://www.interlakeninn.com
74 Interlaken Rd.
84 rooms - $85-295
Pets: In certain rooms w/$10 fee
Creature Comforts: Expansive
resort on Lake Wononskopmuc,
finial beds, reproductions and
bleached rattan furnishings,
CCTV, VCR, a/c, fireplace, kit,
restaurant, pool, sauna, massage,
hlth clb, tennis, racquetball, golf,
boating, lawn games

Wake Robin Inn
(860) 435-2515
http://www.wakerobininn.com
Route 41
40 rooms - $99-260
Pets: Welcome
Creature Comforts: A converted
girls' school, CCTV, VCR, a/c,
fireplace, cont. brkfst

LEDYARD
Applewood Farms Inn
(800) 717-4262, (860) 536-2022
http://www.visitmystic.com/
applewoodfarmsinn
528 Col. Ledyard Hwy.
5 rooms - $115-205
Pets: Welcome
Creature Comforts: 1820's
Colonial on a 33-acre farm, Laura
Ashley fabrics, huge antique king
bed, four poster beds, feather beds,
white washed and wicker
furnishings, Colonial décor, old
canted wood floors, period
furnishings, CCTV, VCR,
fireplaces, refrig, full brkfst,
putting green

Mare's Inn
(860) 572-7556
http://www.bestinns.net/usa/ct/
maresinn.html
333 Col. Ledyard Hwy.
5 rooms - $125-175
Pets: Welcome in two suites
Creature Comforts: Charming
house w/ homey decor, screened
porch, CCTV, a/c, refrig, full
brkfst, trail in woods and nice
lawn

LITCHFIELD
Tollgate Hill Inn
(800) 445-3903, (860) 567-4545
http://www.litchfieldct.com/dng/
tollgate.html
Route 202
20 rooms - $100-189
Pets: Welcome w/$10 fee
Creature Comforts: Nooky and
cranny 1745 Nat'l Hist. Register
inn and restaurant, original
features intact, four poster and
canopy beds, antiques and
reproductions, CCTV, VCR, a/c,
fireplaces, refrig, gourmet
restaurant, great pub, cont. brkfst,
quaint town and xc-skiing nearby

MANCHESTER
Clarion Suites Inn
(800) 252-7466, (860) 643-5811
http://www.clarion.com
191 Spencer St.
104 rooms - $89-175
Pets: Welcome w/$10, $200 dep.
Creature Comforts: CCTV,
VCR, a/c, fireplaces, kit, pool, hlth
clb, whirlpool

Manchester Village Inn
(800) 487-6499, (860) 646-2300
100 E. Center St.
44 rooms - $52-75
Pets: Welcome w/$5 fee
Creature Comforts: CCTV,
VCR, a/c, and refrig

MERIDEN
East Inn
(203) 238-1211
900 E. Main St.
72 rooms - $45-99
Pets: Welcome w/$100 deposit
Creature Comforts: CCTV, a/c,
refrig, cont. brkfst, pool

Ramada Inn
(800) 2-Ramada, (860) 238-2380
http://www.ramada.com
275 Research Pkwy.
149 rooms - $59-129
Pets: Small pets welcome
Creature Comforts: CCTV, a/c,
pool, sauna

Residence Inn
(800) 331-3131, (860s) 634-7770
http://www.residenceinn.com
390 Bee St.
105 rooms - $99-159
Pets: Welcome w/$200 dep.
Creature Comforts: CCTV, a/c,
kit, and cont. brkfst

MILFORD
Red Roof Inn
(800) The-Roof, (203) 877-6060
http://www.redroof.com
10 Rowe Ave.
112 rooms - $40-75
Pets: Small pets welcome
Creature Comforts: CCTV, a/c

MONTVALE
Chesterfield Lodge
(860) 442-0039
1596 Rte. 85
12 rooms - $30-55
Pets: Welcome w/$10 fee
Creature Comforts: CCTV, a/c,
VCR, refrig, micro, cont. brkfst

MYSTIC
Harbour Inne & Cottage
(860) 572-9253
15 Edgemont St.
6 rooms - $80-175
Pets: Welcome w/$10 fee
Creature Comforts: CCTV, a/c,
kit, fireplaces, Jacuzzis, cont.
brkfst

NEW BRITAIN
Ramada Inn
(800) 2-Ramada, (860) 224-9161
http://www.ramada.com
65 Columbus Blvd.
120 rooms - $49-129
Pets: Welcome w/$10 fee
Creature Comforts: CCTV, a/c,
restaurant, cont. brkfst

NEW HAVEN
Motel 6
(800) 4-MOTEL, (203) 469-0343
http://www.motel6.com
270 Foxon Blvd.
58 rooms - $49-59
Pets: Under 30 lbs. welcome
Creature Comforts: CCTV, a/c

Quality Inn
(800) 228-5151, (203) 387-6651
http://www.qualityinn.com
100 Pond Lily Ave.
124 rooms - $80-169
Pets: Welcome
Creature Comforts: CCTV, a/c,
pool

Residence Inn
(800) 331-3131, (203) 777-5337
http://www.residenceinn.com
3 Long Wharf Dr.
110 rooms - $99-189
Pets: Welcome w/$10 fee
Creature Comforts: CCTV, a/c,
kit, cont. brkfst, whirlpool, pool

NEW LONDON
Red Roof Inn
(800) The-Roof, (860) 444-0001
http://www.redroof.com
707 Colman St.
105 rooms - $40-95
Pets: Small pets welcome
Creature Comforts: CCTV,
VCR, a/c

NEW PRESTON
Atha House
(860) 355-7387
http://www.touristguide.com/
connecticut/athahouse
Wheaton Rd., Box 2015
3 rooms - $90-105
Pets: Welcome in breezeway,
resident dog, cat, horses
Creature Comforts: Charming
Cape cottage, CCTV, VCR, a/c,
fireplace, piano, cont. brkfst,
gardens, beautiful landscaping

NIANTIC
Motel 6
(800) 4-MOTEL, (860) 739-6991
http://www.motel6.com
269 Flanders Rd.
93 rooms - $39-55
Pets: Under 30 lbs. welcome
Creature Comforts: CCTV, a/c,
pool

NORFOLK
Blackberry River Inn
(800) 414-3636, (860) 542-5100
http://blackberryriverinn.com
536 Greenwoods Rd.
15 rooms - $100-155
Pets: Welcome in the cottage
Creature Comforts: 1763
Colonial, Nat'l Historic Register,
27 acres, CCTV, a/c, refrig,
fireplaces, Colonial décor, paneled
library, Jacuzzi, full brkfst, pool,
xc-skiing

NORTH HAVEN
Holiday Inn
(800) HOLIDAY, (203) 239-4225
http://www.holiday-inn.com
201 Washington Ave.
140 rooms - $69-99
Pets: Welcome
Creature Comforts: CCTV, a/c,
refrig, restaurant, pool

NORWALK
Garden Park Motel
(203) 847-7303
351 Westport Ave.
21 rooms - $55-80
Pets: Welcome
Creature Comforts: CCTV, a/c

Ramada Inn
(800) 2-Ramada, (203) 853-3477
http://www.ramada.com
789 Connecticut Ave.
230 rooms - $85-125
Pets: Welcome w/$10 fee
Creature Comforts: CCTV, a/c,
restaurant, pool

Silvermine Tavern
(203) 847-4558
194 Perry Ave.
10 rooms - $95-125
Pets: In rooms above store
Creature Comforts: Wonderful
refurbished 1770's inn set along
Silvermine River, CCTV, VCR,
a/c, American antiques, old
portraits, chintzes, canopy beds,
fireplaces, intriguing collectibles,
traditional décor, refrig, restaurant,
country store, cont. brkfst

OLD LYME
Old Lyme Inn
(800) 434-5352, (860) 434-2600
http://www.oldlymeinn.com
85 Lyme St.
13 rooms - $99-170
Pets: Welcome
Creature Comforts: A quaintly
restored 1850's inn with antiques,
Victorian accents, Empire and
Victorian furnishings, CCTV,
VCR, a/c, modern bathrooms w/
brass fixtures, fireplaces, refrig,
restaurant, fun bar, and croquet

OLD SAYBROOK
Sandpiper Motor Inn
(860) 399-7973
1750 Boston Post Rd.
44 rooms - $79-135
Pets: Small pets w/$10 fee
Creature Comforts: CCTV, a/c

PLAINVILLE
Howard Johnson Lodge
(800) I-Go-Hojo, (860) 747-6876
http://www.hojo.com
400 New Britain Ave.
104 rooms - $50-75
Pets: Welcome
Creature Comforts: CCTV, a/c,
restaurant, pool

PUTNAM
King's Inn
(800) 541-7304, (860) 928-7961
5 Heritage Rd.
40 rooms - $60-85
Pets: Welcome
Creature Comforts: CCTV,
VCR, a/c, refrig, restaurant, cont.
brkfst, pool, pond

RIVERSIDE
Howard Johnson Lodge
(800) I-Go-Hojo, (203) 637-3691
http://www.hojo.com
1114 Boston Post Rd.
104 rooms - $49-100
Pets: Welcome w/$50 deposit
Creature Comforts: CCTV, a/c,
cont. brkfst, pool

RIVERTON
Old Riverton Inn
(800) EST-1796, (860) 379-8678
http://www.newenglandinns.com/
inns/riverton/index.html
Route 20
12 rooms - $75-175
Pets: Welcome in ltd. rms
Creature Comforts: 1796 Nat'l
Historic Register inn, Colonial
decor, hand-hewn beamed
ceilings, period furnishings, a/c,
CCTV, claw foot tubs, fireplace,
stereos, refrig, restaurant, full
brkfst, near Hitchcock factory
store, xc-skiing, canoeing

SALISBURY
White Hart
(800) 832-0041, (860) 435-0030
http://www.whitehartinn.com
The Village Green
26 rooms - $75-225
Pets: In certain rms w/$10 fee
Creature Comforts: This classic
inn highlights charming village
common, Waverly chintz, four
poster & canopy beds, vibrant
floral wallpapers, CCTV, a/c,
fireplace, refrig, restaurants,
paneled pub, cont. brkfst, nearby
parks

SHELTON
Ramada Inn
(800) 2-Ramada, (203) 929-1500
http://www.ramada.com
780 Bridgeport Ave.
150 rooms - $99-229
Pets: Small pets welcome
Creature Comforts: CCTV, a/c,
restaurant, pool

Residence Inn
(800) 331-3131, (203) 926-9000
http://www.residenceinn.com
1001 Bridgeport Ave.
95 rooms - $125-195
Pets: $10 fee & CC deposit
Creature Comforts: CCTV, a/c,
kit, cont. brkfst, pool

SIMSBURY
The Ironhorse Inn
(800) 245-9938, (860) 658-2216
http://www.farmval.com/lodging/
ironhrse.htm
969 Hopmeadow St.
28 rooms - $65-85
Pets: Welcome w/$15 fee
Creature Comforts: CCTV, a/c,
kit, cont. brkfst, pool, sauna

SOUTHBURY
Hilton Hotel
(800) HILTONS, (203) 598-7600
http://www.hilton.com
1284 Strongtown Rd.
199 rooms - $89-349
Pets: Small pets w/$50 deposit
Creature Comforts: CCTV, a/c,
restaurant, pool

SOUTHINGTON
Motel 6
(800) 4-MOTEL, (860) 621-7351
http://www.motel6.com
625 Queen St.
126 rooms - $39-45
Pets: Under 30 lbs. welcome
Creature Comforts: CCTV, a/c

VERNON
Howard Johnson
(800) I-Go-Hojo, (860) 875-0781
http://www.hojo.com
451 Hartford Turnpike
63 rooms - $60-85
Pets: Welcome w/$5 fee
Creature Comforts: CCTV, a/c,
cont. brkfst, pool

WATERBURY
House on the Hill
(860) 757-9901
92 Woodlawn Terrace
4 rooms - $100-150
Pets: Welcome
Creature Comforts: 1880's
Victorian mansion, mature
landscaping, antiques, lovely
décor, Oriental rugs, pressed tin
ceilings, CCTV, a/c, fireplace,
patio overlooking garden, paneled
sitting room, refrig, gourmet brkfst

WESTBROOK
Maple's Motel
(860) 399-9345
1935 Boston Post Rd.
18 rooms - $49-75
Pets: Welcome
Creature Comforts: CCTV, a/c,
kit, pool

WEST HAVEN
Super 8 Motel
(800) 800-8000, (203) 932-8338
http://www.super8.com
7 Kimberly Ave.
82 rooms - $45-95
Pets: Welcome
Creature Comforts: CCTV, a/c,
cont. brkfst

WETHERSFIELD
Motel 6
(800) 4-MOTEL6, (860) 563-8900
http://www.motel6.com
1341 Silas Dean Hwy.
146 rooms - $35-49
Pets: Under 30 lbs. welcome
Creature Comforts: CCTV, a/c

Ramada Inn
(800) 2-Ramada, (203) 563-2311
http://www.ramada.com
1330 Silas Deane Hwy.
112 rooms - $55-99
Pets: Welcome
Creature Comforts: CCTV, a/c,
refrig, micro, Jacuzzi, restaurant,
hlth club

WINDSOR
Residence Inn
(800) 31-3131, (860) 688-7474
http://www.residenceinn.com
100 Dunfey Ln.
99 rooms - $89-169
Pets: Welcome w/credit card dep.
Creature Comforts: CCTV, a/c,
fireplace, kit, cont. brkfst

WINDSOR LOCKS

Baymont Inns
(877)BAYMONT, (860) 623-3336
http://www.baymontinns.com
64 Ella T. Crasso Tpke.
105 rooms - $45-69
Pets: Welcome
Creature Comforts: CCTV, a/c,
cont. brkfst

Homewood Suites
(800) 225-5466, (860) 627-8463
http://www.homewoodsuites.com
65 Ella Grasso Tpke.
133 rooms - $99-169
Pets: $10 fee, credit card deposit
Creature Comforts: CCTV, a/c,
fireplaces, kit, pool, hlth club

Motel 6
(800) 4-MOTEL6, (860) 292-6200
http://www.motel6.com
3 National Dr.
101 rooms - $35-49
Pets: Under 30 lbs. welcome
Creature Comforts: CCTV, a/c,
pool

Ramada Inn, Airport
(800) 2-Ramada, (860) 623-9494
http://www.ramada.com
5 Ella Grasso Tpke.
149 rooms - $59-109
Pets: Welcome
Creature Comforts: CCTV, a/c,
restaurant, pool

Sheraton Hotel, Airport
(800) 325-3535, (860) 627-5311
http://www.sheraton.com
1 Bradley Airport Rd.
235 rooms - $85-325
Pets: Small pets welcome
Creature Comforts: CCTV,
VCR, a/c, restaurant, hlth club,
sauna, pool

WOODSTOCK

Elias Child House
(877) 974-9836, (860) 974-9836
http://www.eliaschildhouse.com
50 Perrin Road
4 rooms - $95-125
Creature Comforts: A
charmingly refurbished 1714
home set on 40 acres with old-
fashioned appeal, hardwood floors
covered with colorful area rugs,
Oriental rugs, portraits, family
heirlooms, country antiques, handmade quilts, CCTV, VCR, a/c
fireplaces, refrig, piano, full
brkfst, pool, patio

Delaware

BETHANY BEACH
Westward Pines Motel
(302) 539-7426
http://www.atbeach.com
10 Kent Ave.
14 rooms - $50-99
Pets: Welcome Oct-Mar
Creature Comforts: CCTV, a/c, refrig

BRIDGEVILLE
Teddy Bear B&B
(302) 337-3134
303 Market St.
3 rooms - $45-70
Pets: Welcome
Creature Comforts: CCTV, a/c, refrig, cont. brkfst, fenced yard

CLAYMONT
Hilton Hotel
(800) HILTONS, (302) 792-2700
http://www.hilton.com
630 Naamans Rd.
193 rooms - $99-295
Pets: Under 30 Lbs. w/$50 dep.
Creature Comforts: CCTV, VCR, a/c, restaurant, pool, hlth clb

DEWEY BEACH
Atlantic Oceanside
(800) 422-0481, (302) 227-8811
http://www.atlanticoceanside.com
1700 Rte. 1
60 rooms - $30-150
Pets: Welcome in the off-season w/$5 fee, $25 dep.
Creature Comforts: CCTV, VCR, a/c, refrig, micro, pool

Bellbuoy Motel
(302) 227-6000
21 Van Dyke St.
15 rooms - $40-145
Pets: Welcome w/$5 fee
Creature Comforts: CCTV, a/c, refrig, micro

Best Western Gold Leaf
(800) 528-1234, (302) 226-1100
http://www.bestwestern.com
1400 Rte. 1
75 rooms - $50-199
Pets: Welcome in certain rms
Creature Comforts: CCTV, a/c, refrig, Jacuzzis, cont. brkfst, pool

Sea Esta Motels (I, II)
(800) 436-6591, (302) 227-4343
www.deweybeach.com/sea-esta
1409 & 2306 Rte. 1
63 rooms - $30-125
Pets: Welcome w/$5 fee
Creature Comforts: CCTV, a/c, kit

DOVER
Budget Inn
(302) 734-4433
1246 N. DuPont Hwy.
70 rooms - $40-55
Pets: Small pets welcome
Creature Comforts: CCTV, a/c, kit

Quality Inn
(800) 228-5151, (302) 734-5701
http://www.qualityinn.com
348 N. DuPont Hwy.
133 rooms - $60-85
Pets: Welcome
Creature Comforts: CCTV, a/c, kit, restaurant, pool, hlth clb

FENWICK ISLAND
Atlantic Budget Inn
(302) 539-7673
Ocean Hwy.
49 rooms - $40-109
Pets: Small pets in the off season
Creature Comforts: CCTV, a/c, kit, pool

Iskander's Island
(302) 537-1900
Route 1
60 rooms - $59-165
Pets: 1st floor
Creature Comforts: CCTV, a/c, kit, cont. brkfst, pool

Sands Motel
(302) 539-7745
http://www.beach-net.com/
Sandsmotel.html
Route 1
37 rooms - $75-149
Pets: Welcome w/$3 fee
Creature Comforts: CCTV, a/c, kit, pool

LEWES
Kings Inn
(302) 645-6438
151 Kings Highway
5 rooms - $65-80
Pets: Well mannered pets welcome
Creature Comforts: A charming B&B dating back to 1888, detailed moldings, spacious rooms, CCTV, VCR, a/c, two-person Jacuzzi, stereo, cont. brkfst, and bikes are available

MILLSBORO
Atlantic Budget Inn
(302) 934-6711
210 W. DuPont Hwy.
80 rooms - $60-149
Pets: Small pets w/$25 deposit
Creature Comforts: CCTV, VCR, a/c, pool

NEWARK
Best Western
(800) 528-1234, (302) 738-3400
http://www.bestwestern.com
260 Chapman Rd.
95 rooms - $70-95
Pets: Welcome w/$10 fee
Creature Comforts: CCTV, a/c, cont. brkfst, pool

Comfort Inn
(800) 228-5150, (302) 368-8715
http://www.comfortinn.com
1120 S. College Ave.
100 rooms - $50-69
Pets: Small pets in second flr. rms.
Creature Comforts: CCTV, VCR, a/c, refrig, cont. brkfst, pool

Hampton Inn
(800) Hampton, (302) 737-3900
http://www.hampton-inn.com
3 Concord Ln.
124 rooms - $65-85
Pets: Welcome w/$10 fee
Creature Comforts: CCTV, a/c,
pool

Homestead Village
(888) STAY-HSD, (302) 283-0800
http://www.stayhsd.com
333 Continetal Village
141 rooms - $325-375/wk
Pets: Welcome w/$125 fee
Creature Comforts: CTV, a/c, kit

Howard Johnson Lodge
(800) I-Go-Hojo, (302) 368-8521
http://www.hojo.com
1119 S. College Ave.
144 rooms - $50-125
Pets: Welcome w/$25 dep.
Creature Comforts: CCTV, a/c,
refrig, restaurant, pool, hlth clb

Residence Inn
(800) 331-3131, (302) 453-9200
http://www.residenceinn.com
240 Chapman Rd.
120 rooms - $125-185
Pets: Welcome w/$10 fee
Creature Comforts: CCTV,
VCR, a/c, kit, pool, whirlpool

Travelodge
(800) 578-7878, (302) 737-5050
http://www.travelodge.com
268 E. Main St.
47 rooms - $45-65
Pets: Welcome
Creature Comforts: CCTV, a/c

NEW CASTLE
Days Inn
(800) DAYS-INN, (302) 654-5400
http://www.daysinn.com
3 Memorial Dr.
48 rooms - $45-105
Pets: Welcome
Creature Comforts: CCTV, a/c,
Jacuzzi, cont. brkfst

Motel 6
(800) 4-MOTEL6, (302) 571-1200
http://www.motel6.com
1200 West Ave.
159 rooms - $39-55
Pets: Under 30 lbs. welcome
Creature Comforts: CCTV, a/c,
pool
174

Quality Inn
(800) 228-5151, (302) 328-6666
http://www.qualityinn.com
147 N. DuPont Hwy.
100 rooms - $60-99
Pets: Small pets welcome
Creature Comforts: CCTV,
VCR, a/c, kit, restaurant, pool

Rodeway Inn
(800) 228-2000, (302) 328-6246
http://www.rodeway.com
111 S. DuPont Hwy.
40 rooms - $50-75
Pets: Welcome
Creature Comforts: CCTV, a/c,
refrig, micro, cont. brkfst

Travelodge
(800) 578-7878, (302) 654-5544
http://www.travelodge.com
1213 West Ave.
109 rooms - $38-69
Pets: Welcome
Creature Comforts: CCTV, a/c,
kit, pool

REHOBETH
Airport Motel
(302) 227-6737
Route 1
8 rooms - $65-90
Pets: Welcome w/$10 fee
Creature Comforts: CCTV, a/c,
refrig

Atlantic Budget Inn
(302) 227-9446
154 Rehobeth Ave.
98 rooms - $45-125
Pets: Small pets w/$10 fee
Creature Comforts: CCTV,
VCR, a/c, kit, pool

Atlantic Sands Hotel
(800) 422-0600, (302) 227-2511
http://www.atlanticsandshotel.com
101 N. Boardwalk St.
114 rooms - $150-185
Pets: Welcome in certain rooms
Creature Comforts: CCTV, a/c,
pool, whirlpool

Cape Suites
(302) 226-3342
47 Baltimore Ave.
8 rooms - $105-145
Pets: Welcome w/$5 fee
Creature Comforts: CCTV, a/c,
refrig, micro

Corner Cupboard Inn
(302) 227-8553
www.cornercupboardinn.com
50 Park Ave.
18 rooms - $85-259
Pets: In annex/cottages w/$15 fee
Creature Comforts: Low-key inn
w/restaurant nestled amid pine
grove, short walk to water and
town, intimate courtyard, inviting
decor, charming common room w/
fireplace, intriguing collectibles,
CCTV, a/c, refrig, full brkfst

Renegade Motel
(302) 227-1222
http://www.therenegade.com
Route 1
30 rooms - $85-135
Pets: Welcome w/$25 fee
Creature Comforts: CCTV, a/c,
refrig, cont. brkfst, bar, pool

Sea Esta Motel III
(800) 436-6591, (302) 227-1223
www.deweybeach.com/sea-esta
140 Rehobeth Ave.
12 rooms - $39-125
Pets: Welcome w/$5 fee
Creature Comforts: CCTV, a/c,
refrig, micro

SEAFORD
Comfort Inn
(800) 228-5150, (302) 629-8385
http://www.comfortinn.com
225 N. Dual Hwy.
95 rooms - $60-135
Pets: Small pets
Creature Comforts: CCTV, a/c,
refrig, micro, Jacuzzi, cont. brkfst,
pool, hlth clb

WILMINGTON
Best Western Brandywine
(800) 528-1234, (302) 656-9436
http://www.bestwestern.com
1807 Concord Pike
97 rooms - $65-145
Pets: Welcome
Creature Comforts: CCTV, a/c,
refrig, micro, Jacuzzis, cont.
brkfst, pool, hlth clb

Tally-Ho Motor Lodge
(800) 445-0852, (302) 478-0300
5209 Concord Pike
100 rooms - $40-65
Pets: Welcome w/$10 fee
Creature Comforts: CCTV, a/c,
kit, cont. brkfst

District of Columbia

Baker-Doolittle Mansion
(888) 490-9636, (202) 547-0870
http://www.bakerdoolittle.com
506 E. Capitol St. NE
6 rooms - $85-165
Pets: Welcome
Creature Comforts: Wonderfully inviting 6,500 sq. ft. restored 1865 Victorian mansion, antiques, four poster beds, spacious rooms, elegant decor, CCTV, VCR, a/c, fireplaces, kit, Jacuzzis, cont. brkfst

Best Western New Hampshire
(800) 528-1234, (202) 457-0565
http://www.bestwestern.com
1121 New Hampshire Ave. NW
76 rooms - $169-269
Pets: Welcome in smoking rooms
Creature Comforts: CCTV, VCR, a/c, kit, cont. brkfst, and hlth clb access

The Capitol Hilton
(800) HILTONS, (202) 393-1000
http://www.hilton.com
1001 - 16th St. NW
545 rooms - $165-995
Pets: Welcome
Creature Comforts: CCTV, VCR, a/c, refrig, restaurant, hlth clb, saunas, and whirlpools

Carlyle Suites Hotel
(800) 964-5377, (202) 234-3200
1731 New Hampshire Ave. NE
web site pending
170 rooms - $99-175
Pets: Welcome
Creature Comforts: An Art-Deco hotel, CCTV, a/c, kit, restaurant, hlth clb access

Days Inn Gateway
(800) DAYS-INN, (202) 832-5800
http://www.daysinn.com
2700 New York Ave. NE
195 rooms - $40-85
Pets: Small pets welcome
Creature Comforts: CCTV, a/c, refrig, restaurant, pool

Doubltree Guest Suites
(800) 222-TREE, (202) 785-2000
http://www.doubletree.com
801 New Hampshire Ave. NW
100 rooms - $99-475
Pets: Welcome w/$12 fee
Creature Comforts: CCTV, VCR, a/c, kit, restaurant, and hlth clb access

Doubletree Guest Suites
(800) 222-TREE, (202) 333-8060
http://www.doubletree.com
2500 Pennsylvania Ave. NE
124 rooms - $99-475
Pets: Under 20 lbs. w/$12 fee
Creature Comforts: CCTV, VCR, a/c, kit, restaurant, and hlth clb access

Embassy Row Hotel
(800) HILTONS, (202) 265-1600
http://www.hilton.com
2015 Massachusetts Ave. NW
199 rooms - $120-585
Pets: Welcome
Creature Comforts: CCTV, VCR, a/c, refrig, micro, restaurant, hlth clb, pool

Four Seasons Hotel
(800) 332-3442, (202) 342-0444
http://www.fshr.com
2800 Pennsylvania Ave. NW
195 rooms - $199-2,595
Pets: Welcome (pet program)
Creature Comforts: An intimate yet elegant Georgetown hotel, along the river, floral chintz, Beidermeier-inspired furnishings, CCTV, VCR, a/c, fireplace, kit, Jacuzzis, restaurant, cont. brkfst, pool, hlth clb, sauna, steamrooms, whirlpoo, brick courtyard

Georgetown Suites
(800) 348-7203, (202) 298-1600
http://www.georgetownsuites.com
1000 - 29th St. NW
214 rooms - $150-199
Pets: Under 10 lbs. w/$7 fee
Creature Comforts: Great loaction, contemporary decor combines with functionality and intimate setting, light airy studios, CCTV, a/c, kit, hlth clb

Georgetown Mews
(800) 348-7203, (202) 298-7731
1111- 20th St.
216 rooms - $125-275
Pets: Under 10 lbs. w/$6 fee
Creature Comforts: CCTV, a/c, kit, hlth clb

The Hay-Adams Hotel
(800) 424-5054, (202) 638-6600
http://www.preferredhotels.com
1 Lafayette Sq.
155 rooms - $175-2,400
Pets: Under 25 lbs. w/$150 dep.
Creature Comforts: Classic historic 1927 hotel w/exquisite decor, across from the White House, high Jacobean ceilings, lusturous walnut paneling, English antiques and reproductions, crystal chandeliers, Oriental carpets, French tapestries, CCTV, VCR, a/c, fireplaces, kit, Jacuzzis, restaurant, and hlth clb access

Hereford House B&B
(202) 543-0102
www.bbonline.com/dc/hereford
604 S. Carolina Ave.
4 rooms - $50-75
Pets: Leashed pets welcome
Creature Comforts: Charming Federal-style brick townhouse, charming decor, white wicker accents, CCTV, a/c, garden, and a full brkfst

Holiday Inn
(800) HOLIDAY, (202) 737-1200
http://www.holiday-inn.com
1155 - 14th St. NW
210 rooms - $85-485
Pets: Small pets welcome
Creature Comforts: CCTV, VCR, a/c, refrig, micro, restaurant, pool

Hotel Harrington
(800) 424-8532, (202) 628-8140
http://www.hotel-harrington.com
11th & E Streets NW
260 rooms - $85-159
Pets: Small pets welcome
Creature Comforts: A family owned hotel for over 85 years, CCTV, a/c, refrig, micro, restaurant, and hlth clb access

Hotel Sofitel
(800) 763-4835, (202) 797-2000
http://www.sofitel.com
1914 Connecticut Ave. NW
144 rooms - $185-599
Pets: Small pets w/$50 dep.
Creature Comforts: Lovely hotel w/French décor, set along Embassy Row, CCTV, a/c, refrig, micro, restaurant, hlth clb access

Hotel Tabbard Inn
(202) 785-1277
1739 N St. NW
40 rooms - $65-175
Pets: Welcome w/$20 fee
Creature Comforts: Three historic Victorian townhouses linked together, eclectic furnishings and décor, a/c, fireplaces, refrig, restaurant, cont. brkfst, charming patio, hlth club access

Hotel Washington
(800) 424-9540, (202) 638-5900
http://www.hotelwashington.com
15th & Penn. Ave.
350 rooms - $175-695
Pets: Dogs welcome
Creature Comforts: National historic landmark overlooking White House, host to dozens of U.S. Presidents, elegant ambiance, finial beds, CCTV, a/c, refrig, marble bathrooms, restaurant, hlth clb, sauna

The Jefferson
(800) 368-5966, (202) 347-2200
http://www.slh.com
16th & M streets
100 rooms - $145-850
Pets: Small pets w/$25 fee
Creature Comforts: Intimate, exquisitely appointed centrally-located hotel, Oriental carpets, chintz fabrics, 18th-century canopy beds, original paintings, CCTV, VCR, a/c, refrig, micro, stereos-CDs, antiques, fireplaces, Jacuzzis, intimate restaurant, sauna, hlth clb and golf access

Lincoln Suites
(800) 424-2970, (202) 223-4320
http://www.lincolnhotels.com
1823 L St.
100 rooms - $99-149
Pets: Small pets w/$12 fee
Creature Comforts: CCTV, a/c, kit, restaurant, and hlth clb access

Loews L'Enfant Plaza Hotel
(800) 23-LOEWS, (202) 484-1000
http://www.loewshotels.com
480 L'Enfant Plaza SW
370 rooms - $129-1,250
Pets: Welcome (pet program-Loews Loves Pets: treats & rewards program)
Creature Comforts: Lovely accommodations surrounded by impressive museums and landmarks, French influenced furnishings, European décor, CCTV, VCR, a/c, marble accents, refrig, micro, Jacuzzis, restaurant, pool, hlth clb

The Madison
(800) 424-8577, (202) 862-1600
http://www.dcmadisonhotel.com
1177 - 15th St. NW
355 rooms - $199-475
Pets: Small pets w/$30 daily fee
Creature Comforts: An historic hotel w/Old World charm, elegance, impressive paintings, antiques, CCTV, VCR, a/c, refrig, micro, restaurant, steamroom, sauna, and hlth clb access

Marriott Hotel
(800) 228-9290, (202) 328-2000
http://www.marriott.com
2660 Woodley Rd. NW
1,350 rooms - $175-1,400
Pets: Small pets welcome
Creature Comforts: CCTV, a/c, refrig, restaurant, pool, hlth clb, whirlpool, sauna

Park Hyatt
(800) 233-1234, (202) 789-1234
http://www.hyatt.com
1201 - 24th St. NW
225 rooms - $99-399
Pets: Welcome
Creature Comforts: CCTV, VCR, a/c, refrig, Jacuzzis, restaurant, pool, hlth clb, saunas, steamrooms, whirlpool

Renaissance Hotel
(800) HOTELS-1, (202) 898-9000
http://www.renaissancehotels.com
999 - 9th St. NW
800 rooms - $129-2,025
Pets: Small pets w/$100 dep.
Creature Comforts: CCTV, VCR, a/c, refrig, Jacuzzi, restaurant, cont. brkfst, pool, hlth clb, sauna, steamrooms, and whirlpools

River Inn
(800) 424-2741, (202) 337-7600
http://www.theriverinn.com
924 - 25th St. NW
125 rooms - $125-199
Pets: W/$50 fee & $250 dep.
Creature Comforts: CCTV, VCR, a/c, kit, restaurant, hlth clb access

Savoy Suites Georgetown
(800) 944-5377, (202) 337-9700
web site pending
2505 Wisconsin Ave. NW
145 rooms - $69-199
Pets: Small pets welcome
Creature Comforts: CCTV, a/c, kit, Jacuzzis, restaurant, and hlth clb access

Sheraton Hotel
(800) 325-3535, (202) 328-2000
http://www.sheraton.com
2660 Woodley Rd. NW
1,350 rooms - $145-955
Pets: Welcome
Creature Comforts: CCTV,
VCR, a/c, kit, Jacuzzis, restaurant,
pools, hlth clb, sauna, whirlpool

Swiss Inn
(800) 955-7947, (202) 371-1816
http://www.theswissinn.com
1204 Massachusetts Ave. NW
8 rooms - $65-110
Pets: Selectively welcomed
Creature Comforts: A four-story
brownstone apartment building,
converted to intimate understated
inn, CCTV, VCR, a/c, kit, cont.
brkfst

Travelodge Gateway
(800) 578-7878, (202) 832-8600
http://www.travelodge.com
1917 Bladensburg Rd. NE
148 rooms - $65-89
Pets: Welcome
Creature Comforts: CCTV, a/c,
restaurant, pool

Washington Hilton
(800) HILTONS, (202) 483-3000
http://www.hilton.com
1919 Connecticut Ave. NW
1122 rooms - $129-1,455
Pets: Welcome
Creature Comforts: CCTV,
VCR, a/c, refrig, micro, Jacuzzis,
restaurant, pool, hlth clb, sauna,
steamroom, whirlpool, tennis

Washington Monarch Hotel
(800) 505-9042, (202) 429-2400
www.washingtonmonarch.com
2401 M Street N.W.
425 rooms - $145-1,700
Pets: Under 20 lbs. welcome
Creature Comforts: A light and
airy hotel set in the city's West
End, Italian marble accents, two-
story loggia, floral courtyard,
Beidermeier-inspired furnishings,
CCTV, VCR, a/c, refrig, Jacuzzis,
English reproductions, restaurant,
pool, hlth clb, sauna, steamroom,
whirlpool, racquet ball, squash

Washington Vista Hotel
(800) 445-8667, (202) 429-1700
http://www.hilton.com
1400 M St.
Pets: Welcome
Creature Comforts: CCTV,
VCR, a/c, refrig, Jacuzzis,
restaurants, hlth clb, saunas,
and whirlpools

The Watergate Hotel
(800) 424-2736, (202) 965-2300
http://www.swissotel.com
2650 Virginia Ave. NW
235 rooms - $285-1,900
Pets: Small pets welcome
Creature Comforts: Renowned
Watergate complex offers
luxurious accommodations and
great river views, writing desks,
antiques and Queen Anne
reproductions, festive chintz,
CCTV, VCR, a/c, kit, stereos,
Jacuzzis, restaurants, pool, hlth
clb, sauna, steam rooms,
whirlpools, gardens, river views

Westin Fairfax Hotel
(800) 228-3000, (202) 293-2100
http://www.westin.com
2100 Massachsuetts Ave. NW.
206 rooms - $269-999
Pets: Small pets welcome
Creature Comforts: CCTV, a/c,
refrig, restaurant, hlth clb access,
and a whirlpool

The Willard Hotel
(800) 327-0200, (202) 628-9100
http://hotels.washington.
interconti.com
1401 Pennsylvania Ave NW
340 rooms - $169-2,795
Pets: Small pets w/CC deposit
Creature Comforts: An
architectural 1904 National
landmark w/ wonderful common
areas and lovely guest rooms,
CCTV, VCR, a/c, kit, Jacuzzis,
elegant restaurant, shops, hlth clb

Florida

ALACHUA
Comfort Inn
(800) 228-5150, (904) 462-2414
http://www.comfortinn.com
15405 Martin Luther King Blvd.
90 rooms - $60-124
Pets: Small pets w/$10 fee
Creature Comforts: CCTV, a/c,
refrig, pool

Days Inn
(800) DAYS-INN, (904) 462-3251
http://www.daysinn.com
16301 Martin Luther King Blvd.
60 rooms - $40-145
Pets: Welcome w/$5 fee
Creature Comforts: CCTV, a/c,
refrig, micro, cont. brkfst, pool

Ramada Limited
(800) 2-Ramada, (904) 462-4200
http://www.ramada.com
16305 NW 163 Lane
45 rooms - $60-129
Pets: Small pets w/$5 fee
Creature Comforts: CCTV, a/c

Travelodge
(800) 578-7878, (352) 462-2244
http://www.travelodge.com
Route 1
100 rooms - $40-55
Pets: Welcome w/$10 fee
Creature Comforts: CCTV, a/c,
restaurant, cont. brkfst, pool

ALTAMONTE SPRINGS
Crosby's Inn
(800) 821-6685, (407) 886-3220
1440 W. Orange Blossom Trail
62 rooms - $50-140
Pets: Welcome w/$10 fee
Creature Comforts: CCTV, a/c,
kit, pool

Embassy Suites
(800) 362-2779, (407) 834-2400
http://www.embassy-suites.com
225 E. Altamonte Dr.
210 rooms - $99-149
Pets: Welcome w/$50 dep.
Creature Comforts: CCTV, a/c,
restaurant, pool, lake views

Hampton Inn
(800) Hampton, (407) 869-9000
http://www.hampton-inn.com
151 N. Douglas Ave.
210 rooms - $65-135
Pets: Welcome w/$60 fee
Creature Comforts: CCTV, a/c,
refrig, cont. brkfst, pool, whirlpool

La Quinta Inn
(800) Nu-Rooms, (407) 788-1411
http://www.laquinta.com
150 S. Westmonte Dr.
112 rooms - $60-89
Pets: Small pets welcome
Creature Comforts: CCTV, a/c,
refrig, micro, cont. brkfst, pool

Residence Inn
(800) 331-3131, (407) 788-7991
http://www.residenceinn.com
270 Douglas Ave.
125 rooms - $95-199
Pets: Under 25 lbs. welcome w/$5
fee, $150 dep.
Creature Comforts: CCTV, a/c,
kit, fireplaces, cont. brkfst, pool

AMELIA ISLAND
Florida House Inn
(800) 258-3301, (904) 261-3300
http://www.floridahouse.com
22 S. 3rd St.
12 rooms - $75-160
Pets: Small pets welcome
Creature Comforts: A National
Historic Register gem, 1857 inn
w/claw foot tubs, antique pine
furniture, four poster beds, CCTV,
VCR, a/c, refrig, Jacuzzi,
fireplaces, restaurant, pub,
courtyard w/200 year old oak tree,
full brkfst

APALACHICOLA
The Gibson Inn
(850) 653-2191
100 Market St.
30 rooms - $65-125
Pets: Welcome w/$5 fee
Creature Comforts: A rambling
National Historic Register inn,
antiques, hand-crafted furnishings,
dhurries, four poster beds, detailed
moldings and intricate staircase,
CCTV, a/c, refrig, claw foot tubs,
restaurant

Rainbow Inn
(850) 653-8139
123 Water St.
25 rooms - $60-135
Pets: Welcome w/$5 fee
Creature Comforts: CCTV, a/c,
kit, Jacuzzi, cont. brkfst

Rancho Inn
(850) 653-9435
240 Rte. 98
33 rooms - $40-59
Pets: Welcome w/$4 fee
Creature Comforts: CCTV, a/c

APOLLO BEACH
Ramada Inn Bayside
(800) 2-Ramada, (813) 641-2700
http://www.ramada.com
6414 Surfside Blvd.
102 rooms - $55-165
Pets: Welcome w/$15 dep.
Creature Comforts: CCTV,
VCR, a/c, refrig, micro, restaurant,
pool, beach

APOPKA
Crosby's Motor Inn
(407) 886-3220
1440 W. Orange Blossom Terr.
60 rooms - $45-129
Pets: Small pets w/$10 fee
Creature Comforts: CCTV, a/c,
kit, Jacuzzis, pool

  Florida

ARCADIA
Best Western Inn
(800) 528-1234, (941) 494-4884
http://www.bestwestern.com
504 S. Brevard St.
35 rooms - $50-95
Pets: Small pets w/$10 fee
Creature Comforts: CCTV, a/c, cont. brkfst, pool

BARTOW
Davis Bros Motel
(800) 424-0711, (941) 533-0711
1035 N. Broadway Ave.
25 rooms - $35-60
Pets: Small pets welcome
Creature Comforts: CCTV, VCR, a/c, pool

El Jon Motel
(800) 533-8191, (941) 533-8191
1460 E. Main St.
42 rooms - $40-75
Pets: Welcome
Creature Comforts: CCTV, a/c, pool, golf access

BASEBALL CITY
Days Inn
(800) DAYS-INN, (941) 424-2596
http://www.daysinn.com
Rtes. 4 & 27
121 rooms - $30-125
Pets: Welcome w/$10 fee
Creature Comforts: CCTV, a/c, refrig, pool, whirlpool

BAY HARBOR
Bay Harbor Inn
(305) 868-4141
http://www.bayharborinn.com
9660 E. Bay Harbor Dr.
45 rooms - $80-360
Pets: Welcome w/$12 fee
Creature Comforts: A charming coral stucco building amid toney surroundings, Georgian antiques, Victorian accents, eclectic furnishings, four poster beds, CCTV, a/c, refrig, restaurant, cont. brkfst on yacht, pool, gardens

BOCA RATON
Doubletree Guest Suites
(800) 222-TREE, (561) 997-9500
http://www.doubletreehotels.com
701 NW 53rd St.
180 rooms - $89-219
Pets: Welcome w/$50 fee
Creature Comforts: CCTV, a/c, kit, restaurant, whirlpool, hlth club, pool

Gasparilla Inn
(561) 964-2201
5th at Palm Ave.
160 rooms - $160-255
Pets: Welcome in cottages
Creature Comforts: Classic old Florida inn set on exclusive but low-key island, social season, rms. w/traditional furnishings/tropical color schemes, CCTV, VCR, a/c, fireplace, kit, restaurant, pools, lawn games, tennis, golf, ice cream fountain, game rm-billiards, trails, great shelling on beach

Radisson Suite Hotel
(800) 333-3333, (561) 483-3600
http://www.radisson.com
7920 Glades Rd.
200 rooms - $99-395
Pets: Under 20 lbs. w/$100 fee
Creature Comforts: CCTV, VCR, a/c, refrig, micro, Jacuzzis, restaurant, full brkfst, pool, hlth club access, whirlpool

Residence Inn
(800) 331-3131, (561) 994-3222
http://www.residenceinn.com
525 NW 77th St.
120 rooms - $99-209
Pets: $100-150 fee, CC dep.
Creature Comforts: CCTV, a/c, kit, restaurant, pool, hlth club, country club access, whirlpools

BONIFAY
Best Western Inn
(800) 528-1234, (850) 547-4251
http://www.bestwestern.com
2004 S. Waukesha St.
56 rooms - $40-59
Pets: Welcome w/$3 fee
Creature Comforts: CCTV, VCR, a/c, cont. brkfst, pool

BRANDENTON
Days Inn
(800) DAYS-INN, (941) 746-1141
http://www.daysinn.com
3506 - 1st St. W.
134 rooms - $50-129
Pets: Welcome
Creature Comforts: CCTV, a/c, refrig, restaurant, pool

Econo Lodge
(800) 55-ECONO, (941) 745-1988
http://www.econolodge.com
6727 - 14th St. West
79 rooms - $40-99
Pets: Small pets w/$5 fee
Creature Comforts: CCTV, a/c, refrig, micro, cont. brkfst, pool

Howard Johnson Express
(800) I-Go-Hojo, (941) 756-8399
http://www.hojo.com
6511 - 14th St. West
49 rooms - $45-99
Pets: Welcome w/$5 fee
Creature Comforts: CCTV, a/c, kit, pool

Motel 6
(800) 4-MOTEL6, (941) 747-6005
http://www.motel6.com
660 - 67th St. Circle East
121 rooms - $35-49
Pets: Under 30 lbs.welcome
Creature Comforts: CCTV, a/c, pool

Park Inn Club
(941) 795-4633
4450 - 47th St. West
125 rooms - $85-175
Pets: Small pets w/$6 fee
Creature Comforts: CCTV, a/c, Jacuzzis, cont. brkfst, hlth club access, pool

Super 8 Motel
(800) 800-8000, (941) 756-6656
http://www.super8.com
6516 - 14th St. West
49 rooms - $35-99
Pets: Welcome
Creature Comforts: CCTV, a/c, cont. brkfst, pool

BRADENTON BEACH
Tradewinds Resort
(888) 686-6114, (941) 779-0010
http://www.tradewinds-resort.com
1603 Gulf Drive North
39 rooms - $85-270
Pets: Small pets w/$25 fee
Creature Comforts: CCTV, a/c,
VCR, kitchens, pool, patios-
porches, dock

BRANDON
Behind the Fence B&B
http://www.webbtec.com/bb
(813) 685-8201
1401 Viola Dr.
4 rooms - $45-95
Pets: In cottages w/$10 fee
Creature Comforts: Authentic
replica of 1880's New England
saltbox with Amish décor and
furnishings, antiques, white-
washed wall boards, claw foot
tubs, four poster beds, intriguing
collectibles, oriental rugs, CCTV,
a/c, fireplace, refrig, full brkfst,
and a pool

Brandon Motor Lodge
(813) 689-1261
906 E. Brandon Blvd.
35 rooms - $35-79
Pets: Dogs welcome w/$20 dep.
Creature Comforts: CCTV, a/c,
pool

Red Roof Inn
(800) The Roof, (813) 681-8484
http://www.redroof.com
10121 Horace Ave.
120 rooms - $45-99
Pets: Small pets welcome
Creature Comforts: CCTV, a/c

BROOKSVILLE
Days Inn
(800) DAYS-INN, (352) 796-9486
http://www.daysinn.com
31015 Cortez Blvd.
120 rooms - $50-75
Pets: Welcome w/$6 fee
Creature Comforts: CCTV, a/c,
restaurant, pool

Holiday Inn
(800) HOLIDAY, (352) 796-9481
http://www.holiday-inn.com
30307 Cortez Blvd.
120 rooms - $55-95
Pets: Welcome w/$20 fee
Creature Comforts: CCTV, a/c,
restaurant, pool

BUNNELL
Best Western Plantation Inn
(800) 528-1234, (904) 437-3737
http://www.bestwestern.com
2251 Old Dixie Hwy.
100 rooms - $45-78
Pets: Small pets w/$10 fee
Creature Comforts: CCTV, a/c,
cont. brkfst, pool, whirlpool

BUSHNELL
Best Western Inn
(800) 528-1234, (352) 793-5010
http://www.bestwestern.com
2224 W. Rte. 48
48 rooms - $45-79
Pets: Small pets w/$5 fee
Creature Comforts: CCTV, a/c,
refrig, cont. brkfst, pool

CAPE CORAL
Days Inn
(800) DAYS-INN, (941) 995-0536
http://www.daysinn.com
13353 N. Cleveland Ave.
126 rooms - $40-220
Pets: Welcome w/$10 fee
Creature Comforts: CCTV, a/c,
pool

Del Prado Inn
(800) 231-6818, (941) 542-3151
1502 Miramar St.
100 rooms - $60-89
Pets: Welcome w/$50 dep.
Creature Comforts: CCTV, a/c,
kit, restaurant, pool

Quality Inn
(800) 228-5151, (941) 542-2121
http://www.qualityinn.com
1538 Cape Coral Pkwy
144 rooms - $59-155
Pets: First flr. w/$10 fee
Creature Comforts: CCTV, a/c,
refrig, pool

CAPTIVA ISLAND
"Tween" Waters Inn
(800) 223-5865, (941) 472-5161
http://www.tween-waters.com
15951 Captiva Rd.
128 rooms - $135-495
Pets: Ltd. units w/$10 fee
Creature Comforts: Situated at
the narrowest part of Captiva,
1900's inn and cottages, pickled
wood walls, rattan, CCTV, VCR,
a/c, fireplace, kit, Jacuzzi,
restaurant, cont. brkfst, pool, hlth
clb, sauna, marina-boats, tennis,
lawn games, sandy paths, shelling

CARRABELLE
The Moorings at Carrabelle
(850) 697-2800
1000 Rte. 98
20 rooms - $50-89
Pets: $10 fee, credit card dep.
Creature Comforts: CCTV, a/c,
kit, pool

CEDAR KEY
Dockside Motel
(352) 543-5432
491 Dock St.
10 rooms - $50-79
Pets: Welcome w/$5 fee
Creature Comforts: CCTV, a/c

Park Place Motel
(352) 543-5737
211 - 2nd St.
33 rooms - $65-95
Pets: Welcome w/$5 fee
Creature Comforts: CCTV, a/c,
kit

CHATTAHOOCHEE
Morgan Motel
(850) 663-4336
Rte. 90 East
40 rooms - $39-55
Pets: Welcome w/$10 fee
Creature Comforts: CCTV, a/c,
kit

CHIPLEY
Super 8 Motel
(800) 800-8000, (904) 638-8530
http://www.super8.com
1700 Main St.
40 rooms - $35-59
Pets: Welcome
Creature Comforts: CCTV, a/c,
cont. brkfst

CLEARWATER

Butterfly Motel
(727) 536-1500
http://www.comfortinn.com
12500 Hwy. 19
20 rooms - $40-55
Pets: $5-10 daily fee
Creature Comforts: CCTV, a/c, kit

Comfort Inn
(800) 228-5150, (727) 573-1171
http://www.comfortinn.com
3580 Ulmerton Rd.
120 rooms - $60-124
Pets: Small pets welcome
Creature Comforts: CCTV, a/c, restaurant, pool

Holiday Inn Express
(800) HOLIDAY, (727) 536-7275
http://www.holiday-inn.com
13625 Icot Blvd.
125 rooms - $75-109
Pets: Small pets welcome
Creature Comforts: CCTV, VCR, a/c, restaurant, cont. brkfst, pool, whirlpool

La Quinta, Airport
(800) Nu-Room, (727) 797-8173
http://www.laquinta.com
3301 Ulmerton Rd.
115 rooms - $55-129
Pets: Small pets welcome
Creature Comforts: CCTV, a/c, refrig, cont. brkfst, pool, hlth club, whirlpool

Residence Inn
(800) 331-3131, (727) 573-4444
http://www.residenceinn.com
5050 Ulmerton Rd.
87 rooms - $129-199
Pets: $125-175 fee, CC dep.
Creature Comforts: CCTV, a/c, kit, cont. brkfst, pool, whirlpool, and hlth clb access

CLEARWATER BEACH

Aegan Sands Motel
(800) 942-3432, (727) 447-3464
http://www.travelbase.com/aegean
421 S. Gulfview Blvd.
52 rooms - $55-155
Pets: Small pets w/$25 fee
Creature Comforts: CCTV, a/c, kit, pool, lawn games

Best Western Inn
(800) 528-1234, (727) 441-1722
http://www.bestwestern.com
445 Hamden Dr.
106 rooms - $80-210
Pets: Under 10 lbs. w/CC dep.
Creature Comforts: CCTV, a/c, pool, whirlpool

Clearwater Beach Motel
(800) 292-2295, (727) 441-2425
500 Mandalay Ave.
200 rooms - $65-155
Pets: Under 10 lbs. w/CC dep.
Creature Comforts: CCTV, a/c, kit, pool

Spyglass
(800) 942-3432, (727) 446-8317
www.travelbase.com/aegean
215 S. Gulfview Blvd.
79 rooms - $75-155
Pets: Welcome w/$25 fee
Creature Comforts: CCTV, a/c, kit, pool

CLERMONT

Mulberry Inn B&B
(800) 641-0670, (352) 242-0670
http://www.mulberryinn.com
915 Montrose St.
5 rooms - $55-95
Pets: Welcome w/$50 deposit
Creature Comforts: A charming 1890's home w/wrap-around porch set behind a picket fence, floral accents, four poster beds w/ colorful quilts, CCTV, a/c, kit, cont. brkfst/dinners available

COCOA

Best Western Inn
(800) 528-1234, (407) 632-1065
http://www.bestwestern.com
4225 W. King St.
120 rooms - $50-95
Pets: Small pets w/$5 fee
Creature Comforts: CCTV, micro, refrig, pool

Econo Lodge
(800) 55-ECONO, (407) 632-4561
http://www.econolodge.com
3220 N. Coca Blvd.
144 rooms - $45-75
Pets: Small pets welcome
Creature Comforts: CCTV, VCR, a/c, refrig, micro, restaurant, pool

Ramada Inn
(800) 2-Ramada, (407) 631-1210
http://www.ramada.com
900 Friday Rd.
150 rooms - $50-89
Pets: Small pets w/$25 dep.
Creature Comforts: CCTV, a/c, refrig, micro, restaurant, pool, putting green

COCOA BEACH

Best Western Ocean Inn
(800) 528-1234, (407) 784-2550
http://www.bestwestern.com
5500 N. Atlantic Ave.
100 rooms - $45-70
Pets: Small pets w/$10 fee
Creature Comforts: CCTV, a/c, cont. brkfst, pool, whirlpool

Econo Lodge
(800) 55-ECONO, (407) 783-2252
http://www.econolodge.com
1275 N. Atlantic Ave.
125 rooms - $45-99
Pets: Small pets welcome
Creature Comforts: CCTV, a/c, kit, restaurant, pool

Motel 6
(800) 4-MOTEL6, (407) 783-3103
http://www.motel6.com
3701 N. Atlantic Ave.
151 rooms - $39-55
Pets: Under 30 lbs. welcome
Creature Comforts: CCTV, a/c, pool

Surf Studio Beach Resort
(407) 783-7100
1801 S. Atlantic Ave.
11 rooms - $50-155
Pets: Welcome w/$10 fee
Creature Comforts: CCTV, a/c, kit, pool, on beach

CORAL SPRINGS

La Quinta Inn
(800) Nu-Rooms, (954) 753-9000
http://www.laquinta.com
3701 University Dr.
120 rooms - $60-120
Pets: Small pets welcome
Creature Comforts: CCTV, a/c, refrig, micro, cont. brkfst, pool

Wellesley Inns
(800) 444-8888, (954) 344-2200
http://www.wellesleyinns.com
3100 N. University Dr.
105 rooms - $59-105
Pets: Under 30 lbs. w/$10 fee
Creature Comforts: CCTV, a/c,
refrig, micro, cont. brkfst, pool

CRESTVIEW
Days Inn
(800) DAYS-INN, (850) 682-8842
http://www.daysinn.com
4255 S. Ferdon St.
64 rooms - $40-69
Pets: Welcome w/$10 fee
Creature Comforts: CCTV, a/c,
refrig, micro, cont. brkfst, pool

Holiday Inn
(800) HOLIDAY, (850) 682-6111
http://www.holiday-inn.com
4050 S. Ferdon St.
120 rooms - $55-69
Pets: Small pets welcome
Creature Comforts: CCTV, a/c,
restaurant, pool

Super 8 Motel
(800) 800-8000, (850) 682-9649
http://www.super8.com
3925 S. Ferdon St.
63 rooms - $39-59
Pets: Welcome
Creature Comforts: CCTV, a/c,
kit, hlth clb access, cont. brkfst

CROSS CITY
Carriage Inn
(352) 498-0001
280 E. Main St.
24 rooms - $35-54
Pets: Welcome w/$5 fee
Creature Comforts: CCTV, a/c,
restaurant, pool

CRYSTAL RIVER
Best Western Ocean Inn
(800) 528-1234, (352) 795-3171
http://www.bestwestern.com
614 Rte 19
95 rooms - $75-99
Pets: Welcome w/$3 daily fee
Creature Comforts: CCTV, a/c,
VCR, refrig, restaurant, pool, river

Comfort Inn
(800) 228-5150, (352) 563-1500
http://www.comfortinn.com
4486 N. Suncoast Blvd.
65 rooms - $45-90
Pets: Small pets w/$5 fee
Creature Comforts: CCTV, a/c,
cont. brkfst, pool, tennis

Days Inn
(800) DAYS-INN, (352) 795-2111
http://www.daysinn.com
2380 NW Rte. 19
104 rooms - $45-100
Pets: Welcome w/$7 fee
Creature Comforts: CCTV, a/c,
cont. brkfst, restaurant, pool,
whirlpool

Econo Lodge
(800) 55-ECONO, (352) 795-9447
http://www.econolodge.com
2575 Rte. 19
45 rooms - $39-65
Pets: Small pets w/$5 fee
Creature Comforts: CCTV, a/c,
pool

CUTLER RIDGE
Baymont Inns
(877)BAYMONT, (305) 278-0001
http://www.baymontinns.com
10821 Caribbean Blvd.
105 rooms - $50-85
Pets: Small pets welcome
Creature Comforts: CCTV, a/c,
cont. brkfst, pool

CYPRESS GARDENS
Best Western Admiral's Inn
(800) 528-1234, (941) 324-5950
http://www.bestwestern.com
5665 Cypress Gardens Blvd.
157 rooms - $50-105
Pets: Welcome
Creature Comforts: CCTV, a/c,
refrig, restaurant, pool

DANIA
Motel 6
(800) 4-MOTEL6, (954) 921-5505
http://www.motel6.com
825 E. Dania Beach Blvd.
163 rooms - $44-59
Pets: Under 30 lbs.welcome
Creature Comforts: CCTV, a/c,
pool

Wyndham Hotel
(800) Wyndham, (954) 920-3500
http://www.wyndham.com
1825 Griffin Rd.
255 rooms - $99-499
Pets: Welcome w/$50 fee
Creature Comforts: CCTV, a/c,
refrig, restaurant, whirlpool,
tennis, sauna, hlth club, pool

DAYTONA BEACH
Aruba Inn
(800) 214-1406, (904) 253-5643
1254 N. Atlantic Ave.
33 rooms - $35-79
Pets: Small pets w/$10 fee
Creature Comforts: CCTV, a/c,
kit, beach

Best Western Mayan Inn
(800) 528-1234, (904) 252-0584
http://www.bestwestern.com
103 S. Ocean Ave.
112 rooms - $55-225
Pets: Small pets w/$100 dep.
Creature Comforts: CCTV, a/c,
cont. brkfst, two pools

Breakers Beach Motel
(800) 441-8459, (904) 252-0863
http://www.breakersbeach.com
103 S. Ocean Ave.
22 rooms - $45-99
Pets: Small-med. pets welcome
Creature Comforts: CCTV, a/c,
kit, pool

Budget Host
(800) Bud-Host, (904) 252-1142
http://www.budgethost.com
1305 S. Ridgewood Ave.
24 rooms - $25-55
Pets: Small pets w/$5 fee
Creature Comforts: CCTV, a/c,
and kit

Days Inn
(800) DAYS-INN, (904) 255-0541
http://www.daysinn.com
2900 Int'l Speedway Blvd.
180 rooms - $45-185
Pets: Welcome w/$10 fee
Creature Comforts: CCTV, a/c,
cont. brkfst, restaurant, pool

Days Inn
(800) DAYS-INN, (904) 255-4492
http://www.daysinn.com
1909 S. Atlantic Ave.
191 rooms - $45-125
Pets: Welcome w/$15 fee
Creature Comforts: CCTV, a/c,
cont. brkfst, pool

Driftwood Beach Motel
(800) 490-8935, (904) 677-1331
web site pending
657 S. Atlantic Ave.
44 rooms - $45-75
Pets: Under 15 lbs. w/$10 fee
Creature Comforts: CCTV, a/c,
kit, pool, on the ocean

Holiday Inn
(800) HOLIDAY, (904) 255-4471
http://www.holiday-inn.com
600 N. Atlantic Ave.
333 rooms - $50-255
Pets: Welcome w/$100 dep.
Creature Comforts: CCTV,
VCR, a/c, refrig, micro, Jacuzzis,
restaurant, pool, hlth clb, beach,
and water sports

La Quinta Inn
(800) Nu-Rooms, (904) 255-7142
http://www.laquinta.com
2725 Int'l Speedway Blvd.
144 rooms - $50-89
Pets: Small pets welcome
Creature Comforts: CCTV, a/c,
refrig, micro, cont. brkfst, pool

Radisson Hotel
(800) 333-3333, (904) 239-9800
http://www.radisson.com
640 N. Atlantic Ave.
206 rooms - $70-165
Pets: Welcome w/$25 fee
Creature Comforts: CCTV, a/c,
refrig, restaurant, pool

Ramada Inn
(800) 2-Ramada, (904) 255-2422
http://www.ramada.com
1798 Int'l Speedway Blvd.
127 rooms - $75-275
Pets: Welcome w/$100 dep.
Creature Comforts: CCTV, a/c,
refrig, restaurant, pool

Super 8 Motel
(800) 800-8000, (904) 253-0643
http://www.super8.com
2992 W. Int'l Speedway Blvd.
112 rooms - $40-185
Pets: Welcome
Creature Comforts: CCTV, a/c,
cont. brkfst, pool

White Sands Motel
(904) 253-7461
1122 N. Atlantic Ave.
10 rooms - $35-75
Pets: Small dogs w/$3 fee
Creature Comforts: CCTV, a/c,
kit, pool, beach

DAYTONA BEACH SHORES
Castaways Inn
(800) 407-0342, (904) 254-8480
http://www.visitdaytona.com/
castaways
2043 S. Atlantic Ave.
154 rooms - $85-199
Pets: Welcome w/$6 fee
Creature Comforts: CCTV,
VCR, a/c, refrig, restaurant, pool,
whirlpool, lawn games

Sand Castle Motel
(800) 967-4757
3619 S. Atlantic Ave.
31 rooms - $29-75
Pets: Welcome w/$15 fee
Creature Comforts: CCTV, a/c,
kit, pool

DEERFIELD BEACH
Comfort Suites
(800) 228-5150, (954) 570-8887
http://www.comfortinn.com
1040 E. Newport Center Dr.
70 rooms - $50-175
Pets: Welcome
Creature Comforts: CCTV, a/c,
pool, cont. brkfst, pool, whirlpool

La Quinta Inn
(800) Nu-Rooms , (954) 421-1004
http://www.laquintainn.com
351 W. Hillsboro Blvd.
129 rooms - $50-110
Pets: Small pets welcome
Creature Comforts: CCTV, a/c,
cont. brkfst, pool

Quality Suites
(800) 221-2222, (954) 570-8888
http://www.qualityinn.com
1050 Newport Center Dr.
105 rooms - $75-190
Pets: Welcome
Creature Comforts: CCTV,
VCR, a/c, refrig, micro, restaurant,
cont. brkfst, pool, whirlpool

Ramada Inn Bayside
(800) 2-Ramada, (954) 421-5000
http://www.ramada.com
1401 S. Fed. Hwy.
155 rooms - $55-175
Pets: $10 fee, in smoking rooms
Creature Comforts: CCTV, a/c,
refrig, micro, restaurant, pool

DE FUNIAK SPRINGS
Best Western Inn
(800) 528-1234, (850) 892-5111
http://www.bestwestern.com
Rtes. 10 & 331
100 rooms - $50-75
Pets: Small pets welcome
Creature Comforts: CCTV, a/c,
cont. brkfst, restaurant, pool

Comfort Inn
(800) 228-5150, (850) 892-1333
http://www.comfortinn.com
402 Hugh Adams Rd.
60 rooms - $59-129
Pets: Welcome w/$5 fee
Creature Comforts: CCTV, a/c,
pool

Days Inn
(800) DAYS-INN, (850) 892-6115
http://www.daysinn.com
472 Hugh Adams Rd.
60 rooms - $35-129
Pets: Welcome w/$10 fee
Creature Comforts: CCTV, a/c,
and refrig

DELAND
Holiday Inn
(800) HOLIDAY, (904) 738-5200
http://www.holiday-inn.com
350 E. Int'l Speedway Blvd.
150 rooms - $55-195
Pets: Welcome w/$5 fee
Creature Comforts: CCTV, a/c,
refrig, restaurant, hlth club access,
pool

Quality Inn
(800) 228-5151, (904) 736-3440
http://www.qualityinn.com
2801 E. New York Ave.
110 rooms - $40-275
Pets: On first floor w/$10 fee
Creature Comforts: CCTV,
VCR, a/c, refrig, micro, restaurant,
cont. brkfst, pool

DELRAY BEACH
The Colony Hotel
(800) 552-2363, (561) 276-4123
http://www.thecolonyhotel.com
525 E. Atlantic Ave.
103 rooms - $110-195
Pets: Welcome w/$25 daily fee
Creature Comforts: An historic
Mediterranean-style hotel (just
renovated) white wicker, inviting
ambiance, chintz accents, CCTV,
VCR, a/c, fireplace, refrig, old-
fashioned fixtures, wood blinds,
mahogany furnishings, neat
elevator, restaurant-appropriate
dress, pool, beach club

DESTIN
Days Inn
(800) DAYS-INN, (850) 837-2599
http://www.daysinn.com
1029 Rte. 98
60 rooms - $50-135
Pets: Welcome w/$20 fee
Creature Comforts: CCTV, a/c,
Jacuzzis, refrig, micro, cont.
brkfst, pool

Frangista Beach Inn
(800) 382-2612, (850) 654-5501
4150 Old Hwy. 98
50 rooms - $50-225
Pets: Welcome in the cottage
Creature Comforts: CCTV, a/c,
kit, cont. brkfst, pool

Howard Johnson
(800) I-Go-Hojo, (850) 837-5455
http://www.hojo.com
713 Rte. 98
80 rooms - $40-105
Pets: Small pets w/$20 fee
Creature Comforts: CCTV, a/c,
pool

EAST POINT
Sportsman's Lodge
(850) 670-8423
99 N. Bayshore Dr.
30 rooms - $40-59
Pets: Welcome w/$4 fee
Creature Comforts: CCTV, a/c,
kit, on a bay-dock

ELKTON
Comfort Inn
(800) 228-5150, (904) 829-3435
http://www.comfortinn.com
2625 Rte. 207
63 rooms - $40-129
Pets: Welcome w/$5 fee
Creature Comforts: CCTV, a/c,
cont. brkfst, pool

ELLENTON
Best Western Inn
(800) 528-1234, (941) 729-8505
http://www.bestwestern.com
5218 - 17th St. East
72 rooms - $65-155
Pets: Small pets w/$10 fee
Creature Comforts: CCTV, a/c,
kit, pool

ENGLEWOOD
Days Inn
(800) DAYS-INN, (941) 474-5544
http://www.daysinn.com
2540 S. McCall Rd.
84 rooms - $50-140
Pets: Welcome w/$4 fee
Creature Comforts: CCTV, a/c,
restaurant, pool

Veranda Inn
(800) 633-8115, (941) 475-6533
2073 S. McCall Rd.
38 rooms - $85-119
Pets: Welcome w/$10 fee
Creature Comforts: CCTV,
VCR, a/c, refrig, micro, pool

EUSTIS
Dreamspinner B&B
(888) 474-1229, (352) 589-8082
http://www.dreamspinner.net
117 Diedrich St.
5 rooms - $110-159
Pets: One rm w/$25 fee, $50 dep.
Creature Comforts: A wonderful
old-fashioned 1881 Victorian w/
afternoon tea, antiques, English
chintz, tradtional, CCTV, VCR,
a/c, fireplaces, refrig, full brkfst

EVERGLADES CITY
Rod and Gun Club
(941) 695-2101
200 Riverside Dr.
17 rooms - $50-95
Pets: Welcome
Creature Comforts: Renowned
hunting & fishing club w/cypress
walls, sleepy Everglades town,
host to celebrities and Presidents,
simply decorated cottages, CCTV,
VCR, a/c, fireplace, refrig,
restaurant, intimate bar, pool,
veranda, pool table, overlooks
water and mangroves, dock

Shoney's Inn
(800) 222-2222, (941) 277-2300
http://www.shoneysinn.com
2707 Sadler Rd.
110 rooms - $65-95
Pets: Welcome w/$25 fee
Creature Comforts: CCTV, a/c,
kit, restaurant, pool, and tennis

FLAGLER BEACH
Beach Front Motel
(904) 439-0089
1544 S. A1A
20 rooms - $40-69
Pets: Small pets w/$20 fee
Creature Comforts: CCTV, a/c,
kit, beach

The Topaz
(904) 439-3301
1224 S. Oceanshore Blvd.
49 rooms - $50-150
Pets: Leashed w/$10 fee, $25 dep.
Creature Comforts: Oceanside
hotel with Spanish architecture
and vast array of wonderful
collectibles, beautiful wood floors,
intricate moldings, upscale motel-
style rooms, CCTV, VCR, a/c, kit,
Jacuzzis, restaurant, pool, beach

FLORIDA CITY
Coral Rock
(305) 247-4010
1100 N. Krome Ave.
15 rooms - $39-65
Pets: Welcome w/$50 dep.
Creature Comforts: CCTV, a/c,
kit, pool

Hampton Inn
(800) Hampton, (305) 247-8833
http://www.hampton-inn.com
124 E. Palm St.
122 rooms - $50-119
Pets: Small pets w/$5 fee
Creature Comforts: CCTV, a/c, cont. brkfst, pool

FT. LAUDERDALE
Amerisuites
(800) 833-1516, (954) 763-7670
http://www.amerisuites.com
1851 SE 10th Ave.
126 rooms - $89-199
Pets: Welcome
Creature Comforts: CCTV, a/c, refrig, micro, cont. brkfst

Brick Patio Motel
(954) 563-9540
617 N. Birch Rd.
15 rooms - $29-89
Pets: Welcome w/$10 fee,CC dep.
Creature Comforts: CCTV, a/c, pool

Baymont Inns
(877)BAYMONT, (954) 485-7900
http://www.baymontinns.com
3800 W. Commercial Blvd.
102 rooms - $40-79
Pets: Welcome
Creature Comforts: CCTV, a/c, refrig, micro, cont. brkfst, pool

Doubletree Guest Suites
(800) 222-TREE, (954) 565-3800
http://www.doubletreehotels.com
2670 E. Sunrise Blvd.
229 rooms - $99-229
Pets: Welcome w/$10 fee
Creature Comforts: CCTV, a/c, refrig, micro, restaurant, pool, access to tennis/golf

Doubletree Guest Suites
(800) 222-TREE, (954) 524-8733
http://www.doubletreehotels.com
440 Seabreeze Blvd.
233 rooms - $100-229
Pets: On third floor w/$50 dep.
Creature Comforts: CCTV, refrig, restaurant, pool

La Quinta Inn
(800) Nu-Rooms, (954) 491-7666
http://www.laquinta.com
999 W. Cypress Creek Rd.
144 rooms - $44-149
Pets: Small pets welcome
Creature Comforts: CCTV, a/c, refrig, micro, Jacuzzis, cont. brkfst, pool, whirlpool

Midnight Sea
(800) 910-2357, (954) 463-4827
http://www.midnightsea.com
3005 Alhambra St.
15 rooms - $60-199
Pets: Under 25 lbs. w/$25 fee
Creature Comforts: Art Deco Atrium style guesthouse, rattan & wicker, canopy beds, CCTV, a/c, refrig, micro, Jacuzzi, ceiling fans

Ramada Inn, Airport
(800) 2-Ramada, (954) 584-4000
http://www.ramada.com
2275 Rte. 84
300 rooms - $99-169
Pets: Welcome w/$5 fee, $50 dep.
Creature Comforts: CCTV, a/c, refrig, micro, restaurant, 2 pools

Red Carpet Inn
(800) 251-1962, (954) 792-8181
http://www.reservahost.com
2440 Rte. 84
90 rooms - $45-90
Pets: Small pets $5 fee
Creature Comforts: CCTV, a/c, restaurant, pool

Red Roof Inn
(800) The Roof, (954) 776-6333
http://www.redroof.com
4800 NW 9th Ave.
105 rooms - $50-109
Pets: Welcome w/$5 fee
Creature Comforts: CCTV, a/c, pool

Super 8 Motel
(800) 800-8000, (954) 565-7761
http://www.super8.com
2935 N. Federal Hwy.
50 rooms - $50-85
Pets: Welcome
Creature Comforts: CCTV, a/c

Trevers at the Beach
(800) 533-4744, (954) 564-4341
552 N. Birch Rd.
14 rooms - $39-150
Pets: Welcome w/$50 fee
Creature Comforts: CCTV, a/c, kit, pool

Wellesley Inns
(800) 444-8888, (954) 484-6909
http://www.wellesleyinns.com
5070 N Rte. 7
100 rooms - $59-155
Pets: Under 30 lbs. w/$10 fee
Creature Comforts: CCTV, a/c, refrig, micro, cont. brkfst, pool

Westin Hotel
(800) 228-3000, (954) 772-1331
http://www.westin.com
400 Corporate Way
292 rooms - $99-485
Pets: Under 30 lbs. w/$50 dep
Creature Comforts: Hotel set amid lagoons and manicured grounds, glass façade w/ intimate interiors, soothing color schemes, English antique reproductions, end rooms-curved walls and better views, CCTV, a/c, refrig, two restaurants, hlth clb, sauna, pool, whirlpool, par course, access to tennis/golf

Wish You Were Here Inn
(954) 462-0531
http://www.introweb.com/wishinn
7 N. Birch Rd.
14 rooms - $33-129
Pets: Welcome w/$50-100 fee
Creature Comforts: CCTV, a/c, kit, pool access

FT. MYERS
Baymont Inns
(877)BAYMONT, (941) 275-3500
http://www.baymontinns.com
2717 Colonial Blvd.
125 rooms - $45-99
Pets: Small pets w/$10 fee
Creature Comforts: CCTV, a/c, cont. brkfst, pool

Casa Playa
(800) 569-4876, (941) 765-0510
http://www.casaplayaresort.com
510 Estero Blvd.
115 rooms - $99-275
Pets: Small pets w/$20 daily fee
Creature Comforts: CCTV, a/c, kit, pool

Comfort Suites, Airport
(800) 228-5150, (941) 768-0005
http://www.comfortinn.com
13651 Indian Point Lane
65 rooms - $60-145
Pets: Welcome w/$25 fee
Creature Comforts: CCTV,
VCR, a/c, refrig, micro, Jacuzzis,
cont. brkfst, pool, whirlpool

Days Inn
(800) DAYS-INN, (941) 936-1311
http://www.daysinn.com
11435 S. Cleveland Ave
122 rooms - $40-125
Pets: Welcome w/$6 fee
Creature Comforts: CCTV, a/c,
refrig, pool

Econo Lodge
(800) 55-ECONO, (941) 995-0571
http://www.econolodge.com
13301 N. Cleveland Ave.
79 rooms - $39-89
Pets: Small pets welcome
Creature Comforts: CCTV, a/c,
refrig, cont. brkfst, pool

Golf View Motel
(941) 936-1858
3523 Cleveland Ave.
38 rooms - $40-89
Pets: Small pets w/$4 fee
Creature Comforts: CCTV, a/c,
refrig, pool

La Quinta Inn
(800) Nu-Rooms, (941) 275-3300
http://www.laquinta.com
4850 Cleveland Ave.
129 rooms - $45-139
Pets: Small pets welcome
Creature Comforts: CCTV, a/c,
refrig, micro, cont. brkfst, pool

Motel 6
(800) 4-MOTEL6, (941) 656-5544
http://www.motel6.com
3350 Marinatown Lane
110 rooms - $35-49
Pets: Under 30 lbs. welcome
Creature Comforts: CCTV, a/c,
pool

Radisson Suite Hotel
(800) 333-3333, (941) 466-1200
http://www.radisson.com
20091 Summerlin Rd. SW
155 rooms - $60-185
Pets: Welcome w/$50 fee
Creature Comforts: CCTV, a/c,
refrig, Jacuzzis, restaurant, pool,
whirlpool

Residence Inn
(800) 331-3131, (941) 936-0110
http://www.residenceinn.com
2960 Colonial Blvd.
75 rooms - $95-199
Pets: Welcome w/$25-100 fee
Creature Comforts: CCTV, a/c,
kit, cont. brkfst, pool

Rock Lake Motel
(941) 334-3242
2930 Palm Beach Blvd.
17 rooms - $35-59
Pets: Welcome
Creature Comforts: CCTV, a/c,
kit, and along a lake

Ta Ki-Ki Motel
(941) 334-2135
http://www.cyberstreet.com/takiki
2631 - 1st St.
24 rooms - $40-79
Pets: Welcome w/$6 fee
Creature Comforts: CCTV, a/c,
kit, pool, boat docks

Travelodge
(800) 578-7878, (941) 334-2284
http://www.travelodge.com
2038 W. 1st St.
48 rooms - $35-78
Pets: Welcome
Creature Comforts: CCTV, a/c,
pool, and river views

Wellesley Inns
(800) 444-8888, (941) 278-3949
http://www.wellesleyinns.com
440 Ford St.
105 rooms - $45-129
Pets: Under 30 lbs. w/$10 fee
Creature Comforts: CCTV, a/c,
refrig, micro, cont. brkfst, hlth
club access, pool

FT. MYERS BEACH
Anchor Inn Cottages
(941) 463-2630
285 Virginia Ave.
10 rooms - $345-1,250/wk
Pets: Welcome w/$50 fee
Creature Comforts: CCTV, a/c,
kit, pool

Best Western Inn
(800) 528-1234, (941) 463-6000
http://www.bestwestern.com
684 Estero Blvd.
75 rooms - $85-245
Pets: Small pets w/$10 fee
Creature Comforts: CCTV, a/c,
kit, cont. brkfst, pool, on the
beach-water sports

FT. PIERCE
Days Inn
(800) DAYS-INN, (561) 466-4066
http://www.daysinn.com
6651 Darter Ct.
125 rooms - $39-79
Pets: Welcome w/$10 fee
Creature Comforts: CCTV, a/c,
refrig, pool

Holiday Inn Express
(800) HOLIDAY, (561) 464-5000
http://www.holiday-inn.com
7151 Okeechobee Rd.
99 rooms - $70-109
Pets: Welcome $25 dep.
Creature Comforts: CCTV, a/c,
cont. brkfst, pool

Motel 6
(800) 4-MOTEL6, (561) 461-9937
http://www.motel6.com
2500 Peters Rd.
120 rooms - $30-49
Pets: Under 30 lbs.welcome
Creature Comforts: CCTV, a/c,
pool

FT. WALTON BEACH
Econo Lodge
(800) 55-ECONO, (850) 243-7123
http://www.econolodge.com
1284 Marier Dr.
102 rooms - $39-69
Pets: Small pets w/$5 fee
Creature Comforts: CCTV, a/c,
kit, and water views

Marina Motel
(850) 244-1129
1345 Miracle Strip Pkwy.
39 rooms - $45-109
Pets: $8 fee, credit card deposit
Creature Comforts: CCTV, a/c, kit, cont. brkfst, pool

GAINESVILLE
Apartment Inn Motel
(352) 371-3811
4401 SW 13th St.
36 rooms - $40-59
Pets: Welcome
Creature Comforts: CCTV, a/c

Days Inn
(800) DAYS-INN, (352) 332-3426
http://www.daysinn.com
7516 Newberry Rd.
102 rooms - $40-105
Pets: Welcome w/$5 fee
Creature Comforts: CCTV, a/c, refrig, restaurant, cont. brkfst, pool

Howard Johnson
(800) I-Go-Hojo, (352) 335-6355
http://www.hojo.com
3461 SW Williston Rd.
38 rooms - $35-59
Pets: Small pets welcome
Creature Comforts: CCTV, a/c, cont. brkfst, pool

La Quinta Inn
(800) Nu-Rooms, (352) 332-6466
http://www.laquinta.com
920 NW 69th Terr.
133 rooms - $50-69
Pets: Small pets welcome
Creature Comforts: CCTV, a/c, cont. brkfst, pool

Magnolia Plantation
(352) 375-6653
http://www.magnoliabnb.com
309 SE 7th St.
5 rms/2 cottages - $125-175
Pets: Welcome in cottages
Creature Comforts: Highly recommended, stunning inn w/ beautiful gardens, luxurious amenities, sophisticated decor, French doors, Chippendale furnishings, antiques, CCTV, VCR, Jacuzzi, full brkfst

Motel 6
(800) 4-MOTEL6, (352) 373-1604
http://www.motel6.com
4000 SW 40th Blvd.
122 rooms - $30-48
Pets: Under 30 lbs. welcome
Creature Comforts: CCTV, a/c, pool

Ramada Limited
(800) 2-Ramada, (352) 373-0392
http://www.ramada.com
4021 SW 40th Blvd.
112 rooms - $59-90
Pets: Small pets w/$5 fee
Creature Comforts: CCTV, a/c, pool

Residence Inn
(800) 331-3131, (352) 371-2101
http://www.residenceinn.com
4001 SW 13th St.
82 rooms - $95-169
Pets: Under 40 lbs. w/5 daily fee, $50 cleaning fee, $200 dep.
Creature Comforts: CCTV, a/c, kit, cont. brkfst, pool

Super 8 Motel
(800) 800-8000, (352) 378-3888
http://www.super8.com
4202 SW 40th Blvd.
62 rooms - $40-59
Pets: Welcome
Creature Comforts: CCTV, a/c, refrig, micro, cont. brkfst

Travelodge
(800) 578-7878, (352) 372-4319
http://www.travelodge.com
3103 NW 13th St.
43 rooms - $40-79
Pets: Welcome w/$10 fee
Creature Comforts: CCTV, a/c

HAINES CITY
Best Western Inn
(800) 528-1234, (941) 421-6929
http://www.bestwestern.com
605 B. Moore Rd.
49 rooms - $45-90
Pets: Small pets w/$50 dep.
Creature Comforts: CCTV, a/c, micro, refrig, pool

Econo Lodge
(800) 55-ECONO, (941) 422-8621
http://www.econolodge.com
1504 Rte. 27
120 rooms - $40-79
Pets: Small pets w/$5 fee
Creature Comforts: CCTV, a/c, refrig, micro, pool

HOLIDAY
Best Western Inn
(800) 528-1234, (813) 937-4121
http://www.bestwestern.com
2337 Rte. 19
138 rooms - $60-99
Pets: Small pets w/$5 fee
Creature Comforts: CCTV, a/c, refrig, restaurant, pool

HOLLYWOOD
Comfort Inn
(800) 228-5150, (954) 922-1600
http://www.comfortinn.com
2520 Stirling Rd.
189 rooms - $50-145
Pets: Welcome w/$25 fee
Creature Comforts: CCTV, VCR, a/c, refrig, micro, cont. brkfst, pool

Days Inn
(800) DAYS-INN, (954) 923-7300
http://www.daysinn.com
2601 N. 29th Ave.
114 rooms - $50-139
Pets: Welcome w/$10 fee
Creature Comforts: CCTV, a/c, refrig, cont. brkfst, pool, whirlpool

Green Seas Motel
(954) 923-6564, (954) 927-5707
www.greeenseasmotel.com
1419 S. Federal Hwy.
29 rooms - $40-109
Pets: Smaller pets w/$3 fee
Creature Comforts: CCTV, a/c, kit, pool

Howard Johnson
(800) I-Go-Hojo, (954) 923-1516
http://www.hojo.com
2900 Polk St.
72 rooms - $45-99
Pets: Small pets welcome
Creature Comforts: CCTV, a/c,
pool

Mirador Resort Motel
(954) 922-7581
http://www.miradormotel.com
901 S. Ocean Dr.
41 rooms - $35-75
Pets: Small pets w/$25 fee
Creature Comforts: CCTV, a/c,
kit, restaurant, pool

Montreal Inn
(954) 925-4443
324 Balboa St.
20 rooms - $35-89
Pets: Welcome
Creature Comforts: CCTV, a/c,
kit, pool

HOLMES BEACH
The Inn Between
(941) 778-0751
105 - 66th St.
4 rooms - $395-575/wk
Pets: Welcome w/$20 fee, CC dep.
Creature Comforts: CCTV, a/c,
kit

HOMESTEAD
Days Inn
(800) DAYS-INN, (305) 245-1260
http://www.daysinn.com
51 S. Homestead Blvd.
100 rooms - $45-129
Pets: Welcome
Creature Comforts: CCTV, a/c,
refrig, restaurant, cont. brkfst, pool

Everglades
(305) 247-4117
605 S. Krome Ave.
15 rooms - $35-64
Pets: Small pets welcome
Creature Comforts: CCTV, a/c,
pool

Holiday Inn Express
(800) HOLIDAY, (305) 247-7020
http://www.holiday-inn.com
990 N. Homestead Blvd.
145 rooms - $50-149
Pets: Small pets welcome
Creature Comforts: CCTV, a/c,
pool

Howard Johnson Lodge
(800) I-Go-Hojo, (305) 248-2121
http://www.hojo.com
1020 N. Homestead Blvd.
49 rooms - $45-79
Pets: Small pets welcome
Creature Comforts: CCTV, a/c,
restaurant, pool

Room at the Inn
(305) 246-0492
15830 SW 240th St.
4 rooms - $85-119
Pets: Welcome
Creature Comforts: CCTV, a/c,
fireplace, full brkfst, pool,
whirlpool

HOMOSASSA SPRINGS
Howard Johnson Riverside
(800) I-Go-Hojo, (352) 628-2474
http://www.hojo.com
5297 S. Cherokee Way
72 rooms - $60-125
Pets: Small pets w/$5 fee
Creature Comforts: CCTV, a/c,
restaurant, pool

Ramada Inn
(800) 2-Ramada, (352) 628-4311
http://www.ramada.com
4076 S. Suncoast Blvd.
105 rooms - $69-125
Pets: Small pets w/$5 fee
Creature Comforts: CCTV, a/c,
refrig, restaurant, pool

INDIALANTIC
Baymont Inns
(877)BAYMONT, (407) 779-9994
http://www.baymontinns.com
2900 N. A1A
25 rooms - $35-105
Pets: Small pets w/$10 fee
Creature Comforts: CCTV, a/c,
kit, cont. brkfst

Casablanca Inn
(800) 333-7273, (407) 728-7188
1805 North Highway A-1-A
34 rooms - $40-80
Pets: Small pets w/$5 daily fee
Creature Comforts: CCTV, a/c,
kit, pool

Melbourne Oceanfront Suites
(800) 221-2222, (407) 777-5000
1665 N. A1A
207 rooms - $99-169
Pets: Welcome w/$5 fee, $25 dep.
Creature Comforts: CCTV,
VCR, a/c, refrig, Jacuzzis,
restaurant, cont. brkfst, pool

Oceanfront Cottages
(407) 725-8474
612 Wavecrest Ave.
4 rooms - $90-125
Pets: $10 fee, $100 dep.
Creature Comforts: CCTV, a/c,
kit

INDIAN SHORES
Holiday Villas
(800) 428-4852, (813) 596-4952
19610 Gulf Blvd.
72 villas - $75-105
Pets: Under 15 lbs. w/$50 fee
Creature Comforts: CCTV,
VCR, a/c, kit, pool

INVERNESS
The Crown Hotel
(888) 856-4455, (352) 344-5555
http://www.chronicle-online.com/
crownhotel.htm
109 N. Seminole Ave.
33 rooms - $40-125
Pets: Welcome w/$10 fee
Creature Comforts: 1890's hotel
with Victorian accents and an Old
English flavor, reproductions of
the Royal crown jewels, Queen-
Anne furnishings, antiques,
CCTV, a/c, refrig, restaurant,
English pub-darts, full brkfst, pool

ISLAMORADA
B&B Islamorada
(305) 664-9321
81175 Old Hwy.
3 rooms - $40-78
Pets: Small pets w/$5 fee
Creature Comforts: CCTV, a/c,
refrig, full brkfst

Coconut Grove Resort
(305) 664-0123
84801 Old Hwy.
9 rooms - $49-155
Pets: Under 30 lbs. welcome
Creature Comforts: CCTV, a/c,
kit, restaurant, pool access, ultra
light rentals

Lookout Lodge
(800) 870-1772, (305) 852-9915
http://www.searavendiver.com
87770 Overseas Hwy.
9 rooms - $75-175
Pets: In certain rooms
Creature Comforts: Florida Bay
waterside lodge w/very attractive
tiled bedrms, contemp. furnish,
CCTV, a/c, kit, private beach,
scuba diving, snorkeling, boats

Tropica Vista Motel
(305) 852-8799
90701 Overseas Hwy.
www.floridakeys.sl.us/tropicv.htm
26 rooms - $39-99
Pets: Welcome w/$10 fee
Creature Comforts: CCTV, a/c,
kit, pool, whirlpool

JACKSONVILLE
Admiral Benbow Inn
(904) 741-4254
14691 Duval Rd.
120 rooms - $40-69
Pets: Small pets w/$10 fee
Creature Comforts: CCTV, a/c,
kit, pool

Amerisuites
(800) 833-1516, (904) 737-4477
http://www.amerisuites.com
8277 Western Way Cr.
110 rooms - $89-159
Pets: Welcome w/$10 fee
Creature Comforts: CCTV,
VCR, a/c, kit, Jacuzzis, cont.
brkfst, pool

Best Inns of America
(800) 237-8466, (904) 739-3323
http://www.bestinns.com
8220 Dix Ellis Tr.
108 rooms - $45-68
Pets: Small pets welcome
Creature Comforts: CCTV, a/c,
refrig, cont. brkfst, pool

Baymont Inns
(877)BAYMONT, (904) 268-9999
http://www.baymontinns.com
3199 Hartley Rd.
100 rooms - $45-68
Pets: Small pets welcome
Creature Comforts: CCTV, a/c,
cont. brkfst, pool

Comfort Inn
(800) 228-5150, (904) 739-1155
http://www.comfortinn.com
8333 Dix Ellis Tr.
125 rooms - $60-139
Pets: Small pets w/$20 fee
Creature Comforts: CCTV,
VCR, a/c, micro, refrig, restaurant,
pool, whirlpool

Days Inn
(800) DAYS-INN, (904) 783-7550
http://www.daysinn.com
460 S. Lane Ave.
135 rooms - $30-79
Pets: Welcome w/$5 fee
Creature Comforts: CCTV, a/c,
refrig, restaurant, cont. brkfst, pool

Economy Inns of America
(904) 281-0198
4300 Salisbury Rd.
125 rooms - $40-64
Pets: Small pets welcome
Creature Comforts: CCTV, a/c,
refrig, cont. brkfst, pool

Hampton Inn, Airport
(800) Hampton, (904) 741-4980
http://www.hampton-inn.com
1170 Airport Entrance Rd.
112 rooms - $65-89
Pets: Welcome
Creature Comforts: CCTV, a/c,
pool

Holiday Inn
(800) HOLIDAY, (904) 741-4404
http://www.holiday-inn.com
14670 Duval Rd.
485 rooms - $70-99
Pets: Welcome
Creature Comforts: CCTV, a/c,
restaurant, hlth clb, pool

Homewood Suites
(800) 225-5466, (904) 733-9299
http://www.homewoodsuites.com
8737 Baymeadows Rd.
115 rooms - $119-185
Pets: Welcome w/$75 fee
Creature Comforts: CCTV, a/c,
kit, pool, hlth clb, whirlpool

La Quinta Inn
(800) Nu-Rooms, (904) 731-9940
http://www.laquinta.com
8255 Dix Ellis Tr.
105 rooms - $55-79
Pets: Small pets welcome
Creature Comforts: CCTV, a/c,
refrig, micro, cont. brkfst, pool

La Quinta Inn
(800) Nu-Rooms, (904) 778-9539
http://www.laquinta.com
8555 Blanding Blvd.
120 rooms - $60-79
Pets: Small pets welcome
Creature Comforts: CCTV, a/c,
refrig, micro, cont. brkfst, pool

La Quinta Inn
(800) Nu-Rooms, (904) 751-6960
http://www.laquinta.com
812 Dunn Ave.
128 rooms - $55-78
Pets: Small pets welcome
Creature Comforts: CCTV, a/c,
refrig, micro, cont. brkfst, pool

Microtel Inn
(800) 771-7171, (904) 741-1133
http://www.microtel.com
14585 Duval Rd.
99 rooms - $40-59
Pets: Welcome
Creature Comforts: CCTV, a/c

Microtel Inn
(800) 771-7171, (904) 281-6664
http://www.microtel.com
4940 Mustang Rd.
99 rooms - $40-59
Pets: Welcome
Creature Comforts: CCTV, a/c

Motel 6, Airport
(800) 4-MOTEL6, (904) 757-8600
http://www.motel6.com
10885 Harts Rd.
126 rooms - $35-54
Pets: Under 30 lbs.welcome
Creature Comforts: CCTV, a/c,
pool

Motel 6
(800) 4-MOTEL6, (904) 731-8400
http://www.motel6.com
8285 Dix Ellis Tr.
109 rooms - $39-55
Pets: Under 30 lbs.welcome
Creature Comforts: CCTV, a/c, pool

Motel 6
(800) 4-MOTEL6, (904) 777-6100
http://www.motel6.com
6107 Youngerman Rd.
126 rooms - $35-55
Pets: Under 30 lbs. welcome
Creature Comforts: CCTV, a/c, pool

Ramada Inn
(800) 2-Ramada, (904) 268-8080
http://www.ramada.com
3130 Hartley Rd.
155 rooms - $55-165
Pets: $5 fee & $15 dep.
Creature Comforts: CCTV, a/c, refrig, restaurant, pool

Ramada Inn
(800) 2-Ramada, (904) 737-8000
http://www.ramada.com
5624 Cagle Rd.
132 rooms - $40-119
Pets: $5 fee & $25 dep.
Creature Comforts: CCTV, a/c, refrig, micro, restaurant, pool

Red Roof Inn
(800) The Roof, (904) 741-4488
http://www.redroof.com
14701 Airport Entrance Rd.
104 rooms - $50-76
Pets: $5 fee & $25 dep.
Creature Comforts: CCTV, a/c

Red Roof Inn
(800) The Roof, (904) 777-1000
http://www.redroof.com
6099 Youngerman Rd.
104 rooms - $40-65
Pets: $5 fee & $25 dep.
Creature Comforts: CCTV, a/c

Residence Inn
(800) 331-3131, (904) 733-8088
http://www.residenceinn.com
8365 Dix Ellis Tr.
113 rooms - $95-189
Pets: Welcome w/$50 fee
Creature Comforts: CCTV, a/c, kit, cont. brkfst, hlth club, pool

Super 8 Motel
(800) 800-8000, (904) 751-3888
http://www.super8.com
10901 Harts Rd.
61 rooms - $39-75
Pets: Welcome w/permission
Creature Comforts: CCTV, a/c, cont. brkfst

Travelodge
(800) 578-7878, (904) 731-7317
http://www.travelodge.com
8765 Baymeadows Rd.
119 rooms - $40-75
Pets: Welcome
Creature Comforts: CCTV, a/c, micro, refrig, restaurant, cont. brkfst, pool

JASPER
Days Inn
(800) DAYS-INN, (904) 792-2507
http://www.daysinn.com
Rtes. 6 & 75
55 rooms - $35-79
Pets: Welcome w/$3 fee
Creature Comforts: CCTV, a/c, restaurant, cont. brkfst, pool, whirlpool

Scottish Inns
(800) 251-1962, (904) 792-1234
http://www.reservahost.com
Rte. 3, Box 136
77 rooms - $30-45
Pets: $5 fee, credit card deposit
Creature Comforts: CCTV, a/c, cont. brkfst, pool

JENNINGS
Quality Inn
(800) 228-5151, (904) 938-3501
http://www.qualityinn.com
Rtes. 143 & 75
122 rooms - $45-75
Pets: Welcome w/$10 fee
Creature Comforts: CCTV, a/c, refrig, restaurant, tennis, pool, whirlpool

Jennings House Inn
(904) 938-3305
Rte. 143, Box 179
16 rooms - $25-44
Pets: Welcome
Creature Comforts: CCTV, a/c, refrig, and pool

JUNO BEACH
Holiday Inn Express
(800) HOLIDAY, (561) 622-4366
http://www.holiday-inn.com
13950 Rte. 1
45 rooms - $40-199
Pets: Welcome w/$25 fee
Creature Comforts: CCTV, a/c, micro, refrig, cont. brkfst, pool

KENDALL
Amerisuites
(800) 833-1516, (305) 279-8688
http://www.amerisuites.com
11520 SW - 88th St.
66 rooms - $89-149
Pets: Small pets w/$10 fee
Creature Comforts: CCTV, a/c, refrig, micro, cont. brkfst, pool

Wellesley Inns
(800) 444-8888, (305) 270-0359
http://www.wellesleyinns.com
11750 Mills Dr.
66 rooms - $75-129
Pets: Under 30 lbs. w/$10 fee
Creature Comforts: CCTV, a/c, refrig, micro, cont. brkfst, pool

KEY LARGO
Howard Johnson Resort Hotel
(800) I-Go-Hojo, (305) 451-1400
http://www.hojo.com
Route 1
99 rooms - $99-269
Pets: Welcome w/$10 fee
Creature Comforts: CCTV, a/c, micro, refrig, restaurant, pool, and beach-boating

KEY WEST
Avalon B&B
(800) 848-1317, (305) 294-8233
http://www.avalonbnb.com
1317 Duval St.
10 rooms - $75-195
Pets: Welcome
Creature Comforts: New owners have completely refurbished the inn, new hardwood floors w/ Oriental rugs & dhurrie rugs, white wicker and rattan, four poster canopy beds, CCTV, a/c, refrig, high ceilings, sophisticated décor, romantic cottages, cont. brkfst, and a whirlpool

Alexander Palms Court
(305) 296-6413
715 South St.
12 rooms - $75-379
Pets: Welcome w/$50 fee
Creature Comforts: CCTV, a/c, kit, pool, whirlpool

Boathouse Resort & Marina
(305) 292-0017
1445 S. Roosevelt Blvd.
33 rooms - $175-375
Pets: Welcome w/$200 dep.
Creature Comforts: CCTV, a/c, kit, pool

Caribbean House Motel
(305) 296-1600
226 Petronia St.
10 rooms - $45-85
Pets: Welcome
Creature Comforts: CCTV, a/c, kit, cont. brkfst

Casa Alante Guest Cottages
(305) 293-0702
http://www.casaalante.com
1435 S. Roosevelt Blvd.
10 cottages - $50-175
Pets: Welcome w/$5 fee
Creature Comforts: CCTV, a/c, kit, cont. brkfst

Center Court Inn
(800) 797-8787, (305) 296-9292
http://www.centercourtkw.com
916 Center St.
7 rooms - $99-335
Pets: Welcome w/$10 fee
Creature Comforts: Centrally located charming inn and cottages in a secluded setting, Caribbean color schemes, bleached woods, wicker & oak furnishings, CCTV, VCR, a/c, stereos, kit, Jacuzzi, buffet brkfst, tanning deck, pool, hlth clb, whirlpool, and priv. yards

Chelsea House
(800) 845-8859, (305) 296-2211
http://www.chelseahousekw.com
707 Truman Ave.
15 rooms - $75-295
Pets: Welcome w/$10 daily fee
Creature Comforts: 1870's Victorian mansion w/ Caribbean accents, pastel colors, high ceilings, antiques, wicker and rattan, furnishings, stained glass doors, veranda, CCTV, VCR, a/c, kit, Jacuzzis, pool, cont. brkfst

Courtney's Place
(800) Unwind-9, (305) 294-3480
http://www.keywestparadise.com/courtney.html
720 Whitmarsh Ln.
14 rooms - $99-185
Pets: In first floor and cottages
Creature Comforts: Gingerbread accents and old Key West ambiance, high-energy affable hostess, built on the site of buried treasure, cottages, colorful tropical fabrics, CCTV, VCR, a/c, kit, full brkfst, hlth clb access, pool, access to beach

The Cuban Club
(800) 432-4849, (305) 296-0465
http://www.keywest.com/cubanclb.html
1108 Duval St.
16 rooms - $75-455
Pets: Under 200 lbs. w/$200 dep.
Creature Comforts: A former club for Cubans involved in cigar industry, beautiful, spacious rooms w/intriguing details, four poster beds, French doors lead to wrap-around balconies, elegant decor, CCTV, a/c, refrig, cont. brkfst

Curry Mansion Inn
(800) 253-3466, (305) 294-5349
http://www.currymansion.com
511 Caroline St.
28 rooms - $125-225
Pets: Under 20 lbs. welcome
Creature Comforts: Exquisite 1899 Victorian Mansion on Nat'l Historic Regstr, one of Key West's most desirable inns, elegant décor, antiques and wicker furnishings, Victorian accents, Tiffany glass sliding doors, CCTV, a/c, piano, refrig, cont. brkfst, pool, and a beach club

Days Inn
(800) DAYS-INN, (305) 294-3742
http://www.daysinn.com
3852 N. Roosevelt Blvd.
133 rooms - $99-275
Pets: Welcome w/$15 fee
Creature Comforts: CCTV, a/c, refrig, restaurant, cont. brkfst, pool

Douglas House
(800) 833-0372, (305) 294-5269
http://www.douglashouse.com
419 Amelia St.
15 rooms - $89-189
Pets: Welcome w/$10 fee
Creature Comforts: A pair of quaint Victorian-Bahamian style guest houses, cathedral ceilings and pickled woods, Caribbean color schemes, rooms on upper flrs have garden views, Oriental rugs, crystal chandeliers, CCTV, VCR, a/c, kit, Jacuzzi, cont. brkfst, tropical gardens, 2 pools

Frances Street Bottle Inn
(800) 294-8530, (305) 294-1628
http://www.bottleinn.com
535 Frances St.
7 rooms - $89-169
Pets: Welcome in 2 first flr. rms.
Creature Comforts: Charming Key West decor w/ Carribean colors, antique bottle collection, balconies & brick patio, CCTV, VCR, a/c, kit, Jacuzzi, cont. brkfst

Incentra Carriage House
(305) 296-5565
729 Whitehead St.
8 rooms - $75-295
Pets: Small pets welcome
Creature Comforts: Charming but eclectic alternative lifestyle guest house one block from Hemingway's House, 100 varieties of plant life, hammock, antiques, wicker and rattan, pastel color schemes, sisal rugs, and cathedral ceilings, CCTV, a/c, kit, cont. brkfst, pool

Key Lodge Motel
(800) 458-1296, (305) 296-9915
1004 Duval St.
23 rooms - $75-179
Pets: Welcome w/$10 fee
Creature Comforts: CCTV, a/c, refrig, pool

Nassau House
(800) 296-8513, (305) 296-8513
http://www.nassauhouse.com
1016 Fleming St.
8 rooms - $75-225
Pets: Welcome w/$20 fee
Creature Comforts: Centrally located, the 1894 inn offers unique cottages and suites, antiques, eclectic furnishings and artwork, CCTV, a/c, kit, hearty brkfst, lagoon pool/waterfall, whirlpool

Old Customs House Inn
(305) 294-8507
www.keywest.com/customshs.html
124 Duval St.
6 rooms - $75-200
Pets: Welcome
Creature Comforts: CCTV, VCR, a/c, refrig, restaurant

Ramada Inn
(800) 2-Ramada, (305) 294-5541
http://www.ramada.com
3420 Roosevelt Blvd.
103 rooms - $80-199
Pets: Welcome w/$10 fee
Creature Comforts: CCTV, a/c, kit, restaurant, pool, mini golf

Sea Isle Resort
(305) 294-5188
915 Windsor Lane
24 rooms - $75-149
Pets: Leashed w/$10 fee
Creature Comforts: Encircling a charming courtyard, CCTV, a/c, kit, Jacuzzi, cont. brkfst, pool, and a hlth clb

Speak Easy Inn
(305) 296-2680
http://www.keywestcigar.com
1117 Duval St.
14 rooms - $75-175
Pets: Welcome
Creature Comforts: CCTV, VCR, a/c, refrig, store

Southernmost Point
(305) 294-0715
www.southernmostpoint.com
1327 Duval St.
6 rooms - $55-225
Pets: Welcome
Creature Comforts: An 1855 rambling, shingle-style Victorian mansion, a block from the water, Victorian collectibles, eclectic décor and furnishings, floral accents, high ceilings w/fans, veranda, white wicker, CCTV, a/c, kit, cont. "plus" brkfst

Travelers Palm Garden Cottage
(800) 294-9560, (305) 294-9560
http://www.travelerspalm.com
815 Catherine St.
6 rooms - $95-395
Pets: Small pets welcome
Creature Comforts: CCTV, a/c, kit, pools, hammocks, boating

Whispers Inn
(800) 856-SHHH, (305) 294-5969
http://www.whispersbb.com
409 William St.
7 rooms - $89-185
Pets: Welcome w/$25 fee
Creature Comforts: Lovely Nat'l Hist. Register Victorian-Bahamian house w/antiques, four poster and canopy beds, claw foot tubs, a/c, CCTV, refrig, gourmet brkfst, sauna, steamroom, great gardens, access to a pool, hlth, beach clb

KISSIMMEE
Best Western Inn
(800) 528-1234, (407) 396-0707
http://www.bestwestern.com
5565 W. Irlo Bronson Pkwy.
403 rooms - $40-120
Pets: Under 25 lbs. w/$5 fee
Creature Comforts: CCTV, a/c, tennis, pool, whirlpool

Comfort Inn
(800) 228-5150, (407) 396-7500
http://www.comfortinn.com
7571 W. Irlo Bronson Pkwy.
280 rooms - $35-89
Pets: Small pets w/$10 fee
Creature Comforts: CCTV, a/c, refrig, restaurant, pool

Comfort Suites
(800) 228-5150, (407) 390-9888
http://www.comfortinn.com
7888 W. Irlo Bronson Pkwy.
152 rooms - $75-165
Pets: Small pets w/$10 fee
Creature Comforts: CCTV, a/c, kit, restaurant, cont. brkfst, pool, whirlpool

Days Inn
(800) DAYS-INN, (407) 396-7969
http://www.daysinn.com
5840 W. Irlo Bronson Hwy.
404 rooms - $30-135
Pets: Welcome
Creature Comforts: CCTV, a/c, refrig, restaurant, pool

Days Inn
(800) DAYS-INN, (407) 396-7900
http://www.daysinn.com
5820 W. Irlo Bronson Hwy.
300 rooms - $50-175
Pets: Welcome
Creature Comforts: CCTV, a/c, kit, restaurant, 3 pools

Days Inn
(800) DAYS-INN, (407) 846-8423
http://www.daysinn.com
2095 W. Irlo Bronson Hwy.
122 rooms - $30-99
Pets: Welcome w/$10 fee
Creature Comforts: CCTV, a/c, refrig, restaurant, pool

Fantasy World Club Villas
(800) 874-8047, (407) 396-1808
www.destinationuniversal.com
2935 Hart Ave.
105 rooms - $99-199
Pets: Welcome w/$15 fee
Creature Comforts: CCTV, VCR, a/c, kit, restaurant, 3 pools, spa, tennis, whirlpool

Holiday Inn
(800) HOLIDAY, (407) 396-4488
http://www.holiday-inn.com
5678 W. Irlo Bronson Hwy.
615 rooms - $65-139
Pets: Small pets welcome (pet goodie bag)
Creature Comforts: CCTV, VCR, a/c, refrig, restaurant, tennis, lawn sports, pool

Holiday Inn
(800) HOLIDAY, (407) 846-2713
http://www.holiday-inn.com
2009 W. Vine St.
200 rooms - $49-119
Pets: Small pets w/$10 fee
Creature Comforts: CCTV, a/c, refrig, restaurant, tennis, lawn sports, pool

Homewood Suites
(800) 225-5466, (407) 396-2229
http://www.homewoodsuites.com
3100 Parkway Blvd.
155 rooms - $79-189
Pets: $75 fee & $250 deposit
Creature Comforts: Near Disney World, great family find, large villas w/fireplaces, reproduction country antiques, kit, CCTV, VCR, a/c, cont. brkfst, pool, hlth clb, sports ltd, whirlpool

Howard Johnson
(800) I-Go-Hojo, (407) 846-4900
http://www.hojo.com
2323 E. Irlo Bronson Hwy.
200 rooms - $39-99
Pets: Welcome w/$5 fee
Creature Comforts: CCTV, a/c, refrig, micro, restaurant, pool

Inns of America
(800) 826-0778, (407) 396-7743
http://www.innsamerica.com
2945 Entry Pt. Blvd.
115 rooms - $55-75
Pets: Small pets welcome
Creature Comforts: CCTV, a/c, refrig, micro, cont. brkfst, pool

Motel 6
(800) 4-MOTEL6, (407) 396-6422
http://www.motel6.com
7455 W. Irlo Bronson Hwy.
148 rooms - $39-65
Pets: Under 30 lbs. welcome
Creature Comforts: CCTV, a/c, pool

Ramada Inn
(800) 2-Ramada, (407) 396-1212
http://www.ramada.com
4559 W. Rte. 192
114 rooms - $29-69
Pets: Welcome w/$6 fee
Creature Comforts: CCTV, a/c, refrig, restaurant, pool

Ramada Inn
(800) 2-Ramada, (407) 396-2212
http://www.ramada.com
5055 W. Rte. 192
107 rooms - $35-79
Pets: Welcome w/$6 fee
Creature Comforts: TV, a/c, pool

Red Roof Inn
(800) The Roof, (407) 396-0065
http://www.redroof.com
4970 King's Heath Rd.
101 rooms - $45-90
Pets: Small pets w/$5 fee
Creature Comforts: CCTV, a/c, pool, whirlpool

Summerfield Resort
(407) 847-7222
2422 Summerfield Pl.
38 rooms - $99-189
Pets: Welcome w/$50 fee
Creature Comforts: CCTV, VCR, a/c, kit, pool, whirlpool

LABELLE
The River's Edge Motel
(941) 675-6062
285 N. River Rd.
13 rooms - $50-69
Pets: Welcome
Creature Comforts: CCTV, a/c, kit, pool

LAKE BUENA VISTA
Comfort Inn
(800) 228-5150, (407) 239-7300
http://www.comfortinn.com
8442 Palm Pkwy.
650 rooms - $40-95
Pets: Small pets w/$5 fee
Creature Comforts: CCTV, a/c, restaurant, pool

Days Inn
(800) DAYS-INN, (407) 239-4646
http://www.daysinn.com
12490 Apopka-Vineland Rd.
245 rooms - $49-165
Pets: Small pets w/$10 fee
Creature Comforts: CCTV, a/c, refrig, micro, restaurant, pool

Days Inn
(800) DAYS-INN, (407) 239-0325
http://www.daysinn.com
12799 Apopka-Vineland Rd.
203 rooms - $49-189
Pets: Small pets w/$10 fee
Creature Comforts: CCTV, a/c, refrig, micro, restaurant, pool

Holiday Inn
(800) HOLIDAY, (407) 239-4500
http://www.holiday-inn.com
13351 Rte. 535
505 rooms - $89-199
Pets: Under 25 lbs. welcome
Creature Comforts: CCTV, VCR, a/c, restaurant, pool, whirlpool

Residence Inn
(800) 331-3131, (407) 239-7700
http://www.residenceinn.com
689 rooms - $149-279
Pets: Under 50 lbs. welcome w/ $50 fee and a $150 dep.
Creature Comforts: CCTV, VCR, a/c, kit, restaurant, cont. brkfst, tennis, pool, and whirlpools

LAKE CITY
Best Western Inn
(800) 528-1234, (904) 752-3801
http://www.bestwestern.com
Rtes. 75 & 90
80 rooms - $45-90
Pets: Under 25 lbs. w/$10 fee
Creature Comforts: CCTV, a/c, cont. brkfst, pool, whirlpool

Comfort Inn
(800) 228-5150, (904) 755-1344
http://www.comfortinn.com
4515 Rte. 90
99 rooms - $59-79
Pets: Welcome
Creature Comforts: CCTV, a/c, Jacuzzi, pool

Driftwood Motel
(904) 755-3545
Route 90
20 rooms - $25-44
Pets: Small pets w/$5 fee
Creature Comforts: CCTV, a/c

Econo Lodge
(800) 55-ECONO, (904) 752-7891
http://www.econolodge.com
Rtes. 75 & 90
62 rooms - $35-69
Pets: Small pets w/$3 fee
Creature Comforts: CCTV, VCR, a/c, cont. brkfst, pool

Howard Johnson Lodge
(800) I-Go-Hojo, (904) 752-6262
http://www.hojo.com
Route 13
91 rooms - $35-65
Pets: Welcome
Creature Comforts: CCTV, a/c,
restaurant, pool

Motel 6
(800) 4-MOTEL6, (904) 755-4664
http://www.motel6.com
Hall of Fame Dr.
120 rooms - $29-44
Pets: Under 30 lbs.welcome
Creature Comforts: TV, a/c, pool

Ramada Inn
(800) 2-Ramada, (904) 752-7550
http://www.ramada.com
Route 75
120 rooms - $39-75
Pets: Small pets w/$5 fee
Creature Comforts: CCTV, a/c,
refrig, restaurant, pool, whirlpool

Red Carpet Inn
(800) 251-1962, (904) 755-1707
http://www.reservahost.com
Route 90
54 rooms - $29-69
Pets: Small pets $5 fee
Creature Comforts: CCTV, a/c,
cont. brkfst

Rodeway Inn
(800) 228-2000, (904) 755-5203
http://www.rodeway.com
Route 90
45 rooms - $29-45
Pets: Welcome w/$5 fee
Creature Comforts: CCTV, a/c

Scottish Inns
(800) 251-1962, (904) 755-0230
http://www.reservahost.com
Route 90
33 rooms - $29-38
Pets: Welcome w/$5 fee
Creature Comforts: CCTV, a/c,
cont. brkfst

Travelodge
(800) 578-7878, (904) 755-9505
http://www.travelodge.com
Rtes. 75 & 90
50 rooms - $35-75
Pets: Welcome
Creature Comforts: CCTV, a/c,
restaurant, cont. brkfst

Villager Lodge
(904) 752-9369
Route 90
48 rooms - $29-48
Pets: Welcome w/$5 fee
Creature Comforts: CCTV, a/c,
refrig, micro, cont. brkfst, pool

LAKELAND
Baymont Inns
(877)BAYMONT, (941) 815-0606
http://www.baymontinns.com
4315 Lakeland Park Dr.
107 rooms - $55-89
Pets: Under 50 lbs. in smkng. rms.
Creature Comforts: CCTV, a/c,
kit, cont. brkfst, pool

Comfort Inn
(800) 228-5150, (941) 688-9221
http://www.comfortinn.com
1817 E. Memorial Blvd.
120 rooms - $60-119
Pets: Small pets welcome
Creature Comforts: CCTV, a/c,
restaurant, pool

Days Inn
(800) DAYS-INN, (941) 682-0303
http://www.daysinn.com
508 E. Memorial Blvd.
80 rooms - $30-199
Pets: Welcome w/$10 fee
Creature Comforts: CCTV, a/c,
refrig, restaurant, pool

Motel 6
(800) 4-MOTEL6, (941) 682-0643
http://www.motel6.com
3120 Rte. 98
124 rooms - $35-44
Pets: Under 30 lbs.welcome
Creature Comforts: CCTV, a/c,
pool

Wellesley Inns
(800) 444-8888, (941) 859-3399
http://www.wellesleyinns.com
3520 Rte. 98
105 rooms - $50-169
Pets: Under 25 lbs. w/$10 fee
Creature Comforts: CCTV,
VCR, a/c, refrig, micro, cont.
brkfst, pool

LAKE PLACID
Best Western Inn
(800) 528-1234, (941) 465-3133
http://www.bestwestern.com
2165 Rte. 27
99 rooms - $55-80
Pets: Welcome
Creature Comforts: CCTV, a/c,
restaurant, cont. brkfst, pool, and
access to golf

LAKE WALES
Lantern Motel
(941) 676-4821
3949 Rte. 27
22 rooms - $32-49
Pets: Welcome w/$5 fee
Creature Comforts: CCTV, a/c,
kit, restaurant, pool

LAKE WORTH
Lago Motor Inn
(561) 585-5246
714 S. Dixie Hwy.
18 rooms - $45-79
Pets: Welcome w/$8 fee
Creature Comforts: CCTV, a/c,
kit, pool

Martinique Motor Lodge
(561) 585-2502
801 S. Dixie Hwy.
25 rooms - $35-89
Pets: Small pets welcome w/$8
fee, and a $25 deposit
Creature Comforts: CCTV, a/c,
kit, pool

White Manor Motel
(561) 582-7437
1618 S. Federal Hwy.
14 rooms - $35-69
Pets: Small pets w/$10 fee, and a
credit card deposit
Creature Comforts: CCTV, a/c,
refrig, pool

LANTANA
Inns of America
(800) 826-0778, (561) 588-0456
http://www.innsamerica.com
7051 Seacrest Blvd.
90 rooms - $50-110
Pets: Welcome
Creature Comforts: CCTV, a/c,
refrig, micro, cont. brkfst, pool

Motel 6
(800) 4-MOTEL6, (561) 585-5833
http://www.motel6.com
1310 W. Lantana Rd.
154 rooms - $35-54
Pets: Under 30 lbs.welcome
Creature Comforts: CCTV, a/c, pool

Super 8 Motel
(800) 800-8000, (561) 585-3970
http://www.super8.com
1255 Hypoluxo Rd.
125 rooms - $55-85
Pets: Welcome
Creature Comforts: CCTV, a/c, kit, cont. brkfst, pool

LEESBURG
Shoney's Inn
(800) 222-2222, (352) 787-1210
http://www.shoneysinn.com
1308 N. 14th St.
124 rooms - $39-75
Pets: $10 fee and $50 deposit
Creature Comforts: CCTV, a/c, restaurant, pool

Super 8 Motel
(800) 800-8000, (352) 787-6363
http://www.super8.com
1392 N. Blvd.
53 rooms - $45-69
Pets: Welcome
Creature Comforts: CCTV, a/c, refrig, micro, cont. brkfst, pool

LIVE OAK
Econo Lodge
(800) 55-ECONO, (904) 362-7459
http://www.econolodge.com
Rtes. 129 & 10
52 rooms - $35-80
Pets: Small pets welcome
Creature Comforts: CCTV, a/c, refrig, micro, cont. brkfst, pool

LONGBOAT KEY
Cedars Tennis Club
(800) 433-4621, (941) 383-4621
http://www.visitlongboatkey.com/cedarstennis/
645 Cedars Ct.
96 condos - $850-1,500/wk.
Pets: Welcome in front units
Creature Comforts: Situated on Sarasota Bay amid 33 acres, attractive fully-equipped gray clapboard condos, balloon shades frame windows, rattan, wicker and pickled furnishings, screened lanais, CCTV, VCR, a/c, kit, fireplaces, Olympic pool, tennis program, lawn games, beach

Riviera Beach
(941) 383-2552
http://www.longboatkey.net/riviera
5451 Gulf of Mexico Dr.
11 rooms - $90-190
Pets: Small dogs w/$10 fee
Creature Comforts: CCTV, a/c, kit, pool, lawn games, access to tennis, beach resort

MACCLENNY
Econo Lodge
(800) 55-ECONO, (904) 259-3000
http://www.econolodge.com
Rtes. 121 & 10
53 rooms - $35-89
Pets: Small pets
Creature Comforts: CCTV, a/c, refrig, micro, Jacuzzi, cont. brkfst, pool

MADEIRA BEACH
Sandy Shores Condos.
(813) 392-1281
12924 Gulf Blvd.
55 rooms - $105-135
Pets: Under 20 lbs. w/$15-30 fee
Creature Comforts: CCTV, a/c, kit, pool

Sea Dawn Motel
(813) 391-7500
13733 Gulf Blvd.
8 rooms - $29-69
Pets: Small pets welcome
Creature Comforts: CCTV, a/c, kit

Waves Motel
(813) 391-3641
13343 Gulf Blvd.
14 rooms - $35-75
Pets: Small pets w/$5 fee
Creature Comforts: CCTV, a/c

MADISON
Days Inn
(800) DAYS-INN, (904) 973-3330
http://www.daysinn.com
Route 53
62 rooms - $45-69
Pets: Welcome w/$5 fee
Creature Comforts: CCTV, a/c, refrig, restaurant, cont. brkfst, pool

MARATHON
BoneFish Resort
(305) 743-7107
http://www.bonefishresort.com
Route 1
13 rooms - $40-109
Pets: Welcome w/$5 fee
Creature Comforts: CCTV, a/c, kit, on the ocean

Faro Blanco Marine Resort
(800) 759-3276, (305) 743-9018
1996 Oversees Hwy.
130 units - $60-275
Pets: Welcome in the cottages & houseboats w/an $18 fee
Creature Comforts: Expansive resort w/pink, green, and yellow cottages, natural board walls, dated decor, rqst houseboats w/ charming style, CCTV, a/c, kit, restaurant, pool, marina, fishing charters, on the ocean

Howard Johnson Resort
(800) I-Go-Hojo, (305) 743-8550
http://www.hojo.com
13351 Overseas Hwy.
80 rooms - $80-225
Pets: Welcome w/$10 fee
Creature Comforts: CCTV, a/c, restaurant, pool, access to marina

Pelican Motel
(305) 289-0011
Route 1
9 rooms - $45-85
Pets: Welcome w/$100 dep.
Creature Comforts: CCTV, a/c, refrig, pool

Rainbow Bend Resort
(800) 929-1505, (305) 289-1505
http://www.rainbowbend.com
Route 1
23 rooms - $125-255
Pets: Under 40 lbs. w/$15 fee
Creature Comforts: Charming
bright pink colored cottages,
naturally stained walls, lanais,
rattan & wicker, CCTV, VCR, a/c,
kit, patios, full brkfst, pool, beach,
whirlpool, waterfront, boating

MARCO ISLAND
Boat House Motel
(800) 528-6345, (941) 642-2400
http://theboathousemotel.com
1180 Edington Pl.
22 rooms - $85-240
Pets: $15 one-time fee
Creature Comforts: Waterside
motel & condos, nicely decorated,
request waterview rooms w/decks,
CCTV, VCR, a/c, kit, pool

MARIANNA
Best Western Inn
(800) 528-1234, (850) 526-5666
http://www.bestwestern.com
2086 Rte. 71
80 rooms - $45-69
Pets: Welcome
Creature Comforts: CCTV, a/c,
cont. brkfst, pool

Comfort Inn
(800) 228-5150, (850) 526-5600
http://www.comfortinn.com
2175 Rte 71
80 rooms - $50-79
Pets: Welcome
Creature Comforts: CCTV, a/c,
cont. brkfst, pool

Days Inn
(800) DAYS-INN, (850) 526-4311
http://www.daysinn.com
4132 Lafayette St.
58 rooms - $39-75
Pets: Welcome w/$5 fee
Creature Comforts: CCTV, a/c,
refrig, cont. brkfst, pool

Ramada Inn
(800) 2-Ramada, (850) 526-3251
http://www.ramada.com
4655 Rte. 90
80 rooms - $55-88
Pets: Welcome
Creature Comforts: CCTV, a/c,
kit, restaurant, pool, hlth clb
196

MELBOURNE
Baymont Inns
(877)BAYMONT, (407) 242-9400
http://www.baymontinns.com
7200 George T. Edwards Dr.
105 rooms - $40-89
Pets: Welcome
Creature Comforts: CCTV, a/c,
cont. brkfst, pool

Holiday Inn
(800) HOLIDAY, (407) 768-0200
http://www.holiday-inn.com
200 Rialto Pl.
237 rooms - $99-169
Pets: Small pets w/$50 dep.
Creature Comforts: CCTV, a/c,
restaurant, cont. brkfst, hlth clb,
pool

Super 8 Motel
(800) 800-8000, (407) 723-4430
http://www.super8.com
1515 S. Harbor City Blvd.
55 rooms - $40-75
Pets: Welcome w/$20 dep.
Creature Comforts: CCTV, a/c,
cont. brkfst

Travelodge
(800) 578-7878, (407) 724-5450
http://www.travelodge.com
4505 W. New Haven Ave.
46 rooms - $39-75
Pets: Welcome
Creature Comforts: CCTV, a/c,
pool

MIAMI
Amerisuites
(800) 833-1516, (305) 279-8688
http://www.amerisuites.com
115230 SW 88th St.
68 suites - $130-179
Pets: Under 25 lbs. welcome
Creature Comforts: CCTV,
VCR, a/c, refrig, micro, cont.
brkfst, hlth club, pool, golf access

Baymont Inns (Airport)
(877)BAYMONT, (305) 871-1777
http://www.baymontinns.com
3501 NW Le Jeune Rd.
153 rooms - $60-89
Pets: Welcome in smoking rooms
Creature Comforts: CCTV, a/c,
pool

Club Hotel
(800) 222-TREE, (305) 266-0000
http://www.clubtreehotels.com
1101 NW 57th Ave.
265 rooms - $85-239
Pets: Small pets w/$15 fee
Creature Comforts: CCTV, a/c,
refrig, restaurant, cont. brkfst,
pool, hlth clb

Days Inn
(800) DAYS-INN, (305) 673-1513
http://www.daysinn.com
4299 Collins Ave.
145 rooms - $75-125
Pets: Welcome w/$5 fee
Creature Comforts: CCTV, a/c,
refrig, 2 restaurants, pool

Days Inn
(800) DAYS-INN, (305) 888-3661
http://www.daysinn.com
4767 NW 36 St.
144 rooms - $50-139
Pets: Welcome w/$5 fee
Creature Comforts: CCTV, a/c,
refrig, restaurant, pool

Days Inn
(800) DAYS-INN, (305) 674-0954
http://www.daysinn.com
100 - 21st. St.
172 rooms - $80-159
Pets: Welcome w/$10 fee
Creature Comforts: Oceanfront,
CCTV, a/c, refrig, restaurant, pool

Hampton Inn
(800) Hampton, (305) 854-2070
http://www.hampton-inn.com
2500 Brickell Ave.
70 rooms - $89-135
Pets: Welcome
Creature Comforts: CCTV, a/c,
refrig, pool

Holiday Inn
(800) HOLIDAY, (305) 374-3000
http://www.holiday-inn.com
200 SE 2nd Ave.
255 rooms - $69-199
Pets: $35 fee, credit card dep.
Creature Comforts: CCTV, a/c,
restaurant, hlth clb, pool

Hotel Sofitel
(800) 763-4835, (305) 264-4888
http://www.sofitel.com
5800 Blue Lagoon Dr.
282 rooms - $129-625
Pets: Under 20 lbs. welcome
Creature Comforts: CCTV,
VCR, a/c, refrig, 2 restaurants,
pool, hlth clb, tennis, whirlpool

Howard Johnson Lodge
(800) I-Go-Hojo, (305) 891-7350
http://www.hojo.com
12210 Biscayne Blvd.
95 rooms - $40-89
Pets: Welcome w/$25 fee
Creature Comforts: CCTV, a/c,
refrig, micro, pool

La Quinta Inn
(800) Nu-Rooms, (305) 599-9902
http://www.laquinta.com
7401 NW 36th St.
166 rooms - $80-109
Pets: Small pets welcome
Creature Comforts: CCTV, a/c,
refrig, micro, cont. brkfst, pool

Quality Inn
(800) 228-5151, (305) 251-2000
http://www.qualityinn.com
14501 S. Dixie Hwy.
100 rooms - $65-105
Pets: Small pets welcome
Creature Comforts: CCTV, a/c,
kit, pool

Ramada Inn
(800) 2-Ramada, (305) 595-6000
http://www.ramada.com
7600 Kendall St.
122 rooms - $60-129
Pets: Welcome
Creature Comforts: CCTV, a/c,
cont. brkfst, pool

Red Roof Inn
(800) The Roof, (305) 871-4221
http://www.redroof.com
3401 NW L Jeune Rd.
154 rooms - $60-125
Pets: Small pets w/$10 fee
Creature Comforts: CCTV, a/c,
restaurant, pool

Wellesley Inns
(800) 444-8888, (305) 592-4799
http://www.wellesleyinns.com
8436 NW 36th St.
105 rooms - $55-105
Pets: Under 30 lbs. welcome
Creature Comforts: CCTV, a/c,
refrig, micro, cont. brkfst, pool

MIAMI BEACH
Bay Harbor Inn
(305) 868-4141
9660 E. Bay Harbor Dr.
50 rooms - $80-135
Pets: Small pets on the first flr.
w/a $15 fee
Creature Comforts: A pair of
buildings combining Floridian and
English decors, CCTV, VCR, a/c,
refrig, restaurant, cont. brkfst, pub,
pool, dock/yacht

Brigham Gardens
(305) 531-1331
www.decoweb.com/brigham.htm
1411 Collins Ave.
18 rooms - $50-88
Pets: Welcome w/$6 fee
Creature Comforts: CCTV, a/c,
kit

Fountainebleu Hilton Resort
(800) HILTONS, (305) 538-2000
http://www.hilton.com
4441 Collins Ave.
1205 rooms - $165-899
Pets: Under 25 lbs. w/$25 fee
Creature Comforts: Nestled on
20-acres of lush grounds, CCTV,
a/c, refrig, micro, 2 restaurants,
whirlpool, tennis, pools w/
waterfalls, lawn games, volleyball,
on ocean/boats

Hotel Leon
(305) 673-3767
http://www.hotelleon.com
841 Collins Avenue
18 rooms - $110-395
Creature Comforts: An historic
hotel that was recently renovated,
original features, CCTV, a/c, kit,
mahogany floors, rattan
furnishings, restaurant, bar,
massages

The Kent Hotel
(800) OUTPOST, (305) 531-8800
www.islandoutpost.com/Marlin
1131 Collins Ave.
54 rooms - $95-275
Pets: Welcome w/$150 fee
Creature Comforts: CCTV,
stereo-CDs, a/c, kit, Art Deco
decor, mahogany floors, batik
fabrics, rattan furnishings,
restaurants

The Marlin Hotel
(800) OUTPOST, (305) 531-8800
www.islandoutpost.com/Marlin
1200 Collins Ave.
Pets: Welcome w/$150 fee
50 rooms - $150-450
Creature Comforts: Nestled in
south beach, the hotel is know as
the Rock n' roll hotel for its sound
studio, hosted dozens of
performing notables, CCTV &
web TV, a/c, stereo-CDs, kit, Art
Deco decor, whirlpool, restaurant

Miami Beach Pool Paradise
(305) 532-3666
http://members.aol.com/mbhouse/
mbhouse.html
address provided with rservation
3 rooms - $350
Pets: Welcome w/$25 fee
Creature Comforts: CCTV,
VCR, a/c, kit, vaulted ceilings,
fireplace, Jacuzzi, patio, garden,
pool w/waterfalls

Ocean Front Hotel
(800) 783-1725, (305) 672-2579
http://www.oceanfronthotel.com
1230 Ocean Dr.
27 rooms - $125-525
Pets: Welcome w/$15 fee
Creature Comforts: A trendy
Mediterranean-style hotel
overlooking the ocean in the city's
vibrant Art Deco district, CCTV,
VCR, a/c, kit, stereos, bathrobes,
Jacuzzis, restaurant, ocean views

NAPLES

Baymont Inns
(877)BAYMONT, (941) 352-8400
http://www.baymontinns.com
185 Bedzel Cir.
105 rooms - $45-105
Pets: Small pets welcome
Creature Comforts: CCTV, a/c,
cont. brkfst, pool

Howard Johnson Resort Hotel
(800) I-Go-Hojo, (941) 262-6181
http://www.hojo.com
221 - 9th St. So.
100 rooms - $55-165
Pets: Welcome w/$25 fee
Creature Comforts: CCTV, a/c,
restaurant, kit, pool

Red Roof Inn
(800) The Roof, (941) 774-3117
http://www.redroof.com
1925 Davis Blvd.
155 rooms - $40-140
Pets: Small pets welcome
Creature Comforts: CCTV, a/c,
kit, pool

Wellesley Inns
(800) 444-8888, (941) 793-4646
http://www.wellesleyinns.com
1555 - 5th Ave. So.
102 rooms - $49-175
Pets: Under 30 lbs. w/$10 fee
Creature Comforts: CCTV, a/c,
refrig, micro, cont. brkfst, pool

World Tennis Center
(800) 292-6663, (941) 263-1900
http://www.worldtenniscenter.com
4800 Airport-Pullling Rd.
148 rooms - $80-195
Pets: Small pets w/$5 daily fee
Creature Comforts: Sprawling
Mediterranean-style resort on 82-
acres amid lakes and "friendly"
alligators, terrific condos, indiv.
decorated, CCTV, VCR, a/c, kit,
Jacuzzi, restaurant, pool, hlth clb,
sauna, great tennis program,
whirlpool

NAVARRE

Comfort Inn
(800) 228-5150, (850) 939-1761
http://www.comfortinn.com
8680 Navarre Pkwy
65 rooms - $60-129
Pets: Small pets w/CC dep.
Creature Comforts: CCTV, a/c,
pool
198

NEW PORT RICHEY

Econo Lodge
(800) 55-ECONO, (813) 845-4990
http://www.econolodge.com
7631 Rte. 19
104 rooms - $35-85
Pets: Small pets w/$5 fee
Creature Comforts: CCTV, a/c,
refrig, micro, cont. brkfst, pool

Quality Inn
(800) 228-5151, (813) 847-9005
http://www.qualityinn.com
5316 Rte. 19
135 rooms - $49-75
Pets: Welcome w/$10 fee
Creature Comforts: CCTV, a/c,
refrig, restaurant, pool, whirlpool

NEW SMYRA BEACH

Buena Vista Motel
(904) 428-5565
500 N. Causeway Bridge
8 rooms - $35-70
Pets: Small pets w/$30 dep.
Creature Comforts: CCTV, a/c,
and kit

Smyra Motel
(904) 428-2495
1050 N. Dixie Hwy.
10 rooms - $39-65
Pets: $10 fee, $25 deposit
Creature Comforts: CCTV, a/c,
and refrig

NICEVILLE

Comfort Inn
(800) 228-5150, (904) 678-8077
http://www.comfortinn.com
101 Rte. 85 North
119 rooms - $60-99
Pets: Small pets w/$10 fee
Creature Comforts: CCTV, a/c,
refrig, micro, cont. brkfst, pool,
whirlpool

OCALA

Budget Host
(800) Bud-Host, (352) 732-6940
http://www.budgethost.com
4013 NW Blitchton Rd.
22 rooms - $35-79
Pets: Small pets w/$4 fee
Creature Comforts: CCTV, a/c,
refrig, cont. brkfst

Days Inn
(800) DAYS-INN, (352) 629-7041
http://www.daysinn.com
3811 NW Blichton Rd.
64 rooms - $40-129
Pets: Welcome w/$3 fee
Creature Comforts: CCTV, a/c,
cont. brkfst, pool, whirlpool

Days Inn
(800) DAYS-INN, (352) 867-8399
http://www.daysinn.com
3620 W. Silver Springs Blvd.
100 rooms - $35-85
Pets: Welcome w/$10 fee
Creature Comforts: CCTV, a/c,
cont. brkfst, pool

Holiday Inn
(800) HOLIDAY, (352) 629-0381
http://www.holiday-inn.com
3621 W. Silver Springs Blvd.
272 rooms - $39-89
Pets: Small pets welcome
Creature Comforts: CCTV, a/c,
restaurant, hlth club, pool

Quality Inn
(800) 228-5151, (352) 732-2300
http://www.qualityinn.com
3767 NW Blichton Rd.
122 rooms - $40-83
Pets: Small pets w/$5 fee
Creature Comforts: CCTV, a/c,
refrig, restaurant, pool

Ramada Inn
(800) 2-Ramada, (352) 732-3131
http://www.ramada.com
3810 NW Blichton Rd.
125 rooms - $45-85
Pets: Small pets welcome
Creature Comforts: CCTV, a/c,
refrig, restaurant, pool

Super 8 Motel
(800) 800-8000, (352) 629-8794
http://www.super8.com
3924 W. Silver Springs Blvd.
96 rooms - $35-79
Pets: Welcome
Creature Comforts: CCTV, a/c,
cont. brkfst, pool

Western Motel
(800) 283-4678, (352) 732-6940
4013 NW Blichton Rd.
21 rooms - $35-55
Pets: Welcome
Creature Comforts: CCTV, a/c,
and refrig

OKEECHOBEE

Budget Inn
(941) 763-3185
201 S. Parrott Ave.
22 rooms - $40-99
Pets: Welcome w/$5 fee
Creature Comforts: CCTV, a/c, refrig, micro, pool

Days Inn
(800) DAYS-INN, (941) 763-8003
http://www.daysinn.com
2200 SE Rte. 441
89 rooms - $35-135
Pets: Welcome
Creature Comforts: CCTV, a/c, refrig, pool

Economy Inn
(941) 763-1148
507 N. Parrott Ave.
23 rooms - $30-74
Pets: Small pets w/$5 fee
Creature Comforts: CCTV, a/c

OLD TOWN

Suwannee Gables
(352) 542-7752
Rte. 3, Box 208
22 rooms - $54-125
Pets: Welcome w/$8 fee
Creature Comforts: CCTV, a/c, kit, pool, whirlpool, on the river

ORANGE PARK

Best Western Inn
(800) 528-1234, (904) 264-1211
http://www.bestwestern.com
300 Park Ave.
200 rooms - $60-155
Pets: Under 20 lbs. w/$25 fee
Creature Comforts: CCTV, a/c, pool

Club Continental Suites
(800) 877-6070, (904) 264-6070
2143 Astor St.
38 rooms - $55-85
Pets: Welcome w/$20 fee
Creature Comforts: CCTV, a/c, refrig, Jacuzzis, restaurant, cont. brkfst, 2 pools, and tennis

Holiday Inn
(800) HOLIDAY, (904) 264-9513
http://www.holiday-inn.com
150 Park Ave.
300 rooms - $59-85
Pets: Small pets welcome
Creature Comforts: CCTV, a/c, restaurant, pool

Wilson Inn
(904) 264-4466
4580 Collins Rd.
105 rooms - $40-75
Pets: Welcome w/$25 fee
Creature Comforts: CCTV, a/c, refrig, pool

ORLANDO

Baymont Inns
(877)BAYMONT, (407) 240-0500
http://www.baymontinns.com
2051 Consulate Dr.
126 rooms - $36-69
Pets: Welcome
Creature Comforts: CCTV, a/c, cont. brkfst, pool

Best Western Inn
(800) 528-1234, (407) 841-8600
http://www.bestwestern.com
2041 W. Colonial Dr.
110 rooms - $40-95
Pets: Welcome w/$10 fee
Creature Comforts: CCTV, a/c, refrig, pool

Days Inn
(800) DAYS-INN, (407) 862-2800
http://www.daysinn.com
235 S. Wymore Rd.
150 rooms - $45-99
Pets: Welcome
Creature Comforts: CCTV, a/c, cont. brkfst, pool

Days Inn
(800) DAYS-INN, (407) 644-8000
http://www.daysinn.com
901 N. Orlando Ave.
103 rooms - $40-95
Pets: Welcome
Creature Comforts: CCTV, a/c, cont. brkfst, pool

Days Inn
(800) DAYS-INN, (407) 841-3731
http://www.daysinn.com
2500 W. 33rd St.
200 rooms - $35-119
Pets: Welcome w/$6 fee
Creature Comforts: CCTV, a/c, restaurant, cont. brkfst, pool

Days Inn
(800) DAYS-INN, (407) 351-3800
http://www.daysinn.com
100 Major Blvd.
262 rooms - $45-149
Pets: Small pets w/$10 fee
Creature Comforts: CCTV, a/c, restaurant, cont. brkfst, pool

Days Inn, Airport
(800) DAYS-INN, (407) 859-6100
http://www.daysinn.com
2323 McCoy Rd.
354 rooms - $30-119
Pets: Welcome w/$8 fee
Creature Comforts: CCTV, a/c, pool

Days Inn
(800) DAYS-INN, (407) 351-1200
http://www.daysinn.com
7200 International Dr.
243 rooms - $55-129
Pets: Welcome w/$5 fee
Creature Comforts: CCTV, a/c, cont. brkfst, pool

Days Inn
(800) DAYS-INN, (407) 352-8700
http://www.daysinn.com
9990 International Dr.
218 rooms - $55-110
Pets: Welcome
Creature Comforts: CCTV, a/c, restaurant, pool

Delta Orlando Resort
(800) 634-4763, (407) 351-3340
http://www.deltahotels.com
5715 Major Blvd.
800 rooms - $159-495
Pets: Small pets w/$25 fee
Creature Comforts: An expansive family-oriented resort set on 25-acres by Disney/MGM Studios/Epcot main gate, CCTV, VCR, a/c, kit, Jacuzzis, restaurants-food court, pool, hlth clb, sauna, whirlpool, Wally's Activity Center, tennis, mini-golf, lawn games

Econo Lodge
(800) 55-ECONO, (407) 293-7221
http://www.econolodge.com
3300 Colonial Dr.
102 rooms - $30-79
Pets: Small pets welcome
Creature Comforts: CCTV, a/c, restaurant, pool

Gateway Inn
(800) 327-3808, (407) 351-2000
7050 Kirkman Rd.
354 rooms - $55-109
Pets: Small pets w/$50 dep.
Creature Comforts: CCTV, a/c,
refrig, 2 restaurants, cont. brkfst, 2
pools, lawn games

Homewood Suites
(800) 225-5466, (407) 396-2229
http://www.homewoodsuites.com
3100 Parkway Blvd.
156 rooms - $119-185
Pets: $200 dep, $75 fee
Creature Comforts: CCTV, a/c,
kit, pool, hlth clb, whirlpool

Inns of America
(800) 826-0778, (407) 345-1172
http://www.innsamerica.com
8222 Jamaican Ct.
120 rooms - $49-85
Pets: Small pets welcome
Creature Comforts: CCTV, a/c,
refrig, cont. brkfst, pool

Knights Inn
(800) 843-5644, (407) 425-9065
http://www.knightsinn.com
221 E. Colonial Dr.
77 rooms - $40-85
Pets: Welcome w/$10 fee
Creature Comforts: CCTV, a/c,
kits, restaurant, pool

La Quinta Inn, Airport
(800) Nu-Rooms, (407) 857-9215
http://www.laquinta.com
7931 Daetwyler Dr.
126 rooms - $60-95
Pets: Small pets welcome
Creature Comforts: CCTV, a/c,
refrig, cont. brkfst, pool

La Quinta Inn
(800) Nu-Rooms, (407) 351-1660
http://www.laquinta.com
8300 Jamaican Ct.
199 rooms - $60-89
Pets: Small pets welcome
Creature Comforts: CCTV, a/c,
refrig, micro, restaurant, cont.
brkfst, pool

Motel 6, Universal Studios
(800) 4-MOTEL6, (407) 351-6500
http://www.motel6.com
5909 American Way
112 rooms - $35-49
Pets: Under 30 lbs.welcome
Creature Comforts: CCTV, a/c,
pool

Motel 6, Disney World
(800) 4-MOTEL6, (407) 396-6422
http://www.motel6.com
7455 W. Bronson Hwy.
148 rooms - $39-49
Pets: Under 30 lbs.welcome
Creature Comforts: CCTV, a/c,
pool

Quality Inn
(800) 228-5151, (407) 351-1600
http://www.qualityinn.com
7600 International Dr.
725 rooms - $40-99
Pets: Welcome w/$5 fee
Creature Comforts: CCTV, a/c,
refrig, micro, restaurant, pool, hlth
clb, whirlpool, lawn games

Quality Inn
(800) 228-5151, (407) 345-8585
http://www.qualityinn.com
9000 International Dr.
1025 rooms - $40-99
Pets: Welcome w/$5 fee
Creature Comforts: CCTV, a/c,
refrig, micro, restaurant, pool, hlth
clb, whirlpool, and lawn games

Red Roof Inn
(800) The Roof, (407) 352-1507
http://www.redroof.com
9922 Hawaiian Ct.
135 rooms - $45-99
Pets: Small pets welcome
Creature Comforts: CCTV, a/c,
pool

Rodeway Inn
(800) 228-2000, (407) 351-4444
http://www.rodeway.com
6327 International Dr.
315 rooms - $55-79
Pets: Welcome w/$5 fee
Creature Comforts: CCTV,
VCR, a/c, refrig, 3 restaurants, 2
pools

Travelodge
(800) 578-7878, (407) 851-4300
http://www.travelodge.com
7101 S. Orange Blossom Tr.
162 rooms - $30-85
Pets: Welcome
Creature Comforts: CCTV, a/c,
refrig, micro, cont. brkfst, 2 pools

Travelodge
(800) 578-7878, (407) 423-1671
http://www.travelodge.com
409 N. Magnolia Ave.
75 rooms - $50-89
Pets: Welcome
Creature Comforts: CCTV, a/c,
restaurant, pool

The Veranda B&B
(800) 420-6822, (407) 849-0321
http://www.verandabandb.com
115 N. Summerlin Ave.
9 rooms - $79-139
Pets: Prefer cats
Creature Comforts: Five historic
buildings w/decors ranging from
Victorian to Key West, CCTV, a/c,
cont. brkfst, kit, white wicker,
antiques, Oriental rugs covering
hardwood floors, pool, whirlpool,
lush foliage

Wellesley Inns
(800) 444-8888, (407) 345-0026
http://www.wellesleyinns.com
5635 Windhover Dr.
104 rooms - $45-105
Pets: Under 30 lbs. w/$10 fee
Creature Comforts: CCTV, a/c,
refrig, micro, cont. brkfst, pool

ORMOND BEACH
Comfort Inn
(800) 228-5150, (904) 672-8621
http://www.comfortinn.com
1567 N. Rte. 1
77 rooms - $50-89
Pets: Small pets welcome
Creature Comforts: CCTV, a/c,
cont. brkfst, pool

Comfort Inn
(800) 228-5150, (904) 677-8550
http://www.comfortinn.com
507 S. Atlantic Ave.
50 rooms - $50-155
Pets: Small pets welcome
Creature Comforts: CCTV, a/c,
kit, cont. brkfst, pool, on the beach

Days Inn
(800) DAYS-INN, (904) 672-7341
http://www.daysinn.com
1608 N. Rte. 1
72 rooms - $30-199
Pets: Welcome w/$5 fee
Creature Comforts: CCTV, a/c,
refrig, cont. brkfst, pool

Days Inn
(800) DAYS-INN, (904) 677-6600
http://www.daysinn.com
839 S. Atlantic Ave.
128 rooms - $35-275
Pets: Welcome w/$10 fee
Creature Comforts: CCTV, a/c,
refrig, cont. brkfst, pool, on the
ocean

Driftwood Beach Motel
(800) 490-8935, (904) 677-1331
657 S. Atlantic Ave.
45 rooms - $35-89
Pets: Small pets w/$10 fee
Creature Comforts: CCTV, a/c,
kit, pool, on the ocean

Jamaican Beach Motel
(800) 336-3353, (904) 677-3353
505 S. Atlantic Ave.
42 rooms - $35-155
Pets: Small pets w/$4 fee
Creature Comforts: CCTV, a/c,
kit, pool, on the beach

Makai Motel
(904) 677-8060
http://www.webadept.com/makai
707 S. Atlantic Ave.
110 rooms - $35-75
Pets: Under 20 lbs. w/$5 fee
Creature Comforts: CCTV, a/c,
kit, pool, whirlpool

OSPREY
Ramada Inn
(800) 2-Ramada, (941) 966-2121
http://www.ramada.com
1660 S. Tamiami Tr.
149 rooms - $55-175
Pets: Welcome w/$25 dep.
Creature Comforts: CCTV, a/c,
kit, restaurant, pool, sauna

PALM BAY
Motel 6
(800) 4-MOTEL6, (407) 951-8222
http://www.motel6.com
1170 Malabar Rd. SE
118 rooms - $35-49
Pets: Under 30 lbs.welcome
Creature Comforts: CCTV, a/c,
pool

PALM BEACH
Brazilian Court
(800) 552-0335, (561) 655-7740
http://www.braziliancourt.com
301 Australian Ave.
105 rooms - $275-825
Pets: Welcome w/$75 fee
Creature Comforts: A luxury
1926 hotel, lovely furnishings,
soothing color schemes, CCTV,
VCR, a/c, refrig, micro, restaurant,
pool, fountain courtyard, hlth clb,
access to tennis, massage, and a
whirlpool

The Chesterfield Hotel
(800) 243-7871, (561) 659-5800
http://www.chesterfieldhotel.com
363 Coconut Row
55 rooms - $89-1,175
Pets: Dogs under 40 lbs.
welcome w/$250 deposit
Creature Comforts: A beautifully
refurbished 1926 hotel w/English
country manor decor, lovely
furnishings, marble accents,
Chinese silk screens, CCTV, VCR,
a/c, refrig, micro, restaurant, pool,
library, hlth clb access, sauna,
cigar rm, English tea, whirlpool

Four Seasons Resort
(800) 332-3442, (561) 582-2800
http://www.fshr.com
2800 S. Ocean Blvd.
212 rooms - $199-2,500
Pets: Under 15 Llbs. welcome
Creature Comforts: Exquisite
beachside property, CCTV, VCR,
a/c, fireplace, refrig, micro,
Jacuzzis, restaurant, pool, hlth clb
access, sauna, tennis, massage,
steamrooms, spa,tennis, whirlpool,
kids program, beach, and access to
golf

Heart of Palm Beach Motel
(800) 523-5377, (561) 655-5600
160 Royal Palm Way
88 rooms - $69-275
Pets: Small pets w/CC dep.
Creature Comforts: CCTV,
VCR, a/c, refrig, restaurant, pool

Hibiscus House B&B
(800) 203-4927, (561) 863-5633
http://www.hibiscushouse.com
501 - 30th St.
7 rooms - $55-175
Pets: Welcome in the cottage
Creature Comforts: National
Historic Regstr. B&B w/eleant
ambiance and intriguing antiques
— Oriental and Egyptian antiques,
wood canopy and four poster
beds, Oriental rugs, CCTV, VCR,
a/c, refrig, micro, fireplace, full
brkfst served on crystal and china,
pool, gazebo

Plaza Inn
(800) 233-2632, (561) 832-8666
www.plazainnpalmbeach.com
215 Brazilian Ave.
50 rooms - $85-245
Pets: Small pets welcome
Creature Comforts: Historic
boutique B&B w/Art Deco twist,
four poster bedsteads, lovely
furnishings & antiques, CCTV,
VCR, a/c, refrig, full brkfst, pool,
whirlpoo, pub

PALM BEACH GARDENS
Embassy Suites
(800) 362-2779, (407) 622-1000
http://www.embassy-suites.com
4350 PGA Blvd.
162 rooms - $99-295
Pets: Small pets w/$50 fee
Creature Comforts: CCTV, a/c,
restaurant, cont. brkfst, whirlpool,
tennis, hlth club, pool

Inns of America
(800) 826-0778, (407) 626-4918
http://www.innsamerica.com
4123 Northlake Blvd.
91 rooms - $55-79
Pets: Small pets welcome
Creature Comforts: CCTV, a/c,
refrig, cont. brkfst, pool

PALM BEACH SHORES
Best Western Inn
(800) 528-1234, (561) 844-0233
http://www.bestwestern.com
123 S. Ocean Dr.
50 rooms - $79-149
Pets: Welcome
Creature Comforts: CCTV, a/c,
kit, restaurant, pool, on the beach

PALM COAST
Palm Coast Villas
(904) 445-3525
5454 N. Oceanshore Blvd.
15 rooms - $45-59
Pets: Small pets welcome
Creature Comforts: CCTV, a/c,
kit, pool

PALMETTO
Sea Inn B&B
(941) 721-0365
5515 Rte. 19
8 rooms - $40-64
Pets: Welcome w/$5 fee
Creature Comforts: CCTV, a/c

PALM HARBOR
Knights Inn
(800) 843-5644, (813) 789-2002
http://www.knightsinn.com
34106 Rte. 19
115 rooms - $35-88
Pets: Welcome w/$5 fee
Creature Comforts: CCTV, a/c,
refrig, micro, pool

PANAMA CITY
Best Western Inn
(800) 528-1234, (850) 763-4622
http://www.bestwestern.com
711 W. Beach Dr.
102 rooms - $55-245
Pets: Welcome
Creature Comforts: CCTV, a/c,
refrig, micro, restaurant, pool,
priv. beach

Days Inn
(800) DAYS-INN, (850) 784-1777
http://www.daysinn.com
4111 W. Rte. 98
50 rooms - $40-119
Pets: Welcome w/$2 fee
Creature Comforts: CCTV, a/c,
Jacuzzis, cont. brkfst, pool

Howard Johnson Resort Hotel
(800) I-Go-Hojo, (850) 785-0222
http://www.hojo.com
4601 Rte. 98
80 rooms - $45-89
Pets: Welcome
Creature Comforts: CCTV, a/c,
pool, on the beach

Scottish Inns
(800) 251-1962, (850) 769-2432
http://www.reservahost.com
4907 W. Rte. 98
75 rooms - $30-48
Pets: Welcome w/$2 fee
Creature Comforts: CCTV, a/c,
cont. brkfst, pool

Super 8 Motel
(800) 800-8000, (850) 784-1988
http://www.super8.com
207 Rte. 231
63 rooms - $35-75
Pets: Welcome
Creature Comforts: CCTV, a/c,
pool

PANAMA CITY BEACH
Comfort Inn
(800) 228-5150, (850) 234-6511
http://www.comfortinn.com
9600 S. Thomas Dr.
199 rooms - $60-225
Pets: Small pets w/CC dep.
Creature Comforts: CCTV, a/c,
pool

Howard Johnson Resort Hotel
(800) I-Go-Hojo, (850) 234-3484
http://www.hojo.com
9400 S. Thomas Dr.
153 rooms - $59-275
Pets: Welcome w/CC deposit
Creature Comforts: CCTV, a/c,
kit, pool, on the beach

Surf High Inn on the Cliff
(850) 234-2129
10611 Front Beach Rd.
33 rooms - $35-79
Pets: Welcome w/$5 fee
Creature Comforts: CCTV, a/c,
kit, pool

PEMBROKE PINES
Grand Palms Country Club
(800) 327-9246, (954) 431-8800
110 Grand Palms Dr.
135 rooms - $75-185
Pets: Small pets w/$60 fee
Creature Comforts: CCTV, a/c,
refrig, restaurant, pool, golf

PENSACOLA
Comfort Inn
(800) 228-5150, (850) 478-4499
http://www.comfortinn.com
6919 Pensacola Blvd.
122 rooms - $45-89
Pets: Welcome
Creature Comforts: CCTV, a/c,
pool

Comfort Inn
(800) 228-5150, (850) 455-3233
http://www.comfortinn.com
3 New Warrington Rd.
100 rooms - $50-79
Pets: Welcome w/$25 fee
Creature Comforts: CCTV, a/c,
pool

Days Inn
(800) DAYS-INN, (850) 476-9090
http://www.daysinn.com
7051 Pensacola Blvd.
80 rooms - $40-69
Pets: Welcome w/$5 fee
Creature Comforts: CCTV, a/c,
restaurant, pool

Gulf Beach Inn
(850) 492-4501
web site pending
10655 Gulf Beach Hwy.
1 room - $50-78
Pets: Welcome w/$10 fee
Creature Comforts: CCTV, a/c,
refrig, full brkfst, private beach

La Quinta Inn
(800) Nu-Rooms, (850) 474-0411
http://www.laquinta.com
7750 N. Davis Hwy.
125 rooms - $50-88
Pets: Small pets welcome
Creature Comforts: CCTV, a/c,
refrig, micro, cont. brkfst, pool

Motel 6
(800) 4-MOTEL6, (850) 474-1060
http://www.motel6.com
7226 Plantation Rd.
80 rooms - $35-49
Pets: Under 30 lbs.welcome
Creature Comforts: CCTV, a/c, pool

Motel 6
(800) 4-MOTEL6, (850) 476-5385
http://www.motel6.com
7827 N. Davis Hwy.
108 rooms - $35-49
Pets: Under 30 lbs.welcome
Creature Comforts: CCTV, a/c, pool

Motel 6
(800) 4-MOTEL6, (850) 477-7522
http://www.motel6.com
5829 Pensacola Blvd.
120 rooms - $29-42
Pets: Under 30 lbs.welcome
Creature Comforts: CCTV, a/c, pool

The Pensacola Grand Hotel
(800) 348-3336, (850) 433-3336
www.pensacolagrandhotel.com
200 E. Gregory St.
210 rooms - $95-429
Pets: Small pets w/$50 fee
Creature Comforts: Restored train depot, CCTV, a/c, refrig, restaurant, hlth club, pool

Ramada Inn Bayview
(800) 2-Ramada, (850) 477-7155
http://www.ramada.com
7601 Scenic Hwy.
150 rooms - $65-89
Pets: Small pets w/$5 fee
Creature Comforts: CCTV, a/c, refrig, Jacuzzis, restaurant, pool, whirlpool

Red Roof Inn
(800) The Roof, (850) 476-7960
http://www.redroof.com
7340 Plantation Rd.
105 rooms - $45-79
Pets: Small pets welcome
Creature Comforts: CCTV, a/c

Rodeway Inn
(800) 228-2000, (850) 477-9150
http://www.rodeway.com
8500 Pine Forest Rd.
99 rooms - $35-58
Pets: Welcome w/$6 fee
Creature Comforts: CCTV, a/c, pool

Shoney's Inn
(800) 222-2222, (850) 484-8070
http://www.shoneysinn.com
8080 N. Davis Hwy.
114 rooms - $69-95
Pets: $20 fee, credit card dep.
Creature Comforts: CCTV, a/c, refrig., micro, pool

Super 8 Motel
(800) 800-8000, (850) 457-7277
http://www.super8.com
5 New Warrington Rd.
41 rooms - $50-89
Pets: Welcome w/permission
Creature Comforts: CCTV, a/c, refrig, micro, cont. brkfst, pool

PERRY
Best Budget Inn
(850) 584-6231
2220 Rte. 19
60 rooms - $35-55
Pets: Welcome w/$3 fee
Creature Comforts: CCTV, a/c, pool

Days Inn
(800) DAYS-INN, (850) 584-5311
http://www.daysinn.com
2271 S. Byron Butler Pkwy.
60 rooms - $40-79
Pets: Welcome w/$10 fee
Creature Comforts: CCTV, a/c, restaurant, pool

The Villager Lodge
(850) 584-4221
2238 S. Byron Butler Pkwy.
66 rooms - $40-59
Pets: Welcome
Creature Comforts: CCTV, a/c, refrig, micro, pool, whirlpool

PINELLAS PARK
Days Inn
(800) DAYS-INN, (813) 577-3838
http://www.daysinn.com
9359 Rte. 19
154 rooms - $40-67
Pets: Welcome w/$6 fee
Creature Comforts: CCTV, a/c, refrig, micro, restaurant, pool

La Mark Charles Hotel
(800) 448-6781, (813) 527-7334
6200 - 34th St. N.
95 rooms - $55-125
Pets: $10 fee and $25 deposit
Creature Comforts: CCTV, a/c, kit, restaurant, pool, whirlpool

La Quinta Inn
(800) Nu-Rooms, (813) 545-5611
http://www.laquinta.com
7500 Rte. 19
115 rooms - $50-109
Pets: Small pets welcome
Creature Comforts: CCTV, a/c, refrig, cont. brkfst, pool

PLANTATION
Holiday Inn
(800) HOLIDAY, (954) 472-5600
http://www.holiday-inn.com
1711 N. University Dr.
333 rooms - $85-159
Pets: $20 fee and $25 deposit
Creature Comforts: CCTV, a/c, restaurant, pool

Residence Inn
(800) 331-3131, (954) 723-0300
http://www.residenceinn.com
130 N. University Dr.
135 rooms - $95-199
Pets: Under 25 lbs. w/$200 fee
Creature Comforts: CCTV, a/c, kit, restaurant, cont. brkfst, hlth club, whirlpool, pool

PLANT CITY
Days Inn
(800) DAYS-INN, (813) 752-0570
http://www.daysinn.com
301 S. Frontage Rd.
176 rooms - $40-88
Pets: Welcome w/$10 fee
Creature Comforts: CCTV, a/c, restaurant, pool

Ramada Inn
(800) 2-Ramada, (813) 752-3141
http://www.ramada.com
2011 N. Wheeler St.
260 rooms - $55-89
Pets: Welcome
Creature Comforts: CCTV, a/c,
kit restaurant, pool

POMPANO BEACH
Sea Castle Resort
(800) 331-4466 , (954) 941-2570
730 N. Ocean Blvd.
40 rooms - $55-129
Pets: Welcome w/$10 fee
Creature Comforts: CCTV, a/c,
kit, pool, cont. brkfst

Motel 6
(800) 4-MOTEL6, (954) 977-8011
http://www.motel6.com
1201 NW 31st Ave.
127 rooms - $35-49
Pets: Under 30 lbs.welcome
Creature Comforts: CCTV, a/c,
pool

PORT CHARLOTTE
Days Inn
(800) DAYS-INN, (941) 627-8900
http://www.daysinn.com
1941 Tamiami Tr.
126 rooms - $80-105
Pets: Welcome
Creature Comforts: CCTV, a/c,
refrig, pool

Port Charlotte Motel
(941) 625-4177
3491 Tamiami Tr.
54 rooms - $35-80
Pets: Welcome w/$50 fee
Creature Comforts: CCTV, a/c,
kit, pool

Quality Inn
(800) 228-5151, (941) 625-4181
http://www.qualityinn.com
3400 Tamiami Tr.
105 rooms - $55-119
Pets: Welcome w/$5 fee
Creature Comforts: CCTV, a/c,
refrig, micro, pool

PORT RICHEY
Days Inn
(800) DAYS-INN, (813) 863-1502
http://www.daysinn.com
11736 Rte. 19
156 rooms - $35-99
Pets: Welcome w/$5 fee
Creature Comforts: CCTV, a/c,
kit, restaurant, pool

PORT SALERNO
Pirate's Cove Resort
(561) 287-2500
4307 SE Bayview St.
52 rooms - $80-195
Pets: Welcome w/$100 fee
Creature Comforts: CCTV,
VCR, a/c, refrig, micro, restaurant,
pool, and a marina

PUNTA GORDA
Best Western Waterfront Inn
(800) 528-1234, (941) 639-1165
http://www.bestwestern.com
300 Retta Esplanade
181 rooms - $69-239
Pets: Welcome
Creature Comforts: CCTV, a/c,
refrig, micro, restaurant, cont.
brkfst, pool

Holiday Inn
(800) HOLIDAY, (941) 639-1165
http://www.holiday-inn.com
300 Retta Esplanade
185 rooms - $80-125
Pets: Welcome w/$15 fee
Creature Comforts: CCTV,
VCR, a/c, refrig, micro, Jacuzzis,
restaurant, pool, and a riverfront

Howard Johnson Riverside
(800) I-Go-Hojo, (941) 639-2167
http://www.hojo.com
33 Tamiami Tr.
99 rooms - $40-99
Pets: Welcome w/$20 fee
Creature Comforts: CCTV, a/c,
refrig, micro, Jacuzzis, restaurant,
pool, and lawn games

Motel 6
(800) 4-MOTEL6, (941) 639-9585
http://www.motel6.com
9300 Knights Dr.
114 rooms - $35-49
Pets: Under 30 lbs.welcome
Creature Comforts: CCTV, a/c

QUINCY
Allison House Inn
(888) 875-2511, (850) 875-2511
http://www.travelguides.com/
home/allison_house
215 North Madison St.
20 rooms - $70-95
Pets: Welcome
Creature Comforts: Historic
Georgian dating to 1843 set in the
heart of the historic district,
English-style B&B, CCTV, a/c,
charming decor, brass beds, and
cont. brkfst.

Quincy Motor Inn
(850) 627-8929
368 E. Jefferson St.
20 rooms - $30-39
Pets: Welcome
Creature Comforts: CCTV, a/c,
pool

RIVIERA BEACH
Motel 6
(800) 4-MOTEL6, (561) 863-1011
http://www.motel6.com
3651 W. Blue Heron Blvd.
116 rooms - $35-49
Pets: Under 30 lbs.welcome
Creature Comforts: CCTV, a/c,
pool

SAFETY HARBOR
Safety Harbor Resort
(800) 533-8542, (813) 726-1161
http://www.safetyharborspa.com
105 N. Bayshore Dr.
190 rooms - $99-189
Pets: Under 30 lbs. w/$30 fee
Creature Comforts: Nestled on
Tampa Bay, one of top ten resorts
in the country, CCTV, VCR, a/c,
fireplace, kit, Jacuzzi, restaurants,
cont. brkfst, 3 pools, 50,000 sq. ft.
spa & hlth clb, sauna, mineral
springs, steam-rooms, Outward
Bound Programs, tennis center,
fitness programs,and whirlpools

ST. AUGUSTINE
Barefoot Trace
(904) 471-9212
6240 A1A So.
66 rooms - $675-850/wk
Pets: Welcome w/$40 fee
Creature Comforts: Intruiging
Mediterranean-style condos,
individually decorated, CCTV,
VCR, a/c, kit, pool, spa, tennis

Best Western Inn
(800) 528-1234, (904) 829-1999
http://www.bestwestern.com
2446 Rte. 16
120 rooms - $40-75
Pets: Under 10 lbs. w/$6 fee
Creature Comforts: CCTV, a/c,
cont. brkfst, pool

Days Inn
(800) DAYS-INN, (904) 824-4341
http://www.daysinn.com
2560 Rte. 16
120 rooms - $40-89
Pets: Welcome w/$5 fee
Creature Comforts: CCTV, a/c,
restaurant, pool

Days Inn
(800) DAYS-INN, (904) 829-0135
http://www.daysinn.com
2800 N. Ponce de Leon Blvd.
124 rooms - $40-115
Pets: Welcome w/$10 fee
Creature Comforts: CCTV, a/c,
pool

Econo Lodge
(800) 55-ECONO, (904) 829-5643
http://www.econolodge.com
2535 Rte. 16
138 rooms - $35-125
Pets: Small pets w/$5 fee
Creature Comforts: CCTV, a/c,
restaurant, cont. brkfst, pool

Guest House Lion Inn
(904) 824-2831
420 Anastasia Blvd.
35 rooms - $45-169
Pets: Welcome w/$5 fee
Creature Comforts: CCTV, a/c,
cont. brkfst, pool

ST. AUGUSTINE BEACH
Best Western Inn
(800) 528-1234, (904) 471-8010
http://www.bestwestern.com
3955 A1A
34 rooms - $40-129
Pets: Small pets w/$10 fee
Creature Comforts: CCTV, a/c,
cont. brkfst, pool

Holiday Inn
(800) HOLIDAY, (904) 471-2555
http://www.holiday-inn.com
860 A1A Beach Blvd.
150 rooms - $89-149
Pets: Small pets welcome
Creature Comforts: CCTV, a/c,
restaurant, pool

Howard Johnson Resort
(800) I-Go-Hojo, (904) 471-2675
http://www.hojo.com
300 - A1A Beach Blvd.
144 rooms - $45-155
Pets: Welcome w/$15 fee
Creature Comforts: CCTV, a/c,
restaurant, pool, on the beach

ST. PETE BEACH
Bay Street Villas
(800) 566-8358, (813) 360-5591
7201 Bay St.
22 rooms - $70-125
Pets: Small pets w/$5 fee
Creature Comforts: CCTV, a/c,
kit, pool

Days Inn
(800) DAYS-INN, (813) 577-3838
http://www.daysinn.com
9359 Rte. 19
154 rooms - $40-65
Pets: Welcome w/$6 fee
Creature Comforts: CCTV, a/c,
refrig, micro, pool

Days Inn
(800) DAYS-INN, (813) 522-3191
http://www.daysinn.com
54th Ave. N.
155 rooms - $40-79
Pets: Welcome
Creature Comforts: CCTV, a/c,
restaurant, pool

La Quinta Inn
(800) Nu-Rooms, (813) 527-8421
http://www.laquinta.com
4999 - 34th St.
120 rooms - $45-85
Pets: Under 25 lbs. welcome
Creature Comforts: CCTV, a/c,
refrig, micro, cont. brkfst, hlth clb,
pool

Ritz Motel
(813) 360-7642
4237 Gulf Blvd.
12 rooms - $40-95
Pets: Small pets welcome
Creature Comforts: CCTV, a/c,
kit, pool

Valley Forge Motel
(813) 345-0135
6825 Central Ave.
30 rooms - $40-67
Pets: Welcome w/$3-5 fee
Creature Comforts: CCTV, a/c,
kit, pool

SANFORD
Days Inn
(800) DAYS-INN, (407) 323-6500
http://www.daysinn.com
4650 Rte. 46
120 rooms - $40-99
Pets: Welcome w/$5 fee
Creature Comforts: CCTV, a/c,
restaurant, pool

Marina Hotel
(407) 323-1910
530 N. Palmetto Ave.
99 rooms - $55-139
Pets: Small pets w/$20 fee
Creature Comforts: CCTV, a/c,
two restaurants, pool, lakefront

Super 8 Motel
(800) 800-8000, (407) 323-3445
http://www.super8.com
4750 Rte. 46 W.
104 rooms - $45-89
Pets: Welcome
Creature Comforts: CCTV, a/c,
kit, cont. brkfst, pool

SANIBEL
The Castaways
(800) 375-0152, (941) 472-1252
http://www.castawayssanibel.com/
special.htm
6460 Sanibel-Captiva Rd.
37 cottages - $79-299
Pets: Welcome w/$10 fee
Creature Comforts: New
England-style beachfront cottages,
Old-Floridian architecture,
Caribbean ambiance, CCTV, a/c,
rattan and bleached woods, kit,
pool, marina

Signal Inn
(800) 992-4690, (941) 472-4690
http://www.signalinn.com
1811 Olde Middle Gulf Dr.
16 rooms - $625-2,225/wk
Pets: Crtn. rms w/$10 daily fee
Creature Comforts: Tahitian-style cottages, lush beachside setting, well furnished, CCTV, a/c, kit, Jacuzzi, pool, sauna, whirlpool, book a year in advance

Mitchell's Sand Castles
(941) 472-1282
http://www.eyeware.net/sanibel/island.htm
3951 W. Gulf Dr.
19 cottages - $75-225
Pets: Welcome w/$5 fee
Creature Comforts: Old-fashioned beachside cottages, private, low-key setting, simple beach cottage furnishings, seashell stencils, screened porches, CCTV, a/c, kit, pool, booked a year in advance

SARASOTA
Azure Tides
(800) 326-8433, (941) 388-2101
1330 Ben Franklin Dr.
68 rooms - $135-259
Pets: Welcome w/$50 dep.
Creature Comforts: CCTV, VCR, a/c, kit, pool

Banana Bay Club
(888) 6-Banbay, (941) 346-0113
http://www.bananabayclub.com
8254 Midnight Pass Rd.
6 apartments - $95-225
Pets: Welcome
Creature Comforts: Handful of cottages, lush grounds, calm lagoon, beamed ceilings w/fans, vibrant tropical colors, well appointed, CCTV, a/c, kit, pool, whirlpool, bicycles, boats, access to tennis and golf

The Calais Motel
(941) 921-5797
1735 Stickney Pt. Rd.
25 rooms - $45-95
Pets: Welcome w/$5 fee
Creature Comforts: CCTV, a/c, kit, pool

Coquina on the Beach Resort
(800) 833-2141, (941) 388-2141
1008 Ben Franklin Dr.
33 rooms - $90-325
Pets: Welcome w/$25 fee
Creature Comforts: CCTV, VCR, a/c, kit, pool, on the beach

Days Inn
(800) DAYS-INN, (941) 355-9721
http://www.daysinn.com
4900 N. Tamiami Tr.
121 rooms - $45-115
Pets: Welcome w/$6 fee
Creature Comforts: CCTV, a/c, restaurant, cont. brkfst, pool

Holiday Inn, Airport
(800) HOLIDAY, (941) 355-2781
http://www.holiday-inn.com
7150 N. Tamiami Tr.
175 rooms - $55-125
Pets: Welcome
Creature Comforts: CCTV, a/c, refrig, restaurant, pool

Howard Johnson Inn
(800) I-Go-Hojo, (941) 756-8399
http://www.hojo.com
6511 - 14th St.
50 rooms - $45-95
Pets: Welcome
Creature Comforts: CCTV, a/c, refrig, pool

Quality Inn
(800) 228-5151, (941) 355-7771
http://www.qualityinn.com
8440 N. Tamiami Tr.
100 rooms - $49-109
Pets: Small pets w/$10 fee
Creature Comforts: CCTV, a/c, kit, pool

Ramada Limited
(800) 2-Ramada, (941) 921-7812
http://www.ramada.com
5774 Clark Rd.
61 rooms - $75-109
Pets: Small pets w/$5 fee
Creature Comforts: CCTV, a/c, pool

Wellesley Inns
(800) 444-8888, (941) 366-5128
http://www.wellesleyinns.com
1803 N. Tamiami Tr.
105 rooms - $75-135
Pets: Under 30 lbs. w/$10 fee
Creature Comforts: CCTV, a/c, refrig, micro, cont. brkfst, pool

SATELITE BEACH
Days Inn
(800) DAYS-INN, (407) 777-3552
http://www.daysinn.com
180 A1A
104 rooms - $45-90
Pets: Welcome w/$10 fee
Creature Comforts: CCTV, a/c, refrig, micro, cont. brkfst, pool, and whirlpool

SEBRING
Inn on the Lakes
(800) 531-5253, (941) 471-9400
3100 Golf View Rd.
160 rooms - $65-139
Pets: Welcome w/$15 fee
Creature Comforts: CCTV, a/c, kit, restaurant, pool, massage, lakefront, golf access

SIESTA KEY
Heron Lagoon Club
(941) 346-0617
8212 Midnight Pass Rd.
10 rooms - $75-145
Pets: Welcome
Creature Comforts: Charming coral-colored cottages set amid lush gardens, lanais made from coquina, rattan, wicker and Chippendale reproductions, chintz fabrics, CCTV, VCR, a/c, kit, cont. brkfst, pool, lagoon-dock

Surfrider Beach Apts.
(941) 349-2121
6400 Midnight Pass Rd.
21 rooms - $95-160
Pets: Welcome
Creature Comforts: CCTV, a/c, kit, pool, whirlpool

Tropical Breeze Inn
(800) 300-2492, (941) 349-1125
http://www.tropicalbreezeinn.com
140 Columbus Blvd.
16 rooms - $75-275
Pets: Welcome w/ $40 fee
Creature Comforts: Rooms are decorated around regional themes, rattan and wicker w/floral fabrics, rag rugs, rqst beach suites, CCTV, a/c, kit, pool, Art Deco bathrooms, massage, hlth club, whirlpool, lush gardens, lawn games, beach-boats

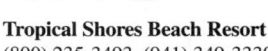

Tropical Shores Beach Resort
(800) 235-3493, (941) 349-3330
http://www.tropicalshores.com
6717 Sarasea Circle
30 rooms - $175-395
Pets: Welcome w/$25 fee
Creature Comforts: CCTV, a/c,
kit, cont. brkfst, pool, whirlpool,
and lawn games

Turtle Beach Resort
(941) 349-4554
http://www.turtlebeachresort.com
9049 Midnight Pass Rd.
6 rooms - $125-295
Pets: $10 fee, credit card dep.
Creature Comforts: Charming,
intimate resort overlooking
Sarasota Bay, silk flowers, rms. w/
Country, Victorian, Southwest,
French and Key West decors,
CCTV, a/c, kit, Jacuzzis, pool, and
a gazebo

SILVER SPRINGS
Days Inn
(800) DAYS-INN, (352) 236-2891
http://www.daysinn.com
5001 E. Silver Springs Blvd.
56 rooms - $40-89
Pets: Welcome w/$5 fee
Creature Comforts: CCTV, a/c,
pool

Holiday Inn
(800) HOLIDAY, (352) 236-2575
http://www.holiday-inn.com
5751 E. Silver Springs Blvd.
102 rooms - $45-99
Pets: Small pets w/$25 fee
Creature Comforts: CCTV, a/c,
refrig, restaurant, pool

Howard Johnson Inn
(800) I-Go-Hojo, (352) 236-2616
http://www.hojo.com
5565 E. Silver Springs Blvd
40 rooms - $45-79
Pets: Small pets w/$5 fee
Creature Comforts: CCTV, a/c,
kit, pool

Sun Plaza Motel
(352) 236-2343
5461 E. Silver Springs Blvd
48 rooms - $35-65
Pets: Welcome w/$5 fee
Creature Comforts: CCTV, a/c,
kit, pool

SOUTH DAYTONA
Red Carpet Inn
(800) 251-1962, (904) 767-6681
http://www.reservahost.com
1855 S. Ridgewood Ave.
32 rooms - $35-155
Pets: Small pets $5 fee
Creature Comforts: CCTV, a/c,
kit, pool

STARKE
Best Western Inn
(800) 528-1234, (904) 964-6744
http://www.bestwestern.com
1290 N. Temple Ave.
50 rooms - $40-95
Pets: Small pets w/$25 fee
Creature Comforts: CCTV, a/c,
refrig, cont. brkfst, pool

Days Inn
(800) DAYS-INN, (904) 964-7600
http://www.daysinn.com
1100 N. Temple Ave.
100 rooms - $40-79
Pets: Welcome w/$10 fee
Creature Comforts: CCTV, a/c,
restaurant, pool

Red Carpet Inn
(800) 251-1962, (904) 964-5590
http://www.reservahost.com
744 N. Temple Ave.
77 rooms - $45-98
Pets: Small pets $5 fee
Creature Comforts: CCTV, a/c,
restaurant, pool

Sleepy Hollow Motel
(904) 964-5006
2317 N. Temple Ave.
14 rooms - $95-240
Pets: Welcome w/$2 fee
Creature Comforts: CCTV, a/c,
refrig, pool

STEINHATCHEE
Steinhatchee Landing Resort
(800) 584-1709, (352) 498-3513
http://steinhatcheelanding.com
Route 51
21 cottages - $109-295
Pets: Welcome w/$250 dep.
Creature Comforts: Moss laden
oaks shade Victorian cottages,
gazebos, footbridges, CCTV,
VCR, stereos, a/c, kit, fireplaces,
screened porches, Jacuzzis,
restaurant, cont. brkfst, hlth club,
tennis, riding, boating, pool bikes,
canoes, trails-wildlife

STUART
Howard Johnson Inn
(800) I-Go-Hojo, (561) 287-3171
http://www.hojo.com
950 Rte. 1
80 rooms - $65-89
Pets: Welcome w/$10 fee
Creature Comforts: CCTV, a/c,
restaurant, cont. brkfst, hlth club
access, pool

Indian River Plantation
(800) 775-5936, (561) 225-3700
www.IndianRiverPlantation.com
585 Northeast Ocean Blvd.
254 rooms - $135-575
Pets: In 1st flr rms. w/$50 fee
Creature Comforts: Terrific
family-oriented 200-acre resort,
bright color schemes and chintz
fabrics, floor-to-ceiling windows,
wicker and Scandinavian-style
furnishings, CCTV, VCR, a/c, kit,
restaurant, pool, hlth clb, tennis,
beach-water crafts, turtles, bike
paths, children's program

SUGAR LOAF KEY
Sugar Loaf Lodge Resort
(305) 745-3211
Mile Marker 17
55 rooms - $65-129
Pets: Welcome w/$10 fee
Creature Comforts: CCTV, a/c,
kit, restaurant, pool, hlth clb,
whirlpool, tennis, boats, mini-golf

SUN CITY CENTER
Sun City Center Inn
(800) 237-8200, (813) 634-3331
1335 Rickenbacker Dr.
99 rooms - $45-99
Pets: Welcome w/$8 fee
Creature Comforts: CCTV, a/c,
restaurant, putting, pool

SUNNY ISLES
Newport Beach Crowne Plaza
(800) HOLIDAY, (305) 949-1300
http://www.crowneplaza.com
16701 Collins Ave.
344 rooms - $125-325
Pets: Under 20 lbs. welcome
Creature Comforts: CCTV,
VCR, a/c, refrig, micro, Jacuzzi,
restaurants, pools, hlth clb, sauna,
whirlpool, water sports

SUNRISE

Baymont Inns
(877)BAYMONT, (954) 846-1200
http://www.baymontinns.com
13651 NW 2nd St.
105 rooms - $60-109
Pets: Small pets welcome
Creature Comforts: CCTV, a/c,
Jacuzzi, cont. brkfst, pool

TALLAHASSEE

Best Inns of America
(800) 237-8466, (850) 562-2378
http://www.bestinns.com
2738 Graves Rd.
77 rooms - $45-79
Pets: Small pets welcome
Creature Comforts: CCTV, a/c,
refrig, cont. brkfst, pool

Collegiate Village Inn
(850) 576-6121
2121 W. Tennessee St.
150 rooms - $35-89
Pets: Small pets welcome
Creature Comforts: CCTV, a/c,
refrig, restaurant, cont. brkfst, pool

Econo Lodge
(800) 55-ECONO, (850) 385-6155
http://www.econolodge.com
2681 N. Monroe St.
82 rooms - $40-78
Pets: Small pets welcome
Creature Comforts: CCTV,
VCR, a/c, refrig, micro, cont.
brkfst

Holiday Inn
(800) HOLIDAY, (850) 562-2000
http://www.holiday-inn.com
2714 Graves Rd.
179 rooms - $65-95
Pets: Small pets w/$10 fee
Creature Comforts: CCTV, a/c,
restaurant, pool

Howard Johnson Express
(800) I-Go-Hojo, (850) 386-5000
http://www.hojo.com
2726 N. Monroe St.
52 rooms - $35-67
Pets: Welcome w/$5 fee
Creature Comforts: CCTV, a/c,
refrig, micro, cont. brkfst, pool

La Quinta Inn
(800) Nu-Rooms, (850) 385-7172
http://www.laquinta.com
2905 N. Monroe St.
155 rooms - $50-79
Pets: Small pets welcome
Creature Comforts: CCTV, a/c,
refrig, micro, cont. brkfst, pool

La Quinta Inn
(800) Nu-Rooms, (850) 878-5099
http://www.laquinta.com
2850 Apalachee Pkwy.
133 rooms - $50-75
Pets: Small pets welcome
Creature Comforts: CCTV, a/c,
refrig, micro, cont. brkfst, pool

Motel 6
(800) 4-MOTEL6, (850) 877-6171
http://www.motel6.com
1027 Apalachee Pkwy.
100 rooms - $35-45
Pets: Under 30 lbs.welcome
Creature Comforts: CCTV, a/c,
pool

Motel 6
(800) 4-MOTEL6, (850) 668-2600
http://www.motel6.com
1481 Timberlane Rd.
153 rooms - $35-49
Pets: Under 30 lbs.welcome
Creature Comforts: CCTV, a/c,
pool

Motel 6
(800) 4-MOTEL6, (850) 386-7878
http://www.motel6.com
2738 N. Monroe St.
101 rooms - $35-49
Pets: Under 30 lbs.welcome
Creature Comforts: CCTV, a/c,
pool

Red Roof Inn
(800) The Roof, (850) 385-7884
http://www.redroof.com
2930 Hospitality St.
108 rooms - $40-77
Pets: Small pets welcome
Creature Comforts: CCTV, a/c

Shoney's Inn
(800) 222-2222, (850) 386-8286
http://www.shoneysinn.com
2801 N. Monroe St.
111 rooms - $45-149
Pets: Welcome
Creature Comforts: CCTV, a/c,
refrig, micro, pool, whirlpool

Travelodge
(800) 578-7878, (850) 224-8161
http://www.travelodge.com
691 W. Tennessee St.
58 rooms - $45-70
Pets: Welcome w/$10 fee
Creature Comforts: CCTV, a/c,
pool

TAMARAC

Baymont Inns
(877)BAYMONT, (954) 485-7900
http://www.baymontinns.com
3800 W. Commercial Blvd.
102 rooms - $50-89
Pets: Small pets welcome
Creature Comforts: CCTV, a/c,
cont. brkfst, pool

Wellesley Inns
(800) 444-8888, (954) 484-6909
http://www.wellesleyinns.com
Rtes. 7 & 441
99 rooms - $55-105
Pets: Under 30 lbs. w/$10 fee
Creature Comforts: CCTV, a/c,
refrig, micro, cont. brkfst, pool

TAMPA

Amerisuites
(800) 833-1516, (813) 282-1037
http://www.amerisuites.com
4811 W. Main St.
126 suites - $89-149
Pets: Small pets w/$10 fee
Creature Comforts: CCTV,
VCR, a/c, refrig, micro, cont.
brkfst, hlth club, pool

Amerisuites
(800) 833-1516, (813) 979-1922
http://www.amerisuites.com
11408 N. 30th St.
125 suites - $99-149
Pets: Small pets welcome
Creature Comforts: CCTV,
VCR, a/c, refrig, micro, cont.
brkfst, hlth club, pool

Baymont Inns
(877)BAYMONT, (813) 626-0885
http://www.baymontinns.com
4811 Rte. 301
101 rooms - $40-95
Pets: Small pets w/$10 fee
Creature Comforts: CCTV, a/c,
cont. brkfst, pool

Baymont Inns, Busch Gardens
(877)BAYMONT, (813) 930-6900
http://www.baymontinns.com
9202 - 30th St. N.
149 rooms - $55-80
Pets: Small pets w/$10 fee
Creature Comforts: CCTV, a/c,
cont. brkfst, pool

Baymont Inns
(877)BAYMONT, (813) 684-4007
http://www.baymontinns.com
602 S. Faulkenburg Rd.
102 rooms - $40-89
Pets: Small pets welcome
Creature Comforts: CCTV, a/c,
cont. brkfst, pool

Days Inn
(800) DAYS-INN, (813) 977-1550
http://www.daysinn.com
701 E. Fletcher Ave.
235 rooms - $45-95
Pets: Welcome w/$6 fee
Creature Comforts: CCTV, a/c,
refrig, micro, cont. brkfst, pool

Days Inn, Busch Gardens
(800) DAYS-INN, (813) 247-3300
http://www.daysinn.com
2520 N. 50th St.
200 rooms - $45-195
Pets: Welcome w/$10 fee
Creature Comforts: CCTV, a/c,
refrig, micro, restaurant, cont.
brkfst, pool

Econo Lodge
(800) 55-ECONO, (813) 933-7681
http://www.econolodge.com
1701 E. Busch Blvd.
238 rooms - $35-59
Pets: Small pets w/$5 fee
Creature Comforts: CCTV, a/c,
refrig, micro, restaurant, cont.
brkfst, pool

Holiday Inn
(800) HOLIDAY, (813) 971-4710
http://www.holiday-inn.com
2701 E. Fowler Ave.
399 rooms - $85-1345
Pets: Small pets welcome
Creature Comforts: CCTV, a/c,
restaurant, pool

Holiday Inn Express
(800) HOLIDAY, (813) 877-6061
http://www.holiday-inn.com
4732 N. Dale Mabry St.
234 rooms - $55-99
Pets: Welcome w/$20 fee
Creature Comforts: CCTV, a/c,
kit, pool

Holiday Inn
(800) HOLIDAY, (813) 621-2081
http://www.holiday-inn.com
2708 N. 50th St.
160 rooms - $60-95
Pets: Small pets w/$25 fee
Creature Comforts: CCTV, a/c,
restaurant, pool, whirlpool

Howard Johnson, Airport
(800) I-Go-Hojo, (813) 875-8818
http://www.hojo.com
2055 N. Dale Mabry St.
135 rooms - $80-109
Pets: Welcome w/$25 dep.
Creature Comforts: CCTV, a/c,
refrig, micro, cont. brkfst, pool

La Quinta Inn
(800) Nu-Rooms, (813) 527-8421
http://www.laquinta.com
4999 - 34th St. N.
122 rooms - $50-90
Pets: Small pets welcome
Creature Comforts: CCTV, a/c,
refrig, micro, cont. brkfst, pool

La Quinta Inn, Airport
(800) Nu-Rooms, (813) 287-0440
http://www.laquinta.com
4730 Spruce St.
124 rooms - $60-85
Pets: Small pets welcome
Creature Comforts: CCTV, a/c,
refrig, micro, cont. brkfst, hlth
club, pool

La Quinta Inn, Busch Gardens
(800) Nu-Rooms, (813) 623-3591
http://www.laquinta.com
2904 Melbourne Blvd.
129 rooms - $50-95
Pets: Small pets welcome
Creature Comforts: CCTV, a/c,
refrig, micro, cont. brkfst, hlth
club, pool

Masters Economy Inn
(800) 633-3434, (813) 621-4681
6010 Rte. 579
115 rooms - $39-55
Pets: Welcome w/$5 fee
Creature Comforts: CCTV, a/c,
refrig, micro, restaurant, pool

Motel 6
(800) 4-MOTEL6, (813) 932-4948
http://www.motel6.com
333 E. Fowler Ave.
150 rooms - $35-49
Pets: Under 30 lbs. welcome
Creature Comforts: CCTV, a/c,
pool

Motel 6
(800) 4-MOTEL6, (813) 628-0888
http://www.motel6.com
6510 N. Rte. 301
108 rooms - $35-49
Pets: Under 30 lbs. welcome
Creature Comforts: CCTV, a/c,
pool

Red Roof Inn
(800) The Roof, (813) 623-5245
http://www.redroof.com
5001 N. Rte. 301
105 rooms - $40-99
Pets: Small pets welcome
Creature Comforts: CCTV, a/c

Residence Inn
(800) 331-3131, (813) 281-5677
http://www.residenceinn.com
3075 N. Rocky Pt. Dr.
175 rooms - $95-199
Pets: Under 30 lbs. welcome w/$5
fee, and a $100 dep.
Creature Comforts: CCTV, a/c,
kit, cont. brkfst, hlth club, pool

Sheraton Four Points Hotel
(800) 325-3535, (813) 626-0999
http://www.sheraton.com
7401 E. Hillsborough Ave.
275 rooms - $100-425
Pets: Welcome
Creature Comforts: CCTV,
VCR, a/c, refrig, micro, restaurant,
pool, hlth clb

Tahitian Inn
(800) 876-1397, (813) 877-6721
601 S. Dale Mabry St.
80 rooms - $49-75
Pets: Welcome w/$25 fee
Creature Comforts: CCTV, a/c,
restaurant, pool

TARPON SPRINGS
Best Western Tahitian Inn
(800) 528-1234, (813) 937-4121
http://www.bestwestern.com
2337 Rte. 19
139 rooms - $60-99
Pets: Small pets w/$10 fee
Creature Comforts: CCTV, a/c,
kit, restaurant, pool

Days Inn
(800) DAYS-INN, (813) 934-0859
http://www.daysinn.com
40050 Rte. 19
204 rooms - $40-99
Pets: Welcome w/$5 fee
Creature Comforts: CCTV, a/c,
restaurant, cont. brkfst, pool

Gulf Manor Motel
(813) 937-4207
548 Whitcomb Blvd.
30 rooms - $45-99
Pets: Small pets w/$5 fee
Creature Comforts: CCTV, a/c,
kit, pool

Scottish Inns
(800) 251-1962, (813) 937-6121
http://www.reservahost.com
110 W. Tarpon Ave.
79 rooms - $30-55
Pets: $5 fee & CC deposit
Creature Comforts: CCTV, a/c,
cont. brkfst, pool

TAVARES
Inn on the Green
(352) 343-6373
700 E. Burleigh Blvd.
75 rooms - $45-149
Pets: Small pets w/$60 dep.
Creature Comforts: CCTV,
VCR, a/c, kit, cont. brkfst, pool,
and lawn games

TEMPLE TERRACE
Residence Inn
(800) 331-3131, (813) 972-4400
http://www.residenceinn.com
13420 N. Telecom Pkwy.
79 rooms - $95-189
Pets: Welcome w/$75 fee
Creature Comforts: CCTV, a/c,
kit, cont. brkfst, pool

TITUSVILLE
Best Western Inn
(800) 528-1234, (407) 269-9100
http://www.bestwestern.com
3455 Cheney Hwy.
125 rooms - $60-99
Pets: Small pets w/$10 fee
Creature Comforts: CCTV, a/c,
cont. brkfst, sauna, hlth club, pool

Days Inn
(800) DAYS-INN, (407) 383-4480
http://www.daysinn.com
3755 Cheney Hwy.
143 rooms - $40-155
Pets: Welcome w/$10 fee
Creature Comforts: CCTV, a/c,
refrig, cont. brkfst, pool

Holiday Inn
(800) HOLIDAY, (407) 269-2121
http://www.holiday-inn.com
4951 S. Washington Ave.
119 rooms - $70-135
Pets: Welcome
Creature Comforts: CCTV, a/c,
refrig, restaurant, pool, playgrnd

Howard Johnson Lodge
(800) I-Go-Hojo, (407) 267-7900
http://www.hojo.com
1829 Riverside Dr.
102 rooms - $60-129
Pets: Welcome
Creature Comforts: CCTV,
VCR, a/c, refrig, micro, hlth club,
pool

TREASURE ISLAND
Seahorse Cottages
(800) 741-2291, (727) 367-2291
http://www.beachdirectory.com/
seahorse
10356 Gulf Blvd.
9 rooms - $55-99
Pets: Small pets w/$5 fee
Creature Comforts: Good value
and appeal, great beachside housekeeping cottages, knotty pine
walls, seaside décor, pine and oak
furnishings, CCTV, a/c, kit, kiddie
pool, sandy beach-barbecue lanais

VENICE
Days Inn
(800) DAYS-INN, (941) 493-4558
http://www.daysinn.com
1710 S. Tamiami Tr.
72 rooms - $50-275
Pets: Welcome w/$15 fee
Creature Comforts: CCTV, a/c,
refrig, cont. brkfst, pool

Inn at the Beach Resort
(800) 255-8471, (941) 484-8471
101 The Esplanade
44 rooms - $99-325
Pets: Under 20 lbs. w/$25 fee
Creature Comforts: CCTV, a/c,
kit, pool, on the beach

Motel 6
(800) 4-MOTEL6, (941) 485-8255
http://www.motel6.com
281 Rte. 41
103 rooms - $35-45
Pets: Under 30 lbs. welcome
Creature Comforts: CCTV, a/c,
pool

VERO BEACH
Best Western Inn
(800) 528-1234, (561) 561-8321
http://www.bestwestern.com
8797 - 20th St.
115 rooms - $65-99
Pets: Small pets welcome
Creature Comforts: CCTV, a/c,
refrig, micro, restaurant, cont.
brkfst, pool, hlth club, lawn games

Days Inn
(800) DAYS-INN, (561) 562-9991
http://www.daysinn.com
8800 - 20th St.
115 rooms - $40-95
Pets: Welcome w/$5 fee
Creature Comforts: CCTV, a/c,
restaurant, pool

Super 8 Motel
(800) 800-8000, (561) 562-9996
http://www.super8.com
8800 - 20th St.
116 rooms - $59-89
Pets: Welcome
Creature Comforts: CCTV, a/c,
pool

WEEKI WATCHEE
Comfort Inn
(800) 228-5150, (352) 596-9000
http://www.comfortinn.com
9373 Cortez Blvd.
65 rooms - $55-89
Pets: Welcome w/$9 fee
Creature Comforts: CCTV, a/c,
refrig, pool

Holiday Inn
(800) HOLIDAY, (352) 596-2007
http://www.holiday-inn.com
6172 Commercial Way
122 rooms - $55-85
Pets: Welcome in hotel's kennel
Creature Comforts: CCTV, a/c,
restaurant, pool

WESLEY CHAPEL
Masters Economy Inn
(800) 633-3434, (813) 973-0155
27807 Rte. 54
120 rooms - $39-55
Pets: Welcome w/$5 fee
Creature Comforts: CCTV, a/c,
refrig, micro, restaurant, pool

WEST PALM BEACH
Comfort Inn
(800) 228-5150, (561) 689-6100
http://www.comfortinn.com
1901 Palm Beach Lakes Blvd.
164 rooms - $49-175
Pets: Welcome w/$10 fee
Creature Comforts: CCTV, a/c,
refrig, restaurant, cont. brkfst, pool

Days Inn
(800) DAYS-INN, (561) 848-8661
http://www.daysinn.com
2700 N. Ocean Dr.
165 rooms - $69-199
Pets: Welcome w/$10 fee
Creature Comforts: CCTV, a/c,
restaurant, pool, whirlpool, private
beach

Days Inn
(800) DAYS-INN, (561) 689-0450
http://www.daysinn.com
2300 - 45th St.
234 rooms - $40-129
Pets: Welcome w/$10 fee
Creature Comforts: CCTV, a/c,
restaurant, pool, whirlpool

Days Inn
(800) DAYS-INN, (561) 686-6000
http://www.daysinn.com
6255 Okeechobee Blvd.
154 rooms - $40-129
Pets: Welcome w/$10 fee
Creature Comforts: CCTV, a/c,
restaurant, pool, hlth club, and a
whirlpool

Knights Inn
(800) 843-5644, (561) 478-1554
http://www.knightsinn.com
2200 - 45th St.
77 rooms - $40-85
Pets: Welcome w/$10 fee
Creature Comforts: CCTV, a/c,
kits, pool

Red Roof Inn
(800) The Roof, (561) 697-7710
http://www.redroof.com
2421 Metro Center Blvd.
128 rooms - $40-99
Pets: Small pets welcome
Creature Comforts: CCTV, a/c,
pool

Residence Inn
(800) 331-3131, (561) 687-4747
http://www.residenceinn.com
2461 Metro Center Blvd.
78 rooms - $95-189
Pets: Welcome w/$200 fee
Creature Comforts: CCTV, a/c,
kit, cont. brkfst, pool

Wellesley Inns
(800) 444-8888, (561) 689-8540
http://www.wellesleyinn.com
1910 Palm Beach Lakes Blvd.
105 rooms - $59-135
Pets: Welcome w/$10 fee
Creature Comforts: CCTV, a/c,
refrig, micro, cont. brkfst, pool

WILDWOOD
Days Inn
(800) DAYS-INN, (352) 748-7766
http://www.daysinn.com
561 E. Rte. 44
130 rooms - $35-85
Pets: Welcome w/$5 fee
Creature Comforts: CCTV, a/c,
cont. brkfst, pool

Red Carpet Inn
(800) 251-1962, (352) 748-4488
http://www.reservahost.com
Route 301
89 rooms - $45-75
Pets: Small pets welcome
Creature Comforts: CCTV, a/c,
pool

WILLISTON
Williston Motor Inn
(352) 528-4801
606 W. Noble Ave.
45 rooms - $30-55
Pets: Welcome w/$5 fee
Creature Comforts: CCTV, a/c,
kit, restaurant, pool

WINTER HAVEN
Best Western Inn
(800) 528-1234, (941) 324-5950
http://www.bestwestern.com
5665 Cypress Gardens Blvd.
155 rooms - $40-109
Pets: Small pets w/CC dep.
Creature Comforts: CCTV, a/c,
refrig, micro, restaurant, cont.
brkfst, pool

Budget Host
(800) Bud-Host, (941) 294-4229
http://www.budgethost.com
970 Cypress Gardens Blvd.
22 rooms - $40-79
Pets: Small pets w/$5 fee
Creature Comforts: CCTV, a/c,
kit, cont. brkfst, pool

Cypress Motel
(941) 324-5867
5651 Cypress Gardens Blvd.
22 rooms - $39-75
Pets: Small pets w/$10 fee
Creature Comforts: CCTV, a/c,
kit, pool

Holiday Inn
(800) HOLIDAY, (941) 294-4451
http://www.holiday-inn.com
1150 Third St. SW
225 rooms - $40-139
Pets: Welcome
Creature Comforts: CCTV, a/c,
refrig, micro, restaurant, pool

Howard Johnson
(800) I-Go-Hojo, (941) 294-7321
http://www.hojo.com
1300 Rte. 17 SW
99 rooms - $45-105
Pets: Small pets welcome
Creature Comforts: CCTV, a/c,
kit, restaurant, pool, lawn games

Scottish Inns
(800) 251-1962, (941) 324-3954
http://www.reservahost.com
1901 Cypress Gardens Blvd.
75 rooms - $30-49
Pets: $5 fee and credit card dep.
Creature Comforts: CCTV, a/c,
cont. brkfst, pool

WINTER PARK
Days Inn
(800) DAYS-INN, (407) 644-8000
http://www.daysinn.com
901 N. Orlando Ave.
103 rooms - $35-99
Pets: Welcome w/$6 fee
Creature Comforts: CCTV, a/c,
refrig, micro, cont. brkfst, pool

YULEE
Days Inn
(800) DAYS-INN, (904) 225-2011
http://www.daysinn.com
3250 Rte. 17
100 rooms - $39-84
Pets: Welcome w/$6 fee
Creature Comforts: CCTV, a/c,
refrig, restaurant, pool

ZEPHYR HILLS
Crystal Springs Motor Inn
(813) 782-1214
6736 Gall Blvd.
32 rooms - $39-64
Pets: Small pets welcome
Creature Comforts: CCTV, a/c,
kit, pool

Georgia

ACWORTH
Best Western Frontier Inn
(800) 528-1234, (770) 974-0116
http://www.bestwestern.com
Route 75
120 rooms - $50-80
Pets: Welcome w/$5 fee
Creature Comforts: CCTV, a/c,
cont. brkfst, pool

Quality Inn
(800) 228-5151, (770) 974-1922
http://www.qualityinn.com
4980 Cowan Rd.
60 rooms - $40-75
Pets: Welcome w/$5 fee
Creature Comforts: CCTV, a/c,
refrig, cont. brkfst, pool

Super 8 Motel
(800) 800-8000, (770) 966-9700
http://www.super8.com
4970 Cowan Rd.
50 rooms - $40-66
Pets: Welcome w/$7 fee
Creature Comforts: CCTV, a/c,
refrig, micro, cont. brkfst, pool

ADAIRSVILLE
Comfort Inn
(800) 228-5150, (770) 773-2886
http://www.comfortinn.com
107 Princeton Blvd.
55 rooms - $40-79
Pets: Small pets welcome
Creature Comforts: CCTV, a/c,
refrig, micro, Jacuzzis, pool

ADEL
Days Inn
(800) DAYS-INN, (912) 896-4574
http://www.daysinn.com
1200 W. 4th St.
80 rooms - $49-60
Pets: Welcome w/$5 fee
Creature Comforts: CCTV, a/c,
restaurant, pool

Howard Johnson
(800) I-Go-Hojo, (912) 896-2244
http://www.hojo.com
1103 W. 4th St.
69 rooms - $35-60
Pets: Small pets w/$4 fee
Creature Comforts: CCTV, a/c,
pool

Scottish Inns
(800) 251-1962, (912) 896-2259
http://www.reservahost.com
911 W. 4th St.
75 rooms - $30-44
Pets: Welcome
Creature Comforts: CCTV, a/c,
pool

Super 8 Motel
(800) 800-8000, (912) 896-4523
http://www.super8.com
1102 W. 4th St.
50 rooms - $40-65
Pets: Welcome w/$5 fee
Creature Comforts: CCTV, a/c,
pool

ALBANY
Econo Lodge
(800) 55-ECONO, (912) 883-5544
http://www.econolodge.com
1806 E. Oglethorpe Blvd.
50 rooms - $45-65
Pets: Welcome
Creature Comforts: CCTV, a/c,
Jacuzzis, cont. brkfst, pool

Holiday Inn
(800) HOLIDAY, (912) 883-8100
http://www.holiday-inn.com
2701 Dawson Rd.
150 rooms - $69-99
Pets: Small pets welcome
Creature Comforts: CCTV, a/c,
restaurant, pool

Knights Inn
(800) 843-5644, (912) 888-9600
http://www.knightsinn.com
1201 Schley Ave.
120 rooms - $40-75
Pets: Welcome w/$10 fee
Creature Comforts: CCTV, a/c,
refrig, micro, pool

Motel 6
(800) 4-MOTEL6, (912) 439-0078
http://www.motel6.com
201 S. Thornton Dr.
100 rooms - $35-39
Pets: Under 30 lbs. welcome
Creature Comforts: CCTV, a/c,
pool

Ramada Inn
(800) 2-Ramada, (912) 883-3211
http://www.ramada.com
2505 N. Slappey Blvd.
160 rooms - $50-99
Pets: Welcome w/$25 dep.
Creature Comforts: CCTV, a/c,
restaurant, pool

Super 8 Motel
(800) 800-8000, (912) 888-8388
http://www.super8.com
2444 N. Slappey Blvd.
62 rooms - $40-64
Pets: Welcome
Creature Comforts: CCTV, a/c,
refrig

ALPHARETTA
Residence Inn
(800) 331-3131, (770) 664-0664
http://www.residenceinn.com
5465 Windward Pkwy.
102 rooms - $80-175
Pets: Small pets w/$150-200 fee
Creature Comforts: CCTV, a/c,
kit, cont. brkfst, pool

AMERICUS
The Cottage Inn
(912) 924-8995, 931-0609
http://webserver.americus.net/
~cottage
Route 49
4 suites - $59-85
Pets: Welcome
Creature Comforts: A lovely
antebellum cottage w/antiques and
sprawling grounds, 18-ft high
ceilings, exquisite paintings,
antique porcelain, Oriental rugs,
four poster beds, brass accents,
period furnishings, handmade
quilts, CCTV, VCR, a/c, fireplace,
kit, Jacuzzi, cont. brkfst, pool,
tennis

1906 Pathway Inn
(800) 889-1466, (912) 928-2078
http://www.bbonline.com/ga/
pathway/index.html#top
501 S. Lee St.
5 rooms - $80-145
Pets: Under 20 lbs. w/$5 fee
Creature Comforts: Lovely
historic 1905 Colonial Revival inn
w/wraparound porches, inviting
decor, elegant ambiance, stained
glass, fireplaces, comforters,
CCTV, VCR, a/c, refrig, Jacuzzis,
full brkfst by candlelight, and
manicured grounds

ASHBURN
Comfort Inn
(800) 228-5150, (912) 567-0080
http://www.comfortinn.com
820 Shoney's Dr.
54 rooms - $40-69
Pets: Small pets w/$5 fee
Creature Comforts: CCTV, a/c,
refrig, micro, Jacuzzis, cont.
brkfst, pool

Days Inn
(800) DAYS-INN, (912) 567-0444
http://www.daysinn.com
823 E. Washington Ave.
68 rooms - $35-70
Pets: Welcome w/$5 fee
Creature Comforts: CCTV, a/c,
cont. brkfst, pool

ATHENS
Best Western Colonial Inn
(800) 528-1234, (706) 546-7311
http://www.bestwestern.com
170 N. Milledge Ave.
69 rooms - $50-75
Pets: Welcome w/$10 fee
Creature Comforts: CCTV, a/c,
refrig, micro, cont. brkfst, pool

Days Inn
(800) DAYS-INN, (706) 546-0410
http://www.daysinn.com
295 E. Dougherty St.
115 rooms - $45-85
Pets: Welcome w/$10 fee
Creature Comforts: CCTV, a/c,
cont. brkfst, pool

Downtowner Inn
(800) 251-1962, (706) 549-2626
1198 S. Milledge Ave.
70 rooms - $30-99
Pets: Welcome
Creature Comforts: CCTV, a/c,
cont. brkfst, pool

Ramada Inn
(800) 2-Ramada, (706) 546-8122
http://www.ramada.com
513 W. Broad St.
158 rooms - $60-119
Pets: Small pets welcome
Creature Comforts: CCTV,
VCR, a/c, refrig, restaurant, pool

Scottish Inns
(800) 251-1962, (706) 546-8161
http://www.reservahost.com
410 Macon Hwy.
70 rooms - $30-55
Pets: Welcome
Creature Comforts: CCTV, a/c,
cont. brkfst, pool

Super 8 Motel
(800) 800-8000, (706) 549-0251
http://www.super8.com
3425 Atlanta Hwy.
40 rooms - $35-55
Pets: Welcome
Creature Comforts: CCTV, a/c,
kit, cont. brkfst, pool, whirlpool

Travelodge
(800) 578-7878, (706) 549-5400
http://www.travelodge.com
898 W. Broad St.
40 rooms - $35-75
Pets: Welcome
Creature Comforts: CCTV, a/c,
kit, Jacuzzis, pool

ATLANTA
Amerisuites
(800) 833-1516, (404) 730-9300
http://www.amerisuites.com
1005 Crestline Pkwy.
150 rooms - $65-155
Pets: Small pets welcome
Creature Comforts: CCTV,
VCR, a/c, refrig, micro, cont.
brkfst, hlth club, pool

Beverly Hills Inn
(800) 331-8520, (404) 233-8520
66 Sheridan Dr. NE
http://www.beverlyhillsinn.com
19 rooms - $99-175
Pets: Small pets w/$50 fee
Creature Comforts: Historic
three-story inn w/pensione
ambiance, English antiques/
reproductions, four poster, finial
beds, floral fabrics, Japanese
screens, CCTV, a/c, kit, cont.
brkfst, access to a pool/hlth club

Best Western Peachtree Inn
(800) 528-1234, (404) 577-6970
http://www.bestwestern.com
330 W. Peachtree St.
110 rooms - $60-155
Pets: Small pets w/CC dep.
Creature Comforts: CCTV, a/c,
kit, cont. brkfst, hlth club

Baymont Inns
(877)BAYMONT, (404) 321-0999
http://www.baymontinns.com
2535 Chantilly Dr. NE
100 rooms - $45-75
Pets: Small pets welcome
Creature Comforts: CCTV, a/c,
cont. brkfst

Best Western Granada Suites
(800) 528-1234, (404) 876-6100
http://www.bestwestern.com
1302 W. Peachtree St.
103 rooms - $69-165
Pets: Small pets w/$50 fee & dep.
Creature Comforts: CCTV, a/c,
hlth club, cont. brkfst

Crowne Plaza
(800)2-CROWNE,(770) 955-1700
http://www.crowneplaza.com
6345 Powers Ferry Rd. NW
296 rooms - $99-229
Pets: Welcome w/$125 fee
Creature Comforts: CCTV, a/c, restaurant, hlth club, pool, and a cont. brkfst

Drury Inn, Airport
(800) Drury Inn, (404) 761-4900
http://www.drury-inn.com
1270 Virginia Ave.
155 rooms - $69-109
Pets: Welcome
Creature Comforts: CCTV, a/c, cont. brkfst, pool, whirlpool

Emory Inn
(404) 712-6700
1641 Clifton Rd.
105 rooms - $89-129
Pets: Welcome w/$25 fee
Creature Comforts: CCTV, a/c, refrig, restaurant, pool

Four Seasons Hotel
(800) 332-3442, (404) 881-9898
http://www.fshr.com
75 - 14th St.
245 rooms - $175-2,100
Pets: Under 15 Lbs. - pet goodies
Creature Comforts: Exquisite hotel in quiet residential neighborhood, lavishly appointed rooms, Jacuzzis, marble accents, English antiques/reproductions, CCTV, VCR, a/c, fireplace, refrig, micro, restaurant, pool, hlth clb, saunas, massage, steamrooms, whirlpools, access to golf/tennis

Grand Hyatt
(800) 233-1234, (404) 365-8100
http://www.hyatt.com
3300 Peachtree Rd.
435 rooms - $175-2,500
Pets: Under 25Lbs. w/$100 fee
Creature Comforts: CCTV, VCR, a/c, refrig, fireplaces, Jacuzzis, restaurant, 3 pools, hlth clb, sauna, whirlpool, and access to tennis and golf

Hawthorne Suites Hotel
(770) 952-9595
1500 Parkwood Circle
220 rooms - $79-229
Pets: Small pets w/$100 fee, credit card dep.
Creature Comforts: CCTV, VCR, a/c, kit, cont. brkfst, pool, hlth clb, whirlpool

Hilton Hotel
(800) HILTONS, (404) 659-2000
http://www.hilton.com
255 Courtland St. NE
1,225 rooms - $119-1,295
Pets: Small pets welcome
Creature Comforts: CCTV, VCR, a/c, refrig, Jacuzzis, 2 restaurants, pool, hlth clb, sauna, whirlpools, tennis

Holiday Inn Central
(800) HOLIDAY, (404) 873-4661
http://www.holiday-inn.com
418 Armour Dr. NE
342 rooms - $69-129
Pets: $25 fee, $125 dep.
Creature Comforts: CCTV, a/c, refrig, Jacuzzis, restaurant, hlth club, pool

Holiday Inn Select
(800) HOLIDAY, (770) 457-6363
http://www.holiday-inn.com
4386 Chamblee-Dunwoody Rd.
249 rooms - $95-169
Pets: $25 fee, $125 dep.
Creature Comforts: CCTV, a/c, refrig, Jacuzzis, restaurant, hlth club, pool

Masters Economy Inn
(800) 633-3434, (404) 696-4690
4120 Fulton Industrial Blvd.
170 rooms - $35-80
Pets: Welcome w/$5 fee
Creature Comforts: CCTV, a/c, refrig, restaurant, pool

Red Roof Druid Hills Inn
(800) The-Roof, (404) 321-1653
http://www.redroof.com
1960 N. Druid Rd.
114 rooms - $40-75
Pets: Small pets welcome
Creature Comforts: CCTV, a/c

Red Roof Six Flags Inn
(800) The-Roof, (404) 696-4391
http://www.redroof.com
4265 Shirley Dr. SW
120 rooms - $40-75
Pets: Small pets welcome
Creature Comforts: CCTV, a/c

Residence Inn
(800) 331-3131, (404) 252-5066
http://www.residenceinn.com
6096 Barfield Rd.
129 rooms - $95-189
Pets: Welcome w/$150 fee
Creature Comforts: CCTV, a/c, kit, cont. brkfst, pool

Residence Inn Buckhead
(800) 331-3131, (404) 239-0677
http://www.residenceinn.com
2960 Piedmont Rd. NE
135 rooms - $135-199
Pets: Welcome w/$150 fee
Creature Comforts: CCTV, a/c, kit, cont. brkfst, pool

Residence Inn Buckhead-Lenox
(800) 331-3131, (404) 467-1660
http://www.residenceinn.com
2222 Lake Blvd.
150 rooms - $95-189
Pets: Welcome w/$150 fee
Creature Comforts: CCTV, a/c, kit, cont. brkfst, pool

Residence Inn Midtown
(800) 331-3131, (404) 872-8885
http://www.residenceinn.com
1041 W. Peachtree St.
65 rooms - $129-199
Pets: Welcome w/$150 fee
Creature Comforts: CCTV, a/c, kit, cont. brkfst, pool

Residence Inn Perimeter East
(800) 331-3131, (404) 455-4446
http://www.residenceinn.com
1901 Savoy Dr.
145 rooms - $69-129
Pets: Welcome w/$100 fee
Creature Comforts: CCTV, a/c, kit, cont. brkfst, pool

Ritz Carlton Hotel
(800) 241-3333, (602) 468-0700
http://www.ritzcarlton.com
3434 Peachtree Road
553 rooms - $275-2,000
Pets: Welcome w/$250 fee
Creature Comforts: Exquisite
hotel set in the midst of a quiet
residential section of Buckhead,
CCTV, VCR, a/c, refrig,
restaurant, pool, sauna, massage,
whirlpool, steamroom, access to
golf

Summerfield Suites
(800) 833-4353, (404) 250-0110
www.summerfieldsuites.com
760 Mt. Vernon Hwy. NE
124 rooms - $99-175
Pets: Welcome w/$100 fee
Creature Comforts: CCTV, a/c,
kit, hlth club, pool, whirlpool

Summerfield Suites
(800) 833-4353, (404) 262-7880
www.summerfieldsuites.com
505 Pharr Rd.
88 rooms - $99-175
Pets: Welcome w/$10 fee, $150
cleaning fee
Creature Comforts: CCTV, a/c,
kit, hlth club, pool, whirlpool

Travelodge
(800) 578-7878, (770) 451-4811
http://www.travelodge.com
3701 Presidential Pkwy.
106 rooms - $35-55
Pets: Welcome w/CC dep.
Creature Comforts: CCTV, a/c,
pool

University Inn
(404) 634-7327
1767 N. Decatur Rd.
50 rooms - $65-140
Pets: Welcome w/$20 fee
Creature Comforts: CCTV, a/c,
kit, cont. brkfst, pool

Westin Peachtree Hotel
(800) 228-3000, (404) 659-1400
http://www.westin.com
210 NW Peachtree St.
1,065 rooms - $129-1,500
Pets: Small pets w/$8 fee
Creature Comforts: CCTV,
VCR, a/c, refrig, 2 restaurants,
hlth club, sauna, 2 pools

Westin Hotel
(800) 228-3000, (404) 762-7676
http://www.westin.com
4736 Best Rd.
499 rooms - $175-650
Pets: Small pets w/$10 fee
Creature Comforts: CCTV, a/c,
refrig, micro, restaurant, sauna,
whirlpool, hlth club, pool

AUGUSTA
Amerisuites
(800) 833-1516, (706) 733-4656
http://www.amerisuites.com
1062 Claussen Rd.
110 rooms - $55-99
Pets: Small pets w/$5
Creature Comforts: CCTV,
VCR, refrig, micro, cont. brkfst,
hlth club, pool, whirlpool

Days Inn
(800) DAYS-INN, (706) 724-8100
http://www.daysinn.com
444 Broad St.
148 rooms - $35-199
Pets: Welcome w/$5 fee
Creature Comforts: CCTV, a/c,
refrig, micro, restaurant, cont.
brkfst, pool

Holiday Inn
(800) HOLIDAY, (706) 737-2300
http://www.holiday-inn.com
2155 Gordon Hwy.
152 rooms - $65-99
Pets: Small pets welcome
Creature Comforts: CCTV, a/c,
pool

La Quinta Inn
(800) Nu-Rooms, (706) 733-2660
http://www.laquinta.com
3020 Washington Rd.
128 rooms - $45-69
Pets: Small pets welcome
Creature Comforts: CCTV, a/c,
refrig, micro, cont. brkfst, pool

Masters Economy Inn
(800) 633-3434, (706) 963-5566
3027 Washington Rd.
165 rooms - $39-85
Pets: Welcome w/$5 fee
Creature Comforts: CCTV, a/c,
refrig, restaurant, pool

Motel 6
(800) 4-MOTEL6, (706) 736-1934
http://www.motel6.com
2650 Center W. Pkwy.
118 rooms - $29-38
Pets: Under 30 lbs. welcome
Creature Comforts: CCTV, a/c,
pool

Radisson Riverfront Hotel
(800) 333-3333, (706) 722-8900
http://www.radisson.com
River Walk & 10th St.
234 rooms - $99-485
Pets: Small pets welcome
Creature Comforts: CCTV, a/c,
refrig, micro, restaurant, sauna,
pool, hlth club, whirlpool

Radisson Suites Hotel
(800) 333-3333, (706) 868-1800
http://www.radisson.com
3038 Washington Rd.
175 rooms - $59-169
Pets: Small pets w/$25 dep.
Creature Comforts: CCTV,
VCR, a/c, Jacuzzis, kit, restaurant,
hlth club access, pool

Ramada Limited
(800) 2-Ramada, (706) 733-8115
http://www.ramada.com
2154 Gordon Hwy.
30 rooms - $39-80
Pets: Small pets w/$25 dep.
Creature Comforts: CCTV, a/c,
and refrig

Red Carpet Inn
(800) 251-1962, (954) 792-8181
http://www.reservahost.com
2440 Rte. 84
90 rooms - $45-90
Pets: Small pets $5 fee
Creature Comforts: CCTV, a/c,
restaurant, pool

Sheraton Hotel
(800) 325-3535, (706) 855-8100
http://www.sheraton.com
2651 Perimeter Pkwy.
180 rooms - $99-399
Pets: Small pets welcome
Creature Comforts: CCTV, a/c,
restaurant, pools, whirlpool,
sauna, hlth clb

 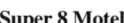

Super 8 Motel
(800) 800-8000, (706) 724-0757
http://www.super8.com
954 - 5th St.
65 rooms - $30-59
Pets: $3 fee and credit card dep.
Creature Comforts: CCTV, a/c,
refrig, micro, cont. brkfst, pool

AUSTELL
Knights Inn
(800) 843-5644, (770) 944-0824
http://www.knightsinn.com
1595 Blair Bridge Rd.
96 rooms - $40-75
Pets: Welcome w/$10 fee
Creature Comforts: CCTV, a/c,
refrig, pool

BAINBRIDGE
Best Western Inn
(800) 528-1234, (912) 246-0015
http://www.bestwestern.com
751 W. Shotwell St.
53 rooms - $40-79
Pets: Under 10 lbs. welcome
Creature Comforts: CCTV, a/c,
cont. brkfst, hlth club, pool

BAXLEY
Pine Lodge Motel
(800) 841-6052, (912) 367-3622
500 S. Main St.
60 rooms - $34-45
Pets: Welcome
Creature Comforts: CCTV, a/c,
refrig, pool

BLAIRSVILLE
7 Creeks Cabins
(706) 745-4753
http://www.7creeks.com
5109 Horseshoe Cove Rd.
6 cottages - $65 ($375/week)
Pets: Must adhere to house rules
Creature Comforts: A 70-acre,
low-key lakeside resort shingled
cottages w/knotty pine walls,
CTV, VCR, fireplace, kit, refrig,
micro, recreational diversions,
floating dock-fishing, lawn games,
near Appalachian Trail

Misty Mountain Cottages
(888) MISTY-MN,(706) 745-4786
http://www.jwww.com/misty
4376 Misty Mountain La.
6 cottages - $55-95
Pets: Welcome w/credit card dep.
Creature Comforts: A secluded
Victorian mountain retreat w/
antiques and private modern
cottages, four poster beds, SATV,
a/c, fireplaces, wrap-around porch,
antiques, Jacuzzis, ceiling fans,
kit, cont. brkfst, ponds,
Appalachian Trail

Nottley Dam Guest House
(706) 745-7939
2266 Nottley Dam Rd.
6 rooms - $65-90
Pets: Small pets welcome
Creature Comforts: CCTV, a/c,
refrig, cont. brkfst

BLUE RIDGE
Blue Ridge Mtn. Cabins
(706) 632-8999
www.blueridgega.com/mtncabins
Rte. 5, Box 1182
42 cabins - $85-155
Pets: $20 fee and $50 deposit
Creature Comforts: Fully-
equipped log cabins set in woods
or on mountainsides w/mtn. and
water views, CCTV, VCR, a/c, kit,
Jacuzzis, whirlpools

Days Inn
(800) DAYS-INN, (706) 632-2100
http://www.daysinn.com
4970 Appalachian Hwy.
60 rooms - $49-99
Pets: Welcome w/$4 fee
Creature Comforts: CCTV, a/c,
refrig, micro, pool

BREMEN
Days Inn
(800) DAYS-INN, (770) 537-4646
http://www.daysinn.com
35 Price Creek Rd.
62 rooms - $49-129
Pets: Welcome w/$5 fee
Creature Comforts: CCTV, a/c,
cont. brkfst, pool

Travelodge
(800) 578-7878, (770) 537-3833
http://www.travelodge.com
1007 Alabama Ave.
78 rooms - $35-139
Pets: Welcome w/$6 fee
Creature Comforts: CCTV, a/c,
refrig, micro, pool

BRUNSWICK
Baymont Inns
(877)BAYMONT, (912) 265-7725
http://www.baymontinns.com
105 Tourist Dr.
101 rooms - $40-75
Pets: Small pets welcome
Creature Comforts: CCTV, a/c,
cont. brkfst, pool

Best Western Inn
(800) 528-1234, (912) 264-0144
http://www.bestwestern.com
5323 New Jesup Hwy.
143 rooms - $45-69
Pets: Small pets welcome
Creature Comforts: CCTV, a/c,
cont. brkfst, pool

Comfort Inn
(800) 228-5150, (912) 264-6540
http://www.comfortinn.com
5308 New Jesup Hwy.
120 rooms - $49-99
Pets: Welcome
Creature Comforts: CCTV,
VCR, a/c, refrig, micro, restaurant,
cont. brkfst, pool

Days Inn
(800) DAYS-INN, (912) 265-8830
http://www.daysinn.com
2307 Gloucester St.
98 rooms - $39-59
Pets: Welcome w/$5 fee
Creature Comforts: CCTV, a/c,
restaurant, cont. brkfst, pool

Embassy Suites
(800) 362-2779, (912) 264-6100
http://www.embassy-suites.com
500 Mall Blvd.
129 rooms - $79-155
Pets: Small pets welcome
Creature Comforts: CCTV, a/c,
Jacuzzis, refrig, micro, hlth club,
pool

Holiday Inn
(800) HOLIDAY, (912) 264-4033
http://www.holiday-inn.com
5252 New Jesup Hwy.
126 rooms - $69-99
Pets: Small pets welcome
Creature Comforts: CCTV, a/c,
restaurant, cont. brkfst, pool

Motel 6
(800) 4-MOTEL6, (912) 264-8582
http://www.motel6.com
403 Butler Dr.
122 rooms - $36-55
Pets: Under 30 lbs. welcome
Creature Comforts: CCTV, a/c,
pool

Ramada Inn Limited
(800) 2-Ramada, (912) 264-3621
http://www.ramada.com
3040 Scarlet St.
212 rooms - $45-99
Pets: Small pets welcome
Creature Comforts: CCTV, a/c,
refrig, restaurant, cont. brkfst, pool

Ramada Inn Downtown
(800) 2-Ramada, (912) 264-8611
http://www.ramada.com
3241 Glynn Ave.
100 rooms - $55-129
Pets: Welcome
Creature Comforts: CCTV, a/c,
refrig, micro, restaurant, cont.
brkfst, hlth club access, pool

Sleep Inn
(800) Sleep-Inn, (912) 261-0670
http://www.sleepinn.com
5272 New Jesup Hwy.
94 rooms - $49-99
Pets: Welcome
Creature Comforts: CCTV,
VCR, a/c, Jacuzzis, cont. brkfst,
pool

Super 8 Motel
(800) 800-8000, (912) 264-8800
http://www.super8.com
5280 New Jesup Hwy.
62 rooms - $45-60
Pets: Welcome
Creature Comforts: CCTV, a/c,
and refrig

BYRON
Best Western Inn
(800) 528-1234, (912) 956-3056
http://www.bestwestern.com
101 Dunbar Rd.
70 rooms - $45-75
Pets: Welcome w/$20 dep.
Creature Comforts: CCTV, a/c,
restaurant, cont. brkfst, hlth club,
and a pool

Econo Lodge
(800) 55-ECONO, (912) 956-5600
http://www.econolodge.com
106 Old Mason Rd.
95 rooms - $30-59
Pets: Welcome w/$5 fee
Creature Comforts: CCTV, a/c,
refrig, micro, cont. brkfst, pool

Passport Inn
(800) 251-1962, (912) 956-5200
Route 75
78 rooms - $35-60
Pets: Small pets welcome
Creature Comforts: CCTV, a/c,
refrig, micro, pool

CAIRO
Best Western Executive Inn
(800) 528-1234, (912) 377-8000
http://www.bestwestern.com
2800 Rte. 84 E.
49 rooms - $45-79
Pets: Under 6 lbs. welcome
Creature Comforts: CCTV, a/c,
restaurant, cont. brkfst, hlth club,
sauna, pool

Days Inn
(800) DAYS-INN, (912) 377-4400
http://www.daysinn.com
35 Rte. 84 E.
34 rooms - $40-65
Pets: Welcome w/$5 fee
Creature Comforts: CCTV, a/c,
cont. brkfst, pool

CALHOUN
Best Western Inn
(800) 528-1234, (706) 629-4521
http://www.bestwestern.com
2261 Rte. 41 NE
40 rooms - $40-69
Pets: Small pets welcome
Creature Comforts: CCTV, a/c,
cont. brkfst, pool, whirlpool

Budget Host
(800) Bud-Host, (706) 629-8644
http://www.budgethost.com
3900 Rte. 53
74 rooms - $35-58
Pets: Small pets welcome
Creature Comforts: CCTV, a/c,
refrig, micro, restaurant, cont.
brkfst, pool

Days Inn
(800) DAYS-INN, (706) 629-8271
http://www.daysinn.com
742 Rte. 53 SE.
120 rooms - $35-80
Pets: Welcome w/$4 fee
Creature Comforts: CCTV, a/c,
refrig, cont. brkfst, pool

Duffy's Motel
(706) 629-4436
1441 Rte. 41 N.
38 rooms - $25-39
Pets: Small pets welcome
Creature Comforts: CCTV, a/c,
pool

Econo Lodge
(800) 55-ECONO, (706) 625-5421
http://www.econolodge.com
1438 Rte. 41
40 rooms - $30-200
Pets: Welcome w/$5 fee
Creature Comforts: CCTV, a/c,
cont. brkfst, pool

Howard Johnson Inn
(800) I-Go-Hojo, (706) 629-9191
http://www.hojo.com
1220 Red Bud Rd.
99 rooms - $45-69
Pets: Small pets w/$5 fee
Creature Comforts: CCTV, a/c,
restaurant, cont. brkfst, hlth club,
pool

Quality Inn
(800) 228-5151, (706) 629-9501
http://www.qualityinn.com
915 Rte. 53 E.
100 rooms - $40-115
Pets: Welcome w/$5 fee
Creature Comforts: CCTV, a/c,
refrig, micro, restaurant, cont.
brkfst, pool

Scottish Inns
(800) 251-1962, (706) 629-8271
http://www.reservahost.com
1510 Red Bud Rd. NE.
77 rooms - $30-94
Pets: Welcome w/$3 fee
Creature Comforts: CCTV, a/c,
cont. brkfst, pool

Super 8 Motel
(800) 800-8000, (706) 602-1400
http://www.super8.com
1446 Rte. 41 N.
46 rooms - $35-65
Pets: Welcome w/permission
Creature Comforts: CCTV, a/c,
cont. brkfst, pool

CAMILLA
Best Western Courtland Inn
(800) 528-1234, (912) 336-0731
http://www.bestwestern.com
600 Rte. 19 S.
52 rooms - $50-75
Pets: Small pets welcome
Creature Comforts: CCTV, a/c,
cont. brkfst, pool

CANTON
Days Inn
(800) DAYS-INN, (770) 479-0301
http://www.daysinn.com
291 Ball Ground Hwy.
40 rooms - $40-65
Pets: Welcome w/$5 fee
Creature Comforts: CCTV, a/c,
refrig, micro, cont. brkfst, pool,
whirlpool

CARROLLTON
Days Inn
(800) DAYS-INN, (770) 830-1000
http://www.daysinn.com
180 Centennial Rd.
58 rooms - $45-75
Pets: Welcome w/$5 fee
Creature Comforts: CCTV, a/c,
cont. brkfst, pool, hlth club

Ramada Inn
(800) 2-Ramada, (770) 834-7700
http://www.ramada.com
1202 S. Park St.
102 rooms - $55-75
Pets: Small pets $10 fee
Creature Comforts: CCTV, a/c,
restaurant, pool

CARTERSVILLE
Budget Host
(800) Bud-Host, (770) 386-0350
http://www.budgethost.com
851 Cass-White Rd.
90 rooms - $39-95
Pets: Welcome w/$4 fee
Creature Comforts: CCTV, a/c,
restaurant, cont. brkfst, pool

Comfort Inn
(800) 228-5150, (770) 387-1800
http://www.comfortinn.com
28 Rte. 294 SE
60 rooms - $39-65
Pets: Welcome w/$5 fee
Creature Comforts: CCTV, a/c,
refrig, micro, Jacuzzis, pool

Days Inn
(800) DAYS-INN, (770) 382-1824
http://www.daysinn.com
5618 Rte. 20 SE
52 rooms - $49-89
Pets: Welcome w/$5 fee
Creature Comforts: CCTV, a/c,
cont. brkfst, pool, whirlpool

Econo Lodge
(800) 55-ECONO, (770) 387-2696
http://www.econolodge.com
35 Cassville Rd.
68 rooms - $30-155
Pets: Welcome
Creature Comforts: CCTV,
VCR, a/c, cont. brkfst, pool

Holiday Inn
(800) HOLIDAY, (770) 386-0830
http://www.holiday-inn.com
2336 Rte. 411 NE
64 rooms - $35-95
Pets: Small pets w/$5 fee
Creature Comforts: CCTV, a/c,
restaurant, cont. brkfst, hlth club,
pool

Howard Johnson Inn
(800) I-Go-Hojo, (770) 386-0700
http://www.hojo.com
25 Carson Loop
99 rooms - $45-69
Pets: Small pets w/$5 fee
Creature Comforts: CCTV, a/c,
restaurant, cont. brkfst, hlth club,
pool

Knights Inn
(800) 843-5644, (770) 386-7263
http://www.knightsinn.com
420 E. Church St.
69 rooms - $39-99
Pets: Small pets welcome
Creature Comforts: CCTV,
VCR, a/c, refrig, micro, cont.
brkfst

Motel 6
(800) 4-MOTEL6, (770) 386-1449
http://www.motel6.com
5657 Rte. 20
50 rooms - $39-48
Pets: Under 30 lbs. welcome
Creature Comforts: CCTV, a/c,
pool

Ramada Limited
(800) 2-Ramada, (770) 382-1515
http://www.ramada.com
45 Rte. 20 Spur SE
49 rooms - $39-109
Pets: Small pets w/$9 fee
Creature Comforts: CCTV, a/c,
refrig, micro, pool

Red Carpet Inn
(800) 251-1962, (770) 382-8000
http://www.reservahost.com
851 Cass-White Rd.
48 rooms - $28-54
Pets: Small pets $4 fee
Creature Comforts: CCTV, a/c,
restaurant, pool

Super 8 Motel
(800) 800-8000, (770) 382-8881
http://www.super8.com
41 Rte. 20 Spur SE
61 rooms - $45-65
Pets: Welcome w/permission
Creature Comforts: CCTV, a/c,
restaurant

CHATSWORTH
Key West Inn
(706) 517-1155
501 GI Maddox Pkwy.
44 rooms - $45-64
Pets: Welcome w/$5 fee
Creature Comforts: CCTV, a/c

CHULA
Red Carpet Inn
(800) 251-1962, (912) 382-2686
http://www.reservahost.com
Route 75
75 rooms - $25-38
Pets: Welcome
Creature Comforts: CCTV, a/c, pool

CLARKSVILLE
Habersham Hollow B&B
(706) 754-5147
Rte. 6, Box 6208
2 cottages - $85-110
Pets: Welcome w/$5 fee
Creature Comforts: A pair of charming cottages wooded setting, knotty pine walls, colorful quilts, dried flowers and wreaths, porches w/woodland views, fireplaces, kit, cont. brkfst

COLLEGE PARK
Baymont Inns, Airport
(877)BAYMONT, (404) 766-0000
http://www.baymontinns.com
2480 Old National Pkwy.
99 rooms - $50-75
Pets: Small pets welcome
Creature Comforts: CCTV, a/c, refrig, micro, cont. brkfst

La Quinta Inn, Airport
(800) Nu-Rooms, (440) 768-1241
http://www.laquinta.com
4874 Old National Hwy.
124 rooms - $60-85
Pets: Small pets welcome
Creature Comforts: CCTV, a/c, cont. brkfst, hlth clb, pool

Marriott Hotel, Airport
(800) 228-9290, (404) 766-7900
http://www.marriott.com
4711 Best Rd.
645 rooms - $75-199
Pets: Under 25 Lbs. w/$50 dep.
Creature Comforts: CCTV, a/c, refrig, restaurant, pool, hlth clb, sauna, racquetball, tennis, spa

Red Roof Inn
(800) The-Roof, (404) 761-9701
http://www.redroof.com
2471 Old National Pkwy.
110 rooms - $45-79
Pets: Small pets welcome
Creature Comforts: CCTV, a/c

COLUMBUS
Baymont Inns
(877)BAYMONT, (706) 323-4344
http://www.baymontinns.com
2919 Warm Springs Rd.
100 rooms - $40-75
Pets: Small pets welcome
Creature Comforts: CCTV, a/c, cont. brkfst, pool

Comfort Inn
(800) 228-5150, (706) 568-3300
http://www.comfortinn.com
3443 Macon Rd.
65 rooms - $55-70
Pets: Small pets welcome
Creature Comforts: CCTV, a/c, refrig, microwave, Jacuzzis, pool, whirlpool

Days Inn
(800) DAYS-INN, (706) 561-4400
http://www.daysinn.com
3452 Macon Rd.
122 rooms - $55-75
Pets: Welcome
Creature Comforts: CCTV, a/c, cont. brkfst, pool

Econo Lodge
(800) 55-ECONO, (706) 682-3803
http://www.econolodge.com
4483 Victory Blvd.
80 rooms - $40-65
Pets: Welcome
Creature Comforts: CCTV, a/c, pool

Howard Johnson
(800) I-Go-Hojo, (706) 322-6641
http://www.hojo.com
1011 Veterans Pkwy.
129 rooms - $49-77
Pets: Small pets welcome
Creature Comforts: CCTV, a/c, restaurant, pool

La Quinta Inn
(800) Nu-Rooms, (706) 568-1740
http://www.laquinta.com
3201 Macon Rd.
125 rooms - $50-80
Pets: Small pets welcome
Creature Comforts: CCTV, a/c, refrig, cont. brkfst, pool

Motel 6
(800) 4-MOTEL6, (706) 687-7214
http://www.motel6.com
3050 Victory Dr.
111 rooms - $39-58
Pets: Under 30 lbs. welcome
Creature Comforts: CCTV, a/c, pool

Super 8 Motel, Airport
(800) 800-8000, (706) 322-6580
http://www.super8.com
2935 Warm Springs Rd.
75 rooms - $45-69
Pets: Welcome w/permission
Creature Comforts: CCTV, a/c, cont. brkfst

COMMERCE
Guest House Inn
(800) 21-GUEST, (706) 335-5147
30934 Rte. 441 S.
74 rooms - $38-47
Pets: Under 15 lbs. welcome
Creature Comforts: CCTV, a/c, cont. brkfst, pool

Holiday Inn Express
(800) HOLIDAY, (706) 335-5183
http://www.holiday-inn.com
30747 Rte. 441 S.
95 rooms - $55-79
Pets: Small pets w/credit card dep
Creature Comforts: CCTV, VCR, a/c, refrig, micro, cont. brkfst, hlth club, pool

Ramada Inn
(800) 2-Ramada, (706) 335-5191
http://www.ramada.com
Rtes. 441 & 85
122 rooms - $45-85
Pets: Welcome
Creature Comforts: CCTV, a/c, refrig, restaurant, cont. brkfst, pool

CONYERS
Comfort Inn
(800) 228-5150, (770) 760-0300
http://www.comfortinn.com
1363 Klondike Rd.
82 rooms - $70-99
Pets: Welcome w/$25 fee
Creature Comforts: CCTV, a/c, refrig, micro, Jacuzzis, sauna, hlth club, pool, whirlpool

Georgia

Ramada Limited
(800) 2-Ramada, (770) 760-0777
http://www.ramada.com
1070 Dogwod Dr.
65 rooms - $60-179
Pets: Small pets w/$5 fee
Creature Comforts: CCTV, a/c,
refrig, micro, cont. brkfst, pool

CORDELE
Colonial Inn
(912) 273-5420
2016 - 16th Ave. E.
90 rooms - $45-75
Pets: Welcome
Creature Comforts: CCTV, a/c,
refrig, micro, cont. brkfst, pool

Days Inn
(800) DAYS-INN, (912) 273-1123
http://www.daysinn.com
Rtes. 75 & 280
126 rooms - $45-65
Pets: Welcome
Creature Comforts: CCTV, a/c,
pool

Econo Lodge
(800) 55-ECONO, (912) 273-2456
http://www.econolodge.com
1618 E. 16th Ave.
45 rooms - $35-55
Pets: Welcome
Creature Comforts: CCTV, a/c,
cont. brkfst

Holiday Inn
(800) HOLIDAY, (912) 273-4117
http://www.holiday-inn.com
1711 E. 16th Ave.
188 rooms - $55-79
Pets: Small pets welcome
Creature Comforts: CCTV, a/c,
restaurant, pool

Passport Inn
(800) 251-1962, (912) 273-4088
http://www.reservahost.com
1602 E. 16th Ave.
70 rooms - $35-50
Pets: Small pets w/$3 fee
Creature Comforts: CCTV, a/c,
refrig, pool

Ramada Inn
(800) 2-Ramada, (912) 273-3390
http://www.ramada.com
2016 E. 16th Ave.
101 rooms - $38-75
Pets: Welcome
Creature Comforts: CCTV, a/c,
refrig, Jacuzzis, restaurant, cont.
brkfst, pool

Rodeway Inn
(800) 228-2000, (912) 273-3390
http://www.rodeway.com
11609 E. 16th Ave.
55 rooms - $39-109
Pets: Welcome
Creature Comforts: CCTV, a/c,
refrig, pool

COVINGTON
Holiday Inn Express
(800) HOLIDAY, (770) 787-4900
http://www.holiday-inn.com
10111 Alcovy Rd.
50 rooms - $65-80
Pets: Small pets w/$25 fee
Creature Comforts: CCTV, a/c,
refrig, micro, cont. brkfst, hlth
club, pool

DALTON
Best Inns of America
(706) 226-1100
1529 W. Walnut Ave.
90 rooms - $45-69
Pets: Small pets welcome
Creature Comforts: CCTV, a/c,
refrig, cont. brkfst, pool

Best Western Inn
(800) 528-1234, (706) 226-5022
http://www.bestwestern.com
2106 Chattanooga Rd.
99 rooms - $45-89
Pets: Small pets welcome
Creature Comforts: CCTV, a/c,
restaurant, pool

Days Inn
(800) DAYS-INN, (706) 278-0850
http://www.daysinn.com
1518 W. Walnut Ave.
145 rooms - $45-66
Pets: Welcome w/$10 fee
Creature Comforts: CCTV, a/c,
cont. brkfst, pool

Holiday Inn
(800) HOLIDAY, (706) 278-0500
http://www.holiday-inn.com
515 Holiday Dr.
198 rooms - $70-99
Pets: Welcome w/$10 dep.
Creature Comforts: CCTV, a/c,
restaurant, hlth club, pool

Motel 6
(800) 4-MOTEL6, (706) 278-5522
http://www.motel6.com
2200 Chattanooga Rd.
67 rooms - $29-42
Pets: Under 30 lbs. welcome
Creature Comforts: CCTV, a/c

Super 8 Motel
(800) 800-8000, (706) 277-9323
http://www.super8.com
236 Connector 3 SW
59 rooms - $45-60
Pets: Welcome w/permission
Creature Comforts: CCTV, a/c,
restaurant, cont. brkfst, pool

DARIEN
Holiday Inn Express
(800) HOLIDAY, (912) 437-5373
http://www.holiday-inn.com
Magnolia Bluff
60 rooms - $55-79
Pets: Welcome w/$5 fee
Creature Comforts: CCTV, a/c,
pool

Open Gates B&B
(912) 437-6985
http://www.inns.com/south/
ga013.htm#ent2404
Vernon Square
4 rooms - $50-75
Pets: Welcome w/permission
Creature Comforts: 1876 B&B
in intimate town square, high
ceilings, family heirlooms,
cheerful colors, antiques, quilts,
baby grand piano, intriguing
collectibles—antique rug and hair
wreath, CCTV, VCR, a/c, refrig,
fireplace, cont. brkfst, pool,
hammock, and lawn games

Super 8 Motel
(800) 800-8000, (912) 437-6660
http://www.super8.com
Rtes. 251 & 95
60 rooms - $40-60
Pets: Welcome w/$10 fee
Creature Comforts: TV, a/c, pool

DECATUR

Holiday Inn
(800) HOLIDAY, (770) 981-5670
http://www.holiday-inn.com
4300 Snapfinger Woods Dr.
166 rooms - $55-99
Pets: Small pets w/credit card dep
Creature Comforts: CCTV, a/c,
pool

Motel 6
(800) 4-MOTEL6, (770) 288-6911
http://www.motel6.com
2565 Wesley Chapel Rd.
100 rooms - $39-57
Pets: Under 30 lbs. welcome
Creature Comforts: CCTV, a/c,
pool

DILLARD

Best Western Inn
(800) 528-1234, (706) 746-5321
http://www.bestwestern.com
Rtes. 441 & 23
66 rooms - $45-129
Pets: Small pets welcome
Creature Comforts: CCTV, a/c,
refrig, cont. brkfst, pool

The Dillard House
(800) 541-0671, (706) 746-5348
http://www.dillardhouse.com
Old Dillard Rd.
65 rooms - $49-155
Pets: Under 25 Lbs. w/$5 fee
Creature Comforts: Informal,
family-oriented resort, cottages,
period furnishings, country
collectibles, CCTV, a/c, Jacuzzis,
fireplaces and woodstoves, kit,
restaurant, lawn games, zoo,
tennis, pool, hiking, riding

DONALSONVILLE

Days Inn
(800) DAYS-INN, (912) 524-2185
http://www.daysinn.com
Route 84
31 rooms - $45-115
Pets: Welcome w/$5 fee
Creature Comforts: CCTV, a/c,
Jacuzzis, cont. brkfst, pool

DOUGLAS

Days Inn
(800) DAYS-INN, (912) 384-5190
http://www.daysinn.com
Route 441
70 rooms - $35-50
Pets: Welcome w/$5 fee
Creature Comforts: CCTV, a/c,
cont. brkfst, pool

Holiday Inn
(800) HOLIDAY, (912) 384-9100
http://www.holiday-inn.com
Route 441
100 rooms - $55-85
Pets: Small pets welcome
Creature Comforts: CCTV, a/c,
refrig, micro, restaurant, pool

Inn at Douglas
(912) 384-2621
1009 N. Peterson Ave.
99 rooms - $45-67
Pets: Small pets welcome
Creature Comforts: CCTV, a/c,
refrig, restaurant, pool

DORAVILLE

Masters Economy Inn
(800) 633-3434, (770) 454-8373
3092 Presidential Pkwy.
89 rooms - $35-70
Pets: Welcome w/$12 fee
Creature Comforts: CCTV, a/c,
refrig, micro, pool

DUBLIN

Holiday Inn
(800) HOLIDAY, (912) 272-7862
http://www.holiday-inn.com
Rtes. 441 & 16
125 rooms - $55-85
Pets: Small pets welcome
Creature Comforts: CCTV, a/c,
refrig, micro, restaurant, hlth club,
pool

DULUTH

Amerisuites
(800) 833-1516, (770) 623-6800
http://www.amerisuites.com
3390 Venture Pkwy.
112 rooms - $65-165
Pets: Small pets w/$10
Creature Comforts: CCTV,
VCR, refrig, micro, cont. brkfst,
hlth club, pool

Amerisuites
(800) 833-1516, (770) 623-5858
http://www.amerisuites.com
11505 Medlock Bridge Rd.
127 rooms - $65-165
Pets: Small pets w/$10 fee
Creature Comforts: CCTV,
VCR, refrig, micro, cont. brkfst,
hlth club, pool

FOLKSTON

Days Inn
(800) DAYS-INN, (912) 496-2514
http://www.daysinn.com
1201 S. 2nd St.
37 rooms - $35-70
Pets: Welcome w/$5 fee
Creature Comforts: CCTV, a/c,
restaurant, pool

FOREST PARK

Super 8 Motel
(800) 800-8000, (404) 363-8811
http://www.super8.com
410 Old Dixie Way
55 rooms - $45-60
Pets: Welcome w/permission
Creature Comforts: CCTV, a/c,
refrig, micro, Jacuzzi, restaurant,
cont. brkfst, pool

FORSYTH

Best Western Hilltop Inn
(800) 528-1234, (912) 994-9260
http://www.bestwestern.com
Rtes. 42 & 75
120 rooms - $40-55
Pets: Small pets w/$25 dep.
Creature Comforts: CCTV, a/c,
cont. brkfst, pool

Days Inn
(800) DAYS-INN, (912) 994-2900
http://www.daysinn.com
Lee Rd. & Rte. 75
100 rooms - $40-85
Pets: Welcome w/$5 fee
Creature Comforts: CCTV, a/c,
cont. brkfst, pool

Econo Lodge
(800) 55-ECONO, (912) 994-5603
http://www.econolodge.com
Rtes. 75 & 83
78 rooms - $30-159
Pets: Welcome w/$5 fee
Creature Comforts: CCTV, a/c,
refrig, micro, restaurant, cont.
brkfst, pool

Hampton Inn
(800) Hampton, (912) 994-9697
http://www.hampton-inn.com
520 Holiday Cir.
125 rooms - $48-60
Pets: Welcome
Creature Comforts: CCTV, a/c,
refrig, cont. brkfst, pool/hlth club
access

Holiday Inn
(800) HOLIDAY, (912) 994-5691
http://www.holiday-inn.com
480 Holiday Circle
122 rooms - $60-99
Pets: Small pets welcome
Creature Comforts: CCTV,
VCR, a/c, refrig, restaurant, pool

Passport Inn
(800) 251-1962, (912) 994-2643
http://www.reservahost.com
Rtes. 75 & 83
70 rooms - $35-65
Pets: Small pets welcome
Creature Comforts: CCTV, a/c

Super 8 Motel
(800) 800-8000, (912) 994-9333
http://www.super8.com
990 Rte. 42
120 rooms - $35-60
Pets: Welcome w/$5 fee
Creature Comforts: CCTV, a/c,
cont. brkfst, pool

GAINSVILLE
Holiday Inn
(800) HOLIDAY, (770) 536-4451
http://www.holiday-inn.com
726 J. Jewell Pkwy.
135 rooms - $70-129
Pets: Small pets welcome
Creature Comforts: CCTV,
VCR, a/c, refrig, micro, restaurant,
pool

Master's Inn Motel
(770) 532-7531
Monroe Dr. & Rte. 129
140 rooms - $35-55
Pets: Welcome w/$2 fee
Creature Comforts: CCTV, a/c,
kit

GARDEN CITY
Masters Economy Inn
(800) 633-3434, (912) 964-4344
4200 Rte. 21
120 rooms - $39-75
Pets: Small pets w/$5 fee
Creature Comforts: CCTV, a/c,
restaurant, pool

GLENNVILLE
Cheeri-o Motel
(912) 654-2176
Rtes. 25 & 301
24 rooms - $35-60
Pets: Small pets welcome
Creature Comforts: CCTV, a/c,
refrig, micro

HAPEVILLE
Residence Inn, Airport
(800) 331-3131, (404) 761-0511
http://www.residenceinn.com
3401 International Blvd.
126 rooms - $90-175
Pets: Small pets w/$100-200 fee
Creature Comforts: CCTV, a/c,
kit, restaurant, cont. brkfst, pool,
whirlpool

HAZLEHURST
The Village Inn
(912) 375-4527
312 Coffee St.
75 rooms - $39-60
Pets: Small pets welcome
Creature Comforts: CCTV, a/c,
refrig, micro, pool

HELEN
Helendorf River Inn
(800) 445-2271, (706) 878-2271
http://www.helendorf.com
33 Munichee Strasse Rd.
98 rooms - $45-120
Pets: In pet rooms w/$10 fee
Creature Comforts: A delightful
Swiss-themed inn set in recreated
Bavarian village, theme murals,
boxed-beamed ceilings, CCTV,
a/c, kit, Jacuzzis, fireplaces, river,
pool, seasonal festivals, access to
rafting, ballooning, riding, hiking

Shoney's Inn
(800) 222-2222, (912) 368-5858
http://www.shoneysinn.com
786 E. Oglethorpe Rd.
163 rooms - $45-69
Pets: Welcome w/$25 dep.
Creature Comforts: CCTV, a/c,
refrig, micro, restaurant, pool

JEFFERSON
Days Inn
(800) DAYS-INN, (912) 945-3785
http://www.daysinn.com
Rtes. 16 & 96
40 rooms - $45-65
Pets: Welcome w/$5 fee
Creature Comforts: CCTV, a/c,
cont. brkfst, pool

JEKYLL ISLAND
Clarion Hotel
(800) 252-7466, (912) 635-2261
http://www.clarioninn.com
85 S. Beachview Dr.
205 rooms - $80-225
Pets: Welcome w/$10 fee
Creature Comforts: CCTV, a/c,
kit, restaurant, pool, beach, hlth
clb, tennis, whirlpool

Comfort Inn
(800) 228-5150, (912) 635-2211
http://www.comfortinn.com
711 N. Beachview Dr.
180 rooms - $75-200
Pets: Welcome
Creature Comforts: CCTV, a/c,
kit, Jacuzzis, restaurant, pool,
beach, sauna, whirlpool

Days Inn
(800) DAYS-INN, (912) 635-3319
http://www.daysinn.com
60 S. Beachview Dr.
155 rooms - $39-79
Pets: Welcome w/$5 fee
Creature Comforts: CCTV, a/c,
restaurant, beach, pool

Holiday Inn
(800) HOLIDAY, (912) 635-3311
http://www.holiday-inn.com
200 S. Beachview Dr.
204 rooms - $65-139
Pets: Small pets w/$8 fee
Creature Comforts: CCTV, a/c,
refrig, micro, restaurant, pool,
tennis

Seafarer Inn
(921) 635-2202
700 N. Beachview Dr.
75 rooms - $45-99
Pets: Welcome w/$10 fee
Creature Comforts: CCTV, a/c, kit, pool

Villas By The Sea
(800) 841-6262, (912) 635-2521
http://www.jekyllislandga.com
1175 N. Beachview Dr.
175 rooms - $85-275
Pets: Welcome w/$50-100 fee
Creature Comforts: Good-sized, well-appointed condos and villas, resort set behind sand dunes, pine and oak furnishings, seaside décor, country accents, CCTV, VCR, a/c, fireplaces, kit, Jacuzzis, restaurant, pool, whirlpool, tennis, hlth club, lawn sports, bicycle paths, golf access

JESUP
Days Inn
(800) DAYS-INN, (912) 427-3751
http://www.daysinn.com
Rtes. 301 & 341
100 rooms - $40-55
Pets: Welcome w/$5 fee
Creature Comforts: CCTV, a/c, cont. brkfst, pool

Western Motel
(912) 427-7600
194 Rte. 301
30 rooms - $39-50
Pets: Welcome w/credit card dep.
Creature Comforts: CCTV, a/c

KENNESAW
Comfort Inn
(800) 228-5150, (770) 419-1530
http://www.comfortinn.com
750 Cobb Place Blvd.
80 rooms - $60-99
Pets: Welcome w/$5 fee
Creature Comforts: CCTV, a/c, pool

Days Inn
(800) DAYS-INN, (770) 419-1576
http://www.daysinn.com
760 Cobb Place
80 rooms - $55-109
Pets: Welcome w/$5 fee
Creature Comforts: CCTV, a/c, cont. brkfst, pool, whirlpool

Red Roof Inn
(800) The-Roof, (770) 429-0323
http://www.redroof.com
520 Roberts Ct. NW
135 rooms - $34-68
Pets: Small pets welcome
Creature Comforts: CCTV, a/c

Rodeway Inn
(800) 228-2000, (770) 590-0519
http://www.rodeway.com
1460 George Busbee Pkwy.
55 rooms - $39-75
Pets: Welcome w/$5 fee
Creature Comforts: CCTV, a/c, refrig, micro, Jacuzzis, pool

KINGSLAND
Best Western Kings Bay Inn
(800) 528-1234, (912) 729-7666
http://www.bestwestern.com
1353 Rte. 40
62 rooms - $50-99
Pets: Welcome w/$30 dep.
Creature Comforts: CCTV, a/c, refrig, micro, Jacuzzis, cont. brkfst, pool

Comfort Inn
(800) 228-5150, (912) 729-6979
http://www.comfortinn.com
111 Edenfield Rd.
129 rooms - $40-85
Pets: Small pets welcome
Creature Comforts: CCTV, VCR, a/c, refrig, micro, Jacuzzis, sauna, hlth club, pool, whirlpool

Days Inn
(800) DAYS-INN, (912) 729-5454
http://www.daysinn.com
1050 E. King Ave.
120 rooms - $40-80
Pets: Welcome w/$5 fee
Creature Comforts: CCTV, a/c, refrig, micro, restaurant, cont. brkfst, pool

Econo Lodge
(800) 55-ECONO, (912) 673-7336
http://www.econolodge.com
1135 E. King Ave.
53 rooms - $45-69
Pets: Welcome w/$25 dep.
Creature Comforts: CCTV, a/c, pool

Holiday Inn
(800) HOLIDAY, (912) 729-3000
http://www.holiday-inn.com
930 Rte. 40
155 rooms - $55-95
Pets: Small pets welcome
Creature Comforts: CCTV, a/c, kit, restaurant, pool, whirlpool

Quality Inn
(800) 228-5151, (912) 729-4363
http://www.qualityinn.com
985 Boone St.
112 rooms - $39-69
Pets: Welcome w/$25 dep.
Creature Comforts: CCTV, a/c, refrig, micro, cont. brkfst, pool

LA GRANGE
Days Inn
(800) DAYS-INN, (706) 882-8881
http://www.daysinn.com
2606 Whitesville Rd.
119 rooms - $45-155
Pets: Welcome w/$5 fee
Creature Comforts: CCTV, a/c, restaurant, cont. brkfst, pool

LAKE PARK
Country Hearth Inn
(912) 559-4939
7008 Bellville Rd.
60 rooms - $45-69
Pets: Small pets welcome
Creature Comforts: CCTV, a/c, pool

Days Inn
(800) DAYS-INN, (912) 559-0229
http://www.daysinn.com
106 Timber Dr.
94 rooms - $35-49
Pets: Welcome w/$2 fee
Creature Comforts: CCTV, a/c, cont. brkfst, pool

Holiday Inn Express
(800) HOLIDAY, (912) 559-5181
http://www.holiday-inn.com
1198 Lake Blvd.
65 rooms - $50-75
Pets: Small pets w/$5 fee
Creature Comforts: CCTV, a/c,
cont. brkfst, pool

Shoney's Inn
(800) 222-2222, (912) 559-5660
http://www.shoneysinn.com
1075 Lakes Blvd.
122 rooms - $40-65
Pets: Small pets welcome
Creature Comforts: CCTV, a/c,
restaurant, pool

Travelodge
(800) 578-7878, (912) 559-0110
http://www.travelodge.com
Route 75
78 rooms - $35-60
Pets: Welcome
Creature Comforts: CCTV, a/c,
cont. brkfst

LAWRENCEVILLE
Days Inn
(800) DAYS-INN, (770) 995-7782
http://www.daysinn.com
731 Duluth Hwy.
56 rooms - $49-105
Pets: Welcome w/$5 fee
Creature Comforts: CCTV, a/c,
kit, cont. brkfst

LITHONIA
La Quinta Inn
(800) Nu-Rooms, (770) 981-6411
http://www.laquinta.com
2859 Panola Rd.
129 rooms - $60-99
Pets: Small pets welcome
Creature Comforts: CCTV,
VCR, a/c, refrig, micro, cont.
brkfst, pool

LOCUST GROVE
Red Carpet Inn
(800) 251-1962, (770) 957-2601
http://www.reservahost.com
4829 Hampton Rd.
85 rooms - $29-40
Pets: Small pets $5 fee
Creature Comforts: CCTV, a/c,
restaurant, cont. brkfst, pool

Scottish Inns
(800) 251-1962, (770) 957-9001
http://www.reservahost.com
4679 Hampton Rd.
69 rooms - $30-99
Pets: Welcome w/$5 fee
Creature Comforts: CCTV, a/c,
restaurant, pool

Super 8 Motel
(800) 800-8000, (770) 957-2936
http://www.super8.com
4605 Hampton Rd.
56 rooms - $40-59
Pets: Welcome
Creature Comforts: CCTV, a/c,
refrig, micro, cont. brkfst, pool

LOUISVILLE
Louisville Motor Lodge
(912) 625-7168
308 Rte. 1
40 rooms - $40-55
Pets: Small pets w/$5 fee
Creature Comforts: CCTV, a/c,
and refrig

MACON
Best Western Inn & Suites
(800) 528-1234, (912) 781-5300
http://www.bestwestern.com
4681 Chambers Rd.
56 rooms - $50-99
Pets: Small pets w/$20 dep.
Creature Comforts: CCTV,
VCR, a/c, refrig, micro, cont.
brkfst, hlth club, whirlpool

Comfort Inn
(800) 228-5150, (912) 746-8855
http://www.comfortinn.com
2690 Riverside Dr.
122 rooms - $55-89
Pets: Small pets w/$50 dep.
Creature Comforts: CCTV, a/c,
refrig, micro, pool

Days Inn
(800) DAYS-INN, (912) 745-8521
http://www.daysinn.com
2737 Sheraton Dr.
120 rooms - $45-69
Pets: Welcome w/$5 fee
Creature Comforts: CCTV, a/c,
refrig, micro, cont. brkfst

Econo Lodge
(800) 55-ECONO, (912) 474-1661
http://www.econolodge.com
4951 Romeiser Dr.
60 rooms - $35-135
Pets: Small pets w/$5 fee and dep.
Creature Comforts: CCTV, a/c,
refrig, micro, cont. brkfst, pool

Hampton Inn
(800) Hampton, (912) 471-0660
http://www.hampton-inn.com
3680 Riverside Dr.
150 rooms - $59-89
Pets: Small pets w/$10 fee
Creature Comforts: CCTV, a/c,
refrig, pool

Howard Johnson
(800) I-Go-Hojo, (912) 746-7671
http://www.hojo.com
2566 Riverside Dr.
122 rooms - $55-75
Pets: Small pets welcome
Creature Comforts: CCTV, a/c,
refrig, micro, restaurant, cont.
brkfst, pool

Holiday Inn Express
(800) HOLIDAY, (912) 743-1482
http://www.holiday-inn.com
2720 Riverside Dr.
95 rooms - $55-79
Pets: Small pets welcome
Creature Comforts: CCTV, a/c,
refrig, micro, cont. brkfst, pool

Holiday Inn
(800) HOLIDAY, (912) 474-2610
http://www.holiday-inn.com
3590 Riverside Dr.
200 rooms - $75-139
Pets: Small pets welcome
Creature Comforts: CCTV, a/c,
refrig, micro, restaurant, cont.
brkfst, pool, whirlpool

Knights Inn
(800) 843-5644, (912) 471-1230
http://www.knightsinn.com
4952 Romeiser Rd.
108 rooms - $35-75
Pets: Small pets w/$5 fee
Creature Comforts: CCTV,
VCR, a/c, refrig, micro, pool

La Quinta Inn
(800) Nu-Rooms, (912) 475-0206
http://www.laquinta.com
3944 River Place Dr.
142 rooms - $69-99
Pets: Small pets welcome
Creature Comforts: CCTV, a/c,
refrig, micro, cont. brkfst, hlth
club, pool, whirlpool

Masters Economy Inn
(800) 633-3434, (912) 788-8910
4295 Rio Nono Ave.
122 rooms - $35-59
Pets: Welcome w/$5 fee
Creature Comforts: CCTV, a/c,
refrig, micro, cont. brkfst, pool

Motel 6
(800) 4-MOTEL6, (912) 474-2870
http://www.motel6.com
4991 Harrison Rd.
103 rooms - $29-42
Pets: Under 30 lbs. welcome
Creature Comforts: CCTV, a/c,
pool

Passport Inn
(800) 251-1962, (912) 474-2665
http://www.reservahost.com
5022 Romeiser Dr.
75 rooms - $29-50
Pets: Welcome w/$5 fee
Creature Comforts: CCTV, a/c,
refrig, pool

Quality Inn
(800) 228-5151, (912) 781-7000
http://www.qualityinn.com
4630 Chambers Rd.
104 rooms - $40-65
Pets: Welcome w/CC dep.
Creature Comforts: CCTV, a/c,
refrig, pool

Ramada Inn
(800) 2-Ramada, (912) 474-0871
http://www.ramada.com
5009 Harrison Rd.
122 rooms - $45-89
Pets: Under 25 lbs. welcome
Creature Comforts: CCTV, a/c,
refrig, micro, restaurant, cont.
brkfst, pool

Rodeway Inn
(800) 228-2000, (912) 781-4343
http://www.rodeway.com
4999 Eisenhower Pkwy.
56 rooms - $49-99
Pets: Welcome w/$20 dep.
Creature Comforts: CCTV,
VCR, a/c, refrig, micro, cont.
brkfst, pool

MADISON
Burnett Place B&B
(706) 342-4034
http://www.innsite.com
317 Old Post Rd.
3 rooms - $75-99
Pets: Welcome
Creature Comforts: Elegant
1830 Federal-style B&B, mature
plantings, pastel hues, Oriental
rugs, antiques, model ships,
pickled floors, four poster beds,
CCTV, VCR, a/c, fireplaces,
refrig, Jacuzzi, full brkfst

Days Inn
(800) DAYS-INN, (706) 342-1839
http://www.daysinn.com
2001 Eaton Hwy.
77 rooms - $49-85
Pets: Welcome w/$5 fee
Creature Comforts: CCTV, a/c,
pool

Ramada Inn
(800) 2-Ramada, (706) 342-2121
http://www.ramada.com
Rtes. 20 & 441
120 rooms - $45-85
Pets: Under 25 lbs. welcome
Creature Comforts: CCTV, a/c,
refrig, micro, cont. brkfst, hlth
club, pool

MARIETTA
Best Inns of America
(800) 237-8466, (770) 955-0004
http://www.bestinns.com
1255 Franklin Rd.
115 rooms - $45-79
Pets: Small pets welcome
Creature Comforts: CCTV, a/c,
refrig, micro, Jacuzzis, cont.
brkfst, pool

Drury Inn
(800) Drury Inn, (770) 612-0900
http://www.drury-inn.com
1170 Powers Ferry Pl.
142 rooms - $69-109
Pets: Small pets welcome
Creature Comforts: CCTV, a/c,
cont. brkfst, pool, whirlpool

Howard Johnson
(800) I-Go-Hojo, (770) 951-1144
http://www.hojo.com
2375 Delk Rd.
101 rooms - $49-99
Pets: Small pets welcome
Creature Comforts: CCTV, a/c,
refrig, micro, Jacuzzis, restaurant,
cont. brkfst, pool

La Quinta Inn
(800) Nu-Rooms, (770) 951-0026
http://www.laquinta.com
2170 Delk Rd.
132 rooms - $60-89
Pets: Small pets welcome
Creature Comforts: CCTV, a/c,
refrig, micro, cont. brkfst, pool

Masters Economy Inn
(800) 633-3434, (770) 951-2005
2682 Windy Hill Rd.
88 rooms - $39-79
Pets: Welcome w/$5 fee
Creature Comforts: CCTV, a/c,
refrig, and micro

Motel 6
(800) 4-MOTEL6, (770) 952-8161
http://www.motel6.com
2360 Delk Rd.
332 rooms - $39-59
Pets: Under 30 lbs. welcome
Creature Comforts: CCTV, a/c,
pool

Ramada Limited
(800) 2-Ramada, (770) 919-7878
http://www.ramada.com
630 Franklin Rd.
45 rooms - $45-100
Pets: Small pets welcome
Creature Comforts: CCTV, a/c,
refrig, micro, Jacuzzis, pool

Super 8 Motel
(800) 800-8000, (770)) 984-1570
http://www.super8.com
2500 Delk Rd.
104 rooms - $40-59
Pets: Welcome w/$15 fee
Creature Comforts: CCTV, a/c,
kit, pool

McDONOUGH
Brittany Motor Inn
(770) 957-5821
1171 Rte. 20
149 rooms - $40-55
Pets: Small pets welcome
Creature Comforts: CCTV, a/c,
pool

Days Inn
(800) DAYS-INN, (770) 957-5261
http://www.daysinn.com
744 Rte. 155
60 rooms - $49-75
Pets: Welcome w/$5 fee
Creature Comforts: CCTV, a/c,
pool

Econo Lodge
(800) 55-ECONO, (770) 957-2651
http://www.econolodge.com
1279 Hampton Rd.
39 rooms - $30-69
Pets: Welcome w/$5 fee
Creature Comforts: CCTV, a/c,
refrig, micro, pool

Holiday Inn
(800) HOLIDAY, (770) 957-5291
http://www.holiday-inn.com
930 Rte. 155
99 rooms - $65-99
Pets: Small pets welcome
Creature Comforts: CCTV, a/c,
restaurant, pool

Red Carpet Inn
(800) 251-1962, (770) 957-2458
http://www.reservahost.com
1170 Hampton Rd.
69 rooms - $30-55
Pets: Small pets welcome
Creature Comforts: CCTV, a/c,
pool

METTER
Days Inn
(800) DAYS-INN, (912) 685-2700
http://www.daysinn.com
720 S. Lewis St.
41 rooms - $39-75
Pets: Welcome w/$10 fee
Creature Comforts: CCTV, a/c,
Jacuzzis, cont. brkfst, pool

MILLEDGEVILLE
Days Inn
(800) DAYS-INN, (912) 453-3551
http://www.daysinn.com
3001 Heritage Rd.
94 rooms - $49-75
Pets: Welcome w/$2 fee
Creature Comforts: CCTV, a/c,
refrig, micro, cont. brkfst, pool

Scottish Inns
(800) 251-1962, (912) 453-9491
http://www.reservahost.com
2474 N. Columbia St.
69 rooms - $30-40
Pets: Welcome
Creature Comforts: CCTV, a/c

MONROE
Days Inn
(800) DAYS-INN, (770) 267-3666
http://www.daysinn.com
Rtes. 78 & 11
47 rooms - $40-175
Pets: Welcome w/$5 fee
Creature Comforts: CCTV, a/c,
restaurant, cont. brkfst, pool

MORROW
Best Western Southlake Inn
(800) 528-1234, (770) 961-6300
http://www.bestwestern.com
6437 Jonesboro Rd.
114 rooms - $50-99
Pets: Small pets welcome
Creature Comforts: CCTV, a/c,
refrig, micro, cont. brkfst, pool

Drury Inn
(800)Drury Inn, (770)960-0500
http://www.drury-inn.com
6520 S. Lee St.
133 rooms - $69-99
Pets: Small pets welcome
Creature Comforts: CCTV, a/c,
cont. brkfst, pool, whirlpool

Red Roof Inn
(800) The-Roof, (770) 968-1483
http://www.redroof.com
1348 S. Lake Plaza Dr.
107 rooms - $35-69
Pets: Small pets welcome
Creature Comforts: CCTV, a/c

Sleep Inn
(800) Sleep-Inn, (770) 472-9800
http://www.sleepinn.com
2185 Mt. Zion Pkwy.
90 rooms - $49-175
Pets: Welcome w/$50 dep.
Creature Comforts: CCTV, a/c,
refrig, micro, Jacuzzi, cont. brkfst,
pool, hlth clb, whirlpool

MOULTRIE
Inn at Moultrie
(912) 985-2200
1713 - 1st Ave. SE
100 rooms - $45-69
Pets: Small pets w/$10 fee
Creature Comforts: CCTV, a/c,
restaurant

NEWNAN
Days Inn
(800) DAYS-INN, (770) 253-8550
http://www.daysinn.com
1344 S. Hwy.
95 rooms - $49-109
Pets: Welcome w/$5 fee
Creature Comforts: CCTV, a/c,
refrig, micro, restaurant, pool

NORCROSS
Amberley Suite Hotel
(800) 365-0659, (770) 263-0515
http://www.travelweb.com
5585 Oakbrook Pkwy.
175 rooms - $59-99
Pets: Welcome w/$50 fee
Creature Comforts: CCTV, a/c,
kit, cont. brkfst, pool, hlth clb,
sauna, whirlpool

Amerisuites
(800) 833-1516, (770) 416-7655
http://www.amerisuites.com
5600 Peachtree Pkwy.
129 rooms - $99-145
Pets: Small pets welcome
Creature Comforts: CCTV,
VCR, a/c, refrig, micro, cont.
brkfst, hlth club, pool

Baymont Inns
(877)BAYMONT, (770) 446-2882
http://www.baymontinns.com
5395 Peachtree Indust. Blvd.
140 rooms - $45-69
Pets: Small pets welcome
Creature Comforts: CCTV, a/c,
cont. brkfst, kit, pool

Drury Inn
(800) Drury-Inn, (770) 729-0060
http://www.drury-inn.com
5655 Jimmy Carter Blvd.
135 rooms - $69-109
Pets: Small pets welcome
Creature Comforts: CCTV, a/c,
cont. brkfst, pool, whirlpool

La Quinta Inn
(800) Nu-Rooms, (770) 448-8686
http://www.laquinta.com
6187 Dawson Blvd.
128 rooms - $65-99
Pets: Small pets welcome
Creature Comforts: CCTV, a/c,
refrig, micro, cont. brkfst, pool

La Quinta Inn
(800) Nu-Rooms, (770) 449-5144
http://www.laquinta.com
5375 Peachtree Indust. Blvd.
128 rooms - $65-75
Pets: Small pets welcome
Creature Comforts: CCTV, a/c,
refrig, micro, cont. brkfst, pool

Motel 6
(800) 4-MOTEL6, (770) 446-2311
http://www.motel6.com
6015 Oakbrook Pkwy.
145 rooms - $39-55
Pets: Under 30 lbs. welcome
Creature Comforts: CCTV, a/c,
pool

Quality Inn
(800) 228-5151, (770) 449-7322
http://www.qualityinn.com
6045 Oakbrook Pkwy.
110 rooms - $45-75
Pets: Small pets w/$5 fee
Creature Comforts: CCTV, a/c,
refrig, pool

Red Roof Inn
(800) The-Roof, (770) 448-8944
http://www.redroof.com
5171 Brook Hollow Pkwy.
115 rooms - $35-69
Pets: Small pets welcome
Creature Comforts: CCTV, a/c

PERRY
Days Inn
(800) DAYS-INN, (912) 987-2142
http://www.daysinn.com
102 Valley Dr.
80 rooms - $45-75
Pets: Welcome w/$5 fee
Creature Comforts: CCTV, a/c,
Jacuzzi, cont. brkfst, pool

Hampton Inn
(800) Hampton, (912) 987-7681
http://www.hampton-inn.com
102 Hampton Ct.
98 rooms - $60-89
Pets: Under 30 lbs. welcome
Creature Comforts: CCTV, a/c,
refrig, cont. brkfst, pool

New Perry Hotel
(800) 877-3779, (912) 987-1000
web site pending
800 Main St.
48 rooms - $35-65
Pets: Welcome w/$5 fee
Creature Comforts: Historic
hotel, CCTV, a/c, restaurant, pool

Passport Inn
(800) 251-1962, (912) 987-9709
http://www.reservahost.com
1519 Sam Nunn Blvd.
75 rooms - $35-65
Pets: Small pets w/$5 fee
Creature Comforts: CCTV, a/c,
refrig, pool

Quality Inn
(800) 228-5151, (912) 987-1345
http://www.qualityinn.com
1504 Sam Nunn Blvd.
72 rooms - $45-79
Pets: Small pets welcome
Creature Comforts: CCTV, a/c,
refrig, micro, restaurant, pool

Ramada Inn
(800) 2-Ramada, (912) 987-8400
http://www.ramada.com
100 Market Place Dr.
60 rooms - $50-89
Pets: Welcome w/$25 fee
Creature Comforts: CCTV, a/c,
refrig, micro, Jacuzzis, cont.
brkfst, pool

Red Carpet Inn
(800) 251-1962, (912) 987-2200
http://www.reservahost.com
105 Carroll Blvd.
86 rooms - $29-55
Pets: Small pets w/$5 fee
Creature Comforts: CCTV, a/c,
pool

Rodeway Inn
(800) 228-2000, (912) 987-3200
http://www.rodeway.com
103 Mashallville Rd.
33 rooms - $39-55
Pets: Welcome
Creature Comforts: CCTV, a/c,
cont. brkfst, pool

Scottish Inns
(800) 251-1962, (912) 987-3622
http://www.reservahost.com
106 Gen Courtney Hodges Blvd.
75 rooms - $30-49
Pets: Welcome w/$3 fee
Creature Comforts: CCTV, a/c,
kit, pool

Super 8 Motel
(800) 800-8000, (912) 987-0999
http://www.super8.com
102 Plaza Dr.
58 rooms - $40-59
Pets: Welcome w/$10 fee
Creature Comforts: CCTV, a/c,
refrig, micro, Jacuzzis, cont.
brkfst, pool

PINE MOUNTAIN
White Columns Motel
(706) 663-2312
19727 Rte. 27
12 rooms - $35-55
Pets: Welcome in certain rooms
Creature Comforts: CCTV, a/c

POOLER
Ramada Inn
(800) 2-Ramada, (912) 748-6464
http://www.ramada.com
301 Gov. Teutlen Dr.
154 rooms - $50-95
Pets: Welcome w/$15 fee
Creature Comforts: CCTV, a/c,
refrig, restaurant, pool

REGISTER
Red Carpet Inn
(800) 251-1962, (912) 852-5200
http://www.reservahost.com
2875 Rte. 301
42 rooms - $45-60
Pets: Small pets welcome
Creature Comforts: CCTV, a/c

RICHMOND HILL
Days Inn
(800) DAYS-INN, (912) 756-3371
http://www.daysinn.com
Rtes. 95 & 17
116 rooms - $50-65
Pets: Welcome w/$5 fee
Creature Comforts: CCTV, a/c,
restaurant, pool

Econo Lodge
(800) 55-ECONO, (912) 756-3312
http://www.econolodge.com
Rtes. 95 & 17
48 rooms - $45-100
Pets: Small pets w/$25 dep.
Creature Comforts: CCTV, a/c,
refrig, micro, cont. brkfst

Motel 6
(800) 4-MOTEL6, (912) 756-3542
http://www.motel6.com
Rtes. 95 & 17
122 rooms - $35-39
Pets: Under 30 lbs. welcome
Creature Comforts: CCTV, a/c,
pool

Travelodge
(800) 578-7878, (912) 756-3325
http://www.travelodge.com
Rtes. 95 & 17
74 rooms - $35-69
Pets: Welcome
Creature Comforts: CCTV, a/c,
cont. brkfst, pool

RINGGOLD
Days Inn
(800) DAYS-INN, (706) 965-5730
http://www.daysinn.com
5436 Alabama Hwy.
58 rooms - $40-115
Pets: Welcome w/$3 fee
Creature Comforts: CCTV, a/c,
Jacuzzis, restaurant, pool

Super 8 Motel
(800) 800-8000, (706) 965-7080
http://www.super8.com
5400 Alabama Hwy.
40 rooms - $40-55
Pets: Welcome w/permission
Creature Comforts: CCTV, a/c,
refrig, micro, Jacuzzis, cont.
brkfst, pool

ROME
Holiday Inn
(800) HOLIDAY, (760) 295-1100
http://www.holiday-inn.com
Rte 411
205 rooms - $55-85
Pets: Welcome
Creature Comforts: CCTV, a/c,
refrig, restaurant, pool, sauna, and
a whirlpool

Super 8 Motel
(800) 800-8000, (760) 234-8182
http://www.super8.com
390 Dodd Blvd. SE
62 rooms - $40-65
Pets: Welcome
Creature Comforts: CCTV, a/c

ROSWELL
Baymont Inns
(877)BAYMONT, (770) 552-0200
http://www.baymontinns.com
575 Old Holcomb Bridge Rd.
105 rooms - $50-75
Pets: Small pets welcome
Creature Comforts: CCTV, a/c,
cont. brkfst, pool

Hampton Inn
(800) Hampton, (770) 587-5161
http://www.hampton-inn.com
9995 Old Dogwood Rd.
130 rooms - $60-89
Pets: Welcome w/$25 fee
Creature Comforts: CCTV, a/c,
refrig, pool

SAUTEE
Royal Windsor B&B
(706) 878-1322
4490 Rte. 356
4 rooms - $95-155
Pets: 1 pet per night w/$10 fee
Creature Comforts: Gracious
English-style cottage on 22 acres,
featured in Southern Living
magazine, antiques, down
comforters, CCTV, VCR, a/c,
fireplace, refrig, English brkfst
and tea, great mtn. views

SAVANNAH
Baymont Inns
(877)BAYMONT, (912) 927-7660
http://www.baymontinns.com
8484 Abercom St.
100 rooms - $45-65
Pets: Small pets welcome
Creature Comforts: CCTV, a/c,
cont. brkfst, pool

Best Western Central Inn
(800) 528-1234, (912) 355-1000
http://www.bestwestern.com
45 Eisenhower Dr.
128 rooms - $50-119
Pets: Small pets w/$5 fee
Creature Comforts: CCTV, a/c,
cont. brkfst, pool

East Bay Inn
(800) 500-1225, (912) 238-1225
http://www.eastbayinn.com
225 East Bay St.
28 rooms - $90-145
Pets: Under 25 lbs. w/$35 fee
Creature Comforts: Wonderfully
refurbished 1853 cotton
warehouse set in historic dist,
exposed brick walls, decorative
plasterwork, Georgian décor,
antique and reproduction
furnishings, brass lamps, Oriental
rugs, CCTV, VCR, a/c, refrig,
micro, fireplace, Jacuzzi,
restaurant, cont. brkfst

Econo Lodge
(800) 55-ECONO, (912) 925-2280
http://www.econolodge.com
7 Gateway Blvd. North
102 rooms - $45-115
Pets: Welcome w/$5 fee
Creature Comforts: CCTV, a/c,
restaurant, pool

Homewood Suites
(800) 225-5466, (912) 353-8500
http://www.homewoodsuites.com
5820 White Bluff Rd.
106 rooms - $89-149
Pets: Welcome w/$70 fee
Creature Comforts: CCTV,
VCR, a/c, kit, cont. brkfst, pool,
hlth clb, whirlpool

Holiday Inn
(800) HOLIDAY, (912) 925-2770
http://www.holiday-inn.com
Route 95
175 rooms - $55-89
Pets: Small pets welcome
Creature Comforts: CCTV, a/c,
refrig, restaurant, pool

Howard Johnson
(800) I-Go-Hojo, (912) 786-0700
http://www.hojo.com
1501 Butler Ave.
41 rooms - $45-95
Pets: Small pets welcome
Creature Comforts: CCTV, a/c,
Jacuzzis, restaurant, pool, at the
beach

Joan's on Jones B&B
(800) 407-3863, (912) 234-3863
http://www.bbonline.com/ga/
savannah/joans
17 W. Jones St.
2 suites - $99-145
Pets: Small dogs w/$50 fee
Creature Comforts: Beautifully
decorated 1883 Victorian
townhouse in National Historic
Landmark District, pastels hues,
Oriental rugs on heart of pine flrs,
antiques, four-poster rice beds,
CCTV, VCR, a/c, fireplace, kit,
cont. brkfst, lush patio/fountain

La Quinta Inn
(800) Nu-Rooms, (912) 355-3004
http://www.laquinta.com
6805 Abercorn St.
155 rooms - $55-80
Pets: Small pets welcome
Creature Comforts: CCTV, a/c,
refrig, micro, cont. brkfst, pool

The Manor House
(800) 462-3595, (912) 233-9597
http://www.bbonline.com/ga/
savannah/manorhouse
201 W. Liberty St.
5 suites - $185-275
Pets: Welcome in courtyard rms
Creature Comforts: A terrific
1830's B&B in historic dist, floor-
to-ceiling windows, pocket doors,
Oriental carpets, handsome color
schemes, English and American
antiques, four-poster beds, CCTV,
VCR, a/c, kit, fireplaces, Jacuzzis,
cont. brkfst

Olde Harbour Inn
(800) 553-6533, (912) 234-4100
http://www.oldeharbourinn.com
508 E. Factors Walk
24 suites - $115-225
Pets: Under 25 lbs. w/$35 fee
Creature Comforts: Historic inn
w/lovely suites nestled along river,
Palladian windows, ornate iron
balconies, English and French
antiques and reproductions,
pastoral and nautical prints, top
floor rooms have 25-ft ceilings
and skylights, four poster rice
beds, Bermuda plaid and floral
fabrics, CCTV, VCR, a/c, kit,
fireplace, restaurant, cont. brkfst

Quality Inn, Airport
(800) 228-5151, (912) 964-1421
http://www.qualityinn.com
1130 Bob Hamon Rd.
170 rooms - $55-75
Pets: Welcome w/$10 fee
Creature Comforts: CCTV, a/c,
refrig, restaurant, pool

Red Carpet Inn
(800) 251-1962, (912) 925-2640
http://www.reservahost.com
1 Fort Argyle Rd.
75 rooms - $45-65
Pets: Small pets $5 fee
Creature Comforts: CCTV, a/c,
restaurant, pool, whirlpool

Shoney's Inn
(800) 222-2222, (912) 925-7050
http://www.shoneysinn.com
17003 Abercom St.
66 rooms - $50-69
Pets: Welcome w/$25 dep.
Creature Comforts: CCTV, a/c,
refrig, micro, cont. brkfst, pool

Super 8 Motel
(800) 800-8000, (912) 927-8550
http://www.super8.com
15 Ft. Argyle Rd.
61 rooms - $40-69
Pets: Welcome w/permission
Creature Comforts: CCTV, a/c,
refrig, micro, Jacuzzis, cont.
brkfst, pool

Travelodge
(800) 578-7878, (912) 927-9830
http://www.travelodge.com
390 Canebrake Rd.
56 rooms - $35-79
Pets: Welcome
Creature Comforts: CCTV, a/c,
cont. brkfst, pool

SENOIA
Culpepper House B&B
(770) 599-8182
35 Broad St.
3 rooms - $75-120
Pets: Leashed pets welcome
Creature Comforts: An 1871
Victorian w/wraparound porch,
original woodwork, stained glass,
antiques, four poster beds, CCTV,
a/c, fireplace, kit, gourmet brkfst-
fine china, golf cart, tandem
bicycles

SMYRNA
Amerihost Inn
(800) 434-5800, (404) 794-1600
5130 S. Cobb Dr.
60 rooms - $55-89
Pets: Welcome w/$10 fee
Creature Comforts: CCTV, a/c,
refrig, micro, cont. brkfst, pool,
hlth clb, sauna, whirlpool

Red Roof Inn
(800) The-Roof, (770) 952-6966
http://www.redroof.com
5171 Brook Hollow Pkwy.
115 rooms - $35-75
Pets: Small pets welcome
Creature Comforts: CCTV, a/c

Residence Inn
(800) 331-3131, (770) 433-8877
http://www.residenceinn.com
2771 Hargrove Rd.
130 rooms - $80-175
Pets: Small pets w/$150-200 fee
Creature Comforts: CCTV, a/c,
kit, cont. brkfst, pool

SPARKS

Red Carpet Inn
(800) 251-1962, (912) 549-8243
http://www.reservahost.com
Rte. 1, Box 212
65 rooms - $40-65
Pets: Small pets welcome
Creature Comforts: CCTV, a/c, pool

STATESBORO

Days Inn
(800) DAYS-INN, (912) 764-5666
http://www.daysinn.com
461 S. Main St.
44 rooms - $35-95
Pets: Welcome w/$5 fee
Creature Comforts: CCTV, VCR, a/c, refrig, micro, pool

Ramada Inn
(800) 2-Ramada, (912) 764-6121
http://www.ramada.com
230 S. Main St.
130 rooms - $50-75
Pets: Welcome
Creature Comforts: CCTV, a/c, refrig, micro, restaurant, cont. brkfst, pool

Statesboro Inn
(800) 846-9466, (912) 489-8628
http://www.statesboroinn.com
106 So. Main St.
18 rooms - $85-135
Pets: Small pets welcome
Creature Comforts: Historic inn w/wrap-around porch, Persian rugs, wicker, hanging plants, floral fabrics, antiques,Victorian accents, CCTV, VCR, a/c, refrig, fireplace, Jacuzzis, restaurant, full brkfst, and lovely gardens

Super 8 Motel
(800) 800-8000, (912) 764-5631
http://www.super8.com
109 N. Main St.
42 rooms - $40-60
Pets: Welcome w/$10 dep.
Creature Comforts: CCTV, a/c, cont. brkfst, pool

STOCKBRIDGE

Amerihost Inn
(800) 434-5800, (770) 507-6500
http://www.amerihostinn.com
100 N. Park Ct.
60 rooms - $55-90
Pets: Welcome w/$10 fee
Creature Comforts: CCTV, a/c, refrig, micro, Jacuzzis, cont. brkfst, sauna, pool, whirlpool

Best Western Frontier Inn
(800) 528-1234, (770) 474-8771
http://www.bestwestern.com
3509 Rte. 138
115 rooms - $40-69
Pets: Under 20 lbs. welcome
Creature Comforts: CCTV, VCR, a/c, refrig, micro, cont. brkfst, pool

Motel 6
(800) 4-MOTEL6, (770) 389-1142
http://www.motel6.com
7233 Davidson Pkwy.
107 rooms - $35-45
Pets: Under 30 lbs. welcome
Creature Comforts: CCTV, a/c, pool

Ramada Inn
(800) 2-Ramada, (770) 474-1700
http://www.ramada.com
7265 Davidson Pkwy.
52 rooms - $55-80
Pets: Small pets welcome
Creature Comforts: CCTV, a/c, whirlpool

SUWANEE

Holiday Inn
(800) HOLIDAY, (770) 945-4921
http://www.holiday-inn.com
2955 Rte. 317
120 rooms - $75-99
Pets: Small pets welcome
Creature Comforts: CCTV, a/c, refrig, Jacuzzis, restaurant, pool, putting green

SWAINSBORO

Bradford Inn
(912) 237-2400
688 S. Main St.
50 rooms - $45-69
Pets: Small pets w/$5 fee
Creature Comforts: CCTV, a/c, and Jacuzzis

Coleman House

(912) 237-9100
323 N. Main St.
7 rooms - $60-90
Pets: Welcome
Creature Comforts: Victorian B&B w/antiques, CCTV, VCR, a/c, fireplaces, refrig, full brkfst

Days Inn
(800) DAYS-INN, (912) 237-9333
http://www.daysinn.com
654 Main St.
32 rooms - $35-75
Pets: Welcome w/$5 fee
Creature Comforts: CCTV, a/c, cont. brkfst

TATE

Tate House
(800) 342-7515, (770) 735-3122
http://www.ngeorgia.com/history/
tate.html
Rte. 53, Box 33
13 units - $90-145
Pets: In cabins w/$50 dep.
Creature Comforts: Set in the foothills of the Blue Ridge Mtns, massive pink marble mansion surrounded by 27-acres of manicured grounds, high ceilings, elegant décor, hand-painted murals, antiques, guests w/pets stay in handsome fully-equipped log cabins w/homey ambiance, CCTV, a/c, refrig, stone fireplaces, Jacuzzis, cont. brkfst, tennis, pool, trails, lawn games

THOMASTON

Days Inn
(800) DAYS-INN, (706) 646-2324
http://www.daysinn.com
1215 Rte. 19
42 rooms - $49-65
Pets: Welcome w/$10 dep.
Creature Comforts: CCTV, a/c, refrig, micro, Jacuzzis, cont. brkfst, pool

THOMASVILLE

Days Inn
(800) DAYS-INN, (912) 226-6025
http://www.daysinn.com
15375 Rte. 19 S.
120 rooms - $39-70
Pets: Welcome w/$5 dep.
Creature Comforts: CCTV, a/c, restaurant, pool

Evans House B&B
(800) 344-4717, (912) 226-1343
http://www.inns.com/south/
ga037.htm#ent2443
725 S. Hansell St.
5 rooms - $75-135
Pets: Welcome - must be crated if
left alone
Creature Comforts: 1898
Victorian set across from 27-acre
park, 12-foot ceilings, stained
glass windows, turn-of-the-
century furnishings, CCTV, VCR,
a/c, claw foot tub, fireplace, kit,
gourmet brkfst, puzzle table,
gardens

Holiday Inn
(800) HOLIDAY, (912) 226-7111
http://www.holiday-inn.com
15138 Rte. 198
149 rooms - $59-89
Pets: Small pets welcome
Creature Comforts: CCTV, a/c,
refrig, restaurant, cont. brkfst,
pool, whirlpool

Susina Plantation Inn
(912) 377-9644
Rte. 3, Box 1010
8 rooms - $125-175 (MAP)
Pets: Welcome
Creature Comforts: A wonderful
6,000 sq. ft mansion, Oriental
rugs, high box-beamed ceilings,
spacious sitting rooms, elegant
furnishings and décor, four poster
canopy beds, CCTV, VCR, a/c,
fireplace, claw foot tubs, refrig,
full brkfst/dinner, pool, lawn
games, tennis, sprawling grounds

Shoney's Inn
(800) 222-2222, (912) 228-5555
http://www.shoneysinn.com
14866 Rte. 19
96 rooms - $35-55
Pets: Welcome w/$25 dep.
Creature Comforts: CCTV, a/c,
restaurant, cont. brkfst, pool

THOMSOM
Best Western White Columns
(800) 528-1234, (706) 595-8000
http://www.bestwestern.com
1890 Washington St.
136 rooms - $50-75
Pets: Small pets welcome
Creature Comforts: CCTV, a/c,
kit, restaurant, cont. brkfst, pool

Days Inn
(800) DAYS-INN, (912) 237-9333
http://www.daysinn.com
654 Main St.
32 rooms - $35-75
Pets: Welcome w/$5 fee
Creature Comforts: CCTV, a/c,
cont. brkfst

TIFTON
Best Western Inn
(800) 528-1234, (912) 386-2100
http://www.bestwestern.com
1103 E. B. Hamilton Dr.
126 rooms - $50-75
Pets: Small pets welcome
Creature Comforts: CCTV, a/c,
refrig, micro, restaurant, cont.
brkfst, pool

Comfort Inn
(800) 228-5150, (912) 382-4410
http://www.comfortinn.com
1104 King Rd.
90 rooms - $50-99
Pets: Small pets w/$3 fee
Creature Comforts: CCTV, a/c,
refrig, pool

Hampton Inn
(800) Hampton, (912) 382-8800
http://www.hampton-inn.com
720 Rte. 319
80 rooms - $55-75
Pets: Small pets welcome
Creature Comforts: CCTV, a/c,
pool

Holiday Inn
(800) HOLIDAY, (912) 382-6687
http://www.holiday-inn.com
Rtes. 75 & 82
190 rooms - $55-89
Pets: Small pets welcome
Creature Comforts: CCTV, a/c,
restaurant, cont. brkfst, pool

Masters Economy Inn
(800) 633-3434, (912) 382-8100
Rtes. 75 & 82
122 rooms - $35-59
Pets: Welcome w/$5 fee
Creature Comforts: CCTV, a/c,
cont. brkfst, pool

Red Carpet Inn
(800) 251-1962, (912) 382-0280
http://www.reservahost.com
1025 W. 2nd St.
80 rooms - $35-49
Pets: Small pets w/$5 fee
Creature Comforts: CCTV, a/c,
restaurant, cont. brkfst, pool

Super 8 Motel
(800) 800-8000, (912) 382-9500
http://www.super8.com
Rte. 75 & W. 2nd St.
70 rooms - $35-55
Pets: Welcome w/$5 fee
Creature Comforts: CCTV, a/c,
cont. brkfst, pool

TOCCOA
Days Inn
(800) DAYS-INN, (912) 282-0907
http://www.daysinn.com
Rtes. 17 & 5
78 rooms - $35-75
Pets: Welcome w/$10 fee
Creature Comforts: CCTV, a/c,
cont. brkfst

TOWNDSEND
Days Inn
(800) DAYS-INN, (912) 832-4411
http://www.daysinn.com
Rtes. 95 & 99
122 rooms - $35-60
Pets: Welcome w/$5 fee
Creature Comforts: CCTV, a/c,
restaurant, cont. brkfst

TUCKER
La Quinta Inn
(800) Nu-Rooms, (770) 496-1317
http://www.laquinta.com
1819 Mountain Indust. Blvd.
129 rooms - $59-80
Pets: Small pets welcome
Creature Comforts: CCTV, a/c,
refrig, micro, cont. brkfst, pool

Masters Economy Inn
(800) 633-3434, (770) 938-3552
1435 Montreal Blvd.
170 rooms - $35-80
Pets: Welcome w/$10 fee
Creature Comforts: CCTV, a/c,
refrig, restaurant, pool

Ramada Inn
(800) 2-Ramada, (770) 939-1000
http://www.ramada.com
2180 Northlake Pkwy.
158 rooms - $50-85
Pets: Welcome w/$25 dep.
Creature Comforts: CCTV, a/c,
pool

Red Roof Druid Hills Inn
(800) The-Roof, (770) 496-1311
http://www.redroof.com
2810 Lawrenceville Hwy
119 rooms - $35-69
Pets: Small pets welcome
Creature Comforts: CCTV, a/c

UNADILLA
Days Inn
(800) DAYS-INN, (912) 627-3211
http://www.daysinn.com
Rtes. 75 & 41
60 rooms - $35-55
Pets: Welcome w/$2 fee
Creature Comforts: CCTV, a/c,
cont. brkfst, pool

Passport Inn
(800) 251-1962, (912) 627-3258
http://www.reservahost.com
Rte. 1, Box 184
44 rooms - $30-48
Pets: Welcome w/$3 fee
Creature Comforts: CCTV, a/c,
pool

Red Carpet Inn
(800) 251-1962, (912) 627-3261
http://www.reservahost.com
101 Roberts St.
69 rooms - $30-44
Pets: Welcome
Creature Comforts: CCTV, a/c

Scottish Inns
(800) 251-1962, (912) 627-3228
http://www.reservahost.com
Rte. 2, Box 82
82 rooms - $29-40
Pets: Welcome w/$3 fee
Creature Comforts: CCTV, a/c,
restaurant, pool

VALDOSTA
Best Western King of the Road
(800) 528-1234, (912) 244-7600
http://www.bestwestern.com
1403 N. St. Augustine Rd.
137 rooms - $45-80
Pets: Small pets welcome
Creature Comforts: CCTV, a/c,
refrig, restaurant, cont. brkfst, pool

Comfort Inn
(800) 228-5150, (912) 242-1212
http://www.comfortinn.com
2799 W. Hill Ave.
140 rooms - $50-75
Pets: Small pets welcome
Creature Comforts: CCTV, a/c,
refrig, micro, restaurant, hlth club,
pool, lawn sports

Days Inn
(800) DAYS-INN, (912) 244-4460
http://www.daysinn.com
Rte. 75 & N. Valdosta Rd.
100 rooms - $35-69
Pets: Welcome w/$5 fee
Creature Comforts: CCTV, a/c,
restaurant, pool

Holiday Inn
(800) HOLIDAY, (912) 242-3881
http://www.holiday-inn.com
1309 St. Augustine Rd.
169 rooms - $55-99
Pets: Welcome
Creature Comforts: CCTV, a/c,
refrig, micro, restaurant, pool

Motel 6
(800) 4-MOTEL6, (912) 333-0047
http://www.motel6.com
2003 W. Hill Ave.
122 rooms - $35-57
Pets: Under 30 lbs. welcome
Creature Comforts: CCTV, a/c,
pool

Quality Inn South
(800) 228-5151, (912) 244-4520
http://www.qualityinn.com
1902 W. Hill Ave.
48 rooms - $40-75
Pets: Welcome
Creature Comforts: CCTV, a/c,
pool

Quality Inn North
(800) 228-5151, (912) 244-8510
http://www.qualityinn.com
1209 St. Augustine Rd.
125 rooms - $60-95
Pets: Small pets welcome
Creature Comforts: CCTV, a/c,
refrig, micro, cont. brkfst, hlth
club, pool

Ramada Inn
(800) 2-Ramada, (912) 242-1225
http://www.ramada.com
2008 W. Hill Ave.
100 rooms - $50-80
Pets: Welcome w/$5 fee
Creature Comforts: CCTV, a/c,
restaurant, pool

Rodeway Inn
(800) 228-2000, (912) 241-1177
http://www.rodeway.com
2015 W. Hill Ave.
85 rooms - $39-99
Pets: Small pets w/$25 dep.
Creature Comforts: CCTV, a/c,
refrig, micro, cont. brkfst, pool

Scottish Inns
(800) 251-1962, (912) 244-7900
http://www.reservahost.com
1114 St. Augustine Rd.
75 rooms - $30-49
Pets: Welcome $6 fee
Creature Comforts: CCTV, a/c,
pool

Shoney's Inn
(800) 222-2222, (912) 244-7711
http://www.shoneysinn.com
1828 W. Hill Ave.
96 rooms - $45-69
Pets: Welcome in smoking rooms
Creature Comforts: CCTV, a/c,
restaurant, pool

Travelodge
(800) 578-7878, (912) 242-3464
http://www.travelodge.com
1330 St. Augustine Rd.
88 rooms - $45-75
Pets: Welcome
Creature Comforts: CCTV, a/c,
restaurant, pool

VIDALIA

Days Inn
(800) DAYS-INN, (912) 537-9251
http://www.daysinn.com
1503 Lyons Hwy.
65 rooms - $49-60
Pets: Welcome w/$10 fee
Creature Comforts: CCTV, a/c,
restaurant, cont. brkfst, pool

Holiday Inn
(800) HOLIDAY, (912) 537-9000
http://www.holiday-inn.com
2619 E. First St.
66 rooms - $45-65
Pets: Small pets welcome
Creature Comforts: CCTV, a/c,
pool

Shoney's Inn
(800) 222-2222, (912) 537-1282
http://www.shoneysinn.com
2505 Lyons Hwy.
128 rooms - $45-74
Pets: Welcome
Creature Comforts: CCTV, a/c,
restaurant, pool

VILLA RICA

Super 8 Motel
(800) 800-8000, (770) 459-8888
http://www.super8.com
195 Rte. 61
62 rooms - $45-75
Pets: Welcome
Creature Comforts: CCTV, a/c,
Jacuzzis, cont. brkfst, pool,
whirlpool

WARNER ROBBINS

Super 8 Motel
(800) 800-8000, (912) 923-8600
http://www.super8.com
105 Woodcrest Blvd.
62 rooms - $45-69
Pets: Welcome
Creature Comforts: CCTV, a/c

WAYCROSS

Days Inn
(800) DAYS-INN, (912) 285-4700
http://www.daysinn.com
2016 Memorial Dr.
56 rooms - $35-69
Pets: Welcome w/$5 fee
Creature Comforts: CCTV, a/c,
cont. brkfst, pool

Holiday Inn
(800) HOLIDAY, (912) 283-4490
http://www.holiday-inn.com
1725 Memorial Dr.
146 rooms - $55-79
Pets: Small pets welcome
Creature Comforts: CCTV,
VCR, a/c, restaurant, cont. brkfst,
hlth. club, pool

Jameson Inn
(912) 283-3800
950 City Blvd.
59 rooms - $45-64
Pets: Welcome in certain rms
Creature Comforts: CCTV, a/c,
pool

Pine Crest Motel
(912) 283-3580
176 Memorial Dr.
30 rooms - $30-44
Pets: Small pets welcome
Creature Comforts: CCTV, a/c,
refrig, pool

WEST POINT

Travelodge
(800) 578-7878, (706) 643-9922
http://www.travelodge.com
1870 State St.
36 rooms - $45-65
Pets: Welcome
Creature Comforts: CCTV, a/c,
refrig, pool

WHITE

Scottish Inns
(800) 251-1962, (770) 382-7011
http://www.reservahost.com
2385 Rte. 411 NE
60 rooms - $30-99
Pets: Welcome w/$5 fee
Creature Comforts: CCTV, a/c,
pool

Hawaii

Hawaii has strict quarantine regulations with regard to pets and a lengthy quarantine period. This makes importation of pets for short-term vacations impractical.

Those who want to bring their pet to Hawaii for a long-term stay should understand that the Department of Agriculture governs rules regarding importation of dogs, cats and other carnivores. There is a mandatory 30-day confinement in the State Animal Quarantine Station. "Specific pre-arrival and post-arrival requirements must be met for pets to qualify for the 30-day quarantine, which is followed by a 90-day post-quarantine observation period where the pet is released to the owner."

The 30-day quarantine regulations are lengthy, involve multiple vaccinations and documentation attesting to the animal's health. It also involves imbedding a microchip under your pet's skin.

For more information you may call the Department of Agriculture at (808) 483-7151 or fax them at (808) 483-7161. You may also write to them at the following address:

Dept. of Agriculture
Animal Quarantine Branch
99-951 Halawa Valley St.
Aiea, Hawaii 96701-3246

Idaho

ALBION
Mtn. Manor B&B
(208) 673-6642
249 W. North St., Box 128
3 rooms - $39-65
Pets: Welcome
Creature Comforts: CCTV, a/c,
refrig, cont. brkfst

AMERICAN FALLS
Hillview Hotel
(208) 226-5151
2799 Lakeview Rd.
33 rooms - $25-49
Pets: Small pets w/$5 fee
Creature Comforts: CCTV, a/c,
refrig, pool

Ronnez Motel
(208) 226-9658
411 Lincoln St.
10 rooms - $29-55
Pets: Small pets welcome
Creature Comforts: CCTV, a/c,
refrig

ARCO
Arco Inn
(208) 527-3100
540 W. Grand St.
12 rooms - $35-60
Pets: Welcome w/$25 deposit
Creature Comforts: CCTV, a/c,
refrig, micro

D. K. Motel
(800) 231-0134, (208) 527-8282
316 S. Front St.
20 rooms - $29-59
Pets: Welcome
Creature Comforts: CCTV, a/c,
refrig, micro

Lazy Motel
(800) 231-0134, (208) 527-8263
Rte. 93, Box 12
19 rooms - $29-50
Pets: Welcome w/$5 fee
Creature Comforts: CCTV, a/c,
refrig, micro

Lost River Motel
(800) 231-0134, (208) 527-3600
405 Hwy. Dr.
15 rooms - $29-59
Pets: Welcome w/$5 fee
Creature Comforts: CCTV, a/c,
kit, whirlpool

ASHTON
Four Seasons Motel
(208) 652-7769
PO Box 848
12 rooms - $30-49
Pets: Welcome
Creature Comforts: CCTV, a/c

Log Cabin Motel
(208) 652-3956
1001 Main St.
10 cabins - $35-60
Pets: Welcome
Creature Comforts: CCTV, a/c,
refrig

Super 8 Motel
(800) 800-8000, (208) 652-7885
http://www.super8.com
1370 Rte. 20 N.
38 rooms - $40-65
Pets: Welcome w/$15 deposit
Creature Comforts: CCTV, a/c,
restaurant

ATHOL
Athol Motel
(208) 683-3476
PO Box 445
8 rooms - $25-49
Pets: Welcome
Creature Comforts: CCTV, a/c,
refrig, micro

BANKS
The Ponderosa
(208) 793-2700
HC 76, Box 1010
3 rooms - $29-39
Pets: Welcome
Creature Comforts: CCTV, a/c,
restaurant

BAYVIEW
Bayview Scenic Motel
(208) 683-2215
6th & Main Sts.
9 rooms - $50-75
Pets: Welcome
Creature Comforts: CCTV, a/c,
kit

MacDonald's Hudson Bay Rsrt
(208) 683-2211
E. 17425 Hudson Bay Rd.
10 cabins - $70-100
Pets: Welcome w/$15 fee
Creature Comforts: CCTV, a/c,
kit, restaurant, water views

Scenic Bay Marina
(208) 683-2243
PO Box 36
4 studios - $55-75
Pets: Welcome
Creature Comforts: CCTV, a/c,
refrig, micro

BELLEVUE
High Country Motel
(208) 788-2050
PO Box 598
10 rooms - $35-70
Pets: Welcome
Creature Comforts: CCTV, a/c

BLACKFOOT
Alder Inn B&B
(208) 785-6968
384 Alder St.
3 rooms - $50-75
Pets: Welcome
Creature Comforts: CCTV, a/c,
refrig, cont. brkfst

Best Western Inn
(800) 528-1234, (208) 785-4144
http://www.bestwestern.com
750 Jensen Grove Dr.
60 rooms - $35-75
Pets: Welcome
Creature Comforts: CCTV, a/c,
refrig, micro, cont. brkfst, hlth
club, pool, whirlpool

Riverside Inn
(208) 785-5000
1229 Park Way Dr., Box 490
80 rooms - $45-100
Pets: Welcome
Creature Comforts: CCTV,
VCR, a/c, refrig, pool

BLISS
Amber Inn
(208) 352-4441
HC 60, Box 1330
30 rooms - $30-45
Pets: Welcome w/$5 fee
Creature Comforts: CCTV, a/c

BOISE
Boulevard Motel
(208) 342-4629
1121 S. Capitol Blvd.
20 rooms - $30-55
Pets: Welcome
Creature Comforts: CCTV, a/c,
kit, cont. brkfst

Best Rest Inn
(800) 733-1418, (208) 322-4404
8002 Overland Rd.
87 rooms - $35-59
Pets: Welcome
Creature Comforts: CCTV,
VCR, a/c, refrig, cont. brkfst,
pool, whirlpool

Budget Inn
(208) 344-8617
2600 Fairview Ave.
44 rooms - $30-62
Pets: Welcome w/$10 fee
Creature Comforts: CCTV, a/c,
refrig, restaurant, pool, whirlpool

Cabana Inn
(208) 343-6000
1600 Main St.
50 rooms - $30-60
Pets: Welcome
Creature Comforts: CCTV, a/c

Capri Motel National 9
(208) 344-8617
2600 Fairview Rd.
44 rooms - $30-55
Pets: Welcome
Creature Comforts: CCTV, a/c,
restaurant, pool

Econo Lodge
(800) 55-ECONO, (208) 344-4030
http://www.econolodge.com
2155 N. Garden St.
52 rooms - $40-55
Pets: Welcome
Creature Comforts: CCTV,
VCR, a/c, refrig, micro, cont.
brkfst

Fall Creek Resort
(208) 653-2242
6633 Overland Rd.
10 rooms - $45-75
Pets: Welcome
Creature Comforts: CCTV, a/c,
refrig, restaurant, hlth clb,
whirlpool, lake/marina

Flying J Inn
(800) 733-1418, (208) 322-4404
8002 Overland Rd.
86 rooms - $34-59
Pets: Welcome
Creature Comforts: CCTV, a/c,
pool, whirlpool

Hampton Inn
(800) Hampton, (208) 331-5600
http://www.hampton-inn.com
3270 S. Shoshone Dr.
65 rooms - $60-99
Pets: Welcome in smoking rooms
Creature Comforts: CCTV, a/c,
refrig, micro, pool, whirlpool

Holiday Inn
(800) HOLIDAY, (208) 344-8365
http://www.holiday-inn.com
3300 Vista Ave.
266 rooms - $60-129
Pets: Small pets welcome
Creature Comforts: CCTV,
VCR, a/c, refrig, restaurant, hlth
club, pool, sauna, whirlpool

Holiday Motel
(208) 376-4631
5416 Fairview Ave.
19 rooms - $30-55
Pets: Welcome
Creature Comforts: CCTV, a/c,
kit, pool

Middle Fork Lodge
(208) 342-7888
PO Box 16278
20 rooms - $400-450/wk
Pets: Welcome
Creature Comforts: Riverside,
CCTV, a/c, kit, restaurant, pool,
hlth clb, whirlpool

Motel 6-Airport
(800) 4-Motel-6, (208) 344-3506
http://www.motel6.com
2323 Airport Way
91 rooms - $35-45
Pets: Under 30 lbs. welcome
Creature Comforts: CCTV, a/c,
pool

Nendels Inn
(800) 547-0106, (208) 344-4030
2155 N. Garden St.
52 rooms - $35-60
Pets: Welcome
Creature Comforts: CCTV, a/c

Owyhee Plaza Hotel
(800) 233-4611, (208) 343-4611
http://boise.org/tour/owy.html
1109 Main St.
100 rooms - $75-385
Pets: Welcome w/$25 dep.
Creature Comforts: 1900's
hotel, recently restored, deluxe
rooms, CCTV, VCR, a/c, refrig,
restaurant, pool, hlth clb, and
whirlpool

Quality Inn
(800) 228-5151, (208) 343-7505
http://www.qualityinn.com
2717 Vista Ave.
80 rooms - $55-99
Pets: Welcome w/$10 fee
Creature Comforts: CCTV,
VCR, a/c, kit, pool

Red Lion Inn - Downtown
(800) RED-LION, (208) 344-7691
http://www.redlion.com
1800 Fairview St.
184 rooms - $60-129
Pets: Small pets welcome
refrig, Jacuzzis, restaurant, pool,
hlth club, whirlpool

Red Lion Inn - Riverside
(800) RED-LION, (208) 344-1871
http://www.redlion.com
2900 Chinden Blvd.
305 rooms - $60-185
Pets: Small pets welcome
Creature Comforts: CCTV, a/c,
refrig, Jacuzzis, restaurant, pool,
sauna, hlth club, whirlpools

Residence Inn
(800) 331-3131, (208) 344-1200
http://www.residenceinn.com
1401 Lusk St.
104 rooms - $95-189
Pets: Welcome w/$10 fee
Creature Comforts: CCTV, a/c,
kit, cont. brkfst, pool, whirlpools

Rodeway Inn
(800) 228-2000, (208) 376-2700
http://www.rodeway.com
1115 N. Curtis Rd.
99 rooms - $60-99
Pets: Welcome w/$25 deposit
Creature Comforts: CCTV, a/c,
refrig, restaurant, cont. brkfst,
sauna, pool, whirlpool

Sawtooth Lodge
(208) 344-6685
1403 E. Bannock Rd.
11 rooms - $35-75
Pets: Welcome
Creature Comforts: CCTV,
restaurant, pool

Seven K Motel
(208) 343-7723
3633 Chinden Blvd.
23 rooms - $35-70
Pets: Welcome
Creature Comforts: CCTV, a/c,
kit, pool

Shilo Inn - Riverside
(800) 222-2244, (208) 344-3521
http://www.shiloinns.com
3031 Main St.
111 rooms - $60-99
Pets: Welcome w/$7 fee
Creature Comforts: CCTV,
VCR, a/c, refrig, micro, cont.
brkfst, pool, hlth clb, steamroom,
sauna, whirlpool

Shilo Inn - Airport
(800) 222-2244, (208) 343-7662
http://www.shiloinns.com
4111 Broadway Ave.
125 rooms - $65-99
Pets: Small pets w/$7 fee
Creature Comforts: CCTV,
VCR, a/c, refrig, micro, cont.
brkfst, pool, hlth clb, steamroom,
sauna, whirlpool

Super 8 Motel
(800) 800-8000, (208) 344-8871
http://www.super8.com
2773 Elder St.
110 rooms - $45-75
Pets: Welcome
Creature Comforts: CCTV, a/c,
pool

West River Inn
(208) 338-1155
3525 Chinden Blvd.
21 rooms - $30-45
Pets: Welcome
Creature Comforts: CCTV, a/c,
kit

BONNERS FERRY
Best Western River Inn
(800) 528-1234, (208) 267-8511
http://www.bestwestern.com
7160 Plaza St.
47 rooms - $69-225
Pets: Welcome
Creature Comforts: CCTV,
refrig, Jacuzzis, restaurant, cont.
brkfst, hlth club, sauna, pool,
whirlpool

Bonners Ferry Resort
(802) 267-2422
Rte. 4, Box 4700
24 rooms - $25-70
Pets: Welcome
Creature Comforts: CCTV, a/c,
kit, restaurant, pool, whirlpool

Deep Creek Resort
(208) 267-2729
Rte. 4, Box 628
10 rooms - $39-55
Pets: Welcome
Creature Comforts: CCTV, a/c,
restaurant

IMA Kootenai Valley Motel
(800) 341-8000, (208) 267-7567
http://www.imalodging.com
Rte. 4, Box 4740
22 rooms - $35-109
Pets: Welcome
Creature Comforts: CCTV, a/c,
kit, whirlpool

Town n' Country Motel
(208) 267-7915
Rte. 4, Box 4664
11 rooms - $40-85
Pets: Welcome
Creature Comforts: CCTV, a/c,
kit, whirlpool

BUHL
Siesta Motel
(208) 543-6427
629 Broadway So.
12 rooms - $29-40
Pets: Welcome
Creature Comforts: CCTV, a/c

BURLEY
Best Western Inn
(800) 528-1234, (208) 678-3501
http://www.bestwestern.com
800 N. Overland Ave.
126 rooms - $50-99
Pets: Small pets welcome
Creature Comforts: CCTV,
VCR, a/c, refrig, Jacuzzis,
restaurant, pool, whirlpools

Budget Motel
(800) 635-4952, (208) 678-2200
900 N. Overland Ave.
140 rooms - $40-79
Pets: Welcome
Creature Comforts: CCTV, a/c,
Jacuzzi, pool, whirlpool

Greenwell Motel
(208) 678-5576
904 E. Main St.
30 rooms - $30-66
Pets: Small pets welcome
Creature Comforts: CCTV, a/c,
kit

Lampliter Motel
(208) 678-0031
304 E. Main St.
16 rooms - $25-65
Pets: Welcome
Creature Comforts: CCTV, a/c,
restaurant

Parish Motel
(208) 678-5505
721 E. Main St.
15 rooms - $25-50
Pets: Welcome
Creature Comforts: CCTV, a/c, kit

Starlite Motel
(208) 678-7766
510 Overland Dr.
9 rooms - $25-50
Pets: Welcome
Creature Comforts: CCTV, a/c, kit

CALDER
St. Jose Lodge
(208) 245-3462
Rte. 3, Box 350
6 rooms - $50-65
Pets: Welcome
Creature Comforts: CCTV, a/c, kit, restaurant

CALDWELL
Best Western Inn
(800) 528-1234, (208) 454-3522
http://www.bestwestern.com
908 Specht Ave.
69 rooms - $55-165
Pets: Welcome w/$50 deposit
Creature Comforts: CCTV, a/c, refrig, cont. brkfst, hlth club, pool, whirlpool

Comfort Inn
(800) 228-5150, (208) 454-2222
http://www.comfortinn.com
901 Specht Ave.
66 rooms - $55-135
Pets: Welcome w/$10 fee
Creature Comforts: CCTV, VCR, a/c, kit, pool, sauna, hlth club, whirlpool

Holiday Motel
(208) 454-3888
512 Frontage Rd.
24 rooms - $28-59
Pets: Welcome
Creature Comforts: CCTV, a/c, restaurant

CAMBRIDGE
Cambridge House B&B at Hunters Inn
(208) 257-3325
PO Box 313
5 rooms - $40-70
Pets: Welcome
Creature Comforts: CCTV, a/c, cont. brkfst

Frontier Motel
(208) 257-3851
PO Box 178
16 rooms - $30-70
Pets: Welcome
Creature Comforts: CCTV, a/c

Hunters Inn
(208) 257-3325
PO Box 313
10 rooms - $25-40
Pets: Welcome
Creature Comforts: CCTV, a/c, cont. brkfst

CASCADE
Arrowhead Cabins
(208) 382-4534
PO Box 337
4 cabins - $30-43
Pets: Welcome
Creature Comforts: CCTV, a/c, hlth clb

Aurora Motel
(800) 554-6175, (208) 382-4948
PO Box 799
10 rooms - $29-55
Pets: Welcome
Creature Comforts: CCTV, a/c, kit

High Country Inn
(208) 382-3315
PO Box 548
11 rooms - $35-60
Pets: Welcome
Creature Comforts: CCTV, a/c, kit

Mountain View Motel
(208) 382-4238
PO Box 1053
26 rooms - $30-55
Pets: Welcome
Creature Comforts: CCTV, a/c, kit, restaurant

North Shore Lodge
(800) 933-3193, (208) 257-2219
175 N. Shoreline Dr.
10 cottages - $50-99
Pets: Welcome
Creature Comforts: Kit, cont. brkfst

Silver Pines Motel
(208) 382-4370
PO Box 70
7 rooms - $35-60
Pets: Welcome
Creature Comforts: CCTV, a/c, kit

Whitewater Guest Ranch
(208) 882-8083
PO Box 70
4 cabins - $50-95
Pets: Welcome
Creature Comforts: Waterfront access, CCTV

CHALLIS
Challis Hot Springs
(208) 879-4442
HC 63, Box 1779
5 rooms - $45-60
Pets: Welcome
Creature Comforts: CCTV, a/c, pool, whirlpool

Challis Motor Lodge
(208) 879-2251
Rte. 93 & Main St
19 rooms - $29-50
Pets: Welcome
Creature Comforts: CCTV, a/c, kit, restaurant

Northgate Motel
(208) 879-2490
Rte. 93, HC 63, Box 1665
55 rooms - $35-50
Pets: $5 fee & $25 dep.
Creature Comforts: CCTV, refrig, micro

The Village Inn
(208) 879-2239
Rte. 93, PO Box 6
54 rooms - $35-60
Pets: Welcome
Creature Comforts: CCTV, a/c, kit, restaurant, whirlpool

CHUBBUCK
Oxbow Motor Inn
(208) 237-3100
4333 Yellowstone Ave.
104 rooms - $40-65
Pets: Welcome w/$5 fee
Creature Comforts: CCTV, a/c,
kit, restaurant, sauna, whirlpool

CLARK FORK
River Delta Resort
(208) 266-1335
Rte 200, Box 128
5 cabins - $50-75
Pets: Welcome
Creature Comforts: Market

COEUR D'ALENE
Bates Motel
(208) 667-1411
2018 Sherman Ave.
11 rooms - $40-50
Pets: Welcome
Creature Comforts: CCTV, a/c

Bennett Bay Inn
(800) 368-8609, (208) 664-6168
Route 90
21 rooms - $35-129
Pets: Welcome
Creature Comforts: CCTV, a/c,
kit, pool, whirlpool

Boulevard Motel
(208) 664-4978
2400 Selice Way
10 rooms - $40-70
Pets: Welcome
Creature Comforts: CCTV, a/c,
kit

Cedar Motel
(208) 664-2278
319 Coeur d' Alene Lake Dr.
16 rooms - $30-109
Pets: Welcome
Creature Comforts: CCTV, a/c,
kit, pool

Coeur d'Alene B&B
(208) 667-7527
906 Foster Ave.
5 rooms - $65-110
Pets: Welcome
Creature Comforts: CCTV, a/c,
cont. brkfst, whirlpool

Coeur d'Alene Inn
(800) 251-STAY, (208) 765-3200
http://www.cdainn.com
414 W. Appleway Ave.
122 rooms - $95-295
Pets: Welcome w/$10 fee
Creature Comforts: Well price
resort w/attractive public areas,
rms. w/Scandinavian furnishings,
CCTV, a/c, refrig, Jacuzzi,
restaurant, pool, hlth clb, sauna,
steamroom, spa, whirlpool, golf,
tennis/rac. courts, marina, longest
floating boardwalk, private beach
& boat

Coeur d'Alene KOA Cabins
(800) KOA-0799, (208) 664-4471
www.KOAkampgrounds.com
10700 Wolf Lodge Bay Rd.
5 rooms - $30-45
Pets: Welcome
Creature Comforts: CCTV, a/c,
kit, pool, whirlpool

Comfort Inn
(800) 228-5150, (208) 765-5500
http://www.comfortinn.com
280 W. Appleway Rd.
52 rooms - $50-225
Pets: Welcome
Creature Comforts: CCTV,
VCR, a/c, Jacuzzis, kit, pool,
sauna, whirlpool

Country Ranch B&B
(208) 664-1189
1495 S. Green Ferry Rd.
2 suites - $90-125
Pets: Welcome
Creature Comforts: CCTV, a/c,
cont. brkfst, whirlpool

Days Inn
(800) DAYS-INN, (208) 667-8668
http://www.daysinn.com
2200 NW Blvd.
61 rooms - $40-85
Pets: Welcome w/$2 fee
Creature Comforts: CCTV, a/c,
cont. brkfst, hlth club, pool,
whirlpool

El Rancho Motel
(208) 664-8794
1915 E. Sherman Ave.
14 rooms - $29-70
Pets: Welcome w/$5 fee
Creature Comforts: CCTV, a/c,
kit

Flamingo Motel & Resort
(208) 664-2159
718 Sherman Ave.
14 rooms - $45-155
Pets: Small dogs w/$10 fee,$25
deposit
Creature Comforts: CCTV, a/c,
kit, pool, whirlpool, park w/tennis

Kingston 5 Ranch B&B
(800) 254-1852, (208) 682-4862
http://www.nidlink.com/~k5ranch
42,297 Silver Valley Rd.
2 rooms - $85-135
Pets: Welcome in dog run
Creature Comforts: Set in Coeur
d'Alene Mtns, charming country
home w/lovely decor, colorful
quilts, four poster beds, French
doors, hardwood floors w/Persian
rugs, CCTV, a/c, fireplaces, refrig,
Jacuzzi, full brkfst, whirlpool

Holiday Inn Express
(800) HOLIDAY, (208) 667-6777
http://www.holiday-inn.com
2209 E. Sherman Ave.
64 rooms - $55-170
Pets: Small pets welcome
Creature Comforts: CCTV,
VCR, a/c, kit, Jacuzzis, sauna,
pool, whirlpool

Monte Vista Motel
(208) 664-8201
320 Coed d'Alene Lake Dr.
9 rooms - $45-85
Pets: Welcome
Creature Comforts: CCTV, a/c

Motel 6
(800) 4-Motel-6, (208) 664-6600
http://www.motel6.com
416 Apple Way
109 rooms - $35-45
Pets: Under 30 lbs. welcome
Creature Comforts: CCTV, a/c,
pool

Rodeway Inn
(800) 228-2000, (208) 664-8244
http://www.rodeway.com
1422 NW Blvd.
66 rooms - $50-159
Pets: Small pets welcome
Creature Comforts: CCTV, a/c,
refrig, restaurant, cont. brkfst,
pool, whirlpool

Scenic Bay Motel
(208) 683-2243
PO Box 36
4 rooms - $60-75
Pets: Welcome
Creature Comforts: CCTV, a/c, kit

Shilo Inn
(800) 222-2244, (208) 664-2300
http://www.shiloinns.com
702 W. Appleway Rd.
138 rooms - $80-159
Pets: Welcome w/$7 fee
Creature Comforts: CCTV, VCR, a/c, kit, cont. brkfst, pool, hlth clb, steamroom, sauna, whirlpool

Summer House by the Lake
(208) 667-9395
1535 Silver Beach Rd.
1 suite - $125-135
Pets: Welcome
Creature Comforts: Lakeside, TV, a/c, kit, cont. brkfst, hlth clb

Super 8 Motel
(800) 800-8000, (208) 756-8880
http://www.super8.com
505 W. Appleway Rd.
95 rooms - $45-79
Pets: Welcome
Creature Comforts: CCTV, a/c

COOLIN
Bishop's Resort & Marina
(208) 443-2191
Box 91
10 rooms - $45-70
Pets: Welcome
Creature Comforts: CCTV, a/c, kit, restaurant, whirlpool, lakefront

DIXIE
Lodgepole Pine Inn
(208) 842-2343
PO Box 71
13 rooms - $35-55
Pets: Welcome
Creature Comforts: CCTV, a/c, kit, restaurant

DONNELLY
Long Valley Motel
(208) 325-8545
161 S. Main St.
8 rooms - $35-75
Pets: Welcome
Creature Comforts: CCTV, a/c, kit

DOWNEY
Downata Hot Springs
(208) 897-5736
www.downatahotsprings.com/
25900 S. Downata Rd.
7 rooms - $50-225
Pets: Welcome
Creature Comforts: CCTV, a/c, kit, restaurant, cont. brkfst, pool, hlth clb, whirlpool

Flag's West Motel
(208) 897-5238
Route 15
12 rooms - $25-36
Pets: Welcome
Creature Comforts: CCTV, a/c, restaurant

DRIGGS
Best Western Inn
(800) 528-1234, (208) 354-2363
http://www.bestwestern.com
476 N. Main St.
40 rooms - $40-85
Pets: Welcome w/permission.
Creature Comforts: CCTV, a/c, kit, Jacuzzis, pool, whirlpool

Pines Motel
(800) 354-2778, (208) 354-2774
105 S. Main St.
10 rooms - $35-55
Pets: Welcome w/$10 fee
Creature Comforts: CCTV, a/c, refrig, micro, whirlpool

DUBOIS
Cross Roads Motel
(208) 374-5258
391 S. Reynolds St.
10 rooms - $29-45
Pets: Welcome
Creature Comforts: CCTV, a/c

EDEN
Amber Inn
(208) 825-5200
1132 E. 1000 South
24 rooms - $30-45
Pets: Welcome w/$3 fee, $10 dep.
Creature Comforts: CCTV, a/c, refrig, micro

ELK CITY
Canterbury House Inn
(208) 842-2591
501 Elk Creek Rd.
2 rooms - $50-85
Pets: Welcome
Creature Comforts: CCTV, a/c, kit, cont. brkfst

Elk City Motel
(208) 842-2452
PO Box 356
15 rooms - $29-59
Pets: Welcome
Creature Comforts: CCTV, a/c, kit, restaurant

Elk City Motel & Lodge
(208) 842-2250
PO Box 143
20 rooms - $25-39
Pets: Welcome
Creature Comforts: CCTV, a/c, kit

Junction Lodge
(208) 842-2459
HC 67, Box 98
6 rooms - $35-44
Pets: Welcome
Creature Comforts: CCTV, a/c, restaurant

Prospector Lodge & Cabins
(208) 842-2557
PO Box 270
12 cabins - $35-75
Pets: Welcome w/$ 5 fee
Creature Comforts: CCTV, VCR, a/c, fireplace, kit, refrig, micro, Jacuzzi, restaurant, cont. brkfst, pool, hlth clb access, sauna, whirlpool

Red River Hot Springs
(208) 842-2587
www.redriverhotsprings.com
Elk City Rd.
10 rms/cabins - $40-100
Pets: Welcome
Creature Comforts: Lodge and rustic cabins, rqst lodge units w/ modern amenities and beam ceilings, CCTV, a/c, fireplace, Jacuzzi, restaurant, pool, whirlpool

Sable Trail Ranch
(208) 842-2672
Red River Rd, Box 21
3 cabins - $10-75
Pets: Welcome
Creature Comforts: Guest ranch
w/bunkhouse

Whitewater Ranch
(208) 926-4231
PO Box 642
10 cabins - $75
Pets: Welcome
Creature Comforts: Restaurant

ELK RIVER
Main Street Cabins
(208) 826-3689
PO Box B
4 cabins - $49-79
Pets: Welcome
Creature Comforts: CCTV, kit,
restaurant

Huckleberry Heaven Lodge
(208) 826-3405
PO Box 165
20 rooms - $55-109
Pets: Welcome
Creature Comforts: CCTV, a/c,
kit, whirlpool

EMMETT
H & H Motel
(208) 365-2482
720 S. John St.
6 rooms - $25-35
Pets: Welcome
Creature Comforts: CCTV, a/c,
kit

Holiday Motel
(208) 365-4479
111 S. Washington St.
20 rooms - $29-55
Pets: Welcome
Creature Comforts: CCTV, a/c

FAIRFIELD
Country Inn
(208) 764-2247
PO Box 393
16 rooms - $35-45
Pets: Welcome
Creature Comforts: CCTV, a/c,
restaurant, hlth clb, whirlpool

FRUITLAND
Elm Hollow B&B
(208) 452-6491
4900 Rte. 95
2 rooms - $45
Pets: Welcome
Creature Comforts: Kit, cont.
brkfst

GARDEN VALLEY
Silver Creek Plunge Motel
(208) 344-8688
HC 76, Box 2377
20 rooms - $35-75
Pets: Welcome
Creature Comforts: Kit, pool

GLENNS FERRY
Redford Motel
(208) 366-2421
612 Main St.
10 rooms - $25-40
Pets: Welcome
Creature Comforts: CCTV, a/c,
kit

GOODING
Gooding Hotel B&B
(888) 260-6656, (208) 934-4374
112 Main St.
6 rooms - $40-65
Pets: Welcome w/deposit
Creature Comforts: On Nat'l
Register of Historic Places, CCTV,
a/c, kit, cont. brkfst

GRANGEVILLE
Elkhorn Lodge
(208) 983-1500
822 SW First St.
20 rooms - $35-49
Pets: Welcome
Creature Comforts: TV, a/c, kit

Monty's Motel
(208) 983-2500
700 Main St.
25 rooms - $35-54
Pets: Small pets welcome
Creature Comforts: CCTV, a/c,
refrig, pool

HAGERMAN
Hagerman Valley Inn
(208) 837-6196
PO Box 480
16 rooms - $39-65
Pets: Welcome
Creature Comforts: CCTV, a/c,
restaurant, whirlpool

Rock Lodge Resort
(208) 837-4822
PO Box 449
11 rooms - $39-85
Pets: Welcome
Creature Comforts: CCTV, a/c,
kit, whirlpool

HAILEY
Airport Inn
(208) 788-2477
820 - 4th Ave. So.
30 rooms - $60-85
Pets: Welcome w/$5 fee
Creature Comforts: CCTV,
VCR, a/c, refrig, micro, whirlpool

Hitchrack Motel
(208) 788-2409
619 S. Main St.
6 rooms - $45-60
Pets: Welcome
Creature Comforts: CCTV, a/c,
kit

HAMMETT
Oasis Ranch Motel
(208) 366-2025
HC 63, Box 6
6 rooms - $25-38
Pets: Welcome
Creature Comforts: CCTV, a/c,
kit

HARRISON
Driftwood Bed and Breakfast
(800) 451-1795, (208) 664-4414
www.nidlink.com/~mikelapd
10200 S. Driftwood Dr.
2 rooms - $115-135
Pets: Welcome
Creature Comforts: Private
home set 600 feet ft. above Lake
Coeur d'Alene, TV, VCR,
fireplace, country brkfst, boating,
hiking

Lakeview Lodge
(208) 689-3318
PO Box 54
21 rooms - $60-120
Pets: Welcome
Creature Comforts: CCTV, a/c,
kit

Peg's B&B Place
(208) 689-3525
202 Garfield Ave.
2 rooms - $45-100
Pets: Welcome
Creature Comforts: CCTV, a/c,
kit, cont. brkfst

Squaw Bay Resort
(208) 664-6450
Rte 2, Box 130
5 cabins - $85-175
Pets: Welcome
Creature Comforts: CCTV, a/c,
kit, restaurant, whirlpool, bay/
marina

HEYBURN
Tops Motel
(208) 436-4724
Rte. 1, Box 1038
16 rooms - $30-49
Pets: Welcome
Creature Comforts: CCTV, a/c,
restaurant

HOMEDALE
Sunnydale Motel
(208) 337-3302
PO Box 935
8 rooms - $25-45
Pets: Welcome
Creature Comforts: CCTV, a/c,
kit

HOPE
Idaho Country Resort
(800) 307-3050, (208) 264-5505
140 Idaho Country Rd.
5 cabins - $80-160
Pets: Welcome
Creature Comforts: CCTV, kit,
whirlpool, waterfront

Red Fir Resort
(208) 264-5287
450 Red Fir Rd.
12 cabins - $75-125
Pets: Welcome
Creature Comforts: CCTV, kit,
waterfront

IDAHO CITY
Idaho City Motel
(208) 392-4290
215 Montgomery St.
5 rooms - $35-50
Pets: Welcome
Creature Comforts: CCTV, a/c

Prospector Motel
(208) 392-4290
517 Main St.
7 rooms - $35-50
Pets: Welcome
Creature Comforts: CCTV, a/c,
kit

IDAHO FALLS
Best Western Stardust Inn
(800) 528-1234, (208) 522-2910
http://www.bestwestern.com
700 Lindsay Blvd.
248 rooms - $50-99
Pets: Welcome
Creature Comforts: CCTV, a/c,
refrig, hlth club, pool, sauna,
whirlpool, riverside

Best Western Driftwood Inn
(800) 528-1234, (208) 523-2242
http://www.bestwestern.com
575 River Pkwy.
74 rooms - $50-129
Pets: Welcome
Creature Comforts: CCTV, a/c,
kit, Jacuzzis, restaurant, pool,
whirlpool, riverside

Bonneville Motel
(208) 522-7847
2000 S. Yellowstone Hwy.
19 rooms - $30-69
Pets: Welcome
Creature Comforts: CCTV, a/c,
kit

Comfort Inn
(800) 228-5150, (208) 528-2804
http://www.comfortinn.com
195 S. Colorado St.
56 rooms - $55-135
Pets: Welcome
Creature Comforts: CCTV, a/c,
refrig, cont. brkfst, pool, whirlpool

Littletree Inn
(800) 521-5993, (208) 523-5993
888 N. Holmes St.
92 rooms - $50-105
Pets: Welcome
Creature Comforts: CCTV, a/c,
restaurant, cont. brkfst, pool, hlth
clb, whirlpool

Motel 6
(800) 4-Motel-6, (208) 522-0112
http://www.motel6.com
1448 W. Broadway St.
80 rooms - $35-50
Pets: Under 30 lbs. welcome
Creature Comforts: CCTV, a/c,
pool

Motel West
(800) 582-1063, (208) 522-1112
1540 W. Broadway St.
80 rooms - $35-55
Pets: Welcome
Creature Comforts: CCTV, a/c,
restaurant, pool, whirlpool

Quality Inn
(800) 228-5151, (208) 523-6260
http://www.qualityinn.com
850 Lindsay Blvd.
127 rooms - $40-79
Pets: Welcome w/$10 fee
Creature Comforts: CCTV, a/c,
restaurant, pool, whirlpool,
waterfront

Shilo Inn
(800) 222-2244, (208) 523-0088
http://www.shiloinns.com
780 Lindsay Blvd.
161 rooms - $89-129
Pets: Welcome w/$7 fee
Creature Comforts: CCTV,
VCR, a/c, refrig, micro, cont.
brkfst, pool, hlth clb, steamroom,
sauna, whirlpool

ISLAND PARK
A-Bar Motel
(800) 286-7358, (208) 558-7358
HC 66, Box 452
8 rooms - $40-95
Pets: Welcome
Creature Comforts: CCTV, a/c,
restaurant

Aspen Lodge
(208) 558-7406
Rtes. 20 & 191, Box 269
5 rooms - $40-90
Pets: Welcome
Creature Comforts: CCTV, a/c,
kit, restaurant

Elk Creek Ranch
(208) 558-7404
PO Box 2
4 rooms - $75
Pets: Welcome
Creature Comforts: CCTV, a/c, restaurant

Mack's Inn Resort
(208) 558-7272
PO Box 10
65 rooms - $29-120
Pets: Welcome
Creature Comforts: CCTV, a/c, kit

Pond's Lodge
(208) 558-7221
PO Box 258
18 cabins - $45-169
Pets: Welcome
Creature Comforts: CCTV, a/c, kit, restaurant, store, waterfront

Sawtell Mountain Resort
(800) 574-0404, (208) 558-9366
PO Box 250
36 rooms - $55-80
Pets: Welcome w/$4 fee
Creature Comforts: CCTV, a/c, restaurant, whirlpool

Staley Springs Lodge
(208) 558-7471
HC 66, Box 102
18 cabins - $60-170
Pets: Welcome
Creature Comforts: CCTV, kit, restaurant, lakefront

Wild Rose Ranch
(208) 558-7201
340 W. 7th St. So.
13 rooms - $55-85
Pets: Welcome
Creature Comforts: CCTV, kit

JEROME
Best Western Inn
(800) 528-1234, (208) 324-9200
http://www.bestwestern.com
3057 S. Lincoln St.
57 rooms - $40-99
Pets: Welcome
Creature Comforts: CCTV, a/c, refrig, micro, cont. brkfst, hlth club, pool, whirlpool

Crest Motel
(208) 324-2670
2983 S. Lincoln St.
18 rooms - $35-55
Pets: Welcome
Creature Comforts: CCTV, a/c

Holiday Motel
(208) 324-2361
401 W. Main St.
23 rooms - $25-65
Pets: Welcome
Creature Comforts: CCTV, a/c

KAMIAH
Clearwater 12 Motel
(800) 935-2671, (208) 935-2671
Cedar St, Box 1168
29 rooms - $45-55
Pets: Welcome w/$5 fee
Creature Comforts: CCTV, a/c, kit, cont. brkfst, hlth clb access, waterfront

Lewis Clark Resort
(208) 935-2556
Rte. 1, Box 17
6 rooms - $45-65
Pets: Welcome w/$5 fee
Creature Comforts: CCTV, VCR, a/c, kit, restaurant, pool, hlth clb, whirlpool

Sundown Motel
(208) 935-2568
Rte. 2, Box 100
14 rooms - $25-33
Pets: Welcome
Creature Comforts: CCTV, a/c

Whitewater Ranch
(208) 935-0631
PO Box 642
4 rooms - $65-75
Pets: Welcome
Creature Comforts: TV

KELLOGG
The Inn at Silver Mtn.
(800) Snow-Fun, (208) 786-2311
305 S. Division St.
9 rooms - $22-39
Pets: Welcome
Creature Comforts: CCTV, a/c, kit, restaurant, whirlpool

Kellogg Vacation Homes
(208) 786-4261
http://www.nidlink.com/
~vacationhomes/homeidx.htm
PO Box 944
20 homes - $55-500
Pets: Welcome w/dep.
Creature Comforts: Fully furnished homes, CCTV, a/c, fireplace, kit, whirlpool

Motel 51
(208) 786-9441
206 E. Cameron Ave.
11 rooms - $29-50
Pets: Welcome
Creature Comforts: CCTV, a/c, kit

Silverhorn Motor Inn
(208) 783-1151
699 W. Cameron Ave.
40 rooms - $55-75
Pets: Welcome
Creature Comforts: CCTV, a/c, restaurant, whirlpool

Sunshine Inn
(208) 784-1186
301 W. Cameron Ave.
16 rooms - $25-44
Pets: Welcome
Creature Comforts: CCTV, a/c, restaurant

Super 8 Motel
(800) 800-8000, (208) 783-1234
http://www.super8.com
601 Bunker Ave.
61 rooms - $45-79
Pets: Welcome
Creature Comforts: CCTV, a/c, refrig, micro, cont. brkfst, pool, whirlpool

Trail Motel
(208) 784-1161
206 W. Cameron Ave.
23 rooms - $29-45
Pets: Welcome
Creature Comforts: CCTV, a/c

KETCHUM
Bald Mtn. Lodge
(800) 892-7407, (208) 726-9963
151 S. Main St, Box 426
30 rooms - $45-110
Pets: Welcome
Creature Comforts: CCTV, a/c, kit, restaurant

Best Western Tyrolean Inn
(800) 333-7912, (208) 726-5336
http://www.bestwestern.com
260 Cottonwood St.
56 rooms - $100-135
Pets: Small pets in smoking rms.
Creature Comforts: CCTV, a/c,
refrig, champagne cont. brkfst,
hlth club, sauna, pool, whirlpool

Christiania Lodge
(800) 535-3241, (208) 726-3351
651 Sun Valley Rd.
37 rooms - $70-95
Pets: Welcome w/$5-10 fee,
signed pet waiver
Creature Comforts: CCTV, a/c,
kit, pool, hot tub

Clarion Inn
(800) 262-4833, (208) 726-5900
http://www.clarioninn.com
PO Box 660
58 rooms - $100-140
Pets: Welcome
Creature Comforts: CCTV,
fireplace, Jacuzzi, restaurant, cont.
brkfst, whirlpool

Elkhorn Resort
(800) 355-4676, (208) 622-4511
http://www.coastalhotel.com
100 Elkhorn Rd., Box 6009
142 rooms - $125-345
Pets: Welcome on first floor of
hotel w/$25 fee
Creature Comforts: An
expansive resort w/hotel rooms
and condos, multimillion $
renovation, CCTV, VCR, a/c,
fireplaces, refrig, Jacuzzis,
restaurant, pool, whirlpool, tennis
center, golf, skiing, lawn games,
kids camp, x-c skiing

Heidelberg Inn
(800) 284-4863, (208) 726-5361
http://www.taylorhotelgroup.com
1908 Warm Springs Rd.
30 rooms - $60-135
Pets: Welcome w/$5 fee
Creature Comforts: CCTV,
VCR, fireplace, kit, restaurant,
cont. brkfst, sauna, whirlpool

Ketchum Korral Motor Lodge
(800) 657-2657, (208) 726-3510
http://www.taylorhotelgroup.com
1908 Warm Springs Rd.
17 rooms - $58-125
Pets: Welcome
Creature Comforts: CCTV, kit,
whirlpool

Ski View Lodge
(208) 726-3441
409 S. Rte. 75
8 rooms - $40-70
Pets: Welcome
Creature Comforts: CCTV, a/c,
kit

Wild Horse Creek Ranch
(208) 588-2575
PO Box 398
10 rooms - $50-130
Pets: Welcome
Creature Comforts: CCTV, a/c,
restaurant, pool, whirlpool

KOOSKIA
Bear Hollow B&B
(800) 831-3713, (208) 926-7146
Rte. 12 - #81, Box 16
3 rooms - $55-90
Pets: Welcome
Creature Comforts: CCTV, a/c,
hlth clb, whirlpool

Ida-Lee Motel
(208) 926-0166
PO Box 592
18 rooms - $29-40
Pets: Welcome
Creature Comforts: CCTV, kit

Mt. Stuart Motel
(208) 926-0166
PO Box 592
16 rooms - $29-50
Pets: Welcome
Creature Comforts: CCTV, a/c,
kit, restaurant

Ryan's Wilderness Inn
(208) 926-4706
HC 75, Box 60
6 rooms - $35-50
Pets: Welcome
Creature Comforts: TV

Three Rivers Resort
(888) 926-4430, (208) 926-4430
http://www.threeriversrafting.com
HC 75, Box 61
15 rooms - $40-109
Pets: Welcome
Creature Comforts: An
outdoorsy resort at the confluence
of 3 rivers, motel/cabins/tent
camping, TV, Jacuzzis, fireplaces,
restaurant, bar, rafting, float trips,
fishing

LAVA HOT SPRINGS
Dempsey Creek Lodge
(208) 776-5000
PO Box 600
2 rooms - $30-55
Pets: Welcome
Creature Comforts: CCTV, a/c,
kit

Lava Hot Springs Inn
(800) 527-5830, (208) 776-5830
94 E. Portneuf Ave.
24 rooms - $59-185
Pets: Welcome
Creature Comforts: CCTV, a/c,
cont. brkfst, whirlpool, mineral
pools, waterfront

Lava Ranch Motel
(208) 776-9917
9611 Rte. 30
10 rooms - $40-79
Pets: Welcome
Creature Comforts: CCTV, a/c,
kit, whirlpool, waterfront

Oregon Trail Lodge
(208) 776-5000
119 E. Main St.
8 rooms - $40-55
Pets: Welcome
Creature Comforts: CCTV, a/c

Riverside Inn/Hot Springs
(800) 733-5504, (208) 776-5504
www.riversideinnhotspring.com/
255 Portneuf Ave.
16 rooms - $65-110
Pets: Welcome w/$6 fee, $50
refundable deposit
Creature Comforts: Historic
1914 inn, elegant ambiance,
colorful quilts, brass beds,
antiques, ceiling fans, CCTV, a/c,
full brkfst, whirlpool, mineral
baths, river front

Tumbling Waters Motel
(208) 776-5589
359 E. Main St.
12 rooms - $49-60
Pets: Welcome
Creature Comforts: CCTV, a/c,
kit

White Wolf B&B
(888) 776-5344, (208) 776-5353
Route 30 East
3 rooms - $55-70
Pets: Welcome
Creature Comforts: CCTV, a/c,
full brkfst, whirlpool

LEADORE
Leadore Inn
(208) 768-2647
PO Box 68
4 rooms - $29-38
Pets: Welcome
Creature Comforts: CCTV, a/c,
kit

LEWISTON
Bel Air Motel
(208) 743-5946
2018 N & S Hwy.
9 rooms - $25-32
Pets: Welcome
Creature Comforts: CCTV, a/c,
kit

Churchill Inns
(208) 743-4501
1021 Main St.
62 rooms - $30-55
Pets: Welcome
Creature Comforts: CCTV, a/c,
kit, pool, whirlpool

El Rancho Motel
(208) 743-8517
2240 - 3rd Ave. No.
24 rooms - $29-38
Pets: Welcome
Creature Comforts: CCTV, a/c,
kit, pool

Hayloft Bed & Breakfast
(208) 746-2363
2031 Powers Ave.
4 rooms - $60-80
Pets: Welcome, horse corral
Creature Comforts: CCTV, a/c,
kit, full brkfst, Jacuzzi

Hollywood Inn
(800) 210-6925, (208) 743-9424
web site pending
3001 N & S Hwy.
41 rooms - $45-65
Pets: Welcome w/$5 fee
Creature Comforts: CCTV, a/c,
restaurant, cont. brkfst, pool

Red Lion Hotel
(800) 232-6730, (208) 799-1000
http://www.redlion.com
621 21st St.
134 rooms - $45-400
Pets: welcome
Creature Comforts: CCTV, a/c,
kit, Jacuzzis, restaurant, pool,
whirlpool, hlth club

Riverview Inn
(800) 806-Room, (208) 746-3311
1325 Main St.
75 rooms - $38-65
Pets: Welcome
Creature Comforts: CCTV, a/c,
refrig, micro, cont. brkfst, pool,
hlth clb, whirlpool

Sacajawea Motor Inn
(800) 333-1393, (208) 746-1393
1824 Main St.
90 rooms - $45-82
Pets: Welcome w/$2 fee
Creature Comforts: CCTV,
VCR, a/c, refrig, micro, Jacuzzis,
restaurant, pool, hlth clb,
whirlpool

Sheep Creek Ranch
(800) 262-8874, (208) 746-6276
http://www.snakeriver
adventures.com
227 Snake River Ave.
1 cabin - $125 nightly fee, $90 fee
for jet boat transportation to cabin
Pets: Leashed pets welcome
Creature Comforts: 1800's
homestead, rustic retreat w/outdoor
shower/toilet, 2 bedrooms,
lanterns, private beautiful setting
w/fishing and hiking

Super 8 Motel
(800) 800-8000, (208) 743-8808
http://www.super8.com
3120 N & S Hwy.
62 rooms - $45-75
Pets: Welcome
Creature Comforts: CCTV, a/c,
kit, hlth club, water views

LOWMAN
New Haven Lodge
(208) 259-3344
Rte 21, Box 3608
6 rooms - $40-119
Pets: Welcome
Creature Comforts: CCTV, a/c,
kit, restaurant, pool, waterfront

Sourdough Lodge
(208) 259-3326
Rte 21, Box 3109
8 rooms - $28-50
Pets: Welcome
Creature Comforts: CCTV,
restaurant

MACKAY
Wagon Wheel Motel
(208) 588-3331
809 W. Custer Rd.
15 rooms - $20-65
Pets: Welcome w/$5 fee
Creature Comforts: CCTV,
fireplace, kit, sport courts

White Knob Motel
(208) 588-2622
Rte 93, Box 180
6 rooms - $25-49
Pets: Welcome
Creature Comforts: CCTV, kit,
pool

MALAD
Village Inn Motel
(208) 766-4761
50 S. 300 East
30 rooms - $35-55
Pets: Welcome
Creature Comforts: CCTV

MCCALL
McCall Accommodation Service
(208) 634-7766
PO Box 1522
85 condos/houses - $75-550
Pets: Welcome w/$50 dep.
Creature Comforts: CCTV, a/c,
fireplace, kit, Jacuzzi, pool, hlth
clb, whirlpool

Best Western Inn
(800) 528-1234, (208) 634-6300
http://www.bestwestern.com
415 - 3rd St.
79 rooms - $60-135
Pets: Small pets welcome
Creature Comforts: CCTV, a/c,
refrig, micro, hlth club, pool,
whirlpool

Brundage Bungalows
(800) 643-2009, (208) 634-2344
http://www.inidaho.com/
bbungalows.htm
400 West Lake
24 rooms - $45-90
Pets: Welcome w/$5 fee
Creature Comforts: CCTV,
VCR, a/c, fireplace, kit

Fircrest Condos.
(208) 634-4528
PO Box 1978
16 condos - $60-175
Pets: Welcome
Creature Comforts: CCTV kit

Lakefork Lodge
(208) 634-3713
Lick Creek Rd., Box 4336
3 rooms - $150-189
Pets: Welcome
Creature Comforts: CCTV, kit,
lakeside

Riverside Motel/Condominiums
(800) 326-5610, (208) 634-5610
http://www.holidayjunction.com/
usa/id/cid0009.html
400 W. Lake St.
27 rooms - $45-125
Pets: Welcome w/$5 fee
Creature Comforts: CCTV, a/c,
fireplace, kit, whirlpool, rvr views

Scandia Inn Motel
(208) 634-7394
401 N. 3rd St.
17 rooms - $45-135
Pets: Welcome w/$ fee
Creature Comforts: CCTV, kit,
sauna

Super 8 Motel
(800) 800-8000, (208) 634-4637
http://www.super8.com
303 S. 3rd St.
60 rooms - $45-79
Pets: Welcome
Creature Comforts: CCTV, a/c,
Jacuzzis, whirlpool

Woodsman Motel
(208) 634-7671
PO Box 884
63 rooms - $30-59
Pets: Welcome
Creature Comforts: CCTV,
restaurant

MONTPELIER
Best Western Inn
(800) 528-1234, (208) 847-1782
http://www.bestwestern.com
243 N. 4th St.
65 rooms - $45-89
Pets: Small pets welcome
Creature Comforts: CCTV,
VCR, a/c, refrig, micro, restaurant,
hlth club, whirlpool

Budget Motel
(208) 847-1273
240 N. 4th St.
24 rooms - $25-42
Pets: Small pets welcome
Creature Comforts: CCTV, a/c,
kit, restaurant

Michelle Motel
(208) 847-1772
401 Boise St.
10 rooms - $25-40
Pets: Welcome
Creature Comforts: CCTV, pool

Park Motel
(208) 847-1911
745 Washington St.
25 rooms - $29-59
Pets: Welcome
Creature Comforts: CCTV,
refrig, micro

MOSCOW
Best Western University Inn
(800) 528-1234, (208) 882-0550
http://www.bestwestern.com
1516 Pullman Rd.
173 rooms - $65-289
Pets: Welcome w/$10 fee
Creature Comforts: CCTV, a/c,
refrig, micro, Jacuzzis, hlth club,
sauna, pool, whirlpool

Hillcrest Motel
(800) 368-6564, (208) 882-7579
web site pending
706 N. Main St.
52 rooms - $30-69
Pets: Welcome w/$5 fee
Creature Comforts: CCTV, kit

Journey's End
(208) 882-5035
1141 Paradise Ridge Rd.
3 rooms - $50-95
Pets: Welcome, horse corral
Creature Comforts: CCTV, kit,
full brkfst

Mark IV Motor Inn
(800) 833-4240, (208) 882-7557
414 N. Main St.
86 rooms - $39-99
Pets: Welcome w/$5 fee
Creature Comforts: CCTV, a/c,
refrig, restaurant, pool, whirlpool

Royal Motor Inn
(208) 882-2581
120 W. 6th St.
38 rooms - $29-75
Pets: Welcome
Creature Comforts: CCTV, a/c,
kit, restaurant, pool

MOUNTAIN HOME
Best Western Foothills Inn
(800) 528-1234, (208) 587-8477
http://www.bestwestern.com
1080 Rte. 20
76 rooms - $50-85
Pets: Welcome w/$50 deposit
Creature Comforts: CCTV, a/c,
kit, Jacuzzis, cont. brkfst, hlth
club, sauna, pool, whirlpool

Hi Lander Motel
(208) 587-3311
615 S. 3rd St. West
34 rooms - $35-55
Pets: Welcome
Creature Comforts: CCTV, a/c,
kit, restaurant, pool

Motel Thunderbird
(208) 587-7927
910 Sunset Strip
27 rooms - $28-40
Pets: Welcome
Creature Comforts: CCTV, a/c, kit, pool

Rosestone Inn
(800) 717-ROSE, (208) 587-8866
495 N. 3rd East
5 rooms - $50-95
Pets: Welcome w/$10 deposit
Creature Comforts: Historic house, CCTV, VCR, a/c, refrig, micro, cont. brkfst

Sleep Inn
(800) Sleep-Inn, (208) 587-9743
http://www.sleepinn.com
1180 Rte. 20
60 rooms - $39-75
Pets: Welcome
Creature Comforts: CCTV, a/c, restaurant, cont. brkfst

Towne Center Motel
(208) 587-3373
410 N. 2nd St. East
31 rooms - $29-45
Pets: Welcome w/$25 deposit
Creature Comforts: CCTV, a/c, refrig, pool

MUD LAKE
B - K's Motel
(208) 663-4578
1073 E. 1500 North
5 rooms - $35-45
Pets: Welcome
Creature Comforts: CCTV, a/c, kit

Haven Motel
(208) 663-4821
1079 E. 1500 North
4 rooms - $35-44
Pets: Welcome
Creature Comforts: CCTV, a/c, kit

NAMPA
Budget Inn
(208) 466-3594
908 - 3rd St. South
41 rooms - $39-50
Pets: Welcome
Creature Comforts: CCTV, a/c, kit, restaurant

Desert Inn
(208) 467-1161
115 - 9th Ave. South
40 rooms - $45-60
Pets: Welcome w/$5 fee
Creature Comforts: CCTV, a/c, refrig, micro, pool

Five Crowns Inn
(208) 466-3594
908 - 3rd St. South
43 rooms - $35-47
Pets: Welcome
Creature Comforts: CCTV, a/c, kit, restaurant, pool, hlth clb, whirlpool

Shilo Inn
(800) 222-2244, (208) 466-8993
http://www.shiloinns.com
617 Nampa Blvd.
61 rooms - $60-80
Pets: Welcome w/$7 fee
Creature Comforts: CCTV, VCR, a/c, refrig, micro, cont. brkfst, pool, steamroom, sauna, whirlpool

Shilo Inn Suites
(800) 222-2244, (208) 465-3250
http://www.shiloinns.com
1401 Shilo Dr.
83 rooms - $70-99
Pets: Welcome w/$7 fee
Creature Comforts: CCTV, VCR, a/c, kit, restaurant, cont. brkfst, pool, steamroom, sauna, hlth club, whirlpool

Starlite Motel
(208) 466-9244
320 - 11th Ave.
16 rooms - $35-50
Pets: Welcome
Creature Comforts: CCTV, a/c, restaurant

Super 8 Motel
(800) 800-8000, (208) 467-2888
http://www.super8.com
24 Nampa Blvd.
62 rooms - $45-60
Pets: Welcome
Creature Comforts: CCTV a/c

NEW MEADOWS
Hartland Inn & Motel
(888) 509-7400, (208) 347-2114
Rtes. 95 and 55
16 rooms - $38-150
Pets: Welcome
Creature Comforts: CCTV, kit, full brkfst, whirlpool, exercise rm.

NORDMAN
Elkin Cabins on Priest Lake
(208) 443-2432
HC 1, Box 40
28 rooms - $89-255
Pets: Welcome
Creature Comforts: CCTV, kit, restaurant, lakefront

Kanisku Resort
(208) 443-2609
HC 1, Box 152
10 rooms - $695-785/week
Pets: Welcome
Creature Comforts: CCTV, kit, restaurant, lakefront

NORTH FORK
North Fork Motel
(208) 865-2412
PO Box 100
30 rooms - $39-50
Pets: Welcome
Creature Comforts: CCTV, kit, restaurant, riverside

River's Fork Inn
(208) 865-2301
Rte. 93, Box 8
7 rooms - $50-80
Pets: Welcome w/$10 fee
Creature Comforts: CCTV, riverside

OROFINO
Helgeson Place Hotel
(208) 476-5729
PO Box 463
19 rooms - $39-59
Pets: Welcome
Creature Comforts: CCTV, a/c, kit, whirlpool

Konkolville Motel
(208) 476-5584
2000 Konkolville Rd.
40 rooms - $35-54
Pets: Welcome
Creature Comforts: CCTV, VCR, a/c, refrig, restaurant, pool, whirlpool

Riverside Motel
(208) 476-5711
10560 Rte. 12
14 rooms - $25-55
Pets: Welcome w/$5 fee
Creature Comforts: CCTV, kit

White Pine Motel
(800) 874-2083, (208) 476-7093
222 Brown St.
18 rooms - $39-60
Pets: Welcome in 1 rm w/$5 fee
Creature Comforts: CCTV, a/c, refrig, micro, whirlpool

PIERCE
Cedar Inn
(208) 464-2704
412 S. Main, Box 494
8 rooms - $22-40
Pets: Welcome
Creature Comforts: CCTV, a/c, restaurant

Key Bar Hotel
(208) 464-2704
Box 494
8 rooms - $20-34
Pets: Welcome
Creature Comforts: CCTV, kit, restaurant

Pierce Motel
(208) 464-2324
509 Main St., Box 96
11 rooms - $29-45
Pets: Welcome
Creature Comforts: CCTV, kit

PINEHURST
Kellogg Vacation Homes
(800) 435-2588, (208) 786-4261
http://onlinenow.com/cda/Kellogg
PO Box 944
12 homes - $65-225
Pets: Welcome
Creature Comforts: CCTV, VCR, a/c, fireplaces, kit, Jacuzzis, whirlpool

PLUMMER
Bonnie's B&B
(208) 686-1165
PO Box 258
52 rooms - $59-70
Pets: Welcome w/$5 fee
Creature Comforts: CCTV, VCR, a/c, cont. brkfst, hlth clb, rec. rm

Hiway Motel
(208) 686-1310
301 - 10th St, Box 179
16 rooms - $35-45
Pets: Welcome
Creature Comforts: CCTV, a/c, kit

POCATELLO
Best Western Cotton Tree
(800) 528-1234, (208) 237-7650
http://www.bestwestern.com
1415 Bench Rd.
149 rooms - $60-119
Pets: Welcome w/$25 deposit
Creature Comforts: CCTV, VCR, a/c, kit, Jacuzzis, restaurant, pool, whirlpool, racquetball

Best Western Weston Inn
(800) 528-1234, (208) 233-5530
http://www.bestwestern.com
745 S. 5th Ave.
60 rooms - $45-80
Pets: Small pets w/$75 deposit
Creature Comforts: CCTV, VCR, a/c, refrig, micro, Jacuzzis, pool, whirlpool

Comfort Inn
(800) 228-5150, (208) 237-8155
http://www.comfortinn.com
1333 Bench Rd.
52 rooms - $55-99
Pets: Welcome w/$10 fee
Creature Comforts: CCTV, a/c, refrig, micro, cont. brkfst, pool, whirlpool

Days Inn
(800) DAYS-INN, (208) 237-0020
http://www.daysinn.com
133 W. Burnside Rd.
115 rooms - $50-75
Pets: Welcome
Creature Comforts: CCTV, a/c, cont. brkfst, sauna, pool, whirlpool

Motel 6
(800) 4-Motel-6, (208) 237-7880
http://www.motel6.com
291 W. Burnside Ave.
134 rooms - $35-45
Pets: Under 30 lbs. welcome
Creature Comforts: CCTV, a/c, pool

Nendel's Inn
(800) 547-0106, (208) 344-4030
4333 Yellowstone Rd.
102 rooms - $30-45
Pets: Welcome
Creature Comforts: CCTV, a/c, kit, restaurant, pool, whirlpool

Quality Inn
(800) 228-5151, (208) 233-2200
http://www.qualityinn.com
1555 Pocatello Creek Rd.
152 rooms - $55-99
Pets: Welcome w/$10 fee
Creature Comforts: CCTV, VCR, a/c, kit, restaurant, cont. brkfst, sauna, hlth club, pool

Rainbow Motel
(208) 232-1451
3020 S. 5th Ave.
9 rooms - $29-40
Pets: Welcome
Creature Comforts: CCTV, a/c

Super 8 Motel
(800) 800-8000, (208) 234-0888
http://www.super8.com
1330 Bench Rd.
80 rooms - $45-69
Pets: Welcome w/$2 fee
Creature Comforts: CCTV, a/c, refrig, micro, Jacuzzis, cont. brkfst

Thunderbird Motel
(208) 232-6330
1415 S. 5th Ave.
45 rooms - $30-45
Pets: Welcome
Creature Comforts: CCTV, VCR, a/c, kit, pool

POLLOCK
R&R Whitewater
Adventure Lodge
(208) 628-3033
1 S. Pollock Rd.
11 rooms - $40-59
Pets: Welcome
Creature Comforts: CCTV, VCR, a/c, whirlpool, riverside

POST FALLS

Best Western Inn
(800) 528-1234, (208) 773-1611
http://www.bestwestern.com
414 E. First Ave.
167 rooms - $60-129
Pets: Welcome
Creature Comforts: CCTV, a/c,
refrig, micro, cont. brkfst, hlth
club, sauna, pool, whirlpool,
hiking trails, tennis, marina/boats

Howard Johnson Inn
(800) I-Go-Hojo, (208) 773-4541
http://www.hojo.com
Pleasant View Rd.
49 rooms - $45-99
Pets: Welcome w/$10 fee
Creature Comforts: CCTV,
VCR, a/c, refrig, micro, Jacuzzis,
full brkfst, pool

Sleep Inn
(800) Sleep-Inn, (208) 777-9394
http://www.sleepinn.com
100 Pleasant View Rd.
84 rooms - $40-85
Pets: Small pets welcome
Creature Comforts: CCTV, pool,
whirlpool

Suntree Inn
(800) 888-6630, (208) 773-4541
3705 W. 56th Ave.
99 rooms - $65-85
Pets: Welcome w/$35 dep.
Creature Comforts: CCTV,
VCR, a/c, refrig, cont. brkfst,
pool, whirlpool

POTLATCH

Rolling Hills B&B
(208) 668-1126
Rte. 1, Box 157
3 rooms - $50-65
Pets: Welcome
Creature Comforts: CCTV, a/c,
refrig, cont. brkfst

PRESTON

Deer Cliff Inn
(208) 852-0643
2106 N. Deer Cliff Rd.
4 cabins - $35-55
Pets: Welcome
Creature Comforts: CCTV, kit,
restaurant

PRIEST LAKE

Hill's Resort
(208) 443-2551
http://www.hillsresort.com
4777 W. Lakeshore Rd.
53 rooms - $85-275
Pets: Welcome
Creature Comforts: Rated #1
Family Cabin Resort by Family
Circle Mag., rqst rustic lakefront
cabins w/exposed panel walls,
CCTV, kit, riverstone fireplaces,
restaurant, whirlpool, tennis,
lakefront/boats

PRIEST RIVER

Selkirk Motel
(208) 448-1112
Rte. 3, Box 441
7 rooms - $40-69
Pets: Welcome
Creature Comforts: CCTV, a/c,
kit, whirlpool

REXBURG

Best Western Inn
(800) 528-1234, (208) 356-4646
http://www.bestwestern.com
450 W. 4th St.
100 rooms - $60-189
Pets: Small pets welcome
Creature Comforts: CCTV,
VCR, a/c, refrig, Jacuzzis, pool,
whirlpool

Calaway Motel
(208) 356-3217
361 S. 2nd St. West
15 rooms - $30-45
Pets: Welcome
Creature Comforts: CCTV, a/c,
kit

Comfort Inn
(800) 228-5150, (208) 359-1311
http://www.comfortinn.com
1513 W. Main St.
52 rooms - $45-99
Pets: Welcome
Creature Comforts: CCTV, a/c,
refrig, micro, pool, whirlpool

Days Inn
(800) DAYS-INN, (208) 356-9222
http://www.daysinn.com
271 S. 2nd West
43 rooms - $40-65
Pets: Welcome w/$2 fee
Creature Comforts: CCTV, a/c,
cont. brkfst, pool

The Lodge Bed & Breakfast
(800) 449-5477, (208) 356-5477
357 W. 400 St. South
10 rooms - $30-58
Pets: Welcome
Creature Comforts: CCTV, a/c

RIGGINS

Bruce Motel
(208) 628-3005
PO Box 208
20 rooms - $35-75
Pets: Welcome
Creature Comforts: CCTV, kit,
riverside

Half Way Inn
(208) 628-3259
HC 75, Box 3760
6 rooms - $25-40
Pets: Welcome
Creature Comforts: River, kit

The Lodge B&B
(208) 628-3863
Rte. 95 at Little Salmon River
4 rooms - $30-60
Pets: Welcome
Creature Comforts: Waterfront,
whirlpool

Pinehurst Resort Cottages
(208) 628-3323
5604 Rte. 95
6 rooms - $35-65
Pets: Welcome w/$3 fee
Creature Comforts: CCTV, kit,
lawn sports, riverside

Riggins Motel
(800) 669-6739, (208) 628-3001
www.rigginsmotel.com
PO Box 1157
19 rooms - $36-89
Pets: Welcome
Creature Comforts: CCTV, kit,
whirlpool

Salmon River Motel
(208) 628-3231
1203 S. Rte. 95
16 rooms - $39-75
Pets: Welcome
Creature Comforts: CCTV,
restaurant

Taylor Motel
(208) 628-3914
206 S. Main St.
5 cabins - $30-45
Pets: Welcome
Creature Comforts: CCTV, kit,
riverside

ROGERSON
Desert Hot Springs
(208) 857-2233
Gen. Delivery
12 rooms - $29-44
Pets: Welcome
Creature Comforts: Restaurant,
pool, whirlpool

RUPERT
Flamingo Lodge Motel
(208) 436-4321
Rte. 1, Box 227
15 rooms - $30-44
Pets: Welcome
Creature Comforts: CCTV, kit

Uptown Motel
(208) 436-4036
Route 24
17 rooms - $29-35
Pets: Welcome
Creature Comforts: CCTV, kit

SAGLE
Bottle Bay Resort
(208) 263-5916
1360 Bottle Bay Rd.
8 cabins - $60-125
Pets: Welcome w/$5 fee
Creature Comforts: CCTV,
VCR, kit, restaurant, lake/marina/
boats

Country Inn
(800) 736-0454, (208) 263-3333
7360 Rte. 95
23 rooms - $35-49
Pets: In smoking rooms w/$10 fee
Creature Comforts: CCTV,
refrig, micro, whirlpool

ST. MARIES
Benewah Resort
(208) 245-3288
Rte. 1, Box 50
5 rooms - $30-38
Pets: Welcome
Creature Comforts: Kit,
restaurant, lakeside

SALMON
Broken Arrow
(208) 865-2241
Route 93
7 cabins - $29-39
Pets: Welcome
Creature Comforts: CCTV,
restaurant, cont. brkfst, waterfront

Indian Creek Ranch
(208) 394-2126
HC 64, Box 105
7 rooms - $125-275 (MAP)
Pets: Welcome
Creature Comforts: Whirlpool
waterfront

Motel Deluxe
(208) 756-2231
112 S. Church St.
24 rooms - $35-55
Pets: Welcome
Creature Comforts: CCTV, a/c,
kit

Suncrest Motel
(208) 756-2294
705 Challis St.
21 rooms - $35-45
Pets: Welcome
Creature Comforts: CCTV, a/c,
kit

Syringa Lodge
(208) 756-4424
2000 Syringa Dr.
8 rooms - $40-95
Pets: Welcome
Creature Comforts: CCTV, a/c,
cont. brkfst, waterfront

Williams Lake Resort
(208) 756-2007
PO Box 1150
26 rooms - $29-125
Pets: Welcome
Creature Comforts: Kit,
restaurant, lakeside

SANDPOINT
Best Spa Motel
(208) 263-3532
521 N. 3rd Ave.
25 rooms - $40-145
Pets: Welcome
Creature Comforts: CCTV,
VCR, a/c, kit, cont. brkfst, pool,
hlth club, whirlpool

Best Western Connie's Inn
(800) 528-1234, (208) 263-9581
http://www.bestwestern.com
323 Cedar St.
53 rooms - $75-275
Pets: Small pets welcome
Creature Comforts: CCTV,
VCR, a/c, refrig, fireplace,
Jacuzzis, restaurant, pool, hlth
club access, whirlpool

Edgewater Resort
(800) 635-2534, (208) 263-3194
http://www.keokee.com/sandida/
edgewater.html
56 Bridge St.
55 rooms - $65-195
Pets: Welcome w/$5 fee
Creature Comforts: CCTV,
VCR, a/c, refrig, micro, Jacuzzis,
restaurant, sauna, whirlpool, lake/
beach/boats

Idaho Country Resort
(800) 307-3050, (208) 264-5505
www.keokee.com/idahoresorts/
141 Idaho Country Rd
6 cabins - $80-175
Pets: Welcome
Creature Comforts: CCTV, kit,
whirlpool, lakeside

K2 Motel
(208) 263-3441
501 N. 4th Ave.
18 rooms - $45-125
Pets: Welcome
Creature Comforts: CCTV, a/c,
kit, whirlpool

Lakeside Inn
(800) 543-8126, (208) 263-3717
http://www.keokee.com/lakeside
106 Bridge St.
60 rooms - $45-135
Pets: In smoking rooms w/$5 fee
Creature Comforts: CCTV,
VCR, a/c, kit, Jacuzzis, cont.
brkfst, hlth clb, sauna, whirlpool,
lake/marina

Monarch West Inn
(800) 543-8193, (208) 263-1222
Route 95
61 rooms - $45-120
Pets: Welcome
Creature Comforts: CCTV, cont.
brkfst, hlth clb, whirlpool

Motel 16
(208) 263-5323
Route 2
16 rooms - $40-109
Pets: Welcome
Creature Comforts: CCTV, a/c, kit, cont. brkfst, pool, hlth clb, whirlpool

Quality Inn
(800) 228-5151, (208) 263-2210
http://www.qualityinn.com
807 N. 5th Ave.
57 rooms - $55-109
Pets: Welcome w/$5 fee
Creature Comforts: CCTV, VCR, a/c, kit, restaurant, pool, whirlpool

Super 8 Motel
(800) 800-8000, (208) 263-2210
http://www.super8.com
3245 Rte. 95
61 rooms - $45-69
Pets: Welcome
Creature Comforts: CCTV, a/c, whirlpool

SHOSHONE
Governor's Mansion
(208) 886-2858
315 S. Greenwood Rd.
7 rooms - $30-65
Pets: Welcome
Creature Comforts: Historic governor's mansion, CCTV, a/c, fireplace, full brkfst

SHOUP
Smith House B&B
(800) 238-5915, (208) 394-2121
49 Salmon River Rd.
1 house - $50-105
Pets: Under 40 lbs. welcome
Creature Comforts: A remote mountain oasis along a river, CCTV, a/c, kit, cont. brkfst, whirlpool, great views

SILVERTON
Molly B'Damm
(208) 556-4391
PO Box 481
17 rooms - $30-55
Pets: Welcome
Creature Comforts: CCTV, VCR, a/c, kit, whirlpool

SODA SPRINGS
Caribou Lodge
(800) 270-9178, (208) 547-3377
110 W. 2nd South
30 rooms - $30-59
Pets: Welcome w/$10 deposit
Creature Comforts: CCTV, a/c, kit, cont. brkfst

Lakeview Motel
(208) 547-4351
341 W. 2nd South
14 rooms - $30-49
Pets: Welcome
Creature Comforts: CCTV, a/c, kit

SPIRIT LAKE
Silver Beach Resort
(208) 632-4842
8350 W. Spirit Lake Rd.
3 cabins - $35-55
Pets: Welcome
Creature Comforts: CCTV, kit, lakeside

STANLEY
Creekside Lodge
(208) 774-2213
PO Box 110
14 rooms - $75-109
Pets: Welcome
Creature Comforts: CCTV, a/c, kit, river views

Danner's Log Cabin Motel
(208) 774-3539
PO Box 196
9 cabins - $55-115
Pets: Welcome
Creature Comforts: Kit

Elk Mtn RV Resort
(208) 774-2202
PO Box 115
1 room - $50-65
Pets: Welcome
Creature Comforts: CCTV, kit, restaurant, river views

Jerry's Country Motel
(800) 972-4627, (208) 774-3566
HC 67, Box 300
9 rooms - $53-74
Pets: Welcome w/$5 fee
Creature Comforts: CCTV, VCR, kit, river views

Mountain Village Resort
(800) 843-5475, (208) 774-3661
Rtes 75 & 21, Box 150
61 rooms - $60-129
Pets: Welcome w/$6 fee
Creature Comforts: CCTV, VCR, refrig, micro, restaurant, whirlpool

Redfish Lake Lodge
(208) 774-3536
PO Box 9
36 rooms - $55-145
Pets: Welcome
Creature Comforts: Restaurant, lake views

Sawtooth Hotel
(208) 774-9947
PO Box 3205
18 rooms - $35-65
Pets: Welcome
Creature Comforts: CCTV, restaurant

Stanley Outpost
(208) 774-3646
Rte 21, Box 131
6 rooms - $5-80
Pets: Welcome
Creature Comforts: CCTV, kit, water views

Triangle C Ranch
(208) 774-2266
Rte 21, Box 69
8 cabins - $60-70
Pets: Welcome
Creature Comforts: CCTV, kit

TETONIA
Teton Mt. View Lodge
(800) 625-232, (208) 456-2741
www.tetonmountainlodge.com
510 Egbert Ave.
25 rooms - $80-115
Pets: Welcome w/$5 fee
Creature Comforts: CCTV, a/c, refrig, cont. brkfst, fireplaces, log furnishings, whirlpool

Teton Ridge Ranch
(208) 456-2650
http://www.ranchweb.com/teton/
index.html
200 Valley View Rd.
7 rooms - $360-485
Pets: Welcome
Creature Comforts: Stunning
ranch housed in 10,000 sq. foot
lodge, cathedral ceilings, rock
fireplaces, wood stoves, CCTV,
refrig, Jacuzzis, store, riding,
fishing, dog sledding, skiing

TWIN FALLS
Best Western Apollo Inn
(800) 528-1234, (208) 733-2010
http://www.bestwestern.com
296 Addison Ave. West
50 rooms - $45-75
Pets: Small pets welcome
Creature Comforts: CCTV, a/c,
refrig, cont. brkfst, pool, whirlpool

Comfort Inn
(800) 228-5150, (208) 734-7494
http://www.comfortinn.com
1893 Canyon Springs Rd.
52 rooms - $55-90
Pets: Welcome
Creature Comforts: CCTV, a/c,
refrig, micro, Jacuzzis, cont.
brkfst, pool, whirlpool

Motel 3
(208) 733-5360
248 - 2nd Ave. West
39 rooms - $25-49
Pets: Welcome
Creature Comforts: CCTV, a/c,
pool

Motel 6
(800) 4-Motel-6, (208) 734-3993
http://www.motel6.com
1472 Blue Lake Blvd. N.
157 rooms - $35-45
Pets: Under 30 lbs. welcome
Creature Comforts: CCTV, a/c,
pool

Shilo Inn
(800) 222-2244, (208) 733-7545
http://www.shiloinns.com
1586 Blue Lakes Blvd.
128 rooms - $70-129
Pets: Welcome w/$7 fee
Creature Comforts: CCTV,
VCR, a/c, refrig, micro, cont.
brkfst, pool, hlth clb, steamroom,
sauna, whirlpool

Weston Inn
(800) 551-3505, (208) 733-6095
906 Blue Lakes Blvd.
97 rooms - $40-60
Pets: Welcome
Creature Comforts: CCTV, a/c,
cont. brkfst, pool, whirlpool

WALLACE
Best Western Inn
(800) 528-1234, (208) 752-1252
http://www.bestwestern.com
100 Front St.
63 rooms - $75-275
Pets: Small pets w/$25 dep.
Creature Comforts: CCTV,
VCR, a/c, refrig, micro, cont.
brkfst, hlth club, sauna,
steamroom, pool, whirlpool

Myles Motel
(208) 556-4391
PO Box 1348
17 rooms - $29-40
Pets: Welcome
Creature Comforts: CCTV, a/c,
kit

Stardust Motel
(208) 752-1213
410 Pine St.
43 rooms - $45-89
Pets: Welcome w/$25 dep.
Creature Comforts: CCTV, a/c,
kit, refrig, micro, pool, hlth clb,
sauna, steamroom, whirlpool

WEISER
Colonial Motel
(208) 549-0150
251 E. Main St.
24 rooms - $35-70
Pets: Welcome
Creature Comforts: CCTV, a/c,
kit

Indianhead Motel
(208) 549-0331
747 Rte 95
8 rooms - $35-75
Pets: Welcome
Creature Comforts: CCTV

State Street Motel
(208) 549-1390
1279 State St.
13 rooms - $39-60
Pets: Welcome
Creature Comforts: CCTV, a/c,
restaurant

Illinois

ALSIP

Baymont Inn
(877)BAYMONT, (708) 597-3900
http://www.baymontinns.com
12801 S. Cicero Ave.
101 rooms - $65-75
Pets: Small pets welcome
Creature Comforts: CCTV, a/c,
refrig, micro, Jacuzzis, cont.
brkfst, pool

ALTAMONT

Best Western Carriage Inn
(800) 528-1234, (618) 483-6101
http://www.bestwestern.com
1304 S. Main St.
46 rooms - $50-70
Pets: $5 fee in smoking rooms
Creature Comforts: CCTV, a/c,
Jacuzzis, kit, restaurant, pool

Super 8 Motel
(800) 800-8000, (618) 483-6300
http://www.super8.com
Rte. 70, Box 296
25 rooms - $40-65
Pets: $8 fee in smoking rms.
Creature Comforts: CCTV, a/c,
cont. brkfst

ALTON

Comfort Inn
(800) 228-5150, (618) 465-9999
http://www.comfortinn.com
11 Crossroads Ct.
62 rooms - $60-99
Pets: Small pets welcome
Creature Comforts: CCTV, a/c,
refrig, micro, Jacuzzis, cont.
brkfst, hlth club, pool

Days Inn
(800) DAYS-INN, (618) 463-0800
http://www.daysinn.com
1900 Homer Adams Pkwy.
117 rooms - $50-80
Pets: Welcome w/$10 fee
Creature Comforts: CCTV, a/c,
restaurant, cont. brkfst, pool,
whirlpool

Holiday Inn
(800) HOLIDAY, (618) 462-1220
http://www.holiday-inn.com
3800 Homer Adams Pkwy.
140 rooms - $80-95
Pets: Small pets w/$35 dep.
Creature Comforts: CCTV,
VCR, a/c, refrig, cont. brkfst,
restaurant, hlth club, sauna, pool

Super 8 Motel
(800) 800-8000, (618) 465-8885
http://www.super8.com
1800 Homer Adams Pkwy.
63 rooms - $45-75
Pets: Welcome w/permission.
Creature Comforts: CCTV, a/c,
cont. brkfst

AMBOY

Amboy Motel
(815) 857-3916
Rtes. 52/30
9 rooms - $40-58
Pets: Welcome w/$50 fee
Creature Comforts: CCTV, a/c,
kit

ANTIOCH

Best Western Regency Inn
(800) 528-1234, (847) 395-3606
http://www.bestwestern.com
350 Rte. 173
68 rooms - $79-125
Pets: Small pets w/$25 deposit
Creature Comforts: CCTV, a/c,
Jacuzzis, kit, cont. brkfst, pool

ARCOLA

Budget Host
(800) Bud Host, (217) 268-3033
http://www.budgethost.com
640 E. Springfield Rd.
30 rooms - $35-80
Pets: Welcome w/$5 fee
Creature Comforts: CCTV, a/c,
micro, refrig, cont. brkfst, pool

Comfort Inn
(800) 228-5150, (217) 268-4000
http://www.comfortinn.com
610 E. Springfield
40 rooms - $75-100
Pets: Welcome
Creature Comforts: CCTV, a/c,
refrig, Jacuzzis, cont. brkfst, pool

ARLINGTON HEIGHTS

Amerisuites
(800) 833-1516, (847) 956-1400
http://www.amerisuites.com
2111 S. Arlington Heights Rd.
112 rooms - $80-135
Pets: Small pets w/$100 deposit
Creature Comforts: CCTV,
VCR, a/c, refrig, micro, cont.
brkfst, hlth club, whirlpool

La Quinta Inn
(800) Nu-Rooms, (847) 253-8777
http://www.laquinta.com
1415 W. Dundee Rd.
123 rooms - $65-105
Pets: Small pets welcome
Creature Comforts: CCTV, a/c,
cont. brkfst, htlth clb, pool

Motel 6
(800) 4-Motel-6, (847) 806-1230
http://www.motel6.com
441 W. Algonquin Rd.
144 rooms - $44-59
Pets: Under 30 lbs. welcome
Creature Comforts: CCTV a/c

Radisson Suite Hotel
(800) 333-3333, (847) 364-7600
http://www.radisson.com
75 W. Algonquin Rd.
200 rooms - $70-389
Pets: Small pets w/$25 fee
Creature Comforts: CCTV, a/c,
refrig, micro, Jacuzzis, restaurant,
pool, hlth club, whirlpool

Red Roof Inn
(800) The Roof, (847) 228-6650
http://www.redroof.com
22 W. Algonquin Rd.
138 rooms - $45-75
Pets: Small pets welcome
Creature Comforts: CCTV, a/c

ATLANTA
Route 66 Motel
(217) 648-2322
103 Empire St.
36 rooms - $50-65
Pets: Welcome in pet rms
Creature Comforts: CCTV, a/c

AURORA
Howard Johnson Hotel
(800) I-Go-Hojo, (630) 892-6481
http://www.hojo.com
306 S. Lincolnway Rd.
110 rooms - $55-85
Pets: Welcome
Creature Comforts: CCTV, a/c,
restaurant, pool

Motel 6
(800) 4-Motel-6, (630) 851-3600
http://www.motel6.com
2380 N. Farnsworth Ave.
118 rooms - $40-49
Pets: Under 30 lbs. welcome
Creature Comforts: CCTV, a/c,
pool

BARRINGTON
Barrington Motor Lodge
(800) 354-6605, (847) 381-2640
405 W. NW Hwy.
52 rooms - $59-89
Pets: Small pets w/$5 fee
Creature Comforts: CCTV, a/c,
refrig, cont. brkfst

Days Inn
(800) DAYS-INN, (847) 381-2640
http://www.daysinn.com
405 W. NW Hwy.
57 rooms - $65-85
Pets: Welcome w/$5 fee
Creature Comforts: CCTV, a/c,
refrig, restaurant, pool, tennis

BEARDSTOWN
Super 8 Motel
(800) 800-8000, (217) 323-5858
http://www.super8.com
Rtes. 67 & 100
40 rooms - $40-70
Pets: Welcome w/permission
Creature Comforts: CCTV, a/c,
Jacuzzis, cont. brkfst, pool

BELLEVILLE
Days Inn
(800) DAYS-INN, (618) 234-9400
http://www.daysinn.com
2120 W. Main St.
80 rooms - $70-85
Pets: Welcome
Creature Comforts: CCTV,
VCR, a/c, refrig, micro, restaurant,
cont. brkfst, pool

Super 8 Motel
(800) 800-8000, (618) 234-9670
http://www.super8.com
600 E. Main St.
42 rooms - $45-100
Pets: Welcome
Creature Comforts: CCTV, a/c,
kit, cont. brkfst, pool

BENTON
Benton Gray Plaza Motel
(618) 439-3113
706 W. Main St.
31 rooms - $40-59
Pets: Small pets welcome
Creature Comforts: CCTV, a/c,
cont. brkfst

Days Inn
(800) DAYS-INN, (618) 439-3183
http://www.daysinn.com
711 W. Main St.
56 rooms - $45-99
Pets: Welcome w/$5 fee
Creature Comforts: CCTV,
VCR, refrig, a/c, restaurant

Super 8 Motel
(800) 800-8000, (618) 438-8205
http://www.super8.com
711 1/2 W. Main St.
54 rooms - $40-55
Pets: Welcome w/permission
Creature Comforts: CCTV, a/c,
micro, refrig

BLOOMINGTON
Best Inns of America
(800) 237-8466, (309) 827-5333
http://www.bestinns.com
1905 W. Market St.
105 rooms - $45-79
Pets: Welcome
Creature Comforts: CCTV, a/c,
refrig, cont. brkfst, pool

Country Inns and Suites
(800) 456-4000, (309) 828-7177
http://www.countryinns.com
923 Maple Hill Rd.
62 rooms - $70-89
Pets: Welcome in smoking rooms
Creature Comforts: CCTV, a/c,
refrig, Jacuzzi, pool

Days Inn, West
(800) DAYS-INN, (309) 829-6292
http://www.daysinn.com
1707 W. Market St.
58 rooms - $45-80
Pets: Welcome
Creature Comforts: CCTV, a/c,
refrig, micro, pool, whirlpool

Guesthouse Inn
(800) 21-GUEST , (309) 663-1361
http://www.guesthouse.net
1803 E. Empire St.
100 rooms - $55-70
Pets: Med. pets w/$10 fee
Creature Comforts: CCTV, a/c,
refrig, micro, cont. brkfst, hlth
club

Howard Johnson Express
(800) I-Go-Hojo, (309) 829-3100
http://www.hojo.com
401 Brock Dr.
32 rooms - $35-60
Pets: Welcome w/permission
Creature Comforts: CCTV, a/c,
pool

Jumer's Chateau
(800) 285-8637, (309) 662-2020
http://www.jumers.com
1601 Jumer Dr.
180 rooms - $85-169
Pets: Welcome w/$25 dep.
Creature Comforts: Reminscent
of French country chateau (w/
plenty of whimsical touches),
public spaces with antiques and
collectibles, bedrooms contain
French-style reproduction
furnishings, four-poster beds, orig.
art, CCTV, a/c, fireplaces, refrig,
Jacuzzis, restaurant, pool, hlth clb,
saunas, whirlpool, game room

Ramada Inn
(800) 2-Ramada, (309) 662-5311
http://www.ramada.com
1219 Holiday Dr.
208 rooms - $55-88
Pets: Welcome
Creature Comforts: CCTV, a/c,
refrig, Jacuzzis, restaurant, sauna,
pool, whirlpool, rec. dome-mini
golf

Super 8 Motel
(800) 800-8000, (309) 663-2388
http://www.super8.com
818 IAA Dr.
61 rooms - $40-78
Pets: Welcome
Creature Comforts: CCTV a/c

BOURBONNAIS
Lees Inns
(800) 733-5337, (815) 932-8080
http://www.leesinn.com
1500 N. Rte. 50
120 rooms - $69-149
Pets: Small pets in first flr rms.
Creature Comforts: CCTV, a/c,
Jacuzzis

Motel 6
(800) 4-MOTEL6, (815) 933-2300
http://www.motel6.com
Route 50
96 rooms - $34-49
Pets: Under 30 lbs. welcome
Creature Comforts: CCTV, a/c,
pool

BREESE
Knotty Pine Motel
(618) 526-4556
Old Rte. 50
10 rooms - $30-43
Pets: Welcome
Creature Comforts: CCTV, a/c

BRIDGEVIEW
Exel Inn
(800) 367-3935, (708) 430-1818
http://www.exelinns.com
9625 S. 76th Ave.
112 rooms - $55-139
Pets: Small pets welcome
Creature Comforts: CCTV, a/c,
kit, Jacuzzis, cont. brkfst.

BUREAU
Ranch House Lodge
(815) 659-3361
Rtes. 26 & 29
17 rooms - $30-40
Pets: Welcome
Creature Comforts: CCTV, a/c

BURR RIDGE
Best Western Inn
(800) 528-1234, (630) 325-2900
http://www.bestwestern.com
300 S. Frontage Rd.
124 rooms - $75-105
Pets: Small pets welcome
Creature Comforts: CCTV, a/c,
refrig, restaurant, spa, pool

CAIRO
Days Inn
(800) DAYS-INN, (618) 734-0215
http://www.daysinn.com
Route 1, Box 10
38 rooms - $28-44
Pets: Welcome
Creature Comforts: CCTV, a/c,
restaurant, pool

CARBONDALE
Best Inns of America
(800) 237-8466, (618) 529-4801
http://www.bestinns.com
1345 E. Main St.
86 rooms - $45-65
Pets: Small pets welcome
Creature Comforts: CCTV, a/c,
refrig, cont. brkfst, pool

Holiday Inn
(800) HOLIDAY, (618) 529-1100
http://www.holiday-inn.com
800 E. Main St.
95 rooms - $65-80
Pets: Welcome
Creature Comforts: CCTV, a/c,
refrig, restaurant, pool, whirlpool

Super 8 Motel
(800) 800-8000, (618) 457-8822
http://www.super8.com
1180 E. Main St.
63 rooms - $45-70
Pets: Welcome w/permission
Creature Comforts: CCTV, a/c,
refrig, micro, cont. brkfst

CARLINVILLE
Carlin Villa Motel
(800) 341-8000, (217) 854-3201
http://www.imalodging.com
Route 4
35 rooms - $45-60
Pets: Welcome w/$5 fee
Creature Comforts: CCTV,
VCR, a/c, refrig, micro, cont
brkfst, Jacuzzi, pool, whirlpool

Holiday Inn
(800) HOLIDAY, (217) 324-2100
http://www.holiday-inn.com
Rtes. 108/I55
100 rooms - $55-169
Pets: Small pets w/$10 fee
Creature Comforts: CCTV,
VCR, a/c, refrig, restaurant, pool,
whirlpool, lake

CARTHAGE
Prairie Winds Motel
(217) 357-3101
Route 136
24 rooms - $34-47
Pets: Welcome
Creature Comforts: CCTV,
VCR, a/c, refrig, pool

CASEY
Comfort Inn
(800) 228-5150, (217) 932-2212
http://www.comfortinn.com
Rtes. 170 & 49
52 rooms - $50-79
Pets: Small pets welcome
Creature Comforts: CCTV,
VCR, a/c, Jacuzzis, kit, cont.
brkfst, hlth club, pool

CASEYVILLE
Best Inns of America
(800) 237-8466, (618) 397-3300
http://www.bestinns.com
2423 Old Country Inn Rd.
85 rooms - $45-79
Pets: Small pets welcome
Creature Comforts: CCTV,
VCR, a/c, refrig, Jacuzzis, cont.
brkfst, pool

CENTRALIA
Bell Tower Inn
(618) 533-1300
200 E. Noleman St.
58 rooms - $45-75
Pets: Small pets welcome
Creature Comforts: CCTV,
VCR, a/c, refrig, micro, pool

CHAMPAIGN
Baymont Inn
(877)BAYMONT, (217) 356-8900
http://www.baymontinns.com
302 W. Anthony Dr.
100 rooms - $50-75
Pets: Small pets welcome
Creature Comforts: CCTV, a/c,
refrig, micro, cont. brkfst, hlth clb

Campus Inn
(217) 359-8888
1701 S. State St.
108 rooms - $40-55
Pets: Small pets welcome
Creature Comforts: CCTV, a/c,
refrig

Chancellor Hotel
(800) 257-6667, (217) 352-7891
1501 S. Neil St.
224 rooms - $65-220
Pets: Welcome
Creature Comforts: CCTV, a/c,
kit, restaurant, pool, hlth clb,
sauna, whirlpools, putting green

Comfort Inn
(800) 228-5150, (217) 352-4055
http://www.comfortinn.com
305 Marketview Dr.
67 rooms - $50-75
Pets: Small pets welcome
Creature Comforts: CCTV, a/c,
refrig, micro, pool, whirlpool

Drury Inn
(800) Drury-Inn, (217) 398-0030
http://www.drury-inn.com
905 W. Anthony Dr.
135 rooms - $75-95
Pets: Welcome
Creature Comforts: CCTV, a/c,
refrig, micro, cont. brkfst, pool,
hlth clb

La Quinta Inn
(800) Nu-Rooms, (217) 359-1601
http://www.laquinta.com
1900 Center Dr.
122 rooms - $55-75
Pets: Welcome
Creature Comforts: CCTV, a/c,
refrig, micro, pool

Red Roof Inn
(800) The-Roof, (217) 352-0101
http://www.redroof.com
22 W. Algonquin Rd.
138 rooms - $45-75
Pets: Small pets welcome
Creature Comforts: CCTV, a/c

Super 8 Motel
(800) 800-8000, (217) 359-2388
http://www.super8.com
202 Marketview Dr.
61 rooms - $45-75
Pets: Welcome in smoking rooms
Creature Comforts: CCTV, a/c,
cont. brkfst

CHARLESTON
Best Western Worthington Inn
(800) 528-1234, (217) 348-8161
http://www.bestwestern.com
920 W. Lincoln Ave.
67 rooms - $60-139
Pets: Under 15 lbs. welcome
Creature Comforts: CCTV, a/c,
Jacuzzis, refrig, micro, restaurants,
pool

Econo Lodge
(800) 55-ECONO, (217) 345-7689
http://www.econolodge.com
810 W. Lincoln Hwy.
53 rooms - $40-69
Pets: Small pets welcome
Creature Comforts: CCTV, a/c,
refrig, cont. brkfst, hlth club, pool

CHENOA
Super 8 Motel
(800) 800-8000, (618) 483-6300
http://www.super8.com
Rte. 70, Box 296
25 rooms - $40-75
Pets: Welcome in smoking rooms
Creature Comforts: CCTV, a/c,
cont. brkfst

CHESTER
Best Western Reids' Inn
(800) 528-1234, (618) 826-3034
http://www.bestwestern.com
2150 State St.
46 rooms - $55-73
Pets: Under 20 lbs. welcome
Creature Comforts: CCTV,
VCR, a/c, refrig, Jacuzzis, hlth
club, pool, whirlpool

CHICAGO
Ambassador West
(800) Wyndham, (312) 787-3700
http://www.wyndham.com
1300 N. State Pkwy.
220 rooms - $150-289
Pets: Small pets welcome
Creature Comforts: A lovely
1924 hotel, beautifully restored,
European ambiance, finial beds,
subtle color schemes, CCTV,
VCR, a/c, refrig, Jacuzzis,
restaurants, and a hlth club

Blackstone Hotel
(800) 622-6330, (312) 427-4300
636 S. Michigan Ave.
305 rooms - $99-169
Pets: Welcome w/$50 dep
Creature Comforts: CCTV, a/c,
hlth clb

Best Western Inn
(800) 528-1234, (773) 244-3435
http://www.bestwestern.com
3434 N. Broadway Ave.
59 rooms - $90-139
Pets: Small pets welcome
Creature Comforts: CCTV, a/c,
refrig, sauna, whirlpool

City Suites Hotel

(888) City-Inns, (312) 404-3400
http://www.cityinns.com
933 W. Belmont Ave.
44 rooms - $110-130
Pets: Welcome w/$250 dep.
Creature Comforts: CCTV,
VCR, a/c, refrig, micro, cont.
brkfst, hlth club access

Claridge Hotel

(800) 245-1258, (312) 787-4980
http://www.claridgehotel.com
1244 N. Dearborn Pkwy.
167 rooms - $150-750
Pets: Welcome
Creature Comforts: Classic
Chicago hotel, lovely interiors,
Queen-Anne furnishings,
sophisticated traditional decor,
duvets, down pillows, CCTV, a/c,
refrig, fireplace, Jacuzzis, cont.
brkfst, restaurant, hlth clb access,
comp. limo service

Clarion Inn

(800) 621-4005, (312) 346-7100
http://www.clarioninn.com
71 E. Wacker Dr.
417 rooms - $155-289
Pets: Small pets welcome
Creature Comforts: CCTV, a/c,
refrig, restaurant, hlth club

Days Inn - Midway Airport

(800) DAYS-INN, (773) 581-0500
http://www.daysinn.com
5400 S. Cicero Ave.
200 rooms - $90-169
Pets: Welcome
Creature Comforts: CCTV, a/c,
cont. brkfst, hlth club

Delaware Towers

(312) 944-4245
25 East Delaware Pl.
146 suites - $140-300
Pets: Welcome
Creature Comforts: Luxury
hotel, CCTV, a/c, kit

Essex Inn

(800) 621-6909, (312) 939-2800
800 S. Michigan Ave.
255 rooms - $90-159
Pets: Welcome w/$50 dep.
Creature Comforts: CCTV, a/c,
refrig, restaurant, pool

Fairmont Hotel

(800) 527-4727, (312) 565-8000
http://www.fairmont.com
200 North Columbus Dr.
690 rooms - $220-1,500
Pets: Under 25 lbs. welcome,
pampered pet program
Creature Comforts: Luxury hotel
w/lake views near Grant Park,
sophisticated decor w/earthtone
colors, CCTV, VCR, a/c, mini-bar,
dressing rm, oversized baths w/
terry robes, fine toiletries, hair
dryers, gourmet restaurants, pool,
hlth clb access

Four Seasons Hotel

(800) 332-3442, (312) 280-8800
http://www.fshr.com
120 E. Delaware St.
342 rooms - $295-2,600
Pets: Under 15 lbs. welcome
Creature Comforts: Luxury
hotel, traditional English motif,
fine antiques, original art,
sophisticated decor, near the lake,
CCTV, VCR, a/c, fireplace, kit,
Jacuzzis, restaurant, pool, hlth clb,
sauna, spa, whirlpool, access to
squash, tennis, and golf

Hilton Hotel - Downtown

(800) HILTONS, (312) 922-4400
http://www.hilton.com
720 S. Michigan Ave.
1,544 rooms - $165-499
Pets: Small pets w/$100 dep.
Creature Comforts: Historic
hotel, CCTV, a/c, refrig, three
restaurants, saunas, hlth club
access, whirlpools

Hilton Hotel - O'Hare Airport

(800) HILTONS, (773) 686-3000
http://www.hilton.com
Rtes 190/Airport Way
858 rooms - $195-395
Pets: Small pets welcome
Creature Comforts: CCTV, a/c,
refrig, restaurants, sauna, hlth
club, indoor golf, pool, whirlpool

Holiday Inn Mart Plaza

(800) HOLIDAY, (312) 836-5000
http://www.holiday-inn.com
350 N. Orleans St.
525 rooms - $40-299
Pets: Small pets welcome
Creature Comforts: CCTV, a/c,
refrig, restaurant, hlth club, pool

Hotel Monaco

(800) 397-7661, (312) 960-8538
225 North Wabash
http://www.hotelmonaco.com
192 rooms - $125-245
Pets: Under 20 lbs. welcome
Creature Comforts: 1930's
French Deco inspired luxury hotel,
painted woodwork, rich colors in
lobby with original art, striking
bedroom decor w/Art Deco
touches, wide striped green and
white wallpaper, whimsical
accents, rich mahogany
furnishings, writing desks,
armoires, CCTV, a/c, VCR, CD,
Jacuzzis in suites, baths w/fine
toiletries, hair dryers, bathrobes,
restaurant, fitness rm, pool

House of Blues

(877) 569-3742, (312) 245-0333
333 North Dearborn St.
http://www.loewshotels.com
367 rooms - $225-425
Pets: Under 40 lbs.
Creature Comforts: Art Deco
hotel in landmark Marina City
Complex, striking and festive
decor, stunning lobby w/stained
glass, unique sculpture and art
objects, bedrooms w/bold colors
and whimsical Art Deco touches,
CCTV, VCR, CD players, minibars, bathrooms w/hair dryers,
robes, toiletries, House of Blues
restaurant, *Crunch* health club,
state-of-the-art bowling center on
site, fitness rm.

Howard Johnson Hotel

(800) I-Go-Hojo, (312) 693-2323
http://www.hojo.com
8201 W. Higgins Rd.
110 rooms - $60-99
Pets: Welcome
Creature Comforts: CCTV, a/c,
restaurant, pool

Marriott Hotel, Downtown

(800) 228-9290, (847) 836-0100
http://www.marriott.com
540 N. Michigan Ave.
1,174 rooms - $155-759
Pets: Welcome w/$50 dep.
Creature Comforts: CCTV,
VCR, a/c, refrig, Jacuzzis,
restaurant, pool, hlth clb, sauna,
whirlpools

Marriott Hotel, O'Hare Airport
(800) 228-9290, (773) 693-4444
http://www.marriott.com
8535 W. Higgins Rd.
680 rooms - $120-210
Pets: Small pets w/$25 dep.
Creature Comforts: CCTV, a/c, refrig, restaurants, pool, hlth clb, sauna, pool, whirlpools

Motel 6
(800) 4-MOTEL6, (312) 787-3580
http://www.motel6.com
162 E. Ontario St.
191 rooms - $80-120
Pets: Under 30 lbs. welcome
Creature Comforts: CCTV, a/c

Palmer House Hilton
(800) 445-8667, (312) 726-7500
http://www.hilton.com
17 E. Monroe St.
1,639 rooms - $145-699
Pets: Welcome
Creature Comforts: Historic hotel, CCTV, VCR, a/c, refrig, restaurants, pool, hlth clb, spa, whirlpool

Park Brompton Inn
(888) City-Inns, (312) 404-3499
http://www.cityinns.com
528 W. Brompton Pl.
50 rooms - $85-139
Pets: Welcome w/$250 dep.
Creature Comforts: CCTV, a/c, kit, hlth club access

Radisson Suite Hotel
(800) 333-3333, (312) 787-2900
http://www.radisson.com
160 E. Huron St.
342 rooms - $120-295
Pets: Small pets w/$25 fee
Creature Comforts: CCTV, a/c, refrig, micro, Jacuzzis, restaurant, pool, hlth club, whirlpool

Renaissance Chicago Hotel
(800) HOTELS-1, (312) 372-7200
http://www.renaissancehotels.com
1 West Wacker Dr.
550 rooms - $220-349
Pets: Under 10 lbs. welcome w/ $45 cleaning fee and signed waiver
Creature Comforts: Award-winning hotel, CCTV, a/c, restaurants, pool, whirlpool, hlth club

Residence Inn
(800) 331-3131, (312) 943-9800
http://www.residenceinn.com
201 E. Walton St.
222 rooms - $129-349
Pets: Two pets per rm. w/$15 fee
Creature Comforts: CCTV, a/c, kit, cont. brkfst, hlth club

Ritz Carlton Hotel
(800) 332-3442, (312) 266-1000
http://www.fshr.com
160 E. Pearson St.
435 rooms - $275-2,500
Pets: Under 15 lbs. welcome
Creature Comforts: Exquisite hotel atop renowned Water Tower Place, stunning city and lake views, rqst lakeview rms, sophisticated decor in rich taupe and mahogany hues, armoires, botanical prints, sumptuous designer fabrics, CCTV, VCR, a/c, fireplace, kit, Jacuzzis, restaurant, pool, hlth clb, sauna, spa, whirlpool, massage, access to golf, squash, tennis

The Surf Hotel
(800) SURF-108, (312) 528-8400
http://www.cityinns.com
555 W. Surf St.
55 rooms - $80-145
Pets: Welcome w/$250 dep.
Creature Comforts: CCTV, a/c, refrig, hlth clb access

The Sutton Place Hotel
(800) 606-8188, (312) 266-2100
http://www.suttonplace.com
21 E. Bellevue Pl.
245 rooms - $225-795
Pets: Under 25 lbs. w/$200 dep.
Creature Comforts: Strikingly sleek modern exterior w/elegant interior spaces and a residential ambiance, contemporary decor w/ bold black and white checked duvetss, CCTV, VCR, stereo w/ CD, a/c, mini-bar, marble baths w/ separate showers and soaking tubs, restaurant, hlth clb, golf access

Tremont Hotel
(800) 621-8133, (312) 751-1900
http://www.slh.com
100 E. Chestnut St.
132 rooms - $220-999
Pets: Welcome w/credit card dep.
Creature Comforts: A lovely boutique hotel w/elegant guest rooms, traditional decor, canopy beds, marble bathrooms, CCTV, VCR, a/c, stereos-CDs, refrig, micro, restaurant

Westin Hotel
(800) 879-5444, (312) 943-7200
http://www.westin.com
909 N. Michigan Ave.
200 rooms - $175-349
Pets: Under 20 lbs. welcome
Creature Comforts: CCTV, VCR, a/c, restaurant, hlth clb sauna, whirlpool, rqst upper level lake view rms.

CHILLICOTHE
Super 8 Motel
(800) 800-8000, (309) 274-2568
http://www.super8.com
615 S. 4th St.
36 rooms - $40-70
Pets: Welcome
Creature Comforts: CCTV, a/c, kit, Jacuzzis, cont. brkfst

CLINTON
Days Inn
(800) DAYS-INN, (217) 935-4140
http://www.daysinn.com
Route 51
56 rooms - $45-85
Pets: Welcome
Creature Comforts: CCTV, a/c, refrig, micro, hlth club, pool

COLLINSVILLE
Drury Inn
(800) Drury-Inn, (618) 345-7700
http://www.drury-inn.com
602 N. Bluff Rd.
125 rooms - $59-85
Pets: Welcome
Creature Comforts: CCTV, a/c, refrig, micro, cont. brkfst, pool

Maggie's B&B
(618) 344-8283
2102 N. Keebler Ave.
5 rooms - $60-90
Pets: Welcome w/$5 fee
Creature Comforts: An historic home, CCTV, VCR, a/c, refrig, micro, fireplaces, full brkfst, whirlpool

Motel 6
(800) 4-MOTEL6, (618) 345-2100
http://www.motel6.com
295-A N. Bluff Rd.
86 rooms - $35-49
Pets: Under 30 lbs. welcome
Creature Comforts: CCTV, a/c, pool

Pear Tree Inn
(800) At-A-Tree, (618) 345-9500
http://www.drury-inn.com
552 Ramada Blvd.
105 rooms - $55-70
Pets: Under 20 lbs. welcome
Creature Comforts: CCTV, a/c, cont. brkfst, pool

Super 8 Motel
(800) 800-8000, (618) 345-8008
http://www.super8.com
2 Gateway Dr.
63 rooms - $45-80
Pets: Welcome w/permission
Creature Comforts: CCTV, a/c, cont. brkfst

CRESTWOOD
Hampton Inn
(800) Hampton, (708) 597-3330
http://www.hampton-inn.com
13330 S. Cicero Ave.
123 rooms - $65-105
Pets: Welcome
Creature Comforts: CCTV, a/c, cont. brkfst, pool, hlth club

CRYSTAL LAKE
Super 8 Motel
(800) 800-8000, (815) 455-2388
http://www.super8.com
577 Crystal Point Dr.
59 rooms - $49-79
Pets: Welcome
Creature Comforts: CCTV, a/c, cont. brkfst

DANVILLE
Best Western Regency Inn
(800) 528-1234, (217) 446-2111
http://www.bestwestern.com
360 Eastgate Rd.
42 rooms - $50-115
Pets: Welcome w/permission
Creature Comforts: CCTV, a/c, refrig, Jacuzzis, restaurant, cont. brkfst, hlth club, whirlpool, pool

Best Western Riverside Inn
(800) 528-1234, (217) 431-0020
http://www.bestwestern.com
57 S. Gilbert St.
42 rooms - $50-105
Pets: Small pets w/$10 dep.
Creature Comforts: CCTV, a/c, refrig, Jacuzzis, cont. brkfst, pool, whirlpool

Comfort Inn
(800) 228-5150, (217) 443-8004
http://www.comfortinn.com
383 Lynch Dr.
56 rooms - $50-109
Pets: Small pets welcome
Creature Comforts: CCTV, a/c, refrig, cont. brkfst, pool

Glo Motel
(217) 442-2086
3617 N. Vermilion Rd.
22 rooms - $35-53
Pets: $4 fee, $10 deposit
Creature Comforts: CCTV, a/c, refrig, pool

Ramada Inn
(800) 2-Ramada, (217) 446-2400
http://www.ramada.com
388 Eastgate Dr.
130 rooms - $55-109
Pets: Welcome
Creature Comforts: CCTV, a/c, kit, restaurant, pool, hlth club, whirlpool

Redwood Motor Inn
(800) 369-1339, (217) 443-3690
411 Lynch Dr.
65 rooms - $39-85
Pets: Welcome
Creature Comforts: CCTV, a/c, kit, pool

Super 8 Motel
(800) 800-8000, (217) 443-4499
http://www.super8.com
377 Lynch Dr.
50 rooms - $45-75
Pets: Welcome
Creature Comforts: CCTV, a/c, kit

DECATUR
Baymont Inn
(877)BAYMONT, (217) 875-5800
http://www.baymontinns.com
5100 Hickory Pt. Frontage Rd.
104 rooms - $45-69
Pets: Small pets welcome
Creature Comforts: CCTV, a/c, refrig, micro, cont. brkfst

Country Inns and Suites
(800) 456-4000, (217) 872-2402
http://www.countryinns.com
5150 Hickory Pt. Frontage Rd.
62 rooms - $70-100
Pets: Welcome in smoking rooms
Creature Comforts: CCTV, a/c, micro, refrig, pool

Days Inn
(800) DAYS-INN, (217) 422-5900
http://www.daysinn.com
333 N. Wyckles Rd.
119 rooms - $45-69
Pets: Welcome
Creature Comforts: CCTV, a/c, cont. brkfst

Holiday Inn
(800) HOLIDAY, (217) 422-8800
http://www.holiday-inn.com
Rte. 36 & Wyckles Rd.
385 rooms - $89-275
Pets: Small pets w/$25 dep.
Creature Comforts: CCTV, VCR, a/c, refrig, Jacuzzis, restaurant, hlth club, sauna, tennis-paddle courts., lawn games, pool

Intown Motel
(217) 422-9080
1013 E. Eldorado St.
12 rooms - $30-45
Pets: Welcome w/$5 fee
Creature Comforts: CCTV, a/c

Red Carpet Inn
(800) 251-1962, (217) 877-3380
http://www.redcarpetinns.com
3035 N. Water St.
44 rooms - $40-65
Pets: Small pets w/$20 dep.
Creature Comforts: CCTV, a/c, refrig.

Super 8 Motel
(800) 800-8000, (217) 877-8888
http://www.super8.com
3141 N. Water St.
62 rooms - $45-70
Pets: Welcome
Creature Comforts: CCTV, a/c

DEERFIELD
Marriott Suites
(800) 457-GOLF, (847) 405-9666
http://www.marriott.com
2 Parkway Blvd.
252 rooms - $129-199
Pets: Welcome w/$50-100 fee
Creature Comforts: CCTV, VCR, a/c, refrig, micro, restaurant, pool, hlth clb, sauna, whirlpool

Residence Inn
(800) 331-3131, (847) 940-4644
http://www.residenceinn.com
530 Lake Cook Rd.
126 rooms - $109-189
Pets: Welcome w/$100-150 fee
Creature Comforts: CCTV, a/c, fireplaces, Jacuzzis, kit, cont. brkfst, hlth club, pool

DEKALB
Motel 6
(800) 4-MOTEL6, (815) 756-3398
http://www.motel6.com
1116 W. Lincoln Hwy.
111 rooms - $34-56
Pets: Under 30 lbs. welcome
Creature Comforts: CCTV, a/c, pool

DES PLAINES
Travelodge
(800) 578-7878, (847) 296-5541
http://www.travelodge.com
3003 Mannheim Rd.
95 rooms - $60-90
Pets: Small pets w/$25 dep.
Creature Comforts: CCTV, a/c, refrig, micro, restaurant, cont. brkfst, hlth club, pool

DIX
Scottish Inns
(800) 251-1962, (618) 266-7254
Route 57
75 rooms - $30-49
Pets: Welcome w/$3 fee
Creature Comforts: CCTV, a/c, cont. brkfst, pool

DIXON
Best Western Brandywine Inn
(800) 528-1234, (815) 284-1890
http://www.bestwestern.com
443 Rte. 2
90 rooms - $60-175
Pets: Small pets w/$25 dep.
Creature Comforts: CCTV, a/c, refrig, restaurant, cont. brkfst, hlth club, pool

DOWNERS GROVE
Marriott Suites
(800) 228-9290, (630) 852-1500
http://www.marriott.com
1500 Opus Place
254 suites - $65-160
Pets: Under 20 lbs., must be crated in your room
Creature Comforts: CCTV, a/c, refrig, micro, pool, health club access

Red Roof Inn
(800) The-Roof, (630) 963-4205
http://www.redroof.com
1113 Butterfield Rd.
135 rooms - $45-75
Pets: Small pets welcome
Creature Comforts: CCTV, a/c

DWIGHT
Super 8 Motel
(800) 800-8000, (815) 584-1888
http://www.super8.com
14 E. Northbrook Dr.
40 rooms - $45-70
Pets: Welcome w/$25 dep.
Creature Comforts: CCTV, a/c, Jacuzzis, cont. brkfst

EAST HAZELCREST
Motel 6
(800) 4-MOTEL6, (708) 957-9233
http://www.motel6.com
17214 Halstead St.
121 rooms - $44-59
Pets: Under 30 lbs. welcome
Creature Comforts: CCTV, a/c, pool

EAST MOLINE
Super 8 Motel
(800) 800-8000, (309) 796-1999
http://www.super8.com
2201 John Deere Expwy.
63 rooms - $45-69
Pets: Welcome w/permission
Creature Comforts: CCTV, a/c, cont. brkfst, hlth club, whirlpool

EAST PEORIA
Motel 6
(800) 4-MOTEL6, (309) 699-7281
http://www.motel6.com
104 W. Camp St.
78 rooms - $40-55
Pets: Under 30 lbs. welcome
Creature Comforts: CCTV, a/c, pool

Super 8 Motel
(800) 800-8000, (309) 698-8889
http://www.super8.com
725 Taylor St.
64 rooms - $45-69
Pets: Welcome
Creature Comforts: CCTV, a/c

EFFINGHAM
Abe Lincoln Motel
(217) 342-4717
Route 32
18 rooms - $35-48
Pets: Welcome
Creature Comforts: CCTV, a/c, refrig

Anthony Acres Resort
(217) 868-2950
RR 2
28 rooms - $60-75
Pets: After Labor Day w/$10 fee
Creature Comforts: a/c, kit

Baymont Inn
(877)BAYMONT, (217) 342-2525
http://www.baymontinns.com
1103 Ave. of Mid-America
122 rooms - $50-75
Pets: Small pets welcome
Creature Comforts: CCTV, a/c, refrig, micro, cont. brkfst

Best Inns of America
(800) 237-8466, (217) 347-5141
http://www.bestinns.com
1209 N. Kellar Dr.
82 rooms - $39-55
Pets: Small pets welcome
Creature Comforts: CCTV, a/c,
pool

Best Western Raintree Inn
(800) 528-1234, (217) 342-4121
http://www.bestwestern.com
Rtes. 70 & 40
60 rooms - $45-60
Pets: Welcome in smoking rooms
Creature Comforts: CCTV, a/c,
refrig, restaurant, cont. brkfst, pool

Budget Host
(800) Bud Host, (217) 342-4133
http://www.budgethost.com
Route 45
25 rooms - $32-45
Pets: Welcome w/$25 dep.
Creature Comforts: CCTV, a/c,
cont. brkfst

Comfort Inn
(800) 228-5150, (217) 347-5050
http://www.comfortinn.com
1304 W. Evergreen Dr.
70 rooms - $65-85
Pets: Welcome
Creature Comforts: CCTV, a/c,
refrig, micro, Jacuzzi, cont. brkfst,
pool, sauna, whirlpool, and an
exercise room

Comfort Suites
(800) 228-5150, (217) 342-3151
http://www.comfortinn.com
1310 W. Fayette Rd.
65 rooms - $70-100
Pets: Welcome
Creature Comforts: CCTV, a/c,
refrig, fireplace, Jacuzzi, pool

Days Inn
(800) DAYS-INN, (217) 342-9271
http://www.daysinn.com
Rtes. 57 & 70
119 rooms - $45-65
Pets: Welcome
Creature Comforts: CCTV, a/c,
cont. brkfst, pool

Econo Lodge
(800) 55-ECONO, (217) 347-7131
http://www.econolodge.com
1205 N. Keller Dr.
74 rooms - $43-79
Pets: Small pets welcome
Creature Comforts: CCTV, a/c,
refrig, cont. brkfst, hlth club, pool

Hampton Inn
(800) Hampton, (217) 342-4499
http://www.hampton-inn.com.com
1509 Hampton Dr.
62 rooms - $54-69
Pets: Welcome in smoking rooms
Creature Comforts: CCTV, a/c,
refrig, Jacuzzis, pool, sauna

Holiday Inn
(800) HOLIDAY, (217) 342-4161
http://www.holiday-inn.com
1600 W. Fayette Ave.
134 rooms - $59-75
Pets: Small pets in smoking rms.
Creature Comforts: CCTV,
VCR, a/c, Jacuzzis, restaurant,
pool

Howard Johnson Express
(800) I-Go-Hojo, (217) 342-4667
http://www.hojo.com
1606 W. Fayette Ave.
54 rooms - $40-69
Pets: Welcome w/permission
Creature Comforts: CCTV,
VCR, a/c, cont. brkfst, pool

Knights Inn
(800) 843-5644, (217) 342-2165
http://www.knightsinn.com
1000 W. Fayette Ave.
32 rooms - $29-49
Pets: Small pets w/$5 fee
Creature Comforts: CCTV, a/c,
cont. brkfst

Quality Inn
(800) 228-5151, (217) 367-6000
http://www.qualityinn.com
1600 W. Fayette Ave.
135 rooms - $65-79
Pets: Small pets welcome
Creature Comforts: CCTV, a/c,
refrig, restaurant, pool

Ramada Inn
(800) 2-Ramada, (217) 342-2131
http://www.ramada.com
Rtes. 57 & 70
175 rooms - $55-139
Pets: Welcome in smoking rooms
Creature Comforts: CCTV, a/c,
kit, Jacuzzis, restaurant, cont.
brkfst, sauna, pool, whirlpool, hlth
club, mini golf, bowling

Super 8 Motel
(800) 800-8000, (217) 342-6888
http://www.super8.com
140 Thelma Kellar Ave.
49 rooms - $45-70
Pets: Welcome
Creature Comforts: CCTV, a/c,
cont. brkfst

ELGIN
Baymont Inn
(800) 4-Budget, (847) 931-4800
http://www.baymontinns.com
500 Toll Gate Rd.
82 rooms - $60-82
Pets: Welcome
Creature Comforts: CCTV, a/c,
refrig, micro, cont. brkfst

ELK GROVE
Exel Inn
(800) 367-3935, (847) 894-2085
http://www.exelinns.com
1000 Devon Ave.
111 rooms - $60-79
Pets: Small pets welcome
Creature Comforts: CCTV,
VCR, a/c, refrig, micro, Jacuzzis,
cont. brkfst.

Exel Inn - O'Hare Airport
(800) 367-3935, (847) 803-9400
http://www.exelinns.com
2881 Touhy Ave.
122 rooms - $69-85
Pets: Small pets welcome
Creature Comforts: CCTV,
VCR, a/c, refrig, micro, Jacuzzis,
cont. brkfst.

Holiday Inn
(800) HOLIDAY, (847) 437-6010
http://www.holiday-inn.com
1000 Busse Rd.
160 rooms - $85-125
Pets: Small pets welcome
Creature Comforts: CCTV, a/c,
refrig, restaurant, hlth club, sauna,
pool, whirlpool

La Quinta Inn
(800) Nu-Rooms, (847) 439-6767
http://www.laquinta.com
1900 Oakton St.
142 rooms - $70-85
Pets: Under 25 lbs. welcome
Creature Comforts: CCTV, a/c,
cont. brkfst, pool

Motel 6
(800) 4-MOTEL6, (847) 981-9766
http://www.motel6.com
1601 Oakton St.
222 rooms - $44-55
Pets: Under 30 lbs. welcome
Creature Comforts: CCTV, a/c

Sheraton Suites Hotel
(800) 325-3535, (847) 290-1600
http://www.sheraton.com
121 NW Point Blvd.
256 rooms - $99-198
Pets: Small pets w/$75 fee
Creature Comforts: CCTV, a/c,
refrig, micro, restaurant, pool, hlth
clb, whirlpool, jogging paths

ELMHURST
Holiday Inn
(800) HOLIDAY, (708) 279-1100
http://www.holiday-inn.com
624 N. York Rd.
228 rooms - $90-100
Pets: Small pets welcome
Creature Comforts: CCTV, a/c,
refrig, Jacuzzis, restaurant, hlth
club, sauna, pool, whirlpool

EL PASO
Super 8 Motel
(800) 800-8000, (309) 527-4949
http://www.super8.com
880 W. Main St.
26 rooms - $45-70
Pets: Welcome
Creature Comforts: CCTV, a/c,
cont. brkfst

EVANSTON
Homestead Hotel
(847) 475-3300
1625 Hinman Ave.
90 rooms - $85-100
Pets: Welcome in ltd. rms
Creature Comforts: CCTV,
VCR, a/c, refrig, restaurant

FAIRVIEW HEIGHTS
Drury Inn
(800) Drury-Inn, (618) 398-8530
http://www.drury-inn.com
12 Ludwig Dr.
105 rooms - $63-85
Pets: Welcome
Creature Comforts: CCTV, a/c,
refrig, cont. brkfst, pool

Ramada Inn
(800) 2-Ramada, (618) 632-4747
http://www.ramada.com
29 Public Sq.
160 rooms - $40-90
Pets: Welcome
Creature Comforts: SATV, a/c,
cont. brkfst, pool

Super 8 Motel
(800) 800-8000, (618) 398-8338
http://www.super8.com
45 Ludwig Dr.
81 rooms - $50-69
Pets: Welcome w/permission
Creature Comforts: CCTV, a/c,
cont. brkfst

Trailway Motel
(618) 397-5757
10039 Lincoln Tr.
30 rooms - $45-70
Pets: Small pets w/$5 fee
Creature Comforts: CCTV, a/c,
refrig

FARMER CITY
Budget Motel
(309) 928-2157
Rte. 54
18 rooms - $40-55
Pets: Welcome w/$3 fee
Creature Comforts: CCTV, a/c,
refrig

Days Inn
(800) DAYS-INN, (309) 928-9434
http://www.daysinn.com
Rte. 74, Box 195
41 rooms - $45-109
Pets: Welcome w/$5 fee
Creature Comforts: CCTV,
VCR, a/c, Jacuzzi, cont brkfst.

FORSYTH
Comfort Inn
(800) 228-5150, (217) 875-1166
http://www.comfortinn.com
134 Barnett Ave.
57 rooms - $60-70
Pets: Welcome
Creature Comforts: CCTV,
VCR, a/c, refrig, micro, pool, hlth
clb.

FRANKLIN PARK
Travelodge
(800) 578-7878, (847) 288-0600
http://www.travelodge.com
3010 N. Mannheim Rd.
80 rooms - $45-65
Pets: Welcome
Creature Comforts: CCTV, a/c,
Jacuzzis, refrig, micro, pool

FREEPORT
Ramada Inn
(800) 2-Ramada, (815) 297-9700
http://www.ramada.com
1300 E. South St.
90 rooms - $65-75
Pets: Welcome
Creature Comforts: CCTV, a/c,
refrig, micro, restaurant, pool

West Motel
(815) 232-4188
2084 W. Galena Ave.
17 rooms - $40-52
Pets: Small pets welcome
Creature Comforts: CCTV, a/c,
refrig

GALENA
Best Western Quiet House
(800) 528-1234, (815) 777-2577
http://www.bestwestern.com
Rte. 20
42 rooms - $90-199
Pets: Welcome in ltd. rms w/
manager's approval
Creature Comforts: CCTV, a/c,
refrig, cont. brkfst, hlth club, pool,
whirlpool

Cottage at Amber Creek Farm
(815) 777-8400
122 South Bench
1 cottage - $99-165
Pets: $25 fee, $100 dep.
Creature Comforts: Charming
cottage surrounded by hundreds of
acres, fireplace, kit, cont. brkfst,
whirlpool

Farster's Executive Inn
(800) 545-8551, (815) 777-9125
305 N. Main St.
8 suites - $80-175
Pets: Smal pets welcome
Creature Comforts: CCTV, a/c,
fireplace, kit, Jacuzzis

GALESBURG
Comfort Inn
(800) 228-5150, (309) 344-5445
http://www.comfortinn.com
907 W. Carl Sandburg Dr.
46 rooms - $50-94
Pets: Small pets welcome
Creature Comforts: CCTV, a/c,
cont. brkfst

Jumer's Continental Inn
(800) 285-8637, (309) 343-7151
http://www.jumers.com
260 S. Soangetaha Rd.
148 rooms - $69-149
Pets: Welcome w/$25 dep.
Creature Comforts: An inn w/
Old World European charm,
antiques, detailed woodworking,
CCTV, VCR, a/c, refrig, micro,
Jacuzzis, restaurant, pool, saunas,
whirlpool, playing fields

Ramada Inn
(800) 2-Ramada, (309) 343-9161
http://www.ramada.com
29 Public Sq.
90 rooms - $55-88
Pets: Welcome
Creature Comforts: CCTV,
VCR, a/c, refrig, restaurant, pool

Regency Hotel
(800) 648-4707, (309) 344-1111
3282 N. Henderson St.
141 rooms - $39-60
Pets: Welcome w/$5 fee
Creature Comforts: CCTV, a/c,
restaurant, pool

GENESEO
Deck Plaza Motel
(309) 944-4651
2181 S. Oakwood Ave.
120 rooms - $30-49
Pets: Welcome in certain rms
Creature Comforts: CCTV, a/c,
restaurant, pool

GENEVA
Oscar Swan Country Inn
(630) 232-0173
1800 W. State St.
8 rooms - $79-150
Pets: Welcome
Creature Comforts: A charming
1900's Colonial Revival mansion
set on spacious grounds amid
shade trees in Fox Valley, CCTV,
VCR, a/c, fireplace, refrig, full
brkfst

GILMAN
Days Inn
(800) DAYS-INN, (815) 265-7283
http://www.daysinn.com
834 Rte. 24
38 rooms - $50-75
Pets: Welcome w/$3 fee
Creature Comforts: CCTV, a/c,
cont. brkfst, pool, whirlpool

Super 8 Motel
(800) 800-8000, (815) 265-7000
http://www.super8.com
1301 S. Crescent St.
52 rooms - $50-75
Pets: Welcome
Creature Comforts: CCTV, a/c,
Jacuzzis, cont. brkfst

GLEN ELLYN
Best Western Four Seasons
(800) 528-1234, (630) 469-8500
http://www.bestwestern.com
675 Roosevelt Rd.
121 rooms - $55-80
Pets: Under 20 lbs. welcome
Creature Comforts: CCTV, a/c,
kit, cont. brkfst

Holiday Inn
(800) HOLIDAY, (630) 629-6000
http://www.holiday-inn.com
1250 Roosevelt Rd.
120 rooms - $75-99
Pets: Welcome w/travel crate
Creature Comforts: CCTV,
VCR, a/c, restaurant, hlth club
access, pool

GLENVIEW
Baymont Inn
(877)BAYMONT, (847) 635-8300
http://www.baymontinns.com
1625 Milwaukee Ave.
148 rooms - $50-69
Pets: Welcome
Creature Comforts: CCTV, a/c,
refrig, micro, cont. brkfst

Motel 6
(800) 4-MOTEL6, (847) 390-7200
http://www.motel6.com
1535 Milwaukee Ave.
111 rooms - $42-55
Pets: Under 30 lbs. welcome
Creature Comforts: CCTV, a/c

GOLCONDA
San Damiano Retreat
(618) 285-3507
Rte. 1, Box 106
26 rooms - $59-129
Pets: Welcome w/$10 fee
Creature Comforts: CCTV, a/c,
kit, fireplaces, Jacuzzi, cont.
brkfst, dining rm, overlook river

GRAYVILLE
Best Western Windsor Oaks
(800) 528-1234, (618) 375-7930
http://www.bestwestern.com
2200 S. Court St.
60 rooms - $59-85
Pets: Welcome from Sept. - May
Creature Comforts: CCTV, a/c,
restaurant, pool

GREENVILLE
Best Western Country View
(800) 528-1234, (618) 864-3030
http://www.bestwestern.com
Rtes. 70 & 127
83 rooms - $39-65
Pets: Small pets welcome
Creature Comforts: CCTV, a/c,
restaurant, cont. brkfst, hlth club,
pool, whirlpool

Budget Host
(800) Bud-Host, (618) 664-1950
http://www.budgethost.com
Rtes. 70 & 127
50 rooms - $33-55
Pets: Small pets w/$5 fee
Creature Comforts: CCTV, a/c,
kit, Jacuzzis, cont. brkfst

Prairie House Country Inn
(618) 664-3003
RR 4, Box 47
6 rooms - $100-125
Pets: Welcome w/travel crate
Creature Comforts: CCTV,
VCR, a/c, refrig, micro, cont.
brkfst, hlth clb access

Super 8 Motel
(800) 800-8000, (618) 664-0800
http://www.super8.com
Rtes. 70 & 127
43 rooms - $40-69
Pets: Welcome w/permission
Creature Comforts: CCTV, a/c,
cont. brkfst

GREENUP
Five Star Motel
(217) 923-5512
Rtes. 40 & 130
30 rooms - $26-32
Pets: Welcome
Creature Comforts: CCTV, a/c

Gateway Inn Motel
(217) 923-3176
716 E. Elizabeth St.
28 rooms - $40-52
Pets: Welcome
Creature Comforts: CCTV, a/c

GURNEE
Baymont Inn
(877)BAYMONT, (847) 662-7600
http://www.baymontinns.com
5688 N. Ridge Rd.
105 rooms - $49-105
Pets: Small pets welcome
Creature Comforts: CCTV, a/c,
refrig, micro, cont. brkfst

HAMEL
Innkeeper Motel
(618) 633-2111
Rtes. 55 & 140
28 rooms - $40-52
Pets: Welcome w/$5 fee
Creature Comforts: CCTV, a/c,
refrig, restaurant, lake

HARRISBURG
Plaza Motel
(618) 253-7651
411 E. Poplar St.
47 rooms - $38-49
Pets: Welcome
Creature Comforts: CCTV, a/c,
refrig

Super 8 Motel
(800) 800-8000, (618) 253-8081
http://www.super8.com
100 E. Seright St.
38 rooms - $50-65
Pets: Welcome w/permission
Creature Comforts: CCTV, a/c,
cont. brkfst

HARVARD
Amerihost Inn
(800) 434-5800, (815) 943-0700
http://www.amerihostinn.com
1701 S. Division St.
58 rooms - $80-150
Pets: Small pets welcome
Creature Comforts: CCTV, a/c,
refrig, micro, cont. brkfst, pool,
hlth clb, sauna, whirlpool

HENRY
Henry Harbor Inn
(309) 364-2365
208 Cromwell Dr.
22 rooms - $60-95
Pets: Welcome
Creature Comforts: CCTV, a/c,
kit, cont. brkfst

HIGHLAND
Cardinal Inn
(618) 654-4433
101 Walnut St.
10 rooms - $45-54
Pets: Welcome
Creature Comforts: CCTV, a/c,
refrig

HILLSIDE
Holiday Inn
(800) HOLIDAY, (708) 544-9300
http://www.holiday-inn.com
4400 Frontage Rd.
250 rooms - $99-189
Pets: Small pets welcome
Creature Comforts: CCTV, a/c,
refrig, restaurant, hlth club, pool

HOFFMAN ESTATES
Amerisuites
(800) 833-1516, (847) 839-1800
http://www.amerisuites.com
2750 Greenspoint Pkwy.
130 rooms - $135-150
Pets: Small pets w/$100 deposit
Creature Comforts: CCTV,
VCR, a/c, refrig, micro, cont.
brkfst, hlth club, pool

Baymont Inn
(877)BAYMONT, (847) 882-8848
http://www.baymontinns.com
2075 Barrington Rd.
100 rooms - $55-73
Pets: Small pets welcome
Creature Comforts: CCTV, a/c,
refrig, micro, cont. brkfst

La Quinta Inn
(800) Nu-Rooms, (847) 882-3312
http://www.laquinta.com
2280 Barrington Rd.
129 rooms - $70-95
Pets: Small pets welcome
Creature Comforts: CCTV, a/c,
refrig, cont. brkfst, pool

Red Roof Inn
(800) The-Roof, (847) 885-7877
http://www.redroof.com
2500 Hassell Rd.
118 rooms - $45-75
Pets: Small pets welcome
Creature Comforts: CCTV, a/c

JACKSONVILLE
Holiday Inn
(800) HOLIDAY, (217) 245-9571
http://www.holiday-inn.com
1717 W. Morton Ave.
116 rooms - $59-129
Pets: Welcome
Creature Comforts: CCTV,
VCR, a/c, refrig, restaurant, hlth
club access, sauna, pool,
whirlpool, rec. dome

Motel 6
(800) 4-MOTEL6, (217) 243-7157
http://www.motel6.com
1716 W. Morton Dr.
77 rooms - $34-40
Pets: Under 30 lbs. welcome
Creature Comforts: CCTV, a/c,
pool

Star Lite Motel
(217) 245-7184
1910 W. Morton Ave.
33 rooms - $34-45
Pets: Small pets welcome
Creature Comforts: CCTV, a/c

JOLIET
Comfort Inn, North
(800) 228-5150, (815) 436-5141
http://www.comfortinn.com
3235 Norman Ave.
64 rooms - $59-169
Pets: Small pets welcome
Creature Comforts: CCTV, a/c,
refrig, cont. brkfst, pool

Comfort Inn, South
(800) 228-5150, (815) 744-1770
http://www.comfortinn.com
135 S. Larkin Ave.
67 rooms - $59-159
Pets: Small pets welcome
Creature Comforts: CCTV, a/c,
refrig, cont. brkfst, pool

Manor Motel
(815) 467-5385
32926 E. Eames Rd.
77 rooms - $45-64
Pets: Welcome w/$10 fee
Creature Comforts: CCTV, a/c,
pool

Motel 6
(800) 4-MOTEL6, (815) 439-1332
http://www.motel6.com
3551 Mall Loop Dr.
121 rooms - $44-59
Pets: Under 30 lbs. welcome
Creature Comforts: CCTV, a/c

Motel 6
(800) 4-MOTEL6, (815) 729-2800
http://www.motel6.com
1850 McDonough Rd.
129 rooms - $34-55
Pets: Under 30 lbs. welcome
Creature Comforts: CCTV, a/c

Red Roof Inn
(800) The-Roof, (815) 843-7663
http://www.redroof.com
1750 McDonough St.
108 rooms - $48-75
Pets: Small pets welcome
Creature Comforts: CCTV, a/c,
refrig, micro

JONESBORO
Trail of Tears Sports Resort
(618) 833-8697
Old Cape Rd.
7 rooms - $50-75
Pets: Welcome
Creature Comforts: CCTV, a/c,
refrig, restaurant, cont. brkfst,
whirlpool, pond, lawn sports

KEITHSBURG
The Keithsburg Motel
(309) 374-2659
Second & Main Sts.
15 rooms - $39-45
Pets: Welcome
Creature Comforts: CCTV, a/c,
refrig

KEWANEE
Kewanee Motor Lodge
(800) 853-4007, (309) 853-4000
400 S. Main St.
28 rooms - $40-53
Pets: Welcome
Creature Comforts: CCTV, a/c,
refrig, micro

KNOXVILLE
Super 8 Motel
(800) 800-8000, (309) 289-2100
http://www.super8.com
Route 74
48 rooms - $45-65
Pets: Welcome
Creature Comforts: CCTV, a/c,
cont. brkfst, pool

LANSING
Holiday Inn
(800) HOLIDAY, (708) 474-6300
http://www.holiday-inn.com
17356 Torrence Ave.
165 rooms - $80-99
Pets: Small pets welcome
Creature Comforts: CCTV, a/c,
refrig, restaurant, pool

Red Roof Inn
(800) The-Roof, (708) 895-9570
http://www.redroof.com
2450 E. 173rd St.
107 rooms - $45-70
Pets: Small pets welcome
Creature Comforts: CCTV, a/c

LE ROY
Super 8 Motel
(800) 800-8000, (309) 962-4700
http://www.super8.com
1 Demma Dr.
41 rooms - $45-65
Pets: Welcome w/$25 dep.
Creature Comforts: CCTV, a/c,
cont. brkfst

LIBERTYVILLE
Best Inns of America
(800) 237-8466, (847) 816-8006
http://www.bestinns.com
1809 W. Milwaukee Ave.
90 rooms - $45-73
Pets: Small pets welcome
Creature Comforts: CCTV, a/c,
refrig, pool

LINCOLN
Comfort Inn
(800) 228-5150, (217) 735-3960
http://www.comfortinn.com
2811 Woodlawn Rd.
52 rooms - $49-75
Pets: Small pets welcome
Creature Comforts: CCTV, a/c,
cont. brkfst, pool

Crossroads Motel
(217) 735-5571
1305 Woodlawn Rd.
29 rooms - $43-50
Pets: Small pets w/$5 fee
Creature Comforts: CCTV, a/c,
refrig, pool

Days Inn
(800) DAYS-INN, (217) 735-1202
http://www.daysinn.com
2011 N. Kickapoo St.
60 rooms - $35-55
Pets: Welcome
Creature Comforts: CCTV, a/c,
cont. brkfst, pool

Holiday Inn Express
(800) HOLIDAY, (217) 735-5800
http://www.holiday-inn.com
130 Olson Rd.
70 rooms - $65-80
Pets: Welcome in smoking rms.
Creature Comforts: CCTV, a/c,
refrig, micro, pool

Super 8 Motel
(800) 800-8000, (217) 732-8886
http://www.super8.com
2809 Woodlawn Rd.
45 rooms - $45-70
Pets: Welcome
Creature Comforts: CCTV, a/c,
Jacuzzi, cont. brkfst, pool

LINCOLNSHIRE
Marriott's Lincolnshire Resort
(800) 228-9290, (847) 634-0100
http://www.marriott.com
10 Marriott Dr.
389 rooms - $99-299
Pets: Welcome w/$25 cleaning fee
Creature Comforts: Expansive
resort set along a lake, CCTV,
VCR, a/c, refrig, Jacuzzis,
restaurants, pool, hlth clb, sauna,
steamrooms, whirlpools, racquet/
tennis cts, golf, boating, hiking

LISLE
Radisson Suite Hotel
(800) 333-3333, (630) 505-0900
http://www.radisson.com
3003 Warrenville Rd.
244 rooms - $75-160
Pets: Under 20 lbs. welcome
Creature Comforts: CCTV, a/c,
refrig, Jacuzzis, restaurant, pool,
hlth club, sauna, whirlpool

LITCHFIELD
Best Western Gardens Inn
(800) 528-1234, (217) 324-2181
http://www.bestwestern.com
413 W. Columbian Blvd. N.
78 rooms - $45-70
Pets: Small pets w/$5 fee
Creature Comforts: CCTV, a/c,
refrig, restaurant, pool

66 Motel
(217) 324-2179
621 N. Sherman St.
28 rooms - $35-46
Pets: Welcome w/$2 fee
Creature Comforts: CCTV, a/c,
refrig

Super 8 Motel
(800) 800-8000, (217) 324-7788
http://www.super8.com
Rtes. 55 & 16
61 rooms - $45-69
Pets: Welcome
Creature Comforts: CCTV, a/c,
cont. brkfst

LOMBARD
Residence Inn
(800) 331-3131, (630) 629-7800
http://www.residenceinn.com
2001 S. Highland Ave.
180 rooms - $129-299
Pets: $6 fee, $100 dep.
Creature Comforts: CCTV,
VCR, a/c, kit, fireplace, cont.
brkfst, hlth club, pool

MACOMB
Days Inn
(800) DAYS-INN, (309) 833-5511
http://www.daysinn.com
1400 N. Lafayette St.
144 rooms - $45-139
Pets: Welcome w/$10 fee
Creature Comforts: CCTV, a/c,
refrig, micro, Jacuzzis, restaurant,
cont. brkfst, pool

MAHOMET
Heritage Inn Motel
(217) 586-4975
Rtes. 74 & 47
25 rooms - $55-65
Pets: Welcome
Creature Comforts: CCTV, a/c

MARION
Best Inns of America
(800) 237-8466, (618) 997-9421
http://www.bestinns.com
2700 W. De Young Rd.
102 rooms - $40-79
Pets: Small pets welcome
Creature Comforts: CCTV, a/c,
refrig, cont. brkfst, pool

Best Western Airport Inn
(800) 528-1234, (618) 993-3222
http://www.bestwestern.com
130 Express Dr.
34 rooms - $45-75
Pets: Welcome
Creature Comforts: CCTV, a/c,
cont. brkfst, pool

Drury Inn
(800) Drury-Inn, (618) 997-9600
http://www.drury-inn.com
2706 W. DeYoung
135 rooms - $65-75
Pets: Welcome, cannot be left
unattended
Creature Comforts: CCTV, a/c,
refrig, micro, cont. brkfst, pool,
exercise rm.

Gray Plaza Motel
(618) 993-2174
Route 13
30 rooms - $30-44
Pets: Welcome w/$5 fee
Creature Comforts: CCTV, a/c,
refrig

Hampton Inn
(800) Hampton, (618) 998-9900
http://www.hampton-inn.com
2710 W. DeYoung
65 rooms - $60-75
Pets: Small pets welcome
Creature Comforts: CCTV, a/c,
pool, exercise rm.

Motel Marion
(618) 993-2101
2100 W. Main St.
50 rooms - $29-36
Pets: Welcome
Creature Comforts: CCTV, a/c,
refrig, micro, pool

Motel 6
(800) 4-MOTEL6, (618) 993-2631
http://www.motel6.com
1008 Halfway Rd.
79 rooms - $34-49
Pets: Under 30 lbs. welcome
Creature Comforts: CCTV, a/c,
pool

Olde Squat Inn
(618) 982-2916
RR 7, Box 246
4 cabins - $33-60
Pets: Welcome
Creature Comforts: TV, stereo,
a/c, fireplace, kit, full brkfst,
whirlpool

Super 8 Motel
(800) 800-8000, (618) 993-5577
http://www.super8.com
2601 W. De Young Rd.
63 rooms - $45-60
Pets: Welcome w/permission
Creature Comforts: CCTV, a/c,
cont. brkfst

Toupal's Country Inn
(618) 995-2074
RR 5
12 rooms - $45-89
Pets: Welcome w/$5 fee
Creature Comforts: CCTV,
VCR, a/c, refrig, Jacuzzi,
restaurant

MARSHALL
Lincoln Motel
(217) 826-2941
Route 40
22 rooms - $28-36
Pets: Small pets welcome
Creature Comforts: CCTV, a/c

MASON CITY
Mason City Motel
(217) 482-3003
701 W. Chestnut St.
17 rooms - $39-48
Pets: Welcome w/$10 dep.
Creature Comforts: CCTV, a/c,
refrig, cont. brkfst

MATTESON

Baymont Inn
(877)BAYMONT, (708) 503-0999
http://www.baymontinns.com
5210 W. Southwick Dr.
115 rooms - $55-75
Pets: Small pets welcome
Creature Comforts: CCTV, a/c,
refrig, micro, cont. brkfst

Peaks Motor Inn
(217) 826-3031
Route 70
48 rooms - $55-70
Pets: Welcome
Creature Comforts: CCTV, a/c,
cont. brkfst

MATTOON

Budget Inn
(217) 235-4011
Rtes. 57 & 45
109 rooms - $45-115
Pets: Welcome
Creature Comforts: CCTV,
VCR, a/c, refrig, Jacuzzi,
steamroom, pool

Ramada Inn
(800) 2-Ramada, (217) 235-0313
http://www.ramada.com
300 Broadway Ave. East
125 rooms - $55-109
Pets: Welcome
Creature Comforts: CCTV,
VCR, a/c, refrig, micro, restaurant,
sauna, whirlpool, pool

Super 8 Motel
(800) 800-8000, (217) 235-8888
http://www.super8.com
Rtes. 15 & 57
61 rooms - $45-60
Pets: Welcome w/permission
Creature Comforts: CCTV, a/c,
cont. brkfst

McLEAN

Super 8 Motel
(800) 800-8000, (309) 874-2366
http://www.super8.com
55 South St.
41 rooms - $45-65
Pets: Welcome w/$25 dep.
Creature Comforts: CCTV, a/c,
cont. brkfst, pool, whirlpool

MENDOTA

Super 8 Motel
(800) 800-8000, (815) 539-7429
http://www.super8.com
508 Rte. 34 East
43 rooms - $45-65
Pets: Welcome w/permission
Creature Comforts: CCTV, a/c,
cont. brkfst

METROPOLIS

Amerihost Players Inn
(800) 434-5800, (618) 524-5678
http://www.amerihostinn.com
203 E. Front St.
122 rooms - $59-99
Pets: Small pets w/$10 fee
Creature Comforts: CCTV, a/c,
refrig, micro, Jacuzzis, cont.
brkfst, pool, hlth clb, sauna,
whirlpool, along river-casino

Best Inns of America
(800) 237-8466, (618) 524-8200
http://www.bestinns.com
2055 E. 5th St.
64 rooms - $45-66
Pets: Small pets welcome
Creature Comforts: CCTV, a/c,
refrig, micro, pool, whirlpool

Isle of View B&B
(618) 524-5838
www.bbonline.com/il/isleofview
205 Metropolis St.
5 rooms - $60-125
Pets: Welcome w/permission
Creature Comforts: Gracious
1889 Victorian mansion near
riverboat casino, beautifully
decorated rms. w/bold colors and
fine antiques, four-poster beds,
fireplace, refrig, Jacuzzis, claw
footed tubs, CCTV, VCR, a/c,
gourmet brkfst/dinner

MINONK

Victorian Oaks B&B
(309) 432-2771
http://www.victorianoaks.com
435 Locust St.
5 rooms - $70-105
Pets: Welcome
Creature Comforts: A lovely
1890's Victorian, romantic setting,
antiques, four-poster beds/quilts,
CCTV, VCR, a/c, fireplace, full
brkfst and dinner on fine linen and
china

MOLINE

Comfort Inn
(800) 228-5150, (309) 762-7000
http://www.comfortinn.com
2600 - 52nd Ave.
63 rooms - $49-95
Pets: Small pets welcome
Creature Comforts: CCTV, a/c,
cont. brkfst, pool

Exel Inn
(800)367-3935, (309) 797-5580
http://www.exelinns.com
2501 - 52nd Ave.
112 rooms - $40-57
Pets: Small pets welcome
Creature Comforts: CCTV, a/c,
refrig, micro, Jacuzzi, cont. brkfst.

Hampton Inn, Airport
(800) Hampton, (309) 762-1711
http://www.hampton-inn.com
6920 - 27th St.
138 rooms - $59-150
Pets: Welcome
Creature Comforts: CCTV, a/c,
refrig, micro, Jacuzzis, cont.
brkfst, pool, hlth club

Holiday Inn
(800) HOLIDAY, (309) 762-8811
http://www.holiday-inn.com
6902 27th St.
215 rooms - $75-150
Pets: Small pets welcome
Creature Comforts: CCTV, a/c,
refrig, micro, Jacuzzis, restaurant,
pool, recreation rm, mini-golf

La Quinta Inn
(800) Nu-Rooms, (309) 762-9008
http://www.laquinta.com
5450 - 27th St.
128 rooms - $59-85
Pets: Under 20 lbs. welcome
Creature Comforts: CCTV, a/c,
refrig, micro, cont. brkfst, pool

Motel 6
(800) 4-MOTEL6, (309) 764-8711
http://www.motel6.com
Quad City Airport Rd.
98 rooms - $35-50
Pets: Under 30 lbs. welcome
Creature Comforts: CCTV, a/c,
pool

MORRIS

Comfort Inn
(800) 228-5150, (815) 942-1433
http://www.comfortinn.com
70 Gore Rd.
50 rooms - $45-98
Pets: Small pets welcome
Creature Comforts: CCTV, a/c,
cont. brkfst, pool

Holiday Inn
(800) HOLIDAY, (815) 942-6600
http://www.holiday-inn.com
200 Gore St.
122 rooms - $60-89
Pets: Small pets welcome
Creature Comforts: CCTV, a/c,
refrig, micro, restaurant, pool

MORTON

Comfort Inn
(800) 228-5150, (309) 266-8888
http://www.comfortinn.com
Rte. 74 & Ashland Ave.
50 rooms - $55-85
Pets: Small pets welcome
Creature Comforts: CCTV, a/c,
refrig, micro, cont. brkfst, pool

The Villager Lodge
(309) 263-2511
128 W. Queenswood Rd.
49 rooms - $39-50
Pets: Welcome
Creature Comforts: CCTV, a/c

MORTON GROVE

Best Western Inn
(800) 528-1234, (847) 965-6400
http://www.bestwestern.com
9424 Waukegan Rd.
54 rooms - $49-80
Pets: Under 20 lbs. welcome
Creature Comforts: CCTV, a/c,
cont. brkfst, hlth club

MT. PROSPECT

Ramada Inn
(800) 2-Ramada, (309) 662-5311
http://www.ramada.com
1219 Holiday Dr.
208 rooms - $55-88
Pets: Welcome
Creature Comforts: CCTV, a/c,
refrig, Jacuzzis, restaurant, sauna,
pool, whirlpool, fun dome-mini
golf

MT. STERLING

Land of Lincoln Motel
(217) 773-3311
403 E. Main St.
26 rooms - $29-44
Pets: Welcome
Creature Comforts: CCTV, a/c,
kit

MT. VERNON

Best Inns of America
(800) 237-8466, (618) 244-4343
http://www.bestinns.com
222 S. 44th St
153 rooms - $45-69
Pets: Welcome
Creature Comforts: CCTV, a/c,
refrig, pool, cont. brkfst.

Daystop
(800) DAYS-INN, (618) 244-3224
http://www.daysinn.com
750 S. 10th St.
41 rooms - $35-55
Pets: Welcome w/$3 fee
Creature Comforts: CCTV, a/c,
cont. brkfst, pool

Drury Inn
(800) Drury-Inn, (618) 244-4550
http://www.drury-inn.com
145 N. 44th St.
80 rooms - $50-75
Pets: Welcome, cannot be left
unattended
Creature Comforts: CCTV, a/c,
refrig, micro, cont. brkfst, pool

Holiday Inn
(800) HOLIDAY, (618) 244-3670
http://www.holiday-inn.com
Rtes. 57 & 5
236 rooms - $50-99
Pets: Welcome w/$10 fee
Creature Comforts: CCTV, a/c,
refrig, micro, restaurant, hlth club,
sauna, pool, whirlpool

Motel 6
(800) 4-MOTEL6, (618) 244-2383
http://www.motel6.com
333 S. 44th St.
78 rooms - $34-49
Pets: Under 30 lbs. welcome
Creature Comforts: CCTV, a/c,
pool

Ramada Inn
(800) 2-Ramada, (618) 244-7100
http://www.ramada.com
222 Potomac Blvd.
188 rooms - $55-95
Pets: Welcome
Creature Comforts: CCTV, a/c,
refrig, restaurant, cont. brkfst,
pool, whirlpool

Super 8 Motel
(800) 800-8000, (618) 242-8800
http://www.super8.com
401 S. 44th St.
63 rooms - $45-65
Pets: Welcome w/permission
Creature Comforts: CCTV, a/c,
cont. brkfst

MUDDY

Days Inn
(800) DAYS-INN, (618) 252-6354
http://www.daysinn.com
Route 45
81 rooms - $35-50
Pets: Welcome
Creature Comforts: CCTV, a/c,
cont. brkfst, pool

MUNDELEIN

Super 8 Motel
(800) 800-8000, (847) 949-8842
http://www.super8.com
1950 S. Lake St.
74 rooms - $45-85
Pets: Welcome w/permission
Creature Comforts: CCTV, a/c,
refrig, micro, cont. brkfst

MURPHYSVILLE

Apple Tree Inn
(800) 626-4356, (618) 687-2345
100 N. 2nd St.
30 rooms - $35-50
Pets: Welcome
Creature Comforts: CCTV, a/c,
refrig, pool, hlth clb, sauna,
whirlpool

NAPERVILLE

Country Inns and Suites
(800) 456-4000, (309) 548-0966
http://www.countryinns.com
1847 W. Diehl Rd.
62 rooms - $70-100
Pets: Welcome in smoking rooms
Creature Comforts: CCTV, a/c,
micro, refrig, pool

Days Inn
(800) DAYS-INN, (630) 369-3600
http://www.daysinn.com
1350 E. Ogden Ave.
122 rooms - $50-75
Pets: Welcome
Creature Comforts: CCTV, a/c,
cont. brkfst

Exel Inn
(800) 367-3935, (630) 357-0022
http://www.exelinns.com
1585 N. Naperville Rd.
122 rooms - $50-69
Pets: Small pets welcome
Creature Comforts: CCTV,
VCR, a/c, refrig, micro, cont.
brkfst.

Homestead Village
(800) 367-3935, (630) 577-0200
1827 Centre Point Circle
136 rooms - $50-85
Pets: Small pets welcome
Creature Comforts: CCTV, a/c,
kit, refrig, micro

Red Roof Inn
(800) The-Roof, (630) 369-2500
http://www.redroof.com
1698 W. Diehl Rd.
120 rooms - $45-69
Pets: Small pets welcome
Creature Comforts: CCTV, a/c

Travelodge
(800) 578-7878, (630) 505-0200
http://www.travelodge.com
1617 N. Naperville/Wheaton Rd.
104 rooms - $50-75
Pets: Welcome w/$10 fee
Creature Comforts: CCTV, a/c,
refrig

NASHVILLE
Best Western U.S. Inn
(618) 478-5341
11640 Rte. 27
50 rooms - $39-70
Pets: Welcome w/$25 dep. in
smoking rms.
Creature Comforts: TV, VCR, a/
c, refrig, micro, kit, Jacuzzi

NAUVOO
IMA Family Motel
(800) 341-8000, (217) 453-6527
http://www.imalodging.com
150 N. Warsaw Rd.
67 rooms - $35-95
Pets: Welcome
Creature Comforts: CCTV, a/c,
refrig, micro, pool

NEWTON
River Park Motel
(618) 783-2327
RR 5
16 rooms - $29-38
Pets: Welcome
Creature Comforts: CCTV, a/c

NILES
Thrift Lodge
(847) 647-9444
http://www.travelodge.com
7247 N. Waukegan Rd.
54 rooms - $50-75
Pets: Welcome
Creature Comforts: CCTV, a/c,
cont. brkfst, pool

NORMAL
Best Western University Inn
(800) 528-1234, (309) 454-4070
http://www.bestwestern.com
6 Trader Circle
100 rooms - $50-70
Pets: Small pets, cannot be left
unattended
Creature Comforts: CCTV, a/c,
refrig, micro, cont. brkfst, pool,
sauna, whirlpool

Comfort Suites
(800) 228-5150, (309) 452-8588
http://www.comfortinn.com
310 Greenbriar Dr.
60 rooms - $69-104
Pets: Small pets welcome
Creature Comforts: CCTV, a/c,
refrig, micro, cont. brkfst, pool

Holiday Inn
(800) HOLIDAY, (309) 452-8300
http://www.holiday-inn.com
8 Traders Cir.
158 rooms - $75-269
Pets: Small pets w/$25 dep.
Creature Comforts: CCTV,
VCR, a/c, refrig, micro, restaurant,
hlth club, pool

Motel 6
(800) 4-MOTEL6, (309) 452-0422
http://www.motel6.com
1600 N. Main St.
98 rooms - $35-49
Pets: Under 30 lbs. welcome
Creature Comforts: CCTV, a/c,
pool

NORTHBROOK
Red Roof Inn
(800) The-Roof, (847) 205-1755
http://www.redroof.com
340 Waukegan Rd.
120 rooms - $49-75
Pets: Small pets welcome
Creature Comforts: CCTV, a/c

OAKBROOK TERRACE
Hilton Suites Hotel
(800) HILTONS, (630) 941-0100
http://www.hilton.com
10 Drury Lane
210 rooms - $99-160
Pets: Small pets welcome
Creature Comforts: CCTV,
VCR, a/c, refrig, restaurant, sauna,
hlth club, pool, whirlpool

La Quinta Inn
(800) Nu-Rooms, (630) 495-4600
http://www.laquinta.com
666 Midwest Rd.
150 rooms - $70-120
Pets: Small pets welcome
Creature Comforts: CCTV, a/c,
cont. brkfst, pool

O'FALLON
Comfort Inn
(800) 228-5150, (618) 624-6060
http://www.comfortinn.com
1100 Eastgate Dr.
96 rooms - $59-99
Pets: Small pets w/$20 dep.
Creature Comforts: CCTV, a/c,
refrig, Jacuzzis, restaurant, pool,
whirlpool

Ramada Inn
(800) 2-Ramada, (618) 628-9700
http://www.ramada.com
1320 Park Plaza Dr.
154 rooms - $55-99
Pets: Welcome
Creature Comforts: CCTV, a/c,
pool

Sleep Inn
(800) Sleep-Inn, (618) 628-8200
http://www.sleepinn.com
140 Venita Dr.
70 rooms - $75-109
Pets: Small pets welcome
Creature Comforts: CCTV, a/c,
Jacuzzis, restaurant, cont. brkfst,
pool, hlth club, whirlpool

OGLESBY
Holiday Inn Express
(800) HOLIDAY, (815) 883-3535
http://www.holiday-inn.com
900 Holiday St.
70 rooms - $65-80
Pets: Welcome in smoking rms.
Creature Comforts: CCTV, a/c,
refrig, micro, Jacuzzis, pool

OKAWVILLE
Super 8 Motel
(800) 800-8000, (618) 243-6525
http://www.super8.com
812 N. Henhouse Rd.
40 rooms - $45-69
Pets: Welcome w/permission
Creature Comforts: CCTV, a/c,
Jacuzzis

OLNEY
Super 8 Motel
(800) 800-8000, (618) 392-7888
http://www.super8.com
Rtes. 130 & North Ave.
41 rooms - $45-60
Pets: Welcome w/permission
Creature Comforts: CCTV, a/c,
Jacuzzis, cont. brkfst

OREGON
VIP Motel
(815) 732-6195
1326 Rte. 2
12 rooms - $45-53
Pets: Welcome
Creature Comforts: CCTV, a/c,
refrig

OTTAWA
Holiday Inn Express
(800) HOLIDAY, (815) 433-0029
http://www.holiday-inn.com
120 W. Stevenson Rd.
70 rooms - $60-70
Pets: Welcome in smoking rms.
Creature Comforts: CCTV, a/c,
refrig, micro, pool

PALATINE
Motel 6
(800) 4-MOTEL6, (847) 359-0046
http://www.motel6.com
1450 E. Dundee Rd.
122 rooms - $44-55
Pets: Under 30 lbs. welcome
Creature Comforts: CCTV, a/c

Ramada Inn
(800) 2-Ramada, (847) 359-6900
http://www.ramada.com
920 E. NW Hwy.
195 rooms - $65-99
Pets: Small pets welcome
Creature Comforts: CCTV, a/c,
refrig, restaurant, pool, saunas,
hlth club, whirlpool

PANA
Rose Bud Motel
(217) 562-3929
Rtes. 16 & 51
12 rooms - $30-42
Pets: Welcome
Creature Comforts: CCTV, a/c,
restaurant

PARIS
Pinnell Motor Inn
(217) 465-6441
130 Olson Rd.
25 rooms - $45-60
Pets: Welcome
Creature Comforts: CCTV, a/c

Super 8 Motel
(800) 800-8000, (217) 463-8888
http://www.super8.com
Route 150
37 rooms - $45-59
Pets: Welcome w/$25 dep.
Creature Comforts: CCTV, a/c,
cont. brkfst

PEKIN
Best Western Pekin Inn
(800) 528-1234, (309) 347-5533
http://www.bestwestern.com
2801 E. Court St.
50 rooms - $55-75
Pets: Small pets w/$25 fee
Creature Comforts: CCTV, a/c,
pool, sauna, whirlpool

Comfort Inn
(800) 228-5150, (309) 353-4047
http://www.comfortinn.com
3240 N. Vandever Ave.
48 rooms - $55-79
Pets: Small pets welcome
Creature Comforts: CCTV, a/c,
cont. brkfst, pool

PEORIA
Comfort Suites
(800) 228-5150, (309) 688-3800
http://www.comfortinn.com
4021 War Memorial Rd.
66 rooms - $65-99
Pets: Small pets welcome
Creature Comforts: CCTV, a/c,
refrig, micro, cont. brkfst, pool

Holiday Inn-Brandywine
(800) HOLIDAY, (309) 686-8000
http://www.holiday-inn.com
440 N. Brandywine Dr.
251 rooms - $79-179
Pets: Welcome w/$25 dep.
Creature Comforts: CCTV,
VCR, a/c, kit, restaurant, hlth club,
sauna, pool, hlth club, whirlpool,
rec. dome

Holiday Inn-City Center
(800) HOLIDAY, (309) 674-2500
http://www.holiday-inn.com
500 Hamilton Blvd.
265 rooms - $79-159
Pets: Welcome w/$25 dep.
Creature Comforts: CCTV,
VCR, a/c, refrig, micro, restaurant,
sauna, pool, hlth club, whirlpool

Hotel Pere Marquette
(800) 447-1676, (309) 637-6500
www.hotelperemarquette.com
501 Main St.
286 rooms - $89-525
Pets: Small pets w/$100 dep.
Creature Comforts: An elegantly
refurbished 1927 historic hotel on
Nat'l Register of Historic Places,
frequented by countless dignitaries
and hollywood personalities,
CCTV, a/c, kit, Jacuzzis,
traditional decor, restaurants,
whirlpool, hlth clb

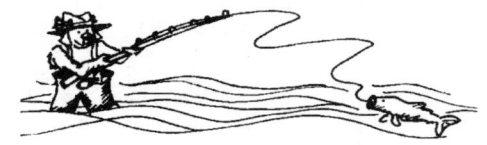

Jumer's Castle Lodge
(800) 285-8637, (309) 673-8040
http://www.jumers.com
117 N. Western Ave.
177 rooms - $85-149
Pets: Small pets w/$25 dep.
Creature Comforts: Bavarian inn
w/Old World charm, European
furnishings, custom woodworking,
CCTV, a/c, refrig, Jacuzzis,
restaurant, pool, saunas,
whirlpool, hlth club access

Mark Twain Hotel
(309) 676-3600
225 NE Adams St.
108 rooms - $79-240
Pets: Welcome
Creature Comforts: CCTV, a/c,
refrig, micro, Jacuzzi, restaurant,
hlth clb, whirlpool

Red Roof Inn
(800) The-Roof, (309) 685-3911
http://www.redroof.com
4031 N. War Memorial Dr.
109 rooms - $40-69
Pets: Small pets welcome
Creature Comforts: CCTV, a/c

Super 8 Motel
(800) 800-8000, (309) 688-8074
http://www.super8.com
4025 W. War Memorial Dr.
70 rooms - $45-60
Pets: Welcome w/permission
Creature Comforts: CCTV, a/c,
cont. brkfst

PERU
Days Inn
(800) DAYS-INN, (815) 224-1060
http://www.daysinn.com
Rtes. 80 & 251
108 rooms - $40-55
Pets: Welcome w/$5 fee
Creature Comforts: CCTV, a/c,
cont. brkfst, pool

Motel 6
(800) 4-MOTEL6, (815) 224-2785
http://www.motel6.com
1900 May Rd.
90 rooms - $34-49
Pets: Under 30 lbs. welcome
Creature Comforts: CCTV, a/c

Super 8 Motel
(800) 800-8000, (815) 223-1848
http://www.super8.com
1851 May Rd.
62 rooms - $40-65
Pets: Welcome w/permission
Creature Comforts: CCTV, a/c,
cont. brkfst

PINCKNEYVILLE
Main Street Inn
(618) 357-2128
112 S. Main St.
26 rooms - $35-49
Pets: Welcome
Creature Comforts: CCTV, a/c

POCAHONTAS
Tahoe Motel
(618) 669-2404
Rtes. 40 & 70
12 rooms - $35-48
Pets: Welcome
Creature Comforts: CCTV, a/c,
refrig

Wikiup Motel
(618) 669-2293
5 Plant St.
22 rooms - $40-52
Pets: Welcome
Creature Comforts: CCTV, a/c

POLO
Village Inn Motel
(815) 946-2229
1007 S. Division St.
12 rooms - $35-46
Pets: Welcome w/$5 fee
Creature Comforts: CCTV, a/c,
refrig

PONTIAC
Comfort Inn
(800) 228-5150, (815) 842-2777
http://www.comfortinn.com
1821 W. Reynolds St.
58 rooms - $55-139
Pets: Small pets welcome
Creature Comforts: CCTV, a/c,
cont. brkfst, pool

Super 8 Motel
(800) 800-8000, (815) 844-6888
http://www.super8.com
601 S. Deerfield Rd.
50 rooms - $45-65
Pets: Welcome w/permission
Creature Comforts: CCTV, a/c,
refrig, cont. brkfst

PONTOON BEACH
Best Western Camelot Inn
(800) 528-1234, (618) 931-2262
http://www.bestwestern.com
1240 Old Chain of Rocks Rd.
54 rooms - $45-70
Pets: Small pets w/$10 fee
Creature Comforts: CCTV, a/c,
refrig, cont. brkfst, pool

PRINCETON
Days Inn
(800) DAYS-INN, (815) 875-3371
http://www.daysinn.com
2238 N. Main St.
87 rooms - $45-90
Pets: Welcome w/$6 fee
Creature Comforts: CCTV, a/c,
refrig, micro, restaurant, cont.
brkfst, pool

Princeton Motor Lodge
(815) 875-1121
Rtes. 80 & 26
22 rooms - $39-50
Pets: Welcome
Creature Comforts: CCTV, a/c

PROSPECT HEIGHTS
Exel Inn
(800) 367-3935, (847) 459-0545
http://www.exelinns.com
540 Milwaukee Ave.
122 rooms - $49-140
Pets: Small pets welcome
Creature Comforts: CCTV,
VCR, a/c, kit, Jacuzzis, cont.
brkfst, whirlpool

QUINCY
Bel-Air Motel
(217) 223-1356
2314 N. 12th St.
21 rooms - $35-45
Pets: Welcome
Creature Comforts: CCTV, a/c,
refrig

Comfort Inn
(800) 228-5150, (217) 228-2700
http://www.comfortinn.com
4100 Broadway St.
58 rooms - $59-85
Pets: Small pets welcome
Creature Comforts: CCTV, a/c,
cont. brkfst, pool

Days Inn
(800) DAYS-INN, (217) 223-6610
http://www.daysinn.com
200 Maine St.
121 rooms - $35-85
Pets: Welcome
Creature Comforts: CCTV, a/c,
Jacuzzis, restaurant, cont. brkfst,
pool

Diamond Motel
(217) 223-1436
4703 N. 12th St.
20 rooms - $25-34
Pets: Welcome
Creature Comforts: CCTV, a/c

Holiday Inn
(800) HOLIDAY, (217) 222-2666
http://www.holiday-inn.com
201 S. 3rd St.
155 rooms - $60-75
Pets: Small pets welcome.
Creature Comforts: CCTV,
VCR, a/c, refrig, hlth club, sauna,
pool, rec. dome

Super 8 Motel
(800) 800-8000, (217) 228-8808
http://www.super8.com
224 N. 36th St.
59 rooms - $45-69
Pets: Welcome w/permission
Creature Comforts: CCTV, a/c,
refrig, micro, Jacuzzis, waterbeds,
cont. brkfst

Travelodge
(800) 578-7878, (217) 222-5620
http://www.travelodge.com
200 S. 3rd St.
68 rooms - $45-65
Pets: Welcome
Creature Comforts: CCTV, a/c,
refrig, micro, restaurant, pool

RANTOUL
Best Western Heritage Inn
(800) 528-1234, (217) 892-9292
http://www.bestwestern.com
420 S. Murray Rd.
48 rooms - $55-75
Pets: Small pets w/$10 fee
Creature Comforts: CCTV, a/c,
pool, sauna, whirlpool

Days Inn
(800) DAYS-INN, (217) 893-0700
http://www.daysinn.com
801 W. Champion St.
81 rooms - $50-65
Pets: Welcome
Creature Comforts: CCTV, a/c,
pool

RICHMOND
Days Inn
(800) DAYS-INN, (815) 678-4711
http://www.daysinn.com
11200 N. Rte. 12
60 rooms - $55-65
Pets: Welcome w/$5 fee
Creature Comforts: CCTV, a/c,
cont. brkfst, pool

Drake Inn
(815) 678-3501
8613 S. Rte. 12
11 rooms - $55-70
Pets: Welcome
Creature Comforts: CCTV, a/c,
refrig

ROBINSON
Best Western Inn
(800) 528-1234, (618) 544-8448
http://www.bestwestern.com
1500 W. Main St.
42 rooms - $50-75
Pets: Welcome w/$5 fee
Creature Comforts: CCTV, a/c,
refrig, cont. brkfst, tennis

ROCHELLE
Amerihost Inn
(800) 434-5800, (815) 562-9530
http://www.amerihostinn.com
333 Lincoln Hwy.
60 rooms - $55-75
Pets: Small pets welcome
Creature Comforts: CCTV, a/c,
refrig, micro, cont. brkfst, pool,
hlth clb, sauna, whirlpool

Holiday Inn
(800) HOLIDAY, (815) 562-5551
http://www.holiday-inn.com
Rtes. 251 & 38
95 rooms - $75-99
Pets: Small pets welcome
Creature Comforts: CCTV,
VCR, a/c, kit, restaurant, hlth club,
pool

ROCK FALLS
Holiday Inn
(800) HOLIDAY, (815) 626-5500
http://www.holiday-inn.com
2105 S. 1st Ave.
117 rooms - $59-89
Pets: Welcome
Creature Comforts: CCTV, a/c,
refrig, restaurant, pool, whirlpool

Super 8 Motel
(800) 800-8000, (815) 626-8800
http://www.super8.com
2100 - 1st Ave.
63 rooms - $45-65
Pets: Welcome w/permission
Creature Comforts: CCTV, a/c

ROCKFORD
Airport Inn
(815) 397-4000
4419 S. 11th St.
114 rooms - $50-65
Pets: Welcome w/$5 fee
Creature Comforts: CCTV, a/c

Best Suites of America
(815) 227-1300
7401 Walton Ave.
96 rooms - $75-125
Pets: Small pets welcome
Creature Comforts: CCTV,
VCR, a/c, refrig, micro, cont.
brkfst, pool, exercise rm.

Best Western Colonial Inn
(800) 528-1234, (815) 398-6050
http://www.bestwestern.com
4850 E. State St.
84 rooms - $75-195
Pets: Welcome w/permission
Creature Comforts: CCTV, a/c,
refrig, restaurant, hlth club

Comfort Inn
(800) 228-5150, (815) 398-7061
http://www.comfortinn.com
7392 Argus Dr.
64 rooms - $59-109
Pets: Small pets welcome
Creature Comforts: CCTV, a/c,
cont. brkfst, pool

Exel Inn
(800) 367-3935, (815) 332-4915
http://www.exelinns.com
220 S. Lyford Rd.
100 rooms - $45-89
Pets: Small pets welcome
Creature Comforts: CCTV, a/c,
kit, Jacuzzis

Motel 6
(800) 4-Motel-6, (815) 398-6080
http://www.motel6.com
3851 - 11th St.
114 rooms - $34-49
Pets: Under 30 lbs. welcome
Creature Comforts: CCTV, a/c, pool

Red Roof Inn
(800) The-Roof, (815) 398-9750
http://www.redroof.com
7434 E. State St.
107 rooms - $45-80
Pets: Small pets welcome
Creature Comforts: CCTV, a/c

Residence Inn
(800) 331-3131, (815) 227-0013
http://www.residenceinn.com
7542 Colosseum Dr.
95 rooms - $89-149
Pets: $5 nightly fee; $100 one-time fee
Creature Comforts: CCTV, a/c, kit, fireplaces, cont. brkfst, hlth club, pool

Six Pence Inn
(815) 398-0066
4205 - 11th St.
122 rooms - $29-34
Pets: Welcome w/$5 fee
Creature Comforts: CCTV, a/c, pool

Super 8 Motel
(800) 800-8000, (815) 229-5522
http://www.super8.com
7646 Colosseum Dr.
50 rooms - $49-75
Pets: Welcome w/permission
Creature Comforts: CCTV, a/c, kit, Jacuzzi, cont. brkfst

Sweden House Lodge
(800) 886-4138, (815) 398-4130
4605 E. State St.
104 rooms - $45-75
Pets: Smoking rooms w/$10 fee
Creature Comforts: CCTV, VCR, a/c, kit, cont. brkfst, pool, hlth clb, whirlpool

ROLLING MEADOWS
Comfort Inn
(800) 228-5150, (847) 259-5900
http://www.comfortinn.com
2801 Algonquin Rd.
104 rooms - $75-99
Pets: Small pets welcome
Creature Comforts: CCTV, a/c, refrig, cont. brkfst, pool

Motel 6
(800) 4-MOTEL6, (847) 818-8088
http://www.motel6.com
1800 Winnetka Cir.
129 rooms - $44-55
Pets: Under 30 lbs. welcome
Creature Comforts: CCTV, a/c, pool

ROSEMONT
Clarion Hotel
(800) 252-7466, (847) 297-8464
http://www.clarioninn.com
6810 N. Mannheim Rd.
190 rooms - $99-169
Pets: Small pets welcome
Creature Comforts: CCTV, a/c, refrig, restaurant, pool, hlth clb, sauna, whirlpool

Holiday Inn, O'Hare
(800) HOLIDAY, (847) 671-6350
http://www.holiday-inn.com
5440 N. River Rd.
505 rooms - $129-199
Pets: Small pets welcome
Creature Comforts: CCTV, VCR, a/c, refrig, restaurant, hlth club, sauna, pool, whirlpool

Hotel Sofitel
(800) SOFITEL, (847) 678-4488
http://www.sofitel.com
5550 N. River Rd.
303 rooms - $139-599
Pets: Under 20 lbs. welcome
Creature Comforts: Gracious, French ambiance w/American decorative twist, traditional homey decor, CCTV, VCR, a/c, refrig, Jacuzzis, restaurant, pool, hlth clb, sauna, whirlpool

Quality Inn - O'Hare Airport
(800) 228-5151, (847) 297-1234
http://www.qualityinn.com
6810-A N. Mannheim Rd.
263 rooms - $99-169
Pets: Small pets welcome
Creature Comforts: CCTV, a/c, refrig, restaurant, pool

SALEM
Continental Motel
(618) 548-3090
1600 E. Main St.
24 rooms - $29-40
Pets: Welcome
Creature Comforts: CCTV, a/c

Comfort Inn
(800) 228-5150, (618) 548-2177
http://www.comfortinn.com
1500 W. Main St.
65 rooms - $55-100
Pets: Small pets welcome
Creature Comforts: CCTV, a/c, refrig, micro, cont. brkfst, pool, whirlpool

Holiday Inn
(800) HOLIDAY, (618) 548-4212
http://www.holiday-inn.com
1812 W. Main St.
98 rooms - $45-65
Pets: Small pets welcome
Creature Comforts: CCTV, VCR, a/c, refrig, micro, restaurant, pool

Motel Lakewood
(618) 548-2785
1500 E. Main St.
20 rooms - $28-39
Pets: Welcome
Creature Comforts: CCTV, a/c, refrig, micro

Restwell Motel
(618) 548-2040
700 W. Main St.
12 rooms - $25-32
Pets: Welcome
Creature Comforts: CCTV, a/c, refrig

Super 8 Motel
(800) 800-8000, (618) 548-5882
http://www.super8.com
118 Paragon Rd.
57 rooms - $45-65
Pets: Welcome w/permission
Creature Comforts: CCTV, a/c, kit, cont. brkfst

SAVANNA
Indian Head Motel
(815) 273-2154
3523 Rte. 84
12 rooms - $27-39
Pets: Welcome
Creature Comforts: CCTV, a/c, refrig, cont. brkfst

Law's Motel
(815) 273-7728
Rtes. 52 & 64
32 rooms - $40-59
Pets: Welcome
Creature Comforts: CCTV, a/c,
refrig, micro, Jacuzzi, cont. brkfst

Radke Hotel
(815) 273-3713
422 Main St.
15 rooms - $30-44
Pets: Small pets welcome
Creature Comforts: CCTV, a/c,
refrig, micro

SAVOY
Best Western Paradise Inn
(800) 528-1234, (217) 356-1824
http://www.bestwestern.com
1001 N. Dunlap Rd.
62 rooms - $50-75
Pets: Small pets w/$3 fee
Creature Comforts: CCTV, a/c,
kit, cont. brkfst, pool

SCHAUMBURG
Amerisuites
(800) 833-1516, (847) 330-1060
http://www.amerisuites.com
1851 McConner Pkwy.
130 rooms - $130-155
Pets: Under 10 lbs. welcome
Creature Comforts: CCTV,
VCR, a/c, refrig, micro, cont.
brkfst, hlth club, whirlpool

Drury Inn
(800) Drury-Inn, (847) 517-7737
http://www.drury-inn.com
600 N. Martingale Rd.
125 rooms - $75-99
Pets: Welcome
Creature Comforts: CCTV, a/c,
refrig, micro, cont. brkfst, pool

Homewood Suites
(800) 225-5466, (847) 605-0400
http://www.homewoodsuites.com
815 E. American La.
105 rooms - $80-129
Pets: Welcome w/$100 dep.
Creature Comforts: CCTV,
VCR, a/c, kit, pool, hlth clb,
whirlpool

La Quinta Inn
(800) Nu-Rooms, (847) 517-8484
http://www.laquinta.com
1730 E. Higgins Rd.
126 rooms - $70-89
Pets: Welcome
Creature Comforts: CCTV, a/c,
cont. brkfst, pool

Marriott Hotel
(800) 228-9290, (847) 240-0100
http://www.marriott.com
50 N. Martingale Rd.
395 rooms - $75-299
Pets: Under 25 lbs. welcome
Creature Comforts: CCTV,
VCR, a/c, refrig, Jacuzzis,
restaurant, pool, hlth clb, sauna,
whirlpools

Summerfield Suites
(800) 833-4353, (847) 619-6677
901 E. Woodfield Office Ct.
112 rooms - $79-168
Pets: $50 fee, $200 dep.
Creature Comforts: CCTV,
VCR, a/c, kit, restaurant, cont.
brkfst, pool, hlth clb, sauna,
whirlpool,tennis

SCHILLER PARK
Motel 6 - O'Hare Airport
(800) 4-MOTEL6, (847) 671-4282
http://www.motel6.com
9408 W. Lawrence Ave.
143 rooms - $44-59
Pets: Under 30 lbs. welcome
Creature Comforts: CCTV, a/c

Residence Inn
(800) 331-3131, (847) 725-2210
http://www.residenceinn.com
9450 W. Lawrence Ave.
170 rooms - $129-475
Pets: Welcome w/$100 fee
Creature Comforts: CCTV, a/c,
kit, cont. brkfst, whirlpool, hlth
club

SHEFFIELD
Days Inn
(800) DAYS-INN, (815) 454-2361
http://www.daysinn.com
Rtes. 40 & 80
50 rooms - $35-65
Pets: Welcome w/$5 fee
Creature Comforts: CCTV, a/c,
refrig, micro, cont. brkfst, hlth
club

SHELBYVILLE
Lithia Resort
(217) 774-2882
www.bmmhnet.com/lithiaresort
Rte. 4, Box 105
12 rooms - $45-120
Pets: Welcome w/$5 fee, $25 dep.
Creature Comforts: CCTV,
VCR, a/c, kit, restaurant, pool

SHOREWOOD
Days Inn
(800) DAYS-INN, (815) 725-2180
http://www.daysinn.com
19747 Frontage Rd.
117 rooms - $50-149
Pets: Welcome
Creature Comforts: CCTV, a/c,
refrig, micro, restaurant, pool

SKOKIE
Holiday Inn
(800) HOLIDAY, (847) 679-8900
http://www.holiday-inn.com
5300 W. Touhy Ave.
245 rooms - $99-199
Pets: Rooms w/outside entrances
Creature Comforts: CCTV,
VCR, a/c, refrig, restaurant, hlth
club, sauna, pool, whirlpool

Howard Johnson Hotel
(800) I-Go-Hojo, (847) 679-4200
http://www.hojo.com
9333 Skokie Blvd.
133 rooms - $95-169
Pets: Welcome
Creature Comforts: CCTV, a/c,
restaurant, hlth club, sauna, pool,
whirlpool

SOUTH HOLLAND
Baymont Inn
(877)BAYMONT, (708) 596-8700
http://www.baymontinns.com
102 rooms - $55-75
Pets: Under 15 lbs. in smkng. rms.
Creature Comforts: CCTV, a/c,
refrig, micro, cont. brkfst

Red Roof Inn
(800) The-Roof, (708) 331-1621
http://www.redroof.com
17301 S. Halstead Rd.
135 rooms - $45-79
Pets: Small pets welcome
Creature Comforts: CCTV, a/c

SPARTA

Mac's Motel
(618) 443-3614
700 S. St. Louis St.
28 rooms - $35-45
Pets: Welcome
Creature Comforts: CCTV, a/c,
refrig

SPRING VALLEY

Riviera Motel
(815) 894-2225
Rtes. 80 & 89
70 rooms - $29-35
Pets: Welcome
Creature Comforts: CCTV, a/c,
refrig, micro

SPRINGFIELD

Best Inns of America
(800) 237-8466, (217) 522-1100
http://www.bestinns.com
500 N. 1st St.
90 rooms - $45-80
Pets: Small pets welcome
Creature Comforts: CCTV, a/c,
refrig, pool

Best Western Lincoln Plaza
(800) 528-1234, (217) 523-5661
http://www.bestwestern.com
101 E. Adams St.
122 rooms - $65-109
Pets: Small pets w/$10 fee
Creature Comforts: CCTV, a/c,
refrig, restaurant, cont. brkfst, hlth
club

Comfort Inn
(800) 228-5150, (217) 787-2250
http://www.comfortinn.com
3442 Freedom Dr.
67 rooms - $60-99
Pets: Small pets welcome
Creature Comforts: CCTV, a/c,
cont. brkfst, pool

Days Inn
(800) DAYS-INN, (217) 529-0171
http://www.daysinn.com
3000 Stevenson Dr.
153 rooms - $55-70
Pets: Welcome
Creature Comforts: CCTV, a/c,
cont. brkfst, hlth club access, pool

Drury Inn
(800) Drury-Inn, (217) 529-3900
http://www.drury-inn.com
3180 S. Dirksen Pkwy.
120 rooms - $65-90
Pets: Welcome
Creature Comforts: CCTV, a/c,
refrig, micro, cont. brkfst, pool

Hampton Inn
(800) Hampton, (217) 529-1100
http://www.hampton-inn.com
3185 S. Dirksen Pkwy.
124 rooms - $60-90
Pets: Small pets welcome
Creature Comforts: CCTV, a/c,
refrig, micro, pool, exercise rm.

Hilton Hotel
(800) HILTONS, (217) 789-1530
http://www.hilton.com
700 E. Adams St.
365 rooms - $99-629
Pets: Small pets w/$100 dep.
Creature Comforts: CCTV, a/c,
refrig, micro, restaurant, saunas,
hlth club, whirlpools

Holiday Inn
(800) HOLIDAY, (217) 529-7171
http://www.holiday-inn.com
3100 S. Dirksen Pkwy.
375 rooms - $75-179
Pets: Small pets welcome
Creature Comforts: CCTV,
VCR, a/c, refrig, Jacuzzis,
restaurant, hlth club, sauna,
whirlpool, pool, rec. dome

Motel 6
(800) 4-MOTEL6, (217) 529-1633
http://www.motel6.com
6010 S. 6th St.
98 rooms - $34-49
Pets: Under 30 lbs. welcome
Creature Comforts: CCTV, a/c,
pool

Pear Tree Inn
(800) Drury Inn, (217) 529-9100
http://www.drury-inn.com
390 S. Dirksen Pkwy.
52 rooms - $49-75
Pets: Welcome
Creature Comforts: CCTV, a/c,
cont. brkfst, pool

Ramada Inn
(800) 2-Ramada, (217) 529-7131
http://www.ramada.com
625 E. St. Joseph St.
99 rooms - $70-99
Pets: Welcome w/$10 fee
Creature Comforts: CCTV, a/c,
Jacuzzis, pool

Red Roof Inn
(800) The-Roof, (217) 753-4302
http://www.redroof.com
3200 Singer Ave.
106 rooms - $33-59
Pets: Small pets welcome
Creature Comforts: CCTV, a/c

Sleep Inn
(800) Sleep Inn, (217) 787-6200
http://www.sleepinn.com
3470 Freedom Dr.
62 rooms - $49-99
Pets: Small pets welcome
Creature Comforts: CCTV, a/c,
cont. brkfst

Super 8 Motel, East
(800) 800-8000, (217) 528-8889
http://www.super8.com
1330 S. Dirksen Pkwy.
65 rooms - $49-65
Pets: Welcome w/permission
Creature Comforts: CCTV, a/c,
cont. brkfst

Super 8 Motel, North
(800) 800-8000, (217) 529-8898
http://www.super8.com
3675 S. 6th St.
122 rooms - $49-65
Pets: Welcome w/permission
Creature Comforts: CCTV, a/c,
cont. brkfst, restaurant

STAUNTON

Super 8 Motel
(800) 800-8000, (618) 635-5353
http://www.super8.com
832 E. Main St.
52 rooms - $40-55
Pets: Welcome w/permission
Creature Comforts: CCTV, a/c,
cont. brkfst

SULLIVAN
Gateway Inn
(217) 728-4314
5 Hamilton St.
40 rooms - $44-50
Pets: Welcome
Creature Comforts: CCTV, a/c

SYCAMORE
Amerihost Inn
(800) 434-5800, (815) 895-4979
http://www.amerihostinn.com
1475 S. Peace Rd.
60 rooms - $55-69
Pets: Small pets welcome
Creature Comforts: CCTV, a/c,
refrig, micro, Jacuzzis, pool, hlth
clb, sauna, whirlpool

TAYLORVILLE
29 West Motel
(217) 824-2216
709 Springfield Rd.
21 rooms - $35-50
Pets: Small pets w/$4 fee
Creature Comforts: CCTV, a/c,
refrig, micro

TINLEY PARK
Baymont Inn
(877)BAYMONT, (708) 633-1200
http://www.baymontinns.com
7255 W. 183rd St.
105 rooms - $50-95
Pets: Small pets welcome
Creature Comforts: CCTV, a/c,
refrig, micro, Jacuzzis, cont.
brkfst, pool

Hampton Inn
(800) Hampton, (708) 633-0602
http://www.hampton-inn.com
18501 N. Creek Dr.
65 rooms - $60-95
Pets: Small pets welcome
Creature Comforts: CCTV, a/c,
refrig, micro, pool

TONICA
Kishauwau on the Vermillion
(815) 442-8453
http://www.kishauwau.com
Route 1
12 cottages - $80-135
Pets: Welcome in 5 cottages
Creature Comforts: Charming
paneled cottages w/quilts and
period furnishings, CCTV, VCR,
a/c, kit, fireplaces, Jacuzzis, trails,
river views/fishing/canoeing

TROY
Scottish Inns
(800) 251-1962, (618) 667-9969
http://www.reservahost.com
909 Edwardsville Rd.
69 rooms - $30-40
Pets: Welcome
Creature Comforts: CCTV, a/c,
cont. brkfst, pool

TUSCOLA
Holiday Inn Express
(800) HOLIDAY, (217) 253-6363
http://www.holiday-inn.com
1201 Tuscola Ave.
80 rooms - $70-85
Pets: Welcome in smoking rms.
Creature Comforts: CCTV, a/c,
pool

Super 8 Motel
(800) 800-8000, (217) 253-5488
http://www.super8.com
Rtes. 57 & 36
64 rooms - $49-69
Pets: Welcome
Creature Comforts: CCTV, a/c,
cont. brkfst

ULLIN
Best Western Cheekwood Inn
(800) 528-1234, (618) 845-3700
http://www.bestwestern.com
Route 57
40 rooms - $45-75
Pets: Small pets welcome
Creature Comforts: CCTV,
VCR, a/c, pool, whirlpool

URBANA
Best Western Cunningham
(800) 528-1234, (217) 367-8331
http://www.bestwestern.com
1907 N. Cunningham Pl.
153 rooms - $55-169
Pets: Small dogs in ltd. rms
Creature Comforts: CCTV, a/c,
refrig, cont. brkfst, hlth club, pool

Jumer's Castle Lodge
(800) 285-8637, (217) 384-8800
http://www.jumers.com
209 S. Broadway St.
128 rooms - $80-169
Pets: Welcome w/$25 dep.
Creature Comforts: French
decor accented w/period pieces,
CCTV, a/c, refrig, Jacuzzis,
restaurant, pool, hlth clb, saunas,
whirlpool

Motel 6
(800) 4-MOTEL6, (217) 344-1082
http://www.motel6.com
1906 N. Cunningham Ave.
103 rooms - $34-45
Pets: Under 30 lbs. welcome
Creature Comforts: CCTV, a/c,
pool

Park Inn
(217) 344-8000
2408 N. Cunningham Ave.
148 rooms - $60-255
Pets: Welcome w/$10 fee
Creature Comforts: CCTV, a/c,
refrig, micro, Jacuzzi, restaurant,
pool, hlth clb

Sleep Inn
(800) Sleep-Inn, (217) 367-6000
http://www.sleepinn.com
1908 N. Lincoln Ave.
65 rooms - $66-109
Pets: Small pets welcome
Creature Comforts: CCTV, a/c,
refrig, hlth club

VANDALIA
Days Inn
(800) DAYS-INN, (618) 283-4400
http://www.daysinn.com
Rtes. 51 & 70
95 rooms - $38-85
Pets: Welcome w/$10 deposit
Creature Comforts: CCTV, a/c,
restaurant, cont. brkfst, pool

Ramada Inn Limited
(800) 2-Ramada, (618) 283-1400
http://www.ramada.com
Route 40
59 rooms - $50-85
Pets: Welcome w/$10 fee
Creature Comforts: CCTV,
VCR, a/c, refrig, micro, pool

Travelodge
(800) 578-7878, (618) 283-2363
http://www.travelodge.com
1500 N. 6th St.
48 rooms - $50-65
Pets: Welcome
Creature Comforts: CCTV, a/c,
pool

VERNON HILLS
Amerisuites
(800) 833-1516, (847) 918-1400
http://www.amerisuites.com
450 N. Milwaukee Ave.
128 rooms - $120-150
Pets: Under 10 lbs.
Creature Comforts: CCTV,
VCR, a/c, refrig, micro, cont.
brkfst, hlth club, whirlpool

VILLA PARK
Motel 6
(800) 4-MOTEL6, (630) 941-9100
http://www.motel6.com
10 W. Roosevelt Rd.
109 rooms - $44-59
Pets: Under 30 lbs. welcome
Creature Comforts: CCTV, a/c,
pool

WARRENVILLE
Amerisuites
(800) 833-1516, (847) 956-1400
http://www.amerisuites.com
2111 S. Arlington Heights Rd.
112 rooms - $80-135
Pets: Under 10 lbs.
Creature Comforts: CCTV,
VCR, a/c, refrig, micro, cont.
brkfst, hlth club, whirlpool

WASHINGTON
Super 8 Motel
(800) 800-8000, (309) 444-8881
http://www.super8.com
1884 Washington Rd.
48 rooms - $45-60
Pets: Welcome
Creature Comforts: CCTV, a/c,
cont. brkfst

WATSEKA
Carousel Inn
(815) 432-4966
1120 E. Walnut St.
25 rooms - $35-54
Pets: Small pets w/$10 fee
Creature Comforts: CCTV, a/c,
refrig, micro

Super 8 Motel
(800) 800-8000, (815) 432-6000
http://www.super8.com
710 W. Walnut St.
41 rooms - $50-75
Pets: Welcome w/permission
Creature Comforts: CCTV, a/c,
Jacuzzis, cont. brkfst

WAUKEGAN
Best Inns of America
(800) 237-8466, (847) 336-9000
http://www.bestinns.com
31 N. Green Bay Rd.
90 rooms - $45-79
Pets: Small pets welcome
Creature Comforts: CCTV, a/c,
cont. brkfst, pool

Best Western Inn
(800) 528-1234, (847) 244-6100
http://www.bestwestern.com
411 S. Greenbay Rd.
52 rooms - $55-109
Pets: Small dogs in ltd. rooms
Creature Comforts: CCTV, a/c,
refrig, cont. brkfst

Super 8 Motel
(800) 800-8000, (847) 249-2388
http://www.super8.com
630 N. Green Bay Rd.
61 rooms - $40-75
Pets: Welcome w/permission
Creature Comforts: CCTV, a/c

Travelodge
(800) 578-7878, (847) 244-8950
http://www.travelodge.com
222 W. Grand Ave.
61 rooms - $50-80
Pets: Welcome
Creature Comforts: CCTV, a/c,
pool

WENONA
Super 8 Motel
(800) 800-8000, (815) 853-4371
http://www.super8.com
Rtes. 39 & 17
36 rooms - $45-60
Pets: Small pets w/$25 dep.
Creature Comforts: CCTV, a/c,
kit, Jacuzzis, cont. brkfst

WEST CHESTER
Hampton Inn
(800) Hampton, (708) 409-1000
http://www.hampton-inn.com
2222 Enterprise Dr.
111 rooms - $69-105
Pets: Small pets welcome
Creature Comforts: CCTV, a/c,
cont. brkfst, whirlpool, hlth club

WEST FRANKFORT
Gray Plaza Motel
(618) 932-3116
1010 W. Main St.
49 rooms - $36-50
Pets: Welcome w/$5 fee
Creature Comforts: CCTV, a/c,
refrig

WESTMONT
Homestead Village
(630) 323-9292
855 Pasquinelli Dr.
139 rooms - $85-120
Pets: Welcome
Creature Comforts: TV, a/c, kit

WILLOWBROOK
Baymont Inn
(877)BAYMONT, (630) 654-0077
http://www.baymontinns.com
855 W. 79th St.
138 rooms - $55-75
Pets: Small pets welcome
Creature Comforts: CCTV, a/c,
refrig, micro, cont. brkfst

Holiday Inn
(800) HOLIDAY, (630) 325-6400
http://www.holiday-inn.com
7800 S. Kingery Hwy.
222 rooms - $79-99
Pets: Small pets welcome
Creature Comforts: CCTV,
VCR, a/c, refrig, restaurant, hlth
club, pool

WINTHROP HARBOR
Sandpiper Inn
(847) 746-7380
301 Sheridan Rd.
25 rooms - $49-79
Pets: Small pets welcome
Creature Comforts: CCTV, a/c,
Jacuzzis

WOODSTOCK
Super 8 Motel
(800) 800-8000, (815) 337-8808
http://www.super8.com
1220 Davis Rd.
60 rooms - $49-80
Pets: Welcome w/$5 fee
Creature Comforts: CCTV, a/c,
Jacuzzis, cont. brkfst

Indiana

ALEXANDRIA
Country Gazebo Inn
(765) 754-8783
http://www.innsites.com
RR 1, Box 323
8 rooms - $45-75
Pets: Welcome
Creature Comforts: CCTV,
VCR, a/c, fireplace, refrig, micro,
full brkfst

ANDERSON
Best Inns of America
(800) 237-8466, (765) 644-2000
http://www.bestinns.com
5706 Scatterfield Rd.
93 rooms - $45-75
Pets: Small pets welcome
Creature Comforts: CCTV, a/c,
cont. brkfst

Comfort Inn
(800) 228-5150, (765) 644-4422
http://www.comfortinn.com
2205 E. 59th St.
56 rooms - $59-139
Pets: Welcome
Creature Comforts: CCTV, a/c,
refrig, micro, cont. brkfst,
whirlpool, pool

Motel 6
(800) 4-MOTEL6, (765) 642-9023
http://www.motel6.com
5810 Scatterfield Rd.
125 rooms - $35-49
Pets: Under 30 lbs.welcome
Creature Comforts: CCTV, a/c,
pool

Ramada Inn
(800) 2-Ramada, (765) 649-0451
http://www.ramada.com
5901 Scatterfield Rd.
114 rooms - $55-169
Pets: Welcome w/$25 dep.
Creature Comforts: CCTV,
VCR, a/c, refrig, Jacuzzis,
restaurant, sauna, pool, whirlpool,
tennis

BEDFORD
Rosemont Motel
(812) 275-5953
1923 M St.
24 rooms - $35-48
Pets: Small pets w/$6 fee
Creature Comforts: CCTV, a/c,
refrig

BLOOMINGTON
Best Western Fireside Inn
(800) 528-1234, (812) 332-2141
http://www.bestwestern.com
4501 E. 3rd St.
96 rooms - $45-120
Pets: Under 20 lbs. welcome
Creature Comforts: CCTV, a/c,
cont. brkfst, pool

Days Inn
(800) DAYS INN, (812) 336-0905
http://www.daysinn.com
200 Matlock Rd.
50 rooms - $65-175
Pets: Welcome
Creature Comforts: CCTV, a/c,
refrig, Jacuzzis, cont. brkfst

Hampton Inn
(800) Hampton, (812) 334-2100
http://www.hampton-inn.com
2100 N. Walnut St.
131 rooms - $65-89
Pets: Welcome
Creature Comforts: CCTV, a/c,
refrig, micro, Jacuzzis, cont.
brkfst, pool, hlth club

Motel 6
(800) 4-MOTEL6, (812) 332-0337
http://www.motel6.com
126 S. Franklin Rd.
91 rooms - $35-49
Pets: Under 30 lbs. welcome
Creature Comforts: CCTV, a/c,
pool

Motel 6, University
(800) 4 MOTEL6, (812) 332-0820
http://www.motel6.com
1800 N. Walnut St.
109 rooms - $35-49
Pets: Under 30 lbs. welcome
Creature Comforts: CCTV, a/c,
pool

Super 8 Motel
(800) 800-8000, (812) 323-8000
http://www.super8.com
1000 W. State Rd.
62 rooms - $39-56
Pets: Small pets w/permission.
Creature Comforts: CCTV, a/c,
refrig, micro, cont. brkfst, pool,
whirlpool

BLUFTON
Budget Inn
(219) 824-0820
1420 N. Main St.
20 rooms - $33-45
Pets: Small pets w/$8 fee
Creature Comforts: CCTV, a/c,
kit

BRAZIL
Howard Johnson Express
(800) I-Go-Hojo, (812) 446-2345
http://www.hojo.com
935 W. Rte. 42
80 rooms - $36-79
Pets: Welcome w/permission
Creature Comforts: CCTV, a/c,
cont. brkfst

CARLISLE
Super 8 Motel
(800) 800-8000, (812) 398-2500
http://www.super8.com
Route 41
37 rooms - $39-56
Pets: Welcome w/permission
Creature Comforts: CCTV, a/c,
cont. brkfst

CENTERVILLE
Super 8 Motel
(800) 800-8000, (765) 855-5461
http://www.super8.com
2407 N. Centerville Rd.
41 rooms - $45-59
Pets: Welcome
Creature Comforts: CCTV, a/c

CLARKSVILLE
Best Western Greentree Inn
(800) 528-1234, (812) 288-9281
http://www.bestwestern.com
1425 Broadway Rd.
105 rooms - $55-79
Pets: Small pets welcome
Creature Comforts: CCTV, a/c,
pool

CLINTON
Renatto Inn
(317) 832-3557
Rtes. 63 & 163
33 rooms - $ 35-58
Pets: Small pets welcome
Creature Comforts: CCTV, a/c,
refrig, micro, restaurant

CLOVERDALE
Quality Inn
(800) 228-5151, (765) 795-3500
http://www.qualityinn.com
1035 N. Main St.
112 rooms - $60-119
Pets: Small pets welcome
Creature Comforts: CCTV, a/c,
refrig, restaurant, pool

COLUMBIA CITY
Columbia City Motel
(219) 244-5103
500 Old Rte. 30
12 rooms - $30-45
Pets: Small pets welcome
Creature Comforts: CCTV, a/c,
refrig

Lees Inns
(800) 733-5337, (219) 244-5300
http://www.leesinn.com
235 Frontage Rd.
52 rooms - $59-139
Pets: Small pets welcome
Creature Comforts: CCTV, a/c,
Jacuzzis

COLUMBUS
Days Inn
(800) DAYS-INN, (812) 376-6183
http://www.daysinn.com
3445 Jonathan Moore Pike
118 rooms - $55-95
Pets: Welcome
Creature Comforts: CCTV, a/c,
refrig, cont. brkfst, pool

Holiday Inn
(800) HOLIDAY, (812) 372-1541
http://www.holiday-inn.com
2480 Jonathan Moore Pike
254 rooms - $69-125
Pets: Welcome
Creature Comforts: CCTV, a/c,
refrig, micro, restaurant, sauna,
hlth club, whirlpool, pool

Ramada Inn
(800) 2-Ramada, (812) 376-3051
http://www.ramada.com
2485 Jonathan Moore Pike
165 rooms - $75-249
Pets: Welcome w/$25 dep.
Creature Comforts: CCTV,
VCR, a/c, refrig, micro, Jacuzzis,
restaurant, sauna, pool, whirlpool,
tennis

Super 8 Motel
(800) 800-8000, (812) 372-8828
http://www.super8.com
110 Brexpark Dr.
62 rooms - $45-75
Pets: Welcome
Creature Comforts: CCTV, a/c,
cont. brkfst

CRAWFORDSVILLE
Holiday Inn
(800) HOLIDAY, (765) 362-8700
http://www.holiday-inn.com
2500 N. Lafayette Rd.
150 rooms - $65-85
Pets: Small pets welcome
Creature Comforts: CCTV,
VCR, a/c, refrig, micro, restaurant,
pool

Super 8 Motel
(800) 800-8000, (765) 364-9999
http://www.super8.com
1025 Corey Blvd.
58 rooms - $48-69
Pets: Welcome w/permission.
Creature Comforts: CCTV, a/c,
cont. brkfst, pool, whirlpool

DALE
Scottish Inns
(800) 251-1962, (812) 937-2816
http://www.reservahost.com
Rtes. 64 & 231
77 rooms - $33-45
Pets: Welcome w/$5 fee
Creature Comforts: CCTV, a/c,
cont. brkfst

DALEVILLE
Super 8 Motel
(800) 800-8000, (317) 378-0888
http://www.super8.com
Rtes. 69 & 67
45 rooms - $45-65
Pets: Welcome w/permission.
Creature Comforts: CCTV, a/c,
cont. brkfst

DECATUR
Days Inn
(800) DAYS-INN, (219) 728-2196
http://www.daysinn.com
1033 N. 13th St.
43 rooms - $45-90
Pets: Welcome w/$3 fee
Creature Comforts: CCTV, a/c,
refrig, whirlpool, pool

ELKHART
Diplomat Motel
(219) 264-4118
3300 Cassopolis Rd.
22 rooms - $29-53
Pets: Welcome w/$5 fee
Creature Comforts: CCTV, a/c,
refrig

Econo Lodge
(800) 55-ECONO, (219) 262-0540
http://www.econolodge.com
3440 Cassopolis St.
36 rooms - $35-99
Pets: Small pets welcome
Creature Comforts: CCTV,
VCR, a/c, Jacuzzis, cont. brkfst

Knights Inn
(800) 843-5644, (219) 264-4262
http://www.knightsinn.com
52188 Rte. 19
120 rooms - $35-80
Pets: Welcome w/$25 dep.
Creature Comforts: CCTV, a/c,
kit, pool

Quality Inn
(800) 228-5151, (219) 295-0280
http://www.qualityinn.com
300 S. Main St.
137 rooms - $45-169
Pets: Small pets welcome
Creature Comforts: CCTV, a/c,
refrig, restaurant, cont. brkfst,
whirlpool, sauna, pool

Ramada Inn
(800) 2-Ramada, (219) 262-1581
http://www.ramada.com
3011 Belvedere Rd.
144 rooms - $78-109
Pets: Welcome w/$10 fee
Creature Comforts: CCTV,
VCR, a/c, refrig, restaurant, sauna,
hlth club, whirlpool, pool

Red Roof Inn
(800) The-Roof, (219) 262-3691
http://www.redroof.com
2902 Cassopolis St.
80 rooms - $45-85
Pets: Small pets welcome
Creature Comforts: CCTV, a/c

Super 8 Motel
(800) 800-8000, (219) 264-4457
http://www.super8.com
345 Windsor Ave.
62 rooms - $45-65
Pets: Welcome w/permission.
Creature Comforts: CCTV, a/c,
cont. brkfst

Turnpike Inn
(219) 264-1108
3500 Cassopolis St.
18 rooms - $30-45
Pets: Small pets w/$3 fee
Creature Comforts: CCTV, a/c,
refrig

EVANSVILLE
Coolbreeze Estate B&B
(821) 422-9635
http://www.coolbreezebb.com
4 rooms - $75-85
Pets: Small well-behaved pets
welcome
Creature Comforts: Historic
1905 home near river w/spacious
corner rooms and antiques, wicker
swing on porch, lovely decor,
sunny library, CCTV, VCR, a/c,
refrig, full brkfst

Comfort Inn
(800) 228-5150, (812) 477-2211
http://www.comfortinn.com
5006 E. Morgan Ave.
52 rooms - $55-99
Pets: Small pets welcome
Creature Comforts: CCTV, a/c,
cont. brkfst, pool

Days Inn
(800) DAYS-INN, (812) 473-7944
http://www.daysinn.com
4819 Tecumsen Ln.
60 rooms - $55-75
Pets: Welcome w/$5 fee
Creature Comforts: CCTV, a/c,
cont. brkfst, whirlpool, pool

Drury Inn
(800) Drury-Inn, (812) 423-5818
http://www.drury-inn.com
3901 Rte. 41
151 rooms - $65-88
Pets: Welcome
Creature Comforts: CCTV, a/c,
refrig, micro, cont. brkfst,
whirlpool, pool

Lees Inns
(800) 733-5337, (812) 477-6663
http://www.leesinn.com
5538 E. Indiana St.
52 rooms - $55-84
Pets: Welcome
Creature Comforts: CCTV, a/c,
refrig, Jacuzzis

Motel 6
(800) 4-MOTEL6, (812) 424-6431
http://www.motel6.com
4321 Rte. 41
102 rooms - $39-49
Pets: Under 30 lbs. welcome
Creature Comforts: CCTV a/c

Studio Plus
(888) 788-3467, (812) 479-0103
http://www.studioplus.com
301 Eagle Crest
72 rooms - $60-99
Pets: Welcome w/credit card dep.
Creature Comforts: CCTV, a/c,
refrig, micro, pool, hlth clb

Super 8 Motel
(800) 800-8000, (812) 476-4008
http://www.super8.com
4600 Morgan Ave.
62 rooms - $50-69
Pets: Welcome
Creature Comforts: CCTV, a/c,
cont. brkfst

FISHERS
The Frederick-Talbott Inn
(800) 566-BEDS, (317) 578-3600
http://www.fredtal.com
13805 Allisonville Rd.
11 rooms - $95-185
Pets: Welcome
Creature Comforts: Lovely blue
green 1870's Gothic farmhouse
with English antiques and friendly
ambiance, CCTV, VCR, a/c,
fireplace, refrig, Jacuzzi, full
brkfst

Holiday Inn
(800) HOLIDAY, (317) 578-9000
http://www.holiday-inn.com
9780 North by Northwest Blvd.
78 rooms - $75-169
Pets: Small pets welcome
Creature Comforts: CCTV, a/c,
refrig, Jacuzzis, restaurant, pool

Holiday Inn Express
(800) HOLIDAY, (317) 578-2000
http://www.holiday-inn.com
9790 North by Northwest Blvd.
77 rooms - $75-99
Pets: Welcome
Creature Comforts: CCTV, a/c,
refrig, Jacuzzis, cont. brkfst

Residence Inn
(800) 331-3131, (317) 842-1111
http://www.residenceinn.com
9765 Crosspoint Blvd.
80 rooms - $115-199
Pets: Welcome w/$150 fee
Creature Comforts: CCTV, a/c,
fireplaces, Jacuzzis, kit, cont.
brkfst, hlth club, pool

FT. WAYNE
Baymont Inns
(800) 4-Budget, (219) 489-2220
http://www.baymontinns.com
1005 W. Washington Cent. Rd.
100 rooms - $50-69
Pets: Small pets welcome
Creature Comforts: CCTV, a/c,
refrig, micro, cont. brkfst

Best Inns of America
(800) 237-8466, (219) 483-0091
http://www.bestinns.com
3017 W. Coliseum Blvd.
104 rooms - $69-94
Pets: Welcome
Creature Comforts: CCTV, a/c,
refrig, cont. brkfst

Comfort Inn
(800) 228-5150, (219) 484-6262
http://www.comfortinn.com
2908 Goshen Rd.
52 rooms - $45-175
Pets: Small pets w/$25 dep.
Creature Comforts: CCTV, a/c,
refrig, Jacuzzis, cont. brkfst, pool

Days Inn
(800) DAYS-INN, (219) 484-9681
http://www.daysinn.com
Route 69
151 rooms - $39-55
Pets: Welcome
Creature Comforts: CCTV, a/c,
restaurant, cont. brkfst, sauna, hlth
club, pool

Days Inn
(800) DAYS-INN, (219) 424-1980
http://www.daysinn.com
3730 E. Washington Blvd.
120 rooms - $39-65
Pets: Welcome w/$4 fee
Creature Comforts: CCTV, a/c,
restaurant, pool

Economy Inn
(219) 489-3588
http://www.economyinns.com
1401 W. Washington Cent. Rd.
48 rooms - $39-80
Pets: Welcome
Creature Comforts: CCTV, a/c,
refrig, cont. brkfst

Hampton Inn
(800) Hampton, (219) 489-0908
http://www.hampton-inn.com
5702 Challenger Pkwy.
90 rooms - $69-85
Pets: Under 25 lbs. welcome
Creature Comforts: CCTV, a/c,
kit, hlth club, pool

Hometown Inn
(219) 749-5058
6910 Rte. 30
80 rooms - $35-95
Pets: Welcome
Creature Comforts: CCTV,
VCR, a/c, kit, Jacuzzis

Knights Inn
(800) 843-5644, (219) 484-2669
http://www.knightsinn.com
2901 Goshen Rd.
100 rooms - $39-75
Pets: Welcome w/$25 dep.
Creature Comforts: CCTV, a/c,
kit, pool

Lees Inns
(800) 733-5337, (219) 489-8888
http://www.leesinn.com
5707 Challenger Pkwy.
73 rooms - $59-145
Pets: Small pets welcome
Creature Comforts: CCTV, a/c,
Jacuzzis

Marriott Hotel
(800) 228-9290, (219) 484-0411
http://www.marriott.com
305 E. Washington Cent. Dr.
224 rooms - $75-149
Pets: Welcome
Creature Comforts: CCTV, a/c,
refrig, restaurant, pool, hlth clb,
whirlpool

Motel 6
(800) 4-MOTEL6, (219) 482-3972
http://www.motel6.com
3003 Coliseum Blvd. West
105 rooms - $35-49
Pets: Under 30 lbs. welcome
Creature Comforts: CCTV, a/c

Red Roof Inn
(800) The-Roof, (219) 484-8641
http://www.redroof.com
2920 Goshen Rd.
78 rooms - $45-75
Pets: Small pets welcome
Creature Comforts: CCTV, a/c

Residence Inn
(800) 331-3131, (219) 484-4700
http://www.residenceinn.com
4919 Lima Rd.
80 rooms - $75-169
Pets: Welcome w/$50-100 fee
Creature Comforts: CCTV,
VCR, a/c, fireplaces, Jacuzzis, kit,
cont. brkfst, hlth club, pool

FRANKLIN
Days Inn
(800) DAYS-INN, (317) 736-8000
http://www.daysinn.com
2180 E. King St.
100 rooms - $49-90
Pets: Welcome
Creature Comforts: CCTV, a/c,
refrig, micro, cont. brkfst, pool

FREEMONT
E & L Motel
(219) 495-3300
35 West Rte. 120
12 rooms - $29-44
Pets: Welcome w/$4 fee
Creature Comforts: CCTV, a/c

FRENCH LICK
Lane Motel
(812) 936-9919
Box 224
43 rooms - $40-80
Pets: Welcome
Creature Comforts: CCTV, a/c,
refrig, micro, Jacuzzi, pool

The Pines at Patoka Lake
(812) 936-9854
Lake Village Dr.
12 cabins - $65-95
Pets: Welcome w/$75 dep.
Creature Comforts: CCTV,
VCR, kit

GOSHEN
Best Western Pines Inn
(800) 528-1234, (219) 533-0408
http://www.bestwestern.com
900 Lincoln East
77 rooms - $60-79
Pets: Small pets welcome
Creature Comforts: CCTV, a/c,
hlth club

GREENCASTLE
College Inn
(317) 653-4167
315 Bloomington St.
22 rooms - $29-44
Pets: Small pets welcome
Creature Comforts: CCTV, a/c, refrig

GREENFIELD
Howard Hughes Motor Lodge
(317) 462-4493
1310 W. Main St.
22 rooms - $35-49
Pets: Small pets welcome
Creature Comforts: CCTV, a/c, refrig

GREENSBURG
Best Western Pines Inn
(800) 528-1234, (812) 663-6055
http://www.bestwestern.com
2317 N. St
74 rooms - $55-79
Pets: Small pets w/$5 fee
Creature Comforts: CCTV, a/c, cont. brkfst, pool, hlth club, whirlpool

Lees Inns
(800) 733-5337, (812) 663-9998
http://www.leesinn.com
2211 N. State Rd. 3
95 rooms - $49-89
Pets: Welcome on 1st floor
Creature Comforts: CCTV, a/c, refrig, whirlpool

GREENWOOD
Comfort Inn
(800) 228-5150, (317) 887-1515
http://www.comfortinn.com
110 Sheek Rd.
74 rooms - $60-225
Pets: Welcome w/$10 dep.
Creature Comforts: CCTV, a/c, refrig, Jacuzzis, cont. brkfst, pool

HAMMOND
Holiday Inn
(800) HOLIDAY, (219) 844-2140
http://www.holiday-inn.com
3830 - 179th St.
154 rooms - $85-125
Pets: Welcome if attended
Creature Comforts: CCTV, a/c, refrig, restaurant, pool

Motel 6
(800) 4-MOTEL6, (219) 845-0330
http://www.motel6.com
3840 - 179th St.
136 rooms - $40-55
Pets: Under 30 lbs. welcome
Creature Comforts: CCTV, a/c, pool

HOBART
Comfort Inn
(800) 228-5150, (219) 947-7677
http://www.comfortinn.com
1915 Mississippi St.
61 rooms - $59-99
Pets: Small pets welcome
Creature Comforts: CCTV, a/c, Jacuzzis, cont. brkfst, whirlpool, pool, whirlpool

HOWE
Super 8 Motel
(800) 800-8000, (219) 562-2828
http://www.super8.com
7333 N. Rte. 9
77 rooms - $50-70
Pets: Welcome
Creature Comforts: CCTV, a/c, refrig, cont. brkfst

HUNTINGTON
Comfort Inn
(800) 228-5150, (219) 356-3434
http://www.comfortinn.com
2205 N. Jefferson St.
64 rooms - $60-135
Pets: Small pets welcome
Creature Comforts: CCTV, a/c, refrig, micro, cont. brkfst, pool, whirlpool

Days Inn
(800) DAYS-INN, (219) 359-8989
http://www.daysinn.com
2996 W. Park Dr.
62 rooms - $49-75
Pets: Welcome w/$20 fee
Creature Comforts: CCTV, a/c, pool

INDIANAPOLIS
Baymont Inns
(800) 4-Budget, (317) 244-8100
http://www.baymontinns.com
2650 Executive Dr.
102 rooms - $45-72
Pets: Welcome
Creature Comforts: CCTV, a/c, refrig, micro, cont. brkfst

Baymont Inns, East
(800) 4-Budget, (317) 897-2300
http://www.baymontinns.com
2349 Post Dr.
105 rooms - $45-70
Pets: Welcome
Creature Comforts: CCTV, a/c, refrig, micro, cont. brkfst

Comfort Inn
(800) 228-5150, (317) 872-3100
http://www.comfortinn.com
3880 W. 92nd St.
58 rooms - $65-275
Pets: Small pets welcome
Creature Comforts: CCTV, a/c, cont. brkfst, pool

Comfort Inn, Downtown
(800) 228-5150, (317) 631-9000
http://www.comfortinn.com
520 S. Capitol Ave.
86 rooms - $85-550
Pets: Small pets welcome
Creature Comforts: CCTV, a/c, kit, Jacuzzis, cont. brkfst, hlth club, pool

Comfort Inn - Northeast
(800) 228-5150, (317) 595-0700
http://www.comfortinn.com
8190 Summit Hill Dr.
130 rooms - $75-385
Pets: Small pets welcome
Creature Comforts: CCTV, a/c, refrig, Jacuzzis, cont. brkfst, hlth club, pool

Days Inn
(800) DAYS-INN, (317) 841-9700
http://www.daysinn.com
8275 Craig St.
161 rooms - $75-99
Pets: Welcome w/$25 fee
Creature Comforts: CCTV, a/c, cont. brkfst, hlth club

Days Inn, East
(800) DAYS-INN, (317) 359-5500
http://www.daysinn.com
7314 E. 21st St.
120 rooms - $43-79
Pets: Welcome w/$10 fee
Creature Comforts: CCTV, a/c,
cont. brkfst, pool

Days Inn-Northwest
(800) DAYS-INN, (317) 293-6550
http://www.daysinn.com
3740 N. High School Rd.
152 rooms - $49-85
Pets: Welcome
Creature Comforts: CCTV, a/c,
restaurant, cont. brkfst, pool

Drury Inn
(800) Drury-Inn, (317) 876-9777
http://www.drury-inn.com
9320 N. Michigan Rd.
112 rooms - $65-89
Pets: Welcome
Creature Comforts: CCTV, a/c,
refrig, micro, cont. brkfst, pool

Hampton Inn
(800) Hampton, (317) 359-9900
http://www.hampton-inn.com
2311 N. Shadel Ave.
125 rooms - $65-89
Pets: Small pets welcome
Creature Comforts: CCTV, a/c,
refrig, pool, whirlpool, hlth club

Holiday Inn, East
(800) HOLIDAY, (317) 359-5341
http://www.holiday-inn.com
6990 E. 21st St.
185 rooms - $85-125
Pets: Welcome
Creature Comforts: CCTV, a/c,
refrig, restaurant, hlth club,
whirlpool, pool

Holiday Inn, Southeast
(800) HOLIDAY, (317) 783-7751
http://www.holiday-inn.com
5120 Victory Dr.
142 rooms - $75-105
Pets: Welcome
Creature Comforts: CCTV, a/c,
refrig, restaurant, pool

Homewood Suites
(800) 225-5466, (317) 253-1919
http://www.homewoodsuites.com
2501 E. 86th St.
115 rooms - $99-129
Pets: Welcome w/$50 dep.
Creature Comforts: CCTV,
VCR, a/c, fireplaces, kit, pool, hlth
clb, sauna, whirlpool

Howard Johnson Express
(800) I-Go-Hojo, (317) 352-0481
http://www.hojo.com
7050 E. 21st St.
116 rooms - $40-69
Pets: Welcome w/permission
Creature Comforts: CCTV, a/c,
cont. brkfst, pool

Howard Johnson Express
(800) I-Go-Hojo, (317) 291-8800
http://www.hojo.com
2602 N. High School Rd.
125 rooms - $35-65
Pets: Welcome w/permission
Creature Comforts: CCTV, a/c,
pool

Howard Johnson Express
(800) I-Go-Hojo, (317) 849-6910
http://www.hojo.com
7202 E. 82nd St.
76 rooms - $45-69
Pets: Welcome w/permission
Creature Comforts: CCTV, a/c,
refrig, micro, Jacuzzis, pool

Howard Johnson Hotel
(800) I-Go-Hojo, (no local tel)
http://www.hojo.com
8401 W. Washington St.
120 rooms - $40-75
Pets: Welcome w/permission
Creature Comforts: CCTV, a/c,
restaurant, cont. brkfst, whirlpool,
sauna, hlth club, pool

Knights Inn
(800) 843-5644, (317) 848-2423
http://www.knightsinn.com
9402 Haver Way
112 rooms - $40-69
Pets: Welcome w/$5 fee
Creature Comforts: CCTV, a/c,
kit, pool

Knights Inn
(800) 843-5644, (317) 788-0125
http://www.knightsinn.com
4909 Knights Way
104 rooms - $65-89
Pets: Welcome w/$5 fee
Creature Comforts: CCTV, a/c,
kit, pool

La Quinta Inn
(800) Nu-Rooms, (317) 359-1021
http://www.laquinta.com
7304 E. 21st St.
122 rooms - $53-78
Pets: Welcome
Creature Comforts: CCTV, a/c,
cont. brkfst, pool

La Quinta Inn, Airport
(800) Nu-Rooms, (317) 247-4281
http://www.laquinta.com
5316 W. Southern Ave.
124 rooms - $65-85
Pets: Welcome
Creature Comforts: CCTV, a/c,
cont. brkfst, pool

Lees Inns
(800) 733-5337, (317) 297-8880
http://www.leesinn.com
5011 N. Lafayette Rd.
76 rooms - $75-195
Pets: Welcome
Creature Comforts: CCTV, a/c,
Jacuzzis

Marriott Hotel
(800) 228-9290, (317) 352-1231
http://www.marriott.com
7202 E. 21st St.
252 rooms - $75-349
Pets: Welcome w/$150 fee
Creature Comforts: CCTV,
VCR, a/c, refrig, Jacuzzis,
restaurant, pool, hlth clb, and a
whirlpool

Motel 6
(800) 4-MOTEL6, (317) 293-3220
http://www.motel6.com
6330 Debonair Ln.
164 rooms - $39-50
Pets: Under 30 lbs. welcome
Creature Comforts: CCTV, a/c

Motel 6, East
(800) 4-MOTEL6, (317) 546-5864
http://www.motel6.com
2851 ShadelAve.
117 rooms - $40-55
Pets: Under 30 lbs. welcome
Creature Comforts: CCTV, a/c

Motel 6, Airport
(800) 4-MOTEL6, (317) 248-1231
http://www.motel6.com
5241 W. Bradbury Ave.
131 rooms - $35-45
Pets: Under 30 lbs. welcome
Creature Comforts: CCTV, a/c,
pool

Pickwick Farms, Airport
(800) RENT-390, (317) 240-3567
1 Pt. Robert Dr.
123 rooms - $69-99
Pets: $10 fee, $150 deposit
Creature Comforts: CCTV,
VCR, a/c, kit

Quality Inn
(800) 228-5151, (317) 787-8341
http://www.qualityinn.com
520 E. Thompson Rd.
184 rooms - $69-199
Pets: Small pets welcome
Creature Comforts: CCTV, a/c,
refrig, restaurant, sauna,
whirlpool, pool, billiards/gm rm

Quality Inn
(800) 228-5151, (317) 897-2000
http://www.qualityinn.com
2141 N. Post Rd.
156 rooms - $65-195
Pets: Small pets welcome
Creature Comforts: CCTV, a/c,
refrig, restaurant, whirlpool, pool,
tennis

Red Roof Inn
(800) The-Roof, (317) 872-3030
http://www.redroof.com
9520 Valparaiso Ct.
107 rooms - $45-75
Pets: Small pets welcome
Creature Comforts: CCTV, a/c

Red Roof Inn
(800) The-Roof, (317) 788-9551
http://www.redroof.com
5221 Victory Dr.
105 rooms - $40-75
Pets: Small pets welcome
Creature Comforts: CCTV, a/c

Red Roof Inn
(800) The Roof, (317) 293-6881
http://www.redroof.com
6415 Debonair Ln.
109 rooms - $40-75
Pets: Small pets welcome
Creature Comforts: CCTV, a/c

Residence Inn
(800) 331-3131, (317) 872-0462
http://www.residenceinn.com
3553 Founders Rd.
88 rooms - $99-199
Pets: $7 fee, $50 cleaning fee
Creature Comforts: CCTV,
VCR, a/c, fireplaces, Jacuzzis, kit,
cont. brkfst, hlth club, pool

Residence Inn
(800) 331-3131, (317) 244-1500
http://www.residenceinn.com
5224 W. Southern Ave.
65 rooms - $115-199
Pets: $7 fee, $50 cleaning fee
Creature Comforts: CCTV,
VCR, a/c, fireplaces, Jacuzzis, kit,
cont. brkfst, hlth club, pool

Super 8 Motel
(800) 800-8000, (317) 895-5402
http://www.super8.com
8850 E. 21st St.
120 rooms - $45-65
Pets: Welcome
Creature Comforts: CCTV, a/c,
refrig, micro, Jacuzzis, cont.
brkfst, pool, whirlpool, hlth club,
pool

Super 8 Motel
(800) 800-8000 - No local tel
http://www.super8.com
McFarlBlvd.
64 rooms - $50-65
Pets: Welcome w/$10 fee
Creature Comforts: CCTV, a/c,
refrig, micro, Jacuzzis, cont.
brkfst, pool, whirlpool, pool

JASPER
Days Inn
(800) DAYS-INN, (812) 482-6000
http://www.daysinn.com
Rtes. 162-164
84 rooms - $55-84
Pets: Welcome w/$5 fee
Creature Comforts: CCTV, a/c,
restaurant, cont. brkfst, pool

JEFFERSONVILLE
Days Inn
(800) DAYS-INN, (812) 288-9331
http://www.daysinn.com
350 Eastern Blvd.
172 rooms - $40-65
Pets: Welcome
Creature Comforts: CCTV, a/c,
cont. brkfst, pool

Motel 6
(800) 4-MOTEL6, (812) 283-7703
http://www.motel6.com
2016 Old Rte. 31
98 rooms - $35-45
Pets: Under 30 lbs. welcome
Creature Comforts: CCTV, a/c,
pool

Ramada Inn
(800) 2-Ramada, (812) 284-6711
http://www.ramada.com
700 W. Riverside Dr.
188 rooms - $78-155
Pets: Welcome w/$5 fee
Creature Comforts: CCTV, a/c,
refrig, restaurant, pool

KENTLAND
Tri-Way Inn
(219) 474-5141
611 E. Dunlap St.
29 rooms - $39-65
Pets: Welcome
Creature Comforts: CCTV, a/c, refrig, micro, pool

KOKOMO
Comfort Inn
(800) 228-5150, (765) 452-5050
http://www.comfortinn.com
522 Essex Dr.
63 rooms - $60-129
Pets: Small pets welcome
Creature Comforts: CCTV, a/c, cont. brkfst, pool

Motel 6
(800) 4-MOTEL6, (765) 457-8211
http://www.motel6.com
2808 S. Reed Rd.
93 rooms - $45-55
Pets: Under 30 lbs. welcome
Creature Comforts: CCTV, a/c

LAFAYETTE
Comfort Inn
(800) 228-5150, (765) 447-0016
http://www.comfortinn.com
31 Frontage Rd.
62 rooms - $65-245
Pets: Small pets welcome
Creature Comforts: CCTV, a/c, refrig, micro, Jacuzzis, cont. brkfst, whirlpool, hlth club, pool

Days Inn
(800) DAYS-INN, (765) 447-4131
http://www.daysinn.com
400 Sagamore Pkwy.
180 rooms - $50-105
Pets: Welcome
Creature Comforts: CCTV, a/c, cont. brkfst, pool

Holiday Inn
(800) HOLIDAY, (317) 449-4808
http://www.holiday-inn.com
201 Frontage Rd.
64 rooms - $75-95
Pets: Welcome
Creature Comforts: CCTV, a/c, Jacuzzis, cont. brkfst

Homewood Suites
(800) 225-5466, (317) 448-9700
http://www.homewoodsuites.com
3939 Rte. 26
85 rooms - $90-245
Pets: Welcome w/$50 dep.
Creature Comforts: CCTV, VCR, a/c, fireplaces, kit, pool, hlth clb, sauna, whirlpool

Knights Inn
(800) 843-5644, (317) 447-5611
http://www.knightsinn.com
4110 Rte. 26
112 rooms - $39-95
Pets: Welcome w/$25 dep.
Creature Comforts: CCTV, VCR, a/c, kit

Loeb House Inn
(765) 420-7737
http://www.qklink.com/loebinn
708 Cincinnati St.
5 rooms - $ 75-185
Pets: Welcome
Creature Comforts: 1882 Grand Italianate-style home overlooking river, historic district, detailed moldings, grand staircase, CCTV, VCR, a/c, fireplaces, Jacuzzis and claw foot tubs, full brkfst

Radisson Hotel
(800) 333-3333, (317) 447-0575
http://www.radisson.com
4343 Rte. 26
125 rooms - $80-159
Pets: Under 15 lbs. welcome
Creature Comforts: CCTV, VCR, a/c, kit, Jacuzzis, restaurant, pool, sauna, hlth club, whirlpool

Red Roof Inn
(800) The-Roof, (317) 448-4671
http://www.redroof.com
4201 Rte. 26
80 rooms - $40-75
Pets: Small pets welcome
Creature Comforts: CCTV, a/c

LA PORTE.
Pine Lake Hotel
(800) 374-6338, (219) 362-4585
444 Pine lake Ave.
145 rooms - $65-109
Pets: Small pets welcome
Creature Comforts: CCTV, a/c, refrig, restaurant, pool, sauna, hlth club, whirlpool, putting green

LEBANON
Comfort Inn
(800) 228-5150, (765) 482-4800
http://www.comfortinn.com
210 Sam Ralston Rd.
57 rooms - $60-199
Pets: Small pets welcome
Creature Comforts: CCTV, a/c, refrig, Jacuzzis, cont. brkfst, hlth club, whirlpool, pool

Holiday Inn
(800) HOLIDAY, (317) 482-0500
http://www.holiday-inn.com
505 S. Rte. 39
205 rooms - $69-95
Pets: Small pets welcome
Creature Comforts: CCTV, a/c, refrig, micro, restaurant, sauna, hlth club, whirlpool, pool, tennis, rec. room

Lees Inns
(800) 733-5337, (317) 482-9611
http://www.leesinn.com
1245 Rte. 32
50 rooms - $65-135
Pets: Welcome
Creature Comforts: CCTV, a/c, refrig, Jacuzzis, full brkfst.

LOGANSPORT
Holiday Inn
(800) HOLIDAY, (219) 753-6351
http://www.holiday-inn.com
3550 E. Market St.
98 rooms - $65-129
Pets: Welcome
Creature Comforts: CCTV, a/c, refrig, restaurant, pool

Super 8 Motel
(800) 800-8000, (219) 722-1273
http://www.super8.com
3801 E. Market St.
40 rooms - $55-75
Pets: Welcome w/$10 fee
Creature Comforts: CCTV, a/c, cont. brkfst, hlth club access

MADISON
Best Western Inn
(800) 528-1234, (812) 273-5151
http://www.bestwestern.com
700 Clifty Dr.
69 rooms - $55-135
Pets: Small pets w/$5 fee
Creature Comforts: CCTV, a/c, hlth club

President Madison Motel
(800) 45-MOTEL, (812) 265-2361
http://www.presidentmotel.com
906 E. 1st St.
25 rooms - $45-59
Pets: Welcome in pet rooms
Creature Comforts: CCTV,
VCR, a/c, refrig, micro, cont.
brkfst, pool

MARION
Comfort Inn
(800) 228-5150, (765) 651-1006
http://www.comfortinn.com
1345 N. Baldwin Ave.
62 rooms - $69-175
Pets: Small pets welcome
Creature Comforts: CCTV, a/c,
Jacuzzis, refrig, micro, cont.
brkfst, sauna, hlth club, pool

Holiday Inn
(800) HOLIDAY, (765) 668-8801
http://www.holiday-inn.com
501 E. 4th St.
122 rooms - $65-99
Pets: Welcome
Creature Comforts: CCTV, a/c,
refrig, micro, restaurant,
whirlpool, pool

Lees Inns
(800) 733-5337, (765) 342-1842
http://www.leesinn.com
50 Bill's Blvd.
50 rooms - $65-99
Pets: Small pets welcome
Creature Comforts: CCTV, a/c,
Jacuzzis

Radisson's Hotel Roberts
(800) 333-3333, (765) 741-7777
http://www.radisson.com
420 S. High St.
132 rooms - $85-259
Pets: Under 20 lbs. w/$50 dep.
Creature Comforts: CCTV,
VCR, a/c, kit, Jacuzzis, restaurant,
pool, hlth club, whirlpool

MERRILLVILLE
Comfort Inn
(800) 228-5150, (219) 947-7677
http://www.comfortinn.com
1915 Mississippi St.
61 rooms - $60-99
Pets: Small pets welcome
Creature Comforts: CCTV, a/c,
Jacuzzis, cont. brkfst, whirlpool,
pool

Knights Inn
(800) 843-5644, (219) 736-5100
http://www.knightsinn.com
8250 Louisiana St.
128 rooms - $37-88
Pets: Welcome
Creature Comforts: CCTV, a/c,
kit, pool

La Quinta Inn
(800) Nu-Rooms, (219) 738-2870
http://www.laquinta.com
8210 Louisiana St.
120 rooms - $53-78
Pets: Welcome
Creature Comforts: CCTV, a/c,
refrig, cont. brkfst, pool

Lees Inns
(800) 733-5337, (219) 942-8555
http://www.leesinn.com
6201 Opportunity Ln.
75 rooms - $59-159
Pets: Welcome in pet rooms
Creature Comforts: CCTV, a/c,
Jacuzzis, hlth club

Motel 6
(800) 4-MOTEL6, (219) 738-2701
http://www.motel6.com
8290 Louisiana St.
125 rooms - $35-50
Pets: Under 30 lbs. welcome
Creature Comforts: CCTV, a/c,
pool

Radisson Hotel
(800) 333-3333, (219) 769-6311
http://www.radisson.com
800 E. 81st Ave.
345 rooms - $85-829
Pets: Under 50 lbs. welcome
Creature Comforts: CCTV,
VCR, a/c, kit, Jacuzzis,
restaurants, pool, sauna, hlth club,
whirlpool, putting green

Red Roof Inn
(800) The-Roof, (219) 738-2430
http://www.redroof.com
8290 Georgia St.
107 rooms - $45-78
Pets: Small pets welcome
Creature Comforts: CCTV, a/c

Residence Inn
(800) 331-3131, (219) 791-9000
http://www.residenceinn.com
8018 Delaware Pl.
79 rooms - $115-199
Pets: $10 fee, $50 deposit
Creature Comforts: CCTV, a/c,
Jacuzzis, kit, cont. brkfst, hlth
club, whirlpool, pool

Super 8 Motel
(800) 800-8000, (219) 736-8383
http://www.super8.com
8300 Louisiana St.
62 rooms - $49-65
Pets: Welcome w/permission
Creature Comforts: CCTV, a/c,
refrig, micro, cont. brkfst

METAMORA
Thorpe House Country Inn
(888) happy-day, (765) 872-9149
www.emetamora.com/thorpehouse
19049 Clayborn St.
7 rooms - $70-129
Pets: Welcome
Creature Comforts: 1840's inn
w/gingerbread trim and a low-key
atmosphere, CCTV, a/c, refrig,
micro, full brkfst, restaurant,
country store

MICHIGAN CITY
Comfort Inn
(800) 228-5150, (219) 879-9190
http://www.comfortinn.com
3801 N. Frontage Rd.
50 rooms - $55-95
Pets: Small pets welcome
Creature Comforts: CCTV, a/c,
cont. brkfst, pool

Knights Inn
(800) 843-5644, (219) 874-9500
http://www.knightsinn.com
201 W. Kieffer Rd.
102 rooms - $39-129
Pets: Welcome w/$25 dep.
Creature Comforts: CCTV, a/c,
kit, pool

Red Roof Inn
(800) The-Roof, (219) 874-5251
http://www.redroof.com
110 W. Kieffer Rd.
80 rooms - $45-70
Pets: Small pets welcome
Creature Comforts: CCTV, a/c

MISHAWAKA
Hampton Inn
(800) Hampton, (219) 273-2309
http://www.hampton-inn.com
445 Univeristy Dr.
63 rooms - $63-139
Pets: Welcome
Creature Comforts: CCTV, a/c,
refrig, micro, pool

MONTICELLO
1887 Black Dog Inn
(219) 583-8297
2830 Untaluti Rd.
6 rooms - $75-99
Pets: Welcome
Creature Comforts: A charming
B&B, CCTV, VCR, a/c, refrig,
micro, cont. brkfst, pool

MOUNT VERNON
Four Seasons Motel
(812) 838-4821
2400 W. 4th St.
42 rooms - $58-99
Pets: Welcome w/$25 dep.
Creature Comforts: CCTV, a/c,
refrig, micro, pool

MUNCIE
Comfort Inn
(800) 228-5150, (765) 282-6666
http://www.comfortinn.com
4011 W. Bethel
66 rooms - $60-129
Pets: Small pets welcome
Creature Comforts: CCTV, a/c,
cont. brkfst, pool

Days Inn
(800) DAYS-INN, (765) 288-2311
http://www.daysinn.com
3509 N. Everbrook Ln.
62 rooms - $45-69
Pets: Welcome
Creature Comforts: CCTV, a/c,
cont. brkfst

Lees Inns
(800) 733-5337, (765) 282-7557
http://www.leesinn.com
3302 Everbrook Lane
52 rooms - $59-165
Pets: Small pets welcome
Creature Comforts: CCTV,
VCR, a/c, refrig, Jacuzzis

Radisson Hotel
(800) 333-3333, (765) 741-7777
http://www.radisson.com
420 S. High St.
129 rooms - $80-239
Pets: Under 20 lbs. w/$50 dep.
Creature Comforts: CCTV, a/c,
refrig, restaurant, pool, hlth club
access, whirlpool

Super 8 Motel
(800) 800-8000, (765) 286-4333
http://www.super8.com
3601 W. Fox Ridge Lane
63 rooms - $45-65
Pets: Welcome
Creature Comforts: CCTV, a/c

NAPPANEE
Victorian Guest House
(219) 773-4383
http://www.victorianb-b.com
302 E. Market St.
6 rooms - $55-99
Pets: Welcome in one room
Creature Comforts: Set in the
heart of Amish country, an 1887
Victorian w/stained glass
windows, charming decor,
Victorian acents, antiques, four
poster beds, collectibles, CCTV,
VCR, a/c, fireplace, refrig, and a
full brkfst

NASHVILLE
Salt Creek Inn
(812) 988-1149
Rte. 46, Box 397
66 rooms - $49-119
Pets: Welcome w/$10 fee
Creature Comforts: CCTV, a/c,
kit

Story Inn
(812) 988-2273
6404 S. Rte. 135
12 rooms - $79-129
Pets: $10 fee, $50 dep.
Creature Comforts: Kit,
restaurant, full breakfast

NEW ALBANY
Holiday Inn Express
(800) HOLIDAY, (812) 945-2771
http://www.holiday-inn.com
411 W. Spring St.
133 rooms - $75-99
Pets: Welcome
Creature Comforts: CCTV, a/c,
refrig, micro, cont. brkfst, pool

NEW CASTLE
Best Western Raintree Inn
(800) 528-1234, (765) 521-0100
http://www.bestwestern.com
2836 S. State Rd. 3
104 rooms - $49-75
Pets: Under 25 lbs. welcome
Creature Comforts: CCTV, a/c,
pool, hlth club, whirlpool

Days Inn
(800) DAYS-INN, (765) 987-7548
http://www.daysinn.com
5343 S. State Rd. 3
83 rooms - $45-75
Pets: Welcome w/$4 fee
Creature Comforts: CCTV, a/c,
cont. brkfst, pool

PLYMOUTH
Days Inn
(800) DAYS-INN, (219) 935-4276
http://www.daysinn.com
2229 N. Michigan St.
36 rooms - $40-65
Pets: Welcome w/$5 fee
Creature Comforts: CCTV, a/c,
restaurant

Holiday Inn
(800) HOLIDAY, (219) 936-4013
http://www.holiday-inn.com
2550 N. Michigan St.
109 rooms - $65-99
Pets: Welcome
Creature Comforts: CCTV, a/c,
refrig, restaurant, pool, hlth club/
golf access

Motel 6
(800) 4-MOTEL6, (219) 935-5911
http://www.motel6.com
235 N. Michigan Ave.
103 rooms - $35-50
Pets: Under 30 lbs. welcome
Creature Comforts: CCTV, a/c, pool

PORTAGE
Days Inn
(800) DAYS-INN, (219) 762-2136
http://www.daysinn.com
6161 Melton Rd.
118 rooms - $55-159
Pets: Welcome
Creature Comforts: CCTV, a/c, Jacuzzi, cont. brkfst, pool

Lees Inns
(800) 733-5337, (219) 763-7177
http://www.leesinn.com
2300 Willow Creek Rd.
52 rooms - $65-159
Pets: Small pets welcome
Creature Comforts: CCTV, a/c, Jacuzzis

Ramada Inn
(800) 437-5145, (219) 762-5546
http://www.ramada.com
6200 Melton Rd.
160 rooms - $65-99
Pets: Small pets welcome
Creature Comforts: CCTV, a/c, refrig, restaurant, pool, hlth clb, sauna, whirlpool

REMINGTON
Carson Inn
(219) 261-2181
13736 S. Rte. 231
99 rooms - $39-50
Pets: Welcome w/$10 fee
Creature Comforts: CCTV, a/c, restaurant, pool

Days Inn
(800) DAYS-INN, (219) 261-3182
http://www.daysinn.com
4252 Rte. 24
99 rooms - $50-75
Pets: Welcome w/$5 fee
Creature Comforts: CCTV, a/c, cont. brkfst, pool

RENSSELAER
Interstate Motel
(219) 866-4146
8530 W. Rte. 114
30 rooms - $35-46
Pets: Welcome w/$10 fee
Creature Comforts: CCTV, a/c

REYNOLDS
Park View Motel
(219) 984-5380
RR1, Box 4
18 rooms - $35-59
Pets: Welcome w/$2 fee
Creature Comforts: CCTV, a/c, refrig

RICHMOND
Best Western Imperial Inn
(800) 528-1234, (765) 966-1505
http://www.bestwestern.com
3020 E. Main St.
44 rooms - $38-75
Pets: Small pets w/$5 fee
Creature Comforts: CCTV, a/c, cont. brkfst, pool

Clarion Inn
(800) 228-7466, (765) 966-5000
http://www.clarioninn.com
900 S. A St.
105 rooms - $69-125
Pets: Welcome
Creature Comforts: CCTV, VCR, a/c, refrig, micro, Jacuzzis, fireplace, restaurant, pool, hlth club

Comfort Inn
(800) 228-5150, (765) 935-4766
http://www.comfortinn.com
912 Mendelson Dr.
52 rooms - $69-99
Pets: Small pets welcome
Creature Comforts: CCTV, a/c, cont. brkfst, pool

Days Inn
(800) DAYS-INN, (765) 966-7591
http://www.daysinn.com
540 W. Eaton Pike
161 rooms - $75-99
Pets: Welcome w/$25 fee
Creature Comforts: CCTV, a/c, cont. brkfst, hlth club

Holiday Inn
(800) HOLIDAY, (765) 966-7511
http://www.holiday-inn.com
5501 National Rd. East
133 rooms - $75-325
Pets: Small pets welcome
Creature Comforts: CCTV, a/c, refrig, micro, Jacuzzis, restaurant, hlth club, whirlpool, pool, rec. dome

Howard Johnson Express
(800) I-Go-Hojo, (765) 962-7576
http://www.hojo.com
2525 Chester Blvd.
75 rooms - $37-75
Pets: Welcome w/$5 fee
Creature Comforts: CCTV, VCR, a/c, pool

Lees Inns
(800) 733-5337, (765) 966-6559
http://www.leesinn.com
6030 E. National Rd.
90 rooms - $65-145
Pets: Small pets welcome
Creature Comforts: CCTV, a/c, refrig, micro, Jacuzzis

Ramada Inn
(800) 2-Ramada, (765) 962-5551
http://www.ramada.com
4700 National Rd. East
157 rooms - $55-89
Pets: Welcome w/$10 fee
Creature Comforts: CCTV, a/c, refrig, restaurant, pool

ROSELAND
Best Inns of America
(800) 237-8466, (219) 277-7700
http://www.bestinns.com
425 Dixie Hwy.
93 rooms - $50-75
Pets: Under 25 lbs. welcome
Creature Comforts: CCTV, a/c, cont. brkfst

Days Inn
(800) DAYS-INN, (219) 277-0510
http://www.daysinn.com
52757 Rte. 31
180 rooms - $55-76
Pets: Under 25 lbs. w/$5 fee
Creature Comforts: CCTV, a/c, refrig, cont. brkfst, pool

Holiday Inn
(800) HOLIDAY, (219) 272-6600
http://www.holiday-inn.com
515 Dixie Way
226 rooms - $95-175
Pets: Small pets welcome
Creature Comforts: CCTV, a/c, refrig, restaurant, sauna, hlth club, whirlpool, pool, mini golf

SCOTTSBURG
Best Western Inn
(800) 528-1234, (812) 752-2212
http://www.bestwestern.com
Rtes. 65 & 56
96 rooms - $60-129
Pets: Small pets welcome
Creature Comforts: CCTV, a/c, cont. brkfst, hlth club

Campbell's Motel
(812) 752-4401
300 N. Gardner Rd.
25 rooms - $25-53
Pets: Welcome w/$5 fee
Creature Comforts: CCTV, a/c, refrig, micro

Mariann Travel Inn
(812) 752-3396
Rtes. 65 & 56
98 rooms - $45-60
Pets: Welcome
Creature Comforts: CCTV, a/c, refrig, restaurant, pool

SEYMOUR
Days Inn
(800) DAYS-INN, (812) 522-3678
http://www.daysinn.com
302 S. Commerce Dr.
120 rooms - $40-109
Pets: Welcome
Creature Comforts: CCTV, a/c, refrig, Jacuzzi, cont. brkfst, pool

Knights Inn
(800) 843-5644, (812) 522-3523
http://www.knightsinn.com
207 N. Sandy Creek Dr.
115 rooms - $39-80
Pets: Small pets welcome
Creature Comforts: CCTV, a/c, kit, pool

Lees Inns
(800) 733-5337, (812) 523-1850
http://www.leesinn.com
2075 E. Tipton St.
75 rooms - $70-99
Pets: Small pets welcome
Creature Comforts: CCTV, a/c, Jacuzzis

Super 8 Motel
(800) 800-8000, (812) 524-2000
http://www.super8.com
Rtes. 65 & 50
51 rooms - $45-65
Pets: Welcome w/$3 fee, $25 dep.
Creature Comforts: CCTV, a/c, cont. brkfst, pool

SHELBYVILLE
Holiday Inn
(800) HOLIDAY, (317) 392-3221
http://www.holiday-inn.com
1810 N. Riley Hwy.
99 rooms - $69-99
Pets: Small pets welcome
Creature Comforts: CCTV, VCR, a/c, refrig, micro, restaurant, pool

Lees Inns
(800) 733-5337, (317) 392-2299
http://www.leesinn.com
2880 Rte. 44
72 rooms - $65-139
Pets: Small pets welcome
Creature Comforts: CCTV, a/c, Jacuzzis

Super 8 Motel
(800) 800-8000, (317) 392-6239
http://www.super8.com
20 Rampart Dr.
61 rooms - $45-69
Pets: Welcome
Creature Comforts: CCTV, a/c, cont. brkfst, sauna, hlth. club

SHIPSHEWANA
Super 8 Motel
(800) 800-8000, (219) 768-4004
http://www.super8.com
470 S. Van Buren St.
46 rooms - $49-65
Pets: Welcome w/$8 fee
Creature Comforts: CCTV, a/c, cont. brkfst

SOUTH BEND
Comfort Inn
(800) 228-5150, (219) 272-1500
http://www.comfortinn.com
52939 Rte. 33
100 rooms - $60-199
Pets: Small pets welcome
Creature Comforts: CCTV, a/c, refrig, micro, cont. brkfst, pool

Days Inn
(800) DAYS-INN, (219) 277-0510
http://www.daysinn.com
52757 Rte. 31
180 rooms - $45-69
Pets: Welcome
Creature Comforts: CCTV, a/c, cont. brkfst, pool

Holiday Inn
(800) HOLIDAY, (219) 272-6600
http://www.holiday-inn.com
515 Dixie Hwy.
222 rooms - $75-129
Pets: Small pets welcome
Creature Comforts: CCTV, a/c, refrig, micro, Jacuzzis, restaurant, sauna, hlth club, whirlpool, pool

Knights Inn
(800) 843-5644, (219) 277-2960
http://www.knightsinn.com
236 Dixie Hwy.
116 rooms - $35-80
Pets: Welcome w/$5 fee
Creature Comforts: CCTV, a/c, kit, cont. brkfst, pool

Motel 6
(800) 4-MOTEL6, (219) 272-7072
http://www.motel6.com
52624 Rte. 31
147 rooms - $39-50
Pets: Under 30 lbs. welcome
Creature Comforts: CCTV, a/c, pool

Oliver Inn
(888) 697-4466, (219) 232-4545
www.michiana.org/users/oliver
630 W. Washington St.
9 rooms - $80-135
Pets: Small pets considered
Creature Comforts: A nicely
refurbished 1886 Victorian (25
rooms) on National Register of
Historic Places, detailed
woodworking, spiral stairs,
Waterford crystal sconces, CCTV,
VCR, a/c, Jacuzzis, fireplaces,
refrig, cont. brkfst, baby grand-CD
player, lawn games, elegant
restaurant next door, golf access

Residence Inn
(800) 331-3131, (219) 289-5555
http://www.residenceinn.com
716 N. Niles Ave.
80 rooms - $65-145
Pets: Welcome w/$100 fee
Creature Comforts: CCTV,
VCR, a/c, kit, cont. brkfst, hlth
club, pool

SULLIVAN
Days Inn
(800) DAYS-INN, (812) 268-6391
http://www.daysinn.com
Rtes. 41 & 154
60 rooms - $45-75
Pets: Welcome
Creature Comforts: CCTV, a/c,
cont. brkfst

TAYLORSVILLE
Comfort Inn
(800) 228-5150, (812) 526-9747
http://www.comfortinn.com
10330 N. Rte. 31
54 rooms - $60-199
Pets: Small pets w/$5 fee
Creature Comforts: CCTV,
VCR, a/c, refrig, micro, Jacuzzis,
cont. brkfst, pool

TELL CITY
Daystop
(800) DAYS-INN, (812) 547-3474
http://www.daysinn.com
Rte. 66 & 14th St.
67 rooms - $40-65
Pets: Welcome w/$10 fee
Creature Comforts: CCTV, a/c,
restaurant, pool

Ramada Inn Limited
(800) 2-Ramada, (812) 547-3234
http://www.ramada.com
235 Orchard Hill Dr.
60 rooms - $60-109
Pets: $7 fee & $25 dep.
Creature Comforts: CCTV, a/c,
refrig, Jacuzzis, hlth club

TERRE HAUTE
Best Western Linden Inn
(800) 528-1234, (812) 234-7781
http://www.bestwestern.com
3325 Rte. 41
97 rooms - $60-95
Pets: Small pets welcome
Creature Comforts: CCTV, a/c,
cont. brkfst, sauna, pool, whirlpool

Comfort Suites
(800) 228-5150, (812) 235-1770
http://www.comfortinn.com
501 E. Margaret Ave.
60 rooms - $69-145
Pets: Welcome
Creature Comforts: CCTV,
VCR, a/c, refrig, micro, cont.
brkfst, pool

Drury Inn
(800) Drury Inn, (812) 238-1206
http://www.drury-inn.com
3040 Rte. 41
152 rooms - $55-88
Pets: Under 20 lbs. welcome
Creature Comforts: CCTV, a/c,
refrig, micro, cont. brkfst,
whirlpool, pool

Holiday Inn
(800) HOLIDAY, (812) 232-6081
http://www.holiday-inn.com
3300 Rte. 41
232 rooms - $89-199
Pets: Welcome
Creature Comforts: CCTV, a/c,
refrig, restaurant, hlth club,
whirlpool, pool

Knights Inn
(800) 843-5644, (812) 234-9931
http://www.knightsinn.com
401 E. Margaret Dr.
124 rooms - $45-69
Pets: Welcome w/$25 dep.
Creature Comforts: CCTV, a/c,
kit, pool

Mid Town Motel
(812) 232-0383
400 S. 3rd St.
70 rooms - $35-50
Pets: Welcome
Creature Comforts: CCTV, a/c,
kit

Motel 6
(800) 4-MOTEL6, (812) 238-1586
http://www.motel6.com
1 W. Honey Creek Dr.
117 rooms - $33-49
Pets: Under 30 lbs. welcome
Creature Comforts: CCTV, a/c,
pool

Pear Tree Inn
(800) At-A-Tree, (812) 234-4268
http://www.drury-inn.com
3050 Rte. 41
66 rooms - $40-69
Pets: Under 20 lbs. welcome
Creature Comforts: CCTV, a/c,
cont. brkfst, pool access

Super 8 Motel
(800) 800-8000, (812) 232-4890
http://www.super8.com
3089 S. 1st St.
118 rooms - $45-73
Pets: Welcome
Creature Comforts: CCTV, a/c

Woodbridge Motel
(812) 877-1571
4545 Wabash Ave.
26 rooms - $33-45
Pets: Welcome w/$10 dep.
Creature Comforts: CCTV, a/c,
refrig, micro, pool

VALPARAISO
Super 8 Motel
(800) 800-8000, (219) 464-9840
http://www.super8.com
3005 John Howell Dr.
58 rooms - $45-59
Pets: Welcome
Creature Comforts: CCTV, a/c,
Jacuzzis, cont brkfst, pool

VINCENNES

Best Western Inn
(800) 528-1234, (812) 882-2100
http://www.bestwestern.com
2500 Old Decker Rd.
40 rooms - $45-75
Pets: Welcome
Creature Comforts: CCTV, a/c,
refrig, pool, sauna, hlth club,
whirlpool

Holiday Inn
(800) HOLIDAY, (812) 886-9900
http://www.holiday-inn.com
600 Wheatland Rd.
133 rooms - $65-95
Pets: Small pets welcome
Creature Comforts: CCTV, a/c,
refrig, restaurant, hlth club,
whirlpool, pool

Super 8 Motel
(800) 800-8000, (812) 882-5101
http://www.super8.com
609 Shirlee St.
39 rooms - $45-59
Pets: Welcome w/$25 dep.
Creature Comforts: CCTV, a/c,
Jacuzzis, cont. brkfst, pool

Vincennes Lodge
(812) 882-1282
1411 Willow St.
40 rooms - $33-44
Pets: Welcome w/$25 dep.
Creature Comforts: CCTV, a/c

WARSAW

Comfort Inn
(800) 228-5150, (219) 267-7337
http://www.comfortinn.com
2605 E. Center St.
60 rooms - $70-139
Pets: Welcome
Creature Comforts: CCTV, a/c,
refrig, Jacuzzis, cont. brkfst, pool

Days Inn
(800) DAYS-INN, (219) 269-3031
http://www.daysinn.com
3521 Lake City Hwy.
80 rooms - $59-225
Pets: Welcome w/$10 fee
Creature Comforts: CCTV, a/c,
Jacuzzis, restaurant, cont. brkfst,
pool

Holiday Inn
(800) HOLIDAY, (219) 269-2323
http://www.holiday-inn.com
2519 E. Center St.
155 rooms - $75-99
Pets: Welcome
Creature Comforts: CCTV, a/c,
refrig, restaurant, sauna, hlth club,
whirlpool, pool

Ramada Inn
(800) 2-Ramada, (219) 269-2432
http://www.ramada.com
2519 E. Center St.
155 rooms - $80-155
Pets: Welcome
Creature Comforts: CCTV,
VCR, a/c, refrig, micro, restaurant,
sauna, pool, whirlpool, hlth club,
golf access

White Hill Manor
(219) 269-6933
2513 E. Center St.
8 rooms - $85-130
Pets: Welcome
Creature Comforts: A lovely
4,000 sq. ft. Tudor manor set atop
a hill, CCTV, VCR, a/c, refrig,
micro, Jacuzzi, fireplace, full
brkfst

WEST LAFAYETTE

Holiday Inn
(800) HOLIDAY, (317) 567-2131
http://www.holiday-inn.com
5600 Rte. 43
152 rooms - $60-95
Pets: Welcome
Creature Comforts: CCTV, a/c,
refrig, restaurant, sauna, pool

Travelodge
(800) 578-7878, (765) 743-9661
http://www.travelodge.com
200 Brown St.
45 rooms - $45-75
Pets: Welcome
Creature Comforts: CCTV, a/c,
pool, hlth club access

Iowa

ADAIR
Best Western Jesse James
(800) 528-1234, (515) 742-5251
http://www.bestwestern.com
Route 80
32 rooms - $40-59
Pets: Small pets welcome
Creature Comforts: CCTV, a/c,
cont. brkfst, whirlpool

Budget Inn
(515) 742-5553
Route 80
33 rooms - $33-48
Pets: Welcome
Creature Comforts: CCTV, a/c

ALGONA
IMA Burr Oak Motel
(800) 341-8000, (515) 295-7213
http://www.imalodging.com
Route 169
42 rooms - $33-50
Pets: Welcome in economy rooms
Creature Comforts: CCTV, a/c

ALBIA
Indian Hills Inn
(515) 932-7181
Route 1
52 rooms - $35-59
Pets: Welcome w/$7 fee
Creature Comforts: CCTV, a/c,
micro, restaurant, pool, sauna,
whirlpool

AMANA
Comfort Inn
(800) 228-5150, (319) 668-2700
http://www.comfortinn.com
Route 80
61 rooms - $45-94
Pets: Welcome
Creature Comforts: CCTV, a/c,
cont. brkfst, whirlpool, pool

Holiday Inn
(800) HOLIDAY, (319) 668-1175
http://www.holiday-inn.com
Route 80
156 rooms - $69-99
Pets: Welcome
Creature Comforts: CCTV, a/c,
refrig, micro, restaurant, cont.
brkfst, whirlpool, pool

AMES
Baymont Inns
(877)BAYMONT, (515) 296-2500
http://www.baymontinns.com
2500 Elwood Dr.
90 rooms - $59-139
Pets: Welcome in kennels
Creature Comforts: CCTV, a/c,
refrig, Jacuzzis, cont. brkfst, pool

Best Western Starlite Village
(800) 528-1234, (515) 232-9260
http://www.bestwestern.com
2601 E. 13th St.
130 rooms - $55-83
Pets: Small pets welcome
Creature Comforts: CCTV,
VCR, a/c, cont. brkfst, sauna, hlth
club, whirlpool, pool

Heartland Inn
(800) 334-3277, (515) 233-6060
Rtes. 30 & 35
87 rooms - $50-175
Pets: In smoking rooms w/$10 fee
Creature Comforts: CCTV, a/c,
refrig, micro, Jacuzzi, cont. brkfst,
sauna, pool

Holiday Inn
(800) HOLIDAY, (515) 292-8600
http://www.holiday-inn.com
Route 30
189 rooms - $90-139
Pets: Welcome in smoking rooms
Creature Comforts: CCTV, a/c,
refrig, restaurant, pool

Howard Johnson Express
(800) I-Go-Hojo, (515) 232-8363
http://www.hojo.com
1709 S. Duff Ave.
73 rooms - $45-69
Pets: Welcome
Creature Comforts: CCTV, a/c,
cont. brkfst, pool

Ramada Inn
(800) 2-Ramada, (515) 232-3410
http://www.ramada.com
1206 S. Duff Rd.
102 rooms - $60-165
Pets: Welcome w/$25 dep.
Creature Comforts: CCTV, a/c,
Jacuzzis, restaurant, pool

Thriftlodge
(800) 525-9055, (515) 233-4444
http://www.travelodge.com
229 S. Duff Ave.
45 rooms - $49-65
Pets: Welcome
Creature Comforts: CCTV, a/c,
cont. brkfst, pool

University Inn
(515) 232-0280
316 S. Duff Rd.
118 rooms - $49-88
Pets: Welcome w/$10 fee
Creature Comforts: CCTV, a/c,
refrig, micro, Jacuzzi, restaurant,
cont. brkfst, pool, hlth clb access

ANKENY
Best Western Starlite Inn
(800) 528-1234, (515) 964-1717
http://www.bestwestern.com
133 SE Delaware Rd.
116 rooms - $55-75
Pets: Small pets w/$3 fee
Creature Comforts: CCTV,
VCR, a/c, Jacuzzis, restaurant,
cont. brkfst, hlth club, pool

Days Inn
(800) DAYS-INN, (515) 965-1995
http://www.daysinn.com
103 NE Delaware Rd.
54 rooms - $45-66
Pets: Welcome w/$5 fee
Creature Comforts: CCTV, a/c,
restaurant

Super 8 Motel
(800) 800-8000, (515) 964-4503
http://www.super8.com
206 SE Delaware Rd.
53 rooms - $40-59
Pets: Welcome w/permission
Creature Comforts: CCTV, a/c,
Jacuzzis, cont. brkfst, whirlpool,
pool

ARNOLDS PARK
Fillenwarth Beach Cottages
(712) 332-5646
http://www.fillenwarthbeach.com
87 Lake Shore Dr.
93 rooms - $475-1,600/wk
Pets: Welcome w/$25 dep.
Creature Comforts: A fun
family-oriented resort w/a host of
amenities, CCTV, VCR, a/c, kit,
pool, tennis, basketball, lawn
sports, amusement park, lake
beach/games/boats, cocktail/
adventure cruises

ATLANTIC
Econo Lodge
(800) 55-ECONO, (712) 243-4067
http://www.econolodge.com
Rtes. 80 & 71
50 rooms - $39-55
Pets: Welcome
Creature Comforts: CCTV, a/c,
pool

AVOCA
Capri Motel
(712) 343-6301
110 E. Pershing St.
25 rooms - $38-59
Pets: Welcome w/$5 fee
Creature Comforts: CCTV, a/c

BETTENDORF
Heartland Inn
(800) 334-3277, (319) 355-6336
815 Golden Valley Dr.
86 rooms - $69-169
Pets: Welcome w/$25 dep.
Creature Comforts: CCTV, a/c,
refrig, Jacuzzis, cont. brkfst, pool

Jumer's Castle Lodge
(800) 285-8637, (319) 359-7141
http://www.jumers.com
900 Spruce Hills Rd.
212 rooms - $80-155
Pets: Welcome w/$25 dep.
Creature Comforts: German-
style castle, four poster beds,
tapestries, custom woodworking,
CCTV, a/c, refrig, micro,
fireplace, Jacuzzis, restaurant, full
brkfst, pool, saunas, hlth club,
whirlpool, lawn games, tennis

Twin Bridge Motor Inn
(319) 355-6451
221 - 15th St.
70 rooms - $39-73
Pets: Welcome w/$25 dep.
Creature Comforts: CCTV, a/c,
refrig, restaurant, cont. brkfst,
pool, whirlpool

BLOOMFIELD HILLS
Southfork Inn
(800) 926-2860, (515) 664-1063
Rtes. 2 & 63
23 rooms - $39-49
Pets: Welcome w/$5 fee
Creature Comforts: CCTV, a/c,
restaurant

BOONE
Super 8 Motel
(800) 800-8000, (515) 432-8890
http://www.super8.com
1715 S. Story St.
56 rooms - $45-65
Pets: Welcome w/permission
Creature Comforts: CCTV, a/c,
cont. brkfst

BURLINGTON
Best Western Pzazz Inn
(800) 528-1234, (319) 753-2223
http://www.bestwestern.com
3001 Winegard Dr.
151 rooms - $60-125
Pets: Welcome
Creature Comforts: CCTV,
VCR, a/c, refrig, micro, Jacuzzis,
restaurant, cont. brkfst, hlth club,
pool

Comfort Inn
(800) 228-5150, (319) 753-0000
http://www.comfortinn.com
3051 Kirkwood Rd.
52 rooms - $39-76
Pets: Small pets welcome
Creature Comforts: CCTV, a/c,
refrig, micro, cont. brkfst, pool

Days Inn
(800) DAYS-INN, (319) 752-1111
http://www.daysinn.com
1601 N. Roosevelt Ave.
44 rooms - $40-68
Pets: Welcome w/$5 fee
Creature Comforts: CCTV, a/c,
cont. brkfst

Ramada Inn
(800) 2-Ramada, (319) 754-5781
http://www.ramada.com
2759 Mt. Pleasant St.
150 rooms - $55-109
Pets: Welcome w/$10 dep.
Creature Comforts: CCTV, a/c,
Jacuzzis, restaurant, sauna,
whirlpool, pool

CARROLL
Best Western Inn
(800) 528-1234, (712) 792-9274
http://www.bestwestern.com
Route 30
33 rooms - $39-139
Pets: Welcome
Creature Comforts: CCTV, a/c,
refrig, micro, cont. brkfst, hlth
club

71-30 Motel
(712) 792-1100
Rtes. 71 & 30
28 rooms - $39-55
Pets: Welcome w/$ fee
Creature Comforts: CCTV, a/c,
refrig, pool

Super 8 Motel
(800) 800-8000, (712) 792-4753
http://www.super8.com
Route 71
30 rooms - $40-59
Pets: Welcome w/permission
Creature Comforts: CCTV, a/c,
cont. brkfst

CEDAR FALLS
Blackhawk Motor Inn
(319) 271-1161
122 Washington St.
14 rooms - $40-54
Pets: Welcome
Creature Comforts: CCTV, a/c, kit

Econo Lodge
(800) 55-ECONO, (319) 277-6931
http://www.econolodge.com
4117 University Ave.
80 rooms - $39-79
Pets: Welcome
Creature Comforts: CCTV, a/c, pool

Holiday Inn
(800) HOLIDAY, (319) 277-2230
http://www.holiday-inn.com
5826 University Ave.
178 rooms - $69-99
Pets: Welcome
Creature Comforts: CCTV, a/c, refrig, Jacuzzis, restaurant, pool

University Inn
(319) 277-1412
4711 University Ave.
50 rooms - $38-69
Pets: Welcome w/$20 dep.
Creature Comforts: CCTV, a/c, Jacuzzis

CEDAR RAPIDS
Collins Plaza Hotel
(319) 393-6600
1200 Collins Rd. NE
222 rooms - $99-155
Pets: Small pets w/$50 fee
Creature Comforts: CCTV, a/c, refrig, micro, Jacuzzi, restaurant, pool, hlth clb, sauna, whirlpool

Comfort Inn North
(800) 228-5150, (319) 393-8247
http://www.comfortinn.com
5055 Rockwell Dr.
59 rooms - $55-95
Pets: Small pets welcome
Creature Comforts: CCTV, a/c, cont. brkfst

Comfort Inn South
(800) 228-5150, (319) 363-7934
http://www.comfortinn.com
390 - 33rd Ave. SW
60 rooms - $49-94
Pets: Small pets welcome
Creature Comforts: CCTV, a/c, cont. brkfst

Days Inn
(800) DAYS-INN, (319) 365-4339
http://www.daysinn.com
3245 Southgate Place SW
40 rooms - $50-75
Pets: Welcome
Creature Comforts: CCTV, a/c, cont. brkfst, whirlpool, pool

Days Inn
(800) DAYS-INN, (319) 365-9441
http://www.daysinn.com
2501 Williams Blvd. SW
184 rooms - $59-89
Pets: Welcome w/$5 fee
Creature Comforts: CCTV, a/c, restaurant, cont. brkfst, whirlpool, sauna, hlth club, pool

Econo Lodge
(800) 55-ECONO, (319) 363-8888
http://www.econolodge.com
622 - 33rd Ave. SW
50 rooms - $49-139
Pets: Welcome
Creature Comforts: CCTV, a/c, Jacuzzis, refrig, micro, pool

Exel Inn
(800) 367-3935, (319) 366-2475
616 - 33rd Ave. SW
95 rooms - $55-229
Pets: Small pets welcome
Creature Comforts: CCTV, a/c, Jacuzzis, cont. brkfst.

Howard Johnson Express
(800) I-Go-Hojo, (319) 363-9999
http://www.hojo.com
3233 Southridge Dr. SW
42 rooms - $49-65
Pets: Welcome
Creature Comforts: CCTV, a/c, Jacuzzis, cont. brkfst, pool

Howard Johnson Express
(800) I-Go-Hojo, (800) 446-4655
http://www.hojo.com
Wright Brothers Blvd.
74 rooms - $55-95
Pets: Welcome
Creature Comforts: CCTV, a/c, Jacuzzis, cont. brkfst, hlth club, whirlpool, pool

Red Roof Inn
(800) The-Roof, (319) 366-7523
http://www.redroof.com
3325 Southgate Ct. SW
109 rooms - $50-75
Pets: Small pets welcome
Creature Comforts: CCTV, a/c

Sheraton Four Points Hotel
(800) 325-3535, (319) 366-8671
http://www.sheraton.com
525 - 33rd Ave. SW
158 rooms - $79-198
Pets: Small pets w/$50 dep.
Creature Comforts: CCTV, a/c, refrig, Jacuzzis, restaurant, pool, sauna, whirlpool

Super 8 Motel
(800) 800-8000, (319) 363-1755
http://www.super8.com
400 - 33rd Ave. SW
62 rooms - $40-59
Pets: Welcome w/permission
Creature Comforts: CCTV, a/c, cont. brkfst

Super 8 Motel
(800) 800-8000, (319) 362-6002
http://www.super8.com
720 - 33rd Ave. SW
61 rooms - $45-59
Pets: Welcome w/permission.
Creature Comforts: CCTV, a/c, Jacuzzis, cont. brkfst

CHARITON
IMA Royal Rest Motel
(800) 341-8000, (515) 774-5961
http://www.imalodging.com
Route 34
28 rooms - $39-82
Pets: Small pets welcome
Creature Comforts: CCTV, a/c, refrig, cont. brkfst

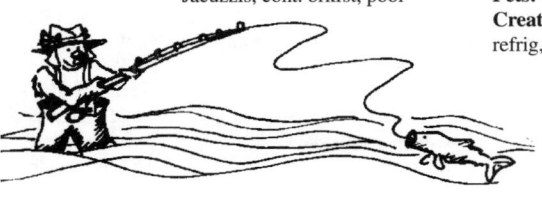

CHARLES CITY
IMA Hartwood Inn
(800) 341-8000, (515) 228-4352
http://www.imalodging.com
1312 Gilbert St.
35 rooms - $39-74
Pets: Small pets in smoking rms.
Creature Comforts: CCTV, a/c, refrig, micro, cont. brkfst, pool

CHEROKEE
Best Western Inn
(800) 528-1234, (712) 225-5701
http://www.bestwestern.com
1401 N. 2nd St.
55 rooms - $55-79
Pets: Small pets welcome
Creature Comforts: CCTV, VCR, a/c, restaurant, cont. brkfst, hlth club, pool

Super 8 Motel
(800) 800-8000, (712) 225-4278
http://www.super8.com
1400 N. Second St.
34 rooms - $45-59
Pets: Welcome w/permission.
Creature Comforts: CCTV, a/c, cont. brkfst, sauna, hlth club

CLEAR LAKE
Best Western Holiday Inn
(800) 528-1234, (515) 357-5253
http://www.bestwestern.com
Rtes. 18 & 35
117 rooms - $55-122
Pets: Welcome
Creature Comforts: CCTV, a/c, restaurant, cont. brkfst, whirlpool, sauna, pool

Budget Inn
(515) 357-8700
1306 N. 25th St.
60 rooms - $44-59
Pets: Welcome
Creature Comforts: CCTV, a/c, cont. brkfst, pool

Heartland Inn
(800) 334-3277, (515) 357-5123
1603 S. Shore Dr.
20 rooms - $69-169
Pets: Welcome w/$10 fee
Creature Comforts: CCTV, a/c, refrig, cont. brkfst

Lake Country Inn
(515) 357-2184
518 Rte. 18
28 rooms - $30-53
Pets: Welcome
Creature Comforts: CCTV, a/c, kit

Super 8 Motel
(800) 800-8000, (515) 357-7521
http://www.super8.com
Route 35
60 rooms - $40-59
Pets: Welcome w/permission.
Creature Comforts: CCTV, a/c, cont. brkfst

CLINTON
Best Western Frontier Inn
(800) 528-1234, (319) 242-7112
http://www.bestwestern.com
2300 Lincolnway
117 rooms - $50-89
Pets: Small pets w/$3 fee
Creature Comforts: CCTV, a/c, refrig, micro, restaurant, cont. brkfst, hlth club, pool

Ramada Inn
(800) 2-Ramada, (319) 243-8841
http://www.ramada.com
1522 Lincolnway
102 rooms - $65-125
Pets: Welcome w/$10 dep.
Creature Comforts: CCTV, VCR, a/c, kit, restaurant, pool

Travelodge
(800) 578-7878, (319) 243-4730
http://www.travelodge.com
302 - 6th Ave. So.
50 rooms - $45-65
Pets: Welcome
Creature Comforts: CCTV, a/c, refrig, restaurant, pool

CLIVE
Baymont Inns
(877)BAYMONT, (515) 221-9200
http://www.baymontinns.com
1390 NW 188th St.
105 rooms - $49-85
Pets: Small pets welcome
Creature Comforts: CCTV, a/c, refrig, pool

Residence Inn
(800) 331-3131, (515) 223-7700
http://www.residenceinn.com
11428 Forest Ave.
112 rooms - $75-159
Pets: Welcome w/CC dep.
Creature Comforts: CCTV, a/c, kit, cont. brkfst, hlth club, pool

COLUMBUS JUNCTION
Columbus Motel
(319) 728-8080
Route 92
25 rooms - $35-59
Pets: Welcome w/$4 fee
Creature Comforts: CCTV, a/c, kit

COOK
Vermillion Dam Lodge
(800) 325-5780
http://www.vdl.com
RR 667, Box 1105
15 cottages - $795-1,200/wk
Pets: Welcome w/$75 fee/wk
Creature Comforts: Knotty pine cottages, fireplaces, kit, pool, lawn sports, volleyball, riveside/lake/boating/beach

CORALVILLE
Best Western Canterbury Inn
(800) 528-1234, (319) 351-0400
http://www.bestwestern.com
704 - 1st Ave.
109 rooms - $60-199
Pets: Small pets welcome
Creature Comforts: CCTV, VCR, a/c, Jacuzzis, fireplaces, restaurant, cont. brkfst, sauna, whirlpools, pool

Best Western Westfield Inn
(800) 528-1234, (319) 354-7770
http://www.bestwestern.com
1895 - 27th Ave..
155 rooms - $59-99
Pets: Small pets welcome
Creature Comforts: CCTV, a/c, restaurant, cont. brkfst, hlth club, whirlpool, pool

Comfort Inn
(800) 228-5150, (319) 351-8144
http://www.comfortinn.com
209 W. 9th St.
56 rooms - $59-109
Pets: Small pets welcome
Creature Comforts: CCTV, a/c, Jacuzzis, cont. brkfst, pool

Heartland Inn
(800) 334-3277, (319) 351-8132
87 - 2nd St.
174 rooms - $60-245
Pets: In smoking rooms w/$10 fee
Creature Comforts: CCTV, a/c, refrig, Jacuzzis, fireplaces, cont. brkfst, pool

Motel 6
(800) 4-MOTEL6, (319) 354-0030
http://www.motel6.com
810 - 1st Ave.
103 rooms - $34-54
Pets: Under 30 Lbs. welcome
Creature Comforts: CCTV, a/c, pool

COUNCIL BLUFFS
Best Western Crossroads
(800) 528-1234, (712) 322-3150
http://www.bestwestern.com
2216 - 27th Ave.
107 rooms - $60-85
Pets: Small pets w/$25 dep.
Creature Comforts: CCTV, a/c, restaurant, cont. brkfst, sauna, whirlpool, hlth club, pool

Days Inn
(800) DAYS-INN, (712) 323-2200
http://www.daysinn.com
3619 - 9th Ave.
40 rooms - $59-85
Pets: Welcome w/$10 fee
Creature Comforts: CCTV, a/c, cont. brkfst, sauna, hlth club, pool

Econo Lodge
(800) 55-ECONO, (712) 366-9699
http://www.econolodge.com
3208 S. 7th St.
62 rooms - $45-109
Pets: Welcome w/$20 dep.
Creature Comforts: CCTV, a/c, hlth club, whirlpools

Heartland Inn
(800) 334-3277, (712) 322-8400
1000 Woodbury Ave.
173 rooms - $60-229
Pets: Welcome w/$8 fee
Creature Comforts: CCTV, a/c, kit, Jacuzzi, cont. brkfst

Motel 6
(800) 4-MOTEL6, (712) 366-2405
http://www.motel6.com
3032 S. Expwy.
84 rooms - $39-55
Pets: Under 30 lbs. welcome
Creature Comforts: CCTV, a/c, pool

Ramada Inn
(800) 2-Ramada, (712) 328-3881
http://www.ramada.com
2325 Ave. N
148 rooms - $60-125
Pets: Welcome w/$25 dep.
Creature Comforts: CCTV, a/c, refrig, restaurant, pool

Super 8 Motel
(800) 800-8000, (712) 322-2888
http://www.super8.com
2712 S. 24th St.
87 rooms - $40-59
Pets: Welcome w/permission.
Creature Comforts: CCTV, a/c, cont. brkfst

Terra Jane Country Inn
(712) 322-4200
http://www.top.net/terrajane
24814 Greenview Rd.
5 rooms - $90-150
Pets: Small pets welcome
Creature Comforts: Historic Victorian w/gingerbread accents, brimming with charm, CCTV, VCR, a/c, fireplace, refrig, brass beds, Jacuzzi, full brkfst, lawn games, volleyball

CRESCO
Cresco Motel
(319) 547-2240
620 - 2nd Ave. SE
22 rooms - $35-73
Pets: Welcome w/$10 fee
Creature Comforts: CCTV, a/c

DAVENPORT
Best Western Steeplegate Inn
(800) 528-1234, (319) 386-6900
http://www.bestwestern.com
100 W. 76th St.
121 rooms - $75-159
Pets: Small pets w/$3 fee
Creature Comforts: CCTV, VCR, a/c, refrig, micro, Jacuzzis, hlth club, pool

Comfort Inn
(800) 228-5150, (319) 391-8222
http://www.comfortinn.com
7222 NW Blvd.
89 rooms - $49-155
Pets: Small pets welcome
Creature Comforts: CCTV, a/c, Jacuzzis, restaurant, cont. brkfst, hlth club

Country Inns
(800) 456-4000, (319) 388-6444
http://www.countryinns.com
140 E. 55th St.
65 rooms - $49-105
Pets: Under "knee-height" are gladly welcomed
Creature Comforts: CCTV, a/c, refrig, fireplace, cont. brkfst, pool

Days Inn
(800) DAYS-INN, (319) 355-1190
http://www.daysinn.com
3202 E. Kimberly Rd.
65 rooms - $45-109
Pets: Welcome w/$5 fee
Creature Comforts: CCTV, a/c, Jacuzzis, cont. brkfst, whirlpool, pool

Econo Lodge
(800) 55-ECONO, (319) 355-6471
http://www.econolodge.com
Rtes. 80 & 71
65 rooms - $49-75
Pets: Small pets welcome
Creature Comforts: CCTV, a/c, refrig, cont. brkfst, pool

Exel Inn
(800) 367-3935, (319) 386-6350
http://www.excelinns.com
6310 N. Brady St.
102 rooms - $45-99
Pets: Small pets in smoking rms.
Creature Comforts: CCTV, a/c, cont. brkfst.

Hampton Inn
(800) Hampton, (319) 359-3921
http://www.hamptoninn.com
3330 E. Kimberly Rd.
133 rooms - $60-165
Pets: Welcome
Creature Comforts: CCTV, a/c, kit, pool

Heartland Inn
(800) 334-3277, (319) 386-8336
6605 N. Brady St.
85 rooms - $50-149
Pets: Welcome in smoking rooms
Creature Comforts: CCTV, a/c, cont. brkfst, pool

Motel 6
(800) 4-MOTEL6, (319) 391-8997
http://www.motel6.com
6111 N. Brady St.
98 rooms - $34-58
Pets: Under 30 lbs. welcome
Creature Comforts: CCTV, a/c, pool

Residence Inn
(800) 331-3131, (319) 391-8877
http://www.residenceinn.com
120 E. 55th St.
79 rooms - $80-159
Pets: $100 fee, $10 daily fee
Creature Comforts: CCTV, a/c, kit, cont. brkfst, hlth club, whirlpool, pool

Super 8 Motel
(800) 800-8000, (319) 388-9810
http://www.super8.com
410 E. 65th St.
61 rooms - $40-59
Pets: Welcome w/permission.
Creature Comforts: CCTV, a/c, cont. brkfst

DECORAH
Super 8 Motel
(800) 800-8000, (319) 382-8771
http://www.super8.com
Rtes. 9 & 52
60 rooms - $40-59
Pets: Welcome w/permission.
Creature Comforts: CCTV, a/c, refrig, micro, cont. brkfst, hlth club, whirlpool

DENISON
Best Western Inn
(800) 528-1234, (712) 263-2898
http://www.bestwestern.com
502 Boyer Valley Rd.
40 rooms - $38-55
Pets: Small pets welcome
Creature Comforts: CCTV, a/c, cont. brkfst

Days Inn
(800) DAYS-INN, (712) 263-2500
http://www.daysinn.com
315 Chamberlin Dr.
43 rooms - $40-79
Pets: Welcome
Creature Comforts: CCTV, a/c, cont. brkfst, whirlpool, hlth club

DES MOINES
Adventureland Park Inn
(800) 532-1286, (515) 265-7321
Rtes. 80 & 65
130 rooms - $49-95
Pets: Small pets in outside rooms
Creature Comforts: CCTV, a/c, refrig, restaurant, pool

Archer Motel
(515) 265-0368
4965 Hubbell Ave.
29 rooms - $38-55
Pets: Welcome
Creature Comforts: CCTV, a/c, cont. brkfst, pool

Best Western Airport Inn
(800) 528-1234, (515) 287-6464
http://www.bestwestern.com
1810 Army Post Rd.
144 rooms - $55-105
Pets: Small pets w/$50 dep.
Creature Comforts: CCTV, a/c, cont. brkfst, pool

Best Western Bavarian Inn
(800) 528-1234, (515) 265-5611
http://www.bestwestern.com
5220 NE 14th St.
103 rooms - $55-225
Pets: Small pets w/$50 dep.
Creature Comforts: CCTV, a/c, cont. brkfst

Best Western Colonial Inn
(800) 528-1234, (515) 265-7511
http://www.bestwestern.com
5020 NE 14th St.
62 rooms - $42-99
Pets: Welcome
Creature Comforts: CCTV, a/c, cont. brkfst, hlth club

Best Western Starlight Inn
(800) 528-1234, (515) 282-5251
http://www.bestwestern.com
929 - 3rd St.
105 rooms - $59-125
Pets: Small pets welcome
Creature Comforts: CCTV, a/c, kit, cont. brkfst, hlth club, pool, whirlpool

Best Western Walnut Creek Inn
(800) 528-1234, (515) 223-1212
http://www.bestwestern.com
1258 - 8th St.
68 rooms - $55-85
Pets: Small pets welcome
Creature Comforts: CCTV, a/c, cont. brkfst, whirlpool, pool

Budget Host
(800) Bud-Host, (515) 276-5401
http://www.budgethost.com
7625 Hickman Ave.
30 rooms - $35-66
Pets: Small pets w/$5 fee
Creature Comforts: CCTV, a/c, refrig, cont. brkfst

Comfort Inn
(800) 228-5150, (515) 287-3434
http://www.comfortinn.com
5231 Fleur Dr.
55 rooms - $59-110
Pets: Small pets welcome
Creature Comforts: CCTV, a/c, cont. brkfst, pool

Days Inn
(800) DAYS-INN, (515) 265-2541
http://www.daysinn.com
3501 E. 14th St.
100 rooms - $49-75
Pets: Welcome
Creature Comforts: CCTV, a/c, restaurant, cont. brkfst, pool

Fort Des Moines Hotel
(800) 532-1466, (515) 243-1161
http://www.hotelfortdm.com
1000 Walnut St.
235 rooms - $70-279
Pets: Welcome
Creature Comforts: CCTV, a/c,
refrig, restaurant, hlth club, pool

Heartland Inn, Airport
(800) 334-3277, (515) 256-0603
1901 Hackney Ave.
132 rooms - $60-275
Pets: Welcome w/$10 fee
Creature Comforts: CCTV, a/c,
refrig, micro, Jacuzzi, cont. brkfst,
and a pool

Heartland Inn, West
(800) 334-3277, (515) 226-0414
11414 Forest Ave.
88 rooms - $59-225
Pets: Welcome w/$10 fee
Creature Comforts: CCTV, a/c,
refrig, Jacuzzi, cont. brkfst

Hickman Motor Lodge
(515) 276-8591
6500 Hickman Rd.
40 rooms - $43-59
Pets: Welcome
Creature Comforts: CCTV, a/c,
and a kit

Holiday Inn
(800) HOLIDAY, (515) 278-0271
http://www.holiday-inn.com
5000 Merle Hay Rd.
144 rooms - $69-139
Pets: Small pets welcome
Creature Comforts: CCTV, a/c,
refrig, restaurant, pool

Howard Johnson Hotel
(800) I-Go-Hojo, (515) 278-4755
http://www.hojo.com
4800 Merle Hay Rd.
217 rooms - $65-105
Creature Comforts: CCTV, a/c,
restaurant, cont. brkfst, sauna,
whirlpool, pool

Marriott Hotel
(800) 228-9290, (515) 245-5500
http://www.marriott.com
700 Grand Ave.
415 rooms - $75-425
Pets: Welcome
Creature Comforts: An
expansive hotel, CCTV, VCR, a/c,
refrig, restaurants, pool, hlth clb

Motel 6, Airport
(800) 4-MOTEL6, (515) 287-6364
http://www.motel6.com
4817 Fleur Dr.
98 rooms - $34-49
Pets: Under 30 lbs. welcome
Creature Comforts: CCTV, a/c

Motel 6, North
(800) 4-MOTEL6, (515) 266-5456
http://www.motel6.com
4940 NE 14th St.
120 rooms - $34-49
Pets: Under 30 lbs. welcome
Creature Comforts: CCTV, a/c,
pool

Savery Hotel & Spa
(800) 798-2151, (515) 244-2151
401 Locust St.
222 rooms - $79-275
Pets: Small pets w/$50 dep.
Creature Comforts: CCTV, a/c,
refrig, restaurant, whirlpool,
sauna, hlth club, pool

Super 8 Motel
(800) 800-8000, (515) 278-8858
http://www.super8.com
4758 Merle Hay Rd.
152 rooms - $48-75
Pets: Welcome w/$10 dep.
Creature Comforts: CCTV, a/c,
refrig, micro, Jacuzzis, cont. brkfst

Super 8 Motel, Airport
(800) 800-8000, no local tel.
http://www.super8.com
50 Hackley Rd.
63 rooms - $49-75
Pets: Welcome w/$10 fee.
Creature Comforts: CCTV, a/c,
Jacuzzis, cont. brkfst, whirlpool,
pool

DESOTO
Edgetowner Motel
(515) 834-2641
Rte. 80
25 rooms - $39-50
Pets: Small pets welcome
Creature Comforts: CCTV, a/c

DUBUQUE
Best Western Midway Inn
(800) 528-1234, (319) 557-8000
http://www.bestwestern.com
3100 Dodge St.
151 rooms - $70-169
Pets: Small pets welcome
Creature Comforts: CCTV,
VCR, a/c, refrig, Jacuzzis, cont.
brkfst, sauna, hlth club, whirlpool,
pool

Comfort Inn
(800) 228-5150, (319) 556-3006
http://www.comfortinn.com
4055 McDonald Dr.
52 rooms - $60-99
Pets: Small pets welcome
Creature Comforts: CCTV, a/c,
cont. brkfst, pool

Days Inn
(800) DAYS-INN, (319) 583-3297
http://www.daysinn.com
1111 Dodge St.
156 rooms - $49-175
Pets: Welcome
Creature Comforts: CCTV, a/c,
restaurant, cont. brkfst, hlth club,
pool

Heartland Inn
(800) 334-3277, (319) 556-6555
2090 Southpark Ct.
60 rooms - $59-135
Pets: Welcome w/$10 fee
Creature Comforts: CCTV, a/c,
refrig, micros, cont. brkfst, cont.
brkfst

Holiday Inn
(800) HOLIDAY, (319) 556-2000
http://www.holiday-inn.com
450 Main St.
192 rooms - $69-165
Pets: Crated pets welcome
Creature Comforts: CCTV, a/c,
kit, restaurant, Jacuzzis, hlth club,
whirlpool, pool

Motel 6
(800) 4-MOTEL6, (319) 556-0880
http://www.motel6.com
2670 Dodge St.
98 rooms - $34-55
Pets: Under 30 lbs. welcome
Creature Comforts: CCTV, a/c

Richards House
(319) 557-1492
www.the-richards-house.com
1492 Locust Ave.
5 rooms - $45-99
Pets: Small pets welcome
Creature Comforts: An 1883
Victorian brick mansion w/stained
glass windows, intricately carved
woodwork, and period antiques,
CCTV, VCR, a/c, claw foot tubs,
fireplace, refrig, gourmet brkfst,
murder mysteries

Super 8 Motel
(800) 800-8000, (319) 582-8898
http://www.super8.com
2730 Dodge St.
61 rooms - $45-64
Pets: Welcome w/permission.
Creature Comforts: CCTV, a/c,
cont. brkfst

Timmerman's Lodge
(800) 336-3181, (815) 747-3181
http://www.timmermans.com
7777 Timmerman Dr.
75 rooms - $79-144
Pets: Welcome
Creature Comforts: An
expansive resort, CCTV, VCR,
a/c, refrig, restaurant, pool,
whirlpool, sauna, golf, access to
skiing and a casino

DYERSVILLE
Colonial Inn
(319) 875-7194
1110 - 9th St. SE
32 rooms - $39-60
Pets: Welcome w/$5 fee
Creature Comforts: CCTV, a/c

EVANSVILLE
Ramada Inn
(800) 2-Ramada, (319) 235-1111
http://www.ramada.com
450 Evansville Dr.
45 rooms - $49-145
Pets: Welcome w/$15 dep.
Creature Comforts: CCTV, a/c,
refrig, micro, Jacuzzis, restaurant,
whirlpool, pool

FAIRFIELD
Best Western Inn
(800) 528-1234, (515) 472-2200
http://www.bestwestern.com
2200 W. Burlington St.
52 rooms - $60-95
Pets: Small pets welcome
Creature Comforts: CCTV, a/c,
Jacuzzis, restaurant, cont. brkfst,
pool

Dream Motel
(515) 472-4161
Route 34
42 rooms - $35-60
Pets: Welcome w/$5 fee
Creature Comforts: CCTV, a/c

FT. DODGE
Best Western Starlite Inn
(800) 528-1234, (515) 573-7177
http://www.bestwestern.com
1513 - 3rd Ave. NW
52 rooms - $53-145
Pets: Small pets in kennel
Creature Comforts: CCTV, a/c,
refrig, micro, Jacuzzis, restaurant,
cont. brkfst, hlth club, sauna,
whirlpool, pool

Comfort Inn
(800) 228-5150, (515) 573-3731
http://www.comfortinn.com
2938 - 5th Ave.
48 rooms - $55-119
Pets: Small pets welcome
Creature Comforts: CCTV, a/c,
Jacuzzis, cont. brkfst, pool

Holiday Inn
(800) HOLIDAY, (515) 955-3621
http://www.holiday-inn.com
2001 Rte. 169
100 rooms - $55-75
Pets: Welcome in smoking rooms
Creature Comforts: CCTV, a/c,
restaurant, whirlpool, pool

FT. MADISON
Best Western Iowan Inn
(800) 528-1234, (319) 372-7510
http://www.bestwestern.com
Route 61
140 rooms - $60-85
Pets: Small pets welcome
Creature Comforts: CCTV, a/c,
cont. brkfst, sauna, whirlpool, pool

The Madison Motel
(319) 372-7740
3440 Ave. L
20 rooms - $40-59
Pets: Welcome w/$5 fee
Creature Comforts: CCTV, a/c,
refrig

GLENWOOD
Bluff View Motel
(712) 622-8191
Rtes. 29 & 34
28 rooms - $35-44
Pets: Welcome w/$35 dep.
Creature Comforts: CCTV,
VCR, a/c, restaurant

Western Inn
(712) 527-3175
707 S. Locust St..
30 rooms - $39-55
Pets: Welcome
Creature Comforts: CCTV, a/c,
hlth clb access

GRINNELL
Best Western Inn
(800) 528-1234, (515) 236-6116
http://www.bestwestern.com
2210 West St.
38 rooms - $49-85
Pets: Caged cats welcome
Creature Comforts: CCTV,
VCR, a/c, restaurant, cont. brkfst,
sauna, hlth club, whirlpool, pool

Days Inn
(800) DAYS-INN, (515) 236-6710
http://www.daysinn.com
Rtes. 80 & 146
41 rooms - $55-85
Pets: Welcome w/$5 fee
Creature Comforts: CCTV, a/c,
cont. brkfst, pool

Super 8 Motel
(800) 800-8000, (515) 236-7888
http://www.super8.com
Rtes. 80 & 146
53 rooms - $59-79
Pets: Welcome w/permission.
Creature Comforts: CCTV, a/c,
cont. brkfst

HAMPTON
Gold Key Motel
(515) 456-2566
1570 Rte. 65
23 rooms - $29-55
Pets: Welcome
Creature Comforts: CCTV, a/c

HUMBOLDT
Super 8 Motel
(800) 800-8000, (515) 332-1131
http://www.super8.com
Route 3
34 rooms - $45-65
Pets: Welcome w/permission.
Creature Comforts: CCTV, a/c,
cont. brkfst, sauna, hlth club

INDEPENDENCE
Super 8 Motel
(800) 800-8000, (319) 334-7041
http://www.super8.com
2000 - 1st West
39 rooms - $45-59
Pets: Welcome w/permission.
Creature Comforts: CCTV, a/c,
Jacuzzis, cont. brkfst

INDIANOLA
Woods Motel
(515) 961-5311
web site pending
906 S. Jefferson St.
15 rooms - $34-49
Pets: Welcome w/$5 fee
Creature Comforts: CCTV, a/c,
refrig

IOWA CITY
Days Inn
(800) DAYS-INN, (319) 354-4400
http://www.daysinn.com
205 - 2nd St.
49 rooms - $49-65
Pets: Welcome
Creature Comforts: CCTV, a/c,
cont. brkfst

Holiday Inn
(800) HOLIDAY, (319) 337-4058
http://www.holiday-inn.com
210 S. Dubuque St.
235 rooms - $89-175
Pets: Welcome w/$10 fee
Creature Comforts: CCTV, a/c,
refrig, micro, Jacuzzis, restaurant,
sauna, whirlpool, hlth club, pool

JEFFERSON
Redwood Motel
(515) 386-3116
209 E. Rte. 30
25 rooms - $38-49
Pets: Welcome
Creature Comforts: CCTV, a/c

Super 8 Motel
(800) 800-8000, (515) 386-2464
http://www.super8.com
Rtes. 30 & 4
34 rooms - $40-59
Pets: Welcome w/permission.
Creature Comforts: CCTV, a/c,
cont. brkfst, hlth club, sauna

JOHNSTON
Best Inns of America
(800) 237-8466, (515) 270-1111
http://www.bestinns.com
5050 Merle Hay Rd.
90 rooms - $55-85
Pets: Small pets welcome
Creature Comforts: CCTV,
VCR, a/c, refrig, micro, cont.
brkfst, whirlpool, a pool

The Inn & Conference Cent.
(515) 276-5411
5055 Merle Hay Rd.
148 rooms - $48-135
Pets: W/$10 fee & CC dep.
Creature Comforts: CCTV, a/c,
kit, restaurant, pool

KEOKUK
Chief Motel
(319) 524-2565
2701 Main St.
18 rooms - $38-50
Pets: Welcome w/$5 fee
Creature Comforts: CCTV, a/c,
refrig

Econo Lodge
(800) 55-ECONO, (319) 524-3252
http://www.econolodge.com
3764 Main St.
59 rooms - $40-69
Pets: Welcome
Creature Comforts: CCTV, pool

Keokuk Motor Lodge
(800) 252-2256, (319) 524-3252
3764 Main St.
60 rooms - $39-55
Pets: Welcome w/$5 fee
Creature Comforts: CCTV, a/c,
micro, cont. brkfst, pool

LE MARS
Amber Inn Motel
(712) 546-7066
635 - 8th Ave. SW
72 rooms - $39-64
Pets: Welcome
Creature Comforts: CCTV, a/c,
cont. brkfst

MAPLETON
Maple Motel
(712) 882-1271
Rtes. 141 & 175
16 rooms - $39-50
Pets: Welcome
Creature Comforts: CCTV, a/c,
restaurant

MARQUETTE
The Frontier Motel
(319) 873-3497
101 S. 1st St.
20 rooms - $39-95
Pets: Small pets w/$5 fee
Creature Comforts: CCTV, a/c

MARSHALLTOWN
Best Western Thunderbird
(800) 528-1234, (515) 752-3631
http://www.bestwestern.com
2009 S. Center St.
30 rooms - $40-90
Pets: Small pets in kennel
Creature Comforts: CCTV, a/c,
cont. brkfst, pool

Best Western Regency Inn
(800) 528-1234, (515) 752-6321
http://www.bestwestern.com
3303 S. Center St.
105 rooms - $60-195
Pets: Welcome w/$10 fee
Creature Comforts: CCTV, a/c,
restaurant, cont. brkfst, whirlpool,
pool

Comfort Inn
(800) 228-5150, (515) 752-6000
http://www.comfortinn.com
2613 S. Center St.
62 rooms - $50-145
Pets: Small pets welcome
Creature Comforts: CCTV, a/c,
refrig, micro, Jacuzzi, cont. brkfst,
pool

Days Inn
(800) DAYS-INN, (515) 753-7777
http://www.daysinn.com
403 E. Church St.
30 rooms - $55-90
Pets: Welcome w/$10 fee
Creature Comforts: CCTV, a/c,
cont. brkfst

MASON CITY
Days Inn
(800) DAYS-INN, (515) 424-0210
http://www.daysinn.com
2301 - 4th St. SW
57 rooms - $45-80
Pets: Welcome
Creature Comforts: CCTV, a/c,
cont. brkfst, whirlpool, pool, on
the water

Holiday Inn
(800) HOLIDAY, (515) 423-1640
http://www.holiday-inn.com
2101- 4th St. SW
135 rooms - $55-169
Pets: Welcome
Creature Comforts: CCTV, a/c,
refrig, Jacuzzis, pool

Thriftlodge
(800) 525-9055, (515) 424-2910
http://www.travelodge.com
24 - 5th St. SW
47 rooms - $45-65
Pets: Welcome
Creature Comforts: CCTV, a/c,
refrig, cont. brkfst, pool

MISSOURI VALLEY
Days Inn
(800) DAYS-INN, (712) 642-4003
http://www.daysinn.com
1967 Rte. 30
48 rooms - $49-95
Pets: Welcome
Creature Comforts: CCTV, a/c,
cont. brkfst, pool, whirlpool, hlth
club, pool

MONTPELIER
Varner's Caboose B&B
(319) 381-3652
204 E. 2nd St., Box 10
1 room - $65-79
Pets: Welcome
Creature Comforts: Neat old
Rock Island line Caboose set
behind hosts' house, refurbished
w/loads of charm, CCTV, VCR,
a/c, kit, full brkfst

MT. PLEASANT
Heartland Inn
(800) 334-3277, (319) 385-2102
800 N. Grand Ave.
59 rooms - $55-75
Pets: Welcome w/$8 fee
Creature Comforts: CCTV, a/c,
refrig, cont. brkfst, pool

Ramada Inn
(800) 2-Ramada, (319) 385-0571
http://www.ramada.com
1200 E. Baker St.
64 rooms - $50-85
Pets: Welcome w/$10 dep.
Creature Comforts: CCTV, a/c,
refrig, Jacuzzis, pool

NEW Hampton
Southgate Inn
(800) 728-4145, (515) 394-4145
2199 McCloud Rd.
56 rooms - $33-59
Pets: Welcome in economy sectn.
Creature Comforts: CCTV, a/c,
refrig, cont. brkfst

NEWTON
Best Western Inn
(800) 528-1234, (515) 792-4200
http://www.bestwestern.com
Rtes. 80 & 14
115 rooms - $50-92
Pets: Welcome
Creature Comforts: CCTV,
VCR, a/c, restaurant, cont. brkfst,
whirlpool, hlth club, sauna, pool,
putting green

Days Inn
(800) DAYS-INN, (515) 792-2330
http://www.daysinn.com
1605 W. 19th St.
59 rooms - $49-83
Pets: Welcome
Creature Comforts: CCTV, a/c,
cont. brkfst

Ramada Limited
(800) 2-Ramada, (515) 792-8100
http://www.ramada.com
1405 W. W. 19th St.
79 rooms - $45-80
Pets: Welcome w/$10 dep.
Creature Comforts: CCTV, a/c,
cont. brkfst, hlth club

Super 8 Motel
(800) 800-8000, (515) 792-8868
http://www.super8.com
1635 S. 12th Ave. West
43 rooms - $45-59
Pets: Welcome w/permission.
Creature Comforts: CCTV, a/c,
cont. brkfst

Terrace Lodge
(800) 383-7722, (515) 792-7722
Rtes. 80 & 14
60 rooms - $55-65
Pets: Welcome
Creature Comforts: CCTV, a/c,
restaurant, cont. brkfst, pool

OKOBOJI
Country Club Motel
(800) 831-5615, (712) 332-5617
1107 Sanborn Ave.
53 rooms - $45-159
Pets: In smoking rms. w/$10 dep.
Creature Comforts: CCTV, a/c,
kit, Jacuzzis, pool

Village East Resort
(800) 727-4561, (712) 332-2161
http://www.ver.com
1405 Rte. 71
97 rooms - $80-175
Pets: Welcome in smoking rooms
Creature Comforts: CCTV, a/c,
refrig, micro, restaurant, hlth club,
tennis/ racquet courts, sauna, pool,
and a whirlpool

ONAWA
Super 8 Motel
(800) 800-8000, (712) 423-2101
http://www.super8.com
Rtes. 29 & 175
80 rooms - $45-65
Pets: Welcome w/permission.
Creature Comforts: CCTV, a/c,
Jacuzzis, cont. brkfst

OSCEOLA
Best Western Regal
(800) 528-1234, (515) 342-2123
http://www.bestwestern.com
1520 Jeffrey's Dr.
35 rooms - $50-75
Pets: Under 40 lbs. welcome
Creature Comforts: CCTV, a/c,
cont. brkfst

Blue Haven Motel
(800) 333-3180, (515) 342-2115
325 S. Main St.
25 rooms - $39-75
Pets: Welcome
Creature Comforts: CCTV, a/c,
refrig, micro, cont. brkfst

OSKALOOSA
Comfort Inn
(800) 228-5150, (515) 672-0375
http://www.comfortinn.com
2401 A Ave.
46 rooms - $55-165
Pets: Welcome
Creature Comforts: CCTV, a/c,
Jacuzzis, cont. brkfst, whirlpool,
hlth club, pool

Red Carpet Inn
(800) 251-1962, (515) 673-8641
http://www.reservahost.com
2278 Rte. 63
45 rooms - $40-69
Pets: Welcome
Creature Comforts: CCTV, a/c,
refrig, pool

Traveler Budget Inn
(515) 673-8333
1210 A Ave. E
28 rooms - $39-70
Pets: Welcome
Creature Comforts: CCTV, a/c

OTTUMWA
Colonial Motor Inn
(515) 683-1661
1534 Albia Rd.
24 rooms - $30-47
Pets: Welcome w/$10 fee
Creature Comforts: CCTV, a/c

Days Inn
(800) DAYS-INN, (515) 682-8131
http://www.daysinn.com
206 Church St.
135 rooms - $45-75
Pets: Welcome w/$5-25 fee
Creature Comforts: CCTV, a/c,
refrig, micro, restaurant, cont.
brkfst, pool

Heartland Inn
(800) 334-3277, (515) 682-8526
125 W. Joseph Ave.
88 rooms - $50-75
Pets: Welcome w/$10 fee
Creature Comforts: CCTV, a/c,
restaurant, cont. brkfst, whirlpool,
pool

PRINCETON
Woodlands Inn
(800) 257-3177, (319) 289-4661
PO Box 127
5 rooms - $65-125
Pets: Selectively welcomed
Creature Comforts: Charming
B&B on 23 acres, traditional
decor, country antiques and
reproductions, CCTV, a/c, refrig,
fireplace, full brkfst, pool, and a
whirlpool

SHENANDOAH
Tall Corn Motel
(712) 246-1550
Rte. 59 & Sheridan Rd.
92 rooms - $39-60
Pets: Welcome
Creature Comforts: CCTV, a/c,
restaurant, cont. brkfst, pool

SIBLEY
Super 8 Motel
(800) 800-8000, (712) 754-3603
http://www.super8.com
1108 - 2nd Ave.
32 rooms - $45-90
Pets: Welcome w/$6 fee
Creature Comforts: CCTV, a/c,
Jacuzzis, cont. brkfst

SIOUX CENTER
Econo Lodge
(800) 55-ECONO, (712) 722-4000
http://www.econolodge.com
86 - 9th St. Cir. NE
55 rooms - $45-66
Pets: Crated pets welcome
Creature Comforts: CCTV, a/c,
refrig, whirlpool

SIOUX CITY
Baymont Inns
(877)BAYMONT, (712) 233-2302
http://www.baymontinns.com
3101 Singing Hills Rd.
65 rooms - $55-109
Pets: Welcome in kennels
Creature Comforts: CCTV, a/c,
refrig, Jacuzzis, cont. brkfst, pool

Best Western City Centre
(800) 528-1234, (712) 277-1550
http://www.bestwestern.com
130 Nebraska St.
114 rooms - $59-85
Pets: Small pets welcome
Creature Comforts: CCTV, a/c,
cont. brkfst, hlth club, pool

Comfort Inn
(800) 228-5150, (605) 232-3366
http://www.comfortinn.com
115 Streeter Dr.
49 rooms - $45-99
Pets: Small pets welcome
Creature Comforts: CCTV, a/c,
Jacuzzis, cont. brkfst, pool

Elmdale Motel
(712) 277-1012
2200 Rte. 75
14 rooms - $28-46
Pets: Welcome w/$3 fee
Creature Comforts: CCTV, a/c,
refrig, micro

Hilton Suites Hotel
(800) HILTONS, (712) 277-4101
http://www.hilton.com
707 - 4th St.
194 rooms - $105-149
Pets: Small pets welcome
Creature Comforts: CCTV,
VCR, a/c, refrig, restaurant, sauna,
hlth club, pool, whirlpool

Holiday Inn
(800) HOLIDAY, (712) 277-3211
http://www.holiday-inn.com
1401 Zenith Dr.
156 rooms - $75-179
Pets: Welcome
Creature Comforts: CCTV, a/c,
refrig, restaurant, pool

Motel 6
(800) 4-MOTEL6, (712) 277-3131
http://www.motel6.com
6166 Harbor Dr.
71 rooms - $34-55
Pets: Under 30 lbs. welcome
Creature Comforts: TV, a/c, pool

Palmer House
(800) 833-4221, (712) 276-4221
3440 E. Gordon Dr.
65 rooms - $40-55
Pets: Welcome w/$25 fee
Creature Comforts: CCTV, a/c,
cont. brkfst

Riverboat Inn
(800) 238-6146, (712) 277-9400
http://www.riverboatinn.com
701 Gordon Dr.
115 rooms - $60-129
Pets: Welcome w/$50 dep.
Creature Comforts: CCTV, a/c,
refrig, micro, Jacuzzis, restaurant,
pool, sauna, whirlpool

Super 8 Motel
(800) 800-8000, (712) 274-1520
http://www.super8.com
4307 Stone Ave.
60 rooms - $45-60
Pets: Welcome
Creature Comforts: CCTV, a/c,
cont. brkfst

SLOAN
Rodeway Inn
(800) 228-2000, (712) 428-4280
http://www.rodeway.com
1862 Rte. 141
52 rooms - $49-65
Pets: Small pets welcome
Creature Comforts: CCTV, a/c

SPIRIT LAKE
Oaks Motel
(712) 336-2940
1701 Chicago St.
12 rooms - $39-90
Pets: Welcome w/$25 dep.
Creature Comforts: CCTV, a/c,
cont. brkfst

Shamrock Inn
(712) 336-2668
2231 - 18th St.
35 rooms - $40-90
Pets: Small pets welcome
Creature Comforts: CCTV, a/c,
pool

STORY LAKE
Cross Roads Motel
(800) 383-1456, (712) 732-1456
Rtes. 3 & 71
21 rooms - $28-59
Pets: Welcome
Creature Comforts: CCTV, a/c,
refrig

Economy Inn
(712) 732-2342
1316 N. Lake Ave.
36 rooms - $32-49
Pets: Small pets w/$3 fee
Creature Comforts: CCTV, a/c

STORY CITY
Super 8 Motel
(800) 800-8000, (515) 733-5281
http://www.super8.com
515 Factory Outlet Dr.
42 rooms - $40-65
Pets: Welcome w/$10 dep..
Creature Comforts: CCTV, a/c,
cont. brkfst

Viking Motor Inn
(800) 233-4306, (515) 733-4306
Route 35
32 rooms - $45-73
Pets: Small pets welcome
Creature Comforts: CCTV, a/c,
refrig, micro, Jacuzzis, pool

STUART
Super 8 Motel
(800) 800-8000, (515) 523-2888
http://www.super8.com
Route 80
49 rooms - $45-63
Pets: Welcome w/permission.
Creature Comforts: CCTV, a/c,
cont. brkfst

TOLEDO
Super 8 Motel
(800) 800-8000, (515) 484-5888
http://www.super8.com
Route 30
49 rooms - $40-85
Pets: Welcome w/permission.
Creature Comforts: CCTV, a/c,
Jacuzzis, cont. brkfst, whirlpool

URBANDALE
Comfort Inn
(800) 228-5150, (515) 270-1037
http://www.comfortinn.com
5900 Sutton Dr.
61 rooms - $55-95
Pets: Small pets welcome
Creature Comforts: CCTV, a/c,
cont. brkfst, pool

Sleep Inn
(800) Sleep-Inn, (515) 270-2424
http://www.sleepinn.com
11211 Hickman Rd.
80 rooms - $55-120
Pets: Small pets welcome
Creature Comforts: CCTV, a/c,
cont. brkfst, pool

WALCOTT
Super 8 Motel
(800) 800-8000, (319) 284-5083
http://www.super8.com
Route 80
60 rooms - $45-59
Pets: Welcome w/$5 fee
Creature Comforts: CCTV, a/c,
cont. brkfst

WALNUT
Super 8 Motel
(800) 800-8000, (712) 784-2221
http://www.super8.com
Route 80
51 rooms - $48-75
Pets: Welcome w/permission.
Creature Comforts: CCTV, a/c,
Jacuzzis, cont. brkfst, pool

Walnut Creek Inn
(800) 711-5409, (712) 784-2233
33246 Antique City Dr.
32 rooms - $42-69
Pets: Welcome w/CC dep.
Creature Comforts: CCTV, a/c,
refrig

WASHINGTON
Super 8 Motel
(800) 800-8000, (319) 653-6621
http://www.super8.com
119 Westview Dr.
56 rooms - $48-69
Pets: Welcome w/$25 fee
Creature Comforts: CCTV, a/c,
cont. brkfst

WATERLOO
Best Western Starlite
(800) 528-1234, (319) 235-0321
http://www.bestwestern.com
214 Washington St.
218 rooms - $55-75
Pets: Welcome w/$5 fee
Creature Comforts: CCTV, a/c,
cont. brkfst, sauna, whirlpool, pool

Comfort Inn
(800) 228-5150, (319) 234-7411
http://www.comfortinn.com
1945 LaPorte Rd.
56 rooms - $55-95
Pets: Small pets welcome
Creature Comforts: CCTV, a/c,
cont. brkfst, pool

Days Inn
(800) DAYS-INN, (319) 233-9191
http://www.daysinn.com
2141 LaPorte Rd.
51 rooms - $50-109
Pets: Welcome
Creature Comforts: CCTV, a/c,
kit, cont. brkfst, whirlpool, hlth
club, pool

Exel Inn
(800) 367-3935, (319) 235-2165
http://www.excelinns.com
3350 University Ave.
105 rooms - $40-139
Pets: Small pets in smokng rms
Creature Comforts: CCTV, a/c,
Jacuzzi, cont. brkfst.

Heartland Inn
(800) 334-3277, (319) 235-4461
1809 La Porte Rd.
115 rooms - $59-145
Pets: Welcome w/$10 fee
Creature Comforts: CCTV, a/c,
kit, fireplace, Jacuzzi, cont. brkfst

Heartland Inn
(800) 334-3277, (319) 232-7467
3052 Marnie Ave.
55 rooms - $55-145
Pets: Welcome w/$10 fee
Creature Comforts: CCTV, a/c,
Jacuzzis, cont. brkfst, pool

Holiday Inn
(800) HOLIDAY, (319) 233-7560
http://www.holiday-inn.com
205 W. 4th St.
229 rooms - $85-225
Pets: Welcome
Creature Comforts: CCTV, a/c,
refrig, Jacuzzis, restaurant,
whirlpool, hlth club access, pool

Super 8 Motel
(800) 800-8000, (319) 233-1800
http://www.super8.com
1825 LaPorte Rd.
62 rooms - $50-75
Pets: Welcome
Creature Comforts: CCTV, a/c,
cont. brkfst

WAVERLY
Amerihost Inn
(800) 434-5800, (319) 352-0399
http://www.amerihost.com
404 - 29th Ave. SW
60 rooms - $60-150
Pets: Small pets w/$50 dep.
Creature Comforts: CCTV, a/c,
refrig, micro, Jacuzzis, pool, hlth
clb, sauna, whirlpool

Best Western Red Fox
(800) 528-1234, (319) 352-5330
http://www.bestwestern.com
Route 3
127 rooms - $65-159
Pets: Small pets welcome
Creature Comforts: CCTV, a/c,
refrig, micro, Jacuzzis, restaurants,
cont. brkfst, whirlpools, tennis,
sport courts, pool

WEBSTER CITY
Super 8 Motel
(800) 800-8000, (515) 832-2000
http://www.super8.com
305 Close Dr.
44 rooms - $48-59
Pets: Welcome w/permission
Creature Comforts: CCTV, a/c,
cont. brkfst, pool

WEST BEND
West Bend Motel
(515) 887-3611
13 - 4th Ave.
18 rooms - $25-45
Pets: Welcome
Creature Comforts: CCTV, a/c

WEST BRANCH
Presidential Motor Inn
(319) 643-2526
711 S. Downey St.
38 rooms - $40-50
Pets: Welcome w/$5-10 fee
Creature Comforts: CCTV, a/c

WEST LIBERTY
Econo Lodge
(800) 55-ECONO, (319) 627-2171
http://www.econolodge.com
1943 Garfield Ave.
37 rooms - $39-55
Pets: Welcome
Creature Comforts: CCTV, a/c,
restaurant, cont. brkfst, pool

WEST UNION
Super 8 Motel
(800) 800-8000, (319) 422-3140
http://www.super8.com
Route 150
39 rooms - $45-65
Pets: Welcome w/$25 dep.
Creature Comforts: CCTV, a/c,
kit, cont. brkfst

WILLIAMS
Best Western Norseman
(800) 528-1234, (515) 854-2281
http://www.bestwestern.com
Route 35
33 rooms - $43-70
Pets: Small pets welcome
Creature Comforts: CCTV, a/c,
cont. brkfst

WILLIAMSBURG
Best Western Quiet House
(800) 528-1234, (319) 668-9777
http://www.bestwestern.com
1708 N. Highland St.
33 rooms - $69-155
Pets: Welcome w/$15 fee
Creature Comforts: CCTV, a/c,
Jacuzzis, cont. brkfst, hlth club,
pool

Crest Motel
(319) 668-1522
340 W. Evans St.
30 rooms - $33-59
Pets: Welcome w/$5 fee
Creature Comforts: CCTV, a/c

Days Inn
(800) DAYS-INN, (319) 688-2097
http://www.daysinn.com
2214 U Ave.
111 rooms - $39-75
Pets: Welcome
Creature Comforts: CCTV, a/c,
cont. brkfst, whirlpool, sauna,
pool, put. green

Ramada Limited
(800) 2-Ramada, (319) 668-1000
http://www.ramada.com
220 Hawkeye Dr.
42 rooms - $55-145
Pets: In smoking rms. w/$25 dep.
Creature Comforts: CCTV, a/c,
kit

Super 8 Motel
(800) 800-8000, (319) 668-9718
http://www.super8.com
1708 N. Highland St.
20 rooms - $55-89
Pets: Welcome w/$15 fee
Creature Comforts: CCTV, a/c,
cont. brkfst

Super 8 Motel
(800) 800-8000, (319) 668-2800
http://www.super8.com
2228 U. Ave.
63 rooms - $40-59
Pets: Welcome w/permission.
Creature Comforts: CCTV, a/c,
cont. brkfst

WINTERSET
Village View
(800) 862-1218, (515) 462-1218
711 E. Rte. 92
16 rooms - $35-58
Pets: Welcome w/$5 fee
Creature Comforts: CCTV,
VCR, a/c

Kansas

ABILENE
Balfour's House B&B
(785) 263-4262
940 - 1900 Ave.
2 rooms - $45-69
Pets: Welcome
Creature Comforts: A host of Southwestern accents, CCTV, a/c, refrig, fireplace, cont. brkfst, pool, whirlpool

Best Western Pride Inn
(800) 528-1234, (785) 263-2800
http://www.bestwestern.com
1709 N. Buckeye Ave.
80 rooms - $49-80
Pets: Small pets w/$20 dep.
Creature Comforts: CCTV, a/c, restaurant, cont. brkfst, hlth club, pool

Best Western President's Inn
(800) 528-1234, (785) 263-2050
http://www.bestwestern.com
2210 N. Buckeye Ave.
64 rooms - $40-75
Pets: Small pets welcome
Creature Comforts: CCTV, a/c, refrig, restaurant, hlth club, pool

Diamond Motel
(785) 263-2360
1407 NW 3rd St.
30 rooms - $28-58
Pets: Small pets w/$5 fee
Creature Comforts: CCTV, a/c, refrig

Super 8 Motel
(800) 800-8000, (785) 359-2388
http://www.super8.com
202 Marketview Dr.
61 rooms - $45-75
Pets: Welcome in smoking rooms
Creature Comforts: CCTV, a/c, cont. brkfst

Spruce House
(785) 263-3900
604 N. Spruce St.
3 rooms - $55-75
Pets: Welcome by arrangement
Creature Comforts: An 1882 Italianate home, hardwood floors covered w/woven rugs, pocket doors, fresh flowers, CCTV, VCR, a/c, refrig, full brkfst

ARKANSAS CITY
Best Western Hallmark Inn
(800) 528-1234, (316) 442-1400
http://www.bestwestern.com
1617 N. Summit St.
47 rooms - $40-75
Pets: Small pets w/$5 fee
Creature Comforts: CCTV, a/c, refrig, micro, cont. brkfst, pool

Regency Court Inn
(800) 325-9151, (316) 442-1400
web site pending
1617 N. Summit St.
88 rooms - $39-99
Pets: Small pets w/$10 fee
Creature Comforts: CCTV, a/c, refrig, restaurant, cont. brkfst, pool, whirlpool

ATCHINSON
Atchinson Motor Inn
(913) 367-7000
401 S. 10th St.
45 rooms - $38-49
Pets: Welcome w/$10 dep.
Creature Comforts: CCTV, VCR, a/c, pool

Comfort Inn
(800) 228-5150, (913) 367-7666
http://www.comfortinn.com
509 S. 9th St.
46 rooms - $49-74
Pets: Small pets welcome
Creature Comforts: CCTV, VCR, a/c, restaurant

AUBURN
Lippincott's Fyshe House
(785) 256-2436
8720 W. 85th St.
2 rooms - $65-80
Pets: Well-behaved pets welcome
Creature Comforts: Charmingly rustic ranch house, CCTV, fireplace, refrig, full brkfst, hot tub

BAXTER SPRINGS
Baxter Inn 4 Less
(316) 856-2106
2451 Military Ave.
32 rooms - $38-60
Pets: Welcome w/$25 dep.
Creature Comforts: CCTV, a/c

BELLEVILLE
Best Western Bel Villa Inn
(800) 528-1234, (785) 527-2231
http://www.bestwestern.com
215 Rte. 36
40 rooms - $44-60
Pets: Small pets welcome
Creature Comforts: CCTV, a/c, restaurant, cont. brkfst, pool

BELOIT
Super 8 Motel
(800) 800-8000, (785) 738-4300
http://www.super8.com
205 W. Rte. 24
40 rooms - $45-69
Pets: Welcome
Creature Comforts: CCTV, a/c, Jacuzzis, cont. brkfst, pool access

Waconda Motel
(800) 538-5998
Rtes. 24 & 14
29 rooms - $34-39
Pets: Welcome
Creature Comforts: CCTV, a/c

CHANUTE
Chanute Safari Inn
(316) 431-9460
3500 S. Santa Fe St.
40 rooms - $38-59
Pets: Welcome w/$5 fee
Creature Comforts: CCTV, a/c, pool

Guest House
(800) 523-6128, (316) 431-0600
1814 S. Santa Fe St.
29 rooms - $30-48
Pets: Welcome
Creature Comforts: CCTV, a/c,
pool

CLAY CENTER
Cedar Court Motel
905 Crawford Rd.
45 rooms - $30-64
Pets: Small pets welcome
Creature Comforts: CCTV,
VCR, a/c, restaurant, pool

COFFEYVILLE
Super 8 Motel
(800) 800-8000, (316) 251-2250
http://www.super8.com
104 W. 11th St.
91 rooms - $45-79
Pets: Welcome
Creature Comforts: CCTV, a/c,
cont. brkfst, pool

COLBY
Best Western Crown Inn
(800) 528-1234, (785) 462-3943
http://www.bestwestern.com
2320 S. Range Ave.
29 rooms - $50-89
Pets: Welcome
Creature Comforts: CCTV, a/c,
pool

Budget Host
(800) Bud-Host, (785) 462-3338
http://www.budgethost.com
1745 W. 4th St.
32 rooms - $37-69
Pets: Welcome
Creature Comforts: CCTV, a/c,
refrig, pool

Comfort Inn
(800) 228-5150, (785) 462-3833
http://www.comfortinn.com
2225 S. Range St.
49 rooms - $50-84
Pets: Small pets w/$5 fee
Creature Comforts: CCTV, a/c,
refrig, Jacuzzis, cont. brkfst, hlth
club, whirlpool, pool

Days Inn
(800) DAYS-INN, (785) 462-8691
http://www.daysinn.com
1925 S. Range St.
44 rooms - $50-79
Pets: Small pets w/$5 fee
Creature Comforts: CCTV, a/c,
pool, whirlpool

Econo Lodge
(800) 55-ECONO, (785) 462-8201
http://www.econolodge.com
1985 S. Range St.
44 rooms - $40-69
Pets: Small pets welcome
Creature Comforts: CCTV, a/c

Super 8 Motel
(800) 800-8000, (785) 462-8248
http://www.super8.com
1040 Zelfer Ave.
63 rooms - $43-70
Pets: Welcome w/permission.
Creature Comforts: CCTV, a/c,
Jacuzzis, cont. brkfst, whirlpool

CONCORDIA
Best Western Thunderbird Inn
(800) 528-1234, (785) 243-4545
http://www.bestwestern.com
89 Lincoln St.
50 rooms - $45-70
Pets: Welcome w/permission.
Creature Comforts: CCTV, a/c,
pool, hlth club, whirlpool

COUNCIL GROVE
Cottage House Hotel
(800) 727-7903, (316) 767-6828
25 N. Neoosho
45 rooms - $40-135
Pets: Welcome w/$9 fee
Creature Comforts: Historic
1870's house w/Victorian flair,
CCTV, VCR, a/c, refrig, Jacuzzis,
cont. brkfst, hlth clb, sauna,
whirlpool

DODGE CITY
Astro Motel
(316) 227-8146
2200 W. Wyatt Earp Blvd.
33 rooms - $33-68
Pets: Welcome
Creature Comforts: CCTV, a/c,
pool

Best Western Silver Spur
(800) 528-1234, (316) 227-2125
http://www.bestwestern.com
1510 W. Wyatt Earp Blvd.
121 rooms - $53-75
Pets: Welcome w/$10 dep.
Creature Comforts: CCTV, a/c,
restaurant, pool

Days Inn
(800) DAYS-INN, (316) 225-9900
http://www.daysinn.com
2408 Wyatt Earp Blvd.
111 rooms - $55-120
Pets: Welcome
Creature Comforts: CCTV, a/c,
restaurant, cont. brkfst, pool,
sauna, hlth club, whirlpool

Econo Lodge
(800) 55-ECONO, (316) 225-0231
http://www.econolodge.com
1610 W. Wyatt Earp Rd.
100 rooms - $53-90
Pets: Small pets welcome
Creature Comforts: CCTV, a/c,
restaurant, pool

Holiday Inn Express
(800) HOLIDAY, (316) 227-5000
http://www.holiday-inn.com
2320 W. Wyatt Earp Blvd.
64 rooms - $65-89
Pets: Small pets welcome
Creature Comforts: CCTV, a/c,
kit, Jacuzzis, pool, hlth club,
whirlpool

Super 8 Motel
(800) 800-8000, (316) 225-3924
http://www.super8.com
108 W. Wyatt Earp Blvd.
64 rooms - $50-78
Pets: Welcome
Creature Comforts: CCTV, a/c,
cont. brkfst, pool

EL DORADO
Best Western Red Coach
(800) 528-1234, (316) 321-6900
http://www.bestwestern.com
2525 W. Central St.
73 rooms - $54-95
Pets: Under 50 lbs. welcome
Creature Comforts: CCTV, a/c,
kit, Jacuzzis, restaurant, hlth club,
sauna, pool

Heritage Inn
(316) 321-6800
2515 W. Central St.
33 rooms - $35-59
Pets: Smkng rms-$5 fee, $10 dep.
Creature Comforts: CCTV, a/c, refrig, Jacuzzis

ELKHART
Elkhart Motel
(316) 697-2168
329 Morton Rd.
20 rooms - $38-69
Pets: Welcome
Creature Comforts: CCTV, a/c

ELLSWORTH
Best Western Garden Prairie
(800) 528-1234, (785) 472-3116
http://www.bestwestern.com
Rtes. 156 & 140
37 rooms - $48-75
Pets: Small pets welcome
Creature Comforts: CCTV, a/c, restaurant, whirlpool, pool

EMPORIA
Best Western Hospitality House
(800) 528-1234, (316) 342-7587
http://www.bestwestern.com
3021 W. Rte. 50
145 rooms - $55-79
Pets: Small pets welcome
Creature Comforts: CCTV, a/c, refrig, Jacuzzis, restaurant, whirlpool, hlth club, sauna, pool

Budget Host
(800) Bud-Host, (316) 343-6922
http://www.budgethost.com
1830 E. Rte. 50
25 rooms - $30-49
Pets: Welcome in smoking rooms
Creature Comforts: CCTV, a/c, refrig, pool

Comfort Inn
(800) 228-5150, (316) 343-7750
http://www.comfortinn.com
2511 W. 18th St.
48 rooms - $40-62
Pets: Small pets w/CC dep.
Creature Comforts: CCTV, a/c, cont. brkfst, whirlpool, pool

Days Inn
(800) DAYS-INN, (316) 342-1787
http://www.daysinn.com
3032 Rte. 50
39 rooms - $43-69
Pets: Welcome
Creature Comforts: CCTV, a/c, Jacuzzis, cont. brkfst, pool, whirlpool

Motel 6
(800) 4-MOTEL6, (316) 343-1240
http://www.motel6.com
2630 W. 18th St.
59 rooms - $35-58
Pets: Under 30 lbs.welcome
Creature Comforts: CCTV, a/c

Super 8 Motel
(800) 800-8000, (316) 342-7567
http://www.super8.com
2913 W. Rte. 50
46 rooms - $43-76
Pets: Welcome w/$10 fee
Creature Comforts: CCTV, a/c, refrig, micro, cont. brkfst, hlth club access

ENTERPRISE
Ehrsam Place B&B
(800) 470-7774, (785) 263-8747
www.ehrsamplace.com
103 S. Grant St., Box 52
3 rooms - $60-90
Pets: In courtyard rooms
Creature Comforts: Historic 14-room Greek Revival mansion set on 20-acres, antiques, original artwork, canopy beds, Native American collectibles, CCTV, VCR, a/c, fireplace, refrig, full brkfst, whirlpool, trails

FLORENCE
Holiday Motel
(316) 878-4246
Rtes. 50 & 77
14 rooms - $39-65
Pets: Welcome
Creature Comforts: CCTV, a/c, refrig.

FORT SCOTT
Best Western Inn
(800) 528-1234, (316) 223-0100
http://www.bestwestern.com
101 State St.
78 rooms - $55-75
Pets: Small pets welcome
Creature Comforts: CCTV, VCR, a/c, refrig, restaurant, whirlpool, sauna, hlth club, pool

Frontier Inn 4 Less
(316) 223-5330
2222 S. Main St.
39 rooms - $50-69
Pets: Small pets welcome
Creature Comforts: CCTV, VCR, a/c

GARDEN CITY
Best Western Red Baron
(800) 528-1234, (316) 275-4164
http://www.bestwestern.com
Rtes. 50 & 83
68 rooms - $49-75
Pets: Welcome
Creature Comforts: CCTV, a/c, refrig, micro, Jacuzzis, restaurant, pool

Best Western Wheat Lands
(800) 528-1234, (316) 276-2387
http://www.bestwestern.com
1311 E. Fulton St.
112 rooms - $50-88
Pets: Welcome
Creature Comforts: CCTV, a/c, refrig, micro, Jacuzzis, restaurant, pool

Budget Host
(800) Bud-Host, (316) 275-0677
http://www.budgethost.com
123 Honey Bee Ct.
34 rooms - $45-63
Pets: Welcome
Creature Comforts: CCTV, a/c, refrig, pool

Continental Inn
(800) 621-0318, (316) 276-7691
1408 Jones Ave.
54 rooms - $30-55
Pets: Welcome w/$5 fee
Creature Comforts: CCTV, a/c, refrig, micro, restaurant, pool

Days Inn
(800) DAYS-INN, (316) 275-5095
http://www.daysinn.com
1818 Commanche Rd.
76 rooms - $49-79
Pets: Welcome
Creature Comforts: CCTV, a/c,
cont. brkfst, pool

National 9 Inn
(316) 276-2394
1502 E. Fulton Rd.
24 rooms - $42-66
Pets: Welcome
Creature Comforts: CCTV, a/c,
refrig, micro, pool

Plaza Inn
(800) 875-5201, (316) 275-7471
web site pending
1911 E. Kansas Ave.
109 rooms - $55-97
Pets: Welcome
Creature Comforts: CCTV,
VCR, a/c, restaurant, pool,
whirlpool, sauna

GARDNER
Super 8 Motel
(800) 800-8000, (913) 856-8887
http://www.super8.com
2001 E. Santa Fe Rd.
55 rooms - $55-75
Pets: Welcome w/permission.
Creature Comforts: CCTV, a/c,
Jacuzzis, cont. brkfst, pool

GOODLAND
Best Western Buffalo Inn
(800) 528-1234, (785) 899-3621
http://www.bestwestern.com
830 W. Rte. 24
93 rooms - $48-84
Pets: Small pets in smoking rms.
Creature Comforts: CCTV, a/c,
refrig, restaurant, whirlpool, pool

Comfort Inn
(800) 228-5150, (785) 899-7181
http://www.comfortinn.com
2519 Enterprise Rd.
49 rooms - $55-83
Pets: Small pets welcome
Creature Comforts: CCTV, a/c,
Jacuzzis, cont. brkfst, hlth club,
pool

Howard Johnson Hotel
(800) I-Go-Hojo, (785) 899-3644
http://www.hojo.com
2218 Commerce Rd.
79 rooms - $47-85
Pets: Welcome
Creature Comforts: CCTV,
VCR, a/c, cont. brkfst, sauna,
whirlpool, pool, and a rec. dome

Motel 6
(800) 4-MOTEL6, (785) 899-5672
http://www.motel6.com
2420 Commerce Rd.
84 rooms - $35-59
Pets: Under 30 lbs.welcome
Creature Comforts: CCTV, a/c,
pool

Super 8 Motel
(800) 800-8000, (785) 899-7566
http://www.super8.com
2520 S. Rte. 27
48 rooms - $49-78
Pets: Welcome w/$25 dep.
Creature Comforts: CCTV, a/c,
cont. brkfst

GREAT BEND
Best Western Angus Inn
(800) 528-1234, (316) 792-3541
http://www.bestwestern.com
2920 - 10th St.
90 rooms - $55-94
Pets: Small pets welcome
Creature Comforts: CCTV,
VCR, a/c, refrig, micro, Jacuzzis,
restaurant, cont. brkfst, sauna, hlth
club, pool

Days Inn
(800) DAYS-INN, (316) 792-8235
http://www.daysinn.com
4701 - 10th St.
43 rooms - $40-75
Pets: Welcome w/permission.
Creature Comforts: CCTV, a/c,
cont. brkfst

Holiday Inn
(800) HOLIDAY, (316) 792-2431
http://www.holiday-inn.com
3017 - 10th St.
175 rooms - $55-87
Pets: Welcome
Creature Comforts: CCTV, a/c,
refrig, Jacuzzis, restaurant,
Jacuzzis, pool, steamroom, sauna,
hlth club, whirlpool

Peaceful Acres B&B
(316) 793-7527
Rte. 5, Box 153
2 rooms - $33-49
Pets: Welcome
Creature Comforts: Farmhouse
on 10 acres, CCTV, fireplace,
refrig, full brkfst

Super 8 Motel
(800) 800-8000, (316) 793-8466
http://www.super8.com
3500 - 10th St.
42 rooms - $43-75
Pets: Welcome w/$10 fee
Creature Comforts: CCTV, a/c,
micro, cont. brkfst, whirlpool,
sauna, pool

GREENSBURG
Best Western J-Hawk Inn
(800) 528-1234, (316) 723-2121
http://www.bestwestern.com
515 W. Kansas Ave.
30 rooms - $57-83
Pets: Small pets welcome
Creature Comforts: CCTV, a/c,
whirlpool, hlth club, pool

Econo Lodge
(800) 55-ECONO, (316) 723-2141
http://www.econolodge.com
800 E. Kansas Ave.
29 rooms - $35-59
Pets: Small pets welcome
Creature Comforts: CCTV, a/c,
restaurant, pool

HAYS
Best Western Vagabond Inn
(800) 528-1234, (785) 625-2511
http://www.bestwestern.com
2524 Vine St.
92 rooms - $65-95
Pets: Small pets welcome
Creature Comforts: CCTV, a/c,
refrig, micro, Jacuzzis, restaurant,
sauna, hlth club, whirlpool, pool

Budget Host Villa
(800) Bud-Host, (785) 625-2563
http://www.budgethost.com
810 E. 8th St.
49 rooms - $35-69
Pets: Welcome
Creature Comforts: CCTV, a/c,
kit, pool

Days Inn
(800) DAYS-INN, (785) 628-8261
http://www.daysinn.com
3205 N. Vine St.
87 rooms - $45-109
Pets: Welcome
Creature Comforts: CCTV, a/c,
restaurant, cont. brkfst, hlth club
access, pool

Hampton Inn
(800) Hampton, (785) 625-8103
http://www.hampton-inn.com
3801 Vine St.
115 rooms - $50-95
Pets: Welcome
Creature Comforts: CCTV,
VCR, a/c, refrig, micro, Jacuzzis,
cont. brkfst, pool, hlth club access

Holiday Inn
(800) HOLIDAY, (785) 625-7371
http://www.holiday-inn.com
3603 Vine St.
190 rooms - $60-89
Pets: Small pets welcome
Creature Comforts: CCTV, a/c,
refrig, Jacuzzis, pool, sauna,
steamroom, hlth club, whirlpool,
rec. dome

Motel 6
(800) 4-MOTEL6, (785) 625-4282
http://www.motel6.com
3404 Vine St.
59 rooms - $39-58
Pets: Under 30 lbs.welcome
Creature Comforts: CCTV, a/c,
pool

HUTCHINSON
Astro Motel
(316) 663-1151
15 E. 4th St.
30 rooms - $33-49
Pets: Small pets welcome
Creature Comforts: CCTV, a/c,
kit, pool

Best Western Sun Dome
(800) 528-1234, (316) 663-4444
http://www.bestwestern.com
11 Des Moines Ave.
95 rooms - $65-99
Pets: Small pets welcome
Creature Comforts: CCTV, a/c,
whirlpool, sauna, hlth club, pool

Comfort Inn
(800) 228-5151, (316) 663-7822
http://www.comfortinn.com
1621 Super Plaza
64 rooms - $59-140
Pets: Small pets welcome
Creature Comforts: CCTV,
VCR, a/c, Jacuzzis, cont. brkfst,
sauna, whirlpool, pool

Days Inn
(800) DAYS-INN, (316) 663-7100
http://www.daysinn.com
100 E. 2nd Ave.
78 rooms - $45-279
Pets: Small pets w/$10 fee
Creature Comforts: CCTV, a/c,
Jacuzzis, cont. brkfst, hlth club,
pool

Quality Inn
(800) 228-5151, (316) 663-1211
http://www.qualityinn.com
15 W. 4th Ave.
97 rooms - $54-139
Pets: Small pets welcome
Creature Comforts: CCTV,
VCR, a/c, refrig, micro, Jacuzzis,
restaurant, pool

Super 8 Motel
(800) 800-8000, (316) 662-6394
http://www.super8.com
1315 E. 11th Ave.
46 rooms - $45-75
Pets: Welcome w/$10 fee
Creature Comforts: CCTV, a/c,
micro, cont. brkfst

INDEPENDENCE
Appletree Inn
(316) 331-5500
201 N. 8th St.
65 rooms - $50-99
Pets: Welcome
Creature Comforts: CCTV, a/c,
refrig, micro, Jacuzzis, pool,
whirlpool

Best Western Prairie Inn
(800) 528-1234, (316) 331-7300
http://www.bestwestern.com
Rtes. 75 & 160
41 rooms - $48-70
Pets: Welcome w/$4 fee
Creature Comforts: CCTV, a/c,
cont. brkfst, pool

IOLA
Best Western Inn
(800) 528-1234, (316) 365-5161
http://www.bestwestern.com
1315 N. State St.
59 rooms - $45-69
Pets: Small pets welcome
Creature Comforts: CCTV, a/c,
refrig, restaurant, pool

JUNCTION CITY
Best Western Jayhawk Inn
(800) 528-1234, (785) 238-5188
http://www.bestwestern.com
110 E. Flinthills Blvd.
48 rooms - $40-78
Pets: Welcome in smoking rooms
Creature Comforts: CCTV, a/c,
kit, cont. brkfst, pool

Dreamland Motel
(785) 238-1108
520 E. Flint Hills Blvd.
25 rooms - $32-49
Pets: Welcome w/$3 fee
Creature Comforts: CCTV, a/c,
refrig, micro, pool

Econo Lodge
(800) 55-ECONO, (785) 238-8181
http://www.econolodge.com
211 W. Flinthills Blvd.
57 rooms - $40-75
Pets: Small pets w/$10 dep.
Creature Comforts: CCTV, a/c,
refrig, cont. brkfst

Super 8 Motel
(800) 800-8000, (785) 238-8101
http://www.super8.com
1001 E. 6th St.
97 rooms - $48-70
Pets: Welcome w/$25 dep.
Creature Comforts: CCTV, a/c,
refrig, micro, cont. brkfst, hlth
club, sauna, whirlpool, pool

Travelodge
(800) 578-7878, (785) 238-5147
http://www.travelodge.com
201 Continental Dr.
40 rooms - $45-79
Pets: Small pets welcome
Creature Comforts: CCTV, a/c, pool

KANSAS CITY
Best Western Inn
(800) 528-1234, (913) 677-3060
http://www.bestwestern.com
501 Southwest Blvd.
113 rooms - $75-109
Pets: Welcome if attended
Creature Comforts: CCTV, a/c, kit, cont. brkfst, whirlpool, pool

LAKIN
Windy Heights B&B
(316) 355-7699
607 Country Heights Rd.
4 rooms - $45-60
Pets: Welcome
Creature Comforts: Quiet home set along golf course, CCTV, a/c, fireplace, refrig, full brkfst

LANSING
Econo Lodge
(800) 55-ECONO, (913) 727-2777
http://www.econolodge.com
504 N. Main St.
40 rooms - $40-65
Pets: Welcome w/$25 dep.
Creature Comforts: CCTV, a/c, refrig, micro

LARNED
Best Western Townsman
(800) 528-1234, (316) 285-3114
http://www.bestwestern.com
123 E. 14th St.
44 rooms - $47-64
Pets: Welcome
Creature Comforts: CCTV, a/c, pool

LAWRENCE
Best Western Hallmark
(800) 528-1234, (785) 841-6500
http://www.bestwestern.com
730 Iowa St.
60 rooms - $56-79
Pets: Welcome in smoking rooms
Creature Comforts: CCTV, a/c, cont. brkfst, pool

Days Inn
(800) DAYS-INN, (785) 843-9100
http://www.daysinn.com
2309 Iowa St.
101 rooms - $50-99
Pets: Welcome
Creature Comforts: CCTV, a/c, restaurant, cont. brkfst, pool, sauna, whirlpool

Holiday Inn
(800) HOLIDAY, (785) 841-7077
http://www.holiday-inn.com
200 MacDonald Dr.
194 rooms - $75-199
Pets: Welcome
Creature Comforts: CCTV, a/c, refrig, restaurant, cont. brkfst, hlth clb, sauna, whirlpool, pool, and a rec. room

Ramada Inn
(800) 2-Ramada, (785) 842-7030
http://www.ramada.com
2222 W. 6th St.
112 rooms - $60-139
Pets: Small pets in smoking rms.
Creature Comforts: CCTV, a/c, refrig, Jacuzzis, restaurant, pool

Super 8 Motel
(800) 800-8000, (785) 842-5721
http://www.super8.com
515 McDonald Dr.
48 rooms - $49-75
Pets: Welcome w/$10 fee
Creature Comforts: CCTV, a/c, micro, cont. brkfst

Travelodge
(800) 578-7878, (785) 842-5100
http://www.travelodge.com
801 Iowa St.
68 rooms - $50-87
Pets: Small pets welcome
Creature Comforts: CCTV, a/c, pool

Westminster Inn
(785) 841-8410
2525 W. 6th St.
60 rooms - $45-64
Pets: Welcome w/$20 dep.
Creature Comforts: CCTV, a/c, pool

LEAVENWORTH
Best Western Hallmark
(800) 528-1234, (913) 651-6000
http://www.bestwestern.com
3211 S. 4th St.
52 rooms - $55-79
Pets: Welcome if attended
Creature Comforts: CCTV, a/c, refrig, cont. brkfst, pool

Ramada Inn
(800) 2-Ramada, (913) 651-5500
http://www.ramada.com
101 S. 3rd St.
98 rooms - $45-83
Pets: Welcome
Creature Comforts: CCTV, a/c, refrig, pool

Super 8 Motel
(800) 800-8000, (913) 682-0744
http://www.super8.com
303 Montana Ct.
60 rooms - $40-69
Pets: Welcome
Creature Comforts: CCTV, a/c, refrig, cont. brkfst

LENEXA
La Quinta Inn
(800) 531-5900, (913) 492-5500
http://www.travelweb.com
9461 Lenexa Dr.
110 rooms - $60-80
Pets: Small pets welcome
Creature Comforts: CCTV, a/c, refrig, pool

LIBERAL
Best Western La Fonda
(800) 528-1234, (316) 624-5601
http://www.bestwestern.com
229 W. Pancake Blvd.
46 rooms - $40-99
Pets: Small pets welcome
Creature Comforts: CCTV, a/c, refrig, micro, pool

Cimarron Inn
(316) 624-6203
564 E. Pancake Blvd.
33 rooms - $35-59
Pets: Welcome w/$5 fee
Creature Comforts: CCTV, a/c, pool

Gateway Inn
(800) 833-3391, (316) 624-0242
720 E. Rte. 54
100 rooms - $40-59
Pets: Welcome
Creature Comforts: CCTV, a/c,
refrig, restaurant, pool, tennis

Liberal Inn
(800) 458-4667, (316) 624-7254
603 E. Pancake Blvd.
123 rooms - $40-105
Pets: Welcome
Creature Comforts: CCTV, a/c,
restaurant, pool, whirlpool

Thunderbird Inn
(316) 624-7271
2100 N. Rte. 83
29 rooms - $33-48
Pets: small pets welcome
Creature Comforts: CCTV, a/c

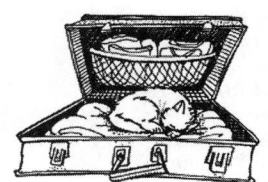

LINDSBORG
Coronado Motel
(913) 227-3943
305 Harrison St.
10 rooms - $32-65
Pets: Welcome
Creature Comforts: CCTV, a/c,
pool

LOUISBURG
Red Maple Inn
(913) 837-2840
201 S. 11th St.
4 rooms - $60-85
Pets: Small pets welcome
Creature Comforts: A charming
inn w/gingerbread accents, CCTV,
VCR, a/c, fireplace, refrig,
Jacuzzi, full brkfst, pool

LYONS
Lyons Inn
(316) 257-5185
817 W. Main St.
28 rooms - $36-59
Pets: Welcome
Creature Comforts: CCTV, a/c

MANHATTAN
Best Western Continental
(800) 528-1234, (785) 776-4771
http://www.bestwestern.com
100 Bluemont St.
92 rooms - $50-75
Pets: Small pets welcome
Creature Comforts: CCTV, a/c,
refrig, micro, Jacuzzis, cont.
brkfst, hlth club, whirlpool, pool

Days Inn
(800) DAYS-INN, (913) 539-5391
http://www.daysinn.com
1501 Tuttle Creek Blvd.
119 rooms - $50-85
Pets: Welcome
Creature Comforts: CCTV, a/c,
refrig, micro, cont. brkfst, pool

Holiday Inn
(800) HOLIDAY, (913) 539-5311
http://www.holiday-inn.com
530 Richards Dr.
198 rooms - $75-249
Pets: Welcome
Creature Comforts: CCTV, a/c,
restaurant, pool, sauna, whirlpool,
rec. dome

Motel 6
(800) 4-MOTEL6, (785) 537-1022
http://www.motel6.com
510 Turtle Creek Blvd.
87 rooms - $35-58
Pets: Under 30 lbs. welcome
Creature Comforts: CCTV, a/c,
pool

Ramada Inn
(800) 2-Ramada, (913) 539-7531
http://www.ramada.com
17th & Anderson Sts.
115 rooms - $85-129
Pets: Small pets welcome
Creature Comforts: CCTV,
VCR, a/c, refrig, restaurant, hlth
club access, pool

MANKATO
Dreamliner Motel
(913) 378-3107
Rte. 36, Box 8
28 rooms - $33-42
Pets: Welcome w/$5 fee
Creature Comforts: CCTV, a/c

MARYSVILLE
Best Western Surf Inn
(800) 528-1234, (785) 562-2354
http://www.bestwestern.com
2005 Center St.
52 rooms - $43-65
Pets: Small pets welcome
Creature Comforts: CCTV, a/c,
refrig, cont. brkfst, whirlpool,
sauna, pool

Thunderbird Motel
(800) 662-2373, (785) 562-2373
Route 36
22 rooms - $30-55
Pets: Welcome
Creature Comforts: CCTV, a/c,
refrig, cont. brkfst

Super 8 Motel
(800) 800-8000, (785) 562-5588
http://www.super8.com
1155 Pony Express Rd.
42 rooms - $44-60
Pets: Welcome w/$20 dep.
Creature Comforts: CCTV, a/c,
Jacuzzis, cont. brkfst, pool

MCPHERSON
Best Western Holiday Manor
(800) 528-1234, (316) 241-5343
http://www.bestwestern.com
2211 E. Kansas Ave.
110 rooms - $54-68
Pets: Small pets welcome
Creature Comforts: CCTV, a/c,
refrig, Jacuzzi, cont. brkfst,
sauna, whirlpool, pool

Super 8 Motel
(800) 800-8000, (913) 241-8881
http://www.super8.com
2110 E. Kansas Rd.
42 rooms - $45-68
Pets: Welcome w/permission.
Creature Comforts: CCTV, a/c,
Jacuzzis, cont. brkfst, pool

MERRIAM
Comfort Inn
(800) 446-4656, (913) 262-2622
http://www.hotelchoice.com
6401 E. Frontage Rd.
100 rooms - $60-86
Pets: Small pets welcome
Creature Comforts: CCTV, a/c,
refrig, micro, pool

Drury Inn
(800) 325-8300, (913) 236-9200
http://www.druryinn.com
9009 Shawnee Mission Pkwy.
115 rooms - $70-89
Pets: Welcome
Creature Comforts: CCTV, a/c,
refrig, micro, pool

NEWTON
Best Western Red Coach
(800) 528-1234, (316) 283-9120
http://www.bestwestern.com
1301 E. First St.
81 rooms - $50-98
Pets: Small pets w/permission.
Creature Comforts: CCTV, a/c,
Jacuzzis, kit, sauna, whirlpool,
pool

Days Inn
(800) DAYS-INN, (316) 283-3330
http://www.daysinn.com
105 Manchester St.
80 rooms - $54-85
Pets: Welcome w/$10 fee
Creature Comforts: CCTV, a/c,
micro, cont. brkfst

Super 8 Motel
(800) 800-8000, (316) 283-7611
http://www.super8.com
1620 E. 2nd St.
38 rooms - $45-68
Pets: Welcome w/$10 fee
Creature Comforts: CCTV, a/c,
Jacuzzis, cont. brkfst, pool

OAKLEY
Annie Oakley Motel
(785) 877-3343
428 Center St.
25 rooms - $29-45
Pets: Small pets welcome
Creature Comforts: CCTV, a/c

Best Western Golden Plains
(800) 528-1234, (785) 672-3254
http://www.bestwestern.com
3506 Rte. 40
26 rooms - $49-74
Pets: Small pets welcome
Creature Comforts: CCTV, a/c,
refrig, pool

First Travel Inn
(785) 672-3226
708 Center Ave.
25 rooms - $33-59
Pets: Welcome w/$4 fee
Creature Comforts: CCTV, a/c,
pool

OBERLIN
Frontier Motel
(913) 475-2203
207 E. Frontier Pkwy.
28 rooms - $29-58
Pets: Welcome
Creature Comforts: CCTV,
VCR, a/c, pool

OLATHE
Best Western Hallmark
(800) 528-1234, (913) 782-4343
http://www.bestwestern.com
211 N. Rawhide Dr.
90 rooms - $40-59
Pets: Small pets welcome
Creature Comforts: CCTV, a/c,
refrig, micro, pool

OSAWATOMIE
Landmark Inn
(913) 755-3051
304 Eastgate Dr.
39 rooms - $42-59
Pets: Small pets in smoking rms.
Creature Comforts: CCTV, a/c,
restaurant

OSBORNE
Camelot Inn
(913) 436-5413
933 N. 1st St.
33 rooms - $37-49
Pets: Welcome w/$10 fee
Creature Comforts: CCTV, a/c

OTTAWA
Best Western Hallmark
(800) 528-1234, (785) 242-7000
http://www.bestwestern.com
2209 S. Princeton Rd.
60 rooms - $49-75
Pets: Small pets in smoking rms.
Creature Comforts: CCTV, a/c,
refrig, pool

Days Inn
(800) DAYS-INN, (785) 242-4842
http://www.daysinn.com
1641 S. Main St.
40 rooms - $45-69
Pets: Welcome
Creature Comforts: CCTV, a/c,
cont. brkfst, whirlpool, pool

Econo Lodge
(800) 55-ECONO, (785) 242-3400
http://www.econolodge.com
2331 S. Cedar St.
57 rooms - $46-69
Pets: Small pets in smoking rms.
Creature Comforts: CCTV,
VCR, a/c, refrig, cont. brkfst, pool

Village Inn
(785) 242-5512
2520 S. Main St.
14 rooms - $29-49
Pets: Welcome
Creature Comforts: CCTV, a/c,
kit, pool, rec. court

OVERLAND PARK
Amerisuites
(800) 833-1516, (913) 451-2553
6801 W. 112th St.
125 rooms - $99-125
Pets: Under 10 Lbs. w/CC dep.
Creature Comforts: CCTV,
VCR, a/c, refrig, micro, cont.
brkfst, pool, and hlth clb access

Doubletree Hotel
(800) 222-TREE, (913) 451-6100
http://www.doubletreehotels.com
10100 College Blvd.
350 rooms - $80-459
Pets: Welcome w/$50 fee
Creature Comforts: Upscale
property, CCTV, a/c, refrig, micro,
Jacuzzi, restaurant, cont. brkfst,
pool, hlth clb, sauna, whirlpool,
hlth club

Drury Inn
(800) 325-8300, (913) 345-1500
http://www.druryinn.com
10951 Metcalf Ave.
160 rooms - $80-99
Pets: Welcome
Creature Comforts: CCTV, a/c,
refrig, micro, cont. brkfst, pool

Holiday Inn
(800) HOLIDAY, (913) 262-3010
http://www.holiday-inn.com
7240 Shawnee Mission Pkwy.
200 rooms - $80-95
Pets: Small pets w/$20 dep.
Creature Comforts: CCTV, a/c,
refrig, micro, cont. brkfst, pool,
hlth clb, sauna, whirlpool

Red Roof Inn
(800) 843-7663, (913) 341-0100
http://www.redroof.com
6800 W. 108th St.
110 rooms - $46-65
Pets: Small pets welcome in the
smoking rooms
Creature Comforts: CCTV, a/c

Residence Inn
(800) 331-3131, (913) 491-3333
http://www.residenceinn.com
6300 W. 110th St.
115 suites - $110-160
Pets: $5 fee, $50-75 dep.
Creature Comforts: CCTV,
VCR, a/c, kit, pool, hlth clb
access, sauna, whirlpools

White Haven Motor Lodge
(800) 752-2891, (913) 649-8200
8039 Metcalf Ave.
80 rooms - $40-75
Pets: Small pets welcome
Creature Comforts: CCTV,
VCR, a/c, kit, pool

Wyndham Garden Hotel
(800) Wyndham, (913) 383-2550
http://www.wyndham.com
7000 W. 108th St.
185 rooms - $65-95
Pets: Small pets welcome
Creature Comforts: CCTV, a/c,
refrig, restaurant, pool, hlth clb

PARSONS
Townsman Motel
(800) 552-4008, (316) 421-6990
Rte 59, Box 813
38 rooms - $33-49
Pets: Welcome
Creature Comforts: CCTV, a/c,
refrig, pool

PEABODY
Jones Sheep Farm B&B
(316) 983-2815
RR 2, Box 185
2 rooms - $50-65
Pets: Welcome
Creature Comforts: A low-key
turn-of-the-century country home,
full farm brkfst

PHILLIPSBURG
Mark V Motel
(800) 219-3149, (785) 543-5223
320 W. State St.
33 rooms - $30-49
Pets: Welcome
Creature Comforts: CCTV, a/c,
pool

PITTSBURG
Sunset Motel
(316) 231-3950
1159 S. 220th St.
6 rooms - $49-67
Pets: Small pets welcome
Creature Comforts: CCTV, a/c

PRATT
Best Western Hillcrest
(800) 528-1234, (316) 672-6407
http://www.bestwestern.com
1336 E. 1st St.
40 rooms - $37-55
Pets: Small pets welcome
Creature Comforts: CCTV, a/c,
refrig, cont. brkfst, pool

Days Inn
(800) DAYS-INN, (316) 672-9465
http://www.daysinn.com
1901 E. 1st St.
47 rooms - $45-79
Pets: Welcome w/$3 fee
Creature Comforts: CCTV, a/c,
refrig, cont. brkfst, pool

Evergreen Inn
(800) 456-6424, (316) 672-6431
20001 W. Rte 54
14 rooms - $36-54
Pets: Welcome
Creature Comforts: CCTV, a/c,
pool

Holiday Inn Express
(800) HOLIDAY, (316) 672-9433
http://www.holiday-inn.com
1400 W. Rte. 54
38 rooms - $58-80
Pets: Small pets welcome
Creature Comforts: CCTV, a/c,
pool, whirlpool

Red Carpet Inn
(800) 251-1962, (316) 672-5588
http://www.reservahost.com
1401 E. First St.
24 rooms - $29-50
Pets: Small pets w/$3 fee
Creature Comforts: CCTV, a/c,
kit

Super 8 Motel
(800) 800-8000, (316) 672-2969
http://www.super8.com
Route 54
45 rooms - $39-58
Pets: Welcome w/permission.
Creature Comforts: CCTV, a/c,
cont. brkfst, whirlpool

QUINTER
Budget Host Q Motel
(800) Bud-Host, (913) 754-3337
http://www.budgethost.com
Rtes. 212 & 70
48 rooms - $40-63
Pets: Welcome w/$5 dep.
Creature Comforts: CCTV, a/c,
refrig, restaurant

ROSE HILL
Queen Anne's Lace B&B
(316) 733-4075
15335 SW Queen Anne's Lace Rd
2 rooms - $45-68
Pets: Crated pets welcome
Creature Comforts: A quiet
wooded country setting, CCTV,
VCR, a/c, fireplace, refrig,
Jacuzzi, full brkfst

RUSSELL
Budget Host Winchester
(800) Bud-Host, (913) 483-6660
http://www.budgethost.com
1225 S. Fossil St.
50 rooms - $40-68
Pets: Welcome w/$5 dep.
Creature Comforts: CCTV, a/c,
refrig, micro, pool

SALINA

Arliner Motel
(785) 827-9315
632 Westport Blvd.
39 rooms - $29-45
Pets: Small pets welcome
Creature Comforts: CCTV, a/c, pool

Best Western Heart of America
(800) 528-1234, (785) 827-9315
http://www.bestwestern.com
632 Westport Blvd.
100 rooms - $50-75
Pets: Welcome w/permission.
Creature Comforts: CCTV, a/c, refrig, cont. brkfst, whirlpool, sauna, pool

Best Western Mid-America
(800) 528-1234, (785) 827-0356
http://www.bestwestern.com
1846 N. 9th St.
108 rooms - $50-75
Pets: Welcome w/permission.
Creature Comforts: CCTV, a/c, refrig, restaurant, cont. brkfst, whirlpool, sauna, pool

Budget Inn Vagabond
(800) Bud-Host, (785) 825-7256
http://www.budgethost.com
217 S. Broadway St.
44 rooms - $30-59
Pets: Welcome w/$25 dep.
Creature Comforts: CCTV, a/c, kit, pool

Comfort Inn
(800) 228-5150, (785) 826-1711
http://www.comfortinn.com
1820 W. Crawford St.
60 rooms - $54-79
Pets: Small pets welcome
Creature Comforts: CCTV, a/c, cont. brkfst, pool

Holiday Inn
(800) HOLIDAY, (785) 823-1739
http://www.holiday-inn.com
1616 W. Crawford St.
196 rooms - $70-99
Pets: Welcome
Creature Comforts: CCTV, a/c, refrig, Jacuzzis, restaurant, pool, hlth club, sauna, steamroom, whirlpool

Howard Johnson
(800) I-Go-Hojo, (785) 827-5511
http://www.hojo.com
2403 S. 9th St.
102 rooms - $55-75
Pets: Small pets welcome
Creature Comforts: CCTV, a/c, refrig, pool

Motel 6
(800) 4-MOTEL6, (785) 827-8397
http://www.motel6.com
635 W. Diamond Dr.
82 rooms - $39-56
Pets: Under 30 lbs.welcome
Creature Comforts: CCTV, a/c, pool

Ramada Inn
(800) 2-Ramada, (785) 825-8211
http://www.ramada.com
1949 N. 9th St.
102 rooms - $55-75
Pets: Welcome w/$10 dep.
Creature Comforts: CCTV, a/c, Jacuzzis, restaurant, pool

Red Carpet Inn
(800) 251-1962, (785) 825-2111
http://www.reservahost.com
2020 W. Crawford St.
115 rooms - $53-79
Pets: Welcome in smoking rooms
Creature Comforts: CCTV, a/c, kit, Jacuzzis, restaurant, hlth club, sauna, whirlpool, pool

Super 8 Motel
(800) 800-8000, (785) 823-9215
http://www.super8.com
1640 W. Crawford St.
61 rooms - $45-68
Pets: Welcome w/permission.
Creature Comforts: CCTV, a/c, cont. brkfst

Super 8 Motel
(800) 800-8000, (785) 823-8808
http://www.super8.com
120 E. Diamond Dr.
49 rooms - $52-68
Pets: Welcome w/$5 fee
Creature Comforts: CCTV, a/c, cont. brkfst, pool, whirlpool

SMITH CENTER

Modern Aire Motel
(800) 727-7332, (785) 282-6644
117 Rte 36
16 rooms - $30-45
Pets: Welcome
Creature Comforts: CCTV, a/c, pool

TOPEKA

Best Western Meadow Acres
(800) 528-1234, (785) 267-1681
http://www.bestwestern.com
2950 S. Topeka St.
83 rooms - $55-75
Pets: Welcome w/$8 fee
Creature Comforts: CCTV, a/c, refrig, Jacuzzis, cont. brkfst, whirlpool, sauna, pool

Comfort Inn
(800) 228-5150, (785) 273-5365
http://www.comfortinn.com
1518 SW Wanamaker Rd.
67 rooms - $55-109
Pets: Small pets welcome
Creature Comforts: CCTV, a/c, refrig, cont. brkfst, whirlpool, pool

Days Inn
(800) DAYS-INN, (785) 272-8538
http://www.daysinn.com
1510 SW Wanamaker Rd.
62 rooms - $45-89
Pets: Welcome
Creature Comforts: CCTV, a/c, refrig, cont. brkfst, whirlpool, pool

Econo Lodge
(800) 55-ECONO, (785) 273-6969
http://www.econolodge.com
1240 SW Wanamaker Rd.
47 rooms - $50-75
Pets: Small pets w/$25 dep.
Creature Comforts: CCTV, VCR, a/c, cont. brkfst, whirlpool, pool

Plaza Inn Hotel
(800) 833-8033, (785) 266-8880
3802 S. Topeka Blvd.
169 rooms - $49-60
Pets: Welcome
Creature Comforts: CCTV, a/c,
refrig, restaurant, pool

Motel 6
(800) 4-MOTEL6, (785) 272-8283
http://www.motel6.com
709 Fairlawn Rd.
101 rooms - $35-50
Pets: Under 30 lbs.welcome
Creature Comforts: CCTV, a/c,
pool

Motel 6
(800) 4-MOTEL6, (785) 273-9888
http://www.motel6.com
1224 Wanamaker Rd. SW
91 rooms - $40-59
Pets: Under 30 lbs.welcome
Creature Comforts: CCTV, a/c

Ramada Inn
(800) 2-Ramada, (785) 234-5400
http://www.ramada.com
420 E. 6th St.
424 rooms - $50-249
Pets: Under 25 lbs. welcome
Creature Comforts: CCTV,
VCR, a/c, refrig, restaurant,
whirlpool, hlth club, pool

Residence Inn
(800) 331-3131, (785) 271-8903
http://www.residenceinn.com
1620 SW Westport Dr.
66 suites - $95-160
Pets: $10 daily fee, $50 one-time
cleaning fee
Creature Comforts: CCTV, a/c,
kit, pool, hlth clb, whirlpools

Super 8 Motel
(800) 800-8000, (785) 273-5100
http://www.super8.com
5968 SW 10th St.
62 rooms - $47-66
Pets: Welcome w/$10 dep.
Creature Comforts: CCTV, a/c,
cont. brkfst

WAKEENEY
Best Western Wheel Inn
(800) 528-1234, (785) 743-2118
http://www.bestwestern.com
Rtes. 70 & 283
50 rooms - $43-70
Pets: Welcome
Creature Comforts: CCTV, a/c,
refrig, pool

WAMEGO
Simmer Motel
(913) 456-2304
1215 Rte. 24
22 rooms - $35-65
Pets: Welcome
Creature Comforts: CCTV, a/c,
refrig, micro, pool

WELLINGTON
Oak Tree Inn
(316) 326-8191
1177 E. 16th St.
58 rooms - $50-60
Pets: Small pets welcome
Creature Comforts: CCTV, a/c

WINFIELD
Comfort Inn
(800) 228-5150, (316) 221-7529
http://www.comfortinn.com
Route 77
51 rooms - $65-170
Pets: Small pets welcome
Creature Comforts: CCTV, a/c,
cont. brkfst, pool

WITCHITA
Best Western Red Coach
(800) 528-1234, (316) 832-9387
http://www.bestwestern.com
915 E. 53rd St.
152 rooms - $65-80
Pets: Under 15 lbs. w/$25 dep.
Creature Comforts: CCTV, a/c,
kit, Jacuzzis, restaurant, sauna,
whirlpool, hlth club, pool

Best Western Red Coach
(800) 528-1234, (316) 942-5600
http://www.bestwestern.com
6815 W. Kellogg St.
130 rooms - $75-99
Pets: Under 15 lbs. w/$25 fee
Creature Comforts: CCTV, a/c,
kit, Jacuzzis, restaurant, sauna,
whirlpool, hlth club, pool

Clarion Hotel
(800) CLARION, (316) 942-7911
http://www.clarioninn.com
5805 W. Kellogg St.
205 rooms - $65-199
Pets: Small pets w/$25 dep.
Creature Comforts: CCTV, a/c,
restaurant, cont. brkfst, whirlpool,
hlth club, pool

Comfort Inn, South
(800) 228-5150, (316) 522-1800
http://www.comfortinn.com
4849 S. Laura St.
114 rooms - $60-79
Pets: Welcome in pet rooms
Creature Comforts: CCTV, a/c,
cont. brkfst, pool

Comfort Suites, Airport
(800) 228-5150, (316) 945-2600
http://www.comfortinn.com
658 Westside Dr.
50 rooms - $85-125
Pets: Small pets welcome
Creature Comforts: CCTV, a/c,
refrig, micro, cont. brkfst, hlth
club, pool

Comfort Inn, East
(800) 228-5150, (316) 686-2844
http://www.comfortinn.com
9525 E. Corporate Hills
58 rooms - $60-99
Pets: Small pets welcome
Creature Comforts: CCTV, a/c,
cont. brkfst, whirlpool, pool

Four Points
(800) 325-3535, (316) 686-7131
http://www.fourpoints.com
549 S. Rock Rd.
262 rooms - $65-369
Pets: $25 fee & $100 dep.
Creature Comforts: CCTV, a/c,
refrig, micro, Jacuzzi, restaurant,
pool, hlth clb, whirlpool

Hampton Inn
(800) Hampton, (316) 686-3576
http://www.hampton-inn.com
9449 E. Corporate Hills Rd.
81 rooms - $70-89
Pets: Welcome
Creature Comforts: CCTV, a/c,
refrig, micro, pool

Holiday Inn, Airport
(800) HOLIDAY, (316) 943-2181
http://www.holiday-inn.com
5500 W. Kellogg Rd.
154 rooms - $75-99
Pets: Small pets welcome
Creature Comforts: CCTV, a/c,
refrig, restaurant, pool, sauna,
whirlpool

Holiday Inn
(800) HOLIDAY, (316) 685-1281
http://www.holiday-inn.com
7335 E. Kellogg Rd.
193 rooms - $75-99
Pets: Small pets welcome
Creature Comforts: CCTV, a/c,
kit, restaurant, pool, sauna,
whirlpool

La Quinta Inn
(800) Nu-Rooms, (913) 681-2881
http://www.laquinta.com
7700 E. Kellogg Rd.
122 rooms - $55-89
Pets: Small pets welcome
Creature Comforts: CCTV, a/c,
refrig, pool

Marriott Hotel
(800) 228-9290, (316) 651-0333
http://www.marriott.com
9100 Corporate Hills Rd.
295 rooms - $85-199
Pets: Smal! pets welcome
Creature Comforts: CCTV,
VCR, a/c, refrig, restaurant, pool,
hlth clb, sauna, whirlpools, hiking
trails

Motel 6
(800) 4-MOTEL6, (316) 945-8440
http://www.motel6.com
5734 W. Kellogg Rd.
146 rooms - $40-59
Pets: Under 30 lbs.welcome
Creature Comforts: CCTV, a/c,
pool

Quality Inn
(800) 228-5151, (316) 772-8730
http://www.qualityinn.com
600 S. Holland St.
105 rooms - $45-67
Pets: Small pets welcome
Creature Comforts: CCTV, a/c,
refrig, restaurants, cont. brkfst,
pool

Red Carpet Inn
(800) 251-1962, (316) 529-4100
http://www.reservahost.com
607 E. 47th St.
32 rooms - $45-68
Pets: Small pets w/$2 fee
Creature Comforts: CCTV, a/c,
Jacuzzis

Red Carpet Inn
(800) 251-1962, (316) 264-2323
http://www.reservahost.com
925 N. Broadway St.
18 rooms - $44-58
Pets: Small pets welcome
Creature Comforts: CCTV, a/c

YATES CENTER
Star Motel
(316) 625-2175
206 S. Fry Rd.
12 rooms - $29-46
Pets: Welcome
Creature Comforts: CCTV, a/c

Townsman Motel
(316) 625-2131
609 W. Mary Rd.
33 rooms - $29-48
Pets: Small pets welcome
Creature Comforts: CCTV, a/c

Kentucky

ASHLAND
Days Inn
(800) DAYS-INN, (606) 928-3600
http://www.daysinn.com
12700 Rte. 180
63 rooms - $49-75
Pets: Welcome
Creature Comforts: CCTV,
VCR, a/c, refrig, cont. brkfst, pool

Knights Inn
(800) 843-5644, (606) 928-9501
http://www.knightsinn.com
7216 Rte. 60
122 rooms - $42-55
Pets: Welcome w/$5 fee
Creature Comforts: CCTV, a/c,
kit, pool

AURORA
Cedar Lane Resort
(502) 474-8042
Route 68
12 rooms - $39-54
Pets: Welcome
Creature Comforts: CCTV, a/c,
kit, pool

Early American Motel
(502) 474-2241
16749 Rte. 68
19 rooms - $42-69
Pets: Welcome w/$7 fee
Creature Comforts: CCTV,
VCR, a/c, kit, pool

Fin n' Feather Lodge
(502) 474-2351
Route 68
8 rooms - $35-45
Pets: Welcome w/$4 fee
Creature Comforts: CCTV, a/c,
kit, pool

BARDSTOWN
Parkview Motel
(800) 732-2384, (502) 348-5983
418 E. Stephen Foster Ave.
39 rooms - $49-89
Pets: Small pets welcome
Creature Comforts: CCTV, a/c,
kit, cont. brkfst, pool

Holiday Inn
(800) HOLIDAY, (502) 348-9253
http://www.holiday-inn.com
Bluegrass Pkwy.
102 rooms - $69-99
Pets: Small pets welcome
Creature Comforts: CCTV,
VCR, a/c, refrig, restaurant, hlth
club, sauna, pool, whirlpool

Old Kentucky Home
(800) 772-1174, (502) 348-5979
414 Stephen Foster Ave.
35 rooms - $36-53
Pets: Small pets welcome
Creature Comforts: CCTV, a/c,
refrig, pool

Ramada Inn
(800) 2-Ramada, (502) 349-0363
http://www.ramada.com
523 N. 3rd St.
40 rooms - $55-89
Pets: Welcome
Creature Comforts: CCTV, a/c,
refrig, pool

Red Carpet Inn
(800) 251-1962, (502) 348-1112
http://www.reservahost.com
1714 New Haven Rd.
25 rooms - $39-58
Pets: Small pets in smoking rms.
Creature Comforts: CCTV, a/c

BEREA
Boone Tavern Hotel
(800) 366-9358, (606) 986-9358
http://www.4berea.com/tavern
100 Main St.
59 rooms - $59-99
Pets: Small pets welcome
Creature Comforts: Historic
southern inn now run by Berea
College students, pleasant rms w/
traditional furnishings handmade
by students, CCTV, a/c, restaurant,
hlth club access

Days Inn
(800) DAYS-INN, (606) 986-7373
http://www.daysinn.com
Rtes. 595 & 75
60 rooms - $49-69
Pets: Welcome w/$5 fee
Creature Comforts: CCTV, a/c,
kit, pool

Econo Lodge
(800) 55-ECONO, (606) 986-9323
http://www.econolodge.com
1010 Paint Lick Rd.
46 rooms - $49-79
Pets: Small pets welcome
Creature Comforts: CCTV,
VCR, a/c, refrig, micro, Jacuzzis,
cont. brkfst

Holiday Motel
(606) 986-9311
100 Jane St.
62 rooms - $49-60
Pets: Small pets w/$5 fee
Creature Comforts: CCTV, a/c,
kit, pool

Knights Inn
(800) 843-5644, (606) 986-2384
http://www.knightsinn.com
715 Chestnut St.
57 rooms - $40-70
Pets: Welcome w/$5 fee
Creature Comforts: CCTV, a/c,
refrig, micro, cont. brkfst

Super 8 Motel
(800) 800-8000, (606) 986-8426
http://www.super8.com
196 Prince Royal Dr.
60 rooms - $39-75
Pets: Welcome w/permission.
Creature Comforts: CCTV,
VCR, a/c, cont. brkfst, pool

BOWLING GREEN

Alpine Lodge
(502) 843-4846
http://travelassist.com/reg/
ky102s.html
5310 Morgantown Rd.
5 rooms - $45-90
Pets: Small pets welcome
Creature Comforts: Swiss Chalet style lodge on 11 buccolic acres, CCTV, a/c, Southern brkfst, pool, whirlpool, gazebo

Baymont Inn
(877)BAYMONT, (502) 843-3200
http://www.baymontinns.com
165 - 3 Springs Rd.
101 rooms - $49-68
Pets: Small pets w/$5 fee
Creature Comforts: CCTV, a/c, cont. brkfst

Drury Inn
(800) Drury-Inn, (502) 842-7100
http://www.drury-inn.com
3250 Scottsville Rd.
142 rooms - $55-89
Pets: Welcome
Creature Comforts: CCTV, a/c, cont. brkfst, pool

Holiday Inn
(800) HOLIDAY, (502) 781-1500
http://www.holiday-inn.com
3240 Scottsville Rd.
106 rooms - $50-119
Pets: Small pets welcome
Creature Comforts: CCTV, a/c, refrig, micro, restaurant, hlth club, pool, whirlpool

Motel 6
(800) 4-MOTEL6, (502) 843-0140
http://www.motel6.com
3199 Scottsville Rd.
91 rooms - $35-49
Pets: Under 30 lbs. welcome
Creature Comforts: CCTV, a/c, pool

News Inn Bowling Green
(800) 443-3701, (502) 781-3460
3160 Scottsville Rd.
54 rooms - $44-69
Pets: Small pets w/$5 fee in the smoking rooms
Creature Comforts: CCTV, a/c, refrig, micro, cont. brkfst, pool

Ramada Inn
(800) 2-Ramada, (502) 781-3000
http://www.ramada.com
4767 Scottsville Rd.
120 rooms - $55-85
Pets: Welcome
Creature Comforts: CCTV, a/c, refrig, restaurant, pool

Scottish Inns
(800) 251-1962, (502) 781-6550
http://www.reservahost.com
3140 Scottsville Rd.
69 rooms - $39-55
Pets: Welcome
Creature Comforts: CCTV, a/c, cont. brkfst, pool

BROOKS

Baymont Inn
(877)BAYMONT, (502) 955-9550
http://www.baymontinns.com
191 Brenton Way
82 rooms - $55-75
Pets: Small pets welcome
Creature Comforts: CCTV, a/c, cont. brkfst

BURKESVILLE

Riverfront Lodge
(502) 864-3300
305 Keen St.
42 rooms - $45-59
Pets: Small pets welcome
Creature Comforts: CCTV, a/c, pool

CADIZ

Country Inn by Carlson
(800) 456-4000, (502) 522-7007
http://www.countryinns.com
5909 Hopkinsville Rd.
49 rooms - $60-75
Pets: Welcome w/$25 dep.
Creature Comforts: CCTV, VCR, a/c, cont. brkfst, pool

Holiday Inn Express
(800) HOLIDAY, (502) 522-3700
http://www.holiday-inn.com
153 Broad Bent Blvd.
50 rooms - $60-70
Pets: Small pets welcome in smoking rms.
Creature Comforts: CCTV, a/c, pool

CAMPBELLSVILLE

Best Western Campbellsville
(800) 528-1234, (502) 465-7001
http://www.bestwestern.com
1400 E. Broadway
59 rooms - $55-65
Pets: Small pets welcome
Creature Comforts: CCTV, a/c, refrig, micro, pool

CARROLLTON

Blue Gables Court
(502) 732-4248
1501 Highland Ave.
20 rooms - $30-49
Pets: Small pets welcome
Creature Comforts: CCTV, a/c, refrig

Days Inn
(800) DAYS-INN, (502) 732-9301
http://www.daysinn.com
Rtes. 71 & 227
84 rooms - $50-79
Pets: Welcome
Creature Comforts: CCTV, a/c, cont. brkfst, pool

Holiday Inn Express
(800) HOLIDAY, (502) 732-6661
http://www.holiday-inn.com
141 Inn Rd.
63 rooms - $65-79
Pets: Small pets welcome
Creature Comforts: CCTV, a/c, micro, pool

Super 8 Motel
(800) 800-8000, (502) 732-9301
http://www.super8.com
130 Slumber Ln.
45 rooms - $50-55
Pets: Welcome
Creature Comforts: CCTV, a/c

CAVE CITY

Comfort Inn
(800) 228-5150, (270) 773-2030
http://www.comfortinn.com
801 Mammoth Cave Rd.
66 rooms - $45-99
Pets: Welcome w/$5 fee
Creature Comforts: CCTV, a/c, refrig, micro, Jacuzzis, cont. brkfst, pool

Days Inn
(800) DAYS-INN, (270) 773-2151
http://www.daysinn.com
Rtes. 65 & 70
110 rooms - $35-69
Pets: Welcome if attended
Creature Comforts: CCTV,
VCR, a/c, refrig, restaurant, cont.
brkfst, whirlpool, pool

Holiday Inn Express
(800) HOLIDAY, (270) 773-3101
http://www.holiday-inn.com
102 Happy Valley St.
105 rooms - $65-79
Pets: Welcome w/$7 fee
Creature Comforts: CCTV, a/c,
refrig, micro, pool

Quality Inn
(800) 228-5151, (270) 773-2181
http://www.qualityinn.com
Mammoth Cave Rd.
99 rooms - $35-80
Pets: Small pets w/$6 fee
Creature Comforts: CCTV, a/c,
refrig, micro, pool

Super 8 Motel
(800) 800-8000, (270) 773-2500
http://www.super8.com
799 Mammoth Cave St.
50 rooms - $35-85
Pets: Welcome w/$5 fee
Creature Comforts: CCTV, a/c,
kit, Jacuzzis, cont. brkfst, pool

CORBIN
Baymont Inn
(877)BAYMONT, (606) 523-9040
http://www.baymontinns.com
174 Adams Rd.
96 rooms - $49-75
Pets: Small pets welcome
Creature Comforts: CCTV, a/c,
kit, cont. brkfst, pool

Holiday Inn
(800) HOLIDAY, (606) 528-6301
http://www.holiday-inn.com
2615 Cumberland Falls Hwy.
142 rooms - $60-85
Pets: Welcome
Creature Comforts: CCTV, a/c,
restaurant, pool

Knights Inn
(800) 843-5644, (606) 523-1500
http://www.knightsinn.com
37 Rte. 770
110 rooms - $37-56
Pets: Welcome w/$6 fee
Creature Comforts: CCTV, a/c,
kit, pool

Super 8 Motel
(800) 800-8000, (606) 528-8888
http://www.super8.com
Route 11
62 rooms - $45-70
Pets: Welcome w/$6 fee
Creature Comforts: CCTV, a/c,
kit, Jacuzzis, cont. brkfst

COVINGTON
Embassy Suites
(800) 362-2779, (606) 261-8400
http://www.embassy-suites.com
10 E. Rivercenter Blvd.
225 rooms - $140-225
Pets: Small pets welcome
Creature Comforts: CCTV, a/c,
refrig, restaurant, pool

Riverview Hotel
(800) 292-2079, (606) 491-1200
http://www.hotelschoice.com
668 Fifth St.
238 rooms - $90-139
Pets: Small pets welcome
Creature Comforts: CCTV, a/c,
refrig, micro, restaurant, hlth club,
whirlpool, pool, game rm.

Sanford House B&B
(888) 291-9133, (606) 291-9133
e-mail: DanRRmiles@aol.com
1026 Russell St.
4 rooms - $55-85
Pets: Welcome w/$10 fee
Creature Comforts: Historic
1820's Victorian B&B on Nat'l
Hist. Register, charming decor,
antiques, CCTV, VCR, a/c,
Jacuzzi, fireplace, kit, full brkfst,
lovely garden

DANVILLE
Days Inn
(800) DAYS-INN, (606) 236-8601
http://www.daysinn.com
Route 127
113 rooms - $59-79
Pets: Welcome
Creature Comforts: CCTV, a/c,
restaurant, pool

Holiday Inn Express
(800) HOLIDAY, (606) 236-8600
http://www.holiday-inn.com
96 Daniel Dr.
64 rooms - $65-79
Pets: Welcome
Creature Comforts: CCTV, a/c,
refrig, pool

Super 8 Motel
(800) 800-8000, (606) 236-8881
http://www.super8.com
3663 Rte. 150
49 rooms - $43-59
Pets: Welcome w/$50 fee
Creature Comforts: CCTV, a/c,
Jacuzzis, cont. brkfst

DRY RIDGE
Super 8 Motel
(800) 800-8000, (606) 824-3700
http://www.super8.com
88 Blackburn Lane
50 rooms - $45-75
Pets: Welcome w/permission.
Creature Comforts: CCTV, a/c,
Jacuzzis

EDDYVILLE
Eddy Bay Lodging
(502) 388-9960
75 Forest Glen Dr.
15 rooms - $65-129
Pets: Welcome w/$3 fee
Creature Comforts: CCTV, a/c,
kit

Holiday Hills Townhouses
(502) 388-7236
5631 Rte. 93
6 rooms - $69-155
Pets: Welcome w/$25 fee
Creature Comforts: CCTV, a/c,
kit, pool

Regency Inn
(502) 388-2281
616 Tanner Ave.
24 rooms - $44-65
Pets: Small pets welcome
Creature Comforts: CCTV, a/c,
pool

ELIZABETHTOWN
Best Western Cardinal Inn
(800) 528-1234, (502) 765-6139
http://www.bestwestern.com
642 E. Dixie Rd.
67 rooms - $45-60
Pets: Welcome w/CC dep.
Creature Comforts: CCTV, a/c,
pool

Comfort Inn
(800) 228-5150, (502) 769-3030
http://www.comfortinn.com
1043 Executive Dr.
132 rooms - $59-105
Pets: Small pet welcome
Creature Comforts: CCTV, a/c,
refrig, micro, Jacuzzis, hlth club,
pool

Days Inn
(800) DAYS-INN, (502) 769-5522
http://www.daysinn.com
2010 N. Mulberry Rd.
121 rooms - $43-59
Pets: Welcome w/$5 fee
Creature Comforts: CCTV, a/c,
restaurant, cont. brkfst, pool

Motel 6
(800) 4-MOTEL6, (502) 769-3102
http://www.motel6.com
Rtes. 62 & 65
98 rooms - $29-49
Pets: Under 30 lbs. welcome
Creature Comforts: CCTV, a/c,
pool

Super 8 Motel
(800) 800-8000, (502) 737-1088
http://www.super8.com
2028 N. Mulberry St.
59 rooms - $40-66
Pets: Welcome w/$5 fee
Creature Comforts: CCTV, a/c,
cont. brkfst, pool

ERLANGER
Baymont Inn
(877)BAYMONT, (606) 746-0300
http://www.baymontinns.com
1805 Airport Exchange Blvd.
115 rooms - $75-95
Pets: Welcome in pet rooms
Creature Comforts: CCTV, a/c,
refrig, micro, cont. brkfst, pool

Comfort Inn
(800) 228-5150, (606) 727-3400
http://www.comfortinn.com
630 Donaldson Rd.
144 rooms - $59-90
Pets: Small pet w/$20 fee
Creature Comforts: CCTV, a/c,
refrig, restaurant, pool

Howard Johnson Express
(800) I-Go-Hojo, (606) 342-6200
http://www.hojo.com
648 Donaldson Rd.
81 rooms - $44-70
Pets: Welcome
Creature Comforts: CCTV,
VCR, a/c, cont. brkfst, pool

Residence Inn
(800) 331-3131, (606) 282-7400
http://www.residenceinn.com
2811 Circleport Dr.
80 rooms - $100-190
Pets: Welcome w/$150 fee
Creature Comforts: CCTV,
VCR, a/c, kit, fireplace, cont.
brkfst, pool, exercise rm.

FAIRDEALING
Cozy Cove Resort
(800) 467-8168, (502) 354-8168
http://www.kentuckylake.com/
cozycove
1917 Reed Rd.
12 cottages - $65-1,600
Pets: Welcome w/$50 fee
Creature Comforts: A dozen log
cabin cottages set along Kentucky
Lake, CCTV, Jacuzzi, brass beds,
country decor, kit, sandy beach,
boat rentals, playground

King Creek Resort
(502) 354-8268
972 King Creek Rd.
9 rooms - $475-1,100/wk
Pets: Welcome w/$20 fee
Creature Comforts: CCTV, kit,
marina, boat rentals

FLORENCE
Amerisuites
(800) 833-1516, (606) 647-1170
http://www.amerisuites.com
300 Meijer Dr.
130 rooms - $115-130
Pets: Welcome w/$50 fee
Creature Comforts: CCTV,
VCR, a/c, refrig, micro, cont.
brkfst, hlth club, whirlpool

Best Western Inn
(800) 528-1234, (606) 525-0090
http://www.bestwestern.com
7821 Commerce Dr.
51 rooms - $65-80
Pets: Welcome
Creature Comforts: CCTV, a/c,
Jacuzzis, cont. brkfst, pool

Knights Inn
(800) 843-5644, (606) 371-9711
http://www.knightsinn.com
8049 Dream St.
115 rooms - $40-69
Pets: Welcome
Creature Comforts: CCTV, a/c,
kit, cont. brkfst, pool

Motel 6
(800) 4-MOTEL6, (606) 283-0909
http://www.motel6.com
7937 Dream St.
79 rooms - $40-65
Pets: Under 30 lbs. welcome
Creature Comforts: CCTV, a/c,
pool

Super 8 Motel
(800) 800-8000, (606) 283-1221
http://www.super8.com
7928 Dream St.
93 rooms - $45-65
Pets: Welcome in pet rooms
Creature Comforts: CCTV, a/c,
refrig, Jacuzzis, cont. brkfst

FT. MITCHELL
Holiday Inn
(800) HOLIDAY, (606) 331-1500
http://www.holiday-inn.com
2100 Dixie Hwy.
215 rooms - $80-139
Pets: Welcome w/$10 fee
Creature Comforts: CCTV, a/c,
refrig, restaurant, hlth club, sauna,
whirlpool, pool

FT. WRIGHT
Days Inn
(800) DAYS-INN, (606) 341-8801
http://www.daysinn.com
1945 Dixie Hwy.
115 rooms - $43-59
Pets: Welcome
Creature Comforts: CCTV, a/c,
cont. brkfst, pool

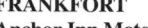

FRANKFORT

Anchor Inn Motel
(502) 227-7404
790 E. Main St.
9 rooms - $35-58
Pets: Welcome
Creature Comforts: CCTV, a/c, refrig

Bluegrass Inn
(800) 322-1802, (502) 695-1800
635 Versailes Rd.
61 rooms - $40-59
Pets: Welcome w/$10 fee
Creature Comforts: CCTV, a/c, kit, pool

Super 8 Motel
(800) 800-8000, (502) 875-3220
http://www.super8.com
1225 Rte. 127
46 rooms - $45-69
Pets: Welcome w/$10 fee
Creature Comforts: CCTV, a/c, cont. brkfst

FRANKLIN

Comfort Inn
(800) 228-5150, (270) 586-6100
http://www.comfortinn.com
3794 Nashville Rd.
54 rooms - $44-79
Pets: Welcome w/$7 fee
Creature Comforts: CCTV, a/c, Jacuzzis, cont. brkfst, pool

Days Inn
(800) DAYS-INN, (270) 598-0163
http://www.daysinn.com
103 Trotter Lane
60 rooms - $39-80
Pets: Welcome w/$5 fee
Creature Comforts: CCTV, a/c, Jacuzzis, cont. brkfst, pool

Holiday Inn Express
(800) HOLIDAY, (270) 586-5090
http://www.holiday-inn.com
3811 Nashville Rd.
55 rooms - $50-65
Pets: Welcome w/$7 fee
Creature Comforts: CCTV, a/c, refrig, Jacuzzis, cont. brkfst, pool

Super 8 Motel
(800) 800-8000, (270) 586-8885
http://www.super8.com
2805 Scottsville Rd.
40 rooms - $39-59
Pets: Welcome w/permission.
Creature Comforts: CCTV, a/c, cont. brkfst

GEORGETOWN

Days Inn
(800) DAYS-INN, (502) 863-5000
http://www.daysinn.com
385 Cherry Blossom Way
67 rooms - $35-109
Pets: Welcome w/$5 fee
Creature Comforts: CCTV, a/c, refrig, Jacuzzis, cont. brkfst, pool

Econo Lodge
(800) 55-ECONO, (502) 863-2240
http://www.econolodge.com
3075 Paris Pike
60 rooms - $32-89
Pets: Welcome
Creature Comforts: CCTV, a/c, Jacuzzis, cont. brkfst, pool

Motel 6
(800) 4-MOTEL6, (502) 863-1166
http://www.motel6.com
401 Cherryblossom Way
98 rooms - $35-55
Pets: Under 30 lbs. welcome
Creature Comforts: CCTV, a/c, pool

Shoney's Inn
(800) 222-2222, (502) 868-9800
http://www.shoneysinn.com
200 Shoney Dr.
105 rooms - $50-74
Pets: Welcome w/$5 fee
Creature Comforts: CCTV, a/c, pool

Super 8 Motel
(800) 800-8000, (502) 863-4888
http://www.super8.com
Rtes. 75 & 62
62 rooms - $45-75
Pets: Welcome w/$6 fee
Creature Comforts: CCTV, VCR, a/c, kit, Jacuzzis, cont. brkfst, pool

GILBERTSVILLE

Moors Resort
(800) 626-5472, (502) 362-8361
http://www.moorsresort.com
Rte. 963 & Moors Rd.
27 rooms - $99-259
Pets: Welcome w/$50 dep.
Creature Comforts: A charming lodge, assorted log cottages, and houseboats are set on Kentucky Lake, inviting ambiance and country decor, brass beds, CCTV, VCR, fireplaces, kit, restaurant, pool, whirlpool, mini golf, beach, marina

Ramada Inn Resort
(800) 2-Ramada, (502) 362-4278
http://www.ramada.com
Route 62
94 rooms - $55-89
Pets: Small pets w/$25 dep.
Creature Comforts: CCTV, a/c, restaurant, pool

GLASGOW

Comfort Inn
(800) 228-5150, (502) 651-9099
http://www.comfortinn.com
210 Calvary Rd.
62 rooms - $55-75
Pets: Welcome w/$5 fee
Creature Comforts: CCTV, a/c, refrig, micro, Jacuzzis, pool

Family Budget Inn
(800) Glascow, (502) 651-1757
http://www.familybudgetinns.com
1003 W. Main St.
80 rooms - $39-60
Pets: Welcome
Creature Comforts: CCTV, a/c, restaurant, cont. brkfst, pool

GRAND RIVERS

Best Western Barkley-Lakes
(800) 528-1234, (502) 928-2700
http://www.bestwestern.com
720 Complex Dr.
80 rooms - $50-85
Pets: Small pets w/$5 fee
Creature Comforts: CCTV, a/c, refrig, Jacuzzis, cont. brkfst

HARLAN
Best Western Inn
(800) 528-1234, (606) 573-3385
http://www.bestwestern.com
2608 S. Rte. 421
62 rooms - $65-85
Pets: Small pets welcome
Creature Comforts: CCTV, a/c,
cont. brkfst, pool

HARRODSBURG
Best Western Inn
(800) 528-1234, (606) 734-9431
http://www.bestwestern.com
1680 Danville Rd.
69 rooms - $55-79
Pets: Small pets welcome
Creature Comforts: CCTV, a/c,
cont. brkfst, pool

HAZARD
Days Inn
(800) DAYS-INN, (606) 436-4777
http://www.daysinn.com
359 Morton Blvd.
60 rooms - $47-69
Pets: Welcome w/$6 fee
Creature Comforts: CCTV, a/c,
cont. brkfst, whirlpool, pool

HEBRON
Radisson Inn, Airport
(800) 333-3333, (606) 371-6166
http://www.radisson.com
Rtes. 275 & 212
215 rooms - $75-169
Pets: Small pets welcome
Creature Comforts: CCTV, a/c,
refrig, restaurant, pool

HENDERSON
Days Inn
(800) DAYS-INN, (502) 826-6600
http://www.daysinn.com
2044 Rte. 41
117 rooms - $54-119
Pets: Welcome
Creature Comforts: CCTV, a/c,
restaurant, pool

Scottish Inns
(800) 251-1962, (502) 827-1806
http://www.reservahost.com
2820 Rte. 41
65 rooms - $39-55
Pets: Welcome w/$5 fee
Creature Comforts: CCTV, a/c,
cont. brkfst, pool

HOPKINSVILLE
Best Western Inn
(800) 528-1234, (502) 886-9000
http://www.bestwestern.com
4101 Ft. Campbell Blvd.
108 rooms - $55-75
Pets: Under 20 lbs. w/$4 fee
Creature Comforts: CCTV, a/c,
cont. brkfst, hlth/racq. club, pool

Econo Lodge
(800) 55-ECONO, (502) 886-5242
http://www.econolodge.com
2916 Ft. Cambell Blvd.
90 rooms - $45-70
Pets: Welcome
Creature Comforts: CCTV, a/c,
cont. brkfst, sauna, whirlpool, pool

Holiday Inn
(800) HOLIDAY, (502) 886-4413
http://www.holiday-inn.com
2910 Ft. Campbell Blvd.
101 rooms - $65-84
Pets: Welcome
Creature Comforts: CCTV, a/c,
restaurant, pool

Rodeway Inn
(800) 228-2000, (502) 885-1126
http://www.rodeway.com
2923 Ft. Campbell Blvd.
55 rooms - $40-59
Pets: Welcome
Creature Comforts: CCTV, a/c,
cont. brkfst, hlth club

HORSE CAVE
Budget Host
(800) Bud-Host, (270) 786-2165
http://www.budgethost.com
Route 65
80 rooms - $35-55
Pets: Small pets w/$5 fee
Creature Comforts: CCTV,
VCR, a/c, kit, cont. brkfst

HURSTBOURNE
Red Roof Inn, East
(800) The-Roof, (502) 426-7621
http://www.redroof.com
9330 Blairwood Rd.
107 rooms - $50-79
Pets: Small pets welcome
Creature Comforts: CCTV, a/c,
restaurant

IRVINE
Oak Tree Inn
(800) 528-1234, (606) 723-2600
1075 Richmond Rd.
28 rooms - $55-60
Pets: Small pets welcome
Creature Comforts: CCTV, a/c,
refrig, micro, exercise room

JEFFERSONTOWN
Amerisuites
(800) 833-1516, (502) 426-0119
http://www.amerisuites.com
701 S. Hurstbourne Pkwy.
125 rooms - $85-120
Pets: Under 10 lbs.
Creature Comforts: CCTV,
VCR, a/c, refrig, micro, cont.
brkfst, hlth club

Days Inn
(800) DAYS-INN, (502) 491-1040
http://www.daysinn.com
1850 Embassy Sq. Blvd.
100 rooms - $45-78
Pets: Welcome w/$6 fee
Creature Comforts: CCTV, a/c,
pool

KUTTAWA
Days Inn
(800) DAYS-INN, (270) 388-5420
http://www.daysinn.com
Factory Outlet Ave.
60 rooms - $55-79
Pets: Welcome w/$10 fee
Creature Comforts: CCTV, a/c,
Jacuzzis, cont. brkfst, pool

LAGRANGE
Days Inn
(800) DAYS-INN, (502) 222-7192
http://www.daysinn.com
Rtes. 71 & 53
90 rooms - $45-65
Pets: Welcome
Creature Comforts: CCTV, a/c,
restaurant, pool

LEBANON
Country Hearth Inn
(800) 528-1234, (502) 692-4445
720 West Main St.
40 rooms - $45-90
Pets: Small pets welcome
Creature Comforts: CCTV, a/c,
refrig, micro, Jacuzzis, cont.
brkfst, pool

LEITCHFIELD

Countryside Inn
(502) 259-4021
315 Commerce Dr.
46 rooms - $39-45
Pets: Welcome
Creature Comforts: CCTV, a/c

LEXINGTON

Best Western Regency
(800) 528-1234, (606) 293-2202
http://www.bestwestern.com
Rtes. 75 & 60
112 rooms - $55-109
Pets: Small pets welcome
Creature Comforts: CCTV, a/c,
refrig, Jacuzzis, cont. brkfst,
whirlpool, sauna, pool

Days Inn
(800) DAYS-INN, (606) 299-1202
http://www.daysinn.com
1987 N. Broadway St.
189 rooms - $43-99
Pets: Welcome w/$7 fee
Creature Comforts: CCTV, a/c,
restaurant, cont. brkfst, pool

Days Inn, South
(800) DAYS-INN, (606) 263-3100
http://www.daysinn.com
5575 Athens Rd.
56 rooms - $42-70
Pets: Welcome w/$3 fee
Creature Comforts: CCTV, a/c,
cont. brkfst

Econo Lodge
(800) 55-ECONO, (606) 231-6300
http://www.econolodge.com
925 Newton Pike
110 rooms - $35-70
Pets: Welcome
Creature Comforts: CCTV, a/c,
refrig, restaurant, cont. brkfst, pool

Econo Lodge
(800) 55-ECONO, (606) 263-5101
http://www.econolodge.com
5527 Athens Rd.
67 rooms - $30-65
Pets: Welcome
Creature Comforts: CCTV, a/c,
refrig, cont. brkfst

Greenleaf Inn
(800) 354-9096, (606) 277-1191
2280 Nicholasville Rd.
111 rooms - $45-65
Pets: Welcome w/$50 dep.
Creature Comforts: CCTV, a/c,
refrig, cont. brkfst, pool

Holiday Inn, North
(800) HOLIDAY, (606) 233-0512
http://www.holiday-inn.com
1950 Newton Pike
302 rooms - $99-179
Pets: Welcome
Creature Comforts: CCTV, a/c,
restaurant, hlth club, sauna, pool,
whirlpool

Holiday Inn, South
(800) HOLIDAY, (606) 263-5241
http://www.holiday-inn.com
5532 Athens Rd.
150 rooms - $70-109
Pets: Small pets welcome
Creature Comforts: CCTV, a/c,
kit, restaurant, hlth club, sauna,
pool, whirlpool, and a rec. dome

Kentucky Inn
(800) 221-6652, (606) 254-1177
525 Walker St.
105 rooms - $50-74
Pets: Welcome w/$50 fee
Creature Comforts: CCTV, a/c,
refrig, restaurant, pool

La Quinta Inn
(800) Nu-Rooms, (606) 231-7551
http://www.laquinta.com
1919 Stanton Way
128 rooms - $59-80
Pets: Small pets welcome
Creature Comforts: CCTV, a/c,
refrig, cont. brkfst, pool

Marriott Griffin Gate
(800) 228-9290, (606) 231-5100
http://www.marriott.com
1800 Newtown Pike
409 rooms - $99-899
Pets: Welcome w/$40 fee
Creature Comforts: Modern, full
service resort w/appealing
amenities, CCTV, VCR, a/c, kit,
refrig, fireplaces, Jacuzzis,
bathrobes, restaurants, expansive
recreational facilities include pool,
hlth clb, sauna, tennis, golf,
whirlpools, solarium, set along the
water

Motel 6
(800) 4-MOTEL6, (606) 293-1431
http://www.motel6.com
2260 Elkhorn Rd.
98 rooms - $35-53
Pets: Under 30 lbs. welcome
Creature Comforts: CCTV, a/c,
pool

Quality Inn
(800) 228-5151, (606) 233-0561
http://www.qualityinn.com
1050 Newtown Pike
99 rooms - $60-75
Pets: Welcome
Creature Comforts: CCTV, a/c,
refrig, micro, cont. brkfst, pool

Radisson Hotel
(800) 333-3333, (606) 231-9000
http://www.radisson.com
369 W. Vine St.
365 rooms - $89-450
Pets: Small pets w/$30 fee
Creature Comforts: CCTV, a/c,
restaurant, hlth club, sauna,
whirlpool, pool

Red Roof Inn, North
(800) The-Roof, (606) 293-2626
http://www.redroof.com
483 Haggard Ln.
105 rooms - $48-80
Pets: Small pets welcome
Creature Comforts: CCTV, a/c

Red Roof Inn, South
(800) The-Roof, (606) 277-9400
http://www.redroof.com
2651 White Dr.
115 rooms - $44-80
Pets: Small pets welcome
Creature Comforts: CCTV, a/c

Residence Inn
(800) 331-3131, (606) 231-6191
http://www.residenceinn.com
1080 Newtown Pike
80 rooms - $99-189
Pets: Welcome $150 fee
Creature Comforts: CCTV,
VCR, a/c, kit, fireplaces, cont.
brkfst, pool, tennis, whirlpools

Shoney's Inn
(800) 222-2222, (606) 269-4999
http://www.shoneysinn.com
2753 Richmond Rd.
103 rooms - $50-74
Pets: Welcome
Creature Comforts: CCTV, a/c,
refrig, pool

Super 8 Motel
(800) 800-8000, (606) 299-6241
http://www.super8.com
2351 Buena Vista Rd.
62 rooms - $45-74
Pets: Welcome
Creature Comforts: CCTV, a/c,
refrig, micro

Wilson Inn & Suites
(800) 945-7667, (606) 293-6113
2400 Buena Vista Dr.
110 rooms - $45-79
Pets: Welcome
Creature Comforts: CCTV, a/c,
cont. brkfst, pool

LIBERTY
Brown Motel
(606) 787-6224
Route 127
22 rooms - $52-75
Pets: Small pets w/$2 fee
Creature Comforts: CCTV, a/c,
refrig, micro, pool

LONDON
Best Western Harvest Inn
(800) 528-1234, (606) 864-2222
http://www.bestwestern.com
207 W. Rte. 80
100 rooms - $45-80
Pets: Small pets welcome
Creature Comforts: CCTV, a/c,
refrig, micro, Jacuzzis, cont.
brkfst, whirlpool, pool

Budget Host Westgate
(800) Bud-Host, (606) 878-7330
http://www.budgethost.com
254 W. Dan. Boone Pkwy.
45 rooms - $40-69
Pets: Welcome
Creature Comforts: CCTV, a/c,
Jacuzzis, cont. brkfst

Days Inn
(800) DAYS-INN, (606) 878-9800
http://www.daysinn.com
2035 West Rte. 192
64 rooms - $36-99
Pets: Welcome w/$4 fee
Creature Comforts: CCTV, a/c,
refrig, micro, cont. brkfst,
restaurant, hlth club, pool

Super 8 Motel
(800) 800-8000, (606) 878-9800
http://www.super8.com
285 West Rte. 80
64 rooms - $49-75
Pets: Welcome w/permission.
Creature Comforts: CCTV, a/c,
refrig, micro, Jacuzzis, cont.
brkfst, pool, exercise rm.

LOUISA
Best Western Village Inn
(800) 528-1234, (606) 638-9417
http://www.bestwestern.com
117 E. Madison St.
28 rooms - $45-69
Pets: Welcome
Creature Comforts: CCTV, a/c,
refrig

LOUISVILLE
Breckinridge Inn
(502) 456-5050
2800 Breckinridge Ln.
122 rooms - $75-99
Pets: Welcome w/$50 dep.
Creature Comforts: CCTV, a/c,
refrig, restaurant, pool, tennis,
sauna, hlth clb.

Days Inn, East
(800) DAYS-INN, (502) 896-8871
http://www.daysinn.com
4621 Shelbyville Rd.
90 rooms - $60-80
Pets: Welcome w/$10 fee
Creature Comforts: CCTV,
VCR, a/c, refrig, micro, cont.
brkfst, pool, hlth clb.

Executive Inn
(800) 626-2708, (502) 367-6161
http://www.executivewest.com
978 Phillips Ln.
466 rooms - $85-129
Pets: Welcome w/$100 fee
Creature Comforts: CCTV,
VCR, a/c, kit, restaurant, pool,
sauna, whirlpool

Executive Inn, West
(800) 626-2708, (502) 367-2251
http://www.executivewest.com
830 Phillips Ln.
612 rooms - $80-129
Pets: Welcome w/$100 fee
Creature Comforts: CCTV, a/c,
refrig, micro, restaurant, pool

Holiday Inn, Airport
(800) HOLIDAY, (502) 452-6361
http://www.holiday-inn.com
1465 Gardiner Ln.
198 rooms - $90-139
Pets: Welcome
Creature Comforts: CCTV, a/c,
refrig, micro, restaurant, pool,
exercise rm., tennis

Holiday Inn, Downtown
(800) HOLIDAY, (502) 582-2241
http://www.holiday-inn.com
120 W. Broadway
285 rooms - $99-179
Pets: Welcome
Creature Comforts: CCTV, a/c,
refrig, micro, restaurant, pool,
exercise rm.

Holiday Inn Rivermont
(800) HOLIDAY, (502) 897-5101
http://www.holiday-inn.com
1041 Zorn St.
119 rooms - $80-129
Pets: Welcome
Creature Comforts: CCTV, a/c,
restaurant, pool

Holiday Inn South, Airport
(800) HOLIDAY, (502) 964-3311
http://www.holiday-inn.com
3317 Fern Valley Rd.
404 rooms - $90-139
Pets: Welcome w/$10 fee
Creature Comforts: CCTV, a/c,
refrig, restaurant, pool, and an
exercise room

Holiday Inn, Southeast
(800) HOLIDAY, (502) 454-0451
http://www.holiday-inn.com
3255 Bardstown Rd.
195 rooms - $90-129
Pets: Small pets w/$50 fee
Creature Comforts: CCTV, a/c, refrig, cont. brkfst, restaurant, hlth club, whirlpool, pool

Holiday Inn, Southwest
(800) HOLIDAY, (502) 448-2020
http://www.holiday-inn.com
4110 Dixie Hwy.
170 rooms - $75-125
Pets: Welcome
Creature Comforts: CCTV, a/c, restaurant, pool, whirlpool, hlth clb.

Mainstay Suites
(800) 660-MAIN, (502) 267-4454
1650 Alliant Ave.
100 rooms - $70-95
Pets: Welcome w/$5 fee
Creature Comforts: CCTV, a/c, kit, cont. brkfst, pool, exercise rm.

Melrose Inn
(502) 228-1136
13306 Rte. 42
40 rooms - $45-69
Pets: Welcome w/$7 fee, $25 dep.
Creature Comforts: CCTV, a/c, refrig, restaurant, pool

Old Louisville Inn
(502) 635-1574
http://www.OldLouInn.com
1359 South Third St.
10 rooms - $95-195
Pets: Welcome w/approval
Creature Comforts: Elegant Victorian inn, circa 1901, set in historic district, antiques, orig. mahogany woodworking and handcut crystal fixtures, hardwood flrs, 12-ft. ceilings, four-poster beds, VCR, a/c, cont. brkfst w/ special popovers, games

Ramada Inn, Airport
(800) 2-Ramada, (502) 456-4411
http://www.ramada.com
1921 Bishop Ln.
150 rooms - $80-99
Pets: Small pets w/$25 fee
Creature Comforts: CCTV, VCR, a/c, restaurant, refrig, pool

Ramada Inn
(800) 2-Ramada, (502) 893-2551
http://www.ramada.com
4805 Brownsboro Rd.
145 rooms - $75-109
Pets: Small pets w/$50 fee
Creature Comforts: CCTV, VCR, a/c, restaurant, refrig, pool

Red Roof Inn, Airport
(800) The-Roof, (502) 968-0151
http://www.redroof.com
4704 Preston Hwy.
108 rooms - $44-95
Pets: Small pets welcome
Creature Comforts: CCTV, a/c

Red Roof Inn
(800) The-Roof, (502) 456-2993
http://www.redroof.com
3322 Red Roof Inn Pl.
112 rooms - $65-88
Pets: Small pets welcome
Creature Comforts: CCTV, a/c

Residence Inn
(800) 331-3131, (502) 425-1821
http://www.residenceinn.com
120 N. Hurstbourne Pkwy.
98 rooms - $99-189
Pets: Welcome $75 fee
Creature Comforts: CCTV, VCR, a/c, kit, cont. brkfst, pool, whirlpools

Rivermont Inn
(502) 897-5101
1041 Zorn Ave.
118 rooms - $99-189
Pets: Welcome
Creature Comforts: CCTV, a/c, restaurant, pool, whirlpools

Rocking Horse Manor
(888) Horse-BB, (502) 583-0408
http://www.bbonline.com/ky/
rockinghorse
1022 S. Third St.
5 rooms - $75-135
Pets: Welcome
Creature Comforts: 1888
Richardson Romanesque mansion, parquet flrs, ornately carved woodwork w/rich patina, stained glass windows, Oriental rugs, four-poster beds, feather beds, handmade quilts, beautifully decorated rooms, CCTV, a/c, robes, full brkfst

Seelbach Hilton
(800) 333-3399, (502) 585-3200
http://www.hilton.com
500 Fourth Ave.
321 rooms - $89-525
Pets: Welcome w/$50 dep.
Creature Comforts: Historic 1905 hotel w/early American accents and restored Victorian antique furnishings, four-poster beds, CCTV, VCR, a/c, refrig, Jacuzzis, gourmet, award-winning restaurant and wine cellar, hlth club access, pool

Sleep Inn Fairgrounds
(800) Sleep-Inn, (502) 368-9597
http://www.sleepinn.com
3330 Preston Hwy.
77 rooms - $45-199
Pets: $5 daily fee & $25 clean fee
Creature Comforts: CCTV, a/c, cont. brkfst

Super 8 Motel
(800) 800-8000, (502) 968-0088
http://www.super8.com
4800 Preston Hwy.
100 rooms - $49-75
Pets: Welcome w/permission.
Creature Comforts: CCTV, a/c, cont. brkfst

Thrifty Dutchman Motel
(502) 968-8124
3357 Fern Valley Rd.
99 rooms - $39-55
Pets: Welcome w/$35 dep.
Creature Comforts: CCTV, VCR, a/c, refrig, micro

Wilson Inn, Airport
(800) WILSONS, (502) 473-0000
http://www.wilsoninns.com
3209 Kemmons Dr.
108 rooms - $34-65
Pets: Welcome
Creature Comforts: CCTV, a/c, cont. brkfst

Wilson Inn
(800) WILSONS, (502) 499-0000
http://www.wilsoninns.com
9802 Bunsen Way
70 rooms - $34-65
Pets: Welcome
Creature Comforts: CCTV, a/c, cont. brkfst

Woodhaven B&B
(888) 895-1011, (502) 895-1011
401 S. Hubbards La.
7 rooms - $70-95
Pets: Welcome
Creature Comforts: A charming
Gothic Revival B&B that dates
back to the 1850s, CCTV, VCR,
a/c, fireplace, refrig, cont. brkfst

MADISONVILLE
Days Inn
(800) DAYS-INN, (502) 821-8620
http://www.daysinn.com
1900 Lantaff Blvd.
143 rooms - $59-170
Pets: Welcome w/$5 fee
Creature Comforts: CCTV, a/c,
restaurant, cont. brkfst, sauna,
pool

MAMMOTH CAVE
Mammoth Cave Hotel
(502) 758-2225
Mammoth Cave Rd.
100 rooms - $39-75
Pets: Welcome
Creature Comforts: TV,
restaurant, tennis

MAYFIELD
Super 8 Motel
(800) 800-8000, (502) 247-8899
http://www.super8.com
1100 Links Lane
47 rooms - $45-69
Pets: Welcome w/permission.
Creature Comforts: CCTV, a/c,
cont. brkfst

MAYSVILLE
Ramada Inn
(800) 2-Ramada, (606) 564-6793
http://www.ramada.com
484 Moody Dr.
120 rooms - $65-85
Pets: Welcome
Creature Comforts: CCTV, a/c,
kit, restaurant, tennis, pool

MIDDLESBORO
Park View Motel
(606) 248-4516
202 - 1/2 N. 12th St.
21 rooms - $35-55
Pets: Welcome
Creature Comforts: CCTV, a/c,
refrig

MORTON'S GAP
Best Western Pennyrile
(800) 528-1234, (502) 258-5201
http://www.bestwestern.com
Pennyrile Pkwy.
60 rooms - $45-65
Pets: Welcome w/$15 deposit
Creature Comforts: CCTV,
VCR, a/c, refrig, cont. brkfst, pool

MT. STERLING
Days Inn
(800) DAYS-INN, (606) 498-4680
http://www.daysinn.com
8705 Maysville Rd.
94 rooms - $32-59
Pets: Welcome w/$5 fee
Creature Comforts: CCTV, a/c,
restaurant, pool

Scottish Inns
(800) 251-1962, (606) 498-3424
http://www.reservahost.com
517 Maysville Rd.
65 rooms - $35-55
Pets: Welcome
Creature Comforts: CCTV, a/c,
cont. brkfst, pool

MT. VERNON
Days Inn
(800) DAYS-INN, (606) 256-3300
http://www.daysinn.com
Route 25
100 rooms - $35-84
Pets: Welcome
Creature Comforts: CCTV, a/c,
cont. brkfst

Econo Lodge
(800) 55-ECONO, (606) 256-4621
http://www.econolodge.com
1630 Richmond St.
35 rooms - $35-85
Pets: Welcome
Creature Comforts: CCTV, a/c,
pool

Kastle Inn Motel
(606) 256-5156
Rtes. 25 & 75
52 rooms - $42-59
Pets: Small pets welcome
Creature Comforts: CCTV,
VCR, a/c, kit, pool

MULDRAUGH
Golden Manor Motel
(502) 942-2800
116 Dixie Hwy.
40 rooms - $40-79
Pets: Small pets w/$10 fee
Creature Comforts: CCTV, a/c,
kit, pool

MUNFORDVILLE
Super 8 Motel
(800) 800-8000, (270) 524-4888
http://www.super8.com
88 Stock Penn Rd.
50 rooms - $39-75
Pets: Welcome
Creature Comforts: CCTV, a/c,
Jacuzzis, cont. brkfst

MURRAY
Days Inn
(800) DAYS-INN, (502) 753-6706
http://www.daysinn.com
517 S. 12th St.
40 rooms - $49-175
Pets: Welcome w/$5 fee
Creature Comforts: CCTV, a/c,
kit, Jacuzzis, cont. brkfst, pool

Murray Plaza Court
(502) 753-2682
12th St. S.
40 rooms - $35-49
Pets: Welcome
Creature Comforts: CCTV, a/c

Shoney's Inn
(800) 222-2222, (502) 753-5353
http://www.shoneysinn.com
1503 N. 12th St.
71 rooms - $50-74
Pets: Welcome w/$5 fee
Creature Comforts: CCTV, a/c,
pool

NEW CONCORD
Missing Hill Resort
(502) 436-5519
HC Box 215
6 cabins - $45-65
Pets: Welcome w/$10 fee
Creature Comforts: CCTV, a/c,
kit, river/beach/fishing

OAK GROVE

Baymont Inn
(877)BAYMONT, (502) 439-0022
http://www.baymontinns.com
12759 Ft. Campbell Blvd.
102 rooms - $45-75
Pets: Welcome
Creature Comforts: CCTV, a/c, refrig, micro, Jacuzzis, cont. brkfst, pool

Days Inn
(800) DAYS-INN, (502) 640-3888
http://www.daysinn.com
212 Auburn St.
74 rooms - $45-99
Pets: Welcome w/$5 fee
Creature Comforts: CCTV, a/c, Jacuzzis, cont. brkfst, pool

OWENSBORO

Days Inn
(800) DAYS-INN, (502) 684-9621
http://www.daysinn.com
3720 New Hartford Rd.
122 rooms - $47-69
Pets: Welcome w/$2 fee
Creature Comforts: CCTV, a/c, restaurant, pool

Holiday Inn
(800) HOLIDAY, (502) 685-3941
http://www.holiday-inn.com
3136 W. 2nd St.
144 rooms - $69-115
Pets: Small pets welcome
Creature Comforts: CCTV, a/c, refrig, Jacuzzis, restaurant, cont. brkfst, hlth club, sauna, pool, whirlpool

Motel 6
(800) 4-MOTEL6, (502) 686-8606
http://www.motel6.com
4585 Frederica St.
90 rooms - $35-54
Pets: Under 30 lbs. welcome
Creature Comforts: CCTV, a/c, pool

Super 8 Motel
(800) 800-8000, (502) 685-3388
http://www.super8.com
1027 Goetz Dr.
52 rooms - $48-69
Pets: Welcome
Creature Comforts: CCTV, a/c, cont. brkfst

Trails End
(502) 771-5590
www.mindspring.com/~jramey
5931 Rte. 56
2 condos - $59-85
Pets: Welcome
Creature Comforts: CCTV, a/c, fireplace, kit, full brkfst, pool, sauna, hlth clb, whirlpool, riding

WeatherBerry B&B
(270) 684-8760
http://members.aol.com/
weatherber/index.html
2731 W. 2nd St.
3 rooms - $60-99
Pets: Welcome
Creature Comforts: Gracious Southern home, circa 1840, once served as weather station, orig. details, 12-foot ceilings, period antiques, gilded 12-ft mirrors, rqst Southern Wildflowers Rm. w/ floral wallpapers and unique antique bed, outside entrance, CCTV, a/c, kit, full Southern brkfst, lily gardens

PADUCAH

Baymont Inn
(877)BAYMONT, (270) 443-4343
http://www.baymontinns.com
5300 Old Cairo Rd.
79 rooms - $49-69
Pets: Welcome in pet rooms
Creature Comforts: CCTV, a/c, cont. brkfst

Best Inns of America
(800) 237-8466, (270) 442-3334
http://www.bestinns.com
5001 Hinckleville Rd.
90 rooms - $49-75
Pets: Welcome
Creature Comforts: CCTV, a/c, refrig, cont. brkfst, pool

Budget Host
(800) Bud-Host, (270) 443-8401
http://www.budgethost.com
1234 Broadway St.
59 rooms - $38-59
Pets: Small pets w/$5 fee
Creature Comforts: CCTV, a/c, refrig, cont. brkfst

Days Inn
(800) DAYS-INN, (270) 442-7501
http://www.daysinn.com
3901 Hinkleville Rd.
122 rooms - $49-85
Pets: Welcome w/$5 fee
Creature Comforts: CCTV, a/c, cont. brkfst, pool

Drury Suites
(800) Drury Inn, (270) 441-0024
http://www.drury-inn.com
120 McBride La.
145 rooms - $80-109
Pets: Welcome
Creature Comforts: CCTV, a/c, cont. brkfst, whirlpool, pool

1857 B&B
(800) 264-5607, (270) 444-3960
127 Market House Sq.
3 rooms - $75-100
Pets: Small pets welcome
Creature Comforts: National registry property w/ Victorian flair, traditional decor, intriguing, collectibles, CCTV, VCR, a/c, refrig, cont. brkfst, whirlpool

Farley Place B&B
(270) 442-2488
http://www.bbonline.com/ky/
farley/
166 Farley Pl.
2 rooms - $65-85
Pets: Welcome w/permission
Creature Comforts: Pre-Civil War era home, Victorian and American country antiques, hardwood floors, CCTV, a/c, fireplace, refrig, full brkfst

Hampton Inn
(800) Hampton, (270) 442-4500
http://www.hampton-inn.com
4930 Hinkleville Rd.
60 rooms - $75-105
Pets: Small pets welcome
Creature Comforts: CCTV, a/c, cont. brkfst, pool

Pear Tree Inn
(800) At-A-Tree, (270) 444-7200
http://www.drury-inn.com
4910 Hinkleville Rd.
124 rooms - $55-79
Pets: Welcome
Creature Comforts: CCTV, a/c, cont. brkfst, whirlpool, pool

Quality Inn
(800) 228-5151, (270) 443-8751
http://www.qualityinn.com
1380 Irvin Cobb Dr.
99 rooms - $43-76
Pets: Welcome
Creature Comforts: CCTV, a/c,
refrig, cont. brkfst, pool

Trinity Hills Farm
(800) 488-3998, (270) 488-3999
www.bbonline.com/ky/trinityhills
10455 Old Lovelace Rd.
5 rooms - $70-135
Pets: Well-behaved, 1st floor rms.
Creature Comforts: Set on 17-
acres amid lakes, gardens, patios,
porches, CCTV, a/c, fireplace,
refrig, full brkfst, kit, and a hot tub

PAINTSVILLE
Days Inn
(800) DAYS-INN, (606) 789-3551
http://www.daysinn.com
512 S. Mayo Trail
73 rooms - $45-95
Pets: Welcome w/$5 fee
Creature Comforts: CCTV, a/c,
refrig, Jacuzzis, cont. brkfst,
whirlpool, hlth club, pool

PARKERS LAKE
Holiday Motor Lodge
(606) 376-2732
Route 90
52 rooms - $44-63
Pets: Welcome
Creature Comforts: CCTV, a/c

PIKEVILLE
Landmark Inn
(800) 831-1469, (270) 432-2545
146 S. Mayo Tr.
102 rooms - $60-75
Pets: Small pets w/$10 fee
Creature Comforts: CCTV, a/c,
kit, restaurant, pool

PRESTONBURG
Holiday Inn
(800) HOLIDAY, (606) 886-0001
http://www.holiday-inn.com
575 S. Rte. 23
119 rooms - $73-99
Pets: Small pets welcome
Creature Comforts: CCTV, a/c,
restaurant, hlth club, whirlpool,
and a pool

Super 8 Motel
(800) 800-8000, (606) 886-3355
http://www.super8.com
196 Prince Royal Dr.
80 rooms - $49-75
Pets: Welcome
Creature Comforts: CCTV, a/c,
Jacuzzis, cont. brkfst

PROSPECT
Melrose Inn
(502) 228-1136
13306 Rte. 42
40 rooms - $40-69
Pets: Welcome w/$25 dep.
Creature Comforts: CCTV, a/c,
kit, pool

RADCLIFF
Econo Lodge
(800) 55-ECONO, (502) 351-4488
http://www.econolodge.com
261 N. Dixie Hwy.
49 rooms - $49-70
Pets: Welcome
Creature Comforts: CCTV, a/c,
refrig, cont. brkfst, pool

Fort Knox Inn
(502) 351-3199
1400 N. Dixie Hwy.
40 rooms - $45-65
Pets: Welcome
Creature Comforts: CCTV, a/c,
pool

Super 8 Motel
(800) 800-8000, (502) 352-1888
http://www.super8.com
395 Redmar Rd.
50 rooms - $49-75
Pets: Small pets w/$ 25 dep.
Creature Comforts: CCTV, a/c,
refrig, cont. brkfst

RICHMOND
Days Inn
(800) DAYS-INN, (606) 624-5769
http://www.daysinn.com
2109 Belmont Dr.
70 rooms - $47-65
Pets: Welcome w/$5 fee
Creature Comforts: CCTV, a/c,
pool

Econo Lodge
(800) 55-ECONO, (606) 623-8813
http://www.econolodge.com
230 Eastern Bypass
96 rooms - $38-55
Pets: Welcome
Creature Comforts: CCTV, a/c,
cont. brkfst, pool

Howard Johnson
(800) I-Go-Hojo, (606) 624-2612
http://www.hojo.com
1688 Northgate Dr.
98 rooms - $44-65
Pets: Welcome
Creature Comforts: CCTV, a/c,
kit, pool

Motel 6
(800) 4-MOTEL6, (606) 623-0880
http://www.motel6.com
1698 Northgate Dr.
124 rooms - $35-49
Pets: Under 30 lbs.welcome
Creature Comforts: CCTV, a/c,
pool

Super 8 Motel
(800) 800-8000, (606) 624-1550
http://www.super8.com
107 N. Keeneland Rd.
63 rooms - $45-69
Pets: Welcome
Creature Comforts: CCTV, a/c,
cont. brkfst

RICHWOOD
Econo Lodge
(800) 55-ECONO, (606) 485-4123
http://www.econolodge.com
11165 Frontage Rd.
56 rooms - $39-115
Pets: Welcome
Creature Comforts: CCTV, a/c,
cont. brkfst, pool

SHELBYVILLE
Best Western Lodge
(800) 528-1234, (502) 633-4400
http://www.bestwestern.com
115 Isaac Shelby Dr.
79 rooms - $49-65
Pets: Small pets welcome
Creature Comforts: CCTV, a/c,
cont. brkfst, pool, whirlpool, hlth
club access

Days Inn
(800) DAYS-INN, (502) 633-4005
http://www.daysinn.com
101 Howard Dr.
64 rooms - $39-57
Pets: Welcome
Creature Comforts: CCTV, a/c,
cont. brkfst

SHEPHERDSVILLE
Best Western South
(800) 528-1234, (502) 543-7097
http://www.bestwestern.com
211 Lakeview Dr.
85 rooms - $54-85
Pets: Small pets welcome
Creature Comforts: CCTV, a/c,
pool, whirlpool

Days Inn
(800) DAYS-INN, (502) 543-3011
http://www.daysinn.com
Rtes. 65 & 44
120 rooms - $39-50
Pets: Welcome
Creature Comforts: CCTV, a/c,
pool

Motel 6
(800) 4-MOTEL6, (502) 543-4400
http://www.motel6.com
144 Paroquet Springs Rd.
98 rooms - $39-55
Pets: Under 30 lbs. welcome
Creature Comforts: CCTV, a/c,
pool

SOUTH WILLIAMSON
Super 8 Motel
(800) 800-8000, (606) 237-5898
http://www.super8.com
65 Rte. 292
59 rooms - $50-75
Pets: Welcome w/permission
Creature Comforts: CCTV, a/c,
refrig, micro, Jacuzzis, cont. brkfst

SMITHS GROVE
Bryce Inn
(502) 563-5141
592 S. Main St.
24 rooms - $40-59
Pets: Small pets welcome
Creature Comforts: CCTV, a/c,
refrig, pool

SOMERSET
Cumberland Motel
(606) 561-5131
6050 Rte. 27
17 rooms - $39-58
Pets: Welcome
Creature Comforts: CCTV, a/c

SPRINGFIELD
Glenmar Plantation
(800) 828-3330, (606) 284-7791
www.win.net/~mainstring/bb/
2444 Valley Hill Rd.
8 rooms - $80-160
Pets: Welcome
Creature Comforts: A handsome
red brick 1785 Georgian manor on
inviting 200-acre property, filled
w/antiques, CCTV, a/c, fireplace,
refrig, full brkfst, massive log
beamed barns-farm animals

VERSAILLES
Rose Hill Inn
(800) 307-0460, (606) 873-5957
http://www.rosehillinn.com
233 Rose Hill Ave.
8 rooms - $80-135
Pets: Welcome in cottage and
apartment (2 Golden Retrieves in
residence)
Creature Comforts: Charming
1823 Kentucky Victorian brick
mansion (7,000 sq. ft) set on 3
acres, four-poster & canopy beds,
windowseat overlooking rose
garden, handmade quilts, some
high ceilings, country antiques,
CCTV, VCR, a/c, double Jacuzzi,
fireplace, kit, claw foot tubs, full
brkfst, request cottage

Tyrone Pike B&B
(800) 736-7722, (606) 873-2408
http://www.bbonline.com/ky/
tyrone/
3820 Tyrone Pike
4 rooms - $100-145
Pets: Welcome
Creature Comforts: Contemp.
B&B w/eclectic furnishings,
sleigh and four-poster beds, claw
foot and soaking tubs, CCTV,
VCR, a/c, kit, full brkfst

WALTON
Days Inn
(800) DAYS-INN, (606) 485-4151
http://www.daysinn.com
11177 Frontage Rd.
137 rooms - $42-68
Pets: Welcome
Creature Comforts: CCTV, a/c,
pool

WILLIAMSBURG
Best Western Inn
(800) 528-1234, (606) 549-1500
http://www.bestwestern.com
Rtes. 75 & 92
81 rooms - $33-58
Pets: Small pets welcome
Creature Comforts: CCTV, a/c,

Holiday Inn Express
(800) HOLIDAY, (606) 549-3450
http://www.holiday-inn.com
30 West Route 92
100 rooms - $55-65
Pets: Small pets welcome in
smoking rms.
Creature Comforts: CCTV, a/c,
pool

WINCHESTER
Best Western Country Squire
(800) 528-1234, (606) 744-7210
http://www.bestwestern.com
1307 W. Lexington Rd.
45 rooms - $60-90
Pets: Small pets w/$5 fee
Creature Comforts: CCTV, a/c,
refrig, micro, Jacuzzis, cont.
brkfst, pool

Holiday Inn
(800) HOLIDAY, (606) 744-9111
http://www.holiday-inn.com
1100 Interstate Dr.
65 rooms - $69-99
Pets: Small pets welcome
Creature Comforts: CCTV, a/c,
refrig, restaurant, pool

Louisiana

ALEXANDRIA
Best Western Inn
(800) 528-1234, (318) 445-5530
http://www.bestwestern.com
2720 W. MacArthur Dr.
153 rooms - $60-85
Pets: Under 20 lbs. welcome
Creature Comforts: CCTV, a/c,
refrig, micro, Jacuzzis, restaurant,
whirlpool, pool, tennis

La Quinta Inn
(800) Nu-Rooms, (318) 442-3700
http://www.laquinta.com
2333 S. Acadian Hwy.
142 rooms - $65-89
Pets: Small pets welcome
Creature Comforts: CCTV, a/c,
refrig, micro

Motel 6
(800) 4-MOTEL6, (318) 445-2336
http://www.motel6.com
546 MacArthur Dr.
113 rooms - $34-45
Pets: Under 30 lbs. welcome
Creature Comforts: CCTV, a/c,
pool

Rodeway Inn
(800) 228-2000, (318) 448-1611
http://www.rodeway.com
742 MacArthur Dr.
120 rooms - $43-69
Pets: Welcome w/$25 dep.
Creature Comforts: CCTV,
VCR, a/c, refrig, pool

Super 8 Motel
(800) 800-8000, (318) 445-6541
http://www.super8.com
700 MacArthur Dr.
79 rooms - $50-79
Pets: Small pets welcome
Creature Comforts: CCTV, AC,
cont. brkfst, pool

ARCADIA
Days Inn
(800) DAYS-INN, (318) 263-3555
http://www.daysinn.com
1061 Rte. 151
34 rooms - $45-83
Pets: Welcome
Creature Comforts: CCTV, a/c,
refrig, micro, pool, whirlpool

BASTROP
Country Inn
(318) 281-8100
1815 E. Madison Ave.
32 rooms - $44-60
Pets: Small pets welcome
Creature Comforts: CCTV, a/c

BATON ROUGE
Baymont Inns
(800) 4-Budget, (225) 291-6600
http://www.baymontinns.com
10555 Rieger Rd.
102 rooms - $48-69
Pets: Small pets welcome
Creature Comforts: CCTV, a/c,
cont. brkfst, pool

Comfort Inn
(800) 228-5150, (225) 927-5790
http://www.comfortinn.com
2445 S. Acadian Hwy.
150 rooms - $65-95
Pets: Welcome
Creature Comforts: CCTV, a/c,
kit, cont. brkfst, pool

La Quinta Inn
(800) Nu-Rooms, (225) 924-9600
http://www.laquinta.com
2333 S. Acadian Hwy.
142 rooms - $65-89
Pets: Small pets welcome
Creature Comforts: CCTV, a/c,
refrig, cont. brkfst, pool

Motel 6
(800) 4-MOTEL6, (225) 924-2130
http://www.motel6.com
9901 Gwen Adele Ave.
178 rooms - $39-48
Pets: Under 30 lbs. welcome
Creature Comforts: CCTV, a/c,
pool

Motel 6
(800) 4-MOTEL6, (225) 291-4912
http://www.motel6.com
10445 Rieger Rd.
110 rooms - $40-59
Pets: Under 30 lbs. welcome
Creature Comforts: CCTV, a/c,
pool

Quality Inn
(800) 228-5151, (225) 293-9370
http://www.qualityinn.com
10920 Mead Frontage Rd.
150 rooms - $55-88
Pets: Small pets welcome
Creature Comforts: CCTV,
VCR, a/c, refrig, cont. brkfst,
restaurant, pool

Red Roof Inn
(800) The-Roof, (225) 275-6600
http://www.redroof.com
11314 Boardwalk Dr.
108 rooms - $50-79
Pets: Small pets welcome
Creature Comforts: CCTV, a/c

Shoney's Inn
(800) 222-2222, (225) 925-8399
http://www.shoneysinn.com
9919 Gwen Adele Dr.
195 rooms - $53-105
Pets: Small pets w/$25 fee
Creature Comforts: CCTV, a/c,
refrig, micro, pool

BOSCO
Boscobel Cottage
(318) 325-1550
185 Cordell Ln.
4 rooms - $80-105
Pets: Welcome
Creature Comforts: Historic
B&B w/lots of appeal, CCTV, a/c,
cont. brkfst

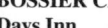

BOSSIER CITY
Days Inn
(800) DAYS-INN, (318) 742-9200
http://www.daysinn.com
200 John Wesley Blvd.
178 rooms - $30-66
Pets: Welcome w/$5 fee
Creature Comforts: CCTV, a/c,
refrig, micro, cont. brkfst, pool

Ramada Limited
(800) 2-Ramada, (318) 746-8410
http://www.ramada.com
750 Isle of Capri Rd.
240 rooms - $51-71
Pets: Small pets w/$15 fee
Creature Comforts: CCTV, a/c,
restaurant, pool

Residence Inn
(800) 331-3131, (318) 747-6220
http://www.residenceinn.com
1001 Gould Dr.
73 rooms - $99-169
Pets: Welcome w/$100-150 fee
Creature Comforts: CCTV, a/c,
kit, cont. brkfst, whirlpool, hlth
club, pool

BREAUX BRIDGE
Best Western Inn
(800) 528-1234, (318) 332-1114
http://www.bestwestern.com
2088 Rees St.
50 rooms - $65-165
Pets: Small pets w/$25 fee
Creature Comforts: CCTV, a/c,
cont. brkfst, pool

CHALMETTE
Quality Inn
(800) 228-5151, (504) 277-5353
http://www.qualityinn.com
5353 Paris Rd.
136 rooms - $55-129
Pets: Welcome w/$25 fee
Creature Comforts: CCTV, a/c,
restaurant, pool, marina access

CROWLEY
Best Western Inn
(800) 528-1234, (318) 783-2378
http://www.bestwestern.com
9571 Egan Hwy.
46 rooms - $65-170
Pets: Small pets w/$10-25 fee
Creature Comforts: CCTV, a/c,
cont. brkfst, pool

DELHI
Best Western Inn
(800) 528-1234, (318) 878-5126
http://www.bestwestern.com
35 Snider Rd.
47 rooms - $49-85
Pets: Under 8 lbs. welcome
Creature Comforts: CCTV, a/c,
pool

DE RIDDER
Best Western Inn
(800) 528-1234, (318) 462-3665
http://www.bestwestern.com
1213 N. Pine St.
75 rooms - $49-80
Pets: Under 10 lbs. welcome
Creature Comforts: CCTV, a/c,
refrig, restaurant, pool

Red Carpet Inn
(800) 251-1962, (318) 463-8605
http://www.reservahost.com
806 N. Pine St.
59 rooms - $33-69
Pets: Welcome
Creature Comforts: CCTV, a/c,
cont. brkfst, pool

FRANKLIN
Best Western Forest Inn
(800) 528-1234, (318) 826-1810
http://www.bestwestern.com
1909 Main St.
82 rooms - $65-89
Pets: Under 25 lbs. welcome
Creature Comforts: CCTV, a/c,
refrig, micro, restaurant, pool

HAMMOND
Best Western Inn
(800) 528-1234, (504) 542-8555
http://www.bestwestern.com
14175 Rte. 190
57 rooms - $49-85
Pets: welcome w/permission
Creature Comforts: CCTV, a/c,
pool

HOUMA
Crochet House B&B
(504) 879-3033
801 Midland Dr.
2 rooms - $49-78
Pets: Welcome in studio
Creature Comforts: CCTV, a/c,
fireplace, kit, cont. brkfst

Maison des Anges B&B
(504) 873-7662
508 Academy St.
6 rooms - $45-150
Pets: Welcome by reservation
Creature Comforts: Lovely 1905
Victorian, built of virgin cypress,
original features, baths w/hand-
painted tiles and claw foot tubs,
CCTV, VCR, kit, full brkfst,
fenced yard

Quality Inn
(800) 228-5151, (504) 879-4871
http://www.qualityinn.com
1400 W. Tunnel Blvd.
153 rooms - $59-175
Pets: Small pets welcome
Creature Comforts: CCTV, a/c,
restaurant, pool

JENNINGS
Days Inn
(800) DAYS-INN, (318) 824-6550
http://www.daysinn.com
2502 Port Dr.
69 rooms - $55-94
Pets: Welcome w/$5 fee
Creature Comforts: CCTV, a/c,
pool

KENNER
Days Inn
(800) DAYS-INN, (504) 469-2531
http://www.daysinn.com
1300 Vets. Mem. Dr.
324 rooms - $55-109
Pets: Welcome w/$10 fee
Creature Comforts: CCTV, a/c,
refrig, restaurant, pool

Sleep Inn
(800) Sleep-Inn, (504) 466-9666
http://www.sleepinn.com
2850 Loyola Dr.
120 rooms - $65-169
Pets: Small pets welcome
Creature Comforts: CCTV, a/c,
cont. brkfst, hlth club

KINDER
Comfort Inn
(800) 228-5150, (318) 738-3240
http://www.comfortinn.com
13894 Rte. 165
63 rooms - $95-150
Pets: Welcome
Creature Comforts: CCTV, a/c,
refrig, Jacuzzis, pool

LAFAYETTE

Best Western Inn
(800) 528-1234, (318) 234-9667
http://www.bestwestern.com
1801 W. Pinhook Rd.
290 rooms - $99-139
Pets: Under 25 lbs. welcome
Creature Comforts: CCTV, a/c,
refrig, hlth club, whirlpool, pool

Bois Des Chenes Inn
(318) 233-7816
http://members.aol.com/
boisdchene/bois.htm
338 N. Sterling St.
5 rooms - $80-120
Pets: Welcome w/CC dep.
Creature Comforts: An 1820's
plantation on Nat'l Historic
Register, surrounded by 500 year
old oak trees, expansive columned
porch, CCTV, a/c, antiques,
country décor, fireplaces, refrig,
full southern brkfst, tour of
acclaimed Mouton Plantation
House

Comfort Inn
(800) 228-5150, (318) 232-9000
http://www.comfortinn.com
1421 SE Evangeline Hwy.
196 rooms - $65-93
Pets: Welcome w/CC dep.
Creature Comforts: CCTV, a/c,
restaurant, cont. brkfst, hlth club,
pool

Days Inn
(800) DAYS-INN, (318) 237-8880
http://www.daysinn.com
1620 N. University St.
120 rooms - $50-75
Pets: Welcome w/$10 fee
Creature Comforts: CCTV, a/c,
cont. brkfst, pool

La Quinta Inn
(800) Nu-Rooms, (318) 233-5610
http://www.laquinta.com
2100 NE Evangeline Hwy.
139 rooms - $55-99
Pets: Small pets welcome
Creature Comforts: CCTV, a/c,
cont. brkfst, pool

Motel 6
(800) 4-MOTEL6, (318) 233-2055
http://www.motel6.com
2724 NE Evangeline Hwy.
101 rooms - $34-45
Pets: Under 30 lbs. welcome
Creature Comforts: CCTV, a/c,
pool

Quality Inn
(800) 228-5151, (318) 232-6131
http://www.qualityinn.com
1605 N. University Ave.
152 rooms - $50-89
Pets: Small pets welcome
Creature Comforts: CCTV, a/c,
refrig, restaurant, pool

Red Roof Inn
(800) The-Roof, (318) 233-3339
http://www.redroof.com
1718 N. University Ave.
105 rooms - $50-79
Pets: Small pets welcome
Creature Comforts: CCTV, a/c

Rodeway Inn
(800) 228-2000, (318) 233-5500
http://www.rodeway.com
1801 NW Evangeline Hwy.
135 rooms - $45-75
Pets: Under 30 lbs. w/$10 fee
Creature Comforts: CCTV, a/c,
micro, restaurant, pool

Super 8 Motel
(800) 800-8000, (318) 232-8826
http://www.super8.com
2224 NE Evangeline Hwy.
71 rooms - $49-75
Pets: Small pets w/permission
Creature Comforts: CCTV, a/c,
cont. brkfst, pool

LAFITTE

Victoria Inn
(800) 689-4797, (504) 689-4757
http://www.victoriainn.com
Rte. 45, Box 545
5 rooms - $60-180
Pets: Welcome in certain rooms
Creature Comforts: A charming
cottage on 6 acres accented w/
gardens, antique and wicker
furnishings, CCTV, VCR, a/c,
fireplace, kit, Creole brkfst on fine
china, lake/dock

LAKE CHARLES

Days Inn
(800) DAYS-INN, (318) 433-1711
http://www.daysinn.com
1010 N. ML King Hwy.
147 rooms - $50-75
Pets: Welcome w/$4 fee
Creature Comforts: CCTV, a/c,
cont. brkfst, pool

LA PLACE

Best Western Inn
(800) 528-1234, (504) 651-4000
http://www.bestwestern.com
4289 Main St.
58 rooms - $75-185
Pets: Small pets welcome
Creature Comforts: CCTV, a/c,
refrig, micro, hlth club, pool

LULING

Comfort Inn
(800) 228-5150, (504) 785-1125
http://www.comfortinn.com
12177 Rte. 90
41 rooms - $65-145
Pets: Welcome
Creature Comforts: CCTV, a/c,
refrig, micro, cont. brkfst, pool

MANSFIELD

Mansfield Inn
(318) 872-5034
1055 Washington Ave.
69 rooms - $42-59
Pets: Small pets welcome
Creature Comforts: CCTV, a/c,
pool

METAIRIE

Doubletree Hotel
(800) 222-TREE, (504) 836-5253
http://www.doubletreehotels.com
3838 N. Causeway Blvd.
212 rooms - $95-189
Pets: Small pets w/$50 fee
Creature Comforts: CCTV, a/c,
refrig, micro, restaurant, cont.
brkfst, pool, sauna, steamroom,
hlth clb, tennis

La Quinta Inn
(800) Nu-Rooms, (504) 835-8511
http://www.laquinta.com
3100 Rte. 10 (Service Rd.)
100 rooms - $79-99
Pets: Small pets w/$25 dep.
Creature Comforts: CCTV, a/c,
cont. brkfst, pool

Quality Inn

(800) 228-5151, (504) 833-8211
http://www.qualityinn.com
2261 N. Causeway Blvd.
204 rooms - $75-189
Pets: Small pets w/$25 dep.
Creature Comforts: CCTV, a/c,
kit, restaurant, hlth club, sauna,
pool

MINDEN
Best Western Inn

(800) 528-1234, (318) 377-1001
http://www.bestwestern.com
1411 Sibley Rd.
40 rooms - $50-85
Pets: Small pets welcome
Creature Comforts: CCTV, a/c,
cont. brkfst, hlth club, pool

MONROE
Best Western, Airport

(800) 528-1234, (318) 345-4000
http://www.bestwestern.com
1475 Garrett Rd.
50 rooms - $59-80
Pets: Small pets welcome
Creature Comforts: CCTV, a/c,
refrig, micro, cont. brkfst, pool
and a whirlpool

Days Inn

(800) DAYS-INN, (318) 345-2220
http://www.daysinn.com
5650 Frontage Rd.
58 rooms - $49-70
Pets: Welcome
Creature Comforts: CCTV, a/c,
refrig, micro, cont. brkfst, pool

La Quinta Inn

(800) Nu-Rooms, (318) 322-3900
http://www.laquinta.com
1035 Rte. 165
128 rooms - $55-79
Pets: Small pets welcome
Creature Comforts: CCTV, a/c,
cont. brkfst, pool

Motel 6

(800) 4-MOTEL6, (318) 322-5430
http://www.motel6.com
1501 Rte. 165
105 rooms - $32-45
Pets: Under 30 lbs. welcome
Creature Comforts: CCTV, a/c,
pool

MORGAN CITY
Holiday Inn

(800) HOLIDAY, (504) 385-2200
http://www.holiday-inn.com
520 Roderick St.
175 rooms - $59-139
Pets: Welcome w/$25 deposit
Creature Comforts: CCTV, a/c,
pool

NATCHITOCHES
Cloutier Town House B&B

(877) 699-8471, (318) 352-5242
http://www.cloutierbandb.com
416 Jefferson St.
2 suites - $95-110
Pets: "Precious pets welcome"
Creature Comforts: Gracious
townhouse in historic district,
antiques, intriguing collectibles,
bedroom furnished w/fine
"Louisiana Empire" antiques,
CCTV, VCR, a/c, fireplace,
Jacuzzi, refrig, micro, Jacuzzi, full
southern. brkfst

Petit Tarn Guest House

(800) 351-7666, (318) 352-5242
http://www.cloutierbandb.com
612 Williams Ave.
3 suites - $95-110
Pets: "Precious pets welcome"
Creature Comforts: Guest house
on Cane River overlooking
historic Front St., French doors,
hardwood flrs, some La. antiques,
four-poster beds, intriguing
collectibles, CCTV, VCR, a/c,
fireplace, Jacuzzi, refrig, micro,
Jacuzzi, cont. brkfst.

Days Inn

(800) DAYS-INN, (318) 352-4426
http://www.daysinn.com
1000 College Ave.
60 rooms - $39-65
Pets: Welcome w/$4 fee
Creature Comforts: CCTV, a/c,
pool

Super 8 Motel

(800) 800-8000, (318) 352-1700
http://www.super8.com
801 Rte. 1
43 rooms - $45-95
Pets: Small pets w/$5 fee
Creature Comforts: CCTV, a/c,
cont. brkfst

NEW IBERIA
Best Western Inn

(800) 528-1234, (318) 364-3030
http://www.bestwestern.com
2714 Rte. 14
104 rooms - $55-99
Pets: Small pets w/$50 dep.
Creature Comforts: CCTV, a/c,
Jacuzzis, restaurant, cont. brkfst,
pool

Holiday Inn

(800) HOLIDAY, (318) 367-1201
http://www.holiday-inn.com
2915 Rte. 14
175 rooms - $59-99
Pets: Small pets welcome
Creature Comforts: CCTV,
VCR, a/c, restaurant, pool

NEW ORLEANS
The Ambassador Hotel

(888) 527-5271, (504) 527-5271
http://www.neworleans.com/
ambassador
535 Tchoupitoulas St.
75 rooms - $95-299
Pets: Welcome w/$CC dep.
Creature Comforts: Three 19th-
century refurbished warehouses,
wrought-iron four poster beds,
hardwood floors, high ceilings,
CCTV, a/c, refrig, restaurant, cont.
brkfst, hlth clb, views of Historic
Riverfront District

Annabelle's House B&B

(504) 899-0701
1716 Milan St.
8 rooms - $85-155
Pets: Welcome in apt.
Creature Comforts: A lovely
1840's Greek Revival home,
CCTV, a/c, kit, cont. brkfst

Best Western Inn

(800) 528-1234, (504) 822-0200
http://www.bestwestern.com
2820 Tulane Ave.
75 rooms - $55-140
Pets: Small pets w/$10 fee
Creature Comforts: CCTV, a/c,
refrig, micro, cont. brkfst, pools,
whirlpool

Chimes B&B
(800) 729-4640, (504) 89-2621
http://www.gnofn.org/~bedbreak
Constantinople & St. Charles Sts.
6 rooms - $80-135
Pets: Small pets in ltd. rms
Creature Comforts: A charming
two-story B&B in historic
neighborhood, brimming w/
antiques, ceiling fans, CCTV,
VCR, a/c, refrig, claw foot tubs,
cont. brkfst, inviting courtyard w/
lovely plantings-hammock

The Columns Hotel
(800) 445-9308, (504) 899-9308
http://www.thecolumns.com
3811 St. Charles Ave.
20 rooms - $90-250
Pets: Small to medium dogs
welcome
Creature Comforts: Landmark
Italiante hotel, intimate yet
gracious, orig. mahogany
woodwork, stained glass
windows, formal antiques, four-
poster beds, CCTV, a/c, fireplace,
refrig, clawfoot tubs, cont. brkfst,
fine dining in restaurant, tea room,
jazz

Hilton Riverside Hotel
(800) HILTONS, (504) 561-0500
http://www.hilton.com
2 Poydras St.
1,600 rooms - $165-399
Pets: Under 20 Lbs. w/$35 fee
Creature Comforts: CCTV, a/c,
refrig, restaurant, pool

Hilton Hotel, Airport
(800) HILTONS, (504) 469-5000
http://www.hilton.com
901 Airline Hwy.
315 rooms - $145-250
Pets: Under 20 lbs. w/$35 fee
Creature Comforts: CCTV, a/c,
refrig, restaurant, pool

La Quinta Inn
(800) Nu-Rooms, (504) 246-5800
http://www.laquinta.com
8400 Rte. 10
105 rooms - $59-135
Pets: Small pets welcome
Creature Comforts: CCTV, a/c,
refrig, cont. brkfst, pool

Le Meridien
(800) 543-4300, (504) 525-6500
http://www.meridienhotel.com
614 Canal St.
494 rooms - $295-2,500
Pets: Under 10 lbs.
Creature Comforts: Luxury hotel
in the French Quarter, CCTV,
VCR, a/c, Jacuzzi, pool, sauna,
whirlpool, hlth clb.

Maison Esplanade Guest House
(800) 892-5529, (504) 523-8080
http://www.maisonesplanade.com
1244 Esplanade Rd.
10 rooms - $80-190
Pets: Welcome w/$100 dep.
Creature Comforts: Restored
Greek Reviva historic landmark
(1846) w/wraparound porches,
13-foot ceilings, fireplace, four
poster beds, fans, CCTV, a/c,
refrig, and a cont. brkfst

Olivier Estates B&B
(800) 429-3240, (504) 949-9600
1425 North Prieur
6 rooms - $85-499
Pets: Small pets welcome
Creature Comforts: An historic
1855 B&B, top 50 B&Bs in U.S.
by LA Times, CCTV, VCR, a/c,
refrig, Jacuzzi, fireplaces, stereo,
cont. brkfst, pool, whirlpool

Rathbone Inn B&B
(800) 947-2101, (504) 947-2100
http://www.rathboneinn.com
1227 Esplanade Rd.
13 rooms - $80-135
Pets: Welcome
Creature Comforts: A lovely
1850's mansion w/handsome
decor, CCTV, VCR, a/c, refrig,
micro, full brkfst, whirlpool in
garden courtyard

Southern Nights B&B
(504) 861-7187
http://www.neworleans.com/
southernnights
1827 S. Carrollton Ave.
5 rooms - $55-85
Pets: Welcome
Creature Comforts: 1890's
haunted mansion w/high ceilings,
antiques, four-poster beds, CCTV,
a/c, 13 fireplaces, refrig, cont.
brkfst, courtyard-lattice and
tropical landscaping, bikes, theme
murder mystery weekends

Windsor Court Hotel
(800) 262-2662, (504) 523-6000
http://windsorcourthotel.com
300 Gravier St.
325 rooms - $250-3,775
Pets: Under 50 lbs. w/$150 fee,
$250 dep.
Creature Comforts: Highly
recommended, named best hotel
in US, elegant and intimate,
spacious townhouses w/ terraces,
impressive antiques, artwork,
CCTV, VCR, a/c, kit, Jacuzzi,
restaurant, pool, hlth clb, sauna,
massage, steamroom, whirlpool

NEW ROADS
River Blossom Inn
(504) 638-8650
300 N. Carolina St.
4 rooms - $60-89
Pets: Small pets welcome
Creature Comforts: A charming
1880's house, CCTV, a/c,
fireplace, refrig, southern brkfst

OPELOUSAS
Best Western Inn
(800) 528-1234, (318) 942-5540
http://www.bestwestern.com
1635 Rte. 49
46 rooms - $65-160
Pets: Small pets w/$10-25 fee
Creature Comforts: CCTV, a/c,
cont. brkfst, pool

PORT ALLEN
Days Inn
(800) DAYS-INN, (504) 387-0671
http://www.daysinn.com
215 Lobdell Hwy.
154 rooms - $40-75
Pets: Welcome w/$6 fee
Creature Comforts: CCTV, a/c,
refrig, restaurant, pool

Motel 6
(800) 4-MOTEL6, (504) 343-5945
http://www.motel6.com
2800 Frontage Rd.
132 rooms - $34-49
Pets: Under 30 lbs. welcome
Creature Comforts: CCTV, a/c,
pool

Super 8 Motel
(800) 800-8000, (504) 381-9134
http://www.super8.com
Rtes. 10 & 415
148 rooms - $49-75
Pets: Small pets welcome
Creature Comforts: CCTV, a/c,
cont. brkfst, pool

RAYVILLE
Cottonland Inn
(800) 528-7732, (318) 728-5985
Rtes. 20 & 137
78 rooms - $33-49
Pets: Small pets welcome
Creature Comforts: CCTV, a/c,
restaurant, pool

RUSTON
Holiday Inn
(800) HOLIDAY, (318) 255-5901
http://www.holiday-inn.com
401 N. Service Rd.
232 rooms - $59-135
Pets: Welcome (kennels avail)
Creature Comforts: CCTV, a/c,
restaurant, pool

ST. FRANCISVILLE
Butler Green Wood B&B
(225) 635-6312
http://www.butlergreenwood.com
8345 Rte. 61
6 cottages - $85-125
Pets: Welcome
Creature Comforts: An exquisite
Antebellum home w/ Victorian
accents, lovely gardens, listed on
National Historic Register, CCTV,
VCR, a/c, kit, fireplaces, four
poster beds, Jacuzzi, claw foot
tubs, cont. brkfst, library,
hammock, pool, tennis, canoeing,
table tennis, tour of mansion

Green Springs B&B
(800) 457-4978, (225) 635-4232
http://www.virtualcities.com/ons/
la/p/lap7603.htm
7463 Tunica Trace
3 cottages- $90-245
Pets: Small pets w/$25 fee
Creature Comforts: Lovely
5,000 sq. ft. country estate on 150
acres that has been in same family
for over 200 years, antiques,
original works of art, charmingly
appointed cottages, CCTV, VCR,
a/c, kit, bar, Jacuzzi, fireplace,
refrig, plantation brkfst

Lake Rosemound Inn
(225) 635-3176
http://www.virtualcities.com/
lakerosemountinn
10473 Lindsey Ln.
4 rooms - 80-120
Pets: Welcome
Creature Comforts: Picturesque
lakeside setting that is ideal for
romantics, CCTV, a/c, fireplace,
common kit, Jacuzzis, country
brkfst, stereo, dart board, pool
table, clubhouse parlor w/ "help
yourself" ice cream parlor, on
lake/beach/fishing

ST. MARTINVILLE
Maison Bleue B&B
(318) 394-1215
417 N. Main St.
4 rooms - $69-85
Pets: Welcome
Creature Comforts: CCTV, a/c,
fireplace, stereo, stocked refrig,
full brkfst

SHREVEPORT
Days Inn
(800) DAYS-INN, (318) 636-0080
http://www.daysinn.com
4935 W. Monkhouse Rd.
148 rooms - $30-60
Pets: Welcome w/$5 fee
Creature Comforts: CCTV, a/c,
cont. brkfst, pool

Econo Lodge
(800) 55-ECONO, (318) 636-0771
http://www.econolodge.com
4911 Monkhouse Dr.
65 rooms - $39-70
Pets: Welcome
Creature Comforts: CCTV, a/c,
refrig, pool

Fairfield Place
(318) 222-0048
http://www.fairfieldbandb.com
2221 Fairfield Ave.
12 rooms - $125-250
Pets: Conditionally welcomed
Creature Comforts: Two elegant
1890's mansions, period details
intact, antiques, wicker, art and
book collection, European feather
beds, four-poster beds, CCTV, a/c,
refrig, Jacuzzi, gourmet brfkst,
very inviting courtyards

Howard Johnson Inn
(800) I-Go-Hojo, (318) 424-6621
http://www.hojo.com
1906 N. Market St.
130 rooms - $45-80
Pets: Welcome
Creature Comforts: CCTV, a/c,
pool

La Quinta Inn
(800) Nu-Rooms, (318) 671-1100
http://www.laquinta.com
6700 Financial Cr.
118 rooms - $65-89
Pets: Small pets welcome
Creature Comforts: CCTV, a/c,
refrig, restaurant, cont. brkfst,
whirlpool, hlth club, pool

Quality Inn
(800) 228-5151, (318) 746-5050
http://www.qualityinn.com
4300 Industrial Dr.
165 rooms - $49-99
Pets: Small pets welcome
Creature Comforts: CCTV, a/c,
Jacuzzis, cont. brkfst, pool

Red Roof Inn
(800) The-Roof, (318) 938-5342
http://www.redroof.com
7296 Greenwood Rd.
107 rooms - $50-79
Pets: Small pets welcome
Creature Comforts: CCTV, a/c

Super 8 Motel
(800) 800-8000, (318) 635-8888
http://www.super8.com
5204 Monkhouse Dr.
143 rooms - $46-78
Pets: Small pets welcome
Creature Comforts: CCTV, a/c,
pool

SLIDELL
Econo Lodge
(800) 55-ECONO, (504) 641-2153
http://www.econolodge.com
58512 Tyler Rd.
57 rooms - $50-99
Pets: Welcome
Creature Comforts: CCTV, a/c,
refrig, micro, cont. brkfst, pool

La Quinta Inn
(800) Nu-Rooms, (504) 643-9770
http://www.laquinta.com
794 Service Rd.
182 rooms - $65-89
Pets: Small pets welcome
Creature Comforts: CCTV, a/c,
refrig, restaurant, cont. brkfst, pool

Motel 6
(800) 4-MOTEL6, (504) 649-7925
http://www.motel6.com
136 Taos St.
153 rooms - $39-59
Pets: Under 30 lbs. welcome
Creature Comforts: CCTV, a/c,
pool

Ramada Limited
(800) 2-Ramada, (504) 643-9960
http://www.ramada.com
798 Service Rd.
150 rooms - $55-80
Pets: Small pets w/$20 dep.
Creature Comforts: CCTV, a/c,
restaurant, pool

SULPHUR
La Quinta Inn
(800) Nu-Rooms, (318) 527-8303
http://www.laquinta.com
2600 S. Ruth St.
105 rooms - $69-99
Pets: Small pets welcome
Creature Comforts: CCTV, a/c,
refrig, restaurant, cont. brkfst, pool

TALLULAH
Super 8 Motel
(800) 800-8000, (318) 574-2000
http://www.super8.com
1604 New Hwy.
58 rooms - $45-70
Pets: Small pets w/$10-30 fee
Creature Comforts: CCTV, a/c,
cont. brkfst, pool

THIBODAUX
Howard Johnson Hotel
(800) I-Go-Hojo, (504) 447-9071
http://www.hojo.com
201 N. Canal Blvd.
118 rooms - $70-150
Pets: Welcome
Creature Comforts: CCTV, a/c,
restaurant, cont. brkfst, tennis,
pool

VINTON
Best Western Delta Downes
(800) 528-1234, (318) 589-7492
http://www.bestwestern.com
2267 Old Rte. 90
92 rooms - $55-90
Pets: Welcome w/$15 dep.
Creature Comforts: CCTV, a/c,
pool

WEST MONROE
Red Roof Inn
(800) THE-ROOF,(318) 388-2420
http://www.redroof.com
102 Constitution Dr.
98 rooms - $50-79
Pets: Small pets welcome
Creature Comforts: CCTV, a/c

WINNSBORO
Best Western Inn
(800) 528-1234, (318) 435-2000
http://www.bestwestern.com
4198 Front St.
30 rooms - $45-89
Pets: Leashed small pets
Creature Comforts: CCTV, a/c,
cont. brkfst, pool

Maine

AUBURN

Auburn Inn
(207) 777-1777
55 Washington St.
118 rooms - $57-99
Pets: Small pets w/$25 dep.
Creature Comforts: CCTV, a/c, restaurant, pool

AUGUSTA

Augusta Hotel
(888) 63-MAINE, (207) 622-6371
390 Western Ave.
95 rooms - $75-205
Pets: Welcome w/$30 dep.
Creature Comforts: CCTV, a/c, kit, restaurant, cont. brkfst, pool, whirlpool

Best Western Senator
(800) 528-1234, (207) 622-5804
http://www.bestwestern.com
284 Western Ave.
103 rooms - $65-199
Pets: Small pets welcome
Creature Comforts: CCTV, a/c, refrig, fireplace, Jacuzzis, restaurant, hlth club, whirlpool, pool, spa

Echo Lake Lodge
(207) 685-9550
Route 17
21 rooms - $85-125
Pets: Welcome
Creature Comforts: Kit, lake w/ beach and boating

Motel 6
(800) 4-MOTEL6, (207) 622-0000
http://www.motel6.com
18 Edison Dr.
71 rooms - $39-59
Pets: Under 30 lbs.welcome
Creature Comforts: CCTV, a/c

BAILEY ISLAND

Driftwood Inn
(207) 833-5461
Washington Ave.
30 rooms - $50-95
Pets: Welcome in cottages
Creature Comforts: Classic shingled cottages on a quiet seaside cove, Spartan décor, CCTV, fireplace, kit, restaurant, pool, beach

BANGOR

Best Western White House
(800) 528-1234, (207) 862-3737
http://www.bestwestern.com
155 Littlefield Ave.
66 rooms - $50-98
Pets: Welcome
Creature Comforts: CCTV, a/c, refrig, cont. brkfst, sauna, pool

Comfort Inn
(800) 228-5150, (207) 942-7899
http://www.comfortinn.com
750 Hogan Rd.
95 rooms - $55-99
Pets: Small pets w/$5 fee
Creature Comforts: CCTV, a/c, refrig, restaurant, cont. brkfst, pool

Days Inn, Airport
(800) DAYS-INN, (207) 942-8272
http://www.daysinn.com
250 Odlin Rd.
101 rooms - $50-98
Pets: Welcome w/$6 fee
Creature Comforts: CCTV, a/c, cont. brkfst, whirlpool, pool

Econo Lodge
(800) 55-ECONO, (207) 945-0111
http://www.econolodge.com
327 Odlin Rd.
130 rooms - $40-79
Pets: Small pets welcome
Creature Comforts: CCTV, a/c, refrig, micro

Holiday Inn
(800) HOLIDAY, (207) 947-0101
http://www.holiday-inn.com
404 Odlin Rd.
205 rooms - $80-129
Pets: Small pets w/$25 dep.
Creature Comforts: CCTV, VCR, a/c, refrig, restaurant, whirlpool, pool

Holiday Inn, Civic Center
(800) HOLIDAY, (207) 947-8651
http://www.holiday-inn.com
500 Main St.
124 rooms - $55-99
Pets: Small pets w/$25 dep.
Creature Comforts: CCTV, a/c, refrig, restaurant, pool

Main Street Inn
(207) 942-5282
480 Main St.
64 rooms - $40-75
Pets: Small pets welcome
Creature Comforts: CCTV, a/c, cont. brkfst

Motel 6
(800) 4-MOTEL6, (207) 947-6921
http://www.motel6.com
1100 Hammond St.
60 rooms - $36-58
Pets: Under 30 lbs.welcome
Creature Comforts: CCTV, a/c

Penobscot Inn
(800) 468-2878, (207) 947-0566
570 Main St.
52 rooms - $49-85
Pets: Welcome
Creature Comforts: CCTV, VCR, a/c, restaurant

Phenix Inn
(207) 947-0411
http://www.maineguide.com/
bangor/phenixinn
20 W. Market Square
33 rooms - $65-145
Pets: Well-behaved pets welcome
Creature Comforts: Refurbished
historic landmark, canopy beds,
reproductions, CCTV, VCR, a/c,
modern bathrooms w/ brass
fixtures, kit, cont. brkfst, hlth club

Riverside Inn
(207) 947-3800
495 State St.
55 rooms - $55-98
Pets: Small pets w/$8 fee
Creature Comforts: CCTV, a/c

Rodeway Inn
(800) 228-2000, (207) 942-6301
http://www.rodeway.com
482 Odlin Rd.
99 rooms - $39-83
Pets: Welcome w/$5 fee
Creature Comforts: CCTV, a/c,
refrig, restaurant

Sheraton Four Points Hotel
(800) 325-3535, (207) 947-6721
http://www.sheraton.com
308 Godfrey Blvd. (airport)
101 rooms - $89-170
Pets: Welcome
Creature Comforts: CCTV, a/c,
refrig, micro, restaurant, pool, hlth
clb, sauna, whirlpool, lawn sports,
and game rooms

BAR HARBOR
Balance Rock Inn
(800) 753-0494, (207) 288-2610
www.barharborvacations.com
21 Albert Meadow St.
16 rooms - $99-495
Pets: Welcome w/$15 fee
Creature Comforts: Waterside
shingle-style mansion, circa 1903,
on magnificent grounds, grand
staircase, elegant decor, four-
poster beds, CCTV, a/c, kit,
marble bathrooms-Jacuzzis, full
brkfst, veranda bar, pool,
fireplaces, hlth clb, steambaths,
walk along famous Shore Path to
see Balance Rock

Bar Harbor Inn
(800) 248-3351, (207) 288-3351
http://www.barharborinn.com
1 Newport Dr.
155 rooms - $69-450
Pets: 1st floor w/$15 nightly fee
Creature Comforts: Eight acre
oceanfront resort overlooking
Frenchman's Bay, Queen-Anne
reproductions, canopy beds,
CCTV, VCR, a/c, fireplace, refrig,
restaurant, cont. brkfst, pool, hlth
club, whirlpool

Days Inn
(800) DAYS-INN, (207) 288-3321
http://www.daysinn.com
120 Eden St.
66 rooms - $60-125
Pets: Welcome
Creature Comforts: CCTV, a/c,
cont. brkfst

Hutchin's Mtn Motel
(800) 775-4833, (207) 288-4833
Rte. 3, Box 1190
22 rooms - $ 42-125
Pets: Welcome
Creature Comforts: CCTV, kit,
fireplace, pool

Ledgelawn Inn
(800) 274-5334, (207) 288-4596
http://www.barharborvacations.
com/llibarharbor.htm
66 Mt. Desert St.
33 rooms - $85-299
Pets: Welcome
Creature Comforts: Historic
Downeast Colonial Revival
"summer cottage," antiques,
reproductions, white wicker,
canopy and brass beds, charming
Carriage House, CCTV, VCR, a/c,
fireplace, refrig, verandas,
Jacuzzis, steambaths, restaurant,
cont. brkfst, sauna, pool, whirlpool

Wonderview Inn
(888) 439-VIEW, (207) 288-3358
http://www.wonderviewinn.com
Rte. 3, Box 25
80 rooms - $60-145
Pets: Welcome w/$10 fee
Creature Comforts: On historic
estate, CCTV, a/c, restaurant, pool,
great views, expansive grounds

BATH
Fairhaven Inn
(888) 443-4391, (207) 443-4391
www.mainecoast.com/fairhaven
N. Bath Rd., Box 85
8 rooms - $65-125
Pets: Selectively welcomed w/$10
fee (had recent bad experiences)
Creature Comforts: A charming
antique 1790's Colonial set on a
bluff, 23 acres, country décor,
antiques, CCTV, VCR, a/c, tavern
room-games, pastry lessons from
hosts, fireplace, refrig, full brkfst,
hiking, xc-skiing

The Inn at Bath
(207) 443-4294
http://www.innatbath.com
969 Washington St.
9 rooms - $79-175
Pets: Leashed pets w/$50 deposit
Creature Comforts: A lovely
1810 Greek Revival home with
beamed ceilings, wide board
floors, antiques, handsome décor,
four-poster and canopy beds,
designer fabrics, CCTV, VCR, a/c,
fireplaces, refrig, micro, Jacuzzis,
full brkfst, pool, hlth clb access,
sauna, whirlpool

Holiday Inn
(800) HOLIDAY, (207) 443-9741
http://www.holiday-inn.com
139 Western Ave.
140 rooms - $55-129
Pets: Welcome
Creature Comforts: CCTV, a/c,
restaurant, pool

Small Point B&B
(207) 389-1716
HC 32, Box 250
3 rooms - $50-89
Pets: Welcome
Creature Comforts: A secluded
1800's coastal farmhouse, CCTV,
a/c, refrig, country brkfst

BELFAST
Admiral's Ocean Inn
(207) 338-4260
192 Northport Ave.
20 rooms - $ 34-95
Pets: Welcome w/$20 dep.
Creature Comforts: CCTV, a/c,
cont. brkfst, pool

Belfast Harbor Inn
(800) 545-8576, (207) 338-5205
http://www.belfastharborinn.com
Rte. 1, Box 5230
60 rooms - $44-129
Pets: Welcome w/$5 fee
Creature Comforts: CCTV, a/c, pool, and bay access

Comfort Inn
(800) 228-5150, (207) 338-2090
http://www.comfortinn.com
Rte. 1, Box 35
52 rooms - $70-175
Pets: Small pets welcome
Creature Comforts: CCTV, a/c, cont. brkfst, sauna, whirlpool, pool

Gull Motel
(207) 338-4030
Rte. 1, Box 5377
14 rooms - $40-85
Pets: Welcome
Creature Comforts: CCTV, a/c, and bay views

Wonderview Cottages
(207) 338-1455
http://www.maineguide.com/belfast/wonderview
Rte. 1, Box 5339
20 cottages - $400-850/wk
Pets: Leashed pets are welcome with a $25 deposit
Creature Comforts: A charming cottage colony set up the hill from the bay, fireplaces, woodstoves, maple furnishings, simple decor, low-key ambiance, kit, lawn sports, sandy beach

BETHEL
Bethel Inn & Country Club
(800) 654-0125, (207) 824-2175
http://www.bethelinn.com
On the Common
100 rooms - $109-450
Pets: Welcome w/$30 fee
Creature Comforts: A classic 1913 New England resort w/a variety of recreational options, traditional furnishings, Vermont quilts, CCTV, VCR, Jacuzzis, fireplace, kit, restaurant, library, pool, hlth clb, sauna, massage, lawn games, tennis, whirlpool, lake/dock, xc-skiing, golf

Briar Lea B&B
(207) 824-4717
http://www.nettx.com/briarlee
150 Mayville Rd.
6 rooms - $49-145
Pets: Small pets w/$10 nightly fee
Creature Comforts: An historic 1850's farmhouse, CCTV, VCR, refrig, fireplace, restaurant, full brkfst

Chapman Inn
(877) 359-1498, (207) 824-2657
http://www.chapmaninn.com
On the Common
10 rooms - $60-119
Pets: Welcome
Creature Comforts: 1865 Federal w/informal atmosphere, CCTV, VCR, fireplace, kit, dining room, full brkfst, game rm-pool table, sauna, priv. beach, boating

L'Auberge Country Inn
(800) 760-2774, (207) 824-2774
www.laubergecountryinn.com
Hill Mill Rd.
6 rooms - $69-129
Pets: Welcome
Creature Comforts: A lovingly restored 1890's barn, high ceilings, maple furnishings, floral wallpapers, some antiques, CCTV, VCR, a/c, fireplace, baby grand piano, full brkfst, restaurant, five acres, and xc-skiing

Sudbury Inn
(800) 395-7837, (207) 824-2174
web site pending
1 Main St.
17 rooms - $65-109
Pets: Welcome
Creature Comforts: CCTV, a/c, fireplace, restaurant, pub, cont. brkfst

BOOTHBAY
Hillside Acres
(207) 633-3411
Adams Pond Rd.
10 rooms - $39-85
Pets: Welcome
Creature Comforts: CCTV, kit, pool

White Anchor Motel
(207) 633-3788
Rte. 27, Box 438
32 rooms - $40-89
Pets: Welcome w/CC dep.
Creature Comforts: CCTV, a/c, and kit

BOOTHBAY HARBOR
Harborside Resort
(800) 235-5402, (207) 633-5381
PO Box 516
33 rooms - $55-125
Pets: Welcome
Creature Comforts: CCTV, a/c, kit, restaurant

Lawnmeer Inn
(800) 633-7645, (207) 633-2544
http://www.lawnmeerinn.com
Rte. 27, Box 505
32 rooms - $69-189
Pets: Welcome w/$10 daily fee
Creature Comforts: CCTV, a/c, water views

Leeward Village
(888) 817-9907, (207) 633-3681
http://www.gwi.net/~leeward
96 Ocean Pt. Rd.
25 rooms - $60-175
Pets: Small pets welcome
Creature Comforts: CCTV

Ocean Pt. Cabin
(207) 633-2981
HC Box 936
2 cabin - $300-375
Pets: Welcome
Creature Comforts: TV, kit, fireplace

The Pines Motel
(207) 633-4555
Sunset Rd., Box 693
32 rooms - $35-89
Pets: Welcome w/permission
Creature Comforts: CCTV, tennis, lawn games, pool

Smuggler's Cove Inn
(800) 633-3008, (207) 633-2800
Rte. 96, Box 837
62 rooms - $65-160
Pets: w/$10 fee & 50 dep.
Creature Comforts: CCTV, refrig, micro, restaurant, cont. brkfst, pool, beach, boat dock

Welch House Inn
(800) 279-7313, (207) 633-3431
www.wiscasset.net/welchhouse
36 McKown St.
15 rooms - $55-165
Pets: Small pets welcome
Creature Comforts: CCTV, a/c,
refrig, cont. brkfst

BREWER
Brewer Motor Inn
(207) 989-4476
359 Wilson St.
32 rooms - $39-67
Pets: Welcome
Creature Comforts: CCTV, a/c,
kit, cont. brkfst
Rodeway Inn

(800) 228-2000, (207) 989-3200
http://www.rodeway.com
448 Wilson St.
78 rooms - $39-65
Pets: Welcome w/$5 fee
Creature Comforts: CCTV, a/c,
cont. brkfst.

BROOKSVILLE
Breezemere Farm Inn
(888) 223-FARM, (207) 326-8628
http://www.bbonline.com/me/
breezemere
RR 1, Box 290
14 rms/cottages - $60-130
Pets: Welcome w/$25 fee
Creature Comforts: Wonderful,
1850's secluded working farm on
Orient Harbor, accepting guests
since 1917, cottages tucked into
woods, stone fireplaces, kit, full
brkfst, beautiful surroundings,
hiking, bird sanctuary, canoeing,
farm animals

Oakland House
(800) 359-Relax, (207) 359-8521
http://www.oaklandhouse.com
435 Herrick Rd, Box 400
16 cottages - $270-1,200 (AP)
Pets: In cottages w/$10 fee
Creature Comforts: A classic
Maine cottage resort set on 50
waterside acres, some rustic
cottages w/neat camp furnishings,
fieldstone fireplaces, some
modern cottages, request
waterviews, CCTV, kit, dining rm,
sandy beach, lawn sports, sailing,
fishing, access to golf

BROWNFIELD
Foothills Farm B&B
(207) 935-3799
RR 1, Box 598
4 rooms - $55-99
Pets: Welcome w/$5 fee
Creature Comforts: CCTV, a/c,
fireplace, kit, full brkfst

BRUNSWICK
Mainline Motel
(207) 725-8761
133 Pleasant St.
50 rooms - $39-95
Pets: Welcome w/$5 fee
Creature Comforts: CCTV, a/c,
and kit

Viking Motor Inn
(800) 429-6661, (207) 729-6661
287 Bath Rd.
29 rooms - $48-96
Pets: Welcome w/$10 fee
Creature Comforts: CCTV, a/c,
kit, lawn games, pool

BUCKSPORT
Best Western Jed Prouty
(800) 528-1234, (207) 469-3113
http://www.bestwestern.com
52 Main St.
40 rooms - $65-130
Pets: Welcome
Creature Comforts: CCTV, a/c,
cont. brkfst

Bucksport Motor Inn
(800) 626-9734, (207) 469-3111
151 Main St.
25 rooms - $39-65
Pets: Welcome
Creature Comforts: CCTV

CALAIS
Calais Motor Inn
(207) 454-7111
293 Main St.
72 rooms - $55-79
Pets: Welcome
Creature Comforts: CCTV, a/c,
restaurant

International Motel
(207) 454-7515
276 Main St.
61 rooms - $50-119
Pets: Welcome
Creature Comforts: CCTV, a/c,
Jacuzzi

CAMDEN
Beloin's Motel
(207) 236-3262
HCR 60, Box 3105
33 rooms - $59-105
Pets: Welcome
Creature Comforts: CCTV, a/c,
kit

Blue Harbor House
(800) 248-3196, (207) 236-3196
http://www.blueharborhouse.com
67 Elm St.
10 rooms - $90-159
Pets: Welcome in carriage house
Creature Comforts: A nooky and
cranny 1810 New England Cape,
short walk to town, canopy, brass,
or four-poster beds, folk art, pine
furnishings, quilts, country
antiques, CCTV, VCR, a/c,
fireplace, Jacuzzis, restaurant, full
brkfst

CAPE ELIZABETH
Inn by The Sea
(800) 888-IBTS, (207) 799-3134
http://www.innbythesea.com
40 Bowery Beach Rd.
43 rooms - $165-485 (EP)
Pets: Welcome (pet goodies)
Creature Comforts: Highly
recommended, shingle-style resort
overlooking ocean, beautiful inn
w/Audubon prints, wicker and
Chippendale furnishings, down
comforters, CCTV, VCR,
fireplace, kit, Jacuzzi, intimate
gourmet restaurant, cont. brkfst,
pool, whirlpool, tennis, lawn
sports, beach, bicycles

CARIBOU
Caribou Inn
(207) 498-3733
Rte. 1, Box 25
72 rooms - $50-129
Pets: Welcome
Creature Comforts: CCTV, a/c,
kit, Jacuzzi, restaurant, pool, hlth
clb, whirlpool

CASTINE
The Manor
(877) Manor-Inn, (207) 326-4861
http://www.manor-inn.com
Battle Ave., Box 873
14 rooms - $125-195
Pets: Small pets are welcome
Creature Comforts: Expansive
1900's manor house w/sloping
lawns, high ceilings, massive rms,
inviting ambiance, Oriental
carpets, Victorian accents, CCTV,
VCR, fireplace, refrig, restaurant,
fun pub, cont. brkfst, game rm,
lawn games, yoga, nature trails

Castine Harbor Lodge
(207) 326-4335
http://www.castinemaine.com
Perkins St, Box 215
10 rooms - $99-155
Pets: Leashed pets welcome
Creature Comforts: Eclectically
appointed, 1893 waterside
"summer cottage," 250 feet of
wrap-around porches, charming
honeymoon cottage, large
expanses of glass, antiques,
reproductions, rattan, CCTV,
fireplace, kit, cont. brkfst, water
views, great honeymoon cottage

Pentagoet Inn
(800) 845-1701, (207) 326-8616
http://www.pentagoet.com
Main St., Box 4
16 rooms - $99-145
Pets: Welcome in certain rooms
Creature Comforts: An historic
1894 Victorian inn set in the heart
of town, Colonial furnishings,
CCTV, fireplace, four poster beds,
porch, refrig, cont. brkfst, and
afternoon tea

CENTER LOVELL
Hewnoaks Cottages
(207) 925-6051
RR 1, Box 65
6 cottages - $75-99
Pets: Welcome
Creature Comforts: CCTV, a/c,
kit, on a lake

CORNISH
Midway Motel
(207) 625-8835
S. Hiram Rd, Box 22
11 rooms - $42-99
Pets: Welcome
Creature Comforts: CCTV, a/c

DAMARISCOTTA
County Fair Motel
(207) 563-3769
Rte. 1, Box 36
21 rooms - $49-77
Pets: Welcome w/$5 fee
Creature Comforts: CCTV cont.
brkfst

DEER ISLE
Pilgrim's Inn
(207) 348-6615
http://www.pilgrimsinn.com
Main St., Box 69
12 rooms - $100 (EP)-220 (MAP)
Pets: Welcome in the cottage
Creature Comforts: A large
wood framed 1793 Colonial listed
on Nat'l Historic Regstr, eight foot
fieldstone fireplaces, beamed
ceilings, country antiques and
wicker, charming cottage w/bead-
board accents, CCTV, VCR, kit,
restaurant-great dining, full brkfst,
decks, view of harbor

EAGLE LAKE
Overlook Motel
(207) 444-4535
N. Main St, Box 347
12 rooms - $48-69
Pets: Small pets welcome
Creature Comforts: CCTV, a/c,
kit

EAST HOLDEN
The Lucerne Inn
(207) 843-5123
http://www.lucerneinn.com
Bar Harbor Rd.
26 rooms - $65-99
Pets: In ltd. rms w/$5 fee
Creature Comforts: CCTV,
VCR, a/c, fireplace, Jacuzzis,
restaurant, cont. brkfst, pool

EASTPORT
The Todd House
(207) 853-2328
1 Capen Ave.
7 rooms - $49-89
Pets: Welcome
Creature Comforts: 1775 inn w/
intriguing history, National
Historic Landmark, period
antiques, finial beds, Colnial
pieces, unusual collectibles,
CCTV, huge stone fireplaces, cont.
brkfst, and nice water views

EAST WINTHROP
Lakeside Motel
(800) 532-6892, (207) 395-6741
www.byme.com/lakeside motel
PO Box 236
32 units - $60-89
Pets: Welcome
Creature Comforts: CCTV, a/c,
kit, on a lake, boat rentals

EDGECOMB
Bay View Inn
(207) 882-6911
web site pending
Rte. 1, Box 117
14 cottages - $55-99
Pets: Welcome w/$5 fee
Creature Comforts: CCTV,
refrig

Edgecomb Inn
(800) 437-5503, (207) 882-6343
http://www.muddyrudder.com
306 Eddy Rd., Box 51
40 rooms - $55-129
Pets: Welcome in cottages
Creature Comforts: CCTV, a/c,
kit, cont. brkfst, restaurant

ELIOT

Farmstead B&B
(207) 439-5033, 748-3145
379 Goodwin Rd.
5 rooms - $59-70
Pets: Welcome
Creature Comforts: Quaint,
1704 Cape, bucolic setting, brass
beds, handmade quilts, country
antiques and décor, CCTV, VCR,
fireplace, refrig, micro, full brkfst

ELLSWORTH

Brookside Motel
(207) 667-2543
Rtes. 1 & 3
52 rooms - $40-95
Pets: Welcome
Creature Comforts: CCTV, a/c,
refrig, pool

Colonial Motor Inn
(207) 667-5548
Bar Harbor Rd.
70 rooms - $65-129
Pets: Welcome
Creature Comforts: CCTV, a/c,
kit, restaurants, whirlpool

Comfort Inn
(800) 228-5150, (207) 667-1345
http://www.comfortinn.com
130 High St.
63 rooms - $50-139
Pets: Small pets w/$25 dep.
Creature Comforts: CCTV, a/c,
cont. brkfst, hlth club

Holiday Inn
(800) HOLIDAY, (207) 667-9341
http://www.holiday-inn.com
215 High St.
102 rooms - $60-155
Pets: Welcome
Creature Comforts: CCTV, a/c,
refrig, restaurant, pool

Jasper's Motel
(207) 667-5318
200 High St.
32 rooms - $45-99
Pets: Small pets welcome
Creature Comforts: CCTV, a/c,
restaurant

Twilite Motel
(800) 395-5097, (207) 667-8165
Rtes. 1 and 3
22 rooms - $39-85
Pets: Welcome w/$20 dep.
Creature Comforts: CCTV, a/c,
cont. brkfst

The White Birches
(207) 667-3621
Rte. 1, Box 743
66 rooms - $45-155
Pets: Welcome
Creature Comforts: CCTV, a/c,
refrig, Jacuzzi, restaurant, and golf

FALMOUTH

Falmouth Inn
(207) 781-2120
209 Rte. 1
32 rooms - $44-89
Pets: Welcome
Creature Comforts: CCTV, a/c,
and kit

FARMINGTON

Mount Blue Motel
(207) 778-6004
4 Wilton Rd.
18 rooms - $43-69
Pets: Welcome w/$8 fee
Creature Comforts: CCTV, a/c

FREEPORT

Eagle Motel
(800) 334-4088, (207) 865-4088
web site pending
291 Rte. 1
20 rooms - $69-99
Pets: Welcome
Creature Comforts: CCTV, a/c,
cont. brkfst

Freeport Inn
(800) 99-VALUE, (207) 865-3106
http://www. freeportinn.com
335 Rte. 1
85 rooms - $55-130
Pets: Welcome
Creature Comforts: CCTV,
VCR, a/c, refrig, restaurant, lawn
games, pool

The Isaac Randall House
(800) 865-9295, (207) 865-9295
http://www.isaacrandall.com
5 Independence Dr.
9 rooms - $69-135
Pets: "We love dogs" - they are
welcome in certain rooms (doggie
treats provided)
Creature Comforts: A lovely
1823 Federal style farmhouse on 6
acres — a short walk to town —
beamed ceilings, handmade quilts,
dried flowers and wreaths, canopy
and brass beds, CCTV, VCR, a/c,
fireplace, kit, Jacuzzi, full brkfst

GLEN COVE

Claddaugh Motel
(207) 594-8479
Rte. 1, Box 101
15 rooms - $65-79
Pets: Welcome
Creature Comforts: CCTV, a/c,
kit, pool

GRAND LAKE STREAM

Leen's Lodge
(207) 796-5575
PO Box 40
10 rooms - $79-99
Pets: Welcome w/$15 fee
Creature Comforts: CCTV, kit

GREENVILLE

Chalet Moosehead Motel
(800) 290-3645, (207) 695-2950
Box 327
15 rooms - $59-110
Pets: Welcome w/$10 fee
Creature Comforts: CCTV, a/c,
kit, lawn games, lake-boats

Greenwood Motel
(207) 695-3321
Rtes. 6 & 15
14 rooms - $45-80
Pets: Welcome w/$5 fee
Creature Comforts: CCTV,
refrig, nature trails, pool, golf
access

Kineo View Lodge
(800) 659-8439, (207) 695-4470
http://www.maineguide.com/
mooshead/kineo.html
Rte. 15, Box 514
12 rooms - $49-85
Pets: Welcome w/$5 fee
Creature Comforts: CCTV,
whirlpool, lawn games, nature
trails/lake

Maine

HANCOCK POINT
Crocker House Country Inn
(207) 422-6806
http://www.maineguide.com/
downeast/crocker
HC 77, Box 171
10 rooms - $79-145
Pets: Welcome
Creature Comforts: Wonderfully secluded 1884 country inn with plenty of charm, Persian carpets, floral fabrics, brass and maple finial beds, wicker, country quilts and antiques, pine floors, CCTV, VCR, a/c, woodstove, refrig, intimate restaurant, full brkfst, whirlpool, moorings access, great waterside walks, bikes, kayaks, access to tennis

HARBORSIDE
Hiram Blake Camp
(207) 326-4951
PO Box 59
15 cottages - $120-175
Pets: Welcome
Creature Comforts: An old-fashioned camp w/weathered shingled cottages set on a peninsula amid 100 acres, fieldstone fireplaces, rattan and pine furnishings, knotty pine walls, Downeast collectibles, kit, dining room, full brkfst, trails, quiet cove-boats

HOULTON
Scottish Inns
(800) 251-1962, (207) 532-2236
Bangor Rd.
44 rooms - $34-59
Pets: Welcome w/$5 fee
Creature Comforts: CCTV, a/c, refrig, cont. brkfst

JACKMAN
Sky Lodge
(207) 668-2171
Rte. 201
19 rooms - $55-109
Pets: Welcome w/$25 fee
Creature Comforts: CCTV, kit, restaurant, pool

JEFFERSON
Housekeeping Cottages
(207) 832-7055
RR 1, Box 820
1 cottage - $240-350/wk
Pets: Welcome
Creature Comforts: Kit

KENNEBUNK
Kennebunk Inn
(207) 985-3351
45 Main St.
28 rooms - $99-165
Pets: Welcome
Creature Comforts: 1790's inn, CCTV, a/c, fireplace, refrig, library, turn-of-the-century ambiance, restaurant, cont. brkfst

Lodge at Kennebunk
(207) 985-9010
Rte. 3
40 rooms - $65-110
Pets: Welcome
Creature Comforts: CCTV, a/c, refrig, cont. brkfst, pool

KENNEBUNKPORT
Cabot Cove Cottages
(800) 962-5424, (207) 967-5424
http://cabotcovecottages.com
7 S. Main St., Box 1082
15 cottages - $95-160 (EP)
Pets: Welcome w/$5 fee
Creature Comforts: Charming shingled cottages w/knotty pine interiors tucked along a tidal cove, CCTV, white wicker, floral fabrics, kit, lawn sports, boats

Captain Jefferds Inn
(800) 839-6844, (207) 967-2311
http://www.captainjefferdsinn.com
Pearl St., Box 691
16 rooms - $99-229
Pets: Welcome w/$20 nightly fee
Creature Comforts: Lovely 1794 Federal mansion, elegant décor, fireplaces, traditionally furnished theme rooms, country quilts, antiques, four-poster beds, Oriental rugs, solarium, beamed ceiling carriage house w/skylight and country decor, CCTV, VCR, refrig, Jacuzzis, claw foot tubs, lovely gardens, full brkfst

The Colony
(800) 552-2363, (207) 967-3331
http://www.thecolonyhotel.com
140 Ocean Ave., Box 511
121 rooms - $199-425
Pets: Welcome w/$25 nightly fee
(pet goodies)
Creature Comforts: A classic family-owned grand hotel with wrap-around porches overlooking craggy coastline, high ceilings, cozy summer ambiance-old Maine charm, and Downeast decor, CCTV, VCR, fireplaces, refrig, micro, restaurant, pool, putting green, lawn games, beach, tennis/golf access

The Green Heron Inn
(207) 967-3315
http://www.greenheroninn.com
Ocean Ave., Box 2578
11 rooms - $70-139
Pets: Welcome in ltd. rooms
Creature Comforts: An intimate inn set along a saltwater creek, charming cottage, intimate rooms, country quilts, CCTV, VCR, a/c, fireplace, kit, cont. brkfst

Lodge at Turbat's Creek
(207) 967-8700
Ocean Ave, Box 2722
25 rooms - $79-115
Pets: Welcome in certain rooms
Creature Comforts: CCTV, a/c, cont. brkfst

The Seaside
(207) 967-4461
http://www.kennebunkbeach.com
Gooch's Beach, Box 631
10 cottages - $85-199
Pets: Welcome in cottages
Creature Comforts: 1756 inn on 20 waterfront acres, CCTV, knotty pine walls, maple and wicker furnishings, bates bedspreads, cozy décor, fireplace, kit, lawn games, beach

345

KINGFIELD
The Herbert
(800) The-Herb, (207) 265-2000
http://www.byme.com/theherbert
Main St, Box 67
20 rooms - $65-175
Pets: Welcome
Creature Comforts: An historic, albeit eclectic, 1918 hotel w/orig. woodwork, old-fashioned décor, brass beds, antiques, restaurant, CCTV, VCR, a/c, fireplace, refrig, Jacuzzis, cont. brkfst, hlth clb, steamroom, whirlpool

KITTERY
Enchanted Nights B&B
(207) 439-1489
http://www.enchanted-nights-bandb.com
29 Wentworth St.
6 rooms - $80-189
Pets: Welcome
Creature Comforts: Appealing 1890 Princess Anne Victorian, woodstoves, antiques and wicker furnish., floral fabrics, four-poster and wrought iron beds, Victorian reproductions, balloon curtains, CCTV, VCR, refrig, Jacuzzis-claw foot tubs, full brkfst on antique china, pet area

Super 8 Motel
(800) 800-8000, (207) 439-2000
http://www.super8.com
85 Rte. 1
56 rooms - $40-99
Pets: Welcome w/permission
Creature Comforts: CCTV, a/c, cont. brkfst, pool

LEE
Dunloggin B&B
(207) 738-5014
Rte. 6, PO Box 306
3 rooms - $55-80
Pets: Welcome
Creature Comforts: Lakeside B&B, CCTV, refrig, full brkfst

LEEDS
Angel Cove Cottages
(207) 524-5041
http://te.com/maine/angell.htm
Bishop Hill Rd, Box 29
9 cottages - $525/wk
Pets: Welcome
Creature Comforts: CCTV, kit, fireplaces, on lake/beach

LEWISTON
Motel 6
(800) 4-MOTEL6, (207) 782-6558
http://www.motel6.com
516 Pleasant St.
66 rooms - $36-55
Pets: Under 30 lbs.welcome
Creature Comforts: CCTV, a/c

LIMERICK
Jeremiah Mason B&B
(207) 793-4858
http://www.maineguide.com/limerick/jeremiah
5 Main St.
7 rooms - $55-79
Pets: Crated small pets
Creature Comforts: CCTV, a/c, cont. brkfst

LINCOLN
Briarwood Motor Inn
(800) 734-6731, (207) 794-6731
PO Box 628
26 rooms - $45-75
Pets: Welcome
Creature Comforts: CCTV, a/c, refrig, restaurant, cont. brkfst

Lincoln House Motel
(207) 794-3096
85 Main St.
20 rooms - $38-59
Pets: Welcome
Creature Comforts: CCTV, a/c, refrig, and micro

LINCOLNVILLE
Pine Grove Cottages
(800) 530-5265, (207) 236-2929
web site pending
Box 714
7 rooms - $55-109
Pets: Welcome w/$7 fee
Creature Comforts: CCTV, a/c, fireplace, kit, and Jacuzzis

LUBEC
Eastland Motel
(207) 733-5501
RR1, Box 220
20 rooms - $40-75
Pets: Small pets w/$4 fee
Creature Comforts: CCTV

MACHIAS
Bluebird Motel
(207) 255-3332
Rte. 1, Box 45
40 rooms - $49-69
Pets: Welcome
Creature Comforts: CCTV, a/c

Machias Motor Inn
(207) 255-4861
26 E. Main St.
34 rooms - $50-89
Pets: Welcome w/$5 fee
Creature Comforts: CCTV, a/c, kit

Maineland Motel
(207) 255-3334
Route 1
32 rooms - $35-59
Pets: Welcome
Creature Comforts: CCTV, a/c

MANSET
Seawall Motel
(800) 248-9250, (207) 244-9250
http://palermo.org/acadiainfo/a160/a160-05.htm
Route 102A
20 rooms - $45-90
Pets: Welcome
Creature Comforts: CCTV, a/c, restaurant, and ocean views

MEDWAY
Gateway Inn
(207) 746-3193
Route 157
39 rooms - $49-109
Pets: Welcome
Creature Comforts: CCTV, a/c, kit, pool

Katahdin Shadows Motel
(800) 794-5267, (207) 746-9349
web site pending
Rte. 153, Box H
11 rooms - $36-45
Pets: Welcome
Creature Comforts: CCTV, a/c, refrig

MILFORD
Milford Motel
(800) 282-3330, (207) 827-3200
http://www.mint.net/milford
154 Rte. 2
20 rooms - $54-95
Pets: Welcome
Creature Comforts: CCTV, a/c, refrig

MILLINOCKET
Atrium Inn & Health Club
(207) 723-4555
740 Central St.
82 rooms - $70-99
Pets: Welcome
Creature Comforts: CCTV, VCR, a/c, refrig, micro, Jacuzzis, cont. brkfst, pool, hlth clb, whirlpool

Best Western Heritage
(800) 528-1234, (207) 723-9777
http://www.bestwestern.com
935 Central St.
49 rooms - $55-99
Pets: Small pets welcome
Creature Comforts: CCTV, a/c, restaurant, hlth club, whirlpool

MONHEGAN ISLAND
The Island Inn
(207) 596-0371
Ocean Ave.
http://www.midcoast.com/
~islandin
35 rooms - $79-215
Pets: Welcome w/$20 fee
Creature Comforts: A large old inn perched on a hillside overlooking the harbor and ocean, great porches, simple furnishings and Downeast decor, restaurant, cont. brkfst

The Trailing Yew
(800) 592-2520, (207) 596-0440
Lobster Cove Rd.
35 rooms - $55-79
Pets: Welcome
Creature Comforts: Secluded island retreat, wonderfully rustic oasis, no heat or electricity, fireplace, Spartan décor, restaurant, great hiking, craggy coastline to explore

MOODY
N'er Beach Motel
(207) 646-2636
Rte. 1, Box 389
50 rooms - $45-120
Pets: Welcome
Creature Comforts: CCTV, a/c, refrig, cont. brkfst

NAPLES
Augustus Bove House
(207) 693-6365
http://www.nettx.com/
augustusbove/
Rtes. 302 & 114
12 rooms - $75-149
Pets: Welcome
Creature Comforts: A handsome 3-story 1856 brick Colonial beside Long Lake, simple decor, CCTV, VCR, a/c, refrig, Jacuzzi, and a full brkfst

NEWPORT
Lovley's Motel
(800) 666-6760, (207) 368-4311
Rtes. 11 & 100
64 rooms - $35-99
Pets: Welcome
Creature Comforts: CCTV, a/c, kit, pool, whirlpool, lawn games

NORTH ANSON
Embden Lake Resort
(207) 642-2687
http://www.vacationspot.com
RR 1, Box 3395
4 cottages - $105-139
Pets: Welcome
Creature Comforts: Lakeside, CCTV, VCR, stereo, woodstove, kit

OGUNQUIT
Capt. Thomas Motel
(207) 646-4600
www.chickadee.com/captthom
305 Rte. 1
75 rooms - $55-239
Pets: Welcome
Creature Comforts: CCTV, a/c, restaurant, indoor pool

Norseman Motor Inn
(207) 646-7024
http://www.norsemanresorts.com
PO Box 896
94 rooms - 55-195
Pets: After Oct 1
Creature Comforts: CCTV, a/c, refrig, restaurant, beach

Studio East Motor Inn
(207) 646-7297
43 Main St.
25 rooms - $44-99
Pets: Welcome w/$5 fee
Creature Comforts: CCTV, a/c, restaurant

West Highland Inn
(207) 646-2181
http://www.westhighland.com
14 Shore Rd., Box 1667
10 rooms - $65-149
Pets: Welcome in certain rooms
Creature Comforts: A lovely 1890 Victorian, in village, Persian rugs, fireplace, antiques, tab curtains, floral fabrics, dried wreaths, brass and maple beds, enclosed porch w/bead-board accents, CCTV, a/c, full brkfst

White Rose Inn
(800) 639-4483, (207) 646-3432
http://www.whiteroseinn.com
Rte 1, P.O. Box 2227
10 rooms - $65-129
Pets: Welcome in certain rooms
Creature Comforts: A cozy inn w/antiques, tab curtains, floral fabrics, dried wreaths, canopy beds, porch, CCTV, a/c, full brkfst

Yellow Monkey B&B
(207) 646-9056
168 Main St.
40 rooms - $90-155
Pets: Welcome
Creature Comforts: CCTV, a/c, refrig, Jacuzzi, cont. brkfst

OLD ORCHARD BEACH
Beau Rivage Motel
(800) 939-4668, (207) 934-4668
http://www.beaurivagemotel.com
54 E. Girard Ave.
59 rooms - $50-229
Pets: Welcome w/$25 dep.
Creature Comforts: CCTV, a/c, kit, Jacuzzis, pool, sauna, whirlpool

Crest Motel
(800) 909-4060, (207) 934-4060
http://www.crestmotel.com
35 E. Grand Ave.
30 rooms - $65-185
Pets: $5 fee in off-season
Creature Comforts: CCTV, a/c,
refrig, micro, pool, beach

Flagship Motel
(800) 486-1681, (207) 934-4866
http://www.nettx.com/
flagshipmotel
54 W. Grand Ave.
25 rooms - $40-115
Pets: Small pets w/$5 fee
Creature Comforts: CCTV, a/c,
refrig, pool, beach

Grand Beach Inn
(800) 834-9696, (207) 934-4621
http://www.oobme.com
198 E. Grand Ave.
85 rooms - $65-189
Pets: In certain rms w/$10 fee
Creature Comforts: CCTV, a/c,
kit, restaurant, pool

Old Colonial Motel
(888) 225-5989 , (207) 934-9862
http://www.customnet.com/
oldcolonial
61 W. Grand Ave.
32 rooms - $55-175
Pets: Welcome in off-season
Creature Comforts: CCTV,
VCR, a/c, kit, pool, on beach

Sea View Motel
(207) 934-4180
65 W. Grand Ave.
50 rooms - $45-175
Pets: Welcome
Creature Comforts: CCTV, a/c,
kit, pool

Waves Motor Inn
(207) 934-4949
87 W. Grand Ave.
140 rooms - $55-165
Pets: Welcome
Creature Comforts: CCTV, a/c,
kit, pool

ORONO
Best Western Black Bear
(800) 528-1234, (207) 866-7120
http://www.bestwestern.com
4 Godfrey Dr.
68 rooms - $60-129
Pets: Welcome
Creature Comforts: CCTV, a/c,
restaurant, cont. brkfst, hlth club,
sauna

University Motor Inn
(800) 321-4921, (207) 866-4921
5 College Ave.
49 rooms - $45-75
Pets: Small pets welcome
Creature Comforts: CCTV, a/c,
restaurant, cont. brkfst, pool

PATTEN
Mt. Chase Lodge
(207) 528-2183
http://www.maineguide.com/
patten/mtchase
Shin Pond Rd.
5 cabins - $69-80
Pets: Welcome
Creature Comforts: Lakeside, kit

Shin Pond Village
(207) 528-2900
http://www.mainerec.com/
shinpond
RR 1, Box 280
10 units - $35-99
Pets: Welcome w/$2 fee
Creature Comforts: CCTV, a/c,
kit, store, restaurant

PORTLAND
Andrews Lodging B&B
(207) 797-9157
http://www.travelguides.com/
home/andrews_lodging/
417 Auburn St.
6 rooms - $85-179
Pets: Welcome w/$10 fee
Creature Comforts: Charming
Colonial w/affable hosts and
welcoming ambiance, Oriental
rugs, Shaker furnishings, folk art
collectibles, sky lights, wicker,
country quilts, kit, CCTV, VCR,
a/c, Jacuzzi, full brkfst, lawn
games, and gardens

The Danforth Inn
(800) 991-6557, (207) 879-8755
http://www.danforthmaine.com
163 Danforth St.
10 rooms - $115-285
Pets: Welcome w/$5 one-time fee
Creature Comforts: Historic
District, beautifully restored 1823
Colonial Revival mansion, high
ceilings, hand-carved moldings,
canopy and four-poster beds,
stained glass windows, floral
fabrics, CCTV, VCR, a/c, library,
cupola w/views, fireplaces, refrig,
cont. brkfst, billiard rm., massage

Days Inn
(800) DAYS-INN, (207) 677-9506
http://www.daysinn.com
Rte. 1, Box 183
42 rooms - $45-75
Pets: Welcome w/$10 fee
Creature Comforts: CCTV, a/c,
cont. brkfst, pool

Doubletree Hotel
(800) 222-TREE, (207) 774-5611
http://www.doubletreehotels.com
1230 Congress St.
152 rooms - $75-170
Pets: Welcome
Creature Comforts: CCTV, a/c,
refrig, restaurant, pool

Holiday Inn
(800) HOLIDAY, (207) 774-5601
http://www.holiday-inn.com
81 Riverside St.
202 rooms - $80-165
Pets: Small pets in smoking rms
Creature Comforts: CCTV, a/c,
refrig, restaurant, pool, sauna

Howard Johnson Hotel
(800) I-Go-Hojo, (207) 774-5861
http://www.hojo.com
155 Riverside Rd.
120 rooms - $65-149
Pets: Welcome
Creature Comforts: CCTV,
VCR, a/c, refrig, Jacuzzis,
restaurant, pool, whirlpool

Howard Johnson Hotel
(800) I-Go-Hojo, (207) 775-5343
http://www.hojo.com
675 Main St.
123 rooms - $70-149
Pets: Welcome
Creature Comforts: TV, a/c, pool

Inn at Portland
(800) 289-6469, (207) 775-3711
1150 Brighton Ave.
123 rooms - $55-125
Pets: In smkng rms w/$10 fee
Creature Comforts: CCTV, a/c,
cont. brkfst, pool

Inn at St. John
(800) 636-9127, (207) 773-6481
http://www.innatstjohn.com
939 Congress St.
31 rooms - $45-129
Pets: Small pets welcome
Creature Comforts: Modest inn
reminiscent of European pensione,
Victorian accents, Oriental
carpets, antiques, cut glass lamps,
CCTV, a/c, refrig, cont. brkfst

Motel 6
(800) 4-MOTEL6, (207) 775-0111
http://www.motel6.com
1 Riverside St.
128 rooms - $40-65
Pets: Under 30 lbs.welcome
Creature Comforts: CCTV, a/c

Radisson Wilshire Hotel
(800) 333-3333, (207) 775-5411
http://www.radisson.com
157 High St.
203 rooms - $89-375
Pets: Small pets w/$100 dep.
Creature Comforts: CCTV, a/c,
refrig, restaurants, sauna, hlth clb

PRESQUE ISLE
Keddy's Motor Inn
(207) 764-3321
Rte. 1, Box 270
154 rooms - $63-79
Pets: Welcome
Creature Comforts: CCTV,
VCR, a/c, restaurant, sauna, pool

Northern Light's Motel
(207) 764-4441
692 Main St.
14 rooms - $29-49
Pets: Welcome w/$10 fee
Creature Comforts: CCTV, a/c

PROSPECT HARBOR
Oceanside Meadows Inn
(207) 963-5557
http://www.oceaninn.com
Rte. 195, Corea Rd.
7 rooms - $90-135
Pets: Welcome w/$8 daily fee
Creature Comforts: An 1860's
sea captain's home nestled on 200
acres along a cove, tranquil,
charming Downeast décor, pastel
color schemes, antiques, Oriental
rugs, ship models, dried flowers,
CCTV, fireplace, refrig, full
gourmet brkfst, croquet, new barn
for music & lectures

RANGELEY
Farmhouse Inn
(207) 864-5805
web site pending
Rte. 4, Box 165
6 rooms - $54-89
Pets: Welcome
Creature Comforts: A low-key
country inn set on 5 acres, CCTV,
fireplace, refrig, full brkfst

Rangeley Motor Inn
(207) 864-3341
http://www.rangleyinn.com
Main St., Box 160
52 rooms - $59-135
Pets: In 1 room w/$8 fee
Creature Comforts: CCTV
restaurant

Town & Country Motel
(207) 864-3755
http://www.byme.com/tl
Main St., Box 47
15 rooms - $45-65
Pets: Welcome w/$5 fee
Creature Comforts: TV, a/c, kit

ROCKLAND
Navigator Motor Inn
(800) 545-8026, (207) 594-2131
520 Main St.
78 rooms - $53-109
Pets: Small pets welcome
Creature Comforts: CCTV, a/c,
kit, restaurant

Oakland Seashore
(207) 594-8104
RFD 1, Box 1449
21 units - $49-69
Pets: Welcome
Creature Comforts: TV, kit, on a
beach

Trade Winds Motor Inn
(207) 596-6661
2 Park View Dr.
142 rooms - $70-139
Pets: Welcome
Creature Comforts: CCTV, a/c,
refrig, pool, hlth club

ROCKWOOD
Abnaki Cottages
(207) 534-7318
http://www.maineguide.com/
moosehead/abnaki
Abnaki Rd., Box 6
5 cottages - $60-79
Pets: Welcome
Creature Comforts: TV, kit

The Birches Resort
(800) 825-WILD, (207) 534-7305
http://www.birches.com
PO Box 41
15 cabins - $85-235
Pets: Welcome w/$8 fee
Creature Comforts: Neat, old-
fashioned hand-hewn log cabin
resort on 11,000 acres of
wilderness preserve, CCTV, VCR,
fireplaces-woodstoves, kit,
Jacuzzi, restaurant, lodge w/35-ton
stone fireplace, hlth clb, sauna,
whirlpool, lake beach/marina/
boats

Maynards in Maine
(207) 534-7703
PO Box 228
13 cottages - $60-175
Pets: Welcome
Creature Comforts: TV,
fireplaces, kit, dining rm, on river

RUMFORD
Linnell Motel
(800) 446-9038, (207) 364-4511
Route 2
52 rooms - $49-75
Pets: Welcome w/$5 fee
Creature Comforts: CCTV, a/c,
kit, restaurant

The Madison 4-Season Resort
(800) 258-6234, (207) 364-7973
Rte. 2, Box 398
60 rooms - $60-145
Pets: Welcome
Creature Comforts: CCTV, a/c,
kit, restaurant, pool

SACO
Classic Motel
(800) 290-3909, (207) 282-5569
http://www.classicmotel.com
21 Ocean Park Rd.
18 rooms - $75-99
Pets: Welcome w/travel crate
Creature Comforts: CCTV, a/c,
Jacuzzis, kit, pool

Crown n' Anchor Inn
(800) 561-8865, (207) 282-3829
121 North St.
6 rooms - $60-105
Pets: Welcome
Creature Comforts: A lovely
1837 Greek Revival mansion,
high ceilings and detailed
moldings, crystal chandeliers,
Victorian antiques, portraits,
CCTV, VCR, a/c, fireplace, refrig,
micro, Jacuzzi, full brkfst

Saco Motel
(207) 284-6952
473 Main St.
25 rooms - $35-74
Pets: Welcome
Creature Comforts: CCTV, a/c,
pool

Tourist Haven Motel
(207) 284-7251
757 Portland Rd.
11 rooms - $39-75
Pets: Welcome w/$5 fee
Creature Comforts: CCTV, a/c

SANFORD
Bar-H Motel
(207) 324-4662
581 Main St.
39 rooms - $45-79
Pets: Welcome
Creature Comforts: CCTV, a/c,
kit, pool

SEARSPORT
Light's Motel
(207) 548-2405
PO Box 349
14 rooms - $39-55
Pets: Welcome
Creature Comforts: CCTV,
restaurant

SKOWHEGAN
Belmont Motel
(800) 235-6669, (207) 474-8315
425 Madison Ave.
35 rooms - $55-108
Pets: Welcome
Creature Comforts: CCTV,
VCR, a/c, refrig, pool, lawn games

Breezy Acres Motel
(207) 474-2703
Rte. 201, Box 1090
12 rooms - $45-69
Pets: Welcome in certain rooms
Creature Comforts: CCTV, a/c,
refrig, pool

SOUTH PORTLAND
Best Western Merry Manor
(800) 528-1234, (207) 774-6151
http://www.bestwestern.com
700 Main St.
151 rooms - $55-129
Pets: Welcome
Creature Comforts: CCTV, a/c,
refrig, restaurant, pool

Howard Johnson Hotel
(800) I-Go-Hojo, (207) 775-5343
http://www.hojo.com
675 Main St.
122 rooms - $85-149
Pets: Welcome
Creature Comforts: CCTV, a/c,
refrig, restaurant, pool

Marriott Hotel
(800) 228-9290, (207) 871-8000
http://www.marriott.com
200 Sable Oaks Dr.
225 rooms - $119-325
Pets: Under 25 lbs. w/$20 fee
Creature Comforts: CCTV, a/c,
refrig, micro, restaurant, pool, hlth
clb, saunas, whirlpools

SPRUCE HEAD
The Craignair Inn
(800) 320-9997, (207) 594-7644
http://www.craignair.com
533 Clark Island Rd.
22 rooms - $49-119
Pets: Welcome w/$9 fee
Creature Comforts: An old
fashioned inn and carriage house
built in 1920s to house granite
quarry workers, simply furnished,
braided rugs, country antiques,
boarding house, CCTV, fireplace,
refrig, restaurant, piano, full
brkfst, adjacent island to explore

STRATTON
Spillover Motel
(207) 246-6571
PO Box 427
19 rooms - $55-75
Pets: Welcome w/$5 fee, $20 dep.
Creature Comforts: CCTV, a/c,
refrig, cont. brkfst

TENANTS HARBOR
East Wind Inn
(800) 241-VIEW, (207) 372-6366
http://www.eastwindinn.com
PO Box 149
29 rooms - $59-275
Pets: With a one-time $10 fee
Creature Comforts: Neat inn
tucked away on the edge of a
small harbor, country antiques,
CCTV, fireplace, intimate lobby
w/piano, refrig, restaurant w/ship
models, charming cottage w/apts.

TRENTON
Days Inn
(800) DAYS-INN, (207) 677-9506
http://www.daysinn.com
Rte. 1, Box 183
42 rooms - $45-75
Pets: Welcome w/$10 fee
Creature Comforts: CCTV, a/c,
cont. brkfst, pool

Sunrise Motel
(800) 419-2473, (207) 667-8452
http://www.acadia-sunrise.com
RR 1, Box 146
24 rooms - $30-109
Pets: Small pets w/$5 fee
Creature Comforts: CCTV, kit,
restaurant, pool

WATERFORD
Kedarburn Inn
(207) 583-6182
e-mail: members@aol.com/
kedar01
Rte. 35, Box 61
7 rooms - $79-149
Pets: Welcome
Creature Comforts: An English
B&B experience set in a charming
1858 home, village location next
to Lake Keoka, handmade quilts,
pastel color schemes, antiques,
brass and four-poster beds, CCTV,
VCR, a/c, fireplace, refrig,
restaurant, high tea, and a full
English brkfst

The Waterford Inne
(207) 583-4037
www.innbook.com/water.html
Chadbourne Rd., Box 149
9 rooms - $79-115
Pets: Welcome w/$10 fee
Creature Comforts: An 1825
farmhouse on 25 acres, antiques,
stenciled wallpapers, primitive
collectibles, CCTV, VCR, a/c,
fireplace, refrig, library, gourmet
dinner, full brkfst, pond, gardens

WATERVILLE
Atrium Motel
(207) 873-2777
332 Main St.
100 rooms - $50-95
Pets: Welcome
Creature Comforts: CCTV, a/c,
refrig, micro, cont. brkfst, pool,
sauna, whirlpool

Best Western Inn
(800) 528-1234, (207) 873-3335
http://www.bestwestern.com
356 Main St.
86 rooms - $55-99
Pets: Welcome
Creature Comforts: CCTV,
VCR, a/c, refrig, micro, restaurant,
hlth club, pool

Budget Host
(800) Bud-Host, (207) 873-3366
http://www.budgethost.com
400 Kennedy Memorial Dr.
44 rooms - $35-85
Pets: Small pets welcome
Creature Comforts: CCTV,
VCR, a/c, refrig, micro, restaurant,
cont. brkfst

Econo Lodge
(800) 55-ECONO, (207) 872-5577
http://www.econolodge.com
455 Kennedy Memorial Dr.
50 rooms - $39-94
Pets: Small pets welcome
Creature Comforts: CCTV, a/c,
cont. brkfst, pool

Holiday Inn
(800) HOLIDAY, (207) 873-0111
http://www.holiday-inn.com
375 Main St.
138 rooms - $80-159
Pets: Small pets welcome
Creature Comforts: CCTV,
VCR, a/c, refrig, restaurant,
whirlpool, pool

WELD
Kawanhee Inn Lakeside Lodge
(207) 585-2000, 778-4306
http://www.lakeinn.com
Route 142, Box 119
21 units - $70-179
Pets: Welcome
Creature Comforts: Neat, 1930's
log lodge and shingled cottages set
along a lake, old-fashioned
furnishings, country antiques,
calico curtains, CCTV, kit, stone
fireplaces, refrig, open beamed-
ceiling restaurant w/ great home
cooking, boating, hiking, access to
tennis and golf

WELLS
Garrison Suites Motel
(800) 646-3497, (207) 646-3497
www.chickadee.com/garrison
1099 Post Rd.
60 rooms - $40-125
Pets: Welcome in the off-season
Creature Comforts: CCTV, a/c,
kit, pool

Ne'r Beach Motel
(207) 646-2636
Rte. 1, Box 389
45 rooms - $38-149
Pets: Welcome
Creature Comforts: CCTV, a/c,
kit, lawn games, pool

Water Crest Cottages
(800) 847-4693, (207) 646-2202
http://wc.watercrestcotages.com
PO Box 37
19 rooms - $56-79
Pets: Welcome
Creature Comforts: CCTV, VCR
a/c, refrig, Jacuzzi, cont. brkfst,
pool, whirlpool, hlth clb

WESTBROOK
Super 8 Motel
(800) 800-8000, (207) 854-1881
http://www.super8.com
208 Larrabee Rd.
104 rooms - $40-89
Pets: Small pets welcome
Creature Comforts: CCTV, a/c,
kit, cont. brkfst

WILTON
Whispering Pines Motel
(207) 645-3721
Rte. 4, Box 649
30 rooms - $43-89
Pets: Welcome w/$4 fee
Creature Comforts: CCTV,
VCR, a/c, kit, boat dock

WINTERPORT
Colonial Winterport Inn
(207) 223-5307
Main St. Box 525
7 rooms - $55-79
Pets: Welcome
Creature Comforts: Nestled
along the Penobscot River, 1834
Colonial, CCTV, a/c, fireplaces,
country décor, Victorian antiques,
refrig, restaurant, full brkfst

YARMOUTH
Down-east Village Motel
(800) STAY-DEV, (207) 846-5161
705 Rte. 1
32 rooms - $59-109
Pets: Welcome
Creature Comforts: CCTV, a/c,
kit, restaurant, pool

YORK
York Commons Inn
(800) 537-5515, (207) 363-8903
Rte. 1, Box 427
88 rooms - $55-119
Pets: Small pets welcome
Creature Comforts: CCTV, a/c,
refrig, micro, cont. brkfst, pool

Maryland

ABERDEEN

Days Inn
(800) DAYS-INN, (410) 272-8500
http://www.daysinn.com
783 W. Bel Air Ave.
49 rooms - $53-79
Pets: Dogs welcome
Creature Comforts: CCTV, a/c,
cont. brkfst, pool

Econo Lodge
(800) 55-ECONO, (410) 272-5500
http://www.econolodge.com
820 W. Bel Air Ave.
51 rooms - $40-57
Pets: Small pets welcome
Creature Comforts: CCTV, a/c,
refrig, restaurant, cont. brkfst, hlth
club, pool

Four Points Hotel
(800) 325-3535, (410) 273-6300
http://www.sheraton.com
980 Hospitality Way
133 rooms - $75-129
Pets: Small pets w/$75 fee
Creature Comforts: CCTV, a/c,
refrig, micro, restaurant, sauna,
hlth club, pool

Holiday Inn
(800) HOLIDAY, (410) 272-8100
http://www.holiday-inn.com
1007 Beards Hill Rd.
124 rooms - $99-129
Pets: Small pets welcome
Creature Comforts: CCTV,
VCR, a/c, kit, restaurant, hlth club,
sauna, pool, whirlpool

Red Roof Inn
(800) The-Roof, (410) 273-7800
http://www.redroof.com
988 Hospitality Way
110 rooms - $65-89
Pets: Small pets welcome
Creature Comforts: CCTV, a/c

Super 8 Motel
(800) 800-8000, (410) 272-5420
http://www.super8.com
1008 Beards Hill Rd.
62 rooms - $45-78
Pets: Welcome w/permission.
Creature Comforts: CCTV, a/c,
refrig, micro, cont. brkfst

ANNAPOLIS

Days Inn
(800) DAYS-INN, (410) 974-4440
http://www.daysinn.com
2520 Riva Rd.
74 rooms - $45-105
Pets: Welcome
Creature Comforts: CCTV, a/c,
cont. brkfst, pool

Econo Lodge
(800) 55-ECONO, (410) 224-4317
http://www.econolodge.com
2451 Riva Rd.
69 rooms - $55-130
Pets: Small pets welcome
Creature Comforts: CCTV, a/c,
refrig, Jacuzzis

Holiday Inn
(800) HOLIDAY, (410) 224-3150
http://www.holiday-inn.com
210 Holiday Ct.
222 rooms - $75-149
Pets: Small pets welcome
Creature Comforts: CCTV,
VCR, a/c, kit, restaurant, hlth club
access, pool

Loews Hotel
(800) 526-2593, (410) 263-7777
http://www.loewshotels.com
126 West St.
217 rooms - $129-425
Pets: Welcome
Creature Comforts: A six-story
brick hotel, short walk to town,
waterfront, and U.S. Naval
Academy, luxurious public spaces,
traditional decor, CCTV, VCR,
a/c, refrig, restaurant, sports bar,
hlth clb access

Jonas Green B&B
(410) 263-5892
http://www.inn-guide.com/
jonasgreen/index.html
124 Charles St.
3 rooms - $79-125
Pets: Welcome
Creature Comforts: Wonderful
1690's home in historic district,
run by orig. owner's descendents,
gracious hosts, antique glass,
Colonial ambiance, some antiques,
CCTV, VCR, a/c, fireplace, refrig,
cont. brkfst

Residence Inn
(800) 331-3131, (410) 573-0300
http://www.residenceinn.com
170 Admiral Cochrane Dr.
101 rooms - $129-199
Pets: Welcome w/$75 fee
Creature Comforts: CCTV, a/c,
kitchens, cont. brkfst, sports ct,
whirlpool, pool

The Scotlaur Inn
(410) 269-6737
http://www.scotlaurinn.com
165 Main St.
10 rooms - $59-95
Pets: Welcome
Creature Comforts: An eclectic
B&B set atop centrally located
landmark restaurant, 1900's decor,
family furnishings, cozy
ambiance, CCTV, a/c, cont. brkfst

BALTIMORE

Admiral Fell Inn
(800) 292-4667, (410) 522-7377
http://www.admiralfell.com
888 S. Broadway St.
79 rooms - $135-225
Pets: Under 30 lbs. w/$35 fee on
1st floor (pet goodies provided)
Creature Comforts: Located in
the historic Fell's Point district
amid antique shops and sea
captain's homes, Federal
reproductions, four-poster beds,
CCTV, VCR, a/c, Jacuzzis,
fireplaces, restaurant, cont brkfst

Biltmore Suites
(800) 868-5064, (410) 728-6550
http://www.biltmoresuites.com
205 W. Madison St.
28 rooms - $99-179
Pets: Welcome w/$25 fee
Creature Comforts: Intimate
hotel near historic sites, traditional
decor, brass beds, festive color
schemes, dried flowers,
reproductions, traditional decor,
CCTV, VCR, a/c, kit, fireplaces,
cont. brkfst, courtyard w/wrought
iron furnishings

Days Inn
(800) DAYS-INN, (410) 882-0900
http://www.daysinn.com
8801 Loch Raven Blvd.
120 rooms - $45-119
Pets: Welcome w/$15 fee
Creature Comforts: CCTV, a/c,
restaurant, cont. brkfst, pool

Holiday Inn Inner Harbor
(800) HOLIDAY, (410) 685-3500
http://www.holiday-inn.com
301 W. Lombard St.
375 rooms - $119-289
Pets: Small pets welcome
Creature Comforts: CCTV, a/c,
refrig, restaurant, pool

Holiday Inn
(800) HOLIDAY, (410) 485-7900
http://www.holiday-inn.com
6510 Frankford Ave.
139 rooms - $79-99
Pets: Small pets welcome
Creature Comforts: CCTV, a/c,
refrig, restaurant, pool

Howard Johnson Express
(800) I-Go-Hojo, (410) 747-8900
http://www.hojo.com
5701 Baltimore National Pike
145 rooms - $53-99
Pets: Welcome
Creature Comforts: CCTV,
VCR, a/c, refrig, pool, whirlpool

Inn at Government House
(410) 539-0566
1125 N. Calvert St.
18 rooms - $95-165
Pets: Welcome
Creature Comforts: Beautifully
restored historic property set in
historic district, fireplaces,
antiques/reprrductions, four-poster
beds, paneled walls, detailed
woodworking, traditional decor,
CCTV, VCR, a/c, refrig, cont.
brkfst

Motel 6
(800) 4-MOTEL6, (410) 265-7660
http://www.motel6.com
1654 Whitehead Ct.
133 rooms - $45-59
Pets: Under 30 lbs. welcome
Creature Comforts: CCTV, a/c,
pool

Tremont Hotel
(800) TREMONT, (410) 576-1200
8 E. Pleasant St.
59 rooms - $99-200
Pets: Welcome w/$5 fee, $50 dep.
Creature Comforts: A centrally
located hotel w/ intimate
ambiance, residential decor,
CCTV, VCR, a/c, kit, restaurant,
cont. brkfst, hlth club access

Tremont Plaza Hotel
(800) TREMONT, (410) 727-2222
222 St. Paul St.
231 rooms - $140-200
Pets: Welcome w/$5 fee, $50 dep.
Creature Comforts: Charming
hotel w/inviting atmosphere and
expansive rooms, residential
ambiance, CCTV, a/c, kit, stereos,
restaurant, cont. brkfst, hlth club,
saunas, pool

BELTSVILLE
Holiday Inn
(800) HOLIDAY, (301) 937-4422
http://www.holiday-inn.com
4095 Powder Mill Rd.
204 rooms - $79-175
Pets: Small pets welcome
Creature Comforts: CCTV, a/c,
refrig, micro, restaurant, hlth club,
pool, whirlpool

BETHESDA
Holiday Inn
(800) HOLIDAY, (301) 652-2000
http://www.holiday-inn.com
8120 Wisconsin Ave.
274 rooms - $95-159
Pets: Small pets welcome
Creature Comforts: CCTV, a/c,
restaurant

Ramada Inn
(800) 2-Ramada, (301) 654-1000
http://www.ramada.com
8400 Wisconsin Ave.
163 rooms - $85-109
Pets: Small pets welcome
Creature Comforts: CCTV, a/c,
refrig, restaurant, pool

Residence Inn
(800) 331-3131, (301) 718-0200
http://www.residenceinn.com
7335 Wisconsin Ave.
188 rooms - $149-199
Pets: $5 daily fee, $100 one-time
cleaning fee
Creature Comforts: CCTV, a/c,
kitchens, cont. brkfst, sauna, hlth
club, cont. brkfst

BOWIE
Econo Lodge
(800) 55-ECONO, (301) 464-0089
http://www.econolodge.com
4502 NW Crain Hwy.
75 rooms - $50-75
Pets: Small pets w/$5 fee
Creature Comforts: CCTV, a/c,
refrig, pool

BUCKEYTOWN
Catoctin Inn
(800) 730-5550, (301) 874-5555
http://www.catoctininn.com
3613 Buckeystown Rd.
8 rooms - $89-160
Pets: In cottages w/$25 fee
Creature Comforts: Charming
1780's home w/wraparound porch
and historic outbuildings, shaded
by magnolias and set on four
acres, charming cottages, gazebo,
antiques, hooked rugs, locally
hand-crafted furnishings, CCTV,
VCR, a/c, fireplaces, refrig,
Jacuzzis, cont. brkfst, whirlpool

CALIFORNIA
Super 8 Motel
(800) 800-8000, (301) 862-9822
http://www.super8.com
22801- 3 Notch Rd.
62 rooms - $48-78
Pets: Welcome w/permission.
Creature Comforts: CCTV, a/c,
refrig, micro, cont. brkfst

CAMP SPRINGS
Days Inn
(800) DAYS-INN, (301) 423-2323
http://www.daysinn.com
5001 Mercedes Blvd.
125 rooms - $59-99
Pets: Welcome
Creature Comforts: CCTV, a/c,
restaurant, cont. brkfst, pool

Motel 6
(800) 4-MOTEL6, (301) 702-1061
http://www.motel6.com
5701 Allentown Rd.
145 rooms - $49-65
Pets: Under 30 lbs.welcome
Creature Comforts: CCTV, a/c

CAPITOL HEIGHTS
Days Inn
(800) DAYS-INN, (301) 336-8900
http://www.daysinn.com
55 Hampton Pk. Blvd.
190 rooms - $60-119
Pets: Welcome
Creature Comforts: CCTV, a/c,
restaurant, cont. brkfst, pool

Motel 6
(800) 4-MOTEL6, (301) 499-0800
http://www.motel6.com
75 Hampton Park Blvd.
122 rooms - $50-79
Pets: Under 30 lbs.welcome
Creature Comforts: CCTV, a/c

CASCADE
Bluebird on the Mtn.
(800) 362-9526, (301) 241-4161
www.bbonline.com/md/bluebird
14700 Eyler Ave.
5 rooms - $115-140
Pets: Well-behaved pets welcome
Creature Comforts: Gracious
refurbished 1900's manor house,
porch w/rocking chairs, Oriental
and braided rugs, four-poster beds,
pastel colors, CCTV, VCR,
fireplace, refrig, claw foot tubs,
Jacuzzis, full brkfst, massage

CHESTERTOWN
The River's Inn
(800) 894-6347, (410) 778-6347
rolphswharfmarina1.bizonthe.net
1008 Rolph's Wharf Rd.
6 rooms - $85-120
Pets: Welcome w/ a $10 fee
Creature Comforts: Refurbished
1830's Victorian farmhouse set on
rolling hills between a farm and a
river, country decor, CCTV, VCR,
a/c, fireplace, refrig, fun
restaurant, cont. brkfst, pool,
beach, marina-boat rentals

CHEVERLY
Howard Johnson Inn
(800) I-Go-Hojo, (301) 779-7700
http://www.hojo.com
5811 Annapolis Rd.
164 rooms - $59-99
Pets: Welcome
Creature Comforts: CCTV, a/c,
cont. brkfst, pool

CHEVY CHASE
Holiday Inn
(800) HOLIDAY, (301) 656-1500
http://www.holiday-inn.com
5520 Wisconsin Ave.
215 rooms - $79-179
Pets: Small pets w/credit card
deposit
Creature Comforts: CCTV, a/c,
refrig, Jacuzzis, restaurant, pool

COLUMBIA
Columbia Inn
(800) 638-2817, (410) 730-3900
http://www.columbia-inn.com
10207 Wincopin Cir.
288 rooms - $129-389
Pets: Welcome w/$75 dep.
Creature Comforts: CCTV,
VCR, a/c, refrig, restaurant, cont.
brkfst, pool, golf/hlth club access

CUMBERLAND
Holiday Inn
(800) HOLIDAY, (301) 724-8800
http://www.holiday-inn.com
100 S. George St.
128 rooms - $79-99
Pets: Welcome
Creature Comforts: CCTV,
VCR, a/c, refrig, restaurant, pool

DELMAR
Rodeway Inn
(800) 228-2000, (410) 896-3434
http://www.rodeway.com
9544 Ocean Hwy.
92 rooms - $45-89
Pets: Welcome
Creature Comforts: CCTV,
VCR, a/c, kit, cont. brkfst, pool

EASTON
Days Inn
(800) DAYS-INN, (410) 822-4600
http://www.daysinn.com
7018 Ocean Gateway
80 rooms - $60-95
Pets: Welcome w/$8 fee
Creature Comforts: CCTV, a/c,
cont. brkfst, pool

Econo Lodge
(800) 55-ECONO, (410) 820-5555
http://www.econolodge.com
8175 Ocean Gateway
48 rooms - $50-65
Pets: Small pets welcome
Creature Comforts: CCTV, a/c,
refrig, cont. brkfst

Tidewater Inn
(800) 237-8775, (410) 822-1300
http://www.tidewaterinn.com
101 E. Dover St.
114 rooms - $75-325
Pets: Dogs in on-site kennel
Creature Comforts: Well-
appointed inn set in historic
district, 18th-century reproduction
furnishings, Colonial decor,
CCTV, VCR, a/c, fireplaces,
refrig, Jacuzzi, restaurant, beamed
ceilinged bar, pool, access to golf
and sailing

EDGEWOOD
Best Western Invitation Inn
(800) 528-1234, (410) 679-9700
http://www.bestwestern.com
162 rooms - $55-95
Pets: Small pets welcome
Creature Comforts: CCTV,
VCR, a/c, refrig, micro, cont.
brkfst, pool

Days Inn
(800) DAYS-INN, (410) 671-9990
http://www.daysinn.com
2116 Emmorton Park Rd.
75 rooms - $50-75
Pets: Smoking rooms w/$10 fee
Creature Comforts: CCTV, a/c,
refrig, micro, cont. brkfst, pool

Motel Edgewood
(410) 676-4466
2209 Pulaski Hwy.
23 rooms - $40-59
Pets: Small pets welcome
Creature Comforts: CCTV, a/c,
refrig, micro

ELKTON
Econo Lodge
(800) 55-ECONO, (410) 392-5010
http://www.econolodge.com
311 Belle Hill Rd.
59 rooms - $40-59
Pets: Small pets welcome
Creature Comforts: CCTV, a/c,
refrig, cont. brkfst

Garden Cottage
(410) 398-5566
234 Blair Shore Rd.
1 cottage - $90-109
Pets: Welcome
Creature Comforts: Charming
rustic cottage w/rough hewn board
walls, rural setting surrounded by
lovely gardens and a 400-year-old
sycamore, brass bed, cozy interior-
country decor, teddy bear
collection, CCTV, a/c, fireplace,
refrig, full brkfst, gazebo, 130
acres

Knights Inn
(800) 843-5644, (410) 392-6680
http://www.knightsinn.com
262 Belle Hill Rd.
122 rooms - $40-85
Pets: Small pets w/$10 fee
Creature Comforts: CCTV, a/c,
kit, and a pool

Motel 6
(800) 4-MOTEL6, (410) 392-5020
http://www.motel6.com
223 Belle Hill Rd.
127 rooms - $40-55
Pets: Under 30 Lbs.welcome
Creature Comforts: CCTV, a/c

Sutton Motel
(410) 398-3830
405 E. Pulanski Hwy.
12 rooms - $35-49
Pets: Small pets welcome
Creature Comforts: CCTV, a/c

FREDERICK
Comfort Inn
(800) 228-5150, (301) 695-6200
http://www.comfortinn.com
420 Prospect Blvd.
118 rooms - $50-88
Pets: Small pets welcome
Creature Comforts: CCTV, a/c,
refrig, micro, cont. brkfst, hlth
club, pool

Days Inn
(800) DAYS-INN, (301) 694-6600
http://www.daysinn.com
5646 Buckeystown Pike
120 rooms - $68-99
Pets: Small pets welcome w$5 fee
& $25 dep.
Creature Comforts: CCTV, a/c,
kit, cont. brkfst, pool

Hampton Inn
(800) Hampton, (301) 698-2500
http://www.hampton-inn.com
5311 Buckeystown Pike
159 rooms - $90-139
Pets: Small pets w/$10 fee
Creature Comforts: CCTV, a/c,
refrig, micro, restaurant, cont.
brkfst, pool

Holiday Inn
(800) HOLIDAY, (301) 694-7500
http://www.holiday-inn.com
5400 Holiday Dr.
155 rooms - $85-109
Pets: Small pets welcome
Creature Comforts: CCTV, a/c,
refrig, restaurant, pool

Holiday Inn
(800) HOLIDAY, (301) 695-2881
http://www.holiday-inn.com
5579 Spectrum Dr.
99 rooms - $65-99
Pets: Small pets w/$25 dep.
Creature Comforts: CCTV, a/c,
refrig, micro, cont. brkfst

Red Horse Inn
(800) 245-6701, (301) 662-0281
996 W. Patrick St.
72 rooms - $45-78
Pets: Small pets welcome
Creature Comforts: CCTV, a/c,
restaurant

Turning Point
(301) 874-2421
http://www.bbonline.com/md/
turningpoint
3406 Urbana Pike
5 rooms - $80-175
Pets: In 1 cottage w/deposit
Creature Comforts: Charming
1910 Edwardian mansion flanked
by mature trees, a pair of cottages,
fireplace, collectibles and
miniatures, country antiques and
decor, CCTV, VCR, a/c,
restaurant, refrig, full brkfst

FROSTBURG
Comfort Inn
(800) 228-5150, (301) 689-2050
http://www.comfortinn.com
11100 New Georges Creek Rd.
100 rooms - $50-79
Pets: Small pets welcome
Creature Comforts: CCTV, a/c,
Jacuzzis, cont. brkfst, hlth club,
pool, golf access

GAITHERSBURG
Comfort Inn
(800) 228-5150, (301) 330-0023
http://www.comfortinn.com
16216 Frederick Rd.
127 rooms - $55-129
Pets: Small pets welcome
Creature Comforts: CCTV, a/c,
refrig, micro, full brkfst, hlth club,
pool

Hilton Hotel
(800) HILTONS, (301) 977-8900
http://www.hilton.com
620 Perry Pkwy.
300 rooms - $75-349
Pets: Small pets welcome
Creature Comforts: CCTV, a/c,
refrig, restaurant, pools

Holiday Inn
(800) HOLIDAY, (301) 948-8900
http://www.holiday-inn.com
2 Montgomery Village Rd.
302 rooms - $105-379
Pets: Small pets welcome
Creature Comforts: CCTV, a/c,
kit, restaurant, hlth club, pool

Red Roof Inn
(800) The-Roof, (301) 977-3311
http://www.redroof.com
497 Quince Orchard Rd.
114 rooms - $45-129
Pets: Small pets welcome
Creature Comforts: CCTV, a/c

Residence Inn
(800) 331-3131, (301) 590-3003
http://www.residenceinn.com
9721 Washington Blvd.
135 rooms - $129-169
Pets: w/$100 fee & $6 daily fee
Creature Comforts: CCTV, a/c,
kitchens, cont. brkfst, sports court,
and a pool

GLEN BURNIE
Days Inn
(800) DAYS-INN, (410) 576-1000
http://www.daysinn.com
6600 Ritchie Hwy.
100 rooms - $75-105
Pets: Welcome
Creature Comforts: CCTV, a/c,
restaurant, cont. brkfst, pool

Holiday Inn
(800) HOLIDAY, (410) 761-8300
http://www.holiday-inn.com
6600 Ritchie Hwy.
99 rooms - $75-109
Pets: Small pets welcome
Creature Comforts: CCTV, a/c,
restaurant, pool

GRANTSVILLE
Holiday Inn
(800) HOLIDAY, (301) 895-5993
http://www.holiday-inn.com
2541 Chestnut Ridge Rd.
100 rooms - $55-85
Pets: Small pets welcome
Creature Comforts: CCTV, a/c,
restaurant, sauna, hlth club, pool
whirlpool

Walnut Ridge B&B
(888) 41-walnut, (301) 895-4248
http://www.walnutridge.net
92 Main St.
4 rooms - $65-130
Pets: Small pets welcome
Creature Comforts: A charming
1864 farmhouse furnished in a
country decor with antiques,
quilts, country collectibles, family
heirlooms, wood-fired hot tub,
porches & gardens, gazebo, piano,
CCTV, VCR, a/c, kit, full brkfst

HAGERSTOWN
Best Western Venice Inn
(800) 528-1234, (301) 733-0830
http://www.bestwestern.com
431 Dual Hwy.
204 rooms - $55-135
Pets: Welcome in poolside rooms
Creature Comforts: CCTV,
VCR, a/c, Jacuzzis, kit, restaurant,
hlth club, pool

Comfort Suites
(800) 228-5150, (301) 733-2700
http://www.comfortinn.com
1101 Dual Hwy.
84 rooms - $50-75
Pets: Small pets welcome
Creature Comforts: CCTV, a/c,
cont. brkfst

Econo Lodge
(800) 55-ECONO, (301) 791-3560
http://www.econolodge.com
18221 Mason Dixon Rd.
56 rooms - $45-68
Pets: Small pets welcome
Creature Comforts: CCTV, a/c,
refrig, cont. brkfst

Four Points
(800) 325-3535, (301) 790-3010
http://www.sheraton.com
1910 Dual Hwy.
109 rooms - $65-169
Pets: Small pets w/$50 dep.
Creature Comforts: CCTV, a/c,
refrig, micro, restaurant, sauna,
hlth club, whirlpool, pool

Motel 6
(800) 4-MOTEL6, (301) 582-4445
http://www.motel6.com
11321 Massey Blvd.
102 rooms - $40-59
Pets: Under 30 lbs. welcome
Creature Comforts: CCTV, a/c,
pool

Stateline Motel
(301) 733-8262
18221 Mason Dixon Rd.
22 rooms - $30-49
Pets: Welcome w/$3 fee
Creature Comforts: CCTV, a/c

Sunday's B&B
(800) 221-4828, (301) 797-4331
http://www.sundaysbnb.com
39 Broadway St.
3 rooms - $50-78
Pets: Welcome w/approval
Creature Comforts: Lovely
Queen-Anne home, CCTV, VCR,
a/c, fireplace, refrig, full brkfst

Super 8 Motel
(800) 800-8000, (301) 739-5800
http://www.super8.com
Rtes. 70 & 40
62 rooms - $45-60
Pets: Welcome w/permission.
Creature Comforts: CCTV, a/c,
cont. brkfst

HANOVER
Holiday Inn, BVI Airport
(800) HOLIDAY, (410) 684-3388
http://www.holiday-inn.com
7481 Ridge Rd.
160 rooms - $75-165
Pets: Welcome
Creature Comforts: CCTV, a/c,
restaurant, cont. brkfst, pool

Red Roof Inn
(800) The-Roof, (410) 712-4070
http://www.redroof.com
7306 Parkway Dr.
107 rooms - $40-85
Pets: Small pets welcome
Creature Comforts: CCTV, a/c

HAVRE DE GRACE
Spencer Silver Mansion
(800) 780-1485, (410) 939-1097
200 S. Union Ave.
4 rooms - $70-140
Pets: Welcome in carriage house
Creature Comforts: Nicely
restored turreted 1812 mansion,
historic district, large porch,
Victorian decor, marble floors,
high ceilings-lovely wallpapers,
antiques, claw foot tubs, two-story
carriage house w/spiral staircase,
fireplace, kit, CCTV, VCR, a/c,
Jacuzzi, full gourmet brkfst

Super 8 Motel
(800) 800-8000, (410) 939-1880
http://www.super8.com
929 Pulaski Hwy.
63 rooms - $45-69
Pets: Welcome w/permission.
Creature Comforts: CCTV, a/c, refrig, micro, cont. brkfst

HUNT VALLEY
Embassy Suites
(800) EMBASSY, (410) 584-1400
http://www.embassy-suites.com
213 International Circle
221 rooms - $135-179
Pets: Welcome
Creature Comforts: CCTV, a/c, restaurant, cont. brkfst, pool

Marriott Hunt Valley Inn
(800) 228-9290, (410) 785-7000
http://www.marriott.com
245 Shawan Rd.
388 rooms - $99-389
Pets: Small pets w/CC dep.
Creature Comforts: CCTV, a/c, refrig, restaurant, pool, hlth clb, sauna, whirlpool, tennis, golf access

Residence Inn
(800) 331-3131, (410) 584-7370
http://www.residenceinn.com
10710 Beaver Dam Rd.
95 rooms - $129-179
Pets: w/$50 fee & $6 daily fee
Creature Comforts: CCTV, a/c, kitchens, cont. brkfst, pool

INDIAN HEAD
Super 8 Motel
(800) 800-8000, (301) 753-8388
http://www.super8.com
Route 210
46 rooms - $49-75
Pets: Welcome w/permission.
Creature Comforts: CCTV, a/c, cont. brkfst

JESSUP
Comfort Inn
(800) 228-5150, (410) 880-3133
http://www.comfortinn.com
8828 Balto-Wash. Blvd.
63 rooms - $65-95
Pets: Welcome
Creature Comforts: CCTV, a/c, refrig, cont. brkfst

Red Roof Inn
(800) The-Roof, (410) 796-0380
http://www.redroof.com
8000 Washington Blvd.
107 rooms - $58-89
Pets: Small pets welcome
Creature Comforts: CCTV, a/c

JOPPA
Super 8 Motel
(800) 800-8000, (410) 676-2700
http://www.super8.com
1015 Pulaski Hwy.
45 rooms - $55-70
Pets: Welcome w/permission.
Creature Comforts: CCTV, a/c, cont. brkfst

LANHAM
Days Inn
(800) DAYS-INN, (301) 459-6600
http://www.daysinn.com
9023 Annapolis Rd.
114 rooms - $55-79
Pets: Welcome
Creature Comforts: CCTV, a/c, Jacuzzis, restaurant, cont. brkfst, whirlpool, pool

Red Roof Inn
(800) The-Roof, (301) 731-8830
http://www.redroof.com
9050 Lanham-Severn Rd.
102 rooms - $45-79
Pets: Small pets welcome
Creature Comforts: CCTV, a/c

LAUREL
Comfort Suites
(800) 228-5150, (301) 206-2600
http://www.comfortinn.com
14402 Laurel Pl.
119 rooms - $79-205
Pets: Small pets welcome
Creature Comforts: CCTV, a/c, refrig, micro, restaurant, cont. brkfst, hlth club, pool

Motel 6
(800) 4-MOTEL6, (301) 497-1544
http://www.motel6.com
3510 Old Annapolis Rd.
126 rooms - $45-59
Pets: Under 30 lbs. welcome
Creature Comforts: CCTV, a/c, pool

Red Roof Inn
(800) The-Roof, (301) 498-8811
http://www.redroof.com
12525 Laurel-Bowe Rd.
118 rooms - $48-83
Pets: Small pets welcome
Creature Comforts: CCTV, a/c

LA VALLE
Super 8 Motel
(800) 800-8000, (301) 729-6265
http://www.super8.com
1301 National Hwy.
63 rooms - $49-80
Pets: Welcome w/permission.
Creature Comforts: CCTV, a/c, refrig, micro, cont. brkfst

LEXINGTON PARK
Days Inn
(800) DAYS-INN, (301) 863-6666
http://www.daysinn.com
60 Main St.
164 rooms - $63-85
Pets: Welcome
Creature Comforts: CCTV, a/c, kit, restaurant, cont. brkfst, pool

LINTHICUM HEIGHTS
Amerisuites
(800) 833-1516, (410) 859-3366
http://www.amerisuites.com
940 International Dr. (BWI)
128 rooms - $89-125
Pets: Small pets w/CC dep.
Creature Comforts: CCTV, a/c, cont. brkfst, pool, and hlth club

Comfort Suites
(800) 228-5150, (410) 691-1000
http://www.comfortinn.com
815 Elkridge Landing
139 rooms - $65-129
Pets: Small pets welcome
Creature Comforts: CCTV, a/c, cont. brkfst

Comfort Inn, Airport
(800) 228-5150, (410) 789-9100
http://www.comfortinn.com
6921 Baltimore-Annapolis Blvd.
188 rooms - $90-170
Pets: Small pets welcome
Creature Comforts: CCTV, a/c, refrig, restaurant, sauna, hlth club, and a whirlpool

Hampton Inn, Airport
(800) Hampton, (410) 850-0600
http://www.hampton-inn.com
829 Elkridge Landing Rd.
142 rooms - $75-109
Pets: Small pets w/$10 fee
Creature Comforts: CCTV, a/c

Holiday Inn, Airport
(800) HOLIDAY, (410) 859-8400
http://www.holiday-inn.com
890 Elkridge Landing Rd.
260 rooms - $115-169
Pets: Small pets welcome
Creature Comforts: CCTV,
VCR, a/c, refrig, restaurant, pool

Motel 6
(800) 4-MOTEL6, (410) 636-9070
http://www.motel6.com
5179 Raynor Ave.
136 rooms - $46-68
Pets: Under 30 lbs.welcome
Creature Comforts: CCTV, a/c,
pool

Red Roof Inn, Airport
(800) The-Roof, (410) 850-7600
http://www.redroof.com
827 Elkridge Landing Rd.
132 rooms - $57-85
Pets: Small pets welcome
Creature Comforts: CCTV, a/c

Sheraton Hotel (airport)
(800) 325-3535, (410) 859-3300
http://www.sheraton.com
7032 Elm Rd.
195 rooms - $80-225
Pets: Small pets w/CC deposit
Creature Comforts: CCTV, a/c,
refrig, micro, restaurants, sauna,
steamroom, hlth club, whirlpool,
and a pool

McHENRY
Comfort Inn
(800) 228-5150, (301) 387-4200
http://www.comfortinn.com
2704 Deep Creek Dr.
76 rooms - $60-105
Pets: Small pets welcome
Creature Comforts: CCTV, a/c,
cont. brkfst

NORTH EAST
Crystal Inn
(800) 631-3803, (410) 287-7100
http://www.crystalinns.com
1 Center Dr.
92 rooms - $80-130
Pets: Small pets w/$50 dep.
Creature Comforts: CCTV, a/c,
cont. brkfst, kit, restaurant, pool,
hlth club, and whirlpool

OCEAN CITY
Bay Sails Inn
(800) 776-5634, (410) 524-5634
102 - 60th St.
64 rooms - $99-135
Pets: Welcome w/$8 fee
Creature Comforts: CCTV, a/c,
pool

Best Western Sea Bay Inn
(800) 528-1234, (410) 524-6100
http://www.bestwestern.com
6007 Coastal Hwy.
92 rooms - $35-189
Pets: Welcome Nov.—Mar.
Creature Comforts: CCTV, a/c,
Jacuzzis, kit, restaurant, pool

Fenwick Inn
(800) 492-1873, (410) 250-1100
http://www.fenwickinn.com
138th St. & Coastal Hwy.
200 rooms - $65-199
Pets: From Oct-Mar w/$10 fee
Creature Comforts: CCTV, a/c,
kit, restaurant, pool, whirlpool

Georgia Belle Suites
(800) 542-4444, (410) 250-4000
www.ocean-city.com/gbhome.htm
12000 Coastal Hwy.
100 rooms - $60-299
Pets: Welcome except July/Aug.
Creature Comforts: CCTV,
VCR, a/c, refrig, micro, restaurant,
pool

Sheraton Fountainbleu Hotel
(800) 325-3535, (410) 273-6300
http://www.sheraton.com
10100 Coastal Hwy.
292 rooms - $89-355
Pets: Small pets w/$20 fee
Creature Comforts: Expansive
beach-front resort, CCTV, a/c, kit,
restaurants, saunas, steam-room,
hlth club, whirlpools, pool, tennis/
golf access

OXFORD
Combsberry B&B
(410) 226-5353
http://www.combsberry.com
4837 Evergreen Road
7 rooms - $250-400
Pets: Welcome in the cottage
Creature Comforts: A Lovely
English country Manor on 9 acres
along the Eastern Shore, CCTV,
kit, fireplace, rattan, brass & four-
poster beds, antiques, floral chintz,
reproductions, full brkfst, sky
lights, Jacuzzi, Oriental rugs,
water views, formal gardens

OXON HILL
Red Roof Inn
(800) The-Roof, (301) 567-8030
http://www.redroof.com
6170 Oxon Hill Rd.
122 rooms - $58-75
Pets: Small pets welcome
Creature Comforts: CCTV, a/c

PERRYVILLE
Comfort Inn
(800) 228-5150, (410) 642-2866
http://www.comfortinn.com
61 Heather Ln.
104 rooms - $50-75
Pets: Small pets welcome
Creature Comforts: CCTV, a/c,
restaurant, cont. brkfst, hlth club

PIKESVILLE
Holiday Inn
(800) HOLIDAY, (410) 486-5600
http://www.holiday-inn.com
1721 Reisterstown Rd.
106 rooms - $75-99
Pets: Small pets welcome
Creature Comforts: CCTV, a/c,
refrig, restaurant, hlth club, pool

POCOMOKE CITY
Days Inn
(800) DAYS-INN, (410) 957-3000
http://www.daysinn.com
1540 Ocean Hwy.
87 rooms - $58-90
Pets: Welcome
Creature Comforts: CCTV, a/c,
refrig, restaurant, cont. brkfst, pool

Quality Inn
(800) 228-5151, (410) 957-1300
http://www.qualityinn.com
825 Ocean Ave.
64 rooms - $55-99
Pets: Small pets welcome
Creature Comforts: CCTV, a/c,
refrig, Jacuzzis, cont. brkfst, pool

PRINCESS ANNE
Econo Lodge
(800) 55-ECONO, (410) 651-9400
http://www.econolodge.com
10936 Market Ln.
52 rooms - $50-90
Pets: Small pets w/$5 fee
Creature Comforts: CCTV, a/c,
kitchenetes, Jacuzzi, pool

Waterloo Country Inn
(410) 651-0883
www.waterloocountryinn.com
28822 Mt. Vernon Rd.
5 rooms - $105-249
Pets: Welcome in one room
Creature Comforts: A charming
1750s waterside country estate
listed on National Historic
Register, TV, a/c, refrig, Jacuzzi,
antiques, lovely decor, spacious
rooms, Victorian accents,
fireplaces, gourmet brkfst, outside
pool, gardens, tidal pond-canoe,
and bikes

RAWLINGS
Diplomat Motel
(301) 729-2311
17012 McMullen Hwy.
14 rooms - $38-53
Pets: Welcome w/$5 fee
Creature Comforts: CCTV, a/c,
refrig, micro

ROCK HALL
Huntingfield Manor B&B
(800) 720-8788, (410) 639-7779
http://www.huntingfield.com
4928 Eastern Neck Rd.
6 rooms - $85-145
Pets: Welcome in the cottage
Creature Comforts: Refurbished
working farm set on 70 acres
dating back to the 1600s, country
decor, affable hosts, sunny library,
great common room, CCTV,
VCR, a/c, refrig, fireplace, cont.
brkfst, kit

ROCKVILLE
Best Western Gateway
(800) 528-1234, (301) 424-4940
http://www.bestwestern.com
1251 W. Montgomery Ave.
165 rooms - $65-119
Pets: Small pets welcome
Creature Comforts: CCTV, a/c,
refrig, micro, cont. brkfst, hlth
club, pool

Comfort Inn
(800) 228-5150, (301) 948-8000
http://www.comfortinn.com
3 Research Ct.
107 rooms - $55-95
Pets: Small pets welcome
Creature Comforts: CCTV, a/c,
cont. brkfst, pool

Ramada Inn
(800) 2-Ramada, (301) 881-2300
http://www.ramada.com
1775 Rockville Pike
158 rooms - $70-139
Pets: Small pets w/$20 fee
Creature Comforts: CCTV, a/c,
refrig, Jacuzzis, restaurant, hlth clb

Woodfin Suite Hotel
(800) 237-8811, (301) 590-9880
http://www.woodfinsuites.com
1380 Piccard Dr.
202 rooms - $93-245
Pets: $50 deposit and $5 daily fee
Creature Comforts: CCTV, a/c,
kitchens, pool

ROYAL OAKS
The Oaks
(410) 745-5053
http://www.the-oaks.com
25876 Royal Oaks Rd.
25 rooms - $65-300
Pets: Welcome in annex
Creature Comforts: Renovated
1784 inn w/great porches, nestled
on 10 acres along Oak Creek,
white wicker, traditional decor,
antiques and reproductions,
CCTV, a/c, fireplace, refrig,
Jacuzzis, cont. brkfst, pool, bikes,
lawn sports, boating

ST. MICHAELS
Inn at Perry Cabin
(800) 722-2949, (410) 745-2200
http://www.perrycabin.com
308 Watkins Rd.
41 rooms - $295-925
Pets: Welcome (pet menu)
Creature Comforts: Lovely
Colonial waterside mansion set on
25 acres, English country house,
restored by Sir Bernard Ashley in
1990 (founder of Laura Ashley),
most of the rooms face the bay,
fireplace, Oriental rugs, exquisite
decor, Laura Ashley accents, a/c,
restaurant, antiques, indoor, heated
pool, hlth club, sauna, steamroom,
croquet, bikes, boating

Kemp House Inn
(410) 745-2243
412 Talbot St.
6 rooms - $75-125
Pets: Welcome in cottage
Creature Comforts: Handsome
1807 Federal brick home w/
country antiques, brick and wide
board floors, handmade quilts,
braided rugs, four-poster rope
bedsteads, period furnishings,
CCTV, a/c, fireplaces, refrig, cont.
brkfst, charming cottage w/
cathedral ceilings, wicker rockers

SALISBURY
Best Western Inn
(800) 528-1234, (410) 546-1300
http://www.bestwestern.com
1735 N. Salisbury Blvd.
101 rooms - $55-139
Pets: Small pets welcome
Creature Comforts: CCTV, a/c,
refrig, micro, cont. brkfst, pool

Comfort Inn
(800) 228-5150, (410) 543-4666
http://www.comfortinn.com
270 N. Salisbury Bld.
96 rooms - $54-109
Pets: Small pets welcome
Creature Comforts: CCTV, a/c,
refrig, micro, Jacuzzis, lawn
games, cont. brkfst

Econo Lodge
(800) 55-ECONO, (410) 749-7155
http://www.econolodge.com
712 N. Salisbury Rd.
92 rooms - $40-75
Pets: Small pets w/$20 dep.
Creature Comforts: CCTV, a/c,
refrig, cont. brkfst, pooll

Howard Johnson Inn
(800) I-Go-Hojo, (410) 742-7194
http://www.hojo.com
2625 N. Salisbury Blvd.
123 rooms - $55-129
Pets: Welcome in certain rooms
Creature Comforts: CCTV, a/c,
cont. brkfst, pool

Super 8 Motel
(800) 800-8000, (410) 749-5131
http://www.super8.com
2615 N. Salisbury Blvd.
48 rooms - $44-75
Pets: Welcome w/permission.
Creature Comforts: CCTV, a/c,
refrig, micro, cont. brkfst

SNOW HILL
River House Inn
(410) 632-2722
http://www.riverhouseinn.com
201 E. Market St.
8 rooms - $100-195
Pets: Cottage w/$20 fee
Creature Comforts: A wonderful
National Register 1860 Victorian
home overlooking river, very
charming, CCTV, VCR, a/c, bikes,
lovely decor, refrig, micro, dock,
Jacuzzi, fireplaces, gardens &
spacious lawn, large porches w/
river views, access to boats

SOLOMONS
Holiday Inn
(800) HOLIDAY, (410) 326-6311
http://www.holiday-inn.com
155 Holiday Dr.
325 rooms - $85-185
Pets: Small pets w/$50 dep.
Creature Comforts: CCTV, a/c,
kit, Jacuzzis, restaurant, pool, hlth
club, sauna, marina

THURMONT
Rambler Motel
(301) 271-2424
Rtes. 15 & 550
32 rooms - $48-70
Pets: Small pets w/$7 fee
Creature Comforts: CCTV, a/c

Super 8 Motel
(800) 800-8000, (301) 271-7888
http://www.super8.com
300 Tippin Dr.
46 rooms - $48-75
Pets: Welcome w/permission.
Creature Comforts: CCTV, a/c,
refrig, micro, waterbeds, and a
cont. brkfst

TILGHMAN ISLAND
Tilghman Island Inn
(800) 866-2141, (410) 886-2141
www.tilghmanisland.com/tii/
End of Coopertown Rd.
12 rooms - $95-165
Pets: In garden rooms w/$15 fee
Creature Comforts: Low-key, 5
acre waterside resort, CCTV,
VCR, a/c, fireplace, refrig,
restaurant, pool, tennis, lawn
sports, dock, short walk to the
village

TIMONIUM
Red Roof Inn
(800) The-Roof, (410) 666-0380
http://www.redroof.com
111 W. Tinonium Rd.
135 rooms - $49-95
Pets: Small pets welcome
Creature Comforts: CCTV, a/c

TOWSON
Days Inn
(800) DAYS-INN, (410) 882-0900
http://www.daysinn.com
8801 Loch Raven Blvd.
148 rooms - $35-135
Pets: Small pets w/$15 fee
Creature Comforts: CCTV, a/c,
micro, restaurant, cont. brkfst

Holiday Inn
(800) HOLIDAY, (410) 823-4410
http://www.holiday-inn.com
1100 Crowmwell Bridge Rd.
138 rooms - $89-129
Pets: Small pets welcome
Creature Comforts: CCTV, a/c,
restaurant, pool

Ramada Inn
(800) 2-Ramada, (410) 823-8750
http://www.ramada.com
8712 Loch Raven Blvd.
122 rooms - $60-109
Pets: Welcome
Creature Comforts: CCTV, a/c,
kit, restaurant, pool, hlth clb

UPPER MARLBORO
Forest Hills Motel
(301) 627-3969
2901 Crain Hwy.
12 rooms - $48-59
Pets: Welcome
Creature Comforts: CCTV, a/c

WALDORF
Days Inn
(800) DAYS-INN, (301) 932-9200
http://www.daysinn.com
11370 Days Ct.
100 rooms - $45-75
Pets: Welcome w/$10 fee
Creature Comforts: CCTV, a/c,
refrig, micro, Jacuzzis, restaurant,
cont. brkfst, pool

Econo Lodge
(800) 55-ECONO, (301) 645-0022
http://www.econolodge.com
11770 Business Park Dr.
88 rooms - $44-68
Pets: Small pets w/$15 fee
Creature Comforts: CCTV, a/c,
refrig, micro, Jacuzzis

Holiday Inn
(800) HOLIDAY, (301) 645-8200
http://www.holiday-inn.com
1 St. Patrick's Dr.
194 rooms - $75-100
Pets: Small pets w/CC dep.
Creature Comforts: CCTV, a/c,
kit, restaurant, pool

Howard Johnson Express
(800)I-Go-Hojo, (301) 932-5090
http://www.hojo.com
3125 Crain Hwy.
110 rooms - $42-69
Pets: Welcome
Creature Comforts: CCTV, a/c,
kit, restaurant, cont. brkfst, pool

Super 8 Motel
(800) 800-8000, (301) 932-8957
http://www.super8.com
3550 Crain Hwy.
59 rooms - $47-65
Pets: Welcome w/permission.
Creature Comforts: CCTV, a/c,
refrig, micro, cont. brkfst

WESTMINSTER
Boston Inn
(410) 848-9095
533 Baltimore Blvd.
114 rooms - $38-66
Pets: Welcome
Creature Comforts: CCTV, a/c,
kit, pool

Comfort Inn
(800) 228-5150, (410) 857-1900
http://www.comfortinn.com
451 WMC Dr.
101 rooms - $57-165
Pets: Small pets welcome
Creature Comforts: CCTV, a/c,
Jacuzzis, cont. brkfst, hlth club,
whirlpool, tennis, pool

Days Inn
(800) DAYS-INN, (410) 857-0500
http://www.daysinn.com
25 S. Cranberry Rd.
96 rooms - $64-85
Pets: Welcome w/$5 fee
Creature Comforts: CCTV, a/c,
refrig, micro, cont. brkfst, hlth
club access, pool

WILLIAMSPORT
Days Inn
(800) DAYS-INN, (301) 582-3500
http://www.daysinn.com
310 E. Potomac St.
100 rooms - $55-85
Pets: Welcome
Creature Comforts: CCTV, a/c,
cont. brkfst, pool

WINGATE
Wingate Manor B&B
(888) 397-8717, (410) 397-8717
http://www.wingatebb.com
2335 Wingate-Bishop's Head Rd.
6 rooms - $80-125
Pets: Well-behaved dogs are
welcome in one room
Creature Comforts: Historic
turn-of-the-cenury home set
amidst rivers, pine forests, islands,
and wetlands, period furnishings
and family heirlooms, woodstove,
piano, CCTV, a/c, full brkfst,
hosts are award-winning chefs,
boats, bikes available - popular
destination for bicyclists

Massachusetts

AMHERST

Howard Johnson Inn
(800) I-Go-Hojo, (413) 586-0114
http://www.hojo.com
401 Russell St.
100 rooms - $65-155
Pets: Welcome
Creature Comforts: CCTV, a/c, refrig, Jacuzzis, cont. brkfst, pool

Lord Jeffery Inn
(800) 742-0358, (413) 253-2576
http://www.pinnacle-inns.com/lordjefferyinn
30 Boltwood Avenue
48 rooms - $79-185
Pets: Small pets welcome with a $15 a day fee
Creature Comforts: A classic 1926 New England inn set amid the charming college town of Amherst, CCTV, VCR, a/c, fireplace, refrig, traditional decor, period reproductions, balconies w/ views of common, restaurant, tavern, and a cont. brkfst

University Lodge
(413) 256-8111
virtual-valley.com/universitylodge
345 N. Pleasant St.
22 rooms - $49-105
Pets: Welcome
Creature Comforts: CCTV, a/c

ANDOVER

Andover Inn
(800) 242-5903, (978) 475-5903
http://www.andoverinn.com
Chapel Ave.
23 rooms - $109-175
Pets: Small pets welcome
Creature Comforts: A traditional brick building set on a prestigious prep school campus, CCTV, VCR, a/c, fireplace, refrig, restaurant, cont. brkfst

Marriott Hotel
(800) 228-9290, (978) 975-3600
http://www.marriott.com
123 Old River Rd.
294 rooms - $165-225
Pets: Small pets w/$35 dep.
Creature Comforts: CCTV, a/c, refrig, restaurant, pool, hlth clb, whirlpools, hiking trail

Ramada Hotel
(800) 2-Ramada, (978) 475-5400
http://www.ramada.com
311 Lowell St.
179 rooms - $95-159
Pets: Small pets welcome
Creature Comforts: CCTV, a/c, refrig, restaurant, pool, hlth club

AUBURN

Baymont Inns
(800) 4-Budget, (508) 832-7000
http://www.baymontinns.com
444 Southbridge Rd.
101 rooms - $57-75
Pets: Small pets in smoking rms.
Creature Comforts: CCTV, a/c, cont. brkfst

BARNSTABLE

Lamb and the Lion Inn
(800) 909-6923, (508) 362-6823
http://www.lambandlion.com
Rte 6A
5 rooms - $95-225
Pets: "Friendly pets" are welcome w/$10 daily fee
Creature Comforts: A lovely 1740's sprawling cape encircling a pool, set on a knol amid 4 acres, fireplaces, common area w/ white wicker, CCTV, VCR, a/c, decks, fireplace, suites w/kit, four poster & finial beds, sunken tub, and a cont. brkfst

BARRE

Jenkins House B&B
(800) 378-7373, (978) 355-6444
www.bbhost.com/jenkinsinn
Rtes. 122 & 32
5 rooms - $95-155
Pets: Welcome w/$5 fee
Creature Comforts: A charming 1834 Victorian set alongside the town common, CCTV, VCR, a/c, fireplace, finial and four poster beds, kit, Jacuzzi, 4-star restaurant, porches-gardens, full brkfst

BEDFORD

Renaissance Bedford Hotel
(781) 275-5500
44 Middlesex Tpk.
284 rooms - $115-245
Pets: Welcome w/credit card dep.
Creature Comforts: CCTV, VCR, a/c, restaurant, pool, hlth club, sauna, tennis

BOSTON

30 Appleton St.
(617) 542-7279
30 Appleton St.
2 studios - $100-135
Pets: Welcome
Creature Comforts: Charming South End row house, nicely appointed w/an assortment of amenities, CCTV, VCR, a/c, kit, bow window, Victorian accents, and a cont. brkfst, front studio is larger but also a little noisier

Back Bay Hilton
(800) HILTONS, (617) 236-1100
http://www.hilton.com
40 Dalton St.
333 rooms - $155-399
Pets: Small pets welcome
Creature Comforts: CCTV, a/c, refrig, restaurant, pool

Boston Harbor Hotel
(800) 752-7077, (617) 439-7000
http://www.bhh.com
70 Rowes Wharf
230 rooms - $199-1,750
Pets: Welcome, pet program w/
food, walking maps, scoopers, etc.
Creature Comforts: A luxury
waterfront hotel, traditional
furnishings, antique maps, CCTV,
VCR, a/c, fireplace, kit, marble
baths, chintz, Jacuzzi, award
winning restaurant, pool, hlth clb,
sauna, steam rm, whirlpool, spa

Chandler Inn
(800) 842-3450, (617) 482-3450
http://www.chandlerinn.com
26 Chandler St.
56 rooms - $79-129
Pets: Welcome w/credit card dep.
Creature Comforts: CCTV, a/c

The Colonnade Hotel
(800) 962-3030, (617) 424-7000
http://www.colonnadehotel.com
120 Huntington Ave.
285 rooms - $195-1,455
Pets: Welcome
Creature Comforts: CCTV,
VCR, a/c, refrig, stereos, Jacuzzis,
restaurant, pool, hlth clb

The Eliot Hotel
(800) 44-ELIOT, (617) 267-1607
http://www.eliothotel.com
370 Commonwealth Ave.
95 rooms - $225-375
Pets: Welcome
Creature Comforts: Highly
recommended, historic hotel w/
lovely European ambiance,
elegant lobby, antique and chintz
furnishings, orig art, intimate
suites, French doors, CCTV, VCR,
a/c, refrig, micro, Italian marble
baths, restaurant, hlth club access

Fairmont Copley Hotel
(800) 527-4727, (617) 267-5300
http://www.fairmont.com
138 St. James St.
380 rooms - $195-1,600
Pets: Under 25 lbs. welcome
Creature Comforts: Boston
landmark set in the heart of the
city, Sheraton-style furnishings,
chintz, CCTV, VCR, a/c,
fireplaces, kit, marble baths,
Jacuzzis, restaurant, hlth clb
access, sauna, spa, whirlpool

Four Seasons Hotel
(800) 332-3442, (617) 338-4400
http://www.fshr.com
200 Boylston St.
287 rooms - $195-2,600
Pets: Under 15 lbs welcome,
excellent pet program - beds,
kibble, biscuits, and pet menu
Creature Comforts: Luxurious
hotel overlooking Pub. Gardens,
fine reproductions, English
antiques, Sheraton-style furnish.,
chintz, very attentive staff,
CCTV, VCR, a/c, fireplaces, kit,
marble baths, Jacuzzis, award
winning restaurant, pool, hlth
clb, sauna, spa, whirlpool

Howard Johnson Hotel
(800) I-Go-Hojo, (617) 267-3100
http://www.hojo.com
575 Commonwealth Ave.
179 rooms - $119-240
Pets: Welcome
Creature Comforts: CCTV, a/c,
pool

Howard Johnson Hotel
(800) I-Go-Hojo, (617) 267-8300
http://www.hojo.com
1271 Boylston St.
94 rooms - $99-195
Pets: Welcome
Creature Comforts: CCTV, a/c,
restaurant, pool

Le Meridien
(800) 543-4300, (617) 451-1900
http://www.lemeridien-hotels.com
250 Franklin St.
326 rooms - $215-1,400
Pets: "Lap dogs" are welcome
Creature Comforts: Located in
the heart of financial district in the
old Federal Reserve building,
CCTV, VCR, a/c, kit, Jacuzzi,
restaurant, cont. brkfst, pool, hlth
clb, sauna, whirlpool

The Ritz Carlton Hotel
(800) 241-3333, (617) 536-5700
http://www.ritzcarlton.com
15 Arlington St.
278 rooms - $275-2,000
Pets: Under 20 Lbs w/$30 fee
Creature Comforts: Classic
Boston hotel, set in Back Bay,
European rooms w/ traditional
furnishings, marble baths, CCTV,
VCR, a/c, fireplace, kit, refrig,
micro, Jacuzzi, rooftop and formal
restaurants, famous bar, cont.
brkfst, pool, hlth clb access, sauna,
whirlpool

Seaport Hotel
(888) SEAPORT, (617) 385-4000
http://www.seaporthotel.com
1 Seaport Lane
425 rooms - $255-1,500
Pets: Under 50 Lbs welcome
Creature Comforts: European
rooms w/ traditional furnishings,
marble baths, CCTV, VCR, a/c,
fireplace, kit, refrig, micro,
Jacuzzi, rooftop and formal
restaurants, cont. brkfst, pool, hlth
clb, sauna, whirlpool, massage

Sheraton Hotel
(800) 325-3535, (617) 236-2000
http://www.sheraton.com
39 Dalton St.
1,180 rooms - $170-299
Pets: Welcome
Creature Comforts: CCTV, a/c,
refrig, micro, restaurants, pool,
hlth clb, sauna, whirlpool

Swissotel
(800) 637-9477, (617) 451-2600
http://www.swissotel.com
1 Ave. de Lafayette
495 rooms - $225-550
Pets: Small pets welcome
Creature Comforts: CCTV,
VCR, a/c, kit, Jacuzzi, restaurant,
pool, hlth clb, sauna, whirlpool

Westin Hotel
(800) WESTIN-1, (617) 262-9600
http://www.westin.com
10 Huntington Ave.
802 rooms - $199-399
Pets: Small pets welcome
Creature Comforts: CCTV, a/c,
refrig, 3 restaurants, cont. brkfst,
pool, hlth clb, sauna, whirlpool

BOURNE
Best Western Inn
(800) 528-1234, (508) 759-0800
http://www.bestwestern.com
100 Trowbridge Rd.
43 rooms - $60-160
Pets: Small pets welcome
Creature Comforts: CCTV, a/c, kit, Jacuzzis, restaurant, pool

Yankee Thrift Motel
(508) 759-3883
114 Trowbridge Rd.
56 rooms - $59-89
Pets: Small pets w/$5 fee
Creature Comforts: CCTV, a/c, kit, pool

BRAINTREE
Days Inn
(800) DAYS-INN, (781) 848-1260
http://www.daysinn.com
190 Wood Rd.
104 rooms - $65-145
Pets: Welcome w/$5 fee
Creature Comforts: CCTV, a/c, cont. brkfst, pool

Motel 6
(800) 4-MOTEL6, (781) 848-7890
http://www.motel6.com
125 Union St.
92 rooms - $65-80
Pets: Under 30 lbs. welcome
Creature Comforts: CCTV, a/c, pool

BREWSTER
Greylin House
(800) 233-6662, (508) 896-0004
http://www.capecodtravel.com/greylin
2311 Main St.
5 rooms - $65-130
Pets: Welcome w/$15 fee
Creature Comforts: Charming 1837 house w/ lots of appeal, CCTV, VCR, a/c, fireplace, kit, cont. brkfst, library, period furnishings & antiques, lawn games

High Brewster
(800) 203-2634, (508) 896-3636
924 Satucket Rd.
6 cottages - $95-220
Pets: Welcome w/$25-50 fee
Creature Comforts: Three pondside acres, rock walls/grdns, antique inn, Cape-style cottages w/eclectic furnishings, CCTV, VCR, a/c, fireplace, kit, gourmet restaurant, full brkfst, lawn games

Pine Hill Cottages
(508) 896-1999
web site pending
PO Box 75
4 cottages - $300-375/wk
Pets: Welcome
Creature Comforts: Kit, trails

BROOKLINE
Beech Tree Inn
(800) 544-9660, (617) 277-1620
http://www.innsite.com/inns/A030640.html
83 Longwood Ave.
10 rooms - $85-150
Pets: Welcome
Creature Comforts: A charming Victorian, residential area, period features, antiques, CCTV, VCR, a/c, fireplace, kit, cont. brkfst

The Bertram Inn
(800) 295-3822, (617) 566-2234
http://www.bertraminn.com
92 Sewall Ave.
12 rooms - $85-240
Pets: Welcome w/credit card dep.
Creature Comforts: A 1907 Victorian, residential area, period features, stained glass, antiques, Oriental rugs, oak paneling, four poster beds, rattan, CCTV, VCR, a/c, fireplace, refrig, micro, and a delux cont. brkfst

BUZZARDS BAY
Bay Motor Inn
(508) 759-3989
www.capecod.com/baymotorinn
223 Main St.
17 rooms - $45-115
Pets: Welcome
Creature Comforts: CCTV, a/c, kit, pool

Shipsway Motel
(508) 888-0206
51 Canal Rd.
20 rooms - $45-75
Pets: Welcome
Creature Comforts: CCTV, kit, pool

CAMBRIDGE
The Charles Hotel
(800) 882-1818, (617) 864-1200
http://www.charleshotel.com
1 Bennett St.
296 rooms - $199-1,525
Pets: Welcome w/credit card dep.
Creature Comforts: An elegant Harvard Sq. hotel w/Shaker accents, antique quilts, contemp. rooms, CCTV, VCR, a/c, refrig, micro, restaurant, pool, hlth clb, sauna, massage, steamroom, whirlpool, jazz bar

Howard Johnson Hotel
(800) I-Go-Hojo, (617) 492-777
http://www.hojo.com
777 Memorial Dr.
205 rooms - $109-250
Pets: Welcome
Creature Comforts: CCTV, a/c, refrig, micro, restaurant, cont. brkfst, pool

Windsor House B&B
(617) 354-3116, 354-7916
283 Windsor St.
2 rooms - $65-85
Pets: Welcome
Creature Comforts: CCTV, VCR, a/c, fireplace, cont. brkfst

CENTERVILLE
Corners Motor Lodge
(800) 242-1137, (508) 775-7223
capecod.com/centervillecorners
369 S. Main St.
49 rooms - $45-135
Pets: Welcome w/$5 fee
Creature Comforts: CCTV, a/c, kit, cont. brkfst, pool, sauna

Lighthouse Village Cottages
(508) 945-5907
http://www.virtualcities.com
Seagull Lane
10 units - $800-995/wk
Pets: Welcome
Creature Comforts: CCTV,
VCR, a/c, kit, on the beach

CHARLESTOWN
The Elms B&B
(617) 241-8067
http://www.homestead.com/elms
address povided w/reservation
3 rooms - $125
Pets: Welcome
Creature Comforts: CCTV,
VCR, a/c, antiques, computer
hook-ups, fax, kit, Jacuzzi, patio
& deck, along the Freedom Trail

CHATHAM
Morgan Waterfront Houses
(508) 945-1870
http://www.capecodtravel.com/
morganwaterfront
444 Old Harbor Rd.
4 houses - $550-3,000/wk
Pets: Welcome
Creature Comforts: Wonderful
homes, CCTV, VCR, Jacuzzis,
fireplace, kit, brick patios, nice
yards, kids play areas, near water

Ocean Front Cottages
(508) 945-5907
Seagull Lane
30 rooms - $800-3,895/wk
Pets: Welcome
Creature Comforts: CCTV,
VCR, a/c, fireplace, kit, beachfrnt

CHELMSFORD
Best Western Inn
(800) 528-1234, (508) 256-7511
http://www.bestwestern.com
187 Chelmsford St.
115 rooms - $75-105
Pets: Small pets welcome
Creature Comforts: CCTV, a/c,
hlth club, whirlpool, sauna, pool

CHICOPEE
Best Western Inn
(800) 528-1234, (413) 592-6171
http://www.bestwestern.com
463 Memorial Dr.
106 rooms - $49-75
Pets: Smaller pets welcome
Creature Comforts: CCTV, a/c,
refrig, pool

Motel 6
(800) 4-MOTEL6, (413) 592-5141
http://www.motel6.com
1 Burnett Rd.
88 rooms - $45-60
Pets: Under 30 lbs. welcome
Creature Comforts: CCTV, a/c,
pool

CONCORD
Best Western Inn
(800) 528-1234, (978) 369-6100
http://www.bestwestern.com
740 Elm St.
106 rooms - $79-129
Pets: Small pets welcome
Creature Comforts: CCTV, a/c,
cont. brkfst, hlth club, whirlpool,
pool

DANVERS
Motel 6
(800) 4-MOTEL6, (978) 774-8045
http://www.motel6.com
65 Newbury St.
109 rooms - $55-70
Pets: Under 30 lbs. welcome
Creature Comforts: CCTV, a/c,
pool

Residence Inn
(800) 331-3131, (978) 777-7171
http://www.residenceinn.com
51 Newbury St.
95 rooms - $189-299
Pets: $100 clean fee, $7 daily fee
Creature Comforts: CCTV,
VCR, a/c, kit, hlth club, tennis,
pool

Super 8 Motel
(800) 800-8000, (978) 774-6500
http://www.super8.com
225 Newbury St.
78 rooms - $49-85
Pets: Welcome
Creature Comforts: CCTV, a/c,
kit, pool

DEDHAM
Hilton Hotel
(800) HILTONS, (781) 329-7900
http://www.hilton.com
25 Allied Dr.
249 rooms - $119-649
Pets: Small pets welcome
Creature Comforts: CCTV,
VCR, a/c, refrig, restaurant, hlth
club, tennis, sauna, pool

DENNIS PORT
Acorn Cottages
(508) 760-2101
927 Main St.
8 houses - $500-950/wk
Pets: Welcome
Creature Comforts: CCTV,
VCR, a/c, fireplace, kit, Jacuzzi,
beach

Lamplighter
(800) 328-8812, (508) 398-8469
http://www.sunsol.com/brentwood
329 Main St.
24 rooms - $33-60
Pets: Welcome w/$20 fee
Creature Comforts: CCTV, a/c,
kit, pool

Marine Lodge Cottages
(508) 398-2963
15 North St.
15 rooms - $385-900/wk
Pets: Welcome w/$2 fee
Creature Comforts: CCTV,
VCR, a/c, fireplace, kit, tennis,
pool, and lawn games

Town Cottages
(800) 328-8812, (508) 398-8469
http://www.sunsol.com/brentwood
319 Main St.
10 cottages - $430-550/wk
Pets: Welcome w/$20 fee
Creature Comforts: CCTV, a/c,
kit, pool

EAST FALMOUTH
Green Harbor Waterfront
(508) 548-4747
http://www.gogreenharbor.com
134 Acapesket Rd.
40 rooms - $80-235
Pets: Welcome w/$10 fee
Creature Comforts: CCTV, a/c,
kit, waterfront-boats, pool, and
lawn games

EASTHAM
Blue Dolphin Inn
(800) 654-0504, (508) 255-1159
www.capecod.net/bluedolphin
5950 Rte. 6
50 rooms - $55-139
Pets: Sept.-June w/$7 fee
Creature Comforts: CCTV, a/c,
kit, pool

Gibson Cottages
(508) 255-0882
www.capecodtravel.com/gibson
80 Depot St, Box 86
7 cottages - $550-1,000
Pets: Welcome
Creature Comforts: CCTV,
VCR, kit, woodstove

Town Crier Motel
(800) 932-1434, (508) 255-4000
http://www.towncriermotel.com
Route 6, Box 457
33 rooms - $49-120
Pets: Sept-June w/$10 fee
Creature Comforts: CCTV,
VCR, a/c, refrig, restaurant, pool

EAST SANDWICH
Cedar Cottages
(508) 888-0464
59 Ploughed Neck Rd.
3 cottages - $475-535/wk
Pets: Welcome
Creature Comforts: CCTV, kit

Earl of Sandwich Motel
(800) 442-3275, (508) 888-1415
378 Rte. 6A
22 rooms - $50-95
Pets: Welcome
Creature Comforts: CCTV, a/c,
refrig, cont. brkfst

Pine Grove Cottages
(508) 888-8179
Route 6A
10 cottages - $360-595/wk
Pets: Welcome
Creature Comforts: CCTV, kit

Wingscorton Farm Inn
(508) 888-0534
http://www.traveldata.co/inns/
data/wingscor.html
11 Wing Blvd.
4 rooms - $120-225
Pets: Welcome w/$10 fee
Creature Comforts: A wonderful
1758 farm on 13 acres, lovely
decor, period features, country
antiques, CCTV, VCR, a/c,
fireplace, kit, full brkfst, bicycles,
and a private beach

EDGARTOWN
Point Way Inn
(888) 711-6633, (508) 627-8633
http://www.pointway.com
Main St. & Pease Point Way
14 rooms - $175-325
Pets: Welcome in recently
redcorated Garden Room w/ a
one-time $25-50 fee
Creature Comforts: A charming
1850's inn set at the top of Main
St, antique furnishings, charming
beach decor, Ralph lauren accents,
four poster beds, CCTV, VCR, a/c,
fireplace, refrig, salon w/games &
puzzles, croquet, and a full brkfst

The Victorian Inn
(508) 627-4784
http://www.thevic.com
24 S. Water St.
14 rooms - $135-325
Pets: Nov-May w/$5 fee
Creature Comforts: A neat old
1820's Victorian inn in the heart of
town, antique furnishings,
charming Victorian decor, CCTV,
VCR, a/c, fireplace, refrig, and a
full gourmet brkfst

FALL RIVER
Days Inn
(800) DAYS-INN, (508) 676-1991
http://www.daysinn.com
332 Milliken Blvd.
102 rooms - $55-105
Pets: Welcome
Creature Comforts: CCTV, a/c,
restaurant, pool

FALMOUTH
Bayberry Inn
(508) 540-2962
226 Trotting Park Rd.
2 rooms - $55-80
Pets: Welcome w/CC deposit
Creature Comforts: A charming
Cape cottage set amid roses and
woodlands, CCTV, VCR, a/c,
woodstove, refrig, cont. brkfst,
pond, English cottage decor, and a
nice yard

Falmouth Inn
(800) 255-4157, (508) 540-2500
http://www.falmouthinn.com
824 Main St.
123 rooms - $50-90
Pets: Welcome
Creature Comforts: CCTV, a/c,
refrig, restaurant, pool, sauna

Mariner Motel
(800) 949-2939, (508) 548-1331
http://www.marinermotel.com
555 Main St.
28 rooms - $49-129
Pets: Welcome w/$5 fee
Creature Comforts: CCTV, a/c,
refrig, pool

Ocean View Motel
(508) 540-4120
263 Grand Ave.
18 rooms - $75-199
Pets: $10 fee/credit card dep.
Creature Comforts: CCTV, a/c,
kit, restaurant, beach

Quality Inn
(800) 847-2211, (508) 540-2000
http://www.qualityinn.com
291 Jones Rd.
99 rooms - $79-185
Pets: Welcome
Creature Comforts: CCTV, a/c,
restaurant, cont. brkfst, pool

FITCHBURG
Royal Plaza Hotel
(978) 342-7100
150 Royal Plaza Dr.
244 rooms - $79-129
Pets: Welcome
Creature Comforts: CCTV,
VCR, a/c, refrig, micro, Jacuzzi,
restaurant, cont. brkfst, pool, hlth
clb, sauna, whirlpool

FLORIDA
Whitcomb Summit Motel
(413) 662-2625
229 Mohawk Trail
19 rooms - $50-90
Pets: Welcome in cabins
Creature Comforts: CCTV,
restaurant, pool

FRAMINGHAM
Motel 6
(800) 4-MOTEL6, (508) 620-0500
http://www.motel6.com
1668 Worcester Rd.
105 rooms - $55-79
Pets: Under 30 lbs. welcome
Creature Comforts: CCTV, a/c

Red Roof Inn
(800) The-Roof, (508) 872-4499
http://www.redroof.com
650 Cochituate Rd.
169 rooms - $47-99
Pets: Small pets welcome
Creature Comforts: CCTV, a/c

GAY HEAD
Duck Inn
(508) 645-9018
Just off State Rd., Box 160
5 rooms - $79-185
Pets: Welcome in first floor room,
cats and pig in residence
Creature Comforts: A 200-year-
old farmhouse w/stone walls and
ocean views, secluded, peaceful,
informal ambiance, health-
oriented, CCTV, fireplaces, refrig,
full farm brkfst, masseuse, hot tub

GLOUCESTER
Cape Anne Motor Inn
(800) 464-VIEW, (978) 281-2900
www.capeannemotorinn.com
33 Rockport Rd.
32 rooms - $65-145
Pets: Welcome
Creature Comforts: CCTV, a/c,
fireplace, kit, cont. brkfst, pool,
beach

The Manor Inn
(978) 283-0614
141 Essex Ave.
26 rooms - $45-109
Pets: Welcome w/$5 fee
Creature Comforts: CCTV, a/c,
overlooks the river

Ocean View Inn
(800) 315-7557, (978) 283-6200
www.oceanviewinnandresort.com
171 Atlantic Rd.
65 rooms - $75-199
Pets: Welcome
Creature Comforts: CCTV,
VCR, a/c, refrig, restaurant, pool,
lawn sports, on 5-1/2 acres and on
the water

GREAT BARRINGTON
Barrington Court Motel
(413) 528-2340
400 Stockbridge Rd.
24 rooms - $75-175
Pets: Welcome w/$10 fee
Creature Comforts: CCTV, a/c,
kit, Jacuzzis, pool

Brook Cove
(413) 274-6653
30 Linda Lane
1 room - $69-90
Pets: Welcome
Creature Comforts: CCTV, a/c,
kit

Chez Gabrielle
(413) 528-2799
320 State Rd.
2 rooms - $85-125
Pets: Welcome w/$10 fee
Creature Comforts: CCTV, a/c,
fireplaces, refrig, cont. brkfst, dog
doors, fenced yard

Chicadee Cottage
(413) 528-0002
27 Division St.
2 rooms - $69-80
Pets: Welcome
Creature Comforts: CCTV, a/c,
cont. brkfst

Wainright Inn
(413) 528-2062
http://www.wainwrightinn.com
518 S. Main St.
8 rooms - $75-185
Pets: Welcome
Creature Comforts: Wonderful
1776 inn, wraparound porches,
former inn and tavern, antiques,
charming dining rm, CCTV, VCR,
a/c, fireplaces, refrig, full brkfst

GREENFIELD
The Brandt House B&B
(800) 235-3329, (413) 774-3329
http://www.brandthouse.com
29 Highland Ave.
8 rooms - $100-190
Pets: Welcome w/$20 fee
Creature Comforts: A
wonderfully refurbished 16-rm
Victorian mansion, down duvets,
fine linens, antiques, CCTV, VCR,
a/c, fireplace, refrig, micro, full
brkfst, billiards, tennis, skating,
xc-skiing, flower gardens & lovely
grounds, charming hostess, ask for
room 8

Candlelight Motor Inn
(888) 262-0520, (413) 772-0101
208 Mohawk Trail
56 rooms - $49-90
Pets: Welcome w/$5 fee
Creature Comforts: CCTV, a/c

Old Tavern Farm
(413) 772-0474
http://www.oldtavernfarm.com
817 Colrain Rd.
3 rooms - $110-185
Pets: Welcome by arrangement
Creature Comforts: Intriguing
historic property dating back to
1746, antiques, family heirlooms,
taproom/livingroom, four poster
beds, braided rugs, ballroom,
CCTV, a/c, kit, fireplaces, and an
assortment ofneat old Americana
collectibles

HADLEY
Clark Tavern B&B
(413) 586-1900
http://www.clarktaverninn.com
98 Bay Road
4 rooms - $95-135
Pets: Welcome w/$15 fee
Creature Comforts: A neat old
wonderfully restored 1740
Colonial tavern, CCTV, VCR, a/c,
refrig, four poster & canopy beds,
fireplaces, pool, hammock, porch,
dining room, and a full breakfast

Howard Johnson
(800) I-Go-Hojo, (413) 586-0114
http://www.hojo.com
401 Russell Rd.
98 rooms - $55-129
Pets: Welcome
Creature Comforts: CCTV, a/c,
refrig, pool

HARWICHPORT
Coachman Lodge
(508) 432-0707
774 Main St.
25 rooms - $65-110
Pets: Welcome
Creature Comforts: CCTV, a/c,
kit, restaurant, pool

Harbor Walk
(508) 432-1675
6 Freeman St.
7 rooms - $450-800/wk
Pets: In cottage, first floor rms.
Creature Comforts: An intimate
1880 Victorian summer house,
Colonial decor, wicker accents,
quilts, four poster beds, painted
floors, pastel color schemes, a/c
CCTV, VCR, fireplace, library,
and a full brkfst

HAVERHILL
Best Western Inn
(800) 528-1234, (978) 373-1511
http://www.bestwestern.com
401 Lowell Ave.
126 rooms - $55-109
Pets: Small pets welcome
Creature Comforts: CCTV,
VCR, a/c, refrig, micro, Jacuzzis,
hlth club

HOLYOKE
Holiday Inn
(800) HOLIDAY, (413) 534-3311
http://www.holiday-inn.com
245 Whiting Farms Rd.
220 rooms - $85-155
Pets: Welcome w/$25 dep.
Creature Comforts: CCTV, a/c,
refrig, restaurant, hlth club, sauna,
whirlpool, pool

HOUSATONIC
Christine's B&B Carriage Hse
(800) 536-1186, (413) 274-6149
http://christinesinn.com
325 North Plain Rd.
4 rooms - $75-165
Pets: Welcome in 1st floor room
Creature Comforts: 1780s
homestead with many of the
original features, CCTV, a/c,
refrig, 3-course breakfast, garden
rm-white wicker, gardens, four
poster & canopy beds, handmade
quits, resident golden retriever

HYANNIS
Glo-min by the Sea
508) 255-0882
http://www.capecod.net/glo-min
182 Sea St.
12 rooms - $45-99
Pets: Welcome
Creature Comforts: CCTV, a/c,
and kit

Hyannis Sands Motel
(508) 790-1700
921 Rte. 132
36 rooms - $45-99
Pets: Welcome
Creature Comforts: CCTV, a/c

Rainbow Motel
(508) 362-3217
Route 132
46 rooms - $50-80
Pets: Welcome
Creature Comforts: CCTV, a/c,
refrig, pool

Snug Harbour Lodge
(800) 345-0130, (508) 771-0699
48 E. Main St.
48 rooms - $69-85
Pets: Welcome w/$10 fee
Creature Comforts: CCTV, a/c,
refrig, pool

HYANNIS PORT
Harbor Village
(508) 775-7581
http://www.harborvillage.com
160 Marston Ave.
20 cottages - $100-175
Pets: welcome w/$100/wk fee
Creature Comforts: Private
weathered shingled cottage colony
set on 17 acres near the water,
beach-country decor, CCTV,
VCR, a/c, fireplaces, kit, deck

Sea Breeze Cottages
(508) 775-4269
337 Sea St.
1 apt. - $450-850/wk
Pets: Welcome
Creature Comforts: TV, a/c, kit

Simmons Inn
(800) 637-1649, (508) 778-4999
http://www.capecodtravel.com/
simmonsinn
288 Scudder Ave.
10 rooms - $140-325
Pets: Welcome w/$20 fee
Creature Comforts: 1820's ship
captain's home w/antiques and
nautical themes, host is car buff,
four poster beds w/country quilts,
CCTV, VCR, a/c, billard room,
ceramic animal collections,
library, fireplaces, refrig, scotch
tastings, and a full brkfst

KINGSTON
Inn at Plymouth Bay
(800) 941-0075, (781) 585-3831
Route 3
65 rooms - $65-125
Pets: Welcome
Creature Comforts: CCTV, a/c,
refrig, micro, restaurant, pool, hlth
clb, sauna, whirlpool

LANESBORO
Mt. View Motel
(413) 442-1009
499 S. Main St.
12 rooms - $40-129
Pets: Small pets in ltd. rms
Creature Comforts: TV, a/c, kit

The Weathervane Motel
(413) 443-3230
475 S. Main St.
15 rooms - $38-120
Pets: Welcome w/$5 fee
Creature Comforts: CCTV, a/c,
kit, pool

LAWRENCE
Hampton Inn
(800) Hampton, (978) 975-4050
http://www.hampton-inn.com
224 Winthrop Ave.
125 rooms - $85-129
Pets: Welcome
Creature Comforts: CCTV, a/c,
cont. brkfst

LEE
Devonfield
(800) 664-0880, (413) 243-3298
http://www.devonfield.com
85 Stockbridge Rd.
10 rooms - $85-275
Pets: Welcome in the cottage
Creature Comforts: A handsome
Federal on 40-acres, antiques,
lovely decor,CCTV, VCR, a/c,
fireplace, Jacuzzi, kit, full brkfst,
pool, tennis, cathedral ceiling cotg

LENOX
Seven Hills Country Inn
(800) 869-6518, (413) 637-0060
http://www.sevenhillsinn.com
40 Plunkett St.
50 rooms - $85-289
Pets: Welcome w/$20 daily fee in
Terrace House (motor lodge)
Creature Comforts: Main inn is
Berkshire "cottage", w/antique
furnishings, leaded glass windows,
high ceilings, large common rms,
guests w/pets stay in motel-type
rms, CCTV, VCR, a/c, refrig,
restaurant, pool, terraced lawns,
lovely gardens, 27 acres

Walker House
(800) 235-3098, (413) 637-1271
http://www.walkerhouse.com
64 Walker St.
8 rooms - $85-195
Pets: Welcome
Creature Comforts: Welcoming
1804 Colonial mansion w/musical
themed rooms, hardwood flrs, four
poster beds, antiques, whimsical
touches, gardens, CCTV, VCR,
a/c, fireplace, new video theater,
refrig, cont. brkfst

LEOMINSTER
Inn on the Hill
(800) 357-0052, (978) 537-1661
450 N. Main St.
99 rooms - $40-59
Pets: Welcome w/$10 fee
Creature Comforts: CCTV, a/c, refrig, restaurant, pool

Motel 6
(800) 4-MOTEL6, (978) 537-8161
http://www.motel6.com
Rtes. 2 & 13
115 rooms - $40-54
Pets: Under 30 lbs. welcome
Creature Comforts: CCTV, a/c, pool

LEXINGTON
Battel Green Inn
(781) 862-6100
1720 Massachusetts Rd.
96 rooms - $59-105
Pets: Welcome
Creature Comforts: CCTV, VCR, a/c, kit, cont. brkfst, pool

LYNN
Diamond District B&B
(800) 666-3076, (781) 599-5122
www.diamonddistrictinn.com
142 Ocean Ave.
9 rooms - $99-245
Pets: Certain rms. w/$10 daily fee
Creature Comforts: Gracious 1911 Georgian-style mansion, one block from water, antiques, family heirlooms, Oriental rugs, CCTV, VCR, a/c, verandah, fireplace, refrig, micro, hlth club access, and a full brkfst

LUDLOW
Misty Meadows B&B
(413) 583-8103
467 Fuller St.
3 rooms - $35-60
Pets: Welcome
Creature Comforts: 200-year old house on 85 acres, CCTV, fireplace, refrig, cont. brkfst, pool

MALDEN
New England Motor Ct.
(800) 334-1043, (781) 321-0505
551 Broadway St.
22 rooms - $49-90
Pets: Welcome
Creature Comforts: CCTV, a/c, refrig, cont. brkfst

MANSFIELD
Motel 6
(800) 4-MOTEL6, (508) 339-2323
http://www.motel6.com
60 Forbes Blvd.
126 rooms - $50-65
Pets: Under 30 lbs. welcome
Creature Comforts: CCTV, a/c, pool

MARBLEHEAD
Sea Gull Inn B&B
(781) 631-1893
http://www.seagullinn.com
106 Harbor Ave.
3 rooms - $95-200
Pets: Welcome
Creature Comforts: Charming B&B on picturesque Marblehead Neck, waterview suites, hand-painted walls, Victorian collectibles, Shaker antiques, four poster beds, country quilts, Oriental rugs, CCTV, VCR, a/c, fireplace, refrig, cont. brkfst, croquet, kyaking, patios, gardens

MARION
Village Landing B&B
(508) 748-0350, Fax:1774
13 South St, Box 477
2 rooms - $85-95
Pets: Welcome
Creature Comforts: CCTV, VCR, a/c, kit, cont. brkfst

MARLBOROUGH
Super 8 Motel
(800) 800-8000, (508) 460-1000
http://www.super8.com
880 Don. J. Lynch Blvd.
64 rooms - $55-73
Pets: Welcome
Creature Comforts: CCTV, a/c, cont. brkfst

MIDDLEBORO
Days Inn
(800) DAYS-INN, (508) 946-4400
http://www.daysinn.com
Rtes. 105 & 495
113 rooms - $69-85
Pets: Welcome
Creature Comforts: CCTV, a/c, cont. brkfst, pool

NANTUCKET
Bartlett's Beach Cottages
(508) 228-3906
PO Box 899
3 rooms - $1,500/wk
Pets: Welcome
Creature Comforts: CCTV, VCR, a/c, fireplaces, kit, on a pond

Boat House & Grey Lady
(800) 245-9552, (508) 228-9552
http://www.nantucket.net/lodging/greylady
15 Old Wharf/34 Centre St.
1 cottage/ 2 rooms - $100-550 or $2,500/week
Pets: Welcome
Creature Comforts: Well appointed cottage on a wharf or charming 1st flr bedrooms, CCTV, VCR, a/c, fireplace, kit, laundry

Corkish Cottages
(508) 228-5686
http://www.nantucket.net/lodging/corkishcottages
320 Polpis Rd.
3 cottages - $1,200-2,800/wk
Pets: Welcome
Creature Comforts: Set on a 73-acre parcel that abuts conservation land, spacious family areas w/ catedral ceilings, sun decks, well appointed for the most part, braided rugs, casual summer cottage decor, SatTV, VCR, a/c, fireplace, kit, laundry

Danforth House
(508) 228-0136
121 Main St.
2 rooms - $75-185
Pets: Welcome in the off season
Creature Comforts: Classic antique home, same family for 3 generations, antiques, horsehair bed in one rm, gracious hostess, CCTV, VCR, a/c, fireplaces, kit, cont. brkfst, pretty gardens

Jared Coffin House
(800) 248-2405, (508) 228-2400
http://www.jaredcoffinhouse.com
29 Broad St.
60 rooms - $60-225
Pets: Welcome w/$15 fee, long-time dog-friendly inn
Creature Comforts: Historic buildings w/antiques, wide pine floors, Oriental rugs, four poster and canopy beds, floral prints and fabrics, some small bedrooms, CCTV, a/c, fireplace, refrig, restaurant, pub, full brkfst

Far Island Cottages
(508) 228-4227
41 Madaket Rd.
2 cottages - $1,200/wk
Pets: Welcome in 1 cottage
Creature Comforts: CCTV, a/c, kit

Halliday's Nantucket House
(508) 228-9450
2 E. York St.
1 cottage - $ 450-550/wk
Pets: Welcome
Creature Comforts: garden cottage w/kit, patio

Nesbitt Inn
(508) 228-0156
21 Broad St.
15 rooms - $50-140
Pets: Welcome in apartments
Creature Comforts: An 1872 Victorian inn, homey decor, comfortable, CCTV, a/c, fireplace, kit, cont. brkfst

Safe Harbor Guest House
(508) 228-3222
2 Harbor View Way
rooms - $145-189
Pets: Welcome
Creature Comforts: CCTV, VCR, a/c, fireplace, refrig, full brkfst

NEW ASHFORD
Carriage House
(413) 458-5359
Rte 7
12 rooms - $40-65
Pets: Welcome
Creature Comforts: CCTV, a/c, and access to a pool

NEWBURYPORT
The Essex St. Inn
(978) 465-3148
7 Essex St.
20 rooms - $80-175
Pets: Welcome in townhouses
Creature Comforts: 1880's bldngs w/eclectically appointed rms, CCTV, VCR, a/c, fireplace, refrig, cont. brkfst

Morrill Place Inn
(888) 594-4667, (978) 462-2808
web site pending
209 High St.
10 rooms - $75-115
Pets: Welcome
Creature Comforts: A lovely 1806 sea captain's mansion, individually decorated rms, hand-painted flrs, four poster beds, antiques, intriguing collectibles, quaint decor, CCTV, VCR, a/c, fireplace, refrig, micro, full brkfst

The Windsor House
(888) trelawny, (978) 462-3778
http://www.virtualcities.com
38 Federal St.
6 rooms - $99-139
Pets: Welcome in ground floor rm
Creature Comforts: Restored 1786 Federal-style brick house w/ 2 ft. thick walls, hardwood flrs, antiques, quilts, high ceilings, neat kitchen/brkfst rm, CCTV, VCR, a/c, fireplace, kit, English brkfst

NORTHAMPTON
Days Inn
(800) DAYS-INN, (413) 586-1500
http://www.daysinn.com
117 Conz St.
58 rooms - $55-125
Pets: Welcome
Creature Comforts: CCTV, a/c, pool, whirlpool

NORTH NEW SALEM
Bullard Farm B&B
(978) 544-6959
89 Elm St.
4 rooms - $70-99
Pets: Welcome w/$20 fee
Creature Comforts: An inviting 200 year-old Colonial B&B w/ country antiques, bucolic setting, pewter pieces, country quilts, Colonial stenciling, collectibles, braided rugs, CCTV, fireplace, kit, cont. brkfst

NORTH TRURO
Outer Reach Resort
(800) 942-5388, (508) 487-9500
http://www.provincetown.com/ptowninn
Route 6
70 rooms - $65-129
Pets: Welcome w/$10 fee
Creature Comforts: CCTV, refrig, restaurant, pool, and tennis

Seascape Motor Inn
(508) 487-1225
web site pending
21 rooms - $94-120
Pets: Leashed pets welcome
Creature Comforts: STV, a/c, kit

OAK BLUFFS
Island Inn
(800) 462-0269, (508) 693-2002
http:///www.islandinn.com
Beach Rd., Box 1585
50 rooms - $75-300
Pets: Welcome during off-season
Creature Comforts: CCTV, a/c, fireplaces, kit, restaurant, pool, tennis, and golf

Tivoli Inn
(508) 693-7928
http://www.mvy.com/tivoli
125 Circuit Ave., Box 1033
6 rooms - $65-150
Pets: Welcome in 1st flr & apt.
Creature Comforts: Victorian gingerbread house, CCTV, a/c, refrig

ORANGE
Bald Eagle Motel
(978) 544-8864
110 Daniel Shay Hwy.
27 rooms - $40-109
Pets: Welcome
Creature Comforts: CCTV, a/c

ORLEANS

Holiday Motel
(800) 451-1833, (508) 255-1514
486 Cranberry Hwy.
46 rooms - $55-129
Pets: In certain rooms w/$10 fee
Creature Comforts: CCTV, a/c,
refrig, pool

Skaket Beach Motel
(800) 835-0298, (508) 255-1020
capecod-orleans.com/skaketbeach
203 Rte. 6A
45 rooms - $49-165
Pets: Welcome in the off-season
with a $9 fee
Creature Comforts: CCTV, a/c,
kit, cont. brkfst, pool

PITTSFIELD

Bonnie Brae Cabins
(413) 442-3754
108 Broadway St.
7 cabins - $50-75
Pets: Welcome
Creature Comforts: Rustic
cabins, refrig, pool

Heart of Berkshires Motel
(413) 443-1255
970 W. Housatonic St.
15 rooms - $48-109
Pets: Small dogs welcome
Creature Comforts: CCTV, a/c,
pool

PROVINCETOWN

Bay Shore
(508) 487-9133
http://www.provincetown.com/
bayshore
493 Commercial St.
19 suites - $115-185
Pets: Welcome w/$10 fee
Creature Comforts: A classic
rambling bayside Cape, beamed
ceilings, rough hewn walls,
international array of furnishings/
seaside collectibles, request a
waterview room, decks, CCTV,
VCR, a/c, fireplace, kit, small
lawn for sunbathing

Breakwater Motor Inn
(800) 487-1134, (508) 487-1134
Rte. 6A
85 rooms - $65-119
Pets: Welcome
Creature Comforts: CCTV, a/c,
kit, restaurant, sauna, pool

Cape Codder Guest House
(508) 487-0131
570 Commercial St.
14 rooms - $45-55
Pets: Welcome in first floor rooms
Creature Comforts: casual
setting, CCTV, fireplace, refrig,
cont. brkfst, sandy beach

Holiday Inn
(800) HOLIDAY, (508) 587-1711
http://www.holiday-inn.com
Route 6A
77 rooms - $95-175
Pets: Welcome
Creature Comforts: CCTV, a/c,
refrig, restaurant, pool

White Sands Motel
(508) 487-0244
Route 6A
52 rooms - $65-275
Pets: Welcome w/$10 fee
Creature Comforts: CCTV, a/c,
kit, cont. brkfst, pool, sauna,
whirlpool

White Wind Inn
888) 449-WIND, (508) 487-1526
http://www.whitewindinn.com
174 Commercial St.
11 rooms - $85-225
Pets: Welcome in 3 rooms with a
$10 nightly fee
Creature Comforts: Refurbished
1825 Victorian, attractive decor,
sm water views, CCTV, VCR, a/c,
refrig, fireplace, cont. brkfst

RANDOLPH

Holiday Inn
(800) HOLIDAY, (781) 961-1000
http://www.holiday-inn.com
1374 Main St.
160 rooms - $125-199
Pets: Small pets welcome
Creature Comforts: CCTV, a/c,
refrig, restaurant, pool

RAYNHAM

Days Inn
(800) DAYS-INN, (508) 824-8647
http://www.daysinn.com
Route 44
75 rooms - $49-60
Pets: Welcome
Creature Comforts: CCTV, a/c,
pool

REHOBOTH

Five Bridges Farm Inn
(508) 252-3190
154 Pine St.
5 rooms - $69-105
Pets: Welcome w/$5 fee
Creature Comforts: Contemp,
beautifully decorated home, 60-
acres in the country, CCTV, VCR,
a/c, fireplace, kit, full brkfst, pool,
tennis, llamas, bucolic setting

REVERE

Howard Johnson Hotel
(800) I-Go-Hojo, (781) 284-7200
http://www.hojo.com
407 Squire Rd.
107 rooms - $75-145
Pets: Welcome
Creature Comforts: CCTV, a/c,
refrig, micro, restaurant, cont.
brkfst, pool

RICHMOND

A B&B in the Berkshires
(800) 795-7122, (413) 698-2817
1666 Dublin Rd.
3 rooms - $65-130
Pets: Welcome
Creature Comforts: Berkshire
hills setting w/pretty gardens &
meadows, CCTV, VCR, a/c,
fireplace, refrig, full brkfst,
hammock, xc-skiing

ROCKLAND

Holiday Inn Express
(800) HOLIDAY, (781) 871-5660
http://www.holiday-inn.com
909 Hingham St.
75 rooms - $75-105
Pets: Welcome (pet welcome kit)
Creature Comforts: CCTV, a/c,
refrig, micro, cont. brkfst, hlth
club access

Ramada Hotel
(800) 2-Ramada, (781) 781-0545
http://www.ramada.com
929 Hingham St.
125 rooms - $99-159
Pets: Small pets welcome
Creature Comforts: CCTV, a/c,
refrig, Jacuzzis, restaurant, pool

ROCKPORT

Blueberry B&B
(978) 546-2838
2 rooms - $75-80
Pets: Welcome
Creature Comforts: CCTV, a/c, kit, period furnishings, handmade quilts, and a full brkfst

Carlson's B&B
(978) 546-2770
43 Broadway
2 rooms - $85-95
Pets: Welcome
Creature Comforts: Quaint Victorian, B&B & art gallery, CCTV, a/c, canopy beds, kit,and a full brkfst

Sandy Bay Motor Inn
(800) 437-7155, (978) 546-7155
173 Main St.
80 rooms - $69-155
Pets: Welcome w/$50 dep.
Creature Comforts: CCTV, a/c, kit, tennis, pool

SALEM

Hawthorne Hotel
(800) 729-7829, (978) 741-0680
http://www.hawthornehotel.com
On the Common
89 rooms - $119-310
Pets: Welcome w/$15 fee
Creature Comforts: A handsome brick building overlooking Salem Common, trad. reproductions, nautical prints, Oriental rugs, CCTV, VCR, a/c, fireplace, refrig, restaurant, cont. brkfst, hlth club

The Salem Inn
(800) 446-2995, (978) 744-0480
http://www.saleminnma.com
7 Summer St.
33 rooms - $95-189
Pets: Welcome in 1 house
Creature Comforts: Three Nat'l Historic Register building w/faux marble walls, pastel color schemes, hand-carved woodwork, antiques, botanical prints, CCTV, VCR, a/c, fireplace, refrig, Jacuzzis, restaurant, cont. brkfst

Stephen Daniels House
(978) 744-5709
1 Daniels St.
6 rooms - $69-129
Pets: Welcome
Creature Comforts: Historic 1667 B&B, sloping wide pine flrs, steep staircases, beamed ceilings, canopy beds, Oriental rugs, period antiques, CCTV, a/c, decoys, huge fireplaces, kit, cont. brkfst

Sandwich Lodge
(800) 282-5353, (508) 888-2275
54 Rte. 6A
70 rooms - $55-130
Pets: Welcome w/$10 fee
Creature Comforts: CCTV, VCR, a/c, refrig, micro, Jacuzzi, cont. brkfst, hlth club, pool, whirlpool

SAUGUS

Colonial Traveler Motor Court
(800) 323-2731, (781) 233-6700
1753 Broadway St.
25 rooms - $49-90
Pets: Welcome
Creature Comforts: CCTV, a/c, refrig, cont. brkfst

SCITUATE

Clipper Ship Lodge
(800) 368-3818, (781) 545-5550
www.clippershiplodge.com
7 Beaver Dam Rd
29 rooms - $75-159
Pets: Welcome w/$10 fee
Creature Comforts: CCTV, a/c, refrig, pool

SEEKONK

Motel 6
(800) 4-MOTEL6, (508) 336-7800
http://www.motel6.com
821 Fall River Ave.
85 rooms - $55-79
Pets: Under 30 lbs. welcome
Creature Comforts: CCTV, a/c

Ramada Inn
(800) 2-Ramada, (508) 336-7300
http://www.ramada.com
940 Fall River Rd.
126 rooms - $65-109
Pets: Small pets welcome
Creature Comforts: CCTV, a/c, refrig, restaurant, full brkfst, pool, sauna, whirlpool, putting green, hlth club

SHEFFIELD

Depot Guest House
(413) 229-2908
PO Box 575
5 rooms - $-55-70
Pets: Welcome in Nov-March
Creature Comforts: CCTV, a/c, kit

Ivanhoe Country House
(413) 229-2143
254 S. Undermountain Rd.
9 rooms - $70-125
Pets: Welcome w/$10 daily fee
Creature Comforts: Expansive 1780's colonial home on 25-acres, homey decor, cozy common rm w/ fireplace, hardwood flrs, claw foot tubs, traditional furnishings, CCTV, VCR, a/c, fireplaces, kit, cont. brkfst, pool

Racebrook Lodge
(888) RB-Lodge, (413) 229-2916
http://www.rblodge.com
864 S. Undermountain Rd.
20 rooms - $80-139
Pets: Welcome in certain rooms with a $25 one-time fee
Creature Comforts: A refurbished 1830's timber-peg barn, stenciling, hand-hewn beams, country quilts, Oriental rugs, country furnishings, CCTV, VCR, a/c, fireplace, refrig, micro, cont. brkfst, jazz concerts

SOMMERSET

Quality Inn
(800) 228-5151, (508) 678-4545
http://www.qualityinn.com
1878 Wilbur Ave.
105 rooms - $60-120
Pets: Welcome w/$50 dep.
Creature Comforts: CCTV, a/c, refrig, Jacuzzis, restaurant, cont. brkfst, pool, whirlpool

SOUTHBOROUGH
Red Roof Inn
(800) The-Roof, (508) 481-3904
http://www.redroof.com
367 Turnpike Rd.
106 rooms - $48-80
Pets: Small pets welcome
Creature Comforts: CCTV, a/c

SOUTH DEERFIELD
Motel 6
(800) 4-MOTEL6, (413) 665-7161
http://www.motel6.com
Rtes. 5 & 10
123 rooms - $45-60
Pets: Under 30 lbs. welcome
Creature Comforts: CCTV, a/c,
pool

SOUTH EGREMONT
Swiss Hutte
(413) 528-6200
Route 23
15 rooms - $79-225
Pets: Welcome
Creature Comforts: CCTV, a/c,
refrig, restaurant, cont. brkfst,
pool, 12 acres/pond, tennis

SOUTH HARWICH
Handkerchief Shoals Motel
(508) 432-2200
Route 28
26 rooms - $45-80
Pets: Welcome
Creature Comforts: CCTV, a/c,
refrig, micro, cont. brkfst, pool

SOUTH WELLFLEET
Green Haven Cottages
(508) 349-1715
www.capecod.net/greenhaven
Rte. 6, Box 486
8 cottages - $85-109
Pets: Welcome w/$200 dep.
Creature Comforts: CCTV, a/c,
kit

SOUTH YARMOUTH
Brentwood Lodge & Cottages
(800) 328-8812, (508) 398-8812
http://www.sunsol.com/brentwood
961 Main St.
56 rooms - $480-900/wk
Pets: Welcome w/$15 fee
Creature Comforts: CCTV,
VCR, a/c, kit, Jacuzzi, cont.
brkfst, pool, sauna

Motel 6
(800) 4-MOTEL6, (508) 394-4000
http://www.motel6.com
1314 Rte. 28
77 rooms - $50-65
Pets: Under 30 lbs. welcome
Creature Comforts: CCTV, a/c,
pool

Wind Jammer Motor Inn
(800) 448-9744, (508) 398-2370
http://www.windjammers.com
192 S. Shore Dr.
52 rooms - $45-140
Pets: Welcome w/$20 fee
Creature Comforts: CCTV, a/c,
refrig, pool

SPENCER
Zucas Homestead Farm
(508) 885-5320
85 Smithfield Rd.
1 room - $95
Pets: Welcome
Creature Comforts: Set on a 100
acre working farm, CCTV, refrig,
Jacuzzi, fireplce in bedroom, and a
full brkfst

SPRINGFIELD
Holiday Inn
(800) HOLIDAY, (413) 781-0900
http://www.holiday-inn.com
711 Dwight St.
244 rooms - $99-229
Pets: Welcome
Creature Comforts: CCTV, a/c,
refrig, micro. restaurant, hlth club,
sauna, whirlpool, pool

STURBRIDGE
Best Western Inn
(800) 528-1234, (508) 347-9121
http://www.bestwestern.com
Route 20
54 rooms - $63-95
Pets: Small pets welcome
Creature Comforts: CCTV, a/c,
refrig, restaurant, sauna, pool

Econo Lodge
(800) 55-ECONO, (508) 347-2324
http://www.econolodge.com
682 Main St.
48 rooms - $55-95
Pets: Welcome
Creature Comforts: CCTV, a/c,
pool

Green Acres Motel
(508) 347-3496
2 Shepard Rd.
16 rooms - $50-135
Pets: Small pets welcome
Creature Comforts: CCTV, a/c,
kit, Jacuzzis, pool

Host Hotel
(800) 582-3232, (508) 347-7393
366 Main St.
241 rooms - $99-295
Pets: Welcome
Creature Comforts: CCTV, a/c,
refrig, fireplaces, 3 restaurants,
pool, hlth clb, sauna, whirlpool,
lawn sports, racquetball, lake/
boating

Publick House Historic Resort
(800) PUBLICK, (508) 347-3313
http://www.publickhouse.com
On the Common
140 rooms - $70-175
Pets: In lodge w/$5 nightly fee
Creature Comforts: A wonderful
old 1771 inn w/terrific old New
England exhibits and theme
weekends, CCTV, a/c, fireplace,
refrig, restaurants, tavern, cont.
brkfst, pool, tennis, and lawn
sports

Sturbridge Motor Inn
(508) 347-7327
66 Old Rte. 15
33 rooms - $50-85
Pets: Welcome w/$15 fee
Creature Comforts: CCTV, a/c,
refrig, cont. brkfst, pool

Super 8 Motel
(800) 800-8000, (508) 347-9000
http://www.super8.com
358 Main St.
56 rooms - $59-85
Pets: Welcome
Creature Comforts: CCTV, a/c,
refrig, cont. brkfst, pool

SUDBURY
Arabian Horse Inn
(800) ARA-BIAN, (978)443-7400
277 Old Sudbury Rd.
56 rooms - $129-255
Pets: Dogs and horses welcome
Creature Comforts: A rambling
house set on a 9-acre horse farm
w/a pond and pasture, four-story
barn, canopy & four poster beds,
fireplace, grand piano, CCTV, a/c,
kit, full brkfst, Jacuzzi, cottage

TEWKSBURY
Residence Inn
(800) 331-3131, (978) 640-1003
http://www.residenceinn.com
1775 Andover St.
128 rooms - $139-199
Pets: Welcome w/$10 fee
Creature Comforts: CCTV,
VCR, a/c, kit, hlth club, pool

TRYINGHAM
Sunset Farm B&B
(413) 243-3229
http://www.sunsetfarminn.com
66 Tryingham Rd.
4 rooms - $80-100
Pets: Small pets w/$15 dep.
Creature Comforts: Nat'l
Historic Register prpty w/Shaker
accents, CCTV, a/c, fireplace,
restaurant, full brkfst, colorful
quilts, on the Appalachian trail

VINEYARD HAVEN
Hidden Hill Cottages
(508) 693-2809
http://www.mvy.com/hddnhill
PO Box 1644
4 rooms - $800-1,050
Pets: Welcome w/$50 fee
Creature Comforts: Cottages set
on 4 acres, CCTV, a/c, fireplace,
cathedral ceilings, kit, sky lights,
outdoor grill, books-games, decks,
meadow, byo linens

WALTHAM
Summerfield Suites
(800) 833-4353, (781) 290-0026
www.summerfield-suites.com
54 Forth Ave.
135 rooms - $99-325
Pets: $150 fee & $10 daily fee
Creature Comforts: CCTV,
VCR, a/c, kit, hlth club, pool

Westin Hotel
(800) WESTIN-1, (781) 290-5600
http://www.westin.com
70 - 3rd Ave.
345 rooms - $105-275
Pets: Small pets welcome
Creature Comforts: CCTV, a/c,
refrig, restaurant, cont. brkfst,
pool, hlth clb

WAREHAM
Little Harbor Guest House
(508) 295-6329
20 Stockton Shortcut Rd.
5 rooms - $60-89
Pets: Welcome
Creature Comforts: Neat 1700's
red Cape Cod cottage, canopy
beds, wicker furnishings, CCTV,
VCR, a/c, fireplace, refrig, cont.
brkfst, pool, whirlpool, putting
green

WELLFLEET
Friendship Cottages
(508) 349-3390
530 Chequessen Neck Rd.
3 cottages - $400-650/wk
Pets: Welcome
Creature Comforts: CCTV,
VCR, a/c, fireplaces, kit

WESTBOROUGH
Marriott Hotel
(800) 228-9290, (508) 366-5511
http://www.marriott.com
5400 Computer Dr.
224 rooms - $85-175
Pets: Welcome
Creature Comforts: CCTV, a/c,
refrig, restaurant, pool, hlth clb,
whirlpool

Residence Inn
(800) 331-3131, (508) 366-7700
http://www.residenceinn.com
25 Connector Rd.
105 rooms - $75-189
Pets: Welcome w/$100 fee
Creature Comforts: CCTV,
VCR, a/c, kit, hlth club, pool,
whirlpool, sport court

WEST DENNIS
Captain Varrieur's Cottages
(800) 647-7126, (508) 394-4338
PO Box 1332
14 cottages - $600-950/wk
Pets: Welcome
Creature Comforts: CCTV,
VCR, a/c, fireplace, kit

Elmwood Inn
(508) 394-2798
57 Old Main St.
6 rooms - $75-85
Pets: Welcome
Creature Comforts: 1890s inn,
CCTV, fireplace, refrig, full brkfst

Pine Cove Inn
(508) 398-8511
Route 28
4 cottages - $300-350
Pets: Welcome
Creature Comforts: CCTV, kit

Woodbine Village on the Cove
(508) 881-1381
Route 28
2 rooms - $375/wk
Pets: Leashed welcome
Creature Comforts: CCTV, kit

WESTFIELD
Country Court Motel
(413) 562-9790
480 Southampton Rd.
12 rooms - $45-65
Pets: Welcome in courtyard rooms
Creature Comforts: CCTV, a/c

WESTFORD
Regency Hotel
(800) 543-7801, (978) 692-8200
www.westforregency.com
219 Littleton Rd.
194 rooms - $115-245
Pets: Welcome W/100 deposit
Creature Comforts: CCTV,
VCR, a/c, refrig, micro, restaurant,
pool, hlth clb, sauna, whirlpool

WEST HARWICH
Barnaby Inn
(800) 439-4764, (508) 432-6789
http://www.barnabyinn.com
36 Main St.
6 rooms - $70-145
Pets: Welcome in first floor room
Creature Comforts: A charming
1796 home, poster beds, based on
English B&Bs, CCTV, VCR,
fireplace, Jacuzzi, refrig, cont.
brkfst, neat cottage, dog area

Claddagh Inn
(508) 432-9628
77 Main St.
6 rooms - $99-150
Pets: Small pets welcome
Creature Comforts: CCTV, a/c,
refrig, restaurant, pool

WESTMINSTER
Wachusett Village Inn
(800) 342-1905, (978) 874-5351
www.wachusettvillageinn.com
Rtes. 2A & 140
35 cottages - $99-135
Pets: Welcome in cottages with a $25 fee and a CC deposit
Creature Comforts: CCTV, refrig, micro, restaurant, pool, hlth clb, tennis

Westminster Village Inn
(800) 342-1905, (978) 874-5351
9 Village Inn Rd.
75 rooms - $90-159
Pets: Welcome
Creature Comforts: CCTV, a/c, kit, restaurant, cont. brkfst, pool

WEST SPRINGFIELD
Econo Lodge
(800) 55-ECONO, (413) 734-8278
http://www.econolodge.com
1533 Elm St.
59 rooms - $40-120
Pets: Welcome
Creature Comforts: CCTV, a/c, Jacuzzis, cont. brkfst

Ramada Inn
(800) 2-Ramada, (413) 781-2300
http://www.ramada.com
21 Baldwin St.
48 rooms - $69-159
Pets: Welcome w/$10 fee
Creature Comforts: CCTV, a/c, refrig, micro, Jacuzzi, cont. brkfst, pool, hlth clb access

Red Carpet Inn
(800) 251-1962, (413) 733-6678
http://www.redcarpetinns.com
560 Riverdale St.
29 rooms - $45-94
Pets: Small pets $10 fee
Creature Comforts: CCTV, a/c, Jacuzzis, kit, pool

Red Roof Inn
(800) The-Roof, (413) 731-1010
http://www.redroof.com
1254 Riverdale St.
112 rooms - $43-86
Pets: Small pets welcome
Creature Comforts: CCTV, a/c

WEST STOCKBRIDGE
Shaker Mill Inn
(800) 958-9942, (413) 232-8596
http://www.shakermillinn.com
2 Oak St.
9 suites- $145-325
Pets: Welcome w/$25 fee.
Creature Comforts: Barn to an early 1800's stagecoach stop, beautifully renovated w/pickled flrs, vaulted ceilings, skylights, contemp. decor, orig. art, antique accents, large screen tv, CCTV, VCR, a/c, stone fireplaces, kit, Jacuzzi, cont. brkfst, swimming-quarry

Pleasant Valley Motel
(413) 232-8511
Route 22
16 rooms - $45-139
Pets: Welcome
Creature Comforts: CCTV, a/c, cont. brkfst, pool

Red Roof Inn
(800) The-Roof, (781) 935-7110
http://www.redroof.com
19 Commerce Way
160 rooms - $59-120
Pets: Small pets welcome
Creature Comforts: CCTV, a/c, pool

The Williamsville Inn
(413) 274-6118
http://www.williamsvilleinn.com
Route 41
16 rooms - $120-285
Pets: Welcome in certain rooms
Creature Comforts: An historic inn w/appeal set on 10 acres, antiques, and affable hostesses, CCTV, VCR, a/c, fireplaces, refrig, restaurant, cont. brkfst, pool, clay tennis court, flower gardens, and art showcases

WEST YARMOUTH
Red Rose Inn
(508) 775-2944
http://www.redroseinn.com
6 New Hampshire Ave.
14 rooms - $65-165
Pets: Small pets welcome
Creature Comforts: Set on the shores of Lewis Bay, CCTV, fireplace, kit, board games, and a full brkfst

Ryan's Cottage
(508) 771-6387
19 Sandy Lane
1 cottage - $500-600/wk
Pets: Small pets welcome
Creature Comforts: CCTV, fireplace, kit

Thunderbird Motel
(800) 247-3006, (508) 775-2692
http://www.thunderbirdmotel.com
Route 28
141 rooms - $60-85
Pets: Welcome
Creature Comforts: CCTV, a/c, refrig, cont. brkfst, pool

Town & Country Lodge
(800) 992-2340, (508) 771-0212
452 Main St.
150 rooms - $55-80
Pets: Small pets w/$5 fee
Creature Comforts: CCTV, a/c, refrig, pool, sauna, whirlpool

Yarmouth Shores
(508) 775-1944
29 Lewis Bay Rd.
13 cottages - $200-500
Pets: Welcome
Creature Comforts: CCTV, fireplace, kit, on the water

WILLIAMSTOWN
Cozy Corner Motel
(413) 458-8006
284 Sand Springs Rd.
12 rooms - $50-93
Pets: Welcome w/$5 fee
Creature Comforts: CCTV, a/c, pool

Jericho Valley Inn
(800) JERICHO, (413) 458-9511
http://www.jerichovalleyinn.com
Rte 43, Box 239
25 rooms - $50-270
Pets: Welcome in cottages
Creature Comforts: An upscale motor inn w/charming knotty pine cottages, CCTV, a/c, fireplace, kit, cont. brkfst, pool, and 350 acres/trails

The Villager Motel
(413) 458-4046
953 Simonds Rd.
14 rooms - $49-85
Pets: Small pets welcome
Creature Comforts: CCTV, a/c

The Williams Inn
(800) 828-0133, (413) 458-9371
On the Green
99 rooms - $90-210
Pets: 1st flr rms w/$10 daily fee
Creature Comforts: Former student dorm, period furnishings, gracious ambiance, CCTV, VCR, a/c, fireplace, refrig, restaurant, cont. brkfst, pool, saunas, whirlpool

WOBURN
Hampton Inn
(800) Hampton, (781) 935-7666
http://www.hampton-inn.com
315 Mishawaum Rd
99 rooms - $75-149
Pets: Small pets welcome
Creature Comforts: CCTV, a/c, cont. brkfst, and hlth club access

Ramada Hotel
(800) 2-Ramada, (781) 935-8760
http://www.ramada.com
15 Middlesex Canal Park
195 rooms - $120-149
Pets: Small pets welcome
Creature Comforts: CCTV, a/c, refrig, restaurant, pool, hlth club

Red Roof Inn
(800) The-Roof, (781) 935-7110
http://www.redroof.com
19 Commerce Way
160 rooms - $59-120
Pets: Small pets welcome
Creature Comforts: CCTV, a/c, pool

WORCESTER
Econo Lodge
(800) 55-ECONO, (508) 852-5800
http://www.econolodge.com
531 Lincoln St.
48 rooms - $45-60
Pets: Welcome
Creature Comforts: CCTV, a/c, cont. brkfst

Hampton Inn
(800) Hampton, (508) 757-0400
http://www.hampton-inn.com
110 Summer St.
99 rooms - $95-129
Pets: Welcome
Creature Comforts: CCTV, a/c, refrig, micro, cont. brkfst

YARMOUTHPORT
The Colonial House
(800) 999-3416, (508) 362-4348
277 Main St.
21 rooms - $70-95
Pets: Welcome w/$5 fee
Creature Comforts: A registered historic landmark dating back to 1730s, CCTV, VCR, a/c, fireplace, refrig, Jacuzzi, restaurant, cont. brkfst, pool, hlth clb, lawn games

Land's End Cottage
(508) 362-5298
268 Main St.
3 rooms - $100-125
Pets: Welcome if they are quiet - on the first floor
Creature Comforts: A wonderful 1720s Cape surrounded flanked by gardens and woods, terrific hostess, antiques, family heirlooms, down comforters, cobblestone patio, CCTV, a/c, fireplace, kit, a full brkfst

The Village Inn
(508) 362-3182
92 Main St., Box 1
10 rooms - $60-95
Pets: Welcome w/$10 nightly fee
Creature Comforts: A terrific 1795 Colonial with loads of ambiance and homey appeal, dark wood paneling, detailed moldings & bookshelves, country kit, copper tub, old-fashioned floral wallpapers, handmade quilts, CCTV, a/c, fireplace, refrig, cont. brkfst, a lovely hostess

Michigan

ACME
Knollwood Motel
(616) 938-2040
5777 Rte 31
14 rooms - $42-95
Pets: Welcome
Creature Comforts: CCTV, a/c

ALBION
Days Inn
(800) DAYS-INN, (517) 629-9411
http://www.daysinn.com
27644 C. Drive North
102 rooms - $59-79
Pets: Welcome
Creature Comforts: CCTV, a/c,
cont. brkfst, whirlpool, hlth club,
pool

ALLEGAN
Budget Host
(800) Bud-Host, (616) 673-6622
http://www.budgethost.com
1580 Lincoln Rd.
20 rooms - $40-99
Pets: Small pets w/$7 fee
Creature Comforts: CCTV, a/c,
kit, Jacuzzis

ALLEN PARK
Best Western Greenfield Inn
(800) 528-1234, (313) 271-1600
http://www.bestwestern.com
3000 Enterprise Rd.
208 rooms - $85-135
Pets: Welcome w/credit card dep.
Creature Comforts: CCTV,
VCR, a/c, refrig, micro, cont.
brkfst, whirlpool, sauna, pool

ALGONAC
Linda's Lighthouse Inn
(810) 794-2992
http://www.lindasbnb.com
5965 Point Tremble Rd.
4 rooms - $85-135
Pets: Welcome w/$15 fee
Creature Comforts: A fun inn
that was formerly a speakeasy,
CCTV, VCR, a/c, refrig, cont.
brkfst, Jacuzzi, whirlpool, ponds,
gardens, balconies overlooking the
water, dock — fishing/swimming

ALMA
Petticoat Inn
(517) 681-5728
2454 W. Monroe Rd.
11 rooms - $30-45
Pets: Welcome
Creature Comforts: CCTV, a/c

ALPENA
Amber Motel
(517) 354-8573
2052 State St.
22 rooms - $39-70
Pets: Welcome
Creature Comforts: CCTV, a/c,
kit, cont. brkfst, pool

Bay Motel
(517) 356-6137
2107 Route 23
23 rooms - $35-155
Pets: Welcome
Creature Comforts: CCTV, a/c,
Jacuzzis, kit

Fletcher Motel
(800) 334-5920, (517) 354-4191
1001 Route 23
98 rooms - $60-105
Pets: Welcome
Creature Comforts: CCTV,
VCR, a/c, kit, Jacuzzi, restaurant,
pool, hlth clb, sauna, whirlpool

Holiday Inn
(800) HOLIDAY, (517) 356-2151
http://www.holiday-inn.com
1000 Route 23
150 rooms - $75-130
Pets: Small pets welcome
Creature Comforts: CCTV, a/c,
kit, restaurant, pool, sauna, rec.
dome, whirlpool, hlth club, putting
green

Parker House Inn
(517) 595-6484
11505 Route 23
14 units - $45-70
Pets: Welcome w/$5 fee
Creature Comforts: CCTV, a/c,
kit, on lake/boat

Water's Edge Motel
(517) 354-5495
1000 State St.
11 rooms - $30-55
Pets: Welcome
Creature Comforts: CCTV, a/c,
kit, Jacuzzis, on a lake

ANN ARBOR
Best Western Wolverine Inn
(800) 528-1234, (734) 665-3500
http://www.bestwestern.com
3505 S. State St.
119 rooms - $59-135
Pets: Welcome
Creature Comforts: CCTV, a/c,
refrig, micro, cont. brkfst,
whirlpool, sauna, pool

Comfort Inn
(800) 228-5150, (734) 973-6100
http://www.comfortinn.com
2455 Carpenter Rd.
126 rooms - $65-149
Pets: Small pets welcome
Creature Comforts: CCTV, a/c,
Jacuzzis, cont. brkfst, pool

Hampton Inn, North
(800) Hampton, (734) 996-4444
http://www.hampton-inn.com
2300 Green Rd.
132 rooms - $75-100
Pets: Under 20 lbs. welcome
Creature Comforts: CCTV, a/c,
refrig, cont. brkfst, pool, hlth club

Holiday Inn
(800) HOLIDAY, (734) 769-9800
http://www.holiday-inn.com
3600 Plymouth Rd.
222 rooms - $95-120
Pets: Small pets welcome
Creature Comforts: CCTV, a/c,
refrig, restaurant, pool, sauna, hlth
club, whirlpool

Red Roof Inn
(800) The-Roof, (734) 996-5800
http://www.redroof.com
3621 Plymouth Rd.
106 rooms - $52-85
Pets: Small pets welcome
Creature Comforts: CCTV, a/c

Residence Inn
(800) 331-3131, (734) 996-5666
http://www.residenceinn.com
800 Victors Way
115 rooms - $135-199
Pets: Welcome w/$50-150 fee
Creature Comforts: CCTV,
VCR, a/c, kit, cont. brkfst, hlth
club access, sport court, whirlpool,
tennis, pool

AUBURN HILLS
Amerisuites
(800) 833-1516, (248) 475-9393
http://www.amerisuites.com
1545 Opdyke Rd.
127 rooms - $60-129
Pets: Small pets welcome
Creature Comforts: CCTV,
VCR, a/c, refrig, micro, hlth club,
pool, whirlpool

Hilton Suites
(800) HILTONS, (248) 334-2222
http://www.hilton.com
2300 Featherstone Rd.
225 rooms - $125-199
Pets: Small pets welcome w/credit
card deposit
Creature Comforts: CCTV, a/c,
refrig, micro, restaurant, hlth club,
whirlpool, sauna, pool

Holiday Inn
(800) HOLIDAY, (248) 373-4550
http://www.holiday-inn.com
1500 Opdyke Rd.
188 rooms - $119-185
Pets: Small pets welcome
Creature Comforts: CCTV, a/c,
refrig, Jacuzzis, restaurant, pool,
hlth club, whirlpool

Motel 6
(800) 4-MOTEL6, (248) 373-8440
http://www.motel6.com
1471 Opdyke Rd.
114 rooms - $44-59
Pets: Under 30 lbs. welcome
Creature Comforts: CCTV, a/c

Residence Inn
(800) 331-3131, (248) 858-8664
http://www.residenceinn.com
3333 Centerpoint Blvd.
115 rooms - $129-199
Pets: Welcome w/$100 cleaning
fee
Creature Comforts: CCTV, a/c,
kit, and a cont. brkfst

AU GRES
Best Western Pinewood Lodge
(800) 528-1234, (517) 876-4060
http://www.bestwestern.com
510 W. Rte 23
30 rooms - $79-119
Pets: Small pets welcome
Creature Comforts: CCTV, a/c,
refrig, Jacuzzis, whirlpool, hlth
club, pool

BARAGA
Carla's Lake Shore Motel
(906) 353-6256
Rte 41, Box 233
11 rooms - $49-60
Pets: Welcome w/$5 fee
Creature Comforts: CCTV
restaurant

Super 8 Motel
(800) 800-8000, (906) 353-6680
http://www.super8.com
790 Michigan Ave.
40 rooms - $48-70
Pets: Welcome
Creature Comforts: CCTV, a/c,
cont. brkfst

BATTLE CREEK
Battle Creek Inn
(800) 232-3405, (616) 979-1100
5050 Beckley Rd.
211 rooms - $64-95
Pets: Welcome
Creature Comforts: CCTV, a/c,
kit, Jacuzzi, restaurant, pub, cont.
brkfst, pool, hlth clb, whirlpool

Baymont Inns
(877)BAYMONT, (616) 979-5400
http://www.baymontinns.com
4725 Beckley Rd.
90 rooms - $49-85
Pets: Small pets in first flr rms.
Creature Comforts: CCTV, a/c,
refrig, cont. brkfst, pool

Days Inn
(800) DAYS-INN, (616) 979-3561
http://www.daysinn.com
4786 Beckley Rd.
88 rooms - $49-75
Pets: Welcome
Creature Comforts: CCTV, a/c,
cont. brkfst, whirlpool

Econo Lodge
(800) 55-ECONO, (616) 965-3976
http://www.econolodge.com
1205 N. Keller Dr.
74 rooms - $43-79
Pets: Small pets welcome
Creature Comforts: CCTV, a/c,
refrig, cont. brkfst, hlth club, pool

Hampton Inn
(800) Hampton, (616) 979-5577
http://www.hampton-inn.com
1150 Riverside Dr.
64 rooms - $63-99
Pets: Under 20 lbs. welcome
Creature Comforts: CCTV, a/c,
cont. brkfst, pool, whirlpool

Holiday Inn Express
(800) HOLIDAY, (616) 965-3201
http://www.holiday-inn.com
2590 Capitol Ave. SW
101 rooms - $85-129
Pets: Small pets welcome
Creature Comforts: CCTV, a/c,
refrig, micro, pool, hlth club,
whirlpool

Knights Inn
(800) 843-5644, (616) 964-2600
http://www.knightsinn.com
2595 Capitol Ave. SW
92 rooms - $43-84
Pets: Small pets w/$5 fee
Creature Comforts: CCTV,
VCR, a/c, Jacuzzis, kit, cont.
brkfst

Michigan Motel
(616) 963-1565
20475 Capitol Ave.
25 rooms - $39-50
Pets: Welcome w/$3 fee
Creature Comforts: CCTV, a/c,
kit, restaurant, cont. brkfst

   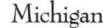

Motel 6
(800) 4-MOTEL6, (616) 979-1141
http://www.motel6.com
4775 Beckley Rd.
77 rooms - $34-57
Pets: Under 30 lbs. welcome
Creature Comforts: CCTV, a/c,
pool

Super 8 Motel
(800) 800-8000, (616) 979-1828
http://www.super8.com
5395 Beckley Rd.
62 rooms - $45-75
Pets: Welcome
Creature Comforts: CCTV, a/c,
refrig, micro, cont. brkfst

BAY CITY
Americinn
(800) 634-3444, (517) 671-0071
3915 Three Mile Rd.
66 rooms - $60-143
Pets: Welcome
Creature Comforts: CCTV, a/c,
Jacuzzis, cont. brkfst, whirlpool,
and a pool

Bay Valley Hotel & Resort
(800) 292-5028, (517) 686-3500
http://webgolfer.com/bayvalley
2470 Old Bridge Rd.
152 rooms - $64-95
Pets: Welcome
Creature Comforts: CCTV, a/c,
whirlpool, sauna, pool, tennis,
golf, x-country skiing

Delta Motel
(517) 684-4490
1000 S. Euclid Ave.
19 rooms - $30-68
Pets: Small pets welcome
Creature Comforts: CCTV, a/c,
kit, restaurant

Holiday Inn
(800) HOLIDAY, (517) 892-3501
http://www.holiday-inn.com
501 Saginaw St.
99 rooms - $85-175
Pets: Welcome
Creature Comforts: CCTV, a/c,
refrig, restaurant, pool, sauna,
whirlpool

BEAR LAKE
Windward Shore Motel
(616) 377-6321
5812 E. Torch Lake
6 rooms - $50-65
Pets: Welcome
Creature Comforts: CCTV, a/c,
refrig

BELLEVILLE
Red Roof Inn
(800) The-Roof, (734) 697-2244
http://www.redroof.com
45501 Rte 94
112 rooms - $52-78
Pets: Small pets welcome
Creature Comforts: CCTV, a/c

BENTON HARBOR
Comfort Inn
(800) 228-5150, (616) 925-1880
http://www.comfortinn.com
1598 Mall Dr.
52 rooms - $39-95
Pets: Small pets welcome
Creature Comforts: CCTV, a/c,
cont. brkfst, pool

Days Inn
(800) DAYS-INN, (616) 925-7021
http://www.daysinn.com
2699 Michigan Rd.
120 rooms - $53-85
Pets: Welcome w/$5 fee
Creature Comforts: CCTV, a/c,
refrig, micro, whirlpool, hlth club,
sauna, pool

Motel 6
(800) 4-MOTEL6, (616) 925-5100
http://www.motel6.com
2063 Pipestone Rd.
109 rooms - $30-44
Pets: Under 30 lbs. welcome
Creature Comforts: CCTV, a/c,
pool

Ramada Inn
(800) 2-Ramada, (616) 927-1172
http://www.ramada.com
798 Ferguson Dr.
116 rooms - $45-105
Pets: Welcome w/$25 fee
Creature Comforts: CCTV, a/c,
refrig, micro, Jacuzzis, restaurant,
whirlpool, pool

Red Roof Inn
(800) The-Roof, (616) 927-2484
http://www.redroof.com
1630 Mall Dr.
105 rooms - $43-70
Pets: Small pets welcome
Creature Comforts: CCTV, a/c

Super 8 Motel
(800) 800-8000, (616) 926-1371
http://www.super8.com
1950 E. Napier Ave.
62 rooms - $45-67
Pets: Welcome
Creature Comforts: CCTV, a/c,
refrig, micro, cont. brkfst

BERGLAND
Northwinds Motel Resort
(906) 575-3557
1497 W. Rte 28
18 rooms - $29-78
Pets: Welcome
Creature Comforts: CCTV, a/c,
kit, cont. brkfst, hlth clb,
whirlpool, on a lake

BEULAH
Pine Knot Motel
(616) 882-7751
171 N. Center St.
10 rooms - $45-95
Pets: Welcome
Creature Comforts: CCTV, a/c,
kit

Sunnywoods Resort
(800) 347-9728, (616) 325-3952
14065 Honor Hwy.
14 cottages - $40-90
Pets: Welcome w/$3 fee
Creature Comforts: CCTV,
fireplaces, kit, on the river

BIRCH RUN
Best Western Frankenmutch
(800) 528-1234, (517) 624-9395
http://www.bestwestern.com
9087 Birch Run
146 rooms - $55-165
Pets: Welcome in ltd. rms.
Creature Comforts: CCTV, a/c,
refrig, restaurant, whirlpool, pool

Super 8 Motel
(800) 800-8000, (517) 624-4440
http://www.super8.com
9235 E. Birch Run Rd.
109 rooms - $42-70
Pets: Welcome
Creature Comforts: CCTV, a/c,
refrig, micro, Jacuzzis, sauna, hlth
club

BLOOMFIELD HILLS
St. Christopher Motel
(810) 647-1800
3915 Telegraph Rd.
22 rooms - $39-53
Pets: Welcome
Creature Comforts: CCTV, a/c

BOYNE FALLS
Boyne Vue Motel
(800) 549-2822, (616) 549-2822
2711 Railroad St.
10 rooms - $35-85
Pets: Welcome
Creature Comforts: CCTV, a/c,
kit, whirlpool

BREVORT
Chapel Hill Motel
(906) 292-5521
4422 W. Route 2
25 rooms - $40-55
Pets: Small pets w/$5 fee
Creature Comforts: CCTV, a/c,
kit, pool

BRIDGEPORT
Baymont Inns
(877)BAYMONT, (517) 777-3000
http://www.baymontinns.com
6460 Dixie Hwy.
103 rooms - $45-73
Pets: Small pets welcome
Creature Comforts: CCTV, a/c,
cont. brkfst

Motel 6
(800) 4-MOTEL6, (517) 777-2582
http://www.motel6.com
6361 Dixie Hwy.
111 rooms - $34-50
Pets: Under 30 lbs. welcome
Creature Comforts: CCTV, a/c

BRIDGMAN
Bridgeman Inn
(616) 465-3187
9999 Red Arrow Hwy.
33 rooms - $35-75
Pets: Welcome
Creature Comforts: CCTV, a/c,
pool

BURTON
Walli's Super 8 Motel
(810) 743-8850
G-1341 S. Center St.
69 rooms - $39-95
Pets: Welcome
Creature Comforts: CCTV, a/c,
Jacuzzis

CADILLAC
Best Western Bill Oliver's
(800) 528-1234, (616) 775-2458
http://www.bestwestern.com
5675 E Rte. 55
66 rooms - $60-106
Pets: Small pets welcome
Creature Comforts: CCTV, a/c,
refrig, fireplaces, restaurant,
whirlpool, sauna, pool, tennis

Cadillac Sand's Resort
(800) 64-SANDS, (616) 775-2407
http://www.cadillacsands.com
Route 55
55 rooms - $55-135
Pets: In rms along hwy w/$10 fee
Creature Comforts: A low-key,
budget family resort, CCTV, a/c,
refrig, Jacuzzis, restaurant, cont.
brkfst, pool, xc-skiing, lawn
games, golf, trails, on lake/beach/
boating

Econo Lodge
(800) 55-ECONO, (616) 775-6700
http://www.econolodge.com
2501 Sunnyside Dr.
31 rooms - $44-95
Pets: Small pets welcome
Creature Comforts: CCTV, a/c,
refrig, restaurant

McGuires Resort
(888) McGuires, (616) 775-9947
http://www.mcguiresresort.com
7880 Mackinaw Tr.
123 rooms - $75-155
Pets: In smoking rooms w/$15 fee
Creature Comforts: An
expansive resort overlooking golf
course and Lake Cadillac, CCTV,
a/c, refrig, Jacuzzis, fireplaces,
restaurant, sauna, whirlpool,
tennis, xc-ski trails, golf, pool

Pilgrim's Village
(616) 775-5412
181 S. Lake Mitchell
123 units - $50-75
Pets: Welcome w/$5 fee
Creature Comforts: CCTV, a/c,
kit, cont. brkfst

Pine Chata Motel
(616) 775-4677
5936 E. Rte 55
12 rooms - $39-70
Pets: Small pets w/$25 dep.
Creature Comforts: CCTV, a/c

Pine Knoll Motel
(616) 775-9471
8072 Mackinaw Tr.
15 rooms - $39-60
Pets: Welcome
Creature Comforts: CCTV, pool

South Shore Resort
(800) 569-8651, (616) 775-1185
web site pending
1246 Sunnyside Dr.
16 rooms - $50-109
Pets: Welcome w/$5 fee
Creature Comforts: CCTV,
refrig, cont. brkfst, beach/boatiing

Sun n' Snow Motel
(616) 775-9961
301 S. Lake Mitchell Dr.
29 rooms - $40-125
Pets: Welcome w/$5 fee
Creature Comforts: CCTV, a/c,
kit, beach, golf access

CANTON
Baymont Inns
(877)BAYMONT, (734) 981-1808
http://www.baymontinns.com
41211 Ford Rd.
101 rooms - $52-79
Pets: Small pets welcome
Creature Comforts: CCTV, a/c,
refrig, cont. brkfst

Motel 6
(800) 4-MOTEL6, (734) 981-5000
http://www.motel6.com
41216 Ford Rd.
107 rooms - $37-75
Pets: Under 30 lbs. welcome
Creature Comforts: CCTV, a/c, pool

CARO
Kings Way Inn
(517) 673-7511
1057 E. Caro Rd.
24 rooms - $32-70
Pets: Welcome
Creature Comforts: CCTV, a/c

CASEVILLE
Surf n' S, Motel
(517) 856-4400
6006 Pt. Austin Rd.
19 rooms - $40-90
Pets: Welcome
Creature Comforts: CCTV, a/c, kit, pool, on a lake

CASS CITY
Wildwood Motel
(517) 872-3366
5986 E. Cass City Rd.
16 rooms - $33-40
Pets: Welcome
Creature Comforts: CCTV, a/c

CEDARVILLE
Comfort Inn
(800) 228-5150, (906) 484-2266
http://www.comfortinn.com
210 W. Route 134
49 rooms - $47-129
Pets: Small pets in ltd. rms
Creature Comforts: CCTV, a/c, Jacuzzis, cont. brkfst, pool

CHARLEVOIX
The Lodge Motel
(616) 547-6565
Route 31
40 rooms - $35-165
Pets: Welcome
Creature Comforts: CCTV, a/c, kit, pool

Sleep Inn
(800) Sleep-Inn, (616) 547-0300
http://www.sleepinn.com
801 Petroskey Ave.
59 rooms - $45-135
Pets: Small pets welcome
Creature Comforts: CCTV, a/c, cont. brkfst, pool

CHARLOTTE
Super 8 Motel
(800) 800-8000, (517) 543-8288
http://www.super8.com
Rtes 69 & 50
50 rooms - $49-90
Pets: Welcome
Creature Comforts: CCTV, a/c, Jacuzzis

CHEBOYGAN
Birch Haus Motel
(616) 627-5862
1301 Mackinaw Ave.
12 rooms - $32-60
Pets: Small pets w/$5 fee
Creature Comforts: CCTV, a/c, refrig, cont. brkfst

Cheboygan Motor Lodge
(616) 627-3129
1355 Mackinaw Ave.
25 rooms - $34-105
Pets: Welcome w/$5 fee
Creature Comforts: CCTV, a/c, kit, pool

Pine River Motel
(616) 627-5119
102 Lafayette St.
16 rooms - $35-60
Pets: Welcome w/$10 fee
Creature Comforts: CCTV, a/c

CLARE
Doherty Motor Hotel
(800) 525-4115, (517) 386-3441
604 McEwan St.
90 rooms - $45-75
Pets: Welcome
Creature Comforts: CCTV, a/c, restaurant, pool, whirlpool

Knights Inn
(800) 843-5644, (517) 386-7201
http://www.knightsinn.com
1110 McEwan St.
35 rooms - $73-125
Pets: Small pets welcome
Creature Comforts: CCTV, a/c, whirlpool, pool

COLDWATER
Econo Lodge
(800) 55-ECONO, (517) 278-4501
http://www.econolodge.com
884 W. Chicago Rd.
46 rooms - $38-65
Pets: Small pets welcome
Creature Comforts: CCTV, a/c, cont. brkfst

Little King Motel
(517) 278-6660
847 E. Chicago Rd.
19 rooms - $34-54
Pets: Welcome
Creature Comforts: CCTV, a/c, pool

Quality Inn
(800) 228-5151, (517) 278-2017
http://www.qualityinn.com
1000 Orleans Blvd.
123 rooms - $63-179
Pets: Small pets welcome
Creature Comforts: CCTV, a/c, Jacuzzis, restaurant, pool

Super 8 Motel
(800) 800-8000, (517) 278-8833
http://www.super8.com
600 Orleans Blvd.
58 rooms - $49-85
Pets: Welcome
Creature Comforts: CCTV, a/c

COPPER HARBOR
Astor House/Minnetonka Resort
(800) 433-2770, (906) 289-4449
http://www.exploringthenorth.com/
minnet/minnet.html
Rtes 41 & 26
25 cottages - $49-95
Pets: Welcome w/$5 fee
Creature Comforts: CCTV, a/c, kit, saunas

King Copper Motel
(800) 833-2470, (906) 289-4214
PO Box 68
34 rooms - $45-65
Pets: Welcome
Creature Comforts: CCTV, xc-skiing, on a lake

Norland Motel
(906) 289-4815
Route 41
8 rooms - $38-59
Pets: Welcome w/$5 fee
Creature Comforts: CCTV, kit

CURTIS
Seasons Motel
(906) 586-3078
Main St.
9 rooms - $40-49
Pets: Welcome
Creature Comforts: CCTV, a/c, kit

DEARBORN
Quality Inn
(800) 228-5151, (313) 565-0800
http://www.qualityinn.com
21430 Michigan Ave.
97 rooms - $55-149
Pets: Small pets welcome
Creature Comforts: CCTV, a/c, Jacuzzis, cont. brkfst, pool

Red Roof Inn
(800) The-Roof, (313) 278-9732
http://www.redroof.com
24130 Michigan Ave.
112 rooms - $49-79
Pets: Small pets welcome
Creature Comforts: CCTV, a/c

Residence Inn
(800) 331-3131, (313) 441-1700
http://www.residenceinn.com
5777 Southfield Service Dr.
128 rooms - $129-199
Pets: Welcome w/$7 daily fee, $100 cleaning fee
Creature Comforts: CCTV, a/c, kit, cont. brkfst, hlth club, sport court, whirlpool, pool

DETROIT
Hotel St. Regis
(800) 848-4810 (313) 873-3000
3071 W. Grand Blvd.
222 rooms - $85-149
Pets: Welcome
Creature Comforts: CCTV, a/c, kit, Jacuzzis, restaurant

Howard Johnson Inn
(800) I-Go-Hojo, (313) 946-1400
http://www.hojo.com
9555 Middlebelt Rd.
123 rooms - $60-145
Pets: Welcome
Creature Comforts: CCTV, a/c, cont. brkfst, hlth club, whirlpool

Omni River Place
(800) 890-9505, (313) 259-9500
http://www.omnihotels.com
1000 River Place
108 rooms - $99-529
Pets: Welcome w/$100 deposit
Creature Comforts: Historic hotel in the heart of the city, CCTV, VCR, a/c, refrig, Jacuzzis, restaurant, pool, hlth clb, saunas, whirlpools, massage, tennis, tanning, croquet

Ramada Inn
(800) 2-Ramada, (313) 962-2300
http://www.ramada.com
400 Bagley Ave.
100 rooms - $60-99
Pets: Welcome
Creature Comforts: CCTV, a/c, refrig, Jacuzzis, restaurant

Shorecrest Motor Inn
(800) 992-9616, (313) 568-3000
http://www.visitdetroit.com
1316 E. Jefferson Ave.
55 rooms - $58-155
Pets: Small pets welcome
Creature Comforts: CCTV, a/c, restaurant

Suburban House
(313) 536-9646
16920 Telegraph Rd.
49 rooms - $33-49
Pets: Welcome
Creature Comforts: CCTV, a/c, kit, pool

Westin Renaissance Hotel
(800) 879-5444, (313) 568-8000
http://www.westin.com
Renaissance Center
1,392 rooms - $165-229
Pets: Welcome
Creature Comforts: CCTV, VCR, a/c, refrig, 3 restaurants, pool, hlth clb access

DRUMMOND ISLAND
Vechell's Cedar View Resort
(906) 493-5381
PO Box 175
9 cabins - $230-365/wk
Pets: Leashed pets welcome
Creature Comforts: CCTV, fireplace, kit, fire pit, golf access, overlooking/boats

Yacht Haven
(800) 543-4743, (906) 493-5232
http://www.michiweb.com/yachthaven
Old Mill Rd.
20 cottages - $80-245
Pets: Welcome
Creature Comforts: Off eastern tip of Michigan's Upper Peninsula, cottages nestled along wooded shoreline, CCTV, a/c, fireplace, kit, whirlpools, restaurant, beach/marina/fishing, xc-skiing, hunting, golf access

EAGLE HARBOR
Shoreline Resort
(906) 289-4441
201 Front St.
8 rooms - $59-75
Pets: Welcome w/$10 dep.
Creature Comforts: CCTV restaurant

EAST CHINA
Marine Bay Lodge
(810) 765-8877/8878
6000 River Rd.
18 rooms - $34-70
Pets: Welcome
Creature Comforts: CCTV, a/c, on a river

EAST POINTE
Eastland Motel
(810) 772-1300
21055 Gratiot Ave.
42 rooms - $32-43
Pets: Welcome
Creature Comforts: CCTV, a/c, kit

Imperial Motel
(810) 771-0560
22055 Gratiot Ave.
22 rooms - $32-44
Pets: Welcome
Creature Comforts: CCTV, a/c, Jacuzzis

EAST TAWAS
Carriage Inn
(800) 666-8493, (517) 362-2831
1500 Rte 23
8 rooms - $35-55
Pets: Welcome
Creature Comforts: CCTV, a/c, hlth clb

ELK RAPIDS
Camelot Inn
(616) 264-8573
10962 Rte 31
12 rooms - $43-95
Pets: Welcome
Creature Comforts: CCTV, kit

ESCANABA
Bay View Motel
(800) 547-1201, (906) 786-2843
Routes 41 & 35
23 rooms - $35-65
Pets: Welcome w/$8 fee
Creature Comforts: CCTV, a/c,
refrig, pool

Days Inn
(800) DAYS-INN, (906) 789-1200
http://www.daysinn.com
2603 N. Lincoln Rd.
123 rooms - $59-79
Pets: Welcome w/$30 dep.
Creature Comforts: CCTV, a/c,
restaurant, whirlpool, pool

Hiawatha Motel
(906) 786-1341
2400 Ludington St.
22 rooms - $40-58
Pets: Welcome
Creature Comforts: CCTV,
VCR, a/c, kit, Jacuzzi

FARMINGTON HILLS
Holiday Inn
(800) HOLIDAY, (248) 477-4000
http://www.holiday-inn.com
38123 W. 10-Mile Rd.
262 rooms - $119-160
Pets: Small pets welcome
Creature Comforts: CCTV,
VCR, a/c, refrig, micro, Jacuzzis,
restaurant, pool, whirlpool, sauna,
rec. dome, putting green

Motel 6
(800) 4-MOTEL6, (248) 471-0590
http://www.motel6.com
38300 Grand Ave.
106 rooms - $40-56
Pets: Under 30 lbs. welcome
Creature Comforts: CCTV, a/c

Red Roof Inn
(800) The-Roof, (248) 478-8640
http://www.redroof.com
24300 Sinacola Ct.
109 rooms - $43-79
Pets: Small pets welcome
Creature Comforts: CCTV, a/c

FENNVILLE
J. Paule's Fenn Inn
(616) 561-2836
e-mail: jpaules@accn.org
2254 S. 58th St.
3 rooms - $65-100
Pets: One welcomed at a time
Creature Comforts: CCTV, a/c,
kit, full brkfst, hlth clb

FLAT ROCK
Sleep Inn
(800) Sleep-Inn, (734) 782-9898
http://www.sleepinn.com
29101 Commerce Dr.
62 rooms - $57-80
Pets: Small pets welcome
Creature Comforts: CCTV, a/c,
cont. brkfst

FLINT
Baymont Inns
(877)BAYMONT, (810) 732-2300
http://www.baymontinns.com
4160 Pier N. Blvd.
90 rooms - $48-69
Pets: Small pets welcome
Creature Comforts: CCTV, a/c,
cont. brkfst

Days Inn
(800) DAYS-INN, (810) 239-4681
http://www.daysinn.com
2207 W. Bristol Rd.
138 rooms - $40-160
Pets: Welcome
Creature Comforts: CCTV, a/c,
refrig, micro, Jacuzzis, restaurant,
cont. brkfst, pool

Howard Johnson Express
(800) I-Go-Hojo, (810) 733-5910
http://www.hojo.com
3277 Miller Rd.
135 rooms - $45-80
Pets: Welcome
Creature Comforts: CCTV, a/c,
Jacuzzis, kit, cont. brkfst, pool

Motel 6
(800) 4-MOTEL6, (810) 767-7100
http://www.motel6.com
2324 Austin Pkwy.
107 rooms - $36-45
Pets: Under 30 lbs. welcome
Creature Comforts: CCTV, a/c,
pool

Red Roof Inn
(800) The-Roof, (810) 733-1660
http://www.redroof.com
G-3219 Miller Rd.
105 rooms - $44-65
Pets: Small pets welcome
Creature Comforts: CCTV, a/c

Super 8 Motel
(800) 800-8000, (810) 230-7888
http://www.super8.com
3033 Claude Ave.
62 rooms - $45-68
Pets: Welcome
Creature Comforts: CCTV, a/c,
cont. brkfst

FOUNTAIN
Christie's Log Cabins
(800) 209-7385, (616) 462-3218
6503 E. Sugar Grove
6 cottages - $49-85
Pets: Welcome
Creature Comforts: Kit, lake/
water sports

FRANKEMUTH
Drury Inn
(800) Drury-Inn, (517) 652-2800
http://www.drury-inn.com
260 S. Main St.
79 rooms - $65-139
Pets: Welcome
Creature Comforts: CCTV, a/c,
refrig, cont. brkfst, whirlpool, pool

FRANKFORT
Bay Valley Inn
(800) 352-7113, (231) 352-7114
1561 Scenic Hwy.
22 rooms - $49-95
Pets: Welcome w/$5-10 fee
Creature Comforts: CCTV,
VCR, a/c, refrig, cont. brkfst

Chimney Corners Resort
(231) 352-7522
1602 Crystal Dr.
29 cottages - $40-119
Pets: Welcome
Creature Comforts: Kit,
fireplace, restaurant, tennis,
woods, on a lake/beach/boat

Hotel Frankfort
(231) 352-4303
http://www.brooksideinn.com/
hotfrk.htm
231 Main St.
18 rooms - $75-175
Pets: Small pets welcome-$10 fee
Creature Comforts: An old world setting w/Victorian ambiance, CCTV, a/c, Jacuzzis, fireplaces, four-poster beds, restaurant, Polynesian spa, sauna, steambath, tanning solarium, and a whirlpool

FREELAND
Freeland Inn and Motel
(517) 695-9646
6840 Midland Rd.
25 rooms - $39-55
Pets: Welcome
Creature Comforts: CCTV

GAYLORD
Best Western Royal Crest
(800) 528-1234, (517) 732-6451
http://www.bestwestern.com
803 S. Otsego Ave.
44 rooms - $55-139
Pets: Welcome
Creature Comforts: CCTV, a/c, refrig, micro, cont. brkfst, whirlpool, sauna, hlth club, pool

Downtown Motel
(517) 732-5010
208 S. Otsego Ave.
22 rooms - $39-75
Pets: Welcome
Creature Comforts: CCTV, a/c, kit

Econo Lodge
(800) 55-ECONO, (517) 732-5133
http://www.econolodge.com
2880 Old Rte 27
36 rooms - $49-85
Pets: Small pets welcome
Creature Comforts: CCTV, a/c, cont. brkfst

Holiday Inn
(800) HOLIDAY, (517) 732-2431
http://www.holiday-inn.com
833 W. Main St.
140 rooms - $79-105
Pets: Small pets welcome
Creature Comforts: CCTV, a/c, refrig, restaurant, whirlpool, pool

Microtel
(888) 808-6331, (517) 731-6331
http://www.microtelinn.com
510 S. Wisconsin St.
102 rooms - 45-95
Pets: Welcome in smkng rms
Creature Comforts: CCTV, a/c, cont. brkfst, pool

Super 8 Motel
(800) 800-8000, (517) 732-5193
http://www.super8.com
1042 W. Main
82 rooms - $49-155
Pets: Welcome
Creature Comforts: CCTV, a/c, Jacuzzis, kit, cont. brkfst, sauna, hlth club, pool

Timberly Motel
(888) 321-2606, (517) 732-5166
881 S. Old Rte 27
30 rooms - $42-80
Pets: Welcome w/$5 fee
Creature Comforts: CCTV, a/c, cont. brkfst

GLADSTONE
Norway Pines Motel
(906) 786-5119
7111 Rte 2
11 rooms - $30-55
Pets: Welcome
Creature Comforts: CCTV, a/c, kit, whirlpool

Sleepy Hollow Motel
(906) 786-7092
7156 Rte 2
18 rooms - $28-50
Pets: Welcome
Creature Comforts: CCTV, a/c, kit

GLADWIN
Gladwin Motor Inn
(517) 426-9661
1003 W. Cedar Ave.
16 rooms - $29-55
Pets: Welcome
Creature Comforts: CCTV, a/c

GRAND BLANC
Scenic Inn
(810) 694-6611
G-8308 S. Saginaw Rd.
17 cottages - $89-125
Pets: Welcome
Creature Comforts: CCTV, a/c, restaurant, cont. brkfst, pool

GRAND MARAIS
Alverson Motel
(906) 494-2681
Randolph Rd., Box 188
14 rooms - $42-54
Pets: Welcome
Creature Comforts: CCTV

Voyageur's Motel
(906) 494-2389
E. Wilson Rd, Box 281
12 rooms - $42-65
Pets: Welcome w/$5 fee
Creature Comforts: CCTV

GRAND RAPIDS
Baymont Inns
(877)BAYMONT, (616) 956-3300
http://www.baymontinns.com
2873 Kraft Ave. SE
102 rooms - $48-99
Pets: Small pets welcome
Creature Comforts: CCTV, a/c, cont. brkfst

Cascade Inn
(616) 949-0850
2865 Broadmoore
64 rooms - $30-49
Pets: Welcome
Creature Comforts: CCTV, a/c, fireplaces, kit, restaurant, pool

Days Inn
(800) DAYS-INN, (616) 235-7611
http://www.daysinn.com
310 Pearl St. NW
175 rooms - $55-115
Pets: Welcome w/$10 fee
Creature Comforts: CCTV, a/c, Jacuzzis, restaurant, cont. brkfst, hlth club, pool

Econo Lodge
(800) 55-ECONO, (616) 965-6601
http://www.econolodge.com
5175 - 28th St. SE
101 rooms - $43-159
Pets: Small pets welcome
Creature Comforts: CTV, VCR, a/c, Jacuzzis, cont. brkfst, pool

Exel Inn
(800)FOR-EXEL, (616) 957-3000
http://www.exelinns.com
4855 - 28th St. SE
112 rooms - $45-109
Pets: Small pets welcome
Creature Comforts: CCTV, a/c, refrig, micro, Jacuzzis, and a cont. brkfst.

Hampton Inn
(800) Hampton, (616) 956-9304
http://www.hampton-inn.com
4981 - 28th St. SE
120 rooms - $68-85
Pets: Under 20 lbs. welcome
Creature Comforts: CCTV, a/c,
refrig, cont. brkfst, pool

Holiday Inn
(800) HOLIDAY, (616) 363-9001
http://www.holiday-inn.com
270 Ann St. NW
165 rooms - $80-99
Pets: Welcome
Creature Comforts: CCTV, a/c,
refrig, restaurant, pool

Homewood Suites
(800) 225-5466, (616) 285-7100
http://www.homewoodsuites.com
3920 Stahl Dr. SE
77 rooms - $99-169
Pets: Welcome
Creature Comforts: CCTV,
VCR, a/c, kit, pool, hlth clb

Motel 6
(800) 4-MOTEL6, (616) 957-3511
http://www.motel6.com
3524 - 28th SE
118 rooms - $34-50
Pets: Under 30 lbs. welcome
Creature Comforts: CCTV, a/c,
pool

New England Suites Hotel
(800) 784-8371, (616) 940-1777
2985 Kraft Ave. SE
40 rooms - $60-85
Pets: Welcome
Creature Comforts: CCTV, a/c,
kit

Peaches B&B
(888) 210-6910, (616) 454-8000
http://www.peaches-inn.com
29 Gay Ave. SE
5 rooms - $80-90
Pets: Dogs only w/$10 daily fee
Creature Comforts: A handsome
1916 Georgian manor original
hardwood floors, woodwork,
traditional decor, white wicker,
four poster beds, CCTV,VCR, a/c,
five fireplaces, exercise rm, pool,
ping-pong & game room, full
brkfst, resident Dalmatian

Red Roof Inn
(800) The-Roof, (616) 942-0800
http://www.redroof.com
5131 - 28th St. SE
106 rooms - $49-75
Pets: Small pets welcome
Creature Comforts: CCTV, a/c

Residence Inn
(800) 331-3131, (616) 957-8111
http://www.residenceinn.com
2701 E. Beltline SE
96 rooms - $109-179
Pets: Welcome w/ a $6 daily fee,
$60 one-time fee
Creature Comforts: CCTV, a/c,
kit, cont. brkfst, pool, hlth club,
whirlpool

Swan Inn Motel
(800) 875-7926, (616) 784-1224
5182 Alpine Ave. NW
40 rooms - $39-60
Pets: Welcome
Creature Comforts: CCTV, a/c,
kit, restaurant, pool

GRAYLING
Cedar Motel
(517) 348-5884
606 N. James Rd.
10 rooms - $30-45
Pets: Welcome
Creature Comforts: CCTV, a/c

Holiday Inn
(800) HOLIDAY, (517) 348-7611
http://www.holiday-inn.com
2650 S. Business Loop
150 rooms - $75-179
Pets: Welcome
Creature Comforts: CCTV,
VCR, a/c, refrig, micro, Jacuzzis,
restaurant, sauna, whirlpool, rec.
dome, pool

North Country Lodge
(800) 475-6300, (517) 348-8471
http://www.grayling-mi.com/
northcountrylodge
Rte 75, Box 290
23 rooms - $45-175
Pets: Welcome
Creature Comforts: CCTV, a/c,
fireplaces, kit, Jacuzzis

Pointe North
(517) 348-5950
Rte 75
21 rooms - $40-79
Pets: Welcome
Creature Comforts: CCTV, a/c,
kit, cont. brkfst

River Country Motor Lodge
(800) 733-7396, (517) 348-8619
http://www.grayling-mi.com/
rivercountry
Route 75
17 rooms - $35-70
Pets: Welcome
Creature Comforts: CCTV, kit,
snowmobiles

Super 8 Motel
(800) 800-8000, (517) 348-8888
http://www.super8.com
5828 N.A. Miles Hwy.
61 rooms - $52-70
Pets: Welcome
Creature Comforts: CCTV, a/c,
Jacuzzis, cont. brkfst

Woodland Motel
(517) 348-9094
267 Rte 75
22 rooms - $35-85
Pets: Welcome
Creature Comforts: CCTV, kit,
snowmobiles

HAGAR SHORES
Sweet Shore Resort
(616) 849-1233
web site pending
3313 Chestnut St.
30 rooms - $60-135
Pets: Welcome
Creature Comforts: CCTV, a/c,
kit, restaurant, pool

HARBOR BEACH
Train Station Motel
(517) 479-3215
2044 N. Lake Shore Rd.
9 rooms - $55-100
Pets: Welcome
Creature Comforts: CCTV,
restaurant, on a lake

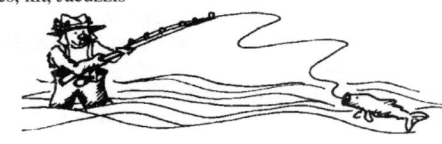

HARBOR SPRINGS
Cottage Inn
(231) 526-5431
http://www.harborsprings-mi.com/
cottage
145 Zoll St.
22 rooms - $69-180
Pets: Welcome w/$5 fee
Creature Comforts: Single level buildings w/warm B&B ambiance, antiques, wicker furnishings, CCTV-VCR, a/c, kit, fireplaces, cont. brkfst, access to boating, fishing, xc-skiing/golf

HARPER WOODS
Parkcrest Inn
(313) 884-8800
20000 Harper Ave.
49 rooms - $60-83
Pets: Small pets welcome
Creature Comforts: CCTV, a/c, kit, Jacuzzis, restaurant, pool

HART
Budget Host Hart Motel
(800) Bud-Host, (616) 873-2151
http://www.budgethost.com
715 State St.
16 rooms - $45-149
Pets: Small pets welcome
Creature Comforts: CCTV, a/c, kit, beach, bike trail

Comfort Inn
(800) 228-5150, (616) 873-3456
http://www.comfortinn.com
2248 Comfort Dr.
61 rooms - $65-155
Pets: Small pets welcome
Creature Comforts: CCTV, a/c, cont. brkfst, refrig, whirlpool, pool

HAZEL PARK
Quality Inn
(800) 228-5151, (248) 399-5800
http://www.qualityinn.com
1 W. 9-Mile Rd.
184 rooms - $65-109
Pets: Small pets welcome
Creature Comforts: CCTV, a/c, restaurant, pool

HESSEL
Lakeview Motel
(906) 484-2474
PO Box 277
18 units - $43-65
Pets: Welcome
Creature Comforts: CCTV, a/c, kit, fireplace, on a lake/beach/dock

HOLLAND
Knights Court
(800) 843-5644, (616) 392-1000
422 E. 32nd St.
71 rooms - $49-115
Pets: Welcome
Creature Comforts: CCTV, a/c, Jacuzzi, brkfst, whirlpool, pool

HOUGHTON
Best Western King's Inn.
(800) 528-1234, (906) 482-5000
http://www.bestwestern.com
215 Shelden Ave.
68 rooms - $54-139
Pets: Welcome
Creature Comforts: CCTV, a/c, refrig, cont. brkfst, whirlpool, pool

Best Western Franklin Sq.
(800) 528-1234, (906) 487-1700
http://www.bestwestern.com
820 Shelden Ave.
103 rooms - $70-139
Pets: Welcome w/$5 fee
Creature Comforts: CCTV, a/c, refrig, restaurant, Jacuzzis, cont. brkfst, pool

HOUGHTON LAKE
Hillside Motel
(517) 366-5711
3419 W. Houghton Lake Dr.
11 rooms - $49-66
Pets: Welcome
Creature Comforts: CCTV, a/c

Holiday on the Lake
(517) 422-5195
100 Clearview Rd.
29 rooms - $39-112
Pets: Welcome w/$10 fee
Creature Comforts: CCTV, a/c, kit, restaurant, beach/boating

Lagoon Resort
(517) 422-5761
6578 W. Houghton Lake Dr.
15 cottages - $35-75
Pets: Welcome
Creature Comforts: CCTV, a/c, kit, pool, on a lake/boating

Valhalla Motel
(517) 422-5137
9869 W. Shore Dr.
12 rooms - $39-85
Pets: Welcome w/$10 fee
Creature Comforts: CCTV, a/c, kit, pool, lawn games

Way North Motel
(517) 422-5523
9052 N. Old Rte 27
13 units- $39-65
Pets: Welcome
Creature Comforts: CCTV, a/c, kit

HUDSON
Sunset Acres Motel
(517) 448-8968
400 S. Meridian St
8 rooms - $35-55
Pets: Welcome
Creature Comforts: CCTV, a/c

IMLAY CITY
Days Inn
(800) DAYS-INN, (810) 724-8005
http://www.daysinn.com
6692 Newark Rd.
60 rooms - $47-135
Pets: Welcome w/$8 fee
Creature Comforts: CCTV, a/c, Jacuzzis, restaurant, cont. brkfst, pool

Super 8 Motel
(800) 800-8000, (810) 724-8700
http://www.super8.com
6951 Newark Rd.
60 rooms - $45-69
Pets: Welcome
Creature Comforts: CCTV, a/c, Jacuzzis, cont. brkfst, whirlpool

INDIAN RIVER
Northwoods Lodge
(616) 238-7729
2390 S. Straits Rd.
15 rooms - $50-105
Pets: Welcome
Creature Comforts: CCTV, a/c, kit, cont. brkfst, sauna, whirlpool, xc-skiing

Reids Motor Court
(616) 238-9353
3977 S. Straits Rd.
14 rooms - $34-55
Pets: Welcome
Creature Comforts: CCTV, a/c, kit

Star Gate Motel
(616) 238-7371
4646 S. Straits Rd.
15 cottages - $35-52
Pets: Welcome
Creature Comforts: CCTV, kit

Woodlands Lodge
(616) 238-4137
5115 S. Straits Rd.
18 cottages - $45-60
Pets: Welcome
Creature Comforts: CCTV, a/c,
kit, xc-skiing

IONIA
Midway Motel
(616) 527-2080
7076 S. State Rd.
18 rooms - $30-55
Pets: Welcome
Creature Comforts: CCTV, a/c

Super 8 Motel
(800) 800-8000, (616) 527-2828
http://www.super8.com
7245 S. State Rd.
73 rooms - $49-96
Pets: Welcome
Creature Comforts: CCTV, a/c,
cont. brkfst, whirlpools

IRON MOUNTAIN
Best Western Executive Inn
(800) 528-1234, (906) 774-2040
http://www.bestwestern.com
1518 S. Stephenson Ave.
57 rooms - $59-79
Pets: Welcome
Creature Comforts: CCTV, a/c,
refrig, cont. brkfst, pool

Days Inn
(800) DAYS-INN, (906) 774-2181
http://www.daysinn.com
8176 S. Rte 2
44 rooms - $46-105
Pets: Welcome w/$7 fee
Creature Comforts: CCTV, a/c,
Jacuzzis, cont. brkfst, whirlpool,
pool

Econo Lodge
(800) 55-ECONO, (906) 774-6220
http://www.econolodge.com
1609 S. Stephenson Ave.
63 rooms - $43-59
Pets: Small pets welcome
Creature Comforts: CCTV, a/c,
Jacuzzis, cont. brkfst, pool

Edgewater Resort
(800) 236-6244, (906) 774-6244
http://www.edgewaterresort.com
N4128 Route 2
9 cottages - $295-465/wk
Pets: Welcome w/$3 fee
Creature Comforts: Cozy log
cabins w/homey country décor set
along a gently running river,
CCTV, kit, dining, living rooms,
river/beach, xc-skiing, hunting/
fishing, access to golf

IRONWOOD
Armata Motel
(906) 932-4421
124 W. Cloverland Dr.
14 rooms - $30-95
Pets: Welcome w/$3 fee
Creature Comforts: CCTV, a/c,
refrig, micro

Budget Host
(800) Bud-Host, (906) 932-1260
http://www.budgethost.com
447 W. Cloverland Dr.
15 rooms - $40-99
Pets: Small pets w/$4 fee
Creature Comforts: CCTV, a/c

Crestview Inn
(906) 932-4845
424 Cloverland Dr.
12 rooms - $30-63
Pets: Welcome w/$10 fee
Creature Comforts: CCTV, a/c,
refrig, micro, sauna

Super 8 Motel
(800) 800-8000, (906) 932-3395
http://www.super8.com
160 E. Cloverland Dr.
42 rooms - $45-65
Pets: Welcome
Creature Comforts: CCTV, a/c

ISHPEMING
Best Western Country Inn
(800) 528-1234, (906) 485-6345
http://www.bestwestern.com
850 Route 41
60 rooms - $53-85
Pets: Under 10 lbs. welcome
Creature Comforts: CCTV, a/c,
refrig, restaurant, cont. brkfst,
whirlpool, pool

JACKSON
Baymont Inns
(877)BAYMONT, (517) 789-6000
http://www.baymontinns.com
2035 N. Service Rd.
68 rooms - $40-74
Pets: Under 50 lbs. welcome
Creature Comforts: CCTV, a/c,
refrig, micro, cont. brkfst

Holiday Inn
(800) HOLIDAY, (517) 783-2681
http://www.holiday-inn.com
2000 Holiday Inn Dr.
185 rooms - $79-129
Pets: Small pets w/$15 fee
Creature Comforts: CCTV, a/c,
refrig, restaurant, pool

Motel 6
(800) 4-MOTEL6, (517) 789-7186
http://www.motel6.com
830 Royal Dr.
95 rooms - $34-58
Pets: Under 30 lbs. welcome
Creature Comforts: CCTV, a/c,
pool

Rodeway Inn
(800) 228-2000, (517) 787-1111
http://www.rodeway.com
901 Rosehill Dr.
90 rooms - $49-120
Pets: Welcome
Creature Comforts: CCTV, a/c,
Jacuzzis, cont. brkfst, pool

JONESVILLE
Pinecrest Motel
(517) 849-2137
516 W. Chicago St.
22 rooms - $30-42
Pets: Welcome
Creature Comforts: CCTV, a/c

KALAMAZOO
Baymont Inns
(877)BAYMONT, (616) 372-7999
http://www.baymontinns.com
2203 S. 11th St.
90 rooms - $45-86
Pets: Small pets in smkng rms.
Creature Comforts: CCTV, a/c

Clarion Inn
(800) 228-7466, (616) 385-3922
http://www.clarioninn.com
3600 E. Cork St.
156 rooms - $65-159
Pets: Small pets welcome
Creature Comforts: CCTV, a/c,
refrig, restaurant, sauna, pool,
whirlpool

Days Inn
(800) DAYS-INN, (616) 382-2303
http://www.daysinn.com
1912 E. Kilgore Rd.
68 rooms - $45-73
Pets: Welcome w/$5 fee
Creature Comforts: CCTV, a/c,
restaurant, pool

Hampton Inn
(800) Hampton, (616) 344-7774
http://www.hampton-inn.com
1550 E. Kilgore Rd.
65 rooms - $68-90
Pets: Small pets welcome
Creature Comforts: CCTV, a/c,
refrig, cont. brkfst, pool

Holiday Inn, Airport
(800) HOLIDAY, (616) 381-7070
http://www.holiday-inn.com
3522 Sprinkle Rd.
145 rooms - $79-129
Pets: Welcome
Creature Comforts: CCTV, a/c,
refrig, restaurant, hlth club, pool

Holiday Inn, West
(800) HOLIDAY, (616) 375-6000
http://www.holiday-inn.com
2747 S. 11th St.
187 rooms - $85-129
Pets: Welcome
Creature Comforts: CCTV, a/c,
refrig, restaurant, hlth club, pool

Motel 6
(800) 4-MOTEL6, (616) 344-9255
http://www.motel6.com
3704 Van Rick Rd.
104 rooms - $34-50
Pets: Under 30 lbs. welcome
Creature Comforts: CCTV, a/c,
pool

Quality Inn
(800) 228-5151, (616) 388-3551
http://www.qualityinn.com
3750 Easy St.
115 rooms - $50-93
Pets: Small pets w/$10 fee
Creature Comforts: CCTV,
VCR, a/c, refrig, and a pool

Red Roof Inn, East
(800) The-Roof, (616) 382-6350
http://www.redroof.com
3701 E. Cork St.
80 rooms - $50-75
Pets: Small pets welcome
Creature Comforts: CCTV, a/c

Red Roof Inn, West
(800) The-Roof, (616) 375-7400
http://www.redroof.com
5425 W. Michigan Ave.
105 rooms - $42-65
Pets: Small pets welcome
Creature Comforts: CCTV, a/c

Residence Inn
(800) 331-3131, (616) 349-0856
http://www.residenceinn.com
1500 E. Kilgore Rd.
85 rooms - $99-175
Pets: $6 fee, $100 one-time fee
Creature Comforts: CCTV, a/c,
kit, cont. brkfst, hlth club access,
sport court, whirlpool, pool

KENTWOOD
Residence Inn
(800) 331-3131, (616) 957-8111
http://www.residenceinn.com
2701 E. Beltline
95 rooms - $99-175
Pets: $6 fee, $60 one-time fee
Creature Comforts: CCTV, a/c,
kit, cont. brkfst, hlth club access,
sport court, whirlpool, pool

LAKE CITY
Northcrest
(616) 839-2075
1341 S. Lakeshore Dr.
24 rooms - $49-75
Pets: Welcome w/$5 fee
Creature Comforts: CCTV, a/c,
pool, whirlpool

LAKESIDE
White Rabbit Inn
(800) 967-2224, (616) 469-4620
http://www.whiterabbitinn.com
14634 Red Arrow Hwy.
8 cabins - $95-225
Pets: Welcome in cabins
Creature Comforts: Charming
knotty pine cabins w/skylights,
low ceilings, bentwood furniture,
CCTV, VCR, a/c, kit, fireplaces,
Jacuzzis, stereo-CDs, cont. brkfst,
whirlpool, access to trails, lake,
antique stores, gourmet dining

LANSING
Best Western Governor's Inn
(800) 528-1234, (517) 393-5500
http://www.bestwestern.com
6133 S. Pennsylvania
131 rooms - $55-99
Pets: Welcome
Creature Comforts: CCTV, a/c,
refrig, restaurant, cont. brkfst,
whirlpool, sauna, pool

Best Western Midway Hotel
(800) 528-1234, (517) 627-8471
http://www.bestwestern.com
7711 W. Saginaw Hwy.
149 rooms - $74-93
Pets: Small pets welcome
Creature Comforts: CCTV, a/c,
refrig, restaurant, cont. brkfst,
whirlpool, sauna, pool

Howard Johnson Express
(800) I-Go-Hojo, (517) 694-0454
http://www.hojo.com
6741 S. Cedar St.
100 rooms - $38-99
Pets: Welcome
Creature Comforts: CCTV, a/c,
Jacuzzis, kit, cont. brkfst, pool

Motel 6, Central
(800) 4-MOTEL6, (517) 484-8722
http://www.motel6.com
112 E. Main St.
118 rooms - $34-50
Pets: Under 30 lbs. welcome
Creature Comforts: CCTV, pool

Motel 6, West
(800) 4-MOTEL6, (517) 321-1444
http://www.motel6.com
7326 W. Saginaw Hwy.
104 rooms - $34-49
Pets: Under 30 lbs. welcome
Creature Comforts: CCTV, a/c,
pool

Red Roof Inn, East
(800) The-Roof, (517) 332-2575
http://www.redroof.com
3615 Dunckel Rd.
82 rooms - $45-80
Pets: Small pets welcome
Creature Comforts: CCTV, a/c

Red Roof Inn, West
(800) The-Roof, (517) 321-7246
http://www.redroof.com
7412 W. Saginaw St.
80 rooms - $46-78
Pets: Small pets welcome
Creature Comforts: CCTV, a/c

Residence Inn, East
(800) 331-3131, (517) 886-5030
http://www.residenceinn.com
922 Delta Commerce Dr.
79 rooms - $85-155
Pets: Welcome w/$10 daily fee,
$25 one-time charge
Creature Comforts: CCTV, a/c,
kit, cont. brkfst, hlth club access,
sport court, whirlpool, pool

Residence Inn, West
(800) 331-3131, (517) 332-7711
http://www.residenceinn.com
1600 E. Grand River
60 rooms - $85-150
Pets: Welcome w/$10 daily fee,
$25 one-time fee
Creature Comforts: CCTV, a/c,
kit, cont. brkfst, hlth club access,
sport court, whirlpool

Travelodge
(800) 578-7878, (517) 337-1621
http://www.travelodge.com
2736 E. Grand River Rd.
82 rooms - $36-54
Pets: Small pets welcome
Creature Comforts: CCTV, a/c,
Jacuzzis, kit, pool

LAPEER
Town & Country Motel
(810) 664-9132
1275 Imlay City Rd.
19 rooms - $40-69
Pets: Welcome
Creature Comforts: TV

LELAND
Falling Waters Lodge
(231) 256-9832
http://www.angelfire.com/mi/fwl/
index.html
200 W. Cedar St
20 rooms - $80-180
Pets: Welcome
Creature Comforts: Set along a
river near the 200-year old historic
Fishtown, beach, CCTV, a/c, kit,
balconies, great lake views

LEWISTON
Fairway Inn
(517) 786-2217
Country Rd. 489
21 rooms - $45-60
Pets: Welcome
Creature Comforts: CCTV, a/c

LUDINGTON
Days Inn
(800) DAYS-INN, (231) 843-2233
http://www.daysinn.com
5095 W. Route 10
43 rooms - $55-105
Pets: Welcome
Creature Comforts: CCTV, a/c,
Jacuzzis, cont. brkfst, whirlpool,
pool

Nader's Lakeshore Lodge
(800) 968-0109, (231) 843-8757
web site pending
612 N. Lakeshore Dr.
26 rooms - $39-90
Pets: Welcome
Creature Comforts: CCTV, a/c,
Jacuzzi, kit, pool, lawn games

Nova Motel
(800) 828-3162, (231) 843-3454
http://www.novamotel.com
472 S. Old Route 31
32 rooms - $32-75
Pets: Welcome
Creature Comforts: CCTV, a/c,
cont. brkfst, pool, whirlpool

Super 8 Motel
(800) 800-8000, (231) 843-2140
http://www.super8.com
5005 W. Route 10
41 rooms - $45-66
Pets: Small pets w/$5 fee
Creature Comforts: CCTV, a/c,
Jacuzzis, cont. brkfst

Timberlane Long Lake Resort
(800) 227-2142, (231) 757-2142
http://www.t-one.net/
timberlaneresort
7410 E. Route 10, Box 68
18 cottages - $45-99
Pets: Welcome w/$5 fee
Creature Comforts: CCTV, a/c,
kit, lake/beach, boating

Ventura Motel
(800) 968-1440, (231) 845-5124
http://www.ventura-motel.com
604 W. Ludington
25 rooms - $35-119
Pets: Welcome w/$5 fee
Creature Comforts: CCTV, a/c,
whirlpool

MACKINAW CITY
American Motel
(616) 436-5231
14351 S. Route 31
12 rooms - $35-75
Pets: Welcome
Creature Comforts: A/C, refrig,
micro

Beachcomber Motel
(800) 968-1383, (616) 436-8451
http://www.mackinawcity.com/
lodging
1011 S. Huron
24 rooms - $45-135
Pets: Small pets w/$3 fee
Creature Comforts: CCTV, a/c,
kit, Jacuzzis, cont. brkfst, pool,
lake/beach, boats

The Beach House
(800) 262-5353, (616) 436-5353
http://www.mackinawcity.com/
beachhouse
1035 S. Huron St.
29 rooms - $39-169
Pets: Small pets w/$10 fee
Creature Comforts: Charming
white clapboard cottages set along
Lake Huron, CCTV, a/c, kit, pool,
cont. brkfst, whirlpool, sandy
beach, playground

Budget Host
(800) Bud-Host, (616) 436-5543
http://www.budgethost.com
517 N. Huron St.
22 rooms - $38-145
Pets: Small pets welcome
Creature Comforts: CCTV, a/c,
kit, Jacuzzis

Capri Motel
(616) 436-5498
801 S. Nicolet St.
28 rooms - $30-73
Pets: Small pets welcome
Creature Comforts: CCTV, a/c,
pool

Econo Lodge
(800) 55-ECONO, (616) 436-5026
http://www.econolodge.com
412 Nicolet St.
32 rooms - $37-149
Pets: Small pets welcome
Creature Comforts: CCTV, a/c,
restaurant

Holiday Inn Express
(800) HOLIDAY, (616) 436-7100
http://www.holiday-inn.com
364 Louvingney Rd.
72 rooms - $45-189
Pets: Welcome w/credit card dep.
Creature Comforts: CCTV, a/c,
refrig, cont. brkfst, hlth club,
sauna, whirlpool, pool

Kings Inn
(616) 436-5322
1020 S. Nicolet St.
24 rooms - $40-189
Pets: Small pet welcome
Creature Comforts: CCTV, a/c,
Jacuzzis, cont. brkfst, pool

La Mirage Motel
(800) 729-0998, (616) 436-5304
699 N. Huron St.
25 rooms - $40-145
Pets: Welcome in corner rooms
Creature Comforts: CCTV, a/c,
refrig, micro, Jacuzzis, pool,
sauna, whirlpool

Lamplighter Motel
(616) 436-5350
303 Jamet St.
11 rooms - $45-70
Pets: Small pets w/$5 fee
Creature Comforts: CCTV, a/c

Motel 6
(800) 4-MOTEL6, (616) 436-8961
http://www.motel6.com
206 Nicolet St.
105 rooms - $40-126
Pets: Under 30 lbs. welcome
Creature Comforts: CCTV, a/c,
pool

Parkside Inn
(800) 827-8301, (616) 436-8301
102 Nicolet St.
45 rooms - $50-95
Pets: Welcome
Creature Comforts: CCTV, a/c,
refrig, pool, whirlpool

Quality Inn
(800) 228-5151, (616) 436-5051
http://www.qualityinn.com
917 S. Huron Dr.
60 rooms - $45-185
Pets: Small pets w$5 fee
Creature Comforts: CCTV,
VCR, a/c, Jacuzzis, pool, sauna,
whirlpool, beach

Ramada Inn
(800) 2-Ramada, (616) 436-5535
http://www.ramada.com
450 S. Nicolet St.
155 rooms - $45-220
Pets: Under 20 lbs w/$50 dep.
Creature Comforts: CCTV, a/c,
refrig, micro, Jacuzzis, restaurant,
sauna, whirlpool, pool

Starlite Budget Inn
(800) 288-8190, (616) 436-5959
116 Old Rte 31
32 rooms - $50-89
Pets: Welcome w/$5 fee
Creature Comforts: CCTV, a/c,
refrig, cont. brkfst, pool

Surf Motel
(800) 822-8314, (616) 436-8831
http://www.mackinawcity.com/
surfmotel
907 S. Huron St.
42 rooms - $35-139
Pets: Small pets w/$20 fee
Creature Comforts: CCTV, a/c,
refrig, micro, cont. brkfst, pool,
whirlpool, on the beach

Super 8 Motel
(800) 800-8000, (616) 436-5252
http://www.super8.com
601 N. Huron Ave.
50 rooms - $40-160
Pets: Welcome
Creature Comforts: CCTV, a/c,
refrig, Jacuzzis, cont. brkfst, hlth
club, sauna, whirlpool, pool

Val-U Motel
(616) 436-7691
14394 Old Rte 31
26 rooms - $29-63
Pets: Welcome
Creature Comforts: CCTV, pool

Vin Del Motel
(616) 436-5273
223 W. Central St.
16 rooms - $38-89
Pets: Welcome w/$10 fee
Creature Comforts: CCTV, a/c,
refrig, micro, pool

MADISON HEIGHTS
Knights Inn
(800) 843-5644, (248) 583-7700
http://www.knightsinn.com
32703 Stephenson Hwy.
150 rooms - $43-74
Pets: Small pets welcome
Creature Comforts: CCTV, a/c,
refrig, cont. brkfst, pool

Motel 6
(800) 4-MOTEL6, (248) 583-0500
http://www.motel6.com
32700 Barrington Rd.
100 rooms - $40-53
Pets: Under 30 lbs. welcome
Creature Comforts: CCTV, a/c

Red Roof Inn
(800) The-Roof, (248) 583-4700
http://www.redroof.com
32511 Concord Dr.
109 rooms - $44-75
Pets: Small pets welcome
Creature Comforts: CCTV, a/c

Residence Inn
(800) 331-3131, (248) 583-4322
http://www.residenceinn.com
32650 Stephenson Hwy.
95 rooms - $140-199
Pets: Welcome w/ a $7 daily fee,
$75 one-time fee
Creature Comforts: CCTV, a/c,
kit, cont. brkfst, hlth club access,
sport court, whirlpool, pool

MANCELONA
Mancelona Motel
(800) 320-1240, (616) 587-8621
8306 N. Rte 131
19 rooms - $40-83
Pets: Welcome
Creature Comforts: CCTV, a/c,
kit, xc-skiing

Rapid River Motel
(616) 258-2604
7530 Rte 131
13 rooms - $35-55
Pets: Welcome
Creature Comforts: CCTV, a/c,
kit, xc-skiing

MANISTEE
Hillside Motel
(800) 234-1250, (616) 723-2584
1599 S. Rte 31
20 rooms - $35-105
Pets: Small dogs w/$8 fee
Creature Comforts: CCTV, a/c,
Jacuzzis, pool

MANISTIQUE
Comfort Inn
(800) 228-5150, (906) 341-6981
http://www.comfortinn.com
726 E. lakeshore Dr.
58 rooms - $55-120
Pets: Small pets w/$5 fee
Creature Comforts: CCTV, a/c,
refrig, Jacuzzis, cont. brkfst, pool,
and a whirlpool

Econo Lodge
(800) 55-ECONO, (906) 341-6014
http://www.econolodge.com
1101 E. lakeshore Dr.
31 rooms - $43-74
Pets: Small pets welcome
Creature Comforts: CCTV, a/c,
cont. brkfst

Holiday Motel
(906) 341-2710
Rte 2, Box 1514
22 rooms - $37-55
Pets: Welcome w/$5 fee
Creature Comforts: CCTV pool

Howard Johnson Express
(800) I-G0-Hojo, (906) 341-6981
http://www.hojo.com
726 E. Lake Shore Dr.
57 rooms - $48-97
Pets: Welcome
Creature Comforts: CCTV, a/c,
whirlpool

Ramada Inn
(800) 2-Ramada, (906) 341-6911
http://www.ramada.com
2 Lakeshore Dr.
42 rooms - $55-89
Pets: Welcome
Creature Comforts: CCTV, a/c,
refrig, micro, Jacuzzis, pool

MANTON
Green Mill Motel
(616) 824-3504
709 N. Rte 131
18 rooms - $34-75
Pets: Welcome
Creature Comforts: CCTV, a/c,
xc-skiing

MARINE CITY
Port Seaway Inn
(810) 765-4033
7623 River Rd.
18 rooms - $35-98
Pets: Welcome
Creature Comforts: CCTV, a/c,
kit, on a river

MARQUETTE
Bavarian Inn
(906) 226-2314
2782 W. Rte 41
25 rooms - $32-50
Pets: Welcome
Creature Comforts: CCTV, a/c,
refrig, restaurant

Birchmont Motel
(906) 228-7538
2090 S. Rte 41
36 rooms - $44-55
Pets: Welcome w/$4 fee
Creature Comforts: CCTV, kit,
pool

Comfort Inn
(800) 228-5150, (906) 228-0028
http://www.comfortinn.com
2463 Rte 41
60 rooms - $79-145
Pets: Small pets welcome
Creature Comforts: CCTV, a/c,
refrig, micro, Jacuzzis, cont.
brkfst, whirlpool, pool

Holiday Inn
(800) HOLIDAY, (906) 225-1351
http://www.holiday-inn.com
1951 Rte 41
202 rooms - $80-99
Pets: Welcome
Creature Comforts: CCTV, a/c,
refrig, restaurant, hlth club, sauna,
whirlpool, pool

Lamplighter Motel
(906) 228-4004
3600 Rte 41
17 rooms - $28-50
Pets: Welcome
Creature Comforts: CCTV, a/c,
xc-skiing

Ramada Inn
(800) 2-Ramada, (906) 228-6000
http://www.ramada.com
412 W. Washington St.
112 rooms - $75-109
Pets: Welcome
Creature Comforts: CCTV, a/c,
refrig, Jacuzzis, restaurant, cont.
brkfst, whirlpool, sauna, pool

Tiroler Hof Motel
(800) 892-9376, (906) 226-7516
web site pending
150 Carp River Hill
44 rooms - $43-64
Pets: Small pets welcome
Creature Comforts: CCTV, a/c,
refrig, restaurant, sauna, xc skiing,
river/lake

Travelodge
(800) 578-7878, (906) 249-1712
http://www.travelodge.com
1010 Rte 28
39 rooms - $39- 55
Pets: Small pets welcome
Creature Comforts: CCTV, a/c,
kit, Jacuzzis, restaurant, cont.
brkfst, hlth club, pool

MARSHALL
Arbor Inn
(800) 424-0807, (616) 781-7772
15435 W. Michigan Ave.
48 rooms - $48-62
Pets: Under 20 Lbs in smkng rms
Creature Comforts: CCTV, a/c,
kit, pool

McMILLAN
Interlaken Lodge
(906) 586-3545
Rte 3, Box 2542
8 cottages - $69-135
Pets: Welcome
Creature Comforts: CCTV, a/c, kit, Jacuzzis, xc skiing, on a lake/beach

MENOMINEE
Howard Johnson Express
(800) I-GO-HOJO,(906) 863-4431
http://www.hojo.com
2561 - 10th St.
50 rooms - $39-80
Pets: Welcome
Creature Comforts: CCTV, a/c, kit, cont. brkfst, whirlpool, sauna, whirlpool, pool

MIDLAND
Fairview Inn
(800) 422-2744, (517) 631-0070
www.fairviewinnmidland.com
2200 W. Wackerly St.
102 rooms - $55-74
Pets: Welcome w/$25 dep.
Creature Comforts: CCTV, VCR, a/c, refrig, cont. brkfst, hlth club, pool

Holiday Inn
(800) HOLIDAY, (517) 631-4220
http://www.holiday-inn.com
1500 W. Wackerly
234 rooms - $85-169
Pets: Welcome in smoking rooms
Creature Comforts: CCTV, VCR, a/c, refrig, micro, Jacuzzis, restaurant, hlth club, sauna, whirlpool, pool

Plaza Suites Hotel
(517) 496-0100
5217 Bay City Rd.
75 rooms - $89-170
Pets: Small pets welcome
Creature Comforts: CCTV, VCR, a/c, refrig

Ramada Inn
(800) 2-Ramada, (517) 631-0570
http://www.ramada.com
1815 S. Saginaw Rd.
82 rooms - $50-129
Pets: Welcome w/$25 dep.
Creature Comforts: CCTV, VCR, a/c, kit, Jacuzzis, restaurant, cont. brkfst, hlth club, pool

Sleep Inn
(800) Sleep-Inn, (517) 837-1010
http://www.sleepinn.com
2100 W. Wackerly St.
80 rooms - $56-80
Pets: Small pets welcome
Creature Comforts: CCTV, a/c, Jacuzzi, cont. brkfst, pool

MILAN
Star Motel
(734) 439-2448
335 E. Lewis Ave.
13 rooms - $38-55
Pets: Welcome
Creature Comforts: TV

MILFORD
Huron Valley Motel
(810) 685-1020
640 N. Milford Rd.
13 rooms - $39-50
Pets: Welcome
Creature Comforts: CCTV, a/c

MONROE
Comfort Inn
(800) 228-5150, (734) 384-9094
http://www.comfortinn.com
6500 E. Albain Rd.
65 rooms - $65-105
Pets: Small pets welcome
Creature Comforts: CCTV, a/c, cont. brkfst, whirlpool, pool

Econo Lodge
(800) 55-ECONO, (734) 289-4000
http://www.econolodge.com
1440 N. Dixie Hwy.
115 rooms - $44-115
Pets: Small pets welcome
Creature Comforts: CCTV, a/c, refrig, micro, cont. brkfst, restaurant, sauna, whirlpool, pool

Holiday Inn
(800) HOLIDAY, (734) 242-6000
http://www.holiday-inn.com
1225 N. Dixie Hwy.
126 rooms - $75-139
Pets: Small pets welcome
Creature Comforts: CCTV, a/c, refrig, restaurant, pool

Hometown Inn
(734) 289-1080
1885 Welcome Way
89 rooms - $38-99
Pets: Welcome
Creature Comforts: CCTV, VCR, a/c, kit, Jacuzzis

MT. PLEASANT
Comfort Inn
(800) 228-5150, (517) 772-4000
http://www.comfortinn.com
2424 S. Mission St.
138 rooms - $65-145
Pets: Small pets welcome
Creature Comforts: CCTV, a/c, Jacuzzis, cont. brkfst, pool

Holiday Inn
(800) HOLIDAY, (517) 772-2905
http://www.holiday-inn.com
5665 E. Piccard Ave.
185 rooms - $70-175
Pets: Small pets welcome
Creature Comforts: CCTV, a/c, kit, Jacuzzis, restaurant, sauna, whirlpool, hlth club, pool, rec. dome

MUNISING
Alger Falls Motel
(906) 387-3536
9427 Route 28
16 rooms - $40-75
Pets: Small pets welcome
Creature Comforts: CCTV, a/c, refrig, micro

Best Western Inn
(800) 528-1234, (906) 387-4864
http://www.bestwestern.com
Rte 28, Box 310
80 rooms - $60-115
Pets: Welcome
Creature Comforts: CCTV, a/c, refrig, micro, cont. brkfst, whirlpool, sauna, pool

Comfort Inn
(800) 228-5150, (906) 387-5292
http://www.comfortinn.com
Route 28
61 rooms - $58-105
Pets: Small pets welcome
Creature Comforts: CCTV, a/c, Jacuzzis, cont. brkfst, pool

Star Lite Motel
(906) 387-2291
500 Rte 28
12 rooms - $38-45
Pets: Welcome
Creature Comforts: CCTV

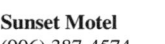

Sunset Motel
(906) 387-4574
1315 Bay St.
16 rooms - $39-65
Pets: Small pets w/$3 fee
Creature Comforts: CCTV, kit, on a lake

Yule Log Resort
(906) 387-3184
122 W. Chocobay
9 cottages - $43-85
Pets: Welcome
Creature Comforts: CCTV, kit, lake/beach

MUSKEGON
Bel Aire Motel
(616) 733-2196
4240 Airline Rd.
16 rooms - $44-78
Pets: Welcome w/$50 dep.
Creature Comforts: CCTV

Quality Inn
(800) 228-5151, (616) 739-9429
http://www.qualityinn.com
150 E. Seaway Dr.
135 rooms - $45-105
Pets: Small pets welcome
Creature Comforts: CCTV, a/c, Jacuzzis, restaurant, pool

Super 8 Motel
(800) 800-8000, (616) 733-0088
http://www.super8.com
3380 Hoyt St.
62 rooms - $45-69
Pets: Welcome
Creature Comforts: CCTV, a/c, refrig, micro, cont. brkfst

NEGAUNEE
Quartz Mt. Inn
(906) 475-7165
791 Rte 41
26 rooms - $33-45
Pets: Welcome
Creature Comforts: CCTV, a/c, kit, cont. brkfst

NEW BALTIMORE
Lodgekeeper Inn
(800) 282-5711, (810) 949-4520
29101 - 23-Mile Rd.
40 rooms - $44-85
Pets: Welcome w/$6 fee
Creature Comforts: CCTV, a/c, kit

NEWBERRY
Gateway Motel
(906) 293-5651
Rte 4, Box 980
11 rooms - $35-58
Pets: Welcome
Creature Comforts: CCTV

Park-A-Way Motel
(906) 293-5771
Rte 4, Box 966
24 rooms - $35-66
Pets: Welcome
Creature Comforts: CCTV, a/c, kit, pool

Rainbow Lodge
(906) 658-3357
Country Rte 423
10 cottages - $35-80
Pets: Welcome
Creature Comforts: CCTV, a/c, kit, restaurant, river/boats

NEW BUFFALO
Comfort Inn
(800) 228-5150, (616) 469-4440
http://www.comfortinn.com
11539 O'Brien Ct.
96 rooms - $50-119
Pets: Small pets welcome
Creature Comforts: CCTV, a/c, refrig, micro, Jacuzzis, cont. brkfst, hlth club, pool

Edgewood Motel
(616) 469-3345
18716 Laporte Rd.
21 rooms - $39-48
Pets: Welcome
Creature Comforts: Playground

Grand Beach Motel
(616) 469-1555
19189 Rte. 12
14 rooms - $30-80
Pets: Welcome w/$5 fee
Creature Comforts: CCTV, a/c, refrig, pool

Sans Souci Inn
(616) 756-3141
http://www.sans-souci.com
19265 S. Lakeside Dr.
9 units - $110-200
Pets: Small pets are selectively welcomed
Creature Comforts: A quiet B&B w/attractive rooms, cottages nestled on 50-acres along Lake Michigan, CCTV, VCR, a/c, gourmet kit, Jacuzzis, fireplaces, cont. brkfst, lawn sports, hiking, lake/beach

NILES
Ramada Inn
(800) 2-Ramada, (616) 684-3000
http://www.ramada.com
930 S. 11th St.
129 rooms - $70-125
Pets: Welcome
Creature Comforts: CCTV, a/c, kit, restaurant, pool

NOVI
Fairlane Motel
(248) 445-8667
45700 Grand River Rd.
7 rooms - $33-47
Pets: Welcome
Creature Comforts: CCTV

ONTONAGON
Best Western Porcupine Mtn.
(800) 528-1234, (906) 885-5311
http://www.bestwestern.com
120 Lincoln St.
71 rooms - $69-125
Pets: Small pets welcome
Creature Comforts: CCTV, VCR, a/c, refrig, restaurant, cont. brkfst, pool

Royal Motel
(906) 885-5348
2900 Rte 64
18 rooms - $45-269
Pets: Welcome w/$5 fee, $25 dep.
Creature Comforts: CCTV, a/c, kit, Jacuzzis, restaurant, cont. brkfst, lake/beach/boating

Scott's Superior Inn
(906) 884-4866
277 Lakeshore Dr.
14 rooms - $43-67
Pets: Welcome w/$5 fee
Creature Comforts: CCTV, a/c, kit, sauna, whirlpool, beach

Sunshine Motel
(906) 884-2187
1442 Rte 64
22 cottages - $30-80
Pets: Welcome
Creature Comforts: CCTV, a/c,
kit, cont. brkfst, river/beach/
boating

Superior Shores Resort
(906) 884-2653
1823 Rte 64
10 cottages - $40-125
Pets: Welcome
Creature Comforts: CCTV, a/c,
kit, lake/beach/boating

OSCODA
Anchorage Cottages Resort
(517) 739-7843
3164 Rte 23
6 cottages - $49-99
Pets: Welcome
Creature Comforts: CCTV, a/c,
kit, lake/beach

Aspen Motor Inn
(800) 89-ASPEN, (517) 739-9152
115 N. Lake St.
22 rooms - $33-55
Pets: Welcome
Creature Comforts: CCTV, a/c

Blue Horizon Court
(800) 524-5201, (517) 739-8487
4208 Rte. 23
16 cottages - $35-60
Pets: Welcome
Creature Comforts: CCTV, a/c,
kit, whirlpool, lake/beach/boating

Cedar Lane Resort
(517) 739-9988
7404 N. Rte 23
12 cottages - $32-75
Pets: Welcome
Creature Comforts: CCTV, a/c,
kit, lake/beach/boating

Rainbow Resort
(517) 739-5695
5764 N. Rte 23
7 cottages - $40-65
Pets: Welcome
Creature Comforts: CCTV, a/c,
kit, lake/beach/boating

Redwood Motor Lodge
(517) 739-2021
3111 N. Rte 23
46 cottages - $55-130
Pets: Welcome
Creature Comforts: CCTV, a/c,
Jacuzzis, kit, pool, sauna,
whirlpool, lake/beach/boating

Surfside Condominiums
(800) 278-5060, (517) 739-5363
www.fishandgame.com/surfside
6504 N. Route 23
35 rooms - $55-169
Pets: Welcome in one unit
Creature Comforts: CCTV, a/c,
fireplaces, kit, Jacuzzis, lake/
beach

OWOSSO
Owosso Motor Lodge
(517) 725-7148
2247 E. Main St.
24 rooms - $35-55
Pets: Welcome
Creature Comforts: CCTV, a/c,
kit

PARADISE
Curley's Motel
(800) 2-For-Fun, (906) 492-3445
web site pending
Rte 123
30 rooms - $40-70
Pets: Welcome
Creature Comforts: CCTV, a/c,
fireplaces, kit, hlth clb, lake/beach/
boating

PAW PAW
Quality Inn
(800) 228-5151, (616) 655-0303
http://www.qualityinn.com
Ampey Blvd.
49 rooms - $55-119
Pets: Small pets welcome
Creature Comforts: CCTV, a/c,
fireplace, cont. brkfst, pool

PERRY
Heb's Inn
(517) 625-7500
2811 Lansing Rd.
14 rooms - $44-59
Pets: Welcome w/$5 fee
Creature Comforts: CCTV, a/c

PETOSKEY
Coach House Motel
(616) 347-2593
2445 Charlevoix Ave.
16 rooms - $55-79
Pets: Small pets welcome
Creature Comforts: CCTV, a/c,
pool

Comfort Inn
(800) 228-5150, (616) 347-3220
http://www.comfortinn.com
1314 Rte 31
64 rooms - $50-200
Pets: Small pets welcome
Creature Comforts: CCTV, a/c,
kit, Jacuzzis, cont. brkfst

Days Inn
(800) DAYS-INN, (616) 347-8717
http://www.daysinn.com
630 W. Mitchell
94 rooms - $45-135
Pets: Welcome w/$10 fee
Creature Comforts: CCTV, a/c,
Jacuzzis, restaurant, cont. brkfst,
whirlpool, pool

Econo Lodge
(800) 55-ECONO, (616) 348-3323
http://www.econolodge.com
1858 Rte 131
59 rooms - $45-120
Pets: Small pets welcome
Creature Comforts: CCTV, a/c,
cont. brkfst, whirlpool, pool

PINCONNING
Trail House Motel
(517) 879-4219
201 S. Rte 13
22 rooms - $38-80
Pets: Welcome
Creature Comforts: CCTV, a/c,
fireplaces, restaurant, beach

PLAINWELL
Comfort Inn
(800) 228-5150, (616) 685-9891
http://www.comfortinn.com
622 Allegan St.
65 rooms - $65-125
Pets: Small pets welcome
Creature Comforts: CCTV, a/c,
Jacuzzis, cont. brkfst, pool

PLYMOUTH
Red Roof Inn
(800) The-Roof, (734) 459-3300
http://www.redroof.com
39700 Ann Arbor Rd.
108 rooms - $46-75
Pets: Small pets welcome
Creature Comforts: CCTV, a/c

PORT AUSTIN
Lakeside Motor Lodge
(517) 738-5201
PO Box 358
30 rooms - $39-65
Pets: Welcome
Creature Comforts: CCTV, a/c,
kit, pool, lake/boating

PORT HURON
Days Inn
(800) DAYS-INN, (810) 984-1522
http://www.daysinn.com
2908 Pine Grove
104 rooms - $45-140
Pets: Welcome w/$5 fee
Creature Comforts: CCTV, a/c,
Jacuzzis, kit, cont. brkfst, pool,
whirlpool, tennis

Knights Inn
(800) 843-5644, (810) 982-1022
http://www.knightsinn.com
2160 Water St.
89 rooms - $49-75
Pets: Small pets welcome
Creature Comforts: CCTV, a/c,
Jacuzzis, refrig, cont. brkfst, pool

Main Street Lodge
(810) 984-3166
514 Huron Ave.
40 rooms - $44-220
Pets: Welcome w/$5 fee
Creature Comforts: CCTV, a/c,
Jacuzzi

PORTLAND
Best Western Heritage
(800) 528-1234, (517) 647-2250
http://www.bestwestern.com
1681 Grand River Ave.
48 rooms - $59-225
Pets: Small pets welcome
Creature Comforts: CCTV,
VCR, a/c, refrig, micro, cont.
brkfst, whirlpool, hlth club, pool

POWERS
Candle Lite Motel
(906) 497-5413
PO Box 195
17 rooms - $28-35
Pets: Welcome
Creature Comforts: CCTV, a/c

REDFORD
Coach & Lantern Motel
(313) 533-4020
25255 Grand River Ave.
65 rooms - $34-50
Pets: Welcome
Creature Comforts: CCTV, a/c,
kit, pool

Dorchester Motel
(313) 533-8400
26825 Grand River Ave.
34 rooms - $39-80
Pets: Welcome
Creature Comforts: CCTV, a/c,
kit, Jacuzzis, whirlpool

ROCHESTER HILLS
Red Roof Inn
(800) The-Roof, (248) 853-6400
http://www.redroof.com
2580 Crooks Rd.
112 rooms - $52-89
Pets: Small pets welcome
Creature Comforts: CCTV, a/c

ROMULUS
Baymont Inns
(877)BAYMONT, (734) 722-6000
http://www.baymontinns.com
9000 Wickham Rd.
102 rooms - $52-79
Pets: Small pets welcome
Creature Comforts: CCTV, a/c,
refrig, cont. brkfst

Crowne Plaza Inn
(800) HOLIDAY, (734) 729-2600
http://www.holiday-inn.com
8000 Meriman Rd.
365 rooms - $129-199
Pets: Small crated pets welcome
Creature Comforts: CCTV,
VCR, a/c, refrig, restaurant, hlth
club, sauna, pool, whirlpool

Days Inn, Airport
(800) DAYS-INN, (734) 946-4300
http://www.daysinn.com
9501 Middlebelt Rd.
127 rooms - $69-135
Pets: Welcome w/$25 dep.
Creature Comforts: CCTV, a/c,
Jacuzzis, restaurant, hlth club,
pool

Howard Johnson Inn
(800) I-Go-Hojo, (734) 946-1400
http://www.hojo.com
9501 Middlebelt Rd.
122 rooms - $65-119
Pets: Welcome w/$10 fee
Creature Comforts: CCTV, a/c,
Jacuzzis, refrig, micro, cont.
brkfst, hlth club

Marriott Hotel
(800) 228-9290, (734) 729-7555
http://www.marriott.com
30559 Flynn Dr.
152 rooms - $65-199
Pets: Welcome w/$50 fee
Creature Comforts: CCTV, a/c,
refrig, restaurant, pool

ROSEVILLE
Baymont Inns
(877)BAYMONT, (810) 296-6910
http://www.baymontinns.com
20675 - 13 Mile Rd.
101 rooms - $48-79
Pets: Small pets welcome.
Creature Comforts: CCTV, a/c,
refrig, cont. brkfst

Georgian Inn
(800) 477-1466, (810) 294-0400
31327 Gratiot Ave.
110 rooms - $69-149
Pets: Welcome
Creature Comforts: CCTV, a/c,
kit, Jacuzzis, restaurant, pool, hlth
club

SAGINAW
Best Western Inn
(800) 528-1234, (517) 793-2080
http://www.bestwestern.com
325 Davenport Ave.
113 rooms - $54-79
Pets: Welcome
Creature Comforts: CCTV, a/c,
refrig, restaurant, cont. brkfst, pool

Four Points Hotel
(800) 325-3535, (517) 790-5050
http://www.sheraton.com
4960 Towne Centre Rd.
155 rooms - $79-120
Pets: Small pets welcome
Creature Comforts: CCTV,
VCR, a/c, refrig, restaurant, pool,
hlth club, pool

Holiday Inn
(800) HOLIDAY, (517) 755-0461
http://www.holiday-inn.com
1408 S. Outer Dr.
159 rooms - $75-129
Pets: Welcome
Creature Comforts: CCTV, a/c,
refrig, restaurant, hlth club, sauna,
whirlpool, raquetball court, pool

Knights Inn, South
(800) 843-5644, (517) 754-9200
http://www.knightsinn.com
1415 S. Outer Dr.
109 rooms - $45-80
Pets: Small pets welcome
Creature Comforts: CCTV,
VCR, a/c, Jacuzzis, kit, cont.
brkfst, pool

Quality Inn
(800) 228-5151, (517) 753-2461
http://www.qualityinn.com
3425 Holland Ave.
95 rooms - $55-116
Pets: Small pets welcome
Creature Comforts: CCTV, a/c,
cont. brkfst, whirlpool, pool

Red Roof Inn
(800) The-Roof, (517) 754-8414
http://www.redroof.com
966 S. Outer Dr.
80 rooms - $38-72
Pets: Small pets welcome
Creature Comforts: CCTV, a/c

Super 8 Motel
(800) 800-8000, (517) 791-3003
http://www.super8.com
4848 Towne Centre Rd.
62 rooms - $45-66
Pets: Welcome
Creature Comforts: CCTV, a/c,
refrig, micro

ST. IGNACE
Bay View Motel
(906) 643-9444
1133 N. State St.
20 rooms - $32-69
Pets: Welcome w/$5 fee
Creature Comforts: CCTV, a/c

Budget Host
(800) Bud-Host, (906) 643-9666
http://www.budgethost.com
700 N. State St.
59 rooms - $48-185
Pets: Small pets w/$20 dep.
Creature Comforts: CCTV, a/c,
refrig, micro, Jacuzzis, cont.
brkfst, whirlpool, pool

Driftwood Motel
(906) 643-7744
590 N. State St.
20 rooms - $34-58
Pets: Welcome w/$5 fee
Creature Comforts: CCTV, a/c,
restaurant

Howard Johnson Express
(800) I-Go-Hojo, (906) 643-9700
http://www.hojo.com
913 Blvd. Dr.
57 rooms - $54-125
Pets: Welcome
Creature Comforts: CCTV, a/c,
Jacuzzis, cont. brkfst, sauna, pool

Rodeway Inn
(800) 228-2000, (906) 643-8511
http://www.rodeway.com
750 Rte 2
42 rooms - $45-139
Pets: Welcome
Creature Comforts: CCTV, a/c,
Jacuzzis, cont. brkfst, pool

ST. JOSEPH
Best Western Golden Link
(800) 528-1234, (616) 983-6321
http://www.bestwestern.com
2723 Niles Ave.
36 rooms - $35-69
Pets: Small pets welcome
Creature Comforts: CCTV, a/c,
kit, Jacuzzis, cont. brkfst, pool

SANDUSKY
Thumb Heritage Inn
(810) 648-4811
405 W. Sanilac Rd.
22 rooms - $39-79
Pets: Welcome
Creature Comforts: CCTV, Jac.

SAUGATUCK
Douglas Dunes Resort
(616) 857-1401
333 Blue Star Hwy.
30 rooms - $65-120
Pets: Welcome
Creature Comforts: CCTV, a/c,
restaurant, pool

Pines Motel
(616) 857-5211
56 S. Blue Star Hwy.
12 rooms - $32-105
Pets: Welcome
Creature Comforts: CCTV

Sherwood Forest B & B
(800) 838-1246, (616) 857-1246
www.sherwoodforestbandb.com
938 Center Street - P.O. Box 315
5 rooms - $85-165
Pets: Selectively welcomed if
small, well mannered, & groomed
Creature Comforts: A neat old
1890s Victorian cottage with a
wrap-around porch, Jacuzzi, pool
w/dolphin mural, Oriental rugs,
antiques, fireplace, breakfasts &
dinners, CCTV, VCR

Ship-n-Shore
(616) 857-2194
528 Water St.
40 rooms - $75-120
Pets: Welcome
Creature Comforts: CCTV, a/c,
pool, whirlpool, lake/river/boating

SAULT ST. MARIE
Admirals Inn
(906) 632-1130
2701 Rte 75
19 rooms - $35-55
Pets: Welcome
Creature Comforts: CCTV, a/c

Bavarian Motor Lodge
(906) 632-6864
2006 Ashmun St.
110 rooms - $54-160
Pets: Welcome w/$10 fee
Creature Comforts: CCTV, a/c,
kit

Biltmore Motel
(906) 632-2119
331 E. Portage Rd.
14 rooms - $38-59
Pets: Welcome
Creature Comforts: CCTV, a/c,
refrig, micro

Crestview Thrifty Inns
(906) 635-5213
1200 Ashmun St.
44 rooms - $42-70
Pets: Welcome in smkng rms
Creature Comforts: CCTV, a/c,
refrig, cont. brkfst

Grand Motel
(906) 632-2141
1100 E. Portage
20 rooms - $28-70
Pets: Welcome
Creature Comforts: CCTV, a/c,
kit, pool, along a river/beach

Imperial Motor Inn
(800) 859-9898, (906) 632-7334
2215 Ashmun St.
14 rooms - $35-64
Pets: Small pets welcome
Creature Comforts: CCTV, a/c,
refrig, micro, cont. brkfst

King's Inn Motel
(906) 635-5061
3755 Rte 75
16 rooms - $32-65
Pets: Welcome
Creature Comforts: CCTV, a/c,
playground

Royal Motel
(906) 632-6323
1707 Ashmun St.
22 rooms - $35-70
Pets: Small pets welcome
Creature Comforts: CCTV, a/c,
playground

Seaway Motel
(800) 782-0466, (906) 632-8201
1800 Ashmun St.
20 rooms - $65-79
Pets: Welcome w/$5 fee
Creature Comforts: CCTV, a/c,
cont. brkfst

Super 8 Motel
(800) 800-8000, (906) 632-8882
http://www.super8.com
3826 Rte 75
61 rooms - $45-75
Pets: Welcome
Creature Comforts: CCTV, a/c,
cont. brkfst

SENEY
Country Inn
(906) 499-3376
307 Route 28
11 rooms - $33-44
Pets: Welcome
Creature Comforts: CCTV, a/c,
restaurant

SMYRNA
Double R Ranch Resort
(616) 794-0520
http://www.doublerranch.com
4424 Whites Bridge Rd.
6 rooms - $38-55
Pets: Leashed pets welcome
Creature Comforts: CCTV, a/c,
fireplace, restaurant

SOMERSET
Motel Somerset
(517) 547-7241
13980 E. Chicago Rd.
14 rooms - $32-69
Pets: Welcome
Creature Comforts: CCTV, a/c

SOUTHFIELD
Econo Lodge
(800) 55-ECONO, (248) 358-1800
http://www.econolodge.com
23300 Telegraph Rd.
66 rooms - $58-89
Pets: Small pets w/credit card dep
Creature Comforts: CCTV, a/c,
refrig, micro, Jacuzzis, cont.
brkfst, pool

Hilton Garden Inn
(800) HILTONS, (248) 357-1100
http://www.hilton.com
26000 American Dr.
198 rooms - $95-199
Pets: Welcome
Creature Comforts: CCTV, a/c,
refrig, restaurant, hlth club,
whirlpool, sauna, pool

Holiday Inn
(800) HOLIDAY, (248) 353-7700
http://www.holiday-inn.com
26555 Telegraph Rd.
416 rooms - $79-259
Pets: Welcome in smoking rooms
Creature Comforts: CCTV, a/c,
refrig, restaurant, hlth club,
whirlpool, pool

Marriott Hotel
(800) 228-9290, (248) 729-7555
http://www.marriott.com
27033 Northwestern Hwy.
222 rooms - $85-209
Pets: Under 20 lbs. welcome
Creature Comforts: CCTV, a/c,
refrig, restaurant, hlth club, pool

Ramada Inn
(800) 2-Ramada, (248) 552-7777
http://www.ramada.com
17017 W. 9-Mile Rd.
252 rooms - $99-189
Pets: Welcome
Creature Comforts: CCTV, a/c,
refrig, restaurant, pool

Red Roof Inn
(800) The-Roof, (248) 353-7200
http://www.redroof.com
27660 Northwestern Hwy.
114 rooms - $59-85
Pets: Small pets welcome
Creature Comforts: CCTV, a/c

Residence Inn
(800) 228-9290, (248) 352-8900
http://www.residenceinn.com
26700 Central Park Blvd.
145 rooms - $99-199
Pets: Welcome w/ a $7 daily fee,
$100 one-time fee
Creature Comforts: CCTV, a/c,
kit, restaurant, pool

SOUTHGATE
Baymont Inns
(877)BAYMONT, (313) 374-3000
http://www.baymontinns.com
12888 Reeck Rd.
101 rooms - $45-85
Pets: Small pets welcome
Creature Comforts: CCTV, a/c,
cont. brkfst

SOUTH HAVEN
Econo Lodge
(800) 55-ECONO, (616) 637-5141
http://www.econolodge.com
09817 Route 140
60 rooms - $45-120
Pets: Small pets welcome
Creature Comforts: CCTV, a/c,
kit, Jacuzzis, restaurant, cont.
brkfst, hlth club, sauna, pool

STANDISH
Standish Motel
(517) 846-9571
Rtes 23 & 76
16 rooms - $35-55
Pets: Welcome
Creature Comforts: CCTV, a/c

STERLING HEIGHTS
Knights Inn
(800) 843-5644, (810) 268-0600
http://www.knightsinn.com
7887 - 17-mile Rd.
102 rooms - $49-85
Pets: Small pets welcome
Creature Comforts: CCTV,
VCR, a/c, Jacuzzis, kit, cont.
brkfst

STEVENSVILLE
Baymont Inns
(877)BAYMONT, (616) 428-9111
http://www.baymontinns.com
2601 W. Marquette Woods Rd.
103 rooms - $55-90
Pets: Under 50 lbs. in smkng rms
Creature Comforts: CCTV, a/c,
cont. brkfst

Hampton Inn
(800) Hampton, (616) 429-2700
http://www.hampton-inn.com
5050 Red Arrow Hwy.
77 rooms - $75-89
Pets: Welcome w/$50 dep.
Creature Comforts: CCTV, a/c,
Jacuzzis, cont. brkfst, pool

Park Inn International
(800) 228-5885, (616) 429-3218
http://www.qtm.net/~parkinn
4290 Red Arrow Hwy.
90 rooms - $45-129
Pets: Welcome
Creature Comforts: CCTV, a/c,
kit, Jacuzzis, restaurant, pool, hlth
clb, sauna, whirlpool

STURGIS
Comfort Inn
(800) 228-5150, (616) 651-7881
http://www.comfortinn.com
1300 S. Centerville Rd.
83 rooms - $60-119
Pets: Small pets welcome
Creature Comforts: CCTV, a/c,
cont. brkfst, pool

TAWAS CITY
North Star Motel
(517) 362-2255
1119 S. Rte 23
19 rooms - $40-75
Pets: Welcome
Creature Comforts: CCTV, a/c,
kit, cont. brkfst, pool

Tawas Motel
(517) 362-3822
1124 Rte 23
22 rooms - $45-79
Pets: Welcome
Creature Comforts: CCTV, a/c,
refrig, micro, Jacuzzis, cont.
brkfst, pool, sauna, whirlpool

TAYLOR
Hoffman's Colonial House
(734) 291-3000
10780 S. Telegraph Rd.
50 rooms - $30-49
Pets: Welcome
Creature Comforts: CCTV, a/c,
restaurant, pool, sauna

Red Roof Inn
(800) The-Roof, (734) 374-1150
http://www.redroof.com
21230 Eureka Rd.
112 rooms - $49-75
Pets: Small pets welcome
Creature Comforts: CCTV, a/c

Super 8 Motel
(800) 800-8000, (734) 283-8830
http://www.super8.com
15101 Huron St.
63 rooms - $49-75
Pets: Welcome
Creature Comforts: CCTV, a/c,
refrig, micro, cont. brkfst

TECUMSEH
Stacy Mansion
(800) 891-8782, (512) 423-6979
http://www.lenawee.net/stacybnb
710 W. Chicago Blvd.
5 rooms - $85-135
Pets: Small w/$10 fee
Creature Comforts: A lovely
1850s Victorian mansion,
antiques-beds (super soft cotton
sheets), reproduction wallpapers,
Oriental carpets, CCTV, a/c,
refrig, fireplace, formal gardens,
gourmet brkfst, grand piano,
library, and music room

Tecumseh Inn
(517) 423-7401
1445 W. Chicago Blvd.
61 rooms - $42-99
Pets: Welcome
Creature Comforts: CCTV, a/c,
Jacuzzis, refrig, bar

THREE RIVERS
Greystone Motel
(616) 278-1695
59271 Rte 131, Box 62
48 rooms - $34-79
Pets: Welcome
Creature Comforts: CCTV, a/c,
cont. brkfst, pool, sauna, whirlpool

Three Rivers Inn
(616) 273-9521
1220 W. Broadway St.
98 rooms - $49-85
Pets: Welcome w/$5 fee
Creature Comforts: CCTV, a/c,
Jacuzzi, restaurant, pool

TRAVERSE CITY
Comfort Inn
(800) 228-5150, (616) 929-4423
http://www.comfortinn.com
96 rooms - $45-149
Pets: Small pets welcome
Creature Comforts: CCTV,
VCR, a/c, Jacuzzis, restaurant,
cont. brkfst, whirlpool, pool

Economy Inn
(616) 938-2080
1582 Route 31
25 rooms - $39-119
Pets: Welcome w/$6 fee
Creature Comforts: CCTV, a/c,
Jacuzzi

Fox Haus Motor Lodge
(616) 947-4450
704 Munson Rd.
80 rooms - $35-185
Pets: Welcome
Creature Comforts: CCTV, a/c,
kit, Jacuzzis, cont. brkfst, pool,
hlth clb, sauna, whirlpool, tennis

Holiday Inn
(800) HOLIDAY, (616) 947-3700
http://www.holiday-inn.com
615 E. Front St.
180 rooms - $85-185
Pets: Welcome
Creature Comforts: CCTV, a/c,
refrig, restaurant, sauna, pool, hlth
club

Main Street Inns
(800) 255-7180, (616) 929-0410
http://www.mainstreetinnsusa.com
618 E. Main St.
93 rooms - $35-199
Pets: Welcome in somking rooms
Creature Comforts: CCTV,
a/c,VCR, kit, Jacuzzis, pool, sauna

Traverse Bay Inn
(800) 968-2646, (616) 938-2646
http://www.traversebayinn.com
2300 Rte 31
25 rooms - $59-179
Pets: Welcome w/$10 fee
Creature Comforts: CCTV,
VCR, a/c, refrig, cont. brkfst,
pool, whirlpool

TROUT LAKE
McGowan Family Motel
(906) 569-3366
Route 123
10 rooms - $43-55
Pets: Small pets welcome
Creature Comforts: CCTV, kit,
restaurant

TROY
Drury Inn
(800) Drury Inn, (248) 528-3330
http://www.drury-inn.com
575 W. Big Beaver Rd.
152 rooms - $79-97
Pets: Welcome
Creature Comforts: CCTV, a/c,
refrig, cont. brkfst, pool

Hilton Hotel
(800) HILTONS, (248) 879-2100
http://www.hilton.com
5500 Crooks Rd.
192 rooms - $89-399
Pets: Welcome w/$25 fee
Creature Comforts: CCTV, a/c,
refrig, restaurant, hlth club, sauna,
pool

Holiday Inn
(800) HOLIDAY, (248) 689-7500
http://www.holiday-inn.com
2537 Rochester Ct.
154 rooms - $55-129
Pets: Welcome
Creature Comforts: CCTV, a/c,
refrig, restaurant, pool, hlth club
access

Red Roof Inn
(800) The-Roof, (248) 689-4391
http://www.redroof.com
2350 Rochester Ct.
108 rooms - $59-95
Pets: Small pets welcome
Creature Comforts: CCTV, a/c

Residence Inn
(800) 331-3131, (248) 689-6856
http://www.residenceinn.com
2600 Livemois Rd.
153 rooms - $135-199
Pets: Welcome w/$7 daily fee,
$75 one-time fee
Creature Comforts: CCTV,
VCR, a/c, kit, cont. brkfst, hlth
club access, whirlpool, pool

UNION PIER
Sweethaven Resort
(616) 469-0332
http://www.sweethavenresort.com
9517 Union Pier Rd.
5 cottages - $135-185
Pets: Welcome
Creature Comforts: Artistic
decor w/handcrafted furnishings,
vaulted ceilings, CCTV, VCR, a/c,
fireplace, kit, stereos-CDs, refrig,
cont. brkfst, whirlpool, 6 acres of
woodlands

UTICA
Baymont Inns
(877)BAYMONT, (810) 731-4700
http://www.baymontinns.com
45311 Park Ave.
109 rooms - $55-90
Pets: Small pets welcome
Creature Comforts: CCTV, a/c,
Jacuzzis, cont. brkfst, pool

WAKEFIELD
Indianhead Mtn. Resort
(800) 3-INDIAN, (906) 229-5181
http://www.indianheadmtn.com
500 Indianhead Rd.
100 rooms - $55-179
Pets: In ltd. rms w/$25 fee
Creature Comforts: Ranked as
one of the top five midwestern ski
resorts, Lodge on top of the mtn.,
CCTV, a/c, fireplaces, kit,
Jacuzzis, restaurant, pool, hlth clb,
sauna, whirlpool, tennis, golf,
sleigh rides, and tubing

WALKER
Motel 6
(800) 4-MOTEL6, (616) 784-9375
http://www.motel6.com
777 - 3 Mile Rd.
102 rooms - $38-52
Pets: Under 30 lbs. welcome
Creature Comforts: CCTV, a/c,
pool

WARREN
Baymont Inns
(877)BAYMONT, (810) 574-0550
http://www.baymontinns.com
30900 Van Dyke Rd.
101 rooms - $45-88
Pets: Small pets welcome
Creature Comforts: CCTV, a/c,
cont. brkfst

Homewood Suites
(800) 225-5466, (810) 558-7870
http://www.homewoodsuites.com
30180 N. Civic Cent. Blvd.
77 rooms - $95-129
Pets: Under 15 Lbs. w/$65 fee
Creature Comforts: CCTV,
VCR, a/c, kit, pool, hlth clb

Motel 6
(800) 4-MOTEL6, (810) 826-9300
http://www.motel6.com
8300 Chicago Rd.
117 rooms - $38-55
Pets: Under 30 lbs. welcome
Creature Comforts: CCTV, a/c

Quality Inn
(800) 228-5151, (810) 264-0100
http://www.qualityinn.com
32035 Van Dyke Ave.
198 rooms - $63-139
Pets: Welcome w/$50 fee
Creature Comforts: CCTV, a/c,
Jacuzzis, restaurant, pool, hlth
club, sport courts, lawn games

Red Roof Inn
(800) The-Roof, (810) 573-4300
http://www.redroof.com
26300 DeQuindre Rd.
136 rooms - $49-75
Pets: Small pets welcome
Creature Comforts: CCTV, a/c

Residence Inn
(800) 331-3131, (810) 558-8050
http://www.residenceinn.com
30120 Civic Center Blvd.
134 rooms - $119-199
Pets: Welcome w/$75 fee
Creature Comforts: CCTV,
VCR, a/c, kit, cont. brkfst, hlth
club access, pool

WATERS
Northland Inn
(517) 732-4470
web site pending
9311 Old Rte 27
17 rooms - $45-75
Pets: Welcome
Creature Comforts: CCTV, a/c,
refrig, cont. brkfst

WATERSMEET
Vacationland Resort
(906) 358-4380
http://www.westernup.com/
vacationland
19636 E. Hebert Rd.
9 cottages - $65-175
Pets: Welcome w/$25 fee
Creature Comforts: Charming
log cabins set along the Cisco
Chain of 15 lakes, CCTV, VCR,
a/c, fireplaces, kit, sauna, tennis,
basketball-volleyball, access to
golf, lake, beach, and water sports

WEST BRANCH
La Hacienda Motel
(517) 345-2345
969 W. Houghton Ave.
14 cottages - $39-72
Pets: Welcome
Creature Comforts: CCTV, a/c,
kit

Super 8 Motel
(800) 800-8000, (517) 345-8488
http://www.super8.com
2596 Austin Way
41 rooms - $49-75
Pets: Welcome
Creature Comforts: CCTV, a/c,
cont. brkfst

Tri-Terrace Motel
(517) 345-3121
2259 Rte 75 Bus.
45 rooms - $42-65
Pets: Welcome
Creature Comforts: CCTV, a/c,
pool

Welcome Motel
(517) 345-2896
3308 W. Rte 76
13 rooms - $32-59
Pets: Welcome w/$ fee
Creature Comforts: CCTV, a/c,
kit

WHITE PIGEON
Plaza Motel
(616) 483-7285
7140 Route 131
18 rooms - $30-50
Pets: Welcome
Creature Comforts: CCTV, a/c

WHITMORE LAKE
The Lakes Motel
(313) 449-5991
8365 Main St.
7 rooms - $39-65
Pets: Welcome
Creature Comforts: CCTV, a/c,
kit, restaurant

WOODHAVEN
Knights Inn
(800) 843-5644, (313) 676-8550
http://www.knightsinn.com
21880 West Rd.
89 rooms - $43-65
Pets: Small pets w/$5 fee
Creature Comforts: CCTV,
VCR, a/c, kit, Jacuzzis, cont.
brkfst

WYOMING
Jim Williams Motel
(616) 241-5461
3821 S. Division Rd.
55 rooms - $32-55
Pets: Welcome
Creature Comforts: CCTV, a/c,
kit

YPSILANTI
Mayflower House Motel
(313) 434-2200
5610 Carpenter St.
20 rooms - $39-98
Pets: Welcome
Creature Comforts: CCTV, a/c,
Jacuzzis, restaurant, whirlpool

Minnesota

AITKIN
Edgewater Resort
(218) 927-2895
RR3, Box 890
7 cabins - $450-675
Pets: Welcome w/$5 fee
Creature Comforts: CCTV, kit,
restaurant, on lake

Forty Club Inn
(800) 682-8152, (218) 927-2903
950 Second St.
40 rooms - $45-79
Pets: Welcome w/$5 fee
Creature Comforts: CCTV,
VCR, Jacuzzis, cont. brkfst, sauna,
whirlpool

Ripple River Motel
(800) 258-3734, (218) 927-3734
701 Minnesota Ave.
29 rooms - $39-72
Pets: Small pets in ltd. rms
Creature Comforts: CCTV, a/c,
refrig, micro, Jacuzzis

ALBERT LEA
Bel Aire Motor Inn
(800) 373-4073, (507) 373-3893
700 Rte. 69
48 rooms - $34-54
Pets: Welcome
Creature Comforts: CCTV,
VCR, a/c, refrig, micro, pool

Best Western Albert Lea
(800) 528-1234, (507) 373-8291
http://www.bestwestern.com
811 E. Plaza St
124 rooms - $53-75
Pets: Welcome w/$5 fee
Creature Comforts: CCTV, a/c,
refrig, restaurant, sauna,
whirlpool, hlth club, pool

Budget Inn
(507) 373-1496
2210 E. Main St.
38 rooms - $30-60
Pets: Welcome
Creature Comforts: CCTV, a/c

Countryside Inn Motel
(800) 341-8000, (507) 373-2448
2102 E. Main St
50 rooms - $40-55
Pets: Welcome w/$3 fee
Creature Comforts: CCTV, cont.
brkfst

Days Inn
(800) DAYS-INN, (507) 373-6471
http://www.daysinn.com
2306 E. Main St
130 rooms - $59-85
Pets: Welcome w/$5 fee
Creature Comforts: CCTV, a/c,
restaurant, pool

Super 8 Motel
(800) 800-8000, (507) 377-0591
http://www.super8.com
2019 E. Main St
60 rooms - $40-63
Pets: Welcome
Creature Comforts: CCTV,
VCR, a/c, refrig, micro, cont.
brkfst

ALEXANDRIA
Country Inn Suites
(800) 456-4000, (320) 763-9900
http://www.countryinns.com
5304 Route 29 S.
64 rooms - $54-80
Pets: Small pets welcome
Creature Comforts: CCTV, a/c,
refrig, micro, Jacuzzis, pool,
sauna, whirlpool

L Motel
(320) 763-5121
910 Rte. 27 W.
16 rooms - $29-49
Pets: Welcome
Creature Comforts: CCTV, a/c,
refrig, cont. brkfst

Skyline Motel
(800) 467-4096, (320) 763-6552
605 - 30th Ave.
12 rooms - $35-55
Pets: Welcome
Creature Comforts: CCTV, a/c,
refrig

Super 8 Motel
(800) 800-8000, (320) 763-6552
http://www.super8.com
4620 Rte. 29 S.
57 rooms - $42-52
Pets: Welcome
Creature Comforts: CCTV, a/c,
cont. brkfst

ANNANDALE
Thayer Inn
(800) 944-6595, (612) 274-8222
http://www.thayers.net
60 Elm St.
11 rooms - $85-145
Pets: Welcome
Creature Comforts: Historic
1895 Victorian railroad house w/
reputed ghost, antiques, four
poster beds, CCTV, a/c, fireplace,
refrig, Jacuzzi, cont. brkfst, sauna,
whirlpool, clawfoot tubs, ghosts/
murder mysteries

ANOKA
Super 8 Motel
(800) 800-8000, (612) 422-8000
http://www.super8.com
1129 Rte. 10
56 rooms - $52-70
Pets: Welcome w/permission
Creature Comforts: CCTV, a/c,
refrig, micro, Jacuzzis, cont. brkfst

APPLETON
Super 8 Motel
(800) 800-8000, (320) 289-2500
http://www.super8.com
900 N. Munsterman Rd.
34 rooms - $42-56
Pets: Welcome
Creature Comforts: CCTV, a/c,
cont. brkfst

APPLE VALLEY
AmericInn Motel
(800) 634-3444, (612) 111-3800
http://www.americinn.com
15000 Glazier Ave.
64 rooms - $75-99
Pets: Small pets welcome
Creature Comforts: CCTV,
VCR, a/c, refrig, micro, Jacuzzis,
sauna, whirlpool, hlth club, pool

AUSTIN
Ausin Motel
(800) 433-9254, (507) 433-9254
805 - 21st St. NE
46 rooms - $25-45
Pets: Welcome w/$3 fee
Creature Comforts: CCTV, a/c,
refrig, micro

Days Inn
(800) DAYS-INN, (507) 433-8600
http://www.daysinn.com
700 - 16th Ave. NW
59 rooms - $49-73
Pets: Welcome
Creature Comforts: CCTV, a/c,
Jacuzzis, restaurant, cont. brkfst,
hlth club, pool

Holiday Inn
(800) HOLIDAY, (507) 433-1000
http://www.holiday-inn.com
1701- 4th St. NW
122 rooms - $65-169
Pets: Small pets welcome
Creature Comforts: CCTV, a/c,
refrig, micro, Jacuzzis, restaurant,
sauna, whirlpool, pool

Rodeway Inn
(800) 228-2000, (507) 437-7774
http://www.rodeway.com
3303 W. Oakland Ave.
55 rooms - $42-90
Pets: Welcome w/$25 dep.
Creature Comforts: CCTV, a/c,
cont. brkfst

Super 8 Motel
(800) 800-8000, (507) 433-1801
http://www.super8.com
1401 NW 14th St
34 rooms - $42-63
Pets: Welcome
Creature Comforts: CCTV, a/c,
cont. brkfst

AVON
AmericInn Motel
(800) 634-3444, (320) 356-2211
http://www.americinn.com
304 Blattner Dr.
28 rooms - $39-53
Pets: Welcome
Creature Comforts: CCTV,
VCR, a/c, fireplace

BABBITT
Timber Bay Lodge
(800) 846-6821, (218) 827-3682
http://www.timberbay.com
8347 Timber Bay Rd.
12 cabins - $675-1,455/week
Pets: Welcome w/$10 daily fee
Creature Comforts: Small resort
on Birch Lake w/knotty pine
cabins, modern houseboats geared
to families, comfy pine
furnishings, CCTV, kit, fireplaces,
lawn games, golf access, kids
programs, water slide, on lake/
sandy beach/marina/boating

BABAUDETTE
Sportsman's Lodge
(800) 862-8602, (218) 634-1342
www.sportsmanslodgelow.com
Rte. 1, Box 167
20 cabins - $50-185
Pets: Welcome in cabins
Creature Comforts: Terrific
lodge, many amenities, CCTV,
a/c, fireplace, kit, restaurants,
pool, whirlpool, on river

BAXTER
Twin Birch Motel
(218) 829-2833
2300 N. Fairview Rd.
15 rooms - $32-54
Pets: Welcome
**Creature Comfo · CCTV, a/c,
cont. brkfst

BECKER
Super 8 Motel
(800) 800-8000, (612) 261-4440
http://www.super8.com
13804 - 1st St.
32 rooms - $42-63
Pets: Welcome w/$10 dep.
Creature Comforts: CCTV, a/c,
refrig, micro, Jacuzzis, cont.
brkfst, whirlpool, sauna

BEMIDJI
Bel Air Motel
(218) 751-3222
1350 Paul Bunyan Dr. NW
22 rooms - $33-62
Pets: Welcome
Creature Comforts: CCTV, a/c,
refrig, micro

Best Western Inn
(800) 528-1234, (218) 751-0390
http://www.bestwestern.com
2420 Paul Bunyan Dr. NW
62 rooms - $45-85
Pets: Small pets welcome
Creature Comforts: CCTV, a/c,
refrig, Jacuzzis, cont. brkfst,
sauna, pool, whirlpool

Comfort Inn
(800) 228-5150, (218) 751-7700
http://www.comfortinn.com
3500 Comfort Dr.
61 rooms - $45-109
Pets: Small pets welcome
Creature Comforts: CCTV, a/c,
cont. brkfst, pool

Edgewater Motel
(218) 751-3600
1015 Paul Bunyan Dr. NE
72 rooms - $36-199
Pets: Small pets welcome
Creature Comforts: CCTV,
VCR, a/c, refrig, micro, sauna,
whirlpool, on lake/beach/boating

Holiday Inn Express
(800) HOLIDAY, (218) 751-2487
http://www.holiday-inn.com
2422 Ridgeway Ave. NW
70 rooms - $65-80
Pets: Small pets welcome
Creature Comforts: CCTV, a/c,
refrig, Jacuzzis, sauna, whirlpool,
hlth club, pool

Ruttger's Birchmont Lodge
(888) RUTTGER, (218) 751-1630
http://www.ruttger.com
530 Beachmont Beach Rd.
32 cabins - $38-179
Pets: In cabins w/$8 fee
Creature Comforts: Lakefront
cedar stone cottages, CCTV, a/c,
fireplaces, kit, Jacuzzis, restaurant,
pools, hlth clb, saunas, whirlpools,
lake/boating, tennis, skating, golf
access, hlth club, xc-skiing

BENSON
Motel 1
(320) 843-4434
620 Atlantic Ave.
8 rooms - $34-42
Pets: Welcome
Creature Comforts: CCTV, a/c, kit

Super 8 Motel
(800) 800-8000, (320) 843-3451
http://www.super8.com
600 - 22nd St. S.
21 rooms - $40-59
Pets: Welcome w/$3 fee
Creature Comforts: CCTV, a/c, cont. brkfst, sauna, hlth club

BIG FORK
Travelodge
(800) 578-7878, (218) 743-4700
http://www.travelodge.com
Rtes 38 & 77
38 rooms - $49-129
Pets: Small pets welcome
Creature Comforts: CCTV, a/c, Jacuzzis, cont. brkfst, pool

BLACK DUCK
AmericInn Motel
(800) 634-3444, (218) 835-4500
http://www.americinn.com
Rte. 71
25 rooms - $45-94
Pets: Welcome
Creature Comforts: CCTV, a/c, refrig, micro, cont. brkfst, Jacuzzi, pool, sauna, hlth club, whirlpool

Drake Motel
(218) 835-4567
305 N. Pine St.
12 rooms - $44-85
Pets: Small pets welcome
Creature Comforts: CCTV, a/c

BLOOMINGTON
Best Western Thunderbird
(800) 528-1234, (612) 854-3411
http://www.bestwestern.com
2201 E. 78th St.
263 rooms - $95-189
Pets: Small pets in smkng rms
Creature Comforts: CCTV, a/c, refrig, Jacuzzis, cont. brkfst, sauna, pools, hlth club, whirlpool

Best Western Seville Plaza
(800) 528-1234, (612) 830-1300
http://www.bestwestern.com
8151 Bridge Rd.
254 rooms - $69-99
Pets: Welcome
Creature Comforts: CCTV, a/c, refrig, Jacuzzis, restaurant, cont. brkfst, sauna, pool, whirlpool

Baymont Inns, Airport
(877)BAYMONT, (612) 881-7311
http://www.baymontinns.com
7815 Nicolet Ave.
189 rooms - $58-75
Pets: Welcome in smoking rooms
Creature Comforts: CCTV, a/c, refrig, micro, cont. brkfst

Comfort Inn, Airport
(800) 228-5150, (612) 854-3400
http://www.comfortinn.com
1321 E. 78th St.
276 rooms - $75-119
Pets: Small pets welcome
Creature Comforts: CCTV, a/c, restaurant, hlth club, pool

Exel Inns
(800) 367-3935, (612) 854-7200
2701 E. 78th St.
205 rooms - $40-57
Pets: Small pets in ltd. rms
Creature Comforts: CCTV, VCR, a/c, refrig, micro, Jacuzzis, cont. brkfst.

Hotel Sofitel
(800) 876-6303, (612) 835-1900
http://www.sofitel.com
5601 W. 78th St.
284 rooms - $135-399
Pets: Under 20 lbs. welcome
Creature Comforts: CCTV, VCR, a/c, refrig, Jacuzzis, restaurant, pool, hlth clb, massage

Marriott Hotel, Airport
(800) 228-9290, (612) 854-7441
http://www.marriott.com
2020 E. 79th St.
479 rooms - $65-189
Pets: Welcome
Creature Comforts: CCTV, VCR, a/c, refrig, restaurant, pool, hlth clb, sauna, whirlpools

Radisson Hotel
(800) 333-3333, (612) 835-7800
http://www.radisson.com
7800 Normandale Blvd.
585 rooms - $99-169
Pets: Under 20 lbs. w/$50 dep.
Creature Comforts: CCTV, a/c, refrig, micro, Jacuzzis, restaurant, pool, hlth club, whirlpool

Select Inn
(800) 641-1000, (612) 835-7400
http://www.selectinn.com
7851 Normandale Blvd.
147 rooms - $39-65
Pets: Welcome w/$25 dep.
Creature Comforts: CCTV, a/c, cont. brkfst, hlth club, pool

Super 8 Motel
(800) 800-8000, (612) 888-8800
http://www.super8.com
7800 - 2nd Ave. S.
147 rooms - $59-75
Pets: Welcome
Creature Comforts: CCTV, a/c, Jacuzzis, waterbeds, cont. brkfst, sauna, whirlpool, hlth club

BLUE EARTH
Super 8 Motel
(800) 800-8000, (507) 526-7376
http://www.super8.com
1120 N. Grove St
40 rooms - $42-63
Pets: Welcome w/permission
Creature Comforts: CCTV, a/c, cont. brkfst, sauna, whirlpool, hlth club

BRAINERD
AmericInn Motel
(800) 634-3444, (218) 829-3080
http://www.americinn.com
600 Delwood Rd.
59 rooms - $55-73
Pets: In certain rooms
Creature Comforts: CCTV, a/c, refrig, micro, Jacuzzis, cont. brkfst, pool, sauna, whirlpool

Country Inns by Carlson
(800) 456-4000, (218) 828-2161
http://www.countryinns.com
1220 Dellwood Dr. N.
45 rooms - $65-115
Pets: Under 25 lbs. welcome
Creature Comforts: CCTV,
VCR, a/c, refrig, micro, Jacuzzi,
pool, sauna, hlth club, whirlpool

Days Inn
(800) DAYS-INN, (218) 829-0391
http://www.daysinn.com
Rtes. 210 & 371
59 rooms - $55-75
Pets: Welcome
Creature Comforts: CCTV, a/c,
cont. brkfst, hlth club access

Dellwood Motel
(218) 829-8756
1302 S. 6th St
20 rooms - $35-49
Pets: Welcome
Creature Comforts: CCTV, a/c

Econo Lodge
(800) 55-ECONO, (218) 828-0027
http://www.econolodge.com
2655 Route 371 S.
34 rooms - $39-105
Pets: Small pets welcome
Creature Comforts: CCTV, a/c,
restaurant, cont. brkfst

Holiday Inn
(800) HOLIDAY, (218) 829-1441
http://www.holiday-inn.com
2115 S. 6th St
150 rooms - $65-99
Pets: Small pets welcome
Creature Comforts: CCTV, a/c,
refrig, restaurant, Jacuzzis, sauna,
tennis, pool

BRECKENRIDGE
Best Inns
(800) BEST-INN, (218) 643-9201
http://www.bestinns.com
821 Rte. 75
27 rooms - $45-85
Pets: Welcome w/$50 dep.
Creature Comforts: CCTV, a/c,
refrig, micro, Jacuzzi, cont. brkfst,
pool, whirlpool

BROOKLYN CENTER
Baymont Inns
(877)BAYMONT, (612) 561-8400
http://www.baymontinns.com
6415 N. James Circle
99 rooms - $50-72
Pets: Small pets welcome
Creature Comforts: CCTV, a/c,
refrig, micro, restaurant, cont.
brkfst

Days Inn
(800) DAYS-INN, (612) 560-7464
http://www.daysinn.com
1600 N. James Circle
60 rooms - $59-105
Pets: Welcome
Creature Comforts: CCTV, a/c,
cont. brkfst, hlth club

Hilton Hotel
(800) HILTONS, (612) 566-8000
http://www.hilton.com
2200 Freeway Blvd.
177 rooms - $99-399
Pets: Welcome
Creature Comforts: CCTV, a/c,
refrig, restaurant, saunas, hlth
club, pool, whirlpools

BUFFALO
Super 8 Motel
(800) 800-8000, (612) 682-5930
http://www.super8.com
303 - 10th Ave. S.
32 rooms - $46-63
Pets: Welcome w/permission
Creature Comforts: CCTV, a/c,
waterbed, cont. brkfst, pool,
whirlpool

BURNSVILLE
Holiday Inn
(800) HOLIDAY, (612) 435-2100
http://www.holiday-inn.com
14201 Nicollet Ave. S.
145 rooms - $85-129
Pets: Small pets in ltd. rms
Creature Comforts: CCTV, a/c,
refrig, micro, Jacuzzis, restaurant,
sauna, whirlpool, hlth club, pool

Red Roof Inn
(800) The-Roof, (612) 890-1420
http://www.redroof.com
12920 Aldrich Ave. S.
85 rooms - $35-75
Pets: Small pets welcome
Creature Comforts: CCTV, a/c

Super 8 Motel
(800) 800-8000, (612) 894-3400
http://www.super8.com
1101 Burnsville Pkwy.
67 rooms - $48-69
Pets: Welcome w/$10 fee
Creature Comforts: CCTV, a/c,
micro, cont. brkfst

CANNON FALLS
Country Quiet Inn
(800) 258-1843, (612) 258-4406
37295 - 112 Ave. Way
2 rooms - $70-130
Pets: Welcome
Creature Comforts: CCTV,
VCR, a/c, fireplace, Jacuzzi,
refrig, full brkfst

CHANHASSEN
Country Inns by Carlson
(800) 456-4000, (612) 937-2424
http://www.countryinns.com
591 W. 78th St.
122 rooms - $80-105
Pets: Under 25 lbs. w/$10 fee
Creature Comforts: CCTV,
VCR, a/c, refrig, micro, Jacuzzi,
pool, sauna, whirlpool

CHATFIELD
Lund's Guest House
(507) 867-4003
218 Winona St.
8 rooms - $50-75
Pets: Welcome
Creature Comforts: CCTV,
homey décor & furnishings,
fireplace, kit, cont. brkfst

CHISAGO CITY
Super 8 Motel
(800) 800-8000, (612) 257-8088
http://www.super8.com
11650 Lake Blvd.
25 rooms - $39-56
Pets: In ltd. rms w/$6 fee
Creature Comforts: CCTV, a/c,
Jacuzzis, refrig, micro, cont.
brkfst, pool, whirlpool

CLEARWATER

Baymont Inns
(877)BAYMONT, (612) 558-2221
http://www.baymontinns.com
945 Rte. 24
28 rooms - $38-65
Pets: Small pets welcome
Creature Comforts: CCTV, a/c, refrig, micro, Jacuzzis, restaurant, sauna, whirlpool

CLOQUET

AmericInn Motel
(800) 634-3444, (218) 879-1231
http://www.americinn.com
111 Big Lake Rd.
51 rooms - $43-89
Pets: Welcome
Creature Comforts: CCTV, a/c, refrig, micro, cont. brkfst, Jacuzzis, pool, whirlpool, sauna

COLD SPRING

AmericInn Motel
(800) 634-3444, (218) 685-4539
http://www.americinn.com
118 - 3rd St.
24 rooms - $42-99
Pets: Welcome
Creature Comforts: CCTV, a/c, refrig, micro, Jacuzzis, whirlpool, pool, sauna

COOK

Vermillion Dam Lodge
(800) 325-5780, (218) 666-5418
http://www.vdl.com
3276 Randa Rd., Box 1105
15 cabins - $695-1,200/wk
Pets: Welcome w/$75 a week fee
Creature Comforts: CCTV, a/c, fireplace, kit, Jacuzzi, pool, lake/marina

COON RAPIDS

Country Inns by Carlson
(800) 456-4000, (612) 780-3797
http://www.countryinns.com
155 Coon Rapids Blvd.
115 rooms - $79-115
Pets: Under 25 lbs. w/CC dep.
Creature Comforts: CCTV, VCR, a/c, refrig, micro, restaurant, cont. brkfst, Jacuzzi, pool, whirlpool

CRANE LAKE

Olson's Borderland Lodge
(800) 777-8392, (218) 993-2233
http://www.bordelandlodge.com
7488 Crane Lake Rd.
14 cabins - $80-480
Pets: Welcome w/$6 daily fee
Creature Comforts: CCTV, fireplace, kit, restaurant, pool

CROOKSTON

Northland Inn
(218) 281-5210
2200 University Ave.
75 rooms - $50-65
Pets: Welcome w/$3 fee
Creature Comforts: CCTV, a/c, restaurant, whirlpool, pool

DEER RIVER

Bahr's Motel
(218) 246-8271
PO Box 614
22 rooms - $30-45
Pets: Welcome
Creature Comforts: CCTV, a/c, kit

Miller's Resort
(218) 246-8951 or 327-4877
RR1, Box 266
3 cabins - 275-350/wk
Pets: Welcome in cabins 2 and 3 w/$25 weekly fee,
Creature Comforts: Family owned cabins on quiet Island Lake, exuberant hostess, loves dogs, clean comfortable cabins, serene, lake views, TV, living rm, kit, fishing, boating, swimming

DEERWOOD

Country Inns by Carlson
(800) 456-4000, (218) 534-3101
http://www.countryinns.com
115 Front St E.
40 rooms - $65-109
Pets: Welcome
Creature Comforts: CCTV, VCR, a/c, refrig, micro, pool, sauna, whirlpool

Deerwood Motel
(218) 534-3163
9 W. Forest Rd.
16 rooms - $38-65
Pets: Welcome
Creature Comforts: CCTV, a/c

DETROIT LAKES

Best Western Holland Inn
(800) 528-1234, (218) 847-4483
http://www.bestwestern.com
615 Route 10 E.
60 rooms - $60-145
Pets: In first floor rooms
Creature Comforts: CCTV, VCR, a/c, refrig, micro, Jacuzzis, sauna, whirlpool, hlth club, pool

Budget Host Inn
(800) Bud-Host, (218) 847-4454
http://www.budgethost.com
895 Route 10 E.
24 rooms - $40-75
Pets: Welcome
Creature Comforts: CCTV, a/c, refrig, micro

Castaway Inn & Resort
(800) 640-3395, (218) 847-4454
http://www.detroitlakes.com/castaway
Rte. 4, Box 15
29 rooms - $60-95
Pets: Welcome w/$10 daily fee
Creature Comforts: CCTV, a/c, kit, whirlpool, beach/boats

Holiday Inn
(800) HOLIDAY, (218) 847-2121
http://www.holiday-inn.com
Route 10 E.
105 rooms - $65-99
Pets: Welcome
Creature Comforts: CCTV, VCR, a/c, refrig, micro, restaurant, sauna, whirlpool, volleyball, pool, rec. dome, dock

Super 8 Motel
(800) 800-8000, (218) 847-1651
http://www.super8.com
400 Morrow Ave.
39 rooms - $45-54
Pets: Welcome
Creature Comforts: CCTV, a/c, cont. brkfst

DEXTER

Mill Inn Motel
(507) 584-6440
PO Box 78
22 rooms - $39-59
Pets: Welcome w/$6 fee
Creature Comforts: CCTV, a/c

DILWORTH
Howard Johnson
(800) I-Go-Hojo, (218) 287-1212
http://www.hojo.com
701 Center Ave. E.
49 rooms - $40-99
Pets: Welcome
Creature Comforts: CCTV,
VCR, a/c, refrig, micro, Jacuzzis,
restaurant, cont. brkfst

DULUTH
Allyndale IMA Motel
(800) 341-8000, (218) 628-1061
http://www.imalodging.com
510 N. 66th Ave. W.
21 rooms - $35-75
Pets: Welcome w/$5 fee
Creature Comforts: CCTV, a/c,
refrig, micro

Best Western
(800) 528-1234, (218) 727-6851
http://www.bestwestern.com
131 W. 2nd St
45 rooms - $40-89
Pets: Small pets welcome
Creature Comforts: CCTV, a/c,
refrig, cont. brkfst

Best Western Edgewater
(800) 528-1234, (218) 728-3601
http://www.bestwestern.com
2400 London Rd.
222 rooms - $54-139
Pets: Small pets welcome
Creature Comforts: CCTV, a/c,
refrig, micro, sauna, whirlpool,
mini golf, lawn games, pool

Best Western
(800) 528-1234, (218) 728-3601
http://www.bestwestern.com
2211 London Rd.
65 rooms - $54-139
Pets: Small pets welcome
Creature Comforts: CCTV, a/c,
refrig, micro, sauna, whirlpool,
pool

Days Inn
(800) DAYS-INN, (218) 727-3110
http://www.daysinn.com
909 Cottonwood Ave.
86 rooms - $49-90
Pets: Welcome
Creature Comforts: CCTV,VCR,
a/c, cont. brkfst

Grand Motel
(800) 472-0841, (218) 624-4821
4312 Grand Ave.
13 rooms - $45-55
Pets: Welcome
Creature Comforts: CCTV, a/c,
refrig

Manor on the Creek B&B
(800) 428-3189, (218) 728-3189
http://www.visitduluth.com/Manor
2215 E. Second St.
3 rooms - $129-199
Pets: Friendly dogs w/$10 fee
Creature Comforts: An
intriguing 15,000 sq. ft mansion
w/original ornate woodworking
rounded ceilings, Victorian
antiques, theme rooms, quilts,
CCTV, VCR, a/c, fireplace, refrig,
Jacuzzi, full brkfst, pool, hlth clb
access, sauna, whirlpool

Motel 6
(800) 4-MOTEL6, (218) 723-1123
http://www.motel6.com
200 S. 27th Ave.
100 rooms - $34-49
Pets: Under 30 lbs. welcome
Creature Comforts: CCTV, a/c

Park Inn International
(800) 777-8560, (218) 727-8821
web site pending
250 Canal Park Dr.
145 rooms - $65-109
Pets: Welcome w/$20 fee
Creature Comforts: CCTV, a/c,
kit, restaurant, pool, sauna,
whirlpool, beach

Radisson Suite Hotel
(800) 333-3333, (218) 727-8981
http://www.radisson.com
505 W. Superior St.
200 rooms - $69-325
Pets: Under 25 lbs. welcome
Creature Comforts: CCTV, a/c,
refrig, restaurant, hlth club access,
sauna, pool, whirlpool

Select Inn
(218) 723-1123
200 S. 27th St
100 rooms - $45-60
Pets: Welcome w/$25 dep.
Creature Comforts: CCTV, a/c,
refrig, cont. brkfst.

Voyageur Lakewalk Inn
(800) 258-3911, (218) 722-3911
http://www.visitduluth.com/
Voyageur
333 E. Superior St.
42 rooms - $45-155
Pets: Welcome w/$10 fee
Creature Comforts: Homelike
décor w/lake views from most
bedrooms, rough-hewn log
furnishings, suite w/ floor-to-
ceiling windows, CCTV, a/c,
fireplaces, kit, Jacuzzis, and a
cont. brkfst

Willard Munger Inn
(800) 982-2453, (218) 624-4818
http://www.mungerinn.com
7408 Grand Ave.
22 rooms - $50-135
Pets: Welcome
Creature Comforts: CCTV, a/c,
fireplaces, kit, Jacuzzi, restaurant,
bikes/canoes, trails

EAGAN
Holiday Inn Express
(800) HOLIDAY, (612) 681-9266
http://www.holiday-inn.com
1950 Rahncliff Ct.
122 rooms - $85-109
Pets: Welcome in smoking rooms
Creature Comforts: CCTV, a/c,
kit, Jacuzzis, full brkfst, whirlpool,
hlth club, pool

Residence Inn
(800) 331-3131, (612) 688-0363
http://www.residenceinn.com
3040 Eagandale Pl.
122 rooms - $129-269
Pets: Small pets w/$100 fee
Creature Comforts: CCTV,
VCR, a/c, fireplaces, kit, cont.
brkfst, pool, hlth club

EAST GRAND FORKS
Comfort Inn
(800) 228-5150, (218) 773-9545
http://www.comfortinn.com
Rte. 2 East
80 rooms - $65-109
Pets: Welcome
Creature Comforts: CCTV, a/c,
refrig, micro, Jacuzzis, cont.
brkfst, sauna, whirlpool, pool

EDEN PRAIRIE
Residence Inn
(800) 331-3131, (612) 829-0033
http://www.residenceinn.com
7780 Flying Cloud Dr.
125 rooms - $129-229
Pets: Welcome w/$50-200 fee
Creature Comforts: CCTV,
VCR, a/c, fireplaces, kit, cont.
brkfst, pool, hlth club

EDINA
Hawthorn Suites
(800) 527-1133, (612) 893-9300
http://www.hawthorn.com
3400 Edinburgh Way
140 rooms - $99-149
Pets: Under 25 lbs. welcome
w/$50 fee and $150 dep.
Creature Comforts: CCTV,
VCR, a/c, kit, Jacuzzis, restaurant,
pool, skating, hlth clb

ELK
AmericInn Motel
(800) 634-3444, (612) 441-8554
http://www.americinn.com
17432 Rte. 10
44 rooms - $50-75
Pets: $3 fee & $50 dep.
Creature Comforts: CCTV, a/c,
VCR, refrig, micro, hlth club,
sauna, pool

Red Carpet Inn
(800) 251-1962, (612) 441-2424
http://www.redcarpetinns.com
17291 Rte. 10
40 rooms - $39-66
Pets: Small pets w/$5 fee
Creature Comforts: CCTV, a/c,
refrig, micro, restaurant, pool

ELY
Blue Heron B&B
(218) 365-4720
http://www.blueheronbnb.com
PO Box 46
3 rooms - $80-115
Pets: Welcome
Creature Comforts: Lakeside log
cabin and yurt on 10 acres along
Boundary Waters Canoe Area
Wilderness, quilts, CCTV,
fireplaces-woodstove, refrig, cont.
brkfst, sauna, canoes, trails

Budget Host Inn
(800) Bud-Host, (218) 365-3237
http://www.budgethost.com
1047 E. Sheridan St.
18 rooms - $39-99
Pets: In ltd. rms w/$5 fee
Creature Comforts: CCTV,
VCR, a/c, refrig

Silver Rapids Lodge
(218) 365-4877
HC 1, Box 2992
22 rooms - $65-95
Pets: 3 units w/$10 fee
Creature Comforts: CCTV, kit,
Jacuzzi, restaurant, xc-skiing, lake

EVELETH
Holiday Inn
(800) HOLIDAY, (218) 744-2703
http://www.holiday-inn.com
701 Hat Trick Ave.
145 rooms - $60-99
Pets: Small pets welcome
Creature Comforts: CCTV, a/c,
restaurant, sauna, whirlpool, pool,
putting green

Koke's Downtown Motel
(218) 744-4500
714 Fayal Rd.
14 rooms - $29-40
Pets: Welcome
Creature Comforts: CCTV, a/c

FAIRFAX
Fairfax Motel
(507) 426-7266
403 E. Lincoln Ave.
14 rooms - $35-50
Pets: Welcome w/CC dep.
Creature Comforts: CCTV, a/c,
kit

FAIRMONT
Comfort Inn
(800) 228-5150, (507) 238-5444
http://www.comfortinn.com
2225 N. State St
40 rooms - $65-122
Pets: Small pets welcome
Creature Comforts: CCTV, a/c,
cont. brkfst, whirlpool, pool

Highland Court Motel
(507) 235-6686
1245 Lake Ave.
30 rooms - $30-59
Pets: Welcome
Creature Comforts: CCTV, a/c,
refrig, micro

Holiday Inn
(800) HOLIDAY, (507) 238-4771
http://www.holiday-inn.com
1201 Torgerson Dr.
106 rooms - $66-99
Pets: Small pets welcome
Creature Comforts: CCTV, a/c,
refrig, Jacuzzis, restaurant, sauna,
whirlpool, hlth club, pool

Super 8 Motel
(800) 800-8000, (507) 238-9444
http://www.super8.com
1200 Torgerson Dr.
47 rooms - $52-73
Pets: Welcome
Creature Comforts: CCTV, a/c,
cont. brkfst

FARIBAULT
AmericInn Motel
(800) 634-3444, (507) 334-9464
http://www.americinn.com
1801 Lavender Dr.
45 rooms - 65-79
Pets: Small pets welcome
Creature Comforts: CCTV,
VCR, a/c, refrig, micro, Jacuzzis,
sauna, pool, whirlpool

Best Western Galaxie
(800) 528-1234, (507) 334-5508
http://www.bestwestern.com
1401 Rte. 60
59 rooms - $45-60
Pets: Welcome in front bldg.
Creature Comforts: CCTV, a/c,
refrig, sauna, whirlpool, pool

Select Inn
(800) 641-1000, (507) 334-2051
http://www.selectinn.com
4040 Rte. 60
68 rooms - $39-60
Pets: Welcome w/$25 dep.
Creature Comforts: CCTV,
VCR, a/c, pool

FERGUS FALLS
AmericInn Motel
(800) 634-3444, (218) 739-3900
http://www.americinn.com
526 Western Ave.
44 rooms - $55-70
Pets: Welcome w/$50 dep.
Creature Comforts: CCTV,
VCR, a/c, refrig, micro, Jacuzzis,
pool, sauna

Days Inn
(800) DAYS-INN, (218) 739-3311
http://www.daysinn.com
610 Western Ave. N.
57 rooms - $45-90
Pets: Welcome
Creature Comforts: CCTV, a/c,
Jacuzzis, cont. brkfst, whirlpool

Super 8 Motel
(800) 800-8000, (218) 739-3261
http://www.super8.com
2454 College Way
32 rooms - $39-54
Pets: Welcome w/permission
Creature Comforts: CCTV, a/c,
cont. brkfst

FINLAYSON
Super 8 Motel
(800) 800-8000, (320) 245-5284
http://www.super8.com
Rtes 35 & 23
30 rooms - $44-58
Pets: Welcome in pet rooms
Creature Comforts: CCTV, a/c,
cont. brkfst, whirlpool

FOREST LAKE
Forest Motel
(612) 464-4077
7 NE 6th Ave.
14 rooms - $35-65
Pets: Welcome
Creature Comforts: CCTV, a/c,
refrig

FOSSTON
Super 8 Motel
(800) 800-8000, (218) 435-1088
http://www.super8.com
Rte. 2 E.
29 rooms - $43-55
Pets: Welcome w/permission
Creature Comforts: CCTV, a/c,
cont. brkfst, whirlpool, sauna

FRANKLIN
Maple Hill Cottage
(507) 557-2403
RR 1, Box 12
Cottages - $50-65
Pets: Welcome
Creature Comforts: CCTV, kit

FRINDLEY
Best Western Kelly Inn
(800) 528-1234, (218) 571-9440
http://www.bestwestern.com
5201 Central Ave. NE
96 rooms - $53-75
Pets: Cats welcome
Creature Comforts: CCTV, a/c,
refrig, Jacuzzis, restaurant, sauna,
whirlpool, pool

GLENCOE
Glencoe Castle B&B
(800) 517-3334, (320) 864-3043
831 - 13th St.
http://members.aol.com/
Schoeneck1/home.htm
3 rooms - $85-175
Pets: Small crated pets welcome,
not allowed in public areas
Creature Comforts: 1895 ornate
Queen-Anne Gothic Victorian
castle w/wraparound porches,
lovely handpainted-murals and
parquet flrs, original woodwork,
rqst Master Suite w/Jacuzzi,
micro, CCTV, VCR, a/c, cont.
brkfst, whirlpool

Super 8 Motel
(800) 800-8000, (320) 864-6191
http://www.super8.com
717 Morningside Dr.
33 rooms - $43-55
Pets: Welcome w/$5 fee
Creature Comforts: CCTV, a/c,
cont. brkfst, whirlpool

GLENWOOD
Hi-view Motel
(320) 634-4541
255 N. Rte. 55
12 rooms - $30-49
Pets: Welcome
Creature Comforts: CCTV, a/c

GRAND MARAIS
Best Western Superior Inn
(800) 528-1234, (218) 387-2240
http://www.bestwestern.com
Rte. 61
50 rooms - $45-175
Pets: Welcome
Creature Comforts: CCTV,
VCR, a/c, refrig, micro, Jacuzzis,
on lake

Clearwater Lodge
(800) 527-0554, (218) 388-2254
http://www.canoe-bwca.com
355 Gunflint Trail
6 cabins - $695-800
Pets: In cabins w/$60 fee
Creature Comforts: Nestled right
on the picturesque BWCA Lake,
the historic lodge offers terrific
secluded log cabins, CCTV,
fireplace, kit, sauna, trails, on lake/
boats-canoe trips, trails

East Bay Motel
(800) 414-2807, (218) 387-2800
Wisconsin St.
41 rooms - $55-160
Pets: Welcome
Creature Comforts: CCTV,
fireplace, refrig, micro, Jacuzzi,
restaurant, massage whirlpool, on
lake

Econo Lodge
(800) 55-ECONO, (218) 387-2547
http://www.econolodge.com
Rte. 61 East
51 rooms - $45-125
Pets: Small pets welcome
Creature Comforts: CCTV, a/c,
Jacuzzis, cont. brkfst, whirlpool,
sauna

Golden Eagle Lodge
(800) 346-2203, (218) 388-2203
http://www.golden-eagle.com
325 Gunflint Trail
11 rooms - $95-125
Pets: Welcome w/$18 fee
Creature Comforts: CCTV, kit, on lake

Gunflint Lodge Resort
(800) 328-3325, (218) 388-2294
http://www.gunflintlodge.com
143 S. Gunflint Lake
24 rooms - $180-375
Pets: Welcome w/$10 fee
Creature Comforts: On Gunflint Lake, neat old fashioned fishing lodge, modern cabins w/Western decor, TV, VCR, kit, fireplaces, stereo-CDs, Jacuzzis, saunas, whirlpools, wilderness canoe trips, xc-skiing, riding, on lake/boating/fishing

Gunflint Pines Resort
(800) 533-5814, (218) 388-4454
http://www.gunflintpines.com
755 Gunflint Trail
6 cabins - $120-135
Pets: Welcome w/$8 fee
Creature Comforts: Modern A-frame cabins on banks of Gunflint Lake, CCTV, kit, fireplace, picture windows-lake views, fishing, xc-skiing/snowshoeing

Little Ollie Lake Cabin
(800) 322-8327, (218) 388-4487
http://www.bounderycountry.com/cabin.html
590 Gunflint Trail
1 cabin - $120-155
Pets: Welcome w/$10 fee
Creature Comforts: Modern two bedroom cabin set in wilderness, CCTV, fireplace, kit, sauna, 32 acres, canoe, bikes, lake/dock, snowshoe/xc-skiing

Nor'wester Lodge
(800) 992-4386 (218) 388-2252
www.boreal.org/norwester
550 Gunflint Trail
10 cabins - $650-1,299/wk
Pets: Welcome in cabins with a $10 daily fee
Creature Comforts: CCTV, kit, fireplaces, restaurant, sauna, lawn games, hunting/fishing, on lake/boating

Sandgren Motel
(800) 387-2975, (218) 387-2975
Rte. 61, Box 1056
8 rooms - $35-63
Pets: Under 20 lbs. welcome
Creature Comforts: CCTV, a/c, kit

Seawall Motel
(800) 245-5806, (218) 387-2095
Rte. 61 & 3rd Ave.
17 rooms - $65-75
Pets: Small dogs w/$5 fee
Creature Comforts: CCTV, a/c, refrig

Super 8 Motel
(800) 800-8000, (218) 387-2448
http://www.super8.com
Route 61
35 rooms - $40-95
Pets: Welcome w/permission
Creature Comforts: CCTV, a/c, refrig, cont. brkfst, sauna, whirlpool

Toteboda Motel
(218) 387-1585
1800 W. Rte. 61
18 rooms - $39-84
Pets: Welcome
Creature Comforts: CCTV, a/c, refrig, sauna, whirlpool

GRAND RAPIDS
Best Western Rainbow Inn
(800) 528-1234, (218) 326-9655
http://www.bestwestern.com
1300 Rte. 169
80 rooms - $50-85
Pets: Welcome w/$50 deposit
Creature Comforts: CCTV, VCR, a/c, refrig, restaurants, sauna, whirlpool, pool

Country Inn Suites
(800) 456-4000, (218) 327-4960
http://www.countryinns.com
2601 Rte. 169
45 rooms - $58-80
Pets: Welcome
Creature Comforts: CCTV, a/c, refrig, micro, pool, sauna, whirlpool

Days Inn
(800) DAYS-INN, (218) 326-3457
http://www.daysinn.com
311 E. Rte. 2
34 rooms - $45-75
Pets: Welcome
Creature Comforts: CCTV, a/c, cont. brkfst

Sawmill Inn
(800) 677-7509, (218) 326-8501
2301 S. Pokegama Ave.
129 rooms - $58-115
Pets: Welcome
Creature Comforts: CCTV, a/c, refrig, Jacuzzis, restaurant, pool, saunas, whirlpools

GRANITE FALLS
Viking Sundance Inn
(320) 564-2411
Routes 212 & 67
22 rooms - $34-49
Pets: Welcome
Creature Comforts: CCTV, a/c

Super 8 Motel
(800) 800-8000, (320) 564-4075
http://www.super8.com
845 Rte. 212
63 rooms - $43-59
Pets: Welcome w/$4 fee
Creature Comforts: CCTV, a/c, refrig, micro, Jacuzzis, cont. brkfst, pool, whirlpool

HIBBING
Days Inn
(800) DAYS-INN, (218) 263-8306
http://www.daysinn.com
1520 Rte. 37 E.
61 rooms - $45-75
Pets: Welcome
Creature Comforts: CCTV, a/c, cont. brkfst

Hibbing Park Hotel
(800) 262-3481, (218) 384-7751
http://www.explorerminneta.com
1402 E. Howard St.
122 rooms - $62-95
Pets: Welcome w/$50 deposit
Creature Comforts: CCTV, VCR, a/c, refrig, restaurant, pool, sauna, whirlpool

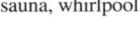

Super 8 Motel
(800) 800-8000, (218) 263-8982
http://www.super8.com
1411 E. 40th St.
49 rooms - $46-69
Pets: Welcome
Creature Comforts: CCTV, a/c,
cont. brkfst

HINCKLEY
Best Western Gold Pine
(800) 528-1234, (320) 384-6112
http://www.bestwestern.com
Routes 48 & 35
50 rooms - $44-80
Pets: Welcome
Creature Comforts: CCTV, a/c,
refrig, Jacuzzis

Days Inn
(800) DAYS-INN, (320) 384-7751
http://www.daysinn.com
Routes 35 & 48
69 rooms - $45-109
Pets: Welcome
Creature Comforts: CCTV,
VCR, a/c, Jacuzzis, cont. brkfst,
pool, sauna

Holiday Inn Express
(800) HOLIDAY, (320) 384-7171
http://www.holiday-inn.com
604 Weber Ave.
101 rooms - $65-139
Pets: Small pets w/$10 fee
Creature Comforts: CCTV, a/c,
refrig, micro, Jacuzzis, cont.
brkfst, sauna, whirlpool, pool

HUTCHINSON
Best Western Victorian
(800) 528-1234, (320) 587-6030
http://www.bestwestern.com
1000 Route 7
52 rooms - $60-99
Pets: Welcome w/$20 fee
Creature Comforts: CCTV, a/c,
kit, Jacuzzis, restaurant, pool

INTERNATIONAL FALLS
Days Inn
(800) DAYS-INN, (218) 283-9441
http://www.daysinn.com
2331 Route 53 S.
58 rooms - $44-62
Pets: Welcome
Creature Comforts: CCTV, a/c,
cont. brkfst, whirlpool, sauna, and
a hlth club

Hilltop Motel
(800) 322-6671, (218) 283-2505
2002 - 2nd Ave.
16 rooms - $45-60
Pets: Welcome
Creature Comforts: CCTV, a/c

Holiday Inn
(800) HOLIDAY, (218) 283-4451
http://www.holiday-inn.com
1500 Route 71
125 rooms - $65-109
Pets: Small pets in smkng rooms
Creature Comforts: CCTV, a/c,
refrig, micro, Jacuzzis, restaurant,
sauna, whirlpool, pool

Island View Lodge
(800) 777-7856, (218) 266-3511
http://www.rainy-lake.com
HCR 8, Box 411
11 cabins - $65-275
Pets: In cabins w/$11 fee
Creature Comforts: Nestled on
Rainy Lake in Voyageurs Nat'l
Park, knotty pine cabins w/ homey
décor, CCTV, a/c, fireplace, kit,
restaurant, store, recreation rm,
beach/boats, fishing

Northernaire Floating Lodges
(800) 854-7958, (218) 286-5221
www.northernet.com/nflhboat
2690 Rte. 94, Box 510
15 boats - $725-2,200/wk
Pets: Welcome
Creature Comforts: Fully-
equipped houseboats on Rainy
Lake, kit, store, fishing

JACKSON
Budget Host Inn
(800) Bud-Host, (507) 847-2020
http://www.budgethost.com
950 Rte. 71
25 rooms - $42-59
Pets: Small pets welcome
Creature Comforts: CCTV, a/c,
refrig

Super 8 Motel
(800) 800-8000, (507) 847-3498
http://www.super8.com
2025 Rte. 71 N.
49 rooms - $49-68
Pets: Welcome
Creature Comforts: CCTV, a/c,
Jacuzzi, cont. brkfst

LAKE CITY
Lake Pepin Lodge
(800) 644-2780, (612) 345-5392
620 Central Point Rd.
16 rooms - $60-95
Pets: Welcome
Creature Comforts: CCTV, a/c,
refrig, micro, Jacuzzi, trails/xc
skiing, on lake/beach

LAKEVILLE
Motel 6
(800) 4-MOTEL6, (612) 469-1900
http://www.motel6.com
11274 - 210th St.
84 rooms - $34-49
Pets: Under 30 lbs. welcome
Creature Comforts: CCTV, a/c

Super 8 Motel
(800) 800-8000, (612) 469-1134
http://www.super8.com
20800 Kenrick Ave.
132 rooms - $50-70
Pets: Welcome w/permission
Creature Comforts: CCTV, a/c,
cont. brkfst, pool, whirlpool

LONG PRAIRIE
Budget Host Inn
(800) Bud-Host, (320) 732-6118
http://www.budgethost.com
417 Lake St.
18 rooms - $37-55
Pets: Welcome
Creature Comforts: CCTV, a/c,
refrig, micro

LUTSEN
Best Western Cliff Dweller
(800) 528-1234, (218) 663-7273
http://www.bestwestern.com
Rte. 61, Box 26
22 rooms - $45-109
Pets: Welcome
Creature Comforts: CCTV, a/c,
refrig, set above lake

Lutsen Resort
(800) 258-8736, (218) 663-7212
http://www.lutsenresort.com
Route 61
105 units - $39-270
Pets: Welcome in the Sea Villas
Creature Comforts: A neat
Scandinavian-style lodge w/ hand-
carved beams and huge stone
fireplaces, charming log cabins w/
cheery décor, CCTV, VCR, a/c,
stereo, woodstoves, kit, restaurant,
bar, pool, whirlpool, sauna, tennis,
on Lake Superior

The Mountain Inn
(800) 686-4669, (218) 663-7244
Ski Hill Rd.
30 rooms - $59-130
Pets: In ltd. rms w/$15 fee
Creature Comforts: CCTV,
VCR, a/c, refrig, micro, cont.
brkfst, sauna, whirlpool, golf
access

Solbakken Resort
(800) 435-3950, (218) 663-7566
HC 3, Box 170
17 rooms - $44-235
Pets: In 12 rms w/$5 fee
Creature Comforts: Refurbished
1930's log cabin lodge, quilts,
CCTV, kit, sauna, whirlpool,
trails/xc skiing, Lake Superior,
lodge to lodge xc-ski prgrm

Thomsonite Beach
(218) 387-1532
Rte. 3, Box 470
10 rooms - $44-155
Pets: Welcome w/$10 fee
Creature Comforts: CCTV, kit,
on lake

LUVERNE
Comfort Inn
(800) 228-5150, (507) 283-9488
http://www.comfortinn.com
801 S. Kniss
44 rooms - $48-80
Pets: Small pets welcome
Creature Comforts: CCTV, a/c,
cont. brkfst, whirlpool, pool

Super 8 Motel
(800) 800-8000, (507) 283-9541
http://www.super8.com
Rtes 90 & 75
36 rooms - $45-70
Pets: Welcome w/permission
Creature Comforts: CCTV, a/c,
cont. brkfst

MANKATO
Best Western Hotel
(800) 528-1234, (507) 625-9333
http://www.bestwestern.com
1111 Range St.
147 rooms - $55-99
Pets: 1 pet per room (limited)
Creature Comforts: CCTV,
VCR, a/c, refrig, micro, restaurant,
sauna, whirlpool, hlth club, pool

Baymont Inns
(877)BAYMONT, (507) 345-8800
http://www.baymontinns.com
111 W. Lind Ct.
65 rooms - $39-60
Pets: Small pets in smoking rms.
Creature Comforts: CCTV, a/c,
refrig, micro, cont. brkfst, sauna,
whirlpool

Comfort Inn
(800) 228-5150, (507) 388-5107
http://www.comfortinn.com
131 Apache Pl.
56 rooms - $59-105
Pets: Small pets welcome
Creature Comforts: CCTV, a/c,
refrig, micro, cont. brkfst,
whirlpool, pool

Days Inn
(800) DAYS-INN, (507) 387-3332
http://www.daysinn.com
Rtes 169 & 14
50 rooms - $44-97
Pets: Welcome
Creature Comforts: CCTV,
VCR, a/c, Jacuzzis, cont. brkfst,
whirlpool, pool, on pond/trail

Holiday Inn
(800) HOLIDAY, (507) 345-1234
http://www.holiday-inn.com
101 E. Main St.
150 rooms - $65-95
Pets: Small pets welcome
Creature Comforts: CCTV, a/c,
refrig, micro, Jacuzzis, restaurant,
sauna, whirlpool, hlth club, pool

Riverfront Inn
(507) 388-1638
1727 N. Riverfront Dr.
20 rooms - $39-175
Pets: Small pets welcome
Creature Comforts: CCTV,
VCR, a/c, fireplace, refrig, micro,
Jacuzzis, sauna, whirlpool

MANTORVILLE
Grand Old Mansion
(507) 635-3231
501 Clay St.
4 rooms - $35-75
Pets: In log house
Creature Comforts: An 1899
Victorian mansion, CCTV, a/c, kit,
full brkfst

MAPLEWOOD
Best Western Inn
(800) 528-1234, (612) 770-2811
http://www.bestwestern.com
1780 E. CR D
118 rooms - $75-155
Pets: Welcome w/$5 fee
Creature Comforts: CCTV,
VCR, a/c, refrig, restaurant, sauna,
whirlpool, hlth club access, pool

MARSHALL
Best Western Inn
(800) 528-1234, (507) 532-3221
http://www.bestwestern.com
1500 E. College Dr.
100 rooms - $57-75
Pets: Welcome
Creature Comforts: CCTV,
VCR, a/c, refrig, micro, Jacuzzis,
restaurant, sauna, whirlpool, hlth
club, pool

Comfort Inn
(800) 228-5150, (507) 532-3070
http://www.comfortinn.com
1511 E. College Dr.
49 rooms - $55-104
Pets: Small pets welcome
Creature Comforts: CCTV,
VCR, a/c, refrig, micro, Jacuzzis,
cont. brkfst, whirlpool, hlth club

Super 8 Motel
(800) 800-8000, (507) 537-1461
http://www.super8.com
1106 E. Main St.
80 rooms - $46-65
Pets: Welcome w/$5 dep.
Creature Comforts: CCTV, a/c,
Jacuzzis, cont. brkfst

Traveler's Choice
(800) 532-5721, (507) 532-5721
http://www.marshallcvb.com
1425 E. College Dr.
90 rooms - $35-50
Pets: In smoking rooms
Creature Comforts: CCTV,
VCR, a/c, cont. brkfst

McGREGOR
Country Meadows Inn
(218) 768-7378
Rtes 65 & 210
34 rooms - $45-72
Pets: In smoking rooms w/$5 fee
Creature Comforts: CCTV, a/c,
fireplace, refrig, micro, Jacuzzis,
whirlpool

MELROSE
Super 8 Motel
(800) 800-8000, (320) 256-4261
http://www.super8.com
231 E. County Rd.
26 rooms - $42-99
Pets: Welcome w/permission
Creature Comforts: CCTV, a/c,
Jacuzzis, cont. brkfst

MILACA
Rodeway Inn
(800) 228-2000, (320) 983-2660
http://www.rodeway.com
215 - 10th Ave.
31 rooms - $54-69
Pets: Welcome w/$25 dep.
Creature Comforts: CCTV,
VCR, a/c, refrig, Jacuzzi,
fireplace, cont. brkfst

MINNEAPOLIS
Best Western Downtown
(800) 528-1234, (612) 370-1400
http://www.bestwestern.com
405 S. 8th St.
159 rooms - $79-95
Pets: Small pets welcome
Creature Comforts: CCTV, a/c,
refrig, cont. brkfst, sauna,
whirlpool, hlth club

Comfort Inn
(800) 228-5150, (612) 785-4746
http://www.comfortinn.com
9052 NW University St.
56 rooms - $50-119
Pets: Small pets welcome
Creature Comforts: CCTV, a/c,
cont. brkfst, pool

Crowne Plaza Northstar
(800) HOLIDAY, (612) 338-2288
http://www.crowneplaza.com
618 S. 2nd Ave.
225 rooms - $85-289
Pets: Under 20 lbs. welcome
Creature Comforts: CCTV,
VCR, a/c, refrig, micro, restaurant,
hlth clb

Hilton Hotel
(800) HILTONS, (612) 566-8000
http://www.hilton.com
2200 Freeway Blvd.
176 rooms - $99-399
Pets: Welcome
Creature Comforts: CCTV, a/c,
refrig, restaurant, saunas, hlth
club, pool, whirlpools

Holiday Inn Metrodome
(800) HOLIDAY, (612) 333-4646
http://www.holiday-inn.com
1500 Washington Ave.
266 rooms - $85-139
Pets: Small pets welcome
Creature Comforts: CCTV, a/c,
refrig, Jacuzzis, restaurant, sauna,
whirlpool, pool

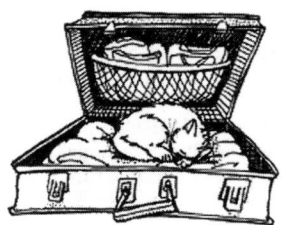

Marquette Minneapolis
(800) HILTONS, (612) 333-4545
http://www.hilton.com
710 Marquette Ave.
278 rooms - $85-199
Pets: Small pets are welcome with
a $100 deposit
Creature Comforts: CCTV, a/c,
Jacuzzi, refrig, restaurant, hlth clb,
access to pool

Marriott Hotel
(800) 228-9290, (612) 349-4000
http://www.marriott.com
30 S. 7th St.
585 rooms - $75-225
Pets: Welcome
Creature Comforts: CCTV,
VCR, a/c, refrig, restaurant, pool,
hlth clb, sauna, steamrooms,
massage, whirlpools

Radisson Plaza Hotel
(800) 333-3333, (612) 339-4900
http://www.radisson.com
35 S. 7th St.
358 rooms - $99-169
Pets: Under 25 lbs. welcome
Creature Comforts: CCTV, a/c,
refrig, micro, Jacuzzis, restaurant,
pool, sauna, massage, hlth club,
whirlpool

Radisson Metrodome Hotel
(800) 333-3333, (612) 379-8888
http://www.radisson.com
615 Washington Ave. SE
303 rooms - $109-399
Pets: Welcome
Creature Comforts: CCTV,
VCR, a/c, refrig, micro, Jacuzzis,
restaurant, pool, hlth club access,
whirlpool

Regal Hotel
(800) 522-8856, (612) 332-6000
http://www.regal-hotels.com
1313 Nicolet Mall
320 rooms - $125-299
Pets: Welcome
Creature Comforts: CCTV,
VCR, a/c, refrig, Jacuzzis,
restaurant, pool, sauna, whirlpool

Rodeway Inn
(800) 228-2000, (612) 871-2000
http://www.rodeway.com
2335 - 3rd Ave. S.
67 rooms - $59-120
Pets: Welcome w/$25 dep.
Creature Comforts: CCTV, a/c,
kit, cont. brkfst, pool

MONTICELLO
Best Western Silver Fox
(800) 528-1234, (612) 295-4000
http://www.bestwestern.com
1114 Cedar St.
65 rooms - $55-99
Pets: Welcome
Creature Comforts: CCTV,
VCR, a/c, refrig, restaurant, sauna,
whirlpool, pool

Comfort Inn
(800) 228-5150, (612) 295-1111
http://www.comfortinn.com
200 E. Oakwood Dr.
33 rooms - $52-105
Pets: Small pets welcome
Creature Comforts: CCTV,
VCR, a/c, refrig, micro, Jacuzzis,
cont. brkfst

MOOREHEAD

Best Western Red River
(800) 528-1234, (218) 233-6171
http://www.bestwestern.com
600 - 30th Ave. S.
172 rooms - $55-85
Pets: Small pets welcome
Creature Comforts: CCTV, a/c,
refrig, restaurant, sauna,
whirlpool, hlth club, pool

Guest House Motel
(218) 233-2471
2107 Main St. SE
22 rooms - $32-44
Pets: Welcome w/$4 fee
Creature Comforts: CCTV, a/c,
refrig, micro

Motel 75
(218) 233-7501
810 Belsly Blvd.
69 rooms - $35-45
Pets: Welcome
Creature Comforts: CCTV, a/c

MORA

Ann River Motel
(612) 679-2972
1819 S. Rte. 65
24 rooms - $36-50
Pets: Small pets welcome
Creature Comforts: CCTV, a/c,
Jacuzzis

Motel Mora
(800) 657-0167, (612) 679-3262
web site pending
301 S. Rte. 65
24 rooms - $35-56
Pets: Welcome w/$5 fee
Creature Comforts: CCTV, a/c,
kit

MORRIS

Best Western Prairie Inn
(800) 528-1234, (320) 589-3030
http://www.bestwestern.com
200 Rte. 28
90 rooms - $40-99
Pets: Welcome w/$ fee
Creature Comforts: CCTV, a/c,
refrig, restaurant, cont. brkfst,
pool, sauna, whirlpool

MORTON

Granite Valley Motel
(507) 697-6205
400 W. Ledge Rd.
40 rooms - $45-58
Pets: Welcome w/$10 fee
Creature Comforts: CCTV, a/c

NEVIS

The Park Street Inn
(800) 797-1778, (218) 652-4500
http://www.parkstreetinn.com
254 Park St.
4 rooms - $55-129
Pets: Welcome
Creature Comforts: An old-
fashioned home on hill built by
banker, CCTV, VCR, a/c,
fireplace, refrig, Jacuzzis, full
country brkfst, hiking trail, water
fall, lake views

NEW ULM

Colonial Inn Motel
(507) 354-3128
1315 N. Broadway St.
25 rooms - $28-50
Pets: Small pets welcome
Creature Comforts: CCTV, a/c

Holiday Inn
(800) HOLIDAY, (507) 359-2941
http://www.holiday-inn.com
2101 S. Broadway St.
125 rooms - $75-135
Pets: Small pets in smkng rms
Creature Comforts: CCTV, a/c,
refrig, restaurant, whirlpool, pool,
sauna

Super 8 Motel
(800) 800-8000, (507) 359-2400
http://www.super8.com
1901 S. Broadway St.
62 rooms - $48-63
Pets: Welcome w/$5 fee
Creature Comforts: CCTV, a/c,
Jacuzzis, refrig, micro, cont. brkfst

NISSWA

Nisswa Motel
(218) 963-7611
1426 Merrill Ave.
18 rooms - $34-70
Pets: Welcome w/$3 fee(1 per rm)
Creature Comforts: CCTV,
VCR, a/c, refrig

NORTH BRANCH

Cross Roads Motel
(800) 422-0160, (612) 674-7074
1118 Main St.
15 rooms - $40-65
Pets: In ltd. rooms w/$5 fee
Creature Comforts: CCTV, a/c,
kit, Jacuzzi

NORTHFIELD

Super 8 Motel
(800) 800-8000, (507) 663-0371
http://www.super8.com
1420 Riverview Dr.
40 rooms - $49-66
Pets: Welcome
Creature Comforts: CCTV, a/c,
refrig, micro, cont. brkfst

OLIVIA

The Sheep Shedde Inn
(320) 523-5000
2425 W. Lincoln Ave.
32 rooms - $39-58
Pets: Small pets welcome
Creature Comforts: CCTV, a/c,
restaurant

ONAMIA

Econo Lodge
(800) 55-ECONO, (320) 532-3838
http://www.econolodge.com
40993 Rte. 169
38 rooms - $35-105
Pets: Small pets welcome
Creature Comforts: CCTV, a/c,
restaurant, cont. brkfst

Lake Mille Lacs Resort
(800) 657-4704, (320) 532-3657
http://www.eddysresorts.com
Routes 169 & 26
82 rooms - $65-129
Pets: Welcome w/$10 daily fee
Creature Comforts: CCTV, a/c,
fireplace, refrig, micro, Jacuzzis,
restaurant, pool, hlth clb, sauna,
whirlpool, marina/fishing

ORR

North Country Inn
(218) 757-3778
4483 Rte. 53
12 rooms - $39-55
Pets: Welcome in ltd. rms
Creature Comforts: CCTV,
VCR, a/c

OWATONNA
Budget Host Inn
(800) Bud-Host, (507) 451-8712
http://www.budgethost.com
745 State Ave.
28 rooms - $35-80
Pets: Small pets welcome
Creature Comforts: CCTV, a/c,
refrig, micro

Country Inn by Carlson
(800) 456-4000, (507) 455-9295
http://www.countryinns.com
130 Allen Ave. NW
52 rooms - $55-90
Pets: Small pets w/$25 dep.
Creature Comforts: CCTV, a/c,
refrig, micro, Jacuzzis, pool,
whirlpool

Oakdale Motel
(507) 451-5480
1418 S. Oak St.
24 rooms - $29-115
Pets: In smoking rooms w/$8 fee
Creature Comforts: CCTV, a/c,
kit, Jacuzzi

Ramada Inn
(800) 2-Ramada, (507) 455-0606
http://www.ramada.com
1212 Rte. 35
117 rooms - $57-80
Pets: Under 20 lbs welcome
Creature Comforts: CCTV, a/c,
refrig, Jacuzzis, restaurant, pool

PARK RAPIDS
Econo Lodge
(800) 55-ECONO, (218) 732-8888
http://www.econolodge.com
Rte. 34 East
40 rooms - $39-55
Pets: Small pets welcome
Creature Comforts: CCTV, a/c,
cont. brkfst, whirlpool

PINE RIVER
Trailside Inn
(800) 450-4499, (218) 587-4499
Rte. 371
30 rooms - $ 55-105
Pets: Welcome
Creature Comforts: CCTV, a/c,
cont. brkfst, hlth clb, sauna,
whirlpool

PIPESTONE
Super 8 Motel
(800) 800-8000, (507) 825-4217
http://www.super8.com
605 - 8th Ave.
40 rooms - $43-79
Pets: In smkng rms w/$20 dep.
Creature Comforts: CCTV, a/c,
refrig, Jacuzzis

PLYMOUTH
Radisson Hotel
(800) 333-3333, (612) 559-6600
http://www.radisson.com
3131 Campus Dr.
244 rooms - $99-169
Pets: Under 40 lbs. welcome
Creature Comforts: CCTV, a/c,
refrig, micro, Jacuzzis, restaurant,
pool, hlth club, whirlpool, tennis,
racquetball

Red Roof Inn
(800) The-Roof, (612) 553-1751
http://www.redroof.com
2600 Annapolis Lane
120 rooms - $35-85
Pets: Small pets welcome
Creature Comforts: CCTV, a/c

PRINCETON
Rum River Motel
(612) 389-3120
510 - 19th Ave. N.
29 rooms - $39-53
Pets: Small pets welcome
Creature Comforts: CCTV, a/c,
refrig, Jacuzzi, cont. brkfst

PROCTOR
AmericInn Motel
(800) 634-3444, (218) 624-1028
http://www.americinn.com
185 Rte. 2
45 rooms - $59-139
Pets: Small pets w/$25 dep.
Creature Comforts: CCTV, a/c,
refrig, micro, Jacuzzis, sauna,
whirlpool, pool

RED WING
AmericInn Motel
(800) 634-3444, (218) 385-9060
http://www.americinn.com
1819 Old Main St.
49 rooms - $59-85
Pets: Small pets welcome
Creature Comforts: CCTV, a/c,
refrig, micro, Jacuzzis, sauna,
whirlpool, hlth club, pool

Best Western Quiet House
(800) 528-1234, (612) 388-1577
http://www.bestwestern.com
Route 61
51 rooms - $75-175
Pets: Small pets w/$15 fee
Creature Comforts: CCTV, a/c,
refrig, whirlpool, hlth club, pool

Days Inn
(800) DAYS-INN, (612) 388-3568
http://www.daysinn.com
955 - 7th St.
48 rooms - $44-90
Pets: Welcome w/$8 dep.
Creature Comforts: CCTV, a/c,
cont. brkfst, whirlpool, pool

REDWOOD FALLS
Comfort Inn
(800) 228-5150, (507) 644-5700
http://www.comfortinn.com
1382 E. Bridge St.
108 rooms - $50-133
Pets: Small pets welcome
Creature Comforts: CCTV, a/c,
cont. brkfst, whirlpool, sauna

RICHFIELD
Motel 6
(800) 4-MOTEL6, (612) 861-4491
http://www.motel6.com
7460 Cedar Ave. So.
103 rooms - $44-59
Pets: Under 30 lbs. welcome
Creature Comforts: CCTV, a/c

ROCHESTER
Best Western Inn
(800) 528-1234, (507) 289-3987
http://www.bestwestern.com
20 NW Fifth Ave.
62 rooms - $50-85
Pets: Welcome w/$5 fee
Creature Comforts: CCTV, a/c,
Jacuzzis, kit, sauna, whirlpool,
pool

Blondell's Motel
(800) 441-5209, (507) 582-9444
1406 - 2nd St. SW
56 rooms - $45-57
Pets: Welcome
Creature Comforts: CCTV, a/c,
kit, refrig, restaurant

Clinic View Inn
(507) 289-8646
9 NW 3rd Ave.
122 rooms - $79-125
Pets: Welcome
Creature Comforts: CCTV, a/c,
kit, restaurant, pool, hlth clb,
sauna, whirlpool

Comfort Inn
(800) 228-5150, (507) 281-2211
http://www.comfortinn.com
1625 S. Broadway St.
164 rooms - $65-138
Pets: Small pets welcome
Creature Comforts: CCTV, a/c,
refrig, micro, Jacuzzis, restaurant,
cont. brkfst, pool

Country Inns by Carlson
(800) 456-4000, (507) 285-3335
http://www.countryinns.com
4323 Rte. 52
64 rooms - $60-85
Pets: Small pets w/$10 fee
Creature Comforts: CCTV, a/c,
refrig, micro, Jacuzzis, pool,
sauna, whirlpool

Days Inn
(800) DAYS-INN, (507) 282-3801
http://www.daysinn.com
6 - 1st Ave.
71 rooms - $50-75
Pets: Welcome
Creature Comforts: CCTV, a/c,
Jacuzzis, restaurant, cont. brkfst

Days Inn, South
(800) DAYS-INN, (507) 286-1001
http://www.daysinn.com
111 SE 28th St.
130 rooms - $49-67
Pets: Welcome
Creature Comforts: CCTV, a/c,
kit, restaurant, cont. brkfst

Daystop
(800) DAYS-INN, (507) 282-2733
http://www.daysinn.com
Rte. 52/2nd St.
49 rooms - $40-69
Pets: Welcome
Creature Comforts: CCTV, a/c,
kit, cont. brkfst

Econo Lodge
(800) 55-ECONO, (507) 288-1855
http://www.econolodge.com
519 - 3rd Ave. SW
62 rooms - $48-62
Pets: Small pets welcome
Creature Comforts: CCTV, a/c,
kit, cont. brkfst

Fiksdal Motel
(507) 288-2671
1215 SW 2nd St.
24 rooms - $40-55
Pets: Welcome
Creature Comforts: CCTV, a/c,
kit

Holiday Inn
(800) HOLIDAY, (507) 288-3231
http://www.holiday-inn.com
220 S. Broadway St.
172 rooms - $70-129
Pets: Small pets welcome
Creature Comforts: CCTV,
VCR, a/c, refrig, micro, restaurant

Holiday Inn
(800) HOLIDAY, (507) 288-1844
http://www.holiday-inn.com
1630 S. Broadway St.
198 rooms - $60-85
Pets: Small pets welcome
Creature Comforts: CCTV, a/c,
kit, Jacuzzis, restaurant, sauna,
whirlpool, hlth club, pool

Howard Johnson
(800) I-Go-Hojo, 507) 289-1617
http://www.hojo.com
111 - 17th Ave. SW
49 rooms - $45-79
Pets: Welcome w/$5 fee
Creature Comforts: CCTV, a/c,
refrig, micro, cont. brkfst, pool

Kahler Hotel
(800) 533-1655, (507) 282-2581
http://www.kahler.com
20 SW 2nd Ave.
699 rooms - $59-1,600
Pets: Welcome in smkng rms
Creature Comforts: Historic
hotel w/English Tudor motif,
CCTV, VCR, a/c, refrig, 6
restaurants, pool, hlth clb, sauna,
whirlpool, rooftop sundeck

Kahler Inn
(800) 533-1655, (507) 289-8646
http://www.kahler.com
9 NW 3rd Ave.
265 rooms - $65-149
Pets: Welcome in smoking rooms
Creature Comforts: CCTV,
VCR, a/c, refrig, restaurant, pool,
hlth clb, sauna, whirlpool

Knights Inn
(800) 843-5644, (507) 282-1756
http://www.knightsinn.com
106 - 21 St SE
82 rooms - $45-89
Pets: Welcome in smoking rooms
Creature Comforts: CCTV, a/c,
refrig, micro, cont. brkfst

Marriott Hotel
(800) 228-9290, (507) 280-6000
http://www.marriott.com
101 - 1st Ave. SW
195 rooms - $135-399
Pets: Welcome on third flr.
Creature Comforts: CCTV,
VCR, a/c, refrig, micro, restaurant,
pool, hlth clb, sauna, whirlpools

Motel 6
(800) 4-MOTEL6, (507) 282-6625
http://www.motel6.com
2107 W. Frontage Rd.
107 rooms - $34-49
Pets: Under 30 lbs. welcome
Creature Comforts: CCTV, a/c,
pool

Quality Inn
(800) 228-5151, (507) 282-8091
http://www.qualityinn.com
1620 - 1st Ave. SE
40 suites - $75-175
Pets: Small pets welcome
Creature Comforts: CCTV, a/c,
kit, cont. brkfst

Radisson Hotel
(800) 333-3333, (507) 281-8000
http://www.radisson.com
150 S. Broadway St.
210 rooms - $89-169
Pets: Welcome
Creature Comforts: CCTV, a/c,
refrig, micro, Jacuzzis, restaurant,
pool, hlth club, whirlpool

Ramada Inn
(800) 2-Ramada, (507) 288-9090
http://www.ramada.com
435 - 16th Ave. NW
120 rooms - $45-63
Pets: Small pets welcome
Creature Comforts: CCTV, a/c,
refrig, cont. brkfst, pool

Super 8 Motel
(800) 800-8000, (507) 288-8288
http://www.super8.com
1230 S. Broadway St.
89 rooms - $53-69
Pets: Welcome w/$10 dep.
Creature Comforts: CCTV, a/c,
refrig, micro, Jacuzzis, cont.
brkfst, whirlpool, pool

Super 8 Motel
(800) 800-8000, (507) 282-9905
http://www.super8.com
1850 S. Broadway St.
62 rooms - $49-65
Pets: Welcome
Creature Comforts: CCTV, a/c,
cont. brkfst

Super 8 Motel, West
(800) 800-8000, (507) 281-5100
http://www.super8.com
1608 - 2nd St. SW
65 rooms - $54-69
Pets: Welcome
Creature Comforts: CCTV, a/c,
refrig, micro, cont. brkfst

Thriftlodge
(800) 525-9055, (507) 337-1621
http://www.travelodge.com
1837 S. Broadway St.
27 rooms - $36-49
Pets: Small pets welcome
Creature Comforts: CCTV, a/c,
cont. brkfst

Travelodge
(800) 578-7878, (507) 289-4095
http://www.travelodge.com
426 - 2nd St. SW
63 rooms - $44-75
Pets: Small pets welcome
Creature Comforts: CCTV, a/c,
Jacuzzis, kit, cont. brkfst, sauna,
whirlpool

ROGERS
AmericInn Motel
(800) 634-3444, (612) 428-4346
http://www.americinn.com
21800 Industrial Blvd.
36 rooms - $48-75
Pets: Small pets w/$5 fee
Creature Comforts: CCTV,
VCR, a/c, refrig, micro, Jacuzzis,
sauna, whirlpool, pool

Super 8 Motel
(800) 800-8000, (612) 428-4000
http://www.super8.com
21130 - 134th Ave. N.
63 rooms - $52-73
Pets: Welcome w/$5 fee
Creature Comforts: CCTV, a/c,
cont. brkfst

ROSEAU
AmericInn
(800) 634-3444, (218) 463-1045
http://www.americinn.com
1090 - 3rd St. NW
34 rooms - $45-65
Pets: Small pets w/$5 fee
Creature Comforts: CCTV, a/c,
refrig, micro, sauna, whirlpool,
pool

Super 8 Motel
(800) 800-8000, (218) 463-2196
http://www.super8.com
318 Westside Rd.
35 rooms - $39-50
Pets: Small pets welcome
Creature Comforts: CCTV, a/c,
restaurant

ROSEVILLE
Motel 6
(800) 4-MOTEL6, (612) 639-3988
http://www.motel6.com
2300 Cleveland Ave. N.
113 rooms - $42-58
Pets: Under 30 lbs. welcome
Creature Comforts: CCTV, a/c,
and a pool

ST. CLOUD
Baymont Inns
(877)BAYMONT, (612) 253-4444
http://www.baymontinns.com
70 S. 37th Ave.
90 rooms - $58-75
Pets: Welcome in smkng rms
Creature Comforts: CCTV, a/c,
refrig, micro. cont. brkfst, sauna,
whirlpool

Best Western Americana Inn
(800) 528-1234, (320) 252-8700
http://www.bestwestern.com
520 S. Rte. 10
63 rooms - $55-110
Pets: Welcome w/$5 fee
Creature Comforts: CCTV, a/c,
kit, Jacuzzis, restaurant, sauna,
whirlpool, pool

Best Western Kelly Inn
(800) 528-1234, (320) 253-0606
http://www.bestwestern.com
Rte. 2 & 4th Ave.
230 rooms - $65-120
Pets: Welcome
Creature Comforts: CCTV,
VCR, a/c, refrig, micro, Jacuzzis,
restaurant, sauna, whirlpool, pool

Days Inn
(800) DAYS-INN, (320) 253-0500
http://www.daysinn.com
420 SE Rte. 10
78 rooms - $45-134
Pets: Welcome
Creature Comforts: CCTV, a/c,
Jacuzzis, cont. brkfst, whirlpool,
pool

Gateway Motel
(320) 252-4050
310 Lincoln Ave. SE
34 rooms - $29-50
Pets: Welcome w/$5 fee
Creature Comforts: CCTV, a/c,
refrig, micro

Holiday Inn
(800) HOLIDAY, (320) 253-9000
http://www.holiday-inn.com
75 - 37th Ave. S.
255 rooms - $65-199
Pets: Small pets welcome
Creature Comforts: CCTV,
VCR, a/c, kit, Jacuzzis, restaurant,
sauna, whirlpool, hlth club, pool

Motel 6
(800) 4-MOTEL6, (320) 253-7070
http://www.motel6.com
815 - 1st St. S.
93 rooms - $34-49
Pets: Under 30 lbs. welcome
Creature Comforts: CCTV, a/c

Ramada Inn
(800) 2-Ramada, (320) 253-3200
http://www.ramada.com
121 Park Ave.
68 rooms - $55-90
Pets: Welcome
Creature Comforts: CCTV, a/c,
refrig, cont. brkfst, hlth club, pool

Super 8 Motel
(800) 800-8000, (320) 253-5530
http://www.super8.com
50 Park Ave. S.
68 rooms - $40-53
Pets: Welcome
Creature Comforts: CCTV, a/c,
cont. brkfst

Thrifty Motel
(320) 253-6320
130 - 14th Ave. NE
50 rooms - $33-69
Pets: Welcome w/4$ fee
Creature Comforts: CCTV,
VCR, a/c, Jacuzzis

ST. JAMES
Super 8 Motel
(800) 800-8000, (507) 375-4708
http://www.super8.com
Route 60
34 rooms - $44-60
Pets: Welcome w/permission
Creature Comforts: CCTV, a/c,
cont. brkfst, hlth club

ST. JOSEPH
Super 8 Motel
(800) 800-8000, (320) 363-7711
http://www.super8.com
Route 75
27 rooms - $42-62
Pets: Small pets welcome
Creature Comforts: CCTV, a/c,
cont. brkfst

ST. PAUL
Best Western Kelly Inn
(800) 528-1234, (612) 227-8711
http://www.bestwestern.com
161 St. Anthony Ave.
126 rooms - $80-120
Pets: Welcome
Creature Comforts: CCTV, a/c,
kit, restaurant, sauna, whirlpool,
pool

Days Inn
(800) DAYS-INN, (612) 292-8929
http://www.daysinn.com
175 W. 7th St.
199 rooms - $65-155
Pets: Welcome
Creature Comforts: CCTV,
VCR, a/c, restaurant, cont. brkfst

Exel Inns
(800) 367-3935, (612) 771-5566
1739 Old Hudson Rd.
100 rooms - $45-75
Pets: Small pets welcome
Creature Comforts: CCTV,
VCR, a/c, refrig, micro, Jacuzzis,
cont. brkfst.

Holiday Inn
(800) HOLIDAY, (612) 731-2220
http://www.holiday-inn.com
2201 Burns Ave.
194 rooms - $90-129
Pets: Small pets w/$25 dep.
Creature Comforts: CCTV, a/c,
refrig, micro, Jacuzzis, restaurant,
sauna, whirlpool, hlth club, pool

Ramada Inn
(800) 2-Ramada, (612) 735-2333
http://www.ramada.com
1870 Old Hudson Rd.
200 rooms - $75-129
Pets: Small pets welcome
Creature Comforts: CCTV, a/c,
refrig, restaurant, pool, sauna, hlth
club, whirlpool

SAUK CENTRE
Econo Lodge
(800) 55-ECONO, (320) 352-6581
http://www.econolodge.com
Route 94
38 rooms - $45-125
Pets: Small pets w/credit card dep
Creature Comforts: CCTV, a/c,
Jacuzzi, restaurant, cont. brkfst

Super 8 Motel
(800) 800-8000, (320) 352-6581
http://www.super8.com
Route 94
38 rooms - $44-60
Pets: Welcome w/$10 dep.
Creature Comforts: CCTV, a/c,
Jacuzzis, waterbeds, restaurant,
cont. brkfst

ST. PETER
AmericInn Motel
(800) 634-3444, (507) 931-6554
http://www.americinn.com
700 N. Minnesota Ave.
43 rooms - $50-75
Pets: First flr. smoking rooms
Creature Comforts: CCTV, a/c,
refrig, micro, Jacuzzis, whirlpool,
pool

SAUK RAPIDS
AmericInn Motel
(800) 634-3444, (320) 352-2800
http://www.americinn.com
1230 Timberlane Rd.
42 rooms - $50-75
Pets: Small pets w/credit card dep
Creature Comforts: CCTV,
VCR, a/c, refrig, micro, Jacuzzis

Econo Lodge
(800) 55-ECONO, (320) 251-9333
http://www.econolodge.com
1420 - 2nd St. N.
51 rooms - $45-135
Pets: Small pets w/$10 fee
Creature Comforts: CCTV, a/c,
Jacuzzis, cont. brkfst

Gopher Prairie Motel
(800) 341-8000, (320) 352-2215
http://www.imalodging.com
Rtes 94 and 71
23 rooms - $35-45
Pets: Welcome
Creature Comforts: CCTV, a/c,
kit, waterbeds

Hillcrest Motel
(800) 858-6333, (320) 352-2215
965 S. Main St.
22 rooms - $29-40
Pets: Welcome w/$5 fee
Creature Comforts: CCTV, a/c

SCHROEDER
Lamb's Resort
(218) 663-7292
http://www.boreal.org/lambsresort
Rte. 61, Lamb's Way
15 cabins- $89-130
Pets: Welcome w/$6 fee
Creature Comforts: Charming family-owned resort on 60 acres w/log cabins, CCTV, kit, Jacuzzi, restaurant, cont. brkfst, pool, hlth clb access, sauna, whirlpool, gift shop, on Lake Superior

SEBEKA
K's Motel
(218) 837-5162
Route 71
12 rooms - $35-42
Pets: Welcome
Creature Comforts:CCTV, refrig

SHAKOPEE
AmericInn Motel
(800) 634-3444, (612) 445-5074
http://www.americinn.com
1251 E. 1st Ave.
56 rooms - $55-80
Pets: Small pets welcome
Creature Comforts: CCTV, VCR, a/c, refrig, micro, Jacuzzis, sauna, whirlpool, hlth club

SILVER BAY
Mariner Motel
(800) 777-8452, (218) 226-8452
46 Outer Dr.
29 rooms - $38-80
Pets: Welcome
Creature Comforts: CCTV, kit, sauna, Jacuzzis

SLEEPY EYE
Best Western Seven Gables
(800) 528-1234, (507) 794-5390
http://www.bestwestern.com
1100 E. Main St.
37 rooms - $56-95
Pets: Welcome w/$6 fee
Creature Comforts: CCTV, VCR, a/c, refrig, whirlpool, pool

SPICER
Northern Inn
(320) 796-2091
154 Lake St.
32 rooms - $49-80
Pets: Small pets w/$8 fee
Creature Comforts: CCTV, a/c, refrig, micro, pool

STAPLES
Super 8 Motel
(800) 800-8000, (218) 894-3585
http://www.super8.com
109 - 2nd Ave. W.
36 rooms - $43-59
Pets: Welcome w/permission
Creature Comforts: CCTV, a/c

STILLWATER
Best Western Inn
(800) 528-1234, (612) 430-1300
http://www.bestwestern.com
1750 W. Frontage Rd.
60 rooms - $53-165
Pets: Small pets welcome
Creature Comforts: CCTV, a/c, refrig, Jacuzzis, whirlpool, hlth club

TAYLORS FALLS
The Springs Inn
(800) 851-4243, (612) 465-6565
90 Government Rd.
28 rooms - $35-60
Pets: Welcome w/$8 fee
Creature Comforts: CCTV, a/c, kit, whirlpool, river views

THIEF RIVER FALLS
Best Western Inn
(800) 528-1234, (218) 681-7555
http://www.bestwestern.com
1060 Rte. 32
78 rooms - $52-74
Pets: Welcome if leashed
Creature Comforts: CCTV, VCR, a/c, refrig, restaurant, whirlpool, pool

C'mon Inn
(800) 950-8111, (218) 681-3000
1586 Rte. 59
45 rooms - $48-89
Pets: Welcome in smoking rooms
Creature Comforts: CCTV, a/c, refrig, cont. brkfst, pool, whirlpool

Super 8 Motel
(800) 800-8000, (218) 681-6205
http://www.super8.com
1915 Rte. 59 SE
46 rooms - $48-64
Pets: Welcome
Creature Comforts: CCTV, a/c, cont. brkfst

TOFTE
Bluefin Bay Motel
(800) BLUE-FIN, (218) 663-7296
http://www.bluefinbay.com
Rte. 61, Box 2125
138 rooms - $75-395
Pets: In ltd. rooms w/$12 fee
Creature Comforts: Units lining the Lake Superior, contemporary decor, CCTV, VCR, a/c, fireplace, kit, Jacuzzi, restaurant, cont. brkfst, pool, hlth clb, sauna, massage, whirlpool, tennis, store

Chateau Le Veaux
(800) 445-5773, (218) 663-7223
http://www.boreal.org/chateau/
6626 Rte. 61, Box 115
34 condos - $60-195
Pets: Welcome in certain rooms with a $10 daily fee
Creature Comforts: Terrific accommodations set in shingled condos-individually decorated, CCTV, a/c, fireplace, kit, Jacuzzi, pool, hlth clb, sauna, whirlpool, library, on Lake Superior, trail

TWO HARBORS
Country Inns by Carlson
(800) 456-4000, (218) 834-5557
http://www.countryinns.com
1204 - 7th Ave.
48 rooms - $59-119
Pets: Small pets welcome
Creature Comforts: CCTV, VCR, a/c, refrig, micro, Jacuzzis, pool, sauna, whirlpool

Superior Shores Resort
(800) 242-1988, (218) 834-5671
http://www.superiorshores.com
10 Superior Shores Rd.
128 rooms - $55-325
Pets: In ltd. rms w/$25 dep.
Creature Comforts: Set along Lake Superior's rocky shoreline, cozy lodge w/ pine walled rooms, down comforters, CCTV, VCR, a/c, stone fireplaces, kit, sky lights, Jacuzzi, restaurant, pool, shop, tennis, trails, xc-skiing

TYLER
Babette's Inn
(507) 537-1632
308 S. Tyler St.
3 suites - $60-75
Pets: Welcome
Creature Comforts: CTV, VCR, a/c, fireplaces, gourmet brkfst

VIRGINIA

Lakeshore Motor Inn
(800) 569-8131, (218) 741-3360
404 N. 6th Ave.
18 rooms - $37-56
Pets: Welcome
Creature Comforts: CCTV, a/c,
Jacuzzis

Ski-View Motel
(218) 741-8918
903 - 17th St. N.
60 rooms - $32-44
Pets: Welcome
Creature Comforts: CCTV, a/c,
sauna

WABASHA

The Anderson House
(800) 535-5467, (651) 565-4524
http://www.theandersonhouse.com
333 W. Main St.
25 rooms - $55-145
Pets: Small pets welcome
Creature Comforts: 1856 inn,
Victorian pictures, antiques, quilts,
marble topped dressers, gardens,
cookie jar, CCTV, a/c, fireplace,
refrig, micro, Jacuzzis, restaurant,
10 resident cats

WACONIA

Super 8 Motel
(800) 800-8000, (612) 442-5147
http://www.super8.com
301 E. Frontage Rd.
26 rooms - $49-66
Pets: Welcome w/permission
Creature Comforts: CCTV, a/c,
Jacuzzis, cont. brkfst, whirlpool

WALKER

Lakeview Inn
(800) 252-5073, (218) 547-1212
PO Box 1359
13 rooms - $45-62
Pets: Welcome w/$5 fee
Creature Comforts: CCTV, a/c,
kit

WARROAD

The Patch Motel
(218) 386-2723
Route 11
82 rooms - $39-50
Pets: Welcome
Creature Comforts: CCTV, a/c,
pool, hlth clb, whirlpool

WHITE BEAR LAKE

Country Inns by Carlson
(800) 456-4000, (612) 429-5393
http://www.countryinns.com
4940 Rte. 61
90 rooms - $80-149
Pets: Small pets welcome
Creature Comforts: CCTV, a/c,
refrig, micro, fireplaces, Jacuzzis,
restaurant, pool, sauna, whirlpool

WILLMAR

Colonial Inn
(800) 396-4445, (320) 235-4444
web site pending
1102 S. 1st St.
22 rooms - $49-89
Pets: Welcome
Creature Comforts: CCTV,
VCR, a/c, refrig, micro, Jacuzzis

Comfort Inn
(800) 228-5150, (320) 231-2601
http://www.comfortinn.com
2200 E. Rte. 12
60 rooms - $53-145
Pets: Small pets welcome
Creature Comforts: CCTV, a/c,
Jacuzzis, cont. brkfst, pool

Days Inn
(800) DAYS-INN, (320) 231-1275
http://www.daysinn.com
225 - 28th St SE
59 rooms - $48-60
Pets: Welcome
Creature Comforts: CCTV, a/c,
Jacuzzis, cont. brkfst, whirlpool,
sauna

Holiday Inn
(800) HOLIDAY, (320) 235-6060
http://www.holiday-inn.com
2100 Rte. 12
99 rooms - $65-99
Pets: Small pets welcome
Creature Comforts: CCTV, a/c,
refrig, restaurant, sauna,
whirlpool, hlth club, pool

Super 8 Motel
(800) 800-8000, (320) 235-7260
http://www.super8.com
2655 S. 1st St.
60 rooms - $42-60
Pets: Welcome
Creature Comforts: CCTV, a/c,
cont. brkfst

WINDOM

Super 8 Motel
(800) 800-8000, (507) 831-1120
http://www.super8.com
222 S. 3rd Ave.
32 rooms - $46-64
Pets: Welcome w/$6 fee
Creature Comforts: CCTV, a/c,
cont. brkfst

WINONA

Best Western Riverport
(800) 528-1234, (507) 452-0606
http://www.bestwestern.com
900 Bruski Dr.
106 rooms - $60-109
Pets: Small pets w/$10 fee
Creature Comforts: CCTV,
VCR, a/c, refrig, micro, Jacuzzis,
restaurant, sauna, whirlpool, hlth
club, pool

Days Inn
(800) DAYS-INN, (507) 454-6930
http://www.daysinn.com
420 Cottonwood Dr.
58 rooms - $44-75
Pets: Welcome
Creature Comforts: CCTV, a/c,
cont. brkfst

Quality Inn
(800) 228-5151, (507) 454-4390
http://www.qualityinn.com
956 Mankato Ave.
112 suites - $60-99
Pets: Small pets welcome
Creature Comforts: CCTV,
VCR, a/c, refrig, micro, restaurant,
cont. brkfst, whirlpool, pool

Sterling Motel
(800) 452-1235, (507) 454-1120
1450 Gilmore Ave.
32 rooms - $35-65
Pets: Welcome w/$5 fee
Creature Comforts: CCTV, a/c,
refrig

Super 8 Motel
(800) 800-8000, (507) 454-6066
http://www.super8.com
1025 Sugar Loaf Rd.
61 rooms - $45-63
Pets: Welcome
Creature Comforts: CCTV,
VCR, a/c, waterbeds, cont. brkfst

WOODBURY
Hampton Inn
(800) Hampton, (612) 578-2822
http://www.hampton-inn.com
1450 Weir Dr.
64 rooms - $65-100
Pets: Under 20 lbs. welcome
Creature Comforts: CCTV, a/c,
cont. brkfst, pool, whirlpool, hlth
club access

Red Roof Inn
(800) The-Roof, (612) 738-7160
http://www.redroof.com
1806 Woodale Dr.
109 rooms - $40-75
Pets: Small pets welcome
Creature Comforts: CCTV, a/c

WORTHINGTON
Best Western Inn
(800) 528-1234, (507) 376-4146
http://www.bestwestern.com
1923 Dover St.
36 rooms - $35-63
Pets: Welcome in smkng rms.
Creature Comforts: CCTV, a/c,
refrig, micro, cont. brkfst.

Budget Host Inn
(800) Bud-Host, (507) 376-6155
http://www.budgethost.com
207 Oxford St.
16 rooms - $39-80
Pets: In smkng rms w/$5 fee
Creature Comforts: CCTV, a/c,
refrig, micro

Holiday Inn
(800) HOLIDAY, (507) 322-2991
http://www.holiday-inn.com
2015 Humiston Ave.
119 rooms - $69-129
Pets: Welcome in smoking rooms
Creature Comforts: CCTV, a/c,
refrig, micro, Jacuzzis, restaurant,
sauna, whirlpool, pool

Super 8 Motel
(800) 800-8000, (507) 372-7755
http://www.super8.com
Rte. 266, Box 98
60 rooms - $46-54
Pets: Welcome w/$10 dep.
Creature Comforts: CCTV, a/c,
refrig, micro, cont. brkfst,
whirlpool

ZUMBROTA
Super 8 Motel
(800) 800-8000, (507) 732-7852
http://www.super8.com
Rtes 52 & 68
30 rooms - $40-59
Pets: Welcome
Creature Comforts: CCTV, a/c,
Jacuzzis, restaurant, cont. brkfst

Mississippi

ABERDEEN
Best Western Inn
(800) 528-1234, (601) 369-4343
http://www.bestwestern.com
801 E. Commerce St.
50 rooms - $49-65
Pets: Small pets welcome
Creature Comforts: CCTV, a/c,
refrig, cont. brkfst, pool

BATESVILLE
Comfort Inn
(800) 228-5150, (601) 563-1188
http://www.comfortinn.com
290 Power Dr.
51 rooms - $48-84
Pets: Small pets welcome
Creature Comforts: CCTV, a/c,
cont. brkfst, pool

BAY ST. LOUIS
Key West Inn
(228) 466-0444
http://www.keywestinn.net
1000 Rte. 90
45 rooms - $65-120
Pets: Small pets w/$5 fee
Creature Comforts: CCTV, a/c

BILOXI
Days Inn
(800) DAYS-INN, (228) 872-8255
http://www.daysinn.com
7305 Washington Ave.
55 rooms - $55-165
Pets: Welcome w/$10 fee
Creature Comforts: CCTV, a/c,
refrig, micro, Jacuzzis, cont.
brkfst, whirlpool, pool

Lofty Oaks Inn
(800) 280-4361, (601) 392-6722
www.bbhost.com/loftyoaksinn
17288 Route 67
4 rooms - $99-135
Pets: Small pets welcome
Creature Comforts: An elegantly
appointed B&B with a homey
ambiance, situated on 6 acres
adjacent to a golf course, theme
rooms, CCTV, VCR, a/c, kit,
Jacuzzi, fireplace, piano, deck,
romantic setting, cont. brkfst, pool

Motel 6
(800) 4-MOTEL6, (601) 388-5130
http://www.motel6.com
2476 Beach Blvd.
100 rooms - $43-55
Pets: Under 30 lbs. welcome
Creature Comforts: CCTV, a/c,
pool

President BroadwaterResort
(800) THE-PRES, (228) 388-2211
www.presidentbroadwater.com
21100 Beach Blvd.
478 rooms - $95-160
Pets: Welcome w/$100 dep.
Creature Comforts: An
expansive resort on 260 acres
along the water, CCTV, a/c, kit,
restaurant, 3 pools, hlth clb, sauna,
whirlpool, tennis, golf, casino,
marina/boating/deep sea fishing

BROOKHAVEN
Claridge Inn
(601) 833-1341
1210 Broackway Blvd.
120 rooms - $42-50
Pets: Small dogs welcome
Creature Comforts: CCTV, a/c,
restaurant, cont. brkfst, pool

CANTON
Econo Lodge
(800) 55-ECONO, (601) 859-2643
http://www.econolodge.com
119 Soldier Colony Rd.
40 rooms - $45-59
Pets: Small pets welcome
Creature Comforts: CCTV, a/c,
cont. brkfst, pool

CLARKSDALE
Days Inn
(800) DAYS-INN, (601) 624-4391
http://www.daysinn.com
1910 Rte. 61
99 rooms - $45-98
Pets: Welcome w/$8 fee
Creature Comforts: CCTV, a/c,
restaurant, cont. brkfst, pool

Hampton Inn
(800) Hampton, (601) 627-9292
http://www.hampton-inn.com
710 S. State St.
93 rooms - $65-89
Pets: Welcome
Creature Comforts: CCTV, a/c,
cont. brkfst, pool, sports ct, hlth
club

CLINTON
Days Inn
(800) DAYS-INN, (601) 925-5065
http://www.daysinn.com
482 Springridge Rd.
40 rooms - $40-125
Pets: Welcome
Creature Comforts: CCTV, a/c,
refrig, micro, Jacuzzis, cont.
brkfst, pool

DURANT
Super 8 Motel
(800) 800-8000, (601) 653-3881
http://www.super8.com
31201 Rte. 12
30 rooms - $45-69
Pets: Welcome w/$10 fee
Creature Comforts: CCTV, a/c,
Jacuzzis, cont. brkfst

FOREST
Best Western Inn
(800) 528-1234, (601) 469-2640
http://www.bestwestern.com
Route 20
82 rooms - $52-69
Pets: Welcome
Creature Comforts: CCTV, a/c,
refrig, micro, pool

Comfort Inn
(800) 228-5150, (601) 469-2100
http://www.comfortinn.com
1250 Rte. 35
51 rooms - $49-65
Pets: Small pets welcome
Creature Comforts: CCTV, a/c,
refrig, micro, cont. brkfst, pool

GREENVILLE

Comfort Inn
(800) 228-5150, (601) 378-4976
http://www.comfortinn.com
3080 Rte. 82
76 rooms - $56-89
Pets: Small pets welcome
Creature Comforts: CCTV, a/c, refrig, micro, cont. brkfst, pool

Days Inn
(800) DAYS-INN, (601) 335-1999
http://www.daysinn.com
2500 Rte. 82
154 rooms - $40-69
Pets: Welcome w/$3 fee
Creature Comforts: CCTV, a/c, refrig, cont. brkfst, pool

Ramada Inn
(800) 2-Ramada, (601) 332-4411
http://www.ramada.com
2700 Rte. 82
122 rooms - $55-89
Pets: Welcome
Creature Comforts: CCTV, a/c, restaurant, pool

GREENWOOD

Comfort Inn
(800) 228-5150, (601) 453-5974
http://www.comfortinn.com
401 Rte. 82
60 rooms - $55-80
Pets: Small pets welcome
Creature Comforts: CCTV, a/c, refrig, micro, cont. brkfst, pool

GRENADA

Best Western Inn
(800) 528-1234, (601) 226-7816
http://www.bestwestern.com
1750 Sunset Dr.
61 rooms - $48-79
Pets: Under 20 lbs. welcome
Creature Comforts: CCTV, a/c, refrig, cont. brkfst, pool

Holiday Inn
(800) HOLIDAY, (601) 226-2851
http://www.holiday-inn.com
1796 Sunset Dr.
132 rooms - $60-94
Pets: Welcome
Creature Comforts: CCTV, a/c, refrig, micro, restaurant, sauna, whirlpool, hlth club, pool

GULFPORT

Best Western Seaway
(800) 528-1234, (228) 864-4650
http://www.bestwestern.com
9475 Rte. 49
178 rooms - $39-95
Pets: Small pets welcome
Creature Comforts: CCTV, a/c, refrig, cont. brkfst

Crystal Inn
(888) 822-9600, (228) 822-9600
http://www.crystalinn.com
9379 Canal Rd.
112 rooms - $55-109
Pets: Welcome w/$25 dep.
Creature Comforts: CCTV, a/c, kit, cont. brkfst, pool, hlth clb, whirlpool

Hampton Inn
(800) Hampton, (228) 868-3300
http://www.hampton-inn.com
Rtes. 49 & 10
155 rooms - $65-99
Pets: Welcome
Creature Comforts: CCTV, a/c, refrig, pool

Holiday Inn, Airport
(800) HOLIDAY, (228) 868-8200
http://www.holiday-inn.com
9415 Rte. 49
154 rooms - $74-99
Pets: Under 20 lbs. w/$100 dep.
Creature Comforts: CCTV, a/c, refrig, restaurant, hlth club, pool

Motel 6
(800) 4-MOTEL6, (228) 863-1890
http://www.motel6.com
9355 Rte. 49
98 rooms - $40-59
Pets: Under 30 lbs. welcome
Creature Comforts: CCTV, a/c, pool

Shoney's Inn
(800) 222-2222, (228) 868-8500
http://www.shoneysinn.com
9375 Rte. 49
80 rooms - $65-99
Pets: Small pets welcome
Creature Comforts: CCTV, a/c, refrig, micro, cont. brkfst, pool

HATTIESBURG

Comfort Inn
(800) 228-5150, (601) 268-2170
http://www.comfortinn.com
6595 Rte. 49
119 rooms - $59-76
Pets: Small pets welcome
Creature Comforts: CCTV, a/c, refrig, micro, restaurant, cont. brkfst, hlth club, pool

Days Inn
(800) DAYS-INN, (601) 544-6300
http://www.daysinn.com
15250 Poole St.
120 rooms - $40-65
Pets: Welcome w/$6 fee
Creature Comforts: CCTV, a/c, refrig, micro, cont. brkfst, pool

Hampton Inn
(800) Hampton, (601) 264-8080
http://www.hampton-inn.com
4301 Hardy St.
154 rooms - $65-79
Pets: Welcome
Creature Comforts: CCTV, a/c, refrig, micro, Jacuzzis, hlth club access, pool

Howard Johnson Inn
(800) I-G0-Hojo, (601) 268-2251
http://www.hojo.com
6553 Rte. 49
180 rooms - $36-95
Pets: Welcome w/$5 fee
Creature Comforts: CCTV, a/c, refrig, micro, cont. brkfst, pool

Motel 6
(800) 4-MOTEL6, (601) 544-6096
http://www.motel6.com
6508 Rte. 49
117 rooms - $36-59
Pets: Under 30 lbs. welcome
Creature Comforts: CCTV, a/c, pool

IUKA

Victorian Inn
(601) 423-9221
199 Rte. 180
60 rooms - $42-64
Pets: Welcome
Creature Comforts: CCTV, a/c, pool

JACKSON

Best Suites of America
(601) 899-8580
5411 Rte. 55
102 rooms - $75-99
Pets: Small pets welcome
Creature Comforts: CCTV, VCR, a/c, refrig, micro, Jacuzzis, pool, hlth clb access, whirlpool

Best Western Metro Inn
(800) 528-1234, (601) 355-7483
http://www.bestwestern.com
1520 Ellis Ave.
158 rooms - $55-85
Pets: Small pets welcome
Creature Comforts: CCTV, a/c, refrig, cont. brkfst, whirlpool, pool

Best Western Northeast Inn
(800) 528-1234, (601) 982-1011
http://www.bestwestern.com
5035 Rte. 55
133 rooms - $55-94
Pets: Small pets w/CC dep.
Creature Comforts: CCTV, a/c, refrig, cont. brkfst, hlth club, pool

Crowne Plaza Hotel
(800) HOLIDAY, (601) 969-5100
http://www.crowneplaza.com
200 E. Amite St.
355 rooms - $85-169
Pets: Under 10 Lbs w/$100 dep.
Creature Comforts: CCTV, a/c, refrig, micro, restaurant, sauna, whirlpool, hlth club, pool

Edison Walthall Hotel
(601) 948-6161
225 E. Capitol St.
209 rooms - $70-199
Pets: Welcome w/$10 fee
Creature Comforts: CCTV, a/c, refrig, restaurant, pool

Harvey Hotel
(601) 366-9411
5075 Rte. 55
225 rooms - $75-99
Pets: W/$25 fee & CC dep.
Creature Comforts: CCTV, a/c, refrig, micro, restaurant, pool

Holiday Inn
(800) HOLIDAY, (601) 355-3472
http://www.holiday-inn.com
2649 Rte. 80
290 rooms - $69-129
Pets: $25 fee, credit card dep.
Creature Comforts: CCTV, a/c, refrig, micro, restaurant, pool

Howard Johnson Inn
(800) I-Go-Hojo, (601) 354-4455
http://www.hojo.com
1065 S. Frontage Rd.
120 rooms - $37-59
Pets: Welcome
Creature Comforts: CCTV, a/c, restaurant, cont. brkfst, pool

La Quinta Inn, North
(800) Nu-Rooms, (601) 957-1741
http://www.laquinta.com
616 Blairwood Rd.
144 rooms - $59-86
Pets: Small pets welcome
Creature Comforts: CCTV, a/c, refrig, cont. brkfst, pool

La Quinta Inn, South
(800) Nu-Rooms, (601) 373-6110
http://www.laquinta.com
150 Angle St.
100 rooms - $58-75
Pets: Small pets welcome
Creature Comforts: CCTV, a/c, refrig, cont. brkfst, pool

Motel 6
(800) 4-MOTEL6, (601) 956-8848
http://www.motel6.com
6145 Rte. 55
100 rooms - $39-48
Pets: Under 30 lbs. welcome
Creature Comforts: CCTV, a/c, pool

Ramada Inn
(800) 2-Ramada, (601) 957-2800
http://www.ramada.com
1001 County Line Rd.
303 rooms - $70-299
Pets: Under 10 lbs. w/$25 fee
Creature Comforts: CCTV, a/c, kit, restaurant, whirlpool, pool

Red Roof Inn, Coliseum
(800) The-Roof, (601) 969-5006
http://www.redroof.com
700 Larson St.
115 rooms - $49-75
Pets: Small pets welcome
Creature Comforts: CCTV, a/c, cont. brkfst

Red Roof Inn
(800) The-Roof, (601) 956-7707
http://www.redroof.com
810 Adcock St.
108 rooms - $49-74
Pets: Small pets welcome
Creature Comforts: CCTV, a/c, cont. brkfst

Residence Inn
(800) 331-3131, (601) 355-3599
http://www.residenceinn.com
881 E. River Pl.
122 rooms - $99-299
Pets: Welcome w/$100 fee
Creature Comforts: CCTV, VCR, a/c, kit, fireplace, cont. brkfst, hlth club, whirlpools, pool

Scottish Inns
(800) 251-1962, (601) 969-1144
http://www.reservahost.com
2263 Rte. 80
55 rooms - $30-42
Pets: Welcome
Creature Comforts: CCTV, a/c, cont. brkfst

KOSCIUSKO

Best Western Parkway Inn
(800) 528-1234, (601) 289-6252
http://www.bestwestern.com
1052 Vet. Memorial Dr.
50 rooms - $48-63
Pets: Small pets w/$4 fee
Creature Comforts: CCTV, a/c, refrig, micro, cont. brkfst, pool

LAUREL

Days Inn
(800) DAYS-INN, (601) 428-8421
http://www.daysinn.com
Rtes. 11 & 59
85 rooms - $39-50
Pets: Welcome w/$5 fee
Creature Comforts: CCTV, a/c, refrig, restaurant, pool

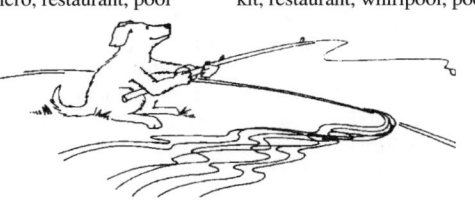

Super 8 Motel
(800) 800-8000, (601) 649-8885
http://www.super8.com
107 Sawmill Rd.
57 rooms - $49-69
Pets: Welcome w/permission
Creature Comforts: CCTV, a/c,
Jacuzzis, cont. brkfst, pool

Macomb
Best Western Inn
(800) 528-1234, (601) 684-5566
http://www.bestwestern.com
2298 Delaware Ave.
150 rooms - $55-109
Pets: Small pets welcome
Creature Comforts: CCTV, a/c,
refrig, cont. brkfst, pool

Holiday Inn
(800) HOLIDAY, (601) 684-6211
http://www.holiday-inn.com
1900 Delaware Ave.
142 rooms - $50-79
Pets: Welcome
Creature Comforts: CCTV, a/c,
refrig, restaurant, pool

Super 8 Motel
(800) 800-8000, (601) 684-7654
http://www.super8.com
100 Commerce St.
41 rooms - $45-59
Pets: Welcome w/travel crate
Creature Comforts: CCTV, a/c,
cont. brkfst

MAGEE
Comfort Inn
(800) 228-5150, (601) 849-2300
http://www.comfortinn.com
5441 Simpson Hwy.
50 rooms - $55-86
Pets: Small pets welcome
Creature Comforts: CCTV, a/c,
refrig, micro, cont. brkfst, pool

MERIDIAN
Budgetel Inn
(800) 4-Budget, (601) 693-2300
http://www.budgetel.com
1400 Roebuck Dr.
101 rooms - $45-65
Pets: Small pets welcome
Creature Comforts: CCTV, a/c,
refrig, cont. brkfst, pool

Days Inn
(800) DAYS-INN, (601) 483-3812
http://www.daysinn.com
530 Rte. 80
115 rooms - $40-99
Pets: Welcome
Creature Comforts: CCTV, a/c,
refrig, cont. brkfst, pool

Econo Lodge
(800) 55-ECONO, (601) 693-9393
http://www.econolodge.com
2405 S. Frontage Rd.
33 rooms - $35-67
Pets: Small pets welcome
Creature Comforts: CCTV, a/c,
cont. brkfst

Holiday Inn Express
(800) HOLIDAY, (601) 693-4521
http://www.holiday-inn.com
1401 Roebuck Dr.
112 rooms - $50-85
Pets: Small pets welcome
Creature Comforts: CCTV, a/c,
refrig, pool

Motel 6
(800) 4-MOTEL6, (601) 482-1182
http://www.motel6.com
2309 S. Frontage Rd.
89 rooms - $32-49
Pets: Under 30 lbs. welcome
Creature Comforts: CCTV, a/c,
pool

Sleep Inn
(800) Sleep-Inn, (601) 485-4646
http://www.sleepinn.com
1301 Hamilton Ave.
55 rooms - $45-67
Pets: Small pets welcome
Creature Comforts: CCTV, a/c,
pool

MOSS POINT
Best Western Flagship
(800) 528-1234, (228) 475-5000
http://www.bestwestern.com
4830 Amoco Dr.
80 rooms - $44-89
Pets: Welcome
Creature Comforts: CCTV, a/c,
refrig, micro, cont. brkfst, pool

Holiday Inn Express
(800) HOLIDAY, (228) 474-2100
http://www.holiday-inn.com
4800 Amoco Dr.
101 rooms - $55-99
Pets: Small pets welcome
Creature Comforts: CCTV, a/c,
refrig, pool

Scholar Inn
(228) 475-8444
6623 Rte. 63
50 rooms - $46-59
Pets: Welcome w/$3 fee
Creature Comforts: CCTV, a/c

NATCHEZ
Cedar Grove Plantation
(601) 445-0585
http://cedargroveplantation.com
617 Kingston Rd.
5 rooms - $70-150
Pets: Welcome in the kennel
Creature Comforts: 1830's
Greek Revival house on National
Historic Register, lovely decor,
Oriental rugs, library, CCTV, a/c,
fireplace, refrig, southern brkfst,
pool, fishing pond, lawn games,
trails, and bikes

Days Inn
(800) DAYS-INN, (601) 445-8291
http://www.daysinn.com
109 Rte. 61
120 rooms - $35-90
Pets: Welcome
Creature Comforts: CCTV, a/c,
refrig, restaurant, cont. brkfst, pool

Guest House Historic Hotel
(601) 442-1054
201 N. Pearl St.
16 rooms - $85-105
Pets: Under 25lbs. w/$25 daily fee
Creature Comforts: An 1840
historic inn appointed w/antiques,
CCTV, a/c, refrig, restaurant, cont.
brkfst

Ramada Inn
(800) 2-Ramada, (601) 446-6311
http://www.ramada.com
130 John R Junkin Dr.
163 rooms - $65-99
Pets: Under 25 lbs. welcome
Creature Comforts: CCTV, a/c,
refrig, restaurant, pool

     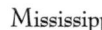

NEWTON
Days Inn
(800) DAYS-INN, (601) 683-6454
http://www.daysinn.com
Rtes. 15 & 20
40 rooms - $45-69
Pets: Welcome w/$8 fee
Creature Comforts: CCTV, a/c,
refrig, cont. brkfst, pool

OCEAN SPRINGS
Sleep Inn
(800) Sleep-Inn, (601) 872-0440
http://www.sleepinn.com
7412 Tucker Rd.
78 rooms - $44-129
Pets: Small pets welcome
Creature Comforts: CCTV, a/c,
Jacuzzis, restaurant, cont. brkfst,
pool, hlth club, whirlpool

OXFORD
Holiday Inn
(800) HOLIDAY, (601) 234-3031
http://www.holiday-inn.com
400 N. Lamar Ave.
122 rooms - $69-99
Pets: Small pets welcome
Creature Comforts: CCTV, a/c,
kit, restaurant, pool

Oliver-Britt House
(601) 234-8043
512 Van Buren Ave.
5 rooms - $50-79
Pets: Small, quiet dogs welcome
Creature Comforts: CCTV, a/c,
refrig, antiques, full southern
brkfst

PASCOGOULA
La Font Inn
(800) 647-6077, (228) 762-7111
http://www.lafont.com
2703 Denny Ave.
194 rooms - $68-99
Pets: Welcome
Creature Comforts: A sprawling
resort near Mississippi Gulf Coast
shopping, CCTV, a/c, kit,
restaurant, olympic pool, hlth clb,
steambaths, sauna, whirlpool,
tennis, lawn games, on 10 acres

PASS CHRISTIAN
Inn at the Pass
(800) 217-2588, (228) 452-0333
125 E. Scenic Dr.
5 rooms - $79-99
Pets: Welcome in the cottage
Creature Comforts: Victorian
inn on Nat'l Hist. Register, CCTV,
a/c, fireplace, refrig, full brkfst,
beach

PHILADELPHIA
Days Inn
(800) DAYS-INN, (601) 650-3590
http://www.daysinn.com
1009 Holland Ave.
40 rooms - $60-80
Pets: Welcome w/$5 fee
Creature Comforts: CCTV, a/c,
refrig, micro, cont. brkfst

Key West Inn
(800) 833-0555, (601) 656-0052
http://www.keywestinn.net
1004 Central Dr.
45 rooms - $59-82
Pets: Welcome w/$5 fee
Creature Comforts: CCTV, a/c,
pool

Ramada Inn
(800) 2-Ramada, (601) 656-1223
http://www.ramada.com
1011 Holland Ave.
48 rooms - $55-85
Pets: Welcome w/$5 fee
Creature Comforts: CCTV, a/c,
refrig, micro, restaurant, cont.
brkfst, pool

PICAYUNE
Days Inn
(800) DAYS-INN, (601) 799-1339
http://www.daysinn.com
450 S. Lofton Ave.
50 rooms - $50-135
Pets: Welcome
Creature Comforts: CCTV, a/c,
refrig, micro, Jacuzzis, cont.
brkfst, hlth club, pool

RICHLAND
Days Inn
(800) DAYS-INN, (601) 932-5553
http://www.daysinn.com
1035 Rte. 49
45 rooms - $60-95
Pets: Welcome w/$5 fee
Creature Comforts: CCTV, a/c,
refrig, micro, Jacuzzis, cont. brkfst

RIDGELAND
Red Roof Inn
(800) The-Roof, (601) 956-7707
http://www.redroof.com
810 Adcock St.
108 rooms - $45-79
Pets: Small pets welcome
Creature Comforts: CCTV, a/c

ROBINSONVILLE
Cottage Inn
(800) 363-2985, (662) 363-2971
http://www.cottageinnchalet.com
4235 Casino Centre Dr., Box 40
20 rooms - $70-189
Pets: Welcome
Creature Comforts: Charming
guest rooms, traditional decor,
vaulted ceilings, period
reproductions, CCTV, a/c,
fireplace, kit, Jacuzzis, cont. brkfst

Key West Inn
(800) 833-0555, (662) 363-0021
http://www.keywestinn.net
Route 61
45 rooms - $50-99
Pets: Welcome w/$5 fee
Creature Comforts: CCTV, a/c

SARDIS
Best Western Inn
(800) 528-1234, (601) 487-2424
http://www.bestwestern.com
410 E. Lee St.
79 rooms - $48-79
Pets: Welcome
Creature Comforts: CCTV, a/c,
refrig, micro, cont. brkfst, hlth
club, whirlpool, pool

STARKVILLE
Holiday Inn
(800) HOLIDAY, (601) 323-6161
http://www.holiday-inn.com
Route 12
175 rooms - $65-98
Pets: Welcome
Creature Comforts: CCTV, a/c,
refrig, restaurant, pool

TUNICA
Hotel Marie
(601) 363-0100
1195 Main St.
30 rooms - $54-109
Pets: Dogs welcome
Creature Comforts: Historic
hotel, CCTV, a/c, restaurant

TUPELO

Amerihost Inn
(800) 434-5800, (601) 844-7660
625 Spicer Dr.
62 rooms - $59-78
Pets: Small pets welcome
Creature Comforts: CCTV, a/c,
refrig, micro, Jacuzzis, cont.
brkfst, pool, hlth clb

Executive Inn
(800) 533-3220, (662) 841-2222
10 N. Gloster Rd.
116 rooms - $59-89
Pets: Welcome w/$15 fee
Creature Comforts: CCTV, a/c,
refrig, micro, restaurant, pool,
sauna, whirlpool

Red Roof Inn
(800) The-Roof, (662) 844-1904
http://www.redroof.com
1500 McCullough Blvd.
100 rooms - $50-85
Pets: Small pets welcome
Creature Comforts: CCTV, a/c,
pool

VICKSBURG

Belle of the Bends
(800) 844-2308, (601) 634-0737
http://www.belleofthebends.com
508 Klein St.
4 rooms - $95-155
Pets: Welcome
Creature Comforts: A restored
1876 mansion overlooking a river,
CCTV, VCR, a/c, antiques, family
heirlooms, high windows, detailed
moldings, fireplaces, Jacuzzis,
memorabillia, refrig, full brkfst

Corners B&B
(800) 444-7421, (601) 636-7421
http://www.thecorners.com
601 Klein St.
16 rooms - $85-165
Pets: Welcome
Creature Comforts: A beautifully
refurbished 1873 Victorian B&B,
listed on the National Historic
Register, CCTV, a/c, fireplaces,
refrig, micro, canopy beds, piano,
handmade quilts, Jacuzzis,
antiques, verandah, full brkfst

Duff Green Mansion
(800) 992-0037, (601) 636-6968
www.duffgrenmansion.com
1114 First East St.
7 rooms - $85-175
Pets: Small pets welcome
Creature Comforts: A palatial
12,000 sq. ft. antebellum mansion,
former hospital for Confederate
soldiers, CCTV, VCR, a/c,
fireplace, poster beds, antiques,
refrig, Jacuzzi, plantation brkfst,
pool, self-serve bar, mansion tour

Hampton Inn
(800) Hampton, (601) 636-6100
http://www.hampton-inn.com
3330 Clay St.
148 rooms - $65-85
Pets: Welcome
Creature Comforts: CCTV, a/c,
refrig, pool, trail

Park Inn
(800) 359-9363, (601) 638-5811
4137 Frontage Rd.
115 rooms - $45-75
Pets: Welcome w/$5 fee
Creature Comforts: CCTV, a/c,
refrig, Jacuzzi, restaurant, cont.
brkfst, pool

Ramada Inn
(800) 2-Ramada, (601) 638-5750
http://www.ramada.com
4216 Washington St.
55 rooms - $45-115
Pets: Welcome
Creature Comforts: CCTV, a/c,
restaurant, cont. brkfst.

Super 8 Motel
(800) 800-8000, (601) 638-5077
http://www.super8.com
4127 Frontage Rd.
62 rooms - $45-68
Pets: Welcome
Creature Comforts: CCTV, a/c,
refrig, micro, cont. brkfst,
whirlpool, pool

Missouri

ARNOLD
Drury Inn
(800) 325-8300, (314) 296-9600
http://www.druryinn.com
1201 Drury Lane
96 rooms - $56-72
Pets: Welcome
Creature Comforts: CCTV, a/c,
refrig, micro, cont. brkfst, pool

White Wing Resort
(314) 338-2318
http://natins.com/motel/white
Box 840
18 rooms - $47-55
Pets: Small short-haired dogs
Creature Comforts: CCTV, a/c,
kit, pool, boat dock

AURORA
Aurora Inn Motel
(417) 678-5035
Route 39
32 rooms - $38-52
Pets: Ltd. rms w/$5 fee
Creature Comforts: CCTV,
refrig

BELLEFONTAINE NGHBRS
Motel 6
(800) 4-MOTEL6, (314) 869-9400
http://www.motel6.com
1405 Dunn Rd.
80 rooms - $30-45
Pets: Small pets welcome
Creature Comforts: CCTV, a/c

BELTON
Econo Lodge
(800) 55-ECONO, (816) 322-1222
http://www.econolodge.com
222 Peculiar Dr.
51 rooms - $40-65
Pets: Small pets welcome
Creature Comforts: CCTV, a/c,
cont. brkfst

BERKELEY
Ramada, Airport
(800) 2-Ramada, (314) 427-7600
http://www.ramada.com
9600 Natural Bridge Rd.
200 rooms - $65-90
Pets: Small pets welcome
Creature Comforts: CCTV, a/c,
refrig, restaurant, cont. brkfst,
pool, hlth clb, sauna, whirlpool

BETHANY
Best Western I-35 Inn
(800) 528-1234, (816) 425-7915
http://www.bestwestern.com
Route 1, Box 249B
78 rooms - $49-57
Pets: Small pets w/$10 fee
Creature Comforts: CCTV, a/c,
cont. brkfst, whirlpool

BLUE SPRINGS
Motel 6
(800) 4-MOTEL6, (816) 228-9133
http://www.motel6.com
901 West Jefferson St.
123 rooms - $36-38
Pets: One small pet per room
Creature Comforts: CCTV, a/c

Ramada Inn
(800) 2-Ramada, (816) 229-6363
http://www.ramada.com
1110 North 7 Rte.
140 rooms - $50-125
Pets: Welcome w/$10 fee
Creature Comforts: CCTV, a/c

BOLIVAR
Super 8
(800) 800-8000, (417) 777-8888
http://www.super8.com
1919 S. Killingsworth Ave.
63 rooms - $46-60
Pets: Welcome with permission
Creature Comforts: CCTV, a/c,
suites w/Jacuzzi, cont. breakfast

Welcome Inn
(417) 326-5268
4710 S. 128th Rd.
25 rooms - $30-40
Pets: Welcome w/$20 deposit
Creature Comforts: CCTV, a/c,
pool

BOURBON
Budget Inn Motel
(314) 732-4080
55 Rte. C
17 rooms - $30-36
Pets: Welcome w/$5 fee, $5
deposit
Creature Comforts: CCTV

BRANSON
Barrington Hotel
(800) 251-1962, (417) 334-8866
263 Shepherd of the Hills Pkwy.
150 rooms - $40-65
Pets: Small pets w/$10 fee
Creature Comforts: CCTV,
VCR, a/c, refrig, Jacuzzi, cont.
brkfst, pool, whirlpool

Baymont Inn and Suites
(800) 789-4103, (417) 336-6161
http://www.baymontinns.com
2375 Green Mtn. Drive
89 rooms - $50-75
Pets: In certain rooms w/$50
deposit - $40 refundable
Creature Comforts: CCTV, a/c,
refrig, pool

Best Western Rustic Oak
(800) 828-0404, (417) 334-6464
http://www.bestwestern.com
403 W. Main St.
108 rooms - $50-72
Pets: Welcome
Creature Comforts: CCTV,
VCR, a/c, suites, refrig, Jacuzzi,
cont. brkfst, pool, sauna, whirlpool

Big Valley Motel
(800) 332-7274, (417) 334-7676
2005 W. Rte. 76
99 rooms - $39-56
Pets: Small pets w/$20 deposit
Creature Comforts: CCTV,
VCR, a/c, refrig, micro, pool

Branson Lodge
(417) 334-3105
Route 165
33 rooms - $42-65
Pets: Welcome w/$10 fee
Creature Comforts: CCTV, a/c,
refrig, suites w/fireplace, kit,
micro, pool

Brighton Place Motel
(417) 334-5510
3516 W. Rte. 76
80 rooms - $40-58
Pets: Small pets w/$10 fee
Creature Comforts: CCTV, a/c,
pool

Colonial Mountain Inn
(417) 272-8414
Route 13
50 rooms - $30-50
Pets: Welcome w/$5 fee
Creature Comforts: CCTV,
restaurant, cont. brkfst, pool

Country Music Inn
(417) 336-3300
3060 Green Mtn. Dr.
82 rooms - $49-50
Pets: Small dogs w/$5 fee
Creature Comforts: CCTV,
fireplace, kit, Jacuzzi, restaurant,
cont. brkfst, pool, hlth club access,
sauna, whirlpool

Days Inn, Branson
(800) DAYS INN, (417) 334-5544
http://www.daysinn.com
3524 Keeter St.
425 rooms - $40-102
Pets: Welcome w $10 fee
Creature Comforts: CCTV, a/c,
refrig, cont. brkfst, pool, whirlpool

Fiddler's Inn
(800) 544-6483, (417) 334-2212
3522 W. Rte. 76
78 rooms - $42-55
Pets: Welcome in ltd. rooms
Creature Comforts: CCTV,
VCR, a/c, cont. brkfst, pool,
whirlpool

Howard Johnson
(800) I-Go-Hojo, (417) 336-5151
http://www.hojo.com
3027 W. Route 76
344 Rooms - $50-65
Pets: Welcome w/$8.50 fee
Creature Comforts: CCTV, a/c,
refrig, micro, cont. brkfst, pool,
whirlpool

Lakeshore Resort
(800) 583-6101, (417) 334-6262
www.branson.com/lakeshore
1773 Lakeshore Dr.
15 cottages - $65-110
Pets: Dogs under 25 lbs. in certain
cottages w/$7.50 daily fee
Creature Comforts: On banks of
Lake Taneycomo, intimate country
resort, family oriented, expansive
grounds, very attractive cottages
w/decks, CCTV, VCR, a/c, kit,
fireplace, full brkfst, pool, boat
rentals, fishing

Ramada Inn
(800) 2-Ramada, (417) 337-5207
http://www.ramada.com
2316 Shepherd of the Hills Expwy
90 rooms - $50-70
Pets: Welcome w/$5 fee
Creature Comforts: CCTV, a/c,
cont. brkfst, pool

Residence Inn
(800) 331-3131, (417) 336-4077
http://www.residenceinn.com
280 Wildwood Dr.
85 Rooms - $50-140
Pets: Welcome w/$5 daily fee,
$25 one-time cleaning fee
Creature Comforts: CCTV, a/c,
refrig, kit, micro, fireplace,
Jacuzzi, cont. brkfst, pool,
basketball court

Rock View Resort
(800) 742-7625, (417) 334-4678
http://www.rockviewresort.com
1049 Park View Dr.
12 rooms - $40-75
Pets: Small dogs w/$6 daily fee,
do not leave alone
Creature Comforts: Lakeside
resort, CCTV, kit, pool, whirlpool,
boat rentals

Rustic Gate
(417) 272-3326
Route 13
65 rooms - $30-35
Pets: Welcome w/$50 deposit
Creature Comforts: CCTV,
Jacuzzi, pool

Settle Inn
(800) 677-6906, (417) 335-4700
http://www.bransonsettleinnn.com
3050 Green Mountain Dr.
300 rooms - $55-130
Pets: Small pets w/$8 fee
Creature Comforts: CCTV, a/c,
refrig, micro, special Jacuzzi
suites, restaurant, cont. brkfst,
pools

Welk Resort
(417) 336-3575
1984 Route 165
160 rooms - $80-85
Pets: Welcome
Creature Comforts: CCTV, a/c,
restaurant, pool, whirlpool

BRIDGETON
Econo Lodge
(800) 55-ECONO, (314) 731-3000
http://www.econolodge.com
4575 N. Lindbergh Blvd.
103 rooms - $45-55
Pets: Welcome w/$5 fee
Creature Comforts: CCTV, a/c,
cont. brkfst, pool

Henry VIII Hotel
(314) 731-3040
4690 N. Lindbergh Blvd.
390 rooms - $80-110
Pets: Small pets w/$50 deposit
Creature Comforts: CCTV,
VCR, a/c, kit, Jacuzzi, restaurant,
2 pools, hlth clb, sauna, whirlpool

Knights Inn
(800) 843-5644, (314) 925-2020
http://www.knightsinn.com
12433 St. Charles Rock Rd.
132 rooms - $40-55
Pets: Welcome
Creature Comforts: CCTV, a/c,
refrig, micro, Jacuzzi, pool

Motel 6
(800) 4-MOTEL6, (314) 291-6100
http://www.motel6.com
3655 Pennridge Dr.
251 rooms - $32-43
Pets: Under 30 lbs. welcome
Creature Comforts: CCTV, a/c, pool

Scottish Inns
(800) 251-1962, (314) 731-1010
www.reservahost.com
4645 N. Lindbergh Blvd.
55 rooms - $35-45
Pets: Welcome
Creature Comforts: CCTV, a/c, restaurant, cont. brkfst

CAMERON
Best Western Acorn Inn
(800) 528-1234, (816) 632-2187
http://www.bestwestern.com
Rtes. 35 & 36
40 rooms - $44-59
Pets: Welcome
Creature Comforts: CCTV, VCR, a/c, refrig, fireplace, kit, micro, restaurant, cont. brkfst, pool

Days Inn
(800) DAYS INN, (816) 632-6623
http://www.daysinn.com
501 Northland Dr.
38 rooms - $40-50
Pets: Welcome with $3 fee
Creature Comforts: CCTV, a/c, cont. brkfst, pool

Rambler Motel
(816) 632-6571
Route 69
35 rooms - $35-45
Pets: Welcome
Creature Comforts: CCTV, a/c, cont. brkfst, pool

CAPE GIRARDEAU
Drury Inn
(800) 325-8300, (573) 334-7151
http://www.druryinn.com
104 S. Vantage Dr.
137 rooms - $67-75
Pets: Welcome
Creature Comforts: CCTV, a/c, refrig, micro, restaurant, expanded cont. brkfst, hlth club privileges, pool

Drury Suites
(800) 325-8300, (573) 339-9500
http://www.druryinn.com
3303 Campster Dr.
85 rooms - $80-85
Pets: Under 20 lbs.
Creature Comforts: CCTV, VCR, a/c, refrig, micro, Jacuzzi, exc. cont. brkfst, hlth club privileges, pool, whirlpool

Hampton Inn
(800) Hampton, (573) 651-3000
http://www.hampton-inn.com
103 Cape West Parkway
82 rooms - $65-80
Pets: Welcome
Creature Comforts: CCTV, a/c, cont. brkfst, hlth clb access

Holiday Inn
(800) HOLIDAY, (573) 334-4491
http://www.holiday-inn.com
Rte. 55 & William St.
186 rooms - $68-100
Pets: Small pets welcome
Creature Comforts: CCTV, VCR, a/c, restaurant, cont. brkfst, pool, sauna, whirlpool, game room, shuffle board, table tennis, billiards, fitness center

Pear Tree Inn
(573) 334-3000
3248 William St.
80 rooms - $60-69
Pets: Welcome w/permission
Creature Comforts: CCTV, a/c, restaurant, cont. brkfst, pool

Victorian Inn Motel
(573) 651-4486
3265 William St.
133 rooms - $55-150
Pets: Small pets welcome
Creature Comforts: CCTV, VCR, a/c, refrig, micro, suite Jacuzzi, pool, hlth clb, sauna, whirlpool, game room

CARTHAGE
Days Inn
(800) DAYS INN, (417) 335-4700
http://www.daysinn.com
2244 Grand Ave.
39 rooms - $40-58
Pets: Small pets welcome, crated when in the room
Creature Comforts: CCTV, VCR, a/c, pool, cont. brkfst

Econo Lodge
(800) 55-ECONO, (417) 358-3900
http://www.econolodge.com
1441 W. Central Ave.
82 rooms - $50-65
Pets: Welcome w/$15 deposit
Creature Comforts: CCTV, VCR, a/c, cont. brkfst, pool, whirlpool

CASSVILLE
Holiday Motel
(417) 847-3163
85 South Main St.
18 rooms - $37-47
Pets: Small dogs w/$5 fee
Creature Comforts: CCTV, a/c, refrig, kit, pool

Super 8
(800) 800-8000, (417) 847-4888
http://www.super8.com
101 S. Rte. 37
46 rooms - $42-54
Pets: Small pets welcome
Creature Comforts: CCTV, VCR, a/c, Jacuzzi, restaurant, cont. brkfst, pool,

Townhouse Motel
(417) 847-4196
Routes 112 and 248
22 rooms - $28-38
Pets: Welcome w/$4 fee
Creature Comforts: CCTV, VCR, a/c, refrig, micro, pool

CHILLICOTHE
Best Western Inn
(800) 528-1234, (660) 646-0572
http://www.bestwestern.com
1020 S. Washington St.
60 rooms - $42-50
Pets: Welcome w/$5 fee
Creature Comforts: CCTV, a/c, refrig, cont. brkfst, pool

Super 8
(800) 800-8000, (660) 646-7888
http://www.super8.com
Old Rte. 36 East
55 rooms - $40-60
Pets: Welcome
Creature Comforts: CCTV, a/c, cont. brkfst

Grand River Inn
(660) 646-6590
606 W. Business 36
60 rooms - $48-56
Pets: Welcome in first flr rms.
Creature Comforts: CCTV, VCR, a/c, refrig, micro, restaurant, cont. brkfst, pool, sauna, whirlpool

Travel Inn Motel
(660) 646-0784
Rte. 3665
25 rooms - $30-40
Pets: Welcome
Creature Comforts: CCTV, a/c

CLARKSVILLE
Clarksville Inn
(573) 242-3324
Route 79
17 rooms - $30-40
Pets: Welcome w/$5 fee
Creature Comforts: CCTV, a/c

CLAYTON
The Danielle Hotel
(800) 325-8302, (314) 721-0101
216 N. Meramec Ave.
90 rooms - $90-120
Pets: Small pets, treats on arrival
Creature Comforts: Intimate hotel near residential area, parks nearby, well appointed rooms, amenities, CCTV, VCR, a/c, kit, fireplace, Jacuzzi, restaurant, cont. brkfst, pool, hlth clb access, sauna, whirlpool

CLINTON
Colonial Motel
(816) 885-2206
Rtes. 7 and 13
30 rooms - $30-55
Pets: Small pets w/$2 fee
Creature Comforts: CCTV, a/c, refrig, micro, pool

Holiday Inn, Clinton
(800) HOLIDAY, (816) 885-6901
http://www.holiday-inn.com
Route 7 at Rives Rd.
100 rooms - $65-115
Pets: Small pets welcome
Creature Comforts: CCTV, a/c, Jacuzzi, restaurant, cont. brkfst, pool, hlth clb, sauna, whirlpool

Safari Motel
(816) 885-3395
1505 N. Second St.
39 rooms - $30-50
Pets: Small pets w/$5 fee
Creature Comforts: CCTV, a/c, pool

COLUMBIA
Baymont Inn and Suites
(800) 789-4103, (573) 445-1899
http://www.baymontinns.com
2500 Rte. 70 Dr. SW
102 rooms - $42-52
Pets: Med. pets welcome
Creature Comforts: CCTV, a/c, micro, refrig

Days Inn Conf. Center
(800) DAYS INN, (573) 445-8511
http://www.daysinn.com
1900 Rte. 70 Drive SW
160 rooms - $60-80
Pets: Welcome w/$5 fee
Creature Comforts: CCTV, VCR, a/c, refrig, micro, Jacuzzi, restaurant, cont. brkfst, pool

Econo Lodge
(800) 800-8000, (573) 442-1191
http://www.econolodge.com
900 Rte. 70 Dr. SW
93 rooms - $35-95
Pets: Welcome w/$4 fee
Creature Comforts: CCTV, a/c, restaurant, cont. brkfst, pool, sauna, whirlpool

Holiday Inn-Holidome
(800) HOLIDAY, (573) 449-2491
http://www.holiday-inn.com
Providence Rd. at Rte. 70
142 rooms - $60-80
Pets: Welcome in outside rooms
Creature Comforts: CCTV, a/c, restaurant, pool, hlth clb, sauna, whirlpool, game room

Holiday Inn Select
(800) HOLIDAY, (573) 445-8531
http://www.holiday-inn.com
2200 Rte. 70 Dr. SW
300 rooms - $65-250
Pets: Welcome
Creature Comforts: CCTV, VCR, a/c, refrig, Jacuzzi, 5-star restaurants, cont. brkfst, pool, hlth clb, sauna, whirlpool

Ramada Inn
(800) 2-Ramada, (573) 449-0051
http://www.ramada.com
1100 Vandiver Dr.
190 rooms - $65-90
Pets: Small pets w/$50 deposit
Creature Comforts: CCTV, a/c, refrig, micro, restaurant, cont. brkfst, pool, hlth clb

Ramada Inn
(800) 2-Ramada, (573) 443-2090
http://www.ramada.com
1111 E. Broadway St.
102 rooms - $50-130
Pets: Small pets w/$50 deposit
Creature Comforts: New 97, CCTV, VCR, a/c, refrig, micro, 4-star restaurant, cont. brkfst, pool, hlth clb access, sauna, whirlpool

Red Roof Inn
(800) 843-7663, (573) 442-0145
http://www.redroof.com
201 E. Texas Ave.
108 rooms - $30-62
Pets: Small pets welcome
Creature Comforts: CCTV, a/c

CONCORDIA
Best Western Heidelberg Inn
(800) 528-1234, (660) 463-2114
http://www.bestwestern.com
406 W. Williams St.
55 rooms - $44-55
Pets: Welcome
Creature Comforts: CCTV, a/c, cont. brkfst, pool

Concordia Inn
(660) 463-7987
200 Main St.
44 rooms - $55-70
Pets: Welcome w/$20 deposit
Creature Comforts: CCTV, a/c, pool, whirlpool

CUBA
Best Western Cuba Inn
(800) 528-1234, (573) 885-7707
http://www.bestwestern.com
Route 2, Box 284
50 rooms - $34-50
Pets: Small pets welcome
Creature Comforts: CCTV, a/c, refrig, restaurant, cont. brkfst, pool

DEFIANCE
Da Gas Haus Nadler
(314) 987-2200
1707 Rte 60W (business)
4 rooms - $75-125
Pets: Welcome
Creature Comforts: CCTV,
VCR, a/c, full brkfst, whirlpool

DIXON
Rock Eddy Bluff
(800) 335-5921, (573) 759-6081
http://www.rockeddy.com
Route 62
4 rooms - $70-110
Pets: Welcome in cottages or cabin
Creature Comforts: 150 mtn.
acres, Contemp. Bluff House w/
French doors, hrdwd flrs, rocking
chrs, quilts, antique beds, fluffy
comforters, CCTV, a/c, rustic
1880's Line Camp Cabin w/
woodstove, hardwood floors,
decks with river views, hot tub,
and horses

DONIPHAN
Days Inn
(800) DAYS INN, (573) 996-2400
http://www.daysinn.com
100 Oaktree Village
27 rooms - $45-65
Pets: Small pets w/$8 fee
Creature Comforts: CCTV, a/c,
Jacuzzi, pool

EAGLE ROCK
Lazy Eagle Resort
(800) 232-4783, (417) 271-3390
P.O. Box 141
15 rooms - $38-40
Pets: Medium pets welcome
Creature Comforts: CCTV, a/c,
refrig, kit, restaurant, pool,
whirlpool

EUREKA
Days Inn
(800) DAYS INN, (314) 938-5565
http://www.daysinn.com
15 Hilltop Village Rd.
198 rooms - $40-150
Pets: Welcome w/$5 fee
Creature Comforts: CCTV, a/c,
refrig, Jacuzzi, restaurant, pool,
whirlpool, sauna, putting green

Oak Grove Inn
(314) 938-4368
1733 W. Fifth St.
60 rooms - $40-70
Pets: Welcome w/$10 fee
Creature Comforts: CCTV, a/c,
pool

Ramada Inn, Six Flags
(800) 2-Ramada, (314) 938-6661
http://www.ramada.com
4901 Allentown Rd.
180 rooms - $75-150
Pets: Small pets welcome
Creature Comforts: CCTV, a/c,
restaurant, pool, sauna, whirlpool

Red Carpet Inn
(800) 251-1962, (314) 938-5348
http://www.redcarpetinns.com
1725 W. Fifth St.
60 rooms - $35-60
Pets: Small pets w/$20 deposit
Creature Comforts: CCTV, a/c,
refrig, pool

ELLINGTON
Scenic Rivers Motel
(573) 663-7722
231 N. Second St.
17 rooms - $34-38
Pets: Small pets welcome
Creature Comforts: CCTV

FENTON
Drury Inn, Southwest
(800) 325-8300, (314) 343-7822
http://www.druryinn.com
1088 S. Rte. Dr.
110 rooms - $65-85
Pets: Welcome
Creature Comforts: CCTV, a/c,
pool

Motel 6
(800) 4-MOTEL6, (314) 349-1800
http://www.motel6.com
1860 Bowles Ave.
110 rooms - $40-50
Pets: Small pets welcome
Creature Comforts: CCTV, a/c,
pool

Pear Tree Inn
(800) 325-8300, (314) 343-8820
http://www.druryinn.com
1100 S. Rte. Dr.
105 rooms - $60-75
Pets: Small pets welcome
Creature Comforts: CCTV, a/c,
pool

FESTUS
Baymont Inn and Suites
(800) 789-4103, (314) 937-2888
http://www.baymontinns.com
1303 Veterans Blvd.
101 rooms - $45-60
Pets: Small pets welcome
Creature Comforts: CCTV, a/c,
refrig, micro, cont. brkfst

Drury Inn
(800) 325-8300, (314) 933-2400
http://www.druryinn.com
1001 Veterans Blvd.
57 rooms - $50-75
Pets: Welcome
Creature Comforts: CCTV, a/c,
refrig, micro, cont. brkfst, pool

FLORISSANT
Red Roof Inn
(800) 843-7663, (314) 831-7900
http://www.redroof.com
307 Dunn Rd.
110 rooms - $40-60
Pets: Small pets welcome
Creature Comforts: CCTV

FORISTELL
Best Western West 70
(800) 528-1234, (314) 673-2900
http://www.bestwestern.com
12 Rte. West
60 rooms - $40-45
Pets: Small pets w/$4 fee
Creature Comforts: CCTV,
VCR, a/c, pool

FULTON
Budget Host Westwoods Motel
(800) Bud-Host, (573) 642-5991
http://www.budgethost.com
422 Gaylord Dr.
21 rooms - $26-85
Pets: Welcome w/$3 fee
Creature Comforts: CCTV, a/c,
refrig, Jacuzzi, pool

GRAIN VALLEY
Travelodge
(800) 578-7878, (816) 224-3420
http://www.travelodge.com
105 Sunny Lane Dr.
42 rooms - $35-50
Pets: Welcome w/$5 fee
Creature Comforts: CCTV, a/c,
kit, pool

HANNIBAL
Days Inn
(800) DAYS INN, (573) 248-1700
http://www.daysinn.com
4070 Market St.
63 rooms - $40-95
Pets: Welcome
Creature Comforts: CCTV, a/c,
Jacuzzi, cont. brkfst, pool, sauna,
whirlpool

Econo Lodge
(800) 55 ECONO, (573) 221-1490
http://www.econolodge.com
612 Mark Twain Ave.
50 rooms - $30-80
Pets: Small pets w/$50 deposit
Creature Comforts: CCTV, a/c,
pool

Ramada Inn
(800) 2-Ramada, (573) 221-4100
http://www.ramada.com
4141 Market St.
247 rooms - $35-125
Pets: Welcome
Creature Comforts: CCTV,
VCR, a/c, refrig, micro, restaurant,
cont. brkfst, pool, hlth clb access,
sauna, whirlpool, tennis courts,
putting green, rec. room

Travelodge
(800) 578-7878, (573) 221-4100
http://www.travelodge.com
502 Mark Twain Ave.
27 rooms - $34-75
Pets: Welcome in special rooms
Creature Comforts: CCTV, a/c,
refrig, pool

HARRISONVILLE
Best Western Inn
(800) 528-1234, (816) 884-3200
http://www.bestwestern.com
2201 Rockhaven Blvd.
30 rooms - $40-65
Pets: Small pets w/deposit
Creature Comforts: CCTV, a/c,
refrig, pool, lawn games

Caravan Motel
(800) 578-7878, (816) 884-4100
1705 Rte. 291 North
24 rooms - $30-45
Pets: Welcome in special rooms
Creature Comforts: CCTV, a/c

Slumber Inn Motel
(800) 578-7878, (816) 884-3100
Route 71
28 rooms - $34-45
Pets: Small pets welcome
Creature Comforts: CCTV,
micro, refrig

HAYTI
Drury Inn
(800) 325-8300, (573) 359-2702
http://www.druryinn.com
Route 84
94 rooms - $50-65
Pets: Welcome
Creature Comforts: CCTV, a/c,
pool

HAZELWOOD
Baymont Inn and Suites
(800) 789-4103, (314) 731-4200
http://www.baymontinns.com
318 Taylor Rd.
110 rooms - $40-50
Pets: Small pets in smoking rms.
Creature Comforts: CCTV, a/c,
refrig, micro, pool

La Quinta (Airport)
(800) Nu-Rooms, (314) 731-3881
http://www.laquinta.com
5781 Campus Ct.
100 rooms - $50-65
Pets: Small pets welcome in
smoking rooms
Creature Comforts: CCTV, a/c,
refrig, micro, pool

HIGGINSVILLE
Best Western Camelot
(800) 528-1234, (816) 584-3646
http://www.bestwestern.com
Route 13
45 rooms - $42-65
Pets: Small pets welcome
Creature Comforts: CCTV, a/c,
restaurant, pool

Super 8 Motel
(800) 800-8000, (816) 584-7781
http://www.super8.com
Route 13
41 rooms - $40-55
Pets: Welcome w/$10 deposit
Creature Comforts: CCTV, a/c

HOLTS SUMMIT
Ramada Inn
(800) 2-Ramada, (37) 896-8787
http://www.ramada.com
150 City Plaza
37 rooms - $50-90
Pets: Small pets welcome
Creature Comforts: CCTV, a/c,
refrig, Jacuzzi, cont. brkfst, and a
hlth club

INDEPENDENCE
Howard Johnson
(800) 446-4656, (816) 373-8856
http://www.hojo.com
4200 S. Noland Rd.
170 rooms - $60-75
Pets: Welcome w/$25 deposit
Creature Comforts: CCTV,
VCR, a/c, refrig, micro, restaurant,
cont. brkfst, 2 pools, sauna,
whirlpool, lawn games

Red Roof Inn
(800) 843-7663, (816) 373-2800
http://www.redroof.com
13712 E. 42nd Terrace
110 rooms - $40-65
Pets: Small pets welcome
Creature Comforts: CCTV, a/c,
hlth clb access

Super 8
(800) 800-8000, (816) 833-1888
http://www.super8.com
4832 S. Lynn Ct.
79 rooms - $40-70
Pets: Welcome in smoking rooms
Creature Comforts: CCTV, a/c

Serendipity B&B
(800) 203-4299, (816) 833-4719
http://www.bbhost.com/
serendipitybb
116 S. Pleasant St.
5 rooms - $45-85
Pets: Welcome in Carriage House suite w/$10 nightly fee
Creature Comforts: 1887 brick Victorian, Cuban mahogany woodwork, antiques, museum-like w/extensive Victorian doll, toy and book collections, music boxes, Carriage Hse stes-Santa Fe w/four poster beds, kitchen, sitting rm; End of Trail suite w/train theme, four poster bed, kit, full candlelit brkfst

JACKSON
Drury Inn and Suites
(800) 325-8300, (573) 243-9200
http://www.druryinn.com
225 Drury Lane
81 rooms - $60-80
Pets: Welcome
Creature Comforts: CCTV, a/c, refrig, micro, cont. brkfst, pool

JAMESPORT
Nancy's Guest Cottage B&B
(660) 684-6156
RR 1, Box 3
2 rooms - $75
Pets: Small pets welcome
Creature Comforts: Set in Amish community, CCTV, a/c, full brkfst

JEFFERSON CITY
Capitol Plaza Hotel
(573) 635-1234
415 W. McCarty St.
260 rooms - $85-110
Pets: Welcome
Creature Comforts: CCTV, VCR, a/c, refrig, Jacuzzi, restaurant, cont. brkfst, pool, hlth clb, sauna, whirlpool

Hotel De Ville
(573) 636-5231
319 W. Miller St.
99 rooms - $55-65
Pets: Welcome w/$25 fee and a $50 deposit
Creature Comforts: CCTV, VCR, a/c, refrig, restaurant, pool, hlth clb access

Howard Johnson
(800) I-Go-Hojo, (573) 636-5101
http://www.hojo.com
422 Monroe St.
154 rooms - $65-75
Pets: Welcome
Creature Comforts: CCTV, a/c, cont. brkfst, pool

Motel 6
(800) 4-MOTEL6, (573) 445-8433
http://www.motel6.com
Stadium Blvd.
100 rooms - $30-46
Pets: Under 30 lbs. welcome
Creature Comforts: CCTV, a/c

Ramada Inn
(800) 2-Ramada, (573) 635-7171
http://www.ramada.com
1510 Jefferson St.
235 rooms - $70-140
Pets: Welcome
Creature Comforts: CCTV, a/c, refrig, restaurant, pool, hlth club

JOPLIN
Best Western Sands Inn
(800) 528-1234, (417) 624-8300
http://www.bestwestern.com
1611 Range Line Rd.
62 rooms - $50-70
Pets: Welcome in smoking rooms
Creature Comforts: CCTV, a/c, pool

Drury Inn
(800) 325-8300, (417) 781-8000
http://www.druryinn.com
3601 Range Line Rd.
115 rooms - $75-85
Pets: Welcome
Creature Comforts: CCTV, a/c, refrig, micro, cont. brkfst, pool, whirlpool

Holiday Inn Hotel
(800) HOLIDAY, (417) 782-1000
http://www.holiday-inn.com
3615 Range Line Rd.
265 rooms - $65-175
Pets: Welcome
Creature Comforts: CCTV, VCR, a/c, restaurant, pool, hlth clb, whirlpool, sauna

Howard Johnson
(800) 446-4656, (417) 623-0000
http://www.hojo.com
3510 Range Line Rd.
115 rooms - $45-65
Pets: Welcome
Creature Comforts: CCTV, VCR, a/c, refrig, micro, pool

Motel 6
(800) 4-MOTEL6, (417) 781-6400
http://www.motel6.com
Range Line Rd.
rooms - $40-75
Pets: Small pets welcome
Creature Comforts: CCTV, a/c, pool

Sleep Inn
(800) 753-3746, (417) 782-1212
http://www.sleepinn.com
Rtes. 44 & 43
63 rooms - $50-60
Pets: Welcome w/$5 fee
Creature Comforts: CCTV, a/c

Super 8
(800) 800-8000, (417) 782-8765
http://www.super8.com
2830 E. 36th St.
50 rooms - $40-60
Pets: Small pets welcome
Creature Comforts: CCTV, a/c, refrig, micro

Westwood Motel
(417) 782-7212
1700 W. 30th
30 rooms - $40-75
Pets: $5 fee/$25 deposit
Creature Comforts: CCTV, a/c, refrig, micro, pool

KANSAS CITY
Baymont Inn and Suites
(800) 789-4103, (816) 822-7000
http://www.baymontinns.com
8601 Hillcrest Rd.
115 rooms - $42-60
Pets: Welcome in smoking rooms
Creature Comforts: CCTV, a/c, refrig, micro, whirlpool

Baymont Inn and Suites
(800) 789-4103, (816) 221-1200
http://www.baymontinns.com
2214 Taney St.
105 rooms - $45-55
Pets: Welcome in smoking rooms
Creature Comforts: CCTV,
VCR, a/c, refrig, micro, cont.
brkfst

Drury Inn - Stadium
(800) 325-8300, (816) 923-3000
http://www.druryinn.com
3830 Blue Ridge Cutoff
135 rooms - $75-85
Pets: Welcome
Creature Comforts: CCTV, a/c,
kit, cont. brkfst, pool, and hlth clb
access

Embassy Suites, Airport
(800) 362-2779, (816) 891-7788
http://www.embassy-suites.com
7640 NW Tiffany Springs Pkwy.
240 rooms - $100-155
Pets: Small pets welcome
Creature Comforts: Atrium
setting, CCTV, a/c, refrig, micro,
restaurant, cont. brkfst, pool, hlth
clb, sauna, whirlpool

Fairmont Hotel
(800) 527-4727, (816) 756-1500
http://www.fairmont.com
401 Ward Pkwy.
400 rooms - $120-1,500
Pets: Under 25 lbs. welcome with
a $50 fee
Creature Comforts: Exceptional
property w/creek and trees
overlooking plaza, beautifully
furnished bedrooms, CCTV, VCR,
a/c, refrig, micro, Jacuzzi, 4-star
restaurant, pool, hlth clb, sauna,
whirlpool

Historic Suites of America
(816) 842-6544
612 Central Ave.
125 rooms - $40-75
Pets: Small pets w/$3 fee, $50 dep
Creature Comforts: Historic-
restored, CCTV, VCR, a/c, kit,
fireplace, Jacuzzi, cont. brkfst,
pool, hlth clb access, sauna, and a
whirlpool

Inn Towne Lodge
(816) 453-6550
2680 NE 43 St.
240 rooms - $35-55
Pets: Small pets w/$5 fee
Creature Comforts: CCTV, a/c,
kit, restaurant, pool

Marriott, Airport
(800) 228-9290, (816) 464-2200
http://www.marriott.com
775 Brasillia Ave.
385 rooms - $65-150
Pets: Small pets welcome
Creature Comforts: CCTV, a/c,
refrig, restaurant, pool, hlth clb,
sauna, whirlpool, hlth club

Marriott Hotel
(800) 228-9290, (417) 623-0391
http://www.marriott.com
200 W. 12th St.
600 rooms - $80-600
Pets: Welcome w/$25 fee
Creature Comforts: CCTV,
VCR, a/c, refrig, restaurant, cont.
brkfst, pool, hlth clb, sauna,
whirlpool

Motel 6
(800) 4-MOTEL6, (816) 33-4468
http://www.motel6.com
6400 E. 87th St.
115 rooms - $35-45
Pets: Small pets welcome
Creature Comforts: CCTV, a/c

Park Place
(800) 821-8532, (816) 483-9900
1601 N. Universal Ave.
330 rooms - $65-130
Pets: Welcome w/$25 deposit
Creature Comforts: CCTV,
VCR, a/c, refrig, restaurant, cont.
pool, hlth club, sauna, whirlpool

Ramada Inn Benjamin Ranch
(800) 2-Ramada, (816) 765-4331
http://www.ramada.com
6101 E. 87th St.
255 rooms - $75-100
Pets: Welcome w/$25 deposit
Creature Comforts: CCTV, a/c,
kit, restaurant, pool, and hlth clb
access

Residence Inn, Airport
(800) 331-3131, (816) 891-9009
http://www.residenceinn.com
9200 NW Prairie View Rd.
115 suites - $130-180
Pets: Small pets-$5 fee, $150 dep
Creature Comforts: CCTV,
VCR, a/c, refrig, micro, kit,
fireplace, Jacuzzi, pool, hlth clb,
sauna, whirlpool, sports facilities

Residence Inn, Union Hill
(800) 331-3131, (816) 561-3000
http://www.residenceinn.com
2975 Main St.
100 suites - $130-180
Pets: $5 fee, $50-75 deposit
Creature Comforts: CCTV,
VCR, a/c, refrig, micro, kit, pool,
hlth clb access, whirlpool

Super 8 Motel, NW
(800) 800-8000, (816) 587-0808
http://www.super8.com
6900 NW 83rd.
55 rooms - $40-55
Pets: Small pets welcome
Creature Comforts: CCTV, a/c,
refrig, micro

Westin Crown Center
(800) 228-3000, (816) 474-4400
http://www.westin.com
1 Pershing Rd.
770 rooms - $110-1,200
Pets: Small pets w/$5 fee, $50 dep
Creature Comforts: CCTV,
VCR, a/c, refrig, restaurant, pool,
hlth clb access, sauna, whirlpool

KIMBERLING CITY
Best Western, Kimberling Arms
(800) 528-1234, (417) 739-2461
http://www.bestwestern.com
Route 13 South
40 rooms - $45-110
Pets: Small pets welcome
Creature Comforts: Lakeside,
CCTV, a/c, kit, fireplace, Jacuzzi,
cont. brkfst, pool

Kimberling Hghts Resort Motel
(417) 779-4158
Route 13
15 rooms - $40-75
Pets: Small pets welcome
Creature Comforts: CCTV,
refrig, kit

Kimberling Inn Resort
(800) 833-5551, (417) 739-4311
www.kimberling.com
Route 13
235 rooms - $40-160
Pets: Welcome w/$100 deposit
Creature Comforts: Lakefront,
CCTV, VCR, a/c, kit, fireplace,
Jacuzzi, restaurants, 4 pools, hlth
clb access, sauna, whirlpool,
tennis courts, mini-golf, marina,
bowling, and boat rentals

King's Kove Resort
(417) 739-4513
Lake Rd.
12 rooms - $60-80
Pets: Small pets w/$25 fee
Creature Comforts: CCTV, kit,
fireplace, pool, hlth clb access,
sauna, whirlpool, marina, and boat
rentals

KIRKSVILLE
Best Western Shamrock
(800) 528-1234, (816) 665-8352
http://www.bestwestern.com
Route 63
50 rooms - $55-60
Pets: Small pets w/$15 fee
Creature Comforts: CCTV, a/c,
pool

Budget Host Village Inn
(800) Bud-Host, (816) 665-3722
http://www.budgethost.com
1304 S. Baltimore Rd.
30 rooms - $45-50
Pets: Welcome w/$5 fee
Creature Comforts: CCTV, a/c,
refrig, micro

Comfort Inn
(800) 228-5150, (816) 665-2205
http://www.comfortinn.com
2209 N. Baltimore Rd.
50 rooms - $45-50
Pets: Welcome
Creature Comforts: CCTV,
refrig, micro, restaurant

Days Inn
(800) DAYS INN, (816) 665-8244
http://www.daysinn.com
Route 63
105 rooms - $60-95
Pets: Small pets welcome
Creature Comforts: CCTV,
VCR, a/c, refrig, micro, Jacuzzi,
restaurant, pool, hlth clb access,
whirlpool

KNOB NOSTER
Whiteman Inn
(816) 563-3000
2340 W. Irish Ln.
90 rooms - $40-55
Pets: Small pets w/$3 fee
Creature Comforts: CCTV, a/c,
refrig

LAKE OZARK
Holiday Inn, Lakeside
(800) HOLIDAY, (573) 365-2334
http://www.holiday-inn.com
Route 54
215 rooms - $60-150
Pets: Welcome w/$10 fee
Creature Comforts: Lovely
grounds on Lake Ozark, CCTV,
VCR, a/c, refrig, restaurant, cont.
2 pools, hlth clb, sauna, whirlpool

LAKE ST. LOUIS
Days Inn
(800) DAYS INN, (314) 993-5600
http://www.daysinn.com
2560 Outer Rd.
65 rooms - $45-60
Pets: $5 fee in smoking rooms
Creature Comforts: CCTV, a/c,
refrig, pool, sauna, whirlpool

LAURIE
Millstone Lodge
(800) 290-2596, (573) 372-5111
State Rd. 0, Box 1157
62 rooms - $69-119
Pets: Welcome w/$10 fee
Creature Comforts: Lake of
Ozarks setting, full-service resort,
kit, restaurant, pool, marina,
tennis, volleyball, lawn games,
playground

LEBANON
Best Western Wyota
(800) 528-1234, (417) 532-6171
http://www.bestwestern.com
1225 Mill Creek Rd.
50 rooms - $40-50
Pets: Small pets welcome
Creature Comforts: CCTV, a/c,
pool

Brentwood Motel
(417) 532-6131
1320 S. Jefferson Rd.
25 rooms - $35-40
Pets: Welcome w/$50 deposit
Creature Comforts: CCTV,
micro, refrig

Econo Lodge
(800) 55 ECONO, (417) 588-3226
http://www.econolodge.com
2073 W. Elm St.
41 rooms - $36-50
Pets: Small pets welcome
Creature Comforts: CCTV, a/c,
cont. brkfst

Quality Inn
(800) 228-5151, (417) 532-7111
http://www.qualityinn.com
2071 W. Elm St.
80 rooms - $42-65
Pets: Small pets welcome
Creature Comforts: CCTV,
VCR, a/c, restaurant

LEE'S SUMMIT
Best Western Summit Inn
(800) 528-1234, (816) 525-1400
http://www.bestwestern.com
625 N. Murray Rd.
100 rooms - $50-100
Pets: Small pets w/$25 deposit
Creature Comforts: CCTV,
VCR, a/c, refrig, micro, restaurant,
cont. brkfst, 2 pools, whirlpool

Comfort Inn
(800) 228-5150, (816) 524-8181
http://www.comfortinn.com
607 SE Oldham Pkwy.
57 rooms - $60-70
Pets: Welcome
Creature Comforts: CCTV, a/c,
refrig, micro, cont. brkfst, pool,
whirlpool

LEXINGTON
Lexington Inn
(816) 259-4641
Route 13
59 rooms - $40-55
Pets: Small pets w/$100 deposit
Creature Comforts: CCTV, a/c,
restaurant, pool

LIBERTY
Best Western Hallmark
(800) 528-1234, (816) 781-8770
http://www.bestwestern.com
209 Route 291 N.
63 rooms - $40-75
Pets: Welcome
Creature Comforts: CCTV, a/c,
refrig, pool

LOUISIANA
River's Edge Motel
(573) 754-4522
201 Mansion St.
30 rooms - $30-50
Pets: Small pets welcome
Creature Comforts: CCTV, a/c,
refrig, micro

MACON
Best Western Inn
(800) 528-1234, (816) 385-2125
http://www.bestwestern.com
28933 Sunset Dr.
48 rooms - $45-55
Pets: Small pets w/$20 deposit
Creature Comforts: CCTV, a/c,
refrig, micro, restaurant, pool

Super 8
(800) 800-8000, (816) 385-5788
http://www.super8.com
3508 Range Line Rd.
64 rooms - $40-75
Pets: Welcome
Creature Comforts: CCTV,
VCR, a/c, refrig, micro

MARYLAND HEIGHTS
Best Western Westport Park
(800) 528-1234, (573) 291-8700
http://www.bestwestern.com
2434 Old Dorsett Rd.
155 rooms - $80-110
Pets: Small pets w/$25 fee
Creature Comforts: CCTV, a/c,
refrig, Jacuzzi, restaurant, pool,
hlth club access, sauna, whirlpool

Comfort Inn Westport
(800) 228-5150, (314) 878-1400
http://www.comfortinn.com
12031 Lackland Dr.
175 rooms - $60-110
Pets: Small pets w/$20 deposit
Creature Comforts: CCTV, a/c,
refrig, pool, hlth clb

Drury Inn, Westport
(800) 325-8300, (314) 576-9966
http://www.druryinn.com
12220 Dorsett Rd.
130 rooms - $80-90
Pets: Welcome
Creature Comforts: CCTV, a/c,
refrig, micro, Jacuzzi, pool, hlth
clb access

Red Roof Inn, Westport
(800) 843-7663, (314) 991-4900
http://www.redroof.com
11837 Lackland Rd.
165 rooms - $40-50
Pets: Small pets welcome
Creature Comforts: CCTV, ac,
health club access

MARYVILLE
Super 8
(800) 800-8000, (816) 582-8088
http://www.super8.com
Route 71
34 rooms - $40-69
Pets: Welcome w/$10 deposit
Creature Comforts: CCTV, a/c,
refrig

MEHLVILLE
Holiday Inn, South I-55
(800) HOLIDAY, (314) 894-0700
http://www.holiday-inn.com
4234 Butler Hill Rd.
165 rooms - $80-110
Pets: Welcome
Creature Comforts: CCTV, a/c,
refrig, micro, restaurant, pool,
whirlpool

Oak Grove Motel
(314) 894-9449
6602 S. Lindbergh Blvd.
100 rooms - $40-70
Pets: Welcome w/$10 fee
Creature Comforts: CCTV,
VCR, a/c, Jacuzzi

MEXICO
Best Western Inn
(800) 528-1234, (573) 581-1440
http://www.bestwestern.com
1010 E. Liberty St.
65 rooms - $35-50
Pets: Small pets w/$25 deposit
Creature Comforts: CCTV, a/c,
refrig, micro, kit, restaurant, pool

MOBELY
Ramada Inn
(800) 2-Ramada, (816) 263-6540
http://www.ramada.com
Routes 24 and 63
100 rooms - $50-70
Pets: Welcome
Creature Comforts: CCTV,
VCR, a/c, refrig, micro, restaurant,
pool, whirlpool

MONETT
Oxford Inn
(417) 235-8039
868 Route 60
42 rooms - $40-50
Pets: Welcome w/$10 fee
Creature Comforts: CCTV, a/c,
refrig, micro, Jacuzzi, pool

MONROE CITY
Econo Lodge
(800) 55 ECONO, (573) 735-4200
http://www.econolodge.com
Routes 24 and 36
50 rooms - $30-65
Pets: Small pets w/$5 fee
Creature Comforts: CCTV,
VCR, a/c, pool

MOUNT VERNON
Best Western Bel Aire
(800) 528-1234, (417) 466-2111
http://www.bestwestern.com
740 E. Mt. Vernon Rd.
45 rooms - $40-55
Pets: Small pets welcome
Creature Comforts: CCTV, a/c,
pool

Budget Host Ranch
(800) Bud-Host, (417) 466-2125
http://www.budgethost.com
Routes 39 and 44
22 rooms - $40-55
Pets: Small pets w/$5 fee
Creature Comforts: CCTV, a/c,
pool

MOUNTAIN GROVE
Best Western Ranch House
(800) 528-1234, (417) 926-3152
http://www.bestwestern.com
111 E. 17th St.
50 rooms - $40-60
Pets: Small pets w/$5 fee
Creature Comforts: CCTV, a/c,
Jacuzzi

Days Inn, Mountain Grove
(800) DAYS INN, (417) 926-5555
http://www.daysinn.com
300 E. 19th St.
40 rooms - $40-50
Pets: Small pets w/$6 fee
Creature Comforts: CCTV, a/c,
pool

NEVADA
Best Western, Rambler
(800) 528-1234, (417) 667-3351
http://www.bestwestern.com
1401 Austin St.
55 rooms - $40-50
Pets: Small pets welcome
Creature Comforts: CCTV, a/c,
refrig, pool

Comfort Inn
(800) 228-5150, (417) 667-6777
http://www.comfortinn.com
1401 E. Austin St.
50 rooms - $40-55
Pets: Small pets w/$25 deposit
Creature Comforts: CCTV, a/c,
refrig, micro, Jacuzzi, pool,
whirlpool

Ramsey's Nevada Motel
(417) 667-5273
1514 E. Austin St.
27 rooms - $30-50
Pets: Small pets w/$5 deposit
Creature Comforts: CCTV, a/c,
refrig, pool

Super 8
(800) 800-8000, (417) 667-8888
http://www.super8.com
2301 E. Austin St.
59 rooms - $40-50
Pets: Welcome in smoking rooms
Creature Comforts: CCTV, a/c,
cont. brkfst, pool, whirlpool

NIXA
Super 8
(800) 800-8000, (417) 725-0880
http://www.super8.com
418 Massey Blvd.
45 rooms - $40-55
Pets: Welcome w/$20 deposit
Creature Comforts: CCTV, a/c,
pool

OAK GROVE
Days Inn
(800) DAYS INN, (816)625-8686
http://www.daysinn.com
101 North Locust Rd.
50 rooms - $40-75
Pets: Welcome
Creature Comforts: CCTV, a/c,
cont. brkfst

Econo Lodge
(800) 55 ECONO, (816) 625-3681
http://www.econolodge.com
410 SE First St.
40 rooms - $50-60
Pets: Small pets welcome
Creature Comforts: CCTV, a/c

OSAGE BEACH
Best Western, Dogwood Hills
(800) 528-1234, (573) 348-1735
http://www.bestwestern.com
Route 54
65 rooms - $45-90
Pets: Welcome w/$25 deposit
Creature Comforts: CCTV, a/c,
refrig, micro, kit, restaurant, cont.
brkfst, pool, hlth clb access,
whirlpool, golf

Scottish Inn
(800) 251-1962, (573) 348-4123
www.reservahost.com
Route 54
24 rooms - $30-60
Pets: Small pets-$5 fee, smkg rms
Creature Comforts: CCTV, a/c,
pool

OZARK
Holiday Inn Express
(800) HOLIDAY, (417) 485-6688
http://www.holiday-inn.com
1900 Evangel St.
50 rooms - $50-60
Pets: Welcome w/$10 fee
Creature Comforts: CCTV, a/c,
refrig, micro, Jacuzzi, cont. brkfst,
pool, whirlpool

Super 8
(800) 800-8000, (417) 581-8800
http://www.super8.com
299 N. 20th St.
61 rooms - $45-60
Pets: Welcome
Creature Comforts: CCTV, a/c,
cont. brkfst, pool

PACIFIC
Holiday Inn Express
(800) HOLIDAY, (314) 257-8400
http://www.holiday-inn.com
1400 W. Osage St.
45 rooms - $60-80
Pets: Small pets-$10 fee, $10 dep
Creature Comforts: CCTV, a/c,
cont. brkfst

PERRYVILLE
Best Western Colonial
(800) 528-1234, (573) 547-1091
http://www.bestwestern.com
1500 Liberty St.
70 rooms - $55-60
Pets: Small pets, 1 per room
Creature Comforts: CCTV, a/c,
pool

Budget Host
(800) Bud-Host, (573) 547-4516
http://www.budgethost.com
221 S. Kings Rte.
20 rooms - $30-40
Pets: Welcome
Creature Comforts: CCTV, a/c,
refrig

PLATTE CITY
Best Western, Airport
(800) 528-1234, (816) 858-4588
http://www.bestwestern.com
Route 29
63 rooms - $42-60
Pets: Small pets welcome
Creature Comforts: CCTV, a/c,
refrig, pool, whirlpool

Comfort Inn
(800) 228-5150, (816) 858-5430
http://www.comfortinn.com
1200 Rte. 92
94 rooms - $40-75
Pets: Small pets welcome
Creature Comforts: CCTV,
VCR, a/c, refrig, pool

POPLAR BLUFF
Drury Inn
(800) 325-8300, (573) 686-2451
http://www.druryinn.com
2200 N. Westwood Blvd.
80 rooms - $60-65
Pets: Welcome
Creature Comforts: CCTV, a/c,
refrig, micro, cont. brkfst, pool,
hlth clb access

Holiday Inn
(800) HOLIDAY, (573) 785-7711
http://www.holiday-inn.com
2115 N. Westwood Blvd.
145 rooms - $45-150
Pets: Welcome
Creature Comforts: CCTV, a/c,
refrig, micro, Jacuzzi, restaurant,
cont. brkfst, pool, whirlpool

Pear Tree Inn
(573) 785-7100
2218 Westwood Blvd
77 rooms - $50-60
Pets: Welcome
Creature Comforts: CCTV, a/c,
pool, hlth clb access

PORTAGEVILLE
Teroy Motel
(573) 379-5461
903 N. Route 61
20 rooms - $30-34
Pets: Welcome
Creature Comforts: CCTV, a/c

RICHMOND HEIGHTS
Residence Inn
(800) 331-3131, (314) 862-1900
http://www.residenceinn.com
1100 McMorrow Ave.
155 rooms - $120-160
Pets: Welcome with a $25 first
night fee, $10 for additional nights
Creature Comforts: CCTV,
VCR, a/c, kit, pool, hlth clb
access, sauna, whirlpool

ROCK PORT
Rock Port Inn
(816) 744-6282
Rtes. 29 & 136
40 rooms - $40-45
Pets: Welcome
Creature Comforts: CCTV, a/c,
refrig, micro, Jacuzzi

ROLLA
Bestway Inn
(573) 341-2158
1631 Martin Springs Dr.
20 rooms - $30-40
Pets: Welcome w/$10 deposit
Creature Comforts: CCTV, a/c,
pool

Best Western Coachlight
(800) 528-1234, (573) 341-2511
http://www.bestwestern.com
1403 Martin Springs Dr.
90 rooms - $50-65
Pets: Small pets welcome
Creature Comforts: CCTV, a/c,
refrig, pool

Days Inn
(800) DAYS INN, (573) 341-3700
http://www.daysinn.com
1207 Kings Highway
40 rooms - $40-60
Pets: Welcome
Creature Comforts: CCTV, a/c,
pool

Drury Inn
(800) 5325-8300, (573) 364-4000
http://www.druryinn.com
2006 N. Bishop Rd.
88 rooms - $65-75
Pets: Welcome
Creature Comforts: CCTV, a/c,
refrig, micro, cont. brkfst, pool,
hlth clb access

Econo Lodge
(800) 55 ECONO, (573) 341-3130
http://www.econolodge.com
1417 Martin Springs Dr.
64 rooms - $40-50
Pets: Small pets in smkng rooms
Creature Comforts: CCTV, a/c,
pool

Howard Johnson Lodge
(800) I-Go-Hojo, (573) 364-7111
http://www.hojo.com
127 H.J. Drive
80 rooms - $60-70
Pets: Welcome in smoking rooms
Creature Comforts: CCTV,
VCR, a/c, refrig, restaurant, cont.
brkfst, 2 pools, whirlpool, sauna

Western Inn
(573) 341-3050
1605 Martin Springs Dr.
40 rooms - $40-60
Pets: Welcome
Creature Comforts: CCTV, a/c,
refrig, micro, kit, pool

ST. CHARLES
Baymont Inn and Suites
(800) 789-4103, (314) 946-6936
http://www.baymontinns.com
1425 S. Fifth St.
140 rooms - $60-70
Pets: Welcome
Creature Comforts: CCTV, a/c,
refrig, micro, pool, hlth clb

Comfort Inn
(800) 228-5150, (314) 949-8700
http://www.comfortinn.com
2750 Plaza Way
120 rooms - $60-75
Pets: Welcome w/$100 deposit
Creature Comforts: CCTV,
VCR, a/c, refrig, micro, cont.
brkfst, pool, hlth clb access,
whirlpool

Knights Inn
(800) 843-5644, (314) 925-2020
http://www.knightsinn.com
3800 Harry S. Truman Dr.
110 rooms - $40-60
Pets: Small pets w/$25 deposit
Creature Comforts: CCTV, a/c,
refrig

Red Roof Inn
(800) 843-7663, (314) 947-7770
http://www.redroof.com
2010 Zumbahl Rd.
110 rooms - $45-70
Pets: Small pets welcome
Creature Comforts: CCTV, a/c,
refrig

ST. CLAIR
Budget Lodging
(314) 629-1000
866 S. Outer Rd.
70 rooms - $40-50
Pets: Welcome w/$5 fee
Creature Comforts: CCTV,
VCR, a/c, kit, Jacuzzi, pool

ST. JAMES
Comfort Inn
(800) 228-5150, (573) 265-5005
http://www.comfortinn.com
110 N. Outer Rd.
60 rooms - $50-80
Pets: Small dogs welcome
Creature Comforts: CCTV,
VCR, a/c, refrig, micro, Jacuzzi,
cont. brkfst, pool, hlth clb,
whirlpool

ST. JOSEPH
Drury Inn
(800)325-8300, (816) 364-4700
http://www.druryinn.com
4213 Frederick Blvd.
140 rooms - $55-75
Pets: Welcome
Creature Comforts: CCTV, a/c,
refrig, micro, cont. brkfst, pool,
hlth clb

Holiday Inn
(800) HOLIDAY, (816) 279-8000
http://www.holiday-inn.com
102 S. Third St.
170 rooms - $45-275
Pets: Welcome
Creature Comforts: CCTV, a/c,
refrig, micro, restaurant, cont.
brkfst, pool, whirlpool, sauna

Ramada Inn
(800) 2-Ramada, (816) 233-6192
http://www.ramada.com
4016 Frederick Ave.
160 rooms - $55-65
Pets: Small pets w/$20 fee
Creature Comforts: CCTV, a/c,
refrig, micro, restaurant, cont.
brkfst, pool, whirlpool

ST. LOUIS
Drury Inn, Airport
(800) 325-8300, (314) 423-7700
http://www.druryinn.com
10490 Natural Bridge Rd.
175 rooms - $80-90
Pets: Welcome
Creature Comforts: CCTV, a/c,
refrig, micro, cont. brkfst, pool,
whirlpool

Drury Inn Covention Center
(800) 325-8300, (314) 231-8100
http://www.druryinn.com
711 N. Broadway St.
190 rooms - $95-105
Pets: Welcome
Creature Comforts: Historic
hotel, CCTV, a/c, refrig, micro,
restaurant, cont. brkfst, pool, hlth
clb access, whirlpool

Drury Inn, Union Station
(800) 325-8300, (314) 231-3900
http://www.druryinn.com
201 S. 20th St.
180 rooms - $105-115
Pets: Welcome
Creature Comforts: CCTV, a/c,
refrig, micro, restaurant, cont.
brkfst, pool, hlth clb, whirlpool

Hampton Inn Union Station
(800) Hampton, (314) 241-3200
http://www.hampton-inn.com
2211 Market St.
63 rooms - $40-75
Pets: Welcome
Creature Comforts: CCTV, a/c,
refrig, micro, restaurant, cont.
brkfst, pool, hlth clb access,
whirlpool

Holiday Inn Convention Center
(800) HOLIDAY, (314) 421-4000
http://www.holiday-inn.com
811 N. 9th St.
300 rooms - $80-120
Pets: Welcome
Creature Comforts: CCTV, a/c,
refrig, Jacuzzi, restaurant, cont.
brkfst, pool, hlth clb access,
whirlpool

Holiday Inn Forest Park
(800) HOLIDAY, (314) 645-0700
http://www.holiday-inn.com
5915 Wilson Ave.
125 rooms - $80-100
Pets: Welcome
Creature Comforts: CCTV, a/c,
refrig, restaurant, pool

Red Roof Inn
(800) 843-7663, (314) 645-0101
http://www.redroof.com
5823 Wilson Ave.
102 rooms - $55-85
Pets: Small pets welcome
Creature Comforts: CCTV, a/c

Regal Riverfront Hotel
(800) 325-7353, (314) 241-9500
http://www.regalstl.com
200 S. Fourth St.
808 rooms - $140-1,000
Pets: Welcome w/$50 deposit
Creature Comforts: Unique
circular bldng, recently renovated,
attractive rooms, ample amenities,
CCTV, a/c, refrig, micro,
restaurant, pools, hlth club

Holiday Inn Riverfront
(800) HOLIDAY, (314) 621-8200
http://www.holiday-inn.com
200 N. 4th St.
455 rooms - $60-110
Pets: Small pets w/$50 deposit
Creature Comforts: CCTV, a/c,
kit, restaurant, pool, hlth clb
access

Marriott, Airport
(800) 228-9290, (314) 423-9700
http://www.marriott.com
Route 70
600 rooms - $100-110
Pets: Welcome w/$25 deposit
Creature Comforts: CCTV,
VCR, a/c, refrig, micro, restaurant,
cont. brkfst, 2 huge pools, hlth
club,

Motel 6, Airport
(800) 4-MOTEL6, (314) 427-1313
http://www.motel6.com
4576 Woodson Rd.
106 rooms - $38-49
Pets: Under 30 lbs. welcome
Creature Comforts: CCTV, a/c,
pool

Motel 6, NE
(800) 4-MOTEL6, (314) 869-9400
http://www.motel6.com
1405 Dunn Rd.
81 rooms - $35-49
Pets: Under 30 lbs. welcome
Creature Comforts: CCTV, a/c,
pool

Motel 6, South
(800) 4-MOTEL6, (314) 892-3664
http://www.motel6.com
6500 S. Lindbergh Ave.
118 rooms - $40-52
Pets: Under 30 lbs. welcome
Creature Comforts: CCTV, a/c,
pool

Red Roof Inn, Hampton
(800) 843-7663, (314) 645-0101
http://www.redroof.com
5823 Wilson Ave.
102 rooms - $55-80
Pets: Small pets welcome
Creature Comforts: CCTV, a/c

Residence Inn
(800) 331-3131, (314) 469-0060
http://www.residenceinn.com
1881 Craigshire Rd.
130 rooms/suites - $125-180
Pets: Welcome w$10 fee and a
$25 deposit
Creature Comforts: CCTV,
VCR, a/c, kit, restaurant, pool,
hlth clb access, sauna, whirlpool,
exercise room

Summerfield Suites
(800) 833-4353, (314) 878-1500
http://.www.summerfield.com
1855 Craigshire Rd.
110 rooms - $100-150
Pets: Welcome w/$6 fee and $75
non-refundable deposit
Creature Comforts: CCTV,
VCR, a/c, kit, fireplace, pool, hlth
clb, sauna, whirlpool

ST. PETERS
Drury Inn
(800) 325-8300, (314) 397-9700
http://www.druryinn.com
80 Mid Rivers Mall Dr.
135 rooms - $60-80
Pets: Welcome
Creature Comforts: CCTV, a/c,
refrig, micro, cont. brkfst, pool,
whirlpool

STE. GENEVIEVE
Family Budget Inns
(573) 543-2272
17030 Bremen Rd.
70 rooms - $40-55
Pets: Small pets welcome w/$3
fee and $20 deposit
Creature Comforts: CCTV, a/c,
refrig, pool

SIKESTON
Best Western Coach House
(800) 528-1234, (573) 471-9700
http://www.bestwestern.com
220 S. Interstate Dr.
60 rooms - $45-80
Pets: Small pets welcome
Creature Comforts: CCTV, a/c,
refrig, hlth clb, pool

Drury Inn
(800) 325-8300, (573) 471-4100
http://www.druryinn.com
2602 E. Malone
80 rooms - $55-70
Pets: Welcome
Creature Comforts: CCTV,
VCR, a/c, refrig, micro, pool,
whirlpool

Hampton Inn
(800) Hampton, (573) 471-3930
http://www.hampton-inn.com
1330 S. Main St.
130 rooms - $50-60
Pets: Welcome
Creature Comforts: CCTV,
VCR, a/c, refrig

Holiday Inn Express
(800) HOLIDAY, (573) 471-8660
http://www.holiday-inn.com
2602 East Rear Malone Rd.
70 rooms - $40-65
Pets: Welcome
Creature Comforts: CCTV,
VCR, a/c, pool

SPRINGFIELD
Best Western Ambassador
(800) 528-1234, (417) 869-0001
http://www.bestwestern.com
2745 N. Glenstone Ave.
100 rooms - $40-50
Pets: Small pets welcome
Creature Comforts: CCTV,
VCR, a/c, refrig, micro, Jacuzzi,
pool

Best Western Coach House
(417) 528-1234, (417) 862-0701
http://www.bestwestern.com
2535 N. Glenstone Ave.
130 rooms - $45-70
Pets: Welcome
Creature Comforts: CCTV,
VCR, a/c, refrig, micro, 2 pools

Best Western Sycamore
(417) 528-1234, (417) 866-1963
http://www.bestwestern.com
203 S. Glenstone Ave.
95 rooms - $40-60
Pets: Welcome
Creature Comforts: CCTV, a/c,
refrig, micro, Jacuzzi, restaurant,
pool

Clarion Inn
(800) 228-5150, (417) 883-6550
http://www.clarioninn.com
3333 S. Glenstone Ave.
200 rooms - $80-150
Pets: Welcome w/$10 fee
Creature Comforts: CCTV, a/c,
restaurant, pool

Comfort Inn
(800) 228-5150, (417) 866-5255
http://www.comfortinn.com
2550 N. Glenstone Ave.
180 rooms - $55-80
Pets: Welcome w/$10 fee
Creature Comforts: CCTV, a/c,
refrig, micro, Jacuzzi, pool

Comfort Suites
(800) 228-5150, (417) 886-5090
http://www.comfortinn.com
1260 E. Independence St.
55 suites - $70-95
Pets: Welcome w/$25 fee
Creature Comforts: CCTV, a/c,
refrig, micro, Jacuzzi, restaurant,
pool, hlth clb, sauna, whirlpool

Days Inn, North
(800) DAYS INN, (417) 865-5511
http://www.daysinn.com
2700 N. Glenstone Ave.
177 rooms - $40-50
Pets: Welcome w/$25 deposit
Creature Comforts: CCTV, a/c,
pool

Days Inn
(800) DAYS INN, (417) 862-0153
http://www.daysinn.com
621 W. Sunshine St.
44 rooms - $55-95
Pets: Welcome w/$10 fee
Creature Comforts: CCTV,
VCR, a/c, Jacuzzi, cont. brkfst,
pool

Holiday Inn, University Plaza
(800) HOLIDAY, (417) 864-7333
http://www.holiday-inn.com
333 John Q. Hammons Pkwy.
275 rooms - $90-115
Pets: Small pets welcome
Creature Comforts: CCTV,
VCR, a/c, refrig, micro, Jacuzzi,
restaurant, 3 pools, hlth clb, sauna,
whirlpool, tennis

Motel 6
(800) 446-8356, (417) 833-0880
http://www.motel6.com
3114 Kentwood North
105 rooms - $26-42
Pets: Under 30 lbs. welcome
Creature Comforts: CCTV, a/c,
pool

Red Roof Inn
(800) 843-7663, (417) 831-2100
http://www.redroof.com
2655 N. Glenstone Ave.
115 rooms - $35-55
Pets: Small pets welcome
Creature Comforts: CCTV, a/c

Residence Inn
(800) 331-3131, (417) 883-7300
http://www.residenceinn.com
1550 E. Raynell St.
80 rooms - $100-140
Pets: Welcome w/$100 deposit
Creature Comforts: CCTV, a/c,
refrig, micro, kit, pool, hlth clb
access, sauna, whirlpool

Scottish Inns
(800) 251-1962, (417) 862-4301
www.reservahost.com
2933 North Glenstone Ave.
35 rooms - $32-48
Pets: Small pets welcome
Creature Comforts: CCTV, a/c,
refrig, micro, pool

Sheraton Hawthorne Park
(800) 325-3535, (417) 831-3131
http://www.sheraton.com
2431 North Glenstone Ave.
210 rooms - $70
Pets: Welcome
Creature Comforts: CCTV, a/c,
refrig, restaurant, 2 pools, hlth clb
access, sauna, whirlpool

Skyline Motel
(417) 866-4356
2120 North Glenstone Ave.
20 rooms - $30-45
Pets: Welcome w/$5 fee
Creature Comforts: CCTV,
VCR, a/c, refrig, pool

Travelodge, Bass Country Inn
(800) 578-7878, (417) 866-6671
http://www.travelodge.com
2610 North Glenstone Ave.
225 rooms - $45-65
Pets: Welcome
Creature Comforts: CCTV, a/c, 2
pools, tennis

STRAFFORD
Super 8 Motel
(800) 800-8000, (417) 736-3883
http://www.super8.com
315 E. Chestnut St.
45 rooms - $40-55
Pets: Welcome
Creature Comforts: CCTV, a/c

SULLIVAN
Best Western Penberthy
(800) 528-1234, (573) 468-3136
http://www.bestwestern.com
307 North Service Rd.
50 rooms - $45-150
Pets: Small pets welcome
Creature Comforts: CCTV,
VCR, a/c, kit, Jacuzzi, pool

Family Motor Inn
(573) 468-4119
209 North Service Rd.
65 rooms - $30-50
Pets: Welcome w/$3 fee
Creature Comforts: CCTV, a/c,
kit, pool, whirlpool

Ramada Inn
(800) 2-Ramada, (573) 468-4172
http://www.ramada.com
309 N. Service Rd.
80 rooms - $50-65
Pets: Small pets welcome
Creature Comforts: CCTV, a/c,
pool, lawn games, game room

SWEET SPRINGS
People's Choice Motel
(816) 335-6315
1001 N. Locust St.
30 rooms - $30-40
Pets: Welcome w/$20 deposit
Creature Comforts: CCTV, a/c

TIPTON
Super 8
(800) 800-8000, (816) 433-5525
http://www.super8.com
452 Route 50 West
25 rooms - $30-35
Pets: Small pets welcome
Creature Comforts: CCTV, a/c,
refrig, micro

VAN BUREN
Hawthorne Motel
(573) 323-4275
Main St.
30 rooms - $25-40
Pets: Welcome
Creature Comforts: CCTV, a/c,
pool

VILLA RIDGE
Best Western Diamond
(800) 528-1234, (314) 742-3501
http://www.bestwestern.com
581 Rte. 100 East
65 rooms - $50-90
Pets: Welcome
Creature Comforts: CCTV, a/c,
cont. brkfst, pool

WAPPAPELLO
Millers Motor Lodge
(573) 222-8579
Route 2
30 rooms - $40-90
Pets: Small pets w/$5 fee
Creature Comforts: Country
setting, some cabins, CCTV, a/c,
refrig, micro, fireplace, pool

WARRENTON
Days Inn
(800) DAYS INN, (314) 456-4301
http://www.daysinn.com
220 Arlington Way
72 rooms - $40-70
Pets: Small pets w/$6 fee
Creature Comforts: CCTV, a/c,
restaurant, cont. brkfst, pool

Motel 6, South
(800) 4-MOTEL6, (314) 456-2522
http://www.motel6.com
804 N. Rte. 47
55 rooms - $33
Pets: Under 30 lbs. welcome
Creature Comforts: CCTV, a/c,
pool

WAYNESVILLE
Best Western Montis
(800) 528-1234, (573) 336-4299
http://ww.bestwestern.com
14086 Rte. Z
50 rooms - $45-60
Pets: Small pets w/$25 deposit
Creature Comforts: CCTV, a/c,
refrig, kit, fireplace, pool

Days Inn
(800) DAYS INN, (573) 336-4299
http://www.daysinn.com
14125 Rte. Z
35 rooms - $40-60
Pets: Welcome w/$5 fee
Creature Comforts: CCTV,
VCR, a/c, refrig, micro, pool

Econo Lodge
(800) 55 ECONO, (573) 336-7272
http://www.econolodge.com
309 Rte. Z
50 rooms - $45-65
Pets: Welcome
Creature Comforts: CCTV,
VCR, a/c, refrig, micro, Jacuzzi,
pool

Ramada Inn
(800) 2-Ramada, (573) 336-2121
http://www.ramada.com
Missouri Ave.
80 rooms - $50-100
Pets: Welcome w/$25 fee
Creature Comforts: CCTV,
VCR, a/c, kit, fireplace, Jacuzzi,
restaurant, cont. brkfst, 2 pools,
hlth clb, sauna, whirlpool, exercise
facilities

WENTZVILLE
Holiday Inn
(800) HOLIDAY, (314) 327-7001
http://www.holiday-inn.com
900 Corporate Pkwy.
140 rooms - $65-105
Pets: Small pets w/$10 fee
Creature Comforts: CCTV,
VCR, a/c, refrig, micro, restaurant,
pool

Howard Johnson
(800) I-Go-Hojo, (314) 327-5212
http://www.hojo.com
1500 Continental Dr.
100 rooms - $35-60
Pets: Welcome
Creature Comforts: CCTV, a/c,
micro, cont. brkfst, pool

Ramada Inn
(800) 2-Ramada, (314) 327-5300
http://www.ramada.com
1400 Continental Dr.
81 rooms - $40-75
Pets: Small pets w/$10 fee
Creature Comforts: CCTV, a/c,
refrig, pool

WEST PLAINS
Best Western Grand Villa
(800) 528-1234, (417) 257-2711
http://www.bestwestern.com
220 Route 63
60 rooms - $50-60
Pets: Medium pets welcome
Creature Comforts: CCTV, a/c,
refrig, micro, restaurant, full
brkfst, pool, hlth clb, whirlpool

Days Inn
(800) DAYS INN, (417) 256-4135
http://www.daysinn.com
2105 Porter Wagoner Blvd.
120 rooms - $40-65
Pets: Welcome w/$5 fee
Creature Comforts: CCTV,
VCR, a/c, refrig, micro, Jacuzzi,
restaurant, pool

Ramada Inn
(800) 2-Ramada, (417) 256-8191
http://www.ramada.com
1301 Preacher Rd.
80 rooms - $40-60
Pets: Welcome
Creature Comforts: CCTV, a/c,
refrig, micro, Jacuzzi, restaurant,
pool

WOODSON TERRACE
Days Inn, Airport
(800) DAYS INN, (314) 423-6770
http://www.daysinn.com
4545 Woodson Rd.
200 rooms - $40-75
Pets: Welcome w/$5 fee
Creature Comforts: CCTV, a/c,
pool

Montana

ANACONDA
Georgetown Lake Lodge
(406) 563-7020
Denton's Point Rd.
10 rooms - $40-60
Pets: Welcome
Creature Comforts: CCTV, a/c

Pintlar Inn
(406) 563-5072
Gerogetown Lake
7 rooms - $30-40
Pets: Welcome
Creature Comforts: CCTV,
restaurant

Seven Gables Resort
(406) 563-5052
www.sevengablesmontana.com
Georgetown Lake
10 rooms - $40-75
Pets: Welcome
Creature Comforts: CCTV, a/c,
restaurant

AUGUSTA
Bunkhouse Inn Motel
(406) 562-3387
122 Main St.
9 rooms - $25-35
Pets: Welcome
Creature Comforts: CCTV, a/c,
restaurant

BAKER
Roy's Motel
(406) 778-3321
327 W. Montana Ave.
21 rooms - $38-55
Pets: Welcome in smkng rms.
Creature Comforts: CCTV, a/c

BELGRADE
Homestead Inn Motel
(800) 272-9500, (406) 388-0800
6261 Jack Rabbit Ln.
70 rooms - $45-65
Pets: Welcome
Creature Comforts: CCTV, a/c,
whirlpool

BIGFORK
O'Duachain Country Inn
(800) 837-7460, (406) 837-6851
www.montanainn.com
675 Ferndale Dr.
5 rooms - $90-110
Pets: Selectively welcomed with
prior approval
Creature Comforts: Log cabin
on five acres w/animal menagerie,
exposed log walls, two-story
living rm, western memorabilia,
CCTV, VCR, kit, fireplace, full
brkfst, hot tub

Swan Lake Guest Cabins
(888) 837-1557, (406) 837-1137
1167 Sylvan Dr.
5 cabins - $75-115
Pets: Welcome
Creature Comforts: New log
cabins in woods, handmade log
furniture, CCTV, VCR, refrig,
micro, sauna, abundant wildlife,
boating, hiking

Timbers Motel
(800) 821-4546, (406) 837-6200
8540 Rte. 40
40 rooms - $35-70
Pets: Welcome w/$5 fee, $50
deposit
Creature Comforts: CCTV, a/c,
whirlpool

Woods Bay Motel
(406) 837-3333
26481 E. Shore Rte.
12 rooms - $40-60
Pets: Welcome
Creature Comforts: CCTV, a/c

BIG SANDY
Q's Motel
(406) 378-2389
Rte. 87
8 rooms - $38-45
Pets: Welcome
Creature Comforts: CCTV, a/c

BIG SKY
Best Western Buck's T-4 Lodge
(800) 528-1234, (406) 995-4111
http://www.bestwestern.com
46625 Gallatin Rd.
75 rooms - $70-110
Pets: Small pets w/$5 fee
Creature Comforts: CCTV, a/c,
kit, Jacuzzi, restaurant, whirlpool

320 Ranch
(800) 243-0320, (406) 995-4283
http://www.gomontana.com/
320guestranch.html
205 Buffalo Horn Creek
6 cabins - $101-135
Pets: Welcome w/$10 nightly fee
Creature Comforts: 1820's ranch
w/beautiful log cabins, comforters,
modern amenities, CCTV, kit.
fireplace, woodstove, dining
room, horseback riding, fishing-
river, xc-skiing, kids program,
minutes from Yellowstone Park

BIG TIMBER
Big Timber Inn B&B
(406) 932-4080
Box 328
2 rooms - $40-60
Pets: Welcome
Creature Comforts: Banks of
Yellowstone River, CCTV, refrig,
micro, full brkfst

The Grand Hotel B&B
(406) 932-4459
www.grand-hotel.com
139 McLeod St.
7 rooms - $60-90
Pets: Quiet pets welcome
Creature Comforts: National
Historic Register 1890s inn,
exposed brick, tin ceilings, parquet
flrs, country antiques, excellent
restaurant, wine cellar, saloon

Sweet Grass Ranch
(406) 537-4477
www.sweetgrassranch.com
Melville Rte., HC 87, Box 2161
4 rms/8 cabins - $600-950/wk pp
Pets: Welcome w/approval
Creature Comforts: Nat'l
Historic Register ranch, striking
riverside loc., family friendly w/
horseback riding, ranch animals,
simple cabins w/woodstoves, all
meals

Super 8
(800) 800-8000, (406) 932-8888
http://www.super8.com
I-90/Rte. 10
115 rooms - $43-50
Pets: Welcome w/$10 fee
Creature Comforts: CCTV,
VCR, a/c

BILLINGS
Airport Metra Inn
(800) 234-6611, (406) 245-6611
403 Main St.
103 rooms - $35-45
Pets: Welcome in certain rooms
Creature Comforts: CCTV, a/c,
refrig, kit, restaurant, pool

Best Western Billings
(800) 528-1234, (406) 248-9800
http://www.bestwestern.com
5610 S. Frontage Rd.
80 rooms - $60-75
Pets: Small pets welcome
Creature Comforts: CCTV, a/c,
refrig, micro, Jacuzzi, pool, sauna,
whirlpool

Best Western Ponderosa
(800) 528-1234, (406) 259-5511
http://www.bestwestern.com
2511 First Ave. N.
130 rooms - $60-70
Pets: Small pets welcome
Creature Comforts: CCTV, a/c,
refrig, micro, Jacuzzi, restaurant,
sauna

Billings Inn Motel
(406) 252-6800
880 N. 29th St.
60 rooms - $40-50
Pets: Welcome
Creature Comforts: CCTV, a/c,
refrig, micro, cont. brkfst

Cherry Tree Inn
(800) 237-5882, (406) 252-5603
823 N. Broadway
65 rooms - $38-42
Pets: Welcome
Creature Comforts: CCTV, a/c,
refrig, kit

Clarion Inn
(800) CLARION, (406) 248-7151
http://www.clarioninn.com
1223 Mullowney Ln.
240 rooms - $47-100
Pets: Welcome
Creature Comforts: CCTV, a/c,
refrig, micro, restaurant, pool,
whirlpool

Comfort Inn
(800) 228-5150, (406) 652-5200
http://www.comfortinn.com
2030 Overland Ave.
60 rooms - $50-70
Pets: Small pets w/$10 fee
Creature Comforts: CCTV, a/c,
refrig, micro, pool

Days Inn
(800) DAYS INN, (406) 252-4007
http://www.daysinn.com
843 Parkway Ln.
46 rooms - $45-65
Pets: Small pets welcome
Creature Comforts: CCTV,
VCR, a/c, refrig, whirlpool

Dude Rancher Lodge
(800) 221-3302, (406) 259-5561
415 N. 29th
57 rooms - $45-60
Pets: Welcome w/$6 fee
Creature Comforts: CCTV, a/c,
refrig, micro, kit, Jacuzzi,
restaurant

Heights Inn Motel
(800) 275-8451, (406) 252-8451
1206 Main St.
33 rooms - $30-41
Pets: Welcome w/deposit
Creature Comforts: CCTV, a/c,
kit

Hilltop Inn
(800) 878-9282, (406) 245-5000
1116 N. 28th St.
45 rooms - $40-50
Pets: Welcome w/$5 fee
Creature Comforts: CCTV, a/c,
refrig, micro

Holiday Inn
(800) HOLIDAY, (406) 248-7701
http://www.holiday-inn.com
5500 Midland Rd.
350 rooms - $60-100
Pets: Welcome in 2-story bldg
Creature Comforts: CCTV, a/c,
refrig, micro, Jacuzzi, restaurant,
cont. brkfst, pool, hlth clb, sauna,
whirlpool

Howard Johnson Express
(800) 446-4656, (406) 248-4656
http://www.hojo.com
1001 S. 27th St.
173 rooms - $40-60
Pets: Welcome w/$100 deposit
Creature Comforts: CCTV, a/c,
cont. brkfst

Juniper Inn Motel
(800) 826-7530, (406) 245-4128
1315 N. 27th St.
47 rooms - $48-80
Pets: Welcome w/$5 fee
Creature Comforts: CCTV, a/c,
refrig, micro, kit, Jacuzzi, cont.
brkfst

Kelly Inn
(800) 635-3559, (406) 252-2700
5425 Midland Rd.
90 rooms - $40-70
Pets: Welcome
Creature Comforts: CCTV, a/c,
refrig, micro, sauna, whirlpool

Lazy KT Motel
(800) 290-2681, (406) 252-6606
1403 First Ave. N.
25 rooms - $30-40
Pets: Welcome w/$10 deposit
Creature Comforts: CCTV, a/c,
refrig, micro

Motel 6, South
(800) 4-MOTEL6, (406) 252-0093
http://www.motel6.com
5400 Midland Rd.
99 rooms - $25-35
Pets: Small pets welcome
Creature Comforts: CCTV, a/c,
pool

Motel 6, North
(800) 4-MOTEL6, (406) 248-7551
http://www.motel6.com
5353 Midland Rd.
118 rooms - $30-40
Pets: Small pets welcome
Creature Comforts: CCTV, a/c, pool

Picture Court Motel
(800) 523-7379, (406) 252-8478
5146 Laurel Rd.
20 rooms - $30-35
Pets: Welcome w/$3 fee per pet
Creature Comforts: CCTV, a/c

Quality Inn
(800) 228-5151, (406) 652-1320
http://www.qualityinn.com
2036 Overland Ave.
120 rooms - $50-70
Pets: Welcome w/$25 deposit
Creature Comforts: CCTV, VCR, a/c, refrig, cont. brkfst, whirlpool

Radisson Northern
(800) 333-3333, (406) 245-5121
http://www.radisson.com
19 N. Broadway
165 rooms - $80-90
Pets: Small pets welcome in smoking rooms
Creature Comforts: CCTV, a/c, refrig, restaurant

Ramada Ltd.
(800) 2-Ramada, (406) 252-2584
http://www.ramada.com
1345 Mullowney Ln.
120 rooms - $60-70
Pets: Welcome w/$20 deposit
Creature Comforts: CCTV, VCR, a/c, refrig, micro, cont. brkfst, pool

Rimrock Inn Motel
(800) 624-9770, (406) 252-7107
1203 N. 27th St.
83 rooms - $35-45
Pets: Welcome w/$2 fee
Creature Comforts: CCTV, a/c, restaurant, cont. brkfst, pool, hlth clb., sauna, whirlpool

Rimview Inn Motel
(800) 551-1418, (406) 248-2622
1025 N. 27th St.
55 rooms - $35-50
Pets: Welcome w/$5 fee
Creature Comforts: CCTV, a/c, refrig, micro, kit, Jacuzzi, cont. brkfst

Sheraton Billings
(800) 325-3535, (406) 252-7400
http://www.sheraton.com
37 N. 27th St.
288 rooms - $80-100
Pets: Welcome
Creature Comforts: CCTV, a/c, restaurant, cont. brkfst, pool, hlth clb access, sauna, whirlpool, game room

Super 8
(800) 800-8000, (406) 248-8842
http://www.super8.com
5400 Southgate Dr.
115 rooms - $60-70
Pets: Welcome w/$20 deposit
Creature Comforts: CCTV, VCR, a/c

War Bonnet Inn
(406) 248-7761
2612 Belknap Ave.
102 rooms - $35-40
Pets: Welcome w/$10 deposit
Creature Comforts: CCTV, a/c, restaurant, pool

BOULDER
Castoria Motel
(406) 225-3549
211 S. Monroe
30 rooms - $25-35
Pets: Welcome
Creature Comforts: CCTV, a/c

O-Z Motel
(406) 225-3364
114 N. Main St.
9 rooms - $25-35
Pets: Welcome
Creature Comforts: CCTV, a/c

BOZEMAN
Alpine Lodge
(888) 922-5746, (406) 586-0356
Rte. 191
24 rms/7 cottages - $30-80
Pets: Welcome
Creature Comforts: Rqst cottages, clean, updated w/kit, sitting area, CCTV, a/c

Blue Sky Motel
(800) 845-9032, (406) 587-2311
1010 E. Main
29 rooms - $35-50
Pets: Welcome w/$5 fee
Creature Comforts: CCTV, a/c, cont. brkfst

Bozeman Inn
(800) 648-7515, (406) 587-3176
1235 N. 7th Ave.
50 rooms - $44-65
Pets: Welcome w/$5 fee
Creature Comforts: CCTV, a/c, refrig, micro, restaurant, cont. brkfst, sauna, whirlpool

Bozeman's Western Heritage
(800) 877-1094, (406) 586-8534
1200 E. Main St.
40 rooms - $45-85
Pets: Small pets w/$7 fee
Creature Comforts: CCTV, a/c, Jacuzzi, restaurant, cont. brkfst, pool, hlth clb., sauna, whirlpool

Days Inn
(800) DAYS INN, (406) 587-5251
http://www.daysinn.com
1321 N. 7th
80 rooms - $50-80
Pets: Welcome w/$25 deposit
Creature Comforts: CCTV, a/c, refrig, micro, kit, sauna, whirlpool

Fairfield Inn
(800) 228-2800, (406) 587-2222
http://www.fairfieldinn.com
828 Wheat Dr.
70 rooms/suites - $40-75
Pets: Welcome
Creature Comforts: CCTV, a/c,
refrig, micro, pool, whirlpool

Holiday Inn
(800) HOLIDAY, (406) 587-4561
http://www.holiday-inn.com
5 Baxter Ln.
180 rooms - $60-90
Pets: Small pets welcome
Creature Comforts: CCTV, a/c,
refrig, Jacuzzi, whirlpool

Hud Cabin
(406) 763-5215
13730 Portnell Rd.
1 rooms - $850/week
Pets: Welcome
Creature Comforts: CCTV, kit,
fireplace

Rainbow Motel
(406) 587-4201
510 N. 7th Ave.
42 rooms - $45-50
Pets: Small pets w/$10 fee
Creature Comforts: CCTV, a/c,
refrig, micro, kit

Ramada Ltd.
(800) 2-Ramada, (406) 585-2626
http://www.ramada.com
2020 Wheat Dr.
50 rooms - $40-120
Pets: Welcome
Creature Comforts: CCTV, a/c,
pool

Royal 7
(406) 587-3103
310 N. 7th Ave.
50 rooms - $35-60
Pets: Welcome in smoking rooms
Creature Comforts: CCTV, a/c,
refrig, micro, kit, whirlpool

Sleep Inn
(800) 753-3746, (406) 585-7888
http://www.sleepinn.com
817 Wheat Dr.
56 rooms - $48-99
Pets: Welcome
Creature Comforts: CCTV, a/c,
cont. brkfst, pool

Super 8
(800) 800-80000, (406) 586-1521
http://www.super8.com
800 Wheat Dr.
110 rooms - $40-70
Pets: Welcome w/$5 fee
Creature Comforts: CCTV,
VCR, a/c

BROADUS
C Bar J Motel
(406) 436-2671
Rte. 212
30 rooms - $40-55
Pets: Welcome
Creature Comforts: CCTV, a/c,
kit

Quarterhorse Motor Inn
(406) 436-2626
Rte. 212
10 rooms - $45-60
Pets: Welcome
Creature Comforts: CCTV, a/c

BROWNING
Glacier Motel
(406) 338-7277
Rte. 2
9 rooms - $40-60
Pets: Welcome
Creature Comforts: CCTV, a/c

Western Motel
(406) 338-7572
121 Central Ave.
15 rooms - $40-60
Pets: Welcome
Creature Comforts: CCTV, a/c

BUTTE
Best Western Copper King
(800) 332-8600, (406) 494-6666
http://www.bestwestern.com
4655 Harrison Ave.
150 rooms - $65-85
Pets: Welcome
Creature Comforts: CCTV, a/c,
Jacuzzi, restaurant, sauna,
whirlpool, tennis

Capri Motel
(800) 342-2772, (406) 723-4391
220 N. Wyoming St.
70 rooms - $32-50
Pets: Welcome w/$5 fee
Creature Comforts: CCTV, a/c,
kits, cont. brkfst, hlth clb access,
whirlpool

Comfort Inn
(800) 442-4667, (406) 494-8850
http://www.comfortinn.com
2777 Harrison Ave.
150 rooms/suites - $50-110
Pets: Welcome w/$5 fee
Creature Comforts: CCTV,
VCR, a/c, refrig, micro, cont.
brkfst, Jacuzzi, sauna, whirlpool

Copper King Mansion
(406) 782-7580
www.butteamerica.com/
copperking.html
219 W. Granite St.
4 rooms - $55-95
Pets: Well behaved pets welcome
Creature Comforts: An 1884
34-room Victorian mansion with
ornately carved woodwork,
stained glass windows, period
antiques, rqst master suite w/
frescoed ceiling, 2 fireplaces,
other rooms w/sleigh beds, Art
Deco furnishings., full brkfst,
access to sauna/whirlpool

Days Inn
(800) DAYS INN, (406) 494-7000
http://www.daysinn.com
2700 Harrison Ave.
74 rooms - $50-85
Pets: Welcome
Creature Comforts: CCTV, a/c,
Jacuzzi, whirlpool

Mile Hi Motel
(406) 494-2250
3499 Harrison Ave.
43 rooms - $40-75
Pets: Welcome
Creature Comforts: CCTV, a/c,
pool

Rocker Inn Motel
(406) 723-5464
122001 W. Brown's Gulch
50 rooms - $37-45
Pets: Welcome
Creature Comforts: CCTV, a/c,
refrig

Rose Motel
(406) 723-4346
920 S. Montana St.
11 rooms - $25-35
Pets: Welcome
Creature Comforts: CCTV, a/c

Skookum Motel
(406) 494-2153
3541 S. Harrison Ave.
39 rooms - $25-40
Pets: Welcome
Creature Comforts: CCTV, a/c

Super 8
(800) 800-8000, (406) 494-6000
http://www.super8.com
2929 Harrison Ave.
104 rooms - $44-55
Pets: Welcome w/$4 fee
Creature Comforts: CCTV,
VCR, a/c

War Bonnet Motel
(800) 443-1806, (406) 494-7800
2100 Cornell Ave.
135 rooms - $58-88
Pets: Small pets w/$10 fee, $50
deposit
Creature Comforts: CCTV, a/c,
refrig, restaurant, pool, hlth clb
access, sauna, whirlpool

CAMERON
West Fork Cabin Camp
(406) 682-4802
1475 287 N.
10 cabins - $40-60
Pets: Welcome
Creature Comforts: CCTV, a/c

CHARLO
Allentown Motel
(406) 644-2588
41000 Rte. 93
10 rooms - $25-35
Pets: Welcome
Creature Comforts: CCTV, a/c,
restaurant

CHINOOK
Chinook Motor Inn
(406) 357-2248
100 Indiana St.
38 rooms - $45-55
Pets: Welcome w/$5 fee
Creature Comforts: CCTV, a/c,
restaurant

CHOTEAU
Big Sky Motel
(800) 466-5318
209 S. Main
14 rooms - $35-54
Pets: Welcome w/$5 fee
Creature Comforts: CCTV, a/c,
refrig, micro, kit

Styren Ranch Guest House
(888) 789-7367, (406) 466-5698
961 - 20th Rd. NW
3 rooms - $75-95
Pets: Welcome
Creature Comforts: Montana
farmhouse, Rocky Mtn. front
range, rural, SATV, kit, fireplace

CLINTON
Rock Creek Lodge
(406) 825-4868
I-90, exit 126
6 rooms - $25-35
Pets: Welcome
Creature Comforts: CCTV, a/c

COLUMBIA FALLS
Glacier Inn Motel
(406) 892-4341
1401 Second Ave.
19 rooms - $40-60
Pets: Welcome
Creature Comforts: CCTV, a/c

Meadow Lake Resort
(800) 321-4653, (406) 892-7601
http://www.meadowlake.com
100 St. Andrews Dr.
115 rms/condos - $90-450
Pets: Small pets w/$15 nightly fee
in the hotel rooms
Creature Comforts: Award
winning luxury resort on 325
acres, inn and condo rms, CCTV,
VCR, a/c, refrig, micro, kit,
fireplace, Jacuzzi, restaurant, cont.
brkfst, pools, hlth clb, whirlpool,
sauna, golf, hiking, tennis,
horseback riding, near Glacier
Nat'l Pk.

Super 8
(800) 800-8000, (406) 892-0888
http://www.super8.com
Rtes. 40 & 206
32 rooms - $40-150
Pets: Welcome
Creature Comforts: CCTV, a/c,
refrig, micro, fireplace, Jacuzzi

COLUMBUS
Super 8
(800) 800-8000, (406) 322-4101
http://www.super8.com
602 - 8th Ave.
72 rooms - $55-65
Pets: Welcome w/$4 fee
Creature Comforts: CCTV,
VCR, a/c, restaurant, cont. brkfst,
sauna, whirlpool

CONRAD
Conrad Motel
(406) 278-7544
210 N. Main
15 rooms - $35-45
Pets: Welcome w/$5 fee in the
smoking rooms
Creature Comforts: CCTV, a/c,
refrig, micro

Northgate Motel
(406) 278-3516
5 N. Main
5 rooms - $30-35
Pets: Welcome
Creature Comforts: CCTV, a/c,
refrig

Super 8 Townhouse
(800) 800-8000, (406) 278-7676
http://www.super8.com
215 N. Main
48 rooms - $44-60
Pets: Welcome w/$5 fee
Creature Comforts: CCTV,
VCR, a/c, kit

COOKE CITY
Elkhorn Lodge
(406) 838-2332
208 Main St.
8 rooms/cabins - $45-52
Pets: Welcome
Creature Comforts: Simple rms
w/some antiques, CCTV, kit

High Country Motel
(406) 838-2272
Rte. 212
15 rooms - $40-65
Pets: Welcome
Creature Comforts: CCTV,
refrig, restaurant

Soda Butte Lodge
(406) 838-2251
210 Rte. 212
32 rooms - $50-85
Pets: Welcome w/$5 fee
Creature Comforts: CCTV,
restaurant, pool, whirlpool

CUT BANK
Corner Motel
(800) 851-5541, (406) 873-5544
1121 E. Railroad St.
12 rooms - $31-40
Pets: Welcome w/$2.50 fee
Creature Comforts: CCTV, a/c,
restaurant, whirlpool

Glacier Gateway Inn
(800) 851-5541, (406) 873-5544
1121 E. Railroad St.
20 rooms - $49-55
Pets: Welcome w/$2.50 fee
Creature Comforts: Unique
property w/theme rooms, CCTV,
VCR, a/c, refrig, microwave,
Jacuzzi, restaurant, cont. brkfst,
hlth clb., whirlpool

Parkway Motel
(406) 873-4582
Rte. 2
5 rooms - $35-40
Pets: Welcome
Creature Comforts: CCTV, a/c

Terrace Motel
(406) 873-5031
Main St.
18 rooms - $30-35
Pets: Small pets welcome
Creature Comforts: CCTV, a/c

DARBY
Triple Creek Ranch
(406) 821-4664
www.triplecreekranch.com
5551 West Fork Stage Rte.
17 cabins - $475-995 (AP)
Pets: Under 20 lbs. welcome with
a $100 deposit
Creature Comforts: Highly
recommended, luxurious ranch w/
log and cedar cabins, some
creekside, beautifully decorated,
gourmet dining, CCTV-VCR, a/c,
refrig, fireplaces, Jacuzzi, pool,
restaurant, whirlpool, putting
green, hlth club, horseback riding,
fishing, hiking, x-c skiing, lawn
games, and a stocked trout pond

Wilderness Motel
(800) 820-2554, (406) 821-3405
Rte. 93
12 rooms - $42-50
Pets: Welcome w/$4 fee
Creature Comforts: CCTV,
refrig, micro

DE BORGIA
Hotel Albert B&B
(800) 678-4303, (406) 678-4303
www.rusticweb.com/hotelalbert
2 Yellowstone Tr.
4 rooms - $55-65
Pets: Small dogs welcome
Creature Comforts: Historic and
classic looking Old West hotel,
simple rms, CCTV, country quilts,
full brkfst, near hiking & xc-skiing

DEER LODGE
Downtowner Motel
(406) 846-1021
5046 4th St.
11 rooms - $40-60
Pets: Welcome
Creature Comforts: CCTV, a/c,
pool

Scharf Motor Inn
(800) 341-8000, (406) 846-2810
819 Main St.
44 rooms - $30-47
Pets: Welcome
Creature Comforts: CCTV, a/c,
refrig, micro, kit, restaurant

Super 8
(800) 800-8000, (406) 846-2370
http://www.super8.com
1150 N. Main
54 rooms - $44-55
Pets: Welcome
Creature Comforts: CCTV,
VCR, a/c

DILLON
Best Western Paradise Inn
(800) 528-1234, (406) 683-4214
http://www.bestwestern.com
650 N. Montana
65 rooms - $50-65
Pets: Welcome w/mangr's aprvl
Creature Comforts: CCTV, a/c,
restaurant, cont. brkfst, pool,
whirlpool

Comfort Inn
(800) 228-5150, (406) 683-6831
http://www.comfortinn.com
450 N. Interchange
50 rooms - $40-60
Pets: Small pets w/$3 fee
Creature Comforts: CCTV,
VCR, a/c, refrig, micro, cont.
brkfst, pool

Creston Motel
(406) 683-2341
335 S. Atlantic St.
22 rooms - $30-40
Pets: Small pets welcome
Creature Comforts: CCTV, a/c,
refrig, micro

Crosswinds Motel
(406) 683-2378
1004 S. Atlantic St.
15 rooms - $25-35
Pets: Welcome
Creature Comforts: CCTV, a/c,
restaurant

Sacajawea Motel
(406) 683-2381
775 N. Montana St.
15 rooms - $25-35
Pets: Welcome
Creature Comforts: CCTV, a/c

Sundowner Motel
(800) 524-9746, (406) 683-2375
500 N. Montana St.
33 rooms - $30-40
Pets: Welcome
Creature Comforts: CCTV, a/c,
refrig, micro

Super 8
(800) 800-8000, (406) 683-4288
http://www.super8.com
550 N. Montana St.
47 rooms - $45-55
Pets: Welcome w/$25 deposit
Creature Comforts: CCTV, a/c,
refrig, micro, cont. brkfst

DRUMMOND
Drummond Motel
(406) 288-3272
170 W. Front St.
9 rooms - $25-35
Pets: Welcome
Creature Comforts: CCTV, a/c

Sky Motel
(800) 559-3206, (406) 288-3206
Front & Broadway
15 rooms - $25-35
Pets: Welcome
Creature Comforts: CCTV, a/c, pool

Wagon Wheel Motel
(406) 288-3201
Front & C Street
11 rooms - $25-35
Pets: Welcome
Creature Comforts: CCTV, a/c, restaurant

EAST GLACIER PARK
Porter's Alpine Motel
(406) 226-4402
147 Montana St.
14 rooms - $40-60
Pets: Welcome
Creature Comforts: CCTV, refrig

Sears Motel
(406) 226-4432
1023 Rte. 49N.
16 rooms - $40-55
Pets: Small pets welcome
Creature Comforts: CCTV

ELLISTON
Last Chance Motel
(406) 492-7250
Rte. 12
4 rooms - $20-30
Pets: Welcome
Creature Comforts: CCTV

EMIGRANT
Querencia B&B
(888) 603-4500, (406) 333-4500
www.queencia.com
MP 36.74, Rte. 89 S., Box 184
5 rooms - $90-125
Pets: Welcome, pet sitting & kennels are available
Creature Comforts: Timber home w/decks, overlooking Yellowstone River, fir floors, wood stove, library, family suite, log bedsteads, overstuffed furniture, Native Am. rugs, kit, cont. brkfst, great restaurant, fishing, hiking

ENNIS
El Western Resort
(800) 831-2773, (406) 682-4217
http://www.elwestern.com
Rte. 287
28 cabins - $55-325
Pets: Welcome w/$5 nightly fee
Creature Comforts: 17 acre creekside setting, 1940's chinked log cabins, barnboard walls, fireplace, pine furnishings, CCTV, kit, fireplace, fly fishing, hiking, swimming, xc skiing, whirlpool

Fan Mountain Motel
(406) 682-5200
204 N. Main
28 rooms - $45-55
Pets: Welcome
Creature Comforts: CCTV, a/c, refrig, micro

Riverside Motel
(800) 535-4139, (406) 682-4240
346 Main St.
12 rooms - $35-50
Pets: Welcome
Creature Comforts: CCTV, micro, kit

Silvertip Lodge
(406) 682-4384
301 Main St.
9 rooms - $20-40
Pets: Welcome
Creature Comforts: CCTV, a/c

Sportsman's Lodge
(406) 682-4242
310 Rte. 287
29 rooms - $40-75
Pets: Welcome
Creature Comforts: CCTV, a/c, restaurant, pool

ESSEX
Denny's Motel
(406) 888-5720
Rte. 2
8 rooms - $39-45
Pets: Small pets w/$5 fee
Creature Comforts: SATV

EUREKA
Ksanka Motor Inn
(406) 296-3127
Hwys 37/93
30 rooms - $45-50
Pets: Welcome w/$5
Creature Comforts: CCTV, a/c, refrig

FAIRVIEW
Korner Motel
(800) 656-7637, (406) 727-5259
217 W. 9th St.
15 rooms - $15-25
Pets: Welcome
Creature Comforts: CCTV

FORSYTH
Best Western Sundowner
(800) 528-1234, (406) 356-2115
http://www.bestwestern.com
1018 Front St.
40 rooms - $55-70
Pets: Small pets w/$3 fee
Creature Comforts: CCTV, a/c, refrig

Montana Inn
(406) 356-7947
659 Front
27 rooms - $25-30
Pets: Welcome
Creature Comforts: CCTV, a/c

Rails Motel
(800) 356-2242, (406) 356-2242
3rd & Front St.
49 rooms - $40-45
Pets: Welcome
Creature Comforts: CCTV, a/c, refrig, full brkfst

Restwell Motel
(800) 548-3442, (406) 356-2771
810 Front St.
18 rooms - $30-40
Pets: Small pets welcome
Creature Comforts: CCTV, a/c, micro

Westwind Motor Inn
(406) 356-2038
W. Main St.
33 rooms - $40-45
Pets: Welcome w/$1 fee
Creature Comforts: CCTV, a/c, refrig

FORT BENTON
Grand Union Hotel
(406) 622-3840
1308 Front St.
28 rooms - $65-110
Pets: Welcome
Creature Comforts: CCTV, a/c,
restaurant

Fort Motel
(406) 622-3312
1809 St. Charles St.
11 rooms - $35-45
Pets: Welcome w/$2 fee per pet
Creature Comforts: CCTV, a/c

FORT SMITH
Bighorn Angler Motel
(406) 666-2233
Rte. 313
9 rooms - $55-60
Pets: Small pets welcome
Creature Comforts: CCTV and
refrig in guest lounge

GALATIN GATEWAY
Castle Rock Inn
(406) 763-4243
Rte. 191
9 rooms - $50-75
Pets: Welcome
Creature Comforts: CCTV, a/c,
kit

GARDINER
Absaroka Lodge
(800) 755-7414, (406) 848-7414
http://www.yellowstonemotel.com
Rte. 89/Yellowstone River Bridge
41 rooms - $80-100
Pets: Welcome w/$5 nightly fee
Creature Comforts: CCTV, a/c,
micro, kit

Best Western Hot Springs
(800) 528-1234, (406) 848-7311
http://www.bestwestern.com
Rte. 89
85 rooms - $50-95
Pets: Welcome w/$3 fee, ltd. rms
Creature Comforts: CCTV,
VCR, refrig, micro, kit, Jacuzzi,
restaurant, sauna, whirlpool

Blue Haven Motel
(406) 848-7719
Rte. 89
8 rms/cabins - $35-50
Pets: Welcome w/$5 one-time fee
Creature Comforts: TV, refrig

Wilson's Yellowstone Rvr Motel
(406) 848-7303
14 E. Park St.
37 rooms - $35-70
Pets: Welcome
Creature Comforts: Riverside
location, CCTV, a/c, refrig

GLASGOW
Campbell Lodge
(406) 228-9328
Rte. 2
31 rooms - $28-32
Pets: Welcome w/$5 fee
Creature Comforts: CCTV, a/c

Cottonwood Inn
(800) 321-8213, (406) 228-8213
Rte. 2
95 rooms - $52-65
Pets: Welcome
Creature Comforts: CCTV, a/c,
refrig, Jacuzzi, restaurant, pool,
sauna, whirlpool

Koski's Motel
(800) 238-8282, (406) 228-8282
Rte. 2
24 rooms - $35-40
Pets: Small pets welcome
Creature Comforts: CCTV, a/c

La Casa Motel
(406) 228-9311
Rte. 2/Third St. North
13 rooms - $35-45
Pets: Welcome
Creature Comforts: TV, a/c, kit

Lakeridge Motel
(406) 526-3597
Rte. 24
5 rooms - $35
Pets: Small pets welcome
Creature Comforts: CCTV, a/c

Star Motel
(406) 228-2494
1023 Rte. 2 West
31 rooms - $30-35
Pets: Welcome
Creature Comforts: CCTV, a/c,
refrig, micro

GLENDIVE
Best Western Jordan Inn
(800) 824-5067, (406) 365-5655
http://www.bestwestern.com
222 N. Kendrick
85 rooms - $55-70
Pets: Small pets w/$5 fee
Creature Comforts: CCTV,
VCR, a/c, refrig, micro, restaurant,
pool, sauna

Budget Host Riverside
(800) Bud-Host, (406) 365-2349
http://www.budgethost.com
Rte. 16
35 rooms - $35-42
Pets: Small pets w/$10 deposit
Creature Comforts: CCTV, a/c,
refrig, kit

Days Inn
(800) DAYS INN, (406) 365-6011
http://www.daysinn.com
2000 N. Merrill
59 rooms - $30-50
Pets: Welcome
Creature Comforts: CCTV, a/c,
cont. brkfst, pool

Kings Inn
(406) 365-5636
Rte. 90
20 rooms - $40-45
Pets: Welcome w/$3-5
Creature Comforts: CCTV, a/c,
restaurant, pool, hot tub

Super 8
(800) 800-8000, (406) 365-5671
http://www.super8.com
1904 N. Merrill Ave.
51 rooms - $40-45
Pets: Welcome
Creature Comforts: CCTV, a/c,
cont. brkfst

GOLD CREEK
LH Ranch Bunk and Biscuit
(406) 288-3436
471 Mullan Trail
2 rooms - 75-85
Pets: Welcome w/$5 fee
Creature Comforts: Seven
generation ranch dating back to
1851, creekside setting log house
w/2 rooms, homey atmosphere,
cont. brkfst, hot tub, hiking trails,
trout fishing

GREAT FALLS

Best Western Heritage Inn
(800) 528-1234, (406) 761-1900
http://www.bestwestern.com
1700 Fox Farm Rd.
240 rooms/suites - $72-105
Pets: Small pets welcome
Creature Comforts: CCTV, a/c,
refrig, restaurant, cont. brkfst,
pool, hlth clb access, sauna,
whirlpool

Best Western Ponderosa
(800) 528-1234, (406) 761-3410
http://www.bestwestern.com
220 Central Ave.
100 rooms - $60-85
Pets: Small pets welcome
Creature Comforts: CCTV, a/c,
refrig, micro, restaurant, sauna

Budget Inn Motel
(800) 362-4282, (406) 453-1602
2 Treasure State Dr.
60 rooms - $45-51
Pets: Welcome
Creature Comforts: CCTV, a/c,
refrig, micro

Central Motel
(406) 453-0161
715 Central Ave.
27 rooms - $35-45
Pets: Small pets welcome
Creature Comforts: CCTV, a/c,
refrig, micro, kit

Comfort Inn
(800) 228-5150, (406) 454-2727
http://www.comfortinn.com
1120 - 9th St.
65 rooms - $60-90
Pets: Welcome w/$5 fee
Creature Comforts: CCTV, a/c,
refrig, micro, cont. brkfst, pool,
spa

Edelweiss Motor Inn
(406) 452-9503
626 Central Ave. W.
20 rooms - $30-35
Pets: Welcome in smkng
Creature Comforts: CCTV, a/c

Great Falls Inn
(406) 453-6000
1400 - 28th St. S.
45 rooms - $40-50
Pets: Welcome w/$5 fee
Creature Comforts: CCTV, a/c,
refrig, micro

Holiday Inn
(800) HOLIDAY, (406) 727-7200
http://www.holiday-inn.com
400 - 10th Ave. S.
171 rooms - $60-85
Pets: Small pets welcome
Creature Comforts: CCTV, a/c,
refrig, restaurant, pool, sauna,
whirlpool

Imperial Inn
(406) 452-9581
601 Second Ave. N.
32 rooms - $38-45
Pets: Welcome w/$10 fee
Creature Comforts: CCTV, a/c

Mid-Town Motel
(800) 457-2411, (406) 453-2411
526 - 2nd Ave. N.
39 rooms - $40-47
Pets: Welcome
Creature Comforts: CCTV, a/c,
Jacuzzi, restaurant

The Old Oak Inn
(888) 727-5782, (406) 727-5782
http://www.mtbba.com/html/
bb_23.html
709 Fourth Ave. N.
6 rooms - $60-95
Pets: Welcom
Creature Comforts: Restored
1909 Victorian Nat'l Historic
Register home, CCTV, VCR, a/c,
fireplace, full brkfst, whirlpool

Plaza Inn
(406) 452-9594
1224 10th Ave. S.
20 rooms - $35-55
Pets: Welcome
Creature Comforts: CCTV, a/c

Sahara Motel
(800) 772-1330, (406) 761-6150
3460 10th Ave. S.
20 rooms - $36
Pets: Welcome
Creature Comforts: CCTV, a/c

Ski's Western Motel
(406) 453-3281
2410 10th Ave.
25 rooms - $38-58
Pets: Small pets w/$5 fee
Creature Comforts: CCTV, a/c

Super 8
(800) 800-8000, (406) 727-7600
http://www.super8.com
1214 - 13th St. S.
117 rooms - $50-55
Pets: Welcome
Creature Comforts: CCTV, a/c

Townhouse Inns
(800) 442-4667, (406) 761-4600
1411 - 10th Ave. S.
108 rooms - $60-77
Pets: Welcome w/$5 fee
Creature Comforts: CCTV, a/c,
kit, restaurant, pool, hlth clb
access, sauna, whirlpool

Triple Crown Motor Inn
(800) 722-8300, (406) 727-8300
621 Central Ave.
50 rooms - $45-50
Pets: Welcome
Creature Comforts: CCTV, a/c

Village Motor Inn
(800) 354-0868, (406) 727-7666
726 - 10th Ave. S.
34 rooms/cottages - $33-40
Pets: Welcome in smoking rooms
Creature Comforts: CCTV, a/c,
refrig, kit

GREENOUGH
Loran's Clearwater Inn
(406) 244-9535
Rtes. 200 & 83
4 rooms - $25-35
Pets: Welcome
Creature Comforts: CCTV, a/c

HAMILTON
Bitteroot Motel
(406) 363-1142
408 S. First St.
10 rooms - $25-40
Pets: Welcome
Creature Comforts: CCTV, a/c

City Center Motel
(406) 363-1651
415 W. Main
14 rooms - $40-60
Pets: Welcome
Creature Comforts: CCTV, a/c

Comfort Inn
(406) 228-1550, (406) 363-6600
http://www.comfortinn.com
1113 N. First St.
65 rooms - $40-85
Pets: Welcome w/$4 fee
Creature Comforts: CCTV,
VCR, a/c, refrig, micro, cont.
brkfst, sauna, whirlpool

Deer Crossing B&B
(800) 763-2232, (406) 363-2232
http://www.wtp.net/go/
deercrossing
396 Hayes Creek Rd.
6 rooms - $45-115
Pets: Welcome in Bunk House
with a $5 fee. They must get along
with ranch animals
Creature Comforts: 25 pine and
pastured acres in Bitterroot Valley,
orig. bunkhouse, country quilts,
antique wood stove, hearty full
ranch brkfast, robes, homemade
treats, fly fishing, horseback
riding, hiking, great valley views

Sportsman Motel
(406) 363-2411
410 N. First St.
18 rooms - $25-40
Pets: Welcome
Creature Comforts: CCTV, a/c,
restaurant

HARDIN
Kendrick House Inn
(406) 665-3035
206 N. Custer Ave.
5 rooms - $55-65
Pets: Welcome w/permission,
prefers first floor rooms during the
off season
Creature Comforts: National
Historic Register house, gracious
1914 boarding hse w/porches, late
Victorian antiques, iron and cherry
beds, full brkfst

Lariat Motel
(406) 665-2683
Center St.
18 rooms - $40-45
Pets: Welcome w/$3
Creature Comforts: CCTV, a/c,
refrig, micro

Western Motel
(406) 665-2296
830 W. Third St.
28 rooms - $40-75
Pets: Welcome w/$2.50 fee
Creature Comforts: CCTV, a/c,
refrig, micro

HARLOWTON
Corral Motel
(406) 632-4331
Rtes. 12 & 191
27 rooms - $35-45
Pets: Welcome
Creature Comforts: CCTV, a/c,
refrig

Countryside Inn
(800) 632-4120, (406) 632-4119
Rte. 12
15 rooms - $44-48
Pets: Small pets welcome
Creature Comforts: CCTV, a/c,
refrig, hot tub, sauna

Troy Motel
(406) 632-4428
Rte. 12
15 rooms - $35-40
Pets: Small pets welcome
Creature Comforts: CCTV, a/c

HAUGAN
Silver $ Motel
(800) 531-1968, (406) 678-4271
Off I-90
40 rooms - $45-50
Pets: Welcome w/$20 deposit
Creature Comforts: CCTV, a/c

HAVRE
Budget Inn Motel
(406) 265-8625
115 Ninth Ave.
16 rooms - $35040
Pets: Welcome
Creature Comforts: CCTV, a/c,
kit

Circle Inn Motel
(406) 265-9655
Rte. 2
12 rooms - $38-42
Pets: Welcome w/$3 fee, ltd. rms
Creature Comforts: CCTV, a/c,
refrig, micro

El Toro Inn
(406) 265-5414
521 First St.
41 rooms - $40-50
Pets: Welcome
Creature Comforts: CCTV, a/c

Rails Inn
(800) 724-5746, (406) 265-1438
537 Second St.
35 rooms - $40
Pets: Welcome w/$10 deposit
Creature Comforts: CCTV, a/c,
refrig, micro

HELENA
Aladdin Motor Inn
(800) 541-2743, (406) 443-2300
2101 E. 11th Ave.
72 rooms/suites - $45-60
Pets: Welcome w/$6 fee
Creature Comforts: CCTV, a/c,
restaurant, pool

Appleton Inn
(800) 956-1999, (406) 449-7492
http://www.appletoninn.com
1999 Euclid
6 rooms - $65-105
Pets: Non-confrontational pets
welcome. Must be quiet, not
allowed in dining room
Creature Comforts: Historic,
restored 1890's Victorian, wrap-
around porch, hand-crafted
furnishings, four posted beds,
country quilts, some antiques,
CCTV, VCR, refrig, fireplace, full
gourmet brkfst, hlth clb access

Barrister B&B
(800) 823-1148, (406) 443-7330
416 N. Ewing
5 rooms - $85-100
Pets: Welcome
Creature Comforts: An 1874
Victorian mansion on National
Historic Register, orig. features,
stained glass windows, Victorian
antiques, 6 fireplaces, sun porch,
four poster beds, high ceilings,
CCTV, a/c, full brkfst, and hors
d'oeuvres

Comfort Inn
(800) 228-5150, (406) 443-1000
http://www.comfortinn.com
750 Fee St.
56 rooms - $60-90
Pets: Welcome w/$10 fee in
smoking rooms
Creature Comforts: CCTV, a/c,
refrig, micro, cont. brkfst, pool,
whirlpool

Days Inn
(406) DAYS INN, (406) 442-3280
http://www.daysinn.com
2001 Prospect Ave.
96 rooms - $40-60
Pets: Welcome w/$25 deposit
Creature Comforts: CCTV, a/c

King's Carriage Inn
(406) 442-6080
910 Last Chance Gulch
70 rooms - $45-60
Pets: Welcome w/$9 fee
Creature Comforts: CCTV, a/c,
refrig, micro, pool

Knights Rest Motel
(406) 442-6384
1831 Euclid Ave.
12 rooms - $35-50
Pets: Welcome
Creature Comforts: CCTV, a/c,
refrig, micro, kit

Park Plaza Hotel
(406) 443-2200
22 N. Last Chance Gulch
72 rooms - $65-80
Pets: Welcome w/$10 fee
Creature Comforts: CCTV, a/c,
refrig, micro, restaurant

Shilo Inn
(800) 222-2244, (406) 442-0320
http://www.shiloinns.com
2020 Prospect Ave.
46 rooms - $60-80
Pets: Welcome w/$7 fee
Creature Comforts: CCTV,
VCR, a/c, refrig, micro, kit, pool,
hlth clb, sauna, whirlpool

Super 8
(800) 800-8000, (406) 892-4341
http://www.super8.com
2200 11th Ave.
102 rooms - $50-55
Pets: Welcome
Creature Comforts: CCTV,
VCR, a/c

HOT SPRINGS
Hot Springs Spa
(406) 741-2283
North Spring St.
18 rooms - $20-40
Pets: Welcome
Creature Comforts: CCTV, a/c,
mineral water baths

HUNGRY HORSE
Hungry Horse Motel
(406) 387-5443
8808 Rte. 2 East
10 rooms - $35
Pets: Welcome w/$5 fee
Creature Comforts: CCTV, kit

Mini Golden Inns
(800) 891-6464, (406) 387-4313
8955 Rte. 2 E.
38 rooms - $48-50
Pets: Welcome
Creature Comforts: CCTV,
VCR, a/c, refrig, micro, kit

KALISPELL
Aero Inn
(406) 755-3798
1830 Rte. 93 S.
62 rooms - $40-90
Pets: Welcome
Creature Comforts: CCTV,
VCR, a/c, refrig, kit, sauna,
whirlpool

Best Western Outlaw Inn
(800) 528-1234, (406) 755-6100
http://www.bestwestern.com
1701 Rte. 93 S.
219 rooms - $65-100
Pets: Welcome w/$4 fee
Creature Comforts: CCTV, a/c,
refrig, Jacuzzi, restaurant, cont.
brkfst, pool, hlth clb access, sauna,
whirlpool, extensive sports
complex

Blue and White Motel
(800) 382-3577, (406) 755-4311
http://www.bluewhite.com
640 E. Idaho
107 rooms - $45-60
Pets: Welcome in smoking rooms
Creature Comforts: CCTV, a/c,
cont. brkfst, pool, sauna, whirlpool

Cavanaugh's at Kalispell Center
(800) THE INNS, (406) 752-6660
http://www.cavanaughs.com
20 N. Main St.
131 rooms - $75-110
Pets: Small pets welcome
Creature Comforts: CCTV, a/c,
restaurant, cont. brkfst, pool,
exercise rm, sauna, whirlpool

Days Inn Kalispell
(800) DAYS INN, (406) 756-3222
http://www.daysinn.com
1550 Rte. 93 N
54 rooms - $40-85
Pets: Small pets welcome
Creature Comforts: CCTV, a/c

Diamond Lil's Motel
(800) 843-7301, (406) 752-3467
http://www.ohwy.commp/d/
diamondl.htm
Rte. 93 S.
62 rooms - $64-75
Pets: Welcome in smoking rooms
Creature Comforts: CCTV, a/c,
refrig, Jacuzzi, pool, whirlpool

Four Seasons Motor Inn
(800) 545-6399, (406) 755-6123
350 N. Main St.
101 rooms - $50-65
Pets: Med. pets welcome
Creature Comforts: CCTV, a/c,
restaurant, whirlpool

Glacier Gateway Motel
(406) 755-3330
264 N. Main St.
23 rooms - $30-70
Pets: Welcome, dogs only
Creature Comforts: CCTV, a/c,
refrig, kit

Kalispell Grand
(800) 858-7422, (406) 755-8100
http://www.kalispellgrand.com
100 Main St.
40 rooms - $64-115
Pets: Welcome
Creature Comforts: Historic
hotel, Victorian details-tin ceiling,
hand-carved staircase, antique
furnishings, CTV, a/c, cont. brkfst,
Jacuzzi, restaurant

Motel 6
(406) 4-MOTEL6, (406) 752-6355
http://www.motel6.com
1540 Rte. 93 S.
115 rooms - $35-50
Pets: Pets under 30 lbs. welcome
Creature Comforts: CCTV, a/c

Red Lion Inn
(800) RED LION, (406) 755-6700
http://www.doubletreehotels.com
1330 Rte. 2 West
65 rooms - $70-95
Pets: Welcome in smoking rooms
Creature Comforts: CCTV, a/c,
whirlpool

Super 8
(800) 800-8000, (406) 755-1888
http://www.super8.com
1341 First Ave. E.
74 rooms - $45-55
Pets: Welcome w/$25 deposit
Creature Comforts: CCTV, a/c,
cont. brkfst

White Birch Motel
(406) 752-4008
17 Shady Ln.
8 rooms - $30-70
Pets: Welcome
Creature Comforts: CCTV, a/c,
refrig, kit

LAUREL
Russell Motel
(406) 628-6513
Main St.
13 rooms - $30-40
Pets: Welcome
Creature Comforts: CCTV, kit

LEWISTON
B&B Motel
(800) 341-8000, (406) 538-5496
520 E. Main St.
35 rooms - $35-42
Pets: Welcome
Creature Comforts: CCTV, a/c,
refrig, kit

Mountain View Motel
(800) 862-5786, (406) 538-3457
1422 W. Main St.
34 rooms - $35-40
Pets: Welcome
Creature Comforts: CCTV, a/c,
kits

Sunset Motel
(406) 538-8741
115 N.E. Main St.
16 rooms - $35-40
Pets: Small pets welcome
Creature Comforts: CCTV, a/c,
kit

Trail's End Motel
(406) 538-5468
216 N.E. Main St.
18 rooms - $35-40
Pets: Welcome w/$5 fee and
credit card dep.
Creature Comforts: CCTV, a/c,
kit

Yogo Inn
(800) 860-YOGO, (406) 538-8721
211 E. Main St.
125 rooms - $55-70
Pets: Welcome w/$5 fee
Creature Comforts: CCTV, a/c,
refrig, restaurant, pool

LIBBY
Budget Host Caboose Motel
(800) Bud-Host, (406) 293-6201
http://www.budgethost.com
714 Rte. 2 W.
28 rooms - $40-50
Pets: Welcome w/$50 fee
Creature Comforts: CCTV, a/c,
refrig

Kootenai Country Inn
(406) 293-7878
http://www.virtualcities.com/ons/
mt/n/mtn75020.htm
264 Mack Rd.
1 suite/1 cottage - $65-85
Pets: Welcome w/approval
Creature Comforts: Set on
Kootenai Rvr, rqst Amish guest
house, lodge pole beds, quilts,
CCTV, VCR, kit, full brkfst

Super 8
(800) 800-8000, (406) 293-2771
http://www.super8.com
448 Rte. 2 W.
41 rooms - $45-65
Pets: Welcome w/$5 fee
Creature Comforts: CCTV, a/c

LINCOLN
Blue Sky Motel
(406) 362-4450
Main St.
9 rooms - $35-40
Pets: Welcome
Creature Comforts: CCTV,
refrig, micro

Leeper's Motel
(406) 362-4333
Rte. 200
15 rooms - $40-45
Pets: Welcome w/$5 fee
Creature Comforts: CCTV, a/c,
refrig, micro, pool, sauna,
whirlpool

Snowy Pines Inn
(406) 362-4481
Rte. 200
10 rooms - $40-45
Pets: Welcome w/$5 fee
Creature Comforts: CCTV,
refrig, micro

Three Bears Motel
(406) 362-4355
Rte. 200
10 rooms - $35-40
Pets: Welcome
Creature Comforts: CCTV,
refrig, micro

LIVINGSTON
Budget Host Parkway Motel
(800) Bud-Host, (406) 222-3840
http://www.budgethost.com
1124 W. Park
28 rooms - $40-65
Pets: Welcome w/$4 fee
Creature Comforts: CCTV, a/c,
refrig, pool

Del Mar Motel
(406) 222-3120
I-90
33 rooms - $30-60
Pets: Welcome w/$5 fee
Creature Comforts: CCTV, a/c,
refrig

Best Western Yellowstone
(800) 826-1214, (406) 222-6110
1515 W. Park
100 rooms - $60-80
Pets: Welcome w/$8 fee
Creature Comforts: CCTV, a/c,
restaurant, pool

Murray Hotel
(406) 222-1350
http://www.murrayhotel.com
201 West Park St.
rooms - $54-100
Pets: Dogs only
Creature Comforts: Historic and classic western hotel, authentic surroundings, turn-of-century furnishings, classic 1900's elevator, rms w/period antiques, orig. baths w/porcelain tubs, neat bar and public areas

Paradise Inn
(406) 222-6320
Park St.
43 rooms - $35-80
Pets: Small pets welcome
Creature Comforts: CCTV, a/c, refrig, whirlpool

Rainbow Motel
(800) 788-2301, (406) 222-3780
5574 Park St.
24 rooms - $45-65
Pets: Welcome
Creature Comforts: Homey, CCTV, a/c, picnic area

River Inn on the Yellowstone
(406) 222-2429
http://www.tp.net/go/riverinn
4950 Highway 89 S.
5 rooms - $45-90
Pets: Welcome in rustic cabin and sheepherder's wagon (summer only)
Creature Comforts: Rustic retreat, 1893 farmhouse, neat riverside cabin, contemporary decor, refrig, braided rugs, gourmet brkfst, hot tub

S-S Motel
(800) 339-0591 (MT),
(406) 339-0591
1 Vista View Dr.
16 rooms - $40-60
Pets: Welcome
Creature Comforts: CCTV, a/c

LOLO
DAYS INN
(800) DAYS INN, (406) 273-2121
http://www.daysinn.com
11225 Rte. 93 S.
40 rooms - $40-60
Pets: Welcome
Creature Comforts: CCTV, a/c, refrig

MARTIN CITY
Abbott Valley Homestead
(406) 387-5330
http://www.abbottvalley.com
Box 98
4 cabins - $90-175
Pets: Welcome w/permission
Creature Comforts: Bucolic valley setting, creekside cabins w/ 1900's atmosphere, hand-hewn log cabins, some w/knotty pine walls others w/exposed beams, nicely decorated but w/character, woodstoves, stereos, kit, hiking, near Glacier Nat'l Park

Middle Fork Motel
(406) 387-5900
Rte. 2
10 rooms - $55-75
Pets: Small pets w/$5 fee
Creature Comforts: CCTV, refrig, micro, kit

MCALISTER
Crossroads Cabins
(406) 682-7652
P.O. Box 155, Rte. 287 N.
6 cabins - $35-45
Pets: Welcome w/$5 fee
Creature Comforts: Kit

MILES CITY
Best Western
(800) 528-1234, (406) 232-4560
http://www.bestwestern.com
1015 S. Haynes
54 rooms - $55-95
Pets: Welcome w/approval
Creature Comforts: CCTV, a/c, refrig, micro, pool, sauna, whirlpool

Buckboard Motel
(800) 525-6303, (406) 232-3550
1006 S. Haynes
57 rooms - $35-40
Pets: Welcome
Creature Comforts: CCTV, a/c, pool, whirlpool

Budget Host's Custer's Inn
(800) Bud-Host, (406) 232-5170
http://www.budgethost.com
1209 S. Haynes
56 rooms - $40-45
Pets: Welcome w/$20 deposit
Creature Comforts: CCTV, a/c, sauna

Days Inn
(800) DAYS INN, (406) 232-3550
http://www.daysinn.com
1006 S. Haynes
55 rooms - $35-50
Pets: Welcome
Creature Comforts: CCTV, a/c, refrig, micro, cont. brkfst, pool

Motel 6
(800) 4-MOTEL6, (406) 232-7040
http://www.motel6.com
1314 S. Haynes
113 rooms - $25-35
Pets: Medium dogs welcome
Creature Comforts: CCTV, a/c, pool

Rodeway Inn
(800) 228-2000, (406) 232-2450
http://www.rodeway.com
501 Main St.
34 rooms - $35-45
Pets: Welcome w/$4 fee
Creature Comforts: CCTV, a/c, restaurant

Super 8
(800) 800-8000, (406) 232-5261
http://www.super8.com
Rte. 59 & I-94
58 rooms - $30-40
Pets: Welcome
Creature Comforts: CCTV, a/c

MISSOULA
4 B's Inn North
(800) 272-9500, (406) 542-7550
4953 N. Reserve
67 rooms - $35-70
Pets: Welcome
Creature Comforts: CCTV, a/c, refrig, micro, whirlpool

4 B's Inn South
(800) 272-9500, (406) 251-2665
3803 Brooks St.
79 rooms - $35-70
Pets: Welcome
Creature Comforts: CCTV, a/c, refrig, Jacuzzi, whirlpool

Best Western Executive
(800) 528-1234, (406) 543-7221
http://www.bestwestern.com
201 E. Main St.
51 rooms - $50-70
Pets: Welcome w/$50 deposit
Creature Comforts: CCTV, a/c, refrig, restaurant

Best Western Grant Creek
(800) 528-1234, (406) 543-0700
http://www.bestwestern.com
I-90/Reserve St.
126 rooms - $60-100
Pets: Small pets w/deposit
Creature Comforts: Newer property w/special features, CCTV, a/c, refrig, cont. brkfst, sauna, whirlpool

Brooks Street Motor Inn
(800) 538-2360, (406) 549-5115
333 Brooks St.
61 rooms - $40-60
Pets: $3 fee in ltd. rms.
Creature Comforts: CCTV, a/c

Brownie's Plus Motel
(800) 543-6614, (406) 543-6614
1540 W. Broadway
25 rooms - $25-35
Pets: Welcome
Creature Comforts: CCTV, a/c, restaurant

Budget Motel/Lodge Riverside
(406) 549-2358
1135 W. Broadway
50 rooms - $25-35
Pets: Welcome
Creature Comforts: CCTV, a/c

Campus Inn Motel
(800) 232-8013, (406) 549-5134
744 E. Broadway
81 rooms - $35-50
Pets: Welcome w/$6 fee
Creature Comforts: CCTV, a/c, refrig, micro, cont. brkfst, pool, whirlpool

Clark Fork Inn
(406) 543-6619
1010 W. Broadway
15 rooms - $40-55
Pets: Welcome
Creature Comforts: CCTV, a/c

Comfort Inn
(800) 228-5150, (406) 542-0888
http://www.comfortinn.com
4545 N. Reserve St.
52 rooms/suites - $52-98
Pets: Welcome w/$5 fee
Creature Comforts: CCTV, a/c, refrig, micro, Jacuzzi, cont. brkfst, pool, whirlpool

Creekside Inn Motel
(800) 551-2387, (406) 549-2387
630 E. Broadway
50 rooms - $50-70
Pets: Welcome w/$50 deposit
Creature Comforts: CCTV, a/c, refrig, kit

Days Inn
(800) DAYS INN, (406) 721-9776
http://www.daysinn.com
Rte. 93/I-90
69 rooms - $50-76
Pets: Welcome w/$5 fee
Creature Comforts: CCTV, VCR, a/c, refrig, whirlpool

Doubletree Edgewater
(800) RED-LION, (406) 728-3100
http://www.doubletreehotels.com
100 Madison
172 rooms - $65-90
Pets: Small pets welcome
Creature Comforts: River views, CCTV, a/c, restaurant, cont. brkfst, pool, whirlpool

Downtown Motel
(800) 549-5191
502 E. Broadway
22 rooms - $30-45
Pets: Welcome w/$5 fee
Creature Comforts: CCTV, a/c

Hampton Inn
(800) Hampton, (406) 549-1800
http://www.hampton-inn.com
4805 N. Reserve St.
60 rooms - $65-75
Pets: Small pets welcome
Creature Comforts: CCTV, VCR, a/c, whirlpool

Holiday Inn, Missoula
(800) HOLIDAY, (406) 721-8550
http://www.holiday-inn.com
200 S. Pattee St.
200 rooms - $70-75
Pets: Welcome
Creature Comforts: CCTV, VCR, a/c, refrig, restaurant, sauna, whirlpool

Hubbard's Ponderosa Lodge
(800) 341-8000, (406) 543-3102
800 E. Broadway
42 rooms - $40-55
Pets: Welcome w/approval
Creature Comforts: CCTV, a/c, refrig

Orange Street Inn
(800) 328-0801, (406) 721-3610
801 N. Orange
81 rooms - $45-50
Pets: $5 fee in ltd. rms.
Creature Comforts: CCTV, VCR, a/c, kit

Red Lion Inn, Missoula
(800) RED LION, (406) 728-3300
http://www.doubletreehotels.com
700 W. Broadway
76 rooms - $45-55
Pets: Small pets w/$5 fee
Creature Comforts: CCTV, a/c, restaurant, cont. brkfst, pool, whirlpool

Redwood Lodge
(800) 874-9412, (406) 728-2110
8060 Rte. 93 N.
40 rooms - $40-75
Pets: Welcome
Creature Comforts: CCTV, a/c, refrig, whirlpool

Royal Motel
(406) 542-2184
338 Washington
12 rooms - $40-75
Pets: Welcome w/$3 fee
Creature Comforts: CCTV, a/c, refrig, micro

Ruby's Reserve Street Inn
(800) 221-2057, (406) 721-0990
4825 N. Reserve
128 rooms - $55-75
Pets: Welcome
Creature Comforts: Riverside location/views, CCTV, VCR, a/c, refrig, micro, kit, restaurant, whirlpool

Sleep Inn
(800) Sleep-Inn, (406) 543-5883
http://www.sleepinn.com
3425 Dore Ln.
59 rooms - $50-75
Pets: $5 fee in smkng rms.
Creature Comforts: CCTV, a/c, refrig, micro, cont. brkfst, pool, whirlpool

Thunderbird Motel
(800) 952-2400, (406) 728-3100
1009 E. Broadway
27 rooms - $40-80
Pets: Small pets w/approval in
first floor rooms
Creature Comforts: CCTV, a/c,
refrig, Jacuzzi, whirlpool

Travelers Inn
(800) 862-7878, (406) 728-8330
4850 N. Reserve
26 rooms - $35-50
Pets: Small pets welcome
Creature Comforts: CCTV, a/c,
refrig

MONTANA CITY
Elkhorn Mountain Inn
(406) 442-6625
1 Jackson Creek
22 rooms - $50-60
Pets: Welcome w/$5 fee
Creature Comforts: CCTV,
VCR, a/c, refrig, Jacuzzi

NEVADA CITY
Nevada City Hotel/Cabins
(800) 648-7588, (406) 843-5377
P.O. Box 62
17 rooms - $55-80
Pets: Welcome w/deposit
Creature Comforts: 1862 hotel
in historic district, museum-like
public spaces, authentic bar, rqst
Victorian rms.

NOXON
Noxon Motel
(406) 847-2600
2 Klakken Rd.
9 rooms - $25-35
Pets: Welcome
Creature Comforts: CCTV, a/c

OVANDO
Lake Upsata Guest Ranch
(800) 594-7687, (406) 793-580
http://www.upsata.com
135 Lake Upsata Rd., Box 6
8 cabins - $190-220 (AP)
Pets: Welcome w/approval
Creature Comforts: Family-
oriented guest ranch, beautiful
lake views, very attractive log
cabins, hearty meals, children's
prgrms, fly fishing, horseback
riding, rafting, cookouts, and lawn
sports

PLAINS
Tops Motel
(406) 826-3412
340 E. Railroad Ave.
9 rooms - $40-60
Pets: Welcome
Creature Comforts: CCTV, a/c

PLENTYWOOD
Sherwood Inn
(406) 765-2810
Main St.
63 rooms - $40-45
Pets: Welcome
Creature Comforts: CCTV, kit

POLSON
Days Inn
(800) DAYS INN, (406) 883-3120
http://www.daysinn.com
914 Rte. 93
25 rooms - $45-75
Pets: Welcome w/$5 fee
Creature Comforts: CCTV, a/c

PRAY
Chico Hot Springs Lodge
(800) hot-wada,(406) 333-4933
www.chicohotsprings.com
1 Chico Rd.
80 rooms - $85-300
Pets: "We're pet friendly, so bring
your four-legged friends along."
$5 one-time fee
Creature Comforts: 1900's lodge
set on 150 acres in foothills of
Absaroka Beartooth mtns., choose
between spacious Lower Lodge
rms, quaint and cozy historic
lodge rms, or rustic cabins, CCTV,
refrig, kit, pool, hot springs,
beautiful herb and flower gardens,
exercise rm, massage, lawn
games, hiking, and a private
landing strip

RED LODGE
Beck's Alpine Motel
(406) 446-2213
Rte. 212
15 rooms - $40-60
Pets: Welcome
Creature Comforts: CCTV, a/c

Best Western Lupine
(800) 528-1234, (406) 446-1321
http://www.bestwestern.com
702 S. Hauser
46 rooms - $50-75
Pets: Welcome
Creature Comforts: CCTV, a/c,
refrig, micro, kit, Jacuzzi, cont.
brkfst, pool, sauna, whirlpool

Comfort Inn
(800) 228-5150, (406) 446-4469
http://www.comfortinn.com
612 N. Broadway
55 rooms - $50-90
Pets: Welcome
Creature Comforts: CCTV, a/c,
refrig, micro, kit, Jacuzzi, cont.
brkfst, pool, sauna, whirlpool

Eagle's Nest Motel
(406) 446-2312
702 S. Broadway
16 rooms - $25-35
Pets: Welcome
Creature Comforts: CCTV, a/c

Super 8
(800) 800-8000, (406) 446-2288
http://www.super8.com
Rte. 212 S.
50 rooms/suite - $50-100
Pets: Welcome
Creature Comforts: CCTV,
VCR, a/c, refrig, micro, kit,
Jacuzzi, whirlpool

Yodeler Motel
(406) 446-1435
601 S. Broadway
22 rooms - $35-75
Pets: Welcome
Creature Comforts: CCTV, a/c,
refrig, micro, kit, Jacuzzi,
whirlpool

RONAN
Starlite Motel
(800) 823-4403, (406) 676-7000
18 Main St. SW
15 rooms - $25-35
Pets: Welcome
Creature Comforts: CCTV, a/c

ROUNDUP
Big Sky Motel
(406) 323-2303
740 Main St.
22 rooms - $35-40
Pets: Welcome
Creature Comforts: CCTV, a/c,
refrig

ST. IGNATIUS
Sunset Motel
(406) 745-3900
32670 Rte. 93
10 rooms - $25-35
Pets: Welcome
Creature Comforts: CCTV, a/c

ST. MARY
St. Mary Lodge/Resort
(800) 368-3689, (406) 732-4431
http://www.glcpark.com
Route 89
76 rooms - $90-250
Pets: Welcome w/$50 fee
Creature Comforts: Stunning
Glacier Park setting, new lodge
rms, hand-hewn log furnishings,
rqst luxury cottages, CCTV, a/c,
kit, fireplace, restaurant

ST. REGIS
Little River Motel
(406) 649-2713
I-90, Exit 33
16 rooms - $25-35
Pets: Welcome
Creature Comforts: CCTV, a/c

Super 8
(800) 800-8000, (406) 649-2422
http://www.super8motel.com
I-90, Exit 33
53 rooms - $45-50
Pets: Welcome w/deposit
Creature Comforts: CCTV, a/c,
whirlpool

ST. XAVIER
Cattle King Motor Inn
(800) 562-2775, (406) 487-5332
Rte. 13 S.
31 rooms - $45-50
Pets: Welcome w/$5 fee
Creature Comforts: CCTV, a/c

SEELEY LAKE
Duck Inn Motel
(800) 237-9978, (406) 677-2335
Rte. 83, MM
9 rooms - $45-50
Pets: Welcome w/$10 deposit
Creature Comforts: Near lake
and state park, CCTV

The Emily A B&B
(800) 977-4639, (406) 677-FISH
www.theemilya.com
Box 350
6 rooms/cabin/teepee - $95-150
Pets: Welcome in the cabins
w/ a $5 dog fee, $10 horse fee
Creature Comforts: Massive
larch log lodge on private lake/160
acres, porches, atrium, fieldstone
fireplace, Western art collection/
period furnishings, quilts, down
comforters, family suite w/kit, full
breakfast, hiking, boating, birding

Wilderness Gateway Inn
(406) 677-2095
Rte. 83 S.
19 rooms - $40-50
Pets: Welcome w/$5 fee
Creature Comforts: CCTV

SHELBY
Comfort Inn
(800) 228-5150, (406) 434-2212
http://www.comfortinn.com
50 Frontage Rd.
72 rooms - $62-90
Pets: Welcome w/$5 fee
Creature Comforts: CCTV,
VCR, a/c, refrig, micro, cont.
brkfst, pool, sauna, whirlpool

Crossroads Inn
(406) 434-5134
Rte. 2
51 rooms - $54-65
Pets: Small pets in smkng rms.
Creature Comforts: CCTV, a/c,
refrig, micro, pool, hlth clb access,
whirlpool

Glacier Motel
(800) 764-5181, (406) 434-5181
744 Rte. 2
17 rooms - $40-45
Pets: Welcome
Creature Comforts: CCTV, a/c,
refrig

O'Haire Manor Motel
(800) 541-5809, (406) 434-5555
204 Second St.
40 rooms - $40-75
Pets: Small pets w/$5 fee
Creature Comforts: CCTV, a/c,
refrig, whirlpool, exercise room

SIDNEY
Lone Tree Motel
(406) 482-4520
900 S. Central
42 rooms - $38-40
Pets: Welcome
Creature Comforts: CCTV, a/c

Richland Motor Inn
(406) 482-6400
1200 S. Central
61 rooms - $50-55
Pets: Small pets welcome
Creature Comforts: CCTV, a/c,
refrig, micro

SILVERGATE
Silvergate Cabins
(406) 838-2371
Rte. 212
10 cabins - $55
Pets: Welcome
Creature Comforts: CCTV, a/c,
kit

Pine Edge Cabins
(406) 838-2222
Box 45
10 cabins- $40-75
Pets: Welcome
Creature Comforts: CCTV, kit

STANFORD
Sundown Motel
(800) 346-2316, (406) 566-2316
Rte. 200 W.
11 rooms - $25-35
Pets: Welcome
Creature Comforts: CCTV,
restaurant

STEVENSVILLE
Mystical Mountain Inn
(406) 642-3464
http://www.rmdbs.net/users/
mystical/Mystical1.html
126 Indian Prairie Loop
6 rooms - $85-115
Pets: Welcome, there are 2
Chinese Pugs in residence
Creature Comforts: 6,000
square-foot contemporary log
home on 17 acres, lodge like
atmosphere, plate glass wndws,
decks, river stone fireplace,
bedrooms w/vaulted ceilings,
Jacuzzis, CCTV, full brkfst,
intimate restaurant, exercise rm,
hot tub, trout ponds

St. Mary's Motel
(800) 624-7015, (406) 777-2838
3889 Rte. 93
16 rooms - $40-50
Pets: Welcome
Creature Comforts: CCTV, a/c,
refrig, micro

SUPERIOR
Budget Host Big Sky Motel
(800) Bud-Host, (406) 822-4831
http://www.budgethost.com
103 Fourth Ave. E.
24 rooms - $40-50
Pets: Welcome
Creature Comforts: CCTV, a/c

Lake Townsend Motel
(800) 856-3461, (406) 226-3461
413 N. Pine
14 rooms - $30-40
Pets: Welcome
Creature Comforts: CCTV, a/c,
refrig, micro, kit

THREE FORKS
Broken Spur Motel
(800) 354-3048, (406) 285-3237
124 West Elm St.
20 rooms - $40-50
Pets: Welcome w/$5 fee
Creature Comforts: CCTV, a/c

Fort Three Forks Motel
(800) 477-5690, (406) 285-3233
10766 Route 287
24 rooms - $40-60
Pets: Small pets w/$5 fee
Creature Comforts: CCTV, a/c

Sacajawea Hotel
(800) 821-7326, (406) 285-6515
http://www.sacajaweahotel.com
5 North Main St.
33 rooms - $70-100
Pets: Welcome w/$5 daily fee
Creature Comforts: 1882 hotel,
wonderful front porch, beamed
ceilings, hardwood flrs, Old West
atmosphere w/period furnishings,
library, clawfoot tubs, restaurant

TOWNSEND
Mustang Motel
(800) 349-3499, (406) 266-3491
412 N. Front St.
22 rooms - $30-40
Pets: Welcome w/$5 fee
Creature Comforts: CCTV, a/c,
refrig, micro

TROUT CREEK
**Blue Spruce Lodge and
Guest Ranch**
(800) 831-4797, (406) 827-4762
http://www.montanalodge.com
451 Marten Creek Rd.
9 rooms - $800-1,500/wk (AP)
Pets: Welcome w/approval
Creature Comforts: 5,000 sq.
foot lodge built of hand-hewn
spruce logs, "barrier free"
buildings for wheelchair access,
beautiful setting, exposed log
walls, simple rms w/pine
furnishings, SATV, dining rm,
exercise rm, hot tub, sauna, pool
table, 200 acres for hiking, fishing,
horseback riding

Trout Creek Motel/RV
(406) 827-3268
Rte. 200
8 rooms - $40-60
Pets: Welcome
Creature Comforts: CCTV, a/c

TWIN BRIDGES
King's Motel
(800) 222-5150, (406) 684-5639
307 S. Main
12 rooms - $25-35
Pets: Welcome
Creature Comforts: CCTV, a/c

Stardust Country Inn
(406) 684-5648
409 N. Main
6 rooms - $25-35
Pets: Welcome
Creature Comforts: CCTV

VALIER
Lake Francis Motel
(800) 551-8332, (406) 279-3476
412 Teton
12 rooms - $30-40
Pets: Welcome
Creature Comforts: CCTV,
refrig, stove

VIRGINIA CITY
Daylight Creek Motel
(406) 843-5377
Box 338
8 rooms - $40-60
Pets: Welcome
Creature Comforts: CCTV, a/c

Fairweather Inn
(406) 843-5377
315 W. Wallace
32 rooms/cabins - $35-45
Pets: Welcome in cabins
Creature Comforts: CCTV

WEST GLACIER
Mtn. Timbers Wilderness Lodge
(800) 841-3835, (406) 387-5830
5385 Rabe Rd., Box 94
7 rms/1cabin - $60-275
Pets: Welcome w/approval
Creature Comforts: Massive log
cabin on over 200 acres, huge
living rm w/extensive library,
plate glass windows w/mtn views,
priv. cabin w/kit, river rock
fireplace, SATV, VCR, refrig,
Jacuzzi, restaurant, full brkfst,
exercise rm, hot tub

River Bend Motel
(406) 888-5662
200 Going to the Sun Rd.
33 rooms - $60-80
Pets: Welcome
Creature Comforts: CCTV, a/c,
restaurant

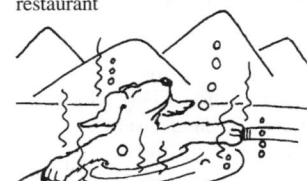

WEST YELLOWSTONE

Bar-N-Ranch
(800) BIG-SKYS, (406) 646-7229
http://www.bar-n-ranch.com
Box 127
8 rooms - $190-200
Pets: Welcome w/$10 daily fee
Creature Comforts: Classic
hand-hewn 1880's stone/timber
lodge and trapper's cabins, main
lodge is 10,000 sq. feet, antiques,
fine art, CCTV, fireplace, Jacuzzi,
hearty brkfst, horseback riding,
hiking, fishing

Best Western Crosswinds
(800) 528-1234, (406) 646-9557
http://www.bestwestern.com
201 Firehole
70 rooms - $35-110
Pets: Welcome
Creature Comforts: CCTV, a/c,
refrig, micro, pool, whirlpool

Best Western Desert Inn
(800) 528-1234, (406) 646-7376
http://www.bestwestern.com
133 Canyon
65 rooms - $32-122
Pets: Welcome
Creature Comforts: CCTV, a/c,
pool, whirlpool

Best Western Executive Inn
(800) 528-1234, (406) 646-7681
http://www.bestwestern.com
236 Dunraven
82 rooms - $58-95
Pets: Welcome w/mngr's approval
Creature Comforts: CCTV, a/c,
restaurant, pool, hlth clb,
whirlpool

Best Western Weston Inn
(800) 528-1234, (406) 646-7373
http://www.bestwestern.com
103 Gibbon St.
65 rooms - $45-90
Pets: Small pets welcome
Creature Comforts: CCTV, a/c,
pool, whirlpool

Buckboard Motel
(406) 646-9020
119 Electric St.
24 rooms - $30-70
Pets: Small dogs only, no cats
Creature Comforts: CCTV, a/c,
whirlpool

Circle R Motel
(406) 646-7461
321 Madison
28 rooms - $40-60
Pets: Welcome
Creature Comforts: CCTV, a/c

Days Inn West Yellowstone
(800) DAYS INN, (406) 646-7656
http://www.daysinn.com
118 Electric St.
45 rooms - $65-85
Pets: Small pets w/$5 fee
Creature Comforts: CCTV, a/c,
refrig, sauna, whirlpool

Evergreen Motel
(800) 488-2750, (406) 646-7655
229 Firehole
16 rooms - $35-80
Pets: Small pets w/$10 fee
Creature Comforts: CCTV,
refrig, micro, kit

Hibernation Station
(800) 580-3557, (406) 646-4200
http://hibernationstation.com
Greywolf Ave.
30 cabins - $99-239
Pets: Welcome in ltd. cabins w/
$10 daily fee
Creature Comforts: Surrounded
by Nat'l Forest, tapestry walls,
handmade log furniture,
fireplaces, Jacuzzis

Kelly Inn Motel
(800) 259-4672, (406) 646-4544
104 S. Canyon St.
78 rooms - $50-100
Pets: Welcome w/$20 deposit
Creature Comforts: CCTV, a/c,
refrig, micro, Jacuzzi, pool, sauna,
whirlpool

Lake View Cabins
(406) 646-7257
15570 Habgen Lake Rd.
6 rooms - $40-60
Pets: Welcome
Creature Comforts: CCTV, a/c,
kit

Ranch Motel
(406) 646-7388
235 Canyon Rd.
27 rooms - $60-80
Pets: Welcome
Creature Comforts: CCTV, a/c,
pool

Three Bear Lodge
(800) 646-7353, (406) 646-7353
217 Yellowstone Ave.
77 rooms - $65-95
Pets: Small pets w/$5 fee
Creature Comforts: CCTV, a/c,
refrig, micro, Jacuzzi, restaurant,
pool, whirlpool

Traveler's Lodge
(800) 831-5741, (406) 646-9561
225 Yellowstone Ave.
43 rooms - $45-150
Pets: Small pets w/$6 fee
Creature Comforts: CCTV, a/c,
refrig, pool, sauna, whirlpool

Weary Rest Motel
(406) 646-7633
Rte. 20
10 rooms - $40-80
Pets: Welcome
Creature Comforts: CCTV

WHITE SULPHUR SPRINGS

Spa Hot Springs Motel
(406) 547-3366
202 W. Main
21 rooms - $25-35
Pets: Welcome
Creature Comforts: CCTV, pool

Tenderfoot/Hiland Motel
(406) 547-3303
301 W. Main
21 rooms - $25-35
Pets: Welcome
Creature Comforts: CCTV

WHITEFISH

Allen's Motel
(406) 862-3995
6540 Rte. 93 S.
17 rooms - $40-60
Pets: Welcome
Creature Comforts: CCTV

Best Western Rocky Mountain
(800) 528-1234, (406) 862-2569
http://www.bestwestern.com
6510 Rte. 93 S.
79 rooms - $60-150
Pets: Small pets welcome
Creature Comforts: CCTV, a/c,
refrig, micro, cont. brkfst, pool,
hlth clb, sauna, whirlpool

Nebraska

AINSWORTH
Lazy A Motel
(402) 387-2600
Route 20 E.
21 rooms - $25-35
Pets: Welcome
Creature Comforts: CCTV, a/c

Skinner's Motor Court
(402) 387-2021
Route 65
12 rooms - $25-35
Pets: Welcome
Creature Comforts: CCTV, a/c

Remington Arms Motel
(800) 248-3971, (402) 387-2220
1000 E. Fourth St.
23 rooms - $35-55
Pets: Welcome
Creature Comforts: CCTV, a/c, restaurant

ALLIANCE
Holiday Inn Express
(800) HOLIDAY, (308) 762-7600
http://www.holiday-inn.com
1420 W. Third Ave.
60 rooms - $60-70
Pets: Welcome w/$20 deposit
Creature Comforts: CCTV, a/c, Jacuzzi, restaurant, cont. brkfst, pool, whirlpool

McCarroll's Motel
(308) 762-3680
1028 E. Third St.
29 rooms - $35-55
Pets: Welcome
Creature Comforts: CCTV, a/c

Sunset Motel
(308) 762-8660
1210 Route 2 E.
20 rooms - $40-75
Pets: Welcome w/$5 fee
Creature Comforts: CCTV, a/c, refrig, micro, Jacuzzi, pool

Super 8
(800) 800-8000, (308) 762-8300
http://www.super8.com
1419 W. Third St.
39 rooms - $50-60
Pets: Welcome w/deposit
Creature Comforts: CCTV, a/c

West Way Motel
(308) 762-4040
1207 W. Third St.
45 rooms - $50-70
Pets: Small pets welcome
Creature Comforts: CCTV, a/c, restaurant

ALMA
Super Out Post Motel
(308) 928-2116
Routes 183 & 136
17 rooms - $25-35
Pets: Welcome
Creature Comforts: CCTV, a/c

Western Holiday Motel
(800) 258-8124, (308) 928-2155
Route 1
23 rooms - $30-35
Pets: Welcome
Creature Comforts: CCTV, a/c

ARAPAHOE
Arapahoe Court
(308) 962-7948
Routes 6 & 34
7 rooms - $35-45
Pets: Welcome
Creature Comforts: CCTV, a/c, restaurant, pool, exercise facilities

Shady Rest Camp Motel
(308) 962-5461
Routes 6 & 34
26 rooms - $35-55
Pets: Welcome
Creature Comforts: CCTV, a/c

AUBURN
Auburn Inn Motel
(800) 272-3143, (402) 274-3141
517 - J St.
30 rooms - $35-40
Pets: Welcome
Creature Comforts: CCTV, a/c, refrig, micro, cont. brkfst

Palmer House Motel
(800) 272-3193, (402) 274-3193
1918 - J St.
22 rooms - $40-48
Pets: Welcome
Creature Comforts: CCTV, a/c, refrig, micro

AURORA
Budget Host Ken's Motel
(800) Bud-Host, (402) 694-3141
1515 Eleventh St.
40 rooms - $25-35
Pets: Small pets in smkng rooms
Creature Comforts: CCTV, a/c, refrig

Hamilton Motor Inn
(402) 694-6961
907 Route 14 S.
26 rooms - $30-50
Pets: Welcome
Creature Comforts: CCTV, a/c, restaurant, pool

BASSETT
Ranchland Motel
(402) 684-3376
Box 366
11 rooms - $30-45
Pets: Welcome
Creature Comforts: CCTV, a/c, restaurant

BEATRICE
Beatrice Inn Motel
(800) 232-8742, (402) 223-4074
3500 N. 6th St.
65 rooms - $38-49
Pets: In first floor smoking room
Creature Comforts: CCTV, a/c, restaurant, pool

Holiday Villa Motel
(402) 223-4036
1820 N. Sixth St.
50 rooms - $30-55
Pets: Welcome
Creature Comforts: CCTV, a/c,
kit

Victorian Inn
(402) 228-5955
1903 N. Sixth St.
30 rooms - $35-44
Pets: Welcome
Creature Comforts: CCTV,
VCR, a/c, cont. brkfst

BEAVER CITY
Furnace County Inn
(308) 268-7705
Route 89 & 10th St.
9 rooms - $25-39
Pets: Welcome
Creature Comforts: CCTV, a/c

BELLEVUE
American Family Inn
(800) 253-2865, (402) 291-0804
1110 Fort Crook Rd.
110 rooms - $40-59
Pets: Under 40 lbs. w/$5 fee
Creature Comforts: CCTV, a/c,
refrig, micro, kit, Jacuzzi,
restaurant, pool, sports courts

Offutt Motor Court
(402) 291-4333
3618 Fort Crook Rd.
15 rooms - $25-38
Pets: Welcome
Creature Comforts: CCTV, a/c

BLAIR
Rath Inn
(402) 426-2340
Route 1
32 rooms - $30-45
Pets: Welcome
Creature Comforts: CCTV, a/c,
restaurant, cont. brkfst, pool

BLOOMFIELD
Four Seasons Motel
(800) 763-1261, (308) 762-3680
Route 3
28 rooms/apt - $35-55
Pets: Welcome
Creature Comforts: CCTV, a/c,
refrig

BREWSTER
Uncle Buck's Lodge
(800) 239-9190, (308) 547-2210
Box 100
6 rooms - $35-57
Pets: Welcome
Creature Comforts: CCTV, a/c,
full brkfst

BRIDGEPORT
Bridgeport Inn
(308) 262-0290
Box 1106
21 rooms - $35-58
Pets: Welcome
Creature Comforts: CCTV, a/c

BROKEN BOW
Wagon Wheel Motel
(800) 770-2433, (308) 872-2433
1545 SE St.
15 rooms - $30-35
Pets: Welcome
Creature Comforts: CCTV, a/c,
pool

Wm. Penn Lodge Motel
(308) 872-2412
853 E. SE St.
28 rooms - $25-40
Pets: Welcome
Creature Comforts: CCTV, a/c

BURWELL
Calamus River Lodge
(308) 346-4331
Box 305
9 rooms - $20-35
Pets: Welcome
Creature Comforts: CCTV,
restaurant

Rodeo Inn
(800) 926-9427, (308) 346-4408
Box 475
14 rooms - $30-36
Pets: Welcome
Creature Comforts: CCTV, a/c,
whirlpool

CALLAWAY
Chesley's Lodge
(308) 836-2658
Route 1
5 rooms - $30-45
Pets: Welcome
Creature Comforts: CCTV, cont.
brkfst

Traveler's Inn Callaway House
(308) 836-4414
Box 189
10 rooms - $35-65
Pets: Welcome
Creature Comforts: CCTV, full
brkfst

CAMBRIDGE
Bunkhouse Motel
(308) 697-4540
Routes 6 & 34
6 rooms - $25-40
Pets: Welcome
Creature Comforts: CCTV, a/c

Medicine Creek Lodge
(308) 697-3774
Route 2, Box 93
5 rooms - $25-39
Pets: Welcome
Creature Comforts: CCTV

CENTRAL CITY
Crest Motel
(888) 879-9201, (308) 946-3077
Route 30
13 rooms - $25-37
Pets: Welcome
Creature Comforts: CCTV, a/c,
pool

CHADRON
Best Western West Hills
(800) 528-1234, (308) 432-3305
http://www.bestwestern.com
1100 W. Tenth St.
67 rooms - $50-79
Pets: Small pets welcome
Creature Comforts: CCTV, a/c,
refrig, micro, Jacuzzi, hlth clb,
whirlpool

Blaine Motel
(308) 432-5568
159 Bordeaux St.
14 rooms - $25-50
Pets: Welcome
Creature Comforts: CCTV, a/c

Economy 9 Motel
(308) 432-3119
1201 W. Rte. 20
45 rooms - $40-65
Pets: Welcome
Creature Comforts: CCTV, a/c,
cont. brkfst, whirlpool

Olde Main Street Inn
(308) 432-3380
www.chadron.com/oldemain
115 Main St., Box 46
7 rooms - $50-75
Pets: Warmly welcomed in certain guest rooms
Creature Comforts: 1890's hotel and saloon, Victorian suites, in process of restoration, CCTV, a/c, fireplace, Jacuzzi, fine restaurant, full brkfst

Round Up Motel
(308) 432-5591
901 E. Third St.
23 rooms - $30-40
Pets: Welcome
Creature Comforts: CCTV, a/c

CODY
Cody's Country Cottage
(402) 823-4182
Route 20
1 cabin - $35-50
Pets: Welcome
Creature Comforts: CCTV, a/c, kit, fireplace

COLUMBUS
Gembel's Motel
(402) 564-2729
3220 Eighth St.
21 rooms - $35-55
Pets: Welcome
Creature Comforts: CCTV, a/c

New World Inn
(800) 433-1492, (402) 387-0700
265 - 33rd Ave.
154 rooms - $40-60
Pets: Small pets welcome
Creature Comforts: CCTV, a/c, restaurant, pool, hlth clb access, whirlpool

Rosebud Motel
(402) 564-3256
154 Lakeshore Dr.
11 rooms - $35-50
Pets: Welcome
Creature Comforts: CCTV, a/c

Seven Knights Motel
(402) 563-3533
2222 - 23rd St.
44 rooms - $35-55
Pets: Small pets welcome, not left unattended
Creature Comforts: CCTV, a/c, whirlpool

COZAD
Budget Host Circle S Motel
(402) Bud-Host, (308) 784-2290
http://www.budgethost.com
440 S. Meridian Rd.
50 rooms - $35-48
Pets: Small pets welcome
Creature Comforts: CCTV, a/c, refrig, restaurant

CRAWFORD
Hilltop Motel
(800) 504-1444, (308) 665-1144
304 McPherson St.
14 rooms - $30-46
Pets: Welcome in smoking rooms
Creature Comforts: CCTV, a/c

Town Line Motel
(800) 903-1450, (308) 665-1450
4070 Market St.
24 rooms - $35-49
Pets: Welcome
Creature Comforts: CCTV, a/c, kit

CREIGHTON
Black Horse Inn
(402) 358-3587
408 Rice St.
30 rooms - $35-55
Pets: Welcome
Creature Comforts: CCTV, a/c, restaurant, cont. brkfst

CRETE
Villa Madrid Motel
(800) 827-0260, (402) 826-4341
Route 33 W.
28 rooms - $30-43
Pets: Welcome w/approval
Creature Comforts: CCTV, a/c, refrig, restaurant

CROFTON
Bogner's Motel
(402) 388-4626
Routes 12 & 121
8 rooms - $25-35
Pets: Welcome
Creature Comforts: CCTV, a/c, restaurant

DAVID CITY
Fiesta Motel
(402) 367-3129
Route 15
18 rooms - $25-38
Pets: Welcome
Creature Comforts: CCTV, a/c

DIXON
The Georges
(402) 584-2625
Route 20
4 rooms - $25-39
Pets: Welcome
Creature Comforts: CCTV, full brkfst

EDGAR
Hotel Edgar
(402) 224-3226
Main St. S.
10 rooms - $25-36
Pets: Welcome
Creature Comforts: CCTV, a/c, restaurant

ELWOOD
J.J.'s Marina
(308) 785-2836
4 Lakeview Acres Dr.
10 rooms - $40-58
Pets: Welcome
Creature Comforts: CCTV, a/c, restaurant, boating

FAIRBURY
Capri Motel
(800) 932-0589, (402) 729-3317
1100 - 14th St.
35 rooms - $30-38
Pets: Welcome w/$5 fee
Creature Comforts: CCTV, a/c, refrig

FALLS CITY
Check In Motel
(402) 245-2433
1901 Fulton St.
19 rooms - $25-39
Pets: Welcome
Creature Comforts: CCTV, a/c

Stephenson Motel
(402) 245-2459
2621 Harlan St.
39 rooms - $30-45
Pets: Welcome
Creature Comforts: CCTV, a/c, pool

FREMONT
Comfort Inn
(800) 228-5150, (402) 721-1109
http://www.comfortinn.com
1649 E. 23rd St.
48 rooms - $55-89
Pets: Welcome
Creature Comforts: CCTV, a/c, refrig, micro, cont. brkfst, pool

Holiday Lodge
(800) 743-ROOM, (402) 727-1110
1220 E. 23rd St.
100 rooms - $50-69
Pets: Small pets welcome
Creature Comforts: CCTV, a/c, restaurant, pool, whirlpool

Super 8
(800) 800-8000, (402) 727-4445
http://www.super8.com
1250 E. 23rd St.
43 rooms - $40-55
Pets: Welcome w/permission
Creature Comforts: CCTV, a/c

FUNK
Uncle Sam's Hilltop Lodge
(308) 995-2204
Route 1
3 rooms - $35-59
Pets: Welcome
Creature Comforts: CCTV, full brkfst

GENOA
Redwood Motel
(402) 993-2817
336 N. Elm St.
5 rooms - $25-44
Pets: Welcome
Creature Comforts: CCTV, a/c

GERING
Cavalier Motel
(308) 635-3176
3655 N. Tenth St.
39 rooms - $30-49
Pets: Welcome
Creature Comforts: CCTV, a/c, restaurant, pool

Circle S Lodge
(308) 436-2157
400 M St.
30 rooms - $35-56
Pets: Welcome
Creature Comforts: CCTV, a/c

GIBBON
Country Inn and Antiques
(800) 887-6324, (308) 468-5256
2432 Lowell Rd.
21 rooms - $25-49
Pets: Welcome
Creature Comforts: CCTV, ac, refrig, cont. brkfst

GORDON
Meadow View Ranch B&B
(308) 282-0679
HC 91, Box 29
4 rooms - $60-80
Pets: Welcome
Creature Comforts: 5,000-acre working cattle farm, 1910 bunkhouse conv. to rooms, SATV, VCR, kit, full brkfst, canoeing

GOTHENBURG
Travel Inn
(308) 537-3638
501 S. Lake St.
32 rooms - $30-49
Pets: Welcome
Creature Comforts: CCTV, a/c, pool

Western Motor Inn
(308) 537-3622
1102 - 21st St.
26 rooms - $35-46
Pets: Welcome
Creature Comforts: CCTV, a/c

GRAND ISLAND
Best Western Riverside
(800) 528-1234, (308) 384-5150
http://www.bestwestern.com
3333 Ramada Rd.
182 rooms - $55-95
Pets: Welcome
Creature Comforts: CCTV, a/c, restaurant, cont. brkfst, pool, exercise room, whirlpool, tennis

Budget Host, Island Motel
(800) Bud-Host, (308) 382-1815
http://www.budgethost.com
2311 S. Locust St.
44 rooms - $28-58
Pets: Small pets w/$3 fee
Creature Comforts: CCTV, a/c, refrig

Conoco Motel
(308) 384-2700
2107 W. Second St.
38 rooms - $40-70
Pets: Small pets welcome
Creature Comforts: CCTV, a/c, refrig, restaurant, pool

Holiday Inn — I-80
(800) HOLIDAY, (308) 384-7770
http://www.holiday-inn.com
Rtes. 80 & 281
214 rooms - $50-90
Pets: Small pets welcome
Creature Comforts: CCTV, a/c, refrig, Jacuzzi, restaurant, pool, hlth club, whirlpool

Lazy V Motel
(800) 735-0772, (308) 384-0700
2703 E. Route 30
26 rooms - $25-36
Pets: Small pets welcome
Creature Comforts: CCTV, a/c, pool

Oak Grove Inn
(800) 435-7144, (308) 384-1333
3205 S. Locust St.
60 rooms - $30-45
Pets: Welcome w/$10 deposit
Creature Comforts: CCTV, a/c

Super 8
(800) 800-8000, (308) 384-4380
http://www.super8.com
2603 S. Locust St.
80 rooms - $40-75
Pets: Welcome
Creature Comforts: CCTV, a/c, refrig, pool, whirlpool

USA Inns of America
(800) 659-4096, (308) 381-0111
7000 S. Nine Bridge Rd.
63 rooms - $40-59
Pets: Welcome w/$5 fee
Creature Comforts: CCTV, VCR, a/c, refrig, micro, Jacuzzi

GREENWOOD
Days Inn Motel
(402) 944-3313
13006 - 238th St.
30 rooms - $25-39
Pets: Welcome
Creature Comforts: CCTV, a/c, cont. brkfst

HARTINGTON
Hillcrest Motel
(402) 254-6850
403 Robinson Ave.
16 rooms - $25-43
Pets: Welcome
Creature Comforts: CCTV, a/c

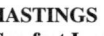

HASTINGS

Comfort Inn
(800) 228-5150, (402) 463-5252
http://www.comfortinn.com
2903 Osborne Dr.
64 rooms - $55-100
Pets: Welcome w/$5 fee
Creature Comforts: CCTV, a/c,
refrig, micro, Jacuzzi, cont. brkfst,
pool, whirlpool

Holiday Inn
(800) HOLIDAY, (402) 463-6721
http://www.holiday-inn.com
2205 Osborne Dr. E.
100 rooms - $55-95
Pets: Welcome
Creature Comforts: CCTV, a/c,
restaurant, pool, whirlpool

Midlands Lodge
(800) 237- 1872, (402) 463-2428
910 West J St.
47 rooms - $30-40
Pets: Small pets welcome
Creature Comforts: CCTV, a/c,
refrig, pool

Rainbow Motel
(800) 825-7424, (402) 463-2989
1400 West J St.
31 rooms - $35-45
Pets: Small pets welcome
Creature Comforts: CCTV, a/c

Super 8
(800) 800-8000, (402) 463-8888
http://www.super8.com
2200 N. Kansas Ave.
50 rooms - $40-75
Pets: Welcome
Creature Comforts: CCTV, a/c,
Jacuzzi

USA Inns
(800) 348-0426, (402) 463-1422
2424 Osborne Dr.
63 rooms - $40-45
Pets: Welcome
Creature Comforts: CCTV,
VCR, a/c, refrig, micro

Wayfair Motel
(402) 463-2434
101 East J St.
14 rooms - $35-50
Pets: Welcome
Creature Comforts: CCTV, a/c

X-L Motel
(800) 341-8000, (402) 463-3148
1400 West J St.
33 rooms - $30-44
Pets: Welcome w/small deposit
Creature Comforts: CCTV, a/c,
refrig, pool, whirlpool

HAYES CENTER

Midway Motel
(308) 286-3253
Route 25
4 rooms - $20-37
Pets: Welcome
Creature Comforts: CCTV, a/c,
restaurant

HEBRON

Riverside Motel
(402) 768-7366
Route 81
12 rooms - $25-46
Pets: Welcome
Creature Comforts: CCTV, a/c

Wayfarer Motel
(402) 768-7226
104 N. 13th St.
23 rooms - $25-39
Pets: Welcome
Creature Comforts: CCTV, a/c,
pool

HOLDREGE

Plains Motel
(800) 341-8000, (308) 995-8646
619 W. Route 6
22 rooms - $35-59
Pets: Welcome
Creature Comforts: CCTV, a/c

KEARNEY

Best Western Tel-Star
(800) 528-1234, (308) 237-5185
http://www.bestwestern.com
1010 Third Ave.
69 rooms - $55-75
Pets: Welcome
Creature Comforts: CCTV,
VCR, a/c, restaurant, exercise
rooms, sauna, whirlpool

Budget Motel South
(308) 237-5991
411 S. Second Ave.
69 rooms - $45-72
Pets: Welcome w/$5 fee
Creature Comforts: CCTV,
VCR, a/c, pool

Holiday Inn
(800) HOLIDAY, (308) 237-3141
http://www.holiday-inn.com
301 S. Second St.
210 rooms - $70-200
Pets: Welcome
Creature Comforts: CCTV, a/c,
restaurant, pool, whirlpool, tennis,
golf

Kearney Inn 4 Less
(308) 237-2671
709 Second Ave.
42 rooms - $40-58
Pets: Welcome w/$10 deposit
Creature Comforts: CCTV,
VCR, a/c

Quality Inn
(800) 228-5151, (308) 234-2541
http://www.qualityinn.com
I-80/South Second
107 rooms - $45-65
Pets: Welcome
Creature Comforts: Spacious
grounds, CCTV, a/c, restaurant,
pool

Western Inn South
(800) 437-8457, (308) 234-1876
510 Third Ave.
43 rooms - $40-67
Pets: Welcome w/$15 deposit
Creature Comforts: CCTV, a/c,
pool, sauna, whirlpool

Western Motel
(800) 234-2408, (308) 234-2408
824 E. 25th St.
20 rooms - $25-44
Pets: Welcome
Creature Comforts: CCTV, a/c

KIMBALL

Finer Motel
(308) 235-4878
Route 30 E.
14 rooms - $30-45
Pets: Welcome
Creature Comforts: CCTV, a/c,
kit

First Interstate Motel
(308) 235-4601
Rtes. 80 & 71
29 rooms - $40-50
Pets: Welcome w/$5 fee
Creature Comforts: CCTV, a/c,
restaurant

Motel Kimball
(308) 235-4606
Route 30 E.
16 rooms - $25-39
Pets: Welcome
Creature Comforts: CCTV, a/c,
restaurant

Super 8
(800) 800-8000, (308) 235-4888
http://www.super8.com
15 W. 8th St.
42 rooms - $45-59
Pets: Welcome w/$10 fee
Creature Comforts: CCTV, a/c,
micro, cont. brkfst, hlth clb access

Western Motel
(308) 235-4622
Route 30
24 rooms - $35-60
Pets: Welcome
Creature Comforts: CCTV, a/c,
refrig, micro

LAUREL
Big Red Motel
(402) 256-9952
202 Route 20
19 rooms - $25-45
Pets: Welcome
Creature Comforts: CCTV, a/c

LEXINGTON
Budget Host Minute Man
(800) Bud-Host, (308) 324-5544
http://www.budgethost.com
801 S. Plum Creek Hwy.
36 rooms - $32-45
Pets: Welcome in smoking rooms
Creature Comforts: CCTV, a/c,
pool

Days Inn
(800) DAYS-INN, (308) 324-6440
http://www.daysinn.com
2506 Plum Creek Pkwy.
30 rooms - $55-85
Pets: Dogs in smkng rms w/$5 fee
Creature Comforts: CCTV, a/c,
refrig, micro, Jacuzzi, cont. brkfst,
hlth clb

Econo Lodge
(800) 55-ECONO, (308) 324-5601
http://www.econolodge.com
Rtes. 80 & 283
50 rooms - $45-69
Pets: Welcome
Creature Comforts: CCTV, a/c,
pool
466

Green Valley Motel
(308) 324-3216
311 W. Fifth St.
14 rooms - $25-39
Pets: Welcome
Creature Comforts: CCTV, a/c

Toddle Inn Motel
(308) 286-3253
2701 Plum Creek Pkwy.
24 rooms - $35-55
Pets: Welcome
Creature Comforts: CCTV, a/c,
pool

LINCOLN
Airport Lodge
(402) 474-1311
2410 NW 12th St.
141 rooms - $30-49
Pets: Welcome
Creature Comforts: CCTV, a/c,
pool

Best Western Airport Inn
(800) 528-1234, (402) 475-9541
http://www.bestwestern.com
3200 NW 12th St.
127 rooms - $55-79
Pets: Welcome
Creature Comforts: CCTV, a/c,
restaurant, pool, hlth clb

Best Western Villager Motor Inn
(800) 528-1234, (402) 464-9111
http://www.bestwestern.com
5200 - O St.
187 rooms - $75-89
Pets: Welcome
Creature Comforts: CCTV, a/c,
restaurant, cont. brkfst, pool,
whirlpool

Comfort Inn
(800) 228-5150, (402) 475-2200
http://www.comfortinn.com
2940 NW 12th St.
66 rooms - $40-67
Pets: Welcome
Creature Comforts: CCTV, a/c,
exercise room, whirlpool

Comfort Suites
(800) 221-222, (402) 464-8080
http://www.comfortinn.com
4231 Industrial Ave.
60 rooms - $60-109
Pets: Small pets welcome
Creature Comforts: CCTV, a/c,
refrig, micro, pool, whirlpool

Congress Inn
(800) 447-2393, (402) 477-4488
2001 West O St.
50 rooms - $50-68
Pets: Welcome
Creature Comforts: CCTV, a/c,
refrig, micro, restaurant, pool

Econo Lodge
(800) 55-ECONO, (402) 474-1311
http://www.econolodge.com
2410 NW 12th St.
138 rooms - $40-68
Pets: Welcome
Creature Comforts: CCTV, a/c,
Jacuzzi, restaurant, cont. brkfst,
pool

Guesthouse Inn
(402) 466-2341
3245 Cornhusker Hwy.
41 rooms - $35-65
Pets: Welcome
Creature Comforts: CCTV, a/c,
pool

Holiday Inn
(800) HOLIDAY, (402) 474-1417
http://www.holiday-inn.com
1010 West Bond St.
106 rooms - $60-85
Pets: Small pets welcome in
smoking rooms
Creature Comforts: CCTV, a/c,
cont. brkfst, pool, whirlpool

Inn 4 Less
(402) 475-4511
1140 W. Cornhusker Hwy.
33 rooms - $30-55
Pets: Welcome
Creature Comforts: CCTV, a/c,
kit

King's Inn Motel
(402) 466-2324
3510 Cornhusker Hwy.
14 rooms - $35-65
Pets: Welcome
Creature Comforts: CCTV, a/c

Motel 6
(800) 4-MOTEL6, (402) 475-3211
http://www.motel6.com
1700 W. Lincolnway
98 rooms - $28-48
Pets: Under 30 lbs. welcome
Creature Comforts: CCTV, a/c

Quality Inn
(800) 228-5151, (402) 475-4971
http://www.qualityinn.com
1101 Bond St.
108 rooms - $66-89
Pets: Welcome
Creature Comforts: CCTV, a/c,
cont. brkfst, pool

Quality Inn
(800) 228-5151, (402) 464-3171
http://www.qualityinn.com
5250 Cornhusker Hwy.
150 rooms - $50-75
Pets: Small pets welcome
Creature Comforts: CCTV, a/c,
restaurant, pool, sauna, whirlpool,
recreation area

Ramada Inn
(800) 2-Ramada, (402) 475-4400
http://www.ramada.com
2310 N. 12th St.
108 rooms - $70-200
Pets: Welcome
Creature Comforts: CCTV, a/c,
restaurant, pool, hlth clb, sauna,
whirlpool

Residence Inn
(800) 331-3131, (402) 483-4900
http://www.residenceinn.com
200 S. 68th Pl.
120 rooms - $90-130
Pets: $50 deposit, $50 fee
Creature Comforts: CCTV,
VCR, a/c, kit, cont. brkfst,
exercise room, pool, whirlpool

Sleep Inn
(800) Sleep-Inn, (402) 475-1550
http://www.sleepinn.com
3400 NW 12th St.
80 rooms - $40-75
Pets: Welcome
Creature Comforts: CCTV, a/c,
cont. brkfst, pool

Starlite Motel
(402) 466-1902
5200 Cornhusker Hwy.
23 rooms - $45-59
Pets: Welcome
Creature Comforts: CCTV, a/c

Stop 'N' Sleep
(402) 423-7111
1140 Calvert St.
51 rooms - $45-59
Pets: Welcome
Creature Comforts: CCTV, a/c

Town House Suites
(800) 279-1744, (402) 475-3000
1744 M St.
53 rooms - $50-69
Pets: Welcome, must sign waiver
Creature Comforts: CCTV, a/c,
refrig, micro

LOUP CITY
Colony Inn
(308) 745-0164
Route 92
16 rooms - $25-45
Pets: Welcome
Creature Comforts: CCTV, a/c,
restaurant

MCCOOK
Best Western Chief Motel
(800) 528-1234, (308) 345-3700
http://www.bestwestern.com
612 West B St.
111 rooms - $50-80
Pets: Small pets welcome
Creature Comforts: CCTV, a/c,
restaurant, pool, whirlpool, hlth
club

Cedar Motel
(800) 352-4489, (308) 345-7091
1400 East C St.
23 rooms - $25-49
Pets: Welcome
Creature Comforts: CCTV, a/c,
restaurant

Red Horse Motel
(308) 345-2800
Routes 6 & 34
35 rooms - $35-49
Pets: Welcome
Creature Comforts: CCTV, a/c,
restaurant

Super 8
(800) 800-8000, (308) 345-1141
http://www.super8.com
1103 East B St.
40 rooms - $45-60
Pets: Welcome w/permission
Creature Comforts: CCTV, a/c,
hlth clb access

NEBRASKA CITY
American Star Inn
(402) 873-6556
1715 S. 11th St.
29 rooms - $45-75
Pets: Welcome
Creature Comforts: CCTV, a/c

Apple Inn
(800) 659-4446, (402) 873-5959
502 S. 11th
60 rooms - $40-60
Pets: Small pets welcome
Creature Comforts: CCTV, a/c,
refrig, Jacuzzi, pool

NELIGH
Deluxe Motel
(402) 887-4628
Route 275 E.
10 rooms - $35-55
Pets: Welcome
Creature Comforts: CCTV, a/c

West Hillview Motel
(402) 887-4186
Route 275
14 rooms - $35-55
Pets: Welcome
Creature Comforts: CCTV, a/c

NIOBRARA
Two Rivers Salon/Hotel
(402) 857-3340
254-12 Park Ave.
3 rooms - $35-65
Pets: Welcome
Creature Comforts: CCTV, a/c,
restaurant

NORFOLK
Blue Ridge Motel
(402) 371-0530
916 S. 13th St.
32 rooms - $20-37
Pets: Welcome
Creature Comforts: CCTV, a/c

Norfolk Country Inn
(800) 233-0733, (402) 371-4430
Routes 275 & 81
127 rooms - $45-55
Pets: Small pets welcome
Creature Comforts: CCTV, a/c,
refrig, restaurant, pool

NORTH PLATTE

Best Western Chalet Lodge
(800) 528-1234, (308) 532-2313
http://www.bestwestern.com
920 N. Jeffers St.
38 rooms - $45-65
Pets: Small pets welcome in
cetrain rooms w/$3 fee
Creature Comforts: CCTV, a/c,
cont. brkfst, pool

Best Western Circle C South
(800) 528-1234, (308) 532-0130
http://www.bestwestern.com
1211 S. Dewey St.
77 rooms - $50-85
Pets: Small pets welcome w/$6 fee
Creature Comforts: CCTV, a/c,
restaurant, 2 pools

Blue Spruce Motel
(308) 534-2600
821 S. Dewey St.
26 rooms - $35-65
Pets: Welcome
Creature Comforts: CCTV, a/c,
whirlpool

Camino Inn
(308) 532-9090
2102 S. Jeffers St.
226 rooms - $60-80
Pets: Welcome
Creature Comforts: CCTV, a/c,
restaurant, cont. brkfst, pool,
sauna, whirlpool

Country Inn
(308) 532-2313
321 S. Dewey
40 rooms - $45-69
Pets: Welcome
Creature Comforts: CCTV, a/c,
pool, whirlpool

First Interstate Inn
(308) 532-6980
Route 80
29 rooms - $35-55
Pets: Small pets w/$5 fee
Creature Comforts: CCTV, a/c,
refrig, micro

Green Acres
(308) 532-6654
4601 Rodeo Rd.
18 rooms - $40-85
Pets: Small pets, ltd rms, $3 fee
Creature Comforts: CCTV, a/c,
kit, pool

Husker Inn
(308) 532-6654
721 E. Fourth St.
24 rooms - $30-48
Pets: Welcome
Creature Comforts: CCTV, kit

Motel 6
(800) 4-MOTEL6, (308) 534-6200
http://www.motel6.com
1520 S. Jeffers St.
61 rooms - $35-45
Pets: Under 30 lbs. welcome
Creature Comforts: CCTV, a/c,
pool

Pioneer Motel
(308) 532-8730
902 S. Dewey St.
20 rooms - $30-44
Pets: Welcome
Creature Comforts: CCTV, a/c,
pool

Rambler Motel
(308) 532-9290
1420 Rodeo Rd.
26 rooms - $25-38
Pets: Small pets welcome
Creature Comforts: CCTV, a/c,
refrig, pool

Sands Motor Inn
(308) 532-0151
501 Halligan Dr.
81 rooms - $35-59
Pets: Welcome w/$10 fee
Creature Comforts: CCTV, a/c,
restaurant, pool

Stanford Motel
(800) 743-4934, (308) 532-9380
1400 E. Fourth St.
30 rooms - $35-49
Pets: Small pets welcome
Creature Comforts: CCTV,
VCR, a/c, refrig, micro

Stockman Inn
(800) 624-4643, (308) 534-3630
1402 S. Jeffers St.
150 rooms - $45-69
Pets: Welcome
Creature Comforts: CCTV, a/c,
refrig, restaurant, pool

Super 8
(800) 800-8000, (308) 532-4224
http://www.super8.com
220 Eugene Ave.
113 rooms - $40-58
Pets: Welcome w/deposit
Creature Comforts: CCTV, a/c,
Jacuzzi, cont. brkfst, hlth clb
access, whirlpool

Travelers Inn
(800) 341-8000, (308) 534-4020
602 E. Fourth St.
32 rooms - $35-45
Pets: Welcome
Creature Comforts: CCTV,
VCR, a/c, refrig

OGALLALA

Best Western Stagecoach
(800) 528-1234, (308) 284-3656
http://www.bestwestern.com
201 Stagecoach Trial
99 rooms - $45-89
Pets: Welcome in certain rooms
Creature Comforts: CCTV,
VCR, a/c, restaurant, cont. brkfst,
pool, hlth clb access, whirlpool

Days Inn
(800) DAYS INN, (308) 284-6365
http://www.daysinn.com
601 Stagecoach Trail
31 rooms - $55-75
Pets: Dogs are fee-smoking rooms
otherwise there is a $5 fee
Creature Comforts: CCTV,
VCR, a/c, refrig, micro

First Interstate Inn
(800) 462-4667, (308) 284-2056
108 Prospector Dr.
40 rooms - $30-49
Pets: Small pets welcome
Creature Comforts: CCTV, a/c

Kingsley Lodge
(800) 883-2775, (308) 284-2775
Route 61
15 rooms - $25-55
Pets: Welcome
Creature Comforts: CCTV,
restaurant

Lakeway Lodge
(308) 284-4431
918 N. Spruce St.
26 rooms - $30-55
Pets: Welcome
Creature Comforts: CCTV, pool

Lazy K Motel
(800) 508-4085, (308) 284-4085
1501 E. First St.
22 rooms - $30-57
Pets: Welcome
Creature Comforts: CCTV, a/c,
pool

Plaza Inn
(308) 284-8416
E. Rte. 30
44 rooms - $40-65
Pets: Welcome
Creature Comforts: CCTV, a/c,
pool, whirlpool

Ramada Ltd.
(800) 2-Ramada, (308) 284-3623
http://www.ramada.com
201 Chuckwagon Rd.
153 rooms - $50-79
Pets: Welcome w/$5 fee
Creature Comforts: CCTV, a/c,
restaurant, pool

Sunset Motel
(308) 284-4264
Route 30 W.
11 rooms - $25-35
Pets: Welcome
Creature Comforts: CCTV, a/c

Super 8
(800) 800-8000, (308) 284-2076
http://www.super8.com
500 East A South
90 rooms - $40-79
Pets: Welcome
Creature Comforts: CCTV, a/c,
cont. brkfst, hlth clb access,
whirlpool

Western Paradise Motel
(308) 284-3684
221 E. First St.
25 rooms - $25-38
Pets: Welcome
Creature Comforts: CCTV, a/c

OMAHA
Ben Franklin Motel
(800) 688-3658, (402) 895-2200
10308 Sapp Brothers Dr.
96 rooms - $45-65
Pets: Welcome w/$5 fee
Creature Comforts: CCTV,
VCR, a/c, refrig, micro, Jacuzzi

Best Western Central
(800) 528-1234, (402) 397-3700
http://www.bestwestern.com
3650 S. 72nd St.
213 rooms - $60-100
Pets: Welcome
Creature Comforts: CCTV, a/c,
refrig, micro, restaurant, pool,
health club

Baymont Inns
(877)BAYMONT, (402) 592-5200
http://www.baymontinns.com
10760 M St.
96 rooms - $55-75
Pets: Welcome in smoking rooms
Creature Comforts: CCTV, a/c,
refrig, micro

Comfort Inn
(800) 228-5150, (402) 592-2882
http://www.comfortinn.com
10919 - J St.
77 rooms - $50-99
Pets: Welcome
Creature Comforts: CCTV,
VCR, a/c, cont. brkfst, pool

Econo Lodge West Dodge
(800) 55-ECONO, (402) 391-7100
http://www.econolodge.com
7833 W. Dodge St.
48 rooms - $40-50
Pets: Welcome
Creature Comforts: CCTV, a/c,
kit, cont. brkfst, whirlpool

Hampton Inn
(800) Hampton, (402) 391-5300
http://www.hampton-inn.com
10728 - L St.
135 rooms - $55-69
Pets: Welcome
Creature Comforts: CCTV, a/c,
refrig, Jacuzzi

Hawthorne Suites
(800) 527-1133, (402) 331-0101
http://www.hyatt.com
11025 M St.
88 rooms - $55-85
Pets: Small pets w/$15 fee
Creature Comforts: CCTV, a/c,
refrig, micro, kit, pool, hlth clb,
whirlpool

La Quinta
(800) 531-5900, (402) 493-1900
http://www.laquinta.com
3330 N. 104th Ave.
130 rooms - $55-65
Pets: Welcome
Creature Comforts: CCTV, a/c,
refrig, micro

Marriott Hotel
(800) 228-9290, (402) 399-9000
http://www.marriott.com
10220 Regency Circle
301 rooms - $95-145
Pets: Welcome
Creature Comforts: CCTV, a/c,
refrig, restaurant, cont. brkfst, hlth
clb access, pool, sauna, whirlpool

Motel 6
(800) 4-MOTEL6, (402) 331-3161
http://www.motel6.com
10708 M St.
103 rooms - $25-32
Pets: Under 30 lbs. welcome
Creature Comforts: CCTV, a/c,
pool

The Offutt House
(402) 553-0951
http://www.virtualcities
140 North 39th St.
7 rooms - $65-105
Pets: Welcome on a limited basis
in two rooms
Creature Comforts: 1894
mansion in historic district,
library, sunporch & patio, antique
filled rooms, piano, CCTV,
fireplace, full brkfst

Park Inn International
(800) 437-7275, (402) 895-2555
http://www.ParkHtls.com
9305 S. 145th St.
56 rooms - $45-65
Pets: Welcome w/$25 deposit
Creature Comforts: CCTV,
VCR, a/c, refrig, micro, restaurant,
whirlpool

Ramada Hotel, Central
(800) 2-Ramada, (402) 397-7030
http://www.ramada.com
7007 Grover St.
214 rooms - $55-69
Pets: Welcome, crate needed
Creature Comforts: CCTV, a/c,
refrig, restaurant, pool, sauna,
whirlpool

Ramada Inn, Airport
(800) 2-Ramada, (402) 342-5100
http://www.ramada.com
2002 Locust St.
149 rooms - $60-79
Pets: Under 10 lbs. w/$10 deposit
Creature Comforts: CCTV,
VCR, a/c, refrig, restaurant, pool,
sauna, whirlpool

Residence Inn
(800) 331-3131, (402) 553-8898
http://www.residenceinn.com
6990 Dodge St.
80 rooms - $100-125
Pets: Welcome w/$25 fee
Creature Comforts: CCTV,
VCR, a/c, kit, cont. brkfst, hlth clb
access, whirlpool

Satellite Motel
(402) 733-7373
6006 - L St.
15 rooms - $35-49
Pets: Welcome w/$2 fee, $20 dep.
Creature Comforts: CCTV, a/c,
refrig

Sheraton Inn Omaha
(800)325-3535, (402) 895-1000
http://www.sheraton.com
4888 S. 118th St.
163 rooms - $40-79
Pets: Welcome
Creature Comforts: CCTV, a/c,
refrig, micro, restaurant, pool,
sauna, whirlpool

Townhouse Inn
(402) 893-3777
140th & West Center Rd.
22 rooms - $35-65
Pets: Welcome
Creature Comforts: CCTV, a/c

O'NEILL
Budget Host Carriage House
(800) Bud-Host, (402) 336-3403
http://www.budgethost.com
929 E. Douglas St.
14 rooms - $30-58
Pets: Welcome
Creature Comforts: CCTV, a/c

Capri Motel
(800) 341-8000, (402) 336-2762
1020 E. Douglas St.
26 rooms - $35-49
Pets: Welcome
Creature Comforts: CCTV, a/c

Elms Motel
(800) 526-9052, (402) 336-3800
Routes 20 & 275
21 rooms - $30-40
Pets: Welcome
Creature Comforts: CCTV, a/c

Golden Hotel
(800) 658-3148, (402) 336-4436
406 E. Douglas St.
34 rooms - $30-49
Pets: Welcome
Creature Comforts: Historic,
CCTV, a/c, kit, whirlpool

ORCHARD
Orchard Motel
(402) 893-2165
Route 20
6 rooms - $20-39
Pets: Welcome
Creature Comforts: CCTV, a/c

OSHKOSH
S&S Motel
(308) 772-3350
Routes 26 & 27
13 rooms - $25-35
Pets: Welcome
Creature Comforts: CCTV, a/c,
restaurant

Shady Rest Motel
(308) 772-4115
Route 26 & Main St.
12 rooms - $30-39
Pets: Welcome
Creature Comforts: CCTV,
refrig

PAWNEE CITY
Pawnee Inn
(402) 852-2238
1021 - F St.
10 rooms - $25-39
Pets: Welcome
Creature Comforts: CCTV,
refrig, restaurant

PAXTON
Days Inn
(800) DAYS INN, (402) 239-4719
http://www.daysinn.com
Route 80
36 rooms - $45-69
Pets: Welcome w/$5 fee
Creature Comforts: CCTV, a/c,
micro, cont. brkfst, pool, game
room

PLATTSMOUTH
Brown's Family Motel
(402) 296-9266
1913 Route 34E
29 rooms - $50-69
Pets: Welcome
Creature Comforts: CCTV, a/c,
refrig

RANDOLPH
Cedar Motel
(402) 337-0500
107 E. Route 20
14 rooms - $30-45
Pets: Welcome
Creature Comforts: CCTV, a/c

RED CLOUD
Elavonis-McFarland Hotel
(402) 746-2329
137 W. Fourth Ave.
13 rooms - $25-40
Pets: Welcome
Creature Comforts: CCTV, a/c,
restaurant

REPUBLICAN CITY
Gateway Motel
(308) 799-2815
Route 136
11 rooms - $25-40
Pets: Welcome
Creature Comforts: CCTV, a/c

RUSHVILLE
Antlers Motel
(308) 327-2444
607 E. Second St.
20 rooms - $30-45
Pets: Welcome
Creature Comforts: CCTV, a/c

Nebraskaland Motel
(308) 327-2487
508 E. Second St.
13 rooms - $30-45
Pets: Welcome
Creature Comforts: CCTV, a/c

ST. PAUL
Keller's Korner Motel
(308) 754-4451
Routes 281 & 92
15 rooms - $20-40
Pets: Welcome
Creature Comforts: CCTV, a/c

Super 8
(800) 800-8000, (308) 754-4554
http://www.super8.com
116 Howard Ave.
37 rooms - $48-59
Pets: Welcome w/damage deposit
Creature Comforts: CCTV, a/c,
restaurant, cont. brkfst

SCHULYER
Johnnie's Motel
(402) 352-5454
1028 E. Third St.
31 rooms - $30-45
Pets: Welcome
Creature Comforts: CCTV, a/c

Valley Court Motel
(402) 352-3326
320 W. 16th St.
13 rooms - $25-40
Pets: Welcome
Creature Comforts: CCTV, a/c

SCOTTSBLUFF
Capri Motel
(800) 642-2774, (308) 635-2057
2424 Ave. I
30 rooms - $35-55
Pets: Welcome w/$3 fee
Creature Comforts: CCTV, a/c,
cont. brkfst

Lamplighter Motel
(800) 341-8000, (308) 632-7108
606 E. 27th St.
40 rooms - $35-55
Pets: Small pets welcome
Creature Comforts: CCTV, a/c,
cont. brkfst, pool

Sands Motel
(800) 535-1075, (308) 632-6191
814 W. 27th St.
19 rooms - $30-50
Pets: Small pets w/$3 fee
Creature Comforts: CCTV, a/c,
refrig

Scottsbluff Inn
(800) 597-3111, (308) 635-3111
1901 21st Ave.
138 rooms - $45-69
Pets: Welcome w/$6
Creature Comforts: CCTV,
VCR, a/c, refrig, restaurant, pool,
hlth clb, sauna, whirlpool

SEWARD
East Hill Motel
(402) 643-3679
131 Rte. 34 E.
19 rooms - $35-45
Pets: Welcome
Creature Comforts: CCTV, a/c

Seward Super 8
(800) 800-8000, (402) 643-3388
http://www.super8.com
Route 15 S.
45 rooms - $48-59
Pets: Welcome w/permission
Creature Comforts: CCTV, a/c,
Jacuzzi, kit, cont. brkfst

SIDNEY
Conestoga Motel
(308) 254-6000
Route 1
14 rooms - $25-35
Pets: Welcome
Creature Comforts: CCTV, a/c

Deluxe Motel
(308) 254-4666
2201 Illinois St.
16 rooms - $30-49
Pets: Welcome
Creature Comforts: CCTV, a/c

El Palomino Motel
(308) 254-5566
2020 Illinois St.
23 rooms - $35-49
Pets: Welcome
Creature Comforts: CCTV, a/c

Fort Sidney Motor Hotel
(800) 642-2774, (308) 635-2057
935 Ninth Ave.
50 rooms - $35-49
Pets: Welcome
Creature Comforts: CCTV, a/c,
refrig, micro, kit, restaurant, pool

Generic Motel
(800) 893-5309, (308) 254-5427
11552 Route 30
11 rooms - $35-48
Pets: Welcome
Creature Comforts: CCTV, a/c

Holiday Inn
(800) HOLIDAY, (308) 254-2000
http://www.holiday-inn.com
664 Chase Blvd.
85 rooms - $75-90
Pets: Welcome w/$10 fee
Creature Comforts: CCTV,
VCR, a/c, Jacuzzi, restaurant,
pool, hlth clb, whirlpool

Sidney Motor Lodge
(308) 254-4581
730 E. Jennifer Ln.
16 rooms - $35-59
Pets: Small pets welcome
Creature Comforts: CCTV,
VCR, a/c, refrig, micro, kit

Super 8
(800) 800-8000, (308) 254-2081
http://www.super8.com
2115 W. Illinois Ave.
60 rooms - $40-50
Pets: Welcome w/permission
Creature Comforts: CCTV, a/c,
cont. brkfst

SOUTH SIOUX CITY
Marina Inn
(800) 798-7980, (402) 494-4000
Fourth and B Streets
182 rooms - $80-99
Pets: Welcome
Creature Comforts: CCTV,
VCR, a/c, refrig, Jacuzzi,
restaurant, whirlpool

Ramada Ltd.
(800) 2-Ramada, (402) 494-8874
http://www..ramada.com
2829 Dakota Ave.
80 rooms - $40-149
Pets: Welcome
Creature Comforts: CCTV, a/c,
refrig, Jacuzzi, sauna

SPENCER
Skyline Motel
(800) 917-1300, (402) 589-1300
Routes 281 & 12
15 rooms - $40-75
Pets: Welcome in smoking rooms
Creature Comforts: CCTV, a/c

STUART
Stuart Village Inn
(402) 924-3133
Box 238
35 rooms - $25-45
Pets: Welcome
Creature Comforts: CCTV, a/c

SUPERIOR
Victorian Inn
(402) 879-3245
Route 14 N.
25rooms - $25-46
Pets: Welcome
Creature Comforts: CCTV, a/c,
cont. brkfst, exercise room

SUTHERLAND
Park Motel
(800) 437-2565, (308) 386-4384
1110 First St.
14 rooms - $40-85
Pets: Welcome
Creature Comforts: CCTV, a/c

SUTTON
Sutton Motel
(402) 773-4803
208 N. French St.
6 rooms - $25-37
Pets: Welcome
Creature Comforts: CCTV, a/c

SYRACUSE
Mustang Motel
(402) 269-2185
940 Park St.
10 rooms - $35-59
Pets: Welcome
Creature Comforts: CCTV, a/c

TABLE ROCK
Hill Haven Lodge
(402) 839-2023
Route 1
3 rooms - $35-49
Pets: Welcome
Creature Comforts: 125-year-old
limestone bldng, CCTV, full brkfst

THEDFORD
Rodeway Inn
(800) 228-2000, (308) 645-2284
http://www.rodeway.com
HC 58, Box ID
42 rooms - $40-65
Pets: Welcome
Creature Comforts: CCTV,
VCR, a/c, Jacuzzi, cont. brkfst

TRYON
Longhorn Motel
(308) 587-2345
Routes 92 & 97
5 rooms - $30-45
Pets: Welcome
Creature Comforts: CCTV, a/c

VALENTINE
Ballard Motel
(402) 376-2922
227 S. Hall St.
10 rooms - $25-39
Pets: Welcome
Creature Comforts: CCTV, a/c

Merritt Resort
(402) 376-3437
Route 97
15 rooms - $45-85
Pets: Welcome
Creature Comforts: CCTV, a/c

Motel Raine
(402) 376-2030
Route 20 W.
34 rooms - $35-55
Pets: Small pets welcome
Creature Comforts: CCTV, a/c,
cont. brkfst

Niobrara Inn
(877) 376-1779, (402) 376-1779
www.nabb1.com/val1779.htm
Main St.
6 rooms - $50-110
Pets: Selectively welcomed
Creature Comforts: Wonderful
Arts & Crafts style 1912 rambling
house, oak woodwork, lovely
front porch, antiques, full brkfst,
beautiful countryside

Trade Winds Lodge
(800) 341-8000, (402) 376-1600
Routes 20 & 83
32 rooms - $35-56
Pets: Welcome
Creature Comforts: CCTV, a/c,
refrig, pool

Valentine Motel
(800) 376-2450, (402) 376-2450
Routes 20 & 83
12 rooms - $35-65
Pets: Welcome
Creature Comforts: CCTV, a/c,
refrig

VERDIGRE
Veridgre Inn
(402) 668-2277
305 W. Third Ave.
3 rooms - $25-40
Pets: Welcome
Creature Comforts: 100-year-old
home, full brkfst

WAHOO
Bill's Wahoo Motel
(402) 443-9933
Route 1
10 rooms - $25-45
Pets: Welcome
Creature Comforts: CCTV

WAUNETA
Wauneta Motel
(308) 394-5434
35 E. Route 6
4 rooms - $25-35
Pets: Welcome
Creature Comforts: CCTV

WAUSA
Commercial Hotel
(402) 586-2377
Main St.
6 rooms - $25-45
Pets: Welcome
Creature Comforts: CCTV, kit

WAYNE
K-D Motel
(402) 375-1770
311 E. Seventh St.
25 rooms - $30-45
Pets: Welcome
Creature Comforts: CCTV, a/c,
cont. brkfst

Sports Club Motel
(402) 375-4222
Route 2
32 rooms - $25-45
Pets: Welcome
Creature Comforts: CCTV, a/c,
cont. brkfst

WEST POINT
Pointers Inn Motel
(402) 372-4291
534 S. Lincoln Hwy.
27 rooms - $35-49
Pets: Welcome
Creature Comforts: CCTV, a/c

Super 8
(800) 800-8000, (402) 372-3998
http://www.super8.com
1211 N. Lincoln
39 rooms - $45-55
Pets: Welcome w/deposit
Creature Comforts: CCTV, a/c,
Jacuzzi, cont. brkfst, hlth club

WILBER
Hotel Wilbur
(888) 494-5237, (402) 821-2020
W. Second & S. Wilbur Sts.
10 rooms - $40-75
Pets: Hunting kennels available
Creature Comforts: 1895 hotel,
CCTV, restaurant

WISNER
Midwest Motel
(402) 529-6910
1612 Ave. E
9 rooms - $25-45
Pets: Welcome
Creature Comforts: CCTV, a/c

WOOD RIVER
Wood River Motel
(308) 583-2256
11774 s. Rte. 11
18 rooms - $35-55
Pets: Welcome
Creature Comforts: CCTV, a/c,
restaurant

WYMORE
D&M Motel
(402) 543-3801
601 S. 14th St.
8 rooms - $25-39
Pets: Welcome
Creature Comforts: CCTV, a/c

YORK
Best Western Palmer Inn
(800) 528-1234, (402) 362-5585
http://www.bestwestern.com
2426 S. Lincoln
41 rooms - $40-69
Pets: Small pets welcome
Creature Comforts: CCTV, a/c,
cont. brkfst, pool

Super 8
(800) 800-8000, (402) 362-3388
http://www.super8.com
Rte. 80
96 rooms - $45-60
Pets: Welcome
Creature Comforts: CCTV, a/c,
cont. brkfst, exercise equip.

USA Inns
(402) 362-6885
4817 S. Lincoln St.
82 rooms - $45-60
Pets: Welcome
Creature Comforts: CCTV, a/c,
refrig, micro, Jacuzzi, restaurant

Nevada

ALAMO
Meadow Lane Motel
(702) 725-3371
Route 93
15 rooms - $30-49
Pets: Welcome
Creature Comforts: CCTV, a/c

AMARGOSA VALLEY
Longstreet Inn, Casino
(775) 372-1777
Route 373
60 rooms - $40-99
Pets: Welcome w/CC deposit
Creature Comforts: CCTV, a/c,
restaurant, and a pond

AUSTIN
Lincoln Motel
(702) 964-2698
28 Main St.
17 rooms - $30-49
Pets: Welcome
Creature Comforts: CCTV, a/c,
kit, restaurant

Mountain Motel
(702) 964-2471
Route 50
12 rooms - $30-58
Pets: Welcome
Creature Comforts: CCTV, a/c

Pony Canyon Motel
(702) 964-2605
Route 50
10 rooms - $35-57
Pets: Welcome
Creature Comforts: CCTV, a/c,
kit

Pony Express House
(702) 964-2306
888 Main St.
2 rooms - $35-54
Pets: Welcome
Creature Comforts: CCTV, a/c,
kit

BAKER
Border Inn
(702) 234-7300
Routes 50 & 6
29 rooms - $30-47
Pets: Welcome
Creature Comforts: CCTV, a/c,
kit, restaurant

Silverjack Motel
(702) 234-7323
Main St.
7 rooms - $31-59
Pets: Welcome
Creature Comforts: CCTV, a/c

BATTLE MOUNTAIN
Bel Court Motel
(775) 635-2569
292 E. Front St.
9 rooms - $20-36
Pets: Welcome
Creature Comforts: CCTV, a/c

Best Western Big Chief
(800) 528-1234, (775) 635-2416
http://www.bestwestern.com
434 West Front St.
58 rooms - $60-99
Pets: Welcome
Creature Comforts: CCTV, a/c,
micro, kit, cont. brkfst, pool,
whirlpool

Broadway Colt Motel
(800) 343-0085, (775) 635-5424
650 West Front St.
72 rooms - $40-63
Pets: Welcome
Creature Comforts: CCTV, a/c,
kit, restaurant, whirlpool

Comfort Inn
(800) 228-5150, (702) 635-5880
www.comfortinn.com
521 E. Front St.
72 rooms - $55-65
Pets: Welcome w/$20 deposit
Creature Comforts: CCTV, a/c,
refrig, restaurant, cont. brkfst,
pool, whirlpool

Ho Motel
(775) 635-5101
150 W. Front St.
12 rooms - $20-39
Pets: Welcome
Creature Comforts: CCTV, a/c,
restaurant

BEATTY
Burro Inn
(800) 843-2078, (775) 553-2225
Route 95
62 rooms - $35-50
Pets: Welcome
Creature Comforts: CCTV, a/c,
restaurant

El Portal Motel
(775) 553-2912
301 Main St.
30 rooms - $30-40
Pets: Welcome
Creature Comforts: CCTV, a/c,
pool

Stagecoach Hotel & Casino
(800) 4BIG-WIN, (775) 553-2548
Route 95
45 rooms - $25-50
Pets: Welcome
Creature Comforts: CCTV, a/c,
restaurant, cont. brkfst, pool,
sauna, whirlpool

BOULDER CITY
Desert Inn of Boulder City
(702) 293-2827
800 Nevada Hwy.
26 rooms - $30-100
Pets: Welcome
Creature Comforts: CCTV, a/c,
kit

Lake Mead Resort
(800) 752-9669, (702) 293-2074
322 Lakeshore Rd.
43 rooms - $50-125
Pets: Welcome
Creature Comforts: CCTV, a/c,
restaurant, pool

Flamingo Inn Motel
(702) 293-3565
804 Nevada Hwy.
15 rooms - $30-58
Pets: Welcome
Creature Comforts: CCTV, a/c, kit

Nevada Inn
(800) 638-8890, (702) 293-2044
1009 Nevada Hwy.
55 rooms - $30-59
Pets: Welcome
Creature Comforts: CCTV, a/c, kit, Jacuzzi, pool

Starview Motel
(702) 293-1658
1017 Nevada Hwy.
22 rooms - $30-89
Pets: Welcome
Creature Comforts: CCTV, a/c, restaurant, pool

CALIENTE
Caliente Hot Springs Motel
(800) 748-4785, (702) 726-3777
Route 93
18 rooms - $35-79
Pets: Winter months only
Creature Comforts: CCTV, a/c, kit, whirlpool

Rainbow Canyon Motel
(702) 726-3291
884 A St.
7 rooms - $31-46
Pets: Welcome
Creature Comforts: CCTV, a/c, kit

Shady Motel
(702) 726-3106
450 Front St.
22 rooms - $35-45
Pets: Welcome
Creature Comforts: CCTV, a/c, kit

CARSON CITY
Best Western Trailside
(800) 528-1234, (775) 883-7300
http://www.bestwestern.com
900 S. Carson St.
68 rooms - $45-139
Pets: Welcome
Creature Comforts: CCTV, a/c, refrig, pool, whirlpool

Carson Motor Lodge
(775) 882-5535
800 N. Carson St.
17 rooms - $30-50
Pets: Welcome
Creature Comforts: CCTV, a/c, kit

Days Inn
(800) DAYS INN, (775) 883-3343
http://www.daysinn.com
3101 N. Carson St.
63 rooms - $40-89
Pets: Small pets w/$5 fee
Creature Comforts: CCTV, a/c, refrig, micro

Desert Hills Motel
(800) Nevada 1, (775) 882-1932
1010 S. Carson St.
33 rooms - $40-87
Pets: Welcome
Creature Comforts: CCTV, a/c, whirlpool

Downtowner Motor Inn
(800) 364-4908, (775) 882-1377
801 N. Carson St.
33 rooms - $35-58
Pets: Med. size pets w/$25 dep.
Creature Comforts: CCTV, a/c

Motel Orleans
(775) 882-2007
2731 S. Carson St.
58 rooms - $30-66
Pets: Welcome w/$50 fee
Creature Comforts: CCTV, a/c, refrig, micro, pool, whirlpool

Motel 6
(800) 4-MOTEL6, (775) 885-7710
http://www.motel6.com
2749 S. Carson St.
82 rooms - $30-46
Pets: Welcome
Creature Comforts: CCTV, a/c, pool

Pioneer Motel
(775) 882-3046
907 S. Carson St.
35 rooms - $30-70
Pets: Welcome
Creature Comforts: CCTV, a/c, pool

Round House Inn
(775) 882-3446
1400 N. Carson St.
39 rooms - $40-76
Pets: Welcome
Creature Comforts: CCTV, a/c, pool

Sierra Vista Motel
(800) Nevada-1, (775) 883-9500
711 S. Plaza St.
24 rooms - $30-78
Pets: Welcome
Creature Comforts: CCTV, a/c, kit

Silver Queen Inn
(800) Nevada-1, (775) 882-5534
201 W. Caroline St.
35 rooms - $30-57
Pets: Welcome
Creature Comforts: CCTV, a/c, kit

Super 8
(800) 800-8000, (775) 883-7800
http://www.super8.com
2829 S. Carson St.
63 rooms - $45-69
Pets: Welcome
Creature Comforts: CCTV, a/c

Westerner Motel
(775) 883-6565
555 N. Stewart St.
102 rooms - $35-56
Pets: Welcome
Creature Comforts: CCTV, a/c, refrig, kit

DENIO
Denio Jct. Motel
(702) 941-0371
Box 10
11 rooms - $30-45
Pets: Welcome
Creature Comforts: CCTV, a/c, restaurant

ELKO
Best Western Elko Inn Express
(800) 528-1234, (775) 738-7261
http://www.bestwestern.com
837 Idaho St.
49 rooms - $60-96
Pets: Small pets welcome
Creature Comforts: CCTV, a/c, refrig, micro, cont. brkfst, pool

Best Western Gold Country
(800) 528-1234, (775) 738-8241
http://www.bestwestern.com
2050 Idaho St.
151 rooms - $50-99
Pets: Small pets welcome
Creature Comforts: CCTV, a/c,
refrig, restaurant, pool

Centre Motel
(775) 738-3226
475 Third St.
22 rooms - $30-54
Pets: Welcome
Creature Comforts: CCTV, a/c

Elko Motel
(775) 738-4433
1243 Idaho St.
32 rooms - $27-64
Pets: Welcome
Creature Comforts: CCTV, a/c

Esquire Motor Lodge
(800) 822-7473, (775) 738-3157
505 Idaho St.
21 rooms - $30-69
Pets: Welcome
Creature Comforts: CCTV, a/c

High Desert Inn
(888) 394-8303, (775) 738-8425
305 Idaho St.
172 rooms - $60-110
Pets: Welcome
Creature Comforts: CCTV, a/c,
refrig,restaurant, pool, hlth club,
and a whirlpool

Holiday Inn Express
(800) HOLIDAY, (775) 777-0990
http://www.holiday-inn.com
3019 E. Idaho St.
77rooms - $80-120
Pets: Welcome
Creature Comforts: CCTV, a/c,
kit, and a cont. brkfst

Louis Motel
(775) 738-3536
2100 W. Idaho St.
23 rooms - $30-47
Pets: Welcome
Creature Comforts: CCTV, a/c

Motel 6
(800) 4 MOTEL6, (775) 738-4337
http://www.motel6.com
3021 Idaho St.
123 rooms - $34-49
Pets: Under 30 lbs. welcome
Creature Comforts: CCTV, a/c,
pool

Red Lion Inn & Casino
(800) RED LION, (775) 738-2111
http://www.redlioninns.com
2065 Idaho St.
223 rooms - $80-275
Pets: Welcome
Creature Comforts: CCTV,
VCR, a/c, refrig, Jacuzzi,
restaurant, pool

Shilo Inn
(800) 222-2244, (775) 738-5522
http://www.shiloinns.com
2401 Mtn. City Hwy.
70 rooms - $55-129
Pets: Welcome w/$7 fee
Creature Comforts: CCTV, a/c,
refrig, micro, pool, hlth clb, sauna,
hlth club

Thunderbird Motel
(775) 738-7115
345 Idaho St.
70 rooms - $40-92
Pets: Medium pets welcome
Creature Comforts: CCTV, a/c,
refrig, micro, pool

Towne House Motel
(775) 738-7269
500 W. Oak St.
19 rooms - $30-59
Pets: Welcome
Creature Comforts: CCTV, a/c

Travelers Motel
(775) 738-4048
1181 Idaho St.
15 rooms - $30-69
Pets: Welcome
Creature Comforts: CCTV, a/c

ELY
Best Western Main
(800) 528-1234, (775) 289-4529
http://www.bestwestern.com
1101 Aultman St.
19 rooms - $50-69
Pets: Small pets welcome
Creature Comforts: CCTV, a/c

Best Western Park-Vue
(800) 528-1234, (775) 289-4497
http://www.bestwestern.com
930 Aultman St.
21 rooms - $50-84
Pets: Small attended pet welcome
Creature Comforts: CCTV,
VCR, a/c, refrig, and a cont. brkfst

El Rancho Motel
(775) 289-3644
1400 Aultman St.
12 rooms - $35-53
Pets: Welcome
Creature Comforts: CCTV, a/c

Fireside Inn
(800) 732-8288, (775) 289-3765
McGill Hwy.
14 rooms - $40-79
Pets: Welcome w/$5 fee
Creature Comforts: CCTV, a/c,
refrig, restaurant

Grand Central Motel
(775) 289-6868
1498 Lyons Ave.
13 rooms - $26-44
Pets: Welcome
Creature Comforts: CCTV, a/c

Great Basin Inn
(775) 289-4468
701 Avenue F
21 rooms - $35-69
Pets: Welcome
Creature Comforts: CCTV, a/c,
pool, whirlpool

Hotel Nevada
(800) 574-8879, (775) 289-6665
501 Aultman
65 rooms - $25-50
Pets: Welcome
Creature Comforts: CCTV, a/c,
refrig, micro, restaurant

Idle Inn Motel
(775) 289-4411
150 Fourth St.
26 rooms - $25-43
Pets: Welcome
Creature Comforts: CCTV, a/c

Lane's Ranch Motel
(775) 238-5246
Route 318, Preston
15 rooms - $30-53
Pets: Welcome
Creature Comforts: CCTV, a/c,
restaurant

Motel 6
(800) 4 MOTEL6, (775) 289-6671
http://www.motel6.com
770 Avenue O
122 rooms - $25-47
Pets: Under 30 lbs. welcome
Creature Comforts: CCTV, a/c, pool

Ramada Copper Queen Hotel
(800) 2-Ramada, (775) 289-4884
http://www.ramada.com
701 Ave. I
64 rooms - $55-129
Pets: Welcome
Creature Comforts: CCTV, a/c, refrig, Jacuzzi, restaurant, pool

Rustic Inn
(775) 289-4404
1555 Aultman St.
12 rooms - $35-60
Pets: Welcome
Creature Comforts: CCTV, a/c, refrig, micro

Sure Rest Motel
(775) 289-2512
1550 High St.
12 rooms - $30-49
Pets: Welcome
Creature Comforts: CCTV, kit, a/c

White Pine Motel
(775) 289-3800
1301 Aultman
29 rooms - $35-59
Pets: Welcome
Creature Comforts: CCTV, a/c

EUREKA
Colonnade Hotel
(775) 237-9988
Clark and Monroe Sts.
15 rooms - $25-39
Pets: Welcome
Creature Comforts: CCTV, a/c

Eureka Motel
(775) 237-5247
10289 Main St.
17 rooms - $28-55
Pets: Welcome
Creature Comforts: CCTV, a/c

Jackson House B&B
(775) 237-5577
10200 Main St.
8 rooms - $40-68
Pets: Welcome
Creature Comforts: CCTV, a/c

Ruby Hill Motel
(775) 237-5339
Route 50
11 rooms - $30-49
Pets: Welcome
Creature Comforts: CCTV, a/c

Sundown Lodge
(775) 237-5334
Main St.
27 rooms - $30-49
Pets: Welcome
Creature Comforts: CCTV, a/c

FALLON
Bonanza Inn & Casino
(775) 423-6031
855 W. Williams Ave.
77 rooms - $45-89
Pets: Welcome
Creature Comforts: CCTV, a/c, refrig, micro, restaurant, pool

Budget Inn
(775) 423-2277
1705 S. Taylor St.
21 rooms - $40-67
Pets: Welcome
Creature Comforts: CCTV, a/c, refrig, micro

Nevada Belle Motel
(775) 423-4648
25 N. Taylor St.
27 rooms - $30-59
Pets: Welcome
Creature Comforts: CCTV, a/c, refrig, micro, pool

Oxbow Motor Inn
(775) 423-7021
60 S. Allen St.
51 rooms - $45-88
Pets: Welcome
Creature Comforts: CCTV, a/c, whirlpool

Value Inn
(775) 423-5151
180 W. Williams St.
22 rooms - $35-59
Pets: Welcome
Creature Comforts: CCTV, a/c, refrig, micro, pool

Western Motel
(775) 423-5118
125 S. Carson St.
22 rooms - $35-450
Pets: Small pets w/$3 fee
Creature Comforts: CCTV, a/c, refrig, pool

FERNLEY
Lahontan Motel
(775) 575-2744
135 E. Main St.
12 rooms - $35-48
Pets: Welcome
Creature Comforts: CCTV, a/c

Rest Rancho Motel
(800) 682-6445, (775) 575-4452
325 Main St.
46 rooms - $25-59
Pets: Welcome
Creature Comforts: CCTV, a/c, refrig, micro, restaurant, pool

GARDNERVILLE
Nenzel Mansion B&B
(775) 782-7644
1431 Ezell St.
5 rooms - $80-120
Pets: Welcome, St. Bernard and Bassett Hound in residence
Creature Comforts: 1910 mansion, porches, renovated w/ period accents intact, great sitting room w/marble fireplace, wicker and brass beds, antique baths, antiques, CCTV, a/c, full brkfst

Topaz Lodge & Casino
(800) 962-0732, (775) 266-3338
1979 Route 395 S.
58 rooms - $39-64
Pets: Welcome w/$5 deposit
Creature Comforts: CCTV, a/c, restaurant, pool

GENOA
Genoa House Inn
(702) 782-7075
Box 141
3 rooms - $115-130
Pets: Dogs only, morning treats
Creature Comforts: 1872 Nat'l Historic Register Victorian, tucked into mountainside, antiques, afternoon wine, full brkfst, Jacuzzi, local hot springs, rqst Garden Rm w/outside entrance, dog-friendly park just across from house

477

HAWTHORNE

Best Western Desert Lodge
(800) 528-1234, (775) 945-2660
http://www.bestwestern.com
1402 E. Fifth St.
39 rooms - $55-86
Pets: Welcome
Creature Comforts: CCTV, a/c, pool, whirlpool

Cliff House Lakeside Resort
(775) 945-2444
1 Cliff House Dr.
12 rooms - $30-45
Pets: Welcome
Creature Comforts: CCTV, a/c, kit, restaurant

El Capitan Lodge & Casino
(775) 945-3321
540 F St.
103 rooms - $30-49
Pets: Welcome w/$10 deposit
Creature Comforts: CCTV, a/c

Hawthorne Motel
(775) 945-2544
72-Sierra Hwy 95
14 rooms - $24-39
Pets: Welcome
Creature Comforts: CCTV, a/c, kit

Holiday Lodge
(775) 945-3316
Fifth and J Sts.
23 rooms - $27-45
Pets: Welcome
Creature Comforts: CCTV, a/c, kit

Monarch Motel
(775) 945-3117
1291 E. Fifth St.
9 rooms - $25-45
Pets: Welcome
Creature Comforts: CCTV, a/c

Rocket Motel
(702) 945-2143
694 Sierra Way
14 rooms - $25-45
Pets: Welcome
Creature Comforts: CCTV, a/c, kit

Wright Motel
(775) 945-2213
West Fifth and I Sts.
9 rooms - $30-48
Pets: Welcome
Creature Comforts: CCTV, a/c

HENDERSON

Bobby Motel
(702) 565-9711
2100 S. Boulder Hwy.
21 rooms - $25-45
Pets: Welcome
Creature Comforts: CCTV, a/c, restaurant

Outpost Motel
(702) 564-2664
1104 N. Boulder Hwy.
20 rooms - $36-49
Pets: Welcome
Creature Comforts: CCTV, a/c, kit

Sky Motel
(702) 564-1534
1713 N. Boulder Hwy.
21 rooms - $35-57
Pets: Welcome
Creature Comforts: CCTV, a/c, refrig, micro, kit, fireplace, Jacuzzi, restaurant, cont. brkfst, pool, hlth clb access, sauna, whirlpool

INDIAN SPRINGS

Indian Springs Motor Hotel
(702) 879-3700
320 E. Tonopah Hwy.
45 rooms - $25-55
Pets: Welcome w/$5 fee
Creature Comforts: CCTV, a/c, refrig, micro, restaurant

JACKPOT

Barton's Club 93
(775) 755-2341
Route 93
60 rooms - $20-55
Pets: Welcome
Creature Comforts: CCTV, a/c, restaurant

Horseshu Hotel & Casino
(775) 755-7777
http://www.ameristars.com
1385 Rte. 93
121 rooms - $30-95
Pets: Welcome
Creature Comforts: CCTV, a/c, pool, whirlpool, golf

JAYBRIDGE

Outdoor Inn
(702) 488-2311
Main St.
15 rooms - $30-69
Pets: Welcome
Creature Comforts: CCTV, a/c, kit, restaurant

LAKE TAHOE, NORTH

Augustus Associates
(800) 40-TAHOE, (702) 831-2846
Box 4030, Incline Vlg.
24 rooms - $100-395
Pets: Welcome
Creature Comforts: CCTV, a/c, pool

Forest Pines Rental Agency
(800) 458-2463, (702) 831-1307
123 Juanita Dr., Incline Vlg.
40 rooms - $95-175
Pets: Welcome
Creature Comforts: CCTV, VCR, a/c, kit, fireplace, Jacuzzi, pool, whirlpool

Lake Tahoe Reservations/ Crystal Management
(800) 424-8988, (702) 831-8988
774 Mays Blvd., Incline Vlg.
57 rooms - $75-1,200
Pets: Welcome
Creature Comforts: CCTV, VCR, a/c, kit, fireplace, Jacuzzi, pool, whirlpool

Lakeside Sales Co.
(800) 831-3099, (702) 831-0752
956 Lakeshore Blvd., Incline Vlg.
25 rooms - $125-560
Pets: Welcome
Creature Comforts: CCTV, VCR, a/c, kit, fireplace, Jacuzzi, pool, whirlpool

Omni Properties
(800) 338-4884, (702) 832-3003
923 Tahoe Blvd., Incline Vlg.
20 rooms - $100-230
Pets: Welcome
Creature Comforts: CCTV, VCR, a/c, kit, fireplace, Jacuzzi, pool, whirlpool

LAKE TAHOE, SOUTH
Glenbrook Resort
(702) 749-5662
2070 Pray Meadow Rd
30 rooms - $235-445
Pets: Welcome
Creature Comforts: Upscale
condominiums, CCTV, VCR, a/c,
kit, fireplace

Zephyr Cove Resort
(702) 588-6644
http://www.tahoedixie2.com/
Resort.html
760 Rte. 50
30 rooms - $65-285
Pets: Welcome w/$5 fee
Creature Comforts: 1900's Lake
Tahoe resort, classic rambling
shingle style main lodge, rustic
cabins, rqst lakefront, family
favorite, CCTV, kit, fireplace,
restaurant, boating, swimming,
paddle boat

LAMOILLE
Breitenstein House B&B
(702) 753-6356
Box 281381
4 rooms - $55-135
Pets: Welcome
Creature Comforts: CCTV, a/c,
restaurant, whirlpool

Pine Lodge/Hotel Lamoille
(702) 753-6363
Lamoille Hi-way
3 rooms - $55-95
Pets: Welcome
Creature Comforts: CCTV, a/c,
restaurant

LAS VEGAS
Alexis Park Resort
(800) 582-2228, (702) 796-3300
http://www.alexispark.com
375 E. Harmon Ave.
500 suites - $80-1,250
Pets: Welcome w/$50 fee
Creature Comforts: CCTV,
VCR, a/c, refrig, kit, Jacuzzi,
fireplaces, 3 pools, hlth club,
whirlpool, and a sauna

Barker Motel
(702) 642-1138
2600 Las Vegas Blvd., N.
26 rooms - $26-80
Pets: Welcome
Creature Comforts: CCTV, a/c,
kit, pool, whirlpool

Best Western Heritage
(800) 528-1234, (702) 798-7736
http://www.bestwestern.com
4975 S. Valley View Blvd.
59 rooms - $70-135
Pets: Welcome
Creature Comforts: CCTV, a/c,
cont. brkfst, pool, hlth clb access,
sauna, whirlpool

Best Western Main Street
(800) 528-1234, (702) 382-3455
http://www.bestwestern.com
1000 N. Main St.
91 rooms - $51-125
Pets: Small pets w/$8 fee
Creature Comforts: CCTV, a/c,
cont. brkfst, pool

Best Western Nellis
(800) 528-1234, (702) 643-6111
http://www.bestwestern.com
5330 E. Craig Rd.
52 rooms - $48-150
Pets: Welcome w/$5 fee, $50 dep
Creature Comforts: CCTV, a/c,
pool

Best Western Parkview
(800) 528-1234, (702) 385-1213
http://www.bestwestern.com
905 Las Vegas Blvd., N.
56 rooms - $45-129
Pets: Small pets w/$8 fee
Creature Comforts: CCTV, a/c,
pool

Center Strip Inn
(702) 739-6066
3688 Las Vegas Blvd.
152 rooms - $30-190
Pets: Welcome
Creature Comforts: CCTV,
VCR, a/c, refrig, micro, cont.
brkfst, Jacuzzi, pool

City Center Motel
(702) 382-4766
700 E. Fremont St.
57 rooms - $35-90
Pets: Welcome
Creature Comforts: CCTV, a/c,
pool

Comfort Inn, North
(800) 228-5150, (702) 399-1500
http://www.comfortinn.com
910 E. Cheyenne Rd.
59 rooms - $80-185
Pets: Small pets welcome
Creature Comforts: CCTV, a/c,
refrig, micro, kit, Jacuzzis, cont.
brkfst, pool, whirlpool

Crowne Plaza
(800) HOLIDAY, (702) 369-4400
http://www.holiday-inn.com
4255 S. Paradise Rd.
201 rooms - $95-195
Pets: Suites w/$200 dep.
Creature Comforts: CCTV, a/c,
micro, restaurant, pool, hlth clb
access, sauna, whirlpool

Daisy Motel & Apartments
(702) 382-0707
415 S. Main St.
151 rooms - $35-65
Pets: Welcome
Creature Comforts: CCTV, a/c,
kit, pool

Desert Star Motel
(702) 382-1066
1210 Las Vegas Blvd.
40 rooms - $35-159
Pets: Welcome
Creature Comforts: CCTV, a/c,
kit, pool

E-Z 8 Motel
(800) 326-6835, (702) 735-9513
5201 S. Industrial Rd.
127 rooms - $25-49
Pets: Welcome
Creature Comforts: CCTV, a/c,
pool

Fergusons Motel
(800) 933-7829, (702) 382-3500
1028 E. Fremont St.
66 rooms - $30-109
Pets: Welcome w/$50 deposit
Creature Comforts: CCTV, a/c,
pool

Gateway Motel
(702) 382-2146
928 Las Vegas Blvd.
46 rooms - $25-60
Pets: Welcome
Creature Comforts: CCTV, a/c

Gatewood Motel
(702) 457-3660
3075 E. Fremont St.
19 rooms - $35-79
Pets: Welcome
Creature Comforts: CCTV, a/c

Glass Pool Inn
(800) 527-7118, (702) 739-6636
4613 Las Vegas Blvd., S.
46 rooms - $30-105
Pets: Welcome
Creature Comforts: CCTV, a/c,
kit, restaurant, pool

Golden Inn Motel
(702) 384-8204
120 Las Vegas Blvd. N.
71 rooms - $20-109
Pets: Welcome
Creature Comforts: CCTV, a/c,
pool

Holiday Inn Express
(800) HOLIDAY, (702) 256-3766
http://www.holiday-inn.com
8669 W. Sahara Ave.
59 rooms - $70-148
Pets: Small pets welcome
Creature Comforts: CCTV, a/c,
refrig, micro, cont. brkfst, Jacuzzi,
pool, sauna, whirlpool

Holiday Royale Apt. Suites
(800) 732-7676, (702) 733-7676
4505 Paradise Rd.
298 rooms - $120-235/wk.
Pets: Welcome
Creature Comforts: CCTV, a/c,
kit, pool

Howard Johnson
(800) I-Go-Hojo, (702) 388-0301
http://www.hojo.com
1401 Las Vegas Blvd.
104 rooms - $50-90
Pets: Welcome
Creature Comforts: CCTV, a/c,
refrig, restaurant, whirlpool

King Albert Motel
(800) 553-7753, (702) 732-1555
185 Albert Ave.
100 rooms - $35-65
Pets: Welcome
Creature Comforts: CCTV, a/c,
kit, pool

Knotty Pine Motel
(702) 642-8300
1900 Las Vegas Blvd.
20 rooms - $22-45
Pets: Welcome
Creature Comforts: CCTV, a/c,
kit

La Quinta Motor Inn
(800) 796-9000, (702) 739-7457
http://www.laquinta.com
3782 Las Vegas Blvd.
114 rooms - $55-95
Pets: Small pets welcome
Creature Comforts: CCTV, a/c,
pool

Lucky Lady Motel
(702) 385-1093
1308 E. Fremont St.
18 rooms - $40-159
Pets: Welcome
Creature Comforts: CCTV, a/c,
kit

Motel 8 - Mr. Deli
(702) 798-7223
3961 Las Vegas Blvd. S.
30 rooms - $25-110
Pets: Welcome
Creature Comforts: CCTV, a/c,
restaurant, pool

Motel 6
(800) 4 MOTEL6, (702) 457-8051
http://www.motel6.com
4125 Boulder Hwy.
161 rooms - $30-58
Pets: Under 30 lbs. welcome
Creature Comforts: CCTV, a/c,
pool

Motel 6
(800) 4 MOTEL6, (702) 739-6747
http://www.motel6.com
5085 S. Industrial Rd.
139 rooms - $30-59
Pets: Under 30 lbs. welcome
Creature Comforts: CCTV, a/c,
pool

Motel 6
(800) 4 MOTEL6, (702) 798-0728
http://www.motel6.com
195 E. Tropicana Ave.
63 rooms - $30-50
Pets: Under 30 lbs. welcome
Creature Comforts: CCTV, a/c,
pool

Regency Motel
(702) 382-2332
700 N. Main St.
30 rooms - $30-54
Pets: Welcome
Creature Comforts: CCTV, a/c,
pool

Residence Inn
(800) 331-3131, (702) 796-9300
http://www.residenceinn.com
3225 Paradise Rd.
192 rooms - $90-260
Pets: Welcome w/$100 deposit
Creature Comforts: CCTV,
VCR, a/c, refrig, micro, kit, pool,
hlth clb access, sauna, whirlpool

Silver Queen
(702) 384-8157
1401 E. Carson St.
14 rooms - $25-50
Pets: Welcome
Creature Comforts: CCTV, a/c,
kit

Super 8
(800) 800-8000, (702) 794-0888
http://www.super8.com
4250 Koval Ln.
290 rooms - $42-60
Pets: Welcome
Creature Comforts: CCTV, a/c,
restaurant, pool, whirlpool

Tam O'Shanter Motel
(800) 727-DICE, (702) 735-7331
3317 Las Vegas Blvd. S.
98 rooms - $40-75
Pets: Welcome
Creature Comforts: CCTV, a/c,
pool

Travel Inn Motel
(702) 384-3040
217 Las Vegas Blvd. N.
57 rooms - $30-120
Pets: Welcome
Creature Comforts: CCTV, a/c,
pool

Vagabond Inn, Center Strip
(800) 828-8032, (702) 735-5102
http://www.vagabondinn.com
1919 E. Fremont St.
126 rooms - $45-139
Pets: Welcome
Creature Comforts: CCTV, a/c,
pool

Vagabond Motel
(702) 387-1650
1919 E. Fremont St.
17 rooms - $30-55
Pets: Welcome
Creature Comforts: CCTV, a/c,
kit, pool

Valley Motel
(702) 384-6490
1313 E. Fremont St.
22 rooms - $30-60
Pets: Welcome
Creature Comforts: CCTV, a/c

Wellesley Inn
(800) 444-8888, (702) 731-3111
www.wellesleyinnandsuites.com
1550 E. Flamingo Rd.
125 rooms - $50-99
Pets: Small pets w/CC dep.
Creature Comforts: CCTV, a/c,
kit, pool, hlth club, cont. brkfst

LAUGHLIN
Bay Shore Inn
(702) 299-9010
1955 W. Casino Dr.
40 rooms - $25-45
Pets: Small pets w/$10 fee
Creature Comforts: CCTV, a/c,
restaurant, pool, hlth clb access,
sauna, whirlpool

Don Laughlins Riverside Rsrt.
(702) 298-2535
1650 S. Casino Dr.
1404 rooms - $39-140
Pets: With $8 fee & $100 deposit
Creature Comforts: CCTV, a/c,
restaurant, pool, whirlpool, casino

LOVELOCK
Cadillac Inn
(702) 273-2798
1395 Cornell Ave.
12 rooms - $20-40
Pets: Welcome
Creature Comforts: CCTV, a/c,
kit

Covered Wagon Motel
(702) 273-2961
945 Dartmouth Ave.
16 rooms - $35-45
Pets: Welcome
Creature Comforts: CCTV, a/c,
kit

Desert Haven Motel
(702) 273-2339
885 Dartmouth Ave.
17 rooms - $25-45
Pets: Welcome
Creature Comforts: CCTV, a/c,
kit

Lovelock Inn
(702) 273-2937
Route 40 W.
37 rooms - $40-65
Pets: Welcome
Creature Comforts: CCTV, a/c,
kit, pool

National 9 Motel
(702) 273-2224
1390 Cornell Ave.
10 rooms - $25-45
Pets: Welcome
Creature Comforts: CCTV, a/c

Sage Motel
(702) 273-0444
1335 Cornell Ave.
7 rooms - $17-39
Pets: Welcome
Creature Comforts: CCTV, a/c

Sierra Motel
(702) 273-2798
14th & Dartmouth Ave.
14 rooms - $20-49
Pets: Welcome
Creature Comforts: CCTV, a/c

Sunset Motel
(702) 273-7366
1145 Cornell Ave.
14 rooms - $20-45
Pets: Welcome
Creature Comforts: CCTV, a/c,
kit

McDERMITT
Diamond A Motel
(702) 532-8551
140 S. Rte. 95
11 rooms - $27-45
Pets: Welcome
Creature Comforts: CCTV, a/c

McDermitt Motel
(702) 532-8588
Route 95
23 rooms - $30-49
Pets: Welcome
Creature Comforts: CCTV, a/c

MESQUITE
Budget Inn & Suites
(702) 346-7444
390 N. Sandhill Dr.
68 rooms - $50-69
Pets: Welcome w/$25 deposit
Creature Comforts: CCTV, a/c,
kit, Jacuzzi, pool, whirlpool

Desert Palms Motel
(702) 346-5756
Mesquite Blvd.
21 rooms - $30-59
Pets: Welcome
Creature Comforts: TV, a/c, kit

Si Redds Oasis Hotel
(800) 621-0187, (702) 346-5232
1137 Mesquite Blvd.
738 rooms - $40-68
Pets: Welcome w/$100 deposit
Creature Comforts: CCTV, a/c,
refrig, micro, Jacuzzi, restaurant,
pool, hlth clb access, sauna,
whirlpool

Valley Inn Motel
(702) 346-5281
791 W. Mesquite Blvd.
17 rooms - $30-65
Pets: Welcome
Creature Comforts: CCTV, a/c,
pool

Virgin River Hotel/Casino
(800) 346-7721, (702) 346-7777
915 Mesquite Blvd.
721 rooms - $20-55
Pets: Welcome w/$25 deposit
Creature Comforts: CCTV, a/c,
restaurant, pool, whirlpool

MILL CITY
Super 8
(800) 800-8000, (702) 538-7311
http://www.super8.com
Route 80
50 rooms - $49-89
Pets: Welcome w/$5 fee
Creature Comforts: CCTV, a/c,
restaurant

MINDEN
Best Western Minden
(800) 528-1234, (775) 782-7766
http://www.bestwestern.com
1795 Ironwood Dr.
81 rooms - $45-129
Pets: Welcome w/$5 fee
Creature Comforts: CCTV, a/c,
pool

Holiday Lodge
(800) 266-2289, (775) 782-2288
1591 Route 395
20 rooms - $30-59
Pets: Welcome w/$3 fee, $20 dep.
Creature Comforts: CCTV, a/c, kit, restaurant, pool

MT. CHARLESTON
Mt. Charleston Resort
(800) 955-1314, (702) 872-5408
Mt. Charleston/Kyle Canyon Rd.
23 rooms - $125-249
Pets: Welcome w/$10 fee
Creature Comforts: New log cabins, porch swings, exposed log walls, immaculate, hand-crafted furniture, quilts, central fireplace, parquet floors, CCTV, Jacuzzi, exc. restaurant, riding stables

MOUNTAIN CITY
Chambers' Motel
(702) 763-6626
Box 188
11 rooms - $30-49
Pets: Welcome
Creature Comforts: CCTV, a/c

Mountain City Motel
(702) 763-6617
Box 102
14 rooms - $30-76
Pets: Welcome
Creature Comforts: CCTV, a/c, kit, restaurant

OASIS
Oasis Motel
(702) 478-5113
I-80, Exit 378
5 rooms - $20-45
Pets: Welcome
Creature Comforts: A/C

OLD NEVADA
Bonnie Springs Motel
(702) 875-4400
One Gunfighter Ln.
50 rooms - $55-135
Pets: Welcome
Creature Comforts: CCTV, a/c, kit, restaurant, pool, sauna, whirlpool

OVERTON
Echo Bay Resort
(800) 752-9669, (702) 394-4000
Route 167
52 rooms - $75-95
Pets: Welcome w/$5 fee, $25 dep.
Creature Comforts: Lakeside setting-Lake Mead, CCTV, a/c, restaurant, boating, swimming, fishing

PAHRUMP
Charlotta Inn Motel
(702) 727-5445
1201 S. Route 160
17 rooms - $28-45
Pets: Welcome
Creature Comforts: CCTV, a/c, pool

Days Inn, Pahrump Station
(800) DAYS INN, (702) 727-5100
http://www.daysinn.com
Route 160 N.
45 rooms - $50-105
Pets: Welcome w/$6 fee
Creature Comforts: CCTV, a/c, Jacuzzi, cont. brkfst, pool

Saddle West Hotel
(775)727-1111
1220 W. Route 160
110 rooms - $40-125
Pets: Small pets w/$100 deposit
Creature Comforts: CCTV, a/c, Jacuzzi, cont. brkfst, restaurant, pool, casino

PIOCHE
Hutchings Motel
(702) 962-5404
Route 93
5 rooms - $30-49
Pets: Welcome
Creature Comforts: CCTV, a/c

Motel Pioche
(702) 962-5551
100 LaCour St.
9 rooms - $30-46
Pets: Welcome
Creature Comforts: TV, a/c, kit

RENO
Bonanza Motor Inn
(800) 808-3303, (775) 322-8632
215 W. Fourth St.
57 rooms - $40-129
Pets: Welcome
Creature Comforts: CCTV, a/c, pool

Castaway Inn
(775) 329-2555
525 W. Second St.
45 rooms - $150-280/wk.
Pets: Welcome
Creature Comforts: CCTV, a/c, kit

Days Inn
(800) DAYS INN, (775) 786-4070
http://www.daysinn.com
701 E. Seventh St.
137 rooms - $35-115
Pets: Welcome w/$10 fee
Creature Comforts: CCTV, a/c, pool

Donner Inn Motel
(775) 323-1851
720 W. Fourth St.
34 rooms - $30-50
Pets: Welcome
Creature Comforts: CCTV, a/c, restaurant, pool

Downtowner Motor Lodge
(775) 322-1188
150 Stevenson St.
38 rooms - $30-50
Pets: Welcome
Creature Comforts: CCTV, a/c, kit, pool

El Patio Motel
(775) 825-6666
3495 S. Virginia St.
53 rooms - $40-59
Pets: Welcome
Creature Comforts: CCTV, a/c, kit, pool

El Ray Motel
(775) 329-6669
330 N. Arlington
23 rooms - $35-129
Pets: Welcome
Creature Comforts: CCTV, a/c

El Tavern Motel
(775) 322-4504
1801 W. Fourth St.
42 rooms - $35-48
Pets: Welcome
Creature Comforts: TV, a/c, kit

Farris Motel
(775) 322-3190
1752 E. Fourth St.
32 rooms - $85-165/wk.
Pets: Welcome
Creature Comforts: TV, a/c, kit

Gatekeeper Inn
(800) 822-3504, (775) 786-3500
221 W. Fifth St.
28 rooms - $36-99
Pets: Welcome w/notice
Creature Comforts: CCTV, a/c

Gateway Inn
(800) 345-2910, (775) 747-4220
1275 Stardust St.
102 rooms - $35-110
Pets: Welcome
Creature Comforts: CCTV, a/c,
restaurant, pool

Gold Coin Motel
(775) 323-0237
2555 E. Fourth St.
16 rooms - $30-65
Pets: Welcome
Creature Comforts: CCTV, a/c,
kit

Holiday Inn, Downtown
(800) HOLIDAY, (775) 786-5151
http://www.holiday-inn.com
1000 E. Sixth St.
rooms - $60-199
Pets: Welcome
Creature Comforts: CCTV,
VCR, a/c, refrig, restaurant, pool

Howard Johnson
(800) I-Go-Hojo, (775) 322-8181
http://www.hojo.com
567 W. Fourth St.
108 rooms - $40-77
Pets: Medium pets w/$35 deposit
Creature Comforts: CCTV, a/c,
refrig, restaurant, pool

Keno Motel
(775) 322-6281
322 N. Arlington St.
20 rooms - $25-38
Pets: Welcome
Creature Comforts: CCTV, a/c

La Quinta Inn
(800) 531-5900, (775) 348-6100
http://www.laquinta.com
4001 Market St.
130 rooms - $55-89
Pets: Small pets welcome
Creature Comforts: CCTV, a/c,
refrig

Motel 500
(775) 786-2777
500 S. Center St.
26 rooms - $25-50
Pets: Welcome
Creature Comforts: CCTV, a/c

Motel 6
(800) 4 MOTEL6, (775) 329-8681
http://www.motel6.com
666 N. Wells Ave.
97 rooms - $30-45
Pets: Under 30 lbs. welcome
Creature Comforts: CCTV, a/c

Motel 6
(800) 4 MOTEL6, (775) 786-9852
http://www.motel6.com
866 N. Wells Ave.
142 rooms - $25-39
Pets: Under 30 lbs. welcome
Creature Comforts: CCTV, a/c

Motel 6
(800) 4 MOTEL6, (775) 747-7390
http://www.motel6.com
1400 Stardust St.
123 rooms - $30-48
Pets: Under 30 lbs. welcome
Creature Comforts: CCTV, a/c

Olympic Apartment Hotel
(775) 323-0726
195 W. Second St.
19 rooms - $45-95
Pets: Under 30 lbs. welcome
Creature Comforts: CCTV, a/c,
kit

Plaza Motor Lodge
(775) 786-1077
11 E. Plaza St.
10 rooms - $30-85
Pets: Welcome
Creature Comforts: CCTV, a/c

Ponderosa Motel
(775) 786-3070
595 Lake St.
25 rooms - $35-78
Pets: Welcome
Creature Comforts: CCTV, kit

Ranch Motel
(775) 851-1129
7400 S. Virginia St.
21 rooms - $25-45
Pets: Welcome
Creature Comforts: CTV, a/c, kit

Residence Inn
(800) 331-3131, (702) 853-8800
http://www.residenceinn.com
9845 Gateway Dr.
120 rooms - $100-165
Pets: With a $6 daily fee and a
$75 cleaning charge
Creature Comforts: CCTV,
VCR, a/c, kit, pool, hlth clb

River House Motor Hotel
(775) 329-0036
2 Lake St.
32 rooms - $50-68
Pets: Welcome
Creature Comforts: CCTV, a/c

Seasons Inn
(800) 322-8588, (775) 322-6000
495 West St.
56 rooms - $40-109
Pets: Welcome w/$10 fee
Creature Comforts: CCTV, a/c

Silver Dollar Motor Lodge
(775) 323-6875
817 N. Virginia St.
26 rooms - $35-49
Pets: Welcome
Creature Comforts: CTV, a/c, kit

Silver State Lodge
(775) 322-1380
1791 W. Fourth St.
57 rooms - $100-225/wk
Pets: Welcome
Creature Comforts: CTV, a/c, kit

Sundance Motel
(800) 438-5660, (775) 329-9248
850 N. Virginia St.
41 rooms - $30-59
Pets: Welcome
Creature Comforts: CCTV, a/c,
kit, pool

Super 8
(800) 800-8000, (775) 825-2940
http://www.super8.com
5851 S. Virginia St.
151 rooms - $45-59
Pets: Welcome
Creature Comforts: CCTV, a/c,
cont. brkfst, pool, whirlpool

Travelodge
(800) 578-7878, (775) 329-3451
http://www.travelodge.com
655 W. Fourth St.
98 rooms - $30-99
Pets: Welcome in pet rooms
Creature Comforts: CCTV, a/c,
pool

Travelodge, Central
(800) 578-7878, (775) 786-2500
http://www.travelodge.com
2050 Market St.
210 rooms - $32-149
Pets: Welcome w/$5 daily fee
Creature Comforts: CCTV, a/c,
kit, restaurant, cont. brkfst, pool,
sauna, whirlpool

Truckee River Lodge
(800) 635-8950, (775) 786-888
501 W. First St.
227 rooms - $35-198
Pets: Welcome
Creature Comforts: CCTV, a/c,
restaurant, hlth clb

Vagabond Inn
(800) 522-1555, (775) 825-7134
http://www.vagabondinn.com
3131 S. Virginia St.
129 rooms - $40-75
Pets: Small pets w/$5 fee
Creature Comforts: CCTV, a/c,
pool

SEARCHLIGHT
El Rey Motel
(702) 457-8051
430 S. Hobson & Rte. 95
21 rooms - $35-59
Pets: Welcome
Creature Comforts: CCTV, a/c

SPARKS
Blue Fountain Inn
(800) 359-0359, (702) 367-7366
1590 Victorian Ave.
68 rooms - $35-57
Pets: Welcome
Creature Comforts: CCTV, a/c

InnCal
(800) 550-0055, (702) 358-2222
255 N. McCarran Blvd.
133 rooms - $25-96
Pets: Welcome
Creature Comforts: CCTV, a/c,
restaurant

Motel 6
(800) 4 MOTEL6, (702) 358-1080
http://www.motel6.com
2405 Victorian Ave.
95 rooms - $33-49
Pets: Under 30 lbs. welcome
Creature Comforts: CCTV,
VCR, a/c, whirlpool

Pony Express Lodge
(702) 358-7110
2406 Prater Way
101 rooms - $30-58
Pets: Welcome
Creature Comforts: CCTV, a/c,
kit

Silver Club Hotel & Casino
(800) 648-1137, (702) 358-4771
1040 Victorian Ave.
206 rooms - $40-76
Pets: Small pets welcome
Creature Comforts: CCTV, a/c,
refrig, restaurant

STATELINE
Super 8
(800) 800-8000, (702) 358-8884
http://www.super8.com
1900 E. Greg Str.
71 rooms - $48-65
Pets: Welcome w/ CC deposit
Creature Comforts: CCTV, a/c,
pool

TONOPAH
Best Western Hi-Desert Inn
(800) 528-1234, (702) 482-3511
http://www.bestwestern.com
320 Main St.
62 rooms - $50-79
Pets: Welcome, no puppies
Creature Comforts: CCTV, a/c,
pool, hlth clb access

Gloden Hills Motel
(702) 482-6238
826 Erie Main St.
40 rooms - $20-42
Pets: Welcome
Creature Comforts: CCTV, a/c,
restaurant

Jim Butler Motel
(800) 635-9455, (702) 482-3577
320 Main St.
25 rooms - $35-49
Pets: Small pets welcome, no cats
Creature Comforts: CCTV, a/c,
refrig, 5 restaurants

Mizpah Hotel & Casino
(800) 646-4641, (702) 482-6202
100 Main St.
45 rooms - $30-66
Pets: Welcome
Creature Comforts: CCTV, a/c,
restaurant

Silver Queen Motel
(702) 482-6291
255 Erie Main St.
85 rooms - $28-48
Pets: Welcome
Creature Comforts: CCTV, a/c,
kit, restaurant, pool

Sundowner Motel
(702) 482-6224
700 Route 95
93 rooms - $25-45
Pets: Welcome
Creature Comforts: CCTV, a/c,
kit, restaurant

Tonopah Motel
(702) 482-3987
325 Main St.
20 rooms - $25-55
Pets: Welcome
Creature Comforts: CCTV, a/c,
kit

UNIONVILLE
Old Pioneer Garden B&B
(702) 538-7585
79 Main St.
9 rooms - $65-89
Pets: Welcome
Creature Comforts: CCTV, a/c,
kit, restaurant

VIRGINIA CITY
Crooked House B&B
(800) 340-6353, (775) 847-4447
8 South "F" Street, Box 646
4 rooms - $75-125
Pets: Selectively welcomed
Creature Comforts: A charing
home built in 1870s, original
features, CCTV, a/c, kit, claw
footed tubs

Gold Hill Hotel
(702) 847-0111
Main St.
13 rooms - $40-85
Pets: Welcome
Creature Comforts: CCTV, a/c,
kit

Silver Queen
(702) 847-0440
28 N. C Street
29 rooms - $40-77
Pets: Welcome
Creature Comforts: CCTV, a/c

Spargo House B&B
(702) 847-7455
395 S. B Street
3 rooms - $60-85
Pets: Welcome
Creature Comforts: CCTV, a/c,
kit, full brkfst

WELLS
Best Western Sage Motel
(800) 528-1234, (702) 752-3353
http://www.bestwestern.com
576 Sixth St.
24 rooms - $40-65
Pets: Small pets w/$5 fee
Creature Comforts: CCTV, a/c,
refrig, micro, pool

Lone Star Motel
(702) 752-3632
676 Sixth St.
10 rooms - $25-55
Pets: Welcome
Creature Comforts: CCTV, a/c,
kit

Motel 6
(800) 4 MOTEL6, (702) 752-2116
http://www.motel6.com
Rtes. 80 & 93
122 rooms - $25-49
Pets: Welcome
Creature Comforts: CCTV, a/c,
pool

Mountain View Motel
(702) 752-3345
134 Sixth St.
14 rooms - $20-39
Pets: Welcome
Creature Comforts: CCTV, a/c

Rest Inn Suites
(702) 752-2277
1250 E. Sixth St.
56 rooms - $40-69
Pets: Small pets w/$6 fee
Creature Comforts: CCTV, a/c,
refrig, micro

Sharon Motel
(702) 752-3232
633 Sixth St.
10 rooms - $20-58
Pets: Welcome
Creature Comforts: CCTV, a/c,
refrig, micro

Shell Crest Motel
(702) 752-3755
575 Sixth St.
12 rooms - $20-59
Pets: Welcome
Creature Comforts: CCTV, a/c,
kit

Super 8
(800) 800-8000, (702) 752-3384
http://www.super8.com
930 Sixth St.
57 rooms - $45-68
Pets: Welcome w/$5 fee
Creature Comforts: CCTV, a/c,
refrig, micro, pool

Wagon Wheel Motel
(702) 752-2151
326 Sixth St.
30 rooms - $20-47
Pets: Welcome
Creature Comforts: CCTV, a/c

Wells Chinatown
(702) 752-2101
455 S. Humboldt St.
19 rooms - $30-55
Pets: Welcome
Creature Comforts: CCTV, a/c

WENDOVER
Super 8
(800) 800-8000, (435) 664-2888
http://www.super8.com
Wendover Blvd.
74 rooms - $45-75
Pets: Welcome
Creature Comforts: CCTV, a/c

Western Ridge Motel
(435) 665-2211
Off Route 80
55 rooms - $30-75
Pets: Small pets welcome
Creature Comforts: CCTV, a/c

WINNEMUCCA
Best Western Gold Country Inn
(800) 528-1234, (775) 623-6999
http://www.bestwestern.com
921 W. Winnemucca Blvd.
72 rooms - $90-180
Pets: Welcome
Creature Comforts: CCTV, a/c,
cont. brkfst, pool

Best Western Holiday Motel
(800) 528-1234, (775) 623-3684
http://www.bestwestern.com
670 W. Winnemucca Blvd.
40 rooms - $60-89
Pets: Welcome
Creature Comforts: CCTV, a/c,
cont. brkfst, pool

Bull Head Motel
(775) 623-3636
500 E. Winnemucca Blvd.
46 rooms - $35-65
Pets: Welcome
Creature Comforts: CCTV, a/c

Cozy Motel
(775) 623-2615
344 E. Winnemucca Blvd.
16 rooms - $30-50
Pets: Welcome
Creature Comforts: CCTV, a/c,
kit

Days Inn
(800) DAYS INN, (702) 623-3661
http://www.daysinn.com
511 W. Winnemucca Blvd.
50 rooms - $65-75
Pets: Welcome w/$10 fee
Creature Comforts: CCTV, a/c,
refrig, micro, pool

Downtown Motel
(775) 623-2394
251 Winnemucca Blvd.
16 rooms - $30-55
Pets: Welcome
Creature Comforts: CCTV, a/c

Frontier Motel
(775) 623-2915
410 Winnemucca Blvd.
30 rooms - $40-69
Pets: Welcome
Creature Comforts: CCTV,
a/c, and a pool

La Villa Motel
(775) 623-2334
Fourth and Aiken Sts.
38 rooms - $35-75
Pets: Welcome
Creature Comforts: CCTV, a/c

Motel T Motel
(800) 645-5658, (775) 623-0222
1122 Winnemucca Blvd.
75 rooms - $35-89
Pets: Welcome
Creature Comforts: CCTV, a/c,
restaurant, pool

Motel 6
(800) 4 MOTEL6, (775) 623-1180
http://www.motel6.com
1600 Winnemucca Blvd.
103 rooms - $30-45
Pets: Under 30 lbs. welcome
Creature Comforts: CCTV, a/c

Nevada Motel
(775) 623-5281
635 W. Winnemucca Blvd.
28 rooms - $25-85
Pets: Welcome
Creature Comforts: CCTV, a/c,
pool

Park Motel
(775) 623-2810
740 Winnemucca Blvd.
19 rooms - $30-49
Pets: Welcome
Creature Comforts: CCTV, a/c,
pool

Pyrenees Motel
(775) 623-1116
714 Winnemucca Blvd.
40 rooms - $40-68
Pets: Welcome
Creature Comforts: CCTV, a/c

Red Lion Inn & Casino
(800) RED LION, (775) 623-2565
http://www.doubletreehotels.com
741 W. Winnemucca Blvd.
107 rooms - $80-125
Pets: Small pets w/$10 fee
Creature Comforts: CCTV,
VCR, a/c, restaurant, pool

Scott Shady Court
(775) 623-3646
400 First St.
70 rooms - $40-85
Pets: Welcome
Creature Comforts: CCTV, a/c

Super 8
(800) 800-8000, (775) 625-1818
http://www.super8.com
1157 W. Winnemucca Blvd.
50 rooms - $40-95
Pets: Welcome
Creature Comforts: CCTV, a/c

Thunderbird Motel
(775) 457-8051
511 Winnemucca Blvd.
50 rooms - $45-85
Pets: Welcome
Creature Comforts: CCTV, a/c,
pool

Val-U Inn
(800) 443-7777, (775) 623-5248
125 E. Winnemucca Blvd.
80 rooms - $55-79
Pets: Small pets w/$5 fee
Creature Comforts: CCTV,
VCR, a/c, refrig, micro, pool,
sauna

Winners Hotel & Casino
(800) 648-4770, (775) 623-2511
185 Winnemucca Blvd.
83 rooms - $38-85
Pets: Small pets welcome
Creature Comforts: CCTV, a/c,
restaurant

YERINGTON
Casino West
(800) 227-4661, (702) 463-2481
11 N. Main St.
65 rooms - $40-65
Pets: Welcome
Creature Comforts: CCTV, a/c,
restaurant, pool

City Center Motel
(702) 463-2135
307 N. Main St.
13 rooms - $30-45
Pets: Welcome
Creature Comforts: CCTV, a/c

In Town Motel
(702) 463-2164
111 S. Main St.
18 rooms - $35-55
Pets: Welcome
Creature Comforts: CCTV, a/c

Ranch House Motel
(702) 463-2200
311 W. Bridge St.
15 rooms - $30-55
Pets: Welcome
Creature Comforts: CCTV, a/c

New Hampshire

ALTON
Joy Cottages
(603) 569-4973
Roberts Cove Rd.
8 cottages - $55-60
Pets: Welcome
Creature Comforts: CCTV,
micro, kit

Horse and Buggy Cottages
(603) 875-5600
Route 28A
20 cottages - $325/wk
Pets: Welcome
Creature Comforts: CCTV, kit

ANTRIM
Maplehurst Inn
(603) 588-8000
67 Main St.
13 rooms - $85-90
Pets: Welcome Mon-Thurs in first
floor room
Creature Comforts: CCTV, a/c,
restaurant, cont. brkfst

ASHLAND
Black Horse Motor Court
(603) 968-7116
Route 3
8 cottages - $470-599/wk
Pets: Welcome
Creature Comforts: CCTV, kit,
fireplace, lake swimming, boating

Haus Trillium B&B
(603) 968-2180
Sanborn Rd.
3 rooms - $50-65
Pets: Welcome w/approval
Creature Comforts: 1880's
farmhouse and barn meadows,
orchards, European ambiance,
down comforters, antiques,
fireplace, full German brkfst,
hiking

BARTLETT
Country Inn at Bartlett
(800) 292-2353, (603) 374-2353
http://www.bartlettinn.com
Route 302
16 rooms - $70-130
Pets: Welcome in cottages, do not
leave unattended
Creature Comforts: 1885
farmhouse and cottages, simple
decor w/maple furnishings, CCTV,
kit, fireplace, full country brkfst,
hot tub

Mountain Home Cabins
(603) 374-2277
Route 302
10 rooms - $40-50
Pets: Welcome
Creature Comforts: Summer
only, rustic cabins, kit, swimming

Villager Motel
(800) 334-6988, (603) 374-2742
http://www.villagermotel.com
Route 302
29 rooms - $50-135
Pets: Welcome w/$6 fee
Creature Comforts: 15-acre
wooded setting on Saco River,
CCTV, a/c, refrig, kit, fireplace

BENNINGTON
Econo Lodge
(800) 55-ECONO, (603) 588-2777
http://www.econolodge.com
634 Francistown Rd.
32 rooms - $60-100
Pets: Welcome in select rooms
Creature Comforts: CCTV, a/c,
cont. brkfst

BERLIN
Traveler Motel
(603) 752-2500
25 Pleasant St.
30 rooms - $40-70
Pets: Small pets w/$25 fee
Creature Comforts: CCTV, a/c,
kit

BETHLEHEM
Pinewood Motel
(800) 328-9307, (603) 444-2075
Route 302
20 rooms - $44-95
Pets: Leashed, not left unattended
Creature Comforts: CCTV, a/c,
kit, fireplace, pool

Sherman Inn
(800) 336-8344, (603) 869-2457
2000 Main St.
24 rooms - $54-60
Pets: Welcome
Creature Comforts: CCTV, kit

Wayside Inn
(800) 448-9557, (608) 869-3364
http://www.thewaysideinn.com
Box 480
26 rooms - $75-120
Pets: Welcome in one motel room
Creature Comforts: Historic inn/
motel, CCTV, fireplace,
restaurant, full brkfst, tennis

CAMPTON VILLAGE
Campton Inn
(603) 726-4449
Main and Owl St.
5 rooms - $65-75
Pets: Welcome during quieter
times, during week and off season
Creature Comforts: Sitting rm,
screened in porch, full brkfst

CENTER HARBOR
Kona Mansion Inn
(603) 253-4900
Jacobs Rd.
4 cottages - $445-520/wk
Pets: Welcome in cottages
Creature Comforts: 130 acres
surround Tudor mansion and
cottages on Lake Winnipesaukee,
clean, simple cottages, pine floors,
calico curtains, tv, restaurant, lake
swimming, boating, golf

Lake Shore Motel/Cottages
(603) 253-6244
Lakeshore Dr.
6 rooms - $55-95
Pets: Welcome in ltd. rooms
Creature Comforts: CCTV, a/c, kit, beach, dock, swimming, boating

Meadows Lakeside Lodging
(603) 253-4347
Route 25
40 rooms - $55-100
Pets: Welcome w/$7 fee
Creature Comforts: CCTV, a/c, fireplace, 200 ft. beach, boat rentals, swimming

Watch Hill B&B
(603) 253-4334
Old Meredith Rd.
4 rooms - $65-80
Pets: Welcome w/notice
Creature Comforts: 1772 hillside cottage, lake views, owner prof. trained chef, sitting rooms w/ American/European antiques, bedrooms w/country furnishings, CCTV, fireplace, gourmet brkfst

CENTER CONWAY
Saco River Motor Lodge
(603) 447-3720
2626 Main St.
16 rooms - $90-200
Pets: Welcome at mngr's discretion -"likeable" dogs only
Creature Comforts: CCTV, a/c, refrig, kit, pool, lake swimming, boating

Sunny Brook Cottages
(603) 447-3922
www.sunnybrookcottages.com/
Route 16
10 rooms - $50-110
Pets: Most pets welcome w/$10 one-time fee
Creature Comforts: Charming 1930's era brookside cottages, beadboard walls, attractive furnishings, quilts, fireplaces, kit, porches, lawn games, swimming

Tanglewood Motel/Cottages
(603) 447-5932
Route 16
8 rooms - $50-100
Pets: Welcome
Creature Comforts: Efficiency cottages, kit, swimming

CENTER OSSIPEE
Hitching Post Village Inn
(603) 539-3360
Old Route 16
9 rooms - $57-67
Pets: Welcome w/notice
Creature Comforts: 1850 Colonial inn, Franklin stove, canopy beds, full brkfst

CENTER SANDWICH
Corner House Inn
(800) 501-6219, (603) 284-6219
Routes 133/109
3 rooms - $80
Pets: Welcome w/approval
Creature Comforts: Operating as inn for 150 years, wonderful public area w/fireplace, intimate restaurant, excellent food, Victorian guest rms., brass beds, handmade quilts, full brkfst

CHESTERFIELD
Chesterfield Inn
(800) 365-5515, (603) 256-3211
www.distninns/chstr/index.html
Route 9
13 rooms - $150-175
Pets: Welcome w/approval
Creature Comforts: Beautiful gardens/terraces, restored historic farmhouse and barn w/exposed beams, country elegance, modern amenities, handmade quilts, CCTV, a/c, refrig, fireplace, gourmet restaurant, full brkfst

CLAREMONT
Claremont Motor Lodge
(603) 542-2540
Beauregard St.
18 rooms - $40-50
Pets: Welcome
Creature Comforts: CCTV, a/c, kit

Del-E-Motel
(603) 542-9567
24 Sullivan St.
20 rooms - $30-50
Pets: Welcome w/$8 fee
Creature Comforts: CCTV, a/c, refrig, micro, kit

COLEBROOK
Colebrook House/Motel
(800) 626-7331, (603) 237-5521
http://www.colebrookhouse.com
132 Main St.
14 rooms - $40-50
Pets: Welcome w/$5 fee
Creature Comforts: CCTV, kit, fireplace, Jacuzzi, full brkfst

Northern Comfort Motel
(603) 237-4440
Route 3
19 rooms - $50-66
Pets: Small pets welcome
Creature Comforts: CCTV, refrig, micro, kit

CONCORD
Brick Tower Motor Inn
(603) 224-9565
414 S. Main St.
51 rooms - $59-65
Pets: Welcome w/$5 fee
Creature Comforts: CCTV, a/c, pool

Comfort Inn
(800) 228-5150, (603) 226-4100
http://www.comfortinn.com
71 Hall St.
100 rooms - $65-150
Pets: Welcome
Creature Comforts: CCTV, a/c, cont. brkfst, pool

Econo Lodge
(800) 55-ECONO, (603) 224-4011
http://www.econolodge.com
Gulf St.
49 rooms - $50-85
Pets: Small pets welcome
Creature Comforts: CCTV, VCR, a/c, cont. brkfst

Holiday Inn
(800) HOLIDAY, (603) 224-9534
http://www.holiday-inn.com
172 N. Main
122 rooms - $90-225
Pets: Small pets welcome
Creature Comforts: CCTV, a/c, restaurant

CONWAY
Sunnybrook Cottages
(603) 447-3922
www.3craft.com/sunnybrook
1901 White Mountain Hwy.
10 cottages - $69-110
Pets: One-time $10 fee
Creature Comforts: Brookside cottages, CCTV, a/c, kit, fireplace, barbecues

Tanglewood Motel/Cottages
(603) 447-5932
Route 16
8 cottages - $50-84
Pets: Welcome, they cannot be left alone
Creature Comforts: Brookside cottages, wooded setting, family friendly, CCTV, a/c, kit, pool

DOVER
Days Inn
(800) DAYS INN, (603) 742-0400
http://www.daysinn.com
481 Central Ave.
63 rooms - $60-120
Pets: Welcome
Creature Comforts: CCTV, a/c, kit, cont. brkfst, pool

ENFIELD
Mary Kean House
(603) 632-4241
Box 5, Lower Shaker Village
5 rooms - $90-130
Pets: Welcome
Creature Comforts: Victorian suites w/antiques, collectibles, CCTV, fireplace, full brkfst

EXETER
Best Western Hearthside
(800) 528-1234, (603) 772-3794
http://www.bestwestern.com
137 Portsmouth Ave.
33 rooms - $50-110
Pets: Welcome w/$10 fee
Creature Comforts: CCTV, a/c, pool

FRANCESTOWN
Inn at Crotched Mountain
(603) 588-6840
www.innbook.com/crotched.html
Mountain Rd.
13 rooms - $40-75
Pets: Welcome w/$5 fee
Creature Comforts: 1820's farmhouse, country antiques/tools, hrdwd floors, fireplaces, mountain views, request fireplace rooms, CCTV, full brkfst, pool

FRANCONIA
Gale River Motel
(800) 255-7989, (603) 823-5655
1 Main St.
13 cottages - $50-82
Pets: Welcome w/$10 fee
Creature Comforts: CCTV, refrig, micro, kit, whirlpool

Horse and Hound
(800) 450-5501, (603) 823-5501
205 Wells Rd.
10 rooms - $80-120
Pets: Welcome w/$9 fee/notice
Creature Comforts: Rambling informal English hunting lodge, eclectic comb. antique/country furnishings, CCTV, fireplace, restaurant, full brkfst

Lovett's Inn by Lafayette Brook
(800) 356-3802, (603) 823-7761
http://www.lovettsinn.com
Route 18
37 rooms - $100-150
Pets: Welcome in cottages
Creature Comforts: 1784 inn w/ modern cottages, well appointed, expansive lawns, pond, CCTV, fireplace, gourmet restaurant, full brkfst, pool

GILMANTON
Temperance Tavern
(603) 267-7349
Old Province Rd.
5 rooms - $75-120
Pets: Welcome
Creature Comforts: 1793 graciously restored inn w/original wallpaper, fixtures, antique furnishings, walk-in fireplaces, gourmet brkfst—authentic decor

FRANKLIN
D.K. Motel
(603) 934-3311
390 North Main St.
10 rooms - $48-58
Pets: Welcome w/$4 fee
Creature Comforts: CCTV, a/c, refrig

GLEN
Red Apple Inn
(603) 383-9680
Route 16
15 rooms - $40-110
Pets: Welcome w/$10 fee
Creature Comforts: CCTV, a/c

GORHAM
Colonial Comfort Inn
(800) 470-4224, (603) 466-2732
370 Main St.
15 rooms - $30-75
Pets: Welcome
Creature Comforts: CCTV, a/c, kit

Gorham Motor Inn
(800) 445-0913, (603) 446-3381
324 Main St.
39 rooms - $35-75
Pets: Welcome w/$6 fee
Creature Comforts: CCTV, a/c

Moose Brook Motel
(603) 466-5400
65 Lancaster Rd.
14 rooms - $35-55
Pets: Small pets in smoking rms.
Creature Comforts: CCTV, a/c, kit

Royalty Inn
(800) 43-RELAX, (603) 466-3312
http://www.royaltyinn.com
130 Main St.
90 rooms - $50-80
Pets: Welcome w/$5 fee
Creature Comforts: CCTV, a/c, refrig, kit, restaurant, pool, hlth clb, whirlpool, racquetball

Topnotch Motor Inn
(800) 228-5496, (603) 466-5496
Main St.
35 rooms - $45-85
Pets: Small pets w/$25 deposit
Creature Comforts: CCTV, VCR, a/c, refrig

Town & Country Motor Inn
(800) 325-4386, (603) 466-3315
www.townandcountryinn.com
Route 2
159 rooms - $45-90
Pets: Welcome
Creature Comforts: CCTV, a/c,
restaurant, pool, hlth clb,
whirlpool

HAMPTON
Lamie's Inn and Tavern
(800) 805-5050, (603) 926-0330
Route 1
31 rooms - $60-105
Pets: Small pets welcome
Creature Comforts: Historic
tavern, Colonial style rooms,
CCTV, a/c, restaurant

Stone Gable Inn
(800) 737-6606, (603) 926-6883
869 Lafayette Rd.
63 rooms - $45-65
Pets: Welcome
Creature Comforts: CCTV, a/c,
refrig, micro

HAMPTON FALLS
Hampton Falls Inn
(800) 356-1729, (603) 926-9545
11 Lafayette Rd.
47 rooms - $40-75
Pets: Small pets welcome
Creature Comforts: CCTV,
VCR, a/c, restaurant, cont. brkfst,
pool, hlth clb access, sauna,
whirlpool

HANOVER
The Hanover Inn
(800) 443-7024, (603) 643-4300
http://www.dartmouth.edu/~inn
On the Green
104 rooms - $210-300
Pets: Welcome w/$15 fee
Creature Comforts: On
Dartmouth College green,
Colonial-style antiques/fabrics,
finial beds, well-aptd baths,
CCTV, a/c, refrig, restaurants,
pool, hlth clb access, sauna,
whirlpool, walking paths

HENNIKER
Henniker Motel
(603) 428-3536
Craney Pond Rd.
20 rooms - $50-75
Pets: Welcome w/$3 fee
Creature Comforts: CCTV,
VCR, a/c, refrig, whirlpool

HILLSBORO
1830 House Motel
(603) 478-3135
626 W. Main St.
13 rooms - $54-59
Pets: Welcome w/$10 deposit
Creature Comforts: CCTV, kit,
pool

INTERVALE
Swiss Chalet
(800) 831-2727, (603) 356-2232
Route 16A
36 rooms - $50-140
Pets: Welcome w/$10 fee
Creature Comforts: CCTV, a/c,
fireplace, Jacuzzi, restaurant, cont.
brkfst, pool, whirlpool

JACKSON
Dana Place Inn
(603) 934-3311
http://www.danaplace.com
Rtes. 16A & 16B
35 rooms - $75-135
Pets: Welcome
Creature Comforts: CCTV, a/c,
fireplace, restaurant, pool, exercise
rm., whirlpool, tennis, xc-country
skiing

Ellis River House
(800) 233-8309, (603) 383-9339
http://www.erhinn.com
Route 16
19 rooms - $70-230
Pets: Welcome in cottage
Creature Comforts: Antique
Colonial farmhouse and cottage
on river, cottage w/sitting rm., loft
bedroom w/country pine, colorful
fabrics, CCTV, refrig, micro,
restaurant, full brkfst, pool,
whirlpool

The Village House
(800) 972-8343, (603) 383-6666
Route 16A
30 rooms - $50-80
Pets: Welcome
Creature Comforts: CCTV, kit,
pool, whirlpool, tennis

Whitney's Inn
(800) 677-5737, (603) 383-8916
http://www.whitneysinn.com
Route 16B
29 rooms - $65-140
Pets: Ltd. rms w/$25 fee
Creature Comforts: 1842 inn/
cottages on Black Mtn., favorite
family inn, cottages top pick for
dogs, CCTV, VCR, a/c, kit,
fireplace, gourmet restaurant,
pond swimming, tennis, hiking,
skiing

JEFFERSON
Applebrook B&B
(800) 545-6504, (603) 586-7713
http://www.applebrook.com
Route 115
12 rooms - $55-90
Pets: Welcome w/$6 fee
Creature Comforts: Rambling
Victorian farmhouse, sunny rooms
w/bright floral fabrics, antique
furnishings/beds, whimsical
touches-gold fish pond in living
rm., CCTV, hearty brkfst,
whirlpool

Evergreen Motel
(603) 586-4449
Route 2
18 rooms - $30-60
Pets: Small pets welcome
Creature Comforts: CCTV

Jefferson Notch Motel/Cabins
(800) 345-3833, (603) 466-3833
http://www.jeffnotchmotel-
cabins.com
Route 2
28 rms/cottages - $50-100
Pets: Welcome, pet pool
Creature Comforts: Kit, pool,
whirlpool

Josselyn's Getaway Log Cabins
(800) 586-4507
North Rd.
7 cabins - $75-90
Pets: Welcome
Creature Comforts: CCTV, kit,
fireplace

KEARSARGE

Issac E. Merrill House
(800) 328-9041, (603) 356-9041
http://www.nhinns.com
Box 8
21 rooms - $60-260
Pets: Welcome in certain rooms
Creature Comforts: Rambling antique home w/modern interior, mtn. setting near N. Conway, casual, ski house atmosphere, CCTV, a/c, fireplace, full brkfst, sister ppty offers pool, hlth clb access, whirlpool

KEENE

Best Western Sovereign Hotel
(800) 528-1234, (603) 357-3038
http://www.bestwestern.com
401 Winchester St.
131 rooms - $80-160
Pets: Welcome
Creature Comforts: CCTV, a/c, restaurant, full brkfst, pool

Days Inn
(800) DAYS INN, (603) 352-7616
http://www.daysinn.com
175 Key Rd.
80 rooms - $70-85
Pets: Small pets welcome
Creature Comforts: CCTV, VCR, a/c, refrig, kit, Jacuzzi, full brkfst, whirlpool

Valley Green Motel
(603) 352-7350
379 West St.
60 rooms - $40-70
Pets: $6 fee, $25 deposit
Creature Comforts: CCTV, a/c, kit

LANCASTER

Lancaster Motor Inn
(603) 788-4921
112 Main St.
36 rooms - $35-50
Pets: Small pets welcome
Creature Comforts: CCTV, a/c, refrig, micro, kit, cont. brkfst

Woodpile Inn Motel
(603) 788-2096
39 Portland St.
15 rooms - $30-50
Pets: Small pets welcome
Creature Comforts: CCTV

LEBANON

Holiday Inn Express
(800) HOLIDAY, (603) 448-5070
http://www.holiday-inn.com
Route 120
50 rooms - $70-120
Pets: Welcome in smoking rms.
Creature Comforts: CCTV, a/c

LINCOLN

Parker's Motel
(603) 745-8341
Route 3
28 rooms - $30-80
Pets: Welcome w/$25 deposit
Creature Comforts: CCTV, a/c, kit

LITTLETON

Eastgate Motor Inn
(603) 444-3971
Route 3
55 rooms - $45-59
Pets: Welcome
Creature Comforts: CCTV, a/c, restaurant, cont. brkfst, pool

Thayer's Inn
(800) 634-8179, (603) 934-3311
136 Main St.
40 rooms - $40-70
Pets: Not left unattended
Creature Comforts: 1850's historic hotel, hand carved staircase/detail, eclectic furnishings/country antiques, casual ambiance, paddle fans, tin ceilings, CCTV, refrig

LYME

Loch Lyme Lodge
(800) 423-2141, (603) 795-2141
Route 10
24 cottages - $450-700/wk
Pets: Welcome w/vaccinations
Creature Comforts: Appealing rustic cottages overlooking lake, family summer camp, kit, fireplace, swimming, boating, hiking, camp library, dining room

MANCHESTER

Comfort Inn
(800) 228-5150, (603) 668-2600
http://www.comfortinn.com
298 Queen City Ave.
100 rooms - $60-135
Pets: Welcome w/$50 deposit
Creature Comforts: CCTV, a/c, refrig, micro, cont. brkfst, pool, hlth club

Econo Lodge
(800) 55-ECONO, (603) 624-0111
http://www.econolodge.com
75 W. Hancock Rd.
113 rooms - $45-65
Pets: Welcome
Creature Comforts: CCTV, a/c, cont. brkfst

Four Points, Sheraton
(800) 325-3535, (603) 668-6110
http://www.sheraton.com
55 John Devine Dr.
125 rooms - $80-105
Pets: Small pets welcome
Creature Comforts: CCTV, a/c, restaurant, pool

Holiday Inn, Center
(800) HOLIDAY, (603) 625-1000
http://www.holiday-inn.com
700 Elm St.
250 rooms - $90-105
Pets: Welcome
Creature Comforts: CCTV, a/c, restaurant, pool

MARLBOROUGH

Peep-Willow Farm
(603) 876-3807
Bixby St.
3 rooms - $50
Pets: Welcome, leash on ppty, cannot disturb farm animals
Creature Comforts: 20-acre thoroughbred horse farm, fireplace, full farm brkfst, hiking, cross-country skiing

MILFORD

Ram in the Thicket
(603) 654-6440
24 Maple St.
9 rooms - $60-75
Pets: Quiet pets w/approval
Creature Comforts: Nooky and cranny inn, antiques, four-poster beds, pretty views, fireplace, gourmet restaurant, cont. brkfst

MERRIMACK

Merrimack Hotel/Conf. Ctr.
(800) The Tara, (603) 424-8000
4 Executive Park Dr.
199 rooms - $60-80
Pets: Welcome
Creature Comforts: CCTV, a/c, restaurant, pool, hlth clb

Residence Inn, Marriott
(800) 331-3131, (603) 934-3311
http://www.residenceinn.com
246 Daniel Webster Hwy.
95 rooms - $110-150
Pets: $5 fee, $50 deposit
Creature Comforts: CCTV, a/c,
refrig, micro, kit, pool

MOULTONBORO
Rob Roy Motor Lodge
(603) 476-5571
Route 25
18 rooms - $50-75
Pets: Welcome
Creature Comforts: CCTV, a/c

NASHUA
Holiday Inn
(800) HOLIDAY, (603) 888-1551
http://www.holiday-inn.com
9 Northeastern Blvd.
166 rooms - $70-135
Pets: Small pets
Creature Comforts: CCTV, a/c,
refrig, micro, restaurant, pool, hlth
clb

Motel 6
(800) 4 Motel 6, (603) 889-4151
http://www.motel6.com
2 Progress Ave.
80 rooms - $50-55
Pets: Under 30 lbs. welcome
Creature Comforts: CCTV, a/c

Nashua Marriott
(800) 228-9290, (603) 880-9100
http://www.marriott.com
2200 Southwood Dr.
240 rooms - $80-120
Pets: Welcome
Creature Comforts: CCTV, a/c,
restaurant, pool

Red Roof Inn
(800) THE ROOF, (603) 888-1893
http://www.redroof.com
77 Spitbrook Rd.
115 rooms - $55-65
Pets: Welcome w/notice
Creature Comforts: CCTV, a/c

NEW LONDON
Twin Lake Village
(603) 526-6460
21 Twin Lake Village Rd.
40 rooms - $340-360 pp/wk
Pets: Welcome in cottages
Creature Comforts: 200-acres
sloping lawns, mtn. views, built in
1896, classic NE family resort,
shingle-style cottages, country
antiques, refrig, kit, fireplace,
restaurant, lake swimming,
boating, tennis, lawn games

NEWPORT
Newport Motel
(603) 863-1440
467 Sunapee St.
18 rooms - $55-75
Pets: Small pets welcome
Creature Comforts: CCTV, a/c,
refrig, pool

Eagle Inn at Coit Mountain
(800) 367-2364, (603) 863-3583
523 North Main St.
6 rooms - $90-130
Pets: Welcome by arrangement
Creature Comforts: Gracious
1790 Georgian-Federal summer
estate, lovely rooms, period
antiques, fireplace, evening
dessert delvrd to rm, TV/VCR on
rqest, gourmet restaurant, hearty
country brkfst

NORTH CONWAY
Maple Leaf Motel
(603) 356-5388
Route 16
15 rooms - $42-60
Pets: Welcome
Creature Comforts: CCTV, a/c,
refrig

North Conway Mountain Inn
(603) 356-2803
Main St.
32 rooms - $40-75
Pets: Welcome w/$50 deposit
Creature Comforts: CCTV, a/c

Stonehurst Manor
(800) 525-9100, (603) 934-3311
http://www.stonehurstmanor.com
Rtes. 302 & 16
24 rooms - $95-150
Pets: Welcome in ltd. rms.
Creature Comforts: CCTV, a/c,
fireplace, full brkfst, restaurant,
swimming, tennis

NORTHWOOD
Lake Shore Farm Resort
(603) 942-5921
273 Jenness Pond Rd.
32 rooms - $110-140 (AP)
Pets: Welcome
Creature Comforts: Rambling
farmhouse, casual resort for
families since 1926, simple
furnishings, emphasis on outdoor
diversions, fireplace, dining room,
family style meals, pond, lawn
games, indoor games

PITTSBURG
The Glen
(800) 445-GLEN, (603) 538-6500
First Connecticut Lake
18 rooms - $130-145 (AP)
Pets: Welcome in cottages
Creature Comforts: Classic
fishing/hunting lodge on First Ct.
Lake, knotty pine cabins, home
cooked meals, camp furnishings,
fishing guides, fireplace, canoeing,
hiking

Lopstick Lodge and Cabins
(800) 538-6659
http://www.lopstick.com
First Connecticut Lake
9 rooms - $68-125
Pets: Welcome w/$10 fee
Creature Comforts: Attractive,
knotty pine cabins and hunting
lodge on First Ct. Lake, TV, VCR,
fireplace, kit

Spruce Cone Cabins
(800) 538-6361, (603) 538-6572
www.spruceconecabins.com
First Connecticut Lake
20 cabins - $40-56
Pets: Welcome w/$10 fee
Creature Comforts: Sporting
lodge on Lake Francis, kit

Tall Timber Lodge
(800) 835-6343, (603) 538-6651
http://www.talltimber.com
231 Beach Rd.
20 cabins - $80-230
Pets: Welcome w/$10 fee
Creature Comforts: Popular,
award-winning 1946 sporting
lodge w/rustic log cabins and
luxury cottages, knotty pine walls,
attractive decor, TV, VCR,
fireplace, kit, swimming, fishing

Timberland Lodge and Cabins
(800) 545-6613, (603) 538-6613
http://www.timberlandlodge.com
First Connecticut Lake
20 cabins - $72-125
Pets: Welcome in most units w/ $10 fee
Creature Comforts: Simple but attractive lakefront 1930's log cabins and some new cabins, sophisticated camp decor, Metallak Shores preferred for family gatherings, woodstove, kit, swimming, fishing, boating

PLYMOUTH
Best Western White Mtn.
(800) 528-1234, (603) 536-3520
http://www.bestwestern.com
Route 3
101 rooms - $50-125
Pets: Welcome
Creature Comforts: CCTV, a/c, refrig, micro, restaurant, pool, hlth clb, sauna, whirlpool

Pilgrim Inn/Cottages
(800) 216-1900, (603) 536-1319
http://www.pilgriminn.com
307 Main St., Route 3 North
20 rms/cottages - $40-90
Pets: Welcome w/permission
Creature Comforts: Request charming small white cottages in rural setting, attractive country decor, floral fabrics, CCTV, a/c, micro, refrig, kit, cont. brkfst

PORTSMOUTH
Anchorage Inn
(800) 370-8111, (603) 431-8111
417 Woodbury Ave.
95 rooms - $50-140
Pets: Welcome
Creature Comforts: CCTV, a/c, refrig, Jacuzzi, cont. brkfst, pool, sauna, whirlpool

The Port Motor Inn
(800) 282-PORT, (603) 436-4378
Portsmouth Circle and Route 1
56 rooms - $45-120
Pets: Welcome
Creature Comforts: CCTV, a/c, refrig, micro, wet bar, cont. brkfst, pool

Wren's Nest Village Inn
(603) 436-2481
3548 Lafayette Rd.
34 rooms - $70-170
Pets: Small pets w/$10 fee
Creature Comforts: CCTV, a/c, refrig, micro, kit

RINDGE
Woodbound Inn
(800) 688-7770, (603) 934-3311
http://www.nhweb.com/woodbound/index.htm
62 Woodbound Rd.
63 rooms - $90-200
Pets: Welcome in cabins
Creature Comforts: 200-acre lakeside setting, 1890's shingled inn w/knotty pine cabins, maple furn., fireplace, refrig, dining rm.

ROCHESTER
Anchorage Inn
(603) 332-3350
Route 125
31 rooms - $46-60
Pets: Welcome
Creature Comforts: CCTV, a/c, kit, pool

SALEM
Holiday Inn
(800) HOLIDAY, (603) 893-5511
http://www.holiday-inn.com
1 Keewaydin Dr.
84 rooms - $75-220
Pets: Welcome w/$50 deposit
Creature Comforts: CCTV, a/c, restaurant, cont. brkfst, pool

Red Roof Inn
(800) Red Roof, (603) 898-6422
http://www.redroof.com
15 Red Roof Ln.
110 rooms - $35-65
Pets: Small pets welcome
Creature Comforts: CCTV, a/c

SALISBURY
Horse Haven B&B
(603) 648-2101
www.bbonline.com/nh/horsehaven
462 Raccoon Hill Rd.
5 rooms - $75
Pets: $5 fee. "Impeccably mannered dogs allowed in the house; others and horses in barn."
Creature Comforts: 1805 farmhouse on 35 acres, TV fireplace/woodstove, cont. brkfst

SHELBURNE
Philbrook Farm Inn
(603) 466-3831
881 North Rd.
15 rooms - $110-140 (MAP)
Pets: Welcome in cottages
Creature Comforts: Family-owned farm since 1853, rambling, classic farmhouse w/traditional cottages near brook, valley/mtn views, family heirlooms, antiques, fireplace, home cooked meals, games, pool, lawn games, hiking

SUGAR HILL
Hilltop Inn
(800) 770-5695, (603) 823-5695
http://www.hilltopinn.com
Route 117
9 rooms - $80-150
Pets: Welcome w/$10 fee, dog sitting avail.
Creature Comforts: Classic NE mountaintop vlg, 1895 Victorian inn w/fine period decor, wonderful hosts, cozy ambiance, TV, VCR, wood stove, dining rm, full gourmet brkfst, hiking, skiing nrby

The Homestead Inn
(800) 823-5564, (603) 823-5564
www.thehomestead1802.com
Route 117
23 rooms - $75-90
Pets: Welcome w/$5 fee in 4 rms.
Creature Comforts: 1802 inn filled w/family antiques, full brkfst, afternoon tea, CCTV in sitting rm.

SUNAPEE
Best Western Sunapee Lake
(800) 606-5253, (603) 763-2010
http://www.sunapeelakelodge.com
1403 Route 103
55 rooms - $70-180
Pets: Welcome in ltd. rooms
Creature Comforts: CCTV, VCR, refrig, micro, Jacuzzi, restaurant, pool, hlth club

Burkehaven Resort
(603) 763-2788
179 Burkehaven Hill Rd.
10 rooms - $69-79
Pets: Welcome
Creature Comforts: CCTV, kit

Dexter's Inn/Tennis Club
(800) 232-5571, (603) 763-5571
http://www.bbhost.com/dextersinn
258 Stagecoach Rd.
18 rooms - $135-175 (MAP)
Pets: Welcome in annex or Holly Cottage w/$10 fee
Creature Comforts: 1803 mountaintop inn w/expansive views, manicured grounds, rooms w/Victorian furnishings, CCTV, fireplace, pool, tennis courts, lawn games, TV, restaurant, hiking

TAMWORTH
Tamworth Inn
(800) 642-7352, (603) 323-7721
http://www.tamworth.com
Main St.
16 rooms - $120-160
Pets: Welcome w/$5 fee, cannot be left unattended
Creature Comforts: 1833 Victorian inn in pristine, historic village on peaceful river, nooks and crannies, country antiques, charming pub, hlth club, restaurant, CCTV, fireplace, hiking, near swimming

TILTON
Tilton Manor B&B
(603) 286-3457
http://www.tiltonmanor.com
40 Chestnut St.
4 rooms - $80-150
Pets: Welcome
Creature Comforts: 1800's Victorian B&B, four acres w/ brook, orig. woodwork, fireplaces, antiques, micro, kit, country brkfst

TROY
Inn at East Hill Farm
(800) 242-6495, (603) 242-6495
http://www.east-hill-farm.com
460 Monadnock St.
52 rooms - $50-80
Pets: Welcome in older cottages
Creature Comforts: Great family cottages, simple rooms w/lots of activities, fireplace, restaurant, cont. brkfst, farm animals, pool

TWIN MOUNTAIN
Charlmont Motor Inn
(603) 846-5549
http://www.musar.comtraveler/
charlmont_motor_inn.html
Route 3
35 rooms - $55-70
Pets: Welcome
Creature Comforts: CCTV, a/c, restaurant, pool

Patio Motor Court
(603) 846-5562
http://www.thepatio.com
Route 3
35 rooms - $55-70
Pets: Welcome in off season
Creature Comforts: CCTV, a/c, restaurant, pool

WENTWORTH
Hilltop Acres
(603) 764-5896
East Side/Buffalo Rd.
5 rooms - $65-80
Pets: Welcome in cottages
Creature Comforts: TV, kit, fireplace

WEST LEBANON
Airport Economy Inn
(800) 433-3466, (603) 298-8888
45 Airport Rd.
55 rooms - $50-65
Pets: Welcome w/$10 fee
Creature Comforts: CCTV, VCR, a/c, refrig, cont. brkfst

Radisson Inn, N. Country
(800) 333-3333, (603) 298-5906
http://www.radisson.com
25 Airport Rd.
125 rooms - $99-110
Pets: Small pets w/$50 deposit
Creature Comforts: CCTV, a/c, restaurant, pool, hlth clb, sauna, whirlpool

WHITEFIELD
The Spalding Inn
(800) 368-VIEW, (603) 837-2572
Mountain View Rd.
46 rooms - $99-109
Pets: Welcome in cottages
Creature Comforts: Classic mtn. summer resort, 200 acres, stunning views, exquisite gardens, simple cottages w/1950s charm, comf. furnishings, CCTV, kit, fireplace, formal restaurant, pool, golf, tennis, walking paths

WILTON CENTER
Stepping Stones B&B
(603) 654-9048
Bennington Battle Trail
3 rooms - $50-65
Pets: Welcome, stay on paths
Creature Comforts: 1700's Greek Revival cottage, mtn. setting w/beautiful gardens, antique furnishings, down comforters, hand-woven rugs/ blankets, country decor, fireplace, bountiful gourmet brkfst, hiking

WINNISQUAM
Lynmere Motel/Cottages
(603) 524-0912
850 Laconia Rd.
15 rooms - $35-85
Pets: Small pets in certain rooms w/$100 dep.
Creature Comforts: CCTV, kit

WOLFEBORO
Allen 'A' Motor Inn
(800) 732-8507, (603) 569-1700
Route 28
43 rooms - $70-100
Pets: Welcome w/$10 fee
Creature Comforts: CCTV, pool, playground

Lake Motel
(888) 569-1110, (603) 569-1100
Route 28
30 rooms - $70-100
Pets: Small pets
Creature Comforts: CCTV, kit

Museum Lodges
(603) 569-1551
http://www.museumlodges.com
32 Gov. Wentworth Hwy.
10 cottages - $90
Pets: Welcome in off season
Creature Comforts: Shingled lakeside cottages, kitchen, living rm, fireplace, deep wtr docks, beach

WOODSVILLE
All Seasons Motel
(603) 747-2157
Route 302
13 rooms - $40-56
Pets: Welcome
Creature Comforts: CCTV, kit

New Jersey

ABESCON
Days Inn
(800) DAYS INN, (609) 652-2200
http://www.daysinn.com
Route 30
102 rooms - $45-180
Pets: Welcome w/$20 daily fee
Creature Comforts: CCTV, a/c,
Jacuzzi, cont. brkfst, pool

ASBURY PARK
The Berkeley-Cateret Hotel
(908) 776-9546
1401 Ocean Ave.
245 rooms - $90-160
Pets: Welcome w/$50 fee
Creature Comforts: CCTV, a/c,
Jacuzzi, restaurant, cont. brkfst,
and a spa

AVALON
The Sealark Bed & Breakfast
(609) 967-5647
http://www.sealark.com
3018 First Avenue
8 rooms - $65-129
Pets: Well-behaved pets welcome
Creature Comforts: An 1890s
Victorian w/ inviting wrap-around
front porch w/rockers, CCTV-
VCR, a/c, refrig, fireplace,
antiques, rattan, ocean views,
brkfst buffet, request Lighthouse
Room, great beach one block from
the B&B

BEACH HAVEN
Engleside Inn
(800) 762-2214, (609) 492-1251
http://www.engleside.com
30 Engleside Ave.
71 rooms - $85-330
Pets: Welcome Sept 15th - April
30th w/$10 daily fee
Creature Comforts: CCTV, a/c,
refrig, micro, kit, Jacuzzi, balcony,
restaurant, pool, sandy beach

BELMAR
Down the Shore B&B
(732) 681-9023
www.belmar.com/downtheshore
201 - 7th Ave.
3 rooms - $85-110
Pets: Wel-behaved pets welcome
Creature Comforts: Low-key
homey ambiance situated a block
from the beach & boardwalk,
inviting porch and parlor, a/c, TV,
fireplace, country quilts, full brkfst

BEVERLY
Whitebriar B&B
(609) 871-3859
1029 South Cooper St.
6 rooms - $50-135
Pets: Orderly pets welcome
Creature Comforts: 1700's
Saltbox-style houses, a/c,
fireplace, Jacuzzi, restaurant, full
brkfst, pool, whirlpool

BLACKWOOD
Howard Johnson
(800) I-Go-Hojo, (609) 652-2200
http://www.hojo.com
832 N. Black Horse Pike
101 rooms - $45-95
Pets: Welcome w/$10 fee
Creature Comforts: CCTV, a/c,
Jacuzzi, restaurant, pool

BORDENTOWN
Best Western Bordentown
(800) 528-1234, (609) 298-8000
http://www.bestwestern.com
1068 Route 206
101 rooms - $65-125
Pets: Small pets welcome
Creature Comforts: CCTV, a/c,
refrig, restaurant, cont. brkfst,
pool, sauna

Days Inn
(800) DAYS INN, (609) 298-6100
http://www.daysinn.com
Route 206 N
131 rooms - $55-69
Pets: Welcome
Creature Comforts: CCTV, a/c,
restaurant, pool

Econo Lodge
(800) 55-ECONO, (609) 298-5000
http://www.econolodge.com
Rtes. 130 & 206
60 rooms - $45-139
Pets: Welcome
Creature Comforts: CCTV, a/c,
restaurant, cont. brkfst, pool

CAPE MAY
Marquis de Lafayette
(800) 257-0432, (609) 652-2200
501 Beach Dr.
73 rooms - $125-310
Pets: Welcome w/$20 daily fee
and CC deposit in certain rooms
Creature Comforts: Contemp.
bldg w/ unobstructed ocean views,
CCTV, a/c, refrig, kit, restaurant,
nearby pet friendly beach and park

The Moffitt House
(800) 498-0915, (609) 898-0915
http://www.moffitthouse.com
715 Broadway
4 rooms - $65-100
Pets: Welcome in one room
Creature Comforts: 1700's
country Victorian, a/c, fireplace,
wide board floors, family
hierlooms, antiques, front porch,
patio, full brkfst, bikes, hammocks

CATERET
Holiday Inn
(800) HOLIDAY, (908) 541-9500
http://www.holiday-inn.com
1000 Roosevelt Ave.
120 rooms - $90-130
Pets: Small pets welcome
Creature Comforts: CCTV, a/c,
restaurant

CHERRY HILL
Holiday Inn
(800) HOLIDAY, (609) 663-5300
http://www.holiday-inn.com
Route 70 & Sayer Ave.
185 rooms - $70-90
Pets: One per room
Creature Comforts: CCTV, a/c,
restaurant, pool, exercise rm,
sauna, whirlpool

Residence Inn
(800) 331-3131, (609) 429-6111
http://www.residenceinn.com
1821 Old Cuthbert Rd.
96 rooms - $125-170
Pets: Welcome w/$50 deposit
Creature Comforts: CCTV,
VCR, a/c, refrig, micro, kit,
fireplace, cont. brkfst, hlth clb

CLIFTON
Howard Johnson
(800) I-Go-Hojo, (973) 471-3800
http://www.hojo.com
680 Rte.3 West
115 rooms - $80-120
Pets: Small pets welcome
Creature Comforts: CCTV, a/c,
restaurant

Ramada Hotel
(800) 2-Ramada, (973) 778-6500
http://www.ramada.com
265 Rte. 3 East
183 rooms - $75-145
Pets: Small pets welcome
Creature Comforts: CCTV, a/c,
kit, restaurant

EAST BRUNSWICK
Motel 6
(800) 4-MOTEL6, (732) 390-4545
http://www.motel6.com
244 Route 18
114 rooms - $50-65
Pets: Under 30 lbs. welcome
Creature Comforts: CCTV,
VCR, a/c, hlth clb access

EAST HANOVER
Ramada Hotel
(800) 2-Ramada, (973) 386-5622
http://www.ramada.com
130 Route 10
255 rooms - $60-130
Pets: Small pets welcome
Creature Comforts: CCTV, a/c,
restaurant

EAST RUTHERFORD
Sheraton Meadowlands
(800) 325-3535, (201) 896-0500
http://www.sheraton.com
2 Meadowlands Plaza
425 rooms - $99-145
Pets: Welcome
Creature Comforts: CCTV, a/c,
and a restaurant

EAST WINDSOR
Days Inn
(800) DAYS INN, (609) 448-3200
http://www.daysinn.com
460 Route 33 East
100 rooms - $60-120
Pets: Welcome
Creature Comforts: CCTV, a/c,
refrig, micro, Jacuzzi, restaurant,
cont. brkfst, pool

EATONTOWN
Crystal Motor Lodge
(800) 562-5290, (732) 542-4900
Route 35
77 rooms - $75-109
Pets: Welcome w/$5 fee
Creature Comforts: CCTV, a/c,
refrig, micro, pool

EDISON
Crowne Plaza (Raritan Ctr.)
(800) HOLIDAY, (732) 225-8300
http://www.crowneplaza.com
125 Raritan Ctr. Pkwy
275 rooms - $110-160
Pets: Welcome in smoking rooms
w/$20 cleaning fee
Creature Comforts: CCTV, a/c,
restaurant

Red Roof Inn
(800) The-Roof, (732) 248-9300
http://www.redroof.com
860 New Durham Rd.
135 rooms - $55-85
Pets: Welcome
Creature Comforts: CCTV, a/c

Wellesley Inn
(800) 444-8888, (732) 287-0171
831 Route 1 S.
100 rooms - $45-125
Pets: Small pets welcome
Creature Comforts: CCTV, a/c,
cont. brkfst

ELIZABETH
Hilton Hotel
(800) HILTONS, (908) 351-3900
http://www.hilton.com
1170 Spring St.
375 rooms - $135-229
Pets: Small pets welcome
Creature Comforts: CCTV, a/c,
restaurant, brkfst buffet

ENGLEWOOD
Radisson Hotel
(800) 333-3333, (201) 871-2020
http://www.radisson.com
401 S. Van Brunt St.
191 rooms - $119-130
Pets: Small pets welcome w/$200
refundable deposit
Creature Comforts: CCTV, a/c,
restaurant

FAIRFIELD
Ramada Inn
(800) 2-Ramada, (973) 575-1742
http://www.ramada.com
38 Two Bridges Rd.
177 rooms - $80-150
Pets: Small pets welcome
Creature Comforts: CCTV, a/c,
Jacuzzis, restaurant, pool,

FLEMINGTON
Ramada Inn
(800) 2-Ramada, (908) 782-7472
http://www.ramada.com
Routes 202 & 31
105 rooms - $80-109
Pets: Welcome w/$10 fee
Creature Comforts: CCTV, a/c,
kit

HASBROUCK HEIGHTS
Crowne Plaza
(800) HOLIDAY, (201) 288-6100
http://www.crowneplaza.com
650 Terrace Ave.
355 rooms - $110-230
Pets: Small pets welcome
Creature Comforts: CCTV, a/c,
refrig, micro, restaurant, saunas

HAZLET
Wellesley Inn
(800) 444-8888, (732) 888-2800
3215 Route 35 N.
90 rooms - $55-80
Pets: Small pets welcome
Creature Comforts: CCTV, a/c

HIGHLANDS
Seascape Manor B&B
(732) 291-8467, 872-7932
http://www.bbianj.com/seascape
3 Grand Tour
4 rooms - $90-160
Pets: Selectively welcomed
Creature Comforts: Hillside
setting overlooking the ocean,
charming 1800's manor house w/
antiques and collectibles, large
porch, fireplace, country quilts,
down comforters, CCTV, a/c,
gourmet brkfst, soaking tubs,
decks and patios overlook Sandy
Hook National Recreation Area
and NYC skyline, lawn games,
boats

HOPE
Inn at Millrace Pond
(800) 746-6467, (908) 459-4884
www.innatmillracepond.com
313 Hwy 519, Box 359
17 rooms - $110-160
Pets: Small dogs in ltd. rooms
Creature Comforts: Highly
recommended, gracious 1760 inn
and grist mill on 23 acres, four
historic buildings, exposed post/
beams, stone walls, wide board
pine floors, Colonial/primitive
reproductions, CCTV, a/c,
gourmet restaurant, Colnial tavern,
cont. brkfst, tennis

JERSEY CITY
Econo Lodge
(800) 55-ECONO, (201) 420-9040
http://www.econolodge.com
750-762 Tonnelle Ave.
38 rooms - $55-79
Pets: Welcome
Creature Comforts: CCTV, a/c,
Jacuzzi, cont. brkfst

LAWRENCEVILLE
Howard Johnson
(800) I-Go-Hojo, (908) 896-1100
http://www.hojo.com
2995 Brunswick Pike
105 rooms - $75-95
Pets: Small pets welcome
Creature Comforts: CCTV, a/c,
refrig, micro, restaurant, and a
cont. brkfst

Red Roof Inn
(800) The-Roof, (609) 459-4884
http://www.redroof.com
3203 Brunswick Pike
150 rooms - $50-82
Pets: Welcome
Creature Comforts: CCTV, a/c

LYNDHURST
Novotel (Meadowlands)
(800) NOVOTEL, (201) 896-6666
http://www.novotel.com
1 Polito Ave.
220 rooms - $80-109
Pets: Welcome
Creature Comforts: CCTV, a/c,
restaurant

MAHWAH
Sheraton Crossroads Hotel
(800) 325-3535, (201) 529-1660
http://www.sheraton.com
One International Blvd.
225 rooms - $90-215
Pets: Welcome
Creature Comforts: CCTV, a/c,
restaurant, pool, sauna, tennis
cont. brkfst

MIDDLETOWN
Howard Johnson
(800) I-Go-Hojo, (732) 671-3400
http://www.hojo.com
750 Rte. 35 South
81 rooms - $70-130
Pets: Welcome w/$5 daily fee
Creature Comforts: CCTV, a/c,
refrig, restaurant

MILLVILLE
Millville Motor Inn
(800) 428-4373, (908) 459-4884
Route 47
150 rooms - $50-60
Pets: Welcome w/$5 fee
Creature Comforts: CCTV, a/c,
refrig, micro, kit, restaurant, pool

MONMOUTH JUNCTION
Red Roof Inn
(800) THE ROOF, (732) 821-8800
http://www.redroof.com
208 New Rd.
120 rooms - $40-85
Pets: Small pets welcome
Creature Comforts: CCTV, a/c

Residence Inn by Marriott
(800) 331-3131, (732) 329-9600
http://www.residenceinn.com
Route 1
210 rooms - $90-160
Pets: Welcome w/$10 fee
Creature Comforts: CCTV, a/c,
kit, pool, hlth clb access,
whirlpool

MOUNT HOLLY
Best Western inn
(800) 528-1234, (609) 261-3800
http://www.bestwestern.com
2020 Route 541
61 rooms - $70-139
Pets: Small pets welcome
Creature Comforts: CCTV, a/c,
kit

Howard Johnson
(800) I-Go-Hojo, (609) 267-6550
http://www.hojo.com
Route 541
90 rooms - $55-99
Pets: Welcome
Creature Comforts: CCTV, a/c,
Jacuzzi, restaurant, cont. brkfst,
sauna, whirlpool

MOUNT LAUREL
Red Roof Inn
(800) THE ROOF, (609) 234-5589
http://www.redroof.com
603 Fellowship Rd.
110 rooms - $45-75
Pets: Small pets welcome
Creature Comforts: CCTV, a/c

Summerfield Suites
(800) 833-4353, (609) 222-1313
www.summerfieldsuites.com
3000 Crawford Rd.
114 rooms - $90-165
Pets: Under 50 lbs. w/$100
cleaning fee; $10 daily fee
Creature Comforts: CCTV, a/c,
kit, pool, hlth club

NEWARK
Sheraton Hotel
(800) 325-3535, (973) 690-5500
http://www.sheraton.com
128 Frontage Rd.
500 rooms - $90-199
Pets: Small pets welcome
Creature Comforts: CCTV, a/c,
restaurant, pool, hlth club

OCEAN CITY
Crossing Motor Inn
(609) 398-4433
3420 Haven Ave.
70 rooms - $50-160
Pets: Welcome in the off season
w/$15 fee
Creature Comforts: CCTV, a/c,
kit, cont. brkfst, pool

PARAMUS
Howard Johnson Lodge
(800) I-Go-Hojo, (201) 265-4200
http://www.hojo.com
Route 17
80 rooms - $70-99
Pets: Small pets welcome
Creature Comforts: CCTV, a/c,
pool

Radisson Inn
(800) 333-3333, (201) 262-6900
http://www.radisson.com
601 From Rd.
120 rooms - $130-150
Pets: Small pets welcome
Creature Comforts: CCTV, a/c,
restaurant, pool, hlth club

PARK RIDGE
Marriott Inn
(800) 228-9290, (201) 307-0800
http://www.marriott.com
300 Brae Blvd.
289 rooms - $95-160
Pets: Small pets, first floor rms.
Creature Comforts: CCTV, a/c,
restaurant, pool, hlth club, sprt crt

PARSIPPANY
Days Inn
(800) DAYS INN, (973) 335-0200
http://www.daysinn.com
3159 Route 46
120 rooms - $80-125
Pets: Welcome
Creature Comforts: CCTV, a/c,
refrig, micro, kit, restaurant, pool

Hilton Inn
(800) HILTONS, (973) 267-7373
http://www.hilton.com
One Hilton Court
510 rooms - $80-160
Pets: Welcome
Creature Comforts: CCTV, a/c,
restaurant, pools, tennis, trail

Ramada Inn Limted
(800) 2-Ramada, (973) 263-0404
http://www.ramada.com
949 Route 46 East
75 rooms - $75-105
Pets: Small pets welcome
Creature Comforts: CCTV, a/c,
pool

Red Roof Inn
(800) THE ROOF, (973) 334-3737
http://www.redroof.com
855 Route 46 East
105 rooms - $55-99
Pets: Welcome
Creature Comforts: CCTV, a/c

PENNS GROVE
Wellesley Inn
(800) 444-8888, (609) 299-3800
517 S. Pennsville-Auburn Rd.
140 rooms - $60-79
Pets: Welcome w/$40 deposit
Creature Comforts: CCTV, a/c,
cont. brkfst, pool, hlth club

PISCATAWAY
Motel 6
(800) 4-MOTEL6, (732) 981-9200
http://www.motel6.com
1012 Stelton Rd.
136 rooms - $45-70
Pets: Under 30 lbs. welcome
Creature Comforts: CCTV, a/c

PLAINFIELD
Pillars B&B
(888) PILLARS, (908) 753-0922
http://cimarron.net/usa/nj/
pillars.html
922 Central Avenue
6 rooms - $95-109
Pets: Well-behaved dogs are
welcome (pet sitting available)
Creature Comforts: A Victorian-
Georgian mansion, mature trees
and gardens, old-fashioned charm,
CCTV, a/c, fireplace, organ, game
table, canopy and four-poster
beds, kit

PRINCETON
Amerisuites
(800) 833-1516, (609) 720-0200
http://www.amerisuites.com
3565 Rte 1
125 rooms - $105-185
Pets: Small pets w/$125 fee
Creature Comforts: CCTV, a/c,
refrig, pool, hlth club, whirlpool

Novotel Princeton Hotel
(800) NOVOTEL, (609) 520-1200
http://www.novotel.com
100 Independence Way
180 rooms - $80-175
Pets: Small pets welcome, crated
if left alone
Creature Comforts: CCTV, a/c,
refrig, pool, restaurant, hlth club,
whirlpool

Peacock Inn
(609) 924-1707
20 Bayard Ln.
17 rooms - $115-145
Pets: Welcome
Creature Comforts: 1775
gambrel roof inn, period details,
intimate bedrooms w/European
antiques, collectibles, CCTV, full
brkfst, gourmet restaurant, close to
Princeton University campus

Residence Inn
(800) 331-3131, (609) 329-9600
http://www.residenceinn.com
4225 Route 1
208 rooms - $150-200
Pets: Welcome w/$10 fee
Creature Comforts: CCTV,
VCR, a/c, kit, pool, hlth clb
access, whirlpool

Summerfield Suites Hotel
(800) 833-4353, (609) 951-0009
www.summerfieldsuites.com
4375 Route 1 South
125 rooms - $90-199
Pets: Small pets w/$8 fee
Creature Comforts: CCTV, a/c,
kit, fireplace, pool

RAMSEY
Howard Johnson
(800) I-Go-Hojo, (201) 327-4500
http://www.hojo.com
1255 Route 17 S.
50 rooms - $55-90
Pets: Small pets w/$5 deposit
Creature Comforts: CCTV, a/c,
refrig, restaurant, cont. brkfst, pool

Inn at Ramsey
(201) 327-6700
1315 Route 17 S.
63 rooms - $40-75
Pets: Welcome
Creature Comforts: CCTV,
VCR, a/c, refrig, micro, Jacuzzi,
cont. brkfst, restaurant

Wellesley Inn
(800) 444-8888, (201) 934-9250
946 Route 17 N.
90 rooms - $55-125
Pets: Welcome w/$5 fee
Creature Comforts: CCTV, a/c,
cont. brkfst, hlth club

RUNNEMEDE
Holiday Inn
(800) HOLIDAY, (609) 939-4200
http://www.holiday-inn.com
109 Ninth Ave.
175 rooms - $79-225
Pets: Welcome in two rooms
Creature Comforts: CCTV, a/c,
restaurant, cont. brkfst, pool

SADDLE BROOK
Holiday Inn
(800) HOLIDAY, (201) 843-0600
http://www.holiday-inn.com
50 Kenney Pl.
145 rooms - $70-109
Pets: Small pets welcome
Creature Comforts: CCTV, a/c,
refrig, restaurant, pool, hlth clb
access

SEACAUCAS
Embassy Suites
(800) 362-2779, (201) 864-7300
http://www.embassy-suites.com
455 Plaza Dr.
260 rooms - $130-239
Pets: Small pets w/$150 deposit
Creature Comforts: CCTV,
VCR, a/c, kit, pool, hlth club

Radisson Suite
(800) 333-3333, (201) 863-8700
http://www.radisson.com
350 Route 3 West
151 rooms - $120-225
Pets: Small pets w/$500 deposit
Creature Comforts: CCTV, a/c,
Jacuzzis, brkfst, restaurant, pool

Red Roof Inn
(800) THE ROOF, (201) 319-1000
http://www.redroof.com
15 Meadowlands Pkwy.
170 rooms - $60-129
Pets: Small pets welcome
Creature Comforts: CCTV, a/c

SOMERS POINT
Residence Inn
(800) 331-3131, (609) 927-6400
http://www.residenceinn.com
900 Mays Landing Rd.
121 rooms - $80-180
Pets: Under 30 lbs. w/$50 fee
Creature Comforts: CCTV,
VCR, a/c, refrig, micro, kit,
fireplace, full brkfst

SOMERSET
Holiday Inn
(800) HOLIDAY, (732) 356-1700
http://www.holiday-inn.com
195 Davidson Ave.
285 rooms - $110-139
Pets: Small pets welcome
Creature Comforts: CCTV, a/c,
restaurant, pool

Ramada Inn
(800) 2-Ramada, (732) 560-9880
http://www.ramada.com
60 Cottontail Ln.
125 rooms - $66-125
Pets: Welcome
Creature Comforts: CCTV, a/c,
kit, restaurant, pool

Summerfield Suites Hotel
(800) 833-4353, (732) 356-8000
260 Davidson
140 rooms - $130-210
Pets: Small welcome w/$5 fee,
$100 deposit
Creature Comforts: CCTV, a/c,
kit, pool

SOUTH PLAINFIELD
Holiday Inn
(800) HOLIDAY, (908) 753-5500
http://www.holiday-inn.com
4701 Stelton Rd.
173 rooms - $70-110
Pets: Small pets welcome
Creature Comforts: CCTV, a/c,
restaurant, pool

SPRINGFIELD
Holiday Inn
(800) HOLIDAY, (973) 376-9400
http://www.holiday-inn.com
304 Route 22 West
195 rooms - $90-108
Pets: Welcome
Creature Comforts: CCTV, a/c,
refrig, restaurant, pool, and a hlth
club

TINTON FALLS
Red Roof Inn
(800) THE ROOF, (732) 389-4646
http://www.redroof.com
11 Centre Plaza
120 rooms - $45-95
Pets: Small pets welcome
Creature Comforts: CCTV, a/c

Residence Inn
(800) 331-3131, (732) 389-8100
http://www.residenceinn.com
90 Park Rd.
96 rooms - $120-145
Pets: Welcome w/$150 fee
Creature Comforts: CCTV, a/c,
kit, pool, hlth club

Sunrise Suites
(732) 389-4800
3 Centre Plaza
96 rooms - $99-160
Pets: Small pets w/$50 fee
Creature Comforts: CCTV, a/c,
and kit

TOMS RIVER
Holiday Inn
(800) HOLIDAY, (732) 244-4000
http://www.holiday-inn.com
290 Route 37 E.
125 rooms - $85-115
Pets: Small pets welcome
Creature Comforts: CCTV, a/c,
VCR, restaurant, pool, hlth club

Howard Johnson
(800) I-Go-Hojo, (732) 244-1000
http://www.hojo.com
955 Hopper Ave.
96 rooms - $70-190
Pets: Welcome w/$15 fee
Creature Comforts: CCTV, a/c,
restaurant, pool

Ramada Inn
(800) 2-Ramada, (732) 905-2626
http://www.ramada.com
2373 Route 9
128 rooms - $70-130
Pets: Welcome
Creature Comforts: CCTV, a/c,
kit, fireplace, Jacuzzi, restaurant,
pool, tennis

VOORHEES
Hampton Inn
(800) Hampton, (609) 346-4500
http://www.hampton-inn.com
121 Laurel Oak Rd.
120 rooms - $90-99
Pets: Welcome
Creature Comforts: CCTV, a/c,
pool, hlth club

WARREN
Somerset Hills Hotel
(800) 688-0700, (908) 647-6700
http://www.shh.com
200 Liberty Corner Rd.
112 rooms - $100-190
Pets: Small pets welcome
Creature Comforts: CCTV, a/c,
kit, Jacuzzi, restaurant, pool, hlth
clb

WEEHAWKEN
Ramada Suite Hotel
(800) 2-Ramada, (201) 617-5600
http://www.ramada.com
500 Harbor Blvd.
245 rooms - $120-420
Pets: Small pets w/$75 deposit
Creature Comforts: CCTV, a/c,
refrig, micro, restaurant, cont.
brkfst, pool, hlth clb

WHIPPANY
Howard Johnson
(800) I-Go-Hojo, (973) 539-8350
http://www.hojo.com
1255 Route 10
108 rooms - $95-135
Pets: Small pets in first floor rms.
Creature Comforts: CCTV,
VCR, a/c, kit, restaurant, cont.
brkfst, pool

WOODCLIFF LAKE
Woodcliff Lake Hilton
(800) HILTONS, (201) 391-3600
http://www.hilton.com
200 Tice Blvd.
335 rooms - $120-195
Pets: Welcome
Creature Comforts: CCTV, a/c,
restaurant, pool, sauna, tennis,
putting green, massage, and a
sport court

New Mexico

ABIQUIU
Casa del Rio B&B
(800) 920-1495, (505) 753-2035
www.bbonline.com/nm/casadelrio
19946 Rte. 84
4 rooms - $100-125
Pets: Horses only, corral, $10 fee
Creature Comforts: Authentic
adobe home, Southwest decor,
kiva fireplace, CCTV, a/c, full
brkfst, Arabian horses

ALAMOGORDO
All American Inn
(505) 437-1850
508 S. White Sands Blvd.
28 rooms - $30-35
Pets: Small pets welcome
Creature Comforts: CCTV, a/c,
refrig

Best Western Desert Aire
(800) 528-1234, (505) 437-2110
http://www.bestwestern.com
1021 S. White Sands Blvd.
99 rooms - $45-60
Pets: Welcome w/$50 deposit
Creature Comforts: CCTV,
VCR, a/c, refrig, micro, kit,
Jacuzzi, pool, whirlpool

Holiday Inn
(800) HOLIDAY, (505) 437-7100
http://www.holiday-inn.com
1401 S. White Sands Blvd.
108 rooms - $65-90
Pets: Welcome w/refundable $50
deposit
Creature Comforts: CCTV, a/c,
refrig, micro, restaurant, pool

La Quinta, Airport
(800) 531-5900, (505) 269-0400
http://www.laquinta.com
1433 Beers School Rd.
125 rooms - $60-75
Pets: Small pets welcome
Creature Comforts: CCTV, a/c,
pool

Motel 6
(800) 4-MOTEL6 (505) 434-5970
http://www.motel6.com
251 Panorama Blvd.
123 rooms - $35-40
Pets: Under 30 lbs. welcome
Creature Comforts: CCTV, VCR,
a/c

Satellite Inn
(505) 437-8454
2224 N. White Sands Blvd.
41 rooms - $35-45
Pets: Welcome
Creature Comforts: CCTV, VCR,
a/c, refrig, micro, kit

Super 8 Motel
(800) 800-8000, (505) 434-4205
http://www.super8.com
3204 N. White Sands Blvd.
57 rooms - $40-50
Pets: Welcome w/permission
Creature Comforts: CCTV, VCR,
a/c, refrig, micro, cont. brkfst

ALBUQUERQUE
Adobe and Roses
(505) 897-2329
1011 Ortega Rd. NW
3 rooms - $50-115
Pets: Welcome w/notice
Creature Comforts: Adobe home
in residential area, beautiful
gardens/trees, Mexican tile floors,
southwestern pottery, weavings,
pierced tin, suites w/beamed
ceilings, sitting areas, kiva
fireplace, full southwestern brkfsts,
CCTV, a/c, kit

Amerisuites
(800) 833-1516, (505) 242-9300
http://www.amerisuites.com
1400 Support Pl. SE
128 rms - $95-110
Pets: Under 20 lbs. welcome
Creature Comforts: CCTV, VCR,
a/c, refrig, micro, full brkfst, pool

Amerisuites
(800) 833-1516, (505) 872-9000
http://www.amerisuites.com
6901 Arvada Ave.
128 rms - $70-110
Pets: Under 20 lbs. welcome
Creature Comforts: CCTV,
VCR, a/c, kit, full brkfst, pool

Amberley Suite Hotel
(800) 333-9806, (505) 823-1300
7620 Pan American Hwy.
171 suites - $80-150
Pets: Welcome w/$5 fee
Creature Comforts: CCTV,
VCR, a/c, refrig, micro, kit,
restaurant, pool, hlth clb access,
sauna, whirlpool

Baymont Inns
(800) Baymont, (505) 242-1555
http://www.baymontinns.com
1511 Gibson Blvd. SE
113 rooms - $65-85
Pets: Welcome
Creature Comforts: CCTV, a/c,
refrig, micro, pool

Baymont Inns
(800) Baymont, (505) 345-7500
http://www.baymontinns.com
7439 Pan American Hwy.
100 rooms - $55-62
Pets: Welcome
Creature Comforts: CCTV, a/c,
refrig, micro, pool

Best Western Airport
(800) 528-1234, (505) 242-7022
http://www.bestwestern.com
2400 Yale Blvd. SE
118 rooms - $60-100
Pets: Welcome
Creature Comforts: CCTV, a/c,
refrig, cont. brkfst, pool

Best Western American
(800) 528-1234, (505) 298-7426
http://www.bestwestern.com
12999 Central Ave.
78 rooms - $55-80
Pets: Welcome w/$2 fee
Creature Comforts: CCTV, a/c,
refrig, micro, kit, restaurant, pool,
whirlpool

Casita Chamisa
(505) 897-4644
850 Chamisal Rd., NW
1 cottage - $95-135
Pets: Welcome w/notice in cottage
Creature Comforts: 1850's
adobe casita on site of
architectural dig, shade trees,
gardens, bucolic setting, gracious
hosts, cottage w/sitting room, two
bedrooms, Southwest decor,
CCTV, kit, cont. brkfst, indoor
pool

Comfort Inn, Airport
(800) 228-5150, (505) 243-2244
http://www.comfortinn.com
2300 Yale Blvd.
115 rooms - $65-80
Pets: Welcome w/$7 fee
Creature Comforts: CCTV,
VCR, a/c, pool, whirlpool

Comfort Inn East
(800) 228-5150, (505) 294-1800
http://www.comfortinn.com
13031 Central Ave. NE
125 rooms - $50-60
Pets: Small pets w/$5 fee
Creature Comforts: CCTV, a/c,
refrig, restaurant, cont. brkfst,
pool, whirlpool

Days Inn
(800) DAYS INN, (505) 294-3297
http://www.daysinn.com
13317 Central Ave.
75 rooms - $60-100
Pets: Small pets w/$5 fee
Creature Comforts: CCTV, a/c,
pool, sauna, whirlpool

Days Inn Eubank
(800) DAYS INN, (505) 275-3297
http://www.daysinn.com
10321 Hotel Circle NE
75 rooms - $45-70
Pets: Welcome w/$5 fee
Creature Comforts: CCTV, a/c,
pool, sauna, whirlpool

Econo Lodge
(800) 55-ECONO, (505) 292-7600
http://www.econolodge.com
13211 Central Ave. NE
58 rooms - $45-85
Pets: Small pets w/$5 fee
Creature Comforts: CCTV, a/c

Hampton Inn - North
(800) Hampton, (505) 344-1555
http://www.hampton-inn.com
5101 Ellison Ave. NE
125 rooms - $60-70
Pets: Welcome
Creature Comforts: CCTV,
VCR, a/c, refrig

Holiday Inn Express
(800) HOLIDAY, (505) 275-8900
http://www.holiday-inn.com
10330 Hotel Ave.
105 rooms - $70-120
Pets: Welcome w/$5 fee
Creature Comforts: CCTV, a/c,
refrig, micro, Jacuzzi, restaurant,
cont. brkfst, pool, hlth clb, sauna,
whirlpool

Holiday Inn
(800) HOLIDAY, (505) 884-2511
http://www.holiday-inn.com
2020 Menaul Ave.
360 rooms - $70-120
Pets: Welcome w/$125 deposit,
$25 non-refundable
Creature Comforts: CCTV, a/c,
restaurant, pool, whirlpool,
exercise rm.

Howard Johnson Express
(800) 446-4656, (505) 828-1600
http://www.hojo.com
7630 Pan American Hwy.
85 rooms - $60-70
Pets: Welcome w/$5 fee
Creature Comforts: CCTV, a/c,
cont. brkfst, pool, hlth clb,
whirlpool

La Quinta, Airport
(800) 531-5900, (505) 243-5500
http://www.laquinta.com
2116 Yale Blvd. SE
110 rooms - $65-75
Pets: Small pets welcome
Creature Comforts: CCTV, a/c,
refrig, cont. brkfst, pool

La Quinta North
(800) 531-5900, (505) 821-9000
http://www.laquinta.com
5241 San Antonio Dr. NE
131 rooms - $65-70
Pets: Small pets welcome
Creature Comforts: CCTV, a/c,
refrig, cont. brkfst, pool

La Quinta San Mateo
(800) 531-5900, (505) 884-3591
http://www.laquinta.com
2424 San Mateo Blvd.
110 rooms - $65-75
Pets: Small pets welcome
Creature Comforts: CCTV, a/c,
refrig, cont. brkfst, pool

Maggie's Raspberry Ranch
(505) 897-1523
9817 Eldridge Rd., NW
3 rooms - $75-95
Pets: Welcome
Creature Comforts: CCTV, a/c,
full brkfst, pool

Motel 6
(800) 4-MOTEL6, (505) 294-4600
http://www.motel6.com
13141 Central Ave. NE
123 rooms - $30-45
Pets: Under 30 lbs. welcome
Creature Comforts: CCTV, a/c,
pool

Motel 6
(800) 4-MOTEL6, (505) 843-9228
http://www.motel6.com
1701 University Ave. NE
118 rooms - $30-44
Pets: Under 30 lbs. welcome
Creature Comforts: CCTV,
VCR, a/c

Motel 6
(800) 4-MOTEL6, (505) 821-1472
http://www.motel6.com
8510 Pan American Freeway NE
125 rooms - $35-49
Pets: Under 30 lbs. welcome
Creature Comforts: CCTV, a/c,
pool

Motel 6
(800) 4-MOTEL6, (505) 243-8017
http://www.motel6.com
1000 Avenida Cesar Chavez SE
97 rooms - $30-45
Pets: Under 30 lbs. welcome
Creature Comforts: CCTV, a/c,
pool

Motel 6
(800) 4-MOTEL6, (505) 831-8888
http://www.motel6.com
5701 Iliff Rd. NW
111 rooms - $30-42
Pets: Under 30 lbs. welcome
Creature Comforts: CCTV, a/c, pool

Motel 6
(800) 4-MOTEL6, (505) 831-3400
http://www.motel6.com
6015 Iliff Rd.
131 rooms - $30-44
Pets: Under 30 lbs. welcome
Creature Comforts: CCTV, a/c, pool, whirlpool

Plaza Inn
(800) 237-1307, (505) 243-5693
900 Medical Arts NE
121 rooms - $70-85
Pets: Small pets welcome
Creature Comforts: CCTV, a/c, refrig, micro, restaurant, pool, exercise rm, whirlpool

Radisson Hotel
(800) 333-3333, (505) 888-3311
http://www.radisson.com
2500 Carlisle NE
150 rooms - $110-130
Pets: Welcome w/$50 deposit
Creature Comforts: CCTV, VCR, a/c, refrig, micro, cont. brkfst, restaurant, pool, whirlpool

Ramada Inn East
(800) 2-Ramada, (505) 271-1000
http://www.ramada.com
25 Hotel Circle NE
200 rooms - $75-85
Pets: Welcome
Creature Comforts: CCTV, a/c, refrig, micro, restaurant, pool, whirlpool

The Ranchette
(800) 374-3230, (505) 877-5140
http://www.vivanewmexico.com/nm/ranchette
2329 Lakeview Dr. SW
3 rooms - $55-85
Pets: Small pets welcome
Creature Comforts: Adobe home w/moumtain views, room w/floral southwestern motif, terry robes, Vegetarian meals

Residence Inn
(800) 331-3131, (505) 881-2661
http://www.residenceinn.com
3300 Prospect Dr NE
115 rooms - $110-180
Pets: Welcome w/$8 fee, $50 deposit
Creature Comforts: CCTV, VCR, a/c, refrig, micro, kit, pool, hlth clb, sauna, whirlpool, racquetball

Sleep Inn
(800) Sleep-Inn, (505) 244-3325
http://www.sleepinn.com
2300 N. International Blvd.
110 rooms - $65-75
Pets: Small pets welcome
Creature Comforts: CCTV, a/c, refrig, micro, kit, pool, whirlpool

Super 8 Motel
(800) 800-8000, (505) 888-4884
http://www.super8.com
2500 University Blvd.
245 rooms - $45-55
Pets: Welcome w/$5 fee
Creature Comforts: CCTV, a/c, refrig, micro

Travelodge I-40
(800) 578-7878, (505) 292-4878
http://www.travelodge.com
13139 Central Ave. NE
41 rooms - $40-100
Pets: Small pets w/$5 fee
Creature Comforts: CCTV, a/c, cont. brkfst

W.E. Mauger Estate
(505) 242-8755
http://www.maugerbb.com
701 Roma Ave. NW
8 rooms - $80-150
Pets: Medium dogs w/$30 one-time fee, stay in rm. w/dog door and private yard
Creature Comforts: 1897 Victorian on Nat'l Hist. Register, simple elegance, recmd. Talbot Rm, furnished w/antiques-some orig. to house, down comforter, sleigh bed, CCTV, a/c, full brkfst

Wyndham Hotel
(800) 227-1117, (505) 843-7000
http://www.wynatabq.com
2910 Yale Blvd., SE
276 rooms - $60-100
Pets: Welcome
Creature Comforts: CCTV, a/c, refrig, micro, restaurant, pool, hlth clb, tennis

ALTO
High Country Lodge
(800) 845-7265, (505) 336-4321
Route 48
33 cottages - $80-130
Pets: Welcome w/$10 fee
Creature Comforts: CCTV, refrig, micro, kit, fireplace, pool, sauna

La Junta Guest Ranch
(800) 443-8243, (505) 336-4361
Box 139
10 cabins - $105-295
Pets: Welcome w/$5 fee
Creature Comforts: New Mexican mtn. cabins w/touch of the bayou, maple furnishings, patchwork quilts, fireplace, kit, recreation rm, hiking

ARTESIA
Artesia Inn
(505) 746-9801
1820 S. First St.
35 rooms - $40-50
Pets: Small pets
Creature Comforts: CCTV, a/c, refrig.

BELEN
Best Western Belen
(800) 528-1234, (505) 861-3181
http://www.bestwestern.com
2111 Sosimo Padilla Blvd.
50 rooms - $70-85
Pets: Welcome
Creature Comforts: CCTV, VCR, a/c, refrig, micro, pool, exercise rm.

BERNALILLO
La Hacienda Grande
(800) 353-1887, (505) 867-1887
http://www.lahaciendagrande.com
21 Baros Ln.
6 rooms - $99-120
Pets: Medium dogs welcome. Must be quiet, not allowed in courtyard
Creature Comforts: Historic territorial style adobe set in agricultural community, interior courtyard, lovely rooms w/kiva fireplaces, tile floors, pine antiques, southwestern art, Jacuzzi, excellent brkfst

BLOOMFIELD
Super 8 Motel
(800) 800-8000, (505) 632-8886
http://www.super8.com
525 W. Broadway St.
45 rooms - $45-60
Pets: Welcome w/$20 deposit
Creature Comforts: CCTV, VCR, a/c, Jacuzzi, cont. brkfst

CARLSBAD
Best Western Stevens Inn
(800) 528-1234, (505) 887-2851
http://www.bestwestern.com
1829 So. Canal St.
200 rooms - $50-65
Pets: Small pets welcome
Creature Comforts: CCTV, VCR, a/c, refrig, micro, kit, Jacuzzi, restaurant, pool

Continental Inn
(505) 887-0341
3820 National Parks Hwy.
60 rooms - $50-65
Pets: Welcome w/$10 fee
Creature Comforts: CCTV, a/c, refrig

Days Inn, Carlsbad
(800) DAYS INN, (505) 887-7800
http://www.daysinn.com
3910 National Parks Hwy.
50 rooms - $40-45
Pets: $5 fee, $10 deposit
Creature Comforts: CCTV, a/c, refrig, micro, pool, whirlpool

Holiday Inn Carlsbad
(800) HOLIDAY, (505) 885-8500
http://www.holiday-inn.com
601 S. Canal St.
150 rooms - $65-75
Pets: Small pets w/$5 fee, $25 deposit
Creature Comforts: CCTV, a/c, refrig, micro, restaurant, cont. brkfst, pool, hlth clb, sauna, whirlpool

Lorlodge
(505) 887-1171
2019 S. Canal St.
30 rooms - $30-45
Pets: Small pets welcome
Creature Comforts: CCTV, VCR, a/c, refrig, micro, pool

Motel 6
(800) 4-MOTEL6, (505) 885-0011
http://www.motel6.com
3824 National Pks Hwy.
80 rooms - $35-48
Pets: Under 30 lbs. welcome
Creature Comforts: CCTV, a/c, restaurant, pool

Quality Inn
(800) 228-5151, (505) 887-2861
http://www.qualityinn.com
3706 National Parks Hwy.
125 rooms - $55-75
Pets: Small pets welcome
Creature Comforts: CCTV, VCR, a/c, refrig, micro, restaurant, pool, whirlpool

Stagecoach Inn
(505) 887-1148
1819 South Canal St.
56 rooms - $35-45
Pets: Welcome
Creature Comforts: CCTV, a/c, refrig, kit, pool, whirlpool

Super 8 Motel
(800) 800-8000, (505) 887-8888
http://www.super8.com
3817 National Parks Hwy.
61 rooms - $45-55
Pets: Small pets welcome
Creature Comforts: CCTV, a/c, refrig, micro, cont. brkfst, pool, whirlpool

CHAMA
Elkhorn Lodge and Cafe
(800) 532-8874, (505) 756-2105
Route 1
33 rooms - $55-90
Pets: Welcome w/$6 fee, leashed on grounds, not left unattended
Creature Comforts: Nestled on banks of Rio Chama, recommend cabins w/knotty pine walls, priv. porches, CCTV, kit, restaurant, playground, lawn games, fishing, hiking

River Bend Lodge
(505) 756-2264
2625 Rte. 64/84
18 rooms - $65-120
Pets: Welcome w/$10 fee
Creature Comforts: CCTV, refrig, fireplace, hot tub

CHIMAYO
La Posada de Chimayó
(505) 351-4605
www.laposadadechimayo.com
Box 463
2 suites - $70
Pets: Welcome, must stay off furniture
Creature Comforts: Historic adobe home, sage and pinon hills, naturalized gardens, private, secluded setting, viga ceilings, tile floors, kiva fireplaces, decorated w/southwestern and Mexican collectibles, gourmet southwestern breakfast, walks in hills, winding rural lanes

CIMARRON
Cimarron Inn
(505) 376-2268
212 E. Tenth St.
13 rooms - $35-40
Pets: Dogs only w/$50 deposit
Creature Comforts: CCTV, refrig, micro

CLAYTON
Best Western Kokopelli
(800) 528-1234, (505) 374-2589
http://www.bestwestern.com
702 S. First St.
45 rooms - $60-90
Pets: Small pets w/$5 fee
Creature Comforts: CCTV, a/c, cont. brkfst

Holiday Motel
(505) 374-2558
Rte. 87 North
31 rooms - $40-65
Pets: Welcome w/$3 fee
Creature Comforts: CCTV, a/c,
cont. brkfst

Super 8 Motel
(800) 800-8000, (505) 374-8127
http://www.super8.com
1425 S. First St.
30 rooms - $45-60
Pets: Welcome
Creature Comforts: CCTV, a/c

CLOVIS
Comfort Inn
(505) 7662-4591
1616 Mabry Dr.
50 rooms - $50-65
Pets: Small pets in smoking rms.
Creature Comforts: CCTV, a/c,
refrig, pool, whirlpool

Days Inn
(800) DAYS INN, (505) 762-2971
http://www.daysinn.com
1720 Mabry Dr.
96 rooms - $40-50
Pets: Welcome
Creature Comforts: CCTV, a/c,
pool

Holiday Inn
(800) HOLIDAY, (505) 762-4491
http://www.holiday-inn.com
2700 Mabry Dr.
125 rooms - $55-65
Pets: Welcome
Creature Comforts: CCTV, a/c,
restaurant, pool, hlth clb access,
whirlpool, sauna

CORRALES
La Mimosa
(505) 898-1354
Box 2008
1 cottage - $50-85
Pets: Welcome
Creature Comforts: Cozy guest
house set on beautiful courtyard,
brick floors, original southwestern
art, Navajo rugs, CCTV, refrig,
coffee maker, full breakfast w/
locally grown produce, jams, walk
along quiet dirt lanes

DEMING
Anselment's Butterfield Motel
(505) 544-0011
309 West Pine St.
12 rooms - $25-35
Pets: Welcome
Creature Comforts: CCTV, a/c,
refrig, pool

Best Western Mimbres Valley
(800) 528-1234, (505) 546-4544
http://www.bestwestern.com
1500 W. Pine St.
40 rooms - $45-50
Pets: Welcome
Creature Comforts: CCTV, a/c,
refrig

Days Inn
(800) DAYS INN, (505) 546-8813
http://www.daysinn.com
1709 E. Spruce St.
58 rooms - $35-50
Pets: Welcome
Creature Comforts: CCTV, a/c,
restaurant, pool

Deming Motel
(505) 546-2737
500 W. Pine St.
28 rooms - $30-35
Pets: Small pets w/$3 fee
Creature Comforts: CCTV, a/c,
refrig, pool

Grand Motor Inn
(505) 546-2631
1721 E. Spruce St.
61 rooms - $45-50
Pets: Small pets welcome
Creature Comforts: CCTV, a/c,
refrig, restaurant, pool

Holiday Inn
(800) HOLIDAY, (505) 546-2661
http://www.holiday-inn.com
Route 10
80 rooms - $50-60
Pets: Welcome
Creature Comforts: CCTV, a/c,
refrig, micro, restaurant, pool

Motel 6
(800) 4-MOTEL6, (505) 546-2681
http://www.motel6.com
Route 10
100 rooms - $35-40
Pets: Under 30 lbs. welcome
Creature Comforts: CCTV, a/c,
pool

Wagon Wheel Motel
(505) 546-2681
1109 W. Pine St.
20 rooms - $25-35
Pets: Small pets welcome
Creature Comforts: CCTV, a/c,
refrig, pool

DULCE
Best Western Jicarilla
(800) 528-1234, (505) 759-3663
http://www.bestwestern.com
Route 64
45 rooms - $60-80
Pets: Small pets w/$20 deposit
Creature Comforts: CCTV, a/c,
refrig, micro, restaurant, pool

ELEPHANT BUTTE
Quality Inn
(800) 228-5151, (505) 744-5431
http://www.qualityinn.com
Route 195
50 rooms - $60-85
Pets: Welcome w/$10 fee
Creature Comforts: CCTV,
VCR, a/c, refrig, restaurant, pool

ESPANOLA
Chamisa Inn
(505) 753-7291
920 N. Riverside Dr.
50 rooms - $40-80
Pets: Welcome w/$10 fee
Creature Comforts: CCTV, a/c,
cont. brkfst, pool

Comfort Inn
(800) 228-5150, (505) 753-2419
http://www.comfortinn.com
247 S. Riverside Dr.
40 rooms - $50-70
Pets: Small pets w/$5 fee
Creature Comforts: CCTV, a/c,
refrig, pool, whirlpool

Super 8 Motel
(800) 800-8000, (505) 753-5374
http://www.super8.com
811 S. Riverside Dr.
51 rooms - $50-60
Pets: Welcome w/$20 deposit
Creature Comforts: CCTV, a/c

Best Western Inn
(800) 528-1234, (505) 327-5221
http://www.bestwestern.com
700 Scott Ave.
195 rooms - $80-110
Pets: Welcome
Creature Comforts: CCTV,
VCR, a/c, refrig, micro, restaurant,
pool, hlth clb., sauna, whirlpool

Comfort Inn
(800) 228-5150, (505) 325-2626
http://www.comfortinn.com
555 Scott Ave.
62 rooms - $50-65
Pets: Welcome w/$5 fee
Creature Comforts: CCTV, a/c,
pool, hlth clb access

Holiday Inn Express
(800) HOLIDAY, (505) 325-2545
http://www.holiday-inn.com
2110 Bloomfield Hwy.
65 rooms - $65-85
Pets: Welcome w/$50 deposit
Creature Comforts: CCTV, a/c,
refrig, micro, Jacuzzi, pool,
whirlpool

Holiday Inn Farmington
(800) HOLIDAY, (505) 327-9811
http://www.holiday-inn.com
600 E. Broadway St.
150 rooms - $70-85
Pets: Welcome w/$50 deposit
Creature Comforts: CCTV, a/c,
refrig, Jacuzzi, restaurant, pool,
hlth clb, sauna, whirlpool

La Quinta, Airport
(800) 531-5900, (505) 327-4706
http://www.laquinta.com
675 Scott Ave.
105 rooms - $60-75
Pets: Small pets welcome
Creature Comforts: CCTV, a/c,
refrig, micro, pool

Motel 6
(800) 4-MOTEL6, (505) 327-0242
http://www.motel6.com
510 Scott Ave.
98 rooms - $30
Pets: Under 30 lbs. welcome
Creature Comforts: CCTV a/c,
restaurant, pool

Motel 6
(800) 4-MOTEL6, (505) 327-0242
http://www.motel6.com
1600 Bloomfield Hwy.
134 rooms - $27-30
Pets: Under 30 lbs. welcome
Creature Comforts: CCTV a/c,
pool

GALLUP
Ambassador Motel
(505) 722-3843
1601 W. Rte. 66
46 rooms - $25-35
Pets: Small pets welcome
Creature Comforts: CCTV a/c,
pool

Best Western Inn and Suites
(800) 528-1234, (505) 722-2221
http://www.bestwestern.com
3009 Rte 66 West
125 rooms - $65-110
Pets: Small pets welcome
Creature Comforts: CCTV, a/c,
refrig, restaurant, pool, exercise
rm., sauna, whirlpool

Best Western Royal Holiday
(800) 528-1234, (505) 722-4900
http://www.bestwestern.com
1903 Rte. 66 W.
50 rooms - $50-150
Pets: Small pets w/deposit
Creature Comforts: CCTV, a/c,
refrig, micro, pool

Blue Spruce Lodge
(505) 863-5211
1119 Rte. 66 East
20 rooms - $25-35
Pets: Small pets welcome in
special rooms
Creature Comforts: CCTV, a/c,
micro, exercise rm.

Comfort Inn
(800) 228-5150, (505) 722-2404
http://www.comfortinn.com
3208 Rte. 66 West
50 rooms - $45-70
Pets: Welcome w/$5 fee
Creature Comforts: CCTV, a/c,
refrig, pool

Days Inn East
(800) DAYS INN, (505) 863-3891
http://www.daysinn.com
1603 Rte. 66 West
78 rooms - $40-60
Pets: Welcome w/$5 fee
Creature Comforts: CCTV, a/c,
refrig, pool

Days Inn West
(800) DAYS INN, (505) 863-6889
http://www.daysinn.com
3201 Rte. 66 West
75 rooms - $40-65
Pets: Welcome w/$5 fee
Creature Comforts: CCTV, a/c,
refrig, micro, Jacuzzi, pool,
whirlpool

Econo Lodge Gallup
(800) 55-ECONO, (505) 722-3800
http://www.econolodge.com
3101 Rte. 66 West
50 rooms - $45-70
Pets: Welcome
Creature Comforts: CCTV, a/c,
refrig, micro

Economy Inn
(505) 863-9301
1709 Rte. 66 West
50 rooms - $25-40
Pets: Small pets welcome
Creature Comforts: CCTV, a/c,
refrig, micro

El Capitan Motel
(505) 863-6828
1300 Rte. 66 East
40 rooms - $30-40
Pets: Small pets welcome
Creature Comforts: CCTV, a/c

El Rancho Hotel
(800) 543-6351, (505) 863-9311
http://www.elranchohotel.com
1000 East Rte. 66
102 rooms - $50-75
Pets: Welcome
Creature Comforts: Classic
Route 66 motel w/historic
Hollywood connection, two-story
lobby w/autographed photos of
film stars, attractive rooms, Native
American art and wagon wheel
headboards, recommend hotel rms
over motel rms, CCTV, a/c

Holiday Inn Hotel
(800) HOLIDAY, (505) 722-2201
http://www.holiday-inn.com
2915 Rte. 66 West
215 rooms - $55-65
Pets: Welcome
Creature Comforts: CCTV, a/c,
refrig, restaurant, pool, hlth clb
access, sauna, whirlpool

Motel 6
(800) 4-MOTEL6, (505) 326-4501
http://www.motel6.com
3306 Route 66 W.
80 rooms - $30
Pets: Under 30 lbs. welcome
Creature Comforts: CCTV a/c,
restaurant, pool

Road Runner Motel
(505) 863-3804
3012 Route 66 East
30 rooms - $30-37
Pets: Small pets w/$20 deposit
Creature Comforts: CCTV a/c,
pool

Roseway Inn
(505) 863-9385
2003 West Rte 66 West
95 rooms - $30-45
Pets: Small pets w/$20 deposit
Creature Comforts: CCTV a/c,
refrig, micro, pool, sauna,
whirlpool

Sleep Inn
(800) Sleep-Inn, (505) 863-3535
http://www.sleepinn.com
3820 Route 66 East
60 rooms - $45-65
Pets: Small pets w/$5 fee
Creature Comforts: CCTV a/c,
restaurant, cont. brkfst, pool,
whirlpool

Travelodge
(800) 578-7878, (505) 287-7800
http://www.travelodge.com
1608 E. Santa Fe Blvd.
60 rooms - $40-60
Pets: Welcome w/$5 dep.
Creature Comforts: CCTV, a/c,
pool, whirlpool

GLENWOOD
Los Olmos Guest Ranch
(505) 539-2311
http://www.gilanet.com/losolmos
Route 180
14 cottages - $60-85
Pets: Welcome w/$5 dep.
Creature Comforts: Rock
cottages, main lodge, restaurant,
pool, hot tub, horseback riding

GRANTS
Best Western Grants Inn
(800) 528-1234, (505) 287-7901
http://www.bestwestern.com
1501 E. Santa Fe Ave.
125 rooms - $65-97
Pets: $50 refundable deposit
Creature Comforts: CCTV,
VCR, a/c, refrig, micro, kit,
restaurant, pool, hlth club, sauna,
whirlpool

Days Inn
(800) DAYS INN, (505) 287-8883
http://www.daysinn.com
1504 E. Santa Fe Ave.
56 rooms - $60-90
Pets: Welcome
Creature Comforts: CCTV, a/c

Holiday Inn Express
(800) HOLIDAY, (505) 285-4676
http://www.holiday-inn.com
1496 E. Santa Fe Ave.
60 rooms - $60-90
Pets: Welcome
Creature Comforts: CCTV, a/c,
refrig, cont. brkfst, pool, whirlpool

Leisure Lodge
(505) 287-2991
1204 E. Santa Fe Ave.
33 rooms - $30-40
Pets: Small pets welcome
Creature Comforts: CCTV, a/c,
refrig, pool

Motel 6
(800) 4-MOTEL6, (505) 863-4492
http://www.motel6.com
3306 West 66
80 rooms - $30-42
Pets: Under 30 lbs. welcome
Creature Comforts: CCTV,
VCR, a/c, pool, restaurant

Sands Motel
(505) 287-2996
112 MacArthur Blvd.
24 rooms - $30-40
Pets: Small pets w/$10
Creature Comforts: CCTV, a/c,
refrig, pool

HOBBS
Best Western Leawood
(800) 528-1234, (505) 393-4101
http://www.bestwestern.com
1301 E. Broadway St.
68 rooms - $45-50
Pets: Small pets welcome
Creature Comforts: CCTV,
VCR, a/c, refrig, restaurant, pool,
exercise rm., whirlpool

Days Inn
(800) DAYS INN, (505) 397-6541
http://www.daysinn.com
211 N. Marland Blvd.
61 rooms - $55-75
Pets: Small pets w/$10 fee
Creature Comforts: CCTV, a/c

Econo Lodge
(800) 55-ECONO, (505) 397-3591
http://www.econolodge.com
619 N. Marland Blvd.
37 rooms - $35-45
Pets: Welcome
Creature Comforts: CCTV, a/c,
restaurant, cont. brkfst, pool

Innkeepers of New Mexico
(505) 397-7171
309 N. Marland Blvd.
64 rooms - $45-50
Pets: Welcome
Creature Comforts: CCTV, a/c,
refrig, pool

Ramada Inn
(800) 2-Ramada, (505) 397-3251
http://www.ramada.com
501 N. Marland Blvd.
75 rooms - $50-60
Pets: Small pets w/$25 deposit
Creature Comforts: CCTV, a/c,
restaurant, pool

Super 8 Motel
(800) 800-8000, (505) 397-7511
http://www.super8.com
722 N. Marland Blvd.
60 rooms - $35-40
Pets: Welcome w/permission
Creature Comforts: CCTV,
VCR, a/c, Jacuzzi, cont. brkfst

Travelodge
(800) 578-7878, (505) 393-4775
http://www.travelodge.com
309 N. Marland Blvd.
63 rooms - $35-45
Pets: Welcome
Creature Comforts: CCTV, a/c,
pool

Zia Motel
(505) 397-3591
619 North Marland Blvd.
40 rooms - $35-40
Pets: Small pets w/$25 deposit
Creature Comforts: CCTV, a/c,
refrig, pool

LAS CRUCES
Baymont Inns
(800) Baymont, (505) 523-0100
http://www.baymontinns.com
1500 Hickory Dr.
88 rooms - $40-45
Pets: Welcome
Creature Comforts: CCTV, a/c,
cont. brkfst, pool

Best Western Mesilla Valley
(800) 528-1234, (505) 524-8603
http://www.bestwestern.com
901 Avenida de Mesilla
165 rooms - $60-70
Pets: Welcome
Creature Comforts: CCTV, a/c,
refrig, micro, restaurant, pool,
whirlpool

Best Western Mission Inn
(800) 528-1234, (505) 524-8591
http://www.bestwestern.com
1765 S. Main St.
68 rooms - $55-65
Pets: Small pets welcome
Creature Comforts: CCTV, a/c,
refrig, restaurant, pool

Days Inn
(800) DAYS INN, (505) 526-4441
http://www.daysinn.com
2600 S. Valley Dr.
130 rooms - $50-70
Pets: Welcome w/$10 fee
Creature Comforts: CCTV, a/c,
refrig, micro, restaurant, pool,
sauna

Desert Lodge
(505) 524-4441
1900 W. Picacho St.
10 rooms - $20-30
Pets: Small pets welcome
Creature Comforts: CCTV, a/c

Hampton Inn
(800) Hampton, (505) 526-8311
http://www.hampton-inn.com
755 Avenida de Mesilla
120 rooms - $60-65
Pets: Welcome
Creature Comforts: CCTV, a/c,
refrig, pool

Hilltop Hacienda
(800) , (505) 382-3556
http://www.zianet.com/hilltop
2600 Westmoreland
3 rooms - $75-85
Pets: Very well behaved pets
welcome, must be supervised
Creature Comforts: Spanish
architecture, adobe brick home w/
stunning views, 18 acre setting,
CCTV, VCR, a/c, farm brkfst

Hilton Inn
(800) HILTONS, (505) 522-4300
http://www.hilton.com
705 S. Telshor Blvd.
203 rooms - $95-115
Pets: Welcome
Creature Comforts: CCTV, a/c,
refrig, Jacuzzi, restaurant, pool

Holiday Inn Las Cruces
(800) HOLIDAY, (505) 526-4411
http://www.holiday-inn.com
201 E. University Ave.
180 rooms - $65-75
Pets: Under 25 lbs. welcome
Creature Comforts: CCTV, a/c,
restaurant, pool

Holiday Inn Express
(800) HOLIDAY, (505) 527-9947
http://www.holiday-inn.com
2200 S. Valley Dr.
55 rooms - $50-85
Pets: Small dogs and cats w/$25
fee
Creature Comforts: CCTV, a/c,
refrig, micro, restaurant, cont.
brkfst, pool, exercise rm.,
whirlpool

La Quinta
(800) 531-5900, (505) 524-0331
http://www.laquinta.com
790 Avenida de Mesilla
99 rooms - $60-65
Pets: Small pets welcome
Creature Comforts: CCTV, a/c,
refrig, Jacuzzi, pool, hlth clb

Lundeen Inn of the Arts
(505) 526-3326
http://www.innofthearts.com
618 S. Alameda Blvd.
20 rooms - $60-85
Pets: Med. dogs welcome in ltd.
rms. w/$15 fee
Creature Comforts: Territorial-
style adobe bldgs and casitas w/art
gallery and inn, Mexican tile
floors, French doors, Palladian
windows, antiques, rooms named
after southwestern artists,
handcrafted furniture, hardwood
floors, CCTV, a/c, gourmet full
brkfst

Motel 6
(800) 4-MOTEL6, (505) 525-1010
http://www.motel6.com
235 La Posada Ln.
118 rooms - $30-42
Pets: Under 30 lbs. welcome
Creature Comforts: CCTV, a/c,
pool

Royal Host Motel
(505) 524-8536
2146 W. Picacho St.
25 rooms - $30-40
Pets: Welcome w/$5 fee
Creature Comforts: CCTV, a/c,
pool

Super 8
(800) 800-8000, (505) 523-8695
http://www.super8.com
245 La Posada
59 rooms - $50-60
Pets: Welcome w/permission
Creature Comforts: CCTV,
VCR, a/c, refrig, micro

Western Inn
(505) 523-5399
2155 W. Picacho rd.
49 rooms - $30-45
Pets: Small pets welcome
Creature Comforts: CCTV, a/c,
kit, pool

LAS VEGAS
El Camino Motel
(505) 425-5994
1152 Grand Ave.
25 rooms - $50-70
Pets: Small pets-$6 fee, $20 dep.
Creature Comforts: CCTV, a/c

Inn on the Santa Fe Trail
(888) 448-8438, (505) 425-6791
www.innonthesantafetrail.com
1133 N. Grand Ave.
33 rooms - $50-70
Pets: Welcome w/$5 deposit
Creature Comforts: Appealing
1930's hacienda style motel w/
central courtyard, southwestern
style rooms, CCTV, a/c, refrig,
micro, restaurant, cont. brkfst,
pool, whirlpool

Plaza Hotel
(800) 328-1882, (505) 425-3591
http://worldplaces.com/plaza
230 Old Town Plaza
36 rooms - $66-120
Pets: Welcome w/$10 fee
Creature Comforts: 1882 hotel
on "Old Town" plaza, Victorian
furnishings, old fashioned bar w/
historic photos, guest rooms filled
w/mix of Victorian and contemp.
furnishings, attractive decor,
CCTV, a/c, refrig, restaurant

LORDSBURG
Best Western American
(800) 528-1234, (505) 542-3591
http://www.bestwestern.com
944 E. Motel Dr.
89 rooms - $50-65
Pets: Welcome w/$50 deposit
Creature Comforts: CCTV,
VCR, a/c, refrig, micro, restaurant,
pool

Best Western Western Skies
(800) 528-1234, (505) 542-8807
http://www.bestwestern.com
1303 S. Main St.
39 rooms - $45-50
Pets: Welcome
Creature Comforts: CCTV, a/c,
restaurant, pool

Days Inn
(800) DAYS INN, (505) 542-3600
http://www.daysinn.com
1100 W. Motel Dr.
56 rooms - $65-75
Pets: Welcome
Creature Comforts: CCTV, a/c,
refrig, micro, pool, exercise rm.

Holiday Inn Express
(800) HOLIDAY, (505) 542-3666
http://www.holiday-inn.com
1408 S. Main
40 rooms - $60-75
Pets: Welcome w/$50 deposit
Creature Comforts: CCTV, a/c,
pool

LOS ALAMOS
Hilltop House Hotel
(800) 462-0936, (505) 662-2441
http://losalamos.com/hilltophouse
400 Trinity Dr.
34 rooms - $75-85
Pets: Welcome
Creature Comforts: CCTV, a/c,
restaurant, cont. brkfst, pool,
exercise rm.

MORIARTY
Days Inn
(800) DAYS INN, (505) 832-4451
http://www.daysinn.com
Rte 66 West
41 rooms - $50-70
Pets: Welcome w/$5 fee
Creature Comforts: CCTV, a/c,
refrig, micro

Sunset Motel
(505) 832-4234
501 Old Rte 66
18 rooms - $37
Pets: Welcome w/$5 fee
Creature Comforts: CCTV, a/c

Super 8 Motel
(800) 800-8000, (505) 832-6730
http://www.super8.com
1611 Route 66 West
70 rooms - $35-45
Pets: Welcome w/$20 deposit
Creature Comforts: CCTV, a/c,
refrig

PLACITAS
Hacienda de Placitas
(505) 867-0082
www.haciendainnofthearts.com
491 Rte. 165
3 suites/2 cottages - $99-159
Pets: Welcome
Creature Comforts: Set on 300
acres atop mesa overlooking mtns,
6,000 sq. ft. hacienda and historic
outbuildings, windmill, stone
walls, fish ponds, original artwork
throughout w/gallery, guests stay
in adobe cottages w/antique beds,
quilts, kiva fireplace, CCTV, a/c,
refrig, micro, terry robes, gourmet
meals, afternoon tea, restaurant,
pool

POJOAQUE
Rancho Jacona
(505) 455-7948
http://www.ranchojacona.com
Route 5, Box 250
6 casitas - $120-195
Pets: Welcome — leashed on
ppty, cannot chase ranch animals
Creature Comforts: A 30-acre
ranch along Pojaque river, lush
landscaping, historic casitas w/
Mexican tile floors, bancos, viga
ceilings, contemp. furnishings
mixed w/native pottery, baskets,
weavings, CCTV, a/c, refrig,
micro, refrig, pond, hiking

PORTALES
Portales Inn
(505) 359-1208
218 W. Third St.
40 rooms - $35-40
Pets: Welcome
Creature Comforts: CCTV, a/c,
restaurant

RATON
Harmony Manor Motel
(505) 445-2763
351 Clayton Rd.
17 rooms - $45-60
Pets: Small pets w/$4 fee
Creature Comforts: CCTV, a/c

Melody Lane Motel
(800) 421-5210, (505) 445-3655
136 Canyon Dr.
30 rooms - $40-50
Pets: Small pets w/$3 fee
Creature Comforts: CCTV, a/c

Motel 6
(800) 4-MOTEL6, (412) 445-2777
http://www.motel6.com
1600 Cedar St.
104 rooms - $30-42
Pets: Under 30 lbs. welcome
Creature Comforts: CCTV, a/c,
pool

Super 8 Motel
(800) 800-8000, (505) 445-2355
http://www.super8.com
1610 Cedar St
49 rooms - $50-60
Pets: Small pets welcome
Creature Comforts: CCTV,
VCR, a/c, refrig

RED RIVER
Tall Pine Resort
(505) 754-2211
211 Beecham Rd.
126 rooms - $35-50
Pets: Under 30 lbs. welcome
Creature Comforts: CCTV, VCR

Terrace Towers Lodge
(800) 695-6343
Box 149
26 rooms - $40-120
Pets: Welcome in main lodge
Creature Comforts: CCTV, hot
tub

RIO RANCHO
Best Western Rio Rancho
(800) 528-1234, (505) 892-1700
http://www.bestwestern.com
1465 Rio Rancho Dr.
120 rooms - $55-70
Pets: Welcome w/$4 fee
Creature Comforts: CCTV,
VCR, a/c, refrig, micro, kit,
Jacuzzi, restaurant, pool, hlth clb,
whirlpool

Days Inn
(800) DAYS INN, (505) 892-8800
http://www.daysinn.com
4200 Crestview Dr.
48 rooms - $45-55
Pets: Welcome
Creature Comforts: CCTV, a/c,
refrig, micro, pool, whirlpool
ROAD FORKS

Desert West Motel
(505) 542-8801
Route 10
60 rooms - $40-50
Pets: Welcome
Creature Comforts: CCTV, a/c,
refrig, kit, pool

ROSWELL
Best Western El Rancho Palacio
(800) 528-1234, (505) 622-2721
http://www.bestwestern.com
2205 N. Main St.
45 rooms - $45-55
Pets: Welcome
Creature Comforts: CCTV, a/c,
pool, whirlpool

Best Western Sally Port Inn
(800) 528-1234, (505) 622-6430
http://www.bestwestern.com
2000 N. Main St.
125 rooms - $65-100
Pets: Welcome
Creature Comforts: CCTV, a/c,
refrig, kit, restaurant, pool, hlth
clb, whirlpool, tennis

Budget Inn, West
(505) 623-3811
2200 West Second St.
125 rooms - $65-100
Pets: Welcome
Creature Comforts: CCTV, a/c,
refrig, kit, restaurant, pool, hlth
clb, whirlpool, tennis

Budget Inn, North
(800) 752-4667, (505) 623-3811
2200 West Second St.
125 rooms - $65-100
Pets: Welcome
Creature Comforts: CCTV, a/c,
refrig, kit, restaurant, pool, hlth
clb, whirlpool, tennis

Days Inn
(800) DAYS INN, (505) 623-4021
http://www.daysinn.com
1310 N. Main St
65 rooms - $45-60
Pets: Welcome
Creature Comforts: CCTV, a/c,
refrig, restaurant, pool, whirlpool

Frontier Motel
(800) 678-1401, (505) 622-1400
3010 N. Main St.
39 rooms - $30-40
Pets: Welcome
Creature Comforts: CCTV, a/c,
refrig, cont. brkfst, pool

National 9 Inn
(800) 524-9999, (505) 622-0110
2001 N. Main St
65 rooms - $30-40
Pets: Welcome
Creature Comforts: CCTV, a/c,
refrig, cont. brkfst, pool

Ramada Inn
(800) 2-Ramada, (505) 623-9440
http://www.ramada.com
2803 W. 2nd St.
60 rooms - $55-60
Pets: Small pets-$15 fee, $25 dep.
Creature Comforts: CCTV, a/c,
restaurant, pool

Roswell Inn
(505) 623-4920
1815 N. Main St.
120 rooms - $55-65
Pets: Small pets w/$10 fee
Creature Comforts: CCTV, a/c,
refrig, restaurant, pool, whirlpool

RUIDOSO
Bestway Inn
(505) 378-8000
2052 Rte. 70 W.
20 rooms - $30-90
Pets: Welcome w/$4 fee
Creature Comforts: CCTV,
VCR, a/c, refrig, micro, whirlpool

Idle Hour Lodge
(800) 831-1186, (505) 257-2711
http://www.idlehourlodge.com
112 Lower Terrace
12 cabins - $62-77
Pets: Welcome w/permission and
$20 fee
Creature Comforts: Rustic,
knotty pine cabins, CCTV, kit,
fireplace, playground

Inn at Pine Springs
(505) 378-8100
Route 70
100 rooms - $49-79
Pets: Welcome
Creature Comforts: CCTV, a/c,
cont. brkfst, pool

Riverside Cottages
(800) 328-2804, (505) 257-4753
101 Flume Canyon
10 cabins - $90-125
Pets: Small pets w/$50 deposit
Creature Comforts: Riverside
cabins, antique decor, CCTV, kit,
fireplace

Swiss Chalet Inn
(800) 477-9477, (505) 258-3333
http://www.innofthehills.com/
swiss.htm
Rte. 48, 1451 Mechem Dr.
82 rooms - $60-135
Pets: Small pets welcome
Creature Comforts: Festive
Swiss-style hotel, window boxes,
traditional cherry and
Scandinavian furnishings, CCTV,
a/c, refrig, micro, Swiss restaurant,
pool, hlth clb, sauna, whirlpool

Village Lodge
(505) 258-5442
1000 Mechem Dr.
26 rooms - $30-90
Pets: Small pets welcome
Creature Comforts: CCTV, a/c,
refrig, micro, kit, whirlpool

SANTA FE
Alexander's Inn
(505) 986-1431
http://www.collectorsguide.com/
sf/l008.html
529 E. Palace Ave.
6 rooms, 4 cottages - $75-180
Pets: Welcome
Creature Comforts: Highly
recommended, 1903 Craftsman-
style home, beautifully landscaped
courtyard w/fruit trees, perennials,
Victorian antiques, traditionally
decorated rms., kiva fireplace,
CCTV, a/c, refrig, micro, kit,
robes, flowers, down comforters,
gourmet brkfst buffet, afternoon
tea/baked treats, hlth clb access,
hiking

Arius Compound
(800) 735-8453, (505) 982-2621
http://www.ariuscompound.com
Box 1111
3 casitas - $90-200
Pets: Welcome w/$5 nightly fee
per pet, in residence a Great
Pyrenees and Bichon Frisee
Creature Comforts: Old
Mexican style casitas set in
compound, on historic Canyon
Rd., courtyard and gardens w/fruit
trees and fountains, tile flrs,
Southwest decor, fireplace, CCTV,
a/c, kit, hot tub

Cactus Lodge
(505) 471-7699
2864 Cerrillos Rd.
25 rooms - $30-90
Pets: Welcome
Creature Comforts: CCTV, a/c

Casapueblo Inn
(800) 955-4455, (505) 471-7699
http://www.casapueblo.com
138 Park Ave.
12 suites - $110-440
Pets: Welcome
Creature Comforts: Luxurious
suites w/kiva fireplaces, viga
ceilings, Southwestern
furnishings, CCTV, a/c, refrig, kit,
good choice for families, affiliated
w/the Eldorado Hotel

Days Inn
(800) DAYS INN, (505) 438-3822
http://www.daysinn.com
3650 Cerrillos Dr.
99 rooms - $50-120
Pets: Small pets welcome
Creature Comforts: CCTV, a/c,
refrig, Jacuzzi, pool, whirlpool

De Romero on Duran Casitas
(877) 205-9235, (505) 988-1422
www.southwesterninns.com/
deromero.htm
132 Duran St.
6 casitas - $80-150
Pets: Well behaved pets welcome
Creature Comforts: Adobe
casitas, in same family for 80
years, Mexican and saltillo tile
floors, CCTV, kit, fireplace, hot
tub

Doubletree Club Hotel
(800) 222-TREE, (505) 473-2800
http://www.doubletreehotels.com
3347 Cerrillos Rd.
210 rooms - $110-155
Pets: Small pets w/$30 deposit
Creature Comforts: CCTV, a/c,
refrig, micro, kit, restaurant, pool,
hlth clb, whirlpool

El Paradero B&B
(505) 988-1177
http://www.elparadero.com
220 W. Manhattan
14 rooms - $65-140
Pets: Dogs welcome w/$10 daily
fee
Creature Comforts: 1800's
Territorial-style inn w/Victorian
accents, eclectic mix of Victorian
and southwestern furnishings,
simple fabrics, skylights, hand-
painted decorative murals, CCTV,
a/c, fireplace, kit, hearty brkfsts

Eldorado Hotel
(800) 955-4455, (505) 988-4455
http://www.eldoradohotel.com
309 W. San Francisco St.
220 rooms - $190-1,000
Pets: Welcome in special rooms
Creature Comforts: Massive,
fortress-like facade reminiscent of
ancient pueblos, impressive art
collection, southwestern rm. decor
w/light stained woods, contemp.
furnishings, lithographs or
weavings decorating walls, robes,
toiletries, CCTV, VCR, a/c, refrig,
Jacuzzi, restaurant, pool, hlth clb,
whirlpool

Fairfield Inn
(800) 228-2800, (505) 474-4442
http://www.farifieldinn.com/
4150 Cerrillos Rd.
56 rooms - $70-90
Pets: Small pets w/$10 fee
Creature Comforts: CCTV, a/c,
pool

Holiday Inn
(800) HOLIDAY, (505) 473-4686
http://www.holiday-inn.com
4048 Cerrillos Rd.
131 rooms - $85-160
Pets: Welcome w/$25 fee
Creature Comforts: CCTV, a/c,
refrig, restaurant, pool, hlth clb,
sauna, whirlpool

Homewood Suites
(800) 225-5466, (505) 988-3000
http://www.homewoodsuites.com/
400 Griffin St.
100 rooms - $120-190
Pets: Welcome w/$10 fee, $50 deposit
Creature Comforts: CCTV, a/c, refrig, micro, kit, fireplace, restaurant, cont. brkfst, pool, hlth clb, sauna, whirlpool

Hotel Santa Fe
(800) 825-9876, (505) 982-1200
http://www.santafe.org/
hotelsantafe
1501 Paseo de Peralta
131 rooms - $120-190
Pets: Welcome w/$50 deposit
Creature Comforts: CCTV, a/c, refrig, micro, restaurant, pool, whirlpool

Inn of the Anazasi
(800) 688-8100, (505) 988-3030
http://www.innoftheanasazi.com/
113 Washington Ave.
59 rooms - $200-400
Pets: Welcome w/$30 fee
Creature Comforts: Gracious intimate adobe hotel just off Plaza, interior feels like ancient pueblo w/sophisticated touches of Native American art, leather chairs, interior waterfall, southwestern style rms. w/adobe walls, kilim pillows, four poster wrought iron beds, CCTV, ac, refrig, terry robes, organic toiletries, kiva fireplace, excellent gourmet restaurant

Inn of the Turquoise Bear
(800) 396-4104, (505) 983-0798
http://www.collectorsguide.com/
sf/l023.html
342 E. Buena Vista St.
11 - $95-290
Pets: Small pets by arrangement, ltd. rms, $20 cleaning fee per pet
Creature Comforts: Wonderful historic Spanish-Pueblo Revival style home, rock terraces, gardens, viga ceilings, lodge pole four poster beds, down comforters, kiva fireplace, terry robes, CCTV, VCR, expanded cont. brkfst, afternoon wine and cheese

Inn on the Alameda
(888) 984-2121, (505) 984-2121
http://inn-alamed.com/index.html
303 East Alameda
72 rooms - $140-350
Pets: Welcome, pet amenity prog w/kibble, dog walk map, treats
Creature Comforts: Pueblo style inn called "most enchanting small hotel in Santa Fe," gracious reception area, courtyards, pickled pine/teak furnishings, hand-carved beds, tables, kiva fireplaces, exposed beams, CCTV, a/c, refrig, lavish cont. brkfst, whirlpool

La Quinta
(800) 531-5900, (505) 471-1142
http://www.laquinta.com
4928 Cerrillos Rd.
128 rooms - $60-95
Pets: Small pets welcome
Creature Comforts: CCTV, a/c, refrig, pool

Las Palomas
(800) 955-4455, (505) 471-1142
http://www.laspalomas.com
4928 Cerrillos Rd.
10 suites - $110-350
Pets: Small pets welcome
Creature Comforts: Beautifully restored historic pueblo-style casitas, courtyards, trees, Southwest decor, feather beds, down comforters, CCTV, VCR, stereo, a/c, kiva fireplace, kit, cont. brkfst, pool

The Madeleine
(888) 321-5123, (505) 982-3465
http://www.prestonhouse.com
106 Faithway St.
15 rooms - $75-170
Pets: Well behaved pets welcome
Creature Comforts: 1886 Queen Anne style house, sister inn to Alexander's Inn, beautiful gardens, sunny rooms w/garden themes, windowseats, floral down comforters, some antiques, CCTV, a/c, fireplace, full country brkfst

Motel 6
(800) 4-MOTEL6, (505) 471-4140
http://www.motel6.com
3695 Cerrillos Rd.
121 rooms - $36-44
Pets: Under 30 lbs. welcome
Creature Comforts: CCTV, a/c, pool

Motel 6
(800) 4-MOTEL6, (505) 473-1380
http://www.motel6.com
3007 Cerrillos Rd.
104 rooms - $36-45
Pets: Under 30 lbs. welcome
Creature Comforts: CCTV, a/c, pool

Quality Inn
(800) 228-5151, (505) 471-1211
http://www.qualityinn.com
3011 Cerrillos Rd.
100 rooms - $65-90
Pets: Welcome
Creature Comforts: CCTV, VCR, a/c, refrig, pool

Residence Inn
(800) 331-3131, (505) 988-7300
http://www.residenceinn.com
1698 Galisteo Dr.
121 rooms - $95-200
Pets: $10 fee, $150 deposit
Creature Comforts: CCTV, VCR, a/c, refrig, micro, kit, fireplace, pool, whirlpool

Rio Vista Suites
(800) 745-9910, (505) 982-6636
320 Artist Rd.
12 suites - $65-140
Pets: Small pets welcome
Creature Comforts: CCTV, VCR, a/c, kit, cont. brkfst

SANTA ROSA
Best Western Adobe
(800) 528-1234, (505) 472-3446
http://www.bestwestern.com
1501 Will Rogers Dr.
60 rooms - $40-60
Pets: Small pets welcome
Creature Comforts: CCTV, a/c, pool

Best Western Santa Rosa
(800) 528-1234, (505) 472-5877
http://www.bestwestern.com
3022 Will Rogers Dr.
45 rooms - $50-55
Pets: Small pets w/$5 fee
Creature Comforts: CCTV, a/c,
refrig, pool

Comfort Inn
(800) 228-5150, (505) 472-5570
http://www.comfortinn.com
3343 Will Rogers Dr., East
45 rooms - $50-60
Pets: Welcome
Creature Comforts: CCTV, a/c

Days Inn
(800) DAYS INN, (505) 472-5985
http://www.daysinn.com
1830 Will Rogers Dr.
50 rooms - $50-65
Pets: Welcome
Creature Comforts: CCTV,
VCR, a/c

Holiday Inn, Express
(800) HOLIDAY, (505) 472-5411
http://www.holiday-inn.com
3300 Will Rogers Dr.
70 rooms - $50-70
Pets: Small pets in smoking rms.
Creature Comforts: CCTV, a/c,
pool

Motel 6
(800) 4-MOTEL6, (505) 472-3045
http://www.motel6.com
3400 Will Rogers Dr.
91 rooms - $35-45
Pets: Under 30 lbs. welcome
Creature Comforts: CCTV, a/c,
pool

Super 8 Motel
(800) 800-8000, (505) 472-5388
http://www.super8.com
1201 Will Rogers Dr.
90 rooms - $40-45
Pets: Welcome w/$20 deposit
Creature Comforts: CCTV,
VCR, a/c

SILVER CITY
Bear Mountain Guest Ranch
(800) 880-2358, (505) 538-2538
http://www.dinfinitiv.com/bear/
Box 1163
10 rooms, 4 cottages - $55-95
Pets: Welcome
Creature Comforts: 160
mountainous acres abutting Gila
National Forest, Territorial-style
ranch house w/outlying cottages,
simple furnishings, family-style
meals, casual atmosphere

Copper Manor Motel
(800) 832-2916, (505) 538-5392
710 Silver Heights
70 rooms - $45-55
Pets: Small pets welcome
Creature Comforts: CCTV, a/c,
restaurant, pool, whirlpool

Drifter Motel
(800) 853-2916, (505) 538-2916
711 Silver Heights Rd.
70 rooms - $45-50
Pets: Small pets welcome
Creature Comforts: CCTV, a/c,
restaurant, pool, whirlpool

Econo Lodge
(800) 55-Econo, (505) 534-1111
http://www.econolodge.com
1120 Rte. 180 E.
65 rooms - $40-70
Pets: Small pets w/$25 deposit
Creature Comforts: CCTV, a/c,
refrig, micro, pool

Holiday Motor Hotel
(505) 538-3711
http://www.holidayhotel.com
3420 Rte. 180 E.
80 rooms - $55-65
Pets: Welcome
Creature Comforts: CCTV, a/c,
restaurant, pool

Super 8 Motel
(800) 800-8000, (505) 388-1983
http://www.super8.com
1040 East Rte. 180
69 rooms - $50-65
Pets: Small pets w/$5 fee
Creature Comforts: CCTV, a/c,
pool, whirlpool

SOCORRO
Econo Lodge
(800) 55-Econo, (505) 835-1500
http://www.econolodge.com
713 California St.
45 rooms - $35-50
Pets: Small pets w/$10 deposit
Creature Comforts: CCTV, a/c,
refrig, micro, pool, whirlpool

Holiday Inn Express
(800) HOLIDAY, (505) 838-0556
http://www.holiday-inn.com
1100 California Ave., NE
80 rooms - $85-105
Pets: Welcome w/$5 fee
Creature Comforts: CCTV, a/c,
refrig, micro, restaurant, pool

Motel 6
(800) 4-MOTEL6, (505) 835-4300
http://www.motel6.com
807 S. Rte. 85
123 rooms - $28-39
Pets: Under 30 lbs. welcome
Creature Comforts: CCTV, a/c,
pool

TAOS
Adobe and Stars
(800) 211-7076, (505) 776-2776
http://www.taosadobe.com
Box 2285
8 rooms - $105-175
Pets: Welcome w/$50 deposit
Creature Comforts: Pueblo-style
home perched on mesa, expansive
views, southwestern decor w/
Navajo blankets, sculpture,
sophisticated yet rustic
furnishings, CCTV, a/c, kiva
fireplace, full brkfst, Jacuzzis

Casa Encantada
(800) 223-8267, (505) 758-7477
http://www.casaencantada.com
416 Liebert Rd.
9 rooms - $75-125
Pets: Welcome w/$10 fee per pet
Creature Comforts: Highly
recommended, adobe walls
surround courtyards and rooms,
tucked away, beautiful gardens,
sophisticated yet simple
Southwest decor, CCTV, VCR,
a/c, fireplace, full brkfst

Del Norte Vista Properties
(800) 258-8436
10 Tecolate Rd.
Houses - $125-600
Pets: Welcome w/varying fees
Creature Comforts: Pet-friendly
properties, CCTV, a/c, kit, living
rm, 1-5 bedrooms,

El Monte Lodge
(800) 828-TAOS, (505) 758-3171
http://www.travelbase.com/
destinations/taos/el-monte
317 Kit Carson Rd.
13 rooms - $75-125
Pets: Welcome w/$6 fee
Creature Comforts: 1930's
traditional Pueblo-style cottages,
parklike setting, Eastern
Americana-style furnishings,
CCTV, a/c, refrig, kit, fireplace

El Pueblo Lodge
(800) 433-9612, (505) 758-8700
http://taoswebb.com/hotel/
elpueblo
412 Paseo del Pueblo Norte
60 rooms - $65-248
Pets: Welcome w/$10 fee
Creature Comforts: Lodge
rooms and condominiums, CCTV,
a/c, refrig, micro, kit, fireplace,
pool, whirlpool

El Rincon Inn
(505) 758-4874
114 Kit Carson Rd.
13 rooms - $65-125
Pets: Welcome w/$5 fee
Creature Comforts: 1800's
adobe inn mixes Native American/
Spanish traditions, colorful wall
murals, stained glass, hand-carved
furnishings in themed rooms, cozy
and personal w/southwestern
touch, CCTV, VCR, stereo,
fireplace, Jacuzzi, cont. brkfst

Fechin Inn
(888) 751-1002, (505) 751-1000
http://www.fechin-inn.com
227 Paseo Del Pueblo Norte
85 rooms - $110-488
Pets: Welcome in first floor rooms
Creature Comforts: Inn built
around famous southwestern
artist's, Nicolai Fechin, historic
adobe home, woodwork mirrors
Fechin's distinctive style, earthen
colors, light pine furnishings, terry
robes, CCTV, a/c, refrig, fireplace,
cont. brkfst, walk to Plaza

Holiday Inn Don Fernando
(800) HOLIDAY, (505) 758-4444
http://www.holiday-inn.com
1005 Paseo del Pueblo Norte
125 rooms - $110-175
Pets: Welcome w/$75 deposit
Creature Comforts: CCTV, a/c,
refrig, fireplace, restaurant, pool,
whirlpool, tennis

Inn on the Rio
(800) 859-6752, (505) 758-7199
http://www.innontherio.com
910 East Kit Carson Dr.
11 rooms - $89-130
Pets: Small dogs w/$10 fee
Creature Comforts: "Best kept
secret in Taos", charming but low
key adobe lodge, viga ceilings,
hardwood flrs, Indian blankets,
murals, ecclectic mix of country
antiques and family favorites,
CCTV, refrig, fireplace, cont.
brkfst, pool

Quality Inn
(800) 228-5151, (505) 758-2200
http://www.qualityinn.com
1043 Paseo del Pueblo Sur
125 rooms - $55-75
Pets: Small pets welcome
Creature Comforts: CCTV,
VCR, a/c, refrig, micro, restaurant,
pool, whirlpool

Rancho Ramada de Taos
(800) 2-Ramada, (505) 758-2900
http://www.ramada.com
615 Paseo del Pueblo
125 rooms - $60-120
Pets: Small pets welcome
Creature Comforts: CCTV, a/c,
refrig, restaurant, cont. brkfst,
pool, whirlpool

Sagebrush Inn
(800) 428-3626, (505) 758-2254
1508 Paseo del Pueblo Sur
100 rooms - $60-110
Pets: Small pets welcome
Creature Comforts: CCTV, a/c,
refrig, micro, fireplace, restaurant,
full brkfst, pool, whirlpool

Sun God Lodge
(800) 821-2437, (505) 758-3162
http://www.sungodlodge.com
919 Paseo del Pueblo Sur
48 rooms - $55-110
Pets: Small pets w/$50 deposit
Creature Comforts: Nice motel
w/adobe exterior, tree-lined plaza,
rooms decorated w/bright colors
in southwestern theme, local art,
weavings, CCTV, VCR, a/c, kit,
kiva fireplace, restaurant, cont.
brkfst, hlth clb access, hot tub

TAOS SKI VALLEY
Alpine Village Suites
(800) 576-2666, (505) 776-8540
taoswebb.com/nmusa/cottams
Box 917
23 suites - $140-280
Pets: Welcome w/$15 fee
Creature Comforts: Slopeside
suites, light lofted spaces w/fully
equipped kits, handcrafted New
Mexican furniture, recommend the
newer buldings luxury suites w/
corner fireplaces and upscale
furnishings, CCTV, VCR, a/c, kit,
fireplace, pool, hlth clb access,
and a hot tub

Austing Haus
(800) 748-2932, (505) 776-2649
http://www.taosweb.com/hotel/
austinghaus/index.html
Taos Ski Valley Rd.
36 rooms - $75-160
Pets: Welcome
Creature Comforts: Swiss chalet
w/traditional timber frame
construction, exposed beams,
massive plate glass windows,
intimate rooms w/beam ceilings,
stenciled walls, Queen-Anne style
furnishings, brass lamps,
recommend rooms in newer
section near hot tub room, CCTV,
VCR, a/c, kit, fireplace, restaurant,
expnded cont. brkfst, hot tub

514

THOREAU
Zuni Mountain Lodge
(505) 862-7616
http://maslow.cia-g.com/~zuniml
40 Perch Dr.
10 rooms - $85
Pets: Welcome only with permission
Creature Comforts: Set at foot of Bluewater Lake, contemp. home in rugged mtn. setting, CCTV, VCR, dining rm

TRUTH OR CONSEQUENCES
Best Western Hot Springs
(800) 528-1234, (505) 894-6665
http://www.bestwestern.com
2270 N. Date St.
41 rooms - $60-65
Pets: Small pets welcome
Creature Comforts: CCTV, a/c, restaurant, pool

Super 8 Motel
(800) 800-8000, (505) 894-7888
http://www.super8.com
2151 North Date St.
39 rooms - $45-52
Pets: Welcome w/$20 deposit
Creature Comforts: CCTV, VCR, a/c

TUCUMCARI
Americana Motel
(505) 461-0431
406 E. Tucumcari Blvd.
15 rooms - $20-40
Pets: Welcome
Creature Comforts: CCTV, a/c

Best Western Aruba
(800) 528-1234, (505) 461-3335
http://www.bestwestern.com
1700 E. Tucumcari Blvd.
35 rooms - $45-55
Pets: Welcome
Creature Comforts: CCTV, a/c, pool

Best Western Pow Wow Inn
(800) 528-1234, (505) 461-0500
http://www.bestwestern.com
801 West Tucumcari Blvd.
65 rooms - $45-65
Pets: Welcome w/$10 fee
Creature Comforts: CCTV, VCR, a/c, refrig, kit, restaurant, pool

Budget Host Royal Palacio
(800) Bud-Host, (505) 461-1212
http://www.budgethost.com
1620 East Tucumcari Blvd.
25 rooms - $30-40
Pets: Small pets w/$3 fee
Creature Comforts: CCTV, VCR, a/c, refrig, kit, restaurant, pool

Comfort Inn
(800) 228-5150, (505) 461-4094
http://www.comfortinn.com
2800 E. Tucumcari Blvd.
60 rooms - $55-60
Pets: Welcome w/$6 fee
Creature Comforts: CCTV, a/c, pool

Days Inn
(800) DAYS INN, (505) 461-3158
http://www.daysinn.com
2623 S. First St.
40 rooms - $40-60
Pets: Welcome
Creature Comforts: CCTV, a/c

Econo Lodge
(800) 55-ECONO, (505) 461-4194
http://www.econolodge.com
3400 E. Tucumcari Blvd.
41 rooms - $35-65
Pets: Welcome
Creature Comforts: CCTV, a/c

Holiday Inn
(800) HOLIDAY, (505) 461-3780
http://www.holiday-inn.com
3716 E. Tucumcari Blvd.
100 rooms - $45-85
Pets: Welcome w/$6 fee
Creature Comforts: CCTV, a/c, restaurant, pool, whirlpool

Motel 6
(800) 4-MOTEL6, (505) 461-4791
http://www.motel6.com
2900 E. Tucumcari Blvd.
122 rooms - $30
Pets: Under 30 lbs. welcome
Creature Comforts: CCTV, a/c, pool

Rodeway Inn, West
(800) 228-2000, (505) 461-3140
http://www.rodeway.com
1302 W. Tucumcari Blvd.
60 rooms - $50-60
Pets: Welcome
Creature Comforts: CCTV, a/c, pool

Safari Motel
(505) 461-3642
722 E. Tucumcari Blvd.
24 rooms - $50-60
Pets: Welcome w/$3 fee
Creature Comforts: CCTV, a/c, pool

Super 8 Motel
(800) 800-8000, (505) 461-4444
http://www.super8.com
4001 E. Tucumcari Blvd.
65 rooms - $40-50
Pets: Small pets w/$25 deposit
Creature Comforts: CCTV, a/c, pool

Tucumcari Travelodge
(800) 578-7878, (505) 461-1401
http://www.travelodge.com
1214 E. Tucumcari Blvd.
37 rooms - $35-45
Pets: Small pets w/$10 deposit
Creature Comforts: CCTV, a/c, pool

VAUGHN
Bel-Air Motel
(505) 584-2241
Rtes. 60 & 285
20 rooms - $30-39
Pets: Small pets w/$10 deposit
Creature Comforts: CCTV, a/c

WHITES CITY
Best Western Cavern Inn
(800) 528-1234, (505) 785-2291
http://www.bestwestern.com
17 Carlsbad Caverns Rd.
65 rooms - $50-80
Pets: Small pets w/$10 fee
Creature Comforts: CCTV, VCR, a/c, Jacuzzi, pool, whirlpool

New York

ACRA
Sleepy Dutchman
(518) 622-2050
Route 23
10 rooms - $45-60
Pets: Welcome w/$2 fee
Creature Comforts: CCTV, a/c, kit

ALBANY
Econo Lodge
(800) 55-ECONO, (518) 456-8811
http://www.econolodge.com
1632 Central Ave
100 rooms - $42-82
Pets: Welcome
Creature Comforts: CCTV, a/c, cont. brkfst

Howard Johnson
(800) I-Go-Hojo, (518) 462-6555
http://www.hojo.com
416 Southern Blvd.
135 rooms - $75-150
Pets: Welcome
Creature Comforts: CCTV, a/c, Jacuzzi, restaurant, cont. brkfst, pool, hlth club

Howard Johnson
(800) I-Go-Hojo, (518) 869-0281
http://www.hojo.com
1614 Central Ave.
103 rooms - $69-100
Pets: Welcome
Creature Comforts: CCTV, a/c, Jacuzzi, restaurant, cont. brkfst, pool

Mansion Hill Inn
(518) 465-2038
http://www.mansionhill.com
115 Philip St.
8 rooms - $95-155
Pets: Welcome
Creature Comforts: Two early 1900's row houses near State House, perennial gardens, attractive rms. w/floral fabrics, uncluttered, CCTV, a/c, new baths, excellent intimate restaurant

Motel 6
(800) 4-MOTEL6, (518) 438-7447
http://www.motel6.com
100 Watervliet St.
98 rooms - $43
Pets: Under 30 lbs. welcome
Creature Comforts: CCTV, a/c

Ramada Inn
(800) 2-Ramada, (518) 489-2981
http://www.ramada.com
1228 Western Ave.
198 rooms - $70-90
Pets: Small pets w/$5 fee
Creature Comforts: CCTV, a/c, restaurant, cont. brkfst, pool, sauna

Red Roof Inn
(800) THE ROOF, (518) 459-1971
http://www.redroof.com
188 Wolf Rd.
115 rooms - $59-69
Pets: Welcome
Creature Comforts: CCTV, a/c

ALEXANDRIA BAY
Riveredge Resort
(800) ENJOY-US, (315) 482-9917
http://www.riveredge.com
17 Holland St.
129 rooms - $75-300
Pets: Small pets w/$10 fee, large dogs must be approved,
Creature Comforts: Attractive red brick hotel overlooking St. Lawrence River, traditionally furnished rooms w/waterfront balconies, full resort amenities, CCTV, VCR, a/c, Jacuzzi suites, gourmet restaurant, pool, hlth clb, sauna, boating, fishing

ALTMAR
Cannon's Place
(315) 298-5054
Box 209
14 rooms - $40
Pets: Small, quiet pets welcome
Creature Comforts: CCTV

Fox Hollow Lodge
(315) 298-2876
www.riconnect.comclande/fox
9 Gerhard Rd.
2 cabins - $60-90
Pets: Welcome
Creature Comforts: CCTV, a/c, micro, kit

AMHERST
Lord Amherst Hotel
(800) 544-2200, (716) 839-2200
5000 Main St.
100 rooms - $60-80
Pets: Welcome
Creature Comforts: CCTV, a/c, refrig, micro, cont. brkfst, pool

Motel 6
(800) 4-MOTEL6, (716) 834-2231
http://www.motel6.com
4400 Maple St.
94 rooms - $40
Pets: Under 30 lbs. welcome
Creature Comforts: CCTV, a/c

Marriott
(800) 228-9290, (716) 689-6900
http://www.marriott.com
1340 Millersport Hwy.
355 rooms - $100-150
Pets: Welcome w/$50 deposit
Creature Comforts: CCTV, a/c, restaurant, pool

Red Roof Inn
(800) THE ROOF, (716) 689-7474
http://www.redroof.com
42 Flint Rd.
108 rooms - $40-65
Pets: Welcome
Creature Comforts: CCTV, a/c

AMSTERDAM
Valley View Motel
(518) 842-5637
Rte. 5 South
60 rooms - $30-50
Pets: Welcome
Creature Comforts: CCTV, a/c, refrig, micro

ANGELICA
Angelica Inn B&B
(716) 466-3063
64 West Main St.
7 rooms - $70-85
Pets: Small pets welcome
Creature Comforts: Queen Anne Victorian, CCTV, a/c, kit, full brkfst

ARMONK
Ramada Inn
(800) 2-Ramada, (914) 273-9090
http://www.ramada.com
94 Business Park Dr.
141 rooms - $100-140
Pets: $6 fee, $100 deposit
Creature Comforts: CCTV, VCR, a/c, refrig, micro, restaurant, pool

AUBURN
Budget Inn
(315) 253-3296
Route 20
20 rooms - $35-75
Pets: Welcome
Creature Comforts: CCTV, a/c

Days Inn
(800) DAYS INN, (315) 252-7567
http://www.daysinn.com
37 William St
51 rooms - $55-70
Pets: Welcome
Creature Comforts: CCTV, a/c, cont. brkfst, hlth club, whirlpool

Holiday Inn
(800) HOLIDAY, (315) 253-4531
http://www.holiday-inn.com
75 North St.
165 rooms - $70-105
Pets: Small pets welcome
Creature Comforts: CCTV, a/c, pool

Irish Rose B&B
(315) 255-0196
102 South Second St.
5 rooms - $65-85
Pets: Small pets welcome
Creature Comforts: An 1872 Victorian inn w/a hand-carved staircase, orig. woodwork, intimate rms w/Irish linens, antiques, brass beds, dried flowers, basket of toiletries, a/c, refrig, full gourmet candlelit brkfst, pool

AVOCA
Caboose Motel
(607) 566-2216
8620 Rte 415
23 rooms - $
Pets: Welcome in ltd. rooms
Creature Comforts: Five caboose car lodgings, CCTV, a/c, restaurant, pool

BATAVIA
Best Western Batavia
(800) 528-1234, (716) 343-1000
http://www.bestwestern.com
8204 Park Rd.
75 rooms - $65-115
Pets: Welcome w/$50 deposit
Creature Comforts: CCTV, a/c, restaurant, pool

Best Western Batavia
(800) 528-1234, (716) 343-1000
http://www.bestwestern.com
8204 Park Rd.
75 rooms - $65-115
Pets: Welcome w/$50 deposit
Creature Comforts: CCTV, a/c, restaurant, pool

Crown Inn
(716) 343-2311
200 Oak St.
20 rooms - $70-80
Pets: Medium pets w/$6 fee and deposit
Creature Comforts: CCTV, a/c

Rodeway Inn
(800) 228-2000, (716) 343-2311
http://www.rodeway.com
8212 Park Rd.
20 rooms - $50-60
Pets: Small pets welcome
Creature Comforts: CCTV, a/c, kit, restaurant, cont. brkfst, pool

BATH
Days Inn
(800) DAYS INN, (607) 776-7644
http://www.daysinn.com
330 W. Morris St.
51 rooms - $45-65
Pets: Welcome
Creature Comforts: CCTV, a/c, restaurant, pool

Old National Hotel
(607) 776-4104
13 E. Steuben St.
24 rooms - $42-45
Pets: Welcome w/$25 deposit
Creature Comforts: CCTV, a/c, restaurant

BELLPORT
Great South Bay Inn
(516) 285-8588
160 S. Country Rd.
6 rooms - $80-95
Pets: Small pets w/$15 fee
Creature Comforts: Intimate 1900's rambling shingled cottage, original woodwork, formal gardens, indiv. decorated rooms w/antiques, brass, Oriental rugs, CCTV, a/c, full brkfst, walk to beach

BERLIN
Sedgwick Inn
(518) 658-2334
Route 22
11 rooms - $65-85
Pets: Welcome in motel w/$5 fee
Creature Comforts: Historic inn and antique store w/attractive gardens, Americana furnishings in character filled motel rms, spotless tiled baths w/toiletries, TV, a/c, gourmet restaurant, full brkfst

BINGHAMTON
Comfort Inn
(800) 228-5150, (607) 722-5353
http://www.comfortinn.com
1156 Front St.
67 rooms - $60-125
Pets: Welcome
Creature Comforts: CCTV, a/c, cont. brkfst

Holiday Inn, Arena
(800) HOLIDAY, (607) 722-1212
http://www.holiday-inn.com
2-8 Hawley St.
240 rooms - $65-80
Pets: Welcome w/$25 fee
Creature Comforts: CCTV, a/c, refrig, micro, restaurant, cont. brkfst, pool, hlth club

Hotel De Ville
(800) 295-5599, (607) 722-0000
80 State St.
60 rooms - $90-200
Pets: Small pets welcome
Creature Comforts: Historic
state house bldng converted to
hotel, period details, city center,
CCTV, a/c, kit, intimate restaurant

Motel 6
(800) 4-MOTEL6, (607) 771-0400
http://www.motel6.com
1012 Front St.
98 rooms - $35-49
Pets: Under 30 lbs. welcome
Creature Comforts: CCTV, a/c

Howard Johnson Express
(800) I-Go-Hojo, (607) 724-1341
http://www.hojo.com
690 Front St.
107 rooms - $40-70
Pets: Welcome
Creature Comforts: CCTV, a/c,
Jacuzzi, cont. brkfst, pool

Super 8, Court St.
(800) 800-8000, (607) 775-3443
http://www.super8.com
Upper Court St.
105 rooms - $45-55
Pets: Welcome
Creature Comforts: CCTV,
VCR, a/c, refrig, micro, Jacuzzi,
restaurant

BOONVILLE
Headwaters Motor Lodge
(315) 942-4493
13524 Rte. 12
37 rooms - $50-65
Pets: Welcome w/$3 fee
Creature Comforts: CCTV, a/c,
refrig, cont. brkfst, hlth clb access

BOWMANSVILLE
Red Roof Inn
(800) THE ROOF, (716) 633-1100
http://www.redroof.com
146 Maple Dr.
109 rooms - $50-75
Pets: Small pets welcome
Creature Comforts: CCTV, a/c

BRIGHTON
Hampton Inn, South
(800) Hampton, (716) 272-7800
http://www.hampton-inn.com
717 E. Henrietta Rd.
115 rooms - $80-90
Pets: Welcome
Creature Comforts: CCTV, a/c

Wellesley Inn, Brighton
(800) 444-8888, (716) 427-0130
http://www.wellesleyinns.com
797 E. Henrietta Rd.
98 rooms - $45-90
Pets: Welcome w/$3 fee
Creature Comforts: CCTV, a/c

BROCKPORT
Econo Lodge
(800) 55-ECONO, (716) 637-3157
http://www.econolodge.com
6575 Fourth Section Rd.
39 rooms - $44-80
Pets: Welcome
Creature Comforts: CCTV, a/c,
restaurant, pool

BUFFALO
Buffalo Motor Lodge
(800) 437-3744, (716) 896-2800
475 Dingens St.
35 rooms - $55-70
Pets: Welcome
Creature Comforts: CCTV, a/c,
restaurant, pool

Hilton, Buffalo
(800) HILTONS, (716) 845-5100
http://www.hilton.com
120 Church St.
470 rooms - $100-170
Pets: Welcome
Creature Comforts: CCTV, a/c,
kit, restaurant, pool

Wellesley Inn, Brighton
(800) 444-8888, (716) 427-0130
http://www.wellesleyinns.com
797 E. Henrietta Rd.
98 rooms - $45-90
Pets: Welcome w/$3 fee
Creature Comforts: CCTV, a/c

CALCIUM
Microtel
(800) 771-7171, (315) 629-5000
http://www.microtelinns.com
8000 Virginia Smith Dr.
99 rooms - $35-45
Pets: Small pets welcome
Creature Comforts: CCTV, a/c,
refrig

CAMBRIDGE
Blue Willow Motel
(518) 677-3552
51 South Park St.
12 rooms - $40-55
Pets: Welcome
Creature Comforts: CCTV, a/c

Cambridge Inn B&B
(518) 677-5741
16 West Main St.
8 rooms - $55-75
Pets: Welcome w/$10 fee
Creature Comforts: CCTV, a/c

Town House Motor Inn
(518) 677-5524
Route 22
10 rooms - $45-55
Pets: Small pets w/$10 fee
Creature Comforts: CCTV, a/c

CANAAN
Inn at Shaker Mill Farm
(518) 794-9345
Route 22
20 rooms - $75-100 pp (MAP)
Pets: Welcome
Creature Comforts: An neat inn
occupying 150-yr.-old mill,
streamside setting surrounded by
12 bucolic acres, stone walls, high
ceilings, Vermont quilts, informal
atmosphere, huge beamed
ceilings, d.r. overlooking stream,
hearty home-cooked meals, great
getaway for hikers/xc-skiers

CANANDAIGUA
Canandaigua Inn on the Lake
(800) 228-2801, (716) 394-7800
770 S. Main St.
130 rooms - $85-300
Pets: Welcome
Creature Comforts: Lakeside
setting w/adjacent parks, attractive
interior public areas and rms. w/
traditional furnishings, CCTV,
VCR, a/c, refrig, micro, restaurant,
pool, hlth clb, lawn games

Econo Lodge Canandaigua
(800) 55-ECONO, (716) 394-9000
http://www.econolodge.com
170 Eastern Blvd.
65 rooms - $47-75
Pets: Welcome
Creature Comforts: CCTV,
VCR, a/c, cont. brkfst

CANASTOTA
Days Inn
(800) DAYS INN, (315) 697-3309
http://www.daysinn.com
Route 13
60 rooms - $65-75
Pets: Welcome
Creature Comforts: CCTV, a/c

CATSKILL
Days Inn
(800) DAYS INN, (518) 943-5800
http://www.daysinn.com
Route 87
75 rooms - $60-125
Pets: Welcome
Creature Comforts: CCTV, a/c,
restaurant, pool, sauna, whirlpool

CAZENOVIA
Lincklaen House
(315) 655-3461
http://www.cazenovia.com/
lincklaen
79 Albany St.
21 rooms - $99-125
Pets: Welcome
Creature Comforts: A landmark
1835 brick hotel, gracious lobby
w/fireplaces, sweeping staircase,
rms. maintain historic feeling but
w/modern amenities, request
quieter rear rooms, stenciled walls,
reproduction antiques, CCTV, a/c,
dining room, tavern, cont. brkfst,
quiet back streets

CHAPPAQUA
Crabtree Kittle House
(914) 666-8044
11 Kittle Rd.
11 rooms - $95
Pets: Welcome
Creature Comforts: 1790
carriage house on estate setting,
most notable for its wine cellar/
restaurant, simply furnished rms.
w/Colonial theme, CCTV, cont.
brkfst

CHATEAUGAY
Banner House Inn
(518) 425-3566
Main St.
13 rooms - $30-60
Pets: Small pets welcome
Creature Comforts: Fireplace,
kit, restaurant, beach, boat, tennis

CHEEKTOWAGA
Holiday Inn, Gateway
(800) HOLIDAY, (518) 896-2900
http://www.holiday-inn.com
601 Dingens
119 rooms - $80-110
Pets: Small pets welcome
Creature Comforts: CCTV, a/c,
restaurant, pool

Wellesley Inn
(800) 444-8888, (716) 631-8966
http://www.wellesleyinns.com
4630 Genesee St
85 rooms - $55-70
Pets: Welcome w/$5 fee
Creature Comforts: CCTV, a/c,
cont. brkfst

West Winds Motel/Cottages
(888) Westwnd, (315) 686-3352
http://www.thousandislands.com/
westwinds/
38267 Rte. 12 E.
Rooms, $45-70; Cottages, $550-
920/wk
Pets: Welcome w/$20 fee
Creature Comforts: Attractive
riverside cottages, CCTV, a/c, kit,
lawn games, boating

CLIFTON PARK
Comfort Inn
(800) 228-5150, (518) 373-0222
http://www.comfortinn.com
Fire Rd., Old Rte. 146
60 rooms - $70-140
Pets: Welcome
Creature Comforts: CCTV,
VCR, a/c, Jacuzzi, cont. brkfst,
pool, hlth clb.

CLINTON
The Hedges B&B
(315) 853-3031
180 Sanford Ave.
5 rooms - $75-100
Pets: Welcome
Creature Comforts: Elegant
Federal w/period antiques, country
cottage w/canopy bed, CCTV, a/c,
Jacuzzi, kit, gourmet brkfst

COBBLESKILL
Best Western
(800) 528-1234, (518) 234-4321
http://www.bestwestern.com
Route 146 & Plank Rd.
76 rooms - $85-140
Pets: Welcome w/$25 deposit
Creature Comforts: CCTV, a/c,
restaurant, pool

COLONIE
Marriott
(800) 228-9290, (518) 458-8444
http://www.marriott.com
189 Wolf Rd.
365 rooms - $100-175
Pets: Welcome
Creature Comforts: CCTV, a/c,
restaurant, pool

Ramada Inn
(800) 2-Ramada, (518) 456-0222
http://www.ramada.com
1630 Central Ave.
100 rooms - $50-60
Pets: Welcome w/$25 deposit
Creature Comforts: CCTV, a/c

COMMACK
Howard Johnson
(800) I-Go-Hojo, (516) 864-8820
http://www.hojo.com
450 Moreland Rd.
109 rooms - $70-120
Pets: Welcome
Creature Comforts: CCTV, a/c,
cont. brkfst, pool

COOPERS PLAINS
Stiles Motel
(607) 962-5221
9239 Victoria Hwy.
16 rooms - $30-50
Pets: Welcome w/$4 fee
Creature Comforts: CCTV, a/c,
refrig

COOPERSTOWN

Best Western Inn at Commons
(800) 528-1234, (607) 547-9439
http://www.bestwestern.com
50 Commons Dr.
62 rooms - $70-160
Pets: Small pets w/$5 fee
Creature Comforts: CCTV, a/c,
restaurant, pool, hlth club

CORNING

Econo Lodge
(800) 55-ECONO, (607) 962-4444
http://www.econolodge.com
200 Robert Dann Dr.
61 rooms - $60-75
Pets: Welcome w/$5 fee
Creature Comforts: CCTV, a/c,
refrig, micro, Jacuzzi, cont. brkfst

Radisson Hotel Corning
(800) 333-3333, (607) 962-5000
http://www.radisson.com
125 Denison Pkwy.
175 rooms - $100-250
Pets: Small pets welcome
Creature Comforts: CCTV,
VCR, a/c, refrig, micro, Jacuzzi,
restaurant, pool

CORTLAND

Comfort Inn
(800) 228-5150, (607) 753-7721
http://www.comfortinn.com
2 1/2 Locust Ave.
66 rooms - $65-95
Pets: Welcome
Creature Comforts: CCTV, a/c,
restaurant, cont. brkfst, hlth club

Econo Lodge
(800) 55-ECONO, (607) 753-7594
http://www.econolodge.com
3775 Rte. 11
72 rooms - $45-90
Pets: Welcome
Creature Comforts: CCTV, a/c,
restaurant, cont. brkfst

Holiday Inn
(800) HOLIDAY, (607) 756-4431
http://www.holiday-inn.com
2 River St.
150 rooms - $75-95
Pets: Welcome w/$15 fee
Creature Comforts: CCTV, a/c,
restaurant, pool

Super 8 Motel
(800) 800-8000, (607) 756-5622
http://www.super8.com
188 Clinton Ave.
58 rooms - $55-60
Pets: Welcome w/permission
Creature Comforts: CCTV,
VCR, a/c

CUBA

Cuba Coachlight Motel
(716) 968-1992
1 North Branch Rd.
28 rooms - $40-50
Pets: Welcome w/$4 fee
Creature Comforts: CCTV, a/c

DANSVILLE

Daystop
(800) DAYS INN, (716) 335-6023
http://www.daysinn.com
Commerce Dr.
20 rooms - $40-50
Pets: Welcome
Creature Comforts: CCTV, a/c,
restaurant

DEBRUCE

De Bruce Country Inn
(914) 439-3900
www.debrucecountryinn.com
Route 23
14 rms/2 suites - $90-120 (MAP)
Pets: Welcome at owner's
discretion w/$25 deposit
Creature Comforts: Rambling,
historic inn set on spectacular
Willowemoc River, casual
atmosphere, revolving art exhibit,
cozy bedrms furnished w/hand-
made quilts, country antiques,
pool, whirlpool, sauna, world
famous trout fishing

DEER PARK

Deer Park Motor Inn
(516) 667-8300
354 Commack Rd.
45 rooms - $55-65
Pets: Welcome w/$25 deposit
Creature Comforts: CCTV, a/c

DELHI

Buena Vista Motel
(607) 746-2135
28 Andes Rd.
33 rooms - $45-55
Pets: Welcome
Creature Comforts: CCTV, a/c,
kit

DEPOSIT

Alexander's Inn-Oquaga Lake
(607) 467-6023
www.tempotek.com/alexinn/
770 Oquaga Lake Rd.
4 rooms - $60-100
Pets: Welcome
Creature Comforts: "1997 Best
B&B in Southern Tier", CCTV,
VCR, a/c, Jacuzzi, fireplace, kit

DIAMOND POINT

Diamond Cove Cottages
(518) 668-5787
Lake Shore Dr.
40 rooms/cottages - $55-120
Pets: Small pets w/$50 deposit
Creature Comforts: CCTV, a/c,
kit, fireplace, restaurant, pool

DOVER PLAINS

Old Drovers Inn
(914) 832-9311
http://www.olddroversinn.com/
Old Route 22
4 rooms - $150-395
Pets: Welcome w/$20 fee, must be
friendly and well behaved
Creature Comforts: 1600s inn w/
museum quality antiques, elegant
fabrics, fine collectibles, authentic
and gracious, fireplace, award-
winning restaurant, acres of woods
and gardens

DUNKIRK

Comfort Inn
(800) 228-5150, (716) 672-4450
http://www.comfortinn.com
3925 Vineyard Dr.
61 rooms - $60-80
Pets: Welcome
Creature Comforts: CCTV,
VCR, a/c, refrig, Jacuzzi, cont.
brkfst

Four Points Hotel
(800) 325-3535, (716) 366-8350
http://www.sheraton.com
30 Lake Shore Dr.
130 rooms - $80-105
Pets: Small pets w/$10 fee
Creature Comforts: CCTV, a/c,
restaurant, pool

Rodeway Inn
(800) 228-2000, (716) 366-2200
http://www.rodeway.com
310 Lakeshore Dr.
48 rooms - $45-70
Pets: Welcome w/$5 fee
Creature Comforts: CCTV, a/c,
cont. brkfst

Southshore Motor Lodge
(800) 228-5150, (716) 366-2822
5040 West Lake Rd.
20 rooms - $45-95
Pets: Dogs only
Creature Comforts: CCTV, a/c,
pool

Vineyard Motel
(716) 366-4400
3929 Vineyard Dr.
40 rooms - $55-65
Pets: Welcome w/$7 fee
Creature Comforts: CCTV, a/c,
restaurant, cont. brkfst

DURHAM
Rose Motel
(518) 239-8496
Route 145
11 rooms - $45-75
Pets: Welcome
Creature Comforts: CCTV, a/c,
kit

EAST HAMPTON
Bassett House Inn
(516) 324-6127
128 Montauk Hwy.
12 rooms - $115-195
Pets: In smoking rooms w/$3 fee
Creature Comforts: An 1830
Colonial decorated in eclectic
style w/funky antiques and Art
Deco collectibles, some CCTV,
a/c, refrig, full brkfst, whirlpool,
attractive gardens, outskirts of
town

East Hampton Point Cottages
(516) 324-9191
http://www.easthamptonpoint.com
295 Three Mile Harbor Rd.
30 cottages - $100-375
Pets: Welcome
Creature Comforts: Highly
recommended, traditional
Hampton cottages surround tree-
shaded courtyards, porches, skylit
rooms, French doors, wicker and
bleached pine furnishings, CCTV,
a/c, kit, Jacuzzi, gourmet
waterside restaurant, pool, marina,
tennis

EAST SYRACUSE
Embassy Suites
(800) 362-2779, (315) 446-3200
http://www.embassy-suites.com
646 Old Collamar Rd.
215 rooms - $99-115
Pets: Small pets welcome
Creature Comforts: CCTV, a/c,
restaurant, pool

Holiday Inn East
(800) HOLIDAY, (315) 437-2761
http://www.holiday-inn.com
6501 College Place
205 rooms - $99-115
Pets: Small pets welcome
Creature Comforts: CCTV, a/c,
restaurant, pool

Holiday Inn, North
(800) HOLIDAY, (315) 457-4000
http://www.holiday-inn.com
6701 Buckley Rd.
188 rooms - $65-80
Pets: Small pets welcome
Creature Comforts: CCTV, a/c,
pool

Marriott Hotel
(800) 228-9290, (315) 432-0200
http://www.marriott.com
6301 Route 298
250 rooms - $80-170
Pets: Small pets w/$100 deposit
Creature Comforts: CCTV, a/c,
restaurant, pool

Microtel
(800) 771-717, (315) 437-3500
http://www.microtelinns.com
6608 Collamer Rd.
99 rooms - $35-40
Pets: Welcome
Creature Comforts: CCTV, a/c

Motel 6
(800) 4-MOTEL6, (315) 433-1300
http://www.motel6.com
6577 Court Street
88 rooms - $36-50
Pets: Under 30 lbs. welcome
Creature Comforts: CCTV, a/c

Residence Inn
(800) 331-3131, (315) 432-4488
http://www.residenceinn.com
6420 Yorktown Circle
102 rooms - $60-160
Pets: $5 fee, $75 deposit
Creature Comforts: CCTV, a/c,
kit, pool, hlth clb access

Super 8 Motel
(800) 800-8000, (315) 432-5612
http://www.super8.com
6620 Old Collamer Rd.
53 rooms - $50-55
Pets: Welcome w/permission
Creature Comforts: CCTV, a/c

EAST WINDHAM
Point Lookout Inn
(518) 734-3381
Route 23
19 rooms - $70-125
Pets: $15 fee, $100 deposit
Creature Comforts: Spectacular
valley views from cliffside perch,
ski lodge exterior w/inviting
interior spaces, massive stone
fireplace, request. valley view
rooms, earth tones and Native
American themes, CCTV,
excellent restaurant, cont. brkfst,
hiking, skiing

ELMIRA
Coachman Motor Lodge
(607) 733-5526
908 Pennsylvania Ave.
18 rooms - $55-70
Pets: Small pets welcome
Creature Comforts: CCTV, a/c

Holiday Inn
(800) HOLIDAY, (607) 734-4211
http://www.holiday-inn.com
760 E. Water St.
150 rooms - $80-90
Pets: Welcome
Creature Comforts: CCTV, a/c,
restaurant, pool

Red Jacket Motor Inn
(800) 562-5808, (607) 734-1616
Route 17
48 rooms - $80-90
Pets: Small pets w/$10 fee
Creature Comforts: CCTV, a/c,
refrig, restaurant, pool

ESSEX
Cupola House & Cottage
(518) 963-7222
http://www.virtualcities.com/
vacation/ny/z/nyz48v1.htm
122 Main St.
52 rooms - $75-135
Pets: Welcome in cottage w/$25
fee
Creature Comforts: 1930's
Morse Cottage on Lake
Champlain, CCTV, a/c, kit

FAIRPORT
Trail Break Motor Inn
(716) 223-1710
7340 Pittsford-Palmyra Rd.
33 rooms - $40-50
Pets: Small pets w/$2 fee
Creature Comforts: CCTV, a/c,
refrig

FALCONER
Motel 6
(800) 4-MOTEL6, (716) 665-3670
http://www.motel6.com
1980 E. Main St.
79 rooms - $38-54
Pets: Under 30 lbs. welcome
Creature Comforts: CCTV, a/c

FLEISCHMANNS
River Run
(914) 254-4884
http://www.bbonline.com/ny/
riverrun/
Main St.
8 rooms - $50-90
Pets: Welcome w/$5 fee, (very
friendly but firm pet policy)
Creature Comforts: One of our
favorites, Catskills riverside B&B,
1887 Victorian w/stained glass
windows, oak floors, country
antiques, many special touches for
guest dogs, CCTV, suite w/kit,
cont. brkfst, pretty riverside
setting, hiking, skiing, fishing

FARMINGTON
Budget Inn
(716) 924-5020
6001 Rte. 96
20 rooms - $40-45
Pets: Small pets welcome
Creature Comforts: CCTV, a/c

FISHER'S LANDING
Island Boat House B&B
(800) 686-6056, (315) 686-2272
http://www.1000islands.com/
occident/occident.htm
Occident Island
2 rooms, 1 boathouse - $140-260
Pets: $3 fee in smkng rms.
Creature Comforts: Private
island on St. Lawrence, historic
fishing lodge and boathouse,
family antiques, refrig, country
brkfst, canoe, fish, sail

FISHKILL
Residence Inn
(800) 331-3131, (914) 896-5210
http://www.residenceinn.com
2841 Route 9
136 rooms - $130-230
Pets: $6 fee, $100 deposit
Creature Comforts: CCTV,
VCR, a/c, kit

Wellesley Inn
(800) 444-8888, (914) 896-4995
http://www.wellesleyinns.com
2477 Rte. 9
140 rooms - $55-85
Pets: In smoking rooms w/$3 fee
Creature Comforts: CCTV, a/c,
refrig, cont. brkfst

FREDONIA
Days Inn
(800) DAYS INN, (716) 673-1351
http://www.daysinn.com
10455 Bennett Rd.
75 rooms - $45-90
Pets: Welcome
Creature Comforts: CCTV, a/c,
whirlpool

FREEPORT
Freeport Motor Inn
(516) 623-9100
445 S. Main St.
61 rooms - $70-85
Pets: Small pets w/$50 dep.
Creature Comforts: CCTV, a/c

FULTON
Fulton Motor Lodge
(315) 598-6100
163 S. First St.
70 rooms - $56-100
Pets: Welcome
Creature Comforts: CCTV, a/c,
pool

Quality Inn
(800) 228-5151, (315) 593-2444
http://www.qualityinn.com
930 S. First St.
69 rooms - $55-150
Pets: Welcome
Creature Comforts: CCTV, a/c,
restaurant, pool

GARDEN CITY
The Garden City Hotel
(800) 547-0400, (516) 747-3000
http://www.gch.com
45 Seventh St.
280 rooms - $175-850
Pets: Under 15 lbs. welcome,
bigger dogs negotiable
Creature Comforts: CCTV, a/c,
refrig, Jacuzzi, restaurant, pool,
hlth clb, sauna, whirlpool

GENEVA
Motel 6
(800) 4-MOTEL6, (315) 789-4050
http://www.motel6.com
485 Hamilton St.
61 rooms - $42-55
Pets: Under 30 lbs. welcome
Creature Comforts: CCTV, a/c

Ramada Lakefront
(800) 2-Ramada, (315) 789-0400
http://www.ramada.com
41 Lakefront Dr.
148 rooms - $90-115
Pets: Welcome w/$10 fee
Creature Comforts: Beautiful
lakeside setting, CCTV, a/c, refrig,
micro, Jacuzzi, restaurant, pool,
hlth clb

GRAND GORGE
Golden Acres Farm Ranch
(800) 847-2151, (607) 588-7329
http://www.goldenacres.com/
Windy Ridge Rd.
300 rooms - $80-330
Pets: Welcome w/$6 fee
Creature Comforts: CCTV, a/c,
refrig, micro, kit, pools, whirlpool,
sauna, horseback riding, tennis

GRAND ISLAND
Chateau Motor Lodge
(716) 773-2868
1810 Grand Island Blvd.
17 rooms - $40-65
Pets: Welcome
Creature Comforts: CCTV, a/c,
refrig, kit, restaurant, refrig, pool,
hlth club, golf, tennis

Cinderella Motel
(716) 773-2872
2797 Grand Island Blvd.
15 rooms - $50-70
Pets: Welcome
Creature Comforts: CCTV, a/c,
kit

GREAT NECK
Inn at Great Neck
(516) 773-2000
http://www.slh.com/slh/pages/e/
eckusaa.html
30 Cutter Mill Rd.
85 rooms - $195-500
Pets: Welcome w/$200 deposit
Creature Comforts: Small luxury
hotel w/Art Deco inspired rooms,
CCTV, VCR, a/c, refrig, marble
baths, Jacuzzi, restaurant, hlth clb

GREECE
Comfort Inn, West
(800) 228-5150, (716) 621-5700
http://www.comfortinn.com
1501 West Ridge Rd.
83 rooms - $59-130
Pets: Welcome
Creature Comforts: CCTV, a/c,
cont. brkfst

Hampton Inn
(800) Hampton, (716) 663-6070
http://www.hampton-inn.com
500 Center Place Dr.
119 rooms - $65-80
Pets: Welcome
Creature Comforts: CCTV, a/c

Marriott, Greentree
(800) 228-9290, (716) 225-6880
http://www.marriott.com
1890 West Ridge Road
215 rooms - $100-115
Pets: Welcome
Creature Comforts: CCTV, a/c,
restaurant, pool

Wellesley Inn
(800) 444-8888, (716) 621-2060
http://www.wellesleyinns.com
1635 West Ridge Road
98 rooms - $50-75
Pets: Welcome w/$3 fee
Creature Comforts: CCTV, a/c

HAGUE
Locust Inn B&B
(518) 543-6035
Lakeshore Dr.
4 rooms - $75-125
Pets: Welcome
Creature Comforts: CCTV, a/c,
kit, full brkfast, beach swimming

HAMBURG
Howard Johnson Express
(800) I-Go-Hojo, (716) 648-2000
http://www.hojo.com
5245 Camp Rd.
117 rooms - $38-77
Pets: Welcome
Creature Comforts: CCTV, a/c,
kit, pool

Holiday Inn
(800) HOLIDAY, (716) 649-0500
http://www.holiday-inn.com
5440 Camp Rd.
130 rooms - $75-150
Pets: Small pets w/$10 fee
Creature Comforts: CCTV, a/c,
refrig, restaurant, pool, hlth club,
sauna

HAMLIN
Sandy Creek Manor House
(800) 594-0400, (716) 964-7528
http://www.sandycreekbnb.com/
1960 Redman Rd.
3 rooms - $65-85
Pets: Small pets w/approval
Creature Comforts: 1900's
English Tudor-style home w/
European ambiance, extensive
perennial gardens, antique
furnishings, Amish quilts, TV,
VCR, a/c, full brkfst, whirlpool,
walking paths, 5 min. to Lake
Ontario, fishing, boating

HAMPTON BAYS
Bowens by the Bay
(800) 533-3139, (516) 728-1158
177 West Montauk Hwy.
9 rms/7 cottages - $75-200
Pets: Welcome in cottages
Creature Comforts: CCTV, a/c,
kit, tennis

HANCOCK
Smith's Colonial Motel
(607) 637-2989
Route 97
13 rooms - $50-70
Pets: Welcome
Creature Comforts: CCTV, a/c

HENRIETTA
Microtel
(800) 771-7171, (716) 334-3400
http://www.microtelinns.com
905 Lehigh Station Rd
99 rooms - $45-50
Pets: Small pets welcome
Creature Comforts: CCTV, a/c

Red Roof Inn
(800) THE ROOF, (716) 359-1100
http://www.redroof.com
4820 W. Henrietta Rd.
110 rooms - $40-50
Pets: Small pets welcome
Creature Comforts: CCTV, a/c

Residence Inn
(800) 331-3131, (716) 272-8850
http://www.residenceinn.com
1300 Jefferson Rd
112 rooms - $100-125
Pets: Welcome w/$250 deposit
Creature Comforts: CCTV, a/c,
kit, pool

HERKIMER
Herkimer Motel
(315) 866-0490
100 Marginal Rd.
61 rooms - $50-70
Pets: Small pets welcome
Creature Comforts: CCTV, a/c,
refrig, kit, pool

Inn Towne Motel
(315) 866-1101
227 N. Washington St.
33 rooms - $40-55
Pets: Small pets w/$6 fee
Creature Comforts: CCTV, a/c,
kit, cont. brkfst

HIGHLAND FALLS
Best Western Palisade
(800) 528-1234, (914) 446-9400
http://www.bestwestern.com
Rtes. 218 & 9W
53 rooms - $75-85
Pets: Welcome w/deposit
Creature Comforts: CCTV, a/c,
cont. brkfst

HILLSDALE
Linden Valley Lodge
(518) 325-7100
Route 23 East
7 rooms - $95-145
Pets: Welcome
Creature Comforts: Pondside
setting w/perennial gardens,
decks, rooms w/traditional cherry
furnishings, immaculate, CCTV,
a/c, refrig, large baths, full brkfst

Swiss Hutte Motel
(518) 325-3333
http://www.swisshutte.com
Route 23 East
126 rooms - $60-75
Pets: Welcome in 2 rooms
Creature Comforts: Attractive
motel set along brook w/perennial
gardens, rooms w/bleached bead
board walls, Scandinavian furn.,
CCTV, a/c, French restaurant,
cont. brkfst, pool, walk to skiing

HORNELL
Econo Lodge
(800) 55-ECONO, (607) 324-0800
http://www.econolodge.com
7464 Old State Route 36
69 rooms - $44-50
Pets: Welcome
Creature Comforts: CCTV, a/c,
restaurant, cont. brkfst

HORSEHEADS
Best Western Marshall Manor
(800) 528-1234, (607) 739-3891
http://www.bestwestern.com
3527 Watkins Glen Rd.
40 rooms - $40-70
Pets: Welcome
Creature Comforts: CCTV, a/c,
refrig, micro, restaurant, cont.
brkfst, pool

Howard Johnson Express
(800) I-Go-Hojo, (607) 739-5636
http://www.hojo.com
2671 Corning Rd.
76 rooms - $50-90
Pets: Welcome
Creature Comforts: CCTV, a/c,
refrig, micro, restaurant, pool

Knights Inn
(800) 843-5644, (607) 739-3807
http://www.knightsinn.com
2707 Westinghouse Rd.
40 rooms - $45-65
Pets: Small pets w/$10 fee
Creature Comforts: CCTV, a/c,
pool

Motel 6
(800) 4-MOTEL6, (607) 739-2525
http://www.motel6.com
4133 Route 17
81 rooms - $38
Pets: Under 30 lbs. welcome
Creature Comforts: CCTV, a/c

HUDSON
St. Charles Hotel
(518) 822-9900
http://www.stcharleshotel.com
16 Park Pl.
34 rooms - $60-99
Pets: Small pets welcome
Creature Comforts: Historic
hotel, recently renovated,
traditional decor, CCTV, VCR,
a/c, cont. brkfst, restaurants, hlth
clb access

HUNTER
Hunter Inn
(518) 263-7777
Main St.
41 rooms - $60-170
Pets: Welcome w/$10 fee
Creature Comforts: CCTV, a/c,
kit, cont. brkfst, hlth clb access

HUNTINGTON
Huntington Country Inn
(800) 739-5777, (516) 421-3900
270 W. Jericho Turnpike
64 rooms - $80-155
Pets: Welcome
Creature Comforts: CCTV, a/c,
kit, cont. brkfst, hlth clb access

ITHACA
Best Western University
(800) 528-1234, (607) 272-6100
http://www.bestwestern.com
1020 Ellis Hollow Rd.
94 rooms - $60-110
Pets: Small pets w/$10 fee
Creature Comforts: CCTV, a/c,
restaurant, pool, hlth clb accss

Collegetown Motor Lodge
(607) 273-3542
312 College Ave
40 rooms - $50-100
Pets: Welcome w/$10 fee
Creature Comforts: CCTV, a/c

Econo Lodge
(800) 55-ECONO, (607) 257-1400
http://www.econolodge.com
2303 N. Triphammer Rd.
72 rooms - $50-95
Pets: Welcome
Creature Comforts: CCTV, a/c,
refrig, micro, Jacuzzi, cont. brkfst

Holiday Inn
(800) HOLIDAY, (607) 272-1000
http://www.holiday-inn.com
222 S. Cayuga St
180 rooms - $80-175
Pets: Small pets w/$15 fee
Creature Comforts: CCTV, a/c,
refrig, micro, restaurant, cont.
brkfst, hlth clb access

La Tourelle Country Inn
(607) 273-2374
1150 Danby Rd.
35 rooms - $79-150
Pets: Welcome in 3 first floor rms.
Creature Comforts: French country estate set on 70 acres atop bluff w/spectacular views, oversized rooms w/French provincial furnishings, fresh flowers, CCTV, a/c, Jacuzzi, restaurant, cont. brkfst, pool, tennis, fishing pond, hiking

Log Country Inn
(800) 274-4771, (607) 589-4771
http://www.logtv.com/inn/
Box 581
3 rooms - $55-200
Pets: Welcome
Creature Comforts: Hand-hewn log lodge w/European country decor, 20-acre wooded setting, handmade quilts, antiques, claw-foot tubs, farm brkfst w/blintzes and Russian pancakes, sauna, hiking

Meadow Court Inn
(607) 273-3885
529 S. Meadow St.
60 rooms - $40-150
Pets: Welcome w/permission
Creature Comforts: CCTV, a/c, restaurant

Ramada Inn
(800) 2-Ramada, (607) 257-3100
http://www.ramada.com
2310 N. Triphammer Rd.
121 rooms - $75-95
Pets: Small pets welcome
Creature Comforts: CCTV, a/c, refrig, micro, restaurant, pool

JAMESTOWN
Comfort Inn
(800) 228-5150, (716) 664-5920
http://www.comfortinn.com
2800 N. Main St.
101 rooms - $63-93
Pets: Welcome
Creature Comforts: CCTV, a/c, Jacuzzi, cont. brkfst

Holiday Inn
(800) HOLIDAY, (716) 664-3400
http://www.holiday-inn.com
150 W. Fourth St
150 rooms - $80-100
Pets: Small pets welcome
Creature Comforts: CCTV, a/c, restaurant, pool

JEFFERSONVILLE
The Griffin House
(914) 482-3371
http://www.zelacom.com/lodging/griffin.htm
178 Maple Ave.
5 rooms - $65-85
Pets: Welcome w/approval
Creature Comforts: 1900's Victorian, TV, a/c, full brkfst

JOHNSON CITY
Best Western
(800) 528-1234, (607) 729-9194
http://www.bestwestern.com
569 Harry L Drive
100 rooms - $55-70
Pets: Welcome w/notice
Creature Comforts: CCTV, a/c, restaurant, pool, hlth clb access

Red Roof Inn
(800) THE ROOF, (607) 729-8940
http://www.redroof.com
590 Fairview St.
107 rooms - $49-59
Pets: Welcome
Creature Comforts: CCTV, a/c

JOHNSTOWN
Holiday Inn
(800) HOLIDAY, (518) 762-4686
http://www.holiday-inn.com
308 N. Comrie Ave.
101 rooms - $60-87
Pets: Welcome
Creature Comforts: CCTV, a/c, restaurant, pool

KINGSTON
Holiday Inn
(800) HOLIDAY, (914) 338-0400
http://www.holiday-inn.com
503 Washington St.
215 rooms - $85-130
Pets: Small pets welcome
Creature Comforts: CCTV, a/c, restaurant, pool

Super 8 Motel
(800) 800-8000, (914) 338-3078
http://www.super8.com
487 Washington Ave.
84 rooms - $51-64
Pets: Welcome w/$7 fee
Creature Comforts: CCTV, a/c, cont. brkfst

LAKE CLEAR
Junction Inn
(518) 891-4632
Junction Rd.
7 rooms - $38-48
Pets: Welcome, leashed
Creature Comforts: Restaurant

Lodge at Lake Clear
(800) 442-2356, (518) 891-1489
http://mountain-air.com/lodge/
Rtes. 186 & 30
6 rooms - $90-190
Pets: Welcome in the cabins
Creature Comforts: Contemp. cabins w/vaulted ceiling and redwood walls, antique and butcher block furn., kit, woodstove, Jacuzzi, grill, picnic table, CCTV, German restaurant, private beach, lake swimming

LAKE GEORGE
Balmoral Motel
(518) 668-2673
444 Canada St.
30 rooms - $35-130
Pets: Welcome w/$10 fee
Creature Comforts: CCTV, a/c

Best Western
(800) 528-1234, (518) 668-5701
http://www.bestwestern.com
Route 87
87 rooms - $55-140
Pets: Small pets w/$5 fee
Creature Comforts: CCTV, a/c, refrig, pool

Fort William Henry
(518) 668-3081
http://www.fortwilliamhenry.com
Route 9
100 rooms - $140-260
Pets: Under 30 lbs. welcome
Creature Comforts: CCTV, VCR, a/c, kit, cont. brkfst, pool, whirlpool, sauna

Green Haven Resort Motel
(518) 668-2489
3136 Lake Shore Dr.
20 rooms - $90-190
Pets: Welcome in the cabins
Creature Comforts: CCTV, a/c,
kit, pool

Travelodge
(800) 578-7878, (518) 668-5421
http://www.travelodge.com
Rte. 9, Canada St.
54 rooms - $37-69
Pets: Welcome
Creature Comforts: CCTV,
VCR, a/c, restaurant

LAKE PLACID
Adirondack Cozy Cabins
(800) 220-1940, (518) 523-4724
http://www.lakeandmountain.com
Whiteface Inn Rd.
12 rooms - $135-300
Pets: Welcome
Creature Comforts: Adirondack
cabins w/fieldstone fireplaces, kit,
lake swimming, boating

Adirondack Escape
(800) 542-2636, (570) 675-7105
www.lakeandmountain.com/
90 Whiteface Inn Rd.
1 condo - $95-150
Pets: Welcome w/restrictions
Creature Comforts: Single
condo unit w/CCTV, a/c, kit,
fireplace, lake swimming, boating

Alpine Inn
(800) 257-4638, (518) 523-2180
http://www.alpine-inn.com/
Route 86
18 rms/cottages - $48-98
Pets: Welcome
Creature Comforts: CCTV, a/c,
kit, fireplace, cont. brkfst,
restaurant, pool

Art Devlin's Olympic Inn
(518) 523-3700
http://artdevlins.com/
350 Main St
40 rooms - $48-108
Pets: Welcome
Creature Comforts: CCTV, a/c,
refrig, cont. brkfst, pool, hlth club,
sauna

Best Western Golden Arrow
(800) 582-5540, (518) 523-3353
http://www.golden-arrow.com
150 Main St.
128 rooms - $99-199
Pets: Welcome w/$10 fee
Creature Comforts: CCTV, a/c,
fireplaces, kit, restaurant, pool,
hlth club, whirlpool, hlth club,
beach

Camp Solitude B&B
(518) 523-3190
http://home.att.net/~gwallace68/
campsolitude/index.html
70 Saranac Ave.
4 cottages - $88-160
Pets: Welcome w/some
restrictions
Creature Comforts: 1890's
classic and rustic Adirondack
camp, cottages w/rustic charm,
simple antiques, stone fireplace,
sauna, canoes, beach swimming

Cascade Inn Motel
(518) 523-2130
Cascade Rd.
11 rooms - $38-45
Pets: Welcome w/$10 fee
Creature Comforts: CCTV, a/c,
restaurant

Cobble Mountain Lodge
(518) 523-2040
81 Wilmington Rd.
15 cabins - $45-100
Pets: Welcome w/$10 fee
Creature Comforts: CCTV, kit,
grills, sauna

Edelweiss Motel
(518) 523-3821
14 Wilmington Rd.
20 rooms - $40-65
Pets: Welcome w/$10 fee
Creature Comforts: CCTV, pool

Edge of the Lake Motel
(800) 523-9430, (518) 523-3821
56 Saranac Ave.
20 rooms - $58-108
Pets: Welcome w/$10 fee
Creature Comforts: CCTV, a/c,
kit, pool, boats

Fourpeaks
(518) 946-7313
http://4peaks.com/fhome.htm
Stonehouse Rd.
5 cottages - $70-130
Pets: Dogs welcome w/$25 one-
time fee, two dog limit per cabin,
dog sitters available
Creature Comforts: Wonderful
authentic Adirondack camps on
700 acre private mountaintop,
classic camp furnishings, colorful
quilts, woodstoves, fieldstone
fireplaces, hot/cold running water
old fashioned tubs, screened-in
porches, hiking, fishing, very dog
friendly

Hilton Lake Placid
(800) 755-5598, (518) 523-2130
http://www.lphilton.com
One Mirror Lake Dr.
178 rooms - $99-199
Pets: Welcome w/restrictions
Creature Comforts: CCTV, a/c,
Jacuzzi, restaurant, pool, sauna,
whirlpool, hlth clb

Howard Johnson
(800) 858-4656, (518) 523-9555
http://www.hojo.com
90 Saranac Ave.
92 rooms - $85-150
Pets: Welcome
Creature Comforts: 1999
Howard Johnson ppty of the year,
CCTV, a/c, restaurant, pool,
whirlpool, boating, tennis

Jackrabbit Inn
(800) 584-7006, (518) 523-0123
http://jackrabbitinn.com
Route 73, Cascade Rd.
8 rooms - $38-180
Pets: Welcome w/restrictions
Creature Comforts: CCTV,
VCR, a/c, kit, restaurant, pool

**Lake & Mountain Properties of
Lake Placid**
(800) 982-2747, (518) 523-9861
www.lakeandmountain.com/
Whiteface Inn Rd.
8 rooms - $135-950
Pets: Welcome
Creature Comforts: Rental
agency w/condos, townhouses,
houses, CCTV, VCR, a/c, kit,
fireplace, hot tub, boating, tennis

Lake Placid Lodge
(518) 523-2700
http://www.lakeplacidlodge.com
Whiteface Inn Rd.
22 rooms - $300-700
Pets: Welcome in Birch and Pine cottages, welcoming goodie bag, pet amenities, special meals
Creature Comforts: Highly recommended, elegant, exclusive 19th-century Adirondack retreat on Lake Placid, private, lavish rooms w/hand-crafted log furniture and luxurious Adirondack ambiance, down comforters, CCTV, a/c, refrig, stone fireplace, marble baths, European toiletries, soaking tubs, five-star restaurant, priv. beach, boating, golf, tennis, mtn. bikes

Lake Placid Resort/Holiday Inn
(800) 874-1980, (518) 523-2556
http://www.lpresort.com
1 Olympic Dr.
209 rooms - $59-400
Pets: Welcome w/restrictions
Creature Comforts: CCTV, a/c, refrig, micro, kit, Jacuzzi, fireplace, restaurant, refrig, pool, hlth club, golf, tennis

Lake Shore Motel
(518) 523-2261
http://www.thelakeshore.com
54 Saranac Ave.
16 rooms - $60-160
Pets: Welcome
Creature Comforts: CCTV, a/c, refrig, kit, boating

Northwoods Inn
(888) 783-3177, (518) 523-1818
http://www.northwoodsinn.com
122 Main St.
52 rooms - $79-229
Pets: Welcome
Creature Comforts: CCTV, a/c, kit, restaurant, cont. brkfst

Paradise Point on Paradox Bay
(518) 523-4433
Saranac Ave.
52 rooms - $70-360
Pets: Well-behaved pets welcome
Creature Comforts: Waterfront apt, CCTV, VCR, a/c, kit, fireplace, boat slip

Placid Bay Inn
(518) 523-2001
http://www.placidbay.com
70 Saranac Ave
21 rooms - $50-95
Pets: Welcome w/restrictions
Creature Comforts: CCTV, a/c, kit, fireplace, pool, boating

Ramada Inn
(800) 2-Ramada, (518) 523-2587
http://www.ramadalp.com
8-12 Saranac Ave.
90 rooms - $70-130
Pets: Welcome
Creature Comforts: CCTV, a/c, fireplaces, restaurant, pools, hlth club, whirlpool

Swiss Acres Inn
(800) 464-4690, (518) 523-3040
http://www.swissacres.com
189 Saranac Ave.
40 rooms - $38-68
Pets: Welcome
Creature Comforts: CCTV, a/c, kit, restaurant, cont. brkfst, whirlpool

Village Motel
(800) 613-2150, (518) 523-2150
11 Cascade Rd.
13 rooms - $38-79
Pets: Welcome
Creature Comforts: CCTV, a/c, kit, pool

Water's Edge Condominiums
(800) 982-3747, (518) 523-9861
http://lake-placid.ny.us/lpcondos
Victor Herbert Rd.
12 rooms - $175-250
Pets: Welcome
Creature Comforts: CCTV, VCR, a/c, kit, fireplace, Jacuzzi, pool, boating

Woodlake Motor Inn
(800) 586-2616, (518) 523-2750
34 Saranac Ave
23 rooms - $40-95
Pets: Welcome
Creature Comforts: CCTV, a/c, kit, restaurant, cont. brkfst, pool

LATHAM
Century House Inn
(888) 674-6873, (518) 785-0931
www.centuryhouse.inter.net/
997 New Loudon Rd.
72 rooms - $90-225
Pets: Welcome w/$10 fee
Creature Comforts: Appealing motor inn resembling Georgetown row houses, terraced gardens, gracious interior, request garden level rooms, Colonial style furnishings, tiled baths, CCTV, a/c, kit, fine dining, full buffet brkfst, pool, tennis, walking paths

Comfort Inn
(800) 228-5150, (518) 783-1900
http://www.comfortinn.com
866 Albany Shaker Rd.
95 rooms - $56-71
Pets: Welcome
Creature Comforts: CCTV, a/c, refrig, micro, restaurant

Hampton Inn
(800) Hampton, (518) 785-0000
http://www.hampton-inn.com
981 New Loudon Rd.
126 rooms - $75-90
Pets: Welcome
Creature Comforts: CCTV, a/c, pool

Holiday Inn, Express
(800) HOLIDAY, (518) 783-6161
http://www.holiday-inn.com
946 New Loudon Rd.
121 rooms - $70-105
Pets: Welcome
Creature Comforts: CCTV, a/c, pool

Microtel
(800) 771-7171, (518) 782-9161
http://www.microtelinns.com
7 Rensselaer Ave.
99 rooms - $40-55
Pets: Welcome
Creature Comforts: CCTV, a/c, refrig, micro

Quality Inn
(800) 228-5151, (518) 785-1414
http://www.qualityinn.com
622 Watervliet-Shaker Rd.
57 rooms - $55-99
Pets: Welcome
Creature Comforts: CCTV, a/c, restaurant, full brkfst, pool

Residence Inn
(800) 331-3131, (518) 783-0600
http://www.residenceinn.com
1 Residence Inn Dr.
112 rooms - $80-175
Pets: Welcome w/$5 fee
Creature Comforts: CCTV, a/c,
kit, pool, hlth club

LEONARDSVILLE
Horned Dorset
(315) 855-7988
Route 8
4 rooms - $75-95
Pets: Welcome
Creature Comforts: Italianate
inn and fine French restaurant in
Fingerlakes farm community, high
ceilings, sweeping staircase,
important antiques, period decor,
a/c, oversized baths, kit, gourmet
restaurant, cont. brkfst

LIBERTY
Holiday Inn, Express
(800) HOLIDAY, (914) 292-7171
http://www.holiday-inn.com
Route 52 East
69 rooms - $60-95
Pets: Welcome w/$5 fee
Creature Comforts: CCTV, a/c,
pool

LITTLE FALLS
Best Western Little Falls
(800) 528-1234, (315) 823-4954
http://www.bestwestern.com
20 Albany St.
40 rooms - $55-65
Pets: Welcome
Creature Comforts: CCTV, a/c,
restaurant

LIVERPOOL
Days Inn
(800) DAYS INN, (315) 451-1511
http://www.daysinn.com
400 Seventh North St.
126 rooms - $60-75
Pets: Welcome
Creature Comforts: CCTV, a/c,
cont. brkfst, pool

Econo Lodge
(800) 55-ECONO, (315) 451-6000
http://www.econolodge.com
401 Seventh North St.
84 rooms - $50-90
Pets: Welcome
Creature Comforts: CCTV, a/c,
cont. brkfst
528

Homewood Suites
(800) 225-5466, (315) 451-3800
http://www.homewoodsuites.com
275 Elwood Davis Rd.
75 rooms - $110-180
Pets: Welcome w/$75 deposit
Creature Comforts: CCTV, a/c,
refrig

Knights Inn
(800) 843-5644, (315) 453-6330
http://www.knightsinn.com
430 Electronics Pkwy.
35 rooms - $45-55
Pets: Welcome w/$5 fee
Creature Comforts: CCTV, a/c,
refrig, cont. brkfst

LIVINGSTON MANOR
Mountain View Inn
(914) 439-5070
913 Chanderly Rd.
9 rooms - $80-90
Pets: Small pets welcome
Creature Comforts: Country inn,
rural location, full brkfst

LONG LAKE
Journey's End Cottages
(518) 624-5381
Route 30
4 rooms - $450-575/week
Pets: Welcome spring/fall only
Creature Comforts: CCTV

MALONE
Dreamland Motel
(518) 483-1806
Route 11
12 rooms - $30-60
Pets: Welcome
Creature Comforts: CCTV, a/c,
pool

Econo Lodge
(800) 55-ECONO, (518) 483-0500
http://www.econolodge.com
227 W. Main St.
38 rooms - $45-55
Pets: Welcome
Creature Comforts: CCTV, a/c,
cont. brkfst, pool

Four Seasons Motel
(518) 483-3490
236 West Main St.
25 rooms - $45-55
Pets: Welcome
Creature Comforts: CCTV, a/c,
pool

Gateway Motel
(800) 551-0611, (518) 483-4200
Finney Blvd.
13 rooms - $36-45
Pets: Welcome
Creature Comforts: CCTV, a/c,
kit, restaurant, pool

Sunset Motel
(518) 483-3367
East Main St.
26 rooms - $36-75
Pets: Welcome
Creature Comforts: CCTV, a/c,
pool

MALTA
Post Road Lodge
(800) 836-2687, (518) 584-4169
Route 9
28 rooms - $69-99
Pets: Welcome w/$5 fee
Creature Comforts: CCTV, a/c,
kit, cont. brkfst

MASSENA
New Flanders Inn
(800) 654-6212, (315) 769-2441
West Orvis & Main Sts.
140 rooms - $58-65
Pets: Welcome w/$15 fee
Creature Comforts: CCTV, a/c

MELVILLE
Huntington Hilton
(800) HILTONS, (516) 845-1000
http://www.hilton.com
598 Broad Hollow Rd.
300 rooms - $95-120
Pets: Small pets welcome
Creature Comforts: CCTV, a/c,
pool

MEXICO
Strike King Lodge
(315) 963-7826
286 State Route 104B
4 rooms - $50-65
Pets: Welcome
Creature Comforts: CCTV, a/c

MIDDLEPORT
Canal Country Inn
(716) 735-7572
4021 Peet St.
5 rooms - $46-58
Pets: Small pets welcome
Creature Comforts: Set on Erie
Canal, full brkfst

MIDDLETOWN
Howard Johnson
(800) I-Go-Hojo, (914) 342-5822
http://www.hojo.com
551 Route 211 East
117 rooms - $60-115
Pets: Welcome
Creature Comforts: CCTV, a/c,
restaurant, pool

Middletown Motel
(914) 342-2535
501 Route 211 E.
100 rooms - $55-70
Pets: Welcome
Creature Comforts: CCTV, a/c,
pool

Super 8 Motel
(800) 800-8000, (914) 692-5828
http://www.super8.com
563 Rte. 211 E
82 rooms - $57-68
Pets: Welcome w/permission
Creature Comforts: CCTV,
VCR, a/c, Jacuzzi

MILLBROOK
Cottonwood Motel
(914) 677-3283
http://www.cottonwoodmotel.com
Route 44
19 rooms - $79-145
Pets: Welcome
Creature Comforts: CCTV, a/c,
refrig

MONTAUK
Sepp's Surf-Sound Cottages
(516) 668-2215
Ditch Plains Rd.
9 cottages - $85-135 daily,
($800-900/wk in July/August)
Pets: Welcome
Creature Comforts: CCTV, kit

MONTGOMERY
Super 8 Motel
(800) 800-8000, (914) 457-3143
http://www.super8.com
207 Montgomery Rd.
96 rooms - $52-55
Pets: Welcome w/permission
Creature Comforts: CCTV,
VCR, a/c, micro

MONTOUR FALLS
Falls Motel
(607) 535-7262
239 Genesee St.
11 rooms - $40-65
Pets: Welcome w/$8 fee
Creature Comforts: CCTV, a/c

Relax Inn
(607) 535-7183
100 Clawson Blvd.
11 rooms - $30-70
Pets: Welcome w/$10 fee
Creature Comforts: CCTV, a/c,
refrig, pool

NEW PALTZ
Mountain Meadows
(914) 255-6144
http://
www.mountainmeadowsbnb.com/
543 Albany Post Rd.
3 rooms - $95-105
Pets: Small, calm, even-tempered
dogs welcome
Creature Comforts: Private
home, CCTV, a/c, refrig, full
brkfst, pool, hot tub

NEW TOWN
Days Inn
(800) DAYS INN, (914) 374-2411
http://www.daysinn.com
Routes 17M & 6
44 rooms - $45-120
Pets: Welcome
Creature Comforts: CCTV, a/c,
pool

NEW YORK CITY
Best Western President Hotel
(800) 528-1234, (212) 246-8800
http://www.bestwestern.com
234 W. 48th St.
351 rooms - $100-200
Pets: Under 15 lbs. welcome
Creature Comforts: CCTV, a/c,
restaurant

The Carlyle
(800) 227-5737, (212) 744-1600
http://www.premierhotels.com/
www/premier/Carlylenewy/
35 East 76th St.
190 rooms - $325-2,400
Pets: Welcome
Creature Comforts: Classic
Manhattan hotel, elegant, intimate
and exquisite foyer, rooms w/
antiques, Oriental rugs, hardwood
floors, chintz fabrics, CCTV,
VCR, a/c, refrig, pantry, baths w/
European toiletries, thick terry
robes, Bemelmans restaurant, hlth
clb, sauna, whirlpool

Crowne Plaza Manhattan
(800) HOLIDAY, (212) 977-4000
http://www.holiday-inn.com
1605 Broadway St.
775 rooms - $225-345
Pets: Small pets welcome
Creature Comforts: CCTV, a/c,
restaurant, pool

Dumont Plaza Suite Hotel
(800) ME-SUITE, (212) 481-6700
150 East 34th St.
250 rooms - $130-300
Pets: Welcome w/$200 deposit
Creature Comforts: CCTV, a/c,
kit, restaurant, hlth clb. access

Four Seasons
(800) 332-3442, (212) 758-5700
http://www.fshr.com
57 East 57th St.
375 rooms - $450-3,030
Pets: Under 15 lbs. welcome
Creature Comforts: Striking I.M.
Pei inspired building, soaring
ceilings, massive flower
arrangements, oversized rooms,
CCTV, a/c, refrig, electronic
draperies, down comforters,
marble baths, European toiletries,
makeup mirror, TV, Jacuzzi tubs,
restaurant, state-of-the-art fitness
center

Hilton, New York
(800) HILTONS, (212) 586-7000
http://www.hilton.com
1335 Ave. of the Americas
2,040 rooms - $195-305
Pets: Welcome
Creature Comforts: CCTV, a/c,
restaurant

Hotel Lucerne
(212) 875-1000
201 West 79th St.
175 rooms - $140-185
Pets: Welcome
Creature Comforts: CCTV, a/c, restaurant

Hotel Plaza Athenee
(800) 447-8800, (212) 734-9100
http://www.plaza-athenee.com/
37 East 64th St.
152 rooms - $410-3,500
Pets: Medium pets welcome
Creature Comforts: Sister hotel to Paris' Plaza Athenee, classic French decor, discreet staff, elegant and subdued room decor, CCTV, a/c, refrig, marble baths, Jacuzzi tubs, fine restaurant, hlth clb access

Iroquois Hotel
(800) 332-7220, (212) 840-3080
http://www.slh.com/pages/n/newiroa.html
49 W. 44th St.
114 rooms - $275-925
Pets: Small to med. pets welcome
Creature Comforts: Boutique hotel, elegant neo-classic residential decor, orig. art, soft earth tones, fireplace, terry robes, marble baths, Jacuzzi, Belgian chocolates, cont. brkfst, afternoon hors d'oeuvres, restaurant, hlth club

The Kimberley
(212) 755-0400
145 E. 50th St.
195 rooms - $175-325
Pets: Welcome
Creature Comforts: CCTV, a/c, kit, restaurant

Le Parker Meridien
(800) 543-4300, (212) 245-5000
http://www.lemeridien-hotels.com
118 West 57th St.
700 rooms -350-425
Pets: Small pets welcome
Creature Comforts: European style hotel, rqst odd number rms w/views of Park, CCTV, a/c, kit, restaurant, rooftop pool, jogging track, hlth clb access

Loews New York Hotel
(800) 23-LOEWS, (212) 752-7000
http://www.loewshotels.com
569 Lexington Ave.
726 rooms - $189-239
Pets: Small pets welcome
Creature Comforts: CCTV, a/c, restaurant, pool, hlth clb

The Lowell
(800) 221-4444, (212) 838-1400
http://www.preferredhotels.com
28 E. 63rd St.
65 rooms - $325-955
Pets: Under 10 lbs. welcome
Creature Comforts: Our favorite boutique hotel, 1926 Art Deco facade, intimate marble foyer w/ French Empire furniture, jewel box bedrooms, Asian and English antiques, chintz fabrics, down comforters, terraces, fireplaces, CCTV, VCR, a/c, kit w/gourmet foods, intimate dining room

Millennium Broadway
(800) 622-5569, (212) 768-4400
www.millenniumbroadway.com/
145 W. 44th St.
752 rooms - $295-625
Pets: Welcome
Creature Comforts: Updated Art Deco-style hotel and contemp. tower w/European flair and service, guest rms w/Art Deco furnishings, walls of windows, down pillows, wool blankets, oversized baths, CCTV, a/c, restaurant, hlth club

The Mark
(800) 843-6275, (212) 744-4300
http://www.themarkhotel.com
25 East 77th St.
180 rooms - $425-2,200
Pets: Under 20 lbs. w/approval
Creature Comforts: 1920's Art Deco facade, Beidermeier furnishings, green and rose tones contemp. furnishings w/traditional details and Asian accents, tailored fabrics, down pillows, Frette sheets, CCTV, VCR, a/c, marble baths w/soaking tubs, heated towel rack, famous Mark bar, hlth clb access

Marriott, La Guardia
(800) 228-9290, (718) 565-8900
http://www.marriott.com
102-05 Ditmars Blvd.
440 rooms - $150-700
Pets: Small pets w/$100 deposit
Creature Comforts: CCTV, a/c, restaurant, pool

Marriott Financial Center
(800) 228-9290, (212) 385-4100
http://www.marriott.com
85 West St.
505 rooms - $140-280
Pets: Small pets welcome
Creature Comforts: CCTV, a/c, restaurant, pool

Marriott Marquis
(800) 228-9290, (212) 398-1900
http://www.marriott.com
1535 Broadway St.
1915 rooms - $190-350
Pets: Small pets welcome
Creature Comforts: CCTV, a/c, restaurant

Mayflower Hotel
(800) 223-4164, (212) 265-0060
http://www.mayflowerhotel.com/
15 Central Park West
565 rooms - $180-210
Pets: Small pets w/approval
Creature Comforts: CCTV, VCR, a/c, refrig, restaurant, hlth club

New York Palace
(800) NY-Palace, (212) 888-7000
http://www.newyorkpalace.com
455 Madison Ave.
900 rooms - $325-375
Pets: Small pets welcome, w/ signed waiver
Creature Comforts: Originally a Helmsley hotel, blending historic brownstones w/contemp. tower, ornately decorated rms, CCTV, VCR, a/c, kit, restaurant

Novotel
(800) NOVOTEL, (212) 315-0100
226 W. 52nd St.
472 rooms - $159-229
Pets: Welcome w/$100 deposit
Creature Comforts: CCTV, VCR, a/c, restaurant

The Pierre
(800) 743-7734, (212) 838-8000
http://www.fourseasons.com/
locations/NewYorkThePierre/
index.html
Fifth Ave. at 61st St.
205 rooms - $355-2,600
Pets: Welcome—excellent
pet program
Creature Comforts: A grand
hotel w/well-preserved features-
cornices, paneled walls, gilded
moldings, Edwardian antiques,
rotunda w/hand-painted frescoes,
residential feeling to bedrooms,
Chippendale and Queen-Anne
furnishings, chintz, CCTV, VCR,
a/c, refrig, marble baths, terry
robes, restaurant, hlth clb access

The Peninsula
(800) 262-9467, (212) 247-2200
http://www.peninsula.com/hotels/
newyork/newyork.html
700 Fifth Ave.
271 rooms - $300-750
Pets: Welcome w/signed waiver
Creature Comforts: Newly
renovated Art Nouveau-style
hotel, classic contemp.
furnishings, CCTV, VCR, a/c,
marble baths, terry robes,
restaurant, rooftop pool, hlth club

The Plaza Hotel
(800) 527-4727, (212) 759-3000
http://www.fairmont.com
Fifth Avenue at Central Park S.
805 rooms - $300-750
Pets: Under 20 lbs. w/$20 fee
Creature Comforts: Landmark
hotel, gracious public spaces,
CCTV, VCR, a/c, min bari, marble
fireplaces, down pillows, terry
robes, restaurants, hlth club, spa

The Regency
(800) 233-2356, (212) 759-4100
http://www.loewshotels.com
540 Park Ave.
375 rooms - $350-750
Pets: Welcome w/signed waiver
Creature Comforts: CCTV,
VCR, a/c, refrig, marble baths,
Jacuzzi, restaurant, hlth club

Renaissance New York
(800) 228-9290, (212) 765-7676
http://www.renaissancehotels.com
714 Seventh Ave.
304 rooms - $325-475
Pets: Welcome w/$60 fee
Creature Comforts: Times
Square location, European
ambiance w/subtle earth tones,
lacquered furnishings, luxury
amenities, CCTV, a/c, restaurant,
hlth club

Royalton Hotel
(212) 869-4400
44 W. 44th St.
205 rooms - $275-425
Pets: Small pets welcome
Creature Comforts: Avante
garde decor, CCTV, VCR, a/c,
fireplace, unique bathrooms w/
tech chrome and glass fixtures, 44
restaurant, htlh club

Sheraton Manhattan
(800) 325-3535, (212) 581-3300
http://www.sheraton.com
790 Seventh Ave.
660 rooms - $180-400
Pets: Welcome
Creature Comforts: CCTV, a/c,
restaurant, pool

Sheraton New York Hotel
(800) 325-3535, (212) 581-1000
http://www.sheraton.com
811 Seventh Ave.
1760 rooms - $180-325
Pets: Welcome
Creature Comforts: CCTV, a/c,
restaurant

Soho Grand Hotel
(800) 965-3000, (212) 965-3000
http://www.sohogrand.com
310 W. Broadway St.
369 rooms - $334-414
Pets: 70 pet-friendly rooms,
luxury amenities, dog walking
Creature Comforts: Very pet
friendly and highly recommended,
reflects hip Soho style, impressive
suspended wire glass and iron
staircase, sophisticated custom-
designed rms w/orig. art and
furnishings, Frette linens, robes,
amenities from Kiehl's pharmacy
(oldest in NY City), CCTV, VCR,
a/c, comp. newspaper, restaurant,
pool, hlth club

Waldorf Towers
(800) HILTONS, (212) 355-3100
http://www.hilton.com
100 E. 50th St.
245 rooms - $375-5,000
Pets: Small pets welcome
Creature Comforts: CCTV, a/c,
restaurant

NEWFANE
Lake Ontario Motel
(716) 7768-5004
3330 Lockport-Olcott Rd.
12 rooms - $45-55
Pets: Welcome
Creature Comforts: CCTV, a/c

NIAGARA FALLS
NEW YORK
Best Western Inn on the River
(800) 528-1234, (716) 283-7612
http://www.bestwestern.com
7001 Buffalo Ave.
150 rooms - $80-140
Pets: Small pets w/notice
Creature Comforts: CCTV, a/c,
refrig, micro, restaurant, pool,
sauna

Best Western Summit Inn
(800) 528-1234, (716) 283-7612
http://www.bestwestern.com
9500 Niagara Falls Blvd.
88 rooms - $50-120
Pets: Small pets w/notice
Creature Comforts: CCTV, a/c,
refrig, micro, restaurant, pool,
sauna

Budget Host, Americana
(800) Bud-Host, (716) 297-2660
http://www.budgethost.com
9401 Niagara Falls Blvd.
27 rooms - $40-90
Pets: Small pets welcome
Creature Comforts: CCTV, a/c,
kit, pool

Coachman Motel
(800) 335-2295, (716) 285-2295
523 Third St.
18 rooms - $40-100
Pets: Welcome w/$50 deposit
Creature Comforts: CCTV, a/c,
refrig

Days Inn
(800) DAYS INN, (716) 285-9321
http://www.daysinn.com
201 Rainbow Blvd.
200 rooms - $60-230
Pets: Welcome w/$7 fee
Creature Comforts: CCTV, a/c,
restaurant

Howard Johnson Inn
(800) I-Go-Hojo, (716) 285-5261
http://www.hojo.com
454 Main St.
80 rooms - $65-135
Pets: Welcome
Creature Comforts: CCTV, a/c,
refrig, micro, Jacuzzi, restaurant,
pool, sauna

Knights Inn
(800) 843-5644, (716) 297-3647
http://www.knightsinn.com
9900 Niagara Falls Blvd.
23 rooms - $45-120
Pets: Welcome
Creature Comforts: CCTV, a/c,
refrig, Jacuzzi, pool

Niagara Rainbow Motel
(716) 283-1760
7900 Niagara Falls Blvd.
25 rooms - $30-90
Pets: Welcome
Creature Comforts: CCTV, a/c,
Jacuzzi, pool

Pelican Motel
(716) 283-2278
6817 Niagara Falls Blvd.
15 rooms - $30-100
Pets: Welcome
Creature Comforts: CCTV, a/c,
kit, pool

Radisson Hotel, Niagara Falls
(800) 333-3333, (716) 285-3361
http://www.radisson.com
Third St.
401 rooms - $50-450
Pets: Welcome w/$50 deposit
Creature Comforts: CCTV, a/c,
restaurant, pool, sauna, whirlpool

Ramada Inn at the Falls
(800) 333-2557, (716) 282-1212
http://www.ramada.com
240 Rainbow Blvd. N.
217 rooms - $60-110
Pets: In certain rooms w/CC dep
Creature Comforts: CCTV, a/c,
restaurant, pool, sauna
532

Sands Motel
(716) 297-3797
9393 Niagara Falls Blvd.
16 rooms - $25-90
Pets: Small pets welcome
Creature Comforts: CCTV, a/c,
restaurant, cont. brkfst, pool,
sauna

Travelers Budget Inn
(716) 297-3228
9001 Niagara Falls Blvd.
25 rooms - $30-80
Pets: Welcome w/$6 fee
Creature Comforts: CCTV, a/c,
kit

NIAGARA FALLS, ONTARIO
Best Western Fallsview
(800) 263-2580, (905) 356-0551
http://www.bestwestern.com
5551 Murray St.
245 rooms - $70-200
Pets: Small pets welcome
Creature Comforts: CCTV, a/c,
pool, restaurant

Camelot Inn
(905) 354-3754
5640 Stanley
55 rooms - $35-75
Pets: Small pets welcome
Creature Comforts: CCTV, a/c,
pool

Comfort Inn North of the Falls
(800) 228-5150, (905) 356-0131
http://www.comfortinn.com
4009 River Rd.
65 rooms - $40-225
Pets: Welcome w/$30 deposit
Creature Comforts: CCTV, a/c,
fireplace, restaurant

Flamingo Motor Inn
(905) 356-4646
7701 Lundys Lane
95 rooms - $40-85
Pets: Small pets w/$10 fee
Creature Comforts: CCTV, a/c,
kit, pool

Glengate Motel
(905) 357-1333
5534 Stanley Ave.
30 rooms - $35-90
Pets: Small pets w/$7 fee
Creature Comforts: CCTV, a/c,
kit, pool

Holiday Inn, By the Falls
(800) HOLIDAY, (905) 356-1333
http://www.holiday-inn.com
5339 Murray Hill Rd.
125 rooms - $55-190
Pets: Small pets welcome
Creature Comforts: CCTV, a/c,
restaurant, pool

Inn on Niagara Parkway
(905) 356-1233
7857 Niagara Pkwy.
55 rooms - $50-130
Pets: Small pets welcome
Creature Comforts: CCTV, a/c,
pool

Niagara Pkwy. Court Motel
(905) 295-3331
3708 Main St.
19 rooms - $50-90
Pets: Small pets welcome
Creature Comforts: CCTV, a/c,
pool

Ramada Coral Resort
(800) 272-6232, (905) 356-6116
http://www.ramadainn.com
7429 Lundys Lane
130 rooms - $55-200
Pets: Small pets w/$10 fee
Creature Comforts: CCTV, a/c,
fireplace, Jacuzzi, restaurant, pool,
hlth clb, sauna, whirlpool

Sheraton Inn, Niagara
(800) 263-2566, (905) 374-4142
http://www.sheraton.com
6045 Stanley Ave.
113 rooms - $60-200
Pets: Small pets welcome
Creature Comforts: CCTV, a/c,
fireplace, Jacuzzi, restaurant, pool,
sauna, whirlpool

Stanley Motor Inn
(905) 358-9238
6220 Stanley Ave.
45 rooms - $40-130
Pets: Small pets w/$5 fee
Creature Comforts: CCTV, a/c,
pool

Sunset Inn
(905) 354-7513
5803 Stanley St.
33 rooms - $35-70
Pets: Small pets welcome
Creature Comforts: CCTV, a/c,
Jacuzzi, pool

Venture Inn
(905) 358-3293
4960 Clifton Hill
181 rooms - $50-170
Pets: Small pets welcome
Creature Comforts: CCTV, a/c,
restaurant, pool

NORWICH
Howard Johnson
(800) I-Go-Hojo, (607) 334-2200
http://www.hojo.com
75 North Broad St.
87 rooms - $60-90
Pets: Welcome
Creature Comforts: CCTV, a/c,
kit, Jacuzzi, restaurant, pool

OGDENSBURG
Days Inn
(800) DAYS INN, (315) 393-3200
http://www.daysinn.com
1200 Paterson St.
29 rooms - $47-55
Pets: Welcome
Creature Comforts: CCTV, a/c,
restaurant

Quality Inn Grand-View
(800) 228-5151, (315) 393-4550
http://www.qualityinn.com
Riverside Dr.
50 rooms - $60-95
Pets: Welcome w/$10 fee
Creature Comforts: CCTV, a/c,
kit, Jacuzzi, restaurant, cont.
brkfst, pool

Rodeway Inn Windjammer
(800) 228-2000, (315) 393-3730
http://www.rodeway.com
68 Riverside Dr.
21 rooms - $50-70
Pets: Welcome w/$10 deposit
Creature Comforts: CCTV, a/c,
kit, pool

Stonefence Hotel
(800) 253-1545, (315) 393-1545
Route 37 S.
40 rooms - $40-135
Pets: Welcome w/$12.50 fee
Creature Comforts: CCTV, a/c,
kit, restaurant, pool, sauna,
whirlpool, tennis, boat rentals, and
lawn games

OLD FORGE
Best Western Sunset Inn
(800) 528-1234, (315) 369-6836
http://www.bestwestern.com
Route 28
52 rooms - $45-145
Pets: Welcome in some rooms
Creature Comforts: CCTV, a/c,
cont. brkfst, pool, sauna,
whirlpool, tennis

ONEONTA
Holiday Inn
(800) HOLIDAY, (607) 433-2250
http://www.holiday-inn.com
Route 23
120 rooms - $85-120
Pets: Small pets welcome
Creature Comforts: CCTV, a/c,
restaurant, pool

Super 8 Motel
(800) 800-8000, (607) 432-9505
http://www.super8.com
Rte. 23, Southside
60 rooms - $60-82
Pets: Welcome w/permission
Creature Comforts: CCTV,
VCR, a/c, cont. brkfst

OSWEGO
Best Western Little Falls
(800) 528-1234, (315) 342-4040
http://www.bestwestern.com
26 East First St.
93 rooms - $85-150
Pets: Small pets welcome
Creature Comforts: CCTV, a/c,
restaurant, pool, hlth clb,
whirlpool

K&G Lodge
(315) 343-8171
94 Creamery Rd.
6 rooms - $50-60
Pets: Welcome
Creature Comforts: CCTV, a/c,
kit, restaurant

Sunset Cabins
(315) 343-2166
Route 89
11 cabins - $55-75
Pets: Welcome
Creature Comforts: CCTV, kit

The Thomas Inn
(315) 343-4900
309 Seneca St.
47 rooms - $52-55
Pets: Welcome w/deposit
Creature Comforts: CCTV, a/c

Twin Pines Cabins
(315) 343-2475
1881 Route 1
16 rooms - $40-60
Pets: Welcome
Creature Comforts: CCTV, a/c,
kit

OWEGO
Sunrise Motel
(607) 687-5666
3778 Waverly Rd.
19 rooms - $35-40
Pets: Welcome w/$3 fee
Creature Comforts: CCTV, a/c

PAINTED POST
Best Western Lodge
(800) 528-1234, (607) 962-2456
http://www.bestwestern.com
Route 146 & Plank Rd.
135 rooms - $50-100
Pets: Welcome
Creature Comforts: CCTV, a/c,
restaurant, pool

Stiles Motel
(800) 331-3920, (607) 962-5221
9239 Victory Hwy.
15 rooms - $35-40
Pets: Welcome w/$3 fee
Creature Comforts: CCTV, a/c

PARISH
Montclair Motel
(315) 625-7100
Route 69
10 rooms - $35-40
Pets: Welcome
Creature Comforts: CCTV, a/c

PARKSVILLE
Best Western Paramount
(800) 528-1234, (607) 292-6700
http://www.bestwestern.com
Tanzman Rd.
185 rooms - $65-135
Pets: Under 20 lbs. welcome
Creature Comforts: CCTV, a/c,
restaurant, pool

PEEKSKILL
Peekskill Inn
(914) 739-1500
634 Main St.
54 rooms - $65-100
Pets: Small pets welcome
Creature Comforts: CCTV, a/c,
restaurant, pool

PEMBROKE
Econo Lodge
(800) 55-ECONO, (716) 599-4681
http://www.econolodge.com
8493 Rte. 77
73 rooms - $44-80
Pets: Welcome
Creature Comforts: CCTV, a/c,
restaurant

PLAINVIEW
Residence Inn
(800) 331-3131, (516) 433-6200
http://www.residenceinn.com
9 Gerhard Rd.
165 rooms - $145-300
Pets: $15 fee, $75 deposit
Creature Comforts: CCTV,
VCR, a/c, kit, pool

PLATTSBURGH
Baymont Inns
(800) 4-Budget, (518) 562-4000
http://www.baymontinns.com
16 Plaza Blvd.
110 rooms - $50-60
Pets: Welcome
Creature Comforts: CCTV, a/c,
pool

Econo Lodge
(800) 55-ECONO, (518) 561-1500
http://www.econolodge.com
528 Route 3
98 rooms - $44-65
Pets: Welcome
Creature Comforts: CCTV, a/c,
cont. brkfst, pool

Howard Johnson
(800) I-Go-Hojo, (518) 561-7750
http://www.hojo.com
446 Route 3
120 rooms - $60-90
Pets: Welcome
Creature Comforts: CCTV, a/c,
refrig, Jacuzzi, restaurant, pool

Ramada Plattsburgh Inn
(800) 431-5145, (518) 561-5000
http://www.ramada.com
412 Route 3
100 rooms - $75-90
Pets: Welcome in some rooms
Creature Comforts: CCTV, a/c,
restaurant, pool, hlth clb access

Super 8 Motel
(800) 800-8000, (518) 562-8888
http://www.super8.com
7129 Rte. 9
61 rooms - $45-50
Pets: Welcome w/deposit
Creature Comforts: CCTV,
VCR, a/c, pool

PORT JERVIS
Comfort Inn
(800) 228-5150, (914) 856-6611
http://www.comfortinn.com
Greenville Trnpke
104 rooms - $44-120
Pets: Welcome
Creature Comforts: CCTV, a/c,
refrig, micro, Jacuzzi, cont. brkfst

PORT ONTARIO
Mannings Port Ontario
(315) 298-2509
Route 3
25 rooms - $44-66
Pets: Welcome
Creature Comforts: CCTV, a/c,
kit

POUGHKEEPSIE
Econo Lodge
(800) 55-Econo, (914) 452-6600
http://www.econolodge.com
426 South Rd.
113 rooms - $60-100
Pets: Welcome
Creature Comforts: CCTV, a/c,
restaurant, cont. brkfst, pool

Holiday Inn Express
(800) HOLIDAY, (914) 473-1151
http://www.holiday-inn.com
341 South Rd.
120 rooms - $80-100
Pets: Small pets welcome
Creature Comforts: CCTV, a/c,
Jacuzzi, restaurant, pool

PULASKI
Clark's Cottages
(315) 298-4778
Route 5
6 cottages - $270-300/wk
Pets: Welcome
Creature Comforts: Rustic
cottages, kit

Double Eagle Lodge
(315) 298-3326
3268 Rte. 13
15 rooms - $25-30
Pets: Small pets welcome
Creature Comforts: CCTV, a/c,
refrig, cont. brkfst

Fish Hawk Lodge
(315) 298-5841
1091 Albion Cross Rd.
4 rooms - $30-40
Pets: Welcome
Creature Comforts: Common
area w/CCTV, refrig, kit

Golden Fish Cabins
(315) 298-6556
Route 3
4 rooms - $50
Pets: Welcome
Creature Comforts: CCTV, kit

Laurdon Heights
(315) 298-6091
Lewis St.
2 apts - $160
Pets: Welcome w/deposit
Creature Comforts: CCTV, kit

Port Lodge Motel
(315) 298-6876
7469 Scenic Hwy.
34 rooms - $49-58
Pets: Welcome
Creature Comforts: CCTV, a/c,
pool

Portly Angler Lodge
(315) 298-4773
Rtes. 2A & 13
39 rooms - $65
Pets: Welcome, must remain
crated in room
Creature Comforts: A/C

Redwood Motel
(315) 298-4717
http://www.salmon-river.com/
redwood
Route 13
50 rooms - $39-46
Pets: Welcome w/$20
Creature Comforts: CCTV, a/c,
pool

QUEENSBURY
Susse Chalet
(518) 793-8891
http://www.sussechalet.com
24 Big Boom Rd.
44 rooms - $55-85
Pets: Small pets welcome
Creature Comforts: CCTV, a/c,
pool

QUOGUE
The Inn at Quogue
(516) 653-6560
47-52 Quogue St.
70 rooms - $100-350
Pets: Welcome in specific rms.
Creature Comforts: Historic inn/
cottages set in exclusive village of
Quogue, lovely gardens,
Hamptons summer cottage feeling
w/chintz, wicker, and hardwood
floors, kit, gourmet dining, cont.
brkfst in season, pool, private
beach, bicycles

RAY BROOK
Pioneer Village
(800) 625-4572, (518) 891-4572
Route 86
20 cottages - $35-70
Pets: Welcome
Creature Comforts: CCTV, a/c,
kit

RHINEBECK
Beekman Arms
(914) 736-8000
http://www.beekmanarms.com
4 Mill St.
59 rooms - $80-150
Pets: Welcome in 4 annex rooms
Creature Comforts: 1844 inn w/
antiques and contemp. comforts,
annex rooms w/French provincial
feeling, armoire, pant press, refrig,
CCTV, a/c, American country
award winning restaurant

WhistleWood Farm B&B
(914) 876-6838
http://www.whistlewood.com
11 Pells Rd.
5 rooms, 1 cottage - $85-120
Pets: Welcome w/$15 fee, credit
card deposit, do not leave alone,
kennels available
Creature Comforts: Hilltop
horse farm, western style ranch
house w/country antiques,
fieldstone fireplace, handmade
quilts, western collectibles, CCTV,
a/c, excellent country brkfst,
lakefront cottage available,
horseback riding, hiking, fishing,
biking

RIPLEY
Budget Host Colonial Squire
(800) Bud-Host, (716) 736-8000
http://www.budgethost.com
Shortman Rd.
120 rooms - $85-120
Pets: Small pets welcome
Creature Comforts: CCTV, a/c,
restaurant, pool

ROCHESTER
Comfort Inn, Central
(800) 228-5150, (716) 436-4400
http://www.comfortinn.com
395 Buell Rd.
73 rooms - $55-100
Pets: Welcome
Creature Comforts: CCTV, a/c,
cont. brkfst

Econo Lodge
(800) 55-ECONO, (716) 427-2700
http://www.econolodge.com
940 Jefferson Rd.
102 rooms - $50-110
Pets: Welcome
Creature Comforts: CCTV, a/c,
Jacuzzi, cont. brkfst

Holiday Inn, Airport
(800) HOLIDAY, (716) 328-6000
http://www.holiday-inn.com
911 Brooks Ave.
281 rooms - $100-120
Pets: Welcome
Creature Comforts: CCTV, a/c,
restaurant, pool, hlth club, sauna

Motel 6
(800) 4-MOTEL6, (716) 436-2170
http://www.motel6.com
155 Buell Rd.
96 rooms - $42
Pets: Under 30 lbs. welcome
Creature Comforts: CCTV, a/c

Ramada Inn
(800) 2-Ramada, (716) 464-8800
http://www.ramada.com
1273 Chili Ave.
156 rooms - $50-65
Pets: Welcome w/$10 fee
Creature Comforts: CCTV, a/c,
refrig, micro, restaurant, cont.
brkfst, pool, sauna

Residence Inn
(800) 331-3131, (716) 433-6200
http://www.residenceinn.com
1300 Jefferson Rd.
112 rooms - $99-140
Pets: Welcome w/$6 daily fee,
$125 one-time fee
Creature Comforts: CCTV,
VCR, a/c, kit, pool, cont. brkfst

Towpath Motel
(716) 271-2147
2323 Monroe Ave.
20 rooms - $45-50
Pets: Small pets w/$25 deposit
Creature Comforts: CCTV, a/c

ROCKVILLE CENTER
Holiday Inn, Airport
(800) HOLIDAY, (516) 678-1300
http://www.holiday-inn.com
173 Sunrise Hwy.
99 rooms - $115-140
Pets: Welcome
Creature Comforts: CCTV, a/c,
restaurant, pool

ROME
Adirondack Thirteen Pines
(315) 337-4930
7357 River Rd.
12 rooms - $35-55
Pets: Welcome
Creature Comforts: CCTV, a/c,
pool

American Heritage
(800) 836-1203, (315) 339-3610
799 Lower Lawrence St.
27 rooms - $40-50
Pets: Welcome
Creature Comforts: CCTV, a/c,
cont. brkfst

535

Beeches-Paul Revere
(315) 336-1776
7900 Turin Rd.
75 rooms - $70-150
Pets: Welcome
Creature Comforts: CCTV, a/c,
kit, Jacuzzi, restaurant, pool

Family Inns of America
(800) 348-3577, (315) 328-6000
145 E. Whitesboro St.
56 rooms - $40-45
Pets: Welcome
Creature Comforts: CCTV, a/c,
refrig

ROSCOE
Huff House
(800) 358-5012, (607) 498-9953
Route 2
46 rooms - $105-150
Pets: Welcome in cottages
Creature Comforts: Special
mountaintop golf retreat, family
run for 45 yrs., peaceful setting,
lovely main house w/golf and
fishing theme, stone fireplace,
very simple cottage rms., CCTV,
a/c, refrig, dining room w/fine
home-cooked meals, famous golf
school, tennis, pool, lawn games,
fly fishing

Roscoe Motel
(607) 498-5220
Old Route 17
20 rooms - $45-55
Pets: Small pets welcome
Creature Comforts: CCTV, a/c,
kit, pool

SARANAC LAKE
Adirondack Motel
(800) 416-0117, (518) 891-2116
23 Lake Flower Ave.
9 rooms - $40-95
Pets: Welcome, leashed
Creature Comforts: CCTV, kit,
cont. brkfst, beach

Cochran's Cabins
(518) 483-3490
303 Kiwassa Rd.
12 rooms - $65-105
Pets: Welcome
Creature Comforts: Fireplace,
kit

Comfort Inn
(800) 228-5150, (518) 891-1970
http://www.comfortinn.com
148 Lake Flower Ave
69 rooms - $50-120
Pets: Welcome
Creature Comforts: CCTV, a/c,
restaurant, pool

Hotel Saranac
(800) 937-0211, (518) 891-2200
http://www.hotelsaranac.com/
101 Main St.
92 rooms - $59-99
Pets: Welcome
Creature Comforts: Historic
hotel, near Saranac Lake w/hotel
school on site, wonderful lobby,
motel rooms w/some character,
small baths, restaurant

The Point
(800) 255-3530, (518) 891-5674
http://www.thepointresort.com/
HCR 1, Box 65
11 rooms - $825-1,300 (AP)
Pets: Welcome
Creature Comforts: Highly
recommended, very exclusive,
Adirondack wilderness lodge on
Saranac Lake, luxurious fabrics
and furnishings fill original
"cottages", down comforters,
Jacuzzi , five-star cuisine, formal
attire, canoes, lake boats, fishing

Townhouse at Saranac Lake
(518) 891-3458
Box 223
5 rooms - $150-200
Pets: Welcome
Creature Comforts: CCTV,
VCR, a/c, kit, beach

SARATOGA SPRINGS
Adirondack Motel
(518) 584-3510
230 West Avenue
27 rooms - $69-110
Pets: Welcome
Creature Comforts: CCTV, a/c,
kit, pool

Best Western
(800) 528-1234, (518) 584-2350
http://www.bestwestern.com
3291 South Broadway St.
37 rooms - $55-170
Pets: Welcome
Creature Comforts: CCTV, a/c,
restaurant, pool

Community Court Motel
(518) 584-6666
248 Broadway St.
42 rooms - $60-75
Pets: Welcome
Creature Comforts: CCTV, a/c,
kit

Country Club Motel
(518) 584-4780
306 Church St.
12 rooms - $69-135
Pets: Welcome w$5 one-time fee
Creature Comforts: CCTV, a/c,
refrig, micro, kit

Grand Union Motel
(518) 584-9000
http://www.grandunionmotel.com
92 South Broadway St.
64 rooms - $77-165
Pets: Welcome w/$15
Creature Comforts: CCTV, a/c,
refrig, pool

Holiday Inn
(800) HOLIDAY, (518) 584-4550
http://www.holiday-inn.com
232 Broadway St.
150 rooms - $85-200
Pets: Welcome
Creature Comforts: CCTV, a/c,
refrig, micro, restaurant, pool, hlth
club

St. Charles Motel
(518) 584-2050
160 Broadway St.
32 rooms - $45-150
Pets: Welcome
Creature Comforts: CCTV, a/c,
refrig, kit

Union Gables B&B
(800) 398-1558, (518) 584-1558
http://www.uniongables.com/
55 Union Ave.
12 rooms - $85-275
Pets: Welcome
Creature Comforts: Gracious
Victorian inn, fully restored,
glowing wood floors/trim, rms. w/
lovely unique decor, hand-painted
furnishings, antiques, CCTV, a/c,
refrig, cont. brkfst, hlth club, hot
tub, tennis, walk to race track

SAUGERTIES
Howard Johnson
(800) I-Go-Hojo, (914) 246-9511
http://www.hojo.com
2764 Route 32
84 rooms - $55-77
Pets: Welcome in certain rooms
Creature Comforts: CCTV, a/c,
restaurant, cont. brkfst, pool

SCHENECTADY
Holiday Inn
(800) HOLIDAY, (518) 393-4141
http://www.holiday-inn.com
100 Nott Terrace
185 rooms - $90-125
Pets: Small pets welcome
Creature Comforts: CCTV, a/c,
restaurant, pool

Ramada Inn
(800) 2-Ramada, (518) 370-7151
http://www.ramada.com
450 Nott St.
175 rooms - $65-75
Pets: Welcome
Creature Comforts: CCTV, a/c,
restaurant, pool, whirlpool

SCHROON LAKE
Blue Ridge Motel
(518) 532-7521
Rtes. 80 & 255
17 rooms - $60-75
Pets: Welcome w/$5 fee
Creature Comforts: CCTV, a/c,
restaurant, cont. brkfst, pool,
sauna

Dun Roamin Cabins
(518) 532-7277
http://www4.webway.com/
dunroamin/
Route 9
9 cabins - $48-85
Pets: Welcome, but shouldn't be
left alone
Creature Comforts: CCTV, kit,
fireplace

Rawlins Motel/Cabins
(518) 532-7907
Route 9, Fowler Ave.
9 rooms - $40-88
Pets: Welcome w/$5
Creature Comforts: CCTV, kit,
fireplace

SHANDAKEN
Shandaken Inn
(914) 688-5100
Route 28
6 rooms - $85-150
Pets: Welcome w/notice
Creature Comforts: Private
Catskills retreat, 1870's shingle-
style home, terraces, fireplaces,
gourmet meals, pool

Sterns Point House
(914) 688-5100
Sterns Point Rd.
6 rooms - $75-130
Pets: Welcome walked off
property/never left alone
Creature Comforts: CCTV, a/c,
cont. brkfst

SOUTHAMPTON
Bayberry Inn
(800) 659-2020, (516) 283-4220
281 County Rd.
35 rooms - $75-130
Pets: Welcome
Creature Comforts: CCTV, a/c,
cont. brkfst, pool

Village Latch Inn
(800) 54-Latch, (516) 283-2160
http://www.villagelatch.com/
101 Hill St.
67 rooms - $175-375
Pets: Cottages w/$20 fee
Creature Comforts: Historic
rambling inn on 5-acre estate
setting, patios, charming rooms w/
collectibles from owners' world
travels, CCTV, a/c, refrig, cont.
brkfst, pool, tennis, bicycle, walk
to town

Cold Springs Bay Resort
(516) 283-7600
Route 27
39 rooms - $45-250
Pets: Welcome
Creature Comforts: CCTV, a/c,
kit, pool

SPRING GLEN
Gold Mountain Chalet Resort
(800) 395-5200, (914) 647-4332
catskillwebpages.comgoldmtn/
Tyce Rd.
30 chalets - $179-249 (AP)
Pets: Welcome in sauna chalets w/
$15 fee and deposit
Creature Comforts: Southwest
decor, valley views, CCTV, a/c,
kit, fireplace, Jacuzzi, pool, tennis,
whirlpool, sauna

STATEN ISLAND
The Harbor House
(800) 626-8096, (718) 876-0056
http://www.bestinns.net/usa/ny/
harborhouse.html
1 Hyland Blvd.
10 rooms - $50-110
Pets: Welcome, large pets must be
approved
Creature Comforts: 1890 home
w/panoramic city/harbor views,
causal interior spaces, CCTV,
VCR, a/c, kit, cont. brkfst

SUFFERN
Wellesley Inn
(800) 444-8888, (914) 368-1900
http://www.wellesleyinns.com
17 N. Airmont Rd.
97 rooms - $78-85
Pets: Welcome w/$5 fee
Creature Comforts: CCTV, a/c

SYRACUSE
Best Western University Tower
(800) 528-1234, (315) 479-7000
http://www.bestwestern.com
701 E. Genesee St.
275 rooms - $50-170
Pets: Small pets welcome
Creature Comforts: CCTV, a/c,
restaurant, pool, sauna

Comfort Inn, Central
(800) 228-5150, (315) 453-0045
http://www.comfortinn.com
7010 Interstate Island Rd.
110 rooms - $70-100
Pets: Welcome
Creature Comforts: CCTV, a/c,
restaurant, cont. brkfst, hlth club

Days Inn
(800) DAYS INN, (315) 437-5965
http://www.daysinn.com
6609 Thompson Rd.
100 rooms - $45-70
Pets: Welcome w/$5 fee
Creature Comforts: CCTV, a/c

Four Points
(800) 325-3535, (315) 457-1122
http://www.sheraton.com
441 Electronics Pkwy.
278 rooms - $65-135
Pets: Welcome
Creature Comforts: CCTV, a/c,
restaurant, pool

Holiday Inn
(800) HOLIDAY, (315) 457-8700
http://www.holiday-inn.com
100 Farrell Rd.
155 rooms - $65-115
Pets: Welcome
Creature Comforts: CCTV, a/c,
restaurant, pool

Ramada Inn
(800) 2-Ramada, (315) 463-0202
http://www.ramada.com
6590 Thompson Rd.
50 rooms - $55-85
Pets: Welcome
Creature Comforts: CCTV, a/c,
cont. brkfst

TARRYTOWN
Marriott Westchester
(800) 228-9290, (914) 631-2200
http://www.marriott.com
670 White Plains Rd.
445 rooms - $120-155
Pets: Welcome
Creature Comforts: CCTV, a/c,
restaurant, pool

TICONDEROGA
Circle Court Motel
(518) 585-7660
440 Montcalm St.
15 rooms - $45-65
Pets: Small pets w/$20 deposit
Creature Comforts: CCTV, a/c

TONAWANDA
Super 8 Motel
(800) 800-8000, (716) 876-4020
http://www.super8.com
1288 Sheridan Dr.
59 rooms - $50-60
Pets: Welcome w/$10 deposit
Creature Comforts: CCTV, a/c,
cont. brkfst

Microtel
(800) 771-7171, (716) 693-8100
http://www.microtelinns.com
1 Hospitality Center Way
100 rooms - $40-45
Pets: Welcome
Creature Comforts: CCTV, a/c

TUPPER LAKE
Cold River Ranch
(518) 359-7559
Corey's
6 rooms - $30-160
Pets: Welcome
Creature Comforts: CCTV, a/c,
pool

Pine Terrace Motel
(518) 359-9258
94 Moody Rd.
25 rooms - $45-75
Pets: Welcome, leashed
Creature Comforts: Fireplace,
kit

Sunset Park Motel
(518) 359-3995
71 Demars Blvd.
11 rooms - $45-60
Pets: Welcome
Creature Comforts: CCTV,
restaurant, beach, boating

Timber Lodge Motel
(518) 359-2320
91 Moody Rd.
11 rooms - $40-100
Pets: Welcome
Creature Comforts: CCTV, pool

The Wawbeek
(800) 953-2656, (518) 359-2656
http://www.wawbeek.com
Panther Mountain Rd.
20 cottages - $100-200
Pets: Welcome
Creature Comforts: Built in
Adirondack Great Camp tradition,
40 wooded lakeside acres, orig.
1900's cottages and some new
cottages, rqest newer units w/
attractive Adirondack furnishings,
vaulted ceilings, kit, stone
fireplace, excellent lakefront
dining, full breakfast, beach,
swimming, boating

UNIONDALE
Marriott Long Island
(800) 228-9290, (516) 794-3800
http://www.marriott.com
101 James Doolittle Blvd.
620 rooms - $120-140
Pets: Small pets welcome
Creature Comforts: CCTV, a/c,
restaurant, pool

UTICA
A-1 Motel
(315) 735-6698
238 N. Genesee St.
20 rooms - $45-55
Pets: Welcome w/$5 fee
Creature Comforts: CCTV, a/c,
pool

Best Western Gateway
(800) 528-1234, (315) 732-4121
http://www.bestwestern.com
175 N. Genesee St.
89 rooms - $70-130
Pets: Welcome
Creature Comforts: CCTV, a/c,
cont. brkfst, hlth club

Happy Journey Motel
(315) 738-1959
300 N. Genesee St.
18 rooms - $40-50
Pets: Welcome w/$5 fee, no cats
Creature Comforts: CCTV, a/c

Holiday Inn
(800) HOLIDAY, (315) 797-2131
http://www.holiday-inn.com
1777 Burrstone Rd.
100 rooms - $99-149
Pets: Small pets welcome
Creature Comforts: CCTV, a/c,
restaurant, pool, hlth club,
whirlpool

Motel 6
(800) 4-MOTEL6, (315) 797-8743
http://www.motel6.com
150 N. Genesee St.
59 rooms - $42-55
Pets: Under 30 lbs. welcome
Creature Comforts: CCTV, a/c

Radisson Hotel
(800) 333-3333, (315) 797-8010
http://www.radisson.com
200 Genesee St.
160 rooms - $75-120
Pets: Welcome w/$20 deposit
Creature Comforts: CCTV, a/c,
restaurant, pool, hlth club

Red Roof Inn
(800) THE ROOF, (315) 724-7128
http://www.redroof.com
20 Weaver St.
112 rooms - $60-80
Pets: Welcome w/notification
Creature Comforts: CCTV, a/c

Super 8 Motel
(800) 800-8000, (315) 797-0964
http://www.super8.com
309 North Genesse St.
40 rooms - $54-60
Pets: Welcome w/permission
Creature Comforts: CCTV, a/c,
Jacuzzi, cont. brkfst

VALATIE
Blue Spruce Motel
(518) 758-9711
Route 9
28 rooms - $50-75
Pets: Welcome
Creature Comforts: CCTV, a/c,
restaurant, pool

VESTAL
Parkway Motel
(607) 785-3311
900 Vestal Pkwy.
70 rooms - $40-60
Pets: Small pets welcome
Creature Comforts: CCTV, a/c,
refrig, micro, restaurant, cont.
brkfst, pool, sauna, whirlpool

Howard Johnson Express
(800) I-Go-Hojo, (607) 729-6181
http://www.hojo.com
3601 Vestal Pkwy.
60 rooms - $40-75
Pets: Welcome
Creature Comforts: CCTV, a/c,
refrig, micro, Jacuzzi, restaurant,
cont. brkfst, pool

Residence Inn
(800) 331-3131, (607) 770-8500
http://www.residenceinn.com
4610 Vestal Pkwy
75 rooms - $85-150
Pets: $10 daily fee, $250 cleaning
Creature Comforts: CCTV, a/c,
kit, pool

VICTOR
Microtel
(800) 771-7171, (716) 924-9240
http://www.microtelinns.com
7498 Main St.
100 rooms - $45-65
Pets: Welcome
Creature Comforts: CCTV, a/c,
refrig, micro

WALLKILL
Audrey's Farmhouse B&B
(914) 895-3440
2188 Brunswick Rd.
5 rooms - $90-110
Pets: Welcome w/notice
Creature Comforts: One of our
favorites-1740's farmhouse set in
countryside, formal and informal
gardens, interior nooks and
crannies w/beautiful country
antiques/southwest collectibles,
down comforters, feather beds,
baths oils, lavish brkfst, pool,
hiking

WATERLOO
Holiday Inn
(800) HOLIDAY, (315) 539-5011
http://www.holiday-inn.com
2468 Rte. 414
150 rooms - $60-100
Pets: Welcome
Creature Comforts: CCTV, a/c,
restaurant, pool

WATERTOWN
Best Western Carriage House
(800) 528-1234, (315) 782-8000
http://www.bestwestern.com
300 Washington St.
161 rooms - $62-82
Pets: Welcome w/deposit
Creature Comforts: CCTV, a/c,
restaurant, pool, hlth club, sauna

City Line Motel
(315) 782-9619
19226 Route 11
15 rooms - $30-55
Pets: Welcome
Creature Comforts: CCTV, a/c,
refrig, micro

Econo Lodge
(800) 55-ECONO, (315) 782-5500
http://www.econolodge.com
1030 Arsenal St.
60 rooms - $55-75
Pets: Welcome
Creature Comforts: CCTV, a/c,
cont. brkfst, pool

New Parrot Motel
(315) 788-5080
19325 Outer Washington St.
27 rooms - $35-55
Pets: Welcome
Creature Comforts: CCTV,
VCR, a/c, pool

Quality Inn
(800) 228-5151, (315) 788-6800
http://www.qualityinn.com
1190 Arsenal St.
96 rooms - $60-70
Pets: Welcome
Creature Comforts: CCTV, a/c,
restaurant, pool

Super 8 Motel
(800) 800-8000, (315) 786-8886
http://www.super8.com
652 Arsenal St.
48 rooms - $30-40
Pets: Welcome w/$5 fee
Creature Comforts: CCTV, a/c

WATKINS GLEN
Chieftain Motel
(607) 535-4759
3815 Route 14
15 rooms - $40-85
Pets: Small pets w/$25 deposit
Creature Comforts: CCTV,
VCR, a/c, kit, pool

WEEDSPORT
Best Western Weedsport
(800) 528-1234, (315) 834-6623
http://www.bestwestern.com
2709 Eerie Dr.
34 rooms - $40-90
Pets: Small pets welcome
Creature Comforts: CCTV, a/c,
refrig, micro, cont. brkfst, pool

WESTMORELAND
Carriage Motor Inn
(315) 853-3561
Route 233
24 rooms - $40-90
Pets: Small pets w/$5 fee, $5 dep.
Creature Comforts: CCTV, a/c,
refrig, micro, cont. brkfst, pool

WHITE PLAINS
Residence Inn
(800) 331-3131, (914) 761-7700
http://www.residenceinn.com
5 Barker Ave.
130 rooms - $150-295
Pets: $15 daily fee, $75 clean dep.
Creature Comforts: CCTV, a/c,
kit, hlth club

WILLIAMSVILLE
Econo Lodge
(800) 55-ECONO, (716) 634-1500
http://www.econolodge.com
7200 Transit Rd.
65 rooms - $40-95
Pets: Welcome
Creature Comforts: CCTV, a/c

Heritage Country Inn
(800) 283-3899, (716) 633-4900
http://www.wnybiz.comheritage
8261 Main St.
61 rooms - $60-100
Pets: Welcome
Creature Comforts: CCTV, a/c,
kit, cont. brkfst

Microtel
(800) 771-7171, (716) 633-6200
http://www.microtelinns.com
50 Freeman Rd.
100 rooms - $40-50
Pets: Small pets w/$5 fee
Creature Comforts: CCTV, a/c

Residence Inn
(800) 331-3131, (716) 632-6622
http://www.residenceinn.com
100 Maple Rd.
115 rooms - $120-150
Pets: Welcome w/$6 fee
Creature Comforts: CCTV,
VCR, a/c, kit, pool

WILMINGTON
Alder Bottoms Lodge
(905) 813-7904
Springfield Rd.
1 lodge - $600-900/wk
Pets: Welcome
Creature Comforts: Waterside
cabin, CCTV, fireplaces, kit,
swimming

Grand View Motel
(518) 946-2209
Route 86
18 rooms - $49-99
Pets: Small pets welcome
Creature Comforts: CCTV, a/c,
pool

Hungry Trout Motor Inn
(800) 766-9137, (518) 946-2217
http://www.hungrytrout.com
Route 86
20 rooms - $69-139
Pets: Small pets welcome
Creature Comforts: CCTV, a/c,
kit, Victorian pub, pool

Ledge Rock at Whiteface
(800) 336-4754, (518) 946-2379
HCR2, Box 34
18 rooms - $50-160
Pets: Welcome w/$8 fee
Creature Comforts: CCTV, a/c,
kit, pool

Mountain Brook Lodge
(518) 946-2262
Route 86
20 rooms - $50-90
Pets: Welcome w/restrictions
Creature Comforts: CCTV, a/c,
pool

North Pole Motor Inn
(800) 245-0228, (518) 946-7733
Route 86
20 rooms - $37-89
Pets: Welcome
Creature Comforts: CCTV, a/c,
refrig, micro, pool

Whiteface Chalet
(800) 932-0859, (518) 946-2207
Springfield Rd.
16 rooms - $50-70
Pets: Welcome
Creature Comforts: CCTV, a/c,
restaurant, pool, hlth club, tennis,
lawn games

Wilderness Inn II
(518) 946-2391
http://www.lakeplacid.net/
wildernessinn
Route 86
8 cottages - $50-75
Pets: Welcome
Creature Comforts: CCTV, kit,
fireplace, restaurant

Willkommen B&B
(800) 541-9119, (518) 946-7669
http://lakeplacid.net/
willkommenhof/
Route 86
18 rooms - $50-160
Pets: Welcome
Creature Comforts: CCTV, full
brkfst, sauna, whirlpool

WOODBURY
Ramada Ltd.
(800) 2-Ramada, (516) 921-8500
http://www.ramada.com
8030 Jericho Tpke
100 rooms - $75-85
Pets: Welcome
Creature Comforts: CCTV, a/c,
pool

North Carolina

ABERDEEN

Best Western Pinehurst
(800) 528-1234, (910) 944-2367
http://www.bestwestern.com
1500 Sandhills Blvd.
50 rooms - $75-89
Pets: One small dog per room
Creature Comforts: CCTV, a/c,
cont. brfkst, pool

Inn at the Bryant House
(800) 453-4019, (910) 944-3300
214 N. Poplar St.
11 rooms - $50-80
Pets: Welcome
Creature Comforts: Charming
inn, airy summer house motif,
handmade quilts, antique
collectibles, rag rugs, rqst first flr.
bdrm, CCTV, a/c, cont. brkfst,
jogging trail, tennis/golf access

Motel 6
(800) 4-MOTEL6, (910) 944-5633
http://www.motel6.com
1408 Sandhills Blvd.
81 rooms - $35-49
Pets: Under 30 lbs. welcome
Creature Comforts: CCTV, a/c,
restaurant

ALBERMARLE

Rodeway Inn
(800) 228-2000, (704) 985-1111
http://www.rodeway.com
200 Henson St.
40 rooms - $45-55
Pets: Welcome w/$50 deposit
Creature Comforts: CCTV, a/c,
restaurant

ARDEN

Comfort Inn
(800) 228-5150, (704) 687-9199
http://www.comfortinn.com
15 Rockwood Rd.
58 rooms - $40-100
Pets: Welcome
Creature Comforts: CCTV, a/c,
refrig, micro, cont. brkfst, pool,
hlth club, whirlpool

ASHEVILLE

Asheville Accommodations
(800) 770-9055, (919) 929-5553
http://www.carolinamornings.com
Rooms/Houses - $60-500
Pets: Welcome
Creature Comforts: Reservation
service-"rustic hideaways to
elegant mansions", indivdual rms
to houses, CCTV, VCR, a/c, kit,
cont. brkfst, pool, hlth clb, sauna,
tennis, whirlpool

Best Inns of America
(828) 298-4000
1435 Tunnel Rd.
85 rooms - $55-65
Pets: Small pets welcome
Creature Comforts: CCTV,
VCR, a/c, refrig, cont. brkfst,
pool, hlth clb access, sauna,
whirlpool

Blake House Inn
(888) 353-5227, (828) 681-5227
http://www.blakehouse.com/
150 Royal Pine Dr.
5 rooms - $110-130
Pets: Welcome w/$10 fee
Creature Comforts: 1847 Gothic
Revival, tradtional furnishings w/
some antiques, down comforters,
rice and iron beds, French doors,
fireplace, CCTV, VCR, gourmet
brkfst

Comfort Inn River Ridge
(800) 228-5150, (828) 298-9141
http://www.comfortinn.com
800 Fairview Rd.
177 rooms - $70-140
Pets: Welcome
Creature Comforts: CCTV, a/c,
Jacuzzi, cont. brkfst, pool

Comfort Suites
(800) 228-5150, (828) 665-4000
http://www.comfortinn.com
890 Brevard Rd.
125 rooms - $50-120
Pets: Welcome
Creature Comforts: CCTV, a/c,
cont. brkfst, pool, hlth club

Days Inn, East
(800) DAYS INN, (828) 298-5140
http://www.daysinn.com
1500 Tunnel Rd.
124 rooms - $35-110
Pets: Welcome w/$4 fee
Creature Comforts: CCTV, a/c,
refrig, kit, restaurant, pool

Dogwood Cottage Inn
(828) 258-9725
40 Canterbury Rd. N.
4 rooms - $100-110
Pets: Well-behaved pets welcome
Creature Comforts: Classic 1900
shingled Carolina mountain home,
wicker, chintz, hrdwd flrs, French
doors, fireplace, Early American
furnishings, CCTV, a/c, full brkfst,
afternoon tea, pool

Econo Lodge
(800) 55-ECONO, (828) 254-9521
http://www.econolodge.com
190 Tunnel Rd.
53 rooms - $45-85
Pets: Small pets welcome
Creature Comforts: CCTV,
VCR, a/c, refrig, micro, cont.
brkfst

Hill House B&B
(800) 379-0002, (828) 232-0345
http://www.bbonline.com/nc/
hillhouse
120 Hillside St.
7 rooms - $125-215
Pets: Welcome by arrangement
Creature Comforts: Victorian
painted lady w/art gallery,
antiques, four-poster beds,
fireplace, Jacuzzis, clawfoot tubs,
gourmet brkfst, rqst "Cottage"

Holiday Inn, Asheville Mall
(800) HOLIDAY, (828) 252-4000
http://www.holiday-inn.com
201 Tunnel Rd.
131 rooms - $49-99
Pets: Small pets welcome
Creature Comforts: CCTV, a/c,
refrig, restaurant, pool

Holiday Inn East
(800) HOLIDAY, (828) 298-5611
http://www.holiday-inn.com
1450 Tunnel Rd.
111 rooms - $90-130
Pets: Small pets welcome
Creature Comforts: CCTV, a/c,
restaurant, pool

Motel 6
(800) 4-MOTEL6, (828) 299-3040
http://www.motel6.com
1415 Tunnel Rd.
106 rooms - $35-49
Pets: Under 30 lbs. welcome
Creature Comforts: CCTV, a/c,
pool

Red Roof Inn, West
(800) THE ROOF, (828) 667-9803
http://www.redroof.com
16 Crowell St.
110 rooms - $50-65
Pets: Small pets welcome
Creature Comforts: CCTV, a/c

Super 8 Motel
(800) 800-8000, (828) 298-7952
http://www.super8.com
1329 Tunnel Rd.
124 rooms - $37-57
Pets: Welcome w/$25 deposit
Creature Comforts: CCTV, a/c,
refrig, micro, cont. brkfst, pool

ATLANTIC BEACH
Sea Gull Motel
(800) 257-2196, (252) 726-3613
http://www.nccoast.com
102 Henderson Rd.
12 rooms - $25-60
Pets: Welcome
Creature Comforts: CCTV, a/c,
refrig, kit

AVON
Avon Cottages
(252) 995-4123
http://www.avoncottages.com/
40279 Younce Rd.
22 cottages - $250-950/wk
Pets: Welcome
Creature Comforts: Weathered
shingle oceanside cottages set
behind dunes, some views,
understated but clean, simply
furnided, rms, rqst oceanfront,
CCTV, a/c, kit, fireplace

Outer Beaches Realty
(800) 627-3150, (252) 995-4477
http://www.outerbeaches.com
Route 12 at Tigrone Blvd.
426 cottages - $350-2,000
Pets: Welcome w/$50 per pet fee
Creature Comforts: CCTV, a/c,
kit, fireplace, Jacuzzi, pool,
whirlpool, sauna, tennis

Surf or Sound Realty
(800) 237-1138, (252) 995-5801
http:www.surforsound.com
Route 12
175 cottages - $350-2,000
Pets: Welcome in 30 units w/a
$60 cleaning fee
Creature Comforts: CCTV, a/c,
kit, fireplace, Jacuzzi, pool,
whirlpool, sauna, tennis,
horseback riding

BANNER ELK
Banner Elk Inn B&B
(828) 898-6223
407 Main St. East
4 rooms - $80-140
Pets: "Loving, housebroken, pets
welcome"
Creature Comforts: Restored
1912 country church, perennial
grdns, international antique and
book collection, engaging hostess/
international traveler, European
down comforters, antique beds,
CCTV, Jacuzzi, full brkfst

Eagle Ridge Log Cabin Rentals
(828) 963-5299
http://eagleridgelogcabins.com
190 McGuire Mtn. Rd.
3 cabins - $140-150
Pets: Welcome in Treetop or
Woodside cabins
Creature Comforts: Log cabins,
CCTV, kit, fireplace, Jacuzzi, hlth
club, sauna

BATTLEBORO
Days Inn
(800) DAYS INN, (252) 446-0621
http://www.daysinn.com
6970 Rte. 4
118 rooms - $46-70
Pets: Welcome w/$6 fee
Creature Comforts: CCTV, a/c,
restaurant, cont. brkfst, pool

Deluxe Inn
(252) 446-2411
Route 1
53 rooms - $35-45
Pets: Welcome w/$5 fee
Creature Comforts: CCTV, a/c

Motel 6
(800) 4-MOTEL6, (252) 977-3505
http://www.motel6.com
Gold Rock Rd.
100 rooms - $26-40
Pets: Under 30 lbs. welcome
Creature Comforts: CCTV, a/c,
pool

Red Carpet Inn
(800) 251-1962, (252) 446-0771
Route 1
100 rooms - $53-73
Pets: Welcome w/$5 fee
Creature Comforts: CCTV, a/c,
kit, pool

Scottish Inns
(800) 251-1962, (252) 446-1831
Route 1
95 rooms - $49-65
Pets: Welcome w/$5 fee
Creature Comforts: CCTV, a/c,
restaurant, pool

Super 8
(800) 800-8000, (252) 442-8075
http://www.super8.com
Route 1
152 rooms - $38-49
Pets: Welcome w$6 fee
Creature Comforts: CCTV, a/c,
pool

BEECH MOUNTAIN
Beech Mountain Chalet Rentals
(800) 368-7404, (828) 387-4231
405 Beech Mtn. Pkwy.
100 chalets - $440-650/wk.
Pets: Welcome in three units
Creature Comforts: CCTV, a/c,
kit, fireplace, hlth clb access

Beech Mountain Slopeside Rntls
(800) 692-2061, (828) 387-4251
503 Beech Mtn. Pkwy.
87 condos - $1,300-1,575/wk
Pets: Welcome in 3 units
Creature Comforts: CCTV, a/c,
kit, fireplace

BISCOE
Days Inn
(800) DAYS INN, (910) 428-2525
http://www.daysinn.com
531 E. Main St.
43 rooms - $80-135
Pets: Welcome
Creature Comforts: CCTV, a/c,
refrig, micro, kit, pool, whirlpool

BLACK MOUNTAIN
Black Mountain Inn
(800) 735-6128, (828) 669-8528
www.blackmountaininn.com
718 Old Hwy 70
7 rms, 1 suites - $88-135
Pets: Well behaved, supervised
pets welcome w/$10 fee
Creature Comforts: Highly
recommended, 1800's inn built as
stagecoach stop, nicely restored
w/orig. features, ceiling fans,
hardwood flrs, antique beds,
quilts, claw foot tubs, gourmet
brkfst

Comfort Inn
(800) 228-5150, (828) 669-9950
http://www.comfortinn.com
585 Rte. 9
57 rooms - $40-140
Pets: Welcome
Creature Comforts: CCTV, a/c,
refrig, micro, cont. brkfst, pool,
hlth club, whirlpool

Super 8 Motel
(800) 800-8000, (828) 669-8076
http://www.super8.com
101 Flat Creek Rd.
85 rooms - $33-77
Pets: Welcome w/$10 deposit
Creature Comforts: CCTV, a/c,
kit, pool, whirlpool

BLOWING ROCK
Cameron's Country Cabins
(800) 251-1962, (828) 295-4836
Route 1, Box 644
8 cabins - $125-150
Pets: Welcome
Creature Comforts: Charming
log cabins on 25 mountain acres
w/spectacular views, some
luxurious amenities, antiques,
wicker, hand-carved beds, stone
fireplaces or woodstoves, CCTV,
kit, Jacuzzi, outdoor hot tub

Peacock Ridge Cabins
(828) 295-3783
374 Charlies Way
3 cottages - $95-135
Pets: Welcome w/$10 fee
Creature Comforts: 20-acre
wooded setting, rough hewn
chestnut/cedar cabins, hrdwd flrs,
Oriental rugs, floral fabrics,
French doors, CCTV, kit, dining
rm, trout pond, creek, hiking trails

BOONE
Cardinal Motel
(800) 222-5638, (828) 264-3630
2135 Blowing Rock Rd.
43 rooms - $43-55
Pets: Welcome w/$5 fee
Creature Comforts: CCTV, a/c,
restaurant, pool

Grandma Jean's B&B
(828) 262-3670
http://www.bbchannel.com/bbc/
p206334.asp
254 Meadowview Rd.
4 rooms - $45-75
Pets: Small pets welcome
Creature Comforts: 1920's
cottage, cont. brkfst, afternoon
tea, CCTV

Scottish Inns
(800) 524-5214, (828) 264-2483
782 Blowing Rock Rd.
47 rooms - $49-55
Pets: Welcome w/$5 fee
Creature Comforts: CCTV, a/c,
kit, pool, sauna

BREVARD
Sunset Motel
(828) 884-9106
415 S. Broad St.
19 rooms - $40-70
Pets: Welcome w/$5 fee
Creature Comforts: CCTV, a/c,
refrig

Willoughby Woods
(828) 877-5588
http://brevardnc.com/business/
wwoods/wwoods.htm
1800 Happy Acres Rd.
5 cabins - $100
Pets: Dogs welcome w/$10 fee,
horses too. PeeWee, the host's
dog, hosts a web page w/special
instructions for visiting pets.
Creature Comforts: Modern
woodland cottages, very clean,
hardwood flrs, contemporary
furnishings, CCTV, VCR, a/c, kit,
fireplace, grill

BRYSON CITY
Mountain Laurel Motel
(828) 488-6641
250 Main St.
18 rooms - $40-50
Pets: Welcome w$5 fee
Creature Comforts: CCTV, hlth
club, whirlpool, sauna

West Oak B&B/Cottages
(828) 488-2438
101 Fryemont St.
5 rms/7cabins - $90-115
Pets: Welcome in cabins
Creature Comforts: CCTV, a/c,
fireplace, kit

BURLINGTON
Comfort Inn
(800) 228-5150, (336) 227-3681
http://www.comfortinn.com
Rtes. 85 & 49
127 rooms - $61-99
Pets: Welcome
Creature Comforts: CCTV, a/c,
cont. brkfst, pool, hlth club.

Motel 6
(800) 4-MOTEL6, (336) 226-1325
http://www.motel6.com
2155 Hanford Rd.
112 rooms - $35-46
Pets: Under 30 lbs. welcome
Creature Comforts: CCTV, a/c,
pool

CANDLER
Days Inn, Ashville West
(800) DAYS INN, (704) 298-8191
http://www.daysinn.com
2551 Smoky Park Hwy.
101 rooms - $55-75
Pets: Welcome
Creature Comforts: CCTV, a/c,
pool

CANTON

Rivermont Cabins
(828) 648-3066
http://www.rivermont.com
162 Rivermont Dr.
9 cabins - $375-875/wk.
Pets: Welcome w/$35 one-time fee
Creature Comforts: Contemp., hand-hewn log cabins, mtn and riverviews, handsomely decorated, handwoven rugs, local crafts, quilts, orig. art, immaculate, SATV, a/c, kit, fireplace or Appalachian stove, whirlpool, golf

CARY

Global Corporate Stay Intl.
(800) 533-2370, (919) 851-1511
6211 St. Regis Circle
100 suites - $75-85
Pets: Welcome w/$100 fee
Creature Comforts: Suites located throughout Raleigh/ Durham area, CCTV, a/c, kit, fireplace, hlth club., whirlpool, sauna

La Quinta Inn/Suites
(800) 531-5900, (918) 254-1626
http://www.laquinta.com
191 Crescent Commons
125 rooms - $79-89
Pets: Small pets welcome
Creature Comforts: CCTV, a/c, refrig, micro, cont. brkfst, pool, whirlpool, sauna

Motel 6
(800) 4-MOTEL6, (919) 467-6171
http://www.motel6.com
1401 Buck Jones Rd.
116 rooms - $43-55
Pets: Under 30 lbs. welcome
Creature Comforts: CCTV, a/c, pool

CASHIERS

Doherty/Wilson Real Estate
(828) 743-3242
Box 480
7 homes - $750-1,500/wk
(monthly rentals in season)
Pets: Welcome
Creature Comforts: CCTV, VCR, a/c, kit, hlth clb, pool

High Hampton Inn
(800) 334-2551, (828) 743-2411
http://www.highhamptoninn.com/
12525 E. 52nd St. S.
125 rooms - $150-188
Pets: Welcome in kennels
Creature Comforts: 1,400-acre Nat. Historic Register resort in Blue Ridge Mtns., classic lodge and cottages, mtn. crafted furniture, fireplaces, CCTV, restaurant, golf, tennis, 30-acre lake, sailing, hiking, swimming

Lakeview Mountain Cabins
(828) 884-9106
http://www.dnet.net/lmc/
Box 471
6 rms/3 cottages - $450-550/wk
Pets: Welcome w/$75 fee
Creature Comforts: SATV, kit, fireplace, tennis, trails

Tumblin' Creek Chalet
(828) 743-2504
Spring Valley Rd.
1 cottage - $375/wk
Pets: Welcome
Creature Comforts: On Troutstram, CCTV, kit, fireplace

The Valley Aire Motel
(828) 743-3998
Route 107 N.
20 rooms - $70-80
Pets: Small pets welcome
Creature Comforts: CCTV

CHAPEL HILL

Carolina Mornings
(800) 770-9055, (919) 929-5553
www.carolinamornings.com/
109 Circadian Way
20 rms/4 cottages - $60-200
Pets: Welcome in ltd. rms.
Creature Comforts: Reservation service for B&Bs, inns, cabins, lodges

The Siena Hotel
(800) 223-7379, (919) 929-4000
http://www.sienahotel.com
1505 E. Franklin St.
80 rooms - $155-225
Pets: One-time $50 fee
Creature Comforts: Award-winning European style hotel, tasteful decor, luxurious rms and amenities, French doors, marble baths, CCTV, a/c, restaurant

CHARLOTTE

AmeriSuites
(800) 833-1516, (704) 522-8400
http://www.amerisuites.com
7900 Forest Point Blvd.
128 rooms - $90-115
Pets: Under 10 lbs. welcome
Creature Comforts: CCTV, VCR, a/c, cont. brkfst, refrig, micro, pool

Best Western Merchandise Mart
(800) 528-1234, (704) 358-3755
http://www.bestwestern.com
3024 E. Independence Blvd.
148 rooms - $63-132
Pets: Small pets welcome
Creature Comforts: CCTV, a/c, restaurant, pool

Comfort Inn
(800) 228-5150, (704) 598-0007
http://www.comfortinn.com
Route 85 and Sugar Creek Rd.
87 rooms - $60-150
Pets: Welcome
Creature Comforts: CCTV, a/c, refrig, micro, Jacuzzi, cont. brkfst, pool, hlth club.

Days Inn, UNCC
(800) DAYS INN, (704) 597-8110
http://www.daysinn.com
1408 W. Sugar Creek Rd.
150 rooms - $55-75
Pets: Welcome w/$5 fee
Creature Comforts: CCTV, a/c, pool

Days Inn
(800) DAYS INN, (704) 333-4733
http://www.daysinn.com
601 N. Tyron Rd.
100 rooms - $50-70
Pets: Welcome w/$5 fee
Creature Comforts: CCTV, a/c, restaurant, pool

ExecuStay
(800) 789-7829, (704) 599-1575
http://www.execustay.com
3301-D Woodpark Blvd.
200 condos - $50-70
Pets: Welcome in ltd. units
Creature Comforts: Fully furnished condos for long-term stays, CCTV, a/c, kit, hlth clb access

Hilton
(800) HILTONS, (704) 527-8000
http://www.hilton.com
Gateway Center
143 rooms - $125-155
Pets: Small pets w/$15 fee, $50 refundable deposit
Creature Comforts: CCTV, a/c, refrig, micro, restaurant, cont. brkfst, pool, hlth clb access, whirlpool, sauna

Hyatt, Charlotte
(800) 233-1234, (704) 554-1234
http://www.hyatt.com
5501 Carnegie Blvd.
262 rooms - $95-175
Pets: Welcome
Creature Comforts: CCTV, a/c, restaurant, pool, hlth club., sauna, whirlpool

La Quinta, Airport
(800) 531-5900, (704) 393-5306
http://www.laquinta.com
3100 S. Rte. 85 Service Rd.
128 rooms - $55-60
Pets: Small pets welcome
Creature Comforts: CCTV, a/c, cont. brkfst, pool

La Quinta, South
(800) 531-5900, (704) 522-7110
http://www.laquinta.com
7900 Nations Ford Rd.
120 rooms - $62-70
Pets: Small pets welcome
Creature Comforts: CCTV, a/c, refrig, micro, cont. brkfst, pool

Microtel Inn, Airport
(800) 840-2972, (704) 398-9601
http://www.microtelinn.com
3412 S. Rte. 85 Service Rd.
99 rooms - $45-60
Pets: Small pets welcome
Creature Comforts: CCTV, a/c

Motel 6, South
(800) 4-MOTEL6, (704) 527-0144
http://www.motel6.com
3430 St. Vardell Ln.
122 rooms - $35-44
Pets: Under 30 lbs. welcome
Creature Comforts: CCTV, a/c, pool

Quality Inn, Central
(800) 228-5151, (704) 377-6961
http://www.qualityinn.com
2400 Wilkinson Blvd.
105 rooms - $70-160
Pets: Welcome
Creature Comforts: CCTV, a/c, restaurant, pool, hlth club.

Quality Inn, Suites
(800) 228-5151, (704) 596-0182
http://www.qualityinn.com
4330 N. Rte. 85
92 rooms - $55-338
Pets: Welcome
Creature Comforts: CCTV, a/c, cont. brkfst, pool, whirlpool

Red Roof Inn, Airport
(800) THE ROOF, (704) 392-2316
http://www.redroof.com
3300 Rte. 85 S.
85 rooms - $45-60
Pets: Small pets welcome
Creature Comforts: CCTV, a/c

Red Roof Inn, Coliseum
(800) THE ROOF, (704) 529-1020
http://www.redroof.com
131 Red Roof Dr.
114 rooms - $55-60
Pets: Welcome
Creature Comforts: CCTV, a/c

Red Roof Inn, University Pl.
(800) THE ROOF, (704) 596-8222
http://www.redroof.com
5116 Rte. 85 N.
110 rooms - $42-70
Pets: Small pets welcome
Creature Comforts: CCTV, a/c

Residence Inn
(800) 331-3131, (704) 547-1122
http://www.residenceinn.com
8503 N. Tyron St.
89 rooms - $100-140
Pets: Welcome w/$200 fee
Creature Comforts: CCTV, a/c, kit

Residence Inn, Tyvola
(800) 331-3131, (704) 527-8110
http://www.residenceinn.com
5800 Westpark Dr.
79 rooms - $140-180
Pets: $5 fee, $100 deposit
Creature Comforts: CCTV, VCR, a/c, kit, pool

Sheraton Airport Plaza
(800) 325-3535, (704) 393-2207
http://www.sheraton.com
3315 Rte. 85
222 rooms - $89-128
Pets: Small pets welcome
Creature Comforts: CCTV, a/c, restaurant, pool

Sleep Inn
(800) Sleep-Inn, (714) 549-4544
http://www.sleepinn.com
Rte. 29 & W.T. Harris Blvd.
121 rooms - $60-100
Pets: Welcome
Creature Comforts: CCTV, a/c, cont. brkfst, pool

Travelodge
(800) 578-7878, (704) 527-8500
http://www.travelodge.com
219 Archdale Dr.
116 rooms - $35-49
Pets: Welcome
Creature Comforts: CCTV, a/c, refrig, micro, pool

CHEROKEE
Comfort Suites
(800) 228-5150, (828) 497-3500
http://www.comfortinn.com
35 Rte. 441 N.
91 rooms - $65-125
Pets: Welcome
Creature Comforts: CCTV, a/c, restaurant, cont. brkfst, pool

Hampton Inn
(800) Hampton, (828) 497-3115
http://www.hampton-inn.com
Rtes. 19 & 441 S.
67 rooms - $50-72
Pets: Small pets w/$25 deposit
Creature Comforts: CCTV, a/c, pool

Pink Motel
(828) 497-3530
34 Rte. 441 N.
20 rooms - $50-75
Pets: Welcome
Creature Comforts: Riverside setting, CCTV, restaurant, pool

Pioneer Motel/Cottages
(828) 497-2435
Rte. 19 S.
34 rooms - $30-65
Pets: Small pets welcome
Creature Comforts: CCTV, a/c, kit, pool

CONCORD

Days Inn
(800) DAYS INN, (704) 786-9121
http://www.daysinn.com
5125 Davidson St.
75 rooms - $40-85
Pets: Welcome w/$5
Creature Comforts: CCTV, a/c,
restaurant, pool

CORNELIUS

Holiday Inn
(800) HOLIDAY, (704) 892-9120
http://www.holiday-inn.com
19901 Holiday Ln.
118 rooms - $85-105
Pets: Welcome
Creature Comforts: CCTV, a/c,
restaurant, pool

Quality Inn/Suites
(800) 228-5151, (704) 896-7622
http://www.qualityinn.com
19521 E. Liverpool Pkwy
60 rooms - $65-170
Pets: Welcome
Creature Comforts: CCTV, a/c,
restaurant, pool

COROLLA

B&B on the Beach
(800) 962-0201, (252) 453-3033
1023 Ocean Trail
360 cottages - $750-2,500/wk
Pets: Welcome w/$45
cleaning fee, 2 dogs
maximum per unit
Creature Comforts: Excellent
selection of house rentals, very pet
friendly, choose Conch Club units,
CCTV, VCR, a/c, kit, fireplace,
Jacuzzi, tennis, hlth clb, pool

Village Realty
(800) 548-9688, (252) 480-2224
http://www.villagerealtyobx.com/
27 condos - $750-3,500/wk
Pets: Welcome w/$75 fee
Creature Comforts: Excellent
selection of pet-friendly rentals,
CCTV, VCR, a/c, kit, fireplace,
Jacuzzi, tennis, hlth clb, pool

CRUSO

Heritage Cove Cabins
(800) 646-4020, (828) 648-4020
http://www.heritagecove.com
101 Heritage Cove Dr.
5 cabins - $700-850/wk
Pets: Welcome $6 fee, not to be
left unattended
Creature Comforts: CCTV, a/c,
kit

CULLOWHEE

Fox Den Cottages
(800) 721-9847, (828) 293-9847
http://www.cat2.com/foxden
501 Regional Rd. S.
4 cottages - $65-100
Pets: Welcome w/$5 fee
Creature Comforts: CCTV, a/c,
fireplace, hlth club., whirlpool,
sauna

DILLSBORO

Woodland Motel
(800) 366-4331, (828) 586-4331
Route 441 S.
12 rooms - $49-79
Pets: Small pets welcome, travel
crates preferred
Creature Comforts: CCTV, a/c,
restaurant, pool

DUCK

Carolina Designs Realty
(800) 368-3825, (252) 261-3934
http://www.carolinadesigns.com
1197 Duck Rd.
190 cottages - $500-2,000/wk
Pets: Welcome w/$60 fee
Creature Comforts: CCTV, a/c,
kit, tennis

R&R Resort Rental Properties
(800) 433-8805, (252) 261-1136
http://www.rrvacations.com
1184 Duck Rd.
325 cottages - $500-2,000/wk
Pets: Welcome w/$60 fee
Creature Comforts: CCTV, a/c,
kit, tennis

DUNN

Best Western Inn
(800) 528-1234, (910) 892-2162
http://www.bestwestern.com
Route 1
142 rooms - $40-60
Pets: Small pets w/$5 fee
Creature Comforts: CCTV, a/c,
restaurant, pool

Ramada
(800) 2-Ramada, (910) 892-8101
http://www.ramada.com
Rtes. 95 & 421
100 rooms - $57-69
Pets: Small pets welcome
Creature Comforts: CCTV, a/c,
pool

DURHAM

Best Western Skyland
(800) 528-1234, (919) 383-2508
http://www.bestwestern.com
5400 Route 70
31 rooms - $55-85
Pets: Welcome w/$5 fee
Creature Comforts: CCTV, a/c,
pool

Carolina Duke Motor Inn
(919) 286-0771
2517 Guess Rd.
180 rooms - $40-45
Pets: Welcome w/$3 fee
Creature Comforts: CCTV, a/c,
refrig, pool

Red Roof Inn
(800) THE ROOF, (919) 471-9882
http://www.redroof.com
2000 Rte. 85 Service Rd.
119 rooms - $55-75
Pets: Under 30 lbs. welcome
Creature Comforts: CCTV, a/c

Red Roof Inn, Chapel Hill
(800) THE ROOF, (919) 489-9421
http://www.redroof.com
5623 Chapel Hill Blvd.
115 rooms - $50-69
Pets: Welcome
Creature Comforts: CCTV, a/c

Red Roof Inn
(800) THE ROOF, (919) 361-5764
http://www.redroof.com
4405 Rte. 55 E.
115 rooms - $35-45
Pets: Welcome
Creature Comforts: CCTV, a/c

Residence Inn
(800) 331-3131, (919) 361-1266
http://www.residenceinn.com
1919 Rte. 54 E.
125 rooms - $110-145
Pets: $200 cleaning fee
Creature Comforts: CCTV, a/c, kit, pool

EDENTON
Coach House Inn
(252) 482-2107
823 Broad St.
34 rooms - $30-42
Pets: Small pets welcome
Creature Comforts: CCTV, a/c

ELIZABETH CITY
Days Inn
(800) DAYS INN, (919) 335-4316
http://www.daysinn.com
308 S. Hughes Blvd.
48 rooms - $55-75
Pets: Welcome w/$10 fee
Creature Comforts: CCTV, a/c, cont. brkfst

EMERALD ISLE
Bluewater Associates
Better Homes & Gardens
(252) 354-2323
http://www.bluewaterassoc.com
200 Mangrove Dr.
95 cottages - $750-2,500/wk
Pets: Welcome w/$60 fee
Creature Comforts: CCTV, a/c, kit, tennis

FAYETTEVILLE
Coliseum Inn
(910) 485-5161
2507 Gillespie St.
68 rooms - $40-49
Pets: Welcome
Creature Comforts: CCTV, a/c

Comfort Inn
(800) 228-5150, (910) 323-8333
http://www.comfortinn.com
1957 Cedar Creek Rd.
120 rooms - $62-65
Pets: Welcome
Creature Comforts: CCTV, a/c, refrig, micro, full brkfst

Days Inn
(800) DAYS INN, (910) 323-1255
http://www.daysinn.com
Rtes. 95 & 13
120 rooms - $55-75
Pets: Welcome w/$6 fee
Creature Comforts: CCTV, a/c, restaurant, cont. brkfst, pool

Holiday Inn Bordeaux
(800) HOLIDAY, (910) 323-0111
http://www.holiday-inn.com
1707 Owen Dr.
290 rooms - $70-85
Pets: Welcome w/$100 deposit
Creature Comforts: CCTV, a/c, restaurant, pool

Howard Johnson
(800) I-Go-Hojo, (910) 323-8282
http://www.hojo.com
1965 Cedar Creek Rd.
168 rooms - $54-93
Pets: Welcome
Creature Comforts: CCTV, a/c, pool, hlth clb access, sauna, whirlpool

Motel 6
(800) 4-MOTEL6, (910) 485-8122
http://www.motel6.com
2076 Cedar Creek Rd.
113 rooms - $32-44
Pets: Under 30 lbs. welcome
Creature Comforts: CCTV, a/c, pool

FONTANA VILLAGE
Fontana Motel
(828) 479-3677
Route 28
6 rooms - $30-80
Pets: Welcome
Creature Comforts: CCTV, a/c, kit

FORT MILL
Days Inn
(800) DAYS INN, (803) 548-8000
http://www.daysinn.com
3482 Carowinds Blvd.
119 rooms - $45-85
Pets: Welcome w/$5 fee
Creature Comforts: CCTV, a/c, cont. brkfst, pool

Ramada
(800) 2-Ramada, (803) 548-2400
http://www.ramada.com
225 Carowinds Blvd.
210 rooms - $67-145
Pets: Welcome
Creature Comforts: CCTV, a/c, cont. brkfst, pool, hlth club.

FRANKLIN
Barber's Motel
(828) 524-2444
3108 Georgia Rd.
19 rooms - $40-49
Pets: Welcome
Creature Comforts: CCTV, a/c, kit, restaurant

Days Inn
(800) DAYS INN, (828) 524-6491
http://www.daysinn.com
1320 E. Main St.
41 rooms - $40-75
Pets: Welcome
Creature Comforts: CCTV, a/c, refrig, micro, cont. brkfst, pool

Dogwood Country Cottages
(828) 524-2558
1115 Lowery Ln.
2 cottages - $50-66
Pets: Welcome w/$50 fee
Creature Comforts: CCTV, kit

Eagle's Nest
(828) 524-3649
128 Sugar Fork Rd.
1 cottage - $???
Pets: Welcome
Creature Comforts: Waterfront, CCTV, kit, fireplace

Gemstone Cottages
(800) 428-9118, (828) 524-9854
http://intertekweb.net/gemstone
196 Gemstone Dr.
15 cottages - $60-69
Pets: Welcome w/$10 fee
Creature Comforts: CCTV, a/c, kit, tennis

Mountain View Cottages
(828) 524-4605
74 Stonehouse Dr.
9 cottages - $65-75
Pets: Small pets welcome
Creature Comforts: Rustic cottages, CCTV, kit, pool

Pine Hill Park
(828) 524-8328
28 Hill St.
3 cottages - $230/wk
Pets: Under 20 lbs.
Creature Comforts: Call a year in advance for summer season, CCTV, kit, pool

Sleepy Hollow Cottages
(828) 524-4311
130 Sleepy Hollow Ln.
6 cabins - $250/wk
Pets: Welcome
Creature Comforts: CCTV, kit

FUQUAY-VARINA
Comfort Inn
(800) 228-5150, (717) 476-1500
http://www.comfortinn.com
7616 Purfoy Rd.
120 rooms - $60-165
Pets: Welcome w/$5 fee
Creature Comforts: CCTV, a/c, cont. brkfst, restaurant, pool, exercise rm.

GARNER
Hampton Inn
(800) Hampton, (919) 772-6500
http://www.hampton-inn.com
10 Drexmore Rd.
68 rooms - $55-70
Pets: Welcome
Creature Comforts: CCTV, a/c, pool

GASTONIA
Days Inn
(800) DAYS INN, (704) 864-9981
http://www.daysinn.com
1700 N. Chester Rd.
71 rooms - $50-120
Pets: Welcome
Creature Comforts: CCTV, a/c, restaurant, cont. brkfst, pool

Motel 6
(800) 4-MOTEL6, (704) 868-4900
http://www.motel6.com
1721 Broadcast St.
80 rooms - $35-44
Pets: Under 30 lbs. welcome
Creature Comforts: CCTV, a/c, pool

GLENDALE SPRINGS
Mountain View Lodge/Cabins
(800) 903-6811, (336) 982-2233
http://www.mtnviewlodge.com/
Blue Ridge Pkwy., Milepost 256
10 cabins - $65-110
Pets: Welcome in cabins w/$7 one-time fee
Creature Comforts: CCTV, VCR, kit, fireplace

GOLDSBORO
Days Inn
(800) DAYS INN, (919) 734-9471
http://www.daysinn.com
2000 Wayne Memorial Dr.
121 rooms - $50-55
Pets: Welcome
Creature Comforts: CCTV, a/c, restaurant, pool, hlth club, Jacuzzi, sauna

Motel 6
(800) 4-MOTEL6, (919) 734-4542
http://www.motel6.com
701 Rte. 70 E. Bypass
86 rooms - $35-48
Pets: Under 30 lbs. welcome
Creature Comforts: CCTV, a/c, pool

Quality Inn
(800) 228-5151, (919) 735-7901
http://www.qualityinn.com
708 Rte 70 E. Bypass
118 rooms - $55-135
Pets: Welcome
Creature Comforts: CCTV, a/c, Jacuzzi, cont. brkfst, pool, hlth club

Ramada
(800) 2-Ramada, (919) 736-4590
http://www.ramada.com
808 W. Grantham St.
128 rooms - $43-79
Pets: Small pets welcome
Creature Comforts: CCTV, a/c, kit, pool

GRASSY CREEK
River House Inn
(336) 982-2109
1896 Old Field Creek Rd.
6 rooms - $90-150
Pets: Welcome
Creature Comforts: Lovely country inn, riverside setting on 170 mountain acres, rock walls, porches, antique-filled rms, stone fireplace, Jacuzzi, CCTV, gourmet restaurant, full brkfst

GREENSBORO
Days Inn
(800) DAYS INN, (336) 688-0476
http://www.daysinn.com
501 Regional Rd. S.
122 rooms - $55-65
Pets: Welcome
Creature Comforts: CCTV, a/c, restaurant, pool

Econo Lodge
(800) 55-ECONO, (336) 852-4080
http://www.econolodge.com
3303 Isler St.
71 rooms - $45-110
Pets: Welcome
Creature Comforts: CCTV, a/c, cont. brkfst

Howard Johnson
(800) I-Go-Hojo, (336) 294-4920
http://www.hojo.com
3030 High Point Rd.
176 rooms - $62-82
Pets: Welcome
Creature Comforts: CCTV, a/c, restaurant, cont. brkfst, pool, hlth clb access, sauna

Motel 6
(800) 4-MOTEL6, (336) 668-2085
http://www.motel6.com
605 S. Regional Rd.
125 rooms - $35-46
Pets: Under 30 lbs. welcome
Creature Comforts: CCTV, a/c, pool

Motel 6, South
(800) 4-MOTEL6, (336) 854-0993
http://www.motel6.com
831 Greenhaven Dr.
149 rooms - $35-44
Pets: Under 30 lbs. welcome
Creature Comforts: CCTV, pool

Red Roof Inn, Airport
(800) THE ROOF, (336) 271-2636
http://www.redroof.com
615 Regional Rd.
112 rooms - $50-85
Pets: Small pets welcome
Creature Comforts: CCTV, a/c

Red Roof Inn, Coliseum
(800) THE ROOF, (336) 852-6560
http://www.redroof.com
2101 W. Meadowview Rd.
108 rooms - $50-65
Pets: Welcome
Creature Comforts: CCTV, a/c

Residence Inn
(800) 331-3131, (336) 294-8600
http://www.residenceinn.com
2000 Veasley St.
130 rooms - $100-125
Pets: $100 cleaning fee
Creature Comforts: CCTV,
VCR, a/c, pool

GREENVILLE
Red Roof Inn
(800) THE ROOF, (919) 756-2792
http://www.redroof.com
301 S.E. Greenville Rd.
148 rooms - $45-54
Pets: Welcome
Creature Comforts: CCTV, a/c,
pool

HAVELOCK
Days Inn
(800) DAYS INN, (919) 447-1122
http://www.daysinn.com
1220 E. Main St.
73 rooms - $50-65
Pets: Welcome
Creature Comforts: CCTV, a/c,
cont. brkfst, pool

HAYESVILLE
Chatuge Mountain Inn
(800) 948-2755, (828) 389-9340
196 Gemstone Dr.
14 rooms - $49-58
Pets: Welcome
Creature Comforts: CCTV, a/c

HENDERSONVILLE
Comfort Inn
(800) 228-5150, (704) 693-8800
http://www.comfortinn.com
206 Mitchell Dr.
85 rooms - $60-165
Pets: Small pets welcome
Creature Comforts: CCTV, a/c,
refrig, micro, cont. brkfst, pool

Mountain Aire Suites
(828) 692-9173
1351 Asheville Hwy.
1 cottage, 3 suites - $50-70
Pets: Welcome w/approval
Creature Comforts: CCTV, a/c,
kit, fireplace, whirlpool, tennis

Quality Inn & Suites
(800) 228-5151, (704) 692-7231
http://www.qualityinn.com
201 Sugarloaf Rd.
149 rooms - $45-155
Pets: Welcome
Creature Comforts: CCTV, a/c,
restaurant, cont. brkfst, pool, hlth
club., whirlpool, sauna

HERTFORD
Beechtree Inn
(252) 426-7815
http://www.albermarle-nc.com/
lodging/beechtr.htm
Pender Rd.
3 cottages - $55-80
Pets: Welcome
Creature Comforts: Historic
property w/14 pre-Civil War
cottages, 3 cottages w/antique and
handmade reprod. furniture,
CCTV, a/c, furniture making
classes, bicycles, table tennis

HICKORY
Econo Lodge
(800) 55-ECONO, (828) 328-2111
http://www.econolodge.com
325 Rte. 70 SW
132 rooms - $44-69
Pets: Welcome
Creature Comforts: CCTV, a/c,
pool

Hickory Motor Lodge
(828) 322-1740
404 Rte. 70 SW
86 rooms - $33-3
Pets: Well-behaved pets welcome
Creature Comforts: CCTV, a/c,
restaurant

Howard Johnson
(800) I-Go-Hojo, (828) 322-1600
http://www.hojo.com
5300 Clarion Blvd.
64 rooms - $55-70
Pets: Welcome
Creature Comforts: CCTV, a/c,
cont. brkfst, pool, hlth club, sauna

Red Roof Inn
(800) THE ROOF, (828) 323-1500
http://www.redroof.com
1184 Lenoir-Rhyne Blvd.
108 rooms - $45-60
Pets: Welcome
Creature Comforts: CCTV, a/c

HIGHLANDS
Fire Mountain Inn and Cabins
(800) 775-4446, (828) 526-4446
http://www.firemountaininn.com
Box 2772
15 rooms/cabins - $100-275
Pets: One dog only, under 40 lbs.
w/$10 fee and $150 deposit, ltd.
cabins
Creature Comforts: Lodge set
on mountaintop, contemp. art and
sculpture, cabins w/cathedral
ceilings, kit, stone fireplaces,
decks, pencil post beds, CCTV,
VCR, Jacuzzis, candlelit cont.
brkfst, hot tub, hiking, bird
sanctuary, gardens

Mountain High Motel
(800) 445-7293, (828) 526-2790
http://www.mountainhigh.com
200 Main St.
55 rooms - $50-175
Pets: Welcome in two rooms
Creature Comforts: CCTV, a/c,
refrig, micro, Jacuzzi

Skyline Lodge/Restaurant
(800) 575-9546, (828) 526-2121
http://www.skylinelodge.com
Flat Mtn. Rd.
9 rooms - $89-110
Pets: Welcome in 4 rooms
Creature Comforts: CCTV, a/c,
fireplace, restaurant, pool, hlth
club, sauna, whirlpool

HIGH POINT

Holiday Inn
(800) HOLIDAY, (336) 886-7011
http://www.holiday-inn.com
236 S. Main St.
173 rooms - $65-155
Pets: Welcome
Creature Comforts: CCTV, a/c,
refrig, micro, restaurant, pool

Motel 6
(800) 4-MOTEL6, (336) 841-7717
http://www.motel6.com
200 Ardale Dr.
83 rooms - $30-44
Pets: Under 30 lbs. welcome
Creature Comforts: CCTV, a/c,
pool

Radisson Hotel-High Point
(800) 333-3333, (336) 889-8888
http://www.radisson.com
135 S. Main St.
252 rooms - $75-250
Pets: Small pets welcome, nearby
kennel for larger pets
Creature Comforts: CCTV, a/c,
restaurant, pool, whirlpool, hlth
clb access

JACKSONVILLE

Onslow Inn
(800) 763-3151, (910) 346-4000
201 Marine Blvd.
92 rooms - $44-80
Pets: Welcome
Creature Comforts: CCTV, a/c,
restaurant, pool

Super 8 Motel
(800) 800-8000, (910) 455-6888
http://www.super8.com
2149 N. Marine Blvd.
60 rooms - $55-65
Pets: Welcome w/$10 fee
Creature Comforts: CCTV, a/c,
refrig, micro, pool

JONESVILLE

Rose's Village Motel
(336) 835-3609
407 N. Bridge St.
23 rooms - $30-40
Pets: Small pets welcome
Creature Comforts: CCTV, a/c,
restaurant, pool

KENLY

Econo Lodge
(800) 55-ECONO, (919) 284-1000
http://www.econolodge.com
Rtes. 301 & 95
60 rooms - $38-58
Pets: Welcome
Creature Comforts: CCTV, a/c,
cont. brkfst, pool

KILL DEVIL HILLS

Anchorage Motel
(252) 441-7226
903 S. Virginia Dare Tr.
17 rms/apts - $33-55
Pets: Welcome w/$4 fee
Creature Comforts: CCTV, a/c,
kit, tennis

Budget Host Inn
(800) Bud-Host, (252) 441-2503
http://www.budgethost.com
1003 S. Croatan Rd.
40 rooms - $40-100
Pets: Welcome w/$10-20 deposit
Creature Comforts: CCTV, a/c,
kit, pool

Ramada Inn Nags Head
(800) 2-Ramada, (252) 441-2151
http://www.ramada.com
1701 Virginia Dare Trail
172 rooms - $54-184
Pets: Small pets welcome
Creature Comforts: CCTV, a/c,
refrig, micro, restaurant, pool,
whirlpool

KITTY HAWK

Kitty Hawk Rentals
(800) 635-1559, (252) 441-7166
http://www.beachrealtync.com
2091 N. Croatan Hwy
600 cottages - $500-5,000/wk
Pets: Welcome w/$50 fee in many
accommodations
Creature Comforts: CCTV,
VCR, a/c, refrig, micro, kit,
fireplace, Jacuzzi, pool, hlth club,
whirlpool, sauna

KURE BEACH

East Wind Cottages
(910) 458-5234
217 Ft. Fisher Blvd.
3 cottages - $60-85
Pets: Welcome
Creature Comforts: CCTV, a/c,
kit

LAKE LURE

Geneva Riverside Motel
(828) 625-4121
Hwys 64/74
31 rooms - $60-65
Pets: Welcome w/$5
Creature Comforts: CCTV, a/c,
kit, pool, boating, fishing

Pine Gables
(828) 625-8846
http://www.lake-lure.com/
pinegables.html
328 Boys Camp Rd.
2 cottages - $75
Pets: Welcome
Creature Comforts: Rustic and
historic log cabins, lakefront, kit,
volleyball, horseshoes, boating

LAUREL SPRINGS

Doughton-Hall B&B
(336) 359-2341
http://www.doughtonhall.com
12668 Hwy. 18 South
4 rooms - $45-80
Pets: May stay inside if inn is
empty, outside if other guests
Creature Comforts: 1896 Queen
Anne Victorian, brass beds,
Jacuzzi, country brkfst

LAURINBURG

Hampton Inn
(800) Hampton, (910) 277-1516
http://www.hampton-inn.com
115 Hampton Circle
50 rooms - $64-70
Pets: Welcome
Creature Comforts: CCTV, a/c,
pool

LENOIR

Days Inn
(800) DAYS INN, (704) 754-0731
http://www.daysinn.com
206 Blowing Rock Rd.
78 rooms - $50-70
Pets: Welcome
Creature Comforts: CCTV, a/c,
cont. brkfst

LINVILLE FALLS
Blue Ridge Lodge/Country Club
(828) 756-0020, (877) 626-0020
http://www.blueridgecc.com
Route 3, Hwy. 221
12 rms, 3 condos - $89-250
Pets: Well-behaved pets welcome
Creature Comforts: Planned golf community w/acres of woodlands, golf villas, condos, SATV, kit, refrig, stone fireplace, hot tub

Humpback Hollow Cabins
(888) 263-3632, (828) 766-6555
www.humpbackhollow.com/
16 Luther Franklin Ln.
3 cabins - $90-125
Pets: Welcome
Creature Comforts: Unique cabins — historic to modern, all have natural board walls, mix of antique/contemp. furnishings, country decor, SATV, VCR, a/c, kit, fireplace

Parkview Lodge
(800) 849-4452, (828) 765-4787
http://www.parkviewlodge.com/
Route 221, MP 317
2 cabins - $45-85
Pets: Welcome w/$10 fee
Creature Comforts: CCTV, a/c, kit, cont. brkfst, pool

LUMBERTON
Best Western Inn
(800) 528-1234, (910) 618-9799
http://www.bestwestern.com
201 Jackson Ct.
63 rooms - $55-85
Pets: Small pets welcome
Creature Comforts: CCTV, a/c, refrig, micro, Jacuzzi, cont. brkfst

Comfort Suites
(800) 228-5150, (910) 739-8800
http://www.comfortinn.com
215 Wintergreen Dr.
93 rooms - $60-100
Pets: Welcome
Creature Comforts: CCTV, a/c, refrig, cont. brkfst, pool, hlth club.

Motel 6
(800) 4-MOTEL6, (910) 738-2410
http://www.motel6.com
2361 Lackey Rd.
83 rooms - $30-45
Pets: Under 30 lbs. welcome
Creature Comforts: CCTV, a/c, pool

Quality Inn
(800) 228-5151, (910) 738-8261
http://www.qualityinn.com
3608 Kahn Dr.
120 rooms - $55-80
Pets: Welcome
Creature Comforts: CCTV, VCR, a/c, cont. brkfst, pool

MAGGIE VALLEY
Abbey Inn Motel
(800) 545-5853, (828) 926-1188
http://www.abbeyinn.com
6375 Soco Rd.
20 rooms - $38-60
Pets: Welcome w/$8 one-time fee
Creature Comforts: CCTV, a/c, kit

Applecover Inn
(800) 787-4788, (828) 926-9100
www.gatewaytothesmokies.com/applecoverinn.htm
4077 Soco Rd.
20 rooms - $40-55
Pets: Welcome
Creature Comforts: CCTV, a/c, refrig, micro,

Bear Run Log Cabin Rentals
(828) 926-7566
www.bearrunlogcabins.com/
1604 Moody Farm Rd.
4 cabins - $115
Pets: Welcome w/approval
Creature Comforts: Modern log cabins, creekside, beautiful views, immaculate, bright country decor, braided rugs, SATV, a/c, kit, fireplace

Country Cabins
(888) 222-4611, (828) 926-0612
http://smokeymountains.net/countrycabins.html
171 Bradley St.
5 cabins - $90-120
Pets: Welcome w/one-time $5 fee
Creature Comforts: Modern and historic log cabins, stream, CCTV, a/c, kit, fireplace

Hearth and Home Inn
(888) 926-1845, (828) 926-1845
http://www.haywood.main.nc.us/~tramey
Route 19
20 rooms - $30-60
Pets: Welcome w/$5 fee
Creature Comforts: CCTV, a/c

Maggie Mountain Villas
(800) 308-1808, (828) 452-4285
http://www.cyberrentals.com/nc/kozinc.html
8 Ivy Ln.
2 villas/1 chalet - $105-255
Pets: Welcome, "no alligators"
Creature Comforts: Villas/chalet w/fine valley views, country decor, light and airy, CCTV, a/c, kit, stone fireplace, hot tub

Mountain Joy Cottages
(828) 926-1257
121 Setzer Cove Rd.
8 cabins - $595-840/wk
Pets: Welcome w/$5, crated if left unattended
Creature Comforts: CCTV, a/c, kit, fireplace

Pioneer Village
(828) 926-1881
219 Campbell Creek Rd.
13 cabins - $65-105
Pets: Welcome in cabins 8,9, 10
Creature Comforts: CCTV, a/c, kit, fireplace

MANTEO
Pirate's Cove
(800) 537-7245, (252) 473-6800
http://www.pirates-cove.com
Hwys 64/264
74 condos/hses - $49-55
Pets: Ltd units w/$60 cleaning fee
Creature Comforts: Private resort complex, modern—well appointed units, cathedral ceilings, some water vws, CCTV, VCR, a/c, stereo, kit, pool, tennis, volleyball

MOOREHEAD CITY
William & Garland Motel
(252) 247-3733
Route 58
11 rooms - $45-55
Pets: Small pets welcome
Creature Comforts: CCTV, a/c, kit

MOORESVILLE
Ramada Ltd.
(800) 2-Ramada, (704) 664-6556
http://www.ramada.com
Rtes. 77 & 150
79 rooms - $65-125
Pets: Small pets welcome
Creature Comforts: CCTV, a/c,
pool

MORGANTON
Cabins in the Laurel
(828) 438-8185
Route 181 N.
6 cabins - $40-55
Pets: Small pets welcome
Creature Comforts: Rustic
cabins or modern house w/a/c, kit,
fireplace, Jacuzzi

MORRISVILLE
Baymont Inns
(800) 789-4103, (919) 481-3600
http://www.baymontinns.com
1001 Aerial Center Pkwy.
122 rooms - $50-65
Pets: Small pets welcome
Creature Comforts: CCTV, a/c,
pool

La Quinta
(800) 531-5900, (919) 461-1771
http://www.laquinta.com
1001 Hospitality Ct.
127 rooms - $80-100
Pets: Small pets welcome
Creature Comforts: CCTV, a/c,
kit, pool, whirlpool, hlth club.,
sauna

MURPHY
Cobb Creek Cabins
(828) 837-0270
Cobb Dr.
4 cabins - 65-95
Pets: Small pets welcome
Creature Comforts: CCTV, a/c,
kit, fireplace, whirlpool

Comfort Inn
(800) 228-5150, (704) 837-8030
http://www.comfortinn.com
114 Rte. 64 W.
56 rooms - $55-109
Pets: Welcome
Creature Comforts: CCTV, a/c,
cont. brkfst, pool

Hamlet O' Cabins
(800) 644-5957, (828) 644-5957
http://www.cherokee/co.com
311 Hilltop Ln.
4 cabins - $50-65
Pets: Welcome w/$5 fee
Creature Comforts: CCTV, a/c,
kit, fireplace

Pine Creek Cabins
(828) 837-4228
1010 Gold Branch Rd.
11 cabins - $60-75
Pets: Welcome w/$10 fee
Creature Comforts: CCTV, a/c,
kit, pool

West Motel
(828) 837-2012
105 Andrews Rd.
34 rooms - $35-45
Pets: Welcome w/$6 fee
Creature Comforts: CCTV, a/c

NAGS HEAD
Carefree Cottages
(252) 441-5340
6721 S. Virginia Dare Tr.
4 cottages - $350-500/wk
Pets: Small pets welcome
Creature Comforts: CCTV, a/c,
kit

Laughing Gull Cottages
(252) 441-5005
Beach Rd, MP 17
8 cottages - $320-1,500/wk
Pets: Welcome w/$30 fee,
extensive pet rules
Creature Comforts: Classic
Nag's Head shingle cottages,
beachfront, simple furnishings,
perfect low-key beachside
destination, CCTV, a/c, VCR, kit,
grills

Toad Hall Cottage
(252) 441-1297
325 W. Soundside Rd.
1 cottage - $450-750/wk
Pets: Welcome w/$40 fee, with
signed waiver
Creature Comforts: Wonderful,
1930's cottage, richly hued pine
walls, hardwood flrs, eaved
bedrooms, classic comfortable
furnishings, some antiques,
CCTV, VCR, stereo, kit

OAK CITY
Southern Comfort B&B
(252) 798-7081
15909 Route 125 N.
2 rooms/1 cabin - $50-65
Pets: Welcome
Creature Comforts: CCTV, a/c,
tennis

OCRACOKE
Anchorage Inn
(252) 928-1101
http://www.anchorageinn.com
Route 12
36 rooms - $65-105
Pets: Welcome in certain rooms
Creature Comforts: CCTV, a/c,
restaurant, pool

Sharon Miller Realty
(800) 955-0630, (252) 928-5711
http://www.ocracoke-island.com
Silver Lake Rd.
150 ctges/condo - $400-$1,700/wk
Pets: Welcome w/up to a $100 fee
Creature Comforts: CCTV, a/c,
kit, fireplace, Jacuzzi, pool,
whirlpool, hlth club, sauna

PINEHURST
Motel 6
(800) 4-MOTEL6, (910) 944-5633
http://www.motel6.com
1408 N. Sandhills Blvd.
81 rooms - $35-48
Pets: Under 30 lbs. welcome
Creature Comforts: CCTV, a/c,
pool

RAEFORD
Days Inn
(800) DAYS INN, (910) 904-1050
http://www.daysinn.com
401 Bypass and Teal Rd.
44 rooms - $45-75
Pets: Welcome w/$4 fee
Creature Comforts: CCTV, a/c,
Jacuzzi, cont. brkfst, pool,
whirlpool

RALEIGH
Days Inn, Crabtree
(800) DAYS INN, (919) 781-7904
http://www.daysinn.com
6329 Glenwood Ave.
122 rooms - $75-85
Pets: Welcome w/$25 fee
Creature Comforts: CCTV, a/c,
restaurant, pool

Fairfield Inn, Crabtree
(800) 228-2800, (919) 881-9800
http://www.marriott.com
2201 Summit Park Ln.
128 rooms - $75-250
Pets: Small pets welcome
Creature Comforts: CCTV, a/c, pool, whirlpool, hlth clb

Howard Johnson
(800) I-Go-Hojo, (919) 231-3000
http://www.hojo.com
3120 New Bern Ave.
73 rooms - $45-60
Pets: Welcome
Creature Comforts: CCTV, a/c, cont. brkfst, pool, whirlpool

La Quinta Suites
(800) 531-5900, (919) 785-0071
http://www.laquinta.com/
2211 Summit Park Ln.
134 rooms - $69-79
Pets: Small pets welcome
Creature Comforts: CCTV, a/c, cont. brkfst, pool

Motel 6
(800) 4-MOTEL6, (919) 782-7071
http://www.motel6.com
3921 Arrow Dr.
63 rooms - $42-53
Pets: Under 30 lbs. welcome
Creature Comforts: CCTV, a/c

Plantation Inn Resort
(800) 521-1932, (919) 876-1411
www.plantationinnraleigh.com/
6401 Capital Blvd.
94 rooms - $58-95
Pets: Welcome in certain rooms
Creature Comforts: Wooded 26-acre setting, CCTV, a/c, restaurant, pool, playground

Red Roof Inn
(800) THE ROOF, (919) 878-9310
http://www.redroof.com
3201 Old Wake Forest Rd.
147 rooms - $50-65
Pets: Welcome
Creature Comforts: CCTV, a/c, pool

Residence Inn
(800) 331-3131, (919) 878-6100
http://www.residenceinn.com
1000 Navaho Rd.
145 rooms - $70-145
Pets: Welcome w/$200 fee
Creature Comforts: CCTV, a/c, kit, pool

Wynne Residential Suites
(800) 477-6922, (919) 781-6922
6008 Triangle Dr.
300 rooms - $1,750-1,900/month
Pets: Welcome
Creature Comforts: Long-term apt. rentals in tri-city area, CCTV, VCR, a/c, kit, pool, hlth clb access, sauna, whirlpool

ROANOKE RAPIDS
Motel 6
(800) 4-MOTEL6, (919) 537-5252
http://www.motel6.com
605 S. Regional Rd.
125 rooms - $35-45
Pets: Under 30 lbs. welcome
Creature Comforts: CCTV, a/c, pool

ROCKY MOUNT
Comfort Inn
(800) 228-5150, (919) 937-7765
http://www.comfortinn.com
200 Gateway Blvd.
125 rooms - $65-71
Pets: Welcome
Creature Comforts: CCTV, a/c, cont. brkfst, pool, hlth club

Comfort Inn, North
(800) 228-5150, (919) 972-9426
http://www.comfortinn.com
Rtes. 95 & 48
50 rooms - $50-75
Pets: Welcome
Creature Comforts: CCTV, a/c, refrig, cont. brkfst, pool

Holiday Inn
(800) HOLIDAY, (919) 937-6300
http://www.holiday-inn.com
5350 Dortches Blvd.
152 rooms - $55-75
Pets: Welcome
Creature Comforts: CCTV, a/c, refrig, micro, pool

Howard Johnson
(800) I-Go-Hojo, (919) 977-9595
http://www.hojo.com
7568 Hwy 48
84 rooms - $30-95
Pets: Welcome
Creature Comforts: CCTV, a/c, restaurant, pool

ROXBORO
Days Inn
(800) DAYS INN, (910) 599-9276
http://www.daysinn.com
1006 N. Madison Blvd.
53 rooms - $50-80
Pets: Welcome
Creature Comforts: CCTV, a/c, cont. brkfst, pool

SALISBURY
Days Inn
(800) DAYS INN, (704) 633-4211
http://www.daysinn.com
1810 Lutheran Synod Dr.
147 rooms - $50-95
Pets: Welcome w/$6 fee
Creature Comforts: CCTV, a/c, cont. brkfst, pool

Econo Lodge
(800) 55-ECONO, (704) 633-8850
http://www.econolodge.com
600 Route 291
85 rooms - $40-65
Pets: Welcome
Creature Comforts: CCTV, a/c, restaurant

Hampton Inn
(800) Hampton, (704) 637-8000
http://www.hampton-inn.com
1001 Klumac Rd.
121 rooms - $55-70
Pets: Welcome w/$6 fee
Creature Comforts: CCTV, a/c, pool

Holiday Inn
(800) HOLIDAY, (704) 637-3100
http://www.holiday-inn.com
530 S. Jake Alexander Blvd.
186 rooms - $65-70
Pets: Welcome w/$10 fee
Creature Comforts: CCTV, a/c, refrig, micro, kit, restaurant, pool

Sleep Inn
(800) Sleep-Inn, (704) 633-5961
http://www.sleepinn.com
321 Bendix Dr.
116 rooms - $48-90
Pets: Welcome
Creature Comforts: CCTV, a/c,
restaurant, cont. brkfst, pool

SANFORD
Palomino Motel
(919) 776-7531
Route 1
90 rooms - $40-49
Pets: Welcome
Creature Comforts: CCTV,
VCR, a/c, refrig, micro, restaurant,
pool, hlth club, whirlpool, sauna

SAPPHIRE
Woodlands Inn
(828) 966-4709
http://www.virtualcities.com/ons/
nc/m/ncm6601.htm
1309 Hwy 64
14 rooms - $70-125
Pets: Under 25 lbs. w/notice
Creature Comforts: In "Land of
the Waterfalls", bedrms w/brass or
iron beds, featherbeds, CCTV, a/c,
refrig, Jacuzzi, fireplace, full
brkfst, pool

SMITHFIELD
Howard Johnson
(800) I-Go-Hojo, (919) 934-7176
http://www.hojo.com
Route 95
60 rooms - $40-85
Pets: Welcome
Creature Comforts: CCTV, a/c,
refrig, micro, cont. brkfst, pool

Log Cabin Motel
(919) 934-1534
Hwy 70 East
60 rooms - $50-55
Pets: Welcome w/$5 fee
Creature Comforts: CCTV, a/c,
restaurant

SOUTHERN PINES
Fairway Motel
(910) 692-2711
1410 Route 1 South
25 rooms - $40-49
Pets: $10 one-time fee
Creature Comforts: CCTV, a/c,
pool, hlth club., whirlpool

STATESVILLE
Red Roof Inn
(800) THE ROOF, (704) 878-2051
http://www.redroof.com
1508 E. Broad St.
115 rooms - $47-65
Pets: Small pets welcome
Creature Comforts: CCTV, a/c

Super 8 Motel
(800) 800-8000, (704) 878-9888
http://www.super8.com
1125 Greenland Dr.
41 rooms - $50-55
Pets: Welcome w/permission
Creature Comforts: CCTV, a/c

SYLVA
Azalea Motel
(828) 586-2051
97 Skyland Dr.
9 rooms - $40-48
Pets: Welcome
Creature Comforts: CCTV, a/c,
restaurant, pool

TAYLORSVILLE
Barkley House B&B
(704) 632-9060
2522 N. Route 16 S.
4 rooms - $55-80
Pets: Small pets welcome
Creature Comforts: Intimate
B&B, CCTV, a/c, cont. brkfst

VALLE CRUCIS
Valle Crucis Log Cabins
(828) 963-7774
Box 554
9 cabins - $125-175
Pets: Welcome w/$35 fee
Creature Comforts: Appalachian
ambiance, hand-hewn cabins,
woodland setting, hand-painted
and antique furniture, collectibles,
CCTV, a/c, kit, fireplace, hot tubs

WADESBORO
Days Inn
(800) DAYS INN, (704) 694-9145
http://www.daysinn.com
209 E. Caswell St.
48 rooms - $45-85
Pets: Welcome w/$4 fee
Creature Comforts: CCTV, a/c,
refrig, micro, restaurant, cont.
brkfst, pool

WASHINGTON
Econo Lodge North
(800) 55-ECONO, (610) 521-3900
http://www.econolodge.com
1220 W. 15th St.
48 rooms - $38-55
Pets: Welcome
Creature Comforts: CCTV, a/c,
cont. brkfst

WAYNESVILLE
Mountain Creek B&B
(800) 557-9766, (828) 456-5509
http://www.bbonline.com/nc/mcbb
100 Chestnut Walk
6 rooms - $90-110
Pets: Welcome on selective
basis w/$20 one-time fee
Creature Comforts: Lodge
setting, six acre setting, stone
house, CCTV, a/c, Jacuzzi,
fireplace, cont. brkfst, pool

WELDON
Days Inn
(800) DAYS INN, (704) 864-9981
http://www.daysinn.com
Route 158 E.
97 rooms - $45-100
Pets: Welcome w/$5 fee
Creature Comforts: CCTV, a/c,
cont. brkfst, pool, whirlpool

WILLIAMSTON
Comfort Inn
(800) 228-5150, (919) 792-8400
http://www.comfortinn.com
Route 64 Bypass
59 rooms - $44-70
Pets: Welcome
Creature Comforts: CCTV, a/c,
cont. brkfst, hlth club

WILMINGTON
219 S. 5th B&B
(800) 219-7634, (910) 763-5539
219 S. 5th St.
4 rooms - $75-115
Pets: Small, well-behaved pets,
cannot leave alone unless in crate
Creature Comforts: 1871 Greek
Revival, antiques, CCTV, VCR,
a/c, fireplace, kit

Anderson Guest House
(888) 265-1216, (910) 343-8128
520 Orange St.
2 rooms - $90
Pets: Welcome
Creature Comforts: 1851
Italianate, antiques, rqst canopy
bed rm w/fireplace and clawfoot
tub, CCTV, a/c, full brkfst

Camellia Cottage B&B
(800) 763-9171, (910) 763-9171
118 S. Fourth St.
4 rooms/1 suite - $135-150
Pets: Welcome
Creature Comforts: Queen Anne
shingle style home, newly
renovated Victorian, Victorian
furnishings, handpainted murals
and tiles, English linens, fireplace,
CCTV, a/c, full brkfst served on
china and crystal

Hampton Inn
(800) Hampton, (910) 256-9600
http://www.hampton-inn.com
1989 Eastwood Rd.
120 rooms - $79-129
Pets: Welcome
Creature Comforts: CCTV, a/c,
fireplace, Jacuzzi, pool, hlth club.

Motel 6
(800) 4-MOTEL6, (910) 762-0120
http://www.motel6.com
Hwys 17/74
113 rooms - $40-52
Pets: Under 30 lbs. welcome
Creature Comforts: CCTV, a/c,
pool

Waterway Lodge
(800) 331-3131, (910) 256-3771
Rtes. 132 & 76
40 rooms - $60-130
Pets: $15 fee in certain rooms
Creature Comforts: CCTV, a/c,
refrig, micro, pool

WILSON
Days Inn
(800) DAYS INN, (704) 864-9981
http://www.daysinn.com
1815 Rte. 301
100 rooms - $62-70
Pets: Welcome
Creature Comforts: CCTV, a/c,
refrig, micro, cont. brkfst, pool

Quality Inn, South
(800) 228-5151, (919) 243-5165
http://www.qualityinn.com
2901 Rte. 301 S.
100 rooms - $55-75
Pets: Welcome
Creature Comforts: CCTV, a/c,
refrig, micro, Jacuzzi, restaurant,
cont. brkfst, pool

Sleep Inn
(800) Sleep-Inn, (919) 234-2900
http://www.sleepinn.com
5011 Hayes Pl.
60 rooms - $55-99
Pets: Welcome
Creature Comforts: CCTV, a/c,
cont. brkfst, pool, whirlpool

WINSTON-SALEM
Augustus T. Zevely Inn
(800) 928-9299, (336) 748-9299
803 S. Main St.
12 rooms - $80-110
Pets: Welcome in one room
Creature Comforts: 1850's
restored brick inn in historic Old
Salem, hand-hewn furnishings,
reproduction antiques, four-poster
beds, CCTV, a/c, fireplace,
Jacuzzi, full gourmet brkfst

Hawthorn Inn
(800) 972-3774, (336) 777-3000
420 High St.
198 rooms - $70-79
Pets: Welcome in certain rooms
Creature Comforts: CCTV, a/c,
kit, restaurant, cont. brkfst, pool,
hlth club, whirlpool

Motel 6
(800) 4-MOTEL6, (336) 661-1588
http://www.motel6.com
3810 Patterson Ave.
103 rooms - $38-46
Pets: Under 30 lbs. welcome
Creature Comforts: CCTV, a/c,
pool

Residence Inn
(800) 331-3131, (336) 759-0777
http://www.residenceinn.com
7835 N. Point Blvd.
88 rooms - $100-125
Pets: Small pets w/$150 fee
Creature Comforts: CCTV, a/c,
kit, fireplace, restaurant, pool, hlth
club, sauna, whirlpool

WRIGHTSVILLE BEACH
Waterway Lodge
(800) 677-3771, (910) 256-3771
7246 Wrightsville Ave.
44 rooms - $85-110
Pets: Welcome w/$15 fee
Creature Comforts: CCTV, a/c,
refrig, micro, kit, pool

YANCEYVILLE
Days Inn
(800) DAYS INN, (336) 694-9494
http://www.daysinn.com
1858 Rte. 86 North
45 rooms - $45-95
Pets: Welcome w/$5 fee
Creature Comforts: CCTV, a/c,
kit, Jacuzzi, cont. brkfst, pool

North Dakota

BEACH
Buckboard Inn Motel
(888) 449-3599, (701) 872-4794
1191 First Ave.
40 rooms - $30-40
Pets: Welcome
Creature Comforts: CCTV, refrig, micro

BISMARCK
Best Western Doublewood
(800) 528-1234, (701) 258-7000
http://www.bestwestern.com
1400 E. Interchange
143 rooms - $55-70
Pets: Welcome w/$25 deposit
Creature Comforts: CCTV, a/c, refrig, micro, restaurant, pool, sauna, whirlpool

Best Western Fleck House
(800) 528-1234, (701) 255-1450
http://www.bestwestern.com
Routes 16 & 94
122 E. Thayer
58 rooms - $45-67
Pets: Welcome
Creature Comforts: CCTV, a/c, refrig, cont. brkfst, pool

Comfort Inn
(800) 228-5150, (701) 223-1911
http://www.comfortinn.com
1030 Interstate Ave.
147 rooms - $45-69
Pets: Welcome
Creature Comforts: CCTV, a/c, refrig, cont. brkfst, pool, whirlpool

Days Inn
(800) DAYS INN, (701) 223-9151
http://www.daysinn.com
1300 E. Capitol Rd.
110 rooms - $40-69
Pets: Welcome
Creature Comforts: CCTV, a/c, cont. brkfst, pool, whirlpool, sauna

Expressway Inn
(800) 456-6388, (701) 223-9077
200 Bismarck Expwy.
163 rooms - $50-60
Pets: Welcome w/$10 fee
Creature Comforts: CCTV, a/c, refrig, micro, cont. brkfst, pool, whirlpool, sauna

Fairfield Inn, North
(800) 228-2800, (701) 223-9077
http://www.marriott.com
1120 Century Rd.
63 rooms - $40-79
Pets: Welcome
Creature Comforts: CCTV, a/c, refrig, micro, cont. brkfst, pool, whirlpool

Fairfield Inn, South
(800) 228-2800, (701) 223-9293
http://www.marriott.com
135 Ivy Ave.
63 rooms - $45-66
Pets: Welcome
Creature Comforts: CCTV, a/c, refrig, micro, cont. brkfst, pool, whirlpool

Holiday Inn
(800) HOLIDAY, (701) 255-6000
http://www.holiday-inn.com
605 E. Broadway Rd.
215 rooms - $70-200
Pets: Welcome
Creature Comforts: CCTV, a/c, Jacuzzi, restaurant, pool, hlth clb, sauna, whirlpool

Kelly Inn
(800) 635-3559, (701) 223-8001
1800 N. Twelfth St.
101 rooms - $40-75
Pets: Welcome
Creature Comforts: CCTV, VCR, a/c, Jacuzzi, restaurant, pool, sauna, whirlpool

Radisson Inn, Bismarck
(800) 333-3333, (701) 258-7700
http://www.radisson.com
800 S. Third St.
306 rooms - $75-190
Pets: Welcome w/$10 fee
Creature Comforts: CCTV, a/c, refrig, micro, Jacuzzi, restaurant, pool, sauna, whirlpool

Select Inn
(800) 641-1000, (701) 223-8060
1505 Interchange Ave.
102 rooms - $35-55
Pets: Small pets w/$25 deposit
Creature Comforts: CCTV, VCR, a/c

Super 8
(800) 800-8000, (701) 255-1314
http://www.super8.com
Routes 16 & 94
61 rooms - $45-50
Pets: Small pets welcome
Creature Comforts: CCTV, VCR, a/c

BOTTINEAU
Turtle Mountain Lodge
(701) 263-4206
10076 Market St.
24 rooms - $45-59
Pets: Welcome w/cc deposit
Creature Comforts: Lakeside location, CCTV, a/c, cafe, pool, marina

BOWMAN
Budget Host 4 U Motel
(800) Bud-Host, (701) 523-3243
http://www.budgethost.com
704 Rte. 12 W.
40 rooms - $30-47
Pets: Welcome
Creature Comforts: CCTV, a/c, sauna

El Vu Motel
(800) 521-0379, (701) 872-4794
Rtes. 85 & 12
16 rooms - $35-47
Pets: Welcome
Creature Comforts: CCTV, a/c

North Winds Lodge
(701) 523-5641
Rtes 16 & 94
16 rooms - $25-39
Pets: Welcome
Creature Comforts: CCTV, a/c,
pool

Super 8 Motel
(800) 800-8000, (701) 523-5613
http://www.super8.com
Rtes. 12 & 85
31 rooms - $42-59
Pets: Welcome w/permission
Creature Comforts: CCTV, a/c,
toast bar

CARRINGTON
Chieftan Motor Lodge
(701) 652-3131
Route 281
50 rooms - $40-57
Pets: Small pets welcome
Creature Comforts: CCTV, a/c,
restaurant

Super 8
(800) 800-8000, (701) 652-3982
http://www.super8.com
Route 281
40 rooms - $45-59
Pets: Welcome w/permission
Creature Comforts: CCTV, a/c,
Jacuzzi

DEVILS LAKE
Comfort Inn
(800) 228-5150, (701) 662-6760
http://www.comfortinn.com
215 Rte. 2 East
60 rooms - $50-68
Pets: Welcome w/$10 deposit
Creature Comforts: CCTV, a/c,
micro, refrig, dlx cont. brkfst,
whirlpool

Days Inn, Devil Lake
(800) DAYS INN, (701) 662-5381
http://www.daysinn.com
Rtes. 2 & 20
45 rooms - $48-59
Pets: Welcome w/$3 fee
Creature Comforts: CCTV, a/c,
refrig, micro, Jacuzzi, cont. brkfst

Super 8
(800) 800-8000, (701) 662-8656
http://www.super8.com
1001 Rte. 2 East
39 rooms - $44-57
Pets: Welcome w/permission
Creature Comforts: CCTV, a/c,
cont. brkfst

Trails West Motel
(800) 453-5011, (701) 662-5011
Rotue 2 West
74 rooms - $35-49
Pets: Welcome w/$10 deposit
Creature Comforts: CCTV, a/c,
cont. brkfst

DICKINSON
Budget Inn
(701) 225-9123
529 12th St.
54 rooms - $40-75
Pets: Welcome
Creature Comforts: CCTV, a/c

Comfort Inn
(800) 228-5150, (701) 264-7300
http://www.comfortinn.com
493 Elks Dr.
115 rooms - $40-55
Pets: Small pets welcome
Creature Comforts: CCTV, a/c,
cont. brkfst, pool, whirlpool

Hartfield Inn
(701) 225-6710
509 Third Ave. W.
4 rooms - $60-90
Pets: Small pets welcome
Creature Comforts: CCTV, a/c,
full brkfst, hot tub

Hospitality Inn/Conf. Center
(800) 422-0949, (701) 227-1853
Route 22
149 rooms - $45-90
Pets: Welcome
Creature Comforts: CCTV, a/c,
Jacuzzi, restaurant, pool, sauna,
whirlpool

Nodak Motel
(701) 225-5119
600 E. Villard St.
26 rooms - $25-43
Pets: Welcome
Creature Comforts: CCTV, a/c,
pool

Rodeway Inn
(800) 228-2000, (701) 225-6703
http://www.rodeway.com
1000 W. Villard St.
35 rooms - $35-70
Pets: Welcome
Creature Comforts: CCTV, a/c,
pool

Select Inn
(800) 641-1000, (701) 227-1891
642 W. 12th St.
59 rooms - $30-40
Pets: $5 fee, $25 deposit
Creature Comforts: CCTV, a/c

Super 8
(800) 800-8000, (701) 227-1215
http://www.super8.com
637 12th St. West
59 rooms - $38-40
Pets: Welcome
Creature Comforts: CCTV, a/c

FARGO
AmericInn Motel
(800) 634-3444, (701) 234-9946
1421 - 35th St. SW
43 rooms - $40-75
Pets: Small pets welcome
Creature Comforts: CCTV,
VCR, a/c, cont. brkfst, pool,
whirlpool, sauna

Best Western Doublewood
(800) 528-1234, (701) 235-3333
http://www.bestwestern.com
3333 13th Ave.
170 rooms - $70-90
Pets: Small pets w/deposit
Creature Comforts: CCTV, a/c,
restaurant, pool, sauna, whirlpool

Best Western Kelly
(800) 528-1234, (701) 282-2143
http://www.bestwestern.com
3800 Main Ave.
133 rooms/suites - $65-180
Pets: Small pets welcome
Creature Comforts: CCTV, a/c,
refrig, micro, Jacuzzi, restaurant,
cont. brkfst, pool, sauna, whirlpool

Comfort Inn West
(800) 228-5150, (701) 282-9596
http://www.comfortinn.com
3825 - 9th Ave. SW
56 rooms - $45-80
Pets: Welcome
Creature Comforts: CCTV, a/c,
cont. brkfst, pool, whirlpool

Comfort Inn East
(800) 228-5150, (701) 280-9666
http://www.comfortinn.com
1407 - 35th St.
66 rooms - $46-80
Pets: Welcome
Creature Comforts: CCTV, a/c,
cont. brkfst, pool, whirlpool

Country Suites by Carlson
(800) 456-4000, (701) 234-0565
1307 35th St. South
100 rooms - $72-140
Pets: Under 15 lbs. welcome w/a
$100 refundable deposit
Creature Comforts: CCTV, a/c,
refrig, micro, whirlpool

Days Inn, Airport
(800) DAYS INN, (701) 232-0000
http://www.daysinn.com
1507 19th Ave. N.
60 rooms - $65-120
Pets: Welcome
Creature Comforts: CCTV, a/c,
cont. brkfst, pool, hlth clb, sauna,
whirlpool

Days Inn W. Fargo
(800) DAYS INN, (701) 382-9100
http://www.daysinn.com
525 E. Main Ave.
62 rooms - $35-100
Pets: Welcome
Creature Comforts: CCTV, a/c,
Jacuzzi, cont. brkfst, pool, sauna,
whirlpool

Econo Lodge
(800) 55 ECONO, (701) 232-3412
http://www.econolodge.com
1401 35th St. S.
67 rooms - $35-49
Pets: Welcome
Creature Comforts: CCTV, a/c,
cont. brkfst

Expressway Inn
(800) 437-0044, (701) 235-3141
Rtes. 94 & 81
116 rooms - $50-65
Pets: Small pets welcome
Creature Comforts: CCTV, a/c,
refrig, micro, Jacuzzi, restaurant,
pool

Flying J Motel
(800) 845-1311, (701) 282-8473
3150 39th St. SW
40 rooms - $35-49
Pets: Welcome w/$25 deposit
Creature Comforts: CCTV, a/c,
sauna

Holiday Inn
(800) HOLIDAY, (701) 282-2700
http://www.holiday-inn.com
3803 13th Ave. S.
300 rooms - $75-100
Pets: Welcome
Creature Comforts: CCTV, a/c,
restaurant, pool, sauna, whirlpool

Holiday Inn Express
(800) 228-5150, (701) 282-2000
http://www.holiday-inn.com
1040 40th St. S.
77 rooms - $55-85
Pets: Welcome
Creature Comforts: CCTV, a/c,
cont. brkfst, pool, sauna, whirlpool

Kelly Inn, 13th St.
(800) 635-3559, (701) 277-8821
4207 13th Ave.
59 rooms - $40-75
Pets: Welcome
Creature Comforts: CCTV, a/c,
refrig, cont. brkfst, pool, sauna,
whirlpool

Motel 6 West
(800) 4-MOTEL6, (701) 232-9251
http://www.motel6.com
1307 - 35th St. South
96 rooms - $40-75
Pets: Under 30 lbs. welcome
Creature Comforts: CCTV, a/c,
pool

Motel 75
(800) 828-5962, (701) 232-1321
3402 14th Ave. S.
102 rooms - $30-48
Pets: Welcome
Creature Comforts: CCTV, a/c,
cont. brkfst

Radisson Hotel Fargo
(800) 228-5150, (701) 232-7363
http://www.radisson.com
201 Fifth St. N.
151 rooms - $70-100
Pets: Welcome w/$25 deposit
Creature Comforts: CCTV, a/c,
restaurant, hlth clb, pool, sauna,
whirlpool

Rodeway Inn
(800) 228-2000, (701)
http://www.rodeway.com
2202 University Dr. S.
93 rooms - $44-95
Pets: Welcome
Creature Comforts: CCTV, a/c,
cont. brkfst, pool, whirlpool

Select Inn
(800) 641-1000, (701) 282-6300
1307 35th St. South
38 rooms - $36-52
Pets: Welcome
Creature Comforts: CCTV, a/c,
cont. brkfst

Super 8
(800) 800-8000, (701) 232-9202
http://www.super8.com
3518 Interstate Blvd.
110 rooms - $45-95
Pets: Welcome w/$3 fee
Creature Comforts: CCTV,
VCR, a/c

GARRISON
Garrison Motel
(701) 463-2858
Route 37
30 rooms - $30-45
Pets: Welcome
Creature Comforts: CCTV, a/c

 North Dakota

GRAFTON
Leonard Motel
(701) 352-1730
Route 17
23 rooms - $30-45
Pets: Small pets welcome
Creature Comforts: CCTV, a/c

GRAND FORKS
Best Western Town House
(800) 528-1234, (701) 746-5411
http://www.bestwestern.com
710 First Ave. N.
114 rooms - $50-75
Pets: Small pets w/$25 deposit
Creature Comforts: CCTV, a/c,
refrig, micro, kit, restaurant, pool,
sauna, whirlpool

Comfort Inn
(800) 228-5150, (701) 775-7503
http://www.comfortinn.com
1030 Interstate Ave.
147 rooms - $45-65
Pets: Welcome
Creature Comforts: CCTV, a/c,
refrig, micro, pool, whirlpool

Country Inn/Suites
(800) 456-4000, (701) 773-9545
Route 2 East
89 rooms - $50-75
Pets: Welcome w/$50 deposit
Creature Comforts: CCTV, a/c,
refrig, cont. brkfst, pool, hlth club,
whirlpool, sauna

Days Inn
(800) DAYS INN, (701) 775-0060
http://www.daysinn.com
3101 S. 34th St.
52 rooms - $45-70
Pets: Welcome
Creature Comforts: CCTV, a/c,
refrig, micro, pool, whirlpool

Econo Lodge
(800) 55 ECONO, (701) 746-6666
http://www.econolodge.com
900 N. 43rd St.
44 rooms - $35-57
Pets: Welcome
Creature Comforts: CCTV, a/c,
refrig

Holiday Inn
(800) HOLIDAY, (701) 772-7131
http://www.holiday-inn.com
1210 N. 43rd St.
150 rooms - $60-85
Pets: Welcome in smoking rooms
Creature Comforts: CCTV,
VCR, a/c, Jacuzzi, restaurant,
pool, hlth clb, whirlpool, sauna

Plainsman Motel
(800) 341-8000, (701) 775-8134
2201 Gateway Dr.
50 rooms - $30-49
Pets: Welcome
Creature Comforts: CCTV, a/c,
cont. brkfst

Rodeway Inn
(800) 228-2000, (701) 795-9960
http://www.rodeway.com
4001 Gateway Dr.
32 rooms - $35-56
Pets: Welcome w/$5 fee
Creature Comforts: CCTV, a/c,
cont. brkfst

Ramada
(800) 2-Ramada, (701) 775-3951
http://www.ramada.com
1205 N. 43rd St.
100 rooms - $65-80
Pets: Small pets welcome
Creature Comforts: CCTV, a/c,
restaurant, pool, whirlpool, sauna

Select Inn
(701) 775-0555
1000 N. 42nd St.
120 rooms - $30-49
Pets: Welcome
Creature Comforts: CCTV,
VCR, a/c, cont. brkfst

Super 8
(800) 800-8000, (701) 775-8138
http://www.super8.com
1122 N. 43rd St.
33 rooms - $45-59
Pets: Welcome in smoking rooms
Creature Comforts: CCTV, a/c,
cont. brkfst

Westward Ho Motel
(701) 775-5341
Route 2
108 rooms - $45-57
Pets: Welcome
Creature Comforts: CCTV,
VCR, a/c, restaurant, pool, sauna

JAMESTOWN
Best Western Dakota
(800) 528-1234, (701) 252-3611
http://www.bestwestern.com
Rtes. 92 & 281 S
123 rooms - $50-100
Pets: Small pets w/$4 fee
Creature Comforts: CCTV, a/c,
Jacuzzi, restaurant, pool,whirlpool

Comfort Inn
(800) 228-5150, (701) 252-7125
http://www.comfortinn.com
811 - 20th St. SW
52 rooms - $45-58
Pets: Small pets welcome
Creature Comforts: CCTV, a/c,
refrig, micro, cont. brkfst, pool,
whirlpool

Gladstone Select Hotel
(800) 641-1000, (701) 252-0700
111 Second St., NE
117 rooms - $45-64
Pets: Welcome w/$25 deposit
Creature Comforts: CCTV,
VCR, a/c, restaurant, pool,
whirlpool

Ranch House Motel
(800) 341-8000, (701) 252-0222
408 Business Loop W.
40 rooms - $30-45
Pets: Welcome
Creature Comforts: CCTV,
VCR, a/c, kit, refrig, pool

LAKOTA
Sunlac Inn
(701) 247-2487
1030 Interstate Ave.
41 rooms - $30-45
Pets: Welcome w/$5 fee
Creature Comforts: CCTV, a/c,
restaurant

MANDAN
Best Western Seven Seas Inn
(800) 528-1234, (701) 663-7401
http://www.bestwestern.com
Route 94
103 rooms - $55-70
Pets: Welcome w/$25 deposit
Creature Comforts: CCTV, a/c,
refrig, micro, restaurant, pool,
whirlpool

River Ridge Inn
(701) 663-0001
2630 Old Red Trail
79 rooms - $45-58
Pets: Welcome w/$25 deposit
Creature Comforts: CCTV, a/c,
restaurant, whirlpool, casino

MINOT
Best Western International
(800) 528-1234, (701) 852-3161
http://www.bestwestern.com
1505 N. Broadway Rd.
270 rooms - $50-75
Pets: Small pets welcome
Creature Comforts: CCTV, a/c,
refrig, restaurant, pool, whirlpool

Best Western Kelly
(800) 528-1234, (701) 852-4300
http://www.bestwestern.com
1510 26th Ave. SW
100 rooms - $50-85
Pets: Small pets welcome
Creature Comforts: CCTV,
VCR, a/c, Jacuzzi, cont. brkfst,
pool, whirlpool

Casa Motel
(701) 852-2352
1900 W. Rte. 2
14 rooms - $55-70
Pets: Welcome
Creature Comforts: CCTV, a/c

Comfort Inn
(800) 228-5150, (701) 852-2201
http://www.comfortinn.com
1515 - 22nd Ave. SW
142 rooms - $48-70
Pets: Welcome
Creature Comforts: CCTV,
VCR, a/c, cont. brkfst, pool,
whirlpool

Dakota Inn
(800) 862-5003, (701) 852-2201
1515 - 22nd Ave. SW
129 rooms - $40-50
Pets: Welcome
Creature Comforts: CCTV, a/c,
pool, whirlpool

Days Inn
(800) DAYS INN, (701) 852-3646
http://www.daysinn.com
2100 Fourth St.
82 rooms - $45-60
Pets: Small pets welcome
Creature Comforts: CCTV,
VCR, a/c, refrig, micro, cont.
brkfst, pool, whirlpool

Holiday Inn
(800) HOLIDAY, (701) 852-2504
http://www.holiday-inn.com
2000 Burdick Expwy E.
175 rooms - $50-75
Pets: Small pets welcome
Creature Comforts: CCTV, a/c,
restaurant, pool, whirlpool, sauna

Select Inn
(800) 641-1000, (701) 255-6000
225 22nd Ave. NW
100 rooms - $35-48
Pets: Small pets w/$25 deposit
Creature Comforts: CCTV, a/c,
refrig, kit

Super 8
(800) 800-8000, (701) 852-1817
http://www.super8.com
1315 N. Broadway
60 rooms - $40-59
Pets: Welcome, leashed at motel
Creature Comforts: CCTV, a/c,
restaurant, cont. brkfst

NEW TOWN
4 Bears Lodge/Casino
(800) 294-5454, (701) 627-4018
Rtes. 16 & 94
40 rooms - $45-59
Pets: Welcome w/$25 deposit
Creature Comforts: CCTV,
VCR, a/c, restaurant

PARSHALL
Parshall Motor Inn
(701) 862-3127
N. Main St.
15 rooms - $35-49
Pets: Welcome
Creature Comforts: CCTV, a/c,
refrig, micro

ROLLA
Northern Lights
(800) 535-6145, (701) 477-6164
Route 5
17 rooms - $35-47
Pets: Welcome w/$5 fee
Creature Comforts: CCTV,
VCR, a/c

RUGBY
Econo Lodge
(800) 55 ECONO, (701) 776-5776
http://www.econolodge.com
Route 2 E.
67 rooms - $35-49
Pets: Welcome w/$5 fee
Creature Comforts: CCTV,
VCR, a/c, Jacuzzi, restaurant,
cont. brkfst, pool, whirlpool

VALLEY CITY
Mid Town Motel
(701) 845-2830
906 E. Main St.
13 rooms - $30-45
Pets: Welcome
Creature Comforts: CCTV, a/c

Wagon Wheel Inn
(701) 845-5333
Route 94
59 rooms - $40-58
Pets: Welcome
Creature Comforts: CCTV,
VCR, a/c, refrig, micro, Jacuzzi,
cont. brkfst, pool, whirlpool

WAHPETON
Comfort Inn
(800) 228-5150, (701) 642-1115
http://www.comfortinn.com
209 - 13th St. S.
46 rooms - $50-69
Pets: Small pets welcome
Creature Comforts: CCTV, a/c,
refrig, micro, Jacuzzi, cont. brkfst,
pool, whirlpool

Super 8 Motel
(800) 800-8000, (701) 642-8731
http://www.super8.com
1001 - 210 Rd.
58 rooms - $42-58
Pets: Welcome w/permission
Creature Comforts: CCTV, a/c,
Jacuzzi, pool, hlth club, whirlpool

WASHBURN
ScotWood Motel
(701) 462-8191
Route 83
25 rooms - $34-47
Pets: Welcome w/$5 fee
Creature Comforts: CCTV, a/c

WATFORD CITY
McKenzie Inn
(701) 842-3980
Route 85 W.
14 rooms - $30-39
Pets: Welcome w/permission
Creature Comforts: CCTV, a/c,
refrig, whirlpool, sauna

WILLISTON
Airport International Inn
(701) 774-0421
Rtes. 2 & 85 North
143 rooms - $35-45
Pets: Welcome w/permission
Creature Comforts: CCTV, a/c,
restaurant, pool, whirlpool

El Rancho Motor Hotel
(800) 433-8529, (701) 572-6321
http://www.super8.com
Rtes. 12 & 85
92 rooms - $35-48
Pets: Welcome w/permission
Creature Comforts: CCTV, a/c,
restaurant

Select Inn
(800) 641-1000, (701) 572-4242
Rtes. 2 & 85 N.
60 rooms - $42-55
Pets: Welcome w/permission
Creature Comforts: CCTV, a/c,
cont. brkfst, pool, whirlpool

Super 8 Motel
(800) 800-8000, (701) 572-8371
http://www.super8.com
2324 Second Ave. W.
82 rooms - $35-46
Pets: Welcome w/permission
Creature Comforts: CCTV, a/c,
cont. brkst, pool, whirlpool

Ohio

AKRON
Days Inn
(800) DAYS INN, (330) 644-1204
http://www.daysinn.com
3237 S. Arlington Rd.
122 rooms - $60-90
Pets: Welcome
Creature Comforts: CCTV, a/c,
cont. brkfst, pool

Hampton Inn
(800) Hampton, (330) 666-7361
http://www.hampton-inn.com
80 Springside Dr.
63 rooms - $63-70
Pets: Welcome
Creature Comforts: CCTV, a/c,
pool

Holiday Inn
(800) HOLIDAY, (330) 644-7126
http://www.holiday-inn.com
Rte. 77 & Arlington St.
130 rooms - $70-196
Pets: Welcome
Creature Comforts: CCTV, a/c,
restaurant, pool

Red Roof Inn, North
(800) THE ROOF, (330) 666-0566
http://www.redroof.com
99 Rothrock Rd.
110 rooms - $40-70
Pets: Small pets welcome
Creature Comforts: CCTV, a/c

Red Roof Inn
(800) THE ROOF, (330) 644-7748
http://www.redroof.com
2939 S. Arlington Rd.
120 rooms - $45-75
Pets: Small pets welcome
Creature Comforts: CCTV, a/c

Super 8 Motel
(800) 800-8000, (330) 666-8887
http://www.super8.com
79 Rothrock Rd.
59 rooms - $45-55
Pets: Welcome w/permission
Creature Comforts: CCTV, a/c

AMHERST
Motel 6
(800) 4-MOTEL6, (440) 988-3266
http://www.motel6.com
704 N. Levitt Rd.
126 rooms - $35-44
Pets: Under 30 lbs. welcome
Creature Comforts: CCTV, a/c,
pool

ASHLAND
Days Inn
(800) DAYS INN, (419) 289-0101
http://www.daysinn.com
County Rd. 1575
61 rooms - $40-80
Pets: Welcome
Creature Comforts: CCTV, a/c,
Jacuzzi, cont. brkfst, pool

Travelodge
(800) 578-7878, (419) 281-0567
http://www.travelodge.com
736 Route 250
65 rooms - $48-70
Pets: Small pets welcome
Creature Comforts: CCTV, a/c,
refrig, kit, pool

ASHTABULA
Cedars Motel
(440) 992-5406
2015 W. Prospect Rd.
15 rooms - $45-75
Pets: Welcome
Creature Comforts: CCTV, a/c

Ho Hum Motel
(440) 969-1136
3801 N. Ridge West
11 rooms - $45-69
Pets: Welcome
Creature Comforts: CCTV, a/c

AURORA
The Aurora Inn
(800) 444-6121, (330) 562-6121
30 E. Garfield Rd.
72 rooms - $99-210
Pets: In one wing w/$50 deposit
Creature Comforts: New
England-style decor, CCTV, a/c,
Jacuzzis, whirlpool, game room,
sauna, restaurant, tennis, pool

AUSTINTOWN
Best Western Inn
(800) 528-1234, (330) 544-2378
http://www.bestwestern.com
870 N. Canfield-Niles Rd.
58 rooms - $49-83
Pets: In smking rooms w/CC dep.
Creature Comforts: CCTV, a/c,
restaurant, and a pool

BARNESVILLE
Georgian Pillars B&B
(888) 425-3741, (740) 425-3741
128 E. Walnut St.
3 rooms - $65-70
Pets: Welcome w/permission
Creature Comforts: CCTV, a/c,
full brkfst

BEACHWOOD
Cleveland Marriott East
(800) 228-9290, (216) 464-5950
http://www.marriott.com
3663 Park East Dr.
403 rooms - $109-169
Pets: Welcome
Creature Comforts: CCTV,
VCR, a/c, restaurant, pool, hlth
club, whirlpool, sauna

Residence Inn
(800) 331-3131, (216) 831-3030
http://www.residenceinn.com
3628 Park E. Dr.
174 rooms - $99-209
Pets: Welcome w/$200 fee
Creature Comforts: CCTV, a/c,
kit, pool, hlth clb access

Ohio

BELLEFONTAINE
Holiday Inn
(800) HOLIDAY, (937) 593-8515
http://www.holiday-inn.com
1134 N. Main St.
100 rooms - $65-75
Pets: Welcome
Creature Comforts: CCTV, a/c, restaurant, pool

BERLIN
Jake n' Ivy's B&B
(330) 893-3215
5409 Township Rd.
3 rooms - $60-65
Pets: Welcome w/permission
Creature Comforts: CCTV, a/c, kit, cont. brkfst

BLUE ASH
Best Western Hotel
(800) 528-1234, (513) 793-4500
http://www.bestwestern.com
5901 Pfieffer Rd.
220 rooms - $80-145
Pets: Under 20 Lbs. welcome
Creature Comforts: CCTV, a/c, refrig, restaurant, and a pool

Main Stay Suites
(800) 660-MAIN, (513) 985-9992
4630 Creek Rd.
100 rooms - $50-100
Pets: $5 fee and a $100 deposit
Creature Comforts: CCTV, a/c, kit, cont. brkfst, and a pool

Red Roof Inn
(800) THE ROOF, (513) 793-8811
http://www.redroof.com
5900 Pfeiffer Rd.
110 rooms - $60-100
Pets: Small pets welcome
Creature Comforts: CCTV, a/c

Residence Inn
(800) 331-3131, (513) 530-5060
http://www.residenceinn.com
5280 Broadmoor Rd.
66 rooms - $99-149
Pets: Welcome w/$200 fee
Creature Comforts: CCTV, a/c, kit

Studio Plus Blue Ash
(513) 793-6750
4260 Hunt Rd.
71 rooms - $75-85
Pets: Welcome w/$75 fee
Creature Comforts: CCTV, a/c, kit, pool

BOARDMAN
Days Inn
(800) DAYS INN, (330) 758-2371
http://www.daysinn.com
8392 Market St.
50 rooms - $50-165
Pets: Welcome w/$5 fee
Creature Comforts: CCTV, a/c, Jacuzzi, cont. brkfst, pool

Economy Inn
(330) 549-3224
10145 Market St.
35 rooms - $35-65
Pets: Small pets w/$5 fee
Creature Comforts: CCTV, a/c, refrig, micro, Jacuzzi, cont. brkfst, pool

Microtel
(888) 771-7171, (330) 758-1816
http://www.microtelinn.com
7393 South Ave.
90 rooms - $40-49
Pets: Welcome w/signed form
Creature Comforts: CCTV, a/c

Wagon Wheel
(330) 758-4551
7015 Market St.
20 rooms - $30-69
Pets: Welcome w/$5 fee
Creature Comforts: CCTV, a/c, refrig, micro, Jacuzzi

BOSTON HEIGHTS
Comfort Inn
(800) 228-5150, (330) 650-2040
http://www.comfortinn.com
6731 Industrial Pkwy.
58 rooms - $75-125
Pets: Welcome
Creature Comforts: CCTV, a/c, Jacuzzi, cont. brkfst, pool, whirlpool

BOWLING GREEN
Best Western Falcon Plaza
(800) 528-1234, (419) 352-4671
http://www.bestwestern.com
1450 E. Wooster St.
74 rooms - $58-99
Pets: Welcome w/mngrs approval
Creature Comforts: CCTV, a/c, restaurant

BROOKVILLE
Days Inn
(800) DAYS INN, (937) 898-4946
http://www.daysinn.com
100 Parkview Dr.
62 rooms - $45-62
Pets: Welcome w/$5 fee
Creature Comforts: CCTV, a/c, cont. brkfst, pool

BUCYRUS
Days Inn
(800) DAYS INN, (419) 562-3737
http://www.daysinn.com
1515 N. Sandusky St.
100 rooms - $50-195
Pets: Welcome w/$10 fee
Creature Comforts: CCTV, a/c, refrig, Jacuzzi, cont. brkfst, pool

BURBANK
Plaza Motel
(330) 624-3012
8450 Garman Rd.
20 rooms - $40-85
Pets: Welcome
Creature Comforts: CCTV, a/c

CALDWELL
Inn at Belle Valley
(740) 732-7333
Route 821
15 rooms - $35-45
Pets: Welcome
Creature Comforts: CCTV, a/c

CAMBRIDGE
Best Western Cambridge
(800) 528-1234, (740) 439-3581
http://www.bestwestern.com
1945 Southgate Pkwy.
95 rooms - $34-94
Pets: Small pets welcome
Creature Comforts: CCTV, VCR, a/c, pool

Cambridge Fairdale Inn
(800) 528-1234, (740) 432-2304
6405 Glen Rte.
19 rooms - $35-50
Pets: Small pets welcome
Creature Comforts: CCTV, pool

Cambridge Travelodge
(800) 578-7878, (740) 432-7375
http://www.travelodge.com
Rtes. 70 & 209
46 rooms - $45-90
Pets: Welcome
Creature Comforts: CCTV, a/c, refrig, pool, sauna, whirlpool

563

Holiday Inn
(800) HOLIDAY, (740) 432-7313
http://www.holiday-inn.com
2248 Southgate Pkwy.
110 rooms - $67-130
Pets: Small pets welcome
Creature Comforts: CCTV, a/c,
restaurant, pool

CANTON
Best Suites of America
(330) 499-1011
3970 Convenience Circle
105 rooms - $75-129
Pets: Small pets welcome
Creature Comforts: CCTV,
VCR, a/c, refrig, micro, cont.
brkfst, pool, exercise room, whrlpl

Days Inn
(800) DAYS INN, (330) 493-8883
http://www.daysinn.com
3970 Convenience Circle
61 rooms - $45-60
Pets: Welcome
Creature Comforts: CCTV,
VCR, a/c, cont. brkfst

Holiday Inn
(800) HOLIDAY, (330) 494-2770
http://www.holiday-inn.com
4520 Everhard Rd.
200 rooms - $70-185
Pets: Small pets welcome
Creature Comforts: CCTV, a/c,
restaurant, pool

Motel 6
(800) 4-MOTEL6, (330) 494-7611
http://www.motel6.com
6880 Sunset Strip Ave. NW
85 rooms - $35-40
Pets: Under 30 lbs. welcome
Creature Comforts: CCTV, a/c,
pool

Parke Suites
(330) 494-2233
4285 Everhart Rd.
25 rooms - $65-100
Pets: Samll pets w/$30 fee
Creature Comforts: CCTV, a/c,
kit

Red Roof Inn
(800) THE ROOF, (330) 499-1970
http://www.redroof.com
5353 Inn Circle Ct.
110 rooms - $50-69
Pets: Small pets welcome
Creature Comforts: CCTV, a/c
564

Residence Inn
(800) 331-3131, (330) 493-0004
http://www.residenceinn.com
5280 Broadmoor Rd.
66 rooms - $99-189
Pets: Welcome w/$200 deposit
Creature Comforts: CCTV, a/c,
kit, pool, hlth club

Super 8 Motel
(800) 800-8000, (330) 492-5030
http://www.super8.com
3950 Convenience Cir, N.W.
101 rooms - $50-85
Pets: Welcome w/permission
Creature Comforts: CCTV, a/c,
cont. brkfst

CHILLICOTHE
Chillicothe B&B
(740) 772-6848
2020 S. Paint St.
4 rooms - $50-60
Pets: Welcome w/permission
Creature Comforts: 1864
Italianate, CCTV, a/c, full brkfst

Christopher Inn
(800) 257-7042, (740) 774-6835
30 N. Plaza Blvd.
61 rooms - $63-90
Pets: Welcome, $6 fee, $100 dep.
Creature Comforts: CCTV, a/c,
refrig, micro, Jacuzzi, cont. brkfst,
pool, sauna, whirlpool

Comfort Inn
(800) 228-5150, (740) 775-3500
http://www.comfortinn.com
20 N. Plaza Blvd.
110 rooms - $60-95
Pets: Welcome
Creature Comforts: CCTV, a/c,
Jacuzzi, restaurant, cont. brkfst,
and a pool

Days Inn
(800) DAYS INN, (740) 775-7000
http://www.daysinn.com
1250 N. Bridge St.
150 rooms - $50-85
Pets: Welcome w/$5 fee
Creature Comforts: CCTV, a/c,
Jacuzzi, restaurant, cont. brkfst,
pool

CINCINNATI
The Cincinnatian Hotel
(800) 942-9000, (513) 381-3000
http://www.cincinnatianhotel.com
601 Vine St.
146 rooms - $210-1,500
Pets: Small pets welcome
Creature Comforts: 1882
National Register of Historic
Places, eight-story skylit atrium,
balconies, old-world atmosphere
w/contemporary works of art,
elegant decor, CCTV, a/c, refrig,
Jacuzzis, fireplaces, vaulted
ceilings, surround sound,
restaurant, sauna, hlth club

Comfort Inn
(800) 228-5150, (513) 771-3400
http://www.comfortinn.com
11440 Chester Rd.
227 rooms - $70-129
Pets: Welcome
Creature Comforts: CCTV, a/c,
cont. brkfst, pool

Comfort Inn
(800) 228-5150, (513) 683-9700
http://www.comfortinn.com
9011 Fields Ertel Rd.
115 rooms - $40-125
Pets: Small pets w/$25 deposit
Creature Comforts: CCTV, a/c,
cont. brkfst, pool

Days Inn
(800) DAYS INN, (513) 528-3800
http://www.daysinn.com
4056 Mt. Carmel & Tobasco Rds.
93 rooms - $50-117
Pets: Welcome
Creature Comforts: CCTV, a/c,
restaurant, pool

Holiday Inn
(800) HOLIDAY, (513) 241-8660
http://www.holiday-inn.com
800 W. Eighth St.
245 rooms - $90-109
Pets: Welcome
Creature Comforts: CCTV, a/c,
restaurant, pool, hlth club

Howard Johnson
(800) I-Go-Hojo, (513) 631-8500
http://www.hojo.com
5410 Ridge Ave.
121 rooms - $62-99
Pets: Welcome
Creature Comforts: CCTV, a/c,
restaurant, pool

Howard Johnson
(800) I-Go-Hojo, (513) 825-3129
http://www.hojo.com
400 Glensprings Dr.
120 rooms - $55-87
Pets: Welcome
Creature Comforts: CCTV, a/c,
cont. brkfst, pool

Motel 6
(800) 4-MOTEL6, (513) 752-2262
http://www.motel6.com
3960 Nine Mile Rd.
108 rooms - $32-35
Pets: Under 30 lbs. welcome
Creature Comforts: CCTV, a/c,
pool

CIRCLEVILLE
Braeburn Farm B&B
(740) 474-7086
6768 Zane Trail Rd.
4 rooms - $75-85
Pets: Welcome
Creature Comforts: 1853 brick
farmhouse on 300 acres, antique-
filled rooms, featherbeds, canopy
and sleigh beds, claw-foot tubs,
fireplace, CCTV, a/c, country
brkfst, lawn games, woodland
walks, farm animals

Knights Inn
(740) 474-6006
Rte. 23 South
75 rooms - $35-109
Pets: Welcome
Creature Comforts: CCTV, a/c,
kit

CLEVELAND
Baymont Inn and Suites
(800) 4-Budget, (216) 251-8500
http://www.baymontinns.com
4222 W. 150th St.
125 rooms - $55-79
Pets: Welcome
Creature Comforts: CCTV, a/c,
cont. brkfst

Cleveland Airport Marriott
(800) 228-9290, (216) 252-5333
http://www.marriott.com
4277 W. 150th St.
379 rooms - $90-160
Pets: Welcome w/$50 fee
Creature Comforts: CCTV, a/c,
restaurant, pool, hlth club

Comfort Inn
(800) 228-5150, (440) 234-3131
http://www.comfortinn.com
17550 Rosbough Dr.
136 rooms - $60-130
Pets: Welcome
Creature Comforts: CCTV, a/c,
cont. brkfst, pool

Rider's Inn
(440) 354-8200
792 Mentor Ave.
11 rooms - $65-99
Pets: Welcome w/permission
Creature Comforts: Historic
stagecoach inn, CCTV, a/c,
restaurant, full brkfst

Ritz-Carlton
(800) 241-3333, (216) 623-1300
http://www.ritzcarlton.com
1515 W. Third St.
210 rooms - $170-500
Pets: Welcome w/$30 deposit
Creature Comforts: Downtown
location, near offices/shopping,
luxurious hotel, recently
renovated, CCTV, a/c, refrig, fine
restaurant, pool, hlth club,
whirlpool, sauna

COLUMBUS
Amerisuites
(800) 833-1515, (614) 846-4355
http://www.amerisuites.com
7490 Vantage Dr.
125 rooms - $100-140
Pets: Small pets w/$20 fee
Creature Comforts: CCTV,
VCR, a/c, refrig, micro, full brkfst,
pool, hlth club

Best Western University Inn
(800) 528-1234, (614) 261-7141
http://www.bestwestern.com
3232 Olentangy River Rd.
95 rooms - $60-85
Pets: Welcome
Creature Comforts: CCTV, a/c,
restaurant, pool, hlth club

Candlelite Lane B&B
(614) 885-8165
1466 Candlelite Ln.
2 rooms - $55-85
Pets: Welcome w/permission
Creature Comforts: CCTV, a/c,
cont. brkfst

Comfort Suites
(800) 228-5150, (614) 529-8118
http://www.comfortinn.com
3831 Park Mill Run Dr.
60 rooms - $75-98
Pets: Welcome
Creature Comforts: CCTV, a/c,
cont. brkfst, pool

Days Inn, Downtown
(800) DAYS INN, (614) 275-0388
http://www.daysinn.com
1559 W. Broad St.
112 rooms - $35-69
Pets: Welcome w/$6 fee
Creature Comforts: CCTV, a/c,
pool

Days Inn, Fairgrounds
(800) DAYS INN, (614) 299-4300
http://www.daysinn.com
1700 Clara Ave.
116 rooms - $40-68
Pets: Welcome w/$5 fee
Creature Comforts: CCTV, a/c

Days Inn University
(800) DAYS INN, (614) 261-0523
http://www.daysinn.com
3160 Olentangy River Rd.
110 rooms - $35-75
Pets: Welcome w/$10 fee
Creature Comforts: CCTV, a/c,
kit, cont. brkfst, pool

Econo Lodge
(800) 55-ECONO, (614) 864-4670
http://www.econolodge.com
5950 Scarborough Blvd.
150 rooms - $45-89
Pets: Welcome
Creature Comforts: CCTV, a/c,
refrig, micro, pool

Econo Lodge
(800) 55-ECONO, (614) 274-8581
http://www.econolodge.com
920 Wilson Rd.
45 rooms - $46-69
Pets: Welcome
Creature Comforts: CCTV, a/c,
refrig

Holiday Inn City Center
(800) HOLIDAY, (614) 221-3281
http://www.holiday-inn.com
175 E. Town St.
240 rooms - $80-139
Pets: Small pets w/$150 deposit
Creature Comforts: CCTV, a/c,
restaurant, pool

Holiday Inn Columbus Airport
(800) HOLIDAY, (614) 237-6360
http://www.holiday-inn.com
750 Stelzer-James Rd.
236 rooms - $75-125
Pets: Small pets w/$10 fee
Creature Comforts: CCTV,
VCR, a/c, refrig, micro, restaurant,
pool, hlth club

Holiday Inn on the Lane
(800) HOLIDAY, (614) 294-4848
http://www.holiday-inn.com
328 W. Lane Ave.
243 rooms - $89-135
Pets: Welcome
Creature Comforts: CCTV, a/c,
restaurant, pool, hlth club

Holiday Inn Worthington
(800) HOLIDAY, (614) 885-3334
http://www.holiday-inn.com
750 Stelzer-James Rd.
316 rooms - $99-110
Pets: Small pets welcome
Creature Comforts: CCTV, a/c,
restaurant, pool, hlth club

Homewood Suites
(800) 225-5466, (614) 785-0001
http://www.homewoodsuites.com
115 Hutchinson Ave.
99 rooms - $99-125
Pets: Welcome w/$8 fee
Creature Comforts: CCTV,
VCR, a/c, kit, cont. brkfst, pool

Howard Johnson
(800) I-Go-Hojo, (614) 486-4554
http://www.hojo.com
1070 Dublin-Grandview Ave.
100 rooms - $40-85
Pets: Welcome
Creature Comforts: CCTV, a/c,
Jacuzzi

Knights Inn East
(800) 843-5644, (614) 864-0600
http://www.knightsinn.com
4320 Groves Rd.
100 rooms - $35-80
Pets: Welcome w/$20 deposit
Creature Comforts: CCTV, a/c,
refrig, micro

Knights Inn North
(800) 843-5644, (614) 864-7635
http://www.knightsinn.com
1300 E. Dublin-Granville Rd.
115 rooms - $33-52
Pets: Welcome
Creature Comforts: CCTV, a/c,
pool

Lansing Street B&B
(800) 383-7839, (614) 444-8488
180 Lansing St.
2 suites - $65-89
Pets: Small pets in carriers,
resident Bouvier
Creature Comforts: Traditional
home in historic neighborhood,
private courtyard, fireplace, early
American furnishings, CCTV, a/c,
full brkfst

Marriott North
(800) 228-9290, (614) 885-1885
http://www.marriott.com
6500 Doubletree Ave.
300 rooms - $59-140
Pets: Welcome in first floor rooms
w/$50 fee
Creature Comforts: CCTV,
VCR, a/c, restaurant, pool, hlth clb
access

Microtel, Worthington
(888) 771-7171, (614) 436-0556
http://www.microtelinn.com
7500 Vantage Dr.
100 rooms - $32-42
Pets: Welcome
Creature Comforts: CCTV, a/c

Motel 6
(800) 4-MOTEL6, (614) 755-2250
http://www.motel6.com
5910 Scarborough Blvd.
100 rooms - $35-40
Pets: Under 30 lbs. welcome
Creature Comforts: CCTV, a/c,
pool

Motel 6
(800) 4-MOTEL6, (614) 846-9860
http://www.motel6.com
1289 E. Dublin-Granville Rd.
91 rooms - $38-40
Pets: Under 30 lbs. welcome
Creature Comforts: CCTV, a/c

Motel 6
(800) 4-MOTEL6, (614) 870-0993
http://www.motel6.com
5500 Renner Rd.
118 rooms - $37-40
Pets: Under 30 lbs. welcome
Creature Comforts: CCTV, a/c,
pool

New England Suites Hotel
(800) 784-8373, (614) 764-0770
3950 Tuller Rd.
42 rooms - $65-75
Pets: Welcome
Creature Comforts: CCTV,
VCR, a/c, refrig, micro, cont.
brkfst

Parke University Hotel
(800) 277-6158, (614) 267-1111
3025 Olentangy River Rd.
204 rooms - $60-125
Pets: Welcome
Creature Comforts: CCTV, a/c,
restaurant, pool

Quality Inn, East
(800) 228-5151, (614) 861-0321
http://www.qualityinn.com
4801 E. Broad St.
148 rooms - $60-119
Pets: Welcome
Creature Comforts: CCTV, a/c,
restaurant, pool

Quality Inn and Suites
(800) 228-5151, (614) 431-0208
http://www.qualityinn.com
10530 Corduroy Rd.
50 rooms - $63-99
Pets: Welcome
Creature Comforts: CCTV, a/c,
refrig, restaurant, cont. brkfst, pool

Ramada University Hotel
(800) 2-Ramada, (614) 267-7461
http://www.ramada.com
3110 Olentangy River Rd.
243 rooms - $90-128
Pets: Small pets welcome
Creature Comforts: CCTV, a/c,
restaurant, pool

Red Roof Inn North
(800) THE ROOF, (614) 846-8520
http://www.redroof.com
750 Morse Rd.
110 rooms - $55-79
Pets: Small pets welcome
Creature Comforts: CCTV, a/c

Red Roof Inn University
(800) THE ROOF, (614) 267-9941
http://www.redroof.com
441 Ackerman Rd.
120 rooms - $55-70
Pets: Small pets welcome
Creature Comforts: CCTV, a/c

Red Roof Inn West
(800) THE ROOF, (614) 878-9245
http://www.redroof.com
5001 Renner Rd.
80 rooms - $45-70
Pets: Small pets welcome
Creature Comforts: CCTV, a/c

Residence Inn, East
(800) 331-3131, (614) 864-8844
http://www.residenceinn.com
2084 S. Hamilton Rd.
80 rooms - $99-159
Pets: $5 fee, $100 deposit
Creature Comforts: CCTV, a/c,
kit, cont. brkfst, pool

Residence Inn, North
(800) 331-3131, (614) 431-1819
http://www.residenceinn.com
6191 W. Zumstein Dr.
95 rooms - $105-149
Pets: Welcome w/$175 fee
Creature Comforts: CCTV, a/c,
kit, pool

Sheraton Suites Columbus
(800) 325-3535, (614) 436-0004
http://www.sheraton.com
201 Hutchinson Rd.
261 rooms - $90-199
Pets: Welcome
Creature Comforts: CCTV, a/c,
restaurant, pool, hlth club

Victorian B&B
(614) 299-1656
5101 W. Creek Rd.
5 suites - $85-100
Pets: Welcome in 2-bedroom suite
Creature Comforts: Victorian
Nat'l Historic Register mansion,
CCTV, a/c, full brkfst

Westin Great Southern
(888) 625-5144, (614) 228-3800
http://www.westin.com
310 S. High St.
198 rooms - $110-375
Pets: Welcome w/$100 fee
Creature Comforts: 1897 hotel,
recent restoration, elegant public
areas, bedrooms w/European
decor, Queen-Anne furnishings,
marble baths, intimate, CCTV, a/c,
refrig, restaurant, hlth clb

COSHOCTON
Travelodge
(800) 578-7878, (740) 622-9823
http://www.travelodge.com
565 Lincoln Way
50 rooms - $60-75
Pets: Small pets welcome
Creature Comforts: CCTV, a/c,
refrig, micro, kit

CURTICE
Econo Lodge
(800) 55-ECONO, (419) 836-2822
http://www.econolodge.com
600 Route 291
58 rooms - $25-79
Pets: Welcome w/$25 deposit
Creature Comforts: CCTV, a/c,
refrig, micro, restaurant

CUYAHOGA FALLS
Sheraton Suites Cuyahoga Falls
(800) 325-3535, (330) 929-3000
http://www.sheraton.com
1989 Front St.
215 rooms - $150-175
Pets: Welcome w/$100 deposit
Creature Comforts: CCTV, a/c,
restaurant, pool

DAYTON
Days Inn
(800) DAYS INN, (937) 898-4946
http://www.daysinn.com
7470 Miller Ln.
102 rooms - $40-70
Pets: Welcome
Creature Comforts: CCTV, a/c,
cont. brkfst, pool

Dayton Marriott
(800) 228-9290, (937) 223-1000
http://www.marriott.com
1414 S. Patterson Blvd.
399 rooms - $89-169
Pets: Welcome
Creature Comforts: CCTV, a/c,
restaurant, pool, hlth clb access

Econo Lodge South
(800) 55-ECONO, (937) 223-0166
http://www.econolodge.com
2140 Edwin C. Moses Blvd.
118 rooms - $40-79
Pets: Welcome
Creature Comforts: CCTV, a/c,
cont. brkfst, pool

Howard Johnson Express
(800) I-Go-Hojo, (937) 454-0550
http://www.hojo.com
7575 Poe Ave.
120 rooms - $60-78
Pets: Welcome w/$50 deposit
Creature Comforts: CCTV, a/c,
cont. brkfst, pool

Motel 6
(800) 4-MOTEL6, (937) 898-3606
http://www.motel6.com
7130 Miller Ln.
98 rooms - $32-45
Pets: Under 30 lbs. welcome
Creature Comforts: CCTV, pool

Quality Inn, South
(800) 228-5151, (937) 435-1550
http://www.qualityinn.com
1944 Miamisburg Centerville
73 rooms - $53-82
Pets: Welcome
Creature Comforts: CCTV, a/c,
cont. brkfst, pool

Ramada Inn North
(800) 2-Ramada, (937) 890-9500
http://www.ramada.com
4079 Little York Rd.
137 rooms - $45-84
Pets: Welcome
Creature Comforts: CCTV, a/c,
restaurant, pool, hlth club

Residence Inn
(800) 331-3131, (937) 898-7764
http://www.residenceinn.com
7070 Poe Ave.
65 rooms - $115-160
Pets: Welcome w/$200 fee
Creature Comforts: CCTV, a/c,
kit, pool

DELAWARE
Travelodge
(800) 578-7878, (740) 369-4421
http://www.travelodge.com
1001 Rte. 23
31 rooms - $45-69
Pets: Under 30 lbs. welcome
Creature Comforts: CCTV, a/c,
restaurant

DOVER
Knights Inn
(800) 843-5644, (330) 364-7724
http://www.knightsinn.com
889 Commercial Pkwy.
100 rooms - $30-85
Pets: Welcome
Creature Comforts: CCTV, a/c,
kit, pool

DUBLIN
Baymont Inn and Suites
(800) 789-4103, (614) 792-8300
http://www.baymontinns.com
6145 Park Center Dr.
104 rooms - $55-89
Pets: Welcome
Creature Comforts: CCTV, a/c

Red Roof Inn
(800) THE ROOF, (614) 764-3993
http://www.redroof.com
5125 Post Rd.
107 rooms - $45-79
Pets: Small pets welcome
Creature Comforts: CCTV, a/c

Residence Inn
(800) 331-3131, (614) 791-0403
http://www.residenceinn.com
435 Metro Place
110 rooms - $120-179
Pets: Welcome w/$100 deposit
Creature Comforts: CCTV, a/c,
kit, pool

Woodfin Suites Hotel
(800) 237-8811, (614) 766-7762
http://www.woodfinsuites.com
4130 Tuller Rd.
88 rooms - $110-190
Pets: Small pets w/$100 deposit
Creature Comforts: CCTV,
VCR, a/c, kit, fireplace, full brkfst,
pool

Wyndham Dublin Hotel
(800) Wyndham, (614) 764-2200
http://www.wyndham.com
600 Metro Place North
217 rooms - $70-160
Pets: Small pets welcome
Creature Comforts: CCTV, a/c,
restaurant, pool, hlth club

EATON
Econo Lodge
(800) 55-ECONO, (937) 456-5959
http://www.econolodge.com
1-70/Hwy 127
51 rooms - $41-55
Pets: Welcome w/$5 fee
Creature Comforts: CCTV, a/c,
cont. brkfst

ELYRIA
Comfort Inn
(800) 228-5150, (440) 324-7676
http://www.comfortinn.com
739 Leona St.
66 rooms - $50-115
Pets: Welcome
Creature Comforts: CCTV, a/c,
Jacuzzi, cont. brkfst, pool,
whirlpool

Howard Johnson Express
(800) I-Go-Hojo, (440) 323-1515
http://www.hojo.com
1724 Lorain Blvd.
36 rooms - $40-88
Pets: Welcome w/$15 fee
Creature Comforts: CCTV, a/c,
Jacuzzi, restaurant

ENGLEWOOD
Holiday Inn Airport
(800) HOLIDAY, (937) 832-1234
http://www.holiday-inn.com
10 Rockridge Rd.
150 rooms - $75-109
Pets: Small pets welcome
Creature Comforts: CCTV, a/c,
restaurant, pool

Motel 6
(800) 4-MOTEL6, (937) 832-3770
http://www.motel6.com
1212 S. Main St.
107 rooms - $30-39
Pets: Under 30 lbs. welcome
Creature Comforts: CCTV, a/c,
pool

ERLANGER
Comfort Inn
(800) 228-5150, (606) 727-3400
http://www.comfortinn.com
640 Donaldson Rd.
146 rooms - $65-81
Pets: Welcome
Creature Comforts: CCTV, a/c,
restaurant, cont. brkfst, pool

FAIRBORN
Homewood Suites
(800) 225-5466, (937) 429-0600
http://www.homewoodsuites.com
2750 Presidential Dr.
128 rooms - $89-129
Pets: Small pets w/$10 fee
Creature Comforts: CCTV, a/c,
kit, cont. brkfst/buffet dinner,
pool, hlth club

Red Roof Inn
(800) THE ROOF, (937) 426-6116
http://www.redroof.com
2580 Colonel Glenn Hwy.
110 rooms - $55-79
Pets: Small pets welcome
Creature Comforts: CCTV, a/c

FAIRLAWN
Residence Inn
(800) 331-3131, (330) 666-4811
http://www.residenceinn.com
120 W. Montrose Ave.
115 rooms - $90-185
Pets: Welcome w/$75-100 deposit
Creature Comforts: CCTV, a/c,
kit, pool

FAIRVIEW PARK
Knights Inn
(800) 843-5644, (440) 734-4500
http://www.knightsinn.com
22115 Brookpark Rd.
78 rooms - $34-55
Pets: Welcome
Creature Comforts: CCTV, a/c,
restaurant, pool

FINDLAY
Econo Lodge
(800) 55-ECONO, (419) 422-0154
http://www.econolodge.com
316 Emma St.
49 rooms - $35-72
Pets: Welcome
Creature Comforts: CCTV, a/c,
Jacuzzi

Ramada
(800) 2-Ramada, (419) 423-8212
http://www.ramada.com
820 Trenton Ave.
140 rooms - $65-80
Pets: Small pets welcome
Creature Comforts: CCTV, a/c,
restaurant, pool

FOREST PARK
Amerisuites
(800) 833-1515, (513) 825-9035
http://www.amerisuites.com
12001 Chase Plaza Dr.
125 rooms - $80-135
Pets: Small pets w/$50 deposit
Creature Comforts: CCTV,
VCR, a/c, micro, full brkfst, pool

Lees Inn & Suites
(800) SEE-LEES, (513) 825-9600
http://www.leesinn.com
11967 Chase Plaza Dr.
80 rooms - $80-105
Pets: Under 20 Lbs. on 1st floor
Creature Comforts: CCTV, a/c,
refrig, Jacuzzis, cont. brkfst, pool,
and a hlth club

FOSTORIA
Days Inn
(800) DAYS INN, (419) 435-6511
http://www.daysinn.com
601 Findlay St.
42 rooms - $47-95
Pets: Welcome
Creature Comforts: CCTV, a/c,
Jacuzzi, cont. brkfst, pool

FRANKLIN
Super 8 Motel
(800) 800-8000, (513) 422-4888
http://www.super8.com
3553 Commerce Dr.
49 rooms - $45-59
Pets: Welcome w/permission
Creature Comforts: CCTV, a/c,
refrig, cont. brkfst

FREDERICKTOWN
Heartland Country Resort
(800) 230-7030, (419) 768-9300
http://www.bbhost.com/heartland
2994 Township Rd.
7 rooms - $80-179
Pets: Welcome w/$12 fee (horses
boarded)
Creature Comforts: 1878
farmhouse on 100-acre ranch,
private country retreat, gracious
hosts and friendly Golden
Retrievers, pristine log cabins w/
cathedral ceilings, full kit,
woodstove, beautiful country
furnishings, quilts, CCTV, a/c,
Jacuzzis, full brkfst, billiards,
pool, horseback riding, lawn
games, farm animals, game room,
hay rides, and massages

FREMONT
Fremont Turnpike Motel
(419) 332-6489
Route 53
20 rooms - $35-95
Pets: Small pets w/$5 fee
Creature Comforts: CCTV, a/c,
pool, hlth club

Holiday Inn
(800) HOLIDAY, (419) 334-2682
http://www.holiday-inn.com
3422 Port Clinton Rd.
160 rooms - $60-145
Pets: Small pets welcome
Creature Comforts: CCTV, a/c,
pool, restaurant

Travelodge
(800) 578-7878, (419) 334-9517
http://www.travelodge.com
1750 Cedar St.
50 rooms - $55-95
Pets: Small pets welcome
Creature Comforts: CCTV, a/c

GALION
Hometown Inn
(800) 578-7878, (717) 264-4187
172 N. Portland Way
30 rooms - $45-150
Pets: Small pets welcome
Creature Comforts: CCTV, a/c

GALLIPOLIS
William Ann Motel
(740) 446-3373
565 Lincoln Way
56 rooms - $45-53
Pets: Small pets welcome
Creature Comforts: CCTV, a/c,
refrig

GIRARD
Econo Lodge
(800) 55-ECONO, (330) 759-9820
http://www.econolodge.com
1615 E. Liberty St.
56 rooms - $36-57
Pets: Welcome
Creature Comforts: CCTV, a/c

Motel 6
(800) 4-MOTEL6, (330) 759-7833
http://www.motel6.com
1600 Motor Inn Dr.
125 rooms - $26-36
Pets: Under 30 lbs. welcome
Creature Comforts: CCTV, a/c,
pool

GRANVILLE
The Porch House
(800) 587-1995, (740) 587-1995
241 E. Maple St.
5 rooms - $65-70
Pets: Welcome w/permission
Creature Comforts: 1903
country Victorian, CCTV, a/c, full
brkfst

GROVE CITY
Best Western Executive
(800) 528-1234, (614) 875-7770
http://www.bestwestern.com
4026 Jackpot Rd.
50 rooms - $50-70
Pets: Welcome w/$6 fee
Creature Comforts: CCTV, a/c,
refrig, pool

Red Roof Inn
(800) THE ROOF, (614) 875-8543
http://www.redroof.com
1900 Stringtown Rd.
106 rooms - $45-80
Pets: Small pets welcome
Creature Comforts: CCTV, a/c

HAMILTON
Hamiltonian Hotel
(800) 522-5570, (513) 896-6200
One Riverfront Plaza
124 rooms - $73-119
Pets: Welcome
Creature Comforts: CCTV, a/c,
restaurant, pool

HEATH
Super 8 Motel
(800) 800-8000, (614) 788-9144
http://www.super8.com
1177 South Hebron Rd.
46 rooms - $50-60
Pets: Welcome w/permission
Creature Comforts: CCTV, a/c,
cont. brkfst

HILLIARD
Comfort Inn
(800) 228-5150, (614) 529-8118
http://www.comfortinn.com
3831 Park Mill Run Dr.
60 rooms - $75-95
Pets: Welcome w/$5 fee
Creature Comforts: CCTV, a/c,
refrig, micro, cont. brkfst, pool,
whirlpool

Homewood Suites
(800) 225-5466, (614) 529-4100
http://www.homewoodsuites.com
3841 Park Mill Run Dr.
66 rooms - $120-1235
Pets: Welcome w/$45 fee
Creature Comforts: CCTV, a/c,
kit, cont. brkfst, hlth club, pool

Motel 6
(800) 4-MOTEL6, (614) 771-1500
http://www.motel6.com
3950 Parkway Ln.
105 rooms - $35-40
Pets: Under 30 lbs. welcome
Creature Comforts: CCTV, a/c,
pool

HILLSBORO
Greystone Motel
(937) 393-1966
8190 Rte. 50 E.
38 rooms - $30-48
Pets: Welcome
Creature Comforts: CCTV, a/c

HIRAM
Hiram Inn
(800) 325-5087, (330) 569-3222
6720 Wakefield Rd.
3 rooms - $55-85
Pets: Welcome w/permission
Creature Comforts: CCTV, a/c,
full brkfst

HOLLAND
Cross Country Inn
(800) 578-7878, (419) 866-6565
1201 E. Mall Dr.
130 rooms - $40-54
Pets: Welcome
Creature Comforts: CCTV, a/c,
pool

Red Roof Inn
(800) THE ROOF, (419) 866-5512
http://www.redroof.com
1214 Corporate Dr.
110 rooms - $45-69
Pets: Small pets welcome
Creature Comforts: CCTV, a/c

Residence Inn
(800) 331-3131, (419) 867-9555
http://www.residenceinn.com
6101 Trust Dr.
95 rooms - $125-150
Pets: Welcome w/$50 fee
Creature Comforts: CCTV, a/c,
kit, pool

HUBER HEIGHTS
Travelodge
(800) 578-7878, (937) 236-9361
http://www.travelodge.com
7911 Brandt Pike
50 rooms - $45-99
Pets: Welcome
Creature Comforts: CCTV, a/c,
cont brkfst, pool

HUDSON
Hudson Inn
(330) 650-1100
344 E. Hines Hill Rd.
210 rooms - $55-89
Pets: Welcome
Creature Comforts: CCTV, a/c,
restaurant, pool

HURON
Plantation Motel
(419) 433-4790
2815 Cleveland Rd.
25 rooms - $30-126
Pets: Welcome w/$7 deposit
Creature Comforts: CCTV, a/c,
kit, pool

INDEPENDENCE
Amerisuites
(800) 833-1515, (216) 328-1060
http://www.amerisuites.com
6025 Jefferson Dr.
130 rooms - $60-130
Pets: Welcome
Creature Comforts: CCTV,
VCR, a/c, refrig, micro, cont.
brkfst, pool, hlth club

Baymont Inn and Suites
(800) 789-4103, (216) 247-1133
http://www.baymontinns.com
6161 Quarry Ln.
100 rooms - $60-93
Pets: Welcome
Creature Comforts: CCTV, a/c

Cleveland Hilton South
(800) HILTONS, (216) 447-1300
http://www.hilton.com
6200 Quarry Ln.
191 rooms - $110-170
Pets: Small pets w/$25 fee
Creature Comforts: CCTV, a/c,
pool, hlth club

Red Roof Inn
(800) THE ROOF, (216) 447-0030
http://www.redroof.com
6020 Quarry Ln.
110 rooms - $49-86
Pets: Small pets welcome
Creature Comforts: CCTV, a/c

Residence Inn
(800) 331-3131, (216) 520-1450
http://www.residenceinn.com
5101 W. Creek Rd.
120 rooms - $99-170
Pets: Welcome w/$200 fee
Creature Comforts: CCTV, a/c,
kit, cont brkfst, pool

JACKSON

Knights Inn
(800) 843-5644, (740) 286-2135
http://www.knightsinn.com
404 Chillicothe Rd.
35 rooms - $42-55
Pets: Welcome
Creature Comforts: CCTV, a/c

KENT

Holiday Inn
(800) HOLIDAY, (330) 678-0101
http://www.holiday-inn.com
4363 Rte. 43
155 rooms - $70-100
Pets: Small pets w$50 deposit
Creature Comforts: CCTV,
VCR, a/c, refrig, micro, restaurant,
pool

Knights Inn
(800) 843-5644, (330) 678-5250
http://www.knightsinn.com
4423 Rte. 43
99 rooms - $37-59
Pets: Welcome
Creature Comforts: CCTV, a/c,
pool

LAKEWOOD

Days Inn
(800) DAYS INN, (216) 226-4800
http://www.daysinn.com
12019 Lake Ave.
66 rooms - $65-78
Pets: Welcome
Creature Comforts: CCTV, a/c,
cont. brkfst

LANCASTER

Best Western Lancaster
(800) 528-1234, (614) 653-3040
http://www.bestwestern.com
1858 Memorial Dr.
168 rooms - $60-79
Pets: Under 20 lbs. welcome
Creature Comforts: CCTV, a/c,
refrig, micro, restaurant, putting
green

Knights Inn
(800) 843-5644, (614) 687-4823
http://www.knightsinn.com
1327 River Valley Rd.
60 rooms - $35-68
Pets: Small pets w/$5 fee
Creature Comforts: CCTV, a/c,
kit, Jacuzzi

LEBANON

Econo Lodge
(800) 55-ECONO, (513) 932-4111
http://www.econolodge.com
674 N. Broadway St.
49 rooms - $40-75
Pets: Welcome
Creature Comforts: CCTV, a/c,
pool

The Queen Anne
(513) 932-3836
102 N. High St.
3 rooms - $50-60
Pets: Welcome w/permission
Creature Comforts: CCTV,
VCR, a/c, cont. brkfst

LIMA

Days Inn
(800) DAYS INN, (419) 227-6515
http://www.daysinn.com
1250 Neubrecht Rd.
118 rooms - $45-79
Pets: Welcome w/$10 fee
Creature Comforts: CCTV, a/c,
cont. brkfst, pool

Econo Lodge
(800) 55-ECONO, (419) 222-0596
http://www.econolodge.com
1201 Neubrecht Rd.
130 rooms - $47-53
Pets: Welcome
Creature Comforts: CCTV, a/c,
restaurant, full brkfst, pool, hlth
club

Holiday Inn
(800) HOLIDAY, (419) 222-0004
http://www.holiday-inn.com
1920 Roschman Ave.
150 rooms - $75-100
Pets: Welcome
Creature Comforts: CCTV, a/c,
restaurant, pool, rec. area

Motel 6
(800) 4-MOTEL6, (419) 228-0456
http://www.motel6.com
1800 Harding Rd.
96 rooms - $35-46
Pets: Under 30 lbs. welcome
Creature Comforts: CCTV, a/c

Super 8 Motel
(800) 800-8000, (419) 227-2221
http://www.super8.com
1430 Bellefontaine Ave.
76 rooms - $38-42
Pets: Welcome w/permission
Creature Comforts: CCTV, a/c,
pool

LODI

Howard Johnson Express
(800) I-Go-Hojo, (330) 769-2053
http://www.hojo.com
I-71/I-76
19 rooms - $40-45
Pets: Welcome
Creature Comforts: CCTV, a/c,
restaurant

LOUDONVILLE

Little Brown Inn
(888) 994-5525, (419) 994-5525
940 S. Market St.
20 rooms - $43-63
Pets: Small pets are selectively
welcomed
Creature Comforts: CCTV, a/c

MACEDONIA

Baymont Inn and Suites
(800) 4-Budget, (330) 468-5400
http://www.baymontinns.com
268 E. Highland Rd.
90 rooms - $55-99
Pets: Welcome in smoking rooms
Creature Comforts: CCTV, a/c,
cont. brkfst, pool

Knights Inn
(800) 843-5644, (330) 467-1981
http://www.knightsinn.com
240 E. Highland Rd.
85 rooms - $40-69
Pets: Welcome
Creature Comforts: CCTV,
VCR, a/c, refrig, micro, pool

Motel 6
(800) 4-MOTEL6, (330) 468-1670
http://www.motel6.com
311 E. Highland Rd.
123 rooms - $35-47
Pets: Under 30 lbs. welcome
Creature Comforts: CCTV, a/c,
pool

MANSFIELD

42 Motel
(419) 884-1315
2444 Lexington Ave.
22 rooms - $38-65
Pets: Welcome
Creature Comforts: CCTV, a/c, refrig, pool

191 Park Place Hotel
(800) 425-7275, (419) 526-2117
191 Park Ave. W.
93 rooms - $55-84
Pets: Welcome w/$10 fee
Creature Comforts: CCTV, a/c, refrig, micro, restaurant

Baymont Inn and Suites
(800) 789-4103, (419) 774-0005
http://www.baymontinns.com
120 Stander Ave.
95 rooms - $50-75
Pets: Welcome
Creature Comforts: CCTV, a/c, cont. brkfst, pool

Best Western Mansfield Inn
(800) 528-1234, (419) 589-2200
http://www.bestwestern.com
880 Laver Rd.
104 rooms - $60-75
Pets: Under 20 lbs. welcome
Creature Comforts: CCTV, a/c, restaurant, pool

Comfort Inn, North
(800) 228-5150, (419) 529-1000
http://www.comfortinn.com
500 N. Trimble Rd.
114 rooms - $45-150
Pets: Welcome
Creature Comforts: CCTV, a/c, refrig, micro, restaurant, cont. brkfst, pool, hlth clb access, sauna, whirlpool

Econo Lodge
(800) 55-ECONO, (419) 589-3333
http://www.econolodge.com
1017 Koogle Rd.
51 rooms - $44-92
Pets: Small pets welcome
Creature Comforts: CCTV, a/c, restaurant, pool

Hampton Inn
(800) Hampton, (419) 747-5353
http://www.hampton-inn.com
1051 N. Lexington-Springmill Rd.
62 rooms - $62-69
Pets: Welcome
Creature Comforts: CCTV, a/c, restaurant, pool

Knights Inn
(800) 843-5644, (419) 529-2100
http://www.knightsinn.com
555 N. Trimble Rd.
88 rooms - $43-54
Pets: Welcome
Creature Comforts: CCTV, a/c, kit, pool

Travelodge
(800) 578-7878, (419) 756-7600
http://www.travelodge.com
90 Hanley Rd.
92 rooms - $41-79
Pets: Welcome
Creature Comforts: CCTV, a/c, kit, pool

Super 8 Motel
(800) 800-8000, (419) 756-8875
http://www.super8.com
2425 Interstate Circle
69 rooms - $45-77
Pets: Welcome w/permission
Creature Comforts: CCTV, VCR, a/c

MARBLEHEAD

Surf Motel
(419) 798-4823
230 E. Main St.
24 rooms - $49-65
Pets: Welcome
Creature Comforts: CCTV, a/c, pool

MARIETTA

Econo Lodge
(800) 55-ECONO, (740) 374-8481
http://www.econolodge.com
702 Pike St.
48 rooms - $38-60
Pets: Welcome
Creature Comforts: CCTV, a/c, restaurant, cont. brkfst, pool

Knights Inn
(800) 843-5644, (740) 373-7373
http://www.knightsinn.com
506 Pike St.
110 rooms - $45-75
Pets: Welcome w/$5 fee
Creature Comforts: CCTV, VCR, a/c, refrig, pool

Lafayette Hotel
(800) 331-9337, (740) 373-5522
http://www.historiclafayette.com
101 Front St.
78 rooms - $65-200
Pets: Welcome w/$100 deposit
Creature Comforts: Nat'l Historic Register, on Ohio River, simple rooms w/Victorian charm, gun collection, old pilot wheel, CCTV, a/c, fine restaurant, pool

MARION

Comfort Inn
(800) 228-5150, (740) 389-5552
http://www.comfortinn.com
256 Jamesway Rd.
56 rooms - $55-100
Pets: Welcome
Creature Comforts: CCTV, a/c, cont. brkfst, pool

Days Inn
(800) DAYS INN, (740) 389-4651
http://www.daysinn.com
1838 Marion-Mt. Gilead Rd.
84 rooms - $44-100
Pets: Welcome w/$5 fee
Creature Comforts: CCTV, a/c, kit, Jacuzzi, cont. brkfst, pool, whirlpool

Travelodge
(800) 578-7878, (740) 389-4671
http://www.travelodge.com
1952 Marion-Mt. Gilead Rd.
90 rooms - $47-86
Pets: Welcome
Creature Comforts: CCTV, a/c, refrig, micro, pool, hlth club

MARYSVILLE

Holiday Inn Express
(800) HOLIDAY, (937) 644-8821
http://www.holiday-inn.com
16510 Square Dr.
75 rooms - $65-99
Pets: Small pets welcome
Creature Comforts: CCTV, a/c, kit, Jacuzzis, hlth club, pool

Super 8 Motel
(800) 800-8000, (614) 873-4100
http://www.super8.com
10220 Rte. 42
30 rooms - $38-58
Pets: Welcome w/$5 fee
Creature Comforts: CCTV,
VCR, a/c, cont. brkfst

MASON
Baymont Inn and Suites
(800) 789-4103, (513) 459-1111
http://www.baymontinns.com
9918 Escort Dr.
95 rooms - $55-125
Pets: Welcome
Creature Comforts: CCTV, a/c,
pool

Best Western Kings Island
(800) 528-1234, (513) 398-3633
http://www.bestwestern.com
9847 Escort Dr.
124 rooms - $45-159
Pets: Welcome
Creature Comforts: CCTV, a/c,
pool

Days Inn
(800) DAYS INN, (513) 398-3297
http://www.daysinn.com
Mason/Montgomery Rd.
124 rooms - $40-107
Pets: Welcome
Creature Comforts: CCTV, a/c,
cont. brkfst, pool

Holiday Inn Express
(800) HOLIDAY, (513) 398-8075
http://www.holiday-inn.com
4859 McKnight Rd.
200 rooms - $70-179
Pets: Welcome
Creature Comforts: CCTV, a/c,
refrig, Jacuzzi, restaurant, full
brkfst, pool, hlth clb access

Red Roof Inn
(800) THE ROOF, (513) 398-3633
http://www.redroof.com
9847 Escort Dr.
124 rooms - $49-155
Pets: Welcome
Creature Comforts: CCTV, a/c,
cont. brkfst, pool

Westin Hotel
(800) 228-3000, (513) 621-7700
http://www.westin.com
Fountain Sq.
448 rooms - $89-199
Pets: Small well-trained pets
Creature Comforts: CCTV, a/c,
refrig, micro, restaurant, pool, hlth
clb access

MAUMEE
Country Inn and Suites
(419) 893-8576
541 W. Dussel Dr.
64 rooms - $70-120
Pets: Small pets welcome
Creature Comforts: CCTV, a/c,
pool

Days Inn
(800) DAYS INN, (419) 893-9960
http://www.daysinn.com
150 Dussel Dr.
120 rooms - $50-69
Pets: Welcome
Creature Comforts: CCTV, a/c,
Jacuzzi, cont. brkfst, pool

Red Roof Inn
(800) THE ROOF, (419) 893-0292
http://www.redroof.com
1570 Reynolds Rd.
110 rooms - $45-75
Pets: Small pets welcome
Creature Comforts: CCTV, a/c

MAYFIELD HEIGHTS
Baymont Inn and Suites
(800) 4-Budget, (216) 442-8400
http://www.baymont.com
1421 Golden Gate Blvd.
103 rooms - $57-89
Pets: Welcome
Creature Comforts: CCTV, a/c,
kit, cont. brkfst

MENTOR
Knights Inn
(800) 843-5644, (440) 953-8835
http://www.knightsinn.com
8370 Broadmoor Rd.
105 rooms - $46-76
Pets: Small pets welcome
Creature Comforts: CCTV, a/c,
pool

MIAMISBURG
Motel 6
(800) 4-MOTEL6, (937) 434-8750
http://www.motel6.com
8101 Springboro Pike
134 rooms - $32-39
Pets: Under 30 lbs. welcome
Creature Comforts: CCTV, a/c,
pool

Red Roof Inn
(800) THE ROOF, (937) 866-0705
http://www.redroof.com
222 Byers Rd.
110 rooms - $45-79
Pets: Small pets welcome
Creature Comforts: CCTV, a/c

Residence Inn
(800) 331-3131, (937) 434-7881
http://www.residenceinn.com
155 Prestige Pl.
95 rooms - $115-135
Pets: Welcome w/$10 fee
Creature Comforts: CCTV, a/c,
pool

MIDDLEBURG HEIGHTS
Comfort Inn
(800) 228-5150, (440) 234-3131
http://www.comfortinn.com
17550 Rosbough Dr.
135 rooms - $70-147
Pets: Welcome w/$25 fee
Creature Comforts: CCTV,
VCR, a/c, Jacuzzi, refrig, cont.
brkfst, pool, hlth club

Motel 6
(800) 4-MOTEL6, (440) 234-0990
http://www.motel6.com
7219 Engle Rd.
95 rooms - $35-48
Pets: Under 30 lbs. welcome
Creature Comforts: CCTV, a/c

Red Roof Inn
(800) THE ROOF, (440) 243-2441
http://www.redroof.com
17555 Bagley Rd.
120 rooms - $45-80
Pets: Small pets welcome
Creature Comforts: CCTV, a/c

Residence Inn
(800) 331-3131, (440) 234-6688
http://www.residenceinn.com
17525 Rosbough Dr.
160 rooms - $125-180
Pets: Welcome w/$200 fee
Creature Comforts: CCTV, a/c, kit, pool

MIDDLETOWN
Manchester Inn/Conf. Center
(800) 523-9126, (513) 422-5481
http://www.manchesterinn.com
1027 Manchester Ave.
80 rooms - $65-140
Pets: Small pets welcome
Creature Comforts: CCTV, a/c, restaurant, cont. brkfst, pool, hlth clb access

Park Way Inn
(513) 423-9403
2425 N. Verity Pkwy.
55 rooms - $35-55
Pets: Welcome
Creature Comforts: CCTV, a/c, pool

MONROE
Econo Lodge
(800) 55-ECONO, (513) 539-9221
http://www.econolodge.com
150 Garver Rd.
105 rooms - $50-79
Pets: Welcome
Creature Comforts: CCTV, a/c, cont. brkfst, pool

MONTPELIER
Holiday Inn
(800) HOLIDAY, (419) 485-5555
http://www.holiday-inn.com
13508 Rte. 15
160 rooms - $85-195
Pets: Small pets welcome
Creature Comforts: CCTV, a/c, restaurant, pool

MORAINE
Super 8 Motel
(800) 800-8000, (937) 298-0380
http://www.super8.com
2450 Dryden Rd.
72 rooms - $40-45
Pets: Welcome w/permission
Creature Comforts: CCTV, a/c

MOUNT GILEAD
Knights Inn
(800) 843-5644, (419) 946-6010
http://www.knightsinn.com
5898 Hwy 95
46 rooms - $47-64
Pets: Welcome w/$50 deposit
Creature Comforts: CCTV, a/c, restaurant

MOUNT VERNON
Dan Emmett House Hotel
(800) 480-8221, (740) 392-6886
150 Howard St.
60 rooms - $60-99
Pets: Welcome
Creature Comforts: CCTV, a/c, Jacuziis, cont. brkfst, restaurant, pool, whirlpool, sauna

Historic Curtis Inn
(800) 93-HOTEL, (740) 397-4334
6 Public Square
72 rooms - $52-69
Pets: Welcome
Creature Comforts: CCTV, a/c, restaurant, hlth club

Mount Vernon Inn
(740) 392-9881
601 W. High St.
13 rooms - $48-83
Pets: Welcome
Creature Comforts: CCTV, a/c, refrig, micro, cont. brkfst

NAPOLEAN
Paramount Hotel
(800) 843-5644, (419) 592-5010
2395 N. Scott St.
80 rooms - $50-58
Pets: Small pets welcome
Creature Comforts: CCTV, a/c, restaurant, pool

NELSONVILLE
Quality Inn
(800) 228-5151, (419) 592-5010
http://www.qualityinn.com
Rtes. 33 & 691
42 rooms - $55-130
Pets: Welcome
Creature Comforts: CCTV, a/c, restaurant, pool

NEW PHILADELPHIA
Motel 6
(800) 4-MOTEL6, (330) 339-6446
http://www.motel6.com
181 Bluebell Dr. SW
83 rooms - $35-45
Pets: Under 30 lbs. welcome
Creature Comforts: CCTV, a/c, pool

Schoenbrunn Inn
(800) 929-7799, (330) 339-4334
1186 W. High Ave.
60 rooms - $60-140
Pets: In first floor rms w/$10 fee
Creature Comforts: CCTV, a/c, refrig, micro, Jacuzzis, full brkfst, pool, hlth club, whirlpool, sauna

Travelodge
(800) 578-7878, (330) 339-6671
http://www.travelodge.com
1256 W. High St.
62 rooms - $42-75
Pets: Welcome
Creature Comforts: CCTV, a/c, kit, pool

NEWARK
Holiday Inn
(800) HOLIDAY, (740) 522-1165
http://www.holiday-inn.com
733 Hebron Rd.
107 rooms - $50-75
Pets: Small pets welcome
Creature Comforts: CCTV, a/c, refrig, restaurant, pool

Howard Johnson
(800) I-Go-Hojo, (740) 522-3191
http://www.hojo.com
775 Hebron Rd.
72 rooms - $52-95
Pets: Welcome
Creature Comforts: CCTV, a/c, refrig, Jacuzzi, restaurant, cont. brkfst, pool, hlth club

NEWTON FALLS
Rodeway Inn
(800) 228-2000, (330) 872-0988
http://www.rodeway.com
4248 Rte. 5
35 rooms - $30-95
Pets: Welcome w/permission
Creature Comforts: CCTV, a/c, cont. brkfst

NORTH LIMA
Davis Motel
(330) 549-2113
10860 Market St.
33 rooms - $30-55
Pets: Welcome w/permission
Creature Comforts: CCTV, a/c,
restaurant

Rodeway Inn
(800) 228-2000, (330) 549-3988
http://www.rodeway.com
10650 Market St.
40 rooms - $35-85
Pets: Small pets w/$5 fee
Creature Comforts: CCTV, a/c,
refrig, micro, cont. brkfst

Super 8 Motel
(800) 800-8000, (330) 549-2187
http://www.super8.com
10076 Market St.
87 rooms - $50-165
Pets: Welcome w/permission
Creature Comforts: CCTV, a/c,
Jacuzzi, pool

NORTH OLMSTEAD
Econo Lodge
(800) 55-ECONO, (440) 734-1100
http://www.econolodge.com
22989 Lorain Rd.
59 rooms - $40-70
Pets: Welcome
Creature Comforts: CCTV, a/c,
restaurant, pool

NORWALK
L K Motel
(800) 282-5711, (419) 668-8255
283 Benedict Ave.
20 rooms - $45-68
Pets: Welcome w/permission
Creature Comforts: CCTV, a/c,
kit

NORWOOD
Quality Inn
(800) 228-5151, (513) 351-6000
http://www.qualityinn.com
1375 W. Route 554747
Montgomery Rd.
146 rooms - $90-135
Pets: Welcome
Creature Comforts: CCTV, a/c,
refrig, micro, restaurant, and pool

OBERLIN
Oberlin Inn
(440) 775-1111
7 N. Main St.
76 rooms - $90-175
Pets: Small pets welcome
Creature Comforts: CCTV, a/c,
restaurant, hlth clb access

OREGON
Comfort Inn
(800) 228-5150, (419) 691-8911
http://www.comfortinn.com
2930 Navarre Ave.
80 rooms - $65-123
Pets: Welcome
Creature Comforts: CCTV,
VCR, a/c, refrig, micro, Jacuzzi,
cont. brkfst, pool

OXFORD
Scottish Inns
(800) 251-1962, (513) 523-6306
5235 College Corner Pike
30 rooms - $35-59
Pets: Welcome w/$5 fee
Creature Comforts: CCTV, a/c,
cont. brkfst, pool

PAINESVILLE
Villa Rosa Motel
(440) 357-7502
2140 North Ridge Rd.
21 rooms - $38-49
Pets: Welcome
Creature Comforts: CCTV, a/c

Rider's 1812 Inn
(440) 354-8200
http://www.ncweb.com/ridersinn
792 Mentor Ave.
10 rooms - $75-105
Pets: Med. pets welcome in the
Den and Innkeeper's Suites
Creature Comforts: 1812 inn,
creaky floors, ghosts reputedly
wander the halls, Victorian
furnishings, antiques, request
innkeeper's suite w/dble bed and
clawfoot tub, CCTV-VCR, full
brkfst, restaurant, pub

PERRYSBURG
Baymont Inn and Suites
(800) 789-4103, (419) 872-0000
http://www.baymontinns.com
1154 Professional Dr.
105 rooms - $50-79
Pets: Small pets welcome
Creature Comforts: CCTV, a/c,
cont. brkfst

Days Inn
(800) DAYS INN, (419) 874-8771
http://www.daysinn.com
10667 Fremont Pike
124 rooms - $65-80
Pets: Welcome
Creature Comforts: CCTV,
VCR, a/c, refrig, micro, cont.
brkfst, pool

Howard Johnson
(800) I-Go-Hojo, (419) 837-5245
http://www.hojo.com
I-280/Hanley Rd.
138 rooms - $38-59
Pets: Welcome
Creature Comforts: CCTV, a/c,
restaurant, pool, hlth club, and a
sauna

Red Carpet Inn
(800) 251-1962, (419) 872-8902
http://www.redcarpetinn.com
2449 Brice Rd.
110 rooms - $55-75
Pets: Small pets welcome
Creature Comforts: CCTV,
VCR, a/c, refrig, micro

PIQUA
Howard Johnson
(800) I-Go-Hojo, (937) 773-2314
http://www.hojo.com
902 Scot Dr.
60 rooms - $45-64
Pets: Welcome
Creature Comforts: CCTV, a/c,
cont. brkfst, pool

POLAND
Red Roof Inn
(800) THE ROOF, (330) 758-1999
http://www.redroof.com
1051 Tiffany South
118 rooms - $39-78
Pets: Small pets welcome
Creature Comforts: CCTV, a/c,
kit

Residence Inn
(800) 331-3131, (330) 726-1747
http://www.residenceinn.com
7396 Tiffany South
75 rooms - $70-165
Pets: Welcome w/$100 fee
Creature Comforts: CCTV, a/c,
kit, pool

PORT CLINTON
Country Hearth Inn
(800) 282-5711, (419) 732-2111
1815 E. Perry St.
66 rooms - $35-155
Pets: Small pets welcome
Creature Comforts: CCTV, a/c,
refrig, micro, kit, pool, lake

PORTSMOUTH
Best Western Inn
(800) 528-1234, (740) 354-2851
http://www.bestwestern.com
3762 Rte. 23
100 rooms - $59-79
Pets: Small pets welcome
Creature Comforts: CCTV, a/c,
restaurant, pool

Ramada
(800) 2-Ramada, (740) 354-7711
http://www.ramada.com
711 Second St.
119 rooms - $53-79
Pets: Welcome, no discounts
Creature Comforts: CCTV, a/c,
refrig, restaurant, cont. brkfst,
pool, hlth club

PUT-IN-BAY
Perry Holiday Hotel
(419) 285-2107
99 Concord Ave.
50 rooms - $70-146
Pets: Small pets welcome
Creature Comforts: CCTV, a/c,
pool

REYNOLDSBURG
Best Western Inn (Airport)
(800) 528-1234, (614) 864-1280
http://www.bestwestern.com
2100 Brice Rd.
143 rooms - $61-79
Pets: Small pets welcome
Creature Comforts: CCTV, a/c,
restaurant, pool

La Quinta
(800) 531-5900, (614) 866-6456
http://www.laquinta.com
2447 Brice Rd.
125 rooms - $50-95
Pets: Small pets welcome
Creature Comforts: CCTV, a/c,
pool

Lenox Inn
(614) 861-7800
13700 Reynoldsburg-Baltimore
150 rooms - $65-80
Pets: Welcome w/$10 fee
Creature Comforts: CCTV, a/c,
restaurant, pool

Super 8 Motel
(800) 800-8000, (614) 866-8000
http://www.super8.com
6201 Oaktree Ln.
92 rooms - $50-60
Pets: Welcome w/$3 fee
Creature Comforts: CCTV, a/c,
refrig, micro

RICHFIELD
Holiday Inn
(800) HOLIDAY, (330) 659-6151
http://www.holiday-inn.com
4742 Brecksville Rd.
216 rooms - $50-109
Pets: Welcome
Creature Comforts: CCTV, a/c,
restaurant, pool, hlth club, and
mini. golf

Howard Johnson
(800) I-Go-Hojo, (330) 659-6116
http://www.hojo.com
5171 Brecksville Rd.
61 rooms - $45-97
Pets: Welcome
Creature Comforts: CCTV, a/c,
restaurant, cont. brkfst

RIO GRANDE
College Hill Motel
(614) 245-5326
10987 Rte. 588
13 rooms - $35-45
Pets: Welcome
Creature Comforts: CCTV, a/c

ST. CLAIRSVILLE
Knights Inn
(800) 843-5644, (740) 695-5038
http://www.knightsinn.com
51260 National Rd.
109 rooms - $35-65
Pets: Welcome in ltd. rms.
Creature Comforts: CCTV,
VCR, a/c, micro, kit, Jacuzzi, pool

Super 8 Motel
(800) 800-8000, (740) 695-1994
http://www.super8.com
68400 Matthews Dr.
62 rooms - $44-58
Pets: Welcome w/permission
Creature Comforts: CCTV, a/c

Red Roof Inn
(800) THE ROOF, (740) 695-4057
http://www.redroof.com
68301 Red Roof Ln.
110 rooms - $45-77
Pets: Small pets welcome
Creature Comforts: CCTV, a/c

SALEM
Timerlanes Inn
(330) 337-9901
544 E. Pershing St.
57 rooms - $50-65
Pets: Welcome
Creature Comforts: CCTV, a/c,
restaurant

SANDUSKY
Clarion Hotel
(800) CLARION, (419) 625-6280
http://www.clarioninn.com
1119 Sandusky Mall Rd.
143 rooms - $75-125
Pets: Welcome
Creature Comforts: CCTV, a/c,
refrig, pool, hlth club

Coronado Motel
(888) 720-STAY, (419) 625-2954
431 Venice Rd.
27 rooms - $30-109
Pets: Welcome w/$10 fee
Creature Comforts: CCTV, a/c,
kit, pool

Four Points by Sheraton
(800) 325-3535, (419) 625-6280
http://www.sheraton.com
1119 Sandusky Mall Blvd.
145 rooms - $50-200
Pets: Small pets welcome
Creature Comforts: CCTV, a/c,
restaurant, pool, hlth club,
whirlpool

Radisson Harbour Inn
(800) 333-3333, (419) 627-2500
http://www.radisson.com
2001 Cleveland Rd.
237 rooms - $59-209
Pets: Small pets w/$50 deposit
Creature Comforts: CCTV,
VCR, a/c, refrig, restaurant, pool,
whirlpool

Wagner's 1844 Inn
(419) 626-1726
230 E. Washington St.
3 rooms - $70-100
Pets: Welcome w/permission
Creature Comforts: CCTV, a/c,
full brkfst

SHARONVILLE
Cincinnati Marriott
(800) 228-9290, (513) 772-1720
http://www.marriott.com
11320 Chester Rd.
350 rooms - $110-150
Pets: Small pets welcome
Creature Comforts: CCTV,
VCR, a/c, refrig, micro, Jacuzzi,
restaurant, cont. brkfst, pool, hlth
clb access

Holiday Inn
(800) HOLIDAY, (513) 563-8330
http://www.holiday-inn.com
3855 Hauck Rd.
275 rooms - $110-130
Pets: Small pets welcome
Creature Comforts: CCTV, a/c,
restaurant, pool, tennis

Holiday Inn, North
(800) HOLIDAY, (513) 771-0700
http://www.holiday-inn.com
2235 Sharon Rd.
409 rooms - $99-140
Pets: Small pets welcome
Creature Comforts: CCTV, a/c,
refrig, micro, Jacuzzi, restaurant,
pool, hlth club, whirlpool, saunas,
domed rec. area

Homewood Suites
(800) 225-5466, (513) 772-8888
http://www.homewoodsuites.com
2670 E. Kemper Rd.
112 rooms - $110-200
Pets: Welcome w/$10 fee
Creature Comforts: CCTV, a/c,
kit, pool

Motel 6
(800) 4-MOTEL6, (513) 563-1123
http://www.motel6.com
3850 Hauck Rd.
110 rooms - $35-40
Pets: Under 30 lbs. welcome
Creature Comforts: CCTV, a/c,
pool

Motel 6
(800) 4-MOTEL6, (513) 772-5944
http://www.motel6.com
2000 E. Kemper Rd.
123 rooms - $35-40
Pets: Under 30 lbs. welcome
Creature Comforts: CCTV, a/c,
pool

Red Roof Inn
(800) THE ROOF, (513) 771-5552
http://www.redroof.com
2301 E. Sharon Rd.
110 rooms - $50-75
Pets: Small pets welcome
Creature Comforts: CCTV, a/c,

Red Roof Inn
(800) THE ROOF, (513) 771-5141
http://www.redroof.com
11345 Chester Rd.
106 rooms - $40-75
Pets: Welcome
Creature Comforts: CCTV, a/c,
hlth club

Residence Inn
(800) 331-3131, (513) 771-2525
http://www.residenceinn.com
11689 Chester Rd.
145 rooms - $90-110
Pets: Welcome w/$75-90 fee
Creature Comforts: CCTV, a/c,
kit, pool

Woodfield Suites
(800) 338-0008, (513) 771-0300
http://www.woodfinsuites.com
11029 Dowlin Dr.
150 rooms - $90-140
Pets: Small pets w/$100 deposit
Creature Comforts: CCTV, a/c,
kit, Jacuzzis, pool, whirlpool, hlth
club,

SHAWNEE
Rodeway Inn
(800) 228-2000, (405) 275-1005
http://www.rodeway.com
12510 Valley View Rd.
28 rooms - $35-49
Pets: Welcome w/permission
Creature Comforts: CCTV, a/c,
cont. brkfst

SHELBY
L K Motel
(800) 282-5711, (419) 347-2141
178 Mansfield Rd.
33 rooms - $35-47
Pets: Welcome w
Creature Comforts: CCTV, a/c,
kit

SIDNEY
Holiday Inn
(800) HOLIDAY, (937) 492-1131
http://www.holiday-inn.com
400 Folkerth Ave.
130 rooms - $65-79
Pets: Small pets welcome
Creature Comforts: CCTV, a/c,
refrig, micro, restaurant, pool

SOUTH POINT
Best Western Southern Hills Inn
(800) 528-1234, (614) 894-3391
http://www.bestwestern.com
803 Solida Rd.
49 rooms - $40-58
Pets: Welcome w/$6 fee
Creature Comforts: CCTV, a/c,
restaurant, pool

SPRINGDALE
Baymont Inn and Suites
(800) 789-4103, (513) 671-2300
http://www.baymontinns.com
12150 Springfield Pike
105 rooms - $50-85
Pets: Small pets welcome
Creature Comforts: CCTV, a/c,
cont. brkfst

Best Western Springdale
(800) 528-1234, (513) 671-6600
http://www.bestwestern.com
11911 Sheraton Lane
267 rooms - $100-120
Pets: Welcome w/$25 fee
Creature Comforts: CCTV, a/c,
refrig, restaurant, cont. brkfst,
pool, hlth club, whirlpool

SPRINGFIELD
Executive Inn
(937) 324-5601
325 W. Columbia Ave.
74 rooms - $37-41
Pets: Welcome
Creature Comforts: CCTV, a/c, restaurant

Knights Inn
(800) 843-5644, (937) 325-8721
http://www.knightsinn.com
2207 W. Main St.
40 rooms - $55-70
Pets: Welcome w/$10 fee
Creature Comforts: CCTV, a/c, kit, pool

Rodeway Inn
(800) 228-2000, (937) 324-5561
http://www.rodeway.com
1715 West North St.
127 rooms - $44-59
Pets: Welcome w/permission
Creature Comforts: CCTV, a/c, cont. brkfst, pool

STEUBENVILLE
Holiday Inn
(800) HOLIDAY, (740) 282-0901
http://www.holiday-inn.com
1401 University Blvd.
120 rooms - $55-75
Pets: Welcome
Creature Comforts: CCTV, a/c, restaurant, pool

STOW
Stow Inn
(330) 688-3508
4601 Darrow Rd.
33 rooms - $65-87
Pets: Welcome
Creature Comforts: CCTV, a/c, refrig, micro

STRONGSVILLE
Days Inn
(800) DAYS INN, (440) 234-3575
http://www.daysinn.com
9029 Pearl Rd.
40 rooms - $45-69
Pets: Welcome w/$5 fee
Creature Comforts: CCTV, a/c, cont. brkfst

Red Roof Inn
(800) THE ROOF, (440) 238-0170
http://www.redroof.com
15385 Royalton Rd.
110 rooms - $50-77
Pets: Small pets welcome
Creature Comforts: CCTV, a/c

TOLEDO
Clarion Hotel Westgate
(800) CLARION, (419) 535-7070
http://www.clarioninn.com
3536 Secor Rd.
305 rooms - $75-275
Pets: Welcome w/$75 fee
Creature Comforts: CCTV, a/c, refrig, Jacuzzis, restaurant, pool

Comfort Inn Westgate
(800) 228-5150, (419) 531-2666
http://www.comfortinn.com
3560 Secor Rd.
70 rooms - $55-69
Pets: Small pets w/$50 deposit
Creature Comforts: CCTV, a/c, cont. brkfst

Crowne Plaza
(800) HOLIDAY, (419) 241-1411
http://www.holiday-inn.com
2 Seagate/Summit St.
240 rooms - $65-89
Pets: Welcome w/$25 deposit
Creature Comforts: CCTV, a/c, restaurant, pool, hlth club, whirlpool

Holiday Inn
(800) HOLIDAY, (419) 865-1361
http://www.holiday-inn.com
2340 S. Reynolds Rd.
220 rooms - $90-120
Pets: Welcome
Creature Comforts: CCTV, a/c, restaurant, pool, hlth club

Motel 6
(800) 4-MOTEL6, (419) 865-2308
http://www.motel6.com
5335 Heatherdowns Blvd.
100 rooms - $35-40
Pets: Under 30 lbs. welcome
Creature Comforts: CCTV, a/c

Radisson Inn
(800) 333-3333, (419) 241-3000
http://www.radisson.com
1010 S. Summit St.
400 rooms - $80-120
Pets: Under 50 lbs. welcome
Creature Comforts: CCTV, a/c, restaurant, hlth club

Ramada
(800) 2-Ramada, (419) 381-8765
http://www.ramada.com
2429 S. Reynolds Rd.
255 rooms - $80-99
Pets: Small pets welcome
Creature Comforts: CCTV, a/c, refrig, micro, restaurant, pool

Red Roof Inn
(800) THE ROOF, (419) 536-0118
http://www.redroof.com
3530 Executive Pkwy.
120 rooms - $60-80
Pets: Small pets welcome
Creature Comforts: CCTV, a/c

TROY
Holiday Inn
(800) HOLIDAY, (937) 332-1700
http://www.holiday-inn.com
60 Troy Town Rd.
66 rooms - $70-99
Pets: Welcome
Creature Comforts: CCTV, a/c, refrig, cont. brkfst, pool, hlth club

Knights Inn
(800) 843-5644, (937) 339-1515
http://www.knightsinn.com
30 Troy Town Rd.
85 rooms - $45-59
Pets: Small pets welcome
Creature Comforts: CCTV, a/c, refrig, micro

Motel 6
(800) 4-MOTEL6, (937) 335-0013
http://www.motel6.com
1210 Brukner Dr.
81 rooms - $30-35
Pets: Under 30 lbs. welcome
Creature Comforts: CCTV, a/c

Quality Inn/Suites
(800) 228-5151, (937) 335-0021
http://www.qualityinn.com
1375 W. Route 55
95 rooms - $55-115
Pets: Small pets w/travel crate
Creature Comforts: CCTV, a/c, refrig, Jacuzzi, restaurant, pool

Residence Inn
(800) 331-3131, (937) 440-9303
http://www.residenceinn.com
87 Troy Town Dr.
96 rooms - $69-99
Pets: Welcome w/$100-200 fee
Creature Comforts: CCTV, a/c,
kitchen, cont. brkfst, pool, hlth clb

URBANA
Logan Lodge Motel
(937) 652-2188
2551 Rte. 68
30 rooms - $60-70
Pets: Welcome w/$15 fee
Creature Comforts: CCTV, a/c

VANDALIA
Park Inn International
(800)437-PARK,(937) 898-8321
75 Corporate Center Dr.
100 rooms - $40-80
Pets: Small pets welcome
Creature Comforts: CCTV, a/c,
kit, pool, hlth club

VAN WERT
Days Inn
(800) DAYS INN, (419) 238-5222
http://www.daysinn.com
820 N. Washington St.
79 rooms - $45-90
Pets: Welcome
Creature Comforts: CCTV, a/c,
cont. brkfst, restaurant, pool

Lodge Keeper
(419) 238-3700
875 N. Washington St.
50 rooms - $45-55
Pets: Small pets welcome
Creature Comforts: CCTV, a/c,
pool

VERMILION
Holiday Inn Express
(800) HOLIDAY, (440) 967-8770
http://www.holiday-inn.com
2417 Rte. 60
68 rooms - $90-139
Pets: Under 40 lbs. w/$40 dep.
Creature Comforts: CCTV, a/c,
refrig, cont. brkfst, pool, hlth club

WAPAKONETA
Days Inn
(800) DAYS INN, (419) 738-2184
http://www.daysinn.com
1659 Bellefontaine St.
80 rooms - $55-94
Pets: Welcome w/$10 fee
Creature Comforts: CCTV, a/c,
kit, cont. brkfst, pool

Holiday Inn
(800) HOLIDAY, (419) 738-8181
http://www.holiday-inn.com
I-75 & Bellefontaine St.
100 rooms - $60-99
Pets: Welcome
Creature Comforts: CCTV, a/c,
refrig, restaurant, cont. brkfst,
pool, hlth club

Super 8 Motel
(800) 800-8000, (419) 738-8810
http://www.super8.com
1011 Lunar Dr.
38 rooms - $44-56
Pets: Welcome w/permission
Creature Comforts: CCTV, a/c,
kit, Jacuzzi, cont. brkfst

WARREN
Best Western Downtown
(800) 528-1234, (330) 392-2515
http://www.bestwestern.com
777 Mahoning Ave.
105 rooms - $55-75
Pets: Welcome
Creature Comforts: CCTV, a/c,
Jacuzzis, cont. brkfst, pool

Park Hotel
(330) 393-1200
136 N. Park Ave.
56 rooms - $60-129
Pets: Welcome w/$100 deposit
Creature Comforts: CCTV, a/c,
refrig, micro, restaurant, Jacuzzis,
cont. brkfst

WARRENSVILLE
Days Inn
(800) DAYS INN, (216) 662-9200
http://www.daysinn.com
4511 Northfield Rd.
87 rooms - $40-56
Pets: Welcome
Creature Comforts: CCTV, a/c,
cont. brkfst

WARRENSVILLE HEIGHTS
Econo Lodge
(800) 55-ECONO, (216) 475-4070
http://www.econolodge.com
4353 Northfield Rd.
80 rooms - $40-70
Pets: Welcome
Creature Comforts: CCTV, a/c

WASHINGTON COURT HSE
Knights Inn
(800) 843-5644, (740) 335-9133
http://www.knightsinn.com
1820 Columbus Ave.
55 rooms - $42-60
Pets: Welcome
Creature Comforts: CCTV, a/c,
refrig, micro, kit

WAUSEON
Arrowhead Motel
(419) 335-5811
8225 Rte. 108
35 rooms - $36-58
Pets: Welcome
Creature Comforts: CCTV, a/c

WESTERVILLE
The College Inn
(888) 794-3090, (614) 794-3090
63 W. College Rd.
3 rooms - $75-90
Pets: Welcome w/permission
Creature Comforts: 1870's
Victorian, CCTV, a/c, full brkfst

Knights Inn Westerville
(800) 843-5644, (614) 890-0426
http://www.knightsinn.com
32 Heatherdown Dr.
109 rooms - $30-165
Pets: Welcome
Creature Comforts: CCTV, a/c,
kit, pool

WESTLAKE
Red Roof Inn
(800) THE ROOF, (440) 892-7920
http://www.redroof.com
29595 Clemens Rd.
100 rooms - $65-85
Pets: Small pets welcome
Creature Comforts: CCTV, a/c

Residence Inn
(800) 331-3131, (440) 892-2254
http://www.residenceinn.com
30100 Clemens Rd.
105 rooms - $140-180
Pets: Welcome w/$200 fee
Creature Comforts: CCTV, a/c,
kit, cont. brkfst, pool, hlth clb
access

WHEELERSBURG
Comfort Inn/Oregon
(800) 228-5150, (740) 574-1046
http://www.comfortinn.com
8226 Ohio River Rd.
52 rooms - $58-105
Pets: Welcome
Creature Comforts: CCTV,
VCR, a/c, Jacuzzi, cont. brkfst,
pool

WICKLIFFE
J&L Motel Wickliffe
(440) 944-2000
29508 Euclid Ave.
15 rooms - $50-75
Pets: Welcome
Creature Comforts: CCTV, a/c

WILMINGTON
Holiday Inn Express
(800) HOLIDAY, (937) 382-5858
http://www.holiday-inn.com
155 Holiday Dr.
60 rooms - $60-90
Pets: Under 20 Lbs. welcome
Creature Comforts: CCTV, a/c,
cont brkfst, refrig, hlth club, pool

WOOSTER
Econo Lodge
(800) 55-ECONO, (330) 264-8883
http://www.econolodge.com
2137 E. Lincoln Way
98 rooms - $40-69
Pets: Welcome w/$5 fee
Creature Comforts: CCTV, a/c,
cont. brkfst, restaurant, pool

Super 8 Motel
(800) 800-8000, (330) 264-6211
http://www.super8.com
969 Timken Rd.
44 rooms - $44-80
Pets: Small pets w/$2 fee
Creature Comforts: CCTV, a/c

WORTHINGTON
Clarion Hotel
(800) CLARION, (614) 436-0700
http://www.clarioninn.com
7007 N. High St.
233 rooms - $85-175
Pets: $25 Cleaning fee and a $10
nightly charge
Creature Comforts: CCTV, a/c,
refrig, Jacuzzi, restaurant, sauna,
pool

Red Roof Inn
(800) THE ROOF, (614) 846-3001
http://www.redroof.com
7474 N. High St.
110 rooms - $55-78
Pets: Small pets welcome
Creature Comforts: CCTV, a/c

XENIA
Allendale Garden Inn
(937) 376-8124
38 S. Allison Ave.
89 rooms - $40-45
Pets: Small pets w/$15 fee
Creature Comforts: CCTV, a/c,
refrig, micro

Best Western Regency Inn
(800) 528-1234, (937) 372-9954
http://www.bestwestern.com
600 Little Main St.
20 rooms - $45-59
Pets: Welcome w/$20 deposit
Creature Comforts: CCTV, a/c

YOUNGSTOWN
Best Western Meander Inn
(800) 528-1234, (330) 544-2378
http://www.bestwestern.com
870 N. Canfield-Niles Rd.
57 rooms - $60-87
Pets: Welcome
Creature Comforts: CCTV, a/c,
restaurant, full brkfst

Days Inn
(800) DAYS INN, (330) 759-3410
http://www.daysinn.com
1610 Motor Inn Dr.
136 rooms - $45-86
Pets: Welcome w/$5 fee
Creature Comforts: CCTV, a/c,
cont. brkfst, pool

Super 8 Motel
(800) 800-8000, (330) 759-0040
http://www.super8.com
4250 Belmont Ave.
48 rooms - $42-50
Pets: Welcome w/permission
Creature Comforts: CCTV, a/c,
whirlpool

ZANESVILLE
Best Western Town Inn
(800) 528-1234, (740) 452-4511
http://www.bestwestern.com
135 N 7th St.
60 rooms - $55-129
Pets: Welcome w/$10 fee
Creature Comforts: CCTV, a/c,
cont brkfst, restaurant

Comfort Inn
(800) 228-5150, (740) 454-4144
http://www.comfortinn.com
739 Leona St.500 Monroe St.
92 rooms - $70-210
Pets: Welcome w/$10 fee
Creature Comforts: CCTV, a/c,
Jacuzzi, cont. brkfst, pool, sauna,
whirlpool

Holiday Inn
(800) HOLIDAY, (614) 453-0771
http://www.holiday-inn.com
4645 E. Pike
130 rooms - $70-170
Pets: Small pets welcome
Creature Comforts: CCTV, a/c,
Jacuzzis, restaurant, pool, sauna,
whirlpool, rec. area

Super 8 Motel
(800) 800-8000, (614) 455-3124
http://www.super8.com
2440 National Rd.
62 rooms - $50-65
Pets: Welcome w/permission
Creature Comforts: CCTV, a/c

Oklahoma

ALTUS
Best Western Altus
(800) 528-1234, (580) 482-9300
http://www.bestwestern.com
2804 N. Main St.
100 rooms - $50-80
Pets: Welcome w/$5 fee
Creature Comforts: CCTV, a/c,
refrig, micro, pool, sauna,
whirlpool

Ramada Inn
(800) 2-Ramada, (580) 477-3000
http://www.ramada.com
2515 E. Broadway St.
122 rooms - $50-105
Pets: Welcome w/$10 fee
Creature Comforts: CCTV,
VCR, a/c, refrig, Jacuzzi,
restaurant, pool

ALVA
Ranger Inn
(580) 327-1981
420 E. Oklahoma Blvd.
40 rooms - $35-45
Pets: Welcome in certain rooms
Creature Comforts: CCTV, a/c,
micro

Wharton's Vista Motel
(580) 327-3232
1330 Oklahoma Blvd.
20 rooms - $35-46
Pets: Welcome
Creature Comforts: CCTV, a/c

ARDMORE
Comfort Inn
(800) 228-5150, (580) 226-1250
http://www.comfortinn.com
2700 W. Broadway St.
110 rooms - $55-75
Pets: Small pets welcome
Creature Comforts: CCTV, a/c,
refrig, Jacuzzi, pool, whirlpool

Days Inn, Ardmore
(800) DAYS INN, (580) 223-7976
http://www.daysinn.com
2432 Veterans Blvd.
65 rooms - $40-75
Pets: Small pets w/$5 fee
Creature Comforts: CCTV, a/c

Dorchester Motel
(580) 226-1761
2614 W. Broadway St.
45 rooms - $30-48
Pets: Small pets welcome
Creature Comforts: CCTV, a/c

Holiday Inn
(800) HOLIDAY, (580) 223-7130
http://www.holiday-inn.com
2705 Holiday Dr.
175 rooms - $50-69
Pets: Welcome
Creature Comforts: CCTV, a/c,
refrig, Jacuzzi, restaurant, cont.
brkfst, pool

Lake Murray Resort
(800) 654-8240, (580) 223-7130
3310 S. Lake Murray Dr.
81 cabins - $60-150
Pets: Welcome
Creature Comforts: Lakeside
cottages, lakeside, refrig, micro,
kitchen, restaurant, pool, boating,
swimming, lawn games

Motel 6
(800) 4-MOTEL6, (580) 226-7666
http://www.motel6.com
120 Holiday Dr.
126 rooms - $25-39
Pets: Small pets — 1 per room
Creature Comforts: CCTV,
VCR, a/c, pool

Super 8 Motel
(800) 800-8000, (580) 223-2201
http://www.super8.com
2120 Veterans Blvd.
52 rooms - $30-48
Pets: Welcome w/$5 fee
Creature Comforts: CCTV, a/c,
cont. brkfst

ATOKA
Best Western Atoka Inn
(800) 528-1234, (580) 889-7381
http://www.bestwestern.com
2101 S. Mississippi
55 rooms - $50-75
Pets: Small pets welcome
Creature Comforts: CCTV, a/c,
refrig, micro, restaurant, pool,
whirlpool

BARTLESVILLE
Best Western
(800) 528-1234, (918) 335-7755
http://www.bestwestern.com
222 Washington Blvd., SE
112 rooms - $55-85
Pets: Welcome w/approval
Creature Comforts: CCTV, a/c,
refrig, Jacuzzi, restaurant, pool

Holiday Inn
(800) HOLIDAY, (918) 333-8320
http://www.holiday-inn.com
1410 Washington Blvd., SE
105 rooms - $48-85
Pets: Small pets welcome
Creature Comforts: CCTV, a/c,
refrig, micro, Jacuzzi, restaurant,
pool, hlth clb, sauna, whirlpool

Super 8 Motel
(800) 800-8000, (918) 335-1122
http://www.super8.com
211 SE Washington Blvd.
40 rooms - $45-75
Pets: Welcome
Creature Comforts: CCTV, a/c,
Jacuzzi, restaurant, whirlpool

BLACKWELL
Comfort Inn
(800) 228-5150, (580) 363-7000
http://www.comfortinn.com
1201 N. 44th St.
60 rooms - $50-75
Pets: Welcome w/$10 fee
Creature Comforts: CCTV, a/c,
pool

Days Inn
(800) DAYS INN, (580) 363-2911
http://www.daysinn.com
4302 W. Doolin Rd.
50 rooms - $40-75
Pets: Welcome
Creature Comforts: CCTV, a/c, micro, pool

BROKEN ARROW
Econo Lodge
(800) 55-ECONO, (918) 258-6617
http://www.econolodge.com
1401 N. Elm St.
40 rooms - $40-55
Pets: In smoking rooms w/$5 fee
Creature Comforts: CCTV, a/c

Holiday Inn, South
(800) HOLIDAY, (918) 258-7085
http://www.holiday-inn.com
2600 N. Aspen Rd.
200 rooms - $60-89
Pets: Welcome
Creature Comforts: CCTV, a/c, refrig, Jacuzzi, restaurant, pool, hlth clb

BROKEN BOW
End of the Trail Motel
(580) 584-3350
N. Park St.
16 rooms - $25-38
Pets: Welcome
Creature Comforts: CCTV, a/c

CHANDLER
Econo Lodge
(800) 55 ECONO, (580) 258-2131
http://www.econolodge.com
600 North Price Rd.
41 rooms - $48-55
Pets: Welcome
Creature Comforts: CCTV, a/c, restaurant, pool

CHECOTAH
Best Western La Donna
(800) 528-1234, (918) 473-2376
http://www.bestwestern.com
Route 40
50 rooms - $40-69
Pets: Welcome
Creature Comforts: CCTV, a/c, pool

Sharpe House B&B
(918) 473-2832
301 NW Second St.
3 rooms - $50-60
Pets: Polite pets welcome
Creature Comforts: Columned house, recently redecorated, family collectibles, CCTV, a/c, fireplace, full brkfst

CHICKASHA
Best Western
(800) 528-1234, (405) 224-4890
http://www.bestwestern.com
2101 South Fourth St.
158 rooms - $40-75
Pets: Small pets welcome
Creature Comforts: CCTV, a/c, pool, whirlpool

Days Inn
(800) DAYS INN, (405) 222-5800
http://www.daysinn.com
2701 South Fourth St.
90 rooms - $35-75
Pets: Small pets welcome
Creature Comforts: CCTV, VCR, a/c, refrig, micro, restaurant, pool

CLAREMORE
Best Western
(800) 528-1234, (918) 341-4410
http://www.bestwestern.com
940 S. Lynn Riggs
52 rooms - $50-80
Pets: Welcome
Creature Comforts: CCTV, a/c, pool

Days Inn
(800) DAYS INN, (918) 343-3297
http://www.daysinn.com
Hwy 66 and Country Club Dr.
65 rooms - $45-75
Pets: Welcome w/$5 fee
Creature Comforts: CCTV, a/c, refrig, cont. brkfst, pool

Motel Claremore
(918) 341-3254
812 E. Will Rogers Blvd.
15 rooms - $35-46
Pets: Small dogs welcome
Creature Comforts: CCTV, a/c

CLINTON
Best Western Tradewinds
(800) 528-1234, (580) 323-2610
http://www.bestwestern.com
2128 Gary Blvd.
70 rooms - $40-75
Pets: Welcome
Creature Comforts: CCTV, a/c, refrig, restaurant, pool, whirlpool

DEL CITY
La Quinta
(800) Nu-Rooms, (405) 672-0067
http://www.laquinta.com
5501 Tinker Diagonal Rd.
105 rooms - $50-80
Pets: Small pets welcome
Creature Comforts: CCTV, a/c, pool

DUNCAN
Duncan Inn
(580) 252-5210
3402 N. Rte. 81
93 rooms - $30-44
Pets: Welcome
Creature Comforts: CCTV, a/c, pool

Holiday Inn
(800) HOLIDAY, (580) 252-1500
http://www.holiday-inn.com
1015 Rte. 81
138 rooms - $45-69
Pets: Welcome
Creature Comforts: CCTV, VCR, a/c, restaurant, pool

DURANT

Best Western Markita Inn
(800) 528-1234, (580) 924-7676
http://www.bestwestern.com
2401 W. Main St.
62 rooms - $45-90
Pets: Small pets welcome
Creature Comforts: CCTV, a/c, pool

Holiday Inn
(800) HOLIDAY, (580) 924-5432
http://www.holiday-inn.com
2121 W. Main St.
81 rooms - $60-75
Pets: Welcome w/$10 fee
Creature Comforts: CCTV, a/c, refrig, micro, restaurant, pool

EDMUND

Ramada Plaza
(800) 2-Ramada, (405) 341-3577
http://www.ramada.com
930 E. Second St.
141 rooms - $80-100
Pets: Welcome w/$15 fee
Creature Comforts: CCTV, a/c, refrig, micro, restaurant, full brkfst, pool, whirlpool

EL RENO

Best Western Hensley's
(800) 528-1234, (405) 262-6490
http://www.bestwestern.com
Rte. 40 & Country Club Dr.
60 rooms - $40-65
Pets: Welcome w/$25 deposit
Creature Comforts: CCTV, a/c, refrig, micro, full brkfst, pool

Days Inn
(800) DAYS INN, (405) 262-8720
http://www.daysinn.com
2700 S. Country Club
50 rooms - $40-65
Pets: Welcome
Creature Comforts: CCTV, a/c, refrig, micro, cont. brkfst, pool

Ramada Hotel
(800) 2-Ramada, (405) 262-1022
http://www.ramada.com
Route 40
43 rooms - $45-80
Pets: Welcome
Creature Comforts: CCTV, a/c, cont. brkfst, pool

Super 8 Motel
(800) 800-8000, (405) 262-8240
http://www.super8.com
2820 Rte. 81 S
50 rooms - $40-55
Pets: Welcome w/$5 fee, $20 dep
Creature Comforts: CCTV, a/c, pool

ELK CITY

Best Western Elk City
(800) 528-1234, (580) 225-2331
http://www.bestwestern.com
2015 W. Third St.
80 rooms - $30-65
Pets: Welcome
Creature Comforts: CCTV, a/c, pool

Days Inn
(800) DAYS INN, (580) 225-9210
http://www.daysinn.com
1100 Rte. 34
110 rooms - $40-80
Pets: Welcome w$5 fee
Creature Comforts: CCTV, a/c, refrig, cont. brkfst, pool

Econo Lodge
(800) 55 ECONO, (580) 225-5120
http://www.econolodge.com
108 Meadow Ridge Rd.
45 rooms - $40-65
Pets: Welcome
Creature Comforts: CCTV, kit

Holiday Inn
(800) HOLIDAY, (580) 225-6637
http://www.holiday-inn.com
Meadow Ridge Rd.
150 rooms - $60-70
Pets: Welcome
Creature Comforts: CCTV, a/c, refrig, Jacuzzi, restaurant, pool, hlth clb, sauna, whirlpool

Knights Inn
(800) 563-5644, (580) 225-2241
http://www.knightsinn.com
2604 E. Route 66
30 rooms - $30-40
Pets: Welcome w/$4 fee
Creature Comforts: CCTV, a/c

Motel 6
(800) 4-MOTEL6, (580) 225-6661
http://www.motel6.com
2500 E. Rte. 66
82 rooms - $25-40
Pets: Under 30 lbs, 1 per room
Creature Comforts: CCTV, a/c, pool

Quality Inn
(800) 228-5151, (580) 225-8140
http://www.qualityinn.com
102 BJ Hughes Access Rd.
50 rooms - $35-60
Pets: Welcome w/$2 fee
Creature Comforts: CCTV, a/c, pool, whirlpool

Ramada Inn
(800) 2-Ramada, (580) 225-0305
http://www.ramada.com
2500 S. Main St.
48 rooms - $33-44
Pets: Small pets w/$5 fee
Creature Comforts: CCTV, a/c, refrig, micro, pool

Super 8 Motel
(800) 800-8000, (580) 225-9430
http://www.super8.com
2801 E. Rte. 66
45 rooms - $38-49
Pets: Welcome
Creature Comforts: CCTV, a/c, refrig, cont. brkfst, pool

Travelodge, Elk City
(800) 578-7878, (580) 243-0150
http://www.travelodge.com
301 Sleepy Hollow Ct.
45 rooms - $30-45
Pets: Welcome
Creature Comforts: CCTV, a/c

ERICK

Comfort Inn
(800) 228-5150, (580) 536-8124
http://www.comfortinn.com
Route 30
50 rooms - $50-80
Pets: Small pets welcome
Creature Comforts: CCTV, cont. brkfst, pool, sauna, whirlpool

Days Inn
(800) DAYS INN, (580) 526-3315
http://www.daysinn.com
Route 80
32 rooms - $40-55
Pets: Welcome w/$3 fee
Creature Comforts: CCTV, a/c

ENID

Holiday Inn
(800) HOLIDAY, (580) 237-6000
http://www.holiday-inn.com
2901 S. VanBuren Ave.
150 rooms - $40-75
Pets: Small pets welcome
Creature Comforts: CCTV, a/c,
restaurant, pool

Ramada Inn
(800) 2-Ramada, (580) 234-0440
http://www.ramada.com
3005 Owen K. Garriott Rd.
125 rooms - $45-65
Pets: Welcome w/$4 fee
Creature Comforts: CCTV,
VCR, a/c, refrig, micro, restaurant,
cont. brkfst, pool, hlth clb

EUFALA

Days Inn
(800) DAYS INN, (918) 689-3999
http://www.daysinn.com
120 rooms - $46-60
Pets: Welcome w/$5 fee
Creature Comforts: New
construction on Lake Eufala,
CCTV, a/c, cont. brkfst

FREDERICK

Scottish Inns
(800) 251-1962, (580) 335-2129
1015 S. Main St.
45 rooms - $28-35
Pets: Welcome w/$4 fee
Creature Comforts: CCTV, a/c

GLENPOOL

Best Western Glenpool
(800) 528-1234, (918) 322-5201
http://www.bestwestern.com
14831 S. Casper St.
64 rooms - $45-70
Pets: Small pets welcome
Creature Comforts: CCTV, a/c,
cont. brkfst, pool

GORE

Fin and Feather Resort
(918) 487-5148
Route 1
80 rooms - $55-150
Pets: Welcome
Creature Comforts: CCTV, a/c,
kit, restaurant, cont. brkfst, pool,
whirlpool, ext. recreation facilities

GUTHRIE

Best Western Territorial
(800) 528-1234, (405) 282-8831
http://www.bestwestern.com
2323 Territorial Tr.
84 rooms - $40-60
Pets: Small pets welcome
Creature Comforts: CCTV, a/c,
restaurant, pool

Harrison House Inn
(800) 375-1001, (405) 282-1000
124 W. Harrison St.
30 rooms - $75-125
Pets: Small pets welcome
Creature Comforts: 1893 Nat'l
Historic Register inn, period
antiques, brass fixtures, period
wallpapers, restaurant, cont. brkfst

GUYMON

Best Western Townsman Inn
(800) 528-1234, (580) 338-6556
http://www.bestwestern.com
212 NE Rte. 54
75 rooms - $50-65
Pets: Small pets welcome
Creature Comforts: CCTV, a/c,
refrig, micro, Jacuzzi, 2 pools,
health club, whirlpool

Econo Lodge
(800) 55 ECONO, (580) 338-5431
http://www.econolodge.com
923 Rte. 54 East
40 rooms - $40-60
Pets: Small pets w/$3 fee
Creature Comforts: CCTV, a/c

Super 8 Motel
(800) 800-8000, (580) 338-0507
http://www.super8.com
1201 Rte. 54 E.
59 rooms - $45-59
Pets: Welcome
Creature Comforts: CCTV, a/c,
cont. brkfst, whirlpool

HENRYETTA

Gateway Inn Motel
(918) 652-4448
Route 75
40 rooms - $30-45
Pets: Welcome w/$25 deposit
Creature Comforts: CCTV, a/c,
pool

Guesthouse Inn and Dome
(800) 21 GUEST, (918) 652-2581
810 Trudgeon St.
85 rooms - $50-75
Pets: Welcome
Creature Comforts: CCTV, a/c,
refrig, micro, Jacuzzi, restaurant,
pool, hlth clb, sauna, whirlpool

KINGSTON

Lake Texoma Resort
(800) 654-8240, (580) 564-2311
http://www.otrd.state.ok.us
Box 41
27 cabins - $65-100
Pets: Welcome in cabins
Creature Comforts: CCTV, a/c,
kit, fireplace, restaurant, pool,
tennis, volleyball, golf

LAWTON

Best Western Sandpiper
(800) 528-1234, (580) 353-0310
http://www.bestwestern.com
2202 Rte. 277 & Rte. 281 N.
125 rooms - $40-79
Pets: Welcome w/$5 fee
Creature Comforts: CCTV,
VCR, a/c, refrig, restaurant, pool

Holiday Inn
(800) HOLIDAY, (580) 353-1682
http://www.holiday-inn.com
3134 Cache Rd.
175 rooms - $50-90
Pets: Small pets welcome
Creature Comforts: CCTV, a/c,
refrig, micro, Jacuzzi, restaurant,
pool

Howard Johnson
(800) I-Go-Hojo, (580) 353-0200
http://www.hojo.com
1125 Gore Blvd.
145 rooms - $45-65
Pets: Small pets w/$25 fee
Creature Comforts: CCTV, a/c,
refrig, micro, Jacuzzi, restaurant, 2
pools, hlth clb, sauna

Ramada Inn
(800) 2-Ramada, (580) 355-7155
http://www.ramada.com
601 N. 2nd St., NW
100 rooms - $40-70
Pets: Small pets w/$15 fee
Creature Comforts: CCTV, a/c,
restaurant, pool

LONE WOLF
Quartz Mountain Inn
(800) 654-8240, (580) 563-2424
Route 1
15 cottages - $50-88
Pets: Welcome
Creature Comforts: Cottage
resort on 6,200 acre Lake Altus,
state park run, hiking, fishing,
boating

MCALESTER
Comfort Inn
(800) 228-5150, (918) 426-0115
http://www.comfortinn.com
1415 George Nigh Exp.
58 rooms - $45-75
Pets: Welcome
Creature Comforts: CCTV, a/c,
refrig, micro, restaurant, cont.
brkfst, pool

Days Inn
(800) DAYS INN, (918) 426-5050
http://www.daysinn.com
1217 S. George Nigh Exp.
100 rooms - $50-70
Pets: Welcome w/$5 fee
Creature Comforts: CCTV, a/c,
refrig, restaurant, cont. brkfst, pool

Holiday Inn
(800) HOLIDAY, (918) 465-4329
http://www.holiday-inn.com
Rte. 69 Bypass
160 rooms - $50-100
Pets: Welcome
Creature Comforts: CCTV, a/c,
restaurant, pool, hlth clb, sauna,
whirlpool, putting green

Super 8
(800) 800-8000, (918) 426-5400
http://www.super8.com
2400 S. Main St.
35 rooms - $30-50
Pets: Small pets welcome
Creature Comforts: CCTV, a/c,
refrig, restaurant, pool

MIAMI
Best Western Inn
(800) 528-1234, (918) 542-6681
http://www.bestwestern.com
2225 E. Steve Owens Blvd.
80 rooms - $40-70
Pets: Small pets welcome
Creature Comforts: CCTV, a/c,
refrig, restaurant, pool

MIDWEST CITY
Comfort Inn
(800) 228-5150, (405) 733-1339
http://www.comfortinn.com
5653 Tinker Diagonal Rd.
145 rooms - $55-70
Pets: Small pets w/$25 deposit
Creature Comforts: CCTV,
VCR, a/c, refrig, micro, pool

Holiday Inn, East
(800) HOLIDAY, (405) 737-4481
http://www.holiday-inn.com
5701 Tinker Diagonal Rd.
160 rooms - $50-70
Pets: Small pets w/$25 deposit
Creature Comforts: CCTV, a/c,
restaurant, pool, hlth clb access,
sauna, whirlpool

Motel 6
(800) 4-MOTEL6, (405) 737-6676
http://www.motel6.com
5701 Tinker Diagonal Rd.
93 rooms - $35-49
Pets: Under 30 lbs. welcome
Creature Comforts: CCTV, a/c,
pool

Super 8
(800) 800-8000, (405) 737-8880
http://www.super8.com
6821 SE 29th St.
42 rooms - $42-55
Pets: Welcome w/permission
Creature Comforts: CCTV, a/c

MOORE
Best Western Crossroads
(800) 528-1234, (405) 794-6611
http://www.bestwestern.com
2600 N. Broadway Rd.
80 rooms - $45-65
Pets: Welcome
Creature Comforts: CCTV, a/c,
restaurant, pool

Days Inn
(800) DAYS INN, (405) 794-5070
http://www.daysinn.com
1701 N. Moore Ave.
50 rooms - $40-50
Pets: Welcome w/$10 fee
Creature Comforts: CCTV, a/c,
refrig, pool

Motel 6
(800) 4-MOTEL6, (405) 799-6616
http://www.motel6.com
1417 N. Moore Ave.
120 rooms - $25-35
Pets: Small pets welcome
Creature Comforts: CCTV, a/c,
pool

Super 8 Motel
(800) 800-8000, (405) 794-4030
http://www.super8motel.com
1520 N. Service Rd.
40 rooms - $45-50
Pets: Welcome w/$8 fee, $25 dep.
Creature Comforts: CCTV, a/c,
Jacuzzi, cont. brkfst

MUSKOGEE
Best Western Tradewinds
(800) 528-1234, (918) 683-2951
http://www.bestwestern.com
534 S. 32nd St.
115 rooms - $40-50
Pets: Small pets w/$5 fee
Creature Comforts: CCTV, a/c,
refrig, micro, pool

Days Inn
(800) DAYS-INN, (918) 683-3911
http://www.daysinn.com
900 S. 32nd St.
45 rooms - $40-56
Pets: Small pets w/$5 fee
Creature Comforts: CCTV, a/c,
refrig, micro, pool

Muskogee Inn
(918) 683-6551
2300 E. Shawnee Rd.
125 rooms - $40-75
Pets: Small pets welcome
Creature Comforts: CCTV, ac,
pool

Ramada Inn
(800) 2-Ramada, (918) 682-4341
http://www.ramada.com
800 S. 32nd St.
140 rooms - $50-65
Pets: Welcome
Creature Comforts: CCTV, a/c,
refrig, restaurant, health club,
pool, sauna

NORMAN

Days Inn
(800) DAYS INN, (405) 360-4380
http://www.daysinn.com
609 N. Interstate
75 rooms - $40-50
Pets: Welcome w/$10 deposit
Creature Comforts: CCTV, a/c,
refrig, micro, pool, whirlpool

Econo Lodge
(800) 55 ECONO, (405) 364-5554
http://www.econolodge.com
100- 26th Dr., SW
44 rooms - $45-65
Pets: Welcome
Creature Comforts: CCTV, a/c,
cont. brkfst

Guest Inns
(405) 360-1234
2543 W. Main St.
110 rooms - $40-55
Pets: Welcome w/$10 fee
Creature Comforts: CCTV, a/c,
refrig, micro, pool

Residence Inn
(800) 331-3131, (405) 366-0900
http://www.residenceinn.com
2681 Jefferson St.
125 rms/suites - $80-120
Pets: Welcome w/$75 deposit
Creature Comforts: CCTV,
VCR, a/c, kit, pool, whirlpool

Stratford House Motel
(405) 329-7194
225 N. Interstate Dr.
40 rooms - $49-60
Pets: Welcome
Creature Comforts: CCTV, a/c,
refrig, Jacuzzi, cont. brkfst, pool

OKLAHOMA CITY

Best Western Saddleback
(800) 528-1234, (405) 947-7000
http://www.bestwestern.com
4300 SW Third St.
220 rooms - $65-85
Pets: Small pets w/$20 deposit
Creature Comforts: CCTV, a/c,
restaurant, cont. brkfst, pool, hlth
clb, sauna, whirlpool

Best Western Tradewinds
(800) 528-1234, (405) 235-4531
http://www.bestwestern.com
1800 E. Reno Rd.
200 rooms - $50-88
Pets: Small pets welcome
Creature Comforts: CCTV, a/c,
refrig, restaurant, pool

Carlyle Motel
(405) 946-3355
3600 NW 39th Exp.
25 rooms - $25-40
Pets: Small pets w/$5 fee
Creature Comforts: CCTV, a/c

Clarion Hotel, Airport
(800) CLARION, (405) 942-8511
http://www.clarioninn.com
801 S. Meridian Rd.
322 rooms - $68-85
Pets: Welcome
Creature Comforts: CCTV, a/c,
restaurant, cont. brkfst, pool, hlth
clb, sauna, whirlpool

Clarion Hotel/Conf. Center
(800) CLARION, (405) 528-2741
http://www.clarioninn.com
4345 N. Lincoln Blvd.
70 rooms - $70-110
Pets: Welcome
Creature Comforts: CCTV,
VCR, a/c, refrig, micro, kit,
Jacuzzi, restaurant, cont. brkfst,
pool, tennis

Comfort Inn
(800) 228-5150, (405) 947-0038
http://www.comfortinn.com
4017 NW 39th Exp.
115 rooms - $40-75
Pets: Welcome
Creature Comforts: CCTV,
VCR, a/c, refrig, micro, kit, cont.
brkfst, pool, hlth clb access, sauna,
whirlpool

Comfort Inn, East
(800) 228-5150, (405) 733-1339
http://www.comfortinn.com
5653 Tinker Diagonal Rd.
145 rooms - $58-80
Pets: Welcome
Creature Comforts: CCTV, a/c,
refrig, micro, restaurant, cont.
brkfst, pool, hlth clb

Comfort Inn, North
(800) 228-5150, (405) 528-6511
http://www.comfortinn.com
4445 N. Lincoln Blvd.
240 rooms - $60-85
Pets: Welcome
Creature Comforts: CCTV, a/c,
restaurant, pool, tennis

Comfort Inn and Suites
(800) 228-5150, (405) 943-4400
http://www.comfortinn.com
4240 W. I-40 Service Rd.
90 rooms - $65-87
Pets: Welcome
Creature Comforts: CCTV, a/c,
cont. brkfst, pool

Days Inn, Airport
(800) DAYS INN, (405) 947-8721
http://www.daysinn.com
4712 W. Rte 40
254 rooms - $43-72
Pets: Welcome
Creature Comforts: CCTV, a/c,
restaurant, cont. brkfst, pool

Days Inn
(800) DAYS INN, (405) 946-0741
http://www.daysinn.com
2801 NW 39th St.
117 rooms - $40-175
Pets: Welcome
Creature Comforts: CCTV, a/c,
restaurant, pool, tennis

Days Inn, South
(800) DAYS INN, (405) 677-0521
http://www.daysinn.com
2616 Rte. 35 S.
152 rooms - $46-175
Pets: Welcome w/$15 fee
Creature Comforts: CCTV, a/c,
restaurant, cont. brkfst, pool,
putting green, golf access

Econo Lodge
(800) 55 ECONO, (405) 787-7051
http://www.econolodge.com
8200 W. Rte. 40 Service Rd.
55 rooms - $34-55
Pets: Welcome
Creature Comforts: CCTV,
VCR, a/c, pool

Econo Lodge, Airport
(800) 55-ECONO, (405) 947-8651
http://www.econolodge.com
820 S. McArthur Blvd.
100 rooms - $35-40
Pets: Welcome
Creature Comforts: CCTV,
VCR, a/c, restaurant, pool

Embassy Suites
(800) 362-2779, (405) 682-6000
http://www.embassy-suites.com
1815 S. Merdian Ave.
235rooms - $99-150
Pets: Small pets welcome
Creature Comforts: CCTV, a/c,
refrig, micro, kit, Jacuzzi,
restaurant, pool, hlth clb, sauna,
whirlpool

Fifth Season Motor Inn
(405) 843-5558
6200 N. Robinson Rd.
200 rooms - $70-100
Pets: Small pets welcome
Creature Comforts: CCTV, a/c,
refrig, micro, Jacuzzi, restaurant,
pool, hlth clb access, sauna,
whirlpool

Hilton Inn, NW
(800) HILTONS, (405) 848-4811
http://www.hilton.com
2945 NW Exp.
215 rooms - $100-150
Pets: Small pets w/$15 fee
Creature Comforts: CCTV,
VCR, a/c, refrig, Jacuzzi,
restaurant, cont. brkfst, pool, hlth
clb, sauna, whirlpool

Holiday Inn, Express
(800) HOLIDAY, (405) 942-8544
http://www.holiday-inn.com
737 S. Meridian
160 rooms - $60-79
Pets: Small pets welcome
Creature Comforts: CCTV, a/c,
refrig, cont. brkfst, pool, hlth clb,
sauna, whirlpool

Holiday Inn, North
(800) HOLIDAY, (405) 478-0400
http://www.holiday-inn.com
12001 NE Expressway
210 rooms - $65-88
Pets: Small pets welcome
Creature Comforts: CCTV, a/c,
restaurant, cont. brkfst, 2 pools,
hlth clb, sauna, whirlpool

Holiday Inn
(800) HOLIDAY, (405) 685-4000
http://www.holiday-inn.com
2101 S. Meridian Rd.
245 rooms - $65-85
Pets: Small pets welcome
Creature Comforts: CCTV, a/c,
restaurant, pool, hlth clb, sauna,
whirlpool

Howard Johnson
(800) I-Go-Hojo, (405) 677-0551
http://www.hojo.com
1629 S. Prospect St.
60 rooms - $35-45
Pets: Welcome w/$25 deposit
Creature Comforts: CCTV, a/c,
pool

Howard Johnson
(800) I-Go-Hojo, (405) 943-9841
http://www.hojo.com
400 S. Meridian Ave.
75 rooms - $50-68
Pets: Welcome
Creature Comforts: CCTV, a/c,
refrig, cont. brkfst, pool

La Quinta, South
(800) Nu-Rooms, (405) 631-8661
http://www.laquinta.com
8315 Rte. 35 S.
120 rooms - $50-69
Pets: Small pets welcome
Creature Comforts: CCTV, a/c,
cont. brkfst, pool

La Quinta, Airport
(800) Nu-Rooms, (405) 942-0040
http://www.laquinta.com
800 S. Meridian Rd.
170 rooms - $60-85
Pets: Welcome
Creature Comforts: CCTV, a/c,
restaurant, pool

Motel 6
(800) 4-MOTEL6, (405) 478-4030
http://www.motel6.com
12121 NE Expressway
98 rooms - $30-49
Pets: Under 30 lbs. welcome
Creature Comforts: CCTV, a/c,
pool

Motel 6, Airport
(800) 4-MOTEL6, (405) 946-6662
http://www.motel6.com
820 S. Meridian Rd.
130 rooms - $30-49
Pets: Under 30 lbs. welcome
Creature Comforts: CCTV, a/c,
pool

Motel 6, West
(800) 4-MOTEL6, (405) 947-6550
http://www.motel6.com
4200 W. Rte. 40
119 rooms - $35-49
Pets: Under 30 lbs welcome
Creature Comforts: CCTV, a/c,
pool, whirlpool

Marriott, Oklahoma City
(800) 228-9290, (405) 842-6633
http://www.marriott.com
3233 NW Expressway
355 rooms - $90-165
Pets: Small pets welcome
Creature Comforts: CCTV,
VCR, a/c, refrig, restaurant, pool,
hlth clb, sauna, whirlpool

Ramada Inn, Airport
(800) 2-Ramada, (405) 947-2351
http://www.ramada.com
3535 NW 39th Exp.
160 rooms - $50-80
Pets: Welcome
Creature Comforts: CCTV, a/c,
refrig, rstaurant, pool

Ramada Plaza
(800) 2-Ramada, (405) 341-3577
http://www.ramada.com
9320 E. Second St.
145 rooms - $70-100
Pets: Welcome w/$15 fee
Creature Comforts: CCTV, a/c,
refrig, restaurant, pool, hlth clb,
whirlpool

Residence Inn
(800) 331-3131, (405) 942-4500
http://www.residenceinn.com
4361 W. Reno Rd.
135 rooms - $100-130
Pets: Welcome w/$50 deposit
Creature Comforts: CCTV,
VCR, a/c, kit, pool, hlth clb,
sauna, whirlpool

Richmond Suites
(800) 843-1440, (405) 840-1440
1600 NW Exp.
50 rooms - $75-125
Pets: Welcome
Creature Comforts: CCTV,
VCR, a/c, refrig, micro, rstaurant,
pool, hlth clb access

Super 8
(800) 800-8000, (405) 947-7801
http://www.super8.com
6000 N. Bryant St.
70 rooms - $35-58
Pets: Welcome w/$25 deposit
Creature Comforts: CCTV, a/c

Quality Inn, North
(800) 228-5151, (405) 528-2741
http://www.qualityinn.com
4070 Market St.
213 rooms - $55-77
Pets: Welcome
Creature Comforts: CCTV, a/c,
Jacuzzi, restaurant, pool, sauna,
whirlpool

Quality Inn Southwest
(800) 228-5151, (405) 632-6666
http://www.qualityinn.com
7800 C.A. Henderson Blvd.
110 rooms - $55-69
Pets: Welcome
Creature Comforts: CCTV, a/c,
cont. brkfst, pool

OKMULGEE
Best Western Inn
(800) 528-1234, (918) 756-9200
http://www.bestwestern.com
3499 N. Wood Dr.
50 rooms/suites - $55-75
Pets: Small pets welcome
Creature Comforts: CCTV,
VCR, a/c, refrig, Jacuzzi,
restaurant, cont. brkfst, pool

Days Inn
(800) DAYS INN, (918) 758-0660
http://www.daysinn.com
1221 S. Wood Dr.
30 rooms - $20-30
Pets: Welcome
Creature Comforts: CCTV, a/c

PAULS VALLEY
Amish Inn Motel
(405) 238-7545
Route 19
30 rooms - $25-39
Pets: Welcome
Creature Comforts: CCTV, a/c

Days Inn
(800) DAYS INN, (405) 238-7548
http://www.daysinn.com
Route 19
55 rooms - $40-65
Pets: Welcome w/$10 deposit
Creature Comforts: CCTV, a/c,
refrig, micro

Four Sands West Motel
(405) 238-6416
Route 19
55 rooms - $45-59
Pets: Small pets welcome
Creature Comforts: CCTV, a/c,
refrig, micro, pool

PERRY
Best Western Cherokee Strip
(800) 528-1234, (405) 336-2218
http://www.bestwestern.com
Route 77
90 rooms - $50-85
Pets: Small pets w/$25 deposit
Creature Comforts: CCTV, a/c,
restaurant, pool

Dan-D-Motel
(405) 336-4463
515 Fir St.
25 rooms - $20-32
Pets: Welcome
Creature Comforts: CCTV, a/c,
refrig, pool

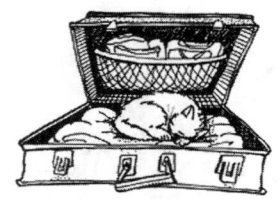

PONCA CITY
Rose Stone B&B
(800) 763-9922, (580) 765-5699
120 S. Third St.
28 rooms - $65-80
Pets: Welcome
Creature Comforts: Luxury
hotel in historic bank, marble
walls, walnut paneling, traditional
decor, CCTV, VCR, a/c, refrig,
micro, restaurant, full brkfst
served on china, hlth club

POTEAU
Best Western Traders Inn
(800) 528-1234, (918) 647-4001
http://www.bestwestern.com
3111 N. Braodway
56 rooms - $45-75
Pets: Small pets w/$20 fee
Creature Comforts: CCTV, a/c,
restaurant, cont. brkfst, pool,
whirlpool

PRYOR
Days Inn
(800) DAYS INN, (918) 825-7600
http://www.daysinn.com
Rtes. 69 & 69A
53 rooms - $32-55
Pets: Welcome w/$5 fee
Creature Comforts: CCTV, a/c,
refrig, micro, restaurant, cont.
brkfst, pool

PURCELL
Econo Lodge
(800) 55 ECONO, (405) 527-5603
http://www.econolodge.com
2500 Route 74, S.
33 rooms - $40-65
Pets: Welcome w/$4 fee
Creature Comforts: CCTV, a/c,
refrig, restaurant

SALISAW
Best Western Blue Ribbon
(800) 528-1234, (918) 775-6294
http://www.bestwestern.com
706 S. Kerr St.
80 rooms - $45-70
Pets: Welcome w/$5 fee
Creature Comforts: CCTV, a/c,
refrig, micro, restaurant, cont.
brkfst, pool, whirlpool

Days Inn
(800) DAYS INN, (918) 775-4406
http://www.daysinn.com
Route 59
75 rooms - $36-49
Pets: Welcome
Creature Comforts: CCTV, a/c,
refrig

Econo Lodge
(800) 55 ECONO, (918) 775-7981
http://www.econolodge.com
2403 E. Cherokee Rd.
42 rooms - $34-45
Pets: Welcome
Creature Comforts: CCTV, a/c

Super 8
(800) 800-8000, (918) 775-8900
http://www.super8.com
924 S. Kerr St.
97 rooms - $35-49
Pets: Welcome w/permission
Creature Comforts: CCTV, a/c,
pool

SAPULPA
Super 8
(800) 800-8000, (918) 227-3300
http://www.super8.com
1505 New Sapulpa Rd.
60 rooms - $35-49
Pets: Welcome
Creature Comforts: CCTV,
VCR, a/c, refrig, Jacuzzi, pool

SAVANNA
Budget Host Colonial Inn
(800) Bud-Host, (918) 548-3506
http://www.budgethost.com
Route 69
30 rooms - $25-37
Pets: Welcome
Creature Comforts: CCTV, a/c

SHAWNEE
Best Western Cinderella
(800) 480-5111, (405) 273-7010
http://www.bestwestern.com
623 Kickapoo Spur
95 rooms - $55-75
Pets: Welcome
Creature Comforts: CCTV,
VCR, a/c, refrig, Jacuzzi,
restaurant, pool, whirlpool

Hampton Inn
(800) Hampton, (405) 275-1540
http://www.hampton-inn.com
4851 Kickapoo
64 rooms - $60-87
Pets: Welcome w/$5 fee
Creature Comforts: CCTV, a/c,
refrig, micro, restaurant, cont.
brkfst, pool

Holiday Inn
(800) HOLIDAY, (405) 275-4404
http://www.holiday-inn.com
4900 N. Harrison St.
110 rooms - $60-90
Pets: Welcome
Creature Comforts: CCTV, a/c,
refrig, restaurant, pool

Motel 6
(800) 4-MOTEL6, (405) 275-5310
http://www.motel6.com
4981 Harrison St.
64 rooms - $35-49
Pets: Small pets welcome
Creature Comforts: CCTV, a/c,
pool

Rodeway Inn
(800) 228-2000, (405) 275-1005
http://www.rodeway.com
12510 Valley View Rd.
28 rooms - $35-55
Pets: Welcome w/$20 deposit
Creature Comforts: CCTV, a/c,
cont. brkfst

STILLWATER
Best Western Stillwater
(800) 528-1234, (405) 377-7010
http://www.bestwestern.com
600 E. McElroy
125 rooms - $50-86
Pets: Small pets welcome
Creature Comforts: CCTV, a/c,
refrig, restaurant, pool, hlth clb,
sauna, whirlpool

Days Inn
(800) DAYS INN, (405) 743-2570
http://www.daysinn.com
5010 W. Sixth St.
80 rooms - $35-65
Pets: Welcome w/$20 deposit
Creature Comforts: CCTV, a/c,
pool

Holiday Inn
(800) HOLIDAY, (405) 372-0800
http://www.holiday-inn.com
2515 W. Sixth St.
140 rooms - $50-75
Pets: Small pets welcome
Creature Comforts: CCTV, a/c,
Jacuzzi, restaurant, pool, hlth clb,
sauna, whirlpool

Motel 6
(800) 4-MOTEL6, (405) 624-0433
http://www.motel6.com
5122 West Sixth
87 rooms - $26-39
Pets: Small pets w/deposit
Creature Comforts: CCTV, a/c,
pool

STROUD
Best Western Stroud
(800) 528-1234, (918) 968-9515
http://www.bestwestern.com
1200 N. 8th Ave.
45 rooms - $50-85
Pets: Small pets welcome
Creature Comforts: CCTV, a/c,
Jacuzzi, restaurant, pool

SULPHUR
Super 8 Motel
(800) 800-8000, (580) 622-6500
http://www.super8.com
2110 W. Sulpher St.
40 rooms - $40-69
Pets: Welcome w/permission
Creature Comforts: CCTV, a/c,
Jacuzzi

TAHLEQUAH
Tahlequah Motor Lodge
(918) 456-2350
Route 60
55 rooms - $40-55
Pets: Small pets w/$5 fee, $20 dep
Creature Comforts: CCTV, a/c,
refrig, restaurant, pool, sauna,
whirlpool

TONKAWA
Western Inn
(580) 628-2577
Route 60
28 rooms - $35-47
Pets: Welcome
Creature Comforts: CCTV, a/c

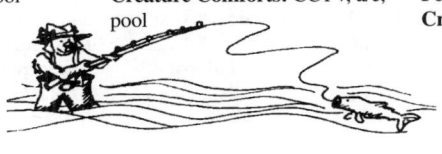

TULSA

Best Western Tradewinds, Cent.
(800) 528-1234, (918) 749-5561
http://www.bestwestern.com
3141 E. Skelly Dr.
170 rooms - $55-72
Pets: Small pets welcome
Creature Comforts: CCTV, a/c,
refrig, Jacuzzi, restaurant, pool,
hlth clb

Best Western Tradewinds East
(800) 528-1234, (918) 743-7931
http://www.bestwestern.com
3337 E. Skelly Dr.
155 rooms - $50-59
Pets: Small pets welcome
Creature Comforts: CCTV, a/c,
restaurant, cont. brkfst, pool

Baymont Inn
(800) 4-Budget, (918) 488-8777
http://www.baymontinns.com
4530 E. Skelly Dr.
110 rooms - $45-50
Pets: Small pets welcome
Creature Comforts: CCTV, a/c,
refrig, micro, pool

Comfort Inn
(800) 228-5150, (918) 622-6776
http://www.comfortinn.com
4717 S. Yale Ave.
109 rooms - $50-60
Pets: Welcome
Creature Comforts: CCTV, a/c,
kit, Jacuzzi, cont. brkfst, pool

Country Inn Suites
(800) 456-4000, (918) 234-3535
1034 N. Garnett Rd.
50 rooms - $55-70
Pets: Welcome w/$20 deposit
Creature Comforts: CCTV, a/c,
refrig, micro, Jacuzzi, pool

Days Inn, West
(800) DAYS INN, (918) 446-1561
http://www.daysinn.com
5525 W. Skelly Dr.
80 rooms - $35-60
Pets: Welcome w/$4 fee
Creature Comforts: CCTV, a/c,
restaurant, pool

Days Inn, Airport
(800) DAYS INN, (918) 438-5050
http://www.daysinn.com
1016 N. Garnett Rd.
75 rooms - $40-45
Pets: Small pets w/$10 fee
Creature Comforts: CCTV, a/c,
cont. brkfst

Doubletree Hotel, Warren Pl.
(800) 222-TREE, (918) 495-1000
http://www.doubletreehotels.com
6110 S. Yale Ave.
370 rooms - $75-160
Pets: Med. pets w/$100 deposit
Creature Comforts: Luxurious
rms, heart of Tulsa, CCTV, a/c,
refrig, Jacuzzi, restaurant, cont.
brkfst, pool, hlth clb access, sauna,
whirlpool

Doubletree Hotel, Downtown
(800) 222-TREE, (918) 587-8000
http://www.doubletreehotels.com
616 W. Seventh St.
63 rooms - $40-75
Pets: Welcome w/$25 fee
Creature Comforts: CCTV,
VCR, a/c, refrig, micro, Jacuzzi,
restaurant, cont. brkfst, pool, hlth
clb, sauna, whirlpool

Holiday Inn, Airport
(800) HOLIDAY, (918) 437-7660
http://www.holiday-inn.com
1010 N. Garnett Rd.
160 rooms - $60-85
Pets: Small pets welcome
Creature Comforts: CCTV, a/c,
restaurant, pool

Holiday Inn Express
(800) HOLIDAY, (918) 459-5321
http://www.holiday-inn.com
E. 71st St.
64 rooms - $65-85
Pets: Med. pets w/$50 deposit
Creature Comforts: CCTV, a/c,
cont. brkfst, pool, whirlpool

La Quinta, Airport
(800) Nu-Rooms, (918) 836-3931
http://www.laquinta.com
35 N. Sheridan Rd.
100 rooms - $55-70
Pets: Small pets welcome
Creature Comforts: CCTV, a/c,
cont. brkfst, pool

La Quinta
(800) Nu-Rooms, (918) 665-0220
http://www.laquinta.com
10829 E. 41st. St.
115 rooms - $55-60
Pets: Small pets welcome
Creature Comforts: CCTV, a/c,
pool

La Quinta, South
(800) Nu-Rooms, (918) 254-1626
http://www.laquinta.com
12525 E. 52nd St. S.
130 rooms - $45-60
Pets: Small pets welcome
Creature Comforts: CCTV, a/c,
pool

Motel 6, East
(800) 4-MOTEL6, (918) 234-6200
http://www.motel6.com
1011 S. Garnett Rd.
153 rooms - $30-35
Pets: Small pets welcome
Creature Comforts: CCTV, a/c,
pool

Motel 6, West
(800) 4-MOTEL6, (918) 445-0223
http://www.motel6.com
5828 W. Skelly Dr.
155 rooms - $32-35
Pets: Small pets welcome
Creature Comforts: CCTV, a/c,
pool

Ramada Tulsa
(800) 2-Ramada, (918) 622-7700
http://www.ramada.com
5000 E. Skelly
320 rooms - $55-55
Pets: Small pets w/$50 deposit
Creature Comforts: CCTV,
VCR, a/c, refrig, whirlpool,
restaurant, pool, hlth club

Residence Inn
(800) 331-3131, (918) 664-7241
http://www.residenceinn.com
8181 E. 41st St.
135 rooms - $99-125
Pets: Welcome $50 fee
Creature Comforts: CCTV, a/c,
kit, pool, hlth clb, sauna, and a
whirlpool

Sheraton Tulsa
(800) 325-3535, (918) 627-5000
http://www.sheraton.com
10918 E. 41st St.
335 rooms - $120-130
Pets: Small pets welcome
Creature Comforts: CCTV, a/c,
refrig, restaurant, pool, hlth clb,
sauna, whirlpool

Super 8, Airport
(800) 800-8000, (918) 836-1981
http://www.super8.com
6616 E. Archer St.
55 rooms - $35-55
Pets: Welcome W/$10 fee
Creature Comforts: CCTV, a/c,
kit

Super 8
(800) 800-8000, (918) 493-7000
http://www.super8.com
1347 E. Skelly Dr.
78 rooms - $35-55
Pets: Small pets w/$5 fee, $20 dep
Creature Comforts: CCTV, a/c,
pool

WAGONOR
Indian Lodge Motel
(918) 485-3184
Route 51
25 cabins - $40-155
Pets: Welcome w/$10 fee, damage
deposit, must be flea-free
Creature Comforts: CCTV, a/c,
kit, pool

Western Hills Guest Ranch
(918) 772-2545
http://www.otrd.state.ok.us
Route 51
100 rms/50 cabins - $40-150
Pets: Small pets in cabins
Creature Comforts: Concrete
block cabins w/simple motel room
decor, CCTV, a/c, VCR, refrig,
micro, kit, restaurant, pool, golf
course, tennis, stables

WATONGA
Roman Nose Resort
(580) 623-7281
Route 8A
10 cabins - $75-95
Pets: Welcome
Creature Comforts: CCTV, a/c,
kit, fireplace, restaurant

WEATHERFORD
Best Western Mark
(800) 528-1234, (405) 772-3325
http://www.bestwestern.com
525 E. Main St.
60 rooms - $45-75
Pets: Welcome
Creature Comforts: CCTV, a/c,
refrig, pool

Scottish Inns
(800) 251-1962, (405) 772-3349
616 E. Main St.
75 rooms - $29-39
Pets: Welcome
Creature Comforts: CCTV, a/c,
pool

WEBBERS FALLS
Super 8
(800) 800-8000, (405) 464-2272
http://www.super8.com
Route 100
40 rooms - $35-57
Pets: Welcome w/permission
Creature Comforts: CCTV, a/c

WOODWARD
Hospitality Inn
(580) 254-2964
4120 Williams Ave.
60 rooms - $30-60
Pets: Welcome w/$7 fee
Creature Comforts: CCTV, a/c,
cont. brkfst

Northwest Inn
(580) 256-7600
Route 270
125 rooms - $50-76
Pets: Welcome
Creature Comforts: CCTV, a/c,
refrig, restaurant, pool

Wayfarer Inn
(580) 256-5553
2901 Williams Ave.
90 rooms - $40-75
Pets: Welcome in kennels
Creature Comforts: CCTV, a/c,
refrig, restaurant, pool

YUKON
Comfort Inn
(800) 228-5150, (405) 324-1000
http://www.comfortinn.com
321 N. Mustang Rd.
110 rooms - $45-70
Pets: Welcome w/$50 dep.
Creature Comforts: CCTV, a/c,
kit, pool

Oregon

AGNESS
Lucas Pioneer Ranch & Lodge
(541) 247-7443
Box 37
4 cabins - $40-60
Pets: Welcome in cabin
Creature Comforts: CCTV, a/c,
and a kit

Singing Springs Resort
(541) 247-6162
Box 68
7 rooms - $40-45
Pets: Small pets welcome
Creature Comforts: Simple
units, some w/kits

ALBANY
Best Western Pony Soldier
(800) 528-1234, (541) 928-6322
http://www.bestwestern.com
315 Airport Rd. SE
72 rooms - $75-95
Pets: Small pets welcome
Creature Comforts: CCTV,
VCR, a/c, refrig, restaurant, cont.
brkfst, pool, hlth club., whirlpool

Comfort Inn
(800) 228-5150, (541) 928-0921
http://www.comfortinn.com
251 Airport Way SE
50 rooms - $70-100
Pets: Welcome
Creature Comforts: CCTV, a/c,
kit, Jacuzzi, cont. brkfst, pool,
whirlpool, sauna

Holiday Inn Express
(800) HOLIDAY, (541) 928-5050
http://www.holiday-inn.com
1100 Price Rd.
75 rooms - $60-90
Pets: Welcome in ltd. rooms
Creature Comforts: CCTV,
VCR, a/c, refrig, micro, restaurant,
pool, hlth clb, whirlpool

Motel Orleans
(800) 626-1900, (541) 926-0170
1212 Price Rd., SE
78 rooms - $40-49
Pets: In certain rooms w/$5 fee
Creature Comforts: CCTV, a/c,
refrig, restaurant, pool

Stardust Motel
(541) 926-4233
2735 E. Pacific Blvd.
30 rooms - $35-47
Pets: Welcome in certain rooms
Creature Comforts: CCTV, a/c,
refrig, micro

ASHLAND
Ashland Motel
(541) 482-2561
1145 Siskiyou Blvd.
27 rooms - $55-76
Pets: Welcome in certain rooms
Creature Comforts: CCTV, a/c,
refrig, pool

Best Western Bard's Inn
(800) 528-1234, (541) 482-0049
http://www.bestwestern.com
132 North Main St
72 rooms - $85-165
Pets: Welcome w/$10 fee
Creature Comforts: CCTV, a/c,
refrig, cont. brkfst, pool

Best Western Heritage Inn
(800) 528-1234, (541) 482-6932
http://www.bestwestern.com
434 Valley View Rd
53 rooms - $70-109
Pets: Welcome
Creature Comforts: CCTV, a/c,
refrig, cont. brkfst, pool, whirlpool

Green Springs Box R Ranch
(541) 482-0614
16799 Route 66
4 cabins - $110-150
Pets: Welcome in cabins
Creature Comforts: Historic
stagecoach stop turned 1,000-acre
working ranch, antique bldgs w/
modern log guest cabins, CCTV,
kit, stone fireplace, hiking

Knights Inn
(800)547-4566, (541) 482-5111
2359 Ashland St.
40 rooms - $40-65
Pets: Small pets w/$6 fee
Creature Comforts: CCTV, a/c,
restaurant, pool, whirlpool

Patterson House B&B
(888) 482-9171, (541) 482-9171
http://www.mind.net/patterson
639 N. Main St.
4 rooms - $60-100
Pets: Your "best friend" is always
welcome, dogs only
Creature Comforts: 1910
Craftsman-style bungalow, for
privacy request cottage, indiv.
decorated rooms w/floral themes,
CCTV, VCR, a/c, refrig, lavish
healthy vegetarian brkfst, pool,
deck

Quality Inn
(800) 228-5151, (541) 488-2330
http://www.qualityinn.com
2520 Ashland St
60 rooms - $50-100
Pets: Welcome w/$6 fee
Creature Comforts: CCTV,
VCR, a/c, kit, restaurant, cont.
brkfst, pool

Rodeway Inn
(800) 228-2000, (541) 482-2641
http://www.rodeway.com
1193 Siskiyou Blvd.
65 rooms - $50-89
Pets: Small pets w/$6 fee
Creature Comforts: CCTV, a/c,
restaurant, pool

Super 8
(800) 800-8000, (541) 388-6888
http://www.super8.com
2350 Ashland St.
67 rooms - $45-55
Pets: Welcome
Creature Comforts: CCTV, pool

Windmill Inn
(800) 547-4747, (541) 482-8310
http://www.windmillinns.com
2525 Ashland St.
230 rooms - $50-275
Pets: Welcome
Creature Comforts: CCTV,
VCR, a/c, refrig, micro, Jacuzzi,
restaurant, cont. breakfast, pool,
whirlpool, tennis

ASTORIA
Crest Motel
(800) 421-3141, (503) 325-3141
5366 Leif Erickson Dr
40 rooms - $45-95
Pets: Welcome
Creature Comforts: CCTV,
refrig, micro, Jacuzzi, cont.
breakfast, pool, whirlpool, river

Lamplighter Motel
(800) 845-8847, (503) 325-4051
131 W. Marine Dr.
29 rooms - $45-78
Pets: Welcome w/$5 fee
Creature Comforts: CCTV,
Jacuzzi, whirlpool

Red Lion Inn
(800) RED-LION, (503) 325-7373
http://www.doubletreehotels.com
400 Industry St.
125 rooms - $65-160
Pets: Welcomew/$10 fee
Creature Comforts: CCTV,
waterfront restaurant, river views

BAKER CITY
Baker City Motel/RV
(800) 931-9229, (541) 523-6381
880 Elm St.
17 rooms - $28-37
Pets: Welcome
Creature Comforts: CCTV, a/c

Bridge Street Inn
(800) 932-9220, (541) 523-6571
134 Bridge St.
40 rooms - $33-48
Pets: Welcome
Creature Comforts: CCTV, a/c

Budget Inn
(800) 547-5827, (541) 523-6324
2205 Broadway St.
35 rooms - $32-40
Pets: Welcome w/$3 fee
Creature Comforts: CCTV, a/c,
restaurant

El Dorado Motel
(800) 537-5756, (541) 523-6494
695 Campbell St.
56 rooms - $48-52
Pets: Welcome
Creature Comforts: CCTV, a/c,
refrig, micro, pool

Geiser Grand Hotel
(888) 434-7374, (541) 523-1889
http://www.geisergrand.com
1996 Main St.
30 rooms - $89-225
Pets: Dogs welcome w/$10 fee
Creature Comforts: Exquisite
1889 hotel, period features
recently restored-immense stained
glass window, ornately carved
wood and plaster work, sweeping
staircases, 100 chandeliers, large
rooms w/period furnishings, great
views from 3rd floor-ten ft. high
windows, historic memorabilia
displayed, canopy beds, CCTV,
VCR, a/c, Jacuzzis, restaurant,
cont. breakfast, hlth clb access

Oregon Trail Motel
(800) 628-3982, (541) 523-5844
211 Bridge St.
54 rooms - $35-38
Pets: Welcome w/$5 fee
Creature Comforts: CCTV,
refrig, restaurant, pool

Quality Inn
(800) 228-5151, (541) 523-2242
http://www.qualityinn.com
810 Campbell St.
54 rooms - $55-60
Pets: Welcome w/$10 fee
Creature Comforts: CCTV, a/c,
cont. brkfst

BANDON
Bandon Beach Motel
(541) 347-4430
1110 - 11th St. SW
28 rooms - $45-75
Pets: Welcome
Creature Comforts: CCTV, kit,
fireplace, pool, whirlpool

Bandon Wayside Motel
(541) 347-3421
1175 Second St.
8 rooms - $36-66
Pets: Welcome
Creature Comforts: CCTV

Best Western Inn at Face Rock
(800) 528-1234, (541) 347-9441
http://www.bestwestern.com
3225 Beach Loop Rd.
55 rooms - $50-134
Pets: Welcome w/$15 fee
Creature Comforts: CCTV, kit,
Jacuzzis, restaurant, cont. brkfst,
pool, sauna, whirlpool

Caprice Motel
(541) 347-4494
Route 101
15 rooms - $35-60
Pets: Small dogs only
Creature Comforts: CCTV, kit

La Kris Motel
(888) 496-3610, (541) 347-3610
Rte. 101 at 9th St.
12 rooms - $42-65
Pets: Welcome
Creature Comforts: CCTV, kit,
restaurant

Sunset Oceanfront
(800) 842-2407, (541) 347-2453
http://www.sunsetmotel.com
1755 Beach Loop Dr. SW
56 rooms - $45-165
Pets: Welcome w/$7 daily fee
Creature Comforts: Seaside
beach houses and motel units,
CCTV, kit, fireplace, restaurant,
whirlpool

Table Rock Motel
(541) 347-2700
840 Beach Loop Rd.
15 rooms - $35-90
Pets: Welcome
Creature Comforts: CCTV, kit

BEAVERTON
Greenwood Inn
(800) 289-1300, (503) 643-7444
http://www.greenwoodinn.com
10700 SW Allen Blvd.
250 rooms - $110-400
Pets: $10 fee, $100 deposit
Creature Comforts: Very nice
rooms, CCTV, refrig, micro,
fireplace, Jacuzzi, restaurant, pool,
hlth clb., sauna, whirlpool

Shilo Inn
(800) 222-2244, (503) 297-2551
http://www.shiloinns.com
9900 SW Canyon Rd.
140 rooms - $95-129
Pets: Welcome w/$7 fee
Creature Comforts: CCTV,
refrig, micro, restaurant, pool, hlth
clb., whirlpool

BEND
Bend Holiday Motel
(800) 252-0121, 541-382-4620
http://www.freeyellow.com:8080/
members8/wayne-schnur
880 S.E. 3rd St.
25 rooms - $55-110
Pets: Dogs with "non-oily coats
are welcome"
Creature Comforts: CCTV, a/c,
kit, whirlpool

Bend Riverside Motel
(800) 284-Bend, (503) 389-Bend
http://bendriversidemotel.com
1565 NW Hill St.
179 rooms - $55-115
Pets: In smoking rooms w/$5 fee
Creature Comforts: CCTV, a/c,
refrig, kit, fireplace, pool, hlth clb,
whirlpool, tennis

Best Western Entrada
(800) 528-1234, (541) 382-4080
http://www.bestwestern.com
19221 Century Dr.
79 rooms - $60-95
Pets: Small pets w/$5 fee
Creature Comforts: CCTV, a/c,
Jacuzzi, cont. brkfst, pool,
whirlpool

Best Western Inn/Suites
(800) 528-1234, (541) 382-1515
http://www.bestwestern.com
721 NE Third St.
102 rooms - $55-96
Pets: Small pets welcom
Creature Comforts: CCTV, a/c,
cont. brkfst, pool, hlth clb access,
whirlpool

Cascade Motel
(800) 852-6031, (503) 382-2612
420 S.E .Third St.
33 rooms - $35-45
Pets: Welcome w/$4 fee
Creature Comforts: CCTV, a/c,
refrig, micro, pool

Cimarron Inn, South
(800) 304-4050, (541) 382-8282
201 N.E. Third St.
118 rooms - $40-57
Pets: Welcome w/$10 fee
Creature Comforts: CCTV, a/c,
kit

Comfort Inn
(800) 228-5150, (541) 388-2227
http://www.comfortinn.com
61200 S Route 97
65 rooms - $80-185
Pets: Welcome w/$5
Creature Comforts: CCTV, a/c,
cont. brkfst, Jacuzzis, sauna, pool

East Lake Resort
(541) 536-2230
22430 East Lake & Paulina Rd.
16 rooms - $40-100
Pets: Welcome
Creature Comforts: CCTV, kit,
restaurant, pool

Hampton Inn
(800) Hampton, (541) 388-4114
http://www.hampton-inn.com
15 NE Butler Market Rd
100 rooms - $65-85
Pets: Welcome
Creature Comforts: CCTV, a/c,
refrig, cont. brkfst, pool, whirlpool

Holiday Inn Express
(800) HOLIDAY, (541) 317-8500
http://www.holiday-inn.com
20615 Grandview Dr.
98 rooms - $65-109
Pets: Welcome
Creature Comforts: CCTV, a/c,
cont. brkfst, Jacuzzis, restaurant,
pool, hlth clb, whirlpool, sundeck

Motel West
(800) 282-3577, (541) 389-5577
228 NE Irving St.
39 rooms - $36-40
Pets: Welcome
Creature Comforts: CCTV, a/c,
kit, restaurant

Palmer's Motel/Cafe
(541) 347-4430
645 NE Greenwood Ave.
8 rooms - $32-36
Pets: Welcome
Creature Comforts: CCTV, a/c,
kit, restaurant

Red Lion Inn, North
(800) RED-LION, (541) 382-7011
http://www.doubletreehotels.com
1415 NE Third St.
75 rooms - $70-99
Pets: Welcome
Creature Comforts: CCTV, a/c,
VCR, restaurant, pool, whirlpool,
sauna

Red Lion Inn, South
(800) RED-LION, (541) 382-8384
http://www.doubletreehotels.com
849 N.E. Third St.
75 rooms - $70-97
Pets: Welcome
Creature Comforts: CCTV,
VCR, restaurant, pool, whirlpool

Riverhouse Resort
(800) 547-3928, (541) 389-3111
http://www.riverhouse.com
3075 N Rte. 97
220 rooms - $65-185
Pets: Welcome in certain rooms
Creature Comforts: Set on banks
of Deschutes River, attractive
complex, request riverside rooms,
CCTV, a/c, VCR, kit, fireplace,
Jacuzzi, restaurant, pool, sauna,
whirlpool, tenis, golf, trails

Rodeway Inn
(800) 228-2000, (541) 382-2211
http://www.rodeway.com
3705 N. Rte. 97
36 rooms - $34-50
Pets: Small pets welcome
Creature Comforts: CCTV, a/c,
cont. brkfst, pool, whirlpool

Shilo Inn
(800) 222-2244, (541) 389-9600
http://www.shiloinns.com
3105 O B Riley Rd.
150 rooms - $80-180
Pets: Welcome w/$7 fee
Creature Comforts: CCTV, kit,
fireplace, Jacuzzis, restaurant,
pool, hlth clb., sauna, whirlpool

Sleep Inn
(800) Sleep-Inn, (541) 330-0050
http://www.sleepinn.com
600 N.E. Bellevue St.
60 rooms - $51-80
Pets: Welcome, if not left alone
Creature Comforts: CCTV, a/c,
cont. brkfst, pool

Super 8
(800) 800-8000, (541) 388-6888
http://www.super8.com
1275 S. Rte. 97
79 rooms - $50-69
Pets: Welcome
Creature Comforts: CCTV,
VCR, restaurant, pool, whirlpool

Travelers Inn
(800) 507-2211, (541) 382-2211
3705 N. Rte. 97
75 rooms - $40-68
Pets: Welcome w/$5 fee
Creature Comforts: CCTV,
refrig, micro, pool

Twin Lakes Resort
(541) 593-6526
Route 42
14 rooms - $45-119
Pets: Welcome w/$5 fee
Creature Comforts: CCTV, kit,
fireplace, restaurant, boating

Westward Ho Motel
(800) 999-8143, (541) 382-2111
904 S.E. Third St.
65 rooms - $44-59
Pets: Welcome
Creature Comforts: CCTV,
refrig, micro, kit, pool, whirlpool

BOARDMAN
Dodge City Inn
(541) 481-2451
First and Front Sts.
40 rooms - $43-49
Pets: Welcome in smoking rooms
Creature Comforts: CCTV, a/c,
refrig, micro, pool

Econo Lodge
(800) 55-ECONO, (541) 481-2375
http://www.econolodge.com
105 SW Front St.
51 rooms - $44-58
Pets: Welcome
Creature Comforts: CCTV, a/c,
refrig, micro, pool

Riverview Motel
(541) 481-2775
200 Front St. NE
20 rooms - $35-40
Pets: Welcome
Creature Comforts: CCTV, a/c

BROOKINGS
Beaver State Motel
(541) 469-5361
437 Chetco St.
17 rooms - $40-55
Pets: Welcome
Creature Comforts: CCTV, kit

Best Western Beachfront
(800) 528-1234, (541) 469-7779
http://www.bestwestern.com
16008 Boat Basin Rd.
78 rooms - $65-175
Pets: Small pets welcome in
oceanfront rooms
Creature Comforts: Oceanfront
motel, CCTV, a/c, kit, Jacuzzi,
pool, whirlpool

Bonn Motel
(541) 469-2161
1216 Chetco St.
37 rooms - $42-52
Pets: Welcome
Creature Comforts: CCTV, kit,
pool, sauna

Harbor Inn Motel
(800) 469-8444, (541) 469-3194
15991 Route 101 South
30 rooms - $45-55
Pets: Welcome w/$5 fee
Creature Comforts: CCTV, cont.
brkfst, pool

Pacific Sunset Motel
(541) 469-2141
1144 Chetco St.
40 rooms - $46-64
Pets: Welcome w/$5 fee
Creature Comforts: CCTV,
micro, cont. brkfst, pool

BURNS
Ponderosa Inn
(800) 528-1234, (541) 573-2047
577 W. Monroe St.
52 rooms - $60-83
Pets: Small pets welcome
Creature Comforts: CCTV, a/c,
cont. brkfst, pool

BonTemps Motel
(541) 347-4430
74 W. Monroe St.
15 rooms - $27-56
Pets: Welcome
Creature Comforts: CCTV, a/c,
kit, restaurant, pool, hlth club.

Royal Inn
(541) 573-5295
999 Oregon Ave.
38 rooms - $50-64
Pets: In certain rooms w/$20 dep.
Creature Comforts: CCTV, a/c,
refrig, micro, Jacuzzi, pool,
whirlpool, sauna

Sea Dreamer Inn
(800) 408-4367, (541) 469-6629
http://www.virtualcities.com/ons/
or/y/ory2801.htm
15167 McVay Lane
4 rooms - $60-85
Pets: Mature well-mannered pets
are welcome w/$10 fee
Creature Comforts: Charming
1912 country Victorian built out of
redwood, spacious yard, views of
the ocean, antiques, libraries, full
brkfst, CCTV

Silver Spur Motel
(800) 400-2077, (541) 573-2077
789 N. Broadway St.
26 rooms - $33-48
Pets: Welcome w/$5 fee
Creature Comforts: CCTV, a/c,
kit, cont brkfst, pool, hlth club.,
whirlpool, and a sauna

CAMP SHERMAN
Black Butte Resort/RV Park
(541) 595-6514
35 Shuttle-Sherman Rd.
6 rooms - $55-65
Pets: Welcome
Creature Comforts: Kitchen

Cold Springs Resort
(541) 595-6271
www.coldsprings-resort.com
25615 Cold Springs Resort Lane
5 rooms - $90-150
Pets: Welcome w/$8 fee
Creature Comforts: Parklike
setting on Metolius River, quaint
cottages, contemporary decor,
walking paths, kit, lofts, fireplace,
covered porches, restaurant, pool

Twin View Resort
(541) 595-6125
13860 SW Forest Svs Rd.
6 rooms - $70-98
Pets: Welcome
Creature Comforts: Kit,
fireplace

CANNON BEACH

Cannon Village Motel
(503) 436-2317
3163 South Hemlock
11 cabins - $70-120
Pets: Welcome w/$5 fee
Creature Comforts: Old fashioned cabins w/yards, CCTV, kit

Ecola Creek Lodge
(800) 873-2749, (503) 436-0562
http://www.at-e.com/ecola
208 - 5th St.
21 rooms - $80-175
Pets: Welcome w/$10 fee
Creature Comforts: Unique motel w/pretty grounds, ponds, across from park and ocean, individually and attractively decorated rms, CCTV, kit, fireplace, restaurant, cont. brkfst

The Guest House Motel
(800) 585-0630, (503) 436-0630
cannon-beach.net/guesthouse
1016 S. Hemlock St.
1 house/1 cottage/1 rm - $135-229
Pets: Welcome
Creature Comforts: Attractive house and cottage w/CCTV, VCR, kit, Jacuzzi, fireplace, block to beach

Hallmark Resort
(888) 448-4449, (503) 436-1566
http://www.hallmarkinns.com
1400 S. Hemlock
133 rooms - $60-425
Pets: Welcome w/$5 fee
(pet amenities)
Creature Comforts: Cliffside loc. overlooking Haystack Rock/Cannon Beach, request ocean view rooms, well appointed, star-bucks coffee, CCTV, VCR, a/c, kit, Jacuzzi, fireplaces, pool, hlth club., sauna, whirlpool, massage

Haystack Resort
(800) 499-2220, (503) 436-1577
http://www.haystackresort.com
3339 S. Hemlock St.
23 rooms - $90-190
Pets: Certain units w/$5 fee
Creature Comforts: Ocean views, condominiums are especially nice, kit, fireplace, CCTV, VCR, kit, Jacuzzi, decks, pool, whirlpool, sauna

Land's End Motel
(800) 793-1477, (503) 436-2264
253 West Second St.
14 rooms - $107-177
Pets: Welcome
Creature Comforts: CCTV, kit, fireplace, whirlpool

McBee Motel Cottages
(800) 238-4107, (503) 436-1392
www.oregoncoastlodgings.com
888 S. Hemlock St.
12 rooms - $35-135
Pets: Welcome w/$5 fee
Creature Comforts: chgarming English style cottages, CCTV, kit, fireplace

Quiet Cannon Lodgings
(503) 436-1405 or 1805
372 N. Spruce St.
2 condos - $85-95
Pets: Welcome w/$5 initial fee
Creature Comforts: Oceanside condos tucked into pine grove, spacious units, nice decor, decks, barbecue, CCTV, kit, fireplace, quiet setting

Sunset Surf Ocean Front
(800) 243-8035, (503) 368-5224
248 Ocean Rd.
41 rooms - $50-120
Pets: Welcome
Creature Comforts: Ocean views, CCTV, kit, Jacuzzi, fireplace, pool, whirlpool

Surf Sand Resort
(800) 547-6100, (503) 436-2274
http://www.surfsand.com
Gower St., Box 219
86 rooms - $99-270
Pets: Welcome w/$5 fee
Creature Comforts: CCTV, VCR, kit, Jacuzzi, fireplace, pool, restaurant, whirlpool, ocean views

Tolvana Inn
(800) 333-8890, (503) 436-2211
http://www.v-v-a.com
3400 S. Hemlock Rd.
176 rooms - $60-240
Pets: Welcome w/$10 fee
Creature Comforts: CCTV, VCR, kit, fireplace, pool, whirlpool, sauna, beach access

CANYONVILLE

Leisure Inn
(541) 839-4278
554 SW Pine St.
37 rooms - $35-50
Pets: Welcome
Creature Comforts: CCTV, a/c, kit, pool

CASCADE LOCKS

Best Western Columbia River
(800) 528-1234, (541) 374-8777
http://www.bestwestern.com
735 Wanapa St.
63 rooms - $60-135
Pets: Small pets welcome
Creature Comforts: CCTV, a/c, refrig, micro, cont. brkfst, pool, hlth club., whirlpool

Econo Inn
(541) 374-8417
Box 217
30 rooms - $40-55
Pets: Small pets that don't shed welcome w/$20 deposit
Creature Comforts: CCTV, a/c, refrig, micro

CASCADE SUMMIT

Shelter Cove Resort
(541) 433-2548
Route 58
8 rooms - $65-155
Pets: One dog welcome per cabin
Creature Comforts: Lakefront cabins/RV park, CCTV, kit, boat rentals

CAVE JUNCTION

Country Hills Resort
(800) 997-8464, (541) 592-3406
7901 Caves Hwy.
5 rooms - $42-65
Pets: Welcome w/$5 fee
Creature Comforts: Motel/RV park on 22 acres, CCTV, a/c, kit

CHARLESTON
Captain John's Motel
(541) 888-4041
8061 Kingfisher Dr.
46 rooms - $42-69
Pets: Welcome
Creature Comforts: CCTV, kit,
restaurant, cont. brkfst

CHEMULT
Crater Lake Motel
(541) 365-2241
Route 97
20 rooms - $35-45
Pets: Welcome
Creature Comforts: CCTV,
refrig

CHILOQUIN
Melita's Motel/Cafe
(541) 783-2401
39500 Route 97 N.
13 rooms - $35-56
Pets: Welcome
Creature Comforts: CCTV,
restaurant

Spring Creek Ranch Motel
(800) 626-1292, (541) 783-2775
47600 Hwy. 97 N.
10 rooms - $28-39
Pets: Welcome
Creature Comforts: Kit,
fireplace

CLACKAMAS
Clackamas Inn
(800) 874-6560, (503) 650-5340
16010 SE 82nd Dr.
45 rooms - $60-99
Pets: Welcome w/$5 daily fee
Creature Comforts: CCTV, a/c,
refrig, micro, Jacuzzi, cont. brkfst,
pool

COOS BAY
Best Western Holiday
(800) 528-1234, (541) 269-5111
http://www.bestwestern.com
411 N. Bayshore Rd.
77 rooms - $60-159
Pets: Small pets w/$10 fee
Creature Comforts: CCTV, a/c,
cont. brkfst, pool, hlth club.,
whirlpool

Coos Bay Manor
(800) 269-1224, (541) 269-1224
http://www.virtualcities.com/ons/
or/c/orc3601.htm
955 South Fifth St.
5 rooms - $65-100
Pets: Welcome, dogs must be well
mannered and get along w/ the
three resident cats ($10 initial fee)
Creature Comforts: Colonial
house on Nat'l Historic Register,
sweeping central staircase, high
ceilings, individually decorated
rooms w/wicker, Victorian
antiques & accents, columned
porches, four-poster beds,
fireplace, full brkfst, balcony,
wonderful fragrance from
wisteria, rhododendrons, and lilacs

Edgewater Inn
(541) 267-0423
275 E. Johnson St.
82 rooms - $67-107
Pets: Small pets w/$8 fee
Creature Comforts: CCTV,
VCR, a/c, refrig, Jacuzzi, cont.
brkfst, pool, hlth club., whirlpool

Itty Bitty Inn
(541) 347-4430
1110 - 11 St. SW
28 rooms - $45-79
Pets: Welcome
Creature Comforts: CCTV, kit,
fireplace, pool, whirlpool

Motel 6
(800) 4-MOTEL6, (541) 267-7171
http://www.motel6.com
Route 101 & Bayshore Rd.
94 rooms - $35-59
Pets: Under 30 lbs. welcome
Creature Comforts: CCTV, a/c,
sauna, whirlpool

Red Lion Inn
(800) RED-LION, (541) 267-4141
http://www.doubletreehotels.com
1313 N. Bayshore Rd.
145 rooms - $70-98
Pets: Welcome
Creature Comforts: CCTV,
VCR, a/c, refrig, Jacuzzi,
restaurant, pool, hlth clb

This Old House B&B
(541) 267-5224
http://bnbweb.com/
thisoldehouse.html
202 Alder Ave.
4 rooms - $85-160
Pets: Selectively welcomed
Creature Comforts: A charming
yellow 1893 Victorian set behind
gardens and a picket fence, 6-
person spa, fireplace, wetbar,
antiques, spacious common areas,
Oriental rugs, CCTV, a/c, refrig,
full brkfst, nice views, hostess
prepares Japanese cuisine

Timber Lodge Motel
(800) 782-7592, (541) 267-7066
1001 N. Bayshore Rd.
53 rooms - $45-70
Pets: Welcome w/$5 fee
Creature Comforts: CCTV, a/c,
refrig, restaurant

COQUILLE
Myrtle Lane Motel
(541) 396-2102
787 N. Central Blvd.
25 rooms - $35-49
Pets: In certain rooms w/$4 fee
Creature Comforts: CCTV,
VCR, a/c, refrig, Jacuzzi,
restaurant, pool, hlth clb

CORVALLIS
Ashwood B&B
(800) 306-5136, (541) 757-9772
2940 NW Ashwood Dr.
3 rooms - $60-70
Pets: Welcome
Creature Comforts: CCTV, a/c,
fireplace

Econo Lodge
(800) 55-ECONO, (541) 752-9601
http://www.econolodge.com
345 N.W. Second St.
61 rooms - $45-59
Pets: Welcome w/$5 fee
Creature Comforts: CCTV, a/c,
restaurant

Jason Inn
(800) 346-3291, (541) 753-7326
800 NW Ninth St.
51 rooms - $35-49
Pets: Welcome w/$4 nightly fee
Creature Comforts: CCTV, a/c,
refrig, restaurant, pool

Shanico Inn
(541) 754-7474
1113 NW Ninth St.
75 rooms - $45-65
Pets: Small pets welcome w/$5
fee in certain rooms
Creature Comforts: CCTV, a/c,
refrig, micros, cont. brkfst, pool,
and a hlth clb.

Super 8
(800) 800-8000, (541) 758-8088
http://www.super8.com
407 N.W. Second St.
101 rooms - $55-69
Pets: Welcome
Creature Comforts: CCTV, a/c,
pool, whirlpool

COTTAGE GROVE
Best Western Village Green
(800) 528-1234, (541) 942-2491
http://www.bestwestern.com
725 Row River Rd.
96 rooms - $80-105
Pets: Welcome
Creature Comforts: CCTV, a/c,
cont. brkfst, fireplace, restaurant,
pool, hlth club., whirlpool, tennis

Comfort Inn
(800) 228-5150, (541) 942-9747
http://www.comfortinn.com
845 Gateway Blvd.
58 rooms - $60-109
Pets: Welcome
Creature Comforts: CCTV, a/c,
Jacuzzi, cont. brkfst, pool

Holiday Inn Express
(800) HOLIDAY, (541) 942-1000
http://www.holiday-inn.com
1601 Gateway Blvd.
40 rooms - $55-125
Pets: Welcome w/$10 fee
Creature Comforts: CCTV, a/c,
refrig, micro, pool, hlth clb, and a
whirlpool

CRATER LAKE
Holiday Village Motel/RV
(541) 365-2394
Route 97
8 rooms - $28-59
Pets: Welcome
Creature Comforts: CCTV, kit

Whispering Pines Motel
(541) 365-2259
Rtes. 97 & 138
11 rooms - $35-66
Pets: Welcome
Creature Comforts: CCTV, kit,
restaurant

Wilson's Cottages
(541) 381-2209
57997 Rte. 62
10 rooms - $40-65
Pets: Welcome
Creature Comforts: CCTV, kit

CRESCENT
Woodsman Country Lodge
(541) 433-2710
Route 97
14 rooms - $35-79
Pets: Welcome w/$5 fee
Creature Comforts: CCTV, kit,
fireplace, Jacuzzi

CRESCENT LAKE
Odell Lake Resort
(541) 433-2540
odelllakeresort.uswestdex.com
Box 72
26 rooms - $40-210
Pets: Welcome in cabins, one pet
per cabin w/$5 fee
Creature Comforts: Rough-hewn
log lodge w/sunny great room and
restaurant, rustic log cabins on
overlooking Odell Lake, request
cabins 6-8, 10, 12, 16, and 17, kit,
fireplace or woodstove, canoe/
motor boat rentals, fishing, hiking
bicycling, xc-skiing

Shelter Cove Resort
(800) 647-2729, (541) 433-2548
http://www.sheltercoveresort.com
Route 97
8 cabins - $65-99
Pets: One dog per cabin w/$5 fee
Creature Comforts: Rqst quaint
100-yr-old log cabin, CCTV, kit,
woodstove, boating, skiing

Willamette Pass Inn
(541) 433-2211
Route 97
12 rooms - $60-75
Pets: Welcome w/$15 fee
Creature Comforts: CCTV, kit,
fireplaces, fruit basket/muffins
delivered in evening

DALLAS
Riverside Inn
(541) 623-8163
517 Main St.
23 rooms - $45-59
Pets: Welcome
Creature Comforts: CCTV, a/c,
kit

DAYVILLE
Fish House Inn
(888) 286-FISH, (541) 987-2124
http://grantcounty.cc/business/
dayville/fishhouse
110 Franklin St.
5 rooms - $60-78
Pets: Welcome in cottage
Creature Comforts: Rooms
decorated around fish & ocean
themes, CCTV, refrig, micro

DEPOE BAY
Inn at Arch Rock
(800) 767-1835, (541) 765-2560
http://www.innatarchrock.com
70 NW Sunset St.
11 rooms - $80-130
Pets: Ltd. rooms w/$10 fee
Creature Comforts: Cliffside
setting w/spectacular views of
Depoe Bay, loads of character,
request room 8 — hardwood flrs,
wood-paneled walls, chintz
fabrics, tiny sitting area, window
seats, CCTV, kit, cont. brkfst

Trollers Lodge
(800) 472-9335, (541) 765-2287
355 SW Rte 101
12 rooms - $59-95
Pets: Welcome w/$5 fee
(welcome biscuits)
Creature Comforts: CCTV, kit

Whale Inn at Depoe Bay
(541) 765-2789
416 Rte. 101 N.
11 rooms - $40-85
Pets: Welcome
Creature Comforts: CCTV, kit,
fireplace

ELKTON

Big K Guest Ranch
(800) 390-BIG-K, (541) 584-2295
http://www.big-k.com
20029 Rte. 138 W.
20 cabins - $200-250 (AP)
Pets: Welcome w/$10 daily fee
Creature Comforts: Umpqua
River ranch, 12,000 square foot
Log Lodge, modern log cabins,
fireplace, Jacuzzi, homecooked
meals, fishing, horseback riding,
hiking across 2,500 acres, rafting

ENTERPRISE

Ponderosa Motel
(541) 426-3186
102 E. Greenwood Rd.
25 rooms - $49-79
Pets: Welcome
Creature Comforts: CCTV, a/c

Troy's Wilderness Retreat
(541) 828-7741
84570 Bartlett Rd.
6 rooms - $35-78
Pets: Welcome
Creature Comforts: Very rustic
cabins, lodge rms., CCTV, a/c, kit

Wilderness Inn
(800) 965-1205, (541) 426-4535
301 W. North St.
29 rooms - $49-69
Pets: Welcome w/$5 nightly fee
Creature Comforts: CCTV, a/c,
kit, Jacuzzi, sauna

EUGENE

Best Western Greentree Inn
(800) 528-1234, (541) 485-2727
http://www.bestwestern.com
1759 Franklin Blvd.
65 rooms - $65-89
Pets: Welcome in certain rooms
Creature Comforts: CCTV, a/c,
kit, cont. brkfst, pool, whirlpool,
and a hlth club

Best Western New Oregon Inn
(800) 528-1234, (541) 683-3669
http://www.bestwestern.com
1655 Franklin Blvd.
128 rooms - $65-89
Pets: Welcome in certain rooms
Creature Comforts: CCTV, a/c,
pool, hlth club., whirlpool, sauna

Campus Inn
(800) 888-6313, (541) 343-3376
390 E. Broadway
60 rooms - $56-72
Pets: Under 25 lbs. w/$25 deposit
Creature Comforts: A/C, brkfst

Country Squire Inn
(541) 484-2000
33100 Van Duyn Rd.
105 rooms - $40-109
Pets: Welcome
Creature Comforts: CCTV, a/c,
refrig, micro, Jacuzzi, restaurant

Courtesy Inn
(541) 345-3391
345 West Sixth Ave.
34 rooms - $40-65
Pets: Welcome
Creature Comforts: CCTV, a/c,
restaurant

Eugene Hilton
(800) HILTONS, (541) 342-2000
http://www.hilton.com
66 E Sixth St.
275 rooms - $120-275
Pets: Welcome
Creature Comforts: CCTV, a/c,
restaurant, cont brkfst, pool, hlth
clb, and a whirlpool

Executive House Motel
(541) 683-4000
1040 W. Sixth Ave.
36 rooms - $32-45
Pets: Welcome
Creature Comforts: CCTV, a/c

Motel 6
(800) 4-MOTEL6, (541) 687-2395
http://www.motel6.com
3690 Glenwood Dr.
59 rooms - $35-48
Pets: Under 30 lbs. welcome
Creature Comforts: CCTV, pool

Quality Inn
(800) 228-5151, (541) 342-1243
http://www.qualityinn.com
2121 Franklin Blvd.
75 rooms - $58-108
Pets: Welcome in smoking rms.
Creature Comforts: CCTV, a/c,
refrig, restaurant, cont. brkfst,
pool, whirlpool, sauna

Ramada Inn
(800) 2-Ramada, (541) 342-5181
http://www.ramada.com
225 Coburg Rd.
150 rooms - $60-88
Pets: Small pets w/$15 fee
Creature Comforts: CCTV, a/c,
refrig, micro, restaurant, cont.
brkfst, pool, whirlpool

Red Lion Inn
(800) RED-LION, (541) 342-5201
http://www.doubletreehotels.com
205 Coburg Rd.
140 rooms - $80-109
Pets: Welcome
Creature Comforts: CCTV, a/c,
restaurant, pool, hlth clb, and a
whirlpool

Travelodge
(800) 444-6383, (541) 342-6383
http://www.travelodge.com
1859 Franklin Blvd.
60 rooms - $61-99
Pets: Welcome in certain rooms
Creature Comforts: CCTV, a/c,
refrig, micro, restaurant, cont.
brkfst, whirlpool, sauna

Valley River Inn
(800) 543-8266, (541) 687-0123
http://www.valleyriverinn.com
1000 Valley River Way
257 rooms - $155-315
Pets: Welcome in ltd. rooms, pet
goodie bag
Creature Comforts: Great
rooms, spacious, contemporary
design, river views, CCTV, a/c,
Jacuzzi, balconies, restaurant,
pool, whirlpool, sauna, walking
trails

FLORENCE

Lighthouse Inn
(541) 997-3221
155 Rte. 101
28 rooms - $55-110
Pets: Welcome
Creature Comforts: CCTV-
VCR, refrig, micro, fireplace

Mercer Lake Resort
(800) 355-3633, (541) 997-3633
88875 Bay Berry Ln.
10 rooms - $55-80
Pets: Welcome
Creature Comforts: Rustic
cabins, kit

Money Saver Motel
(541) 997-7131
170 Rte. 101
40 rooms - $52-78
Pets: Welcome w/$20 deposit
Creature Comforts: CCTV

Ocean Breeze Motel
(800) 753-2642, (541) 997-2642
85165 Rte. 101
12 rooms - $40-55
Pets: Small pets w/$5 fee
Creature Comforts: CCTV, kit, restaurant

Park Motel
(541) 997-2634
85034 Rte. 101
17 rooms - $48-129
Pets: Welcome
Creature Comforts: CCTV, kit

Silver Sands Motel
(541) 997-3459
1449 Rte. 101
50 rooms - $35-69
Pets: Welcome
Creature Comforts: Kit, pool

FORT KLAMATH
Wilson's Cottages
(541) 381-2209
57997 Rte. 62
10 rooms - $40-58
Pets: Welcome
Creature Comforts: Kit

FOSSIL
Bridge Creek Flora Inn
(541) 763-2355
828 Main St.
4 rooms - $60-79
Pets: Welcome
Creature Comforts: CCTV, cont. brkfst

GARIBALDI
Bayshore Inn
(503) 322-2552
227 Garibaldi Ave.
21 rooms - $69-118
Pets: Welcome
Creature Comforts: CCTV, kit

Tilla Bay Motel
(503) 322-3405
805 Garibaldi Ave.
11 rooms - $39-59
Pets: Welcome
Creature Comforts: Kit

GEARHEART
Gearheart by the Sea
(800) 547-0115, (503) 738-8331
http://www.gearhartresort.com
1157 N. Marion St.
80 rooms - $120-199
Pets: Welcome in certain condos w/$11 daily fee
Creature Comforts: Individually owned and furnished condos on the ocean, CCTV, micro, kit, Jacuzzis, fireplace, whirlpool, pool, golf

GLENEDEN BEACH
Beachcombers Haven
(800) 428-5533, (541) 764-2252
7045 NW Glen Ave.
7 rooms - $125-165
Pets: Welcome
Creature Comforts: Beach rentals, CCTV, kit, fireplace, whirlpool

Salishan Lodge
(800) 452-2300, (541) 764-3600
http://www.salishan.com
7760 Highway 101
205 rooms - $120-270
Pets: Welcome w/$25 initial fee
Creature Comforts: Luxurious 700-acre resort nestled on wooded hills above Siletz Bay, villa rooms nestle into forested hillsides, sliding glass doors, decks, original art, CCTV, VCR, refrig, Jacuzzi, stone fireplace, restaurants, pools, hlth clb, whirlpool, sauna, golf, tennis, three-mile-long dog-friendly beach

GLIDE
Steelhead Run B&B
(800) 348-0563, (541) 496-0563
http://www.steelheadrun.com
23049 N. Umpqua Hwy.
5 rooms - $65-105
Pets: In studio w/$15 fee
Creature Comforts: CCTV, a/c, kit, cont. brkfst, pool, game room, deck-views of garden and river, lawn games

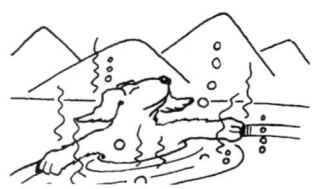

GOLD BEACH
Best Western Beachcomber Inn
(800) 528-1234, (541) 247-6691
http://www.bestwestern.com
1250 S. Rte. 101
49 rooms - $55-105
Pets: Welcome w/approval
Creature Comforts: CCTV, a/c, cont. brkfst, pool, whirlpool

City Center Motel
(541) 247-6675
94200 Harlow Rd.
21 rooms - $40-85
Pets: Certain rooms w/$10 fee
Creature Comforts: CCTV, a/c, micro, kit

Drift In Motel
(800) 424-3833, (541) 247-4547
94250 Port Dr.
23 rooms - $50-64
Pets: Welcome w/$5 fee
Creature Comforts: CCTV, kit, mini golf

Econo Lodge
(800) 55-ECONO, (541) 247-6606
http://www.econolodge.com
29171 S. Ellensburg Ave
41 rooms - $55-95
Pets: Welcome w/$5 fee
Creature Comforts: CCTV, refrig, micro, kit

Ireland's Rustic Cottages
(541) 247-7718
29330 S. Ellensburg Ave.
40 rooms - $45-66
Pets: Welcome w/$5 fee
Creature Comforts: CCTV, kit, fireplace

Jot's Resort
(800) FOR-JOTS, (541) 247-6676
http://www.jotsresort.com
Rte. 101 at Rogue River
121 rooms - $90-300
Pets: Welcome w/$10 nightly fee
Creature Comforts: Nice motor lodge at mouth of Rogue River, water view rooms, sliding glass doors open to decks, Scandinavian style furnishings, CCTV, refrig, kit, fireplace, restaurant, pool, whirlpool, sauna, hlth club, jet boating, guided fish tours

Motel 6
(800) 4-MOTEL6, (541) 247-4533
http://www.motel6.com
94433 Jerry's Flat Rd.
130 rooms - $30-78
Pets: Under 30 lbs. welcome
Creature Comforts: CCTV, a/c,
beach

Sand 'n Sea
(800) 808-SAND, (541) 247-6658
29362 Ellensburg Ave.
43 rooms - $49-82
Pets: In pet rooms w/$5 fee
Creature Comforts: TV, refrig,
and micro

Western Village Motel
(541) 247-6611
29399 Ellensburg Ave.
27 rooms - $50-80
Pets: Welcome w/$5 fee
Creature Comforts: CCTV, kit,
fireplace

GOVERNMENT CAMP
Mt. Hood Inn
(800) 443-7777, (503) 272-3205
http://www.mthoodinn.com
87450 E. Government Camp Loop
57 rooms - $85-165
Pets: Welcome w/$5 daily fee
Creature Comforts: CCTV, kit,
Jacuzzi, cont. brkfst, whirlpool

GRANTS PASS
Best Western Grants Pass
(800) 528-1234, (541) 476-1117
http://www.bestwestern.com
111 NE Agness Rd.
84 rooms - $65-90
Pets: Small pets welcome
Creature Comforts: CCTV, a/c,
restaurant, Jacuzzis, cont. brkfst,
pool, whirlpool

Best Western at the Rogue
(800) 528-1234, (541) 582-2200
http://www.bestwestern.com
8959 Rogue River Hwy.
53 rooms - $50-170
Pets: Small pets w/CC deposit
Creature Comforts: CCTV,
VCR, a/c, restaurant, cont. brkfst,
pool, whirlpool, hlth clb.

Comfort Inn
(800) 228-5150, (541) 479-8301
http://www.comfortinn.com
1889 N.E. Sixth St.
60 rooms - $55-75
Pets: Welcome
Creature Comforts: CCTV, a/c,
refrig, micro, cont. brkfst, pool,
and a whirlpool

Flamingo Inn
(541) 476-6601
728 NW Sixth St.
33 rooms - $30-39
Pets: Welcome
Creature Comforts: CCTV, a/c,
kit, pool

Holiday Inn Express
(800) HOLIDAY, (541)471-6144
http://www.holiday-inn.com
105 NE Agness Rd.
80 rooms - $60-130
Pets: Small pets w/$5 fee
Creature Comforts: CCTV,
VCR, a/c, refrig, micro, Jacuzzi,
cont. brkfst, pool, hlth clb, and a
whirlpool

Mahoney's Rod and Reel Motel
(541) 474-4411
http://www.mahoneyresorts.com
7875 Rogue River Hwy
8 rooms - $39-75
Pets: Welcome
Creature Comforts: CCTV, a/c,
kit, pool, whirlpool

Motel 6
(800) 4-MOTEL6, (541) 474-1331
http://www.motel6.com
1800 NE Seventh St.
122 rooms - $35-63
Pets: Under 30 lbs. welcome
Creature Comforts: CCTV, a/c,
pool

Redwood Motel
(541) 476-0878
815 NE 6th St.
25 rooms - $57-79
Pets: Small pets w/$10 fee
Creature Comforts: CCTV,
VCR, a/c, refrig, micro, Jacuzzi,
pool, whirlpool

Regal Lodge
(541) 479-3305
1400 NW Sixth St.
30 rooms - $30-39
Pets: Welcome
Creature Comforts: CCTV, a/c,
kit, fireplace, restaurant, pool

Riverside Inn Resort
(800) 334-4567, (541) 476-6873
http://www.riverside-inn.com
971 SE 6th St
174 rooms - $65-375
Pets: $15 one-time fee
Creature Comforts: CCTV,
VCR, a/c, kit, fireplace, Jacuzzi,
restaurant, pools, hlth clb access,
whirlpool, overlooks the river

Rogue River Inn
(541) 582-1120
6285 Rogue River Hwy.
21 rooms - $40-79
Pets: Welcome
Creature Comforts: CCTV, kit

Shilo Inn
(800) 222-2244, (503) 479-8391
http://www.shiloinns.com
1880 NW Sixth St.
70 rooms - $70-99
Pets: Welcome w/$7 fee
Creature Comforts: CCTV,
refrig, micro, pool, sauna

Super 8
(800) 800-8000, (541) 474-3358
http://www.super8.com
1949 NE Seventh St.
79 rooms - $50-65
Pets: Welcome w/$25 deposit
Creature Comforts: CCTV, a/c,
pool, whirlpool

Thriftlodge
(800) 525-9055, (541) 476-7793
http://www.travelodge.com
748 SE Seventh St.
35 rooms - $30-65
Pets: Small pets w/$3 fee
Creature Comforts: CCTV, pool

HALFWAY
Clear Creek Farm
(800) 414-5710, (541) 742-2238
www.clearcreekfamilyranch.com
Box 737
6 rooms - $60-79
Pets: Welcome
Creature Comforts: 1000-acre working ranch in bucolic setting w/orchards, pond, stream, bison, farm animals, antique farmhouse w/summer kit, rustic guest barn and cottage, fantastic farm breakfasts, hot tub, hiking, game room, assortment of organized programs, great for kids & dogs

Pine Valley Lodge/Supper Club
(541) 742-2238
http://www.neoregon.net/
pinevalleylodge
Box 712
6 rooms - $55-65
Pets: Welcome w/notice
Creature Comforts: Lodge w/ authentic features, filled w/ western antiques/collectibles, bedrooms set under eaves, furnished w/hand-painted antiques, down comforters & Pendleton blankets on four poster/ oak beds, excellent food in intimate restaurant, located close to Hell's Canyon

HILLSBORO
Best Western, Hallmark
(800) 528-1234, (503) 648-3500
http://www.bestwestern.com
3500 NE Cornell Rd.
123 rooms - $88-135
Pets: Small pets welcome
Creature Comforts: CCTV, a/c, restaurant, brkfst, pool, hlth club.

Candlewood Hotel
(800) 946-6200, (503) 681-2121
3133 NE Shute Rd.
126 rooms - $86-126
Pets: Welcome w/$75 deposit
Creature Comforts: CCTV, a/c, kit, hlth club, whirlpool

Cavanaughs Hotel
(800) 325-4000, (503) 648-3500
http://www.cavanaughs.com
3500 NE Cornell Rd.
122 rooms - $109-159
Pets: Welcome w/CC deposit
Creature Comforts: CCTV, a/c, refrig, Jacuzzis, restaurant, hlth club, whirlpool

Residence Inn
(800) 331-3131, (503) 531-3200
http://www.residenceinn.com
18855 NW Tanasbourne Rd.
125 rooms - $110-180
Pets: Welcome w/$10 fee
Creature Comforts: CCTV, a/c, kit, fireplace, pool, hlth club., whirlpool, sport court

HOOD RIVER
Best Western Hood River Inn
(800) 528-1234, (541) 386-2200
http://www.bestwestern.com
1108 E. Marina Way
149 rooms - $60-179
Pets: Small pets w/approval
Creature Comforts: CCTV, a/c, fireplace, Jacuzzis, restaurant, pool, whirlpool, dock, lawn games

Columbia Gorge Hotel
(800) 345-1921, (541) 386-5566
www.columbiagorgehotel.com
4000 Westcliff Dr.
46 rooms - $150-299
Pets: Welcome, leashed on ppty $25 fee per night
Creature Comforts: Striking cliffside location, lush grounds, historic hotel w/gracious public areas, pleasant rooms w/traditional furnishings, req. west wing near waterfall, CCTV, a/c, fireplace, gourmet restaurant, famous "Farm Brkfst", gardens

Hood River Hotel
(800) 386-1859, (503) 386-1900
http://www.hoodriverhotel.com
102 Oak Ave.
41 rooms - $50-175
Pets: Welcome w/$15 nightly fee
Creature Comforts: Restored historic brick hotel, Victorian antiques, sunny sitting room, charming but simple guest rooms, calico/chintz fabrics, dried flowers, canopy or four-poster beds, CCTV, kit, Northern Italian cafe, Jacuzzis, sauna, hlth clb

Lost Lake Resort
(541) 386-6366
Mt. Hood Nat'l Forest
8 rooms - $40-99
Pets: Welcome
Creature Comforts: Kit, swimming

Meredith Gorge Motel
(541) 386-1515
4300 Westcliff Rd.
21 rooms - $38-55
Pets: Welcome
Creature Comforts: CCTV, a/c, kit

Vagabond Lodge
(541) 386-2992
4070 Westcliff Dr.
39 rooms - $50-88
Pets: Small pets welcome
Creature Comforts: CCTV, a/c, kit, fireplace

JACKSONVILLE
Jacksonville Inn
(800) 321-9344, (541) 899-1900
http://www.jacksonvilleinn.com
175 E. California St.
11 rooms - $80-225
Pets: Welcome w/approval in all but two rooms, own bedding
Creature Comforts: 1862 brick inn set in Historic District, high ceilings, Victorian antique furnishings, sophisticated decor, CCTV, kit, Jacuzzi, cont. brkfst, good restaurant, walking distance of shops/residential area

Stage Lodge
(800) 253-8254, (541) 899-3953
http://www.stagelodge.com
830 N. 5th St.
27 rooms - $72-145
Pets: Welcome w/$10 fee
Creature Comforts: CCTV, a/c, refrig, micro, fireplace, Jacuzzi, fireplace

JOHN DAY
Best Western John Day
(800) 528-1234, (541) 575-1700
http://www.bestwestern.com
315 W. Main St.
39 rooms - $60-105
Pets: Small pets w/$4 fee
Creature Comforts: CCTV, refrig, micro, Jacuzzis, restaurant, pool, hlth club., whirlpool

Budget 8 Motel
(541) 575-2155
315 W. Main St.
14 rooms - $40-55
Pets: Welcome
Creature Comforts: CCTV,
restaurant, pool

Budget Inn
(800) 854-4442, (541) 575-2100
250 E. Main St.
14 rooms - $35-49
Pets: In smoking rooms w/$3 fee
Creature Comforts: CCTV, a/c,
refrig

Dreamers Lodge
(541) 575-0526
144 N. Canyon Blvd.
25 rooms - $45-58
Pets: Welcome
Creature Comforts: CCTV, a/c,
refrig, kit

Sunshine B&B
(541) 575-1153
210 NW Canton Rd.
2 rooms - $45-69
Pets: Welcome
Creature Comforts: CCTV, a/c,
cont. brkfst, pool

Sunset Inn
(800) 452-4899, (541) 575-1462
390 W. Main St.
43 rooms - $47-65
Pets: Welcome
Creature Comforts: CCTV, a/c,
kit, restaurant, pool, whirlpool

JORDAN VALLEY
Sahara Motel
(800) 828-4432, (541) 586-2810
607 North Main St.
22 rooms - $35-47
Pets: Welcome w/$5 fee
Creature Comforts: CCTV, a/c

KERBY
Holiday Motel
(541) 592-3003
24810 Redwood Hwy.
11 rooms - $47-58
Pets: Welcome
Creature Comforts: CCTV, a/c,
kit

KLAMATH FALLS
A-1 Budget Motel
(541) 884-8104
3844 Rte. 97 North
32 rooms - $42-59
Pets: Welcome
Creature Comforts: CCTV, a/c,
kit, cont. brkfst, pool

Best Western Klamath
(800) 528-1234, (541) 882-1200
http://www.bestwestern.com
2627 Sixth St.
71 rooms - $70-90
Pets: Small pets welcome
Creature Comforts: CCTV, a/c,
refrig, micro, cont. brkfst, pool,
hlth club., whirlpool

Cimmaron Motor Inn
(800) 742-2648, (541) 882-4601
3060 S. Sixth St.
163 rooms - $45-59
Pets: Welcome w/$5 fee
Creature Comforts: CCTV, a/c,
refrig, micro, pool

Hill View Motel
(541) 883-7771
5543 S. Sixth St.
16 rooms - $38-47
Pets: Welcome
Creature Comforts: CCTV, a/c

La Vista
(541) 882-8844
3939 Rte. 97 N.
24 rooms - $40-57
Pets: Welcome
Creature Comforts: CCTV, a/c,
kit, restaurant, pool, whirlpool

Maverick Motel
(800) 404-6690, (541) 882-6688
1220 Main St.
49 rooms - $35-42
Pets: Welcome w/$5 one-time fee
Creature Comforts: CCTV, a/c,
cont. brkfst, pool

Motel 6
(800) 4-MOTEL6, (541) 884-2110
http://www.motel6.com
5136 S. Sixth St.
61 rooms - $30-48
Pets: Under 30 lbs. welcome
Creature Comforts: CCTV, a/c,
pool

Olympic Lodge
(541) 883-8800
3006 Green Springs Dr.
32 rooms - $30-58
Pets: Welcome
Creature Comforts: CCTV, a/c,
kit

Oregon Motel 8
(541) 883-3431
5225 Route 97
30 rooms - $35-50
Pets: Small pets w/$5 fee
Creature Comforts: CCTV, a/c,
kit, pool

Quality Inn
(800) 228-5151, (541) 882-4666
http://www.qualityinn.com
100 Main St.
81 rooms - $65-105
Pets: Welcome w/CC deposit
Creature Comforts: CCTV, a/c,
restaurant, cont. brkfst, pool

Red Lion Inn
(800) RED-LION, (541) 882-8864
http://www.doubletreehotels.com
3612 S. 6th St.
110 rooms - $80-99
Pets: Welcome
Creature Comforts: CCTV,
VCR, a/c, refrig, micro, Jacuzzis,
restaurant, pool, hlth clb, and a
whirlpool

Shilo Suites Hotel
(800) 222-2244, (541) 885-7980
http://www.shiloinns.com
2500 Almond St.
145 rooms - $90-153
Pets: Welcome
Creature Comforts: CCTV, kit,
restaurant, pool, hlth clb., and a
whirlpool

Super 8
(800) 800-8000, (541) 884-8880
http://www.super8.com
3805 Route 97 North
61 rooms - $50-59
Pets: Welcome
Creature Comforts: CCTV, a/c,
whirlpool

LA GRANDE
Budget Inn
(541) 963-7116
2215 E. Adams Ave.
34 rooms - $70-89
Pets: Welcome w/$5 fee
Creature Comforts: CCTV, a/c,
refrig, micro, cont. brkfst, hlth clb

Greenwell Motel
(541) 963-4134
305 Adams Ave.
33 rooms - $25-39
Pets: Welcome
Creature Comforts: CCTV, a/c,
kit, pool

Howard Johnson Inn
(800) I-Go-Hojo, (541) 963-7195
http://www.hojo.com
2612 Island Ave.
146 rooms - $70-85
Pets: Small pets welcome
Creature Comforts: CCTV, a/c,
refrig, micro, cont. brkfst, pool,
hlth clb, sauna, whirlpool

Quail Run Motor Inn
(541) 963-3400
2400 Adams Ave.
15 rooms - $27-35
Pets: Welcome
Creature Comforts: CCTV, a/c,
kit, restaurant, cont. brkfst

Stardust Lodge
(541) 963-4166
402 Adams Ave.
30 rooms - $25-49
Pets: Welcome
Creature Comforts: CCTV, a/c,
restaurant, pool

LAKEVIEW
Best Western Skyline Lodge
(800) 528-1234, (541) 947-2194
http://www.bestwestern.com
414 North G St.
38 rooms - $60-85
Pets: Welcome w/$10 fee
Creature Comforts: CCTV, a/c,
micro, brkfst, pool, whirlpool

Interstate 8 Motel
(541) 947-3341
354 N. K St.
32 rooms - $34-44
Pets: Welcome
Creature Comforts: CCTV, a/c,
cont. brkfst, restaurant

Lakeview Lodge Motel
(541) 947-2181
301 N. G Street
40 rooms - $40-69
Pets: Welcome
Creature Comforts: CCTV, a/c,
kit, hlth club, sauna, whirlpool

Rim Rock Motel
(541) 947-2185
727 S. F St.
27 rooms - $30-39
Pets: Welcome
Creature Comforts: CCTV, a/c,
kit, restaurant

LAKE OSWEGO
Best Western Sherwood
(800) 528-1234, (503) 620-2980
http://www.bestwestern.com
15700 SW Upper Boones Ferry
101 rooms - $75-125
Pets: Welcome w/permission
Creature Comforts: CCTV, a/c,
Jacuzzi, pool, sauna

Crowne Plaza
(800) 227-6963, (503) 624-8400
http://www.holiday-inn.com
14811 Kruse Oaks Blvd.
160 rooms - $105-210
Pets: Welcome
Creature Comforts: CCTV,
VCR, a/c, refrig, pool, hlth clb,
whirlpool, sauna, bikes

Residence Inn
(800) 331-3131, (503) 684-2603
http://www.residenceinn.com
15200 SW Bangy Rd.
112 rooms - $115-135
Pets: Welcome w/$10 fee
Creature Comforts: CCTV, a/c,
kit, fireplace, cont. brkfst, pool,
whirlpool

LAPINE
Best Western Newbury Station
(800) 528-1234, (541) 536-5130
http://www.bestwestern.com
16515 Reed Rd.
40 rooms - $55-155
Pets: Under 15 lbs. welcome
Creature Comforts: CCTV, a/c,
refrig, cont. brkfst, fireplace, pool,
hlth clb access, whirlpool

Diamond Stone Guest Lodge
(800) 600-6263, (541) 536-6263
http://www.diamondstone.com
16693 Sprague Loop
3 rooms - $80-139
Pets: Welcome w/$20 daily fee
Creature Comforts: B &B w/
incredible panoramic views of
Cascades, art gallery, attractive
rooms w/quilts, pine furnishings,
suite has wonderful views, CCTV,
VCR, a/c, fireplace, full brkfst, kit,
hors d'oeuvres, hot tub, sauna,
exercise room, 5 acres, and golf

Highlander Motel/RV Park
(541) 536-2131
51511 Rte. 97
9 rooms - $35-49
Pets: Welcome
Creature Comforts: CCTV, a/c,
kit

Pauline Lake Resort
(541) 536-2240
13 miles off Rte. 97
14 cabins - $55-145
Pets: One pet welcome per cabin
Creature Comforts: Lakeside
setting, fully-equipped cabins, kit,
woodstove, restaurant

Timbercrest Inn
(541) 536-1737
52560 Rte. 97
21 rooms - $35-57
Pets: Welcome
Creature Comforts: CCTV, a/c,
kit

West View Motel
(800) 440-2115, (541) 536-2115
Route 97
9 rooms - $40-55
Pets: Welcome in smoking room
Creature Comforts: CCTV

LINCOLN CITY
Anchor Motel
(800) 582-8611, (541) 996-3810
4417 SW Rte. 101
29 rooms - $35-55
Pets: Welcome w/$5-10 fee
Creature Comforts: CCTV,
refrig, kit

Best Western Lincoln Sands
(800) 528-1234, (541) 994-4227
http://www.bestwestern.com
535 NW Inlet Rd.
33 rooms - $90-399
Pets: Small pets welcome
Creature Comforts: CCTV,
VCR, cont. brkfst, kit, Jacuzzis,
pool, hlth club., sauna, whirlpool

Blue Heron Landing Motel
(541) 994-4708
4006 W. Devils Lake Rd.
8 rooms - $60-67
Pets: Welcome
Creature Comforts: CCTV, kit

City Center Motel
(541) 994-2612
1014 NE Rte. 101
15 rooms - $32-55
Pets: Welcome
Creature Comforts: CCTV, a/c,
kit

Coho Inn
(800) 848-7006, (541) 994-3684
1635 NW Harbor Rd.
50 rooms - $60-150
Pets: Small pets w/$6 fee
Creature Comforts: CCTV,
refrig, kit, fireplace, whirlpool,
sauna

Dock of the Bay Motel
(800) 362-5229, (541) 996-3549
116 SW 51st St
30 rooms - $60-150
Pets: Small pets w/$5 fee
Creature Comforts: CCTV, kit,
fireplace, whirlpool, sauna

Enchanted Cottage B&B
(888) 877-1455, (541) 996-4101
http://www.virtualcities.com/ons/
or/z/orz7601.htm
4507 SW Coast Rd.
3 rooms - $100-150
Pets: Small dogs welcome in
California Suite (private entrance)
Creature Comforts: Intimate and
tastefully appointed cottage tucked
into hillside overlooking Siletz
Bay, a short walk to beach,
California Suite w/oak bed, bath
robes, priv. entrance, CCTV,
fireplace, full gourmet brkfst,
homemade smoked salmon, deck

Ester Lee Motel
(888) 996-3606, (541) 996-3606
3803 SW Rte. 101
53 rooms - $65-89
Pets: Welcome
Creature Comforts: CCTV, kit

Hideaway Motel
(541) 994-8874
810 SW Tenth
6 rooms - $70-125
Pets: Welcome w/$5 nightly fee,
limit to 2 pets/room
Creature Comforts: Shake
cottage nestled into cliff in
residential area, recommend
Master Suite for expansive views,
pine paneled walls, maple and oak
furnishings, pleasant decor,
CCTV, kit, fireplace, steps to
ocean

Lincoln City Inn
(541) 996-4400
1091 SE 1st St.
60 rooms - $70-139
Pets: Welcome w/$10 fee
Creature Comforts: CCTV,
VCR, refrig, micro, Jacuzzi,
whirlpool, sauna

Rodeway Inn
(800) 228-2000, (541) 996-3996
http://www.rodeway.com
861 SW 51st St.
41 rooms - $40-148
Pets: Welcome
Creature Comforts:CCTV, brkfst

Sailor Jack Motel
(888) Heave-Ho, (541) 994-3696
1035 NW Harbor Ave.
40 rooms - $60-149
Pets: Welcome
Creature Comforts: CCTV,
refrig, kit, fireplace, sauna

Sea Echo Motel
(541) 994-2575
3510 NE Rte. 101
12 rooms - $42-65
Pets: Welcome
Creature Comforts: CCTV, a/c,
cont. brkfst

Seagull Beachfront Motel
(800) 422-0219, (541) 994-2948
1511 NW Harbor Rd.
25 rooms - $70-180
Pets: Welcome w/$5 fee
Creature Comforts: Oceanview
rms, CCTV, kit, fireplace, Jacuzzi

Shilo Inns
(800) 222-2244, (503) 994-3655
http://www.shiloinns.com
1501 NW 40th Pl.
248 rooms - $60-245
Pets: Welcome w/$7 fee
Creature Comforts: CCTV,
refrig, micro, restaurant, pool, hlth
clb., whirlpool, sauna

Surftides Beach Resort
(800) 994-2191, (541) 994-2191
2945 Jetty Ave.
123 rooms - $54-97
Pets: Welcome
Creature Comforts: CCTV, a/c,
fireplace, restaurant, cont. brkfst,
pool, whirlpool, sauna

Westshore Oceanfront Motel
(800) 621-3187, (541) 996-2001
3127 SW 32nd St.
19 rooms - $75-85
Pets: Welcome w/$5 fee per pet
Creature Comforts: Oceanside,
CCTV, kit, fireplace

Whistling Winds Motel
(541) 994-6155
3264 NW Jetty
15 rooms - $45-85
Pets: Welcome
Creature Comforts: CCTV, a/c,
kit

MADRAS
Best Western Rama Inn
(800) 528-1234, (541) 475-6141
http://www.bestwestern.com
12 SW Fourth St.
46 rooms - $50-100
Pets: Welcome
Creature Comforts: CCTV, a/c,
refrig, micro, cont. brkfst, pool,
hlth club., sauna, whirlpool

Goffy's Motel
(800) 227-6865, (541) 475-4633
600 N. Rte. 26
100 rooms - $50-109
Pets: Small pets w/$20 deposit,
$15 refundable
Creature Comforts: CCTV, a/c,
refrig, micro, Jacuzzi, pool

Juniper Motel
(800) 244-1399, (541) 475-6186
414 N. Rte. 26
22 rooms - $40-59
Pets: Welcome w/$5 fee
Creature Comforts: CCTV, a/c,
refrig, micro

Royal Dutch Motel
(541) 475-2281
1102 SW Rte. 97
10 rooms - $32-58
Pets: Welcome
Creature Comforts: CCTV, a/c

Sonny's Motel
(800) 624-6137, (541) 475-7217
1539 SW Rte. 97
44 rooms - $50-64
Pets: Welcome w/$10 fee
Creature Comforts: CCTV, a/c,
refrig, micro, restaurant, pool,
whirlpool

MAZANITA
Sunset Surf Oceanfront
(800) 243-8035, (541) 368-5224
1539 Rte. 97
41 rooms - $55-119
Pets: Welcome in certain rooms
w/$10 one time fee
Creature Comforts: CCTV, a/c,
kit, fireplace, pool

MAUPIN
Deschutes Motel
(541) 395-2626
616 Mill St.
12 rooms - $45-59
Pets: Welcome
Creature Comforts: CCTV,
VCR, a/c, kit, Jacuzzi, pool, and
whirlpool

The Oasis
(541) 395-2611
609 Rte. 197
10 rooms - $45-69
Pets: Welcome
Creature Comforts: CCTV, a/c,
kit, restaurant

McKENZIE BRIDGE
The Country Place
(541) 822-6008
56245 Delta Dr.
3 cabins - $70-89
Pets: Controlled pets welcome
Creature Comforts: Riverside
cabins, CCTV, a/c, kit, living rm,
and fireplaces

MCMINNVILLE
Paragon Motel
(800) 525-5469, (541) 472-9493
2065 Rte. 99 West
55 rooms - $40-56
Pets: Welcome $6 fee
Creature Comforts: CCTV, a/c,
refrig, kit, pool

MEDFORD
Best Western Pony Soldier Inn
(800) 528-1234, (541) 779-2011
http://www.bestwestern.com
2340 Crater Lake Hwy.
72 rooms - $75-99
Pets: Welcome w/$25 fee
Creature Comforts: CCTV, a/c,
refrig, micro, cont. brkfst, pool,
and whirlpool

Cedar Lodge
(541) 773-7361
2340 Crater Lake Hwy.
80 rooms - $35-68
Pets: Welcome w/$20 deposit
Creature Comforts: CCTV,
VCR, a/c, refrig, micro, kit, pool

Diamond Lake Resort
(800) 733-7593, (541) 793-3333
http://www.diamondlake.net
Route 138
92 rooms - $70-175
Pets: Welcome w/$5 nightly fee
Creature Comforts: CCTV, a/c,
kit, fireplace, restaurant, bikes,
boats-marina

Horizon Inn
(800) 452-2255, (541) 779-5085
1154 E. Barnett Rd.
130 rooms - $69-155
Pets: Welcome w/$10 fee
Creature Comforts: CCTV, a/c,
refrig, micro, Jacuzzi, restaurant,
pool, whirlpool, sauna, hlth club

Motel 6, North
(800) 4-MOTEL6, (541) 779-0550
http://www.motel6.com
2400 Biddle Rd.
116 rooms - $35-52
Pets: Under 30 lbs. welcome
Creature Comforts: TV, a/c, pool

Motel 6, South
(800) 4-MOTEL6, (541) 773-4290
http://www.motel6.com
950 Alba Dr.
167 rooms - $30-55
Pets: Under 30 lbs. welcome
Creature Comforts: TV, a/c, pool

Pear Tree Motel
(800) 645-7332, (541) 535-4445
3730 Fern Valley Rd.
45 rooms - $50-98
Pets: Small pets w/$10 fee
Creature Comforts: CCTV,
VCR, a/c, pool, whirlpool

Red Lion Inn
(800) RED-LION, (541) 779-5811
http://www.doubletreehotels.com
200 N. Riverside Rd.
190 rooms - $55-250
Pets: Welcome w/$50 deposit
Creature Comforts: CCTV,
refrig, Jacuzzi, restaurant, pool,
hlth club.

Reston Hotel
(800) 779-STAY, (541) 779-3141
2300 Crater Lake Hwy.
164 rooms - $50-110
Pets: $10 fee, $25 deposit
Creature Comforts: CCTV,
VCR, a/c, refrig, micro, Jacuzzi,
restaurant, pool
Windmill Inn

(800) 547-4747, (541) 779-0050
http://www.windmillinns.com
1950 Biddle Rd.
123 rooms - $55-90
Pets: Welcome
Creature Comforts: CCTV,
VCR, a/c, kit, Jacuzzi, restaurant,
cont. brkfst, pool, sauna

MILTON-FREEWATER
Out West Motel
(800) 881-6647, (541) 938-6647
84040 Rte. 11
11 rooms - $35-49
Pets: Welcome
Creature Comforts: TV, a/c, kit

MYRTLE CREEK
Quick Stop Motel & Market
(541) 863-4689
6453 Dole Rd.
12 rooms - $32-59
Pets: Welcome
Creature Comforts: CCTV, a/c, kit

MYRTLE POINT
Myrtle Trees Motel
(541) 572-5811
1010 Eight St.
29 rooms - $38-53
Pets: Welcome
Creature Comforts: CCTV

NESKOWIN
Breakers Condominiums
(503) 392-3963
48060 Breakers Blvd.
11 rooms - $165-225
Pets: Welcome
Creature Comforts: CCTV, kit, fireplace

NETARTS
Terimore Lodging by the Sea
(800) 635-1821, (503) 842-4623
5105 Crab Ave.
26 rooms - $35-87
Pets: Welcome w/$5 fee
Creature Comforts: CCTV, refrig, kit, fireplace

Three Capes Inn
(503) 842-4003
4800 Netarts Hwy West
8 rooms - $45-65
Pets: Welcome
Creature Comforts: CCTV, a/c, kit

NEWBURG
Shilo Inn
(800) 222-2244, (503) 537-0303
http://www.shiloinns.com
501 Sitka Ave.
60 rooms - $55-95
Pets: Welcome w/$7 fee
Creature Comforts: CCTV, VCR, a/c, refrig, micro, restaurant, pool, hlth clb., whirlpool, sauna

NEWPORT
Agate Beach Oceanfront Motel
(800) 755-5674, (541) 265-8746
http://www.ohwy.com/or/a/agatebch.htm
175 NW Gilbert Way
10 rooms - $115-150
Pets: Welcome w/$10 fee
Creature Comforts: Private beach access, ocean views, CCTV, kit

City Center Motel
(800) 628-9665, (541) 265-7381
538 SW Coast Hwy.
30 rooms - $45-67
Pets: Medium pets w/$5 fee
Creature Comforts: CCTV, refrig, micro

Driftwood Village Motel
(541) 265-5738
7947 N. Coast Hwy.
12 rooms - $55-125
Pets: Welcome w/$7 fee
Creature Comforts: CCTV, kit, fireplace

Green Gables Bed & Breakfast
(800) 515-9065, (541) 265-9141
http://greengablesbb.com
156 SW Coast Street
2 rooms - $85-105
Pets: "Well-mannered mature pets are welcome if not left alone"
Creature Comforts: Charming Victorian B&B a block from the ocean, CCTV, VCR, refrig, micro, antiques, two-person Jacuzzis, Turret Room has great views and a balcony, cont. brkfst, bookstore

Hallmark Resort
(888) 448-4449, (541) 265-2600
http://www.hallmarkinns.com
744 SW Elizabeth St.
157 rooms - $70-245
Pets: In pet rooms w/$5 fee
Creature Comforts: Spectacular oceanside setting, CCTV, a/c, refrig, micro, Jacuzzis, cont. brkfst, pool, massage, whirlpool

Holiday Inn at Agate Beach
(800) HOLIDAY, (541) 265-9411
http://www.holiday-inn.com
3019 N. Coast Hwy.
148 rooms - $79-155
Pets: Welcome
Creature Comforts: CCTV, restaurant, pool, whirlpool

Money Saver Motel
(541) 265-2277
861 SW Coast Hwy. 101
42 rooms - $44-89
Pets: Welcome
Creature Comforts: CCTV, kit

Newport Motor Inn
(541) 265-8516
1311 N. Coast Hwy. 101
39 rooms - $32-63
Pets: Welcome
Creature Comforts: CCTV, a/c, restaurant

Shilo Inns
(800) 222-2244, (541) 265-7701
http://www.shiloinns.com
536 SW Elizabeth St.
180 rooms - $100-200
Pets: Welcome w/$7 fee
Creature Comforts: CCTV, VCR, kit, restaurant, pool

Starfish Point
(541) 265-3751
http://www.newportnet.com/starfishpoint
140 NW 48th St.
6 rooms - $60-79
Pets: Welcome w/$5 fee-only 2 pets at any one time
Creature Comforts: Stunning cliffside condominiums, tucked into cliffs w/plate glass windows overlooking forest and ocean, request end units, split-level units, cozy & fully equipped w/CCTV, VCR, stereo, kit, fireplace, Jacuzzi, private decks, stereos

Surf N Sand Motel
(541) 265-2215
8143 N. Coast Hwy.
17 rooms - $65-117
Pets: Welcome
Creature Comforts: Fireplace

Val-U-Inn
(800) 443-7777, (541) 265-6203
http://www.valuinn.com
531 SW Fall St.
70 rooms - $65-144
Pets: Small pets w/$5 fee
Creature Comforts: CCTV,
VCR, kit, Jacuzzi, cont. brkfst,
pool, hlth clb., whirlpool, sauna

Vikings Cottages
(800) 480-2477, (541) 265-2477
www.vikingsoregoncoast.com
729 NW Coast St.
39 rooms - $65-225
Pets: Welcome in cottages, not
condominiums
Creature Comforts: CCTV, kit,
fireplace, some w/great views

Waves Motel
(541) 265-4661
820 NW Coast St.
24 rooms - $58-68
Pets: Small pets
Creature Comforts: CCTV, some
oceanview rooms

Whaler Motel
(800) 433-9444, (541) 265-9261
155 SW Elizabeth St.
73 rooms - $90-139
Pets: Small pets in certain rooms
Creature Comforts: CCTV,
VCR, refrig, micro, fireplace,
cont. brkfst

NORTH BEND
City Center Motel
(541) 756-5118
750 Connecticut St.
18 rooms - $32-55
Pets: Welcome
Creature Comforts: CCTV, kit

Plainview Motel/RV Park
(800) 962-2815, (541) 888-5166
2760 Cape Arago Hwy.
12 rooms - $40-99
Pets: Welcome
Creature Comforts: CCTV, kit,
fireplace, cont. brkfst

Pony Village Motor Lodge
(541) 756-3191
Virginia Ave.
119 rooms - $43-79
Pets: Welcome
Creature Comforts: CCTV,
restaurant

NYSSA
Lake Owyhee Resort
(541) 339-2444
1200 Lake Owyhee Dam Rd.
18 rooms - $42-49
Pets: Welcome
Creature Comforts: CCTV, a/c,
kit, pool, hlth club.

OAKLAND
Beckley House B&B
(541) 459-9320
www.makewebs.com/beckley
338 SE Second Street, Box 198
3 rooms - $60-85
Pets: Selectively welcomed in the
Spring Suite
Creature Comforts: A cozy 1898
classic Revival Victorian, listed
on the U.S. National Register of
Historic Home, library w/
collectibles, TV, patio swing,
floral accents, full brkfst

OAKRIDGE
Best Western Oakridge Inn
(800) 528-1234, (541) 782-2212
http://www.bestwestern.com
47433 Rte. 58
40 rooms - $60-89
Pets: Small pets w/$5 fee
Creature Comforts: CCTV, a/c,
cont. brkfst, pool, whirlpool

ONTARIO
Best Western Inn
(800) 528-1234, (541) 889-2600
http://www.bestwestern.com
251 Goodfellow St.
60 rooms - $60-155
Pets: Small dogs only
Creature Comforts: CCTV, a/c,
cont. brkfst, pool, hlth club.

Budget Inn
(800) 505-9047, (541) 889-3101
1737 N. Oregon St.
26 rooms - $30-39
Pets: Welcome
Creature Comforts: CCTV, a/c,
refrig, pool

Carlisle Motel
(800) 640-8658, (541) 889-8658
589 N. Oregon St.
18 rooms - $35-65
Pets: Welcome w/$5 fee
Creature Comforts: CCTV, a/c,
kit,

Holiday Inn
(800) HOLIDAY, (541) 889-8621
http://www.holiday-inn.com
1249 Tapadera Ave.
99 rooms - $60-90
Pets: Welcome
Creature Comforts: CCTV,
VCR, restaurant, pool, whirlpool

Holiday Motel
(541) 889-9188
615 E. Idaho Ave.
71 rooms - $35-48
Pets: Welcome
Creature Comforts: CCTV,
VCR, restaurant, pool

Motel 6
(800) 4-MOTEL6, (541) 889-6617
http://www.motel6.com
275 NE Fourth St.
126 rooms - $29-65
Pets: Under 30 lbs. welcome
Creature Comforts: CCTV, a/c,
pool

Oregon Trail Motel
(541) 889-8633
92 E. Idaho Ave.
30 rooms - $36-45
Pets: Welcome
Creature Comforts: CCTV, a/c,
refrig

Stockman's Motel
(541) 889-4446
81 SW First St.
28 rooms - $34-45
Pets: Welcome
Creature Comforts: CCTV, a/c,
restaurant

Super 8
(800) 800-8000, (541) 889-8282
http://www.super8.com
266 Goodfellow St.
63 rooms - $48-115
Pets: Welcome w/permission
Creature Comforts: CCTV, a/c,
cont. brkfst, pool, hlth club.

OREGON CITY
Budget Inn Gladstone
(800) 655-9368, (503) 656-1955
19240 SE McLoughlin Blvd.
36 rooms - $37-65
Pets: Welcome
Creature Comforts: CCTV, a/c,
kit, restaurant, pool

Rivershore Hotel
(800) 443-7777, (503) 655-7141
http://www.rivershore.com
1900 Clackamette Dr.
120 rooms - $65-79
Pets: Welcome w/$5 fee
Creature Comforts: CCTV, a/c,
refrig, micro, restaurant, pool,
whirlpool, sauna

OTTER ROCK
Alpine Chalet
(541) 765-2572
7045 SW Otter Crest Loop
3 condos - $90-115
Pets: Welcome w/$10
Creature Comforts: CCTV,
VCR, a/c, kit

PACIFIC CITY
Inn at Cape Kiwanda
(888) 965-7001, (503) 965-7001
www.innatcapekiwanda.com
33105 Cape Kiwanda Dr.
35 rooms - $99-289
Pets: Welcome w/$10 nightly fee
Creature Comforts: Great
accommodations set on dunes
overlooking the ocean, CCTV,
fireplace, Jacuzzi, kit, restaurant,
whirlpool, hlth club, decks

Inn at Pacific City
(888) 722-2489, (503) 965-6366
http://www.innatpacificcity.com
35215 Brooten Rd.
16 rooms - $49-99
Pets: Welcome w/$9 nightly fee
Creature Comforts: CCTV, kit

PENDLETON
7 Inn at the Ranch
(800) REG7INN, (541) 276-4711
Route 84
50 rooms - $39-55
Pets: Welcome w/$2 fee
Creature Comforts: CCTV, a/c

Chaparral Motel
(541) 276-8654
620 SW Tutilla Ave.
51 rooms - $40-57
Pets: Small pets w/$5 fee
Creature Comforts: CCTV, a/c,
refrig, kit

Doubletree Hotel
(800) 222-TREE, (541) 276-6111
http://www.doubletreehotels.com
304 SE Nye Ave.
170 rooms - $71-249
Pets: Small pets welcome
Creature Comforts: CCTV, a/c,
refrig, micro, Jacuzzis, balconies,
restaurant, pool, whirlpool, sauna

Let'er Buck Motel
(541) 276-3293
205 SE Dorion Ave.
35 rooms - $28-37
Pets: Welcome
Creature Comforts: CCTV, a/c,
refrig, kit

Longhorn Motel
(541) 276-7531
411 SW Dorion Ave.
36 rooms - $31-56
Pets: Welcome
Creature Comforts: CCTV, a/c

Motel 6
(800) 4-MOTEL6, (541) 276-3160
http://www.motel6.com
325 SE Nye Ave.
122 rooms - $30-49
Pets: Under 30 lbs. welcome
Creature Comforts: CCTV, a/c,
pool

Super 8
(800) 800-8000, (541) 276-8881
http://www.super8.com
601 SE Nye Ave.
50 rooms - $50-59
Pets: Welcome w/$20 deposit
Creature Comforts: CCTV, a/c,
restaurant, cont. brkfst, pool

Tapadera Inn
(800) 722-8277, (541) 276-3231
105 SE Court St.
50 rooms - $40-50
Pets: Welcome w/$5 fee
Creature Comforts: CCTV, a/c,
restaurant

Vagabond Inn
(800) 522-1555, (541) 276-5252
http://www.vagabondinn.com
201 SW Court St.
51 rooms - $38-59
Pets: Welcome
Creature Comforts: CCTV, a/c,
pool, cont. brkfst

Wildhorse Resort
(800) 654-WILD, (541) 276-0355
http://wildhorseresort.com
72779 Rte. 331
99 rooms - $50-135
Pets: In certain 1st floor rooms w/
$10 one-time fee
Creature Comforts: CCTV, a/c,
refrig, micro, Jacuzzi, pool, hlth
clb, whirlpool, sauna, casino, golf

PORT ORFORD
Castaway-by-the-Sea
(541) 332-4502
545 W. Fifth St.
13 rooms - $45-85
Pets: Welcome
Creature Comforts: CCTV, kit

Sea Crest Motel
(541) 332-3040
Route 101
18 rooms - $45-75
Pets: Small pets in certain rooms
Creature Comforts: TV, refrig,
and ocean views

Shoreline Motel
(541) 332-2903
206 Sixth St.
13 rooms - $40-62
Pets: Welcome
Creature Comforts: CCTV, kit,
restaurant

PORTLAND
Aladdin Motor Inn
(800) 292-4466, (503) 246-8241
8905 SW 30th Ave.
52 rooms - $40-75
Pets: Welcome
Creature Comforts: CCTV, a/c,
kit, restaurant, whirlpool

The Benson Hotel
(800) 426-0670, (503) 228-2000
www.westcoasthotels.com/benson
309 SW Broadway Rd.
287 rooms - $145-600
Pets: Welcome w/signed waiver
Creature Comforts: Historic
French baroque hotel, marble
floors, walnut wainscoting, crystal
chandeliers, fine antiques,
sophisticated guest rooms w/
traditional furnishings, fireplace,
taupe and cream colors, botanical
prints, request Benson or corner
rooms, CCTV, a/c, refrig, Jacuzzi,
restaurants, hlth clb access

Best Western, Convention
(800) 528-1234, (503) 233-2677
http://www.bestwestern.com
420 NE Holladay Rd.
95 rooms - $65-109
Pets: Under 20 lbs. in smk. rms
Creature Comforts: CCTV, a/c,
refrig, restaurant

Best Western Imperial
(800) 528-1234, (503) 228-7221
http://www.bestwestern.com
400 SW Broadway St.
134 rooms - $80-125
Pets: Small pets w/$10 fee
Creature Comforts: CCTV, a/c,
refrig, cont. brkfst, hlth club

Best Western Meadows
(800) 528-1234, (503) 286-9600
http://www.bestwestern.com
1215 N Hayden Meadows Dr.
146 rooms - $80-95
Pets: Welcome $22 one-time fee
Creature Comforts: CCTV, a/c,
cont. brkfst, whirlpool

Clarion Hotel, Airport
(800) CLARION, (503) 251-2000
http://www.clarioninn.com
6233 NE 78th
198 rooms - $80-135
Pets: Small pets w/$50 deposit
Creature Comforts: CCTV, a/c,
refrig, restaurant, pool, hlth clb,
whirlpool, sauna

Comfort Inn, Convention
(800) 228-5150, (503) 233-7933
http://www.comfortinn.com
431 N.E. Multnomah Rd.
79 rooms - $65-135
Pets: Welcome
Creature Comforts: CCTV, a/c,
cont. brkfst, pool

Days Inn
(800) DAYS INN, (503) 221-2550
http://www.daysinn.com
3828 NE 82nd Blvd.
75 rooms - $55-80
Pets: Welcome w/$10 fee
Creature Comforts: CCTV, a/c,
pool, hlth club.

Days Inn
(800) DAYS INN, (503) 289-1800
http://www.daysinn.com
9930 N. Whittaker Rd.
213 rooms - $60-78
Pets: Welcome w/$17 fee
Creature Comforts: CCTV, a/c,
kit, cont. brkfst

Doubletree, Columbia River
(800) 222-TREE, (503) 283-2111
http://www.doubletreehotels.com
1401 N. Hayden Island Dr.
350 rooms - $100-330
Pets: Under 20 lbs. w/$35 fee
Creature Comforts: CCTV, a/c,
refrig, micro, Jacuzzi, restaurant,
pool, whirlpool, tennis

Doubletree Hotel, Downtown
(800) 222-TREE, (503) 221-0450
http://www.doubletreehotels.com
310 SW Lincoln St.
230 rooms - $100-375
Pets: Welcome w/$25 deposit
Creature Comforts: CCTV, a/c,
refrig, micro, Jacuzzi, restaurant,
pool, whirlpool, tennis

Fifth Avenue Suites Hotel
(800) 711-2971, (503) 222-0001
http://www.5thavenuesuites.com
506 SW Washington at 5th
220 rooms - $150-625
Pets: Welcome
Creature Comforts: 1900's
historic hotel, intimate rooms,
lovely decor, French doors,
CCTV, a/c, restaurant, cont. brkfst,
and a hlth clb

Four Points Hotel
(800) 325-3535, (503) 221-0711
http://www.sheraton.com
50 SW Morrison Rd.
139 rooms - $90-255
Pets: Small pets w/$10 fee
Creature Comforts: CCTV, a/c,
kit, restaurant, hlth clb access

Hotel Vintage Plaza
(800) 263-2305, (503) 228-1212
http://www.vintageplaza.com
422 SW Broadway
107 rooms - $165-750
Pets: Welcome
Creature Comforts: Historic
downtown hotel, sophisticated
decor, intimate spaces, request
starlight suites w/conservatory
windows, lovely traditional decor,
Jacuzzi, Starlight Room feature
unique conservatory windows,
CCTV, VCR, a/c, refrig, fireplace,
rose petals sprinkled on beds at
turndown-"packages," restaurant,
cont. brkfst, comp. wine tasting,
executive gym

Howard Johnson Hotel, Airport
(800) I-Go-Hojo, (503) 255-6722
http://www.hojo.com/
7101 NE 82nd Ave.
137 rooms - $75-100
Pets: Welcome
Creature Comforts: CCTV, a/c,
restaurant, pool, hlth clb, sauna,
whirlpool

Mallory Hotel
(800) 228-8657, (503) 223-6311
http://www.malloryhotel.com
729 SW 15th St.
124 rooms - $70-150
Pets: Welcome w/$10 fee
Creature Comforts: Historic
hotel, old world charm, Cavernous
lobby with detailed moldings and
columns, reasonable rates, 1930's
Art Deco decor, CCTV, eclectic
furnishings, a/c, kit, restaurant

Mark Spencer
(800) 548-3934, (503) 224-3293
http://www.markspencer.com
729 SW 15th St.
100 rooms - $75-120
Pets: Welcome w/$200 deposit
Creature Comforts: Apartment
hotel, CCTV, a/c, kit, cont. brkfst,
hlth club

Marriott Hotel
(800) 228-9290, (503) 226-7600
http://www.marriott.com
1401 SW Naito Pkwy.
500 rooms - $110-520
Pets: Welcome w/$50 fee
Creature Comforts: CCTV, a/c, refrig, Jacuzzi, restaurant, pool, hlth clb,whirlpool, sauna, massage

Motel 6
(800) 4-MOTEL6, (503) 238-0600
http://www.motel6.com
3104 SE Powell Blvd.
69 rooms - $40-55
Pets: Under 30 lbs. welcome
Creature Comforts: CCTV, a/c, pool

Oxford Suites
(800) 548-7848, (503) 283-3030
http://www.oxfordsuites.com
12226 N. Jantzen Dr.
135 rooms - $70-185
Pets: Under 20 lbs. w/$15 fee
Creature Comforts: CCTV, VCR, a/c, refrig, micro, Jacuzzi, cont. brkfst, pool, hlth clb, and a whirlpool

Quality Inn (airport)
(800) 228-5151, (503) 256-4111
http://www.qualityinn.com
8247 NE Sandy Blvd
120 rooms - $75-139
Pets: Welcome w/$10 fee
Creature Comforts: CCTV, VCR, a/c, restaurant, cont. brkfst, pool

Red Lion (Colliseum)
(800) RED-LION, (503) 235-8311
http://www.doubletreehotels.com
1225 N. Thunderbird Way
212 rooms - $110-160
Pets: Small pets w/$15 fee
Creature Comforts: CCTV, a/c, refrig, Jacuzzi, pool, hlth club.

Residence Inn
(800) 331-3131, (503) 288-1400
http://www.residenceinn.com
1710 NE Multnomah Rd.
170 rooms - $125-190
Pets: Welcome w/$10 fee
Creature Comforts: CCTV, a/c, kit, pool, fireplace, hlth clb access, tennis, whirlpool

RiverPlace Hotel
(800) 227-1333, (503) 228-3233
http://www.riverplacehotel.com
1510 SW Harbor Way
85 rooms - $220-750
Pets: Welcome w/$100 fee
Creature Comforts: Graceful shingle-style hotel overlooking Willamette River, contemporary interior, marble, teak, and oak accents, Nantucket style rooms w/ light woods, pastel colors, luxuriously appointed, down pillows, CCTV, VCR, a/c, refrig, micro, fireplace, marble bath, Jacuzzi, terry robes, restaurants, gourmet cont. brkfst, hlth clb

Rose Manor Motel
(503) 236-4175
4546 SE McCloughin Rd.
75 rooms - $49-68
Pets: Welcome w/$5 fee
Creature Comforts: CCTV, a/c

Rodeway Inn (Convention)
(800) 228-2000, (503) 231-2000
http://www.rodeway.com
1506 NE Second St.
44 rooms - $70-80
Pets: Welcome
Creature Comforts: CCTV, a/c, cont. brkfst

Rodeway Inn (Mall)
(800) 228-2000, (503) 255-0808
http://www.rodeway.com
9225 SE Stark St.
42 rooms - $50-70
Pets: Welcome
Creature Comforts: CCTV, a/c, refrig, micro, cont. brkfst, pool, whirlpool

Sixth Ave. American Hospitality
(503) 226-2979
2221 SW Sixth Ave.
29 rooms - $45-59
Pets: Welcome
Creature Comforts: CCTV, a/c, restaurant

Super 8
(800) 800-8000, (503) 257-8988
http://www.super8.com
11011 N.E. Holman Rd.
80 rooms - $62-78
Pets: Welcome w/permission
Creature Comforts: CCTV, a/c

Travelodge, Airport
(800) 578-7878, (503) 255-1400
http://www.travelodge.com
9727 NE Sandy Blvd.
164 rooms - $55-90
Pets: Welcome w/$25 deposit
Creature Comforts: CCTV, a/c, refrig, cont. brkfst, Jacuzzis

Travelodge (convention)
(800) 578-7878, (503) 231-7665
http://www.travelodge.com
1506 NE 2nd Ave.
44 rooms - $50-125
Pets: Welcome w/$10 fee
Creature Comforts: CCTV, a/c, refrig, cont. brkfst, sauna

Travelodge Suites
(800) 578-7878, (503) 788-9394
http://www.travelodge.com
7740 S.W. Powell Blvd.
39 rooms - $70-95
Pets: Welcome
Creature Comforts: CCTV, a/c, refrig, micro, cont. brkfst, sauna

PRINEVILLE
Rodeway Inn
(800) 228-2000, (541) 447-4152
http://www.rodeway.com
1050 East Third St.
26 rooms - $40-69
Pets: Welcome
Creature Comforts: CCTV, a/c, cont. brkfst

City Center Motel
(541) 447-5522
509 E. Third St.
20 rooms - $34-46
Pets: Welcome
Creature Comforts: CCTV, a/c

Ochoco Inn and Motel
(541) 447-6231
123 East Third St.
46 rooms - $35-65
Pets: Welcome
Creature Comforts: CCTV, a/c

Rustlers Roost Motel
(541) 447-5043
960 West Third St.
20 rooms - $40-52
Pets: Welcome
Creature Comforts: CCTV, a/c, kit, restaurant

REDMOND

Redmond Inn
(800) 833-3259, (541) 548-1091
1545 Route 97 S.
47 rooms - $45-65
Pets: Welcome w/$5 fee
Creature Comforts: CCTV, a/c, kit, cont. brkfst, Jacuzzi, pool

Super 8
(800) 800-8000, (541) 548-8318
http://www.super8.com
3629 - 21st Pl.
85 rooms - $50-65
Pets: Welcome w/$25 deposit
Creature Comforts: CCTV, a/c, restaurant, pool

Travelodge
(800) 578-7878, (541) 548-2101
http://www.travelodge.com
1128 N.W. Sixth St.
30 rooms - $40-78
Pets: Welcome
Creature Comforts: CCTV, a/c, and a kit

REEDSPORT

Anchor Bay Inn
(800) 767-1821, (541) 271-2149
1821 Rte. 101
20 rooms - $37-69
Pets: Small pets w/$5 daily fee
Creature Comforts: CCTV, VCR, cont. brkfst, kit, pool

Best Western Salbasgeon
(800) 528-1234, (541) 271-4831
http://www.bestwestern.com
1400 Rte. 101
56 rooms - $65-130
Pets: Welcome w/approval
Creature Comforts: CCTV, kit, brkfst, pool, hlth club., whirlpool

Economy Inn
(541) 271-3671
1593 Highway Ave. 101
42 rooms - $35-65
Pets: Welcome w/$3 fee
Creature Comforts: CCTV, refrig, micro, kit, pool

Fir Grove Motel
(541) 271-4848
2178 Winchester Ave.
19 rooms - $34-45
Pets: Welcome
Creature Comforts: CCTV, a/c, kit, pool

Salbasgeon Inn of Umpqua
(541) 271-2025
45209 Rte. 38
11 rooms - $55-75
Pets: Welcome w/$5 fee
Creature Comforts: CCTV, kit, boating and putting green

Salty Seagull Motel
(800) 476-8336, (541) 271-3729
45209 Rte. 38
9 rooms - $42-45
Pets: Welcome
Creature Comforts: CCTV, kit

ROCKAWAY BEACH

101 Motel
(503) 355-2420
530 N. Rte. 101
7 rooms - $35-59
Pets: Welcome
Creature Comforts: CCTV, kit

Ocean Locomotion Motel
(503) 355-2093
19130 Alder Ave.
8 rooms - $47-89
Pets: Welcome
Creature Comforts: CCTV, kit, fireplace

Ocean Spray Motel
(503) 355-2237
505 N. Pacific Ave.
8 rooms - $40-79
Pets: Welcome
Creature Comforts: CCTV, kit

Rockaway Getaway Motel
(800) 756-5552, (503) 355-2501
621 S. Pacific Ave.
14 rooms - $40-120
Pets: $15 one-time fee
Creature Comforts: CCTV, VCR, and a kit

Sand Dollar Motel
(503) 355-2301
105 NW 23rd. Ave.
10 rooms - $45-85
Pets: Welcome
Creature Comforts: CCTV, kit

Sea Treasures Inn
(800) 444-1864, (503) 355-8220
301 N. Miller St.
14 rooms - $48-146
Pets: Welcome
Creature Comforts: CCTV, kit

Silver Sands Motel
(800) 457-8972, (503) 355-2206
215 S. Pacific Ave.
65 rooms - $82-135
Pets: Small pets welcome
Creature Comforts: CCTV, kit, fireplace, pool, whirlpool, sauna

Surfside Oceanfront Resort
(800) 243-7786, (503) 355-2312
101 NW 11th St.
90 rooms - $50-150
Pets: Welcome w/$10 initial fee
Creature Comforts: CCTV, kit, fireplace, pool

Tradewinds Motel
(800) 824-0938(503) 355-2112
523 N. Pacific Ave.
20rooms - $50-240
Pets: Small pets w/$10 fee
Creature Comforts: CCTV, refrig, fireplace

ROSEBURG

Best Western Garden Villa
(800) 528-1234, (541) 672-1601
http://www.bestwestern.com
760 NW Garden Valley Blvd
121 rooms - $65-96
Pets: Welcome w/approval
Creature Comforts: CCTV, a/c, cont. brkfst, pool, hlth club., and whirlpool

Dunes Motel
(800) 260-9973, (541) 672-6684
610 W. Madrone Rd.
46 rooms - $43-55
Pets: Welcome
Creature Comforts: CCTV, a/c, kit, cont. brkfst

Holiday Inn Express
(800) HOLIDAY, (541) 673-7517
http://www.holiday-inn.com
375 W. Harvard Blvd
100 rooms - $60-137
Pets: Small pets w/$10 fee
Creature Comforts: CCTV, a/c, refrig, micro, Jacuzzi, pool, hlth clb, whirlpool

Howard Johnson Express
(800) I-Go-Hojo, (541) 673-5082
http://www.hojo.com
978 NE Stephens St.
31 rooms - $50-79
Pets: Welcome
Creature Comforts: CCTV, a/c, kit, Jacuzzi, cont. brkfst, hlth clb

Motel Orleans
(800) 626-1900, (541) 673-5561
427 NW Valley Garden Blvd.
75 rooms - $40-69
Pets: In certain rms. w/$100 dep.
Creature Comforts: CCTV, a/c,
kit, pool

Sycamore Motel
(800) 524-9999, (541) 672-3354
1624 SE Stephens St.
12 rooms - $36-38
Pets: Small pets welcome
Creature Comforts: CCTV, a/c,
refrig

Windmill Inn
(800) 228-5150, (541) 957-1100
http://www.comfortinn.com
1539 Mulholland Dr.
37 rooms - $50-125
Pets: Welcome
Creature Comforts: CCTV, a/c,
cont. brkfst, kit, pool

ST. HELENS
Best Western Oak Meadows
(800) 528-1234, (503) 397-3000
http://www.bestwestern.com
585 S. Columbia River Hwy.
50 rooms - $65-90
Pets: Welcome w/$15 fee
Creature Comforts: CCTV, a/c,
refrig, micro, cont. brkfst, pool,
hlth club., pool

Village Inn
(503) 397-1490
535 S. Rte. 30
45 rooms - $35-53
Pets: In certain rooms w/$3 fee
Creature Comforts: CCTV, a/c

SALEM
City Centre Motel
(800) 289-0121, (503) 364-0121
510 Liberty St. SE
30 rooms - $42-59
Pets: Welcome
Creature Comforts: CCTV, a/c,
cont. brkfstl

Motel 6
(800) 4-MOTEL6, (503) 371-8024
http://www.motel6.com
1401 Hawthorne Ave. NE
115 rooms - $32-60
Pets: Under 30 lbs. welcome
Creature Comforts: CCTV, a/c,
pool

Motel 6
(800) 4-MOTEL6, (503) 588-7191
http://www.motel6.com
2250 Mission St. SE
78 rooms - $32-49
Pets: Under 30 lbs. welcome
Creature Comforts: CCTV, a/c,
pool

Phoenix Inn, South
(503) 588-9220
4370 Commercial SE
89 rooms - $66-125
Pets: Small pets w/$10 fee
Creature Comforts: CCTV, a/c,
refrig, micro, Jacuzzi, cont. brkfst,
pool, hlth clb, whirlpool

Quality Hotel
(800) 228-5151, (503) 370-7888
http://www.qualityinn.com
3301 Market St. SE
150 rooms - $78-88
Pets: Welcome w/$10 fee
Creature Comforts: CCTV, a/c,
restaurant, pool

Super 8
(800) 800-8000, (541) 370-8888
http://www.super8.com
1288 Hawthorne St. N.E.
79 rooms - $55-69
Pets: Welcome w/permission
Creature Comforts: CCTV, a/c,
pool, whirlpool

Tiki Lodge Motel
(800) 438-8458, (503) 581-4441
3705 Market St. NE
50 rooms - $40-49
Pets: Welcome
Creature Comforts: CCTV, a/c,
refrig, pool

Travelodge
(800) 578-7878, (503) 581-2466
http://www.travelodge.com
1555 State St.
42 rooms - $50-90
Pets: Welcome in certain rooms
Creature Comforts: CCTV, a/c

SEASIDE
Aloha Inn
(503) 738-9581
441 - 2nd Ave.
50 rooms - $50-80
Pets: Small pets w/$10 fee
Creature Comforts: CCTV, kit,
Jacuzzi, pool, whirlpool, sauna

Best Western Ocean View
(800) 528-1234, (503) 738-3334
http://www.bestwestern.com
414 N. Prom St.
84 rooms - $65-205
Pets: Small pets w/$15 fee
Creature Comforts: CCTV,
VCR, kit, fireplace, Jacuzzi,
restaurant, cont. brkfst, pool, and a
whirlpool

Coast River Inn
(800) 479-5191, (503) 738-8474
800 S. Holladay Dr.
20 rooms - $71-88
Pets: Welcome w/$5 daily fee
Creature Comforts: CCTV, kit

Comfort Inn, Boardwalk
(800) 228-5150, (503) 738-3011
http://www.comfortinn.com
545 Broadway Rd.
65 rooms - $60-188
Pets: In certain rooms w/$7 fee
Creature Comforts: CCTV,
VCR, refrig, micro, fireplace,
restaurant, cont. brkfst, pool,
whirlpool, sauna

Country River Inn
(800) 605-3337, (503) 738-8049
1020 N. Holladay Dr.
16 rooms - $40-99
Pets: Welcome
Creature Comforts: CCTV, cont.
brkfst

Lanai Oceanfront Condos
(800) 738-2683, (503) 738-6343
3140 Sunset Blvd.
18 rooms - $45-85
Pets: In certain rooms w/$10 fee
Creature Comforts: Oceanviews,
CCTV, kit, pool

Motel 6
(800) 4-MOTEL6, (503) 738-6269
http://www.motel6.com
2369 S. Holladay Dr.
116 rooms - $50-128
Pets: Under 30 lbs. welcome
Creature Comforts: CCTV,
refrig, Jacuzzis, pool

Seaside Inn
(503) 738-9581
441 - 2nd Ave.
50 rooms - $60-145
Pets: Welcome w/$5 daily fee
Creature Comforts: CCTV, kit, pool, and whirlpool

Seaview Inn
(800) 479-5191, (503) 738-5371
120 Ninth Ave.
18 rooms - $58-85
Pets: Welcome w/$5 daily fee
Creature Comforts: Oceanview, CCTV, kit

SISTERS
Best Western Ponderosa Lodge
(800) 528-1234, (541) 549-1234
http://www.bestwestern.com
500 Rte. 20 West
48 rooms - $80-97
Pets: Welcome w/$5 fee
Creature Comforts: CCTV, a/c, refrig, micro, cont. brkfst, pool, whirlpool, trails

Comfort Inn
(800) 228-5150, (541) 549-7829
http://www.comfortinn.com
540 Rte. 20 W
50 rooms - $50-120
Pets: Welcome
Creature Comforts: CCTV, a/c, kit, cont. brkfst, pool, whirlpool

Lake Creek Lodge
(800) 797-6331, (503) 595-6331
http://www.lakecreeklodge.com
Star Route
16 cottages - $60-150
Pets: Welcome w/$10 daily fee
Creature Comforts: Built in 1935, lovely cottage complex in Deschutes Nat. Forest, beautiful grnds, pond, knotty pine walls, simple furnishings, handmade quilts, refrig, fieldstone fireplace, decks, dining room w/brkfst and dinner included, pool, stocked pond, hiking, lawn games, tennis, game room

Squaw Creek B&B
(800) 930-0055, (541) 549-4312
http://www.sisterslodging.com
68733 Junipine Ln.
3 rooms - $80-99
Pets: Welcome w/$20 deposit (lab in residence, kennels available)
Creature Comforts: Charming B&B, Rough hewn timber and stone construction, Native American accents, CCTV-VCR, fireplace, window seats, full brkfst, hot tub, 9 acres, creek, wildlife (deer)

SPRINGFIELD
Motel Orleans
(541) 746-1314
3315 Gateway Rd.
70 rooms - $45-64
Pets: Under 30 lbs. welcome
Creature Comforts: CCTV, a/c, refrig, micro, pool

Motel 6
(800) 4-MOTEL6, (541) 741-1105
http://www.motel6.com
3752 International Ct.
131 rooms - $33-54
Pets: Under 30 lbs. welcome
Creature Comforts: CCTV, a/c, pool

Red Lion Inn
(800) RED-LION, (541) 726-8181
http://www.doubletreehotels.com
3280 Gateway Rd.
235 rooms - $75-285
Pets: Welcome
Creature Comforts: CCTV, a/c, refrig, Jacuzzi, restaurant, cont. breakfast, pool, whirlpool

Rodeway Inn
(800) 228-2000, (541) 746-8471
http://www.rodeway.com
3480 Hutton St.
58 rooms - $80-98
Pets: Welcome
Creature Comforts: CCTV, a/c, cont. brkfst, pool, hlth club.

Shilo Inns
(800) 222-2244, (541) 747-0332
http://www.shiloinns.com
3350 Gateway Rd.
75 rooms - $50-109
Pets: Welcome w/$7 fee
Creature Comforts: CCTV, a/c, restaurant, pool

Village Inn Motel
(541) 747-4546
1875 Mohawk Blvd.
71 rooms - $50-89
Pets: Welcome w/$7 fee
Creature Comforts: CCTV, VCR, kit, Jacuzzis, restaurant, pool, whirlpool

STAYTON
Bird and Hat B&B
(503) 769-7817
http://www.wvi.com/~dhull/bird%26hat.html
717 N. Third St.
3 rooms - $55-75
Pets: Welcome
Creature Comforts: Charming 1907 cottage, w/lovely gardens set in wine country, inviting front porch, rooms w/some farmhouse antiques, four poster beds, CCTV, VCR, a/c, fireplace, balconies

Gardner House B&B
(503) 769-6331
633 North Third St.
1 suite - $75-95
Pets: Totally trained reliable pets
Creature Comforts: CCTV, refrig

SUBLIMITY
Silver Mountain B&B
(800) 952-3905, (503) 769-7127
4672 Drift Creek Rd. SE
2 rooms - $65-75
Pets: Welcome (3 resident dogs)
Creature Comforts: CCTV, fireplace, cont. brkfst, pool, whirlpool, sauna

SUMMER LAKE
The Lodge at Summer Lake
(541) 943-3993
36980 Rte. 31
12 rooms - $40-49
Pets: Welcome
Creature Comforts: CCTV, a/c, restaurant, cont. brkfst, pool

Summer Lake Inn
(800) 261-2778, (541) 943-3983
http://www.summerlakeinn.com
31501 Route 31
50 rooms - $65-265
Pets: Welcome in cabins w/$10
one-time fee
Creature Comforts: 1902 inn set
on 640 acres, request new cabins
w/views of Summer Lake; older
cabins have pond views, beautiful
natural wood walls, lovely décor
w/contemp. furnishings, plate
glass windows, wrap-around
decks, gourmet dining, TV, VCR,
kit, fireplaces, woodstoves,
Jacuzzis, restaurant, pool, hot tub,
in-room massage, hiking, fishing,
birding, discovering petroglyphs

SUTHERLIN
Pennywise Motel
(541) 459-1424
150 Myrtle St.
61 rooms - $55-155
Pets: Welcome w/$4 fee
Creature Comforts: CCTV,
VCR, kit, Jacuzzi, pool, whirlpool

SWEET HOME
The Sweet Home Inn
(541) 367-5137
805 Long St.
28 rooms - $40-83
Pets: Welcome w/$5 fee
Creature Comforts: CCTV,
refrig, Jacuzzi, sauna, whirlpool

THE DALLES
American Hospitality Inns
(541) 296-9111
200 W. Second St.
54 rooms - $39-59
Pets: Welcome
Creature Comforts: CCTV, a/c,
restaurant, pool

Best Western Umatilla House
(800) 528-1234, (541) 296-9107
http://www.bestwestern.com
Second and Liberty Sts.
65 rooms - $70-80
Pets: Welcome w/$5 fee
Creature Comforts: CCTV, a/c,
refrig, micro, Jacuzzi, cont. brkfst,
restaurant, pool, hlth club

Captain Gray's Guest House
(800) 448-4729, (541) 298-8222
210 W. Fourth St.
3 rooms - $55-70
Pets: Welcome
Creature Comforts: CCTV, a/c,
kit, cont. brkfst, whirlpool

Days Inn
(800) DAYS INN, (541) 296-1191
http://www.daysinn.com
2500 W. Sixth St.
70 rooms - $50-75
Pets: Welcome w/$10 fee
Creature Comforts: CCTV, a/c,
pool, whirlpool

Inn at the Dalles
(800) 982-3496, (541) 296-1167
3550 SE Frontage Rd.
44 rooms - $35-70
Pets: Welcome
Creature Comforts: CCTV, a/c,
kit, pool

Lone Pine Motel
(541) 298-2800
351 Lone Pine Rd
55 rooms - $50-73
Pets: Welcome w/$6 fee
Creature Comforts: CCTV,
VCR, refrig, micro, Jacuzzi, pool,
hlth clb, whirlpool

Quality Inn
(800) 228-5151, (541) 298-5161
http://www.qualityinn.com
2114 W. Sixth St.
85 rooms - $55-119
Pets: Welcome
Creature Comforts: CCTV,
VCR, a/c, kit, restaurant, pool,
hlth clb access

Shilo Inns
(800) 222-2244, (541) 298-5502
http://www.shiloinns.com
3223 Bret Clodfelter Way
115 rooms - $55-175
Pets: Welcome w/$7 fee
Creature Comforts: CCTV, a/c,
refrig, micro, Jacuzzi, restaurant,
pool, hlth clb, whirlpool, sauna

TIGARD
Embassy Suites
(800) 362-2779, (541) 644-4000
http://www.embassy-suites.com
9000 SW Washington Sq.
355 rooms - $125-510
Pets: Welcome
Creature Comforts: CCTV,
VCR, a/c, kit, Jacuzzi, cont.
brkfst, pool, whirlpool, sauna,
pond, hlth club

Motel 6
(800) 4-MOTEL6, (503) 620-2066
http://www.motel6.com
17950 SW McEwan Rd.
80 rooms - $38-55
Pets: Under 30 lbs. welcome
Creature Comforts: CCTV, a/c,
pool

Motel 6
(800) 4-MOTEL6, (503) 684-0760
http://www.motel6.com
17959 SW McEwan Rd.
80 rooms - $38-54
Pets: Under 30 lbs. welcome
Creature Comforts: CCTV, a/c,
pool

Quality Inn
(800) 228-5151, (503) 620-3460
http://www.qualityinn.com
8247 N.E. Sandy Blvd
118 rooms - $70-115
Pets: Welcome w/$10 fee
Creature Comforts: CCTV,
VCR, a/c, pool, hlth club.,
whirlpool, sauna

Shilo Inns
(800) 222-2244, (503) 620-4320
http://www.shiloinns.com
10830 SW Greenburg Rd.
75 rooms - $60-119
Pets: Welcome w/$7 fee
Creature Comforts: CCTV,
VCR, a/c, whirlpool, hlth clb.,
whirlpool

TILLAMOOK
Shilo Inns
(800) 222-2244, (503) 842-7971
http://www.shiloinns.com
2515 N. Main St.
100 rooms - $65-155
Pets: Welcome w/$10 fee
Creature Comforts: CCTV,
VCR, refrig, micro, restaurant,
pool, hlth clb, whirlpool, sauna

Western Royal Inn
(503) 842-8844
1125 N. Main St.
42 rooms - $50-99
Pets: Welcome w/$5 fee
Creature Comforts: CCTV,
VCR, refrig, micro, whirlpool

TROUTDALE
Burns West Motel
(503) 667-6212
790 NW Frontage Rd.
60 rooms - $36-48
Pets: Welcome
Creature Comforts: CCTV, a/c,
kit, restaurant

Motel 6
(800) 4-MOTEL6, (503) 665-2254
http://www.motel6.com
1610 NW Frontage Rd.
123 rooms - $32-49
Pets: Under 30 lbs. welcome
Creature Comforts: CCTV, a/c,
pool

Phoenix Inn
(800) 824-6824, (503) 669-6500
http://www.phoenixinn.com
477 NW Phoenix Dr.
72 rooms - $55-85
Pets: Small pets w/$10 fee
Creature Comforts: CCTV, a/c,
refrig, micro, cont. brkfst, Jacuzzi,
pool, whirlpool

TUALATIN
Sweetbriar Inn
(800) 551-9167, (503) 692-5800
7125 SW Nyberg Rd
133 rooms - $70-120
Pets: Welcome w/$40 deposit
Creature Comforts: CCTV, a/c,
kit, restaurant, pool, hlth clb
access

UMATILLA
Heather Inn
(800) 447-7529, (541) 922-4871
705 Willamette Ave.
68 rooms - $40-65
Pets: Welcome
Creature Comforts: CCTV, a/c,
kit, restaurant, pool, hlth club,
whirlpool, sauna

Tillicum Inn
(541) 922-3236
1481 Sixth St.
79 rooms - $39-62
Pets: Welcome
Creature Comforts: CCTV, a/c,
kit, restaurant

UNION
Angle Farm Country Inn
(541) 562-5671
7125 SW Nyberg Rd
133 rooms - $70-100
Pets: Welcome w/$40 deposit
Creature Comforts: CCTV, a/c,
kit, restaurant, pool, hlth clb

VIDA
Wayfarer Resort
(800) 627-3613, (541) 896-3613
http://www.wayfarerresort.com
46725 Goodpasture Rd.
13 cottages - $70-195
Pets: Welcome w/$10 daily fee
Creature Comforts: Low-key,
storybook cottages nestled in
woods on creek, flyfishing haven,
knotty pine cottages w/open beam
ceilings, comfortable furniture,
picture windows, handmade quilts,
request creekside cottages, CCTV,
kit, fireplace, tennis, and great
hiking-biking trails

WALDPORT
Alsea Manor Motel
(541) 563-3249
Route 101
16 rooms - $37-94
Pets: Small pets welcome
Creature Comforts: CCTV

Edgewater Cottages
(541) 563-2240
3978 SW Rte. 101
9 rooms - $60-355
Pets: Welcome w/$5-7 fee, not
left unattended or on furniture
Creature Comforts: Informal
family-owned cottage colony set
on sand dunes overlooking
Pacific, knotty pine walls,
handmade quilts, eclectic but
comfortabe furnishings, CCTV,
kit, fireplaces, woodstoves, great
beach for dogs to explore

Sundown Motel
(800) 535-0192, (541) 563-3018
5050 Rte. 101
8 rooms - $40-99
Pets: Welcome
Creature Comforts: Oceanview,
CCTV, kit

WARRENTON
Shilo Inns
(800) 222-2244, (503) 861-2181
http://www.shiloinns.com
1609 E. Harbor Dr.
64 rooms - $85-245
Pets: Welcome w/$10 fee
Creature Comforts: CCTV,
VCR, a/c, kit, restaurant, hlth clb.,
and a whirlpool

WESTPORT
Westport Motel
(541) 455-2212
Route 30
8 rooms - $45-80
Pets: Welcome
Creature Comforts: CCTV, kit

WHEELER
Wheeler on the Bay Lodge
(800) 469-3204, (503) 368-5858
580 Marine Dr.
11 rooms - $80-115
Pets: Welcome
Creature Comforts: CCTV and
fireplace

WILSONVILLE
Comfort Inn
(800) 228-5150, (503) 682-9000
http://www.comfortinn.com
8855 SW Citizens Rd.
64 rooms - $60-125
Pets: Welcome w/$3 daily fee
Creature Comforts: CCTV, a/c,
refrig, cont. brkfst, pool, whirlpool

Holiday Inn
(800) HOLIDAY, (503) 682-2211
http://www.holiday-inn.com
25425 SW Boones Ferry Rd.
169 rooms - $75-125
Pets: Welcome w/$10 fee
Creature Comforts: CCTV, a/c,
refrig, micro, restaurant, pool, hlth
clb, whirlpool

Motel Orleans
(503) 682-3184
8815 SW Sun Place
75 rooms - $40-74
Pets: Welcome w/CC deposit
Creature Comforts: CCTV, a/c,
refrig, micro, Jacuzzi, pool, and
whirlpool

Super 8
(800) 800-8000, (503) 682-2088
http://www.super8.com
25438 S.W. Parkway Ave.
72 rooms - $50-55
Pets: Welcome w/$25 deposit
Creature Comforts: CCTV, a/c,
restaurant, cont. brkfst, pool

WINCHESTER BAY
Rodeway Inn
(800) 228-2000, (541) 271-4871
http://www.rodeway.com
390 Broadway St.
51 rooms - $55-95
Pets: Welcome
Creature Comforts: CCTV, a/c,
and kit

WOODBURN
Comfort Inn
(800) 228-5150, (503) 982-1727
http://www.comfortinn.com
120 N.E. Arney Rd.
49 rooms - $60-115
Pets: Welcome
Creature Comforts: CCTV, a/c,
kit, restaurant, cont. brkfst, pool,
Jacuzzis, sauna

Fairway Inn Motel
(800) 981-2466, (503) 981-3211
2450 Country Club Rd.
49 rooms - $42-49
Pets: Welcome
Creature Comforts: CCTV, a/c,
kit, pool

Holiday Inn Express
(800) HOLIDAY, (503) 982-6515
http://www.holiday-inn.com
2887 Newburg Hwy.
75 rooms - $60-78
Pets: Welcome in certain rooms
Creature Comforts: CCTV,
VCR, a/c, refrig, micro, restaurant,
pool, hlth clb, whirlpool

Super 8
(800) 800-8000, (541) 981-8881
http://www.super8.com
821 Evergreen Rd.
81 rooms - $50-64
Pets: Welcome w/$25 deposit
Creature Comforts: CCTV, a/c,
restaurant, cont. brkfst, pool

YACHATS
The Adobe Resort
(800) 522-3623, (541) 547-3141
http://www.adoberesort.com
1555 Hwy 101, Box 219
97 rooms - $60-185
Pets: Welcome w/$5 nightly fee
Creature Comforts: Perched on
an oceanside bluff, CCTV, refrig,
fireplace, Jacuzzi, balconies-great
views, restaurant, whirlpool,
sauna, and a hlth club

Fireside Motel
(800) 336-3573, (541) 547-3636
http://www.overleaflodge.com
1881 Hwy 101
44 rooms - $60-139
Pets: Welcome in certain rooms
w/$7 daily fee
Creature Comforts: CCTV,
VCR, refrig, Jacuzzi, fireplace,
ocean views

Holiday Inn Motel
(541) 547-3120
5933 Hwy. 101
7 rooms - $55-65
Pets: Welcome
Creature Comforts: CCTV, kit,
fireplace

Ocean Cove Inn
(541) 547-3900
Prospect & Rte. 101
4 rooms - $55-89
Pets: Welcome
Creature Comforts: CCTV

Rock Park Cottages
(541) 547-3214
431 West Second St.
5 rooms - $60-119
Pets: Welcome
Creature Comforts: Oceanview,
CCTV, kit

Shamrock Lodgettes
(800) 845-5028, (541) 547-3312
http://wwwbeachesbeaches.com/
shamrock.html
105 Hwy 101, Box 346
20 cottages - $65-100
Pets: Welcome w/$3 daily fee
Creature Comforts: Log cabins
in parklike setting, fireplace or
woodstove, camp furnishings,
request water view rooms, CCTV,
kit, stone fireplace, book well in
advance, hot tub, sauna, massage

Silver Surf Motel
(800) 281-5723, (503) 547-3175
www.silversurf-motel.com
3767 N. Rte. 101
24 rooms - $80-130
Pets: Welcome w/$5 fee
Creature Comforts: Oceanview,
CCTV, kit, pool, whirlpool

The See Vue
(541) 547-3227
http://www.seevue.com
95590 Rte. 101
11 rooms - $45-75
Pets: Welcome w/$5 nightly fee,
max of two dogs/room
Creature Comforts: Wonderful
motel w/eclectic and kitschy
interior set on seaside cliffs, cozy
rms w/Southwest, Wild West,
Asian themes, unique furnishings-
antique/hand-crafted, excellent
views, CCTV, kit, hiking nearby

Yachats Inn
(541) 547-3456
331 S. Coast Hwy 101
20 rooms - $65-90
Pets: Welcome
Creature Comforts: CCTV, kit,
fireplace, whirlpool

YAMHILL
Flying M Ranch
(503) 622-3222
http://www.flying-m-ranch.com
23029 NW Flying M Rd.
35 rooms - $60-220
Pets: Welcome, must be leashed
Creature Comforts: 600-acre
ranch near Trask Mtn, massive
timbered main lodge w/stone
fireplace, simple bunkhouse units,
request river view rooms, cabins
w/wood stove or fireplace, living
and dining rooms, kit, riding,
swimming, private air strip

Pennsylvania

ABBOTTSTOWN
Inn at the Altland House
(717) 259-9535
http://www.altlandhouse.com
Center Square
7 rooms - $89-115
Pets: Small pets in ltd. rooms
Creature Comforts: 1790 inn
and cottage, modern
appointments, CCTV, a/c, Jacuzzi,
fireplace, cont. brkfst, known for
its fine restaurant

ADAMSTOWN
Black Forest Inn
(717) 484-4801
500 Lancaster Ave.
19 rooms - $40-100
Pets: Welcome w/$8 fee
Creature Comforts: CCTV, a/c,
pool

ALLENTOWN
Days Inn Conference Center
(800) DAYS INN, (610) 395-3731
http://www.daysinn.com
Rtes. 22 & 309
275 rooms - $50-125
Pets: Welcome w/$15 fee
Creature Comforts: CCTV, a/c,
refrig, micro, cont. brkfst,
restaurant, pool

Holiday Inn
(800) HOLIDAY, (610) 391-1000
http://www.holiday-inn.com
Rtes. 100/78
125 rooms - $50-140
Pets: Welcome
Creature Comforts: CCTV, a/c,
refrig, restaurant, pool, exercise
rm.

Holiday Inn Express
(800) HOLIDAY, (610) 435-7880
http://www.holiday-inn.com
1715 Plaza Ln.
84 rooms - $55-95
Pets: Small pets w/$10 fee
Creature Comforts: CCTV, a/c,
refrig, pool

Howard Johnson
(800) I-Go-Hojo, (610) 439-4000
http://www.hojo.com
3220 Hamilton Blvd.
44 rooms - $75-125
Pets: Welcome w/permission
Creature Comforts: CCTV, a/c,
refrig, micro, Jacuzzi, restaurant,
cont. brkfst, pool

Microtel Inn
(800) 771-7171, (610) 266-9070
http://www.microtel.com
1880 Steelstone Rd.
105 rooms - $40-50
Pets: Welcome
Creature Comforts: CCTV, a/c,
refrig, micro

Red Roof Inn
(800) The Roof, (610) 264-5404
http://www.redroof.com
1846 Catasauqua Rd.
115 rooms - $40-86
Pets: Small pets welcome
Creature Comforts: CCTV, a/c

Sheraton Inn Jetport
(800) 325-3535, (610) 266-1000
http://www.sheraton.com
3400 Airport Rd.
147 rooms - $140-175
Pets: Welcome
Creature Comforts: CCTV,
VCR, a/c, refrig, restaurant, cont.
brkfst, pool, hlth clb, sauna,
whirlpool

ALTOONA
Econo Lodge
(800) 55-ECONO, (814) 944-3555
http://www.econolodge.com
2906 Pleasant Valley Blvd.
70 rooms - $45-70
Pets: Welcome
Creature Comforts: CCTV, a/c,
kit

Hampton Inn
(800) Hampton, (814) 941-3500
http://www.hampton-inn.com
180 Charlotte Dr.
75 rooms - $80-110
Pets: Small pets w/$5 fee
Creature Comforts: CCTV, a/c,
refrig, micro,, pool, exercise rm.

Motel 6
(800) 4-MOTEL6, (814) 946-7601
http://www.motel6.com
1500 Sterling St.
112 rooms - $50-55
Pets: Under 30 lbs. welcome
Creature Comforts: CCTV, a/c,
pool

Super 8
(800) 800-8000, (814) 942-5350
http://www.super8.com
3535 Fairway Dr.
63 rooms - $46-68
Pets: Welcome w/permission
Creature Comforts: CCTV, a/c

ALUM BANK
West Vu Motel
(814) 839-2632
Route 56
16 rooms - $30-40
Pets: Welcome w/$4 fee
Creature Comforts: CCTV, a/c,
refrig

BARKEYVILLE
Days Inn
(800) DAYS INN, (814) 786-7901
http://www.daysinn.com
855 Route 46 East
83 rooms - $55-65
Pets: Welcome
Creature Comforts: CCTV, a/c

BARTONSVILLE
Comfort Inn
(800) 228-5150, (570) 476-1500
http://www.comfortinn.com
Route 611
120 rooms - $60-165
Pets: Welcome
Creature Comforts: CCTV, a/c,
fireplace, Jacuzzi, restaurant, pool

Holiday Inn
(800) HOLIDAY, (570) 424-6100
http://www.holiday-inn.com
Route 611
150 rooms - $40-75
Pets: Under 30 lbs. welcome
Creature Comforts: CCTV, a/c,
Jacuzzi, restaurant, pool

BEAVER FALLS
Holiday Inn
(800) HOLIDAY, (724) 846-3700
http://www.holiday-inn.com
Route 18
155 rooms - $80-90
Pets: Welcome
Creature Comforts: CCTV, a/c,
refrig, micro, restaurant, pool

BEDFORD
Best Western Bedford Inn
(800) 752-8592, (814) 623-9006
http://www.bestwestern.com
Route 220 N.
105 rooms - $50-80
Pets: Welcome w/$50 deposit
Creature Comforts: CCTV,
VCR, a/c, restaurant, pool, hlth
club, whirlpool

Econo Lodge
(800) 55-ECONO, (814) 623-5174
http://www.econolodge.com
Transport St.
32 rooms - $40-65
Pets: Welcome
Creature Comforts: CCTV, a/c,
restaurant

Host Inn
(814) 623-9511
Route 76
18 rooms - $30-35
Pets: Welcome
Creature Comforts: CCTV, a/c

Janey Lynn Motel
(814) 623-9515
Route 76
20 rooms - $26-40
Pets: Small pets w/$4 fee
Creature Comforts: CCTV, a/c,
refrig, micro

Midway Motel
(814) 623-8107
Route 76
34 rooms - $30-50
Pets: Small pets w/$5 fee
Creature Comforts: CCTV, a/c,
refrig, micro, pool

Motel Town House
(800) Try-Town, (814) 623-5138
Rte.220 South
20 rooms - $32-55
Pets: Small pets w/$5 fee
Creature Comforts: CCTV, a/c,
refrig, micro

Quality Inn
(800) 228-5151, (814) 623-5188
http://www.qualityinn.com
Route 76
65 rooms - $60-70
Pets: Welcome
Creature Comforts: CCTV, a/c,
refrig, micro, restaurant, pool

Super 8
(800) 800-8000, (814) 623-5880
http://www.super8.com
Route 220 N.
57 rooms - $45-62
Pets: Welcome w/permission
Creature Comforts: CCTV,
VCR, a/c, refrig, micro, restaurant,
cont. brkfst, hlth club, whirlpool

BELLEFONT
Annie Natt House
(814) 353-1456
http://bellefonte.com/annienatt
127 West Curtain St.
2 suites - $70-99
Pets: Pets w/carriers welcome
Creature Comforts: 1882
Italianate home in quiet
neighborhood, beautifully
preserved details, antiques,
Oriental rugs, CCTV, a/c, kit,
fireplace, gourmet brkfst on
weekends

BENSALEM
Comfort Inn
(800) 228-5150, (215) 245-0100
http://www.comfortinn.com
3660 Street Rd.
140 rooms - $80-120
Pets: Welcome w/$25 deposit
Creature Comforts: CCTV, a/c

BENTON
Red Poppy B&B
(717) 925-5823
Route 82
4 rooms - $70-90
Pets: Welcome
Creature Comforts: Victorian
inn filled w/antiques, casual
atmosphere, fireplaced living
room, ceiling fans, canopy beds,
claw foot tub, full brkfst, refrig

BERWICK
Red Maple Inn
(717) 752-6220
Route 11
18 rooms - $50-70
Pets: Welcome w/$5 fee, deposit
Creature Comforts: CCTV, a/c

BERWYN
Residence Inn
(800) 331-3131, (610) 640-9494
http://www.residenceinn.com
600 W. Swedesford Rd.
90 rooms - $115-125
Pets: $6 fee, $100 deposit
Creature Comforts: CCTV, a/c,
kit, hlth clb access

BETHEL
Comfort Inn
(800) 228-5150, (717) 933-8888
http://www.comfortinn.com
41 Diner Dr.
70 rooms - $50-150
Pets: Welcome w/$10 fee
Creature Comforts: CCTV,
VCR, a/c, refrig, micro, cont.
brkfst, pool, hlth clb

BETHLEHEM
Comfort Inn
(800) 228-5150, (610) 865-6300
http://www.comfortinn.com
3191 Highfield Dr.
116 rooms - $74-95
Pets: Welcome w/$7 fee
Creature Comforts: CCTV,
VCR, a/c, Jacuzzi, cont. brkfst,
pool, hlth clb access, sauna,
whirlpool

Holiday Inn
(800) HOLIDAY, (610) 866-5800
http://www.holiday-inn.com
Rtes. 22 & 512
195 rooms - $110-150
Pets: Small pets welcome
Creature Comforts: CCTV, a/c,
restaurant

BLAKESLEE
Blueberry Mountain Inn
(570) 646-7144
http://blueberrymountaininn.com
Thomas Rd.
6 rooms - $90-115
Pets: Welcome on ltd. basis w/$40 deposit, (4 resident cats)
Creature Comforts: Rambling contemp. house on 400 acres, stunning rooms, request Ivy room on first floor w/own porch, neat great room w/stone fireplace, full brkfst, pool, whirlpool

BLOOMSBURG
Econo Lodge, Bloomsburg
(800) 55-ECONO, (570) 623-5174
http://www.econolodge.com
189 Columbia Mall Rd.
80 rooms - $48-120
Pets: Welcome w/$10 fee
Creature Comforts: CCTV, a/c, refrig, micro

Inn at Buckhorn
(570) 784-5300
5 Buckhorn Rd.
80 rooms - $50-100
Pets: Welcome w/$10 fee in smoking rms.
Creature Comforts: CCTV, a/c, refrig, cont. brkfst

Inn at Turkey Hill
(800) (570) 387-1500
http://www.innatturkeyhill.com
991 Central Rd.
23 rooms - $85-190
Pets: Welcome w/$15 one-time fee
Creature Comforts: Historic inn surrounded by newer rooms in traditional style bldngs, manicured grounds, pond, lovely country decor, hand-painted furnishings, pencil post beds, recommend converted "stable" rooms overlooking fields, CCTV, VCR, a/c, fireplace, Jacuzzi, gourmet restaurant, full brkfst

Magee's Main St.
(800) 331-9815, (570) 784-3200
20 W. Main St.
43 rooms - $65-89
Pets: Welcome
Creature Comforts: CCTV, a/c, restaurant, cont. brkfst

BLUE MOUNTAIN
Kenmar Motel
(717) 423-5915
17788 Cumberland Hwy.
15 rooms - $40-90
Pets: Welcome in ltd. rms. w/$3 fee
Creature Comforts: TV, a/c, refrig

BREEZEWOOD
Comfort Inn
(800) 228-5150, (814) 735-2200
http://www.comfortinn.com
Rte. 70 & Route 30
118 rooms - $40-75
Pets: Small pets w/$5 fee
Creature Comforts: CCTV, a/c, restaurant, cont. brkfst, pool, whirlpool

Ramada Inn
(800) 2-Ramada, (814) 735-4005
http://www.ramada.com
Rtes. 70 & 30
126 rooms - $50-80
Pets: Welcome w/$50 deposit
Creature Comforts: CCTV, VCR, a/c, restaurant, cont. brkfst, pool, hlth club, sauna, whirlpool

BRIDGEVILLE
Knights Inn
(800) 843-5644, (412) 221-8110
http://www.knightsinn.com
111 Hickory Grade Rd.
104 rooms - $44-55
Pets: Welcome
Creature Comforts: CCTV, VCR, a/c, refrig, micro

BROOKVILLE
Budget Host Gold Eagle
(800) Bud-Host, (814) 849-7344
http://www.budgethost.com
250 W. Main St.
29 rooms - $35-50
Pets: Small pets welcome
Creature Comforts: CCTV, a/c, refrig, kit, restaurant

Days Inn
(800) DAYS INN, (814) 849-8001
http://www.daysinn.com
230 Allegheny Blvd.
134 rooms - $45-75
Pets: Welcome
Creature Comforts: CCTV, a/c, restaurant, pool

Holiday Inn Express
(800) HOLIDAY, (814) 849-8381
http://www.holiday-inn.com
235 Allegheny Blvd.
69 rooms - $45-65
Pets: Welcome w/$5 fee
Creature Comforts: CCTV, a/c

Super 8
(800) 800-8000, (814) 849-8840
http://www.super8.com
251 Allegheny Blvd.
56 rooms - $45-55
Pets: Small pets welcome
Creature Comforts: CCTV, a/c

BURNHAM
Clarion Inn
(800) CLARION, (717) 248-4961
http://www.clarioninn.com
Route 322
120 rooms - $60-75
Pets: Welcome
Creature Comforts: CCTV, VCR, a/c, refrig, micro, restaurant, pool

BUTLER
Days Inn
(800) DAYS INN, (724) 287-6761
http://www.daysinn.com
139 Pittsburgh Rd.
133 rooms - $45-90
Pets: Small pets w/$25 fee
Creature Comforts: CCTV, a/c, restaurant, cont. brkfst, pool, whirlpool

Super 8
(800) 800-8000, (717)287-8888
http://www.super8motel.com
Route 8
66 rooms - $40-46
Pets: Welcome w/permission
Creature Comforts: CCTV, VCR, a/c, cont. brkfst

CAMP HILL
Radisson Penn Harris
(800) 333-3333, (717) 763-7117
http://www.radisson.com
1150 Camp Hill By-Pass
250 rooms - $70-90
Pets: Small pets w/$75 deposit
Creature Comforts: CCTV, a/c, refrig, restaurant, pool, hlth clb access, sauna, whirlpool

CANANDENSIS
Merry Inn
(800) 858-4182, (717) 595-2011
Route 390
6 rooms - $80-95
Pets: Welcome in 1 rm. w/$25 dep
Creature Comforts: Early 1940's
Cape-style house, "cozy,
comfortable, and charming," full
brkfst, hot tub

CARLISLE
Days Inn, Carlisle
(800) DAYS INN, (717) 258-4147
http://www.daysinn.com
101 Alexander Spring Rd.
136 rooms - $60-125
Pets: Welcome w/$6 fee
Creature Comforts: CCTV, a/c,
refrig, Jacuzzi, pool, hlth clb
access

Econo Lodge
(800) 55-ECONO, (717) 247-7775
http://www.econolodge.com
1460 Harrisburg Pike
72 rooms - $45-80
Pets: Small pets w/$5 fee
Creature Comforts: CCTV, a/c

Embers Inn
(800) 692-7315, (717) 243-1717
1700 Harrisburg Pike
275 rooms - $45-175
Pets: Welcome
Creature Comforts: CCTV,
VCR, a/c, refrig, micro, restaurant,
pool, hlth clb, whirlpool, sauna,
games

Holiday Inn Carlisle
(800) HOLIDAY, (717) 245-2400
http://www.holiday-inn.com
1450 Harrisburg Pike
100 rooms - $65-105
Pets: Welcome w/$10 fee
Creature Comforts: CCTV, a/c,
restaurant, pool

Motel 6
(800) 4-MOTEL6, (717) 249-7622
http://www.motel6.com
1153 Harrisburg Pike
120 rooms - $45-110
Pets: Under 30 lbs. welcome
Creature Comforts: CCTV, a/c,
refrig, micro, pool

Quality Inn
(800) 228-5151, (717) 243-6000
http://www.qualityinn.com
1255 Harrisburg Pike
95 rooms - $58-120
Pets: Welcome
Creature Comforts: CCTV, a/c,
restaurant, cont. brkfst, pools,
exercise rm.

Rodeway Inn
(800) 228-2000, (717) 249-2800
http://www.rodeway.com
1239 Harrisburg Pike
100 rooms - $50-60
Pets: Small pets welcome
Creature Comforts: CCTV, a/c,
kit, restaurant, cont. brkfst, pool

Sleep Inn
(800) Sleep-Inn, (717) 249-8863
http://www.sleepinn.com
5 East Garland Dr.
100 rooms - $70-80
Pets: Welcome
Creature Comforts: CCTV, a/c,
refrig, micro, pool, exercise rm.

Super 8
(800) 800-8000, (717) 245-9898
http://www.super8.com
100 Alexander Spring Rd.
60 rooms - $50-60
Pets: Welcome
Creature Comforts: CCTV, a/c,
refrig, micro

CHADDS FORD
Brandywine River Hotel
(610) 388-1200
Rtes. 1 & 100
39 rooms - $120-175
Pets: Small pets w/$20 fee, they
need to be crated if left alone
Creature Comforts: Country
Victorian style roadside hotel,
nicely landscaped brick paths,
interiors reflect Colonial theme,
rooms w/reproduction Queen-
Anne furnishings/chintz fabrics,
brass fixtures, CCTV, VCR, a/c,
refrig, fireplace, Jacuzzi, afternoon
tea

CHALK HILL
Lodge at Chalk Hill
(800) 833-4283, (724) 438-8880
Route 40
62 rooms - $75-100
Pets: Welcome w/$5 fee
Creature Comforts: Lakeside,
TV, a/c, kit, cont. brkfst, walking
trails

CHAMBERSBURG
Days Inn
(800) DAYS INN, (717) 263-1288
http://www.daysinn.com
30 Falling Spring Rd.
107 rooms - $60-65
Pets: Welcome
Creature Comforts: CCTV, a/c,
refrig, micro, restaurant, cont.
brkfst

Holiday Inn
(800) HOLIDAY, (717) 263-3400
http://www.holiday-inn.com
1095 Wayne Ave.
140 rooms - $65-75
Pets: Welcome
Creature Comforts: CCTV, a/c,
refrig, restaurant, cont. brkfst, pool

Travelodge
(800) 578-7878, (717) 264-4187
http://www.travelodge.com
565 Lincoln Way
54 rooms - $50-65
Pets: Welcome
Creature Comforts: CCTV, a/c,
refrig, restaurant

CLARION
Days Inn
(800) DAYS INN, (814) 226-8682
http://www.daysinn.com
Rtes. 80 & 68
150 rooms - $45-120
Pets: Welcome
Creature Comforts: CCTV, a/c,
refrig, micro, cont. brkfst, pool,
exercise rm.

Holiday Inn
(800) HOLIDAY, (814) 226-8850
http://www.holiday-inn.com
Route 80 & 68
125 rooms - $80-95
Pets: Welcome
Creature Comforts: CCTV, a/c,
refrig, micro, restaurant, pool

Super 8
(800) 800-8000, (814) 226-4550
http://www.super8.com
Route 68
100 rooms - $50-65
Pets: Welcome
Creature Comforts: CCTV,
VCR, a/c, refrig, kit, cont. brkfst,
pool

CLARKS SUMMIT
Ramada Plaza
(800) 2-Ramada, (570) 586-2730
http://www.ramada.com
Rtes. 80 & 255
108 rooms - $60-150
Pets: Welcome w/$10 fee
Creature Comforts: Recent
rennovation, CCTV, a/c,
restaurant, cont. brkfst, pool,
sauna

Summit Inn
(570) 586-1211
649 Northern Blvd.
33 rooms - $50-70
Pets: Welcome w/$5 fee
Creature Comforts: CCTV, a/c,
refrig, micro

CLEARFIELD
Best Western
(800) 528-1234, (814) 765-2441
http://www.bestwestern.com
Route 879
125 rooms - $50-70
Pets: Small pets welcome
Creature Comforts: CCTV, a/c,
restaurant

Budget Inn
(717) 765-2639
Route 322 E.
30 rooms - $30-40
Pets: Welcome w/$4 fee
Creature Comforts: CCTV, a/c

Cedarwood Lodge
(800) 798-0456, (814) 765-4805
216 South Front St.
1 cabin - $75-100
Pets: Welcome
Creature Comforts: Cabin on 8
acres in Moshannon State Forest,
CCTV, a/c, kit, screened porches,
grill, hiking

Comfort Inn
(800) 228-5150, (814) 768-6400
http://www.comfortinncom
Industrial Park Rd.
71 rooms - $55-70
Pets: Welcome
Creature Comforts: CCTV, a/c,
refrig, Jacuzzis, pool, exercise rm.

Days Inn
(800) DAYS INN, (814) 765-5381
http://www.daysinn.com
Route 879
120 rooms - $40-80
Pets: Small pets welcome
Creature Comforts: CCTV, a/c,
restaurant, pool

Rodeway Inn
(800) 228-2000, (814) 765-7587
http://www.rodeway.com
Route 322
34 rooms - $35-75
Pets: Welcome
Creature Comforts: CCTV, a/c,
refrig, restaurant, cont. brkfst

Super 8
(800) 800-8000, (814) 768-7580
http://www.super8.com
Route 879
50 rooms - $50-75
Pets: Welcome
Creature Comforts: CCTV, a/c

Victorian Loft B&B
(800) 798-0456, (814) 765-1712
216 S. Front St.
2 rooms - $40-100
Pets: Welcome in rooms
w/private bath or suite
Creature Comforts: An 1894
Victorian riverfront house w/
gingerbread trim, antique
furnishings, country charm,
CCTV, a/c, kit, full brkfst

COOKSBURG
Forest View Cabins
(814) 744-8413
855 Route 46 East
3 cabins - $85-95
Pets: Welcome w/$5 fee
Creature Comforts: Two-bedrm
cabins, CCTV, living room, kit

COOPERSBURG
Travelodge
(800) 578-7878, (610) 282-1212
http://www.travelodge.com
Route 309
34 rooms - $40-85
Pets: Welcome
Creature Comforts: CCTV,
VCR, a/c, refrig, micro, Jacuzzi,
cont. brkfst, whirlpool

CORAOPOLIS
Embassy Suites, Airport
(800) 362-2779, (412) 269-9070
http://www.embassy-suites.com
550 Cherrington Pkwy.
225 rooms - $125-160
Pets: Welcome
Creature Comforts: CCTV,
VCR, a/c, refrig, micro, restaurant,
pool, hlth club, sauna, whirlpool

Hampton Inn, Airport
(800) Hampton, (412) 264-0020
http://www.hampton-inn.com
1420 Beers School Rd.
130 rooms - $65-75
Pets: Small pets welcome
Creature Comforts: CCTV, a/c

Holiday Inn, Airport
(800) HOLIDAY, (412) 262-3600
http://www.holiday-inn.com
1406 Beers School Rd.
255 rooms - $40-75
Pets: Welcome
Creature Comforts: CCTV, a/c,
refrig, micro, restaurant, pool,
whirlpool

La Quinta, Airport
(800) Nu-Rooms, (412) 269-0400
http://www.laquinta.com
1433 Beers School Rd.
125 rooms - $60-75
Pets: Small pets welcome
Creature Comforts: CCTV, a/c,
pool

Marriott, Airport
(800) 228-9290, (412) 788-8800
http://www.marriott.com
100 Aten Rd.
315 rooms - $100-165
Pets: Small pets welcome
Creature Comforts: CCTV, a/c,
pool

Motel 6, Airport
(800) 4-MOTEL6, (412) 269-0990
http://www.motel6.com
1170 Thorn Run Rd.
98 rooms - $38-49
Pets: Under 30 lbs. welcome
Creature Comforts: CCTV, a/c

Red Roof Inn, Airport
(800) The Roof, (412) 264-5678
http://www.redroof.com
1454 Beers School Rd.
120 rooms - $55-80
Pets: Small pets welcome
Creature Comforts: CCTV, a/c

Wyndham Garden Hotel
(800) Wyndham, (412) 695-0002
http://www.wyndham.com
Route 60
141 rooms - $120-210
Pets: Small pets welcome
Creature Comforts: CCTV, a/c, pool

CRANBERRY TOWNSHIP
Red Roof Inn
(800) The Roof, (412) 776-5670
http://www.redroof.com
20009 Route 19 & Marguerite Rd.
108 rooms - $50-65
Pets: Under 30 lbs. welcome
Creature Comforts: CCTV, a/c, pool

Holiday Inn Express
(800) HOLIDAY, (412) 772-1000
http://www.holiday-inn.com
20003 Route 19
101 rooms - $70-120
Pets: Welcome
Creature Comforts: CCTV, a/c, pool, whirlpool

Residence Inn
(800) 331-3131, (412) 779-1000
http://www.residenceinn.com
1308 Freedom Rd.
96 rooms - $100-140
Pets: Welcome
Creature Comforts: CCTV, a/c, kit, pool, hlth clb access

DANVILLE
Red Roof Inn
(800) The Roof, (570) 275-7600
http://www.redroof.com
300 Red Roof Inn Rd.
107 rooms - $40-55
Pets: Welcome w/permission
Creature Comforts: CCTV, a/c

DELMONT
Super 8
(800) 800-8000, (724) 468-4888
http://www.super8.com
180 Sheffield Dr.
46 rooms - $48-90
Pets: Welcome w/$5 fee
Creature Comforts: CCTV, a/c, Jacuzzi

DENVER
Black Horse Lodge/Suites
(717) 336-7563
Route 272 N.
75 rooms - $65-260
Pets: Welcome
Creature Comforts: CCTV, VCR, a/c, kit, Jacuzzi, cont. brkfst, pool, whirlpool

Comfort Inn
(800) 228-5150, (717) 336-4649
http://www.comfortinncom
2015 N. Reading Rd.
45 rooms - $70-150
Pets: Small pets w/$8 fee
Creature Comforts: CCTV, a/c, cont. brkfst, hlth club

Pennsylvania Dutch Motel
(717) 336-5559
2275 N. Reading Rd.
20 rooms - $35-50
Pets: Welcome
Creature Comforts: CCTV, a/c

DICKSON CITY
Quality Hotel
(570) 383-9979
1946 Scranton-Carbondale Rte.
85 rooms - $65-75
Pets: Welcome
Creature Comforts: CCTV, VCR, a/c, restaurant

DOUGLASSVILLE
Econo Lodge
(800) 55-ECONO, (610) 385-3016
http://www.econolodge.com
387 Ben Franklin Rte.
25 rooms - $45-100
Pets: Small pets w/$10-20 deposit
Creature Comforts: CCTV, VCR, a/c

DUBOIS
Dubois Manor Motel
(814) 371-5400
525 Liberty Blvd.
45 rooms - $45-55
Pets: Small pets w/$5 fee
Creature Comforts: CCTV, a/c

Holiday Inn
(800) HOLIDAY, (814) 371-5100
http://www.holiday-inn.com
Rtes. 80 & 219
160 rooms - $60-90
Pets: Welcome
Creature Comforts: CCTV, a/c

Ramada Inn
(800) 2-Ramada, (814) 371-7070
http://www.ramada.com
Rtes. 80 & 255
96 rooms - $50-65
Pets: Welcome
Creature Comforts: CCTV, a/c, restaurant, cont. brkfst, pool, sauna, exercise rm.

DUNMORE
Days Inn
(800) DAYS INN, (570) 348-6101
http://www.daysinn.com
1100 O'Neill Rte.
90 rooms - $60-75
Pets: Welcome w/$3 fee
Creature Comforts: CCTV, VCR, a/c, refrig, micro, cont. brkfst

Holiday Inn
(800) HOLIDAY, (570) 343-4771
http://www.holiday-inn.com
200 Tigue St.
140 rooms - $90-135
Pets: Welcome
Creature Comforts: CCTV, a/c, refrig, micro, cont. brkfst, restaurant, pool

EASTON
Days Inn
(800) DAYS INN, (610) 253-0546
http://www.daysinn.com
2555 Nazareth Rd.
84 rooms - $50-75
Pets: Welcome w/$5 fee
Creature Comforts: CCTV, a/c

EBENSBURG
Comfort Inn
(800) 228-5150, (814) 472-6100
http://www.comfortinn.com
Route 22
78 rooms - $55-130
Pets: Welcome
Creature Comforts: CCTV, a/c,
Jacuzzi, cont. brkfst, pool, hlth clb
access

Cottage Inn & Restaurant
(814) 472-8002
Route 22
56 rooms - $45-65
Pets: Welcome
Creature Comforts: CCTV,
VCR, a/c, restaurant, pool

EDINBORO
Ramada Inn
(800) 2-Ramada, (814) 734-5650
http://www.ramada.com
Route 6N
100 rooms - $60-80
Pets: Welcome w/$15 one-time
fee
Creature Comforts: CCTV, a/c,
pool

ENOLA
Quality Inn
(800) 228-5151, (717) 732-0785
http://www.qualityinn.com
501 N. Enola Rd.
72 rooms - $69-89
Pets: Welcome w/deposit
Creature Comforts: CCTV, a/c,
restaurant, cont. brkfst, pool

EPHRATA
Smithton Inn
(717) 733-6094
www.historicsmithtoninn.com
900 West Main St.
8 rooms - $65-175
Pets: Well-behaved dogs
welcome, must stay off furniture
Creature Comforts: Perennial
gardens surround this classic 1760
stone building, beautifully restored
w/antiques and hand-crafted
reproductions, boxed canopy or
four-poster beds, Amish quilts,
CCTV, VCR, a/c, refrig, fireplace,
restaurant, gourmet brkfst

ERIE
Days Inn
(800) DAYS INN, (814) 868-8521
http://www.daysinn.com
7415 Schultz Rd.
113 rooms - $50-80
Pets: Welcome w/$5 fee
Creature Comforts: CCTV, a/c,
Jacuzzi, pool

Hampton Inn
(800) Hampton, (814) 868-6800
http://www.hampton-inn.com
8050 Old Oliver Rd.
100 rooms - $70-110
Pets: Welcome w/$5 fee
Creature Comforts: CCTV, a/c,
refrig, micro, pool, exercise rm.

Holiday Inn
(800) HOLIDAY, (814) 456-2961
http://www.holiday-inn.com
18 West 18th St.
135 rooms - $75-80
Pets: Under 25 lbs., do not leave
unttended
Creature Comforts: CCTV, a/c,
restaurant, pool

Microtel
(800) 771-7171, (814) 864-1010
http://www.microtel.com
8100 Peach St.
100 rooms - $40-55
Pets: Welcome w/$4 fee
Creature Comforts: CCTV, a/c

Motel 6
(800) 4-MOTEL6, (814) 864-4811
http://www.motel6.com
7575 Peach St.
83 rooms - $40
Pets: Under 30 lbs. welcome
Creature Comforts: CCTV, a/c,
pool

Red Roof Inn
(800) The Roof, (814) 848-5246
http://www.redroof.com
7865 Perry Rte.
110 rooms - $38-95
Pets: Small pets welcome
Creature Comforts: TV, a/c

Super 8
(800) 800-8000, (814) 864-4911
http://www.super8.com
8040 B Perry Rte.
93 rooms - $60-65
Pets: Welcome w/permission
Creature Comforts: TV, a/c,
refrig, cont. brkfst, restaurant,
pool, exercise rm.

ERWINNA
Golden Pheasant Inn
(800) 230-7030, (610) 294-9595
http://www.goldenpheasant.com
Route 32
6 rooms - $135-165
Pets: Welcome w/$20 fee in
Cottage Suite
Creature Comforts: Gorgeous
Bucks County country inn,
fabulous food, cottage rests on
Delaware Canal, antique filled
spaces, four-poster beds, sitting
room, chintz and wicker
furnishings

ESSINGTON
Comfort Inn
(800) 228-5150, (610) 521-9800
http://www.comfortinn.com
53 Industrial Hwy.
150 rooms - $65-115
Pets: Welcome
Creature Comforts: CCTV, a/c,
Jacuzzi, restaurant, cont. brkfst,
hlth clb

Holiday Inn, Airport
(800) HOLIDAY, (610) 521-2400
http://www.holiday-inn.com
45 Industrial Hwy.
304 rooms - $70-85
Pets: Welcome
Creature Comforts: CCTV,
VCR, a/c, refrig, restaurant, pool

Motel 6
(800) 4-MOTEL6, (610) 521-6650
http://www.motel6.com
43 Industrial Hwy.
131 rooms - $45-55
Pets: Under 30 lbs. welcome
Creature Comforts: CCTV, a/c

Red Roof Inn
(800) The Roof, (610) 521-5090
http://www.redroof.com
49 Industrial Hwy.
135 rooms - $55-67
Pets: Under 30 lbs. welcome
Creature Comforts: CCTV, a/c

EXTON
Holiday Inn Express
(800) HOLIDAY, (610) 524-9000
http://www.holiday-inn.com
120 N. Pottstown Pike
124 rooms - $65-90
Pets: Welcome
Creature Comforts: CCTV, a/c,
cont. brkfst, pool, hlth club

Holiday Inn
(800) HOLIDAY, (610) 363-1100
http://www.holiday-inn.com
815 N. Pottstown Pike
215 rooms - $70-90
Pets: Welcome
Creature Comforts: CCTV, a/c,
kit, restaurant, full brkfst, pool,
hlth clb access, sauna, whirlpool

FAYETTEVILLE
Rite Spot Motel
(717) 352-2144
5651 Lincoln Way E.
20 rooms - $40-45
Pets: Small pets w/$2 fee
Creature Comforts: CCTV, a/c,
restaurant

FOGELSVILLE
Cloverleaf Motel
(610) 395-3367
327 Star Rd.
30 rooms - $40-60
Pets: Welcome
Creature Comforts: CCTV, a/c

FRACKVILLE
Econo Lodge
(800) 55-ECONO, (570) 874-3838
http://www.econolodge.com
501 S. Middle St.
39 rooms - $50-80
Pets: Welcome w/$6 fee
Creature Comforts: CCTV, a/c,
refrig, micro, cont. brkfst

Granny's Budget Host
(800) Bud-Host, (570) 874-0408
http://www.budgethost.com
115 W. Coal St.
35 rooms - $40-45
Pets: Welcome
Creature Comforts: CCTV, a/c,
restaurant

FRANKLIN
Inn at Franklin
(814) 437-3031
1411 Liberty St.
85 rooms - $65-70
Pets: Small pets w/$10 fee
Creature Comforts: CCTV, a/c,
refrig, Jacuzzis, cont. brkfst,
restaurant

FRYESTOWN
Motel of Fryestown
(717) 933-4613
90 Fort Motel Dr.
12 rooms - $35-45
Pets: Welcome
Creature Comforts: TV, a/c

GALETON
Ox Yoke Inn
(814) 435-6522
Route 6
15 rooms - $40-44
Pets: Welcome
Creature Comforts: CCTV, a/c

Pine Log Motel
(814) 435-6400
120 N. Pottstown Pike
10 rooms - $45-59
Pets: Welcome
Creature Comforts: CCTV,
refrig

GETTYSBURG
Best Inn
(800) 237-8466, (717) 334-1188
301 Steinwehr Ave.
75 rooms - $50-89
Pets: Small pets welcome
Creature Comforts: CCTV, a/c,
kit, cont. brkfst

Heritage Motor Lodge
(717) 334-9281
64 Steinwehr Ave.
35 rooms - $50-85
Pets: Small pets w/$5 fee
Creature Comforts: CCTV, a/c

Holiday Inn, Battlefield
(800) HOLIDAY, (717) 334-6211
http://www.holiday-inn.com
516 Baltimore St.
100 rooms - $85-110
Pets: Welcome
Creature Comforts: CCTV, a/c,
restaurant, pool

GIBSONIA
Comfort Inn
(800) 228-5150, (724) 444-8700
http://www.comfortinn.com
Rte 8
65 rooms - $55-60
Pets: Welcome
Creature Comforts: CCTV, a/c

GLEN MILLS
Sweetwater Farm
(800) Sweetwater, (215) 459-4711
http://www.sweetwaterinn.com
50 Sweetwater Rd.
13 rooms - $140-230
Pets: Welcome in the cottages
Creature Comforts: 1734
Georgian mansion and cottages on
gentleman's farm, main house
filled w/formal antiques, cottages
w/country antiques, French doors,
dhurrie rugs, hand-painted
furniture, kit, full brkfst, pool,
walking/riding trails

GRANTVILLE
Holiday Inn, Harrisburg
(800) HOLIDAY, (717) 469-0661
http://www.holiday-inn.com
604 Station Rd.
200 rooms - $60-200
Pets: Welcome
Creature Comforts: CCTV,
VCR, a/c, refrig, micro, restaurant,
pool, hlth clb, sauna

GROVE CITY
Lynnrose Bed and Breakfast
(724) 458-6425
114 West Main St.
5 rooms - $60-70
Pets: Welcome
Creature Comforts: TV, a/c

HAMLIN

Comfort Inn
(800) 228-5150, (570) 689-4148
http://www.comfortinn.com
Route 191
125 rooms - $60-100
Pets: Welcome w/$5 fee
Creature Comforts: CCTV,
VCR, a/c, refrig, Jacuzzi, cont.
brkfst

HARRISBURG

Baymont Inn
(800) 4-Budget, (717) 540-9339
http://www.baymontinns.com
200 N. Mountain Rd.
65 rooms - $70-85
Pets: Welcome
Creature Comforts: CCTV, a/c,
cont. brkfst

Baymont Inn, Airport
(800) 4-Budget, (717) 939-8000
http://www.baymontinns.com
990 Eisenhower Blvd.
115 rooms - $50-80
Pets: Small pets welcome
Creature Comforts: CCTV, a/c,
refrig, micro

Best Western Capital Plaza
(800) 528-1234, (717) 545-9089
http://www.bestwestern.com
150 Nationwide Dr.
120 rooms - $55-65
Pets: Small pets welcome
Creature Comforts: CCTV,
VCR, a/c, refrig, micro, cont.
brkfst, pool, hlth club

Best Western Harrisburg
(800) 528-1234, (717) 652-7180
http://www.bestwestern.com
300 North Mountain Rd.
50 rooms - $70-90
Pets: Welcome
Creature Comforts: CCTV, a/c,
restaurant, cont. brkfst

Comfort Inn
(800) 228-5150, (717) 540-8400
http://www.comfortinn.com
7744 Linglestown Rd.
80 rooms - $70-100
Pets: Welcome
Creature Comforts: CCTV,
VCR, a/c, refrig, micro, cont.
brkfst, pool, exercise rm.

Comfort Inn, East
(800) 228-5150, (717) 561-8100
http://www.comfortinn.com
4021 Union Deposit Rd.
115 rooms - $70-100
Pets: Welcome
Creature Comforts: CCTV,
VCR, a/c, cont. brkfst, pool

Days Inn, Airport
(800) DAYS INN, (717) 939-4147
http://www.daysinn.com
800 Eisenhower Blvd.
82 rooms - $50-90
Pets: Welcome
Creature Comforts: CCTV, a/c,
refrig, micro, cont. brkfst, pool

Holiday Inn Express
(800) HOLIDAY, (717) 233-1611
http://www.holiday-inn.com
525 S. Front St.
118 rooms - $80-100
Pets: Small pets w/$10 fee
Creature Comforts: CCTV, a/c,
refrig, cont. brkfst, restaurant,
pool, exercise rm.

Howard Johnson
(800) I-Go-Hojo, (717) 233-1611
http://www.hojo.com
473 Eisenhower Blvd.
176 rooms - $40-100
Pets: Welcome
Creature Comforts: CCTV, a/c,
restaurant, cont. brkfst, pool, hlth
clb

Red Roof Inn, North
(800) The Roof, (717) 657-1445
http://www.redroof.com
400 Corporate Circle
105 rooms - $45-69
Pets: Small pets welcome
Creature Comforts: CCTV, a/c

Red Roof Inn, South
(800) The Roof, (717) 939-1331
http://www.redroof.com
950 Eisenhower Blvd.
110 rooms - $35-65
Pets: Welcome
Creature Comforts: CCTV, a/c

Residence Inn
(800) 331-3131, (717) 561-1900
http://www.residenceinn.com
4480 Lewis Rd.
82 rooms - $110-125
Pets: $5 fee, $50 deposit
Creature Comforts: CCTV, a/c,
kit

Sleep Inn
(800) Sleep-Inn, (717) 540-9100
http://www.sleepinn.com
7930 Linglestown Rd.
41 rooms - $45-85
Pets: Welcome w/$5 fee
Creature Comforts: CCTV, a/c

Super 8, North
(800) 800-8000, (717) 233-5891
http://www.super8.com
4125 N. Front St.
57 rooms - $48-65
Pets: Welcome
Creature Comforts: CCTV,
VCR, a/c, refrig, restaurant, pool

Travelodge
(800) 578-7878, (717) 564-3876
http://www.travelodge.com
4125 N. Front St.
58 rooms - $50-70
Pets: Welcome
Creature Comforts: CCTV, a/c,
refrig, restaurant, pool

Wyndham Garden Hotel
(800) Wyndham, (717) 558-9500
http://www.wyndham.com
765 Eisenhower Blvd.
165 rooms - $110-140
Pets: Small pets welcome
Creature Comforts: CCTV, a/c,
refrig, micro, restaurant, pool

HAWLEY

Falls Port Inn
(570) 226-2600
330 Main Ave.
9 rooms - $55-100
Pets: Welcome
Creature Comforts: Historic
1900's inn, charming bedrooms,
some antiques, TV, VCR, a/c,
excellent restaurant, exercise rm.

HAZLETON
Best Western Gennetti
(800) 528-1234, (570) 454-2494
http://www.bestwestern.com
Route 309
90 rooms - $60-150
Pets: Small pets welcome
Creature Comforts: CCTV,
VCR, a/c, refrig, micro, cont.
brkfst, pool

Comfort Inn
(800) 228-5150, (570) 455-9300
http://www.comfortinn.com
Rte. 93 & Kiwanis Blvd.
120 rooms - $70-100
Pets: Welcome
Creature Comforts: CCTV,
VCR, a/c, Jacuzzi, restaurant,
cont. brkfst

Forest Hill Inn
(570) 459-2730
Route 93
40 rooms - $50-55
Pets: Welcome
Creature Comforts: CCTV, a/c

Hazleton Motor Inn
(570) 459-1451
615 E. Broad St.
26 rooms - $35-50
Pets: Welcome
Creature Comforts: CCTV, a/c,
kit

Mount Laurel Motel
(717) 455-6391
1039 S. Church St.
38 rooms - $35-45
Pets: Welcome
Creature Comforts: CCTV, a/c,
refrig

Ramada Inn
(800) 2-Ramada, (570) 455-2061
http://www.ramada.com
Route 309
110 rooms - $55-90
Pets: Welcome
Creature Comforts: CCTV, a/c,
refrig, micro, restaurant, pool

HERMITAGE
Holiday Inn
(800) HOLIDAY, (724) 981-1530
http://www.holiday-inn.com
3200 S. Hermitage Rd.
180 rooms - $40-75
Pets: Small pets welcome
Creature Comforts: CCTV,
VCR, a/c, refrig, restaurant, pool

Royal Motel
(724) 347-5546
301 S. Hermitage Rd.
24 rooms - $40-50
Pets: Small pets w/$5 fee, $10 dep
Creature Comforts: CCTV, a/c

HERSHEY
Holiday Inn Express
(800) HOLIDAY, (717) 583-0500
http://www.holiday-inn.com
610 Walton Ave.
110 rooms - $90-150
Pets: Small pets w/$10 fee
Creature Comforts: CCTV, a/c,
refrig, micro, cont. brkfst, pool,
whirlpool, exercise rm.

HONESDALE
Fife and Drum Motor Inn
(570) 253-1392
100 Terrace St.
30 rooms - $44-70
Pets: Small pets w/$6 fee
Creature Comforts: CCTV, a/c,
refrig, micro

HONEYBROOK
Historic Waynebrook Inn
(610) 273-2444
http://www.honeybrook.com/
waynebrookinn
Rtes. 10 & 322
20 rooms - $90-195
Pets: Small pets welcome
Creature Comforts: Historic inn
set in Amish country, updated rms,
canopy and plantation beds,
armoires, Victorian decor, CCTV,
VCR, a/c, kit, Jacuzzi, restaurant,
full brkfst

HORSHAM
Residence Inn
(800) 331-3131, (215) 443-7330
http://www.residenceinn.com
3 Walnut Grove Dr.
120 rooms - $99-175
Pets: Welcome w/$150 fee
Creature Comforts: CCTV,
VCR, a/c, kit, pool, hlth clb access

HUNTINGDON
Days Inn
(800) DAYS INN, (814) 643-3934
http://www.daysinn.com
Route 22 & Fourth St.
76 rooms - $50-75
Pets: Welcome w/$5 fee
Creature Comforts: CCTV, a/c,
refrig, micro

INDIANA
Best Western University Inn
(800) 528-1234, (724) 349-9620
http://www.bestwestern.com
1545 Wayne Ave.
110 rooms - $50-65
Pets: Welcome
Creature Comforts: CCTV, a/c,
Jacuzzi, restaurant, pool

Holiday Inn Holidome
(800) HOLIDAY, (724) 463-3561
http://www.holiday-inn.com
1395 Wayne Ave.
160 rooms - $75-80
Pets: Welcome
Creature Comforts: CCTV, a/c,
kit, restaurant, pool, exercise rm.

Super 8
(800) 800-8000, (724) 349-4600
http://www.super8.com
111 Plaza Dr.
62 rooms - $48-75
Pets: Pets w/permission
Creature Comforts: CCTV, a/c,
refrig, micro, Jacuzzi

JOHNSTOWN
Comfort Inn
(800) 228-5150, (814) 266-3678
http://www.comfortinn.com
455 Theater Dr.
117 rooms - $60-70
Pets: Welcome w/$5 fee
Creature Comforts: CCTV,
VCR, a/c, restaurant, cont. brkfst,
pool

Days Inn
(800) DAYS INN, (814) 269-3366
http://www.daysinn.com
1540 Scalp Ave.
94 rooms - $50-55
Pets: Welcome w/$25 deposit
Creature Comforts: CCTV, a/c,
restaurant, cont. brkfst, pool,
whirlpool

Holiday Inn
(800) HOLIDAY, (814) 535-7777
http://www.holiday-inn.com
250 Market St.
165 rooms - $70-80
Pets: $10 deposit, must be in
kennel, cannot be left unattended
Creature Comforts: CCTV, a/c,
refrig, micro, restaurant, pool,
exercise rm.

Holiday Inn Express
(800) HOLIDAY, (814) 266-8789
http://www.holiday-inn.com
1440 Scalp Ave.
110 rooms - $65-70
Pets: Supervised pets welcome
Creature Comforts: CCTV, a/c,
refrig, micro

Sleep Inn
(800) Sleep-Inn, (814) 262-9292
http://www.sleepinn.com
453 Theater Dr.
62 rooms - $55-60
Pets: Welcome w/$4 fee
Creature Comforts: CCTV, a/c,
refrig, micro, restaurant, cont.
brkfst

KANE
Kane View Motel
(814) 837-8600
Route 6
20 rooms - $35-49
Pets: Welcome
Creature Comforts: CCTV

KEMPTON
Hawk Mountain Inn
(610) 756-4224
221 Stony Run Valley Rd.
8 rooms - $100-140
Pets: Welcome
Creature Comforts: Native stone
house near Hawk Mtn. Sanctuary,
beautiful views, stone fireplace in
common rm., rms. contain CCTV,
a/c, fireplace, Jacuzzi, country
brkfst, pool, hiking, birdwatching

KITTANNING
Comfort Inn
(800) 228-5150, (724) 543-5200
http://www.comfortinn.com
422 W. Belmont
70 rooms - $75-105
Pets: small pets w/$8 fee
Creature Comforts: CCTV, a/c,
refrig, micro, pool, exercise rm.

Rodeway Inn
(800) 228-2000, (724) 543-1100
http://www.rodeway.com
Rte. 422 East
20 rooms - $45-55
Pets: Welcome
Creature Comforts: CCTV, a/c,
refrig, micro, cont. brkfst

KULPSVILLE
Holiday Inn
(800) HOLIDAY, (215) 368-3800
http://www.holiday-inn.com
1750 Sumneytown Pk.
185 rooms - $65-80
Pets: Small pets w/$20 fee,
mngrs. discretion
Creature Comforts: CCTV,
VCR, a/c, kit, restaurant, pool

KUTZTOWN
Campus Inn
(610) 683-8721
15080 Kutztown Rd.
30 rooms - $50-80
Pets: Small pets welcome
Creature Comforts: CCTV, a/c,
refrig, micro, Jacuzzi, cont. brkfst,
pool

Lincoln Motel
(610) 683-3456
Main St.
15 rooms - $40-80
Pets: Small pets welcome
Creature Comforts: CCTV,
VCR, a/c

LAKE HARMONY
Days Inn
(800) DAYS INN, (610) 683-8721
http://www.daysinn.com
Rte. 940
40 rooms - $75-200
Pets: Welcome w/$5 fee
Creature Comforts: CCTV, a/c,
refrig, Jacuzzi, cont. brkfst

Ramada Inn
(800) 2-Ramada, (814) 443-4646
http://www.ramada.com
Rtes. 76 & 70
140 rooms - $60-175
Pets: Welcome w/$50 deposit
Creature Comforts: CCTV,
VCR, a/c, refrig, Jacuzzis,
restaurant, pool, sauna, whirlpool

LANCASTER
Best Western Eden Resort
(800) 528-1234, (717) 569-6444
http://www.edenresort.com
222 Eden Rd.
275 rooms - $85-150
Pets: Welcome
Creature Comforts: CCTV, a/c,
kit, restaurant, cont. brkfst, pool,
hlth clb access, sauna, whirlpool,
tennis

Comfort Inn
(800) 228-5150, (717) 898-2431
http://www.comfortinn.com
500 Centerville Rd.
166 rooms - $75-150
Pets: Small pets w/$8 fee
Creature Comforts: CCTV, a/c,
refrig, Jacuzzi, restaurant, cont.
brkfst, pool, hlth clb, sauna,
whirlpool

Hotel Brunswick
(717) 397-4801
Chestnut & Queen Streets
225 rooms - $60-85
Pets: Small pets w/$100 dep.
Creature Comforts: CCTV, a/c,
refrig, restaurant, pool, exercise
rm.

Lancaster Host Resort
(800) 233-0121, (717) 299-8971
2300 Lincoln Hwy.
330 rooms - $100-160
Pets: Welcome
Creature Comforts: CCTV, a/c,
refrig, pools, whirlpool, exercise
rm., tennis, golf

Quality Inn
(800) 228-5151, (717) 569-0477
http://www.qualityinn.com
2363 Oregon Pike
82 rooms - $50-150
Pets: Welcome w/$25 deposit
Creature Comforts: CCTV,
VCR, a/c, restaurant, cont. brkfst,
pool

Super 8
(800) 800-8000, (717) 393-8888
http://www.super8.com
2129 Lincoln Rte. East
100 rooms - $47-110
Pets: Small pets w/$25 deposit
Creature Comforts: CCTV, a/c,
refrig, micro

Travel Inn
(717) 299-8971
2151 Lincoln Rte. East
67 rooms - $50-90
Pets: Welcome
Creature Comforts: CCTV, a/c,
pool

Travelodge
(800) 578-7878, (717) 397-4201
http://www.travelodge.com
2101 Columbia Ave.
58 rooms - $42-92
Pets: Welcome
Creature Comforts: CCTV, a/c,
restaurant, cont. brkfst, pool

LANGHORNE
Red Roof Inn
(800) The Roof, (215) 750-6200
http://www.redroof.com
3100 Cabot Blvd.
90 rooms - $50-80
Pets: Small pets welcome
Creature Comforts: CCTV, a/c

LESTER
Econo Lodge
(800) 55-ECONO, (610) 521-3900
http://www.econolodge.com
600 Route 291
134 rooms - $47-62
Pets: Welcome
Creature Comforts: CCTV, a/c,
restaurant, pool

LEWISBURG
Days Inn
(800) DAYS INN, (570) 523-1171
http://www.daysinn.com
Rte 15
110 rooms - $70-135
Pets: Small pets welcome
Creature Comforts: CCTV,
VCR, a/c, refrig, micro

LIGONIER
Lady of the Lake B&B
(724) 238-6955
http://www.lmt1.com/lady/
157 Rte. 30
5 rooms - $90-150
Pets: Small pets w/permission
Creature Comforts: 1800's
farmhouse and cottages set on 60-
acres fronting private lake, French
country decor in main house,
slightly more rustic cottage,
handmade quilts, down
comforters, four-poster beds,
CCTV, Jacuzzi, woodburning
stove, kit, full six-course brkfst,
whirlpool, tennis court, farm
animals

LIONVILLE
Comfort Inn
(800) 228-5150, (610) 524-8811
http://www.comfortinn.com
5 North Pottstown Pike
105 rooms - $60-65
Pets: Welcome w/$5 fee
Creature Comforts: CCTV,
VCR, a/c, refrig, micro, Jacuzzi,
pool, hlth clb

Hampton Inn
(800) Hampton, (610) 363-5555
http://www.hampton-inn.com
4 North Pottstown Pike
122 rooms - $65-85
Pets: Welcome
Creature Comforts: CCTV, a/c

LITITZ
General Sutter Inn
(717) 626-2115
14 East Main St.
14 rooms - $70-100
Pets: Welcome w/notice
Creature Comforts: 1760's brick
inn w/old world feeling, Victorian
crystal/gas parlor lamps, early
American antiques, collectibles,
old-fashioned fabrics, CCTV, a/c,
restaurant

LOCK HAVEN
Best Western
(800) 800-8000, (570) 748-3297
http://www.bestwestern.com
101 East Walnut St.
67 rooms - $50-90
Pets: Welcome w/$5 fee
Creature Comforts: CCTV,
VCR, a/c, refrig, micro, cont.
brkfst, hlth club

LUMBERVILLE
Black Bass Hotel
(215) 297-5815
http://www.blackbasshotel.com
Route 32
9 rooms - $80-150
Pets: Welcome
Creature Comforts: A 1745
riverside tavern w/massive
outdoor patio overlooking
Delaware River, old English pub,
extensive murals, overstuffed
furniture, funky bedrooms have
sloping wood floors, handmade
quilts, country antiques, eclectic
furnishings, excellent restaurant

MALVERN
Great Valley House B&B
(215) 644-6759
http://pages.prodigy.net/
greatvalleyhouse
RD 3, Box 110
3 rooms - $80-95
Pets: Welcome w/$15 fee
Creature Comforts: 1720 stone
farmhouse surrounded by three
acres and boxwood hedges,
careful restoration created living
museum, canopied and antique
brass beds, colorful quilts, down
comforters, walk-in fireplace,
pool, full brkfst

QUAKERTOWN
Rodeway Inn
(800) 228-2000, (215) 536-7600
http://www.rodeway.com
1920 Rte 663
40 rooms - $75-85
Pets: Welcome
Creature Comforts: CCTV, a/c,
kit, refrig, micro, Jacuzzi

MANHEIM
Rodeway Inn
(800) 228-2000, (717) 665-2755
http://www.rodeway.com
2931 Lebanon Rd.
39 rooms - $34-60
Pets: Welcome
Creature Comforts: CCTV, a/c, pool

MANSFIELD
Comfort Inn
(800) 228-5150, (570) 662-3000
http://www.comfortinn.com
300 Gateway Dr.
100 rooms - $55-85
Pets: Welcome
Creature Comforts: CCTV, a/c

Mansfield Inn
(570) 662-2136
26 S. Main St.
25 rooms - $55-65
Pets: Welcome w/$5
Creature Comforts: CCTV, a/c, cont. brkfst

West's Deluxe Motel
(570) 659-5141
Route 15
20 rooms - $35-45
Pets: Welcome
Creature Comforts: CCTV, restaurant, pool

MARS
Days Inn
(800) DAYS INN, (412) 772-2700
http://www.daysinn.com
909 Sheraton Dr.
103 rooms - $55-70
Pets: Welcome
Creature Comforts: CCTV, a/c, cont. brkfst, hlth club

MATAMORAS
Best Western Hunt's Landing
(800) 528-1234, (570) 491-2400
http://www.bestwestern.com
Rtes. 6 & 209
107 rooms - $65-160
Pets: Welcome
Creature Comforts: Riverside setting, CCTV, a/c, refrig, micro, Jacuzzis, restaurant, cont. brkfst, pool
630

MEADVILLE
Days Inn
(800) DAYS INN, (814) 337-4264
http://www.daysinn.com
240 Conneaut Lake Rd.
165 rooms - $55-90
Pets: $5 fee, $25 deposit
Creature Comforts: CCTV, VCR, a/c, restaurant, pool, whirlpool

Motel 6
(800) 4-MOTEL6, (814) 724-6366
http://www.motel6.com
11237 Shaw Ave.
60 rooms - $48-64
Pets: Under 30 lbs. welcome
Creature Comforts: CCTV, a/c

Super 8
(800) 800-8000, (814) 333-8883
http://www.super8.com
17259 Conneaut Lake Rd.
62 rooms - $48-65
Pets: Pets w/permission
Creature Comforts: CCTV, VCR, a/c, cont. brkfst

MECHANICSBURG
Holiday Inn
(800) HOLIDAY, (717) 697-0321
http://www.holiday-inn.com
5401 Carlisle Pk.
218 rooms - $85-120
Pets: Welcome w/$50 deposit
Creature Comforts: CCTV, a/c, refrig, micro, Jacuzzi, restaurant, pool, hlth clb access, lawn games

MERCER
Colonial Inn Motel
(724) 662-5600
383 N. Perry Rte.
20 rooms - $25-35
Pets: Welcome
Creature Comforts: CCTV, a/c

Howard Johnson Lodge
(800) I-Go-Hojo, (724) 748-3030
http://www.hojo.com
835 Perry Rte.
102 rooms - $75-85
Pets: Welcome
Creature Comforts: CCTV, a/c, restaurant, pool, hlth clb, sauna

MIFFLINVILLE
Super 8
(800) 800-8000, (717) 759-6778
http://www.super8.com
Route 80
30 rooms - $45-55
Pets: Welcome w/deposit
Creature Comforts: CCTV, a/c, restaurant

MILESBURG
Holiday Inn
(800) HOLIDAY, (814) 355-7521
http://www.holiday-inn.com
Route 150
115 rooms - $55-95
Pets: Small pets welcome
Creature Comforts: CCTV, VCR, a/c, refrig, micro, restaurant, pool

MILFORD
Milford Motel
(570) 296-6411
Routes 6 & 209
19 rooms - $45-55
Pets: Welcome
Creature Comforts: CCTV, a/c, refrig, pool

Cliff Park Inn and Golf Course
(800) 225-6535, (570) 296-6491
http://www.cliffparkinn.com
155 Cliff Park Rd.
18 rooms - $100-140
Pets: Welcome in one cottage
Creature Comforts: Historic 1820's inn on 600-acre estate, large public rooms w/massive stone hearths, wonderful old-fashioned cottages nicely furnished w/family antiques, CCTV, VCR, refrig, full brkfst, restaurant, pool, whirlpool, 9-hole golf course

Myer Motel
(570) 296-7223
Routes 6/209
18 rooms - $45-75
Pets: Welcome w/$20 dep.
Creature Comforts: CCTV, a/c, kit

Red Carpet Inn
(800) 251-1962, (570) 296-9444
Routes 84 & 6
25 rooms - $55-70
Pets: Welcome w/$5 fee
Creature Comforts: CCTV, a/c

Tourist Village Motel
(570) 491-4414
Routes 6 & 209
17 rooms - $38-58
Pets: Welcome
Creature Comforts: CCTV, a/c, kit

MONROEVILLE
Days Inn
(800) DAYS INN, (412) 856-1610
http://www.daysinn.com
2727 Mosside Blvd.
106 rooms - $55-65
Pets: Welcome w/$5 fee
Creature Comforts: CCTV, a/c

Hampton Inn
(800) Hampton, (412) 380-4000
http://www.hampton-inn.com
3000 Mosside Blvd.
140 rooms - $90-100
Pets: Welcome
Creature Comforts: CCTV, VCR, a/c, refrig, pool

Holiday Inn
(800) HOLIDAY, (412) 372-1022
http://www.holiday-inn.com
2750 Mosside Blvd.
190 rooms - $70-130
Pets: Under 25 lbs. welcome
Creature Comforts: CCTV, a/c, restaurant, pool

Red Roof Inn
(800) The Roof, (412) 856-4738
http://www.redroof.com
2729 Mosside Blvd.
116 rooms - $55-65
Pets: Small pets welcome
Creature Comforts: CCTV, a/c

MOOSIC
Days Inn
(800) DAYS INN, (717) 457-6713
http://www.daysinn.com
4130 Birney Ave.
46 rooms - $45-125
Pets: Welcome w/$5 fee
Creature Comforts: CCTV, a/c, kit, cont. brkfst, whirlpool

MONTROSE
Ridge House
(570) 278-4933
6 Ridge St.
4 rooms - $50-55
Pets: Welcome
Creature Comforts: 1860's Victorian, unique because of octagonal shape, antique furnishings, TV

MORGANTOWN
Holiday Inn
(800) HOLIDAY, (610) 286-3000
http://www.holiday-inn.com
230 Cherry St.
190 rooms - $90-120
Pets: Welcome w/$10 dep.
Creature Comforts: CCTV, VCR, a/c, refrig, micro, restaurant, pool, whirlpool, sauna

MUNCY
Walton House B&B
(717) 546-8114
172 W. Water St.
4 rooms - $50-65
Pets: Welcome w/$25 deposit
Creature Comforts: CCTV, a/c, restaurant, cont. brkfst

NEW CASTLE
Comfort Inn
(800) 228-5150, (724) 658-7700
http://www.comfortinn.com
1740 New Butler Rd.
79 rooms - $65-75
Pets: Small pets w/$6 fee
Creature Comforts: CCTV, a/c, refrig, micro, Jacuzzi, cont. brkfst, hlth club

NEW COLUMBIA
Comfort Inn
(800) 228-5150, (570) 568-8000
http://www.comfortinn.com
106 Blair Blvd.
120 rooms - $60-70
Pets: Welcome
Creature Comforts: CCTV, a/c, refrig, micro, whirlpool, cont. brkfst, restaurant, pool

NEW CUMBERLAND
Days Inn
(800) DAYS INN, (717) 774-4156
http://www.daysinn.com
353 Lewisberry Rd.
62 rooms - $50-65
Pets: Welcome w/$5 fee
Creature Comforts: CCTV, VCR, a/c, restaurant, pool

Holiday Inn
(800) HOLIDAY, (717) 774-2721
http://www.holiday-inn.com
Route 83
195 rooms - $50-120
Pets: Small pets w/$10 fee
Creature Comforts: CCTV, a/c, restaurant, cont. brkfst, pool, whirlpool, exercise rm.

Knights Inn
(800) 843-5644, (717) 774-5990
http://www.knightsinn.com
300 Commerce Dr.
117 rooms - $30-39
Pets: Welcome w/$5 fee
Creature Comforts: CCTV, a/c, refrig, micro, pool

Motel 6
(800) 4-MOTEL6, (717) 774-8910
http://www.motel6.com
200 Commerce Dr.
124 rooms - $35-42
Pets: Under 30 lbs. welcome
Creature Comforts: CCTV, a/c, pool

NEW HOPE
Aaron Burr House
(215) 862-2343
http://www.new-hope-inn.com
80 West Bridge St.
7 rooms - $90-160
Pets: Welcome w/notice, no puppies
Creature Comforts: 1854 Victorian, in-town location, beautifully restored black walnut floors/wainscoting, four poster beds and antique furnishings mixed w/reproductions, fireplace, expanded cont. brkfst

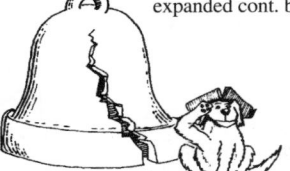

Best Western New Hope
(800) 528-1234, (215) 862-5221
http://www.bestwestern.com
6426 Lower York Rd.
152 rooms - $75-150
Pets: Small pets w/$20 fee
Creature Comforts: CCTV, a/c,
restaurant, pool, hlth clb, tennis,
lawn games

Fox and Hound B&B
(800) 862-5082, (215) 862-5082
http://www.foxhoundinn.com
246 W. Bridge St.
8 rooms - $85-160
Pets: Welcome in Room 1
Creature Comforts: 1850's stone
house, in-town location, pet-
friendly room has sep. outside
entrance, traditional reproductions
in light pine, sitting area, attractive
accents, sofa, CCTV, a/c,
fireplace, full brkfst weekends,
expanded cont. brkfst weekdays

**Wedgewood Collection of
Historic Inns**
(215) 862-2570
http://www.new-hope-inn.com
855 Route 46 East
11 rooms - $75-190
Pets: Welcome in ltd rms-$20 fee
Creature Comforts: Two classic
inns-Victorian and Classic
Revival-with extensive formal
gardens, antiques, sleigh and brass
beds, comforters, private baths w/
English toiletries, expanded cont.
brkfst

NEW KENSINGTON
Clarion Inn
(800) CLARION, (724) 335-9171
http://www.clarioninn.com
300 Tarentum Bridge Rd.
110 rooms - $60-75
Pets: Welcome
Creature Comforts: CCTV, a/c,
refrig, micro, restaurant, pool, hlth
clb.

NEW STANTON
Ramada Inn
(800) 2-Ramada, (724) 925-6755
http://www.ramada.com
110 N. Main St.
150 rooms - $70-105
Pets: Welcome w/$5 fee
Creature Comforts: CCTV, a/c,
refrig, micro, pool

NORTH EAST
Red Carpet Inn
(800) 251-1962, (814) 725-4554
12264 E. Main St.
58 rooms - $68-79
Pets: Welcome
Creature Comforts: CCTV, a/c,
cont. brkfst, pool

Vineyard B&B
(814) 725-5307
10757 Side Hill Rd.
4 rooms - $68-79
Pets: Small pets welcome
Creature Comforts: CCTV, cont.
brkfst

OAKDALE
Comfort Inn
(800) 228-5150, (412) 787-2600
http://www.comfortinn.com
7011 Old Steubenville Pike
74 rooms - $50-100
Pets: Welcome w$5 fee
Creature Comforts: CCTV, a/c,
restaurant, cont. brkfst, hlth club

OAKLAND
Best Western University
(800) 528-1234, (412) 683-6100
http://www.bestwestern.com
3401 Blvd. of the Allies
119 rooms - $85-100
Pets: Welcome
Creature Comforts: CCTV, a/c,
restaurant, pool

Hampton Inn, University
(800) Hampton, (412) 681-1000
http://www.hampton-inn.com
3315 Hamlet St.
132 rooms - $100-110
Pets: Welcome
Creature Comforts: CCTV, a/c

Holiday Inn, Select
(800) HOLIDAY, (412) 682-6200
http://www.holiday-inn.com
100 Lytton Ave.
250 rooms - $120-125
Pets: Small pets welcome
Creature Comforts: CCTV, a/c,
restaurant, pool

OIL CITY
Holiday Inn
(800) HOLIDAY, (814) 677-1221
http://www.holiday-inn.com
One Seneca St.
105 rooms - $70-120
Pets: Welcome
Creature Comforts: CCTV, a/c,
refrig, micro, Jacuzzi, restaurant,
pool, hlth clb access

PHILADELPHIA
Best Western Center City Hotel
(800) 528-1234, (215) 568-8300
http://www.bestwestern.com
501 N. 22nd St.
183 rooms - $90-130
Pets: Under 35 lbs. w/$10 fee
Creature Comforts: CCTV, a/c,
refrig, restaurant, pool, hlth clb
access

**Best Western Independence
Park**
(800) 528-1234, (215) 922-4443
http://www.bestwestern.com
235 Chestnut St.
36 rooms - $125-185
Pets: Welcome w/$10 fee
Creature Comforts: CCTV,
VCR, a/c, refrig, restaurant, cont.
brkfst

Crowne Plaza
(800) HOLIDAY, (215) 561-7500
http://www.holiday-inn.com
1800 Market St.
445 rooms - $175-250
Pets: Welcome
Creature Comforts: CCTV, a/c,
refrig, restaurant, pool, exercise
rm.

Four Seasons Hotel
(800) 332-3442, (215) 963-1500
http://www.fshr.com
One Logan Sq.
365 rooms - $195-1,185
Pets: Under 15 lbs. w/$100
deposit
Creature Comforts: Set on
Logan Circle near science
museums, an oasis in the city w/
indoor atrium, richly hued woods
and marble, luxurious rooms,
Federal-style furnishings, inlaid
mahogany tables, CCTV, a/c,
refrig, restaurants, pool, hlth clb,
sauna, whirlpool

Hilton, Airport
(800) HILTONS, (215) 365-4150
http://www.hilton.com
4509 Island Ave.
330 rooms - $100-115
Pets: Welcome w/$25 fee
Creature Comforts: CCTV, a/c, refrig, restaurant, cont. brkfst, pool, hlth clb access, whirlpool

Marriott, Airport
(800) 228-9290, (215) 492-9000
http://www.marriott.com
I95/Rte. 291
420 rooms - $180-350
Pets: Small pets welcome
Creature Comforts: CCTV, a/c, refrig, restaurant, pool, exercise rm.

Residence Inn, Airport
(800) 331-3131, (215) 492-1611
http://www.residenceinn.com
4630 Island Ave.
105 rooms - $90-170
Pets: $6 fee, $100 dep
Creature Comforts: CCTV, a/c, kit, pool

Rittenhouse
(800) 635-1042, (215) 546-9000
http://www.rittenhouse.com
210 Rittenhouse Sq.
100 rooms - $220-1,300
Pets: Welcome w/notice
Creature Comforts: Modern high rise w/Art Deco interior, coffered ceilings, profusion of flowers and plants, residential qlty to rms., tailored coverlets, Queen Anne reproductions, CCTV, VCR, a/c, refrig, marble baths, soaking tubs, fine restaurants, pool, hlth clb

Ten-Eleven Clinton
(215) 923-8144
http://www.teneleven.com
1011 Clinton St.
7 suites - $125-200
Pets: Dogs welcome
Creature Comforts: Highly recommended, 1836 Federal townhouse, "quiet retreat in heart of big city," hardwood flrs, lovely antique furnishings, chintz fabrics, four poster beds, CCTV, VCR, a/c, fireplaces, kit, courtyard

Travelodge
(800) 578-7878, (215) 755-6500
http://www.travelodge.com
2015 Penrose Ave.
210 rooms - $75-100
Pets: Small pets w/$15 fee
Creature Comforts: CCTV, a/c, refrig, micro, restaurant, pool, hlth clb access

PHILIPSBURG
Harbor Inn
(800) 508-0520, (814) 342-0250
Route 322
64 rooms - $48-60
Pets: Welcome
Creature Comforts: CCTV, a/c, restaurant

Main Liner Motel
(814) 342-2004
Route 322
21 rooms - $38-49
Pets: Welcome w/$6 fee
Creature Comforts: CCTV, a/c, refrig

PINE GROVE
Comfort Inn
(800) 228-5150, (570) 345-8031
http://www.comfortinn.com
Routes 81 & 443
68 rooms - $56-120
Pets: Welcome
Creature Comforts: CCTV, a/c, cont. brkfst, pool, hlth club

Econo Lodge
(800) 55-ECONO, (570) 345-4099
http://www.econolodge.com
Off Route 81
51 rooms - $45-60
Pets: Welcome
Creature Comforts: CCTV, a/c

PITTSBURGH
Amerisuites, Airport
(800) 833-1516, (412) 494-0202
http://www.amerisuites.com
6011 Campbell's Run Rd.
128 rooms - $90-120
Pets: Under 10 lbs., larger pets require deposit or fee
Creature Comforts: CCTV, VCR, a/c, refrig, micro, cont. brkfst, pool, hlth club

Days Inn
(800) DAYS INN, (412) 828-5400
http://www.daysinn.com
Route 28
101 rooms - $55-75
Pets: Welcome
Creature Comforts: CCTV, a/c

Days Inn
(800) DAYS INN, (412) 922-0120
http://www.daysinn.com
100 Kisow Dr.
116 rooms - $41-59
Pets: Welcome
Creature Comforts: CCTV, a/c, refrig., micro, cont. brkfst

Doubletree Hotel
(800) 222-TREE, (412) 281-3700
http://www.doubletreehotels.com
1000 Penn Ave.
615 rooms - $99-175
Pets: Welcome
Creature Comforts: CCTV, a/c, kit, restaurant, pool

Hampton Inn
(800) Hampton, (412) 922-0100
http://www.hampton-inn.com
555 Trumbull Dr.
63 rooms - $69-79
Pets: Welcome
Creature Comforts: CCTV, a/c

Hawthorn Suites
(800) 338-7812, (412) 279-6300
http://www.hawthorn.com
700 Mansfield Ave.
150 rooms - $79-99
Pets: Welcome w/$10 fee (max-2 per room)
Creature Comforts: CCTV, VCR, a/c, kit, fireplace, cont. brkfst, pool, hlth clb

Hilton
(800) HILTONS, (412) 391-4600
http://www.hilton.com
Gateway Center
715 rooms - $130-179
Pets: Dogs welcome w/signed agreement
Creature Comforts: CCTV, a/c, refrig, restaurant

Holiday Inn
(800) HOLIDAY, (412) 366-5200
http://www.holiday-inn.com
4859 McKnight Rd.
150 rooms - $90-130
Pets: Welcome
Creature Comforts: CCTV, a/c,
refrig, micro, restaurant, cont.
brkfst, hlth clb access

Holiday Inn, Central
(800) HOLIDAY, (412) 922-8100
http://www.holiday-inn.com
401 Holiday Dr.
205 rooms - $120-135
Pets: Welcome
Creature Comforts: CCTV, a/c,
refrig, micro, restaurant, cont.
brkfst, pool, hlth club

Holiday Inn, Parkway E.
(800) HOLIDAY, (412) 247-2700
http://www.holiday-inn.com
915 Brinton Rd.
180 rooms - $90-120
Pets: Small pets welcome
Creature Comforts: CCTV, a/c,
refrig, micro, restaurant, pool, hlth
clb access

Holiday Inn, South
(800) HOLIDAY, (412) 833-5300
http://www.holiday-inn.com
164 Ft. Couch Rd.
210 rooms - $75-95
Pets: Welcome
Creature Comforts: CCTV, a/c,
refrig, micro, restaurant, pool, hlth
clb access

Howard Johnson
(800) I-Go-Hojo, (412) 884-6000
http://www.hojo.com
5300 Clarion Blvd.
95 rooms - $75-95
Pets: Welcome
Creature Comforts: CCTV, a/c,
cont. brkfst, pool, hlth clb access

MainStay Suites
(800) 660-MAIN, (412) 490-7343
1000 Park Lane
95 rooms - $75-95
Pets: Welcome w/$10 fee, $50
deposit
Creature Comforts: CCTV, a/c,
kit, cont. brkfst, pool, exercise rm.

Marriott, Greentree
(800) 228-9290, (412) 922-8400
http://www.marriott.com
101 Marriott Dr.
467 rooms - $75-135
Pets: Small pets welcome
Creature Comforts: CCTV, a/c,
restaurant, pool

Motel 6
(800) 4-MOTEL6, (412) 922-9400
http://www.motel6.com
211 Beecham Rd.
126 rooms - $35-53
Pets: Under 30 lbs. welcome
Creature Comforts: CCTV,
VCR, a/c

Red Roof Inn
(800) The Roof, (412) 787-7870
http://www.redroof.com
6404 Steubenville Pk.
120 rooms - $50-65
Pets: Welcome
Creature Comforts: CCTV, a/c

Super 8 Motel
(800) 800-8000, (724) 733-8008
http://www.super8.com
1807 Route 286
49 rooms - $50-90
Pets: Welcome w/permission
Creature Comforts: CCTV,
VCR, a/c, Jacuzzi, cont. brkfst

Westin William Penn
(800) 228-3000, (412) 281-7100
http://www.westin.com
530 William Penn Rd.
595 rooms - $130-155
Pets: Small well-trained pets
Creature Comforts: CCTV, a/c,
restaurant, hlth club, hlth clb
access

PITTSTON
Holiday Inn Express
(800) HOLIDAY, (570) 654-3300
http://www.holiday-inn.com
30 Concorde Dr.
100 rooms - $60-70
Pets: Welcome
Creature Comforts: CCTV, a/c,
refrig, micro cont. brkfst,
restaurant, pool

Howard Johnson
(800) I-Go-Hojo, (570) 654-3301
http://www.hojo.com
307 Route 315
45 rooms - $55-85
Pets: Welcome
Creature Comforts: CCTV, a/c,
restaurant, cont. brkfst, pool

Knights Inn
(800) 843-5644, (570) 654-6020
http://www.knightsinn.com
Route 315
65 rooms - $35-55
Pets: Small pets welcome
Creature Comforts: CCTV,
VCR, a/c, kit, Jacuzzi, cont. brkfst

PLEASANTVILLE
West Vu Motel
(814) 839-2632
Route 96
15 rooms - $30-45
Pets: Under 30 lbs. welcome
Creature Comforts: CCTV, a/c

POTTSTOWN
Comfort Inn
(800) 228-5150, (610) 326-5000
http://www.comfortinn.com
99 Robinson St.
120 rooms - $60-90
Pets: Small pets w/$25 deposit
Creature Comforts: CCTV, a/c,
refrig, micro, pool

Days Inn
(800) DAYS INN, (610) 970-1101
http://www.daysinn.com
29 High St.
60 rooms - $50-90
Pets: Welcome w/$10 fee
Creature Comforts: CCTV, a/c,
refrig, cont. brkfst

Holiday Inn Express
(800) HOLIDAY, (610) 327-3300
http://www.holiday-inn.com
1600 Industrial Rte.
120 rooms - $60-65
Pets: Welcome w/$25 fee
Creature Comforts: CCTV, a/c,
refrig, micro, cont. brkfst, pool

PUNXSUTAWNEY
Country Villa Motel
(814) 938-8330
Route 119
25 rooms - $35-55
Pets: Welcome w/$4 fee
Creature Comforts: CCTV, a/c,
kit, restaurant

Pantall Hotel
(814) 938-6600
135 E. Mahoning St.
55 rooms - $47-105
Pets: Welcome
Creature Comforts: Historic
hotel, Victorian details, CCTV, a/c

READING
Best Western Dutch Colony
(800) 528-1234, (610) 779-2345
http://www.bestwestern.com
4635 Perkiomen Ave.
69 rooms - $60-95
Pets: Small pets w/$5 fee
Creature Comforts: CCTV, a/c,
refrig, micro, restaurant, pool,
whirlpool

Econo Lodge
(800) 55-ECONO, (610) 378-1145
http://www.econolodge.com
2310 Fraver Dr.
48 rooms - $45-60
Pets: Under 25 lbs.
Creature Comforts: CCTV,
VCR, a/c, cont. brkfst

Ramada Inn
(800) RAMADA, (610) 929-4741
http://www.holiday-inn.com
2545 N. Fifth St.
140 rooms - $75-90
Pets: Welcome
Creature Comforts: CCTV,
VCR, a/c, refrig, micro, restaurant,
pool, hlth clb.

RIDGWAY
The Royal Inn
(814) 773-3153
855 Route 46 East
45 rooms - $40-75
Pets: Welcome
Creature Comforts: CCTV, a/c,
refrig

SAYRE
Best Western Grand Victorian
(800) 528-1234, (570) 888-7711
255 Spring St.
100 rooms - $80-95
Pets: Under 25 lbs. w/$25 fee
Creature Comforts: CCTV,
VCR, a/c, refrig, micro, restaurant,
pool, sauna, whirlpool, tennis,
racquetball

SCRANTON
Econo Lodge
(800) 55-ECONO, (570) 348-1000
http://www.econolodge.com
1175 Kane St.
65 rooms - $45-75
Pets: Welcome w/$5 fee
Creature Comforts: CCTV, a/c,
refrig, micro, Jacuzzi, restaurant,
cont. brkfst, pool

SELINSGROVE
Comfort Inn
(800) 228-5150, (717) 374-8880
http://www.comfortinn.com
Routes 11 & 15
61 rooms - $40-90
Pets: Welcome w/$10 fee
Creature Comforts: CCTV, a/c,
VCR

SEWICKLEY
Sewickley Country Inn
(412) 741-4300
801 Ohio River Blvd.
150 rooms - $40-75
Pets: Small pets welcome
Creature Comforts: CCTV, a/c,
restaurant, pool

SHAMOKIN DAM
Days Inn
(800) DAYS INN, (717) 743-1111
http://www.daysinn.com
Routes 11 & 15
151 rooms - $40-80
Pets: Welcome
Creature Comforts: CCTV, a/c,
restaurant, pool

SHARTLESVILLE
Dutch Motel
(610) 488-1479
Route 22
15 rooms - $35-45
Pets: Welcome w/$3 fee
Creature Comforts: CCTV, a/c

SHELOCTA
Charbert Farm B&B
(800) 475-8264, (724) 726-8264
2439 Laurel Rd.
4 rooms - $85-150
Pets: Welcome
Creature Comforts: 1850's
farmhouse set on 100 acres,
antique furnishings w/Victorian
touches, relaxed atmosphere,
down comforters, TV, VCR,
fireplace

SOMERSET
Budget Host
(800) Bud-Host, (814) 445-7988
http://www.budgethost.com
799 N. Center Ave.
30 rooms - $35-70
Pets: Welcome w/$5 fee
Creature Comforts: CCTV, a/c

Budget Inn
(814) 443-6441
736 N. Center Ave.
25 rooms - $85-105
Pets: Welcome
Creature Comforts: CCTV, a/c,
refrig, micro

Days Inn
(800) DAYS INN, (814) 445-9200
http://www.daysinn.com
220 Waterworks Rd.
106 rooms - $50-80
Pets: Small pets welcome
Creature Comforts: CCTV, a/c,
restaurant, cont. brkfst

Dollar Inn
(800) 250-1505, (814) 445-2977
1146 N. Center Ave.
15 rooms - $30-55
Pets: Welcome in ltd rms w/$5 fee
Creature Comforts: CCTV, a/c,
refrig

Holiday Inn
(800) HOLIDAY, (814) 445-9611
http://www.holiday-inn.com
202 Shaffer St.
100 rooms - $70-100
Pets: Small pets welcome
Creature Comforts: CCTV,
VCR, a/c, restaurant, pool

Inn at Georgian Place
(814) 443-1043
http://www.somersetcounty.com/
theinn/
800 Georgian Pl. Dr.
12 rooms - $95-185
Pets: Welcome
Creature Comforts: Gracious
Georgian mansion, circa 1915,
beautifully restored woodwork,
marble, orig. fixtures, rooms
contain sleigh, rice, or canopy
beds, antique Victorian wicker or
traditional cherry furnishings,
CCTV, VCR, a/c, fireplace,
gourmet brkfst

Knights Inn
(800) 843-5644, (814) 445-8933
http://www.knightsinn.com
Rtes. 76 & 70
111 rooms - $45-65
Pets: Welcome
Creature Comforts: CCTV,
VCR, a/c, kit, pool

Ramada Inn
(800) 2-Ramada, (814) 443-4646
http://www.ramada.com
Rtes. 76 & 70
155 rooms - $85-105
Pets: Small pets welcome
Creature Comforts: CCTV,
VCR, a/c, refrig, restaurant, cont.
brkfst, pool, hlth clb access, sauna,
whirlpool

STATE COLLEGE
Autoport Motel
(814) 237-7666
1405 S. Atherton St.
85 rooms - $55-95
Pets: Small pets w/$5 fee
Creature Comforts: CCTV,
VCR, a/c, refrig, micro, restaurant,
pool

Days Inn, Penn State
(800) DAYS INN, (814) 238-8454
http://www.daysinn.com
240 S. Pugh St.
185 rooms - $55-95
Pets: Small pets w/$8 fee
Creature Comforts: CCTV, a/c,
pool

Ginther's B&B
(814) 234-0772
104 Farmstead Ln.
4 rooms - $50-100
Pets: Welcome, crated if left alone
Creature Comforts: Cape Cod
style house w/Pennsylvania Dutch
furnishings, CCTV, a/c, cont.
brkfst

Ramada
(800) 2-Ramada, (814) 238-3001
http://www.ramada.com
1450 S. Atherton St.
287 rooms - $65-75
Pets: Small pets welcome
Creature Comforts: CCTV, a/c,
refrig, micro, Jacuzzi, restaurant,
pool

STRASBURG
Historic Strasburg Inn
(800) 872-0201, (717) 687-7691
www.historicstrasburginn.com
Route 896
102 rooms - $85-160
Pets: Welcome w/$15 fee
Creature Comforts:
Williamsburg style motel on 58
rolling acres, reproduction
furnishings, CCTV, VCR, a/c,
refrig, Jacuzzis, restaurant, cont.
brkfst, pool, hlth club, bicycles,
lawn games, playground

STROUDSBURG
Budget Motel
(800) 233-8144, (570) 424-5451
http://www.silo.com/budget
Route 80
115 rooms - $40-75
Pets: Welcome w/$20 deposit
Creature Comforts: CCTV, a/c,
restaurant, walking trails

Super 8
(800) 800-8000, (570) 424-7411
http://www.super8.com
340 Green Tree Dr.
57 rooms - $55-70
Pets: Welcome w/permission
Creature Comforts: CCTV, a/c

THORNTON
Pace One Inn/Restaurant
(610) 459-3702
www.bbonline.com/pa/paceone
Thornton & Glen Mills Rd.
6 rooms - $75-95
Pets: Welcome w/permission
Creature Comforts: Classic
Brandywine 1740's stone barn,
exposed beams, large bedrooms
w/casual country decor, a/c,
excellent restaurant., cont. brkfst

TREVOSE
Red Roof Inn
(800) Red Roof, (215) 244-9422
http://www.redroof.com
3100 Lincoln Rte.
165 rooms - $35-75
Pets: Small pets welcome
Creature Comforts: CCTV, a/c

UNIONTOWN
Holiday Inn
(800) HOLIDAY, (724) 437-2816
http://www.holiday-inn.com
700 W. Main St.
180 rooms - $70-95
Pets: Welcome
Creature Comforts: CCTV, a/c,
restaurant, cont. brkfst, pool,
tennis

Mount Vernon Inn
(724) 437-2704
180 W. Main St.
45 rooms - $48-80
Pets: Small pets-$10 fee, $25 dep.
Creature Comforts: CCTV, a/c,
refrig, restaurant, exercise rm.

WARREN
Holiday Inn
(800) HOLIDAY, (814) 726-3000
http://www.holiday-inn.com
210 Ludlow St.
110 rooms - $60-75
Pets: Small pets welcome
Creature Comforts: CCTV, a/c,
restaurant, pool, hlth club, sauna

Super 8
(800) 800-8000, 723-8881
http://www.super8.com
204 Struthers St.
55 rooms - $45-59
Pets: Small pets w/$25 deposit
Creature Comforts: CCTV, a/c

WAYNESBORO
Best Western
(800) 528-1234, (717) 762-9113
http://www.bestwestern.com
239 W. Main St.
52 rooms - $60-88
Pets: Welcome in ltd. rms. w/$5 fee
Creature Comforts: CCTV, VCR, a/c, refrig, micro, cont. brkfst

WAYNESBURG
Econo Lodge
(800) 55-ECONO, (412) 627-5544
http://www.econolodge.com
350 Miller Ln.
60 rooms - $45-60
Pets: Welcome
Creature Comforts: CCTV, VCR, a/c, refrig, micro

Super 8
(800) 800-8000, (412) 627-8880
http://www.super8.com
80 Miller Ln.
55 rooms - $45-68
Pets: Welcome
Creature Comforts: CCTV, a/c

WASHINGTON
Holiday Inn, Meadow Lands
(800) HOLIDAY, (724) 222-6200
http://www.holiday-inn.com
Racetrack Rd.
138 rooms - $89-129
Pets: Welcome
Creature Comforts: CCTV, a/c, kit, restaurant, hlth clb access, sauna, whirlpool

Motel 6
(800) 4-MOTEL6, (724) 223-8040
http://www.motel6.com
1283 Motel 6 Dr.
102 rooms - $36-49
Pets: Under 30 lbs. welcome
Creature Comforts: CCTV, a/c, pool

Red Roof Inn
(800) The Roof, (724) 228-5750
http://www.redroof.com
1399 W. Chestnut St.
110 rooms - $40-60
Pets: Small pets welcome
Creature Comforts: CCTV, a/c

WELLSBORO
Canyon Motel
(800) 255-2718, (570) 724-1681
18 East Ave.
30 rooms - $35-50
Pets: Welcome in smoking rms.
Creature Comforts: CCTV, VCR, a/c, refrig, micro, Jacuzzi, pool

WEST CHESTER
Abbey Green Motor Lodge
(610) 692-3310
1036 Wilmington Pike
17 rooms - $40-60
Pets: Welcome
Creature Comforts: CCTV, a/c, kit

Holiday Inn
(800) HOLIDAY, (610) 692-1900
http://www.holiday-inn.com
943 S. High St.
140 rooms - $85-95
Pets: Small pets welcome
Creature Comforts: CCTV, a/c, kit, restaurant

WEST MIDDLESEX
Comfort Inn
(800) 228-5150, (724) 342-7200
http://www.comfortinn.com
Route 18 & Wilson Rd.
60 rooms - $55-70
Pets: Welcome w/$10 fee
Creature Comforts: CCTV, a/c, pool

Radisson Hotel
(800) 333-3333, (724) 528-2501
http://www.radisson.com
Rtes. 80 & 18
151 rooms - $40-75
Pets: Small pets welcome
Creature Comforts: CCTV, a/c, restaurant, cont. brkfst, pool, hlth clb access, sauna, whirlpool

WHITE HAVEN
Days Inn
(800) DAYS INN, (717) 443-0391
http://www.daysinn.com
Route 940
40 rooms - $40-75
Pets: Welcome w/$5 fee
Creature Comforts: CCTV, VCR, a/c, kit, Jacuzzi, cont. brkfst

Ramada Inn
(800) 2-Ramada, (717) 443-8471
http://www.ramada.com
Route 940
135 rooms - $60-140
Pets: Welcome w/$50 deposit
Creature Comforts: CCTV, a/c, refrig, restaurant, pool

WILKES-BARRE
Best Western Genetti
(800) 528-1234, (570) 823-6152
http://www.bestwestern.com
77 E. Market St.
72 rooms - $70-90
Pets: Welcome
Creature Comforts: CCTV, VCR, a/c, restaurant, pool

Days Inn
(800) DAYS INN, (570) 826-0111
http://www.daysinn.com
760 Kidder St.
75 rooms - $48-62
Pets: Welcome
Creature Comforts: CCTV, a/c

Hampton Inn
(800) Hampton, (570) 825-3838
http://www.hampton-inn.com
1063 Route 315
125 rooms - $60-80
Pets: Small pets welcome
Creature Comforts: CCTV, a/c

Holiday Inn
(800) HOLIDAY, (570) 824-8901
http://www.holiday-inn.com
880 Kidder St.
168 rooms - $70-90
Pets: Small pets welcome
Creature Comforts: CCTV, a/c, refrig, micro, restaurant, pool

Red Carpet Inn
(800) 251-1962, (570) 823-2171
400 Kidder St.
55 rooms - $40-60
Pets: Welcome w/$5 fee
Creature Comforts: CCTV, a/c

Red Roof Inn
(800) The Roof, (570) 829-6422
http://www.redroof.com
1035 Route 315
110 rooms - $75-85
Pets: Small pets welcome
Creature Comforts: CCTV, a/c

WILLIAMSPORT

City View Inn
(888) 224-VIEW, (570) 326-2601
Montgomery Pike
36 rooms - $45-50
Pets: Welcome w/$5 fee
Creature Comforts: CCTV, a/c,
restaurant

Econo Lodge
(800) 55-ECONO, (570) 326-1501
http://www.econolodge.com
2401 E. Third St.
99 rooms - $45-55
Pets: Welcome
Creature Comforts: CCTV, a/c,
restaurant

Genetti Hotel & Suites
(800) 321-1388, (570) 326-6600
http://www.genetti.com
200 W. Fourth St.
199 rooms - $45-125
Pets: Welcome
Creature Comforts: CCTV,
VCR, a/c, refrig, micro, Jacuzzis,
restaurant, pool, exercise rm.

Holiday Inn
(800) HOLIDAY, (570) 326-1981
http://www.holiday-inn.com
1840 E. Third St.
157 rooms - $65-75
Pets: Small pets welcome
Creature Comforts: CCTV, a/c,
restaurant, pool

Ridgemont Motel
(570) 321-5300
Route 15 S.
8 rooms - $35-40
Pets: Small pets in ltd. rms.
Creature Comforts: CCTV, a/c,
kit

Sheraton Inn
(800) 325-3535, (570) 327-8231
http://www.sheraton.com
100 Pine St.
150 rooms - $75-85
Pets: Welcome
Creature Comforts: CCTV, a/c,
refrig, micro, restaurant, pool,
exercise rm.

WIND GAP

Travel Inn, Wind Gap
(610) 863-4146
499 Moorestown Rd.
33 rooms - $50-75
Pets: Welcome w/$5 fee
Creature Comforts: CCTV, a/c,
refrig

WYOMISSING

Clarion Inn at Reading
(800) CLARION, (610) 372-7811
http://www.clarioninn.com
1040 Park Rd.
250 rooms - $70-110
Pets: Small pets w/$25 deposit
Creature Comforts: CCTV, a/c,
refrig, pool, exercise rm.

Econo Lodge
(800) 55-ECONO, (610) 378-5105
http://www.econolodge.com
635 Spring St.
85 rooms - $35-80
Pets: Small pets welcome
Creature Comforts: CCTV, a/c

Sheraton Berkshire
(800) 325-3535, (610) 376-3811
http://www.sheraton.com
1741 W. Papemill Rd.
256 rooms - $110-150
Pets: Welcome
Creature Comforts: CCTV, a/c,
restaurant, pool

Wellesley Inn
(800) 444-8888, (610) 374-1500
http://www.wellesleyinn.com
910 Woodland Ave.
110 rooms - $45-75
Pets: Welcome w/$5 fee
Creature Comforts: CCTV, a/c,
refrig, micro, cont. brkfst

YORK

Days Inn Hotel
(800) DAYS INN, (717) 843-9971
http://www.daysinn.com
222 Arsenal Rd.
125 rooms - $50-90
Pets: Welcome w/$10 fee
Creature Comforts: CCTV, a/c,
kit, pool

Holiday Inn East
(800) HOLIDAY, (717) 755-1966
http://www.holiday-inn.com
2600 E. Market St.
120 rooms - $70-85
Pets: Small pets welcome
Creature Comforts: CCTV, a/c,
restaurant, pool

Holiday Inn Holidome
(800) HOLIDAY, (717) 846-9500
http://www.holiday-inn.com
2000 Loucks Rd.
180 rooms - $70-100
Pets: Welcome
Creature Comforts: CCTV, a/c,
restaurant, pool

Motel 6, Airport
(800) 4-MOTEL6, (717) 846-6260
http://www.motel6.com
125 Arsenal Rd.
98 rooms - $34-40
Pets: Under 30 lbs. welcome
Creature Comforts: CCTV, a/c

Super 8
(800) 800-8000, (717) 852-8686
http://www.super8.com
40 Arsenal Rd.
95 rooms - $50-65
Pets: Small pets w/$25 deposit
Creature Comforts: CCTV, a/c

Rhode Island

BLOCK ISLAND
The Blue Dory Inn
(800) 992-7290, (401) 466-5891
http://www.bluedoryinn.com
Box 488
10 rooms - $95-425
Pets: Welcome in cottages and
suites w/$25 daily fee
Creature Comforts: 1889 inn,
shingle style w/Victorian accents,
rms. w/oak and wicker beds, some
antiques, coordinated fabrics,
summer house feel, CCTV, VCR,
cont. brkfst

BRISTOL
Reynolds House Inn
(800) 754-0230, (401) 254-0230
Box 5
6 rooms - $80-150
Pets: Welcome
Creature Comforts: CCTV, a/c,
full brkfst

MIDDLETOWN
Budget Host
(800) Bud-Host, (401) 849-4700
http://www.budgethost.com
1185 W. Main Rd.
77 rooms - $36-115
Pets: Small pets welcome
Creature Comforts: CCTV, a/c

Carlton Pineapple Inn
(401) 847-8400
1225 Aquidneck Ave.
21 rooms - $30-80
Pets: Small pets w/$50 deposit
Creature Comforts: A/C, refrig,
micro

Howard Johnson Inn
(800) I-Go-Hojo, (401) 849-2000
http://www.hojo.com
351 W. Main St.
160 rooms - $65-355
Pets: Welcome
Creature Comforts: CCTV, a/c,
refrig, Jacuzzis, restaurant, cont.
brkfst, pool, whirlpool

Ramada Inn
(800) 2-Ramada, (401) 846-7600
http://www.ramada.com
936 W. Main St.
150 rooms - $99-159
Pets: Welcome w/$10 fee
Creature Comforts: CCTV, a/c,
refrig, cont. brkfst, pool

NEWPORT
Murray House B&B
(401) 846-3337
http://www.murrayhouse.com
1 Murray Pl.
3 rooms - $65-165
Pets: Welcome in one rm.
Creature Comforts: Intimate
B&B, in-town, pretty gardens,
rms. priv. entrances and decorated
wi/Victorian florals, CCTV, refrig,
micro, kit, cont. brkfst, pool

Motel 6
(800) 4-MOTEL6, (401) 848-0600
http://www.motel6.com
249 JT Connell Hwy.
77 rooms - $65-80
Pets: Under 30 lbs. welcome
Creature Comforts: CCTV, a/c

PORTSMOUTH
Founder's Brook Motel
(401) 683-1244
314 Boyd's Ln.
33 rooms - $40-130
Pets: Welcome w/$10 deposit
Creature Comforts: CCTV, a/c,
refrig

PROVIDENCE
The Biltmore
(800) 294-7709, (401) 421-0700
http://www.grandheritage.com
Kennedy Plaza
245 rooms - $120-1,000
Pets: Under 80 lbs. w/deposit
Creature Comforts: An historic
landmark dating back to 1922,
handsoe deocr, writing desks,
finial bedsteads, CCTV, a/c, refrig,
microwaves, restaurant, hlth club

Caddy House
(401) 273-5398
127 Power St.
3 rooms - $80
Pets: Nice dogs welcome
Creature Comforts: 1839
Victorian, antiques, CCTV, a/c,
fireplace, cont. brkfst

Marriott
(800) 228-9290, (401) 272-2400
http://www.marriott.com
One Orms St.
344 rooms - $120-160
Pets: $25 fee, $25 deposit
Creature Comforts: CCTV, a/c,
restaurant, pool

Westin Hotel
(800) 228-3000, (412) 598-8000
http://www.westin.com
One W. Exchange St.
365 rooms - $100-250
Pets: Small pets in carrier
Creature Comforts: CCTV, a/c,
Jacuzzi, restaurant, pool, hlth clb,
sauna, whirlpool

SOUTH KINGSTON
King's Rose B&B
(888) 230-ROSE , (401) 783-5222
1747 Mooresfield Rd.
5 rooms - $75-130
Pets: Well-behaved pets welcome
Creature Comforts: A charming
Williamsburg-style home, library,
sunroom-bar, fireplaces, antiques
and reproductions, full brkfst on
the patio, tennis, and lovely
English gardens

WAKEFIELD
Larchwood Inn
(800) 275-5450, (401) 783-1800
http://www.innbook.com/inns/
larchwd/
521 Main St.
19 rooms - $65-130
Pets: Welcome w/$5 nightly fee
Creature Comforts: 1800's inn
w/shade trees, expansive lawns,
comfortable public rms, simple yet
traditionally furnished rooms, a/c,
fireplace, Scottish tavern and
restaurant

WARWICK
Holiday Inn at the Crossings
(800) HOLIDAY, (401) 732-6000
http://www.holiday-inn.com
801 Greenwich Ave.
265 rooms - $125-525
Pets: Small pets welcome
Creature Comforts: CCTV,
VCR, a/c, refrig, Jacuzzi,
restaurant, pool, hlth clb, sauna,
whirlpool

Master Hosts Inn
(401) 737-7400
2138 Post Rd.
103 rooms - $65-72
Pets: Welcome
Creature Comforts: CCTV, a/c

Residence Inn
(800) 331-3131, (401) 737-7100
http://www.residenceinn.com
500 Kilvert St.
95 rooms - $115-155
Pets: Small pets w/$10 fee
Creature Comforts: CCTV, a/c,
kit, pool

Sheraton Inn
(800) 325-3535, (401) 738-4000
http://www.sheraton.com
1850 Post Rd.
210 rooms - $100-240
Pets: Welcome w/$25 fee
Creature Comforts: CCTV, a/c,
VCR, restaurant, pool, hlth club,
and a whirlpool

South Carolina

AIKEN

Briar Patch B&B
(803) 649-2010
544 Magnolia Ln.
2 rooms - $50
Pets: Welcome w/permission
Creature Comforts: 1900 stables converted to guest rms, canopy beds, attractive decor, some antiques, bay window, fireplace, cont. brkfst, tennis

Comfort Suites
(800) 228-5150, (803) 641-1100
http://www.comfortinn.com
3608 Richland Ave. W.
68 rooms - $50-150
Pets: Welcome
Creature Comforts: CCTV, VCR, a/c, kit, Jacuzzi, cont. brkfst, pool, hlth clb, sauna, whirlpool

Days Inn, Downtown
(800) DAYS INN, (803) 649-5524
http://www.daysinn.com
1204 Richland Ave. W.
42 rooms - $35-50
Pets: Ltd. rms w/$5 fee
Creature Comforts: CCTV, a/c, refrig, micro, restaurant, cont. brkfst

Holiday Inn Express
(800) HOLIDAY, (803) 648-0999
http://www.holiday-inn.com
155 Colony Pkwy.
100 rooms - $75-85
Pets: Welcome w/$25 fee
Creature Comforts: CCTV, a/c, refrig, micro, pool, whirlpool, exercise rm.

Holiday Inn Express
(800) HOLIDAY, (803) 502-0900
http://www.holiday-inn.com
110 E. Frontage Rd.
60 rooms - $75-85
Pets: Welcome w/$25 fee
Creature Comforts: CCTV, a/c, pool

Ramada Ltd.
(800) 2-Ramada, (803) 648-6821
http://www.ramada.com
1850 Richland Ave.
80 rooms - $35-45
Pets: Welcome w/$4 fee
Creature Comforts: CCTV, VCR, a/c, refrig, micro, restaurant, pool

ALLENDALE

Villager Lodge
(803) 584-2184
671 N. Main St.
45 rooms - $30-35
Pets: Small pets w/$10 fee
Creature Comforts: CCTV, a/c, refrig, micro, cont. brkfst

ANDERSON

Days Inn
(800) DAYS INN, (864) 375-0375
http://www.daysinn.com
1007 Smith Mill Rd.
50 rooms - $65-90
Pets: Welcome
Creature Comforts: CCTV, a/c, cont. brkfst, pool, whirlpool

La Quinta
(800) 531-5900, (864) 225-3721
http://www.laquinta.com
3430 Clemson Blvd.
100 rooms - $55-60
Pets: Small pets welcome
Creature Comforts: CCTV, VCR, a/c, refrig, micro, pool

Quality Inn
(800) 228-5151, (864) 226-1000
http://www.qualityinn.com
3509 Clemson Blvd.
119 rooms - $60-104
Pets: Welcome w/$10 deposit
Creature Comforts: CCTV, VCR, a/c, refrig, micro, Jacuzzi, cont. brkfst, pool, hlth clb, sauna

Ramada Inn
(800) 2-Ramada, (864) 226-6051
http://www.ramada.com
3025 N. Main St.
130 rooms - $45-150
Pets: Under 25 lbs.
Creature Comforts: CCTV, VCR, a/c, restaurant, pool

Royal American Motor Inn
(864) 226-7236
4515 Clemson Blvd.
50 rooms - $35-40
Pets: Welcome
Creature Comforts: CCTV, VCR, a/c, refrig, micro

Super 8 Motel
(800) 800-8000, (864) 225-8384
http://www.super8.com
3302 Cinema Ave.
65 rooms - $45-50
Pets: Small pets welcome
Creature Comforts: CCTV, a/c

BEAUFORT

Battery Creek Inn
(843) 521-1441
19 Marina Village Lane
20 villas - $75-99
Pets: Welcome w/$50 fee
Creature Comforts: Villas overlooking Battery Creek, CCTV, a/c, kit

Days Inn Beaufort
(800) DAYS INN, (843) 524-1551
http://www.daysinn.com
1660 Ribaut Rd.
150 rooms - $60-85
Pets: Welcome w/dep.
Creature Comforts: CCTV, a/c, cont. brkfst, pool

Holiday Inn
(800) HOLIDAY, (843) 524-2144
http://www.holiday-inn.com
2001 Boundry St.
150 rooms - $65-70
Pets: Welcome w/$20 fee
Creature Comforts: CCTV, a/c, refrig, micro, restaurant, pool

Howard Johnson Express
(800) I-Go-Hojo, (843) 524-6020
http://www.hojo.com
Route 21
63 rooms - $65-75
Pets: Small pets welcome
Creature Comforts: CCTV, a/c,
cont. brkfst, pool

BENNETTSVILLE
Holiday Inn Express
(800) HOLIDAY, (843) 479-1700
http://www.holiday-inn.com
213 Rtes. 15 & 401 Bypass E.
52 rooms - $59-90
Pets: Welcome in smoking rooms
Creature Comforts: CCTV, a/c,
Jacuzzi, pool

CALHOUN FALLS
Latimer Inn
(864) 391-2747
Hwy 81 N.
4 rooms - $39-49
Pets: Welcome on occasion
Creature Comforts: TV,
a/c, kit, cont. brkfst

CAMDEN
**A Camden, South
Carolina Bed & Breakfast**
(803) 432-236
http://www.tech-tech.com/
b&bonlyweb
127 Union St.
3 rooms - $90-150
Pets: Welcome w/$25 one-time
fee and deposit
Creature Comforts: Antique
filled 1900's B&B, brass and four
poster beds, featherbeds, down
comforters, fireplace in room,
antique quilts, fine amenities,
CCTV, VCR, a/c, bathrobes,
gourmet brkfst

Colony Inn
(803) 432-5508
2020 W. DeKalb St.
53 rooms - $45-55
Pets: Small pets w/$10 fee
Creature Comforts: CCTV, a/c,
restaurant, pool

Lord Camden Inn
(803) 713-9050
http://www.lordcamden-inn.com
1502 Broad St.
3 rooms - $75-110
Pets: Welcome w/$10 fee, two
cats in residence
Creature Comforts: 1832
Southern Plantation-style
mansion, heart pine floors,
original woodwork, mahogany
and walnut English antiques,
Oriental rugs, herb and flower
gardens, CCTV, a/c, full brkfst,
pool

CAYCE
Knights Inn
(800) 843-5644, (803) 794-0222
http://www.knightsinn.com
1987 Airport Blvd.
40 rooms - $35-40
Pets: Welcome w/$10 fee
Creature Comforts: CCTV, a/c,
refrig, micro, cont. brkfst

Masters Economy Inn
(800) 633-3434, (803) 796-4300
2125 Commerce Dr.
112 rooms - $33-40
Pets: Welcome w/$5 fee
Creature Comforts: CCTV, a/c,
refrig, micro, pool

CHARLESTON
Best Western
(800) 528-1234, (843) 571-6100
http://www.bestwestern.com
1540 Savannah Rte.
87 rooms - $50-140
Pets: Small pets welcome
Creature Comforts: CCTV,
VCR, a/c, cont. brkfst, pool

Econo Lodge
(800) 55-ECONO, (843) 747-0961
http://www.econolodge.com
3668 Dorchester Rd.
198 rooms - $42-60
Pets: Small pets-$10 fee, $25 dep
Creature Comforts: CCTV, a/c,
refrig, kit, restaurant, cont. brkfst,
pool

Holiday Inn, Riverview
(800) HOLIDAY, (843) 556-7100
http://www.holiday-inn.com
301 Savannah Rte.
181 rooms - $60-145
Pets: Welcome
Creature Comforts: CCTV, a/c,
refrig, restaurant, pool

Indigo Inn
(800) 845-7639, (843) 577-5900
http://www.aesir.com/indigoinn
1 Maiden Lane
40 rooms - $110-185
Pets: Welcome on 1st floor
w/$20 nightly fee
Creature Comforts: 1850 Indigo
warehouse, inn w/18th century
charm, 4-poster beds, traditional
furnishings, request rooms
overlooking the courtyard, CCTV,
a/c, hunt brkfst

King Charles Inn
(800) 528-1234, (843) 723-7451
www.charlestownmanagement.com
237 Meeting St.
91 rooms - $80-200
Pets: Under 25 lbs. w/deposit
Comforts: Renovated 1830s inn
in historic district, four-poster
beds, period reproductions, CCTV,
a/c, refrig, Jacuzzi, restaurant,
pool

Masters Economy Inn
(800) 633-3434, (843) 744-3530
6100 Rivers Ave.
57 rooms - $42-45
Pets: Welcome w/$5 fee
Creature Comforts: CCTV, a/c,
refrig, micro, pool

Motel 6
(800) 4-MOTEL6, (843) 556-5144
http://www.motel6.com
2058 Savannah Rte.
111 rooms - $34-50
Pets: Under 30 lbs. welcome
Creature Comforts: CCTV, a/c,
pool

Sheraton Hotel
(800) 968-3569, (843) 723-3000
http://www.sheraton.com
170 Lockwood Blvd.
355 rooms - $99-350
Pets: Welcome w/$50 dep.
Creature Comforts: CCTV, a/c,
restaurant, hlth club, pool

Super 8 Motel, Airport
(800) 800-8000, (843)747-7500
http://www.super8.com
4620 Dorchester Rd.
100 rooms - $45-50
Pets: Welcome
Creature Comforts: CCTV, a/c,
refrig, micro, Jacuzzi, cont. brkfst,
pool

Town & Country Inn
(843) 571-1000
2008 Savannah Rte.
122 rooms - $70-120
Pets: Welcome
Creature Comforts: CCTV,
VCR, a/c, micro, restaurant, pool,
exercise rm.

CHERAW
Days Inn
(800) DAYS INN, (843) 537-5554
http://www.daysinn.com
820 Market St.
50 rooms - $40-70
Pets: Welcome w/$5 fee
Creature Comforts: CCTV, a/c,
refrig, micro, cont. brkfst, pool,
whirlpool

Inn Cheraw
(800) 535-8709, (843) 537-7733
501 Cheraw
4 rooms - $53-65
Pets: Welcome
Creature Comforts: CCTV, a/c,
cont. brkfst

Spears Guest House
(888) 424-3729, (803) 537-1094
228 Huger St.
4 rooms - $56
Pets: Welcome
Creature Comforts: CCTV, a/c,
cont. brkfst

CLINTON
Comfort Inn
(800) 228-5150, (864) 833-5558
http://www.comfortinn.com
12785 Rte. 56 N.
81 rooms - $50-85
Pets: Welcome
Creature Comforts: CCTV,
VCR, a/c, refrig, micro, full brkfst,
pool

Days Inn
(800) DAYS INN, (864) 833-6600
http://www.daysinn.com
44 Plumbers Rd.
58 rooms - $45-75
Pets: Welcome
Creature Comforts: CCTV, a/c,
cont. brkfst, pool, whirlpool, sauna

Ramada Inn
(800) 2-Ramada, (864) 833-4900
http://www.ramada.com
I-26 & Rte. 56
103 rooms - $70-130
Pets: Small pets w/$10 fee
Creature Comforts: CCTV, a/c,
refrig, micro, restaurant, pool

COLUMBIA
Adams Mark
(800) 444-Adam, (803) 771-7000
http://www.adamsmark.com/
columbia
1200 Hampton St.
301 rooms - $70-125
Pets: Small pets w/$50 fee
Creature Comforts: CCTV, a/c,
restaurant, pool, whirlpool, hlth
clb

Amerisuites
(800) 833-1516, (803) 736-6666
http://www.amerisuites.com
7525 Two Notch Rd.
112 rooms - $70-100
Pets: Small pets welcome
Creature Comforts: CCTV,
VCR, a/c, refrig, micro, restaurant,
cont. brkfst, pool

Baymont Inns Inn, East
(800) 789-4103, (803) 736-6400
http://www.baymontinns.com
1538 Horseshoe Dr.
100 rooms - $45-60
Pets: Small pets welcome
Creature Comforts: CCTV, a/c,
cont. brkfst, pool

Baymont Inns Inn, West
(800) 789-4103, (803) 798-3222
http://www.baymontinns.com
911 Bush River Rd.
105 rooms - $40-48
Pets: Small pets welcome
Creature Comforts: CCTV, a/c,
cont. brkfst, pool

Comfort Inn
(800) 228-5150, (803) 798-0500
http://www.comfortinn.com
499 Piney Grove Rd.
163 rooms - $45-65
Pets: Welcome w/$25 fee
Creature Comforts: CCTV, a/c,
refrig

Days Inn
(800) DAYS INN, (803) 754-4408
http://www.daysinn.com
133 Plumbers Rd.
44 rooms - $44-55
Pets: Welcome
Creature Comforts: SATV, a/c,
pool

Holiday Inn, Airport
(800) HOLIDAY, (803) 794-9440
http://www.holiday-inn.com
500 Chris Dr.
148 rooms - $75-85
Pets: Welcome w/$25 fee, $100
deposit
Creature Comforts: CCTV, a/c,
restaurant, pool

Holiday Inn at USC
(800) HOLIDAY, (803) 799-7800
http://www.holiday-inn.com
630 Assembly St.
176 rooms - $60-115
Pets: $25 fee for pets over 25 lbs,
under 25 lbs. are free
Creature Comforts: CCTV, a/c,
refrig, micro, restaurant, pool,
exercise rm.

Holiday Inn, NE
(800) HOLIDAY, (803) 736-3000
http://www.holiday-inn.com
7510 Two Notch Rd.
255 rooms - $50-55
Pets: Under 20 lbs. w/$25 fee
Creature Comforts: CCTV, a/c,
restaurant, pool, whirlpool,
exercise rm.

La Quinta Inn
(800) 531-5900, (803)8-9590
http://www.laquinta.com
1335 Garner Ln.
121 rooms - $50-60
Pets: Small pets welcome
Creature Comforts: CCTV, a/c,
refrig, micro, cont. brkfst, pool

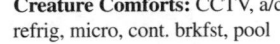

Motel 6
(800) 4-MOTEL6, (803) 798-9210
http://www.motel6.com
1776 Burning Tree Rd.
97 rooms - $36-55
Pets: Under 30 lbs. welcome
Creature Comforts: CCTV, a/c,
pool

Ramada Plaza
(800) 2-Ramada, (803) 736-5600
http://www.ramada.com
8105 Two Notch Rd.
190 rooms - $80-150
Pets: Under 10 lbs. w/notice
Creature Comforts: CCTV,
VCR, a/c, refrig, micro, Jacuzzi,
restaurant, pool, exercise rm.

Red Roof Inn, East
(800) THE ROOF, (803) 736-0850
http://www.redroof.com
7580 Two Notch Rd.
110 rooms - $55-65
Pets: Small pets welcome
Creature Comforts: CCTV, a/c

Red Roof Inn, West
(800) THE ROOF, (803) 798-9220
http://www.redroof.com
10 Berryhill Rd.
120 rooms - $45-65
Pets: Welcome
Creature Comforts: CCTV, a/c

Residence Inn, Marriott
(800) 331-3131, (803) 779-7000
http://www.residenceinn.com
150 Stoneridge Dr.
130 rooms - $100-150
Pets: Welcome w/$200 fee
Creature Comforts: CCTV, a/c,
kit

Sheraton Hotel
(800) 968-3569, (803) 731-0300
http://www.sheraton.com
2100 Bush River Dr.
275 rooms - $99-390
Pets: Small pets w/$CC dep.
Creature Comforts: CCTV, a/c,
refrig, restaurant, hlth club, pool

Super 8, Downtown
(800) 800-8000, (803) 735-0008
http://www.super8.com
5719 Fairfield Rd.
43 rooms - $45-120
Pets: Welcome w/$7 fee
Creature Comforts: CCTV, a/c,
Jacuzzi, cont. brkfst

Super 8, West
(800) 800-8000, (803) 796-4833
http://www.super8.com
2516 Augusta Rd.
88 rooms - $38-50
Pets: Welcome w/$5 fee
Creature Comforts: CCTV, a/c,
pool, restaurant

DILLON
Days Inn
(800) DAYS INN, (843) 774-6041
http://www.daysinn.com
818 Radford Blvd.
121 rooms - $36-70
Pets: Small pets welcome
Creature Comforts: CCTV, a/c,
cont. brkfst, pool

Econo Lodge
(800) 55-ECONO, (843) 774-4181
http://www.econolodge.com
1223 Radford Rd.
46 rooms - $35-95
Pets: Welcome
Creature Comforts: CCTV, a/c,
cont. brkfst

Howard Johnson Express
(800) I-Go-Hojo, (843) 774-5111
http://www.hojo.com
904 Radford Blvd.
78 rooms - $35-115
Pets: Welcome
Creature Comforts: CCTV,
VCR, a/c, cont. brkfst, pool

Super 8
(800) 800-8000, (843) 774-4161
http://www.super8.com
1203 Radford Blvd.
100 rooms - $40-100
Pets: Small pets w/$5 fee
Creature Comforts: CCTV, a/c,
cont. brkfst

EASLEY
Days Inn
(800) DAYS INN, (864) 859-9902
http://www.daysinn.com
Rte. 153 E.
73 rooms - $44-52
Pets: Small pets w/$7 fee
Comforts: CCTV, a/c, refrig,
micro, cont. brkfst, pool

EDGEFIELD
Cedar Grove Plantation B&B
(888) 660-5217, (803) 637-3056
1365 Rte. 25 N.
2 rooms - $60-85

Pets: Welcome, hostess loves
well-behaved dogs, cats, and birds
Creature Comforts: 1790
plantation house on Nat'l Historic
Register, vast acreage, orig. details
intact, lovely gardens, suite w/
sitting rm, fireplaces, French wall
treatments, CCTV, VCR, a/c, full
gourmet brkfst, catered dinners by
rqst, pool, hot tub, gardens and
intriguing wild life

FLORENCE
Days Inn, North
(800) DAYS INN, (843) 665-4444
http://www.daysinn.com
2111 W. Lucas St.
103 rooms - $40-70
Pets: Welcome
Comforts: CCTV, a/c, cont.
brkfst, pool, hlth club, whirlpool

Days Inn, South
(800) DAYS INN, (843) 665-8550
http://www.daysinn.com
Rtes. 95 & 76
120 rooms - $40-60
Pets: Welcome w/$6 fee
Comforts: CCTV, a/c, cont.
brkfst, pool

Econo Lodge
(800) 55-ECONO, (843) 665-8558
http://www.econolodge.com
Rtes. 95 & 52
120 rooms - $40-60
Pets: Welcome
Creature Comforts: CCTV, a/c,
refrig, micro, cont. brkfst, pool,
whirlpool

Holiday Inn
(800) HOLIDAY, (843) 665-4555
http://www.holiday-inn.com
1819 W. Lucas St.
181 rooms - $70-100
Pets: Specific pet rooms available nightly, call hotel directly
Creature Comforts: CCTV, a/c, refrig, restaurant, pool, exercise rm.

Howard Johnson Express
(800) I-Go-Hojo, (843) 664-9494
http://www.hojo.com
3821 Bancroft Rd.
51 rooms - $45-65
Pets: Welcome
Creature Comforts: CCTV, VCR, a/c, Jacuzzi, cont. brkfst, pool

Motel 6
(800) 4-MOTEL6, (843) 667-6100
http://www.motel6.com
1834 W. Lucas Rd.
109 rooms - $34-49
Pets: Under 30 lbs. welcome
Creature Comforts: CCTV, a/c, pool

Park Inn International
(843) 662-9421
831 S. Irby St.
105 rooms - $35-45
Pets: Small pets welcome
Creature Comforts: CCTV, a/c, refrig, restaurant, cont. brkfst, pool

Quality Inn
(800) 228-5151, (843) 669-1715
http://www.qualityinn.com
3024 TV Rd.
95 rooms - $45-55
Pets: Welcome w/$5 fee
Creature Comforts: CCTV, a/c, cont. brkfst, pool

Ramada Inn
(800) 2-Ramada, (843) 669-4241
http://www.ramada.com
2038 W. Lucas St.
179 rooms - $75-85
Pets: Small pets welcome
Creature Comforts: CCTV, VCR, a/c, refrig, Jacuzzi, restaurant, pool, sauna, whirlpool

Red Roof Inn
(800) THE ROOF, (843) 678-9000
http://www.redroof.com
2690 David McLeod Blvd.
115 rooms - $45-79
Pets: Small pets welcome
Creature Comforts: CCTV, a/c

Super 8
(800) 800-8000, (843) 661-7267
http://www.super8.com
1832 W. Lucas St.
67 rooms - $45-75
Pets: Welcome w/permission
Creature Comforts: CCTV, a/c, cont. brkfst

Thunderbird Motor Inn
(843) 669-1611
2004 W. Lucas
135 rooms - $45-55
Pets: Small pets welcome
Creature Comforts: CCTV, a/c, refrig, micro, restaurant, cont. brkfst, pool, hlth clb access

Young's Plantation
(843) 669-4171
Rtes. 95 & 76
121 rooms - $30-44
Pets: Welcome w/$4 fee
Creature Comforts: CCTV, a/c, refrig, micro, cont. brkfst, restaurant, pool

GAFFNEY
Comfort Inn
(800) 228-5150, (864) 487-4200
http://www.comfortinn.com
143 Corona Dr.
83 rooms - $70-95
Pets: Welcome
Creature Comforts: CCTV, VCR, a/c, refrig, micro, cont. brkfst, hlth clb access

Days Inn
(800) DAYS INN, (864) 489-7172
http://www.daysinn.com
Rtes. I-85 & 11
100 rooms - $39-63
Pets: Welcome
Comforts: CCTV, a/c, restaurant, cont. brkfst, pool

GEORGETOWN
Mansfield Plantation
(800) 355-3223, (803) 546-6961
www.mansfieldplantation.com
Route 8, Box 590
8 rooms - $95-125
Pets: Welcome w/approval
Creature Comforts: Highly recommended, 900-acre rice plantation, black oaks laden w/ Spanish moss, Big House and charming guest cottages, family antiques, rqst North Brick House w/sophisticated décor, high ceilings, Oriental rugs, chintz, river views, full brkfst, fishing, hunting, access to tennis and golf, croquet, lawn games

GREENVILLE
Amerisuites
(800) 833-1516, (864) 232-3000
http://www.amerisuites.com
40 W. Orchard Dr.
128 rooms - $90-125
Pets: Small pets w/$25 fee
Creature Comforts: CCTV, VCR, a/c, refrig, micro, cont. brkfst, pool, exercise rm.

Crowne Plaza, Greenville
(800) 2Crowne, (864) 297-6300
http://www.crowneplaza.com
851 Congaree Rd.
208 rooms - $70-150
Pets: Welcome w/$125 deposit, $25 is nonrefundable
Creature Comforts: CCTV, a/c, restaurants, pool, whirlpool, exercise rm.

Days Inn
(800) DAYS INN, (864) 288-6221
http://www.daysinn.com
831 Congaree Rd.
120 rooms - $50-110
Pets: Welcome w/$10 fee
Comforts: CCTV, VCR, a/c, refrig, micro, cont. brkfst, pool

Guesthouse Suites Plus
(800) 21-Guest, (864) 297-0099
http://www.guesthouse.net
48 McPrice Court
150 rooms - $69-129
Pets: $125 fee
Creature Comforts: CCTV, VCR, a/c, kit, fireplace, restaurant, pool, whirlpool, hlth clb access

Holiday Inn I-85
(800) HOLIDAY, (864) 277-8921
http://www.holiday-inn.com
4295 Augusta Rd.
150 rooms - $80-90
Pets: Under 10 lbs. w/$10 fee
Creature Comforts: CCTV, a/c,
restaurant, pool, exercise rm.

Holiday Inn Express, Airport
(800) HOLIDAY, (864) 297-5353
http://www.holiday-inn.com
5009 Pelham Rd.
150 rooms - $80-90
Pets: Under 25 lbs. w/$15 fee
Creature Comforts: CCTV, a/c,
restaurant, cont. brkfst, pool

La Quinta Inn
(800) 531-5900, (864) 297-3500
http://www.laquinta.com
31 Old Country Rd.
125 rooms - $60-70
Pets: Small pets welcome
Creature Comforts: CCTV, a/c,
pool

Microtel Inn
(888) 771-7171, (864) 297-7866
http://www.microtelinn.com
20 Interstate Ct.
125 rooms - $43-52
Pets: Welcome
Creature Comforts: CCTV, a/c,
refrig, micro, pool

Motel 6
(800) 4-MOTEL6, (864) 277-8630
http://www.motel6.com
224 Bruce Rd.
102 rooms - $33
Pets: Under 30 lbs. welcome
Creature Comforts: CCTV, a/c,
pool

The Phoenix Inn
(864) 233-4651
246 N. Pleasantburg Dr.
190 rooms - $65-88
Pets: Small pets welcome
Creature Comforts: Unique hotel
w/rural feeling, CCTV, VCR, a/c,
refrig, micro, four-poster beds,
excellent restaurant, pool, exercise
rm.

Quality Inn
(800) 228-5151, (864) 297-9000
http://www.qualityinn.com
50 Orchard Park Dr.
148 rooms - $61-91
Pets: Welcome w/$5 fee
Creature Comforts: CCTV, a/c,
cont. brkfst, pool

Ramada Inn, Downtown
(800) 2-Ramada, (864) 232-7666
http://www.ramada.com
1001 S. Church St.
141 rooms - $55-115
Pets: Small pets welcome
Creature Comforts: CCTV,
VCR, a/c, refrig, Jacuzzi,
restaurant, pool

Ramada Inn South
(800) 2-Ramada, (864) 277-3734
http://www.ramada.com
1314 S. Pleasantburg Dr.
119 rooms - $39-59
Pets: Small pets w/$25 fee
Creature Comforts: CCTV, a/c,
cont. brkfst, restaurant, pool,
tennis

Red Roof Inn
(800) THE ROOF, (864) 297-4458
http://www.redroof.com
2801 Laurens Rd.
110 rooms - $45-60
Pets: Small pets welcome
Creature Comforts: CCTV, a/c

Residence Inn
(800) 331-3131, (864) 297-0099
http://www.residenceinn.com
48 McPrice Court
78 suites - $100-125
Pets: Welcome-$5 fee, $100 dep
Creature Comforts: CCTV, a/c,
fireplace, kit, cont. brkfst, pool,
whirlpool

Travelodge
(800) 578-7878, (864) 277-8670
http://www.travelodge.com
1465 S. Pleasantburg Dr.
100 rooms - $45-75
Pets: Small pets w/$5 fee
Creature Comforts: CCTV, a/c,
refrig, micro, pool

GREER
Comfort Suites
(800) 228-5150, (864) 213-9331
http://www.comfortinn.com
Route 52
83 rooms - $70-150
Pets: Welcome
Creature Comforts: CCTV, a/c,
cont. brkfst, pool, hlth club

Mainstay Suites
(800) 228-5150, (864) 987-5566
http://www.mainstaysuites.com
2671 Dry Pocket Rd.
99 suites - $70-89
Pets: Welcome w/$5 fee
Creature Comforts: CCTV, a/c,
refrig, micro, cont. brkfst, pool,
exercise rm., tennis

HARDEEVILLE
Days Inn
(800) DAYS INN, (843) 784-2281
http://www.daysinn.com
Rtes. 95 & 17
100 rooms - $36-70
Pets: Welcome w/$5 fee
Comforts: CCTV, a/c, restaurant,
pool

Holiday Inn Express
(800) HOLIDAY, (803) 726-9400
http://www.holiday-inn.com
Rtes. I-95 & 17
108 rooms - $50-110
Pets: Small pets w/$7 fee, contact
hotel directly
Creature Comforts: CCTV,
VCR, a/c, refrig, micro, Jacuzzi,
cont. brkfst, pool

Howard Johnson
(800) I-Go-Hojo, (843) 784-2271
http://www.hojo.com
Rtes. I-95 & 17
128 rooms - $35-70
Pets: Welcome
Creature Comforts: CCTV,
VCR, a/c, restaurant, pool

Ramada Ltd.
(800) 2-Ramada, (843) 784-3192
http://www.ramada.com
1314 S. Pleasantburg Dr.
61 rooms - $40-100
Pets: Welcome w/$5 fee
Creature Comforts: CCTV, a/c,
cont. brkfst

HILTON HEAD

Bayshore of Hilton Head
(888) 842-9494, (843) 842-9494
http://www.bayshorerentals.com
81 Pope Ave.
50 condos - $600-2000/wk
Pets: Welcome w/$200 deposit
Creature Comforts: Fully
equipped condominiums scattered
throughout Hilton Head, CCTV,
VCR, a/c, kit, pool, tennis

Comfort Suites
(800) 228-5150, (843) 842-6662
http://www.comfortinn.com
2 Tanglewood Dr.
153 rooms - $50-160
Pets: Welcome
Creature Comforts: CCTV, a/c,
refrig, micro, cont. brkfst, pool,
hlth club

Motel 6
(800) 4-MOTEL6, (843) 785-2700
http://www.motel6.com
830 William Hilton Pkwy.
116 rooms - $40-54
Pets: Under 30 lbs. welcome
Creature Comforts: CCTV, a/c,
pool

Quality Suites
(800) 228-5151, (843) 681-3655
http://www.qualityinn.com
200 Museum St.
137 rooms - $76-130
Pets: Welcome w/$10 fee
Creature Comforts: CCTV,
VCR, a/c, refrig, micro, restaurant,
pool

Red Roof Inn
(800) THE ROOF, (843) 686-6808
http://www.redroof.com
5 Regency Pkwy.
115 rooms - $50-90
Pets: Small pets welcome
Creature Comforts: CCTV, a/c,
pool

LANCASTER

Days Inn
(800) DAYS INN, (803) 286-6441
http://www.daysinn.com
1100 N. Main St.
120 rooms - $36-55
Pets: Welcome
Comforts: CCTV, a/c, restaurant,
cont. brkfst, pool, exercise rm.

LANDRUM

Red Horse Inn
(864) 895-4968
http://www.theredhorseinn.com
310 N. Campbell Rd.
5 rooms - $110-125
Pets: "Pets may be allowed if
their masters are well behaved,"
$50 dep.
Creature Comforts: Highly
recommended, 190-acre horse
farm w/storybook Victorian
cottages, fine furnishings, ceiling
fans, chintz, four-poster beds,
CCTV, a/c, kit, fireplace, Jacuzzi,
full brkfst, fountain w/koi,
massage

LITTLE RIVER

Days Inn
(800) DAYS INN, (843) 249-3535
http://www.daysinn.com
1564 Rte. 17 N.
50 rooms - $65-95
Pets: Small pets w/$10 fee
Comforts: CCTV, a/c, cont.
brkfst, pool

LUGOFF

Days Inn
(800) DAYS INN, (803) 438-6990
http://www.daysinn.com
529 Rte. 601
47 rooms - $48-75
Pets: Welcome w/$5 fee
Creature Comforts: CCTV, a/c,
cont. brkfst, restaurant, pool,
whirlpool, exercise rm.

MANNING

Comfort Inn
(800) 228-5150, (803) 473-7550
http://www.comfortinn.com
Rtes. 95 & 261
60 rooms - $50-80
Pets: Welcome
Creature Comforts: CCTV, a/c,
pool, exercise rm., tennis

Days Inn
(800) DAYS INN, (803) 473-2913
http://www.daysinn.com
Route 5
77 rooms - $36-70
Pets: Welcome w/$5 fee
Comforts: CCTV, a/c, restaurant,
pool

Manning Economy Inn
(803) 473-4021
Rtes. 95 & 261
56 rooms - $30-50
Pets: Small pets welcome
Comforts: CCTV, a/c, pool

MT. PLEASANT

Comfort Inn
(800) 228-5150, (843) 884-5853
http://www.comfortinn.com
310 Rte. 17 Bypass
122 rooms - $60-140
Pets: Welcome w/$10 fee
Creature Comforts: CCTV,
VCR, a/c, Jacuzzi, cont. brkfst,
pool

Masters Economy Inn
(800) 633-3434, (843) 884-2814
300 Wingo Way
120 rooms - $40-60
Pets: Welcome w/$6 deposit
Creature Comforts: CCTV, a/c,
refrig, cont. brkfst, pool

Red Roof Inn
(800) THE ROOF, (843) 884-1411
http://www.redroof.com
301 Johnnie Dodds Blvd.
125 rooms - $60-100
Pets: Small pets welcome
Creature Comforts: CCTV, a/c,
pool

MYRTLE BEACH

Days Inn, North
(800) DAYS INN, (843) 272-6196
http://www.daysinn.com
3209 Rte. Route 17 S.
44 rooms - $38-45
Pets: Welcome
Comforts: CCTV, a/c, refrig,
micro, cont. brkfst, restaurant,
pool

El Dorado Motel
(843) 626-3559
2800 S. Ocean Blvd.
42 rooms - $30-120
Pets: Small dogs w/$5 fee, off season
Comforts: CCTV, a/c, refrig, micro, kit, pools, whirlpool, sauna

La Quinta Inn/Suites
(800) 531-5900, (843) 916-8801
http://www.laquinta.com
1561 21st Ave. N.
130 rooms - $60-120
Pets: Welcome
Creature Comforts: CCTV, a/c, refrig, micro, cont. brkfst, pool, hlth club, whirlpool

The Mariner
(800) 685-8775, (843) 449-5281
7003 N. Ocean Blvd.
33 rooms - $30-95
Pets: Welcome only in off-season
Creature Comforts: CCTV, a/c, kit

Red Roof Inn
(800) THE ROOF, (843) 626-4444
http://www.redroof.com
2801 S. Kings Rte.
153 rooms - $50-165
Pets: Small pets welcome
Creature Comforts: CCTV, a/c, kit, pool

St. John's Inn
(800) 845-0624, (843) 449-5251
6803 N. Ocean Blvd.
90 rooms - $40-105
Pets: Small pets w/$7 fee, $50 dep.
Creature Comforts: CCTV, a/c, refrig, micro, restaurant, pool, whirlpool

Sea Mist Resort
(800) 654-5613, (843) 448-1551
http://www.seamist.com
1200 South Ocean Blvd.
830 rooms - $30-250
Pets: Welcome w/$50 fee
Creature Comforts: CCTV, a/c, kit, Jacuzzi, restaurant, pool, sauna, whirlpool

Super 8
(800) 800-8000, (843) 293-6100
http://www.super8.com
3450 Rte. 17 S. Bypass
85 rooms - $40-100
Pets: Welcome w/$10 fee
Creature Comforts: CCTV, a/c, pool

Waterside Inn
(843) 448-5935
2000 N. Ocean Blvd.
50 rooms - $35-150
Pets: Small pets w/$7 fee, $65 dep
Creature Comforts: CCTV, a/c, pool

NEWBURY
Best Western Newbury
(800) 528-1234, (803) 276-5850
http://www.bestwestern.com
11701 S. Rte. 34
113 rooms - $40-50
Pets: Small pets welcome
Creature Comforts: CCTV, VCR, a/c, cont. brkfst, pool, hlth club

NORTH CHARLESTON
Comfort Inn, Airport
(800) 228-5150, (843) 554-6485
http://www.comfortinn.com
5055 N. Arco Ln.
122 rooms - $45-95
Pets: Welcome
Creature Comforts: CCTV, VCR, a/c, refrig, micro, cont. brkfst, pool

Days Inn, Airport
(800) DAYS INN, (843) 747-4101
http://www.daysinn.com
2998 W. Montague Ave.
147 rooms - $50-80
Pets: Welcome w/$ 6 fee
Creature Comforts: CCTV, a/c, refrig, restaurant, pool

La Quinta Inn
(800) 531-5900, (843) 797-8181
http://www.laquinta.com
2499 La Quinta Ln.
122 rooms - $55-65
Pets: Small pets welcome
Creature Comforts: CCTV, a/c, refrig, micro, cont. brkfst

Motel 6
(800) 4-MOTEL6, (843) 572-6590
http://www.motel6.com
2551 Ashley Phosphate Rd.
125 rooms - $34-38
Pets: Under 30 lbs. welcome
Creature Comforts: CCTV, a/c, pool

Orchard Inn
(800) 368-4571, (843) 747-3672
4725 Saul White Blvd.
90 rooms - $38-50
Pets: Welcome w/$25 deposit
Creature Comforts: CCTV, a/c, pool

Red Roof Inn
(800) THE ROOF, (843) 572-9100
http://www.redroof.com
7480 Northwoods Blvd.
109 rooms - $50-60
Pets: Small pets welcome
Creature Comforts: CCTV, a/c

Residence Inn
(800) 331-3131, (843) 572-5757
http://www.residenceinn.com
7645 Northwoods Blvd.
90 rooms - $95-150
Pets: Welcome w/$50-75 deposit
Creature Comforts: CCTV, VCR, a/c, kit, restaurant, hlth clb access

Stayover Lodge
(843) 554-1600
2070 McMillan Ave.
97 rooms - $50-60
Pets: Welcome w/permission
Creature Comforts: CCTV, a/c, refrig, micro, pool

Super 8 Motel
(800) 800-8000, (843) 572-2228
http://www.super8.com
2311 Ashley Phosphate Rd.
89 rooms - $45-50
Pets: Welcome w/permission
Creature Comforts: CCTV, a/c, cont. brkfst, pool

ORANGEBURG
Best Western Orangeburg
(800) 528-1234, (803) 534-7630
http://www.bestwestern.com
826 John Calhoun Dr.
105 rooms - $40-50
Pets: Welcome w/$8 fee
Creature Comforts: CCTV, a/c, cont. brkfst, pool, hlth club

Quality Inn
(800) , (803) 531-4600
http://www.qualityinn.com
415 John Calhoun Dr.
100 rooms - $60-70
Pets: Welcome
Comforts: SATV, a/c, refrig,
restaurant, pool, whirlpool,
exercise rm.

Super 8
(800) 800-8000, (803) 531-1921
http://www.super8.com
610 John Calhoun Dr.
45 rooms - $39-45
Pets: Small pets w/$8 fee
Creature Comforts: CCTV, a/c,
refrig, micro, pool

RICHBURG
Days Inn
(800) DAYS INN, (803) 789-5555
http://www.daysinn.com
3217 Lancaster Hwy.
47 rooms - $55-90
Pets: Welcome w/$3 fee
Comforts: CCTV, a/c, cont.
brkfst, pool, whirlpool

Relax Inn
(803) 789-6363
3200 Lancaster Hwy.
30 rooms - $35-45
Pets: Welcome w/$5 fee
Creature Comforts: CCTV, a/c

Super 8
(800) 800-8000, (803) 789-7888
http://www.super8.com
3085 Lancaster Hwy.
58 rooms - $80-90
Pets: Welcome w/$3 fee
Creature Comforts: CCTV, a/c,
refrig, micro, Jacuzzi, cont. brkfst,
pool

RIDGELAND
Best Western Point South
(800) 528-1234, (843) 726-8101
http://www.bestwestern.com
Rtes. 95 & 17
113 rooms - $45-65
Pets: Welcome in smoking rooms
Creature Comforts: CCTV, a/c,
refrig, restaurant, pool, whirlpool

Comfort Inn
(800) 228-5150, (843) 726-2121
http://www.comfortinn.com
Rtes. 95 & 278
100 rooms - $52-68
Pets: Welcome
Creature Comforts: CCTV,
VCR, a/c, restaurant, cont. brkfst,
pool

Econo Lodge
(800) 55-ECONO, (843) 571-1880
http://www.econolodge.com
516 E. Main St.
77 rooms - $45-55
Pets: Welcome in special rms.
Creature Comforts: CCTV, a/c,
Jacuzzi, cont. brkfst

RIDGE SPRING
Southwood Manor B&B
(888) 806-9898, (803) 685-5100
http://www.the-innside-
scoop.com/southwood.htm
100 E. Main St.
4 rooms - $75-125
Pets: Crated pets welcome,
(horses welcome too)
Creature Comforts: Gracious
Georgian Colonial, antiques, four
poster beds, chintz balloon
draperies, a/c, hearty hunt brkfst,
pool, tennis, 2,000 ft. airstrip

ROCK HILL
Best Western
(800) 528-1234, (803) 329-1330
http://www.bestwestern.com
Rte 21
60 rooms - $55-85
Pets: Welcome w/$10 fee
Creature Comforts: CCTV,
VCR, a/c, refrig, Jacuzzi,
restaurant, full brkfst, pool,
whirlpool

Book and Spindle
(803) 328-1913
626 Oakland Ave.
4 rooms - $60-80
Pets: Small pets welcome
Creature Comforts: A 1930's
Georgian style brick house set in
the historic district, hardwood flrs,
period furnishings, English
antiques, rice bed, CCTV, a/c, kit,
fireplace, patios, hearty brkfst

Holiday Inn
(800) HOLIDAY, (803) 329-1122
http://www.holiday.com
2640 N. Cherry St.
125 rooms - $50-60
Pets: Under 20 lbs. welcome
Comforts: CCTV, a/c, refrig,
Jacuzzi, restaurant, pool

Park Avenue Inn
(877) 422-0127, (803) 325-1764
347 Park Ave.
125 rooms - $60-75
Pets: Small pets welcome
Comforts: 1916 Colonial,
Victorian accents, CCTV, a/c,
cont. brkfst

ST. GEORGE
Best Western, St. George
(800) 528-1234, (843) 563-2277
http://www.bestwestern.com
Rtes. 95 & 78
68 rooms - $45-70
Pets: Welcome
Creature Comforts: CCTV, a/c,
restaurant, cont. brkfst, pool

Comfort Inn
(800) 228-5150, (843) 563-4180
http://www.comfortinn.com
Rtes. 95 & 78
104 rooms - $40-80
Pets: Welcome
Creature Comforts: CCTV, a/c,
cont. brkfst, pool

Economy Inn of America
(843) 563-4195
5971 W. Jim Bilton Blvd.
67 rooms - $25-45
Pets: Welcome w/$2 fee
Creature Comforts: CCTV, a/c,
pool

Holiday Inn
(800) HOLIDAY, (843) 563-4581
http://www.holiday-inn.com
6014 W. Jim Bilton Blvd.
122 rooms - $70-95
Pets: "We are a pet friendly hotel
where your furry friends are
welcome"
Creature Comforts: CCTV, a/c,
restaurant, pool

St. George Economy Motel
(843) 563-2360
125 Motel Dr.
35 rooms - $30-45
Pets: Small pets welcome
Creature Comforts: CCTV, a/c, pool

Super 8
(800) 800-8000, (843) 563-5551
http://www.super8.com
114 Winningham Rd.
59 rooms - $40-60
Pets: Welcome w/permission
Creature Comforts: CCTV, a/c, cont. brkfst, pool

SALEM
Sunrise Farm B&B
(888) 991-0121, (864) 944-0121
www.bbonline.com/sc/sunrisefarm
265 Britain St.
6 rooms - $85-120
Pets: Medium pets welcome in cottages, damage deposit, not allowed on furniture, crated if left alone
Creature Comforts: 1890 Victorian and guest cottages on 10-acre farm, family antiques, sophisticated country decor, handmade quilts, TV, VCR, a/c, kit, fireplace, full brkfst, farm animals

SANTEE
Comfort Inn
(800) 228-5150, (803) 854-3221
http://www.comfortinn.com
265 Britain St.
62 rooms - $52-125
Pets: Welcome
Creature Comforts: CCTV, a/c, cont. brkfst, pool

Days Inn
(800) DAYS INN, (803) 854-2175
http://www.daysinn.com
Rtes. 95 & 6
120 rooms - $50-65
Pets: Welcome w/$6 fee
Comforts: CCTV, a/c, restaurant, cont. brkfst, pool

Economy Inn
(803) 854-2107
626 Bass Dr.
43 rooms - $30-40
Pets: Small pets welcome
Creature Comforts: CCTV, a/c, pool

Ramada Inn
(800) 2-Ramada, (803) 854-2191
http://www.ramada.com
Rtes. 95 & 6
117 rooms - $48-58
Pets: Small pets w/$25 fee
Creature Comforts: CCTV, a/c, pool

Super 8
(800) 800-8000, (803) 854-3456
http://www.super8.com
9125 Old Rte. 6
42 rooms - $35-40
Pets: Small pets in smoking rms.
Creature Comforts: CCTV, a/c, Jacuzzi stes, cont. brkfst

SPARTANBURG
Days Inn
(800) DAYS INN, (864) 503-9048
http://www.daysinn.com
1000 Hearon Circle
138 rooms - $70-85
Pets: Welcome
Comforts: CCTV, a/c, pool

Days Inn
(800) DAYS INN, (864) 585-4311
http://www.daysinn.com
578 N. Church St.
82 rooms - $34-52
Pets: Welcome w/$10 fee
Comforts: CCTV, a/c, pool

Motel 6
(800) 4-MOTEL6, (864) 573-6383
http://www.motel6.com
105 Jones Rd.
124 rooms - $32
Pets: Under 30 lbs. welcome
Creature Comforts: CCTV, a/c, pool

Quality Hotel
(800) 228-5151, (864) 503-0780
http://www.qualityinn.com
7136 Asheville Rte.
143 rooms - $50-130
Pets: Welcome w/$10 fee
Creature Comforts: CCTV, a/c, refrig, micro, Jacuzzi, restaurant, full brkfst, pool

Ramada Inn
(800) 2-Ramada, (864) 576-5220
http://www.ramada.com
200 International Dr.
224 rooms - $60-200
Pets: Welcome w/$25 fee
Creature Comforts: CCTV, a/c, refrig, micro, restaurant, cont. brkfst, pool, whirlpool, sauna, exercise rm.

Residence Inn
(800) 331-3131, (864) 576-3333
http://www.residenceinn.com
9011 Fairforest Rd.
88 rooms - $98-125
Pets: Welcome w/$150 fee
Creature Comforts: CCTV, VCR, a/c, kit, cont. brkfst, pool, hlth clb, whirlpool

SUMMERTON
Econo Lodge
(800) 55-ECONO, (803) 485-2865
http://www.econolodge.com
Rtes. 95 & 102
60 rooms - $35-60
Pets: Welcome
Creature Comforts: CCTV, a/c, cont. brkfst, pool

SUMMERVILLE
Econo Lodge
(800) 55-ECONO, (843) 875-3022
http://www.econolodge.com
110 Holiday Inn Dr.
100 rooms - $55-75
Pets: Small pets w/$15 fee
Creature Comforts: CCTV, a/c

Holiday Inn Express
(800) HOLIDAY, (843) 875-3300
http://www.holiday-inn.com
120 Holiday Inn Dr.
125 rooms - $60-100
Pets: Under 20 lbs.-free; over 20 lbs.-$10 fee
Creature Comforts: CCTV, a/c, refrig, cont. brkfst, pool

SUMTER

Magnolia Inn B&B
(888) 666-0296, (803) 775-6694
www.bbonline.com/sc/magnolia/
4 rooms - $75-135
Pets: Welcome w/deposit
Comforts: Greek Revival B&B,
porches, beautiful gardens w/
flowering dogwood, rich period
details, antiques and Victorian
furnishings including oak mansion
bed, stained glass, quilts, CCTV,
a/c, 5 fireplaces, southern brkfst,
pool, porch swing, garden

Ramada Inn
(800) 2-Ramada, (803) 775-2323
http://www.ramada.com
226 N. Washington St.
125 rooms - $60-80
Pets: Welcome w/$50 dep.
Creature Comforts: CCTV, a/c,
kit, restaurant, cont. brkfst, pool

Travelers Inn
(803) 775-2323
Rtes. 521 & 76
125 rooms - $35-50
Pets: Small pets welcome
Creature Comforts: CCTV, a/c,
refrig, cont. brkfst, pool

TRAVELERS REST

Sleep Inn
(800) Sleep Inn, (864) 834-7040
http://www.sleepinn.com
110 Hawkins Rd.
82 rooms - $50-70
Pets: Welcome w/$10 fee
Comforts: CCTV, a/c, cont.
brkfst, pool

UNION

Comfort Inn
(800) 228-5150, (864) 427-5060
http://www.comfortinn.com
315 N. Duncan Hwy.
50 rooms - $55-65
Pets: Welcome w/$10 fee
Creature Comforts: CCTV, a/c,
cont. brkfst, pool

WALTERBORO

Best Western Walterboro
(800) 528-1234, (843) 538-3600
http://www.bestwestern.com
1140 Snider's Hwy.
114 rooms - $50-70
Pets: Small pets welcome
Creature Comforts: CCTV, a/c,
cont. brkfst, pool

Comfort Inn
(800) 228-5150, (843) 538-5403
http://www.comfortinn.com
1245 Sniders Hwy.
106 rooms - $35-115
Pets: Welcome
Creature Comforts: CCTV, a/c,
Jacuzzi, full brkfst, pool, exercise
rm.

Econo Lodge
(800) 55-ECONO, (843) 538-3830
http://www.econolodge.com
1057 Sniders Hwy.
100 rooms - $50-60
Pets: Welcome
Creature Comforts: CCTV, a/c

Holiday Inn
(800) HOLIDAY, (843) 538-5473
http://www.holiday-inn.com
1286 Sniders Hwy.
170 rooms - $50-75
Pets: Small pets w/$10 fee
Creature Comforts: Very nice,
CCTV, a/c, restaurant, pool

Mt. Carmel Farm B&B
(843) 538-5770
Rte. 2
2 rooms - $75
Pets: Welcome, horses boarded
Creature Comforts: Old-
fashioned farm cottage, simple
furnishings, CCTV, a/c, fireplace,
country brkfst, farm animals

Super 8 Motel, Airport
(800) 800-8000, (843) 538-5383
http://www.super8.com
1972 Bells Hwy.
44 rooms - $40-55
Pets: Welcome in smoking rms.
Creature Comforts: CCTV, a/c,
Jacuzzi, pool

WINNSBORO

Days Inn
(800) DAYS INN, (803) 635-1447
http://www.daysinn.com
Rtes. 34 & 321 Bypass
45 rooms - $45-80
Pets: Small pets w/$5 fee
Comforts: CCTV, a/c, cont.
brkfst, pool

Fairfield Motel
(803) 635-4681
115 S. 321 Bypass
62 rooms - $40-55
Pets: Welcome
Creature Comforts: CCTV, a/c,
refrig, micro, pool

YEMASSEE

Days Inn
(800) DAYS INN, (843) 726-8156
http://www.daysinn.com
Rtes. 95 & 17
116 rooms - $40-50
Pets: Welcome w/$10 fee
Comforts: CCTV, a/c, restaurant,
cont. brkfst, pool, hlth club

Holiday Inn Express
(800) HOLIDAY, (843) 726-9400
http://www.holiday-inn.com
40 Frampton Dr.
55 rooms - $50-55
Pets: Welcome
Creature Comforts: CCTV, a/c

YORK

Days Inn
(800) DAYS INN, (803) 684-2525
http://www.daysinn.com
1568 Alexander Love Rte.
41 rooms - $45-120
Pets: Welcome w/$5 fee
Comforts: CCTV, a/c, Jacuzzi,
cont. brkfst, pool, whirlpool

South Dakota

ABERDEEN

Aberdeen Settle Inn
(605) 225-5300
Sixth Ave.
35 rooms - $30-39
Pets: Welcome
Creature Comforts: Request the inner court rooms, CCTV, a/c

Best Western
(800) 528-1234, (605) 229-4040
http://www.bestwestern.com
1400 8th Ave. NW
154 rooms - $65-87
Pets: Welcome
Creature Comforts: CCTV, a/c, refrig, micro, Jacuzzi, restaurant, pool, sauna, whirlpool

Breeze-Inn Motel
(800) 341-8000, (605) 225-4222
1216 - 6th Ave., SW
19 rooms - $30-45
Pets: Small pets welcome
Creature Comforts: CCTV, a/c, refrig, micro

Comfort Inn
(800) 228-5150, (605) 226-0097
http://www.comfortinn.com
2923 Sixth Ave., SE
40 rooms - $55-85
Pets: Welcome w/$6 fee
Creature Comforts: CCTV, a/c, Jacuzzi, cont. brkfst, sauna, whirlpool

Super 8, East
(800) 800-8000, (605) 229-5005
http://www.super8.com
2405 SE Sixth Ave.
108 rooms - $45-59
Pets: Welcome
Creature Comforts: CCTV, a/c, cont. brkfst, hlth clb access, sauna

Super 8, North
(800) 800-8000, (605) 226-2288
http://www.super8.com
770 NW Rte. 281
25 rooms - $38-55
Pets: Welcome
Creature Comforts: CCTV, a/c, cont. brkfst

Super 8, West
(800) 800-8000, (605) 225-1711
http://www.super8.com
714 S. Rte. 281
39 rooms - $35-50
Pets: Welcome
Creature Comforts: CCTV, a/c, cont. brkfst

White House Inn
(800) 225-6000, (605) 225-5000
500 Sixth Ave. SW
96 rooms - $40-55
Pets: Welcome
Creature Comforts: CCTV, a/c, refrig

BADLANDS NAT'L PARK

Badlands Inn
(800) 341-8000, (605) 433-5401
Route 377
24 rooms - $40-58
Pets: Welcome
Creature Comforts: CCTV, a/c, pool

Budget Host Motel
(800) Bud-Host, (605) 433-5335
http://www.budgethost.com
Route 90
17 rooms - $40-55
Pets: Welcome
Creature Comforts: CCTV, a/c

Cedar Pass Lodge
(605) 433-5460
1 Cedar St.
23 cabins - $45-59
Pets: Welcome w/$5
Creature Comforts: CCTV, a/c, kit, restaurant

BELLE FOURCHE

Ace Motel
(605) 892-2612
109 Sixth Ave.
14 rooms - $25-50
Pets: Welcome
Creature Comforts: CCTV, a/c, micro

Best Western Kings Inn
(800) 528-1234, (605) 892-2691
http://www.bestwestern.com
518 National St.
30 rooms - $45-115
Pets: Small pets welcome
Creature Comforts: CCTV, a/c, restaurant, pool

Motel Lariat
(605) 892-2601
1033 Elkhorn Rd.
11 rooms - $30-54
Pets: Welcome w/$3 fee
Creature Comforts: CCTV, a/c

Super 8
(800) 800-8000, (605) 892-3361
http://www.super8.com
501 National St.
43 rooms - $40-59
Pets: Welcome
Creature Comforts: CCTV, VCR, a/c, cont. brkfst

BROOKINGS

Best Western Staurolite Inn
(800) 528-1234, (605) 692-9421
http://www.bestwestern.com
2515 East Sixth St.
102 rooms - $45-65
Pets: Welcome
Creature Comforts: CCTV, a/c, pool

Holiday Inn
(800) HOLIDAY, (605) 692-9471
http://www.holiday-inn.com
2500 E. Sixth St.
125 rooms - $40-75
Pets: Welcome
Creature Comforts: CCTV, VCR, a/c, restaurant, pool, hlth clb, whirlpool

Super 8
(800) 800-8000, (605) 692-6920
http://www.super8.com
3034 LeFevre Rd.
46 rooms - $45-58
Pets: Welcome
Creature Comforts: CCTV,
VCR, a/c, Jacuzzi, cont. brkfst

Wayside Motel
(800) 658-4577, (605) 692-4831
1430 Sixth St.
20 rooms - $25-39
Pets: Welcome
Creature Comforts: CCTV, a/c

BUFFALO
Tipperary Lodge
(605) 375-3721
Route 85
28 rooms - $40-75
Pets: Small pets welcome
Creature Comforts: CCTV, a/c,
refrig, micro, kit

CANISTOTA
Best Western U-Bar Motel
(800) 528-1234, (605) 296-3466
http://www.bestwestern.com
130 Ash St.
28 rooms - $35-65
Pets: Small pets w/mngr approval
Creature Comforts: CCTV, a/c

CHAMBERLAIN
Alewel's Lake Shore Motel
(605) 734-5566
115 N. River St.
37 rooms - $35-54
Pets: Small pets welcome
Creature Comforts: CCTV, a/c

Bel Aire Motel
(605) 734-5595
312 E. King St.
35 rooms - $40-65
Pets: Small pets w/$5 fee
Creature Comforts: CCTV, a/c

Days Inn
(800) DAYS INN, (605) 734-4100
http://www.daysinn.com
I-90, Exit 260
45 rooms - $40-87
Pets: Welcome
Creature Comforts: CCTV, a/c,
pool, whirlpool

Oacoma Inn
(605) 734-5593
Route 90
36 rooms - $35-100
Pets: Welcome w/$20 deposit
Creature Comforts: CCTV,
VCR, a/c

Oasis Inn
(800) 635-3559, (605) 734-6061
Route 90
70 rooms - $40-75
Pets: Welcome w/$3 fee
Creature Comforts: CCTV, a/c,
Jacuzzi, restaurant, cont. brkfst,
sauna, whirlpool, fishing pond,
mini golf

Radisson Resort, Cedar Shore
(800) 333-3333, (605) 734-6376
http://www.radisson.com
1010 George Michelson Dr.
100 rooms - $70-190
Pets: Welcome w/$10 fee
Creature Comforts: New resort,
riverside setting, beautiful atrium,
CCTV, VCR, a/c, refrig, micro,
restaurant, pool, hlth clb access,
sauna, whirlpool, extensive
activities-boating, mtn. biking,
fishing, golf, hiking

CORSICA
Country Corner B&B
(605) 946-5852
RR 2, Box 46
3 rooms - $35-57
Pets: Welcome
Creature Comforts: 1908
restored Victorian, CCTV, a/c,
refrig, micro

CUSTER STATE PARK
American Presidents Resort
(605) 673-3373
Route 16A
45 rooms - $30-200
Pets: Welcome
Creature Comforts: CCTV, a/c,
kit, pool, whirlpool, lawn games

Bavarian Inn Motel
(800) 657-4312, (605) 673-2802
1000 N. Fifth St.
65 rooms - $30-80
Pets: Welcome w/deposit
Creature Comforts: CCTV, a/c,
refrig, Jacuzzi, restaurant, pool,
sauna, whirlpool, tennis

Blue Bell Lodge & Resort
(800) 658-3530, (605) 255-4531
http://www.custerresorts.com
Route 87
29 cabins - $80-165
Pets: Welcome in older cabins
Creature Comforts: Private
retreat in Custer State Park, new
handcrafted log cabins, refrig,
micro, kit, restaurant, home-
cooked meals, hayrides,
chuckwagon cookouts

Chief Motel
(605) 673-2318
120 Mt. Rushmore Rd.
34 rooms - $35-80
Pets: Welcome w/$5 fee
Creature Comforts: CCTV, a/c,
pool, sauna, whirlpool

Legion Lake Resort
(800) 658-3530, (605) 255-4521
http://www.custerresorts.com
Rtes. 87 & 16A
25 cabins - $69-110
Pets: Ltd. cabins w/$5 fee
Creature Comforts: Lakeside
lodge/cabins, low-key setting,
dining room serving local game,
swimming, fishing, paddle boats,
canoeing, swimming, near
Centennial trail

Rocket Motel
(605) 673-4401
211 Mt. Rushmore Rd.
27 rooms - $35-60
Pets: Small pets welcome
Creature Comforts: CCTV, a/c

State Game Lodge/Resort
(800) 658-3530, (605) 255-4541
http://www.custerresorts.com
Route 16A
50 cabins - $85-310
Pets: Welcome in cabins w/$5 fee
Creature Comforts: Stone and
wood lodge w/rustic cabins,
incredible scenery, pristine lake,
kit, fireplace, dining room serving
local game, hiking, paddle
boating, swimming

Sylvan Lake Resort
(800) 658-3530, (605) 255-4561
http://www.custerresorts.com
Route 87
190 rooms - $85-310
Pets: Welcome in cabins w/$5 fee
Creature Comforts: Wonderful,
gracious stone lodge on Nat.
Historic Regstr, Calvin Coolidge's
summer White House, log cabins
in pine grove, kit, fireplace, dining
rm., hiking, boating

The Roost Resort
(605) 673-2326
Route 16A
7 rooms - $40-65
Pets: Welcome
Creature Comforts: CCTV,
refrig

DAKOTA DUNES
Country Inn and Suites
(605) 232-3500
151 Tower Rd.
70 rooms - $65-80
Pets: Small pets w/$15 fee
Creature Comforts: CCTV, a/c,
refrig, micro, Jacuzzi, whirlpool

DEADWOOD
Days Inn
(800) DAYS INN, (605) 578-3476
http://www.daysinn.com
Rtes. 85 & 14A
38 rooms - $40-100
Pets: Welcome
Creature Comforts: CCTV, a/c,
restaurant

Deadwood Gulch Resort
(800) 695-1876, (605) 578-1294
http://www.deadwoodgulch.com
Route 85 S.
98 rooms - $55-95
Pets: Welcome one-time $10 fee
Creature Comforts: CCTV, a/c,
restaurant, casino, pool, whirlpool,
kiddie fun park, horseback riding,
hiking

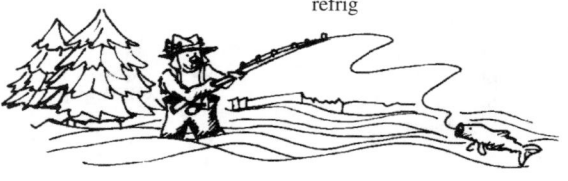

First Gold Hotel
(605) 578-9777
270 Main St.
53 rooms - $60-88
Pets: Welcome w/$50 deposit
Creature Comforts: CCTV,
VCR, a/c, kit, Jacuzzi, restaurant

EAGLE BUTTE
Super 8
(800) 800-8000, (605) 964-8888
http://www.super8.com
Rtes. 212 S & 63S
40 rooms - $45-60
Pets: Welcome
Creature Comforts: CCTV,
Jacuzzi, cont. brkfst

EUREKA
Lake View Motel
(501) 284-2681
Route 10
25 rooms - $30-45
Pets: Welcome
Creature Comforts: CCTV, a/c,
and a kit

FAITH
Prairie Vista Inn
(605) 967-2343
Route 212
27 rooms - $50-69
Pets: Small pets welcome
Creature Comforts: CCTV, a/c,
Jacuzzi, whirlpool, sauna

FAULKTON
Super 8
(800) 800-8000, (605) 598-4567
http://www.super8.com
700 Main St.
20 rooms - $44-59
Pets: Welcome w/permission
Creature Comforts: CCTV,
VCR, a/c, Jacuzzi

FORT PIERRE
Fort Pierre Motel
(605) 223-3111
211 S. First St.
20 rooms - $35-48
Pets: Welcome
Creature Comforts: CCTV,
refrig

FREEMAN
Fensel's Motel
(800) 658-3319, (605) 925-4202
Route 81
10 rooms - $32-43
Pets: Welcome
Creature Comforts: CCTV, a/c

GETTYSBURG
Trail Motel
(605) 765-2482
http://www.trailmotel.com
Route 212
22 rooms - $30-45
Pets: Welcome
Creature Comforts: CCTV, a/c

HILL CITY
Best Western Golden Spike
(800) 528-1234, (605) 574-2577
http://www.bestwestern.com
Rtes. 16 & 385
61 rooms - $40-115
Pets: Welcome w/mngr's approval
Creature Comforts: CCTV, a/c,
refrig, micro, restaurant, pool,
exercise rm, whirlpool, bike
rentals

Lantern Inn Motel
(605) 574-2582
Rtes. 16 & 385
19 rooms - $45-80
Pets: Welcome w/$4 fee
Creature Comforts: CCTV,
VCR, a/c, refrig, pool

Lodge at Palmer Gulch
(800) 562-8503, (605) 574-2525
Route 244
61 rooms - $50-140
Pets: Welcome
Creature Comforts: CCTV,
VCR, a/c, refrig, micro, fireplace,
Jacuzzi, pool, whirlpool

Robins Roost Cabins
(605) 574-2252
12630 Robins Roost Rd.
8 cabins - $35-45
Pets: Welcome in 3 cabins
Creature Comforts: CCTV, a/c,
kit, fireplace

HOT SPRINGS

Best Western Inn by the River
(800) 528-1234, (605) 745-4292
http://www.bestwestern.com
602 W. River St.
32 rooms - $60-100
Pets: Welcome
Creature Comforts: CCTV, VCR, a/c, pool

Bison Motel
(800) 456-5174, (605) 745-5191
Route 385
19 rooms - $50-60
Pets: Welcome
Creature Comforts: CCTV, a/c, cont. brkfst

Comfort Inn
(800) 228-5150, (605) 745-7378
http://www.comfortinn.com
737 S. Sixth St.
51 rooms - $60-150
Pets: Welcome
Creature Comforts: CCTV, VCR, a/c, refrig, Jacuzzi, cont. brkfst, pool, hlth clb access, whirlpool

Hills Inn
(605) 745-3130
640 S. Sixth St.
35 rooms - $50-90
Pets: Small pets welcome
Creature Comforts: CCTV, a/c

Super 8
(800) 800-8000, (605) 745-3888
http://www.super8.com
800 Mammoth St.
44 rooms - $50-65
Pets: Welcome w/$25 deposit
Creature Comforts: CCTV, VCR, a/c, restaurant

HURON

Best Western Huron
(800) 528-1234, (605) 352-2000
http://www.bestwestern.com
2000 Dakota South
52 rooms - $50-65
Pets: Welcome w/permission
Creature Comforts: CCTV, VCR, a/c, cont. brkfst, sauna, whirlpool

Crossroads Hotel
(605) 352-3204
Fourth & Wisconsin SW
100 rooms - $40-75
Pets: Welcome
Creature Comforts: CCTV, a/c, restaurant, pool, sauna, whirlpool

Traveler Motel
(605) 352-6703
241 Lincoln NW
24 rooms - $27-30
Pets: Welcome
Creature Comforts: CCTV, a/c, pool

INTERIOR

Badlands Budget Host
(800) Bud-Host, (605) 433-5335
http://www.budgethost.com
Rtes. 44 & 377
17 rooms - $35-45
Pets: Welcome, crated if left
Creature Comforts: CCTV, a/c, pool

KADOKA

Best Western H&H El Centro
(800) 528-1234, (605) 837-2287
http://www.bestwestern.com
Rte. 90 Bus. Loop
39 rooms - $40-105
Pets: Small pets welcome
Creature Comforts: CCTV, a/c, restaurant, pool, whirlpool

Dakota Inn
(800) 341-8000, (605) 837-2151
Route 90
34 rooms - $45-59
Pets: Welcome
Creature Comforts: CCTV, a/c, pool

Motel Lariat
(800) 341-8000, (605) 837-2151
Rte. 90 Bus. Loop
34 rooms - $30-56
Pets: Welcome w/$3 fee
Creature Comforts: CCTV, a/c, pool

Hilltop Motel
(605) 837-2216
225 Rte. 16
16 rooms - $30-53
Pets: Small pets welcome
Creature Comforts: CCTV, a/c

West Motel
(605) 837-2427
306 Rte. 16W
18 rooms - $30-55
Pets: Welcome w/$3 fee
Creature Comforts: CCTV, a/c

KENNEBEC

Budget Host
(800) Bud-Host, (605) 869-2210
http://www.budgethost.com
Rtes. 90 & 16
16 rooms - $25-48
Pets: Medium-size pets accepted
Creature Comforts: CCTV, a/c

King's Motel
(605) 869-2270
Route 90
10 rooms - $40-65
Pets: Welcome
Creature Comforts: CCTV, a/c

KEYSTONE

Bed and Breakfast Inn
(605) 666-4490
208 First St.
8 rooms - $50-80
Pets: Small pets w/$5 fee
Creature Comforts: Streamside, CCTV, refrig, fireplace, full brkfst

Best Western Four Presidents
(800) 528-1234, (605) 666-4472
http://www.bestwestern.com
250 Winter St.
32 rooms - $65-95
Pets: Small pets w/$10 fee
Creature Comforts: CCTV, VCR, a/c

First Lady Inn
(605) 666-4990
702 Route 16A
40 rooms - $55-85
Pets: Welcome w/$7 fee
Creature Comforts: CCTV, a/c, micro, Jacuzzi, whirlpool

Kelly Inn
(800) 635-3559, (605) 666-4483
Cemetary Rd.
44 rooms - $35-155
Pets: Welcome
Creature Comforts: CCTV, a/c, kit

Powder House Lodge
(800) 321-0692, (605) 666-4646
Route 16A
34 rooms - $48-130
Pets: Ltd. units w/$7 fee
Creature Comforts: Lodge w/log cabins/motel rms, rqst new cabins, barn board walls, immaculate, log beds, CCTV, a/c, refrig, micro, Jacuzzi, restaurant, pool

Rushmore Manor Inn
(800) 456-1878, (605) 666-4443
115 Swanzey St.
63 rooms - $50-100
Pets: First floor rooms w/$10 fee
Creature Comforts: CCTV, a/c, refrig, restaurant, pool, whirlpool

LEAD
Best Western Golden Hills
(800) 528-1234, (605) 584-1800
http://www.bestwestern.com
900 Miners Ave.
100 rooms - $60-105
Pets: Small pets welcome
Creature Comforts: CCTV, a/c, refrig, restaurant, hlth clb

White House Inn
(800) 654-5323, (605) 584-2000
395 Glendale Rd.
70 rooms - $50-110
Pets: Welcome w/$5 fee, $25 dep.
Creature Comforts: CCTV, VCR, a/c, refrig, micro, Jacuzzi, whirlpool

LEMMON
Prairie Motel
(605) 374-3304
115 E. Tenth Ave.
12 rooms - $25-39
Pets: Welcome w/$4 fee
Creature Comforts: CCTV, a/c, refrig, micro, kit

MADISON
Lake Park Motel
(605) 256-3524
Rtes. 34 & 81
40 rooms - $40-55
Pets: Small pets welcome
Creature Comforts: CCTV, a/c, refrig, micro

Super 8 Motel
(800) 800-8000, (605) 256-6931
http://www.super8.com
Rtes. 34 & 81
63 rooms - $35-50
Pets: Welcome w/permission
Creature Comforts: CCTV, a/c

MILLBANK
Lantern Motel
(605) 432-4591
1010 South Dakota St.
30 rooms - $40-53
Pets: Welcome w/$3 fee, $40 dep.
Creature Comforts: CCTV, a/c

Manor Motel
(800) 341-8000, (605) 432-4527
Route 12 E.
30 rooms - $35-48
Pets: Welcome
Creature Comforts: CCTV, a/c, pool, sauna, whirlpool

MITCHELL
Best Western Motor Inn
(800) 528-1234, (605) 996-2376
http://www.bestwestern.com
1001 S. Burr St.
77 rooms - $45-85
Pets: Welcome
Creature Comforts: CCTV, a/c, refrig, cont. brkfst, pool

Econo Lodge
(800) 55-ECONO, (605) 996-6647
http://www.econolodge.com
1313 S. Ohlman Rd.
45 rooms - $40-56
Pets: Welcome
Creature Comforts: CCTV, a/c

Holiday Inn
(800) HOLIDAY, (605) 996-6501
http://www.holiday-inn.com
1525 W. Havens Ave.
153 rooms - $50-85
Pets: Welcome in smoking rooms
Creature Comforts: CCTV, a/c, restaurant, pool, sauna, whirlpool, indoor games

Motel 6
(800) 4-MOTEL6, (605) 996-0530
http://www.motel6.com
1309 S. Ohlman Rd.
96 rooms - $30-47
Pets: Under 30 lbs. welcome
Creature Comforts: CCTV, a/c, pool

Siesta Motel
(800) 424-0537, (605) 996-5544
1210 Havens Rd.
21 rooms - $30-45
Pets: Welcome w/$3 fee
Creature Comforts: CCTV, a/c

MOBRIDGE
Super 8
(800) 800-8000, (605) 845-7215
http://www.super8.com
Route 12 W.
31 rooms - $37-47
Pets: Welcome w/permission
Creature Comforts: CCTV, a/c, Jacuzzi

Wrangler Motor Inn
(605) 845-3641
820 W. Grand Circle
60 rooms - $50-75
Pets: Welcome
Creature Comforts: CCTV, a/c, sauna, whirlpool

MURDO
Best Western Graham's
(800) 528-1234, (605) 669-2441
http://www.bestwestern.com
301 W. Fifth St.
45 rooms - $40-80
Pets: Small pets w/permission
Creature Comforts: CCTV, a/c, pool, bsktball crt, playground

Hospitality Inn
(605) 669-2425
302 W. Fifth St.
30 rooms - $45-90
Pets: Welcome
Creature Comforts: CCTV, a/c, micro

Super 8 Motel
(800) 800-8000, (605) 669-2437
http://www.super8.com
Route 90
50 rooms - $30-45
Pets: Welcome w/$5 fee
Creature Comforts: CCTV, a/c, Jacuzzi

NORTH SIOUX CITY
Super 8 Motel
(800) 800-8000, (605) 232-4716
http://www.super8.com
1300 River Dr.
47 rooms - $50-60
Pets: Welcome w/$5 fee
Creature Comforts: CCTV, a/c, refrig, micro, Jacuzzi

OACOMA

Oasis Inn
(800) 341-800, (605) 734-6061
W. Route 16
69 rooms - $40-65
Pets: Welcome
Creature Comforts: CCTV, a/c, restaurant, sauna, whirlpool, mini-golf, pond

PICKSTOWN

Fort Randall Inn
(800) 340-7801, (605) 487-7801
Rtes. 12 & 281
17 rooms - $35-60
Pets: Welcome
Creature Comforts: CCTV, VCR, a/c, refrig

PIEDMONT

Elk Creek Resort and Lodge
(800) 846-2267, (605) 787-4884
elkcreek.org/ecrweb/index.html
Elk Creek Rd.
18 rooms - $65-150
Pets: Welcome w/$7 fee
Creature Comforts: Serene Black Hills setting near Petrified Frst, clean, rqst mdrn cottages w/ CCTV, loft, dining area, kit, pool, hot tub, hiking

PIERRE

Best Western
(800) 528-1234, (605) 224-6877
http://www.bestwestern.com
920 W. Sioux St.
151 rooms - $60-75
Pets: Welcome
Creature Comforts: CCTV, a/c, refrig, micro, Jacuzzi, restaurant, pool

Budget Host State Motel
(800) Bud-Host, (605) 224-5896
http://www.budgethost.com
640 N. Euclid Rd.
36 rooms - $35-50
Pets: Small pets welcome
Creature Comforts: CCTV, VCR, a/c, kit, cont. brkfst, pool, sauna, exercise rm, whirlpool

Capitol Inn
(800) 658-3055, (605) 224-6387
815 Wells Ave.
104 rooms - $25-40
Pets: Welcome
Creature Comforts: CCTV, VCR, a/c, kit, pool

Days Inn
(800) DAYS INN, (605) 224-0411
http://www.daysinn.com
520 W. Sioux Ave.
78 rooms - $48-58
Pets: Welcome w/$5 fee
Creature Comforts: CCTV, VCR, a/c, refrig, Jacuzzi

Governor's Inn
(800) 341-8000, (605) 224-4200
700 W. Sioux Ave.
81 rooms - $55-100
Pets: Welcome w/$10 fee
Creature Comforts: CCTV, VCR, a/c, refrig, micro, Jacuzzi, pool, whirlpool

Kelly Inn
(800) 635-3559, (605) 224-4140
713 W. Sioux Ave.
48 rooms - $40-45
Pets: Welcome
Creature Comforts: CCTV, a/c, pool, sauna access

Super 8 Motel
(800) 800-8000, (605) 224-1617
http://www.super8.com
320 W. Sioux Ave.
78 rooms - $40-55
Pets: Welcome
Creature Comforts: CCTV, VCR, a/c, cont. brkfst

PLANKINTON

Super 8 Motel
(800) 800-8000, (605) 942-7722
http://www.super8.com
801 S. Main St.
33 rooms - $45-70
Pets: Welcome
Creature Comforts: CCTV, a/c, Jacuzzi

PLATTE

Kings Inn
(605) 337-3385
Route 44
34 rooms - $35-48
Pets: Welcome
Creature Comforts: CCTV, a/c, hot tub

PRESHO

Hutch's Motel
(800) 341-8000, (605) 895-2591
930 E. 9th St.
30 rooms - $35-50
Pets: Welcome w/$5 fee
Creature Comforts: CCTV, a/c

RAPID CITY

Big Sky Motel
(605) 348-3200
4080 Tower Rd.
30 rooms - $30-55
Pets: Small pets welcome
Creature Comforts: CCTV, a/c

Castle Inn
(800) 658-5464, (605) 348-4120
15 North St., East
22 rooms - $35-65
Pets: Welcome w/$5 fee
Creature Comforts: CCTV, a/c, refrig, kit, pool

Days Inn, Downtown
(800) DAYS INN, (605) 343-5501
http://www.daysinn.com
125 Main St.
156 rooms - $45-175
Pets: Welcome w/$15 fee
Creature Comforts: CCTV, a/c, restaurant, pool,

Econo Lodge
(800) 55-ECONO, (605) 342-6400
http://www.econolodge.com
625 E. Disk Dr.
125 rooms - $40-110
Pets: Welcome w/$5 fee
Creature Comforts: CCTV, a/c, refrig, micro, Jacuzzi, pool, whirlpool

Fair Value Inn
(605) 342-8118
1607 LaCrosse St.
25 rooms - $30-65
Pets: Small dogs welcome
Creature Comforts: CCTV, a/c

Foothills Inn
(605) 348-5640
1625 N. LaCrosse St.
65 rooms - $69-89
Pets: Welcome
Creature Comforts: CCTV, a/c, refrig, restaurant, pool

Gold Star Motel
(605) 341-7051
801 E. North St.
25 rooms - $35-70
Pets: Small pets w/$5 fee
Creature Comforts: CCTV, a/c

Holiday Inn
(800) HOLIDAY, (605) 348-1230
http://www.holiday-inn.com
1902 LaCrosse St.
210 rooms - $60-90
Pets: Small pets welcome
Creature Comforts: CCTV,
VCR, a/c, refrig, restaurant, pool,
whirlpool

Holiday Inn, Rushmore Plaza
(800) HOLIDAY, (605) 348-4000
http://www.holiday-inn.com
505 N. Fifth St.
205 rooms - $90-115
Pets: Welcome in smoking rooms
Creature Comforts: CCTV, a/c,
refrig, micro, restaurant, sauna,
health club, whirlpool

Motel 6
(800) 4-MOTEL6, (605) 343-3687
http://www.motel6.com
620 E. Latrobe St.
150 rooms - $30-47
Pets: Under 30 lbs. welcome
Creature Comforts: CCTV, a/c,
pool

Quality Inn
(800) 228-5151, (605) 342-3322
http://www.qualityinn.com
2208 Mt. Rushmore
110 rooms - $30-170
Pets: Welcome
Creature Comforts: CCTV, a/c,
refrig, micro, kit, restaurant

Ramada Inn
(800) 2-Ramada, (605) 342-1300
http://www.ramada.com
1721 N. LaCrosse St.
140 rooms - $55-170
Pets: Small pets w/$10 fee
Creature Comforts: CCTV,
VCR, a/c, refrig, Jacuzzi, pool,
hlth clb access, sauna, whirlpool

Super 8
(800) 800-8000, (605) 348-8070
http://www.super8.com
2124 LaCrosse St.
119 rooms - $35-60
Pets: Welcome
Creature Comforts: CCTV,
VCR, a/c, cont. brkfst

Thrifty Motor Inn
(605) 342-0551
1303 LaCrosse St.
25 rooms - $25-65
Pets: Small pets welcome
Creature Comforts: CCTV, a/c

Tip-Top Motor Hotel
(605) 343-3901
405 St. Joseph St.
62 rooms - $40-110
Pets: Welcome w/$10 fee
Creature Comforts: CCTV,
VCR, a/c, refrig, kit, pool

SELBY
Super 8
(800) 800-8000, (605) 649-7979
http://www.super8.com
5000 Rtes. 12 & 83
35 rooms - $40-75
Pets: Welcome w/$5 fee and dep.
Creature Comforts: CCTV, a/c,
refrig, micro, Jacuzzi

SIOUX FALLS
Baymont Inn
(800) 4-BUDGET, (605)
http://www.baymontinns.com
3200 Meadow Ave.
80 rooms - $50-70
Pets: Welcome in smoking room
Creature Comforts: CCTV, a/c,
refrig, micro, pool, whirlpool

Best Western
(800) 528-1234, (605) 336-0650
http://www.bestwestern.com
2400 N. Louise Ave.
226 rooms - $80-100
Pets: Welcome
Creature Comforts: CCTV, a/c,
restaurant, pool, hlth clb, sauna,
whirlpool

Bismark Inn
(605) 332-2000
3200 W. Russell St.
110 rooms - $40-75
Pets: Welcome
Creature Comforts: CCTV, a/c,
whirlpool

Comfort Inn, North
(800) 228-5150, (605) 331-4490
http://www.comfortinn.com
5100 N. Cliff Ave.
81 rooms - $45-75
Pets: Welcome w/$10 fee
Creature Comforts: CCTV,
VCR, a/c, Jacuzzi, cont. brkfst,
pool, hlth clb

Comfort Inn, South
(800) 228-5150, (605) 361-2822
http://www.comfortinn.com
3216 S. Carolyn Ave.
67 rooms - $55-90
Pets: Welcome
Creature Comforts: CCTV, a/c,
refrig, micro, cont. brkfst, pool

Comfort Suites
(800) 228-5150, (605) 362-9711
http://www.comfortinn.com
3208 S. Carolyn Ave.
61 rooms - $65-100
Pets: Welcome
Creature Comforts: CCTV,
VCR, a/c, refrig, micro, kit, cont.
brkfst, pool

Exel Inn
(800) 356-8103, (605) 331-5800
1300 W. Russell St.
105 rooms - $40-57
Pets: Small pets welcome
Creature Comforts: CCTV,
VCR, a/c, refrig, micro, Jacuzzi

Fairfield Inn
(800) 228-2800, (605) 361-2211
http://www.marriott.com/
fairfieldinn
4501 W. Empire Pl.
65 rooms - $45-60
Pets: Welcome in smoking rooms
Creature Comforts: CCTV, a/c,
refrig, micro, pool, whirlpool

Kelly Inn
(800) 635-3559, (605) 338-6242
3101 Russell St.
45 rooms - $50-60
Pets: Welcome w/$5 fee
Creature Comforts: CCTV,
VCR, a/c, refrig, micro, Jacuzzi,
health club access, sauna,
whirlpool

Motel 6
(800) 4-MOTEL6, (605) 336-7800
3009 Russell St.
87 rooms - $30-45
Pets: Under 30 lbs. welcome
Creature Comforts: CCTV, a/c, pool

Ramada Inn
(800) 2-Ramada, (605) 336-1020
http://www.ramada.com
1301 W. Russell St.
200 rooms - $60-95
Pets: $5 fee in smoking rooms
Creature Comforts: CCTV, a/c, restaurant, pool, hlth clb access

Ramada Limited
(800) 2-Ramada, (605) 330-0000
http://www.ramada.com
407 Lyons Ave.
66 rooms - $40-75
Pets: Welcome w/$15 deposit
Creature Comforts: CCTV, VCR, a/c, refrig, micro, Jacuzzi, pool, whirlpool

Residence Inn
(800) 331-3131, (605) 361-2202
http://www.residenceinn.com
4509 W. Empire Rd.
65 rooms - $90-170
Pets: Welcome w/$5 fee, $25 dep.
Creature Comforts: CCTV, VCR, a/c, refrig, micro, kit, fireplace, cont. brkfst, whirlpool

Rodeway Inn
(800) 228-2000, (605) 336-0230
http://www.rodeway.com
809 West Ave. N.
83 rooms - $50-100
Pets: Welcome
Creature Comforts: CCTV, a/c, refrig, micro, cont. brkfst, pool, whirlpool

Select Inn
(800) 641-1000, (605) 361-1864
3500 S. Gateway Rd.
100 rooms - $35-49
Pets: Small pets w/$25 deposit
Creature Comforts: CCTV, VCR, a/c, refrig, micro, kit

Sleep Inn
(800) Sleep Inn, (605) 339-3992
http://www.sleepinn.com
1500 N. Kiwanis Ave.
66 rooms - $55-60
Pets: Welcome
Creature Comforts: CCTV, VCR, a/c, pool, whirlpool

Super 8
(800) 800-8000, (605) 339-9330
http://www.super8.com
1508 W. Russell Rd.
95 rooms - $45-50
Pets: Welcome
Creature Comforts: CCTV, a/c

SISSETON
Holiday Motel
(605) 698-7644
Route 10 East
19 rooms - $35-40
Pets: Welcome
Creature Comforts: CCTV, a/c

I-29 Motel
(605) 698-4314
Route 10
30 rooms - $40
Pets: Welcome w/$5
Creature Comforts: CCTV, a/c

Viking Motel
(605) 698-7663
Route 10 West
24 rooms - $30-35
Pets: Welcome
Creature Comforts: CCTV, a/c

SPEARFISH
Best Western Downtown
(800) 528-1234, (605) 642-4676
http://www.bestwestern.com
346 W. Kansas Rd.
35 rooms - $35-90
Pets: One small pet per room
Creature Comforts: CCTV, a/c, cont. brkfst, pool, whirlpool

Holiday Inn
(800) HOLIDAY, (605) 642-4683
http://www.holiday-inn.com
Route 90
144 rooms - $70-115
Pets: Welcome w/$10 fee
Creature Comforts: CCTV, a/c, refrig, Jacuzzi, restaurant, pool, exercise rm., whirlpool

Kelly Inn
(800) 635-3559, (605) 642-7995
540 E. Jackson St.
51 rooms - $45-85
Pets: Welcome w/$5 fee
Creature Comforts: CCTV, a/c, Jacuzzi, sauna, whirlpool

Queen's Motel
(605) 642-2631
305 Main St.
12 rooms - $30-49
Pets: Small pets welcome
Creature Comforts: CCTV, a/c

Royal Rest Motel
(605) 642-3842
444 Main St.
12 rooms - $30-65
Pets: Welcome
Creature Comforts: CCTV, a/c

Sherwood Lodge
(605) 642-4688
Jackson Blvd.
22 rooms - $45-59
Pets: Welcome w/$5
Creature Comforts: CCTV, a/c

STURGIS
Best Western Sturgis
(800) 528-1234, (605) 347-3604
http://www.bestwestern.com
2431 S. Junction Ave.
56 rooms - $40-95
Pets: Welcome
Creature Comforts: CCTV, VCR, a/c, refrig, restaurant, pool, sauna, whirlpool

National 9
(605) 347-2506
2426 Junction Ave.
50 rooms - $35-65
Pets: Welcome w/$5 fee
Creature Comforts: CCTV, a/c, refrig

Super 8
(800) 800-8000, (605) 347-4447
http://www.super8.com
Route 90
59 rooms - $40-57
Pets: Welcome w/deposit
Creature Comforts: CCTV, a/c, refrig, micro, Jacuzzi, hlth clb, sauna, whirlpool

VERMILLION

Comfort Inn
(800) 228-5150, (605) 624-8333
http://www.comfortinn.com
701 W. Cherry St.
46 rooms - $40-75
Pets: Welcome w/$5 fee
Creature Comforts: CCTV, a/c,
kit, pool, hlth clb, sauna,whirlpool

Super 8
(800) 800-8000, (605) 624-8005
http://www.super8.com
1208 E. Cherry St.
40 rooms - $40-50
Pets: Welcome w/$5 fee
Creature Comforts: CCTV, a/c,
cont. brkfst, pool, sauna, whirlpool

WALL

Best Western Plains Motel
(800) 528-1234, (605) 279-2145
http://www.bestwestern.com
712 Glenn St.
74 rooms - $50-100
Pets: Welcome w/$5 fee
Creature Comforts: CCTV, a/c,
pool

Elk Motel
(605) 279-2127
1000 South Blvd.
47 rooms - $35-70
Pets: Welcome
Creature Comforts: CCTV, a/c

Kings Inn Motel
(605) 279-2121
608 Main St.
26 rooms - $40-60
Pets: Small pets welcome
Creature Comforts: CCTV, a/c

Sands Motor Inn
(800) 341-8000, (605) 279-2121
804 Glenn St.
49 rooms - $35-80
Pets: Small pets welcome
Creature Comforts: CCTV, a/c

WATERTOWN

Best Western Inn
(800) 528-1234, (605) 886-8011
http://www.bestwestern.com
1901 Ninth Ave. SW
101 rooms - $60-90
Pets: Welcome
Creature Comforts: CCTV, a/c,
refrig, micro, Jacuzzi, restaurant,
pool, sauna, whirlpool

Comfort Inn
(800) 228-5150, (605) 886-3010
http://www.comfortinn.com
800 - 35th St. Cir
60 rooms - $50-100
Pets: Welcome w/$10 fee
Creature Comforts: CCTV, a/c,
Jacuzzi, cont. brkfst, pool,
whirlpool

Guest House Inn
(605) 886-8061
101 North Broadway
57 rooms - $35-49
Pets: Welcome w/$20 deposit
Creature Comforts: CCTV, a/c,
refrig, restaurant, pool

Travel Host Motel
(605) 886-6120
1714 Ninth Ave. SW
31 rooms - $35-49
Pets: Welcome
Creature Comforts: CCTV, a/c

WEBSTER

Super 8
(800) 800-8000, (605) 345-4701
http://www.super8.com
Box 592
26 rooms - $35-47
Pets: Welcome w/permission
Creature Comforts: CCTV, a/c

WINNER

Buffalo Trail Motel
(800) 341-8000, (605) 842-2212
Rtes.18 & 44
30 rooms - $40-100
Pets: Welcome
Creature Comforts: CCTV, a/c

Super 8
(800) 800-8000, (605) 842-0991
http://www.super8.com
902 E. Route 44
25 rooms - $36-70
Pets: Welcome
Creature Comforts: CCTV,
VCR, a/c, cont. brkfst

Warrior Inn Motel
(800) 658-4705, (605) 842-3121
Rtes. 44 & 118
39 rooms - $40-55
Pets: Welcome
Creature Comforts: CCTV, a/c,
cont. brkfst, pool

YANKTON

Best Western Kelly Inn
(800) 528-1234, (605) 665-2906
http://www.bestwestern.com
1607 E. Route 50
123 rooms - $60-90
Pets: Welcome
Creature Comforts: CCTV, a/c,
Jacuzzi, restaurant, pool,
whirlpool, sauna, racquetball, hlth
club

Broadway Motel
(605) 665-7805
1210 Broadway St.
37 rooms - $50-65
Pets: Welcome w/$5 fee
Creature Comforts: CCTV, a/c,
restaurant, expanded cont. brkfst,
pool

Comfort Inn
(800) 228-5150, (605) 665-8053
http://www.comfortinn.com
2118 Broadway St.
45 rooms - $45-65
Pets: Welcome
Creature Comforts: CCTV, a/c,
whirlpool

Lewis and Clark Resort
(605) 665-2680
Route 52
35 rooms/cabins - $40-135
Pets: Welcome
Creature Comforts: CCTV,
VCR, a/c, kit

Super 8
(800) 800-8000, (605) 665-6510
http://www.super8.com
Route 4
58 rooms - $40-55
Pets: Welcome w/permission
Creature Comforts: CCTV, a/c

Best Western Yankton Inn
(605) 665-2906
1607 E. Rte. 50
123 rooms - $55-69
Pets: Welcome
Creature Comforts: CCTV,
VCR, a/c, refrig, micro, restaurant,
pool, hlth clb access, sauna,
whirlpool

Tennessee

ATHENS
Days Inn
(800) DAYS INN, (423) 745-5800
http://www.daysinn.com
2541 Decatur Pike
55 rooms - $40-59
Pets: Small pets welcome
Creature Comforts: CCTV, a/c,
refrig, micro, Jacuzzi

Homestead Inn East
(423) 744-9002
1827 Holiday Dr.
45 rooms - $30-54
Pets: Welcome
Creature Comforts: CCTV, a/c,
fireplace, kit, pool, whirlpool

Homestead Inn West
(423) 745-9002
2808 Decatur Pike
41 rooms - $40-59
Pets: Small pets w/$5 fee
Creature Comforts: CCTV, a/c,
kit, Jacuzzi, pool

Knights Inn
(800) 843-5644, (423) 744-8200
http://www.knightsinn.com
2620 Decatur Pike
90 rooms - $35-49
Pets: Small pets w/$3 fee
Creature Comforts: CCTV, a/c,
refrig, pool

Ramada Inn
(800) 2-Ramada, (423) 745-1212
http://www.ramada.com
115 Route 247
92 rooms - $50-89
Pets: Welcome
Creature Comforts: CCTV, a/c,
pool

Scottish Inns
(800) 251-1962, (423) 745-4880
http://www.reservahost.com
712 Congress Pkwy.
46 rooms - $30-59
Pets: Welcome w/$5 fee
Creature Comforts: CCTV, a/c,
refrig, micro, pool

Super 8 Motel
(800) 800-8000, (423) 745-4500
http://www.super8.com
2539 Decatur Pike
55 rooms - $35-55
Pets: Small pets welcome
Creature Comforts: CCTV, a/c,
refrig, micro, Jacuzzi, pool

BOLIVAR
The Boulivar Inn
(901) 658-3372
626 W. Market St.
40 rooms - $27-50
Pets: Small pets w/$5 fee
Creature Comforts: CCTV, a/c,
kit

BLOUNTVILLE
Super 8 Motel
(800) 800-8000, (423) 323-4155
http://www.super8.com
131 Airport Circle
92 rooms - $40-100
Pets: Welcome
Creature Comforts: CCTV, a/c,
restaurant, pool, hlth clb access

BRENTWOOD
Amerisuites
(800) 833-1515, (615) 661-9477
http://www.amerisuites.com
202 Summit View Dr.
126 rooms - $90-108
Pets: Small pets w/$10 fee
Creature Comforts: Panoramic
view, CCTV, VCR, a/c, kit, pool

Baymont Inn
(800) 4-Budget, (615) 376-4666
http://www.baymontinns.com
108 Westpark Rd.
92 rooms - $55-89
Pets: Small pets welcome
Creature Comforts: CCTV, a/c,
refrig, pool, hlth club

English Manor B&B
(888) 264-4690, (615) 373-4627
http://www.englishmanor.com
6304 Murray Rd.
7 rooms - $75-125
Pets: "Everything Suite" only
Creature Comforts: Bucolic
five-acre horse farm, Colonial
home w/country decor, wicker and
trad. furnishings, potted plants,
CCTV, VCR, a/c, fireplaces, full
brkfst, hand-made candy

Hilton Suites
(800) 445-8667, (615) 370-0111
http://www.hilton.com
9000 Overlook Blvd.
203 rooms - $100-145
Pets: Small pets welcome
Creature Comforts: CCTV,
VCR, a/c, refrig, micro, restaurant,
pool, hlth clb access, sauna,
whirlpool

Residence Inn by Marriott
(800) 331-3131 , (615) 371-0100
http://www.residenceinn.com
206 Ward Circle
110 rooms - $120-170
Pets: Welcome
Creature Comforts: Adjacent
small pond, CCTV, a/c, kit, pool,
hlth clb access, sports court,
whirlpool

BRISTOL
Days Inn
(800) DAYS INN, (423) 968-9119
http://www.daysinn.com
3281 State St.
88 rooms - $50-69
Pets: Welcome
Creature Comforts: CCTV, a/c,
refrig, pool

Hojo Inn
(800) I-Go-Hojo, (423) 968-9474
http://www.hojo.com
975 Volunteer Parkway
40 rooms - $50-135
Pets: Small pets w/$5 fee
Creature Comforts: CCTV,
VCR, a/c, pool

BROWNSVILLE

Best Western Travelers Inn
(800) 528-1234, (901) 779-2389
http://www.bestwestern.com
110 Sunny Hill Cove
44 rooms - $40-89
Pets: Small pets welcome
Creature Comforts: CCTV, a/c,
cont. brkfst, Jacuzzis

Days Inn
(800) DAYS INN, (901) 772-3297
http://www.daysinn.com
2530 Anderson Ave.
43 rooms - $45-67
Pets: Small pets w/$5 fee
Creature Comforts: CCTV, a/c

BUCHANAN

Cypress Bay Resort
(901) 232-8221
110 Cypress Resort Loop
9 cabins - $55-73
Pets: Welcome w/$5 fee
Creature Comforts: CCTV, a/c,
kit

Shamrock Resort
(800) 852-7885, (901) 232-8211
220 Shamrock Rd.
16 cottages - $50-69
Pets: Welcome
Creature Comforts: CCTV, a/c,
kit, pool, tennis

CAMDEN

**Birdsong Resort/Marina
Campground**
(800) 225-7469, (901) 584-7880
255 Marina Rd.
8 rooms - $50-150
Pets: Welcome w/$5 fee
Creature Comforts: CCTV, a/c,
fireplace, kit, pool, whirlpool

Passport Inn
(800) 238-6161, (901) 584-3111
http://www.reservahost.com
Route 70E
41 rooms - $40-70
Pets: Welcome
Creature Comforts: CCTV, a/c,
pool

CARYVILLE

Budget Host Inn
(800) Bud-Host, (423) 562-9595
http://www.budgethost.com
115 Woods Ave.
22 rooms - $25-40
Pets: Welcome
Creature Comforts: CCTV

Super 8 Motel
(800) 800-8000, (423) 562-8476
http://www.super8.com
200 John McGhee Blvd.
98 rooms - $40-69
Pets: Small pets w/$5 fee
Creature Comforts: CCTV, a/c,
and a pool

CELINA

Cedar Hill Resort
(800) 872-8393, (931) 243-3201
2371 Cedar Hill Rd.
26 rooms - $35-175
Pets: Welcome
Creature Comforts: a/c, kit,
restaurant, pool

CENTERVILLE

Bucksnort Travelodge
(800) 578-7878, (931) 729-5450
http://www.travelodge.com
Route 40
34 rooms - $35-76
Pets: Welcome W/$10 deposit
Creature Comforts: CCTV, a/c,
restaurant

Buffalo Inn
(800) 841-5813, (931) 296-7647
Route 40
80 rooms - $44-78
Pets: Dogs welcome w/deposit
Creature Comforts: CCTV, a/c.
cont. brkfst, restaurant, pool

CHATTANOOGA

Best Western Airport Inn
(800) 528-1234, (423) 894-1860
http://www.bestwestern.com
6650 Ringgold Rd.
123 rooms - $40-100
Pets: Small pets welcome
Creature Comforts: CCTV, a/c,
pool

Best Western Royal Inn
(800) 528-1234, (423) 821-6840
http://www.bestwestern.com
3644 Cummings Hwy
54 rooms - $45-120
Pets: Under 10 lbs. welcome
Creature Comforts: CCTV, a/c,
restaurant, cont. brkfst, pool

Comfort Inn
(800) 228-5150, (423) 894-5454
http://www.comfortinn.com
7717 Lee Hwy.
64 rooms - $65-89
Pets: Welcome w/$5 fee
Creature Comforts: CCTV, a/c,
refrig, micro, Jacuzzi, pool

Days Inn
(800) DAYS INN, (423) 821-6044
http://www.daysinn.com
3801 Cummings Hwy.
82 rooms - $40-78
Pets: Welcome w/$5 fee
Creature Comforts: CCTV, a/c,
cont. brkfst, and a pool

Holiday Inn Express
(800) HOLIDAY, (423) 490-8560
http://www.holiday-inn.com
7024 McCutcheon Rd.
51 rooms - $70-99
Pets: Small pets welcome
Creature Comforts: CCTV,
VCR, a/c, pool

Holiday Inn I-75 Airport
(800) HOLIDAY, (423) 855-2898
http://www.holiday-inn.com
2345 Shallowford Village
131 rooms - $70-97
Pets: Small pets welcome
Creature Comforts: CCTV, a/c,
refrig, restaurant, pool, hlth clb

Kings Lodge Motel
(800) 251-7702, (423) 698-8944
2400 Westside Dr.
162 rooms - $40-65
Pets: Small pets welcome
Creature Comforts: CCTV, a/c,
kit, restaurant, pool

La Quinta Inn
(800) 531-5900, (423) 855-0011
http://www.laquinta.com
7015 Shallowford Rd.
134 rooms - $55-90
Pets: Small pets welcome
Creature Comforts: CCTV, a/c,
refrig, cont brkfst, pool, hlth clb

Microtel
(888) 771-7171, (423) 510-0761
http://www.microtelinn.com
7014 McCutcheon Rd.
100 rooms - $40-65
Pets: Welcome
Creature Comforts: CCTV, a/c

Motel 6
(800) 466-8356, (423) 892-7707
http://www.motel6.com
7707 Lee Hwy.
97 rooms - $35-73
Pets: Under 30 lbs. welcome
Creature Comforts: CCTV, a/c,
cont. brkfst, pool

Ramada Inn South
(800) 2-Ramada, (423) 894-6110
http://www.ramada.com
6639 Capehart Lane
138 rooms - $44-89
Pets: Welcome w/$5 fee
Creature Comforts: CCTV, a/c,
Jacuzzis, restaurant, pool,
whirlpool

Red Roof Inn
(800) The Roof, (423) 899-0143
http://www.redroof.com
7014 Shallowford Rd.
112 rooms - $40-69
Pets: Small pets welcome
Creature Comforts: CCTV, a/c

Super 8 Motel
(800) 800-8000, (423) 892-3888
http://www.super8.com
1401 Mack Smith Rd.
260 rooms - $45-66
Pets: Welcome
Creature Comforts: CCTV, a/c,
kit, pool

CLARKSVILLE
A&W Motel
(931) 647-3545
1505 Madison St.
27 rooms - $25-49
Pets: Small, pets w/$5 fee
Creature Comforts: CCTV, a/c

Comfort Inn
(800) 228-5150, (931) 358-2020
http://www.comfortinn.com
1112 Route 76
95 rooms - $35-70
Pets: Welcome w/$4 fee
Creature Comforts: CCTV, a/c,
refrig, pool

Days Inn
(800) DAYS INN, (931) 358-3194
http://www.daysinn.com
1100 Hwy 76 Connector Rd.
84 rooms - $45-67
Pets: Welcome
Creature Comforts: CCTV, a/c,
refrig, micro, pool

Hachland Hill Inn
(931) 647-4084
1601 Madison St.
8 rooms - $70-110
Pets: Welcome w/$10 fee
Creature Comforts: Colonial inn
filled w/antiques, bedrooms w/
fireplaces, known for cozy guest
rms and fine food, beautiful
grounds

Holiday Inn
(800) HOLIDAY, (931) 648-4848
http://www.holiday-inn.com
3095 Wilma Rudolph Blvd.
144 rooms - $45-100
Pets: Welcome
Creature Comforts: CCTV,
VCR, a/c, refrig, restaurant, pool,
hlth clb access, sauna, whirlpool

Ramada Inn Riverview
(800) 2-Ramada, (931) 552-3331
http://www.ramada.com
50 College St.
155 rooms - $55-85
Pets: Welcome w/$25 deposit
Creature Comforts: CCTV, a/c,
refrig, Jacuzzi, pool, hlth clb
access, sauna, whirlpool

Ramada Limited
(800) 2-Ramada, (931) 552-0098
http://www.ramada.com
3100 Wilma Rudolph Blvd.
42 rooms - $45-70
Pets: Welcome
Creature Comforts: CCTV, a/c,
refrig, micro

Travelodge
(800) 578-7878, (931) 645-1400
http://www.travelodge.com
3075 Wilma Rudolph Blvd.
127 rooms - $45-64
Pets: Welcome
Creature Comforts: CCTV, a/c,
refrig, micro, restaurant, pool,
whirlpool

CLEVELAND
Baymont Inn
(800) 4-Budget, (423) 339-1000
http://www.baymontinns.com
107 Interstate Dr. NW
102 rooms - $65-70
Pets: Small pets welcome
Creature Comforts: CCTV, a/c,
refrig, micro, pool

Best Western Cleveland Inn
(800) 528-1234, (423) 472-5566
http://www.bestwestern.com
156 James Asberry Dr.
52 rooms - $55-100
Pets: Small pets w/$5 fee
Creature Comforts: CCTV, a/c,
kit, cont. brkfst, pool

Colonial Inn
(423) 472-6845
1555 - 25th St.
26 rooms - $25-39
Pets: Small pets welcome
Creature Comforts: CCTV, a/c

Days Inn
(800) DAYS INN, (423) 476-2112
http://www.daysinn.com
2550 Georgetown Rd.
57 rooms - $45-75
Pets: Welcome w/$5 fee
Creature Comforts: CCTV, a/c,
refrig, Jacuzzi, pool

Holiday Inn
(800) HOLIDAY, (423) 472-1504
http://www.holiday-inn.com
2400 Executive Park Dr.
146 rooms - $65-90
Pets: Welcome
Creature Comforts: CCTV, a/c,
refrig, restaurant, pool

Quality Inn
(800) 221-2222, (423) 476-8511
http://www.qualityinn.com
2595 Georgetown Rd.
96 rooms - $55-125
Pets: Small pets welcome
Creature Comforts: CCTV, a/c,
kit, restaurant, pool

Ramada Inn
(800) 2-Ramada, (423) 479-4531
http://www.ramada.com
Rtes 75 & 64
145 rooms - $45-75
Pets: Welcome
Creature Comforts: CCTV,
VCR, a/c, refrig, restaurant, pool

Red Carpet Inn
(800) 251-1962, (423) 476-6514
http://www.redcarpetinn.com
1501 - 25th St.
80 rooms - $25-49
Pets: Welcome
Creature Comforts: CCTV, a/c,
pool, whirlpool

COLLIERVILLE
Comfort Inn
(800) 228-5150, (901) 853-1235
http://www.comfortinn.com
1230 W. Poplar Rd.
95 rooms - $55-79
Pets: Welcome w/$10 nightly fee
and a $35 one-time cleaning fee
Creature Comforts: CCTV, a/c,
refrig, micro, Jacuzzis, pool

COLUMBIA
Econo Lodge
(800) 55-ECONO, (931) 381-1410
http://www.econolodge.com
1548 Bear Creek Pike
40 rooms - $45-75
Pets: Small pets welcome
Creature Comforts: CCTV, a/c,
Jacuzzi

James J. Polk Motel
(931) 388-4913
1111 Nashville Hwy.
50 rooms - $35-49
Pets: Small pets w/$5 fee
Creature Comforts: CCTV, a/c,
refrig, pool

Ramada Inn
(800) 2-Ramada, (931) 388-2720
http://www.ramada.com
1208 Nashville Hwy.
155 rooms - $45-85
Pets: Small pets welcome
Creature Comforts: CCTV, a/c,
refrig, micro, restaurant, pool

COOKEVILLE
Alpine Lodge
(931) 526-3333
2021 E. Spring St.
65 rooms - $35-54
Pets: In certain rooms w/$5 fee
Creature Comforts: CCTV, a/c,
refrig, Jacuzzis, cont brkfst, pool

Best Western Thunderbird
(800) 528-1234, (931) 526-7115
http://www.bestwestern.com
900 S. Jefferson Rd.
60 rooms - $40-69
Pets: Welcome
Creature Comforts: CCTV,
VCR, a/c, refrig, pool

Days Inn
(800) DAYS INN, (931) 528-1511
http://www.daysinn.com
1292 Bunker Hill Rd.
100 rooms - $40-69
Pets: Small pets w/$10 deposit
Creature Comforts: CCTV,
VCR, a/c, refrig, Jacuzzi, pool

Eastwood Inn
(931) 526-6158
1646 E. Spring St.
20 rooms - $30-39
Pets: Welcome w/$5 fee
Creature Comforts: CCTV, a/c,
kit, pool

Hampton Inn
(800) Hampton, (931) 520-1117
http://www.hampton-inn.com
340 Interstate Dr.
65 rooms - $55-85
Pets: Welcome
Creature Comforts: CCTV, a/c,
refrig, Jacuzzi, pool, whirlpool

Holiday Inn
(800) HOLIDAY, (931) 526-7125
http://www.holiday-inn.com
970 S. Jefferson
200 rooms - $65-99
Pets: Welcome
Creature Comforts: CCTV, a/c,
refrig, micro, restaurant, pool, hlth
clb access, whirlpool

Howard Johnson Motor Lodge
(800) I-Go-Hojo, (931) 526-3333
http://www.hojo.com
2021 E. Spring St.
64 rooms - $40-79
Pets: Welcome w/$5 fee
Creature Comforts: CCTV,
VCR, a/c, refrig, Jacuzzi, pool,
whirlpool

Star Motor Inn
(800) 842-1685, (931) 526-9511
1115 S. Willow Ave.
79 rooms - $35-55
Pets: Welcome
Creature Comforts: CCTV, a/c,
restaurant, pool

CORDOVA
Best Suites of America
(877) 877-6810, (901) 386-4600
http://www.bestinn.com
8166 Varnavas Dr.
102 rooms - $75-105
Pets: Small pets welcome
Creature Comforts: CCTV,
VCR, a/c, refrig, micro, Jacuzzi,
pool, hlth clb access, whirlpool

CORNERSVILLE
Econo Lodge
(800) 55-ECONO, (931) 293-2111
http://www.econolodge.com
3731 Pulaski Hwy.
40 rooms - $39-55
Pets: Welcome w/$5 fee
Creature Comforts: CCTV, a/c,
and a pool

COVINGTON
Best Western Inn
(800) 528-1234, (901) 476-8561
http://www.bestwestern.com
873 Rte. 51 N
73 rooms - $45-68
Pets: Small pets welcome
Creature Comforts: CCTV, a/c,
kit, pool

CROSSVILLE
Days Inn
(800) DAYS INN, (931) 484-9691
http://www.daysinn.com
3114 N. Main St.
61 rooms - $50-65
Pets: Welcome
Creature Comforts: CCTV, a/c,
restaurant, pool

Ramada Inn
(800) 2-Ramada, (931) 484-7581
http://www.ramada.com
Route 127
137 rooms - $60-99
Pets: Small pets welcome
Creature Comforts: CCTV, a/c,
restaurant, pool

Scottish Inns
(800) 251-1962, (931) 484-8122
http://www.reservahost.com
3406 N. Main St.
24 rooms - $30-53
Pets: Small petsw/$10 deposit
Creature Comforts: CCTV, a/c

Villager Lodge Motel
(800) 972-4061, (931) 484-7561
70 Burnett St.
146 rooms - $30-49
Pets: Welcome
Creature Comforts: CCTV, a/c

CUMBERLAND GAP
Cumberland Gap Inn
(423) 869-9172
630 Brooklyn St.
31 rooms - $70-89
Pets: Small pets w/$15 fee
Creature Comforts: CCTV, a/c,
refrig, micro, Jacuzzi, pool

Holiday Inn
(800) HOLIDAY, (423) 869-3631
http://www.holiday-inn.com
US Hwy 25E
147 rooms - $55-89
Pets: Welcome w/$25 fee
Creature Comforts: CCTV, a/c,
refrig, micro, Jacuzzi, restaurant,
pool, whirlpool

DANDRIDGE
Mountain Harbor Inn
(865) 397-3345
http://mountainharborinn.com
1199 Hwy 139
12 rooms - $60-135
Pets: Welcome w/$8 deposit
Creature Comforts: Lakeside
setting w/mountain views, inn rms
w/antiques, handmade quilts,
CCTV, a/c, kit, full brkfst, fine
dining, boat dock, porches

Tennessee Mountain Inn
(800) 235-9440, (865) 397-9437
531 Patriot Dr.
89 rooms - $40-109
Pets: Small pets-$ 10 fee, $10 dep
Creature Comforts: CCTV, a/c,
Jacuzzi, pool, whirlpool

DAYTON
Best Western Dayton Inn
(800) 528-1234, (423) 775-6560
http://www.bestwestern.com
7835 Rhea County Hwy.
81 rooms - $45-119
Pets: Small pets w/$5 fee
Creature Comforts: CCTV,
VCR, a/c, kit, Jacuzzis, restaurant,
pool, hlth clb access, whirlpool

Days Inn
(800) DAYS INN, (423) 775-9718
http://www.daysinn.com
3914 Rhea City Hwy.
25 rooms - $45-89
Pets: Small pets w/$5 fee
Creature Comforts: CCTV, a/c,
kit, cont. brkfst, Jacuzzi

DENMARK
Econo Lodge
(800) 55-ECONO, (901) 427-2778
http://www.econolodge.com
196 Providence Rd.
53 rooms - $49-75
Pets: Welcome w/$5 fee
Creature Comforts: CCTV,
VCR, a/c, cont. brkfst

DICKSON
Comfort Inn
(800) 228-5150, (615) 446-2423
http://www.comfortinn.com
2325 Rte. 46S
51 rooms - $45-75
Pets: Small pets w/$5 fee
Creature Comforts: CCTV, a/c,
refrig, micro, Jacuzzis

Days Inn
(800) DAYS INN, (615) 446-7561
http://www.daysinn.com
Rtes. 46 & 40
67 rooms - $40-99
Pets: Welcome w/$5 fee
Creature Comforts: CCTV, a/c,
cont. brkfst, pool

Holiday Inn
(800) HOLIDAY, (615) 446-9081
http://www.holiday-inn.com
2420 Rte. 46 S.
110 rooms - $60-79
Pets: Welcome
Creature Comforts: CCTV, a/c,
refrig, micro, restaurant, pool, and
a hlth club

DYERSBURG
Days Inn
(800) DAYS INN, (901) 287-0888
http://www.daysinn.com
2600 Lake Rd.
59 rooms - $40-69
Pets: Small pets welcome
Creature Comforts: CCTV, a/c,
refrig, micro

ELKTON
Economy Inn
(931) 468-2594
Rte. 65 & Bryson Rd.
20 rooms - $29-56
Pets: Welcome
Creature Comforts: CCTV, a/c

FARRAGUT
Baymont Inns
(800) 789-4103, (423) 671-1010
http://www.baymontinns.com
11341 Campbell Lakes Dr.
100 rooms - $60-99
Pets: Welcome
Creature Comforts: CCTV, a/c,
refrig, micro, pool, hlth clb access,
sauna

FAYETTEVILLE
Best Western Fayetteville Inn
(800) 528-1234, (931) 433-0100
http://www.bestwestern.com
3021 Thornton Taylor Pkwy.
64 rooms - $55-90
Pets: Small pets welcome
Creature Comforts: CCTV, a/c,
refrig, micro, restaurant, pool, hlth
clb access

Days Inn
(800) DAYS INN, (931) 433-6121
http://www.daysinn.com
1651 Huntsville Hwy.
51 rooms - $40-79
Pets: Welcome
Creature Comforts: CCTV, a/c,
restaurant, pool

FRANKLIN
Amerisuites
(800) 833-1515, (615) 771-8900
http://www.amerisuites.com
650 Bakers Bridge Ave.
125 rooms - $95-129
Pets: Small pets welcome
Creature Comforts: CCTV, a/c,
cont. brkfst, pool, hlth club

Baymont Inns
(800) 789-4103, (615) 791-7700
http://www.baymontinns.com
4207 Franklin Commons Court
106 rooms - $55-89
Pets: Small pets welcome
Creature Comforts: CCTV, a/c,
refrig, micro, pool, whirlpool

Best Western Franklin Inn
(800) 528-1234, (615) 790-0570
http://www.bestwestern.com
1308 Murfreesboro Rd.
142 rooms - $55-79
Pets: Small pets welcome
Creature Comforts: CCTV, a/c,
pool

Comfort Inn
(800) 228-5150, (615) 791-6675
http://www.comfortinn.com
4206 Franklin Commons Court
59 rooms - $60-99
Pets: Small pets welcome
Creature Comforts: CCTV, a/c,
Jacuzzi, pool

Days Inn
(800) DAYS INN, (615) 790-1140
http://www.daysinn.com
4217 S. Carothers Rd.
60 rooms - $50-95
Pets: Small pets w/$5 fee
Creature Comforts: CCTV, a/c,
refrig, micro, Jacuzzis

Goosecreek Inn
(615) 794-7200
2404 Goose Creek
82 rooms - $45-65
Pets: Welcome
Creature Comforts: CCTV, a/c,
pool

Holiday Inn Express
(800) HOLIDAY, (615) 794-7591
http://www.holiday-inn.com
4202 Franklin Commons Ct.
98 rooms - $77-126
Pets: Welcome w/$15 fee
Creature Comforts: CCTV, a/c,
cont brkfst, pool, hlth clb access

Namaste Acres Country Ranch
(615) 791-0333
http://www.bbonline.com/tn/
namaste/
5436 Leipers Creek Road
4 suites - $75-85
Pets: Small pets welcome
Creature Comforts: Horse ranch
in scenic Leipers Fork valley,
interesting theme suites in log
cabin or lodge w/western
memorabilia, handcarved beds and
furniture, CCTV, VCR/CD, claw
foot tubs, refrig, country brkfst,
deck, rock garden, horseback
riding, pool, hot tub, pond-fishing

GALLATIN
Shoney's Inn
(800) 222-2222, (615) 452-5433
221 W. Main St.
86 rooms - $40-59
Pets: Welcome
Creature Comforts: CCTV, a/c,
restaurant, pool

GATLINBURG
Alto Motel
(423) 436-5175
404 Airport Rd.
22 rooms - $60-85
Pets: Welcome
Creature Comforts: CCTV, a/c,
refrig, restaurant

Bon Air Mountain Inn
(800) 848-4857, (423) 436-4857
950 Parkway Rd.
74 rooms - $45-95
Pets: Welcome
Creature Comforts: CCTV, a/c,
restaurant, pool, whirlpool

Grandview Inn
(800) 578-4330, (423) 436-3161
www.grandviewgatlinburg.com
335 E. Holly Ridge
8 cottages - $85-135
Pets: Welcome in two cottages
Creature Comforts: Knotty pine
cottages, festive country decor,
floral fabrics, CCTV, a/c,
fireplaces, kit, Jacuzzis, balcony,
pool, hot tub

Highland Motor Inn
(800) 635-8874, (423) 436-4110
131 Parkway Rd.
46 rooms - $30-85
Pets: Welcome w/$5 fee
Creature Comforts: CCTV,
VCR, a/c, refrig, micro, pool

Holiday Inn Resort
(800) HOLIDAY, (423) 436-9201
http://www.holiday-inn.com
520 Airport Rd.
402 rooms - $50-250
Pets: Welcome
Creature Comforts: CCTV, a/c,
restaurant, pool, hlth clb access,
whirlpool, golf, tennis

Margie's Chalets
(800) 264-9475, (423) 436-9475
http://www.thesmokies.com/
margies_chalets
P.O. Box 288
21 chalets - $90-105
Pets: "Your pet deserves a
vacation, even if you have two,"
welcome w/$25 deposit
Creature Comforts: Mtn. view
Chalets, og cabins, CCTV, a/c,
stone fireplace, charming decor,
full kit, Jacuzzi, pool, hot tub

Microtel
(888) 771-7171, (423) 436-0107
http://www.microtelinn.com
211 Airport Rd.
102 rooms - $40-90
Pets: Small pets welcome
Creature Comforts: CCTV, a/c

Ramada Limited
(800) 2-Ramada, (865) 436-7881
http://www.ramada.com
756 Parkway Rd.
154 rooms - $80-129
Pets: Welcome
Creature Comforts: CCTV, a/c,
fireplace, refrig, restaurant, pool

River Terrace Resort
(800) 251-2040, (865) 436-5161
http://www.riverterrace.com
240 River Rd.
205 rooms - $59-135
Pets: Welcome w/$50 deposit
Creature Comforts: CCTV,
VCR, a/c, refrig, fireplaces,
Jacuzzis, cont. brkfst, restaurant,
pool, whirlpool, traditional rooms
& log cabins, riverside-fishing

GERMANTOWN

Best Inns of America
(877) 877-6810, (901) 757-7800
http://www.bestinn.com
873 Rte. 51 N
80 rooms - $60-85
Pets: Small pets welcome
Creature Comforts: CCTV,
VCR, a/c, refrig, pool, whirlpool

Hometown Suites
(901) 751-2500
7855 Wolf River Parkway
92 rooms - $100-125
Pets: Welcome w/$100 fee
Creature Comforts: CCTV, a/c,
kit, pool, hlth clb, sports court

GOODLETTSVILLE

Baymont Inns
(800) 4-Budget, (615) 851-1891
http://www.baymontinns.com
120 Cartwright Court
102 rooms - $60-95
Pets: Small pets welcome
Creature Comforts: CCTV, a/c,
refrig, micro

Econo Lodge Rivergate
(800) 55-ECONO, (615) 859-4988
http://www.econolodge.com
320 Long Hollow Pike
107 rooms - $40-69
Pets: Small pets welcome
Creature Comforts: CCTV, a/c,
kit, pool

Motel 6
(800) 4-MOTEL6, (615) 859-9674
http://www.motel6.com
323 Cartwright St.
94 rooms - $35-56
Pets: Under 30 lbs.
Creature Comforts: CCTV, a/c,
pool

Red Roof Inn
(800) The Roof, (615) 859-2537
http://www.redroof.com
110 Northgate Dr.
109 rooms - $45-69
Pets: Small pets welcome
Creature Comforts: CCTV, a/c

Rodeway Inn
(800) 228-2000, (615) 859-1416
650 Wade Circle
30 rooms - $35-59
Pets: Small pets w/$5 fee
Creature Comforts: CCTV, a/c,
pool

GREENEVILLE

Days Inn
(800) DAYS INN, (423) 639-2156
http://www.daysinn.com
935 E. Andrew Johnson Hwy.
60 rooms - $35-89
Pets: Welcome w/$10 nightly fee
Creature Comforts: CCTV, a/c,
kit

HAMPSHIRE

**Natchez Trace B&B
Reservation Service**
(800) 377-2770, (615) 285-2777
http://www.bbonline.com/
natcheztrace
P.O. Box 193
25 B&Bs - $50-150
Pets: Welcome in certain B&Bs
Creature Comforts: 25 B&Bs
along Natchez Trace, Nashville,
Leiper's Fork, Franklin, Fairview,
Hohenwald, Columbia south to
Natchez, MS; CCTV, a/c,
fireplace, full brkfst

Ridgetop B&B
(800) 377-2770, (615) 285-2777
http://www.bbonline.com/ridgetop
Route 412
3 Cottage/cabin - $75-90
Pets: Welcome
Creature Comforts: Contemp.
home set on 170 acres, antique
furnishings, 1830 log cabin,
CCTV, a/c, fireplace, kit, country
decor-quilts, full brkfst, hiking
trails, pond, patio

HARRIMAN

Best Western Sundancer
(800) 528-1234, (423) 882-6200
http://www.bestwestern.com
120 Childs Rd.
50 rooms - $45-90
Pets: Small pets w/$2 fee
Creature Comforts: CCTV, a/c,
hlth clb access

Holiday Inn
(800) HOLIDAY, (423) 882-5340
http://www.holiday-inn.com
1845 S. Roane St.
49 rooms - $50-75
Pets: Welcome
Creature Comforts: CCTV, a/c,
pool

Super 8 Motel
(800) 800-8000, (423) 882-6600
http://www.super8.com
1867 S. Roane St.
48 rooms - $30-69
Pets: Welcome
Creature Comforts: CCTV, a/c,
pool

HERMITAGE

Hermitage Inn
(615) 883-7444
4144 Lebanon Rd.
70 rooms - $35-69
Pets: Small pets welcome
Creature Comforts: CCTV, a/c,
refrig, micro, pool

Ramada Ltd. Airport
(800) 2-Ramada, (615) 889-8940
http://www.ramada.com
5770 Old Hickory Blvd.
100 rooms - $40-79
Pets: Small pets w/$5 fee
Creature Comforts: CCTV, a/c,
Jacuzzi, pool

HUNTSVILLE

Holiday Inn Express
(800) HOLIDAY, (423) 663-4100
http://www.holiday-inn.com
11597 Scott Hwy.
49 rooms - $50-75
Pets: Small pets welcome
Creature Comforts: CCTV, a/c,
and a pool

HURRICANE MILLS

Best Western Inn
(800) 228-1234, (931) 296-4251
http://www.bestwestern.com
Rtes. 40 & 13
89 rooms - $40-110
Pets: Welcome
Creature Comforts: CCTV, a/c,
restaurant, pool

Days Inn
(800) DAYS INN, (931) 296-7647
http://www.daysinn.com
15415 Rte. 13S
78 rooms - $40-69
Pets: Welcome
Creature Comforts: CCTV, a/c,
restaurant, pool

667

Holiday Inn Express
(800) HOLIDAY, (931) 296-2999
http://www.holiday-inn.com
15368 Route 13
50 rooms - $50-75
Pets: Small pets welcome
Creature Comforts: CCTV, a/c,
Jacuzzis, pool

Super 8 Motel
(800) 800-8000, (931) 296-2432
http://www.super8.com
Rtes. 40 & 13
44 rooms - $30-59
Pets: Welcome
Creature Comforts: CCTV, a/c,
pool

JACKSON
Baymont Inn
(800) 4-Budget, (901) 664-1800
http://www.baymontinns.com
2370 N. Highland Ave.
102 rooms - $45-85
Pets: Small pets welcome
Creature Comforts: CCTV, a/c,
refrig, micro, pool

Best Western Old Hickory Inn
(800) 528-1234, (901) 668-4222
http://www.bestwestern.com
1849 RTe. 45 bypass
144 rooms - $50-89
Pets: Welcome
Creature Comforts: CCTV, a/c,
refrig, micro, Jacuzzi, restaurant,
pool

Days Inn
(800) DAYS INN, (901) 668-3444
http://www.daysinn.com
1919 Rte. 45 bypass
120 rooms - $35-85
Pets: Welcome
Creature Comforts: CCTV, a/c,
pool

Days Inn-West
(800) DAYS INN, (901) 668-4840
http://www.daysinn.com
2239 Hollywood Dr.
95 rooms - $45-79
Pets: Welcome
Creature Comforts: CCTV, a/c,
kit, pool

Garden Plaza Hotel
(800) 3-Garden, (901) 664-6900
1770 Route 45 Bypass
168 rooms - $80-119
Pets: Welcome
Creature Comforts: CCTV, a/c,
cont. brkfst, pool, whirlpool, and a
hlth clb

Super 8 Motel
(800) 800-8000, (901) 668-1145
http://www.super8.com
2295 N. Highland Ave.
95 rooms - $45-70
Pets: Welcome
Creature Comforts: CCTV, a/c,
cont. brkfst, hlth clb access

Travelers Motel
(901) 668-0542
2247 N. Highland Ave.
21 rooms - $30-79
Pets: Welcome
Creature Comforts: CCTV, a/c

JELLICO
Best Western Holiday Plaza
(800) 528-1234, (423) 784-7241
http://www.bestwestern.com
133 Holiday Plaza Dr.
50 rooms - $35-86
Pets: Small pets welcome
Creature Comforts: CCTV, a/c,
restaurant, pool

Days Inn
(800) DAYS INN, (423) 784-7281
http://www.daysinn.com
Rtes. 75 & 25 W.
128 rooms - $50-89
Pets: Welcome w/$4 fee
Creature Comforts: CCTV, a/c,
restaurant, pool, playground

JOHNSON CITY
Comfort Inn
(800) 228-5150, (423) 928-9600
http://www.comfortinn.com
1900 S. Roan St.
43 rooms - $60-140
Pets: Welcome w/$40 deposit
Creature Comforts: CCTV, a/c,
refrig, micro, Jacuzzi, pool

Days Inn
(800) DAYS INN, (423) 282-2211
http://www.daysinn.com
2312 Browns Mill Rd.
102 rooms - $50-85
Pets: Welcome w/$15 fee
Creature Comforts: CCTV, a/c,
refrig, micro, Jacuzzi, pool

Garden Plaza Hotel
(800) 342-7336, (423) 929-2000
211 Mockingbird Lane
187 rooms - $90-135
Pets: Welcome
Creature Comforts: CCTV,
VCR, a/c, refrig, restaurant, pool,
hlth clb access, whirlpool

Holiday Inn
(800) HOLIDAY, (423) 282-4611
http://www.holiday-inn.com
101 W. Springbrook Dr.
205 rooms - $80-115
Pets: Small pets welcome
Creature Comforts: CCTV,
VCR, a/c, refrig, restaurant, pool,
hlth clb access

Red Roof Inn
(800) The Roof, (423) 282-3040
http://www.redroof.com
210 Broyles Dr.
115 rooms - $40-84
Pets: Small pets welcome
Creature Comforts: CCTV, a/c,
hlth clb access

Super 8 Motel
(800) 800-8000, (423) 282-8818
http://www.super8.com
108 Wesley St.
63 rooms - $45-85
Pets: Welcome
Creature Comforts: CCTV, a/c

KIMBALL
Days Inn
(800) DAYS INN, (423) 837-7933
http://www.daysinn.com
130 Main St.
100 rooms - $47-79
Pets: Welcome w/$6 fee
Creature Comforts: CCTV, a/c,
cont. brkfst, pool

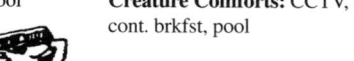

KINGSPORT

Comfort Inn
(800) 228-5150, (423) 378-4418
http://www.comfortinn.com
100 Indian Center Court
122 rooms - $65-150
Pets: Welcome w/$8 fee
Creature Comforts: CCTV,
VCR, a/c, refrig, Jacuzzi, pool,
hlth clb access, sauna, whirlpool

Econo Lodge
(800) 55-ECONO, (423) 245-0286
http://www.econolodge.com
1704 E. Stone Dr.
48 rooms - $40-72
Pets: Welcome
Creature Comforts: CCTV, a/c

La Quinta Inn
(800) 531-5900, (423) 323-0500
http://www.laquinta.com
10150 Airport Parkway
118 rooms - $55-90
Pets: Small pets welcome
Creature Comforts: CCTV, a/c,
refrig, pool, hlth clb access

Microtel
(888) 771-7171, (423) 378-9220
http://www.microtelinn.com
1708 E. Stone Dr.
87 rooms - $40-80
Pets: Welcome w/$10 fee
Creature Comforts: CCTV, a/c,
refrig, micro, hlth clb access

KINGSTON

Days Inn
(800) DAYS INN, (423) 376-2069
http://www.daysinn.com
495 Gallagher Rd.
42 rooms - $40-75
Pets: Welcome w/$5 fee
Creature Comforts: CCTV, a/c,
refrig, pool

KINGSTON SPRINGS

Best Western Harpeth Inn
(800) 528-1234, (615) 952-3961
http://www.bestwestern.com
116 Luy Ben Hills Rd.
44 rooms - $60-90
Pets: Welcome w/$10 fee
Creature Comforts: CCTV, a/c,
refrig, micro, pool

Econo Lodge
(800) 55-ECONO, (615) 952-2900
http://www.econolodge.com
123 Luyben Hills Rd.
26 rooms - $35-79
Pets: Welcome
Creature Comforts: CCTV, a/c,
restaurant, pool

Scottish Inns
(800) 251-1962, (615) 952-3115
http://www.reservahost.com
116 Luyben Hills Rd.
25 rooms - $35-69
Pets: Welcome w/$4 fee
Creature Comforts: CCTV, a/c

KNOXVILLE

Baymont Inns
(800) 789-4103, (865) 671-1010
http://www.baymontinns.com
I40/75 at Campbell Station Rd.
100 rooms - $50-99
Pets: Welcome
Creature Comforts: CCTV, a/c,
pool, hlth clb access

Best Western Inn
(800) 528-1234, (865) 675-7666
http://www.bestwestern.com
500 Lovell Rd.
104 rooms - $45-75
Pets: Welcome w/$8 fee
Creature Comforts: CCTV, a/c,
refrig, micro, pool, hlth clb access

Days Inn-Conference Center
(800) DAYS INN, (865) 687-5800
http://www.daysinn.com
5335 Central Ave. Pike
110 rooms - $55-90
Pets: Small pets w/$5 fee
Creature Comforts: CCTV, a/c,
refrig, restaurant, pool

Days Inn-West
(800) DAYS INN, (865) 966-5801
http://www.daysinn.com
200 Lovell Rd.
120 rooms - $45-85
Pets: Small pets w/$6 fee
Creature Comforts: CCTV, a/c,
refrig, pool

Hampton Inn
(800) 426-7866, (865) 689-1101
http://www.hampton-inn.com
9128 Executive Park
180 rooms - $60-90
Pets: Under 25 Lbs. welcome
Creature Comforts: CCTV, a/c,
refrig, pool, hlth club

Holiday Inn-West
(800) HOLIDAY, (865) 584-3911
http://www.holiday-inn.com
1315 Kirby Rd.
242 rooms - $80-125
Pets: Small pets welcome
Creature Comforts: CCTV, a/c,
refrig, micro, restaurant, pool, hlth
clb access, whirlpool

Howard Johnson Motor Lodge
(800) I-Go-Hojo, (865) 688-3141
http://www.hojo.com
118 Merchant Dr.
213 rooms - $70-95
Pets: Welcome w/$25 deposit
Creature Comforts: CCTV, a/c,
refrig, micro, pool, whirlpool

Hyatt Hotel
(800) 233-1234, (865) 637-1234
http://www.hyatt.com
500 Hill Ave. SE
384 rooms - $125-399
Pets: Small pets w/$35 fee
Creature Comforts: CCTV, a/c,
restaurant, pool, hlth clb, sauna

La Quinta Inn
(800) 531-5900, (865) 690-9777
http://www.laquinta.com
258 Peters Rd. N.
123 rooms - $55-95
Pets: Welcome
Creature Comforts: CCTV, a/c,
refrig, pool, hlth clb access

Microtel
(888) 771-7171, (865) 531-8041
http://www.microtelinn.com
309 N. Peters Rd.
105 rooms - $45-85
Pets: Welcome
Creature Comforts: CCTV, a/c

Motel 6
(800) 4-MOTEL6, (865) 675-7200
http://www.motel6.com
402 Lovell Rd.
113 rooms - $40-84
Pets: Small pets welcome
Creature Comforts: CCTV, pool

Quality Inn North
(800) 221-2222, (865) 689-6600
http://www.qualityinn.com
6712 Central Ave. Pike
129 rooms - $45-80
Pets: Small pets w/$5 fee
Creature Comforts: CCTV, a/c,
Jacuzzi, restaurant, pool

Ramada Limited
(800) 2-Ramada, (865) 456-7271
http://www.ramada.com
722 Breakbill Rd.
61 rooms - $40-95
Pets: Welcome w/$20 deposit
Creature Comforts: CCTV, a/c,
pool, whirlpool

Red Roof Inn, North
(800) The Roof, (865) 689-7100
http://www.redroof.com
5640 Merchant Center Blvd.
84 rooms - $40-75
Pets: Small pets welcome
Creature Comforts: CCTV, a/c,
hlth clb access

Red Roof Inn-West
(800) The Roof, (865) 691-1664
http://www.redroof.com
209 Advantage Place
115 rooms - $40-69
Pets: Small pets welcome
Creature Comforts: CCTV, a/c

Rodeway Inn
(800) 228-2000, (865) 687-3500
6730 Central Ave. Pike
92 rooms - $30-$65
Pets: Welcome w/$6 fee
Creature Comforts: CCTV, a/c,
restaurant, pool

Scottish Inns
(800) 251-1962, (865) 693-6061
http://www.reservahost.com
9340 Park West Blvd.
45 rooms - $40-80
Pets: Welcome
Creature Comforts: CCTV, a/c,
pool

Scottish Inns, North
(800) 251-1962, (865) 689-7777
http://www.reservahost.com
301 Callahan Dr.
40 rooms - $35-75
Pets: Welcome
Creature Comforts: CCTV, a/c,
cont. brkfst, pool

Super 8 Motel
(800) 800-8000, (865) 584-8511
http://www.super8.com
6200 Papermill Rd.
139 rooms - $35-65
Pets: Welcome
Creature Comforts: CCTV, a/c,
kit, pool, whirlpool

LAKE CITY
The Lamb's Inn
(423) 426-2171
602 N. Main St.
34 rooms - $30-45
Pets: Welcome
Creature Comforts: CCTV, a/c,
cont. brkfst, pool

LAKELAND
Super 8 Motel
(800) 800-8000, (901) 372-4575
http://www.super8.com
9779 Huff Puff Rd.
75 rooms - $35-65
Pets: Welcome w/$5 fee
Creature Comforts: CCTV, a/c,
cont. brkfst, pool, whirlpool

LAWRENCEBURG
Best Western Inn
(800) 528-1234, (931) 762-4448
http://www.bestwestern.com
2126 N. Locust Ave.
48 rooms - $50-89
Pets: Small pets welcome
Creature Comforts: CCTV, a/c,
cont. brkfst, pool

LEBANON
Comfort Inn
(800) 228-5150, (615) 444-1001
http://www.comfortinn.com
829 S. Cumberland St.
74 rooms - $40-73
Pets: Welcome w/$5 fee
Creature Comforts: CCTV, a/c,
refrig, Jacuzzi, pool, hlth clb, and
a sauna

Days Inn
(800) DAYS INN, (615) 444-5635
http://www.daysinn.com
231 Murfreesboro Rd.
52 rooms - $35-55
Pets: Welcome w/$5 fee
Creature Comforts: beachfront,
CCTV, a/c, refrig, Jacuzzi, pool

Hampton Inn
(800) 426-7866,(615) 444-7400
http://www.hampton-inn.com
704 S. Cumberland
87 rooms - $55-99
Pets: Small pets welcome
Creature Comforts: CCTV, a/c,
refrig, micro, Jacuzzi, pool, sauna,
whirlpool

Super 8
(800) 800-8000, (614) 444-5637
http://www.super8.com
914 Murfreesboro Rd.
48 rooms - $35-50
Pets: Welcome w/$5 fee
Creature Comforts: CCTV, a/c,
refrig, Jacuzzi, pool

LOUDON
Holiday Inn Express
(800) HOLIDAY, (423) 458-5668
http://www.holiday-inn.com
12452 Hwy 72N
52 rooms - $50-70
Pets: Small pets welcome
Creature Comforts: CCTV, a/c,
pool

Knights Inn
(800) 843-5644, (423) 458-5855
http://www.knightsinn.com
15100 Hwy 72
44 rooms - $35-65
Pets: Small pets w/$3 fee
Creature Comforts: CCTV, a/c,
refrig, pool

MADISON
Rodeway Inn
(800) 228-2000, (615) 865-2323
http://www.rodeway.com
625 N. Gallatin Rd.
30 rooms - $45-66
Pets: Welcome w/$4 fee
Creature Comforts: CCTV, a/c,
cont. brkfst, pool

MANCHESTER
Ambassador Inn
(800) 237-9228, (931) 728-2200
Rte. 6
153 rooms - $35-75
Pets: Welcome
Creature Comforts: CCTV, a/c,
refrig, pool, hlth clb access

Days Inn
(800) DAYS INN, (615) 728-6023
http://www.daysinn.com
890 Interstate Dr.
51 rooms - $40-50
Pets: Welcome w/$3 fee
Creature Comforts: CCTV, a/c,
refrig, Jacuzzi, pool

Hampton Inn
(800) Hampton, (615) 728-3300
http://www.hampton-inn.com
I-24 Hwy 53
54 rooms- $60-70
Pets: Welcome
Creature Comforts: CCTV, a/c,
Jacuzzi, cont. brkfst, pool

Holiday Inn
(800) HOLIDAY, (615) 728-9651
http://www.holiday-inn.com
126 Expressway Dr.
141 rooms - $55
Pets: Welcome
Creature Comforts: CCTV, a/c,
refrig, micro, restaurant

Ramada Inn
(800) 2-Ramada, (615) 728-0800
http://www.ramada.com
2314 Hillsboro Highway
80 rooms - $40-85
Pets: Welcome w/$5 fee
Creature Comforts: CCTV, a/c,
refrig, Jacuzzi, restaurant, pool

Scottish Inns
(800) 251-1962, (615) 728-0506
http://www.reservahost.com
2457 Hillsboro Hwy
92 rooms - $30-55
Pets: Welcome w/$4 fee
Creature Comforts: CCTV, a/c,
kit, pool

Super 8 Motel
(800) 800-8000, (615) 728-9720
http://www.super8.com
2430 Hillsboro Hwy.
50 rooms - $40-75
Pets: Small pets welcome
Creature Comforts: CCTV, a/c,
refrig, Jacuzzi, pool

MARTIN
University Lodge
(800) 748-9480, (901) 587-9577
Rtes. 43 & 431 (University St.)
56 rooms - $45-75
Pets: Welcome w$10 fee
Creature Comforts: CCTV, a/c,
restaurant, pool

McKENZIE
Briarwood Inn
(901) 352-1083
16180 N. Highland Dr.
28 rooms - $34-68
Pets: Welcome
Creature Comforts: CCTV, a/c,
and a pool

McKenzie Motor Inn
(901) 352-3325
121 Highland Dr.
43 rooms - $30-54
Pets: Welcome w/$2 fee
Creature Comforts: CCTV, pool

McMINNVILLE
Scottish Inns
(800) 251-1962, (931) 473-2181
http://www.reservahost.com
1105 Sparta St.
35 rooms - $30-68
Pets: Welcome
Creature Comforts: CCTV, a/c,
pool

Shoney's Inn
(800) 222-2222, (931) 473-4446
508 Sunnyside Heights
61 rooms - $40-85
Pets: Small pets welcome
Creature Comforts: CCTV, a/c,
cont. brkfst, refrig, micro, pool

MEMPHIS
Amerisuites
(800) 833-1515, (901) 680-9700
http://www.amerisuites.com
1220 Primacy Pkwy.
128 rooms - $95-178
Pets: Small pets w/$50 fee
Creature Comforts: CCTV, a/c,
cont. brkfst, kit, restaurant, pool

Baymont Inn, East
(800) 789-4103, (901) 377-2233
http://www.baymontinns.com
6020 Shelby Oaks Dr.
102 rooms - $60-99
Pets: Welcome in smoking rooms
Creature Comforts: CCTV, a/c,
refrig, micro, cont. brkfst, pool

Baymont Inn, Airport
(800) 789-4103, (901) 396-5411
http://www.baymontinns.com
3005 Millbranch Rd.
102 rooms - $60-79
Pets: Welcome
Creature Comforts: CCTV, a/c,
cont. brkfst

Best Western Travelers Inn
(800) 528-1234, (901) 363-8430
http://www.bestwestern.com
5024 Rte. 78
52 rooms - $65-116
Pets: Under 10-15 lbs. welcome
Creature Comforts: CCTV, a/c,
restaurant, pool

Comfort Inn Airport/Graceland
(800) 228-5150, (901) 345-3344
http://www.comfortinn.com
1581 E. Brooks Rd.
60 rooms - $45-85
Pets: Welcome
Creature Comforts: CCTV, a/c,
pool, whirlpool

Comfort Inn, East
(800) 228-5150, (901) 767-6300
http://www.comfortinn.com
5877 Poplar St.
126 rooms - $55-85
Pets: Welcome
Creature Comforts: CCTV, a/c,
restaurant, pool, hlth clb access

Comfort Inn Memphis
International Airport
(800) 228-5150, (901) 332-2370
http://www.comfortinn.com
2411 Winchester Rd.
211 rooms - $50-75
Pets: Welcome
Creature Comforts: CCTV, a/c,
restaurant, pool, hlth clb access,
tennis

Country Suites by Carlson
(800) 456-4000, (901) 366-9333
4300 American Way
120 rooms - $65-87
Pets: Welcome w/$100 fee
Creature Comforts: CCTV, a/c,
kit, cont. brkfst, pool, hlth clb
access, whirlpool

Days Inn
(800) DAYS INN, (901) 346-5500
http://www.daysinn.com
3839 Elvis Presley Blvd.
60 rooms - $65-85
Pets: Welcome w/$5 fee
Creature Comforts: CCTV, a/c,
Jacuzzi, cont. brkfst, pool

Days Inn Riverbluff
(800) DAYS INN, (901) 948-9005
http://www.daysinn.com
340 W. Illinois Ave.
100 rooms - $55-70
Pets: Welcome w/$20 deposit
Creature Comforts: CCTV, a/c,
restaurant, pool, casino, sports
court, boating, bowling

Drury Inn
(800) 325-8300, (901) 373-8200
http://www.drury-inn.com
1556 Sycamore View
123 rooms - $80-109
Pets: Welcome
Creature Comforts: CCTV, a/c,
cont. brkfst, pool, whirlpool, hlth
club

Guest House Inn & Suites
(901) 366-9333
4300 American Way
120 rooms - $70-99
Pets: Welcome
Creature Comforts: CCTV, a/c,
kit, pool, whirlpool

Holiday Inn, East
(800) HOLIDAY, (901) 682-7881
http://www.holiday-inn.com
5795 Poplar Ave.
243 rooms - $90-130
Pets: Welcome
Creature Comforts: CCTV, a/c,
Jacuzzi, restaurant, pool, hlth clb
access, sauna, whirlpool

Holiday Inn Medical Center
(800) HOLIDAY, (901) 278-4100
http://www.holiday-inn.com
1837 Union Ave.
170 rooms - $70-99
Pets: Welcome
Creature Comforts: CCTV, a/c,
restaurant

Homewood Suites
(800) 225-5466, (901) 763-0500
http://www.homewoodsuites.com
5811 Poplar Ave.
140 rooms - $90-150
Pets: Welcome w/$150 fee
Creature Comforts: CCTV, a/c,
kit, cont. brkfst, pool

Howard Johnson Express
(800) I-Go-Hojo, (901) 388-1300
http://www.hojo.com
1541 Sycamore View St.
96 rooms - $50-95
Pets: Welcome
Creature Comforts: CCTV, a/c,
refrig, micro, restaurant, pool

La Quinta Inn, Airport
(800) 531-5900, (901) 396-1000
http://www.laquinta.com
2745 Airways Blvd.
122 rooms - $70-105
Pets: Under 25 lbs. welcome
Creature Comforts: CCTV, a/c,
fireplace, refrig, micro,brkfst, pool

La Quinta Inn, East
(800) 531-5900, (901) 382-2323
http://www.laquinta.com
6068 Macon Cove
130 rooms - $50-95
Pets: Welcome
Creature Comforts: CCTV, a/c,
cont. brkfst, pool

La Quinta Inn, Medical Center
(800) 531-5900, (901)526-1050
http://www.laquinta.com
42 S. Camilla Rd.
130 rooms - $45-105
Pets: Welcome
Creature Comforts: CCTV, a/c,
cont. brkfst, pool

Memphis Inn, East
(800) 770-4667, (901) 373-9898
6050 Macon Cove Rd.
105 rooms - $35-69
Pets: Welcome
Creature Comforts: CCTV, a/c,
kit, pool

Motel 6, East
(800) 4-MOTEL6, (901) 382-8572
http://www.motel6.com
1321 Sycamore View Rd.
100 rooms - $40-89
Pets: Under 30 lbs. welcome
Creature Comforts: CCTV, a/c,
pool

Motel 6, Graceland
(800) 4-MOTEL6, (901) 346-0992
http://www.motel6.com
1117 E. Brooks Rd.
125 rooms - $30-69
Pets: Under 30 lbs. welcome
Creature Comforts: CCTV, a/c,
pool

Red Roof Inn, East
(800) The Roof, (901) 388-6111
http://www.redroof.com
6055 Shelby Oaks Dr.
110 rooms - $40-79
Pets: Welcome
Creature Comforts: CCTV, a/c

Red Roof Inn, Medical Center
(800) The Roof, (901) 528-0650
http://www.redroof.com
210 S. Pauline Rd.
120 rooms - $40-79
Pets: Small pets welcome
Creature Comforts: CCTV, a/c

Red Roof Inn, South
(800) The Roof, (901) 363-2335
http://www.redroof.com
3875 American Way
109 rooms - $40-79
Pets: Welcome
Creature Comforts: CCTV, a/c

Residence Inn by Marriott
(800) 331-3131, (901) 685-9595
http://www.residenceinn.com
6141 Old Poplar Dr.
105 rooms - $115-169
Pets: Under 25 lbs. w/$100 fee
Creature Comforts: CCTV, a/c,
kit, fireplaces, pool, hlth clb
access, sports court, whirlpool

Super 8 Motel
(800) 800-8000, (901) 373-4888
http://www.super8.com
6015 Macon Cove Rd.
70 rooms - $50-69
Pets: Welcome
Creature Comforts: CCTV, a/c

Super 8 Motel, Graceland
(800) 800-8000, (901) 345-1425
http://www.super8.com
3280 Elvis Presley Blvd.
120 rooms - $40-75
Pets: Small pets w/$5 fee
Creature Comforts: CCTV, a/c,
cont. brkfst, pool

Super 8 Memphis, Airport-East
(800) 800-8000, (901) 362-0011
http://www.super8.com
4060 Lamar Ave.
48 rooms - $65-79
Pets: Welcome w/$5 fee
Creature Comforts: CCTV, a/c,
refrig, micro, Jacuzzi, cont. brkfst,
pool

MILAN
Ramada Limited
(800) 2-Ramada, (901) 686-3345
http://www.ramada.com
3022 S.First St.
57 rooms - $60-86
Pets: Welcome w/$10 deposit
Creature Comforts: CCTV, a/c,
refrig, micro, restaurant, pool

MILLINGTON
Best Western Inn
(800) 528-1234, (901) 873-2222
http://www.bestwestern.com
7726 Rte. 51 N.
77 rooms - $45-86
Pets: Small pets welcome
Creature Comforts: CCTV,
VCR, a/c, refrig, micro, pool

Econo Lodge
(800) 55-ECONO, (901) 873-4400
http://www.econolodge.com
8193 Rte. 51 N.
55 rooms - $45-79
Pets: Small pets w/$3 fee
Creature Comforts: CCTV,
VCR, a/c, refrig, micro, pool

MONTEAGLE
Adams Edgeworth Inn
87-RelaxInn, (931) 924-4000
http://www.innjoy.com
Monteagle Assembly
13 rooms - $70-200
Pets: On first floor w/deposit
Creature Comforts: Elegant
1895 Nat'l Historic Register
Victorian inn, verandas, French
doors, lustrous wood floors,
handmade quilts, rice and brass
beds, claw-foot tubs, CCTV, a/c,
fireplace, kit, gourmet candlelit
dinners, cont. brkfst

Days Inn
(800) DAYS INN, (931) 924-2900
http://www.daysinn.com
102 College St.
58 rooms - $25-83
Pets: Welcome
Creature Comforts: CCTV, a/c,
restaurant, pool

**Jim Oliver's Smokehouse
Motor Lodge**
(800) 489-2091, (931) 924-2268
Rtes. 64 & 41A
96 rooms - $25-150
Pets: Welcome
Creature Comforts: CCTV, a/c,
fireplace, kit, restaurant, pool,
tennis

MORRISTOWN
Days Inn
(800) DAYS INN, (423) 587-2200
http://www.daysinn.com
2512 E. Andrew Johnson Hwy.
63 rooms - $35-65
Pets: Small pets welcome
Creature Comforts: CCTV, a/c,
refrig, micro, Jacuzzi

Ramada Inn
(800) 2-Ramada, (423) 587-2400
http://www.ramada.com
Rtes. I-81 and 25E
112 rooms - $60-125
Pets: Welcome
Creature Comforts: CCTV, a/c,
restaurant, pool, hlth clb access

Super 8 Motel
(800) 800-8000, (423) 586-8880
http://www.super8.com
2430 E. Andrew Johnson Hwy.
63 rooms - $35-59
Pets: Welcome
Creature Comforts: CCTV, a/c

MT. JULIET
Natureview Inn B&B
(800) 758-7972, (615) 758-4439
http://www.bbonline.com/tn/
natureview
3354 Old Lebanon Dirt Rd
4 rooms - $75-109
Pets: Well-behaved dogs welcome
Creature Comforts: Small B&B
in a country setting, 5 acres of
pastures, filled w/memorabilia and
collectibles, a/c CCTV, fireplace,
full southern brkfst, kit, pool,
horse stalls & riding

MOUNTAIN CITY
Days Inn
(800) DAYS INN, (423) 727-7311
http://www.daysinn.com
Route 421
40 rooms - $40-79
Pets: Small pets w/$6 fee
Creature Comforts: CCTV, a/c,
Jacuzzi, pool

MURFREESBORO
Best Western Chaffin Inn
(800) 528-1234, (615) 895-3818
http://www.bestwestern.com
168 Chaffin Place
50 rooms - $40-66
Pets: Small pets w/$6 fee
Creature Comforts: CCTV, a/c,
refrig, Jacuzzis, cont. brkfst, pool

Garden Plaza Hotel
(800) 342-7336, (615) 895-5555
1850 Old Fort Parkway
168 rooms - $80-120
Pets: Small pets welcome
Creature Comforts: CCTV, a/c,
refrig, restaurant, pool, hlth clb
access, whirlpool

Holiday Inn Holidome
(800) HOLIDAY, (615) 896-2420
http://www.holiday-inn.com
2227 Old Fort Parkway
180 rooms - $55-79
Pets: Small pets welcome
Creature Comforts: CCTV, a/c,
restaurant, pool, hlth clb access,
sauna, whirlpool

Howard Johnson Lodge
(800) I-Go-Hojo, (615) 896-5522
http://www.hojo.com
2424 S. Church St.
80 rooms - $30-94
Pets: Small pets-$5 fee, $10 dep.
Creature Comforts: CCTV,
VCR, a/c, refrig, micro, Jacuzzis,
cont. brkfst, and a pool

Motel 6
(800) 4-MOTEL6, (615) 890-8524
http://www.motel6.com
114 Chaffin Place
85 rooms - $30-55
Pets: Under 30 lbs. welcome
Creature Comforts: CCTV, a/c

Murfreesboro Motel
(615) 893-2100
1150 N.W. Broad St.
65 rooms - $30-54
Pets: Welcome
Creature Comforts: CCTV, a/c, kit, restaurant, pool

Quality Inn
(800) 221-2222, (615) 848-9030
http://www.qualityinn.com
118 Westgate Blvd.
78 rooms - $35-99
Pets: Welcome w/$5 fee
Creature Comforts: CCTV, a/c, refrig, micro, Jacuzzi, pool

Ramada Limited
(800) 2-Ramada, (615) 896-5080
http://www.ramada.com
1855 S. Church St.
80 rooms - $50-99
Pets: Welcome
Creature Comforts: CCTV, a/c, cont. brkfst, pool, playground

Scottish Inns
(800) 251-1962, (615) 896-3211
http://www.reservahost.com
2029 S. Church St.
100 rooms - $25-64
Pets: Welcome
Creature Comforts: CCTV, pool

Travelodge
(800) 578-7878, (615) 896-2320
http://www.travelodge.com
2025 S. Church St.
105 rooms - $40-49
Pets: Small pets w/$10 fee
Creature Comforts: CCTV, a/c, refrig, pool

NASHVILLE
Baymont Inn, Airport
(800) 789-4103, (615) 885-3100
http://www.baymontinns.com
531 Donelson Pike
150 rooms - $50-89
Pets: Small pets welcome
Creature Comforts: CCTV, a/c, refrig, micro

Baymont Inn, Nashville West
(800) 789-4103, (615) 353-0700
http://www.baymontinns.com
5612 Lenox Ave.
110 rooms - $50-89
Pets: Small pets welcome
Creature Comforts: CCTV, a/c, pool

Best Suites of America
(877) 877-6810, (615) 391-3919
http://www.bestinn.com
2521 Elm Hill Pike
95 rooms - $80-105
Pets: Small pets welcome
Creature Comforts: CCTV, VCR, a/c, refrig, micro, Jacuzzi, restaurant, pool, hlth clb access

Best Western Calumet Inn
(800) 528-1234, (615) 889-9199
http://www.bestwestern.com
701 Stewarts Ferry Pike
80 rooms - $45-99
Pets: Small pets w/$10 fee
Creature Comforts: CCTV, a/c, refrig, micro, Jacuzzi, pool

Days Inn
(800) DAYS INN, (615) 731-7800
http://www.daysinn.com
I-24/Bell Rd.
112 rooms - $45-100
Pets: Welcome w/$6 fee
Creature Comforts: CCTV, a/c, cont. brkfst, pool

Days Inn
(800) DAYS INN, (615) 228-5977
http://www.daysinn.com
1400 Brick Church Rd.
108 rooms - $35-85
Pets: Welcome w/$7-10 fee
Creature Comforts: CCTV, a/c, kit, pool, golf

Drury Inn, Airport
(800) 325-8300, (615) 361-6999
http://www.drury-inn.com
837 Briley Parkway
144 rooms - $70-95
Pets: Welcome
Creature Comforts: CCTV, a/c, refrig, micro, pool, hlth clb access, sauna, whirlpool

Drury Inn, South
(800) 325-8300, (615) 834-7170
http://www.drury-inn.com
341 Harding Place
130 rooms - $70-95
Pets: Welcome
Creature Comforts: CCTV, a/c, refrig, micro, pool

Econo Lodge
(800) 55-ECONO, (615) 226-9805
http://www.econolodge.com
2403 Brick Church Pike
38 rooms - $30-90
Pets: Welcome
Creature Comforts: CCTV, a/c, cont. brkfst

Econo Lodge, Opryland
(800) 55-ECONO, (615) 889-0090
http://www.econolodge.com
2460 Music Valley Dr.
86 rooms - $45-95
Pets: Welcome
Creature Comforts: CCTV, a/c, pool

Econo Lodge Southeast
(800) 55-ECONO, (615) 833-6860
http://www.econolodge.com
97 Wallace Rd.
127 rooms - $40-69
Pets: Welcome
Creature Comforts: CCTV, a/c, cont. brkfst, pool

Embassy Suites
(800) 362-2779, (615) 871-0033
http://www.embassy-suites.com
10 Century Blvd.
296 rooms - $140-175
Pets: Small pets welcome
Creature Comforts: CCTV, a/c, kit, restaurant, pool, hlth clb access, sauna, whirlpool

Guest House Inn
(615) 329-1000
1909 Hayes St.
110 rooms - $75-109
Pets: Small pets welcome
Creature Comforts: CCTV, a/c, refrig

Hampton Inn
(800) 426-7866, (615) 871-0222
http://www.hampton-inn.com
2350 Elm Hill Pike
120 rooms - $70-105
Pets: Small pets welcome
Creature Comforts: CCTV, a/c, pool

Hillsboro House B&B
(800) 228-7851, (615) 292-5501
www.bbonline.com/tn/hillsboro
1933 - 20th Ave., S.
3 rooms - $85-110
Pets: Welcome by arrangement
Creature Comforts: Cozy 1904
Victorian, lovely traditional decor,
antiques, piano, feather beds,
CCTV, a/c, fireplace, full brkfst,
gardens

Holiday Inn Express
(800) HOLIDAY, (615) 226-4600
http://www.holiday-inn.com
2401 Brick Church Pike
172 rooms - $45-89
Pets: Welcome
Creature Comforts: CCTV, a/c,
refrig, pool

Holiday Inn Vanderbilt
(800) HOLIDAY, (615) 327-4707
http://www.holiday-inn.com
2613 West End Ave.
300 rooms - $80-160
Pets: Under 40 Lbs. w/$65 fee
Creature Comforts: CCTV, a/c,
restaurant, pool, hlth clb access

Holiday Inn - The Crossings
(800) HOLIDAY, (615) 731-2361
http://www.holiday-inn.com
201 Crossings Place
140 rooms - $75-120
Pets: Small pets welcome
Creature Comforts: CCTV, a/c,
restaurant, pool, hlth clb access

Homestead Village
(888) STAY-HSD, (615) 316-9020
http://www.homesteadvillage.com
727 McGavock Pike
140 rooms - $75-120
Pets: Welcome w/$75 fee
Creature Comforts: CCTV, a/c,
kit, hlth clb

La Quinta Inn - Airport
(800) 531-5900, (615) 885-3000
http://www.laquinta.com
2345 Atrium Way
136 rooms - $65-109
Pets: Small pets welcome
Creature Comforts: CCTV, a/c,
refrig, micro, pool

La Quinta Inn, Metro Center
(800) 531-5900, (615) 259-2130
http://www.laquinta.com
2001 Metro Center Blvd.
121 rooms - $75-109
Pets: Small pets welcome
Creature Comforts: CCTV, a/c,
restaurant, cont. brkfst, pool

La Quinta Motor Inn, South
(800) 531-5900, (615) 834-6900
http://www.laquinta.com
4311 Sidco Dr.
130 rooms - $70-105
Pets: Small pets welcome
Creature Comforts: CCTV, a/c,
pool

Loews Vanderbilt Plaza
(800) 23-LOEWS, (615) 320-1700
http://www.loewshotels.com
2100 West End Ave.
345 rooms - $160-330
Pets: Under 30 lbs. welcome, over
30 lbs w/approval & CC deposit
Creature Comforts: CCTV,
VCR, a/c, micro, restaurant, pool,
spa, hlth club, and children's
program

Motel 6, Airport
(800) 466-8356, (615) 833-8887
http://www.motel6.com
420 Metroplex Dr.
87 rooms - $35-56
Pets: Under 30 lbs. welcome
Creature Comforts: CCTV, a/c,
pool

Motel 6, North
(800) 466-8356, (615) 227-9696
http://www.motel6.com
311 W. Trinity Lane
125 rooms - $30-49
Pets: Under 30 lbs. welcome
Creature Comforts: CCTV, a/c,
pool

Motel 6, South
(800) 466-8356, (615) 333-9933
http://www.motel6.com
96 Wallace Rd.
125 rooms - $30-49
Pets: Under 30 lbs. welcome
Creature Comforts: CCTV, a/c,
pool

Nashville Medical Center Inn
(615) 329-1000
1909 Hayes St.
108 rooms - $75-89
Pets: $25 fee, $50 deposit
Creature Comforts: CCTV, a/c,
refrig, micro

Pear Tree Inn, South
(800) 282-8733, (615) 834-4242
http://www.peartreeinn.com
343 Harding Place
109 rooms - $55-68
Pets: Welcome
Creature Comforts: CCTV, a/c,
pool

Quarters Motor Inn
(615) 731- 5990
1100 Bell Rd.
41 rooms - $55-69
Pets: Small pets welcome
Creature Comforts: CCTV, a/c,
refrig, Jacuzzi

Ramada Inn Suites
(800) 2-Ramada, (615) 883-5201
http://www.ramada.com
2425 Atrium Way
120 rooms - $60-100
Pets: Welcome w/$10 fee
Creature Comforts: CCTV, a/c,
cont. brkfst, kit, pool

Red Roof Inn
(800) The Roof, (615) 872-0735
http://www.redroof.com
510 Claridge Dr.
120 rooms - $45-75
Pets: Small pets welcome
Creature Comforts: CCTV, a/c

Red Roof Inn, South
(800) The Roof, (615) 832-0093
http://www.redroof.com
4271 Sidco Dr.
85 rooms - $40-73
Pets: Small pets welcome
Creature Comforts: CCTV, a/c

Residence Inn
(800) 331-3131, (615) 889-8600
http://www.residenceinn.com
2300 Elm Hill Pike
168 rooms - $100-165
Pets: Welcome w/$150 fee
Creature Comforts: CCTV, a/c,
fireplace, kit, restaurant, pool,
sports court, whirlpool

Sheraton Music City Hotel
(800) 325-3535, (615) 885-2200
http://www.sheraton.com
777 McGavock Pike
412 rooms - $160-500
Pets: Welcome
Creature Comforts: Beautiful and expansive grounds surround luxury hotel, CCTV, VCR, a/c, refrig, Jacuzzis, restaurant, cont. brkfst, pool, hlth clb access, sauna, whirlpool, tennis

Shoney's Inn
(800) 222-222, (615) 885-4030
2420 Music Valley Dr.
185 rooms - $80-125
Pets: Small pets w/$100 deposit
Creature Comforts: CCTV, a/c, pool, whirlpool

Super 8 Motel
(800) 800-8000, (615) 834-0620
http://www.super8.com
350 Harding Place
216 rooms - $60-85
Pets: Small pets w/$20 deposit
Creature Comforts: CCTV, a/c, refrig, micro, Jacuzzi, pool, hlth clb access

Super 8 Motel
(800) 800-8000, (615) 356-0888
http://www.super8.com
412 Robertson Rd.
73 rooms - $50-80
Pets: Welcome
Creature Comforts: CCTV, a/c, refrig, micro

Union Station Hotel
(800) 331-2123, (615) 726-1001
http://www.wyndham.com
1001 Broadway
124 rooms - $75-175
Pets: Under 25 lbs. welcome
Creature Comforts: Nat'l Historic Register, restored historic train station, stained glass windows, classic woodwork/trim, high ceilings, unique guest rms, CCTV, a/c, fine restaurant, hlth clb access

Westin Hermitage Hotel
(800) 228-3000, (615) 244-3121
http://www.westin.com
231 - 6th Ave.
122 rooms - $129-450
Pets: Welcome w/approval
Creature Comforts: CCTV, VCR, a/c, refrig, restaurant, cont. brkfst, hlth clb access

Wyndham Garden Hotel
(800) Wyndham, (615) 889-9090
1112 Airport Center Dr.
180 rooms - $75-125
Pets: Small pets w/$25 deposit
Creature Comforts: CCTV, a/c, refrig, restaurant, pool, hlth clb access, whirlpool

NEWPORT
Best Western Inn
(800) 528-1234, (423) 623-8713
http://www.bestwestern.com
1015 Cosby Hwy.
111 rooms - $45-135
Pets: Small pets welcome
Creature Comforts: CCTV, a/c, Jacuzzi, restaurant, pool, whirlpool

Holiday Inn
(800) HOLIDAY, (423) 625-8622
http://www.holiday-inn.com
Rtes. 32 & 40
154 rooms - $60-105
Pets: Small pets welcome
Creature Comforts: CCTV, a/c, refrig, restaurant, pool, whirlpool

Relax Inn
(423) 625-1521
1848 W. Knoxville Hwy.
18 rooms - $25-89
Pets: Small pets w/$10 fee deposit
Creature Comforts: CCTV, a/c

NORMANDY
Parish Patch Farm & Inn
(800) 876-3017, (615) 857-3017
http://bbonline.com/tn/parishpatch
1100 Cortner Rd.
21 rooms - $110-195
Pets: Welcome
Creature Comforts: Wonderful historic site that feels like a private estate, mature trees, gristmill, beefalo farm, classically decorated rms w/pencil post four-poster beds, reproduction antiques, CCTV, VCR, a/c, fireplace, kit, country brkfst, restaurant, pool

OAK RIDGE
Comfort Inn
(800) 228-5150, (423) 481-8200
http://www.comfortinn.com
433 S. Rutgers Ave.
122 rooms - $70-95
Pets: Welcome
Creature Comforts: CCTV, VCR, a/c, refrig, micro, pool, hlth clb access

Days Inn
(800) DAYS INN, (423) 483-5615
http://www.daysinn.com
206 S. Illinois Ave.
80 rooms - $50-75
Pets: Welcome w/$3 fee
Creature Comforts: CCTV, a/c, kit, pool, playground

Garden Plaza Hotel
(800) 342-7336, (423) 481-2468
215 S. Illinois Ave.
168 rooms - $90-125
Pets: Small pets welcome
Creature Comforts: CCTV, a/c, refrig, micro, restaurant, pool, whirlpool

Super 8 Motel
(800) 800-8000, (423) 483-1200
http://www.super8.com
1590 Oak Ridge Turnpike
56 rooms - $50-89
Pets: Welcome w/$5 fee
Creature Comforts: CCTV, a/c, refrig, pool

ONEIDA
The Galloway Inn
(423) 569-8835
4525 Rte. 27 S.
10 rooms - $35-49
Pets: Welcome
Creature Comforts: CCTV, a/c, refrig

OOLTEWAH
Super 8 Motel
(800) 800-8000, (423) 238-5951
http://www.super8.com
5111 Hunter Rd.
63 rooms - $40-59
Pets: Small pets welcome
Creature Comforts: CCTV, a/c, Jacuzzi, pool

PARIS

Avalon Motel
(901) 642-4121
1315 Wood St.
40 rooms - $30-59
Pets: Welcome w/$4 fee
Creature Comforts: CCTV, a/c, refrig

Best Western Travellers Inn
(800) 528-1234, (901) 642-8881
http://www.bestwestern.com
1297 E. Wood St.
98 rooms - $45-70
Pets: Small pets w/$25 deposit
Creature Comforts: CCTV, a/c, refrig, pool

PIGEON FORGE

Baymont Inn
(800) 4-Budget, (423) 428-7305
http://www.baymontinns.com
2179 Parkway
132 rooms - $40-99
Pets: Small pets welcome
Creature Comforts: CCTV, a/c, refrig, cont brkfst, and a pool

The Grand Resort Hotel
(800) 251-4444, (423) 453-1000
http://www.grandresorthotel.com
3171 N. Parkway
425 rooms - $50-139
Pets: Small pets w/$10 deposit
Creature Comforts: CCTV, a/c, fireplace, kit, cont. brkfst, Jacuzzis, restaurant, pool, and whirlpools

Heartland Country Resort
(800) 453-4106, (423) 453-4106
2385 Parkway
160 rooms - $30-125
Pets: Welcome w/$20 fee
Creature Comforts: CCTV, a/c, pool, whirlpool, game room

Holiday Inn
(800) HOLIDAY, (423) 428-2700
http://www.holiday-inn.com
3230 Parkway
212 rooms - $40-100
Pets: Under 20 lbs. welcome
Creature Comforts: CCTV, a/c, kit, Jacuzzi, restaurant, cont. brkfst, and a pool

Microtel
(888) 771-7171, (423) 429-0150
http://www.microtelinn.com
202 Emert St.
100 rooms - $35-85
Pets: Small pets welcome
Creature Comforts: CCTV, a/c, refrig, micro, pool

PORTLAND

Budget Host Inn
(800) Bud-Host, (615) 325-2005
http://www.budgethost.com
5339 Long Rd.
50 rooms - $45-70
Pets: Welcome w/$5 fee
Creature Comforts: CCTV, VCR, a/c, refrig, micro, pool

POWELL

Comfort Inn
(800) 228-5150, (423) 938-5500
http://www.comfortinn.com
323 E. Emory Rd.
72 rooms - $50-80
Pets: Small pets w/$30 deposit
Creature Comforts: CCTV, a/c, refrig, micro, Jacuzzi, pool

PULASKI

Super 8 Motel
(800) 800-8000, (615) 363-4501
http://www.super8.com
2400 Route 64
40 rooms - $40-65
Pets: Welcome w/$5 fee
Creature Comforts: CCTV, a/c, refrig, pool

Super 8 Motel
(800) 800-8000, (615) 363-4501
http://www.super8.com
2400 Rte. 64
40 rooms - $45-70
Pets: Welcome w/$5 fee
Creature Comforts: CCTV, a/c, kit, restaurant, pool

RICEVILLE

Relax Inn
(423) 745-5893
3803 Rte. 39W
18 rooms - $25-49
Pets: Welcome w/$8 fee
Creature Comforts: CCTV, a/c, refrig

SAMBURG

Bill Nation's Camp
(901) 538-2177
244 W. Lakeview Dr.
8 rooms - $48-59
Pets: Welcome
Creature Comforts: CCTV, a/c, kit, fishing

Blue Bank Resort
(901) 538-2112
Route 2122
30 rooms - $45-89
Pets: Welcome w/$100 deposit
Creature Comforts: CCTV, a/c, kit, restaurant, pool, marina, boating

Hamilton's Resort
(901) 538-2325
4992 Hamilton Rd.
13 rooms - $45-67
Pets: Welcome
Creature Comforts: kit, pool

SAVANNAH

Shaws Komfort Motel
(901) 925-3977
2302 Wayne Rd.
31 rooms - $30-55
Pets: Welcome
Creature Comforts: CCTV, a/c, refrig

SEVIERVILLE

Best Western Dumplin Valley
(800) 528-1234, (423) 933-3467
http://www.bestwestern.com
3426 Winfield Dunn Parkway
82 rooms - $40-105
Pets: Small pets w/$5 fee
Creature Comforts: CCTV, a/c, fireplace, refrig, Jacuzzi, pool

High Valley Rentals
(800) 636-0608, (423) 428-0608
http://www.knoxville-online.com/high.htm
630 Thomas Loop Rd.
14 rooms - $75-105
Pets: Welcome w/$40 fee and a $50 deposit
Creature Comforts: Fully-furnished mountain log cabins, country decor, CCTV, a/c, kit, fireplace, Jacuzzi, whirlpool, wrap-arouund decks

Spring Gap Log Cabins
(423) 453-0829
3054 Kulpan Way
5 rooms - $85-109
Pets: Small pets w/$25 fee
Creature Comforts: CCTV, a/c,
refrig, micro, Jacuzzi

SHELBYVILLE
Best Western Celebration Inn
(800) 528-1234, (931) 684-2378
http://www.bestwestern.com
724 Madison St.
58 rooms - $60-165
Pets: Small pets w/$10 fee
Creature Comforts: CCTV, a/c,
Jacuzzi, restaurant, hlth clb access

Shelbyville Inn
(931) 684-6050
317 N.Cannon Blvd.
76 rooms - $55-69
Pets: Small pets welcome
Creature Comforts: CCTV, a/c,
refrig, micro, restaurant, pool

SMYRNA
Days Inn
(800) DAYS INN, (615) 355-6161
http://www.daysinn.com
1300 Plaza Dr.
60 rooms - $55-115
Pets: Small pets w/$10 fee
Creature Comforts: CCTV, a/c,
refrig, micro, Jacuzzi, pool

SPRING HILL
Holiday Inn
(800) HOLIDAY, (615) 486-1234
http://www.holiday-inn.com
104 Kedron Rd.
46 rooms - $60-100
Pets: Small pets welcome
Creature Comforts: CCTV, a/c,
kit, Jacuzzi, cont. brkfst, pool

SPRINGFIELD
Best Western Springfield
(800) 528-1234, (615) 384-1234
http://www.bestwestern.com
2001 Memorial Blvd.
80 rooms - $55-69
Pets: Small pets w/$10 fee
Creature Comforts: CCTV, a/c,
refrig, micro, Jacuzzi, pool

Howell's Resort
(615) 642-7442
Rte 1 Box 261
9 rooms - $25-40
Pets: Welcome
Creature Comforts: CCTV, a/c,
kit

Mansard Island Resort
(615) 642-5590
Rte 1, Box 261
39 rooms - $48-70
Pets: Welcome w/$25 deposit
Creature Comforts: CCTV, a/c,
kit, restaurant, pool, tennis

SWEETWATER
Best Western Inn
(800) 528-1234, (423) 337-3541
http://www.bestwestern.com
1421 Murray's Chapel Rd.
137 rooms - $55-155
Pets: Small pets welcome
Creature Comforts: CCTV, a/c,
kit, restaurant, pool, whirlpool

Budget Host Inn
(800) Bud-Host, (423) 337-9357
http://www.budgethost.com
207 Rte. 68
62 rooms - $35-69
Pets: Welcome w/$2 fee
Creature Comforts: CCTV, a/c,
refrig, micro

Comfort Inn
(800) 228-5150, (423) 337-6646
http://www.comfortinn.com
803 S. Main St.
60 rooms - $40-69
Pets: Welcome w/$5 fee
Creature Comforts: CCTV, a/c,
pool

Comfort Inn West
(800) 228-5150, (423) 337-3353
http://www.comfortinn.com
Route 75
54 rooms - $40-75
Pets: Small pets w/$5 fee
Creature Comforts: CCTV,
VCR, a/c, refrig, micro, Jacuzzis,
pool, whirlpool

Days Inn
(800) DAYS INN, (423) 337-4200
http://www.daysinn.com
229 Rte. 68
36 rooms - $35-59
Pets: Welcome w/$5 fee
Creature Comforts: CCTV, a/c,
refrig, micro, Jacuzzi, pool

Sweetwater Hotel
(423) 337-3511
Rte. 75 & SR 68
135 rooms - $40-62
Pets: Small pets welcome
Creature Comforts: CCTV, a/c,
refrig,cont. brkfst, restaurant, pool,
whirlpool

TIPTONVILLE
Ray's Camp
(901) 253-7765
Rte. 1, Box 5
4 rooms - $39-54
Pets: Small pets welcome
Creature Comforts: CCTV, a/c,
kit

TOWNSEND
Best Western Valley View Lodge
(800) 528-1234, (865) 448-2237
http://www.bestwestern.com
Route 321
85 rooms - $45-135
Pets: Small pets welcome
Creature Comforts: CCTV, a/c,
fireplace, kit, Jacuzzi, pool,
whirlpool, gardens

Carnes' Log Cabins
(865) 448-1021
http://www.carneslogcabins.com
Box 153
7 cabins - $85-155
Pets: Small pets welcome
Creature Comforts: Wonderful
log cabins w/porches overlooking
woods, stone fireplace, CCTV, a/c,
kit, hot tub

Days Inn
(800) DAYS INN, (865) 448-9111
http://www.daysinn.com
Route 321
47 rooms - $30-89
Pets: Small pets welcome
Creature Comforts: CCTV, a/c,
refrig, micro, Jacuzzi, pool

Pearl's of the Mountains Cabins
(800) 324-8415, (865) 448-8801
Box 378
3 cabins - $70-95
Pets: Welcome
Creature Comforts: Smoky mtn cabins w/river vws, CCTV, VCR, a/c, kit, fireplace, Jacuzzi

Wear's Motel Cottages
(865) 448-2296
8270 Rte. 73
18 rooms - $45-80
Pets: Small pets w/$10 fee
Creature Comforts: CCTV, a/c, kit, no phones, pool, tennis

UNION CITY
Super 8 Motel
(800) 800-8000, (901) 885-4444
http://www.super8.com
1400 Vaden Ave.
62 rooms - $50-75
Pets: Welcome w/$25 deposit
Creature Comforts: CCTV, a/c, refrig, micro

WALLAND
Twin Valley Ranch B&B
(800) 872-2235, (865) 984-0980
http://www.bbonline.com/tn/
twinvalley/
2848 Old Chihowee Rd.
2 rms/1 cabin - $75-95
Pets: Welcome on limited basis in the cabin, horses stabled
Creature Comforts: Log home B&B and modern log cabin on 263 acres, attractive but simply furnished rooms-country decor, CCTV, kit, fieldstone fireplace, horseback riding, farm animals, and fishing pond

WHITE PINE
Days Inn
(800) DAYS INN, (423) 674-2573
http://www.daysinn.com
3670 Roy Messer Hwy.
76 rooms - $50-59
Pets: Welcome w/$7 fee
Creature Comforts: CCTV, a/c, refrig, micro

WILDERSVILLE
Best Western Crossroads Inn
(800) 528-1234, (901) 968-2532
http://www.bestwestern.com
210 S. Hwy 22 W
40 rooms - $40-60
Pets: Small pets w/$10-25 fee
Creature Comforts: CCTV, a/c, pool, playground

Texas

ABILENE

Best Western Colonial Inn
(800) 528-1234, (915) 677-2683
http://www.bestwestern.com
3210 Pine St.
100 rooms - $55-60
Pets: Welcome w/$5 fee
Creature Comforts: CCTV, a/c,
refrig, restaurant, cont. brkfst, pool

Best Western Mall South
(800) 528-1234, (915) 695-1262
http://www.bestwestern.com
3950 Ridgemont Dr.
61 rooms - $50-68
Pets: Small pets welcome
Creature Comforts: CCTV, a/c,
refrig, whirlpool

Clarion Hotel
(800) 252-7466, (915) 695-2150
http://www.clarioninn.com
5403 S. First St.
183 rooms - $65-90
Pets: Welcome w/$25 one-time
fee
Creature Comforts: CCTV, a/c,
restaurant, pool, whirlpool, sauna

Comfort Inn
(800) 228-5150, (915) 676-0203
http://www.comfortinn.com
1758 Rte. 20E
49 rooms - $55-80
Pets: Welcome
Creature Comforts: CCTV, a/c,
cont. brkfst, pool, hlth clb access

Days Inn
(800) DAYS INN, (915) 672-6433
http://www.daysinn.com
1702 Rte. 20E
98 rooms - $40-50
Pets: Small pets welcome
Creature Comforts: CCTV, a/c,
restaurant, cont. brkfst, pool

Econo Lodge
(800) 55-ECONO, (915) 673-5424
http://www.econolodge.com
1633 W. Stamford St.
34 rooms - $35-50
Pets: Small pets w/$10 deposit
Creature Comforts: CCTV, a/c

Embassy Suites Hotel
(800) 362-2779, (915) 698-1234
http://www.embassy-suites.com
4250 Ridgemont Dr.
176 rooms - $85-90
Pets: Small pets w/$15 fee
Creature Comforts: CCTV, a/c,
restaurant, pool

Hampton Inn
(800) Hampton, (915) 695-4192
http://www.hamptoninn.com
3917 Ridgemont Dr.
64 rooms - $60-85
Pets: Welcome
Creature Comforts: CCTV, a/c,
pool

Holiday Inn Express
(800) HOLIDAY, (915) 673-5271
http://www.holiday-inn.com
1625 Rte. 351
160 rooms - $65-90
Pets: Welcome w/$10 fee
Creature Comforts: CCTV, a/c,
pool

La Quinta Inn
(800) Nu-Rooms, (915) 676-1676
http://www.laquinta.com
3501 W. Lake Road
106 rooms - $65-90
Pets: Small pets welcome
Creature Comforts: CCTV, a/c,
refrig, micro, cont. brkfst, pool

Motel 6
(800) 4-MOTEL6, (915) 672-8462
http://www.motel6.com
4951 W. Stamford St.
118 rooms - $30-45
Pets: Welcome
Creature Comforts: CCTV, a/c,
pool

Quality Inn
(800) 228-5151, (915) 676-0222
http://www.qualityinn.com
505 Pine St.
118 rooms - $55-69
Pets: Welcome w/$10 fee
Creature Comforts: CCTV,
VCR, a/c, restaurant, cont. brkfst,
pool

Ramada Inn
(800) 2-Ramada, (915) 695-7700
http://www.ramada.com
3450 S. Clack St.
146 rooms - $70-75
Pets: Small pets w/$15 fee
Creature Comforts: CCTV, a/c,
restaurant, pool

Royal Inn
(800) 588-4386, (915) 692-3022
5695 S. First St.
145 rooms - $30-49
Pets: Small pets-in rms. or kennel
Creature Comforts: CCTV, a/c,
micro, restaurant, pool

Super 8 Motel
(800) 800-8000, (915) 673-5251
http://www.super8.com
1525 E Rte. 20
97 rooms - $45-50
Pets: Welcome w/$2 fee
Creature Comforts: CCTV, a/c,
refrig, micro, cont. brkfst, pool

ADDISON
Crowne Plaza
(800) 8895-2896, (972) 788-2758
http://www.bristolhotels.com
14315 Midway Rd.
429 rooms - $70-90
Pets: Welcome
Creature Comforts: CCTV, a/c,
restaurant, pool, whirlpool, hlth
clb

Hampton Inn
(800) Hampton, (972) 991-2800
http://www.hamptoninn.com
4555 Beltway Dr.
160 rooms - $60-85
Pets: Welcome
Creature Comforts: CCTV, a/c,
pool

Harvey Hotel
(800) 922-9222, (972) 980-8877
14315 Midway Road
429 rooms - $165-180
Pets: Welcome
Creature Comforts: CCTV, a/c,
restaurant, pool, hlth clb access

Homewood Suites
(800) 225-5466, (972) 788-1342
http://www.homewoodsuites.com
4451 Beltline Road
120 rooms - $85-135
Pets: Welcome w/$50 fee
Creature Comforts: CCTV, a/c,
pool

Motel 6
(800) 4-MOTEL6, (214) 386-4577
http://www.motel6.com
4325 Beltline Road
158 rooms - $35-49
Pets: Under 30 lbs. welcome
Creature Comforts: CCTV,
VCR, a/c

ALICE
Days Inn
(800) DAYS INN, (512) 664-6615
http://www.daysinn.com
555 N. Johnston St.
97 rooms - $50-60
Pets: Welcome w/$5 fee
Creature Comforts: CCTV, a/c,
restaurant, cont. brkfst, pool

ALPINE
Antelope Lodge
(800) 880-8106, (915) 837-2451
2310 W. Rte. 90
27 rooms - $35-60
Pets: Welcome w/$3 fee
Creature Comforts: CCTV, a/c

Best Western Alpine Classic Inn
(800) 528-1234, (915) 837-1530
http://www.bestwestern.com
2401 E. Rte. 90
64 rooms - $55-115
Pets: Under 30 lbs. welcome
Creature Comforts: CCTV, a/c,
restaurant, pool, whirlpool

The Corner House
(800) 585-7795, (915) 837-7161
801 East Ave. E
6 rooms - $30-65
Pets: Welcome
Creature Comforts: CCTV, a/c,
tennis

Highland Inn
(915) 837-5811
1404 East Rte. 90
49 rooms - 40-70
Pets: Welcome
Creature Comforts: CCTV, a/c,
restaurant, pool

Holland Hotel
(800) 535-8040, (915) 837-3844
209 W. Holland Ave.
12 rooms - $40-75
Pets: Welcome
Creature Comforts: 1928
historic hotel, antiques, CCTV, a/c

Ramada Limited
(800) 2-Ramada, (915) 837-1100
http://www.ramada.com
2800 West Rte. 90
61 rooms - $60-95
Pets: Welcome w/$25 deposit
Creature Comforts: CCTV, a/c,
refrig, cont. brkfst

Sunday House Motel
(800) 510-3363, (915) 837-3363
E. Rte. 90
80 rooms - $40-45
Pets: Welcome
Creature Comforts: CCTV, a/c,
pool

ALVIN
Country Hearth Inn
(881) 331-0335
1588 S. Highway
40 rooms - $55-70
Pets: Welcome
Creature Comforts: CCTV, a/c,
pool

AMARILLO
Amarillo East Travelodge
(800) 578-7878, (806) 372-8171
http://www.travelodge.com
Rte. 40E at Tee Anchor Blvd.
96 rooms - $45-50
Pets: Small pets welcome
Creature Comforts: CCTV, a/c,
refrig, restaurant, pool

Amarillo Residence Inn
(800) 331-3131, (806) 354-2978
http://www.residenceinn.com
6700 Interstate 40 West
78 rooms - $80-140
Pets: Welcome w/$50 fee
Creature Comforts: CCTV, a/c,
kit, pool

Amarillo West Travelodge
(800) 578-7878, (806) 353-3541
http://www.travelodgewest.com
2035 Paramount Blvd.
100 rooms - $45-70
Pets: Small pets welcome
Creature Comforts: CCTV, a/c,
pool

Best Western Amarillo
(800) 528-1234, (806) 358-7861
http://www.bestwestern.com
1610 Coulter Dr.
103 rooms - $70-90
Pets: Small pets w/$10 fee
Creature Comforts: CCTV, a/c,
refrig, micro, restaurant, pool,
whirlpool

Best Western Santa Fe
(800) 528-1234, (806) 372-1885
http://www.bestwestern.com
4600 Rte. 40 East
57 rooms - $55-65
Pets: Small pets w/$35 deposit
Creature Comforts: CCTV, a/c,
pool

Big Texan Inn
(800) 657-7177, (806) 372-5000
7701 Rte. 40 East
54 rooms - $35-95
Pets: Small pets w/$20 deposit
Creature Comforts: Old West
theme, CCTV, VCR, a/c, Jacuzzi,
restaurant, pool

Bronco Motel
(806) 355-3321
6005 Amarillo Blvd. West
28 rooms - $35-40
Pets: Welcome w/$10 deposit
Creature Comforts: CCTV, a/c, kit, pool

Budget Host La Paloma Inn
(800) Bud-Host, (806) 372-8101
http://www.budgethost.com
2915 Rte. 40 East
92 rooms - $30-60
Pets: Small pets w/$10 fee
Creature Comforts: CCTV, a/c, Jacuzzi, pool, whirlpool

Comfort Inn
(800) 228-5150, (806) 358-6141
http://www.comfortinn.com
2100 S. Coulter Rd.
117 rooms - $55-70
Pets: Small pets welcome
Creature Comforts: CCTV, a/c, kit, pool

Crowne Plaza
(800) 817-0521, (806) 358-6161
3100 Rte. 40 West
265 rooms - $100-130
Pets: Welcome w/$15 fee
Creature Comforts: CCTV, a/c, restaurant, pool, whirlpool

Econo Lodge
(800) 55-ECONO, (806) 335-1561
http://www.econolodge.com
1803 Lakeside Dr.
87 rooms - $50-60
Pets: Welcome w/$5 fee
Creature Comforts: CCTV, a/c, kit, pool

Hampton Inn
(800) Hampton, (806) 372-1425
http://www.hamptoninn.com
1700 Rte. 40 East
116 rooms - $55-75
Pets: Welcome
Creature Comforts: CCTV, a/c, pool

Homegate Studios and Suites
(888) 456-GATE, (806) 358-7943
http://www.homegate.com
6800 IH-40 West
125 rooms - $42-62
Pets: Welcome
Creature Comforts: CCTV, a/c, pool, exercise rm.

Holiday Inn
(800) HOLIDAY, (806) 372-8741
http://www.holiday-inn.com
1911 Rte. 40 at Ross-Osage
247 rooms - $70
Pets: Welcome
Creature Comforts: CCTV, a/c, restaurant, pool

La Quinta Inn, Medical Center
(800) Nu-Rooms, (806) 352-6311
http://www.laquinta.com
2108 So. Coulter Rd.
129 rooms - $55
Pets: Under 25 lbs.
Creature Comforts: CCTV, a/c, refrig, micro, cont. brkfst, pool

La Quinta Inn, East
(800) Nu-Rooms, (806) 373-7486
http://www.laquinta.com
1708 Rte. 40 East
130 rooms - $60-65
Pets: Under 25 lbs.
Creature Comforts: CCTV, a/c, refrig, micro, cont. brkfst, pool

Motel 6
(800) 4-MOTEL6, (806) 355-6554
http://www.motel6.com
2032 Paramount Blvd.
116 rooms - $35-45
Pets: Welcome
Creature Comforts: CCTV, a/c, pool

Motel 6
(800) 4-MOTEL6, (806) 374-6444
http://www.motel6.com
3930 Rte. 40 East
151 rooms - $30-45
Pets: Welcome
Creature Comforts: CCTV, a/c, pool

Motel 6
(800) 4-MOTEL6, (806) 373-3045
http://www.motel6.com
4301 Rte. 40 East
121 rooms - $30-45
Pets: Welcome
Creature Comforts: CCTV, a/c, pool

Motel 6
(800) 4-MOTEL6, (806) 359-7651
http://www.motel6.com
6030 Rte. 40 West
100 rooms - $35-60
Pets: Welcome
Creature Comforts: CCTV, a/c, pool

Quality Inn Suites
(800) 228-5151, (806) 847-6556
http://www.qualityinn.com
1803 Lakeside Rd.
102 rooms - $50-100
Pets: Welcome
Creature Comforts: CCTV, a/c, restaurant, pool, tennis

Ramada Inn
(800) 2-Ramada, (806) 379-6555
http://www.ramada.com
2501 Rte. 40 East
185 rooms - $75-85
Pets: Welcome w/$10 fee
Creature Comforts: CCTV, VCR, a/c, restaurant, pool

Sleep Inn Amarillo
(800) Sleep-Inn, (806) 372-6200
http://www.sleep-inn.com
2401 Rte. 40 East
55 rooms - $50-65
Pets: Small pets w/$20 deposit
Creature Comforts: CCTV, a/c, pool, whirlpool

ANGLETON
Country Hearth Inn
(409) 849-2465
1235 N. Velasco Rd.
40 rooms - $55-70
Pets: Welcome
Creature Comforts: CCTV, a/c, restaurant, pool

ANTHONY
Super 8 Motel
(800) 800-8000, (915) 886-2888
http://www.super8.com
100 Park North Dr.
49 rooms - $40-90
Pets: Welcome w/$10 fee
Creature Comforts: CCTV, a/c

ARLINGTON

Amerisuites
(800) 833-1516, (817) 649-7676
http://www.amerisuites.com
2380 E. Rd to Six Flags
116 rooms - $59-129
Pets: Welcome
Creature Comforts: CCTV, a/c,
pool, exercise rm.

Baymont Inn
(800) 789-4103, (817) 633-2400
http://www.baymontinns.com
360 Six Flagg Dr.
107 rooms - $50-85
Pets: One pet under 50 lbs, 2 pets
under 15 lbs. in first flr smkng
rms; cannot leave unattended
Creature Comforts: CCTV, a/c,
pool

Best Western, Great Southwest
(800) 528-1234, (817) 640-7722
http://www.bestwestern.com
3501 E. Division St.
122 rooms - $45-75
Pets: Small pets welcome
Creature Comforts: CCTV, a/c,
refrig, micro, restaurant, pool,
whirlpool, playground

Days Inn
(800) DAYS INN, (817) 649-8881
http://www.daysinn.com
1195 N. Watson Rd.
124 rooms - $40-70
Pets: Small pets w/$5 fee
Creature Comforts: CCTV, a/c,
pool

Days Inn Six Flags
(800) DAYS INN, (817) 261-8444
http://www.daysinn.com
910 N. Collins St.
92 rooms - $30-95
Pets: Welcome w/$10 fee
Creature Comforts: CCTV, a/c,
refrig, micro, pool

Hawthorn Suites, Arlington
(800) 527-1133, (817) 640-1188
http://www.hawthorn.com
2401 Brookhollow Plaza
125 rooms - $110-170
Pets: Welcome $5 per day $50 fee
Creature Comforts: CCTV, a/c,
kit, fireplace, hlth club, pool, hot
tub

Howard Johnson
(800) I-Go-Hojo, (817) 633-4000
http://www.hojo.com
117 S. Watson Rd.
192 rooms - $50-70
Pets: Welcome
Creature Comforts: CCTV, a/c,
pool

La Quinta Inn
(800) Nu-Rooms, (817) 640-4142
http://www.laquinta.com
825 N. Watson Rd.
340 rooms - $70-95
Pets: Small pets welcome
Creature Comforts: CCTV, a/c,
refrig, micro, pool, hlth clb access,
whirlpool

Motel 6
(800) 4-MOTEL6, (817) 649-0147
http://www.motel6.com
2626 E. Randall Mill Rd.
121 rooms - $35-59
Pets: Under 30 lbs. welcome
Creature Comforts: CCTV, a/c,
pool

Park Inn
(817) 860-2323
703 Benge Dr.
58 rooms - $40-50
Pets: Small pets w/$10 deposit
Creature Comforts: CCTV, a/c,
refrig, pool

ATHENS

The Flame Motel
(903) 675-5194
205 Dallas Highway
100 rooms - $30-49
Pets: Welcome
Creature Comforts: CCTV, a/c,
pool, hlth clb access

Spanish Trace Inn Motel
(800) 488-5173, (903) 675-5173
716 E. Tyler St.
80 rooms - $45-70
Pets: Welcome
Creature Comforts: CCTV, a/c,
restaurant, pool

ATLANTA

The Butler's Inn
(903) 796-8235
1100 West Main St.
58 rooms - $40-65
Pets: Small pets welcome
Creature Comforts: CCTV, a/c,
refrig, pool

AUSTIN

Amerisuites
(800) 833-1516, (512) 231-9437
http://www.amerisuites.com
3612 Tudor Blvd.
128 rooms - $70-150
Pets: Welcome
Creature Comforts: CCTV, a/c,
pool, exercise rm.

Baymont Inn
(800) 301-0200, (512) 246-2800
http://www.baymontinns.com
150 Parker Dr.
93 rooms - $54-87
Pets: Welcome
Creature Comforts: CCTV, a/c,
pool

Best Western, Atrium North
(800) 528-1234, (512) 339-7311
http://www.bestwestern.com
7928 Gessner Dr.
122 rooms - $50-100
Pets: Welcome
Creature Comforts: CCTV, a/c,
restaurant, cont. brkfst, pool,
sauna

Best Western Seville Plaza Inn
(800) 528-1234, (512) 447-5511
http://www.bestwestern.com
4323 S. Rte. 35
96 rooms - $60-85
Pets: Welcome
Creature Comforts: CCTV, a/c,
refrig, micro, restaurant, pool

The Brook House B&B
(800) 649-3370, (512) 459-0534
www.governorsinnaustin.com
609 West 33rd St.
6 rooms - $75-100
Pets: Welcome in cottage
Creature Comforts: Grey
clapboard main house w/adj.
cottage, country furnishings, oak
antiques and bed, a/c, kit, living
room, cont. brkfst, resident dog-
Ernie the black lab

Carrington's Bluff
(800) 871-8908, (512) 479-0638
www.governorsinnaustin.com
1900 David St.
6 rooms - $75-110
Pets: Welcome, must be flea
free (pet walking/sitting avail)
Creature Comforts: 1877
farmhouse on bluff, secluded,
English country hse motif, hrdwd
flrs, four poster or white iron beds,
country quilts, CCTV, a/c,
fireplace, cont. brkfst

Clarion Inn and Suites
(800) 434-7378, (512) 444-0561
http://www.clarioninn.com
2200 Route 35 S.
156 rooms - $65-129
Pets: Small pets
Creature Comforts: CCTV, a/c,
refrig, micro, restaurant, pool, hlth
clb access

Days Inn, University
(800) DAYS INN, (512) 478-1631
http://www.daysinnn.com
3105 Rte. 35 N.
63 rooms - $55-99
Pets: Welcome
Creature Comforts: CCTV, a/c,
restaurant, cont. brkfst, pool

Doubletree Guest Suites
(800) 222-TREE, (512) 478-7000
http://www.doubletreehotels.com
303 West 15th St.
189 rooms - $110-135
Pets: Small pets w/$10 fee
Creature Comforts: CCTV, a/c,
restaurant, pool

Doubletree Hotel
(800) 222-TREE, (512) 454-3737
http://www.doubletreehotels.com
6505 Rte. 35N
350 rooms - $70-200
Pets: Welcome
Creature Comforts: CCTV, a/c,
restaurant, pool, hlth clb access

Drury Inn Highland Mall
(800) 325-8300, (512) 454-1144
http://www.druryinn.com
919 E. Koenig Lane
136 rooms - $85-99
Pets: Under 20 lbs. welcome
Creature Comforts: CCTV, a/c,
cont. brkfst, pool

Drury Inn North
(800) 325-8300, (512) 467-9500
http://www.druryinn.com
6511 Rte. 35N
152 rooms - $80-99
Pets: Under 20 lbs. welcome
Creature Comforts: CCTV, a/c,
cont. brkfst, pool

Exel Inn
(800) 356-8013, (512) 462-9201
http://www.exelinns.com
2711 S. Rte. 35
89 rooms - $50-75
Pets: Welcome in smoking rooms
Creature Comforts: CCTV, a/c,
cont. brkfst, pool

Four Points Sheraton
(800) 325-3535, (512) 836-8520
http://www.sheraton.com
7800 S. Rte. 35
188 rooms - $65-99
Pets: Welcome
Creature Comforts: CCTV, a/c,
restaurant, pool, hlth clb.

Four Seasons Hotel
(800) 332-3442, (512) 478-4500
http:/www.fshr.com
98 San Jacinto Blvd.
290 rooms - $200-1,200
Pets: Under 15 lbs., leashed in
public areas, pet program, dog
walking, biscuits
Creature Comforts: Luxury hotel
on bluff, beautiful grnds, interior
w/lavish "Ralph Lauren" decor,
luxurious rms w/trad. reprod,
CCTV, a/c, refrig, gourmet
restaurant, pool, hlth clb

Governor's Inn B&B
(800) 871-8908, (512) 477-0711
www.governorsinnaustin.com
611 W. 22nd St.
10 rooms - $80-110
Pets: Welcome w/notice, pet
walking is available
Creature Comforts: Neoclassic
1897 Victorian, wraparound
porches, request first flr rm w/
oversized windows, four-poster
bed w/duvet, faux fireplace, dried
flowers, canopy beds, bedrooms
furnished w/country antiques,
private third floor family suite,
CCTV, a/c, hearty breakfast

Habitat Suites Hotel
(800) 535-4663, (512) 467-6000
500 Highland Mall
96 rooms - $85-150
Pets: Welcome
Creature Comforts: CCTV, a/c,
pool

Hawthorn Suites Central
(800) 527-1133, (512) 459-3335
http://www.hawthorn.com
935 La Posada Dr.
71 rooms - $110-160
Pets: Welcome
Creature Comforts: CCTV, a/c,
pool, tennis

Hawthorn Suites South
(800) 527-1133, (512) 440-7722
http://www.hawthorn.com
4020 S. Rte. -35
120 rooms - $70-180
Pets: Welcome
Creature Comforts: CCTV, a/c,
pool

Heart of Texas Motel
(512) 892-0644
5303 Hwy 290 W.
30 rooms - $50-65
Pets: Welcome
Creature Comforts: CCTV, a/c,
pool

Holiday Inn, Airport/Mall
(800) HOLIDAY, (512) 459-4251
http://www.holiday-inn.com
6911 Rte. 35N
293 rooms - $70-110
Pets: Welcome
Creature Comforts: CCTV, a/c,
restaurant, pool

Holiday Inn, Austin South
(800) HOLIDAY, (512) 448-2444
http:/www.holiday-inn.com
3401 S. Rte. 35
210 rooms - $70-120
Pets: Welcome
Creature Comforts: CCTV, a/c,
restaurant, hlth clb access, sauna,
whirlpool, tennis, golf

Holiday Inn Northwest Plaza
(800) HOLIDAY, (512) 343-0888
http://www.holiday-inn.com
8901 Business Park Dr.
193 rooms - $75-105
Pets: Welcome
Creature Comforts: CCTV, a/c,
restaurant, pool, hlth clb access,
sauna, whirlpool

Howard Johnson Plaza Hotel
(800) I-Go-Hojo, (512) 837-7900
http://www.hojo.com
9106 N. Rte. 35
120 rooms - $45-85
Pets: Welcome
Creature Comforts: CCTV, a/c,
restaurant, cont. brkfst, pool

HomeGate Studios/Suites
(888) 456-GATE, (512) 219-6500
http://www.homegate.com
12424 Research Blvd.
126 rooms - $70-99
Pets: Under 10 lbs. w/deposit
Creature Comforts: Attractive
suite hotel, CCTV, a/c, living rm,
kit, pool

HomeGate Studios/Suites
(888) 456-GATE, (512) 833-0898
http://www.homegate.com
2700 Gracy Farms Ln.
116 rooms - $62-99
Pets: Under 10 lbs. w/deposit
Creature Comforts: Attractive
suite hotel, CCTV, a/c, living rm,
kit, pool

HomeGate Studios/Suites
(888) 456-GATE, (512) 339-6005
http://www.homegate.com
8221 Route 35 N.
121 rooms - $62-99
Pets: Under 10 lbs. w/deposit
Creature Comforts: Attractive
suite hotel, CCTV, a/c, living rm,
kit, pool

HomeGate Studios/Suites
(888) 456-GATE, (512) 326-0100
http://www.homegate.com
1001 Rte 35 S.
150 rooms - $62-99
Pets: Under 10 lbs. w/deposit
Creature Comforts: Attractive
suite hotel, CCTV, a/c, living rm,
kit

La Quinta Inn, Ben White
(800) Nu-Rooms, (512) 443-1774
http://www.laquinta.com
4200 Rte. 35S
130 rooms - $60-120
Pets: Under 25 lbs. welcome
Creature Comforts: CCTV, a/c,
pool

La Quinta Inn, Capitol
(800) Nu-Rooms, (512) 476-1166
http://www.laquinta.com
300 E. 11th St.
145 rooms - $75-90
Pets: Small pets welcome
Creature Comforts: CCTV, a/c,
pool

La Quinta Inn, Airport
(800) Nu-Rooms, (512) 459-4381
http://www.laquinta.com
5812 Rte. 35-N
122 rooms - $60-120
Pets: Under 25 lbs. welcome
Creature Comforts: CCTV, a/c,
pool

La Quinta North
(800) Nu-Rooms, (512) 452-9401
http://www.laquinta.com
7100 Rte. 35-N
115 rooms - $60-120
Pets: Under 25 lbs. welcome
Creature Comforts: CCTV, a/c,
pool

La Quinta Oltorf
(800) Nu-Rooms, (512) 447-6661
http://www.laquinta.com
1603 E. Oltorf Blvd.
132 rooms - $60-120
Pets: Under 25 lbs. welcome
Creature Comforts: CCTV, a/c,
pool

Lake Austin Spa Resort
(800) 847-5637, (512) 372-7300
http://www.lakeaustin.com
1705 S. Quinlan Park Rd.
40 rooms - $280-425
Pets: Welcome w/$100 fee
Creature Comforts: Luxurious
spa, *Travel and Leisure* voted it
"top 50 best kept secrets in the
world", sophsiticated Southwest
decor, orig art, down comforters,
meditation patios, soaking tubs,
CCTV, a/c, restaurant, pool, full
spa and recreation facilities,
highly recommended

Motel 6, Airport
(800) 4-MOTEL6, (512) 467-9111
http://www.motel6.com
5330 Interregional Highway N
109 rooms - $40-65
Pets: Under 30 lbs. welcome
Creature Comforts: CCTV, a/c,
pool

Motel 6, Central
(800) 4-MOTEL6, (512) 837-9890
http://www.motel6.com
8010 Rte. 35N
112 rooms - $40-65
Pets: Under 30 lbs. welcome
Creature Comforts: CCTV, a/c,
pool

Motel 6, North
(800) 4-MOTEL6, (512) 339-6161
http://www.motel6.com
9420 N. Rte. 35
158 rooms - $40-75
Pets: Under 30 lbs. welcome
Creature Comforts: CCTV, a/c,
pool

Motel 6, South
(800) 4-MOTEL6, (512) 444-5882
http://www.motel6.com
2702 Inter-Regional Rte. S.
109 rooms - $40-75
Pets: Under 30 lbs. welcome
Creature Comforts: CCTV, a/c,
restaurant, pool

Ramada Inn, South
(800) 2-Ramada, (512) 447-0151
http://www.ramada.com
1212 W. Ben White Blvd.
103 rooms - $55-90
Pets: Welcome
Creature Comforts: CCTV, a/c,
restaurant, pool

Ramada Limited
(800) 2-Ramada, (512) 451-7001
http://www.ramada.com
5526 N. Rte. 35
140 rooms - $55-75
Pets: Welcome
Creature Comforts: CCTV, a/c,
pool

Red Lion Hotel Airport
(800) RED-LION, (512) 323-5466
http://www.doubletreehotels.com
6121 Rte. 35N at Rte. 290
300 rooms - $125-135
Pets: Dogs only
Creature Comforts: CCTV, a/c,
restaurant, pool, hlth clb access,
whirlpool

Renaissance Austin Hotel
(800) 468-3571
http://www.renaissancehotels.com
9721 Arboretum Blvd.
478 rooms - $105-197
Pets: Welcome
Creature Comforts: CCTV, a/c,
cont. brkfst, pool, hlth clb

Residence Inn, Northwest
(800) 331-3131, (512) 502-8200
http://www.residenceinn.com
3713 Tudor Blvd.
84 rooms - $120-140
Pets: Welcome w/$5 daily fee,
$50 one-time fee
Creature Comforts: CCTV, a/c,
kit, cont. brkfst, pool, hlth clb
access, sauna, whirlpool, sports
court

Residence Inn, South
(800) 331-3131, (512) 912-1100
http://www.residenceinn.com
4537 South Rte. 35
66 rooms - $110-130
Pets: Welcome w/$50 fee
Creature Comforts: CCTV, a/c,
kit, cont.brkfst, pool, hlth clb
access, sauna, whirlpool, sports
club

BALLINGER
Desert Inn Motel
(915) 365-2518
2101 Hutchings Ave.
24 rooms - $30-49
Pets: Welcome
Creature Comforts: CCTV, a/c,
pool

BANDERA
Cool Water Acres
(830) 796-4866
http://home.netcom.com/~jwd2/
Rte 1, Box 785
1 cabin - $80
Pets: One dog permitted w/$5 fee
Creature Comforts: Unique 1870
cabin set on 55 acres and 7-acre
spring-fed lake w/waterfall, cabin
w/orginal open beamed ceilings,
stone fireplace, CCTV, a/c,
separate bedroom, kit, swimming

Hackberry Lodge
(903) 675-5194
205 Dallas Highway
100 rooms - $30-49
Pets: Welcome
Creature Comforts: CCTV, a/c,
pool, hlth clb access

River Front Motel
(800) 870-5671, (830) 460-3690
Main St. at the River Bridge
11 rooms - $45-78
Pets: Welcome
Creature Comforts: CCTV, a/c

River Oak Inn
(830) 796-7751
www.texashillcountrymall.com/
river-oak/inn.htm
1203 Main St., Hwy 16 N.
28 rooms - $40-100
Pets: Welcome
Creature Comforts: Riverfront
motel, CCTV, a/c, refrig, micro

BAYTOWN
Best Western Baytown Inn
(800) 528-1234, (281) 421-2233
http://www.bestwestern.com
5021 Rte. 10 E
50 rooms - $50-69
Pets: Small pets welcome
Creature Comforts: CCTV, a/c,
refrig, micro, Jacuzzi, pool

Baymont Inn
(800) 4-Budget, (281) 421-7300
http://www.baymontinns.com
5215 Rte. 10 East
105 rooms - $45-75
Pets: Welcome
Creature Comforts: CCTV, a/c,
pool

Holiday Inn Express
(800) 465-4329
http://www.holiday-inn.com
5222 Route 10 E.
62 rooms - $58-74
Pets: Small pets welcome
Creature Comforts: CCTV, a/c,
cont. brkfst, pool

La Quinta Inn
(800) Nu-Rooms, (281) 421-5566
http://www.laquinta.com
4911 I-10E
130 rooms - $55-60
Pets: Small pets welcome
Creature Comforts: CCTV, a/c,
refrig, pool

Motel 6
(800) 4-MOTEL6, (281) 576-5777
http://www.motel6.com
8911 Rte. 146
124 rooms - $35-55
Pets: Small pets welcome
Creature Comforts: CCTV, a/c,
pool

BEAUMONT
Best Western Beaumont
(800) 528-1234, (409) 898-8150
http://www.bestwestern.com
2155 N. 11th St.
152 rooms - $55-68
Pets: Welcome
Creature Comforts: CCTV, a/c,
restaurant, pool

Best Western Jefferson Inn
(800) 528-1234, (409) 842-0037
http://www.bestwestern.com
1610 Rte. 10S
120 rooms - $55-60
Pets: Small pets welcome
Creature Comforts: CCTV, a/c,
refrig, micro, cont. brkfst, pool

Days Inn
(800) DAYS INN, (409) 838-0581
http://www.daysinn.com
30 Rte. 10N
150 rooms - $33-55
Pets: Welcome w/$5 fee
Creature Comforts: CCTV, a/c,
pool

Hilton Hotel
(800) HILTONS, (409) 842-3600
http://www.hilton.com
2355 Rte. 10S
150 rooms - $90-120
Pets: Welcome w/$100 deposit
Creature Comforts: CCTV, a/c,
restaurant, pool, hlth clb access

Holiday Inn Beaumont Plaza
(800) HOLIDAY, (409) 842-5995
http://www.holiday-inn.com
3950 Rte. 10 S
253 rooms - $69-125
Pets: Welcome w/$10 deposit
Creature Comforts: CCTV, a/c,
restaurant, pool

Holiday Inn Midtown
(800) HOLIDAY, (409) 892-2222
http://www.holiday-inn.com
2095 N. 11th St.
190 rooms - $70-109
Pets: Welcome w/$100 deposit
Creature Comforts: CCTV, a/c,
pool

La Quinta Inn
(800) Nu-Rooms, (409) 838-9991
http://www.laquinta.com
220 Rte. 10N
122 rooms - $65-95
Pets: Small pets welcome
Creature Comforts: CCTV, a/c,
refrig, micro, cont. brkfst, pool

Quality Inn
(800) 228-5151, (409) 892-7722
http://www.qualityinn.com
1295 N. 11th St.
125 rooms - $65-78
Pets: Welcome
Creature Comforts: CCTV, a/c,
refrig, micro, pool

Ramada Inn Spindletop
(800) 2-Ramada, (409) 898-2111
http://www.ramada.com
2525 N. 11th St.
120 rooms - $50-79
Pets: Welcome
Creature Comforts: CCTV, a/c,
refrig, micro, restaurant, cont.
brkfst, pool

Ramada Ltd.
(800) 2-Ramada, (409) 842-1111
http://www.ramada.com
4085 Rte. 10 South
136 rooms - $45-95
Pets: Welcome
Creature Comforts: CCTV, a/c,
Jacuzzi, cont. brkfst, pool

Ramada Inn
(800) 2-Ramada, (409) 892-7722
http://www.ramada.com
1295 N. 11th St.
122 rooms - $70-95
Pets: Welcome
Creature Comforts: CCTV, a/c,
restaurant, full brkfst, pool

BEDFORD
Holiday Inn
(800) 465-4329
http://www.holiday-inn.com
3005 W. Airport Fwy.
243 rooms - $60-130
Pets: Small pets welcome
Creature Comforts: CCTV, a/c,
restaurant, pool, hlth clb.

La Quinta Inn
(800) Nu-Rooms, (817) 267-5200
http://www.laquinta.com
1450 Airport Fwy.
116 rooms - $60-90
Pets: Small pets welcome
Creature Comforts: CCTV, a/c,
cont. brkfst, pool

BEEVILLE
Best Western Drummers Inn
(800) 528-1234, (361) 358-4000
http://www.bestwestern.com
400 Rte. 181S
60 rooms - $50-70
Pets: Small pets welcome
Creature Comforts: CCTV, a/c,
restaurant, pool

Executive Inn
(512) 358-0022
1601 N. St. Mary St.
68 rooms - $45-80
Pets: Welcome w/$5 fee
Creature Comforts: CCTV, a/c,
refrig, pool

BELLMEAD
Motel 6
(800) 4-MOTEL6, (254) 799-4957
http://www.motel6.com
1509 Hogan Lane
143 rooms - $30-65
Pets: Under 30 lbs. welcome
Creature Comforts: CCTV, a/c,
pool

BELTON
Best Western River Forest Motel
(800) 528-1234, (254) 939-5711
http://www.bestwestern.com
1414 E. Sixth Ave.
48 rooms - $50-80
Pets: Welcome w/$10 fee
Creature Comforts: CCTV, a/c,
pool

Budget Host, The Belton Inn
(800) Bud-Host, (254) 939-0744
http://www.budgethost.com
1520 S. Rte. 35
51 rooms - $45-85
Pets: Welcome
Creature Comforts: CCTV,
VCR, a/c, refrig, micro, pool

Ramada Limited
(800) 2-Ramada, (254) 939-3745
http://www.ramada.com
1102 E. 2nd Ave.
64 rooms - $40-80
Pets: Welcome
Creature Comforts: CCTV, a/c,
micro, cont. brkfst, pool,
playground

BIG BEND NATIONAL PARK
Big Bend Motor Inn
(800) 848-BEND
http://www.bigbendlodging.com
Hwy. 118 and Hwy. 170
84 rooms - $60-70
Pets: Welcome
Creature Comforts: CCTV, a/c,
restaurant, pool

Chisos Mountains Lodge
(915) 477-2291
Basin Rural Station
72 rooms - $61-81
Pets: Welcome
Creature Comforts: CCTV, a/c,
restaurant

BIG SPRING
Econo Lodge
(800) 55-ECONO, (915) 263-5200
http://www.econolodge.com
804 Rte. 20W
50 rooms - $45-65
Pets: Welcome
Creature Comforts: CCTV, a/c,
restaurant, cont. brkfst, pool

Motel 6
(800) 4-MOTEL6, (915) 267-1695
http://www.motel6.com
600 W. Rte. 20
92 rooms - $30-55
Pets: Under 30 lbs. welcome
Creature Comforts: CCTV, a/c,
pool

Ponderosa Motor Inn
(915) 267-5237
2701 Gregg St.
27 rooms - $35-50
Pets: Small pets welcome
Creature Comforts: CCTV, a/c,
restaurant

BLANCO
Creekwood Country Inn
(830) 833-2248
P.O. Box 1357
2 rooms - $75-95
Pets: Welcome w/approval
Creature Comforts: Nature
sanctuary-like setting, cottage w/
antiques, four poster beds, CCTV,
a/c, porch refrig, weekend-full
brkfst

My Little Guest House
(830) 833-5264
Box 67
1 cottage - $75-95
Pets: Friendly dogs welcome, not
allowed on furniture
Creature Comforts: Pretty
shingled two-rm cottage on
Blanco Rvr, massive oaks, iron
bed/floral quilt, milk painted furn,
CCTV, a/c, stocked refrig, kit

BOERNE
Best Western Texas Country Inn
(800) 528-1234, (830) 249-9791
http://www.bestwestern.com
35150 Rte. 10
81 rooms - $55-75
Pets: Welcome w/$10 fee
Creature Comforts: CCTV,
VCR, a/c, cont. brkfst, pool

BONHAM
Days Inn
(800) DAYS INN, (903) 583-3121
http://www.daysinn.com
1515 Old Ector Road
53 rooms - $45-70
Pets: Small pets welcome
Creature Comforts: CCTV, a/c,
refrig, cont. brkfst, pool

BORGER
The Inn Place of Borger
(806) 273-9556
100 Bulldog Blvd.
92 rooms - $45-80
Pets: Small pets welcome
Creature Comforts: CCTV, a/c,
kit

BOWIE
Days Inn
(800) DAYS INN, (940) 872-5426
http://www.daysinn.com
Rtes. 59 & 287
60 rooms - $40-45
Pets: Welcome w/$5 fee
Creature Comforts: CCTV, a/c,
refrig, pool

Parks Inn
(940) 872-1111
708 Park Ave.
40 rooms - $40-45
Pets: Welcome
Creature Comforts: CCTV, a/c,
refrig

BRADY
Best Western Brady Inn
(800) 528-1234, (915) 597-3997
http://www.bestwestern.com
2200 S. Bridge St.
40 rooms - $45-75
Pets: Small pets welcome
Creature Comforts: CCTV, a/c,
refrig, micro, Jacuzzi, cont. brkfst,
pool, whirlpool

Sunset Inn
(915) 597-0789
2108 S. Bridge St.
44 rooms - $45-75
Pets: Small pets welcome
Creature Comforts: CCTV, a/c,
refrig, cont. brkfst, pool

BRENHAM
Ramada Ltd.
(800) 2-Ramada, (409) 836-1300
http://www.ramada.com
2217 S. Market St.
94 rooms - $45-79
Pets: Welcome w/$5 fee
Creature Comforts: CCTV, a/c,
cont. brkfst, pool

Regency Inn
(409) 830-0030
2855 Hwy . 290
90 rooms - $25-55
Pets: Welcome
Creature Comforts: CCTV, a/c,
restaurant, pool

BROADDUS
Country Inn Motel
(409) 872-3691
Route 147
11 rooms - $35-49
Pets: Small pets welcome
Creature Comforts: Neat, rustic
motel in rural setting w/SATV, a/c

BROWNFIELD
Best Western Caprock Inn
(800) 528-1234, (806) 637-9471
http://www.bestwestern.com
321 Lubbock Road
50 rooms - $50-69
Pets: Welcome
Creature Comforts: CCTV, a/c,
restaurant, pool

BROWNSVILLE
Four Points by Sheraton
(800) 325-3535, (956) 350-9191
http://www.sheraton.com
377 N. Expwy.
145 rooms - $90-225
Pets: Small pets welcome
Creature Comforts: CCTV, a/c,
refrig, Jacuzzi, restaurant, pool,
whirlpool

Holiday Inn Fort Brown Hotel
(800) HOLIDAY, (956) 546-2201
http://www.holiday-inn.com
1900 E. Elizabeth St.
168 rooms - $70-98
Pets: Small pets welcome
Creature Comforts: CCTV, a/c,
restaurant, pool, tennis

La Quinta Inn
(800) Nu-Rooms, (956) 546-0381
http://www.laquinta.com
55 Sam Perl Blvd.
100 rooms - $45-80
Pets: Small pets welcome
Creature Comforts: CCTV, a/c,
cont. brkfst, pool

Motel 6
(800) 4-MOTEL6, (956) 546-4699
http://www.motel6.com
2255 N. Expressway
190 rooms - $35-49
Pets: Under 30 lbs. welcome
Creature Comforts: CCTV, a/c,
pool

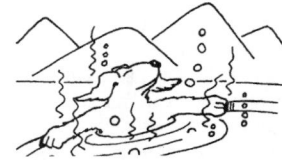

BROWNWOOD
Best Western Brownwood
(800) 528-1234, (915) 646-3511
http://www.bestwestern.com
410 E. Commerce St.
80 rooms - $45-57
Pets: Welcome
Creature Comforts: CCTV, a/c,
pool

Gold Key Inn Motel
(800) 646-0912, (915) 646-2551
515 E. Commerce St.
137 rooms - $45-50
Pets: Small pets welcome
Creature Comforts: CCTV, a/c,
restaurant, pool

BRYAN
Preference Inn
(409) 822-6196
1601 S. Texas Ave.
114 rooms - $45-79
Pets: Welcome w$5 fee
Creature Comforts: CCTV, a/c,
refrig, restaurant, pool

BUFFALO
Best Western Craig's Inn
(800) 528-1234, (903) 322-5831
http://www.bestwestern.com
Rtes. 45 & 79
59 rooms - $50-88
Pets: Small pets welcome
Creature Comforts: CCTV, a/c,
restaurant, pool

BURLESON
Days Inn
(800) DAYS INN, (817) 447-1111
http://www.daysinn.com
329 S. Burleson Blvd.
43 rooms - $60-90
Pets: Welcome w/$10 fee
Creature Comforts: CCTV, a/c,
refrig, micro, cont. brkfst

CALDWELL
Sunset Inn
(409) 567-4661
705 Rte. 36N
56 rooms - $40-75
Pets: Small pets welcome
Creature Comforts: CCTV, a/c,
refrig, micro, cont. brkfst, pool

The Surrey Inn
(409) 567-3221
403 E. Rte. 21
25 rooms - $35-55
Pets: Welcome
Creature Comforts: CCTV, a/c,
refrig, micro, restaurant, pool

CALVERT
Pin Oak B&B
(888) 367-8096, (409) 364-2935
http://www.texassleepaways.com/
pinoak/
503 Pin Oak
5 rooms - $85-90
Pets: Small pets welcome
Creature Comforts: 1901 home
w/11-foot ceilings, orig. featurs,
hardwood flrs, stained glass,
fireplaces, sleigh and brass beds,
antiques, porches, a/c, full brkfst

CAMERON
Varsity Motel
(817) 697-6446
1004 E. 1st St.
40 rooms - $40-55
Pets: Welcome
Creature Comforts: CCTV, a/c,
refrig, pool

CANTON
Best Western Canton Inn
(800) 528-1234, (903) 567-6591
http://www.bestwestern.com
2251 M. Trade Days Blvd.
82 rooms - $45-75
Pets: Small pets welcome
Creature Comforts: CCTV, a/c,
refrig, pool

Days Inn
(800) DAYS INN, (903) 567-6588
http://www.daysinn.com
Rtes. 19 & 20
43 rooms - $48-99
Pets: Under 20 lbs. w/$10 fee
Creature Comforts: CCTV, a/c,
cont. brkfst, pool

CANYON
Holiday Inn Express
(800) 465-4329
http://www.holiday-inn.com
2901 Fourth Ave.
66 rooms - $60-150
Pets: Small pets welcome
Creature Comforts: CCTV, a/c,
refrig, micro, pool, hlth clb.

CANYON LAKE
Maricopa Ranch Resort
(830) 964-3731
Box 1659
23 rooms - $57-85
Pets: Welcome
Creature Comforts: CCTV, a/c,
pool

Maricopa Lodge
(800) 460-8891, (830) 964-3600
www.maricopariversidelodge.com
12381 Rte. 306
19 rooms - $50-107
Pets: Welcome on occasion
Creature Comforts: Riverviews,
CCTV, a/c, pool

CARROLLTON
Red Roof Inn
(800) THE ROOF, (972) 245-1700
http://www.redroof.com
1720 S. Broadway St.
137 rooms - $45-50
Pets: Small pets welcome
Creature Comforts: CCTV, a/c

CASTROVILLE
Best Western Alsatian Inn
(800) 528-1234, (830) 538-2262
http://www.bestwestern.com
1650 Rte. 90W
40 rooms - $70-95
Pets: Welcome w/$5 fee
Creature Comforts: CCTV, a/c,
restaurant, pool

CENTER

Best Western Center Inn
(800) 528-1234, (409) 598-3384
http://www.bestwestern.com
1005 Hurst St.
72 rooms - $40-80
Pets: Small pets welcome
Creature Comforts: CCTV, a/c,
kit, pool

CENTERVILLE

Days Inn
(800) DAYS INN, (903) 536-7175
http://www.daysinn.com
Rtes. 45 & 7
40 rooms - $47-75
Pets: Welcome w/$7 fee
Creature Comforts: CCTV, a/c,
cont. brkfst

CHANNELVIEW

Best Western Houston East
(800) 528-1234, (713) 452-1000
http://www.bestwestern.com
15919 Rte. 10E
98 rooms - $35-65
Pets: Small pets w/$20 deposit
Creature Comforts: CCTV, a/c,
restaurant, pool

CHILDRESS

Best Western Classic Inn
(800) 528-1234, (940) 937-6353
http://www.bestwestern.com
1805 Ave. F NW
65 rooms - $55-69
Pets: Small pets welcome
Creature Comforts: CCTV,
VCR, a/c, cont. brkfst, pool

Comfort Inn
(800) 228-5150, (940) 937-6363
http://www.comfortinn.com
1804 Ave. F. NW
46 rooms - $55-79
Pets: Welcome
Creature Comforts: CCTV, a/c,
pool, sauna, whirlpool

Econo Lodge
(800) 55-ECONO, (940) 937-3695
http://www.econolodge.com
1612 Ave. F. NW
28 rooms - $45-68
Pets: Welcome w/$5 fee
Creature Comforts: CCTV, a/c,
restaurant, cont. brkfst, pool

CISCO

Rodeway White Elephant Inn
(800) 228-2000, (254) 442-3735
http://www.rodeway.com
1898 Rte. 206 W
31 rooms - $45-59
Pets: Welcome w/$25 deposit
Creature Comforts: CCTV, a/c,
pool

CLAUDE

L A Motel
(806) 226-4981
200 E. 1st St.
15 rooms - $30-48
Pets: Small pets welcome
Creature Comforts: CCTV, a/c,
restaurant

CLEBURNE

Budget Host Inn
(800) Bud-Host, (817) 556-3631
http://www.budgethost.com
2107 N. Main St.
28 rooms - $45-60
Pets: Small pets w/$4 fee
Creature Comforts: CCTV, a/c,
pool

Days Inn
(800) DAYS INN, (817) 645-4813
http://www.daysinn.com
101 N. Ridgeway Dr.
45 rooms - $45-70
Pets: Welcome
Creature Comforts: CCTV, a/c,
pool

CLIFTON

The River's Bend B&B
(817) 675-4936
P.O. Box 228
3 rooms - $75-150
Pets: Welcome w/approval,
including horses
Creature Comforts: Farmhouse
on 240 acres, bird lovers paradise,
porches w/swing and rocking
chairs, stone fireplace in great rm.,
antiques, CCTV, VCR, a/c, kit
stocked w/brkfst makings

CLUTE

La Quinta Inn
(800) Nu-Rooms, (409) 265-7461
http://www.laquinta.com
1126 Rte. 332 W
136 rooms - $50-90
Pets: Welcome
Creature Comforts: CCTV, a/c,
pool

Motel 6

(800) 4-MOTEL6, (409) 265-4764
http://www.motel6.com
1000 Rte. 332W
76 rooms - $30-85
Pets: Under 30 lbs. welcome
Creature Comforts: CCTV, a/c,
pool

COLDSPRING

San Jacinto Inn
(409) 653-3008
Rte. 150 W.
13 rooms - $38-41
Pets: Welcome w/$10 fee
Creature Comforts: CCTV, a/c,
refrig

COLLEGE STATION

Comfort Inn
(800) 221-2222, (409) 846-7333
http://www.comfortinn.com
104 Texas Ave. S
114 rooms - $60-90
Pets: Welcome w/$25 deposit
Creature Comforts: CCTV, a/c,
refrig, micro, pool, whirlpool

Hilton Hotel Conference Center
(800) HILTONS, (409) 693-7500
http://www.hilton.com
801 University Dr. E.
303 rooms - $120-165
Pets: Small pets w/$10 fee
Creature Comforts: CCTV, a/c,
kit, restaurant, pool

Holiday Inn - College Station
(800) HOLIDAY, (409) 693-1736
http://www.holiday-inn.com
1503 S. Texas Ave.
126 rooms - $60-85
Pets: Small pets welcome
Creature Comforts: CCTV, a/c,
restaurant, pool

La Quinta Inn
(800) Nu-Rooms, (409) 696-7777
http://www.laquinta.com
607 Texas Ave.
176 rooms - $70-95
Pets: Small pets welcome
Creature Comforts: CCTV, a/c,
refrig, micro, cont. brkfst, pool

Manor House Motor Inn
(800) 231-4100, (409) 764-9540
2504 Texas Ave. S.
116 rooms - $60-85
Pets: Small pets w/$10 fee
Creature Comforts: CCTV, a/c, pool

Motel 6
(800) 4-MOTEL6, (409) 696-3379
http://www.motel6.com
2327 Texas Ave. South
110 rooms - $35-60
Pets: Under 30 lbs. welcome
Creature Comforts: CCTV, a/c, pool

Ramada Inn Motor Hotel
(800) 2-Ramada, (409) 693-9891
http://www.ramada.com
1502 Texas Ave. South
167 rooms - $60-95
Pets: Small pets w/$10 fee
Creature Comforts: CCTV, VCR, a/c, refrig, restaurant, pool, whirlpool

COLORADO CITY
Days Inn
(800) DAYS INN, (915) 728-2638
http://www.daysinn.com
Rtes. 20 & 208
52 rooms - $40-75
Pets: Welcome
Creature Comforts: CCTV, a/c, cont. brkfst, pool

Villa Inn Motel
(915) 728-5217
2310 Hickory St.
40 rooms - $35-55
Pets: Welcome
Creature Comforts: CCTV, a/c, cont. brkfst, pool

COLUMBUS
Columbus Inn
(409) 732-5723
2208 Rte. 71
72 rooms - $50-65
Pets: Welcome w/$10 fee
Creature Comforts: CCTV, a/c, Jacuzzi, pool

COMANCHE
Heritage Hill Bed Breakfast
(915) 356-3397
Rtes. 36 East & 3
4 rooms - $70-100
Pets: Welcome
Creature Comforts: CCTV, a/c

COMFORT
Motor Inn at Comfort
(830) 995-3822
32 Hwy 87 N.
41 rooms - $60-85
Pets: Welcome
Creature Comforts: CCTV, a/c

CONROE
Heather's Glen B&B
(800) 665-2643, (409) 441-6611
http://www.heathersglen.com
200 E. Phillips St.
5 rooms - $70-195
Pets: Welcome w/$25 fee
Creature Comforts: Recently restored Victorian, heart of pine flrs, beamed ceilings, sweeping staircase, period antiques, Oriental rugs, a/c, Jacuzzi, full brkfst

Holiday Inn
(800) HOLIDAY, (409) 756-8941
http://www.holiday-inn.com
1601 Rte. 45 South
137 rooms - $80-85
Pets: Small pets welcome
Creature Comforts: CCTV, a/c, refrig, restaurant, pool, hlth clb access

Motel 6
(800) 4-MOTEL6, (409) 760-3159
http://www.motel6.com
820 Rte. 45 South
123 rooms - $35-49
Pets: Under 30 lbs. welcome
Creature Comforts: CCTV, a/c, pool

Ramada Inn
(800) 2-Ramada, (409) 756-8939
http://www.ramada.com
1520 Frazier St.
79 rooms - $65-90
Pets: Welcome
Creature Comforts: CCTV, a/c, cont. brkfst, pool

CORPUS CHRISTI
Best Western Garden Inn
(800) 528-1234, (361) 241-6675
http://www.bestwestern.com
11217 Rte. 37
40 rooms - $60-88
Pets: Small pets welcome
Creature Comforts: CCTV, a/c, refrig, micro, cont. brkfst, pool, sauna, playground

Best Western Sandy Shores
(800) 528-1234, (361) 883-7456
http://www.bestwestern.com
3200 Surfside Blvd.
247 rooms - $70-130
Pets: Welcome in Garden units
Creature Comforts: CCTV, a/c, restaurant, pool, hlth clb.

Days Inn
(800) DAYS INN, (361) 888-8599
http://www.daysinn.com
901 Navigation Blvd.
121 rooms - $45-80
Pets: Small pets w/$6 fee
Creature Comforts: CCTV, a/c, refrig, micro, restaurant, pool, playground

Drury Inn
(800) 325-8300, (361) 289-8200
http://www.druryinn.com
2021 N. Padre Island Dr.
105 rooms - $55-80
Pets: Welcome
Creature Comforts: CCTV, a/c, pool

Embassy Suites Hotel
(800) 362-2779, (361) 853-7899
http://www.embassy-suites.com
4337 S. Padre Island Dr.
150 rooms - $100-140
Pets: Welcome w/$10 fee
Creature Comforts: CCTV, a/c, restaurant, pool

Gulf Beach - II Motor Inn
(361) 882-3500
3500 Surfside Blvd.
139 rooms - $59-85
Pets: Welcome
Creature Comforts: CCTV, a/c, refrig

Hampton Inn
(800) Hampton, (361) 289-5861
http://www.hamptoninn.com
5501 Rte. 37 & McBride Lane
157 rooms - $55-90
Pets: Welcome
Creature Comforts: CCTV, a/c,
restaurant, pool, hlth clb access

Holiday Inn - Emerald Beach
(800) HOLIDAY, (361) 883-5731
http://www.holiday-inn.com
1102 S. Shoreline Blvd.
368 rooms - $140-150
Pets: Welcome
Creature Comforts: CCTV, a/c,
restaurant, pool

Holiday Inn - Padre Island Dr.
(800) HOLIDAY, (361) 289-5100
http://www.holiday-inn.com
5549 Leopard St.
247 rooms - $70-95
Pets: Small pets welcome
Creature Comforts: CCTV, a/c,
restaurant, pool, hlth clb access

Holiday Inn, North Padre Island
(800) HOLIDAY, (361) 949-8041
http://www.holiday-inn.com
15202 Windward Drove
148 rooms - $70-185
Pets: Small pets w/$10 fee
Creature Comforts: Beachfront,
CCTV, VCR, a/c, refrig, micro,
restaurant, pool, sauna, health clb
access, whirlpool, bicycles, fishing

Howard Johnson
(800) I-Go-Hojo, (361) 883-2951
http://www.hojo.com
224 Rte. 37 North
112 rooms - $30-80
Pets: Welcome
Creature Comforts: CCTV, a/c,
restaurant, pool

La Quinta Inn - North
(800) Nu-Rooms, (361) 888-5721
http://www.laquinta.com
5155 Rte. 37 North
121 rooms - $65-90
Pets: Small pets welcome
Creature Comforts: CCTV, a/c,
refrig, micro, cont. brkfst, pool

La Quinta Inn - South
(800) Nu-Rooms, (361) 991-5730
http://www.laquinta.com
358 Expwy. Airline Road
129 rooms - $70-95
Pets: Small pets welcome
Creature Comforts: CCTV, a/c,
refrig, micro, cont. brkfst, pool

Motel 6 - East
(800) 4-MOTEL6, (361) 991-8858
http://www.motel6.com
8202 S. Padre Island Dr.
26 rooms - $40-80
Pets: Under 30 lbs. welcome
Creature Comforts: CCTV, a/c,
pool

Motel 6 - West
(800) 4-MOTEL6, (361) 289-0280
http://www.motel6.com
845 Lantana St.
124 rooms - $35-80
Pets: Welcome
Creature Comforts: CCTV, a/c,
pool

Racetrack Hotel/Suites
(800) 723-2738
6255 Hwy 37
150 rooms - $40-150
Pets: Welcome w/$7 fee
Creature Comforts: CCTV, a/c,
restaurant, pool

Red Roof Inn
(800) THE ROOF, (361) 289-6925
http://www.redroof.com
630 Rte. 37
142 rooms - $40-70
Pets: Welcome
Creature Comforts: CCTV, a/c,
restaurant, pool

Residence Inn by Marriott
(800) 331-3131, (361) 985-1113
http://www.residenceinn.com
5229 Blanche Moore Dr.
66 rooms - $90-140
Pets: Welcome w/$10 daily fee,
$75 one-time fee
Creature Comforts: CCTV, a/c,
fireplace, kit, restaurant, cont.
brkfst, pool, hlth clb access, sauna,
whirlpool, sports court

Surfside Condominium
(800) 548-4585, (361) 949-8128
15005 Windward Dr.
34 rooms - $75-110
Pets: Small pets w/$3 fee, $50 dep
Creature Comforts: CCTV, a/c,
kit, pool

Travelodge Airport
(800) 578-7878, (361) 289-5666
http://www.travelodge.com
910 Corn Products Road
170 rooms - $50-90
Pets: Welcome
Creature Comforts: CCTV, a/c,
refrig, restaurant, cont. brkfst,
pool, hlth clb access

COTULLA
Rodeway Inn
(800) 228-2000, (210) 879-2311
http://www.rodeway.com
1100 W. Rte. 468
28 rooms - $50-90
Pets: Welcome w/$5 fee
Creature Comforts: CCTV, a/c,
kit, pool, game room

CROCKETT
Crockett Inn
(800) 633-9518, (409) 544-5611
1600 Loop 304 E.
82 rooms - $50-85
Pets: Welcome
Creature Comforts: CCTV, a/c,
restaurant, pool, whirlpool

DALHART
Best Western
(800) 528-1234, (806) 249-2311
http://www.bestwestern.com
1110 W. Rte. 468
28 rooms - $45-85
Pets: Small pets w/$5 fee
Creature Comforts: CCTV, a/c,
kit, pool

Comfort Inn
(800) 228-5150, (806) 249-8585
http://www.comfortinn.com
Rte. 54E
36 rooms - $45-75
Pets: Small pets welcome
Creature Comforts: CCTV, a/c,
refrig, cont. brkfst, pool

Days Inn
(800) DAYS INN, (806) 249-5246
http://www.daysinn.com
701 Liberal St.
43 rooms - $45-90
Pets: Small pets welcome
Creature Comforts: CCTV, a/c, refrig, cont. brkfst, pool, hlth clb access

Econo Lodge
(800) 55-ECONO, (806) 249-6464
http://www.econolodge.com
123 Liberal St.
46 rooms - $35-60
Pets: Small pets w/$20 deposit
Creature Comforts: CCTV, a/c

Sands Motel
(806) 249-4568
301 Liberal St.
36 rooms - $30-59
Pets: Small pets welcome
Creature Comforts: CCTV, a/c, refrig, pool

Super 8 Motel
(800) 800-8000, (806) 249-8526
http://www.super8.com
E. Rte. 54
45 rooms - $45-65
Pets: Welcome w/$25 deposit
Creature Comforts: CCTV, a/c, sauna, whirlpool

DALLAS
Best Western North
(800) 528-1234, (972) 241-8521
http://www.bestwestern.com
13333 N. Stemmons Fwy.
186 rooms - $60-90
Pets: Welcome w/$25 deposit
Creature Comforts: CCTV, a/c, restaurant, pool, hlth clb access, whirlpool

Bristol Suites
(800) 922-9222, (972) 233-7600
7800 Alpha Road
295 rooms - $150-190
Pets: Welcome
Creature Comforts: CCTV, a/c, restaurant, pool, hlth clb access

Days Inn
(800) DAYS INN, (972) 224-3196
http://www.daysinn.com
8312 S. Lancaster Road
50 rooms - $60-90
Pets: Welcome w/$100 fee
Creature Comforts: CCTV, a/c, pool

Days Inn Central
(800) DAYS INN, (972) 827-6080
http://www.daysinn.com
4150 N. Central Expwy.
80 rooms - $50-100
Pets: Small pets w/$35 fee
Creature Comforts: CCTV, a/c, cont. brkfst, pool

Drury Inn - Dallas North
(800) 325-8300, (972) 484-3330
http://www.druryinn.com
2421 Walnut Hill Lane
130 rooms - $70-95
Pets: Welcome
Creature Comforts: CCTV, a/c, cont. brkfst, pool

Econo Lodge
(800) 55-ECONO, (972) 243-5500
http://www.econolodge.com
Rte. 35N at Valley View Lane
110 rooms - $45-80
Pets: Welcome
Creature Comforts: CCTV, a/c, pool

Embassy Suites Hotel - Dallas/ Park Central
(800) 362-2779 , (972) 234-3300
http://www.embassy-suites.com
13131 N. Central Expwy.
279 rooms - $100-195
Pets: Small pets w/$25 fee
Creature Comforts: CCTV, a/c, kit, restaurant, pool

Grand Hotel
(214) 747-7000
1914 Commerce St.
712 rooms - $139-169
Pets: Small pets w/$50 fee
Creature Comforts: CCTV, a/c, refrig, micro, restaurant, whirlpool

Hampton Inn
(800) 426-7866, (972) 742-5678
http://www.hamptoninn.com
1015 Elm St.
311 rooms - $85-125
Pets: Welcome
Creature Comforts: CCTV, a/c, pool, hlth clb access

Hampton Inn - Dallas North
(800) 426-7866, (972) 484-6557
http://www.hamptoninn.com
11069 Composite Dr.
279 rooms - $100-175
Pets: Small pets w/$25 fee
Creature Comforts: CCTV, a/c, kit, pool

Harvey Hotel Dallas
(800) 922-9222, (972) 960-7000
7815 LBJ Fwy. at Coit Road
313 rooms - $60-95
Pets: $125 deposit, $100 refundbl
Creature Comforts: CCTV, a/c, restaurant, pool

Hawthorn Suites
(800) 527-1133, (972) 688-1010
http://www.hawthorn.com
7900 Brookriver Dr.
97 rooms - $130-179
Pets: Small pets w/$30 fee
Creature Comforts: CCTV, a/c, pool

Hotel Crescent Court
(800) 654-6541, (214) 871-3200
http://www.rosewood-hotels.com
400 Crescent Court
200 rooms - $195-1,750
Pets: Welcome w/$50 deposit
Creature Comforts: Dramatic, award-winning structure, lavish public areas, bedrooms w/French doors, trad. reproductions, orig. art, marble/brass baths, CCTV, a/c, gourmet restaurant, pool, spa, hlth clb

La Quinta Inn - Central
(800) Nu-Rooms, (972) 821-4220
http://www.laquinta.com
4440 N. Central Expwy.
101 rooms - $60-85
Pets: Small pets welcome
Creature Comforts: CCTV, a/c, cont. brkfst, pool

La Quinta Inn - East
(800) Nu-Rooms, (972) 324-3731
http://www.laquinta.com
8303 East R.L. Thornton Fwy.
102 rooms - $60-85
Pets: Small pets welcome
Creature Comforts: CCTV, a/c, cont. brkfst, pool

La Quinta Inn Northpark
(800) Nu-Rooms, (972) 361-8200
http://www.laquinta.com
10001 N. Central Expressway
128 rooms - $55-85
Pets: Small pets welcome
Creature Comforts: CCTV, a/c,
refrig, micro, cont. brkfst, pool,
hlth clb access

La Quinta Inn Regal Row
(800) Nu-Rooms, (972) 630-5701
http://www.laquinta.com
1625 Regal Row
132 rooms - $55-80
Pets: Small pets welcome
Creature Comforts: CCTV, a/c,
pool

Le Meridien
(800) 543-4300, (214) 979-9000
http://www.forte-hotels.com
650 N. Pearl St.
432 rooms - $259-505
Pets: Small pets w/$50 fee
Creature Comforts: CCTV, a/c,
refrig, micro, concierge level w/
snack basket and cont. brkfst,
restaurant, hlth club.

Mansion on Turtle Creek
(800) 527-5432, (214) 559-2100
http://www.rosewood-hotels.com
2821 Turtle Creek Blvd.
151 rooms - $250-1,500
Pets: Under 30 lbs. w/$50 fee,
Creature Comforts: 16th-century
Italian Renaissance-style mansion,
terraced gardens, lavish details-
marble staircase, inlaid wood
ceilings, parquet flrs, French doors
in bedrooms open to private
balconies, chintz spreads, down
pillows, mahogany furnishings,
CCTV, a/c, refrig, gourmet
restaurant, cont. brkfst, pool,
sauna, whirlpool, spa

Motel 6
(800) 4-MOTEL6, (972) 484-9111
http://www.motel6.com
2660 Forest Lane
117 rooms - $40-69
Pets: Under 30 lbs. welcome
Creature Comforts: CCTV, a/c,
pool

Motel 6
(800) 4-MOTEL6, (972) 620-2828
http://www.motel6.com
2753 Forest Lane
100 rooms - $40-70
Pets: Under 30 lbs. welcome
Creature Comforts: CCTV, a/c,
pool

Motel 6
(800) 4-MOTEL6, (972) 296-3331
http://www.motel6.com
4220 Independence Dr.
129 rooms - $30-59
Pets: Under 30 lbs. welcome
Creature Comforts: CCTV, a/c,
restaurant, pool

Motel 6
(800) 4-MOTEL6, (972) 386-4579
http://www.motel6.com
4325 Beltline Road
161 rooms - $45-59
Pets: Under 30 lbs. welcome
Creature Comforts: CCTV, a/c,
pool

Quality Inn
(800) 228-5151, (972) 9049955
http://www.qualityinn.com
2830 West Northwest Highway
rooms -$100-150
Pets: Small pets welcome
Creature Comforts: CCTV, a/c,
cont. brkfst, pool, hlth clb access

Radisson Central
(800) 333-3333, (214) 750-6060
http://www.radisson.com
6060 N. Central Expressway
288 rooms - $85-129
Pets: Small pets w/$50 fee
Creature Comforts: CCTV, a/c,
restaurant, pool

Radisson Hotel Suites Dallas
(800) 333-3333, (972) 351-4477
http://www.radisson.com
2330 W. Northwest Highway
198 rooms - $100-180
Pets: Small pets w/$50 deposit,
$25 fee
Creature Comforts: CCTV, a/c,
restaurant, pool, hlth clb access

Radisson Mockingbird West
(800) 333-3333, (972) 634-8850
http://www.radisson.com
1893 W. Mockingbird Lane
304 rooms - $50-130
Pets: Welcome
Creature Comforts: CCTV, a/c,
restaurant, pool, hlth clb access

**Ramada Hotel Downtown
Convention Center**
(800) 2-Ramada, (214) 421-1083
http://www.ramada.com
1011 S. Akard St.
236 rooms - $90-150
Pets: Welcome
Creature Comforts: CCTV, a/c,
refrig, Jacuzzi, restaurant, pool,
hlth clb access, whirlpool

Red Roof Inn, Dallas East
(800) THE ROOF, (972) 388-8741
http://www.redroof.com
8108 East R.L. Thornton Fwy.
109 rooms - $50-60
Pets: Small pets welcome
Creature Comforts: CCTV, a/c

Red Roof Inn, Market Center
(800) THE ROOF, (214) 638-5151
http://www.redroof.com
1550 Empire Central Dr.
111 rooms - $55-65
Pets: Small pets welcome
Creature Comforts: CCTV, a/c

Red Roof Inn, Northwest
(800) THE ROOF, (972) 506-8100
http://www.redroof.com
10335 Gardner Road
112 rooms - $50-60
Pets: Small pets welcome
Creature Comforts: CCTV, a/c

Renaissance Dallas Hotel
(800) 228-9898, (214) 631-2222
2222 Stemmons Fwy.
540 rooms - $90-210
Pets: Small pets welcome
Creature Comforts: CCTV, a/c,
refrig, Jacuzzi, restaurant, pool,
hlth clb access, sauna, whirlpool

Residence Inn, Central-N. Park
(800) 331-3131, (972) 750-8220
http://www.residenceinn.com
10333 N. Central Expressway
103 rooms - $90-135
Pets: Welcome w/$50 fee
Creature Comforts: CCTV, a/c,
kit, pool

Residence Inn - Market Center
(800) 331-3131, (214) 631-2472
http://www.residenceinn.com
6950 Stemmons Fwy.
142 rooms - $120-160
Pets: Welcome w/$50 fee
Creature Comforts: CCTV, a/c,
kit, pool

Residence Inn - North
(800) 331-3131, (972) 669-0478
http://www.residenceinn.com
13636 Goldmark Dr.
70 rooms - $115-160
Pets: Small pets w/$60 fee
Creature Comforts: CCTV, a/c,
pool

Sheraton Park Central
(800) 325-3535, (972) 385-3000
http://www.sheraton.com
12720 Merit Dr.
545 rooms - $105-175
Pets: Small pets welcome
Creature Comforts: CCTV, a/c,
restaurant, pool

Travelodge
(800) 578-7878, (972) 357-1701
http://www.travelodge.com
3140 W. Mockingbird Lane
42 rooms - $45-69
Pets: Welcome
Creature Comforts: CCTV, a/c,
restaurant, cont. brkfst, pool

The Westin Hotel Galleria
(800) 228-3000, (972) 934-9494
http://www.westin.com
13340 Dallas Parkway
431 rooms - $160-260
Pets: Small pets welcome
Creature Comforts: CCTV, a/c,
restaurant, pool

DECATUR
Best Western Inn
(800) 528-1234, (940) 627-5982
http://www.bestwestern.com
1801 S. Rte. 287
46 rooms - $45-70
Pets: Small pets welcome
Creature Comforts: CCTV, a/c,
refrig, micro, cont. brkfst, pool

Comfort Inn
(800) 228-5150, (940) 627-6919
http://www.comfortinn.com
1709 Rte. 287 S
44 rooms - $55-85
Pets: Small pets welcome
Creature Comforts: CCTV, a/c,
refrig, micro, Jacuzzi, cont. brkfst,
pool, hlth clb access, sauna,
whirlpool

DEL RIO
Angler's Lodge
(830) 775-1586
Rte. 90 W.
24 rooms - $45-50
Pets: Welcome
Creature Comforts: CCTV, a/c

Best Western Inn of Del Rio
(800) 528-1234, (830) 775-7511
http://www.bestwestern.com
810 Ave. F
62 rooms - $55-85
Pets: Welcome w/$5 fee
Creature Comforts: CCTV, a/c,
refrig, restaurant, cont. brkfst,
pool, whirlpool

Best Western La Siesta
(800) 528-1234, (830) 775-6323
http://www.bestwestern.com
2000 Ave. F
58 rooms - $55-85
Pets: Welcome w/$5 fee
Creature Comforts: CCTV, a/c,
refrig, micro, restaurant, cont.
brkfst, pool

Days Inn
(800) DAYS INN, (830) 775-0585
http://www.daysinn.com
3808 Ave. F
96 rooms - $50-75
Pets: Small pets welcome
Creature Comforts: CCTV, a/c,
kit, cont. brkfst, pool, whirlpool

Del Rio Motor Lodge
(800) 882-9826, (830) 775-2486
1300 Ave. F
35 rooms - $40-60
Pets: Welcome w/$50 deposit
Creature Comforts: CCTV, a/c,
pool

Holiday Inn Express
(800) HOLIDAY, (830) 775-2933
http://www.holiday-inn.com
3616 Ave. F
60 rooms - $50-90
Pets: Small pets welcome
Creature Comforts: CCTV, a/c,
pool

La Quinta Inn
(800) Nu-Rooms, (830) 775-7591
http://www.laquinta.com
2005 Ave. F
100 rooms - $60-85
Pets: Small pets welcome
Creature Comforts: CCTV, a/c,
cont. brkfst, pool

Lakeview Inn
(800) 344-0109, (830) 775-9521
Rte. 90 W, HCR 3
34 rooms - $40-65
Pets: Welcome
Creature Comforts: CCTV, a/c,
refrig, pool

Motel 6
(800) 4-MOTEL6, (830) 775-0585
http://www.motel6.com
2115 Ave. F
122 rooms - $30-60
Pets: Under 30 lbs. welcome
Creature Comforts: CCTV, a/c,
pool

Ramada Inn
(800) 2-Ramada, (830) 775-1511
http://www.ramada.com
2101 Ave. F
153 rooms - $60-130
Pets: Welcome
Creature Comforts: CCTV,
VCR, a/c, Jacuzzi, cont. brkfst,
pool, sauna

Rough Canyon Inn
(830) 774-6266
Rte. 277 N, RR 2
24 rooms - $27-75
Pets: Welcome
Creature Comforts: CCTV, a/c,
kit

Super 8
(800) 800-8000, (830) 775-7414
3811 Rte. 90 W
98 rooms - $45-70
Pets: Welcome w/$25 deposit
Creature Comforts: CCTV,
VCR, cont. brkfst, pool

DENISON
Ramada Inn
(800) 2-Ramada, (903) 465-6800
http://www.ramada.com
1600 Eisenhower Parkway
100 rooms - $50-90
Pets: Welcome w/$35 deposit
Creature Comforts: CCTV, a/c, restaurant, pool

DENTON
Exel Inn of Denton
(800) 356-8013, (940) 383-1471
http://www.exelinns.com
4211 I-35E North
114 rooms - $40-65
Pets: Small pets welcome
Creature Comforts: CCTV, a/c, micro, Jacuzzi, cont. brkfst, pool

La Quinta Inn
(800) Nu-Rooms, (940) 387-5840
http://www.laquinta.com
700 Fort Worth Dr.
99 rooms - $65-80
Pets: Small pets welcome
Creature Comforts: CCTV, a/c, refrig, micro, cont. brkfst, pool

Motel 6
(800) 4-MOTEL6, (940) 566-4798
http://www.motel6.com
4125 Rte. 35N
85 rooms - $30-59
Pets: Under 30 lbs. welcome
Creature Comforts: CCTV, a/c, restaurant, pool

DESOTO
Holiday Inn
(800) HOLIDAY, (972) 224-9100
http://www.holiday-inn.com
1515 N. Beckley Rd.
149 rooms - $75-235
Pets: Welcome
Creature Comforts: CCTV, a/c, restaurant, pool, hlth clb access

DUMAS
Best Western Dumas Inn Motel
(800) 528-1234, (806) 935-6441
http://www.bestwestern.com
1712 S. Dumas Ave.
101 rooms - $55-89
Pets: Welcome
Creature Comforts: CCTV, a/c, restaurant, pool

Econo Lodge Old Town Inn
(800) 55-ECONO, (806) 935-9098
http://www.econolodge.com
1719 S. Dumas Ave.
41 rooms - $35-69
Pets: Welcome w/$2 fee
Creature Comforts: CCTV, a/c, refrig, micro, pool, whirlpool

Holiday Inn
(800) HOLIDAY, (806) 935-4000
http://www.holiday-inn.com
1525 S. Dumas Ave.
54 rooms - $55-69
Pets: Welcome
Creature Comforts: CCTV, a/c, Jacuzzi, cont. brkfst, pool, hlth clb access

Super 8 Motel
(800) 800-8000, (806) 935-6222
http://www.super8.com
119 W. 17th St.
30 rooms - $50-80
Pets: Welcome w/$5 fee
Creature Comforts: CCTV, a/c

DUNCANVILLE
Hampton Inn
(800) Hampton, (972) 298-4747
http://www.hamptoninn.com
4154 Preferred Place
119 rooms - $60-85
Pets: Welcome w/$50 deposit
Creature Comforts: CCTV, a/c, refrig, micro, cont. brkfst, pool

Holiday Inn - Dallas SW
(800) HOLIDAY, (972) 298-8911
http://www.holiday-inn.com
711 E. Camp Wisdom Road
123 rooms - $65-95
Pets: Small pets w/$25 fee
Creature Comforts: CCTV, a/c, restaurant, pool

Motel 6 - Duncanville
(800) 4-MOTEL6, (972) 296-0345
http://www.motel6.com
202 Jellison Blvd.
76 rooms - $40-75
Pets: Under 30 lbs. welcome
Creature Comforts: CCTV, a/c, pool

EAGLE PASS
Best Western Eagle Pass
(800) 528-1234, (830) 758-1234
http://www.bestwestern.com
1923 Rte. 431
40 rooms - $70-99
Pets: Small pets welcome
Creature Comforts: CCTV, a/c, refrig, micro, cont. brkfst, pool

Holly Inn
(800) 424-8125, (830) 773-9261
2421 Main St.
85 rooms - $44-59
Pets: Welcome w/$50 deposit
Creature Comforts: CCTV, a/c, refrig, restaurant, pool

La Quinta Inn
(800) Nu-Rooms, (830) 773-7000
http://www.laquinta.com
2525 Main St.
130 rooms - $55-77
Pets: Small pets welcome
Creature Comforts: CCTV, a/c, refrig, micro, cont. brkfst, pool

Super 8 Motel
(800) 800-8000, (830) 773-9531
http://www.super8.com
2150 Rte. 277
56 rooms - $50-60
Pets: Small pets welcome
Creature Comforts: CCTV, a/c, kit, restaurant, pool

EASTLAND
Econo Lodge
(800) 55-ECONO, (254) 629-3324
http://www.econolodge.com
2001 I-20W
46 rooms - $40-45
Pets: Welcome
Creature Comforts: CCTV, a/c, pool

Super 8 Motel
(800) 800-8000, (254) 629-3336
http://www.super8.com
3900 Rte. 20E
30 rooms - $40-65
Pets: Welcome w/$2 fee
Creature Comforts: CCTV, a/c, pool

EL PASO

Americana Inn
(915) 852-3025
14387 Gateway W.
50 rooms - $45-60
Pets: Welcome w/$20 fee
Creature Comforts: CCTV, a/c, pool

Baymont Inn
(800) 428-3438, (915) 585-2999
http://www.baymontinns.com
7620 N. Mesa St.
107 rooms - $45-85
Pets: Welcome
Creature Comforts: CCTV, a/c, kit, cont. brkfst, pool

Baymont Inn East
(800) 428-3438, (915) 591-3300
http://www.baymontinns.com
7944 Gateway E.
107 rooms - $50-80
Pets: Small pets welcome
Creature Comforts: CCTV, a/c, kit, cont. brkfst, pool

Best Western Airport Inn
(800) 528-1234, (915) 779-7700
http://www.bestwestern.com
7144 Gateway E.
175 rooms - $50-90
Pets: Small pets welcome
Creature Comforts: CCTV, a/c, restaurant, pool

Budget Lodge Motel
(915) 533-6821
1301 N. Mesa Rd.
48 rooms - $25-39
Pets: Welcome
Creature Comforts: CCTV, a/c

Camino Real Hotel
(800) 722-6466, (915) 534-3000
http://www.caminoreal.com/
elpaso/index.htm
101 S. El Paso St.
360 rooms - $95-950
Pets: Small pets welcome
Creature Comforts: Lavish 1923 hotel, gold coffered ceilings, Tiffany stained glass dome, serpentine marble, bedrooms w/ alcoves, southwestern art, Queen Anne reproductions, CCTV, a/c, refrig, restaurant, pool, hlth clb access, whirlpool, sauna

Comfort Inn Airport East
(800) 228-5150, (915) 594-9111
http://www.comfortinn.com
900 N. Yarbrough St.
200 rooms - $50-60
Pets: Small pets w/$25 deposit
Creature Comforts: CCTV, a/c, cont. brkfst, pool, whirlpool

Days Inn El Paso
(800) DAYS INN, (915) 593-8400
http://www.daysinn.com
9125 Gateway W.
115 rooms - $60-85
Pets: Small pets welcome
Creature Comforts: CCTV, a/c, pool

Econo Lodge
(800) 55-ECONO, (915) 778-3311
http://www.econolodge.com
6363 Montana St.
58 rooms - $50-85
Pets: Welcome
Creature Comforts: CCTV, a/c, cont. brkfst, pool

Embassy Suites Hotel
(800) 362-2779, (915) 779-6222
http://www.embassy-suites.com
6100 Gateway E.
185 rooms - $110-149
Pets: Welcome w/$50 fee
Creature Comforts: CCTV, a/c, pool

Hilton - El Paso Airport
(800) HILTONS, (915) 778-4241
http://www.hilton.com
2027 Airway Blvd.
271 rooms - $135-180
Pets: Welcome w/$100 deposit
Creature Comforts: CCTV, a/c, restaurant, cont. brkfst, pool, hlth clb access, sauna, whirlpool

Howard Johnson Lodge
(800) I-Go-Hojo, (915) 591-9471
http://www.hojo.com
8887 Gateway W.
140 rooms - $65-89
Pets: Welcome
Creature Comforts: CCTV, a/c, restaurant, pool

International Hotel
(800) 668-3466, (915) 544-3300
113 W. Missouri St.
200 rooms - $45-125
Pets: Welcome w/$10 fee
Creature Comforts: CCTV, a/c, restaurant, pool

La Quinta Inn, Airport
(800) Nu-Rooms, (915) 778-9321
http://www.laquinta.com
6140 Gateway Blvd. E.
121 rooms - $45-78
Pets: Small pets welcome
Creature Comforts: CCTV, a/c, refrig, cont. brkfst, pool

La Quinta Inn - Lomaland
(800) Nu-Rooms, (915) 591-2244
http://www.laquinta.com
11033 Gateway W.
138 rooms - $55-75
Pets: Small pets welcome
Creature Comforts: CCTV, a/c, cont. brkfst, pool

La Quinta Inn - West
(800) Nu-Rooms, (915) 833-2522
http://www.laquinta.com
7550 Remcon Circle
130 rooms - $55-85
Pets: Small pets welcome
Creature Comforts: CCTV, a/c, refrig, cont. brkfst, pool

Marriott - El Paso
(800) 228-9290, (915) 779-3300
http://www.marriott.com
1600 Airway Blvd.
296 rooms - $85-140
Pets: Welcome
Creature Comforts: CCTV, a/c, restaurant, pool, hlth clb access

Motel 6
(800) 4-MOTEL6, (915) 592-6386
http://www.motel6.com
1330 Lomaland Dr.
121 rooms - $30-55
Pets: Under 30 lbs. welcome
Creature Comforts: CCTV, a/c, pool

Motel 6 - Central
(800) 4-MOTEL6, (915) 533-7521
http://www.motel6.com
4800 Gateway Blvd. E.
200 rooms - $30-55
Pets: Under 30 lbs. welcome
Creature Comforts: CCTV, a/c, restaurant, pool

Motel 6 - East
(800) 4-MOTEL6, (915) 594-8533
http://www.motel6.com
11049 Gateway Blvd. W.
146 rooms - $30-55
Pets: Under 30 lbs. welcome
Creature Comforts: CCTV, a/c, pool

Quality Inn
(800) 228-5151, (915) 778-6611
http://www.qualityinn.com
6201 Gateway Blvd. W.
307 rooms - $50-55
Pets: Welcome
Creature Comforts: CCTV, a/c, restaurant, pool

Red Roof Inn West
(800) THE ROOF, (915) 587-9977
http://www.redroof.com
7530 Remcon Circle
123 rooms - $50-75
Pets: Small pets welcome
Creature Comforts: CCTV, a/c, pool

ELGIN
The Ragtime Ranch Inn
(800) 800-9743, (512) 285-9599
http://www.bestinns.net/usa/tx/
ragtimeranch.html
P.O. Box 575
4 rooms - $95
Pets: Welcome w/$20 deposit, horses too, lots of space for pets
Creature Comforts: Horse-friendly ranch on 37 acres of shade trees and pastures, ranch house w/large, very attractive bedrms, handmade quilts, CCTV, a/c, refrig, fireplaces, cont. brkfst, pool, riding, walking trails, stocked ponds

ENNIS
Quality Inn
(800) 228-5151, (972) 875-9641
http://www.qualityinn.com
Rtes. 45 & 34
69 rooms - $50-80
Pets: Welcome
Creature Comforts: CCTV, a/c, restaurant, pool

EULESS
La Quinta Inn - DFW West
(800) Nu-Rooms, (915) 833-2522
http://www.laquinta.com
1001 W. Aiport Blvd.
130 rooms - $55-85
Pets: Small pets welcome
Creature Comforts: CCTV, a/c, cont. brkfst, pool

Motel 6, Airport
(800) 4-MOTEL6, (817) 545-0141
http://www.motel6.com
110 W. Airport Fwy.
120 rooms - $30-55
Pets: Under 30 lbs. welcome
Creature Comforts: CCTV, a/c, pool

Ramada Inn - DFW West
(800) 2-Ramada, (817) 283-2400
http://www.ramada.com
2155 W. Airport Fwy.
147 rooms - $50-125
Pets: Welcome w/$25 deposit
Creature Comforts: CCTV, a/c, refrig, micro, Jacuzzi, restaurant, cont. brkfst, pool

FALFURRIAS
Days Inn
(800) DAYS INN, (512) 325-2515
http://www.daysinn.com
208 Rte. 281 S.
31 rooms - $60-85
Pets: Small pets welcome
Creature Comforts: CCTV, a/c, refrig, micro, cont. brkfst, hlth clb access

FARMERS BRANCH
Best Western Oak Tree Inn
(800) 528-1234, (972) 241-8521
http://www.bestwestern.com
13333 N. Stemmons Fwy.
186 rooms - $65-95
Pets: Small pets welcome
Creature Comforts: CCTV, a/c, restaurant, pool

Econo Lodge Dallas Airport
(800) 55-ECONO, (972) 243-5500
http://www.econolodge.com
2275 Valley View Lane
108 rooms - $50-75
Pets: Small pets welcome
Creature Comforts: CCTV, a/c, refrig, micro, pool

La Quinta Inn Northwest
(800) Nu-Rooms, (972) 620-7333
http://www.laquinta.com
13235 Stemmons Fwy. N.
121 rooms - $50-75
Pets: Small pets welcome
Creature Comforts: CCTV, a/c, cont. brkfst, pool

FORT DAVIS
Hotel Limpia
(800) 662-5517, (915) 426-3237
http://wwwvirtualcities.com/ons/
tx/e/txe16010.htm
On the Town Square
33 rooms - $70-125
Pets: Welcome w/$10 fee
Creature Comforts: 1912 pink limestone hotel, Victorian Old West feeling, wrap-around glass porch, pressed tin ceilings, oak antique and reproduction furnishings, CCTV, a/c, restaurant

FORT HANCOCK
Fort Hancock Motel
(800) 553-4654, (915) 769-3981
Rte. 10 E. 72
27 rooms - $45-70
Pets: Welcome
Creature Comforts: CCTV, a/c, pool

FORT STOCKTON
Best Western Swiss Clock Inn
(800) 528-1234, (915) 336-8521
http://www.bestwestern.com
3201 W. Dickinson Blvd.
112 rooms - $50-90
Pets: Welcome w/$20 deposit
Creature Comforts: CCTV, a/c, restaurant, cont. brkfst, pool

Comfort Inn
(800) 228-5150, (915) 336-8531
http://www.comfortinn.com
3200 W. Dickinson Blvd.
95 rooms - $50-75
Pets: Welcome w/$5 fee
Creature Comforts: CCTV, a/c, pool

Days Inn
(800) DAYS INN, (915) 336-7500
http://www.daysinn.com
1408 Rte. 285
50 rooms - $55-75
Pets: Small pets welcome
Creature Comforts: CCTV, a/c, cont. brkfst, pool, whirlpool

Econo Lodge
(800) 55-ECONO, (915) 336-9711
http://www.econolodge.com
800 E. Dickinson Blvd.
86 rooms - $55-80
Pets: Small pets w/$8 fee
Creature Comforts: CCTV, a/c,
refrig, micro, restaurant, cont.
brkfst, pool

La Quinta Inn
(800) Nu-Rooms, (915) 336-9781
http://www.laquinta.com
2601 Rte. 10W
97 rooms - $60-80
Pets: Small pets welcome
Creature Comforts: CCTV, a/c,
refrig, micro, restaurant, cont.
brkfst, pool

Motel 6
(800) 4-MOTEL6, (915) 366-9737
http://www.motel6.com
3001 W. Dickinson Blvd.
139 rooms - $30-55
Pets: Under 30 lbs. welcome
Creature Comforts: CCTV, a/c,
pool

FORT WORTH
Best Western West Branch Inn
(800) 528-1234, (817) 244-7444
http://www.bestwestern.com
7301 W. Fwy.
118 rooms - $50-90
Pets: Small pets welcome
Creature Comforts: CCTV, a/c,
restaurant, cont. brkfst, pool

Days Inn Southwest
(800) DAYS INN, (817) 923-1987
http://www.daysinn.com
4213 Rte. 35 West South Fwy.
55 rooms - $45-85
Pets: Welcome w/$20 deposit
Creature Comforts: CCTV, a/c,
restaurant, cont. brkfst, pool

Days Inn
(800) DAYS INN, (817) 246-4961
http://www.daysinn.com
8500 Las Vegas Trail
121 rooms - $40-65
Pets: Welcome w/$5 fee
Creature Comforts: CCTV, a/c,
cont. brkfst, pool

Green Oaks Inn
(800) 772-7341, (817) 738-7311
6901 W. Fwy.
282 rooms - $65-80
Pets: Welcome w/$25 deposit
Creature Comforts: CCTV, a/c,
restaurant, pool

Hampton Inn
(800) Hampton, (817) 346-7845
http://www.hamptoninn.com
4799 SW Loop 820
78 rooms - $75-99
Pets: Small pets w/$50 fee
Creature Comforts: CCTV, a/c,
pool

Holiday Inn S, South
(800) HOLIDAY, (817) 293-3088
http://www.holiday-inn.com
100 Altamesa E. Blvd.
247 rooms - $70-96
Pets: Small pets welcome
Creature Comforts: CCTV, a/c,
restaurant, pool, sauna, whirlpool

La Quinta Inn West
(800) Nu-Rooms, (817) 246-5511
http://www.laquinta.com
7888 Rte. 30W
106 rooms - $65-75
Pets: Small pets welcome
Creature Comforts: CCTV, a/c,
cont. brkfst, pool

Motel 6 - East
(800) 4-MOTEL6, (817) 834-7361
http://www.motel6.com
1236 Oakland Blvd
96 rooms - $35-48
Pets: Under 30 lbs. welcome
Creature Comforts: CCTV, a/c,
pool

Motel 6 - North
(800) 4-MOTEL6, (817) 625-4359
http://www.motel6.com
3271 Rte. 35W
106 rooms - $40-45
Pets: Under 30 lbs. welcome
Creature Comforts: CCTV, a/c,
pool

Motel 6 - South
(800) 4-MOTEL6, (817) 293-8595
http://www.motel6.com
6600 S. Fwy.
147 rooms - $40-55
Pets: Under 30 lbs. welcome
Creature Comforts: CCTV, a/c,
pool

Motel 6 - SE
(800) 4-MOTEL6, (817) 921-4900
http://www.motel6.com
4433 S. Fwy.
103 rooms - $40-55
Pets: Under 30 lbs. welcome
Creature Comforts: CCTV, a/c,
pool

Motel 6 - West
(800) 4-MOTEL6, (817) 244-9740
http://www.motel6.com
8701 Rte. 30 West
118 rooms - $40-55
Pets: Under 30 lbs. welcome
Creature Comforts: CCTV, a/c,
restaurant, pool

Radisson Plaza Hotel
(800) 333-3333, (817) 870-2100
http://www.radisson.com
815 Main St.
517 rooms - $170-325
Pets: Small pets w/$100 deposit
Creature Comforts: CCTV, a/c,
restaurant, pool

Ramada Hotel Midtown
(800) 2-Ramada, (817) 336-9311
http://www.ramada.com
1401 S. University Dr.
184 rooms - $75-99
Pets: Welcome w/$10 fee
Creature Comforts: CCTV, a/c,
restaurant, pool

Residence Inn by Marriott
(800) 331-3131, (817) 870-1011
http://www.residenceinn.com
1701 S. University Dr.
120 rooms - $110-120
Pets: Small pets w/$5 fee
Creature Comforts: CCTV, a/c,
kit, pool, hlth clb access

Royal Western Suites
(817) 560-0060
8401 Rte. 30 West
113 rooms - $50-69
Pets: Welcome w/$25 deposit
Creature Comforts: CCTV, a/c,
kit, pool

Worthington Hotel
(800) 433-5677, (817) 870-1000
200 Main St.
504 rooms - $190-215
Pets: Small pets welcome
Creature Comforts: CCTV, a/c,
restaurant, pool

FREDERICKSBURG
Alfred Haus B&B
(830) 997-5612
http://www.ktc.net/GSchmidt/
alfredha.htm
231 W. Main St.
1 house - $75-89
Pets: Welcome
Creature Comforts: Yellow
farmhouse on 240-acre working
ranch, shade trees, lake, country
decor, woodstove, patchwork quilt
beds, old fashioned bath, CCTV,
VCR, a/c, kit

Best Western Sunday House Inn
(800) 529-1234, (830) 997-4484
http://www.bestwestern.com
501 E. Main St.
124 rooms - $60-125
Pets: Small pets w/$10 fee
Creature Comforts: CCTV, a/c,
restaurant, pool

Budget Host Deluxe Inn
(800) Bud-Host, (830) 997-3344
http://www.budgethost.com
901 E. Main St.
25 rooms - $40-78
Pets: Small pets welcome
Creature Comforts: CCTV, a/c,
kit

Comfort Inn
(800) 228-5150, (830) 997-9811
http://www.comfortinn.com
908 S. Adams St.
46 rooms - $65-79
Pets: Welcome
Creature Comforts: CCTV, a/c,
refrig, cont. brkfst, pool, tennis

Dietzel Motel
(830) 997-3330
909 W. Main St.
20 rooms - $40-65
Pets: Welcome w/$5 fee
Creature Comforts: CCTV, a/c,
pool

Econo Lodge
(800) 55-ECONO, (830) 997-3437
http://www.econolodge.com
810 S. Adams St.
36 rooms - $40-77
Pets: Welcome
Creature Comforts: CCTV, a/c,
restaurant, cont. brkfst, pool,
whirlpool

Fredericksburg Inn and Suites
(800) 446-0202, (830) 997-0202
201 S. Washington
51 rooms - $70-90
Pets: Welcome w/$10 fee
Creature Comforts: CCTV, a/c,
pool

Heidi's Riverview Guest Ranch
(830) 997-0132
110 N. Milam St.
6 rooms - $60-110
Pets: Welcome
Creature Comforts: CCTV, a/c,
pool, tennis

Magnolia House B&B
(800) 880-4374, (830) 997-0306
101 E. Hackberry Rd.
6 rooms - $85-125
Pets: Welcome
Creature Comforts: CCTV, a/c

Miller's Inn Motel
(830) 997-2244
910 E. Main St.
20 rooms - $35-80
Pets: Welcome
Creature Comforts: CCTV, a/c,
restaurant

Peach Tree Inn
(800) 843-4666, (830) 997-2177
401 S. Washington
34 rooms - $30-100
Pets: Welcome
Creature Comforts: CCTV, a/c,
restaurant, pool

Schmidt Barn B&B
(830) 997-8282
http://www.ktc.net/GSchmidt/
schmibn.htm
231 West Main St.
1 room - $75-89
Pets: Small pets w/permission
Creature Comforts: 1860's stone
barn, sweeping lawns, mature
trees, beamed ceilings, braided
rugs, woodstove, country quilts,
CCTV, a/c, stereo

Settler's Crossing
(800) 874-1020, (830) 997-2722
Route 1376
9 rooms - $95-135
Pets: Very well behaved dogs
Creature Comforts: Historic
cottages on 35 acres, beautifully
restored, sophisticated decor w/
antiques, American folk art,
fireplaces, four-poster beds,
country quilts, CCTV, VCR, a/c,
cont. brkfst

Strackbein-Roeder
Sunday Haus B&B
(830) 997-5612
http://www.ktc.net/GSchmidt/
strackbe.htm
414 West Austin St.
2 rooms - $100-120
Pets: Welcome w/special
permission and $15 fee
Creature Comforts: 1870
"Sunday" house, antique tables,
wide plank flrs, exposed beams,
outdoor fireplace, CCTV, VCR,
a/c, fireplace, kit

Sunset Inn
(830) 997-9581
900 S. Adams St.
26 rooms - $40-55
Pets: Small pets welcome
Creature Comforts: CCTV, a/c,
kit

Watkins Hill Guest House
(800) 899-1672, (830) 997-6739
http://www.watkinshill.com
608 E. Creek St.
7 rooms - $110-165
Pets: Welcome
Creature Comforts: Wonderful
historic property w/elegantly
electic guest houses, sophisticated
decor, Oriental rugs, many
original features intact, 1840 main
lodge, rqst romantic Violets and
Ivy w/brass bed or Bluebonnet
Cottage w/4-poster bed,
woodstove and orig art

West Main Haus B&B
(830) 997-5612
http://www.ktc.net/GSchmidt/
strackbe.htm/westmain.htm
714 W. Main St.
2 rooms - $75-85
Pets: Welcome w/$10 fee
Creature Comforts: 1860's well
preserved limestone house, blue
and yellow hues, hardwood flrs,
whimsical touches, stenciled
walls, CCTV, VCR, a/c, kit

FREEPORT
Country Hearth Inn
(800) 848-5767, (409) 239-1602
1015 W. 2nd
40 rooms - $55-75
Pets: Small pets welcome
Creature Comforts: CCTV, a/c,
pool

FULTON
Bay Front Cottages
(512) 729-6693
309 S. Fulton Beach Rd.
26 cottages - $45-59
Pets: Welcome w/$5 fee
Creature Comforts: Simple and
rustic cottages, CCTV, a/c, kit

Best Western Inn by the Bay
(800) 528-1234, (512) 729-8351
http://www.bestwestern.com
72 rooms - $65-89
Pets: Small pets welcome
Creature Comforts: CCTV, a/c,
kit, cont. brkfst, pool

Kontiki Beach Resort Motel
(800) 242-3407, (512) 729-4975
2290 Fulton Beach Road
40 rooms - $75-89
Pets: Welcome w/$5 fee
Creature Comforts: CCTV, a/c,
kit, pool, tennis, boat dock

Sportsman's Manor
(800) 224-6684, (512) 729-5331
4170 Rte. 35 N
56 rooms - $45-65
Pets: Welcome
Creature Comforts: CCTV, a/c,
kit, pool, lighted fishing pier

GAINESVILLE
Best Western South Winds
(800) 528-1234, (940) 665-7737
http://www.bestwestern.com
W. Frontage Road
35 rooms - $45-80
Pets: Small pets welcome
Creature Comforts: CCTV, a/c,
refrig, micro, cont. brkfst, pool

Budget Host
(800) Bud-Host, (940) 665-2856
http://www.budgethost.com
Rte 2, Box 120
23 rooms - $35-50
Pets: Welcome
Creature Comforts: CCTV, a/c,
pool

Comfort Inn
(800) 228-5150, (940) 665-5599
http://www.comfortinn.com
1936 Rte. 35N
61 rooms - $40-65
Pets: Welcome
Creature Comforts: CCTV, a/c,
cont. brkfst, pool

Days Inn
(800) DAYS INN, (940) 665-5555
http://www.daysinn.com
Route 35
60 rooms - $45-65
Pets: Welcome
Creature Comforts: CCTV, a/c,
cont. brkfst, pool

GALVESTON
Harbor House
(800) 874-3721, (409) 763-3321
Pier 21
40 rooms - $135-175
Pets: Under 25 lbs. welcome
Creature Comforts: CCTV, a/c,
marina

Hilltop Motel
(409) 744-4423
8828 Seawall Blvd.
40 rooms - $30-75
Pets: Welcome
Creature Comforts: CCTV, a/c,
restaurant, pool

Hotel Galvez
(800) 392-4285, (409) 765-7721
2024 Seawall Blvd.
230 rooms - $130-450
Pets: Under 20 lbs. welcome
Creature Comforts: CCTV, a/c,
refrig, restaurant, pool, hlth clb
access, whirlpool

La Quinta Inn
(800) Nu-Rooms, (409) 763-1224
http://www.laquinta.com
1402 Seawall Blvd.
118 rooms - $65-125
Pets: Small pets welcome
Creature Comforts: CCTV, a/c,
pool

Motel 6
(800) 4-MOTEL6, (409) 740-3794
http://www.motel6.com
7404 Ave. J Broadway St.
114 rooms - $40-70
Pets: Welcome
Creature Comforts: CCTV, a/c,
pool

GARLAND
Days Inn
(800) DAYS INN, (972) 226-7621
http://www.daysinn.com
6222 Belt Line Road
120 rooms - $45-70
Pets: Small pets w/$10 fee
Creature Comforts: CCTV, a/c,
pool

La Quinta Inn
(800) Nu-Rooms, (972) 271-7581
http://www.laquinta.com
12721 Rte. 635
122 rooms - $60-75
Pets: Small pets welcome
Creature Comforts: CCTV, a/c,
refrig, micro, cont. brkfst, pool

Motel 6
(800) 4-MOTEL6, (972) 226-7140
http://www.motel6.com
436 W. Rte. 30
110 rooms - $30-55
Pets: Under 30 lbs. welcome
Creature Comforts: CCTV, a/c,
restaurant, cont. brkfst, pool

GATESVILLE
Best Western Chateau Ville
(800) 528-1234, (254) 865-2281
http://www.bestwestern.com
2501 E. Main St.
56 rooms - $45-67
Pets: Small pets welcome
Creature Comforts: CCTV, a/c,
restaurant, pool

GEORGETOWN
Comfort Inn
(800) 228-5150 , (512) 863-7504
http://www.comfortinn.com
1005 Leander Road
55 rooms - $60-86
Pets: Small pets welcome
Creature Comforts: CCTV, a/c,
pool

Days Inn
(800) DAYS INN, (512) 863-5572
http://www.daysinn.com
209 N. Rte. 35
55 rooms - $45-85
Pets: Welcome
Creature Comforts: CCTV, a/c,
pool

La Quinta Inn
(800) Nu-Rooms, (512) 869-2541
http://www.laquinta.com
333 Rte. 35N
99 rooms - $70-98
Pets: Small pets welcome
Creature Comforts: CCTV, a/c,
refrig, micro, restaurant, cont.
brkfst, pool, whirlpool

GIDDINGS
Best Western Classic Inn
(800) 528-1234, (409) 542-5791
http://www.bestwestern.com
3556 E. Austin Road
60 rooms - $45-70
Pets: Small pets welcome
Creature Comforts: CCTV, a/c,
pool, whirlpool

Giddings Sands Motel
(409) 542-3111
1600 E. Austin Road
51 rooms - $40-60
Pets: Small pets welcome
Creature Comforts: CCTV, a/c,
refrig, micro, cont. brkfst, pool

Hideaway Country Cabin
(254) 823-6606
Route 2, Box 148
5 cabins - $85-100
Pets: $10 one-time fee
Creature Comforts: Oak shaded
150-acre ranch, priv. cabins w/
porches, CCTV, a/c, fireplace, kit,
refrig, micro, cont. brkfst, hot tubs

GLEN ROSE
Country Woods Inn
(888) 84-WOODS
http://www.hcnews.com/~cwinn/
420 Grand Ave.
5 rooms - $80-135
Pets: Welcome w/$5 fee
Creature Comforts: Quaint
farmhouse on Paluxy River,
bedrms range from country
antique w/floral accents to simple
and rustic cottages, country brkfst,
afternoon treats, 40 acres for
swimming, canoeing, tennis,
corrals and kennels, croquet

GRAHAM
Gateway Inn
(940) 549-0222
1401 Rte. 16 S
77 rooms - $35-55
Pets: Welcome w/$5 fee
Creature Comforts: CCTV, a/c,
restaurant, pool

GRANBURY
Best Western Classic Inn
(800) 528-1234, (817) 573-8874
http://www.bestwestern.com
1209 N. Plaza Dr.
42 rooms - $50-85
Pets: Small pets welcome
Creature Comforts: CCTV, a/c,
refrig, micro, restaurant, pool

Days Inn of Granbury
(800) DAYS INN, (817) 573-2691
http://www.daysinn.com
1339 N. Plaza Dr.
67 rooms - $50-80
Pets: Small pets welcome
Creature Comforts: CCTV, a/c,
pool

Derrick-Hoffman Farm
(800) 573-9953, (817) 837-6200
8540 Rte. 40
4 rooms - $80-90
Pets: Welcome
Creature Comforts: 265-acre
farm, antique cottage, CCTV, a/c,
country antiques, full brkfst,
walking paths

Lodge of Granbury
(817) 573-2606
401 E. Pearl St.
60 rooms - $90-165
Pets: Welcome
Creature Comforts: CCTV, a/c,
refrig, micro, pool, whirlpool,
tennis

Plantation Inn on the Lake
(800) 422-2402, (817) 573-8846
http://www.hcnews.com/~planinn
1451 E. Pearl St.
53 rooms - $65-90
Pets: Small pets w/$5 fee
Creature Comforts: CCTV, a/c,
refrig, micro, Jacuzzi, cont. brkfst,
pool

GRAND PRAIRIE
La Quinta Inn
(800) Nu-Rooms, (972) 641-3021
http://www.laquinta.com
Rte. 30 & 19th St.
122 rooms - $65-85
Pets: Small pets welcome
Creature Comforts: CCTV, a/c,
refrig, micro, cont. brkfst, pool

Motel 6
(800) 4-MOTEL6, (972) 642-9424
http://www.motel6.com
406 E. Safari Blvd.
129 rooms - $40-60
Pets: Under 30 lbs. welcome
Creature Comforts: CCTV, a/c,
pool

GREENVILLE
Holiday Inn
(800) HOLIDAY, (903) 454-7000
http://www.holiday-inn.com
1215 E Rte. 30
137 rooms - $45-87
Pets: Welcome w/$25 deposit
Creature Comforts: CCTV, a/c,
restaurant, pool

Motel 6
(800) 4-MOTEL6, (903) 455-0515
http://www.motel6.com
5109 Rte. 30
94 rooms - $25-45
Pets: Under 30 lbs. welcome
Creature Comforts: CCTV, a/c, pool

GROVES
Motel 6
(800) 4-MOTEL6, (409) 962-6611
http://www.motel6.com
5201 E. Parkway Rd.
124 rooms - $30-45
Pets: Under 30 lbs. welcome
Creature Comforts: CCTV, a/c, pool

HAMILTON
Hamilton Guest Hotel B&B
(800) 876-2502, (817) 386-8977
109 N. Rice Rd.(US 281)
6 rooms - $70-89
Pets: Welcome
Creature Comforts: CCTV, a/c, cont. brkfst

Value Lodge Inn
(817) 386-8959
Rte. 281 N.
16 rooms - $35-46
Pets: Welcome
Creature Comforts: CCTV, a/c, refrig

Western Motel
(254) 386-3141
1208 S. Rice St.
25 rooms - $35-49
Pets: Small pets w/$20 deposit
Creature Comforts: CCTV, a/c, refrig, micro, pool

HARLINGEN
Best Western Harlingen Inn
(800) 528-1234, (956) 425-7070
http://www.bestwestern.com
6779 Rte. 83 W
102 rooms - $45-85
Pets: Small pets w/$25 deposit
Creature Comforts: CCTV, a/c, restaurant, pool

La Quinta Inn
(800) Nu-Rooms , (956) 428-6888
http://www.laquinta.com
1002 Rte. 83 S.
130 rooms - $70-95
Pets: Small pets welcome
Creature Comforts: CCTV, a/c, refrig, micro, cont. brkfst, pool

Motel 6
(800) 4-MOTEL6, (956) 421-4200
http://www.motel6.com
224 Rte. S. 77
81 rooms - $30-49
Pets: Welcome
Creature Comforts: CCTV, a/c, pool

Super 8 Motel
(800) 800-8000, (956) 412-8873
http://www.super8.com
1115 S. Rte. 77
59 rooms - $55-75
Pets: Small pets welcome
Creature Comforts: CCTV, a/c, Jacuzzi, cont. brkfst, pool

HASKELL
Bevers House on Brick St. B&B
(800) 580-3284, (817) 864-3284
http://www.westex.net/rturner
311 North Avenue F
6 rooms - $55-100
Pets: Welcome
Creature Comforts: Attractive 1904 home w/Colonial antiques, 2-bedroom cottage w/kit and dog run, CCTV, a/c, pool

HEARNE
Executive Inn
(409) 279-5345
Route 6
60 rooms - $55-75
Pets: Welcome w/$5 fee
Creature Comforts: CCTV, a/c, pool

HEBRONVILLE
Texas Executive Inn
(800) 870-7689, (512) 527-4082
1302 N. Smith St.
36 rooms - $45-59
Pets: Welcome
Creature Comforts: CCTV, a/c, refrig, restaurant, full brkfst

HENDERSON
Best Western Inn of Henderson
(800) 528-1234, (903) 657-9561
http://www.bestwestern.com
1500 Rte. 259 S
80 rooms - $50-79
Pets: Small pets welcome
Creature Comforts: CCTV, a/c, cont. brkfst, pool

HEREFORD
Best Western Red Carpet Inn
(800) 528-1234, (806) 364-0540
http://www.bestwestern.com
830 W. 1st St.
90 rooms - $40-90
Pets: Small pets welcome
Creature Comforts: CCTV, a/c, kit, pool

HILLSBORO
Best Western Hillsboro Inn
(800) 528-1234, (254) 582-8465
http://www.bestwestern.com
307 Rte. 35
52 rooms - $60-85
Pets: Small pets welcome
Creature Comforts: CCTV, a/c, pool

Ramada Inn
(800) 2-Ramada, (254) 582-3493
http://www.ramada.com
I-35 Rte. 22
94 rooms - $60-85
Pets: Small pets welcome
Creature Comforts: CCTV, a/c, restaurant, pool

HONDO
Whitetail Lodge
(800) 375-4065, (830) 426-3031
Rte. 90 & 173
52 rooms - $40-68
Pets: Welcome w/$10 fee
Creature Comforts: CCTV, a/c, pool

HOUSTON
Comfort Inn
(800) 228-5150, (713) 943-0035
http://www.comfortinn.com
9000 Airport Blvd.
40 rooms - $55-89
Pets: Welcome w/$5 fee
Creature Comforts: CCTV, a/c, pool

Days Inn Med Center
(800) DAYS INN, (713) 523-3777
http://www.daysinn.com
4640 Main St.
150 rooms - $65-85
Pets: Welcome w/$50 deposit
Creature Comforts: CCTV, a/c,
restaurant, pool

Days Inn Houston North
(800) DAYS INN, (281) 820-1500
http://www.daysinn.com
9025 North Fwy.
100 rooms - $40-75
Pets: Small pets w/deposit
Creature Comforts: CCTV, a/c,
restaurant, cont. brkfst, pool

Days Inn
(800) DAYS INN, (281) 820-1500
http://www.daysinn.com
9535 Katy Fwy.
157 rooms - $50-75
Pets: Welcome w/$5 fee
Creature Comforts: CCTV, a/c,
refrig, micro, restaurant, cont.
brkfst, pool

Doubletree Guest Suites
(800) 222-TREE, (713) 961-9000
http://www.doubletreehotels.com
5353 Westheimer Road
335 rooms - $130-210
Pets: Welcome w/$10 fee
Creature Comforts: CCTV, a/c,
restaurant, pool

Doubletree Hotel, Allen Center
(800) 222-TREE, (713) 759-0202
http://www.doubletreehotels.com
400 Dallas St.
341 rooms - $90-160
Pets: $25 fee, $75 deposit
Creature Comforts: CCTV, a/c,
refrig, restaurant, hlth clb access

Drury Inn
(800) 325-8300, (713) 963-7007
http://www.drury-inn.com
1615 West Loop
134 rooms - $85-105
Pets: Welcome
Creature Comforts: CCTV, a/c,
cont. brkfst, pool, whirlpool

Drury Inn Houston Hobby
(800) 325-8300, (713) 941-4300
http://www.drury-inn.com
7902 Mosley Road
134 rooms - $70-99
Pets: Welcome
Creature Comforts: CCTV, a/c,
cont. brkfst, pool, whirlpool

Drury Inn I -10 West
(800) 325-8300, (281) 467-4411
http://www.drury-inn.com
1000 N. Rte. 6
120 rooms - $70-99
Pets: Welcome
Creature Comforts: CCTV, a/c,
cont. brkfst, pool, whirlpool

Four Seasons Hotel
(800) 332-3442, (713) 650-1300
http://www.fshr.com
1300 Lamar St.
399 rooms - $195-1,000
Pets: Under 15 lbs., must remain
leashed in public areas, pet sitters,
dog walkers, canine/feline cuisine
Creature Comforts: Large, lavish
hotel w/intimate public areas, rms
w/trad. reproductions, rqst pool/
garden views, CCTV, a/c, marble
baths, gourmet restaurant, pool,
hlth club., sauna, whirlpool

Hampton Inn I-10 E
(800) Hampton, (713) 673-4200
http://www.hamptoninn.com
828 Mercury Dr.
90 rooms - $60-79
Pets: Welcome
Creature Comforts: CCTV, a/c,
cont. brkfst, pool

Harvey Suites - Medical Center
(800) 922-9222, (713) 528-7744
6800 Main St.
285 rooms - $70-180
Pets: $25 fee, $125 deposit
Creature Comforts: CCTV, a/c,
kit, restaurant, pool

Hawthorn Suites Hotel
(800) 527-1133, (713) 785-3415
http://www.hawthorn.com
6910 Southwest Fwy.
151 rooms - $140-160
Pets: Small pets w/$5 fee, $25 dep
Creature Comforts: CCTV, a/c,
kit, cont. brkfst, pool

Holiday Inn Hobby Airport
(800) HOLIDAY, (713) 943-7979
http://www.holiday-inn.com
9100 Gulf Fwy.
288 rooms - $110-130
Pets: Small pets w/$50 deposit
Creature Comforts: CCTV, a/c,
restaurant, pool

Holiday Inn Hotel Suites
(800) HOLIDAY, (713) 681-5000
http://www.holiday-inn.com
7787 Katy Fwy.
218 rooms - $60-110
Pets: Welcome w/$25 fee
Creature Comforts: CCTV, a/c,
Jacuzzi, restaurant, pool

Holiday Inn - Houston Airport
(800) HOLIDAY, (281) 449-2311
http://www.holiday-inn.com
15222 JFK Blvd.
401 rooms - $130-140
Pets: Welcome
Creature Comforts: CCTV, a/c,
restaurant, pool, tennis

Holiday Inn - Medical Center
(800) HOLIDAY, (713) 797-1110
http://www.holiday-inn.com
6701 S. Main St.
296 rooms - $90-100
Pets: Small pets welcome w/$25
fee, $125 deposit
Creature Comforts: CCTV, a/c,
restaurant, pool

Holiday Inn Select
(800) HOLIDAY, (713) 523-8448
http://www.holiday-inn.com
2712 Southwest Fwy.
355 rooms - $60-120
Pets: $25 fee, $100 dep
Creature Comforts: CCTV, a/c,
restaurant, pool, whirlpool

Howard Johnson Express Inn
(800) I-Go-Hojo, (713) 666-1411
http://www.hojo.com
9604 S. Main St.
142 rooms - $45-90
Pets: Welcome w/$10 fee
Creature Comforts: CCTV, a/c,
restaurant, cont. brkfst, pool, hlth
clb access

Interstate Motor Lodge
(713) 453-6353
13213 East Fwy.
76 rooms - $45-50
Pets: Welcome w/$20 deposit
Creature Comforts: CCTV, a/c,
refrig, micro, cont. brkfst, pool,
whirlpool, playground

JW Marriott Houston
(800) 228-9290, (713) 961-1500
http://www.marriott.com
5150 Westheimer Road
503 rooms - $200-450
Pets: Small pets w/$50 deposit
Creature Comforts: CCTV, a/c,
kit, restaurant, pool

Lancaster Historic Hotel
(800) 231-0336, (713) 228-9500
701 Texas at Louisiana
93 rooms - $120-885
Pets: Small pets-$50 fee, $50 dep
Creature Comforts: 1926 hotel,
residential qlty, traditional English
decor, bedrms w/flr to ceiling
wndws, formal decor, marble
baths, CCTV, VCR, a/c, CD
player, gourmet restaurant

La Quinta Inn - Astrodome
(800) Nu-Rooms, (713) 668-8082
http://www.laquinta.com
9911 Buffalo Speedway
115 rooms - $65-80
Pets: Small pets welcome
Creature Comforts: CCTV, a/c,
refrig, cont. brkfst, pool, whirlpool

La Quinta Inn, Airport
(800) Nu-Rooms, (713) 447-6888
http://www.laquinta.com
6 N. Belt E.
122 rooms - $70-85
Pets: Small pets welcome
Creature Comforts: CCTV, a/c,
cont. brkfst, pool

La Quinta Inn - Loop 1960
(800) Nu-Rooms, (281) 444-7500
http://www.laquinta.com
17111 N. Fwy.
138 rooms - $65-85
Pets: Small pets welcome
Creature Comforts: CCTV, a/c,
cont. brkfst, pool

La Quinta Inn - Brookhollow
(800) Nu-Rooms, (713) 688-2581
http://www.laquinta.com
11002 Northwest Fwy.
122 rooms - $70-85
Pets: Small pets welcome
Creature Comforts: CCTV, a/c,
cont. brkfst, pool

La Quinta Inn - Cy Fair
(800) Nu-Rooms, (281) 469-4018
http://www.laquinta.com
13290 Rte. 1960W
130 rooms - $65-85
Pets: Small pets welcome
Creature Comforts: CCTV, a/c,
refrig, cont. brkfst, pool

La Quinta Inn - East
(800) Nu-Rooms, (713) 453-5425
http://www.laquinta.com
11999 E. Fwy.
122 rooms - $60-80
Pets: Small pets welcome
Creature Comforts: CCTV, a/c,
refrig, cont. brkfst, pool

La Quinta Inn - Greenway
(800) Nu-Rooms, (713) 623-4750
http://www.laquinta.com
4015 Southwest Fwy.
131 rooms - $65-80
Pets: Small pets welcome
Creature Comforts: CCTV, a/c,
cont. brkfst, pool

La Quinta Inn - Hobby Airport
(800) Nu-Rooms, (713) 941-0900
http://www.laquinta.com
9902 Gulf Fwy.
129 rooms - $65-85
Pets: Small pets welcome
Creature Comforts: CCTV, a/c,
refrig, cont. brkfst, pool

La Quinta Inn SW Fwy/Beltway
(800) Nu-Rooms, (713) 270-9559
http://www.laquinta.com
10552 Southwest Fwy.
114 rooms - $70-85
Pets: Small pets welcome
Creature Comforts: CCTV, a/c,
refrig, micro, cont. brkfst, pool,
whirlpool

La Quinta Inn - West
(800) Nu-Rooms, (713) 932-0808
http://www.laquinta.com
11113 Katy Fwy.
176 rooms - $65-80
Pets: Small pets welcome
Creature Comforts: CCTV, a/c,
refrig, micro, cont. brkfst, pool

La Quinta Inn - Wirt Road
(800) Nu-Rooms, (713) 688-8941
http://www.laquinta.com
8017 Katy Fwy.
100 rooms - $70-88
Pets: Small pets welcome
Creature Comforts: CCTV, a/c,
cont. brkfst, pool

Lovett Inn - Historic B&B
(800) 779-5224, (713) 522-5224
http://www.lovettinn.com
501 Lovett Blvd.
8 rooms - $75-150
Pets: Welcome in four rms.
Creature Comforts: Gracious
Federal-style home in quiet city
nghbrhd, lovely grdns, romantic,
period frnshings, four-poster beds,
suites, CCTV, a/c, refrig, micro,
Jacuzzi, cont. brkfst, pool,
whirlpool

Marriott - By the Galleria
(800) 228-9290, (713) 960-0111
http://www.marriott.com
1750 W. Loop S.
302 rooms - $90-160
Pets: Small pets welcome
Creature Comforts: CCTV,
VCR, a/c, refrig, restaurant, pool,
hlth clb access, sauna, whirlpool

Medallion Hotel Houston
(800) 688-3000, (713) 688-0100
3000 N. Loop W.
382 rooms - $160-250
Pets: Small pets welcome
Creature Comforts: CCTV, a/c,
restaurant, pool, whirlpool

Motel 6
(800) 4-MOTEL6, (281) 497-5000
http://www.motel6.com
28673 Rte. 45 N
135 rooms - $40-55
Pets: Under 30 lbs. welcome
Creature Comforts: CCTV, a/c,
restaurant, pool

Motel 6
(800) 4-MOTEL6, (713) 937-7056
http://www.motel6.com
16884 NW Fwy.
119 rooms - $40-55
Pets: Under 30 lbs. welcome
Creature Comforts: CCTV, a/c,
restaurant, pool

Motel 6
(800) 4-MOTEL6, (281) 290-9188
http://www.motel6.com
2900 W. Sam Houston Parkway
121 rooms - $45-59
Pets: Under 30 lbs. welcome
Creature Comforts: CCTV, a/c,
restaurant, pool

Motel 6
(800) 4-MOTEL6, (713) 664-6425
http://www.motel6.com
3223 S. Loop W
111 rooms - $40-55
Pets: Under 30 lbs. welcome
Creature Comforts: CCTV, a/c,
pool

Motel 6
(800) 4-MOTEL6, (713) 682-8588
http://www.motel6.com
5555 W. 34th St.
118 rooms - $40-55
Pets: Under 30 lbs. welcome
Creature Comforts: CCTV, a/c,
restaurant, pool

Motel 6
(800) 4-MOTEL6, (713) 941-0990
http://www.motel6.com
8800 Airport Blvd.
124 rooms - $40-55
Pets: Under 30 lbs. welcome
Creature Comforts: CCTV, a/c,
pool

Motel 6
(800) 4-MOTEL6, (713) 778-0008
http://www.motel6.com
9638 Plainfield Road
205 rooms - $40-55
Pets: Under 30 lbs. welcome
Creature Comforts: CCTV, a/c,
restaurant, pool

Omni Hotel Houston
(800) The-Omni, (713) 871-8181
http://www.omnihotels.com
Four Riverway
381 rooms - $200-1,000
Pets: Under 25 lbs. w/$50 fee
Creature Comforts: Contemp.
hotel surrounded by dense
woodlands, indoor grdns/streams,
rqst odd number rms w/pool, lake,
meadow vws, well appointed rms,
CCTV, VCR, a/c, gourmet
restaurant, pool, hlth clb access,
sauna, whirlpool, tennis, bicycles

Quality Inn, Airport
(800) 228-5151, (281) 446-9131
http://www.qualityinn.com
6115 Will Clayton Parkway
152 rooms - $65-80
Pets: Welcome w/$15 fee
Creature Comforts: CCTV, a/c,
restaurant, pool, tennis

Ramada Hotel Astrodome
(800) 2-Ramada, (713) 797-9000
http://www.ramada.com
2100 S. Braeswood Blvd.
331 rooms - $60-90
Pets: Small pets w/$10 fee
Creature Comforts: CCTV, a/c,
restaurant, pool

Ramada Limited 1960
(800) 2-Ramada, (281) 893-5224
http://www.ramada.com
15725 Bammel Village Dr.
60 rooms - $50-95
Pets: Welcome w/$5 daily fee,
$25 one-time fee
Creature Comforts: CCTV, a/c,
kit, Jacuzzi, cont. brkfst, pool, hlth
clb access, whirlpool

Ramada Plaza Hotel
(800) 2-Ramada, (713) 462-9977
http://www.ramada.com
12801 Northwest Fwy.
292 rooms - $105-155
Pets: Welcome
Creature Comforts: CCTV, a/c,
restaurant, pool

Red Roof Inn
(800) THE ROOF, (713) 943-3300
http://www.redroof.com
9005 Airport Blvd.
151 rooms - $50-75
Pets: Small pets welcome
Creature Comforts: CCTV, a/c,
pool

Red Roof Inn Houston West
(800) THE ROOF, (713) 579-7200
http://www.redroof.com
15701 Park Ten Place
123 rooms - $45-65
Pets: Small pets welcome
Creature Comforts: CCTV, a/c

Red Roof Inns
(800) THE ROOF, (713) 939-0800
http://www.redroof.com
12929 Northwest Fwy.
123 rooms - $50-80
Pets: Small pets welcome
Creature Comforts: CCTV, a/c,
pool

Residence Inn - Astrodome
(800) 331-3131, (713) 660-7993
http://www.residenceinn.com
7710 S. Main St.
285 rooms - $90-125
Pets: Small pets w/$5 fee, $25 dep
Creature Comforts: CCTV, a/c,
kit, pool

Residence Inn - Clear Lake
(800) 331-3131, (281) 486-2424
http://www.residenceinn.com
525 Bay Area Blvd.
110 rooms - $124-150
Pets: Welcome w/$6 fee, $50 dep
Creature Comforts: CCTV, a/c,
refrig, micro, restaurant, pool, hlth
clb.

Robin's Nest B&B
(800) 622-8343, (713) 528-5821
http://www.e-bnb.com/
4104 Greeley Rd.
4 rooms - $75-100
Pets: "Depends on size, age,
training, and disposition of both
the pet and the owner!"
Creature Comforts: Renovated
1898 Queen Anne Victorian,
beautiful and creative interior
design w/international tones,
bedrooms w/custom fabrics and
antiques, featherbeds, claw-foot
tubs, full brkfst, CCTV, a/c, full
brkfst

Sheraton Brookhollow
(800) 325-3535, (713) 688-0100
http://www.sheraton.com
3000 N. Loop W
382 rooms - $90-160
Pets: Welcome
Creature Comforts: CCTV, a/c,
restaurant, hlth clb access

Shoney's Inn - Astrodome
(800) 222-2222, (713) 799-2436
http://www.shoneysinn.com
2364 S. Loop W
130 rooms - $90-149
Pets: Welcome w/$25 fee
Creature Comforts: CCTV, a/c,
refrig, micro, pool

Shoney's Inn Suites
(800) 222-2222, (713) 776-2633
http://www.shoneysinn.com
12323 Katy Fwy.
115 rooms - $55-85
Pets: Welcome w/$25 fee
Creature Comforts: CCTV, a/c,
refrig, micro, pool

Shoney's Inn Houston, SW
(800) 222-2222, (713) 776-2633
http://www.shoneysinn.com
6687 Southwest Fwy.
115 rooms - $50-85
Pets: Welcome w/$25 deposit
Creature Comforts: CCTV, a/c,
kit, pool

Shoney's Inn - Tidwell
(800) 222-2222, (713) 690-1493
http://www.shoneysinn.com
7887 W. Tidwell Road
115 suites - $65-90
Pets: Small pets w/$50 deposit
Creature Comforts: CCTV, a/c,
kit, pool

TownePlace Suites, Marriott
(281) 286-2132
1050 Bay Area Blvd.
95 rooms - $59-109
Pets: Welcome
Creature Comforts: CCTV, a/c,
pool, exercise rm.

Travelodge
(800) 578-7878, (713) 587-9171
http://www.travelodge.com
4726 FM 1960 W
70 rooms - $45-80
Pets: Welcome
Creature Comforts: CCTV, a/c,
restaurant, pool, golf

Travelodge Houston West
(800) 578-7878, (281) 859-2233
http://www.travelodge.com
4204 Rte. 6 N
60 rooms - $40-60
Pets: Welcome
Creature Comforts: CCTV, a/c,
pool, whirlpool

HUNTSVILLE
Econo Lodge
(800) 55-ECONO, (409) 295-6401
http://www.econolodge.com
1501 Rte. 45N
53 rooms - $45-60
Pets: Small pets w/$10 deposit
Creature Comforts: CCTV, a/c,
pool

Motel 6
(800) 4-MOTEL6, (409) 291-6927
http://www.motel6.com
1607 Rte. 45
122 rooms - $35-50
Pets: Under 30 lbs. welcome
Creature Comforts: CCTV, a/c,
pool

Rodeway Inn
(800) 228-2000, (409) 295-7595
http://www.rodeway.com
3211 Rte. 45
40 rooms - $40-80
Pets: Small pets welcome
Creature Comforts: CCTV, a/c,
pool

Sam Houston Inn
(800) 395-9151, (409) 295-9151
3296 Rte. 45S
76 rooms - $50-75
Pets: Welcome
Creature Comforts: CCTV, a/c,
cont. brkfst, pool

INGRAM
Hunter House Motor Inn
(800) 655-2377, (830) 367-2377
310 Rte. 39W
24 rooms - $50-80
Pets: Welcome
Creature Comforts: CCTV, a/c,
pool

IRVING
Comfort Inn DFW Airport
(800) 228-5150, (972) 929-0066
http://www.comfortinn.com
8205 Esters Road
152 rooms - $70-95
Pets: Small pets w/$15 fee
Creature Comforts: CCTV, a/c,
refrig, micro, cont. brkfst, pool

Drury Inn - DFW Airport
(800) 325-8300, (972) 986-1200
http://www.druryinn.com
4210 W. Airport Fwy.
129 rooms - $75-99
Pets: Small pets welcome
Creature Comforts: CCTV, a/c,
cont. brkfst, pool

Four Seasons Resort and Club
(800) 332-3442, (972) 717-0700
http://www.fshr.com
4150 N. MacArthur Blvd.
357 rooms - $291-1,000
Pets: Under 15 lbs.
Creature Comforts: Sprawling
luxury resort w/extensive athletic
facilities, rqst villas, earth tones/
natural woods, plantation shutters,
CCTV, a/c, Jacuzzi, restaurants,
pool, lap pools, hlth clb, spa, 12
tennis courts, 2 championship golf
courses

Hampton Inn - DFW
(800) Hampton, (972) 986-3606
http://www.hamptoninn.com
4340 West Airport Fwy.
81 rooms - $80-99
Pets: Welcome
Creature Comforts: CCTV, a/c,
pool

Harvey Hotel - DFW Airport
(800) 922-9222, (972) 929-4500
4545 John Carpenter Fwy.
506 rooms - $175-185
Pets: Welcome
Creature Comforts: CCTV, a/c,
restaurant, pool, hlth clb access

707

Harvey Suites
(800) 922-9222, (972) 929-4499
4550 W. John Carpenter Fwy.
164 rooms - $70-165
Pets: Small pets w/$25 fee, $125 deposit
Creature Comforts: CCTV, a/c, refrig, micro, restaurant, cont. brkfst, pool, hlth clb access, sauna, whirlpool

Homewood Suites Las Colinas
(800) 225-5466, (972) 556-0665
http://www.homewoodsuites.com
4300 Wingren Road
136 rooms - $85-190
Pets: Welcome w/$50 fee
Creature Comforts: CCTV, a/c, pool

La Quinta Inn - DFW, East
(800) Nu-Rooms, (972) 252-6546
http://www.laquinta.com
4105 W. Airport Fwy.
169 rooms - $60-90
Pets: Small pets welcome
Creature Comforts: CCTV, a/c, cont. brkfst, pool

Motel 6
(800) 4-MOTEL6, (972) 438-4227
http://www.motel6.com
510 S. Loop 12
76 rooms - $30-55
Pets: Under 30 lbs. welcome
Creature Comforts: CCTV, a/c

Motel 6
(800) 4-MOTEL6, (972) 915-3993
http://www.motel6.com
7800 Heathrow Dr.
120 rooms - $45-59
Pets: Under 30 lbs. welcome
Creature Comforts: CCTV, a/c, pool

Omni Mandalay - Las Colinas
(800) 843-6664, (972) 556-0800
221 E. Las Colinas Blvd.
410 rooms - $100-210
Pets: Welcome w/$50 fee
Creature Comforts: CCTV, a/c, restaurant, pool

Red Roof Inn - DFW Airport
(800) THE ROOF, (972) 929-0020
http://www.redroof.com
8150 Esters Blvd.
158 rooms - $50-75
Pets: Small pets welcome
Creature Comforts: CCTV, a/c
708

Red Roof Inn - DFW South
(800) THE ROOF, (972) 570-7500
http://www.redroof.com
2611 W. Airport Fwy.
126 rooms - $65-70
Pets: Small pets welcome
Creature Comforts: CCTV, a/c, pool

Residence Inn by Marriott
(800) 331-3131, (972) 580-7773
http://www.residenceinn.com
950 W. Walnut Hill Lane
120 rooms - $80-160
Pets: Welcome w/$50-75 fee
Creature Comforts: CCTV, a/c, kit, pool

Sheraton Grand Hotel
(800) 325-3535, (972) 929-8400
http://www.sheraton.com
Rte. 114 Esters Blvd.
300 rooms - $80-160
Pets: Small pets w/$200 deposit
Creature Comforts: CCTV, a/c, restaurant, pool

Wilson World Motor Hotel
(800) 333-9457, (972) 513-0800
4600 West Airport Fwy.
200 rooms - $70-109
Pets: Small pets welcome
Creature Comforts: CCTV, a/c, restaurant, pool

JACKSBORO
Jacksboro Inn
(940) 567-3751
704 S. Main St.
49 rooms - $40-59
Pets: Small pets welcome
Creature Comforts: CCTV, a/c, pool

JACKSONVILLE
Best Western Inn of Jacksonville
(800) 528-1234, (903) 586-9841
http://www.bestwestern.com
1407 E. Rusk St.
94 rooms - $65-95
Pets: Under 6 lbs. welcome
Creature Comforts: CCTV, a/c, restaurant, pool

JASPER
Best Western Inn of Jasper
(800) 528-1234, (409) 384-7767
http://www.bestwestern.com
205 W. Gibson St
59 rooms - $50-80
Pets: Small pets welcome
Creature Comforts: CCTV, a/c, refrig, micro, restaurant, pool, whirlpool

Ramada Inn
(800) 2-Ramada, (409) 384-9021
http://www.ramada.com
239 E. Gibson St.
100 rooms - $55-90
Pets: Small pets welcome
Creature Comforts: CCTV, a/c, restaurant, pool

JEFFERSON
Best Western Inn
(800) 528-1234, (903) 665-3983
http://www.bestwestern.com
400 S. Walcott St.
65 rooms - $65-95
Pets: Under 20 lbs. w/$25 deposit
Creature Comforts: CCTV, a/c, restaurant, pool

JOHNSON CITY
Dream Catcher B&B
(830) 868-4875
Rte 1, Box 345
1 rm/2tipis - $60-95
Pets: Welcome w/$10 fee, leashed, must ignore livestock
Creature Comforts: Creekside setting, Native American tipis and southwestern bunkhouse, whimsical sculptures on ppty, bunkhouse w/iron bed, patchwrk quilt, TV, VCR, a/c, refrig, micro, cont. brkfst; neat tipis w/futons, cook tent, electric, running water

Save Inn
(830) 868-4044
107 Rte. 281-290
53 rooms - $40-59
Pets: Welcome
Creature Comforts: CCTV, a/c, restaurant, pool

JUNCTION

Carousel Inn
(915) 446-3301
1908 Main St.
30 rooms - $30-49
Pets: Welcome
Creature Comforts: CCTV, a/c, pool

Days Inn
(800) DAYS INN, (915) 446-3730
http://www.daysinn.com
111 S. Martinez St.
50 rooms - $55-69
Pets: Welcome w/$4 fee
Creature Comforts: CCTV, a/c, pool

The Hills Motel
(915) 446-2567
1520 Main St.
27 rooms - $40-48
Pets: Small pets welcome
Creature Comforts: CCTV, a/c, restaurant, pool

La Vista Motel
(915) 446-2191
2040 N. Main St.
9 rooms - $30-39
Pets: Welcome
Creature Comforts: CCTV, a/c

KATY

Best Western Houston West Inn
(800) 528-1234, (281) 392-9800
http://www.bestwestern.com
22455 Rte. 10
104 rooms - $50-89
Pets: Small pets welcome
Creature Comforts: CCTV, a/c, kit, pool

Super 8 Motel
(800) 800-8000, (281) 395-5757
http://www.super8.com
22157 Katy Fwy.
30 rooms - $45-65
Pets: Welcome
Creature Comforts: CCTV, a/c, Jacuzzi, cont. brkfst

KERRVILLE

Best Western Sunday House Inn
(800) 528-1234, (830) 896-1313
http://www.bestwestern.com
2124 Sidney Baker St.
97 rooms - $65-100
Pets: Welcome w/$10 fee
Creature Comforts: CCTV, a/c, pool

Flagstaff Inn
(830) 792-4449
Route 27
20 rooms - $30-49
Pets: Welcome
Creature Comforts: CCTV, a/c, refrig

Hillcrest Inn
(830) 896-7400
Route 16
37 rooms - $35-53
Pets: Welcome w/$5 fee
Creature Comforts: CCTV, a/c, refrig, pool

Holiday Inn - Y.O. Ranch Hotel
(800) HOLIDAY, (830) 257-4440
http://www.holiday-inn.com
2033 Sidney Baker St.
200 rooms - $90-120
Pets: Small pets welcome
Creature Comforts: CCTV, a/c, restaurant, pool, tennis

Inn of the Hills River Resort
(800) 292-5690, (830) 895-5000
http://www.innofthehills.com
1001 Junction Rte.
177 rms/condos - $65-225
Pets: Med-size pets in smkng rms.
Creature Comforts: Low-key, family resort, native stone/cypress wood lodge rms, well-appointed condos ovrlkng river, CCTV, a/c, kit, Jacuzzi, restaurants, pool, hlth clb, sauna, whirlpool, tennis, putting green, racquetball, bowling, canoeing, paddleboats

Save Inn Motel
(800) 219-8158, (830) 896-8200
1804 Sidney Baker St.
45 rooms - $40-64
Pets: Small pets welcome
Creature Comforts: CCTV, a/c, restaurant, pool

Wittlinger's Turtle Creek Lodge
(800) 219-8158, (830) 896-8200
http://www.turtlecreeklodge.com
1520 Upper Turtle Creek Rd.
4 rooms - $150-250
Pets: Welcome w/notice
Creature Comforts: Private guest house, creekside setting, stone fp in massive great rm., beautiful decor, 4 bedrooms, CCTV, a/c, kit, floating dock, swimming

KILGORE

Ramada Inn
(800) 2-Ramada, (903) 983-3456
http://www.ramada.com
3501 Rte. 259 N
80 rooms - $55-90
Pets: Welcome
Creature Comforts: CCTV, a/c, refrig, restaurant, pool

KILLEEN

La Quinta Inn
(800) Nu-Rooms, (254) 526-8331
http://www.laquinta.com
1112 Fort Hood St.
105 rooms - $65-85
Pets: Small pets welcome
Creature Comforts: CCTV, a/c, refrig, micro, cont. brkfst, pool

KINGSVILLE

Holiday Inn
(800) HOLIDAY, (512) 595-5753
http://www.holiday-inn.com
3430 Rte. 77 S
75 rooms - $65-99
Pets: Small pets welcome
Creature Comforts: CCTV, a/c, restaurant, pool

Holiday Inn
(800) HOLIDAY, (512) 595-5753
http://www.holiday-inn.com
3430 Rte. 77 S
75 rooms - $50-99
Pets: Small pets welcome
Creature Comforts: CCTV, a/c, refrig, restaurant, pool, hlth clb access, sauna, whirlpool

Motel 6
(800) 4-MOTEL6, (512) 592-5106
http://www.motel6.com
101 N. Rte. 77
86 rooms - $35-58
Pets: Under 30 lbs. welcome
Creature Comforts: CCTV, a/c, pool

LA PORTE

La Quinta Inn
(800) Nu-Rooms, (713) 470-0760
http://www.laquinta.com
1105 Rte. 146S
114 rooms - $60-85
Pets: Small pets welcome
Creature Comforts: CCTV, a/c, refrig, cont. brkfst, pool, hlth clb access

LAKE JACKSON
Best Western Lake Jackson Inn
(800) 528-1234, (409) 297-3031
http://www.bestwestern.com
915 Rte. 332
107 rooms - $45-70
Pets: Welcome w/$5 fee
Creature Comforts: CCTV, a/c,
refrig, micro, pool

Ramada Inn
(800) 2-Ramada, (409) 297-1161
http://www.ramada.com
925 Rte. 332 W
147 rooms - $110-140
Pets: Under 25 lbs. welcome
Creature Comforts: CCTV, a/c,
restaurant, cont. brkfst, pool

LAKE LBJ
**Tropical Hideaway Beach
Resort**
(800) 662-4431, (210) 598-9896
604 Highcrest Dr.
50 rooms - $100-125
Pets: Welcome w/$25 deposit
Creature Comforts: CCTV, a/c,
kit, restaurant, pool, marina,
tennis, volleyball

LA MESA
Shiloh Inn
(800) 222-2244, (806) 872-6721
1707 Lubbock Rte.
50 rooms - $45-70
Pets: Welcome w/$10 fee
Creature Comforts: CCTV, a/c,
pool

LAMPASAS
Circle Motel
(800) 521-5417, (512) 556-6201
1502 S. Key Ave.
43 rooms - $45-75
Pets: Welcome
Creature Comforts: CCTV, a/c,
refrig, pool

Country Inn
(800) 556-2322, (512) 556-5616
21 South St.
17 rooms - $45-65
Pets: Welcome
Creature Comforts: CCTV, a/c,
cont. brkfst

LAREDO
Best Western Fiesta Inn
(800) 528-1234, (956) 723-3603
http://www.bestwestern.com
5240 San Bernardo Ave.
150 rooms - $65-76
Pets: Welcome
Creature Comforts: CCTV, a/c,
pool

Family Gardens Inn
(800) 292-4053, (956) 723-5300
5830 San Bernardo Ave.
191 rooms - $55-69
Pets: Welcome
Creature Comforts: CCTV, a/c,
refrig, micro, pool, hlth clb access

La Quinta Inn
(800) Nu-Rooms, (956) 722-0511
http://www.laquinta.com
3610 Santa Ursula Ave.
152 rooms - $70-85
Pets: Small pets welcome
Creature Comforts: CCTV, a/c,
cont. brkfst, pool

Motel 6- North
(800) 4-MOTEL6, (956) 722-8133
http://www.motel6.com
5920 San Bernardo Ave.
109 rooms - $40-60
Pets: Under 30 lbs. welcome
Creature Comforts: CCTV, a/c,
pool

Motel 6 - South
(800) 4 MOTEL6, (956) 725-8187
http://www.motel6.com
5310 San Bernardo Ave.
94 rooms - $40-65
Pets: Under 30 lbs. welcome
Creature Comforts: CCTV, a/c,
pool

LEAKEY
Whiskey Mountain Inn
(800) 370-6797, (830) 232-6797
www.whiskeymountaininn.com
HCR 1, Box 555
6 rooms - $50-80
Pets: Welcome, "we've never had
a pet smoke inside or leave wet
towels on the floor"
Creature Comforts: Unusual,
rustic cypress farmhouse, tree
trunk porch, w/various cabins,
covered porches, charming but
simple, CCTV, a/c, cont. brkfst,
and hiking trails

LEWISVILLE
Comfort Suites
(800) 228-5150, (972) 315-6464
http://www.comfortinn.com
755 Vista Ridge Mall Dr.
60 rooms - $75-89
Pets: Welcome w/$50 fee
Creature Comforts: CCTV, a/c,
kit, pool

Country Inn Suites
(800) 456-4000, (972) 315-6565
755 B Vista Ridge Mall Dr.
64 rooms - $65-95
Pets: Welcome w/$10 deposit
Creature Comforts: CCTV, a/c,
cont. brkfst, pool

Days Inn
(800) DAYS INN, (972) 436-0080
http://www.daysinn.com
1401 S. Stemmons Fwy.
104 rooms - $50-85
Pets: Small pets welcome
Creature Comforts: CCTV, a/c,
kit, pool

La Quinta Inn
(800) Nu-Rooms, (972) 221-7525
http://www.laquinta.com
1657 S. Stemmons Fwy.
128 rooms - $50-75
Pets: Small pets welcome
Creature Comforts: CCTV, a/c,
refrig, micro, cont. brkfst, pool

LITTLEFIELD
Crescent Park Motel
(800) 658-9960, (806) 385-4464
2000 Hall Ave.
46 rooms - $30-65
Pets: Welcome
Creature Comforts: CCTV, a/c,
pool

LLANO
Best Western
(800) 528-1234, (915) 247-4101
http://www.bestwestern.com
901 W. Young St.
41 rooms - $50-75
Pets: Small pets welcome
Creature Comforts: CCTV, a/c,
refrig, micro, pool

LONGVIEW

Comfort Suites
(800) 228-5150, (903) 663-4991
http://www.comfortinn.com
3307 N. 4th St.
60 rooms - $70-99
Pets: Welcome w/$20 deposit
Creature Comforts: CCTV, a/c, pool

Hampton Inn
(800) Hampton, (903) 758-0959
http://www.hamptoninn.com
112 S. Access Rd.
82 rooms - $70-89
Pets: Welcome w/approval
Creature Comforts: CCTV, VCR, a/c, refrig, micro, Jacuzzi, cont. brkfst, pool, hlth clb access, whirlpool

Holiday Inn
(800) HOLIDAY, (903) 758-0700
http://www.holiday-inn.com
3119 Estes Parkway
189 rooms - $60-95
Pets: Welcome
Creature Comforts: CCTV, a/c, micro, restaurant, pool, whirlpool

La Quinta Inn
(800) Nu-Rooms, (903) 757-3663
http://www.laquinta.com
502 S. Access Road
106 rooms - $60-85
Pets: Small pets welcome
Creature Comforts: CCTV, a/c, cont. brkfst, pool

Longview Inn
(800) 733-1139, (903) 753-0350
605 Access Road
100 rooms - $45-65
Pets: Welcome
Creature Comforts: CCTV, a/c, pool

Motel 6
(800) 4-MOTEL6, (903) 745-5541
http://www.motel6.com
909 - 66th St.
178 rooms - $30-65
Pets: Welcome
Creature Comforts: CCTV, a/c, pool, tennis

LUBBOCK

Best Western Lubbock Regency
(800) 528-1234, (806) 745-2208
http://www.bestwestern.com
6624 Rte. 27
164 rooms - $65-95
Pets: Small pets welcome
Creature Comforts: CCTV, a/c, refrig, micro, restaurant, cont. brkfst, pool, sauna, whirlpool

Holiday Inn Civic Center
(800) HOLIDAY, (806) 763-1200
http://www.holiday-inn.com
801 Ave. Q
293 rooms - $85-110
Pets: Welcome
Creature Comforts: CCTV, a/c, restaurant, pool

Holiday Inn - Lubbock Plaza Hotel
(800) HOLIDAY, (806) 797-3241
http://www.holiday-inn.com
3201 Loop 289S
202 rooms - $100-140
Pets: Small pets welcome
Creature Comforts: CCTV, a/c, restaurant, pool

Motel 6
(800) 4-MOTEL6, (806) 745-5541
http://www.motel6.com
909 - 66th St.
178 rooms - $30-45
Pets: Under 30 lbs. welcome
Creature Comforts: CCTV, a/c, pool

Residence Inn by Marriott
(800) 331-3131, (806) 745-1963
http://www.residenceinn.com
2551 S. Loop 289
80 rooms - $70-135
Pets: Welcome w/$75 fee
Creature Comforts: CCTV, a/c, kit, pool, tennis

Sheraton Inn
(800) 325-3535, (806) 747-0171
http://www.sheraton.com
505 Ave. Q
145 rooms - $70-95
Pets: Welcome
Creature Comforts: CCTV, a/c, restaurant, pool, hlth clb access, tennis

Super 8 Motel
(800) 800-8000, (806) 762-8726
http://www.super8.com
501 Ave. Q
36 rooms - $50-65
Pets: Small pets w/$25 deposit
Creature Comforts: CCTV, a/c

Super 8 Motel
(800) 800-8000, (806) 762-8400
http://www.super8.com
5410 Rte. 27
64 rooms - $60-80
Pets: Welcome w/$6 fee, $25 dep
Creature Comforts: CCTV, a/c, refrig, micro, Jacuzzi, cont. brkfst, pool, hlth clb access, whirlpool

LUCKENBACH

Luckenbach Inn B&B
(800) 997-1124, (830) 997-2205
http://www.luckenbachtx.com
HC 13, Box 9
6 rooms - $95-125
Pets: Welcome-$10 fee, $10 dep
Creature Comforts: 12 acre creekside ranch w/1800's log cabin, request smokehouse w/Hill Country decor, CCTV, VCR, a/c, fireplace, kit

LUFKIN

Best Western Expo Inn
(800) 528-1234, (409) 632-7300
http://www.bestwestern.com
4200 N. Medford Dr.
83 rooms - $50-89
Pets: Small pets w/$20 fee
Creature Comforts: CCTV, a/c, pool

Days Inn
(800) DAYS INN, (409) 639-3301
http://www.daysinn.com
2130 S. lst St.
124 rooms - $50-65
Pets: Welcome
Creature Comforts: CCTV, a/c, restaurant, pool

Holiday Inn
(800) HOLIDAY, (409) 639-3333
http://www.holiday-inn.com
4306 S. 1st St.
102 rooms - $50-89
Pets: Welcome w/$5 fee
Creature Comforts: CCTV, a/c, refrig, restaurant, cont. brkfst, pool, hlth clb access, tennis, golf

La Quinta Inn
(800) Nu-Rooms, (409) 634-3351
http://www.laquinta.com
2119 S. 1st St.
106 rooms - $55-78
Pets: Small pets welcome
Creature Comforts: CCTV, a/c,
refrig, micro, cont. brkfst, pool

Motel 6
(800) 4 MOTEL6, (409) 637-7850
http://www.motel6.com
1110 S. Timberland Dr.
107 rooms - $30-45
Pets: Under 30 lbs. welcome
Creature Comforts: CCTV, a/c,
restaurant, pool

LYTLE
Best Western La Villa
(800) 528-1234, (210) 772-4777
http://www.bestwestern.com
19525 McDonald St.
40 rooms - $45-67
Pets: Welcome
Creature Comforts: CCTV, a/c,
restaurant, pool

MADISONVILLE
Best Western of Madisonville
(800) 528-1234, (409) 348-3606
http://www.bestwestern.com
3305 E. Main
54 rooms - $45-65
Pets: Small pets welcome
Creature Comforts: CCTV, a/c,
restaurant

MARATHON
The Gage Hotel
(800) 884-4243, (915) 386-4396
http://www.gagehotel.com
102 Rte. 90 W.
40 rooms - $65-125
Pets: Welcome
Creature Comforts: Historic
hotel w/neat Mexican feeling-
portales, courtyards, simple yet
attactive southwestern rms w/
Native American influence, a/c,
fireplace, restaurant, pool

MARBLE FALLS
Best Western Marble Falls Inn
(800) 528-1234, (830) 693-5122
http://www.bestwestern.com
1403 Rte. 281 N
61 rooms - $60-95
Pets: Welcome w/$20 deposit
Creature Comforts: CCTV, a/c,
refrig, micro, Jacuzzi, cont.
brkfst, pool, whirlpool

MARSHALL
Best Western of Marshall
(800) 528-1234, (903) 935-1941
http://www.bestwestern.com
5555 E. End Blvd. South
100 rooms - $65-85
Pets: Small pets w/$10 fee
Creature Comforts: CCTV, a/c,
restaurant, pool

Days Inn
(800) DAYS INN, (903) 927-1718
http://www.daysinn.com
4911 E. End Blvd. S.
46 rooms - $50-85
Pets: Small pets w/$10 fee
Creature Comforts: CCTV, a/c,
refrig, pool

Motel 6
(800) 4-MOTEL6, (903) 935-4393
http://www.motel6.com
300 Rte. 20E
121 rooms - $30-55
Pets: Under 30 lbs. welcome
Creature Comforts: CCTV, a/c,
pool

Super 8
(800) 800-8000, (903) 935-1184
http://www.super8.com
40 rooms - $45-69
Pets: Welcome in smoking rooms
Creature Comforts: CCTV, a/c,
cont. brkfst, pool

McALLEN
Drury Inn
(800) 325-8300, (956) 687-5100
http://www.drury-inn.com
612 W. Rte. 83
89 rooms - $75-99
Pets: Welcome
Creature Comforts: CCTV, a/c,
cont. brkfst, pool

Hampton Inn
(800) Hampton, (956) 682-4900
http://www.hamptoninn.com
300 W. Rte. 83
91 rooms - $80-109
Pets: Welcome
Creature Comforts: CCTV, a/c,
pool

Holiday Inn Airport
(800) HOLIDAY, (956) 686-1741
http://www.holiday-inn.com
2000 S. 10th St.
150 rooms - $65-99
Pets: Small pets welcome
Creature Comforts: CCTV, a/c,
pool

Holiday Inn Civic Center
(800) HOLIDAY, (956) 686-2471
http://www.holiday-inn.com
200 Expwy 83W
173 rooms - $80-129
Pets: Small pets welcome
Creature Comforts: CCTV, a/c,
restaurant, pool

La Quinta Inn
(800) Nu-Rooms, (956) 687-1101
http://www.laquinta.com
1100 S. 10th St.
120 rooms - $65-95
Pets: Small pets welcome
Creature Comforts: CCTV, a/c,
pool

Motel 6
(800) 4-MOTEL6, (956) 687-3700
http://www.motel6.com
700 W. Rte. 83
93 rooms - $40-85
Pets: Welcome
Creature Comforts: CCTV, a/c,
pool

McKINNEY
Comfort Inn
(800) 228-5150, (972) 548-8888
http://www.comfortinn.com
2104 N. Central Expressway
82 rooms - $55-89
Pets: Small pets welcome
Creature Comforts: CCTV, a/c,
refrig, micro, pool

Woods Motel
(972) 542-4469
1431 N. Tennessee St.
38 rooms - $35-75
Pets: Small pets welcome
Creature Comforts: CCTV, a/c,
pool

MEMPHIS
Best Western Deville
(800) 528-1234, (806) 259-3583
http://www.bestwestern.com
Rte. 287 NW
37 rooms - $50-96
Pets: Welcome
Creature Comforts: CCTV, a/c,
restaurant, pool

MERCEDES
Days Inn
(800) DAYS INN, (956) 565-3121
http://www.daysinn.com
Mile 2 - W. Rte. 83
50 rooms - $45-95
Pets: Welcome w/$25 deposit
Creature Comforts: CCTV, a/c,
restaurant, pool

MESQUITE
Days Inn
(800) DAYS INN, (972) 279-6561
http://www.daysinn.com
3601 Rte. 80 E
119 rooms - $40-88
Pets: Small pets w/$5 fee
Creature Comforts: CCTV, a/c,
restaurant, pool

MIDLAND
Best Western Inn
(800) 528-1234, (915) 699-4144
http://www.bestwestern.com
3100 W. Wall St
125 rooms - $60-90
Pets: Small pets welcome
Creature Comforts: CCTV, a/c,
restaurant, pool, hlth clb access

Hampton Inn
(800) Hampton, (915) 697-9900
http://www.hamptoninn.com
3904 W. Wall St.
110 rooms - $50-65
Pets: Welcome
Creature Comforts: CCTV, a/c,
pool, hlth clb access, whirlpool,
sauna

Hilton Hotel
(800) HILTONS, (915) 683-6131
http://www.hilton.com
117 W. Wall St.
249 rooms - $95-160
Pets: Small pets w/$25 deposit
Creature Comforts: CCTV, a/c,
restaurant, pool

Holiday Inn Country Villa
(800) HOLIDAY, (915) 697-7754
http://www.holiday-inn.com
Rte. 80 West & Midland Dr.
280 rooms - $60-170
Pets: Welcome
Creature Comforts: CCTV, a/c,
Jacuzzi, restaurant, pool, hlth clb
access, sauna, whirlpool, and a
playground

Motel 6
(800) 4-MOTEL6, (915) 697-3197
http://www.motel6.com
1000 S. Midkiff Road
87 rooms - $30-45
Pets: Under 30 lbs. welcome
Creature Comforts: CCTV, a/c,
pool

Ramada Inn Airport
(800) 2-Ramada, (915) 561-8000
http://www.ramada.com
100 Airport Plaza
95 rooms - $70-95
Pets: Welcome
Creature Comforts: CCTV, a/c,
refrig, micro, restaurant, pool, hlth
clb access

Super 8 Motel
(800) 800-8000, (915) 684-8888
http://www.super8.com
1000 W. Rte. 20
55 rooms - $40-60
Pets: Welcome w/$6 fee
Creature Comforts: CCTV, a/c,
refrig, cont. brkfst, pool

MIDLOTHIAN
Best Western Midlothian Inn
(800) 528-1234, (972) 775-1891
http://www.bestwestern.com
220 N. Rte. 67
40 rooms - $55-78
Pets: Welcome w/$20 deposit
Creature Comforts: CCTV, a/c,
Jacuzzi, cont. brkfst, pool

MINERAL WELLS
Budget Host Inn Mesa Motel
(800) Bud-Host, (940) 325-3377
http://www.budgethost.com
3601 E. Rte. 180
40 rooms - $35-60
Pets: Welcome
Creature Comforts: CCTV, a/c,
pool

Days Inn
(800) DAYS INN, (940) 325-6961
http://www.daysinn.com
3701 E. Hubbard Rd.
72 rooms - $45-69
Pets: Welcome w/$6 fee
Creature Comforts: CCTV, a/c,
cont. brkfst, pool

Hojo Inn
(800) I-Go-Hojo, (940) 328-1111
http://www.hojo.com
2809 Rte. 180 West
30 rooms - $45-65
Pets: Welcome
Creature Comforts: CCTV, a/c,
restaurant, cont. brkfst, pool

MONAHANS
Best Western Colonial Inn
(800) 528-1234, (915) 943-4345
http://www.bestwestern.com
702 W. Rte. 20
90 rooms - $40-85
Pets: Welcome
Creature Comforts: CCTV, a/c,
restaurant, pool

MOUNT PLEASANT
Days Inn
(800) DAYS INN, (903) 577-0152
http://www.daysinn.com
2501 W. Ferguson Rd.
102 rooms - $40-70
Pets: Welcome w/$6 fee
Creature Comforts: CCTV, a/c,
refrig, micro, cont. brkfst, pool

MULESHOE
Heritage House Inn
(800) 253-5896, (806) 272-7575
2301 W. American Blvd.
51 rooms - $40-75
Pets: Welcome
Creature Comforts: CCTV, a/c,
pool

NACOGDOCHES

Eagle's Aerie B&B
(800) 754-3906, (409) 560-4900
12 E. Lake Estates, Rte 3
2 rooms - $55-75
Pets: Well trained dogs welcome
Creature Comforts: Garden level apartment in a log home, lakeside, American antiques, country collectibles, CCTV, a/c, kit, cont. brkfst, lake swimming

Econo Lodge
(800) 55-ECONO, (409) 569-0880
http://www.econolodge.com
2020 NW Loop 224
68 rooms - $35-69
Pets: Welcome
Creature Comforts: CCTV, a/c, restaurant, cont. brkfst, pool

Fredonia Historic Hotel
(409) 564-1234
200 N. Fredonia St.
115 rooms - $60-175
Pets: Welcome
Creature Comforts: CCTV, a/c, restaurant, full brkfst, pool

Hardeman Guest House B&B
(800) 884-1947, (409) 569-1947
316 N. Church St.
4 rooms - $65-89
Pets: Well behaved dogs, "who don't know they're animals" are most welcome
Creature Comforts: 1892 Nat'l Historic Register home, wrap-around porch, country antiques, Oriental rugs, English, French, Asian theme rooms, full brkfst

La Quinta Inn
(800) Nu-Rooms, (409) 560-5453
http://www.laquinta.com
3215 South St.
106 rooms - $55-85
Pets: Small pets welcome
Creature Comforts: CCTV, a/c, refrig, micro, cont. brkfst, pool

NEDERLAND

Best Western Airport Inn
(800) 528-1234, (409) 727-1631
http://www.bestwestern.com
200 Memorial Rte.
115 rooms - $45-75
Pets: Small pets w/$20 deposit
Creature Comforts: CCTV, a/c, pool

NEW BOSTON

Best Western Inn
(800) 528-1234, (903) 628-6999
http://www.bestwestern.com
1024 N. Center St.
49 rooms - $50-90
Pets: Small pets w/$20 fee
Creature Comforts: CCTV, a/c, cont. brkfst, pool

NEW BRAUNFELS

Camp Huaco Springs Cabins
(800) 553-5628, (830) 625-5411
4481 River Road
1 cabin - $120-179
Pets: Welcome
Creature Comforts: Simple cabin, rustic lean-to, a/c, refrig, micro, rafting

Holiday Inn
(800) HOLIDAY, (830) 625-8017
http://www.holiday-inn.com
1051 Rte. 35E
140 rooms - $65-90
Pets: Small pets welcome
Creature Comforts: CCTV, a/c, restaurant, pool, sauna, whirlpool

Kuebler-Waldrip Haus B&B
(800) 299-8372, (830) 625-8372
http://www.nbtexas.com/
kueblerwaldrip/
1620 Hueco Springs Loop
10 rooms - $90-200
Pets: Welcome in Danville School
Creature Comforts: Historic schoolhse on 43 acres, near Guadalupe River, rough hewn walls, tile floors, CCTV, kit, Jacuzzi, candlelit full brkfst, and horseback riding

Rodeway Inn
(800) 967-1168, (830) 629-6991
http://www.rodewayinn.com
130 rooms - $45-100
Pets: Small pets welcome
Creature Comforts: CCTV, a/c, kit, cont. brkfst, pool, whirlpool

NOCONA

Nocona Hills Motel Resort
(940) 825-3161
100 E. Huron Circle
18 rooms - $30-49
Pets: Small pets w/$5 fee
Creature Comforts: CCTV, a/c, refrig, micro

NORTH RICHLAND HILLS

La Quinta Inn Northeast
(800) Nu-Rooms, (817) 485-2750
http://www.laquinta.com
7920 Bedford-Euless Road
102 rooms - $65-95
Pets: Small pets welcome
Creature Comforts: CCTV, a/c, cont. brkfst, pool

Lexington Inn - DFW West
(800) 656-8886, (817) 656-881
8709 Airport Fwy.
114 rooms - $60-85
Pets: Small pets w/$15 fee
Creature Comforts: CCTV, a/c, refrig, micro, restaurant, cont. brkfst, pool, whirlpool

Motel 6
(800) 4-MOTEL6, (817) 485-3000
http://www.motel6.com
7804 Bedford Euless Road
84 rooms - $35-49
Pets: Welcome
Creature Comforts: CCTV, a/c, pool

ODEM

Days Inn
(800) DAYS INN, (512) 368-2166
http://www.daysinn.com
1505 Voss Ave.
24 rooms - $45-70
Pets: Small pets welcome
Creature Comforts: CCTV, a/c, refrig, pool, whirlpool

ODESSA

Best Western Garden Oasis
(800) 528-1234, (915) 337-3006
http://www.bestwestern.com
110 W. Rte. 12
118 rooms - $50-90
Pets: Welcome
Creature Comforts: CCTV, a/c, refrig, restaurant, pool, sauna, whirlpool

Days Inn
(800) DAYS INN, (915) 335-8000
http://www.daysinn.com
3075 E. Business Loop 20
96 rooms - $45-85
Pets: Welcome
Creature Comforts: CCTV, a/c, pool

Econo Lodge
(800) 55-ECONO, (915) 333-1486
http://www.econolodge.com
1518 S. Grant St.
38 rooms - $35-60
Pets: Small pets w/$20 deposit
Creature Comforts: CCTV, a/c,
pool

Holiday Inn, Centre
(800) HOLIDAY, (915) 362-2311
http://www.holiday-inn.com
6201 E. Business I-20
273 rooms - $55-160
Pets: Welcome
Creature Comforts: CCTV, a/c,
Jacuzzi, pool, whirlpool

La Quinta Inn
(800) Nu-Rooms, (915) 333-2820
http://www.laquinta.com
5001 E. Business Loop
122 rooms - $60-85
Pets: Small pets welcome
Creature Comforts: CCTV, a/c,
cont. brkfst, pool

Motel 6 - South
(800) 4-MOTEL6, (915) 333-4025
http://www.motel6.com
200 E Rte. 20
95 rooms - $30-55
Pets: Welcome
Creature Comforts: CCTV, a/c,
pool

Parkway Inn
(800) 926-6760, (915) 332-4224
3071 E. Business 20
80 rooms - $35-55
Pets: Welcome w/$15 deposit
Creature Comforts: CCTV, a/c,
cont. brkfst, pool

Super 8 Motel
(800) 800-8000, (915) 363-8281
http://www.super8.com
6713 Business 20 E
47 rooms - $40-55
Pets: Welcome w/$5 fee
Creature Comforts: CCTV, a/c

Villa West Inn
(915) 335-5055
300 W. Pool Road
40 rooms - $30-45
Pets: Small pets welcome
Creature Comforts: CCTV, a/c,
cont. brkfst

ORANGE
Best Western Inn of Orange
(800) 528-1234, (409) 883-6616
http://www.bestwestern.com
2630 Rte. 10
60 rooms - $60-85
Pets: Welcome
Creature Comforts: CCTV, a/c,
refrig, pool

Holiday Inn
(800) HOLIDAY, (409) 988-0110
http://www.holiday-inn.com
2900 Rte. 10
97 rooms - $75-99
Pets: Welcome w/$10 fee
Creature Comforts: CCTV, a/c,
pool

Motel 6
(800) 4-MOTEL6, (409) 883-4891
http://www.motel6.com
4407- 27th St.
126 rooms - $30-45
Pets: Welcome
Creature Comforts: CCTV, a/c,
restaurant, pool

Ramada Inn
(800) 2-Ramada, (409) 883-0231
http://www.ramada.com
2610 Rte. 10
125 rooms - $70-135
Pets: Welcome
Creature Comforts: CCTV, a/c,
refrig, micro, Jacuzzi, restaurant,
pool

OZONA
Daystop
(800) 329-7466, (915) 392-2631
http://www.daysinn.com
820 Loop 466 West
24 rooms - $45-60
Pets: Welcome
Creature Comforts: CCTV, a/c

PALESTINE
Best Western Palestine Inn
(800) 528-1234, (903) 723-4655
http://www.bestwestern.com
1601 W. Palestine Ave.
66 rooms - $40-89
Pets: Welcome
Creature Comforts: CCTV, a/c,
refrig, restaurant, pool, playground

Days Inn
(800) DAYS INN, (903) 729-3151
http://www.daysinn.com
1100 E. Palestine Ave.
75 rooms - $41-135
Pets: Welcome
Creature Comforts: CCTV, a/c,
pool, tennis

Ramada Inn
(800) 2-Ramada, (903) 723-7300
http://www.ramada.com
1101 E. Palestine Ave.
96 rooms - $60-95
Pets: Welcome
Creature Comforts: CCTV, a/c,
Jacuzzi, restaurant, pool, hlth club.

PARIS
Best Western Inn of Paris
(800) 528-1234, (903) 785-5566
http://www.bestwestern.com
3755 NE Loop 286
80 rooms - $45-65
Pets: Small pets welcome
Creature Comforts: CCTV, a/c,
pool

Holiday Inn
(800) HOLIDAY, (903) 785-5545
http://www.holiday-inn.com
3560 NE Loop 286
124 rooms - $75-95
Pets: Small pets w/$50 fee
Creature Comforts: CCTV, a/c,
restaurant, pool

Victorian Inns
(800) 935-0863, (903) 785-3871
425 NE 35th St.
40 rooms - $40-55
Pets: Welcome
Creature Comforts: CCTV, a/c

PASADENA
Econo Lodge
(800) 55-ECONO, (713) 477-4266
http://www.econolodge.com
823 W. Pasadena Fwy.
40 rooms - $50-75
Pets: Small pets w/$25 fee
Creature Comforts: CCTV, a/c

Ramada Inn
(800) 2-Ramada, (713) 477-6871
http://www.ramada.com
114 S. Richey at Rte. 225
140 rooms - $65-90
Pets: Welcome
Creature Comforts: CCTV, a/c,
restaurant, pool

PEARSALL

Executive Inn
(830) 334-3693
613 N. Oak St.
21 rooms - $40-65
Pets: Welcome w/$5 fee
Creature Comforts: CCTV, a/c, kit

PECOS

Best Western Swiss Clock Inn
(800) 528-1234, (915) 447-2215
http://www.bestwestern.com
900 W. Palmer St.
104 rooms - $50-80
Pets: Small pets welcome
Creature Comforts: CCTV, a/c, restaurant, cont. brkfst, pool

Motel 6
(800) 4-MOTEL6, (915) 445-9034
http://www.motel6.com
3002 S. Cedar St.
96 rooms - $30-55
Pets: Under 30 lbs. welcome
Creature Comforts: CCTV, a/c, pool

PITTSBURG

Carson House Inn & Grille
(888) 302-1878, (903) 856-2468
http://www.carsonhouse.qpg.com/
302 Mt. Pleasant St.
6 rooms - $70-80
Pets: Welcome on case by case basis, well-behaved, owner resp. for damages
Creature Comforts: Charming 1878 Victorian, antique filled rms, CCTV, a/c, excellent restaurant, full brkfst

PLAINVIEW

Best Western Conestoga Inn
(800) 528-1234, (806) 293-9454
http://www.bestwestern.com
600 N Rte. 27
82 rooms - $60-98
Pets: Small pets welcome
Creature Comforts: CCTV, a/c, pool

Days Inn
(800) DAYS INN, (806) 293-2561
http://www.daysinn.com
3600 Olton Road
49 rooms - $40-59
Pets: Welcome w/$4 fee
Creature Comforts: CCTV, a/c, cont. brkfst, pool

Holiday Inn
(800) HOLIDAY, (806) 293-4181
http://www.holiday-inn.com
4005 Olton Road
97 rooms - $50-98
Pets: Small pets welcome
Creature Comforts: CCTV, VCR, a/c, refrig, micro, cont. brkfst, pool

PLANO

Amerisuites
(800) 833-1516, (972) 378-3997
http://www.amerisuites.com
3100 Dallas Pkwy
128 rooms - $59-134
Pets: Welcome
Creature Comforts: CCTV, a/c, pool, exercise rm.

Best Western Park Suites Hotel
(800) 528-1234, (972) 578-2243
http://www.bestwestern.com
640 Park Blvd. E
84 rooms - $75-100
Pets: Small pets welcome
Creature Comforts: CCTV, a/c, refrig, micro, Jacuzzi, cont. brkfst, pool, hlth clb access, whirlpool

Comfort Inn
(800) 228-5150, (972) 424-5568
http://www.comfortinn.com
621 Central Parkway E
102 rooms - $60-79
Pets: Small pets welcome
Creature Comforts: CCTV, a/c, cont. brkfst, pool

Harvey Hotel
(800) 922-9222, (972) 578-8555
1600 N. Central Expressway
279 rooms - $80-140
Pets: $25 fee, $150 deposit
Creature Comforts: CCTV, a/c, restaurant, pool, whirlpool

La Quinta Inn
(800) Nu-Rooms, (972) 423-1300
http://www.laquinta.com
1820 N. Central Expressway
114 rooms - $70-92
Pets: Small pets welcome
Creature Comforts: CCTV, a/c, refrig, micro, cont. brkfst, pool, hlth clb access

Motel 6
(800) 4-MOTEL6, (972) 578-1626
http://www.motel6.com
2550 N. Central Expressway
118 rooms - $35-55
Pets: Welcome
Creature Comforts: CCTV, a/c

PORT ARANSAS

Beachgate Condominiums
(512) 749-5900
2000 On the Beach
12 rooms - $75-85
Pets: Welcome w/$5-10 fee
Creature Comforts: Bedroom/ living rm, CCTV, a/c, kit

Belle's Inn Motel
(512) 749-6138
710 Station at Ave. G
7 rooms - $40-60
Pets: Welcome w/$10-20 fee
Creature Comforts: CCTV, a/c, kit, pool

Belles by the Sea
(512) 749-6138
1423 S. 11th St.
15 rooms – $50-75
Pets: Welcome w/$10-20 fee
Creature Comforts: Simple motel 350 yrds from beach, CCTV, a/c, pool

Executive Keys Apt. Motel
(800) 248-1095, (512) 749-6272
820 Access Road 1A
51 rooms - $40-185
Pets: Welcome w/$5 fee
Creature Comforts: CCTV, a/c, kit, pool

Paradise Isle Motel
(512) 749-6993
314 Cutoff Road
52 rooms - $40-69
Pets: Welcome w/$10 fee
Creature Comforts: CCTV, a/c, refrig, kit, pool

Rock Cottages
(512) 749-6360
603 Ave. G
27 rooms - $32-48
Pets: Welcome w/$7 fee
Creature Comforts: CCTV, a/c, kit

Sea Horse Lodge
(512) 749-5513
503 Ave. G
12 cottages - $70-80
Pets: Small pets w/$5 fee
Creature Comforts:
Housekeeping units, CCTV, a/c,
kit

Sea and Sand Cottages
(512) 749-5191
http://www.tarpon.net/seasand
410 - 10th St.
6 cottages - $65-78
Pets: Welcome
Creature Comforts: CCTV, a/c,
kit, porches

Tropic Island Motel
(512) 749-6128
315 Cutoff Road
42 rooms - $49-79
Pets: Welcome w/$5 fee
Creature Comforts: CCTV, a/c,
refrig, kit

PORT ARTHUR
Ramada Inn
(800) 2-Ramada, (409) 962-9858
http://www.ramada.com
3801 Rte. 73
125 rooms - $70-135
Pets: Welcome
Creature Comforts: CCTV, a/c,
restaurant, pool

PORT ISABEL
Southwind Inn
(956) 943-3392
600 Davis St.
17 rooms - $40-89
Pets: Welcome w/$5 fee
Creature Comforts: CCTV, a/c,
kit, pool

PORTLAND
Comfort Inn
(800) 228-5150 , (512) 643-2222
http://www.comfortinn.com
1703 N. Rte. 181
40 rooms - $60-94
Pets: Small pets welcome
Creature Comforts: CCTV, a/c,
refrig, micro, restaurant, cont.
brkfst, pool, sauna, whirlpool

RICHARDSON
Clarion Hotel
(800) 285-3434, (972) 644-4000
http://www.clarioninn.com
1981 N. Central Expressway
296 rooms - $135-185
Pets: Small pets w/$50 fee
Creature Comforts: CCTV, a/c,
refrig, micro, restaurant, pool, hlth
clb access, saunas

Hawthorn Suites Hotel
(800) 527-1133, (972) 669-1000
http://www.hawthorn.com
250 Municipal Dr.
72 rooms - $120-189
Pets: Small pets w/$50 fee
Creature Comforts: CCTV, a/c,
kit, pool

La Quinta Inn
(800) Nu-Rooms, (972) 234-1016
http://www.laquinta.com
13685 N. Central Expressway
120 rooms - $55-85
Pets: Small pets welcome
Creature Comforts: CCTV, a/c,
refrig, micro, cont. brkfst, pool

Sleep Inn
(800) Sleep-Inn, (972) 470-9440
http://www.sleepinn.com
2458 N. Central Expressway
65 rooms - $55-79
Pets: Welcome
Creature Comforts: CCTV, a/c

RICHMOND
Executive Inn
(281) 342-5387
26035 Southwest Fwy.
50 rooms - $40-65
Pets: Welcome w/$5 fee
Creature Comforts: CCTV, a/c,
kit, pool

ROBSTOWN
Days Inn
(800) DAYS INN, (512) 387-9416
http://www.daysinn.com
320 Rte. 77 S
24 rooms - $50-85
Pets: Small pets welcome
Creature Comforts: CCTV, a/c,
refrig, pool, whirlpool

Econo Lodge
(800) 55-ECONO, (512) 387-9444
http://www.econolodge.com
2225 Rte. 77 N
32 rooms - $50-80
Pets: Welcome
Creature Comforts: CCTV, a/c,
cont. brkfst, pool

ROCKPORT
Anthony's by the Sea B&B
(800) 460-2557, (512) 729-6100
http://www.rockport-fulton.org
732 Pearl St.
6 rooms - $75-95
Pets: Welcome
Creature Comforts: CCTV,
VCR, a/c, kit, full brkfst, pool

Best Western by the Bay
(800) 528-1234, (512) 729-8351
http://www.bestwestern.com
3902 N. Rte. 35
73 rooms - $65-80
Pets: Welcome
Creature Comforts: CCTV, a/c,
restaurant, pool

Days Inn
(800) DAYS INN, (512) 729-6379
http://www.daysinn.com
1212 Rockport
29 rooms - $55-99
Pets: Under 25 lbs. welcome
Creature Comforts: CCTV, a/c,
cont. brkfst, pool

Hunt's Castle-Motel Suites
(512) 729-2273
725 S. Water St.
67 rooms - $50-125
Pets: Welcome
Creature Comforts: CCTV, a/c,
pool

Laguna Reef Apartment Motel
(800) 248-1057, (512) 729-1742
http://www.lagunareef.com
1021 Water St.
85 rooms - $50-230
Pets: Under 30 lbs. welcome w/
$5 fee, $40 deposit
Creature Comforts: CCTV, a/c,
pool

Pelican Reef Motel
(800) 248-1057, (512) 729-3837
1011 E. Market St.
70 rooms - $60-169
Pets: Welcome w/$5 fee
Creature Comforts: CCTV, a/c,
refrig, kit, cont. brkfst, pool,
fishing pier

Sand Dollar Motel
(512) 729-2381
Off Rte. 35
50 rooms - $47-69
Pets: Welcome w/$5 fee
Creature Comforts: CCTV, a/c,
and kit

Sandra Bay Cottages
(512) 729-6257
1801 Broadway St.
19 rooms - $50-69
Pets: Welcome w/$5 fee
Creature Comforts: CCTV, a/c,
kit, pool

Sun Tan Motel
(512) 729-2179
1805 Broadway
23 rooms - $39-53
Pets: Welcome w/$5 fee
Creature Comforts: CCTV, a/c,
kit, lighted fishing pier

The Village Inn
(512) 729-1742
503 N. Austin Rd.
25 rooms - $45-100
Pets: $6 fee, $20 deposit
Creature Comforts: CCTV, a/c,
kit, restaurant, pool

ROSENBERG
Best Western Sundowner Motel
(800) 528-1234, (281) 342-6000
http://www.bestwestern.com
28382 Southwest Fwy.
104 rooms - $45-60
Pets: Welcome w/$10 deposit
Creature Comforts: CCTV, a/c,
pool

ROUND ROCK
La Quinta Inn
(800) 528-1234, (512) 255-6666
http://www.laquinta.com
2004 Rte. 35N
115 rooms - $85-108
Pets: Welcome w/$25 deposit
Creature Comforts: CCTV, a/c

SAN ANGELO
Best Western Inn of the West
(800) 528-1234, (915) 653-2995
http://www.bestwestern.com
415 W. Beauregard Rd.
75 rooms - $55-80
Pets: Small pets welcome
Creature Comforts: CCTV, a/c,
restaurant, cont. brkfst, pool

Days Inn
(800) DAYS INN, (915) 658-6594
http://www.daysinn.com
4613 S. Jackson St.
113 rooms - $45-80
Pets: Small pets welcome
Creature Comforts: CCTV, a/c,
cont. brkfst, pool

El Patio Motel
(800) 677-7735, (915) 655-5711
1901 W. Beauregard St.
100 rooms - $40-70
Pets: Welcome w/$5 fee
Creature Comforts: CCTV, a/c,
pool

Holiday Inn Convention Center
(800) HOLIDAY, (915) 658-2828
http://www.holiday-inn.com
441 Rio Concho Dr.
148 rooms - $95-155
Pets: Welcome
Creature Comforts: CCTV, a/c,
restaurant, pool

Inn of the Conchos
(800) 621-6041, (915) 658-2811
2021 N. Bryant Blvd.
125 rooms - $50-85
Pets: Welcome
Creature Comforts: CCTV, a/c,
pool

La Quinta Inn
(800) Nu-Rooms, (915) 949-0515
http://www.laquinta.com
2307 Loop 306
170 rooms - $60-90
Pets: Small pets welcome
Creature Comforts: CCTV, a/c,
refrig, micro, cont. brkfst, pool,
whirlpool

Motel 6
(800) 4-MOTEL6, (915) 658-8061
http://www.motel6.com
311 N. Bryant St.
106 rooms - $30-55
Pets: Under 30 lbs. welcome
Creature Comforts: CCTV, a/c,
pool

Santa Fe Junction Motor Inn
(800) 634-2599, (915) 655-8101
410 West Ave. L
82 rooms - $30-59
Pets: Welcome
Creature Comforts: CCTV, a/c,
pool

Super 8 Motel
(800) 800-8000, (915) 653-1323
http://www.super8.com
1601 S. Bryant
84 rooms - $50-69
Pets: Welcome
Creature Comforts: CCTV, a/c,
cont. brkfst, pool, whirlpool

SAN ANTONIO
Aloha Inn
(800) 752-6354, (210) 828-0933
1435 Austin Highway
65 rooms - $35-59
Pets: Welcome
Creature Comforts: CCTV, a/c,
pool

Best Western Fiesta Inn
(800) 528-1234, (210) 697-9761
http://www.bestwestern.com
13535 Rte. 10 West
60 rooms - $50-76
Pets: Under 10 lbs. welcome
Creature Comforts: CCTV, a/c,
refrig, micro, restaurant, pool, hlth
clb access, whirlpool

Best Western Ingram Park Inn
(800) 528-1234, (210) 520-8080
http://www.bestwestern.com
6855 NW Loop 410
78 rooms - $45-150
Pets: Welcome
Creature Comforts: CCTV, a/c,
restaurant, pool

Brackenridge House
Blansett Barn
(800) 221-1412, (210) 271-3442
www.brackenridgehouse.com
230 Madison St.
5 rooms/1barn - $125-300
Pets: Small dogs in Blansett Barn
Creature Comforts: Greek
Revival house and barn in historic
dist, residential feeling, CCTV,
lvng rm, kit, bedrooms w/country
quilts, dried flwrs, kit

Coachman Inn Brooks Field
(210) 337-7171
3180 Goliard Road
120 rooms - $45-69
Pets: Small pets w/$5 fee
Creature Comforts: CCTV, a/c,
pool

Comfort Inn Airport North-East
(800) 228-5150, (210) 653-9110
http://www.comfortinn.com
2635 NE Loop 410
203 rooms - $50-98
Pets: Small pets w/$25 deposit
Creature Comforts: CCTV, a/c,
cont. brkfst, pool

Comfort Inn I-10 East
(800) 228-5150, (210) 333-9430
http://www.comfortinn.com
4403 Rte. 10E
120 rooms - $45-89
Pets: Welcome w/$5 fee
Creature Comforts: CCTV, a/c,
refrig, pool, whirlpool

Comfort Inn Sea World
(800) 228-5150, (210) 684-8606
http://www.comfortinn.com
4 Plano Place
55 rooms - $50-105
Pets: Welcome w/$10 fee
Creature Comforts: CCTV, a/c,
Jacuzzi, cont. brkfst, pool,
whirlpool

Comfort Suites
(800) 228-5150, (210) 646-6600
http://www.comfortinn.com
6350 Rte. 35 N
105 rooms - $60-140
Pets: Welcome w/$10 fee
Creature Comforts: CCTV, a/c,
refrig, micro, Jacuzzi, cont. brkfst,
pool, hlth clb access, whirlpool

Days Inn
(800) DAYS INN, (210) 696-7922
http://www.daysinn.com
11790 Rte. 10 West
62 rooms - $60-134
Pets: Welcome w/$50 deposit
Creature Comforts: CCTV, a/c,
Jacuzzi, pool

Days Inn Downtown Laredo St.
(800) DAYS INN, (210) 271-3334
http://www.daysinn.com
1500 Rte. 35S (Jnct.Rte. 10)
91 rooms - $55-100
Pets: Small pets w/$10 fee
Creature Comforts: CCTV, a/c,
pool

Days Inn Northeast
(800) DAYS INN, (210) 225-4521
http://www.daysinn.com
3443 Rte. 35N
122 rooms - $60-85
Pets: Welcome
Creature Comforts: CCTV, a/c,
pool

Days Inn Windcrest
(800) DAYS INN, (210) 650-9779
http://www.daysinn.com
9401 Rte. 35 North
61 rooms - $55-75
Pets: Welcome w/$10 fee
Creature Comforts: CCTV, a/c,
refrig, micro, Jacuzzi, cont. brkfst,
pool

Drury Inn Suites
(800) 325-8300, (210) 366-4300
http://www.druryinn.com
8811 Jones Maltsberger Road
139 rooms - $80-100
Pets: Small pets welcome
Creature Comforts: CCTV, a/c,
cont. brkfst, pool

Drury Inn East
(800) 325-8300, (210) 654-1144
http://www.druryinn.com
8300 Rte. 35N
105 rooms - $65-80
Pets: Welcome
Creature Comforts: CCTV, a/c,
cont. brkfst, pool

Drury Suites, Airport
(800) 325-8300, (210) 308-8100
http://www.druryinn.com
95 NE Loop 410
146 rooms - $80-118
Pets: Welcome
Creature Comforts: CCTV, a/c,
cont. brkfst, pool

Executive Guesthouse Hotel
(800) 362-8700, (210) 494-7600
12828 Rte. 281N
124 rooms - $85-119
Pets: Welcome-$50 fee, $50 dep
Creature Comforts: CCTV, a/c

Family Gardens Country Suites
(800) 314-3424, (210) 599-2404
2383 NE Loop 410
190 rooms - $60-79
Pets: Welcome w/$50 deposit
Creature Comforts: CCTV, a/c,
refrig, micro, pool, hlth clb access,
whirlpool

Hampton Inn Airport
(800) Hampton, (210) 366-1800
http://www.hamptoninn.com
8818 Jones Maltsberger Road
120 rooms - $70-120
Pets: Welcome
Creature Comforts: CCTV, a/c,
pool

Hampton Inn East
(800) Hampton, (210) 657-1107
http://www.hamptoninn.com
4900 Crestwind Dr.
81 rooms - $70-85
Pets: Welcome
Creature Comforts: CCTV, a/c,
pool

Hawthorn Suites
(800) 527-1133, (210) 561-9660
http://www.hawthorn.com
4041 Bluemel Road
128 rooms - $80-120
Pets: Welcome w/$50 fee
Creature Comforts: CCTV, a/c,
kit, cont. brkfst, dinner buffet
weekdays, pool

Hilton Hotel, Airport
(800) HILTONS, (210) 340-6060
http://www.hilton.com
611 NW Loop 410
387 rooms - $110-185
Pets: Welcome
Creature Comforts: CCTV, a/c,
restaurant, pool, hlth clb access

Hilton Palacio Del Rio
(800) HILTONS, (210) 222-1400
http://www.hilton.com
200 S. Alamo St.
482 rooms - $180-365
Pets: Small pets welcome
Creature Comforts: CCTV, a/c,
restaurant, pool

Holiday Inn, Market Square
(800) HOLIDAY, (210) 225-3211
http://www.holiday-inn.com
318 W. Durango St.
315 rooms - $70-120
Pets: Small pets welcome
Creature Comforts: CCTV, a/c,
restaurant, pool

Holiday Inn Express, Airport
(800) HOLIDAY, (210) 308-6700
http://www.holiday-inn.com
95 NE Loop 410
154 rooms - $75-99
Pets: Welcome
Creature Comforts: CCTV, a/c,
pool

Holiday Inn, Northeast
(800) HOLIDAY, (210) 226-4361
http://www.holiday-inn.com
3855 Rte. 35N
202 rooms - $60-119
Pets: Small pets welcome
Creature Comforts: CCTV, a/c,
restaurant, pool

Holiday Inn, Riverwalk
(800) HOLIDAY, (210) 224-2500
http://www.holiday-inn.com
217 N. St. Mary's St.
313 rooms - $120-180
Pets: Small pets welcome
Creature Comforts: CCTV, a/c,
restaurant, pool

Howard Johnson
(800) I-Go-Hojo, (210) 558-7152
http://www.hojo.com
13279 Rte. 10 West
53 rooms - $60-89
Pets: Small pets welcome
Creature Comforts: CCTV, a/c,
pool

La Mansion del Rio
(800) 292-7300, (210) 225-2581
http://www.lamansion.com
112 College St.
337 rooms - $130-2,000
Pets: Welcome w/$100 deposit
Creature Comforts: Historic
Spanish/Colonial hotel w/lovely
courtyards, overlkng Riverwalk,
sophis. yet authentic spaces, ell-
shaped rms, earth tones, request
rooms w/French doors and priv.
balconies, CCTV, VCR, a/c, award
winning restaurant, pool

La Quinta Inn, Airport East
(800) Nu-Rooms, (210) 828-0781
http://www.laquinta.com
333 NE Loop 410
197 rooms - $60-85
Pets: Welcome
Creature Comforts: CCTV, a/c,
restaurant, cont. brkfst, pool

La Quinta Inn, Airport West
(800) Nu-Rooms, (210) 342-4291
http://www.laquinta.com
219 NE Loop 410
100 rooms - $60-85
Pets: Small pets welcome
Creature Comforts: CCTV, a/c,
cont. brkfst, pool

La Quinta Inn, Ingram Park
(800) Nu-Rooms, (210) 680-8883
http://www.laquinta.com
7134 NW Loop 410
195 rooms - $60-85
Pets: Small pets welcome
Creature Comforts: CCTV, a/c,
refrig, micro, cont. brkfst, pool

La Quinta Inn, Lackland
(800) Nu-Rooms, (210) 674-3200
http://www.laquinta.com
6511 Military Dr.
176 rooms - $55-80
Pets: Small pets welcome
Creature Comforts: CCTV, a/c,
refrig, micro, cont. brkfst, pool

La Quinta Inn Market Square
(800) Nu-Rooms, (210) 271-0001
http://www.laquinta.com
900 Dolorosa Rd.
124 rooms - $80-100
Pets: Small pets welcome
Creature Comforts: CCTV, a/c,
pool

La Quinta Inn, South
(800) Nu-Rooms, (210) 922-2111
http://www.laquinta.com
7202 S. Pan American Expwy.
122 rooms - $60-85
Pets: Small pets welcome
Creature Comforts: CCTV, a/c,
refrig, cont. brkfst, pool

La Quinta Inn, Vance Jackson
(800) Nu-Rooms, (210) 734-7931
http://www.laquinta.com
5922 NW Expressway
111 rooms - $55-84
Pets: Small pets welcome
Creature Comforts: CCTV, a/c,
cont. brkfst, pool

La Quinta Inn Windsor Park
(800) Nu-Rooms, (210) 553-6619
http://www.laquinta.com
6410 Rte. 35N
130 rooms - $55-90
Pets: Small pets welcome
Creature Comforts: Beachfront,
CCTV, a/c, cont. brkfst, pool

La Quinta Inn Wurzbach
(800) Nu-Rooms, (210) 593-0338
http://www.laquinta.com
9542 Rte. 10W
106 rooms - $60-85
Pets: Welcome
Creature Comforts: CCTV, a/c,
refrig, micro, cont. brkfst, pool

Marriott Rivercenter
(800) 228-9290, (210) 223-1000
http://www.marriott.com
101 Bowie St.
1000 rooms - $220-875
Pets: Welcome w/signed waiver
Creature Comforts: Massive,
striking city cntr hotel, atrium
lobby, attractive rms w/trad.
reproductions, Concierge level,
CCTV, a/c, minibars, restaurant,
pool, hlth clb, sauna, whirlpool

Marriott Riverwalk
(800) 228-9290, (210) 224-4555
http://www.marriott.com
711 E. Riverwalk
500 rooms - $160-250
Pets: Welcome
Creature Comforts: CCTV, a/c,
restaurant, pool, hlth clb access,
sauna, whirlpool

Monarch House B&B
(800) 851-3666, (210) 733-3939
http://www.monarchhouse.com
128 W. Mistletoe
5 rooms - $75-125
Pets: Welcome in Carriage House
Creature Comforts: Arts and
Crafts home, carriage house w/
sophisticated cowboy ambiance,
coral-colored walls, pine
furnishings, iron beds, CCTV,
VCR, a/c, gourmet brkfst

Motel 6, East
(800) 4-MOTEL6, (210) 333-1850
http://www.motel6.com
138 N.W. White Road
101 rooms - $45-70
Pets: Under 30 lbs. welcome
Creature Comforts: CCTV, a/c,
pool

Motel 6, Fiesta
(800) 4-MOTEL6, (210) 697-0731
http://www.motel6.com
16500 Rte. 10 W
123 rooms - $50-65
Pets: Under 30 lbs. welcome
Creature Comforts: CCTV, a/c,
pool

Motel 6, Ft. Sam Houston
(800) 4-MOTEL6, (210) 661-8791
http://www.motel6.com
5522 N. Pan Am Expressway
156 rooms - $35-60
Pets: Under 30 lbs. welcome
Creature Comforts: CCTV, a/c,
pool

Motel 6, Northeast
(800) 4-MOTEL6, (210) 653-8088
http://www.motel6.com
4621 E. Rittiman Road
112 rooms - $35-60
Pets: Under 30 lbs. welcome
Creature Comforts: CCTV, a/c,
pool

Motel 6, North
(800) 4-MOTEL6, (210) 650-4419
http://www.motel6.com
9503 Rte. 35N
113 rooms - $45-70
Pets: Under 30 lbs. welcome
Creature Comforts: CCTV, a/c,
pool

Motel 6, Northwest
(800) 4-MOTEL6, (210) 593-0013
http://www.motel6.com
9400 Wurzbach Road
117 rooms - $50-75
Pets: Under 30 lbs. welcome
Creature Comforts: CCTV, a/c,
pool

Motel 6, Riverwalk
(800) 4-MOTEL6, (210) 225-1111
http://www.motel6.com
211 N. Pecos St.
118 rooms - $55-80
Pets: Under 30 lbs. welcome
Creature Comforts: CCTV, a/c,
pool

Motel 6, West
(800) 4-MOTEL6, (210) 673-9020
http://www.motel6.com
2185 SW Loop 410
122 rooms - $40-80
Pets: Under 30 lbs. welcome
Creature Comforts: CCTV, a/c,
pool

Oak Motor Lodge
(800) 395-9568, (210) 826-6368
150 Humphreys Ave.
22 rooms - $35-70
Pets: Small pets w/$5 fee
Creature Comforts: CCTV, a/c,
kit, pool

OCasey's Bed and Breakfast
(800) 738-1378
http://www.ocaseybnb.com
225 West Craig Place
7 rooms - $65-110
Pets: Pets in good health welcome
in Clare Cottage and Blarney
Lodge
Creature Comforts: 1904
gracious home and carriage house
w/large suites, hardwood flrs,
orig. woodwork, fireplaces,
porches, antiques, quilts,
charming decor, CCTV, kit, full
brkfst

Painted Lady Inn on Broadway
(210) 220-1092
http://www.bestinns.net/usa/tx/
paintedlady.html
620 Broadway St.
8 rooms - $79-189
Pets: Welcome w/$10 fee
Creature Comforts: 1920's
Southern Colonial, strong
southwest colors, antiques,
luxurious amenities, fireplaces,
CCTV, VCR, a/c, refrig, micro,
Jacuzzi, cont. brkfst in rm.

Pear Tree Inn
(800) 282-8733, (210) 366-9300
1243 NE Loop 410
125 rooms - $55-80
Pets: Welcome
Creature Comforts: CCTV, a/c,
cont. brkfst, pool

Plaza San Antonio Hotel
(800) 421-1172, (210) 229-1000
http://www.marriott.com/marriott/
SATPL/index.htm
555 S. Alamo
252 rooms - $225-750
Pets: Small pets welcome
Creature Comforts: Some
historic bldngs on 6 acres w/
gardens, coutryards, fountains,
intimate public areas, rqst interior
courtyrd rms, trad. reproductions,
CCTV, a/c, fine amenities,
restaurant, pool, hlth clb access,
sauna, whirlpool, tennis, bicycles

Quality Inn Suites
(800) 228-5151, (210) 224-3030
http://www.qualityinn.com
3817 Rte. 35 N
124 rooms - $40-100
Pets: Welcome w/$25 deposit fee
Creature Comforts: CCTV, a/c,
restaurant, pool

Ramada Limited Windsor Park
(800) 2-Ramada, (210) 646-6336
http://www.ramada.com
6370 Rte. 35N
89 rooms - $50-75
Pets: Small pets w/$10 fee
Creature Comforts: CCTV, a/c,
cont. brkfst, pool, whirlpool

Relay Station Motel
(800) 735-2981, (210) 662-6691
5530 I-10E at Ackerman Road
142 rooms - $45-70
Pets: Welcome w/$5 fee
Creature Comforts: CCTV, a/c,
restaurant, pool

Residence Inn
(800) 331-3131, (210) 231-6000
http://www.residenceinn.com
628 S. Santa Rosa Rd.
66 rooms - $120-155
Pets: Small pets w/$5 fee, $25 dep
Creature Comforts: CCTV, a/c,
kit, pool

Rodeway Inn
(800) 228-2000, (210) 223-2951
http://www.rodeway.com
900 N. Main St.
128 rooms - $60-125
Pets: Small pets w/$50 deposit
Creature Comforts: CCTV, a/c,
restaurant, cont. brkfst, pool

Rodeway Inn Crossroads
(800) 228-2000, (210) 734-7111
http://www.rodeway.com
6804 Northwest Expressway
100 rooms - $40-70
Pets: Small pets welcome
Creature Comforts: CCTV, a/c,
pool

Rodeway Inn, Fiesta Park
(800) 228-2000, (210) 698-3991
http://www.rodeway.com
19793 Rte. 10 W
77 rooms - $55-120
Pets: Small pets w/$50 deposit
Creature Comforts: CCTV, a/c,
refrig, micro, restaurant, cont.
brkfst, pool

Seven Oaks Resort
(800) 346-5866, (210) 824-5371
1400 Austin Rte.
189 rooms - $50-90
Pets: Welcome w/$5 fee
Creature Comforts: CCTV, a/c,
refrig, micro, cont. brkfst, pool,
hlth clb access

Super 8 Motel
(800) 800-8000, (210) 637-1033
http://www.super8.com
11027 Rte. 35 N
62 rooms - $40-70
Pets: Welcome
Creature Comforts: CCTV, a/c,
cont. brkfst, pool

Super 8 Motel Downtown North
(800) 800-8000, (210) 227-8888
http://www.super8.com
3617 N. Pan Am Expressway
92 rooms - $50-75
Pets: Small pets welcome
Creature Comforts: CCTV, a/c,
pool

Super 8 Fiesta
(800) 800-8000, (210) 696-6916
http://www.super8.com
5319 Bella Rd.
71 rooms - $45-65
Pets: Welcome w/$5 fee
Creature Comforts: CCTV, a/c,
cont. brkfst, pool

Terrell Castle Country Inn
(800) 356-1605, (210) 271-9145
950 E. Grayson Rd.
9 rooms - $70-200
Pets: Welcome w/approval
Creature Comforts: 1894 castle,
impressive orig. features-parquet
flrs, ornate fireplaces, hexagonal
rms, themed decors, CCTV, a/c,
fireplace, gourmet brkfst

Thrifty Inn Northwest
(210) 696-0810
9806 Rte. 10 West
93 rooms - $45-75
Pets: Welcome
Creature Comforts: CCTV, a/c,
pool

SAN MARCOS
Best Western San Marcos
(800) 528-1234, (512) 754-7557
http://www.bestwestern.com
917 Rte. 35N
49 rooms - $60-97
Pets: Small pets w/$20 deposit
Creature Comforts: CCTV, a/c,
refrig, micro, cont. brkfst, pool,
whirlpool

Comfort Inn
(800) 228-5150, (512) 396-5665
http://www.comfortinn.com
1611 Rte. 35 North
54 rooms - $55-99
Pets: Welcome w/$25 fee
Creature Comforts: CCTV, a/c,
refrig, micro, Jacuzzi, cont. brkfst,
pool, whirlpool

Crystal River Inn
(888) 396-3739, (512) 396-3739
http://www.crystalriverinn.com/
326 W. Hopkins St.
13 rooms - $75-150
Pets: Welcome in cottages by
advance arrangement
Creature Comforts: Highly
recommended, early 1900's
Victorian mansion and historic
outbuildings, lovely gardens,
atrium dining room, cottages w/
intriguing handcarved
Southwestern furniture, English
antiques, fireplace or woodstove,
CCTV, a/c, full brkfst, dinner,
luxurious

Days Inn
(800) DAYS INN, (512) 353-5050
http://www.daysinn.com
1005 IH 35N
63 rooms - $55-80
Pets: Small pets welcome
Creature Comforts: CCTV, a/c,
kit, cont. brkfst, pool

Howard Johnson
(800) I-Go-Hojo, (512) 353-8011
http://www.hojo.com
1635 Aquarena Springs Dr.
100 rooms - $60-90
Pets: $10 fee, $50 dep
Creature Comforts: CCTV, a/c,
pool

La Quinta Inn
(800) Nu-Rooms, (512) 392-8800
http://www.laquinta.com
1619 Rte. 35 N
117 rooms - $75-95
Pets: Small pets welcome
Creature Comforts: CCTV, a/c,
refrig, micro, cont. brkfst, pool

Lonesome Dove B&B
(800) 690-DOVE, (512) 392-2921
http://www.ccsi.com/yeeha/kim/
index.html
8 rooms - $85-105
Pets: Flea-free, housebroken,
well-behaved pets w/$10 fee
Creature Comforts: Charming
Old West cottages, w/colorful
trim, rough hewn walls, wood flrs,
festive decor and amenities,
western collectibles, claw foot
tubs, TV, kit, refrig

Motel 6
(800) 4-MOTEL6, (512) 396-8705
http://www.motel6.com
1321 Rte. 35 West
126 rooms - $35-60
Pets: Under 30 lbs. welcome
Creature Comforts: CCTV, a/c,
pool

Rodeway Inn
(800) 228-2000, (512) 353-1303
http://www.rodeway.com
801 Rte. 35 North
44 rooms - $70-125
Pets: Welcome w/$25 fee
Creature Comforts: CCTV, a/c,
pool

San Marcos Ramada
(800) 2-Ramada, (512) 395-8000
http://www.ramada.com
1701 Rte. 35 North
38 rooms - $55-85
Pets: Welcome w/$5 fee
Creature Comforts: CCTV, a/c,
micro, Jacuzzi, cont. brkfst, pool

SANDERSON
Desert Air Motel
(915) 345-2572
Rtes. 90 & 285
16 rooms - $35-49
Pets: Welcome
Creature Comforts: CCTV, a/c,
refrig

SCHULENBURG
Oakridge Motor Inn
(409) 743-4192
P.O. Box 43
71 rooms - $40-67
Pets: Welcome
Creature Comforts: CCTV, a/c,
restaurant, pool

SEALY
Rodeway Inn
(800) 228-2000, (409) 885-7407
http://www.rodeway.com
2021 Meyers St.
51 rooms - $35-49
Pets: Welcome
Creature Comforts: CCTV, a/c,
pool

SEGUIN
Best Western of Seguin
(800) 528-1234, (830) 379-9631
http://www.bestwestern.com
1603 Rte. 10 (Junct. Rte. 46)
83 rooms - $50-86
Pets: Small pets welcome
Creature Comforts: CCTV, a/c,
pool

SEMINOLE
Raymond Motor Inn
(915) 758-3653
301 West Ave.
37 rooms - $35-49
Pets: Small pets welcome
Creature Comforts: CCTV, a/c,
kit

Seminole Inn
(800) 658-9985, (915) 758-9881
2200 Hobbs Highway
40 rooms - $40-69
Pets: Welcome w/$5 fee
Creature Comforts: CCTV, a/c,
refrig, micro, pool

SHAMROCK
Best Western Irish Inn
(800) 528-1234, (806) 256-2106
http://www.bestwestern.com
301 Rte. 40 East
157 rooms - $60-95
Pets: Welcome
Creature Comforts: CCTV, a/c,
refrig, restaurant, pool, whirlpool,
golf

Econo Lodge
(800) 55-ECONO, (806) 256-2111
http://www.econolodge.com
1006 E. 12th St.
78 rooms - $35-85
Pets: Welcome
Creature Comforts: CCTV, a/c,
kit, cont. brkfst, pool, golf

The Western Motel
(806) 256-3244
104 E. 12th St.
24 rooms - $35-64
Pets: Small pets welcome
Creature Comforts: CCTV, a/c,
restaurant, pool, golf

SHERMAN
Best Western Grayson House
(800) 528-1234, (903) 892-2161
http://www.bestwestern.com
2105 Texoma Parkway
147 rooms - $70-95
Pets: Small pets welcome
Creature Comforts: CCTV, a/c,
restaurant, pool

Holiday Inn
(800) HOLIDAY, (903) 868-0555
http://www.holiday-inn.com
3605 Rte. 75S
142 rooms - $65-90
Pets: Welcome w/$50 deposit
Creature Comforts: CCTV, a/c,
restaurant, pool, hlth clb access,
whirlpool

La Quinta Inn
(800) Nu-Rooms, (903) 870-1122
http://www.laquinta.com
2912 Rte. 75 North
115 rooms - $65-95
Pets: Welcome
Creature Comforts: CCTV, a/c,
refrig, micro, cont. brkfst, pool,
hlth access, whirlpool

SMITHVILLE
The Katy House B&B
(800) The-Katy, (512) 237-4262
http://www.katyhouse.com
201 Ramona St.
4 rooms - $65-99
Pets: Welcome w/approval
Creature Comforts: Italianate-
style home w/Georgian columns,
comfortably furnished, extensive
collection of railroad memorabilia,
rqst Carriage House w/western
motif, quilts, CCTV, a/c, kit,
nearby lake swimming

SNYDER
Great Western Inn
(915) 573-1166
800 E. Coliseum Dr.
56 rooms - $30-58
Pets: Welcome
Creature Comforts: CCTV, a/c,
restaurant, pool

Purple Sage Motel
(800) 545-5792, (915) 573-5491
1501 E. Coliseum Dr.
45 rooms - $35-65
Pets: Welcome
Creature Comforts: CCTV, a/c,
health clb access

Wagon Wheel Guest Ranch
(915) 573-2348
http://www.wagonwheel.com/
Box 880
16 rooms - $40 pp/pd
Pets: Welcome
Creature Comforts: Historic
dude ranch, attractive
accommodations in bunk house/
lodge, stone fireplace, some
antiques, CCTV, horseback riding,
swimming

Willow Park Inn
(800) 854-6818, (915) 573-1961
1137 E. Rte. 180
43 rooms - $45-95
Pets: Welcome
Creature Comforts: CCTV, a/c,
restaurant, pool, hlth clb access,
whirlpool

SONORA
Days Inn
(800) DAYS INN, (915) 387-3516
http://www.daysinn.com
Rte. 10 (Golf Course Road)
99 rooms - $45-65
Pets: Welcome w/$2 fee
Creature Comforts: CCTV, a/c,
restaurant, pool

Twin Oaks Motel
(915) 387-2551
907 N. Crockett Ave.
53 rooms - $35-65
Pets: Small pets welcome
Creature Comforts: CCTV, a/c

SOUTH PADRE ISLAND
Best Western Fiesta Isles
(800) 528-1234, (956) 761-4913
http://www.bestwestern.com
5701 Padre Blvd.
58 rooms - $50-129
Pets: Welcome w/$25 deposit
Creature Comforts: CCTV, a/c,
pool

Castaways, Continental,
La International-Apartments
(800) 221-5218, (956) 761-1903
3700 Gulf Blvd.
75 apts. - $100-145
Pets: Welcome in some apts.
Creature Comforts: Fully
furnished apts w/living rm, 1-2
bedrooms, CCTV, a/c, kit, pool

Days Inn
(800) DAYS INN, (956) 761-7831
http://www.daysinn.com
3913 Padre Blvd.
57 rooms - $60-154
Pets: Welcome w/$20 deposit
Creature Comforts: CCTV, a/c,
kit, pool

Motel 6
(800) 4-MOTEL6, (956) 761-7911
http://www.motel6.com
4013 Padre Blvd.
52 rooms - $55-75
Pets: Under 30 lbs. welcome
Creature Comforts: CCTV, a/c,
pool

The Tiki Apartment Hotel
(956) 761-2694
6608 Padre Blvd.
131 rooms - $80-135
Pets: Small pets w/$15 fee
Creature Comforts: CCTV, a/c,
kit, restaurant, pool

SPRING
Motel 6
(800) 4-MOTEL6, (281) 350-6400
http://www.motel6.com
19606 Cypresswood Ct.
108 rooms - $40-64
Pets: Under 30 lbs. welcome
Creature Comforts: CCTV, a/c,
pool

STAFFORD
La Quinta Inn
(800) Nu-Rooms, (713) 240-2300
http://www.laquinta.com
12727 Southwest Fwy.
129 rooms - $70-90
Pets: Small pets welcome
Creature Comforts: CCTV, a/c,
cont. brkfst, pool

STEPHENVILLE
Best Western Cross Timbers
(800) 528-1234, (254) 968-2114
http://www.bestwestern.com
1625 South Loop
50 rooms - $50-85
Pets: Welcome w/mngr's aprvl
Creature Comforts: CCTV, a/c,
restaurant, pool

Budget Host Texan Motor Inn
(800) Bud-Host, (254) 968-5003
http://www.budgethost.com
3030 W. Washington St.
30 rooms - $40-70
Pets: Small pets w/$3 fee
Creature Comforts: CCTV, a/c

Days Inn
(800) DAYS INN, (254) 968-3392
http://www.daysinn.com
701 S. Loop
60 rooms - $45-70
Pets: Welcome w/$25 fee
Creature Comforts: CCTV, a/c,
refrig, micro, restaurant, pool

Holiday Inn
(800) HOLIDAY, (254) 968-5256
http://www.holiday-inn.com
2865 W. Washington St.
100 rooms - $50-150
Pets: Welcome
Creature Comforts: CCTV, a/c,
restaurant, pool, whirlpool, golf

SULPHUR SPRINGS
Holiday Inn
(800) HOLIDAY, (903) 885-0562
http://www.holiday-inn.com
1495 E. Industrial Dr.
98 rooms - $50-80
Pets: Small pets welcome
Creature Comforts: CCTV, a/c,
restaurant, pool, golf, tennis, and
racquetball

SURFSIDE BEACH
Anchor Motel
(409) 239-3543
1302 Bluewater Highway
32 rooms - $40-75
Pets: Welcome
Creature Comforts: CCTV, a/c,
restaurant

SWEETWATER

Best Western Sunday House Inn
(800) 528-1234, (915) 235-4853
http://www.bestwestern.com
701 SW Georgia Ave.
131 rooms - $55-85
Pets: Welcome
Creature Comforts: CCTV, a/c,
restaurant, pool

Holiday Inn
(800) HOLIDAY, (915) 236-6887
http://www.holiday-inn.com
500 NW Georgia Ave.
107 rooms - $50-89
Pets: Welcome
Creature Comforts: CCTV, a/c,
restaurant, pool

Motel 6
(800) 4-MOTEL6, (915) 235-4387
http://www.motel6.com
510 NW Georgia Ave.
79 rooms - $30-55
Pets: Under 30 lbs. welcome
Creature Comforts: CCTV, a/c,
pool

Mulberry Mansion
(800) 235-3811, (915) 235-3811
1400 Sam Houston St.
6 rooms - $60-195
Pets: Welcome
Creature Comforts: 1913
Trammel Mansion, restored in
1992, ornate decor w/French
antiques, Oriental rugs, window
swags, CCTV, a/c, Roman tubs,
four-course brkfst, private dinners
for two, chauffered Model A

Ranch House Motel
(800) 622-5361, (915) 236-6341
301 SW Georgia Ave.
49 rooms - $35-60
Pets: Welcome
Creature Comforts: CCTV, a/c,
restaurant, pool

TEMPLE
Best Western Inn
(800) 528-1234, (254) 778-5511
http://www.bestwestern.com
2625 S. 31st St.
129 rooms - $65-89
Pets: Small pets welcome
Creature Comforts: CCTV, a/c,
refrig, restaurant, pool

Econo Lodge
(800) 55-ECONO, (254) 771-1688
http://www.econolodge.com
1001 N. General Bruce Dr.
60 rooms - $40-63
Pets: Small pets welcome
Creature Comforts: CCTV, a/c,
cont. brkfst, pool

Howard Johnson
(800) I-Go-Hojo, (254) 778-5521
http://www.hojo.com
1912 S. 31st St.
48 rooms - $30-65
Pets: Welcome
Creature Comforts: CCTV, a/c,
refrig, cont. brkfst, pool

La Quinta Inn
(800) Nu-Rooms, (254) 771-2980
http://www.laquinta.com
1604 W. Barton
106 rooms - $60-80
Pets: Small pets welcome
Creature Comforts: CCTV, a/c,
refrig, micro, pool

Motel 6
(800) 4-MOTEL6, (254) 778-0272
http://www.motel6.com
1100 North General Bruce Dr.
95 rooms - $35-60
Pets: Under 30 lbs. welcome
Creature Comforts: CCTV, a/c,
pool

Super 8 Motel
(800) 800-8000, (254) 778-0962
http://www.super8.com
5505 S. General Bruce Dr.
96 rooms - $45-60
Pets: Welcome
Creature Comforts: CCTV, a/c,
refrig, micro, pool

TERLINGUA
Chisos Mining Company Motel
(915) 371-2254
Rte. 170
28 rooms - $50-65
Pets: Welcome
Creature Comforts: CCTV, a/c,
kit, refrig

TERRELL
Best Western La Piedra Inn
(800) 528-1234, (972) 563-2676
http://www.bestwestern.com
309 Rte. 20 East
60 rooms - $45-65
Pets: Small pets w/$4 fee
Creature Comforts: CCTV, a/c,
refrig, pool

Days Inn
(800) DAYS INN, (972) 551-1170
http://www.daysinn.com
1618 Rte. 34S
40 rooms - $45-70
Pets: Welcome w/$5 fee
Creature Comforts: CCTV, a/c,
refrig, micro, Jacuzzi, cont. brkfst,
pool, whirlpool

TEXARKANA
Best Western Kings Row Inn
(800) 528-1234, (903) 774-3851
http://www.bestwestern.com
4200 N. Stateline Ave.
114 rooms - $50-75
Pets: Small pets welcome
Creature Comforts: CCTV, a/c,
refrig, restaurant, pool

Best Western Northgate
(800) 528-1234, (903) 793-6565
http://www.bestwestern.com
400 W. 53rd St.
64 rooms - $55-76
Pets: Small pets w/$10 fee
Creature Comforts: CCTV, a/c,
refrig, restaurant, cont. brkfst,
pool, sauna, putting green

Baymont Inn
(800) 4-Budget, (903) 773-1000
http://www.baymontinns.com
5102 N. Stateline Ave.
106 rooms - $45-78
Pets: Welcome
Creature Comforts: CCTV, a/c,
pool

Comfort Inn
(800) 228-5150, (903) 792-6688
http://www.comfortinn.com
5105 N. Stateline Ave.
79 rooms - $50-75
Pets: Welcome
Creature Comforts: CCTV, a/c,
Jacuzzi, cont. brkfst, pool

La Quinta Inn
(800) Nu-Rooms, (903) 794-1900
http://www.laquinta.com
5201 Stateline Ave.
130 rooms - $50-80
Pets: Small pets welcome
Creature Comforts: CCTV,
refrig, micro, cont. brkfst, pool

Motel 6
(800) 4-MOTEL6, (903) 793-1413
http://www.motel6.com
1924 Hampton Road
100 rooms - $30-60
Pets: Under 30 lbs. welcome
Creature Comforts: CCTV, a/c,
restaurant, pool

Shoney's Inn
(800) 222-2222, (870) 772-0070
http://www.shoneysinn.com
5210 N. Stateline Road
72 rooms - $50-80
Pets: Small pets welcome
Creature Comforts: CCTV, a/c,
refrig, micro, Jacuzzi, cont. brkfst,
pool, hlth clb access, golf

TEXAS CITY
La Quinta Inn
(800) Nu-Rooms, (409) 948-3101
http://www.laquinta.com
1121 Rte. 146N
121 rooms - $60-80
Pets: Small pets welcome
Creature Comforts: CCTV, a/c,
pool

THE WOODLANDS
Drury Inn Houston Woodlands
(800) 325-8300, (281) 362-7222
http://www.druryinn.com
28099 Rte. 45 N
152 rooms - $75-99
Pets: Welcome
Creature Comforts: CCTV, a/c,
pool

La Quinta Inn
(800) Nu-Rooms, (281) 367-7722
http://www.laquinta.com
28671 Rte. 45N
116 rooms - $75-95
Pets: Small pets welcome
Creature Comforts: CCTV, a/c,
cont. brkfst, pool

Red Roof Inn
(800) THE ROOF, (281) 367-5040
http://www.redroof.inn
24903 Rte. 45N
85 rooms - $50-74
Pets: Small pets welcome
Creature Comforts: CCTV, a/c,
pool

THREE RIVERS
Nolan Ryan's Bass Inn
(800) 803-3340, (512) 786-3521
78071 HCR 71, Box 390
31 rooms - $50-80
Pets: Small pets welcome
Creature Comforts: CCTV, a/c,
kit, pool

TULIA
Best Western Inn
(800) 528-1234, (806) 995-3248
http://www.bestwestern.com
Rte 1, Box 60
37 rooms - $55-85
Pets: Small pets w/$5 fee
Creature Comforts: CCTV, a/c,
restaurant, cont. brkfst, pool

TYLER
Best Western Inn Suites
(800) 528-1234, (903) 595-2681
http://www.bestwestern.com
2828 N. NW Loop
90 rooms - $50-75
Pets: Welcome w/$5 fee
Creature Comforts: CCTV, a/c,
refrig, micro, Jacuzzi, cont. brkfst,
pool, hlth clb access

Days Inn
(800) DAYS INN, (903) 595-2451
http://www.daysinn.com
3300 Mineola Hwy.
138 rooms - $55-75
Pets: Welcome
Creature Comforts: CCTV, a/c,
refrig, micro, Jacuzzi, cont. brkfst,
pool, hlth clb access, whirlpool

Holiday Inn Southeast Crossing
(800) HOLIDAY, (903) 593-3600
http://www.holiday-inn.com
3300 Troup Highway
160 rooms - $70-125
Pets: Welcome
Creature Comforts: CCTV, a/c,
restaurant, pool

La Quinta Inn
(800) Nu-Rooms, (903) 561-2223
http://www.laquinta.com
1601 W. SW Loop
130 rooms - $60-90
Pets: Small pets welcome
Creature Comforts: CCTV, a/c,
cont. brkfst, pool

Motel 6
(800) 4-MOTEL6, (903) 596-6691
http://www.motel6.com
3238 Brady Gentry Parkway
103 rooms - $30-55
Pets: Under 30 lbs. welcome
Creature Comforts: CCTV, a/c,
restaurant, pool

Residence Inn by Marriott
(800) 331-3131, (903) 595-5188
http://www.residenceinn.com
3303 Troup Highway
128 rooms - $80-105
Pets: Welcome w/$50 fee
Creature Comforts: CCTV, a/c,
kit, pool

Rodeway Inn
(800) 228-2000, (903) 531-9513
http://www.rodeway.com
2729 W NW Loop
50 rooms - $50-65
Pets: Small pets w/$25 deposit
Creature Comforts: CCTV, a/c,
pool

Sheraton Tyler Hotel
(800) 325-3535, (903) 561-5800
http://www.sheraton.com
5701 S. Broadway
185 rooms - $65-90
Pets: Small pets w/$25 fee
Creature Comforts: CCTV, a/c,
restaurant, pool

Super 8 Motel
(800) 800-8000, (903) 593-8361
http://www.super8.com
2616 N. NW Loop 323
125 rooms - $45-79
Pets: Welcome
Creature Comforts: CCTV, a/c,
refrig, micro, pool

UNCERTAIN

Mossy Brake Lodge B&B
(800) 607-6002, (903) 780-3440
http://www.texs.com/caddo/
mossy.htm
Rte 2, Box 63 AB
1 room - $65-79
Pets: Welcome, well trained
Creature Comforts: Lakeside,
SATV, VCR, a/c, cont. brkfst,
private bath

UNIVERSAL CITY

Clarion Suites Hotel
(800) 221-2222, (210) 655-9491
http://www.clarioninn.com
13101 E. Loop, 1604N
103 rooms - $85-140
Pets: Welcome w/$25 fee
Creature Comforts: CCTV, a/c,
kit, cont. brkfst, pool, hlth clb
access, whirlpool

UVALDE

Best Western Continental Inn
(800) 528-1234, (830) 278-5671
http://www.bestwestern.com
701 E. Main St.
87 rooms - $35-65
Pets: Small pets welcome
Creature Comforts: CCTV, a/c,
kit, pool

VAN HORN

Best Western American Inn
(800) 528-1234, (915) 283-2030
http://www.bestwestern.com
1309 W. Broadway
33 rooms - $45-70
Pets: Welcome
Creature Comforts: CCTV,
VCR, a/c, refrig, cont. brkfst, pool

Best Western Inn of Van Horn
(800) 528-1234, (915) 283-2410
http://www.bestwestern.com
1705 W. Broadway St.
60 rooms - $45-75
Pets: Welcome
Creature Comforts: CCTV, a/c,
refrig, restaurant, pool

Economy Inn
(800) 826-0778, (915) 283-2754
P.O. Box 622, Rte. 80W
16 rooms - $25-65
Pets: Welcome
Creature Comforts: CCTV, a/c

Freeway Inn
(915) 283-2939
505 Van Horn Dr.
15 rooms - $25-40
Pets: Small pets welcome
Creature Comforts: CCTV, a/c

Holiday Inn Express
(800) HOLIDAY, (915) 283-7444
http://www.holiday-inn.com
1905 Frontage Road
45 rooms - $50-90
Pets: Small pets welcome
Creature Comforts: CCTV, a/c,
refrig, cont. brkfst, pool

Howard Johnson
(800) I-Go-Hojo, (915) 283-2804
http://www.hojo.com
200 Golf Course Dr.
98 rooms - $35-50
Pets: Welcome
Creature Comforts: CCTV,
VCR, a/c, cont. brkfst, pool

Super 8 Motel
(800) 800-8000, (915) 283-2282
http://www.super8.com
1807 E. Service Road
41 rooms - $40-60
Pets: Welcome w/$10 deposit
Creature Comforts: CCTV, a/c

VEGA

Best Western Country Inn
(800) 528-1234, (806) 267-2131
http://www.bestwestern.com
1800 W. Vega Blvd.
41 rooms - $60-90
Pets: Small pets welcome
Creature Comforts: CCTV, a/c,
restaurant, pool

VERNON

Best Western Village Inn
(800) 528-1234, (940) 552-5417
http://www.bestwestern.com
1615 Rte. 76384
47 rooms - $50-65
Pets: Small pets welcome
Creature Comforts: CCTV, a/c,
restaurant, pool

Days Inn
(800) DAYS INN, (940) 552-9982
http://www.daysinn.com
3110 Frontage Road
50 rooms - $45-60
Pets: Welcome
Creature Comforts: CCTV, a/c,
cont. brkfst, pool

Econo Lodge
(800) 55-ECONO, (940) 553-3384
http://www.econolodge.com
4100 Rte. 287 NW
50 rooms - $40-60
Pets: Welcome w/$10 deposit
Creature Comforts: CCTV, a/c,
refrig, pool

Greentree Inn
(800) 600-5421, (940) 552-5421
3029 Morton St.
30 rooms - $40-65
Pets: Small pets welcome
Creature Comforts: CCTV, a/c,
pool

Super 8 Motel
(800) 800-8000, (940) 552-2531
http://www.super8.com
1829 Expressway Highway 287
55 rooms - $40-55
Pets: $5 fee, $20 deposit
Creature Comforts: CCTV, a/c

Western Motel
(940) 552-2531
715 Wilbarger St.
28 rooms - $30-45
Pets: Welcome
Creature Comforts: CCTV, a/c,
pool, playground

VICTORIA

Comfort Inn
(800) 228-5150, (512) 574-9393
http://www.comfortinn.com
1906 Houston Rte.
43 rooms - $60-105
Pets: Small pets welcome
Creature Comforts: CCTV, a/c,
pool

Fairfield Inn by Marriott
(800) 228-2800, (512) 582-0660
http://www.fairfieldinn
7502 Navarro St.
64 rooms - $65-99
Pets: Small pets welcome
Creature Comforts: CCTV, a/c,
pool

Hampton Inn
(800) Hampton, (512) 578-2030
http://www.hamptoninn.com
3112 E. Houston Rte.
102 rooms - $65-90
Pets: Small pets welcome
Creature Comforts: CCTV, a/c,
pool

Holiday Inn Holidome
(800) HOLIDAY, (512) 575-0251
http://www.holiday-inn.com
2705 E. Houston Rte.
226 rooms - $60-95
Pets: Small pets welcome
Creature Comforts: CCTV, a/c, restaurant, pool

La Quinta Inn
(800) Nu-Rooms, (512) 572-3585
http://www.laquinta.com
7603 N. Navarro
130 rooms - $65-80
Pets: Small pets welcome
Creature Comforts: CCTV, VCR, a/c, refrig, micro, cont. brkfst, pool

Motel 6
(800) 4-MOTEL6, (512) 573-1273
http://www.motel6.com
3716 Houston Hwy.
80 rooms - $35-60
Pets: Under 30 lbs. welcome
Creature Comforts: CCTV, a/c, pool

Ramada Inn
(800) 2-Ramada, (512) 578-2723
http://www.ramada.com
3901 E. Houston Hwy.
126 rooms - $50-65
Pets: Small pets welcome
Creature Comforts: CCTV, a/c, restaurant, pool

WACO
Best Western Old Main Lodge
(800) 528-1234, (254) 753-0316
http://www.bestwestern.com
35 - 4th St.
84 rooms - $65-80
Pets: Small pets welcome
Creature Comforts: CCTV, a/c, refrig, micro

Best Western Waco Mall
(800) 528-1234, (254) 776-3194
http://www.bestwestern.com
6624 Rte. 84 West
55 rooms - $60-98
Pets: Small pets welcome
Creature Comforts: CCTV, a/c, refrig, micro, cont. brkfst, pool, whirlpool

Days Inn
(800) DAYS INN, (254) 799-8585
http://www.daysinn.com
1504 Rte. 35
60 rooms - $70-89
Pets: Welcome w/$6 fee
Creature Comforts: CCTV, a/c, cont. brkfst, pool

Econo Lodge
(800) 55-ECONO, (254) 756-5371
http://www.econolodge.com
500 Rte. 35
46 rooms - $40-63
Pets: Welcome
Creature Comforts: CCTV, a/c, cont. brkfst

Hilton Inn
(800) HILTONS, (254) 754-4848
http://www.hilton.com
113 S. University Parks Dr.
199 rooms - $70-120
Pets: Welcome w/signed waiver
Creature Comforts: CCTV, a/c, refrig, pool, hlth access, whirlpool, tennis

Holiday Inn , Waco I-35
(800) HOLIDAY, (254) 753-0261
http://www.holiday-inn.com
1001 Martin Luther King Blvd.
171 rooms - $75-97
Pets: Welcome
Creature Comforts: CCTV, a/c, kit, restaurant, pool

La Quinta Inn
(800) Nu-Rooms, (254) 752-9741
http://www.laquinta.com
1110 S. 9th St.
102 rooms - $70-89
Pets: Small pets welcome
Creature Comforts: CCTV, a/c, refrig, micro, cont. brkfst, pool

Motel 6 Premier
(800) 4-MOTEL6, (254) 662-4622
http://www.motel6.com
3120 Jack Kultgen Fwy.
110 rooms - $35-50
Pets: Under 30 lbs. welcome
Creature Comforts: CCTV, a/c, pool

WAXAHACHIE
Comfort Inn
(800) 228-5150, (972) 937-4202
http://www.comfortinn.com
200 N. Rte. 35E
61 rooms - $60-85
Pets: Small pets welcome
Creature Comforts: CCTV, a/c, refrig, pool

Ramada Limited
(800) 2-Ramada, (972) 937-4982
http://www.ramada.com
795 S. Rte. 35E
90 rooms - $45-70
Pets: Welcome w/$25 deposit
Creature Comforts: CCTV, a/c, pool

WEATHERFORD
Best Western Santa Fe Inn
(800) 528-1234, (817) 594-7401
http://www.bestwestern.com
1927 Santa Fe Dr.
45 rooms - $55-70
Pets: Small pets welcome
Creature Comforts: CCTV, a/c, restaurant, pool

Comfort Inn
(800) 228-5150, (817) 599-8683
http://www.comfortinn.com
809 Palo Pinto St.
42 rooms - $55-75
Pets: Small pets welcome
Creature Comforts: CCTV, a/c, refrig, micro, cont. brkfst, pool

Super 8 Motel
(800) 800-8000, (817) 594-8702
http://www.super8.com
111 W. Rte. 20
80 rooms - $40-55
Pets: Welcome w/$5
Creature Comforts: CCTV, a/c, pool

WEBSTER
Homegate Studios and Suites
(888) 456-GATE, (281) 338-7711
720 West Bay Area Blvd.
85 rooms - $89-99
Pets: Under 10 lbs. welcome
Creature Comforts: CCTV, a/c, refrig, micro, restaurant, pool, exercise rm.

Motel 6
(800) 4-MOTEL6, (281) 332-4581
http://www.motel6.com
1001 W. NASA Rd. 1
122 rooms - $40-55
Pets: Under 30 lbs. welcome
Creature Comforts: CCTV, a/c,
restaurant, pool

WEST COLUMBIA
Country Hearth Inn
(409) 345-2399
714 Columbia Dr.
40 rooms - $55-65
Pets: Welcome
Creature Comforts: CCTV, a/c,
pool

WESTLAKE
Marriott Solana Dallas/FW
(800) 228-9290, (817) 430-3848
http://www.marriott.com
5 Village Circle
198 rooms - $80-160
Pets: Welcome
Creature Comforts: CCTV, a/c,
restaurant, pool

WICHITA FALLS
Best Western Towne Crest Inn
(800) 528-1234, (940) 322-1182
http://www.bestwestern.com
1601 - 8th St.
42 rooms - $45-69
Pets: Welcome
Creature Comforts: CCTV, a/c

Comfort Inn
(800) 228-5150, (940) 322-2477
http://www.comfortinn.com
1750 Maureen St.
66 rooms - $60-85
Pets: Welcome w/$50 deposit
Creature Comforts: CCTV, a/c,
pool

Days Inn
(800) DAYS INN, (940) 723-5541
http://www.daysinn.com
1211 Central Expressway
101 rooms - $45-60
Pets: Welcome w/$5 fee
Creature Comforts: CCTV, a/c,
pool
La Quinta Inn
(800) Nu-Rooms, (940) 322-6971
http://www.laquinta.com
1128 Central Fwy. North
139 rooms - $65-80
Pets: Small pets welcome
Creature Comforts: CCTV, a/c,
refrig, micro, cont. brkfst, pool

Motel 6
(800) 4-MOTEL6, (940) 322-8817
http://www.motel6.com
1812 Maureen St.
82 rooms - $30-55
Pets: Under 30 lbs. welcome
Creature Comforts: CCTV, a/c,
restaurant, pool

WIMBERLEY
Homestead Cottages B&B
(800) 918-8788, (512) 847-8788
http://www.homestead-tx.com
Box 1034
12 cottages - $85-99
Pets: Welcome in Cottages 5-8
w/$10 fee
Creature Comforts: Traditional
Hill Country cabins set along tree-
lined creek, CCTV, a/c, kit, stone
fireplace, Jacuzzi, cont. brkfst, hot
springs

Southwind B&B, Cabins
(800) 508-5277
2701 FM 3237
5 rooms - $75-99
Pets: Welcome
Creature Comforts: CCTV, a/c

WINNIE
Best Western Gulf Coast Inn
(800) 528-1234, (409) 296-9292
http://www.bestwestern.com
46310 Rte. 10E
66 rooms - $45-75
Pets: Welcome w/$25 deposit
Creature Comforts: CCTV, a/c,
restaurant, cont. brkfst, pool

ZAPATA
Best Western Inn by the Lake
(800) 528-1234, (956) 765-8403
http://www.bestwestern.com
78076 Star Route 1, Box 252
50 rooms - $45-75
Pets: Small pets welcome
Creature Comforts: CCTV, a/c,
kit, restaurant, cont. brkfst, pool

Utah

BEAVER
Best Western Paice Inn
(800) 528-1234, (435) 438-2438
http://www.bestwestern.com
161 S. Main St.
24 rooms - $50-65
Pets: Small pets in pet rooms
Creature Comforts: CCTV, pool,
sauna, whirlpool

Best Western Paradise
(800) 528-1234, (435) 438-2455
http://www.bestwestern.com
1451 N. 300 West
53 rooms - $45-70
Pets: Small pets welcome
Creature Comforts: CCTV,
restaurant, pool, whirlpool

Country Inn
(8000 754-2484, (435) 438-2484
1450 N. 300 West
40 rooms - $35-45
Pets: Welcome
Creature Comforts: CCTV,
restaurant

Delano Motel
(435) 438-2418
480 N. Main St.
11 rooms - $30-40
Pets: Small pets w/$5 fee
Creature Comforts: CCTV, a/c

Grenada Inn
(435) 438-2292
75 S. Main St.
20 rooms - $30-40
Pets: Welcome
Creature Comforts: CCTV a/c,
kit

Sleepy Lagoon Motel
(435) 438-5681
882 S. Main St.
20 rooms - $30-45
Pets: Small pets welcome-pet rms.
Creature Comforts: CCTV, a/c,
pool

Stag Motel
(435) 438-2411
370 N. Main St.
8 rooms - $30-40
Pets: Welcome
Creature Comforts: CCTV, a/c

BICKNELL
Aquarius Motel
(800) 833-5379, (435) 425-3835
http://www.ediguide.com/UT/801/
a_inn/aquarius.html
240 W. Main St.
27 rooms - $25-50
Pets: Small pets w/$5 fee, $25 dep
Creature Comforts: CCTV,
VCR, a/c, kit, restaurant, pool

Sunglow Motel
(435) 425-3821
63 E. Main St.
17 rooms - $35-49
Pets: Welcome
Creature Comforts: CCTV,
restaurant

BIG WATER
Warm Creek Motel
(800) 748-5065, (435) 675-9199
Ethan Allen Rte. 89
39 rooms - $50-75
Pets: Welcome
Creature Comforts: CCTV,
restaurant

BLANDING
Best Western Gateway
(800) 528-1234, (435) 678-2278
http://www.bestwestern.com
88 East Center St.
60 rooms - $36-70
Pets: Welcome
Creature Comforts: CCTV, a/c,
cont. brkfst, pool

Blanding Sunset Inn
(435) 678-3323
88 West Center St.
17 rooms - $35-50
Pets: Welcome
Creature Comforts: CCTV, a/c,
kit, whirlpool

Cliff Palace Motel
(800) 553-8093, (435) 678-2264
132 S. Main St.
16 rooms - $35-50
Pets: Welcome
Creature Comforts: CCTV, a/c

Four Corners Inn
(800) 574-3150, (435) 678-3186
131 E. Center St.
32 rooms - $47-62
Pets: Small pets w/$5 fee
Creature Comforts: CCTV,
refrig, micro, kit, cont. brkfst

BLUFF
Kokopelli Inn
(800) 541-8854, (435) 672-2322
Rte. 191
26 rooms - $35-50
Pets: Welcome w/$10 fee
Creature Comforts: CCTV, a/c

Recapture Lodge
(435) 672-2281
Rte. 191
34 rooms - $40-48
Pets: Welcome
Creature Comforts: CCTV,
refrig, micro, kit, pool, whirlpool

BOULDER
Boulder Mtn. Lodge
(800) 556-3446, (435) 335-7460
http://www.boulder-utah.com
Rte. 12 & Burr Trail
20 rooms - $60-135
Pets: In first flr. rms w/$10 fee
Creature Comforts: Eclectic yet
stunning timber and stone, tin-
roofed lodge on 11-acre private
lake, remote setting, rms. w/
exposed timber beams, sandstone
fireplace, attractive craftsman
style furnishings, quilts, a/c, refrig,
micro, Hell's Backbone Grill,
hiking, birding

Boulder Mountain Ranch
(435) 335-7480
http://www.boulderutah.com/bmr
Hell's Backbone Rd.
3 cabins - $65-85
Pets: Welcome w/$8 fee,
great open spaces for dogs to run
Creature Comforts: Rustic but
appealing cabins and main log
lodge on 160-acre working ranch,
beautiful rugged country,
woodstove, cont. brkfst, hiking,
horseback riding, pack trips

Circle Cliffs Motel
(800) 730-7422, (435) 335-7422
246 S. Main St.
3 rooms - $35-45
Pets: Welcome
Creature Comforts: CCTV, kit

BRIAN HEAD
Lodge at Brian Head
(800) 386-5634, (435) 677-3222
314 Hunter Ridge Rd.
40 rooms - $50-115
Pets: Welcome w/$50 deposit
Creature Comforts: CCTV, a/c,
restaurant, pool, sauna, whirlpool,
hlth club

BRIGHAM CITY
Bushnell Lodge
(800) 586-2605, (435) 723-8575
115 East 700 South
24 rooms - $35-65
Pets: Welcome
Creature Comforts: CCTV, a/c,
kit

Crystal Inn
(800) 408-0440, (435) 723-0440
580 Westland Dr.
52 rooms - $55-100
Pets: Welcome w/$20 deposit
Creature Comforts: CCTV,
VCR, a/c, refrig, micro, restaurant,
buffet brkfst, pool, hlth club,
sauna, whirlpool

Howard Johnson
(800) I-Go-Hojo, (435) 723-8511
http://www.hojo.com
1167 S. Main St.
44 rooms - $50-60
Pets: Small pets welcome
Creature Comforts: CCTV, a/c,
restaurant, cont. brkfst, pool,
whirlpool

BRYCE CANYON
Best Western Ruby's Inn
(800) 528-1234, (435) 834-5341
http://www.rubysinn.com
Route 63
369 rooms - $45-125
Pets: Small pets w/deposit
Creature Comforts: CCTV, a/c,
Jacuzzi, restaurant, pool,
whirlpool, sauna

Bryce Junction Inn
(800) 437-4361, (435) 676-2221
Rtes. 89 & 12
32 rooms - $35-70
Pets: Small pets welcome
Creature Comforts: CCTV,
whirlpool

CANNONVILLE
Galloping Tortoise B&B
(435) 679-8664
Box 32
2 rooms - $50-75
Pets: Welcome
Creature Comforts: Kitchen

CASTLE DALE
Village Inn Motel
(435) 381-2309
Box 1244
21 rooms - $40-55
Pets: Welcome
Creature Comforts: CCTV, kit

CEDAR CITY
Astro Budget Inn
(435) 586-6557,
4672 Drift Creek Rd. SE
30 rooms - $35-50
Pets: Welcome
Creature Comforts: CCTV, a/c,
restaurant, pool

Comfort Inn
(800) 228-5150, (435) 586-2082
http://www.comfortinn.com
250 N. 1100 West
110 rooms - $50-80
Pets: Small pets welcome
Creature Comforts: CCTV, a/c,
kit, pool, whirlpool

Days Inn
(800) DAYS INN, (435) 867-8877
http://www.daysinn.com
1204 S. Main
55 rooms - $45-75
Pets: Small pets w/$5 fee
Creature Comforts: CCTV, a/c,
cont. brkfst, pool, whirlpool

Holiday Inn
(800) HOLIDAY, (435) 586-8888
http://www.holiday-inn.com
1575 W. 200 North
100 rooms - $60-95
Pets: Welcome w/$25 fee
Creature Comforts: CCTV,
VCR, a/c, Jacuzzi, restaurant,
pool, hlth club, whirlpool , sauna

Motel 6
(800) 4-MOTEL6, (435) 586-9200
1620 W. 200 North
79 rooms - $30-35
Pets: Under 30 lbs. welcome
Creature Comforts: CCTV, a/c

Rodeway Inn
(800) 228-2000, (435) 586-9916
http://www.rodeway.com
281 S. Main St.
48 rooms - $46-70
Pets: Welcome
Creature Comforts: CCTV, a/c,
restaurant, pool, sauna

Super 8 Motel
(800) 800-8000, (435) 586-8880
http://www.super8.com
145 North 1550 W.
55 rooms - $48-55
Pets: Welcome
Creature Comforts: CCTV, a/c,
Jacuzzi, cont. brkfst

Travelodge
(800) 578-7878, (435) 586-7435
http://www.travelodge.com
2555 N. Main St.
54 rooms - $40-85
Pets: Welcome
Creature Comforts: CCTV, a/c,
pool, whirlpool

Valu-Inn
(435) 586-9114
190 S. Main St.
29 rooms - $30-50
Pets: Small pets w/$10 fee
Creature Comforts: CCTV, a/c, kit

CLEARFIELD
Super 8 Motel
(800) 800-8000, (801) 825-8000
http://www.super8.com
572 N. Main St.
58 rooms - $45-50
Pets: Welcome w/permission
Creature Comforts: CCTV, a/c, Jacuzzi

DELTA
Best Western Motor Inn
(800) 528-1234, (435) 864-3882
http://www.bestwestern.com
527 E. Topaz Blvd.
82 rooms - $52-60
Pets: Welcome w/$10 deposit
Creature Comforts: CCTV, a/c, restaurant, pool, whirlpool

Budget Motel
(435) 864-4533
75 S. 350 East
30 rooms - $30-35
Pets: Welcome
Creature Comforts: CCTV, a/c, kit

Diamond D Motor Lodge
(435) 864-2041
234 W. Main St.
20 rooms - $25-30
Pets: Welcome
Creature Comforts: CCTV, a/c, kit

DRAPER
Econo Lodge
(800) 55-ECONO, (801) 571-1122
http://www.econolodge.com
12605 Minuteman Dr.
55 rooms - $50-70
Pets: Welcome
Creature Comforts: CCTV, a/c

DUCK CREEK VILLAGE
Duck Creek Village Inn
(800) 55-ECONO, (435) 682-2565
Route 14
9 rooms - $50-60
Pets: Small pets w/$6
Creature Comforts: CCTV, VCR, kit, restaurant

Falcon's Nest Cabins
(800) 240-4930, (435) 682-2556
60 Movie Ranch Rd.
10 cabins - $50-70
Pets: Welcome
Creature Comforts: CCTV, kit, restaurant

Pinewoods Mtn Resort
(800) 848-2525, (435) 682-2512
116 Color Country Rd.
6 condos - $60-100
Pets: Small pets in certain condos
Creature Comforts: CCTV, kit, restaurant, whirlpool

EPHRAIM
Iron Horse Motel
(435) 283-4223
670 N. Main St.
10 rooms - $40-55
Pets: Welcome
Creature Comforts: CCTV

ESCALANTE
Circle D Motel
(435) 826-4297
475 W. Main St.
29 rooms - $40-55
Pets: Welcome
Creature Comforts: CCTV, a/c, restaurant

Quiet Falls Motel
(435) 826-4250
75 S. 100 West
19 rooms - $45-55
Pets: Welcome
Creature Comforts: CCTV, kit

Rainbow Country B&B
(800) 252-UTAH, (435) 826-4567
585 E. 300 South
4 rooms - $45-65
Pets: Small pets welcome
Creature Comforts: CCTV, a/c, kit, whirlpool

FILLMORE
Best Western Paradise
(800) 528-1234, (435) 743-6895
http://www.bestwestern.com
1025 N. Main St.
80 rooms - $45-70
Pets: Small pets welcome
Creature Comforts: CCTV, a/c, restaurant, pool, whirlpool

Fillmore Motel
(435) 743-5454
61 N. Main St.
20 rooms - $25-40
Pets: Welcome
Creature Comforts: CCTV, a/c, kit

FRY CANYON
Fry Canyon Lodge
(435) 259-5334
90 W. Rte. 95
5 rooms - $40-100
Pets: Small pets welcome in one room w/$25 dep
Creature Comforts: Basic motel, no a/c, telephones or tv

GARDEN CITY
Eagle Feather Inn
(435) 946-2846
Box 262
2 rooms - $50-65
Pets: Welcome
Creature Comforts: CCTV, VCR, kit, whirlpool

Harbor Village Inn
(800) 324-6840, (435) 946-3448
900 N. Bear Lake Rd.
28 condos rooms - $50-60
Pets: Welcome
Creature Comforts: CCTV, VCR, a/c, kit, fireplace, restaurant, pool, hlth club, sauna, whirlpool

GREEN RIVER

Budget Host Brook Cliff
(800) Bud-Host, (435) 564-3406
http://www.budgethost.com
395 E. Main St.
78 rooms - $30-85
Pets: Small pets w/$5 fee
Creature Comforts: CCTV, a/c,
restaurant, pool

Budget Inn
(435) 564-3441
60 S. Main St.
30 rooms - $35-55
Pets: Welcome
Creature Comforts: CCTV, a/c

Carter's Oasis Motel
(435) 564-3471
118 W. Main St.
20 rooms - $30-48
Pets: Welcome
Creature Comforts: CCTV, a/c,
restaurant

Motel 6
(800) 4-MOTEL6, (435) 564-3436
946 E. Main St.
103 rooms - $35-50
Pets: Under 30 lbs. welcome
Creature Comforts: CCTV, pool

National 9 Inn
(800) 524-9999, (435) 564-8237
456 W. Main St.
30 rooms - $35-45
Pets: Welcome
Creature Comforts: CCTV, a/c

Robber's Roost Motel
(435) 564-3452
225 W. Main St.
20 rooms - $35-45
Pets: Welcome
Creature Comforts: CCTV, a/c,
pool

Super 8 Motel
(800) 800-8000, (435) 564-8888
http://www.super8.com
1248 E. Main St.
68 rooms - $40-45
Pets: Welcome w/permission
Creature Comforts: CCTV, a/c,
cont. brkfst, pool

HATCH

New Bryce Motel
(435) 735-4265
227 W. Main St.
20 rooms - $49-57
Pets: Welcome
Creature Comforts: TV, a/c,
restaurant

Riverside Motel
(800) 824-5651, (435) 735-4223
594 Rte. 89
14 rooms - $30-58
Pets: Welcome on occasion, short-
haired, clean w/$5 fee and deposit
Creature Comforts: CCTV, a/c,
restaurant

HEBER CITY

Danish Viking Lodge
(800) 544-4066, (435) 654-2202
989 S. Main St.
34 rooms - $35-125
Pets: Welcome in certain rooms
Creature Comforts: CCTV,
VCR, a/c, kit, pool, whirlpool

Heber Valley RV Park/Resort
(435) 654-4049
7000 N. Old Rte. 40
4 cabins - $35
Pets: Under 30 lbs. welcome
Creature Comforts: CCTV

Swiss Alps Inn
(435) 654-0722
167 S. Main St.
13 rooms - $40-75
Pets: Small pets welcome
Creature Comforts: CCTV, a/c,
pool

HUNTSVILLE

Jackson Fork Inn
(800) 255-0672, (801) 745-0051
http://www.bbgetaways.com/
JacksonForkInn/
7345 E 900 South
8 rooms - $50-115
Pets: Welcome w/$20 fee
Creature Comforts: 1930's dairy
barn converted to an inn, unusual
rms w/first floor sitting area and
spiral staircase to bedrooms,
Jacuzzis, CCTV, restaurant, cont.
brkfst, whirlpool

HURRICANE

Best Western Lamplighter
(800) 528-1234, (435) 635-4647
http://www.bestwestern.com
280 West State St.
63 rooms - $50-65
Pets: Welcome w/$5 fee
Creature Comforts: CCTV, a/c,
cont. brkfst, pool, whirlpool

Motel 6
(800) 4-MOTEL6, (435) 635-4010
http://www.motel6.com
650 W. State St.
46 rooms - $40-45
Pets: Under 30 lbs. welcome
Creature Comforts: CCTV, a/c,
kit, pool

Super 8 Motel
(800) 800-8000, (435) 635-0808
http://www.super8.com
65 South 700 West
65 rooms - $65-70
Pets: Welcome w/deposit
Creature Comforts: CCTV, a/c,
Jacuzzi, cont. brkfst, pool,
whirlpool

JUNCTION

Junction Motel
(435) 577-2629
300 S. Main St.
5 rooms - $30-48
Pets: Welcome
Creature Comforts: CCTV, kit

KANAB

Aiken's Lodge-National 9
(800) 524-9999, (435) 644-2625
79 W. Center Rte.
31 rooms - $50-65
Pets: Small pets welcome
Creature Comforts: CCTV, a/c,
pool

Brandon Motel B&B
(800) 473-2164, (435) 644-2631
233 W. Center St.
20 rooms - $35-55
Pets: Small pets w/$5 fee
Creature Comforts: CCTV, a/c,
kit, pool

Color Country Inn
(800) 473-2164, (435) 644-2164
1550 S. Rte. 89
13 rooms - $35-55
Pets: Small pets w/$5 fee
Creature Comforts: CCTV,
VCR, a/c

Four Seasons Motel
(435) 644-2635
36 N. 300 West
41 rooms - $35-58
Pets: Welcome
Creature Comforts: CCTV, a/c,
restaurant, pool, whirlpool

K Motel
(435) 644-2611
300 S. 100 East
23 rooms - $37-55
Pets: Small pets w/$50 deposit
Creature Comforts: CCTV, a/c,
pool

Kanab Mission Motel
(435) 644-5373
386 E. 300 South
65 rooms - $35
Pets: Small pets welcome
Creature Comforts: CCTV, a/c

Parry Lodge
(800) 748-4104, (435) 644-2601
89 E. Center St.
89 rooms - $45-65
Pets: Welcome w/$5 fee
Creature Comforts: CCTV, a/c,
restaurant, pool

Riding's Quail Park Lodge
(435) 644-5094
125 Rte. 89 North
13 rooms - $30-55
Pets: In pet rooms w/$8 fee
Creature Comforts: CCTV, a/c,
kit, pool

Shilo Inn
(800) 222-2244, (435) 644-2562
296 W. 100 North
118 rooms - $50-95
Pets: Welcome w/$7 fee
Creature Comforts: CCTV,
VCR, a/c, kit, pool, whirlpool

Sun-N-Sand Motel
(800) 654-1868, (435) 644-5050
http://expressweb.sunsand.com
347 S. 100 East
18 rooms - $30-50
Pets: Small pets-$10 dep, pet rms.
Creature Comforts: CCTV, a/c,
kit, pool, whirlpool

Treasure Trail Motel
(435) 644-2687
150 W. Center St.
30 rooms - $40-55
Pets: Small pets w/$5 fee
Creature Comforts: CCTV, a/c,
pool

LAKE POWELL
Bullfrog's Defiance House
(800) 528-6154, (435) 684-3000
Box 4055, Bullfrog Rd.
56 rooms - $70-110
Pets: Welcome
Creature Comforts: CCTV,
VCR, a/c, kit, restaurant

City Center
(435) 684-7000
Route 276
20 rooms - $90-150
Pets: Small pets w/$25 deposit
Creature Comforts: CCTV, a/c,
kit

Hall's Crossing
(435) 684-7000
Hall's Crossing Marina
20 rooms - $75-115
Pets: Welcome
Creature Comforts: CCTV, a/c,
kit

Hite Family Units
(435) 684-2278
Hite Marina
4 rooms - $75-110
Pets: Welcome
Creature Comforts: CCTV,
VCR, a/c, kit

LAYTON
La Quinta
(800) 531-5900, (801) 776-6700
1965 N. 1200 West
100 rooms - $75-115
Pets: Welcome
Creature Comforts: CCTV, a/c,
pool, hlth club, whirlpool, sauna

Valley View Motel
(801) 825-1632
1560 N. Main St.
12 rooms - $35-50
Pets: Welcome
Creature Comforts: CCTV, a/c,
kit

LEHI
Best Western Timpanogos
(800) 528-1234, (801) 768-1400
http://www.bestwestern.com
Rtes. 95 S & 850 E
59 rooms - $68-86
Pets: Welcome w/$5 deposit
Creature Comforts: CCTV,
VCR, a/c, buffet brkfst, pool, hlth
clb access, sauna, whirlpool

Super 8 Motel
(800) 800-8000, (801) 766-8800
http://www.super8.com
1807 Route 286
49 rooms - $50-60
Pets: Welcome w/permission
Creature Comforts: CCTV, a/c,
Jacuzzi, cont. brkfst, pool, hlth
club, whirlpool

MANILA
Vacation Inn
(800) 662-4327, (801) 266-2811
Route 43
22 rooms - $46-52
Pets: Welcome
Creature Comforts: CCTV, kit

MANTI
Manti Motel & Outpost
(435) 835-8533
445 N. Main St.
11 rooms - $30-62
Pets: Welcome
Creature Comforts: CCTV, kit

MARYSVALE
Big Rock Candy Mtn. Resort
(888) 560-ROCK, (435) 326-2000
http://BigRockCandyMtn.com
Route 89
17 rooms - $60-90
Pets: Small dogs in smoking rm.
Creature Comforts: CCTV,
VCR, a/c, kit, restaurant, hlth club,
whirlpool

Lizzy & Charlie's RV Park
(435) 326-4213
300 E. Rio Grande Ave.
32 cabins - $25-50
Pets: Welcome
Creature Comforts: Simple
cabins and RV parking

MEXICAN HAT
Burch's Trading Co.
(435) 683-2246
Route 163
41 rooms - $50-75
Pets: Welcome
Creature Comforts: CCTV,
restaurant

San Juan Inn
(800) 447-2022, (435) 683-2220
Route 163
36 rooms - $40-65
Pets: Welcome
Creature Comforts: CCTV,
VCR, a/c, restaurant, hlth club,
whirlpool

Valley of the Gods B&B
(970) 749-1164
http://www.apc.net/daniel/
vog.htm
Box 310307
4 rooms - $90-110
Pets: Welcome, not allowed in
rooms but on porches or in Green
Room
Creature Comforts: Neat stone
and timber ranch house, set in
360,000 acre recreation area,
CCTV, VCR, a/c, kit, cont. brkfst,
hiking, fishing, horseback riding

MIDVALE
Homewood Suites
(800) Call-Home, (801) 561-5999
844 E. North Union Ave.
97 rooms - $110-140
Pets: Welcome
Creature Comforts: CCTV,
VCR, a/c, kit, cont. brkfst, pool,
and a whirlpool

La Quinta, Midvale
(800) Nu-Rooms, (801) 566-3291
http://www.laquinta.com
530 Catalta St.
122 rooms - $76-85
Pets: Small pets welcome
Creature Comforts: CCTV, a/c,
refrig, micro, cont. brkfst, pool

Motel 6, Midvale
(800) 4-MOTEL6, (801) 561-0058
496 N. Catalpa St.
128 rooms - $40-52
Pets: Under 30 lbs. welcome
Creature Comforts: CCTV, a/c

MOAB
Apache Motel
(800) 228-6882, (435) 259-5727
http://www.grand.k12ut.us/Moab/
Apache.html
166 S 400 East
32 rooms - $30-65
Pets: Welcome
Creature Comforts: CCTV, a/c,
kit, pool

Bowen Motel
(800) 874-5439, (435) 259-7132
http://www.moab-utah.com/
bowen/mo.html
169 N. Main St.
40 rooms - $40-65
Pets: Small pets welcome
Creature Comforts: CCTV,
VCR, a/c, kit, pool

Cedar Breaks Condos
(800) 505-5343, (435) 259-7830
Hite Marina
6 condos - $55-85
Pets: Welcome
Creature Comforts: CCTV, a/c,
kit

Comfort Suites
(800) 228-5150, (435) 259-5252
http://www.comfortinn.com
800 S. Main St.
75 rooms - $70-125
Pets: Welcome w/$10 fee
Creature Comforts: CCTV, a/c,
pool

Entrada Ranch
(435) 259-5796
http://www.entrada-ranch.com
Entrada Ridge Rd., Mile 9
5 cabins - $50-125
Pets: Welcome
Creature Comforts: CCTV,
VCR, a/c, kit, restaurant

Heather Lane B&B
(435) 259-5928
4381 Heather Ln.
2 rooms - $40-65
Pets: Welcome
Creature Comforts: CCTV,
whirlpool

Kokopelli Lodge
(800) 259-7615, (435) 684-2278
http://www.moab.net/reservations
52 S 100 East
8 rooms - $35-65
Pets: Welcome
Creature Comforts: CCTV, a/c

Moab Valley Inn
(800) 831-6622, (435) 259-4419
711 S. Main St.
127 rooms - $60-125
Pets: Small pets in pet rms.
Creature Comforts: CCTV, a/c,
kit, pool

Pack Creek Ranch
(435) 259-5505
http://www.packcreekranch.com
La Sal Pass Rd.
10 cabins - $75-110
Pets: Welcome
Creature Comforts: Neat open
beamed log lodge and rustic but
charming cabins, on 300 acres, kit,
fireplace, full brkfst, pool, sauna,
whirlpool, horseback riding

Pioneer Springs B&B
(435) 259-4663
http://www.bbonline.com/ut/
pioneer
1275 S. Boulder Rd.
3 rooms - $35-100
Pets: Welcome
Creature Comforts: CCTV, pool,
whirlpool

Ramada Inn
(800) 2-Ramada, (435) 259-7141
http://www.ramada.com
182 S. Main St.
82 rooms - $35-100
Pets: Welcome in queen rooms
Creature Comforts: CCTV, a/c,
restaurant, pool, whirlpool

Red Stone Inn
(435) 259-3500
http://www.moabutah.com/
redstoneinn
535 S. Main St.
50 rooms - $35-65
Pets: Small pets w/$5 fee
Creature Comforts: CCTV, a/c,
kit

Rustic Inn
(800) 231-8184, (435) 259-6177
http://www.moabutah.com/
rusticinn
120 E 100 South
34 rooms - $30-65
Pets: Small pets w/$5 fee in
smoking rms.
Creature Comforts: CCTV, a/c,
kit, pool

Silver Sage Inn
(435) 259-4420
840 S. Main St.
17 rooms - $30-55
Pets: Welcome
Creature Comforts: CCTV, kit

Sleep Inn
(800) Sleep-Inn, (435) 259-4655
http://www.sleepinn.com
1051 S. Main St.
61 rooms - $55-90
Pets: In pet rms w/$10 fee
Creature Comforts: CCTV, a/c,
pool, whirlpool

Virginian Motel
(800) 261-2063, (435) 259-5951
70 E. 200 South
37 rooms - $75-110
Pets: Welcome
Creature Comforts: CCTV, a/c,
refrig, kit

MONTICELLO
Canyonlands Motor Inn
(800) 952-6212, (435) 587-2266
197 N. Main St.
32 rooms - $35-65
Pets: Welcome
Creature Comforts: CCTV, s/c,
kit, pool, sauna, whirlpool

MT. CARMEL JCT.
Best Western Thunderbird
(800) 528-1234, (435) 645-2203
http://www.bestwestern.com
Rtes. 89 & 9
61 rooms - $40-85
Pets: Small pets welcome
Creature Comforts: CCTV, a/c,
restaurant, pool

Golden Hills Motel
(800) 648-2268, (435) 648-2268
125 E. State St.
30 rooms - $35-55
Pets: Small pets in pet rooms
Creature Comforts: CCTV, a/c,
restaurant, pool

MURRAY
Quality Inn, Midvalley
(800) 268-5801, (801) 268-2533
http://www.qualityinn.com/
4465 Century Dr.
131 rooms - $60-110
Pets: Welcome w/$6 fee
Creature Comforts: CCTV, a/c,
kit, restaurant, pool, whirlpool

Reston Hotel
(801) 264-1054
3400 NW 12th St.
98 rooms - $60-75
Pets: Welcome w/$30 fee
Creature Comforts: CCTV,
VCR, a/c, restaurant, pool,
whirlpool

NEPHI
Best Western Paradise
(800) 528-1234, (435) 623-0624
http://www.bestwestern.com
1025 S. Main St.
40 rooms - $45-70
Pets: Small pets welcome
Creature Comforts: CCTV, a/c,
refrig, pool, whirlpool

Motel 6
(800) 4-MOTEL6, (35) 623-0666
http://www.motel6.com
2195 S. Main St.
43 rooms - $40-55
Pets: Under 30 lbs. welcome
Creature Comforts: CCTV, a/c,
pool

Safari Motel
(435) 623-1071
413 S. Main St.
28 rooms - $35-45
Pets: Small pets w/$3 fee
Creature Comforts: CCTV, a/c,
pool

Starlite Motel
(800) 528-1234, (435) 645-2203
675 S. Main St.
24 rooms - $25-65
Pets: Welcome
Creature Comforts: CCTV, a/c,
kit, pool

OGDEN
Best Rest Inn
(800) 343-8644, (801) 393-8644
1206 W. 2100 South
101 rooms - $45-50
Pets: Welcome w/deposit
Creature Comforts: CCTV, a/c,
refrig, micro, restaurant, pool

Best Western High Country
(800) 528-1234, (801) 394-9474
http://www.bestwestern.com
1335 W. 1200 South
111 rooms - $65-75
Pets: Welcome w/$25 deposit
Creature Comforts: CCTV,
VCR, a/c, refrig, Jacuzzi,
restaurant, cont. brkfst, pool,
whirlpool

Best Western Ogden Park
(800) 528-1234, (801) 627-1190
http://www.bestwestern.com
247 - 24th St.
288 rooms - $100-175
Pets: Welcome w/$25 deposit
Creature Comforts: CCTV, a/c,
refrig, micro, restaurant, cont.
brkfst, pool, hlth club, whirlpool

Big Z Motel
(801) 394-6632
1123 W. 2100 South
32 rooms - $45-50
Pets: Small pets w/$20 deposit
Creature Comforts: CCTV, a/c,
kit, restaurant

Comfort Suites
(800) 228-5150, (801) 621-2545
http://www.comfortinn.com
1150 W. 2150 South
142 rooms - $75-105
Pets: Small pets w/$50 deposit
Creature Comforts: CCTV, a/c,
restaurant, pool

Millstream Motel
(801) 394-9425
1450 Washington Blvd.
46 rooms - $35-60
Pets: Welcome
Creature Comforts: CCTV, a/c,
kit, restaurant, hlth club

Motel 6
(800) 4-MOTEL6, (801) 627-4560
http://www.motel6.com
1455 Washington Blvd.
70 rooms - $32-50
Pets: Under 30 lbs. welcome
Creature Comforts: CCTV, a/c

Mt. Lomond Motel
(801) 782-7477
755 Harrisville Rd.
24 rooms - $75-105
Pets: Welcome
Creature Comforts: CCTV, a/c,
kit, restaurant

Sleep Inn
(800) Sleep-Inn, (801) 731-6500
http://www.sleepinn.com
1155 S. 1700 West
66 rooms - $45-75
Pets: Small pets in smoking rms.
Creature Comforts: CCTV,
VCR, a/c, restaurant, cont. brkfst,
whirlpool

Super 8 Motel
(800) 800-8000, (801) 731-7100
http://www.super8.com
1508 W. 2100 S. Ogden Rd.
60 rooms - $40-45
Pets: Welcome w/deposit
Creature Comforts: CCTV, a/c

Travelodge
(800) 578-7878, (801) 394-4563
http://www.travelodge.com
2110 Washington Blvd.
78 rooms - $30-90
Pets: Welcome
Creature Comforts: CCTV, a/c,
pool, hlth club

Western Colony Inn
(801) 627-1332
234 - 24th St.
14 rooms - $40-45
Pets: Small pets w/$20 deposit
Creature Comforts: CCTV, a/c,
refrig, micro

PANGUITCH
Adobe Sands Motel
(800) 497-9261, (435) 676-8874
390 N. Main St.
33 rooms - $35-60
Pets: Small pets in pet rooms
Creature Comforts: CCTV, pool

Cameron Motel
(800) 537-9212, (435) 676-8840
78 W. Center St.
17 rooms - $35-60
Pets: Welcome
Creature Comforts: CCTV, a/c,
kit

Color Country Motel
(800)225-6518, (435) 676-2386
http://www.inforwest.com/
ccmotel/
180 West 400 South
26 rooms - $30-55
Pets: Small pets w/$5 fee
Creature Comforts: CCTV, a/c,
pool, whirlpool

Horizon Motel
(800) 776-2651, (435) 676-2651
730 N. Main St.
16 rooms - $50-75
Pets: Small pets w/$10 fee
Creature Comforts: CCTV,
VCR, a/c, whirlpool

Marianna Inn Motel
(800) 331-7407, (435) 676-8844
699 N. Main St.
24 rooms - $25-70
Pets: Welcome
Creature Comforts: CCTV,
whirlpool

Nelson Motel
(435) 676-8441
308 Main St.
13 rooms - $35-65
Pets: Welcome
Creature Comforts: CCTV, kit

Outdoorsman Inn
(435) 521-3900
600 Route 291
134 rooms - $30-40
Pets: Welcome
Creature Comforts: CCTV,
VCR, kit

Patriarchs Motel/Cabins
(435) 648-2154
12120 W. Rte. 9
10 cabins - $35-50
Pets: Welcome
Creature Comforts: CCTV,
restaurant

Purple Sage Motel
(800) 241-6889, (435) 676-2659
104 E. Center St.
15 rooms - $50-99
Pets: Welcome
Creature Comforts: CCTV, a/c

Sportsman's Paradise
(888) 678-8348, (435) 676-8348
600 Route 291
1 cabin - $30-40
Pets: Welcome
Creature Comforts: CCTV

William Prince
(888) 676-2525, (435) 676-2325
http://www.onlinepages.net/
williamprince/
185 S. 300 East
4 rooms - $50-70
Pets: Welcome
Creature Comforts: 1870 brick
house in historic distric, set behind
picket fence, wonderful guest rms
decorated around beautiful
handmade quilts, antique iron
beds, claw foot tubs, a few TVs,
cont. brkfst

PANGUITCH LAKE
Bear Paw Lake View Resort
(435) 676-2650
905 S. Rte. 143
10 cabins - $50-75
Pets: Welcome
Creature Comforts: CCTV, kit

Deer Trail Lodge
(435) 676-2211
Clear Creek Canyon
9 cabins - $50-125
Pets: Welcome
Creature Comforts: CCTV, kit

Panguitch Lake Resort
(435) 676-2657
791 S. Lake Shore Dr.
15 rooms - $50-75
Pets: Welcome
Creature Comforts: CCTV, kit,
restaurant

Rustic Lodge
(800) 427-8345, (435) 676-2627
186 S. Westshore Rd.
11 cabins - $50-75
Pets: Welcome
Creature Comforts: CCTV, kit,
restaurant

PARK CITY
Best Western Hornes
(800) 528-1234, (435) 649-7300
http://www.bestwestern.com
6560 Landmark Dr.
100 rooms - $70-165
Pets: Welcome w/$25 deposit
Creature Comforts: CCTV, a/c,
refrig, Jacuzzi, restaurant, pool,
hlth club, sauna, whirlpool,
fishing, horseback riding

Blue Church Lodge
(800) 626-5467, (801) 649-8009
http://www.virtualcities.com/ons/
ut/k/utk3501.htm
424 Park Ave.
3 rms/3 condos - $150-250
Pets: Small dogs on a ltd. basis
Creature Comforts: 1897
Mormon church, now listed on
Nat'l Historic Register, indiv.
decorated condos-country antique
to casual mtn. decors, CCTV,
VCR, CD players, a/c, fireplaces,
cont. brkfst

Central Reservations Park City
(800) 243-2932, (435) 649-6606
http://www.CENTRALRES.com
750 Kearns Blvd.
600 condos - $125-500
Pets: Welcome in some units
Creature Comforts: CCTV,
VCR, a/c, kit, fireplace, Jacuzzi,
pool, hlth clb, sauna, whirlpool

Olympia Park Hotel
(800) 234-9003, (435) 649-2900
http://www.olympiahotel.com
1895 Sidewinder Dr.
191 rms/condos - $250-1,000
Pets: Welcome w/$10 fee
Creature Comforts: Newly
redecorated lodge rms, rqst
specialty suites w/four-poster beds
and living areas, CCTV, VCR, a/c,
refrig, micro, kit, fireplace,
Jacuzzi, pool, hlth clb, sauna,
whirlpool

Radisson Park City
(800) 333-3333, (435) 649-5000
http://www.radisson.com
2121 Park Ave.
131 rooms - $120-190
Pets: Small pets w/$15 fee
Creature Comforts: CCTV, a/c,
kit, restaurant, cont. brkfst, pool,
sauna, whirlpool

PAROWAN
Ace Motel
(435) 477-3384
92 N. Main St.
8 rooms - $35-50
Pets: Welcome
Creature Comforts: CCTV, a/c,
kit

Best Western Swiss Village
(800) 528-1234, (435) 477-3391
http://www.tcd.net/~jbixman
580 N. Main St.
28 rooms - $45-65
Pets: Welcome w/$5 fee
Creature Comforts: CCTV, a/c,
restaurant, pool, whirlpool

Days Inn
(800) DAYS INN, (435) 477-3473
http://www.daysinn.com
625 W. 200 South
44 rooms - $40-65
Pets: Welcome w/$8 fee
Creature Comforts: CCTV, a/c,
cont. brkfst, restaurant

Jebediah's Inn
(435) 477-3326
200 S. 600 W. Holyoak Ln.
40 rooms - $35-45
Pets: Welcome
Creature Comforts: CCTV,
restaurant

PAYSON
Comfort Inn
(800) 228-5150, (801) 465-4861
http://www.comfortinn.com
830 N. Main St.
62 rooms - $75-115
Pets: Welcome w/$10 deposit
Creature Comforts: CCTV,
VCR, a/c, refrig, kit, Jacuzzi, pool

PEOA
Peoa Vacation Cottage
(435) 783-5339
5880 N. Rte. 32
1 cottage - $75-125
Pets: Welcome
Creature Comforts: CCTV, kit

PINE VALLEY
Pine Valley Lodge
(435) 574-2544
960 E. Main St.
10 rooms - $25-45
Pets: Welcome
Creature Comforts: Restaurant

PRICE
Budget Host
(800) Bud-Host, (435) 637-2424
http://www.budgethost.com
145 N. Carbonville Rd.
32 rooms - $35-45
Pets: $10 fee, $20 dep
Creature Comforts: CCTV, a/c,
kit, restaurant, pool

Greenwell Inn
(800) 666-3520, (435) 637-3520
www.castlenet.com/greenwell
655 E. Main St.
125 rooms - $40-50
Pets: Welcome w/$10
Creature Comforts: CCTV, a/c,
restaurant, cont. brkfst, pool, hlth
club, whirlpool

National 9
(800) 524-9999, (435) 637-7000
641 W. Price River Dr.
97 rooms - $35-55
Pets: Welcome w/$5 fee
Creature Comforts: CCTV,
VCR, a/c, cont. brkfst

Shaman Lodge
(800) 710-7842, (435) 637-7489
http://www.shamanlodge.com
3769 W. Garden Creek Rd.
6 rooms - $100-175
Pets: Welcome
Creature Comforts: Wonderful, upscale yet casual Western log lodge, on 12 acres abutting BLM lands, 5,400 sq. ft. w/theme bedrooms-Country Inn, Cowboy, Garden, Indian, Hunter/Fishing rms, SATV, full gourmet brkfst, horseback riding

PROVO
Comfort Inn
(800) 228-5150, (801) 374-6020
http://www.comfortinn.com
1555 Canyon Rd.
100 rooms - $50-85
Pets: Small pets w/$25 deposit
Creature Comforts: CCTV, VCR, a/c, refrig, micro, Jacuzzi, cont. brkfst, pool, whirlpool

Days Inn
(800) DAYS INN, (801) 375-8600
http://www.daysinn.com
1600 S. University Ave.
49 rooms - $59-69
Pets: Small pets w/$5 fee
Creature Comforts: CCTV, a/c, kit, pool

Econo Lodge, Airport
(800) 55-ECONO, (801) 373-0099
http://www.econolodge.com
1625 E. Century St.
30 rooms - $50-55
Pets: Small pets w/$25 deposit
Creature Comforts: CCTV, a/c, restaurant, pool

Hampton Inn
(800) Hampton, (801) 377-6396
http://www.hampton-inn.com
1511 S. 40 East
90 rooms - $65-85
Pets: Small pets welcome
Creature Comforts: CCTV, a/c, pool

Motel 6
(800) 4-MOTEL6, (801) 375-5064
http://www.motel6.com
1600 S. University Ave.
119 rooms - $35-59
Pets: Under 30 lbs. welcome
Creature Comforts: CCTV, a/c, pool

National 9 Inn
(800) 524-9999, (801) 374-6800
1380 S. University Ave.
80 rooms - $40-65
Pets: Welcome w/$4 fee, $15 dep.
Creature Comforts: CCTV, a/c, kit, cont. brkfst, pool, sauna, whirlpool

Residence Inn
(800) 97-PROVO, (801) 374-1000
http://www.residenceinn.com
252 W. 2230 North
114 rooms - $125-175
Pets: Small pets w/$200 deposit
Creature Comforts: CCTV, VCR, a/c, kit, pool, fitness cntr, jogging trail

Sleep Inn
(800) Sleep-Inn, (801) 377-6579
http://www.sleepinn.com
1505 S. 40 East
55 rooms - $55-65
Pets: Welcome w/notice, no cats
Creature Comforts: CCTV, a/c

Uptown Motel
(801) 373-8248
469 W. Center St.
29 rooms - $40-57
Pets: Small pets w/$4 fee
Creature Comforts: CCTV, a/c, refrig, kit

RICHFIELD
Best Western AppleTree
(800) 528-1234, (435) 896-5481
http://www.bestwestern.com
145 S. Main St.
62 rooms - $50-80
Pets: Welcome w/$6 fee
Creature Comforts: CCTV, a/c, buffet brkfst, pool, whirlpool

Budget Host Knights Inn
(800) Bud-Host, (435) 896-8228
http://www.budgethost.com
69 S. Main St.
50 rooms - $35-50
Pets: Small pets welcome
Creature Comforts: CCTV, a/c, refrig, micro, restaurant, pool

Days Inn
(800) DAYS INN, (435) 896-6476
http://www.daysinn.com
333 N. Main St.
51 rooms - $50-95
Pets: Welcome w/mngr's apprvl
Creature Comforts: CCTV, a/c, restaurant, pool, hlth club, whirlpool, sauna

New West Motel
(800) 278-4076, (435) 896-4076
http://www.inquo.net/~alphaman/newwest
447 S. Main St.
15 rooms - $30-45
Pets: Welcome w/$5 fee
Creature Comforts: CCTV, a/c

Romanico Inn
(800) 948-0001, (435) 896-8471
1170 S. Main St.
29 rooms - $35-47
Pets: Small pets w/$3 fee
Creature Comforts: CCTV, a/c, refrig, micro, whirlpool

Weston Inn
(800) 333-STAY, (435) 896-9271
647 S. Main St.
40 rooms - $30-45
Pets: Welcome
Creature Comforts: CCTV, a/c, pool, whirlpool

RIVERDALE
Motel 6, Riverdale
(800) 4-MOTEL6, (801) 627-2880
http://www.motel6.com
1500 W. Riverdale Rd.
109 rooms - $35
Pets: Under 30 lbs. welcome
Creature Comforts: CCTV, a/c, pool

ROOSEVELT

Best Western Inn
(800) 528-1234, (435) 722-4644
http://www.bestwestern.com
East Rte. 40
40 rooms - $60-95
Pets: Small pets welcome
Creature Comforts: CCTV, a/c,
restaurant, pool, hlth club,
whirlpool

Frontier Motel
(800) 4-MOTEL6, (435) 722-2201
http://www.motel6.com
75 S. 200 East
54 rooms - $40-55
Pets: Small pets welcome
Creature Comforts: CCTV, a/c,
pool, whirlpool

ST. GEORGE

Olde Penny Farthing B&B
(435) 673-7755
http://www.sunreservations.com/
penny.html
278 N. 100 West
5 rooms - $50-100
Pets: Welcome w/$20 deposit,
crated preferred
Creature Comforts: Charming
historic Victorian inn, pioneer
antiques, Morning Dove best for
dogs, down comforter, peeler log
bed, plank ceiling, saltillo tile
floors, CCTV, full English brkfst

Bloomington Townhomes
(435) 673-6172
144 Brigham Rd.
33 condos - $75-125
Pets: Under 30 lbs. welcome
Creature Comforts: CCTV, a/c,
pool

The Bluffs Motel
(435) 628-6699
1140 S. Bluff Rd.
61 rooms - $60-90
Pets: Small pets in certain rooms
Creature Comforts: CCTV, a/c,
Jacuzzi, pool, whirlpool

Budget Inn/Suites
(800) 929-0790, (435) 673-6661
60 S. Main
115 rooms - $35-55
Pets: Welcome w/$10
Creature Comforts: CCTV, a/c,
kit, pool, hlth club, whirlpool

Days Inn Thunderbird
(800) DAYS INN, (435) 673-6123
http://www.daysinn.com
150 N. 100 East
99 rooms - $50-85
Pets: Welcome w/$20 deposit
Creature Comforts: CCTV, a/c,
cont. brkfst, pool, hlth club,
whirlpool

Econo Lodge
(800) 55-ECONO, (435) 673-4861
http://www.econolodge.com
460 E. St. George St.
54 rooms - $40-70
Pets: Welcome
Creature Comforts: CCTV, a/c,
restaurant, pool

Hilton, St. George
(800) 662-2525, (435) 628-0463
http://www.hilton.com
1450 S. Hilton Dr.
100 rooms - $70-120
Pets: Welcome w/$25 deposit
Creature Comforts: CCTV,
VCR, a/c, restaurant, cont. brkfst,
pool, sauna, whirlpool

Motel 6
(800) 4-MOTEL6, (435) 628-7979
http://www.motel6.com
205 N. 1000 East St.
103 rooms - $30
Pets: Under 30 lbs. welcome
Creature Comforts: CCTV, a/c,
pool

Red Cliffs
(888) Red Cliff, (435) 673-3537
912 Red Cliffs Dr.
46 rooms - $40-70
Pets: Small pets w/$10 deposit
Creature Comforts: CCTV, a/c,
Jacuzzi, cont. brkfst, pool,
whirlpool

Singletree Inn
(800) 528-8890, (435) 673-6161
http://www.singletreeinn.com
260 E. St. George Blvd.
48 rooms - $40-60
Pets: Small pets welcome
Creature Comforts: CCTV, a/c,
refrig, micro, cont. brkfst, pool,
whirlpool

Southside Inn
(888) 628-9081, (435) 628-9000
750 E. St. George Blvd.
38 rooms - $90-130
Pets: Welcome
Creature Comforts: CCTV, a/c,
pool, whirlpool

Sun Time Inn
(800) 237-6253, (435) 673-6181
420 E. St. George Blvd.
46 rooms - $35-50
Pets: Welcome
Creature Comforts: CCTV,
VCR, a/c, kit, pool

Super 8 Motel
(800) 800-8000, (435) 628-4251
http://www.super8.com
915 S. Bluff St.
81 rooms - $35-45
Pets: Welcome
Creature Comforts: CCTV, a/c,
cont. brkfst, pool

Travelodge
(800) 578-7878, (435) 673-4621
http://www.travelodge.com
175 N. 1000 East
40 rooms - $35-80
Pets: Welcome
Creature Comforts: CCTV, a/c,
refrig, micro, pool

SALINA

Budget Host Scenic Hills
(800) Bud-Host, (435) 529-7483
http://www.budgethost.com
75 E. 1500 South
39 rooms - $45-60
Pets: Welcome
Creature Comforts: CCTV, a/c,
kit, restaurant

Henry's Hideway
(435) 529-7467
60 N. State St.
32 rooms - $40-50
Pets: Welcome w/$20 deposit
Creature Comforts: CCTV, a/c,
refrig, micro, pool, whirlpool

Safari Motel
(435) 529-7447
1425 S. State St.
28 rooms - $40-55
Pets: Welcome
Creature Comforts: CCTV, a/c,
restaurant, pool

SALT LAKE CITY

Alpine Executive Suites
(801) 533-8184
150 S. 900 East
5 rooms - $75-100
Pets: Small dogs w/$300 deposit, no cats
Creature Comforts: CCTV

Colonial Village Motel
(800) 228-5150, (801) 486-8171
1530 S. Main St.
34 rooms - $30-48
Pets: Welcome
Creature Comforts: CCTV, a/c, kit

Comfort Inn, Airport
(800) 228-5150, (801) 537-7444
http://www.comfortinn.com
200 N. Admiral Byrd Rd.
154 rooms - $75-150
Pets: Welcome
Creature Comforts: CCTV, a/c, restaurant, pool

Days Inn, Airport
(800) DAYS INN, (801) 539-8538
http://www.daysinn.com
1900 W. North Temple St.
110 rooms - $70-110
Pets: Welcome w/deposit
Creature Comforts: CCTV, a/c, cont. brkfst

Days Inn, Central
(800) DAYS INN, (801) 486-8780
http://www.daysinn.com
315 W. 33rd St.
101 rooms - $60-95
Pets: Welcome
Creature Comforts: CCTV, a/c, refrig, Jacuzzi, cont. brkfst, pool, whirlpool

Doubletree Hotel
(800) 222-TREE, (801) 328-2000
http://www.doubletreehotels.com
255 SW Temple St.
495 rooms - $115-175
Pets: Small pets welcome
Creature Comforts: CCTV, a/c, kit, restaurant, pool

Econo Lodge
(800) 55-ECONO, (801) 363-0062
http://www.econolodge.com
715 West North Temple St.
120 rooms - $55-75
Pets: Welcome
Creature Comforts: CCTV, a/c, restaurant, pool

Hilton, Airport
(800) HILTONS, (801) 539-1515
http://www.hilton.com
5151 Wiley Post Way
287 rooms - $80-95
Pets: Small pets w/$25 deposit
Creature Comforts: CCTV, a/c, refrig, micro, restaurant, pool, hlth clb access, whirlpool

La Quinta, Airport
(800) Nu-Rooms, (801) 366-4444
http://www.laquinta.com
4905 W. Wiley Post
114 rooms - $80-85
Pets: Small pets welcome
Creature Comforts: CCTV, a/c, refrig, micro, cont. brkfst, pool, hlth club

Motel 6, Airport
(800) 4-MOTEL6, (801) 364-1053
http://www.motel6.com
1990 W. North Temple St.
104 rooms - $40
Pets: Under 30 lbs. welcome
Creature Comforts: CCTV, a/c, pool

Motel 6, Downtown
(800) 4-MOTEL6, (801) 531-1252
http://www.motel6.com
176 W. Sixth South St.
109 rooms - $41-48
Pets: Under 30 lbs. welcome
Creature Comforts: CCTV, a/c

Quality Inn
(800) 228-5151, (801) 521-2930
http://www.qualityinn.com
154 W 600 South
312 rooms - $70-100
Pets: Welcome w/$6 fee
Creature Comforts: CCTV, VCR, a/c, refrig, restaurant, pool, hlth club, whirlpool

Ramada Ltd. Suites
(800) 2-Ramada, (801) 539-5005
http://www.ramada.com
315 N. Admiral Byrd Blvd.
60 rooms - $60-95
Pets: Welcome
Creature Comforts: CCTV, a/c, pool, hlth club

Residence Inn
(800) 331-3131, (801) 532-5511
http://www.residenceinn.com
765 E. 400 South
128 rooms - $130-185
Pets: Small pets w/$8 fee
Creature Comforts: CCTV, VCR, a/c, kit, fireplace, pool, hlth clb, whirlpool

Royal Executive Inn
(800) 228-5151, (801) 521-3450
121 N 300 West
95 rooms - $45-75
Pets: Small pets w/$20 deposit
Creature Comforts: CCTV, VCR, a/c, refrig, micro, cont. brkfst, pool

Skyline Inn
(801) 582-5350
2475 E. 1700 South
24 rooms - $60-95
Pets: Small pets welcome
Creature Comforts: CCTV, a/c, pool, whirlpool

Super 8 Motel
(800) 800-8000, (801) 534-0808
http://www.super8.com
915 S. Bluff St.
81 rooms - $36-45
Pets: Welcome
Creature Comforts: CCTV, a/c, cont. brkfst, pool

Super 8 Motel, Airport
(800) 800-8000, (801) 533-8878
http://www.super8.com
223 N. Jimmy Doolittle Rd.
75 rooms - $65-70
Pets: Welcome w/deposit
Creature Comforts: CCTV, a/c,
Jacuzzi, cont. brkfst, pool, hlth
club, whirlpool

Travelodge
(800) 578-7878, (801) 533-8200
http://www.travelodge.com
144 West N. Temple St.
55 rooms - $60-85
Pets: Welcome w/$25 fee in
smoking rooms
Creature Comforts: CCTV, a/c

**Wasatch Front Ski
Accommodations**
(800) 762-7606, (541) 488-2330
http://www.wsa.com.com/
2020 E 3300 South
75 condos - $125-350
Pets: Welcome in some condos
Creature Comforts: CCTV,
VCR, a/c, refrig, kit, restaurant,
cont. brkfst, pool

SANDY
Best Western CottonTree
(800) 528-1234, (801) 523-8484
http://www.bestwestern.com
10695 S. Auto Mall Dr.
110 rooms - $80-100
Pets: Small pets welcome
Creature Comforts: CCTV, a/c,
refrig, micro, cont. brkfst, pool,
hlth club, whirlpool

Residence Inn
(800) 331-3131, (801) 561-5005
http://www.residenceinn.com
270 W. 10000 South
102 rooms - $110-140
Pets: Small pets w/$100 fee
Creature Comforts: CCTV, a/c,
kit, fireplace, Jacuzzi, restaurant,
cont. brkfst, pool, jogging trail

Super 8 Motel
(800) 800-8000, (801) 553-8888
http://www.super8.com
10722 S. 300 West Jordan
62 rooms - $60-75
Pets: Welcome w/deposit
Creature Comforts: CCTV, a/c,
cont. brkfst, pool, hlth club,
whirlpool

SPANISH FORK
Holiday Inn Express
(800) HOLIDAY, (801) 798-9400
http://www.holiday-inn.com
632 Kirby Ln.
47 rooms - $50-75
Pets: Small pets w/$10 deposit
Creature Comforts: CCTV, a/c,
kit, hlth clb access, whirlpool

SPRING CITY
Horseshoe Mountain B&B
(888) 242-2871, (801) 462-2871
310 S. Main St.
3 rooms - $30-48
Pets: Welcome
Creature Comforts: CCTV, a/c,
kit, cont. brkfst

SPRINGDALE
Best Western Driftwood Lodge
(800) 528-1234, (435) 772-3262
http://www.bestwestern.com
1515 Zion Park Blvd.
47 rooms - $90-130
Pets: Small pets welcome
Creature Comforts: CCTV, a/c,
pool, whirlpool

Canyon Ranch Motel
(435) 772-3357
668 Zion Park Blvd.
22 rooms - $40-70
Pets: Welcome
Creature Comforts: CCTV, a/c,
kit, pool, whirlpool

Cliffrose Lodge
(800) 243-8824, (435) 772-3234
http://www.cliffroselodge.com
281 Zion Park Blvd.
36 rooms - $45-150
Pets: Small pets w/$10 fee
Creature Comforts: Bordering
spectacular Zion Nat'l Park, very
attractive, modern motel rms and
uniquely lush gardens, riverside
setting, CCTV, a/c, pool

Desert Pearl Inn
(888) 828-0898, (435) 772-8888
707 Zion Park Blvd.
61 rooms - $50-110
Pets: Welcome
Creature Comforts: CCTV,
VCR, a/c, kit, pool, whirlpool

El Rio Lodge in Zion
(888) 772-3205, (435) 772-3205
995 Zion Park Blvd.
10 rooms - $30-60
Pets: Welcome
Creature Comforts: CCTV, a/c

Zion Park Inn Resort
(800) 934-7275, (435) 772-3200
1215 Zion Park Blvd.
120 rooms - $70-95
Pets: Small pets w/$25 fee
Creature Comforts: CCTV,
VCR, a/c, kit, restaurant, pool,
whirlpool

TOOELE
Oquirrh Motor Inn
(801) 250-0118
8740 N. Rte. 36
41 rooms - $25-45
Pets: Welcome
Creature Comforts: CCTV, a/c

TOQUERVILLE
Your Inn Toquerville B&B
(435) 635-9964
476 Spring Dr.
4 rooms - $45-80
Pets: Welcome
Creature Comforts: CCTV, a/c

TORREY
Capitol Reef Inn
(435) 425-3271
360 W. Main St.
10 rooms - $30-48
Pets: Welcome
Creature Comforts: A/C, restaurant, whirlpool

Cockscomb Inn/Cottage
(800) 530-1038, (435) 425-3511
http://xmission.com/capreef/.com
97 S. State St.
4 rooms - $50-100
Pets: Welcome
Creature Comforts: CCTV, a/c, kit

TREMONTON
Marble Motel
(435) 257-3524
116 N. Tremont St.
10 rooms - $35-40
Pets: Welcome w/$20 deposit
Creature Comforts: CCTV, a/c

Sandman Motel
(435) 257-5675
585 W. Main St.
38 rooms - $40-55
Pets: Small pets w/$20 deposit
Creature Comforts: CCTV, a/c

TROPIC
Bryce Country Cabins
(435) 679-8643
320 N. Rte. 12
8 cabins - $50-65
Pets: Welcome
Creature Comforts: A/C

Bryce Pioneer Village
(800) 222-0381, (435) 679-8546
600 Route 291
44 rooms - $40-65
Pets: Welcome
Creature Comforts: CCTV, VCR, a/c, whirlpool

Doug's Country Motel
(435) 679-8600
121 N. Main St.
29 rooms - $30-55
Pets: Small pets w/$10 fee
Creature Comforts: CCTV, a/c, restaurant

World Host Bryce Valley Inn
(800) 442-1890, (435) 679-8811
200 N. Main St.
65 rooms - $50-115
Pets: Small pets w/$5 fee
Creature Comforts: CCTV, a/c, restaurant

VERNAL
Econo Lodge
(800) 55-ECONO, (435) 789-2000
http://www.econolodge.com
311 E. Main St.
50 rooms - $45-50
Pets: Small pets w/$5 fee
Creature Comforts: CCTV, a/c

Rodeway Inn
(800) 228-2000, (801) 789-8172
http://www.rodeway.com
590 W. Main St.
42 rooms - $35-65
Pets: Small pets w/$20 deposit
Creature Comforts: CCTV, a/c, kit, restaurant

Sage Motel
(800) 760, (801) 954-9292
54 W. Main St.
26 rooms - $40-45
Pets: Welcome in certain rooms
Creature Comforts: CCTV, a/c, restaurant

WELLINGTON
National 9 Inn
(800) 524-9999, (435) 637-7980
50 S. 700 East
50 rooms - $35-50
Pets: Welcome w/$5 fee
Creature Comforts: CCTV, a/c, restaurant, pool

WENDOVER
Days Inn
(800) DAYS INN, (435) 665-3332
http://www.daysinn.com
685 E. Wendover Blvd.
80 rooms - $50-80
Pets: Welcome
Creature Comforts: CCTV, a/c, cont. brkfst, pool, hlth club, whirlpool

Heritage Motel
(800) 457-5927, (435) 665-7744
505 E. Wendover St.
50 rooms - $35-55
Pets: Welcome
Creature Comforts: CCTV, a/c, hlth club

Vermont

ANDOVER
Inn at High View
(802) 875-2724
http://www.innathighview.com
753 East Hill Rd.
8 rooms - $95-155
Pets: Welcome in two suites
Creature Comforts: Secluded
1789 farmhouse on 72 acres,
stunning valley views, country
pine antiques w/contemp. touches,
Vt. quilts, suites w/sitting rms.,
full brkfst, gourmet dinners, pool,
cross-country skiing, hiking

ARLINGTON
Cut Leaf Maples Motel
(802) 375-2725
http://www.virtualvermont.com/
cutleafmaples
3420 Route 7A
8 rooms - $80-110
Pets: Welcome
Creature Comforts: CCTV, a/c

Roaring Branch
(802) 375-6401
Sunderland Hill Rd.
14 cabins - $575-675/wk
Pets: Welcome
Creature Comforts: Kit,
fireplace, swimming

Valhalla Motel
(800) 258-2212, (802) 375-2212
http://www.virtualcities.
com/ons/vt/g/vtg9602.htm
Route 7A
12 rooms - $38-70
Pets: Welcome, do not leave
unattended
Creature Comforts: CCTV, a/c,
refrig, pool

AVERILL
Quimby Country
(802) 822-5533
Forest Lake Rd.
15 cottages - $100-133 PP/AP
Pets: Welcome, do not leave
unattended
Creature Comforts: Cottages
and 1894 lodge set on 650 acres
in NE Kingdom, secluded, rustic,
all meals included, summer camp
atmosphere for families and pets

BARNET
Inn at Maplemont Farm
(800) 230-1617, (802) 633-4880
Route 5, South
4 rooms - $70-95
Pets: Welcome in S. Peacham and
Barnet Suites
Creature Comforts: 1800's
working horse farm on 43 acres
overlkng Conn. Rvr, tin ceilings,
orig, woodwork, bdrms w/
pastoral views, country brkfst,
friendly Bernese Mtn. dog-Max

BARRE
Budget Inn
(800) 446-4656, (802) 479-0529
573 North Main St.
24 rooms - $39-89
Pets: Small pets welcome
Creature Comforts: CCTV

Hollow Inn and Motel
(800) 998-9444, (802) 479-9313
http://www.hollowinn.com
278 South Main St.
40 rooms - $80-110
Pets: Welcome in motelw/$7 fee
Creature Comforts: CCTV,
VCR, a/c, refrig, micro, kit, cont.
brkfst, pool, exercise rm, sauna,
whirlpool

BARTON
Pine Crest Motel and Cabins
(802) 525-3472
http://www.virtualvermont.com/
cabins/indl.html
Route 5
12 cabins - $50-65
Pets: Welcome
Creature Comforts: Small cabins
on 11 acres w/river, CCTV, refrig,
micro

BENNINGTON
Apple Valley Inn and Cafe
(802) 442-6588
Route 7 South
20 rooms - $35-70
Pets: Welcome
Creature Comforts: CCTV, a/c,
Jacuzzi, restaurant, pool

Bennington Motor Inn
(800) 359-9900, (802) 442-5479
http://www.thisisvermont.com/
pages/bennmotorinn.html
143 West Main St.
30 rooms - $55-80
Pets: Ltd. rms. w/$10 fee
Creature Comforts: CCTV, a/c,
refrig.

Darling Kelly's Motel
(802) 442-2322
Route 7 South
21 rooms - $40-80
Pets: Welcome in ltd. rooms
Creature Comforts: CCTV, a/c,
cont. brkfst, pool

Fife N' Drum
(802) 442-4074
http://www.sover.net/~toberua/
Rte. 7 South
18 rooms - $45-100
Pets: Small pets w/$5 fee
Creature Comforts: CCTV, a/c,
refrig, kit, pool

Knotty Pine Motel
(802) 442-5487
http://www.bennington.com/
knottypine
130 Northside Dr.
17 rooms - $45-68
Pets: Welcome
Creature Comforts: CCTV, a/c,
refrig, kit, restaurant, pool

Pleasant Valley Motel
(802) 442-6222
Pleasant Valley Rd.
11 rooms - $40-50
Pets: Welcome
Creature Comforts: CCTV, a/c,
pool

South Gate Motel
(802) 447-7525
Route 7 South
20 rooms - $40-85
Pets: Welcome w/$5 fee
Creature Comforts: CCTV, a/c,
refrig, pool

Ramada Inn
(800) 2-Ramada, (802) 442-8145
http://www.ramada.com
Route 7/Kocher Dr.
101 rooms - $72-105
Pets: Welcome
Creature Comforts: CCTV, a/c,
restaurant, pool, exercise rm.,
sauna, whirlpool

Vermonter Motor Lodge
(800) 382-3175, (802) 442-2529
Route 9, West Rd.
31 rooms - $50-90
Pets: Welcome w/$25 fee
Creature Comforts: 1930s
cottages recommended, CCTV,
a/c, refrig, restaurant, cont. brkfst,
pond swimming

BETHEL
Greenhurst Inn
(800) 510-2553, (802) 234-9474
http://www.innsandouts.com/
property/greenhurstinn.html
RR 2, Box 60
13 rooms - $50-90
Pets: Friendly dogs welcome
Creature Comforts: National
Register Victorian mansion, well
preserved orig. features, vintage
furnishings, rqst large rooms in
main house, European soaps/
toiletries, cont. brkfst, tennis,
croquet

BRADFORD
Bradford Motel
(802) 222-4467
Route 5
15 rooms - $35-60
Pets: Welcome
Creature Comforts: CCTV, a/c,
refrig, kit

BRANDON
Brandon Motor Lodge
(800) 675-7614, (802) 247-9594
Route 7 South
18 rooms - $50-78
Pets: Polite pets w/$5 fee
Creature Comforts: CCTV, a/c,
refrig

Gingerbread House B&B
(802) 247-3380
Route 73 East
1 suite - $50-60
Pets: Welcome w/$5 fee
Creature Comforts: CCTV, kit,
living rm., cont. brkfst

Hivue B&B
(800) 880-3042, (802) 247-3042
Highpond Rd.
5 rooms - $50
Pets: Medium-size dogs welcome
Creature Comforts: CCTV, a/c,
refrig

Moffett House
(800) 394-7239, (802) 247-3843
http://www.brandon.org/
moffett.htm
69 Park St.
7 rooms - $70-140
Pets: Welcome w/fee
Creature Comforts: Victorian
inn w/200 teddy bears and other
collectibles, comfortable and cozy
bedrms, one w/Jacuzzi, full brkfst

BRATTLEBORO
Colonial Motel
(802) 257-7733
889 Putney Rd.
74 rooms - $65-80
Pets: Welcome
Creature Comforts: CCTV, a/c,
refrig, kit, restaurant, pool, and a
hlth club

Econo Lodge
(800) 55-ECONO, (802) 254-2360
http://www.econolodge.com
243 Canal St.
42 rooms - $49-105
Pets: Welcome
Creature Comforts: CCTV, a/c,
cont. brkfst, pool

Molly Stark Motel
(802) 254-2440
829 Marlboro Rd.
14 rooms - $37-75
Pets: Welcome
Creature Comforts: CCTV, a/c

Motel 6
(800) 4-MOTEL6, (802) 254-6007
1254 Putney Rd.
59 rooms - $38-50
Pets: Under 30 lbs. welcome
Creature Comforts: CCTV, a/c

BRIDGEWATER
The Corners Inn /Restaurant
(802) 672-9968
http://www.onisland.
com/lodging/cornersinn
318 Upper Rd.
5 rooms - $55-85
Pets: Well-behaved medium dogs
at owner's discretion
Creature Comforts: Sitting rm.
w/CCTV, restaurant

BRISTOL
Firefly Ranch
(802) 453-2223
http://bbonline.com/vt/firefly
Box 152
3 rooms - $75-140 (MAP)
Pets: Small pets welcome
Creature Comforts: Rural B&B
and guest ranch, attractive rms w/
country quilts, full country brkfst,
four-course dinner, horseback
riding, swimming pond, (if the inn
is full, you may pitch a tent)

BROOKFIELD
Birch Meadow Luxury Cabins
(802) 276-3156
http://bbhost.com/birchmeadow
294 East St.
3 cabins - $95-110
Pets: Welcome w/$30 fee
Creature Comforts: Log cabins,
CCTV, a/c, kit, wood-burning
stoves

BROWNSVILLE
Millbrook B&B
(802) 484-7283
Route 44
59 rooms - $90-150
Pets: Under 30 lbs. welcome
Creature Comforts: Log cabins,
CCTV, a/c, micro, kit, fireplace

Pond House B&B
(802) 484-0011
http://www.windsor.k12.vt.us/
pondhse.html
Box 234
3 rooms - $135-150 (MAP)
Pets: Dogs only welcome w/$10
fee, must be neutered w/rabies and
vaccination certificates
Creature Comforts: 1830's cape
farmhouse on 10 acres, stone
walls, country cottage furnishings,
wide pumpkin pine flrs, down
comforters, gourmet meals,
spring-fed swimming pond

BURLINGTON
Anchorage Inn
(800) 336-1869, (802) 863-7000
http://www.vtanchorageinn.com
108 Dorset St.
90 rooms - $45-90
Pets: Welcome w/$50 deposit
Creature Comforts: CCTV, a/c,
refrig, micro, cont. brkfst, pool,
sauna, whirlpool

Bel-Aire Motel
(888) 282-4533, (802) 863-3116
111 Shelburne Rd.
14 rooms - $40-85
Pets: Ltd. rms w/$6 fee
Creature Comforts: CCTV, a/c,
refrig, micro, cont. brkfst

Best Western Windjammer
(800) 371-1125, (802) 863-1125
http://www.bestwestern.com
1076 Williston Rd.
177 rooms - $60-150
Pets: Welcome in ltd. rms.
Creature Comforts: CCTV,
Nintendo, a/c, restaurant, cont.
brkfst, restaurant, 2 pools, exercise
rm., sauna, whirlpool

Ho Hum Motel
(800) 228-7031, (802) 863-4551
1660 Williston Rd.
36 rooms - $65-80
Pets: Welcome
Creature Comforts: CCTV, a/c,
refrig, pool

Holiday Inn, Burlington
(800) HOLIDAY, (802) 863-6363
http://www.holiday-inn.com
1068 Williston Rd.
175 rooms - $70-145
Pets: Welcome
Creature Comforts: CCTV, a/c,
restaurant, 2 pools, whirlpool,
exercise rm.

Howard Johnson
(800) I-Go-Hojo, (802) 863-5541
http://www.innvermont.com
1 Dorset St.
89 rooms - $49-99
Pets: Welcome in smoking rooms
Creature Comforts: CCTV, a/c,
cont. brkfst, pool, sauna, whirlpool

Ramada
(800) 2-Ramada, (802) 658-0250
http://www.ramada.com
1117 Willston Rd.
127 rooms - $79-140
Pets: Welcome w/deposit and
cannot be left alone in rm.
Creature Comforts: Motel rms.
w/country charm, CCTV, a/c,
restaurant, pool, hlth club

Sheraton, Burlington
(800) 325-3535, (802) 865-6600
http://www.sheraton.com
870 Williston Rd.
310 rooms - $135-175
Pets: Small pets welcome
Creature Comforts: SATV, a/c,
restaurant, pool, hlth club,
whirlpool

Super 8 Motel
(800) 800-8000, (802) 862-6421
http://www.super8.com
1016 Shelburne Rd.
53 rooms - $45-70
Pets: Welcome in smoking rms.
Creature Comforts: CCTV, a/c,
kit, Jacuzzi, restaurant, cont.
brkfst, pool

Town and Country Motel
(802) 862-5786
490 Shelburne Rd.
53 rooms - $45-70
Pets: Dogs only w/$5 fee
Creature Comforts: CCTV, a/c,
kit, Jacuzzi, restaurant, cont.
brkfst, pool

Ramada
(800) 2-Ramada, (802) 658-0250
http://www.ramada.com
Route 260
130 rooms - $60-95
Pets: Small pets welcome
Creature Comforts: CCTV, a/c,
pool, hlth club

COLCHESTER
Days Inn
(800) DAYS INN, (802) 655-0900
http://www.daysinn.com
Route 15
72 rooms - $75-140
Pets: Welcome
Creature Comforts: CCTV, a/c,
refrig, pool, hlth club, whirlpool

Hampton Inn
(800) Hampton, (802) 655-6177
http://www.hamptoninn.com
8 Mountain View Dr.
188 rooms - $75-85
Pets: Welcome
Creature Comforts: CCTV,
VCR, a/c, refrig, micro, kit,
Jacuzzi, pool, and a hlth club

CRAFTSBURY
Craftsbury Outdoor Center
(800) 729-7751
http://www.craftsbury.com
Lost Nation Rd.
40 rooms - $125
Pets: Welcome
Creature Comforts: Simple rms.
from doubles to dorms, meals
inclusive, recreation ctr w/biking,
walking, horseback riding trails,
swimming, canoeing, sailing

Inn on the Common
(800) 521-2233, (802) 586-9619
http://www.innonthecommon.com
Main St.
17 rooms - $220-270 (MAP)
Pets: Welcome w/$15 fee
Creature Comforts: Gracious
historic inn w/stunning views and
perennial gardens, elegant antique
furnishings, handmade quilts,
chintz fabrics, gourmet dining,
exceptional wine cellar, pool,
tennis court, croquet, hlth clb and
recreational facility access

DANVILLE
Indian Joe Court
(802) 684-3430
Route 2
10 cabins - $245-450/wk.
Pets: Welcome
Creature Comforts: Set on Joe's
Pond, CCTV, kit, boating, fishing

DORSET
Barrows House
(800) 639-1620, (802) 867-4455
http://www.barrowshouse.com
Route 30
28 rooms - $155-250 (MAP)
Pets: Welcome in ltd.
cottages w/$10 fee
Creature Comforts: Landmark
property w/traditional white
clapboard bldgs, 12 acres of
trees/lawns, rms. w/simple pine
furnishings, CCTV, a/c, refrig,
kit, pool, sauna, tennis courts,
lawn games, bicycles

EAST BURKE
Old Cutter Inn
(800) 295-1943, (802) 626-5152
http://pbpub.com/cutter.htm
RR 1, Box 62
10 rooms - $55-125
Pets: Always welcome
Creature Comforts: 1845 red
shingled farmhouse,
breathtaking views of valley and
distant Lake Willoughby,
excellent restaurant w/
Continental cuisine, reqst.
carriage hse suites or apt. w/
sitting rm and views, CCTV, kit,
fireplace, pool

ESSEX JUNCTION
The Wilson Inn
(800) 521-2334, (802) 879-1515
http://www.wilsoninn.com
10 Kellogg Rd.
32 suites - $94-140
Pets: Welcome w/$10 fee
Creature Comforts: Very
attractive small suite hotel, near
Burlington, CCTV, a/c, kit,
living rm, dining rm, cont.
brkfst, welcome snack, pool

FAIRLEE
Silver Maple Lodge
(800) 666-1946, (802) 333-4326
www.silvermaplelodge.com
520 Route 5, South
15 rooms - $55-85
Pets: Welcome in cottages
Creature Comforts: Antique
farmhouse/attractive 1950s
cottages, request Cottages 18 &
19, knotty pine walls, maple and
camp-style furnishings, CCTV,
a/c, kit, fireplace, cont. brkfst

GLOVER
Lakeside Haven B&B
(802) 525-3196
http://www.virtualvermont.com
RFD 2, Box 19
2 rooms - $55-65
Pets: Welcome
Creature Comforts: CCTV,
refrig, micro, grill, full brkfst

HARDWICK
Brick House
(802) 472-5512
2 Brick House Rd.
4 rooms - $60-75
Pets: Welcome
Creature Comforts: Authentic
1840's brick Victorian,
incredible herb gardens, some
antiques, eclectic furnishings,
cozy rms., English brkfst tray

ISLAND POND
Lakefront Motel
(802) 723-6507
Cross St.
22 rooms - $60-175
Pets: Small pets w/$5 fee
Creature Comforts: CCTV, a/c,
kit

JEFFERSONVILLE
Deer Run Motor Inn
(800) 354-2728, (802) 644-8866
Rte. 15
25 rooms - $45-60
Pets: Small pets w/$7 fee
Creature Comforts: CCTV, a/c,
pool

Highlander Motel/Dormitory
(800) 367-6471, (802) 644-2725
Rte. 108
12 rooms - $45-65
Pets: Welcome
Creature Comforts: CCTV, a/c,
refrig, pool

JERICHO
Homeplace B&B
(802) 899-3984
Box 96
3 rooms - $55
Pets: Welcome w/$25 deposit
Creature Comforts: Contemp.
hse on 100 acres, CCTV, farm
animals, hiking

KILLINGTON
Cascades Lodge
(800) 345-0113, (802) 422-3731
http://www.cascadeslodge.com
Killington Rd.
46 rooms - $60-175
Pets: Allowed in two rooms w/
$25 fee, summer and fall when
not busy
Creature Comforts: CCTV,
VCR, a/c, refrig, restaurant,
cont. brkfst, pool, whirlpool,
sauna

Cortina Inn
(800) 451-6108, (802) 773-3333
http://www.cortinainn.com
Route 4
97 rooms - $120-20
Pets: Welcome in first floor rms.
Creature Comforts: Full service hotel on lovely grounds, request rooms in new wing overlooking back of ppty, chintz fabrics, reproduction mahogany furnishings, CCTV, a/c, refrig, fireplace, restaurant, cont. brkfst, pool, exercise rm., whirlpool

Edelweiss Motel/Chalets
(800) 479-2863, (802) 775-5577
Route 4
40 rooms - $42-95
Pets: Welcome w/$5 fee
Creature Comforts: CCTV, a/c, refrig, pool, whirlpool, sauna

Val Roc Motel
(800) 238-8762, (802) 422-3881
http://killingtoninfo.com/valroc
Route 4
25 rooms - $50-100
Pets: Welcome w/$5 fee
Creature Comforts: CCTV, a/c, refrig, micro, kit, cont. brkfst, pool, whirlpool, tennis

Wise Vacation Rentals
(800) 642-1147
http://www.wisevacations.com
Box 231, Killington Rd.
10 houses - $2,500-4,500/wk
Pets: $250 cleaning fee
Creature Comforts: CCTV, a/c, kit, fireplace, Jacuzzi, whirlpool

LAKE WILLOUGHBY
Green Acres Cabins
(802) 525-3722
RR 2, Box 424, (Orleans)
5 cottages - $400/wk
Pets: Small pets w/fee
Creature Comforts: Overlooking Lake Willoughby, kit, grill, small beach, dock

WilloughVale Inn
(800) 594-9102, (802) 525-4123
http://www.willoughvale.com
Route 5A, (Westmore)
12 rooms - $80-200
Pets: Welcome
Creature Comforts: Historic inn overlooking spectacular Lake Willoughby, handcrafted furnishings, some antiques, request waterside cottages w/ private docks, kit, fireplaces, gourmet restaurant, dock, boating, fishing

LONDONDERRY
Frog's Leap Inn
(877) Frogs-Leap, (802) 824-3019
http://www.frogsleapinn.com
Route 100
17 rooms - $120-215
Pets: Welcome in "Tad Pool" House, $10/day
Creature Comforts: Classic Vt. country inn on 32 acres, pet-friendly cottage w/2 bedrooms, living rm, kit, nicely decorated, down comforters, hearty Vt. brkfst, evening turndown w/ Godiva chocolates and Pellegrino water, gourmet restaurant, pool, tennis, lawn games

White Pine Lodge
(802) 824-3909
Route 11
5 apts - $50-120
Pets: Well behaved pets w/$7 fee
Creature Comforts: CCTV, a/c, living rm., kit, fireplace

LUDLOW
Cavendish Pointe Hotel
(800) 438-7908, (802) 226-7688
Route 103
70 rooms - $55-82
Pets: Small pets w/$100 deposit
Creature Comforts: CCTV, a/c, refrig, Jacuzzi, restaurant, pool, whirlpool

Coombes Family Inn
(800) 822-8799, (802) 228-8799
http://www.combesfamilyinn.com
953 East Lake Rd.
11 rooms - $55-120
Pets: Welcome
Creature Comforts: 1880 farmhouse w/motel units in rural setting, CCTV, fireplace, farm animals, full brkfst

Timber Inn Motel
(802) 228-8666
Main St.
19 rooms - $45-130
Pets: Dogs welcome in summer
Creature Comforts: CCTV, a/c, kit

MANCHESTER
Avalanche Motel
(800) 592-2622, (802) 362-2622
Routes 11 and 30
23 rooms - $55-70
Pets: Welcome in ltd. rms.
Creature Comforts: CCTV, a/c, refrig, pool

Brittany Inn
(802) 362-1033
/www.thisisvermont.com/brittany
Route 7A
12 rooms - $51-72
Pets: Small pets in ltd. rms.
Creature Comforts: Very attractive small motel w/ immaculate rms, CCTV, a/c, refrig

MARLBORO
Whetstone Inn
(802) 254-2500
Route 7A
12 rooms - $55-90
Pets: Welcome w/approval
Creature Comforts: 1785 tavern in heart of Marlboro village, pond, original features include wide pine flrs/country quilts, painted antiques, collectibles, CCTV, a/c, kit, full country brkfst, cross country skiing on ppty

MENDON
Econo Lodge
(800) 992-9067, (802) 773-6644
http://www.travelbase.com
Route 4
30 rooms - $48-105
Pets: Welcome
Creature Comforts: CCTV, a/c, cont. brkfst, whirlpool, pool

Mendon Mountainview Resort
(800) 368-4311, (802) 773-4311
http://mountainview-resort.com
Route 4, East
40 rooms - $79-135
Pets: Welcome in smoking rms.
Creature Comforts: CCTV, a/c, refrig, fireplace, Jacuzzi, restaurant, pool, whirlpool, sauna

Red Clover Inn
(800) 752-0571, (802) 775-2290
http://www.redcloverinn.com
7 Woodward Rd.
12 rooms - $125-225
Pets: Welcome in carriage house
Creature Comforts: Award
winning inn, historic buildings,
sunny sitting rms. w/fireplaces,
beautifully decorated bdrms w/Vt.
quilts, antiques, gracious owners,
CCTV, a/c, refrig, fireplace,
Jacuzzi, gourmet restaurant, pool,
lawn games, skiing

MIDDLEBURY
Middlebury Inn
(800) 842-4666, (802) 388-4961
http://www.middleburyinn.com
Route 7
78 rooms - $90-280
Pets: Welcome in motel w/$6 fee
Creature Comforts: 1788 inn w/
nicely decorated modern motel
units, floral wallpapers, antique
reproductions, fine toiletries,
CCTV, a/c, restaurant, walk to
college

Sugarhouse Motel
(800) 784-2746, (802) 388-2770
Route 7
14 rooms - $69-79
Pets: Welcome in motel w/$8 fee
Creature Comforts: CCTV, a/c,
refrig, micro

NEWFANE
Four Columns Inn
(800) 787-6633, (802) 365-7713
http://www.fourcolumnsinn.com
230 West St.
15 rooms - $110-275
Pets: Well behaved dogs
welcome, cannot be left alone
Creature Comforts: 1830 Greek
Revival mansion w/lovely grnds/
gardens, inn has exposed hand-
hewn beams, beautifully decorated
rms., brass or hand-carved canopy
beds, antiques, a/c, gourmet
restaurant, fireplace, pool, stream,
hiking

NEWPORT
Top Of the Hills Motel
(800) 258-6748, (802) 334-6748
Route 105
15 rooms - $60-70
Pets: Motel rooms w/$10 fee
Creature Comforts: CCTV

NORTH HERO
Shore Acres
(802) 372-8722
http://www.shoreacres.com
Route 2
23 rooms - $80-135
Pets: Welcome w/$5-10 fee
Creature Comforts: 50-acre
lakeside setting, distant mtn views,
cheerful lakeview rms w/bead
board walls, Scandinavian
furnishings, CCTV, a/c, restaurant,
lawn games, private beach, lake
swimming, boat, sailboard, golf,
relaxed family destination

PERU
Johnny Seesaw's
(800) 424-CSAW, (802) 824-5533
http://www.jseesaw.com
16 rooms - $70-150
Pets: Selectively welcomed
Creature Comforts: Funky, fun
lodge w/great atmosphere and
food, simple country antiques,
some Waverly fabrics, cottages
utilitarian but nice, CCTV, refrig,
fireplace, restaurant, full brkfst,
pool, tennis, hiking, skiing

PITTSFIELD
Clear River Inn and Tavern
(800) 746-7916, (802) 746-7916
Route 100 North
30 rooms - $40-70
Pets: Welcome
Creature Comforts: TV, refrig,
restaurant

POULTNEY
Tower Hall B&B
(800) 894-4004, (802) 287-4040
http://www.sover.net/~towerhal
Bentley Ave.
5 rooms - $60-80
Pets: Welcome in hardwood flr.
rms w/permission, owner
concerned about allergies
Creature Comforts: CCTV, a/c,
refrig, pool, full brkfst, pool,
tennis, hiking, skiing

PROCTORSVILLE
Okemo Lantern Lodge
(802) 226-7770
Box 247
11 rooms - $80-120
Pets: Welcome w/notice
Creature Comforts: 1800's
Victorian inn, wraparound porch,
rqst front rms., Victorian
wallpapers, wicker and oak
furnishings, collectibles, CCTV,
a/c, full country brkfst

PUTNEY
Putney Inn
(800) 653-5517, (802) 387-5517
http://www.putney.net/inn
Depot Rd.
26 rooms - $68-138
Pets: Welcome w/$10 fee
Creature Comforts: 1790s
farmhouse, CCTV, VCR, a/c,
restaurant, full brkfst

QUECHEE
Quality Inn Quechee Gorge
(800) 228-5151, (802) 295-7600
http://www.qualityinn.com
Route 4
59 rooms - $60-125
Pets: Welcome in ltd. rms.
Creature Comforts: CCTV, a/c,
restaurant, pool

Queechee Lakes Rentals
(800) 745-0042, (802) 295-1970
http://www.pbpub.com/
quecheelakes
Rte. 4, The Farmhouse
3 condos - $750-1,500/wk.
Pets: Ltd. units w/$150 deposit
Creature Comforts: CCTV, a/c,
kit, fireplace, restaurant, pool

READING
Bailey's Mills B&B
(800) 639-3437
http://www.bbonline.com/vt/
baileysmills/index.html
Bailey's Mills Rd.
3 rooms - $75-135
Pets: Small polite dogs w/
approval. Small fee.
Creature Comforts: 1820 home
and barn in rural setting, paths and
ponds, traditional Vt. decor,
country quilts/antiques, fireplaced
library, afternoon tea, CCTV, a/c,
full brkfst, pool

ROCHESTER
Harvey's Mountain View
(802) 767-4273
RR 1, Box 53
1 chalet - $550/wk
Pets: Welcome in chalet
Creature Comforts: Dairy farm
on Vt. hillside w/beautiful views,
fireplace, pool, walking trails

RUTLAND
Econo Lodge Pico
(800) 55-ECONO, (802) 773-2784
http://www.econolodge.com
238 S. Main
54 rooms - $45-54
Pets: Welcome
Creature Comforts: CCTV, a/c,
kit, fireplace, restaurant, full brkfst

Green Mont Motel
(800) 774-2575, (802) 775-2575
138 North Main St.
30 rooms - $40-100
Pets: Welcome w/$5 fee
Creature Comforts: CCTV,
VCR, a/c, refrig, micro, pool

Highlander Motel
(800) 884-6069, (802) 773-6069
203 North Main St.
30 rooms - $70-100
Pets: Welcome
Creature Comforts: CCTV,
VCR, a/c, refrig, hearty cont.
brkfst, whirlpool, pool

Holiday Inn Centre of Vermont
(800) HOLIDAY, (802) 775-1911
http://www.holiday-inn.com
411 South Main St.
150 rooms - $100-200
Pets: Welcome, cannot be left
alone in room
Creature Comforts: CCTV,
VCR, a/c, refrig, micro, restaurant,
pool, exercise rm., whirlpool,
sauna

Howard Johnson
(800) I-Go-Hojo, (802) 775-4303
http://www.hojo.com
378 South Main St.
96 rooms - $60-130
Pets: Welcome w/$10 fee
Creature Comforts: CCTV, a/c,
cont. brkfst, pool, sauna

Ramada Ltd.
(800) 2-Ramada, (802) 773-3361
http://www.ramada.com
253 S. Main St.
60 rooms - $69-90
Pets: Small pets welcome
Creature Comforts: CCTV, a/c,
cont. brkfst, pool

Royal Motel
(802) 775-4348
Route 4
30 rooms - $40-95
Pets: Welcome w/$5 fee
Creature Comforts: CCTV, a/c,
refrig, kit, Jacuzzi, pool

SAXTON'S RIVER
Inn at Saxtons River
(802) 869-2110
http://www.innsaxtonsriver.com
16 rooms - $98-108
Pets: Welcome
Creature Comforts: 1900's
Victorian hotel, original features,
intimate sitting rms, Victorian
antiques and wallpapers, rqst rms
to back of hotel, restaurant/pub

Red Barn Guest House
(802) 869-2566
http://www.sover.net/~luring/
rdbrn.html
Hatfield Lane
2 apts - $75-90
Pets: Welcome
Creature Comforts: CCTV, a/c,
kit, full brkfst

ST. ALBANS
Econo Lodge
(800) 55-ECONO, (802) 524-5956
http://www.econolodge.com
287 S. Main St.
30 rooms - $55-87
Pets: Welcome
Creature Comforts: CCTV, a/c,
cont. brkfst

ST. JOHNSBURY
Aime's Motel
(802) 748-3194
http://www.virtualcities.com/
1sttravelerschoice
Route 2
16 rooms - $42-70
Pets: Welcome
Creature Comforts: CCTV, a/c

Fairbanks Inn
(802) 748-5666
32 Western Ave.
46 rooms - $70-115
Pets: Welcome w/$5 fee
Creature Comforts: CCTV, a/c,
pool, putting grn, hlth clb access

Holiday Motel
(802) 748-8192
25 Hasting St.
16 rooms - $42-70
Pets: Welcome
Creature Comforts: CCTV, a/c,
restaurant, pool

Maple Center Motel
(802) 748-2393
20 Hastings St.
34 rooms - $42-85
Pets: Small pets w/$5 fee
Creature Comforts: CCTV, a/c,
restaurant

SHAFTSBURY
Hillbrook Motel
(802) 447-7201
Route 7A
21 rooms - $40-70
Pets: Small pets welcome
Creature Comforts: CCTV, a/c,
pool

Kimberly Farms Cottage
(802) 442-4354
http://geocities.com/Yosemite/
Trails/8897/kimfarm.htm
Meyers Rd.
1 cottage - $50-75
Pets: Welcome
Creature Comforts: CCTV, cont.
brkfst

Serenity Motel
(800) 644-6490, (802) 442-6490
http://www.thisisvermont.com/
pages/serenity.html
Route 1, Box 281
8 cottages - $45-65
Pets: Welcome
Creature Comforts: CCTV, a/c,
refrig

SHELBURNE
Econo Lodge
(800) 55-ECONO, (802) 985-3377
http://www.econolodge.com
1961 Shelburne Rd.
53 rooms - $50-110
Pets: Welcome
Creature Comforts: CCTV, a/c,
restaurant, cont. brkfst

Shelburne Inn and Motel
(802) 985-3305
Route 7
53 rooms - $50-110
Pets: Welcome
Creature Comforts: CCTV, a/c,
restaurant, cont. brkfst

SHOREHAM
Indian Trail Farm
(802) 897-5292
Smith St.
3 rooms - $60
Pets: Welcome
Creature Comforts: 1830 home
on 200 acres overlooking Lake
Champlain, full brkfst, orchards,
pool

SOUTH HERO
Sandbar Motor Inn
(802) 372-6911
Route 2
37 rooms - $65-125
Pets: Welcome
Creature Comforts: CCTV, a/c,
restaurant

SOUTH WOODSTOCK
Kedron Valley Inn
(800) 836-1193, (802) 457-4469
http://www.kedronvalleyinn.com
Route 106
27 rooms - $99-261 (MAP)
Pets: Quiet dogs welcome,
leashed on ppty
Creature Comforts: Highly
recommended, antique Federal
inn, beautifully decorated rms.,
hardwood flrs, collection of
antique quilts, English fabrics,
four-poster beds, woodstoves,
fireplaces, fine dining, pond
swimming, hiking, cross-country
skiing

SPRINGFIELD
Abby Lyn Motel
(802) 886-2223
Routes 106/10
26 rooms - $49-65
Pets: Welcome
Creature Comforts: CCTV, a/c

Holiday Inn Express
(800) HOLIDAY, (802) 885-4516
http://www.holiday-inn.com
818 Charlestown Rd.
88 rooms - $75-115
Pets: Welcome
Creature Comforts: CCTV, a/c,
pool

STOWE
All Seasons Rentals
(800) 54-STOWE, (802) 253-7353
1800 Mountain Rd.
Condos/Apts/Calets - $150-1,000
Pets: Welcome in some units
Creature Comforts: CCTV, a/c,
kit, fireplace, pool, whirlpool

Andersen Lodge
(800) 253-7336, (802) 253-7336
http://www.stoweinfor.com/saa/
andersens
3430 Mountain Rd.
20 rooms - $72-120
Pets: Welcome
Creature Comforts: Tyrolean
inn, CCTV, VCR, a/c, refrig,
restaurant, pool, whirlpool, sauna,
tennis court

Burgundy Rose Motel
(800) 989-7768, (802) 253-7768
Route 11
12 rooms - $50-75
Pets: Dogs welcome w/$5 fee
Creature Comforts: CCTV, a/c,
kit, pool

Commodore's Inn
(800) 447-8693, (802) 253-7131
http://www.stoweinfo.com/saa/
commodores
Route 100
50 rooms - $88-138
Pets: Welcome w/$10 fee
Creature Comforts: CCTV, a/c,
refrig, micro, restaurant, pool,
whirlpool

Country Village Rentals
(800) 320-8777, (802) 253-8777
http://www.cvrandr.com
1003 Main St.
Antque hmes-condos - $100-1,000
Pets: Welcome in some units
Creature Comforts: CCTV, a/c,
kit, fireplace, pool, whirlpool

Evans Realty Associates
(800) 639-6084, (802) 253-4144
http://www.evansrealty
1348 Mountain Rd.
26 rooms - $125-500
Pets: Welcome in some units
Creature Comforts: CCTV, a/c,
kit, fireplace, pool, whirlpool

Green Mountain Inn
(800) 445-6629, (802) 253-7301
www.greenmountaininn.com
Main St., Box 60
72 rooms - $89-329
Pets: Well-mannered dogs
welcome in annex rms.
Creature Comforts: 1833 inn
Nat'l Historic Register inn,
Colonial-style bedrooms, canopy
beds, coordinated fabrics, recently
renovated, CCTV, a/c, excellent
restaurants, pool, hlth clb,
whirlpool, sauna

Hob Knob Inn
(800) 245-8540, (802) 253-8549
http://stoweinfo.com/saa/hobknob
2364 Mountain Rd.
20 rooms - $50-145
Pets: Welcome w/$10 fee
Creature Comforts: CCTV, a/c,
kit, fireplace, Jacuzzi, restaurant,
pool

Honeywood Country Lodge
(800) 659-6289, (802) 253-4124
http://hometown.aol.com/
honeywd/home3
4527 Mountain Rd.
14 rooms - $69-199
Pets: Welcome in ltd. rms.
Creature Comforts: Attractive
lodge w/canopy and brass beds,
Vt. quilts, CCTV, a/c, kit, micro,
pool, whirlpool

Innsbruck Inn
(800) 225-8582, (802) 253-8582
stoweinfo.com/saa/innsbruck
4361 Mountain Rd.
25 rooms - $60-170
Pets: Welcome
Creature Comforts: CCTV, VCR, a/c, micro, kit, Jacuzzi, restaurant, pool, exercise rm., whirlpool, sauna

Miguel's Stoweaway
(800) 245-1240, (802) 253-7574
http://www.miguels.com
3148 Mountain Rd.
9 rooms - $45-120
Pets: Welcome
Creature Comforts: CCTV, a/c, restaurant, full American/Mexican brkfst

Mountain Road Resort
(800) For-MTRD, (802) 253-4566
http://www.stowevtusa.com
Route 108
30 rooms - $80-395
Pets: Small "domestic companions" accepted by advance reservation with a one-time $20 cleaning fee
Creature Comforts: Mini-resort/motor lodge, well landscaped, attractive rms. w/country pine beds, French Provincial fabrics, CCTV, VCR, a/c, refrig, micro, fireplace, Jacuzzi, buffet brkfst, pool, exercise rm., sauna, whirlpool

Notch Brook
(800) 253-4882, (802) 253-4882
http://www.stoweinfo.com/saa/notchbrook
1229 Notch Brook Rd.
66 rooms/condos - $70-290
Pets: Welcome
Creature Comforts: Four-season condos, mountain views, well appointed, Scandinavian furnishings, CCTV, VCR, a/c, kit, fireplace, cont. brkfst, pool, sauna, whirlpool, tennis

Raspberry Patch
(800) 624-0639, (802) 253-4145
http://www.bizindex.com/raspberrypatch
606 Randolph Rd.
4 rooms - $50-95
Pets: Welcome
Creature Comforts: Mountain view B&B, down comforters, antiques, CCTV, a/c, cont. brkfst

Salzburg Inn
(800) 448-4554, (802) 253-8541
4441 Mountain Rd.
48 rooms - $58-98
Pets: Welcome w$10 fee
Creature Comforts: CCTV, a/c, pool, whirlpool, sauna

Stowe Country Rentals
(800) 639-1990
135 Luce Hill Rd.
100s of condos - $140-900
Pets: Welcome in some units
Creature Comforts: CCTV, a/c, kit, fireplace, pool, whirlpool

Stowe Inn at Little River
(800) 227-1108, (802) 253-4836
123 Mountain Rd.
30 condos - $150-350
Pets: Ltd. rms w/$10 fee
Creature Comforts: Riverside condos in cntr of Stowe, modern amenities, beautiful grnds, CCTV, a/c, woodstove, exc. restaurant, pool

Ten Acres Lodge
(800) 327-7357, (802) 253-7638
14 Barrows Rd.
18 rooms - $110-275
Pets: Welcome in 2 cottages
Creature Comforts: Antique inn w/fine dining, charming country cottages w/2-3 bdrms., living rm, pine flrs, oak antiques, down comforters, CCTV, kit, fireplace, full brkfst, pool

Topnotch at Stowe
(800) 451-8686, (802) 253-8585
http://www.topnotch-resort.com
4000 Mountain Rd.
110 rooms - $210-600
Pets: Well behaved dogs welcome, dog-sitting available
Creature Comforts: Fine resort and luxurious spa, beautiful landscaping, striking views, beautifully decorated rms. w/patchwork quilts, French Provincial fabrics, chocolates, CCTV, a/c, refrig, fine toiletries, restaurant, pools, hlth clb, whirlpool, sauna, tennis, croquet, walking paths

WalkAbout Creek Lodge
(800) 426-6697, (802) 253-7354
www.alkaboutcreeklodge.com
199 Edson Hill Rd.
17 rooms - $70-150
Pets: Welcome w/$10 fee
Creature Comforts: Log and fieldstone lodge, fireplace, full brkfst, restaurant, pool, whirlpool, tennis

Ye Olde England Inne
(800) 477-3771, (802) 253-7558
http://www.oldeenglandinne.com
433 Mountain Rd.
30 rooms - $120-395
Pets: Welcome
Creature Comforts: Authentic English pub, charming rms w/Laura Ashley prints, four poster beds, CCTV, a/c, kit, Jacuzzi, restaurant, pool

SWANTON
Country Essence B&B
(802) 868-4247
http://www.countryessence.com
Route 2, Box 95
2 rooms - $60
Pets: Welcome
Creature Comforts: 1850's home on 12 acres, pool

Blue Ford Motel
(802) 868-4147
Route 78
9 rooms - $51-67
Pets: Small pets w/$10 fee
Creature Comforts: CCTV, a/c, kit

TOWNSHEND
Boardman House B&B
(802) 365-4086
http://www.virtualcities.com/
~virtual/ons/vt/t/vtt3010.htm
On the Green
6 rooms - $65-85
Pets: Welcome except during foliage season, not left alone, not allowed on the furniture
Creature Comforts: 1800's farmhouse, full brkfst

UNDERHILL
Four Pause B&B
(802) 899-3927
354 Pleasant Valley Rd.
4 rooms - $55-70
Pets: Small pets w/restrictions
Creature Comforts: Small B&B on 28 acres in foothills, cont. brkfst

VERGENNES
Basin Harbor Club
(800) 622-4000, (802) 475-2311
http://www.basinharbor.com
77 cottages - $135-395 (AP)
Pets: Small, well-trained pets welcome in cottages w/$6.50 fee
Creature Comforts: Highly recommended, classic century-old inn lakeside inn, gracious family resort, charming cottages w/ hardwood flrs, fieldstone fireplace, wicker and pine furnishings, lakefront dining rm., supervised children's activities, boating, swimming, golf, tennis, pool

Whitford House
(800) 746-2704, (802) 788-2704
bbonline.com/vt/whitford
RR 2, Box 1490
5 rooms - $100-150
Pets: Welcome w/advance reservations
Creature Comforts: Beautifully restored antique farmhouse w/ sweeping mtn views, secluded, antiques, extnsv library, down comforters, request carriage house suite, full gourmet brkfst, dinner by request

WAITSFIELD
The Garrison
(800) 766-7829, (802) 496-2352
http://www.madriver.com/lodging/
garrison.html
Route 17
14 condo/motel rooms - $48-125
Pets: Welcome w/deposit
Creature Comforts: CCTV, a/c, kit, pool

Millbrook Inn and Restaurant
(802) 496-2405
http://www.millbrookinn.com
Route 17
7 rooms - $100-140 (MAP)
Pets: Welcome in specific rms, cannot leave alone in rm.
Creature Comforts: 1850's farmhouse, cozy and charming, stenciled walls, antique furnishings, quilts, gourmet country restaurant, full brkfst, skiing Mad River Glen

WARREN
Golden Lion Riverside Inn
(802) 496-3084
Route 100
35 rooms - $26-44
Pets: Welcome w/ltd. rms.
Creature Comforts: CCTV, full brkfst, whirlpool

Powderhound Resort
(802) 496-5100
http://www.powderhoundinn.com
Route 100
50 rooms - $70-120
Pets: Welcome w/$5 fee
Creature Comforts: CCTV, kit, restaurant, pool, whirlpool, tennis

Sugarbush Resort
(800) 53-SUGAR, (802) 583-3333
http://www.sugarbush.com
RR 1
300 condos - $75-1,000
Pets: Welcome in some units
Creature Comforts: CCTV, kit, fireplace, pool, whirlpool, hlth clb access

Sugarbush Village
(800) 451-4326, (802) 583-3000
http://www.Madriver.com
RR 1, Box 68-12
200 condos - $120-500
Pets: Welcome in some units
Creature Comforts: CCTV, kit, fireplace, pool, whirlpool, hlth clb access

WATERBURY
1836 Cabins
(802) 244-8533
Route 100
10 cabins - $79-99
Pets: Welcome
Creature Comforts: 200-acre setting, 1-2 bedroom modern cabins, CCTV, kit, fireplace

Holiday Inn
(800) HOLIDAY, (802) 244-7822
http://www.holiday-inn.com
Blush Hill Rd.
80 rooms - $90-150
Pets: Welcome w/$50 deposit
Creature Comforts: CCTV, a/c, refrig, micro, kit, restaurant, pool, sauna, whirlpool

Old Stagecoach Inn
(800) 262-2206, (802) 244-5056
18 N. Main St.
11 rooms - $45-130
Pets: Well-behaved dogs welcome
Creature Comforts: 1826 meeting house/stagecoach stop-turned Victorian inn, glowing hardwood floors/moldings, stained glass windows, Victorian furnishings, CCTV, a/c, kit, fireplace, tavern, full buffet brkfst

WELLS RIVER
Wells River Motel
(802) 757-2191
36 Main St.
11 rooms - $42-58
Pets: Welcome
Creature Comforts: CCTV, a/c

WEST DOVER
Snow Goose Inn
(888) 604-7964, (802) 464-3984
Box 366, Route 100
11 rooms - $42-58
Pets: Welcome w/$25 fee and
$300 refundable deposit
Creature Comforts: Fabulous
inn w/many historic features,
perennial gardens, period antique
furniture, luxurious rooms w/
featherbeds, fireplaces, Jacuzzis,
priv. decks, comp. wine/hors
d'oeuvres, gourmet brkfst,
children welcome too

WESTON
Darling Family Inn
(802) 824-3223
Route 100
7 rooms - $70-110
Pets: Welcome in cottages
Creature Comforts: 1800's inn
on rolling acreage, intimate
cottages ovrlkg pastures, country
furnishings, gingham curtains, Vt.
quilts, kit, full gourmet brkfst

WHITE RIVER JUNCTION
Best Western at the Jct.
(800) 528-1234, (802) 295-3015
http://www.bestwestern.com
Route 5, South
110 rooms - $60-130
Pets: Welcome w/$10 fee
Creature Comforts: CCTV,
VCR, a/c, refrig, micro, restaurant,
pool, hlth club

Hampton Inn
(800) Hampton, (802) 296-2800
http://www.hamptoninn.com
180 Rte.5
95 rooms - $70-110
Pets: Welcome w/$20 fee
Creature Comforts: CCTV, a/c,
pool

Holiday Inn-White River Jct.
(800) HOLIDAY, (802) 295-3000
http://www.holiday-inn.com
Holiday Inn Dr.
140 rooms - $75-125
Pets: Welcome
Creature Comforts: CCTV, a/c,
restaurant, pool, hlth club, sauna,
and a whirlpool

Hotel Coolidge
(800) 622-1124, (802) 295-3118
In the Village
33 rooms - $39-89
Pets: Welcome w/$100 deposit
Creature Comforts: CCTV, a/c

Pleasant View Motel
(802) 295-3485
65 Woodstock Rd.
16 rooms - $29-59
Pets: Welcome
Creature Comforts: CCTV

WILDER
Wilder Motel
(802) 295-9793
319 Hartford Ave.
9 rooms - $40-48
Pets: Welcome
Creature Comforts: CCTV, a/c,
refrig, pool

WILLIAMSTOWN
Autumn Crest Inn
(802) 433-6627
Clark Rd.
18 rooms - $75-125
Pets: Welcome
Creature Comforts: 1815 inn,
CCTV, a/c, full brkfst

WILLISTON
Residence Inn
(800) 331-3131, (802) 878-2001
http://www.residenceinn.com
1 Hurricane Lane
95 rooms - $105-145
Pets: Welcome w/$100 fee
Creature Comforts: CCTV, a/c,
kit, pool

WILMINGTON
Inn at Quail Run
(800) 343-7227, (802) 464-3362
http://www.bbonline.com/vt/
quailrun
106 Smith Rd.
11 rooms - $105-150
Pets: Welcome w/$15 fee, limit of
2 dogs at the inn at any time
Creature Comforts: Lovely
grnds, culinary inst. chef, country
antiques/brass beds, fireplace, full
country brkfst, pool, whirlpool,
sauna, hiking

Vintage Motel
(800) 899-9660, (802) 464-8824
195 Rte. 9 West
18 rooms - $49-89
Pets: Welcome
Creature Comforts: CCTV, a/c,
cont. brkfst, pool

WOODSTOCK
Applebutter Inn
(802) 457-4158
Route 78
6 rooms - $125-135
Pets: Well groomed small dogs in
2 rms, own bedding
Creature Comforts: 1830 home,
fine linens, down comforters, full
brkfst

Braeside Motel
(800) 303-1366, (802) 457-1366
http://vermontel.com/~braeside
Route 4, East
10 rooms - $48-88
Pets: Welcome
Creature Comforts: CCTV, a/c,
cont. brkfst, pool

Three Church Street
(800) 457-1925, (802) 457-1366
http://www.pbpub.com/vermont/
3church.htm
3 Church St.
11 rooms - $75-115
Pets: Welcome w/approval
Creature Comforts: 1830
Federal inn, informal, homey
furnishings, sitting rm. with tv/
woodstove, full brkfst, pool, tennis

Winslow House
(802) 457-1820
http://www.pbpub.com/
winslowhouse/index
38 Route 4
4 rooms - $75-115
Pets: Welcome
Creature Comforts: CCTV, a/c,
full brkfst

Virginia

ABINGDON

Comfort Inn
(800) 228-5150, (540) 676-2222
http://www.comfortinn.com
170 E. Jonesboro Rd.
82 rooms - $59-129
Pets: Small pets w/$50 deposit
Creature Comforts: CCTV, a/c, refrig, and a pool

ALEXANDRIA

Comfort Inn
(800) 228-5150, (703) 922-9200
http://www.comfortinn.com
5716 S. Van Dorn St.
187 rooms - $60-75
Pets: Small pets w/$10 fee
Creature Comforts: CCTV, a/c, refrig, pool, hlth clb access

Comfort Inn Mount Vernon
(800) 228-5150, (703) 765-9000
http://www.comfortinn.com
7212 Richmond Hwy.
92 rooms - $45-60
Pets: Small pets w/$10 fee
Creature Comforts: CCTV, a/c, kit, pool

Days Inn
(800) DAYS-INN, (703) 354-4950
http://www.daysinn.com
110 S. Bragg St.
200 rooms - $55-80
Pets: Welcome w/$6 fee
Creature Comforts: CCTV, a/c, pool

Days Inn
(800) DAYS-INN, (703) 329-0500
http://www.daysinn.com
6100 Richmond Hwy.
107 rooms - $60-70
Pets: Small pets w/$10 fee
Creature Comforts: CCTV, a/c, refrig, restaurant, pool

Doubletree Suites
(800) 424-2900, (703) 370-9600
http://www.doubletreehotels.com
100 S. Reynolds St.
225 rooms - $100-150
Pets: $10 fee, $200 deposit
Creature Comforts: CCTV, a/c, refrig, micro, restaurant, pool, hlth clb access, sun deck

Econo Lodge
(800) 55-ECONO, (703) 780-0300
http://www.econolodge.com
105 rooms - $70-80
Pets: $25 fee, $50 dep.
Creature Comforts: CCTV, VCR, a/c, kit, restaurant

Econo Lodge, Old Town
(800) 55-ECONO, (703) 836-5100
http://www.econolodge.com
700 N. Washington St.
39 rooms - $55-80
Pets: $25 fee, $50 dep.
Creature Comforts: CCTV, a/c

Executive Club Suites
(800) 535-CLUB,(703)739-CLUB
http://www.execlubdc.com
610 Bashford Lane
78 rooms - $105-155
Pets: $50 clean. fee and $250 dep.
Creature Comforts: CCTV, VCR, a/c, kit, cont. brkfst, pool, hlth club, saunas

Guest Quarters Suite Hotel
(800) 424-2900, (703) 370-9600
http://www.doubletreehotels.com
100 S. Reynolds St.
225 rooms - $110-130
Pets: Welcome w/$10 fee
Creature Comforts: CCTV, VCR, a/c, refrig, micro, kit, pool, hlth club

Holiday Inn, Old Town
(800) HOLIDAY, (703) 549-6080
http://www.holiday-inn.com
480 King St.
227 rooms - $160-170
Pets: Welcome
Creature Comforts: CCTV, a/c, refrig, Jacuzzi, restaurant, pool, hlth clb access, sauna

Holiday Inn, Eisenhower Metro
(800) HOLIDAY, (703) 960-3400
http://www.holiday-inn.com
2460 Eisenhower Ave.
202 rooms - $90-120
Pets: Welcome
Creature Comforts: CCTV, a/c, refrig, restaurant, pool, hlth clb access, sun deck

Howard Johnson Hotel
(800) 446-4656, (703) 329-1400
http://www.hojo.com
5821 Richmond Hwy.
156 rooms - $70-100
Pets: Welcome
Creature Comforts: CCTV, a/c, refrig, Jacuzzi, restaurant, pool, hlth clb access, sauna, whirlpool

Ramada Plaza Hotel, Old Town
(800) 2-Ramada, (703) 683-6000
http://www.ramada.com
258 rooms - $90-109
Pets: Welcome
Creature Comforts: CCTV, a/c, kit, restaurant, pool, hlth clb access

Ramada Plaza, Pentagon
(800) 2-Ramada, (703) 751-4510
http://www.ramada.com
4641 Kenmore Ave.
193 rooms - $70-130
Pets: Welcome w/$100 deposit
Creature Comforts: CCTV, a/c, refrig, Jacuzzi, restaurant, pool, hlth clb access, whirlpool

Red Roof Inn
(800) The Roof, (703) 960-5200
http://www.redroof.com
5975 Richmond Hwy.
115 rooms - $60-65
Pets: Small pets welcome
Creature Comforts: CCTV, a/c

Sheraton Suites
(800) 325-3535, (703) 836-4700
http://www.sheraton.com
801 N. St. Asaph St.
249 rooms - $100-175
Pets: Welcome
Creature Comforts: CCTV, a/c,
refrig, micro, restaurant, pool,
cont. brkfst, hlth clb, sun deck,
and a whirlpool

ALTAVISTA
Comfort Suites Hotel
(800) 228-5150, (804) 369-4000
http://www.comfortinn.com
1558 Main St.
65 rooms - $68-90
Pets: Welcome
Creature Comforts: CCTV,
VCR, a/c, refrig, micro, Jacuzzi,
pool, hlth clb access

AMELIA
Benita's B&B at the Grove
(804) 768-9300
www.bbonline.com/va/benita
16620 Amelia Ave.
4 rooms - $65-75
Pets: Welcome
Creature Comforts: Gracious
antebellum house, wraparound
porch, family antiques, homey
atmosphere, CCTV, a/c, fireplace,
refrig, Southern-style brkfst

APPOMATTOX
Budget Inn
(804) 352-7451
714 Confederate Blvd.
20 rooms - $40-65
Pets: Small pets welcome
Creature Comforts: CCTV, a/c,
refrig, and a pool

Super 8 Motel
(800) 800-8000, (804) 352-2339
http://www.super8.com
Rtes. 460 & 24
46 rooms - $50-65
Pets: Welcome w/permission
Creature Comforts: CCTV, a/c,
refrig, micro, cont. brkfst

ARLINGTON
Best Western Arlington
(800) 528-1234, (703) 979-4400
http://www.bestwestern.com
2480 S. Glebe Rd.
325 rooms - $60-120
Pets: Small pets w/refundable $50
deposit
Creature Comforts: CCTV, a/c,
refrig, micro, Jacuzzi, restaurant,
pool, hlth clb access

**Rosslyn-Key Bridge
Best Western Hotel**
(800) 528-1234, (703) 522-0400
http://www.bestwestern.com
1850 N. Fort Myer Drive
178 rooms - $70-170
Pets: Welcome
Creature Comforts: CCTV, a/c,
restaurant, pool, hlth clb access

Quality Hotel Courthouse Plaza
(800) 228-5150, (703) 524-4000
1200 N. Courthose Rd.
397 rooms - $75-150
Pets: Small pets w/$25 fee
Creature Comforts: CCTV,
VCR, a/c, kit, Jacuzzi, restaurant,
pool, hlth clb access, sauna

ASHLAND
Comfort Inn
(800) 228-5150, (804) 352-7451
http://www.comfortinn.com
101 Cottage Greene Drive
126 rooms - $55-75
Pets: Welcome
Creature Comforts: CCTV, a/c,
pool, hlth clb access, sauna

BASYE
Sky Chalet Country Inn
(540) 856-2147
http://www.skychalet.com
Route 263
8 cabins - $35-85
Pets: Welcome
Creature Comforts: Rustic
mountaintop retreat, fireplaces,
cont. brkfst, trails

BEDFORD
Best Western Terrace House
(800) 528-1234, (540) 783-2144
http://www.bestwestern.com
921 Blue Ridge Ave.
78 rooms - $50-75
Pets: Small pets w/$5 fee
Creature Comforts: CCTV, a/c,
refrig, restaurant, pool

BERRYVILLE
The Lost Dog B&B
(540) 955-1181
http://www.thelostdog.com
211 South Church St.
3 rooms - $55-125
Pets: Welcome w/permission
Creature Comforts: Lovely 1880
home w/many original features,
high ceilings, hardwood flrs,
charming rms. w/handmade quilts,
antiques, CCTV, a/c, Jacuzzi,
gourmet brkfst

BIG STONE GAP
Country Inn Motel
(540) 523-0374
627 Gilley Ave.
42 rooms - $35-47
Pets: Small pets welcome
Creature Comforts: CCTV, a/c,
refrig, micro

BLACKSBURG
Best Western Red Lion Inn
(800) 528-1234, (540) 552-7770
http://www.bestwestern.com
900 Plantation Rd.
104 rooms - $60-105
Pets: Small pets welcome
Creature Comforts: CCTV,
VCR, a/c, restaurant, cont. brkfst,
pool, tennis, volleyball

Comfort Inn
(800) 228-5150, (540) 951-1500
http://www.comfortinn.com
3705 S. Main St.
80 rooms - $90-100
Pets: Welcome w/$5 fee
Creature Comforts: CCTV,
VCR, a/c, refrig, Jacuzzi, pool,
hlth clb access

Donaldson Brown Resort
(540) 231-9485
200 Otey St.
125 rooms - $69-75
Pets: Welcome
Creature Comforts: CCTV, a/c,
refrig, micro, restaurant

Holiday Inn
(800) HOLIDAY, (540) 951-1330
http://www.holiday-inn.com
3503 Holiday Lane
98 rooms - $50-60
Pets: Welcome
Creature Comforts: CCTV, a/c,
restaurant, pool

Four Points Sheraton
(800) 325-3535, (540) 552-7001
http://www.sheraton.com
900 Prices Fork Rd.
148 rooms - $75-149
Pets: Welcome w/damage waiver
Creature Comforts: CCTV, a/c,
refrig, micro, restaurant, pool

BLAND
Big Walker Motel
(540) 688-3331
Route 77
20 rooms - $35-45
Pets: Welcome
Creature Comforts: CCTV, a/c

BRACEY
Days Inn
(800) DAYS-INN, (804) 689-2000
http://www.daysinn.com
2850 Hwy 903
65 rooms - $45-60
Pets: Under 10 lbs., "no snakes"
Creature Comforts: CCTV, a/c,
kit

BRISTOL
Econo Lodge
(800) 55-ECONO, (540) 466-2112
http://www.econolodge.com
912 Commonwealth Ave.
48 rooms - $45-79
Pets: Small pets w/$5 fee
Creature Comforts: CCTV, a/c,
refrig, micro

La Quinta Inn
(800) 531-5900, (540) 669-9353
http://www.laquinta.com
1014 Old Airport Rd.
123 rooms - $55-90
Pets: Small pets welcome
Creature Comforts: CCTV, a/c,
pool

Ramada Inn
(800) 2-Ramada, (540) 669-7171
http://www.ramada.com
2221 Euclid Ave.
122 rooms - $55-79
Pets: Welcome w/$10 fee
Creature Comforts: CCTV, a/c,
micro, restaurant, pool

Red Carpet Inn
(540) 669-1151
15589 Lee Hwy.
60 rooms - $40-115
Pets: Small pets welcome
Creature Comforts: CCTV, a/c,
restaurant, pool

Super 8 Motel
(800) 800-8000, (540) 466-8800
http://www.super8.com
2139 Lee Hwy.
62 rooms - $45-120
Pets: Welcome w/$10 fee
Creature Comforts: CCTV, a/c,
refrig, micro

BUCHANAN
Wattstull Inn
(540) 254-1551
Rte 614, Box 21
26 rooms - $45-65
Pets: Welcome
Creature Comforts: CCTV, a/c,
restaurant, pool

BUENA VISTA
Buena Vista Motel
(540) 261-2138
447 E. 28th St.
18 rooms - $40-69
Pets: Welcome w/$5 fee
Creature Comforts: CCTV, a/c,
restaurant

CAPE CHARLES
Days Inn
(800) DAYS-INN, (757) 331-1000
http://www.daysinn.com
29106 Lankford Hwy.
102 rooms - $50-100
Pets: Welcome w/$5 fee
Creature Comforts: CCTV, a/c,
restaurant, pool

Picket's Harbor B&B
(757) 331-2212
28288 Goffigon Lane
6 rooms - $75-129
Pets: Welcome with approval
Creature Comforts: Colonial set
on 27 acres, bay views, private
beach, CCTV, full breakfast

Sunset Beach Inn
(757) 331-4786
Rte. 13
80 rooms - $59-70
Pets: Welcome w/$10 fee
Creature Comforts: CCTV, a/c,
cont. brkfst, pool

CHANTILLY
Marriott, Dulles Airport
(800) 228-9290, (703) 471-9500
http://www.marriott.com
333 W. Service Rd.
367 rooms - $65-135
Pets: Small pets w/$50 deposit
Creature Comforts: CCTV, a/c,
refrig, restaurant, pool, hlth clb
access, sauna, whirlpool, tennis

CHARLOTTESVILLE
Best Western Cavalier Inn
(800) 528-1234, (804) 296-8111
http://www.bestwestern.com
105 Emmet St. N.
118 rooms - $60-85
Pets: Small pets welcome
Creature Comforts: CCTV, a/c,
refrig, restaurant, pool

Best Western Mount Vernon
(800) 528-1234, (804) 296-6249
http://www.bestwestern.com
1613 Emmet St.
110 rooms - $50-80
Pets: Welcome
Creature Comforts: CCTV,
VCR, a/c, kit, pool

Comfort Inn
(800) 228-5150, (804) 293-6188
http://www.comfortinn.com
1807 Emmet St.
64 rooms - $60-100
Pets: Small pets welcome
Creature Comforts: CCTV, a/c,
pool

Days Inn
(800) DAYS-INN, (804) 293-9111
http://www.daysinn.com
1600 Emmet St.
130 rooms - $55-119
Pets: Welcome
Creature Comforts: CCTV, a/c,
restaurant, pool

Econo Lodge
(800) 55-ECONO, (804) 296-2104
http://www.econolodge.com
400 Emmet St.
60 rooms - $40-70
Pets: Small pets w/$5 fee
Creature Comforts: CCTV, a/c,
pool

Econo Lodge North
(800) 55-ECONO, (804) 295-3185
http://www.econolodge.com
2014 Holiday Drive
47 rooms - $40-69
Pets: Welcome w/$20 deposit
Creature Comforts: CCTV, a/c,
refrig, micro

Holiday Inn North
(800) HOLIDAY, (804) 293-9111
http://www.holiday-inn.com
1600 Emmet St.
129 rooms - $75-98
Pets: Welcome
Creature Comforts: CCTV, a/c,
refrig, micro, restaurant, pool, hlth
clb access, sauna

Knights Inn
(800) 843-5644, (804) 793-8133
http://www.knightsinn.com
1300 Seminole Trail
115 rooms - $50-70
Pets: Welcome
Creature Comforts: CCTV,
VCR, a/c, refrig, pool

Omni Charlottesville
(800) 843-6664, (804) 971-5500
235 W. Main St.
204 rooms - $85-150
Pets: Welcome w/$100 deposit
Creature Comforts: CCTV, a/c,
refrig, micro, restaurant, pool, hlth
clb access, sauna, whirlpool, golf
privileges

Quality Inn
(800) 221-2222, (804) 971-3746
http://www.qualityinn.com
1600 Emmet St.
69 rooms - $60-70
Pets: Welcome w/$5 fee
Creature Comforts: CCTV, a/c,
refrig, pool, hlth clb access

Residence Inn by Marriott
(800) 331-3131, (804) 923-0300
http://www.residenceinn.com
1111 Millmont St.
108 rooms - $90-120
Pets: Welcome w/$150 fee
Creature Comforts: CCTV, a/c,
kit, cont. brkfst, pool, hlth clb
access, sports court

Super 8 Motel
(800) 800-8000, (804) 973-0888
http://www.super8.com
390 Greenbrier Drive
65 rooms - $55-70
Pets: Welcome
Creature Comforts: CCTV, a/c

CHESAPEAKE
Econo Lodge
(800) 55-ECONO, (804) 488-4963
http://www.econolodge.com
4725 W. Military Hwy.
53 rooms - $40-55
Pets: Welcome w/$5 fee
Creature Comforts: CCTV, a/c,
refrig, micro

Motel 6
(800) 4-MOTEL6, (757) 420-2976
http://www.motel6.com
701 Woodlake Drive
80 rooms - $45-55
Pets: Under 30 lbs. welcome
Creature Comforts: CCTV, a/c

Red Roof Inn
(800) The Roof, (757) 523-0123
http://www.redroof.com
724 Woodlake Drive
108 rooms - $45-70
Pets: Small pets welcome
Creature Comforts: CCTV, a/c,
refrig, micro

Super 8 Motel
(800) 800-8000, (757) 547-8880
http://www.super8.com
100 Red Cedar Court
62 rooms - $45-65
Pets: Welcome
Creature Comforts: CCTV, a/c,
refrig, micro, cont. brkfst

Wellesley Inn
(800) 444-8888, (757) 366-0100
http://www.wellesleyinn.com
1750 Sara Drive
106 rooms - $60-100
Pets: Welcome w/$5 fee
Creature Comforts: CCTV, a/c,
refrig, micro, pool, hlth clb access

CHESTER
Comfort Inn
(800) 228-5150, (804) 751-0000
http://www.comfortinn.com
2100 W. Hundred Rd.
123 rooms - $70-90
Pets: Small pets welcome
Creature Comforts: CCTV, a/c,
refrig, micro, Jacuzzi, restaurant,
pool, hlth clb access

Days Inn
(800) DAYS-INN, (804) 748-5871
http://www.daysinn.com
2410 W. Hundred Rd.
172 rooms - $55-95
Pets: Small pets w/$6 fee
Creature Comforts: CCTV, a/c,
kit, pool, playground

Howard Johnson
(800) I-Go-Hojo, (804) 748-6321
http://www.hojo.com
2401 W. Hundred Rd.
166 rooms - $55-95
Pets: Small pets welcome
Creature Comforts: CCTV, a/c,
refrig, restaurant, pool, hlth clb
access

Super 8 Motel
(800) 800-8000, (804) 748-0050
http://www.super8.com
2421 South Drive
45 rooms - $50-60
Pets: Welcome
Creature Comforts: CCTV, a/c,
cont. brkfst

CHRISTIANBURG
Days Inn
(800) DAYS-INN, (540) 382-0261
http://www.daysinn.com
Rtes. 460 & 11
121 rooms - $55-90
Pets: Welcome
Creature Comforts: CCTV, a/c,
pool, playground

Econo Lodge
(800) 55-ECONO, (540) 382-6161
http://www.econolodge.com
2430 Roanoke St.
68 rooms - $40-65
Pets: Small pets welcome
Creature Comforts: CCTV, a/c,
pool

Howard Johnson
(800) I-Go-Hojo, (540) 381-0150
http://www.hojo.com
100 Bristol Drive
68 rooms - $45-95
Pets: Small pets w/$3 fee
Creature Comforts: CCTV,
VCR, a/c, refrig, micro, Jacuzzi

Super 8 Motel
(800) 800-8000, (540) 382-5813
http://www.super8.com
55 Laurel St. NE
50 rooms - $50-75
Pets: Small pets welcome
Creature Comforts: CCTV, a/c,
refrig, micro

CLAYPOOL HILL
Super 8 Motel
(800) 800-8000, (540) 964-9888
http://www.super8.com
Rtes. 460 & 19
46 rooms - $55-65
Pets: Welcome
Creature Comforts: CCTV, a/c,
refrig, micro

CLIFTON FORGE
Longdale Inn
(800) 862-0386, (540) 862-0892
http://www.longdale-inn.com
6209 Longdale Furnace Rd.
11 rooms - $90-140
Pets: First floor suite and cottage
Creature Comforts: Restored 22-
rm. Victorian mansion and cottage
on 12 acres, many period features,
CCTV, a/c, fireplaces, large rooms
w/high ceilings & windows, kit,
Victorian & southwest accents,full
country brkfst and dinner, dog run

COLLINSVILLE
Dutch Inn Motel
(540) 647-3721
633 Virginia Ave.
148 rooms - $55-75
Pets: Welcome w/$5 fee
Creature Comforts: CCTV, a/c,
refrig, micro, restaurant, pool, hlth
clb access, sauna, whirlpool

Econo Lodge
(800) 55-ECONO, (540) 647-3941
http://www.econolodge.com
800 S. Virginia Ave.
47 rooms - $45-135
Pets: Small pets w/$7 fee
Creature Comforts: CCTV, a/c

Fairystone Motel
(540) 647-3716
626 Virginia Ave.
40 rooms - $45-50
Pets: Welcome
Creature Comforts: CCTV, a/c,
kit, pool

Knights Inn
(800) 843-5644, (540) 647-3716
http://www.knightsinn.com
2357 Virginia Ave.
40 rooms - $45-59
Pets: Welcome in certain rooms
Creature Comforts: CCTV, a/c,
refrig, micro, pool

COLONIAL BEACH
Days Inn
(800) DAYS-INN, (804) 224-0404
http://www.daysinn.com
30 Colonial Ave.
60 rooms - $55-89
Pets: Small pets w/$5 fee
Creature Comforts: On Potomac
River, CCTV, a/c, refrig, micro,
pool, beach

COLONIAL HEIGHTS
Days Inn
(800) DAYS-INN, (804) 224-0404
http://www.daysinn.com
2310 Indian Hill Rd.
122 rooms - $65-80
Pets: $5 fee, $5 deposit
Creature Comforts: CCTV, a/c,
cont. brkfst, pool

COVINGTON
Best Western Mountainview
(800) 528-1234, (540) 962-4951
http://www.bestwestern.com
820 E. Madison St.
79 rooms - $75-100
Pets: Welcome w/$10 fee
Creature Comforts: CCTV, a/c,
refrig, restaurant, pool

Budget Inn Motel
(540) 962-3966
Monroe Ave.
21 rooms - $35-50
Pets: Welcome w/$5 fee, $50
refundable deposit
Creature Comforts: CCTV, a/c,
refrig, micro

Comfort Inn
(800) 228-5150, (540) 962-2141
http://www.comfortinn.com
203 Interstate Drive
98 rooms - $70-80
Pets: Welcome w/$10 fee
Creature Comforts: CCTV,
VCR, a/c, refrig, pool, whirlpool

Highland Motel
(540) 962-3901
720 S. Highland Ave.
18 rooms - $38-45
Pets: Welcome w/$7 fee
Creature Comforts: CCTV, a/c,
refrig

Knights Inn
(800) 843-5644, (540) 962-7600
908 Valley Ridge Rd.
74 rooms - $60-65
Pets: Welcome w/$5 fee
Creature Comforts: CCTV, a/c,
kit

Milton Hall B&B
(877) 7-MILTON,(540) 965-0196
http://www.milton-hall.com
207 Thorny Lane
6 rooms - $95-155
Pets: Welcome w/deposit
Creature Comforts: Classic
1870's English manor house in
Alleghany Highlands, 44 acres,
terraced lawns/gardens, French
doors, large bedrooms w/sitting
areas, CCTV, fireplaces, full
English brkfst, Victorian
bedsteads, hiking, boating, and
skiing nearby

CULPEPER
Comfort Inn
(800) 228-5150, (540) 825-4900
http://www.comfortinn.com
890 Willis Lane
49 rooms - $60-85
Pets: Small pets w/$5 fee
Creature Comforts: CCTV, a/c,
kit, pool

Holiday Inn
(800) HOLIDAY, (540) 825-1253
http://www.holiday-inn.com
791 James Madison Rd.
159 rooms - $60-85
Pets: Small pets welcome
Creature Comforts: CCTV, a/c,
refrig, pool

Super 8 Motel
(800) 800-8000, (540) 825-8088
http://www.super8.com
889 Willis Lane
61 rooms - $50-69
Pets: Welcome
Creature Comforts: CCTV, a/c,
refrig, micro, cont. brkfst

DALEVILLE
Best Western Coachman
(800) 528-1234, (540) 992-1234
http://www.bestwestern.com
235 Roanoake Rd.
99 rooms - $45-90
Pets: Small pets in smking rooms
Creature Comforts: CCTV,
VCR, a/c, refrig, restaurant, pool

DANVILLE
Days Inn
(800) DAYS-INN, (804) 836-6745
http://www.daysinn.com
1390 Piney Forest Drive
46 rooms - $45-55
Pets: Small pets w/$5 fee
Creature Comforts: CCTV, a/c,
cont. brkfst

Stratford Inn
(800) 326-8455, (804) 793-2500
2500 Riverside Dr.
156 rooms - $60-165
Pets: Welcome
Creature Comforts: CCTV, a/c,
refrig, micro, Jacuzzi, full brkfst,
pool, hlth clb access, whirlpool,
sauna

Super 8 Motel
(800) 800-8000, (804) 799-5845
http://www.super8.com
2385 Riverside Drive
57 rooms - $50-65
Pets: Welcome
Creature Comforts: CCTV, a/c,
refrig, micro, cont. brkfst

DOSWELL
Best Western-Kings Quarters
(800) 528-1234, (804) 876-3321
http://www.bestwestern.com
16102 Theme Park Way
248 rooms - $30-150
Pets: Small pets welcome
Creature Comforts: CCTV,
VCR, a/c, refrig, restaurant, pool

DUMFRIES
Holiday Inn Express
(800) HOLIDAY, (703) 221-1141
http://www.holiday-inn.com
17133 Dumfries Rd.
186 rooms - $65-89
Pets: Small pets welcome
Creature Comforts: CCTV,
VCR, a/c, refrig, micro, pool, hlth
clb access

EMPORIA
Best Western Inn
(800) 528-1234, (804) 634-3200
http://www.bestwestern.com
1100 W. Atlantic Ave.
98 rooms - $55-90
Pets: Small pets welcome
Creature Comforts: CCTV,
VCR, a/c, refrig, cont. brkfst,
Jacuzzis, pool

Comfort Inn
(800) 228-5150, (804) 348-3282
http://www.comfortinn.com
1411 Skippers Rd.
96 rooms - $50-70
Pets: Welcome
Creature Comforts: CCTV, a/c,
refrig, micro, Jacuzzi, restaurant,
pool, playground

Days Inn
(800) DAYS-INN, (804) 634-9481
http://www.daysinn.com
921 W. Atlantic St.
121 rooms - $50-85
Pets: Small pets w/$5 fee
Creature Comforts: CCTV, a/c,
refrig, pool, playground

Econo Lodge
(800) 55-ECONO, (804) 535-8535
http://www.econolodge.com
3173 Susset Drive
54 rooms - $45-65
Pets: Welcome
Creature Comforts: CCTV, a/c,
refrig, micro, restaurant, cont.
brkfst, pool

Hampton Inn
(800) Hampton, (804) 634-9200
http://www.hampton-inn.com
1207 W. Atlantic St.
115 rooms - $65-75
Pets: Welcome
Creature Comforts: CCTV, a/c,
refrig, micro, pool

Holiday Inn
(800) HOLIDAY, (804) 634-4191
http://www.holiday-inn.com
311 Florida Ave.
144 rooms - $60-95
Pets: Welcome
Creature Comforts: CCTV, a/c,
pool, playground

Red Carpet Inn
(800) 251-1962, (804) 634-4181
1586 Skipper Rd.
42 rooms - $35-45
Pets: Welcome w$3
Creature Comforts: CCTV, a/c,
restaurant, pool

ETLAN
Dulaney Hollow at
Old Rag Mountain
(540) 923-4470
Route 231
7 rooms - $80-110
Pets: In 1 cabin w/$25 fee
Creature Comforts: Cabins
furnished w/primitive and
collectible antiques, set on pond,
no electricity, heated by antique
woodstove, central bath, full brkfst

FAIRFAX
Holiday Inn
(800) HOLIDAY, (703) 591-5500
http://www.holiday-inn.com
3535 Chain Bridge Rd.
127 rooms - $100-170
Pets: Under 20 lbs. welcome
Creature Comforts: CCTV, a/c,
refrig, micro, restaurant, pool

Holiday Inn Fair Oaks
(800) HOLIDAY, (703) 352-2525
http://www.holiday-inn.com
11787 Lee Jackson Hwy.
312 rooms - $80-355
Pets: Small pets welcome
Creature Comforts: CCTV,
VCR, a/c, refrig, restaurant, pool,
hlth clb access, sauna

Hyatt Fair Lakes
(800) 233-1234, (703) 818-1234
http://www.hyatt.com
12777 Fair Lakes Circle
316 rooms - $80-100
Pets: Welcome w/approval
Creature Comforts: CCTV, a/c,
refrig, restaurant, pool, hlth clb
access, sauna, whirlpool

Wellesley Inn
(800) 444-8888, (703) 359-2888
http://www.wellesleyinn.com
10327 Lee Hwy.
83 rooms - $65-80
Pets: Small pets w/$5 fee
Creature Comforts: CCTV,
VCR, a/c, refrig, micro

FALLS CHURCH
Marriott Hotel
(800) 228-9290, (703) 849-9400
http://www.marriott.com
3111 Fairview Park Drive
398 rooms - $55-175
Pets: Welcome w/approval
Creature Comforts: CCTV, a/c,
refrig, restaurant, cont. brkfst,
pool, hlth clb access, sauna,
whirlpool

FANCY GAP
Cascades Mountain Inn
(540) 728-2300
Rte. 2, Box 36
19 rooms - $45-58
Pets: Welcome w/$5 fee
Creature Comforts: CCTV, a/c,
kit, no phones, restaurant, pool,
tennis, playground, basketball

Doe Run Lodge
(800) 325-6189, (540)398-2212
http://www.doerunlodge.com
Blue Ridge Parkway, mile 189
148 rooms - $89-250
Pets: Welcome w/$25 fee
Creature Comforts: Mountain
setting, nice interiors, CCTV, a/c,
kit, restaurant, pool, saunas,
tennis, fishing, and sport shooting
access

FARMVILLE
Super 8 Motel
(800) 800-8000, (804) 392-8196
http://www.super8.com
Route 15S
42 rooms - $50-65
Pets: Welcome w/permission
Creature Comforts: CCTV, a/c,
refrig, micro, cont. brkfst

FORT HAYWOOD
Inn at Tabb's Creek Landing
(804) 725-5136
Route 14, P.O. Box 219
3 rooms - $100-135
Pets: Welcome in suite w/$20 fee
Creature Comforts: 1820's
Antebellum house on 40 acres,
extensive rose grdns, magnolia
trees, cottage suites w/water view,
full Southern brkfst, pool

FREDERICKSBURG
Best Western Inn
(800) 528-1234, (540) 371-5050
http://www.bestwestern.com
2205 William St.
107 rooms - $50-69
Pets: Small pets w/$20 deposit
Creature Comforts: CCTV, a/c,
refrig, pool

Best Western Johnny Appleseed
(800) 528-1234, (540) 373-0000
http://www.bestwestern.com
543 Warrenton Rd.
86 rooms - $50-77
Pets: Welcome w/$5 fee
Creature Comforts: CCTV, a/c,
and a pool

Best Western Thunderbird Inn
(800) 528-1234, (540) 786-7404
http://www.bestwestern.com
3000 Plank Rd.
76 rooms - $45-60
Pets: Small pets w/$20 deposit
Creature Comforts: CCTV, a/c

Days Inn - North
(800) DAYS-INN, (540) 373-5340
http://www.daysinn.com
14 Simpson Rd.
120 rooms - $30-55
Pets: Welcome w/$5 fee
Creature Comforts: CCTV, a/c,
pool, restaurant

Days Inn - South
(800) DAYS-INN, (540) 898-6800
http://www.daysinn.com
5316 Jefferson Davis Hwy.
156 rooms - $30-57
Pets: Welcome w/$5 fee
Creature Comforts: CCTV, a/c,
kit, pool

Dunning Mills Inn
(540) 373-1256
2305 Jefferson Davis Hwy.
44 rooms - $60-79
Pets: $10 fee, $50 deposit
Creature Comforts: CCTV, a/c,
kit, dining room, living room, pool

Econo Lodge South
(800) 55-ECONO, (540) 898-5440
http://www.econolodge.com
5321 Jefferson Davis Hwy.
175 rooms - $35-60
Pets: Small pets w/$5 fee
Creature Comforts: CCTV, a/c,
refrig, micro, pool

Hampton Inn
(800) Hampton, (540) 371-0330
http://www.hampton-inn.com
2310 William St.
166 rooms - $60-95
Pets: Small pets w/$10 fee
Creature Comforts: CCTV, a/c,
pool

Heritage Inn
(800) 787-7440, (540) 898-1000
5308 Jefferson Davis Hwy.
100 rooms - $39-69
Pets: Small pets w/$5 fee
Creature Comforts: CCTV, a/c,
pool

Holiday Inn - South
(800) HOLIDAY, (540) 898-1102
http://www.holiday-inn.com
5324 Jefferson Davis Hwy.
198 rooms - $60-85
Pets: Small pets welcome
Creature Comforts: CCTV,
VCR, a/c, refrig, restaurant, pool,
hlth clb access, sauna, whirlpool

Holiday Inn - North
(800) HOLIDAY, (540) 371-5550
http://www.holiday-inn.com
564 Warrenton Rd.
150 rooms - $40-75
Pets: Small pets welcome
Creature Comforts: CCTV, a/c,
refrig, micro, restaurant, pool

Howard Johnson Hotel
(800) I-Go-Hojo, (540) 898-1800
http://www.hojo.com
5327 Jefferson Davis Hwy.
133 rooms - $50-90
Pets: Small pets welcome
Creature Comforts: CCTV, a/c,
refrig, pool

Motel 6
(800) 4-MOTEL6, (540) 371-5443
http://www.motel6.com
401 Warrenton Rd.
119 rooms - $35-45
Pets: Under 30 lbs. welcome
Creature Comforts: CCTV, a/c, pool

Ramada Inn
(800) 2-Ramada, (540) 786-8361
http://www.ramada.com
Rtes 95 & 3
129 rooms - $55-70
Pets: Small pets w/$25 deposit
Creature Comforts: CCTV, a/c, refrig, micro, pool

Sheraton Inn
(800) 325-3535, (540) 786-8321
http://www.sheraton.com
2801 Plank Rd.
193 rooms - $80-99
Pets: Small pets welcome
Creature Comforts: CCTV, a/c, refrig, Jacuzzi, balcony or patio, restaurant, pool, hlth clb access, tennis

Super 8 Motel
(800) 800-8000, (540) 786-8881
http://www.super8.com
3002 Mall Court
62 rooms - $50-65
Pets: Welcome
Creature Comforts: CCTV, a/c, refrig, micro

FRONT ROYAL
Bluemont Inn
(540) 635-9447
1525 N. Shenandoah Ave.
28 rooms - $34-70
Pets: Welcome.
Creature Comforts: CCTV, a/c, refrig

Budget Inn
(540) 635-2196
1122 N. Royal Ave.
21 rooms - $25-50
Pets: Small pets w/$3 fee, $5 dep.
Creature Comforts: CCTV, a/c, refrig

Scottish Inns
(800) 251-1962, (540) 636-6168
533 S. Royal Ave.
20 rooms - $40-86
Pets: Welcome w/$4 fee
Creature Comforts: CCTV, a/c, restaurant

Super 8 Motel
(800) 800-8000, (540) 636-4888
http://www.super8.com
111 South St.
63 rooms - $45-59
Pets: Welcome w/$5 fee
Creature Comforts: CCTV, a/c, refrig

Twilite Motel
(540) 635-4148
Route 340
19 rooms - $34-115
Pets: Small pets w/$4 fee
Creature Comforts: CCTV, a/c, refrig, micro, cont. brkfst, pool

GLEN ALLEN
Amerisuites
(800) 833-1516, (804) 747-9644
http://www.amerisuites.com
4100 Cox Rd.
126 rooms - $75-125
Pets: Small pets w/$10 fee
Creature Comforts: CCTV, VCR, a/c, kit, pool, hlth clb access

Courtyard by Marriott
(800) 321-2211, (804) 346-5427
www.marriott.com/courtyard
3950 Westerre Pkwy
155 rooms - $95-125
Pets: $75 fee & $10 daily fee
Creature Comforts: CCTV, VCR, a/c, kit, pool, hlth clb

Homewood Suites
(800) Call-Home, (804) 217-8000
http://www.homewoodsuites.com
4100 Innslake Dr.
122 rooms - $120-145
Pets: Welcome w/$100fee
Creature Comforts: CCTV, VCR, a/c, kit, pool, hlth clb

Homestead Village
(888) 782-9473, (804) 747-8898
http://www.stayhsd.com
10961 W. Broad St.
140 rooms - $65-99
Pets: Under 35 lbs. w/$100 fee
Creature Comforts: CCTV, VCR, a/c, kit, hlth clb

Residence Inn by Marriott
(800) 331-3131, (804) 762-9852
http://www.residenceinn.com
3940 Westerre Pkwy.
105 rooms - $80-189
Pets: $6 fee, $100 deposit
Creature Comforts: CCTV, VCR, a/c, fireplace, kit, pool, whirlpool, playground, sports court

GORDONSVILLE
Norfields Farm B&B
(800) 754-0105, (540) 832-2952
http://bbonline.com/va/norfields
1982 James Madison Hwy.
3 rooms - $75-85
Pets: Welcome
Creature Comforts: 1850 dairy farm, bright and pretty interior, country antiques, handmade quilts, stenciled walls, CCTV, a/c, full country breakfast

Sleepy Hollow Farm B&B
(800) 215-4804, (540) 832-5555
16280 Blue Ridge Turnpike
www.sleepyhollowfarmbnb.com
6 rms - $75-145
Pets: Cottage w/$10 fee
Creature Comforts: 18th-century homestead in hollow of Blue Ridge mtns., charming cottage w/ 3 suites, antiques, canopy beds, CCTV, a/c, woodstove and fireplace, Jacuzzi, kit, gourmet brkfst, swimming pond, lawn games, farm animals

GOSHEN
The Hummingbird Inn
(800) 397-3214, (540) 997-9065
http://www.hummingbirdinn.com
30 Wood Lane
5 rooms - $75-185
Pets: Dogs w/$20 fee
Creature Comforts: 1853 Carpeter Gothic, perennial grdns, hardwood flrs, antique four-poster/ brass beds, wicker furnishings, quilts, down comforters, fireplace, Jacuzzis, a/c, full brkfst

HAMPTON
Arrow Inn
(800) 833-2520, (757) 865-0300
7 Semple Farm Rd.
58 rooms - $40-65
Pets: Welcome w/$5 fee
Creature Comforts: CCTV, a/c, kit

Days Inn
(800) DAYS-INN, (757) 826-4810
http://www.daysinn.com
1918 Coliseum Drive
144 rooms - $45-90
Pets: Small pets w/$6 fee
Creature Comforts: CCTV, a/c,
refrig, restaurant, pool

Econo Lodge Coliseum
(800) 55-ECONO, (757) 826-8970
http://www.econolodge.com
2708 W. Mercury Blvd
72 rooms - $40-60
Pets: Small pets w/$5 fee
Creature Comforts: CCTV, a/c,
refrig, micro, Jacuzzi, pool

Hampton Inn
(800) Hampton, (757) 838-8484
http://www.hampton-inn.com
1813 W. Mercury Blvd.
132 rooms - $75-95
Pets: Small pets welcome
Creature Comforts: CCTV, a/c,
refrig, pool, hlth clb access

Holiday Inn
(800) HOLIDAY, (757) 838-0200
http://www.holiday-inn.com
1815 W. Mercury Blvd.
321 rooms - $70-120
Pets: Small pets w/deposit
Creature Comforts: CCTV,
VCR, a/c, refrig, micro, Jacuzzi,
restaurant, pool, hlth clb access,
sauna, whirlpool

La Quinta Inn
(800) 531-5900, (757) 827-8680
http://www.laquinta.com
2138 W. Mercury Blvd.
129 rooms - $50-99
Pets: Welcome
Creature Comforts: CCTV, a/c,
refrig, micro, pool, hlth clb access

Quality Inn
(800) 221-2222, (757) 838-5011
http://www.qualityinn.com
1809 W. Mercury Blvd.
190 rooms - $70-110
Pets: Welcome w/$10 fee
Creature Comforts: CCTV, a/c,
refrig, micro, restaurant, pool, hlth
clb access

Red Roof Inn
(800) The Roof, (757) 838-1870
http://www.redroof.com
1925 Coliseum Drive
103 rooms - $40-67
Pets: Small pets welcome
Creature Comforts: CCTV, a/c,
refrig, micro

HARDYSVILLE
River's Rise B&B
(804) 776-7521
Route 652
1 room - $90-105
Pets: Small pets welcome
Creature Comforts: Private suite,
refrig, micro, cont. brkfst

HARRISONBURG
Comfort Inn
(800) 228-5150, (540) 433-6066
http://www.comfortinn.com
1440 E. Market St.
60 rooms - $70-99
Pets: Welcome
Creature Comforts: CCTV, a/c,
cont. brkfst, pool

Days Inn
(800) DAYS-INN, (540) 433-9353
http://www.daysinn.com
89 rooms - $45-90
Pets: Small pets w/$5 fee
Creature Comforts: CCTV, a/c,
refrig, micro, pool, hlth clb access,
whirlpool

Econo Lodge
(800) 55-ECONO, (540) 433-2576
http://www.econolodge.com
Rtes. 33 & 81
88 rooms - $40-90
Pets: Welcome
Creature Comforts: CCTV, a/c,
cont. brkfst, pool

Howard Johnson Inn
(800) I-Go-Hojo, (540) 434-6771
http://www.hojo.com
605 Port Republic Rd.
134 rooms - $50-76
Pets: Welcome
Creature Comforts: CCTV, a/c,
refrig, restaurant, pool

Motel 6
(800) 4-MOTEL6, (540) 433-6939
http://www.motel6.com
10 Linda Lane
113 rooms - $35-50
Pets: Under 30 lbs welcome
Creature Comforts: CCTV, a/c,
pool

Ramada Inn
(800) 2-Ramada, (540) 434-9981
http://www.ramada.com
1 Pleasant Valley Rd.
130 rooms - $50-90
Pets: Small pets welcome
Creature Comforts: CCTV, a/c,
refrig, pool, hlth clb access

Red Carpet Inn
(800) 251-1962, (540) 434-6704
3210 S. Main St.
161 rooms - $45-55
Pets: Welcome
Creature Comforts: CCTV, a/c,
restaurant, pool

Rockingham Motel
(540) 433-2538
4035 S. Main St.
20 rooms - $35-40
Pets: Welcome w/$3 fee
Creature Comforts: CCTV, a/c,
refrig, micro

Sheraton Inn
(800) 325-3535, (540) 433-2521
http://www.sheraton.com
1400 E. Market St.
138 rooms - $75-119
Pets: Welcome
Creature Comforts: CCTV, a/c,
restaurant, pool, sauna, whirlpool

Super 8 Motel
(800) 800-8000, (540) 433-8888
http://www.super8.com
3330 S. Main St.
50 rooms - $50-105
Pets: Small pets welcome
Creature Comforts: CCTV, a/c,
refrig, micro

Village Inn
(800) 736-7355, (540) 434-7355
Rte. 1, Box 76
37 rooms - $45-65
Pets: Welcome
Creature Comforts: CCTV,
VCR, a/c, kit, Jacuzzi, restaurant,
pool

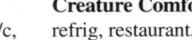

HERNDON
Hilton Hotel Airport
(800) HILTONS, (703) 478-2900
http://www.hilton.com
13869 Park Center Rd.
301 rooms - $85-150
Pets: Welcome w/$100 deposit
Creature Comforts: CCTV, a/c,
refrig, restaurant, pool, hlth clb
access, sauna, whirlpool, tennis,
racquetball

Holiday Inn Express
(800) HOLIDAY, (703) 478-9777
http://www.holiday-inn.com
485 Elden St.
115 rooms - $65-85
Pets: Under 25 Lbs. w/$25 fee
Creature Comforts: CCTV, a/c,
refrig, micro

Hilton Hotel Dulles
(800) HILTONS, (703) 478-2900
http://www.hilton.com
13869 Park Center Rd.
294 rooms - $149-249
Pets: Welcome w/$100 deposit
Creature Comforts: CCTV, a/c,
refrig, restaurant, cont. brkfst,
pool, hlth clb, sauna, whirlpool

Residence Inn by Marriott
(800) 331-3131, (703) 435-0044
http://www.residenceinn.com
315 Elden St.
168 rooms - $125-160
Pets: $6 fee, $100 deposit
Creature Comforts: CCTV,
VCR, a/c, fireplace, kit, pool,
whirlpool, playground, sports
court

Summerfield Suites Hotel
(800) 833-4353, (703) 713-6800
13700 Copper Mine Rd.
112 rooms - $160-200
Pets: Welcome w/$50-100 deposit
Creature Comforts: CCTV,
VCR, a/c, fireplace, kit, pool, hlth
clb access, whirlpool, sports court

HILLSVILLE
Doe Run Lodge
(800) 325-6189, (540) 398-2212
http://www.doerunlodge.com
Blue Ridge Parkway, milepost 189
25 chalets - $109-219
Pets: Welcome w/$25 fee
Creature Comforts: Appalachian
stone and timber lodge w/rustic
but charming cottages, kit,
fieldstone fireplace, Jacuzzi, fine
restaurant, pool, saunas, tennis

Econo Lodge
(800) 55-ECONO, (540) 728-9118
http://www.econolodge.com
Route 77
41 rooms - $55-89
Pets: Welcome
Creature Comforts: CCTV, a/c,
restaurant, cont. brkfst

Holiday Inn Express
(800) HOLIDAY, (540) 728-2120
http://www.holiday-inn.com
85 Airport Rd.
81 rooms - $60-105
Pets: Small pets w/$5 fee
Creature Comforts: CCTV, a/c,
refrig, micro, Jacuzzi, pool

HOT SPRINGS
Roseloe Motel
(540) 839-5373
590 N. Rte 220
14 rooms - $44-70
Pets: Welcome w/$5 fee
Creature Comforts: CCTV, a/c,
kit

Vine Cottage Inn
(800) 410-9755, (540) 839-2422
innsite.com/inns/A003460.html
Box 918
15 rooms - $55-90
Pets: Welcome in ltd. rms-$15 fee
Creature Comforts: 1906
Victorian, antiques, down
comforters, CCTV, VCR, parlor,
siting, room, full brkfst

INDEPENDENCE
The Farmhouse on Elk Creek
(540) 655-4413
6957 Peak Bottom Rd, Box 578
1 house - $300-350/week
Pets: Welcome
Creature Comforts: CCTV, a/c,
kit

IRVINGTON
Hope and Glory Inn
(800) 497-8228, (804) 438-6053
www.theinnmeetingplace.com
P.O. Box 425
11 rooms - $100-175
Pets: In cottages for a $15 fee
Creature Comforts: Highly
recommended, award-winning
inn, 1890 schoolhouse restored to
elegant inn, English cottage
gardens, priv. cottages w/French
doors, porches, hrdwd flrs,
country antiques, CCTV, a/c, kit,
gourmet meals, full brkfst,
swimming

The Tides Inn
(800) 843-3746, (804) 438-5000
http://www.tidesinn.com
King Carter Drive
111 rooms - $191-630
Pets: Garden House w/$10 fee
Creature Comforts: Inn w/old
world charm and sophistication,
25 acres on Rappahannock River,
gracious staff, formal atmosphere,
traditionally decorated rms, fine
amenities, CCTV, a/c, kit, Jacuzzi,
restaurants, pool, beach, marina,
playground, tennis, golf, boating,
fishing, paddleboats, sailboats,
bicycles, lawn games, game room

Tides Lodge
(800) 843-3746,(804) 438-6000
http://www.tidesinn.com
1 St. Andrews Lane
60 rooms - $130
Pets: Small pets w/$10 fee
Creature Comforts: Sister hotel
to Tides Inn, 175-acre waterfront
resort, weathered shingle main
bldng w/lodge rms, Scottish theme
w/reproduction English antiques,
CCTV, a/c, refrig, restaurant, pool,
hlth clb access, sauna, playground,
golf, tennis, boating, lawn games

KEYSVILLE
Sheldon's Motel
(804) 736-8434
Rtes 15 & 360
39 rooms - $45-59
Pets: Welcome
Creature Comforts: CCTV, a/c,
refrig, restaurant

LEESBURG

Best Western Leesburg
(800) 528-1234, (703) 777-9400
http://www.bestwestern.com
726 E. Market St.
99 rooms - $70-89
Pets: Small pets w/$25 fee
Creature Comforts: CCTV, a/c,
restaurant, hlth clb access, pool

Days Inn
(800) DAYS-INN, (703) 777-6622
http://www.daysinn.com
721 E. Market St.
81 rooms - $55-65
Pets: Welcome w/$6 fee
Creature Comforts: CCTV, a/c,
cont. brkfst

Holiday Inn
(800) HOLIDAY, (703) 771-9200
http://www.holiday-inn.com
1500 E. Market St.
125 rooms - $80-170
Pets: Welcome
Creature Comforts: CCTV, a/c,
refrig, restaurant, pool, hlth club

Laurel Brigade Inn
(703) 777-1010
20 W. Market St.
6 rooms - $40-90
Pets: Welcome in ltd. rooms
Creature Comforts: Restaurant

Norris House Inn
(800) 644-1806, (703) 777-1806
http://www.norrishouse.com
108 Loudoun St., SW
6 rooms - $100-145
Pets: Welcome w/notice
Creature Comforts: 1760 inn in
historic district, formal public
rooms overlooking award winning
gardens, bedrooms w/antique
canopy and brass beds, feather
beds, a/c, fireplaces, Stone House
Tea Room

LEXINGTON

Applewood Inn
(800) 463-1902, (540) 463-1962
http://www.applewoodbb.com
Buffalo Bend Rd.
6 rooms - $80-130
Pets: Dogs—1st flr rm. w/$20 fee
Creature Comforts: Attractive,
contemp. home set in Blue Ridge
mtns on 36 acres, solar energy,
antiques, quilts, original art, four-
poster bed, fireplace, CCTV, VCR,
Jacuzzi, full brkfst, pool, hot tub,
llama treks

Best Western at Hunt Ridge
(800) 528-1234, (540) 464-1500
http://www.bestwestern.com
Rte 7
100 rooms - $55-109
Pets: Small pets w/ CC/dep &
permission (in certain rooms)
Creature Comforts: CCTV, a/c,
restaurant, pool

Comfort Inn
(800) 228-5150, (540) 463-7311
http://www.comfortinn.com
Rtes. 64 & 11
80 rooms - $60-90
Pets: Small pets welcome
Creature Comforts: CCTV, a/c,
refrig, pool

Days Inn
(800) DAYS-INN, (540) 463-2143
http://www.daysinn.com
325 W. Midland Tr.
53 rooms - $50-75
Pets: Lrge dogs charged $5 fee
Creature Comforts: CCTV, a/c,
refrig

Econo Lodge
(800) 55-ECONO, (540) 463-7371
http://www.econolodge.com
Rtes. 11 & 64
48 rooms - $35-80
Pets: Welcome
Creature Comforts: CCTV, a/c,
cont. brkfst

Holiday Inn
(800) HOLIDAY, (540) 463-7351
http://www.holiday-inn.com
Rtes. 11 & 64
72 rooms - $65-115
Pets: Small pets welcome
Creature Comforts: CCTV, a/c

Howard Johnson Inn
(800) I-Go-Hojo, (540) 463-9181
http://www.hojo.com
Route 11
100 rooms - $45-80
Pets: Welcome
Creature Comforts: CCTV, a/c,
restaurant, pool

Lexington Lodge
(540) 463-2151
820 S. Main St.
44 rooms - $37-48
Pets: Welcome w/$10 fee
Creature Comforts: CCTV, a/c

Ramada Inn
(800) 2-Ramada, (540) 463-6666
http://www.ramada.com
Rtes. 81 & 11
80 rooms - $60-70
Pets: Welcome
Creature Comforts: CCTV, a/c,
pool

Super 8 Motel
(800) 800-8000, (540) 463-7858
http://www.super8.com
Rte. 7, Box 99
50 rooms - $50-65
Pets: Welcome w/permission
Creature Comforts: CCTV, a/c,
refrig, micro, cont. brkfst

Tom Bradshaw's Cabin
(540) 463-2521
7 N. Main Street
1 Cabin - $150-175
Pets: Welcome
Creature Comforts: A wonderful
2 bedroom cabin set on 3 acres in
the hilll, modern kit, Jacuzzi,
porches, fireplace, charcoal grill,
lawn games

The Keep B&B
(540) 463-3560
116 Lee Ave.
3 rooms - $80-110
Pets: Small pets welcome
Creature Comforts: CCTV,
VCR, full brkfst

LINCOLN
Creek Crossing Farm
(540) 338-7550, (540) 338-4548
Box 18
4 rooms - $95 -145
Pets: Welcome (horses too)
Creature Comforts: 1773
farmhouse w/wraparound porch,
shade trees, 50-acre horse farm w/
25 acres of woods, vibrant hostess,
period antiques, relaxing
atmosphere, beautifully furnished
rms, down comforters, flannel
sheets, fireplaces, full brkfst, a/c,
many repeat canine clients, black
lab in residence

LOCUST DALE
Inn at Meander Plantation
(800) 385-4936, (540) 672-4912
http://www.meander.net
HC 5, Box 460
8 rms/stes - $95-195
Pets: Welcome in three cottages
Creature Comforts: Fabulous
80-acre estate, beautiful grnds,
historic main hse and outbldngs,
Summer Kitchen filled w/
antiques, fireplac, Slave Quarters
w/fireplace, fine linens, brass
beds, armoires, full brkfst

LORTON
Comfort Inn
(800) 228-5150, (703) 643-3100
http://www.comfortinn.com
8180 Silverbrook Rd.
128 rooms - $60-129
Pets: Small pets w/$25 fee
Creature Comforts: CCTV, a/c,
refrig, micro, and a pool

LURAY
Best Western Intown of Luray
(800) 528-1234, (540) 743-6511
http://www.bestwestern.com
410 W. Main St.
40 rooms - $50-105
Pets: Under 20 lbs. w/$20 fee
Creature Comforts: CCTV, a/c,
restaurant, pool

Intown Motor Inn
(540) 743-6511
410 W. Main St.
40 rooms - $45-90
Pets: Welcome w/$10 fee
Creature Comforts: CCTV, a/c,
restaurant, pool, playground

Ramada Inn
(800) 2-Ramada, (540) 743-4521
http://www.ramada.com
Rte. 211
101 rooms - $65-105
Pets: Welcome
Creature Comforts: CCTV,
VCR, a/c, Jacuzzi, restaurant,
pool, volleyball, mini. golf,
outdoor fitness stations

Shenandoah River Inn
(540) 743-1144
201 Stagecoach Lane
3 chalets/cabins - $135-155
Pets: Welcome w/$20 fee
Creature Comforts: CCTV, a/c,
kit, fireplace, Jacuzzi, restaurant

LYNCHBURG
Comfort Inn
(800) 228-5150, (804) 847-9041
http://www.comfortinn.com
3125 Albert Lankford Drive
120 rooms - $55-90
Pets: Small pets welcome
Creature Comforts: CCTV, a/c,
refrig, micro, restaurant, pool

Holiday Inn
(800) HOLIDAY, (804) 847-4424
http://www.holiday-inn.com
3436 Odd Fellows Rd.
248 rooms - $65-80
Pets: Small pets w/$25 deposit
Creature Comforts: CCTV, a/c,
refrig, micro, restaurant, pool, hlth
clb access

Holiday Inn Select
(800) HOLIDAY, (804) 528-2500
http://www.holiday-inn.com
601 Main St.
243 rooms - $70-99
Pets: Welcome
Creature Comforts: CCTV, a/c,
refrig, micro, restaurant, pool, hlth
clb access

Howard Johnson
(800) I-Go-Hojo, (804) 845-7041
http://www.hojo.com
Route 29
70 rooms - $55-77
Pets: Welcome w/notice
Creature Comforts: CCTV, a/c,
restaurant, pool

MANASSAS
Best Western Battlefield
(800) 528-1234, (703) 361-8000
http://www.bestwestern.com
10820 Balls Ford Rd.
120 rooms - $65-89
Pets: Small pets w/$10 daily fee
Creature Comforts: CCTV, a/c,
refrig, hlth club, restaurant, pool

Red Roof Inn
(800) The Roof, (703) 335-9333
http://www.redroof.com
Route 66 & Settlee Rd.
119 rooms - $45-89
Pets: Small pets welcome
Creature Comforts: CCTV, a/c

MARION
Best Western Marion
(800) 528-1234, (540) 783-3193
http://www.bestwestern.com
1424 N. Main St.
119 rooms - $65-79
Pets: Welcome w/$10 deposit
Creature Comforts: CCTV, a/c,
refrig, micro, restaurant, cont.
brkfst, pool

Econo Lodge
(800) 55-ECONO, (540) 783-6031
http://www.econolodge.com
1426 N. Main St.
40 rooms - $45-75
Pets: Welcome
Creature Comforts: CCTV, a/c,
and refrig

Virginia House Motor Inn
(540) 783-5112
1419 N. Main St.
38 rooms - $45-65
Pets: Welcome w/$2-5 fee
Creature Comforts: CCTV, a/c,
pool

MARTINSVILLE
Best Western Inn
(800) 528-1234, (540) 632-5611
http://www.bestwestern.com
Route 220 N (business)
97 rooms - $50-78
Pets: Welcome
Creature Comforts: CCTV, a/c,
refrig, micro, restaurant, pool, hlth
clb access

Super 8 Motel
(800) 800-8000, (540) 666-8888
http://www.super8.com
960 N. Memorial Blvd.
54 rooms - $45-59
Pets: Welcome
Creature Comforts: CCTV, a/c,
refrig, micro

MAX MEADOWS
Gateway Motel
(540) 637-3119
Rte. 3, Box 488
10 rooms - $38-50
Pets: Small dogs in smoking rms.
Creature Comforts: CCTV, a/c

MCLEAN
Best Western Tysons Westpark
(800) 528-1234, (703) 734-2800
http://www.bestwestern.com
8401 Westpark Drive
301 rooms - $70-130
Pets: Welcome w/$8 fee
Creature Comforts: CCTV, a/c,
refrig, restaurant, pool, hlth clb
access, sauna, whirlpool

MEADOWS OF DAN
Woodberry Inn
(540) 593-2567
Milepost 908, Blue Ridge Pkwy.
16 rooms - $65-79
Pets: Well trained, non-shedding
Creature Comforts: TV,
restaurant

MELFA
Captain's Quarters Motel
(757) 787-4545
Rte. 13, Box D
22 rooms - $55-69
Pets: Welcome
Creature Comforts: CCTV, a/c,
kit, restaurant

MILLBORO
Douthat State Park
(800) 933-7275, (540) 862-8100
Rte. 1, Box 212
30 cabins - $40-65
Pets: Welcome in cabins w/$5 fee
Creature Comforts: Fireplace,
kit

MOUNT JACKSON
Best Western Inn
(800) 528-1234, (540) 477-2911
http://www.bestwestern.com
250 Conickville Blvd
98 rooms - $60-85
Pets: Welcome
Creature Comforts: CCTV, a/c,
restaurant, pool, sport crt, tennis

Widow Kip's Country Inn
(800) 478-8714, (540) 477-2400
http://www.widowkips.com
355 Orchard Drive
7 rooms - $85-100
Pets: Welcome in two cottages
Creature Comforts: Restored
1830 Colonial home, two cottages
set around pretty courtyard,
English country décor, wicker,
floral fabrics, CCTV, VCR, a/c,
kit, gourmet brkfst, pool, bicycles,
hiking

NASSAWADOX
Anchor Motel
(757) 442-6363
7120 Lankford Hwy.
41 rooms - $45-69
Pets: Welcome w/$10 deposit
Creature Comforts: CCTV, a/c,
kit

NATURAL BRIDGE
Budget Inn
(540) 291-2896
4331 S. Lee Hwy.
21 rooms - $30-70
Pets: Small pets w/$5 fee
Creature Comforts: CCTV, a/c,
refrig

Fancy Hill Motel
(540) 291-2143
Rte. 11, Box 590
15 rooms - $30-68
Pets: Small pets welcome
Creature Comforts: CCTV, a/c

Natural Bridge Hotel
(800) 533-1410, (540) 291-2121
http://www.naturalbridgeva.com
Rte 11, Box 57
30 cottages - $59-89
Pets: Welcome in cottages-$5 fee
Creature Comforts: CCTV, a/c,
restaurant, cont. brkfst, pool

Wattsull Inn
(540) 254-1551
Blue Ridge Parkway, Exit Rte 43
26 rooms - $48-60
Pets: Welcome w/$2 fee
Creature Comforts: CCTV, a/c,
restaurant, pool

NELLYSFORD
Acorn Inn
(804) 361-9357
http://www.acorninn.com
P.O. Box 431
10 rooms/1 cottage - $40-95
Pets: Welcome in cottage-$10 fee
Creature Comforts: European
B&B, cottage w/CCTV, a/c, kit,
cont. brkfst

NEW CHURCH
Garden and the Sea
(800) 824-0672, (757) 824-0672
http://www.gardenandseainn.com
4188 Nelson Rd.
6 rooms - $60-165
Pets: Welcome w/$50 deposit
Creature Comforts: 1802
Victorian home and 1870's
farmhouse, hrdwd flrs, Victorian
antiques, canopied beds, armoires,
a/c, refrig, Jacuzzi, intimate
restaurant, hearty cont. brkfst

NEW MARKET
Budget Inn
(800) 296-6835, (540) 740-3105
2192 Old Valley Pike
14 rooms - $30-65
Pets: Welcome w/$4 fee, $5 dep
Creature Comforts: CCTV, a/c,
refrig, playground

Days Inn
(800) DAYS-INN, (540) 740-4100
http://www.daysinn.com
9360 George Collins Parkway
85 rooms - $45-70
Pets: Welcome
Creature Comforts: CCTV, a/c,
restaurant, pool

NEWPORT NEWS
Comfort Inn
(800) 228-5150, (757) 249-0200
http://www.comfortinn.com
12330 Jefferson Ave.
124 rooms - $70-89
Pets: Welcome
Creature Comforts: CCTV,
VCR, a/c, refrig, micro, pool, hlth
clb access

Days Inn
(800) DAYS-INN, (757) 874-0201
http://www.daysinn.com
14747 Warwick Blvd.
117 rooms - $40-69
Pets: Welcome w/$5 fee
Creature Comforts: CCTV, a/c,
kit, pool

Host Inn
(800) 747-3303, (757) 599-3303
985 J. Clyde Morris Blvd.
50 rooms - $45-50
Pets: Welcome w/$5 fee, $15 dep.
Creature Comforts: CCTV,
VCR, a/c, refrig, micro, pool

Motel 6
(800) 4-MOTEL6, (757) 595-6336
http://www.motel6.com
797 J. Clyde Morris Blvd.
117 rooms - $35-49
Pets: Under 30 lbs. welcome
Creature Comforts: CCTV, a/c

Newport News Inn
(757) 826-4500
6128 Jefferson Ave.
160 rooms - $50-69
Pets: Under 50 lbs. w/permission
Creature Comforts: CCTV, a/c,
refrig, pool

Ramada Inn
(800) 2-Ramada, (757) 599-4460
http://www.ramada.com
950 J. Clyde Morris Blvd
219 rooms - $55-105
Pets: Small pets w/$150 deposit
Creature Comforts: CCTV, a/c,
refrig, micro, Jacuzzi, restaurant,
pool, hlth clb access

Super 8 Motel
(800) 800-8000, (757) 595-8888
http://www.super8.com
945 J. Clyde Morris Blvd.
61 rooms - $50-69
Pets: Welcome
Creature Comforts: CCTV, a/c,
refrig, micro, cont. brkfst

Travelodge
(800) 578-7878, (757) 826-4500
http://www.travelodge.com
6128 Jefferson Ave.
162 rooms - $55-77
Pets: Welcome
Creature Comforts: CCTV, a/c,
refrig, micro, restaurant, pool

TDY Suites
(800) 282-8849, (757) 888-6667
15910 Warwick Blvd.
48 suites - $55-75
Pets: Welcome w/$50 fee
Creature Comforts: CCTV, a/c,
kit

NORFOLK
Comfort Inn Town Point
(800) 228-5150, (757) 623-5700
http://www.comfortinn.com
930 Virginia Beach Blvd.
168 rooms - $80-109
Pets: Small pets welcome
Creature Comforts: CCTV, a/c,
kit, pool

Days Inn, Marina
(800) DAYS-INN, (757) 583-4521
http://www.daysinn.com
1631 Bayville St.
117 rooms - $55-65
Pets: Welcome
Creature Comforts: On
Chesapeake Bay, CCTV, a/c,
refrig, micro, pool

Days Inn Military Circle
(800) DAYS-INN, (757) 461-0100
http://www.daysinn.com
5701 Chambers St.
161 rooms - $48-87
Pets: Welcome w/$6 fee
Creature Comforts: CCTV, a/c,
restaurant, pool

Econo Lodge Military Circle
(800) 55-ECONO, (757) 461-4865
http://www.econolodge.com
865 N. Military Hwy.
73 rooms - $60-75
Pets: Small pets w/$5 fee
Creature Comforts: CCTV, a/c

Econo Lodge West Ocean View
(800) 55-ECONO, (757) 480-9611
http://www.econolodge.com
9601 Fourth View St.
71 rooms - $50-74
Pets: Welcome w/$50 deposit
Creature Comforts: CCTV, a/c,
kit

Motel 6
(800) 4-MOTEL6, (757) 461-2380
http://www.motel6.com
853 N. Military Hwy.
151 rooms - $35-48
Pets: Under 30 lbs. welcome
Creature Comforts: CCTV, a/c,
pool

Norfolk Waterside Marriott
(800) 228-9290, (757) 627-4200
http://www.marriott.com
235 E. Main St.
405 rooms - $120-140
Pets: Welcome w/$35 fee
Creature Comforts: CCTV,
VCR, a/c, refrig, restaurant, pool,
hlth clb access, sauna, whirlpool

Sheraton Waterside Hotel
(800) 325-3535, (757) 622-6664
http://www.sheraton.com
777 Waterside Drive
446 rooms - $90-225
Pets: Welcome
Creature Comforts: CCTV, a/c,
refrig, micro, restaurant, cont.
brkfst, pool, hlth clb access

Quality Inn
(800) 228-5151, (757) 461-6251
http://www.qualityinn.com
6280 Northampton Blvd.
304 rooms - $70-160
Pets: Welcome w/$25 fee
Creature Comforts: CCTV, a/c,
kit, restaurant, pool, tennis, golf

Ramada Inn Madison Hotel
(800) 2-Ramada, (757) 622-6682
http://www.ramada.com
345 Granby St.
124 rooms - $70-150
Pets: Welcome w/mngr's approval
Creature Comforts: CCTV, a/c,
restaurant

NORTON
Holiday Inn
(800) HOLIDAY, (540) 679-7000
http://www.holiday-inn.com
551 Rte 58
122 rooms - $80-100
Pets: Small pets welcome
Creature Comforts: CCTV, a/c,
refrig, restaurant, pool

Super 8 Motel
(800) 800-8000, (540) 679-0893
http://www.super8.com
425 Wharton Lane
58 rooms - $50-65
Pets: Welcome w/permission
Creature Comforts: CCTV, a/c,
refrig, micro

ONLEY
Anchor Motel
(757) 787-8000
25597 Coastal Blvd.
36 rooms - $45-64
Pets: Welcome
Creature Comforts: CCTV, a/c,
kit

ORANGE
Willow Grove Inn
(800) 949-1778, (757) 672-5982
http://www.willowgroveinn.com
14079 Plantation Way
5 cottages - $275-330 (MAP)
Pets: Welcome in cottages
Creature Comforts: Historic
southern manor house on 37 acres,
great cottages, wide pine floors,
elaborate moldings, American and
English antiques, four-poster and
brass beds, down comforters,
hearty brkfst, fabulous Sunday
brunch, CCTV, lawn games

PENDRAGONDALE
Canterbury Cottage
(540) 364-3970
http://www.thatching.com
bbcottage.htm
12055 Crest Hill Rd.
3 rooms - $90-110
Pets: Welcome, 4 Russian
wolfhounds, English Spaniel in
residence
Creature Comforts: Enchanting
and authentic thatched-roof
cottage on 20 acres, comforters
made from her sheep's wool,
antiques, CCTV, a/c, fireplaces,
down comforters, Jacuzzi, pool,
full brkfst, pool, animal menagerie

PETERSBURG
American Inn
(804) 733-2800
2209 County Drive
113 rooms - $37-49
Pets: Welcome w/$35 fee
Creature Comforts: CCTV, a/c,
kit, pool

Best Western Inn
(800) 528-1234, (804) 733-1776
http://www.bestwestern.com
405 E. Washington St.
124 rooms - $50-117
Pets: Small pets w/$5 fee
Creature Comforts: CCTV, a/c,
refrig, micro, Jacuzzi, restaurant,
pool, hlth clb access

Comfort Inn
(800) 228-5150, (804) 732-2900
http://www.comfortinn.com
11974 Crater Rd.
96 rooms - $40-86
Pets: Welcome
Creature Comforts: CCTV, a/c,
kit, Jacuzzi, pool

Days Inn
(800) DAYS-INN, (804) 733-4400
http://www.daysinn.com
12208 Crater Rd.
154 rooms - $45-75
Pets: Welcome w/$5 fee
Creature Comforts: CCTV, a/c,
kit, restaurant, pool, hlth clb
access

Econo Lodge South
(800) 55-ECONO, (804) 862-2717
http://www.econolodge.com
16905 Parkdale Rd.
90 rooms - $35-49
Pets: Welcome w$5 fee
Creature Comforts: CCTV, a/c,
cont. brkfst, pool

High Street Inn
(888) 733-0505, (804) 733-0505
http://www.highstreetinn.com
405 High St.
5 rooms - $75-115
Pets: Small pets w/$10 nightly fee
Creature Comforts: 1895 Queen
Anne Victorian, original fixtures,
hardwood flrs, orig. woodwork,
fireplaces, large rooms, beautiful
gardens, lawn games, full brkfst

Quality Inn
(800) 228-5151, (804) 733-0600
http://www.qualityinn.com
12205 S. Crater Rd.
139 rooms - $40-75
Pets: Welcome w/$5 fee
Creature Comforts: CCTV, a/c,
refrig, micro, restaurant, pool, hlth
clb access, playground, putting
green, tennis

Ramada Inn
(800) 2-Ramada, (804) 733-0730
http://www.ramada.com
501 E. Washington St.
214 rooms - $50-75
Pets: Small pets welcome
Creature Comforts: CCTV, a/c,
refrig, micro, restaurant, pool, hlth
clb access

Travelodge - North
(800) 578-7878, (804) 733-0000
http://www.travelodge.com
380 E. Washington St.
200 rooms - $45-70
Pets: Welcome
Creature Comforts: CCTV, a/c,
refrig, micro, restaurant, pool

PORTSMOUTH
Holiday Inn Waterfront
(800) HOLIDAY, (757) 393-2573
http://www.holiday-inn.com
8 Crawford Parkway
270 rooms - $90-125
Pets: Welcome
Creature Comforts: Marina
setting, CCTV, a/c, refrig,
restaurant, pool, hlth clb access

PULASKI
Red Carpet Inn
(800) 251-1962, (540) 980-2230
I-81, Exit 94
60 rooms - $50-60
Pets: Welcome w/$5 fee
Creature Comforts: CCTV, a/c

RADFORD
Best Western Inn
(800) 528-1234, (540) 639-3000
http://www.bestwestern.com
1501 Tyler Ave.
72 rooms - $55-89
Pets: Small pets welcome
Creature Comforts: CCTV,
VCR, a/c, refrig, restaurant, pool,
sauna, whirlpool

Comfort Inn
(800) 228-5150, (540) 639-4800
http://www.comfortinn.com
1501 Tyler Ave.
34 rooms - $60-89
Pets: Small pets welcome
Creature Comforts: CCTV, a/c,
refrig, cont. brkfst, Jacuzzi, pool

Dogwood Lodge
(540) 639-9338
7073 Lee Hwy.
15 rooms - $35-40
Pets: Welcome
Creature Comforts: CCTV, a/c

Super 8 Motel
(800) 800-8000, (540) 731-9355
http://www.super8.com
1600 Tyler Ave.
58 rooms - $50-65
Pets: Welcome w/permission
Creature Comforts: CCTV, a/c,
refrig, micro, cont. brkfst

RAPHINE
Days Inn
(800) DAYS-INN, (540) 377-2604
http://www.daysinn.com
West Service Rd.
86 rooms - $40-70
Pets: Welcome
Creature Comforts: CCTV,
VCR, a/c, restaurant, pool

REEDVILLE
Morris House
(804) 453-7016
http://eaglesnest.net/morrishouse
Main St.
5 rooms - $80-150
Pets: Welcome-Waterside Cottage
Creature Comforts: Fabulous
1895 Queen Anne Victorian, all
period details intact, wraparound
porches, waterviews, antiques,
sophisticated decor, four-poster or
canopy beds, quilts, CCTV, a/c,
kit, Jacuzzis or claw foot tubs,
gourmet brkfst, rqst Turret Suite

RICHMOND
Amerisuites Arboretum
(800) 833-1516, (804) 222-4200
http://www.amerisuites.com
201 Arboretum Place
128 rooms - $60-125
Pets: Under 10 Lbs. welcome
Creature Comforts: CCTV,
VCR, a/c, refrig, pool, hlth clb

Days Inn
(800) DAYS-INN, (804) 353-1287
http://www.daysinn.com
1600 Robin Hood Rd.
99 rooms - $40-70
Pets: Small pets w/$3 fee
Creature Comforts: CCTV, a/c,
restaurant, pool

Days Inn West Broad
(800) DAYS-INN, (804) 282-3300
http://www.daysinn.com
2100 Dickens Rd.
179 rooms - $55-85
Pets: Small pets w/$6 fee
Creature Comforts: CCTV, a/c,
refrig, pool, hlth clb access

Econo Lodge Midlothian
(800) 55-ECONO, (804) 276-8241
http://www.econolodge.com
71 rooms - $35-50
Pets: Welcome w/$5 fee
Creature Comforts: CCTV, a/c,
refrig, micro

Holiday Inn Airport
(800) HOLIDAY, (804) 222-6450
http://www.holiday-inn.com
5203 Williamsburg Rd.
230 rooms - $80-85
Pets: Welcome
Creature Comforts: CCTV, a/c,
refrig, micro, restaurant, pool

Holiday Inn Bells Rd.
(800) HOLIDAY, (804) 275-7891
http://www.holiday-inn.com
4303 Commerce Rd.
166 rooms - $80-95
Pets: Small pets welcome
Creature Comforts: CCTV, a/c,
refrig, micro, restaurant, pool,
playground

Holiday Inn Central
(800) HOLIDAY, (804) 359-9441
http://www.holiday-inn.com
3207 N. Blvd.
184 rooms - $75-95
Pets: Small pets welcome
Creature Comforts: CCTV, a/c,
refrig, micro, restaurant, pool, hlth
clb access

Holiday Inn Crossroads
(800) HOLIDAY, (804) 359-6061
http://www.holiday-inn.com
2000 Staples Mill Rd.
147 rooms - $60-65
Pets: Small pets welcome
Creature Comforts: CCTV, a/c,
refrig, restaurant, pool, hlth clb
access

The Jefferson Hotel
(800) 424-8014, (804) 788-8000
http://www.jefferson-hotel.com
Franklin and Adams Sts.
274 rooms - $120-465
Pets: Welcome w/$25 fee
Creature Comforts: A five-star
national historic landmark hotel
that dates back to 1895, gracious
southern hospitality, traditional
decor, lovely setting, CCTV, VCR,
a/c, refrig, micro, Jacuzzis, pool,
hlth clb, whirlpool

La Quinta Inn
(800) 531-5900, (804) 745-7100
http://www.laquinta.com
6910 Midlothian Turnpike
130 rooms - $55-90
Pets: Welcome
Creature Comforts: CCTV, a/c,
refrig, micro, restaurant, pool

Ramada Ltd.
(800) 2-Ramada, (804) 266-7603
http://www.ramada.com
5221 Brook Rd.
118 rooms - $53-79
Pets: Welcome w/$5 fee
Creature Comforts: CCTV, a/c,
refrig, restaurant, cont. brkfst, pool

Ramada Inn, South
(800) 2-Ramada, (804) 271-1281
http://www.ramada.com
2126 Willis Rd.
98 rooms - $65-75
Pets: Welcome
Creature Comforts: CCTV, a/c,
refrig, micro, restaurant, pool

Ramada Inn, West
(800) 2-Ramada, (804) 285-9061
http://www.ramada.com
1500 E. Ridge Rd.
87 rooms - $50-69
Pets: Small pets welcome
Creature Comforts: CCTV, a/c,
refrig, micro, pool, hlth clb access

Red Roof Inn
(800) The Roof, (804) 745-0600
http://www.redroof.com
100 Greshamwood Place
81 rooms - $40-76
Pets: Small pets welcome
Creature Comforts: CCTV, a/c

Red Roof Inn South
(800) The Roof, (804) 271-7240
http://www.redroof.com
4350 Commerce Rd.
108 rooms - $40-65
Pets: Small pets welcome
Creature Comforts: CCTV, a/c,
refrig, micro

Residence Inn by Marriott
(800) 228-9290, (804) 285-8200
http://www.residenceinn.com
2121 Dickens Rd.
80 rooms - $130-169
Pets: Welcome w/$50 fee
Creature Comforts: CCTV,
VCR, a/c, refrig, micro, pool, hlth
clb access, whirlpool, sports court

Sheraton Airport Inn
(800) 325-3535, (804) 226-4300
http://www.sheraton.com
4700 S. Laburnum Ave.
151 rooms - $110-125
Pets: Small pets welcome
Creature Comforts: CCTV, a/c,
refrig, Jacuzzi, restaurant, pool,
hlth clb access, sauna, whirlpool

Super 8 Motel, Airport
(800) 800-8000, (804) 222-8008
http://www.super8.com
5110 Williamsburg Rd.
51 rooms - $55-68
Pets: Welcome w/permission
Creature Comforts: CCTV, a/c,
refrig, micro

Super 8 Chamberlayne
(800) 800-8000, (804) 262-8880
http://www.super8.com
5615 Chamberlayne Rd.
61 rooms - $55-65
Pets: Welcome w/permission
Creature Comforts: CCTV, a/c,
cont. brkfst

Super 8 Midlothian
(800) 800-8000, (804) 320-2823
http://www.super8.com
8260 Midlothian Turnpike
73 rooms - $50-65
Pets: Welcome w/permission
Creature Comforts: CCTV, a/c,
refrig, micro, cont. brkfst

Super 8 Motel
(800) 800-8000, (804) 672-8128
http://www.super8.com
7200 W. Broad St.
49 rooms - $55-65
Pets: Welcome w/permission
Creature Comforts: CCTV, a/c,
refrig, micro, restaurant, cont.
brkfst

RINER
River's Edge
(888) 786-9418, (540) 381-4147
http://www.river-edge.com
6208 Little Camp Rd.
4 rooms - $140-160
Pets: Welcome in the Orchard
Room w/$10 fee, must sign pet
waiver
Creature Comforts: Contemp.
yet traditional home w/oversized
windows overlooking orchards
and river, hardwood flrs, sophis.
decor, four-poster beds, down
comforters, CCTV, a/c, fireplace,
gourmet brkfst, dinner, canoeing,
hiking, bicycles

ROANOKE
Amerisuites
(800) 833-1516, (540) 366-4700
http://www.amerisuites.com
5040 Valley View Blvd.
128 rooms - $89-109
Pets: Under 10 lbs. w/$30 fee
Creature Comforts: CCTV,
VCR, a/c, refrig, micro, cont.
brkfst, pool, hlth club

Clarion Hotel Roanoke Airport
(800) CLARION, (540) 362-4500
http://www.clarioninn.com
2727 Ferndale Drive
154 rooms - $65-109
Pets: Small pets w/$50 deposit
Creature Comforts: CCTV, a/c,
refrig, micro, restaurant, pool, hlth
clb access, whirlpool, tennis,
volleyball

Comfort Inn, Airport
(800) 228-5150, (540) 563-0229
http://www.comfortinn.com
3695 Thirlane Rd.
138 rooms - $45-59
Pets: Welcome w/$15 fee
Creature Comforts: CCTV, a/c,
refrig, restaurant, cont. brkfst,
pool, whirlpool

Days Inn
(800) DAYS-INN, (540) 342-4551
http://www.daysinn.com
535 Orange Ave.
165 rooms - $60-109
Pets: Welcome
Creature Comforts: CCTV, a/c,
refrig, micro, Jacuzzi, pool, tennis

Holiday Inn Tanglewood
(800) HOLIDAY, (540) 774-4400
http://www.holiday-inn.com
4468 Starkey Rd.
196 rooms - $70-135
Pets: Welcome w/$10 fee
Creature Comforts: CCTV, a/c,
restaurant, cont. brkfst, pool, hlth
clb access

Howard Johnson Express
(800) I-Go-Hojo, (540) 344-0981
http://www.hojo.com
320 Kimball Ave.
60 rooms - $48-120
Pets: Small pets welcome
Creature Comforts: CCTV, a/c,
refrig, micro, balcony, restaurant,
cont. brkfst, pool

Marriott Hotel
(800) 228-9290, (540) 563-9300
http://www.marriott.com
2801 Hershberger Rd.
320 rooms - $80-145
Pets: Small pets w/$10 fee
Creature Comforts: CCTV, a/c,
restaurant, pool, hlth clb access,
sauna, whirlpool, tennis

Ramada Inn Rivers Edge
(800) 2-Ramada, (540) 343-0121
http://www.ramada.com
1927 Franklin Rd.
125 rooms - $45-85
Pets: Welcome
Creature Comforts: CCTV, a/c,
restaurant, pool, hlth clb access

Rodeway Inn
(800) 228-2000, (540) 981-9341
http://www.rodeway.com
526 Orange Ave.
102 rooms - $40-50
Pets: Welcome w/$10 fee
Creature Comforts: CCTV, a/c,
restaurant, cont. brkfst

Super 8 Motel
(800) 800-8000, (540) 563-8888
http://www.super8.com
6616 Thirlane Rd.
61 rooms - $50-65
Pets: Welcome w/permission
Creature Comforts: CCTV, a/c,
refrig, micro, cont. brkfst

ROCKY MOUNT
Franklin Motel
(800) 775-3506, (540) 483-9962
Route 220
22 rooms - $30-55
Pets: $10 deposit, $5 fee
Creature Comforts: CCTV, a/c,
refrig, and a Jacuzzi

RUTHER GLEN
Days Inn
(800) DAYS-INN, (804) 448-2011
http://www.daysinn.com
24320 Rogers Clark Blvd.
124 rooms - $50-109
Pets: Welcome
Creature Comforts: CCTV, a/c,
refrig, restaurant, pool

SALEM
Baymont Inns
(800) 4-Budget, (540) 562-2717
http://baymontinns.com
140 Sheraton Drive
114 rooms - $55-95
Pets: Welcome in smkng rms.
Creature Comforts: CCTV, a/c,
refrig, micro, restaurant, pool

Budget Host Inn
(800) Bud-Host, (540) 380-2080
http://www.budhost.com
5399 West Main St.
14 rooms - $30-70
Pets: Welcome w/$5 fee
Creature Comforts: CCTV, a/c,
kit, pool

Holiday Inn
(800) HOLIDAY, (540) 389-7061
http://www.holiday-inn.com
1671 Skyview Rd.
102 rooms - $50-95
Pets: Small pets welcome
Creature Comforts: CCTV, a/c,
restaurant, pool

Knights Inn
(800) 843-5644, (540) 389-0280
http://www.knightsinn.com
3801 Wildwood Rd.
66 rooms - $45-57
Pets: Welcome
Creature Comforts: CCTV, a/c,
refrig, micro

Quality Inn
(800) 228-5151, (540) 562-1912
http://www.qualityinn.com
179 Sheraton Drive
120 rooms - $55-76
Pets: Small pets w/$5 fee
Creature Comforts: CCTV,
VCR, a/c, refrig, micro, restaurant,
pool, hlth clb access

Super 8 Motel
(800) 800-8000, (540) 389-0297
http://www.super8.com
300 Wildwood Rd.
62 rooms - $35-49
Pets: Small pets welcome
Creature Comforts: CCTV, a/c,
refrig, micro

SANDSTON
Best Western Airport Inn
(800) 528-1234, (804) 222-2780
http://www.bestwestern.com
5700 Williamsburg Rd.
122 rooms - $45-55
Pets: Welcome w/$25 deposit
Creature Comforts: CCTV, a/c,
pool

Days Inn Airport
(800) DAYS-INN, (804) 222-2041
http://www.daysinn.com
5500 Williamsburg Rd.
100 rooms - $45-90
Pets: Small pets w/$6 fee
Creature Comforts: CCTV, a/c,
refrig, restaurant, pool

Econo Lodge Airport
(800) 55-ECONO, (804) 222-1020
http://www.econolodge.com
5408 Williamsburg Rd.
53 rooms - $45-90
Pets: Small pets w/$5 fee
Creature Comforts: CCTV, a/c,
refrig, micro

Legacy Inn
(804) 226-4519
5252 Airport Square Lane
126 rooms - $35-55
Pets: Welcome w/$5 fee
Creature Comforts: CCTV, a/c,
refrig, micro, pool

Motel 6
(800) 4-MOTEL6, (804) 222-7600
http://www.motel6.com
5704 Williamsburg Rd.
119 rooms - $35-45
Pets: Under 30 lbs. welcome
Creature Comforts: CCTV, a/c,
pool

SCOTTSVILLE
High Meadows Inn B&B
(800) 232-1832, (804) 286-2218
http://www.highmeadows.com
High Meadows Lane
13 rooms - $85-295
Pets: First floor rms. w/$20 fee
Creature Comforts: 1832 Nat'l
Historic Register home, mahogany
burlwood trim, ornamental
plasterwork, beamed ceilings,
period antiques, four-poster beds,
CCTV, VCR, a/c, Jacuzzi,
restaurant, English brkfst, spring
fed ponds, vineyards, canoeing

SKIPPERS
Econo Lodge
(800) 55-ECONO, (804) 634-6124
http://www.econolodge.com
Rtes. 95 & 629
96 rms - $40-70
Pets: Welcome
Creature Comforts: CCTV, a/c,
cont. brkfst, pool

SMITHFIELD
Four Square Plantation B&B
(757) 365-0749
13357 Four Square Rd.
3 rooms - $80-105
Pets: Small dogs w/permission,
cats in residence
Creature Comforts: 1807
plantation home set on five acres,
listed on National Historic
Register, massive trees, antiques,
four-poster beds, fireplace,
evening turndown, a/c, Southern
brkfst

SOUTH BOSTON

Best Western
(800) 528-1234, (804) 572-4311
http://www.bestwestern.com
200 Seymour Drive
52 rooms - $60-95
Pets: Small pets welcome
Creature Comforts: CCTV, a/c,
refrig, restaurant, pool, hlth clb
access

Super 8 Motel
(800) 800-8000, (804) 572-8868
http://www.super8.com
1040 Bill Tuck Hwy.
58 rooms - $50-55
Pets: Small pets welcome
Creature Comforts: CCTV, a/c,
refrig, micro

SOUTH HILL

Best Western South Hill
(800) 528-1234, (804) 447-3123
http://www.bestwestern.com
Rtes. 58 & 85
152 rooms - $65-79
Pets: Welcome w/$10 fee
Creature Comforts: CCTV, a/c,
refrig, micro, restaurant, pool, hlth
clb access

Econo Lodge
(800) 55-ECONO, (804) 447-7116
http://www.econolodge.com
623 Atlantic St.
53 rooms - $45-70
Pets: Welcome
Creature Comforts: CCTV, a/c,
refrig, micro, pool, hlth clb access

Super 8 Motel
(800) 800-8000, (804) 447-7655
http://www.super8.com
922 E. Atlantic St.
50 rooms - $50-65
Pets: Welcome
Creature Comforts: CCTV, a/c

SPERRYVILLE

The Conyers House B&B
(540) 987-8025
http://www.bnb-n-va.com/
conyers.htm
Slate Mills Rd.
9 rooms - $140-250
Pets: Welcome in cottages and
Cellar Kitchen w/$30 fee
Creature Comforts: Charming
18th-century hunt-country inn,
stone walls, beamed ceilings, fmly
antiques, four-pstr bds, Oriental
rugs, antique clocks, CCTV, VCR,
fireplace, kit, Jacuzzi, gourmet
brkfst/dinner, riding

SPRINGFIELD

Comfort Inn Springfield
(800) 228-5150, (703) 922-9000
http://www.comfortinn.com
6560 Loisdale Court
112 rooms - $80-130
Pets: Welcome
Creature Comforts: CCTV, a/c,
kit, pool, hlth clb access

Hampton Inn
(800) Hampton, (703) 9249444
http://www.hampton-inn.com
6550 Loisdale Court
153 rooms - $80-130
Pets: Small pets welcome
Creature Comforts: CCTV, a/c,
refrig, micro, pool, hlth clb access

Ramada Inn
(800) 2-Ramada, (703) 644-5311
http://www.ramada.com
6868 Springfield Blvd.
193 rooms - $85-125
Pets: Small pets w/$10 fee
Creature Comforts: CCTV, a/c,
refrig, Jacuzzi, hlth clb access

STANDARDSVILLE

The Lafayette Hotel
(804) 985-6345
http://www.thelafayette.com
146 Main Street
10 rooms - $80-100
Pets: Welcome
Creature Comforts: 1840s
Georgian-style hotel, historic
landmark, country decor,
fireplace, a/c, restaurant, full
brkfst

STAUNTON

Armstrong Motel
(540) 337-2611
Route 2
25 rooms - $40-50
Pets: Small pets welcome
Creature Comforts: CCTV, a/c,
restaurant, pool

Ashton Country House
(800) 296-7819, (540) 885-7819
www.bbhost.com/ashtonbnb
Route 2
6 rooms - $80-125
Pets: On 1st flr, weekdays prefrd.
Creature Comforts: 1860 Greek-
Revival hse on 25 acres, period
details and furnishings, sleigh and
four-poster beds, flannel sheets,
country quilts, porches, CCTV,
a/c, gourmet brkfst

Comfort Inn
(800) 228-5150, (540) 886-5000
http://www.comfortinn.com
1302 Richmond Ave.
98 rooms - $50-80
Pets: Small pets welcome
Creature Comforts: CCTV, a/c,
refrig, micro, Jacuzzi, pool

Days Inn
(800) DAYS-INN, (540) 337-3031
http://www.daysinn.com
Route 2
121 rooms - $50-77
Pets: Welcome
Creature Comforts: CCTV, a/c,
cont. brkfst, pool

Econo Lodge
(800) 55-ECONO, (540) 885-5158
http://www.econolodge.com
1031 Richmond Ave.
88 rooms - $45-64
Pets: Welcome
Creature Comforts: CCTV,
VCR, a/c, refrig, micro, restaurant

Super 8 Motel
(800) 800-8000, (540) 886-2888
http://www.super8.com
1015 Richmond Ave.
63 rooms - $45-68
Pets: Welcome
Creature Comforts: CCTV,
VCR, a/c, refrig, hlth clb access

Ingleside Resort
(540) 248-1201
Route 11
165 rooms - $69
Pets: In crtn rms w/$10 fee
Creature Comforts: CCTV, a/c,
refrig, restaurant, pool

STEELE'S TAVERN
Oceola Mill Country Inn
(540) 377-MILL
http://www.symweb.com/osceola
2 cabins - $375-475
Pets: Welcome in cabins
Creature Comforts: Log cabins
w/panoramic vws, CCTV, VCR,
kit, stone fireplace, Jacuzzi

Sugartree Inn
(800) 377-2197, (540) 377-2197
http://www.sugartree.com
Rte. 56
11rms/1 cottage - $100-150
Pets: Welcome in Creek House
Creature Comforts: Creekside
log inn on 28 acres, cottage w/two
bedrooms, attractively furnished,
kit, dining rm.

STEPHENS CITY
Comfort Inn
(800) 228-5150, (540) 869-6500
http://www.comfortinn.com
167 Town Run Lane
59 rooms - $50-90
Pets: Small pets w/$2 fee
Creature Comforts: CCTV,
VCR, a/c, refrig, micro, Jacuzzis,
pool

STERLING
Hampton Inn Dulles Airport
(800) Hampton, (703) 471-8300
http://www.hampton-inn.com
45440 Holiday Drive
127 rooms - $85-135
Pets: Welcome w/$10 fee
Creature Comforts: CCTV,
VCR, a/c, refrig, pool, hlth clb
access

Holiday Inn Washington Dulles
(800) HOLIDAY, (703) 471-7411
http://www.holiday-inn.com
1000 Sully Rd.
296 rooms - $125-180
Pets: Small pets welcome
Creature Comforts: CCTV,
refrig, micro, Jacuzzi, restaurant,
pool, hlth clb access, sauna,
whirlpool
774

STRASBURG
Budget Inn
(540) 465-5298
28999 Old Valley Pike
14 rooms - $45-59
Pets: Welcome w/$5 fee
Creature Comforts: CCTV, a/c,
refrig

Hotel Strasburg
(800) 348-8327, (540) 465-9191
201 Holliday St.
27 rooms - $70-165
Pets: Welcome w/signed waiver
Creature Comforts: Circa 1890,
Victorian decor/furnishings, brass,
iron or canopy beds, lace curtains,
request suites or rm. 210, CCTV,
a/c, suites w/Jacuzzi, restaurant

SUFFOLK
Holiday Inn
(800) HOLIDAY, (757) 934-2311
http://www.holiday-inn.com
2864 Pruden Blvd.
100 rooms - $65-89
Pets: Small pets welcome
Creature Comforts: CCTV, a/c,
refrig, micro, restaurant, pool

SYRIA
Graves Mountain Lodge
(540) 923-4231
http://www.gravesmountain.com
Route 670
53 rooms - $100-200 (AP)
Pets: Welcome in all rooms but
motel units and 3 cottages
Creature Comforts: Rural mtn.
setting w/300 acres of orchards,
farm animals, informal resort w/
rustic cottages, kit, fireplace,
dining room, game room, pool,
tennis, lawn games, hiking

THORNBURG
Holiday Inn Express
(800) HOLIDAY, (540) 582-1097
http://www.holiday-inn.com
6409 Dan Bell Lane
55 rooms - $70-105
Pets: Welcome w/$10 fee
Creature Comforts: CCTV, a/c,
refrig, Jacuzzis, and a pool

TRIANGLE
Ramada Inn
(800) 2-Ramada, (703) 221-1181
http://www.ramada.com
4316 Inn St.
145 rooms - $55-89
Pets: Welcome w/$10 fee
Creature Comforts: CCTV, a/c,
refrig, micro, restaurant, pool

US Inn
(703) 221-1115
4502 Inn St.
79 rooms - $48-55
Pets: Welcome w/$35 deposit
Creature Comforts: CCTV, a/c,
refrig, restaurant, pool

TROUTVILLE
Comfort Inn
(800) 228-5150, (540) 992-5600
http://www.comfortinn.com
2654 Lee Hwy.
72 rooms - $55-90
Pets: Small pets welcome
Creature Comforts: CCTV, a/c,
refrig, micro, pool

Travelodge
(800) 578-7878, (540) 992-6700
http://www.travelodge.com
2444 Lee Hwy.
108 rooms - $45-69
Pets: Welcome w/$6 fee
Creature Comforts: CCTV, a/c,
kit, pool, playground, volleyball

VIENNA
Comfort Inn Tysons Corner
(800) 228-5150, (703) 448-8020
http://www.comfortinn.com
1587 Springhill Rd.
250 rooms - $70-100
Pets: Welcome w/$ fee
Creature Comforts: CCTV, a/c,
refrig, micro, cont. brkfst, pool,
hlth clb access

Residence Inn Marriott
(800) 331-3131, (703) 893-0120
http://www.residenceinn.com
8616 Westwood Center Drive
96 rooms - $150-1220
Pets: Small pets w/$5 fee, $25 dep
Creature Comforts: CCTV,
VCR, a/c, fireplace, kit, pool,
whirlpool, sport court

Vienna Wolftrap Motel
(703) 281-2330
430 Maple Ave, W.
120 rooms - $49-67
Pets: Welcome w/$100 deposit
Creature Comforts: CCTV, a/c

VIRGINIA BEACH
Days Inn
(800) DAYS-INN, (757) 428-7233
http://www.daysinn.com
Atlantic Ave & 32nd St.
122 rooms - $50-255
Pets: Small pets on 1st floor
Creature Comforts: CCTV, a/c,
kit, Jacuzzis, restaurant, pool
and whirlpool

Econo Lodge Expressway
(800) 55-ECONO, (757) 486-5711
http://www.econolodge.com
3637 Bonney Rd.
53 rooms - $40-80
Pets: Small pets w/$5 fee
Creature Comforts: CCTV, a/c,
refrig, micro

Econo Lodge Northampton
(800) 55-ECONO, (757) 460-1000
http://www.econolodge.com
5819 Northampton Blvd.
104 rooms - $35-75
Pets: Welcome w/$25 deposit
Creature Comforts: CCTV,
VCR, a/c, kit, Jacuzzi

Executive Inn
(800) 678-3466, (757) 420-2120
717 S. Military Hwy.
101 rooms - $30-70
Pets: Small pets w/$5 fee
Creature Comforts: CCTV, a/c,
refrig, micro, pool

Flagship Motel
(757) 425-6422
512 Atlantic Ave.
55 rooms - $35-155
Pets: Welcome w/$25 fee
Creature Comforts: CCTV, a/c,
kit, pool

La Quinta Motor Inn
(800) 531-5900, (757) 497-6620
http://www.laquinta.com
192 Newtown Rd.
129 rooms - $50-70
Pets: Small pets welcome
Creature Comforts: CCTV, a/c,
refrig, pool, hlth clb access

Ocean Holiday Hotel
(757) 425-6920
2417 Atlantic Ave.
105 rooms - $40-169
Pets: Welcome w/$10 fee
Creature Comforts: CCTV,
VCR, a/c, refrig, Jacuzzi, pool,
beach, hlth clb access

Ramada Inn, Airport
(800) 2-Ramada, (757)464-9351
http://www.ramada.com
5725 Northampton Blvd.
172 rooms - $60-99
Pets: Welcome w/$10 fee
Creature Comforts: CCTV, a/c,
kit, restaurant, pool

Red Roof Inn
(800) The Roof, (757) 490-0225
http://www.redroof.com
196 Ballard Court
108 rooms - $40-75
Pets: Small pets welcome
Creature Comforts: CCTV, a/c

Stargate Oceanfront
(757) 425-0650
20th St. & Oceanfront St.
60 rooms - $79-99
Pets: Welcome w/$25 fee
Creature Comforts: CCTV, a/c,
kit, pool

Thunderbird Motor Lodge
(800) 633-6669, (757) 428-3024
3410 Atlantic Ave.
63 rooms - $35-135
Pets: Small pets w/$10 fee
Creature Comforts: Oceanfront,
CCTV, a/c, balcony, restaurant,
pool, beach

Travelodge
(800) 578-7878, (757) 473-9745
http://www.travelodge.com
4600 Bonney Rd.
106 rooms - $45-80
Pets: Small pets welcome
Creature Comforts: CCTV,
VCR, a/c, refrig, micro, pool

WARM SPRINGS
Anderson Cottage B&B
(540) 839-2975
Old Germantown Rd.
5 rooms - $65-125
Pets: Small, well-behaved pets
Creature Comforts: Historic log
home and cottage on warm spring
stream, beautiful perennial grdns,
beamed ceilings, sloping wood
floors, Oriental rugs, family
antiques, fireplace, cottage w/kit,
country brkfst, lawn games,
hiking, hammock

Three Hills Inn
(888) 23-HILLS, (540) 839-5381
http://www.3hills.com
Route 220, P.O. Box 9
12 rms, 2 ctgs - $80-190
Pets: Welcome in certain rooms
w/$10 fee
Creature Comforts: Stately 1913
home set on hillside, surrounded
by 40 acres w/sweeping valley
views, CCTV, a/c, elegant foyer,
high ceilings, spacious rooms w/
homey ambiance, fireplace, kit,
restaurant

WARRENTON
Comfort Inn
(800) 228-5150, (540) 349-8900
http://www.comfortinn.com
6633 Lee Hwy.
97 rooms - $55-85
Pets: Small pets w/$10 fee
Creature Comforts: CCTV, a/c,
kit, Jacuzzi, pool, hlth clb access

Hampton Inn
(800) Hampton, (540) 349-4200
http://www.hampton-inn.com
4522 Richmond Rd.
100 rooms - $45-84
Pets: Welcome
Creature Comforts: CCTV,
VCR, a/c, refrig, micro, pool, hlth
clb access

Howard Johnson Inn
(800) I-Go-Hojo, (540) 347-4141
http://www.hojo.com
6 Broadview Ave.
80 rooms - $40-80
Pets: Welcome
Creature Comforts: CCTV, a/c,
refrig, micro, pool

WARSAW

Best Western Warsaw
(800) 528-1234, (804) 333-1700
http://www.bestwestern.com
4522 Richmond Rd.
35 rooms - $60-80
Pets: Under 30 lbs. welcome
Creature Comforts: CCTV, a/c,
restaurant, pool

WASHINGTON

Bleu Rock Inn
(540) 987-3190
12567 Lee Hwy.
5 rooms - $125-195
Pets: Welcome w/approval
Creature Comforts: Set on 80
acres of rolling hills, vineyards,
lake, charming guest rooms, iron
and brass beds, white wicker,
dried flowers, nice views, gourmet
French restaurant w/3 dining rms

Gay Street Inn
(540) 675-3288
http://www.gaystreetinn.com
160 Gay St.
4 rooms - $95-135
Pets: Welcome
Creature Comforts: A restored
1860 farmhouse on quiet street,
affable hosts from Nantucket, pine
furnishings, period pieces,
canopy-pencil post beds, down
comforters, fireplace, CCTV, kit,
full gourmet brkfst

WATERFORD

Pink House B&B
(540) 882-3453
1 Main St.
1 suite - $100-115
Pets: Well trained dogs welcome
Creature Comforts: Charming
Bermudian pink antique house w/
three-rm suite, 18th-century
antiques, handpainted mural,
Oriental rugs, CCTV, a/c, Jacuzzi,
full English brkfst

Milltown Farms Inn
(888) 747-3942, (540) 882-4470
http://www.milltownfarms.com
14163 Milltown Rd.
4 rooms - $100-135
Pets: Welcome in one room w/
private entrance
Creature Comforts: Gracious
1765 log and stone home, period
antiques and original art, Oriental
rugs, handmade quilts, feather
beds, fireplaces, gourmet brkfst

WAYNESBORO

Best Western Inn
(800) 528-1234, (540) 932-3060
http://www.bestwestern.com
15 Windigrove Drive
56 rooms - $65-99
Pets: Under 10 lbs. welcome
Creature Comforts: CCTV, a/c,
restaurant, pool, hlth clb access

Comfort Inn
(800) 228-5150, (540) 942-1171
http://www.comfortinn.com
640 W. Broad St.
75 rooms - $55-79
Pets: Small pets welcome
Creature Comforts: CCTV, a/c,
refrig, micro

Days Inn
(800) DAYS-INN, (540) 943-1101
http://www.daysinn.com
2060 Rosser Ave.
98 rooms - $60-78
Pets: Welcome w/$6 fee
Creature Comforts: CCTV, a/c,
refrig, micro, restaurant, pool

Deluxe Budget Inn
(540) 949-8253
2112 W. Main St.
23 rooms - $30-67
Pets: Small pets w/$4 fee
Creature Comforts: CCTV, a/c,
pool, playground

Super 8 Motel
(800) 800-8000, (540) 943-3888
http://www.super8.com
2045 Rosser Ave.
50 rooms - $45-65
Pets: Small pets welcome
Creature Comforts: CCTV, a/c,
refrig, micro

WILLIAMSBURG

Best Western Colonial Capital
(800) 528-1234, (757) 253-1222
http://www.bestwestern.com
111 Penniman Rd.
86 rooms - $60-118
Pets: Small pets w/$5 fee
Creature Comforts: CCTV, a/c,
refrig, micro, restaurant, pool,
playground

Best Western Patrick Henry Inn
(800) 528-1234, (757) 229-9540
http://www.bestwestern.com
249 E. York St.
301 rooms - $50-165
Pets: Small pets welcome
Creature Comforts: CCTV,
VCR, a/c, refrig, micro, Jacuzzi,
restaurant, pool, playground

Best Western Virginia Inn
(800) 528-1234, (757) 229-1655
http://www.bestwestern.com
900 Capital Ling Rd.
89 rooms - $50-80
Pets: Small pets w/$10 deposit
Creature Comforts: CCTV, a/c,
refrig, micro, pool, playground

Best Western Williamsburg
(800) 528-1234, (757) 229-3003
http://www.bestwestern.com
Rtes. 60 & 199
134 rooms - $69-124
Pets: Small pets welcome
Creature Comforts: CCTV, a/c,
restaurant, pool

**Best Western Williamsburg
Westpark Hotel**
(800) 528-1234, (757) 229-1134
http://www.bestwestern.com
1600 Richmond Rd.
163 rooms - $30-100
Pets: Welcome
Creature Comforts: CCTV, a/c,
restaurant, pool

Comfort Inn
(800) 228-5150, (757) 229-2000
http://www.comfortinn.com
120 Bypass Rd.
152 rooms - $30-90
Pets: Small pets w/$10 fee
Creature Comforts: CCTV, a/c,
pool

Days Inn
(800) DAYS-INN, (757) 229-5060
http://www.daysinn.com
902 Richmond Rd.
102 rooms - $70-90
Pets: Welcome w/$15 fee
Creature Comforts: CCTV, a/c,
cont. brkfst, restaurant, pool

Days Inn Pottery
(800) DAYS-INN, (757) 565-0090
http://www.daysinn.com
6488 Richmond Rd.
73 rooms - $80-109
Pets: Welcome w/$5 fee
Creature Comforts: CCTV, a/c,
restaurant, pool

Econo Lodge Pottery
(800) 55-ECONO, (757) 564-3341
http://www.econolodge.com
7051 Richmond Rd.
75 rooms - $35-135
Pets: Small pets welcome
Creature Comforts: CCTV, a/c,
cont brkfst, and a pool

Governor's Inn
(800) 447-4329, (757) 229-1000
506 N. Henry St.
200 rooms - $45-100
Pets: Welcome
Creature Comforts: CCTV, a/c,
refrig, pool

Heritage Inn
(757) 229-6220
1324 Richmond Rd.
54 rooms - $40-75
Pets: Small pets welcome
Creature Comforts: CCTV, a/c,
pool

Holiday Inn Patriot
(800) HOLIDAY, (757) 565-2600
http://www.holiday-inn.com
3032 Richmond Rd.
160 rooms - $50-136
Pets: Small pets w/$5 fee, $45 dep
Creature Comforts: CCTV,
VCR, a/c, refrig, micro, restaurant,
pool, whirlpool, golf

Hotel Colonial American
(757) 565-1000
6483 Richmond Rd.
189 rooms - $69-79
Pets: $10 fee, $50 deposit
Creature Comforts: CCTV, a/c,
refrig, Jacuzzi, restaurant, cont.
brkfst, pool,

Howard Johnson, West
(800) I-Go-Hojo, (757) 229-2781
http://www.hojo.com
1800 Richmond Rd.
77 rooms - $40-80
Pets: $5 fee, $10 dep.
Creature Comforts: CCTV, a/c,
pool

Inn at 802
(800) 672-4086, (757) 564-0845
http://www.innat802.com
802 Jamestown Rd.
4 rooms - $125-155
Pets: Selectively welcomed
Creature Comforts: Colonial
style B&B with lovely interiors,
period furnishings, library, fireplace, sun room w/rattan, formal
dining room, four-poster beds,
down comforters, country quilts,
ceiling fans, antiques, CCTV,
VCR, stereo, near village

Ramada Inn
(800) 444-4678, (757) 220-1410
500 Merrimac Trail
250 rooms - $69-120
Pets: Welcome w/$10 fee
Creature Comforts: CCTV,
VCR, a/c, refrig, restaurant, cont.
brkfst, pool, sauna, whirlpool

Travelodge
(800) 578-7878, (757) 229-2981
http://www.travelodge.com
1420 Richmond Rd.
109 rooms - $30-150
Pets: Small pets w/$5 fee
Creature Comforts: CCTV, a/c,
refrig, micro, pool

Williamsburg Center Hotel
(800) 492-2855, (757) 220-2800
www.williamsburgcenter.com
600 Bypass Rd.
140 rooms - $40-105
Pets: In 1st flr smk rms. $25 fee
Creature Comforts: CCTV, a/c,
refrig, micro, Jacuzzis, sauna,
whirlpool, and a pool

WILLIS WHARF
Ballard House B&B
(757) 442-2206
http://www.bbchannel.com/bbc/
p205747.asp
12527 Ballard Drive
5 rooms - $60-75
Pets: Welcome w/$5 fee
Creature Comforts: Turn of the
century B&B w/ homey ambiance,
play room, hot tub, front porch
swing, family heirlooms, healthy
southern brkfst, CCTV, hammock,
bikes,

WINCHESTER
Baymont Inns
(800) 789-4103, (540) 678-0800
http://www.baymontinns.com
800 Millwood Ave.
106 rooms - $55-65
Pets: Welcome
Creature Comforts: CCTV, a/c,
refrig, micro

Best Western Lee Jackson
(800) 528-1234, (540) 662-4154
http://www.bestwestern.com
711 Millwood Ave.
140 rooms - $50-69
Pets: Small pets welcome
Creature Comforts: CCTV, a/c,
kit, Jacuzzi, restaurant, pool, hlth
clb

Days Inn
(800) DAYS-INN, (540) 667-1200
http://www.daysinn.com
2951 Valley Ave.
66 rooms - $35-69
Pets: Small pets w/$3 fee
Creature Comforts: CCTV, a/c,
refrig, micro, restaurant, pool

Echo Village Motel
(540) 869-1900
Route 11
66 rooms - $30-39
Pets: Small pets welcome
Creature Comforts: CCTV, a/c

Holiday Inn
(800) HOLIDAY, (540) 667-3300
http://www.holiday-inn.com
1017 Millwood Pike
175 rooms - $70-75
Pets: Small pets welcome
Creature Comforts: CCTV, a/c,
refrig, micro, restaurant, pool, hlth
clb access, tennis

Mohawk Motel
(540) 667-1410
2754 Northwestern Pike
11 rooms - $30-39
Pets: Welcome
Creature Comforts: CCTV, a/c

Quality Inn East
(800) 228-5151, (540) 667-2250
http://www.qualityinn.com
603 Millwood Ave.
96 rooms - $45-65
Pets: Welcome w/$5 fee
Creature Comforts: CCTV, a/c,
refrig, micro, pool, sauna

Super 8 Motel
(800) 800-8000, (540) 665-4450
http://www.super8.com
1077 Millwood Pike
62 rooms - $45-65
Pets: Welcome w/$5 fee
Creature Comforts: CCTV, a/c

Travelodge
(800) 578-7878, (540) 665-0685
http://www.travelodge.com
160 Front Royal Pike
149 rooms - $55-70
Pets: Welcome w/$5 fee
Creature Comforts: CCTV,
VCR, a/c, refrig, micro, Jacuzzi,
pool, hlth clb access

WOODBRIDGE
Comfort Inn
(800) 228-5150, (703) 494-0300
http://www.comfortinn.com
1109 Horner Rd.
94 rooms - $65-90
Pets: Welcome
Creature Comforts: CCTV, a/c,
refrig, micro, Jacuzzi, pool

Days Inn Potomac Mills
(800) DAYS-INN, (703) 494-4433
http://www.daysinn.com
14619 Potomac Mills Rd.
176 rooms - $75-100
Pets: Small pets welcome
Creature Comforts: CCTV, a/c,
refrig, micro, Jacuzzi, pool, hlth
clb access

Econo Lodge
(800) 55-ECONO, (703) 491-5196
http://www.econolodge.com
13317 Gordon Blvd.
65 rooms - $55-70
Pets: In crtn. rms w/$5 fee
Creature Comforts: CCTV, a/c,
refrig, micro

Friendship Inn
(800) 453-4511, (703) 494-4144
13964 Jefferson Davis Hwy.
39 rooms - $30-49
Pets: Welcome w/$5 fee
Creature Comforts: CCTV, a/c,
refrig, micro

Quality Inn
(800) 221-2222, (703) 494-0300
http://www.qualityinn.com
1109 Horner Rd.
95 rooms - $65-90
Pets: Small pets w/$10 fee
Creature Comforts: CCTV,
VCR, a/c, kit, Jacuzzis, pool

WOODSTOCK
Budget Host Inn
(800) Bud-Host, (540) 494-4086
http://www.budhost.com
1290 South Main St.
43 rooms - $40-49
Pets: Welcome
Creature Comforts: CCTV, a/c,
pool

WYTHEVILLE
Best Western Wytheville Inn
(800) 528-1234, (540) 228-7300
http://www.bestwestern.com
355 Nye Rd.
100 rooms - $40-59
Pets: Welcome w/$10 fee
Creature Comforts: CCTV, a/c,
refrig, Jacuzzi, pool

Days Inn
(800) DAYS-INN, (540) 228-5500
http://www.daysinn.com
150 Malin Drive
118 rooms - $45-79
Pets: Welcome w/$5 fee
Creature Comforts: CCTV, a/c

Econo Lodge
(800) 55-ECONO, (540) 228-5517
http://www.econolodge.com
1190 E. Main St.
72 rooms - $40-85
Pets: Small pets w/$5 fee
Creature Comforts: CCTV, a/c,
refrig, micro

Holiday Inn
(800) HOLIDAY, (540) 228-5483
http://www.holiday-inn.com
1800 E. Main St.
199 rooms - $50-85
Pets: Welcome
Creature Comforts: CCTV, a/c,
refrig, restaurant, pool

Interstate Motor Lodge
(540) 228-8618
705 Chapman Rd.
42 rooms - $30-58
Pets: Small pets welcome
Creature Comforts: CCTV, a/c,
restaurant

Motel 6
(800) 4-MOTEL6, (540) 228-7988
http://www.motel6.com
220 Lithia Rd.
109 rooms - $35-49
Pets: Under 30 lbs. welcome
Creature Comforts: CCTV, a/c,
pool

Ramada Inn
(800) 2-Ramada, (540) 228-6000
http://www.ramada.com
955 Peppers Ferry Rd.
154 rooms - $60-98
Pets: Welcome
Creature Comforts: CCTV, a/c,
refrig, micro, restaurant, pool

Red Carpet Inn
(800) 251-1962, (540) 228-5525
280 Lithia Rd.
34 rooms - $35-90
Pets: Welcome w/$5 fee
Creature Comforts: CCTV, a/c

Super 8 Motel
(800) 800-8000, (540) 228-6620
http://www.super8.com
130 Nye Circle
95 rooms - $45-55
Pets: Welcome w/$25 deposit
Creature Comforts: CCTV, a/c

Washington

ABERDEEN
Flamingo Motel
(360) 532-4103
1120 E. Wishkah
20 rooms - $32-45
Pets: Welcome
Creature Comforts: CCTV

Hearthstone Lodge
(360) 533-0100
1700 S. Boone
66 rooms - $40-80
Pets: Welcome
Creature Comforts: CCTV,
restaurant

Nordic Inn Motel
(800) 442-0101
1700 S. Boone St.
66 rooms - $40-70
Pets: Welcome
Creature Comforts: CCTV

Olympic Inn
(360) 533-4200
616 W. Heron St.
55 rooms - $50-80
Pets: Small pets w/$5 fee
Creature Comforts: CCTV, kit

Red Lion Inn
(800) RED-LION, (360) 532-5210
http://www.doubletreehotels.com
521 W. Wishkah
67 rooms - $84-94
Pets: Welcome w/$10 fee
Creature Comforts: CCTV, a/c,
refrig, micro, cont. brkfst

Thunderbird Motel
(360) 532-3153
410 W. Wishkah
36 rooms - $50-64
Pets: Welcome
Creature Comforts: CCTV,
whirlpool

Towne Motel
(360) 533-2340
712 W. Wishkah St.
24 rooms - $30-55
Pets: Welcome
Creature Comforts: CCTV

Travelure Motel
(360) 532-3280
623 W. Wishkah St.
24 rooms - $35-60
Pets: Welcome
Creature Comforts: CCTV

AIRWAY HEIGHTS
Lantern Park Motel
(509) 244-3653
W. 13820 Sunset Hwy.
13 rooms - $35-62
Pets: Welcome
Creature Comforts: CCTV, a/c

ANACORTES
Albatross B&B
(800) 622-8864
5708 Kingsway W.
4 rooms - $70-95
Pets: Welcome
Creature Comforts: CCTV, full
brkfst

Anaco Inn
(888) 293-8833, (360) 293-8833
905 20th
8 rooms - $44-99
Pets: Welcome
Creature Comforts: CCTV, a/c,
kit, fireplace, Jacuzzi, full brkfst

Anacortes Inn
(800) 327-7976, (360) 293-3153
3006 Commercial Ave.
44 rooms - $50-100
Pets: Dogs welcome, no cats
Creature Comforts: CCTV,
refrig, micro, kit, Jacuzzi, pool

Fidalgo Country Inn
(800) 244-4179, (360) 293-3494
http://www.NWcountryinns.com
1250 Rte. 20
50 rooms - $70-190
Pets: Ltd. rms. w/$10-20 fee
Creature Comforts: Motor lodge
w/country inn ambiance, some
water view rms, attractive décor,
rqst suites w/separate sitting rms,
CCTV, a/c, terry robes, cont.
brkfst, pool, whirlpool

Islands Inn
(360) 293-4644
3401 Commercial Ave.
36 rooms - $50-120
Pets: Welcome
Creature Comforts: CCTV, a/c,
cont. brkfst, pool, whirlpool

Lake Campbell Motel
(360) 293-5314
1377 Rte. 20
10 rooms - $40-70
Pets: Welcome
Creature Comforts: CCTV, a/c,
cont. brkfst

Old Brook Inn B&B
(360) 293-4768
http://www.oldbrookinn.com
530 Old Brook Ln.
2 rooms - $80-90
Pets: Welcome, no pythons please
Creature Comforts: Charming
storybook stone and wood B&B
on 10 secluded forested acres,
surrounded by 1868 orchards,
brook, bay/woods views, cozy
bedrooms w/family antiques,
homey atmosphere, CCTV, cont.
brkfst

Ship Harbor Inn
(800) 852-8568, (360) 293-5177
http://www.shipharborinn.com
5316 Ferry Terminal Rd.
26 rooms - $70-95
Pets: Welcome in 4 rooms
Creature Comforts: CCTV

ARLINGTON

Arlington Motor Inn
(360) 652-9595
2214 Rte. 530
42 rooms - $50-65
Pets: Small pets w/$25 fee
Creature Comforts: CCTV, a/c,
refrig, whirlpool

Smokey Point Motor Inn
(360) 652-9595
17329 Smokey Point Dr.
54 rooms - $44-65
Pets: Small pets w/$5 fee
Creature Comforts: CCTV, a/c,
kit, pool

ASHFORD

Cabins at the Berry
(360) 569-2628
37718 Rte. 706 E.
2 rooms - $65-125
Pets: Welcome w/permission
Creature Comforts: CCTV, kit,
fireplace

Mounthaven Resort
(360) 569-2594
38210 Rte. 706 E.
12 cabins - $50-160
Pets: Welcome
Creature Comforts: Kit,
fireplace

Mt. Ranier Country Cabins
(800) 678-3942, (360) 569-2355
38624 Rte. 706 E.
10 rooms - $45-75
Pets: Welcome
Creature Comforts: CCTV, a/c,
restaurant

Wildberry Cabins
(360) 569-2628
37721 Rte. 706 E.
1 cabin - $63-105
Pets: Welcome
Creature Comforts: CCTV,
restaurant

AUBURN

Howard Johnson
(800) I-Go-Hojo, (253) 939-5950
http://www.hojo.com
1521 D. St. NE
66 rooms - $75-90
Pets: Small pets w/$20 fee
Creature Comforts: CCTV, a/c,
refrig, micro, pool

Val-U Inn
(253) 735-9600
9 14th Ave. NW
96 rooms - $60-105
Pets: Welcome w/$5 fee
Creature Comforts: CCTV,
VCR, a/c, refrig, micro, cont.
brkfst, whirlpool

BAINBRIDGE ISLAND

Bainbridge Inn
(206) 842-7564
9200 Hemlock Ave. NE
2 rooms - $75-100
Pets: Welcome w/permission
Creature Comforts: CCTV,
whirlpool

Island Country Inn
(800) 842-8429, (206) 842-6861
http://nwcountryInns.com/island
920 Hildebrand Ln. NW
46 rooms - $70-150
Pets: Welcome w/$10 fee
Creature Comforts: CCTV, a/c,
refrig, kit, restaurant, cont. brkfst,
pool, whirlpool

Monarch Manor B&B
(206) 780-0112
http://www.monarchmanor.com
7656 Madrona Drive, NE
4 cottages - $125-250
Pets: Welcome w/non-refundable
deposit
Creature Comforts: 1930's
manor house, family estate,
charming cottages set into hill
leading to beach, 2 bedrooms in
manor house, Carriage House w/
sleeping loft, The Stable has
panoramic views of Seattle, rqst.
waterside Cabana, CCTV, a/c, full
brkfst, hot tub, sailboards, kayaks

Waterfront B&B
(206) 842-2431
3314 Crystal Springs Dr., NE
1 room - $50-70
Pets: Welcome
Creature Comforts: CCTV, full
brkfst

BELLEVUE

Best Western Bellevue Inn
(800) 528-1234, (425) 455-5240
http://www.bestwestern.com
11211 Main St.
181 rooms - $125-160
Pets: Welcome w/$30 one-time
fee
Creature Comforts: CCTV, a/c,
restaurant, pool, hlth club

La Residence Suites
(425) 455-1475
475 100th Ave. NE
24 rooms - $135
Pets: Welcome w/$
Creature Comforts: CCTV, a/c,
restaurant, pool, hlth club

Doubletree Hotel, Bellevue Ctr
(800) 222-TREE, (425) 455-1515
http://www.doubletreehotels.com
818 112 Ave. SE
208 rooms - $120-154
Pets: Small pets w/$30 deposit
Creature Comforts: CCTV, a/c,
kit, restaurant

Residence Inn, East
(800) 331-3131, (425) 882-1222
http://www.residenceinn.com
14455 29th Ave. NE
120 rooms - $110-210
Pets: Welcome w/$10 fee
Creature Comforts: CCTV, a/c,
kit, pool

West Coast Bellevue Hotel
(425) 455-9444
625 - 116th Ave. NE
176 rooms - $75-105
Pets: Small pets w/$10 fee
Creature Comforts: CCTV, a/c,
restaurant, pool, hlth club

BELLINGHAM

Aloha Motel
(360) 733-4900
315 N. Samish Way
28 rooms - $30-65
Pets: Welcome
Creature Comforts: CCTV, a/c,
cont. brkfst

Best Western Lakeway
(800) 528-1234, (360) 671-1011
http://www.bestwestern.com
714 Lakeway Dr.
132 rooms - $72-99
Pets: Small pets w/$5 fee
Creature Comforts: CCTV,
VCR, a/c, restaurant, brkfst buffet,
pool, hlth club, whirlpool

Cascade Inn
(360) 733-2520
208 N. Samish Way
44 rooms - $32-50
Pets: Welcome
Creature Comforts: CCTV, a/c,
restaurant, whirlpool

Days Inn
(800) DAYS INN, (360) 671-6200
http://www.daysinn.com
125 E. Kellog Rd.
70 rooms - $40-90
Pets: Small pets w/$10 fee
Creature Comforts: CCTV, a/c,
refrig, kit, Jacuzzi, cont. brkfst,
pool, whirlpool

Mac's Motel
(360) 734-7570
1215 E. Maple
30 rooms - $30-50
Pets: Welcome
Creature Comforts: CCTV, a/c

Motel 6
(800) 4-MOTEL6, (360) 671-4494
http://www.motel6.com
3701 Byron
60 rooms - $30-43
Pets: Under 30 lbs. welcome
Creature Comforts: CCTV, a/c,
pool

Quality Inn, Baron Suites
(800) 228-5151, (360) 647-8000
http://www.qualityinn.com
100 E. Kellogg Rd.
86 rooms - $60-100
Pets: Small pets w/$5 fee
Creature Comforts: CCTV,
VCR, a/c, refrig, micro, cont.
brkfst, pool, hlth club

Rodeway Inn
(800) 228-2000, (360) 738-6000
http://www.rodeway.com
3710 Meridian St.
75 rooms - $45-60
Pets: Small pets welcome
Creature Comforts: CCTV, a/c

Shamrock Motel
(360) 676-1050
4133 W. Maplewood Ave.
38 rooms - $28-35
Pets: Welcome
Creature Comforts: CCTV, a/c

Shangri-La Motel
(360) 733-7050
611 E. Holly St.
20 rooms - $35-45
Pets: Welcome
Creature Comforts: CCTV, a/c,
cont. brkfst

Travelers Inn
(360) 671-4600
3750 Meridian St.
124 rooms - $40-80
Pets: Welcome
Creature Comforts: CCTV, a/c,
refrig, pool, whirlpool

Val-U Inn
(360) 671-9600
805 Lakeway Dr.
82 rooms - $52-75
Pets: Welcome
Creature Comforts: CCTV,
VCR, a/c, refrig, micro, cont.
brkfst, pool, whirlpool

BINGEN
The Bingen Haus
(509) 493-4888
706 W. Steuben
6 rooms - $40-85
Pets: Welcome
Creature Comforts: CCTV, full
brkfst, whirlpool

BLAINE
Inn at Semiahmoo
(800) 770-7992, (360) 371-2000
http://www.semiahmoo.com/inn
9565 Semiahmoo Pkwy
198 rooms - $99-500
Pets: Welcome w/$75 fee
Creature Comforts: Luxurious
resort, beautifully decorated rms.
w/light natural woods, CCTV, a/c,
refrig, fireplace, Jacuzzi,
restaurants, pool, hlth club,
whirlpool, golf, tennis, boating,
nature trails

Motel International
(360) 332-8222
758 Peace Portal Dr.
23 rooms - $35
Pets: Welcome
Creature Comforts: CCTV, a/c,
restaurant

Westview Motel
(360) 332-5501
1300 Peace Portal Dr.
13 rooms - $30-40
Pets: Welcome
Creature Comforts: CCTV, a/c

BOTHELL
Residence Inn, East
(800) 331-3131, (425) 485-3030
http://www.residenceinn.com
11920 NE 195th St.
120 rooms - $130-180
Pets: Welcome w/$10 fee
Creature Comforts: CCTV, a/c,
kit, pool

Wagon Wheel Motel
(425) 486-6631
8042 NE Bothell Way
15 rooms - $44-95
Pets: Welcome
Creature Comforts: CCTV, a/c

BREMERTON
Belfair Motel
(360) 275-4485
NE 23322 Rte. 3
28 rooms - $50-60
Pets: Welcome
Creature Comforts: CCTV, a/c

Best Western Bremerton Inn
(800) 528-1234, (360) 405-1111
http://www.bestwestern.com
4303 Kitsap Way
103 rooms - $60-150
Pets: Small pets welcome
Creature Comforts: CCTV, a/c,
refrig, micro, restaurant, cont.
brkfst, pool, whirlpool

Dunes Motel
(360) 377-0093
3400 11th St.
64 rooms - $50-60
Pets: Welcome w/$20 fee
Creature Comforts: CCTV, a/c,
refrig, micro, kit, brkfst, whirlpool

Flagship Inn
(360) 479-6566
4320 Kitsap Way
29 rooms - $60-85
Pets: Small pets w/$5 fee
Creature Comforts: CCTV, a/c

Illahee Manor and Cottages
(800) 693-6680, (360) 698-7555
comstation.com/illaheemanor
6690 Illahee Rd., NE
5 suites/2 cottages - $115-275
Pets: Welcome in cottages
Creature Comforts: 1920's
waterfront manor and cottages on
six acres, Beach House built of
cedar w/floor-to-ceiling windows,
3 bedrooms, kit, hot tub; 1918
Honeymoon Cabin more rustic but
charming w/living rm, kit, Jacuzzi,
CCTV, VCR, a/c, priv. beach

Midway Inn
(360) 479-2909
2909 Wheaton Way
60 rooms - $55-75
Pets: Welcome w/$20 fee
Creature Comforts: CCTV,
VCR, a/c, refrig, kit, cont. brkfst

Oyster Bay Inn
(360) 377-5510
4412 Kitsap Way
78 rooms - $60-125
Pets: Welcome w/$20 fee
Creature Comforts: CCTV,
VCR, a/c, refrig, micro, kit,
restaurant, cont. brkfst

Quality Inn Bremerton
(800) 228-5151, (360) 405-1111
http://www.qualityinn.com
4303 Kitsap Way
103 rooms - $60-150
Pets: Small pets welcome
Creature Comforts: CCTV,
VCR, a/c, refrig, micro, kit, cont.
brkfst, pool, hlth club whirlpool

Super 8 Motel
(800) 800-8000, (360) 377-8881
http://www.super8.com
5066 Kitsap Way
77 rooms - $50-65
Pets: Welcome w/permission
Creature Comforts: CCTV, a/c

BREWSTER
Brewster Motel
(509) 689-2625
801 S. Bridge Hwy.
10 rooms - $35-60
Pets: Welcome w/permission
Creature Comforts: CCTV, a/c,
pool

BRIDGEPORT
Y Motel
(509) 686-2002
2138 Columbia
18 rooms - $35-53
Pets: Welcome w/permission
Creature Comforts: CCTV, a/c

BUCKLEY
Mountain View Inn
(360) 829-1100
29405 Rte. 10 E
41 rooms - $45-55
Pets: Small pets w/$10 fee
Creature Comforts: CCTV, a/c,
Jacuzzi, cont. brkfst, pool,
whirlpool

CAMANO ISLAND
Peifferhaus B&B
(877) 623-8497, (360) 629-4746
http://www.peifferhaus.com
1462 E. Larkspur Ln.
3 rooms - $85-105
Pets: Welcome
Creature Comforts: Charming
farmhouse on five acres,
wonderful rooms, antique
furnishings, vibrant handmade
quilts, great turret room w/green
accents, blue and yellow room
sunlit room w/sitting area,
gourmet brkfst, hot tub

CARSON
Carson Mineral Hot Springs
(800) 607-3678, (509) 427-8292
One St. Martine Rd.
15 rooms/cabins - $35-60
Pets: Welcome w/permission
Creature Comforts: Casual rustic
resort, restaurant, hot mineral
baths, massage

Columbia Gorge Motel
(509) 427-7777
1261 Wind River Rd.
10 rooms - $45-65
Pets: Welcome w/permission
Creature Comforts: CCTV, a/c

CASTLE ROCK
Mt. St. Helens Motel
(360) 274-7721
1340 Mt. St. Helens Way NE
32 rooms - $48-78
Pets: Welcome w/$5 fee
Creature Comforts: CCTV, a/c

Timberland Inn/Suites
(360) 274-6002
1271 Mt. St. Helens Way
40 rooms - $45-120
Pets: Welcome w/$5 fee
Creature Comforts: CCTV, a/c,
refrig, micro, Jacuzzi

CATHLAMET
Nassa Point Motel
(888) 763-7438, (360) 795-3941
851 E. Rte. 4
6 rooms - $35
Pets: Welcome
Creature Comforts: CCTV

CENTRALIA
Days Inn
(800) DAYS INN, (360) 736-2875
http://www.daysinn.com
702 Harrison
87 rooms - $54
Pets: Welcome w/$10 fee
Creature Comforts: CCTV, a/c,
pool

Ferryman's Inn
(360) 330-2094
1003 Eckerson Rd.
84 rooms - $48
Pets: Welcome w/$5 fee
Creature Comforts: CCTV, a/c,
kit, pool, whirlpool, cont. brkfst

Lake Shore Motel
(800) 666-8701, (360) 736-9344
1325 Lakeshore Dr.
34 rooms - $37-41
Pets: Welcome w/$5 fee
Creature Comforts: CCTV, a/c

Motel 6
(800) 4-MOTEL6, (360) 330-2057
http://www.motel6.com
1310 Belmont Ave.
119 rooms - $30-40
Pets: Under 30 lbs. welcome
Creature Comforts: CCTV, a/c, pool

Park Motel
(360) 736-9333
1011 Belmont Ave.
30 rooms - $33
Pets: Welcome
Creature Comforts: CCTV, a/c

Peppertree West Motor Inn
(360) 736-1124
1208 Alder St.
25 rooms - $35-55
Pets: Welcome w/$5 fee
Creature Comforts: CCTV, a/c, refrig, kit, restaurant

CHEHALIS
Relax Inn
(360) 748-8608
550 SW Parkland Dr.
29 rooms - $45-60
Pets: Welcome w/$5 fee
Creature Comforts: CCTV, a/c, refrig, micro, cont. brkfst

CHELAN
Cabana Motel
(509) 682-2223
420 Manson Rd.
12 rooms - $68-164
Pets: Welcome w/$5 fee
Creature Comforts: CCTV, a/c, pool

Kelly's Resort
(509) 687-3220
http://www.kellysresort.com
12801 S. Lakeshore Dr.
14 cottages - $120-200
Pets: Welcome
Creature Comforts: Cottages, kit, fireplace, swimming

Midtowner Motel
(509) 682-4051
721 E. Woodin
46 rooms - $45-110
Pets: Welcome w/$5 fee
Creature Comforts: CCTV, a/c, pool, whirlpool

CHENEY
Bunker's Resort
(509) 235-5212
S 36402 Bunker Landing Rd.
4 rooms - $45-55
Pets: Welcome
Creature Comforts: CCTV, a/c, swimming

Rosebrook Inn
(509) 235-6538
304 W. First St.
12 rooms - $36-55
Pets: Welcome
Creature Comforts: CCTV, a/c

Willow Springs Motel
(509) 235-5138
5 B St.
44 rooms - $37-56
Pets: Welcome w/$5 fee
Creature Comforts: CCTV, a/c, cont. brkfst

CHEWELAH
Nordlig Motel
(509) 935-6704
101 W. Grant St.
14 rooms - $36-52
Pets: Welcome w/$5 fee
Creature Comforts: CCTV, a/c, refrig, micro

Winona Beach Resort
(509) 937-2231
33022 Winona Beach Rd.
7 rooms - $14-25
Pets: Welcome
Creature Comforts: CCTV

CLARKSTON
Astor Motel
(509) 758-2509
1201 Bridge St.
8 rooms - $26
Pets: Welcome
Creature Comforts: CCTV, a/c

Golden Key Motel
(509) 758-5566
1376 Bridge St.
16 rooms - $30-40
Pets: Welcome
Creature Comforts: CCTV, a/c, refrig, micro

Hacienda Lodge Motel
(888) 567-2287, (509) 758-5583
812 Bridge St.
30 rooms - $26-42
Pets: Welcome
Creature Comforts: CCTV, a/c

Highland House B&B
(509) 758-3126
707 Highland
5 rooms - $40-80
Pets: Welcome w/$5 fee
Creature Comforts: CCTV, full brkfst

Motel 6
(800) 4-MOTEL6, (509) 758-1631
http://www.motel6.com
222 Bridge St.
85 rooms - $30-40
Pets: Under 30 lbs. welcome
Creature Comforts: CCTV, a/c, pool

Sunset Motel
(800) 845-5223, (509) 758-2517
1200 Bridge St.
10 rooms - $35-50
Pets: Small pets welcome
Creature Comforts: CCTV, a/c

CLE ELUM
Aster Inn/Antiques
(509) 674-2551
521 East First St.
9 rooms - $30-75
Pets: Small pets welcome
Creature Comforts: CCTV, a/c

Cascade Mountain Inn
(509) 674-2380
906 East First St.
47 rooms - $45-95
Pets: Welcome w/$5 fee
Creature Comforts: CCTV, a/c, refrig, whirlpool

Cedars Motel
(509) 674-5535
1001 East First St.
34 rooms - $35-65
Pets: Welcome w/$5 fee
Creature Comforts: CCTV, a/c, refrig, micro

Chalet Motel
(509) 674-2320
800 East First St.
11 rooms - $35-50
Pets: Welcome w/$5 fee
Creature Comforts: CCTV, a/c

Stewart Lodge
(509) 674-4548
805 West First St.
36 rooms - $43-70
Pets: Small pets w/$5 fee
Creature Comforts: CCTV, a/c, refrig, cont. brkfst, pool, whirlpool

Timber Lodge Motel
(509) 674-5966
301 West First St.
35 rooms - $50-60
Pets: Small pets w/$10 deposit
Creature Comforts: CCTV, VCR, a/c, refrig, micro, cont. brkfst, whirlpool

Wind Blew Inn
(509) 674-2294
811 Rte. 970
8 rooms - $40
Pets: Welcome
Creature Comforts: CCTV, a/c

CLINTON
Home by the Sea B&B
(360) 321-2964
2388 E. Sunlight Beach Rd.
3 cottages - $155-175
Pets: Welcome in one cottage
Creature Comforts: Wonderfully charming waterside cottage, natural wood walls, feather bed, living room, dining room, fireplace, CCTV, full brkfst basket, whirlpool, kayaks, canoe

Sunset Beach Cottage
(360) 579-1590
7359 S. Maxwelton Beach Rd.
1 cottage - $125
Pets: Welcome w/permission
Creature Comforts: CCTV, full brkfst

Sweetwater Cottage
(360) 341-1604
http://whidbey.com/sweetwater
6111 S. Cultus Bay Rd.
1 cottage - $120
Pets: Dogs and horses w/$10 fee
Creature Comforts: Attractive and private, two-bedroom cottage set on 22 acres of meadows and forests, very nicely furnished w/ country decor, living room, CCTV, woodstove, kit, full farm brkfst (can gather own eggs), decks, Finish sauna, hiking trails,

COLVILLE
Beaver Lodge
(509) 684-5657
2430 Rte. 20 E.
40 rooms - $25-40
Pets: Welcome
Creature Comforts: Cont. brkfst, swimming

Benny's Colville Inn
(800) 680-2517, (509) 684-2517
http://www.colvilleinn.com
915 S. Main St.
106 rooms - $40-105
Pets: Welcome w/$5 fee
Creature Comforts: CCTV, a/c, refrig, cont. brkfst, pool, hlth club, whirlpool

CONCONULLY
Conconully Motel
(509) 826-1610
402 N. Main St.
4 rooms - $35
Pets: Welcome
Creature Comforts: TV

CONNELL
M&M Motel
(509) 234-8811
730 S. Columbia Ave.
43 rooms - $26
Pets: Welcome
Creature Comforts: CCTV, a/c

Tumbleweed Motel
(509) 234-2081
433 S. Columbia Ave.
20 rooms - $23-38
Pets: Welcome
Creature Comforts: CCTV, a/c

CONCRETE
Ovenells Heritage Inn
(360) 853-8494
http://www.ovenells-inn.com
46276 Concrete Sauk V.R.
4 rooms/1 cottage - $75-115
Pets: Welcome
Creature Comforts: Farmhouse on 750-acre ranch w/spectacular views and open spaces, brass, wicker and oak antiques, fireplace, farm brkfst, trout pond

COPALIS BEACH
Beachwood Resort
(360) 289-2177
3009 Rte. 109
2 rooms - $65-79
Pets: Welcome
Creature Comforts: CCTV, pool, whirlpool

Iron Springs Ocean Resort
(360) 276-4230
http://www.ironspringsresort.com
3707 Rte. 109
28 rooms - $66-104
Pets: Welcome w/$10 fee
Creature Comforts: Beachside cottages w/expansive ocean views, pine walls/ceilings, comfortably furnished, refrig, stone fireplace, kitchen, fireplace, crabbing, and fishing

Linda's Low Tide Motel
(360) 289-3450
Box 551
12 rooms - $60-125
Pets: Small pets welcome
Creature Comforts: CCTV, restaurant

COULEE CITY
The Main Stay B&B
(509) 632-5687
110 West Main
2 rooms - $40
Pets: Welcome
Creature Comforts: CCTV, a/c, cont. brkfst

COULEE DAM
Coulee House Motel
(800) 715-7767, (509) 633-1101
110 Roosevelt Way
61 rooms - $55-120
Pets: Welcome
Creature Comforts: Overlooking laser light show, CCTV, a/c, kit, restaurants, pool, whirlpool, sauna

COUPEVILLE
Tyee Hotel and Motel
(360) 678-6616
733 S. Roberts Bluff Rd.
9 rooms - $50
Pets: Welcome
Creature Comforts: CCTV, a/c

Victorian B&B
(360) 678-5303
110 Roosevelt Way
3 rooms - $60-100
Pets: Welcome in garden cottage
w/$100 deposit
Creature Comforts: Italianate
home w/priv. guest house, pretty
gardens, antiques, country
furnishings, CCTV, a/c, kit

DARRINGTON
Stagecoach Inn
(360) 436-1776
1100 Seaman
20 rooms - $55-69
Pets: Welcome
Creature Comforts: CCTV

DAYTON
Blue Mountain Motel
(509) 382-3040
414 W. Main St.
23 rooms - $36-75
Pets: Welcome
Creature Comforts: CCTV, a/c

Purple House B&B
415 E. Clay St.
5 rooms - $85-135
Pets: Welcome
Creature Comforts: 1882
Victorian w/European ambiance,
Asian antiques, French doors,
fireplace, private Carriage House
suite, CCTV, a/c, kit, full brkfst w/
homemade breads

Weinhard Hotel
(509) 382-4032
http://www.weinhard.com
235 E. Main St.
15 rooms - $70-125
Pets: Welcome
Creature Comforts: 1800's
Victorian lodge, eclectic antique
furnishings, rooftop garden,
CCTV, a/c, cafe, cont. brkfst

DEER PARK
Love's Victorian B&B
(509) 276-6939
N. 31317 Cedar Rd.
2 rooms - $75-98
Pets: Welcome w/permission
Creature Comforts: Victorian
mansion, period antiques,
Victorian wallpaper and curtains,
CCTV, a/c, fireplace, full brkfst,
hot tub

DEMING
The Logs Resort
(509) 599-2711
235 E. Main St.
15 rooms - $65-110
Pets: Welcome
Creature Comforts: Heavily
forested, moss-covered trees lead
to resort, log cabins set on river
bank, natural wood walls, timber
ceilings, simple décor, CCTV, a/c,
kit, cont. brkfst, stone fireplace,
pool, lawn games, fishing

EAST WENATCHEE
Cedars Inn
(800) 358-2074, (509) 886-8000
80 Ninth St. NE
94 rooms - $61-122
Pets: Welcome w/$6 fee
Creature Comforts: CCTV, a/c,
cont. brkfst, pool, whirlpool

Four Seasons Inn
(509) 884-6611
11 W. Grand Rd.
100 rooms - $52-70
Pets: Welcome
Creature Comforts: CCTV, a/c,
pool, whirlpool

EATONVILLE
Eagles Nest Motel
(360) 569-2533
52120 Mountain Hwy. East
10 rooms - $48
Pets: Welcome
Creature Comforts: CCTV, a/c,
restaurant

EDMONDS
Edmonds Harbor Inn
(425) 771-5021
130 W. Dayton St.
60 rooms - $64-130
Pets: Small pets w/$10 fee
Creature Comforts: CCTV, a/c,
refrig, micro, cont. brkfst, hlth
club

Hudgens Haven
(425) 776-2002
9313 190 SW
1 room - $60
Pets: Welcome
Creature Comforts: CCTV, a/c,
full brkfst

Traveler's Lodge
(425) 771-8008
23825 Rte. 99
58 rooms - $40-50
Pets: Welcome
Creature Comforts: CCTV, a/c,
restaurant

ELBE
Hobo Inn
(360) 569-2500
54104 Mountain Hwy. E.
8 rooms - $70-85
Pets: Welcome w/permission
Creature Comforts: CCTV, full
brkfst

ELLENSBURG
Best Western Inn
(800) 528-1234, (509) 925-9801
http://www.bestwestern.com
1700 Canyon Rd.
105 rooms - $37-77
Pets: Welcome
Creature Comforts: CCTV, a/c,
refrig, restaurant, cont. buffet,
pool, hlth club, whirlpool

Comfort Inn
(800) 228-5150, (509) 925-7037
http://www.comfortinn.com
1722 Canyon Rd.
52 rooms - $50-95
Pets: Welcome
Creature Comforts: CCTV, a/c,
refrig, micro, restaurant, cont.
brkfst, pool, whirlpool

I-90 Motel
(509) 925-9844
1390 Dollar Way
72 rooms - $38-58
Pets: Small pets welcome
Creature Comforts: CCTV, a/c,
refrig, micro

Nites Inn
(509) 962-9600
1200 S. Ruby
72 rooms - $45-55
Pets: Small pets w/$6 fee
Creature Comforts: CCTV, a/c,
refrig, micro

Super 8 Motel
(800) 800-8000, (509) 962-6888
http://www.super8.com
1500 Canyon Rd.
101 rooms - $50-60
Pets: Welcome w/permission
Creature Comforts: CCTV, a/c,
pool, whirlpool

Thunderbird Motel
(800) 843-3492, (509) 962-9856
403 W. 8th Ave.
72 rooms - $38-100
Pets: Welcome w/permission
Creature Comforts: CCTV, a/c,
pool

Waites Motel
(509) 962-9801
601 N. Water
60 rooms - $32-60
Pets: Welcome w/permission
Creature Comforts: CCTV, a/c,
pool

ELMA
Parkhurst Motel
(360) 482-2541
208 E. Main St.
14 rooms - $45-65
Pets: Welcome w/permission
Creature Comforts: CCTV, a/c

ENUMCLAW
Best Western Park Center
(800) 528-1234, (360) 825-4490
http://www.bestwestern.com
1000 Griffen Ave.
40 rooms - $58-73
Pets: Welcome w/$10 fee
Creature Comforts: CCTV, a/c,
refrig, micro, restaurant, whirlpool

EPHRATA
Columbia Motel
(509) 754-5226
1257 Basin
16 rooms - $38-70
Pets: Welcome
Creature Comforts: CCTV, a/c,
cont. brkfst, whirlpool

Lariat Motel
(509) 754-2437
1639 Basin St. SW
42 rooms - $35-55
Pets: Welcome
Creature Comforts: CCTV, a/c,
pool

EVERETT
Everett Inn
(425) 347-9099
12619 Fourth Ave. W.
72 rooms - $50-80
Pets: Welcome
Creature Comforts: CCTV, a/c,
cont. brkfst, restaurant, pool

Holiday Inn
(800) HOLIDAY, (425) 337-2900
http://www.holiday-inn.com
101 128th St. SE
249 rooms - $89-119
Pets: Welcome w/$20 fee
Creature Comforts: CCTV, a/c,
refrig, micro, restaurant, pool,
whirlpool

Motel 6, North
(800) 4-MOTEL6, (425) 347-2060
http://www.motel6.com
I-5 at Exit 189
119 rooms - $35-45
Pets: Under 30 lbs. welcome
Creature Comforts: CCTV, a/c,
pool

Motel 6, South
(800) 4-MOTEL6, (425) 353-8120
http://www.motel6.com
I-5 at Exit 186
100 rooms - $35-50
Pets: Under 30 lbs. welcome
Creature Comforts: CCTV, a/c

Royal Motor Inn
(425) 259-5517
952 N. Broadway
35 rooms - $37-56
Pets: Welcome
Creature Comforts: CCTV, a/c,
pool

Travelodge, Everett Mall
(800) 578-7878, (425) 259-6141
http://www.travelodge.com
9602 19th Ave. SE
116 rooms - $59-79
Pets: Welcome w/$20 fee
Creature Comforts: CCTV, a/c,
kit, pool, whirlpool

Travelodge, Broadway
(800) 578-7878, (425) 259-6141
http://www.travelodge.com
3030 Broadway
29 rooms - $49-62
Pets: Small dogs w/$5 fee, no cats
Creature Comforts: CCTV, a/c

FEDERAL WAY
Best Western Federal Way
(800) 528-1234, (253) 941-6000
http://www.bestwestern.com
31611 20th Ave. S
137 rooms - $70-130
Pets: Small pets w/$20 deposit
Creature Comforts: CCTV, a/c,
refrig, micro, restaurant, whirlpool

Roadrunner Motel
(800) 828-7202, (253) 838-5763
1501 S. 35th St.
59 rooms - $30-38
Pets: Welcome
Creature Comforts: CCTV, a/c

Stevenson Motel
(253) 927-2500
33330 Pacific Hwy S.
22 rooms - $33
Pets: Welcome
Creature Comforts: CCTV, a/c

Super 8
(800) 800-8000, (253) 838-8088
http://www.super8.com
1688 S. 348th St.
90 rooms - $55-60
Pets: Welcome
Creature Comforts: CCTV, a/c

FERNDALE
Scottish Lodge Motel
(360) 384-4040
5671 Riverside Dr.
95 rooms - $39
Pets: Welcome w/permission
Creature Comforts: CCTV, a/c,
pool

Super 8 Motel
(800) 800-8000, (360) 384-8881
http://www.super8.com
1500 Canyon Rd.
101 rooms - $50-60
Pets: Welcome w/permission
Creature Comforts: CCTV, a/c,
pool

FIFE
Best Western Executive Inn
(800) 528-1234, (253) 922-0080
http://www.bestwestern.com
5700 Pacific Hwy E
139 rooms - $85-145
Pets: Welcome w/$20 deposit
Creature Comforts: CCTV, a/c,
refrig, micro, restaurant, full
brkfst, pool

Days Inn
(800) DAYS INN, (253) 922-3500
http://www.daysinn.com
3021 Pacific Hwy
185 rooms - $45-60
Pets: Welcome w/$5 fee
Creature Comforts: CCTV, a/c

Econo Lodge
(800) 55-ECONO, (253) 922-0550
http://www.econolodge.com
3518 Pacific Hwy E
81 rooms - $50-55
Pets: Small pets w/$10 fee
Creature Comforts: CCTV, a/c

Glacier Motel
(253) 922-5882
3401 Pacific Hwy E.
25 rooms - $35-50
Pets: Small pets w/$10 fee
Creature Comforts: CCTV, a/c

Motel 6
(800) 4-MOTEL6, (253) 922-1270
http://www.motel6.com
I-5 at Exit 137
120 rooms - $35-45
Pets: Under 30 lbs. welcome
Creature Comforts: CCTV, a/c, pool

Royal Coachman Inn
(800) 422-3051, (253) 922-2500
5805 Pacific Hwy E
94 rooms - $35-45
Pets: Welcome w/$25 deposit
Creature Comforts: CCTV, a/c, refrig, micro, kit, Jacuzzi, restaurant, whirlpool

FIR ISLAND
South Fork Moorage
(360) 445-4803
http://www.virtualcities.com/ons/wa/f/waf3501.htm
2187 Mann Rd.
2 houseboats - $80-115
Pets: Small pets w/$5 fee
Creature Comforts: Charming houseboats tucked into river bank, Japanese teaboat w/sitting rm, galley, bedroom, window seats, lovely décor; cedar-shingled Karma w/stained glass, Palladian windows, window seats, bedroom, CCTV, refrigs stocked w/champagne

FORKS
Bagby's Town Motel
(800) 742-2429, (360) 374-6231
1080 S. Forks Ave.
20 rooms - $34-40
Pets: Welcome
Creature Comforts: CCTV, hlth club

Forks Motel
(800) 544-3416, (360) 374-6243
351 Forks Ave.
73 rooms - $68-75
Pets: Small pets welcome
Creature Comforts: CCTV, a/c, kit, pool

Hoh Humm Ranch
(360) 374-5337
Rte. 101
2 rooms - $35-45
Pets: Welcome
Creature Comforts: CCTV, full brkfst

Kalaloch Lodge
(360) 962-2271
http://www.visitkalaloch.com
157151 Rte. 101
18 rooms/40 cabins - $55-187
Pets: Cabins w/$10 fee
Creature Comforts: Bluffside weathered-shingle lodge and cabins, wild and remote, cabins w/brass beds, kit, Franklin-style fireplaces, Jacuzzi, hexagonal restaurant, dog-friendly beaches

Manitou Lodge B&B
(360) 374-6295
http://www.manitoulodge.com
Box 600, Kilmer Rd.
6 rooms - $80-105
Pets: Welcome in Eagle Cottage w/$10 fee
Creature Comforts: Timber lodge, attractive rms w/country decor, CCTV, stone fireplace, full brkfst, whirlpool, pristine beaches

Miller Tree Inn
(360) 374-6806
www.northolympic.com/millertree
654 E. Division St.
7 rooms - $50-150
Pets: Welcome
Creature Comforts: 1916 historic farmhouse, pretty rms. furnished w/country antiques, CCTV, full brkfst, hot tub

FREELAND
Harbour Inn
(360) 331-6900
1606 E. Main St.
20 rooms - $58-83
Pets: Welcome in ltd. rms w/$6 fee
Creature Comforts: CCTV, kit

Mutiny Bay Resort/Motel
(360) 331-4500
5856 S. Mutiny Bay Rd.
9 rooms - $60-125
Pets: Welcome
Creature Comforts: CCTV, whirlpool

GARFIELD
RC McCroskey House B&B
(509) 635-1459
Fourth & Manring St.
2 rooms - $75
Pets: Welcome in ltd. rms w/$6 fee
Creature Comforts: CCTV, full brkfst

GIG HARBOR
Best Western Wesley Inn
(888) 462-0002
http://www.bestwestern.com
6575 Kimball Dr.
53 rooms - $79-139
Pets: Small pets w/$5 fee
Creature Comforts: CCTV, a/c, restaurant, cont. brkfst, pool, whirlpool

No Cabbages' B&B
(253) 858-7797
7712 Goodman Dr. N.
2 rooms - $55-75
Pets: Welcome w/permission
Creature Comforts: CCTV, full brkfst

Harborside B&B
(253) 851-1795
8708 Goodman Dr. NW
4 rooms - $80-120
Pets: Welcome
Creature Comforts: CCTV, a/c, full brkfst

787

Olalla Orchard B&B
(253) 857-5915
12530 Orchard Ave. SE
1 room - $95
Pets: Welcome w/permission
Creature Comforts: CCTV, full
brkfst, whirlpool

Westwynd Motel
(800) 468-9963, (253) 857-4047
6703 144th St. NW
24 rooms - $44-72
Pets: Welcome
Creature Comforts: CCTV, a/c

GLACIER
Glacier Creek Lodge
(360) 599-2991
10036 Mt. Baker Hwy.
21 rooms - $40-135
Pets: Welcome
Creature Comforts: CCTV,
restaurant, whirlpool

Mt. Baker Chalet
(360) 599-2405
9857 Mt. Baker Hwy.
23 rooms - $75-150
Pets: Welcome
Creature Comforts: CCTV,
restaurant, pool, whirlpool

GOLDENDALE
Bachris Motel
(888) 713-6197, (509) 773-4325
128 N. Academy
9 rooms - $35-45
Pets: Welcome
Creature Comforts: CCTV, a/c

Ponderosa Motel
(509) 773-5842
775 E. Broadway St.
28 rooms - $36-70
Pets: Welcome
Creature Comforts: CCTV, a/c,
refrig, micro, kit

GRAND COULEE
Center Lodge Motel
(509) 633-0770
508 Spokane Way
17 rooms - 35-75
Pets: Welcome
Creature Comforts: CCTV, a/c

Trail West Motel
(509) 633-3155
108 Spokane Way
26 rooms - $39-70
Pets: Welcome
Creature Comforts: CCTV, a/c,
pool

GRANDVIEW
Apple Valley Motel
(509) 882-3003
903 W. Wine Country Rd.
16 rooms - $28-45
Pets: Welcome
Creature Comforts: CCTV, a/c,
pool

Grandview Motel
(509) 882-1323
522 E. Wine Country Rd.
20 rooms - $28-45
Pets: Welcome
Creature Comforts: CCTV, a/c,
pool

GRANITE FALLS
Mountain View Inn
(360) 691-6668
32005 Mt. Loop Hwy.
6 rooms - $40-45
Pets: Welcome w/permission
Creature Comforts: CCTV

GRAYLAND
Grayland Motel
(360) 267-2395
2013 Rte. 105
15 rooms - $40-45
Pets: Welcome w/$10 fee in ltd.
rooms
Creature Comforts: CCTV, kit

Ocean Spray Motel
(360) 267-2205
1757 Rte. 105
10 rooms - $45-65
Pets: Welcome
Creature Comforts: CCTV,
refrig, micro, kit

Surf Motel & Cottages
(360) 267-2244
2029 Hwy 105
7 rooms - $39-67
Pets: Welcome
Creature Comforts: CCTV

GREEN ACRES
Alpine Motel
(509) 928-2700
18815 E. Cataldo
18 rooms - $35-79
Pets: Small pets w/$5 fee
Creature Comforts: CCTV, a/c,
full brkfst, pool

HOQUIAM
Sandstone Motel
(360) 533-6383
2424 Aberdeen Ave.
24 rooms - $35-65
Pets: Welcome
Creature Comforts: CCTV

Timberline Inn
(360) 533-8048
415 Perry Ave.
25 rooms - $30-45
Pets: Welcome
Creature Comforts: CCTV

Westwood Inn
(360) 532-8161
910 Simpson Ave.
65 rooms - $45-150
Pets: Welcome
Creature Comforts: CCTV

ILWACO
Columbia Pacific Motel
(360) 532-5265
Box 34
16 rooms - $60
Pets: Welcome
Creature Comforts: CCTV

Heidi's Inn
(360) 642-2387
126 Spruce St.
26 rooms - $39-70
Pets: Welcome
Creature Comforts: CCTV,
whirlpool

INCHELIUM
Hartman's Log Cabin Resort
(509) 722-3543
5744 S. Twin Lakes Access
59 rooms - $36-50
Pets: Welcome
Creature Comforts: CCTV, a/c

Rainbow Beach Resort
(509) 722-5901
N. Twin Lake
24 rooms - $35-55
Pets: Welcome
Creature Comforts: CCTV, a/c

ISSAQUAH
Motel 6
(800) 4-MOTEL6, (425) 392-8405
http://www.motel6.com
1885 15th Pl. NW
103 rooms - $40-53
Pets: Under 30 lbs. welcome
Creature Comforts: CCTV, a/c,
pool

KALAMA
Columbia Inn Motel
(360) 673-2855
600 N. Frontage St.
44 rooms - $35-45
Pets: Welcome
Creature Comforts: CCTV, a/c

KELSO
Best Western Aladdin
(800) 528-1234, (360) 425-9660
http://www.bestwestern.com
310 Long Ave.
78 rooms - $47-85
Pets: Small pets w/$5 fee
Creature Comforts: CCTV,
VCR, a/c, refrig, micro, kit, pool,
whirlpool

Budget Inn
(360) 636-4610
505 N. Pacific Ave.
52 rooms - $37-61
Pets: Small pets w/$5 fee
Creature Comforts: CCTV, a/c

Doubletree Motel
(360) 636-4400
510 Kelso Dr.
162 rooms - $80-150
Pets: Welcome
Creature Comforts: CCTV, a/c,
restaurant, pool, whirlpool

Motel 6
(800) 4 MOTEL6, (360) 425-3229
I-5 at Exit 39
60 rooms - $30-45
Pets: Welcome
Creature Comforts: CCTV, a/c,
pool

Super 8 Motel
(800) 800-8000, (360) 423-8880
http://www.super8.com
250 Kelso Dr.
49 rooms - $50-60
Pets: Welcome w/permission
Creature Comforts: CCTV, a/c,
pool, whirlpool

KENNEWICK
Casablanca Bed &Breakfast
(888) 627-0676, (509) 627-0676
http://www.casablancabb.com
94806 E Granada Ct.
3 rooms - $65-85
Pets: Welcome w/permission
Creature Comforts: CCTV,
VCR, a/c, cont. brkfst

Cavanaugh's at Columbia
(800) 325-4000, (509) 783-0611
http://www.cavanaughs.com
1101 N. Columbia Center
162 rooms - $73-300
Pets: Welcome w/permission
Creature Comforts: CCTV, a/c,
refrig, micro, pool

Clearwater Inn
(509) 735-2242
5616 W Clearwater Ave.
59 rooms - $50-65
Pets: Welcome w/permission
Creature Comforts: CCTV, a/c,
cont. brkfst

Comfort Inn
(800) 228-5150, (509) 735-2242
http://www.comfortinn.com
7801 Quinault Ave.
56 rooms - $52-125
Pets: Welcome w/$5 fee
Creature Comforts: CCTV, a/c,
refrig, micro, Jacuzzi, restaurant,
cont. brkfst, pool, whirlpool

Holiday Inn Express
(800) HOLIDAY, (509) 736-3326
http://www.holiday-inn.com
4220 W. 27th Place
53 rooms - $60-100
Pets: Small pets welcome
Creature Comforts: CCTV,
VCR, a/c, refrig, micro, kit,
Jacuzzi, restaurant, cont. brkfst,
pool, whirlpool, sauna

Shaniko Suites Motel
(509) 735-6385
321 N. Johnson St.
47 rooms - $41-64
Pets: Welcome
Creature Comforts: CCTV, a/c,
cont. brkfst, pool

Silver Cloud
(509) 735-6100
7901 W. Quinault Ave.
125 rooms - $46-110
Pets: Small pets w/$10 fee, $50
deposit
Creature Comforts: CCTV, a/c,
Jacuzzi, cont. brkfst, pool, hlth
club, pool, whirlpool

Super 8
(800) 800-8000, (509) 736-6888
http://www.super8.com
626 N. Columbia Ctr. Blvd.
95 rooms - $50-65
Pets: Welcome w/$25 deposit
Creature Comforts: CCTV, a/c,
pool, whirlpool

Tapadera Budget Inn
(800) 722-8277, (509) 783-6191
300 N. Ely St.
61 rooms - $45-60
Pets: Welcome w/$5 fee
Creature Comforts: CCTV, a/c,
restaurant

KENT
Golden Kent Motel
(253) 872-8372
22203 84th Ave. S.
22 rooms - $48-55
Pets: Welcome w/permission
Creature Comforts: CCTV, a/c

Days Inn, South Seattle
(800) DAYS INN, (253) 854-1950
http://www.daysinn.com
1711 W. Meeker St.
82 rooms - $53-119
Pets: Welcome w/$5 fee
Creature Comforts: CCTV, a/c,
cont. brkfst

Howard Johnson
(800) I-Go-Hojo, (253) 852-7224
http://www.hojo.com
1233 N. Central
85 rooms - $58-96
Pets: Welcome w/$10 fee
Creature Comforts: CCTV, a/c,
refrig, pool, hlth club, whirlpool

Val U Inn
(800) 443-7777, (253) 8720-5525
22420 84th Ave. S.
92 rooms - $60-65
Pets: Welcome w/$10 fee
Creature Comforts: CCTV,
VCR, a/c, refrig, micro, cont.
brkfst, whirlpool

KETTLE FALLS
Bull Hill Ranch and Resort
(877) Bull-Hill, (509) 732-6135
http://www.bullhill.com
3738 Bull Hill Rd.
20 cabins - $70-125 (AP)
Pets: Welcome w/$25 deposit
Creature Comforts: Guest ranch,
rustic wood frame or tent cabins,
handcrafted furniture, dining rm.,
horseback riding, fly fishing

Kettle Falls Inn
(800) 701-1927
http://publiconline.com/-wainns
205 E. Third, Rte. 395
24 rooms - $36-56
Pets: Welcome
Creature Comforts: CCTV, a/c,
refrig, kit, Jacuzzi

KINGSTON
Smiley's Colonial Motel
(360) 297-3622
11067 Rte. 104
17 rooms - $40-45
Pets: Welcome
Creature Comforts: CCTV, a/c

KIRKLAND
La Quinta
(800) Nu-Rooms, (425) 828-6585
http://www.laquinta.com
10530 Northeast Northup
118 rooms - $73-135
Pets: Small pets welcome
Creature Comforts: CCTV, a/c,
refrig, micro, cont. brkfst, pool

Motel 6
(800) 4 MOTEL6, (425) 821-5618
12010 120th Pl, NE
123 rooms - $30-45
Pets: Welcome
Creature Comforts: CCTV, a/c,
pool

LA CONNER
Art's Place
(360) 466-3033
511 Talbot St.
1 room - $60
Pets: Welcome
Creature Comforts: CCTV,
cont. brkfst

La Conner Country Inn
(888) 466-4113, (360) 466-3101
http://www.laconnerlodging.com
107 S. Second St.
28 rooms - $89-112
Pets: Welcome in ltd. rooms
Creature Comforts: Motor lodge
w/attractive shingled exterior, rms.
w/Victorian and traditional
furnishings, brass beds, some
fireplaces, CCTV, a/c, library,
cont. brkfst, restaurant

LACEY
Super 8
(800) 800-8000, (360) 459-8888
http://www.super8.com
4615 Martin Way
100 rooms - $53-69
Pets: Welcome
Creature Comforts: CCTV, a/c,
pool

LAKEWOOD
Best Western, Lakewood
(800) 528-1234, (253) 584-2212
http://www.bestwestern.com
6125 Motor Ave. SW
75 rooms - $70-85
Pets: Small pets w/$6 fee
Creature Comforts: CCTV,
VCR, a/c, refrig, micro

Madigan Motel
(800) 228-5151, (253) 588-8697
12039 Pacific Hwy
23 rooms - $35-65
Pets: Small pets welcome
Creature Comforts: CCTV, a/c,
full brkfst

Nights Inn
(253) 582-7550
9325 S. Tacoma Way
75 rooms - $30-50
Pets: Small pets w/$20 deposit
Creature Comforts: CCTV,
VCR, a/c, refrig, kit, Jacuzzi

Quality Inn
(800) 228-5151, (253) 588-5241
http://www.qualityinn.com
9920 S. Tacoma Way
102 rooms - $45-65
Pets: Small pets welcome
Creature Comforts: CCTV, a/c,
kit, Jacuzzi, cont. brkfst

LANGLEY
Inverness Inn
(360) 321-5521
2479 State Rte. 525
6 rooms - $65-90
Pets: Welcome
Creature Comforts: CCTV

Island Tyme B&B
(800) 898-8966, (360) 221-5078
http://www.moriah.com/island-
tyme/index.html
4940 S. Bayview Rd.
5 rooms - $95-140
Pets: Welcome in Keepsake Rm.
w/$10 deposit
Creature Comforts: Modern
Victorian home filled w/antiques
from hosts' antique store,
Keepsake Rm. traditionally
furnished, fireplace, CCTV, VCR,
Jacuzzi, fireplace, gourmet brkfst,
afternoon baked goodies, billiards

LEAVENWORTH
Bayern On the River
(509) 548-5875
1505 Alpensee Strasse St.
26 rooms - $69-98
Pets: Welcome
Creature Comforts: CCTV, pool,
whirlpool

Bindlestiffs Motel
(509) 548-5015
1600 Rte. 2
8 cabins - $58-69
Pets: Welcome
Creature Comforts: CCTV, kit,
cont. brkfst

Bosch Garten B&B
(509) 548-6900
http://www.boschgarten.com/
9846 Dye Rd.
3 rooms - $98-105
Pets: Welcome
Creature Comforts: Private
home, CCTV, full brkfst,
whirlpool

Cougar Inn
(509) 763-3354
8695 Larson Rd.
9 rooms - $45-115
Pets: Welcome
Creature Comforts: CCTV, a/c,
full brkfst

Der Ritterhof Motor Inn
(800) 255-5845, (509) 548-5845
190 Rte. 2
51 rooms - $68-98
Pets: Welcome
Creature Comforts: CCTV, a/c,
kit, full brkfst, pool, whirlpool

Evergreen Inn
(800) 327-7212, (509) 548-5515
http://www.evergreen.com
1117 Front St.
56 rooms - $68-98
Pets: Welcome
Creature Comforts: CCTV, a/c,
refrig, micro, kit, fireplace, cont.
brkfst, pool, whirlpool

Lake Wenatchee Hide-A-Ways
(800) 883-2611, (509) 763-0108
http://www.bluegrouse.com
19944 Rte. 207
15 cabins - $140-175
Pets: Welcome in 5 cabins,
including the Naughty Dog
Creature Comforts: Fully
equipped cabins along river and
lake, CCTV, kit, hot tub

Natapoc Lodging
(888) Natapoc, (509) 763-3313
http://www.natapoc.com
12338 Bretz Rd.
7 rooms - $160-325
Pets: With permission, a $10 fee,
and must follow the pet rules
Creature Comforts: Charming
log cabins and cottages, some
along river, beautifully decorated
w/handmade quilts, country
antiques, TV, VCR, fireplace, kit,
hot springs

Obertal Motor Inn
(800) 537-9382, (509) 548-5204
http://www.obertal.com
922 Commercial St.
25 rooms - $57-109
Pets: Welcome
Creature Comforts: CCTV,
fireplace, pool, whirlpool

Phippens B&B
(800) 666-9806
10285 Ski Hill Dr.
3 rooms - $39-101
Pets: Welcome
Creature Comforts: CCTV, a/c,
fireplace, cont. brkfst, whirlpool

River's Edge Lodge
(509) 548-7612
185 Rte. 2
22 rooms - $57-77
Pets: Welcome in ltd. rooms
Creature Comforts: CCTV, a/c,
kit

Rodeway Inn
(800) 228-2000, (509) 548-7992
http://www.rodeway.com
185 Rte. 2
75 rooms - $45-60
Pets: Welcome w/$10 fee
Creature Comforts: CCTV, a/c,
refrig, Jacuzzi, full brkfst, pool

Saimons Hide-a-Ways
(800) 537-9382, (509) 548-5204
16408 River Rd.
7 cabins - $95-145
Pets: Welcome
Creature Comforts: CCTV,
whirlpool

Squirrel Tree Inn
(509) 763-3157
15251 Rte. 2
6 rooms - $50
Pets: Welcome
Creature Comforts: CCTV, a/c

Tyrolean Ritz
(800) 854-6365, (509) 548-5455
http://www.tyrolritz.com
633 Front St.
16 rooms - $50-125
Pets: $10 fee, $20 deposit
Creature Comforts: CCTV, a/c,
refrig, micro, whirlpool

LILLIWAUP
Mike's Beach Resort
(800) 231-5324, (360) 877-5324
N. 38470 Rte. 101
8 rooms - $40-95
Pets: Welcome
Creature Comforts: CCTV

LONG BEACH
Anchorage Cottages
(360) 642-2351
2209 N. Blvd.
9 rooms - $60-120
Pets: Welcome w/$6 fee
Creature Comforts: CCTV, kit

Arcadia Court
(360) 642-2613
401 N. Ocean Beach Blvd.
8 rooms - $35-83
Pets: Welcome
Creature Comforts: CCTV

Boulevard Motel
(360) 642-2434
301 Ocean Blvd. N.
22 cottages - $45-75
Pets: Welcome w/permission
Creature Comforts: CCTV, kit,
pool

The Breakers Motel/Condo
(800) 219-9833, (360) 642-4414
http://breakerslongbeach.com
26th St. & Rte. 103
14 condos - $59-225
Pets: Welcome w/$10 fee, deposit
Creature Comforts: Oceanview,
attractive condo units, CCTV,
VCR, kit, stone fireplace,
restaurant, pool, whirlpool

Chautaqua Lodge
(800) 869-8401
304 - 14 St. NW
180 rooms - $55-160
Pets: Welcome w/$10 fee, deposit
Creature Comforts: CCTV, kit,
fireplace, pool

Edgewater Inn
(800) 561-2456, (360) 642-2311
409 - 10th St.
84 rooms - $49-104
Pets: Welcome w/$8 fee
Creature Comforts: CCTV,
refrig, micro, fireplace, restaurant,
pool

Lighthouse Motel
(360) 642-3622
12415 Pacific Way
9 rooms - $47-64
Pets: Welcome w/$5 fee
Creature Comforts: CCTV

Long Beach Motel/Cottages
(888) 789-2287, (360) 642-3500
1200 Pacific Ave. South
9 cabins - $47-64
Pets: Welcome
Creature Comforts: CCTV,
refrig, micro, kit, fireplace

Ocean Lodge
(360) 642-2777
101 Blvd. St. N.
65 rooms - $50-90
Pets: Welcome
Creature Comforts: CCTV, pool,
whirlpool

Our Place at the Beach
(800) 538-5107, (360) 642-3793
1309 South Blvd.
28 rooms - $54-59
Pets: Welcome w/$5 fee
Creature Comforts: CCTV,
VCR, kit, fireplace, hlth club,
whirlpool, sauna

Pacific View Motel
(800) 238-0859, (360) 642-2415
203 Bolstad St.
11 rooms - $40-96
Pets: Welcome w/$5 fee
Creature Comforts: CCTV

Sands Motel
(360) 642-2100
12211 Pacific Way
5 rooms - $33-50
Pets: Welcome
Creature Comforts: CCTV

Shaman Motel
(800) 753-3750, (360) 642-3714
115 - 3rd St. SW
42 rooms - $65-120
Pets: Welcome w/$5 fee
Creature Comforts: CCTV, kit,
fireplace, pool

Whales Tale
(360) 642-3455
620 S. Pacific Hwy.
9 rooms - $29-99
Pets: Welcome
Creature Comforts: CCTV, hlth
club, whirlpool

LONGVIEW
Budget Inn
(360) 423-6980
1808 Hemlock St.
32 rooms - $27-45
Pets: Welcome
Creature Comforts: CCTV, a/c,
cont. brkfst

Holiday Inn Express
(800) HOLIDAY, (360) 414-1000
http://www.holiday-inn.com
723 - 7th Ave.
50 rooms - $60-79
Pets: Welcome w/$15 fee
Creature Comforts: CCTV, a/c,
kit, cont. brkfst, pool, whirlpool

Hudson Manor Motel
(360) 425-1100
1616 Hudson St.
25 rooms - $34
Pets: Welcome w/$10 deposit
Creature Comforts: CCTV, a/c,
refrig, micro

Town Chalet Motor Hotel
(360) 423-2020
1822 Washington Way
24 rooms - $30-53
Pets: Welcome w/$25 deposit
Creature Comforts: CCTV, a/c,
micro, kit

Town House Motel
(360) 423-1100
744 Washington Way
28 rooms - $30-50
Pets: Welcome w/$15 deposit
Creature Comforts: CCTV, a/c,
refrig, micro, pool

LOOMIS
Chopaka Lodge
(509) 223-3131
1995 Loomis Orville Hwy.
3 rooms - $45-50
Pets: Welcome
Creature Comforts: CCTV, a/c

LOON LAKE
Robbins Cottages
(509) 233-2130
40750 Robbins Rd.
2 rooms - $300-350/wk
Pets: Welcome
Creature Comforts: CCTV, a/c,
kit

LOPEZ ISLAND
FenWold Cottage & Gardens
(360) 468-3062
80 Port Stanley Rd.
1 cottage - $98
Pets: Welcome
Creature Comforts: Cottage w/
beautiful gardens, CCTV, full
brkfst, full brkfst

LYNDEN
Windmill Inn Motel
(360) 354-3424
8022 Guide Meridien St.
15 rooms - $35-50
Pets: Small dogs w/$5 fee, no cats
Creature Comforts: CCTV, a/c,
kit

LYNNWOOD
Best Western Seattle North
(800) 528-1234, (425) 775-7447
http://www.bestwestern.com
4300 - 200th St. S.W.
100 rooms - $35-50
Pets: Small pets w$10 fee
Creature Comforts: CCTV, a/c,
refrig, micro, restaurant, cont.
brkfst, pool

Residence Inn
(800) 331-3131, (425) 771-1100
http://www.residenceinn.com
18200 Alderwood Mall
120 rooms - $145-199
Pets: Welcome w/$10 fee
Creature Comforts: CCTV, a/c,
kit, fireplace, cont. brkfst

Rose Motel
(425) 744-5616
20222 Rte. 99
10 rooms - $32-35
Pets: Welcome
Creature Comforts: CCTV, a/c

Silver Cloud Lynnwood
(425) 775-7600
19332 - 36th Ave. W
167 rooms - $68-99
Pets: Small pets w/$5 fee
Creature Comforts: CCTV, a/c,
cont. brkfst, pool, hlth club

MAPLE FALLS
Mount Baker Lodging
(800) 709-7669, (360) 599-2453
http://www.mtbakerlodging.com
7425 Mt. Baker Hwy.
25 houses - $99-235
Pets: Welcome w/$100 deposit
Creature Comforts: Riverside
homes and cabins, CCTV, a/c, kit,
fireplace, Jacuzzi, whirlpool

Thurston House B&B
(360) 599-2261
9512 Silver Lake Rd.
2 rooms - $50-65
Pets: Welcome w/$10 fee
Creature Comforts: CCTV, a/c,
full brkfst, whirlpool

MARYSVILLE
Best Western Tulalip
(800) 528-1234, (360) 659-4488
http://www.bestwestern.com
6128 - 33rd Ave.
69 rooms - $69-109
Pets: Small pets welcome
Creature Comforts: CCTV, a/c,
refrig, micro, Jacuzzi, restaurant,
whirlpool

Village Motor Inn
(360) 659-0005
235 Beech St.
45 rooms - $52-130
Pets: Small pets w/$12 fee
Creature Comforts: CCTV, a/c,
refrig, micro, Jacuzzi, cont. brkfst

MAZAMA
Lost River Resort
(800) 996-2537
672 Lost River Rd.
12 rooms - $50-65
Pets: Welcome w/$10 fee
Creature Comforts: CCTV

MOCLIPS
Barnacle Motel
(360) 276-4318
4816 Pacific Ave.
2 rooms - $45-65
Pets: Welcome
Creature Comforts: CCTV

Hi-Tide Ocean Beach Resort
(800) MOCLIPS, (360) 276-4142
http://www.hi-tide-resort.com/
4890 Railroad Ave.
33 condos - $80-164
Pets: Welcome w/$10 fee, towels
provided
Creature Comforts: Oceanfront,
well maintained condos, great
views, CCTV, VCR, kit, fireplace,
sauna

Moclips Motel
(360) 276-4228
4852 Pacific Ave.
11 rooms - $38-65
Pets: Welcome
Creature Comforts: CCTV

Moonstone Beach Motel
(360) 276-4346
4849 Pacific Ave.
8 rooms - $45-64
Pets: Welcome
Creature Comforts: CCTV

MONROE
Best Western Baron
(800) 528-1234, (360) 794-3111
http://www.bestwestern.com
19233 Rte. 2
58 rooms - $48-150
Pets: Small pets w/$15 fee
Creature Comforts: CCTV, a/c,
refrig, micro, kit, restaurant, cont.
brkfst, pool, hlth clb., whirlpool

Fairgrounds Inn
(360) 794-5401
18950 Rte. 2
60 rooms - $35-40
Pets: Welcome w/$5 nightly fee
Creature Comforts: CCTV, a/c

MORTON
Evergreen Motel
(360) 496-5407
121 Front St.
12 rooms - $30-50
Pets: Welcome
Creature Comforts: CCTV

Seasons Motel
(360) 496-6835
200 Westlake Ave.
50 rooms - $55-65
Pets: Small pets w/ $5 fee
Creature Comforts: CCTV, a/c

St. Helens Manorhouse B&B
(800) 551-3290
7476 Rte. 12
4 rooms - $65-95
Pets: Welcome
Creature Comforts: CCTV, a/c,
whirlpool

Sultner Motel
(360) 496-5103
250 Morton Rd.
7 rooms - $30-35
Pets: Welcome
Creature Comforts: CCTV, a/c

MOSES LAKE
Best Western Hallmark
(800) 528-1234, (509) 635-4555
http://www.bestwestern.com
3000 Marina Dr.
161 rooms - $64-140
Pets: Welcome
Creature Comforts: CCTV, a/c,
refrig, kit, Jacuzzi, restaurant,
pool, hlth clb., whirlpool, sauna,
tennis boating

El Rancho Motel
(800) 341-8000, (509) 765-9173
http://www.imalodging.com
1214 S. Pioneer Way
20 rooms - $32-60
Pets: Welcome
Creature Comforts: CCTV, a/c,
pool

Holiday Inn Express
(509) 766-2000
http://www.holiday-inn.com
1745 East Kittleson St.
75 rooms - $68-100
Pets: Welcome in smoking rooms
Creature Comforts: CCTV, a/c,
cont. brkfst, pool, hlth club,
whirlpool

Interstate Inn
(509) 765-1777
2801 W. Broadway St.
30 rooms - $36-49
Pets: Welcome
Creature Comforts: CCTV, a/c,
pool, whirlpool

Maples Motel
(509) 765-5665
1006 W. Third Ave.
22 rooms - $35-85
Pets: Welcome
Creature Comforts: CCTV, a/c

Moses Lake Travelodge
(800) 578-7878, (509) 765-8631
http://www.travelodge.com
316 S Pioneer Way
40 rooms - $42-60
Pets: Welcome w/$5 fee, no cats
Creature Comforts: CCTV, a/c,
pool

Motel 6
(800) 4-MOTEL6, (509) 766-0250
http://www.motel6.com
2822 Wapato Dr.
111 rooms - $32-44
Pets: Under 30 lbs. welcome
Creature Comforts: CCTV, a/c,
pool

Oasis Budget Inn
(509) 765-8638
466 Melva Ln.
40 rooms - $38-65
Pets: Welcome
Creature Comforts: CCTV, a/c,
pool, whirlpool

Shilo Inn
(800) 222-2244, (509) 765-9317
http://www.shiloinn.com
1819 East Kittleson St.
100 rooms - $65-89
Pets: Welcome
Creature Comforts: CCTV, a/c,
cont. brkfst, pool, hlth club,
whirlpool

Sunland Motor Inn
(800) 220-4403
309 E. Third Ave.
22 rooms - $32-52
Pets: Welcome
Creature Comforts: CCTV, a/c

Super 8 Motel
(800) 800-8000, (509) 765-8886
http://www.super8.com
449 Melva Ln.
62 rooms - $51-71
Pets: Welcome w/permission
Creature Comforts: CCTV, a/c,
pool

MOUNT VERNON
Best Western College Way
(800) 528-1234, (360) 424-4287
http://www.bestwestern.com
300 West College Way
66 rooms - $45-75
Pets: Welcome w/$5 fee
Creature Comforts: CCTV, a/c,
refrig, kit, cont. brkfst

Best Western Cottontree
(800) 528-1234, (360) 428-5678
http://www.bestwestern.com
2300 Market St.
121 rooms - $59-89
Pets: Small pets w/$10 fee
Creature Comforts: CCTV, a/c,
refrig, micro, cont. brkfst, pool,
exercise rm

Comfort Inn, Mt. Vernon
(800) 228-5150, (360) 428-7020
http://www.comfortinn.com
1910 Freeway Dr.
68 rooms - $59-69
Pets: Welcome
Creature Comforts: CCTV, a/c,
kit, cont. brkfst, pool, whirlpool

Days Inn
(800) DAYS INN, (360) 424-4141
http://www.daysinn.com
2009 Riverside Dr.
67 rooms - $50-65
Pets: Welcome w/$5 fee
Creature Comforts: CCTV, a/c,
restaurant

Hillside Motel
(360) 445-3252
2300 Bonnie View Rd.
6 rooms - $39-50
Pets: Welcome
Creature Comforts: CCTV, a/c

Tulip Inn
(360) 428-5969
2200 Freeway Dr.
40 rooms - $35-60
Pets: Welcome
Creature Comforts: CCTV, a/c

West Winds Motel
(360) 424-4224
2020 Riverside Dr.
40 rooms - $32-50
Pets: Welcome
Creature Comforts: CCTV, a/c

NAHCOTTA
Moby Dick Hotel/Oyster Farm
(360) 665-4543
http://www.nwplace.com/
mobydick.html
Sandridge Rd.
9 rooms - $75-95
Pets: Welcome w/$10 fee
Creature Comforts: 1929 yellow
stucco hotel, simple exterior w/
distinctive interior spaces, water
views, Art Deco décor w/ocean,
wildlife, or literary themes, CCTV,
a/c, full gourmet brkfst, restaurant

Our House in Nahcotta
(360) 665-6667
Box 33
2 rooms - $95
Pets: Welcome
Creature Comforts: CCTV, a/c,
cont. brkfst

NEAH BAY
Cape Motel
(360) 645-2250
Bayview Ave.
10 rooms - $45-65
Pets: Welcome
Creature Comforts: CCTV

Silver Salmon Resort
(360) 645-2388
Bayview and Roosevelt
9 rooms - $44-65
Pets: Welcome
Creature Comforts: CCTV

Tyee Motel
(360) 645-2223
Box 193
42 rooms - $35-95
Pets: Welcome
Creature Comforts: CCTV

NEWPORT
Golden Spur Motor Inn
(509) 447-3823
924 W. Rte. 2
24 rooms - $45-50
Pets: Small pets w/$10 fee
Creature Comforts: CCTV, a/c,
restaurant

Newport City Inn
(509) 447-3463
220 N. Washington St.
13 rooms - $38-56
Pets: Welcome
Creature Comforts: CCTV, a/c

OAK HARBOR
Acorn Motor Inn
(360) 675-6646
31530 Rte. 20
32 rooms - $42-62
Pets: Welcome
Creature Comforts: CCTV, a/c, cont. brkfst

Best Western Harbor Plaza
(800) 528-1234, (360) 679-4567
http://www.bestwestern.com
33175 Rte. 20
80 rooms - $69-129
Pets: Welcome w/$10 fee
Creature Comforts: CCTV, a/c, refrig, micro, cont. brkfst, pool, exercise rm, whirlpool

OCEAN CITY
Pacific Sands Motel
(360) 289-3588
2687 Rte. 109
9 rooms - $40-56
Pets: Welcome
Creature Comforts: CCTV, pool

Westwinds Resort Motel
(360) 675-6646
2537 Rte. 109
10 rooms - $36-100
Pets: Welcome
Creature Comforts: CCTV

OCEAN SHORES
Beach Front Vacation Rentals
(800) 544-8887
Box 685
60 rooms - $65-250
Pets: Welcome w/deposit
Creature Comforts: CCTV, kit, pool, whirlpool

Discovery Inn
(360) 289-3371
1031 Discovery Ave., SE
21 rooms - $52-78
Pets: Welcome
Creature Comforts: CCTV, kit, pool, whirlpool

Grey Gull
(800) 562-9712, (360) 289-3381
http://www.thegreygull.com
651 Ocean Shores Blvd NW
37 condos - $98-315
Pets: Welcome in ltd. units
Creature Comforts: CCTV, VCR, micro, kit, fireplace, pool, whirlpool, sauna

The Nautilus
(800) 221-4541, (360) 289-2722
835 Ocean Shores Blvd, NW
23 rooms - $98-315
Pets: Welcome w/$10 fee
Creature Comforts: CCTV, VCR, refrig, micro, kit, fireplace, whirlpool

Ocean Shores Motel
(360) 289-3351
681 Ocean Shores Blvd, N
40 rooms - $40-110
Pets: Welcome w/$5 fee
Creature Comforts: CCTV

Ocean View Resort Homes
(800) 927-6394, (360) 289-4416
http://oceanshores.com/lodging/homes/index.shtml
164 Ocean View Blvd.
12 rooms - $75-225
Pets: Welcome
Creature Comforts: CCTV, kit, fireplace, whirlpool

Polynesian Condominiums
(360) 289-3361
615 Ocean Shores Blvd.
71 rooms - $79-179
Pets: Small pets w/$15 fee in ltd. rooms
Creature Comforts: CCTV, VCR, refrig, micro, kit, fireplace, restaurant, pool, whirlpool, sauna

The Sands Resort
(800) 841-4001, (360) 289-2444
oceanshores.com/lodging/sands2
801 Ocean Shores Blvd.
79 rooms - $48-95
Pets: Small pets w/$10 fee
Creature Comforts: SATV, VCR, fireplace, Jacuzzzi, kit, pool, whirlpool, sauna

Sands Royal Pacific Motel
(800) 562-9748
781 Ocean Shores Blvd.
47 rooms - $80-160
Pets: Welcome
Creature Comforts: CCTV, pool, whirlpool

Surfview Condos
(360) 289-3077
757 Ocean Court
5 rooms - $55-80
Pets: Welcome
Creature Comforts: CCTV, kit

OCEAN PARK
Coastal Cottages
(800) 200-0424, (360) 665-4658
1511 264th Pl.
3728 Pacific Way
4 cottages - $30-70
Pets: Welcome
Creature Comforts: CCTV

Harbor View Motel
(360) 665-4959
3306 281st St.
7 rooms - $45-55
Pets: Welcome
Creature Comforts: CCTV

Ocean Park Resort
(360) 665-4585
25904 R St.
14 rooms - $54-110
Pets: Small pets w/$7 fee
Creature Comforts: CCTV, kit

Shakti Cove Cottages
(360) 665-4000
253rd at Park St.
1o cottages - $60-70
Pets: Welcome
Creature Comforts: CCTV, kit

Sunset View Resort
(360) 665-4494
25517 Park Ave.
52 rooms - $65-185
Pets: Welcome
Creature Comforts: CCTV, whirlpool, sauna

Westgate Motel
(360) 665-4211
20803 Pacific Hwy.
45 rooms - $45-60
Pets: Welcome
Creature Comforts: CCTV, kit

OKANOGAN

Cedars Inn
(509) 422-6431
One Appleway Rd.
78 rooms - $45-57
Pets: Welcome
Creature Comforts: CCTV, a/c,
refrig, pool

Ponderosa Motor Lodge
(509) 422-0400
1034 S. Second Ave.
25 rooms - $37-44
Pets: Welcome
Creature Comforts: CCTV,
VCR, refrig, micro, kit

U&I Rivers Edge Motel
(509) 422-2920
838 Second Ave.
9 rooms - $35-50
Pets: Welcome
Creature Comforts: CCTV

OLYMPIA

Bailey Motor Inn
(360) 491-7515
3333 Martin Way
48 rooms - $40-45
Pets: Welcome
Creature Comforts: CCTV, a/c

Best Western Aladdin
(800) 528-1234, (360) 352-7200
http://www.bestwestern.com
900 S. Capitol Way
99 rooms - $50-65
Pets: Small pets w/$5 fee
Creature Comforts: CCTV, a/c,
restaurant, pool hlth club,
whirlpool

Cinnamon Rabbit B&B
(360) 357-5520
1304 Seventh Ave. W.
2 rooms - $55-80
Pets: Welcome if they don't
disturb the rabbits
Creature Comforts: Tiny
cottage-like home, beautiful grdns,
CCTV, a/c, vegetarian brkfst

Holiday Inn Select
(800) HOLIDAY, (360) 943-4000
http://www.holiday-inn.com
2300 Evergreen Park Dr.
177 rooms - $69-175
Pets: Welcome w/$25 fee
Creature Comforts: CCTV, a/c,
restaurant, pool, whirlpool

Holly Motel
(360) 943-3000
2816 Martin Way
37 rooms - $35-41
Pets: Welcome
Creature Comforts: CCTV, a/c

Puget View Guesthouse
(360) 459-1676
bbonline.com/wa/pugetview
7924 - 61st NE
1 cottage - $89
Pets: Welcome
Creature Comforts: Wonderful
guest cottage on forested seaside
bluff, beautiful gardens, English
country cottage motif, CCTV, a/c,
refrig, cont. brkfst, canoe, hiking
at adjacent nature preserve

Tyee Hotel
(800) 386-8933, (360) 352-0511
500 Tyee Dr.
146 rooms - $73-150
Pets: Welcome w/$8 fee
Creature Comforts: CCTV, a/c,
refrig, micro, pool, whirlpool

OMAK

Leisure Village Motel
(509) 826-4442
630 Okoma Dr.
33 rooms - $30-100
Pets: Small pets w/$5 fee
Creature Comforts: CCTV, a/c,
refrig, micro, kit, cont. brkfst,
pool, whirlpool, sauna

Motel Nicholas
(509) 826-4611
527 E. Grape Ave.
20 rooms - $30-45
Pets: Welcome
Creature Comforts: CCTV, a/c

Omak Inn
(800) 204-4800, (509) 826-2980
912 Koala Dr.
50 rooms - $55-70
Pets: Small pets w/$10 fee
Creature Comforts: CCTV, a/c,
refrig, micro, Jacuzzi, full brkfst,
pool, hlth club

Royal Motel
(509) 826-5715
514 E. Riverside Dr.
10 rooms - $30-35
Pets: Welcome w/$20 deposit
Creature Comforts: CCTV, a/c

Thriftlodge
(800) 525-9055, (509) 826-0400
http://www.travelodge.com
122 N. Main St.
59 rooms - $30-50
Pets: Welcome
Creature Comforts: CCTV, a/c,
pool

ORCAS ISLAND

Bartwood Lodge
(360) 376-2242
Rte. 2 (Eastsound)
16 rooms - $50-180
Pets: Welcome w/$5 fee
Creature Comforts: CCTV, a/c,
fireplace, restaurant, pool, tennis,
boating

Deer Harbor Inn
(877) 377-4110, (360) 376-4110
sanjuanweb.com/DeerHarborInn
Deer Harbor Rd.
3 cottages - $99-199
Pets: Well-behaved dogs welcome
in cottages
Creature Comforts: 1915 main
lodge w/attractive ranch cottages
set in apple orchard, knotty pine
walls, down quilts on pine beds,
chicken and egg ranch, CCTV,
fireplace, restaurant, brkfst basket,
whirlpool

North Beach Inn
(360) 276-2660
Box 80 (Eastsound)
11 cabins - $95-170
Pets: Welcome w/$10 fee
Creature Comforts: Weathered
cottages on 100 acres, beach and
upland, casual family-oriented
cabins w/eclectic furnishings, kit,
fireplace, barbecue, CCTV, a/c,
pool, whirlpool

North Shore Cottages
(360) 376-5131
http://www.northshore4kiss.com
271 Sunset Ave. (Eastsound)
3 cottages - $165-245
Pets: "If your dog will vouch for
YOU, you're welcome to stay."
Creature Comforts: Waterview
cottages, rqst architectural gem-
Heron Cottage, intimate,
hardwoods, copper brass, some
nautical themes, antiques wicker,
CCTV, VCR, kit, fireplace,
whirlpool

    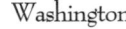
West Beach Resort
(877) West-Bch, (360) 376-2240
http://www.westbeachresort.com/
190 Waterfront Way
15 cottages - $135-180
Pets: Welcome in ltd. cottages w/
$10 fee, signed pet agreement,
refundable damage deposit, not
allowed in deluxe cottages
Creature Comforts: Beachfront
cottages, CCTV, kit, woodstove,
pond, swimming, boating, fishing,
kayaking

OROVILLE
Canary Motel
(509) 476-3684
1320 Main St.
38 rooms - $35-55
Pets: Welcome
Creature Comforts: CCTV, a/c,
pool

Red Apple Inn
(509) 476-3694
1815 Main St.
37 rooms - $36-65
Pets: Welcome
Creature Comforts: CCTV, a/c,
pool

OTHELLO
Aladdin Motor Inn
(509) 488-5671
1020 E. Cedar St.
52 rooms - $35-44
Pets: Welcome
Creature Comforts: CCTV, a/c,
refrig, micro, cont. brkfst, pool

Cimarron Motel
(509) 488-6612
1450 E. Main St.
20 rooms - $32-43
Pets: Welcome
Creature Comforts: CCTV, a/c

PACIFIC BEACH
Sand Dollar Inn
(360) 276-4525
53 Central Ave.
11 rooms - $40-105
Pets: Welcome
Creature Comforts: CCTV,
whirlpool

Sandpiper Beach Resort
(800) 567-4737, (360) 276-4580
http://www.sandpiper-resort.com/
4159 Rte. 109
30 condo suites - $55-100
Pets: Welcome w/$10 fee
Creature Comforts: Great family
find, well designed suites w/ocean
views, nicely decorated, kit,
fireplace, Jacuzzi, electric towel
warmers, espresso bar/gift shop,
long sandy beach to explore

PACKWOOD
Crest Trail Lodge
(800) 477-5339
http://www.mountsthelens.com/
crest_trail_lodge.html
12729 Rte. 12
25 rooms - $50-65
Pets: Welcome
Creature Comforts: CCTV, a/c,
refrig, cont. brkfst, whirlpool

Hotel Packwood
(360) 494-5431
Box 130
9 rooms - $20-38
Pets: Welcome
Creature Comforts: CCTV, a/c

Mountain View Lodge
(360) 494-5555
13163 Rte. 12
24 rooms - $31-73
Pets: Welcome
Creature Comforts: CCTV, a/c,
pool, whirlpool

Tatoosh Meadows Resort
(800) 294-2311, (360) 494-2311
http://www.tmcproperties.com
Box 487
25 homes - $145-300
Pets: $25 one-time fee
Creature Comforts: Various
condos and homes, some
riverfront, CCTV, VCR, kit,
fireplace, whirlpool, sauna

Tatoosh Motel
(360) 494-5321
12880 Rte. 12
14 rooms - $29-125
Pets: Welcome
Creature Comforts: CCTV, a/c,
cont. brkfst, whirlpool

Timberline Village Resort
(360) 494-9224
13807 Rte. 12
21 rooms - $34-44
Pets: Welcome w/$5 fee
Creature Comforts: CCTV, a/c

PASCO
Airport Motel
(509) 545-1460
2532 N. Fourth
42 rooms - $28-40
Pets: Welcome
Creature Comforts: CCTV, a/c,
cont. brkfst, pool

Doubletree Hotel-Pasco
(800) 222-TREE, (509) 547-0701
http://www.doubletreehotels.com
2525 N. 20th Ave.
279 rooms - $75-115
Pets: Welcome
Creature Comforts: CCTV, a/c,
restaurant, pool, exercise rm,
whirlpool

Hallmark Motel
(509) 547-7766
720 Lewis St.
55 rooms - $28-48
Pets: Welcome
Creature Comforts: CCTV, a/c,
pool

King City Truck Stop
(509) 547-3475
2100 E. Hillsboro Rd.
36 rooms - $32-59
Pets: Welcome
Creature Comforts: CCTV, a/c

Motel 6
(800) 4-MOTEL6, (509) 546-2010
http://www.motel6.com
Rtes. 12 & 395
120 rooms - $25-35
Pets: Under 30 lbs. welcome
Creature Comforts: CCTV, a/c,
pool

Sage 'N Sun Motel
(800) 391-9188, (509) 547-2451
1232 S. Tenth Ave.
32 rooms - $28-55
Pets: Welcome
Creature Comforts: CCTV, a/c,
pool

Starlite Motel
(800) 786-8854, (509) 547-7531
2634 N. Fourth Ave.
18 rooms - $28-45
Pets: Welcome
Creature Comforts: CCTV, a/c

Travel Inn Motel
(509) 547-7791
725 W. Lewis St.
38 rooms - $25-32
Pets: Welcome
Creature Comforts: CCTV, a/c

Vineyard Inn
(509) 547-0791
1800 W. Lewis St.
165 rooms - $45-60
Pets: Welcome
Creature Comforts: CCTV, a/c,
pool, whirlpool

PATEROS
Lake Pateros Motor Inn
(800) 444-1985, (509) 923-2203
115 Lake Shore Dr.
30 rooms - $57-79
Pets: Welcome
Creature Comforts: CCTV, a/c,
pool

PEHASTIN
Timberline Motel
(509) 548-7415
8284 Rte. 2
6 rooms - $30-60
Pets: Welcome
Creature Comforts: CCTV, a/c

POINT ROBERTS
Cedar House Inn
(360) 945-0284
1534 Gulf Rd.
6 rooms - $36-49
Pets: Welcome
Creature Comforts: CCTV, a/c,
full brkfst

POMEROY
Pioneer Motel
(509) 843-1559
1201 Main St.
11 rooms - $38-55
Pets: Welcome
Creature Comforts: CCTV, a/c,
whirlpool

PORT ANGELES
Chinook Motel
(360) 452-2336
1414 E. First St.
53 rooms - $40-45
Pets: Welcome w/$5 fee
Creature Comforts: CCTV, a/c,
kit

Doubletree Hotel
(800) 222-TREE, (360) 452-9215
http://www.doubletreehotels.com
221 North Lincoln St.
187 rooms - $59-155
Pets: Welcome w/$35 deposit
Creature Comforts: CCTV, a/c,
refrig, restaurant, pool, whirlpool

Flagstone Motel
(360) 457-9494
415 First St.
45 rooms - $36-90
Pets: Small pets welcome
Creature Comforts: CCTV,
refrig, micro, cont. brkfst, pool

Historic Lake Crescent Lodge
(360) 928-3211
416 Lake Crescent Rd.
53 rooms - $59-155
Pets: Welcome w/$35 deposit
Creature Comforts: Simple
accommodations, spectacular
natural surroundings, wonderful
1916 log and stone lodge w/
massive stone fireplace, open
timbers, glassed-in porch, rqst
1937 Roosevelt Fireplace
Cottages, or simpler Singer Tavern
cottages, water views, CCTV, a/c,
refrig, restaurant, lake swimming,
boating

Log Cabin Resort
(360) 928-3325
http://www.logcabinresort.net/
3183 E. Beach Rd.
28 rooms - $75-118
Pets: Welcome in cabins w/$6 fee
Creature Comforts: Rustic 1928
cabins w/lake or mtn. views

Maple Rose B&B
(800) 570-2007, (360) 457-ROSE
http://www.northolympic.com/
maplerose
112 Reservoir Rd.
5 rooms - $79-147
Pets: Welcome w/$15 fee
Creature Comforts: Small inn w/
many special amenities (plaid
nightshirts/robes), sophisticated
country decor, CCTV, kit, Jacuzzi,
full gourmet brkfst, pool, exercise
rm, whirlpool

Ocean Crest B&B
(800) 570-2007, (360) 452-4832
http://www.northolympic.com/
oceancrest/
402 S. 'M'
2 rooms - $65-85
Pets: Welcome w/$15 fee
Creature Comforts: CCTV, full
brkfst, exercise rm.

Pond Motel
(360) 452-8422
1425 W. Rte. 101
12 rooms - $27-59
Pets: Welcome
Creature Comforts: CCTV,
refrig

Sol Duc Hot Springs
(360) 327-3583
Olympic Nat'l Park
32 rooms - $87-147
Pets: Welcome
Creature Comforts: CCTV,
whirlpool, hot springs

Sportsmen Motel
(360) 457-6196
2909 E. Hwy 101
32 rooms - $45-75
Pets: Welcome
Creature Comforts: CCTV,
restaurant

Super 8 Motel
(800) 800-8000, (360) 452-8401
http://www.super8.com
2104 E. First St.
62 rooms - $60-88
Pets: Welcome w/permission
Creature Comforts: CCTV, a/c

Uptown Motel
(360) 457-9434
101 E. Second St.
35 rooms - $59-155
Pets: Welcome w/$35 deposit
Creature Comforts: CCTV,
refrig, micro, kit, cont. brkfst,
whirlpool

PORT LUDLOW
Inn at Ludlow Bay
(360) 437-0411
One Heron Rd.
37 rooms - $135-450
Pets: Small pets in ltd. rooms w/
$50 deposit
Creature Comforts: Very
attractive contemporary shingle
style resort on peninsula, lovely
public spaces, rms w/Mission style
furnishings and Art Deco décor,
oversized pillows, down duvets,
terry robes, fine toiletries, CCTV,
refrig, fireplaces, Jacuzzi,
restaurant, cont. brkfst, famous
totem pole at end of peninsula

PORT TOWNSEND
Aladdin Motor Inn
(360) 385-3747
2333 Washington St.
30 rooms - $60-99
Pets: Welcome
Creature Comforts: CCTV

Annapurna Inn
(800) 868-ANNA, (360) 385-2909
http://seattle2000.com/annapurna
538 Adams St.
6 rooms - $75-108
Pets: With notice and non-
refundable deposit
Creature Comforts: Storybook
cottage in residential area,
beautiful gardens, hand-stenciled
walls, individually decorated
rooms w/country furnishings,
health-oriented B&B w/organic
vegan cuisine, full brkfst, sauna/
steam bath, yoga, therapeutic
massage

Bishop Victorian Guest Suites
(800) 942-5960, (360) 385-6122
http://www.waypt.com/bishop/
bishop.htm
714 Washington St.
14 suites - $70-140
Pets: Welcome
Creature Comforts: 1890 brick
building, suites w/"West Country"
Victorian motif, original art,
memorabilia, exposed brick walls,
brass beds, dried flowers, CCTV,
kit, fireplaces, soaking tubs, cont.
brkfst

Harborside Inn
(800) 942-5960, (360) 385-7909
330 Benedict St.
63 rooms - $64-175
Pets: Small pets in smoking
rooms
Creature Comforts: CCTV,
refrig, micro, cont. brkfst, pool,
whirlpool

Heritage House Inn
(360) 385-6800
305 Pierce St.
6 rooms - $85-140
Pets: Welcome
Creature Comforts: CCTV, full
brkfst

Old Alcohol Plant Resort
(800) 785-7030
http://www.alcoholplant.com/lace
310 Alcohol Loop Rd.
28 rooms - $44-225
Pets: Welcome w/$10 fee
Creature Comforts: CCTV, kit,
fireplace, Jacuzzi, restaurant, cont.
brkfst, exercise rm.

Palace Hotel
(800) 962-0741
http://www.olympus.net/palace
1004 Water St.
15 rooms - $45-149
Pets: Small pets w/$20 fee
Creature Comforts: CCTV,
refrig, micro, kit, Jacuzzi,
restaurant, cont. brkfst

Point Hudson Resort/Marina
(800) 826-3854, (360) 385-2828
103 Hudson St.
29 rooms - $45-125
Pets: Welcome
Creature Comforts: CCTV, full
brkfst, hlth club

Port Townsend Inn
(360) 385-2211
http://www.olympus.net/bji
2020 Washington St.
33 rooms - $48-98
Pets: Welcome in ltd. rooms
Creature Comforts: CCTV,
VCR, refrig, micro, kit, full brkfst,
pool, whirlpool

Salmonberry Farm
(360) 385-6800
http://olympus.net/getaways/SF/
2404 - 35th St.
1 rooms - $90
Pets: Welcome
Creature Comforts: CCTV,
living rm, fireplace, kit, full brkfst

The Swan Hotel
(360) 385-1718
http://www.waypt.com/bishop/
swan.htm
222 Monroe St.
9 rooms - $90-400
Pets: Welcome w/$10 fee
Creature Comforts: Wonderful
shingled hotel w/wraparound
porches, in historic district, rqst
quaint cottages for privacy or
suites for water views, beautifully
decorated w/pine beds, bright
colors, paddle fans, CCTV, refrig,
micro, kit, Jacuzzi, full brkfst

Water Street Hotel
(800) 735-9810, (360) 385-5467
635 Water St.
16 rooms - $45-125
Pets: $10 fee, $50 deposit
Creature Comforts: CCTV,
refrig, kit

POULSBO
Poulsbo Inn
(800) 597-5151, (360) 779-3921
http://amouse.net/poulsboinn/
18680 Rte. 305
73 rooms - $55-110
Pets: Small pets w/$5 fee
Creature Comforts: Great motel
CCTV, VCR, a/c, refrig, pool,
whirlpool, playground

PROSSER

Best Western Prosser Inn
(800) 528-1234, (509) 786-7977
http://www.bestwestern.com
225 Meriot Dr.
49 rooms - $56-71
Pets: Welcome w/$10 fee, $50 deposit
Creature Comforts: CCTV, a/c, Jacuzzi, pool

Prosser Motel
(509) 786-2555
1206 Wine Country Rd.
16 rooms - $27-46
Pets: Welcome
Creature Comforts: CCTV, a/c

PULLMAN

American Travel Inn
(509) 334-3500
515 S. Grand Ave.
35 rooms - $45-59
Pets: Small pets welcome
Creature Comforts: CCTV, a/c, refrig, pool

Best Western Heritage Inn
(800) 528-1234, (509) 332-0928
http://www.bestwestern.com
928 NW Olsen St.
49 rooms - $56-69
Pets: $10 fee, $50 deposit
Creature Comforts: CCTV, kit, restaurant, cont. brkfst, pool, exercise rm, whirlpool, sauna

Country Bed and Breakfast
(509) 334-4453
http://www.pullman-wa.com/housing/counin.htm
2701 Staley Rd.
5 rooms - $40-100
Pets: Welcome
Creature Comforts: Simple B&B, CCTV, a/c, fireplace, cont. brkfst, play room

Holiday Inn Express
(800) HOLIDAY, (509) 334-4437
http://www.holiday-inn.com
1190 Bishop Blvd.
130 rooms - $79-99
Pets: Welcome
Creature Comforts: CCTV, a/c, pool

Manor Lodge Motel
(509) 334-2511
455 SE Paradise
31 rooms - $37-60
Pets: Welcome
Creature Comforts: CCTV, a/c, refrig

Nendels Motor Inn
(509) 332-2646
915 SE Main St.
60 rooms - $35-49
Pets: Welcome
Creature Comforts: CCTV, a/c

Quality Inn Paradise Creek
(509) 332-0500
SE 1050 Bishop Blvd.
66 rooms - $55-135
Pets: Welcome ltd. rms
Creature Comforts: CCTV, a/c, refrig, micro, Jacuzzi, pool, whirlpool, sauna

PUYALLUP

Best Western Park Plaza
(800) 528-1234, (253) 848-1500
http://www.bestwestern.com
620 S. Hill Park Dr.
100 rooms - $82-99
Pets: Small pets welcome
Creature Comforts: CCTV, a/c, cont. brkfst, pool, hlth clb access

Motel Puyallup
(253) 845-8825
1412 S. Meridian St.
63 rooms - $48-65
Pets: Welcome
Creature Comforts: CCTV, a/c, cont. brkfst

Northwest Motor Inn
(253) 841-2600
1409 S. Meridian St.
51 rooms - $41-60
Pets: Welcome w/$5 fee
Creature Comforts: CCTV, a/c, kit, cont. brkfst, whirlpool

QUILCENE

Maple Grove Motel
(360) 765-3410
61 Maple Grove Rd.
12 rooms - $40-50
Pets: Welcome w/$5 fee
Creature Comforts: CCTV

Quilcene Hotel
(800) 570-0529
Quilcene Ave./Rodgers St.
9 rooms - $50-60
Pets: Welcome
Creature Comforts: CCTV, cont. brkfst, restaurant

QUINAULT

Lake Quinault Lodge
(800) 56-6672, (360) 288-2900,
http://visitlakequinault.com/
1409 S. Meridian St.
92 rooms - $99-210
Pets: Annex rms w/$10 fee
Creature Comforts: Magnificent 1926 shingled lodge on Lake Quinault, Native American themes, massive fireplace, lots of character, annex rooms have cabin-like quality, paneled walls, brass and wicker furnishings, CCTV, a/c, kit, cont. brkfst, pool, whirlpool, sauna, lake swimming, fishing, hiking-rain forest

QUINCY

Sundowner Motel
(509) 787-3587
414 F St. SE
24 rooms - $38-75
Pets: Welcome
Creature Comforts: CCTV, a/c, pool

Traditional Inns
(509) 841-2600
500 SW F St.
24 rooms - $40-78
Pets: Welcome
Creature Comforts: CCTV, a/c

RANDLE

Mt. Adams Motel
(360) 497-7007
9514 Rte. 12
16 rooms - $35-45
Pets: Welcome
Creature Comforts: CCTV, a/c, cont. brkfst, hlth club

Tall Timber Motel
(360) 497-2991
10023 Rte. 12
12 rooms - $33-45
Pets: Welcome
Creature Comforts: CCTV, a/c, full brkfst

RAYMOND
Maunu's Mountcastle Motel
(360) 942-5571
524 Third St.
27 rooms - $40-60
Pets: Welcome w/$5 fee
Creature Comforts: CCTV,
refrig, micro

Willis Motel
(360) 943-5313
425 Third St.
2 rooms - $25-35
Pets: Welcome
Creature Comforts: CCTV

REDMOND
**Homestead Village, Extended
Stay**
(425) 885-6675
15805 NE 28th St.
162 rooms - $315-427
Pets: Welcome
Creature Comforts: CCTV,
VCR, kit, refrig, cont. brkfst,
whirlpool

RENTON
Nendel's Inn
(425) 251-9591
3700 E. Valley Rd.
130 rooms - $60-65
Pets: Welcome w/$3 fee
Creature Comforts: CCTV,
VCR, kit, refrig, cont. brkfst,
whirlpool

REPUBLIC
Frontier Inn Motel
(509) 775-3361
979 S. Clark Ave.
30 rooms - $34-51
Pets: Welcome
Creature Comforts: CCTV, cont.
brkfst, exercise rm, whirlpool

K-Diamond-K
(509) 775-3536
404 Rte. 21 S
4 rooms - $65-105
Pets: Dogs and horses welcome
Creature Comforts: Ranch
focusing on horseback riding,
CCTV, full brkfst

Northern Inn
(509) 775-3371
852 S. Clark St.
25 rooms - $36-48
Pets: Welcome
Creature Comforts: CCTV

Tiffanys Resort
(509) 775-3152
1026 Tiffany Rd.
19 rooms - $43-120
Pets: Welcome
Creature Comforts: CCTV,
swimming

RICHLAND
Bali Hi Motel
(509) 943-3101
1201 George Washington Way
44 rooms - $37-47
Pets: Welcome
Creature Comforts: CCTV, pool,
whirlpool

Best Western Tower Inn
(800) 528-1234, (509) 946-4121
http://www.bestwestern.com
1515 George Washington Way
195 rooms - $70-80
Pets: Welcome w/$5 fee
Creature Comforts: CCTV, a/c,
restaurant, pool, whirlpool

Desert Gold Motel
(509) 627-1000
611 Columbia Dr. SW
28 rooms - $30-50
Pets: Welcome
Creature Comforts: CCTV, a/c,
pool

Doubletree Hotel, Hanford
(800) 222-TREE, (509) 946-7611
http://www.doubletreehotels.com
802 George Washington Way
150 rooms - $57-119
Pets: Welcome
Creature Comforts: CCTV, a/c,
restaurant, pool, whirlpool

Shilo Inn
(800) 222-2244, (509) 946-4661
http://www.shiloinns.com
50 Comstock St.
150 rooms - $65-99
Pets: Small pets w/$7 fee
Creature Comforts: CCTV, a/c,
kit, restaurant, full brkfst, pool,
hlth club, whirlpool

Vagabond Inn
(800) 522-1555, (509) 946-6117
515 George Washington Way
41 rooms - $37-80
Pets: Small pets welcome
Creature Comforts: CCTV, a/c,
refrig, micro, kit, full brkfst, pool

RIMROCK
Game Ridge Motel/Lodge
(509) 672-2212
27350 Rte. 12
14 rooms - $42-140
Pets: Welcome w/$5 fee
Creature Comforts: CCTV,
restaurant, pool, whirlpool

Silver Beach Resort
(509) 672-2500
40350 Rte. 12
17 rooms - $30-60
Pets: Welcome
Creature Comforts: CCTV,
whirlpool

RITZVILLE
Best Western Heritage
(800) 528-1234, (509) 659-1007
http://www.bestwestern.com
1513 Smitty's Blvd.
42 rooms - $47-145
Pets: Welcome w/$5 fee
Creature Comforts: CCTV, a/c,
restaurant, pool, whirlpool

Colwell Motor Inn
(800) 341-8000, (509) 659-1620
http://www.angelfire.com/wa/
ColwellMotorInn/
501 West First Ave.
25 rooms - $40-65
Pets: Welcome w/$5 fee
Creature Comforts: CCTV, a/c,
pool

Empire Motel
(509) 659-1030
101 W. First St.
19 rooms - $27-47
Pets: Welcome
Creature Comforts: CCTV, a/c

Top Hat Motel
(509) 659-1100
210 E. First St.
11 rooms - $46-60
Pets: Welcome w/$5 fee
Creature Comforts: CCTV, a/c

West Side Motel
(800) 559-1164, (509) 659-1164
407 W. First St.
11 rooms - $28-46
Pets: Welcome
Creature Comforts: CCTV, a/c,
cont. brkfst

ROCKPORT
Totem Trail Motel
(360) 873-4535
5551 Rte. 20
8 rooms - $45-55
Pets: Welcome
Creature Comforts: CCTV, a/c,
pool

ROSLYN
Roslyn Inns
(509) 649-2936
106 Fifth St.
3 rooms - $48-290
Pets: Small pets welcome
Creature Comforts: CCTV

SAN JUAN ISLAND
Blair House
http://www.karuna.com/blair/
(800) 899-3030, (360) 378-5907
345 Blair Ave.
7 rms/1 cottage - $75-155
Pets: Welcome in cottage
Creature Comforts: 800 sq.-foot
cottage, great for children and
pets, attractive decor, CCTV,
VCR, kit, woodstove, grill, full
brkfst, pool, hot tub

Friday Harbor House
(360) 378-8455
www.fridayharborhouse.com
130 West St.
20 rooms - $125-275
Pets: Ltd. rooms w/$100 deposit
Creature Comforts: Idyllic
waterside setting, rqst rooms in
main blding, Asian theme to
subtly luxurious rms, European
mattresses and duvets, cherry
furnishings, CCTV, refrig, Jacuzzi,
fine toiletries, intimate restaurant,
cont. brkfst

Harrison House Suites
(800) 407-7933, (360) 378-3587
http://www.san-juan-lodging.com
235 C St.
5 suites - $65-240
Pets: By arrangement
Creature Comforts: 1905
Craftsman, ovrlkg harbor, some
antiques, CCTV, VCR, fireplace,
Jacuzzi, gourmet brkfst, cafe,
whirlpool

The Inns at Friday Harbor
(800) 752-5752, (360) 378-3031
http://www.theinns.com
410 Spring St.
80 rooms - $70-150
Pets: By arrangement
Creature Comforts: CCTV,
refrig, micro, pool, hlth club,
whirlpool, sauna

Snug Harbor Resort/Marina
(360) 378-4762
http://www.snugresort.com
2371 Mitchell Bay Rd.
10 rooms - $70-125
Pets: Welcome w/$5 fee
Creature Comforts:
Housekeeping cottages w/CCTV,
kit, moorings, boat and sea kayak
rentals

Tucker House
(800) 965-0123, (360) 378-2783
http://www.san-juan.net/tucker/
260 B Street
3 cottages - $125-195
Pets: Small dogs in cottages by
arrangement w/fee
Creature Comforts: 1898
Victorian house/cottages, country
decor, kit, woodstove, CCTV/
VCR, gourmet brkfst, hot tub

SEATAC
Airport Plaza Hotel
(206) 433-0400
18601 International Blvd.
121 rooms - $44-85
Pets: Small pets welcome
Creature Comforts: CCTV, a/c,
refrig, restaurant, whirlpool, sauna

Best Western Execútel
(800) 528-1234, (206) 878-3300
http://www.bestwestern.com
20717 International Blvd.
137 rooms - $90-125
Pets: Welcome w/$50 deposit
Creature Comforts: CCTV, a/c,
refrig, Jacuzzi, restaurant, cont.
brkfst, pool, hlth club, whirlpool,
sauna

Doubletree Hotel, Hanford
(800) 222-TREE, (206) 246-8600
http://www.doubletreehotels.com
18740 International Blvd.
825 rooms - $110-150
Pets: Small pets w/$50 deposit
Creature Comforts: CCTV, a/c,
restaurant, pool

Econo Lodge
(800) 55-ECONO, (206) 244-0810
http://www.econolodge.com
13910 Pacific Hwy S.
47 rooms - $54-84
Pets: Welcome
Creature Comforts: CCTV, a/c,
refrig, cont. brkfst, hlth club,
whirlpool

La Quinta
(800) Nu-Rooms, (206) 241-5211
http://www.laquinta.com
2824 S. 188th St.
142 rooms - $65-75
Pets: Small pets welcome
Creature Comforts: CCTV, a/c,
refrig, micro, full brkfst, pool,
whirlpool

Motel 6
(800) 4-MOTEL6, (206) 246-4101
http://www.motel6.com
I-55 at Rte. 518
112 rooms - $35-49
Pets: Under 30 lbs. welcome
Creature Comforts: CCTV, a/c

Motel 6
(800) 4-MOTEL6, (206) 241-1648
http://www.motel6.com
I-5 at Exit 152
146 rooms - $35-50
Pets: Under 30 lbs. welcome
Creature Comforts: CCTV, a/c,
pool

Rodeway Inn
(800) 228-2000, (206) 246-9300
http://www.rodeway.com
2930 S. 176th
59 rooms - $40-80
Pets: Welcome
Creature Comforts: CCTV, a/c,
cont. brkfst

SeaTac Crest Motor Inn
(206) 433-0999
18845 Pacific Hwy S.
46 rooms - $42-65
Pets: Welcome
Creature Comforts: CCTV, a/c,
cont. brkfst

Seattle Airport Hilton
(800) HILTONS, (206) 244-4800
http://www.hilton.com
17620 International Blvd.
180 rooms - $110-125
Pets: Small pets welcome
Creature Comforts: CCTV, a/c,
refrig, restaurant, pool, hlth club,
whirlpool

Seattle Marriott
(800) 228-9290, (206) 241-2000
http://www.marriott.com
3201 South 176th St.
460 rooms - $140-155
Pets: Welcome
Creature Comforts: CCTV, a/c,
restaurant, pool

Super 8 Seatac
(800) 800-8000, (206) 433-8188
http://www.super8.com
3100 S. 192nd
119 rooms - $70-82
Pets: Welcome w/permission
Creature Comforts: CCTV, a/c

Westcoast SeaTac Hotel
(800) 426-0670, (206) 246-5535
18220 International Blvd.
146 rooms - $90-114
Pets: Welcome w/permission
Creature Comforts: CCTV, a/c

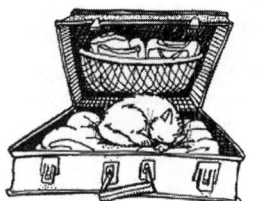

SEATTLE
Alexis Hotel
(800) 426-7033, (206) 624-4844
1007 First Ave.
109 rooms - $180-380
Pets: Welcome w/signed damage
waiver
Creature Comforts: Highly
recommended—small, luxurious,
service-oriented hotel, European
charm and sophistication,
individually decorated rms,
antiques, orig. art, CCTV, a/c, kit,
marble baths, terry robes, gourmet
restaurant, cont. brkfst, exercise
rm, whirlpool

Aurora Seafair Inn
(206) 522-3754
9100 Aurora N.
63 rooms - $60-90
Pets: Small pets w/$5 fee
Creature Comforts: CCTV, a/c,
kit

Beech Tree Manor
(206) 281-7037
http://www.virtualcities.com/ons/
wa/s/was3501.htm
1405 Queen Anne Ave., N.
6 rooms - $70-145
Pets: Welcome
Creature Comforts: 1900's
Victorian filled w/antiques and
exquisite linens, orig. art, chintz
furnishings, brass or ebony beds,
English country house feeling,
gourmet brkfst

Cavanaugh's on Fifth Ave.
(800) 325-4000, (206) 971-8000
http://www.cavanaughs.com
1415 Fifth Ave.
297 rooms - $155-195
Pets: Welcome
Creature Comforts: CCTV, a/c,
restaurant, hlth club

Days Inn Town Center
(800) DAYS INN, (206) 448-3434
http://www.daysinn.com
2205 7th Ave.
90 rooms - $69-135
Pets: Small pets w/$4 fee
Creature Comforts: CCTV, a/c,
restaurant

Doubletree Seattle
(800) 222-TREE, (206) 246-8600
http://www.doubletreehotels.com
18740 Pacific Hwy S.
850 rooms - $150-180
Pets: Welcome
Creature Comforts: CCTV, a/c,
restaurant, pool, exercise rm,
whirlpool

Emerald Inn
(206) 522-5000
8512 Aurora Ave.
43 rooms - $50-95
Pets: Small pets w/$10 fee
Creature Comforts: CCTV, a/c

Executive Residence
(800) 428-3867, (206) 329-8000
http://executiveresidence.com
2400 Elliott
50 rooms - $55-105
Pets: Welcome w/$150 fee
Creature Comforts: CCTV, a/c,
living rm, kit

Four Seasons, Olympic
(800) 332-3442, (206) 621-1700
http://www.fshr.com
411 University St.
450 rooms - $200-1,250
Pets: Welcome, over 50 lbs. must
receive special permission, pet
amenities
Creature Comforts: Highly
recommended, luxurious and
grand 1924 Italian-Renaissance
hotel w/ornately carved plaster
and woodwork, rooms w/
Henredon furnishings, orig. art,
triple sheeted beds, refrig, gourmet
goodies, CCTV, VCR, a/c,
gourmet restaurants, pool, hlth clb

Homewood Suites
(800) 225-5466, (206) 433-8000
http://www.homewoodsuites.com
6955 Fort Dent Way
106 rooms - $109-179
Pets: Welcome w/$50 deposit
Creature Comforts: CCTV, a/c,
pool, whirlpool

Hotel Monaco
(206) 621-1770
1101 Fourth Ave.
189 rooms - $195-450
Pets: Welcome
Creature Comforts: CCTV,
VCR, a/c, Jacuzzi, restaurant, hlth
club

Motel 6
(800) 4-MOTEL6, (206) 824-9902
http://www.motel6.com
I-5, Exit 51
119 rooms - $35-50
Pets: Under 30 lbs. welcome
Creature Comforts: CCTV, a/c, pool

Pensione Nichols
(206) 441-7125
http://www.calbertgroup.com/
nicholspension/
1923 First Ave.
12 rms - $85-160
Pets: Small pets welcome, negotiable on larger ones
Creature Comforts: Reminiscent of European pensione, enormous living rm w/water views, simple furnishings w/one or two antique pieces, comforters, bright colors, whimsical doorstops, suites have most space w/living rm, sleeping alcove, kit

Ramada Inn Seattle
(800) 2-Ramada, (206) 365-0700
http://www.ramada.com
I-5, Northgate Exit
169 rooms - $99-159
Pets: Welcome
Creature Comforts: CCTV, a/c, refrig, micro, kit, full brkfst, pool, hlth club, whirlpool

Residence Inn, Lake Union
(800) 331-3131, (206) 624-6000
http://www.residenceinn.com
800 Fairview Ave. North
234 rooms - $110-350
Pets: Welcome w/$10 fee
Creature Comforts: CCTV, a/c, kit, pool, hlth club, whirlpool

Sun Hill Motel
(206) 525-1205
8517 Aurora Ave. N
25 rooms - $40-45
Pets: Small pets welcome
Creature Comforts: CCTV, a/c

Travelodge Space Needle
(800) 578-7878, (206) 441-7878
http://www.travelodge.com
200 6th Ave.
88 rooms - $79-139
Pets: Small pets w/$5 fee
Creature Comforts: CCTV, a/c, cont. brkfst, pool, whirlpool

Vagabond Space Needle
(800) 522-1555, (206) 522-1555
325 Aurora Ave.
58 rooms - $59-109
Pets: Welcome
Creature Comforts: CCTV, a/c, cont. brkfst, pool, whirlpool

Westin Hotel
(800) 228-3000, (206) 728-1000
http://www.westin.com
1900 5th Ave.
865 rooms - $220-750
Pets: Small pets welcome
Creature Comforts: CCTV, VCR, a/c, refrig, micro, Jacuzzi, restaurant, pool, hlth clb, whirlpool

SEAVIEW
Historic Sou-wester Lodge
(800) 269-6378, (360) 642-2542
Beach Access Rd., 38th Place
18 rms/" - $35-100
Pets: Welcome in cottages and "Tch, tch" trailers
Creature Comforts: Delightful, albeit eclectic, hodgepodge of cottages, inn rms, and curved chrome trailers, creatively furnished, artistic décor, a unique and special find just a block off the water, paths to beach

Seaview Coho Motel
(360) 642-2531
3701 Pacific Way
13 rooms - $35-120
Pets: Welcome
Creature Comforts: CCTV

Seaview Motel
(360) 642-2450
3728 Pacific Way
16 rooms - $30-70
Pets: Welcome
Creature Comforts: CCTV

SEDRO-WOOLLEY
Skagit Motel
(800) 269-6378
1977 Rte. 20
46 rooms - $32-65
Pets: Welcome w/permission
Creature Comforts: CCTV, a/c

Three Rivers Inn
(360) 855-2626
210 Ball St.
40 rooms - $50-70
Pets: Welcome w/$10 deposit
Creature Comforts: CCTV, a/c, refrig, restaurant, full brkfst, pool, whirlpool

SEKIU
Bay Motel
(360) 963-2444
15562 Rte. 112 West
16 rooms - $45-69
Pets: Welcome w/permission
Creature Comforts: CCTV

Curley's Resort
(800) 542-9680
23831 Vashon Hwy. SW
21 rooms - $35-85
Pets: Welcome w/permission
Creature Comforts: CCTV

Straitside Resort
(360) 963-2100
241 Front St.
7 rooms - $45-85
Pets: Welcome w/permission
Creature Comforts: CCTV

SEQUIM
Best Western Sequim Bay
(800) 528-1234, (360) 683-0691
http://www.bestwestern.com
268522 Rte 101
54 rooms - $55-72
Pets: Welcome w/$5 fee
Creature Comforts: CCTV, a/c

Econo Lodge
(800) 55-Econo, (360) 683-7113
http://www.econolodge.com
801 E. Washington St.
44 rooms - $55-80
Pets: Small pets w/$15 fee
Creature Comforts: CCTV, VCR, a/c, refrig, micro, cont. brkfst

Great House Motel
(800) 475-7272
740 E. Washington
20 rooms - $32-75
Pets: Welcome w/permission
Creature Comforts: CCTV, a/c, cont. brkfst

Juan de Fuca Cottages
(360) 683-4433
http://www.dungeness.com/
juandefuca/14.htm
182 Marine Dr.
6 cottages - $100-105
Pets: Small pets w/approval
Creature Comforts: Intimate
cottage colony on windswept bluff
overlooking Dungeness Bay,
cottages w/honey-colored walls,
country décor, homey touches,
CCTV, VCR, kit, gazebo

Rancho Lamro B&B
(360) 683-8133
1734 Woodcock Rd.
2 rooms - $65
Pets: Welcome w/permission
Creature Comforts: CCTV, a/c,
cont. brkfst

Red Ranch Inn
(360) 683-4195
830 W. Washington
55 rooms - $50-85
Pets: Small pets w/$6 fee
Creature Comforts: CCTV, a/c,
kit

Sundowner Motel
(360) 683-5532
364 W. Washington St.
33 rooms - $45-70
Pets: Small pets w/$4 fee
Creature Comforts: CCTV, a/c,
kit

SHELTON
City Center Best Rates Motel
(360) 426-3397
364 W. Washington St.
13 rooms - $39-46
Pets: Welcome w/permission
Creature Comforts: CCTV

Rest Full Farm B&B
(360) 426-8774
http://www.ohwy.com/wa/r/
restfubb.htm
W. 2230 Shelton Valley Rd.
2 rooms - $50-60
Pets: Welcome w/permission
Creature Comforts: CCTV, full
brkfst

Shelton Inn Motel
(360) 426-4468
628 Railroad Ave.
30rooms - $40
Pets: Small pets w/$5 fee
Creature Comforts: CCTV,
refrig, micro, kit, pool

Super 8
(800) 800-8000, (360) 426-1654
http://www.super8.com
2943 Northview Circle
38 rooms - $47-69
Pets: Welcome w/$25 fee
Creature Comforts: CCTV, a/c,
refrig

SILVER CREEK
Lake Mayfield Motel
(360) 985-2484
2911 Rte. 12
8 rooms - $40-50
Pets: Welcome
Creature Comforts: CCTV

SILVERDALE
Cimarron Motel
(800) 273-5076, (360) 692-7777
9734 NW Silverdale Way
63 rooms - $49-59
Pets: Welcome
Creature Comforts: CCTV, cont.
brkfst

SKYKOMISH
Sky River Inn
(800) 367-8194, (360) 677-2261
333 E. River Dr.
18 rooms - $50-85
Pets: Welcome w/$3 fee
Creature Comforts: CCTV, a/c,
refrig, micro, kit, restaurant

SNOHOMISH
Snohomish Grand Valley Inn
(360) 568-8854
11910 Springetti Rd.
5 rooms - $60-85
Pets: Welcome
Creature Comforts: CCTV, full
brkfst, exercise rm, whirlpool

Snohomish Inn at Snohomish
(800) 548-9993
323 Second St.
21 rooms - $49-95
Pets: Welcome
Creature Comforts: CCTV,
restaurant

SNOQUALMIE
Idyll Inn on the River
(425) 868-2000
4548 Tolt River Rd.
2 rooms - $85-210
Pets: Welcome w/permission
Creature Comforts: CCTV, a/c

Salish Lodge/Spa
(800) 826-6124, (425) 888-2556
http://www.salish.com
6501 Railroad Ave.
2 rooms - $85-210
Pets: First floor rms w/$50 fee
Creature Comforts: Highly
recommended, wonderful timber
lodge next to thundering
Snoqualimie Falls, lodge uses
native woods and stone to create
country manor atmosphere,
luxurious rms w/sophisticated
décor, CCTV, a/c, refrig stocked
w/champagne, fireplaces, Jacuzzi
soaking tubs, baskets of gourmet
treats, gourmet restaurant, spa and
hlth clb

SNOQUALMIE PASS
Snoqualmie Summit Inn
(800) 557-STAY, (425) 434-6300
Rte. 906
82 rooms - $59-175
Pets: Welcome w/permission
Creature Comforts: CCTV, a/c

SOAP LAKE
Royal View Motel
(509) 246-1831
Rte. 17
19 rooms - $39
Pets: Welcome
Creature Comforts: CCTV

SPOKANE
Apple Tree Inn
(509) 466-3020
9508 N. Division St.
71 rooms - $48-81
Pets: Small pets in ltd. rooms
Creature Comforts: CCTV, a/c,
refrig, micro, kit, cont. brkfst, pool

Bel-Air Motel 7
(509) 535-1677
E. 1303 Sprague St.
17 rooms - $35-45
Pets: Dogs only w/$6 fee
Creature Comforts: CCTV, a/c,
refrig

Bell Motel
(800) 223-1388, (509) 624-0852
9030 West Sunset Hwy
13 rooms - $30
Pets: Welcome
Creature Comforts: CCTV, a/c,
refrig

Best Western Pheasant Hill
(800) 528-1234, (509) 926-7432
http://www.bestwestern.com
12415 E. Mission at Pines
105 rooms - $79-139
Pets: Small pets welcome
Creature Comforts: CCTV, a/c,
micro, refrig, cont. brkfst, pool,
whirlpool

Best Western Thunderbird
(800) 528-1234, (509) 747-2011
http://www.bestwestern.com
120 West Third Ave.
89 rooms - $54-81
Pets: Small dogs, no cats
Creature Comforts: CCTV, a/c,
refrig, Jacuzzi, pool, hlth club,
whirlpool

Best Western Trade Winds
(800) 528-1234, (509) 326-5500
http://www.bestwestern.com
3033 North Division St.
63 rooms - $56-190
Pets: Small pets w/$20 deposit
Creature Comforts: CCTV, a/c,
refrig, Jacuzzi, pool, hlth club,
whirlpool

Broadway Motel
(888) 888-6630
6317 East Broadway
34 rooms - $50-80
Pets: Welcome
Creature Comforts: CCTV, a/c,
pool

Budget Saver Motel
(509) 534-0669
1234 East Sprague St.
16 rooms - $28-32
Pets: Welcome
Creature Comforts: CCTV, a/c

Cavanaugh's Fourth Ave.
(800) 325-4000, (509) 838-6101
http://www.cavanaughs.com
110 East Fourth Ave.
152 rooms - $60-86
Pets: Small pets welcome
Creature Comforts: CCTV, a/c,
refrig, restaurant, pool
806

Cavanaugh's Inn at the Park
(800) 325-4000, (509) 326-8000
http://www.cavanaughs.com
W. 303 N. River Dr.
402 rooms - $89-199
Pets: Small pets welcome
Creature Comforts: Large hotel
w/open and airy public spaces,
newly redecorated rms w/
contemp. flair, luxury level rms,
w/fireplaces, Jacuzzis, CCTV, a/c,
refrig, restaurant, pool, hlth clb,
great dog parks nearby

Cavanaugh's Resident Court
(800) 325-4000, (509) 624-4142
http://www.cavanaughs.com
1203 West Fifth Ave.
56 rooms - $39-68
Pets: Small pets welcome
Creature Comforts: CCTV, a/c,
kit, pool, whirlpool

Cavanaugh's River Inn
(800) 325-4000, (509) 326-5577
http://www.cavanaughs.com
700 North Division St.
244 rooms - $60-225
Pets: Welcome
Creature Comforts: CCTV, a/c,
refrig, restaurant, full brkfst, pool,
hlth club, whirlpool

Cedar Village Motel
(509) 838-8558
5415 West Sunset Hwy.
28 rooms - $28-60
Pets: Small pets welcome
Creature Comforts: CCTV, a/c

Comfort Inn, Broadway
(800) 228-5150, (509) 535-7185
http://www.comfortinn.com
6309 East Broadway
35 rooms - $50-65
Pets: Welcome
Creature Comforts: CCTV,
VCR, a/c, refrig, micro, kit, cont.
brkfst, pool

Days Inn, Spokane
(800) DAYS INN, (509) 926-5399
http://www.daysinn.com
1919 North Hutchinson
92 rooms - $47-72
Pets: Small pets welcome
Creature Comforts: CCTV, a/c,
refrig

Doubletree Hotel, City Center
(800) 222-TREE, (509) 455-9600
http://www.doubletreehotels.com
322 N. Spokane Falls Ct.
379 rooms - $99-119
Pets: Small pets welcome
Creature Comforts: CCTV,
VCR, a/c, refrig, Jacuzzi,
restaurant, pool, whirlpool, sauna

Doubletree Hotel
(800) 222-TREE, (509) 924-9000
http://www.doubletreehotels.com
1100 North Sullivan St.
237 rooms - $69-120
Pets: Small pets w/$3 fee
Creature Comforts: CCTV, a/c,
refrig, Jacuzzi, restaurant, full
brkfst, pool, whirlpool

Eastgate Motel
(509) 922-4556
10625 East Trent
9 rooms - $35-75
Pets: Welcome
Creature Comforts: CCTV, a/c

Hampton Inn
(800) Hampton, (509) 747-1100
http://www.hampton-inn.com
2010 South Assembly Rd.
131 rooms - $66-225
Pets: Welcome
Creature Comforts: CCTV, a/c,
pool, whirlpool

Motel 6
(800) 4-MOTEL6, (509) 459-6120
http://www.motel6.com
I-90 at Exits 277 and 277A
121 rooms - $42-53
Pets: Under 30 lbs. welcome
Creature Comforts: CCTV, a/c

Oslo's B&B
(888) 838-3157
1821 East 39th
2 rooms - $55-70
Pets: Welcome w/permission
Creature Comforts: CCTV, a/c,
full brkfst

Park Lane Motel
(800) 533-1626
4412 E. Sprague Ave.
28 rooms - $40-90
Pets: Welcome
Creature Comforts: CCTV, a/c, cont. brkfst

Quality Inn Oakwood
(800) 228-5151, (509) 467-4900
http://www.qualityinn.com
7919 N. Division
132 rooms - $62-225
Pets: Welcome
Creature Comforts: CCTV, VCR, a/c, Jacuzzi, pool

Quality Inn Valley Suites
(800) 228-5151, (509) 928-5218
http://www.qualityinn.com
8923 E. Mission St.
127 rooms - $79-300
Pets: Small pets w/$100 deposit
Creature Comforts: CCTV, VCR, a/c, refrig, kit, Jacuzzi, restaurant, cont. brkfst, pool, whirlpool, sauna

Ramada Inn
(800) 2-Ramada, (509) 838-5211
http://www.ramada.com
Spokane International Airport
166 rooms - $80-87
Pets: Small pets welcome
Creature Comforts: CCTV, a/c, Jacuzzi, restaurant, pool

Ranch Motel
(509) 456-8919
1609 South Lewis St.
10 rooms - $30-35
Pets: Small pets welcome
Creature Comforts: CCTV, a/c

Rodeway Inn City Center
(800) 228-2000, (509) 838-8271
http://www.rodeway.com
827 W. First Ave.
79 rooms - $45-69
Pets: Welcome
Creature Comforts: CCTV, a/c, restaurant, cont. brkfst, pool, hlth club, whirlpool

Select Inn Tiki Lodge
(509) 838-2026
W. 1420 Second Ave.
54 rooms - $38-52
Pets: Welcome
Creature Comforts: CCTV, a/c, pool

Shangri-La Motel
(800) 234-4941, (509) 747-2066
2922 W. Government Way
20 rooms - $35-65
Pets: Small dogs w/$15 deposit, no cats
Creature Comforts: CCTV, a/c, kit, cont. brkfst, pool

Shilo Inn
(800) 222-2244, (509) 535-9000
http://www.shiloinn.com
923 East Third Ave.
105 rooms - $69-99
Pets: Welcome w/$7 fee
Creature Comforts: CCTV, VCR, a/c, restaurant, cont. brkfst, pool, hlth clb, whirlpool

Sierra Hotel Spokane
(509) 747-2021
4212 West Sunset Rd.
136 rooms - $52-80
Pets: Welcome
Creature Comforts: CCTV, a/c, pool

Skyline Motel
(509) 747-2021
4212 S. Geiger Blvd.
26 rooms - $25-35
Pets: Welcome w/$7 fee
Creature Comforts: CCTV, a/c

Solar World Estates
(509) 468-1207
20 E. Pineridge Ct.
56 rooms - $35-90
Pets: Welcome
Creature Comforts: CCTV, a/c

Suntree 8 Inn
(800) 888-6630, (509) 838-6630
123 South Post Rd.
46 rooms - $40-60
Pets: Welcome
Creature Comforts: CCTV, a/c, cont. brkfst

Suntree Inn
(800) 888-6630, (509) 838-6630
S. 211 Division St.
80 rooms - $45-70
Pets: Welcome
Creature Comforts: CCTV, a/c, cont. brkfst, pool, whirlpool

Super 8 Motel
(800) 800-8000, (509) 838-4888
http://www.super8.com
2020 Argonne Rd.
190 rooms - $45-65
Pets: Small pets w/$25 deposit
Creature Comforts: CCTV, a/c

Super 8 West
(800) 800-8000, (509) 838-8800
http://www.super8.com
W. 11102 Westbow Blvd.
80 rooms - $45-70
Pets: Welcome w/$30 deposit
Creature Comforts: CCTV, VCR, a/c, pool

Tradewinds Motel
(800) 586-5397, (509) 838-2091
907 West Third Ave.
59 rooms - $36-66
Pets: Welcome w/$20 deposit
Creature Comforts: CCTV, a/c, cont. brkfst, pool, hlth club, whirlpool

SPRAGUE
Last Roundup Motel
(509) 257-2583
312 E. First St.
22 rooms - $35-70
Pets: Welcome
Creature Comforts: CCTV, a/c

Purple Sage Motel
(509) 257-2507
409 West First St.
7 rooms - $28-42
Pets: Welcome
Creature Comforts: CCTV, a/c

SULTAN
Dutch Cup Motel
(800) 844-0488
918 Main St.
59 rooms - $36-66
Pets: Welcome w/$6 fee
Creature Comforts: CCTV, a/c, refrig

SUNNYSIDE
Sun Valley Inn
(509) 837-4721
724 Yakima Valley Hwy.
40 rooms - $25-75
Pets: Welcome w/$5 fee
Creature Comforts: CCTV, a/c, pool

Sunnyside Travelodge
(800) 578-7878, (509) 837-7878
http://www.travelodge.com
408 Yakima Valley Hwy.
73 rooms - $40-100
Pets: Welcome
Creature Comforts: CCTV, a/c,
pool

Town House Motel
(509) 837-5500
509 Yakima Valley Hwy.
21 rooms - $36-50
Pets: Welcome
Creature Comforts: CCTV, a/c

TACOMA
Best Western Executive Inn
(800) 528-1234, (253) 922-0080
http://www.bestwestern.com
5700 Pacific Hwy. East
139 rooms - $79-127
Pets: Small pets welcome
Creature Comforts: CCTV,
VCR, a/c, restaurant, pool,
whirlpool

Best Western Tacoma
(800) 528-1234, (253) 535-2880
http://www.bestwestern.com
8726 S. Hosmer St.
149 rooms - $54-92
Pets: Welcome w/$50 deposit
Creature Comforts: CCTV, a/c,
restaurant, pool, hlth club,
whirlpool

Colonial Motel
(253) 589-3261
12117 Pacific Hwy SW
34 rooms - $35-75
Pets: Welcome
Creature Comforts: CCTV, a/c,
whirlpool

Comfort Inn
(800) 228-5150, (253) 926-2301
http://www.comfortinn.com
5601 Pacific Hwy E
40 rooms - $49-69
Pets: Welcome
Creature Comforts: CCTV, a/c,
refrig, cont. brkfst

Days Inn
(800) DAYS INN, (253) 475-5900
http://www.daysinn.com
6802 Tacoma Mall Blvd.
123 rooms - $67-129
Pets: Small pets w/$15 fee
Creature Comforts: CCTV, a/c,
refrig, pool

Eveline's Old World B&B
(800) 495-4293
723 N. Cushman
3 rooms - $55-95
Pets: Welcome
Creature Comforts: CCTV, a/c,
full brkfst

La Quinta
(800) Nu-Rooms, (253) 383-0146
http://www.laquinta.com
1425 E. 27th St.
158 rooms - $64-89
Pets: Small pets welcome
Creature Comforts: CCTV, a/c,
refrig, micro, restaurant, cont.
brkfst, pool, whirlpool

Motel 6
(800) 4-MOTEL6, (253) 473-7100
http://www.motel6.com
I-5 at Exits 128/129
119 rooms - $35-50
Pets: Under 30 lbs. welcome
Creature Comforts: CCTV, a/c,
pool

Ramada Hotel Tacoma Dome
(800) 2-Ramada, (253) 572-7272
http://www.ramada.com
2611 East "E" St.
160 rooms - $65-225
Pets: Small pets welcome
Creature Comforts: CCTV, a/c

Royal Coachman Inn
(800) 422-3051
7414 S. Hosmer
94 rooms - $65-130
Pets: Small pets welcome
Creature Comforts: CCTV, a/c,
restaurant, Jacuzzi, whirlpool

Sheraton Tacoma
(800) 325-3535, (253) 572-3200
http://www.sheraton.com
1320 Broadway Plaza
319 rooms - $65-130
Pets: Small pets welcome
Creature Comforts: CCTV, a/c,
refrig, Jacuzzi, restaurant, pool

Shilo Inn
(800) 222-2244, (253) 475-4020
http://www.shiloinn.com
7414 Hosmer St.
132 rooms - $69-99
Pets: Welcome w/$7 fee
Creature Comforts: CCTV, a/c,
cont. brkfst, pool, hlth club,
whirlpool

TOKELAND
Tradewinds on the Bay
(800) 222-2244, (253) 475-4020
4305 Pomeroy Ave.
17 rooms - $45-60
Pets: Welcome
Creature Comforts: CCTV

TONASKET
Red Apple Inn
(509) 486-2119
Route 97
21 rooms - $37-55
Pets: Welcome
Creature Comforts: CCTV, a/c

Spectacle Falls Resort
(509) 223-3433
879 Loomis Hwy.
5 rooms - $45-60
Pets: Welcome
Creature Comforts: CCTV,
restaurant

TOPPENISH
Oxbow Motor Inn
(509) 865-5800
511 S. Elm St.
44 rooms - $31-42
Pets: Welcome
Creature Comforts: CCTV,
restaurant

Toppenish Inn Motel
(509) 865-7444
515 S. Elm St.
44 rooms - $44-105
Pets: Welcome
Creature Comforts: CCTV, cont. brkfst, pool, hlth club, whirlpool

TROUT LAKE
Llama Ranch B&B
(509) 395-2786
1980 Rte. 141
5 rooms - $80-199
Pets: Welcome
Creature Comforts: Unique llama farm, CCTV, kit, full brkfst

Trout Lake Country Inn
(509) 395-2894
15 Guler Rd.
4 rooms - $55-85
Pets: Welcome
Creature Comforts: CCTV, full brkfst

TUKWILA
Best Western Southcenter
(800) 528-1234, (425) 226-1812
15901 W. Valley Rd.
146 rooms - $84-99
Pets: Welcome
Creature Comforts: CCTV, a/c, refrig, micro, Jacuzzi, restaurant, pool, hlth club, whirlpool, sauna

Residence Inn, South
(800) 331-3131, (425) 226-5500
http://www.residenceinn.com
16201 West Valley Hwy.
144 rooms - $125-200
Pets: Welcome w/$10 fee, max of two pets per rm.
Creature Comforts: CCTV, a/c, kit, pool, whirlpool

Towne and Country Suites
(800) 545-2323, (206) 246-2323
14800 Interurban Ave. South
89 rooms - $59-100
Pets: Welcome w/permission
Creature Comforts: CCTV, a/c, pool, sauna

TUMWATER
Best Western Tumwater
(800) 528-1234, (360) 956-1235
5188 Capitol Blvd.
89 rooms - $70-80
Pets: Small pets w/$5 fee
Creature Comforts: CCTV, a/c, refrig, micro, Jacuzzi, cont. brkfst, pool, hlth club, whirlpool, sauna

Motel 6
(800) 4-MOTEL6, (360) 754-7320
http://www.motel6.com
I-5, Exit 102
119 rooms - $35-45
Pets: Under 30 lbs. welcome
Creature Comforts: CCTV, a/c, pool

Shalimar Suites
(360) 943-8391
5895 Capitol Blvd. S.
29 rooms - $26-48
Pets: Welcome
Creature Comforts: CCTV, a/c

TWISP
Idle-A-While Motel
(509) 997-3222
505 N. Rte. 20
24 rooms - $50-68
Pets: Dogs only w/$3 fee
Creature Comforts: CCTV, VCR, a/c, kit, whirlpool, sauna

UNION
Alderbrook Resort
(800) 622-9370, (360) 898-2200
7101 Rte. 106 East
80 rms/18 cottages - $70-180
Pets: Small pets w/$8 fee, $25 deposit
Creature Comforts: CCTV, a/c, refrig, micro, fireplace, whirlpool, swimming, boating, golf, tennis

Robin Hood Village
(360) 898-2163
E. 6780 Rte. 106
4 rooms - $73-183
Pets: Welcome
Creature Comforts: CCTV, a/c, whirlpool

UNION GAP
Days Inn
(800) DAYS INN, (509) 248-9700
http://www.daysinn.com
2408 Rudkin Rd.
118 rooms - $45-60
Pets: Welcome w/$10 fee
Creature Comforts: CCTV, a/c, pool

Super 8 Motel
(800) 800-8000, (509) 248-8880
http://www.super8.com
2605 Rudkin Rd.
95 rooms - $47-52
Pets: Welcome w/permission
Creature Comforts: CCTV, a/c, pool

VANCOUVER
Best Western Ferryman's Inn
(800) 528-1234, (360) 574-6635
7901 NE Sixth Ave.
132 rooms - $63-73
Pets: Welcome w/$3 fee
Creature Comforts: CCTV, a/c, cont. brkfst, pool

Doubletree Hotel at the Quay
(800) 222-TREE, (360) 694-8341
http://www.doubletreehotels.com
100 Columbia St.
160 rooms - $92-113
Pets: Small pets welcome
Creature Comforts: CCTV, a/c, restaurant, pool, hlth club

Quality Inn
(800) 228-5151, (360) 696-0516
http://www.qualityinn.com
7001 NE Rte. 99
72 rooms - $54-95
Pets: Welcome
Creature Comforts: CCTV, a/c, refrig, micro, kit, cont. brkfst, pool, whirlpool

Residence Inn Vancouver
(800) 331-3131, (360) 253-4800
http://www.residenceinn.com
8005 NE Parkway Dr.
120 rooms - $110-160
Pets: Welcome w/$10 fee
Creature Comforts: CCTV, a/c, kit

Riverside Motel
(360) 693-3677
4400 Lewis & Clark Hwy
17 rooms - $40-50
Pets: Welcome w/$5 fee
Creature Comforts: CCTV, a/c,
refrig

Rodeway Inn
(800) 228-2000, (360) 256-7044
http://www.rodeway.com
221 NE Chkalov Dr.
120 rooms - $48-95
Pets: Welcome w/$15 fee
Creature Comforts: CCTV, a/c,
refrig, Jacuzzi, cont. brkfst, pool,
whirlpool

Shilo Inn, Hazel Dell
(800) 222-2244, (360) 573-0511
13206 Rte 99
65 rooms - $59-85
Pets: Welcome w/$7 fee
Creature Comforts: CCTV, a/c,
kit, pool

Shilo Inn, Vancouver
(800) 222-2244, (360) 696-0411
http://www.shiloinn.com
401 E. 13th St.
118 rooms - $65-99
Pets: Welcome w/$7 fee
Creature Comforts: CCTV,
VCR, a/c, refrig, micro, cont.
brkfst, pool, hlth club, whirlpool,
sauna

Vancouver Lodge
(360) 693-3668
601 Broadway
45 rooms - $42-85
Pets: Welcome
Creature Comforts: CCTV, a/c

VASHON ISLAND
Angels of the Sea B&B
(800) 798-9249, (206) 463-6980
http://www.angelsofthesea.com
26431 99th Ave. SW
3 rooms - $75-125
Pets: Negotiable
Creature Comforts: Quaint 1917
church converted to intimate inn,
country decor, some antiques,
orig. art, CCTV, VCR, a/c, refrig,
Jacuzzi, gourmet brkfst to harp
music

Castle Hill B&B
(206) 463-5491
26734 94th Ave. SW
3 rooms - $65-85
Pets: Welcome
Creature Comforts: CCTV, a/c,
full brkfst

**Edson House Overlooking
Quartermaster Harbor**
(800) 269-6378
23831 Vashon Hwy. SW
2 rooms - $85-210
Pets: Welcome w/permission
Creature Comforts: CCTV, a/c

Swallow's Nest Cottages
(800) Any-Nest, (206) 463-2646
www.vashonislandcottages.com/
6030 SW 248th St.
8 cottages - $75-170
Pets: Welcome in some cottages
Creature Comforts: CCTV, kit,
living rm, bedroom, full brkfst, hot
tub, massage

WALLA WALLA
A&H Motel
(800) 528-1234, (509) 525-4700
http://www.bestwestern.com
2599 Isaacs
9 rooms - $20-35
Pets: Welcome
Creature Comforts: CCTV, a/c

Best Western Walla Walla Suites
(800) 528-1234, (509) 525-4700
http://www.bestwestern.com
7 East Oak St.
78 rooms - $62-90
Pets: Welcome w/$5 fee
Creature Comforts: CCTV, a/c,
cont. brkfst, pool, hlth club,
whirlpool

Capri Motel
(800) 451-1139
2003 Melrose St.
40 rooms - $32-65
Pets: Welcome
Creature Comforts: CCTV, a/c,
pool

City Center Motel
(509) 529-2660
627 W. Main St.
17 rooms - $33-49
Pets: Welcome
Creature Comforts: CCTV, a/c,
pool

Colonial Motel
(509) 529-1220
2279 E. Isaacs
61 rooms - $32-60
Pets: Welcome
Creature Comforts: CCTV, a/c

Hawthorn Inn and Suites
(800) 527-1133, (509) 525-2522
http://www.hawthorn.com
520 N 2nd Ave.
61 rooms - $59-79
Pets: Welcome
Creature Comforts: CCTV,
VCR, a/c, pool, whirlpool,
exercise rm.

Howard Johnson Express
(800) I-Go-Hojo, (509) 529-4360
http://www.hojo.com
325 E. Main St.
85 rooms - $72-90
Pets: Welcome
Creature Comforts: CCTV, a/c,
refrig, micro, kit, Jacuzzi, cont.
brkfst, pool, hlth club, sauna,
whirlpool

Super 8 Motel
(800) 800-8000, (509) 525-8800
http://www.super8.com
2315 Eastgate St. N.
100 rooms - $50-57
Pets: Welcome w/$25 deposit
Creature Comforts: CCTV, a/c,
pool

Tapadera Budget Inn
(509) 529-2580
Box 1234
30 rooms - $31-54
Pets: Welcome w/permission
Creature Comforts: CCTV, a/c,
cont. brkfst, pool

Vagabond Inn
(800) 522-1555
305 N. Second Ave.
35 rooms - $30-70
Pets: Small pets welcome
Creature Comforts: CCTV, a/c,
pool, whirlpool

WASHOUGAL

Economy Lodge
(800) 55-ECONO, (360) 835-8591
http://www.econolodge.com
544 Sixth St.
26 rooms - $52-56
Pets: Welcome
Creature Comforts: CCTV, a/c

WENATCHEE

Avenue Motel
(800) 733-8981, (509) 663-7161
720 N. Wenatchee Ave.
26 rooms - $45-58
Pets: Welcome
Creature Comforts: CCTV, a/c,
kit

Best Western Heritage
(800) 528-1234, (509) 664-6565
http://www.bestwestern.com
1905 N. Wenatchee Ave.
65 rooms - $59-79
Pets: Welcome w/$50 deposit
Creature Comforts: CCTV, a/c,
refrig, micro, Jacuzzi, kit, cont.
brkfst, pool, whirlpool, sauna

Chieftain Motel
(509) 663-8141
1005 N. Wenatchee Ave.
105 rooms - $50-75
Pets: Welcome
Creature Comforts: CCTV, a/c,
pool

Comfort Inn
(800) 228-5150, (509) 662-1700
http://www.comfortinn.com
815 N. Wenatchee Ave.
81 rooms - $65-83
Pets: Welcome w/$15
Creature Comforts: CCTV, a/c,
cont. brkfst, pool, sauna, whirlpool

Doubletree Hotel
(800) 222-TREE, (509) 663-0711
http://www.doubletreehotels.com
1225 N. Wenatchee Ave.
149 rooms - $69-89
Pets: Welcome
Creature Comforts: CCTV, a/c,
restaurant, pool, whirlpool

Holiday Lodge
(509) 663-8167
610 N. Wenatchee Ave.
59 rooms - $38-75
Pets: Small pets welcome
Creature Comforts: CCTV, a/c,
restaurant, pool, whirlpool

Orchard Inn
(509) 662-3443
1401 N. Miller Ave.
103 rooms - $46-63
Pets: Small pets welcome
Creature Comforts: CCTV, a/c,
refrig, micro, pool

Starlite Motel
(509) 662-8115
1640 N. Wenatchee Ave.
34 rooms - $40-60
Pets: Small pets welcome
Creature Comforts: CCTV, a/c,
pool

Uptowner Motel
(509) 663-8516
101 N. Mission St.
22 rooms - $32-70
Pets: Small pets welcome
Creature Comforts: CCTV, a/c,
pool

Vagabond Inn
(800) 522-1555, (509) 663-8133
700 N. Wenatchee Ave.2
40 rooms - $40-80
Pets: Welcome w/$10 fee
Creature Comforts: CCTV, a/c,
refrig, micro, cont. brkfst

Westcoast Wenatchee Hotel
(509) 662-1234
201 N. Wenatchee Ave.
103 rooms - $46-63
Pets: Small pets welcome
Creature Comforts: CCTV, a/c,
refrig, micro, pool

Welcome Inn
(509) 663-7121
232 N. Wenatchee Ave.
38 rooms - $49-65
Pets: Welcome
Creature Comforts: CCTV, a/c,
pool

Westcoast Wenatchee Center
(800) 426-0670, (509) 663-8133
1640 N. Wenatchee Ave.
147 rooms - $95-195
Pets: Welcome w/$50 deposit
Creature Comforts: CCTV, a/c,
restaurant, full brkfst, pool,
exercise rm, whirlpool

WESTPORT

Albatross Motel
(360) 268-9233
200 E. Dock St.
13 rooms - $38-62
Pets: Welcome
Creature Comforts: CCTV

Chinook Motel
(360) 268-9623
707 N. Montesano
10 rooms - $30-35
Pets: Welcome
Creature Comforts: CCTV

Harbor Resort
(360) 268-0169
871 Needle Rose Dr.
13 rms/cottages - $59-110
Pets: Welcome w/$10 fee
Creature Comforts: CCTV,
refrig, kit

Ken's Kourt Motel
(360) 268-9633
2339 Nyhus
17 rooms - $35-55
Pets: Welcome
Creature Comforts: CCTV

Ocean Ave. Inn
(888) 692-5262
275 Ocean Ave.
12 rooms - $49-135
Pets: Welcome
Creature Comforts: CCTV

Seagull's Nest Motel
(360) 268-9711
830 N. Montesano
16 rooms - $40-45
Pets: Welcome
Creature Comforts: CCTV,
refrig

WHITE SALMON
Inn of the White Salmon
(800) 972-5226, (509) 493-2335
http://www.gorge.net/lodging/iws
172 W. Jewett Blvd.
16 rooms - $75-135
Pets: Welcome
Creature Comforts: Brick
hillside inn w/Victorian charm,
some antiques, carved wood beds,
common area w/CCTV, VCR,
stereo, gourmet brkfst, wonderful
baked goods, whirlpool

WILBUR
Eight Bar B Motel
(509) 647-2400
718 E. Main
15 rooms - $30-65
Pets: Welcome
Creature Comforts: CCTV, pool

Settle Inn Motel
(509) 647-2100
303 NE Main
11 rooms - $30-36
Pets: Welcome
Creature Comforts: CCTV

WINTHROP
Best Western Cascade Inn
(800) 528-1234, (509) 996-3100
http://www.bestwestern.com
960 Rte. 20
63 rooms - $50-100
Pets: Welcome w/$10 fee
Creature Comforts: CCTV, a/c,
cont. brkfst, pool, whirlpool

Riverun Inn
(800) 757-2709, (509) 996-2173
27 Rader Rd.
17 rooms - $55-90
Pets: Welcome w/$5 fee
Creature Comforts: CCTV, a/c,
refrig, micro, kit, pool, whirlpool

The Virginian Resort
(509) 996-2535
808 N. Cascade Hwy.
39 rooms - $55-85
Pets: Welcome w/$5 fee
Creature Comforts: CCTV, a/c,
kit, pool, whirlpool

Winthrop Resort
(800) 444-1972, (509) 996-2217
960 Rte. 20
30 rooms - $45-85
Pets: Welcome w/$10 fee
Creature Comforts: CCTV, a/c,
refrig, micro, kit, cont. brkfst,
pool, whirlpool

Wolfridge Resort
(800) 237-2388, (509) 996-2828
412 Wolf Creek Rd.
17 rooms - $59-149
Pets: Welcome w/$10 fee
Creature Comforts: CCTV, a/c,
pool, whirlpool

WOODLAND
Lewis River Inn
(800) 543-4344, (360) 225-6257
110 Lewis River Rd.
149 rooms - $39-62
Pets: Welcome w/$7 fee
Creature Comforts: CCTV, a/c

Scandia Motel
(360) 225-8006
1123 Hoffman St.
13 rooms - $35-45
Pets: Welcome w/$6 fee
Creature Comforts: CCTV, a/c,
refrig, micro

Woodlander Inn
(800) 444-9667, (360) 225-6548
1500 Atlantic St.
61 rooms - $42-65
Pets: Welcome w/$10 fee
Creature Comforts: CCTV, a/c,
refrig, micro, pool, whirlpool

YAKIMA
All Star Motel
(509) 452-7111
1900 N. First St.
50 rooms - $30-35
Pets: Welcome on occasion in
ltd. rooms
Creature Comforts: CCTV, a/c,
pool

Bali Hai Motel
(509) 452-7178
710 N. First St.
28 rooms - $25-38
Pets: Welcome
Creature Comforts: CCTV, a/c,
pool

Cavanaugh's at Yakima Center
(800) 325-4000, (509) 248-5900
http://www.cavanaughs.com
607 E. Yakima
153 rooms - $65-200
Pets: Small pets w/$10 fee
Creature Comforts: CCTV, a/c,
Jacuzzi, restaurant

Cavanaugh's Gateway Hotel
(800) 325-4000, (509) 248-5900
http://www.cavanaughs.com
9 North Ninth St.
171 rooms - $65-95
Pets: Small pets w/$10 fee
Creature Comforts: CCTV, a/c,
pool, whirlpool

Doubletree Hotel, Yakima
(800) 222-TREE, (509) 248-7850
http://www.doubletreehotels.com
1507 N. First St.
208 rooms - $79-135
Pets: Small pets welcome
Creature Comforts: CCTV, a/c,
Jacuzzi, restaurant, pool

El Corral Motel
(509) 865-2365
61731 Rte. 97
17 rooms - $36-45
Pets: Welcome
Creature Comforts: CCTV, a/c

Nendels
(509) 453-8981
1405 N. First St.
53 rooms - $40-45
Pets: Small pets welcome
Creature Comforts: CCTV, a/c,
cont. brkfst, pool, whirlpool

Pepper Tree Inn
(509) 453-8898
1614 N. First St.
75 rooms - $59-69
Pets: Welcome w/$5 fee
Creature Comforts: CCTV, a/c,
refrig, micro, cont. brkfst, pool

Red Carpet Motor Inn
(509) 457-1131
1608 Fruitvale Blvd.
29 rooms - $32-65
Pets: Small pets w/$5 fee
Creature Comforts: CCTV, a/c,
kit, pool

Red Lion Inn
(800) RED-LION, (509) 453-0391
http://www.doubletreehotels.com
818 N. First St.
58 rooms - $54-99
Pets: Welcome w/$10 fee
Creature Comforts: CCTV, a/c,
refrig, micro, cont. brkfst, pool

Tourist Motor Inn
(509) 452-6551
1223 N. First St.
70 rooms - $27-70
Pets: Welcome
Creature Comforts: CCTV, a/c,
cont. brkfst, pool

Vagabond Inn
(800) 522-1555, (509) 457-6155
510 North First St.
63 rooms - $36-70
Pets: Welcome w/$10 fee
Creature Comforts: CCTV, a/c,
refrig, cont. brkfst

YELM
Prairie Motel
(360) 458-8300
700 Prarie Park Ln.
19 rooms - $50-100
Pets: Welcome
Creature Comforts: CCTV, a/c,
whirlpool

West Virginia

BARBOURSVILLE
Comfort Inn
(800) 228-5150, (304) 733-2122
http://www.comfortinn.com
249 Mall Rd.
58 rooms - $55-96
Pets: Welcome
Creature Comforts: CCTV, a/c,
cont. brkfst, pool, whirlpool

BECKLEY
Best Western Four Seasons
(800) 528-1234, (304) 252-0671
http://www.bestwestern.com
1939 Harper Rd.
80 rooms - $48-70
Pets: Welcome w/$5 fee
Creature Comforts: CCTV, a/c,
Jacuzzis, cont. brkfst

Budget Motel
(304) 253-8318
223 S. Heber St.
27 rooms - $40-45
Pets: Welcome in ltd. rms
Creature Comforts: CCTV, a/c,
refrig

Comfort Inn
(800) 228-5150, (304) 255-2161
http://www.comfortinn.com
1909 Harper Rd.
130 rooms - $59-92
Pets: Welcome w/$25 dep.
Creature Comforts: CCTV, a/c,
refrig, micros, cont. brkfst, hlth
club

Howard Johnson Express
(800) I-Go-Hojo, (304) 255-5900
http://www.hojo.com
1907 Harper Rd.
50 rooms - $59-80
Pets: Welcome
Creature Comforts: CCTV, a/c,
refrig, Jacuzzis, cont. brkfst, pool

Super 8 Motel
(800) 800-8000, (304) 253-0802
http://www.super8.com
2014 Harper Rd.
68 rooms - $49-65
Pets: Welcome w/permission
Creature Comforts: CCTV, a/c,
cont. brkfst

BERKELEY SPRINGS
Gamekeeper's Cottage
(304) 258-1375
http://www.berkeleysprings.com/
gamekeepers
Rte 2, Box 156
1 cottage - $135
Pets: Welcome w/$50 deposit
Creature Comforts: Enchanting
1798 log cabin overlooking pond,
antiques, down comforters, CCTV,
a/c, woodstove, gourmet brkfst
makings, local mineral spa, hiking

The Gatehouse at Sleepy Creek
(304) 258-9282
http://www.The-Gatekeeper.com
126 Harmison Dr.
1 house - $85-125
Pets: Welcome
Creature Comforts: Civil War
era farmhouse on 27 acres, three
bedrooms, TV, VCR, a/c, kit, grill,
wonderful for pets and families

BLUEFIELD
Econo Lodge
(800) 55-ECONO, (304) 327-8171
http://www.econolodge.com
3400 Cumberland Rd.
49 rooms - $40-69
Pets: Welcome w/$5 fee
Creature Comforts: CCTV, a/c,
refrig, micros

Holiday Inn
(800) HOLIDAY, (304) 325-6170
http://www.holiday-inn.com
Rtes. 460 & 52
122 rooms - $70-109
Pets: Welcome
Creature Comforts: CCTV, a/c,
refrig, restaurant, pool

Ramada Inn
(800) 2-Ramada, (304) 325-5421
http://www.ramada.com
3175 E. Cumberland Rd.
99 rooms - $49-75
Pets: Welcome w/$50 dep.
Creature Comforts: CCTV, a/c,
refrig, restaurant, cont. brkfst,
pools, hlth club, whirlpool, sauna

BRIDGEPORT
Holiday Inn
(800) HOLIDAY, (304) 842-5411
http://www.holiday-inn.com
100 Lodgeville Rd.
159 rooms - $55-109
Pets: Welcome
Creature Comforts: CCTV, a/c,
refrig, micros, restaurant, hlth club
access, pool

Knights Inn
(800) 843-5644, (304) 842-7115
http://www.knightsinn.com
1235 W. Main St.
115 rooms - $45-60
Pets: Welcome
Creature Comforts: CCTV,
VCR, a/c, kit, pool

Sleep Inn
(800) Sleep-Inn, (304) 842-1919
http://www.sleepinn.com
115 Tolley Rd.
73 rooms - $55-96
Pets: Welcome
Creature Comforts: CCTV, a/c,
cont. brkfst

BUCKHANNON
Baxa Hotel
(304) 472-2500
21 N. Kanawha St.
39 rooms - $35-45
Pets: Welcome
Creature Comforts: Renovated
motel rms, CCTV, a/c, refrig

Centennial Motel
(304) 472-4100
22 N. Locust
25 rooms - $40-45
Pets: Welcome
Creature Comforts: CCTV, ac

Colonial Motel
(304) 472-3000
24 N. Kanawha St.
40 rooms - $45-50
Pets: Welcome
Creature Comforts: CCTV, a/c, refrig

BURNSVILLE
Motel 79
(304) 853-2918
Main St.
20 rooms - $40-45
Pets: Welcome w/$4 fee
Creature Comforts: CCTV, a/c

CHAPMAN
Rodeway Inn
(800) 228-2000, (304) 855-7182
http://www.rodeway.com
Rtes. 10 & 119
45 rooms - $53-75
Pets: Welcome
Creature Comforts: CCTV, VCR, a/c, refrig, cont. brkfst

CHARLESTON
Days Inn
(800) DAYS-INN, (304) 925-1010
http://www.daysinn.com
6400 MacCorkle Ave.
80 rooms - $50-105
Pets: Small pets welcome
Creature Comforts: CCTV, a/c, cont. brkfst

Hampton Inn
(800) Hampton, (304) 746-4646
http://www.hampton-inn.com
1 Prefered Place
105 rooms - $73-104
Pets: Small pets welcome
Creature Comforts: CCTV, a/c, kit, pool, hlth clb, whirlpool

Holiday Inn
(800) HOLIDAY, (304) 344-4092
http://www.holiday-inn.com
600 E. Kanawha Blvd.
255 rooms - $85-145
Pets: Small pets welcome
Creature Comforts: CCTV, a/c, refrig, restaurant, hlth club, pool

Knights Inn
(800) 843-5644, (304) 925-0451
http://www.knightsinn.com
6401 MacCorkle Ave.
132 rooms - $53-74
Pets: Welcome w/$10 dep.
Creature Comforts: CCTV, VCR, a/c, kit

Motel 6
(800) 4-MOTEL6, (304) 925-0471
http://www.motel6.com
6311 MacCorkle Ave.
104 rooms - $39-50
Pets: Under 30 lbs.welcome
Creature Comforts: CCTV, a/c

Red Roof Inn
(800) The-Roof, (304) 925-6953
http://www.redroof.com
6305 SE MacCorkle Ave.
109 rooms - $49-70
Pets: Small pets welcome
Creature Comforts: CCTV, a/c

CHARLES TOWN
Turf Motel
(800) 422-8873, (304) 725-2081
608 E. Washington St.
45 rooms - $45-60
Pets: Small pets w/$50 deposit
Creature Comforts: CCTV, ac, micro, restaurant

CROSS LANES
Motel 6
(800) 4-MOTEL6, (304) 776-5911
http://www.motel6.com
330 Golf Mtn. Rd.
111 rooms - $39-50
Pets: Under 30 lbs.welcome
Creature Comforts: CCTV, a/c, pool

DAVIS
Black Bear Resort
(800) 553-BEAR, (304) 866-4391
black _bear _resort.com
RR1, Box 55
86 units - $105-159
Pets: In ltd. units w/$35 fee
Creature Comforts: CCTV, a/c, fireplace, kit, Jacuzzis

Budget Host Highlander Lodge
(800)BUD-HOST, (304) 259-5551
http://www.budgethost.com
Route 32 & William Ave.
20 rooms - $35-55
Pets: Welcome w/$10 fee
Creature Comforts: CCTV, a/c, restaurant

Deerfield Resort
(800) 342-3217, (304) 866-4698
http://www.deerfieldvillage.com
1 Cortland Ave.
125 villas - $129-189
Pets: Welcome w/$50 fee
Creature Comforts: Charming cottages w/ contemporary decor, lots of windows, CCTV, VCR, a/c, fireplace, kit, Jacuzzis, restaurants, cont. brkfst, pool, hlth clb, tennis, sport courts, lawn games, fishing pond, bikes, mini. golf

DUNBAR
Super 8 Motel
(800) 800-8000, (304) 768-6888
http://www.super8.com
911 Dunbar Ave.
63 rooms - $48-65
Pets: Welcome w/permission
Creature Comforts: CCTV, a/c, refrig, micros, cont. brkfst

ELKINS
Best Western Inn
(800) 528-1234, (304) 636-7711
http://www.bestwestern.com
Rtes 250 & 219
63 rooms - $49-109
Pets: Small pets w/$5 fee
Creature Comforts: CCTV, a/c, cont. brkfst

Cheat River Lodge
(304) 636-2301
http://wvweb.com/cheatriverlodge
Rte. 1, Box 115
6 rms/6 hses - $58-150
Pets: $5 fee, 1 pet per cabin
Creature Comforts: Neat fieldstone and cedar main lodge w/simply decorated cottages along river, log walls, woodstoves, CCTV, a/c, kit, hot tub, gourmet restaurant, country store

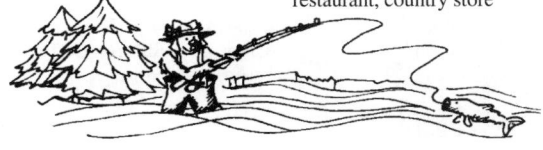

Days Inn
(800) DAYS-INN, (304) 637-4667
http://www.daysinn.com
1200 Harrison Ave.
40 rooms - $59-82
Pets: Welcome
Creature Comforts: CCTV, a/c,
kit, Jacuzzis, restaurant, cont.
brkfst

Econo Lodge
(800) 55-ECONO, (304) 636-6311
http://www.econolodge.com
Route 33
73 rooms - $44-85
Pets: Welcome w/$5 fee
Creature Comforts: CCTV, a/c,
refrig, micros, pool, whirlpool

Super 8 Motel
(800) 800-8000, (304) 636-6500
http://www.super8.com
350 Beverly Pike
44 rooms - $46-65
Pets: Welcome w/permission
Creature Comforts: CCTV, a/c,
refrig, micros, waterbeds, cont.
brkfst

FAIRMONT
Comfort Inn
(800) 228-5150, (304) 367-1370
http://www.comfortinn.com
1185 Airport Rd.
100 rooms - $59-96
Pets: Welcome
Creature Comforts: CCTV, a/c,
cont. brkfst, pool, hlth club

Country Club Lodge
(304) 366-4141
1499 Locust Ave.
30 rooms - $25-35
Pets: Welcome w/$10 fee
Creature Comforts: CCTV, a/c

Econo Lodge
(800) 55-ECONO, (304) 366-5995
http://www.econolodge.com
226 Middletown Rd.
42 rooms - $47-72
Pets: Small pets welcome
Creature Comforts: CCTV, a/c,
refrig, restaurant

Holiday Inn
(800) HOLIDAY, (304) 366-5500
http://www.holiday-inn.com
Rtes. 310 & 79
105 rooms - $45-99
Pets: Welcome
Creature Comforts: CCTV, a/c,
refrig, micros, restaurant, pool

Red Roof Inn
(800) The-Roof, (304) 366-6800
http://www.redroof.com
50 Middletown Rd.
107 rooms - $39-58
Pets: Small pets welcome
Creature Comforts: CCTV, a/c

Super 8 Motel
(800) 800-8000, (304) 363-1488
http://www.super8.com
2208 Pleasant Valley Rd.
54 rooms - $53-75
Pets: Welcome w/permission
Creature Comforts: CCTV, a/c,
Jacuzzis, cont. brkfst

FAYETTEVILLE
The White Horse B&B
(304) 574-1400
http://wvweb.com/www/
white_horse_bb.html
120 Fayette Ave.
6 rms/1 ctg - $85-110
Pets: Small pets welcome
Creature Comforts: Gracious
1906 Nat'l Historic Regis. home
on 27 acres, antiques, hardwood
flrs, hand-painted mural, CCTV,
restaurant, full brkfst

Comfort Inn
(800) 228-5150, (304) 574-3443
http://www.comfortinn.com
Rtes. 19 & 60
106 rooms - $48-99
Pets: Welcome
Creature Comforts: CCTV, a/c,
restaurant, cont. brkfst, pool

GHENT
Econo Lodge
(800) 55-ECONO, (304) 787-3250
http://www.econolodge.com
Route 77
49 rooms - $45-69
Pets: Welcome w/$5 fee
Creature Comforts: CCTV, a/c,
refrig, cont. brkfst

HILLSBORO
The Current B&B
(304) 653-4722
HCR 64, Box 135
4 rooms - $50-75
Pets: Small dogs on ltd basis
Creature Comforts: Farmhouse
in pastoral setting, oak woodwork,
family heirlooms, fresh flowers,
CCTV, VCR, a/c, full brkfst

HUNTINGTON
Days Inn
(800) DAYS-INN, (304) 733-4477
http://www.daysinn.com
64 - 29th St.
139 rooms - $59-80
Pets: Welcome
Creature Comforts: CCTV, a/c,
refrig, micros, cont. brkfst

Econo Lodge
(800) 55-ECONO, (304) 529-1331
http://www.econolodge.com
3325 Rte. 60
110 rooms - $42-63
Pets: Welcome w/$10 fee
Creature Comforts: CCTV, a/c,
refrig, restaurant, pool

Red Roof Inn
(800) The-Roof, (304) 733-3737
http://www.redroof.com
5190 Rte. 60
106 rooms - $45-66
Pets: Small pets welcome
Creature Comforts: CCTV, ac

Uptowner Motel
(800) 828-9016, (304) 525-7741
1415 Fourth Ave.
138 rooms - $65-100
Pets: Welcome
Creature Comforts: CCTV, ac,
restaurant, pool, hlth club.

HURRICANE
Ramada Inn Limited
(800) 2-Ramada, (304) 562-3346
http://www.ramada.com
419 Hurricane Creek Rd.
145 rooms - $46-75
Pets: Welcome w/$5 fee
Creature Comforts: CCTV, a/c,
refrig, cont. brkfst

Red Roof Inn
(800) The-Roof, (304) 757-6392
http://www.redroof.com
Rtes. 64 & 35
79 rooms - $45-66
Pets: Small pets welcome
Creature Comforts: CCTV, a/c

JANE LEW
Wilderness Plantation Inn
(304) 884-7806
Route 79
40 rooms - $50-75
Pets: Welcome w/$6 fee
Creature Comforts: CCTV,
VCR, a/c

KEYSER
Econo Lodge
(800) 55-ECONO, (304) 788-0913
http://www.econolodge.com
Route 220
45 rooms - $48-70
Pets: Welcome
Creature Comforts: CCTV,
VCR, a/c, refrig, restaurant

LEWISBURG
Brier Inn
(304) 645-7722
540 N. Jefferson St.
160 rooms - $49-85
Pets: Small pets w/$10 fee
Creature Comforts: CCTV,
VCR, a/c, kit, Jacuzzi, restaurant,
hlth clb access, pool

Days Inn
(800) DAYS-INN, (304) 645-2345
http://www.daysinn.com
635 N. Jefferson St.
26 rooms - $54-99
Pets: Welcome w/$10 fee
Creature Comforts: CCTV, a/c,
cont. brkfst

The General Lewis Inn
(800) 628-4454 , (304) 645-2600
http://www.generallewisinn.com
301 E. Washington St.
25 rooms - $69-120
Pets: First flr rms w/$10 fee
Creature Comforts: Charming
1834 country inn, inviting
ambiance, fine antiques, intriguing
display of historic collectibles,
four-poster/canopy beds,
traditional furnishings, hrdwd flrs,
CCTV, a/c, fireplaces, restaurant,
cont. brkfst

Super 8 Motel
(800) 800-8000, (304) 647-3188
http://www.super8.com
550 N. Jefferson St.
54 rooms - $48-63
Pets: Under 20 Lbs welcome
Creature Comforts: CCTV, a/c,
refrig, micros, cont. brkfst

LOGAN
Super 8 Motel
(800) 800-8000, (304) 752-8787
http://www.super8.com
316 Riverview Ave.
59 rooms - $54-76
Pets: Welcome w/permission
Creature Comforts: CCTV, a/c,
Jacuzzis, cont. brkfst

MARLINTON
Marlinton Motor Inn
(304) 799-4711
Route 219
70 rooms - $50-55
Pets: Welcome w/$5 fee
Creature Comforts: CCTV, a/c,
restaurant, pool

MARTINSBURG
Days Inn
(800) DAYS-INN, (304) 263-1800
http://www.daysinn.com
209 Viking Way
63 rooms - $69-85
Pets: Welcome
Creature Comforts: CCTV, a/c,
cont. brkfst

Econo Lodge
(800) 55-ECONO, (304) 274-2181
http://www.econolodge.com
Route 81
45 rooms - $48-70
Pets: Welcome
Creature Comforts: CCTV, a/c,
refrig, restaurant, pool

Hampton Inn
(800) Hampton, (304) 267-2900
http://www.hampton-inn.com
978 Foxcroft Ave.
99 rooms - $69-99
Pets: Small pets welcome
Creature Comforts: CCTV, a/c,
refrig, pool

Holiday Inn
(800) HOLIDAY, (304) 267-5500
http://www.holiday-inn.com
301 Foxcroft Ave.
120 rooms - $70-105
Pets: Welcome
Creature Comforts: CCTV, a/c,
refrig, restaurant, sauna, hlth club,
tennis, whirlpool, 2 pools

Knights Inn
(800) 843-5644, (304) 267-2211
http://www.knightsinn.com
1599 E. Miller Blvd.
60 rooms - $54-75
Pets: Welcome
Creature Comforts: CCTV,
VCR, a/c, kit

Krista Lite Motel
(304) 263-0906
Route 1
20 rooms - $30-35
Pets: Welcome
Creature Comforts: CCTV, a/c

Scottish Inns
(800) 251-1962, (304) 267-2935
1024 Winchester Ave.
19 rooms - $38-59
Pets: Welcome w/$5 fee
Creature Comforts: CCTV, a/c,
pool

MORGANTOWN
Econo Lodge
(800) 55-ECONO, (304) 599-8181
http://www.econolodge.com
3506 Monoongahela Blvd.
71 rooms - $65-89
Pets: Welcome
Creature Comforts: CCTV, a/c,
refrig, restaurant, cont. brkfst.

Friendship Inn
(800) 453-4511, (304) 599-4850
http://www.rodeway.com
452 Country Club Rd.
30 rooms - $44-60
Pets: Welcome
Creature Comforts: CCTV, a/c,
kit, cont. brkfst

Holiday Inn
(800) HOLIDAY, (304) 599-1680
http://www.holiday-inn.com
1400 Saratoga Ave.
146 rooms - $52-89
Pets: Welcome
Creature Comforts: CCTV, a/c,
refrig, restaurant, pool

MT. NEBO
Days Inn
(800) DAYS-INN, (304) 872-5151
http://www.daysinn.com
Route 19
102 rooms - $43-99
Pets: Welcome w/$3 fee
Creature Comforts: CCTV, a/c,
Jacuzzis, restaurant, pool

NEW CREEK
Toll Gate Motel
(304) 788-5100
HCR 72, Box 121
17 rooms - $30-35
Pets: Welcome w/$5 fee
Creature Comforts: CCTV, a/c,
refrig

NITRO
Best Western Inn
(800) 528-1234, (304) 755-8341
http://www.bestwestern.com
4115 - 1st Ave.
42 rooms - $48-79
Pets: Small pets welcome
Creature Comforts: CCTV, a/c,
kit, cont. brkfst

PARKERSBURG
Best Western Inn
(800) 528-1234, (304) 485-6551
http://www.bestwestern.com
Rtes. 77 & 50
67 rooms - $45-75
Pets: Small pets welcome
Creature Comforts: CCTV, a/c,
cont. brkfst, pool

Clarion Inn
(800) CLARION, (304) 422-3131
http://www.clarioninn.com
320 Market St.
103 rooms - $75-99
Pets: Welcome
Creature Comforts: CCTV, a/c,
restaurant, cont. brkfst

Red Roof Inn
(800) The-Roof, (304) 485-1741
http://www.redroof.com
3714 - 7th St.
109 rooms - $49-70
Pets: Small pets welcome
Creature Comforts: CCTV, a/c

Stables Lodge Motel
(304) 424-5100
3604 - 7th St.
150 rooms - $40-48
Pets: Welcome w/$5 fee
Creature Comforts: CCTV, a/c,
refrig, micros, pool

PENCE SPRINGS
Pence Springs Hotel
(800) 826-1829, (304) 445-2606
http://www.wvweb.com/www/
Pence_Springs_Hotel
PO Box 90
15 rooms - $70-100
Pets: Welcome w/$10 fee
Creature Comforts: 1897 Nat'l
Historic Regis mansion set on 400
acres, 1920's décor, fireplace,
wicker, jukebox, restaurant, full
brkfst, lawn games, trails, access
to biking, canoeing

PETERSBURG
Smoke Hole Lodge
(304) 257-4442
Box 953
1 house - $70
Pets: Welcome
Creature Comforts: CCTV, kit

PRINCETON
Days Inn
(800) DAYS-INN, (304) 425-8100
http://www.daysinn.com
Rte. 460
124 rooms - $59-95
Pets: Welcome
Creature Comforts: CCTV, a/c,
Jacuzzis, refrig, micros, restaurant,
cont. brkfst, pool

Sleep Inn
(800) Sleep-Inn, (304) 431-2800
http://www.sleepinn.com
1015 Oakville Rd.
81 rooms - $45-83
Pets: Welcome
Creature Comforts: CCTV, a/c,
refrig, micros, cont. brkfst, pool,
whirlpool

Town n' Country Motel
(304) 425-8156
805 Oakvale Rd.
38 rooms - $35-55
Pets: Welcome w/$10 fee
Creature Comforts: CCTV, a/c,
pool

RAVENSWOOD
Scottish Inns
(800) 251-1962, (304) 273-2830
Rte. 2, Box 33
33 rooms - $34-59
Pets: Welcome w/$10 dep.
Creature Comforts: CCTV, a/c

RICHWOOD
Four Seasons Lodge
(304) 846-4605
39-55 Marlinton Rd.
27 rooms - $46-50
Pets: Welcome
Creature Comforts: CCTV, a/c,
refrig

RIPLEY
Super 8 Motel
(800) 800-8000, (304) 372-8880
http://www.super8.com
102 Duke Dr.
44 rooms - $48-65
Pets: Welcome w/permission
Creature Comforts: CCTV, a/c,
waterbeds, cont. brkfst

SOUTH CHARLESTON
Microtel
(800) 771-7177, (304) 744-4900
http://www.microtelinn.com
600 - 2nd St.
101 rooms - $35-55
Pets: Welcome
Creature Comforts: CCTV, a/c

Ramada Inn
(800) 2-Ramada, (304) 744-4641
http://www.ramada.com
2nd Ave. & B St.
244 rooms - $70-169
Pets: $10 fee, $50 dep
Creature Comforts: CCTV, a/c,
refrig, Jacuzzis, restaurant, cont.
brkfst, pool, hlth club, whirlpool

Red Roof Inn
(800) The-Roof, (304) 744-1500
http://www.redroof.com
4006 MacCorkle Ave. SW
135 rooms - $42-65
Pets: Small pets welcome
Creature Comforts: CCTV, a/c,
hlth club access

SUMMERSVILLE
Best Western Lake Lodge
(800) 528-1234, (304) 872-6900
http://www.bestwestern.com
1203 S. Broad St.
59 rooms - $44-70
Pets: Small pets welcome
Creature Comforts: CCTV,
VCR, a/c, cont. brkfst

Comfort Inn
(800) 228-5150, (304) 872-6500
http://www.comfortinn.com
903 Industrial Dr.
99 rooms - $55-85
Pets: Welcome
Creature Comforts: CCTV, a/c,
refrig, micros, cont. brkfst, pool,
racquetball

Sleep Inn
(800) Sleep-Inn, (304) 872-4500
http://www.sleepinn.com
701 Professional Park
97 rooms - $50-79
Pets: Welcome
Creature Comforts: CCTV, a/c,
cont. brkfst, pool

Super 8 Motel
(800) 800-8000, (304) 269-1086
http://www.super8.com
1 Market Pl.
62 rooms - $48-69
Pets: Welcome w/permission
Creature Comforts: CCTV, a/c,
refrig, micros, cont. brkfst

SUITTON
Elk Motor Court
(304) 765-7173
35 Camden Ave.
12 rooms - $23-31
Pets: Welcome
Creature Comforts: CCTV, a/c

WEIRTON
Best Western Inn
(800) 528-1234, (304) 723-5522
http://www.bestwestern.com
350 3 Springs Dr.
114 rooms - $65-90
Pets: Small pets welcome
Creature Comforts: CCTV, a/c,
restaurant, cont. brkfst, lawn
games

WESTON
Comfort Inn
(800) 228-5150, (304) 269-7000
http://www.comfortinn.com
Rtes. 79 & 33
60 rooms - $43-75
Pets: Welcome
Creature Comforts: CCTV, a/c,
restaurant, cont. brkfst, pool

WHEELING
Days Inn
(800) DAYS-INN, (304) 547-0610
http://www.daysinn.com
Rte. 70 & Dalls Pike
106 rooms - $54-130
Pets: Welcome
Creature Comforts: CCTV,
VCR, a/c, Jacuzzis, cont. brkfst,
pool

Wilson Lodge on Ogleby
(800) 624-6988, (304) 243-4000
Route 88
49 cottages - $650-750/wk
Pets: Welcome in cottages
Creature Comforts: CCTV, a/c,
kit, fireplace, swimming, boating

WHITE SULPHUR SPRINGS
Old White Motel
(304) 536-2441
865 E. Main St.
25 rooms - $45-50
Pets: Welcome
Creature Comforts: CCTV, a/c,
restaurant, pool

Wisconsin

ABBOTSFORD
Cedar Crest Motel
(715) 223-3661
207 N. 4th St.
12 rooms - $24-38
Pets: Welcome w/approval
Creature Comforts: CCTV, a/c

Home Motel
(715) 223-6343
412 N. 4th St. & Rte. 13N
18 rooms - $32-40
Pets: Welcome w/$4 fee
Creature Comforts: CCTV, a/c

ALGOMA
Algoma Beach Motel
(920) 487-2828
1500 Lake St.
28 rooms $55-65
Pets: $5 fee in ltd. rms.
Creature Comforts: CCTV, a/c,
kit, Jacuzzi, pool

Barbie Ann Motel
(920) 487-5561
533 Fourth St.
12 rooms - $40-50
Pets: Welcome
Creature Comforts: CCTV, a/c

River Hills Motel
(800) 236-3451, (920) 487-2031
820 N. Water St., Hwy 42
30 rooms - $40-50
Pets: Welcome w/$5 fee
Creature Comforts: Riverside,
CCTV, a/c, boating, fishing,
snowmobiling

Scenic Shore Inn
(920) 487-3214
2221 Lake St.
13 rooms - $45-50
Pets: Welcome w/approval
Creature Comforts: Lakeside,
CCTV, a/c, restaurant

Westwind Shore Cottages
(920) 487-5867
N6870 Rte. 42
5 cottages - $52-87
Pets: Welcome
Creature Comforts: Lakeside,
CCTV, kit, swimming, fishing,
boating

ALLENTON
Addison House B&B
(414) 629-9993
6373 Rte. 175
4 rooms - $65-90
Pets: Welcome
Creature Comforts: A/C, full
brkfst

ALMA
Reidt's Motel and Cabins
(608) 685-4843
S 1638 State Rd. 35
9 rooms - $30-$65
Pets: Welcome w/approval
Creature Comforts: CCTV, a/c,
kit

AMERY
Amery's Camelot Motel
(800) 899-7014, (715) 268-8194
359 Keller Ave S.
18 rooms - $25-40
Pets: Welcome w/approval
Creature Comforts: CCTV, a/c,
snowmobiling

Forrest Inn Motel
(800) 763-1263, (715) 268-4100
1045 River Place Dr.
21 rooms - $40-65
Pets: Welcome w/approval
Creature Comforts: CCTV, a/c,
whirlpool, kit, snowmobiling

ANTIGO
Super 8 Motel
(800) 800-8000, (715) 623-4188
http://www.super8.com
535 Century Ave.
52 rooms - $55-65
Pets: Welcome w/approval
Creature Comforts: CCTV, a/c,
whirlpool, pool, sauna, fishing,
golf, xc-skiing, snowmobiling

APPLETON
Best Western Midway Hotel
(800) 528-1234, (920) 731-4141
http://www.bestwestern.com
3033 W. College Ave.
105 rooms - $85-100
Pets: Welcome w/approval
Creature Comforts: CCTV, a/c,
refrig, micro, restaurant, pool, hlth
clb access, sauna, whirlpool

Baymont Inns
(800) 4-Budget, (920) 734-6070
http://www.baymontinns.com
3920 W. College Ave.
102 rooms - $50-75
Pets: Small pets w/approval
Creature Comforts: CCTV, a/c,
refrig, micro, pool, tennis courts,
volleyball court

Comfort Suites
(800) 228-5150, (920) 730-3800
http://www.comfortinn.com
3809 W. Wisconsin Ave.
130 r ooms - $90
Pets: Welcome
Creature Comforts: CCTV, a/c,
refrig, micro, kits, pool, sauna,
hlth clb access, whirlpool

Exel Inn of Appleton
(800) 367-3935, (920) 733-5551
http://www.exelinns.com
210 N. Westhill Blvd.
105 rooms - $45-55
Pets: Small pets welcome
Creature Comforts: CCTV, a/c,

Residence Inn
(800) 331-3131, (920) 954-0570
http://www.residenceinn.com
(800) 331-3131
310 Metro Dr.
66 rooms - $90-140
Pets: Welcome w/$10-25 fee
Creature Comforts: CCTV, a/c,
kit, pool, hlth clb access,
whirlpool

Roadstar Inn
(920) 731-5271
3623 W. College Ave.
102 rooms - $40-50
Pets: Small pets w/$25 deposit
Creature Comforts: CCTV, a/c,
refrig

Snug Inn Motel
(800) 236-4444, (920) 739-7316
3437 N. Richmond
35 rooms - $35-65
Pets: Welcome w/approval
Creature Comforts: A/C, kit,
restaurant, playground

Woodfield Suites
(800) 338-0008, (920) 734-7777
3730 W. College Ave.
98 rooms - $90-125
Pets: Small pets welcome
Creature Comforts: CCTV,
VCR, a/c, kit, pool, hlth clb
access, sauna, whirlpool, steam
room

ARBOR VITAE
Buckhorn Lodge/Motel
(715) 356-5090
1720 Buckhorn Rd.
8 rooms - $50-150
Pets: Welcome w/approval
Creature Comforts: CCTV,
VCR, a/c, kit, fireplace, pool,
whirlpool, swimming

ARCADIA
RKD Motel
(888) 812-3338, (608) 323-3338
915 E. Main, Rte. 95
27 rooms - $30-45
Pets: Small pets welcome
Creature Comforts: CCTV, a/c,
playground, golf, tennis,
snowmobiling

ASHLAND
Anderson's Motel
(800) 727-2776, (715) 682-4658
2200 W. Lakeshore Dr.
18 rooms - $27-60
Pets: Small pets, one pet per room
Creature Comforts: Lakeside,
CCTV, a/c, refrig, fishing,
snowmobiling

Ashland Motel
(877) 682-5503, (715) 682-5503
2300 W. Lakeshore Dr.
34 rooms - $35-65
Pets: Welcome
Creature Comforts: Lakeside,
CCTV, a/c, restaurant,
snowmobiling

Bayview Motel
(800) 249-3200, (715) 682-5253
2419 Lake Shore Dr. E.
8 rooms - $25-45
Pets: Welcome
Creature Comforts: Lakeside,
CCTV, a/c, kit, fishing, boating,
snowmobiling

Best Western Holiday House
(800) 528-1234, (715) 682-5235
http://www.bestwestern.com
Rte. 2 Lakeshore Dr.
65 rooms - $44-90
Pets: Small pets welcome
Creature Comforts: Lakeside,
CCTV, a/c, refrig, restaurant, pool,
sauna, whirlpool, snowmobiling,
fishing

Crest Motel
(800) 657-1329, (715) 682-6603
115 Sanborn Ave.
22 rooms - $35-65
Pets: Welcome
Creature Comforts: CCTV, a/c,
playground, snowmobiling

Harbor Motel
(715) 682-5211
1206 W. Lakeshore Dr.
17 rooms - $25-55
Pets: Welcome
Creature Comforts: CCTV, a/c,
fishing, boating, snowmobiling

Hotel Chequamegon
(800) 946-5555, (715) 682-9095
101 Lakeshore Dr.
65 rooms - $75-140
Pets: Welcome w/$25 fee
Creature Comforts: Lakeside,
CCTV, a/c, refrig, micro,
restaurant, pool, sauna, whirlpool,
fishing, snowmobiling

Super 8 Motel
(800) 800-8000, (715) 682-4551
http://www.super8.com
1610 W. Lakeshore Dr.
70 rooms - $50-85
Pets: Small pets w/approval
Creature Comforts: Lakeside,
CCTV, a/c, pool, whirlpool,
fishing, boating, golf, xc-skiing,
skiing, snowmobiling

BAILEY'S HARBOR
Baker's Sunset Motel
(920) 839-2218
8404 Highway 57
11 rooms - $40-70
Pets: Welcome w/approval
Creature Comforts: CCTV,
refrig, wading pool, playground,
badminton, croquet, horseshoes,
volleyball

Journey's End Motel
(800) 944-3582, (920) 839-2887
8271 Journey's End Lane
10 rooms - $45-55
Pets: Welcome w/approval
Creature Comforts: CCTV, a/c,
playground

Ridges Resort Guest House
(800) 328-1710, (920) 839-2127
http://www.ridges.com/
8252 Rte. 57
23 rooms - $43-165
Pets: Welcome w/$10 fee in
cottages and 2 Guest House suites
Creature Comforts: Quiet
wooded spot w/seven miles of
trails; prefer Guest House suites
w/vaulted ceilings, attractive
decor, CCTV, refrig, micro,
fireplaces and Jacuzzis; cottages
more rustic housekeeping units,
hlth clb access, whirlpool,
playground, xc-skiing,
snowmobiling, bicycles

BALDWIN
Colonial Motel
(715) 684-3351
I-94 US 63
21 rooms - $30-50
Pets: Welcome w/approval
Creature Comforts: CCTV,
whirlpool

BALSAM LAKE
Balsam Lake Motel
(800) 919-1141, (715) 485-3857
501 W. Main St.
10 rms - $35-50
Pets: Welcome w/approval
Creature Comforts: CCTV, a/c,
kit, playground, xc-skiing,
snowmobiling, fishing

Fox Den Motel Resort
(715) 485-3857
101 County Rd. 1
8 rooms - $35-80
Pets: Welcome w/approval
Creature Comforts: Lakeside,
CCTV, a/c, kit, pool, boating,
fishing, waterskiing,
snowmobiling

BARABOO
4 Winds Motel
(608) 356-9481
S 4090 Rte. 12
20 rooms - $35-100
Pets: Welcome w/approval
Creature Comforts: CCTV, a/c,
kit, pool, playground

Campus Inn Motel
(800) 421-4748, (608) 356-8366
750 W. Pine St.
53 rooms - $40-200
Pets: Welcome w/approval
Creature Comforts: CCTV, a/c,
pool, whirlpool, sauna, hlth clb
access

Quality Inn
(800) 355-6422, (608) 356-6422
http://www.qualityinn.com
626 W. Pine St.
84 rooms - $55-150
Pets: Welcome w/approval
Creature Comforts: CCTV, a/c,
micro, refrig, restaurant, pool, hlth
clb access, sauna, whirlpool

Silver Dale Resort
(608) 356-4004
E 11878 Rte. DL
15 cottages - $65-85
Pets: Welcome w/approval
Creature Comforts: CCTV, a/c,
kit, restaurant

Spinning Wheel Motel
(608) 356-3933
809 8th St.
25 rooms - $35-85
Pets: Welcome w/approval
Creature Comforts: CCTV, a/c

Thunderbird Motor Inn
(800) 233-0827, (608) 356-7757
1013 8th St.
31 rooms - $40-85
Pets: Welcome w/approval
Creature Comforts: CCTV, a/c,
restaurant

BAYFIELD
Apple Tree Inn
(800) 400-6532, (715) 779-5572
http://northland.com/appletree
Rte. 13 S.
4 rooms - $70-85
Pets: Welcome w/approval
Creature Comforts: CCTV, kit

Baywood Place B&B
(715) 779-3690
20 North 3rd St.
4 rooms - $60-75
Pets: Welcome
Creature Comforts: No a/c, no
phones

Harbor's Edge Motel
(715) 779-3962
33 N. Front St.
20 rooms - $45-100
Pets: Welcome w/approval
Creature Comforts: Lakeside,
CCTV, kit

Seagull Bay Motel
(715) 779-5558
Rtes. 13 & S. 7th St.
25 rooms - $35-65
Pets: Welcome w/approval
Creature Comforts: Lakeside,
cottages, CCTV, a/c, kit, xc-
skiing, snowmobiling

Winfield Inn
(715) 779-3252
Rte. One, Box 33
31 rooms - $35-125
Pets: Welcome w/approval
Creature Comforts: Lakeside,
CCTV, a/c, kit, snowmobiling

BEAVER DAM
Grand View Motel
(920) 885-9208
1510 N. Center St., Rte. 33
22 rooms - $30-40
Pets: Welcome w/approval
Creature Comforts: CCTV, a/c

Super 8 Motel
(800), 800-8000, (920) 887-8880
http://www.super8.com
711 Park Ave.
50 rooms - $50-65
Pets: Welcome w/$50 deposit
Creature Comforts: CCTV,
VCR, a/c

BELGIUM
Quarry Inn Motel
(414) 285-3475
690 Rte. D
10 rooms - $30-60
Pets: Welcome w/approval
Creature Comforts: CCTV, a/c,
kit, restaurant

BELOIT
Comfort Inn
(800) 228-5150, (608) 362-2666
http://www.comfortinn.com
2786 Milwaukee Rd.
56 rooms - $55-85
Pets: Welcome w/approval
Creature Comforts: CCTV, a/c,
refrig, micro

Driftwood Motel
(608) 364-4081
1826 Riverside Dr.
10 rooms - $30-40
Pets: Welcome w/approval
Creature Comforts: riverside,
CCTV, a/c, fishing, boating,
waterskiing

Econo Lodge
(800) 55-ECONO, (608) 364-4000
http://www.econolodge.com
2956 Milwaukee Rd.
80 rooms - $50-60
Pets: Welcome
Creature Comforts: CCTV, a/c,
restaurant, pool

Ike's Motel
(608) 362-3424
114 Dearborn Ave.
16 rooms - $30-60
Pets: Welcome w/approval
Creature Comforts: Lakeside,
CCTV, a/c, kit, restaurant, fishing,
boating

BERLIN
Traveler's Rest Motel
(800) 555-7954, (414) 361-4411
227 Ripon Rd., Rte. 49
16 rooms - $40-50
Pets: Welcome w/approval
Creature Comforts: CCTV

BLACK RIVER FALLS
American Heritage Inn
(715) 284-4333
919 Rte. 54
86 rooms - $55-70
Pets: Small pets welcome
Creature Comforts: CCTV, a/c,
refrig, micro, pool, sauna,
whirlpool

Best Western-Arrowhead Lodge
(800) 528-1234, (715) 354-7706
http://www.bestwestern.com
I-94 & Rte. 54
144 rooms - $55-85
Pets: Welcome
Creature Comforts: CCTV, a/c,
fireplace, kit, refrig, micro,
restaurant, pool, sauna, whirlpool,
fishing, snowmobiling, xc-skiing

Falls Economy Motel
(715) 284-9919
512 E. 2nd St. E
18 rooms - $30-50
Pets: Welcome w/approval
Creature Comforts: CCTV, a/c,
pool, playground, xc-skiing,
snowmobiling

Pines Motor Lodge
(800) 345-PINE, (715) 284-5311
Rte. 12 & I-94
20 rooms - $35-50
Pets: Welcome w/approval
Creature Comforts: Riverside,
CCTV, a/c, fireplace, kit, pool,
sauna, restaurant, playground,
fishing, boating, waterskiing,
tennis, xc-skiing, snowmobiling

River Crest Resort
(800) 863-4764, (715) 284-4763
N6978 Rte. 12
4 rooms - $60-80
Pets: Welcome w/approval
Creature Comforts: Riverside,
CCTV, a/c, fireplace, kit,
playground, fishing, boating,
waterskiing

BLOOMER
Bloomer Inn & Suites
(800) 322-7995, (715) 568-3234
Rtes. 53 & 40
30 rooms - $36-75
Pets: Small pets welcome
Creature Comforts: CCTV, a/c,
kit, refrig, restaurant, playground

Twi-Lite Motel
(715) 568-5200
18981 Rte. 40
10 rooms -$25-40
Pets: Welcome w/approval
Creature Comforts: CCTV, a/c

BOSCOBEL
Hubl's Motel
(608) 375-4277
41120 Hwy. 60
10 rooms - $25-75
Pets: Welcome w/approval
Creature Comforts: Riverside,
CCTV, a/c, kit, playground,
fishing, boating

BOULDER JUNCTION
Wildcat Lodge
(715) 385-2421
http://www.fishinginfo.com/go/
wildcatlodge
P6500 Rte. M
16 cottages - $90-160
Pets: Welcome w/$5 fee
Creature Comforts: Informal
1920's lakeside lodge, old-
fashioned cottages, CCTV, a/c, kit,
fireplace, restaurant, pool,
whirlpool, playground, sandy
beach, boating, fishing, tennis,
lawn games, xc-skiing

Zastrow's Lynx Lake Lodge
(800) 882-LYNX, (715) 686-2249
P.O. Box 277
10 rooms - $249/wk
Pets: Welcome
Creature Comforts: Lakeside,
CCTV, a/c, kit, restaurant, pool,
meeting rooms - playground,
boating, fishing, golf, xc-skiing,
snowmobiling

BRANTWOOD
Palmquist's Farm
(800) 519-2558, (715) 564-2558
http://www.northcoast.com/
pqfarm/ski
Rte. 1, Box 134
4 cabins/8 rooms - $85-90
Pets: Welcome w/$5 fee
Creature Comforts: Known for
cross-country skiing, neat Finnish
lodge w/antiques, friendly
proprietors, cabins w/living rms,
fireplaces, multiple bedrooms,
Finnish wall decorations, copper
lights, full brkfst, dinner available
as well, sauna

BRILLION
Sandman Motel
(920) 756-2106
550 W. Ryan St.
14 rooms - $30-50
Pets: Welcome w/approval
Creature Comforts: CCTV, a/c

BROOKFIELD
Motel 6
(800) 4-MOTEL6, (414) 786-7337
http://www.motel6.com
20300 W. Bluemound
146 rooms - $30-40
Pets: Small pets welcome
Creature Comforts: CCTV, pool

Residence Inn by Marriott
(800) 228-9290, (414) 782-5990
http://www.residenceinn.com
950 S. Pinehurst Ct.
104 rooms - $150-200
Pets: Welcome w/$175 fee
Creature Comforts: CCTV, a/c,
kit, pool, whirlpool

CABLE
Lakewoods Resort
(800) 255-5937, (715) 794-2561
http://www.lakewoodsresort.com
HC 73, Box 715
82 rooms - $65-215
Pets: Welcome w/$25 deposit
Creature Comforts: Lakeside lodge/cottages in natural setting w/ beach, CCTV, a/c, fireplace, kit, restaurant, pool, sauna, whirlpool, playground, sailboats, kayaks, bicycles, boating, fishing, waterskiing, golf, tennis, xc-skiing, snowmobiling

CAMBRIDGE
Bison Trail B&B
(920) 648-5433
W9443 E. Kroghville Rd.
2 rooms - $50-70
Pets: Small pets w/$5-10 fee
Creature Comforts: CCTV, a/c, refrig, micro, fireplace

CAMP DOUGLAS
K&K Motel
(608) 427-3100
219 Rtes. 12 & 16
14 rooms - $35-55
Pets: Small pets w/$5-10 fee
Creature Comforts: CCTV, a/c, refrig, micro

CAMPBELL-SPORT
Mielke-Mauk House B&B
(920) 533-8602
W977 Rte. F
5 rooms - $65-90
Pets: Welcome w/approval
Creature Comforts: Wonderful 1860's rambling log house, lakeside, hardwood flrs, handmade quilts, romantic, CCTV, a/c, fireplace, kit, fishing, boating, waterskiing

CASCADE
Hoeft's Resort & Campground
(262) 626-2221
W9070 Crooked Lake Dr.
6 cottages - $300-350/wk
Pets: Welcome w/approval
Creature Comforts: Lakeside, cottages, CCTV, a/c, kit, restaurant, playground, fishing, boating

CASSVILLE
Eagles Roost Resort
(608) 725-5553
1034 Jack Oak Rd.
14 rooms - $40-125
Pets: Welcome w/approval
Creature Comforts: Riverside, cottages, CCTV, pool, playground, boating, fishing, waterskiing

Sand Bar Motel
(608) 725-5300
1115 East Bluff St.
10 rooms - $40-60
Pets: Welcome w/approval
Creature Comforts: CCTV

CHETEK
Red Lodge Resort
(715) 924-4113
400 Russell St.
51 cottages - $65-120
Pets: Welcome w/approval
Creature Comforts: Lakeside, kit, swimming

Wildwood Resort
(715) 924-3259
865 Rte. 23
14 rooms - $35-55
Pets: Small pets w/$5-10 fee
Creature Comforts: CCTV, a/c, refrig, fireplace, swimming

CHILTON
Thunderbird Motel
(920) 849-4216
121 E. Chestnut
15 rooms - $30-56
Pets: Welcome w/approval
Creature Comforts: CCTV a/c

CHIPPEWA FALLS
Americinn Motel
(715) 723-5711
11 W. South Ave.
62 rooms - $55-105
Pets: Small pets welcome
Creature Comforts: Cozy lobby w/fireplace, CCTV, a/c, refrig, micro, Jacuzzis

Country Villa Motel
(715) 288-6376
Rte 3, Box 40
23 rooms - $30-40
Pets: Welcome w/approval
Creature Comforts: CCTV, a/c, kit, playground

Indianhead Motel
(800) 341-8000, (715) 723-9171
501 Summit Ave.
27 rooms - $40-45
Pets: Welcome
Creature Comforts: CCTV, a/c

Lake Aire Motel
(800) 236-2231, (715) 723-2231
5732 Sandburst Lane
17 rooms - $35-45
Pets: Welcome, small dogs only
Creature Comforts: CCTV, a/c, kit, micro, playground

CLINTONVILLE
Clintonville Motel
(715) 823-6565
297 S. Main St.
26 rooms - $30-45
Pets: Welcome w/approval
Creature Comforts: CCTV, a/c

Landmark Motel
(800) 223-5503, (715) 823-7899
5 N. Main St.
22 rooms - $45-65
Pets: Welcome
Creature Comforts: CCTV, a/c

CRANDON
Lakeland Motel
(715) 478-2423
400 S. Lake Ave.
10 rooms - $30-40
Pets: Welcome
Creature Comforts: CCTV, a/c

Rustic Haven Resort
(715) 478-2255
Rte. 1, Box 93
12 rooms - $50-90
Pets: Welcome w/approval
Creature Comforts: Lakeside, cottages, CCTV, a/c, kit, pool, playground, fishing, boating, snowmobiling

CRIVITZ
Bonnie Bell Motel
(715) 854-7395
1450 Rte. 141
8 rooms - $30-60
Pets: Welcome w/approval
Creature Comforts: CCTV, a/c, kit, snowmobiling

The Pines Motel
(715) 854-7987
N7968 Rte. 141 N
10 rooms - $30-60
Pets: Welcome w/approval
Creature Comforts: CCTV, a/c, kit, playground

Shaffer Park Motel
(715) 854-2186
7217 Shaffer Rd.
28 rooms - $45-50
Pets: Welcome
Creature Comforts: Riverside, CCTV, a/c, restaurant, pool, playground, tennis, horseshoes

CUMBERLAND
Island Inn Motel
(715) 822-8540
Rte. 63 N.
21 rooms - $35-60
Pets: Welcome w/approval
Creature Comforts: CCTV, a/c

DARLINGTON
Towne Motel
(608) 776-2661
245 W. Harriet St.
5 rooms - $30-40
Pets: Welcome w/approval
Creature Comforts: Riverside, CCTV, a/c

DICKEYVILLE
Plaza Motel
(800) 545-4061, (608) 568-7562
203 S. Main
21 rooms - $25-50
Pets: Welcome w/approval
Creature Comforts: CCTV, a/c

DODGEVILLE
Best Western Quiet House
(800) 528-1234, (608) 935-7739
http://www.bestwestern.com
1130 N. Johns St
39 rooms - $65-145
Pets: Welcome w/ limitations
Creature Comforts: CCTV, a/c, pool, hlth clb access, whirlpool

Super 8 Motel
(800) 800-8000, (608) 935-3888
http://www.super8.com
1308 Johns St.
43 rooms - $50-60
Pets: Welcome w/ deposit
Creature Comforts: CCTV, a/c, refrig

DRESSER
Valley Motel
(800) 545-6107, (715) 755-2781
211 State Rd. 35
24 rooms - $35-75
Pets: Welcome w/approval
Creature Comforts: CCTV, a/c, kit, whirlpool

DUNBAR
Richards' Motel
(715) 324-5444
11466 W. Rte. 8
15 rooms - $35
Pets: Welcome w/$5 fee
Creature Comforts: CCT, a/c

DYCKESVILLE
Sunset Beach Motel/Condos
(920) 866-2978
N8931 Rte. 57
35 rooms - $40-130
Pets: Welcome w/approval
Creature Comforts: Lakeside, cottages, kit, pool, playground, boating, fishing, waterskiing, xc-skiing, snowmobiling

EAGLE RIVER
7 Mile Pinecrest Resort
(800) 358-4467, (715) 479-8118
11899 Knapp Rd.
13 cottages - $50-195
Pets: Welcome w/approval
Creature Comforts: CCTV, fireplace, swimming, boating

Afterglow Lake Resort
(715) 545-2560
http://www.wisvacations.com/afterglowresort/
5050 Sugar Maple Rd.
15 rms - $390-1,200/wk
Pets: Welcome w/approval
Creature Comforts: 240-wooded acres on pristine Afterglow Lake, housekeeping cottages, CCTV, kit, fireplace, whirlpool, sauna, swimming, lawn games, extensive indoor recreation, tennis, hiking, xc-skiing, snowmobiling

Days Inn
(800) DAYS INN, (715) 479-5151
http://www.daysinn.com
844 Railroad St.
93 rooms - $60-105
Pets: Welcome
Creature Comforts: CCTV, a/c, refrig, micro, Jacuzzi, cont. brkfst, pool

Edgewater Inn and Resort
(888) 334-3987, (715) 479-4011
http://www.edgeinn.com
5054 Rte. 70 W.
21 rms/cottages - $40-190
Pets: Welcome w/$10 fee
Creature Comforts: Knotty pine lodge/simple cottages, waterside, CCTV, kit, porches, play area, hiking, fishing, xc-skiing

Gypsy Villa Resort
(800) 232-9714, (715) 479-8644
950 Circle Dr.
33 cottages - $70-310
Pets: Welcome w/approval
Creature Comforts: Lakeside, cottages, CCTV, a/c, fireplace, kit, pool, hlth clb access, sauna, whirlpool, playground, boating, fishing, waterskiing, xc-skiing, snowmobiling

Pine-Aire Resort Campground
(800) 597-6777, (715) 479-9208
http://www.pine-aire.com
4443 Chain O'Lakes
6 cottages - $75-140/wk
Pets: Welcome in off-season
Creature Comforts: Lakeside cottages, beach, kit, restaurant, marina, boating, fishing

White Eagle Motel
(800) 782-6488, (715) 479-9208
4948 Rte. 70 W
22 rooms - $40-55
Pets: Welcome w/$5 fee
Creature Comforts: CCTV, sauna, whirlpool, boat dock, fishing, paddleboats

EAU CLAIRE
Best Western White House Inn
(800) 528-1234, (715) 832-8356
http://www.bestwestern.com
1828 S. Hastings Way
66 rooms - $40-60
Pets: Welcome w/approval
Creature Comforts: CCTV, a/c, pool, sauna, whirlpool

825

Comfort Inn
(800) 228-5150, (715) 833-9798
http://www.comfortinn.com
3117 Craig Rd.
56 rooms - $50-90
Pets: Welcome w/$5 fee
Creature Comforts: CCTV, a/c,
refrig, micro, pool, whirlpool

Days Inn, West
(800) DAYS INN, (715) 874-5550
http://www.daysinn.com
6319 Truax Lane
74 rooms - $55-70
Pets: Welcome w/$25 deposit
Creature Comforts: CCTV, a/c,
refrig, micro, pool, whirlpool

Exel Inn of Eau Claire
(800) 367-3935, (715) 834-3193
http://www.exelinns.com
2305 Craig Rd.
101 rooms - $40-50
Pets: Small pets welcome
Creature Comforts: CCTV, a/c,
kit

Highlander Inn
(715) 835-2261
1135 W. MacArthur Ave.
41 rooms - $30-35
Pets: Welcome w/approval
Creature Comforts: CCTV, a/c

Holiday Inn
(800) HOLIDAY, (715) 835-2211
http://www.holiday-inn.com
2703 Craig Rd.
137 rooms - $70
Pets: Welcome
Creature Comforts: CCTV, a/c,
refrig, micro, restaurant, pool,
whirlpool

Holiday Inn Convention Center
(800) HOLIDAY, (715) 835-6121
http://www.holiday-inn.com
205 S. Barstow St.
122 rooms - $70-80
Pets: Welcome
Creature Comforts: CCTV, a/c,
restaurant, pool, hlth clb access

Maple Manor Motel
(800) 624-3763, (715) 834-2618
2507 S. Hastings Way
34 rooms - $35-45
Pets: Small pets welcome
Creature Comforts: CCTV, a/c,
refrig, micro, restaurant

Quality Inn
(800) 221-2222, (715) 834-6611
http://www.qualityinn.com
809 W. Clairemont Ave.
120 rooms - $70-130
Pets: Welcome w/$5 fee
Creature Comforts: CCTV, a/c,
refrig, micro, restaurant, pool,
sauna, whirlpool

Roadstar Inn
(715) 832-9731
1151 W. MacArthur Ave.
62 rooms - $35-40
Pets: Welcome w/$ 25 deposit
Creature Comforts: CCTV, a/c,
refrig

Super 8 Motel
(800) 800-8000, (715) 874-6868
http://www.super8.com
6260 Texaco Dr.
31 rooms - $40-55
Pets: Welcome w/$5 fee
Creature Comforts: CCTV, a/c,

EDGERTON
Towne Edge Motel
(608) 884-9328
1104 N. Main St.
18 rooms - $25-40
Pets: Welcome w/approval
Creature Comforts: CCTV, a/c,
restaurant, snowmobiling

EGG HARBOR
The Alpine Resort
(920) 868-3000
http://www.alpineresort.com/
7715 Alpine Rd.
61 rms/cottages - $125-271
Pets: Small pets in housekeeping
homes w/$7 fee
Creature Comforts: Swiss
hospitality on 300 wooded and
beachfront acres, 1-5 bedroom
housekeeping homes, clean but
simply furnished, CCTV, a/c,
VCR, kit, restaurant, swimming,
tennis, golf, lawn games, boating

Shallows Resort
(800) 257-1560, (920) 868-3458
http://www.shallows.com/
7353 Horseshoe Bay Rd.
20 rms/cottages - $65-290
Pets: Non-shedding dogs
under 20 lbs. welcome
Creature Comforts: Wonderful
family resort on Horseshoe Bay,
beautiful grounds, rqst Gatehouse
suites, charming Eagles Nest, or
the Studio (neat fieldstone
cottage), CCTV, a/c, refrig, micro,
kit, fireplace, pool, whirlpool,
swimming, boating, tennis, golf

ELROY
Elroy Valley Inn
(608) 462-8251
Rtes. 80 & 82
30 rooms - $30-50
Pets: Welcome w/approval
Creature Comforts: CCTV, a/c,
restaurant, playground

FENNIMORE
Fennimore Hills Motel
(608) 822-3281
5814 Rte. 18 W.
24 rooms - $46-125
Pets: Small pets welcome
Creature Comforts: extended
country views, CCTV, a/c, refrig,
Jacuzzi

FIFIELD
Boyd's Mason Lake Resort
(715) 762-3469
N12351 Boyd's Rd.
18 cottages - $62-85
Pets: Welcome w/approval
Creature Comforts: CCTV,
fireplace, restaurant, swimming,
fishing

FENNIMORE
Fenmore Hills Motel
(608) 822-3281
5814 Rte. 18 W.
24 rooms - $50-60
Pets: Small pets welcome
Creature Comforts: extended
country views, CCTV, a/c, refrig,
Jacuzzi

FIFIELD
Boyd's Mason Lake Resort
(715) 762-3469
N12351 Boyd's Rd.
18 cottages - $62-85
Pets: Welcome w/approval
Creature Comforts: CCTV,
fireplace, restaurant, swimming,
fishing

FOND DU LAC
Baymont Inns
(800) 4-Budget, (920) 921-4000
http://www.baymontinns.com
77 Holiday Lane
80 rooms - $50-105
Pets: Welcome
Creature Comforts: CCTV, a/c,
refrig, micro, Jacuzzis, pool,
whirlpool

Holiday Inn
(800) HOLIDAY, (920) 923-1440
http://www.holiday-inn.com
625 W. Rolling Meadows Dr.
142 rooms - $90-140
Pets: Welcome
Creature Comforts: CCTV, a/c,
refrig, micro, restaurant, pool, hlth
clb access, sauna, whirlpool

Northway Motel
(888) 276-1580, (920) 921-7975
301 S. Pioneer Rd.
19 rooms - $45-80
Pets: Welcome w/$7 fee
Creature Comforts: CCTV, a/c,
kit, restaurant, playground

Pioneer Motel
(920) 921-2181
195 N. Pioneer Rd.
28 rooms - $25-55
Pets: Welcome
Creature Comforts: CCTV, a/c,
kit

Stretch, Eat, and Sleep
(920) 923-3131
Rtes. 41 & 100
35 rooms - $22-29
Pets: Welcome
Creature Comforts: CCTV,
restaurant

Super 8 Motel
(800) 800-8000, (920) 922-1088
http://www.super8.com
391 Pioneer Rd., US 41
48 rooms - $45-60
Pets: Welcome w/$20 deposit
Creature Comforts: CCTV, a/c,
refrig, micro

FREDERIC
Frederic Motel
(715) 327-4496
Rte. 35
9 rooms - $32-45
Pets: Welcome
Creature Comforts: CCTV

FRIENDSHIP
Island Resort
(608) 339-6725
306 Hillwood Ln.
6 cottages - $30-70
Pets: Welcome w/approval
Creature Comforts: CCTV, kit,
boating

GILLETT
Sleepy Hollow Motel
(920) 855-2727
http://www.ci.gillett.wi.us/
sleepy.htm
5 Rte. 22 E.
20 rooms - $40-58
Pets: Welcome
Creature Comforts: CCTV, kit,
fireplace

GILLS ROCK
Harbor House Inn
(920) 854-5196
12666 Rte. 42
14 rooms - $75-130
Pets: Welcome w/$10 fee
Creature Comforts: Charming
restored 1904 Victorian cottage,
on the harbor w/park-like grounds,
no phones, kit, beach, sauna,
whirlpool, bicycles, rowboat

Windside Cottages
(920) 854-4871
12714 Rte. 42
4 cottages - $60-100
Pets: Welcome w/approval
Creature Comforts: Fireplace,
kit, boating, fishing, xc-skiing

GLENDALE
Baymont Inn, Northeast
(800) 4-Budget, (414) 964-8484
http://www.baymontinns.com
5110 N. Port Washington Rd.
106 rooms - $50-65
Pets: Small pets welcome
Creature Comforts: CCTV, a/c,
kits

Exel Inn Northeast
(800) 367-3935, (414) 961-7272
http://www.exelinns.com
5485 N. Port Washington Rd.
125 rooms - $50-65
Pets: Small pets welcome
Creature Comforts: CCTV, a/c,
refrig, micro, Jacuzzis

Residence Inn by Marriott
(800) 331-3131, (414) 352-0070
http://www.residenceinn.com
7275 N. Port Washington Rd.
96 rooms - $150-185
Pets: $6 fee, $175 deposit
Creature Comforts: some
penthouse bi-level suites, CCTV,
a/c, fireplace, kits, pool

GRANTSBURG
Cedar Point Resort
(715) 488-2224
12480 Cedar Point Ln.
10 cottages - $55-75
Pets: Welcome w/approval
Creature Comforts: CCTV, kit,
swimming, boating

Wood River Inn
(715) 463-2541
703 Rte. 70
21 rooms - $45-50
Pets: Welcome
Creature Comforts: CCTV, a/c,
refrig, restaurant, pool, hlth clb
access, sauna, whirlpool,
xc-skiing, snowmobiling

GREEN BAY
A-1 Tower Motel
(920) 468-1242
2625 Humboldt Rd.
17 rooms - $36-60
Pets: Welcome
Creature Comforts: CCTV

Arena Motel
(920) 494-5636
871 Lombardi Ave.
19 rooms - $40-54
Pets: Welcome
Creature Comforts: CCTV

Bay Motel
(877) 229-7799, (920) 494-8260
1301 S. Military Ave.
53 rooms - $45-60
Pets: Welcome w/$5 fee
Creature Comforts: CCTV, a/c,
refrig, restaurant

Baymont Inn
(800) 4-Budget, (920) 494-7887
http://www.baymontinns.com
2840 S. Oneida St.
80 rooms - $60-65
Pets: Small pets welcome
Creature Comforts: CCTV, a/c,
refrig, micro

Best Western Downtowner
(800) 528-1234, (920) 437-8771
http://www.bestwestern.com
321 S. Washington St.
134 rooms - $60-90
Pets: Welcome
Creature Comforts: CCTV, a/c,
kits, restaurant, wading pool,
sauna, whirlpool

Comfort Inn, Green Bay
(800) 228-5150, (920) 498-2060
http://www.comfortinn.com
2841 Ramada Way
60 rooms - $55-100
Pets: Small pets welcome
Creature Comforts: CCTV, a/c,
refrig, micro, pool, whirlpool

Days Inn, Lambeau Field
(800) DAYS INN, (920) 498-8088
http://www.daysinn.com
1978 Gross Ave.
77 rooms - $40-100
Pets: Small pets welcome
Creature Comforts: CCTV, a/c,
refrig, pool, whirlpool

Days Inn, City Centre
(800) DAYS INN, (920) 435-4484
http://www.daysinn.com
406 N. Washington St.
98 rooms - $65-100
Pets: Small pets welcome
Creature Comforts: overlooking
the Fox River, CCTV, a/c, refrig,
micro, dining room, pool

Exel Inn
(800) 367-3935, (920) 499-3599
http://www.exelinns.com
2870 Ramada Way
104 rooms - $45-55
Pets: Small pets welcome
Creature Comforts: CCTV a/c

Holiday Inn, City Centre
(800) HOLIDAY, (920) 437-5900
http://www.holiday-inn.com
200 Main St.
149 rooms - $70-100
Pets: Welcome w/approval
Creature Comforts: riverside,
CCTV, a/c, restaurant, pool, sauna,
whirlpool, boating, fishing,
waterskiing

Motel 6
(800) 4 MOTEL6, (920) 494-6730
http://www.motel6.com
1614 Shawano Ave.
103 rooms - $30-35
Pets: Under 30 lbs. welcome
Creature Comforts: CCTV,
VCR, a/c

Residence Inn by Marriott
(800) 331-3131, (920) 435-2222
http://www.residenceinn.com
335 W. St. Joseph St.
96 rooms - $85-150
Pets: Welcome w/$5 daily fee,
$150 one-time fee
Creature Comforts: Suites,
CCTV, a/c, kit, fireplace, cont.
brkfst, hlth clb access

Super 8 Motel
(800) 800-8000, (920) 494-2042
http://www.super8.com
2868 S. Oneida St.
84 rooms - $55-65
Pets: $25 fee, $10 deposit
Creature Comforts: CCTV, a/c,
sauna, whirlpool

HARSHAW
Smitty's Idlewild Bar
(715) 277-2314
5320 Lakewood Rd.
8 cottages - $50-65
Pets: Welcome w/approval
Creature Comforts: CCTV, kit,
fireplace, swimming, boating

HAYWARD
Americinn Motel
(800) 634-3444, (715) 634-2700
http://haywardlakes.com/
americinn.htm
15601 Rte. 63 North
38 rooms - $60-75
Pets: Welcome
Creature Comforts: CCTV, a/c,
refrig, micro, Jacuzzi, cont. brkfst,
pool, whirlpool

Best Western Northern Pine
(800) 528-1234, (715) 634-4959
http://www.bestwestern.com
Rte. 6, Box 6489
39 rooms - $45-80
Pets: Welcome w/$7 fee
Creature Comforts: CCTV, a/c,
kit, fireplace, pool, whirlpool,
sauna

Ghost Lake Lodge
(715) 462-3939
http://www.ghostlakelodge.com
Rte. 7, Box 74501
15 cottages - $98-230
Pets: $60 weekly fee per pet
Creature Comforts: Rustic yet
attractive log cabins on private
lake, wilderness setting, fieldstone
fireplaces, screened porch, CCTV,
kit, pool, recreation rm.,
babysitting, tennis, swimming,
boating, fishing

Herman's Landing
(715) 462-3626
8255 N. County Rd.
11 cottages - $95-450
Pets: Welcome w/approval
Creature Comforts: CCTV,
restaurant, boating

Musky Run Resort
(715) 462-3445
12503 N. Town Hall Rd.
6 cottages - $65-160
Pets: Welcome w/approval
Creature Comforts: CCTV, kit,
swimming, boating

Nelson Lake Lodge
(715) 634-3750
http://haywardlakes.com/
nllodge.htm
Rte. 3, Nelson Lake
14 cabins - $53-150
Pets: $25 weekly fee per pet
Creature Comforts: CCTV, kit,
swimming, boating

Nielson's Pine Crest Resort
(715) 462-3297
http://haywardlakes.com/
pinecrest.htm
12459 N. Town Hall Rd.
6 cottages - $65-105
Pets: Welcome w/approval
Creature Comforts: On Little
Spider Lake, CCTV, kit,
restaurant, swimming, boating

Northland Lodge
(715) 462-3379
http://haywardlakes.com/
northland.htm
9181 West Brandt Rd.
19 houses - $475-1,590/wk
Pets: Welcome w/fee
Creature Comforts: Intimate,
family resort, log cottages on Lost
Land Lake, some country
antiques, CCTV, kit, fireplace,
swimming, boating, fishing,
playground, game rm.

Northwoods Motel
(800) 232-9202, (715) 634-8088
9854 N. State Rte. 27
9 rooms - $40-70
Pets: Welcome w/$7 fee
Creature Comforts: CCTV, kit

Park Island Resort
(715) 634-2591
http://haywardlakes.com/
parkisland.htm
Rte. 27
11 cottages - $50-90
Pets: Only by arrangement
Creature Comforts: CCTV, kit,
swimming, boating

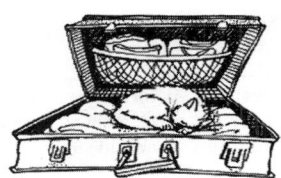

Ross' Teal Lake Lodge
(715) 462-3631
http://www.rossteal.com
Rte. 7A, Ross Rd.
25 rooms - $130-250
Pets: Welcome w/approval
Creature Comforts: Lakeside
cottages/guest homes, neat old
main log lodge, CCTV, refrig,
micro, fireplace, restaurant, pool,
beach, sauna, whirlpool, Audubon
Signature 18-hole golf course,
tennis, boat dock, bicycles,
paddleboats, fishing, xc-skiing

Sunset Lodge
(715) 462-3757
8450 West State Rd.
7 cottages - $65-165
Pets: Welcome w/approval
Creature Comforts: CCTV, kit,
fireplace, boating

Totem Pole Lodge
(715) 462-3367
http://hayward lakes.com/
totem.htm
9216 West Brandt Rd.
9 cottages - $450-760/wk
Pets: Welcome w/$75 fee
Creature Comforts: 1920's lodge
and cottages on Lost Land Lake,
CCTV, kit, restaurant, swimming
beach, boating

Virgin Timber Resort
(715) 462-3269
10820 N. Moose Lake Rd.
7 cottages - $91-162
Pets: $50 fee, only w/pre-approval
Creature Comforts: Great family
resort, 1920's rustic log cabins on
Moose Lake, stone fireplaces,
hardwood flrs, country antiques,
CCTV, kit, fireplace, play area,
swimming, boating, kayaks

Super 8 Motel
(800) 800-8000, (715) 634-2646
http://www.super8.com
317 South Dakota Ave.
46 rooms - $45-60
Pets: Small pets welcome
Creature Comforts: CCTV,
Jacuzzis, pool

Wilderness Haven Resort
(715) 634-1060
http://www.wildernesshaven.com
9293 North Country Rd.
4 cabins - $65-95
Pets: Welcome w/approval
Creature Comforts: CCTV, kit,
swimming, boating

HILES
Little Pine Motel
(715) 649-3431
Rte. 32
13 cottages - $32-75
Pets: Welcome
Creature Comforts: CCTV, kit,
boating

HUDSON
Comfort Inn
(800) 228-5150, (715) 386-6355
http://www.comfortinn.com
811 Dominion Dr.
60 rooms - $55-65
Pets: Small pets w/$50 deposit
Creature Comforts: CCTV, a/c,
Jacuzzis, pool, whirlpool

J.R. Ranch
(800) 386-6190, (715) 386-6190
736 Rte. 12
30 rooms - $30-95
Pets: Welcome
Creature Comforts: CCTV,
fireplace, restaurant, whirlpool

Jefferson-Day House
(715) 386-7111
http://jeffersondayhouse.com
1109 third St.
5 suites - $99-180
Pets: Only by arrangement
Creature Comforts: Lovely 1857
Italianate Antibellum home,
recently restored, parklike
grounds, hardwood flrs, orig.
features, formal setting, traditional
antiques, rms. w/antique walnut
and cherry beds, quilts, fireplace,
terry robes, Jacuzzi, four-course
brkfst

Royal Inn
(715) 386-2366
1509 Coulee Rd.
30 rooms - $31-60
Pets: Welcome
Creature Comforts: CCTV

HURLEY
Days Inn
(800) DAYS INN, (715) 561-3500
http://www.daysinn.com
850 10th Ave.
70 rooms - $45-80
Pets: Small pets welcome
Creature Comforts: CCTV, a/c,
micro, refrig, Jacuzzis, pool,
sauna, whirlpool

Eagle Bluff Condo Rentals
(800) 336-0973, (715) 561-2787
990 10th Ave. North
27 condos - $42-235
Pets: Welcome w/deposit
Creature Comforts: CCTV, kit,
fireplace

Holiday Inn
(800) HOLIDAY, (715) 561-3030
http://www.holiday-inn.com
1000 10th Ave.
100 rooms - $65-75
Pets: Welcome
Creature Comforts: CCTV, a/c,
restaurant, pool, sauna, whirlpool

IRON RIVER
Delta Lodge
(715) 372-4299
Rte. 2
10 cottages - $50-100
Pets: Welcome w/approval
Creature Comforts: CCTV, kit,
fireplace, swimming, boating

Hermitage Supper Club/Resort
(715) 372-4580
Country Hwy. H
3 cottages - $55-75
Pets: Welcome w/approval
Creature Comforts: CCTV, kit,
fireplace, restaurant, boating

JANESVILLE
Baymont Inns
(800) 4-Budget, (608) 758-4545
http://www.baymontinns.com
616 Midland Rd.
107 rooms - $50-70
Pets: Welcome w/$10 fee
Creature Comforts: CCTV, a/c,
micro, refrig, pool, whirlpool

Motel 6
(800) 4 MOTEL6, (608) 756-1742
http://www.motel6.com
3907 Milton Ave.
118 rooms - $40
Pets: Small pets welcome
Creature Comforts: CCTV a/c

Select Inn
(800) 641-1000, (608) 754-0251
http://www.selectinn.com
3520 Milton Ave.
63 rooms - $40-50
Pets: Small pets w/$25 deposit
Creature Comforts: CCTV, a/c,
refrig, restaurant

Super 8 Motel
(800) 800-8000, (608) 756-2040
http://www.super8.com
3430 Milton Ave.
48 rooms - $55-65
Pets: Welcome
Creature Comforts: CCTV a/c

JOHNSON CREEK
Days Inn
(800) DAYS INN, (920) 699-8000
http://www.daysinn.com
4545 W. Linmar Lane
45 rooms - $55-90
Pets: Welcome w/$50 fee, $50
deposit
Creature Comforts: Set high on
a hill w/panoramic views, CCTV,
a/c, micro, refrig, pool, hlth clb
access, whirlpool

KAUKAUNA
Settle Inn
(800) 831-4785, (920) 766-0088
1201 Maloney Dr.
46 rooms - $50-55
Pets: Small pets w/$3 fee
Creature Comforts: CCTV, a/c,
micro, refrig, Jacuzzis, pool,
whirlpool

KENOSHA
Baymont Inns
(800) 4-Budget, (262) 857-7911
http://www.baymontinns.com
7540 118th Ave.
95 rooms - $50-70
Pets: Small pets welcome
Creature Comforts: CCTV a/c

Days Inn
(800) DAYS INN, (262) 857-2311
http://www.daysinn.com
12121 75th St.
96 rooms - $60-95
Pets: Welcome
Creature Comforts: CCTV, a/c,
refrig, restaurant, pool, whirlpool

Knights Inn West
(262) 857-2622
7221 122 Ave.
113 rooms - $50-55
Pets: Welcome
Creature Comforts: CCTV, a/c,
kit

LA CROSSE
Days Inn
(800) DAYS INN, (608) 783-1000
http://www.daysinn.com
101 Sky Harbour Dr.
148 rooms - $65-90
Pets: Small pets w/$5 fee
Creature Comforts: CCTV, a/c,
refrig, micro, Jacuzzis, restaurant,
pool, sauna, whirlpool

Edgewater Motel
(608) 783-2286
N5326 Hilltop Dr.
7 rooms - $25-60
Pets: Welcome
Creature Comforts: CCTV,
boating

Exel Inn
(800) 367-3935, (608) 781-0400
http://www.exelinns.com
2150 Rose St.
102 rooms - $40-55
Pets: Small pets welcome
Creature Comforts: CCTV, a/c,
refrig, micro, whirlpool

Radisson Hotel
(800) 333-3333, (608) 784-6680
http://www.radisson.com
200 Harborview Plaza
170 rooms - $100-150
Pets: Welcome
Creature Comforts: Riverside,
CCTV, a/c, refrig, restaurant, pool,
hlth clb access, whirlpool

Roadstar Inn
(608) 781-3070
2622 Rose St.
110 rooms - $45-50
Pets: Welcome w/$ 25 deposit
Creature Comforts: CCTV, a/c,
refrig

Super 8 Motel
(800) 800-8000, (608) 781-8880
http://www.super8.com
1625 Rose St.
82 rooms - $70
Pets: Welcome w/$ 5 fee
Creature Comforts: CCTV, a/c,
restaurant, pool, whirlpool

LA POINTE
Madeline Island Motel
(715) 747-3000
Col Woods Ave.
11 rooms - $40-70
Pets: Small dogs only
Creature Comforts: Micro,
refrig, no phones, xc-skiing

Woods Manor
(800) 966-3756, (715) 747-3102
Nebraska Row
10 cottages - $109-209
Pets: Welcome w/approval
Creature Comforts: Gracious
1920's manor house on historic
Madeline Island, beamed ceilings,
fine antiques, nicely furnished
rms. w/French doors, down
comforters, quilts, cont. brkfst,
pool, sauna, whirlpool

LAC DU FLAMBEAU
Dillman's Sand Lake Lodge
(715) 588-3143
3305 Sand Lake Lane
10 rooms - $55-400
Pets: Welcome w/approval
Creature Comforts: CCTV, kit,
whirlpool, swimming, boating

Ty-Bach B&B
(715) 588-7851
3104 Simpson Lane
2 rooms - $65-75
Pets: Welcome w/approval
Creature Comforts: Small B&B
on lake, refrig, full brkfst, hot tub

LADYSMITH
AmericInn Motel
(800) 634-3444, (715) 532-6650
800 West College Ave.
38 rooms - $60-75
Pets: Welcome w/$6 fee, $50 dep.
Creature Comforts: CCTV, a/c,
kit, pool, whirlpool

Best Western El Rancho Motel
(800) 528-1234, (715) 532-6666
http://www.bestwestern.com
8500 W. Flambeau Ave.
27 rooms - $50-55
Pets: Welcome
Creature Comforts: CCTV, a/c,
restaurant, pool, xc-skiing,
snowmobiling

Evergreen Motel
(715) 532-3168
1201 W. Lake Avenue
20 rooms - $30-50
Pets: Welcome w/approval
Creature Comforts: CCTV,
snowmobiling

LAKE GENEVA
Alpine Motel
(262) 248-4264
682 Wells St.
9 rooms - $30-120
Pets: Welcome w/approval
Creature Comforts: CCTV, kit,
pool

Budget Host Diplomat
(800) Bud-Host, (262) 248-1809
http://www.budgethost.com
1060 Wells St.
22 rooms - $41-106
Pets: Welcome w/approval k
Creature Comforts: CCTV, pool

Eleven Gables Inn
(800) 362-0395, (262) 248-8393
http://www.lkgeneva.com
493 Wrigley Dr.
9 rooms - $89-255
Pets: Welcome in the Country
Cottage and Peach
Creature Comforts: Inn on Lake
Geneva w/outbuildings, rustic
cottage w/plank walls, fireplace,
Jacuzzi, refrig, micro and two
bedrooms; The Peach has an iron
and brass bed, private balcony,
cont. brkfst

Lake Geneva Motel
(262) 248-3464
524 Wells St.
21 rooms - $40-110
Pets: Welcome w/approval
Creature Comforts: CCTV, kit,
restaurant, swimming

Lakewood Inn Motel
(262) 248-6773
1150 Wells St.
12 rooms - $25-130
Pets: Welcome w/approval
Creature Comforts: CCTV, kit

Pine Tree Motel
(262) 248-4988
903 Wells St.
28 rooms - $30-100
Pets: Welcome w/approval
Creature Comforts: CCTV, kit

T.C. Smith Historic Inn
(800) 423-0233, (262) 248-1097
http://wwte.com/tcinn.htm
865 Main St.
8 rooms - $95-350
Pets: Welcome
Creature Comforts: Highly
recommended, Nat'l Historic
Register, circa 1845, lakeside,
19th-century antiques, Persian
carpets, ornate woodwork, Tiffany
chandeliers; CCTV, a/c, fireplace,
Jacuzzi

LAND O' LAKES
Sunrise Lodge
(800) 221-9689, (715) 547-3684
5894 W. Shore Dr.
23 cottages - $52-150
Pets: Welcome
Creature Comforts: Family-
oriented, lakeside destination,
simple modern cottages and large
house, kit, restaurant, beach,
exercise rm, golf, tennis, boating,
playground, basketball, fishing

Whispering Pines Resort
(715) 547-3600
5932 W. Shore Rd.
10 cottages - $60-105
Pets: Welcome w/approval
Creature Comforts: CCTV, kit,
swimming, boating

LODI

Lodi Valley Suites
(608) 592-7331
N 1440 Rte. 113
26 rooms - $40-115
Pets: Welcome w/approval
Creature Comforts: CCTV, a/c, restaurant, pool

Sunset Resort
(608) 592-4880
N2849 Lake Point Dr.
6 cottages - $65-175
Pets: Welcome w/approval
Creature Comforts: CCTV, kit, swimming, boating

LUCK

Luck Country Inn
(800) 544-7396, (715) 472-2000
Rtes. 35 & 48
37 rooms - $55-80
Pets: Welcome
Creature Comforts: CCTV, a/c, refrig, restaurant, pool, sauna, whirlpool, fishing, boating, waterskiing, tennis, cross-country alpine skiing, snowmobiling

MADISON

Baymont Inns
(800) 4-Budget, (608) 831-7711
http://www.baymontinns.com
8102 Excelsior Dr.
130 rooms - $75-95
Pets: Welcome
Creature Comforts: CCTV, a/c, refrig, micro, pool, hlth clb access, sauna, whirlpool

Best Western West Towne Suites
(800) 528-1234, (608) 833-4200
http://www.bestwestern.com
650 Grand Canyon Dr.
102 rooms - $70-90
Pets: Small pets welcome
Creature Comforts: CCTV, a/c, refrig, pool, hlth club access

Collins House B&B
(608) 255-4230
http://www.collinshouse.com
704 E. Gorham St.
5 rooms - $85-140
Pets: Welcome on occasion w/approval
Creature Comforts: Lovely, 1911 Nat'l Historic Register Prairie School style house, lake views, glowing hardwood flrs, antique Arts and Crafts furnishings, CCTV, VCR, refrig, Jacuzzi, fireplace-woodstove, gourmet brkfst, exceptional baked goodies

Country Inn and Suites
(800) 456-4000, (608) 221-0055
400 River Place
87 rooms - $64-89
Pets: Welcome w/approval
Creature Comforts: CCTV, kit, fireplace, Jacuzzi, pool, exercise rm, whirlpool

Crowne Plaza
(800) HOLIDAY, (608) 244-4703
http://www.holiday-inn.com
4402 E. Washington Ave.
227 rooms - $90-125
Pets: Welcome w/approval
Creature Comforts: CCTV, a/c, Jacuzzis, restaurant, hlth clb access

Days Inn, Southeast
(800) DAYS INN, (608) 233-1800
http://www.daysinn.com
402 E. Broadway Service Rd.
68 rooms - $60-85
Pets: Welcome w/$50 deposit
Creature Comforts: CCTV, a/c, kits, pool, whirlpool

East Towne Suites
(800) 950-1919, (608) 244-2020
4801 Annamark Dr.
123 rooms - $50-150
Pets: Welcome w/$20 deposit
Creature Comforts: CCTV, a/c, refrig, micro, Jacuzzis, restaurant, pool, hlth clb access, whirlpool, playground

Edgewater Hotel
(800) 922-5512, (608) 256-9071
666 Wisconsin Ave.
116 rooms - $80-170
Pets: Welcome w/approval
Creature Comforts: Lakeside, CCTV, kit, restaurant, fishing

Edgewood Motel
(800) 732-8492, (608) 222-8601
101 W. Broadway
14 rooms - $36-49
Pets: Welcome w/approval
Creature Comforts: CCTV

Exel Inn
(800) 356-8013, (608) 241-3861
http://www.exelinns.com
4202 East Towne Blvd.
102 rooms - $45-60
Pets: Small pets welcome
Creature Comforts: CCTV, a/c, micro, refrig, Jacuzzis, hlth club access

Gilman St. Rag
(608) 257-6560
http://www.hawkhill.com/gilmanbb.html
125 E. Gilman St.
2 rooms - $70-90
Pets: Welcome
Creature Comforts: 1885 Queen Anne home, fine art collectibles, some antiques, traditionally furnished bedrooms, sunny brkfst rm., CCTV, a/c, refrig, cont. brkfst

Madison Concourse Hotel
(800) 356-8293, (608) 257-6000
http://www.concoursehotel.com
One W. Dayton St.
356 rooms - $100-180
Pets: Small pets welcome
Creature Comforts: Top floors offer lake or capitol views, CCTV, a/c, micro, refrig, restaurant, pool, hlth clb access, sauna, whirlpool

Motel 6, North
(800)4 MOTEL6, (608) 241-8101
http://www.motel6.com
1754 Thierer Rd.
91 rooms - $30-45
Pets: Under 30 lbs. welcome
Creature Comforts: CCTV, a/c, pool

Motel 6, South
(800) 4 MOTEL6, (608) 466-8356
http://www.motel6.com
6402 E. Broadway
118 rooms - $30-40
Pets: Under 30 lbs. welcome
Creature Comforts: CCTV, a/c, pool

Quality Inn South
(608) 222-5501
4916 E. Broadway
156 rooms - $70-75
Pets: Welcome
Creature Comforts: CCTV, a/c, refrig, restaurant, pool, whirlpool

Ramada Limited
(800) 2-Ramada, (608) 244-2481
http://www.ramada.com
3841 E. Washington St.
194 rooms - $70-90
Pets: Small pets w/ $10 fee
Creature Comforts: CCTV, VCR, a/c, refrig, micro, Jacuzzi, restaurant, pool, whirlpool

Red Roof Inn
(800) THE ROOF, (608) 241-1787
http://www.redroof.com
4830 Hayes Rd.
108 rooms - $35-70
Pets: Small pets welcome
Creature Comforts: CCTV, a/c

Residence Inn by Marriott
(800) 331-3131, (608) 244-5047
http://www.residenceinn.com
4862 Hayes Rd.
66 rooms - $100-150
Pets: Welcome w/$50 fee
Creature Comforts: CCTV, a/c, kit, pool, hlth clb access, whirlpool

Select Inn
(608) 249-1815
4845 Hayes Rd.
100 rooms - $40-50
Pets: Small pets w/$25 deposit
Creature Comforts: CCTV, a/c, refrig, restaurant

Super 8 Motel
(800) 800-8000, (608) 258-9575
http://www.super8.com
1602 West Beltline Hwy.
89 rooms - $60-70
Pets: Welcome w/$50 deposit
Creature Comforts: CCTV, a/c, pool, whirlpool

University Inn
(608) 285-8040
441N. Frances St.
45 rooms - $70-75
Pets: Welcome w/$25 deposit
Creature Comforts: CCTV, a/c, refrig, restaurant

MANITOWISH WATERS
RM Sleight's Wildwood
(715) 543-2140
Wildwood Rd.
10 rooms - $25-100
Pets: Welcome
Creature Comforts: Kitchen, fireplace, boating

MANITOWOC
Comfort Inn
(800) 228-5150, (920) 683-0220
http://www.comfortinn.com
2200 S. 44th St.
47 rooms - $60-85
Pets: Welcome
Creature Comforts: CCTV, a/c, micro, refrig, whirlpool

Days Inn
(800) DAYS INN, (920) 682-8271
http://www.daysinn.com
908 Washington St.
53 rooms - $40-125
Pets: Welcome w/deposit
Creature Comforts: CCTV, a/c, Jacuzzis

Inn on Maritime Bay
(800) 654-5353, (920) 682-7000
101 Maritime Dr.
107 rooms - $80-115
Pets: Welcome w/$25 fee
Creature Comforts: Lakeside, CCTV, a/c, refrig, restaurant, pool, sauna, whirlpool, fishing, boating

Westmoor Motel - IMA
(800) 424-6126, (920) 684-3374
4626 Calumet Ave.
20 rooms - $30-70
Pets: Welcome w/approval
Creature Comforts: CCTV, a/c

MARINETTE
Chalet Motel
(715) 735-6687
1301 Marinette Ave.
21 rooms - $35-45
Pets: Welcome w/approval
Creature Comforts: CCTV, a/c, refrig

Super 8 Motel
(800) 800-8000, (715) 735-7887
http://www.super8.com
1508 Marinette Ave.
68 rooms - $45-55
Pets: Welcome
Creature Comforts: CCTV, VCR, a/c, refrig, micro, cont. brkfst, whirlpool, sauna

MARSHFIELD
Best Western Marshfield
(800) 528-1234, (715) 387-1761
http://www.bestwestern.com
2700 S. Roddis
100 rooms - $50-60
Pets: Welcome w/approval
Creature Comforts: CCTV, a/c, restaurant, pool, whirlpool, snowmobiling

Downtown Motel
(715) 387-1111
750 S. Central Ave.
37 rooms - $40-60
Pets: Welcome w/approval
Creature Comforts: CCTV, a/c, refrig, micro, private picnic area w/basketball court, playground grills

Marshfield Inn
(800) 851-8669, (715) 387-6381
116 W. Ives
32 rooms - $40-55
Pets: Small pets welcome
Creature Comforts: CCTV, a/c, micro, refrig, whirlpool

MAUSTON
Alaskan Motor Inn
(800) 835-8268, (608) 847-5609
I-90 & Rte. 82
48 rooms - $27-60
Pets: Welcome
Creature Comforts: CCTV, a/c, kit, restaurant

City Center Motel
(608) 847-5634
315 E. State Rte. 12
23 rooms - $25-50
Pets: Welcome
Creature Comforts: CCTV

Woodside Ranch Resort
(800) 626-4275, (608) 847-4275
W 3940 Rte. 82
36 rms/ctgs - $30-125
Pets: Welcome w/approval
Creature Comforts: CCTV,
fireplace, pool, sauna, boating

MEDFORD
Medford Inn
(715) 748-4420
321 N. 8th St.
23 rooms - $30-40
Pets: Welcome w/approval
Creature Comforts: CCTV, a/c

MENOMONIE
Best Western Holiday Manor
(800) 528-1234, (715) 235-9651
1815 N. Broadway
138 rooms - $44-114
Pets: Welcome
Creature Comforts: CCTV, a/c,
Jacuzzi, cont. brkfst, pool,
whirlpool

Bolo Country Inn
(800) 553-2656, (715) 235-5596
207 Pine Ave. W.
25 rooms - 50-80
Pets: Welcome w/approval
Creature Comforts: Nestled
amid pines, CCTV, Jacuzzis,
restaurant

Super 8 Motel
(800) 800-8000, (715) 235-8889
http://www.super8.com
1622 N. Broadway
81 rooms - $50-65
Pets: Small pets w/$50 deposit
Creature Comforts: CCTV, a/c

MEQUON
Breeze Inn to Chalet Motel 40
(800) 343-4510, (262) 241-4510
10401 N. Port Washington Rd.
40 rooms - $50-70
Pets: Welcome w/approval
Creature Comforts: CCTV, a/c,
micro, refrig, restaurant

Port Zedler Motel
(262) 241-5850
10036 N. Port Washington Rd.
16 rooms - $40-70
Pets: Welcome w/$5 fee
Creature Comforts: CCTV, a/c,
micro refrig

MERCER
Voyageur Inn Tavern
(715) 476-0013
http://www.mercerwi.com/
voyageurinn
4514 Lake of the Falls Rd.
6 cottages - $40-80
Pets: Welcome w/approval
Creature Comforts: CCTV, kit,
fireplace, pool, whirlpool,
swimming, boating

MILTON
Chase on the Hill B&B
(608) 868-6646
http://www.cruising-america.com/
chaseonthehill
11624 N. State Rd. 26
3 rooms - $60-75
Pets: Welcome w/approval
Creature Comforts: Farmhouse,
circa 1846, hardwood floors,
Oriental rugs, grand piano,
woodstove, canopy beds, country
brkfst, hiking, biking, fishing, xc-
skiing, farm animals

MILWAUKEE
Baymont Inns
(800) 4-Budget, (414) 762-2266
http://www.baymontinns.com
7141 S. 13th St.
102 rooms - $40-55
Pets: Welcome w/approval
Creature Comforts: CCTV, a/c

Baymont Inns
(800) 4-Budget, (414) 535-1300
http://www.baymontinns.com
5442 N. Lovers Lane Rd.
142 rooms - $50-75
Pets: Small pets welcome
Creature Comforts: CCTV, a/c,
micro, refrig

Exel Inn, Northeast
(800) 367-3935, (414) 961-1721
http://www.exelinns.com
5485 N. Port Washington Rd.
125 rooms - $45-70
Pets: Welcome w/approval
Creature Comforts: CCTV, a/c,
whirlpool

Exel Inn, South
(800) 367-3935, (414) 764-1776
http://www.exelinns.com
1201 W. College Ave.
110 rooms - $40-70
Pets: Welcome w/approval
Creature Comforts: CCTV, a/c,
whirlpool

Exel Inn, West
(800) 367-3935, (414) 257-0140
http://www.exelinns.com
115 N. Mayfair Rd.
123 rooms - $35-50
Pets: Welcome w/approval
Creature Comforts: CCTV, a/c,
whirlpool, exercise rm.

Holiday Inn, South
(800) HOLIDAY, (414) 764-1500
http://www.holiday-inn.com
6331 S. 13th St.
159 rooms - $60
Pets: Small pets welcome
Creature Comforts: CCTV, a/c,
restaurant, wading pool, sauna,
playground

Hotel Wisconsin
(414) 271-4900
720 N. Old World Third St.
125 rooms - $50-70
Pets: Welcome w/approval
Creature Comforts: CCTV, kit

Knights Inn, South
(800) 843-5644, (414) 764-1776
9420 S. 20th St.
112 rooms - $51-66
Pets: Welcome w/approval
Creature Comforts: CCTV, a/c,
kit

Motel 6, Airport
(800) 4-MOTEL6, (414) 482-4414
http://www.motel6.com
5037 S. Howell Ave.
117 rooms - $30-35
Pets: Under 30 lbs. welcome
Creature Comforts: CCTV, a/c,
pool

Plaza Hotel
(800) 340-9590, (414) 276-2101
1007 N. Cass St.
78 rooms - $45-69
Pets: Welcome w/approval
Creature Comforts: CCTV, kit

Port Zedler Motel
(414) 241-5850
http://www.execpc.com/~zedler
10036 N. Port Washington Rd.
16 rooms - $30-70
Pets: Welcome w/approval
Creature Comforts: CCTV, a/c,
restaurant

Ramada Inn Airport, South
(800) 2-Ramada, (414) 764-5300
http://www.ramada.com
6401 S. 13th St.
190 rooms - $30-88
Pets: Welcome w/approval
Creature Comforts: CCTV,
VCR, a/c, restaurant, pool, sauna,
whirlpool

Select Inn
(800) 641-1000, (414) 786-6015
http://www.selectinn.com
2510 Plaza Cort
101 rooms - $38-67
Pets: Welcome w/approval
Creature Comforts: CCTV, a/c

Sleepy Hollow Motel
(800) 341-8000, (414) 782-8333
12600 W. Bluemound Rd.
31 rooms - $40-110
Pets: Welcome w/approval
Creature Comforts: CCTV, a/c,
pool

Super 8 Motel, Airport
(800) 800-8000, (414) 481-8488
http://www.super8.com
5253 S. Howell Ave.
116 rooms - $40-55
Pets: Welcome w/$5 fee
Creature Comforts: CCTV, a/c,
micro, refrig, whirlpool

Super 8 Motel
(800) 800-8000, (414) 354-5354
http://www.super8.com
8698 N. Servite Dr.
109 rooms - $40-55
Pets: Welcome w/approval
Creature Comforts: CCTV, a/c,
kit

Woodfield Suites
(800) 338-0008, (414) 962-6767
1201 W. College Ave.
109 rooms - $100-160
Pets: Welcome w/deposit
Creature Comforts: CCTV, a/c,
kit, Jacuzzi, pool, whirlpool,
exercise rm.

MINOCQUA
Aqua Aire Motel
(715) 356-3433
806 Rte. 51 N
10 rooms - $25-60
Pets: Welcome w/approval
Creature Comforts: Lakeside,
CCTV, a/c, restaurant, pool,
playground, boating, fishing,
waterskiing, tennis,
snowmobiling

Best Western-Lakeview Lodge
(800) 528-1234, (715) 356-5208
http://www.bestwestern.com
311 Park St.
41 rooms - $50-100
Pets: Welcome w/$6 fee
Creature Comforts: Lakeside,
CCTV, a/c, pool, whirlpool,
playground, boating, fishing,
waterskiing, snowmobiling

Comfort Inn
(800) 228-5150, (715) 358-2588
http://www.comfortinn.com
8729 Rte. 51 N
51 rooms - $55-75
Pets: Welcome w/$25 deposit
Creature Comforts: CCTV, a/c,
refrig, micro, Jacuzzi, pool,
whirlpool

Cross Trails Motor Lodge
(800) 841-5261, (715) 356-5202
8644 Rte. 51N
17 rooms - $50-70
Pets: Welcome
Creature Comforts: CCTV, a/c,
restaurant, xc-skiing,
snowmobiling

Super 8 Motel
(800) 800-8000, (715) 356-9541
http://www.super8.com
Rtes. 51 & 70 W
34 rooms - $75
Pets: Welcome
Creature Comforts: CCTV, a/c

MONTELLO
Sundowner Motel
(608) 297-2121
510 Underwood Ave.
14 rooms - $35-50
Pets: Welcome
Creature Comforts: CCTV, kit

MOSINEE
Lakeview Log Cabin Resort
(715) 868-3000
2391 Rte. DB
3 units - $45-100
Pets: Welcome w/approval
Creature Comforts: CCTV,
swimming, boating

NEENAH
Fox Valley Inn
(920) 734-9872
2000 Holly Rd.
95 rooms - $25-60
Pets: Welcome
Creature Comforts: CCTV, a/c,
kit, restaurant

NEILSVILLE
Fannies Motel/Supper Club
(715) 743-2169
W 3741 Rte. 10
12 rooms - $27-42
Pets: Welcome w/approval
Creature Comforts: CCTV,
restaurant

Heartland Motel
(715) 743-4004
7 S. Hewett St.
8 rooms - $35-50
Pets: Welcome w/approval
Creature Comforts: CCTV

NEW GLARUS
Swiss-Aire Motel
(608) 527-2138
1200 Rte. 69
26 rooms - $35-60
Pets: Welcome w/$2 fee
Creature Comforts: On Sugar
River bike trails, CCTV, a/c, pool

NEW LISBON
Edge O' The Wood Motel
(800) 638-4929, (608) 562-3705
W 7396 Frontage Rd.
13 rooms - $30-45
Pets: Small pets welcome
Creature Comforts: CCTV, a/c,
refrig, pool, playground,
snowmobiling

NEW LONDON
Rainbow Motel
(888) 588-9147, (920) 982-4550
1140 N. Shawano St.
24 rooms - $32-50
Pets: Welcome w/approval
Creature Comforts: CCTV, a/c

NEW RICHMOND
AmericInn Motel
(800) 634-3444, (715) 246-3993
1020 S. Knowles Ave.
45 rooms - $48-110
Pets: Welcome w/approval
Creature Comforts: CCTV, pool,
whirlpool, sauna

OAK CREEK
Red Roof Inn
(800) THE ROOF, (414) 764-3500
http://www.redroof.com
6360 S. 13th St.
108 rooms - $50-70
Pets: Small pets welcome
Creature Comforts: CCTV, a/c

Knights Inn, South
(414) 761-3807
9420 S. 20th St.
115 rooms - $45-50
Pets: Welcome w/$25 deposit
Creature Comforts: CCTV, a/c,
refrig, micro

ONALASKA
Comfort Inn
(800) 228-5150, (608) 781-7500
http://www.comfortinn.com
1223 Crossing Meadows Dr.
70 rooms - $45-100
Pets: Welcome
Creature Comforts: CCTV, a/c,
refrig, micro, pool, whirlpool

Onalaska Inn, IMA
(800) 341-8000, (608) 783-2270
651 2nd Ave. S.
12 rooms - $35-45
Pets: Small pets welcome
Creature Comforts: CCTV, a/c,
kit

Shadow Run Lodge, IMA
(800) 657-4749, (608) 783-0020
710 2nd Ave. N.
20 rooms - $35-45
Pets: Small pets welcome
Creature Comforts: CCTV, a/c,
kit

OSCEOLA
River Valley Inn/Suites
(888)791-2200, (715) 294-4060
1030 Cascade St.
32 rooms - $60-105
Pets: Welcome
Creature Comforts: CCTV, a/c,
pool, whirlpool

OSHKOSH
Baymont Inns
(800) 4-Budget, (920) 233-4190
http://www.baymontinns.com
1950 Omro Rd.
100 rooms - $50-60
Pets: Small pets welcome
Creature Comforts: CCTV, a/c

Howard Johnson
(800) 1-Go-Hojo, (920) 233-1200
http://www.hojo.com
1919 Omro Rd.
100 rooms - $40-80
Pets: Welcome w/approval
Creature Comforts: CCTV, a/c,
restaurant, pool, whirlpool

Park Plaza Hotel
(800) 365-4458, (920) 231-5000
http://www.hilton.com
1 N. Main St.
179 rooms - $95
Pets: Welcome
Creature Comforts: CCTV,
VCR, a/c, refrig, micro, restaurant,
pool, hlth clb access, whirlpool

Super 8 Motel
(800) 800-8000, (920) 426-2885
http://www.super8.com
1581 W. Park Ave.
61 rooms - $50-65
Pets: Welcome
Creature Comforts: CCTV,
VCR, a/c, sauna, whirlpool

OSSEO
Budget Host Ten-Seven Inn
(800) 888-2199, (715) 597-3114
1994 E. 10th St.
19 rooms - $30-50
Pets: Welcome w/approval
Creature Comforts: CCTV, a/c,
xc-skiing snowmobiling

Rodeway Inn, Alan House Motel
(800) 228-2000, (715) 597-3175
N/W Rtes. 10 & I-94
50 rooms - $40-55
Pets: Welcome w/approval
Creature Comforts: CCTV, a/c,
restaurant

PARK FALLS
Northway Motor Lodge
(800) 844-7144, (715) 762-2406
Rte. 13 South
31 rooms - $50-55
Pets: Small pets welcome
Creature Comforts: CCTV, a/c,
restaurant, hlth clb access, sauna,
whirlpool, racquetball,
snowmobiling

Super 8 Motel
(800) 800-8000, (715) 762-3383
http://www.super8.com
1212 Rte. 13S
30 rooms - $50-60
Pets: Welcome
Creature Comforts: CCTV, a/c,
whirlpool, snowmobiling

PEMBINE
Grand Motel
(715) 324-5417
Rtes 8 & 141
20 rooms - $35-50
Pets: Welcome
Creature Comforts: CCTV, a/c,
refrig, micro, playground
snowmobiling

PHILLIPS
Skyline Motel
(800) 596-0407, (715) 339-3061
804 N. Lake Ave.
28 rooms - $40-60
Pets: Welcome w/approval
Creature Comforts: CCTV, a/c,
restaurant, whirlpool, xc-skiing,
snowmobiling

Timber Inn
(800) 844-4521, (715) 339-3071
606 N. Lake Ave.
22 rooms - $50-55
Pets: Small pets welcome
Creature Comforts: Lakeside,
CCTV, a/c, kit, restaurant,
snowmobiling

PLATTEVILLE
Best Western Governor Dodge
(800) 528-1234, (608) 348-8579
http://www.bestwestern.com
W Rte. 151
74 rooms - $70-75
Pets: Welcome
Creature Comforts: CCTV,
VCR, a/c, refrig, Jacuzzi,
restaurant, pool, sauna, whirlpool

Mound View Inn
(608) 348-9518
1755 E. Rte. 151
32 rooms - $40-60
Pets: Welcome w/$20 deposit
Creature Comforts: CCTV, a/c,
Jacuzzi, whirlpool

Super 8 Motel
(800) 800-8000, (608) 348-8800
http://www.super8.com
100 Rte. 80-81S
46 rooms - $55-60
Pets: Welcome w/approval
Creature Comforts: CCTV, a/c,
kit, Jacuzzi, restaurant, sauna,
whirlpool

PLOVER
Days Inn
(800) DAYS INN, (715) 341-7300
http://www.daysinn.com
5253 Harding Ave.
101 rooms - $40-95
Pets: Welcome
Creature Comforts: CCTV,
VCR, a/c, refrig, cont. brkfst

PLYMOUTH
52 Stafford
(800) 421-4667, (920) 893-0552
http://www.classicinns.com
52 Stafford St.
19 rooms - $80-120
Pets: Welcome
Creature Comforts: 1892
Victorian, Irish guest house w/
Victorian inspired antique-filled
rms, four poster beds, well
appointed, CCTV, Jacuzzi,
intimate restaurant, cozy pub

PORT WASHINGTON
Best Western Harborside
(800) 528-1234, (414) 284-9461
http://www.bestwestern.com
135 E. Grand Ave.
96 rooms - $60-105
Pets: Welcome w/approval
Creature Comforts: Lakeside,
CCTV, a/c, Jacuzzi, restaurant,
pool, sauna, whirlpool, fishing

Driftwood Motel
(414) 284-4113
3415 N. Green Bay Rd.
10 rooms - $32-54
Pets: Welcome w/approval
Creature Comforts: CCTV, a/c,
kit

PORTAGE
Porterhouse Motel
(608) 742-2186
1721 New Pinery Rd.
35 rooms - $26-69
Pets: Small pets welcome
Creature Comforts: CCTV, a/c,
restaurant

Ridge Motor Inn
(608) 742-5306
2900 New Pinery Rd.
114 rooms - $45-90
Pets: Small pets welcome
Creature Comforts: CCTV, a/c,
kit, Jacuzzi, restaurant, pool, hlth
clb access, sauna, whirlpool,
xc-skiing, snowmobiling

POYNETTE
Bayview Lodge Resort
(800) 369-6333, (608) 635-4089
N3135 Rte. V
8 units - $60
Pets: Welcome w/approval
Creature Comforts: CCTV,
restaurant, boating

Happy Hollow Resort
(608) 635-4032
N3769 Tipperary Rd.
10 cottages - $55-75
Pets: Welcome w/approval
Creature Comforts: CCTV, kit,
swimming, boating

PRAIRIE DU CHIEN
Best Western Suites
(800) 528-1234, (608) 326-4777
http://www.bestwestern.com
Rtes. 18 & 35 S
42 rooms - $75-115
Pets: Welcome w/$15 fee
Creature Comforts: CCTV, a/c,
Jacuzzi, pool, hlth clb access,
sauna, whirlpool

Bridgeport Inn
(800) 234-6082, (608) 326-6082
Highways 18 & 35 South
50 rooms - $70-100
Pets: Welcome w/approval
Creature Comforts: CCTV, a/c,
Jacuzzi, pool, hlth clb access,
whirlpool

Brisbois Motor Inn
(800) 356-5850, (608) 326-8404
533 N. Marquette Rd.
46 rooms - $45-90
Pets: Welcome w/$7 fee
Creature Comforts: CCTV, a/c,
refrig, micro, pool

Delta Motel
(608) 326-4951
Rtes. 18 & 35 South
16 rooms - $30-60
Pets: Welcome w/approval
Creature Comforts: CCTV, a/c,
refrig

Holiday Motel
(800) 962-3883, (608) 326-2448
1010 S. Marquette Rd.
18 rooms - $30-60
Pets: Small pets welcome
Creature Comforts: CCTV, a/c,
refrig, Jacuzzi

Prairie Motel
(608) 326-6461
1616 N. Marquette Rd.
32 rooms - $30-60
Pets: Welcome
Creature Comforts: CCTV, a/c,
refrig, micro, pool, playground

Super 8 Motel
(800) 800-8000, (608) 326-8777
http://www.super8.com
Rtes. 18 & 35 South
30 rooms - $60-70
Pets: Small pets w/$15 fee
Creature Comforts: CCTV, a/c,
refrig, micro

PRENTICE
Countryside Motel
(715) 428-2333
Granberg Rd.
23 rooms - $40-45
Pets: Welcome w/$10 fee
Creature Comforts: CCTV,
VCR, a/c, snowmobiling

RACINE
Holiday Inn-Riverside
(800) HOLIDAY, (262) 637-9311
http://www.holiday-inn.com
3700 Northwestern Avenue
110 rooms - $55-90
Pets: Small pets welcome
Creature Comforts: CCTV, a/c,
refrig, micro, restaurant, pool, hlth
clb access

Knights Inn
(800) 843-5644, (262) 886-6667
1149 Oakes Rd.
107 rooms - $39-63
Pets: Welcome
Creature Comforts: CCTV, a/c,
kit

Marriott Hotel
(800) 228-9290, (262) 886-6100
http://www.marriott.com
7111 Washington Ave.
224 rooms - $125
Pets: Small pets welcome
Creature Comforts: CCTV, a/c,
refrig, restaurant, pool, hlth clb
access, sauna, whirlpool

Super 8 Motel
(800) 800-8000, (262) 326-8777
http://www.super8.com
7141 Kinzie Ave.
61 rooms - $55-80
Pets: Welcome
Creature Comforts: CCTV, a/c

REEDSBURG
Copper Springs Motel
(800) 341-8000, (608) 524-4312
Rtes. 23 & 33
14 rooms - $35-50
Pets: Welcome
Creature Comforts: CCTV, a/c,
refrig, micro

Motel Reedsburg
(800) 52-MOTEL, (608) 524-2306
1133 E. Main St.
31 rooms - $40-60
Pets: Welcome
Creature Comforts: CCTV, a/c,
refrig, micro

RHINELANDER
Best Western-Claridge Motor
(800) 528-1234, (715) 362-7100
http://www.bestwestern.com
70 N. Stevens St.
81 rooms - $65-80
Pets: Small pets welcome
Creature Comforts: CCTV, a/c,
kit, restaurant, pool, hlth clb
access, whirlpool

Buck Haven Bar/Resort
(715) 277-2341
4743 Wilderness Ln.
4 cottages - $60-90
Pets: Welcome w/approval
Creature Comforts: CCTV, kit,
swimming, boating
838

Feases' Shady Rest Lodge
(800) 477-3229, (715) 282-5231
Shady Rest Rd.
19 rooms - $60-90
Pets: Welcome w/approval
Creature Comforts: Lakeside,
cottages, CCTV, a/c, fireplace, kit,
restaurant, pool, playground,
fishing, boating, waterskiing,
tennis

Holiday Acres Resort
(800) 261-1500, (715) 369-1500
4060 S. Shore Dr.
56 rooms - $70-90
Pets: Welcome w/$6 fee
Creature Comforts: Lakeside,
cottages, CCTV, VCR, a/c,
fireplace, kit, Jacuzzi, restaurant,
pool, sauna, beach, tennis, boat
dock, playground, fishing, xc-
skiing, snowmobiling, sailboats,
pontoon boats, bicycles, horseback
riding

Kafka's Resort
(800) 426-6674, (715) 369-2929
4281 W. Lake George Rd.
10 rooms - $360-450 weekly
Pets: Welcome
Creature Comforts: Lakeside,
cottages, CCTV, no phones, refrig,
beach, dock, boating, fishing, xc-
skiing

Super 8 Motel
(800) 800-8000, (715) 369-5880
http://www.super8.com
667 W. Kemp St.
43 rooms - $45-60
Pets: Welcome
Creature Comforts: CCTV, a/c,
cross-country and alpine skiing,
snowmobiling

RICE LAKE
Currier's Lakeview Resort
(800) 433-5253, (715) 234-7474
2010 E. Sawyer St.
19 rooms - $40-80
Pets: Welcome
Creature Comforts: Lakeside,
CCTV, VCR, a/c, kit, pool,
playground, rental boats, fishing,
boating, snowmobiling

Pullman Motel
(715) 234-7919
903 Hammond
18 rooms - $30-52
Pets: Small pets welcome
Creature Comforts: CCTV, a/c,
kit

Super 8 Motel
(800) 800-8000, (715) 234-6956
http://www.super8.com
2401 S. Main St.
47 rooms - $60-70
Pets: Small pets welcome
Creature Comforts: CCTV,
VCR, a/c

RICHLAND CENTER
Starlite Motel
(608) 647-6158
Rtes. 2 & 14 East
19 rooms - $60-70
Pets: Welcome w/$5 fee
Creature Comforts: CCTV, a/c,
pool

Super 8 Motel
(800) 800-8000, (608) 647-8988
http://www.super8.com
100 Foundry Dr.
45 rooms - $55-60
Pets: Small pets w/$50 deposit
Creature Comforts: CCTV,
VCR, a/c, refrig, micro, Jacuzzi,
pool, hlth clb access

RIVER FALLS
Super 8 Motel
(800) 800-8000, (715) 425-8388
http://www.super8.com
1207 St. Croix
48 rooms - $60-70
Pets: Welcome
Creature Comforts: CCTV,
VCR, a/c, refrig, micro, Jacuzzi,
pool, whirlpool

ST. CROIX FALLS
Dalles House Motel
(800) 341-8000, (715) 483-3206
Rtes. 8 & 35 South
50 rooms - $46-85
Pets: Welcome w/approval
Creature Comforts: CCTV, a/c,
Jacuzzi, restaurant, pool,
whirlpool, sauna

ST. GERMAIN
Elbert Resort/Condos
(800) 545-8293, (715) 479-1034
1056 Elbert Rd.
14 cottages - $80-300
Pets: Welcome w/approval
Creature Comforts: CCTV, kit,
fireplace, pool, whirlpool

St. Germain B&B
(715) 479-8007
170 Rte. 70
4 rooms - $50-80
Pets: Welcome
Creature Comforts: CCTV, pool

St. Germain Motel
(715) 542-3535
170 Rte. 70
6 rooms - $36-76
Pets: Welcome
Creature Comforts: CCTV,
boating

SAYNER
Froelich's Sayner Lodge
(800) 553-9695, (715) 542-3261
3221 Plum Lake Dr.
10 cottages - $60-100
Pets: Welcome w/approval
Creature Comforts: Lakeside,
cottages, CCTV, a/c, fireplace,
restaurant, pool, playground,
boating, fishing, waterskiing,
tennis

Woodlands Resort-Plum Lake
(715) 542-2474
8553 Camp Highland Rd.
7 cottages - $75-125
Pets: Welcome w/approval
Creature Comforts: CCTV, kit,
fireplace, pool, boating

SHAWANO
Cecil Fireside Inn
(800) 325-5289, (715) 745-6444
400 Lake St.
29 rooms - $30-119
Pets: Welcome
Creature Comforts: CCTV, pool,
whirlpool, sauna

Super 8 Motel
(800) 800-8000, (715) 526-6688
http://www.super8.com
211 Waukechon St.
$40-75
Pets: Welcome w/approval
Creature Comforts: CCTV, a/c,
Jacuzzi, sauna, whirlpool,
snowmobiling

SHEBOYGAN
Baymont Inn
(800) 4-Budget, (920) 457-2321
http://www.baymontinns.com
2932 Kohler Memorial Dr.
97 rooms - $50-60
Pets: Small pets welcome
Creature Comforts: CCTV,

Comfort Inn
(800) 228-5150, (920) 457-7724
http://www.comfortinn.com
4332 N. 40th St.
59 rooms - $55-80
Pets: Welcome w/$25 deposit
Creature Comforts: CCTV,
VCR, a/c, refrig, micro, Jacuzzi,
pool, whirlpool

Parkway Motel
(800) 341-8000, (920) 458-8338
3900 Motel Rd.
32 rooms - $42-64
Pets: Welcome w/approval
Creature Comforts: CCTV,
VCR, a/c, refrig, micro

Select Inn
(800) 641-1000, (920) 458-4641
http://www.selectinn.com
930 N. 8th St.
53 rooms - $32-57
Pets: Small pets w/$25 deposit
Creature Comforts: CCTV, a/c

Super 8
(800) 800-8000, (920) 458-8080
http://www.super8.com
3402 Wilgus Rd.
60 rooms - $40-63
Pets: Welcome w/permission
Creature Comforts: CCTV, a/c,
pool

SHELL LAKE
Aqua Vista Resort
(800) 889-2256, (715) 468-2256
412 E. Rte. B
4 rooms - $30-98
Pets: Welcome
Creature Comforts: CCTV, a/c,
kit, swimming

SIREN
Pine Wood Motel
(715) 349-5225
23862 State Rd. 35
14 rooms - $35-45
Pets: Small pets w/approval
Creature Comforts: CCTV, a/c,
refrig

SPARTA
Best Nights Inn
(608) 269-3066
http://www.bestnightsinn.com
303 W. Wisconsin St.
28 rooms - $28-90
Pets: Small pets welcome
Creature Comforts: CCTV, a/c,
refrig, micro

Country Inn by Carlson
(800) 456-4000, (608) 269-3110
737 Avon Rd.
61 rooms - $60-70
Pets: Small pets w/$5 fee
Creature Comforts: CCTV,
VCR, a/c, kit, Jacuzzi, whirlpool

Downtown Motel
(608) 269-3138
509 S. Water St.
17 rooms - $40-45
Pets: Welcome
Creature Comforts: CCTV

Heritage Motel
(800) 658-9484, (608) 269-6991
704 W. Wisconsin Ave.
22 rooms - $35-55
Pets: Welcome
Creature Comforts: CCTV, a/c,
pool, whirlpool

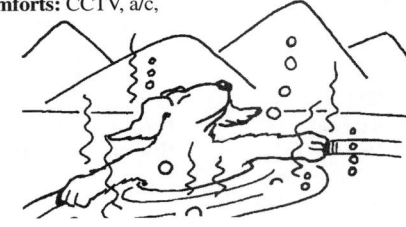

Justin Trails B&B
(800) 488-4521, (608) 269-4522
http://www.justintrails.com
7452 Kathryn Ave.
4 rooms – 80-300$70-170
Pets: Welcome w/$10 fee
Creature Comforts: Highly
rated, "top ten country escapes"
for families, 1920's farmhouse and
Scandinavian style log cabins,
beautiful hand-crafted furnishings,
stone fireplace, CCTV, VCR, kit,
Jacuzzi, full brkfst, xc-skiing

SPOONER
American Heritage Inn
(715) 635-9770
101 Maple St.
45 rooms - $60-75
Pets: Small pets welcome
Creature Comforts: CCTV, a/c,
kit, Jacuzzi, pool, sauna, whirlpool

Country House Motel
(715) 635-8721
http://www.spoonerwi.com/
motel.htm
717 S. River St.
22 rooms - $35-70
Pets: Small pets w/$3 fee
Creature Comforts: CCTV, a/c,
restaurant

Green Acres Motel
(800) 373-5293, (715) 635-2177
N4809 Rte. 63
21 rooms - $45-90
Pets: Welcome w/approval
Creature Comforts: CCTV, a/c,
playground snowmobiling

STEVENS POINT
Baymont Inn
(800) 4-Budget, (715) 344-1900
http://www.baymontinns.com
4917 Main St.
78 rooms - $45-60
Pets: Small pets welcome
Creature Comforts: CCTV, a/c,
refrig, micro

Holiday Inn
(800) HOLIDAY, (715) 341-1340
http://www.holiday-inn.com
1501 N. Point Dr.
275 rooms - $70-90
Pets: Welcome w/approval
Creature Comforts: CCTV, a/c,
restaurant, pool, whirlpool,
children's play park, golf, tennis

Point Motel
(800) 344-3093, (715) 344-8312
209 Division St.
44 rooms - $40-45
Pets: Small pets w/$5 fee
Creature Comforts: CCTV, a/c,
refrig, restaurant, playground

Traveler Motel
(800) 341-8000, (715) 344-6455
3350 Church St.
17 rooms - $35-50
Pets: Small pets welcome
Creature Comforts: CCTV, a/c,
refrig

SPRING GREEN
Spring Green Motel
(888) 647-4410, (608) 588-2141
Rte. 14
4 rooms - $28-70
Pets: Welcome
Creature Comforts: CCTV, kit

STEVENS POINT
Baymont Inn
(800) 4-Budget, (715) 344-1900
http://www.baymontinns.com
170 Rte. 70
79 rooms - $42-50
Pets: Welcome
Creature Comforts: CCTV, a/c,
pool, whirlpool

Holiday Inn
(800) HOLIDAY, (715) 341-1340
http://www.holiday-inn.com
1501 N. Point Dr.
295 rooms - $79-109
Pets: Welcome
Creature Comforts: CCTV, a/c,
restaurant, pool, exercise rm,
whirlpool, sauna

Point Motel
(800) 344-3093, (715) 344-8312
209 Division St.
44 rooms - $35-50
Pets: Welcome
Creature Comforts: CCTV, a/c

STURGEON BAY
Carl's Old Bridge Motel
(920) 743-1245
114 N. Madison Ave.
12 rooms - $30-70
Pets: Welcome w/approval
Creature Comforts: CCTV, a/c

Cherryland Motel/Cottages
(920) 743-3289
1309 Green Bay Rd.
21 rooms - $45-95
Pets: Welcome w/approval
Creature Comforts: CCTV,
VCR, kit, swimming, tennis, golf

Comfort Inn
(800) 228-5150, (920) 743-7846
http://www.comfortinn.com
923 Gren Bay Rd.
52 rooms - $45-125
Pets: Small pets only
Creature Comforts: CCTV, a/c,
refrig, micro, Jacuzzi, whirlpool

Holiday Motel
(920) 743-5571
29 N. 2nd Ave.
18 rooms - $25-75
Pets: Welcome w/approval
Creature Comforts: CCTV, a/c

Nightengale Motel
(920) 743-7633
1547 Egg Harbor Rd.
34 rooms - $25-65
Pets: Welcome w/approval
Creature Comforts: CCTV, a/c

Pembrooke Inn
(920) 746-9776
412 Iowas St.
6 rooms - $80-120
Pets: Welcome
Creature Comforts: Restored
1886 inn w/English country house
ambiance, beautifully decorated,
canopy beds, fireplaces, private
balconies, Jacuzzis, cont. brkfst

Snug Harbor Inn
(800) 231-5767, (920) 743-2337
1627 Memorial Dr.
15 rooms - $50-150
Pets: Welcome w/approval
Creature Comforts: Lakeside,
cottages, CCTV, a/c, fireplace, kit,
Jacuzzi, playground, boating,
fishing, waterskiing, xc-skiing

SUN PRAIRIE
McGovern's Motel Suites
(608) 837-7321
820 W. Main St.
54 rooms - $45-75
Pets: Small pets w/$5 fee
Creature Comforts: CCTV, a/c,
refrig, micro

SUPERIOR
Best Western Bay Walk Inn
(800) 528-1234, (715) 392-7600
http://www.bestwestern.com
1405 Susquehanna
50 rooms - $50-120
Pets: Small pets welcome
Creature Comforts: CCTV,
VCR, a/c, refrig, micro, Jacuzzi,
pool, sauna, whirlpool

Driftwood Inn
(715) 398-6661
2200 E. 2nd St.
12 rooms - $35-65
Pets: Small pets w/$4 fee
Creature Comforts: CCTV, a/c,
refrig, restaurant, snowmobiling

Stockade Motel
(715) 398-3585
1610 E. 2nd St.
17 rooms - $35-55
Pets: Small pets welcome
Creature Comforts: CCTV, a/c,
snowmobiling

Superior Inn
(715) 394-7706
525 Hammond Ave.
69 rooms - $60-90
Pets: Welcome
Creature Comforts: CCTV, a/c,
refrig, micro, Jacuzzi, pool, sauna,
whirlpool

THREE LAKES
Maple Shores Resort
(715) 546-3111
1660 Superior St.
7 cottages - $45-115
Pets: Welcome w/approval
Creature Comforts: CCTV, kit,
fireplace, pool, swimming,
boating

Oneida Village Inn
(800) 374-7443, (546-3373)
1785 Superior St.
47 rooms - $30-80
Pets: Welcome w/approval
Creature Comforts: CCTV, a/c,
kit, restaurant

TOMAH
Budget Host Daybreak Inn
(800) 999-7088, (608) 372-5946
215 E. Clifton St.
32 rooms - $40-70
Pets: Small pets w/$5 fee
Creature Comforts: CCTV, a/c,
refrig, micro

Comfort Inn
(800) 228-5150, (608) 372-6600
http://www.comfortinn.com
305 Wittig Rd.
52 rooms - $40-80
Pets: Welcome
Creature Comforts: CCTV,
VCR, a/c, Jacuzzi, restaurant, pool

Econo Lodge
(800) 55-ECONO, (608) 372-9100
http://www.econolodge.com
2005 N. Superior Ave.
77 rooms - $50-60
Pets: Welcome
Creature Comforts: CCTV,
VCR, a/c, refrig, micro, Jacuzzi,
pool, whirlpool

Howard Johnson
(800) I-Go-Hojo, (608) 372-4500
http://www.hojo.com
I-90 Rte. 131
24 rooms - $40-60
Pets: Welcome w/$3 fee
Creature Comforts: CCTV, a/c,
refrig, micro

Lark Inn
(800) 447-5275, (608) 372-5981
http://www.larkinn.com
229 N. Superior Ave.
25 rooms - $55-80
Pets: Welcome w/$5 fee
Creature Comforts: 1900's
Dutch Colonial inn and log cabins,
attractive country style inn rms w/
quilts, decorative wall hangings,
well appointed, CCTV, VCR, a/c,
refrig, micro, restaurant

Park Motel
(608) 372-4655
1515 Kilbourne Ave.
14 rooms - $30-50
Pets: Small pets welcome
Creature Comforts: CCTV, a/c,
no phones

Super 8 Motel
(800) 800-8000, (608) 372-3901
http://www.super8.com
I-94 Rte. 21
64 rooms - $55-65
Pets: Welcome
Creature Comforts: CCTV,
VCR, a/c, refrig, Jacuzzi

TOMAHAWK
Duck Point Resort
(715) 453-3489
W5930 Duck Point Rd.
22 cottages - $70-150
Pets: Welcome w/approval
Creature Comforts: Fireplace,
kit, swimming, boating

Pine Pointe Resort
(715) 453-3392
West 4249 Sandy Lane
4 cottages - $70
Pets: Welcome w/approval
Creature Comforts: Kit,
swimming, boating

Tomahawk Lodge/Resort
(715) 453-3452
N10985 County
6 cottages - $60-80
Pets: Welcome w/approval
Creature Comforts: Kit,
restaurant, swimming, boating

TREMPEALEAU
Riverview Motel
(608) 534-7784
First and Main Sts
8 rooms - $30-65
Pets: Welcome
Creature Comforts: CCTV,
whirlpool, boating

TWO RIVERS
Cool City Motel
(800) 729-1520, (920) 793-2244
3009 Lincoln Ave.
21 rooms - $25-45
Pets: Welcome w/approval
Creature Comforts: CCTV, a/c,
kit, playground

Village Inn Motel
(800) 551-4795, (920) 794-8818
3310 Memorial Dr.
28 rooms - $55-75
Pets: Small pets w/$5 fee
Creature Comforts: CCTV, a/c,
refrig, micro, restaurant, pool,
whirlpool, miniature golf

VIROQUA
Doucette's Hickory Hill Motel
(608) 637-3104
Rtes. 14, 16, 27 & 82
25 rooms - $30-65
Pets: Welcome
Creature Comforts: CCTV, a/c, kit, pool

WASHBURN
Redwood Motel Chalets
(715) 373-5512
26 W. Bayfield St.
18 rooms - $45-65
Pets: Welcome w/$3 fee
Creature Comforts: CCTV, a/c, kit, charter fishing, snowmobiling

Super 8 Motel
(800) 800-8000, (715) 373-5671
http://www.super8.com
Harborview Dr.
35 rooms - $50-75
Pets: Welcome w/$25 deposit
Creature Comforts: CCTV, a/c, sauna, whirlpool

WASHINGTON ISLAND
Dor-Cros Chalet Motel
(920) 847-2126
P.O. Box 249
7 rooms - $45-69
Pets: Welcome w/approval
Creature Comforts: Cottages, CCTV, a/c, kit, playground

Findlay's Holiday Inn
(920) 847-2526
Detroit Harbor
28 rooms - $60-100
Pets: Welcome w/approval
Creature Comforts: Lakeside, CCTV, a/c, fireplace, kit

WATERTOWN
Candle-Glo Motel
(920) 261-2281
1200 N. Fourth St.
12 rooms - $25-45
Pets: Welcome w/approval
Creature Comforts: CCTV, a/c

Flags Inn Motel
(920) 261-9400
N627 Rte. 26
19 rooms - $30-50
Pets: Welcome w/approval
Creature Comforts: CCTV, a/c, restaurant, xc-skiing, snowmobiling

Super 8 Motel
(800) 800-8000, (920) 261-1188
http://www.super8.com
1730 S. Church St.
45 rooms - $55-65
Pets: Welcome w/$5 fee, $50 dep
Creature Comforts: CCTV, VCR, a/c, refrig, micro, Jacuzzi, pool, whirlpool

WAUPACA
Best Western Grand Seasons
(800) 528-1234, (715) 258-9212
http://www.bestwestern.com
110 Grand Seasons Dr.
90 rooms - $50-70
Pets: Welcome w/approval
Creature Comforts: CCTV, a/c, fireplace, Jacuzzi, restaurant, pool, hlth clb access, sauna, whirlpool, boating, fishing, waterskiing, golf, xc-skiing, snowmobiling

Park Motel
(715) 258-3225
E. 3621 Rtes. 10 & 49
30 rooms - $32-90
Pets: Welcome w/approval
Creature Comforts: CCTV, a/c, kit

WAUSAU
Best Western Midway Hotel
(800) 528-1234, (715) 842-1616
http://www.bestwestern.com
2901 Martin Ave.
98 rooms - $90-100
Pets: Small pets w/$20 fee
Creature Comforts: CCTV, a/c, refrig, micro, restaurant, pool, sauna, whirlpool, playground, volleyball, basketball

Baymont Inn
(800) 4-Budget, (715) 842-0421
http://www.baymontinns.com
1910 Stewart Ave.
96 rooms - $50-60
Pets: Small pets welcome
Creature Comforts: CCTV, a/c, refrig, micro, whirlpool

Exel Inn of Wausau
(800) 367-3935, (715) 842-0641
http://www.exelinns.com
116 S. 17th Ave.
123 rooms - $45-55
Pets: Small pets welcome
Creature Comforts: CCTV, a/c, refrig, micro, Jacuzzi

Marlene Motel
(715) 845-6248
2010 Stewart Ave.
14 rooms - $35-40
Pets: Welcome
Creature Comforts: CCTV, a/c, refrig

Rib Mountain Inn
(715) 848-2802
http://www.ribmtn.com
2900 Rib Mountain Way
24 rooms - $55-125
Pets: Welcome w/$5 fee, $50 dep.
Creature Comforts: at base of ski hill, CCTV, VCR, a/c, kit, whirlpool, sauna

Wausau Inn Conference Center
(800) 928-7281, (715) 842-0711
2001 N. Mountain Rd.
120 rooms - $65-75
Pets: Welcome
Creature Comforts: CCTV, VCR, a/c, restaurant, pool, hlth clb access, whirlpool putting green

WAUSAUKEE
Bear Point Motel
(715) 856-5921
Rte. 180
6 rooms - $25-40
Pets: Welcome w/approval
Creature Comforts: Boating, ski mobiling

WEST BEND
Super 8 Motel
(800) 800-8000, (414) 335-6788
http://www.super8.com
2433 W. Washington St.
49 rooms - $55-65
Pets: Welcome w/approval
Creature Comforts: CCTV, a/c, Jacuzzi, pool, whirlpool

WESTBY
Central Express Inn
(608) 634-2235
Rtes. 27 & 14
21 rooms - $30-60
Pets: Welcome w/approval
Creature Comforts: CCTV, kit, restaurant, whirlpool

Old Towne Motel
(800) 605-0276, (608) 634-2111
Rtes. 27 & 14
21 rooms - $35-50
Pets: Welcome w/approval
Creature Comforts: CCTV, kit, restaurant

WHITE LAKE
Jesse's Wolf River Lodge
(715) 882-2182
http://www.innsite.com/inns/
A002158.html
North 2119 Taylor Rd.
10 rms/ctges - $80-160
Pets: Welcome w/approval
Creature Comforts: Featured as one of the "15 Best Wilderness Getaways", historic lodge and and riverside cottages filled w/ eclectic antiques and memorabilia, a/c, kit, river stone fireplaces, restaurant, whirlpool, playground, fishing, boating, xc-skiing

WHITEWATER
White Horse Inn
(414) 473-4777
W. 4890 Tri County Line Rd.
34 rooms - $42-44
Pets: Welcome
Creature Comforts: CCTV, restaurant

WINDSOR
Super 8 Motel
(800) 800-8000, (608) 846-3971
http://www.super8.com
4506 Lake Circle
54 rooms - $45-50
Pets: Welcome w/$20 deposit
Creature Comforts: CCTV, a/c

WISCONSIN DELLS
Baker's Sunset Bay Resort
(800) 435-6515, (608) 254-8406
http://www.dells.com/
sunsetbay.html
921 Canyon Rd.
75 rooms - $45-185
Pets: Welcome w/approval
Creature Comforts: CCTV, kit, fireplace, pool, whirlpool, exercise rm, swimming, boating

Delton Oaks Resort
(800) 374-6257, (608) 253-4092
730 E. Hiawatha Dr.
31 rooms - $40-210
Pets: Welcome w/approval
Creature Comforts: CCTV, kit, fireplace, whirlpool, swimming

International Motel
(608) 254-2431
1311 E. Broadway St.
45 rooms - $30-130
Pets: Welcome w/approval
Creature Comforts: CCTV, a/c, kit, restaurant, pool, playground

Sands Motel
(608) 254-7447
124 Wisc. Dells Pkwy S.
18 rooms - $30-60
Pets: Welcome w/approval
Creature Comforts: CCTV, kit, swimming

Super 8 Motel
(800) 800-8000, (608) 254-6464
http://www.super8.com
800 Rte. H
122 rooms - $50-85
Pets: Welcome
Creature Comforts: CCTV, VCR, a/c, pool, sauna, whirlpool

Surfside Motel
(608) 254-7594
231 Wisconsin Dells Pkwy.
18 rooms - $40-95
Pets: Welcome w/approval
Creature Comforts: CCTV, whirlpool, swimming

WISCONSIN RAPIDS
Best Western - Rapids Motor
(800) 528-1234, (715) 423-3211
http://www.bestwestern.com
911 Huntington St
43 rooms - $55-90
Pets: Welcome w/manager's approval
Creature Comforts: CCTV, a/c, refrig, whirlpool

Camelot Motel
(715) 325-5111
9210 Rte. 13 S
14 rooms - $40-45
Pets: Welcome
Creature Comforts: CCTV, VCR, a/c, refrig, pool

Hotel Mead
(800) 843-6323, (715) 422-7001
451 E. Grand Ave.
154 rooms - $65-100
Pets: Small pets w/$15 fee
Creature Comforts: CCTV, a/c, restaurant, pool, hlth clb access, sauna, whirlpool

Super 8 Motel
(800) 800-8000, (715) 423-8080
http://www.super8.com
3410 - 8th St. South
48 rooms - $45-60
Pets: Small pets w/$15 fee
Creature Comforts: CCTV, a/c

Wyoming

AFTON
The Corral Motel
(307) 886-5424
161 Washington St.
15 rooms - $40-50
Pets: Welcome w/$2 fee
Creature Comforts: CCTV,
refrig, kit

Best Western Hi-Country Inn
(800) 528-1234, (307) 886-3856
http://www.bestwestern.com
689 S. Washington St.
30 rooms - $55-85
Pets: Small pets welcome
Creature Comforts: CCTV, pool,
whirlpool

Lazy B Motel
(307) 885-3187
219 Washington
26 rooms - $40-60
Pets: Welcome
Creature Comforts: CCTV, kit

Mountain Inn Motel
(307) 886-3156
83542 Route 89
20 rooms - $45-69
Pets: Welcome w/$3 fee
Creature Comforts: CCTV,
sauna, whirlpool

ALPINE
Alpen Haus
(800) 343-6755, (307) 654-7545
http://www.alpenhaus.com
Routes. 89 & 26
45 rooms - $55-125
Pets: Very small pets welcome
Creature Comforts: CCTV,
VCR, refrig, restaurant, cont.
brkfst, whirlpool

Alpine Inn
(307) 654-7644
Route 89
18 rooms - $45-55
Pets: Welcome
Creature Comforts: CCTV, a/c

Best Western Flying Saddle
(800) 528-1234, (307) 654-7561
http://www.bestwestern.com
Rtes. 89 & 26
26 rooms - $80-165
Pets: Small pets welcome
Creature Comforts: Ralph
Lauren decor, cottages, riverside
setting, spectacular scenery,
CCTV, refrig, micro, Jacuzzi,
restaurant, pool, whirlpool, tennis

Lakeside Motel
(307) 654-7507
Route 89
11 rooms - $35-45
Pets: Welcome
Creature Comforts: CCTV, a/c,
kit, **restaurant**

Three Rivers Motel
(307) 654-7551
Route 89
22 rooms - $45-56
Pets: Welcome
Creature Comforts: CCTV, a/c,
kit

ATLANTIC CITY
Atlantic City Mercantile
(307) 332-5143
100 Main St.
4 cabins - $50-60
Pets: Small pets in cabins
Creature Comforts: CCTV, kit,
restaurant

Miner's Delight B&B
(888) 292-0248, (307) 332-0248
http://www.holidayjunction.com/
usa/wy/cwy0051.html
290 Atlantic City Rd.
3 rooms/4 cabins - $60-75
Pets: Welcome
Creature Comforts: Historic
hotel in remote ghost town, rms in
hotel and rustic cabins, full brkfst

BAGGS
Drifters Inn
(307) 383-2015
Route 789
51 rooms - $35-40
Pets: Welcome, if well behaved
Creature Comforts: CCTV, a/c,
refrig, micro, restaurant

BASIN
Lilac Motel
(307) 568-3355
710 West C St.
9 rooms - $35-40
Pets: Welcome, loves animals
Creature Comforts: Cute, old-
fashioned motel, CCTV, a/c,
refrig, micro

BONDURANT
Hoback Village Motel
(307) 654-7551
14272 Routes 189-191
7 rooms - $45-60
Pets: Welcome
Creature Comforts: CCTV, a/c,
restaurant

Smiling S
(307) 733-3457
Box 171
7 rooms - $35-45
Pets: Welcome
Creature Comforts: CCTV

BUFFALO
Arrowhead Motel
(307) 684-9453
749 Fort St.
17 rooms - $25-65
Pets: Welcome w/$5 fee
Creature Comforts: CCTV, a/c,
refrig, micro, kit

Blue Gables Motel
(888) 684-0753, (307) 684-2574
662 N. Main St.
17 rooms - $50-65
Pets: Welcome
Creature Comforts: CCTV, a/c,
pool

Buffalo Motel
(307) 684-5230
370 N. Main St.
19 rooms - $25-45
Pets: Welcome
Creature Comforts: CCTV, a/c

Canyon Motel
(800) 231-0742, (307) 684-2957
997 Fort St.
18 rooms - $40-55
Pets: Welcome w/$3 fee
Creature Comforts: CCTV, a/c,
kit

Comfort Inn
(800) 228-5150, (307) 684-9564
http://www.comfortinn.com
65 Route 16 E.
41 rooms - $40-118
Pets: Welcome in second flr rms.
Creature Comforts: CCTV, a/c,
cont. brkfst, kit, whirlpool

Crossroads Inn
(307) 684-2256
65 North Bypass Rd.
60 rooms - $45-55
Pets: Welcome w/$10 fee
Creature Comforts: CCTV, a/c,
refrig, restaurant, pool

Econo Lodge
(800)55-ECONO, (307) 684-2219
http://www.econolodge.com
333 Hart St.
44 rooms - $35-70
Pets: Welcome
Creature Comforts: CCTV, a/c,
refrig, micro, kit

Mountain View Motel
(307) 684-2881
http://www.buffalowyoming.com
585 Fort St.
14 cabins - $30-45
Pets: Welcome
Creature Comforts: CCTV, a/c,
refrig, micro, kit

South Fork Inn
(307) 267-2609
Route 16
10 cabins - $45-85
Pets: Welcome w/$5 fee
Creature Comforts: Some rustic
cabins w/o baths, 1 w/fireplace,
restaurant

Super 8
(800) 800-8000, (307) 684-2531
http://www.super8.com
655 E. Hart St.
48 rooms - $45-75
Pets: Welcome w/$6 fee
Creature Comforts: CCTV, a/c

Wyoming Motel
(800) 666-5505, (307) 684-5505
http://www.buffalowyoming.com
610 E. Hart St.
27 rooms - $30-150
Pets: Welcome in 5 rooms
Creature Comforts: CCTV, kit,
fireplace, Jacuzzi, restaurant, cont.
brkfst, pool, whirlpool

Z-Bar Motel
(800) 341-8000, (307) 684-5535
www.imalodging.com
626 Fort St.
26 rooms - $35-65
Pets: Welcome w/$4 fee
Creature Comforts: CCTV, a/c,
refrig, micro, kit

CASPER
All American Inn
(307) 235-6688
5755 CY Ave.
38 rooms - $35-48
Pets: Welcome
Creature Comforts: CCTV, a/c,
kit

Best Western Inn
(800) 528-1234, (307) 234-3541
http://www.bestwestern.com
2325 E. Yellowstone St.
42 rooms - $45-80
Pets: Welcome with the
manager's approval
Creature Comforts: CCTV, a/c,
refrig, kit, cont. brkfst, pool

Comfort Inn
(800) 228-5150, (307) 235-3038
http://www.comfortinn.com
480 Lathrop St.
56 rooms - $40-75
Pets: Welcome
Creature Comforts: CCTV, a/c,
refrig, micro, cont. brkfst, pool,
whirlpool

First Interstate Inn
(307) 234-9125
20 SE Wyoming St.
60 rooms - $40-60
Pets: Small pets w/$5 fee
Creature Comforts: CCTV, a/c,
refrig

Hampton Inn
(800) Hampton, (307) 235-6668
http://www.hamptoninn.com
400 West F St.
122 rooms - $65-80
Pets: Welcome
Creature Comforts: CCTV, a/c,
restaurant, cont. brkfst, pool

Holiday Inn
(800) HOLIDAY, (307) 235-2531
http://www.holiday-inn.com
300 West F St.
200 rooms - $75-175
Pets: Welcome
Creature Comforts: CCTV, a/c,
refrig, micro, kit, Jacuzzi,
restaurant, cont. brkfst, pool,
whirlpool, sauna

Kelly Inn
(800) 635-3559, (307) 266-2400
821 N. Poplar St.
103 rooms - $40-50
Pets: Welcome
Creature Comforts: CCTV,
VCR, a/c, sauna, Jacuzzi

Motel 6
(800) 4 MOTEL6, (307) 234-3903
http://www.motel6.com
1150 Wilkins Circle
130 rooms - $28-35
Pets: Small pets welcome
Creature Comforts: CCTV, a/c,
pool

National 9 Inn Showboat
(800) 524-9999, (307) 235-2711
100 West F St.
45 rooms - $35-50
Pets: Welcome w/$10 deposit
Creature Comforts: CCTV, a/c

Parkway Plaza
(800) 270-STAY, (307) 235-1777
123 West E St.
230 rms - $40-180
Pets: Welcome w/$25 deposit
Creature Comforts: CCTV, a/c,
refrig, kit, Jacuzzi, restaurant,
pool, sauna, whirlpool, hlth club

Radisson Hotel
(800) 333-3333, (307) 266-6000
http://www.radisson.com
800 N. Poplar St.
229 rooms - $65-80
Pets: Small pets w/$25 deposit
Creature Comforts: CCTV, a/c,
refrig, micro, Jacuzzi, restaurants,
pool, exercise rm.

Ranch House Motel
(307) 266-4044
1130 F St.
11 rooms - $75/wk
Pets: Small dogs welcome
Creature Comforts: CCTV, a/c

Royal Inn
(800) 967-6925, (307) 654-7507
440 East A St.
36 rooms - $25-38
Pets: In certain rooms w/$2 fee
Creature Comforts: CCTV, a/c,
refrig, pool

Shilo Inn
(800) 222-2244, (307) 237-1335
http://www.shiloinns.com
Curtis Rd.
100 rooms - $60-80
Pets: Welcome w/$6 fee
Creature Comforts: CCTV,
VCR, a/c, refrig, micro, restaurant,
sauna, whirlpool

Super 8 Lodge
(800) 800-8000, (307) 266-3480
http://www.super8.com
3838 Cy Ave.
66 rooms - $44-50
Pets: Welcome w/$3 fee
Creature Comforts: CCTV,
VCR, a/c, cont. brkfst

Westridge Motel
(307) 234-8911
955 Cy Ave.
29 rooms - $36-55
Pets: Small pets w/$4 fee
Creature Comforts: CCTV, a/c

Yellowstone Motel
(307) 234-9174
Yellowstone Hwy.
18 rooms - $30-40
Pets: Welcome
Creature Comforts: CCTV, a/c,
refrig, micro, kit, picnic areas

CENTENNIAL
Centennial Valley Trading Post
(307) 721-5074
Route 130
2 cabins - $35-45
Pets: Welcome
Creature Comforts: CCTV, a/c,
kit, restaurant

Friendly Fly Motel
(307) 742-6033
2758 Rte. 130
8 rooms - $40-52
Pets: Welcome
Creature Comforts: TV

Old Corral Mountain Lodge
(307) 745-5918
Main St.
18 rooms - $50-60
Pets: Welcome
Creature Comforts: TV, a/c

CHEYENNE
A. Drummonds Ranch B&B
(307) 634-6042
cruising-america.com/drummond
399 Happy Jack Rd.
4 rooms - $65-175
Pets: Welcome in the arena,
rubber mats provided
Creature Comforts: 120-acre
contemp. ranch w/farm animals,
antique-filled rooms, terry robes,
fresh flowers, CCTV, full gourmet
brkfst srvd on china/silver, request
Carriage House Loft w/priv. deck,
hot tub, fireplace, steam shower,
stocked pantry, horseback riding,
hiking, mountain biking

Adventurers' Country B&B
(307) 632-4087
http://www.cruising-america.com/
country
3803 Route 80 S. Service Rd.
5 rooms - $55-125
Pets: Welcome in kennel boxes in
barn w/$10 fee
Creature Comforts: Set on 120-
acre Raven Cry Ranch, CCTV,
refrig, fireplace, Jacuzzi, full ranch
brkfst, sauna, restaurant, riding

Avenue Rose B&B
(307) 632-0274
100 E. 27th St.
3 rooms - $45-70
Pets: Welcome
Creature Comforts: 1900s
Victorian, holistic atmosphere,
gardens, full brkfst

Best Western Hitching Post
(800) 528-1234, (307) 638-3301
http://www.bestwestern.com
1700 W. Lincolnway
166 rooms - $70-200
Pets: Welcome
Creature Comforts: Upscale
newly renovated property, CCTV,
a/c, refrig, micro, Jacuzzi,
restaurant, cont. brkfst, pool, hlth
clb, sauna, whirlpool, tennis,
playground

Bit-O-Wyo B&B
(307) 638-8340
http://www.bitowyo.com
470 Happy Jack Rd.
6 rooms - $65-80
Pets: Welcome, horses too
Creature Comforts: Rustic log
house w/attractive, homey decor,
CCTV, full brkfst, hlth clb access,
sauna, whirlpool, horseback
riding, fishing

Cheyenne Motel
(307) 778-7664
1601 E. Lincolnway
30 rooms - $25-40
Pets: Welcome
Creature Comforts: CCTV, a/c,
kit

Comfort Inn
(800) 228-5150, (307) 638-7202
http://www.comfortinn.com
2245 Etchepare Dr.
77 rooms - $46-150
Pets: Welcome
Creature Comforts: CCTV,
VCR, a/c, restaurant, cont. brkfst,
pool

Days Inn
(800) DAYS INN, (307) 778-8877
http://www.daysinn.com
2360 W. Lincoln Way
71 rooms - $55-75
Pets: Welcome
Creature Comforts: CCTV, a/c,
cont. brkfst, sauna, whirlpool

Fairfield Inn
(800) 228-2800, (307) 637-4070
http://www.fairfieldinn.com
1415 Stillwater Ave.
62 rooms - $40-80
Pets: Welcome
Creature Comforts: CCTV, a/c, pool

Firebird Motel
(307) 632-5505
1905 E. Lincolnway
49 rooms - $45-65
Pets: Welcome
Creature Comforts: CCTV, a/c, pool

Fleetwood Motel
(307) 638-8908
3800 E. Lincolnway
21 rooms - $36-43
Pets: Welcome w/$3 fee
Creature Comforts: CCTV, a/c, pool

Frontier Motel
(307) 634-7961
1400 W. Lincolnway
42 rooms - $25-35
Pets: Welcome
Creature Comforts: CCTV, a/c

Holiday Inn
(800) HOLIDAY, (307) 638-4466
http://www.holiday-inn.com
204 W. Fox Farm Rd.
244 rooms - $70-125
Pets: Welcome
Creature Comforts: CCTV, a/c, restaurant, cont. brkfst, pool, sauna, whirlpool

Howdy Pardner B&B
(307) 634-6493
http://www.cruising-america.com/howdy.html
1920 Tranquility Rd.
3 rooms - $65-105
Pets: Welcome, loves pets
Creature Comforts: Modern ranch house on 10 acres, vaulted ceiling common room w/stone fireplace, iron beds, beautiful handmade quilts, sheeperherder wagon also available, CCTV, a/c, refrig, micro, kit, fireplace, gourmet ranch brkfst

La Quinta
(800) 531-5900, (307) 632-7117
http://www.laquinta.com
2410 W. Lincolnway
105 rooms - $50-90
Pets: Small pets welcome
Creature Comforts: CCTV, a/c, refrig, micro, and a pool

Lincoln Court
(800) 221-0125, (307) 638-3301
1700 W. Lincolnway
67 rooms - $45-165
Pets: Welcome
Creature Comforts: CCTV, a/c, refrig, pool, hlth clb, sauna, whirlpool, tennis, playground

Nagle Warren Mansion
(800) 811-2610, (307) 637-3333
www.naglewarrenmansion.com
222 E. 17th St.
12 rooms - $70-200
Pets: Welcome in carriage house
Creature Comforts: 1888 Victorian inn and carriage house, ornate woodwork, parquet floors, stained glass, decorated w/ Victorian antiques, Oriental rugs, sleigh beds, library, afternoon tea, gourmet brkfst, hlth club, hot tub, and massage

Motel 6
(800) 4-MOTEL6, (307) 635-6806
http://www.motel6.com
1735 Westland Rd.
108 rooms - $30-44
Pets: Small pets welcome
Creature Comforts: CCTV, a/c, pool

Porch Swing B&B
(307) 778-7182
http://www.cruising-america.com/porch.html
712 E. 20th St.
3 rooms - $45-85
Pets: Welcome w/permission
Creature Comforts: Historic 1907 home, herb gardens, antiques, simple rooms, handmade quilts, CCTV, refrig, fireplace, full gourmet brkfst, lawn games

Quality Inn
(800) 228-5151, (307) 632-8901
http://www.qualityinn.com
5401 Walker Rd.
105 rooms - $40-175
Pets: Welcome
Creature Comforts: CCTV, a/c, refrig, micro, restaurant, pool

Ranger Motel
(307) 634—7995
909 W. Lincolnway
22 rooms - $25-45
Pets: Welcome
Creature Comforts: CCTV, a/c

Rodeo Inn
(800) 843-5644, (307) 634-2171
http:///www.knightsinn.com
3839 E. Lincolnway
66 rooms - $25-35
Pets: Welcome
Creature Comforts: CCTV, a/c, kit

Sapp Bros. Big C Motel
(307) 632-6600
Route 80
20 rooms - $35-40
Pets: Welcome w/$20 deposit
Creature Comforts: TV, a/c

Super 8
(800) 800-8000, (307) 635-8741
http://www.super8.com
1900 W. Lincolnway
61 rooms - $44-47
Pets: Welcome
Creature Comforts: CCTV, VCR, a/c, refrig, micro

Windy Hills Guest House
(307) 632-6423
http://www.windyhillswyo.com
393 Happy Jack Rd.
2 suites/2 houses - $75-135
Pets: Welcome
Creature Comforts: Charming and cozy guest houses w/views of Medicine Bow Nat'l Forest, request private Guest House or Log House-each w/two rooms, Jacuzzi, fireplace, hand-hewn log beds, fresh flowers, chocolates, kit, Jacuzzi, cont. brkfst

Wyoming Motel
(307) 632-8104
1401 Lincolnway
30 rooms - $25-45
Pets: Welcome
Creature Comforts: CCTV, a/c, kit

CHUGWATER
Super 8
(800) 800-8000, (307) 422-3248
700 Swan Ave.
23 rooms - $40-60
Pets: Small pets welcome
Creature Comforts: CCTV, a/c, restaurant, pool

CLEARMONT
RBL Bison Ranch B&B
(307) 758-4387
Rtes. 14 & 16
3 cabins - $45-55
Pets: Welcome
Creature Comforts: CCTV, a/c, restaurant

CODY
Best Western Sunrise
(800) 528-1234, (307) 587-5566
http://www.bestwestern.com
1407 - 8th St.
40 rooms - $42-99
Pets: Welcome w/mngr's aprvl
Creature Comforts: CCTV, a/c, cont. brkfst, pool

Best Western Sunset
(800) 624-2727, (307) 587-4265
http://www.bestwestern.com
1601 - 8th St.
122 rooms/suites - $45-130
Pets: Small pets preferred
Creature Comforts: CCTV, a/c, restaurant, pool, hlth clb access, whirlpool

Big Bear Motel
(800) 325-7163, (307) 587-3117
139 W. Yellowstone Hwy.
42 rooms - $25-59
Pets: Welcome
Creature Comforts: CCTV, pool

Breteche Creek Ranch
(307) 587-3844
http://www.guestranches.com/breteche
269 RD6FU, Box 596
10 rooms - $825-975/wk
Pets: Welcome, there are lots of dogs on the premises
Creature Comforts: Working cattle ranch on 7,000 high mtn. acres, spectacular scenery, neat tent cabins w/flannel lined sleeping bags, gourmet western fare in central lodge pole lodge, riding, hiking

Carter Mountain Motel
(307) 587-4295
1701 Central Ave.
25 rooms - $30-85
Pets: Welcome
Creature Comforts: CCTV, a/c, kit

Elk Valley Inn
(307) 587-4149
3256 North Fork Hwy.
11 rooms - $40-75
Pets: Welcome
Creature Comforts: CCTV, a/c, kit, restaurant

Gateway Motel
(307) 587-2561
203 Yellowstone Ave.
10 rooms - $25-60
Pets: Welcome
Creature Comforts: CCTV, a/c, kit

Goff Creek Lodge
(800) 859-3985, (307) 587-3753
http://www.goffcreek.com
995 E. Yellowstone Hwy.
17 cabins - $60-110
Pets: Welcome, cannot be left alone in the room
Creature Comforts: Authentic hunting lodge atmosphere w/ cabins nestled at 6,000 feet, pine and fir forest w/stream, knotty pine log cabins, western memorabilia, CCTV, kit, stone fireplace, excellent homestyle cooking, horseback riding, hiking, fishing, lawn games, pack trips

House of Burgess B&B
(307) 283-2800
1508 Alger Ave.
3 rooms - $60-90
Pets: Some pets w/prior approval
Creature Comforts: 1928 Victorian in historic district, CCTV, a/c, expanded cont. brkfst

Hunter Peak Ranch
(307) 587-3711
http://www.nezperce.com/ranchhp.html
Route 296, Box 1731
10 lodge/cabins - $80-110
Pets: Welcome w/$10 daily or $25 one-time fee
Creature Comforts: Incredible views, riverside location, historic 1909 lodge, modern cabins w/kit, woodstove, dining rm., horseback riding, hiking, fishing, swimming

K-Z Guest Ranch
(307) 587-4410
3477 Crandall Rd.
7 rooms - $65-85
Pets: Welcome
Creature Comforts: CCTV, kit, fireplace, restaurant, pool, horseback riding, fishing, hiking, lawn games, xc-skiing

Kelly Inn
(800) 635-3559, (307) 527-5505
2513 Greybull Hwy.
50 rooms - $55-99
Pets: Welcome
Creature Comforts: CCTV, a/c, refrig, micro, Jacuzzi, cont. brkfst, sauna, whirlpool

Mountain View Lodge
(307) 587-2081
2776 N. Fork Hwy.
31 rooms - $35-49
Pets: Welcome
Creature Comforts: CCTV, kit

Parkway Inn
(307) 587-4208
720 Yellowstone
38 rooms - $35-50
Pets: Welcome
Creature Comforts: CCTV, pool

Seven K's Motel
(800) 223-9204, (307) 587-5890
http://www.imt.net/—rodeo/
7k.html
232 W. Yellowstone Ave.
16 rooms - $25-50
Pets: Welcome
Creature Comforts: CCTV, a/c,
refrig, pool

Skyline Motor Inn
(800) 843-8809, (307) 587-4201
1919 - 17th St.
46 rooms - $32-64
Pets: Welcome
Creature Comforts: CCTV, a/c,
pool

Stage Stop
(307) 587-2804
502 Yellowstone Ave.
7 rooms - $30-60
Pets: Welcome
Creature Comforts: CCTV

Super 8
(800) 800-8000, (307) 527-6214
http://www.super8.com
730 Yellowstone Rd.
64 rooms - $45-55
Pets: Welcome
Creature Comforts: CCTV, a/c,
cont. brkfst

Trail Inn
(307) 587-3741
2750 Yellowstone Hwy.
10 rooms - $40-65
Pets: Welcome
Creature Comforts: CCTV, a/c,
kit

Trout Creek Inn
(307) 587-6288
Yellowstone Hwy 14
21 rooms - $28-63
Pets: Welcome
Creature Comforts: CCTV, a/c,
kit, restaurant, pool, whirlpool

Uptown Motel
(307) 587-4245
1562 Sheridan Ave.
10 rooms - $30-64
Pets: Welcome w/mngr's approval
Creature Comforts: CCTV, a/c

Western 6 Gun Motel
(307) 587-4835
423 Yellowstone Ave.
40 rooms - $35-69
Pets: Welcome
Creature Comforts: CCTV, a/c,
kit

Wise Choice Inn
(307) 587-5004
2908 N. Fork Hwy.
17 rooms - $26-55
Pets: Welcome
Creature Comforts: CCTV, a/c

Yellowstone Valley Inn
(888) 705-7703, (307) 587-3961
http://www.westerntravel.com/ye
3324 Yellowstone Hwy., Box 515
36 rooms - $40-95
Pets: Welcome
Creature Comforts: CCTV, a/c,
kit, restaurant, cont. brkfst, pool,
whirlpool

COKEVILLE
Hideout Motel
(307) 279-3281
245 S. Hwy.
11 rooms - $45-55
Pets: Welcome
Creature Comforts: CCTV, kit

Valley Hi Motel
(307) 279-3251
Route 30
22 rooms - $40-49
Pets: Welcome in certain rooms
Creature Comforts: CCTV

DIAMONDVILLE
Energy Inn
(307) 877-6901
Routes 30
42 rooms - $45-56
Pets: Welcome
Creature Comforts: CCTV, a/c,
kit

DOUGLAS
Alpine Inn
(307) 358-4780
2310 E. Richards St.
40 rooms - $33-40
Pets: Welcome w/$5 fee
Creature Comforts: CCTV

Best Western Douglas Inn
(800) 528-1234, (307) 358-9790
http://www.bestwestern.com
1450 Riverbend Dr.
116 rooms - $60-85
Pets: Small pets welcome
Creature Comforts: CCTV, a/c,
restaurant, pool, hlth clb, sauna,
whirlpool

Chieftan Motel
(307) 358-2673
815 Richards St.
21 rooms - $40-45
Pets: Welcome w/deposit
Creature Comforts: CCTV,
refrig, micro

First Interstate Motel
(307) 358-2833
2349 E. Richards St.
44 rooms - $40-60
Pets: Small pets w/$5 fee
Creature Comforts: CCTV, a/c

Plains Motel
(307) 358-4484
628 Richards St.
50 rooms - $30-35
Pets: Welcome
Creature Comforts: CCTV, a/c,
kit

DUBOIS
Bald Mtn. Inn
(800) 682-9323, (307) 455-2844
1349 W. Ramshorn St.
15 rooms - $45-85
Pets: Welcome w/$5 fee
Creature Comforts: CCTV, kit,
fireplace, playground

Black Bear Country Motel
(800) 873-BEAR, (307) 455-2344
505 N. Ramshorn St.
16 rooms - $35-45
Pets: Dogs welcome, no cats
Creature Comforts: CCTV,
refrig

Branding Iron Motel
(900) 341-8000, (307) 455-2893
401 W. Ramshorn St.
23 rooms - $30-72
Pets: Welcome
Creature Comforts: CCTV,
refrig, kit, restaurant

Chinook Winds Mt. Lodge
(307) 455-2987
640 S. First St.
17 rooms - $35-84
Pets: Welcome w/$5 fee
Creature Comforts: CCTV,
refrig, kit, whirlpool, lawn games

Lakes Lodge
(888) 655-LAKE, (307) 455-2171
One Fir Rd.
4 rooms - $35-49
Pets: Welcome
Creature Comforts: CCTV,
restaurant

Lazy L&B Ranch
(800) 453-9488, (307) 455-2839
1072 E. Fork Rd.
12 cabins - $950 pp/wk (AP)
Pets: Welcome
Creature Comforts: 2,000-acre
ranch, restaurant, children's
prgrms, hiking, swimming

Pinnacle Buttes Lodge
(307) 455-2506
3577 Route 26
13 rooms/cabins - $60-75
Pets: Welcome w/$10 fee
Creature Comforts: CCTV, kit,
restaurant, pool, whirlpool

Riverside Inn
(307) 455-2337
Route 26
14 rooms - $35-45
Pets: Welcome
Creature Comforts: CCTV, kit,
pool

Stagecoach Motor Inn
(800) 455-5090, (307) 455-2303
103 Ramshorn St.
50 rooms - $40-75
Pets: Welcome w/$5 fee
Creature Comforts: CCTV,
refrig, kit, pool

Wind River Motel
(307) 455-2611
519 Ramshorn St.
12 rooms - $35-50
Pets: Welcome in certain rooms
Creature Comforts: CCTV, a/c,
kit

EDGERTON
Teapot Motor Lodge
(307) 437-6541
Route 387
20 rooms - $35-40
Pets: Welcome
Creature Comforts: CCTV, a/c

ENCAMPMENT
Riverside Cabins
(307) 327-5361
Route 230
9 cabins - $38-45
Pets: Welcome
Creature Comforts: Hsekpng
cottages, kit, fireplace

Rustic Mountain Lodge
(307) 327-5539
Route 230
4 rooms - $65-74
Pets: Welcome
Creature Comforts: Working
ranch w/comfortable bedrooms,
horseback riding, fishing and
rafting trips

Vecher's Bighorn Lodge
(888) 327-5110, (307) 327-5110
508 McCaffrey St.
12 rooms - $40-45
Pets: Welcome w/$10 fee
Creature Comforts: CCTV,
refrig, kit

EVANSTON
Alexander Motel
(307) 789-2346
Bear River Dr.
19 rooms - $25-30
Pets: Welcome
Creature Comforts: CCTV, pool

Days Inn
(800) DAYS INN, (307) 789-2220
http://www.daysinn.com
339 Wasatch Rd.
92 rooms - $45-90
Pets: Small pets welcome
Creature Comforts: CCTV, a/c,
kit, whirlpool, cont. brkfst, and a
restaurant

Economy Inn
(307) 789-2777
www.innsofamerica.com
1710 Harrison Dr.
42 rooms - $40-45
Pets: Welcome w/$10 fee
Creature Comforts: CCTV, a/c,
kit, restaurant

Hillcrest DX Motel
(307) 789-1111
1725 Harrison Dr.
42 rooms - $40-49
Pets: Welcome w/$10 fee
Creature Comforts: CCTV, a/c,
restaurant

Motel 6
(800) 4-MOTEL6, (307) 789-0791
http://www.motel6.com
261 Bear River Dr.
90 rooms - $30-47
Pets: Small pets welcome
Creature Comforts: CCTV, a/c,
pool, whirlpool

National 9 Inn
(800) 524-9999, (307) 789-9610
1724 Harrison Dr.
87 rooms - $40-55
Pets: Welcome
Creature Comforts: CCTV, a/c

Prairie Inn Motel
(307) 789-2920
264 Bear River Dr.
30 rooms - $40-57
Pets: Welcome w/$5 fee
Creature Comforts: CCTV

Super 8
(800) 800-8000, (307) 789-7510
http://www.super8.com
70 Bear River Dr.
89 rooms - $40-55
Pets: Welcome
Creature Comforts: CCTV, a/c,
refrig, cont. brkfst

Weston Plaza Hotel
(800) 255-9840, (307) 789-0783
1983 Harrison Dr.
101 rooms - $55-90
Pets: Welcome in 2 rooms
Creature Comforts: CCTV, a/c,
refrig, micro, cont. brkfst, pool,
whirlpool

Weston Super Budget Motel
(800) 255-9840, (307) 789-2810
1936 Harrison Dr.
112 rooms - $40-59
Pets: Welcome in certain rooms
Creature Comforts: CCTV, a/c,
restaurant, full brkfst, pool

EVANSVILLE
Shilo Inn
(800) 222-2244, (307) 237-1335
http://www.shiloinns.com
Rte. 25 and Curtis Rd.
100 rooms - $65-99
Pets: Welcome w/$7 fee
Creature Comforts: CCTV, a/c,
refrig, micro, restaurant, pool,
whirlpool, sauna, whirlpool, steam
room

FORT BRIDGER
Wagon Wheel Motel
(307) 782-6361
270 N. Main St.
56 rooms - $35-45
Pets: House trained med. dogs in
rms, outside area for larger dogs
Creature Comforts: CCTV, a/c,
refrig, kit, restaurant

GILLETTE
Arrowhead Motel
(307) 686-0909
202 S. Emerson Ave.
32 rooms - $35-58
Pets: Welcome
Creature Comforts: CCTV, a/c,
kit

Best Western Tower West Lodge
(800) 528-1234, (307) 686-2210
http://www.bestwestern.com
109 N. Route 1-16
63 rooms - $40-85
Pets: Welcome
Creature Comforts: CCTV, a/c,
restaurant, pool, hlth clb, sauna,
whirlpool

Circle L Motel
(307) 682-9375
410 E. Second St.
32 rooms - $35-58
Pets: Welcome
Creature Comforts: CCTV, a/c,
kit

Days Inn
(800) DAYS INN, (307) 682-3999
http://www.daysinn.com
910 E. Boxelder Rd.
138 rooms - $45-70
Pets: Small pets welcome
Creature Comforts: CCTV, a/c

Econo Lodge
(800) 55-ECONO, (307) 682-4757
http://www.econolodge.com
409 Butler Spaeth Rd.
62 rooms - $40-79
Pets: Welcome w/$6 fee, $25
refundable deposit
Creature Comforts: CCTV, a/c,
cont. brkfst

Holiday Inn
(800) HOLIDAY, (307) 686-3000
http://www.holiday-inn.com
2009 S. Douglas Hwy.
158 rooms - $79-110
Pets: Small pets welcome
Creature Comforts: CCTV, a/c,
restaurant, pool, hlth clb access,
sauna, whirlpool, arcade room,
playground

Motel 6
(800) 4-MOTEL6, (307) 686-8600
http://www.motel6.com
2105 Rodgers Dr.
74 rooms - $22-28
Pets: Small pets welcome
Creature Comforts: CCTV, a/c,
sauna, whirlpool

National 9
(800) 524-9999, (307) 464-1510
1020 Rte. 51
79 rooms - $40-75
Pets: Small pets welcome
Creature Comforts: CCTV, a/c,
restaurant, pool

Ramada Limited
(800) 2-Ramada, (307) 682-9341
http://www.ramada.com
608 E. 2nd St.
74 rooms - $40-70
Pets: Under 100 lbs. in smkng rms
Creature Comforts: CCTV, a/c,
refrig, micro, cont. brkfst, pool,
hlth clb access

Super 8
(800) 800-8000, (307) 682-8078
http://www.super8.com
208 S. Decker Court
60 rooms - $40-50
Pets: $5 fee in smoking rooms
Creature Comforts: CCTV, a/c,
cont. brkfst, pool

Thrifty Inn
(800) 621-2182, (307) 682-2616
1004 E. Hwy. 14-16
74 rooms - $35-50
Pets: Welcome
Creature Comforts: CCTV, a/c

GLENROCK
All American Inn
(307) 436-2772
500 W. Aspen St.
23 rooms - $30-45
Pets: Welcome w/$20 deposit
Creature Comforts: CCTV, a/c,
refrig, micro, restaurant

GRAND TETON NAT'L PARK
Colter Bay Cabins
(800) 628-9988, (307) 543-2855
Rtes. 89 & 287
208 rooms/cabins - $61-120
Pets: Welcome
Creature Comforts: Rustic
cabins, restaurant/store, lake
swimming, boating, fishing,
marina, horseback riding

Flagg Ranch Resort
(800) 443-2311, (307) 543-2861
http://www.flaggranch.com
Routes 89 & 191
148 rooms - $77-130
Pets: Welcome in 10 smkng. rms.
Creature Comforts: Located at
entrance to Grand Teton Park,
CCTV, refrig, micro, restaurant,
extensive recreational activities:
hiking, biking, fishing, lawn
games, rafting, xc-skiing

Jackson Lake Lodge
(800) 628-9988, (307) 543-2811
http://www.gtlc.com
Routes 89 & 287
380 rooms - $95-175
Pets: Welcome in first floor rooms
Creature Comforts: Expansive
grounds, Teton views, CCTV,
refrig, micro, Jacuzzi, restaurant,
ext. recreational activities: hiking,
fishing, horseback riding, boating

Signal Mountain Lodge
(307) 543-2831
http://www.signalmtnlodge.com
Routes 89 & 287
115 rooms/cabins - $75-175
Pets: Welcome
Creature Comforts: On Jackson Lake in Grand Teton Park, rqst log cabins w/fireplace, hand-hewn furnishings, quilts, incredible views, refrig, micro, restaurant, beach, extensive rec. activities: swimming, fishing, boating

GREEN RIVER
Coachman Inn
(307) 875-3681
470 E. Flaming Gorge Way
18 rooms - $35-50
Pets: Welcome
Creature Comforts: CCTV, a/c, micro, and a pool

Desmond Motel
(307) 875-3701
140 North Seventh W.
8 rooms - $35-45
Pets: Small pets welcome
Creature Comforts: CCTV, a/c, refrig

Flaming Gorge Motel
(307) 875-4190
316 E. Flaming Gorge Way
17 rooms - $35-45
Pets: Welcome
Creature Comforts: CCTV, a/c, kit

Oak Tree Inn
(307) 875-3500
1170 Flaming Gorge Way
190 rooms - $35-45
Pets: Welcome
Creature Comforts: CCTV, a/c, restaurant

Super 8
(800) 800-8000, (307) 875-9330
http://www.super8.com
280 W. Flaming Gorge
35 rooms - $35-50
Pets: Small pets w/$25 deposit
Creature Comforts: CCTV, a/c

Western Motel
(307) 875-2840
890 Flaming Gorge Way
30 rooms - $35-40
Pets: Welcome w/$25 deposit
Creature Comforts: CCTV, a/c, micro

GREYBULL
K-Bar Motel
(877) 765-4426, (307) 765-4426
300 Greybull Ave.
18 rooms - $30-69
Pets: Small pets w/$3 fee
Creature Comforts: CCTV, a/c

Sage Motel
(307) 765-4443
1135 N. 6th St.
18 rooms - $30-65
Pets: Welcome
Creature Comforts: CCTV, a/c, refrig

Wheels Motel
(307) 765-2105
1324 N. Sixth St.
22 rooms - $40-65
Pets: Welcome
Creature Comforts: CCTV, a/c

Yellowstone Motel
(307) 765-4456
247 Greybull Ave.
33 rooms - $40-80
Pets: Small pets w/$5 fee
Creature Comforts: CCTV, a/c, kit, and a pool

GUERNSEY
Bunkhouse Hotel
(307) 836-2356
350 W. Whalen Rd.
30 rooms - $30-67
Pets: Welcome
Creature Comforts: CCTV, a/c, refrig

HELL'S HALF ACRE
Hell's Half Acre Motel
(307) 472-0018
Route 2026
10 rooms - $30-45
Pets: Welcome
Creature Comforts: TV, a/c

HULETT
Hulett Motel
(800) 451-4332, (307) 467-5220
202 Main St.
10 rooms - $45-62
Pets: Welcome
Creature Comforts: CCTV, a/c

Motel Pioneer
(307) 467-5656
Route 24
15 rooms - $45-58
Pets: Small pets welcome
Creature Comforts: TV, a/c

JACKSON
Alpine Motel
(307) 739-3200
70 Jean St.
18 rooms - $67-128
Pets: Welcome
Creature Comforts: CCTV, a/c, Alps decor, kit, pool

Antler Inn
(800) 522-2406, (307) 733-2535
43 W. Pearl St.
100 rooms - $50-120
Pets: Welcome
Creature Comforts: CCTV, a/c, fireplace, sauna, whirlpool

Cache Creek Motel
(800) 843-4788, (307) 733-7781
www.cachecreekmotel.com
390 N. Glenwood
37 rooms - $50-155
Pets: Welcome
Creature Comforts: CCTV, a/c, kit, whirlpool

Cottages at Snow King
(307) 733-3480
470 King St.
18 rooms - $45-75
Pets: Welcome
Creature Comforts: CCTV, a/c

Country Inn
(307) 733-2364
Box 1255
45 rooms - $48-128
Pets: Welcome
Creature Comforts: CCTV, a/c, kit, sauna, whirlpool

Elk Country Inn
(800) 4-TETONS, (307) 733-2364
480 W. Pearl St.
44 rooms - $56-145
Pets: Welcome in ltd. rms
Creature Comforts: CCTV, a/c, kit

Flat Creek Motel
(800) 438-9338, (307) 733-5276
Route 89
75 rooms - $70-85
Pets: Welcome with a $10 cleaning fee and $40 deposit
Creature Comforts: CCTV, a/c, refrig, micro, kit, cont. brkfst, sauna, whirlpool

JH Development
(800) 342-0833, (307) 733-7072
Box 1569
6 rooms - $80-450
Pets: Welcome
Creature Comforts: CCTV, a/c, refrig, micro, kit, fireplace, pool

Jackson Hole Lodge
(800) 604-9404, (307) 733-2992
http://www.jacksonholelodge.com
420 W. Broadway St.
59 rooms - $70-299
Pets: Welcome w/$50 deposit
Creature Comforts: A 1940's hunting lodge, modern rooms, CCTV, a/c, refrig, micro, kit, fireplace, Jacuzzi, pool, sauna, whirlpools

Mad Dog Ranch
(800) 99 CABIN, (307) 733-3729
http://www.maddogranch.com
Box 7737
9 cabins - $110-170
Pets: Welcome in 2 cabins, horses
Creature Comforts: On five acres, two-bedroom cabins w/ knotty pine walls and vaulted ceilings, lodge pole furnishings, down comforters, CCTV, kit, woodstove, hot tub, sleeping loft, grills, porches

Motel 6
(800) 4-MOTEL6, (307) 733-1620
http://www.motel6.com
1370 W. Broadway
155 rooms - $30-66
Pets: Smal pets welcome in first floor non-smoking rooms
Creature Comforts: CCTV, a/c, restaurant, pool

Old West Cabins
(307) 733-0333
Star Route Box 11
14 rooms - $86-125
Pets: Welcome
Creature Comforts: CCTV

Painted Buffalo Inn
(800) 288-3866, (307) 733-4340
400 W. Broadway St.
135 rooms - $79-140
Pets: Small pets w/$10 fee
Creature Comforts: CCTV, a/c, refrig, restaurant,hlth clb, massage

Prospector Motel
(800) 851-0070, (307) 733-4858
www.jacksonprospector.com
155 N. Jackson St.
20 rooms - $40-125
Pets: Small pets welcome
Creature Comforts: CCTV, a/c, refrig, micro, cont. brkfst, and a whirlpool

Quality Forty-Niner Inn
(800) 451-2980, (307) 733-7550
http://www.qualityinn.com
330 W. Pearl St.
144 rooms - $68-190
Pets: Welcome
Creature Comforts: CCTV, a/c, refrig, micro, fireplace, Jacuzzi, restaurant, cont. brkfst, sauna, whirlpool, hlth club,

Ranch Inn
(800) 348-5599, (307) 733-6363
45 E. Pearl St.
57 rooms - $40-125
Pets: Welcome
Creature Comforts: CCTV, a/c, kit

Rawhide Motel
(800) 835-2999, (307) 733-1216
75 S. Millward
23 rooms - $40-125
Pets: Small pets welcome
Creature Comforts: CCTV, a/c, kit

Red Lion Wyoming Inn
(800) 844-0035, (307) 734-0035
http://www.redlion.com
930 W. Broadway
73 rooms/suites - $80-400
Pets: Welcome
Creature Comforts: Boutique hotel, country-style lodge, impressive lobby w/ornate woodwork and river rock fireplace, luxury rooms w/hand-carved beds, armoires, wool blankets, feather pillows, CCTV, a/c, refrig, kit, fireplace, Jacuzzi, cont. brkfst, pool, hlth clb access, sauna, whirlpool

Sassy Moose Inn
(800) 356-1277, (307) 733-1277
http://www.sassymoose.com
3859 Miles Rd.
5 rooms - $99-140
Pets: "We take pets, we have yet to have a dog drink too much or break anything."
Creature Comforts: Log ranch house near Jackson Hole, Teton views, vaulted ceilings, request Rendezvous Room w/river rock fireplace, down comforters, lodge pole beds, some antiques, CCTV, gourmet brkfst, afternoon tea, hot tub, next to golf course

Snow King Resort
(800) 522-5464, (307) 733-5200
http://www.snowking.com
400 E. Snow King Ave.
254 rooms - $90-500
Pets: Small pets welcome in first floor non-smoking rooms w/$50 fee and $50 deposit
Creature Comforts: Full service, Snow King Mtn. condo/hotel resort, on 500 acres, lobby w/ massive stone fireplace, CCTV, a/c, refrig, micro, kit, fireplace, restaurant, pool, hlth clb, sauna, whirlpools, xc skiing, bikes

Sundance Inn
(888) 478-6326, (307) 733-3444
Box I
28 rooms/suites - $60-130
Pets: Welcome
Creature Comforts: CCTV, a/c, kit, restaurant

Teton Gables Motel
(307) 733-3723
Box 1038
36 rooms - $40-79
Pets: Welcome
Creature Comforts: CCTV, a/c, restaurant

Twin Mntn. River Ranch B&B
(307) 733-1168
1424 Central Ave.
13 rooms - $35-45
Pets: Med. pets welcome
Creature Comforts: Mtn. lodge, CCTV, a/c, hot tub

KAYCEE
Cassidy Inn Motel
(307) 738-2250
326 Nolan St.
19 rooms - $35-44
Pets: Welcome
Creature Comforts: CCTV, a/c

Siesta Motel
(307) 738-2291
255 Nolan Ave.
13 rooms - $30-45
Pets: Welcome
Creature Comforts: CCTV, a/c

KEMMERER
Antler Motel
(307) 877-4461
419 Pine St.
58 rooms - $30-45
Pets: Welcome
Creature Comforts: CCTV, a/c, refrig, micro

Bon Rico
(307) 877-4503
Route 189
24 rooms - $30-45
Pets: Welcome
Creature Comforts: CCTV, a/c, kit, restaurant

Fairview Motel
(307) 877-4461
61 Rte. 30 North
60 rooms - $30-45
Pets: Welcome
Creature Comforts: CCTV, a/c, kit

Fossil Butte Motel
(307) 877-3996
1424 Central Ave.
13 rooms - $35-49
Pets: Med. pets welcome
Creature Comforts: CCTV, a/c, refrig, micro

Lake Viva Marina Motel
(307) 877-9669
Route 233
34 cabins - $25-40
Pets: Welcome
Creature Comforts: Heated cabins, kit, restaurant

Railway Inn Motel
(307) 877-3544
1427 Fifth West Ave.
20 rooms - $35-55
Pets: Welcome
Creature Comforts: CCTV, a/c, refrig, micro

LA GRANGE
Bear Mountain Back Trails
(307) 834-2281
Route 85
1 house - $55 per person (AP)
Pets: Welcome
Creature Comforts: Ranch w/2-bedroom guest house, all meals included

LANDER
Best Western Inn at Lander
(800) 528-1234, (307) 332-2847
http://www.bestwestern.com
260 Grand View Dr.
46 rooms - $55-120
Pets: Welcome w/supervision
Creature Comforts: CCTV, a/c, cont. brkfst, pool

Budget Host Pronghorn Lodge
(800) Bud-Host, (307) 332-3940
http://www.budgethost.com
150 E. Main St.
54 rooms - $40-85
Pets: Welcome in certain rooms
Creature Comforts: CCTV, a/c, refrig, micro, cont. brkfst, whirlpool

Bunkhouse B&B
(800) 582-5262, (307) 332-5624
http://www.landerllama.com/
fbunkhouse.html
2024 Mortimore Ln.
1 house - $75-85
Pets: Must be under complete control and supervised
Creature Comforts: Neat rustic lodge pole hse w/country antiques on Popo Agie river, informal atmosphere, brkfst makings, a/c, kit, great family destination, llamas to feed, llama pack trips

Downtown Motel
(307) 332-3171
569 Main St.
16 rooms - $40-55
Pets: Welcome w/$5 fee
Creature Comforts: CCTV, a/c, refrig, micro

Holiday Lodge
(800) 624-1974, (307) 332-2511
210 McFarlane St.
40 rooms - $35-50
Pets: Welcome w/$5 fee
Creature Comforts: CCTV, a/c, refrig, whirlpool

Piece of Cake B&B
(307) 332-7608
http://www.wyomingbnb-ranchrec.com/PieceofCake.html
2343 Baldwin Creek Rd.
6 rooms/4 cabins - $50-99
Pets: Welcome
Creature Comforts: Set near Wind River Range, small log cabins w/simple furnishings, beautiful views, CCTV, refrig, micro, fireplace, Jacuzzi, western brkfst, hiking, fishing, bikes

Resort at Louis Lake
(888) 422-2246, (307) 332-5549
http://www.wyoming.com/
~louislake
1811 Louis Lake Rd.
7 cabins - $65-145
Pets: Friendly dogs welcome
Creature Comforts: "Rustic, remote, in Wind River Range, 5 log cabins built in 1937 as hunting lodge, two more modern cabins, simple furnishings, cookstove, dry sink, separate bath facilities, beautiful views, canoeing, fishing, horseback riding

Silver Spur Motel
(307) 332-5189
1240 Main St.
25 rooms - $30-49
Pets: Welcome w/$3 fee
Creature Comforts: CCTV, a/c, refrig, micro, kit, pool

Teton Motel
(307) 332-3582
Sixth and Main Sts.
16 rooms - $35-46
Pets: Welcome w$6 fee
Creature Comforts: CCTV, a/c, refrig, micro

LARAMIE
Best Western Foster's Inn
(800) 528-1234, (307) 742-8371
http://www.bestwestern.com
1561 Snowy Range Rd.
112 rooms - $50-95
Pets: Welcome
Creature Comforts: CCTV, a/c, refrig, restaurant, whirlpool

Best Western Gas Lite
(800) 528-1234, (307) 742-6616
http://www.bestwestern.com
960 N. Third St.
30 rooms - $40-80
Pets: Welcome
Creature Comforts: CCTV, a/c

Downtown Motel
(307) 742-6671
165 N. Third St.
30 rooms - $35-65
Pets: Welcome
Creature Comforts: CCTV, a/c

Econo Lodge
(800) 55-ECONO, (307) 745-8900
http://www.econolodge.com
1370 McCue St.
55 rooms - $40-100
Pets: Welcome w/$5 fee
Creature Comforts: CCTV, a/c, refrig, pool

Holiday Inn
(800) HOLIDAY, (307) 742-6611
http://www.holiday-inn.com
2313 Soldier Springs Rd.
100 rooms - $60-105
Pets: Welcome
Creature Comforts: CCTV, a/c, micro, refrig, restaurant, pool

First Inn Gold
(800) 642-4212, (307) 742-3721
421 Boswell Dr.
80 rooms - $40-90
Pets: Welcome w/$8 fee
Creature Comforts: CCTV, VCR, a/c, refrig, restaurant, pool

Motel 6
(800) 4-MOTEL6, (307) 742-2307
http://www.motel6.com
621 Plaza Ln.
122 rooms - $26-32
Pets: Under 30 pounds welcome
Creature Comforts: CCTV, a/c

Motel 8
(307) 745-4856
501 Boswell St.
143 rooms - $35-45
Pets: Welcome/$5 fee
Creature Comforts: CCTV, a/c, kit

Prairie Breeze B&B
(800) 840-2170, (307) 745-5482
http://prairiebreezebandb.com
718 Ivinson Ave.
4 rooms - $60-80
Pets: Welcome w/approval
Creature Comforts: 1888 Victorian listed on Nat'l Historic Register, many original features, charming cottage feeling, handmade quilts, four-poster beds, claw foot tubs, CCTV, a/c, expanded cont. brkfst

Ranger Motel
(307) 742-6677
453 N. Third St.
50 rooms - $30-35
Pets: Medium pets welcome
Creature Comforts: CCTV, a/c, refrig, micro

Sunset Inn
(307) 742-3741
1104 S. Third St.
50 rooms - $40-90
Pets: Small pets welcome
Creature Comforts: CCTV, a/c, refrig, micro, pool, whirlpool

University Inn
(307) 721-8855
1720 Grand St.
37 rooms - $45-55
Pets: Welcome w/$10 fee
Creature Comforts: CCTV, a/c, refrig, micro

LOVELL
Horseshoe Bend
(307) 548-2221
375 E. Main St.
21 rooms - $30-59
Pets: Welcome
Creature Comforts: CCTV, a/c, kit, and a pool

Super 8
(800) 800-8000, (307) 548-2725
http://www.super8.com
595 E. Main St.
33 rooms - $30-49
Pets: Dogs welcome
Creature Comforts: CCTV, a/c

Western Motel
(307) 548-2781
1080 W. Main St.
25 rooms - $32-48
Pets: Welcome
Creature Comforts: CCTV, a/c, kit

LUSK
Rawhide Motel
(307) 334-2440
805 S. Main St.
18 rooms - $38-49
Pets: Welcome
Creature Comforts: CCTV, a/c, refrig, micro

Sage and Cactus Village
(307) 663-7653
http://cruising-america.com/sageandcactus/index.html
Star Route 1
8 tipis - $30-45
Pets: Welcome
Creature Comforts: Authentic Lakota Sioux style teepees located on open ranchlands, evening campfire, full brkfst cooked on open fire, unique family experience

Towhouse Motel
(307) 334-2376
525 S. Main St.
20 rooms - $35-59
Pets: Welcome w/$5 fee
Creature Comforts: CCTV, a/c, refrig

Trail Motel
(800) 333-LUSK, (307) 334-2530
305 W. 8th St.
21 rooms - $36-70
Pets: Small pets w/$5 fee
Creature Comforts: CCTV, a/c, refrig, pool

LYMAN
Valley West Motel
(307) 787-3700
106 E. Clark
40 rooms - $37-48
Pets: Welcome w/$10 fee
Creature Comforts: CCTV, a/c, refrig

MEDICINE BOW
Trampas Lodge
(307) 379-2280
Route 30
18 rooms - $30-39
Pets: Welcome
Creature Comforts: CCTV, refrig

Virginian Historic Hotel
(307) 379-2377
Lincoln Hwy.
33 rooms - $25-47
Pets: Welcome
Creature Comforts: 1908 hotel, CCTV, some suites w/sitting rm, claw-foot tubs, restaurant

MEETEETSE
Oasis Motel
(307) 868-2551
1702 State St.
12 rooms - $35-46
Pets: Welcome w/$7 fee
Creature Comforts: CCTV, a/c, refrig

Vision Quest Motel
(888) 281-9866, (307) 868-2512
2207 State St.
14 rooms - $30-69
Pets: Welcome
Creature Comforts: CCTV, a/c, kit

MOORCROFT
Cozy Motel
(307) 756-3486
219 W. Converse St.
23 rooms - $30-59
Pets: Welcome
Creature Comforts: CCTV, a/c

Keyhole Marina
(307) 756-9259
213 McKean
6 rooms - $35-56
Pets: Welcome
Creature Comforts: CCTV, a/c

Moorcourt Motel
(307) 756-3411
420 Yellowstone
30 rooms - $48-59
Pets: Med. pets welcome
Creature Comforts: CCTV, a/c, refrig, micro

NEWCASTLE
Auto Inn Motel
(307) 746-2734
2503 W. Main St.
21 rooms - $40-49
Pets: Welcome in smoking rooms
Creature Comforts: CCTV, a/c, refrig

Fountain Inn Crystal Park
(800) 882-8858, (307) 746-4426
2 Fountain Plaza
86 rooms - $53-65
Pets: Welcome w/$5 fee
Creature Comforts: Extensive lawns and pond, CCTV, a/c, refrigerator, stove, restaurant, pool

Flying V Cambria Inn
(307) 283-2800
http://w3.trib.com/~flyingv
23726 Route 85
10 rooms - $45-79
Pets: Welcome
Creature Comforts: Historic 1923 sandstone building, CCTV, a/c, full brkfst

Four Corners Inn & Store
(307) 746-4776
24713 Route 85
9 rooms - $35-49
Pets: Very well-behaved small pet
Creature Comforts: Simple rms, lounge w/tv, restaurant

Hilltop Motel
(307) 746-4494
1121 S. Summit St.
15 rooms - $35-44
Pets: Welcome
Creature Comforts: CCTV, a/c, refrig

Morgan Motel
(307) 746-2715
205 S. Spokane
9 rooms - $35-45
Pets: Welcome
Creature Comforts: CCTV, a/c

Pines Motel
(307) 746-4334
248 E. Wentworth St.
11 rooms - $42-66
Pets: Very well-behaved pets
Creature Comforts: CCTV, a/c, refrig, whirlpool

Sage Motel
(307) 746-2724
1227 S. Summit St.
13 rooms - $35-47
Pets: Welcome w/$5 fee
Creature Comforts: CCTV, a/c

Sundowner Inn
(307) 746-2796
451 W. Main St.
32 rooms - $33-38
Pets: Welcome in ltd. rms
Creature Comforts: CCTV, a/c, refrig

PAINTER
Hunter Peak Ranch
(307) 587-3711
4027 Crandall Dr.
8 rooms/cabins - $40-75
Pets: Welcome
Creature Comforts: Riverside, CCTV, refrig, kit, dining room, horseback riding, hiking, fishing

PINE BLUFFS
Gator's Travelyn Motel
(307) 245-3226
515 W. Seventh St.
31 rooms - $35-47
Pets: Welcome
Creature Comforts: CCTV, a/c

Sunset Motel
(307) 245-3591
316 W. Third St.
14 rooms - $35-49
Pets: Welcome
Creature Comforts: CCTV, a/c, kit

PINEDALE

Best Western Pinedale
(800) 528-1234, (307) 367-6869
http://www.bestwestern.com
850 W. Pine St.
59 rooms - $40-99
Pets: Welcome
Creature Comforts: CCTV, refrig, micro, whirlpool

The Chambers House
(800) 567-2168, (307) 367-2168
http://www.travelassist.com/reg/wy404s.html
111 W. Magnolia St.
4 rooms - $50-99
Pets: Welcome w/$10 fee
Creature Comforts: Historic log house, some antiques, bedrooms w/fireplace, full brkfst

Camp O'The Pines
(307) 367-4536
38 N. Fremont St.
14 rooms - $48-59
Pets: Welcome w$3 fee
Creature Comforts: CCTV, kit

Half Moon Motel
(307) 367-2851
46 N. Sublet
19 rooms - $46-58
Pets: Welcome
Creature Comforts: CCTV, refrig

Lakeside Lodge Resort
(307) 367-2221
http://www.lakesidelodge.com
99 FS 111
12 rooms - $65-130
Pets: Welcome
Creature Comforts: Rustic and new lakeside cabins w/attractive decor, kit, restaurant

Log Cabin Motel
(307) 367-4579
49 E. Magnolia
10 rooms - $50-65
Pets: Med. pets welcome
Creature Comforts: CCTV, a/c, refrig, micro

Pine Creek Inn
(307) 367-2191
650 West Pine St.
20 rooms - $35-45
Pets: Welcome
Creature Comforts: TV, a/c, kit

Pole Creek Ranch B&B
(307) 367-4433
www.bbonline.com/wy/polecreek
244 Pole Creek Rd., Box 278
3 rooms, 1 teepee - $50-55
Pets: Welcome, horse boarding
Creature Comforts: CCTV, a/c, refrig, micro, fireplace, full brkfst, hot tub

Rivera Lodge
(307) 367-2424
422 W. Marilyn
8 rooms - $49-80
Pets: Welcome
Creature Comforts: CCTV, kit

Sundance Motel
(307) 367-4336
148 E. Pine St.
22 rooms - $40-75
Pets: Welcome
Creature Comforts: CCTV, kit

Teton Court Motel
(307) 367-4317
123 E. Magnolia St.
17 rooms - $40-45
Pets: Welcome
Creature Comforts: CCTV, kit

Window on the Winds B&B
(307) 367-2600
http://www.cruising-america.com/windowonwinds
10151 Rte. 191
4 rooms - $60-95
Pets: Welcome
Creature Comforts: Rustic log house w/western decor, lodge pole pine beds, down comforters, CCTV, fireplace, full brkfst, and a hot tub

POWELL

Best Choice Motel
(800) 308-8447, (307) 754-2243
337 E. Second St.
20 rooms - $30-45
Pets: Small pets welcome
Creature Comforts: CCTV, a/c, refrig

Best Western Kings Inn
(800) 528-1234, (307) 654-7551
http://www.bestwestern.com
777 East 2nd St.
49 rooms - $40-82
Pets: Welcome in smoking rooms
Creature Comforts: CCTV, a/c, refrig, restaurant, pool

Joann Ranch
(307) 754-4233
137 Rd. 8VE
4 cabins - $40-59
Pets: Welcome
Creature Comforts: Sleep in restored 1800's cabins or teepees, fishing, hiking, swimming

Park Motel
(800) 506-7383, (307) 754-2233
737 E. Second St.
18 rooms - $30-65
Pets: Welcome
Creature Comforts: CCTV, a/c, kit

Super 8
(800) 800-8000, (307) 754-7231
http://www.super8.com
845 E. Coulter
35 rooms - $35-60
Pets: Welcome
Creature Comforts: CCTV, a/c, pool

RANCHESTER

Historic Old Stone House B&B
(307) 655-9239
http://www.cruising-america.com/oldstone.html
135 Wolf Creek Rd.
4 rooms - $60-100
Pets: Welcome in cottage
Creature Comforts: A neat 1899 Craftsman-style house and cottage on ten acres, mountain views, massive parlor, antiques, unique architectural details, twin fireplace chimneys inset with stained glass window, afternoon tea, full brkfst w/linen, china and crystal

Ranchester Western Motel
(800) 341-8000, (307) 655-2212
350 Dayton St.
18 rooms - $30-55
Pets: Welcome in smoking rooms
Creature Comforts: CCTV, a/c, pool

RAWLINS

Best Western Cottontree Inn
(800) 528-1234, (307) 654-7551
http://www.bestwestern.com
23rd at Spruce
122 rooms - $65-90
Pets: Welcome in smoking rooms
Creature Comforts: CCTV, VCR, a/c, restaurant, pool, sauna, whirlpool, hlth club

Bridger Inn
(307) 328-1401
1904 E. Cedar St.
50 rooms - $35-46
Pets: Welcome
Creature Comforts: CCTV, a/c

Days Inn
(800) DAYS INN, (307) 324-6615
http://www.daysinn.com
2222 E. Cedar St.
120 rooms - $45-77
Pets: Small pets welcome
Creature Comforts: CCTV,
VCR, a/c, restaurant, pool

Rawlins Motel
(307) 3240-3456
905 W. Spruce St.
25 rooms - $25-56
Pets: Welcome w/$5 fee
Creature Comforts: CCTV, a/c,
refrig, micro

Sleep Inn
(800) Sleep-Inn, (307) 328-1732
http://www.sleepinn.com
1400 Higley Blvd.
80 rooms - $50-66
Pets: Welcome in smoking rooms
Creature Comforts: CCTV,
VCR, a/c, Jacuzzi, sauna

Sundowner Station
(800) 874-1116, (307) 328-1732
1616 N. Federal St.
59 rooms - $45-55
Pets: Welcome,
Creature Comforts: CCTV,
VCR, a/c, Jacuzzi, pool, sauna

Sunset Motel
(307) 324-3448
1302 W. Spruce St.
19 rooms - $25-47
Pets: Welcome w/$4 fee
Creature Comforts: CCTV, a/c,
refrig

Weston Inn
(800) 255-9840, (307) 789-0783
1801 E. Cedar St.
101 rooms - $45-59
Pets: Welcome
Creature Comforts: CCTV, a/c,
refrig, micro, cont. brkfst, pool,
whirlpool

RIVERTON
Days Inn
(800) DAYS INN, (307) 856-9677
http://www.daysinn.com
909 W. Main St.
32 rooms - $35-65
Pets: Welcome w/$4 fee
Creature Comforts: CCTV, a/c,
refrig, micro

Driftwood Inn
(307) 856-4811
611 W. Main St.
28 rooms - $35-59
Pets: Welcome
Creature Comforts: CCTV, a/c

Hi-Lo Motel
(307) 856-9223
414 N. Federal St.
23 rooms - $34-45
Pets: Medium pets welcome
Creature Comforts: CCTV, a/c,
refrig, micro

Holiday Inn
(800) HOLIDAY, (307) 856-8100
http://www.holiday-inn.com
900 E. Sunset St.
121 rooms - $45-56
Pets: Small pets welcome
Creature Comforts: CCTV, a/c,
refrig, restaurant, pool, rec. dome

Inn El Rancho
(307) 856-7455
211 S. Federal St.
24 rooms - $35-57
Pets: Welcome
Creature Comforts: CCTV, a/c

Jackpine Motel
(307) 856-9251
120 S. Federal St.
19 rooms - $35-55
Pets: Welcome w/$4 fee
Creature Comforts: CCTV, a/c,
pool

Mountain View Motel
(307) 856-2418
720 W. Main St.
19 rooms - $35-50
Pets: Welcome
Creature Comforts: CCTV, a/c

Sundowner Station Motel
(800) 874-1116, (307) 856-9677
1616 N. Federal St.
60 rooms - $35-55
Pets: Welcome
Creature Comforts: CCTV, a/c,
restaurant, pool

Super 8
(800) 800-8000, (307) 857-2400
http://www.super8.com
1040 N. Federal St.
32 rooms - $35-59
Pets: Small pets w/$6 fee
Creature Comforts: CCTV, a/c,
refrig

Thunderbird Motel
(307) 856-9201
302 E. Fremont St.
50 rooms - $35-49
Pets: Welcome w/$4 fee
Creature Comforts: CCTV, a/c,
refrig

ROCK SPRINGS
Comfort Inn
(800) 228-5150, (307) 382-9490
http://www.comfortinn.com
1670 Sunset Dr.
102 rooms - $55-90
Pets: Welcome w/$10 fee
Creature Comforts: CCTV, a/c,
cont. brkfst, pool, whirlpool, and
an exercise room

Days Inn
(800) DAYS INN, (307) 362-5646
http://www.daysinn.com
1545 Elk St.
110 rooms - $50-69
Pets: Welcome
Creature Comforts: CCTV, a/c,
refrig, micro

Econo Lodge
(800) 55 ECONO, (307) 382-4217
http://www.econolodge.com
1635 N. Elk St.
95 rooms - $40-74
Pets: Welcome
Creature Comforts: CCTV, a/c,
restaurant, cont. brkfst, pool, and a
whirlpool

Holiday Inn
(800) HOLIDAY, (307) 382-9200
http://www.holiday-inn.com
1675 Sunset Dr.
115 rooms - $55-79
Pets: Welcome w/$10 deposit
Creature Comforts: CCTV, a/c,
restaurant, pool, whirlpool

Inn at Rock Springs
(307) 362-9600
2518 Foothill Blvd.
150 rooms - $55-65
Pets: Welcome w/$15 fee
Creature Comforts: CCTV, a/c,
refrig, Jacuzzi, restaurant,
whirlpool

Motel 6
(800) 4-MOTEL6, (307) 362-1850
http://www.motel6.com
2615 Commercial Way
125 rooms - $40-45
Pets: Under 30 pounds welcome
Creature Comforts: CCTV, a/c

Ramada Limited
(800) 2-Ramada, (307) 362-1770
http://www.ramada.com
2717 Dewar Dr.
130 rooms - $45-75
Pets: Small pets welcome
Creature Comforts: CCTV, a/c

Rodeway Inn
(800) 228-2000, (307) 362-6673
http://www.rodeway.com
1004 Dewar Dr.
33 rooms - $45-58
Pets: Welcome
Creature Comforts: CCTV, a/c,
refrig, micro

Springs Motel
(307) 362-6683
1525 Ninth St.
22 rooms - $35-65
Pets: Small pets welcome
Creature Comforts: CCTV, a/c

Thunderbird Motel
(307) 362-3739
1556 Ninth St.
20 rooms - $35-40
Pets: Welcome
Creature Comforts: CCTV, a/c,
restaurant

SARATOGA
Hacienda Motel
(307) 326-5751
1116 S. 1st Street
32 rooms - $45-70
Pets: Welcome
Creature Comforts: CCTV,
refrig, kit

Riviera Lodge
(307) 326-5651
Saratoga St.
30 rooms - $38-59
Pets: Welcome
Creature Comforts: CCTV,
refrig

Sage and Sand Motel
(307) 326-8339
311 S. First St.
17 rooms - $35-46
Pets: Welcome
Creature Comforts: CCTV,
refrig

Saratoga Inn
(307) 326-5261
http://www.saratogainn.com
Pick Pike Rd.
50 rooms - $138-158
Pets: Welcome
Creature Comforts: Highly
recommended, newly renovated
lodge, sophisticated room decor,
feather beds on lodge pole frames,
Pendleton wool blankets,
chocolate chip cookies, CCTV,
VCR, a/c, gourmet restaurant,
pool, hot tubs, spa, telescope, golf,
horseback riding, fishing

Silver Moon Motel
(307) 326-5974
412 Bridge St.
14 rooms - $40-49
Pets: Welcome
Creature Comforts: CCTV, kit

SHERIDAN
Alamo Motel
(307) 672-2455
1326 N. Main St.
19 rooms - $35-45
Pets: Welcome on ltd. basis
Creature Comforts: CCTV, a/c

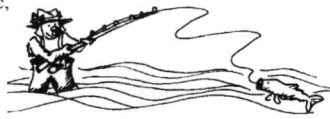

Apple Tree Inn
(800) 670-2428, (307) 672-2428
1552 Coffeen Ave.
19 rooms - $35-43
Pets: Welcome
Creature Comforts: CCTV, a/c

Aspen Inn
(307) 672-9064
1744 N. Main St.
24 rooms - $35-49
Pets: Welcome
Creature Comforts: CCTV, a/c

Bramble Motel
(307) 674-4902
2366 N. Main St.
12 rooms - $30-45
Pets: Welcome w/$25 deposit
Creature Comforts: CCTV, a/c

Comfort Inn
(800) 228-5150, (307) 672-5098
http://www.comfortinn.com
1450 E. Brundage Ln.
45 rooms - $50-85
Pets: Welcome
Creature Comforts: CCTV, a/c

Evergreen Inn
(307) 672-9757
580 E. Fifth St.
28 rooms - $42-49
Pets: Med. pets welcome
Creature Comforts: CCTV, a/c,
refrig

Guest House Motel
(800) 226-9405, (307) 674-7496
2007 N. Main St.
43 rooms - $30-48
Pets: Welcome w/$5 fee
Creature Comforts: CCTV, a/c

Holiday Inn
(800) HOLIDAY, (307) 654-7551
http://www.holiday-inn.com
1809 Sugarland St.
212 rooms - $50-140
Pets: Welcome
Creature Comforts: CCTV, a/c,
refrig, restaurant, pool, exercise
facilities, sauna, whirlpool

Holiday Lodge
(307) 672-2407
625 Coffeen Ave.
22 rooms - $38-45
Pets: Medium size dogs
Creature Comforts: CCTV, a/c,
refrig, micro

Parkway Motel
(307) 674-7259
2112 Coffeen Ave.
14 rooms - $32-39
Pets: Welcome
Creature Comforts: CCTV, a/c, kit

Rock Trim Motel
(307) 672-2464
449 Coffeen Ave.
18 rooms - $28-60
Pets: Small pets welcome
Creature Comforts: CCTV, a/c, refrig, micro, kit

Stage Stop Motel
(307) 672-3459
2167 N. Main St.
19 rooms - $40-59
Pets: Welcome
Creature Comforts: CCTV, a/c, sauna, whirlpool

Super 8
(800) 800-8000, (307) 672-9725
http://www.super8.com
2435 N. Main St.
40 rooms - $40-55
Pets: In smoking rooms w/$2 fee
Creature Comforts: CCTV, a/c

Super Saver Inn
(307) 672-0471
1789 N. Main St.
38 rooms - $33-49
Pets: Welcome w$4 fee
Creature Comforts: CCTV, a/c

Triangle Motel
(307) 674-8031
540 Coffeen St.
7 rooms - $20-35
Pets: Welcome
Creature Comforts: CCTV, a/c

SHOSHONI
Desert Inn Motel
(307) 876-2273
605 W. Second St.
31 rooms - $42-58
Pets: Welcome
Creature Comforts: CCTV, a/c, kit

Shoshoni Motel
(307) 876-2216
503 West Second St.
12 rooms - $35-49
Pets: Welcome w/$4 fee
Creature Comforts: CCTV, a/c

STORY
Piney Creek Inn B&B
(307) 683-2911
http://www.pineycreekinn.com
11 Skylark Ln.
3 rms/2 cabins - $65-150
Pets: Dogs only
Creature Comforts: Bucolic mtn. retreat, rqst cabins w/gnarled pine stairs, Western decor, handmade quilts, casual, fireplace, kit, full brkfst

Wagon Box Supper Club Inn
(307) 683-2444
6 miles off Route 90
6 cabins - $55-95
Pets: Welcome
Creature Comforts: Kit, fireplace, restaurant

SUNDANCE
Bear Lodge Motel
(800) 341-8000, (307) 283-1611
218 Cleveland Ave.
33 rooms - $40-68
Pets: Small pets welcome
Creature Comforts: CCTV, a/c, whirlpool

Best Western Inn
(800) 528-1234, (307) 283-2800
http://www.bestwestern.com
Route 26
40 rooms - $45-99
Pets: Small pets w/$20 deposit
Creature Comforts: CCTV, a/c, sauna, whirlpool

Dean's Pineview Motel
(307) 283-2800
117 N. Eighth St.
18 rooms - $30-47
Pets: Welcome
Creature Comforts: CCTV, a/c, kit

Sundance Mountain Inn
(307) 283-3737
26 Route 585
42 rooms - $40-99
Pets: Welcome
Creature Comforts: CCTV, a/c, cont brkfst, pool, sauna, whirlpool

TEN SLEEP
Log Cabin Motel
(307) 366-2320
Route 16
8 rooms - $30-45
Pets: Welcome w/$10 fee
Creature Comforts: CCTV, refrig, micro, comforters on beds

Meadowlark Lake Resort
(800) 858-5672, (307) 366-2424
Route 16
28 rooms - $45-75
Pets: Welcome in certain rooms
Creature Comforts: Rustic cabins, cottages, motel rooms, CCTV, restaurant

TETON VILLAGE
Crystal Springs Inn
(307) 733-4423
3285 W. McCollister Dr.
15 rooms - $86-99
Pets: Welcome
Creature Comforts: CCTV

The Hostel
(307) 733-3415
Teton Village
54 rooms - $35-45
Pets: Welcome
Creature Comforts: Basic motel rooms — no telephones or tv

THERMOPOLIS
Best Western Moonlighter Inn
(800) 528-1234, (307) 864-2321
http://www.bestwestern.com
600 Broadway
25 rooms - $40-75
Pets: Small pets welcome
Creature Comforts: CCTV, a/c, and a pool

Coachman Inn
(307) 864-3141
112 Route 20
19 rooms - $35-45
Pets: Welcome
Creature Comforts: CCTV, a/c

El Rancho Motel
(307) 864-2341
924 Shoshone St.
13 rooms - $35-40
Pets: Welcome
Creature Comforts: CCTV, a/c

Holiday Inn of the Waters
(800) HOLIDAY, (307) 864-3131
http://www.holiday-inn.com
115 E. Park, Box 1323
80 rooms - $45-110
Pets: Welcome
Creature Comforts: CCTV,
VCR, a/c, restaurant, pool, sport
facilities, sauna, whirlpool,
massage, hot mineral springs

Rainbow Motel
(800) 554-8815, (307) 864-2129
408 Park St.
17 rooms - $40-50
Pets: Welcome w/$5 fee
Creature Comforts: CCTV, a/c,
refrig

Roundtop Mountain Motel
(307) 864-3126
Mondale and Sixth St.
7 rooms/5 cabins - $45-59
Pets: Welcome
Creature Comforts: CCTV, a/c,
kit

Wind River Motel
(307) 283-2800
501 S. Sixth St.
16 rooms - $30-49
Pets: Welcome
Creature Comforts: CCTV, a/c

TORRINGTON
Blue Lantern Motel
(307) 532-8999
1402 Main St.
14 rooms - $25-39
Pets: Welcome
Creature Comforts: CCTV, a/c

King's Inn
(307) 532-4011
1555 Main St.
50 rooms - $40-76
Pets: Welcome w/$4 fee
Creature Comforts: CCTV, a/c,
restaurant

Maverick Motel
(307) 532-4064
Routes 26 & 85
10 rooms - $30-40
Pets: Small pets welcome
Creature Comforts: CCTV, a/c,
refrig, kit

Oregon Trail Lodge
(307) 532-2101
710 E. Valley Rd.
21 rooms - $20-35
Pets: Welcome
Creature Comforts: CCTV, a/c,
kit

UPTON
Upton Motel
(307) 468-9282
440 First St.
13 rooms - $30-48
Pets: Welcome
Creature Comforts: CCTV, a/c

Weston Inn Motel
(307) 468-2401
1601 Hwy. 16
26 rooms - $30-49
Pets: Welcome
Creature Comforts: CCTV, a/c,
restaurant

WAPITIPI
Elephant Head Lodge
(307) 587-3980
www.elephantheadlodge.com
1170 Yellowstone Hwy.
10 rooms - $64-155
Pets: Welcome, likes dogs
Creature Comforts: Cabins built
by Buffalo Bill's niece, nicely
updated, simple yet charming, kit,
fireplace, restaurant, horseback
riding, fishing, hiking

WHEATLAND
Best Western Torchlite
(800) 528-1234, (307) 322-4070
http://www.bestwestern.com
1809 N. 16th St.
51 rooms - $50-80
Pets: Welcome w/deposit
Creature Comforts: CCTV, a/c,
refrig, whirlpool

Blackbird Inn
(307) 322-4540
http://wyomingbnb-
ranchrec.com/BlackbirdInn.html
1101 - 11th St.
5 rooms - $50-75
Pets: Small dogs welcome
Creature Comforts: Victorian
house, full brkfst

Motel Westwinds
(307) 322-2705
1756 South Rd.
30 rooms - $35-60
Pets: Welcome
Creature Comforts: CCTV, a/c

Plains Motel
(307) 322-3416
208 - 16th St.
11 rooms - $38-42
Pets: Welcome
Creature Comforts: CCTV, a/c,
refrig, micro

Vimbo's Motel
(307) 322-3842
203 - 16th St.
38 rooms - $40-77
Pets: Small pets welcome
Creature Comforts: CCTV, a/c

Wyoming Motel
(307) 322-5383
1101 - 9th St.
26 rooms - $34-40
Pets: Welcome in two rms w/$25
Creature Comforts: CCTV, a/c,
refrig

WORLAND
Best Western Settlers Inn
(800) 528-1234, (307) 347-8201
http://www.bestwestern.com
2200 Big Horn Ave.
45 rooms - $45-60
Pets: Welcome
Creature Comforts: CCTV, a/c,
refrig

Days Inn
(800) DAYS INN, (307) 347-4251
http://www.daysinn.com
500 N. 10th St.
43 rooms - $30-75
Pets: Welcome
Creature Comforts: CCTV, a/c,
refrig, micro

Super 8
(800) 800-8000, (307) 347-9236
http://www.super8.com
2500 Big Horn Ave.
35 rooms - $35-60
Pets: Welcome w/permission
Creature Comforts: CCTV, a/c,
refrig

Town and Country Motel
(307) 347-3249
1021 Russell Ave.
22 rooms - $35-57
Pets: Welcome
Creature Comforts: CCTV, a/c,
kit

Town House Motor Inn
(307) 347-2426
119 N. Tenth St.
23 rooms - $45-79
Pets: Welcome
Creature Comforts: CCTV, a/c,
pool

WRIGHT
National 9
(800) 524-9999, (307) 464-1510
519 Latigo St.
27 rooms - $40-75
Pets: Small pets welcome
Creature Comforts: CCTV, a/c,
refrig, kit

**YELLOWSTONE
NATIONAL PARK**
Please check the Yellowstone
National Park rules. Pets are
allowed in few areas in the park.

Lake Lodge/Cabins
(307) 297-2757
http://www.ynp-lodges.com
Box 165
186 rooms - $46-99
Pets: Welcome
Creature Comforts: Lodge w/
cafeteria, request the spacious
Western cabins, hiking, open June-
Sept.

Lake Yellowstone Hotel
(307) 297-2757
http://www.ynp-lodges.com
Box 165
296 rooms - $73-149
Pets: Welcome
Creature Comforts:
Yellowstone's premier hotel, built
in the 1920s and listed in National
Historic Register, renovated to
former grandeur, charming hotel
rooms, simple motel-style cabins,
lakeside dining, boating, hiking,
open May-Oct.

Mammoth Hot Springs
(307) 297-2757
http://www.ynp-lodges.com
Box 165
222 rooms/cottages - $40-75
Pets: Welcome in cottages
Creature Comforts: Built in
1937, simple motel style cottages,
no tv or radios allowed, restaurant,
open May-Oct.

Old Faithful Lodge Cabins
(307) 344-7311
http://www.ynp-lodges.com
Box 165
132 rooms - $26-52
Pets: Welcome
Creature Comforts: Neat stone
lodge w/views of Old Faithful,
rustic cabins, cafeteria, no
television or radios, open May-
September

Roosevelt Lodge Cabins
(307) 344-7311
http://www.ynp-lodges.com
Box 165
80 rooms - $30-45
Pets: Welcome
Creature Comforts: Log lodge
and neat, old fashioned rustic
cabins heated by woodburning
stoves, main lodge w/family-style
restaurant, gift shop, horseback
riding, open June through Sept.

National and State Parks
Pet Rules and Regulations

Alabama's
National and State Park Regulations

National and state park regulations are the same in Alabama. Dogs are welcome in most national and state parks/recreation areas provided they are on a leash under six feet in length. They are not permitted into buildings or by swimming areas. For more information, please telephone the Alabama's National Forest Office at (800) 879-4496 or the Bureau of Tourism and Travel at (800) 252-2262. The following parks and recreation areas **do not allow** pets:

First Creek
Frank Jackson
Holt Lake
Jackson County Park
Lewis Smith lake

Pickensville Recreation Area
S.W. Taylor Park
Sumter Landing
Warrior Lake

Alaska's
National and State Park Regulations

National and state park regulations are essentially the same in Alaska. Pets are welcome in national and state parks/recreation areas as long as they are on a leash six feet in length. They are not permitted into buildings or swimming areas or on many of the trails. They cannot be left alone at any time. For more information, please telephone the Alaska's National Forest Office at (800) 280-2267 or the National Park Offices at (907) 456-0527.

Arizona's
National and State Park Regulations

National and state park regulations are the same in Arizona. With one exception, pets are welcome in all national and state parks/recreation areas provided: They are on a leash no longer than six feet in length. They are not permitted into buildings or swimming areas. Dogs are not permitted on national monument trails. For more information, please telephone the Arizona's National and State Parks Office at (602) 542-4174 or the Office of Tourism at (888) 520-3434. The only Arizona recreation area that **does not** welcome pets is:

Red Rock State Park

Arkansas's
National and State Park Regulations

Pets are welcome in most national and state parks/recreation areas provided they are on a leash. For more information, please telephone the Arkansas Dept. of Parks and Tourism at (800) 628-8725 or the US forest Service at (800) 280-2267. The only parks and recreation areas that **do not** welcome pets are:

Lake Conway
Lake Maumelle

Logoly Park

864

California's
Recreation Areas, National and State Parks

All of the National Parks and Forests listed below allow pets on their trails and in their wilderness areas. Pets older than 4 months must have a certificate stating they have been vaccinated against rabies within the last year. They may be on or off-leash, but if they are off-leash they must be under voice control at all times. For further information please call the Division of Tourism at (800) 862-2543. You may also call the National Forest service at (800) 280-2267 or (800) 444-PARK.

The following parks and recreation areas **allow pets** on a leash:

Anderson Marsch National and State Park
Andrew Molera National and State Park
Angeles National Forest
Annadel National and State Park
Anthony Chabot Regional Park
Anza Borrego Desert National and State Park
Armstrong Redwoods National and State Park
Auburn National and State Park
Austin Creek National and State Park
Benbow Lake National and State Park
Bethany Reservoir National and State Park
Big Basin Redwoods National and State Park
Big Lagoon Park
Brannan Island National and State Park
Butano National and State Park
Calaveras Big Trees National and State Park
Castaic Lake National and State Park
Castle Crags National and State Park
Caswell Memorial National and State Park
Cayucos Beach
Clear Lake National and State Park
Cleveland National Forest
Columbia National and State Historic Park
Colusa-Sacramento River National and State Park
Contra Loma Park
Cow Mountain Park
Cuyamaca Rancho National and State Park
D.L. Bliss National and State Park
Death Valley National Monument
Del Norte Coast Redwoods National and State Park
Del Valle Park
Devil's Postpile National Monument
Doran Park
Eagle Lake Park
East Mojave Park National Conservation Area
Eldorado National Forest
Freemont Peak National and State Park
George J. Hatfield National and State Park
Golden Gate Park
Golden Gate Recreational Area
Griffith Park
Grizzly Creek Redwoods National and State Park
Gualala Point Park
Hendy Woods National and State Park
Henry Cowell Redwoods National and State Park

Henry W. Coe National and State Park
Humboldt Lagoons National and State Park
Inyo National Forest
Jedediah Smith Redwoods National and State Park
King Range National Conservation Area
Klamath National Forest
Lake Berryessa
Lake Casitas
Lake Elsinore National and State Park
Lake Nacimiento
Lake Perris National and State Park
Lake Tahoe Basin Management Unit
Lassen National Forest
Lassen Volcanic National Park
Loch Lomand Park
Los Baños Creek Reservoir National and State Park
Los Padres National Forest
MacKerricher National and State Park
Malakoff Diggins National and State Park
Manresa Beach National and State Park
Martinez Shoreline Park
McArthur-Burney Falls Memorial National and State Park
McConnell National and State Park
Mendocino National Forest
Millerton Lake National and State Park
Mission Bay Park
Mondoc National Forest
Moro Strand Beach National and State Park
Mt. San Jacinto Wilderness National and State Park
Napa Valley National and State Park
Palomar Mtn. National and State Park
Patrick's Point National and State Park
Plumas National Forest
Plumas-Eureka National and State Parks
Point Mugu National and State Park
Point Pinole Shoreline
Portola National and State Park
Prairie Creek Redwoods National and State Park
Pyramid Lake National and State Park
Redwood National Park
Richardson Cove National and State Park
Russian Gulch National and State Park
San Bernardino National Forest
San Bernardino Recreation Area

San Leandro Bay Shoreline	Squaw Lake
Santa Monica Mountains	Stanislaus National Forest
Senator Wash Reservoir	Sunol Wilderness
Sequoia and Kings Canyon National Park	Tahoe National Forest
Sequoia National Forest	Temescal Park
Shadow Cliffs Park	Toiyabe National Forest
Shasta-Trinity National Forest	Vasona Park
Sierra National Forest	Whiskeytown-Shasta/Trinity Recreation Area
Six Rivers National Forest	Will Roger's National and State Historic Park
Smith River Recreation Area	Yosemite
South Yuba River Project National and State Park	
Spring Lake	

Colorado's
National and State Park Regulations

Pets are welcome in most national and state parks/recreation areas provided they are on a leash under six feet in length. For more information, please telephone the Colorado's National Forest Office at (800) 280-2267 or the Parks and Recreation Dept. at (303) 866-3437. The following parks and recreation areas **do not allow** pets:

John Martin Reservoir
Harvey Gap
Schryver Park

Connecticut
National and State Park Regulations

Pets and riding animals, including but not limited to dogs and horses, are prohibited in the following areas of state parks and forests at all times: all buildings, swimming areas and other areas so posted. No pet or riding animals shall enter a water body in which there is a DEP swimming area from anywhere on the DEP property containing that swimming area or from any contiguous DEP property. Riding animals are permitted in all other areas, and pets are permitted in all other areas provided they are on a leash no longer than seven feet and are under the control of their owner or keeper. Pets are permitted in state forest camp grounds, no more than one pet shall be allowed per campsite. Pets are prohibited from National and State Park campgrounds and beaches. For more information, please telephone Dept. of Environmental Protection at (860) 424-3200 or the The Dept. of Economic Development at (800) 282-6863.

The following parks and recreation areas **welcome pets**:

American Legion National and State Park	Osbornedale
Burr Pond National and State Park	Pachaug
Cockaponset National and State Park	Peoples
Day Pond National and State Park	Putnam Memorial
Gay City National and State Park	Quaddick
Hurd National and State Park	Sleeping Giant
Mansfield Hollow	Southford Falls
Mt. Tom	Stanley Quarter Park
Natchaug	Stratton Brook
	Wadsworth Falls
	Wharton Brook

Delaware
National and State Park Regulations

Pets are welcome in all national and state parks/recreation areas provided they are on a leash under six feet in length. For more information, please telephone the Delaware's Div. of Parks & Recreation at (302) 739-4702 or the Tourism Office at (800) 441-8846.

District of Columbia
National and State Park Regulations

Pets are welcome in most national and state parks/recreation areas provided they are on a leash under six feet in length. For more information, please telephone the National Park Service at (202) 619-7222 or the National Capitol Park Service, (202) 619-PARK.

Florida
National and State Park Regulations

Florida is unusual, in that they technically allow pets in the national parks, national forests, along with all state parks and recreation areas, provided they are kept on a six-foot, hand-held leash and are well behaved at all times. The unusual part comes into play because their access to trails, beaches, and the wilderness is severely limited, if not completely restricted. (For instance, dogs can technically enter the Everglades National Park, but cannot walk on the trails, have access to the water, etc.) Pets are not permitted in camping areas, on bathing beaches, or near concession facilities. They may also be restricted to certain areas within most parks. For more information, please telephone the Division of Recreation at (904) 488-9872 or the Office of Tourism at (850) 487-1462.

Pets **are permitted** in the following state parks and recreation areas (with very few limitations):

Bulow Plantation Ruins
Collier-Seminole
Cayo Costa
Delanor-Wiggins Pass
Don Pedro Island
Edward Ball Wakulla Springs
Fort Pierce Inlet
Gasparilla Island
Honeymoon Island
Hugh Taylor Birch
Ichetucknee Springs
John D. MacArthur Beach
John U. Lloyd Beach
Lake Manatee
Lake Talquin

Little Manatee River
North Shore
Ochlockonee River
Paynes Creek
Ponce de Leon Springs
Withlacoochee
Alexander Springs
Fort De Soto
Juniper Springs
Lake Dorr
Maximo Park
Quiet Waters
Topeekeegee Yugnee
Tradewinds
Tree Tops

Georgia
National and State Park Regulations

Pets are welcome in most national and state parks/recreation areas in designated regions provided they are on a leash under six feet in length. They are not permitted in any cottages or lodges within the parks, nor are they allowed on the state beaches. For more information, please telephone the Dept. of Parks & Recreation at (404) 656-3530 or the Dept. of Tourism at (800) 847-4842. The following parks and recreation areas **do not permit pets**:

Cumberland Island National Seashore

Franklin D. Roosevelt Park
Lake Winfield Scott
National Seashore

Idaho
National and State Park Regulations

Pets are welcome in most national and state parks/recreation areas provided they are on a leash under six feet in length. For more information, please telephone the Parks & Recreation Dept. at (800) 635-7820 or the National Forest Office at (800) 879-4496. The following parks and recreation areas **do not permit pets:**

Bear Lake
Eagle Island
Harriman Historic Park

Malad Gorge
C.J. Strike Reservoir

Illinois
National and State Park Regulations

Pets are welcome in almost all national and state parks/recreation areas provided they are on a leash under six feet in length. For more information, please telephone the Bureau of Tourism at (800) 226-6632 or the National Forest Office at (800) 280-2267. The following parks and recreation areas **do not permit pets**:

Lake Springfield Park

Indiana
National and State Park Regulations

Pets are welcome in most national and state parks/recreation areas provided they are on a leash under six feet in length. For more information, please telephone the Tourism Div. at (800) 289-6646 or the National Forest Office at (800) 280-2267. The following parks and recreation areas do not permit pets:

Bass Lake Beach	Marengo Cave Nat. Landmark
Brookville Lake	McCormick's Creek
Brown County Park	Mississinewa Lake
Cagles Mill Lake	Mounds Park
Cecil Harden Lake	Muscatatuck County Park
Chain O' Lakes	Oabache Park
Clark Park	Pokagon Park
Clem's Lake	Potato Creek
Crooked Lake	Salamonie Lake
Deam Lake	Shakamak Park
Eby Pines	Spring Mill
Greene -Sullivan Park	Starve Hollow Beach
Hardy Lake	Summit Lake
Harrison-Crawford Park	Turkey Run
Huntington Lake	Versailles
Indiana Dunes	Washington Park
Kimmell Park	Waveland Lake
Lake Monroe	White Water

Iowa
National and State Park Regulations

Pets are welcome in almost all national and state parks/recreation areas provided they are on a leash under six feet in length. For more information, please telephone the Div. of Tourism at (800) 345-4692 or the Recreation Dept. at (515) 281-5145. The following parks and recreation areas **do not permit pets**:

Crystal Lake Park	Kearney Park
Don Williams Park	Pine Ridge Rec. Area
Eldred Sherwood Park	Smith Lake County Park
Frank A. Gotch Park	Spring Lake
J.F. Kennedy Memorial	West Lake Park
Jon Sheldon Park	

Kansas
National and State Park Regulations

Pets are welcome in almost all national and state parks/recreation areas provided they are on a leash under six feet in length. For more information, please call the Dept. of Tourism at (800) 252-6727 or the Dept. of Wildlife and Parks at (316) 672-5911. The following parks and recreation areas **do not permit** pets:

Forest Park	Louisburg-Middle Creek Lake
Kirwin Reservoir	Marais des Cygnes Refuge
La Cygne Lake	Riverside Park
Lake Fort Scott	Santa Fe Park
Lake Garnett	Warnock Lake
Lake Parsons	

Kentucky
National and State Park Regulations

Pets are welcome in almost all national and state parks/recreation areas provided they are on a leash under six feet in length. For more information, please telephone the Dept. of Travel Dev. at (800) 225-8747 or the National Forest Dept. at (800) 280-2267. The following parks and recreation areas that **do not permit pets**:

Big Double Creek	Lake Shelby
Great Meadow	Rodburn Hollow
Guist Creek Lake	S-Tree Park
Hemlock Grove	Sawyer Park
Herrington Lake	Turkey Foot

Louisiana
National and State Park Regulations

Pets are welcome in almost all national and state parks/recreation areas provided they are on a leash under six feet in length. For more information, please telephone the Office of Tourism at (800) 334-8626 or the Office of Recreation at (504) 342-8111. The following parks and recreation areas **do not permit pets**:

Buhow Lake	Cross Lake
Caddo Lake	Kincaid Lake
Cotie Reservoir	Lake End

Maine
National and State Park Regulations

No pets are allowed on beaches or in the Sebago Lake National and State Park campground. Pets are allowed only under suitable restraint and must not be left unattended. Pets must be on a leash not exceeding four feet in length. Pet owners must immediately clean up any fecal deposits left by their pets. Pet owners may be assigned picnic or campsites in a less congested area of the park. For more information please telephone the Maine Publicity Bureau at (207) 623-0363. The following parks and recreation areas **do not permit pets:**

Baxter Park	Outlet Beach
Crescent Beach	Scarborough Beach
Mahoosucs Park	Sebago Lake

Maryland
National and State Park Regulations

Pets are welcome in most national and state parks/recreation areas provided they are on a leash under six feet in length. For more information, please telephone the State and National Park Services at (800) 830-3874 or the Office of Tourism at (800) 394-5725. The following parks and recreation areas **welcome pets**:

Assateague Island
Big River Park
Brunswick Campsite
Deep Creek Lake
Elk Neck Park
Green Ridge National and State Forest
Louise F. Cosca Park
Patapsco Park

Point Lookout
Potamac National and State Forest
Rock Creek
Rocky Gap
Savage River National and State Forest
Susequehanna Park
Swallow Falls

Massachusetts
National and State Park Regulations

Leashed pets are welcome in all state forests and parks <u>except</u> those listed below. For more information, please telephone the Office of Travel & Tourism (800) 447-6277 or the Div. of Parks & Forests at (617) 727-3180. The following parks and recreation areas **do not permit pets**:

Borderland Park
Cape Cod national Seashore
Dighton Rock
DW Field Park
Gallop Island
George's Island
Great Brook Farm
Halibut Pt.

Lake Dennison
Look Memorial Park
Maudslay Park
Mt. Tom
Natural Bridge
R.T. Crane Memorial Reservation
Rocky Woods Reservation
South Cape Beach
Walden Pond

Michigan
National and State Park Regulations

Pets are welcome in almost all national and state parks/recreation areas provided they are on a leash no longer than six feet in length. They are not permitted to be in public buildings or on the beaches. For more information, please telephone the Dept. of Natural Resources at (517) 373-1214 or the Travel Bureau at (800) 543-2937. The parks and recreation areas that **do not permit pets** in the following:

Ella Sharp Park
Fox Memorial
Isle Royale Park
John Henes Park
Metro Beach
Van Buren Park
Wilson Park

Minnesota
National and State Park Regulations

Pets are welcome in most national and state parks/recreation areas provided they are on a leash six feet in length or in a portable carrier. They must not disrupt other visitors, must have their owners clean up and properly dispose of their waste, and must not enter lodge buildings or beaches areas. For more information, please telephone the Dept. of Natural Resources at (612) 296-6157 or the National Forest Dept. at (800) 280-2267. The following parks and recreation areas **do not permit pets**:

Delagoon
Falls Creek Park
Franz Jevne Park
Lake Winona

Pebble Lake
Shager Park
Tipsinah Mounds
Voyageurs

Mississippi
National and State Park Regulations

Pets are welcome in most national and state parks/recreation areas provided they are on a leash under six feet in length. For more information, please telephone the National Forest at (800) 280-2267 or the Div. of Tourism at (800) 927-6378. The following parks and recreation areas **will not accept pets**:

Delta Park
Desoto Park
Holly Springs
Homochitto Park
Tombigbee Park
Blue Bluff
Jamie Whitten Park
Piney Grove
Waverly Ferry Park
Atwood Water Park
Bogue Chitto Water Park
Burnside Lake Park
Columbia Water Park
Crossroads Water Park
D'Lo Water Park
Flint Creek Water Park
Holmes Water Park
Kemper Park
Lake Bogue Homa
Lake Bolivar
Lake Claude Bennett

Lake Columbia
Lake Jeff Davis
Lake Lamar Bruce
Lake Lincoln
Lake Mary Crawford
Lake Mike Conner
Lake Monroe
Lake Perry
Lake Ross Barnett
Lake Tom Bailey
Lake Walthall
Luxapallia Creek
McLeod Park
Merit Water Park
Meshoba Legion Lake
Oktibbeha County Lake
Pelahachie Lake
Ross Barnett Reservoir
Simpson County Legion lake
Tippah County Lake
Walker's Bridge Water Park
Walkiah Bluff Water Park

Missouri
National and State Park Regulations

Pets are welcome in almost all national and state parks/recreation areas provided they are restrained at all times and on a leash no longer than six feet in length. For more information, please telephone the Dept. of Natural Resources at (800) 334-6946 or the Div. of Tourism at (800) 877-1234. The following parks and recreation areas **do not permit pets**:

Binder Park
Cole County
Fleming Park

Hough Park
Little Prairie Lake

Montana
National and State Park Regulations

Pets are welcome in almost all national and state parks/recreation areas provided they are on a leash no longer than six feet in length. They are not permitted to be in public buildings or on the beaches. For more information, please telephone the US Forest Service at (800) 280-2267 or the Travel Promotion Div. at (800) 847-4868. The following parks and recreation areas **do not permit pets**:

Lolo National Park
Bitterroot Lake
James Kipp Park

Judith Landing
Riverfront Park

Nebraska
National and State Park Regulations

Pets are welcome in almost all national and state parks/recreation areas provided they are on a leash no longer than six feet in length. They are not permitted to be in public buildings or on the beaches. For more information, please telephone the Parks Commission at (402) 471-0641 or the Tourism Bureau at (800) 228-4307. The following parks and recreation areas **do not permit pets**:

Elkhorn River Crossing
Glenn Cunningham Park
Holmes Lake
Ogala National Grassland

Salt Valley Lakes
Standing Bear Lake
Wehrspann Lake
Zorinsky Lake

Nevada
National and State Park Regulations

Pets are welcome in all national and state parks/recreation areas provided they are on a leash no longer than six feet in length. They are not permitted to be in public buildings or on the beaches. For more information, please telephone the Division of National and State Parks at (800) 237-0774 or the Commission on Tourism at (800) 638-2328.

New Hampshire
National and State Park Regulations

Pets are welcome on all national and state parks/recreation areas provided they are on a leash no longer than six feet in length. They are not permitted to be in public buildings or on the beaches. If any pet creates a disturbance or threatens park patrons, it will be removed from the park. For more information, please telephone the National Forest Service Dept. at (800) 280-2267 or the Office of Travel & Tourism at (800) 386-4664. The following parks and recreation areas **welcome pets**:

Androscoggin
Annett
Bear Brook
Bedell Bridge
Blackwater Dam
Cardigan
Chesterfield (dog walk areas)
Coleman Park
Crawford Notch
Dixville Notch
Edward McDowell Lake
Franconia
Franklin Falls Dam
Gardner
Greenfield
Honey Brook

Kearsarge: Rollins & Winslow National and State Parks
Lake Francis
Milan Hill
Moore Reservation
Moose Brook
Mt. Sunapee
Mt. Washington
Nansen
Pillsbury
Pillsbury Park
Risgah
Rollins
White Mountain National Forest
Winslow

New Jersey
National and State Park Regulations

Pets are welcome on all national and state parks/recreation areas provided they are on a leash no longer than six feet in length. They are not permitted to be in public buildings or on the beaches. For more information, please telephone the Div. of Parks & Forestry at (609) 292-2797 or the Div. of Travel & Tourism at (800) 537-7397. The only park that **does not welcome** pets is:

Cape May County Park

New Mexico
National and State Park Regulations

National and state park regulations are the same in New Mexico. With two exceptions, dogs are welcome in all national and state parks/recreation areas provided they are on a leash no longer than ten feet in length. They are not permitted into buildings or swimming areas. Dogs are not permitted on national monument trails. For more information, please telephone the National and State Parks & Recreation Dept. at (888) 667-2757 or the Department of Tourism at (800) 545-2040. The following parks and recreation areas that **do not** welcome pets are:

Blue Hole
Coyote Creek
El Malpais
Fenton Lake
Fort Stanton
James-Wallace Memorial
Leasburg Dam

Orilla Verde Park
Rio Grande Nature Center
Santa Clara Canyon
Sugarite Canyon
The Living Desert Zoo
Wild Rivers

New York
National and State Park Regulations

Pets are welcome on all national and state parks/recreation areas provided they are on a leash no longer than six feet in length. They are not permitted to be in public buildings or on the beaches. For more information, please telephone the Office of Parks & Recreation at (518) 474-0456 or the Div. of Tourism at (800) 225-5697. The following parks and recreation areas that **do not welcome pets** are:

Adirondack Park
Ausabale Pt. Park
Belmont Lake
Bethpage Park
Braddock Bay
Breezy Pt. Park
Catskill Forest Preserve
Cherry Plain Park
Clarence Fahnestock Memorial
Connetquot Preserve
Darien Lake
Evangola park
Harriman Park
Heckscher Park
Hempstead lake
Hither Hill
Jacques Cartier Park
James Baird Park
Jones Beach
Lake Colby

Lake Erie Rec. Area
Lake Flower
Lake Taghkanic
Long Pt.
Margaret Lewis Norris Park
Mary Island
Montauk Pt. Nature Trails
Newton Battlefield Reservation
Orient Beach
Robert Moses Park
Rockland Lake
Sunken Meadow Park
Taconic-Copake Falls
Taconic-Rudd Pond
Valcour Landing
Wildwood Reserve
Saranac Lake

North Carolina
National and State Park Regulations

Dogs are permitted in the Great Smoky Mountains National Park and are also allowed in <u>all</u> of North Carolina's state parks and recreation areas, provided they are on a 6-foot leash. They are not permitted in the any of the cabins or bath houses that are located within the state parks. For more information, please telephone Travel & Tourism Bureau at (800) 847-4862 or the Div. of Parks (919) 733-7275. The following parks and recreation areas **do not permit pets**:

Badin Lake	Cedar Point
Cape Lookout National Seashore	Neuse River

North Dakota
National and State Park Regulations

Pets are welcome in almost all national and state parks/recreation areas provided they are restrained at all times and on a leash no longer than six feet in length. For more information, please telephone the Parks & Recreation Dept. at (701) 328-5357 or the Tourism Dept. at (800) 435-5663. The following parks and recreation areas **do not permit pets**:

Arrowhead Nat. Wildlife Refuge	Tetrault Woods
Mayville City Park	Walhala Riverside Park
Memorial Park	

Ohio
National and State Park Regulations

Pets are welcome in almost all national and state parks/recreation areas provided they are restrained at all times and on a leash no longer than six feet in length. For more information, please telephone the Div. of Parks & Recreation at (614) 265-6561 or the Div. of Travel & Tourism at (800) 282-5393. The following parks and recreation areas **welcome pets**:

A.W. Marion Park	Geneva Park
Alum Creek	Harrison Lake
Barkcamp	Hueston Woods
Beaver Creek Park	Independence Dam
Blue Rock	Indian Lake
Buck Creek	Jefferson Lake
Caesar Creek	Kelly's Island
Cowan Lake	Lake Alma
Cuyahoga Valley Rec. Area	Lake Hope
Deer Creek	Malabar Farm
Delaware Park	Maumee Bay
Dillon Park	Muskingum River
East Fork Park	Paint Creek
Findley Park	Portage Lakes
Forked Run	Punderson Park

Oklahoma
National and State Park Regulations

Pets are welcome in almost all national and state parks/recreation areas provided they are restrained at all times and on a leash no longer than six feet in length. For more information, please telephone the National and State Park Reservations at (800) 654-8240 or the Tourism & Recreation Dept. at (800) 652-6552. The following parks and recreation areas **do not permit pets**:

Adair Park
Ardmore City lake
Atoka Reservoir
Beaver Park
Black Mesa Park
Blue River Rec. Area
Boggy Depot
Chandler City Lake
Crowder Lake
Disney Park
Dustin City Lake
Foss Lake
Henryetta City Lake
Holdenville City Lake
Hominy City Lakes
J.W. Taylor Lakes
Lake Carl Etling
Lake Claremore
Lake John Wells
Lake McMurty
Lake Perry
Lake Talihina

Liberty Lake
McGee Creek
Nanih Waiya Lake
Nichols Park Lake
Okemah Lake
Ozzie Cobb Lake
Pauls Valley Park
Pawnee City Lake
Pennington Creek
Ponca City Lake
Purcell City Lake
Sayre City Park
Skip-out Lake
Sportsman Lake
Spring Creek Lake
Stroud lake
Thunderbird Lake
Twin Lakes
Washita Wildlife Ref.
Wayne Wallace Lake
Weleetka City Lake
Wetumka Lake

Oregon's
National and State Park Regulations

Pets are allowed in all of Oregon's National Forests and areas run by the Army Corps of Engineers. For further information please call the National Forest Service at (800) 280-2267 or the Dept. of Parks & Recreation at 452-5687. The following parks and recreation areas **do not allow** pets:

Bastendorff Beach
Beverly Beach
Pioneer Park

Pennsylvania's
National and State Park Regulations

Pets are welcome in almost all national and state parks/recreation areas provided they are restrained at all times and on a leash no longer than six feet in length. For more information, please telephone the National Forest Info. at (800) 280-2267 or the Bureau of Travel Marketing at (800) 847-4872. The following parks and recreation areas **do not permit pets**:

Bald Eagle Park
Black Moshannon Park
Blue Marsh Lake
Chapman Park
Cherry Springs Park
Colton Pt. Park
Hills Creek
Hugh Moore Park
Hyner Run
Kettle Creek
Leaser lake
Leonard Harrison Park
Little Pine Park

Locust Lake
Lyman Run
Mauch Chunk Lake
Ole Bull Park
Parker Dam
Patterson Park
Poe Paddy Park
Poe Valley
Prouty Place
Raymond Winter Park
Ricketts Glen
S.B. Elliott Park

Rhode Island
National and State Park Regulations

Leashed pets are allowed in some of the parks and recreation areas, however, they are not allowed on the beaches in season during the peak hours, only early in the morning or late in the evening. During the off-season pets are allowed on the beach any time of day. For more information, please telephone the Tourism Division at (800) 556-2484 or the Div. of Environmental Management at (800) 280-2267. The following parks and recreation areas **welcome pets**:

Colt Park
Fort Adams
Goddard Park

Lincoln Woods
Pulaski Memorial

South Carolina
National and State Park Regulations

Pets are welcome in all of the state parks and recreation areas except two, provided they are kept on a six-foot leash. They are welcome in the camping areas, but are not allowed in the recreational cabins. The regulations for dogs on beaches varies from one county to the next. For more information, please telephone Div. of Tourism at (800) 346-3646 or the Dept. of Parks, Recreation, and Tourism at (803) 734-0127. The two recreation areas that **do not welcome** pets are:

Lake Murray
Prestwood Lake

South Dakota
National and State Park Regulations

Pets are welcome in almost all national and state parks/recreation areas provided they are restained at all tmes and on a leash no longer than six feet in length. For more information, please telephone the National Forest Info. at (800) 280-2267 or the Dept of Tourism at (800) 732-5682. The following parks and recreation areas **do not permit pets:**

Amsden Park
Johnson's Pt.
Lake Alvin
Lake Hendricks
N.W. Peican Park
Rosehill Park

S. Blue Dog Park
Sand Creek
Sica Hollow
Swan Creek
Tabor Park
Wall Lake

Tennessee
National and State Park Regulations

Pets are welcome in all national and state parks/recreation areas provided they are restained at all tmes and on a leash no longer than six feet in length. For more information, please telephone the Bureau of National and State Parks at (888) 867-2757 or the Dept of Tourist Development at (800) 491-8366.

Texas
National and State Park Regulations

National and state park regulations are the same in Texas. Attended pets on a six foot leash are welcome in most parks and recreation areas provided they are not permitted into buildings or swimming areas. Dogs are not permitted on national monument trails. Pets that are noisy, viscous, or dangerous are not permitted. For more information, please telephone the Texas' Travel & Tourism Division at (800) 452-9292 or Texas Parks and Wildlife: (800) 792-1112. The parks and recreation areas that **do not allow** pets are:

Big Bend Ranch Park
Big Thcket National Preserve
Falls on the Brazos
Hubbard Creek Lake

Lake Fort Phanton Hill
Lake Leon
Pace Bend Park
Sabine Lake
Ziller Park

Utah
National and State Park Regulations

Pets are welcome in all national and state parks/recreation areas provided they are restrained at all times and on a leash no longer than six feet in length. For more information, please telephone the Bureau of National and State Parks at (801) 538-7221 or the Travel Council at (801) 538-1030. The only recreation area that **does not welcome** pets is:

Great Salt Lake Beach

Vermont
National and State Park Regulations

For the comfort and safety of our human visitors, pets are not allowed in day use areas (beaches or picnic areas) or parking lots unless they are guide animals. The state's genral guidelines are:

1) Owners must have, and show upon entering any park, a proof of rabies vaccination for each pet within last 30 months and be free of infectious diseases. 2) Quiet hours for everyone, including pets, are between 10PM and 7AM. 3) Domesticated or trained animals must be kept on a leash no longer than ten feet and must be attended at all times. 4) Pets are not allowed in any day use areas. 5) Pet owners are responsible for repairing damage caused by and cleaning up after their animals.

For more information, please telephone the Dept. of Forests, Parks, and Recreation at (802) 241-3655 or the Dept. of Tourism at (800) 837-6668. The following parks and recreation areas **do not welcome** pets:

Allis Park
Bell Mtn. Dam
Camp Plymouth
Crystal Lake
Granville Gulf
Kamp Kill Kare
Kingsland Bay
Knight Point

N. Hartland Dam
N. Springfield Park
Sand Bar Park
Shaftsbury Park
Stoughton Pond
Townshend Park
Union Vilage Dam
Wrightsville Dam

Virginia
National and State Park Regulations

Pets are welcome in all national and state parks/recreation areas provided they are restained at all tmes and on a leash no longer than six feet in length. For more information, please telephone the Dept. of Conservation and Recreation at (800) 933-7275 or the Div. of Tourist at (800) 847-4882. The parks and recreation areas that **do not welcome** pets are:

Bear Creek Lake
Burke Lake Park
Ellinore C. Lawrence Park

Lake Accotinik Park
Lake Fairfax Park
River Bend Park

Washington
National and State Park Regulations

Pets are **not allowed** in most of Washington's National Parks, recreation areas, or lands run by the Army Corps of Engineers. Animals are not allowed in ferry terminals, above the car decks, or on the passenger ferries unless they are in a container. For more information, please telephone the Travel Development Dept. at (206) 461-5840 or the Parks & Recreation Comm. at (800) 233-0321. The following parks and recreation areas **do not allow** pets:

Carl Precht Memorial Park
Cascade Park
Chief Looking Glasss
Columbia Park
Connelly Park
Entiat Park
Ice Harbor Lock/Dam
Lake Chelan
Lake Gillette
Lake Sacajawea
Lighthouse Marine Park
Little Goose Lock/Dam
Lower Monumental Lock/Dam
Lowr Granite Lock/Dam
Mayfield Lake County Park
McNary Loch/Dam
Montlake Park
Moses Lake Park

Mt. Baker
Mt. Ranier
North Cascades
Oak Harbor Beach
Olympic
Phil Simon Park
Pt. Defiance Park
Ross Lake
Samish Park
Semiahmoo County Park
Silver Lake County Park
Skamokawa Vista Park
Sunny Beach Point
Thornton A. Sullivan Park
Washington Park
Wenatchee Chief Joseph Dam
Wynoochee Lake

West Virginia
National and State Park Regulations

Pets are welcome in all national and state parks/recreation areas provided they are restained at all tmes and on a leash no longer than six feet in length. For more information, please telephone the National Forest Srvice at (800) 280-2267 or the Div. of Tourism and Parks at (800) 225-5982. The parks and recreation areas that **welcome** pets are:

Beech Fork
Beech Fork Lake
Bluestone Lake
Brooke Hills
Burnsville Lake
Chief Logan Park
E. Lynn Lake
Lake Sherwood
Lake Stephens
Mononngahela Nat. Forest
New River Gorge

Oglebay Park
Plum Orchard Lake
Pringle Tree Park
RD Bailey Lake
Spruce Cob Park
Stonewall Jackson Lake
Sutton Lake
Tomilson Run
Tygart Lake
Wheeling Park

Wisconsin
National and State Park Regulations

Pets are welcome in all but two national and state parks/recreation areas provided they are on a leash except for designated areas. They are not accepted in public buildings, on beaches, or in picnic areas. For more information, please telephone the National Forest Service at (800) 228-2267 or the Dept. of Tourism at (800) 372-2737. The following parks and recreation areas **do not permit pets**:

Horicon Marsh
Shawano Lake

Wyoming
National and State Park Regulations

Pets are welcome in many parks and recreation areas provided they are on a leash. They are not accepted in public buildings, on beaches, or in picnic areas. For more information, please telephone the Div. of National and State Parks at (307) 777-6223 or the Div. of Tourism at (800) 225-5996. The following parks and recreation areas **do not permit pets**:

Black Hills Nat. Forest
Bridger-Teton Nat. Forests

National Hotel and Motel Groups
Toll Free Numbers and Internet Addresses

National Hotel and Motel Groups
Toll Free Numbers and Internet Addresse

Amerisuites	(800) 833-1516	http://www.amerisuites.com
Baymont Inns & Suites	(877) BAYMONT	http://www.baymontinns.com
Best Western	(800) 780-7234	http://www.bestwestern.com
Budgetel	(800) 4-BUDGET	http://www.baymontinns.com
Clarion	(800) CLARION	http://www.clarioninn.com
Comfort Inns	(800) 228-5150	http://www.hotelchoice.com
Courtyard	(800) 321-2211	http://www.courtyard.com
Canadian Pacific Hotels	(800) 441-1414	http://www.cphotels.ca
Clarion	(800) 252-7466	http://www.hotelchoice.com
Days Inn	(800) DAYS-INN	http://www.daysinn.com
Delta Hotels	(800) 268-1133	http://www.DeltaHotels.com
Doubletree	(800) 222-TREE	http://www.doubletreehotels.com
Econo Lodge	(800) 55-ECONO	http://www.hotelchoice.com
Embassy Suites	(800) 362-2779	http://www.embassy-suites.com
Fairfield Inn	(800) 228-2800	http://www.fairfieldinn.com
Fairmont Hotels	(800) 527-4727	http://www.fairmont.com
Four Seasons	(800) 332-3442	http://www.fshr.com
Guest Quarters	(800) 424-2900	http://www.guestquarters.com
Hampton Inns	(800) HAMPTON	http://www.hamptoninn.com
Hawthorne Suites	(800) 527-1133	http://www.hawthorn.com
Hilton Hotels	(800) HILTONS	http://www.hilton.com
Holiday Inn	(800) HOLIDAY	http://www.holidayinn.com
Homewood Suites	(800) CALL-HOME	http://www.homewoodsuites.com
Howard Johnson	(800) 446-4656	http://www.hojo.com
Hyatt Hotels	(800) 233-1234	http://www.hyatt.com
La Quinta	(800) 531-5900	http://www.laquinta.com

National Hotels and Motels		Internet Addresses
Loews Hotels	(800) 445-6937	http://www.loewshotels.com
MainStay Suites	(800) 660-MAIN	http://www.hotelchoice.com
Marriott Hotels	(800) 228-9290	http://www.marriott.com
Motel 6	(800) 4-MOTEL-6	http://www.motel6.com
Quality Inns	(800) 228-5151	http://www.qualityinns.com
Radisson Hotels	(800) 333-3333	http://www.radisson.com
Ramada Inns	(800) 2-RAMADA	http://www.ramada.com
Red Lion Inns	(800) RED-LION	http://www.redlion.com
Red Roof Inns	(800) 843-7663	http://www.redroof.com
Residence Inns	(800) 331-3131	http://www.residenceinn.com
Ritz-Carlton	(800) 241-3333	http://www.ritzcarlton.com .
Rodeway	(800) 228-2000	http://www.rodeway.com
Sheraton Hotels	(800) 325-3535	http://www.sheraton.com
Shilo Inns	(800) 222-2244	http://www.shiloinn.com
Shoney's Inns	(800) 222-2222	http://www.shoneysinn.com
Sleep Inn & Suites	(800) 753-3746	http://www.sleepinn.com
Summerfield Suites	(800) 833-4353	http://www.summerfieldsuites.com
Super 8	(800) 800-8000	http://www.super8motels.com
Travelodge	(800) 578-7878	http://www.travelweb.com
Wellesley Inns	(800) 444-8888	http://www.wellesleyinnandsuites.com
Westin	(800) 228-3000	http://www.westin.com
Wyndham	(800) WYNDHAM	http://www.wyndham.com

Ordering Information

Dawbert Press books are available through book, pet, and gift stores and the Internet. If you have difficulty locating any of our books, you may contact us directly:

Internet at http://www.dawbert.com
E-mail: dawbert@mindspring.com
Telephone: (800) 93-DAWBERT, (781) 934-7202
Fax: (781) 934-2945
Dawbert Press, Order Dept., P.O. Box 67, Duxbury, Massachusetts, 02331

On The Road Again with Man's Best Friend
United States
by Dawn and Robert Habgood

This tome contains over 18,000 accommodations that welcome man's best friend *and* feline. Each entry contains essential facts as well as web site information, pet policies, and a variety of creature comforts. Its authors award special designations to, and brief reviews of, the country's most unique places to stay with a pet. This book was recently nominated by the Dog Writers Association of America as the best general reference book.

0-933603-11-8 $19.95   896 pages

On The Road Again With Man's Best Friend
Eastern United States
Western United States
by Dawn and Robert Habgood

The authors have traveled across the country to select the finest and most unique bed and breakfasts, inns, hotels, and resorts for in-depth reviews. This is a book for anyone who wants the inside scoop on the best places to stay with their pet. The authors' personal insights provide a richness of detail unmatched today in pet travel writing. Each description provides an overview of the accommodation, followed by details on room furnishings and amenities; the best rooms in the inn and those to avoid; as well as other creature comforts. Finally, they suggest the area's best pet pastimes that will appeal to both you and your pet.

Eastern United States
0-933603-32-0 $19.95   Spring, 2000   840 pages

Western United States
0-933603-31-2 $19.95   Fall, 2000   840 pages